# WORLD AUTHORS
## 1900–1950

## Biographical Reference Books
## from The H. W. Wilson Company

Greek and Latin Authors 800 B.C.–A.D. 1000
European Authors 1000–1900
British Authors Before 1800
British Authors of the Nineteenth Century
American Authors 1600–1900
World Authors 1950–1970
World Authors 1970–1975
World Authors 1975–1980
World Authors 1980–1985
World Authors 1985–1990
Spanish American Authors: The Twentieth Century

The Junior Book of Authors
More Junior Authors
Third Book of Junior Authors
Fourth Book of Junior Authors and Illustrators
Fifth Book of Junior Authors and Illustrators
Sixth Book of Junior Authors and Illustrators
Seventh Book of Junior Authors and Illustrators

Great Composers: 1300–1900
Composers Since 1900
Composers Since 1900: First Supplement
Musicians Since 1900
American Songwriters

American Reformers

World Artists 1950–1980
World Artists 1980–1990

Facts About the Presidents
Facts About the British Prime Ministers
Facts About the Supreme Court
Facts About Congress

Nobel Prize Winners

World Film Directors: Volumes I, II

# WORLD AUTHORS

## 1900–1950

*The Wilson Authors Series*

Volume Four
Saki–Zweig

Editors

## Martin Seymour-Smith

and

## Andrew C. Kimmens

The H.W. Wilson Company
New York · Dublin

1996

H.W. Wilson, 950 University Ave., Bronx, NY 10452.
H.W. Wilson web site: http://www.hwwilson.com

Library of Congress Cataloging-in-Publication Data
World authors, 1900–1950 / [editors] Martin Seymour-Smith, Andrew Kimmens .
p.   cm.—(Wilson authors series)
Rev. ed. of: Twentieth century authors, 1942 and its First supplement, 1955.
Includes bibliographical references.
Summary: Provides almost 2700 articles on twentieth-century authors from all over the world who wrote in English or whose works are available in English translation.
ISBN 0-8242-0899-4
1. Literature, Modern—20th century—Bio-bibliography.
2. Literature, Modern—20th century—History and criticism.
[1. Literature, Modern—20th century—History and criticism.]
I. Seymour-Smith, Martin II. Kimmens, Andrew C. III. Twentieth century authors: a biographical dictionary of modern literature. IV. Twentieth century authors: a biographical dictionary of modern literature. First supplement. V. Series.
PN451.W674 1996
809'.04—dc20                                                          96-16380
                                                                           CIP
                                                                           AC

Acknowledgments for the use of copyrighted material and credits for photographs appear at the end of volume four.

PRINTED IN THE UNITED STATES OF AMERICA

# WORLD AUTHORS

## 1900–1950

**"SAKI" (pseudonym of HECTOR HUGH MUNRO)** (December 18, 1870–November 13, 1916), British short story writer, novelist, dramatist, journalist, and satirist of Edwardian life, was born in Akyab, Burma, the son of Charles Augustus Munro, an officer in the British military police, and his wife, the former Mary Frances Mercer, daughter of a rear-admiral. Both parents were descended from Highlands Scots. His  mother went to Devonshire in the west of England in the winter of 1872 to have her fourth child, but was charged by a runaway cow and was killed, along with the baby she was carrying.

Charles Augustus took a house at Pilton, a village near Barnstaple in Devon, and there ensconced his three children, in the charge of his widowed mother, Lucy Jones Munro, and her two spinster sisters, who have, owing to their nephew's accounts, gone down in literary history as two quite horrible women. It appears that Munro's accounts had a strong basis in fact.

The spinsters, Charlotte (nicknamed, bizarrely, "Tom") and Augusta Munro, like their martial brother out in Burma, believed in the myth of benign British rule over brutish "natives"—and they also believed that children resembled such natives. The child, they reasoned, required total repression for its own good: so that it could grow up British, responsible, and "clean." The avenue of escape for Hector and his elder sister lay in the fact that the grandmother was in herself gentle, and that her two daughters loathed each other and spent most of the time scoring pyrrhic victories over each other. The air in the house at Pilton was fetid; the children were not much trusted to go outdoors—and, most important of all, they were discouraged from expressing or demonstrating emotion. The birch and whip were frequently used, but Hector suffered less from these on account of the fact that he had been pronounced by the doctor as the most likely to die first. Munro developed his talent for sketching in his childhood, and continued with it for the rest of his life.

All this is invaluable in helping to explain the background to, and indeed much of the foreground of, Saki's unique fiction, for much of it is based on the clever games which Munro invented in order to maintain his own identity, and in the sadistic fantasies he invented in which he punished the aunts. These games included dressing-up, many pranks, mimicry (of which he proved an early master), and the invention of a wolf (which, transformed, would feature in his work) which frequently devoured his aunts. Walter Allen, in *The English Novel*, having discussed three contemporaries of Saki who enjoyed a temporary popularity in their lifetimes—William de Morgan, May Sinclair, and F. W. Rolfe ("Baron Corvo")—wrote: "These writers, it seems to me, stand far less chance of being read in any foreseeable future than such avowedly 'frivolous' novelists as 'Saki' and the Irish

ladies Edith Somerville and 'Martin Ross.'" Apart from a small cult for Rolfe, and markedly unsuccessful attempts to bring Sinclair (who was certainly a serious writer) back into print, this prophecy (1954) has turned out to be correct. However, apart from short tributes by Graham Greene and V. S. Pritchett, and, notably, the long overdue (1981) full-length critical biography by the American writer A. J. Langguth, there has been little serious criticism of Saki.

Munro, unlike his brother and sister, was kept from a dame's private school in Barnstaple, owing to his "delicacy" of health: he did not in fact get much formal schooling at all, although he did attend Pencarwick School in Exmouth for a term, and a small public school, Bedford Grammar School, for four terms. Then his father, who had retired from military service, "took him over." The family travelled in Germany and France, and made trips to other parts of Europe. One place they stayed for a time—Ethel was now a good-looking girl, while Charlie was being trained for the army—was Davos, in Switzerland. There lived the English man of letters and scholar John Addington Symonds, who maintained a wife and children. Symonds was candid and open about his sexuality toward those who shared his preference for young men; young Hector visited him often, and there seems no doubt that Symonds was a catalyst for the younger man's own emergent attitudes. Munro's homosexuality, as well as the nature of his childhood, and his sympathy with his genial father's political ideas, offers the other key to his work. As John Lauritsen asserts in the *Encyclopedia of Homosexuality*, Munro "accepted Symonds as his mentor in matters of literary style as well as sexual philosophy" (however, Munro goes unmentioned in Symonds's *Memoirs*).

In 1891 Charles Augustus settled in Devon, near Barnstaple, and started a new career as a schoolteacher. Hector spent two years there, undertaking sporadic study under the eye of his father, and playing intricate practical jokes. He had by then developed inner resources—some of them of an intricately cruel nature—that enabled him to survive more or less intact. Within a decade he would find himself able to build a formidable body of minor, but classic and exquisite, writing around his sense of those resources.

Then in 1893 he went, very unwillingly, to Burma, in order to take up a post with the police. Stationed in Singu district, he took little interest in his duties (which were not onerous), and, after fourteen months and a bout of malaria, was invalided out. Then (1896) he went to London—armed with an introduction to a then well-known cartoonist in behalf of the Liberal Party, Sir Francis Carruthers Gould—to become a writer. He did not do so well at first, but established a reputation as a witty and well-dressed man. His first effort was *The Rise of the Russian Empire* (1900), in which he aspired to Gibbonian heights, both of sweep and anti-Christianity, but which, as Langguth writes, "echoes with the frustrations of an adventurer's soul locked in the body of a clerk." It received mixed reviews in England, and markedly hostile ones in America.

Munro now turned to the cartoonist, Gould. He also took a pen-name: "Saki," he well knew, had homosexual overtones: not only did it imply the "cupbearer" familiar from Fitzgerald's *Rubaiyat*, then at the height of its popularity, but also the "desirably beautiful boy" from the (translated) poems of Hafiz, from Goethe's "oriental" poems, and elsewhere. He started as a political satirist and parodist on the *Westminster Gazette*. His "Alice" series, parodies of Lewis Carroll ("Have you ever seen an Ineptitude?" one begins), established him, and from the time of the publication of a collection of them, *The Westminster Alice* (1902), he did not have to look back as a journalist. Gould's illustrations represented the best of his cartoon work.

For a couple of years Saki became a foreign correspondent for the high Tory *Morning Post*—in the Balkans, Poland, Russia, and Paris. He maintained residences in London and in a cottage in nearby Surrey (run for him by his sister Ethel, who now assumed a dominant position in his life). He published his first work of fiction, the story collection *Reginald*, in 1904. Five more collections of stories, two novels, and three plays followed before Munro, a volunteer who had refused a commission, was killed in action by a sniper at Beaumont Hamel in France. His last words were: "Put that damned cigarette out!"

In the stories (more than a hundred) and the two novels, *The Unbearable Bassington* and *When William Comes* (a picture of the upper classes under an imagined Prussian boot, and his most mature book), Saki remarkably combines, as Geoffrey Grigson put it in his *Concise Encyclopedia*, "the conflict between the old and the new worlds, that of the Empire Builders and of an anticipation of the disillusioned 1920s. He is usually docketed with Wilde . . . and the young playwright Maugham, and so, via Firbank, with Evelyn Waugh. . . . the sense of apartness which in another generation turned Orwell to prodigies of bleak panache, drove Saki to bite the hands that fed him in clubs and country houses, but of course the bite was much enjoyed—and at last to remain by choice in the ranks [a reference to Munro's war service]."

The stories are full of coded references to homosexuality: Reginald compares himself with Ganymede (yet another cupbearer and beautiful boy of mythology), and takes an interest in boys of all kinds, including choirboys. Clovis Sangrail of *The Chronicles of Clovis* is similar, and is a frequenter, like his creator, of London baths. V. S. Pritchett wrote: "Saki writes like an enemy. Society has bored him to the point of murder. Our laughter is only a note or two short of a scream of fear." In this fiction a "clear soup is more important than a clear conscience," and prigs, snobs and others whom their creator not only remotely resembled, are made victims. However, in introducing the *Penguin Complete Saki*, Noel Coward (who had encountered some of the same problems that Saki had encountered) wrote: "Many writers who raise youthful minds to a high pitch of enthusiasm are liable, when re-read . . . to lose much of their original magic. Saki does not belong in this category . . . his fiction is dated only by the fact that it describes a society which vanished . . . the green carnations, long since withered, exuded in their day a special fragrance. . . ."

PRINCIPAL WORKS: *Collections*—The Works of Saki, 8 vols. 1926–27; The Complete Saki, 1976 (as The Penguin Complete Saki, 1982). *Selection*—Greene, G. (ed.) The Best of Saki, 1950. *Short stories*—Reginald, 1904; Reginald in Russia, 1910; The Chronicles of Clovis, 1912; Beasts and Super-Beasts, 1914; The Toys of Peace, 1919; The Square Egg and Other Sketches, and Three Plays, 1924; Langguth, A. J. Saki, 1981. *Novels*—The Unbearable Bassington, 1912; When William Came, 1914. *History*—The Rise of the Russian Empire, 1900. *Parodies*—The Westminster Alice, 1902.

ABOUT: Coward, N. in The Penguin Complete Saki, above; Greene, G. *in* The Best of Saki, 1950; Gillen, G. H. Saki, 1969; Grigson, G. The Concise Encyclopedia of World Literature, 1963; Langguth, A. J. Saki: A Life of Hector Hugh Munro, 1981; Munro, E. *in* The Square Egg, 1924; Pritchett, V. S. The Working Novelist, 1965; Spears, G. J. The Satire of Saki, 1963. *Periodicals*—Atlantic Monthly 166 1940; Bookman (London) 71, 1927; London Mercury 12 1925; Texas Quarterly 7 1964.

**SALINGER, J(EROME) D(AVID)** (January 1, 1919– ), American novelist and short story writer, wrote: "Born in New York City. Have lived in and around New York most of my life. Educated in Manhattan public schools, a military academy in Pennsylvania, three colleges (no degrees). A happy tourist's year in Europe when I was eighteen and nineteen. In the army from '42 to '46, two and a half years overseas (in Europe). I was with the Fourth Infantry Division, as a staff sergeant, through five campaigns, from D-Day to the end of the war. I'm now [1955] living in Westport, Connecticut.

"I've been writing since I was fifteen or so. Published my first story in 1940, when I was twenty-one, in *Story*.

"At the time, it seemed like a late start. My short stories have appeared in a number of magazines over the last ten years (*Harper's, Saturday Evening Post, Collier's, Esquire, Cosmopolitan, Story, Good Housekeeping, Mademoiselle*), mostly—and most happily—in the *New Yorker*.

"I'd like to say who my favorite fiction writers are, but I don't see how I can do it without saying why they are. So I won't.

"I'm aware that a number of my friends will be saddened, or shocked, or shocked-saddened, over some of the chapters in *The Catcher in the Rye*. Some of my best friends are children. In fact, all of my best friends are children. It's almost unbearable to me to realize that my book will be kept on a shelf out of their reach."

---

J. D. Salinger has lived in virtual seclusion in his home in a remote location near Cornish, New Hampshire since the 1960s. He remains a paradoxical figure: the author of a novel considered one of the classics of twentieth-century American literature, but a man whose iconoclastic withdrawal is, at best, seen as a "life-imitating-art" embodiment of the alienation he depicts in his later work.

Martin Seymour-Smith, in *Who's Who in Twentieth Century Literature*, called Salinger an "immensely popular American fiction writer whose work is based so precariously on the knife-edge between fluent sensibility and psychological superficiality that he has lapsed into near-silence." True to the comment in the autobiographical statement above, some of Salinger's only contacts with the outside world since his rise to prominence have been with young people: his last published interview was with a teenage-girl reporter for a local high-school newspaper in 1953.

In *The Catcher in the Rye*, a coming-of-age novel that remains Salinger's best-known work, he employs as narrator a New York would-be dropout named Holden Caulfield, a teenaged character introduced in an earlier short story. The novel was a huge popular and critical success, and Caulfield is still one of the most recognizable narrative voices in all of American fiction, an inhabitant of the pantheon with Natty Bumppo, Huck Finn, or Ishmael, as a prototype of a uniquely American sensibility. The novel shocked readers when it was written, although its scenes are considered tame by today's standards. It was perhaps the quintessential American novel of the immediate postwar period, of an America thrust suddenly onto the stage as a world power, in which a "teenage culture" first appeared as a class unto itself. The pressures and anxieties of young people growing up in the atomic age were personified by Holden Caulfield as by no other character in postwar fiction. This work, and its "Glass family saga" successors, have come under increasing fire from critics who argue that Salinger created little more than vapid, transparent characters who are so self-absorbed that they have little of lasting value to say—though Salinger may have wanted merely to reflect the culture's self-absorption.

Salinger was born in New York City on New Year's Day, 1919, the second child and only son of Sol Salinger, a cheese importer of Jewish heritage, and Miriam (Jillich) Salinger, of Scots heritage. The family was upwardly mobile and, by the early 1930s, was living on Park Avenue in Manhattan. As a teenager, Salinger was sent to Valley Forge Military Academy, which was fictionalized into Pencey Prep in *The Catcher in the Rye*. At Valley Forge, Salinger was an average student who contributed to the school's literary magazine and dramatic and glee clubs and wrote a school song that began "Hide not your tears on this last day/Your sorrow has no shame." He was remembered by another student for his somewhat pretentious mannerisms and a "sort of sardonic wit."

After graduation, he applied to New York University and in 1937 spent five months in Europe, which included a visit to the ancestral city of Bydgoszcz, Poland, and to Vienna, where he experienced Nazism at first hand. In the fall of 1938, he enrolled at Ursinus College, at which he wrote a

column in the school's weekly newspaper with a "cool, world-weary note," in the words of Ian Hamilton, his would-be biographer.

Salinger's first fiction was published in *Story* in 1940, then in the *Saturday Evening Post* and *Esquire*, at a time when all three magazines were renowned for publishing high-quality short fiction; the last story published under his name was "Hapworth 16, 1924" in *The New Yorker* in 1965. This quarter-century period was considered the heyday of the short story in American "middlebrow" magazines. There are, however, persistent rumors that he has published more recent works under carefully guarded pseudonyms.

During World War II, Salinger was drafted into the infantry and was involved in the invasion of Normandy and in counterintelligence operations; he saw serious combat and, according to Hamilton, was hospitalized for stress—an experience that undoubtedly informed his celebrated short story "For Esmé—With Love and Squalor," in which a fatigued American soldier is reinvigorated through his correspondence with a thirteen-year-old British girl he had met. In 1945 Salinger married a French woman named Sylvia, of whom little is known except that she may have been a physician or a psychologist. They were divorced the following year. In 1955, he married Claire Douglas, the daughter of the British art critic Robert Langton Douglas; they had two children and were divorced in 1967.

Some of the stories Salinger published in the *New Yorker* and *Collier's* immediately after the war became grist for the later novels, especially for *The Catcher in the Rye*. Salinger published seven stories in *The New Yorker* from 1946 to 1951. In one of them, "A Perfect Day for Bananafish" (1948), Seymour Glass was introduced. This character appears only in this one story—and commits suicide—but his presence dominates many of the author's later works known informally as the "Glass cycle." In these stories, members of the Glass family are portrayed dealing with relationships, crises of identity, and frustrated aspirations as they gather psychically around the spectre of the self-destructed Seymour. The last story in the cycle, *Hapworth 16, 1924*, is written in the form of a letter from summer camp, in which the seven-year-old Seymour weaves a precocious and erudite portrait of him and his younger brother, Buddy, who emerges as the narrator in several of the stories. Eudora Welty, wrote: "J. D. Salinger's writing is original, first rate, serious, and beautiful . . . they [the nine stories] are paradoxes. From the outside, they are often very funny; inside, they are about heartbreak, and convey it; they can do this because they are pure."

*The Catcher In the Rye*, the novel most identified with Salinger, was published in 1951 and immediately became a Book-of-the-Month Club selection (when the choice was made, Salinger is reputed to have said "That's good, is it?"). Even at this point, the author began to exhibit some of the reclusiveness that was to mark his later years. He tried to discourage publicity and even asked that his photograph not be used in connection with the book.

He did allow a trusted colleague, William Maxwell, to interview him for the *Book-of-the-Month Club News* in July 1951. In it, he was quoted as saying "I think writing is a hard life. But it's brought me enough happiness that I don't think I'd even deliberately dissuade anybody (if he had talent) from taking it up. The compensations are few, but when they come, if they come, they're very beautiful."

*The Catcher in the Rye* caused an immediate stir in the United States, and quickly secured a place on the *New York Times* best-seller list, but Salinger decided to escape the glare of the spotlight by escaping to Britain for a two-month trip. Reviews were mixed, though the *New Yorker* predictably offered a five-page paean by S. N. Behrman, and the *New York Times* called it "an unusually brilliant first novel." The *Catholic World*, also predictably, found fault with its "excessive use of amateur swearing and coarse language" (a sentiment echoed in the *New York Herald Tribune Book Review*). But, on the whole, most critics believed that a landmark novel of sorts had been written—perhaps one that would be a benchmark for writing by and about a new postwar generation.

The novel takes its title from Holden Caulfield's misquote of a line by Robert Burns, in which he sees himself as a "catcher in the rye" who must keep the world's children from falling off "some crazy cliff," variously interpreted as a metaphor for the perils of adulthood in an anxiety-ridden world. The novel follows young Holden Caulfield in a picaresque ramble around the streets of Manhattan during his Christmas break. The young narrator is on the verge of dropping out—or flunking out—of Pencey Prep, and he sees his odyssey as an affirmation of youthful integrity against the phoniness of the adult world, a cry that would resonate throughout America's schools and universities a decade later. This Rousseauian affirmation of a young person's sensibility immediately resonated with adolescent readers of all ages, who made *Catcher* required reading as a "rite-of-passage" Baedeker for their own journeys—a book all the more alluring because it was banned by so many squeamish school districts, and still is.

The novel's notoriety increased during the 1950s, as Salinger published other stories in the Glass family saga in the *New Yorker*, culminating with the Kennedy-era publication of *Franny and Zooey* and *Raise High the Roof Beam, Carpenters* and *Seymour: An Introduction*, a single-volume compilation of two of the stories in the Glass cycle. Critics are fond of pointing out the symbolic references in Salinger's nomenclature—"Glass" implying transparency, "Seymour" implying insight ("See More"), and Zooey implying both life and animalistic chaos. Others stress Caulfield's and the Glasses' quest for spiritual meaning, noting that Salinger's works are kind of prose echoes of the Beat poets' fascination with Zen Buddhism and eastern forms of mysticism—an especially ironic symbolism given that it flies in the face of 1950s American conformity.

At the time, Salinger's works were immensely popular, and his new works were awaited with eagerness. Critic Alfred Kazin wrote in the *Atlantic* after the publication of *Franny and Zooey*: "This book's final episode, both in the cuteness of its invention and in the cuteness of speech . . . helps us to understand Salinger's wide popularity. I am sorry to have to use the word 'cute' . . . but there is absolutely no other word that for me so accurately typifies the self-conscious charm and prankishness of his own writing and his extraordinary cherishing of his favorite Glass characters. . . . "

Although Salinger's name became a "household word" in America during the 1950s and 1960s, Salinger the man became more and more reclusive—and occasionally litigious—emerging from his hermitage only to snipe at publishers he thought were trying to appropriate his work. In 1974, he condemned the unauthorized publication of the two-volume *Complete Uncollected Short Stories of J. D. Salinger*. In 1986, he got an injunction against Random House's publication of an unauthorized biography of him by Ian Hamilton, a critic for the London *Sunday Times*. Salinger especially took issue with the book's extensive quoting of personal letters, which he and his lawyers felt went beyond the "fair use" doctrine. Random House was forced by controversial court decisions to ask Hamilton to rewrite the book without quoting from the letters.

In the rewritten version, published as *In Search of J. D. Salinger*, Hamilton expressed Salinger's self-concealment in these words: "He didn't want there to be a record" and "he was passionate in his contempt for the whole business of 'literary biography.'" But Hamilton also admits that "he was, in any real-life sense, invisible, as good as dead, and yet for many he still held an active mythic force. He was famous for not wanting to be famous."

Not all critics agreed with Hamilton's attempts to smoke Salinger out, however. Mordecai Richler, in a *New York Times Book Review* piece (June 5, 1988), called *In Search of J. D. Salinger* a "vengeful" book and scored Hamilton's use of the "royal we" and his referrals to himself in the third person. The article also shed some light on Salinger's reclusive habits: It quoted a neighbor in Cornish who reported that Salinger rose at five or six each morning, walked "down the hill to his studio, a tiny concrete shelter with a translucent plastic roof" to spend fifteen or sixteen hours a day at his typewriter or watching movies.

Salinger's seclusion was further interrupted in the fall of 1992 when a fire broke out at his Cornish hermitage, destroying his "fastidiously preserved seclusion," reported the *New York Times*, which commented how Salinger and his third wife Colleen scurried away like "fleet chipmunks" when reporters approached. If Salinger has adopted a literary credo for the last three decades of his life, it is perhaps to be found in a statement he made to Lacey Fosburgh, a *New York Times* correspondent, upon the unauthorized 1974 publication of his *Complete Uncollected Short Stories*: "There is a marvelous peace in not publishing. Publishing is a terrible invasion of my privacy. I like to write. I love to write. But I write just for myself and my own pleasure."

PRINCIPAL WORKS: The autobiographical material quoted above was written for Twentieth Century Authors First Supplement, 1955. *Novels*—The Catcher in the Rye, 1951; Franny and Zooey, 1961; Raise High the Roof Beam, Carpenters and Seymour: An Introduction, 1963. *Short stories*—Nine Stories (in U.K.: For Esmé—with Love and Squalor, and Other Stories) 1953; The Complete Uncollected Short Stories of J. D. Salinger, 1974.

ABOUT: The autobiographical material quoted above was written Twentieth Century Authors First Supplement, 1955. Bloom, H. (ed.), J. D. Salinger: Modern Critical Views, 1987; Grunwald, H. A. (ed.), Salinger: A Critical and Personal Portrait, 1962; Gwynn, F. L. and Blotner, J. L. The Fiction of J. D. Salinger; Hamilton, I. In Search of J. D. Salinger, 1988; Lundquist, J. J. D. Salinger, 1979; Seymour-Smith, M. Guide to Modern World Literature, 1986; Who's Who in Twentieth Century Literature, 1976. *Bibliography*—Beebe, M. and Sperry, J. Criticism of J. D. Salinger: A Selected Checklist, 1966; Sublette, J. R., J. D. Salinger: An Annotated Bibliography 1938–1981, 1984. *Periodicals*—Antioch Review, Fall 1986; Atlantic Monthly August 1961; Esquire December 1981; Newsweek May 30, 1960; November 18, 1974; July 30, 1979; New York Herald Tribune Book Review August 19, 1951; New York Review of Books October 27, 1988; New York Times, October 23, 1992; New York Times Book Review February 25, 1962, November 1, 1987; June 5, 1988; Publishers Weekly February 26, 1988; Saturday Review of Literature July 14, 1951; February 16, 1952; November-December 1985.

## SALMINEN, SALLY

**SALMINEN, SALLY** (April 25, 1906–July 18, 1976), Finnish novelist who wrote in Swedish, wrote: "Born in Wardo in the Aaland Islands, belonging to the Republic of Finland. [Most of the Aaland Islanders are of Swedish descent, and her mother was Swedish by birth.] My father was a postman and real-estate broker, who was killed when I was seven years old. I was educated in the general people's schools, and by correspondence

courses [in writing and literature]. At sixteen I started to work in a real-estate office. Soon after I went to Sweden and worked in a store. From 1928 to 1930 I worked in a co-operative store in Marienamn, in Aaland. In 1930 I emigrated to the United States. I worked as a 'general houseworker' until 1936. Then with my novel *Katrina*, which I wrote while I was working, I won the first prize in a prize novel contest offered by a publisher in Stockholm and Helsingfors [Helsinki]. In 1936 I returned to Finland. In 1940 I married the artist (painter) Johannes Dührkop, and became a Danish citizen. Now I live in Copenhagen. Swedish is my mother tongue and I always write in that language."

She added: "There is hardly anything to add [to the 1942 profile], as no other books have been translated into English. Perhaps it would be of interest to mention that after the war, from 1946 until 1951, S. S. has, at short intervals, mostly lived in France. A novel, which is going to have the title 'Prins Efflam' and is laid in a fishing village in Brittany, is at this time (January 1953) under preparation and will during this year appear in four of the Scandanavian languages."

The novel *Katrina* was translated into some ten languages. Yet Sally Salminen has not been considered by the critics of Finno-Swedish literature to be a writer of particular literary significance. Such modernist contemporaries of hers as Rabbe Enckell (1903–1974) and Henry Parland (1908–1930) are more important, and the novels of Tito Colliander (1904) received far more critical attention. Yet *Katrina* was its decade's great success—both in Finland and internationally—and made Salminen's name far better known that that of such contemporaries. The playwright Harold Brighouse, reviewing it in the *Manchester Guardian*, wrote: "The book is written with detachment; dispassionately it narrates how Katrina lived and makes no comment. When Miss Salminen wrote [it] she was working as kitchen-maid in the house of an American millionaire. And *Katrina* is unembittered."

The eponymous *Katrina* is a young Finnish girl who leaves her home, a cosy farm, to marry a vainglorious sailor from Aaland. He takes her to a bleak cabin on a rock and goes off to join his ship, leaving her to do domestic work for the rich landowners of the region. Katrina resigns herself to her lot, raises children, and even forms a tolerance for her empty and selfish husband. The *New Republic* reviewer thought that the characters possessed "absolute genuineness"; and the *Times Literary Supplement* thought the book "much more than an interesting story. . . . It has, too, at times the distinction of real poetic intensity of phrase."

Salminen went on to become a prolific writer; there was one untranslated novel before *Mariana* (1940), which was immediately put into English. This, like *Katrina* and many other of Salminen's novels, was set in the Aaland Islands. It is a *bildungsroman*, i.e., novel of growth, depicting the coming to maturity of a woman, Mariana Nilsson, in the second decade of the century. *Commonweal* thought it uneven: capable of sharp insight but also of being as "banal as one of the woman's magazines."

*Prins Efflam* (1953) appeared in English in the year following its publication in Swedish, as *The Prince from the Sea*. This is part of a cycle of novels dealing with Brittany, and was of most interest, outside Scandinavia, to French readers. Two more novels by Salminen appeared in French, but no more were translated into English. She continued to write with some success in Scandinavia (publishing sometimes in Copenhagen, but usually in Helsinki), and in 1968 brought out her reminiscences of America: *Min amerikanska saga*. She also published a book (1971) about her travels in Israel. Her two final books, the last appearing two years before her death, were also autobiographical.

PRINCIPAL WORKS IN ENGLISH TRANSLATION: Katrina (tr. N. Walford) 1937; Mariana (tr. B. Mussey) 1940; A Prince from the Sea (tr. E. Ramsden) 1954.

ABOUT: The autobiographical matterial quoted above was written for Twentieth Century Authors, 1942 and Twentieth Century Authors First Supplement, 1955. Columbia Dictionary of Modern European Literature, 1980. *Periodicals*— Commonweal May 24, 1940; Manchester Guardian September 28, 1937; New Republic October 20, 1937; Times Literary Supplement November 20, 1937.

**"SALTEN, FELIX"** (pseudonym of SIEG-FRIED SALZMANN) (September 6, 1869–October 8, 1945), Austrian journalist, novelist, and  writer of animal stories, wrote: "My parents were very poor, hence I had to cut short my studies. I have spent my whole life in Vienna, where my parents moved from Budapest when I was three weeks old. I am self-taught, and have written since my seventeenth year. Since I was eighteen years old I have been busily engaged as a journalist. My knowledge, which is fairly complex, I have considerably enlarged on the historical side. For the rest, I am an observer, and have no head for philosophy. Maupassant, and later Gottfried Keller, had the greatest influence on my literary development. My activity as a publicist, which speedily became very great, also accustomed me to concentrated work. Very early I formed friendships with Hugo von Hofmannsthal, Arthur Schnitzler, and Hermann Bahr. Later I came in touch with George Courteline, still later with John Galsworthy. I have traveled in England, France, Italy, Egypt, and Palestine, and spent three months in the United States as the beneficiary of a Carnegie endowment. Since then I have loved America and the Americans, and have known the role of leadership to which in the future this people will be called.

"I was honorary president of the Vienna P.E.N. Club, was an honorary citizen of the city of Vienna, and in March of 1939 left forever the unhappy Fatherland, which once was dear to me. As interesting episodes of my life, I may mention the friendship which bound me to the Archdukes of Tuscany, and further, the freeing of Princess Louise of Coburg from the insane asylum and the rehabilitation of her lover, Geza von Mattatich. In New York I was greatly impressed by President Butler of Columbia University, and in Detroit by Henry Ford. Besides this I must mention the friendship which I have enjoyed from the beginning with Max Reinhardt, whom for decades I have placed in the ranks of the leading critics.

"As for my works, which include a great many volumes, I name here my book on Palestine, *Neue Menschen auf alter Erde* [*New Men on the Old Earth*], and the book on my journey through the United States, *Fünf Minuten Amerika* [*Five Minutes of America*]. With books in the field of belles lettres I have had varying success: *Bambi* was a best-seller in America. My books have been translated into many languages, *Bambi* even into Hebrew and Chinese."

---

Best know by the pseudonym he used for his children's books, Salten also wrote—mainly journalism—as Martin Finder. A contemporary of Arthur Schnitzler, and a personal friend of Theodor Herzl (also born in Budapest, but then living in Austria),

Salten became one of the central figures of fin de siècle Vienna, succeeding Herzl as drama critic and feuilleton editor on the *Neue freie Presse*.

He grew in authority and reputation following publication, in 1902, of an impressive obituary of Emile Zola. After this, his critical opinions—though now seen as fairly conventional—were considered influential. For many years Salten wrote adult novels and plays, none of which gained any following outside Austria, although a translation of a one-act play, *Moral Courage (The Gravity of Life)*, did appear in an anthology of 1928. In view of the fact that Salten is the reputed author of *Jozephine Mutzenbacher (Oh! Oh! Josephine)*, an infamous "pornographic" novel (it now reads tamely) of the period (1906), it is ironic that the book which eventually earned him a world-wide reputation was a children's story.

*Bambi: Eine Lebensgeschichte aus dem Walde* (1922), first published in English translation in 1928, tells the story of a young deer growing up in a German forest. The increasing awareness of harshness in the environment as Bambi becomes older and more experienced, and the cruel intrusion of the human presence, clearly have an allegorical layer of meaning that touches on Salten's personal experience. The book was turned into a Walt Disney cartoon in 1942, since which time Salten's name has been associated with the rather over-whimsical interpretation given to his book. He did collaborate on the adaptation, while living in Switzerland, in exile from the Nazis, but the characterization of the deer is much more detailed and realistic in the novel than it is in the film. The story continues to capture young people's imaginations and is effective as anti-hunting propaganda.

Salten applied a similar theme to a story about rabbits, *Funfzehn Hasen: Schicksale in Wald und Feld* (1930, *Fifteen Rabbits*), in which Hops and Plana, the two central rabbits, are followed through the seasons of the year. Bambi made a brief reappearance in this book, but there was also the full-length sequel *Bambis Kinder* (1939). In these, and other narratives about specific animals (he wrote about a horse called "Florian," a squirrel called "Perri" and a dog called "Renni") Salten won the sympathy of the reader through the power of storytelling, while the analogies between animal and human life became ever more explicit. *Freunde aus Aller Welt: Roman eines Zoologischen Gartens (The City Jungle)*, a protest about the captivity of animals, was open propaganda, and some of the later animal stories stood too self-consciously as fables to appeal directly to children.

Salten died in Zurich in 1945. He had traveled widely, particularly in Europe and Palestine, and, spent three months in America courtesy of a Carnegie grant. His travel book about the States, *Fünf minuten Amerika* (1931), has not been translated.

PRINCIPAL WORKS IN ENGLISH TRANSLATION: *Fiction*—Bambi (tr. W. Chambers) 1928; Fifteen Rabbits (tr. W. Chambers) 1930; The Hound of Florence (tr. H. Paterson) 1930; Samson and Delilah (tr. W. Chambers) 1931; The City Jungle (tr. W. Chambers) 1932; Florian: An Emperor's Horse (tr. N. Gullick) 1934; Perri (tr. B. Mussey) 1938; Bambi's Children (tr. B. Fles)

1939; Renni the Rescuer (tr. K. C. Kaufman) 1940; A Forest World (trs. P. R. Milton and S. J. Greenburger) 1942; Good Comrades (tr. P. R. Milton) 1942; Little World Apart, 1947; Jibby the Cat (tr. R. Levin) 1948; Oh! Oh! Josephine, 2 vols., 1973; Prisoner Thirty-three: A Fantasy of Today (tr. H. Nagel). *Drama*—Moral Courage *in* Shay, F. (ed.) Fifty More Contemporary One-Act Plays, 1928.

ABOUT: Abbramson G. (ed.) Blackwell Companion to Jewish Culture, 1989; Columbia Dictionary of Modern European Literature, 1947; Contemporary Authors Vol. 108, 1983; Vol. 137, 1922; Doyle B. (ed.) Who's Who of Children's Literature 1968; Fischer, M. Who's Who in Children's Books, 1975; Garland H. and M. Oxford Companion to German Literature, 1986; Segel, H. B. (ed.) The Vienna Coffeehouse Wits, 1993. *Periodicals*—Natural History June. 1993; New York Times October 9, 1945; Times (London) October 10, 1945.

**SALTER, (JAMES) ARTHUR** (March 15, 1881–June 27, 1975), English civil servant, economist, academic, and politician, was born in Oxford,  the eldest of four sons of James Edward Salter, a prominent Oxford boat builder and politician, and Julia Maria (Millin) Salter. He was educated at Oxford City High School and Brasenose College, Oxford, where he took a degree in classics (1903). He entered the British Civil Service in 1904, and spent his first seven years in the Transport Department of the Admiralty. In 1911 he was transferred to a staff assigned to implement the national health insurance plan introduced by Lloyd George; in 1913 he was promoted to Assistant Secretary of the British National Insurance Commission. In the years that followed, Salter held so many high-level government posts that he was dubbed "the civil servant par excellence."

Salter was recalled to the Admiralty (later known as the Ministry of Shipping) during World War I. As Assistant Director of Transports (1915) and Director of Ship Requisitioning (1917), he introduced innovative methods of allocating Britain's overburdened merchant fleets. In the latter part of the war, he helped set up the Allied Maritime Transport Council and served as chairman of the Allied Maritime Transport Executive. His World War I experiences provided the material for *Allied Shipping Control*, a monograph published under the auspices of the Carnegie Endowment for International Peace.

In 1919 he dealt with reparations and refugees as a secretary of the Supreme Economic Council in Paris. When the League of Nations was formed, Salter was chosen to head the Economic and Financial Section of the secretariat, a post he held in Geneva in 1919 and 1920, and again from 1922 to 1931. From 1920 to 1922, he was General-Secretary of the Reparations Committee. Salter came to prominence as an author after leaving the League of Nations. *Recovery: The Second Effort*, which analyzes the worldwide economic crisis of the 1920s in language accessible to the layman, was praised by critics on both sides of the Atlantic. "No one is

better qualified than Sir Arthur Salter to diagnose the causes of the world's economic disease and to prescribe remedies, and he has fulfilled this most important task with consummate skill," the *Spectator* commented. Walter Lippmann, one of the book's most enthusiastic American reviewers, remarked in the *New York Herald Tribune*, "The special quality of this book is its perspective and proportion . . . I think that nothing dealing with the world crisis has yet been written which so nearly represents the consensus of informed opinion throughout the world." His next book, *The Framework of an Ordered Society*, based on a series of lectures he delivered at Cambridge University in 1933, argues in favor of government intervention in the economic sphere. *The United States of Europe* consists of a collection of papers devoted to such issues as regional confederations, economic sanctions, and the relation of the United States to the League of Nations. For ten years beginning in 1934, Salter was the Gladstone Professor of Political Theory and Institutions at Oxford University. In 1937 he won the seat as an Independent member of Parliament representing Oxford University. He held that seat in Parliament until 1950, when the university's franchise was abolished.

*Security: Can We Retrieve It?*, published on the eve of World War II, is an examination of British national security in which Salter decried Great Britain's lack of military preparedness. In the early stages of World War II, he served as Parliamentary Secretary to the Ministry of Shipping, and from 1941 to 1943 was head of the British Merchant Shipping Mission in Washington, D.C. Just as he had done during World War I, he persuaded American officials to undertake a large-scale shipbuilding program. In Washington he was assisted by his American-born wife, Ethel Mather Bullard, whom he had married in 1940.

From 1951 to 1953, Salter represented Ormskirk in Parliament as a Conservative. During that same period, he served as a very junior minister in Winston Churchill's government. In 1953 he was awarded a peerage, becoming the first Baron of Kidlington. In *Memoirs of a Public Servant*, he provides a detailed account of his life and career up through the middle 1950s. His last book, *Slave of the Lamp*, which he called "a personal narrative, but not an autobiography," mingles anecdote, character sketches of various world leaders, and reflections on the British Civil Service, the League of Nations, and other institutions in which Salter served.

Knighted in 1922 and elevated to Knight Grand Cross of the Order of the British Empire in 1944, Salter was also honored by the governments of France, Italy, Belgium, and China.

PRINCIPAL WORKS: *International affairs and economics*—Allied Shipping Control: An Experiment in International Administration, 1921; A Scheme for an Economic Advisory Organisation in India, 1931; Recovery: The Second Effort, 1932, rev. ed. 1933; The Framework of an Ordered Society, 1933; Modern Mechanization and Its Effects on the Structure of Society, 1933; The United States of Europe, and Other Papers (ed. W. Arnold Forster)1933; China and the Depression: Impressions of a Three Months Visit, 1934 (reissued in condensed form as

China and Silver, 1934); World Trade and Its Future, 1936; Security: Can We Retrieve It? 1939. *Biography*—Personality and Politics: Studies of Contemporary Statesmen, 1947. *Memoirs*—Memoirs of a Public Servant, 1961; Slave of the Lamp: A Public Servant's Notebook, 1967.

ABOUT: Current Biography 1944; Dictionary of National Biography, 1971–1980, 1986; Who's Who 1975. *Periodicals*—New York Herald Tribune April 7, 1932; Saturday Review of Literature July 31, 1948; Spectator April 9, 1932; Times (London) June 30, 1975.

## SALTUS, EDGAR (EVERTSON) (October 8, 1855–July 31, 1921), American novelist and essayist, was born in New York City, the son of Francis

Henry and Eliza Howe (Evertson) Saltus. "The circumstances of Edgar Saltus's emergence," as Eric L. McKitrick wrote in the *New York Review of Books*, "were those incident to upper-class New York life: old Dutch origins; St. Paul's, Yale, Columbia Law, and a *wanderjahr* at Heidelberg in the Seventies; a Grace Church wedding in 1883 to the daughter of a Morgan partner, all of which should have meant certain 'advantages,' and doubtless did."

While very much a product of his time and milieu, Saltus spent a lifetime rebelling against it, although with more self-conscious dilettantism than emotional robustness. He entered Yale in 1872, but never graduated; he received an L.L.B. from Columbia in 1880, but never practiced law. His marriage to Helen Sturgis Read in 1883, a society event, led to an acrimonious divorce eight years later, and caused a public scandal. Saltus's rebellion took the form of an exaggerated hedonism, to which he came early in life, and from which (not excepting the theosophy to which his third and last wife Marie Giles, converted him) he never seriously deviated. Nor was he, in any real sense, a very serious man. In his person Saltus played, influenced by his reading of Baudelaire, the part of the dandy. His literary career exemplified his dictum that "in literature only three things count: style, style polished, style repolished."

Saltus's first book was a biography of Balzac, which, "being utterly detestable," as he wrote, "was widely praised." It was followed by "the gloomiest and worst book ever published," *The Philosophy of Disenchantment*, an enthusiastic exposition of the pessimism of Schopenhauer and of its popularization by von Hartmann, which, despite his own disclaimer, was described by Clair Sprague as "an energetic, vivacious presentation of a melancholy, apparently resigned doctrine . . . Saltus's most effective expositional work." "Out of sheer laziness," Saltus then produced "a history of atheism, *The Anatomy of Negation*, which has been honoured by international dislike." In fact, *The Anatomy of Negation* was one of Saltus's few well praised works, notwithstanding its prefatory proviso, "To avoid misconception, it may be added that no attempt has

been made to prove anything." Carl Van Vechten, a connoiseur of the neurasthenic, considered *The Anatomy of Negation* "Saltus's masterpiece in his early manner. . . . Never was any book, so full of erudition and ideas, written by a true sceptic, so easy to read." This was a characteristically ironic exaggeration.

In 1887, three years after publishing *Balzac*, Saltus brought out *Mr. Incoul's Misadventure*, the first and perhaps best of his sixteen novels. In *Tulane Studies in English* Morse Peckham called this story of an adulterous liaison ending in murder and suicide "a fairly successful effort to present that inherent human viciousness which justifies pessimism and negation. For it is a story of how a proud American aristocrat revenges himself upon his wife and her lover, and is both undetected and unpunished." Like many other critics, Peckham preferred Saltus's nonfiction to his fiction ("His novels, together with his extremely voluminous journalistic essays, are . . . a commercialization of both his style and his philosophy, a condition that necessarily softened the latter"), but it is generally agreed that his earlier novels had a fin-de-siècle piquancy. His later works of fiction, according to Harry Levin, "are spun out increasingly thin. Their mounting reliance on artifice and sensation, on perfumes and poisons, on bejewelled luxury and operatic vice, points directly to the detective story."

The culminating work of Saltus's early period—which is to say, of his career, for as his popularity declined after 1900 he could only repeat himself with less conviction—was *Imperial Purple*, a half-admiring study of decadence in the Roman Empire. Even H. L. Mencken, who considered Saltus's "books of 'philosophy' . . . feeble and superficial, his novels . . . facile improvisations, full of satanic melodrama and wooden marionettes," exempted *Imperial Purple* from his general condemnation: "A certain fine glow is still in it; it has gusto if not profundity; Saltus's worst faults do not damage it appreciably. . . . *Imperial Purple* remains Saltus's best book. It remains also, alas, his only good one."

Although Saltus continued to write fairly prolifically into the new century, his literary moment had passed, and he died almost forgotten. A brief Saltus revival, led by Carl Van Vechten and, from Great Britain, Arthur Symons, occurred in the 1920s and all his works were reprinted by AMS in the 1960s; but he remains of interest far less for what he accomplished than for what he tried to be. "The values of the culture in which he functioned were specious and he knew it," wrote Eric L. McKitrick in the *New York Review of Books*, "but the fashioning of an alternative sensibility . . . was a task to which neither his resources nor his fortitude was equal."

However, this enigmatic figure is still occasionally being appraised in the current revival of interest in American literary decadence of the early 1900s. Edward Lutz's 1991 book, *American Nervousness*, which—with other similar publications—examined the prevalence of the neurasthenic temperament in turn-of-the-century America, devoted a chapter to analysis of "Hamlin Garland's Despair and Edgar

Saltus's Disenchantment." Lutz chose the two figures to show how neurasthenia could affect the genteel Garland as well as Saltus, "a celebrated debauchee who wrote irony- and absinthe-soaked stories of terror, corruption, and paranoia."

Lutz's analysis is helpful in understanding how Saltus envisioned the role of the novel as self-therapy rather than mere entertainment. "His work has been called a 'comic supplement to Veblen's *Theory of the Leisure Class*,'" writes Lutz, "and we could say that in its ironic supplementarity to Veblen's ironic text, Saltus managed to produce the negation of a negation, an invalid notion of invalid leisure. Or we could say that he sounds like an ironic, neurasthenically inverted Descartes when he declares, in *The Philosophy of Disenchantment*: 'I am, therefore I suffer.' In that phrase, with all its self-pity and all its ironic undercutting of self-pity, neurasthenia had found one of its most succinct expressions." Saltus was buried in Sleepy Hollow cemetery, Tarrytown, New York, in the same plot with Mrs. Saltus's dog Toto.

Most of Saltus's papers are in the Collection of American Literature at Yale University.

PRINCIPAL WORKS: *Novels*—Mr Incoul's Misadventure, 1887; The Truth about Tristrem Varick, 1888; Eden: An Episode, 1888; A Transaction in Hearts: An Episode, 1889; A Pace That Kills: A Chronicle, 1889; Mary Magdalen: A Chronicle, 1891 (in U.K.: Mary of Magdala); The Facts in the Curious Case of H. Hyrtl, Esq., 1892; Madam Sapphira, 1893; Enthralled: A Story of International Life, 1894; When Dreams Come True: A Story of Emotional Life, 1894; The Perfume of Eros: A Fifth Avenue Incident, 1905; Vanity Square: A Story of Fifth Avenue Life, 1906; Daughters of the Rich, 1909; the Monster, 1912; The Paliser Case, 1919; The Ghost Girls, 1922. *Short stories*—A Transient Guest and Other Episodes, 1889; Purple and Fine Women, 1902. *History, philosophy, and essays*—Balzac, 1884; The Philosophy of Disenchantment, 1885; The Anatomy of Negation, 1886; Love and Lore, 1890; Imperial Purple, 1892; The Pomps of Satan, 1904; Historia Amoris: A History of Love, Ancient and Modern, 1906; The Lords of the Ghostland: A History of the Ideal, 1907; Oscar Wilde: An Idler's Impression, 1917; The Imperial Orgy: An Account of the Tsars from the First to the Last, 1920; The Uplands of Dream (ed. C. Honce) 1925. *Poetry*—(with M. Saltus) Poppies and Mandragora, 1926. *As compiler*—The Lovers of the World, 3 vols., 189–?

ABOUT: Dictionary of American Biography, Vol. 8, 1935; Levin, H. Grounds for Comparison, 1972; Lutz, E. American Nervousness, 1991; Mencken, H. L. Prejudices, Fifth Series, 1926; Saltus, M. Edgar Saltus, the Man, 1925; Sprague, C. Edgar Saltus, 1968; Twentieth Century American Literature, vol. 6 (ed. H. Bloom) 1987; Twentieth Century Literary Criticism vol. 8, 1982; Van Vechten, C. The Merry-Go-Round, 1918. *Periodicals*—American Quarterly Spring 1951; New York Review of Books November 5, 1970; Tulane Studies in English 1978.

**\*SALVEMINI, GAETANO** (September 8, 1873–September 6, 1957), Italian-born American historian, educator, and biographer, was born in Molfetta in Puglia province, southern Italy. He was educated in church schools until the age of seventeen. He completed his doctorate at the University of Florence in 1894 and became a teacher. He taught in the gymnasium at Palermo (1895–1896) and in the lyceums of Faenza (1896–1898), Lodi (1898–1900), and Florence (1900–1901). In 1901 he became professor of medieval and modern history at the University of Messina and remained in that

*sahl vay MEE nee

position until 1908. He lost his wife and four children in the Messina earthquake (1901). In 1910–1916 he taught at the University of Pisa, and in the latter year he became professor of modern history at the University of Florence. He held this position until resigning under pressure from Italy's fascist government in 1925. Escaping into France without a passport, he made his way to England and thence to the United States, where he became a visiting professor at Harvard (1930–1931) and at Yale (1931–1932). In 1933 he became Lauro de Bossis lecturer at Harvard in the history of Italian civilization. He continued to teach at Harvard until 1948, becoming a naturalized United States citizen in 1940.

Interest in Salvemini's writings has been stimulated by his life-long resistance to fascism and by his insistence that the study of history should elucidate observable political relationships and not be limited to the purely academic. One Italian critic, Giuseppe Prezzolini, commenting on Salvemini's early work in *Rassegna italo-britannica*, said: "He feels led to relate the history of class conflicts in the middle ages because he takes part in the class conflict of the modern age." A socialist who was fully aware of the neglect the south suffered under the union of Italy, Salvemini led the constitutional fight of Puglian peasants against the union of great landholders and government forces, and was their parliamentary candidate in 1911—losing only through the corruption of his opponents. He founded, and for many years edited, the small but influential weekly *L'Unita*. In 1919 he was elected to the Italian parliament as an independent. There he fought against both nationalism and emergent fascism until 1921, when he left parliament to pursue his efforts through teaching.

Salvemini expanded his political and intellectual associations, working in Italy with such active anti-fascists as Emilio Lusso, cofounder of the periodical *Giustizia e Libertà*, Carlo Rosselli and Nello Tarchiani.

In 1925, on being arrested by Mussolini's regime and forced to resign his academic position in Florence, Salvemini composed a letter of resignation to the rector of the university. In his letter he asserted that teaching "loses all its independence and, therefore, all its dignity. It must, therefore, cease to be the instrument of a free education in the life of the citizen and abase itself to servile adulation of the dominant party, or it must become a dry exercise in erudition, alien to the conscience both of master and pupil. . . . I shall return to serve my country in the university when we have regained a government worthy of a civilized country."

In exile Salvemini became a leading figure in providing detailed factual analysis of the society, economy, and politics of fascist Italy. In *What to Do with Italy* he wrote: "The accomplishments of a regime must, after all, be measured not by palaces, stadiums, roads, and military barracks thrown up in a few years by the reckless spending of the people's resources. They are rather to be judged by the result obtained in improving the political, economic, social, and cultural life of a nation."

Contemporary critics noted the thoroughness of his scholarship and the strength of his feelings. A *New York Times* reviewer held that his *Fascist Dictatorship in Italy* "is designed to demolish the moral basis of Mussolini's power. It succeeds. At its conclusion Fascismo stands stripped of all its justification." The review concludes, however, "so edged with hatred is this volume that in content it is somewhat confusing." C. G. Bowers in the *New York World* described the same work as "vivid and damning," while H. R. Spencer in the *Yale Review* said of *Under the Axe of Fascism*: "His statistical facts are inexorable and conclusive." The *Christian Science Monitor* reviewer accepted his polemical style: "Mr. Salvemini is a man of profound antifascist feeling. But his occasional passages of satire seem to emerge quite naturally out of the scholarly text."

While advocating the confiscation of large properties and the nationalization of monopolistic industrial concerns, Salvemini also supported a government by a freely elected parliament and the private ownership of small businesses. He condemned communism as strongly as he did fascism: "The great majority in the country has no desire to fall from the frying pan of the dictatorship of the fascist minority into the fire of the dictatorship of a communist minority."

Even after he became a United States citizen, Salvemini could not abandon his poltical commitment to Italy, and he continued to comment on developments there, writing, for example, in *What to Do with Italy*, "What the British Foreign Office and the American State Department want to set up in Italy is a fascist regime without Mussolini in place of the fascist regime with Mussolini." Salvemini's influence remained considerable in Italy. After Mussolini's downfall, the initial program of the Action party, published in 1943, was quite closely patterned on Salvemini's precepts, He finally retired to Italy in 1954.

PRINCIPAL WORKS IN ENGLISH AND ENGLISH TRANSLATION: The Fascist Dictatorship in Italy, 1927; Under the Axe of Fascism, 1936; (with George La Piana) What to Do with Italy, 1943; The French Revolution (tr. I. M. Rawson) 1954; Mazzini (tr. I. M. Rawson) 1957.

ABOUT: Origo, I. A Need to Testify, 1984. *Periodicals*—Encounter April 1978; Journal of Modern History December 1989; New Statesman February 1985; Rassegna italobritannica 7 1918; Times Literary Supplement April 20, 1984.

## SALZMANN, SIEGFRIED. See SALTEN, FELIX

## SAMPSON, GEORGE (April 6, 1873–February 1, 1950), English educator, editor, and literary historian, was born at Greenwich, London. A distinguished man of letters of his time, he is now chiefly remembered for his successful rewriting and condensing of the fourteen-volume *Cambridge History of English Literature* into the single volume, *The Concise Cambridge History* (1941). This is not an original work, nor was Sampson an original critic; but he was a sound and therefore a very useful historian, who provided generations of students with just what they needed, a scholarly but readable introduction to English literature.

His early life had been difficult. He was the youngest child of a sailor, Thomas Sampson, and his wife Sarah Ann (Hows). Ill health (from which he was never free) prevented his getting to school until he was ten; but by the time he reached school he was already an omnivorous reader. He was eventually trained as an elementary schoolteacher, became a headmaster (1910) and (1925) an inspector of schools. Before that Cambridge had recognized his worth by conferring upon him an honorary M. A. degree.

He wrote or compiled many books, most of them editions of such writers as Coleridge and Keats. He was interested in music and the theater, and wrote pungently on Mendelssohn, Bach, Henry Irving, and scores of others. He exerted an influence on education in England with his *English for the English* (1921), justly described by S. C. Roberts, in the *Dictionary of National Biography*, as "a tract for the times" which became a "minor classic." Here Sampson argued that "a sound educational system must be based upon the great means of human intercourse—human speech and written word."

Sampson was commissioned to write the concise version of the *Cambridge History* in 1921, but bad health prevented his completing it until 1941. Then it was hailed as a tour de force, the greatest tribute to it coming, perhaps, from Lionel Trilling, reviewing it in the *Nation*: "It is not a great history, it has no shaping critical idea . . . but then neither has it any philosophical solemnity . . . It is fresh, lively, frequently witty." The *Times Literary Supplement* said that while it "preserved all the marrow of the original," Sampson had "given it the stamp of his own powerful mind and decisive temper."

Sampson married Grace (Alldis) in 1907. He was a convivial clubman, and became friendly with such writers as Arnold Bennett and H. G. Wells. His later years in retirement at Hove (in Sussex), wrote his friend S. C. Roberts, "were darkened by persistent insomnia."

PRINCIPAL WORKS: As editor—The Works of George Berkeley, 3 vols. 1897–1898; Burke's French Revolution, 1900; Newman's University Sketches, 1903; Newman's Select Essays, 1903; The Lyrical Ballads, 1903; More's Utopia and Roper's Life of More, 1903; Walton's Lives, 1904; The Golden Asse, 1904; George Herbert's Poems, 1904; Keats, 2 vols. 1904; Works of Emerson, 5 vols. 1904; Bagehot's Essays, 2 vols. 1911; The Cambridge Book of Verse and Prose, 1924; The Concise Cambridge History of English Literature, 1941. *Continuation*—Stopford Brooke's Primer of English of English Literature, 1924. *Essays and tracts*—English for the English, 1921; Seven Essays, 1947.

ABOUT: Dictionary of National Biography, 1941–1950, 1959; Who's Who 1950. *Periodicals*—Nation November 29, 1941; Times February 3, 1950; Times Educational Supplement March 10, 1950; Times Literary Supplement August 16, 1941.

## SAMPSON, RICHARD HENRY (pseudonym "RICHARD HULL") (September 6, 1896–1973), English mystery story writer, wrote: "Richard Hull (Richard Henry Sampson) is the youngest son of S. A. Sampson and Nina Hull—hence his pen-name. He was born in London and educated at Rugby School, from which he obtained mathematical exhibitions on leaving. He was to have gone to Trinity, Cambridge, but instead obtained a commission

on his eighteenth birthday. He remained in the army for the rest of the [First World] War, serving for about three years in France, first with an infantry battalion and then with the Machine Gun Corps. At the end of the war he was articled to a firm of chartered accountants, and after qualifying remained on their staff for some years before setting up in practice for himself.

"It can't be said that he was ever a very successful chartered accountant, and in 1933 he began to think that he would be more interested in writing. The decision to do so and to concentrate mainly on a particular type of detective fiction was made after reading Francis Iles' *Malice Aforethought*. Thereafter chartered accountancy, though not abandoned, faded into the background.

"During all this time, Mr. Sampson kept up his interest in soldiering, and up to 1929 served on the active list of the Territorial Battalion to which he had originally been commissioned in 1914. Even after retiring he kept in close touch with them, and was recalled by them on September 1, 1939. . . .

"In fiction he specializes in unpleasant characters because he says there is more to say about them and that he finds them more amusing. For preference he writes in the first person. In life he pleads a kind heart as a set-off to an occasional flash of temper and an endless flow of conversation. For many years he lived almost entirely in a London club, qualifying, as he says, as the club bore. He is convinced that his photograph would be detrimental to his sales."

---

In the late 1930s and early 1940s, Richard Henry Sampson, always known as Richard Hull, enjoyed a high place among mystery novelists in Great Britain. His debut novel, *The Murder of My Aunt*, is still held by mystery aficionados to be a minor classic of the genre. The central character is an effete and foppish young man, the narrator, forced by straitened financial circumstances to live with his rich aunt in a small town in Wales. Loathing his aunt, the town, and its inhabitants, he concocts various plots to murder the old woman and inherit her fortune. The unpleasantness of the narrator is brought out with great and humorous skill. But the aunt proves to be more perspicacious than the young man imagined, and so his schemes are continually thwarted. A *Times Literary Supplement* reviewer praised the novel as "[a] brilliant piece of serious following." In his book *Murder for Pleasure*, a history of the detective story, Howard Haycraft called it "a classic of its kind, an intellectual shocker par excellence." Because most of the novel is narrated by the malefactor (a brief concluding section is narrated by the aunt), and deals with events leading up to the crime—which in this case is never accomplished—Haycraft labeled *The Murder of My Aunt* a prime example of the "inverted" mystery story.

Sampson went on to publish fourteen subsequent mystery novels, none of which lived up to the standards set by *The Murder of My Aunt*. But they were all highly competent, and widely read in their time. Although "by preference" he wrote in the first person, and has often been categorized as a leading practitioner of the "inverted" story, he experimented with a variety of formulas and points of view. In his third novel, *Murder Isn't Easy*, the murder is seen from the perspective of several suspects. In *The Murderers of Monty*, many people are plotting independently to kill one person. Some of his novels, such as *The Ghost It Was* and *And Death Came Too*, are conventional murder mysteries related in the third person and solved by a detective. He created only one detective of any note, Inspector Fenby, who appears in *The Ghost It Was* and *Excellent Intentions*, a courtroom thriller in which the moral ambiguity is compounded by the utter worthlessness of the victim. His oft-praised wicked sense of humor is perhaps most evident in *My Own Murderer*, a complex, psychological thriller in which one of the villains has the same name as his creator—Richard Henry Sampson. A *New Yorker* critic "[r]ecommended [it] for readers who like to follow things to the bitter end," and E. R. Punshon (another crime writer) noted in the *Manchester Guardian*, "it is a tribute to his literary skill that he manages to present extremely disagreeable people in a way that keeps the reader always interested and often chuckling."

Sampson's literary career was interrupted by World War II, during which he briefly served in the Territorial Battalion. After the war, he was employed as an accountant by the Admiralty. His six postwar novels, none of which appeared in the United States, are inferior to his earlier work.

PRINCIPAL WORKS: As "Richard Hull"—The Murder of My Aunt, 1934; Keep It Quiet, 1935; Murder Isn't Easy, 1936; The Ghost It Was, 1936; The Murderers of Monty, 1937; Excellent Intentions, 1938 (in U.S.: Beyond Reasonable Doubt); And Death Came Too, 1939; My Own Murderer, 1940; The Unfortunate Murderer, 1942; Left-Handed Death, 1946; Last First, 1947; Until She Was Dead, 1949; A Matter of Nerves, 1950; Invitation to an Inquest, 1950; The Martineau Murders, 1953.

ABOUT: The autobiographical material quoted above was written for Twentieth Century Authors, 1942 and Twentieth Century Authors First Supplement, 1955. DeAndrea, W. Encyclopedia Mysteriosa: A Comprehensive Guide to the Art of Detection in Print, Radio, and Television, 1994; Haycraft, H. Murder for Pleasure: The Life and Times of the Detective Story, enl. ed., (ed. 1968; Twentieth-Century Crime and Mystery Writers, 3rd ed. L. Henderson) 1991. *Periodicals*—Manchester Guardian March 15, 1940; New Yorker August 31, 1940; Times Literary Supplement October 4, 1934.

**SAMUEL, MAURICE** (February 8, 1895–May 4, 1972), American journalist, novelist, and man of letters, wrote: "The place of my birth is Macin, a townlet in Rumania, opposite Braila on the Danube; the city of my boyhood and youth is Manchester, in England; and I have lived my adult life with New York as a base, Palestine (now Israel) as its opposite, and a lot of countries and cities popping in and out of my life. One would think that with all the traveling I have done—fifty to seventy-five thousand miles in a normal year—I must have a wanderer's blood in me. But except for the exhaustion it sometimes brings, I could swear that it is the world which passes in panorama before me while I observe and note and write. . . .

"The dominating interest of my life has been the riddle of the Jewish episode—some three or four thousand years old now—in the history of the planet. Most of my books have been devoted to one facet or another of this riddle. I have written about Jews lightly, seriously, grimly, satirically, passionately, lovingly—but always in the form of essays. In these essays I pose the question of the meaning of the Jew, his place in the ethical evolution of society, and his self-fulfillment in his communities and in his reconstructed homeland, and the continuation of his trajectory into the future.

"When I break away from this dominating interest, I usually write novels; and afterwards I discover that the theme had had something to do with a moral problem which occupied me in one of my Jewish essays. Thus critics of my novel *Beyond Woman* observed that the non-Jewish characters were Jewish. And in the Italian Renaissance novel *Web of Lucifer* I was actually concerned with the birth of modern Fascism—the matrix of anti-Semitism—as exemplified in Macchiavelli and Cesare Borgia. My . . . novel, *The Devil That Failed*, is a parable of the man trapped in a totalitarian state and unable to establish his identity; but it might also be the parable of the Jew trapped by history and struggling to find out what and who he is.

"In addition to the portentous foregoing works I have some lighter literary essays, like *The World of Sholom Aleichem* and *Prince of the Ghetto*, in which I try to reconstruct the vanished Yiddish-speaking civilization of Europe from the works of its leading writers. In these, as in my other books, my preoccupation is with the meaning behind realities, the spirit which speaks through the acts and characters of men and women. . . ."

---

In his various capacities as author, translator, and itinerant lecturer, Maurice Samuel was, as Robert Alter said in *Commentary* (1964), "a kind of one-man educational movement in American Jewish life." Raised in a traditional, though not Orthodox, Jewish household, he was the son of Isaac Samuel and Fanny (Acker) Samuel. He attended Victoria University of Manchester, but never earned a degree. Samuel came to the United States in 1914, served in the U.S. Army during World War I, worked as an interpreter at postwar peace conferences, and became a naturalized American citizen in 1921. He began his intensive study of Jewish tradition as a young adult, after abandoning a youthful allegiance to socialism. Many of his books contain pronounced autobiographical elements, Samuel's way of sharing his own process of discovery with his readers. Praising this technique in his *Commentary* (1964) review of *Little Did I Know*, a collection of autobiographical essays, Robert Alter wrote, "This necessity to reconstruct the past through painstaking effort qualified him perfectly to recreate it for others. . . . Samuel at his best is really brilliant in his ability to explain a world alien to Western readers by locating it on cultural coordinates familiar to them."

The Yiddish humorist whose stories inspired the hit play *Fiddler on the Roof* is the subject of Samuel's most famous book, *The World of Sholom Aleichem*. Through an examination of Aleichem's fictional town of Kasrielevky and its inhabitants, Samuel evoked the almost forgotten culture from which Aleichem sprang—that of the Russian-Jewish Shtetl of the late nineteenth century. Praised by critics, the book won the Anisfield-Wolf Award in 1943 and the annual award of the *Saturday Review of Literature* in 1944. Similarly, in *Prince of the Ghetto*, Samuel explores the lives of Polish Jews as reflected in the work of another Yiddish-language writer, Isaac Loeb Peretz. In a *Partisan Review* notice of the book, Isaac Rosenfeld commented, "Samuel continues the very good work of bringing an undeservedly dying literature to a possible resuscitation with the English reader, . . . who can have no other contact with it."

Samuel translated more than twenty books, mostly from the Yiddish, by authors such as I. J. Singer and Sholem Asch. He spent much of his time in Israel, and helped Chaim Weizmann, the country's first president, to write his memoirs. From 1953 to 1971, Samuel was a regular panelist, along with Mark Van Doren, on the NBC radio program "Words We Live By." *In Praise of Yiddish*, the last of his books published during his lifetime, was described by *Commentary* (1971) reviewer Lucy Dawidowicz as "a capstone to his career as translator and Jewish cultural mediator."

In one of the essays in *Little Did I Know*, Samuel wrote, "I see myself as one of the *Maggidim*, the wandering preachers of Eastern European Jewry. . . . I do not pretend to be merely a purveyor of information. I have an axe to grind." That "axe" is most apparent in such works as *The Professor and the Fossil*, in which he aptly criticizes Arnold Toynbee's hostile treatment of the Jews in *A Study of History*. In her introduction to *The Worlds of Maurice Samuel*, a posthumously published selection of his writings, Cynthia Ozick declared, "Maurice Samuel is above all a polemicist, assuredly the best of our time. . . . For Samuel the Jewish view is almost never yielded up through simple declaration or exposition; it is wrested out of the engagement with, and finally a disengagement from, an alternative world view." He remained intellectually active until the end of his life.

PRINCIPAL WORKS: *Judaica and nonfiction*—You Gentiles, 1924; I, the Jew, 1927; What Happened in Palestine: the Events of August, 1929, Their Background and Their Significance, 1929; On the Rim of the Wilderness: The Conflict in Palestine, 1930; Jews on Approval, 1932; The Great Hatred, 1940; The World of Sholom Aleichem, 1943; Harvest in the Desert, 1944; Prince of the Ghetto, 1948; Level Sunlight, 1953; Certain People of the Book, 1955; The Professor and the Fossil: Some Observations on Arnold J. Toynbee's A Study of History, 1956; Our Jewish Youth: What Can We Offer Them?, 1957; Blood Accusation: The Strange History of the Beiliss Case, 1966; Light on Israel, 1968; In Praise of Yiddish, 1971; (with M. Van Doren) In the Beginning, Love: Dialogues on the Bible (ed. E. Samuel)

1973; (with M. Van Doren) The Book of Praise: Dialogues on the Psalms (ed. E. Samuel) 1975. *Novels*—The Outsider, 1921; Whatever Gods, 1923; Beyond Woman, 1934; Web of Lucifer, a Novel of the Borgia Fury, 1946; The Devil that Failed, 1952; The Second Crucifixion, 1960. *Autobiography*—The Gentleman and the Jew, 1950; Little Did I Know: Recollections and Reflections, 1963. *Selections*—The Worlds of Maurice Samuel: Selected Writings (ed. M. Hindus) 1977. *As translator*—The Jewish Anthology (by E. Flegg) 1925; Selected Poems (by C. Bialik) 1926; Europe (by H. Keyserling) 1928; Schlump: The Story of a German Soldier Told by Himself, 1929; Childhood in Exile (by S. Levin) 1929; Youth in Revolt (by S. Levin) 1930; The Plough Woman: Records of the Pioneer Women of Palestine (ed. R. Katzenelson-Rubashov) 1932; The Arena (by S. Levin) 1932, The Sinner (Yoshe Kalb) (by I. J. Singer) 1933 (reissued as Yoshe Kalb, 1965); The Brothers Ashkenazi (by I. J. Singer) 1936; The Fishmans (by H. W. Katz) 1938; The River Breaks Up: A Volume of Stories, 1938; The Nazarene (by S. Asch) 1939; East of Eden (by I. J. Singer) 1939; Heil Hunger! Health Under Hitler (by M. Grumpert) 1940; The Lights Go Down (by E. Mann) 1940; Theodore Herzl, a Biography (by A. Bein) 1940; Roosevelt: A Study in Fortune and Power (by E. Ludwig) 1941; What I Believe (by S. Asch) 1941; Haggadah of Passover, 1942; Children of Abraham: The Short Stories of Sholem Asch, 1942; The Apostle (by S. Asch) 1943.

ABOUT: The autobiographical material quoted above was written for Twentieth Century Authors First Supplement, 1955. *Periodicals*—Commentary March 1964, December 1971; New York Times May 5, 1972; Partisan Review February 1949; Times (London) May 6, 1972.

## SANBORN, PITTS (October 19, 1879–March 7, 1941), American music critic, novelist, and journalist, was born John Pitts Sanborn in Port Huron,

Michigan, the son of John Pitts and Mary Ann (Wastell) Sanborn. Educated at Harvard (A.B. 1900, A.M. 1902), he was a newspaperman for more than thirty-five years—and was considered one of the deans of the New York music critics. From 1905 to 1923, he was the music editor of the *New York Globe*. He joined the staff of the *New York Evening Mail* as musical editor in 1923, and retained that post through a series of mergers with the *New York Telegram*, the *New York Evening World*, and the *New York World-Telegram*, the paper he was writing for at the time of his death. Between 1912 and 1923, he was a European correspondent, often in France, for the *Globe* and the *Evening Mail*. An authority on grand opera, he was as well acquainted with the major opera houses of Europe as he was with the Metropolitan in New York. His critical acumen and his efforts to popularize serious European music were recognized by two governments: he was made a Cavalier of the Order of the Crown of Italy in 1932, and decorated as a Knight of the Legion of Honor (France) in 1936. From 1939 until his death, he was the program annotator for the New York Philharmonic Symphony.

Sanborn was a frequent contributor to various musical journals and encyclopedias, and sometimes worked as a radio commentator on musical subjects. He published one collection of verse and two novels. *Prima Donna*, his first novel, follows the triumphant career of an Ohio-born opera singer. His major work, however, was *The Metropolitan Book of the Opera*, written in collaboration with Emil Hilb, and published under the auspices of the Metropolitan Opera Association. Sanborn contributed synopses of the operas in the Metropolitan repertory and biographical sketches of some of the composers. "There could have been no better choice than Pitts Sanborn to undertake a work of this sort," Alexander Smallens wrote in a *New York Herald Tribune Books* review of the volume. Before his sudden death Sanborn had signed a contract with Macmillan to write a biography of the Norwegian soprano Kirsten Flagstad.

PRINCIPAL WORKS: *Poetry*—Vie de Bordeaux, 1916. *Novels*—Prima Donna, a Novel of the Opera, 1929; Greek Night, 1933. *Music*—(with E. Hilb) The Metropolitan Book of the Opera, 1937; Beethoven and His Nine Symphonies, 1939 (reissued as Ludwig von Beethoven, 1951); Brahams and Some of his Works, 1940.

ABOUT: Current Biography 1941; Who Was Who in America, Vol. 1: 1897–1942, 1942. *Periodicals*—Musical America March 10, 1941; New York Herald Tribune Books December 12, 1937; New York Times March 8, 1941.

## SÁNCHEZ FERLIOSO, RAFAEL (December 14, 1927– ), Spanish novelist and short story writer, was born in Rome, the son of Rafael Sánchez Mazas, a minor poet and novelist who was also an early and eager member of the Falange, and of the fervently Roman Catholic group *Cruz y Reya*. Sánchez Mazas was at the time of his son's birth serving as Spanish consul in Rome; later he would have the honor of serving in Franco's (second) 1939 government as a Minister Without Portfolio. A cultivated man, well known for his journalism and his fine high style, he encouraged his son to follow literary pursuits. Sánchez Ferlioso's mother was Italian by birth.

In his mid-twenties Sánchez Ferlioso published a fantasy called *Industries y andanzas de Alfanhuí* (1951; translated as *The Projects and Wanderings of Alfanhuí*). This has been praised, sometimes—as by Paul West—at the expense of the much better known work by which he gained his reputation, *El Jarama* (1955, translated as *The One Day of the Week*), and for which he was awarded the coveted Premio Nadal.

*Alfanhuí* is an episodic, Barrie-like fantasy, based squarely on such works as Carroll's *Alice* books, the Arabian Nights, Kenneth Grahame—and, above all, to an almost plagiaristic extent, on the surrealist tales of the French poet Jules Supervielle. Paul West called it "evocative of the frail stories that appeared in the *Yellow Book* . . . . it traces not only the dawn of self-awareness but also the sudden sense of release into the fertile springs of a previously unknown cosmos . . . . slight as the piece is, it is miraculously judged . . . . *Alfanhuí*, then, is a novel of awareness and a standing rebuke to the young cataloguers, not because lists are bad in themselves, but because compiling them mindlessly is."

In *El Jarama*, described by G. O. Brown as an "incredibly patient record of the conversation of a host of uninteresting people" and as "no doubt intentionally . . . one of the most boring works in the history of the novel," little happens: on a summer Sunday eleven young people go for a picnic and a swim in the River Jarama; a couple kiss; at the end one of the youngsters is drowned. West remarks: "their prattle is at least idiomatic and pert . . . . [but] the inertia of the young passes into the quasi-structure."

Why, then, did this novel once have such a high reputation? The answer, apart from the fact that it appeared when the cult of the French *nouveau roman* was at its height, is because it was alleged to possess "symbolic depths" and to have "subtle recourse to realms of mystery and poetry." *El Jarama* was written at a bad time for literature in Spain. The ablest defense of the book is to be found in an article by E. C. Riley published in the 1963 number of *Filologia* (Barcelona), "Sobre del arte de Sánchez Ferlioso" ("On the art of Sánchez Ferlioso").

In 1961 Sánchez Ferlioso added to his Alfanhuí saga by publishing the original with some additions, including two unrelated short stories, one of which, "Dientes, pólvora, Febrero" ("Teeth, gunpowder, February"), reverts to the matter-of-fact technique of *El Jarama*.

It is hard to write about boredom, and it is indisputable that, in terms of intellect and of linguistic elegance, Sánchez Ferlioso is highly talented. The questions would seem to be: how much so in the context of such other Spanish novelists as Jarnés, Sender, the two Goytisolos, Martín Santos, Cela, and many others; whether the Spanish novel in its more familiarly robust form has by now quite passed him by; and the extent to which, if of course at all, his work is emotionally deficient.

In 1950 Sánchez Ferlioso married the novelist Carmen Martin Gaite (herself a winner of the Nadal Prize in 1957).

PRINCIPAL WORKS IN ENGLISH TRANSLATION: The One Day of the Week (tr. J. M. Cohen) 1962; The Projects and Wanderings of Alfanhuí (tr. R. Danald) 1975.

ABOUT: Brown, G. O. A Literary History of Spain: The Twentieth Century, 1972; Danald, R. *in* The Projects and Wanderings of Alfanhuí, 1975; Seymour-Smith, M. Macmillan Guide to Modern World Literature, 1986; West, P. The Modern Novel, 2 vols., 1963.

**SANDBURG, CARL** (January 6, 1878–July 22, 1968), American poet, biographer, prose writer, and folk-song collector, was born in Galesburg, Illinois, the son of Swedish immigrant parents: August Sandburg (who had changed his name from Johnson), a railroad blacksmith, and the former Clara Anderson. Both parents were devout Lutherans, and the household was poor. Carl was educated at public schools until he was thirteen—he had wanted to be a writer since the age of six—and then began a long series of manual jobs: shifting scenery in a theater, porter in a barbershop, laborer. He served for eight months in Puerto Rico, in the 6th Illinois Volunteers, during the Spanish-American war, but saw no combat. Then he entered Lombard College in his home town and did well as an all-round student. He owed his beginnings as a writer

to a teacher there, Philip Green Wright, who encouraged him to pursue his fascination with Abraham Lincoln, and who himself typeset Sandburg's first book of poems in his cellar, a thirty-nine-page paperbound pamphlet, *In Reckless Ecstasy* (1904), of which only a handful of copies survive. This early poetry is conventional, and not written in the full-flowing free verse or rhythmic prose that he later became known for; but in it and other early publications, the germs of the florid later poet may be glimpsed.

After he left college, Sandburg started a series of better-paid jobs: traveler for a stereoptician slides firm, labor organizer for the Wisconsin Social-Democrats, journalist on the Milwaukee *Leader*. On June 15, 1908, he married a schoolteacher, Lillian Steichen, sister to the noted photographer Edward Steichen; they had three daughters. Sandburg then became secretary to the Mayor of Milwaukee (1910–12). In 1912 he moved to Chica-  go, where he started work with the *Daily News*. By this time his socialistic journalism was beginning to attract attention, and he was working hard on amassing information for a biography on Lincoln. Philip Yannella's 1996 book *The Other Carl Sandburg* focuses on the political aspects of these early years, when Sandburg wrote a series of articles, many anonymously, for the *International Socialist Review*. In 1918, the poet spent a month in Sweden, and was questioned upon his return by Federal authorities who accused him of supporting the Bolsheviks in Russia by acting as a conduit for propaganda and funds. Drawing information from military intelligence files, Yannella recounts how Sandburg moved from being a rather native participant in these activities to became a "belligerent patriot" through his support of the American Alliance for Labor and Democracy, which supported American participation in World War I. It was soon afterwards that Sandburg emerged as "a 100 percent American poet, the singer of the greatness and grandeur of the country's rolling heartland, the thoughtful patriot who knew how its ordinary folk would sacrifice themselves to save the world for democracy."

Sandburg owed his growing reputation as a poet during these early years to Harriet Monroe's *Poetry*, which began to publish his poems in 1914—and stuck by him when his *Chicago Poems* (1916) were reviled for vulgarity and technical incompetence. He had, through the magazine, discovered the imagists; although he never was one himself, he took up some imagist methods, in particular the free-verse techniques.

Sandburg, with *Smoke and Steel* (1920) and later collections, became a very popular poet. Critics, especially American academic ones, have never had much to say about him, for obvious enough reasons. He was at his best as an orator, the rhetorical embracer of a democratic America centered on Lincoln. As M. L. Rosenthal put it, his power was "real" but "secondary." He was a genuine "people's poet," but his work is dated. He was wholly without subtlety, and the only edge he achieved ("Why is there always a secret singing / When a lawyer cashes in? / Why does a hearse horse snicker / Hauling a lawyer away?") was achieved in rather better style by Edgar Lee Masters and Sherwood Anderson. However, he is sincere, never contrived, and always enjoyable to read if the reader is not looking for compression, epigram, or concentration. "Poetry," he wrote, "is the achievement of the synthesis of hyacinths and biscuits." He learned most of his business from Whitman—and from the Lincoln of the Gettysburg Address—but could not achieve Whitman's pure lyricism, nor generate the sheer and irresistible excitement that the elder poet generated. Yet no one has much liked to criticize Sandburg. Alfred Kazin wrote that his *Collected Poems* witnessed "the vast unrealized possibilities of a native American radicalism that has never found its fullest expression."

As a poet, Sandburg belongs, in a generation younger than that of Whitman, to a trio of midwesterners who helped to transform the Anglo-American poetic tradition into an American one: Vachel Lindsay, Edgar Lee Masters, and himself. Lindsay was the most gifted and the least sophisticated, Masters the least gifted and the least unsophisticated; Sandburg comes in between. Lindsay poisoned himself, Masters's gifts evaporated in a cloud of populist fury; only Sandburg could survive. His belief in "the people" was absolute, but he was no political thinker; he lacked intellectual curiosity, but he was decent and he believed in decency—and he did have power, "secondary" though it certainly was. He compiled the vital anthologies *The American Songbag* and *The New American Songbag*, and he could assimilate the poetry in them, even if he could not refine it. He was, if not quite a master, then a great assimilator of, the American folk idiom: "Poets, lawyers, ad men, mason contractors, smart-alecks discussing educated jackasses, here they put crabs into their balloon faces, / here sit the heavy balloon face women lifting crimson lobsters into their crimson faces. . ." —or, "You come along . . . tearing your shirt . . . yelling about Jesus. / Where do you get that stuff? / What do you know about Jesus?" This is, conceded Rosenthal, in a brilliant judgment, "a half-poetry which . . . few of us would wish to do without."

Sandburg's life of Lincoln was published in six volumes (1926–1939). That it is not taken seriously by professional historians need not be held against it. All the historians have read it, in any case: for all its longueurs and errors of interpretation, it is still the most sheerly readable biography of Lincoln, and one of the few that stirs the blood.

Sandburg, showered with honors and honorary degrees, served his country and its media well. He became a national institution of sorts, acting as narrator of the radio program "Cavalcade of America," doing many wartime broadcasts, and writing a patriotic syndicated newspaper column for the *Chicago Times* (1941–1945). In 1945 he moved to Connemara Farm near Flat Rock, North Carolina. In 1959, on the occasion of the 150th anniversary of Lincoln's birth, he became the first private citizen ever to deliver an oration to a joint session of Congress. He won the gold medal for poetry from the Poetry Society of America (1953) and many other honors. For twenty years between the wars Sandburg had travelled widely, reading his poetry (best when recited), accompanying himself on a guitar. His place even as a minor poet is now hardly secure among academics; he usually lacks the edge of Masters in *Spoon River*, and does not achieve the poetry of Lindsay; yet his place as America's outstanding twentieth-century poet of the people is established. There is a Carl Sandburg Association, and most of his major work is in print.

PRINCIPAL WORKS: *Novel*—Remembrance Rock, 1978. *Poetry*—In Restless Ecstasy, 1904; The Plaint of the Rose, 1905; Joseffy, 1910; Chicago Poems, 1916; Cornhuskers, 1918; Smoke and Steel, 1920; Slabs of the Sunburnt West, 1922; West, R. (ed.) Selected Poems, 1926; Good Morning, America, 1928; The People, Yes, 1936; Complete Poems, 1950 (rev. 1970); Van Doren, M. (ed.) Harvest Poems 1910-1960, 1960; Six New Poems and a Parable, 1961; Honey and Salt, 1963. *Nonfiction*—Incidentals (essays) 1904; The Chicago Race Riots, 1919; Abraham Lincoln, 6 vols, 1927-39; Steichen, the Photographer, 1929; (with P. M. Angle) Mary Lincoln, Wife and Widow, 1932; Storm Over the Land, 1942; Abraham Lincoln (condensed), 1954; Fetherling D. and D. (eds.) Carl Sandburg at the Movies, 1985. *Juvenile*—Rootabaga Stories, 1920; Rootabaga Pigeons, 1932; Abe Lincoln Grows Up, 1928; Potato Face, 1930; Early Moon, 1930; A Sandburg Treasury: Prose and Poetry for Young People, 1970. *Autobiography*—Always the Young Strangers, 1952; Sandburg, M. and Hendrik, G. (eds.) Ever the Winds of Chance, 1983. *Letters*—Mitgang, H. (ed.) The Letters of Carl Sandburg, 1968; Sandburg, M. (ed.) The Poet and the Dream Girl: The Love Letters of Lillian Steichen and Carl Sandburg, 1987. *As editor*—The American Songbag, 1927; A Lincoln and Whitman Miscellany, 1938; The New American Songbag, 1950.

ABOUT: Allen, G. W. Carl Sandburg, 1972; Callahan, N. Carl Sandburg: Lincoln of Our Literature, 1970; Carl Sandburg: His Life and Works, 1987; Crowder, R. Carl Sandburg, 1964; D'Allessio, G. Old Troubadour, 1987; Detzer, K. W. Carl Sandburg: A Study in Personality and Background, 1941; Golden, H. Carl Sandburg, 1961; Haas, J. and Lovietz, G. Carl Sandburg: A Pictorial Biography, 1967; Niven, P. Carl Sandburg, 1991; Perry, L. S. My Friend Carl Sandburg, 1981; Salwak, D. (ed.) Carl Sandburg: A Reference Guide, 1988; Sandburg, H. A Great and Glorious Romance: The Story of Carl Sandburg and Lillian Steichen, 1978; Steichen, E. Sandburg: Photographer's View, 1966; Van Doren, M. Sandburg, 1969 (with bibliography); Yannella, P. R. The Other Carl Sandburg, 1996. *Periodicals*—American Literature, March 1991; New York Times July 23, 1967; New York Times Book Review October 27, 1966; Time December 4, 1950.

## SANDERSON, IVAN (pseudonym "TERRENCE ROBERTS") (January 30, 1911– February 19, 1973), British born American naturalist, wrote: "Born in Edinburgh. Educated at Eton and learned sufficient facts at Cambridge to obtain a B.A. in zoology, geology, and botany. After leaving Eton at the age of seventeen, traveled around the world eastwards via Egypt and India to the Malay states and the Dutch East Indies, where a one-man (or one-boy) zoological expedition was carried through to obtain specimens of small animals for the British Museum. Thence traveled in Indo-

China, China, Japan, and reached America and finally England after a year. No note-worthy achievement at Cambridge due to lack of interest in athletics. Literary accomplishments: one article in a varsity newspaper on 'Women,' which was roundly condemned by the authorities.

"Two days after leaving Cambridge sailed as leader of small Percy Sladen Memorial Fund Expedition to the Cameroons, West Africa, on behalf of the British Museum, Cambridge and London Universities. A year spent in the field carrying out research upon and collecting small animals. Returned to London with all the animals and data that had been sought. This initiated a period of zoological studies in museums and the publication of some technical work on zoology. Married in 1934.

"Carried on a small interior decorating business specializing in restaurants and cabarets; studied, wrote and lectured upon African art, culture and dancing and music. The necessity of doing some literary work arose through these latter activities. Literary inferiority complex partially overcome in late 1935, resulting in a book entitled *Animal Treasure* about our work in Africa, which, surprisingly, was a Book-of-the-Month Club selection. The proceeds were invested in a zoological expedition to the West Indies and in the following year another to Dutch Guiana. These gave birth to a second book. . . .

" . . . No claim is made to the title of *author*. Rather is recognition sought in the fields of experimental zoology, natural history, and possibly the art of animal illustration."

---

Ivan T. Sanderson was the son of Arthur Buchanan Sanderson, a whiskey manufacturer, and the former Stella W. W. Robertson. His father established the first game reserve in Kenya, and was killed while filming a rhinoceros there in 1924. Ivan Sanderson had already traveled extensively with his parents, and was left with a strong desire to see, and learn more of the natural world.

The result of Sanderson's Cameroons expedition, *Animal Treasure* was received as a readable alternative to more academic accounts of scientific exploration. "*Animal Treasure* was something of a novelty," wrote the author's obituarist in the *New York Times*, "in that it focused on anecdotes concerning the animals." It was, moreover, written with wit and charm, and A. C. Moore called it "one of the most fascinating and satisfying books about animal life that I have ever read" (*Atlantic*).

However, one fellow scientist, Arthur Loveridge, berated Sanderson's light-hearted approach, dismissing "misinterpretation, exaggeration, sentimentalism and emotionalism" (*Scientific Monthly*); nor did he lack ammunition for his attack. However, in a letter to the scientific periodical *Nature*, the

author responded calmly. "*Animal Treasure* has never been claimed by me to be a purely scientific work," he said, "but as a popular introduction to the public of some of the wild life of West Africa." He capitalized on its popularity with two sequels, illustrated like the first with his own drawings. G. S. Reid, writing for the *Boston Transcript*, said that *Caribbean Treasure* was "exciting, fascinating and beautifully written," and Clifton Fadiman concluded that "Mr. Sanderson's prose, his ideas and his illustrations are equally clean edged" (*New Yorker*).

*Living Treasure*, an account of an expedition to the West Indies and Central America, was praised for its warmth and humor. W.A. Roberts described its author as "a keen observer who writes with an infectious enthusiasm and who also draws uncommonly well" (*New York Herald Tribune Books*).

During the Second World War Sanderson served with the rank of commander for British naval intelligence, in the Caribbean. He then spent two years in New York as Overseas Press Analyst for the British government. He decided to stay in the United States, and became an American citizen. Working as science editor at the Chilton Book Company in Philadelphia, and on *Argosy*, he also began to broadcast on radio and television. He presented a series of extremely popular wildlife programs, including, on CBS, the world's first regularly scheduled color television show, *The World Is Yours*. The expeditions continued, and Sanderson established a roadside zoo in New Jersey to house his unique collection of wild animals. Sadly, the zoo and the entire collection were destroyed by floods in 1955.

Sanderson also continued to write. Futher publications included a straightforward introduction to zoology, *Living Mammals of the World*, of which A. C. Ames remarked "If you want an animal book to read, get Sanderson. If you don't, get it anyway" (*Chicago Sunday Tribune*). *Follow the Whale* was an account of whaling through the ages, and *The Dynasty of Abu* was a study of elephants and all their relatives. Sanderson also wrote a number of books for children, welcomed as "excellent and useful in every way" (*Library Journal*).

In later years Sanderson became increasingly interested in the supernatural. In 1965 he founded the Society for the Investigation of the Unexplained, and remained its trustee and administrative director. He published several books on the subject, most of them rather coolly received. Reviewing *Abominable Snowmen* in the *Saturday Review*, H. R. Rays found that "the author's tendency to rail repeatedly against the closed minds of zoologists becomes an irritating mannerism."

Ivan T. Sanderson was a Fellow of the Royal Geographical Society, the Zoological Society, and the Linnean Society. He received an honorary M.A. from Cambridge University in 1969.

PRINCIPAL WORK: *Natural history*—Animal Treasure, 1937; Caribbean Treasure, 1939; Living Treasure, 1941; Inside Living Animals, 1949; Living Mammals of the World, 1955; Follow the Whale , 1956; Monkey Kingdoms; An Introduction to the Primates, 1957; The Continent We Live On, 1961 (in U.K.: The Natural Wonders of North America); The Dynasty of Abu; A History and Natural History of the Elephants and

Their Relatives, 1962; Exploring East Africa, 1962; Ivan Sanderson's Book of Great Jungles, 1965; This Treasured Land, 1966 (in U.K.: The USA); Green Silence: Travels Through the Jungles of the Orient (ed. S. W. Sanderson) 1974. *Juvenile*—Animals Nobody Knows, 1940; (as Terence Roberts) Mystery Schooner, 1941 (fiction); How to Know the American Mammals, 1951; Silver Mink, 1952 (fiction); John and Juan in the Jungle 1953 (fiction); (as Terence Roberts) The Status Quo, 1956 (fiction). *Supernatural*—Abominable Snowmen; legend Come to Life, 1962; Uninvited Visitors; A Biologist Looks at Ufos, 1967; Things, 1967; More Things, 1969 Invisible Residents: A Disquisition Upon Certain Matters Maritime, and the Possibility of Intelligent Life Under the Waters of this Earth, 1970; Investigating the Unexplained; A Compendium of Disquieting Mysteries of the Natural World, 1972. *Travel*—A Guide to Trinidad, 1951. *As editor*—Animal Tales: An Anthology of Animal Literature of All Countries 1946.

ABOUT: The autobiographical material quoted above was written for Twentieth Century Authors, 1942. Burke, W. J. And Howe, W. D. American Authors and Books, 1972; Commire, A. Something About the Author vol. 6, 1974; Contemporary Authors vols. 37–40, 1979; vols. 41–44, 1979; Herzberg, M.J. The Readers Encyclopedia of American Literature, 1963; Mahoney, B. E. (comp.) Illustrators of Childrens Books, 1958; National Cyclopedia of American Biography, 1977; Ward, M. E. and Marquardt, D. A. Authors of Books for Young People, 1964. *Periodicals*—Atlantic December 1937; Boston Transcript November 17, 1939; Chicago Sunday Tribune November 6, 1955; Christian Science Monitor November 13, 1961; Library Journal November 15, 1951; Nature Magazine April 1, 1939; New York Herald Tribune Books April 20, 1911; New York Times February 21, 1973; Publishers Weekly April 23, 1973; Saturday Review October 21, 1961; Scientific Monthly January, 1938.

**SANDOZ, MARI** (May 11, 1896–March 10, 1966), American historian and novelist, wrote: "I was born at what was then Sandoz post office, Sheridan County, Nebraska, the eldest of six children of Jules A. Sandoz of Neuchatel, Switzerland, and Mary Elizabeth (Fehr) Sandoz of Schaffhausen, Switzerland. I grew up on the architectural scheme of the cowboy—height five feet and a half inch weight 105 pounds. Also weatherbeaten. In the home of 'Old Jules' Sandoz, trapper, locater, horticulturist, and community builder, I grew up speaking German, hearing French, Polish, and Czech, and English, which I learned after I started to school, at nine. I went to rural school four and a half years, took the rural teachers' examination, taught five years in western Nebraska, and attended the University of Nebraska three and one half years, working in a drug laboratory and as English assistant at the university to pay my way.

"I began writing stories as soon as I learned to put letters together. Had several of these published in the junior page of the *Omaha Daily News*. Perhaps my earliest literary influences were Joseph Conrad, whose sea seemed to me so like the sandhills about me, and Hardy, whose recognition of chance and circumstance in the shaping of human destiny seemed very true to the fairly violent life about me. Later I discovered the work of Shakespeare, of the Russians, and finally the Greeks. Aristophanes and

portions of the Old Testament are my favorite material for re-reading.

"In college I wrote seventy-eight short stories, won honorable mention in a *Harper's* contest in 1926, and wrote a bad novel that, fortunately, no one would publish. When a publisher returned *Old Jules* with a curt rejection letter in 1933, I quit. Starved out, my confidence in even my critical faculties gone, I gave up writing permanently. But in less than a month I was writing a novel that I had been thinking about doing for nine or ten years. It was *Slogum House*.

"By the time the rough draft was done, I was offered work at the State Historical Society, in Lincoln, as associate editor of the *Nebraska History Magazine*. I made a new copy of *Old Jules* and started it on its alphabetical rounds of the publishers again. On its fourteenth trip out it was accepted—and won the *Atlantic* non-fiction prize in 1935.

"I never begin to write even a two-page article—let alone a story or a book—without making first a simple, declarative statement of the theme, to be tacked up before my eyes for the duration of the work. Then I go through my notes of pertinent material and begin making drafts, with almost endless revisions.

"I always come back to the Middle West. There's a vigor here, and a broadness of horizon. Besides, I believe that the creative worker must not wander too far from the earth of his emotional identity. I, at least, am Anteus-footed.

"Politically, I suppose that I am what might be called an independent liberal, as the Sandoz family seems to have been for seven hundred years.

"Now I am working on my two Indian biographies that have taken up some of my time and much of my thought for five or six years—a Cheyenne biography and one of a Sioux. These will require five or six more years for completion, I anticipate.

"Since 1942 I have published several books and added to my shorter publications, which had varied from *North American Review* to *Ladies' Home Journal*.

"Since my college days I have worked with students of writing courses, later on the staff of writers' conferences, and, from 1947 on, I have conducted the advanced short story and novel writing courses in the eight-weeks' Writers' Institute at the University of Wisconsin in their summer sessions. In 1950 the University of Nebraska gave me an honorary Doctor of Literature. I am a member of the Authors Guild of the Authors League of America; the Association on American Indian Affairs, and on the board of associate editors of their *The American Indian*; the New York Posse of The Westerners, etc."

---

In the introduction to her biography, *Mari Sandoz: Story Catcher of the Plains*, Helen Winter Stauffer states that not only was her subject recognized as a novelist, historian, and biographer, but also as an authority on the Native Americans of the Great Plains. Stauffer continues that "her work varies in quality, her novels usually considered least successful, and her histories, particularly her biographies, most trenchant. In the latter she fused her skill as a writer, her mastery of historical research, and her empathy for her subjects to create works of unique and lasting value."

*Old Jules*, published as a book in 1935, was the first in Sandoz's Great Plains or Trans-Missouri series. It is a portrait of her father, a rough and tumble pioneer described by William Allen White, in the *Atlantic Book Shelf*, as a "strong, unwashed, passionate, contentious, domineering, amorous old male." It is also the story of a way of life, suggested the *Yale Review*: "Throughout the turmoil of Old Jules's life may be heard the deeper murmur of the nation's battle with the frontier. . . . In brief, the march of civilization westward is the ground-tone of the book." Reviewers praised Sandoz for her realistic portrait of the frontier and the harsh realities of life there, as well as her descriptions of its wild beauty. The reviewer claimed that "surely never, save perhaps in the novels of Miss Willa Cather, has the sinister enchantress, the frontier, seemed so real as in this narrative of the Swiss frontiersman Old Jules," although this is a minority view.

Sandoz continued her series with *Crazy Horse*, a biography of the Oglala Sioux chieftain, and *Cheyenne Autumn*, an account of the infamous mistreatment of the Cheyenne people. "While other writers had stressed the Indian point of view, the language of the white author almost always interfered with the atmosphere of the Indian culture portrayed in the story," her biographer M. W. Stauffer wrote. "It is by means of her particular use of language in her Indian books that Mari Sandoz brings the reader to greater understanding and perhaps even identification with her Indian heroes."

*The Buffalo Hunters, The Cattlemen,* and *The Beaver Men* shift the chronicle to those who took from the land. *The Battle of the Little Big Horn* was published posthumously.

Sandoz's nonfiction, is more important than her fiction, but her novel *Slogum House*, an epic tale of the Nebraska frontier and one woman's overwhelming ambition and greed, almost equals it. Stauffer suggests in her biography that Sandoz "intended it to be an allegorical study of a domineering nation using force to overcome opposition. . . . She wanted to demonstrate the evil of greed, to her the worst of sins, and to study other effects of megalomania, which fascinated her during the years of the great dictators, Hitler, Mussolini, and Stalin."

In 1943 Sandoz moved to New York City to be near her publishers, as well as the museums and archives of the East. Archival material is held by the Mari Sandoz Collection at the University of Nebraska, Lincoln; the Mari Sandoz Corporation, Gordon, Nebraska; and the Mamie Meredith Collection at the Nebraska State Historical Society.

PRINCIPAL WORKS: *Nonfiction*—Old Jules, 1935; Crazy Horse: The Strange Man of the Oglalas, 1942; Cheyenne Autumn, 1953; The Buffalo Hunters: The Story of the Hide Men, 1954; The Cattlemen from the Rio Grande Across the Far Marias, 1958; Hostiles and Friendlies: Selected Short Writings, 1959; Love Song to the Plains, 1961; These Were the Sioux, 1961; The Beaver Men: Spearheads of Empire, 1964; Old Jules Country: A Selection from Old Jules and Thirty Years of Writing Since the Book Was Published, 1965; The Battle of the Little Big Horn, 1966; The Christmas of the Phonograph Records: A Recollection, 1966; Sandhill Sundays and Other Recollections, 1970. *Novels*—Slogum House, 1937; Capital City, 1939; The Tom-Walker, 1947; Winter Thunder, 1954; Miss Morissa: Doctor of the Gold Trail, 1955; The Horsecatcher, 1957; Son of the Gamblin' Man: The Youth of an Artist, 1960; The Story Catcher, 1963; Foal of Heaven, 1993. *Short stories*—Victorie and Other Stories, 1986.

ABOUT: The autobiographical material quoted above was written for Twentieth Century Authors, 1942 and Twentieth Century Authors First Supplement, 1955. Contemporary Literary Criticism Vol. 28, 1984; Dictionary of American Biography, Suppl. 8, Faulkner, V. (ed.) Roundup: A Nebraska Reader, 1957; Greenwell, S. L. Descriptive Guide to the Mari Sandoz Collection, 1980; Notable American Women: The Modern Period, 1980; Pifer, C. S. Gordon Journal Letters of Mari Sandoz, 1992; Pifer, C. S. The Making of an Author: From the Mementoes of Mari Sandoz, 1972; Something About the Author Vol. 5, 1973; Stauffer, H. W. (ed.) Letters of Mari Sandoz, 1992; Stauffer, H. W. Mari Sandoz, 1984; Stauffer, H. W. Mari Sandoz: Story Catcher of the Plains, 1982; Villiger, L. R. Mari Sandoz: A Study in Post-Colonial Discourse, 1994. *Periodicals*—Atlantic Book Shelf November 1935; New York Herald Tribune Books November 28, 1937; New York Times March 11, 1966; New York Times Book Review July 3, 1966; Yale Review December 1935.

**SANSOM, WILLIAM** (January 18, 1912–April 20, 1976), English novelist and short story writer, was born in Camberwell, London. His parents— Mabel (Clark) and Ernest Brooks Sansom, a naval architect—named the boy, their third son, Norman Trevor; "William" was adopted at a later date. Sansom's upbringing included much European travel with his father, and an education at Uppingham School. Following a period of study in Bonn, intended to prepare him for a career in commerce, Sansom joined an Anglo-German bank in London. But he soon left to work for an advertising agency, as a copywriter. At this period, in his early twenties, his creative energies were directed towards show business. He played the piano in jazz clubs, and wrote songs and revue sketches. According to John Lehmann's 1960 profile of Sansom, "he had a waltz accepted for the Folies Bergères in Paris." New friendships—notably with Norman Cameron, the poet, who worked in the same office—awakened Sansom's interest in literature.

At the outbreak of World War II, he joined the fire service as a full-time fireman and, during the height of his experiences in the London blitz, turned to writing serious stories. Encouraged by John Lehmann and Cyril Connolly, who published his work in *Penguin New Writing* and *Horizon*, Sansom wrote with an increasing intensity during the war years. His debut in book-form was the idiosyncratic *Fireman Flower, And Other Stories* (1944), a volume which collected together several of his fire service stories and reflected both his reactions to war-torn London and his initial preference for an allegorical rather than naturalistic approach to fiction.

Immediately welcomed as a promising talent, and praised by people whose literary judgment was respected, Sansom did not have to return to the commercial world for long after the war. (He did spend a short time working for a film company). A two-year grant awarded by the Society of Authors (the money—£200 a year—was actually provided by the publisher Hodder & Stoughton) and a traveling scholarship helped to finance the early stages of his career. Thereafter, he supported his writing of fiction with travel commissions. Those who admire Sansom solely as a short-story writer take the view that his novel writing was undertaken only as a financial imperative, and he personally confirmed as much.

Sansom's early work is frequently described as Kafkaesque, but in stories such as "The Peach-House Potting Shed" (in which an old gardener is informed by the Estate Office that his solitude is to be invaded by another gentleman), "The Wall" (a compact description of a fireman's perceptions as he realizes that the wall of a five-story warehouse is on the point of collapse), and "Fireman Flower" (the most openly allegorical, in which a crew of firemen search an inferno for the heart of the blaze), the emblematical layering is too contrived and clinical to be entirely successful. Philip Toynbee, reviewing Sansom's first collection in the *New Statesman*, observed: "Where Kafka wrote in symbols which expressed the deepest and most tormented regions of his own soul, his pupil's symbolism is far more directly allegorical, more superficial." As Sansom was to acknowledge, in terms of his development as a writer, he was not an allegorist by instinct, but he continued to adopt a nonrealistic style, lingering on details with what he admitted was a fascination derived from the surrealists.

The stories in *Something Terrible, Something Lovely* confirmed that Sansom was less interested in character and plot than in rendering the quality of a chosen situation. This rendering is at its most successful in the title story (two girls plot their revenge for something terrible written on a wall); in "Various Temptations" (an inadequate and ugly single girl becomes involved with a serial killer); and "The Vertical Ladder" (a young man, dared to climb to the top of a gasometer, finds that the ladder stops short of the platform). These three had each been previously published before appearing in book form, but it became clear to Sansom that he could not earn a living solely from the short story. Two semi-fictional travel-collections appeared in 1948 and 1950; between these Sansom published his first novel.

*The Body*, like nearly all Sansom's novels, focuses on an unsatisfactory male-female relationship. A psychological novel, depicting its narrator, the forty-five-year-old Henry Bishop, in the grip of an obsessive and deluded jealousy, the book showed that Sansom might well become capable of applying his stylistic intensity to the demands of the novel. The obsession takes root in the striking opening chapter,

in which Bishop, while attempting to douse a fly with insecticide squirted from a syringe, sees a neighbor, as he believes, peeping at his wife Madge as she washes in the bathroom. An aspect of *The Body's* effectiveness is the contrast between the intensity of emotion built up and the comfortably bourgeois suburban setting. Bernard Bergonzi called it "a mannered book, which deliberately works in a narrow compass; but what it achieves within it is remarkable." Paulette Michel-Michot, at the end of her detailed study *William Sansom, A Critical Assessment*, concluded that both Sansom and [Henry] Green "share the same concern with the trivial and try to heighten it into something attractive, pleasant, or beautiful. . . . Both are interested in the situation itself, not in its temporal-causal aspect. Their characters are not intellectuals, they are ordinary creatures who sense life with their blood and nerves." She also attributed their failure in some books to the same cause—an attempt to transmute the uninteresting and trivial into something worthy of a reader's attention which does not always come off.

In Sansom's case another factor contributed to the ineffectiveness of some of his novels. For all his traveling, he remained a very English writer, and was at his best when writing about suburban streets, back gardens, cafes, and pubs. In those novels which transpose the characters to a continental setting—*The Face of Innocence* and *A Bed of Roses* were the first to do this—the emotional situation takes on the atmosphere of magazine fiction. With *The Loving Eye*, Sansom once more achieved the form he had hit with *The Body*, although in this book the predominant effect is achieved by his treatment of London back-streets and gardens rather than the story, which borders on the whimsical. The hero of the book is typical of Sansom's central male characters—a fussy bachelor in his late thirties, physically feeble (Matthew Ligne suffers from a stomach ulcer) but with a correspondingly abundant imaginative energy. Equally, Lily, the object of Matthew's obsessive interest, confirms what the previous three novels had told the reader about Sansom's view of female character as mysterious, unpredictable, irrational, unfathomable, and irreconcilably different from the male.

Sansom's most successful female character is Marie in *The Cautious Heart*. Her continuing attachment to the hanger-on, Colin, is a puzzle to herself, as well as to the reader, but utterly true-to-life. Sansom makes no attempt to explain her character, prompting Edwin Muir, in his review of the book in *The Observer*, to say, "All these riddles only make the characters more convincing, telling us that they are not diagrams, and that they are extraordinary though in appearance quite ordinary."

Sansom played no part in the angry-young-men scene of the fifties; the sixties proved antithetical to both his temperament and creative concerns. He married, in his early forties, Ruth Grundy (an actress) and settled into a mildly eccentric persona, becoming something of a dandy in terms of his dress-sense. Thirty-three of his stories were published in a collected edition in 1963. They were introduced by Elizabeth Bowen and enthusiastically reviewed by Eudora Welty who defined the key quality of Sansom's work as one of "reflective contemplation. There is an odd contrast, and its pull is felt in the stories between the unhurriedness of their actual events and their racing intensity."

Although he continued to publish during the sixties and early seventies Sansom's energies were increasingly diffused into freelance work. In addition to travel assignments he published a short illustrated book on Proust (in the Writers and their World series), collections of essays, books for children and, in 1972, *The Birth of a Story*, a detailed account of his working method which presents and accounts for the manuscript corrections to the story "No Smoking On The Apron," from *The Ulcerated Milkman*. He worked, this book tells us, in a room which looked out on his garden, for three and a half hours, between ten and one-thirty, averaging five hundred words a day. Such a scrupulous approach to his talent (he was equally careful with his financial affairs) does not make him a favorite with readers who look for rumbustious energy in an author. As one reviewer in the *Times Literary Supplement* put it, "One ungratefully longs for an occasional Pickwickian animation to stir these silent textures." But Sansom, reserving his lighter vein for song lyrics and light musical compositions, did make those silent textures his own, rendering them with a brilliance and intensity which give to his work a unique tone.

PRINCIPAL WORKS: *Novels*—The Body, 1949; The Face of Innocence, 1951; A Bed of Roses, 1954; The Loving Eye, 1956; The Cautious Heart, 1958; The Last Hours of Sandra Lee, 1961; Goodbye, 1966; Hans Feet in Love, 1971; A Young Wife's Tale, 1974. *Short stories*—Fireman Flower and Other Stories, 1944; Three, 1946; Something Terrible, Something Lovely, 1948; South, 1948; The Passionate North, 1950; A Touch of the Sun, 1952; Lord Love Us, 1954; A Contest of Ladies, 1956; Among the Dahlias and Other Stories, 1957; The Stories of William Sansom, 1963; The Ulcerated Milkman, 1966; The Marmalade Bird, 1973. *Juvenile*—It Was Really Charlie's Castle, 1953; The Light That Went Out, 1953; Skimpy, 1974. *Nonfiction*—(with J. Gordon and S. Spender) Jim Braidy: The Story of Britain's Firemen, 1943; Westminster in War, 1947; Pleasures Strange and Simple, 1953; The Icicle and the Sun, 1958; Blue Skies, Brown Studies, 1961; Away to It All, 1964; Christmas, 1968 (in U.S.: A Book of Christmas); Grand Tour Today, 1968; The Birth of a Story, 1972; Proust And His World, 1973. *Ballads*—Lord Love Us, 1954.

ABOUT: Bergonzi, B. Wartime and Aftermath, 1993; Chalplin, L. William Sansom, 1980; Contemporary Authors Vol 42, 1994; Lehmann, J. William Sansom, 1960; Michel-Michot, P. William Sansom A Critical Assessment, 1971; Who's Who 1976–1977. *Periodicals*—New Statesman February 19, 1944; New York Times June 30, 1963; April 21, 1976; Observer October 26, 1958; Queen March 1960; Times (London) April 21, 1976; Times Literary Supplement April 13, 1956; Washington Post April 24, 1976.

**SANTAYANA, GEORGE** (December 16, 1863–September 26, 1952), American-Spanish philosopher, wrote: "The only remarkable thing about my career is that I should have spent the better part of my life in the United States, and written my books in the English language, while retaining my Spanish nationality and sentiment, and figuring in the English-speaking world as a sort of permanent guest, familiar, appreciative and I hope discreet,

but still foreign. This is no less true of me intellectually than it is socially, and should not be ignored in considering my work. It all came from the fact that my maternal grandfather, José Borrás of Reus in Catalonia, was a younger son with an adventurous disposition and emancipated views, such that when in 1823 the French marched into Spain to restore the absolute monarchy, he left the country, wandered to Scotland, where my  mother was born, and later to Virginia, where she spent her early childhood. The consequence was that she could speak English and always retained a fundamental respect and affection for Americans; and she eventually married one of them, George Sturgis, of Boston, a merchant established in Manila. For the changing fortunes of her father had eventually taken her to the Philippine Islands, where his death in 1847 had left her an orphan. Ten years later she became a widow, and went to live in Boston with her three children, according to a promise that she had made to their father. On the outbreak of the Civil War, however, she returned to Spain and there married my father, Augustin Ruiz de Santayan y Reboiro, who had also been for many years in the Philippines and had known her there.

"I was born in Madrid on December 16, 1863, and remained in Spain until 1872, when my father and I sailed from Liverpool for Boston in the Cunard S.S. 'Samaria,' of 3,000 tons. My mother had preceded us with her other children three years earlier, and lived at 302 Beacon Street, then one of the last houses, amid vast vacant lots, on the Mill Dam. In this narrow high house, with a view (and smell) of the Back Bay in the rear, I spent my boyhood, going to the Boston Latin School. At first I was rather unhappy, but in the last two years I found my level and made the first of those many close but scattered friendships that have been the chief personal interest of my bachelor life. Harvard College followed, and two years in Berlin, with a return to Harvard, where I served as a member of the philosophical department from 1889 to 1912.

"Almost all my summers, and the three winters when I had leave of absence during these years, I spent in Europe, principally in Spain and England, within a small but constant circle of relations and friends. I have had the melancholy privilege of surviving most of them; but even now, at the age of seventy-five, I live contentedly in an atmosphere of travel and study, always in hotels, but not without books and friends and the fresh air of the great world and of changing opinions keeping me spiritually young. The dismay that has fallen of late upon so many minds has not touched me. I have never had any illusions about the world's being rationally guided or true to any ideals; reason and ideals arise in doing well something that at bottom there was no reason for doing. This is naturalism, as I understand it; and perhaps I feel myself spiritually young only because I accept beforehand the maxims of the spiritually very old, and expect nothing better. I am not a believer in any religion, literally understood; but I am a man of priestly disposition and think that it is possible to live nobly in this world only if we live in another world ideally.

"There have been short seasons in my life when nevertheless I have been attracted into an unfeigned participation in social pleasures and in political hopes. They are represented by two of my books: *Soliloquies in England* and *The Last Puritan*. These are therefore the most approachable of my writings for the general reader; but even here, though some interest may be aroused, I doubt that the unconverted or unconvertible will find much ultimate satisfaction.

"The *Soliloquies* represent my feelings during the years 1914–1918, when I was living in England, under the incubus of war, yet enjoying a springtime of free thinking and the to me rather novel influences of rural nature. The English people never seemed to me more admirable than under that trial which made a fresh bond between persons and classes that peace and prosperity might have divided. Some memories of that time have run over into *The Last Puritan*; but the chief source for this second book was my experiences in the 1890's of the pleasanter sides of Harvard and Boston. I was then still young enough to sympathize with youth, but already old enough to understand it; and I had read and traveled enough to play at culture and aestheticism without being yet tired of them. It was a pleasant intelligent life on the outskirts of a plutocracy that felt itself perfectly safe and virtuous. For me this cultivated society happened to contain little but youths and ladies; the older men seemed animals of another species; and it must be confessed that not all the youths were cultivated nor all the ladies young. I was myself growing too old to be held by the charms of mere kindness and personality. I feel those charms still, also that of youth, but I am not held by them.

"My American critics are partial to *The Life of Reason* and think it better inspired than my later books. That is a legitimate judgment philosophically; but if the point were, as in this sketch, to catch the salient characters of my life and mind, I think *The Life of Reason* would seem rather an episode, an academic task I had set myself rather than an overflow of my spontaneous philosophy. It is a treatise on possible human progress, a Utopia in substance though in form a criticism of morals, arts, and opinions. It loosely follows, in modern terms, the *Republic* of Plato and the *Ethics* of Aristotle. Like those two works it is programmatic and judicial ostensibly, but really retrospective and in the air. My later philosophy, though not descriptive of so many past things, hugs reality more closely and looks at life in its true history rather than in its good intentions. I have never been a blind lover of life, as the world lives it. My heart has been in religion, or in a philosophy that, like religion, signifies a change of heart. A pig may prefer his pigsty to the open; but would he, if he were a philosopher? I like

to regard society as a part of nature, and to see it as an incident against its non-human ground; and this is not merely cosmically, because that background is older and wider, but also inwardly, because that ground is deeper in human nature itself."

———

George Santayana (he was christened Jorge Ruiz Santayana y Borras, but never used that form of his name) sprang a surprise upon everyone when his novel *The Last Puritan* became a popular bestseller. Competent and interesting although this is, no one has yet quite been able to explain its phenomenal success: it topped the best-seller lists for many months.

Santayana's verse was the least distinguished of his output, and may be dealt with briefly. He did not learn English until he was nine, and so, while he acquired a mastery of the literary language, he lacked spontaneity. His poetry is essentially a skilled pastiche of Shakespeare or romantics such as Shelley and Keats. But this verse is not quite forgotten: a critical collected edition of it, carefully edited by William Holzberger, appeared as late as 1979 from the Bucknell University Press.

Santayana, a homosexual, in private had a disdain for heterosexuality: he called it "breeding." But as a younger man he hid his feelings, and maintained a detached attitude. When the President of Harvard, Charles W. Eliot, criticized his "unworldliness," he and everyone else knew exactly what he was saying. (Santayana himself commented that his "relations with President Eliot and other influential persons had always been strained.")

Santayana was, however, very popular with students. He lectured well and clearly, had a melodious voice, and acquired an excellent reputation as a teacher and as a man of what the poet Lionel Johnson, who met him in London, called "singular charm." In 1909 T. S. Eliot (as well as Conrad Aiken) took his course in "Ideals of Society, Religion, Art and Science in their Historical Development," and Herbert Howarth in his *Notes on Some Figures Behind T. S. Eliot* thought that both Eliot's appreciative references to Spinoza and his feeling that he could never prosper in America owed much to Santayana.

Santayana's philosophy and literary criticism are his most enduring contributions to culture; few now read *The Last Puritan*, although more are becoming acquainted with his absorbing memoirs *Persons and Places*, and with his *Letters*. Read carefully, like his autobiographical statement written for *World Authors*, all this material—unlike his verse—scrupulously avoids concealment. The odd and unusual mixture in his philosophy of hedonism, ethics, love of beauty, idealism, and materialism, is largely explained by his unhappy predicament.

Santayana's philosophy resists categorization; it is not in the mainstream, and some have cast fierce scorn upon it; but it was influential, is important in the history of American thinking, and is interesting in particular for its bearing on literature. His philosophy is quite as interesting, for example, as that of Heidegger—and a good deal more lucidly expressed; but it is not now as widely discussed. However, it is a mistake to conclude that his reputation has faded: on the contrary, he is still widely read, if not in the most modish circles. Simon Blackburn does not wish to exclude him from his *Oxford Dictionary of Philosophy* (an eminently fair book), and properly refers to him as a man of letters as well as a philosopher. He adds that, after following a "naturalistic, psychological method" Santayana had recourse to an "idiosyncratic combination of Platonism and materialism." John Passmore sums him up as an episodic thinker, remarkable for his aperçus rather than for sustained philosophical effort. His power lies in his capacity to shock, illuminatingly, a particular reader; and just at what point the illumination will come depends on the "'set' of the reader's mind . . . That he wrote a widely read novel . . . is not in the least surprising."

One might, from a non-technical point of view, describe Santayana's philosophy as typically *fin de siècle*. But, if that is true, it is by no means pejorative; unlike many of the now forgotten idealists of that time, his philosophy is, if only in discrete parts and its own special way, rigorous.

Santayana was, first and foremost, a thoroughgoing skeptic; however, oddly in such circumstances, he was also, just as thoroughgoingly, a Platonist. Famously, he denied that the existence of anything could be proved, referring to such attempts as "irrational animal faith." Thus, his attachment to Roman Catholicism (he died, tended by nuns, in a retreat in Rome) on aesthetic and historical grounds was, he insisted, "entirely divorced from faith." What Santayana did was to marry a Platonic theory of essences to materialism: his chief work, although not his most accessible or readable one ("full of dark hints," writes Passmore, justifiably), is in the four volumes of *Realms of Being* (1927–40), in which he explores, successively, the realms of essence, matter, truth, and spirit. The necessary introduction to this series is *Scepticism and Animal Faith* (1923). His argument, inasmuch as it can be summed up in brief, is that all rational processes are expressions of animal compulsions to believe in certain things (the influence of William James's pragmatism is by no means absent here): this explains why we believe that matter exists. However, only a grasp of essences enables us to elucidate existence satisfactorily.

In *Scepticism and Animal Faith* Santayana argued that the only data we can be sure of consists of "essence." He even criticized Plato for excluding from the realm of essence anything that is "lowly." In a rather tortuous way, which earned him many critics (he was, after all, trying to combine realism and idealism at a crucial time for both), he tried to establish that the "rational animal," his hero, could use essences as signs: essence is our index to reality (here he made use of arguments already employed by Charles Sanders Peirce). And his own rather bitter experience undoubtedly influenced his view of how the rational man ought to behave: he should be cool, detached—in fact (here he rejected James's

cheerful and hopeful pragmatism, which recommended energy and action), Schopenhaueran—and indeed, Schopenhauer could be claimed as the fundamental influence upon him. The only life for Santayana is that of the spirit. He was conservative only inasmuch as he believed that rationality had lived best in the well established institutions. His philosophy is at its best when it emerges from such literary books as *Interpretations of Poetry and Religion, The Genteel Tradition at Bay* and the valuable posthumous collection *Essays in Literary Criticism.* "As compared with William James's vigor and easy masculinity," writes Ralph Ross in his introduction to the 1967 reprint of *Soliloquies in England and Later Soliloquies,* "Santayana too often sounds finicky, afraid to soil his hands with the world's hot blood." But, he added, "his literary criticism . . . is based on omnivorous reading and a chameleon's sensitivity. He feels every writer's internal temperature, sees the world as he does, and describes it as he might if he wrote Santayana's expository prose. . . . It is a method that might be called impressionism except for Santayana's thoroughness and rigor. . . . " As James Ward Smith wrote in *Concise Encyclopedia of Western Philosophy and Philosophers,* Santayana "as an intellect sought to be 'hard'; but emotionally he was extremely 'soft'." This was a unique mixture in so well developed a mind, and now of course that we know a little more about it, it has its own poignancy. For in his materialistic aspect he emphasized the helplessness of human beings, the result (he, like Russell, believed) of a chance collision of atoms. Yet his Catholicism was, emotionally, very real indeed to him, and so was his disappointment at early discovering that the only kind of love he could feel was a prohibited one.

*The Last Puritan* is not a great or even a major novel; but, like most books Santayana published, it is very well written and engaging, and possesses a quiet excellence. It arose from his dislike of what he found most antipathetic in American life: Calvinism and Transcendentalism. In his hero Oliver Alden, puritanism has worked itself out to its logical end. The heir of a wealthy and now degenerate family—his father Peter is a hedonistic drug addict who wanders the world in his yacht with a young male paid companion—he grows up without love or enlightenment. He turns into a handsome and athletic critic of his decadent surroundings. He fails in love, and finally, having become neurotic and febrile, is killed in World War I.

Santayana was already over seventy when *The Last Puritan* appeared. Emotionally immersed in his Catholicism in Rome, tended by the English sisters of the Little Company of Mary, his intellect revenged itself against this lapse of rationality by writing one of his least effective books, *The Idea of Christ in the Gospels.* He was much criticized for being happy to remain in Mussolini's Italy throughout World War II; but he was an old man, and had in any case never been really sensitive to the cruel realities of politics. His papers are divided: some are at Harvard, others at the Humanities Research Center in Texas, and still more at Columbia, Princeton, and Virginia.

PRINCIPAL WORKS: *Philosophy and Literary Criticism*—The Sense of Beauty, 1896; Interpretations of Poetry and Religion, 1900; The Life of Reason, 5 vols. 1905–07; Three Philosophical Poets: Lucretius, Dante and Goethe, 1910; Winds of Doctrine, 1913; Egotism in German Philosophy, 1916; Character and Opinion in the United States, 1920; Little Essays, 1920; Soliloquies in England and Later Soliloquies, 1922; Scepticism and Animal Faith, 1923; Dialogues in Limbo, 1925, rev. 1948; Platonism and the Spiritual Life, 1927; The Realms of Being, 4 vols., 1928–40 (one vol. ed. 1942); The Genteel Tradition at Bay, 1931; Some Turns of Thought in Modern Philosophy, 1931; Obiter Scripta, 1936; The Idea of Christ in the Gospels, 1946; Dominations and Powers, 1951. *Verse*—Sonnets and Other Verses, 1894; Lucifer: A Theological Tragedy, 1899; The Hermit of Karmel, 1901; Poems, 1923; Holzberger, W. (ed.) Complete Poems, 1979. *Novel*—The Last Puritan, 1936. *Memoirs*—Persons and Places, 3 vols. 1944–53, 1986–87. *Correspondence*—Cory, D. (ed.) Letters, 1955. *Selections*—Cardiff, I. D. (ed.) Atoms of Thought, 1950; Erdman, I. (ed.) Philosophy, 1953; Singer, I. (ed.) Essays in Literary Criticism, 1956; Cory, D. (ed.) The Idler and his Works, 1957; Ballowe J. (ed.) George Santayana's America, 1967; Wilson, D. (ed.) The Genteel Tradition, 1967; Lyon, R. D. (ed.). Santayana on America, 1968.

ABOUT: The autobiographical material quoted above was written for Twentieth Century Authors, 1942. Arnett, W. E. George Santayana, 1968; Carter, D. A. George Santayana, 1992; Cory, D. Santayana: The Later Years: A Portrait with Letters, 1963; Dynes, W. (ed.) Encyclopedia of Homosexuality, 2 vols. 1990; Howarth, H. Notes on Some Figures Behind T. S. Eliot, 1965; Hughson, L. Thresholds of Reality: George Santayana and Modernist Poetics, 1977; Lach, J. George Santayana, 1988; Levinson, H. S. Santayana, Pragmatism, and the Spiritual Life, 1992; McCormick, J. George Santayana: A Biography, 1988; Santayana, G. Persons and Places, above; Schilpp, P. A. (ed.) The Philosophy of George Santayana, 1940; Sprigge, T. L. S. Santayana: An Examination of his Philosophy, 1974; Stallknecht, N. P. George Santayana, 1971; Woodward, A. Living in the Eternal: A Study of George Santayana, 1988. *Periodicals*—Contemporary Review June 1992; Journal of American Studies August 1976; Journal of Philosophy March 26, 1953; Journal of Religion January 1984, July 1987; Newsweek May 7, 1951; Time October 6, 1952.

**SANTEE, ROSS** (August 16, 1888–June 25, 1965), American regionalist and novelist, wrote: "Born in Iowa, Thornburg—five miles north of  What Cheer and twenty miles east of Oskaloosa; family Quakers on both sides. My father died when I was a baby. Mother and two older sisters made up the family, it was an integrated group. Father's people had gone to Iowa in a covered wagon. There were several long tables of the Santee clan at the Old Settlers picnics at Coal Creek. Mother was a Penrose from Ohio. Mother had gone out to Iowa to visit a sister, that was where she met my Dad. Father's people laughed a lot, but on Mother's side they were the stiff-necked variety.

"Raised the usual juvenile disturbances as a boy; interested in any kind of athletics, but I think hunting and trapping were the real love as a boy. Always liked to draw, but about the only pictures I saw were McCutcheon's cartoons in the old *Chicago Record.*

"Moved to Moline, Ill, when I was sixteen; spent the last two years of high school there. Athletics and learning to shoot a good game of pool were my main interest, although the library in Moline was a joy since it was the first one I'd ever been in.

"The river, of course, meant Huck Finn, Tom Sawyer. It was there I first read everything Mark Twain had written. The river itself was something in those days; the log rafts were still coming down and I came to know many of the old men who spent their lives on the river. Among other things I flunked in high school was drawing. I had no interest in drawing flowers and still life setups when I could see the old river rolling from the classroom.

"I spent four years at the Chicago Art Institute, went there with the idea of becoming a cartoonist; worked backstage in most every theatre in the Loop; slung hash in as many places; worked a broom at the Institute for my tuition. New York was the next move.

"Frank Casey, art editor of *Colliers*, bought the first drawing I sold in New York. I sold a few to *Judge*, peddled some to the newspapers. That first year was tough. I interviewed more office boys than I did editors. Worse yet, I'd lost interest in doing cartoons.

"At night I'd prowl the streets of New York, then try to put down what I'd remembered with a brush. One morning Tom Benton saw a lot of these sketches on the floor. He didn't like the cartoons I was doing any more than I did, but these sketches interested him since they were simple, forthright statements. He sent me down to the public library to look up Daumier. That changed everything. When I walked back up to the old Lincoln Square Arcade that night I knew I was through making any drawings except what I wanted to do.

"For several years Mother had been living with a married sister in Globe, Arizona; they'd been wanting me to come. I had no idea of ever going to work for a cow outfit, but I had to have a job.

"I wrangled horses mostly, and the doggone country had got hold of me. I wasn't exactly strange to cowboys, either. As a small boy in Iowa, one of our nearest neighbors owned a big stock farm; they brought in the Longhorns from Montana, sometimes by the trainload; sometimes half a dozen cowpunchers wintered there, mostly Texans via Montana, I heard all the old songs, and I can still remember the scrape of the fiddle when they sang, 'Natchez Under the Hill.'

"Things rocked along for several years—with a year out, killing mosquitoes at Camp Bowie, Texas, in the first unpleasantness of World War I, where I got eight dollars and ten cents a month and never made Pfc. But along with my weakness for pool I had a liking for poker, both stud and draw. So I got out of the army with six hundred dollars. I worked through the fall roundup; went up to Chicago 'to winter,' as the cowboys say, and O'Donnell, editor of a little magazine, *Cartoons*, bought most everything submitted.

"The late George Bellows was teaching at the Art Institute that winter so I went to one of his night classes. He liked the drawings I was making and talked me into trying New York again. So I went back to Arizona, worked through the spring and fall roundups; bought a cap, a pair of flat-heeled shoes, tightened my belt and headed for New York.

"Frank Casey was now editor of *Life*; Charles Dana Gibson had just bought the magazine. Frank was one of the few art editors I'd remembered who left a good taste in my mouth, so I went up to see him. Frank bought some drawings and, besides, he talked me into going down to see Crump, who was editor of *Boy's Life* at that time. Mr. Crump wanted me to do some stories. At first I said No; Tom Craven was a friend of mine and Tom had written ten years and made just twenty dollars. I said it was bad enough to be a lousy artist without taking on more misery. But Crump was insistent; so I wrote a little incident that had happened at the ranch and made a couple of drawings for it—that was what he wanted, something to tie the drawings down. He gave me twenty-five dollars for the piece.

"About that time I went into old *Leslies* to try to peddle some drawings. William Morris Houghten, who was editor, liked the drawings and asked if I'd ever written anything. I laughed, told him I'd just sold two lousy stories to a boy's magazine. He said, 'Bring in one of those "lousy" stories and let me see it.'

"Then *Century* bought six or seven pages of drawings without any text. And about that time Spike Hunt came back from Europe. Spike has older-brothered me ever since we met in Chicago in 1908. I talked Spike into going back to Arizona with me and doing a story about a real cow outfit, and the Rodeo at Payson where they built the corral at the head of the street and turned the calves right down the street; they rode the broncs there, too, and had the horse races down the main street. Spike was high on the idea, and he was coming home with me. Then he was sent to Haiti and the whole thing blew up.

"When I went over to *Century* to pick up some drawings they asked what I was going to do when I went home. I said, 'First thing is the Rodeo at Payson, then I'm going back to the ranch to work. When I told them a little about Payson Rodeo they asked me not only to make the pictures but to write the piece. Well, this is the way it all started.

"Until I was married, in 1926, I split the time between the ranch in Arizona and New York. I never worked for any outfits except the Bar F Bar and the Cross S. Most of their range was on the San Carlos Apache Reservation. In the early 20s both outfits went broke—with the drouth, and the drop in prices. Then the range was turned back to the Apaches, and the white outfits all moved off. . . .

"This Arizona country, Globe and Gila Country, has been the setting for most everything I've ever written—most of the short stories, 'Men and Horses,' 'Cowboy,' 'Apache Land,' and 'The Bubbling Spring'; the setting of 'Hardrock and Silver Sage.' Only the hills haven't changed. It's almost forty years since I rode up the old trail that evening to the Bar F Bar—and, after all, forty years is a long time."

In his monograph on Ross Santee, Neal B. Houston writes that although the "West-That-Was is no more. . . . Santee's books remain to provide themes of the true education, life, and mystique of the cowboy; to tell in the language of the cowboy, the honest humanity of the cowboy; and to reveal, with feeling and pathos, the real lives of real cowboys, friends of Santee who knew that he could tell their stories as they lived them." Although Santee is remembered more for his art than his writing, the two were complementary; he illustrated most of his own words, as in his first book, *Men and Horses*, which used text and illustrations to capture the life of cowboys. "Mr. Santee's stories of cow punchers are good, but his pictures of man and beast are better," was the *Nation's* assessment.

In *Cowboys*, his second book, he describes the life he led as teen-age cowpoke. The *Boston Transcript* claimed he "fills the room with the acid smell of the branding iron, and narrates a little known chapter of Western life." Santee continued his reminiscences in the final books published in his lifetime: *Lost Pony Tracks* and *Dog Days*.

Santee lived the life of an Arizona cowboy with periodic trips to New York City; the National Gallery exhibited his etchings in 1922. It was on one of these trips that he met Eve Farrell. They married in 1926 and built a studio and home in Arden, but made extended trips to Arizona. In 1936 Ross took the directorship of the source book *Arizona State Guide*, a part of the Federal Writers Project of which he became State Supervisor.

Eventually the Santees moved back to Delaware, where they lived for twenty years, until Eve's death in 1963. Ross returned to Arizona to spend his last years in Globe.

In its review of *Apache Lands*, a collection of true stories, the *New York Times* (1947) bemoaned the fact that Santee hadn't published more since "he gave up all notion of becoming a cartoonist and returned to Arizona and the life of a horse-wrangler and cowboy," and went on to state that "few men have known the dry ranges more intimately; fewer have written of them or sketched them more entirely."

PRINCIPAL WORKS: *Nonfiction*—Men and Horses, 1926; Apache Land, 1947; Wranglers and Rounders: The Cowboy Lore of Ross Santee, 1981. *Fiction*—The Pooch, 1931 (reissued as Spike: The Story of a Cowpuncher's Dog, 1931); The Bar X Golf Course, 1933; Sleepy Black: The Story of a Horse, 1933; The Bubbling Spring, 1949 (rev. ed. as Rusty: A Cowboy of the Old West, 1950); Hardrock and Silver Sage, 1951; The Rummy Kid Goes Home, and Other Stories of the Southwest, 1965. *Memoirs*—Cowboy, 1928; Lost Pony Tracks, 1953; Dog Days, 1955.

ABOUT: The autobiographical material quoted above was written for Twentieth Century Authors First Supplement, 1955. Contemporary Authors vol. 108 1983; Houston, N. B. Ross Santee, 1968; Reynolds, J. E. The West of Ross Santee, 1961; Tuska, J. And Piekarski, V. (eds.) Encyclopedia of Frontier and Western Fiction, 1983. *Periodicals*—Boston Transcript November 3, 1928; Nation August 18, 1926; New York Times November 9, 1947; July 1, 1965.

**SAPIR, EDWARD** (January 26, 1884–February 4, 1939), American anthropologist and linguist, was born in the Pomeranian town of Lauenburg, Prussia (now Lebork, Poland), the son of Jacob David Sapir, a synagogue cantor, and Eva (Seagal) Sapir. The Sapirs migrated to England when Edward was five, and several years later moved to the United States, settling first in Richmond, Virginia, and finally, in 1894, in New York City. His family was quite poor, but Sapir, a brilliant student, won first place in a city-wide scholarship competition, which supported his education through high school and Columbia College, where he took a B.A. in 1904.

As an undergraduate and master's candidate, Sapir's major subject was Germanic philology. His course work with Franz Boas—the foremost ethnographer of the early twentieth century, who had pioneered work on American Indian culture, and was Columbia's first professor of anthropology—persuaded him to concentrate, instead, in the anthropological study of language. Inspired by Boas, and under his direction, Sapir traveled to Washington state to conduct field research on the language and culture of the Wishram Indians. He then conducted field studies of Takelma, a language spoken in Oregon (the subject of his masterful doctoral dissertation of 1909), Yana, spoken in California, and Paiute, spoken in Utah.

In 1907–1908 Sapir was a research assistant at the University of California, Berkeley, after which he spent two years teaching anthropology at the University of Pennsylvania. From 1910 to 1925—the most productive period of his life—he lived in Ottawa, Canada, where he was chief of the division of anthropology in the Geological Survey of the Canadian National Museum, his first really important post. In 1925 he joined the faculty of the University of Chicago, and, from 1931 until his death, he was Sterling Professor of Anthropology and Linguistics at Yale.

Sapir was a talented linguist. Yiddish was his first language, but he effectively grew up as a native English speaker. He learned Hebrew as a child, and later studied and mastered many other languages, both ancient and modern, Indo-European and non-Indo-European. In his introduction to *Selected Writings of Edward Sapir*, David Mandelbaum wrote, "He had a truly phenomenal knowledge of languages; linguists have commented that his command of the facts . . . was unsurpassed among linguistic scientists." Sapir is still remembered for his innovative system of classifying Amerindian languages, the study of which continued to occupy him throughout his career.

Sapir was a man of extraordinarily wide-ranging interests. He wrote verse, composed music, and dabbled in literary criticism. His more than merely theoretical work in linguistics and anthropology, although rigorously scientific, is informed by a deeply felt humanism. Much of his work might be classified as cultural criticism in the broadest sense. In *Edward Sapir: Linguist, Anthropologist, Humanist*, Regna Darnell wrote, "He has consistently been labeled a *genius*—a term that fails to address the range and working style of his mind . . . . His

lucid prose, virtually devoid of jargon, remains fascinating; he ties together topics that are, on the surface, quite disparate . . . . His intellectual descendants tend to be considerably narrower in scope than Sapir himself . . . . There sometimes seem to be as many Sapirs as there are linguists and anthropologists claiming continuity with his work." Like the philosopher Charles Sanders Peirce, Sapir left behind him a vast body of unedited material, much of it precious.

Sapir established his reputation as a theorist with the 1916 monograph *Time Perspective in Aboriginal American Culture*, which remained a classic of anthropological literature for several generations. Written before the development of modern archaeological dating techniques, *Time Perspective* provided a theoretical framework for the historical reconstruction of the languages and cultures of non-literate peoples.

*Language: An Introduction to the Study of Speech*, his only publication that can be described as a full book, was also a product of his Canadian years. One of the central premises of *Language* is that there is no such thing as a "primitive" language: "The lowliest South African Bushman speaks in the forms of a rich symbolic system that is in essence perfectly comparable to the speech of the cultivated Frenchman." This now a commonplace, made especially so by the work of Noam Chomsky; in Sapir's day it was far from being this—and despite the many advances in linguistics since its publication, *Language* remains a useful introduction to the subject, and a paperback edition is still in print.

One of Sapir's most important contributions to linguistics was a phonemic analysis, or the study and classification of meaningful sound units in language. In his 1925 paper "Sound Patterns in Language" Sapir showed how any particular phoneme—for example, the sound of "wh" in the English word "when"—attains meaning only through its relation to other phonemes (in that language); moreover, he insisted, the process by which that meaning is created must be viewed as a cultural phenomenon. He argued that a phoneme must be distinguished from other sounds (human or non-human), however similar—such as the "wh" sound of blowing out of a candle—because the latter play no part in a meaning-generating system.

Today Sapir is probably best known, at least among non-linguists, as one of the originators of the so-called Sapir-Whorf hypothesis, sometimes called "the linguistic relativity principle." Sapir's and Whorf's hypothesis, at which they arrived independently, was that the nature of a particular language, i.e., its syntax and lexicon, shapes thought of the speaker, and hence plays a crucial role in the molding of culture. Sapir pointed out, for example, that in the Hopi Indian language verbs do not designate the time when an action occurs, but rather show the degree of validity a speaker attaches to an utterance. Thus, according to the Sapir-Whorf hypothesis, a Hopi Indian and a native English speaker would display fundamentally different approaches to such things as chronology, cause, and effect. The up-to-date version of the hypothesis, which has a "strong" and a "weak" form, has it that in some way, not yet entirely decided, language- and thought-processes have a peculiar identity. As such, the theory now has many adherents. Sapir's belief in "linguistic drift," a sort of evolutionary disrection in the development of language, was opposed by the more mechanistic view of another titan of linguistics, Leonard Bloomfield, who believed Sapir to be soft and sentimental in his general theorisings. Until after World War II Bloomfield's views were in the ascendant; since then the balance has tipped in Sapir's direction.

Sapir was a relentless critic of racism in all of its guises. In his essay "Culture, Genuine and Spurious"—one of his major contributions to cultural criticism—he ridiculed the notion that American civilization was the apogee of human achievement.

The interplay of culture and personality was the focus of much of Sapir's later work. During his years at the University of Chicago and Yale, he was a leader in the movement toward a more interdisciplinary approach to the social sciences. He collaborated with psychologists, psychiatrists, sociologists, and experts from other disciplines, while at the same time he worked to strengthen the theoretical foundations of linguistics and anthropology. Sapir pointed anthropological researchers in new directions in such later essays as "Cultural Anthropology and Psychiatry" and "The Emergence of the Concept of Personality in a Study of Cultures." He was elected to the National Academy of Sciences in 1934, and served as president of the Linguistic Society of America (1933) and the American Anthropological Association (1938). His two marriages—to Florence Delson (who died in 1924) and Jean Victoria McClenaghan—produced five children. One of his sons, James David Sapir, became a linguistic anthropologist.

Sapir published dozens of monographs and essays, and wrote one highly regarded book on general linguistics, but—perhaps because he died relatively young—there was no magnum opus. Nonetheless, social scientists from a variety of disciplines still have to maintain a keen interest in his work. The publisher Mouton de Gruyter began in 1990 issuing a sixteen-volume edition collecting his works to preserve the *inedita* in the best possible form.

PRINCIPAL WORKS: *Linguistics and anthropology*—Takelma Texts, 1909; Wishram Texts . . . Together with Wasco Tales and Myths, Collected by Jeremiah Curtin and Edited by Edward Sapir, 1909; Yana Texts . . . Together with Yana Myths Collected by Roland B. Dixon, 1910; The Takelma Language of Southwestern Oregon, 1912; Abnormal Types of Speech in Nootka, 1915; Noun Reduplication in Comox, a Salish Language of Vancouver Island, 1915; A Sketch of the Social Organization of the Nass River Indians, 1915; Time Perspective in Aboriginal American Culture; A Study in Method, 1916; The Position of Yana in the Hokan Stock, 1917; Yana Terms of Relationship, 1918; Language: An Introduction to the Study of Speech, 1921; The Fundamental Elements of Northern Yana, 1922; (with S. Matthews, E. Tittle, and others) Religious Life, 1929; Totality, 1930; (with L. Spier) Wishram Ethnography, 1930; (with H. Shenton and O. Jespersen) International Communication: A Symposium on the Language Problem, 1931; The Southern Paiute Language, 3 vols., 1931; (with M.

Swadesh) The Expression of Ending-Point Relation in English, French, and German (ed. A. Morris) 1932; Songs for a Comox Dancing Mask (ed. L. Spier) 1939; (with L. Spier) Notes on the Culture of the Yana, 1943; (with M. Swadesh) Native Accounts of Nootka Ethnography, 1955; (with M. Swadesh) Yana Dictionary (ed. M. Haas) 1960; (with H. Hoijer) The Phonology and Morphology of the Navaho Language, 1967; Linguistic Convergence: An Ethnography of Speaking at Fort Chipewyan, Alberta (eds. R. Scollon and S. Scollon) 1979. *Poetry*—Dreams and Gibes, 1917. *Correspondence*—Letters from Edward Sapir to Robert H. Lowie (ed. L. Lowie) 1965; Edward Sapir's Correspondence: An Alphabetical and Chronological Inventory, 1910–1925 (ed. L. Dallaire) 1984; The Sapir-Kroeber Correspondence (ed. V. Golla) 1984. *As editor*—(with M. Barbeau) Folk Songs of French Canada, 1925; (with M. Swadesh) Nootka Texts: Tales and Ethnological Narratives, with Grammatical Notes and Lexical Materials, 1939; (with H. Hoijer) Navaho Texts, 1942. *Selected writings*—Selected Writings of Edward Sapir in Language, Culture and Personality (ed. D. Mandelbaum) 1949 (abridged and reissued as Culture, Language, and Personality: Selected Essays, 1949). *Collected writings*—Collected Works of Edward Sapir, 16 vols., 1990.

ABOUT: Cowan, W., Foster, M., and Koerner, K. (eds.) New Perspectives in Language, Culture and Personality: Proceedings of the Edward Sapir Centenary Conference, 1984; Darnell, R. Edward Sapir: Linguist, Anthropologist, Humanist, 1990; Denine, E. and others (eds.) Thinkers of the Twentieth Century: A Biographical, Bibliographical and Critical Dictionary, 1983; Dictionary of American Biography, Suppl. 2, 1958; Dictionary of Literary Biography, Vol. 92, 1990; Koerner, K. (ed.) Edward Sapir: Appraisals of His Life and Work, 1984; Potraits of Linguists: A Biographical Source Book for the History of Western Linguistics, Vol. 2 (ed. T. Sebeok) 1966; Spier, L., and others (eds.) Language, Culture, and Personality: Essays in Memory of Edward Sapir, 1941. *Periodicals*—American Anthropologist July–September 1939; December 1992; Anthropological Quarterly January 1989; International Journal of American Linguistics October 1984; New York Times February 5, 1939; Times Literary Supplement August 24–30, 1990.

## "SAPPER" (pseudonym of HERMAN CYRIL McNEILE), (September 28, 1888–August 14, 1937), English novelist and short story writer, was born in Bodmin, Cornwall, the son of Malcolm McNeile, a naval officer, and Christiana Mary (Slogett) McNeile. He attended Cheltenham College and the Royal Military Academy in Woolrich. In 1907 he joined the Royal Engineers, and served during World War I as a lieutenant-colonel. In 1914 he married Violet Baird.

Sapper began writing sketches and stories during the war, deriving his pen name from the unofficial title of engineers whose duties included tunneling under and mining enemy lines. Half a dozen volumes of his short fiction were published before he wrote his first novel. But it was his second novel that brought him real renown in 1920, when the character of Bulldog Drummond made his debut. The book carried the  revealing subtitle "The Adventures of a Demobilized Officer Who Found Peace Dull"—thus explaining both the author's reason for writing the book and its nine sequels, and their vast popularity—especially with former soldiers. Although the sequels generally lacked many of the merits of the first book, they were all excellent as escape fiction, abounding in improbable but nonstop adventure. After Sapper's death, Gerard Fairlie (a fellow novelist) wrote additional Bulldog Drummond novels. Sapper and Gerald Du Maurier adapted the character for the stage, with Du Maurier creating the title role to excellent reviews in London and A. E. Matthews to similar praise in New York. Ronald Coleman appeared as Bulldog Drummond in one of the first full-length sound motion pictures in 1929. Although Sapper wrote other novels and numerous short stories which were also popular, he is remembered chiefly as Bulldog Drummond's creator and for his racist and cheerfully fascist opinions. His fiction lacked pretentions, employing a time-tested formula that "invested his picaresque hero with daring, wit, ingenuity, and the ability to turn out on the right side of the law in the long run," according to the *New York Times*.

PRINCIPAL WORKS: *Novels*—Mufti, 1919; Bulldog Drummond, 1920; The Black Gang, 1922; Jim Maitland, 1924; The Third Round, 1924; The Final Count, 1926; The Female of the Species, 1928; Temple Tower, 1929; Tiny Carteret, 1930; Guardians of the Treasure, 1931; Bulldog Drummond Returns, 1932; Bulldog Drummond Strikes Back, 1933 (in U.K.: Knock-Out); Ronald Standish, 1933; Bulldog Drummond at Bay, 1935; Ask for Ronald Standish, 1936; Challenge, 1937. *Short stories*—The Lieutenant and Others, 1915; The Fatal Second, 1916; Men, Women and Guns, 1916; Michael Cassidy, Sergeant, 1916 (in U.K.: Sergeant Michael Cassidy); No Man's Land, 1917; The Human Touch, 1918; The Man in Ratcatcher, 1921; The Dinner Club, 1923; Out of the Blue, 1925; Word of Honour, 1926; The Finger of Fate, 1931; Sapper's War Stories, 1932; 51 Stories, 1934. *Drama*—(with G. Du Maurier) Bulldog Drummond, 1925.

ABOUT: Reilly, J. M. (ed.) Twentieth-Century Crime and Mystery Writers, 1985. *Periodicals*—New York Times August 15, 1937; Times (London) August 16, 1937.

**SARETT, LEW R.** (May 16, 1888–August 17, 1954), American poet, wrote: "I was born in Chicago. My father and mother came to America from  Southeastern Europe. They were of healthy peasant stock, courageous, honest, and industrious. When I was a little boy we moved to Marquette, Michigan. The region was wild and beautiful. Before I was ten I knew a good deal about the woods. Later, as a result of family trouble, my mother and I found ourselves in Chicago alone. We knew bitter poverty and hunger. At the age of twelve I supported my mother and myself with various jobs that paid a pittance: as a bundle boy in a department store, a newsboy, an errand boy in a sweatshop, as employees' lavatory attendant under 'the world's most busy corner' at State and Madison Streets. In this dark period the poet in me was born, and my passion for nature. That passion, born in this period of frustration, is a vital element in my life and work.

"There was a lucky turn in our family affairs and we moved to Benton Harbor, Michigan. There I attended high school and every minute I was free

from school was spent in the woods. When I was eighteen I became a lifesaver on a municipal swimming beach in Chicago. The next year I determined to get a college education. I started at the University of Michigan, but in a year I shifted to Beloit College. I worked my way through these and later through the University of Illinois and Harvard Law School by many jobs: as a guide in the Canadian Woods, as a Forest Ranger in the Rockies, an instructor in a sportsmen's camp in Northern Wisconsin, a guide in Northern Minnesota. . . . In 1911 I received my B.A. from Beloit, and in 1916 my LL. B. from the University of Illinois. From 1912 to 1920 I taught English and public speaking at Illinois. In 1914 I married Margaret Elizabeth Husted; we have a son and a daughter.

"It was while I was teaching at Illinois that I began to write poetry. I was encouraged and helped much in counsel by Stuart P. Sherman, Harriet Monroe, and Carl Sandburg. In 1920 I accepted a position on the faculty of Northwestern University School of Speech. . . . In 1930 I returned to Northwestern, to a full professorship and a full teaching schedule, living in Ravinia, Illinois. Part of each year I give to the woods. Part of the year I do platform work from coast to coast. In 1922 I won the Levinson Prize in Poetry; my *Slow Smoke* was awarded the prize offered by the Poetry Society of America for the best volume of poetry published in America in 1925.

"I like everything rooted in earth, and everything that walks or crawls on earth. I like all people who are simple, natural, and honest. I like gardens and gardening, dogs and horses, trout-fishing, the study of botany and zoology, good books, good painting, and good music. And I like young people and I like the privilege of teaching them.

"In 1953 I became professor emeritus at Northwestern University and established my home in Gainsville, Florida. I am now serving as visiting professor of speech at the University of Florida. My first wife, Margaret Husted, died February 27, 1941. On April 19, 1946, I married my present wife, Alma Johnson."

Through such friends as Carl Sandburg and *Poetry* editor Harriet Monroe, Sarett was loosely affiliated with the Chicago Group of the 1910s and 1920s. As Leonard Nathan noted in a *Poetry* (1957) review of his posthumously published collection *Covenant with Earth*, "Sarett . . . can justifiably be linked to the poets of the midwest who consciously sought out American themes and a folk idiom in which to embody them. But Sarett, unlike [Vachel] Lindsay or Sandburg . . . , turned from the society of cities and farms to what remained of the great northwest wilds. He was not of the calibre of Lindsay, or Sandburg, but was a worthy and excellent poet, and an inspiring teacher."

The two most salient themes in Sarett's poetry are the American wilderness and the American Indian. He was well-acquainted with the Ojibwa (or Chippewa) people of the Lake Superior region. In one of his best-known poems, "The Box of God" (the title piece of his second collection), he reflects upon their forced conversion to Christianity: "The black-robed curés put your pagan Indian / Soul in their white man's House of God, to lay / Upon your pagan lips new songs, to swell / The chorus of amens and hallelujahs."

Sarett won some praise in his lifetime. In a *Literary Review* notice of *The Box of God*, William Rose Benét wrote, "Mr. Sarett's study of his red men has been sincere and intuitive."

In his foreword to Sarett's *Collected Poems*, Carl Sandburg remarked, "Books say Yes to life. Or they say No. *The Collected Poems of Lew Sarett* says Yes." Reviewing the volume in *Poetry* (1941), Leo Shapiro noted, "It is a testimony to Mr. Sarett's poetry that it achieved the popularity it did during the post-war decades, precisely when 'romantic' poetry of this kind was least in demand because of the interest in hollow men and waste lands." While Shapiro regarded Sarett as "a brilliant and original contemporary American poet," the more discerning Leonard Nathan, writing in the same journal sixteen years later, questioned the poet's originality: "Sarett's personal reaction to nature is somewhere between John Muir's and William Cullen Bryant's: simple mysticism tinged with a gentle romantic melancholy . . . in diction, verse pattern, and tone, his personal lyrics seem to arise from the English Romantics rather than from a fresh feeling for or perception of nature."

PRINCIPAL WORKS: *Poetry*—Many Many Moons: A Book of Wilderness Poems, 1920; The Box of God, 1922; Slow Smoke, 1925; Wings Against the Moon, 1931; The Collected Poems of Lew Sarett, with a foreword by Carl Sandburg, 1941; Covenant with Earth: A Selection from the Poetry of Lew Sarett, Including Six Poems Not Previously Published (ed. A. Sarett) 1956. *Speech*—(with W. Foster) Basic Principles of Speech, 1936, 4th rev. ed. (also with A. Sarett) 1966 (reissued as Personal Power through Speech, 1937; rev. ed. reissued as Speech, 1946); (with W. Foster and J. McBurney) Speech, a High School Course, 1943. *As editor*—(with W. Foster) Modern Speeches on Basic Issues, 1939.

ABOUT: The autobiographical material quoted above was written for Twentieth Century Authors, 1942 and Twentieth Century Authors First Supplement, 1955. Untermeyer, L. American Poetry Since 1900, 1923. *Periodicals*—American Magazine February 1926, March 1926; Literary Review January 6, 1923; New York Times August 8, 1954; Poetry December 1931; December 1941; August 1957.

**SAROYAN, WILLIAM** (August 31, 1908–May 18, 1981), American short story writer, novelist, and playwright, was born in Fresno, California (the home of many Armenian refugees from Turkish persecution) of Armenian parents who had reached California in the early years of the century. His father, Armenag, a Presbyterian minister and writer, worked in the vineyards and died of peritonitis when the boy was two years old, and young Williams and his older brother and two sisters were obliged to spend some years in the Fred Finch Orphanage at Oakland, California. But in

1915 his mother, Takoohi, obtained work in a Fresno cannery, and he was able to grow up at home from the age of seven. He discovered that he was a writer at a very early age, and transferred from the Longfellow Junior High School in Fresno to the Technical School (1921) in order to learn to type.

Saroyan began selling newspapers at seven, and worked all his way through school to bring in money. His first significant writing (a story called "The Broken Wheel," written under the name of Sirak Goryan) appeared in 1933 in an Armenian journal, *Hairenik*. He next worked as an office manager at the San Francisco Telegraph Company. He was twenty-six before he achieved fame, almost overnight, with the publication, in *Story* magazine, of what is still probably his most famous work, "The Daring Young Man on the Flying Trapeze" (after the popular song), which soon gave the title to his first bestselling collection. This fame stayed with him until the late 1940s: from the early 1950s his reputation went into a tailspin from which—with the exception of a few devoted fans—it never recovered. Sometimes his considerable achievement is lost sight of by critics who tend to put too much emphasis on the sharpness of his decline. Brian Darwent, his English editor and now one of his chief critics, said of the later work, that Saroyan "wrote about his own and other people's lives in random fragments and off the top of his head. Through the 1960s and 1970s he published, mainly only in America, a long series of these autobiographical sketchbooks, as they might be called. What came up from his memory, unbidden, seemed to be more important and valid to him in artistic terms than what had actually happened. For his last book in the series, *Obituaries*, he specifically asked his publishers not to correct the facts."

But failure was a long way in front of Saroyan when Random House published *The Daring Young Man on the Flying Trapeze*. The royalties financed a trip to Europe and to Armenia. This visit made a profound impression upon him, and he became an expert in the literature of the still-oppressed Armenians. Readers compared the seeming effortlessness of Saroyan's prose in the twenty-six tales of his first book with that of Sherwood Anderson. The *Saturday Review of Literature* conceded that he "rambled," but praised his ability to "make his rambling interesting and not boring. He is intensely conscious of himself, but it is a self of some subtlety." The reviews in fact were not at first particularly good, and Louis Kroenenberger sounded a warning note in the *Nation*: "At the moment Mr. Saroyan is most of the things a serious artist is not. He is an exhibitionist, a verbalist, a poseur, and nose-thumber, a prima donna, and a victim of genius mania. Those are harsh words to throw, in place of a helping hand, to a newcomer; but if the one other thing Mr. Saroyan happens to be—a young writer with talent—is to survive, they must be thrown. He is up to his neck at present in cleverness, and if he persists in being so clever he will end as either a fifth-rater or a bore." Saroyan did not take this or like advice, but he did "survive": he went on writing "off the top of his head," producing some works of genius, but more that was "fifth-rate." But he was a hit-or-miss writer by nature, and must be taken as he was, or not at all. Not a few critics put a high value upon his wild and often conceited stream-of-consciousness prose, even while they deplore his egoism and "genius mania." Moreover, although not read as widely as some of his most ardent admirers claim, he is read, and his is a living name.

Saroyan followed *The Daring Young Man* with more stories, collected in *Inhale and Exhale*. Horace Gregory, a reliable critic, insisted in *Books* that the author tended to "defeat his own ends," but thought that a "touch of pathos" ran all through his egoism and his "bid for immortality"; he predicted, however, that Saroyan would "achieve immortality of a specific kind."

Saroyan continued to dazzle the reading public, if not all the critics, with his novels, stories, and plays. Notable among the plays were *My Heart's in the Highlands* and the most famous and successful of all, *The Time of Your Life* (both 1939). Like the prose, the plays are a formless blend of optimism, ebullience, and sentimentality (that, however, their author always recognizes as such). They were at their most successful in the years of the Depression and World War II, when audiences looked for this kind of material. Saroyan's high reputation was interwoven with the Roosevelt years of upbeat hope against poverty and despair. When they ended, his reputation was finished as well. He served in the U.S. army from 1942 until 1945; he wrote, of the period immediately following, "After the war all that I had was a condition of simple madness, the consequence of having been subjected to unremitting chicken"; "Three years in the Army and a stupid marriage had all but knocked me out of the picture, and, if the truth is told, out of life itself. Suicide was suicide, divorce was divorce . . . I flipped a coin, and it came up divorce."

He kept custody of his children in spite of his then heavy drinking and gambling. Much of his work thereafter consisted of the sort of grumbling and railing that most people, even writers, keep to themselves. Yet he managed to rehabilitate himself: he removed himself from the immediate attention of the revenue services (to whom he owed $50,000) by taking an apartment in Paris, and he worked hard there. He could not, however, renounce gambling, and so often had to rush books off to pay his debts to bookmakers. His last resounding success was the screenplay for *The Human Comedy*, which he wrote just before joining the Signal Corps and which was filmed by Clarence Brown in 1943; it won an Oscar. It is a sentimental tale of life in a small American town, featuring Mickey Rooney, and was called everything from "puerile" to "moving." It is in fact a highly effective "war effort" movie (the novel, his first, that Saroyan made from it coincided with the release of the film) and belongs to its time. Nothing else he did for the theater or screen was ever really as successful.

The setting of his hit play *The Time of Your Life* is a San Francisco honky-tonk in October of 1939. Consisting of disparate episodes centered on a

melodramatic plot, it is a fluent hymn to the American Dream: "In the time of your life, live, so that in that good time there shall be no ugliness or death for yourself or for any life your life touches." Awarded the Pulitzer Prize for it, Saroyan declined it on the grounds that commerce should not patronize the arts. Unlike as in O'Neill's *The Iceman Cometh*, also set in a saloon, Saroyan's central character dispenses optimism and light. Subsequent attempts at drama were, for him, unsuccessful, except for one of his many one-acters, *Hello Out There* (1942). In this bitter play a gambler is in jail on a rape charge falsely laid by a woman whom he deserted. He now falls in love with the prison cook, who tries to save him from a lynch-mob, but he is shot by the husband of his accuser.

The plain and simple, if diffuse, style Saroyan had cultivated in his early years failed to develop, and became sentimental and arch, as his (London) *Times* obituarist (who knew and liked him) commented. A reader indignantly demanded of him: "How could you write so much good stuff and still write such bad stuff? And why the hell hasn't your writing improved with age?" Saroyan proudly quoted this. While his rhapsodic style went out of fashion, his life disintegrated owing to his compulsive gambling and his huge debt to the American tax authorities. His marriage to Carol Marcus (who became Mrs. Walter Matthau)—he married her in 1943, they were divorced in 1949, remarried in 1951, and divorced again in the following year—was difficult. They had two children, Aram (a poet) and Lucy (an actress).

Saroyan's memorial service was attended by the likes of Henry Kissinger and New York's Mayor Koch, and the mourners were addressed by Kurt Vonnegut. His ashes were divided between Armenia and Fresno, to which he had returned in his final years, made painful by cancer and disappointment. Yet he had himself recommended: "Try to be alive, you'll be dead soon enough," and he retained until the end his courage and sense of humor.

PRINCIPAL WORKS: *Novels*—The Human Comedy, 1943 (rev. 1966); The Adventures of Wesley Jackson,1949; The Twin Adventures: The Adventures of William Saroyan, A Diary; the Adventures of Wesley Jackson, 1950; Rock Wagram, 1951; Tiger Tiger, 1967; The Laughing Matter, 1953; Mama I Love You, 1956 (sometimes listed as The Bouncing Ball); Papa You're Crazy, 1957; Boys and Girls Together, 1963; One Day in the Afternoon of the World, 1964. *Short stories*—The Daring Young Man on the Flying Trapeze, 1934; Inhale and Exhale, 1936; Three Times Three, 1936; Little Children, 1937; A Gay and Melancholy Flux, 1937; Love, Here is My Hat, 1937; A Native American, 1938; The Trouble with Tigers, 1938; Peace,It's Wonderful, 1939; Three Fragments and a Story, 1939; My Name is Aram, 1940; Saroyan's Fables, 1941; The Insurance Salesman, 1941; 48 Saroyan Stories, 1942; 31 Selected Stories, 1943; Some Day I'll Be a Millionaire: 34 More Great Stories, 1943; Dear Baby, 1944; The Saroyan Special, 1948; The Fiscal Hoboes, 1949; The Assyrian, 1950; The Whole Voyald, 1956; Love, 1959; After Thirty Years, 1964 (includes essays); Best Stories of Saroyan, 1964; My Kind of Crazy Wonderful People, 1966 (contains one play); Man with the Heart in the Highlands, 1968; My name is Saroyan, 1983; Darwent, B. (ed.) The New Saroyan Reader, 1984. *Fictionalized memoirs*—The Time of Your Life, 1939; Hilltop Russians in San Francisco, 1941; The Bicycle Rider in Beverly Hills, 1952; Here Comes, There Goes, You Know Who, 1961; Me, 1963 (for children); I Used to Believe I Had Forever: Now I'm Not So Sure, 1968; Letters from 74 rue Taibout, 1969; Famous Faces and Other Friends, 1976; Sons Come and Go, Mothers Hang in Forever, 1976; Chance Meetings, 1978; Obituaries,1979; Births, 1981; Darwent,B.(ed.) Saroyan Memoirs 1994. *Plays*— The Man With the Heart in the Highlands, 1938; The Time of Your Life, 1939; The Hungerers, 1929; A Special Announcement, 1940; Three Plays, 1940; Subway Circus, 1940; Three Plays, 1941; Razzle Dazzle, 1942 (includes Hello Out There); Get Away Old Man, 1944; Don't Go Away Mad, 1949.

ABOUT: Floan, H. R. William Saroyan, 1966; Foard, E. C. William Saroyan: A Reference Guide, 1989; Foster, E.H. William Saroyan, 1984; William Saroyan: A Study of the Short Fiction, 1991; Rigson, G. (ed.) Concise Encyclopedia of Modern World Literature, 1963; Harmalian, L. William Saroyan: The Man and the Writer Remembered, 1987; Lee, L. and Gifford, B. William Saroyan, A Biography, 1984; Saroyan, A. William Saroyan, 1983; Seymour-Smith, M. Guide to Modern World Literature, 1986. *Bibliography*—Kherdian, D. A Bibliography of Saroyan 1934–1963, 1965. *Periodicals*—Books February 23, 1936; Current Biography November 1972; Nation November 7, 1934; New Republic November 4, 1957; Saturday Review of Literature October 20, 1934.

## SARTON, GEORGE ALFRED LÉON (August 31, 1884–March 22, 1956), American historian of science, wrote: "George Sarton was born in Ghent

(Belgium). Educated at the Athenaeum and University of Ghent. After obtaining his doctorate in mathematics in 1911, he dedicated his life to the study of the history and philosophy of science. In 1915, he came to the United States; in 1918, he was appointed an associate of the Carnegie Institution of Washington and could devote all his time to his chosen work. From 1916 on, he did some teaching in Harvard University, but it was the Carnegie Institution which made the accomplishment of his task possible. . . .

"He founded *Isis*, an international quarterly concerning his studies, in 1912, and was its editor until 1952; in 1936, he founded *Osiris* to accommodate longer memoirs on the subject."

———

With a degree in celestial mechanics—his dissertation had been on Newtonian physics—George Alfred Léon Sarton had the advantage of being conversant with scientific method; but he always remained a humanist scholar, equally at home in the laboratory and the study. Although his name does not figure in such reference works as the *Dictionary of the History of Science*, Sarton did much to establish the history of science as a specialized discipline in America.

In 1911, Sarton married Eleanor Mabel Elwes of London, who died in 1950. Their only daughter, the poet and writer May Sarton, wrote appreciatively of her father's upbringing in a series of essays in the *New Yorker*. "In My Father's House—" (January 7, 1952) sketches her father's bourgeois childhood in the "remembered aroma" of the "rather sombre" house in Ghent inhabited only by George

and his reclusive father, widowed when George's mother died soon after childbirth. She describes the adolescent Sarton's forays through the cafes of Ghent. "Here he wandered," she wrote, "smoking and composing the early romantic books he wrote under the name of Dominique de Bray, when he thought he would be a poet, and with no idea yet that he would soon be getting a doctorate in celestial mechanics." Sarton spent part of 1931 and 1932 in the Near East, where he learned enough Arabic to consult in the original the scientific classics written in that language.

Throughout his career, Sarton attempted to endow his works with the finesse of a literary stylist: he wanted to bridge the gulf between the sciences and the liberal arts by always treating the former as inextricably woven with the culture and world view of the period under discussion. Though this methodology was rooted in rationality, he never denied the irrational its role as a compelling force in human affairs.

Although his first book, the *Introduction to the History of Science*, appeared in 1927, he did not live to complete the projected eight- or nine-volume series that he believed would be necessary to trace the discipline from ancient until modern times. The first volume appeared in 1952; the second was published posthumously in 1959.

Both volumes were well regarded by reviewers. The first book was praised by the *Times Literary Supplement* for being a "sustained and inspiring narrative . . . that never fails to convey adequately to his readers not only the nature of the cultures that preceded and contributed to Greek thought, but also the spirit of that remarkable civilization that produced the Greek miracle and formulated so many of the problems that are still fundamental to philosophy. . . ."

John Pfeiffer, however, in the *New York Times* called it "a poorly written book." But of its successor Pfeiffer conceded that it offered "a great deal to the serious student of scientific history, for whom style may be a secondary consideration and who will presumably know what to skip and what to read."

In the *Dictionary of American Biography*, Arnold Thackray and Robert K. Merton wrote that "Sarton was culturally oriented toward universal history and those progressivist philosophies that found their basis in positive science and their end in the imminent brotherhood of man. Yet in his thinking he was indebted to Condorcet as well as to Comte. The lines of English thought that led from Herbert Spencer to the Webbs were also important to his vision of the goals to be served by that new synthesis of knowledge to which the history of science was the essential key." Sarton's enduring contribution, they believed, "lay in his success in validating the history of science as an intellectual discipline." Thackray and Merton ended by declaring that "his presence at Harvard was crucial to the later creation and legitimation of a department that is one of the world's major centers of the discipline. The history of science is now firmly institutionalized. It was Sarton's particular gift both to create necessary building materials and to act as the first deliberate architect of this field in America."

PRINCIPAL WORKS: The autobiographical material quoted above was written for Twentieth Century Authors First Supplement, 1955. Introduction to the History of Science, vol. 1, From Homer to Omar Khayyam, 1927; The History of Science and the New Humanism, 1931, rev. 1937; Introduction to the History of Science, vol. 2, From Rabbi Ben Ezra to Roger Bacon, 1931; Study of the History of Mathematics, 1936; Life of Science, 1948; Guide to the History of Science, 1952; History of Science, 1952; Appreciation of Ancient and Medieval Science During the Renaissance, 1954; Galen of Pergamon, 1954; Six Wings; Men of Science in the Renaissance, 1956.

ABOUT: Current Biography 1942; Sarton, Among the Usual Days, a Portrait, 1993. Periodicals—New Yorker, November 28, 1952; January 9, 1954; February 6, 1954; April 3, 1954; Isis, vol. 44 1953; vol. 70 1979; vol. 75 1984; vol. 76 1985; Times Higher Education Supplement, November 30, 1984.

**SARTON, MAY** (May 3, 1912–July 16, 1995), American poet and novelist, wrote: "I was born in Wondelgem, Belgium, but I do not remember any-thing about Belgium then as we were driven out as refugees from the German invasion in 1914. My father, Belgian by birth, [was] the historian of science, George Sarton. My mother was English. We became naturalized Americans in 1924. It is strange to me to think that I would be a writer in French, if it had not been for World War I. As it was I soon forgot my French, as we spoke English at home for my father's sake, and I had to learn French later like any other American child. Belgian writers are divided into those 'of the Flemish tongue' and those of 'the French tongue.' George Sarton and I seem to be Belgian writers 'of the English tongue.' I believe this was all lucky as I'm convinced that English is the best language for poetry in the world.

"My chief education was at the Shady Hill School in Cambridge [Massachusetts], at that time an open-air school. Writing in mittens perhaps explains the illegibility of my hand. But I had the great good fortune there as a small child to be taught poetry by a genius, Agnes Hocking. Poetry became my passion then and has never ceased to be so. From Shady Hill School I went on to high school at the Cambridge High and Latin. My graduation in 1929 was the end of any formal education, because for the next eight years I thought that theatre was to be my life. I entered Eva Le Galienne's Civic Repertory Theatre in New York City as an apprentice when I was seventeen, worked there in small parts and finally became a member of the company and director of the Apprentice Group. When the Civic Repertory closed [in 1933], I tried to keep together a group of the students and we rehearsed and played together as the Associated Actors Theatre for the next three years. All this was a kind of education, different perhaps from college, but I believe now immensely valuable to me as a writer, and I do not regret it.

"The year my little company disbanded my first book of poems came out, and from that time on I have been wholly concerned with writing. I have had all kinds of jobs, from film script writing at the Office of War Information to extensive lecturing on poetry in colleges all over the country, and more recently . . . Briggs-Copeland Instructor in Composition at Harvard University. But these jobs were only for the purpose of buying time for my own writing.

"I believe that poetry and novels are a good combination. Poetry comes in spurts whereas after the initial imaginative creation, a novel can and perhaps must be written day after day on a very regular schedule. The novels, so far, have all been laid in Europe where I have gone back many times to find those old roots. But I believe passionately in America and, as time goes on, hope perhaps to build a bridge the other way, and to be one of those writers who contribute to the understanding of the United States in Europe."

———

During a writing career that spanned more than sixty years, May Sarton produced nineteen novels and fifteen books of poetry, as well as several journals and children's books, continuing to write prolifically and publish almost to the time of her death of breast cancer. Three significant works appeared after her eightieth birthday, her Collected Poems 1930-1993, her last collection of poems, Coming into Eighty, and her final journal, Encore: A Journal of the 80th Year. "She was best known and most highly regarded as a poet," wrote Mel Gussow, her New York Times obituarist. Sarton herself once said "If I were in solitary confinement, I'd never write another novel, and probably not keep a journal, but I'd write poetry, because poems, you see, are between God and me." Several years before her death, she wrote in Encore: A Journal of the Eightieth Year that "I write poems, have always written them, to transcend the painfully personal and reach the universal. I think possibly the poem, if it is a good one, may be like a goal, to which I try to climb, and reach it if I think hard enough about what I have been feeling." By the time of her death, Sarton had achieved somewhat of a minor cult following among American readers who found her verse accessible and her voice gentle if provocative. Many women—and not all of them "feminist"— appreciated her affirmation of feelings once dismissed as worthy of serious poetry; her self-avowed lesbianism made her a heroine to others. Sarton repeatedly made it clear that her compass was drawn close to the heart. "My business is the analysis of feeling," she once said, as if fearing the consequences of the line in "She Shall Be Called Woman" in her first collection, Encounter in April: "And then one day/all feeling/slipped out from her skin/until no finger's consciousness remained." Still, she was neither activist nor polemicist, and rarely expressed radical notions in her verse, whose tone was more calming than corrosive.

A 1937 New England newspaper review of Encounter in April captured this mood in words that really could have been written about her work at any stage in her career: "Here may be found, not the bitterness nor the strife of love—the frequent theme of modern poets—but its possible quietness and comfort."

Her work did not fit into the orthodox modernism of her time, and she was never taken seriously by major critics—William Rose Benét and Martha Bacon of the *Saturday Review* were among her most ardent champions in the early years—nor did she win major prizes like the Pulitzer or the National Book Award, but she was a member of the American Academy of Arts and Sciences and was the recipient of eighteen honorary degrees. This occurred despite her often expressed disdain for academic life, which she once called "a breeding ground for prima donnas." A 1941 letter to essayist Rollo Walter Brown, another of her champions, expands on this theme: "So I have been writing quite a lot of new [poems] in a different sphere, meditative, though not personal. I enclose the latest 'The Sacred Order,' collected in *The Lion and the Rose*, with the words 'Never forget this when the talk is clever:/ Wisdom must be born in the flesh or wither,' which is really against the Academics who always poison history and literature . . . " Perhaps William Stafford summed it up best when he wrote this encomium to the *Collected Poems*: "In May Sarton the private citizen has a champion, one who takes the missiles that the years fling at us all: she parries them, survives, and lives as a model, not of the unusual but of the usual, the person beleaguered but staunch. The big abstractions—war, pain, age, disappointments—find a lodging in one life and are there considered and confronted in an exemplary way."

Sarton was a voracious reader and often shared with her correspondents her admiration for whatever writer she happened to be enamoured with at the moment—there were hundreds. Of course, she did not mean to write serious criticism, but a reading of her many letters give a picture of how her literary temperament evolved over the years, though they also open her to the charge of namedropping. In her twenties, while in England, she met both Edna St. Vincent Millay ("a delightful but slightly spoiled child") and Virginia Woolf ("it was really most extraordinary because one couldn't help falling into this stream of consciousness conversation" and—chillingly premonitory—"Woolf looking like a seahorse, delicate and fabulous and exactly as she should be . . . the room affected her as being underwater and the rest of the evening was *Waves*-ian"). During the war years, she was in turn enchanted by Rilke then Mauriac, then Tolstoy, Flaubert, George Eliot, Huxley, Dinesen, Henry James, and Mistral; immediately after the war, she turned for sustenance to philosophers, like Kierkegaard or Maritain. Of the Russians, she favored Tchekov, Turgenev, and Tolstoy—the latter "a class apart like a great mountain"—over the "self-intoxicated" Dostoievsky.

A deepening sense of concern for the role of the woman writer pervaded much of Sarton's thinking. A letter to Louise Bogan in 1954 is self-revelatory; in it, she writes how she is struck by Robert Graves's commentary about Juana Ines de la Cruz: "Though the burden of poetry is difficult enough for a man to bear, he can always humble himself before an incarnate muse and seek instruction from her—The case of a woman poet is a thousand times worse; since she is herself the Muse, a Goddess without an external power to guide or comfort her, if she strays even a finger's breadth from the path of divine instinct, she must take violent self-vengeance."

Although Sarton wrote nineteen novels, few of them excited critical interest, and she herself felt that her true voice was to be found in poetry. Among the novels, *Faithful are the Wounds* was an exception. It was a fictionalized account that alluded to the struggles of critic F. O. Mattheissen, the self-avowed homosexual Christian and socialist at Harvard who died a suicide in 1950. Written at the end of the contentious McCarthy era, the novel was praised by reviewers who admired its forthright topicality during a period when freedom of expression was threatened. The *New York Herald Tribune Book Review* called it "essentially a *pièce à these*, a blow struck for the freedom of mind that, at this juncture in our history, is in jeopardy. There is always the danger that in a novel of ideas the ideas may overshadow and dominate their spokesmen. To a certain extent this is true of 'Faithful are the Wounds.' But Miss Sarton is enough of an artist and a story-teller to enlist her readers' sympathies." And her ever-loyal *Saturday Review* said bluntly, "This novel leaves a scar. Its readers (they should be legion) will have an increased involvement in the dilemmas of their time." Sarton's 1965 novel, *Mrs. Stevens Hears the Mermaids Singing*, is a prescient and semi-autobiographical fiction about a renowned poet in her seventies who is pursued by two younger reporters seeking to "uncover the provenance of her poetic inspiration." This time, reviewers were not so kind; the *Saturday Review*, for once, was unimpressed ("sensitive to the point of fussiness, and totally without humor") and *Book Week* was downright hostile ("What goes on among half-people whose nether regions are fused and fishily armored has damned little to do with the rest of us, who are bifurcated below and vulnerable all over"). She also used the novel as an opportunity to defend sexual diversity, as seen in a 1965 letter to Basil de Selincourt who was "dismayed" by the publication of *Mrs. Stevens*. "Dearest Basil," Sarton wrote, "please look into your heart and discover whether you really believe the Almighty would have consigned Socrates and Shakespeare to the flames? . . . it looks as if it [homosexuality] really were a part of this mysterious creation from the start . . . "

By the late 1950s, Sarton was writing works that waxed nostalgic for her childhood and young girlhood. There was her popular *I Knew a Phoenix: Sketches for an Autobiography*, the title from the poem by Yeats ("I knew a phoenix in my youth, so let them have their day"). Sarton always admired Yeats; in a 1959 letter to Katharine Davis, she wrote "I do not think that he was a great person, but I do think he was a great poet." Reviwers praised the memoir for its "finely limned and gracefully illuminated" sketches, its charm, its magic, and its gentle nostalgia. The *New York Times* gushed, "Every chapter is illumined by the poet's vision of life, the response of an ardent mind and a generous heart." The book is full of anecdotes about her and her father, and about her early teachers. Sarton had from the beginning preferred traditional metrical forms, such as the Shakespearean sonnet and the quatrain. Writing in the *Christian Science Monitor* in 1966, she declared the usefulnesss of these forms, in which "All is held solid and clear and contained; there is nothing ragged or spilled over." But about the same time, she began experimenting with free verse and irregular rhymes, as in her wide-ranging collection *A Private Mythology*, which included poems on her travels to Greece, India, and Japan, as well as elegies for departed friends and pastorals on country living. Occasional references to recent world events—the war in Vietnam, the deaths of Martin Luther King and two Kennedys—are found in some of the poems in her next collection, *A Grain of Mustard Seed* (1971), but, true to form, she casts them in an elegiac tone: Protestors would never use them as chants in an antiwar demonstration. The increasing solitude of old age, with infirmities treated not as burdens but as opportunities for deeper insight, marks the two collections she published in her seventies: *Letters from Maine*, in 1984; and *The Silence Now*, in 1988. Her published journals of this period are affirmations of growth in the midst of decline, offering an intimate snapshot of her life on the Maine coast, enjoying the sustenance of friends, gardening, and Mozart and, of course, writing poetry. In the last entry (Wednesday, June 24) for *Encore: A Journal of the Eightieth Year*, she writes: "And where have I been in this journal? Through a thicket of ill health into an extraordinary time of happiness and fulfillment, more than I ever dreamed possible, and here it is. In my old age, the recognition I longed for, a rare kind of love shared with Susan, and even enough money to be able to give a lot away! But far more reason for happiness even than these, the sovereign reason is that I am writing a poem almost every day." She closed the journal by quoting three stanzas from George Herbert's "The Flower," in which are found the words "And now in age I bud again." For her envoi in *The Silence Now*, a collection of poems published in 1988, she chose to return to another of her favorite images of regeneration, with a poem entitled "The Phoenix Again."

PRINCIPAL WORKS: *Poetry*—Encounter in April, 1937; Inner Landscape, 1939; The Lion and the Rose, 1948; The Land of Silence, 1953; In Time Like Air, 1958; Letters from Maine, 1983; As Does New Hampshire, and Other Poems, 1987; Coming Into Eighty, 1994. *Novels*—The Single Hound, 1938; The Bridge of Years, 1949; Shadow of a Man, 1950; A Shower of Summer Days, 1952; Faithful Are the Wounds, 1955; Birth of a Grandfather, 1957; Fur Person, 1957; The Small Room, 1961; Joanna and Ulysses: A Tale, 1963; Mrs. Stevens Hears the Mermaids Singing, 1965; Miss Pickthorn and Mr. Hare, 1966; The Poet and the Donkey, 1969; Kinds of Love, 1970; As We Are Now, 1973; Punchs Secret, 1974; Crucial Conversations, 1975; A Walk through the Woods, 1976; A Reckoning, 1978; Anger, 1982; The Magnificent Spinster, 1985; The Education of Harriet Hatfield, 1989. *Essays and journals*—The New

Yorker, January 9, 1952; April 3, 1954; February 6, 1954; I Knew a Phoenix: Sketches for an Autobiography, 1959; Plant Dreaming Deep, 1968; A World of Light: Portraits and Celebrations, 1976; The House by the Sea, 1977; Recovering, a Journal, 1980; At Seventy: A Journal, 1984; Journal of a Solitude, 1985; After the Stroke: A Journal, 1989; Endgame: A Journal of the Seventy-Ninth Year, 1992; A Journal of the Eightieth Year, 1993; Among the Usual Days: Unpublished Poems, Letters, Journals, and Photographs, 1993; Collected Poems, 1930–1993, 1993. *Anthologies*—Daziel, B. D. (ed.), An Anthology of the Journals, Novels, and Poems of May Sarton, 1991; Simpson, M. and Wheelock, M. (ed.), May Sarton: A Self-Portrait, 1986.

ABOUT: The autobiographical material quoted above was written for Twentieth Century Authors First Supplement, 1955. Blouin, L. May Sarton: A Bibliography, 1978; Cornillon, S. K., Images of Women in Fiction, 1972; Hunting, C. (ed.), May Sarton: Woman and Poet, 1982; Rule, J., Lesbian Images, 1975. *Periodicals*—Atlantic January 1953; June 1975; Book Week October 24, 1965; Commonweal July 4, 1975; Hudson Review summer 1967; New York Times November 20, 1983; July 18, 1995; New York Times Book Review March 15, 1939; September 8, 1957; November 24, 1963; October 24, 1965; November 12, 1978; March 27, 1988; Saturday Review March 27, 1937; April 17, 1948; May 19, 1955; October 23, 1965; Sewanee Review, Spring 1958; Springfield Republican April 18, 1937.

**SARTRE, JEAN-PAUL**(June 21, 1905–April 15, 1980), French novelist, dramatist, philosopher, critic, and polemicist, the only man to decline the Nobel Prize for Literature (1964) of his own free will (later he wanted the money, but did not get it), was born in Paris; his father, Jean-Baptiste, was a naval officer who died when Jean-Paul was young. Through his mother, the former Anne-Marie Schweitzer, he was a great nephew of Albert Schweitzer.

Sartre attended the Lycée Louis-le-Grand, after which he studied philosophy at the famous École Normale. He graduated in 1930 and began teaching secondary school in various places in France. Also during this time, 1929–1934, he traveled and studied in Egypt, Greece, and Italy. In Germany (1933–1934), he absorbed the ideas of the phenomenologist philosopher Edmund Husserl and of Martin Heidegger. He also studied the works of Kierkegaard, considered by some to be the founder of the modern existential movement. From these, and from his conviction that "sadness and boredom" lie at the bottom of existence, he derived the bases of his philosophy.

In 1935 Sartre returned to Paris. He took a teaching position and in his free time began frequenting the Left Bank cafés, soon attracting around him a group of intellectuals. Although his writings of this time were unique psychological studies of imagination and human emotion, they did not attract much notice. What did win him a certain amount of recognition was a series of essays he had written for the journal *La Nouvelle Revue Française*. Through these he did much to call attention to American novelists such as Hemingway, Faulkner, and Steinbeck. In 1938 Sartre published his first novel, *La Nausée* (*Nausea*). It was followed, a year later, by a collection of short stories, *Le Mur* (*The Wall*). Both reflect the bitter pessimism and despair of a man who finds himself in a universe where "nothing, absolutely nothing, justifies his existence." These two first works were translated and published nearly ten years later in the United States to mixed, and often poor, reviews. In *The New York Times*, Nabokov commented on *Nausea*: "When an author inflicts his idle and arbitrary philosophic fancy on a helpless person he has invented for that purpose, a lot of talent is needed to make the trick work. One has no special quarrel with [the main character] when he decides that the world exists. But the task to make the world exist as a work of art was beyond Sartre's powers." Of *The Wall*, *Time* remarked that Sartre's style was a "thin derivative brew of Hemingway, Faulkner, Dos Passos and simplified Joyce. It is hard to feel sorry for his gallery of modern misfits . . . he has simply wrenched them out of life's context to illustrate his philosophy of despair."

Sartrean existentialism, much heeded in Europe and highly influential there, was the culmination of a tendency that went back to Max Stirner, Nietzsche, and Kierkegaard, and to Unamuno and Ortega in Spain. It also had roots in many literary works of the past—in particular Tolstoy's *The Death of Ivan Ilyich*—and went back to Pascal and St. Augustine before that, and to gnosticism before Augustine. But in the aftermath of World War II, existentialism became for a decade or so associated almost exclusively with Sartre and with his lifelong companion Simone de Beauvoir. This excited the young and enraged the conventional, and was not taken seriously by those philosophers in the Anglo-Saxon tradition.

After his return from Germany, Sartre taught for a while, then joined the army, and was taken prisoner in 1940. While in prison he wrote and directed plays for his fellow prisoners. Released in 1941, he then joined the Resistance, writing for such underground publications as *Les Lettres Françaises* and *Combat*. In 1943, his first play *Les Mouches* (*The Flies*) was produced in Paris. This retelling of the Orestes story—a man who has taken on the responsibility of avenging his father's death—with its powerful message of freedom in the face of tyranny, somehow escaped the notice of Nazi censors. A year later came the production of *Huis Clos* (*No Exit*), in which Hell is portrayed as a dingy hotel room in which three people—two women and a man—are made to spend eternity "forever condemned to each other's presence." At about this time Sartre published his 700-page philosophical treatise *L'Être et le néant* (*Being and Nothingness*) as well as the pamphlet *L'existentialisme est un humanisme* (*Existentialism Is Humanism*), giving some concrete definition of his philosophy to his ever-expanding circle of disciples. In 1945 he founded the magazine *Les Temps Modernes.*

In the 1950s he wrote the plays *Le Diable et le bon Dieu* (*The Devil and the Good Lord*) about the complacency of a group of feudal peasants; *Kean*,

about an actor who needs an audience—even off stage—to convince him of the reality of his existence; and *Les Séquestrés d'Altona*, (*The Condemned of Altona*) about a former Nazi tormented by his past and the significance history will place on it. This last piece expressed Sartre's views on French military suppression of the independence movement in Algeria, then a French colony. He also applied existential psychoanalysis to racial issues, as in *Réflexions sur la question Juive* (*Anti-Semite and Jew*), and to literary biography, as in *Baudelaire* and *Saint-Genêt*. Leftist to the core, he was never a member of any communist party, and was not a true Marxist inasmuch as, for him, existentialist freedom always came first. He was philosophically critical of Marx's attitude to the future. Beginning in 1949 with his *What Is Literature?*, Sartre became more and more committed to social and political action and concentrated less on creating new literary works. He supported a string of anti-Stalinist causes, and spoke out on behalf of freedom for Hungarians in 1956 and Czechs in 1968. In 1960 Sartre demanded, though it did not happen, to be arrested (as others had been) for signing a declaration of solidarity with young men refusing to fight in Algeria. In 1967 he headed the International War Crimes Tribunal set up by Bertrand Russell to judge American military conduct in Indochina, and in 1968 he supported the cause of student rioters in Paris. In 1971, Sartre and Beauvoir temporarily assumed the editorship of the left-wing papers *La Cause du Peuple* and *Tout* after the editors were jailed. They, too, were jailed briefly for distributing the publications. Blind and ailing for many years, he lived mostly in hotel rooms supported by Beauvoir, his life-long companion. The two had met at the University of Paris and pledged mutual loyalty in times of need, though they permitted "contingent loves."

Sartre dominated most areas of French literature for a quarter of a century, and, certainly, was gifted enough to do so. Eventually his brand of existentialism was overtaken by "structuralism" and then by "deconstructionism"—both in essence quite fruitful ways of investigating old matters. He tried hard to become a true Marxist, but could not manage it; the effort eventually prevented him from writing fiction or plays, which in the long run is to be regretted. He was most distinguished as a writer of fiction, but was also a fine dramatist whose plays will survive.

His short stories, collected in *Intimacy*, are gloomily effective accounts of the various ways in which human beings remain trapped in boredom and other obstructions to "authenticity"—the discovery of oneself. His first novel analyzes these ways at greater length and with detailed imaginative perception. But the unfinished trilogy *Les Chemins de la liberté* (*The ways of liberty*) is his greatest achievement. It is a very good novel whether it is "existentialist" or not. The writing of it caught Sartre in full indecision between individualism and collectivism. His hero, Matthieu, goes in the direction of commitment, following the direction of his creator's intention. However, his impulses towards individualism are as energetically and as sympathetically described as are those towards political cohesion. Thus, as a true representation of the intellectuals of Sartre's generation (Matthieu, like Sartre, has studied philosophy and is a teacher), the novel transcends its thesis. Sartre drew on what suited his imaginative rather than his intellectual convenience: the "simultaneism" of Romains and Dos Passos, the epic structure of Zola (a far more potent influence than has been generally allowed), the demotic language of Céline. Matthieu's personal drama of freedom, culminating in what was often taken as his death (but his creator later stated, for what that may be worth, that he was not killed), is played against that of many of the characters, and that in turn is related to France's descent into the shame of Vichy and defeat by Germany—and that in its turn is related to national events and the selling-out of the Czechs, a symbol here of the individual's almost desperate need (compare Ortega's philosophy in particular) to imprison himself. That Sartre could never bring himself to describe Matthieu's final "leap" into "authenticity" is significant.

Nearly all Sartre's plays were written from the point of view of a man prepared to "dirty his hands" in the interests of the future of society. But always they display concern with individualist scruples, and it is to the author's credit and profit as an effective and stimulating dramatist that this should be so. The human drama is really more absorbing than the theses—emphasizing that Sartre lost himself creatively when he became a theorist and a critic. No play by him remotely illustrates how a human being can become "authentic."

Sartre and Camus clashed famously over the realities of communist ideologies in postwar Europe; their debate was certainly central to the concerns of its time.

PRINCIPAL WORKS IN ENGLISH TRANSLATION: *Drama*—The Flies (tr. S. Gilbert) 1943; No Exit (tr. P. Bowles) 1946; The Red Gloves (tr. K. Black) 1948; The Chips Are Down (tr. L. Varese) 1948; Kean (tr. K. Black) 1954; Nekrassov (tr. S. and G. Leeson) 1957; Loser Wins (tr. S. and G. Leeson) 1960; The Respectful Prostitute (tr. K. Black) 1965. *Other*—The Emotions (tr. B. Frechtman) 1948; Existentialism and Humanism (tr. P. Mairet) 1948; Being and Nothingness (tr. H. Barnes) 1956; Imagination (tr. F. Williams) 1962; Search for a Method (tr. H. Barnes) 1963; The Words (tr. B. Frechtman) 1964; Transcendence of the Ego (tr. F. Williams and R. Kirkpatrick) 1965; The Philosophy of Jean-Paul Sartre (ed. and tr. R. D. Cummings) 1965, 1967.

ABOUT: Bentley, E. R. The Playwright as Thinker, 1946; Dempsey, P. The Psychology of Sartre, 1950; Desan, W. D. Tragic Finale, 1960; Garaudy, R. Literature of the Graveyard, 1948; Grene, M. Dreadful Freedom, 1948; Murdoch, I. Sartre, Romantic Rationalist, 1953; Natanson, M. A Critique of Jean Paul Sartre's Ontology, 1953; Columbia Dictionary of Modern European Literature; Current Biography 1947; Dictionnaire Biographique Français Contemporain; Life June 17, 1946; New York Times Magazine February 2, 1947; January 30, 1949; New Yorker March 16, 1946; August 2, 1947; Partisan Review November 1952; Saturday Review of Literature July 9, 1949; January 20, 1951; Time January 28, 1946; Virginia Quarterly Review Spring 1947; Yale Review Winter 1953.

**SASSOON, SIEGFRIED (LORAINE)** (September 8, 1886–September 1, 1967), English poet, novelist, and memoirist, was born at Weirleigh, his family's estate near Matfield, in the Weald of Kent. He was the second of three sons of Sir Alfred Ezra Sassoon, member of a Jewish merchant family, originally from Baghdad ("the Rothschilds of the East"), and Theresa Georgina (Thornycroft) Sassoon, an artist. His parents separated when  Sassoon was five; four years later his father died of tuberculosis. One of Sassoon's maternal uncles was Sir Hamo Thornycroft, a noted sculptor who was close to him in his youth and encouraged his ambition to write poetry. This Siegfried Sassoon did from an early age; his first published poem, "The Extra Inch," appeared in *Cricket* in April 1903. After attending Marlborough College (1902–1905), where he became student organist—at the same time excelling in sports—Sassoon entered Clare College, Cambridge, in 1906. Because writing and reading poetry engaged his interest far more than law or history, and because all the rest of his attention was given to golf, he was sent down within two years. Possessed of a private income, he was able to lead a dilettante life for the next several years, first at Weirleigh, later in London, riding, hunting, playing cricket, and continuing to write.

Sassoon's first nine little volumes of poetry, conventional bucolic lyrics about the English countryside, were issued anonymously and printed at his own expense, beginning in the year he entered Cambridge. Then, having discovered John Masefield, he wrote *The Daffodil Murderer*, a long narrative poem that starts off as a parody of *The Everlasting Mercy* (1911) but "about half-way through, had forgotten to be satire and was rather good Masefield" (Robert Graves). It was Sassoon's first commercially published work, but appeared under the name of its protagonist, "Saul Kain," one of several uses of a pseudonym in the course of his career. The poem was much admired by Edmund Gosse, who opened the doors to London literary circles by introducing Sassoon to Robert Ross, staunch friend of Oscar Wilde, and to Edward Marsh, the anthologist and editor (and later private secretary to Winston Churchill).

Sassoon met Rupert Brooke, whose influence is seen in his first idealistic, romanticizing war poems. Just before World War I was declared, Sassoon enlisted as a private in the Sussex Yeomanry; in 1915 he accepted a commission in the Royal Welsh Fusiliers, an infantry regiment, and was sent to France. One of his fellow officers was the poet Robert Graves, whose *Good-Bye to All That* records the beginning of their friendship. The death of Sassoon's younger brother, Hamo, at Gallipoli, and of his friend Lt. David Thomas in 1916, and his own experiences of trench warfare led to a profound change of outlook and literary style. He had been (in his own words) "waiting for the spark from heaven to fall" and ignite his art. In 1916 Sassoon crossed no-man's-land to rescue some wounded comrades and was awarded a Military Cross for valor; unofficially, the exploit earned his nickname "Mad Jack." Later in the year, having taken a German trench single-handed, he was nominated for the Victoria Cross.

Then, stricken with gastroenteritis, Sassoon was invalided home to recuperate in a hospital at Oxford. While there he was invited to Lady Ottoline Morrell's famous house parties at nearby Garsington, and began to meet some of the intellectuals protesting the war; subsequent meetings with Bertrand Russell confirmed his pacifism. On his return to the front, Sassoon was wounded and evacuated again to England. In May 1917, *The Old Huntsman, and Other Poems* was published by W. H. Heinemann, with a dedication to Thomas Hardy. The collection takes its title from the lengthy blank-verse poem recounting the huntsman's memories of youthful days riding out with the hounds. In marked contrast to this, and to several shorter pastoral lyrics, are the first of the poems that so bitterly express the realities of warfare in spare, direct, graphic images, without benefit of simile or metaphor. Sassoon never equalled these.

In June 1917 Sassoon wrote "A Soldier's Declaration," made "as an act of wilful defiance of military authority, because I believe that the War is being deliberately prolonged by those who have the power to end it. . . . I have seen and endured the sufferings of the troops, and I can no longer be a party to prolonging those sufferings for ends which I believe to be evil and unjust."

As a further gesture of protest, Lt. Sassoon threw his M.C. into the Mersey River. The statement was printed in the *London Times*, and read out in the House of Commons; Robert Graves's cleverly planned appeal to the authorities—that Sassoon was ill from shell-shock—saved him from court-martial.

Instead, as Graves had suggested, Sassoon was sent to Craiglockhart War Hospital for Nervous Disorders, outside Edinburgh, and placed under the care of Dr. W. H. R. Rivers, who soon realized that his new charge was completely sane and who, reluctantly, gave in to Sassoon's determination to return to the fighting and not betray his men. While there he met Wilfred Owen, whom he encouraged to persevere with his poetry.

After his discharge from "Dottyville" (as he called it), Sassoon served in Ireland and Palestine before returning once more to France; in July 1918 he was accidentally shot in the head by one of his own troops. That year *Counter-Attack and Other Poems* was published: Sassoon's vision of "the hell where youth and laughter go" ("Suicide in the Trenches").

John Middleton Murry wrote off *Counter-Attack* as merely "a cry of pain"; "the comprehension does not go far enough" (*Nation*); but few critics have agreed with this judgment; Virginia Woolf did claim that Sassoon had deserted art to express the intolerable, but acknowledged that "his contempt for palliative . . . is the raw stuff of poetry" (*Times Literary Supplement*). Wilfred Owen, in a letter to Sassoon from the trenches (October 1918), echoed posterity's judgment when he protested that his senses were "charred" by such poems as the title poem.

Sassoon was discharged from the army in March 1919. In the same year the poems from *The Old Huntsman* and *Counter-Attack* were collected in *The War Poems of Siegfried Sassoon*. This was followed by *Picture Show*, the last blast of what Edmund Blunden termed Sassoon's "splendid war on the war," which ends with lines of lyric release celebrating the Armistice:

> Everyone suddenly burst out singing;
> And I was filled with such delight
> As prisoned birds must find in freedom . . . .
> . . . . O, but Everyone
> Was a bird; and the song was wordless; the
>     singing will never be done.

As Winfield Townley Scott summed it up in a review of the 1949 edition of the *Collected Poems*, far different from Rupert Brooke's "romantic piety" or Owen's pity is Sassoon's "terrible dismay and anger at the waste of life, and it is these emotions which give his war poetry its power" (*Poetry*).

For a short period in 1919 Sassoon worked as literary editor of a new publication, the socialist *Daily Herald*, in which capacity he gave reviewing to his poorer friends, such as Graves. Most of the following year he spent in the United States, where he gave a series of antiwar talks and poetry readings. There, too, he met some of the younger American poets. Upon learning of Owen's death in the last week of the war, Sassoon had obtained from the poet's mother copies of his work with a view to their publication. Now, in 1920, they were issued, with Sassoon's introduction. As Osbert Sitwell (although never a great friend) acknowledged in *Noble Essences*: "to Siegfried Sassoon belongs the glory of having discovered Wilfred Owen, and of having helped him and launched him."

Over the next decade Sassoon divided his time between social life in London, hunting and cricket in Wiltshire, and travel to the continent. Among a succession of handsome and younger lovers, his affairs with the actor Glen Byam Shaw and the artist Stephen Tennant (from 1927 to 1933) were the longest lasting. But lovers and friends, of an assured income, and no need to work were little avail against his anxieties about his homosexuality and rootlessness. Increasingly he seemed to retreat into the past, looking back on his own life in the manner of Enoch Arden. Although he went on writing subdued and seldom good verse, much of his work from 1928 on consisted of autobiographical fiction or prose memoirs. The novel *Memoirs of a Fox-Hunting Man*, published anonymously, is a first-person narrative of the life of "George Sherston," from his orphaned childhood, brought up by an aunt in the beautiful Kent countryside to service in the war. Sherston's passionate devotion to riding is the core of the book, which has been called an elegy to a vanished way of life. At the same time, some critics have discerned an aura of satire in the nostalgia. As Graves noted, he "leaves his readers to decide for him whether the book is sincere or ironical" (*Saturday Review of Literature*). It won both the Hawthornden and the James Tait Black prizes in 1928. *Memoirs of an Infantry Officer* followed. Contemporary reviews took note of the somewhat detached yet at the same time introspective tone, and of the irony with which Sherston's war exploits are related. "The chief value of these beautiful and rather sombre *Memoirs*, " Morton Dauwen Zaubel wrote, "is that they convey . . . a sense of the tragic frustration which certain forces are constantly devising for the humiliation and defeat of youth" (*Poetry*). A *Times Literary Supplement* article published in 1973 called it "his one real masterpiece," a work of "candid, critical, and humourous" self-scrutiny. *Sherston's Progress* concludes the trilogy with an account of the hero's hospitalization for shell shock and his further service—again in the detached, yet vividly descriptive prose of the other volumes. All three were published together as *The Complete Memoirs of George Sherston*, and then, many years later, abridged and reissued as *Siegfried Sassoon's Long Journey*.

Shortly after Stephen Tennant left him, Sassoon married Hester Gatty, daughter of a former chief justice of Gibraltar, and settled at Heytesbury, near Warminster, Wiltshire, where he lived for the rest of his life. Their son, George, was born in 1936. The Sassoons separated amicably in 1943, but were never divorced. He now took a closer look at his life in three volumes of true autobiography: *The Old Century and Seven More Years* (his own favorite among his writings), *The Weald of Youth*, and *Siegfried's Journey, 1916–1920*. Fiction and memoirs have their source in the diaries he kept meticulously from wartime on, mingling sharp, sure vignettes of his surroundings and experiences with passages that record moods and yearnings. Three volumes of these diaries, for the critical decade 1915–1925, have been edited by Sir Rupert Hart-Davis; many more manuscript volumes dealing with intimate matters remain unpublished.

Sassoon's first postwar poetry expresssed his bemusement and then bored disgust at the world about him. *Satirical Poems* was criticized for the lack of real feeling underlying its cynicism.

Anticipating later critical views, Stanley Kunitz dismissed Sassoon's later spiritual verse as "a poetry sincere, pathetic, grey, monotonous, and deadening" (*Poetry*).

In 1957, the year after the publication of *Sequences*, more of the same, Sassoon was received into the Roman Catholic Church; thereafter he wrote devotional verse in the main—as in *The Path to Peace*, twenty-nine poems dedicated to Mary Immaculate and printed (as were several of his later works) by the nuns of Stanbrook Abbey.

In addition to his encouragement of Owen's writing, and his tribute to the "sensitive and vigorous mind" of the other great war poet Isaac Rosenberg (in the Introduction to *The Collected Works of Isaac Rosenberg*, 1937), Sassoon wrote two independent works of literary criticism. *On Poetry*, developed from a lecture given at the University of Bristol in 1939, defends his own simple, direct style and rejects modernist ambiguity. Pound and Eliot, Auden, Spender, Edith Sitwell, and Wallace Stevens fail to make his canon, and the book failed to make an impression. *Meredith* is an unassuming biography and introduction to the work of his favorite nineteenth-century author.

By the late 1950's, with his conscious retreat from contemporary verse styles, Siegfried Sassoon's work began to be ignored; over the years, little of his quite large output has been anthologized.

But in recognition of his war poetry, Sassoon was made an honorary fellow of Clare College and in 1965 received an honorary doctorate from Oxford. He was created CBE in 1951. He is buried in the churchyard at Mells, Somerset, near another friend, the Roman Catholic chaplain of Oxford, Msgr. Ronald Knox. Sassoon's papers are housed in the McFarlin Library at the University of Tulsa (Oklahoma) and in the Edmund Blunden Collection at the University of Iowa.

PRINCIPAL WORKS: *Poetry*—Poems, 1906; Orpheus in Diloeryum, 1908 one-act verse play; Sonnets, 1909; Sonnets and Verses, 1909; Twelve Sonnets, 1910; Poems, 1911; Hyacinth, an Idyll, 1912; Melodies, 1912; An Ode for Music, 1912; The Daffodil Murderer: Being the Chantrey Prize Poem, by Saul Kain (pseud.) 1913; Discoveries, 1915; Morning-Glory, 1916; The Old Huntsman, and Other Poems, 1917; Counter-Attack and Other Poems, 1918; Picture Show, 1919 (in U.S.: Picture-Show); The War Poems of Siegfried Sassoon, 1919; Recreations, 1923; Lingual Exercises for Advanced Vocabularians, 1925; Selected Poems, 1925; Satirical Poems, 1926 (enl. ed. 1933); The Heart's Journey, 1928; Poems by Pinchbeck Lyre (pseud.) 1931; The Road to Ruin, 1933; Vigils, 1935; Poems Newly Selected, 1916–1935, 1940; Rhymed Ruminations, 1940; Collected Poems, 1947; The Tasking, 1954; Sequences, 1956; Lenten Illuminations and Sight Sufficient, 1958; Poems, 1958; The Path to Peace, 1960; Collected Poems, 1908–1956, 1961; An Octave: 8 September 1966, 1966. *Fiction*—Memoirs of a Fox-Hunting Man, 1928; Memoirs of an Infantry Officer, 1930; Sherston's Progress, 1936; The Complete Memoirs of George Sherston, 1937; (in U.S.: The Memoirs of George Sherston). *Nonfiction*—The Old Century and Seven More Years, 1938; On Poetry, 1939 (Arthur Skemp Memorial Lecture . . . Univ. of Bristol 16th March 1939); The Flower Show Match and Other Pieces, 1941; The Weald of Youth, 1942; Siegfried's Journey, 1916–1920, 1945; Meredith, 1948; Something about Myself . . . Aged Eleven (illus. M. Adams) 1966; Letters to a Critic (introd. and notes M. Thorpe) 1976; Siegfried Sassoon Diaries, 1920–1922 (ed. R. Hart-Davis) 1981; Siegfried Sassoon Diaries, 1915–1918 (ed. R. Hart-Davis) 1983; Siegfried Sassoon Diaries, 1923–1925 (ed. R. Hart-Davis) 1985; Letters to Max Beerbohm with a Few Answers (ed. R. Hart-Davis) 1986.

ABOUT: Bergonzi, B. Heroes' Twilight: A Study of the Literature of the Great War, 1965; Blunden, E. Undertones of War, 1928; Corrigan Dame Felicitas (ed.) Siegfried Sassoon: A Poet's Pilgrimage, 1973; Fleishman, A. Figures of Autobiography: The Language of Self-Writing in Victorian and Modern England, 1983; Fussell, P. The Great War and Modern Memory, 1975; Fussell, P. (ed.) Siegfried Sassoon's Long Journey: Selections from the Sherston Memoirs, 1983; Graves, R. Good-Bye to All That, 1929; Hoare, P. Serious Pleasure: The Life of Stephen Tennant, 1990; Jackson, S. The Sassoons, 1968; Johnston, J. H. English Poetry of the First World War: A Study in the Evolution of Lyric and Narrative Form, 1964; Keynes, G. L. A Bibliography of Siegfried Sassoon, 1962 (Soho Bibliographies); Lane, A. E. An Adequate Response: The War Poetry of Wilfred Owen and Siegfried Sassoon, 1972; Pinto, V. de S. The City That Shone: An Autobiography (1895–1922) 1969; Sassoon, S. Letters to a Critic (introd. and notes M. Thorpe)

1976; Sassoon, S. Letters to Max Beerbohm with a Few Answers (ed. Sir R. Hart-Davis) 1986; Sassoon, S. The Old Century and Seven More Years, 1938; Sassoon, S. Siegfried Sassoon Diaries, 1915–1918 (ed. R. Hart-Davis) 1983; Sassoon, S. Siegfried Sassoon Diaries, 1920–1922 (ed. R. Hart-Davis) 1981; Sassoon, S. Siegfried Sassoon Diaries, 1923–1925 (ed. R. Hart-Davis) 1985; Sassoon, S. Siegfried's Journey, 1916–1920, 1945; Sassoon, S. Something about Myself . . . Aged Eleven (illus. M. Adams) 1966; Sassoon, S. The Weald of Youth, 1942; Seymour Smith, M. Robert Graves: His Life and Work, 1995; Silkin, J. Out of Battle: The Poetry of the Great War, 1972; Sitwell, Sir O. Noble Essences: A Book of Characters, 1950; Swinnerton, F. A. The Georgian Literary Scene, 1951; Thorpe, M. Siegfried Sassoon: A Critical Study, 1966. Periodicals—Nation July 1918; New York Times September 3, 1967; Poetry August 1929; August 1936; April 1949; Saturday Review of Literature February 23, 1929; Times (London) September 4, 1967; Times Literary Supplement July 11, 1918; June 3, 1926; December 7, 1973; August 31, 1974.

## SAUNDERS, MARSHALL (April 13, 1861– February 15, 1947), Canadian novelist and writer of stories for children, wrote: "I was born [Margaret

Marshall Saunders] near Liverpool, Nova Scotia, the daughter of the Rev. Edward M. Saunders and Maria K. (Freeman) Saunders, descended on both sides from Mayflower Pilgrims. My father's parish was in the Annapolis Valley, near the home of Evangeline. When I was six he was called to a Baptist church in Halifax. I was educated there and in Edinburgh and Orléans, France, returning to Canada in 1879. My father encouraged me to write, saying I 'had some talent.' Then one day I met that king of dogs, Beautiful Joe, spent six months with him and his family, and wrote a book about him. It took a prize in Boston in 1893, and ever since that old dog has been barking his way around the world. For years I wrote other books and traveled in Europe and America. Then I settled down in Toronto with my younger sister. She had her dog and I have my birds—wild ones in the shrubbery and more than two hundred tame ones in the house."

It was Saunders's enchanting tale of a dog's life, *Beautiful Joe*, that gave her a wide reputation. The dog Joe, whose "beauty" is in his loyal and gentle nature, tells of his maltreatment by a former master, that master's comeuppance, and Joe's subsequent adventures. The style, simple and engaging, sometimes avoids the sentimentality that often mars such stories. *Beautiful Joe* won a competition aimed at finding a companion to Anna Sewell's children's classic *Black Beauty*. It has much in common with that plea for humanity to animals. "Together these two tales have done an immense amount to promote the idea of kindness to animals among children of many lands," wrote a reviewer for the *Times* (London). An immediate success, *Beautiful Joe* became one of the most widely read works by any Canadian author, translated into some twenty languages, and filmed in 1947.

Saunders later experimented with a handful of adult novels. *Rose À Charlitte*, a romance centering on an American in Nova Scotia, was thought to have good local color, but to descend into melodrama. *Deficient Saints* is an over-contrived tale of small-town life. More successful, perhaps, because it deals with an issue close to the author's heart, was the later *The Girl From Vermont*. It is the story of a young teacher fighting against the economic exploitation of children, driven by an "everpresent inner consciousness of the misery of our little white slaves." Overt didacticism is ameliorated by a romantic subplot, though not enough for some reviewers: "it limps as fiction," was the opinion of the *New York Times* (1910).

After the turn of the century Saunders went back to doing what she did best, producing numerous books of animal biography. All displayed a sound knowledge of animal behavior, and a passionate interest in their welfare. *Princess Sukey*, the tale of a pigeon rescued by a little boy, "might well be a tract promulgated jointly by the societies for the prevention of cruelty to animals and children," mused one reviewer (*New York Times* 1905).

She wrote nothing after 1927, although she continued to make lecture tours. In 1934 she was created Commander of the Order of the British Empire, and there were many other honors and awards, including an honorary degree from Acadia University.

PRINCIPAL WORKS: Juvenile—Beautiful Joe; An Autobiography, 1894; Daisy; A Tale, 1894; Charles and His Lamb, 1895; For the Other Boy's Sake, and Other Stories, 1896; The King of the Park, 1897; For His Country, and Grandmother and the Crow, 1900; Tilda Jane, 1901; Beautiful Joe's Paradise, 1902; The Story of the Graveleys, 1903; Nita: The Story of an Irish Setter, 1904; Princess Sukey: The Story of a Pigeon and Her Human Friends, 1905; Alpatok: The Story of an Eskimo Dog, 1906; My Pets; Real Happenings in My Aviary, 1908; Tilda Jane's Orphans, 1909; Pussy Blackface: The Story of a Kitten and Her Friends, 1912; The Wandering Dog, 1916; Golden Dicky: The Story of a Canary and His Friends, 1919; Bonnie Prince Fetlar: The Story of a Pony and His Friends, 1920; Jimmie Gold-Coast: The Story of a Monkey and His Friends, 1923; Esther de Warren: The Story of a Mid-Victorian Maiden, 1927. Novels—My Spanish Sailor: A Love Story 1889 (revised as Her Sailor; A Love Story in 1899), The House of Armour, 1897; Rose À Charlitte: An Acadian Romance (also published as Rose of Acadie), 1898; Deficient Saints; A Tale of Maine, 1899; The Girl From Vermont: The Story of a Vacation School Teacher, 1910.

ABOUT: The autobiographical material quoted above was written for Twentieth Century Authors, 1942. Blain, V. (and others) The Feminist Companion to Literature in English, 1990; Buck, C. (ed.) Bloomsbury Guide to Women's Literature, 1992; Dictionary of Literary Biography Vol. 92, 1990; Literary History of Canada, 1965; Oxford Companion to Canadian Literature, 1983; Oxford Companion to Children's Literature, 1991; Sylvestre, G. and Others (eds.) Canadian Writers, 1966; Who's Who 1947. Periodicals—Bookman December 1916; Canadian Bookman December 1930; Times London February 18, 1947; New York Times July 1, 1905; March 26, 1910; November 6, 1927; February 17, 1947; Saturday Night (Toronto) March 1, 1947; School April 1947; Times (London) February 18, 1947.

**SAURAT, DENIS** (October 7, 1890–June 8, 1958), French critic and professor, was born in Toulouse. He was educated at the Universities of Lille and Paris; by 1922, after a stint as lecturer at Glasgow University, he held the Chair of English at the University of Bordeaux. Being virtually bilingual, he taught English literature in France—and then, for most of his life, vice versa. In 1924, he became Director of the Institut Français du Royaume Uni; and in 1926 he moved to London as Professor of French Language and Literature at King's College. He held that position until 1950, when he became Professor Emeritus. His last eight years were spent in Nice, as Director of the Centre international d'études françaises. He was a very well-known spokesman, during World War II, for the Gaullist cause.

Saurat, a charismatic figure who drew large audiences as a lecturer, is not now, in general, much read, although his *Les Dieux du peuple* (1947), *Gods of the People*, was reprinted twice in the 1970s. But during his lifetime some of his books, notably *Milton, Man and Thinker*, were much discussed. He is also still read as a respected scholar of the occult tradition in literature; in that capacity his writings on Blake and Victor Hugo, as well as on Milton, are frequently consulted.

Saurat's London *Times* obituarist recorded that occultism "was the link between his main interests . . . it became a preoccupation which inspired a number of works, poised, sometimes uneasily, often hypnotically, between philosophy and poetry, theology and the more exotic fields of scientific speculation." As a historian of literature he drew the general reader's attention to the merits of such rarities, in literary terms, as Gurdjieff's *Tales of Beelzebub* and the works of the gifted Mauritian poet and prosewriter, Malcolm Chazal (1902–1981). This tendency towards occultism put some critics and readers off, but it fascinated many others.

Saurat's view that Milton drew, through Robert Fludd, on the cabalistic notion of the *tsimtsum* in *Paradise Lost*, was controversial; but it has been quietly influential, and will certainly still bear open-minded investigation. His works on Blake and Milton were criticized for relying on very poor sources (*Saturday Review of Literature*); but the best received and most discussed of all his books, *Milton: Man and Thinker*, was welcomed, even when it was disagreed with. Its aim was to strip Milton of his puritanism, and substitute an esoteric but undogmatic version of the writer. Kenneth Burke, writing in the *Dial*, thought it "decidedly peripheral to those aspects of Milton's poetry which recommend it to modern readers"; George Saintsbury, writing in the *Nation and Athenaeum*, called it "crammed with interest"; the scholar and poet Alan Porter wrote in the *Spectator* that "it is hard to think that a better introduction to Milton could have been written."

Saurat's *Modern French Literature* remains a valuable guide, even though the author's dislikes (of, for example, Gide) are given full but scarcely satisfactory ventilation. *The Guardian* (then still the *Manchester Guardian*), wrote that Saurat was "most stimulating on authors whom he admires—Zola, Loti, France, Proust, Rolland. It is a pity he has so little sympathy with other significant writers . . . who have considerable literary importance . . . this lucid if unkind presentation should be handled with care . . . ." Those of Saurat's books that are likely to survive are the ones on the esoteric subjects that really preoccupied him at the expense of his literary work.

Denis Saurat, who was a member of the French Legion of Honour, was married to the former Ella Bocquet-Smith, with whom he had three daughters and a son.

PRINCIPAL WORKS IN ENGLISH TRANSLATION: Milton, Man and Thinker, 1925; Blake and Modern Thought, 1929; Literature and Occult Traditions (tr. D. Bolton), 1930; A History of Religions, 1934; Blake and Milton, 1935; The End of Fear, 1938; The Christ at Chartres, 1940; French War Aims, 1940; Death and the Dreamer, 1946; Gods of the People, 1947; Modern French Literature, 1870–1940, 1946; Atlantis and the Giants, 1957.

ABOUT: Moore, J. Gurdjieff, 1991. *Periodicals*—Dial November 1925; Manchester Guardian January 7, 1947; Nation and Athenaeum May 9, 1925; New York Times June 10, 1958; Saturday Review of Literature October 11, 1924; Spectator November 14, 1925; Times (London) June 10, 1958.

**SAUSER-HALL, FREDERIC.** See **CENDRARS, BLAISE**

**SAUSSURE, FERDINAND DE** (November 26, 1857–February 22, 1913), Swiss linguist, was born in Geneva, the son of a well-known naturalist whose Huguenot family had emigrated from Lorraine in the late sixteenth century, during the French religious wars. The young Ferdinand was led into the study of language at an early age by a philologist and family friend, Adolphe Pictet. By fifteen he had learned not only French and German but also English, Latin, and Greek—and was already working on a "general system of language." He was also studying Sanskrit.

Saussure studied physics and chemistry at the University of Geneva (1875–1876); then, feeling his time was being wasted, he enrolled at the University of Leipzig (1876–1880), where he could learn Indo-European languages. Leipzig was the center of the young linguistic historians called *Junggrammmatiker*, young "neo-grammarians": these linguists brought (as Saussure himself put it) "the results of comparative study" into "historical sequence." Saussure gained his doctorate from Leipzig—and a reputation. He also attended courses at the University of Berlin during his last two years at Leipzig. In 1878, when he was only twenty-one, he published *Mémoire sur la systéme primitif de voyelles dans les langues indo-européennes* (Memoir on the primitive system of vowels in the Indo-European languages). One linguist—quoted, but not named, by Jonathan Culler in his exposition of Saussure—called this "the most splendid work of comparative philology ever written." It is worth noting that its conclusions were verified by archeological evidence in 1925. But Saussure's most enduring fame, as one of the fathers of modern linguistics and (with Lévi-Strauss and Lévi-Strauss's

French predecessor Émile Durkheim) of the movements called structuralism and semiology (theory of signs), was to arise from a book he never wrote.

Before becoming Professor of Linguistics at Geneva he was (1881–1891) Maitre de Conferences at the École Practique de Hautes Études in Paris. He had not liked Germany, but enjoyed France and teaching Old High German and Sanskrit. Married, with two sons, he was made a Chevalier de la Légion d'Honneur.

In his own time Saussure was thought of as a philological historian in the German "neogrammarian" tradition. He seemed, wrote Jonathan Culler, to be, around 1906, settling into "a decent provincial obscurity." He worked at Lithuanian and wearied of ever being able to express his conviction that "not a single term in linguistics . . . has any meaning for me."

He attained his present high status only because at the University of Geneva, where he was the Professor, he gave (1907–1913), three series of lectures on general linguistics. He had been obliged to do so because in 1906, on the death of a colleague, he had been assigned responsibility for the teaching of general linguistics. These lectures became the basis of the *Course*.

After his early death Saussure's colleagues and two of his students decided that this material should not be lost: hence, in 1916, the publication of the *Cours de linguistique générale*, which appeared in English, in Wade Baskin's version, in 1959—but it had started to exert its influence long before that.

The *Course* was decisive in shifting the emphasis from a historical (diachronic) to a sociological (synchronic) approach to the study of language. We cannot, Saussure insisted, investigate a language fully in terms of its history: for its speakers, it has no history. To describe a language in terms of how it communicates, we need initially, not to investigate its history but, rather, how its various components relate to one another *now*. Thus, in a famous comparision, Saussure suggested that language resembled chess: a person, coming upon a chess positon, does not initially view it in terms of the moves already made, but in those of the potentialities of the position *now*. As for the pieces: these could be replaced by lumps of chalk, coal, and wooden chips—just so long as the players and the observers agree as to their functions in the game.

This, then, is the first Saussurian principle: diachrony (the existence of which he does not, of course, deny) versus synchrony. The second principle is what he called *langue* versus *parole*. *Langage* for Saussure was linguistic ability, the capacity to communicate by means of language present, by heredity, in us all. *Langue* is the *system*, the totality of any language, "the sum of work-images stored in the minds of individuals"; *parole* is the actual *performance*, the concrete act of a person speaking—and thus a dynamic, ongoing, social act ineluctably fixed in a frame of time and place. The total knowledge of the English language I carry within me is thus sharply differentiated from my actual performance in typing these words at a specific moment in a particular place. One is general, the other absolutely specific. Like any speaker of a language, my own "competence" (a much-used term) is far less than the perfect competence of the *langue* itself.

Saussure's third principle, which distinguishes "syntagmatic" from "associative" (or "paradigmatic"), is as follows: a sentence consists of a sequence of signs, each one of which makes a contribution to the meaning of the whole; when these signs are seen as a linear sequence then the relationship is syntagmatic, as in "the man→ can→ leave"; however, when the sign, whatever one it is, is seen as contrasting with all the other signs in the given language, then the relationship is associative or, as is now more usually said, paradigmatic.

From this paradigmatic approach we thus get "The man→can→leave" contrasted with (for example) "The man / woman / cat / fish→ can / may / will / will not →leave / go / hate / love / die." The complex web thus created by these two distinct approaches is a linguistic system.

The exact degree to which Saussure influenced future studies has always been a matter of controversy. An awareness that meanings are established by contrasts, by mutual relationships, rather than by the elements of language themselves, was already implicit in the writings of Franz Boas, while the French sociologist Émile Durkheim's view of society must have influenced Saussure in his view of language as an organism. Thus Saussure's influence on linguistics may not have been as decisive as those of Roman Jakobson and Noam Chomsky (both of whom have implied that they believe Saussure to have over-simplified matters in the interests of gallic lucidity); his influence on structuralism, however—a movement emanating largely from France, and now largely supplanted by its offshoot, deconstructionism—was decisive, and was fully acknowledged by the structuralist *par excellence*, Claude Lévi-Strauss.

Saussure and the great attention paid to his *Course* has deeply affected literature—both criticism and, thus, too, the imaginative works from which it feeds. The *Course* has an obvious if vexed relationship, too, to the more recent notion that no meaning resides in a text—until this meaning is constructed by the reader. Texts viewed in this manner have no existence unless they are read. It was but a short step from this to the even more recent notion of *deconstruction* of texts, a process by which a text is completely divorced from its mere author, who did not know what he was doing. But there is left the possibility of an infinite regress of deconstructions—and the now acknowledged fact of even the deconstructive texts themselves being deconstructed. One of the major figures behind all these and the many other related developments, all of them germane to literature and its making (or abolition), is certainly Ferdinand de Saussure. (He also stands, with Nicholas Troubetzkoy and a few others, including Roland Barthes in more recent times, behind the modern study of semiology.)

The best brief introductions to Saussure have

been written by Geoffrey Sampson in *Thinkers of the 20th Century* and *Makers of Modern Culture.* Jonathan Culler's monograph could be accused of attributing too much importance to Saussure, but offers a clear guide. The standard full-length works are those of E.F.K. Koerner, and the matters are put into context in the book edited by Godel.

PRINCIPAL WORK: Course in General Linguistics (tr. W. Baskin) 1959.

ABOUT: Culler, J. Saussure, 1976; Godel, R. (ed.) A General School Reader in Linguistics, 1969; Koerner, E.F.K. An Annotated, Classified Bibliography of the Background, Development, and Actual Relevance of Ferdinand de Saussure's General Theory of Language, 1972; Koerner, E.G.K. Ferdinand de Saussure: Origin and Development of His Linguistic Thought, 1973; Sampson, G. in Makers of Modern Culture, 1981; Sampson G in Thinkers of the Twentieth Century, 1985; Starobinski, J. Words Upon Words, 1979.

## SAVAGE, D(EREK) S(TANLEY) (March 6, 1917– ),

British poet and critic, wrote: "My parents were of the artisan class; but my father became a small business man, prospered. I was born at Harlow, in Essex, my father then serving in the Army Transport Corps. We moved to Cheshunt, in Hertfordshire, where my father owned two shops, so I had a semi-rural upbringing, and have never loved cities. There was no love or knowledge of art in our family. We children were brought up to 'know the value of money' and to appreciate something called 'security.' My temperament is fundamentally rebellious and freedom-loving, and as a consequence I have always lived in poverty, and have a certain contempt for security. An injury, with complications, at thirteen interrupted my schooling (but I learned nothing at school) and prevented my becoming a merchant sailor as I desired. I went to a commercial college, and was an office-clerk for a time. I worked in a bottle factory, a copper refinery, a bookshop. I became a 'red' and a pacifist and spoke vehemently at street-corners. My poems began to be published from my sixteenth year.

"I formally accepted the Christian faith, after a phase of militant atheism, in 1937, and was confirmed in St. Paul's Cathedral. I married the same year—we have five children. When war came I refused military service as a conscientious objector. I wrote my first book of criticism, *The Personal Principle*, in a condemned cottage, without sanitation or water-supply; when the nearby pumps froze we scraped snow from the ground. Unemployed, lived on the dole for a time, until I obtained work in a hospital. Persecuted by neighbours, payment for the book enabled us to moved to Herefordshire, where I worked on the land and wrote the greater part of *The Withered Branch*. In 1947 I was given a two-hundred pound Atlantic Award (Rockefeller Foundation). The house we rented being sold over our heads, we were ejected by the new owners, and came to Cornwall, where we have lived ever since.

"My spiritual bent may be indicated by a life-long preference over the other books in the Bible for the Apocalypse: also Ecclesiastes. A memorable early experience was a reading of *The Pilgrim's Progress* immediately following the painful extraction of several teeth: a sort of initiation. Russian writers have influenced me profoundly. When, at twenty, I first read Berdyaev's *Freedom and the Spirit*, I knew that my own obscure intuitions were for the first time being developed and expressed for me.

"I have not made literature my career, for I have no career. However, my life and writing are in intimate relation. I write slowly, because I do not care to write like a journalist or a teacher, from my being, but like a poet or seer, from my becoming: in my writing, I am in advance of myself, therefore. I've been working for several years on a very exhaustive study of *Hamlet*, entitled 'The Underground Man': and I am just preparing for publication a study of the writer and politics, 'Caesar's Laurel Crown.'"

———

Not long after he wrote the above for *World Authors* (1955), D. S. Savage more or less gave up writing for publication; but he did not give up writing. He had always been exceedingly particular about issuing work with which he was not fully satisfied— an earlier version of *Hamlet and the Pirates* was already in the advanced stages of production when he withdrew it in order to rewrite it.

Throughout the 1970s, 1980s, and 1990s Savage has lived quietly in Cornwall. His single published book since 1950 is the now much consulted *The Cottager's Companion* (1975), called *Self-Sufficient Country Living* in the United States, where it appeared in 1978. Savage (as he makes clear in his statement above) has never written with his reputation in mind; he has written, rather, in order to make an exact record of a spiritual journey based on an eclectic, practical Christianity still not too far from that practiced by Nicholas Berdyaev who fired his imagination so long ago. Savage's book reviews, in the days (of the 1950s and 1960s) when he undertook them for journals such as the *New Statesman, Spectator* and, notably, *Poetry Chicago* (which published much of his poetry and criticism), showed his sympathy with such thinkers as Gurdjieff and Rudolph Steiner. There is a strong element of mysticism in his religious thinking; but, except possibly sometimes in poetry (which he gave up publishing many years ago), he is not the kind of writer who would think it proper to indulge himself in religious self-revelation. His major interests were always religion, philosophy, psychology, social reform, total disarmament and "encouragement of small-scale husbandry." Thus, *The Cottager's Companion* is quite as vital to him as any of his literary studies. He had become well known as an advisor to those (many of them writers) in search of self-sufficiency long before he published *The Cottager's Companion*: the American poet Robert Creeley wrote to him in that capacity in the early 1950s. Since then many grateful readers who have wanted to "contract out" have consulted the book, which has quietly acquired the status of a classic.

Savage was quite influenced by the clearness of the writing, and the independence, of Robert Graves, whom he knew; there was serious discussion of a plan in which Savage would go to Mallorca—where Graves lived—in 1951, and help to educate their large families, at that time consisting of nine children in all; but it came to nothing.

Savage's somber and elegiac poetry, hardly anthologized—he appears in few directories of poets—was very much of its time, the 1930s and wartime 1940s. The best of it was in his collections *The Autumn World* and *A Time to Mourn.* Some of the individual poems were published in *Poetry Chicago.*

Savage's most influential book, which, like *The Personal Principal,* has been reprinted in America more than once and by more than one press, is *The Withered Branch.* This is a study of six novelists: Ernest Hemingway, E. M. Forster, Virginia Woolf, the now almost forgotten but once quite widely read Welsh novelist Margiad Evans, Aldous Huxley, and James Joyce. Savage was said by most reviewers to "disapprove" of them all, and, undoubtedly, there is a slightly strained, awkward (but at the same time painfully sincere) and moralistic tinge to the book; but, as the critic Stanley Edgar Hyman conceded in a hostile and scornful review of it in *New Mexico Quarterly,* Savage was castigating himself as much as he was castigating his six novelists. Hyman found Savage's confession of this fact embarrassing. The thesis of the book is that society is sick—just in the sense that, as an apt example in the case of such an author, Tolstoy asserted that it was sick—and that the novelists under scrutiny have not cured themselves. Paul Engle and Maxwell Geismar, in the *Chicago Sunday Tribune* and the *Saturday Review* respectively, were equally irritated, but even Engle, (then at least) a believer in the essential correctness of the academic criticism of modernism ("one can only suggest that Savage does not read closely enough in the modern critical way, so that he loses the higher meanings"), after expressing his annoyance, wrote that *The Withered Branch* was "an illuminating and insightful study." Geismar went further: "D. S. Savage is an excellent, original and sometimes infuriating critic. These six essays contain some of the best things I have read lately in the field of literary criticism. Mr. Savage is distressing, I suppose, because just on the edge of real achievement, he will take a dizzy jump into the absolute."

Along the years Savage has spoken of various plans for books: one about writers and politics to have been called "Caesar's Laurel Crown," another on Alain-Fournier's novel *Le Grande Meaulnes,* and yet another on the English novelists of the 1930s. None of these has yet appeared.

Savage is a member of Amnesty International, the Anglican Pacifist Fellowship (of which he was general secretary 1960–1962), and the Fellowship of Reconciliation.

PRINCIPAL WORKS: *Poetry*—The Autumn World, 1939; Don Quixote, 1939; A Time to Mourn, 1943; And Also Much Cattle: Scenario for Four Voices, 1975 (broadcast by the British Broadcasting Corporation November 4, 1956). *Criticism*—The Personal Principle, 1944 (reprinted twice in U. S. A. 1975); Mysticism and Aldous Huxley: An Examination of the Heard-Huxley Theories, 1947 (reprinted in U. S. A. 1979); Hamlet and the Pirates: An Exercise in Literary Detection, 1951 (reprinted in U. S. A. 1977); The Withered Branch, 1950 (reprinted in U. S. A. 1974, 1975, 1976). *Husbandry*—The Cottager's Companion, 1975 (in U. S. A. as Self-Sufficient Country Living, 1978).

ABOUT: The autobiographical material quoted above was written for Twentieth Century Authors First Supplement, 1955. *Periodicals*—Chicago Sunday Tribune February 17, 1952; New Mexico Quarterly Winter 1952; Partisan Review 1, 1942; Saturday Review August 2, 1952; Sewanee Review 54, 1946.

**SAWYER, RUTH (ESTELLE)** (August 5, 1880–June 3, 1970), American folklorist, writer of books for children, novels, and short stories, wrote: "One has to be born; I was, in Boston. My father was Francis Milton Sawyer, my mother Ethelinda J. Smith, of old Lexington stock. Went to private school in New York City—Annie C. Brackett's; then to Packer Institute, Brooklyn and the Garland Kindergarten Training School in Boston; and then to Cuba to help organize kindergartens. Finished with a scholarship at Columbia University—degree B.S. in Education. Had an itinerant position on the *New York Sun* doing feature articles. Went to Ireland on commission, and started collecting folktales. Have been collecting them ever since. Began professional story-telling for the New York Public Lecture Bureau, under Dr. Henry M Leipziger. Finally got married in 1911—husband, Albert C. Durand, M.D. We have a son and a daughter—both a great improvement on their parents.

"Began writing Irish folktales for the *Outlook* (then edited by Lyman Abbott) and the *Atlantic Monthly.* Since then have contributed some two hundred short stories, articles, poems, and serials to current magazines. My book, *Roller Skates,* won the Newbery Award in 1937. *The Primrose Ring* was made into a silent picture by Paramount, and Morosco put on *Seven Miles to Arden* as a play. One of my short stories went into one of the O. Henry Prize volumes.

"As a family we take to the water, sailing and running a cruiser. I was born a Unitarian. I . . . spend three-fourths of the year lecturing and telling stories. Also am becoming a good printer . . ."

_____

Ruth Sawyer was the youngest of the five children of a wealthy importer, and the only girl in the family. The Sawyers left Boston's Back Bay for New York City a year after her birth, and settled on the Upper East Side. Her parents, both from old

New England families, were devoted but exacting. However, they traveled abroad a great deal and, by the time she was ten, Ruth Sawyer was roller skating about the city alone. Her father died in 1894, plunging the family into financial insecurity.

During her lonely childhood, Ruth Sawyer's favorite companion was her Irish nurse, Johanna, who entertained her with an endless fund of stories learned in her native Donegal. Thus began Sawyer's lifelong fascination with folktales and folklore. She studied folklore at Teachers College, Columbia University, where she heard and learned from the work of the British storyteller Marie Shedlock. In 1905 came her first trip to Ireland. She trotted around Donegal on a pony, met both traditional storytellers and writers like James Stephens and Padraic Colum, and told stories in the hospitable home of "Æ" (George Russell)—who was to inspire, in due course, P. L. Travers, creator of Mary Poppins. In 1910 she initiated the first storytelling program for children at the New York Public Library, beginning a long friendship with its innovative children's librarian Anne Carroll Moore. After Sawyer's marriage, she and her husband settled in Ithaca, New York, where Dr. Durand practiced as an ophthalmologist. Her son was born in 1912, her daughter in 1916. She continued her public storytelling, and began to publish her own work.

Sawyer's first book was a novel for adults, *The Primrose Ring*, in which a nurse invokes the powers of magic primroses to prevent the closure of a children's ward. It was widely praised for its sensitive blending of poignancy and humor. A reviewer for the *Boston Transcript* (1915) called it "a delightfully charming modern fairy tale for grown-ups," and although *The Primrose Ring* lacked any significant artistic weight, others agreed that it was "a pretty, happy little tale" (*Independent*).

Sawyer's adult fiction, sometimes sentimental, was nevertheless popular. It is, however, for her contribution to children's literature that she is remembered. In 1931, her delight in the Spanish stories of Washington Irving drew her to that country. She spent a year there, traveling and collecting stories, as she later did in many parts of the world. Three books came out of the Spanish experience, beginning with her first notable book for children, *Tono Antonio*. A fictionalized portrait of a young boy encountered on her travels, J. W. Maury found it "quaint and delightful" (*Boston Transcript* 1934), and it was in Currie Cabot's view "a beautifully written and moving story" (*Saturday Review of Literature*). *Picture Tales from Spain* collected eleven traditional stories, and *My Spain* gives a charming account of the country and its people as she saw them.

International renown came with *Roller Skates*. Here the author, who had learned to skate before she was four, drew on her own excited exploration of the New York City of 1890, as the tomboyish "Lucinda Wyman" describing the characters she met, the sense of freedom she discovered. This story has been credited with introducing urban themes into literature for children. Universally praised for its characterization, vitality, and humor, it also stirred controversy with its tough-minded approach to death. *Horn Book* (1936) claimed that "by confronting a sordid murder and the death of a tiny child, . . . and by integrating these experiences with other aspects of Lucinda's year of discovery and growth, the book, in fact, deals more fully and frankly with the child's experience of death than do many of the books turned out these days."

After the death of Francis Sawyer, the family had been obliged to live for a year at their summer cottage in Maine. This was the subject of a second work of fictionalized biography, *The Year of Jubilo*, continuing—partly through letters—the story of "Lucinda Wyman." It evoked comparisons with the work of Louisa May Alcott, and was described by the *Library Journal* as "a wise and understanding story of a real girl." Further publications for children included the popular *Journey Cake, Ho!*, a rewriting of an old American folktale, and *The Enchanted Schoolhouse*.

The significance of Sawyer's contribution to both oral and written forms of storytelling has been widely recognized. Her guide to the art, *The Way of the Storyteller*, became a standard text for practitioners. In her biography of the author, Virginia Haviland emphasizes "the teller's oral gifts. She was ever the storyteller, 'the way' shining through everything she had to say."

In 1965 Sawyer received the Laura Ingalls Wilder Medal of the American Library Association for her "substantial and lasting contribution to literature for children," and a storytelling festival was held in her honor in Provincetown, Massachusetts.

Ruth Sawyer was a warm, lively woman, who enjoyed spending time with her family. Her daughter Margaret was married to the children's writer Robert McCloskey.

PRINCIPAL WORKS: *Juvenile*—The Tale of the Enchanted Bunnies, 1923; Tono Antonio, 1934; Picture Tales From Spain, 1936; Roller Skates, 1936; The Year of Jubilo, 1940 (in U.K.: Lucinda's Year of Jubilo, 1965); The Least One, 1941; Old Con and Patrick, 1946; The Little Red Horse, 1950; Journey Cake, Ho!, 1950; A Cottage for Betsy, 1954; The Enchanted Schoolhouse, 1956; Dietrich of Berne and the Dwarf-King Laurin; Hero Tales of the Austrian Tirol, 1963; Daddles, the Story of a Plain Hound Dog, 1964. *Christmas stories*—This Way to Christmas, 1916; The Long Christmas, 1941; The Christmas Anna Angel, 1944; This Is the Christmas; A Serbian Folk Tale, 1945; Maggie Rose, Her Birthday Christmas, 1952; The Year of the Christmas Dragon, 1960; Joy to the World, 1966. *Verse*—A Child's Year Book, 1917. *Adult fiction*—The Primrose Ring, 1915; Seven Miles to Arden, 1916; Herself, Himself and Myself, 1917; Doctor Danny, 1918 (stories); Leerie, 1920; Gladiola Murphy, 1923; Four Ducks on a Pond, 1928; Folkhouse; The Autobiography of a Home, 1932; The Luck of the Road, 1934; Gallant: The Story of Storm Veblen, 1936. *Drama*—The Sidhe of Ben-Mor: An Irish Folk Play, 1910; The Awakening, 1918. *Recordings*—Ruth Sawyer, Storyteller, 1965. *Other*—The Way of the Storyteller, 1942, rev. ed. 1977; How to Tell a Story, 1962; My Spain; A Storyteller's Year of Collecting, 1967.

ABOUT: The autobiographical material quoted above was written for Twentieth Century Authors, 1942. Burke, W. J. (and others) American Authors and Books, 1972; Commire, A. Something About the Author Vol. 17, 1976; Haviland, V. Ruth Sawyer, 1965; Kunitz, S. J. and Haycraft, H. (eds.) Junior Book of Authors rev. ed. 1951; Meigs, C. (and others) A Critical History of Children's Literature, 1969; Miller, B. E. and Field, E.

W. (eds.) Newbery Medal Books 1922–1955, 1955; Notable American Women; The Modern Period, 1980; Oxford Companion to Children's Literature, 1991; Twentieth Century Children's Writers 3rd ed., 1989; Ward, M. E. and Marquardt, D. A. Authors of Books for Young People, 1964. *Periodicals*— American Library Association Booklist December 1917; Atlantic November 1936; Book Week December 3, 1944; Boston Transcript June 30, 1915; November 21, 1934; Horn Book January 1936, November 1941, December 1956, October 1965, August 1970, August 1979; Independent May 17, 1915; Library Journal October 15, 1940; New York Herald Tribune Books April 17, 1932; New York Times November 15, 1936; June 6, 1970; Saturday Review of Literature November 17, 1934.

**SAXON, LYLE** (September 4, 1891–April 9, 1946), American journalist and novelist, was born in Baton Rouge, Louisiana, the son of Hugh Saxon

and Katherine (Chambers) Saxon. He had an idyllic childhood on his parents' four thousand-acre plantation. After graduating from Louisiana State University in 1912, he went into newspaper work in New Orleans and Chicago. From 1918 to 1926 he was a feature writer for the New Orleans Times-Picayune.

Saxon's first book, *Father Mississippi*, was based in part on a series of articles he had written for *Century Magazine* concerning the catastrophic floods in 1927. *Father Mississippi* was, however, as much social history and personal reminiscence as it was journalism, and most reviewers responded favorably to the mixture. *New York Herald Tribune Books* called it "a fine piece of work done by a man of great vitality, with the vision of a creative artist, valuable not only for its exact and pertinent information but also for the interest of the personal vision."

Saxon was a regionalist, and his next two books, *Fabulous New Orleans* and *Old Louisiana*, chronicled with his by now accustomed mixture of informality and journalistic thoroughness the city and state with which he was always identified. Of *Old Louisiana*, Stark Young wrote in the *New Republic*, "The book is, by its own inner compulsion, all one piece; and though there is always a sense of passing, there is curiously no sense of death. This is one of the gifts that has fallen to the author, and that endows his book with so gentle and friendly a relish for life. It is a happy, wistful, busy, engaging book, persuasive and rich, full of lovely reminders and full of good sense." Saxon's reputation as (in Edward Dreyer's words) "the best known interpreter of Louisiana in general, and New Orleans, in particular, of his generation," made him a logical choice for the directorship (1935 to 1942) of the Louisiana section of the Federal Writers' Project. Among the publications he supervised or edited in that capacity were *The New Orleans City Guide*, *The Louisiana Guide*, and *Gumbo Ya-Ya: A Collection of Louisiana Folk-Tales*, the last of which Eudora Welty, writing in the *New York Times Book*

*Review*, likened to "an old desk belonging to no-telling-who, so outlandish, occasionally, are the stuffings of the pigeon-holes; the accumulation is curious and interesting, but only some of it worth keeping. Still, there is a romantic, or a hilarious, or a wild note here and there that justifies your looking through the book."

Although Saxon published a handful of short stories in anthologies, his only full-length work of fiction was *Children of Strangers*, a novel about a romantically and socially disappointed mulatto woman living in the plantation country of Louisiana. The *Times Literary Supplement* wrote of it, "One may feel that the portraits of the white plantation owners and their friends are less lovingly done than those of both mulattoes and negroes; but objectivity never really fails, and the book's abiding effect is one of unusual poise, of authentic tragic beauty, of material fined and refined until every episode, every word, has its place in an artistic whole."

A "skilled raconteur who also possessed an extraordinary personal charm," as Dreyer described him, Saxon lived comfortably in Melrose, Louisiana, and New Orleans on the proceeds of his writing and on the considerable sum he received for selling the motion picture rights to his biography *Lafitte, the Pirate* (it was filmed by Cecil B. De Mille as *The Buccaneer* in 1939). He was weakened in his last years by his heavy drinking.

PRINCIPAL WORKS: *Journalism and biography*—Father Mississippi, 1927; Fabulous New Orleans, 1928; Old Louisiana, 1929; Lafitte, the Pirate, 1930; (with E. Dreyer) The Friends of Joe Gilmore, and Some Friends of Lyle Saxon, 1948. *Novels*— Children of Strangers, 1937. *As compiler*—(with others) Gumbo Ya-Ya: A Collection of Louisiana Folk-Tales, 1945.

ABOUT: Dreyer, E. (with L. Saxon) The Friends of Joe Gilmore, and Some Friends of Lyle Saxon, 1948. *Periodicals*—New Republic December 4, 1929; New York Herald Tribune Books December 11, 1927; New York Times October 10, 1946; New York Times Book Review January 20, 1946; Times Literary Supplement December 4, 1937.

**SAYERS, DOROTHY L(EIGH)** (June 13, 1893–December 17, 1957), English writer of detective fiction, dramatist, Dante adapter, and Christian apologist, was born in Oxford, the only child of the Rev. Henry Sayers, an Anglican clergyman and headmaster of the Cathedral Choir School, and Helen Mary (Leigh) Sayers. When she was a child the family moved to Bluntisham in East Anglia, where her father had been appointed rec-

tor. The bleak Fen country in which she grew up is the setting for *The Nine Tailors*, probably her best book. Educated first at home, then at Godolphin School in Salisbury, in 1912 she won a scholarship to the then most prestigious of the Oxford women's colleges, Somerville. In 1915 Sayers took first class honors in modern languages. The following year she published her first book, a verse collection titled *Op.I*; two years later *Catholic Tales and Christian Songs*, with its adaptations of medieval verse forms, appeared. In 1920 Sayers was one of the first group of women to be granted degrees from Oxford University. After a period as a teacher, in Yorkshire and in France, and as a reader for an Oxford publishing house, she moved to London, where she worked as an advertising copywriter (1922–31). Soon after joining the agency, she finished her first mystery, *Whose Body?*, which introduced her famous protagonist, Lord Peter Wimsey, and his Jeeves-like "man," Bunter. In the course of ten more Wimsey novels, the character of the young detective changes. The former war hero, dashing, witty, equipped with cane and monocle, more than slightly callow, develops into a man of conscience and moral responsibility. Crime detection at first seems to him a lark; by the time of *Unnatural Death* Wimsey realizes the consequences of his stepping in to expose the truth. In *Busman's Honeymoon* he weeps for the murderer he has brought to justice. It is this ethical dimension to her work that sets Sayers apart from Agatha Christie, her rival in what is called the Golden Age of English mystery writing. She wrote far better prose than Christie, although never to everyone's taste.

In that period, the early 1920s, Sayers had several unhappy love affairs, including one with the Russian-born novelist John Cournos; a collection of her letters to him is housed at Harvard University. In 1924, after another liaison, she had a son, managing to keep his birth and the identity of his father a secret for many years. He was brought up by her cousin, with Sayers providing for him financially, and was named (John) Anthony Fleming—although Sayers and her eventual husband, Oswald Atherton Fleming, never adopted the child. She and Captain Fleming, a journalist, were married in 1926, the year after she published her second Wimsey novel, *Clouds of Witness*. Like *Murder Must Advertise* after it (a send-up of her experiences at Benson's), it is one of the few detective stories written with authentic humor. With a group of other writers including G. K. Chesterton, Christie, and Fr. Ronald Knox, Sayers founded, in 1929, the Detection Club; they were dedicated, in a light-hearted way, to practicing their craft according to certain rules—the chief one of which was that cases would be solved solely by the detective's powers of deduction.

By 1929 the income from her writing made it possible for Sayers to purchase a home at Witham, in Essex; and in 1931 she was able to devote herself to writing full time. Wimsey and Bunter do not figure in *The Documents in the Case*, written with the collaboration of Dr. Eustace R. Barton; this is a particularly grim story of a murder investigation (Sayers was increasingly fascinated with pathological details), narrated in epistolary style. Lord Peter returns, however, in *Strong Poison*, which also introduces Harriet Vane, Oxford graduate and mystery writer, who has herself been charged with murder. The love interest, thus introduced, builds—from *Have His Carcase*, with the couple working on a case together, to the two books that are considered

Sayers's best. In *The Nine Tailors: Changes Rung on an Old Theme in Two Short Touches and Two Full Peals*, Wimsey comes up against a bizarrely complicated death in a Fenland village. The solution depends—as the subtitle hints—on the art of change ringing. Unfortunately, the author's disquisitions on the subject almost swamp her plot, but its ingenuity and the eerie atmosphere made the book a memorable one except for those—and there were many—put off by Sayers's mannered and sometimes facetious style.

Not until the next book, *Gaudy Night*, does Lord Peter win Harriet Vane's hand, amid Oxford cloisters whose usual serenity has been disturbed by evidence of evil mischief and threat of violence. Many mystery fans have found the novel a disappointment; the critic Mary McCarthy called it "a thorough-going, dismal flop" (*Nation*). At last on their wedding trip, in *Busman's Honeymoon*, the detective couple have to deal with a corpse found in their honeymoon retreat; this is the last of the Wimsey series, although he does appear in several of her short stories.

Thereafter, Sayers turned to other genres, drama to begin with. Her last novel had been adapted from the play of the same name written with her Oxford friend Muriel St. Clare Byrne in 1936, and produced that year at the Comedy Theatre, London. With one other exception (*Love All*, a farce), all her plays were religious dramas, written in not very poetic blank verse. For the Canterbury Festival in 1937 she wrote *The Zeal of Thy House*, about the twelfth-century architect William of Sens who rebuilt the cathedral choir. For the 1939 Festival at the cathedral she wrote *The Devil to Pay*, a retelling of the Dr. Faustus story. Both were subsequently staged in London, as was her last theater piece, *The Emperor Constantine*, produced first at Colchester for the Festival of Britain in 1951. For the BBC she had written the very successful one-act nativity play *He That Should Come*. Early in the war she wrote *The Man Born to Be King*, a twelve-part series on the life of Christ. First aired in 1941–42 and repeated many times annually thereafter, it successfully defied the ban on representations of divinity outside a church setting and the outcry against her use of colloquial speech. Popular in its day, it is now outdated.

A devout Anglo-Catholic, Sayers was for many years a friend of the Oxford writers known as the Inklings, whose spiritual convictions she shared (although she was not a "member" of their group): C. S. Lewis, J. W. Tolkien, and Charles Williams. She expressed her own spiritual and social beliefs in the lectures and essays to which she enthusiastically devoted her time from the 1930s on. As war began her publisher, Gollancz, asked her to set down her thoughts on how to prepare for the eventual days of reconstruction. *Begin Here* was the result, typical of the trenchant, vigorous style of her contemplative writing. *Creed or Chaos? and Other Essays in Popular Theology* argues with wit and common sense for the place of dogma in today's morally confused world. Perhaps most notable of all her writing in this was *The Mind of the Maker*, Sayers's attempt to explain the trinitarian nature of God, the Divine Creator, by analogy with the three-fold activity of the creative artist—involving idea, energy, and power. The scholar Jacques Barzun found the argument "well conceived and . . . at once dramatic and persuasive" (*Nation*), but others were less impressed, and the book is little read now.

While a student at Oxford, Sayers had begun a translation of the medieval French *Song of Roland*; it was not published, however, until the year of her death. In her early London years she had translated *Tristan in Brittany*, a twelfth-century Anglo-Norman romance. During the days of the blitz she was urged by the poet Charles Williams, of the Oxford University Press, to read Dante for escape and consolation. Captured by it, she taught herself Italian in order to read it in the original, and set out to share her delight with others by means of a translation and lectures on the poet's theology and imagery; the latter were later published in two series of papers on Dante. For her three-volume *Comedy of Dante Alighieri the Florentine* she set herself the challenge of using his terza rima verse form. The result is a fast-paced text, in Victorian-style verse, which takes many liberties with the original. Her tendency to add words for clearer meaning has been much criticized. It appeared in Penguin, and after several decades of holding the field, was replaced by a more accurate version.

Dorothy L. Sayers was awarded a Litt.D. by the University of Durham in 1950. Some claim that she brought the "whodunit" (in her case always more the "howdunit") up to the standards of the legitimate novel, although if that is so, her novels have lacked criticism as such. Masterpiece Theatre television dramatizations of some of her mysteries in the 1970s led to a temporary renewed interest in her work, which remains available through numerous reprintings; some of the nonfiction is to be found scattered in specialized collections.

Sayers's papers are housed in the Marion E. Wade Collections at Wheaton College, Wheaton, Illinois. There is also an archive of memorabilia, first editions, and other material at the Dorothy L. Sayers Historical and Literary Society in Witham, founded in 1976. The society sponsors annual seminars and the *Sayers Review* (started in Los Angeles in 1976) publishes articles on her work; but she is today more of a cult figure among Anglo-Catholic theologians and elderly feminists than a serious writer.

PRINCIPAL WORKS: *Fiction*—Whose Body?, 1923; Clouds of Witness, 1925; Unnatural Death, 1927 (in U.S: The Dawson Pedigree; Lord Peter Views the Body, 1928 (short stories); The Unpleasantness at the Bellona Club, 1928; (with R. Eustace) The Documents in the Case, 1930; Strong Poison, 1930; The Five Red Herrings, 1931 (in U.S.: Suspicious Characters); (with members of the Detection Club) The Floating Admiral, 1931; Have His Carcase, 1932; (with members of the Detection Club) As a Policeman, 1933; Hangman's Holiday, 1933 (short stories); Murder Must Advertise, A Detective Story, 1933; The Nine Tailors: Changes Rung on an Old Theme in Two Short Touches and Two Full Peals, 1934; Gaudy Night, 1935; Busman's Honeymoon: A Love Story with Detective Interruptions, 1937; (with members of the Detection Club) Double Death: A Murder Story 1939; In the Teeth of the Evidence, and Other Stories, 1939; The Collected Edition of Detective Stories by Dorothy L. Sayers, 15 vols., 1969–1975; Lord Peter: A Collectin of All the Lord Peter Wimsey Stories (comp. and with introd. by J. Sandoe; Coda by Carolyn Heilbrun; Codetta by E. C. Bentley) 1971; Striding Folly, Including Three Final Lord Peter Wimsey Stories, 1972. *Drama*—Busman's Honeymoon: A Detective Comedy in Three Acts (with M. St. C. Byrne) 1937; The Zeal of Thy House, 1937; The Devil to Pay: Being the Famous History of John Faustus . . . , 1939; He That Should Come: A Nativity Play in One Act, 1939; The Man Born to Be King, a Play-Cycle on the Life of Our Lord and Saviour Jesus Christ . . . 1943; The Just Vengeance: The Litchfield Festival Play for 1946, 1945; The Emporor Constantine, A Chronicle, 1951; (with M. St. C. Byrne) Love All: A Comedy of Manners, 1985. *Poetry*—Op. I, 1916; Catholic Tales and Christian Songs, 1918. *Nonfiction*—Strong Meat, 1939; Begin Here: A War-Time Essay, 1940 (in U.S.: Begin Here: A Statement of Faith); The Mind of the Maker, 1941; Unpopular Opinions, 1946; Creed or Chaos? And Other Essays in Popular Theology, 1947; Introductory Papers on Dante 1954; Further Papers on Dante, 1957; The Poetry of Search and the Poetry of Statement, and Other Posthumous Essays on Literature, Religion, and Language, 1963; Christian Letters to a Post-Christian World: A Selection of Essays (ed. R. Jellema) 1969 (also pub. as The Whimsical Christian: Eighteen Essays, 1978); Are Women Human? (with The Human-Not-Quite-Human; introd. M. McD. Snideler) 1971; A Matter of Eternity: Selections from the Writings of Dorothy L. Sayers (ed. R. K. Sprague) 1973; Wilkie Collins: A Critical and Biographical Study (ed. E. R. Gregory) 1977; Spiritual Writings (comp. A. Loades) 1993. *As editor*—Great Short Stories of Detection, Mystery and Horror, 3 ser. 1929–1934 (in U.S.: The Omnibus of Crime); Tales of Detection, 1936; Essays Presented to Charles Williams, 1947. *As translator*—Tristan in Brittany, Being the Fragments of the Romance of Tristan . . . by Thomas the Anglo-Norman (introd. G. Saintsbury) 1929; The Comedy of Dante Alighieri the Florentine, Cantica I: Hell; Cantica II: Purgatory; Cantica III: (with B. Reynolds) Paradise, 1949–1962; The Song of Roland, 1957.

ABOUT: Brabazon, J. Dorothy L. Sayers: A Biography (pref. Anthony Fleming; foreword P. D. James) 1981; Brunsdale, M. Dorothy L. Sayers: Solving the Mystery of Wickedness, 1990; Contemporary Authors Vol. 119, 1986; Coomes, D. Dorothy L. Sayers: A Careless Rage for Life, 1992; Dale, S. Maker and Craftsman: The Story of Dorothy L. Sayers, 1978, rev. ed. 1992; Dale. A. S. (ed.) Dorothy L. Sayers: The Centenary Celebration, 1993; Dictionary of Literary Biography Vol. 10, pt. 2, 1982; Vol. 36, 1985; Vol. 77, 1989; Vol. 100, 1990; Dictionary of National Biography 1951–1960; Talking of Dorothy L. Sayers, 1977; Durkin, M. B. Dorothy L. Sayers, 1981; Hall, T. H. Dorothy L. Sayers: Nine Literary Studies, 1980; Hannay, M. P. (ed.) As Her Whimsy Took Her, 1979; Harmon, R. B. (with M. A. Burger) An Annotated Guide to the Works of Dorothy L. Sayers, 1977; Hitchman, J. Such a Strange Lady: A Biography of Dorothy L. Sayers, 1975; Hone R. E. Dorothy L. Sayers: A Literary Biography, 1979; Kenney, C. M. The Remarkable Case of Dorothy L. Sayers, 1990; Larsen, G. Dorothy and Agatha, 1990; Lewis, T. L. Dorothy L. Sayers' Wimsey and Interwar British Society, 1994; Mann, J. Deadlier than the Male, 1981; Reilly, J. M. (ed.) Twentieth-Century Crime and Mystery Writers, 1985; Reynolds, B. Dorothy L. Sayers: Her Life and Soul, 1993; Reynolds, B. The Passionate Intellect: Dorothy L. Sayers' Encounter with Dante, 1989; Symons, J. Mortal Consequences: A History from the Detective Story to the Crime Novel, 1973; Tischler, N. M. P. Dorothy L. Sayers, A Pilgrim Soul, 1980; Twentieth-Century Literary Criticism 2, 1979; 15, 1985; Youngborg, R. T. Dorothy L. Sayers, a Reference Guide. *Bibliography*—Gilbert, C. B. A Bibliography of the Works of Dorothy L. Sayers, 1978. *Periodicals*—American Scholar Spring 1968; Commonweal October 15, 1937; Nation April 18, 1936; February 21, 1942; Times (London) December 19, 1957; April 2, 1993.

**SCARBOROUGH, DOROTHY** (January 27, 1878–November 7, 1935), American novelist and folklorist, was born in Mount Carmel, Texas, the  daughter of John B. Scarborough, a lawyer and judge, and Mary (Ellison) Scarborough. She received bachelor's and master's degrees from Baylor University in Waco, Texas, and taught English there from 1905 to 1914. After doing graduate work at the University of Chicago and Oxford University, she went to New York City, where she was awarded a Ph.D. from Columbia University in 1917. Her dissertation, *The Supernatural in Modern English Fiction*, was a lively work of scholarship (though lacking in analytical rigor), and she found a commercial publisher for it almost immediately. It was not as a literary scholar, however, but as a folklorist and novelist that Scarborough achieved a temporary prominence.

Her two principal works as a folklorist brought together a wealth of American folk songs and the lore surrounding them. The first, *On the Trail of Negro Folk-Songs*, which included musical transcriptions by Ola Lee Gulledge, classified songs as ballads, lullabies, work songs, dance songs, and so on, and traced their origins to English and Scottish sources. Despite Scarborough's paternalistic attitude) toward African Americans, which was equally apparent in her fiction and which precluded her from considering the African sources of black folk songs, the book was a contribution to its subject. "To the specialist this book commends itself as a document of permenant authority," wrote a reviewer in the *New Republic*. "Other readers will value the volume as highly for its musical and poetical substance, for the humor and enthusiasm of Dr. Scarborough's comments, and for the charmed style in which she relates her quest."

Scarborough's second volume of folklore studies, *A Song Catcher in Southern Mountains: American Folk-Songs of British Ancestry*, was published posthumously in 1937. This book continued the methodology of its predecessor and was written with the same informality that reviewers of *On the Trail of Negro Folk-Songs* found so appealing. In the *New York Herald Tribune Books* (1937), John Lomax, her fellow folklorist and musicologist, wrote of *A Song Catcher in Southern Mountains*, "For those of us who knew Miss Scarborough well, this handsome volume, so full of her bright, alert self, will remind us of one of her happy letters—a delightful letter to all her friends setting forth the story of a busy summer among the purest-bred Americans this country affords."

As a novelist, Scarborough employed the Texas milieus that attracted her as a folklorist. Her knowledge of Southern agrarian life was so extensive that her fiction sometimes reads like sociology rather than fiction. For example, a critic in the *New York Herald Tribune Books* (1929) wrote of *Can't Get a Red Bird*, the story of a struggling Texas cotton farmer who prevails over poverty and self-doubt, "Miss Scarborough has marshalled her statistics like so much ammunition, she discourses learnedly and appositely upon the cotton market, tick fever and animal industry, diversification, the Texas homestead law, farm organization and cooperation. But as for relating the romance of cotton, or conveying its strange fascination as a crop and a gamble, Miss Scarborough has signally failed."

The most praised of the novels was *Impatient Griselda*, which described the marriage and remarriage of a widowed clergyman and, perhaps because of its concentration on purely domestic matters, escaped the didacticism that marred her other works of fiction. The *Saturday Review of Literature* wrote, "The book is both spacious and gracious; it abounds in 'homely' characters and familiar incidents; it covers the love life of two generations and the years are filled from end to end with 'doings,' [and] the central theme disappears again and again under this efflorescence of detail."

From 1916 until her death Scarborough was, in turn, instructor of English, lecturer, assistant professor, and associate professor at Columbia University, where she offered a notable storytelling class, attended by, among others, Tess Slesinger.

PRINCIPAL WORKS: *Poetry*—Fugitive Verses, 1912. *Criticism, essays, and folklore*—The Supernatural in Modern English Fiction, 1917; From a Southern Porch, 1919; (with O. L. Gulledge) On the Trail of Negro Folk-Songs, 1925; A Song Catcher in Southern Mountains: American Folk-Songs of British Ancestry, 1937. *Novels*—In the Land of Cotton, 1923; The Wind, 1925; Impatient Griselda, 1927; Can't Get a Red Bird, 1929, The Stretch-Berry Smile, 1932. *Juvenile*—The Story of Cotton, 1933. *As editor*—Famous Modern Ghost Stories, 1921; Humorous Ghost Stories, 1921; Selected Short Stories of Today, 1935.

ABOUT: American Women Writers, 1981; Dictionary of American Biography, Suppl. 1, 1944. *Periodicals*—New Republic December 30, 1925; New York Herald Tribune Books November 17, 1929; February 7, 1937; New York Times Book Review April 15, 1923; Saturday Review of Literature October 1, 1927.

**SCARFE, FRANCIS HAROLD** (September 18, 1911–March 1, 1986), English critic, translator, poet, novelist, academic, and administrator, wrote: "I was born in South Shields, in Durham, England. Descended from sea-faring stock I felt myself to be destined for the sea, but perhaps the fact that I could not walk properly for some years owing to rickets gave me an angle on life which turned me into a writer. My father was lost at sea  in 1916, and in 1921 or 1922 I was sent to the Royal Merchant Seamen's Orphanage in Berkshire, where I spent four years. Those years are described fictionally in my first novel, *Promises*—a book I should like to write closer to fact, which in this case was more interesting than fiction.

"I received my University education at Durham,

Cambridge and Paris, and subsequently became senior lecturer in French in Glasgow University. . . .
My first prose book, *Auden and After*, was written
in a hurry and had the success that often comes to
one's least careful work. I had published a year earlier my first poems, *Inscapes*, and in 1942 *Poems
and Ballads*. Being a late developer, and delayed by
war service (lieutenant-colonel in the Army Educational Corps), it was not until 1949 that I found myself able to express anything properly in prose. I
refer to my novels *Promises* and *Single Blessedness*,
which were for me only exercises written with a
view to learning techniques. I have since written
two other novels, *Man's Desiring* and *Violet-Anne*,
the first which I do not intend to publish, the second to appear I hope soon. My life is a constant
struggle to keep a balance between my job and my
writing. To consolidate the first I've recently written a long book on Paul Valéry, whom I met and
admired in 1936; but on the whole I regret having
to do anything which prevents me from writing my
own stuff. I regard those who have no responsibilities, and who can give themselves entirely to writing, as very fortunate.

"My view of the novel is that one's job is not to
turn fact into fiction, but to turn fiction into fact.
By this I mean I regard the novelist's task as imaginative; the realistic novel is washed-up; political
novels are only journalism; the time has arrived
now for what I would call the *poetic novel*.

"I still write poems sometimes (see *Underworlds*), but they tend to be personal. I revolt
against the 'impersonal' theories of Eliot and others
but haven't space to say why. But I think there will
always be some readers who will realise that the
thought and feeling of one man affect all men.

"I have blue eyes and wavy lips, if that interests
anybody, also short ears and thick hair and a voice
on the whole quiet."

---

Francis Scarfe is now most highly valued for his
magisterial translations of the symbolist French
poet Charles Baudelaire, which he first made for
Penguin Books in 1961, as a selection; he subsequently revised and expanded it, rendering it complete, in 1986. Perhaps these versions are all the
more distinguished because, although he had once
been an ambitious poet himself, Scarfe rendered
them into a scholarly, scrupulous, and literal English prose—thus doing more for the understanding
of Baudelaire in English-speaking countries than
any of the numerous translations into verse, however notable.

Scarfe's critical *Auden and After: The Liberation
of Poetry 1930–1941* was written in a hurry (as he
was always at pains to point out). *Auden and After*
is a lively discussion of the poetry of Auden and his
contemporaries such as Spender, MacNeice, and
Prokosch—and of other younger poets such as Symons, Roughton, and Scarfe himself. It tended to
take the poets who were its subject at their own
high valuation of themselves; it lacked a single
point of view; it was very much a young man's
book. It nevertheless exerted an influence whose

legacy is still evident. For all its inadequacies and
omissions, and the fact that it is not a critically coherent book, its sheer sense of excitement about poetry itself fired more young people into enthusiasm
than any other similar book of the 1940s and 1950s.

Scarfe had a distinguished academic career, and
was as highly respected by his colleagues as by his
students. He left Glasgow in 1959 to take up an appointment as Director of the British Institute in
Paris, a post which he held for the next nineteen
years. As his London *Times* obituarist remarked, he
helped to transform the British Institute; and he
"met, with great calm and understanding, the consequences of the upheavals that raged throughout
the Latin Quarter" in 1968. From 1965 until 1978
he was also professor of French in the University of
London; after that he was professor emeritus. It was
a great triumph when, in 1968, Scarfe succeeded in
persuading the University of London to incorporate
the Institute into the British university system. In
the year of his retirement Scarfe was made Chevalier de la Légion d' Honneur, a decoration he particularly appreciated.

He began with high poetic ambitions, and in a
manner unusual in Britain at the time. So interested
was he in French literature that he nearly became
one of the very few British surrealist poets. Scarfe
was associated not with the best known of these,
David Gascoyne, but with the less well known Roger Roughton, who edited the magazine *Contemporary Poetry and Prose*, which had been inspired by
the 1936 Surrealist Exhibition in London. Both
Scarfe and Kenneth Allot contributed surrealist poems to this periodical, which lasted for ten numbers
before failing after just a year. Roughton gassed
himself in Dublin in 1941, and Scarfe wrote a moving elegy for him—one of his most successful poems, the best of which were simple, graceful, and
without pretentiousness.

Scarfe's earlier, surrealist poetry, although inconsequential, possessed great charm. He quoted
from some of it in his *Auden and After*, at the same
time fully recognizing its slightness. Surrealist poems, and some more traditional, appeared in Julian
Symons's magazine *Twentieth Century Verse*
(1937–1939). Like many young poets of that time,
Scarfe went on to publish his early volumes, *Inscapes* and *Forty Poems and Ballads*, with the Fortune Press, whose notorious proprietor, R. J. Caton,
generally charged his poets some (or all, or even
more than all) of the cost of production. But the poets Caton published, among them Kingsley Amis,
Christopher Middleton, and Julian Symons himself,
as well as Scarfe, did thus find an audience. A later
volume, *Underworlds* (1950), was published in a
normal trade edition—but, ironically, interest in
Scarfe's poetry had by then diminished, and this
collection was read much less widely than the first
two had been. Scarfe's later poems, all written in
the single year 1982–1983, were collected in
*Grounds for Conceit* (1984). As Trevor Tolley
wrote in the *Oxford Companion to Twentieth-
Century Poetry*, "his best poems are notable for
their simple and direct handling of personal
themes." This was a quality already evident in his
elegy for his friend Roughton.

Scarfe's other work is more specialized, and deals exclusively with the subject he knew best: French poetry. His Baudelaire, in its final version of 1986, will remain standard. His summary of the life and achievement of T. S. Eliot, written in French—*La Vie et l'oeuvre de T. S. Eliot* (1964)—remains a standard introductory volume in France. In 1961, After his edition of the works of André Chénier—the poet executed during the French Revolution—appeared in 1961, he issued a full critical biography, *André Chénier: His Life and Work 1762-1794* (1965). The *Times Literary Supplement* reviewer called it "reliable," "discriminating," "impressive," and "scholarly and sensitive." Scarfe also wrote a study of Paul Valéry, whom he had met in 1936, and three novels, all of which were well received at the time. Only a few days before his death, remarked his *Times* (London) obituarist, he was reading his translations of La Fontaine to the students at the Institute.

In 1938 Scarfe married Margarete M. Geisler. They had one son.

PRINCIPAL WORKS: *Poetry*—Inscapes, 1940; Forty Poems and Ballads, 1941; Underworlds, 1950; Grounds for Conceit, 1984. *As editor*—Chénier, 1961. *As translator*—Reflections on the World Today (by P. Valery) 1948; Selected Verse (by C. Baudelaire) 1961, (rev. and exp. as The Complete Verse, 1986). *Criticism*—Auden and After: The Liberation of Poetry 1930-1941, 1942; W. H. Auden, 1947; The Art of Paul Valéry, 1954. *Novels*—Promises, 1950; Single Blessedness, 1951; Unfinished Women, 1954.

ABOUT: The autobiographical material quoted above was written for Twentieth Century Authors First Supplement, 1955. Hamilton. I. (ed.) Oxford Companion to Twentieth-Century Poetry, 1994; Who's Who 1985. *Periodicals*—American History Review April 1966; Times (London) March 3, 1986; Times Literary Supplement September 9, 1965.

## SCHACHNER, NATHAN (January 16, 1895–October 2, 1955), American biographer, historian, and novelist, wrote:

"I was born in New York City and attended its public and high schools. I suppose I was somewhat precocious as a child, since by the age of thirteen read with avidity if not complete understanding such works as the *Divine Comedy, Faust, Paradise Lost,* Shakespeare complete, the Greek dramatists, Shelley, Keats and Byron. In spite of these literary passions and the editorship of high school and college magazines, my first turn was toward the sciences. I majored in chemistry, graduating from City College of New York as a Bachelor of Science.

"After several years as a chemist with the New York Board of Health and private concerns I shifted to law and, in spite of the interruption of my legal studies by an interval of army life during World War I, received the degree of Juris Doctor from New York University. Thereafter I spent sixteen years as a busy and fairly successful lawyer; but continued to read more in literature and history than in reported cases.

"About 1930, on a dare, I dashed off a story for a science fiction magazine and lo, it was accepted with a request for more. I was fairly launched on a pulp writing career, snatching moments from my law practice to write hundreds of science, detective, mystery, western and adventure stories. Meanwhile my reading concentrated more and more on history, particularly the medieval scene and early America. The former flowered in a history of the *Mediaeval Universities* which, published simultaneously in England and the United States, achieved a *succès d'estime* if not undue financial rewards.

"My appetite thus whetted, I dropped law and devoted full time to writing. With the single exception of a novelized life of Dante in *The Wanderer,* I have consistently engaged in an examination of American life: including full length biographies of Aaron Burr, Alexander Hamilton and Thomas Jefferson, and a series of historical novels, numerous articles for the general magazines (paid for), learned articles for the learned quarterlies (unpaid for) and assorted book reviews.

"During World War II, I joined the staff of the American Jewish committee as magazine liaison and editorial consultant in a campaign to promote better group relations in this country and headed an editorial board of prominent writers which offered prizes for the magazine stories best directed toward that end.

"My major avocations besides armchair reading and research have been development of jet propulsion, travel and photography. I was a founder and charter member of the American Rocket Society, as well as its president. . . . "

A man of many interests and talents, Nathan Schachner was known primarily for his biographies of Burr, Hamilton, and Jefferson; much less for his historical novels on such subjects as the Civil War and Bacon's Rebellion in 1676. His first book, *Aaron Burr,* courted controversy with its legalistic defense of Burr's unsavory actions and personality; indeed, Henry Steele Commager, writing in the *New York Herald Tribune Books,* accused Schachner of accepting "most of Burr's words as holy writ. . . . His book is one long brief for the defense, at times learned and persuasive, at times clever and disingenuous, but mostly passionate and prejudiced."

Schachner's subsequent biographies were more even-handed, and *Alexander Hamilton,* in particular, was praised for its skillful and balanced integration of a vast array of primary and secondary sources. The *Saturday Review of Literature* wrote, "The quickest way to describe this biography is to say that it is a fresh narrative, well supported by primary sources, and distinctly objective in character. It is not an interpretation but a story. It moves briskly in a way which Hamilton himself would have approved of." On the subject of Jefferson, Schachner was less successful. His two-volume *Thomas Jefferson,* was thought to be a useful compilation of facts, but, as the *United States Quarterly Book Review* put it, "all the facts put together come nowhere near adding up to the whole man, particularly one as subtle and complex as Jefferson."

Schachner's four historical novels were for the most part conscientious interpretations of the past. As a historical novelist he might have been too much a historian and too little a novelist, as the *New York Herald Tribune Weekly Book Review* suggested. Reviewing *The Sun Shine Wests*, the story of a young couple caught up in the turmoil of "bleeding Kansas" just before the Civil War, the paper suggested "So broad and diversified historical development that it necessitates frequent interruption of the personal drama and tends for long periods to overshadow it. Jonathan and Delia become less real than the events that are shaping them. None the less the final tragic climax of their story carries with it the full impact of truth, for it had stemmed directly from the conflict engendered by their clashing personalities."

For the last year of his life Schachner served as public relations director for the National Council of Jewish Women.

PRINCIPAL WORKS: *History and biography*—Aaron Burr: A Biography, 1937; The Mediaeval Universities, 1938; Alexander Hamilton, 1946; The Price of Liberty: A History of the American Jewish Committee, 1948; Thomas Jefferson: A Biography 2 vols., 1951; The Founding Fathers, 1954. *Historical novels*—By the Dim Lamps, 1941; The King's Passenger, 1942; The Sun Shines West, 1943; The Wanderer: A Novel of Dante and Beatrice, 1951. *Science fiction*—Space Lawyer, 1953. *Juvenile*—Alexander Hamilton, Nation Builder, 1952.

ABOUT: The autobiographical material quoted above was written for Twentieth Century Authors First Supplement, 1955. National Cyclopaedia of American Biography Vol. 43, 1961; Twentieth Century Science Fiction Writers, 3rd ed., 1991. *Periodicals*—New York Herald Tribune Books October 3, 1937; New York Herald Tribune Weekly Book Review October 17, 1943; New York Times October 3, 1955; New York Book Review March 2, 1941; Saturday Review of Literature June 15, 1946; United States Quarterly Book Review March 1952.

## SCHAUFFLER, ROBERT HAVEN (April 8, 1879–November 24, 1964), American biographer, essayist, poet, and anthologist, was born in Bruenn,

Austria, the son of American missionaries, Rev. Henry A. Schauffler, D.D., and Clara Eastham (Gray) Schauffler. He arrived in the United States at the age of two. He attended Northwestern University (1898–1899), but his B.A. came from Princeton, where he edited the *Nassau Literary Magazine*. From 1903 to 1904 he was music editor of the *Independent*. After graduating from Princeton Schauffler studied two years at the University of Berlin. Meanwhile he studied the cello with three famous teachers: Steindel, Schroeder, and Hekking.

Schauffler was a special contributor to *Collier's Weekly* in Italy and Greece, in 1906; to the *Century* and *Outlook* in Germany, in 1907; and to *Success* in the West in 1909 and 1910. For the next three years he served in a similar capacity for the *Atlantic*

*Monthly*, the *Metropolitan Magazine*, and *Century Magazine*. Not only was Schauffler a writer on musical topics, but a practicing musician as well. From 1906 to 1909 he and his wife, Katharine de Normandie Wilson, joined with the blind violinist Edwin Grasse to form the Grasse Trio.

In 1929 Schauffler wrote *Beethoven: The Man Who Freed Music*, a two-volume biography that includes a study of the composer's method of composition. "Mr. Schauffler's book may be considered an important move for brighter Beethoven biographies," the *New York Times* critic noted (1930). "Though it is by no means lacking in thoroughness or in seriousness of intention, it is written in a very human style and keeps close to the ground of human interest and level common sense." In 1932 it was abridged under the title *The Mad Musician*. The following year Schauffler published *The Unknown Brahm*. *New York Herald Tribune Books* said "in some respects Mr. Schauffler's study is the most important work that has yet appeared concerning Brahms, because with infinite care and sympathetic insight it examines the Brahms who, if not entirely 'unknown,' has in any case been mainly ignored." Schauffler also published biographies of Robert Schumann and Franz Schubert, but only the Beethoven and Brahms works have remained in print.

Schauffler once called the public library a "most kindly nurse which saw [him] safe from kilts to long trousers and from Palmer Cox to Robert Louis Stevenson." He also stated: "I dote upon librarians in general and librarians love me like a brother. I have saved them a million hours of running around"—chiefly to find the holiday material he conveniently and prolifically collected in his volumes of poetry and prose anthologies, the individual titles of which appeared as the *Our American Holidays* series.

He wrote much ephemeral material in order to earn a living, and only a short selection from this is listed below. Schauffler also indulged athletic and artistic interests. He was decorated by the Queen of Italy for winning the national tennis doubles championship in Rome in 1906. He competed in the Athenian Olympics that same year, and won the Austrian handicap tennis doubles in 1931. He also tried his hand at sculpture.

Robert Haven Schauffler lived for most of his life in Greenwich Village, New York City.

PRINCIPAL WORKS: *Nonfiction*—The Musical Amateur: A Book on the Human Side of Music, 1911; The Joyful Heart, 1914; Beethoven: The Man Who Freed Music, 1929 (abridged as The Mad Musician, 1932); The Unknown Brahms: His Life, Character and Works Based on New Material, 1933; Arturo Toscanini: A Photobiography, 1943; (with M. Gross) Brahms: The Master, 1943; Florestan: The Life and Work of Robert Schumann, 1945; Christmas Cavalcade: A Spiritual Record of Our Time, 1949; Franz Schubert: The Ariel of Music, 1949. *As editor*—Christmas: Its Origin, Celebration and Significance as Related in Prose and Verse, 1907; Thanksgiving: Its Origin, Celebration and Significance as Related in Prose and Verse, 1907; Through Italy With the Poets, 1908; Arbor Day: Its History, Observance, Spirit and Significance: With Practical Suggestions on Tree-Planting and Conservation and a Nature Anthology, 1909; Lincoln's Birthday: A Comprehensive View of Lincoln as Given in the Most Noteworthy Essays . . . and in Lincoln's Own Writings, 1909; Washington's Birthday: Its

History, Observance, Spirit, and Significance as Related in Prose and Verse with a Selection of Washington's Speeches and Writings, 1910; Memorial Day (Decoration Day): Its Celebration, Spirit, and Significance as Related in Prose and Verse with a Nonsectional Anthology of the Civil War, 1911; Flag Day: Its History, Origin, and Celebration as Related in Song and Story, 1912; Independence Day: Its Celebration, Spirit and Significance as Related in Prose and Verse, 1912; (with S. T. Rice) Mother's Day: Its History, Origin, Celebration, Spirit, and Significance as Related in Prose and Verse, 1915; (with S. T. Rice) Easter: Its History, Celebration, Spirit, and Significance as Related in Prose and Verse, 1916; (with S. T. Rice) "Mother" in Verse and Prose: A Book of Rememberance, 1916; Our Flag in Verse and Prose, 1917; The Poetry Cure: A Pocket Medicine Chest of Verse, 1925; (with A. P. Sanford) Armistice Day: An Anthology of the Best Prose and Verse on Patriotism, the Great War, the Armistice: Its History, Observance Spirit and Significance: Victory, the Unknown Soldier and His Brothers, and Peace: With Fiction, Drama, Pageantry and Programs for Armistice Day Observance, 1927; (with A. P. Sanford) Plays for Our American Holidays, 1927; (with A. P. Sanford) Little Plays for Little People, 1929; (with A. P. Sanford) The Magic of Books: Anthology for Book Week, 1929; (with A. P. Sanford) Graduation Day: An Anthology of Verse and Prose for the Use of Students and Teachers in Preparation for Graduation Exercises in All Schools and Colleges: Consisting of the Best Addresses and Orations, Special Articles, Readings, Baccalaureate Sermons, Plays, Pageantry and Graduation Programs, 1930; The Junior Poetry Cure: A First-Aid Kit of Verse for the Young of All Ages, 1931; A Manthology: Songs That Are Fit for Men—and a Few Women, 1931; (with A. P. Sanford) Christmas Plays: A Supplement to Plays for Our American Holidays (Vol. 1), and to Little Plays for Little People, 1932; (with H. Paulmier) Roosevelt Day: The Best Prose and Verse About T. R. as Boy, Young Man, Public Servant, Rancer, Soldier, President, Explorer, and World Citizen: With Anecdoted, Programs for the Days' Observance, and an Original Sketch of His Life, 1932; Hallowe'en: Its Origins, Spirit, Celebration, and Significance as Related in Prose and Verse, Together with Hallowe'en Stories, Plays, Pantomimes: And Suggestions for Games, Stunts, Parties, Feasts, and Decorations, 1933; The Magic of Music: An Anthology for Music Weeks and Days: Music Week, Its Origin and Observance; Musical Memory Contests, Games and Entertainment; Music Study; the Music Cure; Stories; Plays; with an Anthology of the Best Prose and Verse on Music from Plato to Millay, 1935; (with H. Paulmier) Columbus Day: The Best Prose and Verse About Columbus and the Discovery of America: With Tributes, Anecdotes, Plays, Poems, Tableaux, Exercises, and Programs for the Day's Observance, 1938; The Days We Celebrate, 1940– ; (with H. Paulmier) Democracy Days: An Anthology of the Best Prose and Verse on Democracy, Tolerance and Liberty: Plays, Poems, Essay Material, Speeches, and Sayings for Jefferson Day, I'm An American Day, Good Will Day, Brotherhood Week, and Bill of Rights Week, 1942; (with H. Paulmier) Pan-American Day: An Anthology of the Best Prose and Verse on Pan Americanism and the Good Neighbor Policy: Plays, Poems, Essay Material, Speeches, Exercises, and Sayings for Pan American Day and for Year-Round Study in the Schools, 1943; (with H. Paulmier) Peace Days: Poems, Plays, Prose Selections, Essay Material, Anecdotes and Stories, Speeches and Sayings for the Observance of V-Day, Good Will Day, and United Nations Day in the Schools and for Year-Round Observance of the Promotion of Lasting Peace and International Good Will, 1946; (with H. Paulmier) Good Will Days: Poems, Plays, Prose Selections, Essay Material, Anecdotes and Stories, Speeches and Sayings for the Promotion of Racial Good Will, 1947. Verse—Scum o' the Earth, and Other Poems, 1912; The White Comrade, and Other Poems, 1920; Selected Poems of Robert Haven Schauffler, 1922; Magic Flame and Other Poems, 1923; Hobnails in Eden: Poems of a Maine Vagabond, 1929; New and Selected Poems, 1942. Fiction—Where Speech Ends: A Music Maker's Romance, 1906. Memoirs—Fiddler's Luck: The Gay Adventures of a Musical Amateur, 1920, rev. ed. 1941; Fiddler's Folly and Encores, 1942.

ABOUT: Periodicals—Boston Transcript December 18, 1920; Christian Century April 15, 1942; New York Herald Tribune Books January 21, 1934; New York Times January 5, 1930; March 29, 1942; November 25, 1964.

**SCHELLING, FELIX EMANUEL** (September 3, 1858–December 15, 1945), American scholar and critic, was born in New Albany, Indiana, the son of Felix Schelling, a music teacher and later Director of the St. Louis Conservatory of Music, and Rose (White) Schelling. He was the (much) older brother of Ernest H. Schelling, the pianist, composer, and conductor; Felix himself was a gifted pianist, but chose not to make music his vocation.  Owing to frail health Schelling was educated by private tutors and by his mother. Between 1881 and 1884 he took his B.A., L.L.B., and M.A. degrees from the University of Pennsylvania. He then practiced law until 1886, when he became an English instructor at his alma mater. In 1893 he was named the John Welsh Centennial Professor of English Literature, a position he held until 1929, when he was honored with the Felix E. Schelling Professorship.

Schelling's tenure at the University of Pennsylvania was distinguished by provocative teaching and innovative scholarship. According to Arthur Hobson Quinn in his preface to the Schelling Anniversary Papers, Schelling was given a charge in 1888 to "propose a plan by which the scope of the English courses would be broadened and the teaching of the subject be made more effective. . . . His scheme of organization defined the basic principles upon which the Department of English was for the first time really organized."

Schelling was known in his time as one of the greatest living authorities on Elizabethan literature—and on the Tudor period generally; his books reflected this, and much has remained in print. His best known book is Elizabethan Drama, 1558–1642; a two-volume study highly praised by critics, it laid one of the foundations for modern work. Dial reviewer M. W. Sampson called the book "a notable contribution to American scholarship," and a "book for the intelligent layman as well as for the reader." Arthur Hobson Quinn wrote that "for many years all other work was but a by product to his [Schelling's] study of the Elizabethan dramatists." Two years later Schelling published another work, English Literature During the Lifetime of Shakespeare. His last book, Shakespeare Biography and Other Papers, Chiefly Elizabethan, drew a New York Herald Tribune Books review which offers an apt description of the Schelling style: "There is a benign serenity about everything that Professor Schelling writes which is very pleasant in these days of loud-voiced hustle and bustle. He speaks with the soft accent of another age. But beneath the smooth surface of his essays there is the firm substratum of scholarship; and if he speaks softly he speaks none the less with authority."

Schelling retired from the University in 1934 and became curator of the Horace Howard Furness Memorial Library of Shakespeareana in Mount Vernon, New York, a collection devoted to sixteenth- and seventeenth-century works.

PRINCIPAL WORKS: Nonfiction—Two Essays on Robert Browning, 1890; Modern Novelists, 1891; Poetic and Verse Criticism of the Reign of Elizabeth, 1891; The Life and Writings of George Gascoigne, with Three Poems Heretofore Not Reprinted, 1893; Ben Jonson and the Classical School, 1898; The English Chronicle Play: A Study in the Popular Historical Literature Environing Shakespeare, 1902; Humanities Gone and to Come, 1902; Some Features of the Supernatural as Represented in Plays of the Reigns of Elizabeth and James, 1903; The Queen's Progress and Other Elizabethan Sketches, 1904; Elizabethan Drama, 1558–1642: A History of the Drama in England from the Accession of Queen Elizabeth to the Closing of the Theaters, to Which Is Prefixed a Résumé of the Earlier Drama from Its Beginnings, 1908; English Literature During the Lifetime of Shakespeare, 1910, rev. ed. 1927; The English Lyric, 1913; English Drama, 1914; The Tragedies of Shakespeare, 1915; Appraisements and Asperities as to Some Contemporary Writers, 1922; Foreign Influences in Elizabethan Plays, 1923; Summer Ghosts and Winter Topics, 1924; Elizabethan Playwrights: A Short History of the English Drama from Mediaeval Times to the Closing of the Theatres in 1642, 1925; Shakespeare and "Demi-Science": Papers on Elizabethan Topics, 1927; Pedagogically Speaking: Essays and Addresses on Topics More or Less Educational, 1929; The Significance of Shakespeare, 1929; Shakespeare, 1930; Shakespeare Biography and Other Papers, Chiefly Elizabethan, 1937. Verse—Thor, and Some Other War Rhymes, 1918. As editor—A Book of Elizabethan Lyrics, 1895; A Book of Seventeenth Century Lyrics, 1899; The Merchant of Venice, 1903; Shakespeare's Macbeth, 1911; Beaumont and Fletcher, 1912; Typical Elizabethan Plays by Contemporaries and Immediate Successors of Shakespeare, 1926, rev. ed. 1931; The Complete Plays of Ben Jonson, 1934; Elizabethan and Seventeenth-Century Lyrics, 1938.

ABOUT: Dictionary of American Biography, Suppl. 3, 1973; Schelling Anniversary Papers, 1923. Periodicals—Dial July 1, 1908; Nation December 8, 1910; New York Herald Tribune Books May 9, 1937; New York Times December 16, 1945.

## SCHENDEL, ARTHUR FRANCISKUS EMIL VAN (March 5, 1874–September 11, 1946), Dutch novelist, short story writer, playwright, and poet, was born in Batavia (now Djakarta), Dutch East Indies (now Indonesia). He received his education in Amsterdam, where he grew up. He spent two years training and teaching in England before returning to Holland, where, in his twenty-second year, he published his first short novel, Drogon. This, set in the middle ages and with a romantic young nobleman as its protagonist, was determinedly Pre-Raphaelite in its tone. Van Schendel had been exposed to the English poetry of Dante Gabriel Rossetti and William Morris as well as to Dutch influences, and the atmosphere of Drogon is very much that of Morris's poem "The Haystack in the Floods." But there were also elements of Van Schendel's great senior, Louis Couperus, in the peculiarly Dutch way in which the theme of Fate is handled. One of the great strengths of Dutch literature—a small literature, but a great one, and still undervalued in Europe—is the powerful means by which its major writers, from the twelfth-century mystic Hadewijch through Shakespeare's near-contemporary, the poet Jacob Cats, to Louis Couperus, van Schendel, Slauerhoff, and Achterberg, demonstrate that human beings have an in-

eluctable Fate which, paradoxically, they can only change by accepting. (It amounts to a creative variation on the Calvinism in which so many of them were raised.) Thus, one of the chief features of this extraordinary and admirable literature is its tough mystical quality. This is found in abundance in van Schendel, who became, eventually, one of the best loved of all Dutch authors, not only in Holland but also in Flanders.

Although van Schendel later changed his manner, dropping many of the overly lush features evident in Drogon (and its immediate successor De schoone jacht, 1897, The beautiful chase), the "germ of his later work," as Martin Seymour-Smith claims, "is contained in his first story: a dreamy, eccentric young man is 'fated' to seduce his brother's wife" (while the brother is at the crusades). Nor did van Schendel's increasing reversion to the Zola-esque naturalism against which he had initially reacted in his fiction diminish to any significant degree his Dutch-style preoccupation with Fate. In that, if in that alone, he resembles Couperus, the reading of whom must have influenced him. If the fiction of the first of the three phases through which he is usually reckoned to have passed (the "Dutch" period, until 1921, and the two sections of the "Italian" period, 1921–1938 and from 1938 until his death) is not his best, it demonstrated one fact: that he was one of the Dutch masters of prose style, being proficient in making words do what he wanted them to do.

Een zwerver verliefd (1904, A wanderer in love—there is a French translation), perhaps influenced by its author's marriage (1902) to Bertha Jacoba Zimmermann (in 1908 he was married again, to Annie de Boers), tells of a monk's struggles against sexual desire; this theme is continued in Een zwer verdwaald (1907, A lost wanderer). After 1913 and De berg van droomen (The mountain of dreams), there is, claims Seymour L. Flaxman in the 1980 Columbia Dictionary, a change: "the romantic longing and sexual passion . . . becomes attached to a more definite, concrete object; it becomes something more practical—a search of happiness in love." Flaxman is right to detect the change, which is, essentially, a shift from the expression of youthful yearning to that of a more mature, and a more complex, outlook.

The medieval nature of van Schendel's fiction was now beginning to pall, and he himself started to tire of it. In 1921 he went to live in Italy, and his outlook and style began to change, although he always preserved his oneiric quality and his concern with the various ways in which men "live out their fates." The change is first evident in Angiolino en le dente (1923, translated as Angiolino in the Spring), which is set in Italy. Here van Schendel begins to adopt a more realistic approach. But the peak of this decisive second phase in his writing, which was prolific, only came with Het fregatschip Johanna Maria (1930, translated five years later as The Johanna Maria). By means of this novel he gradually gained an international reputation, especially as the English translation was introduced by Sir Arthur Quiller-Couch, whose own robust historical entertainments then had a popular following.

Van Schendel, away from Holland and able to view it with more detachment, now changed his milieu, to his own country as it had been when he was very young. *The Johanna Maria* is the biography of a sailing vessel, launched from the yard at Oostenburg in Amsterdam in February 1865. Jacob Brouwer, its sailmaker, throws his lot in with her forever, and is determined above all to own her. A novel much more subtle in its treatment of the nature of Fate than appears at an initial reading, *The Johanna Maria* tells of how Brouwer realizes his dream—and is then destroyed just as the wooden ship is destroyed. Writing in the *Spectator*, the Irish novelist and short story writer—also an eminently reliable critic—Séan O'Faoláin called it "a remarkable novel . . . slow and steady as a sturdy ship . . . as lovely as a Dutch landscape . . . sad . . . with its suggestion of vanished times and vanished men . . . one of the loveliest books of the sea that the heart could desire." Yet, even in this profound and beautiful book, van Schendel had not yet expressed his full genius. He excelled himself in both *De waterman* (1933, *The Waterman*) and the grim, remorseless *Een Hollandsche drama* (1935, *The House in Harlem*), this latter being for many the most gripping of all his books. In *The Waterman* even the self-sacrificing Maarten Rossaert cannot avoid his destiny as he weaves and bobs his way through the maze of canals and water-alleys which he prefers to the people he is nonetheless sturdily determined to serve. In *The House in Harlem*, which in some respects is reminiscent of Federigo Tozzi's great short novel *Tre Croci*, the keeper of a shop tries, by giving up everything, to save both his self-esteem and his weak nephew, and fails dismally in both. The dark atmosphere here, and sense of doom, are conveyed with a memorable and poetic mastery. What a Dutch critic has faulted as van Schendel's "lack of biological directness" functions here with great power, as a sense of brooding inevitability: as, precisely, a numbing lack of ability to act against Fate.

The on-the-surface more cheerful and humorous *De wereld een dansfeest* (1938, *The earth, a joy of dancing*) marks the beginning of van Schendel's third, and most mystical, period, in which his rich and musical style becomes even more important. This last group of novels has not yet been subjected to sufficient critical investigation, and none of them, with the exception of *De grauwe vogels* (1937, *Grey Birds*), has yet been translated. At this point van Schendel felt that he needed the medium of verse, in which, as his patriotic long poem *De Nederlanden* (1945) demonstrates, he was not adept. The final prose has even been dismissed as too distant from reality, but the true verdict remains to be given, and may be a very different one, since what van Schendel aimed for was always subtle and refined to a high degree. His autobiographical writings, together with some (more interesting) poetry, were edited in *Herdenkingen* (1950, *Memorials*). His collected works appeared in eight volumes between 1976 and 1978. His stories, of which he published several collections, were as highly regarded as his novels. He was awarded the prestigious P. C.

Hooft Prize posthumously (1947). Among his many interesting works are fictional lives of Jesus Christ, Shakespeare, and Verlaine.

PRINCIPAL WORKS IN ENGLISH TRANSLATION: The Johanna Maria (tr. B. Downs) 1935; Grey Birds (tr. M. S. Stephens) 1939; The House in Haarlem (tr. M. S. Stephens) 1939; Angiolino in the Spring (tr. W. C. Niuewenhuis) in Greshoff, J. (ed) Harvest of the Lowland, 1945; The Waterman (tr. N. C. Clegg) 1963; John Company (tr. E. Beekman) 1983.

ABOUT: Columbia Dictionary of Modern European Literature, 1947, 1980; Greshoff, J. Over van Greshendel, 1942 (in Dutch); Meijer, R. P. The Literature of the Low Countries, 1971; Seymour-Smith, M. Macmillan Guide to Modern World Literature, 1986. *Periodicals*—Dichter und Leser, 1972; New York Times September 15, 1946; Pacific Affairs Summer 1984; Proceedings of the IVth Congress of the International Comparative Literature Association, I 1966.

**SCHEVILL, FERDINAND** (November 12, 1868–December 10, 1954), American historian, was born in Cincinnati, Ohio, the son of Ferdinand Schevill and Johanna (Hartmann) Schevill. After receiving a B.A. at Yale in 1889, he pursued graduate study in Germany, taking his Ph.D. at the University of Freiburg in 1892. That same year he became a member of the original faculty of the newly founded University of Chicago, where he taught history until his retirement in 1935. (He initially retired in 1924, but was persuaded to return in 1930 to help reorganize the university's humanities curriculum.) An authority on European history, both medieval and modern, Schevill was a popular teacher whose texts were widely used in university classrooms during the first half of the twentieth century. Renaissance Italy and the development of modern Germany were his two areas of special interest.

Among his early works to receive favorable critical attention were (the still consulted) *Siena, the Story of a Mediaeval Commune* and *Karl Bitter*, a biography of his brother-in-law, a sculptor. *A History of Europe from the Reformation to the Present Day*, his most successful textbook, was in print for many years and underwent numerous revisions. While the early versions of this work focused primarily on political history, later editions "broadened to include economic, social, and humanistic material appropriate to what was coming to be known as the 'new' history," as written in the *Journal of Modern History* tribute to him on his death. In the introduction to *History of Florence*, his most ambitious book, Schevill praised the expanding scope of historical inquiry, but rejected the notion that history could ever aspire to the status of an "abstract science": "But let us make no mistake: scholarship is a portal, not a goal. . . . the modern historian, though he must be refreshed at the well of scholarship and emancipated from the narrow older methods, is still required, like the classical historians, the original inventors of this form of literature, to prove himself as an artist."

PRINCIPAL WORKS: *History*—(with O. Thatcher) Europe in the Middle Age, 1897; History of Modern Europe, 1898; (with O. Thatcher) A General History of Europe (350–1900), 1900; A Political History of Modern Europe from the Reformation to the Present Day, 1907, rev. ed. 1921; Siena, the Story of a Mediaeval Commune, 1909; The Making of Modern Germany: Six Public Lectures Delivered in Chicago in 1915, 1916; The History of the Balkan Peninsula, from the Earliest Times to the Present Day, 1922, rev. ed. 1933 (in U.K.: The Balkan Peninsula and the Near East); A History of Europe from the Reformation to the Present Day, 1925, rev. ed. 1951; The First Century of Italian Humanism, 1928; (with J. Thompson and others) The Civilization of the Renaissance, 1929; History of Florence from the Founding of the City through the Renaissance, 1936 (reissued as Medieval and Renaissance Florence, 1961); (with others) The Foundations of a More Stable World (ed. W. Laves) 1941; The Medici, 1949; Six Historians, 1956. *Biography*—Karl Bitter, 1917; The Great Elector, 1947.

ABOUT: *Periodicals*—Journal of Modern History March 1955; New York Times December 11, 1954.

**\*SCHICKELE, RENÉ** (August 4, 1883–January 31, 1940), German novelist, critic, poet, and playwright, was born at Oberehnheim in Alsace, of a German father, Anton Schickele, and a French mother, Marie (*née* Férard). He was for the whole of his useful and intense life against war, and against both French and German nationalism. Although his name was never on everyone's lips, he was so respected that his complete works were edited in Germany (1960–1961) by no less than Hermann Kesten—and books are still being written about him. His vision of a united Europe, and the nature of his misery at Europe's divisions, are still influential. He is also well known as the single non-English critic to have written an indispensable book on D. H. Lawrence.

Schickele's poetry, though interesting as well as competent in technique, is the least well remembered of his prolific work. Little or none of it (except in obscure and now hard-to-find magazines) has been translated into English (more of it is to be found, scattered in periodicals, in French translation). This verse gained him the reputation of being an expressionist; but, although he remained committed to this movement, his own work outside poetry and the drama was hardly influenced by it. Yet, as John Willett points out in his authoritative *Expressionism*, with his close friend the great poet Ernst Stadler (slaughtered in the First World War) "he helped root the beginnings of literary Expressionism in a European soil."

Schickele had tried his hand at an expressionist novel, *Das Fremde* (*The foreigner*) in 1909, but his first good novel, an unusual one, was *Benkal, der Fruentröster* (1914, *Benkal the consoler of women*), about a sculptor who, feeling incapable of love, destroys his masterpieces and drinks a toast to life.

In 1913 Franz Blei founded the periodical *Die weissen Blätter* (*The white papers*); in the same year the now dominant publisher Kurt Woolf took this on, with Schickele as its editor. Publication ceased on the outbreak of war in August 1914, but Walter Hasenclever, prompted by his friends Martin Buber and others, wrote to Schickele asking him to carry it on, from Switzerland, "as a power to *overcome* the national darkness." That, as Willett writes, "is what it now became." Schickele emigrat-
\*SHIK eh leh

ed to Zürich in 1915, and made the periodical a rallying point for anti-militarism and anti-imperialism. He published it from Switzerland between 1916 and 1918, when he took it back to Germany, where it appeared until 1920. It published many notable writers, including Kafka, Duhamel, and Klabund.

After the war Schickele returned to Berlin and greeted the new republic. But, like so many others, he soon became disillusioned with its muddleheadedness, and withdrew. His chief work, the trilogy *Das Erbe am Rhein* (*The Rhineland heritage*, 1925–1931), he wrote in the Black Forest. The first two parts have been translated: *Maria Capponi* (1925, translated under its original title) and *Blick auf die Vorgesen* (1927; translated as *Heart of Alsace*). The final—and many assert best—part, *Der Wolf in der Hürde* (*The wolf in the fold*, 1931), has yet to appear in an English version. Of the English translation of the second part, V. S. Pritchett, writing in the *Spectator*, said that, while it was "not convincing," and even "tedious and annoying," it did, when read with a proper patience, disclose a "fervent and delicate mind." Other reviewers felt, along with Pritchett, that the facts from which the book had been taken had not had "sufficient refashioning in the imagination." The third part was better received in Germany, but some such complaints were seldom absent from discussion of Schickele's fiction. Yet there has not been a better epic of Alsace than this story of an ex-German soldier and his first love (the Italian marchesa Maria Capponi), and then of his fight for Alsatian autonomy. Thomas Mann praised it in glowing terms: "It can stand forever," he said, "as a standard work, written with the fine and firm hand of an artist, a classic of Alsatian country and soul. It put him where he has since remained, in the front rank of German literature."

In 1933 Schickele was forced to flee yet again from Germany, this time because the Nazi takeover had made him a marked man. In France he wrote the bitterest of all his novels, *Die Flaschenpost* (*Man in a bottle*, 1937), about an individualist who cannot find peace until he reaches a mental hospital. He had settled in Provence, and died there, near Vence, of the asthma which had plagued him for decades. There are books devoted to him in German and French, and a bibliography.

PRINCIPAL WORKS IN ENGLISH TRANSLATION: Maria Capponi (tr. H. Waller) 1928; The Heart of Alsace (tr. H. Waller) 1931.

ABOUT: Columbia Dictionary of Modern European Literature, 1947 and 1980; Dictionary of Literary Biography, Vol. 66, 1988; Seymour-Smith, M. Macmillian Guide to Modern World Literature, 1986; Willett, J. Expressionism, 1970. *Periodicals*—Modern Language Review April 1991; New Statesman May 5, 1929; New York Herald Tribune Books March 4, 1928; February 10, 1929; Spectator August 31, 1929.

**SCHIFF, SYDNEY.** See **HUDSON, STEPHEN**

**SCHLESINGER, ARTHUR MEIER** (February 27, 1888–October 30, 1965), American historian, wrote: "I was born in the rural Ohio town of Xenia, the youngest child of parents who had migrated from Germany some twenty years before. My boyhood was a happy one in a household that loved books and among school friends who loved the outdoors. After going through the Xenia public schools I went on to the state university fifty miles away. There, in due course, I became editor of the college newspaper, and for a time thought I was headed for a career in journalism. But the example of some of my professors persuaded me that it was my destiny to report the events of the past, not of the present. Graduating in 1910 and securing a fellowship at Columbia University, I proceeded there for advanced training in history under Osgood, Robinson, and Beard. Eventually I received my Ph.D. in 1918, but meantime, in 1912, I had begun my teaching career at the Ohio State University. Since 1919 I have taught at the State University of Iowa and at Harvard, where I have been since 1924. In 1914 I married Elizabeth Bancroft; we have two sons. The only real interruption of this uneventful career occurred in 1933–1934, when I took my family on a year's trip round the world.

"I have always enjoyed historical research and writing and have produced a modest number of books. I early became dissatisfied with the view  that history is merely past politics, and in my writing and teaching I have done all I could to disseminate the idea that history should be as inclusive as life itself. Since example is more potent than precept, I joined Dixon Ryan Fox in 1927 in editing a collaborative twelve-volume work, *A History of American Life*, which, I believe, has exerted a strong missionary influence in the intended direction. My *Colonial Merchants and the American Revolution* won the Justin Winsor Prize of the American Historical Association in 1918.

"I have been fortunate in my teachers, my friends, and my students, and to them I attribute any success I may have attained. Politically I have always been an independent, but in practice this has usually caused me to vote the Democratic national ticket."

---

According to his son, Arthur M. Schlesinger, Jr., Arthur Meier Schlesinger attempted throughout his career "to raise social history 'from the status of sheer antiquarianism and impressionistic description to the status of a genuine historical discipline.'" Further, he wanted "to bring certain forces, hitherto neglected, into the mainstream of American history. Thus he placed special emphasis . . . on the city as a major factor in American development. He also wanted to give women, half the population, their rightful place in the growth of American civilization. . . . And he sought full recognition of the role of ethnic minorities in American life—not as a problem but as a process."

The methodology that Schlesinger used to explore American social history was, by later standards, somewhat primitive—Richard Hofstadter

accused him and his followers, with good reason, of "trying to write a kind of sociological history without having any sociological ideas"—but Schlesinger's rejection of what he called the "fife and drum" approach to history did, despite this failing, anticipate the general direction of American historiography for some years to come.

The most influential of his social historical studies was *The Rise of the City, 1878–1898*, his own contribution to the comprehensive *History of American Life* series that he edited with Dixon Ryan Fox. The book was criticized for its overoptimistic point of view and for its apparent absence of theoretical framework, but Terrence J. McDonald, in *Reviews in American History*, claimed that few of its contemporary reviewers perceived "the breadth of concern, sparkling wit, and prodigious research that make this book so much worth another reading. There is no doubt that Schlesinger captured the dynamism and multiplicity that were—and always will be—the hallmarks of the American city. He also both claimed too much for urbanization and specified that process too little."

Schlesinger explored a variety of social and political topics in his nine major monographs: the role of the merchant class and of the popular press during the American Revolution (*The Colonial Merchants and the American Revolution, 1763–1776*; *Prelude to Independence: The Newspaper War on Britain, 1764–1776*), the reform impulse in American life (*The American as Reformer*), even changing fashions in etiquette (*Learning How to Behave: A Historical Study of American Etiquette Books*).

But Schlesinger played a far more important role as a teacher than as a writer. He supervised sixty-nine doctoral dissertations at Harvard, many of them by students who would become leading historians of their generation. He also exercised considerable influence as a historian-activist, by fighting the anti-communist hysteria of Senator Joseph McCarthy, by attempting to bring attention to the plight of American Indians, and by serving on the Massachusetts United Labor Committee and the Commission on Freedom of the Press. "As a scholar," wrote his son, "he helped bring the common life of the people, their habits, beliefs, anxieties, and dreams, into the center of the historical enterprise. As a citizen, he incarnated a tempered and steadfast liberalism, skeptical of pretensions and dogmas, soberly, indestructibly optimistic about the future of the country he loved."

Schlesinger was president of the American Historical Association in 1942 and the recipient of honorary degrees from the University of Chicago, Kenyon College, and Brandeis University. He retired as Francis Lee Higginson Professor at Harvard in 1954, but continued to write history until his death. His papers are in the Oral History Archive at Columbia University.

PRINCIPAL WORKS: *History*—Colonial Appeals to the Privy Council, 1913; (with H. C. Hockett) A Syllabus of United States History, 1915; The Colonial Merchants and the American Revolution, 1763–1776, 1918; New Viewpoints in

American History, 1922; (with H. C. Hockett) A New Syllabus of American History, 1925; Political and Social History of the United States, 1829–1925, 1925; Political and Social Growth of the United States, 1852–1933, 1933; The Rise of the City, 1878–1898, 1933; The New Deal in Action, 1933–1938, 1939; The New Deal in Action, 1933–1939, 1940; Political and Social Growth of the American People, 1865–1940, 1941; Learning How to Behave: A Historical Study of American Etiquette Books, 1946; Paths to the Present, 1949; The American as Reformer, 1950; The Rise of Modern America, 1865–1951, 1951; Prelude to Independence: The Newspaper War on Britain, 1764–1776, 1958; The Birth of the Nation: A Portrait of the American People on the Eve of Independence, 1968; Nothing Stands Still: Essays, 1969. *Autobiography*—In Retrospect: The History of a Historian, 1963. *As editor*—(with D. R. Fox) A History of American Life, 13 vols., 1927–1948; (with D. R. Fox) The Cavalcade of America, 1937; The Atlantic Migration, 1607–1860: A History of the Continuing Settlement of the United States (by M. L. Hansen) 1940; The Immigrant in American History (by M. L. Hansen) 1940.

ABOUT: The autobiographical material quoted above was written for Twentieth Century Authors, 1942. Dictionary of American Biography, Suppl. 7, 1981; Hofstadter, R. and Lipset, S. M. (eds.) Sociology and History: Methods, 1968; Schlesinger, A. M., Jr. *introduction to* Nothing Stands Still (by A. M. Schlesinger) 1969. *Periodicals*—New York Times October 31, 1965; Reviews in American History September 1992.

## SCHLESINGER, ARTHUR MEIER JR. (October 15, 1917– ), American historian wrote: "I was born in Columbus, Ohio. My father was profes-

sor of American history successively at Ohio State, Iowa and Harvard; and I grew up in an academic environment, living from 1924 on in Cambridge, Massachusetts. I went to the Cambridge public schools, then to Phillips Exeter Academy and Harvard, graduating *Summa cum laude* in 1938. I spent the next year—the year between Munich and the war—as a Henry Fellow at Cambridge University; then, for three years I was a member of the Society of Fellows at Harvard University. In the summer of 1942 I went to Washington to work, first for the Office of War Information and then for the Office of Strategic Services. I went overseas for O.S.S. in the spring of 1944, remaining in Europe for a year and a half and serving in London, Paris and Germany. I was deputy chief of the O.S.S. Reports Board in Paris, and, in the meantime, attained the high rank of corporal in the United States Army.

"My senior honors essay at Harvard provided the basis for my first book, *Orestes A. Brownson: A Pilgrim's Progress*, a selection of the Catholic Book Club in 1939. As a member of the Society of Fellows, I completed a first draft of a book on Andrew Jackson and his times; this was accepted for publication shortly before I left for Europe in 1944 and was finally published as *The Age of Jackson* in 1945. It won the Pulitzer prize for history.

"After the war, I spent some time in Washington as a freelance writer, contributing to such magazines as *Life, Fortune, Saturday Evening Post* and *Colliers*. In the fall of 1947 I returned to Cambridge

as associate professor of history at Harvard. In the meantime, I had come to feel the urgent necessity for the development of an organization of American liberals which would recognize the true nature of the Communist threat at home and abroad and would at the same time continue the fight for freedom and social progress. In 1946 I wrote a full-length exposure and indictment of the American Communist Party for *Life* magazine. I participated in the founding convention of Americans for Democratic Action in 1947 and have served since as a national vice-chairman. In an effort to explain the importance of an anti-Communist liberal position, I wrote *The Vital Center* in 1949. . . . "

---

Arthur M. Schlesinger, Jr., began his ongoing study of the American presidency with *The Age of Jackson*, a work that fundamentally challenged the consensus on the significance of Andrew Jackson's presidency and, not incidentally, provided a rationale for the liberal, presidential activism that Schlesinger so much admired in Franklin D. Roosevelt. In fact, Schlesinger was criticized for portraying Jackson as an incipient New Dealer, and his dismissal of the role of frontier individualism in Jacksonian democracy was hotly contested. However, few critics disputed Schlesinger's ability to write narrative history in the grand manner. Writing in the *New York Times Book Review* (1945), Allan Nevins called *The Age of Jackson* "Crisply written, full of pungent comment and quotation, and abounding in vivid thumbnail sketches of important figures," adding, "It perhaps overemphasizes the East as against the West. . . . It is excessively hostile to Whig leaders and Whig ideas. . . . It sometimes rides its thesis a bit too hard. But it is a remarkable piece of analytical history, full of vitality, rich in insights and new facts, and casting a broad shaft of illumination over one of the most interesting periods of our national life."

Schlesinger's most ambitious work on the presidency was *The Age of Roosevelt*, published in three volumes—*The Crisis of the Old Order*, *The Coming of the New Deal*, and *The Politics of Upheaval*—between 1957 and 1960; as of 1995 it had not been completed. More than any other president, Roosevelt personified for Schlesinger the wisdom of the "vital center," the nonideological liberal position that Schlesinger described as the democratic ideal in his 1949 book of that title. In later years, Schlesinger's moderate, pragmatic liberalism came under increasing attack from both the right and the left; but the critical response to *The Age of Roosevelt* was, for the most part, unusually sympathetic. Reviewing *The Politics of Upheaval* in the *New York Times Book Review* (1960), D.W. Brogan wrote, "It is one of the many merits of this brilliant book . . . that Arthur M. Schlesinger Jr. does not indulge in foresight, does not project into the future the often harassed, sometimes nearly despondent, uncertain leader who found that the honeymoon of the New Deal was over. . . . The first and, in many ways, the most masterly achievement of Mr. Schlesinger is his combination of the historian's viewpoint above the battle and the reporters eye of the contemporary witness."

*A Thousand Days: John F. Kennedy in the White House* was Schlesinger's third study of presidential politics and his second book to win the Pulitzer Prize. Having served as a speech writer and adviser to President Kennedy, Schlesinger was not only a witness to but also a participant in the events he described, and some reviewers felt that his impartiality as a historian was fatally compromised. The same could be said of *Robert Kennedy and His Times*, a nine-hundred-page biography of a man who might have been president and whom Schlesinger also served as adviser and admired as a friend. As against their fairly obvious partiality, both books provided a vivid, behind-the scenes view of the use and occasional abuse of political power. While he remained unconvinced by Schlesinger's depiction of Robert Kennedy's gradual conversion from a somewhat brutal realpolitik to a tempered idealism, Gary Wills wrote of the later book in the *New York Times Book Review* (1978), "One comes to respect Mr. Schlesinger's confidence that Robert Kennedy does not need special pleading. All Kennedy critics are quoted frequently and fairly. The challenging, somewhat prickly charm of Mr. Kennedy is by this means more forcefully conveyed than in more protective works."

Richard Nixon, whom Schlesinger discussed at length in *The Imperial Presidency*, was emphatically not Franklin D. Roosevelt or John F. Kennedy. This analysis of the abuse of presidential power was written during the height of the Watergate crisis and received very favorable reviews ("I cannot imagine anyone not learning much from the book," Wills wrote, again in the *New York Times Book Review* [1973]), but more than anything it testified to Schlesinger's disillusion with the course of American politics since the assassination of Robert Kennedy. With his notion of a flourishing liberalism continually frustrated, Schlesinger turned to a theme first advanced by his father, the eminent Harvard historian who shared his name. In *The Cycles of American History* Schlesinger maintained that shifts from liberalism to conservatism and back again were generational and predictable and that by the late 1980s a leftward swing of the pendulum was past due. *The Cycles of American History* was one of the most highly regarded of his later books, but unfortunately for Schlesinger, the theory does not seem to have been born out by recent events. "Ultimately, the dwindling public support for conventional liberal values, policies, and candidates may be a political trend that Schlesinger's cyclical theory of American history may be incapable of addressing," wrote Stephen P. Depoe.

Whatever his personal disappointment in the apparent collapse of the liberal tradition, Schlesinger has continued analyzing American history and politics in a steady stream of books, articles, and reviews, and, since 1966, has trained legions of graduate students in the lessons of history as Albert Schweitzer Professor in the Humanities at the City University of New York. With his familiar bow tie

and horn rim glasses, he is a conspicuous presence at many of Manhattan's more glittering galas. Though Schlesinger's critics on the right and left would hardly agree, Alan Brinkley described him in the *New Republic* as one of his profession's "most important voices" and enumerated the reasons why: "It is not simply because he possesses a literary grace that few American scholars can match, and not simply because the range of his interests and knowledge far exceeds that of most historians in this age of narrow specialization. It is because he possesses a rare ability to make history seem important, because he is willing to argue that the search for an understanding of the past is not simply an aesthetic exercise but a path to the understanding of our own time."

PRINCIPAL WORKS: *History, criticism, and biography*—Orestes A. Brownson: A Pilgrims Progress, 1939 (reissued as A Pilgrims Progress: Orestes A. Brownson, 1966); The Age of Jackson, 1945; The Vital Center: The Politics of Freedom, 1949 (in U.K.: The Politics of Freedom, 1950); (with R. H. Rovere) The General and the President and the Future of American Foreign Policy, 1951 (revised as The MacArthur Controversy and American Foreign Policy, 1965); The Crisis of the Old Order, 1919–1933, 1957; The Coming of the New Deal, 1959; The Politics of Upheaval, 1960; Kennedy or Nixon: Does It Make Any Difference?, 1960; The Politics of Hope, 1963; A Thousand Days: John F. Kennedy in the White House, 1965; The Bitter Heritage: Vietnam and American Democracy, 1941–1966, 1967; The Crisis of Confidence: Ideas, Power, and Violence in America, 1969; The Imperial Presidency, 1973; Robert Kennedy and His Times, 1978; The Cycles of American History, 1986; The Disuniting of America, 1991. *As editor*— (with Q. Howe) Guide to Politics, 1954, 1954; (with M. White) Paths of American Thought, 1963; History of American Presidential Elections, 1789–1968, 4 vols., 1971; The Dynamics of World Power: A Documentary History of United States Foreign Policy, 1945–1973, 5 vols., 1973; History of U.S. Political Parties, 4 vols., 1973; (with R. Bruns) Congress Investigates: A Documented History, 1792–1974, 5 vols., 1975; The Almanac of American History, 1983; The Disuniting of America, 1991; (with others) Running for President: The Candidates and Their Images, 2 vols., 1992.

ABOUT: The autobiographical material quoted above was written for Twentieth Century Authors First Supplement, 1955. Contemporary Authors New Revision Series 28 1989; Contemporary Literary Criticism vol. 84, 1995; Current Biography 1979; Depoe, S. P. Arthur M. Schlesinger, Jr., and the Ideological History of American Liberalism, 1994; Dictionary of Literary Biography vol. 17, 1983. *Periodicals*—New Republic December 1, 1986; New York Times Book Review September 16, 1945; September 11, 1960; November 18, 1973; November 12, 1978.

## SCHLOSS, ARTHUR DAVID. See WALEY, ARTHUR

## SCHMITT, BERNADOTTE E(VERLY) (May 19, 1886–March 22, 1969), American diplomatic historian, wrote: "Bernadotte Schmitt was born in Strasburg, Virginia, the son of Cooper Davis Schmitt and Rose Vernon (Everly) Schmitt. Two ancestors on each side of the family fought in the American Revolution, two more in the War of 1812; both grandfathers served in the Confederate Army in the Civil War. Cooper D. Schmitt was professor of mathematics in the University of Tennessee from 1889 to his death in 1910 and dean of the college from 1907 to 1910.

"Bernadotte Schmitt was graduated from the University of Tennessee in 1904 and the next year went to Oxford as the second Rhodes Scholar from Tennessee. He received the B.A. from Oxford in 1908, gaining a First Class in Modern History. The next two years were spent at the University of Wisconsin, from which he received the Ph.D. degree in 1910.

"From 1910 to 1924 he taught at Western Reserve University; in the latter year he transferred to the University of Chicago as professor of modern history. . . . From 1932 to 1936 he was chairman of the department of history; since 1929 he has edited the *Journal of Modern History*, published by the University of Chicago Press.

" . . . In 1931–32, he was professor of diplomatic history at the Institut Universitaire des Hautes Études Internationales in Geneva. In 1927 he was awarded a Guggenheim Fellowship. In 1937 he became a Fellow of the American Academy of Arts and Sciences. . . .

"Apart from teaching, his chief interest has been writing. The first book, *England and Germany: 1740–1914*, appeared in 1916 and set the course for the future. . . . After

World War I the opening of foreign office archives made possible the rewriting of the diplomatic history of Europe prior to 1914, and Schmitt devoted some years to this task. In 1930 he published two volumes entitled *The Coming of the War, 1914*, which was awarded the George Louis Beer Prize of the American Historical Association for 1930 and the Pulitzer Prize for history in 1931. . . . Other contributions include a chapter in *The Cambridge History of Poland* (1941) and a chapter on Munich in *Czecho-Slovakia: Twenty Years of Independence* (1940).

"In 1943, Schmitt joined the U.S. government for war service, first as special consultant to the Secretary of War, then as a member of the Office for Strategic Services, and next as a special adviser in the division of Historical Policy Research in the Department of State. In 1949 he was appointed United States editor-in-chief of *Documents on German Foreign Policy*, 1918–1945, a tripartite enterprise of the British, French, and United States governments for publishing the captured archives of the German Foreign Office, and served until his retirement in July 1952.

"In 1946 he became professor emeritus at the University of Chicago and resigned as editor of the *Journal of Modern History*.

"In 1945 he edited *Poland* in the United Nations Series, contributing one chapter. He also contributed one chapter to *Yugoslavia* in the same series (1949). While serving as historical adviser in the Department of State, he edited two volumes of official documents, one relating to the Treaty of Versailles, the other to the United Nations Conference in San Francisco."

Bernadotte E. Schmitt originally hoped to follow family tradition by embarking on a science-related career. His grandfather had been a pharmacist, and his father was a mathematics professor at the University of Tennessee, from which young Bernadotte graduated at the age of 18. He decided, however, that he was "not deft enough" in science and in 1905 accepted a Rhodes Scholarship to Oxford. Visiting Germany the following year, he was so "disagreeably impressed by evidences of militarism" that he thereafter devoted his intellectual life to study of the complex political map of Europe during both world wars and the uneasy peace in their interim. This first impression was to color his attitude throughout his career as a diplomatic historian, during which he urged that Germany be held responsible and punished severely for instigating both world wars. In 1969, his *New York Times* obituarist recalled, under the subtitle "Prophet of Disaster," how Schmitt's "student distrust grew into a professor's dogma."

The "prophet of disaster" designation referred to a lecture in Cleveland in January 1914, at which the young scholar joined Lord Northcliffe, publisher of the London *Times*, to warn of Germany's impending offensive. Years later, in the *New Republic*, H. E. Barnes praised the prescience of this "youthful pedagogue" who understood that "Germany was about to spring like a tiger in the jungle upon a pacific and unsuspecting world." Barnes, however, dismissed Schmitt's lack of objectivity in a 1930 review of *The Coming of the War: 1914*, claiming that Schmitt's book was "not the result of an unbiased effort to find where the mountain of newly revealed facts lead us. It is the last frantic effort of the American leader of the Salvagers so to select, present and interpret these facts as to confirm his prophetic intuitions of pre-war vintage. . . . Not a single major contention in this last and final effort of the 'Salvagers' to rehabilitate the Entente legend possesses the slightest validity."

Schmitt, because of his slight build, was not accepted into the U.S. Army until nearly the end of the war, when he was commissioned as a second lieutenant; he never saw overseas duty.

Schmitt's first book, *England and Germany: 1740–1914*, was a detailed overview of relations between the two powers from the accession of George II, the second Hanoverian, to the outbreak of hostilities in the First World War. The book was not well received. The *Nation* reviewer took Schmitt to task for "bias in favor of England that led him more than once to a false perspective of German affairs, to inconsistencies of statement, and even to direct errors."

Soon after accepting the professorship of modern history at the University of Chicago in 1925, Schmitt embarked on a tour of eastern Europe, where he met several leaders, including President Masaryk of Czechoslovakia and King Alexander of Yugoslavia. His observations on these personalities, and on Lord Grey, Raymond Poincaré, and the exiled Kaiser Wilhelm, were included in his book *Interviewing the Authors of the War*, privately printed in 1930. In 1935, he met with Asian political and military leaders in an extensive tour through Japan, China, Manchuria, and Siberia.

Several of Schmitt's books were used as textbooks in modern diplomatic history, notably *The Coming of the War: 1914*. Schmitt's *New York Times* obituary quoted Winston Churchill's evaluation of this work as "a masterly book, which made the Anti-Versaillists sick at heart."

Critical reaction to this book was much more favorable than it was to his first effort. Though a few scholars felt compelled to point out the anti-German bias that informed the work, most were laudatory, such as W. L. Langer, who wrote in *Books* that "Professor Schmitt's book is very complete and there is very little about the crisis of 1914 that cannot be found in these two volumes."

Schmitt became editor of the *Journal of Modern History* in 1929, and in 1936 became an editor of a series of the *Cambridge Modern History*, which assembled scholarly monographs on eastern European diplomatic topics. During and after World War II, Schmitt was one of the academics enlisted by the U.S. government to advise on historical matters dealing with Germany and plans for the United Nations. In 1945, he served as a special assistant to the secretary general at the San Francisco conference at which the UN was established. In 1945, he edited an extensive 500-page volume on *Poland* for the United Nations series. The book, which traced the history of that nation from 1918 to 1939, was praised by Hans Kohn in the *New York Times* as being "a highly scholarly and timely volume on the political, economic, and cultural life of Poland between the two wars."

Schmitt left unfinished *The World in the Crucible, 1914–1919*. It was published in 1984, with Harold C. Vedeler as co-author.

PRINCIPAL WORKS: England and Germany: 1740–1916, 1916; The Coming of the War, 1914, 1930; Triple Alliance and Triple Entente, 1934; The Annexation of Bosnia, 1908–1909, 1937; The Origins of the First World War, 1958; The Fashion and Future of History, 1960; (with H. C. Vedeler) The World in the Crucible, 1914–1919, 1984. *As editor*—Some Historians of Modern Europe, 1942; Poland, 1945; Documents on German Foreign Policy, 1918–45, Volumes III–IV, 1950–53; Journal of Modern History, 1929–46.

ABOUT: The autobiographical material quoted above was written for Twentieth Century Authors, 1942 and Twentieth Century Authors, 1955. Cochran, M. H. Germany Not Guilty in 1914; Current Biography 1942; 1969. *Periodicals*—New York Times, March 24, 1969; Washington Post, March 24, 1969.

**SCHMITT, GLADYS** (May 31, 1909–October 3, 1972), American novelist, was born in Pittsburgh, Pennsylvania, the first of three children of Henry H. And Leonore (Link) Schmitt. Of her early years she wrote: "I took my intellectual nourishment, and perhaps the foreshadowings of my style, from Lutheran doctrine, Lutheran hymns, the Bible, and such glimpses of literature as one gets in the readers of a public grade school and from kind teachers who are amazed to find in a somewhat colorless pupil a natural concern about grammar." She began writing verse (some of it prize-winning) in grammar school and started her first novel at fifteen. At the University of Pittsburgh, she majored in Eng-

lish and continued to write, now concentrating primarily on fiction. She received her B.A., *magna cum laude*, in 1932 and proceeded to graduate work in English. Meanwhile she had a story accepted by Whit Burnett of *Story* magazine ("House Divided," later developed into the novel *The Gates of Aulis*); a second story was bought by the *Atlantic Monthly*.

In 1933 Schmitt left college, in the middle of the depression, to take a job as typist in the Pittsburgh offices of *Scholastic* magazine. In her spare time she worked away at her short stories and at novels. When *Scholastic* moved its editorial offices to New York in 1939, she went along, by now associate editor of the magazine. Dividing her time between her editorial duties and her writing—she was a meticulous writer, given to slow and careful  revision and polishing—she managed to complete her first novel, *The Gates of Aulis*. She submitted the manuscript to the Dial Press, which was offering a $1,000 prize for a novel "of high literary quality that concerns itself realistically with the problems of adjustment which face the young men and women of America today." *The Gates of Aulis* was the unanimous choice of the judges, and it was published in 1942 with considerable critical fanfare. The story of an American family in Pittsburgh, and of their deep personal devotion to each other (the title refers to the sacrifice of Iphigenia in classical legend), the novel was an immediate success.

Schmitt followed *The Gates of Aulis* with another popular success, *David the King*, a massive retelling of the Biblical story. She returned to a contemporary setting in her third novel, *Alexandra*, but this story of an American actress's self-destruction failed to match her first two books. She returned to the long historical novel in *Confessors of the Name*, set in third-century Rome. *New York Herald Tribune Books* found that she had "produced a large crowded and colorful panorama of the far past and again, however costumed and staged, her central interest is the drama of personality."

Schmitt wrote two more contemporary novels, *The Persistent Image* and *A Small Fire*, but they, too, were overshadowed by her historical works. In *I Could Be Mute: The Life and work of Gladys Schmitt*, Jan Cohn describes the reaction of reviewers to Schmitt's fiction: "It has been . . . customary to judge the two sets of novels differently: to find the relatively shorter stories of contemporary life sensitive, subtle, but finally failed; to find the longer and more lavish novels set in the past, grand, profound, distinguished."

This assessment of Schmitt's historical fiction does not mean that her work has held up with the passing of time. In the introduction to *I Could Be Mute* . . . Anita Brostoff points out that Schmitt, a "woman of extraordinary intellectual power and remarkable artistic talent, who published nine novels and many short stories and poems, never gained a substantial and sustained reputation as a writer, either with the literary world or with the reading public." One reason put forward is the excessiveness, of "words, passion, psychology, or philosophy," in many of her big novels. Another is to be found in the limits of the genre itself. Cohn points out that the "historical novel remains essentially an entertainment and has, in recent decades, taken on only pseudo-seriousness in those works that attempt to recreate Biblical or early Christian life," and goes on to state that "Schmitt brought genuine seriousness to the form, genuine psychology and philosophical weight, elegant and studied language." For Cohn "these attributes of elite fiction rest uneasily on the structures of the popular form, so that despite the considered achievement of *David the King*, *Confessor of the Name*, and *Rembrandt*, the novels fail to last, to serve as adequate vehicles for the richness and darkness of Schmitt's imagination."

Soon after the publication of *The Gates of Aulis* Schmitt returned to Pittsburgh to take a professorship of English and fine arts at the Carnegie Institute of Technology (later Carnegie-Mellon University); in 1970 she was named the first Thomas S. Baker Professor of Literature.

PRINCIPAL WORKS: *Novels*—The Gates of Aulis, 1942; David, the King, 1946; Alexandra, 1947; Confessors of the Name, 1952; The Persistent Image, 1955; A Small Fire, 1957; Rembrandt, 1961; Electra, 1965; The Godforgotten, 1972. *Verse*—Sonnets for an Analyst, 1973. *Juvenile*—The Heroic Deeds of Beowulf, 1962; Boris, the Lopsided Bear, 1966.

ABOUT: The autobiographical material quoted above was written for Twentieth Century Authors First Supplement, 1955. Brostoff, A. (ed.) I Could Be Mute: The Life and Work of Gladys Schmitt, 1973; Contemporary Authors Vols. 37–40, 1979; Current Biography 1943; Warfel, H. American Novelists of Today, 1951. *Periodicals*—New York Herald Tribune Books October 26, 1952; New York Times October 3, 1972.

## SCHMITZ, ETTORE. See SVEVO, ITALO

**SCHNEIDER, ISIDOR** (August 25, 1896– August 3, 1977), American poet, novelist, and critic, wrote: "I remember nothing of my birthplace, Horodenko, a small town in Western Ukraine, then in Austro-Hungary, later in Poland, and now [in 1942] in the Soviet Ukraine. I arrived in this country at the age of five.

"My father was a man's tailor, but mass production had practically eliminated his trade; he turned to ladies' tailoring, which soon also went under as

a trade. He tried a number of other ways of earning a living, chiefly running little cleaning and pressing stores, all without success. I was one of five children. The fact that my elder brother went to work made it possible for me to go to college (College of the City of New York), though I earned my way by teaching English to foreigners, helping out in my father's store, and working during summer vacations.

"The one thing I wanted most during my growing years was to escape the sort of life I was living. In my writing I went headlong into fantasy. It was not until many years had passed that I was able to look at the years of my childhood without aversion, and to recall that alongside the privations and the overhanging dread there had been courage to see, and endurance and patience and the constant generosity toward each other of workers, expressed in their wonderful neighborliness common in all trades and in all nationalities. For a long time I looked away from my past, which I would have had to re-enter if I wanted to write realistically.

"My first book was *Dr. Transit*, a fantastic novel in which the scientist hero was simultaneously idealized as the man with power to change the world, satirized because he failed to exercise his power, and Satanized as the arch-realist. In my first book of poems, *The Temptation of Anthony*, the title poem was part of a projected and still unfinished fiction, *The Temple*, which is part poetry and part prose and set out to be a sort of biography of God, that is, the successive goals of man's creative longings.

"All my experience of life, in later happier times as well as in my childhood, made me feel that social changes to eliminate want and insecurity were necessary before a defensible culture could develop in our mechanized world. After 1929 this was the almost unanimous sense of American writers, the exceptions being the few who for some strange reasons found beauty in a landscape of human ruins, or found order in it, since order meant hierarchy with themselves in the upper ranks. The painful but instructive depression years turned me into a 'left' writer and a realist. I was now able to examine my own past without rigging up any mechanism of fantasy.

"In addition to novels and poems I have written short stories, some articles, and many book reviews. I have been awarded a Guggenheim Fellowship and renewal. I have traveled twice to Europe, first in 1928, staying mostly in France and again in 1937 and 1938, staying mostly in the U.S.S.R. I have made my living in publishing houses and on magazines and newspapers, writing publicity and advertising copy. I am married and have a daughter, named for Emily Dickinson.

"Direct experience with socially conscious writing as writer, critic and editor has altered my former thinking about it. I have observed that conscious application of one's writing to social ends results in stiff, self-conscious, and more often than not, feeble work. While long-range advancement is served, in various ways, by good writing of every sort, immediate social objectives can be served by a writer only at risk of restricting and ephemeralising his work. I now feel that a writer can discharge his social responsibility, like other men of whatever profession, best as a citizen."

As his autobiographical statement indicates, Isidor Schneider repudiated much of the "socially conscious writing" with which he was associated. Nevertheless, his ideological verse, novels, and essays from the 1920s to the 1940s were widely read and heatedly debated by fellow leftist writers and intellectuals in their time. The small extent to which he is remembered is owed to his contribution to the literary and political debates of those decades.

Schneider's contention that "conscious application of one's writing to social ends results in stiff, self conscious, and more often than not, feeble work," was exactly the criticism lodged most frequently against his own writing. For example, Allan Gutmann (writing in the collection *Proletarian Writers of the Thirties*) cited a poem from *Comrade, Mister* as an instance of the "partisan fallacy, the assumption that political orthodoxy suffices for artistic success" which Schneider only too often exemplified:

> Ten years ago:
> Boss America was fat,
> belched across the world and was applauded. . . .

Of the same volume, William Rose Benét wrote in the *Saturday Review of Literature*, "Mr. Schneider's attempts at revolutionary poetry are simply not very distinguished. I know he is a sincere man, and apparently it uplifts him to follow Comrade Lenin. His is really the search for a faith to believe in. But one would have to be converted to his particular faith to be more than merely interested in these poems as the biography of one man."

However, a few reviewers, less discerning, found a powerful authenticity in Schneider's fiction, however imperfectly expressed. Reviewing *From the Kingdom of Necessity*, a semi-autobiographical account of a young immigrant's coming of age in New York City, the leftist R. M. Coates wrote in the *New Republic*, "It is a hard, bitter, ugly life he writes about, a life so cruelly beset by oppressive forces, so degraded by filth and poverty and wretchedness as to force those who must submit to it almost below human levels. But Mr. Schneider's personal philosophy and his own understanding are broad enough to encompass them, and the result is a book of undeniable emotional power and great social value."

Aside from his nine books, which included an English-language version of Maxim Gorky's autobiography, and the editorship of three literary anthologies, Schneider was a frequent contributor to the *New Masses*, the *New Republic*, and the *Nation*.

PRINCIPAL WORKS: *Novels*—Doctor Transit, 1925; From the Kingdom of Necessity, 1935; The Judas Time, 1947. *Poetry*—The Temptation of Anthony: A Novel in Verse, and Other Poems, 1928; Comrade, Mister: Poems, 1934. *As editor*—(with others) Proletarian Literature in the United States, 1936; The World of Love, 1964; The Enlightenment: The Culture of the Eighteenth Century, 1965. *As translator*—The Autobiography of Maxim Gorky, 1952.

ABOUT: The autobiographical material quoted above was written for Twentieth Century Authors, 1942 and Twentieth Century Authors First Supplement, 1955. Madden, D. (ed.) Proletarian Writers of the Thirties, 1968. *Periodicals*—New Republic January 1, 1936; New York Herald Tribune Weekly Book Review March 30, 1947; New York Times August 6, 1977; Saturday Review of Literature November 24, 1934.

**SCHNITZLER, ARTHUR** (May 15, 1862–October 21, 1931), Austrian dramatist, novelist, short story writer, and critic, was born in Vienna, the son of a distinguished Jewish throat specialist. Classified, along with Hofmannsthal, Wasserman, and Kraus as a member of the so-called Jung Wein (Young Vienna) group of romantic-decadent writers, Schnitzler has often been, on account of the psychologically penetrating nature of his plays and novels, thought of as the creative equivalent par excellence of his friend Sigmund Freud. There is much merit in this, although it fails to account for his importance in the history of European modernism. Schnitzler followed in the footsteps of his father and qualified in medicine (1885) at the University of Vienna. For some years he held a hospital post, but showed little interest in pursuing medicine as a vocation; he was, however, and remained, deeply interested in psychology and what became psychoanalysis. He lived the life of a man about town, keeping a variety of mistresses— some of them simultaneously; but it was his experiences with Marie Reinhard between 1894 and 1899 upon which he drew most extensively for the writings of his first phase. He had started writing as a boy, with poetry that was published in a prominent newspaper. At the age of thirty-one he gave up his hospital post and retired from medicine, except that he kept a few private patients, personal friends who interested him.

Schnitzler started to write plays in the early 1890s, the chief of these being a series of seven (later expanded to eight) dialogues called *Anatol* (1893, translated under that title), signing himself "Loris," one of his early pseudonyms. The piece gives a cynical but delicate self-portrait of an irresponsible young man-about-town, a philanderer, Anatol, who is prey to melancholy and fear of death and dissolution, and who seeks solace in erotic encounters.

These plays were presented, in Czech, in Prague in 1893, but were not seen in their entirety in their original language until 1912, when they were given in Vienna. They quickly attracted the attention of the literary world, but with the three-act *Libelei* (1895, translated as *Light o' Love*), presented at the Burgtheater in December of 1895, he became famous all over Austria and Germany. Set in contemporary Vienna, the play tells of the (implied) suicide of a girl after her lover has been killed in a duel over another woman. Not all Schnitzler's plays were successful (those in verse in particular were unfortunate, since Schnitzler was not gifted with the ability to write in poetic language), and they suffer from severe limitations: static situations, similarity of plot, and—or so most dramatic critics assert—"lack of unity." His fiction is ultimately more important, although there are few of his plays that would not play well today (they have been successfully adapted for British television). A possible exception to the usual strictures is the last of his important plays, quite likely to be his best: the uncharacteristic (and semi-autobiographical) *Professor Bernhardi* (1912, translated under that title). It is about a distinguished physician who refuses to allow a priest to see a girl who is dying as a result of an abortion; the ensuing scandal gives rise to anti-Semitic feelings, and the doctor is charged with "religious obstruction." He wins through, and even makes a friend of the priest—but at that point he refuses to submit to the system. What can be said without reservation about Schnitzler's plays is that as a whole they give the most realistic and thorough portrait of the Vienna of the pre-World-War I years; indeed, of the closing years of the Hapsburg Empire. And then there is the immortal *Der Reigen* (1900, translated as *The Dance of Love* but most famous as the French movie *La Ronde*). Schnitzler's achievement may not be all that profound here, but of what it is—a light-hearted counterpointing of the love-and-death theme—the play is an almost perfect example.

In fiction Schnitzler's range was wider. In the so far untranslated novel *Sterben* (1895, *Dying*), he gave a memorable description of a dying man; here already he was becoming one of the earliest practitioners of the "stream of consciousness" technique later made famous by Joyce. For the deadly accuracy of the celebrated *Leutnant Gustl* (translated as *None But the Brave*), Schnitzler was actually removed from the reserve list of the Austrian Medical Corps because this tale of a poor young officer who, unable to satisfy his "honor," kills himself, was held to insult the whole Army (which it very properly did—Schnitzler might be the great portraitist of the work of the Empire, but he was no approver of it).

The dramatist Frank Wedekind called this Schnitzler's best work, and Heinrich Mann wrote of it : "Gustl is under pressure either to commit suicide or to resign from the service owing to some bad luck. He is saved by a new and most unlikely occurrence. But one cannot always count on such luck since at a certain point Fortune tires of ever cheerful, thoroughly spoiled Lieutenant Gustl. His creator already understood this. Only occasionally are we saved. Because we grow old, danger remains and increases. Old age is in itself a misfortune: it is precisely this which Schnitzler perceived."

The short novel *Der Weg ins Freie* (1908, translated as *The Road to the Open*) has probably attracted more attention. It is the story of a Jew, Georg von Wergenthin, a composer who has real gifts but lacks drive, and of his affair with a non-Jewish girl. Anti-Semitism, as well as the ending of a romantic relationship, is the theme of the book, in which the author's portrayal of his society is once again impeccably objective.

The best work of Schnitzler's final phase, after the Empire had collapsed, is in the long short story. Probably the best of his extended tales, and a translated one (it also appeared in an outstandingly good

television adaptation) is *Fräulein Else* (1926, translated along with some other stories in the unfortunately entitled *Viennese Novelettes*). This is the memorably poignant monologue of a girl forced into genteel prostitution by her family's debts; there was little better short fiction written in Europe in its time than this beautifully observed, tragic and above all humane tale. Schnitzler's earlier work was excellent and always well executed, but often lush; his later, often neglected outside German-speaking countries, was altogether sharper. Hofmannsthal's early and shrewd judgment is possibly now endorsed by the majority of critics, that "several of his small works of art—tales and plays—emerge, through the magic irony, as his greatest." It must be added that Schnitzler brought to bear a profound clinical knowledge of psychological states, which added yet another dimension to his achievement. A huge interest is now taken in him by critics and commentators on pre-World War I Austria.

PRINCIPAL WORKS IN ENGLISH TRANSLATION: *Drama*—Anatol ("paraphrased" Granville-Barker) 1911; The Lonely Way (tr. E. Bjrkman), 1915; Comedies of Words (tr. P. Loving) 1917; Reigen, The Affairs of Anatol and Other Plays (tr. G. I. Colbron) 1933. *Fiction*—The Road to the Open (tr. H. Samuel) 1923; Dr Graesler (tr. E. C. Slade) 1924; Fräulein Else (tr. R. L. Simon) 1925; None But the Brave (tr. R. L. Simon) 1926; Daybreak (tr. W. A. Drake) 1927; Rhapsody: A Dream Novel (tr. O. P. Schinnerer) 1927; Theresa (tr. O. P. Schinnerer) 1928; Little Novels (tr. E. Sutton) 1929; Flight into Darkness (tr. W. A. Drake) 1931; Viennese Novelettes (tr. various) 1931. *Autobiography*—My Youth in Vienna (tr. F. Morton) 1971. *Letters*—Letters to Hermann Bahr (tr. D. Daviau) 1978.

ABOUT: Badman, G. Arthur Schnitzler, 1973; Columbia Dictionary of Modern European Literature, 1947, 1980; Keiser, B. Deadly Dishonor: The Duel and Honor Code in the Works of Arthur Schnitzler, 1990; Luprecht, M. "What People Call Pessimism": Sigmund Freud, Arthur Schnitzler, and Nineteenth-Century Controversy at the University of Vienna Medical School, 1991; Schnitzler, A. My Youth in Vienna, 1971; Seymour-Smith, M. Guide to Modern World Literature, 1986; Swales, M. Arthur Schnitzler: A Critical Biography, 1971; Urbach, R. Arthur Schnitzler (tr. D. Daviau), 1973; Yates, W. E. Schnitzler, Hofmannsthal, and the Austrian Theater, 1992. *Bibliography*—Berlin, J. An Annotated Arthur Schnitzler Bibliography, 1978. *Periodical*—Time January 14, 1957.

**SCHOLES, PERCY ALFRED** (July 24, 1877–July 31, 1958), English musicologist, was born at Headingley, Leeds. His early interest in and knowledge of music was acquired in haphazard study at home, where he was often confined and kept away from school because of bronchitis. After spending his early twenties teaching, first in Kent, and then in South Africa, Scholes eventually resumed his own formal education on his  return to England, gaining his music degree at St. Edmund Hall, Oxford, in 1908. In the same year he married and began editing *The Music Student*, the journal of the Home Music Study Union, an organization which Scholes had founded. Moving to London in 1912, he began to earn his living as a journalist, working as a critic for the *Evening Standard* from 1913 to 1920, and for the *Observer* from 1920 to 1925. (Fifty-four of Scholes's *Observer* pieces are collected in the book *Crotchets.*)

During the war years (1939–1945) he devised and organized a series of lectures about music for the troops, and his first substantial publication, *The Listener's Guide to Music*, was a direct outcome of this work. The popularity of this short explanatory volume encouraged him to embark on a fuller exposition of musical history, and the more ambitious, but still lucidly written, *The Listener's History of Music* appeared in three volumes between 1923 and 1929. Scholes's aim was "to 'tidy-up' the mind of the music-lover," and, in his introduction to the first volume, cross-examined himself thus: "Have I left out enough to make easy reading for the reader I have in mind? Have I left out the right things? Have I, after all my omissions, presented in what remains a simple, connected generalization of the subject? I hope I have!"

Quick to realize the educational potential of radio, Scholes worked for the BBC as a critic and adviser and, after leaving the *Observer*, edited the *Radio Times* from 1926 to 1928, in which year he decided to make his home in Switzerland. For the rest of his life he worked assiduously, helped by his wife and a team of typists, gathering material for numerous short-term and long-term projects. The work for which he is best-known, *The Oxford Companion to Music*, appeared in 1933, and all modern editions of this book have been based on his original publication. Edward Sackville-West, writing in the *New Statesman* on the book's first appearance, said, "The style of the book is urbane, impartial, eminently readable and sometimes (e.g. on music under the Nazi regime) slyly amusing." Scholes himself (three years before his death) revised the title for its ninth edition, and the first subsequent revision (the tenth edition, edited by John Owen Ward) appeared in 1970, altering, as it happens, the line taken by Scholes on the Nazi influence on German music.

Excellent as this and other of his handbooks are, Scholes's character as a writer and his passion for his subject are best in evidence in two works of more discursive character, *The Puritans and Music* and *The Great Dr. Burney*. The first of these disentangles, with legalistic brio, the true picture of the Puritans' attitude towards music from a torrent of misrepresentations. His method in this book is to quote at length from allusions to the Puritans in a variety of texts, and one by one to undermine their authority. Quoting a long paragraph from Macaulay's *History of England*, he remarks, "There is no history here; we have merely an eloquent catalogue of imaginary attributes." And the book as a whole he describes as "false from beginning to end." Demonstrating historical inconsistencies in Hawthorne's story "The Maypole of Merry Mount" as compared with his novel *The Scarlet Letter*, Scholes is left exclaiming, "It is no use trying to gather history from a Hawthorne!"

Liberal quotation is also the hallmark of the two-volume biography of Charles Burney who, in his *History of Music* (1766), was, according to Scholes, one of the prime movers of the calumnious notion that the Puritans were music-haters. Richly illustrated, and wide-ranging in its biographical focus, the *Times Literary Supplement* described it as "an immense, leisurely two-volume scrapbook of the most entertaining kind." As such, it has served as a rich source of anecdotes and curious facts for those studying a variety of aspects of late eighteenth-century life, but especially for those interested in Johnson and his circle.

Much of the work for the Burney biography, which won the James Tait Black memorial prize, was undertaken during World War II, which Scholes spent back in Britain, living at Aberystwyth and at Oxford. In 1942 he published *God Save the King!*, a brief history of the national anthem, much expanded in *God Save the Queen!* A permanent return to Switzerland was prevented by a devaluation of the pound in 1950, although Scholes did continue to spend every winter there for the sake of his health. He died at Vevey in the summer of 1958, his last works having been, in addition to the revised *Companion*, *The Concise Oxford Dictionary of Music*, *The Oxford Junior Companion to Music*, and a life of Sir John Hawkins. Amongst a variety of offices held, Scholes had been an inspector of music in schools, president of the Society of Recorder Players, vice-president of the Vegetarian Society, and was a keen patron of the League for the Prohibition of Cruel Sports.

PRINCIPAL WORKS: The Listener's Guide to Music, 1919; The Book of the Great Musicians, 1920; The Beginner's Guide to Harmony, 1922; The Listener's History of Music, 1923–1929; Crotchets, 1924; The First Book of the Gramophone Record, 1924; Everybody's Guide to Broadcast Music, 1925; The Columbia History of Music through Ear and Eye, 1930–1938; The Puritans and Music in England and New England, 1934; The Radio Times Music Handbook, 1935; The Oxford Companion to Music, 1938; God Save the King!, 1942; The Mirror of Music 1844–1944, 1947; The Great Dr. Burney, 1948; The Concise Oxford Dictionary of Music, 1952; The Life and Activities of Sir John Hawkins, 1953; God Save the Queen!, 1954; The Oxford Junior Companion to Music, 1955.

ABOUT: Dictionary of National Biography, 1951–1960; Oxbury, H. F. Great Britons, 1985; Who's Who 1958. *Periodicals*— New York Times August 3, 1958; Time July 9, 1956; August 11, 1958; Times (London) August 2, 1958; Times Literary Supplement September 4, 1948.

## SCHOPHER, JEAN. See ANET, CLAUDE

## SCHORER, MARK (May 17, 1908–August 11, 1977), American novelist, critic, and biographer, wrote: "I was born in Sauk City, Wisconsin, the second of four children of Anna and William Schorer, and educated in the local public schools, the University of Wisconsin (1925–1929), and Wisconsin again (1931–1936). . . . I began writing short stories for publication in 1933 (*Scribner's, Harper's, Story*, etc.) and published a novel, *A House Too Old*, in the year before I took my Ph.D. This novel, like the early stories, used Sauk City as background, but since 1936, I have seldom drawn on that material.

"From the beginning, people have been eager to help me to write. As an undergraduate, I held one of the Zona Gale Fellowships that Miss Gale for a certain period of her life personally administered in the interest of young writers at the university. In my last year as a graduate student, I held the Mary L. Adams Fellowship, which made possible the first sketch of a book I later published on William Blake. Teachers were helpful, too, in their confidence, notably Helen C. White and Clinch Calkins at Wisconsin, and later, at Harvard, Robert Hillyer, who did me the greatest service a teacher of writing can do: he begged me not to go on with a novel that was clearly headed for catastrophe. I didn't.

"In the summer of 1936, I was married to Ruth Page of Madison, Wisconsin, and we have two children, Page and Suzanne. The first was born while I was an instructor in Dartmouth College (1936–1937), the second, in my second year as an instructor in Harvard College, where I taught until 1945 as one of the Briggs-Copeland instructors—writers who also wanted to teach; or vice versa. At Harvard, I wrote a novel called *The Hermit Place.* That year I was awarded the Guggenheim Fellowship for the Blake book, which was started in Laguna Beach, California, continued on a sheep ranch outside Roswell, New Mexico, on a renewal of my Guggenheim, completed in Cambridge, and published in 1946. In the meantime, I had been publishing stories in many magazines, but chiefly the *New Yorker*, and literary articles in the quarterlies, and book reviews in the newspapers. Thirty-two of these stories were published in book form under the title *The State of Mind* in 1947.

"By that time I was a professor of English in the University of California, Berkeley, chiefly teaching contemporary literature, critical theory, and story writing. In 1948 I had another Guggenheim renewal to work on a novel in progress and to begin a book on the theory of the novel. I began to be interested in the question of what a novel is as a Fellow of the Kenyon School of English at Kenyon College (now the School of Letters at Bloomington, Indiana), and my work then took the form of a series of lectures delivered before the Princeton Seminar in Literary Criticism in the spring of 1950. The work progresses, but to find out what a novel is, you have to read a great many novels. . . . "

---

Mark Schorer, who became chairman of the English Department at Berkeley (1960–1965), was ultimately more distinguished as critic and biographer than as novelist; but, as he wrote in a tailpiece to the material quoted above, he wrote criticism "rapidly, fiction very slowly." However, "I can obviously not afford to put any faith in the old notion that the two do not get along amiably together, or even in the witty remark about 'Those who can,' etc."

Schorer's creative gifts, were not negligible, and his novels and stories may fairly be classed as the more than merely worthy creative writings of a critic of "omnivorous intelligence." His novel *The Wars of Love* (currently in print in two editions) was often described as "remarkable." It still has its admirers.

Schorer's first critical work was on William Blake: *William Blake: The Politics of Vision.* This, on a notoriously difficult subject, has seldom been quoted from in subsequent books about Blake. However, it is sufficiently useful to have been kept in print over a long period of years.

But Schorer's massive biography, *Sinclair Lewis,* was quite another matter. Reviewers and critics alike complained at the time of its great length, but few pointed out that it was nevertheless readable—even if some of the biographical material was, as Marius Bewley thought, excessive and trivial. It has survived and prospered, largely no doubt because, as Bewley wrote, Schorer had the courage to concede at the beginning that it was "futile to approach any Lewis novel as a work of art." The eminent critic Irving Howe, in his review of the book for the *New York Times,* found it "extremely impressive [in its] piling on of the evidence." Schorer went a long way towards convincingly explaining why, and just how, Lewis failed—and why, and to what extent, he succeeded in certain novels.

Schorer's essay "Technique as Discovery" (1947), a plea that prose fiction deserves and should receive the attention given by the New Criticism to poetic texts, was often anthologized and discussed, although it was not sufficiently thought through to become a critical classic.

The undoubted compulsion to (sometimes) excessive detail which characterizes his *Sinclair Lewis* also adversely affected Schorer's fiction. But, as Albert Guerard wrote in *Contemporary Novelists,* it nonetheless "deserve[d] a wider public" than it found in Schorer's lifetime.

Schorer himself dismissed his first novel, *A House Too Old,* published before he was thirty, as "a lugubrious historical chronicle." After that, he wrote, the interest of his fiction lay in "the psychological complexities, chiefly destructive, of human relationships, and in the difficulties of self-recognition."

*The Hermit Place* reflected this, taking (it was thought by its more discerning critics) as its main model a latter-day practitioner of Jamesian techniques, Elizabeth Bowen. The *Saturday Review* wrote that it was "absorbing" but "uneven": "full of dissonances, of moments of preciosity and of sometimes almost amateurish dialogue." It was nevertheless "curiously fascinating"; "a novel of the inner life," it possessed "the kind of psychological subtlety that gave the literature of the twenties a quality that one misses in most novels of today."

In *The Wars of Love,* his most accomplished novel, Schorer came close to Ford Madox Ford's masterpiece *The Good Soldier.* As it stands, it is a little over-dependent upon Ford's techniques and approach; but these are applied with high intelligence and some wit. The narrator of this grim tale of the brutalities exchanged between four complacent people is himself initially oblivious to his own meanness of spirit, although he finally discovers himself in an ironic ending.

Schorer's short stories, which often appeared in the *New Yorker*, were regarded as graceful and well-crafted, and a few have appeared in anthologies.

At the time of his untimely death from a blood infection following an operation, Schorer was working on a biography of the choreographer Georges Balanchine.

PRINCIPAL WORKS: *Novels*—A House Too Old, 1935; The Hermit Place, 1941; The Wars of Love, 1954. *Short stories*—The State of Mind: Thirty-Two Stories, 1947; The State of Mind: Twenty-Two Stories, 1956; Colonel Markeson and Less Pleasant People, 1966; Pieces of Life, 1977. *Criticism and other*—(with others) Direct Communication, Written and Spoken, 1943; William Blake: The Politics of Vision, 1946; Sinclair Lewis: An American Life, 1963; D. H. Lawrence, 1968; The World We Imagine: Selected Essays, 1968. *As editor*—(with J. Miles and G. McKenzie) Criticism: The Foundations of Modern Literary Judgment, 1948; The Story: A Critical Anthology, 1950; Society and Self in the Novel, 1956; (with P. Durham and E. L. Jones) Harbrace College Reader, 1959; Modern British Fiction, 1961; Sinclair Lewis: A Collection of Critical Essays, 1962; (with others) American Literature, 1965; Galaxy: Literary Modes and Genres, 1967; (with R. M. Ludwig) The Literature of America: Twentieth Century, 1970.

ABOUT: The autobiographical material quoted above was written for Twentieth Century Authors First Supplement, 1955. Bewley, M. Masks and Mirrors: Essays in Criticism, 1970; Dictionary of Literary Biography Vol. 103, 1991; Vinson, J. (ed.) Contemporary Novelists, 1976. *Periodicals*—New Republic September 16, 1946; April 14, 1947; New York Times August 18, 1977; New York Times Book Review March 21, 1954; October 1, 1961; Saturday Review of Literature June 7, 1941; Times Literary Supplement February 26, 1954.

## SCHREINER, OLIVE EMILIE ALBERTINA

(March 24, 1855–December 12, 1920), South African novelist and polemical essayist, was born at

Wittebergen in Basutoland, daughter of Gottlob Shreiner, a Lutheran missionary of German descent, who had been sent to South Africa by the London Missionary Society, and Rebecca Lyndall, from London. She came from a large family, and one of her brothers, William Philip Schreiner, was to become prime minister of the Cape Colony. Schreiner's childhood was miserable, spend on remote mission stations. She received virtually no formal education, but was an avid reader and attempted to educate herself. The death of one of her sisters, when Schreiner was nine, challenged her conventional Christian beliefs and led to a very early espousal of free-thinking, an attitude that alienated her from her parents. Her greatest wish was to become a doctor, and her interest in medical matters shows through in her fiction, but this ambition was impossible to fulfill. At the age of twelve she left home to act as a housekeeper for her older brothers and sisters, and at fifteen she became a nursery governess for various Boer farming families. At sixteen she was seduced, then abandoned. During this period she was deeply influenced by the works of such writers as Darwin, Mill, and Herbert Spencer, whose *First Principles* she was given by a visitor. "I always think that when Christianity burst open upon the dark Roman world it was what that book was to me."

While a teenager, Schreiner began writing the semi-autobiographical novel for which she is famous, *The Story of an African Farm*. Her description of the Karoo, a barren plateau, outstanding for its vivid depiction and spiritual intensity, is especially notable. The book tells the story of two cousins, Lyndall and Em, and their childhood friend Waldo, whose individual searches for truth and understanding create a tale of spiritual and emotional enquiry. A rare work for its period for its overt political tone, its advocacy of female emancipation, and its outright rejection of Christianity, the novel is a brilliant but flawed piece of fiction, by turns comic, insightful, agonizingly introspective, and didactic and highbrow.

Unable to find a South African publisher, Schreiner left for England in 1881, where, after a year, it was accepted by Chapman & Hall. The publisher's reader, George Meredith, suggested revisions, and it was duly published under the pseudonym of Ralph Iron, provoking high praise and, when it was discovered that the author was a young woman, further attention and controversy. Schreiner remained in London until 1889, but despite her fame was very unhappy. She made a few friends, among them a close, probably unconsummated relationship with the sexologist Havelock Ellis, with whom she fell deeply in love. "I think of you like a tall angel," she wrote. Havelock remembered her "short sturdy vigorous body in loose shapeless clothes . . . the beautiful head with the large dark eyes, at once so expressive and so observant." They remained friendly for the rest of her life. During these years she suffered from constant ill-health, some of it psychosomatic, and wrote anguished letters in which she reveals intense mental torture. "Oh, it isn't my chest, it isn't my legs, it's me, myself. What shall I do? Where shall I go?"

Returning to South Africa, despite once having claimed that to do so would, metaphorically, be the death of her, she grew happier. There, she married a lawyer politician, Samuel Cron Cronwright, who added her name to his, gave up his work and became her literary assistant and, after her death, her literary executor. Theirs was an uneasy relationship, but evidence suggests that Schreiner found greater contentment with Cronwright-Schreiner than with anyone else.

Now a celebrity following her first novel, Schreiner wrote polemical journalism, strongly anti-imperialist in tone, and supportive of the Boers. She was a radical liberal, devoted to the rights of mankind and a fierce champion, of the underdog. Nothing she wrote, however, equalled the psychological power or lyrical descriptions of *The Story of an African Farm*, and her unfinished novel, *From Man to Man*, lay untouched after her return from England. An ambitious, complex novel, published posthumously, it dealt, again, with sexual mores and hypocrisy. The critic Dan Jacobson commented that "It is impossible to read *From Man to Man* without feeling an almost overwhelming sense of talents wasted and frustrated in what appears to be a perversely deliberate way." Although Schreiner subsequently wrote several works of nonfiction, none is exceptional. *Woman and Labor*, her feminist tract on the need for equality, written in occasionally Marxist terms, was widely praised on publication, but, despite setting Schreiner apart as an early proponent of the women's movement, is not distinctive. Perhaps the most significant of her later works was *Dreams*, a series of descriptive writings and allegories, published by her husband after her death and described by the *International Book Review* as revealing "the soul and the mind of a woman who saw deeply and felt tremendously, and who carried her vision to the end unmarred."

A tormented, questing, unsatisfied visionary, Olive Schreiner died in 1920. She was buried under a rock sarcophagus above the Karoo Desert. She will be remembered as a fervent thinker and idealist, immersed in politics and causes, whose unhappy early experience of life was to mark her deeply and provide her with her most passionate central theme: that the influence of childhood is profoundly felt in later life.

PRINCIPAL WORKS: *Novels*—The Story of an African Farm, 1883; From Man to Man, 1926; Undine, 1928 (juvenile). *Miscellaneous*—Dreams, 1891; Dream Life and Real Life, 1893; Trooper Peter Halket of Mashonaland, 1897; The South African Question, 1899; Woman and Labor, 1911; Stories, Dreams and Allegories, 1923; Thoughts on South Africa, 1923; The Letters of Olive Schreiner, 1924; A Track to the Water's Edge, 1974.

ABOUT: Berkman, J. A. Olive Schreiner: Feminism on the Frontier, (1979); Berkman, J. A. The Healing Imagination of Olive Schreiner 1989; Clayton, C. (ed.) Olive Schreiner 1980; S. C. Cronwright-Schreiner, The Life of Olive Schreiner, 1924; Ellis, H O. Schreiner, My Other Self: The Letters of Olive Schreiner and Havelock Ellis, 1884–1920, 1992; First, R. and Scott, A. Olive Schreiner: A Biography, 1989; Friedmann, M. V. Olive Schreiner: A Study in Latent Meanings, 1954; Gray, S. Southern African Literature: An Introduction, 1979; Horton, S. R. Difficult Women, Artful Lives: Olive Schreiner and Isak Dinesen, In and Out of Africa, 1995; Jacobson, D. *introduction to* The Story of An African Farm, 1971; G. K. Kmetz, Woman of the Karroo, 1977; Lessing, D. Afterword to the Story of an African Farm, 1968; Schreiner, O. The Letters of Olive Schreiner, 1924; Vivan, I. The Flawed Diamond: Essays on Olive Schreiner, 1991. *Periodicals*—Boston Transcript, April 30, 1927; Contemporary Review, April 1947, International Book Review, March 1923.

**SCHRIFTGIESSER, KARL** (November 12, 1903–August 20, 1988), American historian, wrote: "Karl Schriftgiesser was born in Boston, Massachusetts. His grandfather published a daily and weekly German language newspaper and his father, who died when he was five, was a reporter on Boston newspapers. His mother was of Yankee and Russian ancestry and one of the early kindergarten teachers in that city. Brought up by his Yankee grandmother on the Maine coast and in old Boston, and educated at the famous Roxbury Latin School and for three years in a 'seminary' in Barre, Vermont, his New England background outweighed his European antecedents and led him to his interests in American

history and politics about which he has written extensively.

"At seventeen he quit school to become a copy boy on the *Boston Post*. In 1924 he became a feature writer for the magazine section of the famous old *Boston Evening Transcript*.  For the next ten years he wrote feature articles on every conceivable subject, covered many of the big news events in New England of the 1920s, and contributed articles to such magazines as the *American Mercury*, the *New Yorker*, and the *New Republic*. Through most of this period he assisted the late Edwin Francis Edgett in editing the *Transcript's* book section, interviewing scores of writers for its columns, and writing many critical articles on contemporary literature.

"Shortly after the inauguration of Franklin D. Roosevelt as President he went to Washington to write editorials and a signed column for the *Washington Post*. There he continued his writing about books, but began concentrating more on the contemporary political scene. A difference of political opinion with the publisher led to his resignation, and after a summer spent proving he had no talents as a novelist he joined the reportorial staff of the *New York Times*.

"Assigned to the writing of advance obituaries he wrote hundreds of biographical sketches of leading world citizens, a job of research and writing which led naturally to the writing of his first two books. *Families* was a study of ten outstanding American families, from the Adams family to the Roosevelts. This was followed by *The Amazing Roosevelt Family*, the first over-all history of the famous family which produced two Presidents. His main interests, however, were in the political history of the nation and, in 1944, he wrote a highly critical biography, *The Gentleman from Massachusetts*, of the late Senator Henry Cabot Lodge, the man most responsible for the defeat of the League of Nations by the U.S. Senate.

"This led to a fuller study of the twelve years of Republican rule in Washington, *This Was Normalcy*, in which Schriftgiesser evaluated the administrations of Harding, Coolidge, and Hoover. In the meantime he had become the book critic for *Newsweek*, a post he held for six years. His research on the politics of the 1920s led him to undertake a study of the pressure groups which influence legislation and the results were published, in 1951, in *The Lobbyists*. During this period and since he wrote extensively, for the *New York Times Book Review*, and elsewhere, on the New Deal and Franklin D. Roosevelt. His liberalism was not acceptable to the post-war management of *Newsweek* and he resigned, in 1950, to devote his time to historical research and writing (mainly on a projected history of the New Deal), and to magazine articles for the *Atlantic Monthly*, *Collier's*, and the *New York Times Magazine*.

"He is married to the former Ruth Mansfield of Boston, has one daughter, and lives on an old farm near Londonderry, Vermont."

---

Karl Schriftgiesser provided an impressive example of one who could combine the pursuit of historical studies with journalism without abandoning seriousness. The *Atlantic*, reviewing his first book, *Families*, summed up the general nature of his achievement when it wrote: "These short sketches . . . are done with a straightforward, sometimes dogmatic directness. No punches are pulled, and the author's opinions are seldom in doubt. The chapters are readable and informative, if necessarily compressed." The *New Yorker* went a little further, calling the book a "remarkable group biography"; its author was described as one who combined "a nice sense of historical balance with a gift for neat and fluent statement."

Schriftgiesser's lively books were generally well received, although reviewers occasionally carped at his "lack of sobriety" or "judicial tone"; however, quite as many praised his "restraint." Perhaps the most outstanding of his works were his study of the Roosevelt family, his biography of Henry Cabot Lodge, and his pungently critical account of the concept of "normalcy" during the Republican reign of 1920–1932.

*The Amazing Roosevelt Family 1613–1942* was praised for the sheer amount of erudite detail it gave, but attacked by some for its recourse to material of the "gossipy type" (*Commonweal*). However, the *New York Herald Tribune Books* reviewer found this "easy and pleasant reading."

*The Gentleman from Massachusetts: Henry Cabot Lodge* is a thorough and fair biography of Theodore Roosevelt's older friend. Because of his "quiet restraint," G. W. Johnson believed (*Weekly Book Review*) that Schriftgiesser's book was "all the more deadly."

*This Was Normalcy*, a "severe indictment" (*American History Review*), was felt by Gerald Johnson of the *New York Herald Tribune Weekly Books Review* to establish its point: "the bare facts are enough." Schriftgiesser retired in 1969, and lived out his final years in Londonderry, Vermont.

PRINCIPAL WORKS: Families, 1940; The Amazing Roosevelt Family 1613–1942, 1942; Oscar of the Waldorf, 1943; The Gentleman from Massachusetts: Henry Cabot Lodge, 1944; This Was Normalcy: An Account of Party Politics During Twelve Republican Years 1920–1932, 1948; The Lobbyists: The Art of Business of Influencing Lawmakers, 1951; The Farmer from Merner: The Biography of George J. Mercherla and a History of the State Farm Insurance Companies of Bloomington, Illinois, 1955; Business Comes of Age, 1960; Business and the American Government, 1964; Business and Public Policy: The Role of the Committee for Economic Development 1942–1967, 1967.

ABOUT: The autobiographical material quoted above was written for Twentieth Century Authors First Supplement, 1955. Who's Who in the East, 1979. *Periodicals*—American History Review October 1948; Atlantic February 1941; Books April 19, 1942; Commonweal 12 June, 1942; New Yorker October 26, 1940; New York Herald Tribune Book Review April 25, 1948; New York Times August 20, 1988; Weekly Book Review September 10, 1944.

**SCHULBERG, BUDD** (March 27, 1914– ), American novelist, screenwriter, and dramatist, wrote: "I was born in New York City, but I never think of New York as my source. . . . My home town, and for better or worse, the spring that feeds most of my work, is Hollywood, California. My father, B. P. Schulberg, was one of the motion picture pioneers, one of the very first screen writers, associated with the first American direc-tor, Porter, as well as with Zukor and Lasky in 1912. Before I was ready for the first grade we were living in Hollywood, where B. P. had gone to take charge of Paramount Studios. From that time, about 1920, until I was ready to come East to prep school and college, some seventeen years later, Hollywood was the only world I knew. The studio backlot was my playground and hundreds of nights I went off to sleep with the drone of interminable story conferences as my lullaby music.

"As a child I suffered from a rather severe speech impediment, and perhaps it was for this reason that I began writing poems and stories at an early age. Somewhere in my files I still have a short story written when I was eleven. My mother had founded the first progressive school in Hollywood and was strong for self-expression; she encouraged me. My father, despite his preoccupation with moviemaking, had been a newspaperman and still boasted of the short-story prize he had won in a citywide contest while he was at City College in New York. In other words, he had never lost his interest in the printed word, and I can remember his reading aloud (that lost entertainment!) the works of Melville, Conrad, Dickens and Stevenson. At Los Angeles high school I was better at editing the daily paper and at writing little stories than I was at running the half mile, a feat to which I gave considerable time and effort. In 1932 I came east to Deerfield Academy, by way of preparing for Dartmouth College. It was a significant move for me. I looked around in some wonderment at this green world of the Connecticut Valley. Until that time I must have believed that Western Civilization had its center at the corners of Vine Street and Hollywood Boulevard.

"At Deerfield and at Dartmouth I continued to edit the newspaper and to write. In my senior year at Dartmouth I won a prize in an inter-collegiate short-story contest. I published a few short stories in little magazines, including a novel *Story* titles 'Passport To Nowhere.' From this time on, although there were to be a number of Hollywood detours, I considered myself primarily a writer of fiction.

"From 1937 to 1939 I served a term as a sort of apprentice screen writer for movie producers David O. Selznick and Walter Wanger. But during this same period I was writing a series of Hollywood short stories which were published in *Liberty, Col-*

liers and the *Saturday Evening Post*. One of the first
of these was a story called 'What Makes Sammy
Run?' In 1939 I left Hollywood, returned to the
now familiar Connecticut River, and at Norwich,
Vermont, just across from Dartmouth College, I
completed my first novel, using the title of the short
story mentioned above. Much to my surprise, and
to that of my publisher, it proved both critical and
a commercial success . . .

"After the publication of this novel I spent a half-
vacation, half-work year in Mexico writing screenplays, followed by three years in the Navy, working
for the Office of Strategic Services in Washington,
and in Europe. I was in charge of gathering photographic evidence for the Nuremberg Trials, and
was returned to the inactive reserve in 1946. . . .

"I have written two more novels one against a
background of the prize-fight business, which has
always interested me, *The Harder They Fall*, and
more recently, *The Disenchanted*, which was
drawn from my experience as a 'junior writer assigned to collaborate with a number of older and
well established novelists and playwrights.' Although the protagonist of *The Disenchanted* was
generally identified as F. Scott Fitzgerald, and although I had worked with Mr. Fitzgerald and regarded his work with enthusiasm, I actually had
made a list of fifteen established American writers
whom I had known in Hollywood and whose trials
as film writers contributed to my study of a famous
American author offering up pieces of himself for
money. The theme of success has always fascinated
me; each of my novels has been concerned with it;
I believe Hollywood is rather an ideal microcosm
in which to study it. . . .

"My hobbies, in no particular order, are fishing,
tennis, reading, drinking with friends, jazz, prize-
fights, racing pigeons, family vacations to the Caribbean. I like all forms of writing, from articles to
motion pictures, but of them all I prefer the novel.
In a day of increasing taboos, I think it may represent the final redoubt of a truly free enterprise. I
like the feeling that it is up to me, that make or
break, it is all mine."

---

Budd Schulberg is known primarily for his first
three novels and his screenplay for the 1954 Academy Award-winning movie *On the Waterfront*. Of
the three novels, *What Makes Sammy Run?*, the
story of Sammy Glick, a guttersnipe press agent
who bamboozles his way to success as a powerful
movie producer, probably remains the most admired. Despite its occasional clichés and crudities,
it provides what is still one of the most memorable
depictions of Hollywood sleaze ever written. Reviewing it in the *Nation*, H. P. Lazarus wrote, "It
is a pleasure to watch the author write through and
past what really is his 'first novel to find his own
form and content.' Toward the end Mr. Schulberg
does say what he wants to say, the writing is good,
the plot blooms, and the form is there. Hollywood . . . is more honestly, amusingly, and in-
structively covered than in any other book I know."

In Schulberg's second novel, *The Harder They

*Fall*, the story concerns a talented but unworldly
young fighter from Argentina (Schulberg's model
was the young, Primo Carnero) who is ruthlessly
exploited by a criminal boxing promoter. "Budd
Schulberg's new book is a hard-boiled successor to
his first and tough little novel, *What Makes Sammy
Run?*," wrote John Horn in the *New York Times
Book Review*. "Just as full of heels and no-goods,
and as fast, slangy and wisecracking, *The Harder
They Fall* is in many ways a much better novel than
*Sammy*." The book remains, technically, the best
novel about boxing ever written.

Despite Schulberg's disclaimer, *The Disenchanted*, the story of a once-revered novelist now sunk
in alcohol and reduced to co-writing a musical for
a college revue, took for its model F. Scott Fitzgerald. Bruce Cook, writing in the *Washington Post*,
considered it "a fine, honest, solid novel, one that
is deeply respectful of its hero and treats the writer's vocation with . . . dignity and seriousness,"
but other critics thought it less successful than its
two predecessors. "It has no overtones, only a spate
of fugitive generalizations about the artist and
America, about Hollywood and the artist, about the
literature of the twenties versus the literature of the
thirties, about life, and so on, as the dialogue flows
hither and thither," wrote Ernest Jones in the *Nation* (1950). Despite its mixed reception, *The Disenchanted* was the last of Schulberg's novels whose
publication was treated as a significant event.
Adapted by the author and Harvey Breit, *The Disenchanted* became a successful Broadway play starring Jason Robards, Jr.

Schulberg's screenplay for *On the Waterfront*,
the story of a former prize fighter working as a stevedore on the corruption-ridden waterfront of New
Jersey, was certainly a brilliant place of work; but
the tremendous success of that landmark Elia Kazan film starring Marlon Brando, added little to his
reputation as a novelist. Indeed, *Waterfront*, the
novel expanded from the screenplay in 1955, was
overshadowed by the movie, even though some
critics considered it a distinguished work in itself.
In general, the books Schulberg published after the
1960s have had comparatively slight impact, and
two of his later novels, *Sanctuary V* and *Everything
That Moves*, were dismissed as, essentially, potboilers. However, several of his nonfiction works, such
as a biography of Muhammad Ali (*Loser and Still
Champion*), a study of six American novelists and
their relationship to success (*The Four Seasons of
Success*), and a memoir of his childhood as a "Hollywood prince" (*Moving Pictures*) received largely
favorable reviews. For example, a critic in the *New
Republic* wrote of *The Four Seasons of Success*, "It
is this very personal urgency and sense of shared
fate pervading these pages which gives a modest
collection of literary profiles so keen an edge. It is
both a grave and an exuberant little book. The rivet
at its center is hard truth about our worship of fame
and fortune, how it has poisoned some of the best
American artists."

PRINCIPAL WORKS: *Novels*—What Makes Sammy Run? 1941;
The Harder They Fall, 1947; The Disenchanted, 1950; Waterfront, 1955; Sanctuary V, 1969; Everything That Moves, 1980.

Short stories—Some Faces in the Crowd, 1953; Love, Action, Laughter, and Other Sad Tales, 1989. Drama—(with H. Breit) The Disenchanted, 1959. Screenplays—A Face in the Crowd: A Play for the Screen, 1957; Across the Everglades: A Play for the Screen, 1958; On the Waterfront: Original Story and Screenplay, 1980. Biography—Loser and Still Champion: Muhammad Ali, 1972. Memoirs—Moving Pictures: Memories of a Hollywood Prince, 1981. Criticism—The Four Seasons of Success, 1972 (revised as Writers in America: The Four Seasons of Success, 1983). Other—Swan Watch, 1975. As editor—From the Ashes: The Voices of Watts, 1967.

ABOUT: The autobiographical material quoted above was written for Twentieth Century Authors First Supplement, 1955. Contemporary Authors New Revision Series 19 1987; Contemporary Literary Criticism vol. 7 1977; vol. 48 1988; Contemporary Novelist 5th ed., 1991; Current Biography 1951; Dictionary of Literary Biography vol. 6 1980; vol. 26 1984; vol. 28 1984. Periodicals—Gentlemen's Quarterly April 1994; Nation April 19, 1941; November 25, 1950; New Republic November 18, 1972; New York Times Book Review August 10, 1947; Washington Post March 2, 1975.

## SCHUMAN, FREDERICK L(EWIS) (February 22, 1904–May 19, 1981), American political scientist and historian, was born in Chicago, the son

of August Schuman, a letter carrier, and Ella (Schulze) Schuman. He was educated at the University of Chicago (Ph.B. 1924, Ph.D. 1927). He taught political science at Chicago (1927–1936). In 1936 he went to Williams College as a professor of political science, and two years later was named Woodrow Wilson Professor of Government, a position he held until his retirement in 1968.

Schuman's speciality was modern European and international politics; his first book on the subject, American Policy toward Russia since 1917, was published in 1928. In the view of the Annals of the American Academy of Political and Social Science, three factors distinguished him as a political scientist: "In the first place, Schuman is an academician endowed with an unusual ability to write in a very exciting style. . . . Secondly, Schuman belongs to the younger group of political scientists who . . . are trying to rejuvenate the old-fashioned purely descriptive and legalistic approach to Political Science by injections of the recent discoveries of the dynamic aspects of the other social sciences. . . . In the third place Schuman is gifted with a unique ability to sponge up an enormous amount of material . . . digest it, and present it in sweeping judgments."

Roucek could have added that Schuman's writing was also distinguished by his left-of-center stance, which led him to an early recognition of the full horrors of fascism—but caused him to mitigate the more unsavory aspects of the Soviet political system. On balance, however, Schuman was, as Joseph Barnes wrote in the New York Herald Tribune Weekly Book Review in 1947, "one of the appallingly few American scholars in the social sciences equipped to work on Russian materials." Indeed, it was his "habitual courage [in] analyzing a desper-

ately difficult problem instead of offering to eat a Russian alive," as Stringfellow Barr wrote in the Saturday Review, that got him into trouble with the House Un-American Activities Committee and Senator Joseph McCarthy in the 1940s. Both the committee and the senator accused him of having a record of "Communist affiliations," but unlike many other victims of anticommunist hysteria, Schuman waged a successful and principled campaign in his defense, and his career was largely unaffected by the smears brought against him.

Outstanding among Schuman's thirteen books were The Nazi Dictatorship, a perceptive analysis of the pathology of Hitlerism; Europe on the Eve and Night over Europe, two studies in diplomatic crisis and failure written just before and just after the outbreak of World War II; Soviet Politics, at Home and Abroad, an interpretation of the Russian Revolution and its aftermath; and The Commonwealth of Man, a theoretical "inquiry into power politics and world government." Most received favorable reviews, although many quarreled with Schuman's particular judgments and conclusions. For example, a reviewer in the Atlantic found that in Night over Europe Schuman was "inclined to overrate Soviet military power and to underrate Stalin's aversion to an understanding with the democracies," but Vincent Sheean, writing in the Saturday Review of Literature, thought the same book "a valuable précis of the course of events in world diplomacy from Munich to the present month, arranging events and documents, speeches and negotiations and catastrophes, in the order of their time and logic, the whole thing scholarly in a high degree without being, thank God, the least bit impartial." Again, virtually all of these books were written, according to the American Political Science Review, "with all the fire, the force, and the eloquence that one has come to expect from Schuman," but as Fainsod observed of Soviet Politics, at Home and Abroad, they sometimes manifested "weaknesses of analysis" that were "not altogether obscured by [their] rhetorical brilliance."

After retiring from Williams Schuman moved to Portland, Oregon, where he taught for three years at Portland State University and where he lived with his son for the remaining years of his life.

PRINCIPAL WORKS: Political science and history—American Policy Toward Russia Since 1917: A Study of Diplomatic History, International Law and Public Opinion, 1928; War and Diplomacy in the French Republic: An Inquiry into Political Motivations and the Control of Foreign Policy, 1931; International Politics: An Introduction to the Western State System, 1933, 7th ed. 1969; The Nazi Dictatorship: A Study in the Social Pathology and the Politics of Fascism, 1935 (in U.K.: Hitler and the Nazi Dictatorship, 1936); Germany since 1918, 1937; Europe on the Eve: The Crisis of Diplomacy, 1933–1939, 1939; Design for Power: The Struggle for the World, 1941; Night over Europe: The Diplomacy of Nemesis, 1939–1940, 1941; Soviet Politics, at Home and Abroad, 1946; The Commonwealth of Man: An Inquiry into Power Politics and World Government, 1952; Russia since 1917: Four Decades of Soviet Politics, 1957; Government in the Soviet Union, 1961; The Cold War: Retrospect and Prospect, 1962.

ABOUT: Contemporary Authors Vols. 45–48, 1974; Vol. 135, 1992. Periodicals—American Political Science Review June 1946; Annals of the American Academy of Political and Social Science March 1942; Atlantic March 1941; New York Herald

Tribune Weekly Book Review February 10, 1946; New York Times May 30, 1981; Saturday Review October 13, 1962; Saturday Review of Literature February 1, 1941.

## SCHÜTZE, GLADYS HENRIETTA (RAPHAEL) (pseudonyms "HENRIETTA LESLIE" and "GLADYS MENDL") (1881?–July 19,

1946), English novelist, was born in London and educated at home, where she was often confined to her sickbed. As a child she studied music, taking piano and singing lessons. Her delicate health, however, prevented her taking up a professional singing career. Instead she turned to writing, completing her first novel at the age of twenty.

She married Louis Mendl in 1902, but left him after having become involved in what was then called the British Suffragette movement (to be distinguished historically from the British Suffragist movement). She knew, and was influenced by, two pacifist and feminist authors—the South African, Olive Schreiner, who was resident in England during World War I, and Violet Paget ("Vernon Lee"). In 1913 she married again. Her second husband was Dr. Harrie Schütze, a bacteriologist born and educated in Melbourne, Australia. His Germanic surname was enough, however, to cause casual acquaintances to jump to conclusions, and the xenophobia she experienced during the war as a result of this stereotyping inspired her most successful and best-known novel, *Mrs. Fischer's War*. This was a book society choice on both sides of the Atlantic, and carried a foreword by John Galsworthy. The majority of reviewers found that, in this instance, the power and authenticity of the theme compensated for the wooden and didactic style which weighed down her other novels. The *Times Literary Supplement* called the war novel "a tiny but authentic contribution to the truth of things," and another reviewer remarked that the book "teems with a hundred details which should bring a blush of reminiscent shame to any reader who remembers the fate of the 'alien enemies' and their families in his own community."

Several of the novels reflected the writer's involvement in the women's movement. *A Mouse with Wings* concerns the interplay of pacifism and feminism, and later novels focus on the tensions between career and marriage, but in a manner which became increasingly lush and sentimental.

Schütze was a professional journalist before and after World War I, working for the *Daily Herald* as art critic and special reporter from 1919 to 1923, after which she spent nearly a decade as a campaigner for the Save The Children Fund, traveling widely. This provided her with experiences which led to the publication of a light and self-deprecating travel book, *Where East Is West*, about the Balkans. She collaborated in the writing of several London stage productions, including a dramatization of *Mrs. Fischer's War*, and published an autobiography—under the pseudonym Henrietta Leslie—*More Ha'pence than Kicks*, in 1943.

PRINCIPAL WORKS: (as "Gladys Mendl") The Straight Road, 1911; (as "Gladys Mendl") Roundabout, 1912; (as "Gladys Mendl") Parentage, 1913; Where Runs The River, 1916; A Mouse with Wings, 1920; Conflict, 1921; Belsavage, 1921; Other People's Property, 1922; Dedication, 1923; Hirelle, 1925; The Road to Damascus, 1929; Who Are You?, 1929; After Eight O'Clock, 1930; Mrs. Fischer's War, 1931; Naomis' Child, 1932 (in U.S.: Desired Haven); Where East Is West, 1933; Mother of Five, 1934; Daughters Defiant, 1935; Martin, Come Back!, 1936; No Spring Till Now, 1938; Good Neighbors, 1939; Mistress of Merle, 1940. Autobiography—(as "Henrietta Leslie") More Ha'pence than Kicks, 1943.

ABOUT: Blain, V. Clements, P., and Grundy, I. (eds.) The Feminist Companion to Literature in English, 1990. Periodicals—New York Herald Tribune Books February 22, 1931; Times Literary Supplement September 18, 1930.

## SCHWARTZ, DELMORE (December 8, 1913–

July 11, 1966), American poet, critic, short story writer, and verse dramatist, was born in Brooklyn, New York, the son of Harry Schwartz (who was of Romanian origin) and the former Rose Nathanson. Delmore experienced a miserable childhood, as his parents did not get on together; when the boy was nine his father left for good. Schwartz gave a brilliant and moving account of

his boyhood in his story "In Dreams Begin Responsibilities," which gave him the title for his first book, a mélange of prose and poems. He attended the University of Wisconsin (1931–1933), New York University (1933–1935), and the Harvard School of Philosophy (1935–1937), from which he graduated.

Schwartz is now a well discussed legend, partly because his friend Saul Bellow devoted his novel *Humboldt's Gift* (1975) to a remarkably accurate picture of him. *Humboldt's Gift* is a profound psychological study of a gifted but paranoid personality

Schwartz was also written about, memorably, by two of his fellow "mad" (and alcoholic) poets: John Berryman and Robert Lowell. Thus was built up a legend of a "romantic" poet whose life was wrecked—and ended—by mental illness and very heavy drinking.

Schwartz held, with increasing unhappiness and insecurity, teaching positions at Harvard, Kenyon, Princeton, and Syracuse. He married (1938) and divorced Gertrude Buckman, and then was married again, to Elizabeth Pollet (1949), who did her best to stand by him. Schwartz was a fine looking man, legendarily witty and funny, and altogether a "compelling presence." But he deteriorated through illness and drink, and, after many interludes in sanatoria, he found himself without employment. His paranoia increased to the extent that not even his closest friends were able to have anything to do with him. He checked into a Times

Square hotel in the early summer of 1966, was known there as a "pleasant guest" who worked at his typewriter—but on July 11, by then quite alone, was found dead in his room, apparently of heart failure.

Schwartz's first book, *In Dreams Begin Responsibilities*, was also his best and was welcomed in all quarters: by Wallace Stevens, John Crowe Ransom, T. S. Eliot, Ezra Pound, and Allen Tate, who called it "the first real innovation we've had since Eliot and Pound." Some half-dozen poems have survived as at least potentially major, among them "In the Naked Bed, in Plato's Cave," a complex, ironic and highly allusive and yet lyrical poem, which begins:

> In the naked bed, in Plato's cave,
> Reflected headlights slowly slid the wall,
> Carpenters hammered under the shaded window,
> Wind troubled the window curtains all night long,
> A fleet of trucks strained uphill, grinding,
> Their freights covered, as usual.
> The ceiling lightened again, the slanting diagram
> Slid slowly forth.

This, and "The Heavy Bear Who Goes With Me," in the same volume, are Schwartz's two best-known poems. The prose pieces in *In Dreams Begin Responsibilities*, including the title story, are even more accomplished.

Mental illness began to assail Schwartz with sickening regularity during the mid-fifties. Meanwhile, the publication of his volume of poetry *Summer Knowledge*, in 1959, brought him the Bollingen Prize. Irving Howe then called him, rather than Lowell or Berryman, the "poet of the historical moment."

Schwartz's verse play *Shenandoah*, about the naming rites of a Jewish child in the Bronx, received mixed reviews, and was not much of a success when it was produced after his death. But, in his capacity as editor of *Partisan Review* (1943–1947), and then as associate editor (1947–1955), his critical pieces in the magazine received wide attention, especially the articles "The Isolation of Modern Poetry" and "The Vocation of the Poet in the Modern World." When the *Selected Essays* was posthumously published, Philip Rahv in the *New York Review of Books* (1971) wrote: "Sound in his literary judgments, he wrote without pretention or solemnity and without ever divesting himself of his fine and highly original sense of humor . . . only now . . . can his critical aptitudes and inclinations . . . be properly appreciated." Jonathan Raban, however, writing in the *New Statesman*, was more skeptical, calling Schwartz only effective on such as Thomas Hardy, where there were "no fireworks"; "this immodestly got-up volume holds its contents more like a tomb than a showcase."

Schwartz, as a critic of historical and often intrinsic importance, as the author of a few moving poems, and, above all, as a writer of brilliantly comic stories—many of them satirizing his own milieu—will certainly not be forgotten. His papers are in the Beinecke Library at Yale.

PRINCIPAL WORKS: *Poetry*—Vaudeville for a Princess, 1950; Summer Knowledge: New and Selected Poems 1938–1958, 1959 reissued as Selected Poems: Summer Knowledge 1938–1958 1967; Phillips, R. (ed.) Last and Lost Poems of Delmore Schwartz, 1979 rev. 1989; Dunn, D. (ed.) What It Is to Be Given: Selected Poems, 1976. *Poetry and Prose*—In Dreams Begin Responsibilities, 1938; Genesis, Book One, 1943. *Short stories*—The World Is a Wedding, 1948; Successful Love, 1961; Atlas, J. (ed.) In Dreams Begin Responsibilities and Other Stories, 1978. *Criticism*—Dike, D. A. and Zucker, D. H. (eds.) Selected Essays, 1970. *Drama*—Shenandoah, or The Naming of the Child, 1941. *As editor*—(with J. C. Ransom and J. H. Wheelock) American Poetry at Mid-Century, 1958; Syracuse Poems 1964, 1965. *As translator*—Arthur Rimbaud's Season in Hell (bilingual) 1939. *Juvenile*—I Am Cherry Alive, the Little Girl Sang, 1979. *Correspondence and journals*—Phillips, R. (ed.) The Letters of Delmore Schwartz, 1985; Pollet, E. (ed.) Portrait of Delmore: Journals and Notebooks, 1986.

ABOUT: Atlas, J. Delmore Schwartz: The Life of an American Poet, 1977; Hamilton, I. (ed) Oxford Companion to Twentieth-Century Poetry, 1994; McDougal, Schwartz, 1974; Rosenthal, M. L. The Modern Poets, 1960; Simpson, E. Poets *in* Their Youth, 1982; Wald, A. M. The New York Intellectuals, 1987. *Periodicals*—Atlantic June 1983; Books March 5, 1939; Commentary December 1950; Nation June 11, 1963; New Statesman March 19, 1971; New York Review of Books July 14, 1966, May 20, 1971; Paris Review Winter 1986; Partisan Review Summer 1990; Time December 5, 1977.

**SCHWARTZ, JOZUA MARIUS WILLEM VAN POORTEN.** See **MAARTEN, MAARTENS**

**SCHWEITZER, ALBERT** (January 14, 1875–September 4, 1965), German theologian, philosopher, musician, musicologist, doctor, surgeon, and medical missionary, was born in Kaysersberg, Alsace (French territory then occupied by Germany), the son of a liberal Lutheran minister, Louis Schweitzer, and Adele (Schillinger) Schweitzer. He did not show any particular academic promise in his early school years, except in music. At the age of five he started to learn the piano, and at eight the organ, proving himself an excellent improviser, but reluctant to spend hours practicing set pieces, and thus, according to one of his organ teachers, "the thorn in my flesh." Educated briefly at the local school in Gunsbach, he was sent at the age of ten to Mulhausen, where he lived with his schoolmaster uncle under strict supervision and enjoyed little respite from studies except for his music.

He went on to study theology and philosophy at Strasbourg University, his degree broken by a spell in the army. During military service he closely read the New Testament in Greek, which inspired the first steps of inquiry into a subject that was later to form what is probably his most significant, and certainly most influential, work, *Von Reimarus zu Wrede: Eine Geschichte der Leben-Jesu-Forschung* (1906, translated as *The Quest*  *of the Historical Jesus*). He then studied philosophy briefly at the Sorbonne in Paris, at the same time receiving free organ lessons from the celebrated French organist and composer Charles-Marie Widor. In 1899 he took a Ph.D. in philosophy, his thesis being *Die Religionsphilosophie Kant's: Der Reinen Vernunft bis zur Religion Innerhalb der*

*Grentzen der Blossen Vernunft* (The religious philosophy of Kant from the critique of pure reason to religion within the limits of reason alone). Kant's methodology was to form a significant influence on his thought, although he strongly disagreed with many of Kant's conclusions. In 1902 he became a lecturer in the faculty of theology at Strasbourg University, and in the following year principal of the Theological College of St. Thomas.

By this time Schweitzer was famous throughout Europe on several counts: as an exceptional performer and critic of Bach (at the age of twenty-eight he became organist of the Paris Bach Society, and his edition of Bach's organ works became the standard text), as well as an influential organ-builder whose published works were to change the pattern of organ restoration and installation. He was also renowned as a theologian and philosopher, whose unorthodox ideas about the need for reason and truth within Christian dogma were earning him controversy and praise. "The more I studied the history of Christianity, the more I realized the extent of the errors and disagreement which started because men from the first generation to this day played up faith and piety at the expense of reason, and so put asunder what God had joined together harmoniously." Schweitzer's intellectual position demanded rigorous honesty in all matters; "I think the most important quality in a person concerned with religion is absolute devotion to truth." It was his belief that the Church and Christianity could withstand any probing into historical accuracy, and would in fact be strengthened by such investigations. The Church establishment, however, in the wake of such statements, began to view him with great suspicion.

The publication in 1906 (1910 in English) of *The Quest of the Historical Jesus* marked a landmark in Christian theology. Schweitzer looked freshly at the Synoptic gospels and tried to understand exactly what Jesus really believed. Placing him firmly within the Judaic framework of his period, he concluded that Jesus emphatically believed that a new order would soon begin on earth, an order in which the ethic of love was central. Late in his career, however, Schweitzer revised his opinion that Jesus had any concept about his role in atoning for mankind's sins. Nearly a century after the publication of *The Quest*, it still remains an, essential starting point for subsequent studies into the historicity of the Christian faith.

In 1896, when his scholastic career was flourishing, Schweitzer decided that he could not live a life purely devoted to scholarship and ease. He would continue with his academic career until he was thirty, at which point he would devote his life to the world. "I decided that I would make my life my argument," he said, intending to act out his beliefs rather than just preach them. So at thirty, despite the disapproval of his family and many of his friends, he enrolled at Strasbourg University as a medical student, continuing to teach and play the organ to fund himself through his courses. He graduated as a fully qualified doctor in 1913, with a specialization in tropical diseases, and began to raise funds for the establishment of a hospital in equatorial Africa. To him, the story of Lazarus and Dives was a representation of the disparity between the decadent West and the underdeveloped world, and he felt it was the white man's duty to atone for the damage he had done to the black world.

Although his unorthodox theology led to disapproval by most mission societies, he was finally allowed to go out to Africa by the Paris Missionary Society, who gave him land on which to build his hospital. This he did, with the help of his wife, Helene Bresslau, who had qualified as a nurse to help with his mission. Theirs was a marriage of commitment to the Christian cause rather than a romantic attachment; it is said that Schweitzer first kissed Helene only on their wedding day, in June 1912.

The Schweitzers set up their hospital in Lambaréné, part of French equatorial Africa, where the climate was fiercely tropical. Converting a chicken coop into an operating theater, Schweitzer began to treat the first of thousands of patients. He turned Lambaréné into a sort of medical village, where patients could bring along relatives to cook for them while they recovered. Animals and children roamed through its streets, and sanitation and hygeine seemed to many outsiders to be unacceptably primitive. His medical methods were criticized for their unorthodoxy. Schweitzer believed, however, that in blending African culture with his own techniques he was addressing the needs of the population better than by imposing a purely Western style upon them; certainly, the affection and trust he inspired in those who came to him for treatment and the success of his hospital over the years would seem to confirm this view. He was called "Oganga"—the fetishman—a term of respect. According to one commentator, discussing Schweitzer's relationship with the local people, he "tried to help them on their own terms." By the time of his death, the compound consisted of about seventy buildings, with a leper colony close by, and attracted medical staff from all around the world.

In 1915 Schweitzer evolved the crucial heart of his ethical system, which he termed Reverence for Life, and out of which all his philosophy stemmed. He believed that "Christian theologians confine Christianity to the human form of life." "Man's ethics," he said, "must not end with man, but should extend to the universe." In his view, everything on earth is equally sacred; you should flip an overturned beetle onto its feet, or remove a worm from someone's path before it is crushed. He elaborated this theory in his later works, and exemplified it in his own life, refusing to kill insects or any creature unless it was absolutely essential. Part of the responsibility of this approach, he knew, was the need to accept that in some situations killing is necessary.

Another fresh attitude, and one which was radical for its time, was his conviction that "the spirit of the universe is at once creative and destructive . . . we must inevitably resign ourselves to this." For him, it was up to mankind to invest living with moral value, since nature and the universe were neutral.

On the outbreak of World War I he and his wife, both German citizens, were for four months placed under house arrest, as prisoners of war. During this time Schweitzer worked on *Verfall und Wiederaufbau der Kultur* (1923, Philosophy of civilization). In 1917 they were taken to an internment camp in France, where they stayed until the end of the war. Helene's health never recovered from this experience, and Schweitzer entered a long period of depression, which he later identified as a nervous breakdown brought about partly because of despair at the inhumanity the war had engendered. Despite therapy with the eminent Swiss psychotherapist Dr. Oscar Pfister it took him five years to recover fully.

Returning to Lambaréné in 1924, Schweitzer rebuilt the hospital on a new site, and spent the rest of his life devoted to its development, traveling regularly to Europe to give concerts to raise funds. Because of her health, Helene now visited Lambaréné only during the dry season. In 1919 she gave birth to their only child, Rhena, who was later to train as a laboratory technician so she could work alongside her father at the hospital. More than half the Schweitzers' married life was spent apart, a fact both he and Helene regretted but accepted.

World War II further heightened Schweitzer's belief that mankind was in a period of unprecedented spiritual decadence. Prior to the outbreak of war, he lectured in Germany at some personal risk, and realized it was no longer safe to visit the country under its Nazi rulers. His ideas, however, provided inspiration for those such as Dietrich Bonhoeffer, who resisted Nazism (and died for his beliefs).

During this war the hospital at Lambaréné had to retrench its activities, and by 1945 was in a parlous state. It was only with the intervention of the Unitarian Service Committee in America that it was saved from closure.

Essentially nonpolitical, Schweitzer has been derisively termed "the last of the great white fathers" by critics who found his outdated colonialist attitude to native Africans offensive. The doctor, who sometimes appeared to treat the natives like children, once commented of the local orange trees that "the good Lord has protected the trees. He made the Africans too lazy to pick them bare." He also stated that "there can be no question with these people of real independence, but only whether it is better for them to be delivered over to the mercies, tender or otherwise, of rapacious native tyrants, or to be governed by officals of European states."

The civil rights leader Dr. W. E. B. Du Bois attacked Schweitzer's notion of repaying Africa for white man's misdeeds through a colonial-style system, and said that he represented the reactionary influences that had undermined the African. Schweitzer, though, however dated his political theory, was not acting out of a desire to repress the natives, or to stamp his own authority upon them, but simply believed that the system he used was the most beneficial for them. In this he was increasingly anachronistic, but never deliberately obstructive.

Schweitzer was awarded the 1952 Nobel Peace Prize, the money from which he put towards building a leper colony near the hospital. In 1957 his wife died, and thereafter he remained at Lambaréné. "Others must go and talk now; my Africans would not understand if I left them at the end." But instead of retreating into silence, he became increasingly outspoken on the issue of nuclear weapons, joining with some of the greatest intellects in the world to discuss and denounce the spread of lethal arsenals. In 1958 he made three radio appeals from Oslo entitled "Peace or Atomic War?," and until the end of his life he welcomed visiting journalists or politicians who wished to discuss this issue with him.

He died, peacefully, in 1965, and was buried alongside his wife at Lambaréné. A man of immense humanity, whose authoritarianism sprang from the desire to do as much good for those around him as possible in the manner he thought best, he was a lonely, spiritually tormented figure, profoundly saddened by the nature of the world around him, but determined to bring people around to a fresh way of viewing life. He was summed up by Einstein, with whom he corresponded but never met: "He did not preach and did not warn and did not dream that his example would be ideal and a comfort to innumerable people. He simply acted out of inner necessity."

PRINCIPAL WORKS IN ENGLISH TRANSLATION: *Autobiography*—On the Edge of the Primeval Forest (tr. C. T. Campion) 1922; Memoirs of Childhood and Youth (tr. C. T. Campion) 1925; Forest Hospital at Lambaréné (tr. C. T. Campion) 1931, 1948; More from the Primeval Forest 1931, 1948 (in U.K.); Out of My Life and Thought, An Autobiography (tr. C. T. Campion) 1933, 1949; From My African Notebook (tr. C.E.B. Russell) 1938, (in U.S.: African Notebook) 1938. *Nonfiction*—The Quest of the Historical Jesus (tr. W. Montgomery) 1910, 1949; J. S. Bach, 1911; Paul and His Interpreters (tr. W. Montgomery) 1912; The Mystery of the Kingdom of God (tr. W. Lowry) 1914; Christianity and the Religions of the World, 1923; The Decay and Restoration of Civilization, 1923; Civilization and Ethics, 1923; The Mysticism of Paul the Apostle (tr. W. Montgomery) 1931; Indian Thought and its Development (tr. C.E.B. Russell) 1933; Albert Schweitzer: An Anthology (ed. C. R. Joy) 1947–1948; Goethe (tr. C. R. Joy) 1948; A Psychiatric Study of Jesus (tr. C. R. Joy) 1948; Philosophy of Civilization (tr. C. T. Campion) 1949; Animal World (tr. and ed. C. R. Joy) 1951; Music in the Life of Albert Schweitzer (tr. C. R. Joy) 1951; Peace or Atomic War?, 1958; The Teaching of Reverence for Life (trs. R. and C. Winston) 1965; The Kingdom of God and Primitive Christianity (tr. L. A. Garard) 1968; Reverence for Life (tr. R. H. Fuller) 1970.

ABOUT: Bentley, J. Albert Schweitzer, the Enigma, 1992; Brabazon, J. Albert Schweitzer, 1975; Clark, H. The Ethical Mysticism of Albert Schweitzer, 1962; Cousins, N. Albert Schweitzer's Mission, 1965; Cranford, G. Albert Schweitzer, 1990; Cremaschi, A. Albert Schweitzer, 1985; Current Biography 1948 and 1965; Ensslin, W. Reverence for Life, 1983; Ferschotte, J. Albert Schweitzer, 1954; Franck, F. Days With Albert Schweitzer, 1959; Gollomb, J. Albert Schweitzer, Genius in the Jungle, 1949; Hagedorn, H. Albert Schweitzer: Prophet in the Wilderness, 1962; Ice, J. L. Schweitzer, Prophet of Radical Theology, 1971; Johnson, S. The Value of Dedication, 1979; Joy, C. and Arnold, M. The Africa of Albert Schweitzer, 1948; Kerby, M. Albert Schweitzer, 1991; Knight, V. Verdict on Schweitzer, 1964; Kraus, O. Albert Schweitzer, 1947; Langfeld, G. Albert Schweitzer, A Study of His Philosophy of Life, 1960; McKnight, G. Verdict on Schweitzer: The Man Behind the Legend of Lambaréné, 1964; Marshall, G. An Understanding of Albert Schweitzer, 1966; Marshall, G. and

Poling, D. Schweitzer: A Biography, 1971; Montague, J. F. The Why of Albert Schweitzer, 1965; Mozley, E. N. The Theology of Albert Schweitzer, 1950; Murray, M. Albert Schweitzer, Musician, 1994; Murry, J. Middleton The Challenge of Schweitzer, 1948; Ratter, M. C. Albert Schweitzer, Life and Message, 1950; Robles, H. Albert Schweitzer, an Adventurer for Humanity, 1994; Schulze, G. Shadow of a Star, 1993; Schweitzer, A. Forest Hospital at Lambaréné, 1931; Schweitzer, A. Out of My Life and Thought, 1933, 1949; Schweitzer, A. African Notebook, 1939; Schweitzer, A. Memoirs of Childhood and Youth, 1949; Seaver, G. Albert Schweitzer, Christian Revolutionary, 1944; Seaver, G. Albert Schweitzer, The Man and His Mind, 1947; Seaver, G. Albert Schweitzer, A Vindication. *Periodicals*—Atlantic Monthly November 1961; Ecumenical Review Winter 1950; Etude December 1950; The Humanist March/April 1993; Life October 6, 1947; July 25, 1949; New York Times September 1965; New York Times Magazine January 13, 1952; New Yorker November 20, 1954; Rotarian March 1952; Saturday Review of Literature June 17, 1950; May 2, 1953; March 16, 1963; September 25, 1965; Spectator February 18, 1949; November 6, 1953; Time July 11, 1949; June 21, 1963; World Press Review March 1986.

## SCOLLARD, CLINTON (September 18, 1860–November 19, 1932), American poet and novelist, was born in Clinton, New York, the son of James

Isaac Scollard, a physician, and Elizabeth (Stephens) Scollard. After graduating in 1881 from Hamilton College in Clinton, he began teaching English at the Brooklyn Polytechnic Institute. In 1883 he resigned and spent the next five years traveling (to California, England, and the Middle East) and pursuing graduate studies at Harvard and Cambridge universities. He returned to Hamilton as a professor of English in 1888, remaining there until 1896; thereafter he supported himself by writing.

Scollard's first collection, *Pictures in Song*, was published in 1884. "The work is derivative, but in looking it over one cannot but remark the technical facility which it shows," was the verdict of Jessie Belle Rittenhouse, the poet and anthologist whom he married in 1924, the same year in which he obtained a divorce from his first wife. Although Rittenhouse considered *Pictures in Song* juvenilia, her comment about that work could be applied to almost all of Scollard's poetry. Summarizing the view of many, the *Christian Century* wrote of *The Singing Heart*, a posthumous selection of poems, "Clinton Scollard wrote much, and it was always good—tuneful, graceful, sensitive, sometimes stirring, nearly always lyrical. It was always acceptable . . . but it never took the world by storm."

Scollard also wrote six novels, most of them historical romances set in colonial America or medieval Italy. Of *The Vicar of the Marches*, a reviewer wrote in the *Nation*, "If the occasional clank of machinery makes a jarring note in the story, and if we find both hero and villain even more prodigious in their respective qualities than is usual in tales of the type, *The Vicar of the Marches* is, none the less, good reading enough, and the spirit of old romance

is softened here and there by a poetic note, the echo of its author's familiar verse."

PRINCIPAL WORKS: *Verse*—Pictures in Song, 1884; With Reed and Lyre, 1886; Old and New World Lyrics, 1888; Giovio and Guilia: A Metrical Romance, 1892; Songs of Sunrise Lands, 1892; Under Summer Skies, 1892; Hills of Song, 1895; The Boy's Book of Rhyme, 1896; Skenandoa, 1896; The Lutes of Morn, 1901; Lyrics of the Dawn, 1902; (with W. Rice) Ballads of Valor and Victory, 1903; The Lyric Bough, 1904; Lyrics and Legends of Christmas-Tide, 1904; Odes and Elegies, 1905; Easter-Song: Lyrics and Ballads of the Joy of Springtime, 1906; Blank Verse Pastels, 1907; Voices and Visions, 1908; Pro Patria: Verses Chiefly Patriotic, 1909; Chords of the Zither, 1910; From the Lips of the Sea, 1911; Songs of a Syrian Lover, 1912; Lyrics from a Library, 1913; Matins, 1913; Poems, 1914; Sprays of Shamrock, 1914; The Vale of Shadows and Other Verses of the Great War, 1915; Ballads, Patriotic and Romantic, 1916; Let the Flag Wave, with Other Verses Written in Wartime, 1917; War Voices and Memories, 1919; The Epic of Golf, 1923; The Crowning Years, 1929; Lyrics of Florida, 1929; Songs out of Egypt, 1930; Songs from a Southern Shore, 1932; The Singing Heart: Selected Lyrics and Other Poems (ed. J. B. Rittenhouse) 1934. *Novels*—A Man-at-Arms: A Romance of the Days of Gran Galeazzo Visconti, the Great Viper, 1898; A Knight of the Highway, 1901; The Son of a Tory: A Narrative of the Experiences of William Aubrey in the Mohawk Valley and Elsewhere during the Summer of 1777, 1901; The Cloistering of Ursula: Being Certain Chapters from the Memorial of Andrea, Marquis of Uccelli, and Count Castelpulchio, 1902; Count Falcoln of the Eyrie: A Narrative Wherein Are Set forth the Adventures of Guido Orrabelli dei Falchi During a Certain Autumn of His Career, 1903; The Vicar of the Marches, 1911. *As editor*—The Broken Heart (by J. Ford) 1895; The Poems of Frank Dempster Sherman, 1917; (with J. B. Rittenhouse) The Bird-Lovers' Anthology, 1930; (with J. B. Rittenhouse) Patrician Rhymes: A Résumé of American Society Verse from Philip Freneau to the Present Day, 1932. *Other*—On Sunny Shores, 1893; Footfarings, 1904.

ABOUT: Dictionary of American Biography, 1935; Rittenhouse, J. B. *introduction to* The Singing Heart (by C. Scollard) 1934. *Periodicals*—Christian Century June 6, 1934; Nation December 22, 1910; New York Times November 20, 1932.

## SCOTT, DUNCAN (August 2, 1862–December 19, 1947), Canadian poet, short story writer, and editor, wrote: "My father was a minister of the

Methodist Church in Ottawa, Ontario, where I was born. Until I was seventeen I suffered the vicissitudes of the Methodist itinerant system, living here and there in Canada, and getting what education I could from the public schools and at Stanstead College, Quebec. Then I

entered the Civil Service of Canada, in the Department of Indian Affairs, and remained attached to that department until my retirement, as Deputy Superintendent General, in 1932. During my service I was instrumental in settling a number of vexed Indian questions between the Provinces and the Dominion and introduced improvements in the Medical and Educational Divisions. For this administrative work I was made a Companion of the Order of St. Michael and St. George by George V in 1934.

"It will be gathered that I belong to a type not

unknown in Great Britain and the United States—the public servant who devotes his leisure to literary or artistic pursuits. I had, as a child, shown an aptitude for music and cultivated it strenuously. My interest in the intellectual and artistic life of the Dominion has been constant. I was elected a fellow of the Royal Society of Canada in 1899, and was its Honorary Secretary for eleven years and President in 1921. The University of Toronto and Queens University, Kingston, have honored me with doctorates. I am a Fellow of the Royal Society of Literature of Great Britain. Greatly interested in the drama, I am a Governor of the Dominion Drama Festival. . . ."

———

Duncan Campbell Scott was the only son and youngest child of William Scott and the former Isabella Campbell MacCallum, a Scottish-born pianist. Duncan himself became an accomplished pianist, and developed an educational interest in art but clearly had no thoughts of being anything other than a civil servant until, in his mid-twenties, he met Archibald Lampman, then a leading light in Canadian poetry. They became friends, taking extended canoeing trips together in the Quebec wilderness. Lampman encouraged Scott to write, and in 1892 they both collaborated with Winfred Campbell on a series of weekly literary articles for the *Toronto Globe*. The following year Scott's first volume of poetry was published.

The poems collected in *The Magic House* were, predictably, heavily shaded by the Tennysonian brand of late-Victorian English romanticism that was so much in evidence in the work of Lampman and the other Confederation poets. This group, which included Charles G. D. Roberts and Bliss Carman, were so called because, writing in an era that followed the formal establishment of the Canadian Dominion, they sought to develop a sense of national identity for their country. *The Magic House*, though it was relatively un-Canadian in content, is best known for a particularly regional poem—the dramatic narrative "At the Cedars," which describes the drowning of a Quebec lumberjack. "At the Cedars" was, for its time, experimental in form; stripped of Tennysonian decoration, it makes use of internal and end rhymes, but eschews regular meter, fitting rhythm to action:

The whole drive was jammed
In that bend at the cedars,
The rapids were dammed
with the logs tight rammed
and crammed; you might know
The Devil had clinched them below.

Most of the poems in *The Magic House* are more formally conventional and feature, as Desmond Pacey says, "natural description of an intensely colorful sort touched here and there with magic and mystery" (*Ten Canadian Poets*).

In 1894 Scott married his first wife, a violinist. His father had by this time died, and his mother and two sisters were so hostile to the union that he remained estranged from them for the rest of his life. In 1895 a daughter was born, Elizabeth Duncan, to whom Scott became devoted.

The following year Scott published a collection of short stories, *In the Village of Viger*. Light and dream-like stories about the inhabitants of a village in Quebec, they drew on his experience of the region. Often humorous, always tender and nostalgic, they portray a close-knit community facing the threat of industrialization at the end of the nineteenth century. Reviewers praised Scott's sensitivity and artistry, Gordon Johnston in an essay in *Canadian Writers and Their Works*, finding the stories "polished in method and assured in tone."

Scott's second volume of poetry was *Labour and the Angel*. After *The Magic House* it was, in Pacey's words, "something of a disappointment." Marred as it was by a strong strain of didacticism, the volume was notable only for its inclusion of Scott's first two poems about the Indians he worked with, and of one of his most famous works, "The Piper of Arll." A romantic ballad, resonant with echoes of Coleridge's "Rime of the Ancient Mariner," it tells of a lonely shepherd who is bewitched by the "music" of a mysterious ship; it won praise from the future English Poet Laureate John Masefield, and William Archer called it "a singularly beautiful fantasy, full of jewel-like colour and tenuous, unearthly melody." Scott was, he continues, "a poet of many gifts," but "before everything a colourist" (*Poets of the Younger Generation*).

In 1899 Archibald Lampman died, only thirty-eight years old. It was one of the great sadnesses of Scott's life, and he determined to keep his friend's name alive through his work. He published a memorial edition of Lampman's poems in 1900, and two more editions followed later. He was also editing a series of biographies, jointly with Pelham Edgar, entitled Makers of Canada. In 1905 his own contribution appeared, a volume on John Grave Simco. In the same year he published a critical and biographical sketch of the painter Walter J. Phillips, and his third collection of poetry.

*New World Lyrics and Ballads* was full of the poems of Indian life upon which Scott's reputation ultimately rests. His work for the Department of Indian Affairs frequently took him to the northern wilderness, which was familiar territory to him. His first-hand knowledge of Indian history, culture, and folklore enabled him to produce accurate, unsentimental and unprejudiced accounts of the people and their terrain. The volume contains one of the best known of all Canadian poems, "The Forsaken," telling the story of an elderly woman left to die in the wilderness, according to her people's tradition. The poet's attitude is detached and interested, but Roy Daniells noted that these pieces are far more than ethnographical studies; Scott's enduring theme is the contrast and conflict inherent in the wild, natural world. "Their ultimate meaning," he said, "is the resolution of violence, either into the calm of nature or into nature's own impersonal fury" (*Literary History of Canada*). *New Worlds Lyrics and Ballads* is a vital, intense work, in which narrative forms play out the drama of life in the Canadian north. A reviewer for *Nation* remarked upon its "keen poetic tang," and Pacey found in it "reassuring proof that Scott's poetic inspiration was far from exhausted."

In 1907 Scott and his wife traveled to Spain for a vacation, leaving their daughter in a French convent on the way. A few days later they received a telegram at their hotel in Madrid. It read: "Elizabeth morte." Scott was devastated by the death of his daughter, and wrote nothing for several years.

*Lundys Lane and Other Poems*, when it did arrive, was not well received. Raymond Knister, in an essay in Dragland's book, found it "comparatively speaking at least, a failure, with surprisingly ill-considered inclusions. . . . Yet there is a measure always, which. . . . would make one believe Scott incapable of really bad verse." Pacey concedes that the poems contain some engaging imagery and lyricism, but considered the volume as a whole "embarrassingly bad." *Beauty and Life*, which followed, was more successful. In poems like "Ode for the Keats Centenary," Scott skillfully evokes atmosphere, the varied hues of environment and experience. "His observation of nature is all through his work," said a reviewer for the *Saturday Review of Literature*, "there is a fragrance of balsam and pine about it."

A second collection of short stories, *The Witching of Elspie*, is set in the Hudson Bay region. These stories are much darker and starker than those from *In the Village of Viger*, depicting the wild and violent side of life amongst trappers, traders, and travelers in nineteenth-century Canada. A reviewer for the *New York Times* (1923) felt that "there is a certain vividness of characterization and action that sets these stories apart."

A complete collection of Scott's poetry was followed by *The Green Cloister, Later Poems*. The volume contains the famous "At Gull Rock: 1810." This poem, as Gary Gadder commented in *Colony and Confederation*, is "a dramatic *tour de force*," rescued from melodrama by a typically calm resolution.

*The Circle of Affection*, published in the year of Scott's death, collected poems, short stories, and essays, old and new. Pacey pointed to the new poems as evidence of continuing artistic excellence.

Much has been written about the lack of critical attention given to Scott during his lifetime. He was an extremely shy, modest man who, unlike the other Confederation poets, chose to disappear behind a poetic mask which spoke little of the self. Daniells pointed out that his technique, "more astringent and more uncertain than that of his contemporaries, delayed recognition of his achievement." That achievement has now been reappraised, and Scott's versatility, diversity, and boldness have been recognized. In Gadder's opinion, "he is, in fact, the one breath of fresh air escaping from the mixed bag of Confederation poets." Glenn Clever, in an essay in *The Duncan Campbell Scott Symposium*, affirmed the poet's position as "a primary author of the consciousness of Canada and a watershed author between the old ways and the new in literature."

PRINCIPAL WORKS: *Poetry*—The Magic House and Other Poems, 1893; Labour and the Angel, 1898; New World Lyrics and Ballads, 1905; Via Borealis, 1906; Lundys Lane and Other Poems, 1916; Beauty and Life, 1921; Complete Poems, 1926; The Green Cloister, Later Poems, 1935; Selected Poems (ed. E. K. Brown) 1951. *Short stories*—In the Village of Viger, 1896; The Witching of Elspie, 1923; Selected Stories (ed. G. Clever) 1972. *As editor*—The Poems of Archibald Lampman, 1900; (with P. Edgar) The Makers of Canada, 20 vols., 1903–1908; Amelia Anne Paget, The People of the Plains, 1909; Archibald Lampman, Lyrics of Earth, Sonnets and Ballads, 1925; Selected Poems of Archibald Lampman, 1947. *Other*—John Graves Simco, 1905; The Administration of Indian Affairs in Canada, 1931; Walter J. Phillips, 1947; The Circle of Affection, and Other Pieces in Prose and Verse, 1947; Some Letters of Duncan Campbell Scott, Archibald Lampman and Others (ed. A. S. Bourinot) 1959; More Letters of Duncan Campbell Scott (ed. A. S. Bourinot) 1960; Untitled Novel, ca. 1905, 1979.

ABOUT: The autobiographical material quoted above was written for Twentieth Century Authors, 1942. Archer, W. Poets of the Younger Generation, 1969; Bailey, A. G. And others (eds.) Literary History of Canada, 1965; Brown, E. K. On Canadian Poetry, rev. ed. 1973; Contemporary Authors Vol. 104, 1982; Dictionary of Literary Biography Vol. 91, 1990; Dragland, S. L. (Ed.) Duncan Campbell Scott; A Book of Criticism, 1974; Jones, D. G. Butterfly on Rock: Images in Canadian Literature, 1970; Karsh, V. Karsh Canadians, 1978; Lecker, R. And others (eds.) Canadian Writers and Their Works, 1983; Mandel, E. (ed.) Contexts of Canadian Criticism, 1971; McDougall, R. (ed.) Our Living Tradition 1959; New, W. H. A History of Canadian Literature, 1989; Oxford Companion to Canadian History and Literature, 1967; Oxford Companion to Canadian Literature, 1983; Pacey, D. Ten Canadian Poets, 1958; Percival, W. P. (ed.) Leading Canadian Poets, 1948; Ross, M. (ed.) Poets of the Confederation, 1960; Stich, K. P. (ed.) The Duncan Campbell Scott Symposium, 1980; Sylvestre, G. And others (eds.) Canadian Writers, 1964; Twentieth Century Literary Criticism Vol. 6, 1982; Vinson, J. Great Writers of the English Language: Poets, 1979; Who's Who 1947; Woodcock, G. (ed.) Colony and Confederation, 1974. *Periodicals*—Canadian Forum August 1948; Canadian Literature Winter 1986, Summer 1944; Nation April 19, 1906; New York Times November 18, 1923; December 20, 1947; Publishers Weekly January 10, 1948; Saturday Review of Literature July 16, 1927; Wilson Library Bulletin February 1948.

**SCOTT, EVELYN** (January 17, 1893–August 3, 1963), American novelist, poet, and memoirist, wrote: "I [am] at forty-six years old [1942], arrived at a most interesting period of life. The very young remind me of fish in individual aquariums, gazing, through a medium alien to other species, toward an outer world not yet more than theoretically a fact. Minnows never emerge from the sensory confines of water; but humans, sometimes, after laboriously reaching forty, become capable of a degree of extra-emotional vision. I aspire to such a vision today, though I realize detachment and perspective are not acquired without effort, even in middle life. I think any individual's acceptance of a theory of universals and universal perfection is contingent on inescapable emotional needs, which are the undeliberated outcome of that individual's life experiences. If my mother, Southern from the seventeenth century, had not married a Yankee whose ancestors were from Boston and New York State, I might not have been impelled, as I was, to protest the lingering antebellum tradition under which I grew up. I was born in Tennes-

see, and educated for the most part in New Orleans, by tutors, and at Newcomb Preparatory School, Newcomb College, and the Newcomb School of Art. But I never completed my college course, and I educated myself with precocious reading, which inspired me with simultaneous ambitions to become a writer, a painter, an actress, and a disciple of Pavlowa, Tolstoy, Schopenhauer, Nietzsche, Bergson, and Karl Marx—all at once. Transported by great art, passionately wishing to understand all religions and philosophies, the Puritan side of my descent afflicted me additionally with an ardor for social reform. For this reason I early resolved to do my bit to insure the political and economic equality of races, thus finally safeguarding individual freedom.

"Saturated in Russian, French, and Scandinavian literature, I rejected the idea of being a Southern belle like everybody else, and ran away from home, thus flouting convention with a high-mindedness not all readers of *Escapade* appreciate even today. But it was during my first six early years in the tropics that I came to grips with bedrock actuality in a primitive scene, and learned, through a geographical remoteness from social stimuli, the full value of self-dependence and an 'inner life.'

"I have been married twice; I have a son of twenty-four of whose talents as a painter I am proud; and I have written eighteen books, and am now at work on the nineteenth, a novel of the French Revolution, which I began to write in 1933. Until three years ago, when I settled down again in the United States, I lived mainly abroad, very often in the English country. My present husband, John Metcalfe, British short story writer and novelist, is now serving with the Royal Air Force, where he did duty during the First World War. Altogether, it can be said with accuracy that, 'both literally and metaphorically,' I have traveled far from the South of my childhood. But I owe it to the general aristocratic pretensions of the South, that I still prize most, in myself and in others, a man's control of his own spirit and mind—man's self-direction in the development of an inner life. And I owe it to the South that I never did, and do not now, see virtue in any proposal to make other people 'good' by force. The frail Puritan in me has died, and I hope will never be reborn.

"That is why I do not like philosophies that see man's salvation in terms of complete industrialization and a mechanized culture. Both World Revolutions and National Socialism seem to me theories without realism in any connection except that of acquiring power for dictators or bureaucracies. The present stressing of economics to the exclusion of everything else will eventually make us all spiritual imbeciles. I believe in the 'middle way': in the human as against the mechanized."

--------

Evelyn Scott, whose given name was Elsie Dunn, was born in Clarksville, Tennessee, the only child of Seely Dunn, a railroad executive, and Maude (Thomas) Dunn. At seventeen she was secretary of the Louisiana Women's Suffrage Party. At twenty she left for England with Frederick Creighton Wellman, a married man almost twice her age, dean of the School of Tropical Medicine at Tulane University. To escape the scandal that had followed them across the ocean, they moved to Brazil and adopted the names Cryil and Evelyn Scott. They never actually married. Years afterward Scott described the poverty and ill-health that characterized their residence in Brazil in her harrowing memoir, *Escapade*. It was in Brazil that her only child, Creighton, was born and that she began to publish in avant-garde literary magazines.

Returning to the United States in 1919, the Scotts settled in New York, where Evelyn threw herself into the Greenwich Village literary scene, befriending such writers as Lola Ridge and Kay Boyle and having affairs with William Carlos Williams and Waldo Frank. The aggressive bohemianism she adopted annoyed Cyril Scott. He remained with her until the 1930s; but her behavior permanently alienated her from her son, who regarded her (not without justice) ever after as a monster of egotism. Despite the frenetic social pace she kept up, she began to establish herself as a writer in 1921 with the publication of her first novel, *The Narrow House*. (A volume of imagist poems, *Precipitations*, had been published the year before, but few believed, then or now, that Scott had merit as a poet.) This story of an extended family locked inside the "moral cellar" of their loveless and unchanging relationships was declared a "literary event" by Sinclair Lewis, but its unremitting harshness prevented it from reaching a wide readership. However, Elizabeth Hardwick later wrote of it, "The observation of life in *The Narrow House* is unrelenting in its picture of private encirclement, but never does one feel it is untrue to its setting and its time as an American family portrait."

*The Narrow House* turned out to be the first volume in a trilogy of domestic defeat concerning three generations of an American family. Although the other two volumes, *Narcissus* and *The Golden Door*, received generally favorable reviews, they were not the sort of books that large numbers of the public delighted to read. The closest Scott ever came to commercial success was with her Civil War novel in 1929, *The Wave*. (This was the middle volume of a trilogy of American life in 1859–1914, very clearly influenced by Dos Passos: its predecessor was *Migration*, its successor *A Calendar of Sin*.)

*The Wave* is not an especially easy read either, consisting of myriads of interlocking stories and lacking any identifiable hero or heroine. Yet it was proclaimed by some unwary reviewers as the finest Civil War novel to that date, and for a time it gave Scott's name such currency that William Faulkner's publisher solicited from her a laudatory and perceptive preface to *The Sound and the Fury*, which was used as a key selling point in the promotion of that book. (Faulkner returned the favor, if equivocally, eleven years later by telling an interviewer who had asked which—if any—female writers he admired, "Well, Evelyn Scott was pretty good for a woman.") In *The Wave*, wrote Clifton Fadiman in the *Nation*, Scott "has set in motion a veritable army of characters, each provided with a complete background, as if each were originally conceived as the central figure of a novel. Indeed, Mrs. Scott's insight into and curiosity about her own creations are so vital and enthusiastic that it is only with great difficulty that she avoids . . . her major difficulty: that of so subordinating the tragedies and comedies of her individuals as to give the reader a continuous sense of the great national drama."

*The Wave* suffered from the flaws common to all Scott's fiction: prolixity, overwriting, formlessness. "Though *The Wave* is riveting," wrote Margo Jefferson in the *New York Times Book Review*, "it undercuts fine vernacular speech by putting slang expressions in quotes, favors gaudy nature descriptions and treats the lowliest whites with imaginative respect while offering the lowliest blacks (and there are none but the lowliest) histrionic pity. Evelyn Scott did not write masterpieces. She did write some real and vital novels that deserve to be read."

Scott did write two memoirs which, as good critics once argued, deserve to be read more than her ephemeral fiction. The first of these, *Escapade*, described with unusual candor the physical hardships and psychological stress of her first three years in Brazil. Henry Seidel Canby wrote, in the *Literary Review of the New York Evening Post*, that "her acute sensitiveness to external detail made [her] novels oppressive; here, where her nerves have a strange tropic world to play upon, a luminescence, as of the rays of a searchlight reflected from ocean, tree, mountain, and plain, is the result." Scott described her second memoir, *Background in Tennessee*, as recounting "a sixteen year love affair with Tennessee, disturbed at intervals by a deep unhappiness, later disillusion."

Scott's final book, *The Shadow of the Hawk*, is, according to D. A. Callard, "an idiosyncratic, though technically unexperimental, attempt at satire which . . . was doomed by her deficient sense of humor." By the time of its publication in 1941 she had already entered upon the slow decline that ended with her living, in Callard's words, "as a forgotten woman subsisting on the lowest rung of genteel poverty." Unable to publish a novel of the French Revolution, and convinced that left-wing conspirators were plotting against her, she spent her last decade in a shabby apartment building on the Upper West Side of Manhattan with her second husband, John Metcalfe, a English crime writer and reviewer who had himself seen better days. To Louise Bogan, a former acquaintance whom she encountered one day in the mid-1950s, Scott had become "not only frayed and dingy (she must have been a beauty in her youth) but silly and more than a little mad." She died of lung cancer. Several of her books have been reprinted in recent years, but despite Peggy Bach's assertion in the *Southern Review* that "she was a demonstrably important writer, who may one day again be perceived as major," no full-scale revival has yet occurred.

Scott's manuscripts are in the Humanities Research Center of the University of Texas; other papers are at Smith College and at the International Institute of Social History, Amsterdam.

PRINCIPAL WORKS: *Poetry*—Precipitations, 1920; The Winter Alone, 1930. *Novels*—The Narrow House, 1921; Narcissus, 1922 (in U.K.: Bewilderment); The Golden Door, 1925; Migrations: An Arabesque in Histories, 1927; The Wave, 1929; A Calendar of Sin: American Melodramas, 1931; Eva Gay: A Romantic Novel, 1933; Breathe upon These Slain, 1934; Bread and a Sword, 1937; The Shadow of the Hawk, 1941. *Short stories*—Ideals: A Book of Farce and Comedy, 1927. *Memoirs*—Escapade, 1923; Background in Tennessee, 1937. *Juvenile*—(with C. K. Scott) In the Endless Sands: A Christmas Book for Boys and Girls, 1925; Witch Perkins: A Story of the Kentucky Hills, 1929; (as "Ernest Souza") Blue Rum, 1930; Billy, the Maverick, 1934; The Fourteen Bears, Summer and Winter, 1973.

ABOUT: The autobiographical material quoted above was written for Twentieth Century Authors, 1942. American Women Writers (ed. L. Mainiero) 1981; Bloom, H. (ed.) Twentieth Century Literary Criticism Vol. 6, 1987; Bogan, L. What the Woman Lived: Selected Letters of Louise Bogan, 1920–1970, 1973; Callard, D. A. "Pretty Good for a Woman": The Enigmas of Evelyn Scott, 1985; Contemporary Authors Vol. 104, 1982; Contemporary Literary Criticism Vol. 43, 1987; Dictionary of Literary Biography Vol. 9, 1981; Vol. 48, 1986; Hardwick, E. introduction to The Narrow House, 1977. *Periodicals*—Literary Review of the New York Evening Post September 8, 1923; Nation July 31, 1929; New York Herald Tribune Books October 17, 1937; New York Times Book Review March 2, 1986; Southern Review Autumn 1982.

**SCOTT, WINFIELD TOWNLEY** (April 30, 1910–April 28, 1968), American poet, wrote: "The question, though irrelevant, is so frequent that perhaps I should begin by answering it: No, I am not related to the famous U.S. general whose name I bear. Some of my American ancestry dates from 1620, but for the most part it is Scots-English—farmers and mill workers who settled in New England in, I think, the 1840s. Nobody  even remotely literary or even 'artistic,' barring Job Townsend and John Goddard, cabinetmakers now revered by antiquarians. One of my grandfathers was a good shoe manufacturer, the other a good hardware storekeeper, and my father at various times in his life was employed by both.

"Like Mark Twain, I was born under Halley's Comet (a few days after he also died under it). That was in Haverhill, Massachusetts, but I lived my first ten years in Newport, Rhode Island. Then back to Haverhill. I attended public schools in both cities. I believe I was a very quiet little boy for there were always old ladies who told me stories: I must have sat a great deal. I became a very bookish little boy and soon—I don't know how soon, but before I was ten—I began scribbling stories and had only the one ambition, to 'to be an author.' In Haverhill High School the ambition became specific when we were assigned *The Rime of the Ancient Mariner*. I was dazzled as by sudden revelation. Then and there I thought poetry the most wonderful thing in the world, and I still think so. My own first poems (*not* among the most wonderful, however I may have then felt about them) were printed in the high school paper and, presently, in *Scholastic* magazine.

"My year of graduation from Brown University, 1931, was a year of frightening economic depression, but I had the great luck of a part-time job assisting the literary editor of the *Providence Journal*, for which, as an undergraduate, I had been writing book reviews; and though now and then I had other part-time work—such as ghost-writing speeches and a brief spell of teaching at Brown—I continued on the *Journal* in its book and movie, and radio departments for twenty years, the last ten as its literary editor. In 1951 I resigned to have my writing time to myself. I still do a few book reviews for various publications and now and then a literary essay, but my principal concern continues to be poetry.

"I have had—and I think this is generally true in the field—neither extremes of fortune: some difficulties of publication, but so far temporary ones; some awards and honors. I take it as axiomatic that the attempt to create poetry, as a career, never receives indubitable proof of success; never, certainly, in one's lifetime. . . ."

---

Winfield Townley Scott drew much of his poetic material from the landscapes, characters, and speech patterns of his native New England. His once widely praised "Mr. Whittier," for example, is a portrait of the nineteenth-century New England poet. In a *New York Times* (1948) review of *Mr. Whittier and Other Poems*, Selden Rodman commented, "it is encouraging to find a real craftsman working in the main stream of American poetry—and working it steadily toward mature accomplishment."

But critics more discerning than Rodman found Scott's plainspoken style lame and unevocative. In a *Sewanee Review* notice of his previous collection, *To Marry Strangers*, Robert Lowell wrote, "Scott has no ear. His lyrics are slow, unpretentious, professional and pedestrian." Although he had become a respected literary journalist—having made the *Providence Journal* book page into one of the finest outside New York—and had won praise from such fellow poets as Horace Gregory and William Carlos Williams, Scott was plagued with doubts about the value of his work, and endured frustrating periods of writer's block. From 1948 to 1958, he published poems in various magazines, but not a single book.

His 1946 marriage to the independently wealthy Eleanor Metcalf effectively ended his financial insecurity. In 1954 the couple and their children moved to Santa Fe, New Mexico; it was the first time Scott had lived outside New England. Four years later he published his most ambitious work, *The Dark Sister*, a long narrative poem that recounts a Norse voyage from Greenland to Vinland (North America), led by Freydis, the power-mad half-sister of Leif Ericson. It won a mixed but mostly favorable critical reception. The late poet and critic James Wright summed up posterity's judgment when he complained of "the failure of its language to attain any deep intensity, and complex excitement."

Scott's next collection, *Scrimshaw*, contains one of his better-known poems, "Come Green Again."

After evoking images of Thoreau, Hawthorne, Melville, Twain, and Whitman, the poet concludes:

What I have learned enough
To have as air to breathe
Returns as memory
Of undiminished love:
That no man's creation
But enlarges me.
O all come green again."

In a personal letter, William Carlos Williams lavished praise on the work: "A triumph of poetry, it fairly springs from the page at me . . . I think such writing has a permanent value.

Scott's *Collected Poems* was nominated for a 1963 National Book Award. In 1966 he received the Harriet Monroe *Poetry* prize. In a *Poetry* (1968) review of *New and Selected Poems*, a collection that appeared shortly before Scott's death, Hayden Carruth gallantly declared "He has a splendid talent for story poems and biographical poems, to my mind a talent equal to Frost's and probably greater, yet he has used it sparingly." Toward the end of his life, Scott was mired in depression and drink. He died of an overdose of alcohol and sleeping pills; since he left no final note, was in the midst of several projects, and had been abusing drink and pills for some time, it is not clear whether or not he meant to take his own life. In a *New York Times Book Review* notice of Scott's posthumously-published literary notebooks," Webster Schott claimed that Scott "wrote superbly in the great middle of American poetry—the tradition that includes Emily Dickinson, Edward Arlington Robinson, possibly Frost. But during his lifetime [his work] could not yield what he needed above all else—an absolute conviction of his own worth."

Eleanor Scott edited the collection of prose and poetry, *Alpha Omega*, which appeared after her husband's death. There is a collection of Scott's papers in the John Hay Library at Brown University.

PRINCIPAL WORKS: *Poetry*—Elegy for Robinson, 1936; Biography for Traman, 1937; Wind the Clock, 1941; The Sword on the Table: Thomas Dorr's Rebellion, 1942; To Marry Strangers, 1945; Mr. Whittier and Other Poems, 1948; The Dark Sister, 1958; Scrimshaw, 1959; Collected Poems: 1937–1948, 1962; Change of Weather, 1964; New and Selected Poems (ed. E. Scott) 1967. *Essays*—Exiles and Fabrications, 1961; Alpha Omega (ed. E. Scott) 1971. *Notebooks*—"a dirty hand": The Literary Notebooks of Winfield Townley Scott (ed. M. Armitage) 1969. *As editor*—The Man with the Calabash Pipe (by O. La Farge) 1966; Poems of Robert Herrick, 1967; Judge Me Tenderley: Selected Poems of Emily Dickinson, 1968.

ABOUT: The autobiographical material quoted above was written for Twentieth Century Authors First Supplement, 1955. Contemporary Authors New Revision Series 7 1982; Ciardi, J. (ed.) Mid-Century American Poets, 1950; Donaldson, S. Poet in America: Winfield Townley Scott, 1972; Elliott, G. (ed.) Fifteen Modern American Poets, 1956; Hanulton, I. (ed.) The Oxford Companion to Twentieth-Century American Poetry, 1994. *Periodicals*—New York Times November 7, 1948; April 29 1968; New York Times Book Review September 16, 1979; Ohio Review no. 51 1994; Poetry October 1958, September 1968; Saturday Review April 12, 1958; Sewanee Review Winter 1946.

## SCOTT-MONCRIEFF, CHARLES KENNETH

**SCOTT-MONCRIEFF, CHARLES KENNETH** (September 25, 1889–February 28, 1930), Scottish translator and poet, was born into a distin-

guished but unprosperous family in Stirlingshire. He was the youngest of the three sons of William George Scott-Moncrieff, Sheriff-Substitute of County Lanark. The boy went to Inverness College and as a scholar to Winchester, where (in 1908) he rashly published a homosexual story. At Edinburgh University he was graduated in 1914 with first class honors in English. Mobilized that August into the King's Own Scottish Borderers, he was promoted to captain in 1915. Two years later, he was severely wounded in the leg on the Somme, under circumstances that earned him a Military Cross for gallantry.

Invalided home, Scott-Moncrieff spent the rest of the war on administrative duties at the War Office. In his spare time he translated the medieval French epic *Chanson de Roland*, and contributed reviews and patriotic poems to magazines. He was a tiresomely patriotic versifier, but a brilliant *pasticheur*.

Scott-Moncrieff was a strikingly handsome man, with dark blue eyes and a soft deep voice. According to Dominic Hibberd, biographer of Wilfred Owen, he was also promiscuous, jealous, and quarrelsome, with a talent for making enemies. These included Siegfried Sassoon, whose poems he savaged, and the Sitwells, whom he villified in the *New Witness*. He also caused much offense and distress with a review of Wilfred Owen's poems that referred to his alleged "loss of morale" while shellshocked. This was odd, since Scott-Moncrieff was in love with Owen, wooed him with sub-Shakespearian sonnets—and tried to pull strings at the War Office to avert his return to the Front. (He failed, and Owen was killed a week before the war ended.)

In 1920 Scott-Moncrieff became secretary to Lord Northcliffe, afterwards working on the magnate's flagship, the *Times*, until he persuaded Chatto & Windus to commission a translation of Marcel Proust's *À la recherche du temps perdu*. Scott-Moncrieff shipped his books to Italy, perhaps partly to escape the demands of indigent relatives—the only recreation he listed in *Who's Who* is "nepotism." He was in Pisa until 1927, then Rome. He never recovered from the effects of the war, and died at forty.

Scott-Moncrieff published notable translations of Stendhal, Pirandello, and others, but his reputation stands on his version of Proust's masterpiece, of which he had translated all but the last volume when he died. George Painter in his biography of Proust called it "a great translation which, although not free from elementary but important errors, is a masterly re-creation of the original." Scott-Moncrieff believed that, in translating, it is more important to have a perfect command of one's own language than that of the original. He did as much as anyone to raise the art of the translator to an honorable estate.

PRINCIPAL WORKS: Memories and Letters (eds. J. M. Scott-Moncrieff and L. W. Lunn) 1931. *As translator of Marcel Proust*—Remembrance of Things Past (6 of 7 volumes), 1922–1931 (in U.K.: 7 of 8 volumes). *As translator of "Stendhal" (Henri Beyle)*—The Abbess of Castro and Other Tales, 1926; Armance, 1928; The Charterhouse of Parma, 1937; The Red and Black, 1937 (in U.K.: Scarlet and Black; The Shorter Novels of Stendhal, 1946. *As translator of others*—The song of Roland, 1919; Widsith, Beowulf, Finnsburgh, Waldere, Deor, 1921; Shoot! (by L. Pirandello) 1926; The Old and the Young (by L. Pirandello) 1928; Memoirs of the Duc de Lauzun, 1928; The Adventures of Zeloide and Amanzarifdine (by A. P. de Moncrif) 1929; "—& Co." (by J. R. Bloch) 1929; The Letters of Abelard and Heloise, 1942. *As compiler*—Marcel Proust: An English Tribute, 1924.

ABOUT: Hibberd, D. Owen the Poet, 1986; Hibberd, D. Wilfred Owen: The Last Year, 1992; Painter, G. Marcel Proust: a Biography, 1989; Pearson, J. Façades: Edith, Osbert, and Sacheverell Sitwill, 1978; Scott-Moncrieff, C. K. Memories and Letters (eds. J. M. Scott Moncrieff and L. W. Lunn) 1931; Who Was Who 1916–1928 (for father); Who's Who 1930. *Periodical*—London Mercury April 1930.

## SEABROOK, WILLIAM BUEHLER

**SEABROOK, WILLIAM BUEHLER** (February 22, 1886–September 20, 1945), American occultist and travel writer, was born in Westminster, Maryland, the son of Wil-

liam Levin Seabrook, an itinerant Lutheran minister, and Myra Phelps (Buehler) Seabrook. After graduating from Newberry College in South Carolina, he took a job as cub reporter on the Augusta, Georgia, *Chronicle*, later becoming city editor. He made his first trip to Europe around 1908 and returned to the United States to work on the *Atlanta Journal* before cofounding an advertising agency. During World War I he served overseas as an ambulance driver for the American Field Service and was gassed at Verdun. After the war he spent time as a gentleman farmer on a plantation outside Atlanta. Then he went to New York and worked as a reporter for the *New York Times*, followed by a job as a writer for King Features Syndicate.

In 1924 Seabrook visited the Middle East; three years later he recounted his experiences in his first book *Adventures in Arabia*, which, according to *New York Herald Tribune Books* (1927), was "written with sincerity and persuasive charm." Next Seabrook set his sights on a book about voodoo and spent two years living in Haiti: *The Magic Island* was published in 1929 and became a best-seller. The *New York Evening Post* called it the "best and most thrilling book of exploration that we ever have read. Mr. Seabrook has investigated Voodooism, not with the rigid superiority of the average white man delving into native lore but humbly, respectfully, as an initiate himself."

Seabrook next journeyed to Africa and gathered material for his third book, *Jungle Ways*. This time reviews were mixed. The *Saturday Review of Literature* called it a "book that you will hate to lay down. . . . It will certainly shock you—but you will finish it." *New York Herald Tribune Books* (1931), however, condemned Seabrook for being "clamorously autobiographical, so tiresomely self-revealing, so exclusively concerned with what he's rightly sure is *Hot Stuff*, that Africa becomes obscured." Among the "hot stuff" related in the book is an account in which Seabrook describes eating the flesh of a young man, "who had not been murdered," offered to him by cannibals. In his autobiography *No Hiding Place*, he later revealed that the tribe had tricked him by substituting the meat of an ape. However, he went on to claim (almost certainly falsely) that in France he eventually did consume human flesh, taken from the body of a human killed in an accident.

Seabrook's second ex-wife, the novelist Marjorie Worthington, supported Seabrook's claim in her 1966 memoir *The Strange World of Willie Seabrook*, but unconvincingly. She went on to describe the years she and Seabrook lived in France and their exotic travels together; she also discussed Seabrook's heavy drinking and his sexually sadistic tendencies, although she points out that "in spite of the sexual pattern that he let dominate his life, he was no Marquis de Sade. He was a fine, intelligent, and lovable man, with a touch of genius as well as madness." In Irving Wallace's sensationalist book *Intimate Sex Lives of Famous People*, Seabrook's lifelong fetish is described as "soft sadism," taking the form of chaining or tying women up, but never hurting or making love to them. By the 1930s Seabrook's colorful travels had made him famous. His acute alcoholism, however, forced him to check into Bloomingdale Hospital, White Plains, New York, for a seven-month stay, an interlude he candidly described in his memoir, *Asylum*.

In 1941 Seabrook returned to the occult in *Witchcraft*, a not thorough study of black magic in different parts of the world; again, reviews were mixed. While the *New York Times* found it "interesting," the *Atlantic Monthly*, more accurately, called it a "mediocre jerry-built affair . . . haphazard, poorly executed, vulgar in style." Seabrook's next book was *Doctor Wood*, a biography of the American physicist Robert Williams Wood. Of the author's efforts to present aspects of Wood's unconventional behavior, including his pranks, the *Christian Century* declared that "Seabrook, habituated to writing about wild men, seems to feel that his present subject belongs in the series."

William Seabrook was a contributor to the *Reader's Digest* and other publications. His acquaintances included Gertrude Stein, Aleister Crowley, Aldous Huxley, Isadora Duncan, Man Ray, Emma Goldman, Thomas Mann, and Jean Cocteau. His last book was his autobiography *No Hiding Place*; the title proved prophetic: he was unable to escape his own demons, including alcohol. He took his own life with an overdose of barbiturates at his farm near Rhinebeck, New York.

PRINCIPAL WORKS: *Nonfiction*—Adventures in Arabia Among the Bedouins, Druses, Whirling Dervishes and Yezidee Devil-Worshipers, 1927; The Magic Island, 1929 (also published as The Voodoo Island, 1929); Jungle Ways, 1931; Air Adventure: Paris—Sahara—Timbuctoo, 1933; The White Monk of Timbuctoo, 1934; These Foreigners, 1938 (in U.K.: Americans All: A Human Study of America's Citizens from Europe); Witchcraft: Its Power in the World Today, 1940; Doctor Wood: Modern Wizard of the Laboratory: The Story of an American Small Boy Who Became the Most Daring and Original Experimental Physicist of Our Day—But Never Grew Up, 1941. *Memoirs*—Asylum, 1935; No Hiding Place, 1942.

ABOUT: Current Biography 1940; Dictionary of Literary Biography vol. 4, 1980; Neagoe, P. (ed.) Americans Abroad, 1932; Wallace, I. (et. al.) Intimate Sex Lives of Famous People, 1981; Worthington, M. The Strange World of Willie Seabrook, 1966. *Periodicals*—Atlantic Monthly October 1940; Christian Century November 19, 1941; New York Evening Post January 12, 1929; New York Herald Tribune Books September 4, 1927; April 19, 1931; New York Times September 15, 1940; Saturday Review of Literature April 4, 1931.

**SEAGER, ALLAN** (February 5, 1906–May 10, 1968), American novelist and short story writer, wrote: "I was born in Adrian, Michigan, a small town. Both my grandfathers had settled in the region after the Civil War. Beauman Seager, a Vermonter and a cousin of President Benjamin Harrison, had taken up bounty land. John Allan, an English orphan boy educated at the Blue Coat School had come to this country as a bricklayer in  time to be a soldier. My father was a traveling salesman who knew the whole Mississippi Valley. Sherwood Anderson said he was one of the best storytellers he ever heard and 'if you have any talent, it comes from him.' It was my mother, however, who read to me young and gave me an interest in books. None of my kinfolk was literary in any sense.

"When I was about ten, we moved to Memphis, Tennessee. Hating the place as a Yankee, solemnly reading a hundred pages a day aside from my school work, composing a few worthless, unshowable poems, I wanted to write but I thought there was a special way to do it that someone could show me. No one did (no one ever does) either there or at the University of Michigan where it is not study or classrooms I remember, rather a frieze of pretty girls and long aimless journeys in cars at night. I did, however, make Phi Bete and a Rhodes Scholarship in my senior year.

"From my English grandfather I had expected a journey to England to be, in a sense, a return. I was mistaken. It was foreign country more so than the France, Spain, Germany, and Switzerland I visited in the holidays. It was at an English pub, however, that I began to write, The Crown, East Hanney, Berks. I was stuck there the summer because I had no money and I spent it on a story Sir John Squire bought for the *London Mercury*. I felt then I had a start.

"Returning to New York in the midst of the depression I was fortunate to be hired as an assistant to Frank Crowninshield on *Vanity Fair*. The magazine was dying but I published several stories in it and I learned enough about New York from Crownie's assignments to know that it was not my city. I came to teach part-time at the University of Michigan and except for one year at Bennington College and a year in Hollywood I have been there ever since. Meeting students, young, hopeful, uncorrupt, is a continuing refreshing experience from which I have learned any amount.

"Once I would have hesitated to say that the novel is the conscience of the middle class but when I remember my own, *Equinox, The Inheritance,* and *Amos Berry,* I discover that I believe it. A pleasure of middle-age is the acceptance of one's own origins, whatever one has pretended, however ambivalent the bonds. If I can say anything about the sources of my own work, I believe they lie in the tensions of that ambivalence.

"I live in a village full of maple trees, Tecumseh, Michigan, and I drive the twenty-six miles to Ann Arbor three times a week. My wife, whom I married in 1939, is a beautiful, patient woman, the mother of two beautiful little girls from whom I am learning everything I know all over again."

---

"Allan Seager is one of those shadowy figures, 'the minor writer,' whose neglect at the hands of both public and critics has been lamented but never remedied," wrote Stephen E. Connelly in the preface to his monograph *Allan Seager.* Connelly believed that chief among the reasons for this neglect was Seager's bad luck: the best-seller status of *Equinox* was cut short by the World War II paper shortage; *Death in Anger* was released with little fanfare by a publishing house that was going under; and *The Glass House,* his biography of poet Theodore Roethke, suffered because of his disagreements with Roethke's widow. Seager's emphasis on ideas, his lack of self-publicity, and his choice of settings and subject matter, i.e. the Midwest and the middle class, also contributed to his "shadowy figure" status. Nevertheless, Malcolm Cowley, James Dickey, Robert Penn Warren, and Carl Sandburg were among the admirers of his work.

Connelly describes *Equinox,* Seager's first novel, as containing virtually all his recurring motifs: the "individual's loss of control over his own life, the paralysis of the will, the inability of individuals to see, let alone alter, the forces controlling their lives. It has the central Seager concern: the 'basic American theme' of man trying to be free." The novel's main character is foreign correspondent Richard Miles, who returns to New York where his seventeen-year-old daughter Mary makes a home for him and worships him. "Into this innocent concurrence of dreams come stupid or malicious hints, warning Miles that her devotion is somewhat extrafilial," Marjorie Farber wrote in the *New York Times* (1943). "This unnatural label 'incest,' pinned on a complex human reality, precipitates tragedy." The tragedy comes in the form of Mary's suicide. Of all Seager's novels, *Equinox* garnered the largest readership, yet, as with his later novels, the reviews were mixed. The *Yale Review's* Orville Preston

called it "phoney and cheaply vulgar," but went on to declare that "Seager writes with such elan, such verve, power, and gusto, and creates such tense drama and such wonderful minor characters that *Equinox* is impressive and astonishing stuff."

Throughout his career Seager continued to dramatize what the *New York Times* (1968) called "dark psychological tensions and themes of social protest." *Amos Berry* concerns the strained relationship between an aspiring poet and his corporate executive father, who murders his boss and commits suicide. *Hilda Manning* is a story of murder and adultery set in a Midwestern town. Infidelity and the ultimate acceptance of an unhappy life are central themes in *Death of Anger,* the story of a man unable to break away from his marriage.

Allan Seager was a prolific writer of short stories and essays, published in such periodicals as *Cosmopolitan, Esquire,* the *New Yorker,* and the *Saturday Evening Post.* He was a professor of English at the University of Michigan at his death.

PRINCIPAL WORKS: *Novels*—Equinox, 1943; The Inheritance, 1948; Amos Berry, 1953; Hilda Manning, 1956; Death of Anger, 1960. *Short stories*—The Old Man of the Mountain, and Seventeen Other Stories, 1950. *Nonfiction*—They Worked for a Better World, 1939; A Frieze of Girls: Memoirs as Fiction, 1964; The Glass House: The Life of Theodore Roethke, 1968.

ABOUT: The autobiographical material quoted above was written for Twentieth Century Authors, 1955. Connelly, S. E. Allan Seager, 1983; Contemporary Authors 1994. *Periodicals*—New York Times August 22, 1943; May 11, 1968; Yale Review Autumn 1943.

**SEAMAN, OWEN** (September 18, 1861–February 2, 1936), English parodist and editor of *Punch,* was born in London and educated at Mill Hill and Shrewsbury, where he became captain of the school. At Clare College, Cambridge, he studied classics, and was a collaborator with his friends Henry Ford and Horace Munro on the publication of *Paulopost-prandials,* a skit on university manners. After university, he worked for  a time as a schoolmaster at Rossall and then became professor of literature at Durham College of Science.

He was called to the bar in 1897, the same year in which he joined the staff of *Punch,* having been submitting contributions for some time (notably "The Rhyme Of The Kipperling," a Kipling send-up which appeared in 1894) and already having published a number of parody collections, including *Horace at Cambridge* and *The Battle of the Bays.* Seaman became an assistant editor of *Punch* in 1902, and editor (succeeding Sir Francis Burnand) in 1906. His period at the helm spanned more than a quarter of a decade.

Seaman, who was knighted in 1914, published three wartime collections—*War-time* (1915), *Made in England* (1916), and *From the Home Front* (1918)—which showed him as capable of poor patriotic dignity as of robust ridicule. After the war, he published only one more volume, *Interludes of an Editor*. His time at *Punch*, in terms of the magazine's outward appearance, was marked by the addition of the color red to the front cover "to make it more prominent on the bookstalls." Otherwise, the publication remained a bastion of stability in a period of momentous change. "We are not fond of change in England," the obituary in the *New York Times* quoted him as having said. He viewed humor and parody as the essential neutralizers of self-righteous ostentation. "The function of humor is that of a solvent against shame and hypocrisies. It is a corrective against vulgarities and extravagancies. It clears the air."

Seaman was a Browning enthusiast and, as a young man, had frequently lectured on the poet. He was an active patron of good causes, those who benefited including the training ship HMS *Implacable* and the Chailey Heritage school for the disabled. He retired as editor in 1932, when he underwent a serious operation, recovering sufficiently to enjoy a short spell of active retirement. Because of his never having married, the baronetcy, which was granted to him in 1933, terminated with his death.

*Punch's* own obituary commented on Seaman's editorial qualities: "If there was a tinge of academician in his love of logic and dislike of irrelevance, he was at any rate a master of technique, and in an age progressively inclined to claim poetic license in form as well as matter, he maintained in his own work and demanded from his contributors a high standard of workmanship." A few years earlier, Seaman himself had written, in a farewell editorial, about "the price editorship with its heartbreaking armoury of rejection-forms and, in the case of a critical paper like *Punch*, the obligation it lays upon an Editor to encourage the correction and even the ridicule of better men than himself."

Readers missed him most for his own rhymes of ridicule, printed invariably on a left-hand page and signed "O.S." Most were amusing for their topical reference, but a few have stood the test of time as lasting parodies: "A Ballad of a Bun" (taking off John Davidson's "A Ballad of a Nun"), "To Julia Under Lock and Key" (a pastiche of Herrick), and "The Rhyme of the Kipperling."

PRINCIPAL WORKS: Horace at Cambridge, 1895; Tillers of the Sand, 1895; The Battle of the Bays, 1896; In Cap and Bells, 1900; Borrowed Plumes, 1902; A Harvest of Chaff, 1904; Salvage, 1908; War-time, 1915; Made in England, 1916; From the Home Front, 1918; Interludes of an Editor, 1929.

ABOUT: Adlard, J. Owen Seaman: His Life and Work, 1977; Dictionary of National Biography, 1931–1940, 1949; Graves, C. L. (ed.) Owen Seaman, a Selection, 1937; Who's Who 1935. *Periodicals*—New York Times February 3, 1936; Punch January 13, 1894; November 9, 1932; February 12, 1936; Times (London) February 3, 1936.

**SEAVER, EDWIN** (January 18, 1900– ), American novelist and critic, wrote: "I was born in Washington, D.C., spent my childhood in Philadelphia, went to Worcester Academy, Worcester, Massachusetts, and to college at Harvard (class of 1922). . . . At Harvard I studied the catalogue as-

siduously to find out what the easiest courses were . . . and spent most of my time reading all the good books I had ever wanted to read in the most comfortable chairs provided by the Widener Library and the Harvard Union. I was one of the editors of the *Harvard Monthly*, founded in opposition to what seemed to me then the deadly dull *Harvard Advocate*. . . . Also I was an editor of a short-lived but very lively four-page sheet called the *Proletarian*, which was likewise an opposition sheet, there being at that time another short-lived but decidedly not lively four-page sheet called the *Aristocrat*. I also took Professor Briggs' course in poetry, from which I learned that I didn't want to be a polite poet; refused to take Professor Copeland's writing course because I didn't want anybody to teach me how to write; but petitioned Irving Babbitt to be allowed to take his graduate course in literary criticism, although I was only a sophomore then, and learned more about letters from the 'reactionary' Professor Babbitt than from all my liberal professors.

"I should mention finally that my first two months at Harvard were spent in the Students' Army Training Corps, learning how to stick a bayonet in a dummy, and ending with an honorable discharge from the U.S. Army. I am afraid I was not a very good soldier. A year later came the Boston Police strike, and the monstrous distortions of fact in that set-up, as reported in the press, helped me to understand what happened when Sacco and Vanzetti became sacrificial victims on the altar of Massachusetts justice.

"Coming down to New York in 1922, I got my first job with a big publicity outfit. I was fired for asking for a raise, and became publicity director for the American Civil Liberties Union, and at the same time joined the staff of the *New York Call*, Socialist daily, later going over to the *New York Leader*, which inherited the *Call*. I was likewise on the staff of *Advance*, weekly newspaper of the Amalgamated Clothing Workers. It was about this time that I began reviewing for the *New Republic*, the *Nation*, the *Freeman*, the *Dial*, and other magazines.

"In 1923 I married Anna Vera Bass and in 1924 we went to live in the artists' colony in Woodstock, N.Y. There we founded and edited the little magazine *1924*. Among our contributors were Hart Crane, Ezra Pound, William Carlos Williams, Yvor Winters, Waldo Frank, and Kenneth Burke. Returning to New York at the end of 1925 I took another publicity job with a public utilities corporation for a year, and then returned to Woodstock on the invitation of a number of artists who asked me to tutor their children.

"It was at this time that I began writing what was later to become my first book, but which I then thought of as a series of sketches about white collar workers. . . . Our daughter was born in 1927 and the following year we returned to New York, where I took a job as assistant publicity director for the Federation of Jewish Charities. At the same time I was on the reviewing staffs of the New York *Sun* and *Evening Post*, having a regular weekly column in the latter paper. I helped to found the *New Masses* and was also editor-in-chief of the monthly magazine *Soviet Russia Today* and later literary editor of the *Daily Worker*, contributing a column daily and a page on Sundays. I should perhaps add that I was *not* a member of the Communist Party and have always thought it odd that people assumed I was, whereas nobody ever charged me with being a member of the Republican Party when I was writing for the *Evening Post* and the *Sun*. I also was one of the founders of the League of American Writers and participated actively in the first Writers' Congress.

"From 1937 to 1939 I was a radio book reviewer for radio station WQXR, New York, and lectured at the New School for Social Research. About 1938 I joined the reading staff of the Book of the Month Club. . . . "

Edwin Seaver's literary debut, *The Company*, a novel consisting of a series of sketches on white-collar life in New York, was a success. Reviewing it in the *New York Herald Tribune Books*, Horace Gregory wrote, "Quite in his own fashion Edwin Seaver has written the *Winesburg, Ohio* of the American business office." However, his second novel, *Between the Hammer and the Anvil*, which dramatizes the lives of impoverished tenement dwellers, met with almost universal disapprobation. James T. Farrell, writing in the *Nation*, called it "intellectually pretentious," and the *New York Times* critic Alfred Kazin noted, "Sections of it are deeply moving; but a good many others are ragged and shrill." Seaver never published another novel.

In an effort to acquaint the public with material not found in either the commercial magazines or the "little" magazines, Seaver created and edited *Cross-Section*, four anthologies of previously unpublished prose, poetry, and drama by a diverse group of American writers. While some of his contributors were established authors, many more—including Ralph Ellison, Arthur Miller, and Norman Mailer—were at that time little-known. In the late 1940s, Seaver was forced to resign from the Book of the Month Club because of the anti-Communist hysteria generated by the House Un-American Activities Committee. He later went to work in the publicity and advertising department of the Boston publisher Little, Brown.

Seaver's memoir, *So Far So Good: Recollections of a Life in Publishing*, his first book in almost forty years, appeared when he was eighty-six. As a *Library Quarterly* reviewer noted, "Despite its subtitle, *So Far So Good* is a personal, not an intellectual or professional, memoir." Seaver himself calls it a "random chronicle," and touches variously on aspects of his youth, family, and early literary activities as a "fellow traveler." His parents were Jewish immigrants from Eastern Europe, and Seaver marvels at how remarkably "incurious" he must have been never to learn their country of origin or his own mother's maiden name. He records his left-wing sympathies, but details his disagreements with doctrinaire Marxists. By the 1940s, he insists, he was "politically a neuter." Recalling an appearance he was forced to make before Senator McCarthy's committee, he writes, "The defenders of our national innocence must have been scraping the bottom of the barrel when they subpoenaed anybody as unimportant to their purposes as I was. I had thought that my commie past was buried under some twenty years of indifference, not to mention unawareness that I even existed" (*So Far So Good*).

PRINCIPAL WORKS: *Novels*—The Company, 1930; Between the Hammer and the Anvil, 1937. *Law*—(with W. Weeks) All in the Racket, 1930. *As editor*—Cross-Section: A Collection of New American Writing, 1944; 1945; 1947; 1948; Worlds Great Love Novels, 1944; Pageant of American Humor, 1948. *Memoirs*—So Far So Good: Recollections of a Life in Publishing, 1986.

ABOUT: The autobiographical material quoted above was written for Twentieth Century Authors, 1942. *Periodicals*—Library Quarterly April 1988; Nation March 13, 1937; New York Herald Tribune Books March 23, 1930; New York Times February 21, 1937; Publishers Weekly August 22, 1986.

**SEAWELL, MOLLY ELLIOT** (October 23, 1860–November 15, 1916), American novelist, was born on a plantation in Gloucester County, Virginia, the daughter of John Tyler Seawell, a lawyer, who was the nephew of President John Tyler, and Frances (Jackson) Seawell. She was educated at home; on the death of Mr. Seawell the family moved to Norfolk and then to Washington, D.C., where she lived for the rest of her life.

"I was but little past my twenty-first birthday when, on the strength of having earned about seven hundred dollars by my pen, I rashly assumed the support, by literature, of my family," she wrote in *The Ladies' Battle*. "The rashness, ignorance, and presumption of this can only be excused by the secluded life I led in the library of an old Virginia country house, and in a community where conditions more nearly resembled the eighteenth than the  nineteenth century. In the course of time I became through literature alone, a householder, a property-owner, a taxpayer, and the regular employer of five persons." In Washington Seawell became a political correspondent for several New York papers. One of her first successful ventures into fiction was *Hale-Weston*, a novel published in *Lippincott's Monthly Magazine* in 1899; it proved quite successful and was translated into German. Seawell also won a number of literary prizes, including $3,000 from the *New York Herald* in 1895 for her novelette *The Sprightly Romance of Marsac*. She was a popular and prolific writer, known in particular for her historical romances.

According to *The Feminist Companion to Literature in English* her "plots favour fallen aristocrats and the dilemmas of a man or woman in love with two suitors at once." In 1906 the *Outlook* called her novel, *The Loves of the Lady Arabella,* an "old fashioned romance, with its familiar types and conventional action," but also alleged that she possessed traits which lifted her above the mediocre, noting that the book was "charming because of its literary style and generally artistic workmanship."

Seawell also wrote plays and children's books. From an uncle she heard stories of seafaring exploits which she later utilized in her popular *Young Heroes of Our Navy Series.* Her book *Twelve Naval Captains* was used as a text at the U.S. Naval Academy. In addition to *The Ladies' Battle,* an anti-women's suffrage book, her political writing included *Despotism and Democracy: A Study in Washington Society and Politics.*

Seawell also wrote under the pen name "Foxcroft Davis."

PRINCIPAL WORKS: *Novels*—The Berkeleys and Their Neighbors, 1888, rev. ed. 1892; Hale-Weston, 1888; Throckmorton, 1890; Children of Destiny, 1893; Through Thick and Thin, and The Midshipmen's Mess: A Soldier Story and a Sailor Story, 1893; Decatur and Somers, 1894; The Sprightly Romance of Marsac, 1896; The Strange, Sad Comedy, 1896; A Virginia Cavalier, 1896; The History of Lady Betty Stair, 1897; The Loves of the Lady Arabella, 1898; The Rock of the Lion, 1898; The Lively Adventures of Gavin Hamilton, 1899; The House of Egremont, 1900; Papa Bouchard, 1901; Francezka, 1902; The Fortunes of Fifi, 1903; (as "Foxcroft Davis") Mrs. Darrell, 1905; The Chateau of Montplaisir, 1906; The Victory, 1906; The Secret of Toni, 1907; (as "Foxcroft Davis") The Whirl: A Romance of Washington Society, 1909; The Marriage of Theodora, 1910; The Jugglers, 1911; The Last Duchess of Belgarde, 1911; The Lost Battle, 1911; Betty's Virginia Christmas, 1914; The Diary of a Beauty, 1915; Betty at Fort Blizzard, 1916. *Short stories*—Maid Marian, and Other Stories, 1891; Quarterdeck and Fok'sle: Stories of the Sea, 1895; (with H. Pyle, W. Packard, et. al.) Strange Stories of the Revolution, 1907. *Nonfiction*—Twelve Naval Captains: Being a Record of Certain Americans Who Made Themselves Immortal, 1897; Despotism and Democracy: A Study in Washington Society and Politics, 1903; The Ladies' Battle, 1911. *Juvenile*—Little Jarvis, 1890; Midshipman Paulding, 1891; Paul Jones, 1893; (with J. Barnes, E. D. Deland, et. al.) Boys on the Railroad, 1900; Laurie Vane, and Other Stories, 1901; The Great Scoop, 1903; The Imprisoned Midshipmen, 1908; The Son of Columbus, 1912.

ABOUT: Blain, V., Grundy, I., and Clements, P. The Feminist Companion to Literature in English, 1900; Dictionary of American Biography Vol. 16, 1935. *Periodicals*—New York Times November 16, 1916; Outlook December 15, 1906.

## SECOND, HENRY. See HARRISON, HENRY SYDNOR

## SEDGWICK, ANNE DOUGLAS (March 28, 1873–July 19, 1935), Anglo-American novelist, was born in Englewood, New Jersey, the daughter of George Stanley Sedgwick and Mary (Douglas) Sedgwick. She spent most of her childhood living with her family in England and France. She was educated at home by a governess, then studied art in Paris for five years. In 1908 she married the writer Basil De Selincourt and settled in Kingham, Oxfordshire, England.

Sedgwick's literary career had its roots in the long stories she told to her sisters. After she wrote one of them down her father discovered the manuscript and submitted it to a publisher; *The Dull Miss Archinard* was published in 1898. Sedgwick soon took up writing in earnest.

Elizabeth Bowen states in *Collected Impressions* that Sedgwick's "novels were the Edwardian novel at its best: one cannot too much honour her skill, their integrity—for integrity they must have, or their charm would make one uneasy. She delighted in personality, and in drawing round it an unfaltering moral line." The London *Times* commented on her "power of visualization, which she communicates to the reader so that he sees her

characters 'in their habit as they lived,'" as well as her "gift for making her characters illustrate themselves in action and conversation. She does not need to tell us about them; they reveal themselves in the course of a narrative where the incident, which is never forced, shapes itself into the mould of art."

*Tante,* Sedgwick's ninth novel, was her first major success; it tells the story of Madame Okraska, a great pianist "who feeds her genius on the best products of her nature and gives the waste to a group of adoring friends." The story was dramatized, and made a fine vehicle for the actress Ethel Barrymore. *The Little French Girl,* Sedgwick's most popular novel, offers a contrast of French and English social standards through the story of a French girl who goes to England seeking a marriage of convenience but finds true love instead.

At her death the *Times* declared that the "best of her novels will survive and present to future generations an extraordinarily vivid, intimate and truthful picture of her time." In 1950 Elizabeth Bowen wrote that Sedgwick "inspires nostalgia already, her novels are monuments, minor monuments, but they are cut cleanly and the stone is good."

PRINCIPAL WORKS: *Novels*—The Dull Miss Archinard, 1898; The Confounding of Camelia, 1899; The Rescue, 1902; Paths of Judgement, 1904; The Shadow of Life, 1906; A Fountain Sealed, 1907 (in U.K.: Valerie Upton); Amabel Channice, 1908; Franklin Winslow Kane, 1910 (in U.K.: Franklin Kane); Tante, 1911; The Encounter, 1914; The Third Window, 1920; Adrienne Toner, 1921; The Little French Girl, 1924; The Old Countess, 1927; Dark Hester, 1929; Philippa, 1930. *Short stories*—The Nest and Other Stories, 1912; Christmas Roses and Other Stories, 1920 (in U.K.: Autumn Crocuses). *Nonfiction*—A Childhood in Brittany Eighty Years Ago, 1919.

ABOUT: Blain, V., Clements, P., and Grundy, I. The Feminist Companion to Literature in English: Women Writers from the Middle Ages to the Present, 1990; Bowen, E. Collected Impressions, 1950; De Sélincourt, B. Anne Douglas Sedgwick: A Portrait in Letters, 1936. *Periodical*—Times (London) July 22, 1935.

## SEEGER, ALAN (June 22, 1888–July 4, 1916), American poet, was born in New York City, the son of Charles Louis Seeger, a businessman who made his money refining sugar in Mexico, and Elise Simmons (Adams) Seeger. He grew up on Staten Island in a cultured, prosperous family; his brother

Charles became a well-known musicologist and was the father of the folk singer and political activist Pete Seeger. He attended Staten Island Academy

and the Horace Mann School in Manhattan, and was twelve when his family moved to Mexico City, where they produced a home magazine called the *Prophet*. Seeger entered the Hackley School, Tarrytown, New York, in 1902 and Harvard in 1906. He became editor of, and contributed poetry to, the *Harvard Monthly*.

After taking his B.A. in 1910 he moved back to New York City, where his confused idealism led him to seek what he believed was the beauty of love, the pleasure of the senses, and the benefit of humanity. In *How Can I Keep From Singing* ( a biography of Pete Seeger) David King Dunawat wrote that Alan Seeger "lived among bohemians in Greenwich Village, writing poetry and sleeping on the couch of his pro-Bolshevik classmate John Reed, author of *Ten Days That Shook the World*."

Seeger did not find what he wanted in New York and so, in 1912, headed to Paris, where he wrote and worked in the Latin Quarter. He was one of the first Americans to enlist (1914) in the French Foreign Legion. He is quoted in T. Sturge Moore's *Some Soldier Poets* as declaring, "I have always thirsted for this kind of thing, to be present where the pulsations are the liveliest. Every minute here is worth weeks of ordinary experience . . . . This will spoil one for any other kind of life . . . . Death is nothing terrible after all." Seeger's most famous poem—stark, impressive, moving in the circumstances, but in no way mature—*I Have a Rendezvous With Death*, closes with the lines

> But I've a rendezvous with Death
> At midnight in some flaming town,
> When Spring trips north again this year;
> And I to my pledged word am true,
> I shall not fail that rendezvous.

Seeger kept that rendezvous during the storming of Belloy-en-Santerre. In words Seeger would have approved of, one of his comrades described the "last charge" in Paul Ayres Rockwell's *American Fighters in the Foreign Legion 1914-1918*: "In an irresistible sublime dash, we hurled ourselves to the assault, offering our bodies as target. It was at this moment that Alan Seeger fell heavily wounded in the stomach. His comrades saw him fall and crawl into the shelter of a shell-hole. Since that minute nobody saw him alive."

At his tragically early death Seeger was no more than a promising poet. His scorn of convention did not extend to avoiding the use of ordinary verse forms, or indulging in standard romanticism. His stiff-upper-lip fatalism and heroic glorification of the ultimate human conflict were soon rendered obsolete by the horrors of the trenches. Of his collected poems the *Bookman* wrote, "Imaginative beauty and much nobility of expression mark all of these poems, but their viewpoint is always that of a conventional romantic."

Alan Seeger was buried in a mass grave and posthumously awarded the Croix de Guerre and the Medaille Militaire. As late as the 1970s a street in Biarritz was renamed for him. David King Dunaway wrote: "Thin, energetic, an idealist, Alan Seeger always said life was not worth living past thirty. Everything was the moment for him, and war attracted him like a beacon."

The Houghton Library, Harvard University; the Library of Congress; and the New York Public Library all have collections of Alan Seeger's papers.

PRINCIPAL WORKS: *Poetry*—Poems, 1916. *Letters*—Letters and Diary of Alan Seeger, 1917.

ABOUT: Dictionary of American Biography vol. 16, 1935; Dunaway, D. K. How Can I Keep From Singing: Pete Seeger, 1981; Moore, T. S. Some Soldier Poets, 1919; Rockwell, P. A. American Fighters in the Foreign Legion 1914-1918, 1930; Rubin, M. Men without Masks, 1980; Weinstein, I. Sound No Trumpet: The Life and Death of Alan Seeger, 1967. *Periodical*—Bookman January 1917.

**SEELEY, MABEL (HODNEFIELD)** (March 25, 1903– ), American detective story writer, wrote: "No one ever mistakes me for anything but what I am, a Middle

Westerner. The first six years of my life were spent in Minnesota—I was born there, at Herman—the next five in Illinois, the next five in Iowa, the next three in Wisconsin. In 1921, as a high school senior, I was back in Minnesota, happy to be there. Except for a few years in Chicago, between 1926 and 1929, I stayed in Minnesota until 1949.

"In my family I early discovered the uses of story telling; as the eldest of six children it was soon my job to ride herd. My father is a librarian with a scholarly love for books and language, my mother a member of a clan whose delight is to gather in swarms for family meals and family yarning-sessions. No other stories in the world, for me, have the flavor of those told by the descendants of Norwegian pioneers. What I learned at the family knee was that the most absorbing, the most amazing, the most amusing of all organisms are *people*, and experience hasn't changed this attitude.

"An early taste of being read came at Ellsworth, Wisconsin, where I wrote 'High School News and Notes' for the Ellsworth *Record*. . . . At [the University of] Minnesota I was on the board of the *Minnesota Quarterly*, and in 1926, on graduating, was married to a fellow editor, Kenneth Seeley.

"The two of us set sail for Chicago, he to do graduate work at the University of Chicago, I to take a copy job in advertising. Millions of words later, in 1936, I retired from a profession paced too fast for me, determined never to put pencil to yellow paper again. A year later I was at work on *The Listening House*.

"Why did I choose mysteries for a major interest? Perhaps because I'd found them such a useful anodyne, perhaps because I have a natural relish for horror. If I had a premise, it was that terror would be more terrible, horror more horrible, when visited on people the reader would feel were real, in places he would recognize as real. This hasn't changed, either.

"Mysteries exist only within very rigid limitations; sometimes I find these confining. Twice so far I've tried out the wider spaces of the straight novel; I've enjoyed the freedom. But I've never been able to say 'no more of the other.'"

---

In keeping with her premise that "terror would be more terrible" when it unfolded in places and among people the reader could "recognize as real," Mabel Seeley set her novels in commonplace locales and devoted considerable attention to the elaboration of local color.

*The Listening House,* her first novel, takes place in a run-down boarding house in a Midwestern city, and *The Whispering Cup,* perhaps her most effective mystery, is set in a small Minnesota farming community. Both are narrated by women and—like most of her novels—combine elements of naturalism, romance, and the hard-boiled detective thriller. These early mysteries received glowing reviews and prompted Howard Haycraft, in his book *Murder for Pleasure,* to compare Seeley to Alfred Hitchcock, and to herald her as "a White Hope who will pilot the American-feminine detective story out of the doldrums of its own formula-bound monotony."

The plots of Seeley's mystery novels are intricate. She was sometimes faulted for her overuse of the "had I but known" contrivance; or, as Haycraft remarked, "She indulges in more 'ifs' and premonitory shudders than she has any need to." Her later mystery novels were less well-received than her early work. In a *San Francisco Chronicle* review of *The Beckoning Door,* E. D. Doyle complained, "This is NOT the Mabel Seeley of yore. . . . She's as painstaking as ever in her wonderful descriptions of Midwestern life but she's not as painstaking as ever in the fashioning of her puzzle." *Woman of Property* and *The Stranger Beside Me,* Seeley's "straight" (i.e., non-mystery) novels, portray the conflicts of ambitious and financially successful American women.

PRINCIPAL WORKS: *Novels*—The Listening House, 1938; The Crying Sisters, 1939; The Whispering Cup, 1940; The Chuckling Fingers, 1941; Eleven Came Back, 1943; Woman of Property, 1947; The Beckoning Door, 1950; The Stranger Beside Me, 1951; The Whistling Shadow, 1954 (reissued as The Blonde with the Deadly Past, 1955).

ABOUT: The autobiographical material quoted above was written for Twentieth Century Authors First Supplement, 1955. Barzun, T. and Taylor, W. T. A Catalogue of Crime, rev. and enl. ed., 1989; DeAndrea, W. Encyclopedia Mysteriosa, 1994; Haycraft, H. Murder for Pleasure: The Life and Times of the Detective Story, 1941; Henderson, L. (ed.) Twentieth-Century Crime and Mystery Writers, 3d ed., 1991. *Periodical*—San Francisco Chronicle March 5, 1950.

**"SEGHERS, ANNA" (pseudonym of NETTY RADVANYI)** (November 19, 1900–June 2, 1983), German novelist and essayist, was born as the only child of cultured and respected Jewish parents, who kept an antique shop in Mainz, in the Rhine Valley. Seghers was one of the most capable and lucid of those European left-wing novelists who adhered to the creed of "socialist realism," which sought to use art to promote the Communist  cause. As D. S. Low stated in August Closs's *Twentieth Century German Literature,* although she "has consistently written from an ideological viewpoint," this "has not . . . diminished the literary quality of her writing." And he added that the "masterly" *The Seventh Cross* is "rightly regarded as a classic of its sort."

Seghers, under the tutelage of her father, gained an early and sophisticated interest in art. She chose the history of art as her main subject at the University of Cologne. After graduating, she gained her Ph.D. from the University of Heidelberg (at which she studied sinology as well as art) for a learned thesis on *Jews and Jewry in the Work of Rembrandt.* It was in Heidelberg that she met her husband Ladislaus Radvanyi, a Hungarian sociologist who had just received his own doctorate. Radvanyi was already a member of the Communist party. She joined it in 1929. She began publishing (in 1926) with a story in the *Frankfurter Zeitung;* it was signed, simply, "Seghers," and for some time her work was thought to be that of a man.

The publication of her vivid—if crude and immature—first short novel, *Aufstand der Fischer von St. Barbara* (1928; translated as *The Revolt of the Fishermen* and then again later as *The Revolt of the Fishermen of Santa Barbara*), brought her instant success in the form of high sales and the award of the prestigious Kleist Prize. But in the eyes of the Nazis, then rising in influence and power, Seghers was a marked woman: a Communist and a Jew. She followed her first novel with a collection of stories and a further novel (untranslated), neither of which endeared her to those who already had her marked out. She became well-known throughout Germany as an antifascist. When Hitler gained power, therefore, she and her husband and their two small children—a son and a daughter—fled to Paris. They actively helped the anti-Franco forces in the Spanish civil war. Then, on the Nazi capture of France, she managed to escape to Mexico—but not before her husband had been pitched by the French into a concentration camp, Le Vernet, where he spent some months. For some years Seghers lived in Mexico City, one of a noted group of antifascists. She helped there to found the magazine *Free Germany* and the Heinrich Heine Club for Free German Culture. She returned to Germany in 1947 as an honored author; indeed, she became a "literary idol" of East Germany.

Although *Revolt of the Fishermen* can hardly be described as being without a political thesis—the revolt of Breton fishermen over a monopoly to which they object collapses because fishermen at other ports fail to support it—it contains great literary merit and promise: Seghers was a born storyteller; she wrote with great vitality; and her characterization was balanced, convincing, and uninfluenced by her political beliefs. The *New York World* reviewer found the novel "noteworthy" because it dealt with "the most profound problems of human life" and yet was "truthful," and did not "sentimentalize." The *Nation* (1930) believed it to have "elements of greatness": "firm character studies, fine narration and a sentiment of beauty." But the same critic found that a "sense of remoteness" dulled "the force of the picture." The book was filmed, in Moscow, by Erwin Piscator in 1934.

However, Seghers's fiction in this period (1933–1947) was to deepen and become yet subtler. Always a dedicated Communist, there was also in Seghers a genuine yearning for a better life, and a concern for human suffering (the main subject of her work). *Das Kopflohn* (The ransom, 1933; translated as *A Price on His Head*), written speedily and with burning indignation, describes German peasant characters and a young Socialist as he flees from the Gestapo.

During her fourteen years of exile from her native Germany, Seghers came to regard the German workers as having succumbed too easily to Hitler and his propaganda. She advocated the formation of a Socialist underground, consisting of people—not necessarily Communist by conviction—who really did care for others. But, whatever her own creed, her fiction, when it depicts people united in a common cause against bestiality and psychotic tyranny, is compassionate and convincing.

*The Seventh Cross*, a thrilling adventure story by any standard, is about seven prisoners who escape from a concentration camp; six of them are recaptured and die on a cross—but one, George Heisler, gets away. The Gestapo man who vainly pursues him finally and regretfully defines him as "not just a single being, but a featureless and inexhaustible force." The *Atlantic* had no doubt of the merits of this laconic novel, which in translation became a best-seller: "Noble simplicity of style and story, relentless march of incident, and complete absence of comment make this novel of prewar Nazi Germany intensely engrossing and powerfully moving." Many reviewers, such as Dorothy Hillyer in the *Boston Globe*, believed that in this book they had read their "most impressive account of Nazi Germany to date." Certainly few others had matched it. It was made into a memorable movie by Fred Zinnemann in 1944.

But Seghers was to achieve more before her return to Germany. Many critics, themselves politically uncommitted, believe that in *Transit* (1943; translated under that title), which did not appear in German until 1948, she achieved her masterpiece, although hard-line Marxist critics have regarded it as merely "atypical." Certainly it is not "socialist-realist," as the rest of her work more or less uniformly is. For the German publication she changed the text to provide a more "uplifting" ending. But, it could be argued, *Transit* is by Seghers the artist, not by Seghers the doctrinaire Marxist. Set in Marseilles—whither a young German, Seidler, on the run from a concentration camp, has come—it portrays a city teeming with refugees of all sorts. Seidler manages to get hold of the papers of a writer who has killed himself in Paris, and to assume his identity. More than one reviewer was reminded of Kafka; the mysterious and brilliantly conveyed sense of fogginess and *ennui*, of people groping for meaning and identity, which envelops the book must have had its origin in Seghers's state of mind as she wrote it in a strange city and a strange country. In the *Nation* (1941), Diana Trilling failed to understand it at all: its "cruel joke of a plot" had her puzzled and dismayed. Other reviewers thought it dull and disappointing after *The Seventh Cross*. Some later critics, however, have found in it a strong expression and affirmation of Seghers's belief in dignity and human freedom.

In both *Das Vertrauen* (Trust, 1968) and *Überfahrt* (Crossing, 1971), later "Party" novels, there is implied criticism of the Marxist state of East Germany. There well may, too, be an element of ironic self-criticism in the latter, in which a Brazilian-born doctor returns voluntarily to East Germany because of a "grey-eyed" girl and because it is a "home of men of goodwill."

Seghers's last book that may be appreciated as a coherent artistic whole was written while she was still in exile: *Die Toten bleiben jung* (*The Dead Stay Young*, 1949), a panorama of Germany in the period 1918–1945. This was also the last book by her to be translated while she was still living; it is significant that it was the last story she wrote before she accepted the role of "state writer." Among its extra-literary qualities are its value as an accurate historical guide to the circumstances that led to the rise of the Nazis and to the nature of their rule. Notwithstanding this, Robert Pick wondered, reviewing it in the *Saturday Review of Literature*, whether the author had not been "forced" "to compress the historical background material to the utmost. . . . We are entitled to wonder whether Anna Seghers, by reducing the conflict almost entirely to the Communist vs. Fascist issue, has done justice to the whole picture." The *San Francisco Chronicle*, however, thought it "moving and credible": "people you can know and understand live and act and die."

Seghers's international reputation declined after her return to Germany. She won the National Prize twice (1951, 1959), and the Lenin Peace Prize. Because of this she was accused of falling into a "shallow ideology," but the comparative weakness of her later fiction was also owing to the fact that after a hard and dedicated life, her creative energies had decreased. Her travel books, essays, and parts of her novels are lucidly written; she retained her original simplicity and capacity for objective reporting. She will thus play a legitimate part in any appraisal of twentieth-century German literature. Her *Times* (London) obituarist noted: "Anna Seghers's later novels were certainly 'socialist realist' but in her case this mattered little because she was naturally a straightforward narrative writer—and at all times it was the brotherhood of man, and justice, rather than Marxist . . . dogma that appealed to and inspired her. Most Western readers have felt this appeal and responded to it. . . . All her writings abound in vitality."

PRINCIPAL WORKS IN ENGLISH TRANSLATION: *Omnibus*—Revolt of the Fishermen of Santa Barbara and A Price on His Head (trs. J. and R. Mitchell, and E. Wulff) 1960. *Novels*—The Revolt of the Fishermen (tr. M. Goldsmith) 1929; The Seventh Cross (tr. J. A. Galston) 1942; The Dead Stay Young (tr. anon.) 1950. *Short stories*—Benito's Blue and Nine Other Stories (tr. J. Becker) 1973.

ABOUT: Bangerter, L. A. The Bourgeois Proletarian: A Study of Anna Seghers, 1980; Closs, A. Twentieth Century German Literature, 1969; Columbia Dictionary of Modern European Literature, 1947, 1980; Current Biography 1942; 1983; Dämmrich, H. S. and Hänicke, D. H. (eds.) The Challenge of German Literature, 1971; Huebener, T. The Literature of East Germany, 1970; LaBahn, K. J. Anna Seghers's Exile Literature, 1986; Rosenberg, H. Discovering the Present: Three Decades in Art, Culture and Politics, 1973; Ruhle, J. Literature and Revolution, 1969; Seymour-Smith, M. Macmillan Guide to Modern World Literature, 1986; Seymour-Smith, M. Studies in Short Fiction III, 1966. *Periodicals*—Atlantic October 1942; Books Abroad Winter 1974; Boston Globe September 23, 1943; Explicator Summer 1989; Nation March 26, 1930; New York Times July 2, 1983; New York World March 23, 1930; San Francisco Chronicle July 31, 1950; Saturday Review of Literature July 29, 1950; Times (London) July 3, 1983.

## SEID, RUTH. See SINCLAIR, JO

## SEIGNY, BERNARD. See BAZIN, RENÉ

**SEITZ, DON C(ARLO)** (October 24, 1862– December 4, 1935), American journalist and biographer, was born in Portage, Ohio, the son of Josiah Augustus Seitz, a Universalist minister, and Rebecca (Brown) Seitz. After graduating from the Liberal Institute in Norway, Maine, he began working as a reporter for the *Brooklyn Eagle* in 1880. From there he wrote for the *Eagle*, becoming its city editor in 1892. After a succession of other newspaper jobs, he spent twenty-five years as business manager of the *New York World* (1898–1923). He then managed the *New York Evening World* (1923– 1926), and, after assistant editorship at *Outlook* (1926–1927) and the *Churchman* (1929–1932), retired from journalism.

In the midst of his busy newspaper career, Seitz published many books on a variety of subjects: histories of the Reconstruction era, piracy and dueling  (*The Dreadful Decade, Under the Black Flag, Famous American Duels*); informal travel sketches of Europe, Japan, and Newfoundland (*Discoveries in Every-Day Europe, Surface Japan, The Great Island*); biographies of Lincoln, Artemus Ward, and Senator Charles Curtis; and even several volumes of (undistinguished) verse (*The Buccaneers, In Praise of War, Farm Voices*).

Seitz was neither a distinctive or a distinguished stylist. However, his three biographies of American newspapermen—*Joseph Pulitzer, Horace Greeley*, and *The James Gordon Bennetts*—received much praise, and, together, constitute his achievement.

Most outstanding was his Pulitzer biography. Seitz knew him well and had worked under him at the *New York World*, and his treatment was regarded as well informed and balanced. "Seitz has done an admirable piece of work," wrote O. G. Villard in the *Saturday Review of Literature*. "Although he was and is bound to Mr. Pulitzer and to his memory ties of friendship and admiration . . . he has been able to write critically and with genuine detachment. He has given us a clear biography which makes easy a complete understanding of the character of a man who will remain one of the most interesting figures in American journalism." The same attitude, of critical admiration, informed reviews of *Horace Greeley, Founder of the New York Tribune* and *The James Gordon Bennetts, Father and Son, Proprietors of the New York Herald*. Of the former, W. A. White wrote in the *Nation*, "Seitz has written most entertainingly and with intelligence and courage about men and events of our American Victorian period. He has not made a bronze statue for the park; rather he has pictured an earnest man, more than reasonably honest, whose intelligence is directed rather by his courage than by insight which should come from the wide information."

An unwavering liberal and an able controversialist, Seitz helped to make the *New York World* one of the most influential liberal dailies of its time; it is as a newspaperman that he is remembered.

PRINCIPAL WORKS: *Journalism and biography*—Discoveries in Every-Day Europe: Vagrant Notes of a Rapid Journey, 1907; Elba and Elsewhere, 1910; Surface Japan: Short Notes of a Swift Survey, 1911; Training for the Newspaper Trade, 1916; Artemus Ward (Charles Farrar Browne): A Biography and Bibliography, 1919; Braxton Bragg: General of the Confederacy, 1924; Joseph Pulitzer: His Life and Letters, 1924; Uncommon Americans: Pencil Portraits of Men and Women Who Have Broken the Rules, 1925; Under the Black Flag, 1925; The Dreadful Decade: Detailing Some Phases in the History of the United States from Reconstruction to Resumption, 1869–1879, 1926; The Great Island: Some Observations in and about the Crown Colony of Newfoundland, 1926; Horace Greeley, Founder of the New York Tribune, 1926; The Also Rans: Great Men Who Missed Making the Presidential Goal, 1928; From the Kaw Teepee to Capitol: The Life Story of Charles Curtis, Indian, Who Has Risen to High Estate, 1928; The James Gordon Bennetts, Father and Son, Proprietors of the New York Herald, 1928; Famous American Duels: With Some Account of the Causes that Led up to Them and the Men Engaged, 1929; Lincoln the Politician: How the Rail-Splitter and Flatboatman Played the Great American Game, 1931. *Poetry*—The Buccaneers: Rough Verse, 1912; In Praise of War: Military and Sea Verse, 1917; Farm Voices, 1918. *As editor*—Letters from Francis Parkman to E. G. Squier, 1911; Whistler Stories (by J.A.M. Whistler) 1913; Paul Jones: His Exploits in the English Seas during 1778–1780, 1917; Monogatari: Tales from Old and New Japan, 1924; The Tryal of William Penn and William Mead, 1919; The Tryal of Capt. William Kidd, 1936.

ABOUT: Dictionary of American Biography Suppl. 1, 1944. *Bibliography*—Writings by and about James Abbott McNeil Whistler, 1910. *Periodicals*—Nation January 5, 1927; New York Herald Tribune Books November 18, 1928; New York Times December 5, 1935; Saturday Review of Literature December 20, 1924.

**SELDES, GEORGE (HENRY)** (November 16, 1890–July 2, 1995), American journalist, wrote: "I was born in a sort of Utopian colony founded by my

father, George S. Seldes. It was a failure. But one of my childhood memories is the letters father received from Count Tolstoy and Prince Kropotkin on how to run a cooperative idealistic colony. I got a job in Pittsburgh at the time of the graft trials; corruption was my introduction to city politics . . . During the First World War, I was a member of the press section of the American Army. We had special privileges, equal to those of a general on Pershing's staff—and an automobile. Those who wanted to went to the trenches. I was at St. Mihiel; the Signal Corps got lost, when and Pershing got there three hours later, I was hailed as the captor of the town.

"After the war I went to the *Chicago Tribune* foreign news service . . . For ten years I worked in thirty-seven countries in Europe, Asia, and North Africa. I have interviewed three kings and all the dictators of my time except Kemel Pasha. I have been expelled from Russia, Italy, Fiume (and just escaped it in Romania), for sending out news the truth of which could not be questioned. Other correspondents smuggled out news, or refrained from sending out unfavorable stories, but it was my policy to play the game openly.

"In 1928 I resigned from the *Tribune* and wanted to paint pictures. I did in fact paint more than 150 canvases between then and 1933. But I lost in 1929 the few dollars I had saved up, and it was lucky for me that a publisher asked me to write a book of my experiences. *You Can't Print That!* kept me going for a year, and since then I have been very busy getting out an annual volume. . . . I have only one rule: Let the facts speak for themselves. (The man who said that first was Euripides.) So far I have had only one important error pointed out to me, and that has been corrected. Frequently reviewers make blanket charges that I am biased, prejudiced, one-sided, etc. My answer is this: in almost every book I produce 80 percent or more of unchallengeable facts. The rest of the book is my interpretation of the facts. This is open to criticism. If the 80 percent contains errors they will be corrected.

"*Sawdust Caesar* was turned down by twenty-four publishers. Ten wrote me they were afraid of Mussolini. Only one said he did not like the book. . . .

"I belong to no party, but do not know whether the term 'liberal' or 'progressive' is strong enough to explain my views. In 1936 I went to Spain . . . I found that on the Loyalist side there were various groups and parties frequently fighting each other. That was their tragedy. But the idea of a united or popular front of all liberal, left, progressive elements, such as we also had in France for a short time, is my idea of the only way to upset reaction and Fascism. The trouble with democrats and liberals is that they are too sectarian. I am for the united front of all men of good will in America. And for death to Fascism in all its forms."

———

Like his younger brother, the journalist and critic Gilbert Seldes, George Seldes spent much of his childhood in the utopian community founded by his father in Alliance, New Jersey. He attended high schools in Vineland, New Jersey, and Pittsburgh, Pennsylvania, where at the age of eighteen he landed his first job as a reporter—with the *Pittsburgh Leader* for $3.50 a week. He went to Harvard as a non-degree student in 1912–1913, after which he returned to full-time journalism. A renowned foreign correspondent during World War I, he was an early critic of Fascism in the inter-war years.

Seldes established his reputation as a press critic and a muckraker—a label he always wore with pride—during the 1930s, with the publication of such books as *Can These Things Be!, Iron, Blood and Profits,* and *Freedom of the Press.* Seldes maintained that America's biggest and most influential newspapers had a demonstrably conservative, pro-corporate bias. In *Lords of the Press,* one of his best-selling and most controversial volumes, he documented the connection between that bias and the financial-political interests of powerful publishers. While John Dewey and Charles Beard expressed admiration for the book, a typical complaint was voiced by *New York Times* reviewer Allan Nevins: "In his eagerness to see the worst side of our newspapers, Mr. Seldes has given a distorted and unreal view."

From 1940 to 1950, Seldes wrote, edited, and published *In fact,* a four-page weekly newsletter devoted to investigative exposes and press criticism. "Indeed," Jay Walljasper wrote in an *Utne Reader* profile of Seldes, "you could call him the grandfather of the alternative press. *In fact* helped shape the modern techniques of investigative journalism and Seldes helped elevate the practice of press criticism from mere kitchen-table kvetching to a major component of contemporary journalism." The FBI spied on Seldes and various *In fact* subscribers, and Selde's relentless critique of the Cold War (in *In fact* and elsewhere) earned him an appearance before Senator Joseph McCarthy's committee in 1953. (Seldes was never a member of the Communist Party.)

Seldes retired to Vermont, where he continued to produce an occasional book. Having interviewed many early Soviet leaders, he appeared as a "witness" in Warren Beatty's 1981 film *Reds.* At the age of ninety-six, he published the well-received *Witness to a Century,* a chronicle of the issues and personalities that engaged him during his long career as a journalist. "[T]his is a lighthearted book," James Boylan wrote in the *Columbia Journalism Review,* "and . . . this buoyancy might lead a generation unacquainted with the earlier Seldes to underestimate his seriousness, his contribution to changing the American press for the better. . . . " At the age of 100, Seldes decided against writing one final book, and gave away the Royal manual typewriter he had used since 1930. "I figure I've written everything," he remarked to *Nation* interviewer Morton Mintz. But he remained active, and when he was 104, Barricade Books published *The George Seldes Reader*, an anthology of articles he wrote over his long career.

PRINCIPAL WORKS: *Journalism and politics*—You Can't Print That! The Truth Behind the News, 1918–1928 (in U.K.: The Truth Behind the News, 1918–1933, 1933, rev. ed. 1935; Iron Blood and Profits: An Exposure of the World-Wide Munitions Racket, 1934; The Vatican: Yesterday, Today, Tomorrow, 1934; Freedom of the Press, 1935; Sawdust Caesar: The Untold History of Mussolini and Fascism, 1935; Lords of the Press, 1938; You Can't Do That: A Survey of the Forces Attempting, in the Name of Patriotism, to Make a Desert of the Bills of Rights, 1938; The Catholic Crisis, 1939; Witch Hunt: The Technique and Profits of Red-Baiting, 1940; The Facts Are: A Guide to Falsehood and Propaganda in the Press and Radio, 1942; Facts and Fascism, 1943; One Thousand Americans, 1947; The People Don't Know: The American Press and the Cold War, 1949; Never Tire of Protesting, 1968; Even the Gods Can't Change History; The Facts Speak for Themselves, 1976. *Memoirs*—Tell the Truth and Run, 1953; Witness to a Century: Encounters with the Noted, the Notorious, and Three SOBs, 1987. *Selected writings*—The George Seldes Reader (ed. R. Holhut) 1994. *As editor*—The Great Quotations, 1960; The Great Thoughts, 1985.

ABOUT: The autobiographical material quoted above was written for Twentieth Century Authors, 1942 and First Supplement, 1955. Biographical Dictionary of American Journalism (ed. J. McKerns) 1989; Contemporary Authors, New Revision Series, Vol. 2, 1981; Current Biography 1941; Heald, M. Transatlantic Vistas: American Journalists in Europe, 1900–1940, 1988. *Periodicals*—Columbia Journalism Review May/June 1987; Nation March 11, 1991; New York Times December 4, 1938; Progressive June 1987; February 1989; Utne Reader July/August 1989.

## SELDES, GILBERT (VIVIAN) (January 3, 1893–September 29, 1970), American critic, journalist, and novelist, was born in Alliance, New Jersey, the son of George Sergius and Anna (Saphro) Seldes—and younger brother of the journalist George Seldes. He was educated at Central High School in Philadephia and at Harvard University, from which he graduated in 1914. He was a music critic for the *Philadelphia Evening Ledger* from 1914 to 1916, a freelance foreign correspondent covering World War I, and the American political correspondent for *L'Echo de Paris* in Washington during 1918. The following year he became associate editor of *Collier's Weekly*, and in the 1920s he was recruited by his Harvard friends Scofield Thayer and James Sibley Watson, Jr. to be managing editor for the influential literary journal, *The Dial*. Michael Kammen in his biography of Seldes, *The Lively Arts: Gilbert Seldes and the Transformation of Cultural Criticism in the United States*, stated that " *The Dial* enjoyed its greatest visibility and prestige in the years 1920–23, while Seldes served as managing editor";

an ironic statement, said Arthur Schlesinger Jr. in a review of the book, because "in view of his later career, Seldes began as what today would be invidiously termed an elitist." Seldes wrote about twenty books over the course of a career that also included stints as a columnist for the *New York Journal* (1931–1937), program director for the Columbia Broadcasting System (1937–1945), and dean of the Annenberg School of Communications at the University of Pennsylvania (1959–1963). He was known, however, less for his political journalism, social history, and fiction than for his three studies of the popular arts: *The Seven Lively Arts*, *The Great Audience*, and *The Public Arts*.

The "seven lively arts," according to Seldes, were the circus, the comic strip, the movies, jazz, vaudeville, musical theater, and newspaper satire. He argued passionately—sometimes intemperately—for their artistic validity and cultural importance, pointing to such figures as Charlie Chaplin and George Herriman (the creator of *Krazy Kat*) as examples of individual genius comparable to that of any "highbrow" artist. Although some readers felt that Seldes was carried away by his enthusiasms, the book made a temporary critical splash. Edmund Wilson wrote of it, "To read his book is to live again the last ten years of vaudeville and revue, newspapers and moving pictures, but in a purified and concentrated form. . . . As for the trained dogs, the melodramtic playlet and the sentimental soloist, they, too, become entertaining through the wit of our guide's comments. If he were only a little less fanatical about magnifying the importance of the whole affair, he would make the perfect companion."

Twenty-six years after *The Seven Lively Arts*, Seldes brought out *The Great Audience*, a rather more measured assessment of the impact of the popular arts (television, radio, and film) on mass culture. *The Great Audience* was notably less optimistic than *The Seven Lively Arts*, reflecting as it did Seldes's views on the increasing homogenization of the popular arts. Wilson considered this "solid and sober report" a more impressive work than its predecessor: "It is a critical essay, the most comprehensive and searching I know, on mass entertainment in the United States. . . . This is the first time, so far as I know, that a man of intelligence and taste, with a sound enough education to give him cultural and historical perspective, who has at the same time a practical grasp of the technical and financial aspects of the entertainment business, has set out to attack the whole subject."

*The Public Arts*, the last of the three volumes, was largely concerned with television: "its techniques, its impact, its political implications, and the responsibilities of those who control and manage it," as Leo Rosten wrote in the *New York Herald Tribune Book Review*. Hollis Alpert, writing in the *Saturday Review*, felt that in this book "Seldes raises throughout more questions than he answers, and it is sometimes difficult to distinguish whether he is pro, con, or on the fence—but this is undoubtedly by design, for it is the massed voice of the responsible public which must eventually make the decisions."

A lively and opinionated man, friend to Wilson, F. Scott Fitzgerald, and others, Seldes was married and had two children, one of whom, Marian Seldes, became an actress. In 1996 there appeared Michael Kammen's biography *The Lively Arts: Gilbert Seldes and the Transformation of Cultural Criticism in the United States*. Reviewing the work in *The New York Times Book Review*, Arthur Schlesinger, Jr. praised it as "a rich and stimulating work and a long overdue account of the intelligent and energetic man who almost single-handedly changed American attitudes toward the popular arts." Schlesinger describes Seldes as "an exuberant man, generous and funny, overflowing with charm, curiosity, wit and passion."

Kammen's book pointed out the vast influence Seldes had on reforming the distinctions between "elite" and "popular" cultures from the age of jazz and vaudeville through radio and television. He quotes Seldes as saying, "I suggest that we take the producers of the mass media at their word. Let us accept the basic statement that they give the public what the public wants and let us try to make the public want a great deal more."

PRINCIPAL WORKS: *Criticism, history, and journalism*—The United States and the War, 1917; The Seven Lively Arts, 1924, rev. ed. 1957; The Stammering Century, 1928; An Hour with the Movies and the Talkies, 1929; The Future of Drinking, 1930; The Years of the Locust: America, 1929–1932, 1933; Mainland, 1936; The Movies Come from America, 1937 (in U.K.: Movies for the Millions); Your Money and Your Life: A Manual for the Middle Classes, 1938; Proclaim Liberty! 1942; The Great Audience, 1950; Writing for Television, 1952; The Public Arts, 1956; You and the Mass Media, 1957 (reissued as The New Mass Media, 1962). *Novels*—(as "Foster Johns") The Victory Murders, 1927; (as "Foster Johns") The Square Emerald, 1928; The Wings of the Eagle, 1929. *As editor*—This Is New York: The First Modern Photographic Book of New York, 1934; The Portable Ring Lardner, 1946. *As adapter and translator*—(with G. S. Seldes) Plays of the Moscow Art Theatre Musical Studio, 1925; Lysistrata (by Aristophanes) 1934.

ABOUT: Contemporary Authors vols. 29–32, 1978; Dictionary of American Biography, Suppl. 8, 1988; Kammen, M. The Lively Arts: Gilbert Seldes and the Transformation of Cultural Criticism in the United States, 1996; McKerns, J. P. (ed.) Biographical Dictionary of American Journalism, 1989; Wilson, E. The Shores of Light: A Literary Chronicle of the Twenties and Thirties, 1952. *Periodicals*—New York Herald Tribune Book Review July 15, 1956; New York Times September 30, 1970, May 5, 1996; Saturday Review July 21, 1956.

**SÉLINCOURT, ERNEST DE.** See **DE SÉLINCOURT, ERNEST**

**SELKIRK, JANE.** See **CHAPMAN, MARISTAN**

**SELTZER, CHARLES ALDEN** (August 15, 1875–February 9, 1942), American writer of Western novels and stories, was born in Janesville, Wisconsin, the son of Lucien Bonaparte Seltzer and Oceanna (Hart) Seltzer. His family moved to Columbus, Ohio, the following year, and he attended the public schools there. While still a child, Seltzer went west to live with an uncle on a New Mexico ranch. From that time to his early manhood he roamed the West from the Rio Grande to the Columbia River. Late in the 1890s he returned to the East to work as a carpenter and contractor. His education had been confined to the fundamentals of reading and writing, but he began doggedly to write stories of the West. Ella Alberts, whom he married in 1896, helped her husband to obtain an education and advised him on his work during a dozen or so years of apprenticeship and rejection slips. Seltzer supported his family during this period by working as a newspaper editor, building inspector for the city of Cleveland, and tax consultant. In his later years, when he was living in North Olmstead, Ohio, he served as councilman and then as mayor of that city for two terms (1926–1932).

Seltzer's first book, a collection of Western stories titled *The Range Riders*, was published in 1911; it cannot be said to have added much to an already limited genre dominated by writers like Owen Wister and Zane Grey, and indeed his forty or more novels were for the most part pure formula. His books described "a West that never was and never will be," as a critic in the *New York Times Book Review* (1911) wrote of *The Two-Gun Man*; but their lack of verisimilitude was no deterrent—indeed, it aided his intentions—to popular success. During his life an estimated million and a half copies of his books were sold, and a dozen and a half of them remain in print. Undoubtedly, Seltzer's fans asked no more of him than what he usually gave them: "A lively, swift, thrilling, absorbing tale of the old West combining adventure and romance in approved fashion," as a critic in the *New York Times Book Review* described *Silverspurs*, a novel of 1935.

PRINCIPAL WORKS: *Short stories*—The Range Riders, 1911; The Triangle Cupid, 1912. *Novels*—The Two-Gun Man, 1911; The Coming of the Law, 1912; The Trail to Yesterday, 1913; The Boss of the Lazy Y, 1915; The Range Boss, 1916; The Vengeance of Jefferson Gawne, 1917; "Firebrand" Trevison, 1918; The Ranchman, 1919; The Trail Horde, 1920; "Beau" Rand, 1921; "Drag" Harlan, 1921; Square Deal Sanderson, 1922; West! 1922; Brass Commandments, 1923; Channing Comes Through, 1924; The Way of the Buffalo, 1924; Lonesome Ranch, 1924; Last Hope Ranch, 1925; Trailing Back, 1925; The Valley of the Stars, 1926; The Gentleman from Virginia, 1926; Slow Burgess, 1926; Land of the Free, 1927; The Mesa, 1928; Mystery Range, 1928; The Raider, 1929; The Red Brand, 1929; Pedro the Magnificent, 1929; Gone North, 1930; A Son of Arizona, 1931; Double Cross Ranch, 1932; War on Wishbone Range, 1932; Breath of the Desert, 1932; Clear the Trail, 1933; West of Apache Pass, 1934; Silverspurs, 1935; Kingdom of the Cactus, 1937; Parade of the Empty Boots, 1937; Arizona Jim, 1939; Treasure Ranch, 1940; So Long, Sucker, 1942.

ABOUT: Twentieth Century Western Writers, 2nd ed., 1991. *Periodicals*—New York Times February 10, 1942; New York Times Book Review November 26, 1911; September 8, 1935.

**\*"SERGE, VICTOR" (pseudonym of VICTOR LVOVICH KIBALCHICH)** (1890–November 18, 1947), French-Russian writer and revolutionary, was born in Brussels, Belgium, the son of Russian political exiles. His father, Leo Kibalachich, a *SAR gay noncommissioned cavalry officer, was affiliated with the underground People's Will (Narodnik) party, which assassinated Tsar Alexander II in 1881.  Serge grew up in extreme poverty in England and Belgium, where his father was an itinerant university instructor. Although he had no real formal education, he read voraciously from his parents' well-stocked library. He left home at the age of thirteen, eking out a living in Brussels as an apprentice photographer and draftsman. At fifteen he joined the socialist *Jeunes Gardes* movement.

By the age of eighteen, when he moved to Paris, he had become a committed anarchist. In 1911 he became an editor there of the journal *L'Anarchie*. Serge's radical politics, and his association with members of the *bande à Bonnot*, notorious anarchists, led to his arrest and imprisonment in 1912. Soon after his release in 1917, he left Paris for Barcelona, where he joined the anarchist uprising, which failed, and first signed an article with his pseudonym of Victor Serge. He then returned to Paris with the intention of traveling to revolutionary Russia, but found himself detained in a French concentration camp until the end of World War I.

In January 1919 he arrived in Petrograd, then still in the throes of civil war. Although never a true, committed Bolshevik, Serge decided to align himself with them, and was soon appointed by Grigori Zinoviev to the executive of the Third International, or Comintern. He joined the Communist party and during the early 1920s worked closely with high-level party officials. However, with the ending of the civil war, and especially after the ruthlessly suppressed Kronstadt uprising of 1921, Serge became increasingly critical of the regime's use of terror and secret police to quell dissent. He was on the editorial staff of *Inprekorr*, the Comintern press agency, from 1922 to 1925, serving first in Berlin and later in Vienna. Upon his return to the Soviet Union he publicly associated himself with Leon Trotsky and the Left Opposition to Stalin's regime, despite the leading role Trotsky had taken in repressing the Kronstadt Revolt.

In 1928, after publishing a series of articles on China containing criticisms of Stalin's policies, Serge was arrested and jailed for a short time. Having almost died of a severe stomach ailment during his interrogation, he resolved to devote the rest of his life to serious writing. Between 1930 and his death seventeen years later, Serge produced some twenty books—novels, historical studies, biography, and an autobiography—as well as dozens of essays and many poems. All of his work deals in one way or another with the revolutionary struggle in which he participated. His first novel, *Men in Prison*, arose from his experience of French prisons. His next two novels, *Birth of Our Power* and *Conquered City*, deal respectively with the anarchist

uprising in Spain and the civil war in Petrograd. Serge wrote primarily in French, and most of his work was first published in Paris. All of his books were banned in the Soviet Union. In most cases, English translations appeared years after the original French editions.

Arrested again in 1933, Serge was sentenced to internal exile in the city of Orenburg, where he was denied work and nearly starved. A vigorous campaign by left-wing French intellectuals, André Malraux and André Gide among them, led to his release in 1936. He was then stripped of his Soviet citizenship and expelled from the country.

From 1936 to 1940, Serge lived in Brussels and Paris, supported himself by working in print shops, agitated on behalf of anti-Stalinist leftists in Spain and the Soviet Union, and continued to write voluminously. He came to the attention of British and American readers with *From Lenin to Stalin* and *Russia Twenty Years After*, his first two books translated into English. Edmund Wilson (*Nation*, 1937) welcomed the latter book as "one of the most important works that have yet been published on the Soviet Union. . . . the first inside report by a Russian that has reached the outside world." Another work dating from this period is the novel *Midnight in the Century*. Set in one of modern history's darkest periods—with Hitler triumphant in Germany and Stalin having consolidated his hold over the Soviet Union—it examines the plight of jailed and persecuted Russian dissidents, many of them heroes of the 1917 revolution. When the Nazis conquered France in the spring of 1940, Serge was forced to flee. He made his way to Marseilles, and from there to Mexico, the only country that would offer him refuge. Stateless and impoverished, he died in Mexico City after suffering a heart attack in a taxi.

Serge's merits were not mainly literary—his verse is negligible—but he was a vivid documentarist. Two of his better works—the novel *The Case of Comrade Tulayev* and his autobiography, *Memoirs of a Revolutionary*—appeared posthumously. Now usually regarded as his best work, *The Case of Comrade Tulayev* is set against the backdrop of the Stalinist purges and show trials. It has often been compared to Arthur Koestler's *Darkness at Noon*, but, owing to its stylistic and psychological deficiencies, has never achieved similar influence or recognition.

An anarchist in his youth, and later a Bolshevik and a Trotskyite, Serge ultimately embraced a sort of politically confused libertarian, ahumanistic type of "non-Marxist communism." In *Memoirs of a Revolutionary*, he recounts his tumultuous political life, and provides revealing personal portraits of those he struggled with and against. Reviewing *Memoirs* in the *New Republic*, Irving Howe commented, "Serge was never a Marxist theoretician. . . . He was primarily an observer, a superior journalist from whose books there emanates the heat and turmoil of historical immediacy."

In his introduction to *Memoirs*, translator Peter Sedgwick notes that Serge always resisted the easy appeal of "historical fatalism": "[He] had been one of the first people . . . to use the word 'totalitarian' of the Soviet state, but unlike some Western thinkers he did not mean it to imply a finished, impervious, and stable structure."

Serge remains a figure of considerable interest whose career and writing remain important to students of the Soviet Union.

PRINCIPAL WORKS IN ENGLISH TRANSLATION: *Politics and history*—From Lenin to Stalin (tr. R. Mannheim) 1937; Russia Twenty Years After (tr. M. Schachtman) 1937 (in U.K.: Destiny of a Revolution); Year One of the Russian Revolution (tr. and ed. P. Sedgwick) 1972; What Everyone Should Know About Repression, 1979; (with L. Trotsky) The Serge-Trotsky Papers: The Correspondence and Other Writings Between Victor Serge and Leon Trotsky, 1936–1939 (ed. D. Cotterill) 1994. *Biography*—(with N. S. Trotsky) The Life and Death of Leon Trotsky (tr. A. Pomerans) 1975. *Autobiography*—Memoirs of a Revolutionary, 1901–1941 (tr. and ed. P. Sedgwick) 1963. *Novels*—The Long Dusk (tr. R. Mannheim) 1946; The Case of Comrade Tulayev (tr. W. Trask) 1950; Birth of Our Power (Naissance de notre force) (tr. R. Greeman) 1967; Men in Prison (tr. R. Greeman) 1969; Conquered City (tr. R. Greeman) 1975; Midnight in the Century (tr. R. Greeman) 1982. *Poetry*—Resistance: Selected Poems (tr. J. Brook) 1989.

ABOUT: Bell, D., Johnson, D., and Morris, P. (eds.) Biographical Dictionary of French Political Leaders Since 1870, 1990; Marshall, B. Victor Serge: The Uses of Dissent, 1992; Steinberg, J. (ed.) Verdict of Three Decades: From the Literature of Individual Revolt Against Soviet Communism, 1917–1950, 1950. *Periodicals*—Dissent Winter 1984; Journal of European Studies June 1986; Massachusetts Review Autumn 1981; Nation November 13, 1937; October 23, 1989; New Republic March 7, 1964; New York Times November 20, 1947.

## SERNA, RAMÓN GÓMEZ DE LA. See GÓMEZ DE LA SERNA, RAMÓN

## SERVICE, ROBERT W(ILLIAM) (January 26, 1876–September 11, 1958), Canadian verse writer and novelist, wrote: "I was born in Preston, England, of Scotch-English parentage, and soon after taken to Scotland, where I grew up. I lived in Glasgow until my twenty-first year, being educated at Hillhead High School, and attending classes at Glasgow University. I joined the Commercial Bank of Scotland, in which I served my apprenticeship in banking. On coming of age I found the lust of adventure too strong for me, and resigning from the bank emigrated to Canada. I traveled steerage, landing in Victoria, B.C., with just five dollars in my pocket. For the next seven years I took a course in the College of Hard Knocks, graduating without enthusiasm. I traveled all up and down the Pacific slope, generally on freight trains, and worked in a score of different occupations. Afterwards I went to the Yukon, where I was employed at White Horse and Dawson by the Canadian Bank of Commerce for eight years. There, influenced by Kipling, I began to write, and was greatly surprised to find my work acceptable. I came to Europe to report the Balkan War for the *Toronto Star*, spending a short time with the Turkish army. After that I went to France, which I liked so much I settled there. Then came the Great War, for which I immediately volunteered, and in which I served for two years as an ambulance driver. Last summer the present war caught me in Russia, and I escaped from Warsaw the first day of the bombardment.

Now, in my sixty-seventh year, I feel I have had enough of trouble and excitement, and only ask to be allowed to pass the rest of my days in peace and quiet, far from and, if possible, forgetting this world of strife as I cultivate the roses in my garden."

---

In a 1921 *Texas Review* essay, W. A. Whatley divided Robert W. Service's work into two periods. The first consisted of verse written prior to World War I, when Service earned fame and fortune as the "Kipling of the Northwest": "The major theme of the verse of this period is the interpretation of the life of the Great North, with its pendulum-sweep from the heroic to the mean, and its direct contact with the primary forces of Nature." Service's first collection of verse, *Songs of a Sourdough*, was published in Toronto in 1907, and became one of the most successful debuts in publishing—if not in literary—history. That it was an immediate phenomenon is described in Arthur L. Phelps's *Canadian Writers*: "In the composing room the men who set up the words got so enthusiastic that they went about reciting them like crazy schoolboys. They took sheets home, spouted them to their spouses, and shouted them to their neighbors over the garden fences. . . . Rarely has there been such a riot of glee over the publishing of a book. And to the amazement of the publishers, before the book actually came out, many thousands of advance copies were sold." The book went through fifteen printings in its first year and was released in the United States under the title *The Spell of the Yukon*, garnering even more popularity and, by 1940, sales in excess of two million copies.

The collection contains two of Service's best known verses, "The Shooting of Dan McGrew" and "The Cremation of Sam McGee," both examples of the rugged rhythmic narrative style which drew the enthusiastic attention of the general reading public, but failed to have the same effect with literary critics. The narrator of "The Shooting of Dan McGrew" begins by stating:

> A bunch of the boys were whooping it up in the
> Malemute saloon;
> The kid that handles the music-box was
> hitting a rag-time tune;
> Back of the bar, in a solo game, sat Dangerous Dan
> McGrew,
> And watching his luck was his light-o'-love, the
> lady that's known as Lou.

A sub theme of the poem is the harsh reality of a miner's life and the "growing hunger of lonely men for a home and all that it means," but the climax is a gunfight between Dan and a miner "crazed with 'hooch'": "Then I ducked my head, and the lights went out, and two guns blazed in the dark,/ And a woman screamed, and the lights went up, and two men lay stiff and stark."

The rough life of the miner is also at the core of "The Cremation of Sam McGee," along with a rich vein of "macabre humor." McGee is a prospector who is "always cold, but the land and gold seemed to hold him like a spell." Near death McGee gets the narrator to promise to help him avoid the "icy grave" by cremating his body. After McGee dies the narrator stuffs him into a roaring furnace, later opening the door to check only to find the deceased sitting there "looking cool and calm" and demanding that the door be closed again: "It's fine in here, but I greatly fear you'll let in the cold and storm—/ Since I left Plumtree, down in Tennessee, it's the first time I've been warm."

Whatley described Service's second period as encompassing his poems of World War I. In *My Mate* Service wrote:

Jim as lies there in the dugout wiv's blanket round 'is 'ead
To keep 'is brains from mixin' wiv the mud;
And 'is face as white as putty, and 'is overcoat all red,
Like 'e's' spilt a bloomin' paint-pot—but it's blood.

The self-evident source, again, is Kipling, but Service did not have the capacity to write what Orwell called "good bad verse."

Service also wrote six novels. His first, *The Trail of '98*, was written during his Yukon years; his aim was, as he put it, to write the "only fictional record of the gold rush." Stanley Atherton, in a *Canadian Literature* essay called it a "contrived pot-boiler," but went on to say that it is "nevertheless a significant contribution to literature about the Canadian North. It is one of the earliest attempts to make a myth of the north, to capture the spirit of the land and make it comprehensible."

Service never returned to the Yukon after leaving to become a foreign correspondent for the *Toronto Star*. He eventually settled in the Latin Quarter of Paris and flirted with the Bohemian lifestyle; in 1913 he married Germaine Bourgoin, a French woman. His second novel, *The Pretender: A Story of the Latin Quarter*, concerns an American author who ends up in Paris avoiding marriage, getting married, and struggling to become a serious writer.

In 1931 the Services moved to Nice, where Robert's hopes of "forgetting this world of strife" were dashed in 1940 by the advancing German army. After fleeing to Canada the Services settled in Hollywood for the duration. In 1942 Service appeared in the film *The Spoilers*, which starred Randolph Scott, John Wayne, and Marlene Dietrich.

After the war the Services lived in Monte Carlo. Carl F. Klinck, in his biography *Robert Service*, points out that the verse of Service's later years has "considerable biographical and critical value, for it rounds out, on Service's own terms, the story of his life and thought." Klinck describes this work as displaying a "growing tendency to make explicit attacks upon war, political injustices, and oppression of the poor. The realism with which he now went to the heart of a matter was sharper then the realism of setting in the thrillers, or the realism of human activity in the earlier vignettes." Despite historical interest in this later work, Service's great popularity was behind him, forever linked to the verse he produced as the "Bard of the Yukon," the verse that made him a rich man. When Service was

"crowding eighty-four," he wrote the following lines on the back of a photograph he sent to his publisher: "Alas! My belly is concave,/My locks no longer wavy;/But though I've one foot in the grave/The other's in the gravy."

"Whatever may be said of Service's poetry it made a section of the North in the pioneer days live for many people," Lorne Pierce wrote in 1927. "Some have said that it is not true to the spirit of the Yukon, that there was little gun play and outlawry. However, he has limned in vivid and occasionally vulgar phrase a memorable picture of strong men, mastering passions, and malignant climate."

PRINCIPAL WORKS: *Verse*—Songs of Sourdough, 1907 (reissued as The Spell of the Yukon, and Other Verse, 1907); Ballads of a Cheechako, 1909; Rhymes of a Rolling Stone, 1912; Rhymes of a Red Cross Man, 1916; Selected Poems, With Some Account of His Life and Experiences, 1917; Ballads of a Bohemian, 1921; The Complete Poetical Works of Robert W. Service, 1921 (reissued as The Complete Poems of Robert W. Service, rev. eds. 1938 and 1942; in U.K.: Collected Verse of Robert Service); Twenty Bath-Tub Ballads, 1939; Bar-Room Ballads: A Book of Verse, 1940; Songs of a Sun-Lover, 1949; Rhymes of Roughneck, 1950; Lyrics of a Low Brow, 1951 (in U.K.: Lyrics of a Lowbrow: A Book of Verse); Rhymes of a Rebel, 1952; The Best of Robert Service, 1953; Songs for My Supper, 1953; Carols of an Old Codger: Verse, 1954; More Collected Verse, 1955; Rhymes for My Rags, 1956; Rhyme and Romance: A Robert Service Anthology, 1958; Songs of the High North, 1958; Later Collected Verse, 1965; Yukon Poems of Robert W. Service, 1967; More Selected Verse of Robert Service, 1971; The Song of the Campfire, 1978; Best Tales of the Yukon, 1983. *Novels*—The Trail of '98: A Northland Romance, 1910; The Pretender: A Story of the Latin Quarter, 1914; The Poisoned Paradise: A Romance of Monte Carlo, 1922; The Roughneck, 1923; The Master of the Microbe: A Fantastic Romance, 1926; The House of Fear, 1927. *Nonfiction*—Why Not Grow Young? or, Living for Longevity, 1928. *Memoirs*—Ploughman of the Moon: An Adventure Into Memory, 1945; Harper of Heaven: A Record of Radiant Living, 1948 (in U.K.: Harper of Heaven: A Further Adventure Into Memory).

ABOUT: The autobiographical material quoted above was written for Twentieth Century Authors, 1942. Contemporary Authors 1994; Dictionary of American Biography Suppl. 6; Dictionary of Literary Biography vol. 92 1990; The Dictionary of National Biography, 1951–1960; Hellman, G. T. How to Disappear for an Hour, 1947; Klinck, C. F. Robert Service, 1976; Percival, W. (ed.) Leading Canadian Poets, 1948; Phelps, A. L. Canadian Writers, 1951; Pierce, L. An Outline of Canadian Literature: French and English, 1927; Something About the Author vol. 20 1980; Thomas, C. Canadian Novelists: 1920–1945, 1946; Twentieth-Century Literary Criticism vol. 15 1985. *Periodicals*—Alaska Review Fall 1965; Canadian Literature Winter 1971; New York Times September 13, 1958; Texas Review July 1921; Times (London) September 13, 1958.

**SETON, ANYA** (January 23, 1904–November 8, 1990), American novelist, wrote: "I was born in New York City in the old Beaux Arts Studio Apartments behind the Public Library, which may explain my early and growing passion for libraries and research! I think that every idea, productive one, that I've ever had, has come to me while standing bemused in the stacks of some library, and to the patience and efficiency of librarians I am extremely grateful.

"I was born into a writing family. My father, Ernest Thompson Seton, wrote (and illustrated) some forty books. My mother, Grace Gallatin Seton, has written a dozen. So the career had no glamor for me whatsoever, and I determined to be a physician instead. This ambition died early, for I married at eighteen and at once produced two babies, but all my life I have had a lively interest in medicine and worked in hospitals and clinics particularly mental hygiene clinics, social service—and I was a nurse's aide for some years during and after the war.

"I was an only child and had a rather unorthodox upbringing. It included life (with Indians and Boy Scouts and Woodcraft) on my father's large estate  in Cos Cob, Connecticut, five extended trips to Europe, and three to the Far West. I learned French before I did English, was taught by governesses, travel, and a really formidable amount of reading, until I finally reached a private school and graduated from it. College plans were also erased by the early marriage, but I then lived two years at Oxford with my husband and took courses there.

"During my twenties I experimented rather drearily with short stories and verse, but it was not until 1937 that I suddenly determined to write and sell. It took nineteen months of effort and disappointment until I sold my first short story, and then a few more. But short stories are not natural media for me and it wasn't until I conceived the idea of *My Theodosia*, a biographical novel about the daughter of Aaron Burr, that I found what I wanted to do.

"Research is a joy to me, and the interpretation of actual characters in the light of actual events: the authentic, and I hope vivid, reconstruction of certain phases of the past. . . .

"Willa Cather's work has probably influenced me more than any other writer, yet there is Katherine Mansfield, and Dickens, and the inimitable Jane [Austen]. My life is predominantly domestic. I married (Hamilton M. Chase) a second time, and we have a daughter, and except for necessary travel in search of material, I live in a little house on the Sound in the same Connecticut town where I lived as a child."

Anya Seton reaped popular success and some measure of reviewers' praise for her carefully researched historical and biographical novels. Her work was widely translated, and most of it remains in print in the United States. Readers have delighted in her eventful, sometimes melodramatic, narratives; reviewers often commended her accurate rendering of period detail and her careful depiction of physical setting. Travel was as crucial to her research as extensive reading, and Seton had firsthand knowledge of all the places she wrote about. Her fiction focuses primarily on the lives of women, both real and imaginary. She placed them in a variety of historical and geographic settings.

Seton had her first best-seller with *Dragonwyck*, a lurid gothic-style novel set in New York City and the Hudson Valley during the 1830s and 1840s. The first of her novels to be filmed, it was adapted for the screen by Joseph L. Mankiewicz in his directorial debut. *The Turquoise*, a historical romance set in the American Southwest and New York in the latter part of the nineteenth century, features a heroine with pronounced psychic abilities. *New Yorker* (1946) critic Edmund Wilson predicted (correctly) that *The Turquoise* would be a commercial success, but he dismissed it as a "typical American novel written by a woman for women." Decrying the characters' lack of "even a crude human motivation," Wilson complained, "The whole thing is as synthetic, as arbitrary, as basically cold and dead, as a scenario for a film." The heroine of *Foxfire* is a cultured Easterner trying to adapt to rural Western life after marrying a mining engineer of Apache descent. Despite its poor critical reception, the novel sold well and became the second of Seton's novels to be filmed.

*Katherine*, probably Seton's least melodramatic novel, is a fictionalized biography of Katherine Swynford, a sister-in-law of Geoffrey Chaucer, and the wife of John of Gaunt. *The Winthrop Woman*, which was a major best-seller, is a fictional portrait of Elizabeth Fones, the thrice-married niece (and at one point the daughter-in-law) of John Winthrop, Sr., the first governor of the Massachusetts Bay Colony. It portrays a woman enmeshed in a finely delineated historical context.

*Devil Water*, set in eighteenth-century England and America, concentrates on the lives of Charles Radcliffe, grandson of King Charles II, and Radcliffe's daughter, Jenny. Juvenile works include *The Mistletoe and Sword*, a historical novel, and the biographical study *Washington Irving*.

Christened Ann Seton, the author was known for most of her life as Anya, a diminutive form of Anutika (meaning "cloud-gray eyes"), a name bestowed upon her during childhood by a Sioux Indian friend of her father. She donated her papers to the Historical Society of the Town of Greenwich.

PRINCIPAL WORKS: *Novels*—My Theodosia, 1941; Dragonwyck, 1944; The Turquoise, 1946; The Hearth and the Eagle, 1948; Foxfire, 1950; Katherine, 1954; The Winthrop Woman, 1958; Devil Water, 1962; Avalon, 1965; Green Darkness, 1972. *Juvenile*—The Mistletoe and Sword: A Story of Roman Britain, 1955; Washington Irving, 1960; Smouldering Fires, 1975.

ABOUT: The autobiographical material quoted above was written for Twentieth Century Authors First Supplement, 1955. Current Biography 1953; 1991; Henderson, L. (ed.) Twentieth-Century Romance and Historical Writers, 1990; Something About the Author vol. 3, 1972; Who's Who 1990. *Periodicals*—New York Times November 10, 1990; New Yorker February 16, 1946; May 12, 1962; Saturday Review October 9, 1954; February 15, 1958; Times (London) November 12, 1990.

**SETON, ERNEST THOMPSON** (August 14, 1860–October 23, 1946), American author, naturalist, and illustrator, was born Ernest Evan Thompson in South Shields, Durham, England, the twelfth of fourteen children of Joseph Logan Thompson, a partner in a shipbuilding firm, and Alice (Snowdon) Thompson. One of his father's forebears, a

Scottish Jacobite, had assumed the name Thompson after fleeing to England in the mid-eighteenth century. Ernest began using the surname Seton—after  George Seton, Earl of Winton, one of his father's titled ancestors—in the 1880s. In 1901 he had his name legally changed to Ernest Thompson Seton, though some of his early work appeared under the names Ernest E. Thompson and Ernest Thompson-Seton. In 1866, following the bankruptcy of his father's business, the family immigrated to Canada, settling first on a farm near Lindsay, Ontario, where Seton fell in love with nature and the study of wildlife. In 1870 they moved to Toronto, and Seton attended that city's Collegiate High School. Seton had resolved to become a naturalist, but his father (whom he always detested) insisted that he prepare for an art career.

Apprenticed to a portrait painter in 1876, he later enrolled at the Ontario School of Art. He went to London to study drawing in 1879 and in 1880 was awarded a generous scholarship to the Royal Academy of Painting and Sculpture, but attended classes there for less than one year. Upon returning to Canada in late 1881, he set out for his brother's farm near Carberry, Manitoba. His Manitoba years, among the happiest of his life, were spent exploring the prairie wilderness, collecting specimens, and making wildlife sketches, particularly of birds. After 1883, he was often in New York City, where he studied for a time with the Art Students League, took jobs as a free-lance illustrator, and worked on *The Birds of Manitoba*.

In 1890 Seton traveled to Paris for further study in anatomical drawing. In the following year one of his oil paintings, "The Sleeping Wolf," was shown in the French Academy's Salon. Returning to North America from Paris in 1893 he took a job as a wolf-hunter on a New Mexico ranch. That experience inspired one of his earliest and best known nature short stories, "Lobo, King of the Currumpaw," about an enormous and wily gray wolf who falls to hunters' traps only after its mate is killed. "Lobo," published in *Scribner's Magazine* in 1894 and later included in Seton's popular collection *Wild Animals I Have Known*, set the tone for many of his subsequent animal "biographies." In these, a human narrator (usually Seton himself) makes the acquaintance of a particular (often hunted) wild animal. Although his animals are endowed with a host of human attributes—they have names, and their actions exemplify such traits as bravery, loyalty, or compassion—the narrator provides a scrupulously detailed account of the animal's life in the wild, and every effort is made to see the world through the eyes of that animal. In her book *Survival*, a study of Canadian literary attitudes, Margaret Atwood has noted the distinctively Canadian perspective in Seton's work: the death of the animal "is seen as tragic or pathetic, because the stories are told from the point of view of the animal." Only the first of more than a dozen novelistic animal "biographies" and story collections Seton published, *Wild Animals I Have Known* was a runaway bestseller when it first appeared, and has continued to be popular. In his introduction to a 1977 edition of the book, Alec Lucas observed, "In all probability [it] has outsold any other book by a Canadian author. . . . the book established, if it did not originate, a new literary genre, the realistic animal story."

During the first decade of the twentieth century, Seton's books and lectures brought him international renown and considerable financial success. Among his detractors, perhaps none offered a more penetrating analysis than the critic, poet, and naturalist John Burroughs. In "Real and Sham Natural History," a 1903 essay in the *Atlantic Monthly*, Burroughs called the stories in *Wild Animals I Have Known* "artistic and pleasing," but convincingly debunked the author's assertion that they were "true" accounts of the behavior and capabilities of wild animals. "[T]he line between fact and fiction," Burroughs insisted, "is repeatedly crossed." Moreover, "Fact and fiction are so deftly blended in his work that only a real woodsman can separate them." Seton went to great lengths to persuade Burroughs that he (Seton) was a serious naturalist, and he did eventually gain recognition as such with the publication of two works of popular natural history: *Life—Histories of Northern Animals*, a two-volume study, and *Lives of Game Animals*, a four volume work that received the John Burroughs Bronze Medal in 1927.

Seton's admiration for American Indians prompted him to found (in 1902) the Woodcraft Indians, later known as the Woodcraft League of America, a sort of precursor to the Boy Scouts. Seton promoted the League through a regular column in *Ladies' Home Journal*, and by publishing a series of books on outdoor life and activities designed to help American boys, and those in other industrialized countries, emulate the Native American. Seton was among the founders of the Boy Scouts of America in 1910, but left that organization five years later to protest its increasingly militaristic bent.

In 1930 Seton sold the Connecticut estate he had lived in since 1902 and relocated to a 2,500-acre ranch in New Mexico. His new home—"Seton Castle" and its adjacent "Seton Village"—became a mecca for a variety of conservationists and back-to-nature activists. Seton became an American citizen only in 1931 (having spent his life prior to that time as a British citizen, despite his long residence in Canada). In 1935, soon after divorcing his first wife, Grace Callatin (an author in her own right and the mother of the novelist Anya Seton), he married Julia M. Buttree, a student of Indian lore some thirty years his junior. In 1938, the couple adopted a baby daughter.

Seton published more than forty books, his wild animal stories, which he illustrated himself, being the most popular. Although much of his work appealed primarily to boys, Seton was read by juveniles and adults of both sexes. His autobiography,

*Trail of an Artist-Naturalist,* appeared during his eighty-first year.

PRINCIPAL WORKS: *Art*—Studies in the Art Anatomy of Animals: Being a Brief Analysis of the Visible Forms of the More Familiar Animals and birds, 1896. *Short stories*—Wild Animals I Have Known, 1898 (selections reissued as Lobo, Rag, and Vixen, 1899); Lives of the Hunted, Containing a True Account of the Doings of Five Quadrupeds and Three Birds, 1901 (selections reissued as Krag and Johnny Bear, 1902); Animal Heroes: Being the Histories of a Cat, a Dog, a Pigeon, a Lynx, Two Wolves and a Reindeer, 1905; Wild Animals at Home, 1913; Wild Animal Ways, 1916 (in U.K.: Billy and Other Stories from Wild Animal Ways); Chink, Woolly Coated Little Dog, 1929 (selections from Lives of the Hunted and Wild Animals at Home, pub. in U.K. only); Johnny Bear, Lobo, and Other Stories, 1935; Great Historic Animals: Mainly About Wolves, 1937 (in U.K.: Mainly About Wolves). *Novels*—The Trail of the Sandhill Stag, 1899; The Biography of a Grizzly, 1900; Monarch, the Big Bear of Tallac, 1904; The Biography of a Silver-Fox; or, Domino Reynard of Goldur Town, 1909; The Preacher of Cedar Mountain: A Tale of the Open Country, 1917; Bannertail: The Story of a Gray Squirrel, 1922; The Biography of an Arctic Fox, 1937; Santana, the Hero Dog of France, 1945. *Juvenile*—Two Little Savages: Being the Adventures of Two Boys Who Lived as Indians and What They Learned, 1903; Woodmyth and Fable, 1905; Rolf in the Woods: The Adventures of a Boy Scout with Indian Quonab and Little Dog Skookum, 1911; Woodland Tales, 1921. *Wildlife and nature*—The Birds of Manitoba, 1891; The Natural History of the Ten Commandments, 1907 (also pub. as The Ten Commandments in the Animal World); Life-Histories of Northern Animals: An Account of the Mammals of Manitoba, 2 vols., 1909 (reissued in abridged 1 vol. ed. as Animals Worth Knowing, 1925, and as Animals, 1926; ed. R. M. McCurdy); The Forester's Manual; or, The Forest Trees of North America, 1912; Lives of the Game Animals: An Account of Those Land Animals in America, North of the Mexican Border, Which Are Considered "Game," Either Because They Have Held the Attention of Sportsmen, or Received the Protection of the Law, 4 vols., 1925–1928. *Travel*—The Arctic Prairies: A Canoe Journey of 2,000 Miles in Search of the Caribou: Being an Account of the Voyage to the Region North of Aylmer Lake, 1911. *Games, activities, outdoor life*—The Wild Animal Play for Children, with Alternate Reading for Very Young Children, 1900; How to Play Indian: Directions for Organizing a Tribe of Boy Indians and Making Their Teepees in True Indian Style, 1903 (reissued as The Red Book, 1904); The Birch-Bark Roll of the Outdoor Life: Containing the Standards, Games, Constitution, and Laws of the Woodcraft Indians, 1908 (enl. and reissued as The Book of Woodcraft and Indian Lore, 1912); The American Boy Scout: The Official Hand-Book of Woodcraft for the Boy Scouts of America, 1910 (8th ed. of The Birch-Bark Roll); The Woodcraft Manual for Girls, 1916 (the Fifteenth Birch-Bark Roll); Animal Tracks and Hunter Signs, 1958. *Autobiography*—Trail of an Artist-Naturalist: The Autobiography of Ernest Thomas Seton, 1940. *Miscellaneous*—Sign Talk: A Universal Signal Code, 1918; The Buffalo Wind, 1938. *As illustrator*—Four-Footed Americans and Their Kin (by M. O. Wright; ed. F. M. Chapman) 1898; Bird-Life: A Guide to the Study of Our Common Birds (by F. M. Chapman) 1901; (with L. A. Fuertes) Third Reader: Stories of Birds and Beasts (by M. O. Wright) 1904; The Rhythm of the Red Man: In Song, Dance and Decoration (by J. M. Buttree) 1930; The Indian Costume Book (by J. M. Seton) 1938. *As editor*—Famous Animal Stories: Animal Myths, Fables, Fairy Tales, Stories of Real Animals, 1932; (with J. M. Seton) The Gospel of the Red Man: An Indian Bible, 1936; The Animal Story Book, 1953. *Collections*—The Library of Pioneering and Woodcraft, 6 vols. 1911–1912; Ernest Thompson Seton's Trail and Camp-Fire Stories 1940; The Best of Ernest Thompson Seton (ed. W. K. Robinson) 1949; Ernest Thompson Seton's America: Selections from the Writings of the Artist-Naturalist (ed. F. A. Wiley) 1954; The Worlds of Ernest Thompson Seton (ed. J. G. Samson) 1976; Selected Stories from Ernest Thompson Seton (ed. P. Morley) 1977.

ABOUT: Anderson, H. A. The Chief: Ernest Thompson Seton and the Changing West, 1986; Atwood, M. Survival: A Thematic Guide to Canadian Literature, 1972; Current Biography 1943; 1946; Dictionary of American Biography, Suppl. 4, 1946–1950, 1974; Dictionary of Literary Biography Vol. 92, 1990; Keller, B. Black Wolf: The Life of Ernest Thompson Seton, 1984; Twentieth-Century Literary Criticism Vol. 31, 1989; Who's Who 1946. *Periodicals*—Atlantic Monthly March 1903; New York Times October 24, 1946; Times (London) October 24, 1946.

**SEUSS, DR.** See **GEISEL, THEODORE SEUSS**

**SEYMOUR, BEATRICE KEAN** (1888–October 31, 1955), English novelist, was born Beatrice Stapledon in London, where, unusual for the period, she went to a coeducational school. She always kept her exact date of birth a secret. After attending King's College she worked for a brief time as a typist. Married to William Kean Seymour, parodist and verse dramatist, she published fiction consistently from the 1920s to the 1950s.

A prolific popular novelist, writing about modern relationships, Seymour never achieved the big audience to which her adopted style and subject matter were suited. Her type of fiction has now been superseded by television soap opera. One of her better books was her fifth, *The Last Day,* about half a dozen friends holidaying in Devon, and set in a fictional "Salton at the end of the Stonebridge estuary." L. P. Hartley, who  reviewed several of Seymour's books for the *Saturday Review,* found in *The Last Day* "an unusually just and lively sense of the interplay of passionate relationships." He also, perhaps rashly, praised its "unfailing selectiveness," a quality by no means always evident in Seymour's novels. Rebecca West, writing about the earlier *Intrusion,* had said, "The idea that art is a selective process as well as a response to life, and demands treatment as well as statement of situations, is not present in Mrs. Seymour's mind."

In the 1930s she produced a trilogy—*Maids and Mistresses, Interlude for Sally,* and *Summer of Life* (later published collectively as *The Chronicles of Sally*)—about a parlor maid, Sally Dunn, in which the love affairs of above and below stairs were rather earnestly compared. Her 1940s trilogy—*Buds of May, Tumbled House,* and *The Children Grow Up*—sought to hold a mirror up to English family life in the first half of the twentieth century. In her later work she favored panoramic sagas such as *The Unquiet Field,* which, echoing a theme adopted by her friend Storm Jameson—a vastly superior novelist—followed a Liverpool ship-owning family through four generations. The *Library Journal* pronounced her next book, *Fool of Time,* "dated" and stated bleakly, "No popular demand may be anticipated." Her penultimate novel, *The Wind Is Poured,* something of a departure, remains of interest for being based, as many other novels have been, on an actual crime case known as the Bravo Mystery—a celebrated late-Victorian poisoning.

Several of her novels concern themselves with the plight of women. *The Unquiet Field* tackles the masculine bias of marriage law, *The Second Mrs. Cornford* is about aspects of discrimination against women in higher education, and *The Hopeful Journey* was given a book-jacket description as "a cool study for feminism—the theme of sex-life versus work-life."

One title of Seymour's that has been reprinted (1974) is her study of Jane Austen, written to dispute the view of Austen as a placid spinster who had experienced nothing of excitement in her personal life.

PRINCIPAL WORKS: *Fiction*—Invisible Tides, 1919; Intrusion, 1921; The Hopeful Journey, 1923; The Romantic Tradition, 1925; Unveiled, 1925; The Last Day, 1926; Three Wives, 1927; Youth Rides Out, 1928; False Spring, 1929; But Not for Love, 1930; Maids and Mistresses, 1932; Daughter to Philip, 1933; Interlude for Sally, 1934; Frost at Morning, 1935; Summer of Life, 1936; The Happier Eden, 1937; Fool of Time, 1940; The Chronicles of Sally, 1940; The Unquiet Field, 1940; Happy Ever After, 1941; Return Journey, 1942; Buds of May, 1943; Joy as It Flies, 1944; Tumbled House, 1946; Family Group, 1947; The Children Grow Up, 1949; The Second Mrs. Cornford, 1951; The Wine Is Poured, 1953; The Painted Lath, 1955. *Nonfiction*—Jane Austen, a Study for a Portrait, 1937.

ABOUT: Blain, V., Clements, P. and Grundy, I. (eds.) The Feminist Companion to Literature in English, 1990; Everyman's Dictionary of Literary Biography; Who Was Who 1951–1960. *Periodicals*—Library Journal June 1, 1941; New Statesman June 11, 1921; Saturday Review March 6, 1926.

## SHALOM ALEICHEM. See RABINOWITZ, SOLOMON J.

## SHANNON, FRED ALBERT (February 12, 1893–February 4, 1963), American historian, wrote: "I was born in Sedalia, Missouri, of a family of long pioneer-farmer extraction that had just shortly before been starved out of Kansas by grasshoppers, hail storms, drought, and horse thieves. At six months I was taken to Indiana, where I lived except for one year in Memphis, Tennessee, until 1919. I graduated from the Indiana State Teachers' College (then Normal School) in 1914, and started teaching in the grade schools of Brazil, Indiana. I went there because my new bride, Edna Jones, lived there and her father got me a job. From 1916 to 1919 I was principal of the high school at Reelsville, Indiana. In 1918 I got an M.A. degree at Indiana University. From 1919 to 1923 I was professor of history at Iowa Wesleyan College, from which position I was virtually fired for giving the daughters of the president and dean low grades. Then I finished my formal education at the University of Iowa, getting a Ph.D. in 1924. . . .

"I taught history at the Iowa State Teachers' College, 1924–1926; Kansas State College, 1926–1938; economic history at Williams College, 1938–1939; and have been associate professor of history at the University of Illinois since 1939. I also taught summers at Cornell College (Iowa), Ohio State University, West Virginia University, University of Missouri, and Harvard. I am one of the editors of the *American Economic History Series*.

"My interest in economic and social history probably dates from working in school vacations since the age of eleven in sawmills, grist mills, iron foundries, glass factories, stamping mills, Western wheat fields, carrying papers, clerking in grocery stores, and what have you. You learn a lot that way. . . . "

———

A full professor at the University of Illinois from 1941 until his retirement in 1961, Fred Albert Shannon was a historian of the American Civil War, but is better known for his more original and valuable contributions to the history of American agriculture. His two-volume study *The Organization and Administration of the Union Army* was awarded the Justin Windsor Prize of the American Historical Association in 1928, and the 1929 Pulitzer Prize for history—a rare distinction for a first book. A Midwesterner who grew up under straitened financial circumstances, Shannon possessed an innate sympathy with the common man, a perspective that informed and animated such works as *Economic History of the People of the United States* and *The Farmer's Last Frontier*. In a *Saturday Review of Literature* notice of the latter work, Russell Lord disparaged Shannon's lapses into "stiffly scholarly" prose, but noted, "his blazing indignation at the whirl of social thuggery which makes up so much of our history in respect to land acquisition and use . . . enliven[s] his work enormously."

Shannon relished scholarly controversy and was not afraid to attack his colleagues' work. Most notable in this regard is *An Appraisal of Walter Prescott Webb's The Great Plains*, a scathing critique of the Texas historian's influential book. Active in a variety of professional organizations, Shannon was elected president of the Mississippi Valley Historical Association in 1953. He died in Wickenburg, Arizona. There is a collection of his papers at the archives of the University of Illinois.

PRINCIPAL WORKS: *History*—The Organization and Administration of the Union Army, 1861–1865, 2 vols., 1928; Economic History of the People of the United States, 1934 (revised and reissued as America's Economic Growth, 1940); An Appraisal of Walter Prescott Webb's The Great Plains: A Study in Institutions and Environment, 1940; The Farmer's Last Frontier, 1860–1897, 1945; American Farmers' Movements, 1957; The Centennial Years: A Political and Economic History of America from the 1870s to the Early 1890s (ed. R. Jones) 1967. *As editor*—The Civil War Letters of Sergeant Onley Andrus, 1947.

ABOUT: The autobiographical material quoted above was written for Twentieth Century Authors, 1942. Dictionary of American Biography, Suppl. 7, 1961–1965, 1981. *Periodicals*—Agricultural History April 1963; American Historical Review July 1963; New York Times February 7, 1963; Saturday Review of Literature October 13, 1945.

**SHAPIRO, KARL** (November 10, 1913– ), American poet, wrote: "I was born in Baltimore, Maryland. Baltimore was the birthplace of my parents [Joseph and Sarah (Omansky) Shapiro] and of my brother and sister. Our grandparents emigrated from East Europe in the 1880s.

"I attended public schools in Baltimore, Virginia, and Chicago, and these places have remained home to me off and on during my life. I entered high

school in Norfolk, Virginia, and graduated from one in Baltimore. I matriculated at the University of Virginia in 1932 but continued, several years later, at Johns Hopkins in Baltimore. My army training took place in Virginia in a section of the state which I had been familiar with since childhood. Part of my early schooling took place in Chicago; in later years I returned there to teach in Chicago universities and to edit *Poetry, a Magazine of Verse*.

"My interest in poetry dates back to my high school years. We possessed a large undiversified library in our home, and it was a natural occupation for us to read and try to write. My brother, who was a year older than I, had won several literary prizes for essays, fiction and poetry while in high school and at college. I emulated him. The first poem of any seriousness which I can remember writing was a sonnet in praise of Gandhi. Later, at the University of Virginia, I did poorly in my studies because of my greater interest in writing verses. On leaving the university, which I did against the protests of my family, I devoted myself to this pursuit. I was permitted to study alone for several years, and it was during this unusual period of freedom that I began to develop my work in my own way.

"During this time of self-study I wrote many long poems and plays in verse, nearly all of which I later destroyed. In 1935 I collected a few of my shorter poems and had them published at the Waverly Press in Baltimore. The volume bore the title *Poems* and it was not reviewed or noticed by writers.

"From 1935 to 1937 I worked at various jobs in Baltimore and in 1936 traveled for a short period to Tahiti. The following year, through the assistance of Dr. Hazelton Spencer at Johns Hopkins, I received a scholarship to continue my studies at that university. After two years, however, I found it necessary to raise money to continue, and I enrolled as a salaried library student at the Pratt Library in Baltimore. Toward the end of my first year at the Library I was drafted (March, 1941) into the Army, no deferment being permitted at that time.

"During my first year in the Army I completed a series of poems which I had begun in 1938; these I now began to publish in literary magazines. New Directions offered to publish this group of poems in an anthology for young poets, and I consented. My war service took me overseas in 1942 and I served three years abroad in Australia, New Guinea and the surrounding islands.

"During my overseas life, my fiancée, Evalyn Katz, moved to New York in order to find a publisher for my work. At this venture she was extraordinarily successful. In 1942 she edited *Person, Place and Thing* for Reynal and Hitchcock. In 1944 she edited a new collection to be called *V-Letter*, a book which won the Pulitzer prize the following year. A third volume, *Essay on Rime*, was printed in 1945. Meanwhile, I had published a limited edition of a small collection of my own in Sydney; it was called *The Place of Love*. This book contained a number of poems which appeared in my American books and more which I felt were not worth reprinting. In addition to supervising the publication of my books, Evalyn Katz acted as my literary agent in sending poems to magazines, appearing at literary functions in my behalf, and generally furthering my literary career. On my return to America in 1945 we were married in Baltimore.

"The book called *Essay on Rime* perhaps merits a note. It is a critique of modern poetry, written in blank verse. It was written in New Guinea and in the Dutch East Indies. Part of the pleasure of writing the essay lay in recollecting notes which I had gathered before the war and trying to piece them together into a coherent whole. Certain errors of fact in the poem can be laid to this manner of composition also. By and large, the essay is a comment on the pretentiousness of modern poetry vis-à-vis its myth-making, its self-consciousness about culture and history, and its techniques of symbolism and metaphysics. The book was widely acclaimed on the whole, but it aroused the enmity of the literary avant garde—as, in fact, it was calculated to do.

"In 1947, after living a year in Connecticut, I was appointed to the Library of Congress as Consultant in Poetry. This was an annual appointment, and the following year I was invited to join the faculty of the Johns Hopkins University as lecturer. *Trial of a Poet* was published in 1947 and contained a masque about the plight of the poet who comes into conflict with society.

"In 1950 I was invited to edit *Poetry*, and I resigned my post as associate professor in writing at Hopkins and moved to Chicago. In that city I also taught writing classes at Loyola University and later at the University of Iowa. In 1952 I lectured in Austria at the Salzburg Seminar in American Studies. In 1953 I delivered a series of lectures at the University of Nebraska which were published as a book under the title of *Beyond Criticism*. These lectures elaborate the thesis of *Essay on Rime* and fix as the two chief schools of modernism which seem to me deleterious: Mythic and Historic Poets, the one using poetry as a substitute religion and the other as social propaganda. In opposition to these I posit 'human' poetry, or poetry which is the fullest expression of personality. In 1953 I received a Guggenheim Fellowship and lived in Rome with my family for several months. A volume *Poems 1940–53* was published at that time. . . . "

In his review of *Person, Place and Thing* in the *New Republic* in 1942, Selden Rodman wrote: "Shapiro's style is on the classical side. The images are often violent but are always contained in a strict pattern." A good example is the often-anthologized poem "Auto Wreck":

> The traffic moves around with care,
> But we remain, touching a wound
> That opens to our richest horror.
> Already old, the question Who shall
>     die?
> Becomes unspoken Who is innocent?
> For death in war is done by hands;
> Suicide has cause and stillbirth,
>     logic;
> And cancer, simple as a flower, blooms.
> But this invites the occult mind,
> Cancels our physics with a sneer,
> And spatters all we knew of denouement
> Across the expedient and wicked stones.

Many of the poems of *V-Letter* were based on Shapiro's experiences during World War II. Conrad Aiken noted in the *New Republic* in 1944 that "Shapiro thinks with his feelings, thinks with his imagination," and Louis Untermeyer observed in the *Yale Review* that "his poems are the best which . . . this war has produced." In "The Progress of Faust" (from *Trial of a Poet*) Shapiro showed his moral concern that the atomic bomb used to end the war might in effect be a pact with the devil: "He hid, appearing on the sixth to pose / In an American desert at War's end / Where, at his back, a dome of atoms rose."

Shapiro edited *Poetry* magazine from 1950 to 1956 and the *Newberry Library Bulletin* from 1953 to 1955. In 1955 he lectured for the U.S. State Department in India, and during the next few years was a visiting lecturer at the University of California (1955–1956) and Indiana University (1956–1957). He received a Kenyon School of Letters fellowship in 1956–1957. In 1956 he was appointed professor of English at the University of Nebraska, and editor of the *Prairie Schooner*. He held these posts until 1966 when he resigned from both of them, specifically over his freedom to publish in the journal what he wanted. But his sharp attack on the state of twentieth-century poetry in the fourteen essays of *In Defense of Ignorance* had, he felt, alienated him from much of the academic community. Richard Ellmann wrote in the *New York Times Book Review* that Shapiro "sets out to be reckless. His irritations so far exceed his capacity to organize them that the essays, though they share resentments, sometimes oppose each other. . . . He opposes the literature of his time with a romanticism for which he is temperamentally unfitted." In short, Shapiro argued that mainstream American poetry owed far more to Walt Whitman and William Carlos Williams than to Ezra Pound and T. S. Eliot, both already regarded as icons of modern poetry.

Shapiro's own verse, however, was less controversial. Many of the lyrics of *Poems of a Jew* attempted to define his feelings and his place as a Jewish American. In *A Bourgeois Poet* he revealed his attraction to the Beat poetry of Allen Ginsberg and others. Using Whitman-like free verse he offered at times a mocking but fundamentally honest attempt at self-analysis.

Shapiro taught at the University of Illinois at Chicago Circle for two years (1966–1968) before moving to the University of California, Davis. He received the Eunice Tietjens Memorial Prize in 1961 and the Oscar Blumenthal Prize from *Poetry* in 1963. In 1967 he divorced his first wife and married Teri Kovach. *White-Haired Lover*, which celebrated in a cycle of twenty-nine love poems this new relationship, was awarded the Bolingen Prize (shared with John Berryman) in 1968. The poems of *Adult Book Store* were characterized by a high level of technical skill and emotional firmness. Shapiro also wrote a novel, *Edsel*, and (with Ernst Lert) the libretto for *The Tenor*, a one-act opera with music by Hugo Weisgall. His later books include *Collected Poems*, *The Poetry Wreck: Selected Essays*, and two volumes of autobiography, *The Younger Son* and *Reports of My Death*. Shapiro is a member of the National Institute of Arts and Letters.

Karl Shapiro's papers are at Wayne State University in Detroit, the Lilly Library at Indiana University, and the Library of Congress.

PRINCIPAL WORKS: *Poetry*—Poems, 1935; Person, Place and Thing, 1942; The Place of Love, 1942; V-Letter, 1944; Essay on Rime, 1945; Trial of a Poet, 1947; Poems: 1940–1953, 1953; The House, 1957; Poems of a Jew, 1958; The Bourgeois Poet, 1964; Selected Poems, 1968; White-Haired Lover, 1968; Adult Book Store, 1976; Collected Poems: 1948–1978, 1978; Love and War, Art and God, 1984; Adam and Eve (ed. J. Wheatcroft), 1986; New and Selected Poems: 1940–1986, 1987. *Drama*—(with E. Lert) The Tenor, 1956 (opera libretto; music by H. Weisgall). *Fiction*—Edsel, 1970. *Nonfiction*—English Prosody and Modern Poetry, 1947; A Bibliography of Modern Poetry, 1948; Beyond Criticism, 1953, reissued as A Primer for Poets, 1965; In Defense of Ignorance, 1960; (with J. E. Miller and B. Slote) Start with the Sun: Studies in Cosmic Poetry, 1960; (with R. Ellison) The Writer's Experience, 1964; (with R. Beum) A Prosody Handbook, 1965; Randall Jarrell, 1967; To Abolish Children, 1968 (essays); The Poetry Wreck: Selected Essays, 1950–1970, 1975. *Autobiography*—The Younger Son, 1988; Reports of My Death, 1990. *As editor*—(with L. Untermeyer and R. Wilbur) Modern American and Modern British Poetry, 1955; American Poetry, 1960; Prose Keys to Modern Poetry, 1962; (with R. Phillips) Letters of Delmore Schwartz, 1984.

ABOUT: The autobiographical material quoted above was written for Twentieth Century Authors First Supplement, 1955. Malkoff, K. Contemporary American-Jewish Literature, 1973; Reino, J. Karl Shapiro, 1981; Stepanchev, S. American Poetry since 1945, 1965. *Bibliography*—Bartlett, L. Karl Shapiro: A Descriptive Bibliography, 1979. *Periodicals*—New Republic December 21, 1942; October 23, 1944; New York Times Book Review May 8, 1960; Prairie Schooner Fall 1981; Tri-Quarterly Fall 1978; Yale Review Winter 1945.

**SHAPLEY, HARLOW** (November 2, 1885–October 20, 1972), American astronomer and writer, was born in Nashville, Missouri, the son of Willis Harlow Shapley, a farmer and schoolteacher, and Sarah (Stowell) Shapley. Shapley's youthful education was spotty; he became a full-time newspaper reporter while still a teenager. However, at the age of twenty-one he entered the University of Missouri, where he quickly demonstrated his brilliance in astronomy, a field he chose only after discovering that the courses he had planned to take in journalism were not available. After receiving his B.A. in

1910 and his M.A. the following year, Shapley was awarded a fellowship to Princeton University, from which he received his Ph.D. in 1913. His dissertation, "A Study of the Orbits of Eclipsing Binaries," was an outstanding contribution to the understanding of double stars, and on its basis he obtained a position as an astronomer at the Mount Wilson Observatory in Pasadena, California.

Shapley published more than a hundred significant papers during his eight years at the Mount Wilson Observatory. His most important findings  concerned the stars known as Cepheid variables, from whose pulsations he derived a more accurate way of measuring sidereal distances. The startling conclusion Shapley drew from these new measurements was that the earth and sun occupied a position on the periphery of the galaxy. Bart J. Bok claimed in *Biographical Memoirs of the National Academy of Sciences* that "Shapley . . . . placed our sun and earth in the outskirts of the Milky Way system. He proved . . . . that our sun and earth are definitely not located close to the center of our galaxy."

In 1921 Shapley was named director of the Harvard College Observatory in Cambridge, Massachusetts, a position he held until his retirement in 1952. In his three decades there he turned the Harvard Observatory into one of the leading centers of astronomical research in the world and, not incidentally, provided a haven for many refugee scientists from Europe. Although his truly pioneering work was behind him by the time he left the Wilson Observatory, during his Harvard years he began publishing books intended for general readers, as well as for scientists. Perhaps the most successful of these was *Flights from Chaos: A Survey of Material Systems from Atoms to Galaxies*, which a critic in the *Saturday Review of Literature* characterized as "an astronomical sonnet," adding that professional scientists as well as astronomically inclined general readers "will profit by this succinct natural history of molecules, meteors, moons, stars, galaxies, and the 'Cosmopolasma.'" Of a later volume, *Of Stars and Men: The Human Response to an Expanding Universe*, another critic in the *Saturday Review* wrote, "Not all of the conclusions in this little book—whose intellectual dimensions are so large—will be immediately embraced by other scientists. But neither are Professor Shapley' convictions the product of slap-happy speculation. They represent the sober assessment by a respected astronomer of evidence drawn not only from his special field but also from physics, chemistry, geology, biochemistry, biology, and . . . mathematics. This evidence is presented—in language meant for the literate layman—with persuasion, wit, and at times a sort of cosmic poetry."

With the advent of World War II Shapley devoted increasing amounts of time to political and cul-

tural activities. An outspoken internationalist and advocate of scientific interchange with the Soviet Union, he was denounced by the House Un-American Activities Committee in 1946—only to be elected, in a deliberate retort by the scientific community, to the American Association for the Advancement of Science the following year. He was especially proud of his involvement in the founding of UNESCO, the United Nations Educational, Scientific, and Cultural Organization. According to Kirtley F. Mather in the *American Scholar*, "It was Shapley who almost singlehandedly prevented the deletion of the S from UNESCO" in the deliberations over the charter in 1945.

In his many years of scientific research, Shapley was assisted by his wife Martha Betz, a philologist and mathematician who was herself, according to Bart J. Bok, "an experienced and expert analyst of orbits of eclipsing binaries." Several of their children also became distinguished scientists. Shapley was greatly admired by his peers and received many of the awards the scientific community had to give: the Gold Medal of the Royal Astronomical Society, the Draper medal of the National Academy of Sciences, and the Rumford Medal of the American Academy of Arts and Sciences, among others. His manuscripts are in the Harvard University Archives.

PRINCIPAL WORKS: *Science and astronomy*—Starlight, 1926; Flights from Chaos: A Survey of Material Systems from Atoms to Galaxies, 1930; Galaxies, 1943, 3rd ed. 1972; The Inner Metagalaxy, 1957; Of Stars and Men: The Human Response to an Expanding Universe, 1958; The View from a Distant Star: Man's Future in the Universe, 1963; Beyond the Observatory, 1967. *Autobiography*—Through Rugged Ways to the Stars, 1969. *As editor*—(with C. H. Payne) Radio Talks from the Harvard Observatory: The Universe of Stars, 1926; (with H.E. Howarth) A Source Book in Astronomy, 1929; (with S. Rapport and H. Wright) A Treasury of Science, 1943 (revised as The New Treasury of Science, 1965); Climatic Change: Evidence, Causes, and Effects, 1953; Science Ponders Religion, 1960; Source Book in Astronomy, 1900–1950, 1960.

ABOUT: Biographical Memoirs of the National Academy of Science vol. 49, 1978; Current Biography 1952; Dictionary of American Biography, Suppl. 9, 1994; Dictionary of Scientific Biography vol. 12, 1975. *Periodicals*—American Scholar Summer 1971; New York Times October 21, 1972; Saturday Review May 17, 1958; Saturday Review of Literature February 21, 1931.

**SHARP, DALLAS LORE** (December 13, 1870– November 29, 1929), American naturalist, was born in Haleyville, New Jersey, the son of Reuben Lore and Mary Den (Bradway) Sharp. He  graduated from Brown University in 1895 and was ordained a pastor in the Methodist Episcopal Church in the same year. In 1899 he received a bachelor's degree in theology from Boston University, but in the same year he resigned his pastorship in Brockton Heights, Massachusetts, to become a librarian (later instructor in English and professor of English) at Boston University. Sharp joined the editorial staff of the *Youth's Companion* in 1900 and the following year brought out his first book, *Wild Life Near Home*.

Like his first book, most of the subsequent ones were small-scale, delicate observations of nature that had originally been published as essays in the *Youth's Companion* and *Atlantic Monthly*. Taking a cue from John Burroughs, the homespun naturalist whose biography he was to write in 1921 (*The Seer of Slabsides*), Sharp wrote not of grand vistas but of the backyard delights he enjoyed with his wife and four children in suburban Boston. For all his interest in nature, wrote Peter J. Schmitt, "Sharp was neither scientist nor transcendental philosopher. He was a cultured, middle-class family man, a commuter happily integrating his philosophy and his family into an Arcadian design. . . . Sharp idealized the 'door-yard universe' in which all things related to himself and his family in the subdued nature of back pasture and woodlot. For him the nature movement did not begin with men like Wilson and Audubon, who mastered the wilderness, but with Emerson and Bryant, who traveled near at home and not alone."

Almost all of Sharp's nature books received favorable reviews; some sold in excess of one hundred thousand copies. "He loves hills and bees and open fires," the *Independent* wrote of the 1916 volume *The Hills of Hingham*. "He has a sense of words, a sense of humor and a sense of the infinite. He writes with charm and sincerity of the little things of life, and of the big things." Sharp stated his own credo succinctly in *The Fall of the Year*, a leisurely account of the changing seasons at his farm in Hingham, Massachusetts: "This is a divinely beautiful world, a marvelously interesting world, the best conceivable sort of a world to live in, notwithstanding its gypsy moths, tornadoes, and germs, its laws of gravity, and of cause and effect; and my purpose . . . is to help my readers to come by this belief."

A Democrat who once sought his party's nomination for the United States Senate, Sharp turned to social and political matters in two books advocating the abolition of private schools as contrary to the spirit of American egalitarianism, *Patrons of Democracy* and *Education in Democracy*. Unlike his nature studies, these books courted controversy, and received it. On the other hand, his two posthumous and completely orthdox works of theology, *Christ and His Time* and *Romances from the Old Testament*, offended no one and pleased many. Undoubtedly, however, remembrance of Dallas Lore Sharp derives almost exclusively from his nature writing.

PRINCIPAL WORKS: *Nature studies*—Wild Life Near Home, 1901; A Watcher in the Woods, 1903; Roof and Meadow, 1904; The Lay of the Land, 1908; The Face of the Fields, 1911; The Fall of the Year, 1911; The Spring of the Year, 1911; Ways of the Woods, 1912; Winter, 1912; Beyond the Pasture Bars, 1914; Summer, 1914; Where Rolls the Oregon, 1914; The Hills of Hingham, 1916; The Year Out of Doors, 1917; Highlands and Hollows, 1923; The Magical Chance, 1923; The Spirit of the Hive: Contemplations of a Beekeeper, 1925; Sanctuary! Sanctuary! 1926; The Better Country, 1928. *Biography*—The Seer of Slabsides, 1921. *Social criticism*—Patrons of Democra-

cy, 1920; Education in a Democracy, 1922. *Theology*—Romances from the Old Testament, 1932; Christ and His Time, 1933. *Juvenile*—The Boys' Life of John Burroughs, 1928.

ABOUT: Dictionary of American Biography, vol. 9, 1935; Renehan, E. J., Jr., John Burroughs: An American Naturalist, 1992; Schmitt, P. J. Back to Nature: The Arcadian Myth in Urban America, 1969. *Periodicals*—Independent May 29, 1916; New York Times November 30, 1929.

**SHARP, LUKE.** See **BARR, ROBERT**

**SHARP, MARGERY** (January 25, 1905–March 14, 1991), English novelist, playwright, and children's writer, was born on Malta, the third daughter of J. H. Sharp. She was educated at Streatham High School, where she wrote and sold poems for pocket money, and at Bedford College, London University. Graduating in French, she traveled widely. In 1929, she was a member of the British Universities' Women's Debating Team on its first visit to the United States. She was a popular speaker because of her ability to make her audience laugh—however weighty the debate.

Margery Sharp showed the same talent in her novels. The first of these, *Rhododendron Pie*, appeared in 1930. Its young heroine, born into a wealthy English family of snobbish "bohemian" aesthetes, outrages them all by choosing to marry a bank clerk rather than to have an affair with an artist. The book was widely welcomed as a witty if kindly satire, which showed the merits as well as the pretensions of her highbrow characters.

After five more very English domestic comedies, all mixing satire and sentiment in palatable proportions, came Margery Sharp's first best-seller, *The Nutmeg Tree*. Julia Packett is a forty-ish vaudeville entertainer, warm-hearted but less virtuous than she would like to be. She goes to the south of France to escape some pressing debts and to further her priggish daughter's romance with an unsuitable suitor, in whom Julia promptly recognizes a kindred spirit. "Julia is delightful," wrote Forrest Reid in the *Spectator*. "So, for that matter, is the novel—an unusually attractive one, neither high-brow or low-brow, but very human and very intelligent." Subsequent adventures in the *Saturday Evening Post* brought Julia thousands of new admirers, but *Lady in Waiting*, Sharp's stage version of her novel, had only brief runs in London and New York.

Margery Sharp was married in 1938 to Geoffrey L. Castle. He served as an artillery major in World War II, while Sharp herself worked for the Armed Forces Education Program. She continued to publish, in British and American magazines, as well as in book form, and had her second major success with *Cluny Brown*. Cluny, a parlormaid with a penchant for plumbing, "don't know her place," but finds it in the arms of a Polish literary lion. She is a heroine as unconventional and irresistible as Julia Packett. Rose Feld wrote that "with the raffish gayety that is her own special gift, Miss Sharp has produced a character who is blood sister to all the lovable women who achieve distinction by the guilelessness with which they pursue their self-appointed course" (*Weekly Book Review*).

*Britannia Mews*, which was made into a successful film, chronicles the changing fortunes of a woman who rebels against her Victorian family. She elopes with her drunken drawing teacher to a slum, but lives long enough to see it converted into fashionable town houses. Some critics consider this the most serious and substantial of Margery Sharp's novels; others that it attempted too much for her real but slight talent. Leonard Bacon called it "a parable, and by no means a dull one, of all England. If the figures of her fancy had as much reality as the background against which they move, and as much vitality as her symbolic overtones, *Britannia Mews* would have been something more than a clever book" (*Saturday Review of Literature*).

In the late 1950s, Margery Sharp began to write for children. She took readily to this form, she told Roy Newquist, finding in it "a complete release of the imagination" (*Counterpoint*). Sharp is best known, in America, for a series of books about an elegant, sophisticated, and intrepid white mouse, Miss Bianca, president of a mouse society devoted to the comfort and rescue of prisoners. These "books for the connoisseur" have achieved a cult readership among adults as well as discriminating children.

The first two in the Miss Bianca series were filmed with huge success by Walt Disney Productions as *The Rescuers*. Two other novels, as well as *Britannia Mews*, were made into movies—*The Nutmeg Tree* as *Julia Misbehaves*, starring Greer Garson, and *Cluny Brown* with Jennifer Jones and Charles Boyer, under the direction of Ernest Lubitsch.

A modest woman, Margery Sharp once declined to participate in a popular television panel game, explaining that she did not want to be recognized every time she went into Marks & Spencer's.

PRINCIPAL WORKS: Rhododendron Pie, 1930; Fanfare for Tin Trumpets, 1932; The Nymph and the Nobleman, 1932; The Flowering Thorn, 1933; Sophy Cassmajor, 1934; Four Gardens, 1935; The Nutmeg Tree, 1937; Harlequin House, 1939; The Stone of Chastity, 1940; Three Companion Pieces (Sophy Cassmajor, The Tigress on the Hearth, The Nymph and the Nobleman) 1941; Cluny Brown, 1944; Britannia Mews, 1946; The Foolish Gentlewoman, 1948; Lisse Lillywhite, 1951; The Gipsy in the Parlour, 1954; The Tigress on the Hearth, 1955; The Eye of Love, 1957 (republished as Martha and the Eye of Love, 1969); Something Light, 1960; Martha in Paris, 1962; Martha, Eric and George, 1964; The Sun in Scorpio, 1965; In Pious Memory, 1967; Rosa, 1969; The Innocents, 1971; The Faithful Servants, 1975; Summer Visits, 1977. Short stories—The Lost Chapel Picnic and Other Stories, 1973. Drama—Lady in Waiting, 1941; The Foolish Gentlewoman, 1950. The "Miss Bianca" series—The Rescuers, 1959; Miss Bianca, 1962; The Turret, 1963; Miss Bianca in the Salt Mines, 1966; Miss Bianca in the Orient, 1970; Miss Bianca in the Antarctic, 1971; Miss Bianca and the Bridesmaid, 1972; Bernard the Brave, 1976; Bernard into Battle, 1979. Juvenile—Mélisande, 1960; Lost at the Fair, 1965; The Children Next Door, 1974; The Magical Cockatoo, 1974.

ABOUT: Contemporary Authors vols. 21–22, 1969; Contemporary Novelists, 1982; Newquist, R. Counterpoint, 1964; Third Book of Junior Authors, 1972; Todd, J. (ed.) Dictionary of British Women Writers, 1989; Twentieth-Century Children's Writers, 1978; Who's Who 1990. *Periodicals*—Christian Science Monitor May 4, 1967; National Review June 27, 1967; New Republic June 3, 1978; New Yorker June 22, 1967; March 6, 1978; New York Times Book Review November 29, 1959; October 21, 1962; May 4, 1975; Saturday Review of Literature June 29, 1946; Times (London) March 15, 1991; Times Literary Supplement November 3, 1972; September 5, 1975; Weekly Book Review August 27, 1944.

**SHAW, GEORGE BERNARD** (July 26, 1856–November 2, 1950), Irish dramatist, critic, music-critic (as "Corno di Bassetto"), novelist, and reformer, was born in Dublin.

He liked to claim family connections with both Oliver Cromwell and the Macduff who killed Macbeth. The Shaws went from Hampshire to Ireland late in the seventeenth century. Respectable middle-class or minor gentry, they had a strong sense of family pride. However, Shaw's paternal grandfather, a solicitor and stockbroker, was ruined by an absconding partner. He collapsed and died, leaving his widow almost destitute to raise the eleven surviving children.

One of these hungry children was Shaw's father, George Carr Shaw. He was an amiable, impractical man with a highly developed sense of the ridiculous, which his son inherited. Through family influence, he was given a sinecure in the Dublin law courts, and when that was abolished, a small pension. He capitalized this and entered the wholesale grain trade, of which he knew nothing. The business survived but never prospered.

George Carr Shaw was thirty-seven when he married Lucinda Elizabeth Gurly, then twenty-one. The daughter of an impoverished landowner, very strictly raised by an aunt, she was educated and imaginative, chilly and strong-willed. She accepted Shaw to escape problems at home. On their honeymoon in Liverpool, she learned that her husband, an avowed teetotaller, was actually a remorseful drunkard. She ran off to the docks, meaning to take passage as a stewardess, but was frightened back by interested longshoremen. For this unsuitable marriage, she was disinherited by her aunt. Bessie Shaw turned to music. She had a fine mezzo-soprano voice, and around 1855 began to take lessons from George John Lee, a charismatic and unorthodox singing teacher and conductor.

George Bernard Shaw was the youngest of three children. He and his two sisters grew up in something close to genteel poverty in an unfashionable part of Dublin, but were taught to despise people in retail trade. They saw little of their parents and were brought up mostly by servants, who could be hired for a few pounds a year. Shaw's early discovery of his father's drunkenness made him a teetotaller and a skeptic.

Meanwhile, Bessie Shaw had become "general musical factotum" to Lee, her teacher. In about 1866, the family moved to a better neighborhood, sharing their house in Hatch Street and its costs with Lee. The latter dominated the household. He converted Shaw to his own contempt for the medical profession, and his faith in open windows and brown bread. Summers were spent at Lee's cottage at Dalkey, where Shaw first discovered nature and its beauties.

After some lessons with a governess and a clerical uncle, Shaw went at ten to the Wesleyan Connexional School in Dublin. He hated it and was a poor and lazy student, accused of diverting his peers from their work with comic stories. In 1868 he was moved to a private school near Dalkey, then, to his shame and horror, to Dublin's Central Model School, attended by children who were not only working class but Roman Catholic. The shame was more snobbish than theological. Shaw's Protestant faith was never very passionately held, and around this time he stopped saying his prayers. His formal education was concluded at the Dublin English Scientific and Commercial Day School.

Shaw could never learn anything that did not interest him. On the other hand, he could not remember a time when he was unable to read. He devoured Robinson Crusoe and Pilgrim's Progress at five or six, and Shakespeare and Dickens before he was ten. Shy and timid in reality, Shaw led a rich imaginative life, fed by his reading, in which he was heroic. Thanks to Lee, the house was always full of musicians and of music, which was always even more important to Shaw than literature. By the time he was fifteen, he could sing or whistle by heart the major works of many classical composers, and later he taught himself piano. He also haunted the National Gallery of Ireland, adding a self-taught knowledge of painting to his accomplishments.

In 1871, Shaw went to work as junior clerk at Townshend's, land agents. Soon after, for disputed reasons, Lee moved suddenly to London. He became George John Vandaleur (or Vandeleur) Lee, and set himself up as a musical guru to rich young ladies. Bessie Shaw wanted to work as a music teacher and Lee was her best hope, for this at least. She followed him to London with her two daughters. George Carr Shaw, who had been frightened into sobriety by a fit, could not leave his always declining business, and moved into lodgings with his son. He sent his wife what little money he could, but saw her again but once. When he died in 1885, neither she nor his children bothered to attend his funeral.

Although he despised office work, Shaw was good at it. By the time he was sixteen, he was Townshend's cashier, earning a decent salary and terrified of being trapped into bourgeois respectability. His younger sister died of tuberculosis in 1876, and this spurred him to act. The same year he went to London, joining his mother, by then teaching music, and his surviving sister Lucy, who was beginning to make a career as a singer. He did not return to Ireland for nearly thirty years.

In his preface to Immaturity, Shaw recalls a conversation with a clerk at Townshend's which made him realize "that I never thought I was to be a great man simply because I had always taken it as a matter of course." London was where Irishmen went to become great, but Shaw did not yet know what form his greatness was to take. His first job (1876–1877) was ghosting for Vandaleur Lee as music critic of a satirical magazine, The Hornet. Shaw spent most of the next two years in the reading room of the British Museum, looking at pictures in the National Gallery, or wandering London, desperately poor and shabby. He studied counterpoint, imbibed revolutionary thoughts from the poetry of Shelley, but produced almost nothing and became depressed and hypochondriac.

In 1879 Shaw got a short-lived job with the Edison Telephone Company. The same year he wrote his semi-autobiographical first novel, appropriately called Immaturity. The book is long, shapeless, and often tedious. No one would publish it, or, at first, any of the four somewhat more original novels Shaw wrote over the following four years. The Irrational Knot, a study of marriage, was followed by Love Among the Artists. Its hero is a composer of genius who, like Shaw himself, places art and ideas above almost everything else, including love. The most readable of the novels is Cashel Byron's Profession, a melodrama with a happy ending about a boxer's romance with an heiress. Robert Louis Stevenson called it "horrid fun," which is more than could be said for the oddly ambiguous political novel An Unsocial Socialist. Shaw's novels introduced characters, incidents, and ideas later used to better effect in the plays. That he persisted with fiction in the face of endless rejection was a triumph of self-discipline. It is only surprising that it took him so long to recognize that his gift was not for narrative but for drama. His fiction today is hardly read even by admirers and scholars.

Much more than the novels was happening during these years. Shaw was re-inventing himself, with a ferocious energy that he attributed to his conversion (via Shelley) to vegetarianism. (He was also an anti-vivisectionist and anti-smoker, as well as a teetotaller.) When he arrived in London, he was hopelessly gauche and shy—too shy even to meet people who might have helped him. If he did find himself in company, he became bumptious and rude in self-defense. Shaw studied some books on etiquette, and in 1880 he joined a debating society. Shaking with fear, too numb with it to read his own notes, he forced himself to speak at every meeting. He confronted his physical timidity just as directly by taking boxing lessons at a London gymnasium; it supplied background for Cashel Byron's Profession.

In 1882, Shaw found a subject worthy of his growing skill as a public speaker. A pamphlet by the economist Henry George made a socialist of him. He read other economists, including Marx, and began to preach socialism at public meetings, in public parks, on street corners. For the next twelve years, Shaw spoke somewhere, on average, three times a week. He learned to combine his polemics and wit with a common touch that made him one of the most sought-after orators in England, capable of filling the largest hall to overflowing. In 1884 he joined the recently formed Fabian Society. He was soon the central figure in this influential group of middle-class socialist intellectuals. One immediate effect was that his novels began to be serialized in various socialist magazines. Book publication followed gradually. And there were other benefits.

Shaw in his late twenties was tall, thin, and pale, with red hair and a red beard grown to conceal the effects of an attack of smallpox. With his fierce, upgrowing moustache and eyebrows, he resembled Mephistopheles, who had fascinated him as a child—but a Mephistopheles with a wild sense of humor, liable to double up and sway with laughter. Everything he did gave an impression of energy and audacity. In 1881 Shaw fell romantically in love with a student nurse, Alice Lockett, but it was not until his twenty-ninth birthday that he lost his virginity, to an older woman, Mrs. Jenny Patterson. That accomplished, he embarked on ten years of rather pallid philandering, initially with such socialist comrades as Annie Besant and Edith Nesbit. Shaw was also making important friendships, notable with William Morris, Sidney and Beatrice Webb, and William Archer, whom he met in 1883 in the British Museum reading room.

A distinguished drama critic, Archer was a champion of Ibsen, as Shaw soon became also. Archer found work for Shaw as a reviewer with the *Pall Mall Gazette*, later as an art critic for the *World*. In 1888–1890, Shaw was music critic for a daily newspaper, the *Star*, writing as "Corno di Bassetto." Mozart and Wagner were adulated, Brahms and his followers excoriated. For Shaw, all of the arts, including music, were to be assessed not only aesthetically, but ethically and politically as well. As he later wrote in *The Sanity of Art*, "art should refine our sense of character and conduct, of justice and sympathy . . . making us intolerant of baseness, cruelty, injustice." Shaw's musical judgments, often brilliantly perceptive and original, were sometimes foolish or simply, deliberately provocative. "Corno di Bassetto" wanted attention. He wrote his reviews in plain English, free of critics' jargon, in a style that was personal, irreverant and jauntily dogmatic. In a similar spirit, he attended concerts not in the required frock-coat and silk hat but in yellow tweed knickerbockers with a bright red tie. These essays, collected in *London Music*, are still a pleasure to read.

In 1884, meanwhile, Archer and Shaw had tried to collaborate on a play. It was abandoned after two acts, but completed by Shaw seven years later. In December 1892, J.T. Grein gave it two performances at his Independent Theatre Club. In *Widowers' Houses*, the idealistic young Dr. Trench falls in love on vacation, then learns that his fiancée Blanche is the daughter of a slum landlord, a ruthless exploiter of the poor. She will not renounce her father's money and breaks off the engagement. Trench discovers that part of his own income derives from the same slums. "Morally beggared," he embraces both "tainted wealth" and Blanche.

*Widowers' Houses* began Shaw's almost solitary struggle to challenge the escapism of the nineteenth-century British theater with an Ibsenite theater of ideas. More than a Fabian tract against capitalism, it show that we all share moral responsibility for social evils, and rejects the easy solutions of romantic theater. The hero does not stick nobly to his principles, but sells them out. The heroine is greedy and an erotic bully.

Contemporary reviewers were outraged, though some acknowledged the play's vigorous theatricality, the vitality of its diaglogue and characterization. However, Shaw's friend A. B. Walkley, while praising the play's "power of cogent argument, a terse and trenchant style, a really fine irony," complained that the characters "are not really dramatic characters at all, they are embodied arguments" (*Speaker*). This has remained the commonest criticism of Shaw's theater—that he can create amusing Dickensian caricatures, like Sartorius and Lickcheese in *Widowers' Houses*, but not flesh-and-blood people. His plays tend to pit an intellectual superman resembling the author against skillfully personified ideas, set up to be knocked down by the hero's brilliant paradoxes. Shaw's admirers agree (most of them) that he knew and cared less than Shakespeare did about the roots of human emotion. They point out that Shaw, like Brecht, was more concerned to make us think than feel—and that he succeeded in doing that in his time. "Life would be duller without him," Robert Graves, not an admirer, used to say.

A less serious piece followed, *The Philanderer*, drawing on the author's activities in that field as well as Ibsen's ideas of individual morality (already commended by Shaw in *The Quintessence of Ibsenism*.) Shaw could be as wildly self-critical as he was breathtakingly arrogant and, rereading this play later, found it "a combination of mechanical farce with realistic filth which quite disgusted me." That was said in 1896 in the course of his long "epistolary romance" with the actress Ellen Terry. *The Philanderer* had to wait fourteen years for public production, and *Mrs. Warren's Profession* was banned until 1925 (though there was an American production in 1905, received with horror). The latter play argues passionately that prostitution is rooted, not in the wickedness of women, but in their economic dependency. It also introduces the taboo subject of incest. Even in these early plays, Shaw was attacking convention and hypocrisy, as he did all his life.

The three "unpleasant" plays were followed by four "pleasant" ones—comedies that seek to instruct by entertaining rather than indicting their audiences. Thus, *Arms and the Man*—one of his most enduring plays—is set in the Balkans in order to outflank British jingoism. Its heroine's naive admiration for military glory, and for her absurdly gallant betrothed, is deconstructed by Captain Bluntschli, a Swiss mercenary who would rather live than fight. A funny and highly efficient "well-made" play, it was staged in 1894 in both London and New York, and gave Shaw his first small success. It was plagiarized for the operetta *The Chocolate Soldier*.

*Arms and the Man*, like *Widowers' Houses* and many of the later plays, turns upside down the audience's romantic expectations. Indeed, Bertolt Brecht, whose "alienation effect" was, if only to a limited extent, a Shavian device, wrote that "Probably every single feature of all Shaw's characters can be attributed to his delight in dislocating our stock associations" (*Brecht on Theatre*). However, it is also true and often said that Shaw could not write convincing love scenes, perhaps because the emotional coldness of his upbringing had limited his own capacity for romantic love (as distinct from "philandering"). He nevertheless adored his chilly mother, who has been seen as the model for all the "strong women" in his play.

There is such a woman in the best of the other "pleasant" plays, *Candida*. It is about the wife of a popular Christian socialist clergyman, and what happens when a young poet, Marchbanks, seeks to rescue Candida from her husband and children. For Marchbanks (as for Shaw at that time), domesticity is the death of poetry and the spirit, but it is not so for Candida. She puts herself up for auction, saying that she will choose the weaker of the two men. This device, while teaching her complacent husband to recognize his weakness, shows Marchbanks his strength, enabling him to move on in pursuit of his singular destiny. As Shaw wrote in the *Radio Times*, the play was conceived "as a counterblast to Ibsen's *Doll House*, showing that in the real typical doll's house it is the man who is the doll." There are no villains in *Candida*, and yet it is as rich in drama as in comedy. Using a small cast and one set, with no costume changes, it is also a triumph of structural economy.

Popular as it eventually became, *Candida* was slow to achieve even provincial production. In an 1895 letter to Henry Arthur Jones, Shaw admitted his frustration at his lack of success, and at being taken, if at all, as merely a witty cynic. However, being "a man who habitually thinks of himself as one of the great geniuses of all time," he remained confident that "the public twenty years hence will see feeling and reality where they see nothing now but intellectual swordplay and satire." Undeterred, he went on writing plays. Even geniuses have to live, however, and 1895 Shaw became drama critic of Frank Harris's *Saturday Review*. There, among many other things, he mounted a ferocious campaign against the reactionary Sir Henry Irving, then the most powerful man in the British theater. (See Shaw's *Our Theatres in the Nineties*, 1932).

Shaw had by no means relinquished his active involvement in politics. In 1888, he had edited *Fabian Essays in Socialism*, and in 1893 he collaborated with Keir Hardie in writing the party program for the new Independent Labour party. Shaw was co-founder with the Webbs of the London School of Economics, and launched the petition against the imprisonment of Oscar Wilde—one of his many actions against injustice. In 1897 he entered local government, working for women's rights, women's lavatories, and other public health measures as a vestryman of the London borough of St. Pancras. At the same time, Shaw was slaving over the publication of his *Plays Pleasant and Unpleasant*. He devoted infinite pains to the printing and layout of the two volumes, which embodied his own theories of punctuation and spelling. Since he could not secure proper production of his plays, he supplied them with descriptions of scenes, characters, and actions that would bring them to life for the reader. He added the first of the famous prefaces in which he expanded, not only on the play and its themes and staging, but on himself, his theories, and anything else that occurred to him. Some of the prefaces are twice as long as the works they introduce.

Near the end of this hectic decade, Shaw became exhausted and ill, prone to accidents. Through the Webbs, he had met a wealthy Anglo-Irishwoman, Charlotte Payne-Townshend, prepared to nurse him back to health. They were married on June 1, 1898, when both were over forty. Based on mutual respect and convenience rather than romantic love, the marriage was celibate from early on, but for the most part congenial. However, Arnold Silver, in *Bernard Shaw: The Darker Side*, suggests that the predatory Ann Whitefield in *Man and Superman* is a well-disguised portrait of Charlotte Shaw, and that the play's whole argument is Shaw's attempt "to reconcile himself to his strange marriage." At any rate, married to a rich woman, Shaw was at last making money on his own account. *The Devil's Disciple*, inverting the melodrama of *A Tale of Two Cities*, and set in America during the War of Independence, was a success in New York. It freed him from Grub Street once and for all.

Shaw admired Shakespear (as he always called him) as a master of language, but thought he had failed in the artist's duty of optimism. Shaw's *Caesar and Cleopatra*, in which Julius Caesar teaches a teen-aged Cleopatra the art of government, was in part a response to the romantic defeatism of Shakespeare's *Antony and Cleopatra*, in part a commentary on contemporary politics. Shaw's Caesar is a Lincolnesque statesman of great humanity and humor, a superman who, like the Sphinx, is "part brute, part woman, and part god." Shaw had come to believe that the masses were helplessly reactionary; that exceptional men—"higher evolutionary types"—offered the only hope for progress. This led him later to a short-lived admiration for dictators like Stalin and Mussolini.

After several lesser pieces came what many regard as Shaw's most profound play, *Man and Superman*. Jack Tanner is a wealthy socialist, and a spokesman for Shaw's own political and moral beliefs. (Tanner's "Revolutionist's Handbook" is conveniently printed with the play.) He becomes guardian to the young Ann Whitefield. Being a vehicle of the "Life Force," she decides that he must marry her, since he is intellectually and ethically suitable to father her children. Tanner is too unworldly to recognize this threat to his freedom but is warned by his chauffeur Straker, a pragmatic "New Man." He escapes to Spain, pursued by Ann.

In Spain (Act Three), Tanner dreams that he is Don Juan, in Hell—a Don Juan who does not pursue women but is pursued by them. He debates, with the Devil and others, many of Shaw's favorite themes, in particular his developing theory of Creative Evolution. If we can learn to cooperate with the Life Force, a vulgarization of Bergson's *élan vital*, we can play our part in Creative Evolution, which seeks a heightening of consciousness and through it a better world. These optimistic theories, all of which derive from simplifications of the works of Nietszsche and Schopenhauer, as well as Bergson and Lamarck, Wagner and Samuel Butler, reconcile Tanner to his destiny as Ann's husband: "a father for the Superman." Shaw remained a socialist, and an opponent of what he called "Crosstianity," but his faith in the political process was waning; *Man and Superman* is as religious a play as Shaw ever managed. By then, for Shaw, "the sole hope for human salvation lies in teaching Man to regard himself as an experiment in the realization of God. He must regard God as a helpless longing, which *longed* him into existence by its desperate need for an executive organ" (*Collected Letters, 1898–1910*).

*Don Juan in Hell*, ninety minutes long, is sometimes produced separately as a play in its own right, and is often omitted from productions of *Man and Superman*, although it explains the theories that the rest of the play exemplifies. Louis Kronenberger wrote that "nowhere in English during the twentieth century has there been a more dazzlingly sustained discussion of ideas in dialogue form."

Shaw was forty-eight when the tide turned for him. In 1904, Harley Granville-Barker took over the Royal Court Theatre in Sloane Square and, with J. E. Vedrenne as business manager, launched a deliberate challenge to the commercialism of the London stage. There was at last a theater and an audience ready for Shaw. His Irish play, *John Bull's Other Island*, had enormous success, easily surpassed by *Man and Superman*. *Major Barbara* followed, another gripping discussion play. Barbara Undershaft, a dedicated and fearless officer of the Salvation Army, learns from her demonic father, a manufacturer of armaments, that money and power can be better weapons against evil than love. *The Doctor's Dilemma* rides one of Shaw's favorite hobby horses—the hypocrisy and general uselessness of the medical profession.

In real life, though he could be tactless, sometimes deliberately, Shaw was charming, generous, and considerate. However, for most of his writing life, he had been busily creating a false public persona, the arrogant and deliberately perverse intellectual mountebank who signed himself "G. B. S." This was primarily a device to draw the reluctant world's attention to what he had to say, partly a mask for his shyness. Shaw became trapped in that mask. Increasingly it cost him the respect of his intellectual peers, though his public fame grew and grew.

There were major plays still to come. *Pygmalion* is not major but disconcertingly charming, cunningly deriving a Cinderella story from Shaw's interest in phonetics. It was written for the actress Mrs. Patrick Campbell, for whom Shaw had worked up a false passion. It was the basis for a film and, later, the musical *My Fair Lady*, for which a

more romantic ending than Shaw's was created. Soon after this triumph, Shaw's 1914 essay "Common Sense About the War," misunderstood as unpatriotic, did massive damage to his new-found popularity. *Heartbreak House* was written during this interlude in the wilderness, and blamed the war on the spiritual impoverishment of the pre-war ruling class. It is uncharacteristically Chekhovian in tone, symbolist in manner, ramshackle in structure. Shaw called it his "King Lear," and thought it his masterpiece, an opinion not universally shared. *Back to Methuselah* followed, a cycle of five rather directionless plays on the theme of Creative Evolution. In 1921, Shaw met a young American, Molly Tompkins, and a romance of sorts developed. According to Michael Holroyd in his biography it was almost but not quite consummated when Shaw was seventy.

Shaw's reputation, shattered by his outspokenness about the war, gradually recovered. It was finally mended in 1924 by his marathon *Saint Joan*, received with awed enthusiasm by many, including Pirandello, who called it "a work of poetry from beginning to end" (*New York Times*). Others shared the opinion of T. S. Eliot, who thought that Shaw had turned Joan into "a great middle-class reformer" (*Criterion*). The Shaw industry revived, and made up for lost time. New plays appeared, notably *The Apple Cart* and *Too True to Be Good*. There were essays and books—*The Intelligent Woman's Guide to Socialism, Everybody's Political What's What.* There were Gabriel Pascal's film versions of *Pygmalion, Major Barbara, Caesar and Cleopatra.* In 1926 Shaw received the Nobel Prize for literature. He was by then the world's most famous living dramatist, widely regarded as "a second Shakespeare" who, single-handed, had revolutionized British theater. He was also Britain's Grand Old Man of Letters, an all-purpose professional genius, with predictably colorful opinions on everything.

Shaw died in 1950, at the former rectory in the Hertfordshire village of Ayot St. Lawrence, where he and Charlotte had settled in 1906. He was ninety-four and had outlived his friends and his wife, who died in 1943. At the news of Shaw's passing, Broadway lowered its lights; Nehru adjourned a meeting of the Indian Cabinet.

Stephen Spender agreed with Edmund Wilson and others that Shaw had learned from music, and especially from Mozart, "the secret of external form and progression and sequence" and "the art of instrumentation by which dialogue is interwoven, like woodwind and strings," but concluded that "he has not learned the inwardness of Mozart. His [two-dimensional] art is the direction of dialogue from the outside, not the creation of character from within" (*Nation*). T. S. Eliot damned him with faint praise as "the intellectual stimulant and the dramatic delight of twenty years" (*Criterion*).

PRINCIPAL WORKS: The Works of Bernard Shaw, 30 vols., 1930–1932 (revised as Ayot St. Lawrence Edition, 1931–1932; Standard Edition, 36 vols., 1947–1952). *Drama*—Widowers' Houses, 1893; Man and Superman, 1903; The Devil's Disciple, 1906; You Can Never Tell, 1906; Captain Brassbound's Conversion, 1906; The Doctor's Dilemma, 1908; The Admirable Bashville, 1909; The Shewing-Up of Blanco Posnet, 1909; Press Cuttings,

2387 SHAW, G. B.

1909; Arms and the Man, 1913 (definitive ed., 1977); Mrs. Warren's Profession, 1913; Candida, 1913; John Bull's Other Island, 1913; The Philanderer, 1913; Major Barbara, 1913; Caesar and Cleopatra, 1913; Getting Married, 1913; Overruled, 1915; Pygmalion, 1920 (definitive ed., 1982); Back to Methuselah, 1921 (definitive ed., 1977) Saint Joan, 1923; The Apple Cart, 1930; Geneva, 1939; "In Good King Charles's Golden Days," 1939; Buoyant Billions, 1949; Androcles and the Lion, 1951; Heartbreak House, 1964. *Collections*—Plays Pleasant and Unpleasant (Widowers' Houses, The Philanderer, Mrs. Warren's Profession, Arms and the Man, Candida, The Man of Destiny, You Can Never Tell) 2 vols., 1898; Three Plays for Puritans (The Devil's Disciple, Caesar and Cleopatra, Captain Brassbound's Conversion) 1901; John Bull's Other Island (with Major Barbara, How He Lied to Her Husband) 1907; The Doctor's Dilemma (with Getting Married, The Shewing-Up of Blanco Posnet) 1911; The Man of Destiny (with How He Lied to Her Husband) 1913; Misalliance (with The Dark Lady of the Sonnets, Fanny's First Play) 1914; Androcles and the Lion (with Overruled, Pygmalion) 1916; Heartbreak House (with Great Catherine, Playlets of the War), 1919; The Complete Plays of Bernard Shaw, 1931; Saint Joan (with the Apple Cart) 1933; Three Plays (Too True to Be Good, Village Wooing, On the Rocks) 1934; How He Lied to Her Husband (with The Admirable Bashville) 1935; Nine Plays, 1935; The Simpleton of the Unexpected Isles (with the Six of Calais, The Millionairess) 1936; Six Plays, 1941; Geneva (revised version, with Cymbeline Refinished, "In Good King Charles's Golden Days") 1946; Selected Plays, 1948–1957; Buoyant Billions (with Farfetched Fables, Shakes Versus Shaw) 1951; Selected Plays and Other Writings, 1956; Four Plays (The Devil's Disciple, Candida, Caesar and Cleopatra, Man and Superman) 1965; Selected One-Act Plays, 1965; The Devil's Disciple (with Major Barbara, Saint Joan) 1966; Seven Plays, 1966; Pygmalion and Other Plays, 1967; Three Shorter Plays (The Man of Destiny, The Admirable Bashville, Fanny's First Play) 1968; The Bodley Head Bernard Shaw, 7 vols., 1970–1974 (in U.S.: Collected Plays with Their Prefaces); Selected Plays, 1981; Early Texts: Play Manuscripts in Facsimile (ed. G. Laurence) 12 vols., 1981; Selected Shorter Plays (definitive ed.) 1987. *Fiction*—Cashel Byron's Profession, 1886 (definitve ed., 1979); An Unsocial Socialist, 1887; Love Among the Artists, 1900; The Irrational Knot, 1905; Immaturity, 1931; The Adventures of the Black Girl in Her Search for God, 1932; Short Stories, Scraps and Shavings, 1934 (republished as The Black Girl in Search of God, and Some Lesser Tales, 1964); Selected Novels (The Irrational Knot, Cashel Byron's Profession, An Unsocial Socialist) 1946; An Unfinished Novel (ed. D. Weintraub) 1958. *Drama criticism and prefaces*—The Quintessence of Ibsenism, 1891 (revised as Shaw and Ibsen; ed. J. L. Wisenthal, 1979); Dramatic Opinions and Essays, 1906; Major Critical Essays, 1932; Our Theatres in the Nineties, 1932; Prefaces, 1934; Plays and Players (ed. A. C. Ward) 1952; Shaw on the Theatre (ed. E. J. West) 1958; Shaw's Dramatic Criticism: 1895–1898 (ed. J. F. Matthews) 1959; Shaw on Shakespeare (ed. E. Wilson) 1961; The Complete Prefaces of Bernard Shaw, 1965. *Music criticism*—The Perfect Wagnerite, 1898; Music in London, 1890–1894, 1932; London Music in 1888–1889, 1937; Shaw on Music (ed. E. Bentley) 1955; How to Become a Musical Critic (ed. D. F. Laurence) 1960; G. B. S. on Music, 1962; Collected Music Criticism, 1973; The Great Composers: Reviews and Bombardments (ed. L. Crompton) 1978; Shaw's Music (ed. D. H. Laurence) 3 vols., 1981. *Politics, society and religion*—(as ed.) Fabian Essays in Socialism, 1889; (as ed.) Fabianism and the Empire, 1900; The Common Sense of Municipal Trading, 1904; On Going to Church, 1905; Socialism and Superior Brains, 1910; Peace Conference Hints, 1919; Imprisonment, 1925 (republished as The Crime of Imprisonment, 1946); The Socialism of Shaw (essays and lectures; ed. J. Fuchs) 1926; The Intelligent Woman's Guide to Capitalism and Socialism, 1928 (revised as The Intelligent Women's Guide to Socialism, Capitalism, Sovietism, and Fascism, 1965); Bernard Shaw and Karl Marx: A Symposium, 1884–1889, 1930; What I Really Wrote About the War, 1931; Doctor's Delusions, Crude Criminology, and Sham Education, 1932; Essays in Fabian Socialism, 1932; American Boobs, 1933 (also published as The Political Madhouse in America; in U.S.:

The Future of Political Science in America); Everybody's Political What's What, 1944; The Illusions of Socialism (with Socialism: Principles and Outlook) 1956; Platform and Pulpit (ed. D. H. Laurence) 1961; The Matter with Ireland (eds. D. H. Laurence and D. H. Greene) 1962; Religious Speeches (ed. W. S. Smith) 1963; Shaw on Religion (ed. W. S. Smith) 1967; The Road to Equality: Ten Unpublished Lectures and Essays (ed. L. Crompton) 1971; Bernard Shaw's Practical Politics (ed. L. J. Hubenka) 1976. *Other*—The Sanity of Art, 1908; The Wisdom of Bernard Shaw (ed. C. F. Shaw) 1913; Translations and Tomfooleries, 1926; Pen Portraits and Reviews, 1932; Major Critical Essays, 1932; William Morris As I Knew Him, 1936; Selected Prose (ed. D. Russell) 1952; Shaw on Vivisection (ed. G. H. Bowker) 1949; A Prose Anthology (ed. H. M. Burton) 1959; On Language (ed. A. Tauber) 1963; Bernard Shaw: Selections of His Wit and Wisdom (ed. C. T. Harnsberger) 1965; Bernard Shaw's Ready-Reckoner (ed. N. H. Leigh-Taylor) 1965; Non-Dramatic Literary Criticism (ed. S. Weintraub) 1972; The Portable Bernard Shaw (ed. S. Weintraub) 1977; Lady, Wilt Thou Love Me? (18 love poems to Ellen Terry, attributed to Shaw; ed. J. Werner) 1980; The Collected Screenplays of Bernard Shaw (ed. B. F. Dukore) 1980; Shaw on Dickens (eds. L. and M. Quinn) 1984. *Autobiography, diaries, and letters*—Table-Talk of G. B. S. (ed. A. Henderson) 1925; Ellen Terry and Bernard Shaw: A Correspondence (ed. C. St. John) 1931; Some Unpublished Letters of Bernard Shaw (ed. J. Park) 1939; Shaw Gives Himself Away: An Autobiographical Miscellany, 1939; Florence Farr, Bernard Shaw, and W. B. Yeats (ed. C. Bax) 1942; Sixteen Self Sketches, 1949; Bernard Shaw and Mrs. Patrick Campbell: A Correspondence (ed. A. Dent) 1952; Advice to a Young Critic, and Other Letters (ed. E. J. West) 1955; Bernard Shaw's Letters to Harley Granville-Barker (ed. C. B. Purdom) 1956; My Dear Dorothea: A Practical System of Education for Females, Embodied in a Letter to a Young Person of That Sex, 1956; To a Young Actress: Letters to Molly Tompkins (ed. P. Tompkins) 1960; Collected Letters (ed. D. H. Laurence) 4 vols., 1965–1988; Shaw: An Autobiography (ed. S. Weintraub) 2 vols., 1969–1970; Bernard Shaw and Alfred Douglas: A Correspondence (ed. M. Hyde) 1982; The Playwright and the Pirate: Bernard Shaw and Frank Harris: A Correspondence (ed. S. Weintraub) 1982; Agitations: Letters to the Press, 1875–1950 (ed. D. H. Laurence) 1985; Bernard Shaw's Letters to Siegfried Trebitsch (ed. S. A. Weiss) 1986; The Diaries, 1885–1897 (ed. S. Weintraub) 1985; Shaw, Lady Gregory and the Abbey: A Correspondence and a Record (ed. D. H. Laurence) 1993.

ABOUT: Bentley, E. Bernard Shaw, 1957; Bevan, E. D. Concordance to the Plays and Prefaces of Bernard Shaw, 10 vols., 1971; Chesterton, G. K. George Bernard Shaw, 1909; Ervine, St. J. Bernard Shaw: His Life, Work and Friends, 1956; Evans, T. F. Shaw: The Critical Heritage, 1976; Gibbs, A. M. Shaw: Interviews and Recollections, 1990; Henderson, A. George Bernard Shaw: Man of the Century, 1956; Holroyd, M. Shaw (4 vols., authorized biography) 1988–1993; Irvine, W. The Universe of G. B. S., 1949; MacCarthy, D. Shaw, 1951; Mander, R. and Mitcheson, J. A Theatrical Companion to Shaw, 1977; Meisel, M. Shaw and the Nineteenth-Century Theater, 1963; Pearson, H. Bernard Shaw: His Life and Personality, 1942; Purdom, C. B. A Guide to the Plays of Bernard Shaw, 1963; Rattray, R. F. Bernard Shaw: A Chronicle, 1951; Rossett, B. C. Shaw of Dublin: The Formative Years, 1964; Silver, A. Bernard Shaw: The Darker Side, 1982; Strauss, E. Bernard Shaw: Art and Socialism, 1978; Weintraub, S. Journey to Heartbreak: The Crucible Years of Bernard Shaw, 1914–1918, 1971; Weintraub, S. Bernard Shaw: A Guide to Research, 1992; West, A. A Good Man Fallen Among Fabians, 1974; Wilson, C. Bernard Shaw: A Reassessment, 1969. *Bibliography*—Laurence, D. H. Bernard Shaw: A Bibliography (The Soho Bibliographies, 2 vols.) 1983; Shaw: An Annotated Bibliography of Writings About Him (1871–1930, ed. J. P. Wearing; 1957–1978, ed. D. C. Haberman) 1986. *Periodicals*—Criterion October 1924; Nation April 30, 1949; New York Times January 13, 1924; Radio Times April 12, 1946; Republic November 26, 1959; Shaw Review (formerly Shaw Bulletin) 1950– ; Speaker December 17, 1892.

**SHAW, IRWIN** (February 27, 1913–May 16, 1984), American novelist, short story writer, playwright, and screenwriter, wrote: "I was born in  New York City and was educated in Brooklyn, in the public schools and in Brooklyn College, from which I was graduated with a B.A. in 1934. I played football there for four years, wrote a column for three years for the school newspaper (my first published work), and wrote plays that were put on by the dramatic society. I was expelled in my freshman year for failure in calculus, worked for a year at various jobs around New York, in a cosmetics factory, an installment furniture house, and a department store. To make money when I got back into school I tutored children, worked in the school library, typed manuscripts, wrote theses in English for students in New York University.

"When I got out of school I started writing for the radio serials for two years, among them 'The Gumps' and 'Dick Tracy,' comic-strip dramatizations. I wrote *Bury the Dead* while still writing for the radio, quit the radio for good and all after finishing the play. I've written screen plays in Hollywood on four different occasions, all of them of no consequence. *Siege*, my second play, was a gloomy and immediate failure. *The Gentle People*, produced in 1939, was fairly successful, ran for four and a half months. Another play, *Quiet City*, was tried out in an experimental production by the Group Theatre for two performances, [and] closed before the critics were allowed in. I've also written many short stories, for the *New Yorker*, *Esquire*, *Collier's*, *Story*, the *Yale Review*, other magazines.

"I'm married, live in New York City. My most recent production was *Retreat to Pleasure* (1940), a comedy. My political convictions are liberal.

"*Bury the Dead* is included in Gassner's *Twenty Best Plays of the Modern Theatre*, [and] has been done a great many times all over the country by almost every little theatre group, and has been done in England and Ireland and by the Habima Players of Palestine in a Hebrew translation. *The Gentle People* was produced professionally in London and Copenhagen. Stories of mine are in the 1940 O. Henry and O'Brien collections.

"During the war I served in Africa, England, France, and Germany. After the war, produced two plays, *The Assassins* and, with Peter Viertel, *The Survivors*. Both failed. In the field of the novel I've published *The Young Lions* and *The Troubled Air*. In addition I've published four books of short stories. A short story of mine 'Walking Wounded' won the O. Henry Memorial Prize in 1944 . . ."

---

Irwin Shaw was born in the Bronx, the son of William Shamforoff and Rose (Tompkins) Shamforoff, who changed their family's name to Shaw and moved to Brooklyn, where he spent most of his childhood and attended Brooklyn College. He was expelled in his freshman year for failing calculus, but he returned to become quarterback of the varsity football team and receive his B. A. degree in 1934. After graduation, he wrote radio scripts while working on plays and short stories in his spare time.

At twenty-three, Shaw achieved early and sudden notoriety as a socially conscious playwright when his first play, *Bury the Dead* (1936), a tragic one-act anti-war fable in which six soldiers killed in battle rise up and refuse to be buried, was produced on Broadway to much critical acclaim. With it, Shaw became a firebrand of the left-leaning experimental Group Theatre of the 1930s. The device of slain soldiers refusing to die is not wholly original, however; Austrian playwright Hans Chlumberg used it in his *Miracle at Verdun* (1931). Of Shaw's production, Stark Young wrote in the *New Republic* of the play's powerful imagery: "A myth is created, a veritable fable is established." The play "was too well written to be ignored, and Shaw was embarked upon a promising career," wrote Bergen Evans in the *English Journal.* But some critics doubted the sincerity of Shaw's pacifism and believed he was merely a follower of popular intellectual fashion. He had a modest success with *The Gentle People* (1939), a three-act fable set in Brooklyn, where the meek triumph over the violent, which was produced by the Group Theatre, starring Sylvia Sidney and Franchot Tone. Shaw's other stage offerings were commercial as well as critical flops, and when *The Assassin* (1946) closed early due to negative reviews, he all but abandoned playwriting, but not before publishing a diatribe that lashed out against all those associated with the theater—from drama critics to electricians. The outburst probably led the *New Republic* to hire him as drama critic from September 1947 until March 1948, Evans claimed.

Shaw also wrote for radio, and he went to Hollywood in 1936 to write screenplays. But he is most remembered today for his achievements as the author of the "socially conscious" short story. Many of the more than two dozen stories he published in the *New Yorker* in the late 1930s and 1940s are considered twentieth-century American classics as enduring as those by John Cheever, John O'Hara, or J. D. Salinger.

His first two collected volumes, *The Sailor Off the Bremen* (1939) and *Welcome to the City* (1942), contain some of his best ones, such as "The Sailor Off the Bremen," "The Girls in Their Summer Dresses," "Second Mortgage," and "The Eighty-Yard Run." Three themes predominate in his stories, according to James R. Giles in *Irwin Shaw* (1983): "the effects of the depression on the middle and lower classes; the threat to American values inherent in the rise of fascism at home and abroad; and the moral shallowness at the core of the American success story."

By the end of his career, Shaw had published eighty-four short stories "all with a more powerful realism and cohesiveness than is evident in any of his novels" and "an imaginative record of a turbulent half-century," wrote Giles. In a review of *Mixed Company: Collected Short Stories* (1950), William Peden in the *Saturday Review* compared Shaw to Dickens in his ability to create memorable characters and capture the gritty authenticity of a variety of scenes, from the decrepit atmosphere of a third-rate New York hotel to the oppressive heat of an Army newspaper office in Algiers. "As opposed to other short story writers who were content in depicting a mood or offering a plotless insight, Shaw was that rare thing, a short story writer who was a storyteller," wrote Hubert Saal in the *Saturday Review*. But his considerable talent with the short form "thins out and becomes flat when applied to the longer and more integrated genre of the novel," wrote William Startt in *Midwest Quarterly*.

Shaw's career as a novelist began after he was drafted into the Army in 1942. During World War II, he served in North Africa and Europe and was present at the liberation of Paris. His first novel, *The Young Lions* (1948), was a panorama of the conflict in Europe told from the distinct perspectives of one German and two American soldiers. Published three years after Shaw's discharge from the army, it was assailed by John W. Aldridge in *After the Lost Generation* (1951) and by other critics for its obvious structural flaws and an ending that Aldridge considered Hollywood melodrama. However, its defenders found lasting value in the book as a study of good and evil and as a profounder war novel than either Norman Mailer's *The Naked and the Dead* or James Jones's *From Here to Eternity*. The novel was made into a movie starring Montgomery Clift and Marlon Brando.

Shaw's second novel, *The Troubled Air* (1951), also had literary defects, with writing that "is lathered up with a lot of wisecracking drivel," wrote David Goldknopf in the *New Republic*. Lionel Trilling wrote in *Saturday Review of Literature* that "Irwin Shaw's best work is still in the short story—this is the medium that allows his particular gifts of observation and sentiment to appear to their best advantage." The best-selling novel showed Shaw's concern about the rise of McCarthyism, although he himself was only mildly bruised by the anti-Communist mania that destroyed many of his Hollywood contemporaries.

In 1951, Shaw left the United States for what would become a twenty-five year residency in Paris. He would spend the rest of his life trying, with only intermittent success, to disprove the dictum that no writer should leave his literary roots, wrote Michael Shnayerson in *Irwin Shaw: A Biography* (1989). The slant of his fiction became noticeably different as he became an international literary celebrity. The underdog American everyman that had given his earlier stories such a realistic punch had basically vanished, to be replaced with wealthy expatriates in glamour spots such as Cannes, Paris, and Rome. Led by Aldridge in articles in the *New York Times* and Leslie A. Fiedler, who in a 1956 *Commentary* review called Shaw's writing "half-art," many critics wrote scathingly of how he had sold out and how he had settled for being a superfi-

cial observer of American society whose aesthetics lacked sincerity. Saal found that most of the stories in *Tip on a Dead Jockey* (1957) were disappointing in the absence of the salty spunk of his earlier stories, where "Shaw cared, and his characters cared, about politics and injustice and loneliness and love and growing up and growing old. . . . Against wrong, Shaw spoke up. Again and again, with true tragic dignity, his characters rose up at the last, refused to submit, protested, did something. Now, it seemed, they only shared their disillusionment."

Despite this kind of negative critical assessment, Shaw's works were popular successes: most of his novels became best sellers, and three became television mini-series. Critics who continued to find merit in his work appreciated its underlying morality and concern for the inherently American struggle to find inner strength and decency in the midst of a chaotic world. But these opinions were the minority. Older readers who remembered and admired his early work bemoaned his descent into commercialism.

When his Jordache family saga, *Rich Man, Poor Man* (1970), was televised in 1977, it prompted a more successful second printing of the novel as well as the reissuing of his older novels. Overnight, television was able to beam Shaw's name to millions who had heard it dimly before, if at all. Shaw had nothing to do with the miniseries, but he could hardly argue with the fresh wave of fame, and the money, and the new readers that its success conferred upon him, Shnayerson wrote. Shaw, notorious for living the good life, left Paris in 1976 and began dual residency in Southampton, Long Island, and in Klosters, Switzerland. *The New York Times* reported that by the end of 1981, fourteen million copies of his books were in print in both hard and soft-cover editions.

In a 1981 *Saturday Review* essay-interview, Ross Wetzsteon summed up the official post-war literary assessment of Shaw: "Irwin Shaw has come to represent big bucks and bad books. The unexamined consensus among the quality controllers of American literature is that Shaw was an exceptionally gifted short-story writer who published a promising first novel and then betrayed his promise. According to the official line, with his laconically pointed dialogue, his controlled tough-guy lyricism, and his anti-rhetorical skepticism, he could have been the heir to Hemingway. Instead, by turning increasingly to beautiful-people potboilers, full of sex and violence, set against the cardboard backdrops of Hollywood and Cannes, he did little more than provide source material for TV mini-series starring washed-up ladies' men and failed *Charlie's Angels*. Ten pages into one of his novels and you can hear the cameras dollying in." But Wetzsteon also held that in *Bread Upon the Waters* (1981), the story of a mid-life crisis told with unadorned moral severity, Shaw had returned to telling tales of ordinary people and that the much publicized decline of Irwin Shaw was a myth.

Shaw died of a heart attack in Davos, Switzerland.

PRINCIPAL WORKS: *Novels*—The Young Lions, 1948; The Troubled Air, 1951; Lucy Crown, 1956; Two Weeks in Another Town, 1960; Voices of a Summer Day, 1965; Rich Man, Poor Man, 1970; Evening in Byzantium, 1973; Nightwork, 1975; Beggarman, Thief, 1977; The Top of the Hill, 1979; Bread Upon the Waters, 1981; Acceptable Losses, 1982. Plays: Bury the Dead, 1936; Second Mortgage, 1938; The Gentle People: A Brooklyn Fable, 1939; The Shy and the Lonely, 1941; Sons and Soldiers, 1944; The Assassin, 1946; Children from Their Games, 1962; In the French Style, 1963; A Choice of Wars, 1967. *Screenplays*—The Big Game, 1936; (with D. Fuchs and J. Wald) The Hard Way, 1942; (with others) The Talk of the Town, 1942; Commandos Strike at Dawn, 1942; (with C. Erskine and D. Shaw) Take One False Step, 1949; (with C. Schnee) Easy Living, 1949; I Want You, 1951; Act of Love, 1954; (with others) Ulysses, 1955; Fire Down Below, 1957; (with R. Clement) This Angry Age, 1958; Desire Under the Elms, 1958; The Big Gamble, 1961; In the French Style, 1963; Survival 1967, 1968. *Short stories*—Sailor off the Bremen and Other Stories, 1939; Welcome to the City and Other Stories, 1942; Act of Faith and Other Stories, 1946; Mixed Company: Collected Short Stories, 1950; Tip on a Dead Jockey and Other Stories, 1957; Selected Short Stories, 1961; Short Stories, 1966; Love on a Dark Street and Other Stories, 1970; Retreat and Other Stories, 1970; Whispers in Bedlam: Three Novellas, 1972; God Was Here But He Left Early, 1973; Five Decades, 1978. *Other*—Report on Israel, 1950; In the Company of Dolphins, 1964; Paris!, 1977.

ABOUT: The autobiographical material quoted above was written for Twentieth Century Authors, 1942 and Twentieth Century Authors First Supplement, 1955. Aldridge, J. W. After the Lost Generation; Giles, J. R. Irwin Shaw: A Study of the Short Fiction; Plimpton, G. (ed.) Writers at Work: The Paris Review Interviews; Shnayerson, M. Irwin Shaw: A Biography. *Periodicals*—Commentary July 1956; English Journal November 1951; Midwest Quarterly Summer 1961; New Republic May 13, 1936; July 2, 1951; New York Times July 28, 1962; May 17, 1984; Saturday Review November 18, 1950; August 3, 1957; August 1981; Saturday Review of Literature June 9, 1951.

## SHAW, THOMAS EDWARD. See LAWRENCE T. E.

## SHEARING, JOSEPH. See LONG, G. M. V. C.

## SHEDD, MARGARET COCHRAN (1900–March 9, 1986), American novelist, wrote: "Born in Urumia, Persia, where my parents, and my grandparents before that, were Presbyterian missionaries. My childhood was more than usually happy because it was free, and so it remains in my memory set there far away and lovely in the dark frame of the violence which came immediately after I was sent away to the United States for school—the First World War which, for that part of the world, meant massacre by the Kurds and Turks, death of my parents, and extermination of the native people that I had grown up with and loved, and destruction of the place which had been our family home. I believe this search for another home has motivated much of my writing. Living in Persia also gave me the respect for bi-linguality and, retroactively, some understanding of its effect on a writer and on writing. This probably motivates the work I am presently doing in Mexico.

"I was educated in the United States, went to Stanford University. In 1931 I began to write. At that time we (my husband, Oliver Michael Kisich, one child, and I) lived in the deep bush in British Honduras. There was nothing at all for me to do. Writing seemed a better alternative. The first piece I wrote was for *Theatre Arts* magazine, and it was accepted; and so, with this little encouragement, the thing began which has been happening to me for twenty-two years now—the certainty that life without writing doesn't amount to much and that conversely, the life of a writer is the happiest there is. I wrote a first book, about British  Honduras and its lonely, terrible and beautiful jungles, under contract to a publishing house which went broke before the book was published. I then wrote my first novel, *Hurricane Caye*, without contract and in great discouragement, and it was published in 1941. Meantime we had been living in Central America and the West Indies as much as we had in the United States. Bringing up children (three total) in primitive places does not leave much time for writing. I had got into short stories, which in many ways are the medium I love most of all.

"The Latin countries became a substitute for the childhood home I lost, perhaps because the people are very lovable, maybe because of the multitude of dogs barking at night or because roofs are flat and usable, both in Persia and in these countries. Anyway in 1950 I got interested in working with Mexican and American writers in a bi-lingual writing enterprise. I am presently Director of Centro Mexicano de Escritores, which is largely sponsored by the Rockefeller Foundation. This takes about half the year. We have both creative writers, including some of the best in Mexico, and research fellows. The Centro is presently expanding into some experiment in the theatre and into bi-lingual publishing.

"However, the main thing for me remains my own writing. . . . I might add to the above that precisely because I had lived so much outside the United States, I used . . . *Return to the Beach*, to explore what may be called, in cliché, the American heritage. Living half time out of the United States gives me an especial appreciation of my own country, maybe; anyway I wanted very much to understand what it is we believe in as Americans. My own ancestors were involved in every war and every westward push America has had. I wanted to know what they and I believed and believe in."

———

*Hurricane Caye*, set on a palm plantation in tropical Central America, was welcomed as a first novel of individuality and promise. There was general praise for the sensitivity and sophistication Margaret Shedd brought to her accounts of three very different love affairs, and for her powerful portrayal of the climactic hurricane. *Inherit the Earth* describes the struggles of peons against Falangists in a similar country. F. H. Bullock in *Weekly Book Review* found the peons a little too good to be true, the baddies too unrelievedly bad, and the book's organization excessively neat and pat. Nevertheless, Bullock wrote, "one feels that every person, every incident in the story had been known first hand or shrewdly observed. . . ."

Two of the places important in Margaret Shedd's life no longer exist as such. Urumia, Persia, has become Rezaiyeh, Iran; British Honduras is now Belize. As she says, she found a new home in Mexico, but turned in her fiction to explore "the American heritage," apparently with little enthusiasm. *Return to the Beach*, a sad love story whose hero is dying of wounds received in World War II, presents a hostile portrait of her pioneer ancestors in the predatory patriarch Abel Goade. *Run* is hardly kinder about its small Californian community, whose hysterical suspicions drive an innocent boy to headlong flight from accusations of murder. Anthony Boucher found "psychological and symbolic depths beyond the sensational action," but concluded that the novel worked best as a "suspenseful and surprising" thriller (*New York Times*). Later books included a fictionalized account of the relationship between Cortés and his Indian translator and mistress, Malinche.

PRINCIPAL WORKS: Hurricane Caye, 1942; Inherit the Earth, 1944; Return to the Beach, 1950; Run, 1956; Hosannah Tree, 1967; Malinche and Cortés, 1971; A Silence in Bilbao, 1974.

ABOUT: The autobiographical material quoted above was written for Twentieth Century Authors First Supplement, 1955. Contemporary Authors Vol. 118, 1986. *Periodicals*—Houston Chronicle March 14, 1986; Los Angeles Times March 15, 1986; New York Times January 15, 1956; Weekly Book Review October 15, 1944.

**SHEEAN, VINCENT** (December 5, 1899– March 15, 1975), American essayist and novelist, wrote: "I was born James Vincent Sheean in Pana,

Illinois. My parents were both of Irish parentage. My mother, Susan MacDermott, was the daughter of a Fenian rebel who came to America after the revolt of 1867; my father, William Charles Sheean, was the son of a Southern Irish peasant family which migrated westward after the great potato famine in Ireland in 1848. These are different but representative examples of the Irish migrations, the political and the economic. It was something my Fenian grandmother used to tell—a song and one or two stories about the Irish Brigade, Clares, at the Battle of Fontenoy—which survived in my mind years later and directed me towards the subject around which I wrote a novel, *A Day of Battle*.

"I was educated—so to speak—in Pana and at the University of Chicago. Even though I may have received little formal education there—learned little, worked little—I am sure the exposure to the influences of culture must have had a decisive effect upon my very inexperienced mind. When I left the university—without a degree—I worked for a while on the *Chicago Daily News*, then on the *New York Daily News*, and finally on the *Chicago Tribune*, in Paris. I was a correspondent in Europe for the *Tribune* for the better part of three years, and after I left them in 1925 I was never again regularly employed on a newspaper. At certain crises, such as 1927 in China, 1929 in Palestine, and 1938 in Spain, I returned to newspaper correspondence for brief periods, sending dispatches to the North American Newspaper Alliance mainly. In Spain I sent them to the *New York Herald Tribune*. But for the greater part of the last fifteen years I have employed myself in other forms of writing, political journalism and short stories for magazines, as well as novels and a kind of writing exemplified in my books, *Personal History* and *Not Peace but a Sword*. This kind of writing is not easy to classify; it is a sort of semiautobiographical political journalism, the external world and its graver struggles seen from the point of view of an observer who is not indifferent to them. . . .

"My general political view tends to be that of what is called 'the left.' I believe firmly in the future of a working class movement, but the parties now in existence do not seem to me to place the general proletarian interest very high. I find it hard to imagine any possible set of circumstances in which I might take part in a political movement, so my opinions are merely literary interest (if that).

"I am excessively fond of music, and used often to go without food to buy tickets to concerts and opera. I have a great weakness for Wagner, in spite of the fact that the intellectual content of his works makes no appeal to me. Among the great writers of the past, I admire most the Russian and French novelists (Tolstoy, Dostoevsky, Balzac, Stendhal, and Proust, chiefly) and the English poets. I think I have something more than the conventional regard for Dante. Once during a fairly long residence in Naples I acquired a great admiration for Benedetto Croce, most of whose work I have read and still value highly. Stray enthusiasms of mine at various times have been the plays of Synge, Shaw, and O'Casey, the dialogues of Plato in Jowett's translations, Trotsky's *History of the Russian Revolution*, the polemical papers of Lenin, critical works by Sainte Beuve and Taine, and the wonderful memoirs of the Duc de Saint-Simon. Among writers of my own generation I am particularly sensitive to the work of Ernest Hemingway, Frank O'Connor (in Ireland), André Malraux (in France).

"I was married in 1935, in Vienna, to Diana Forbes Robertson, youngest daughter of Sir Johnston Forbes-Robertson, of the famous family of actors. We have two daughters."

---

As his London *Times* obituarist remarked, Vincent Sheean's *Personal History* (1935), probably his most enduring book, "is still recognized as a source book for the understanding of the events which led to the Second World War, the growth of national liberation movements throughout the world, the fascination and disillusionment of many intellectuals with Marxism, the origins of the Communist revolution in China and the conflict in the Middle East." It was reissued in 1969. When it first appeared, Edward Weeks, reviewing it in *Atlantic Bookshelf*, gently put his finger on a number of its faults: "I have heard [George] Sokolsky deny the accuracy of Sheean's chapter on China and George Hyman shoot the Palestine description full of holes. But Sheean is a romantic, and unintentionally is won to whatever cause appeals to him most." Walter Duranty, although aware of what Weeks had spotted, was more generous when he reviewed the book in the *New York Herald Tribune Books*: "His account of the Rif campaign is one of the finest pieces of newspaper writing I have ever read anywhere. He succeeds in doing what all good reporters try to do . . . to make the reader see and share what he saw, to convey, as Aristotle said, the emotions of pity and terror, than which there is no higher art. I could wish, however, that this book had been a novel rather than a 'personal history because it contains the essence of romance, the spirit of curiosity and adventure,' the 'young man going places and seeing things and taking risks and living a full life. . . . ' Most of it is superbly written and the narrative interest never flags." Mary MacCarthy, in the *Nation*, found it "heartwarming." Malcolm Cowley, in the *New Republic*, commended the "clean narrative style," and praised the book for being a "purely individual drama of ambitions and ideas"; this, he believed, made it "vastly more appealing than the usual war correspondent's memoirs of things romantically seen and dangers escaped." One of Sheean's complaints in later life was that the adventurous role he ascribed to himself in the book caused him to be miscast by editors and publishers, who expected "adventures" from him, rather than more serious work. But it might be said that he had too much of the romantic in him to resist the role cast upon him.

However, *Personal History* is an excellent early example of "book journalism," and its reader today, whatever his or her political views, could not possibly fail to profit from its vividness. *Not Peace But a Sword*, the successor to *Personal History*, gave Sheean's view of the period March 1938–March 1939. Louis Kronenberger, reviewing it for the *New Yorker*, incidentally made a judicious summary of the nature of the author's achievements: "Sheean's best book since *Personal History*. His novels seem to me to lack go; his merit lies in creating a vigorous and graphic picture with himself in the foreground but not dominating it. His subjective approach to big events does not, to be sure, much illumine them. But it is the very sense of his living through great moments as quiveringly, as wonderingly, and sometimes as myopically, as would you or I that gives to this book its human perspective and blunt reality."

The deliberately controversial *This House Against This House*, after giving a personal analysis of the Versailles Treaty, went on to describe Sheean's World War II experiences. The *New Republic* (1946) thought it "journalism of the highest order," but it infuriated others such as the reviewer for *Time* (1946), who thought it "pretentious" in its title, and simply "the mixture as before: part tract, part treatise, part I-was-right-there testimony. . . . Not up to pre-war quality."

*Lead Kindly Light*, a tribute to Mahatma Gandhi, was better received. The Indian V. L. Pandit wrote of it in the *New York Herald Tribune*: "Sheean, besides his close grasp of the essence of Hinduism, has shown remarkable insight into Hinduism as practiced by the masses." Later Sheean wrote a brief life of Gandhi for a series ("Great Lives in Brief"): the *Library Journal* recommended this, too, as an "excellent introduction."

Sheean was obliged for financial reasons to write a number of potboilers, lives of Verdi, Oscar Hammerstein, Edna St. Vincent Millay, and others: all these, while they had no kind of permanence, were readable and reasonably accurate. In *Dorothy and Red*, however, about Sinclair Lewis and his wife, he approached his best. It drew on the accounts of the marriage given to him by his good friend, Dorothy Thompson, and on her letters and diaries. It had a mixed reception, but is now essential reading for anyone who wishes to understand Lewis and the reasons for his decline. Sheean told all, yet, as Edward Weeks wrote in the *Atlantic*, the book was "full of the stress of living and warm with love." Others, at a time when biographical writing tended to the polite rather than the candid or particularly truthful, were deeply offended by the frank revelations of the marriage.

PRINCIPAL WORKS: *Autobiography and political commentary*—Personal History, 1935, new ed. 1969; Not Peace but a Sword, (1939 in U.K.: The Eleventh House); Between the Thunder and the Sun, 1943; This House Against This House, 1946; First and Last Love, 1956. *Political journalism, biography, and history*—An American Among the Riffi, 1926; The New Persia, 1927; Lead Kindly Light, 1949; Thomas Jefferson, Father of Democracy, 1953; Mahatma Gandhi, 1954; Oscar Hammerstein I: The Life and Exploits of an Impresario, 1956 (in U.K.: The Amazing Oscar Hammerstein); Orpheus at Eight: Giuseppe Verdi, 1958; Nehru: The Years of Power, 1960; Dorothy and Red, 1963. *Fiction*—The Anatomy of Virtue, 1927; Gog and Magog, 1930; The Tide, 1933; Sanfelice, 1936; A Day of Battle, 1938; Bird of Wilderness, 1941; A Certain Rich Man, 1947; Rage of the Soul, 1952; Lily, 1954; Beware of Caesar, 1965. *Short stories*—The Piece of a Fan, 1937.

ABOUT: The autobiographical material quoted above was written for Twentieth Century Authors, 1942. Current Biography 1975; Good, H. The Journalist as Biographer, 1993; Morrell, H. Transatlantic Vistas: American Journalists in Europe 1900–1940, 1988; Murrow, E. This I Believe, 1954; Sheean, V. First and Last Love, 1956. *Periodicals*—Atlantic December 1963; Atlantic Bookshelf April 1935; Book Week April 11, 1943; Commonweal April 2, 1943; Nation March 6, 1935; New Republic February 20, 1935; April 1, 1946; New York Herald Tribune July 17, 1949; New York Herald Tribune Books February 10, 1935; New York Times March 17, 1975; New Yorker July 29, 1939; Newsweek June 1, 1959; Saturday Review of Literature July 16, 1949; Time April 15, 1946; March 1, 1975; Times (London) March 18, 1975.

**SHEEN, FULTON JOHN** (May 8, 1895–December 9, 1979), American Roman Catholic bishop, university professor, and television personality, was born in El Paso, Illinois, the son of Newton Morris Sheen, a farmer, and Delia (Fulton) Sheen.

The family moved to Peoria, Illinois, when he was very young, and he was educated, first at St. Mary's School and the Spalding Institute, and then  at St. Viator College in Kankakee, from which he received his M.A (1919). He was ordained a priest for the Diocese of Peoria in 1919. He attended St. Paul Seminary, Minnesota (1919), for a year, and then the Catholic University of America, at Washington, D.C., from which he obtained two theological degrees (S.T.B. and J.C.B.). In 1923, he earned his Ph.D. from Louvain University in Belgium.

Sheen, who from 1926 until 1950 taught philosophy and theology at the Catholic University of America (he ended up as professor of philosophy there), made good progress through the hierarchy of his Church. From 1950 until 1966 he was the national director of the Society for the Propagation of the Faith. From 1966 until 1969 he was Bishop of Rochester, New York. He claimed many famous converts, among them Clare Boothe Luce and the violinist Fritz Kreisler, and first became famous to the American public when he hosted the National Broadcasting Company's radio program "Catholic Hour" in the 1930s. When television came into vogue he became even more famous for his weekly "Life Is Worth Living" programs. Good-looking, fluent, sure of himself, something of a hark-back to the "muscular Christian" of the nineteenth century in style, he was a born broadcaster. He was also a born stirrer up of controversy, and thoroughly enjoyed the attention it brought him.

Sheen's opinions were in general "right-wing": he espoused both corporal and capital punishment. He saw communism in all liberalism, and took Franco's side in the Spanish civil war without knowing about many of the issues involved. Yet he was himself in many ways liberal and kindly and generous. He was so forthright in his support of the poor and needy as Bishop of Rochester—he wanted to give five percent of church revenue to the poor—that it was widely believed that he had been "asked to retire" before his proper time was up, and even that he had been denied a cardinal's hat on the grounds that his kind of generosity threatened the ecclesiastical establishment. In 1967 he openly opposed the escalation of the war in Vietnam. He later supported Nixon when, in the face of public opinion, he agreed to gradual withdrawal.

John Jay Hughes, in his *America* (1980) review of Sheen's autobiography, stated that Sheen "was a . . . blend of intellectual brilliance, uncontrolled romanticism and total naivete about practical affairs." During World War II, Sheen was naive enough to want to withdraw aid to Soviet Russia until that country "gave up atheism."

Sheen's books vary from the very popular to the more learned and serious. Thus, of *Religion Without God*, written before Sheen became a public figure, the *Times Literary Supplement* critic noted,

"This indictment of the conception of God in modern philosophy . . . [is] permeated with all the learning and acuteness of the school of Louvain [from which Sheen acquired his doctorate], and if there is plenty of hard hitting in his work, there is also a perception of when and where to strike." Of *The Philosophy of Science, America* (1934) wrote: "Since Harvey Wickham's . . . death we have had no writer who could deal so devastatingly with Unrealists, Misbehaviorists and Impuritans. . . . He is easier to read than . . . Wickham . . . because he has enjoyed . . . a long and careful training in the rational principles enunciated by Aristotle. . . . All this accumulated wisdom of the centuries Dr. Sheen hands on to us in . . . impeccable English."

Sheen's later books became more popular and less scholarly. Of his *Communism and the Conscience of the West*, *Canadian Forum* perhaps well summed up the general opinion: " [The author's] main points are strong ones. . . . But his picture of liberalism is a vulgar caricature. . . . there is little evidence here of the humble and contrite heart which some people think the essential test of a man's Christian faith."

PRINCIPAL WORKS: *Selections*—The Wit and Wisdom of Bishop Fulton J. Sheen (ed. B. Adler) 1968; The Fulton J. Sheen Treasury, 1969; A. Fulton J. Sheen Reader, 1979. *Religious*—God and Intelligence in Modern Philosophy, 1925; Religion Without God, 1928; The Life of All Living, 1929; The Divine Romance, 1930; Old Errors and New Labels, 1931; Moods and Truths, 1932; The Way of the Cross, 1932; The Seven Last Words, 1933; Hymn of the Conquered, 1933; The Eternal Galilean, 1934; The Philosophy of Science, 1934; The Mystical Body of Christ, 1935; Calvary and the Mass, 1936; The Moral Universe, 1936; The Cross and the Beatitudes, 1927; Communism: The Opium of the People, 1937; The Cross and the Crisis, 1938; Liberty Equality and Fraternity, 1938; The Rainbow of Sorrow, 1938; Victory Over Vice, 1953; Whence Comes Wars, 1940; The Seven Virtues, 1940; Freedom Under God, 1940; War and Guilty, 1941; For God and Country, 1941; Peace, 1942; God and War, 1942; The Divine Verdict, 1943; The Armour of God, 1943; Love One Another, 1944; Seven Words to the Cross, 1944; Seven Pillars of Peace, 1944; Seven Words of Jesus and Mary, 1945; You, 1945; Preface to Religion, 1946; Light Your Lamps, 1947; Love on Pilgrimage, 1947; Communism and the Conscience of the West, 1948; Life Is Worth Living, 5 vols., 1953–1957; The Life of Christ, 1958; Science, Psychiatry and Religion, 1962; Love, Marriage and Children, 1963; The Church, Communism and Democracy, 1964; Guide to Contentment, 1967; The Electronic Christian, 1979. *Autobiography*—Treasure in Clay, 1980.

ABOUT: Baker, G. I Had to Know, 1951; Nizer, L. Between You and Me, 1948; Sheen F. J. Treasure in Clay, 1980. *Periodicals*—America November 8, 1980; January 9, 1934; Canadian Forum August 1948; New York Times December 10, 1979; Newsweek December 24, 1979; Time May 6, 1946; Times Literary Supplement January 19, 1929.

**SHELDON, CHARLES MONROE** (February 26, 1857–February 24, 1946), American clergyman and author, was born in Wellsville, New York, the son of Stewart Sheldon, a Congregational minister, and Sarah (Ward) Sheldon. After early childhood, during which his father preached at a succession of churches, he was raised on a homestead farm near Yankton, South Dakota. Sheldon returned to the east for his education, graduating from Phillips Academy (1879) and then from Brown University (1883). He earned a Bachelor of Divinity degree from Andover Theological Seminary (1886) and, following ordination in the Congregational Church, began a two-year ministry in Waterbury, Vermont.

In 1889 Sheldon moved to Topeka, Kansas to become minister of that city's newly-formed Central Congregational Church, a position he held until  1919. (From 1912 to 1915, he was minister-at-large.) Topeka was, by the time of Sheldon's arrival, a bustling industrial and transportation center; with its large working-class immigrant population and its sizable black ghetto, the city was beset by a host of social and economic tensions. Sheldon, hoping to lure parishioners, began to compose stories—which he incorporated into his sermons—designed to illustrate how Christians could cope with contemporary problems. Many were published serially in the *Advance*, a Congregationalist periodical. Later they were collected.

They attracted little attention until the publication of *In His Steps*, which became one of the best-selling books of all time. Its story is simple: well-to-do members of a Protestant congregation in a Midwestern city vow to govern their lives by the question "What would Jesus do?" Initial sales of *In His Steps* were brisk, but when a copyright defect was discovered, numerous publishers rushed to produce cheap pirated editions of the novel. Sales exploded. While precise sales figures are impossible to determine—Sheldon probably exaggerated when he claimed that thirty million copies had been sold—the novel reached a huge audience, was translated into more than twenty languages, inspired a 1936 film, and remained on several publishers' lists nearly one hundred years after its original appearance. Sheldon was besieged by letters from all over the world asking that he do "what Jesus would do" and share his profits with the less fortunate. In fact, however, because of the piracy, he probably got only a few hundred dollars. The book possesses no literary merit whatsoever, but is regarded as a quintessential expression of the Social Gospel, a reform-minded, mostly middle class, Protestant movement that sought to apply biblical teachings to the social upheavals associated with rapid urbanization and industrialization. In a "reappraisal" of the novel published in the *American Quarterly*, Paul S. Boyer conceded its "abysmal literary quality," and insisted, "*In His Steps* is concerned only minimally with religion, social injustice or reform, but . . . *is* concerned, almost obsessively, with certain psychological and emotional problems troubling the American middle class at the close of the nineteenth century."

An episode from *In His Steps* prompted an unusual journalistic experiment. In March 1900 the new publisher of the *Topeka Daily Capital* invited Sheldon to edit four issues of the newspaper as he (Sheldon) thought Jesus Christ would have done it. Sheldon eliminated all advertising he considered unfit (patent medicines, tobacco products, alcohol, and corsets) and dropped most of the stories on crime and violent sporting events (particularly boxing). He filled the paper instead with religious stories and inspirational material. Subscriptions to the paper during Sheldon's brief editorial tenure skyrocketed from 15,000 copies daily to about 384,000, reaching readers all over the United States and in London. But the experiment was not an unqualified success. Reviewers from both the secular and religious press were unkind, and Sheldon later realized that Frederick Popenoe, the paper's publisher, had exploited his reputation in an effort to increase circulation and pay off debts.

Sheldon published more than forty other books, including novels, religious tracts—and an autobiography. From 1920 to 1925, he was editor-in-chief of the *Christian Herald*, a New York-based Protestant monthly.

PRINCIPAL WORKS: *Fiction*—Richard Bruce; or, The Life That Now Is, 1892; Robert Hardy's Seven Days: A Dream and Its Consequences, 1893; The Twentieth Door, 1893; The Crucifixion of Philip Strong, 1894; His Brother's Keeper; or, Christian Stewardship, 1896; In His Steps: "What Would Jesus Do?," 1897; One of the Two, 1898; The Redemption of Freetown, 1898; Malcolm Kirk: A Tale of Moral Heroism in Overcoming the World, 1898; Lend a Hand, 1899; John King's Question Class, 1899; The Miracle at Markham: How Twelve Churches Became One, 1899; For Christ and the Church, 1899; Born to Serve, 1900; Edward Blake: College Student, 1900; Who Killed Joe's Baby?, 1901; The Reformer, 1902; His Mother's Prayers, 1903; The Narrow Gate, 1903; The Heart of the World: A Story of Christian Socialism, 1905; The Spirit's Power; or, The Revival, 1906 (reissued as Modern Pagans, 1917); Paul Douglas—Journalist, 1909; The High Calling, 1911; The Builder of Ships: The Story of Brander Cushing's Ambition, 1912; "Jesus Is Here!": Continuing the Narrative of In His Steps (What Would Jesus Do?) 1914; Of One Blood, 1916; Howard Chase, Red Hill, Kansas, 1918; All the World, 1919; Heart Stories, 1920; The Richest Man in Kansas, 1921; The Thirteenth Resolution, 1928; He Is Here, 1931. *Religion*—The First Christian Daily Paper and Other Sketches, 1900; A Charles Sheldon Yearbook, 1909; A Little Book For Every Day, 1914; In His Steps To-Day: What Would Jesus Do in Solving the Problems of Present Political, Economic and Social Life?, 1921; The Mere Man and His Problems, 1924; God's Promises, 1927; Life's Treasure Book, Past, Present, and Future, 1929; Let's Talk It Over, 1929; What Did Jesus Really Teach?, 1930; The History of "In His Steps," 1938; The Golden Book of Bible Stories: Favorite Stories from the Old and New Testaments Retold for Children, 1941; Dr. Sheldon's Scrapbook, 1942. *Autobiography*—Charles M. Sheldon: His Life Story, 1925. *As editor*—The Everyday Bible, 1924; The Life of Jesus, 1926.

ABOUT: Bowden, H. (ed.) Dictionary of American Religious Biography, 2nd ed. 1993; Dictionary of American Biography, Suppl. 4, 1946–1950, 1974; Ferre, J. A Social Gospel for Millions: The Religious Bestsellers of Charles Sheldon, Charles Gordon, and Harold Bell Wright, 1988; Melton, G. (ed.) Religious Leaders of America, 1991; Miller, T. Following in His Steps: A Biography of Charles M. Sheldon, 1987; Mott, F. Golden Multitudes: The Story of Best Sellers in the United States, 1947; National Cyclopaedia of American Biography Vol. 34, 1948; Who's Who 1946. *Periodicals*—American Quarterly Spring 1971; American Studies Spring 1990; Journalism Quarterly Spring 1974; New York Times February 25, 1946; Times (London) February 26, 1946.

**SHELDON, EDWARD (BREWSTER)** (February 4, 1886–April 1, 1946), American playwright, was born in Chicago, Illinois, the son of Theodore  Sheldon, a prominent attorney, and Mary (Strong) Sheldon. His mother encouraged his interest in the theater, and he was already an ardent playgoer by the age of fourteen, when he entered the Hill School in Pottstown, Pennsylvania. At Harvard, from which he graduated in 1908, he studied playwriting under George Pierce Baker.

Sheldon achieved fame at the age of twenty-two, with the New York opening of his play *Salvation Nell*, the story of a lowly saloon charwoman who redeems her shattered life by joining the Salvation Army. The title role was played by veteran actress Minnie Maddern Fiske, who had appeared in American productions of dramas by Henrik Ibsen, an important early influence on Sheldon. Like most of his subsequent plays, *Salvation Nell* combines elements of romance and melodrama, but is scrupulously realistic in its portrayal of characters' speech, dress, and environment. Years after its premiere, Eugene O'Neill wrote to Sheldon, "Your *Salvation Nell* . . . was what first opened my eyes to the existence of the real theatre as opposed to the unreal."

Sheldon's second play, *The Nigger*, which had its premiere at New York's experimental New Theatre in December 1909, became an instant *cause célèbre*. George Jean Nathan, who gave the play a glowing review in the *Smart Set*, later (in a 1948 *Cosmopolitan* article) dubbed it one of "the ten dramatic shocks of the century." Morrow, the protagonist, wins the governorship of a southern state as a white supremacist, but later learns that one of his grandparents was black. Instead of denying his heritage, he decides to devote the rest of his life to the betterment of the black race. Notwithstanding its melodramatic aspects, and its "politically incorrect" title—*The Nigger* was one of the first American plays openly to confront such issues as racism, interracial marriage, and lynching. Loren K. Ruff, one of Sheldon's biographers, has called *Salvation Nell*, *The Nigger*, and two other early works—*The Boss* and *The High Road*—"sociorealistic dramas," unique because "their broad spectrum of social problems best reflected the social, political, and economic climate of the Progressive era."

Sheldon reached the peak of his success with *Romance*, which opened in New York at the Maxine Elliott Theatre on February 10, 1913, and was later performed all over the world. (It was revived in 1948 as the musical *My Romance* in the MGM film adaptation of which Greta Garbo starred.) The play centers on a love affair between an Episcopal rector and a fiery diva, who eventually leaves the churchman so as not to impede his career. Dorsi Keane, the star of *Romance*, broke off an engagement to another man to marry Sheldon before the play's premiere.

During the second half of the 1910s, Sheldon concentrated on adaptations of others' works. His 1914 *Song of Songs* is an adaptation of Hermann Sudermann's sentimental best-seller *Das hohe Lied*. *The Jest*, which achieved great success with John Barrymore in the lead role, is an adaptation of the Italian playwright Sem Benelli's *La Cena della Beffe*. From about 1915, Sheldon was afflicted with a virulent and debilitating form of arthritis. His 1921 play *The Lonely Heart*—an introspective drama in which the protagonist is examined in the course of four crises—was his last solo effort. Thereafter, he wrote a number of plays in collaboration with others, notably *My Lulu Belle*, with Charles MacArthur, and *Dishonored Lady*, with Margaret Ayer Barnes. Increasingly, however, he was confined to his penthouse on East Eighty-Fourth Street, and by 1930 was completely immobilized, and had to be fed through a tube. By 1931 he was blind. In her introduction to *The Man Who Lived Twice*, Eric Wollencott Barnes's biography of Sheldon, Anne Morrow Lindbergh recalled a visit to the bedridden playwright: "He was immaculately dressed as if he were lying down for a few minutes only. His eyes were bandaged. He greeted you with a rather breathless whisper." Yet, Lindbergh noted, "After five minutes one never noticed [his afflictions] again. . . . they simply ceased to exist, so overshadowed were they by the personality of the man."

Despite the severity of his illness, Sheldon maintained an active behind-the-scenes role. In 1941 a *New York Times* reporter wrote, "If America has a theatrical center, it is a little known one, the New York apartment of Ned Sheldon. . . . To his bedside come the theatre greats, for inspiration and advice, and his informal salon is a kind of hub for the best theatre of the country." Sheldon received regular visits from such theatrical luminaries as John Gielgud and Paul Robeson, and he often took an interest in advising lesser-known talents. His numerous literary friends included W. Somerset Maugham, Thornton Wilder, and Edith Wharton (whose novel *The Age of Innocence* he helped adapt for the stage). His legendary friendship with John Barrymore is the subject of Sheldon Rosen's 1977 play *Ned and Jack*.

PRINCIPAL WORKS: *Drama*—Salvation Nell: A Play in Three Acts, 1908; "The Nigger," an American Play in Three Acts, 1910; Egypt: A Play in Four Acts, 1912; Romance, a Play in Three Acts with a Prologue and an Epilogue, 1913; The Garden of Paradise, . . . Based on "The Little Mermaid" by Hans Andersen, 1915; (with C. MacArthur) My Lulu Belle: A Play in Four Acts, 1925.

ABOUT: Barnes, E. The Man Who Lived Twice: The Biography of Edward Sheldon; with an Introduction by Anne Morrow Lindbergh, 1956; Canadian Playwrights: A Biographical Guide, 1980; Current Biography 1946; Dictionary of Literary Biography Vol. 7, 1981; National Cyclopaedia of American Biography Vol. 34, 1948; Ruff, L. Edward Sheldon, 1982. *Periodicals*—New York Times April 2, 1946; Times (London) April 3, 1946.

SHELLABARGER, SAMUEL (pseudonym "JOHN ESTEVEN") (May 18, 1888–March 21, 1954), American biographer and novelist, wrote: "I

was born in Washington, D.C., and, since my parents died during my infancy, was brought up there in the house of my paternal grandfather, the Hon. Samuel Shellabarger, a member of Congress during the Civil War, for a time Minister to Portugal, and a well-known lawyer. My grandfather was born in 1817 and my grandmother in 1828, so that, during my boyhood, I was especially under the influence of that generation with its traditional standards and with its memories which extended to the early days of the Republic. I consider this influence paramount in my life.

"Two events of my youth are perhaps worth recording because they helped to determine my later interests. As a boy of twelve, I attended a performance of Sardou's *Dante*, with Sir Henry Irving in the title role. For some reason or other, I decided then, if possible, to become a writer; and, unlike most boyish enthusiasms, this remained constant throughout the years. Afterwards, in 1903, I first toured Europe; and the impressions of London, Paris and Rome at the turn of the century became indelible in my mind and have left nostalgia for the past which has colored my historical writing.

"Educated at private schools, I graduated from Princeton in 1909, and, having chosen the academic profession, set out for Germany in order to study for a doctor's degree. A couple of years later, however, it seemed more expedient to obtain this degree in America, and I entered the graduate school at Harvard in 1911.

"From 1914 until 1917, I was an instructor in English at Princeton. During the First World War, I served in the Ordnance and Military Intelligence and spent a year at the end of the war as assistant military attaché to our legation in Stockholm. Upon returning to Princeton, I spent the next four years as assistant professor in English. In 1922, I resigned from the university and moved with my family to Lausanne, Switzerland, where I remained for the ensuing five years, occupied with writing and travel. Two additional years were spent in France and England. During this period, I wrote a biography, *The Chevalier Bayard*, and a couple of novels.

"Upon returning to America in 1931, we resided for a while in Washington, then settled in Princeton, where I continued for the next seven years to write biography and fiction: the life of Lord Chesterfield, a number of mystery stories and romances. In 1938, I was appointed headmaster of the Columbus School for Girls in Columbus, Ohio. I have always been interested in education and I consider the eight years I spent there as among the most creative and valuable of my life. My duties, however, did not prevent continued writing. It was during this period that I wrote *Captain from Castile*. I re-

turned to Princeton in 1946. Since then I have written two novels: *Prince of Foxes* and *The King's Cavalier*. I am now engaged on another historical novel laid in the eighteenth century.

"In 1915, I married Vivian G. L. Borg, a native of Sweden. We have had two sons and two daughters. My first son, Robert, died in infancy. My second son, John Eric, was killed in World War II."

---

Samuel Shellabarger's popular biographies garnered reviewers' praise and have remained in print, but it was his swashbuckling, romantic historical fiction which earned him fame and fortune. The *New York Times* called Shellabarger "one of the most popular historical novelists of modern times," and *Captain from Castile*, *Prince of Foxes*, *The King's Cavalier*, and *Lord Vanity* earned their author over $1.5 million.

During World War II Shellabarger wrote the epic *Captain from Castile* for his son John Eric, who was killed in action in Germany just months after receiving a pre-publication copy, and two days before V-E Day. Set in sixteenth-century Spain and Mexico, the story follows the dashing young Pedro de Varga, who flees the Spanish Inquisition to the New World, where he joins Cortes. *Saturday Review of Literature* critic Harrison Smith wrote that Shellabarger's "narrative style is lively and simple; his characters, although they are necessarily stereotyped, are not period costumes with sawdust inside, but something resembling flesh and blood; his knowledge of the Spain of that day and of the almost legendary conquest of Mexico must have been gained at the expense of years of study." Indeed, Shellabarger's meticulous research, if not his style, earned him respect. For example, in researching whether Cortes moved his horses to Mexico below or above deck, Shellabarger wrote forty letters to various authorities and spent days doing library research. The *New York Times* went on to say that he "never settled the question to his satisfaction, and finally made the reluctant decision, on his own, that the horses were carried on deck." *Captain from Castile* and *Prince of Foxes* were later made into motion pictures, both starring Tyrone Power.

Shellabarger also wrote now forgotten novels under the pen names John Esteven and Peter Loring. He was a worthy popular historical novelist, who never claimed that his work possessed literary merit.

PRINCIPAL WORKS: As "John Esteven"—The Door of Death: A Mystery Story, 1928; The Black Gale, 1929; Voodoo: A Murder Mystery, 1930; By Night at Dinsmore, 1935; While Murder Waits: Shudders and Chills in a Hair-Raising Story of Death in a Lighthouse, 1937; Graveyard Watch, 1938. Novels—(as "Peter Loring") Grief Before Night, 1938; (as "Peter Loring") Miss Rolling Stone, 1939; Captain from Castile, 1945; Prince of Foxes, 1947; The King's Cavalier, 1950; Lord Vanity, 1953; The Token, 1955; Tolbecken, 1956. Nonfiction—The Chevalier Bayard: A Study in Fading Chivalry, 1928; Lord Chesterfield, 1935 (reissued as Lord Chesterfield and His World, 1951); Lord Chesterfield and Manners, 1938.

ABOUT: The autobiographical material quoted above was written for Twentieth Century Authors First Supplement, 1955. Current Biography 1945; Vinson, J. (ed.) Twentieth-Century

Romance and Gothic Writers, 1982; Warfel, H. R. *American Novelists of Today*, 1951. *Periodicals*—Chicago Sunday Tribune August 19, 1956; New York Times March 22, 1954; Saturday Review of Literature January 27, 1945.

## SHEPARD, BENJAMIN HENRY JESSE FRANCIS. See GRIERSON, FRANCIS

## SHEPARD, ODELL (July 22, 1884–July 19, 1967), American essayist, poet, editor, historian, and educator, was born in Sterling, Illinois, the son of William Orville Shepard, a bishop in the Methodist Church, and Emily (Odell) Shepard. At twenty he was a student in the Northwestern School of Music, remaining until 1904, and also taking courses at Northwestern University from 1902 to 1904. In his last year at Northwestern he was city editor of the *Evanston Index*. Shepard received the degree of Bachelor of Philosophy at the University of Chicago in 1907. In Chicago he was organist in various churches, and a reporter on the *Chicago Tribune* at various times from 1905 to 1907. Shepard, however, did not have printer's ink in his veins. According to the *New York Times* (1967), one of his contemporaries reported that "he walked out on a double murder in Chicago . . . saying it was a sordid business not worth more than a paragraph and he did not intend to put up in his life with such shoddy affairs."

After receiving his master's degree Shepard was an instructor in English at Smith Academy, St. Louis, for a year. From 1909 to 1914 he was professor  of English at the University of Southern California. He earned a Ph.D. from Harvard in 1916 and stayed on as instructor in English there and at Radcliffe College. In 1917 he was appointed Goodwin Professor of English at Trinity College, Hartford, Connecticut. He spent a year abroad in 1927–1928 as a Fellow of the John Simon Guggenheim Memorial Foundation.

Shepard's first published work was *Shakespeare Questions: An Outline for the Study of the Longer Plays*, which appeared in 1916. The next year he published *A Lonely Flute*, a collection of homey poems such as *Evening Rod Song*: "It's a long road and a steep road / And a weary road to climb. / The air bites chill on the windy hill. / At home it is firelight time."

In 1923 Shepard produced a study of Bliss Carman's poetry, and four years later a volume of essays under the title *The Harvest of a Quiet Eye*. *New York Times* (1927) critic Brooks Atkinson wrote that the "pleasant flavor that makes this volume such good reading comes chiefly from Mr. Shepard's discussions on small towns, on the structure of urban living, on farmers in the fields, on the cracker-barrel gossips of Fairford post office, on fishing, on the rhythms of a brook and on science and spirit." The book remains in print as does a collection of meditations titled *The Joys of Forgetting*; Walter de la Mare wrote in the foreword that Shepard "never preaches or attempts to proselytize. There is no trace of a we in his I. He teaches nothing but how to learn, and even as a lecturer he confesses that he sits in spirit among his own audience, and smiles at both." The London *Times* called the collection "serenely gay, carrying a mellow wisdom beneath its irony and pleasant humor."

In 1937 Shepard published *Pedlar's Progress*, a biography of the teacher and philosopher Bronson Alcott. "His book is not perfect," Henry Seidel Canby wrote in *Saturday Review of Literature*. Alcott's unhappy style, sententious, involved, abstract, has had its reaction on Mr. Shepard's own style, which is sometimes inflated, though often also excellent." Mark Van Doren declared in *New York Herald Tribune Books* that "Mr. Shepard has done all that can be done for Alcott with respect to any phase of his activity throughout eighty-eight years." Like Canby, other critics had reservations; H. M. Jones, of the *Yale Review*, found the book "full and authentic as fact, but once beyond the admirable opening chapters, Alcott's life diffuses itself past the power of Mr. Shepard, laboring heavily in the rear, to canalize its flow." The Pulitzer jury apparently had no reservations, for they selected *Pedlar's Progress* for a Pulitzer Prize—as one of the two best biographies of the year in 1938; Shepard shared the honor with Marquis James, author of a two-volume biography of Andrew Jackson.

In 1939 Shepard published *Connecticut: Past and Present*, a miscellany that the *New Yorker* called a "most engrossing mixture of history, geography, topography, and sentimentality." The book caught the eye of Robert A. Herley, who asked Shepard to be his running mate in his successful bid for the governorship of Connecticut. Shepard served as Herley's Lieutenant Governor from 1940 to 1943.

In 1946, after twenty-five years on the faculty, Shepard resigned from Trinity College over a dispute involving the college's president; however, he did continue to lecture there until shortly before his death. After his resignation he collaborated with his son Willard in writing two historical novels. The first of these, *Holdfast Gains*, covers the period of the American Revolution to the early 1800s, its hero being a young Indian, raised by a white family, who must deal with divided loyalties. The second collaboration was *Jenkins' Ear*, an account of the War of Jenkins' Ear as told from the point of view of the eighteenth-century English man-of-letters Horace Walpole—an elaborate and fanciful framework for a richly detailed historical narrative.

Shepard considered *The Lore of the Unicorn* his best work; it remains in print. He was a regular contributor to the *Christian Science Monitor*, the *Nation*, and the *Yale Review*. At his death the *New York Times* noted that "as a teacher, poet, essayist and historian, Mr. Shepard had an impact on the world of letters that brought him a quiet fame that he accepted with grace and mild skepticism."

PRINCIPAL WORKS: *Nonfiction*—Shakespeare Questions: An Outline for the Study of the Leading Plays, 1916; Thomas Wharton and the Historical Point of View in Criticism, 1917; Bliss Carman, 1923; The Harvest of a Quiet Eye: A Book of Digressions, 1927; The Joys of Forgetting: A Book of Bagatelles, 1928; The Lore of the Unicorn, 1930; Thy Road and Thy Creel, 1930; Pedlar's Progress: The Life of Bronson Alcott, 1937; Connecticut: Past and Present, 1939. Novels—(with W. Shepard) Holdfast Gaines, 1946; (with W. Shepard) Jenkins' Ear: A Narrative Attributed to Horace Walpole, Esq., 1951. Poetry—A Lonely Flute, 1917. As editor—A Week on the Concord and Merrimack Rivers (by H. D. Thoreau) 1921; Essays of 1925, 1926; The Heart of Thoreau's Journals, 1927; (with R. Hillyer) Essays of Today: 1926–1927, 1928; (with A. Adams) In Honor of the Ninetieth Birthday of Charles Frederick Johnson, Professor of English in Trinity College, 1883–1906: Papers, Essays, and Stories by His Former Students, 1928; The Three Musketeers (by A. Dumas) 1928; Contemporary Essays, 1929; (with R. Hillyer) Prose Masterpieces of English and American Literature, 1931; (with P. S. Wood) English Prose and Poetry: 1660–1800, 1934; Representative Selections (by H. W. Longfellow) 1934; The Journals of Bronson Alcott, 1938; (with F. A. Manchester) Irving Babbit: Man and Teacher, 1941; The Best of W. H. Hudson, 1949.

ABOUT: Contemporary Authors 1994. Periodicals—New York Herald Tribune Books May 9, 1937; New York Times June 19, 1927; July 20, 1967; New Yorker June 3, 1939; Saturday Review of Literature May 8, 1937; Times (London) February 7, 1929; Yale Review Summer 1937.

## SHERIDAN, CLARE CONSUELO (FREWEN) (September 9, 1885–May 31, 1970),

English sculptor, journalist, and novelist, was born in London, the only daughter of Moreton Sheridan, landowner and sportsman, and Clara Jerome, an American socialite. She had two brothers, and was largely educated at home by governesses, one of whom (so she claimed) was relentlessly cruel. She was later educated at a convent school in Paris and a finishing school in Germany. Her family life was erratic, her parents frequently running out of money, and bailiffs a common sight on the premises. Neither her mother nor father showed her affection, being more absorbed by their own pursuits, in her father's case a succession of affairs, including one with Lillie Langtry. Her family's friends included Rudyard Kipling, Henry James, and George Moore. The last named encouraged her early writing with intentionally damning praise.

Against her parents' approval, in 1910 Clare married Wilfred Sheridan, great-great-grandson of Richard Brinsley Sheridan, the playwright, and widely known as "the best-looking man in England." She had three children by him, Margaret, Elizabeth, and Richard. Elizabeth died in infancy, and Richard was born days after his father's death at the Battle of Loos. Meanwhile, Clare grew interested in sculpture, which was soon to become both an obsession and a way of earning an income. She quickly established a reputation, doing portrait busts of such figures as Winston Churchill, her cousin and lifelong friend, and of Asquith. An intrepid, vibrant, outspoken personality, she accepted an invitation from the Soviet politician Lev Kamenev in

1920 to visit Moscow to make busts of Trotsky and Lenin. This aroused such opprobrium in England that, on her return, she was severely rebuked, and in 1921 she left for America with her children.

There, in 1922, she was commissioned by Herbert Swope, editor of the New York World, to travel throughout Europe and send in reports of its postwar condition. She gained access to some of the most prominent international figures of the time, such as Mussolini and Kemal Ataturk. Her journalism brought her considerable acclaim and led to further, similar commissions. These journeys also gave her the basis of several travel books, the first of which was From Mayfair to Moscow (published in Great Britain as Russian Portraits). She had written her first novel at the age of eighteen (unpublished), and was to write several others, none of them distinguished for anything except the author's natural vivacity. Even she regarded them as "potboilers" and admitted to watching the clock while she wrote them, hoping it would soon be lunchtime. The New York Times dismissed Substitute Bride as "distinctly amateurish," while Stella Defiant, transparently and unkindly based on her brother-in-law, was summed up by the Springfield Republican as "clumsy and disjointed." Her volumes of autobiography and those works directly based on her travels were generally considered shallow, sometimes prejudiced, but were somewhat redeemed by their vivid descriptions and verve.

A willful woman, who revelled in flouting convention, she enjoyed numerous liaisons, including a short friendship with Charlie Chaplin. But she was a devoted, if often selfish mother. Her daughter Margaret later commented that "she was lovely but embarrassing; as a mother impossible, as a person enchanting." Although a mediocre author, she was a clever sculptor and, above all, a fascinating character, who once commented that "if my sins were many they were interesting."

PRINCIPAL WORKS: Novels—Stella Defiant, 1925; The Thirteenth, 1925; Green Amber, 1929; El Caid, 1931; Substitute Bride, 1931; Genetrix, 1935; Offspring, 1936; The Mask, 1942. Autobiography—Nuda Veritas, 1927; Naked Truth, 1928; My Crowded Sanctuary, 1943; To the Four Winds, 1954. Nonfiction—Russian Portraits, 1921; My American Diary, 1922; In Many Places, 1923; West and East, 1923; (with L. Reau, A. Levinson, C. Farrere, and A. Antoine) Faces of Russia, 1924; Across Europe with Satanella, 1925; A Turkish Kaleidoscope, 1926; Arab Interlude, 1936; Redskin Interlude, 1938; Without End, 1939.

ABOUT: Leslie, A. Cousin Clare, 1976; Oxbury, H. E. Great Britons, 1985; Schafer, B. (comp.) They Heard His Voice, 1952. Periodicals—New York Times June 3, 1970; Times (London) June 2, 1970; Wilson Library Bulletin April 1932.

## SHERMAN, STUART PRATT (October 1, 1881–August 21, 1926), American literary critic,

was born in Anita, Iowa, the son of John Sherman, a druggist and farmer, and Ada Martha (Pratt) Sherman. He was raised on a farm near Rolfe, Iowa, in Los Angeles, and—after his father's death from tuberculosis in 1882—in Dorset, Vermont, in the home of his paternal grandfather. After attending Troy Conference Academy in Vermont and Williamstown High School in Williamstown, Massachusetts, he entered Williams College, from which he graduated in 1902. He earned an M.A. (1904) and a Ph.D. (1906) in English literature at Harvard, where he was influenced by the tradition-minded New Humanism of Irving Babbitt and Paul Elmer More.

Sherman began his teaching career as an instructor at Northwestern University, but found an academic home at the University of Illinois, where he

became full professor in 1911 and head of the English department several years later. He taught both Carl and Mark Van Doren as undergraduates; in a speech delivered at the university more than thirty years after Sherman's death, Mark Van Doren recalled him as "the finest teacher I ever had anywhere." Never content with a strictly academic audience, he was a frequent contributor of literary essays to the *Nation* (which also published his verse), the *New Evening Post*, the *Atlantic Monthly*, and other periodicals. He achieved some measure of notoriety for "Graduate Schools and Literature," a scathing critique of American graduate education published in a 1908 edition of the *Nation*. In collaboration with W. P. Trent, John Erskine, and Carl Van Doren (who praised Sherman's intellectual generosity in his memoir *Three Worlds*), he edited *The Cambridge History of American Literature*.

Sherman's debt to Matthew Arnold is evident in his first book—*Matthew Arnold: How to Know Him*—as well as in his second, *On Contemporary Literature* (a collection of his *Nation* essays), in which he tried to employ Arnoldian standards to attack Theodore Dreiser, H. G. Wells, George Moore, and others he deemed guilty of practicing literary naturalism. *Americans*, his third book, traces the Puritan tradition in the work of Franklin, Emerson, and other seminal American figures. It also contains one of Sherman's numerous broadsides against H. L. Mencken, his prime literary adversary. For Sherman, Puritanism—which he defined very broadly—was a "liberative tradition"; consequently, he viewed Mencken's anti-Puritanism and Anglophobia as reckless iconoclasm. Mencken, in a *Smart Set* retort to *Americans*, chided "Prof. Dr. Sherman" for his chauvinism and his ignorance of "the new literature of the Republic, . . . [which] tends more and more to be written by fellows bearing such ghastly names as Ginsberg, Gohlinghorst, Casey, Mitnick, and Massaccio."

In 1924 Sherman moved to New York to edit *Books*, the new incarnation of the *New York Herald Tribune* weekly book review. *Points of View*, in which he expresses admiration for Dreiser, signaled a revision in his critical outlook. In *Critical Woodcuts* (a collection of his *Books* essays), the last volume published before his death, Sherman praised Wells, Sherwood Anderson, and D. H. Lawrence, all of whom he had formerly dismissed. In the essay "H. L. Mencken as Liberator," he took one final swipe at his long-time opponent, even though he had come to respect and agree with many of Mencken's critical judgments.

Sherman's death cut short what promised to be a continuing evolution in his literary ideas. Many of his books remain in print, though his long-term influence has been slight, perhaps because of the fervid nationalism he exhibited early in his career, and perhaps because of his mid-life critical reversal, none of which was profound. A few of Sherman's contemporaries, however, considered him to be America's foremost critic. That, he was not; but he had the courage to change his mind, and is still respected for it.

PRINCIPAL WORKS: *Literary criticism*—Matthew Arnold: How to Know Him, 1917; On Contemporary Literature, 1917; Americans, 1922; The Significance of Sinclair Lewis, 1922; The Genius of America: Studies in Behalf of the Younger Generation, 1923; My Dear Cornelia, 1924; (with T. Spicer-Simson) Men of Letters of the British Isles, 1924; Points of View, 1924; Critical Woodcuts, 1926; The Main Stream, 1927; Shaping Men and Women: Essays on Literature and Life (ed. J. Zeitlin) 1928; (with S. Haardt and E. Clark) Ellen Glasgow: Critical Essays, 1929; The Emotional Discovery of America and Other Essays, 1932. *As editor*—Stevenson's Treasure Island, 1911; The Tragedy of Coriolanus (by W. Shakespeare) 1912; A Book of Short Stories, 1914; 'Tis a Pity She's a Whore and The Broken Heart (by J. Ford) 1915; (with W. P. Trent, J. Erskine, and C. Van Doren) The Cambridge History of American Literature, 4 vols., 1917–1921; The Scarlet Letter (by N. Hawthorne) 1919; Essays and Poems of Emerson, 1921; The Poetical Works of Joaquin Miller, 1923; Letters to a Lady in the Country, Together with Her Replies (by Paul and Caroline) 1925.

ABOUT: Drake, W. (ed.) American Criticism, 1926; Nolte, W. H. L. Mencken: Literary Critic, 1964; Van Doren, C. Three Worlds, 1936; Zeitlin, J. and Woodbridge, H. Life and Letters of Stuart P. Sherman, 2 vols., 1929. *Periodicals*—New York Herald Tribune Books April 18, 1926; New York Times August 22, 1926; School and Society June 7, 1958; Sewanee Review January–March 1927; Smart Set March 1923.

## SHERRIFF, R(OBERT) C(EDRIC)

**SHERRIFF, R(OBERT) C(EDRIC)** (June 6, 1896–November 13, 1975), English playwright, novelist, and screenwriter, was born at Hampton Wick, Surrey, the only child of Herbert Hankin Sherriff and the former Constance Winder. He grew up in Kingston-on-Thames, near London, and was educated at the local grammar school. His main interest there was in sports—he was captain of rowing and cricket, and a keen soccer player.

At seventeen, Sherriff followed his father into the insurance business as a clerk with the Sun Assurance Company. A few months later, he enlisted in the army. At eighteen he was commissioned in the 9th East Surrey Regiment, and saw much action until he was severely wounded at Ypres in 1917. He was discharged with the rank of Captain.

Sherriff returned to the Sun Assurance Company as a claims adjuster. His first amateur plays were comedies, written mostly for the Kingston-on-Thames Rowing Club, which staged an annual production to raise funds. By the seventh year, Sherriff had run out of comedy ideas suitable for an all-male cast. He remembered how starkly dramatic had been his introduction to battle as a young subaltern at Vimy Ridge. His mother had kept his letters, and he used them as the basis for *Journey's End*.

The play, beyond the talents of Sherriff's club, was turned down by professional agents and producers. In December 1928, however, it was given two performances by the Stage Society of London. A young unknown actor named Laurence Olivier played the lead. Harold Monro of the Poetry Bookshop saw the play and recommended it to his friend Maurice Browne, then contemplating a career in management. It opened at the Savoy Theatre on January 21, 1929.

*Journey's End* is set entirely in an officer's dug-out in the front-line trenches before St. Quentin, on the Somme. It is March 1918. Captain Stanhope, a combat veteran at twenty-one, returns from leave to find that a new young subaltern has joined his company. This is Lieutenant Raleigh, who had idolized him at school, and whose sister Stanhope loves. Stanhope is not pleased, fearing that Raleigh will tell her about his heavy drinking, which is all that preserves his sanity. An older officer is killed and another feigns illness. Raleigh takes a prisoner and loses his innocent enthusiasm for battle. The play is built from only a few incidents, some tragic, some comic. There is a party of sorts. The next morning a great German offensive begins. Raleigh is hit, and dies in the dug-out just before it is blown to pieces.

The play ran for 594 performances in London. It played for more than a year in New York, and four companies toured it all over the United States. It was stages in twenty countries Einstein helped to arrange a gala performance in Berlin, film versions were made in English and in German, and it was adapted as a novel.

*Journey's End* was successfully published at a time (1929) the year when war reminiscences such as Graves's *Goodbye to All That* began to be popular. Bernard Shaw said of it: "useful as a corrective to the romantic conception of war. . . . This judgment does insufficient justice to Sherriff's skill in setting up his situation, building up tension, varying the intensity, timing his climaxes." Stark Young wrote that the most striking thing about it is its "underlying poetic feeling" (*New Republic*). Sherriff could have said of his play what Wilfred Owen said of his poems: "My subject is War, and the pity of War. The Poetry is in the pity." Recent revivals of *Journey's End*, dated slang and all, have proved its surprising durability.

Sherriff was a modest man. He was astonished to find himself a rich and world-famous writer, but accepted his destiny and left the insurance business. In 1931 he fulfilled an old ambition by going up to New College, Oxford University. His subject there, history, fed into a growing interest in archeology. He took up rowing again until illness ended that and also his chance of a degree. In 1937 he founded a scholarship at New College.

Often regarded as a one-play man, Sherriff in fact wrote nine others, several showing a preoccupation with various kinds of "journeys' ends." None approached the success of his single masterpiece, but all showed his professionalism, and his unfailing ear for dialogue. Most critics agree that the best of them were *St. Helena*, written with the actress Jeanne de Casalis, about Napoleon's last days; the suspenseful domestic thriller *Home at Seven*; and *The Long Sunset*, set at the end of the Roman occupation of Britain.

Sherriff also wrote several novels, notably *Fortnight in September*, a gently affectionate account of the annual vacation of a very ordinary English family, and *Greengates*, about the troubled retirement of a suburban insurance clerk. L.A.G. Strong, reviewing the former, found "more simple goodness and understanding in this book than in anything I have read for years" (Spectator). A more ambitious novel, *The Hopkins Manuscript*, describes a cataclysm that destroys civilization, and what follows. It had a mixed critical reception but caught the imagination of science fiction enthusiasts. Unlike the other novels, it has been several times republished.

Apart from *Journey's End*, Sherriff had his greatest success with the screenplays he began to write in the 1930s. The best remembered of his films are *The Invisible Man* (1933), *Goodbye, Mr. Chips* (1939), *The Four Feathers* (1939), *That Hamilton Woman* (1941), *Odd Man Out* (with F. L. Green, 1945), and *The Dam Busters* (1955). Sherriff also wrote some radio and television plays, and an autobiography, *No Leading Lady*.

Devoted to his mother, Sherriff had indeed no other "leading lady." He was a slim, dark-haired man, sweet-natured and shy, who liked the outdoors and stayed well clear of literary London. He bought a farm in Dorset and a house called "Rosebriars" in Esher, Surrey. There he would single-handedly act out his plays to get a sense of stage movements and dialogue. He was a Fellow of the Society of Antiquaries and of the Royal Society of Literature.

PRINCIPAL WORKS: *Drama*—Journey's End, 1929; Badger's Green, 1930; Windfall, 1933; (with J. de Casalis) St. Helena, 1934; Miss Mabel, 1949; Home at Seven, 1951; The White Carnation, 1953; The Long Sunset, 1956; The Telescope, 1957; A Shred of Evidence, 1961. *Novels*—(with Vernon Bartlett) Journey's End, 1930; Fortnight in September, 1931; Greengates, 1936; The Hopkins Manuscript, 1939 (revised as The Cataclysm, 1958); Chedworth, 1944; Another Year, 1948; King John's Treasure, 1954 (juvenile); The Wells of St. Mary's, 1962; The Siege of Swayne Castle, 1973. *Screenplays*—Quartet: Stories by W. Somerset Maugham (all four screenplays by Sherriff) 1948; Trio: Stories by W. Somerset Maugham (screenplays by Sherriff and others) 1950; (with F. L. Green) Odd Man Out in Manvell, R. (ed.) Three British Screenplays, 1950. *Autobiography*—No Leading Lady, 1968.

ABOUT: Dictionary of National Biography, 1971–1980, 1986; Nightingale, B. Fifty Modern British Plays, 1982; Stern, G. B. And Did He Stop and Speak to You? 1958; Who's Who 1974–1975. *Periodicals*—Christian Science Monitor Magazine July 29, 1950; New Republic April 10, 1929; New York Times November 18, 1975; Observer January 11, 1970; Punch August 7, 1968; Spectator October 17, 1931; Times (London) November 18, 1975; Times Literary Supplement September 19, 1968.

**SHERWOOD, ROBERT E(MMET)** (April 4, 1896–November 14, 1955), American playwright, historian, and novelist, was born in New Rochelle,  New York, the son of Rosina Emmet Sherwood, an artist and illustrator, and Arthur Murray Sherwood, a highly successful stockbroker. He was educated at Milton Academy in Massachusetts and entered Harvard University in 1914. Although he took a relaxed attitude toward his studies and left Harvard without a degree in 1917, it was there that he wrote his first play, a farce for the Hasty Pudding Club titled *Barnum Was Right*. He also wrote a parody of *Vanity Fair* for the *Harvard Lampoon* which so impressed Frank Crowinshield, *Vanity Fair*'s editor, that Crowinshield offered him a job upon graduation. Before he could accept the offer, however, World War I intervened. Sherwood, who was rejected from the United States Army because of his height (he was six feet seven), enlisted in the Canadian Black Watch Regiment in 1917, served in Britain and France, and was twice wounded. The horror and waste of trench warfare affected him profoundly, and he became a tireless advocate for pacifism until the rise of Hitler, when he switched positions dramatically and lobbied for early American military intervention in World War II. Returning to the United States in 1919, he began working for *Vanity Fair* and formed close friendships with two other young staff writers there, Robert Benchley and Dorothy Parker. All three soon left the magazine over an editorial dispute, and in 1920 Sherwood joined the staff of *Life* magazine. He remained at *Life* as a film critic (one of the first film critics to write for an American publication) and editor until 1928, by which time he had established himself as a playwright.

*The Road to Rome*, Sherwood's comedy about a vacillating Hannibal at the gates of Rome, opened in January of 1927 and ran for nearly four hundred performances. Somewhat reminiscent of Shaw's *Caesar and Cleopatra*, *The Road to Rome* was a mixture of sophisticated repartee and anti-war polemic. It received mixed reviews ("*The Road to Rome* is actable comedy . . . but it is essentially a false, rather than a theatrical play," wrote a critic in *Theatre Arts Monthly*), but it was far more successful than Sherwood's next three or four plays, none of which lasted for more than a few performances. In 1931 he recouped his fortunes with another comedy, *Reunion in Vienna*, which concerned the romantic imbroglios of a Viennese psychiatrist, his elegant wife, and her former lover, a deposed European monarch now reduced to driving a taxicab. A great vehicle for Alfred Lunt and Lynn Fontanne, *Reunion in Vienna* received better reviews for the acting than for the writing, but it was certainly one of Sherwood's most accomplished works. Eleanor Flexner called it "one of the most brilliantly witty of our comedies in recent

years. . . . The comedy is two-edged, for the writer is mocking, not only the faded glamour of Viennese imperial glory, but the cocksureness of the new psychology, which presumes to weigh human emotion with chemical accuracy, and admits of no incalculabilities."

Sherwood's next major play, most famous because of its movie version, starring Leslie Howard and the young Humphrey Bogart, *The Petrified Forest*, was a doom-ridden portrait of various character types—the disillusioned intellectual, the idealistic young girl, the amoral but purposeful gangster—stranded in a roadside cafe on the edge of the Arizona desert. Today it is remembered less for its allegorical musings on the aimlessness of modern life than for having introduced Bogart to the world in the role of the cold-hearted killer Duke Mantee. In general Sherwood's more ambitious plays all suffered from the portentousness so evident in *The Petrified Forest*. Walter J. Meserve maintained that "something in the man caused him to avoid the more searching complexities of life and, instead, face great issues with a guileless spontaneity which bore more evidence of an honest concern than a thoughtful analysis." Nevertheless, the three Pulitzer Prize-winning plays that followed *The Petrified Forest—Idiot's Delight*, *Abe Lincoln in Illinois*, and *There Shall Be No Night*—all dealt unselfconsciously with great issues of social import. Of the three, *Abe Lincoln in Illinois* was probably the most celebrated; it remains one of the very few Sherwood plays to be revived from time to time. Like the other two plays, it was written with the European crisis much in mind, and Lincoln's climactic acceptance of his destiny to lead the nation was meant at least in part to inspire Americans to assume their burden in the coming war. Although the characterization was hardly free from sentimentality (its primary source was Carl Sandburg's hagiographic biography), Sherwood's Lincoln, wrote R. Baird Shuman, "is a compelling protagonist. . . . As hero, Lincoln is warm, humorous at times, sincere, and infinitely human. It is Lincoln's humanity that Sherwood capitalizes on in this play. . . . He goes forth to occupy a position which must be filled with honor and dedication. He leaves behind him all thought of ever again enjoying the privacy which he so much desires."

The subject of *There Shall Be No Night*, Sherwood's last major play, was the response of various Finnish characters to the invasion of their country by the Soviet Union. By the time of its production in 1940 Sherwood had become more involved in interventionist politics (he donated all his royalties from the play to Red Cross relief in Finland) than in playwriting. In the same year he took out a full-page advertisement in newspapers across the country proclaiming "Stop Hitler Now!" Embraced by the Roosevelt administration, he served as director of the Overseas Branch of the Office of War Information from 1942 to 1944 and became one of the president's chief speechwriters. After the war, with his inspiration as a playwright flagging, he turned historian, composing a monumental study of President Roosevelt and his influential adviser Harry L.

Hopkins. *Roosevelt and Hopkins: An Intimate History* earned for Sherwood his fourth Pulitzer Prize as well as the Bancroft Prize for Distinguished Writing in American History. Writing in the *New York Herald Tribune Weekly Book Review,* Joseph Barnes called *Roosevelt and Hopkins* the best book "yet written about the political strategy of the war. . . . It is told in terms of the strange relationship between two men . . . who played great but puzzling parts in the shaping. It is told by a third who was their friend, but who has paid debts in this book only to the old and decent business of writing truly and simply."

Concurrent with his career as a dramatist, Sherwood was a skillful Hollywood screenwriter. (Among his credits were *The Scarlet Pimpernel* and *Rebecca*). Indeed, his screenplay for *The Best Years of Our Lives,* which won seven Academy Awards in 1946, was considerably more successful than the minor plays he wrote or attempted to write after *There Shall Be No Night.* Famous for his mordant sense of humor and unfailing generosity, he nevertheless dried up, creatively, after World War II. He died of a heart attack in New York. Walter J. Meserve's judgment that Sherwood was "never a great playwright" is certainly true, and in the not very selective company of significant American dramatists he occupies a distinctly secondary place. All the same, wrote Meserve, "he spoke intensely and with wit and integrity during a period in history when such plays as his were needed. He provided excellent plays for the moment, out of the moment. . . . This was his greatness, and he was well paid by a grateful generation." He was also a brilliantly accomplished stage craftsman.

The American Academy of Arts and Letters, to which Sherman was admitted in 1950, is the primary repository of his papers.

PRINCIPAL WORKS: *Drama*—The Road to Rome, 1927; The Queen's Husband, 1928; Waterloo Bridge: A Play in Two Acts, 1930; This Is New York: A Play in Three Acts, 1931; Reunion in Vienna: A Play in Three Acts, 1932; The Petrified Forest, 1935; Idiot's Delight, 1936; Abe Lincoln in Illinois: A Play in Twelve Scenes, 1939; There Shall Be No Night, 1940; (with P. Barry) Second Threshold, 1951; Small War on Murray Hill: A Comedy in Two Acts, 1957. *Adaptation*—Tovarich: A Play in Three Acts (by J. Deval) 1938. *Novel*—The Virtuous Knight, 1931 (in U.K.: Unending Crusade). *History*—Roosevelt and Hopkins: An Intimate History, 1948.

ABOUT: Brown, J. M. The Worlds of Robert E. Sherwood: Mirror to His Times, 1896–1939, 1965; Current Biography 1940; Dictionary of American Biography, Suppl. 5, 1977; Dictionary of Literary Biography, Vol. 7, 1981; Vol. 27, 1984; Flexner, E. American Playwrights, 1918–1938, 1938; Meserve, W. J. Robert E. Sherwood: Reluctant Moralist, 1970; Shuman, R. B. Robert E. Sherwood, 1964; Twentieth Century American Literary Criticism: The Chelsea House Library of Literary Criticism Vol. 6, 1987. *Periodicals*—New York Herald Tribune Weekly Book Review October 24, 1948; New York Times November 15, 1955; Theatre Arts Monthly January 1939.

**SHIELS, GEORGE** (June 24, 1886–September 19, 1949), Irish playwright, who wrote for the Abbey Theatre in Dublin, was born in Ballymoney, County Antrim, the son of Robert and Eileen (MacSweeney) Shiels. He was educated at the primary school. Although essentially an autodidact, he acquired a detailed knowledge of Irish and foreign drama. At about the age of twenty Shiels left for North America, where he spent seven years working at laboring jobs in Montana and on the Canadian Pacific Railway. In 1913, badly injured in a railroad accident, he returned to Ballymoney.

For the rest of his life Shiels was confined to a wheelchair; he never even got to Dublin—and only once, in 1928, was able to see the Abbey perform one of his plays, when they were on tour at the Belfast Opera House. He was, however, able to hear a number of his plays performed on the radio, broadcast by the BBC and Radio Eireann.

After his return to Ireland, Shiels began writing short stories based on his American experiences: about life in the mining camps and forests. Several of them were published in popular magazines. In his early thirties he began to write plays under the name George Morshiel. *Away from the Moss,* produced by the Ulster Literary Theatre in Belfast in 1918, was probably his earliest; but neither it nor its successor, *Felix Reid and Bob*  (staged by the Ulster Literary Theatre in 1919), survives in printed form.

In June 1921 Shiels's long connection with the Abbey Theatre began, with the production of his one-act comedy *Bedmates.* Its light, amusing satire touches on a serious subject: England's exploitation of Irish religious differences. He established his reputation with *Paul Twyning,* a romantic comedy about an itinerant craftsman (a stock Irish rural type), staged by the Abbey in October 1922. From then on, for over twenty-five years, he wrote a series of box office hits for the company, comedies (so titled) that reflect, with varying degrees of seriousness, on Ireland's problems. Shiels, a Roman Catholic who once described himself as "an Irish peasant," gives an authentic picture of rural and town life in Northern Ireland at the beginning of the twentieth century. Never well known abroad—although some of his plays were brought to London and New York by the Abbey—he became (according to his friend and fellow dramatist T. C. Murray) one of Ireland's most popular playwrights. As the obituary article in the *Irish Weekly and Ulster Examiner* noted: "His plays were as popular in Belfast as in Dublin, and there was hardly an amateur dramatic society in Ireland that had not at some time staged a George Shiels play." Another particularly successful early comedy was *Professor Tim* (staged in 1925), about an emigrant who returns home disguised as a tramp to test, and prove, his family's hypocritical attitudes.

Shiels's Abbey contemporaries, Murray, Lennox Robinson, and W. B. Yeats, advised him that realism, not romantic comedy, was his forte; during the 1930s his tone darkened. His later plays acknowledge the presence of greed, superstition, corruption, and lawlessness in everyday life. This play, with its touches of grim humor, is an uncompromis-

ingly forthright comment on small-town Irish life
and a family held together by mutual greed.

Shiels's most powerful play was *The Rugged
Path*, which—despite its painful revelations about
Irish ambivalence toward law and order, specifically in dealing with informers—had a record run of
over fifty performances when first put on in Dublin
in 1940. Here, a family's decision to report a band
of outlaws brands them as informers and exposes
them to retaliation at the hands of their neighbors.
In the sequel, *The Summit* (1941), not as successful
a play, the neighbors join in support of the "informers" and restore law and order. A *Threshold* article
on him proposes that the two plays reflect the larger question of Irish neutrality in World War II,
with a warning about fascist brutality. "Long after
anything in [them] has ceased to be topical the plays
will be alive, both as works of creative imagination
and as treasuries of good counsel," the *Times Literary Supplement* suggested.

Intending to do a drama about the Great Famine
and the iniquities of land occupation that preceded
it, Shiels set to work on a long and complex chronicle play; the Abbey rejected his first effort. The rewritten and considerably toned down version,
*Tenants at Will*, about a poor peasant farmer, was
finally produced in 1945.

A collection of Shiels's papers is housed in the
National Library of Ireland, Dublin.

PRINCIPAL WORKS: Bedmates: A Play in One Act, 1922; Professor
Tim: A Comedy in Three Acts, 1927 (also published as Profes-
sor Tim and Paul Twyning, Comedies in Three Acts, 1927);
Two Irish Plays: Mountain Dew, a Play in Three Acts and Car-
tney and Kevney, a Comedy in Three Acts, 1930; The New
Gossoon: A Comedy in Three Acts, 1936; The Passing Day, A
Play in Six Scenes and The Jailbird, a Comedy in Three Acts,
1937; The Rugged Path and The Summit: Plays in Three Acts,
1942; Three Plays: Professor Tim, Paul Twyning, The New
Gossoon, 1945; The Fort Field, a Comedy in Three Acts, 1947;
Give Him a House: A Comedy in Three Acts, 1947; Grogan
and the Ferret, a Comedy in Three Acts, 1947; The Old
Broom: A Comedy in Three Acts, 1947; Quin's Secret: A Com-
edy in Three Acts, 1947; Tenants at Will: A Comedy in Three
Acts, 1947; The Caretakers: A Comedy, 1948.

ABOUT: Deane, S. (ed.) The Field Day Anthology of Irish Writing, Vols. 2 and 3, 1991; Hogan, R. After the Irish Renaissance:
A Critical History of the Irish Drama since The Plough and
the Stars, 1967; Murray, T. C. George Shiels, Brinsley McNamara, etc. *in* The Irish Theatre (ed. L. Robinson) 1939. *Periodicals*—The Irish Times (Dublin) September 20, 1949; The Irish
Weekly and Ulster Examiner (Belfast) September 24, 1949;
New York Times September 21, 1949; Threshold Summer
1974; Times Literary Supplement July 13, 1942.

**\*SHIRER, WILLIAM L(AWRENCE)** (February 23, 1904–December 28, 1993), American journalist, radio news commentator, and novelist, was
born in Chicago, the son of Samuel Smith Shirer, a
lawyer, and Bessie Josephine (Tanner) Shirer. He
was raised in Cedar Rapids, Iowa, and attended
Coe College there; he received his B.A. in 1925.
While a student he got his first newspaper job as
sportswriter for the *Cedar Rapids Republican*. Determined upon graduation to spend some time in
Europe and write fiction and poetry, he borrowed
funds and worked his way over on a cattle boat.
The same year he obtained a job on the copy desk
of the Paris edition of the *Chicago Tribune* (James

°SHY rer

Thurber and Elliot Paul were among his desk-
mates) and took courses in European history at the
Collège de France. In 1927 Shirer became the *Tribune*'s foreign correspon-
dent, covering events
such as Lindbergh's land-
ing in Paris and peace
talks in Geneva. Between
1929 and 1932 he was as-
signed to Vienna as chief
of the *Tribune's* Central
European bureau, and in
the course of those years
traveled to India where
he became acquainted

with Gandhi and interested in the civil disobedi-
ence movement. *Gandhi: A Memoir*, written over
forty years later, chronicles their friendship. In
1931 he was married to Theresa Stiberitz, an Austrian artist; they had two daughters. The marriage
was dissolved in 1970.

Injured while skiing in the Alps in 1932, Shirer
lost the sight of one eye. He left the *Tribune* to recuperate in Spain and work as a free-lance writer.
Back in Paris in 1934, he became European correspondent for the Paris edition of the *New York
Herald Tribune*, following which he worked in
Berlin (1935–1937) as a correspondent for the Universal News Service. He was then invited by Edward R. Murrow, chief of the CBS radio foreign
staff, to open an office for CBS in Vienna. For the
next three years he broadcast from Vienna, Prague,
and Berlin, reporting to the American public on the
spread of totalitarianism. His observations of the
events leading up to World War II became the basis
of his two best-known books, combining brilliant
reportage and an unusual command of history: *Berlin Diary* (1941) and *The Rise and Fall of the Third
Reich* (1960). Both were bestsellers, and were translated into many languages. The diary covers January 1934 to December 1940, when Shirer had to
leave Germany under threat of expulsion as a spy;
he managed to smuggle the manuscript out hidden
under a pile of old radio scripts. "He writes
with . . . the anger and pity that come straight
from the incandescent movements he lived
through," Edward Weeks said, in the *Atlantic
Monthly*. "He lets the evidence speak, and his stark
quotation of the German headlines is one of his
most skillful strokes." Max Fischer, on the other
hand, questioned the book's authority: "I myself
lived in Germany till the fall of 1935 . . . Reading
*Berlin Diary, 1934–1941*, I am of course eager to
learn how the . . . atmosphere has changed since
the days of my farewell"; but he found no answers.
"These things are not in the headlines. And Mr. Shirer is just the typical newspaperman. . . . I admit
he is an excellent reporter, but his book seems to me
rather sterile" (*Commonweal*). Taking the middle
course, George N. Shuster recommended it "because it presents with honesty and firmness truth
that must be known now if [we] are to survive"
(*New York Times*). The sequel, *End of a Berlin Diary*, carries the account through to the end of the
war. In his first published novel, *The Traitor*, Shirer

dealt with the activities of those who turned against their own side and created propaganda for the Germans. "As a primer of European history, between 1932 and 1945, this book is excellent . . . his presentation never lacks fire," the historian Richard Plant observed. But often Shirer "seems so overwhelmed by his materials that his characters change into mere mouthpieces of different shades of opinion" (*New York Times*).

Shirer, who had continued to work for CBS as a commentator based in the United States during the war years, returned to Europe to cover the Nuremberg Trials; his less than optimistic ruminations on the immediate postwar state of affairs form the substance of *Midcentury Journey: The Western World through Its Years of Conflict*. In 1947 he left CBS. According to his own account—in *A Native's Return*, the third volume of his memoirs, collectively titled *Twentieth Century Journey*—his liberal views had displeased a sponsor, and Murrow (by then a vice president) did not defend him to the CBS management. For their part, the producers contended that Shirer's ratings had declined. Only in later years did Shirer and Murrow renew their friendship. In 1947 Shirer went over to the Mutual Broadcasting System, doing news commentary for the next two years. Then, during the McCarthy era in the early 1950s, he was blacklisted as a Communist sympathizer for his earlier support of the so-called Hollywood 10. Although he denied the allegation, "I became unemployable," as he told a *New York Times* interviewer in 1977. "I was broke. . . . Some of my friends were editors and would pay me for a piece, but nothing was ever published. . . . I spent almost five years when my sole income was from . . . one-night lecturer stands stands at universities. They were almost the only place in the country that still had some sort of respect for freedom of speech." His books continued to be published, however: they include *Stranger Come Home*, a roman á clef about a foreign correspondent who returns to America after the war to broadcast news for a network of which his former boss is now vice president; *The Challenge of Scandinavia*; and *The Consul's Wife*, a novel.

During the time he was blacklisted from the radio, Shirer was able to do the research on and write his major work, *The Rise and Fall of the Third Reich*, a long history of National Socialism from the end of World War I to the end of the second war. As he somewhat self-deprecatingly described it, it is "the work of a newspaperman, not a university scholar." It is in fact an objective, straightforward composite of Shirer's own news stories, pertinent anecdotes, diary extracts, confiscated German documents, and Nuremberg Trials testimony—an enormous mass of information very ably organized. The then Professor of Modern History at Oxford, Hugh Trevor-Roper, who specialized in the field, reviewing it in the *New York Times*, declared that it was "a splendid work of scholarship . . . sound in judgment, inescapable in its conclusions." Most reviewers agree that it would be an indispensable sourcebook, though recognizing some limitations: that Shirer gave no original interpretations of the

facts and that, in his concern with political and military history, he left out the effect of Nazism on the German people themselves. German critics contended that the book oversimplified the situation and indicated that all Germans had supported the regime. The book received the National Book Award and a Sidney Hillman Fund Award, both in 1961. Shirer's belief in making history alive to readers led to two successful juvenile books: a shortened version of *The Rise and Fall*, retitled *The Rise and Fall of Adolf Hitler*, and *The Sinking of the Bismarck*, a vividly realistic account of the destruction of a German battleship by the British Navy in 1941.

In 1976 Shirer published the first volume of a three-volume memoir with the overall title *Twentieth-Century Journey: A Memoir of the Life and the Times*. The first volume, *The Start*, takes him from boyhood to the start of his newspaper days, with anecdotes about the expatriate circle in Paris, especially Gertrude Stein. The second is *The Nightmare Years 1930–1940*; and the final volume, published in 1990, *A Native's Return*, tells of his life from 1945 to 1988, the year he married his second wife, Irina Lugovskaya, a Russian emigrée. His last book, *Love and Hatred: The Troubled Marriage of Leo and Sonya Tolstoy*, which was published the year after the author's death is an attempt to find the reason for Tolstoy's abandonment of home and wife before his strange death.

William L. Shirer was a Chevalier of the French Legion of Honor, a member of the Authors Guild (president from 1953 to 1957) and of PEN. He received a George Foster Peabody Award for outstanding news analysis in 1947, and a Wendell Willkie One World Award in 1948.

PRINCIPAL WORKS: *Fiction*—The Traitor, 1950; Stranger Come Home, 1954; The Consul's Wife, 1956. *Nonfiction*—Berlin Diary: The Journal of a Foreign Correspondent, 1934–1941, 1941 (repr. 1993); End of a Berlin Diary 1946; Midcentury Journey: The Western World through Its Years of Conflict, 1952; The Challenge of Scandinavia: Norway, Sweden, Denmark, and Finland in Our Time, 1955; The Rise and Fall of the Third Reich: A History of Nazi Germany, 1960; The Rise and Fall of Adolf Hitler (in U.K.: All about the Rise and Fall of Adolf Hitler) 1961; The Sinking of the Bismarck, 1962; The Collapse of the Third Republic: An Inquiry into the Fall of France in 1940, 1969; Twentieth Century Journey: A Memoir of a Life and the Times, 3 vols., 1976–1990 (vol. 1: The Start, 1904–1930; vol. 2: The Nightmare Years, 1930–1940; vol. 3: A Native's Return, 1945–1988); Gandhi: A Memoir, 1979; Love and Hatred: The Troubled Marriage of Leo and Sonya Tolstoy, 1994.

ABOUT: Contemporary Authors New Revision Series 7, 19; Current Biography 1962; Dictionary of Literary Biography vol. 4, 1980; Heald, M. Transatlantic Vista: American Journalists in Europe, 1900–1940, 1988; McKerns, J. P. (ed.) Biographical Dictionary of American Journalism, 1989; Shirer, W. L. Berlin Diary: The Journal of a Foreign Correspondent, 1934–1941, 1941; Shirer, W. L. End of a Berlin Diary, 1947; Shirer, W. L. Gandhi: A Memoir, 1979; Shirer, W. L. Twentieth Century Journey: A Memoir of a Life and the Times, 3 vols., 1976–1990. *Periodicals*—American Heritage June/July 1984; Atlantic Monthly September 1941, December 1969; Commonweal August 1, 1941, June 18, 1954; Journal of Contemporary History January 1994; New York Times June 22, 1941; November 12, 1950; October 16, 1960; October 10, 1976; July 24, 1977; December 29, 1993; July 24, 1994; New Yorker August 8, 1994; Spectator November 18, 1960; Times (London) December 30, 1993.

## SHOLOKHOV, MIKHAIL ALECKSAN-DROVICH

(May 24, 1905–February 24, 1984), Russian novelist and dramatist, was born in  Kruzhilin, Russia, in the Don region near Voronezh, the son of a farmer and powder-mill owner, Alexander Mikhailovich Sholokhov, and the former Anastasia Chernikova, "an illiterate maid" of Ukrainian and perhaps Turkish origin, to whom he was not married, but who did live in his household as his "servant." Later his mother taught herself to read and write, since she wanted to be able to communicate with her bright son. Sholokhov was not a Cossack by origin; but his mother had hastily been married off by Sholokhov's family to an elderly Cossack, and so upon his birth he inherited all the rights and privileges—which were considerable—of a Cossack. However, the old Cossack died in 1912, and his real parents married—and so the seven-year-old boy suddenly lost his special status.

Sholokhov was educated at a school in Boguchar (Voronezh) until 1918, when the Russian Civil War came to the region. He was a close witness to the anti-Bolshevik uprising, but, always sincerely sympathetic to its aims, began to work for the Bolshevik regime as soon as it was established.

A tax-inspector, clerk, and teacher, he fought for the Reds—probably as machine-gunner—against the anti-Soviet guerrillas. In October 1922 he became an associate, although not a member, of the Komsomol group of writers ("The Young Guard"). He had tried his hand at plays and sketches (none of them now available for scrutiny) before 1922, and had also engaged on a course of prodigious reading; but he began his career as a writer in earnest when he started to attend seminars in creative writing conducted by Osip Brik and Victor Shklovsky, one of the most eminent of critics. By the first part of the 1930s Sholokhov had become the leading writer of the Soviet establishment. He was much maligned, in particular by Solzenhitsyn, who, with others, tried unsuccessfully to demonstrate that he did not write the works for which he is famous.

In 1923 Sholokhov returned to his native province to get married. For a short while he tried living in Moscow, but he found he could not write there, and settled back at home. His first published story, "Ispytanie" (The test), appeared in a Komsomol newspaper in the same year as his marriage to Maria Gromoslavskaya (a teacher, with whom he had four children). In 1926 he published his first two books, collections of tales called Donskie rasskazy (translated as Tales from the Don) and Lazorevaya step (The tulip), and these brought him to the immediate attention of critics. In that year he started work on the epic And Quiet Flows the Don that brought him fame. It took him fourteen years to complete it.

Sholokhov joined the Communist Party in 1932. In the following year he personally persuaded Stalin to send grain to the Don region. In 1938 the police concocted a false case against Sholokhov—but Stalin, after some hesitation, intervened to save him.

During World War II Sholokhov acted as a front-line reporter, and was thus able to publish little. His never finished novel Oni srazhalis za rodinu (1943, 1944, 1969, They fought for their country) is more inspired journalism than fiction, and has never been considered important. Indeed, despite passages from Virgin Soil Upturned, his second epic, Sholokhov the novelist is essentially a single-volume master; to be added to his achievement, however, are his first stories. Many of these show a complete objectivity as they trace the human results of the struggles taking place in the Don region during the period of his own youth there. Anti-Communist American reviewers reviled the stories on their reappearance in 1962; but Mark Slonim, writing in the New York Times Book Review, knew better when he wrote that the collection "contains all the elements that later made Sholokhov a master of representational narrative: tense dramatic plots, fresh landscape, catching humor, and a racy, uninhibited popular humor."

Sholokhov's masterpiece, And Quiet Flows the Don, probably deserved the Nobel Prize as much as any other deliberately pre-modernist, representational twentieth-century novel. His research for it was as thorough as it was intelligent. Set between 1912 and 1922, it gives an incomparable picture of what life was like for the Cossacks in that fateful decade. The protagonist, Grigory Melekhov, suffers loss in love, and in the end surrenders to the Bolshevik cause, which is never really favored. The author shows him as a classic Russian hero, destroyed not by his failings, but by his virtues. Often compared to Tolstoy and to the Russian nineteenth-century novel in general, And Quiet Flows the Don is in fact more original.

Liberals, though, could not have it that this dedicated communist had such virtues. Picking up on a rumor started against him by the secret police in 1928, they ascribed the best of his work to another Don writer called Fyodor Kryukov, who had died while on retreat with the Whites in 1920. The hypothesis was shown to be undoubtedly false; computer analysis carried out by a group of objective Scandinavian scholars destroyed it.

Virgin Soil Upturned, in its first part, is a far more mixed affair. Its textual history is largely unknown, and the second part is simply a ragbag of sketches sewn together. There is no interesting central character. Yet it remains a major fictional description of collectivisation.

Sholokhov recorded the destruction of the Cossack way of life, but hardly realizsed that with its passing went his own creative life. In Schiller's sense, Sholokhov was a "naive" writer, caught up in an age which he could not understand with his intellect, but whose workings he could observe with an often unique exactitude.

PRINCIPAL WORKS IN ENGLISH TRANSLATION: *Novels*—And Quiet Flows the Don (tr. S. Garry), 1941; Virgin Soil Upturned and Harvest on the Don (tr. S. Garry) 1935–1960. *Tales*—Tales from the Don (tr. H. C. Stevens), 1961. *Short stories*—Short Stories (tr. various) 1984. *Articles*—One Man's Destiny (tr. H. C. Stevens) 1957.

ABOUT: Carlisle, O. Voices in the Snow, 1962; Ermolaev, H. Mikhail Sholokhov and His Art, 1982; Matthewson, R. W. Jr., The Positive Hero in Russian Literature, 1975; Medvedev, R. Problems in the Literary Biography of Mikhail Sholokhov, 1977; Mukherjee, G. Mikhail Sholokhov, 1992; Simmons, E. J. Russian Fiction and Soviet Ideology, 1958; Slonim, M. Modern Russian Literature, 1953; Sofronov, A. V. Meetings With Sholokhov, 1985; Stedwart, D. H. Mikhail Sholokhov, 1967. *Periodicals*—New York Review of Books March 4, 1962; Slavic Review Summer 1984.

## SHORTER, CLEMENT KING (July 19, 1857– November 19, 1926), English editor and biographer, was born in London, at Southwark. His fa-

ther, a carrier, went to Australia while Clement was still a boy, to try and make good a living ruined by competition from the railways, but soon after died in Melbourne. Clement, the youngest of three sons, attended school in Norfolk, leaving at the age of fourteen. After several years working for various booksellers and publishers, Shorter settled into secure employment at Somerset House, working as a clerk in the exchequer and audit department. He worked there until his early thirties, continuing his education by attending evening classes at the Birkbeck Institute.

Shorter's journalistic career began around 1888, with a weekly column about books for the *Star*, and an evening shift as sub-editor for the *Penny Illustrated Paper*. In 1890 he was able to give up his clerical position at Somerset House and concentrate on journalism. He was quickly made editor of the *Illustrated London News*; in 1893 he launched the *Sketch*, a weekly aimed at a less serious-minded readership. In the same year appeared the first book of the Irish poet and sculptor, Dora Sigerson, who became Shorter's wife in 1896. By the following year Shorter had become the editor of no less than five papers. Parting from his associate on the *Illustrated London News*, William James Ingram, the enterprising Shorter founded the *Sphere* in 1900, and the *Tatler* three years later.

By this time his main interest had become the collection of manuscripts and effects relating to his favorite authors, in particular the Brontës. The manner in which he acquired, and then held on to, some of the Brontë correspondence (particularly Charlotte's letters to Ellen Nussey) has in recent times been the subject of some suspicion. Tom Winnifrith, in particular, described Shorter's methods as "villainy," although he has had to recant suggestions that Shorter tried to pass off some of Branwell Brontë's work as Charlotte's. Shorter's indiscretions, in comparison with those of his unprincipled associate, T. J. Wise, could be attributed by the charita-

ble to the over-enthusiasm and compulsiveness of a collector. The general opinion of his books is that they contain nothing of critical merit, being in the main mere compendia of correspondence, not too competently put together. But they were significant publications in their time, if only because of the new light shed on their subjects by previously unavailable material. Shorter's editorial work (he produced editions of the Brontë sisters' poems in separate volumes and several works by Mrs. Gaskell) has no scholarly status.

Shorter's first wife died in 1918, after completing a sculpture commemorating the patriots of the Easter rebellion. His second wife (whom he married in 1920), the daughter of a Cornish shipowner, had privately printed after his death an autobiographical fragment entitled *C.K.S.*, edited by J. M. Bulloch.

PRINCIPAL WORKS: Charlotte Brontë and Her Circle, 1896 (published as The Brontës and Their Circle, 1914); Sixty Years of Victorian Literature, 1897; Charlotte Brontë and Her Sister, 1905; Immortal Memories, 1907; The Brontës: Life and Letters, 1908; Highways and Byways in Buckinghamshire, 1910; George Borrow and His Circle, 1913 (published as The Life of George Borrow, 1919); C.K.S.: An Autobiography (ed. J. M. Bulloch), 1927. *As editor*—The Complete Poems of Emily Brontë, 1910; The Complete Poems of Anne Brontë, 1924; The Complete Poems of Charlotte Brontë, 1924.

ABOUT: Dictionary of National Biography, 1922–1930; Seymour-Smith, M. Hardy, 1994; Who's Who 1926; Winnifrith, T. The Brontës and Their Background, 1973. *Periodicals*—New York Times November 20, 1926; Philological Quarterly Spring 1989; Times (London) November 20, 1926.

## SHOTWELL, JAMES T(HOMSON) (August 6, 1874–July 15, 1965), Canadian-American historian, proponent of international organizations, and

poet, was born in Strathroy, Ontario, where he attended the local elementary and high schools. He entered the University of Toronto as a freshman in 1894. After graduation in 1898, Shotwell went on to Columbia University for postgraduate study in medieval history, in the department

of James Harvey Robinson. In 1899 he was given his first opportunity for European travel, when the family of a boy he was tutoring invited him to accompany them on their summer vacation. He found himself in Paris during the retrial of the Dreyfus case, and witnessed the anti-Semitic rioting this provoked, which gave him an appetite for contemporary history, and when back at Columbia he became an enthusiastic disciple of Robinson's "New History," with its emphasis on the use and interpretation of source material. After gaining his doctorate (with a dissertation on the history of the eucharist), Shotwell was appointed to the Columbia University teaching staff and maintained his association with the history department until 1942.

Shotwell's first important commission arose when in 1904 he was invited to become general editor of the eleventh (and best) edition of the *Ency-*

clopaedia Britannica. The Britannica offices were on the third floor of the Times building, and Shotwell, with his colleagues, began to set up a card index of people and events featured in the newspaper, to keep the encyclopaedia articles up to date. This was the origin of the Times Index. Of his own contributions to the encyclopaedia, the essay on "History" in the eleventh edition emphasizes the impact of science and technology on the modern world. His Introduction to the History of History treated the new approach to history as just another branch of scientific research. Many of the articles in the eleventh edition have become famous, and most reference-book experts keep it for consultation.

Shotwell's involvement in international diplomacy began during World War I. In 1917 he served as a committee member on the inquiry set up to study the political, economic, legal, and historical issues that would present themselves at the conclusion of the war, and in 1919 he was on the advisory team accompanying Woodrow Wilson to the Versailles Peace Conference, an experience he later wrote about both in At the Paris Peace Conference and in his autobiography. His accounts contain interesting cameos of T. E. Lawrence and Clemenceau.

After the war Shotwell undertook the massive task of editing the Economic and Social History of the World War (eventually consisting of 152 volumes) for the Carnegie Endowment, and in 1924 became director of the Endowment's Division of Economics and History. Shotwell's involvements gave his writings an air of authority. For example, War as an Instrument of National Policy was widely read on its publication in 1929; it followed successful personal lobbying with the foreign minister of France, Aristide Briand, which had led in 1928 to the signing of the Kellogg-Briand Peace Pact, a declaration renouncing war. Shotwell devoted much of his energies during the thirties and forties to organizing a means of enforcing such declarations. In his Autobiography he wrote: "I drew the conclusion that war between highly industrialized nations is from now on, by its very nature, international and not merely bi-national, for there are no nations that can wage a major war entirely on their own resources. It, therefore, tends to draw neutrals into belligerency in spite of themselves. Thus war spreads like a contagion and ceases to be directable."

World War II reinforced this view and Shotwell became an enthusiastic supporter of the United Nations. From the 1950s onwards he turned more of his attention to writing, principally to a long, panoramic analysis of political evolution.

PRINCIPAL WORKS: Nonfiction—The Religious Revolution of Today, 1913; An Introduction to the History of History, 1922; War as an Instrument of National Policy, 1929; The Heritage of Freedom, 1934; On the Rim of the Abyss, 1936; At the Paris Peace Conference, 1937; Turkey at the Straits, 1940; What Germany Forgot, 1940; The Great Decision, 1944; The Long Way to Freedom, 1960. Verse—Poems, 1953. Memoirs—The Autobiography of James T. Shotwell, 1961.

ABOUT: Current Biography 1944; Dictionary of American Biography, 1961–1965; Who's Who 1965. Periodicals—New York Times July 17, 1965; Times (London) July 17, 1965.

*SHRIDHARANI, KRISHNALAL JETHALAL (September 16, 1911–July 23, 1960), Indian man of letters, wrote: "The only unusual thing about my career is that through literary pursuits I have become a man of two worlds; it is the fate of high caste Hindus to become 'twice born,' but my rebirth has been unconventional. I acquired some recognition as a Gujarati (one of the major Aryan languages of India) poet and playwright  at the age of twenty when my The Banyan Tree (Vadalo, written in jail) came out, but by the time I was twenty-five and in America, English, which was my second language from kindergarten, had become my medium of expression. Even today, six years after the native's return, I continue to write in English and only occasionally in Gujarati, which gives me a much wider reading public not only in the English-speaking world but also in India; even Gujaratis read English. . . . ; I continue to write poems in Gujarati and stories in English. This dual literary nationality often makes me fall between two stools, but often enough it brings to my English writings the flavor of the East, and to my Gujarati writings the cerebrations of the West.

"It was at the height of the Gandhian Age in Gujarati literature and when I was eleven that my first poem was accepted by a literary magazine. The fact needs underscoring because my writings both in Gujarati and in English up to 1947, the year India became independent, echo the throbs of the new movement led by Gandhi to revive ancient springs of emotion and to equate our heritage with those of the proudest peoples in the West. Not that what I wrote was propaganda and not art. But even art became suspect in the eye of the ruling race and the press that printed and published my play, A Flicker of the Flame (Zabakjyot), had to pay a heavy security for better behaviour in future. My novel, I Shall Kill the Human in You (Insan Mita Dunga, a story of jail life) was proscribed.

" . . . At poet Rabindranath Tagore's Santiniketan (abode of peace) I wrote The Suttee (Padmini), a play based on a fable from our Rajput history which dramatizes the conflict of ethical values and arrives at a conclusion diametrically opposite to the one reached by Maurice Maeterlinck in Monna Vanna. The poems written during this period show Tagore's influence in their musical cadence if not in their imageries.

" . . . I had the greatest fun writing My India, My America amidst the sky-scraping canyons which squeeze the New York sky into narrow ribbons. Three years of notes required two additional years of writing down comparisons and contrasts between the East and West in the intimate terms of my experience. It was a deeply disturbing experience also, as the balance is slow in coming. But the balance happily is slowly coming not only within me but to our age whose main problem is not dicta-
*shrid ha RAH nee

torship and the like but the impact of one culture on another."

---

Born in the northwestern Indian province of Gujarat, Krishnalal Shridharani was the son of Jethalal Nagji Shah, a prosperous lawyer, and Laheribai Popatlal (Sheth) Shah. (He dropped the abbreviated surname Shah in favor of Shridharani, which alludes to his illustrious Aryan forbears.) In 1930, while a student at Gandhi's National University in Ahmedabad, he was jailed for participating in Gandhi's famous march to the sea, a protest against the British salt tax. But Shridharani had already exhibited signs of a marked individuality—much to the dismay of his family—over his repeated refusal to accept an arranged marriage. "What I remember most vividly about this period," he wrote in an essay "My Boyhood in India," printed in *Asia*, "[was] the battle I fought to stay unmarried and unbetrothed." Elsewhere in this detailed essay, Shridharani describes his coming-of-age in an India suspended between an ancient culture of "saints and shrines . . . on the borderline between the old and the new, where the past ended and the modern world began."

Although his teachers encouraged his poetry writing during his boarding school years, it was not until his three-month imprisonment, following Gandhi's Salt March, that he began to write in earnest, inspired by memories evoked by a banyan tree visible from his cell. Thus his play, *The Banyan Tree*, was written. This later became known to a whole generation of Indian schoolchildren. His prison stay also produced a short novel, *I Shall Kill the Human in You*, based on interviews with his fellow prisoners; the book was banned by the British authorities but circulated clandestinely. Of this experience Shridharani wrote, "a few months after I came out of prison I had become a real author."

In 1932 he took a degree in English at Visva-Bharati (or Santiniketan—"the abode of peace"), a university founded by the Indian Nobel Prize winner Rabindranath Tagore. Shridharani was one of the few Indians of his generation to study in the United States: he earned an M.A. (1935) in sociology from New York University, as well as an M.S. (1936) in journalism and a Ph.D. (1940) in political theory, both from Columbia University.

*My India, My America*, the most successful of his books in English, is part memoir, part history lesson, and part sociological investigation. Shridharani lectured throughout the United States, and was a frequent contributor to the *New York Times* and other periodicals. He courted controversy with *Warning to the West*, a collection of essays defending Indian nationalism and criticizing Western attitudes and policies toward Asia. Praising the book in the *Saturday Review of Literature*, Norman Cousins wrote, "It will be said that it seeks to instigate and confuse rather than to enlighten. Don't believe it." *The Mahatma and the World* is a biography of Mohandas Gandhi.

Although best known in the West for his journalism and nonfiction, Shridharani was esteemed in India for his verse, fiction, plays, and children's books—as well as for his ardent devotion to the nationalist cause. Shridharani's verse was not distinguished enough to endure). He returned to India in 1946, worked for a time in the Ministry of External Affairs, and became a correspondent for *Amrita Bazar Patrika*. In 1958 he was awarded the Ranjitram Gold Medal in honor of his contributions to Indian literature.

PRINCIPAL WORKS IN ENGLISH TRANSLATION: *History and nonfiction*—War Without Violence: A Study of Gandhi's Method and Its Accomplishments, 1939; My India, My America, 1941 (in U.K.: My India, My West); Warning to the West, 1942; Story of the Indian Telegraphs: A Century of Progress, 1953; (with P. Jain) The Journalist in India: A Study of the Press Corps, 1956; Smiles from Kashmir, 1959. *Biography*—The Mahatma and the World, 1946; The Big 4 of India, 1951. *Reference*—(with S. C. Chatterjeee and S. Kumar) General Knowledge Encyclopaedia, 1949. *Juvenile*—The Adventures of the Upside-Down Tree, 1957.

ABOUT: The autobiographical material quoted above was written for Twentieth Century Authors First Supplement, 1955. Current Biography 1942; Encyclopedia of Indian Literature Vol. 5, 1992. *Periodicals*—Asia October 1941; New York Times July 24, 1960; Saturday Review of Literature December 12, 1942.

**SHUSTER, GEORGE NAUMAN** (August 27, 1894–January 25, 1971), American educator and writer, was born in Lancaster, Wisconsin, the son of Anthony Shuster and Elizabeth (Nauman) Shuster. His father's family were German Catholics, his great grandfather having come to the United States in 1848 from revolutionary Germany. His mother's family were German Lutherans who had originally settled in Pennsylvania. He wrote:
"My secondary education was received at St. Lawrence's College, Fond du Lac, Wisconsin, which was a German Gymnasium transplanted to the New World. We studied Latin and Greek incessantly, but we also learned modern languages, German and French. Notre Dame was my college—then a small institution, with a football team on the first rung of the ladder of fame. My dream was to enter West Point, but when the war came I turned instead to journalism and spent one hectic year trying to be a reporter. Then came 1917, military service, and thereupon eighteen months of life with the A.E.F. first as a member of the Intelligence Section, G.H.Q., serving at the front during almost all the major battles in which the American Army was engaged, and then as an interpreter in the Army of Occupation. Subsequently I attended the University of Poitiers, France, emerging with a Certificat d'Aptitude. Therewith I began my deep interest in modern Europe. I had seen a good deal of post-war Germany—fighting in the streets, the first electoral campaign, hunger, the heavy pressure of the Armistice terms. . . .

"A call came to teach English at Notre Dame, and I answered it, thinking that the quiet life I had known on the campus would help me to recuperate. . . . The president of the University, the Rev. Father James Burns, and I became fast friends. I took my master's degree in French literature, became head of the department of English, and remained at the University until my marriage to Doris Parks Cunningham in 1924. The principal literary product of those years was *The Catholic Spirit in Modern English Literature* (1922). Going to New York for graduate study at Columbia, I came into contact quite accidentally with the newly-formed *Commonweal* group. By the end of the year 1924 the magazine had begun publication, and I had started writing editorials for it.

"The amount of work required during the next twelve years was tremendous, but I retained some teaching connections, usually giving a course of lectures in some New York college. Books written during these years included one or two on Catholic subjects. More and more, however, my thinking and reading were concerned with modern Germany, which I visited for long periods after 1929. Translations from the German likewise followed in almost-too-rapid succession. During 1937 the Carnegie Corporation awarded me a very beguiling two-year fellowship in the study of the Weimar Republic and in particular of the Center Party. I spent most of the following two years abroad, witnessing among other things the taking over of Austria and the development of the Czechoslovak crisis. . . .

"The Board of Higher Education of the City of New York invited me, in 1939, to become academic dean and acting president of Hunter College. After a year of service I became president. Meanwhile the degree of doctor of philosophy had been earned at Columbia University. I shall hope that the tasks, and they are many, of guiding an educational institution will not deflect me from the pursuits of rose-growing, carpentry and tennis in which I remain interested."

---

George Nauman Shuster was one of the most original and eclectic of twentieth-century American interpreters of Roman Catholicism. He was on the liberal wing of his Church, and was one of the first to give a qualified endorsement to contraception; he believed that the Vatican ought to change its traditional views. One year after he resigned from Hunter College in 1960 he became assistant to the President of Notre Dame at South Bend, Indiana. He was the managing editor of the Catholic weekly *Commonweal* from 1929 until 1937.

Because of his intimate knowledge of Germany, Shuster played a major part in its postwar reeducation. From 1929 on, he had visited Germany frequently, studying at universities and living there from 1937 until 1939. During World War II he served on the Enemy Aliens Board in New York City. He was chairman of the Historical Commission to Germany (1945), a delegate to the UNESCO Conferences in Paris in both 1946 and 1958, and chairman of the U.S. National Commission in 1954. His advice to the American Delegation to the Lon-

don Conference on International Education was much valued, and well heeded. He did much to bring UNESCO itself into being. At Notre Dame he was the director of the Center for the Study of Man in Contemporary Society, a body which pursued interdisciplinary research into the humanities and the social sciences. Its report on the state of Catholic education was extremely critical: it called it "scandalously unorganized." Shuster, always an outspoken opponent of the Nazis, later congratulated Konrad Adenauer for his attempts to stamp out anti-Semitism; but he sounded a cautionary note about the educational policy of laying emphasis on Germany's criminal past: this might, he believed, do more harm than good in the long run.

Shuster's active life did not prevent him from being very accessible to students: his obituarist in the *New York Times* noted that "it was not unusual for him to step out on the stage of the college auditorium and read poetry to the assembly, or, in grease paint and costume, act in a faculty show of melodrama or horse opera." It was typical of his humor and capacity for self-criticism to have described himself, in his student days, as "a budding gawky oaf . . . who mooned over Sherwood Anderson, sighed over early Yeats, and sat up nights with *Jean-Christophe*, the then popular novel by Romain Rolland."

He received many honorary degrees as well as the 1954 Butler Medal of Columbia University for service to education. Upon his retirement he declared: "All my life I have been tormented by two demons. In the first place, I cannot stop writing. This is a disease as chronic and as ravaging as malaria. Then, too, I feel a deep desire to concern myself with what strength will remain, with the basic institutions and ideas which are shaping the future destiny of mankind."

Shuster's books included *The Catholic Spirit in English Literature*, which concentrated on the writings of Catholic authors such as Belloc and Chesterton. The *Catholic World* called it "magnificent"; but the *Literary Review* was far less welcoming: Lawrence Mason castigated the author for a general lack of "rigorous thinking-the-thing-through." But this was a comparatively young man's work, and of the more mature *The Catholic Spirit in America* the *Saturday Review of Literature* commented that it was "exceedingly timely" and that Shuster was due for gratitude for "lifting his level of argument above the politics of the day." Of *The Germans* W. K. Stewart wrote, in the *New York Herald Tribune Books*, that it was "so admirable in spirit that one is willing to overlook . . . minor defects. . . . Like a good journalist of the higher sort, he adapts the style and tone to the grade of intelligence somewhat above the average."

Shuster's study of the ode, *The English Ode from Milton to Keats*, was at once a more scholarly and less popularly directed book, and it ranks as an exception among his works. G. F. Whicher in *Books* (1941) was grateful that it was by no means a mere "ant hill of erudition," as it could so easily have been: instead, the reader of the "learned pages" had "the added grace of witty comment which constantly illuminates whatever it touches." Other reviewers and critics were equally enthusiastic.

Shuster's fiction was always well received; for example, *The Hill of Happiness*, a collection of stories about the lives of Franciscan brothers in a monastery (prefaced by Padraic Colum), was described by the *Times Literary Supplement* as written in "happy, tender and gravely humorous terms."

PRINCIPAL WORKS: *Catholicism and literature*—The Catholic Spirit in English Literature, 1922; English Literature, 1926; The Catholic Spirit in America, 1927; The Catholic Church and Current Literature, 1930; Brother Flo: an Imaginative Biography, 1938; The English Ode from Milton to Keats, 1940; Education and Moral Wisdom, 1960. *Novel*—Look Away!, 1939. *Short stories*—The Hill of Happiness, 1926. *Autobiography*—The Ground I Walked On: Memoirs of a College President 1961, enlarged 1969. *Politics*—The Germans, 1932; Strong Man Rules: an Interpretation of Germany Today, 1934; Like a Mighty Army: Hitler Versus Established Religion, 1935; Germany: A Short History, 1944; Cultural Cooperation and the Peace: The Difficulties and Objectives of International Cultural Understanding, 1953; Religion Behind the Iron Curtain, 1954; In Silence I Speak: The Story of Cardinal Mindszenty Today and of Hungary's "New Order," 1956. *As editor*—The World's Great Catholic Literature, 1942, enlarged 1964; The Problem of Population, vol. 2, 1964–1965; St Thomas Aquinas, 1969; (with R. E. Thorson) Evolution in Perspective, 1970.

ABOUT: The autobiographical material quoted above was written for Twentieth Century Authors, 1942. Current Biography 1950; Finkelstein, L. (ed.) American Spiritual Autobiographies, 1948; Hoehn, M. (ed.) Catholic Authors, 1948; Lannie, V. P. (ed.) On the Side of Truth: George N. Shuster, 1974; Romig, W. (ed.) The Book of Catholic Authors, 1948; Shuster, G. N. The Ground I Walked On; Zweig, F. M. Greatness Revisited, 1971. *Periodicals*—Catholic World October 22, 1922; Commonweal February 12, 1960; March 15, 1968; Literary Review September 9, 1922; New York Herald Tribune Books February 28, 1932; January 19, 1941; New York Times January 25, 1977; Time February 7, 1977; Times Literary Supplement December 16, 1926.

## "SHUTE, NEVIL" (pseudonym of NEVIL SHUTE NORWAY) (January 17, 1899–January 12, 1960), English-Australian novelist, was born in

Ealing, Middlesex. His father was Arthur Hamilton Norway, C.B., assistant secretary of the General Post Office in London, and his mother was the former Mary Louisa Gadsden. He was educated at schools in Oxford, Shrewsbury, and Woolwich. In 1916 he witnessed the Easter Rising in Dublin, and won commendation for his volunteer work as a stretcher-bearer with the Red Cross. Postponing his entry into Balliol College, Oxford, he passed into the Royal Military Academy, but he failed the final medical exam. He spent the remaining months of First World War on Home Service as a private in the Suffolk Regiment.

After the war Shute returned to Oxford, and graduated with a third class honors degree in engineering science in 1922. While he was at university he began to write short stories and novels, but he was unable to find a publisher. He developed a particular interest in aeronautical engineering, and

learned to fly while working for aircraft manufacturing firms during the holidays. In 1922 he joined the de Havilland Aircraft Company, and two years later he left to work on the Rigid Airship R100 project, becoming its deputy chief engineer in 1928. The project folded following the 1930 R101 disaster.

In 1931 Shute founded Airspeed Ltd., an airplane manufacturing company. In the same year he married Frances Mary Heaton, a doctor, with whom he had two daughters. His first novel, *Marazan*, received little attention, but he enjoyed some success with *So Disdained* and *Lonely Road*. In 1938 he sold the film rights of *Lonely Road* and *Ruined City* and decided to resign as managing director of Airspeed, which by then employed about a thousand people, and devote himself to writing.

Shute's books draw heavily on his professional experience and expertise, technical detail lending authenticity to his naturalistic, fast-moving narratives. His knowledge of weaponry inspired *What Happened to the Corbetts?*, a prophetic story centering on a Southampton family whose home is destroyed during an air bombardment of Britain. *Landfall: A Channel Story* and *An Old Captivity* both recount the adventures and misadventures of an English aviator. His next novel, *Pied Piper*—one of his three great successes—was an extremely popular account of one man's journey, with a group of children, from occupied France to England, and then to safety in America. *Pied Piper* was filmed, and with its successors *Pastoral* and *Most Secret*, also set against the backdrop of the Second World War, it established Nevil Shute as a household name in England.

In 1940 Shute joined the Royal Naval Volunteer Reserve as a sub-lieutenant, rising to lieutenant-commander the following year. In 1944 he was sent to Normandy as a correspondent for the Ministry of Information, and in 1945 he went to Burma, again as a Ministry correspondent. In 1948 he flew his own plane to Australia in search of novelistic material, and in 1950 he decided to move to that country permanently, settling on a two-hundred-acre farm at Langwarrin, Victoria. Most of his subsequent books are set, at least partially, in Australia, most notably *A Town Like Alice*, his second big success. Centering on a London typist, the novel follows Jean Paget through her experiences in Japanese-occupied Malaya, and her eventual journey to the Australian outback, to visit the man who had befriended her then. Reviewers found the story moving, lively, and skillfully written. "Mr. Shute can still tell the story at hand as well as any one writing today," wrote Ruth Chaplin for the *Christian Science Monitor*.

Shute used an Australian setting to particular advantage in *On the Beach* (1957), a cautionary tale of nuclear apocalypse, in which ordinary people, probably the last human beings left alive, wait quietly for a radioactive cloud to reach their remote corner of the earth and finish them off too. Although some reviewers suggested that these unexceptional Australians might actually be dying of boredom, most readers felt that the very ordinariness of the characters added immediately to the ee-rie horror of their predicament. The book was widely discussed and made into a notable film by the director Stanley Kramer.

Shute's autobiography, a candid account of his life up until 1938, when he left the aircraft indus-try, appeared in 1954. He never viewed himself as a professional author, but in terms of sales, he was outstandingly successful. An unpretentious novelist, without elegance or psychological gifts, he de-served his success as a storyteller. He was also a no-table figure in the aeronautical world, and a fellow of the Royal Aeronautical Society.

PRINCIPAL WORKS: *Novels*—Marazan, 1926; So Disdained, 1928 (in U.S.: The Mysterious Aviator); Lonely Road, 1932; Ruined City, 1938 (in U.S.: Kindling); What Happened to the Corbet-ts? 1939 (in U.S.: Ordeal); An Old Captivity, 1940; Landfall: A Channel Story, 1940; Pied Piper, 1942; Pastoral, 1944; Most Secret, 1945; Vinland the Good, 1946; The Chequer Board, 1947; No Highway, 1948; A Town Like Alice, 1950 (in U.S.: The Legacy); Round the Bend, 1951; The Far Country, 1952; In the Wet, 1953; Requiem for a Wren, 1955 (in U.S.: The Breaking Wave); Beyond the Black Stump, 1956; On the Beach, 1957; The Rainbow and the Rose, 1958; Trustee from the Toolroom, 1960; Stephen Morris, 1961. *Autobiography*—Slide Rule, 1954. *Omnibus volume*—A Nevil Shute Omnibus, 1973.

ABOUT: Contemporary Authors vols. 93–96, 1980; vol. 102, 1981; Current Biography 1942; Dictionary of National Biogra-phy, 1951–1960, 1972; Longman Companion to Twentieth Century Literature, 1970; The New Century Handbook of English Literature, rev. ed. 1967; The Oxford Companion to Australian Literature, 1985; The Readers Encyclopedia, 2nd ed., 1965; Shute, N. Slide Rule, 1954; Smith, J. Nevil Shute, 1976; Twentieth Century Writing: A Reader's Guide to Con-temporary Literature, 1969; Who's Who 1959. *Periodicals*—Book-of-the-Month Club News March 1939; Christian Science Monitor June 10, 1950; Illustrated London News January 23, 1960; Journal of British Studies Spring 1977; New York Times January 13, 1960; Newsweek January 25, 1960; Publishers Weekly January 25, 1960; Saturday Review April 2, 1960; Time October 7, 1940; January 25, 1960; Wilson Library Bul-letin May 1939, March 1960.

## SHY, TIMOTHY. See LEWIS, D. B. W.

## SIDGWICK, ETHEL (December 20, 1877–April 29, 1970), English novelist, was born in Rugby into a wealthy and distinguished family. She was edu-cated at Oxford High School, and privately studied music and literature. She lived in Oxford for most of her life, and never married. In her early writing career she was greatly praised, her observational approach likened to that of Henry James; almost all reviewers remarked on the brilliance and skill of her technique.

Her first novel, *Promise* (1910), indicated the area she was to adopt as her own. The story of a child prodigy, which she continued in a sequel, *Succession* (1913), the novel is a sensitive, subtle ex-amination of genius and expectation. Subsequently she also explored the nuances of family relation-ships and tensions. Although her plots were slight and contained little action, her characters and situ-ations were compelling. The *New York Times* com-mented of *Promise*: "It would be hard to find in recent fiction anywhere a more complete, lifelike and brilliant characterization than this."

Increasingly digressive, her later books lacked

the charm of the earlier ones, and became irritating for their plethora of detail and overly stylized dia-logues. She remained, however, adept at capturing English country life, most notably in *Dorothy's Wedding* (1931, in U.S.: *The Tale of Two Vil-lages*). The ephemeral nature of her talent is captured by the response of one reviewer in the *Boston Transcript* follow-ing the publication of *A Lady of Leisure*: "We put the book down rather

stunned with as brilliant a piece of writing as we will find in any novel of the season, only to discover after the book is laid aside an almost blank recollec-tion of what the four hundred and seventy-one pages have been about." Ethel Sidgwick also wrote several plays for younger children in the form of traditional fairy tales.

PRINCIPAL WORKS: *Novels*—Promise, 1910; Le Gentleman, 1911; Herself, 1912; Succession, 1913; A Lady of Leisure, 1914; Duke Jones, 1914; The Accolade, 1915; Hatchways, 1916; Jamesie, 1917; Madam, 1921; Restoration, 1923; Laura, 1924; When I Grow Rich, 1927; The Bells of Shoreditch, 1928; Dorothy's Wedding, 1931 (in U.S.: The Tale of Two Villages). *Drama*—Four Plays for Children, 1913; Plays for Schools, 1922; Fairy-tale Plays, 1926. *Nonfiction*—Mrs. Henry Sidgw-ick a Memoir, 1938.

ABOUT: *Periodicals*—Bookman January 1929; Boston Tran-script October 24, 1914; Current Opinion February 1916; New York Times September 15, 1912.

## SIEGFRIED, ANDRÉ (April 21, 1975–March 28, 1959), French scholar, political and social scien-tist, was born at Le Havre, the son of a Third Re-public French cabinet minister, Jules Siegfried. He was educated at the Lycée Condorcet and then at the Sorbonne. Siegfried is best remem-bered as an interpreter of the French to other na-tions, in particular to Great Britain and Ameri-ca. His book on England, *L'Angleterre au-*

*jourd'hui, son évolution économique et politique* (1924; translated as *Post-War Britain*), aroused much comment in the British press. Siegfried wrote over forty more books, one of which, about La Fon-taine (1949), is of literary interest, although it has never been translated.

Siegfried was professor of economic geography at the École Libre des Sciences Politiques, Paris (1911–1933), and then, from 1933, held the same position at the Collège de France. He married Paule Lereche, whose father was a deputy, in 1907; they had one daughter. Siegfried was one of the most celebrated of European economists, a man both learned and yet also an author of popular and comprehensible books, and much respected even by those—such as his compatriot, the markedly left-wing André Gide—who disagreed with his opinions. This was because, as his London *Times* obituarist put it, "no French man of his time brought a better trained mind or more objective temper, greater sobriety or candour" to either his economic analyses of England and America or to his representation of his own country to the League of Nations, or to its successor the United Nations. Whatever his own opinions, he never failed to grasp realities. He was also famous for his political articles in the French newspaper *Le Figaro*—of which he was a member of the Board of Directors—which "attracted attention for their clarity and sound sense" *(Times)* in the fifteen years after World War II.

Siegfried's first book, the result of a visit he had made to New Zealand, was *Le Démocratie en Nouvelle-Zealand* (1904). When it appeared in English, in 1914, as *Democracy in New Zealand*, the *Spectator* called it "useful and impartial," and the *Nation* did not believe that time had impaired its value. It is now inevitably dated; but, full of common sense, it was an auspicious beginning for an economist.

*Post-War Britain*, an analysis of the economic and political changes in Great Britain over the decade prior to the election of the first Labour administration (1924), was praised almost everywhere for its lucidity; the English radical economic historian R. H. Tawney in the *New Republic* called it "at once learned and entertaining . . . By far the best study of the economic and political life of England in moderate compass that has appeared in many years." This was praise indeed from a writer whose books had already helped to form many opinions. *America Comes of Age*, a general survey of the United States, attracted similar praise: H. L. Mencken in the *Nation* (1927) thought it "so good that it seems almost incredible," "the most accurate, penetrating and comprehensive survey . . . ever written." The *New Statesman* called it a "better book than *Post-War Britain*." "It has two conspicuous merits. Most of the more important aspects of the United States are brought under review, and the author combines with his lucidity and easy movement a marked freedom from partisanship." Evans Clark in the *New York Times* thought it "the most uncannily penetrating and the most exciting commentary on America that has been produced since this country strode into the center of the world's attention." The *Times Literary Supplement* review, too, considered it to be almost "uncanny" in its insights into American life.

*England's Crisis*, which, although sympathetic and always Anglophile in its attitudes, blamed the conditions of the English economic depression on certain alleged national characteristics, met with a more mixed reception. The reviewer in the *American Political Science Review* found it "sensational" and politically superficial, but praised much of its "sound argument." Harold J. Laski, an influential left-wing English thinker, writing about it in the *Saturday Review of Literature* (1931), praised its "pungency" and its "solid air of unmistakeable veracity," but found its "sins of omission . . . too serious to make it an adequate picture of the problems it seeks to depict." Respect for Siegfried was always apparent, however, whatever the degree of disagreement with his conclusions in his many books.

Siegfried wrote other similar studies, many of them translated, on, for example, Suez and Panama, Canada, and Switzerland. Siegfried's contribution to what Peter Woolstencroft called in *Thinkers of the Twentieth Century* "the field of 'electoral geography'" is important. This combination of science and art attempts, with some success, to determine what environments support what political tendencies.

Siegfried is considered a major contributor to social, cultural, and political analysis. There is a French study, *L'Oeuvre scientifique d'André Siegfried* (The scientific work of Siegfried, 1977), about his contribution to electoral geography, but so far there has been no book on him in English.

PRINCIPAL WORKS IN ENGLISH TRANSLATION: The Race Question in Canada (tr. H. Sapstead) 1907, Democracy in New Zealand (tr. E. V. Burns) 1914, Post-War Britain (tr. H. H. Hemming) 1924; America Comes of Age (tr. H. H. Hemming) 1927; France: A Study in Nationality (written in English) 1930; England's Crisis (tr. H. H. and D. Hemming) 1931; Impressions of Latin America (tr. H. H. and D. Hemming) 1933; Europe's Crisis (tr. H. H. and D. Hemming) 1935; Canada (tr. H. H. and D. Hemming) 1937 (rev. ed. tr. by D. Hemming, 1949); Suez and Panama (tr. H. H. and D. Hemming) 1940; What the British Empire Means to Western Civilization (written in English) 1940; The Mediterranean (tr. D. Hemming) 1948; Switzerland: A Democratic Way of Life (tr. E. Fitzgerald) 1950; Nations Have Souls (tr. E. Fitzgerald) 1952; America at Mid-Century (tr. M. Ledésert) 1955; Routes of Contagion (tr. J. Henderson and M. Clarasó) 1965 (in U.K.: Germs and Ideas).

ABOUT: Devine, E., Held, M. Vinson, J., and Walsh, G. (eds.) Thinkers of the Twentieth Century, 1985. *Periodicals*—American Political Science Review August 1931; Nation October 29, 1914, May 11, 1927; New Republic February 18, 1925; New Statesman July 9, 1927; New York Time April 10, 1927; Newsweek April 13, 1959; Saturday Review of Literature June 13, 1931: June 11, 1955; Spectator October 17, 1914; Time April 13, 1959; Times (London) March 30, 1959; Times Literary Supplement May 5, 1927.

**SIERRA, GREGORIO MARTÍNEZ.** See **MARTÍNEZ SIERRA, GREGORIO**

**SIGERSON, DORA SHORTER MARY** (August 16, 1866–January 6, or 16, 1918), Irish sculptor and poet, was born in Dublin, the eldest daughter of Dr. George Sigerson, a surgeon, historian, and Gaelic scholar, and Hester Varian, a novelist and verse-writer whose only novel, *A Ruined Place*, was published in 1889. Educated privately at home, Dora Sigerson initially turned to art rather than writing, but took up poetry in her twenties, and quickly revealed a minor but not negligible lyric talent. Although a vivacious personality, she tended to be melancholy and introverted in her work, particularly as a younger writer, and her work is deeply pervaded by the theme of death. Titles such as "The Woman Who Went to Hell" and "The Sad Years" indicate the nature of her preoccupations.

A strikingly handsome woman, likened by her friend and fellow poet Katharine Tynan to "the Greek Hermes," she attracted the attention of the critic Clement King Shorter, editor of the *Sketch*, who first saw her photograph in his magazine.

They married in 1896, and Dora moved to England, where she spent the rest of her life. Deeply homesick, she retained her Catholicism and fervent patriotism; Irish subjects continued to provide her inspiration. In the opinion of the scholar Douglas Hyde, first president of the Republic of Ireland, "Her very absence from Ireland has made her . . . more Irish than if she had never left it."

During the Easter Rebellion of 1916 she worked to help both prisoners and accused; her sentiments were aptly caught in *Sixteen Dead Men and Other Poems of Easter Week* (1919). She was also distressed by World War I, which severely affected her spirits in her last years.

The novelist George Meredith, one of her friends, considered her to be "the best ballad writer since Scott." This is greatly exaggerated praise, but

she did possess a gifted turn of phrase, and, while her scope was narrow, it could be exquisitely intense. The *Macmillan Dictionary of Irish Literature* concludes: "A few of her folk poems and simple ballads are quite striking, especially 'A Ballad of Marjorie,' 'The Wind on the Hills' and 'The Banshee.'"

She died in Buckinghamshire, but was buried in Dublin alongside a memorial sculpture she had herself sculpted of the Irish patriots.

PRINCIPAL WORKS: *Novels*—The Country House Party, 1905. *Poetry*—The Fairy Changeling and Other Poems, 1897; Ballads and Poems, 1898; My Lady's Slipper, and Other Verses, 1899; The Father Confessor, 1900; The Woman Who Went to Hell, 1902; As the Sparks Fly Upward, 1904; The Story and Song of Black Roderick, 1906; Through Wintry Terrors, 1907; Collected Poems, 1907 (introduction by George Meredith); The Troubadour and Other Poems, 1910; New Poems, 1912; Madge Linsey and Other Poems, 1913; Do Well and Do Little: A Fairy Tale, 1913; Love of Ireland: Poems and Ballads, 1916; Poems of the Irish Rebellion, 1916; Kittie's Toys: A Child's Song, 1917; The Sad Years, 1918; A Legend of Glendalough and Other Ballads, 1919; Sixteen Dead Men and Other Poems of Easter Week, 1919. *Drama*—A Dull Day in London and Other Sketches, 1920.

ABOUT: Hyde, D. A. A Treasury of Irish Poetry, 1899; Hogan, R. (ed.) MacMillan Dictionary of Irish Literature; O'Conor, N. changing Ireland: Literary Backgrounds of the Irish Free State, 1972; Tynan, K. Memories, 1924. *Periodicals*—Bookman August 1919, April 1922, August 1922, February 1923; Bookman (London) February 1918; Catholic World May 1934, February 1936; Irish Monthly February 1920.

**\*SILLANPÄÄ, FRANS EEMIL** (September 16, 1888–June 3, 1967), Finnish novelist and short story writer, was born in the parish of Hämeenkyrö, in southwestern Finland, not far from the large industrial city of Tampere. His father was a poor tenant farmer whose family had declined from relative prosperity, but Frans had a happy although lonely childhood (he was the only one of three children to survive). He was never inclined to studies, and, although a more than able student, only managed to graduate from his school in Tampere.

In 1908, with money borrowed from friends, Sil-

\*SILL on pah, frants AY meel

lanpää set off for the Imperial Alexander University at Helsinki to study natural sciences. There he learned to drink—his capacity for alcohol, especially when he was with his friend the composer Sibelius, became legendary in his own country—and to get into debt. He did not follow the curriculum except when it interested him, and left five years later without a degree. But he had absorbed as much science as he needed for his purposes as a writer.

The influences upon Sillanpää were not at all unusual at that time. Like other young Finnish writers, he fell under the sway of the so-called Young Finland ("Nuori Suomi") movement, which had arisen some eight years before his birth. This movement, which developed from earlier nationalistic beginnings, was anti-Swedish (because the ruling classes had until comparatively recently been Swedish-speaking and Finno-Swedish literature had been in the ascendant), nationalistic, and essentially romantic. It looked back to the example of one of the greatest of all Finnish writers, Alexis Kivi, who had died at the early age of thirty-eight in 1874, and whose work in the Finnish language was the main inspiration to the members of Young Finland.

Juhani Aho, whom Sillanpää got to know well, was one of the leading lights of the Young Finland movement. He had been to Paris, and his reading of his impressionistic prose sketches (called in Finnish *lastut*), *Lastuja*, which he began to write in 1891, was decisive in Sillanpää's early development. As well as assimilating Aho's romantic realism, Sillanpää—who, like most Finns, spoke Swedish and could therefore understand the other Scandinavian languages—read and admired the work of Strindberg and, in particular, that of the Norwegian Knut Hamsun.

But what made him rather different from his contemporaries was the outlook he had absorbed from his readings in science: like Jack London and many others of the time, he was deeply affected by the popular books of the biologist and evolutionist Ernst Haeckel. There was nothing profound in Haeckel's thinking—it came to be called "biological monism"—which derived from that of T. H. Huxley, and was agnostic (or atheistic) in its import. Sillanpää endowed these ideas with his own rural mysticism. This vague, inconsequential but deeply felt mysticism was reinforced in his mind by his excited reading of the Belgian symbolist poet and playwright Maurice Maeterlinck, then enormously influential all over Europe.

Sillanpää first made a high reputation for himself as a writer with impressionistic stories and sketches published in magazines. These were collected in the volume *Ihmislapsia elämän saatossa* (Children in life's procession, 1917). A publisher then approached him to write a novel on the strength of the attention these stories had attracted. He signed a contract, but preferred drinking and carousing with his friends to working at the commissioned novel. The tale of how the enterprising publisher put him up in a hotel with strict instructions neither to serve him with alcohol nor let him out until he had completed the novel has entered Finnish literary lore.

The result, *Elämä ja aurinko* (Life and sun, 1916), was successful with the small but appreciative Finnish reading public. A story about a young man who loves two different girls throughout a single summer, it reflected both Sillanpää's view of existence—nature dominates, and the affairs are but mirrored within its stately progress—and his personal life. For in 1916 he had also married Sigrid Maria Salomäki. "She was a housemaid," he later wrote, "very good-looking in those days. . . . Before she was twenty-nine we had six children."

Sillanpää's next novel, *Hurskas kurjuus* (1919, translated as *Meek Heritage*), is more mature and deeply felt. Highly topical at the time it appeared, it begins with the execution of a peasant, Jussi Toivola, by the White Army, which had just won a bitter civil war against the Russian-backed Red Army. Like Sibelius and most other Finns not committed to the left, Sillanpää had supported General Mannerheim's German-backed White Army, but largely because he did not like or trust the left. Because of the Tsarist campaign of "russification," suddenly started in the 1890s, Finns tended to regard the Russians, communist or otherwise, as Asiatic barbarian oppressors.

In *Meek Heritage*, Sillanpää took neither side, but rather revealed the extent of the tragedy to Finland as a whole. In it he reflected the opinion of most of the enlightened Finns who had supported the White Army: that the repression of the Red Army—after its shattering defeat of May 1918—had gone too far and had been too bloody. *Meek Heritage* reviews the passive fatalist Jussi's entire existence: his birth into poverty in 1857, his endurance of hardship and personal blows (the death of his wife, his daughter's suicide, his closeness to bankruptcy), his embroilment in a Red Army plot of which he has no real inkling, and, finally, his execution for a murder that he not only did not commit, but could not have committed.

*Meek Heritage* was not translated until 1938, but it then made some impact. John Cournos, writing for the *New York Times* (1938), called it "a marvel of concision. . . . There is pathos here, and pity, and tenderness, which come . . . from comprehension." However, in the *New Yorker* (1938), Clifton Fadiman thought that the "Sillanpää affair [was] a little dull, but rather imposing as man-with-the-hoe novels so often are."

At this point, Sillanpää began to read Osvald Spengler's *Decline of the West* and embraced Spengler's idea about civilizations—that they had life cycles like plants. This concept, and the animal-mysticism of Maeterlinck, influenced Sillanpää's thinking to the extent that he planned an enormous work that, set at the beginning of the Christian era,

would demonstrate the truth of Spengler's morphological theories. But need for money, convivial habit, and perhaps good sense prevailed: he wrote the compact *Hiltu ja Ragna* (Hilda and Ragnar, 1923) instead. This novel, more tendentious than its predecessors, describes how a city boy drives a country girl to suicide.

After a series of novels and stories—the latter always more finished than the former—Sillanpää published the story that gave him a European reputation: *Nuorene nukkunut* (1931, translated in England as *Fallen Asleep While Young: The History of an Offshoot of an Old Family Tree* and in the U.S. as *The Maid Silja*). In technique this resembled his first novel: it begins with a woman's death of tuberculosis and then ranges back over the thirty years of her life, which includes the period of the Civil War.

Sillanpää published more stories and novels, but not even his receipt of the Nobel Prize in 1939 attracted more translators to his work—until 1966, when Alan Blair made a rendering of the 1934 series of vignettes *Ihmiset suviyössä*, as *People in the Summer Night*. The *Times Literary Supplement* reviewer, repeating frequently made comparisons with D. H. Lawrence, noted how "tidily balanced" the themes were.

In 1939 Sillanpää's first wife died. In that year he married his secretary Ann Armia von Hertzen, but they parted in 1940. He now wrote much less—although there were two more novels, some stories and a couple of volumes of memoirs. He entered, quite self-consciously, into his final role: a black-capped, white-bearded peasant-sage—he was a huge bear of a man—broadcasting Christmas tales to children as "Taata" ("Grandpa").

Although there are several books on Sillanpää in Finnish, there is no full-scale study of him in English. He was translated into eighteen languages—there is more by him in French and German than there is in English.

PRINCIPAL WORKS IN ENGLISH TRANSLATION: *Novels*—Meek Heritage (tr. A. Matson) 1938 (revised by J. R. Pitkin, 1971); The Maid Silja: The History of the Last Offshoot of an Old Family Tree (tr. A. Matson) 1933 (in U.K.: Fallen Asleep While Young); People in the Summer Night (tr. A. Blair) 1966. ABOUT: Ahokas, J. A History of Finnish Literature, 1973; Columbia Dictionary of Modern European Literature, 1980; Seymour-Smith, M. Macmillan Guide to Modern World Literature, 1986; Wasson, T. Nobel Prize Winners, 1987. *Periodicals*—American Scandinavian Review March 1940; New York Times November 19, 1933; September 18, 1938; June 3, 1966; New Yorker September 17, 1938; June 3, 1967; Poet Lore Winter, 1940; Saturday Review November 11, 1933; June 11, 1966; Times Literary Supplement May 28, 1938; April 28, 1966.

**SIMENON, GEORGES** (February 13, 1903– September 4, 1989), Francophone Belgian novelist, was born in Liège, Belgium, the son of an insurance clerk. As an adolescent he worked for a baker and a bookseller in Liège; then in 1922 he went to France and began to write pulp crime novels under many pseudonyms. After consulting Colette the writer, who told him he was "too literary" for the mass market, he began to write more serious ones, beginning with *Pierre-le-Letton (The Strange Case* *of Peter Lett)* in 1929. By the end of the 1930s he was the firm favorite of such famous writers as André Gide, Ford Madox Ford (in one of whose last novels, *Vive Le Roy*, he is mentioned in the first pages), Robert Graves, and other literary personalities.

Unlike the later and rather more ambitious novels, the early novels are no more, technically, than police procedurals, but they are by a long chalk the  most inspired ones ever created. However, as is the case with so many commercial successes, Simenon's Paris publisher Fayard was initially dubious. The factor that made them catch on was that the protaginist, Jules Maigret, seemed not to be a fictional detective. His ordinariness was almost emphasised by his creator. He did not carry a gun, he had no opinions, he was not particularly clever: he was just a plodder doing a job. From the start, Simenon, although he told tales of love and passion and mayhem, was entirely devoid of sentimentality.

With a very few exceptions, Simenon is the only crime writer who is universally conceded to have consistent literary qualities. Needless to say, he has been accused of "breaking the requirements" of the genre. Ironically, when Simenon tried to exclude crime from his narratives, he was not often very successful. After writing some 500 novels and short novels, he gave up fiction. He devoted himself to taping his extensive memoirs, which begin with the major tragedy of his life: the suicide of his daughter. This, although by no means a true account, proved to be the best seller of his life.

Simenon was not a happy man. His fiction as whole reflects what he himself called the tragedy of lack of communication between people. Since he wrote so many novels, it would be impracticable to list them all below: the bibliography has therefore been limited to omnibus volumes which contain almost all his best work. The translators are various.

PRINCIPAL WORK IN ENGLISH TRANSLATION: The Short Cases of Inspector Maigret, 1959; Pedigree (tr. R. Baldick), 1962; The Simenon Omnibus, Penguin, 13 vols, 1970–78; Complete Maigret Short Stories, 1979; Intimate Memoirs (tr. J. Stewart), 1984.

ABOUT: Becker, F. F. Georges Simenon, 1977; Benstock, B. Art in Crime Writing, 1983; Frank, F. Simenon's Paris, 1870; Mauriac, C. The New Literature (tr. S. I. Stone) 1959; Marnham, P. The Man Who Wasn't Maigret, 1993; Narjerac, T. The Art of Simenon (tr. C. Rowland) 1952; Young, T. Georges Simenon, 1976; Raymond, R. Simenon in Court, 1968.

**\*SIMMEL, GEORG** (March 1, 1858–September 26, 1918), German sociologist and philosopher, was born in Berlin, the youngest of seven children. His parents were of Jewish descent but had been converted to Christianity; Simmel himself was baptized a Lutheran but did not practice any religion in later life. His father, a manufacturer, died when he was a boy; a family friend, appointed as guard-

°ZIM mel

ian, left him a considerable fortune, which enabled him to lead the life of an independent scholar. At the University of Berlin he studied history, psychology, and philosophy, and received his Ph.D. in 1881 with a dissertation on the nature of matter according to Kant's theory of monadology. From 1885 to 1900 Simmel was a privatdozent (unpaid lecturer) in philosophy at the university, continuing on there from 1900 to 1914 as an honorary pro-fessor (*Extraordinarius*). In 1890 he married Gertrud Kinel, a writer on philosophy; their home became a gathering place for the cultural elite of Berlin, among them Lou Andreas-Salomé and the poets Stefan George and Rainer Maria Rilke. In 1914 he was called to the University of Strasbourg as a paid professor (*Ordinarius*) of philosophy, and he taught there until his death four years later. A prolific writer who contributed hundreds of articles to the learned journals—on the philosophy of history, ethics and aesthetics, psychology, art and literature, as well as sociology—he was also celebrated as a lecturer. The sheer variety of themes and ideas he dealt with earned him a reputation as a dilettante. This, coupled with jealousy of his popularity and the latent anti-Semitism in German academic circles (despite Simmel's nominally Protestant identity), kept him from a full professorship for many years. He did, however, receive an honorary doctorate from Heidelberg in 1911.

Simmel's first major writing was devoted to philosophy: *Die Probleme de Geschichtsphilosophie* (1892; *The Problems of the Philosophy of History*); and *Einleitung in die Moralphilosophie: Eine Kritik der ethischen Grundbegriffe* (Introduction to moral philosophy: a critique of ethical principles, 1892–1893). Both reflect his attempt to apply Kant to contemporary questions. These works were followed by what is considered to be his most profound book, *Philosophie des Geldes* (1900; *The Philosophy of Money*). Defining money as "a social function become a substance," Simmel speculates in this work on the effects of a money economy on the individual in modern society: on the one hand, the freedoms made possible by this system of exchange; on the other hand, its role in social alienation. Although Émile Durkheim (in a review in *L'Année sociologique*) thought the book was "replete with illegitimate speculation," most of Simmel's contemporaries received it favorably. Max Weber, who felt that almost all of Simmel's work "abound[ed] in important theoretical ideas and the most subtle observations," was influenced by it in the writing of his own classic study, *The Protestant Ethic and the Spirit of Capitalism* (1907–1908).

About 1887 Simmel began to introduce sociological concepts into his lectures (he was apparently the first to teach sociology in a German university); and in 1890 he wrote his first lengthy essay in the field: "Über soziale Differenzierung" (On social differentiation). A later, shorter article, "Das Problem der Soziologie" (1894), was translated into English as "The Problem of Sociology." Both pieces represent his attempt to define the still relatively new discipline and stake out its program in ways profoundly different from the positivism of Auguste Comte, the founder of sociology, and the social Darwinism of Herbert Spencer. Simmel's sociology, in contrast, is an abstract discipline, concerned with the analysis of forms of human interaction, cooperative or conflictive, among them: exchange, subordination or domination, conflict, division of labor, space (or social distance), and sociability. Simmel is thus often regarded as the pioneer of "formal sociology." Central to his methodology was his distinction between form and content, form being the principles that give structure to content, which is defined as the underlying motive power of purposes or interests. Many of his critics have objected to his insistence on this dichotomy. Simmel's analyses are based on descriptions of everyday social interactions, observed, not tested by experiment. The approach is nonprescriptive (he does not propose social changes) and ahistorical (he believed that the same forms of social relationships might operate in different times and cultures). His style is difficult: a tendency to pile up examples and his dialectical presentation often obscure his arguments.

His major work, *Soziologie: Untersuchungen über die Formen der Vergesellschaftung* (Sociology: Investigations of the forms of association), was published in 1908. About half of the work has been translated into English in Kurt H. Wolff's *The Sociology of Georg Simmel* and in *Conflict [and] The Web of Group-Affiliations*. It incorporates material from articles written decades earlier together with more recent thinking. David Frisby's *Georg Simmel* provides a helpful outline (in English), with original publication dates of the chapters and an indication of which parts have been translated. Simmel himself characterized his *Soziologie* as "wholly fragmentary, incomplete," but at the same time "dominated by one, methodologically certain, problem-idea." Among this seemingly unsystematic collection of essay-chapters, with their diverse themes and perspectives, is one on the spatial structures of society. It relates to one of his best-known essays (not included in the book), "The Metropolis and Mental Life," which draws upon his own experiences as a resident of modern Berlin. In this he offers his much-quoted definition of a city: "not a spatial entity with social consequences, but a sociological entity that is formed spatially."

The period of Simmel's greatest involvement with sociology was roughly from 1889 to 1909, the year he helped found the German Sociological Association. For the remainder of his time in Berlin he offered few courses in the subject. Significantly, in 1899, in a letter to a colleague of Durkheim's, he complained that "it is . . . painful to me to find that I am only recognized abroad as a sociologist—whereas . . . I see philosophy as my life-task and engage in sociology really only as a subsidiary discipline." His return to his "life-task" began in 1905 with a complete revision of *The Problems of the Philosophy of History*. In 1907 he wrote a treatise on Schopenhauer and Nietzsche, and in 1911 *Philosophische Kultur* (The philosophy of culture), a collection of essays on art and aesthetics, religion, and philosophy, was published. The last book published in his lifetime (in 1918) was *Lebensanschauung: Vier metaphysische Kapital*, metaphysical observations on human life (in four chapters).

Simmel once stated: "I know that I shall die without spiritual heirs"; in a sense he was correct. Regarded, together with Durkheim and Weber, as one of the seminal theorists of twentieth-century sociology, he founded no school, and with the partial exception of Weber and the Marxist political theorist and literary critic György Lukács (his favorite student), he influenced later sociologists only indirectly. He did, however, have an impact on the urban sociology of the early Chicago School; between 1896 and 1910 nine of his essays were translated in the *American Journal of Sociology*. With the translation of more of his work, beginning in the 1950s, interest in his thought has continued.

PRINCIPAL WORKS IN ENGLISH TRANSLATION: The Problem of Sociology *in* Annals of the American Academy of Political and Social Science November 1895; The Metropolis and Mental Life (tr. E. A. Shils) *in* Syllabus and Selected Readings, Second-Year Course in the Study of Contemporary Society [Univ. of Chicago] 5th ed., 1936; The Sociology of Sociability (tr. E. C. Hugher) *in* American Journal of Sociology November 1949; The Sociology of Georg Simmel (tr. and ed. K. H. Wolff) 1950; Conflict [and] The Web of Group-Affiliations (trs. K. H. Wolff and R. Bendix) 1955; Georg Simmel, 1858–1918: A Collection of Essays, with Translations and a Bibliography (ed. K. H. Wolff) 1959; Sociology of Religion (tr. C. Rosenthal) 1959; The Conflict in Modern Culture, and Other Essays (tr. K. P. Etzkorn) 1968; On Individuality and Social Forms: Selected Writings (ed. D. N. Levine) 1971 (The Heritage of Sociology); Readings from Simmel's Works (tr. D. E. Jenkinson and others) *in* P. A. Lawrence, Georg Simmel: Sociologist and European, 1976 (The Making of Sociology ser.); The Problems of the Philosophy of History: An Epistemological Essay (tr. and ed. G. Oakes) 1977; The Philosophy of Money (trs. T. Bottomore and D. Frisby; ed. D. Frisby) 1978 (2nd ed. 1990); Essays on Interpretation in Social Science (tr. and ed. G. Oakes) 1980; Georg Simmel: On Women, Sexuality, and Love (ed. and tr. G. Oakes) 1984; Schopenhauer and Nietzsche (tr. H. Loiskandl and others) 1986.

ABOUT: Abraham, J. H. The Origins and Growth of Sociology, 1973; Coser, L. A. (ed.) Georg Simmel, 1965 (Makers of Modern Social Science); Coser, L. A. Masters of Sociological Thought, 1971; Frisby, D. Georg Simmel, 1984 (Key Sociologists ser.); Frisby, D. Simmel and Since: Essays on George Simmel's Social Theory, 1992; Frisby, D. Sociological Impressionism: A Reassessment of George Simmel's Social Theory, 1981 (2nd. ed. 1992); Green, B. S. Literary Methods and Sociological Theory: Case Studies of Simmel and Weber, 1988; International Encyclopedia of Social Sciences Vol. 14, 1968; Kaern, M. (ed., with others) Georg Simmel and Contemporary Sociology, 1990; Lawrence, P. A. Georg Simmel: Sociologist and European, 1976 (The Making of Sociology ser.); Levin, D. N. Simmel and Parsons: Two Approaches to the Study of Society, 1980; Park, R. E. (with E. W. Burgess) Introduction to the Science of Sociology, 1921; Poggi, G. Money and the Modern Mind: Georg Simmel's Philosophy of Money, 1993; Ray L. J. Formal Sociology: The Sociology of Georg Simmel, 1991; Sellerberg, A.-M. A Blend of Contradictions: Georg Simmel in Theory and Practice, 1994; Spykman, N. J. The Social Theory of Georg Simmel, 1925 (reissued 1964); Thinkers of the Twentieth Century (ed. R. Turner) 2nd ed., 1987 Weingartner, R. H. Experience and Culture: The Philosophy of Georg Simmel, 1962; Weinstein, D. (with M. A. Weinstein) Postmodern(ized) Simmel, 1993; Wintle, J. (ed.) Makers of Modern Culture, 1981; Wolff, K. H. (ed.) Georg Simmel,

1858–1918: A Collection of Essays, with Translations and a Bibliography, 1959; Wolff, K. H. Introduction to The Sociology of Georg Simmel (tr. and ed. K. H. Wolff) 1950; Wolff, K. H. Trying Sociology, 1974. *Periodicals*—American Journal of Sociology vol. 51 1945; May 1958; January and March 1976; Contemporary Sociology July 1979; New York Times September 9, 1984; Sociological Quarterly August 1994; Sociological Review February 1988; August 1989.

## SIMMONS, E(RNEST) J(OSEPH) (December 8, 1903–May 3, 1972), American critic of Russian literature, wrote: "It is sometimes true that acade-

micians are often frustrated writers, and it occasionally happens that writers are frustrated academicians—Gogol had ambitions to be a famous professor of history, but he failed and became a great writer instead. Whatever the degree of frustration involved on both scores, I have managed to write a sizable number of books while at the same time leading a very active life as a professor of Russian literature at a large university. Of course, the two are not incompatible, and for some, writing had better remain an avocation in a world where its devotees may face the risk of penury as the price of commercial failure.

"The desire for security, no doubt, played an unconscious part in the selection of a profession with a salary, for a very insecure childhood in a large poverty-stricken family left its scars and its fears. It is more than a twice-told tale of American life. One of five children of emigrant English and Scotch parents [Mark Simmons and the former Annie McKinnon], I was born in Lawrence, Massachusetts, a mill town of mixed population and unstable economy. The death of my father, when I was five, threw the whole burden of the support of the family on my mother, an heroic Scotch woman, who never flinched in her duty to her children. Perhaps as an escape from dull, impoverished surroundings, I sought refuge in the luxury of omnivorous, undisciplined reading. A new world opened up. I began to scribble poetry and short stories, getting them published in the high school paper. I became a fiery defender of the downtrodden, the condemned, the atheist. At fifteen I wrote a small book, with the pretentious title—'Three Great Iconoclasts: Spinoza, Paine, and Ingersoll.' Fortunately, no publisher found it irresistible, though apparently a theological student at Harvard did years later, for he purloined the manuscript.

"The glittering grail of a college education obsessed me. Getting through high school had meant odd jobs late afternoons and evenings; surviving through seven years of Harvard from the A.B. to the Ph.D. was a feat of financial legerdemain, made possible only by part-time work, scholarships, and hard physical labor during the summers. Then came teaching in English and Russian literature at Harvard, Cornell, and finally at Columbia, where I am head of the department of Slavic languages

and professor of Russian literature at the Russian Institute.

"The writing itch does not always survive such competition, but I was determined. Research trips to Russia during its more interesting early phases of revolutionary development (1928, 1932, 1935, 1937) provided me with rich experiences, and close study of the great Russian classics gave me plenty of inspiration. I continued to turn out arty but unsalable short stories and then a long novel, based on my experiences in Russia, which had in it perhaps more of Dostoevsky than the stuff of contemporary life. My literary agent liked it, the publishers didn't and ordered revisions; in the end no one was satisfied.

"After publishing a purely scholarly book, I turned to biographical writing which had always fascinated me. In those days the Strachey school of biography had reached the point of the widely popularized studies of Maurois, such as his *Ariel*, the biography of Shelley. Fact was often sacrificed to subjective impressionism and the reality of life to sheer sensationalism. It seemed to me that a biography did not have to be dull simply because it was factual and the product of exhaustive research. All the art of the novelist could be employed but in such a way as never to falsify the objective facts of life in constructing a narrative pattern that would be at once absorbing without being unfaithful to the subject.

"In this spirit I wrote my biography of the great poet Pushkin, after three years of research, part of it conducted in Russia. . . .

"I next turned to literary criticism in an extensive study of the notebooks of Dostoevsky in an effort to describe in much detail the creative art of a great writer. This book was an exciting task, for I learned a great deal about the art of writing in moving around so intimately in the creative laboratory of a genius such as Dostoevsky. Meanwhile I had embarked on what was to be a major effort—to put my biographical theories to the test in writing a definitive life of Leo Tolstoy. Seven years of exacting research and endless writing and polishing went into this behemoth, and the result was a book of some eight hundred pages, just about half of what I originally wrote. And this had further to be boiled down to about half again for its serialization in the *Atlantic Monthly*. But it was all worth it, for apart from the material rewards, I obtained much spiritual and intellectual satisfaction in portraying faithfully and objectively, in all its magnificent proportions and accomplishments, the life of one of the greatest men in modern times . . . ."

E. J. Simmons's most important book today is his conscientious and highly accessible pioneer biography of Aleksandr Pushkin (1799–1837), remains the best introduction to the great Russian poet and prose writer. The scholar and translator Avrahm Yarmolinsky, who had edited the first substantial edition of Pushkin's works in English translation (*Poems, Prose and Plays of Pushkin*) in the previous year, writing in the *Nation* (1937), welcomed it thus: "The book has considerable merit and indeed supersedes the only existing biography of Pushkin in English, that by D. S. Mirsky. It is on the whole a scholarly performance, and not without lively moments, for Pushkin's story is quick with human interest." William L. Phelps, reflecting the reactions of the intelligent reader who knew little of Russian literature but wanted to know more, wrote in the *Saturday Review of Literature*: "I have been waiting forty years for this book: Dr. Simmons has written not only a valuable, but an indispensable book." For many English-speaking readers Simmons opened the doors to Pushkin. Antony Wood, the author of the most successful English version of Pushkin's *Little Tragedies*, is firmly of this opinion.

Simmons's study of Dostoevsky, only a little less distinguished, is still valuable. John Cournos, reviewing it in the *New York Times* (1940), wrote: "The two best books on Dostoevsky in English have so far been Avrahm Yarmolinsky's life of him . . . and Edward Hallet Carr's biography. . . . To these must now be added Mr. Simmons's excellent study."

Simmons produced useful, honorable, and dispassionate work. Of the collection of essays he edited, *Through the Glass of Soviet Literature*, B. D. Wolfe, a respected authority on the Soviet Union, wrote that "as a whole" it provided "a valuable analysis both of Soviet literature and of Soviet life. No specialist in the field will want to miss it, and, unlike most university publications made up of doctoral theses, this one can be confidently recommended to the general reader as a book which gives a much better close-up of life in the Soviet Union and the trials of its men of letters than most 'I Was There' books can."

Simmons's *Russian Fiction and Soviet Ideology* remains an illuminating study of three very different Soviet writers, all possessed of genius in some measure, who decided to go along with Stalin: Fedin, Leonov, and Sholokhov. Alexander Werth wrote in the *Nation* (1958): "Having met all three of Ernest Simmons's heroes, I found his book particularly fascinating and—let me say right away—acute and penetrating in its assessment of the more or less tragic dilemma all three of them have faced in the past quarter-century."

The view taken of Simmons's biography of Chekhov by Marc Slonim, a distinguished Russian critic (and author of *Soviet Russian Literature: Writers and Problems 1917–1953*), is indicative of the respect that his fellow scholars liked to pay him. Writing in the *New York Times Book Review*, Slonim said that Simmons's book "might be called bulky and conservative" by some; but it was, he thought, "fascinating reading" and fulfilled its purpose: it brought us "very close to a live, human Chekhov." Howard Moss observed (in the *New Yorker*) that the book was too "conscientious," yet he described it as "invaluable as documentation."

Modest, affable, and helpful to his colleagues, Simmons was able to convey much of his own excitement to his reader. On the political side, he was quietly but firmly anti-communist, but he also disliked American anti-communism in its McCarthyite manifestations and kept an open mind.

Simmons, who was consultant to the Ford Foundation (1961–1963), and who was awarded an honorary L.H.D. degree from Northwestern University in 1968, was in June 1940 married to the former Winifred McNamara, with whom he had one son. His chief works remain in print.

PRINCIPAL WORKS: *Criticism, literary history, and biography*—English Literature and Culture in Russia, 1935; Pushkin, 1937; Dostoievsky: The Making of a Novelist, 1940; An Outline of Modern Russian Literature 1880–1940, 1943; Leo Tolstoy, 1946; Russian Fiction and Soviet Ideology, 1958; Chekhov: A Biography, 1962; Introduction to Russian Realism, 1965; Introduction to Tolstoy's Writings, 1968; Fedor Dostoevsky, 1969; Tolstoy, 1973. *As editor*—(with S. H. Cross) Centennial Essays for Pushkin, 1937; (with A. Kaun) Slavic Studies. 1943; Through the Glass of Soviet Literature, 1953.

ABOUT: The autobiographical material quoted above was written for Twentieth Century Authors First Supplement, 1955. Dictionary of Literary Biography vol. 103, 1991. *Periodicals*—Nation February 20, 1937; May 10, 1958; New York Herald Tribune Book Review August 9, 1953; New York Times December 1, 1940, June 5, 1972; New Yorker March 2, 1963; Russian Review October 1972; 1972; Saturday Review of Literature February 13, 1937.

**SIMONDS, FRANK HERBERT** (April 5, 1878–January 23, 1936), American journalist and historian who specialized in military and diplomat-ic history, was born in Concord, Massachusetts, the only son of William Henry Simonds, a railway conductor, and Jennie E. (Garty) Simonds. The proximity of his birthplace to the site where the American Revolutionary War broke out in 1775 nurtured in him from boyhood an interest  in military tactics and strategy. As a boy, he read Creasy's *The Fifteen Decisive Battles of the World*—a book still read by modern military leaders—and played at reconstructing the battles with toy soldiers. After brief military service in the Spanish-American War in 1898, he graduated from Harvard University in 1900. He moved to New York and served as president of the University Settlement for one year. There he met and married Mary Frances Gledhill in 1902.

Simonds became a political reporter on several New York newspapers, serving as the *Tribune*'s Washington and Albany correspondents. He also covered the state legislature for the *Evening Post* and wrote editorials for the *Evening Sun*, which he edited from 1913 to 1914. Returning to the *Tribune* in 1915 as associate editor, he found that his talent in interpreting military strategy made his commentary immensely popular in the United States; before long, his articles were being syndicated in more than a hundred American newspapers. An editorial he wrote in 1916 to commemorate the first anniversary of the sinking of the *Lusitania* won him a Pulitzer prize. His expertise was enhanced by the many walking tours of northern France he had taken before the war, giving him a unique familiarity with the topography of the theater of conflict. In 1936, his *New York Times* obituarist wrote of those early expeditions: "He measured by his footsteps the extent of ancient battlefields, which were to become battlefields again. He knew the distances by winding white stone roads from hamlet to hamlet, little villages that were to become famous names, and he wrote about the country in which the battles were being fought."

After the war, Simonds went to France to cover the Versailles conference. From there he wrote a story attacking President Wilson's plans to pledge American forces to keep the peace in Europe. This revelation helped fuel public opposition to the League of Nations in the United States. Yet he was later honored by European governments, many of which conferred on him their highest honors available to a foreigner: He was a Chevalier of the (French) Legion of Honor and a Commander of the Order of Phoenix of Greece, among others.

From 1914 through 1920, he published a five-volume series entitled *History of the Great War*, which included reprints of some of the newspaper columns he had written during those years. Although he was a journalist and by no means an academic historian, the *American Historical Review* paid tribute to his expertise: "His book . . . is essentially a popular work. But it is more. Because of the author's ability to grasp the essential factors in the struggle, because he writes as an eye-witness to some of its most significant incidents, and because of his close association with the French and British staffs, his account is a valuable contribution to the military history of the war." At a time when most Americans—politicians, journalists, as well as the general public—sought a return to "normalcy" by isolating themselves from European issues, Simonds was almost alone in trying to explain the importance of international issues in his books.

By 1933, Simonds had become convinced that another European war was imminent. In that year, his *America Faces the Next War* warned an apathetic public of the conflict that was to come. The *New York Times* reviewer wrote, "Not only is Mr. Simonds convinced beyond the slightest doubt that another mighty conflict in Europe is certain soon to break forth, but he expects it possibly within another year." Although Hitler did not invade Poland until 1939, conflicts in Spain and Ethiopia during the mid-1930s are now seen as precursors to the larger war.

Simonds spent the last three years of his life writing about the links between economic nationalism and military conflict. He now found himself held in higher regard by the academic community. He was asked to deliver the Albert Shaw lectures on diplomatic history at Johns Hopkins in 1935. These were later published as *American Foreign Policy in the Post-War Years*. His basic thesis, as pointed out in a commentary in the *Saturday Review*, was that "every administration from Wilson's to Roosevelt's has bungled its foreign policy. . . . he offers this prescription, 'For peace, arbitration; for security, naval parity; for prosperity, protective tariffs; and

for armaments, limitations.'" Samuel Flagg Bemis, in the *American Historical Review*, urged professional historians to take notice, saying that "Every academic person will do well to take heavy counsel from so perspicuous an analysis of the relation of the United States to the agitated world of today. The scholar should not quarrel with the author for a few careless and inaccurate historical allusions; he should fix his thought on the main arguments of the lectures, which ought to be read by every citizen thoughtful of foreign problems."

Simonds's London *Times* obituarist called him "the journalist whose brilliant interpretations in the *New York Tribune* during the war of military and political events abroad won him an international reputation."

PRINCIPAL WORKS: Great War: The First Phase, 1914; Great War: The Second Phase, 1915; They Shall Not Pass, 1916; History of the World War (vols. 1–3, 1918; Vols. 4–5, 1920 U.K.; How Europe Made Peace Without America, 1927; Can Europe Keep the Peace?, 1931; They Won the War, 1931; Can America Stay at Home?, 1932; A B C of War Debts, and the Seven Popular Delusions About Them 1933; (in U.K.: America Must Cancel), America Faces the Next War, 1933; American Foreign Policy in the Post-War Years, 1935; (with B. Emeny) The Great Powers in World Politics, 1935; (with B. Emeny) The Price of Peace: The Challenge of Economic Nationalism, 1935.

ABOUT: Periodicals—Current History January 1936; Forum January 1929; Nation, February 5, 1936; New York Herald Tribune February 3, 1935; New York Times, January 24, 1936; New York Tribune August 14, 1917; Newsweek February 1, 1936.

## SIMONOV, KIRIL MIKHAILOVICH. See SIMONOV, KONSTANTIN

## "SIMONOV, KONSTANTIN" (pseudonym of KIRIL MIKHAILOVICH SIMONOV) (November 28, 1915–August 28, 1979), Soviet novelist, playwright, editor, essayist, screenwriter, and poet, was born in Petrograd (which became Leningrad), the son of a man who failed to return from World War I and was presumed killed. He was one of the more talented of the Soviet writers; but as Helen Segall writes in her article on him in *Handbook of Russian Literature*, he was, as secretary of the Union of Soviet Writers, undoubtedly "active in establishing its conservative policies." His attacks on Alexander Solzenhitsyn were described as "nauseatingly hypocritical." He received the most favorable critical reception at the end of the thirties, for earlier work, such as his (untranslated) poem about Nikolai Ostrovsky; his later books, more famous in the West—owing to the wartime alliance with Russia—were popular, and were skilfully written, but they were not taken as seriously by critics as his early poetry had been.

After some elementary schooling at Saratov on the Volga, the fifteen-year-old Simonov went to work to support his widowed mother and himself. From 1930 until 1935 he worked in a factory as a lathe operator; but as a budding poet of quite evident melodious talent, as well as correct proletarian credentials, some of his work was posted on the walls of his place of work. Encouraged, he began publishing poetry in magazines in 1934, and in

1935 his poem "Dom" (The house) appeared. He graduated from the Gorki Literary Institute in 1938, in which year also appeared his first substantial collection of poetry, *Nastoyaschiye Iyudi* (Real men).

Although Simonov was undoubtedly an establishment toady (he won six Stalin Prizes and one Lenin Prize, and was made a Hero of Socialist La-

bor) who turned a blind eye to Soviet excesses, his work clearly shows that he possessed a conscience, that he was interested in the truth (so far as he could stretch this under Stalin and his successors), and that he would have liked to have been well thought of by those who were not Communist literary bureaucrats. In common with others like him, he underwent periods of severe disfavor—and in 1954, after Stalin's death, he became a dissident for a time. Made editor of the literary magazine *Novy Mir* in 1946, he was dismissed in 1950 for publishing a "decadent love poem." He was reinstated in 1956, but once again dismissed in the following year—this time for publishing Dudintsev's *Not By Bread Alone*. In later years he was to be criticized for "flirting with religious morality."

A poem which made Simonov quite well known during the course of World War II, "Ty pomnish, dorogi Aloisha" (1941, "You Remember, Aloisha"; translated in *Soviet Literature* XII, 1956), movingly reflects the semi-mystical Russian mood of that time, of a wish to return to the soil. It is sentimental, but has the genuine ring of what George Orwell called "good-bad" popular poetry.

But Simonov first made his name as the war correspondent for the army newspaper *Krasnaya Zvedzda* (Red star). He was sent in 1939 to cover the battle of the River Khalkhin Gol in Outer Mongolia (May-September, in which the Mongolian-Soviet forces under General Zhukov—Mongolia was until 1990 a puppet state of the Soviet Union—repulsed the Japanese under Ueda) and reported it brilliantly, although he took the official line that the Russians suffered only 9,824 casualties (whereas the figure was nearer to the admitted Japanese losses of 17,405). His novel *Tovarishichi po oruzhiya* (Comrade in arms, 1952) also deals with these engagements.

In June 1941 he was sent to the front, and during the next four years became one of the most famous of war correspondents; his vivid accounts of the battles appeared in *Pravda* as well as in *Krasnaya*. Some of this material was translated as *No Quarter* in 1943. The *Saturday Review of Literature* wrote that the book "lived up to its title. . . . tense, packed, vivid and often brutal"; the *New Yorker* (1943) praised it as "written with a sensitivity and penetration that suggest both a more vigorous Bunin and a far more subtle Babel. . . . One of the pieces . . . belongs to the grand tradition of Russian literature." This latter was vast over-praise,

since Simonov's work never at any time came near in quality to that of either Bunin or Babel, but it demonstrates the enthusiasm with which the book was received.

While he was acting as war reporter, Simonov began to write a series of war novels on the subject of World War II, beginning with *Comrade in Arms*. The best, and by far the most discussed in the West, was *Dom i nochi* (1943, translated as *Days and Nights*), which has as its main theme the struggle for (the then) Stalingrad. John Hersey wrote in the *New Yorker* (1945) that the novel would "almost certainly be the first work of a Soviet writer to be sold in greater numbers in America than in Russia. . . . It is the best Soviet book so far published here about what the Russians call 'The Great Patriotic War.' . . . I think there will eventually be greater and even truer books on the subject"—and he added that Simonov might well be the man who would write them. But Simonov did not.

Simonov's later novels were more ambitious in scope. *Zhivyye i miotvyye* (translated in U.S.: *The Living and the Dead* and in U.K.: *Victims and Heroes*) describes the first six months of the war as seen by his hero, Vanya Sintsov. Tom Wolfe, reviewing it in the *New York Herald Tribune Books*, put his finger on its deficiencies without being unfair to its undoubted skills: "Military historians may find something of interest in Mr. Simonov's detailed battle descriptions. Literary historians, however, will note quite something else: the fact that this extraordinarily wooden and old-fashioned war novel, by a prominent 47-year-old Soviet writer, was written . . . during the period of the so-called 'Thaw.' . . . The patriotic novel Mr. Simonov wrote about the siege of Stalingrad [*Days and Nights*] was pro-Stalin . . . at the right time. *The Living and the Dead* was anti-Stalin . . . at the right time. Thaw or no thaw, Konstantin Simonov and a whole generation of Soviet novelists like him . . . have had their eye on the directives of the Union of Soviet Writers too long to take a look at the human condition at this late date." George Reavey, writing about the novel in the *Saturday Review*, found it "stark and revealing," but "not without its faults as a novel. The main characters . . . are convincing enough in action or when discussing immediate topics, but they seem to lack inner dimension and personal background."

Simonov was also a successful playwright. All in all, he was a highly talented entertainer who might, under different circumstances, if he could have been free of the shackles of "socialist realism," have achieved more as a writer than, ultimately, he did. He was, however, one of the more important reporters of the war period. The English versions of his later works, by unknown hands, mostly appeared in Moscow, and were little heeded in the West.

PRINCIPAL WORKS IN ENGLISH TRANSLATION: *Novels and reportage*—On the Petsamo Road, 1942; Stalingrad Fights On, 1942; The Russian People, 1942; No Quarter, 1943; Days and Nights, (tr. J. Barnes) 1945; Friendship Is the Most Important Thing in the World (tr. anon) 1946; The Whole World Over, 1947; Friends and Foes, 1951; The Living and the Dead (tr. R. Ainstzein) 1963 (in U.K.: Victims and Heroes); Liberation, 1974. *Drama*—The Russians, 1943; The Russian Question, 1947.

ABOUT: Alexandrova, V. A History of Soviet Literature 1917–1962, 1963; Brown, E. J. Russian Literature Since the Revolution, 1982; Slonim, M. Soviet Russian Literature, Writers and Problems 1917–1977, 1977; Struve, G. Russian Literature Under Lenin and Stalin 1917–1953, 1971; Terras, V. (ed.) Handbook of Russian Literature, 1985. Periodicals—New Yorker Herald Tribune Books November 25, 1962; New York December 18, 1943; November 3, 1945; Saturday Review October 27, 1962; Saturday Review of Literature January 1, 1944; Times (London) August 29, 1979.

**SIMPSON, GEORGE GAYLORD** (June 16, 1902–October 6, 1984), American paleontologist and science writer, wrote: "I was born in Chicago,  youngest of three children and only son of Joseph A. and Helen (Kinney) Simpson, but we soon moved to Wyoming and then to Colorado. My earliest memories are of Denver, where most of my formative years were spent. My father was engaged principally in land development, irrigation, and mining in Utah and Colorado. Trips with him and summers spent in the mountains gave me wide knowledge and enduring love of the Rocky Mountain region, which I still consider my real home. Except for one year in Piedmont, California, I attended the Denver public schools, and I entered the University of Colorado in 1918. Family reverses caused me to leave the university in 1919 and to spend a year working in Chicago and then bumming my way from one job to another in the South and West. In 1920 I was able to return to the University of Colorado, and in 1922 I transferred to Yale University, where I was graduated in 1923.

"Doting elders thought I had a talent for writing and especially for versifying. I accepted their judgment and entered college with the naïve notion of learning to be a poet. I soon found that for me, at least, knowledge is more important than self-expression and that substance in writing is more important than manner. The learning of new truths is far more satisfying than the restating of old ones, and I was increasingly drawn to scientific research as a career. As an undergraduate I was determined to study the history of life and the principles of its evolution, the subjects to which I have ever since devoted myself with no regrets. This aim motivated transfer to Yale, where I continued in the graduate school and was given a Ph.D. in 1926. After a year of post-doctorate research abroad, mostly in the British Museum, I joined the staff of the American Museum of Natural History, New York. . . .

"At the museum I busied myself especially with basic paleontological research, collecting, identifying, and describing fossils, mostly fossil mammals. This work involved numerous expeditions throughout the United States and South America. Most interesting, perhaps, were two long journeys through the heart of Patagonia (1930–31, 1933–34) and another to the then virtually unknown and still wild and beautiful forests and peaks of Venezuelan Guiana (1938–39). Research produced a great deal of scientific rather than literary writing, the number of my technical articles now being well over three hundred.

"As the years have passed, my interests have not changed in focus but have broadened in scope. I have not lost sight of basic technical research, but I have tended more and more to seek a synthesis of knowledge of life and its history and to try to present such knowledge to a wider audience than that of my specialized colleagues. If the label 'author' fits me at all, it is for several books written from this point of view. My career, such as it is, has been scientific rather than literary and has been symbolized by the usual tokens of reasonably successful research: honorary degrees (Yale, Princeton, Glasgow, Durham, Oxford), medals (from the National Academy of Sciences, Geological Societies of America and of France, and others), and fellowships or honorary memberships (National Academy of Sciences, American Philosophical Society, American Academy of Arts and Sciences, Academy of Sciences of Venezuela, Zoological Society of London, and others). I have lectured widely in the United States and also in Argentina, Venezuela, Australia, Egypt, England, and France.

"Aside from more than twenty-five years on the staff of *American Museum*, I have taught as a part-time professor at Columbia University since 1945. I also spent two unpleasant years as an intelligence officer (captain and major) in combat zones in the Mediterranean.

"I have been married twice, secondly and permanently to Dr. Anne Roe, a research psychologist. Thanks to four daughters, our stock of grandchildren is rapidly increasing. We have built a home in the mountains of New Mexico, where we spend as much time as my duties permit."

---

Simpson worked as a curator at the American Museum of Natural History until the late 1950s. He undertook several expeditions, the first being two long journeys into Patagonia, which inspired his first book, *Attending Marvels*, an informal travel journal.

*Tempo and Mode in Evolution* (1944) was followed by the less technical *The Meaning of Evolution* (1949). This important and successful book (his best-known) took a mechanical, materialist view of the universe, arguing cogently against the crude and racist "social Darwinism" of such writers as William Graham Sumner and against the view of evolution tending inexorably towards increasing sophistication and progress. As for the notions of "struggle" and "survival of the fittest," Simpson asserted that "Advantage in differential reproduction is usually a peaceful process in which the concept of struggle is really irrelevant. . . . It was a crude concept of natural selection to think of it simply as something imposed on the species from the outside. It is not, as in the metaphor often used with reference to Darwinian selection, a sieve through which organisms are sifted, some variations passing (surviving) and some being held back (dying). It is rather a process intricately woven into the whole life of the group, equally present in the life and death of the individuals, in the associative relationships of the population, and in their extraspecific adaptations." This book was influential in lending needed perspective to the notion of social Darwinism in America.

The part played by "associative relationships" in evolutionary changes had, for Simpson, clear ethical implications, giving to humans responsibilities which render some actions moral and others immoral. And the shifting ground of evolutionary existence meant that all absolutes and religious certainties were illusory. Simpson's ethical position was very much a relativistic and humanistic one, as much in tune with the decades in which he wrote as the attitudes of Darwinians had been in theirs.

*Horses: The Story of the Horse Family in the Modern World and Through Sixty Million Years of History*, based on a long-term study undertaken by the Museum, was an explication of the way evolutionary processes advance in a haphazard, opportunistic manner. On his resignation from the Museum in 1959, and from the associated role as professor of vertebrate paleontology at Columbia University, Simpson took up a position at Harvard. He continued traveling, and wrote a large number of articles in addition to his books. In the sixties he was a vocal critic of space-race budgets, arguing that the proper arena for exploration and study was our own planet. In his capacity as field-worker he was associated with several newsworthy discoveries, including, in 1953, the skulls of eight "Dawn Horses"; he was also with Louis and Mary Leakey in Africa when they made one of their important discoveries of early hominid remains.

PRINCIPAL WORKS: American Mesozoic Mammalia, 1929; Attending Marvels, 1934; Quantitative Zoology, 1939; Tempo and Mode in Evolution, 1944; The Principles of Classification and a Classification of Mammals, 1945; The Meaning of Evolution, 1949; Horses, The Story of the Horse Family in the Modern World and Through Sixty Million Years of History, 1951; Life in the Past, 1953; (with C. S. Pittendrigh and L. H. Tiffany) Life: An Introduction to Biology, 1957; Principles of Animal Taxonomy, 1961; This View of Life, the World of an Evolutionist, 1964; Periscope View: A Professional Autobiography, 1972; Penguins Past and Present, Here and There, 1976; Fossils and the History of Life, 1983; Discoverers of the Lost World, 1984; Simple Curiosity, Letters from George Gaylord Simpson to His Family 1921–1970, 1987.

ABOUT: The autobiographical material quoted above was written for Twentieth Cenutry Authors First Supplement, 1955. Abbott, D. (ed.) Biographical Dictionary of Scientists, 1984; Current Biography 1964; Simpson, G. Periscope View, 1972. Periodicals—New York Times October 8, 1984; February 14, 1988; Washington Post October 13, 1984.

## SIMPSON, HELEN (DE GUERRY) (December 1, 1897–October 15, 1940), Australian-born English detective story writer and novelist, was born in Sydney, the daughter of a solicitor, Edward Percy Simpson and Anne (de Lauret) Simpson. Her maternal grandfather, the Marquess Guerry de Lauret, had settled in Australia in the 1840s; her great-grandfather, Piers Simpson, was a navy commander and surveyor of New South Wales with Sir Thomas Mitchell. Helen Simpson was educated at Rose Bay Convent and Abbotsleigh, Waharoonga,

and went on to study music at Oxford University. She was forced to leave before taking her degree, however, since the university objected to her appearance in amateur theatricals at the home of the poet John Masefield.

A lively, humorous woman, she wrote her first novel, *Aquittal*, in three weeks as the result of a bet. Continuing her interest in the world of theater, she collaborated with the actress and playwright Clemence Dane on three mysteries: the highly popular, lighthearted *Enter Sir John*, where the amateur detective Sir John sets out to prove a young actress innocent of murder; *Re-enter Sir John*, a sequel, and *Author Unknown*, a satire  on the literary establishment. Some critics considered that the melting of talents marred the books, but they were generally enthusiastically received. Simpson and Dane also wrote a frothy comedy, *Gooseberry Fool*, which was successfully staged at London's Players Theatre.

In 1927 Simpson married the surgeon Denis Browne, nephew of the Australian writer Rolf Boldrewood, and had a daughter with him. She wrote further detective stories and also produced historical novels, such as *Henry VIII* and *The Spanish Marriage*, both of which received mixed reviews. Her *Saraband for Dead Lovers* was about Sophia Dorothea, electress of Hanover, who was confined for a large part of her life for adultery. Simpson's frank descriptions caused the *Times Literary Supplement* to sniff at its "double-bedroom scenes, which are not pretty." Her novel *Cups, Wands and Swords*, about a pair of English twins, revealed her interest in the otherworldly and attracted Cyril Connolly's attention: "The theme is as old as Electra and Orestes, and is managed so well as to make the supernatural a part of the story both credible and moving." Also concerned with the supernatural was *Baseless Fabric*, an early collection of stories which led the *New Statesman* to wax lyrical about one story: "In *Young Magic* she actually gets something of the effect of uncanniness and remoteness at which Mr. De La Mare aims."

The works for which Simpson is best known, however, are *Boomerang*, winner of the James Tait Memorial Prize in 1932, and *Under Capricorn*, both using Australia as their setting and both ambitious and, to a limited extent, successful fictions. *Under Capricorn* was later filmed by Hitchcock. In all her work, Simpson displayed a talent for description, dialogue, and humor. Her flaws lay in unevenness of tone, longueurs, and, in her detective stories, plots that were too thin.

PRINCIPAL WORKS: Novels—Aquittal, 1925; Cups, Wands and Swords, 1927; (with C. Dane) Enter Sir John, 1928; The Desolate House, 1929; Desires and Devices, 1930; ( with C. Dane) Author Unknown, 1930; The Prime Minister Is Dead, 1931; Boomerang, 1932; (with C. Dane) Re-enter Sir John 1932; The Woman on the Beast, 1933; The Spanish Marriage, 1933; Henry VIII, 1934; Saraband for Dead Lovers, 1935; Under Capricorn, 1937; The Female Felon, 1935; Maid No More, 1940. *Short stories*—The Baseless Fabric, 1925. *Drama*—(with C. Dane) Gooseberry Fool 1929; A Man of his Time, 1923; Pan in Pimlico, 1923. *Miscellaneous*—The Cold Table 1935, (Recipes); Heartsease and Honesty (tr. from French), 1935; A Woman Among Wild Men, 1938.

ABOUT: Roderick, C. A. Twenty Australian Novelists, 1947; Dictionary of Autralian Biography, 1949. *Periodicals*—Fornightly Review January 1941; New Statesman, december 12, 1925; November 5, 1927; New York Times October 16, 1940; Times Literary Supplement, Feb 7 1935.

## SINCLAIR, BERTHA. See BOWER, B. M.

## SINCLAIR, HAROLD AUGUSTUS (May 8, 1907–May 24, 1966), American novelist, wrote: "So far as I know, none of my family was ever famous for anything except working hard and minding their own business and never making very much money. I think I got to somewhere around the third year in high school, and have been getting an education ever since, but not inside any cloistered walls. I have lived in Florida, where I saw the hurricane of 1926; in Texas, where I saw very little worth remembering; and in Chicago, where I knew the Dill Pickle and what passed for bohemianism. Have done a great many things in order to make a living, including being a telegraph operator for Western Union, pushing a wheelbarrow on a construction gang, and playing the trumpet in ham dance orchestras hither and yon. I've read more books than I can ever remember, and have wanted to be a writer since I was first able to read, though now I'm approaching that objective it's not all like what I always supposed it would be. Have really been trying to write for some years, but except for some newspaper reviews and a very bad poem in an obscure magazine [had] never published anything until *Journey Home*. Next to reading, my favorite recreations are music and convivial drinking. . . . My favorite modern authors are Thomas Wolfe, William McFee, and Claude Houghton, in just about that order.

"I am not a very social person and have very few close friends, but those few are most excellent ones. I think of myself as being about one-third incurable romanticist, one-third cynical realist and one-third a somewhat vague blank. I'd like to write at least one book that would stand comparison with the best in America . . . and I'd like my children to remember me as a swell guy whether I am or not."

---

Harold Sinclair was born in Chicago, the son of Walter Guy Sinclair, a railroad fireman who abandoned the family when Harold was a young boy, and Violet (Wishard) Sinclair. He was raised primarily by an aunt and uncle in Bloomington, Illinois, a city he used as the basis for the fictional "Everton" in his three-volume historical saga, *American Years, The Years of Growth,* and *Years of Illusion.* After the extended period of bumming about described above, and his marriage in 1933 to Ethel Moran, Sinclair took the job as a department-store salesman that supported the writing of his first two novels.

The first, *Journey Home,* was a semi-autobiographical account of a jobless man's wanderings through depression-era America that pleased many critics. Writing in the *New York Herald Tribune Books,* Alfred Kazin called it "an adventure story, carelessly heroic and readable. . . . It is an uncomplicated narrative, full of high jinks, rural romance and aspirations toward the higher life."

Sinclair's second novel, *American Years*—a chronicle of an Illinois town in the thirty years preceding the election of President Lincoln and the outbreak of the Civil War—was a more ambitious work. It too received favorable reviews and was, according to Robert Bray in the *Illinois Historical Journal,* "the book that made Harold Sinclair as a writer." Focusing on the town of Everton itself, *American Years,* claimed Bray, not

only "lack[ed] a hero, but among the panoply of voices, many fascinating and all having their say, none was privileged. . . . [Sinclair's] artistry pushed point of view beyond third-person omniscience. At its best *American Years* sounded like history talking."

Bray felt that the succeeding volumes in the trilogy "abandoned 'history talking' in favor of more conventional plotting and fictional characterization. . . . Perhaps as a result neither *Years of Growth* nor *Years of Illusion* was as fresh and original as the first volume, nor did they sell as well." A critic in the *Saturday Review of Literature,* reviewing *The Years of Growth,* put it this way: "Mr. Sinclair's writing is rarely distinguished or exciting. It is never invertebrate or shoddy, never sensational or meretricious, but there is a jogging commonplaceness which is often too soothing, and which dims the brilliance of his fine pageant of the years."

The years between 1936 and 1942 were Sinclair's most productive. In addition to *Journey Home* and the Everton trilogy, he wrote what a few considered his best historical novel, *Westward the Tide*—an account of the early years of the frontiersman George Rogers Clark—and a history of New Orleans from 1699 to 1942, *The Port of New Orleans.*

After this period Sinclair's productivity and his popularity declined pretty much in tandem. Nevertheless, his three remaining novels were not without interest or admirers. *Music Out of Dixie* took as its protagonist a young black musician and was described in the *New York Times Book Review* as "a strong and honest novel . . . derived from the rich materials of New Orleans jazz." *The Horse Soldiers,* a fictionalized account of a Civil War raid, was praised even more highly and was made into a 1959 movie by John Ford starring John Wayne and William Holden. Its sequel, *The Cavalryman,* was a critical and commercial failure. By the time of its publication in 1958, alcoholism and disappointed hopes had taken their toll. Sinclair published nothing more until his death, in Bloomington, at the age of fifty-nine. "Drink had debilitated him as a writer," wrote Bray, "and cancer finished him off."

PRINCIPAL WORKS: *Novels*—Journey Home, 1936; American Years, 1938; The Years of Growth, 1861–1893, 1940; Westward the Tide, 1940; Years of Illusion, 1941; Music Out of Dixie, 1952; The Horse Soldiers, 1956; The Cavalryman, 1958. *History*—The Port of New Orleans, 1942; The Daily Pantagraph, 1846–1946, 1976.

ABOUT: The autobiographical material quoted above was written for Twentieth Century Authors, 1942. Contemporary Authors vols. 5–8, 1970; Warfel, H. R. American Novelists of Today, 1951. *Periodicals*—Illinois Historical Journal Autumn 1989; New York Herald Tribune Books September 13, 1936; New York Times May 25, 1966; New York Times Book Review May 25, 1952; Saturday Review February 18, 1956; Saturday Review of Literature February 24, 1940.

## "SINCLAIR, JO" (pseudonym of RUTH SEID)

(July 1, 1913–April 4, 1995), American novelist and playwright, wrote: "I was born in Brooklyn, New York. My parents were still scuffling for a living in the 'Promised Land,' a struggle which had begun for them in Russia the day they were born. Poverty, persecutions, hope; these must have been the whips that changed their lives.

"Emigration was a frightening but insistent dream to Jews in those days. My father, a carpenter, and my mother, a seamstress, went with a large  group from their village to the Argentine, in South America, to work land belonging to a wealthy baron who paid all expenses and promised a living. Their first child was born there, and the living stayed harsh. They went back to Russia. There another child was born, and there, somehow, the dream was replenished. Persecution, poverty, hope; the old words were still there, made a louder and louder sound until the next step was taken. The carpenter and his family came to the United States, to a big city this time. Three more children were born, and the living stayed harsh.

"When I was three, the carpenter took his last step of wandering. We landed in Cleveland, Ohio, and stayed. The rest is uneventful: a family becomes part of a community. We went to school, we graduated and went to work the following day; no money or energy enough for college. . . .

"I was the youngest child. I grew up in the melting-pot neighborhood of a large industrial city, played and went to school with other second-generation kids. Our parents had come from Russia, Italy, Hungary—and from Atlanta, Georgia. We were white and colored, and whereas the dreams were shouted in the dirty stone streets in many languages and slurred dialects, and we kids knew all of them, our own dreams were told in our own language—English, Midwest near-slums variety.

"What makes a person want to write? The old

wandering in the bloodstream? . . . I started writing in high school, and I've been trying ever since.

"For a living, I typed and filed, I made boxes in a knitting mill and read proof for telephone directories, edited a trade magazine, worked on W.P.A. editing and writing projects, was secretary to a calendar-and-novelty boss, wrote publicity for the American Red Cross during a war. Evenings and weekends, I wrote short stories . . . The carpenter was amazed, incredulous, full of a kind of jeering laughter. A writer? The carpenter's wife shrugged: who had ever heard of such a thing?

"One day the first novel was published. It had won a literary contest, it had made quite a bit of money. The carpenter and his wife, much older and very tired with all the struggling and scuffling, held the book in their hands. They looked at the money. Then they said, with a kind of dazed happiness: 'In America, anything can happen.'

"Maybe the old dream had run its gamut, finally. Such dreams can move worlds, they say."

---

*Wasteland*, Sinclair's first and best known novel, tells the story of John Brown (born Jake Braunowitz), an American photographer who disdains his Russian-Jewish immigrant parents, and who is tortured by a denial of his own heritage. With the help of a psychoanalyst, Brown is finally able to accept his family and his roots. The book was awarded the $10,000 Harper Novel Prize in 1946 as the year's best study of some aspect of American life. The published novel went on to become a Book of the Month Club selection, but met with a mixed reception. Wallace Stegner, writing in the *Atlantic*, expressed cautious approval of *Wasteland* as a character study, but added, "there is the suspicion . . . that one function of the book is to justify and demonstrate psychoanalysis, and whenever that suspicion intrudes, the book suffers."

Sinclair's third novel, *The Changelings*, examines the nature and varieties of racial prejudice by portraying the upheavals that ensue when blacks decide to move into a white ethnic neighborhood in a large Ohio city, especially as the changes affect a young women, Judith Vincent. Although Eastern European immigrants—especially women—are at the center of much of her work, Sinclair is concerned with how people from a variety of backgrounds confront their past, and how they cope with the difficult process of becoming Americans. Her short stories appeared in a number of anthologies, and *The Long Moment*, one of her several plays, was produced by the Cleveland Playhouse in 1951. *The Changelings* and *Anna Teller* have recently been reissued.

Sinclair's literary output after *Wasteland* reflected a growing preoccupation with the impact of social forces on the emotional lives of women. *Sing at My Wake* (1951) examined the psychology of a young woman's search for maturity and fulfillment in the face of a failed marriage. *Anna Teller* (1961) depicts how an elderly, forceful Hungarian woman who emigrates to the United States after the 1956 uprising is forced to reexamine her role as woman and mother in an unfamiliar environment. Critics thought that Sinclair was poor at male characterizations, and that the structure of the long novel was clumsy; but some praised her ability to create a strong woman protagonist. The *New York Herald Tribune Book Review* thought that "to the portrait of the woman, Miss Sinclair brings the touch and pigments that portray her in the rich color and depth of her strength and individuality . . . Only with patience that is willing to wade through much that is dull and banal . . . is the reader rewarded by a final knowledge of its splendid heroine."

In 1963, Sinclair was deeply affected by the death of her longtime friend and mentor Helen Buchman. She worked through her sense of pain and loss by keeping a journal recounting daily events around the time of her friend's passing. These memoirs were published in 1992, under the title *The Seasons: Death and Transfiguration.*

This rediscovery of Sinclair's post-*Wasteland* work in recent years has led to a reappraisal by some feminist critics, who admire her work because of its tenacity in focusing exclusively on the painful situation and transformation of strong female characters. However, this praise tends to ignore her poor sense of structure and the longueurs which have combined to relegate her to the ranks of minor novelists.

PRINCIPAL WORKS: *Novels*—Wasteland, 1946; Sing at My Wake, 1951; The Changelings, 1955; Anna Teller, 1960. *Memoirs*—The Seasons: Death and Transfiguration, 1993.

ABOUT: The autobiographical material quoted above was written for Twentieth Century Authors First Supplement, 1955. Contemporary Authors Vols. 5–8, 1969; Current Biography 1941; Dictionary of Literary Biography vol. 28 1984. *Periodicals*—Atlantic April 1946; Library Journal September 15, 1992; New York Herald Tribune Book Review, August 21, 1960; New York Times Book Review January 6, 1946.

## "SINCLAIR, MAY" (pseudonym of MARY AMELIA ST. CLAIR SINCLAIR) (August 24, 1863–November 14, 1946), English novelist, critic,

and philosophical writer, was born at Rock Ferry, Cheshire, the sixth child and only daughter of William Sinclair and his wife Amelia. Her father was a Scot who had once been a wealthy and prosperous shipowner, but a combination of alcoholism and business failure caused his bankruptcy in 1870. He and his wife separated, and May went to live with her mother—who was, however, cold and antipathetic towards her—until the latter's death in 1901. She took over responsibility for the family while in her very early twenties, after her father and four of her brothers died in quick succession.

Sinclair spent only one year at Cheltenham Ladies' College, but while she was there she received invaluable encouragement from the headmistress, Dorothy Beale, who introduced her to the works of the idealist philosopher T. H. Green. He influenced her to the extent that she later wrote two exceptionally well-received books based on his thinking: *A Defence of Idealism* and *The New Idealism.*

Sinclair's private education was impressive, comprising German philosophy, the classics in Latin and Greek, and English literature. Her first publication was a privately issued pamphlet of poetry, *Nakiketas* (1886); another such collection, *Essays in Verse,* followed in 1891. These are immature and unimportant except as a guide to her main preoccupations. Her first novel, *Audrey Craven* (1897), on the other hand, is mature and has even been cited as an anticipation of modernism. It is an interesting and revealing tale of a woman who goes through phases of trying to give herself up to love, art, and religion—but cannot give herself wholly to any of them. This theme, of a certain type of woman's inability to fulfill herself, would become one of Sinclair's predominant preoccupations.

While writing her earlier novels, Sinclair became involved with the women's suffrage movement, wrote a pamphlet called *Feminism* (1912), and pursued the theme of self-transcendence through a combined study of Freudian psychoanalysis (she was one of the founders of the Medico-Psychological Clinic of London in 1913) and the metaphysics to which Dorothy Beale had introduced her. She was elected to the Aristotelian Society (1917). Her interest in idealist philosophy led her into intelligent investigations of supernatural phenomena and the part these played in people's lives. During World War I she spent a few months in an ambulance corps in Belgium and, although aged over fifty, drove an ambulance at the front—about which she wrote a book, *A Journal of Impressions in Belgium.*

Sinclair's reputation was made—even more securely in America than in England—with her novel *The Divine Fire* (1904), which is about a poet, Keith Rickman, much resembling Francis Thompson, but who, unlike Thompson, finally achieves recognition in his lifetime. It is a curious mixture of overbearing theory and sharp caricature. The "divine fire" is the consuming one of genius. Although by no means Sinclair's best novel, this one is still interesting for its portrayal of a man who can write great poetry and yet "drops his aitches"—to the pained embarrassment of the girl who loves him. Rickman's genius is made convincing, which is no mean achievement: as F. M. Colby wrote, reviewing the novel in the *Bookman,* the author "has accomplished the difficult feat of taking a genius for . . . hero and making him seem plausible." But even at the height of its success, critics and reviewers alike reprimanded Sinclair for her "literary shop talk" and her "diffuseness."

As well as being interested in idealist philosophy and the supernatural (in her last long and painful illness she became a spiritualist), Sinclair was affected by the European naturalist movement and therefore by the novels of Zola—and of Thomas Hardy, whom she knew quite well, and who liked and respected her. The naturalists put extreme emphasis upon the effects of heredity and environment. This interest led her to write several "naturalist" novels, including *The Helpmate*, which first appeared in serial form in the *Atlantic*, and which dealt—often with telling irony—with the plight of a woman who puts herself spiritually above her dissolute husband while sacrificing her body to him.

All of these and other novels have their excellencies as well as their longueurs, and it may well be that too few of them are in print for the poor reason that they have been read by too few critics and intelligent publishers. But Sinclair's best work is almost certainly to be found in three other novels: *The Three Sisters*, suggested by her research into the lives of the Brontë sisters, *Mary Olivier: A Life*, and *The Life and Death of Harriet Frean*. All these have been put back into print in recent years.

In 1912 Sinclair published *The Three Brontës*, a biography which met with a mixed reception: it was faulted for its incompleteness and its journalistic style, but praised for the manner in which it communicated the part passion played in the lives of its subjects. The novel that followed in 1914 attracted greater and more universal praise, and was especially noted for its power of psychological penetration, especially into the mind of the Brontë father, the vicar, here named James Cartaret.

*Mary Olivier* is, with *Harriet Frean*, Sinclair's chief essay in "stream-of-consciousness." But it is also influenced, in that regard, by some of the aims of the Imagist poets, most of whom—such as Richard Aldington and H. D.—she knew. Sinclair sought in it to present experience directly—the manner employed by the Imagists. The book is her most overtly autobiographical, and is thus less prone to deal with aspects of life of which she had little or no experience. It was much attacked in America for being "unmoral," but a few reviewers, such as the novelist Gertrude Atherton in the *New York Times*, were able to appreciate it at the time. Atherton wrote: "The style is telegraphic [this had been one of the main aims of the Imagists], short sentences often without subject or predicate. Some critics of English object bitterly to this departure from the good old rules, but for my part I cannot see that anything but results matter, and Miss Sinclair certainly gets results." And the reviewer for *Outlook* thought it "a triumph of intense impressionism and painstaking workmanship. It has at once taken its place as one of the most important (and most puzzling) works of fiction of the season."

The shorter (133 pages) *The Life and Death of Harriet Frean* has been less well studied, but is in some ways wider in range. It tells the story from babyhood to old age of Harriet Frean, whose parents exhorted her to "behave beautifully" whatever circumstances she found herself in. Raymond Mortimer, one of the more critical of the British reviewers of the time, had some just and well-considered words to say of it in the *Dial*: "A well-conceived study carefully planned, modern, and thoughtful in its psychology. And Miss Sinclair is right in the title of her book. For Harriet's death, although it only occupies a couple of pages, is given with a fine intensity which makes the book worth reading for it alone. Miss Sinclair's skill is astonishing, her brilliance never failing, but she writes *a priori*. She is an academic artist in the truest and least insulting sense."

One of the last books Sinclair was able, owing to her poor health, to write at her full powers was *The New Idealism* (a more serious and considered work than her earlier *Defence of Idealism*). It is some tribute to the powers of her mind that it should have elicited from Bertrand Russell the following praise in the *Nation and Athenaeum*: "The present reviewer considered that the book is one of the best defences of idealism that have appeared in recent years. It shows admirable patience in mastering books with which the author does not agree [some of these are by Russell himself], and does complete justice to their merits. Particularly, the well-deserved tribute to Professor [Samuel] Alexander shows a generous appreciation which is not as common in philosophy as it ought to be."

Once regarded as important on both sides of the Atlantic, Sinclair's works became neglected from about 1930. Nor is this, as it has been called, "an enigma": it is because, since she suffered from Parkinson's disease from the mid-1920s, her last three or four novels—from *The Rector of Wyck* onwards—were undoubtedly weak, and, as more or less all critics concur, over-concerned with psychoanalysis. Sherard Vines wrote that she was "philosophical by study and naive in her views of life." Not a major novelist, she was at her best, for all the "sentimentalities, ultra-heroisms and shaky military details" (Vines), an interesting and in certain respects pioneering and experimental one. She did not, as we have been assured more than once, "invent" the term "stream-of-consciousness" (this derives from William James), but she did make an attempt to achieve this in her fiction, and she probably was the first literary critic to apply the term specifically to literature. Her chief fault was that her novels subordinated character to ideas. Her ideas were never superficial, but none of her experiments were completely successful—possibly owing to what Vines called her naïveté about life, and to her brave over-willingness to write about aspects of it to which (she freely admitted) she had never been exposed.

PRINCIPAL WORKS: *Novels*—Audrey Craven, 1897; Mr. and Mrs. Nevill Tyson, 1898 (in U.S.: The Tysons); Two Sides of a Question, 1901 (in U.S.: Superseded); The Divine Fire, 1904; The Helpmate, 1907; The Judgment of Eve, 1907; Kitty Tailleur, 1908; The Creators, 1910; The Flaw in the Crystal, 1911; The Combined Maze, 1913; The Three Sisters, 1914; Tasker Jevons: The Real Story, 1916 (in U.S.: The Belfry); The Tree of Heaven, 1917; Mary Olivier: A Life, 1919; The Romantic, 1920; Mr. Waddington of Wyck, 1921; The Life and Death of Harriet Frean, 1922; Anne Severn and the Fieldings, 1922; A Cure of Souls, 1923; Arnold Waterlow, 1924; The Rector of Wyck, 1925; Far End, 1926; The Allinghams, 1927; The History of Anthony Waring, 1927; Fame, 1929. *Short stories*—The Return of the Prodigal, 1912; Uncanny Stories, 1923; Tales Told by Simpson, 1930; The Intercessor, 1931. *Verse*—Nakiketas, 1886; Essays in Verse, 1891; The Dark Night, 1924. *Other*—The Three Brontës, 1912; A Journal of Impressions in Belgium, 1915; A Defence of Idealism, 1917; The New Idealism, 1922.

ABOUT: Boll, T.E.M. Miss May Sinclair, Novelist, 1973; Brewster, D. and Birrell, A. Dead Reckonings in Fiction, 1924; Kaplan, S. J. Feminine Consciousness in the Modern British Novel, 1975; Klein, L. S. (ed.) Encyclopaedia of World Literature in the 20th Century, 1986; Seymour-Smith, M. Macmillan Guide to Modern World Literature, 1986; Vines, S. 100 Years of British Literature, 1950; Zegger, H. D. May Sinclair, 1976. *Periodicals*—Bookman March 1905; Dial May 22, 1922; Nation and Athenaeum August 5, 1922; New York Times September 7, 1919; Outlook October 1919.

## SINCLAIR, UPTON (BEALL) (September 20, 1878–November 25, 1968), American novelist and polemicist, was born in Baltimore, Maryland, the

son of Upton Beall Sinclair, a salesman in wholesale liquor, and his wife, the former Priscilla Harden. When his father's business failed he moved (1888) to New York and became a hat salesman. Young Upton worked his way through schools and ended up at the City College of New York (1893–1897) and Columbia (1897–1901).

Sinclair belongs less to the history of literature than to that of American socialism and Utopianism; to him the novel was merely a journalistic weapon, and it is on his virtues as a journalist, and not as a literary figure, that he should be judged. He was nominated for the Nobel Prize for Literature in 1932, but the committee is said to have felt that the award itself, for all their admiration, would be carrying matters too far. Still, Sinclair was "an event in nature," and he was a genuine reformer. Like his friend Carl Sandburg, he was ultimately respected, even if he was not always agreed with.

From 1892 Sinclair supported himself by writing, at first for adventure papers and comic strips. Meanwhile he taught himself the major European languages. For years before trying out a "serious" novel, *Springtime and Harvest* (later called *King Midas*, 1901), he was grinding out juvenile fiction; he claimed to have written almost two million words per year.

Sinclair quit Columbia before graduating, and went to live in a shack in Quebec: at this time he was very romantic, and still inspired by poetry, specifically by "Jesus, Hamlet, and Shelley"; he eschewed the materialism of America. His *The Journal of Arthur Stirling* (1903) was accepted by the few that read it as the true thoughts of a young decadent poet, as it was published under the name of Stirling. Then Sinclair's thoughts turned to socialism. He had been reading the novels of Jack London, and with London himself he founded (1905) the Intercollegiate Socialist Society. In 1906 he was heavily defeated when he ran as socialist candidate for the U.S. House of Representatives from New Jersey.

Sinclair achieved overnight fame with the publication of *The Jungle*. Refused by five publishers, he had it published himself. It is one of the most directly influential books ever issued in that it spurred progressive legislators to establish meat-inspection standards. The novel's protagonist is Jurgis Rudkus, a poor Lithuanian immigrant, whose work life in the Chicago stockyards is related with memorably repulsive, but absolutely accurate, realism. Indignation wrote this book for Sinclair, and he never equaled it. Its lack of literary virtue perhaps enhances its reformist effectiveness. It had two main theses. First, it demonstrated that the Beef Trust was keeping the wages of its employees down to a bare minimum; secondly, it showed that the Trust was knowingly selling diseased beef to the public. President Theodore Roosevelt read the book and sent for its author. Sinclair gave him hard evidence, and he pressed for passage of the Pure Food and Drug Act (1906). Dr. H. W. Wiley, a chemist in the department of agriculture, proved the deleterious effect of preservatives in canned food (in the novel a finger is found in a can of meat). As a result, conditions in the stockyards were improved. When the idealistic Sinclair, started to give the president further advice, Roosevelt famously said: "Tell him to go home and let me run the government." The book sold in the millions.

Sinclair put all his *Jungle* royalties into the founding of Helicon Hall, the Helicon Home Colony, near Englewood, New Jersey. Of those who joined the utopian community, the young Sinclair Lewis was to become the most notable. Among its visitors were William James and John Dewey, who approved it in principle, though it was unjustly thought by many of the public to be merely a nest for "free love." One of the more indignant of them probably burned it down (1907)—the origins of the fire are still disputed.

Much later (1933), when Sinclair joined the Democratic Party in order to run for the governorship of California on an End Poverty ticket (he won the nomination but lost the election), he wrote *I, Governor of California and How I Ended Poverty*, a utopian novel. Theodore Dreiser supported him in his bid for office; Franklin D. Roosevelt liked him and might well have taken note of his reforming ideas, but, as Samuel Eliot Morison put it in his *Oxford History of the American People*, the "fat cats" of California thought otherwise, and they put Sinclair forward as a "communist." In fact, unlike so many other left-wing Americans, he never fell for Stalin at all.

Sinclair formed a traveling theater for the performance of socialist drama, and began to associate himself with the ideas of the economist Henry George. His next important fictional polemic was *King Coal* (1917), in which he tried to do for the coal mines what he had already done for the meat industry; in this he was less successful. Although a pacifist, he supported American entrance into World War I, and thus found himself at odds with the socialists. He became more and more a muckraker, and in 1922 in *The Goose Step* presented the universities not as the hotbeds of sedition that they were supposed by many to be, but rather as centers of reaction and "literary annexes to Wall Street."

Sinclair does not require literary appraisal. His more important novels after *The Jungle*, some of them well and vividly written in his journalistic way, include *Boston* (1928), in which an elderly Brahmin woman acquires a conscience and goes to work in a factory, where she meets Sacco and Vanzetti. The book is a moving account of one of the greatest miscarriages of justice of the twentieth century.

Sinclair also created a kind of superman troubleshooter, Lanny Budd, who first appeared in *World's End* (1940). Lanny is the illegitimate son of a munitions millionaire who becomes intimate with most of the world's leading politicians and businessmen. A secret agent, he voices Sinclair's own naive but kindly notions about world affairs. The dozen or so books about him were widely translated, and sold in the hundreds of thousands. The 1942 installment, *Dragon's Teeth*, won its author a Pulitzer Prize.

There is a portrait of Sinclair in Floyd Dell's novel *An Old Man's Folly* (1926). He wrote on pretty well every subject (telepathy, alcoholism, economics, and Jesus are among them). The chief objection to the consideration of him as a literary writer has been, and continues to be, that his characters are in no way real, that they are but puppets in his scheme to popularize socialism.

Sinclair was undoubtedly an earnest man. (His 1903 statement, "My Cause is the Cause of a man who has never yet been defeated, and whose whole being is one all-devouring, God-given holy purpose" has been held against him in this regard, but his courage and determination were never in question. Gandhi, Shaw, Kennedy, and countless others as eminent, were all obliged to take him seriously. Sinclair's books and manuscripts are at the Lilly Library, Indiana University.

PRINCIPAL WORKS: *Novels*—The Jungle, 1906; The Moneychangers, 1908; King Coal, 1917; Oil!, 1927; Boston, 1928; World's End, 1940 (Lanny Budd); Dragon's Teeth, 1942 (Lanny Budd); The Return of Lanny Budd, 1953. *Other*—The Bourgeois Literature, 1905; The Helicon Home Colony, 1906; The Overman, 1907; The Fasting Cure, 1911; The Sinclair-Aston Letters: Famous Correspondence Between Socialist and Millionaire, 1914; The Brass Check, 1919; This World of 1949 and What To Do About It, 1949; Mental Radio, 1962; The Autobiography of Sinclair, 1962. *As editor*—The Cry for Justice, 1915.

ABOUT: Blinderman, A. (ed.) Critics Upon Upton inclair, 1975; Cook, F. J. Muckrakers, 1972; French, W. (ed.) 20th Century American Literature, 1980; Harte, J. L. This is Sinclair, 1938; Gottesman, R. and Silet, C. L. P. The Literary Manuscripts of Sinclair, 1972; Harris, L. Sinclair: American Rebel, 1975; Kazin, A. On Native Grounds, 1942; Yoder, J. A. (ed.) Sinclair, 1975. *Bibliography*—Gottesman, R. Sinclair: An Annotated Checklist, 1973. *Periodical*—New York Times December 27, 1968.

---

**SINGER, ISRAEL JOSHUA** (November 30, 1893–February 10, 1944), Polish-American Yiddish novelist, wrote: "I was born in the town of Bilgeray, a part of Poland, which was then in the Russian Empire. My father was a Rabbi. When I was a mere infant my family moved to Leoncyzn and there I spent my childhood. Later, we moved to Warsaw, where I was prepared for a rabbinical career.

"At the age of eighteen I decided that I did not want to be a clergyman and I gave up on my theological studies. I wanted to have a modern education and proceeded to acquire one by taking casual lessons with inexpensive private tutors while earning my livelihood by doing all kinds of odd jobs.

"In 1915 the German army occupied Warsaw, and for some time I was compelled to do manual labor for the military conquerors. In 1917, right after the outbreak of the Russian Revolution, I moved on to Kiev, Ukraine, where I succeeded in obtaining employment as a proofreader on a Yiddish newspaper. It was in Kiev that I started to write short stories in my spare time. In 1918 I married Genia Kupfersteck, who, like myself, had come to Kiev from Poland. We have one son. [Later another was born.]

"We lived in Russia up to the end of 1921, and those years were a period of continuous civil war and pogroms attended by starvation. Towards the end of 1921 we returned to Warsaw, which in the meantime had become the capital of the independent Polish Republic.

"Back in Warsaw I published a collection of short stories under the title of the opening story, *Pearls*. When the book reached New York this story was brought to the attention of Abraham Cahan, editor of the *Jewish Daily Forward*. Mr. Cahan reprinted the story and I was invited to become a regular contributor to the *Forward*, both as a writer of fiction and as a news correspondent. I have contributed to it ever since.

"In the fall of 1926 I made an extensive trip through Soviet Russia as a special traveling correspondent of the *Forward*, a trip which lasted several months. Upon my return to Poland I wrote and published a book called *The New Russia*.

"In the summer of 1932 I landed on the shores of the United States for the first time. I came to New York for a three months' visit in connection with a stage version of my novel, *Yoshe Kalb*, which was produced by Maurice Schwartz at the Yiddish Art Theatre in the fall of that year. In 1933 the novel was published in an English translation entitled *The Sinner*. In the winter of 1934 I returned to the United States with my wife and son and made New York our home. Here I wrote *The Brothers Ashkenazi*, a novel which has been translated into English, Danish, Swedish, and Dutch. A stage version was subsequently produced by the Yiddish Arts Theatre. My own dramatization of *East of Eden* was produced in the fall of 1939 by Jacob Ben-Ami at the National Theatre, New York . . . Politically I am a believer in the democratic system of government. Among my favorite writers I give first place without hesitation to Stendhal, Flaubert, and Tolstoy."

---

Israel Joshua Singer was the elder brother of the more widely known Nobel Prize winner Isaac Bashevis Singer (1908–1991), and the younger brother of the novelist Esther Kreitman (1891–1954). He was the son of Bathsheba and Pinchos Mendel Singer. Both of his grandfathers had been rabbis. For long, until Isaac Bashevis Singer began to attract really widespread attention (this was after Israel's death), he was regarded as the leading writer of his prolific family. While markedly narrower in range, and markedly less intellectual than Isaac, Israel was a considerable writer. In terms of Yiddish literature, he is a major figure; in international terms he is also important, most particularly for his *chef d'oeuvre* and most objective work, *The Brothers Ashkenazi*. He was a writer of raw, uncompromising power; his emotionalism, with his relish for the sordid, was typical of one who was in essence a naturalist—and he was gifted both as a teller of tales and as a penetrating psychologist. He developed from a skillful traditionally Yiddish storyteller, writing in a contrivedly archaic mode, to an often elegant and always verbally economic one. In this aspect at least he is as important as Isaac Bashevis: as a Yiddish author who helped to preserve this vigorous and colorful language from the death with which it has for so long been threatened.

Singer was both more politically engaged than his brother and more directly and specifically influenced by the European naturalist movement, initiated by the fiction of Zola and his many followers in other countries. He was hotly concerned, especially in his earlier books, with the (frequently zestful) portrayal of squalor. By nature rebellious and dissatisfied, he had run away, at eighteen, from the education and ideas offered to him by his parents.

During his years in Kiev Singer became increasingly disillusioned with the Soviet system. This turned to an extreme bitterness, later expressed in two novels, *Shtol un azyn* (1933; translated as *Blood Harvest* and then again, this time by his son Joseph, as *Blood and Steel*) and in *Khaver Nakhmen* (1939; translated as *East of Eden*). The latter is in two parts, the first about a poverty-stricken Polish peddler, Mattes Ritter, the second about his brother Nachmann, who, like the author, was an idealist attracted by the Soviet experiment, but who grew to detest it. Louis Kroenenberger, writing in the *New York Times*, found it disappointing after the major and much praised novel *The Brothers Ashkenazi*, which had appeared in English in 1936; but he applauded its "vigorous presentation," and thought it "human and interesting." The *Times Literary Supplement* (1933) thought it "almost too well written in that the reader cannot fail to enter in imagination the lowest depths of mental and physical agony." What useful end could be served, the reviewer asked—but conceded that this was a difficult question to answer "with justice."

Singer's first novel to appear in English had been *Yoshe Kalb* (1932, translated as *The Sinner*), the novel upon which his play of the same title was based—indeed, it appeared so quickly in its English version because of the play's great success in New York. He had previously almost given up on writing, but his mentor Abraham Cahan encouraged him to persevere with this book—and then published it for him serially in the *Forward* before it was issued in book form. Like the earlier tales, it had a hasidic setting: among rabbis of nineteenth-century Galicia. It was Singer's harshest and most

bitter portrayal of the state into which the hasidic movement was beginning to decline by the late nineteenth century: from the inspired and genuinely mystical sect of the previous century into a set of cliques squabbling for power and influence. The novel was preferred by most reviewers to the play, which Alter Brody in the *Nation* (1933) described as a "vulgarized . . . adaptation." Brody criticized the "one-sided picture of Chassidism," but admitted that most of the types were "individually authentic"; he endorsed in particular the portrait of the lascivious and greedy Rabbi Melech. Harold Strauss in the *New York Times* (1933) was rather more positive: "Like most historical epics, *The Sinners* has the feeling of being an anonymously created folk-tale handed on by word of mouth from person to person. . . . Written often with shrewd humor, always with intense and cynical realism, it is at once a hysterical bit of self-mockery and a narrative forged to heroic proportions. If it often leaves us dissatisfied with its human motivation, it compensates us with the grandeur of its epic moods." Critics almost always found it hard to deal with the extent of Singer's deep bitterness. This translation of the novel was re-issued in 1965 as *Yoshe Kolb*, with an invaluable introduction by Isaac Bashevis Singer. Apart from *The Bothers Ashkenazi*, which is his undoubted masterpiece, other translations of Singer's works are available: one of these, of his last novel *Di Mishpokhe Karnovski* (translated as *The Family Carnovsky*), is often regarded as the best of his remaining work. It deals with the disastrous effect of the "Enlightenment" ("Haskalah": a movement among late eighteenth- and nineteenth-century Jewry to acquire modern European culture and to achieve "assimilation"). The story of three generations of originally Polish Jews, and of their experiences in Germany and America, it is an examination of the incompatibility of Germanness and Jewishness. In *Library Journal*, S. L. Simon wrote of *The Family Carnovsky*: "[Singer develops] a study of a Jewry bent on assimilation, and blindly ignoring the signs indicating doom . . . [it is] a big engrossing novel which this reviewer kept likening to *Ship of Fools* [by Katherine Anne Porter]."

Some of Israel Singer's best stories, including the famous "Perl" ("Pearls")—a wonderfully evocative and eloquent tale of a hypochondriacal miser—may be read in *The River Breaks Up* (1938). Harold Strauss, this time writing in the *Nation* (1938), commented that "Singer, in casting off archaism, has not cast out his Jewish heritage. . . . He understands not only environmental reactions but also the symbols by which men live. Therein lies his power, a power that is not to be measured in terms of Yiddish literature alone."

The majestic and powerful three-volumed *The Brothers Ashkenazi*—"the most important novel of Jewish life so far published in English" claimed Philip Rahv in the *Nation* (1936)—for which Singer will be chiefly remembered, is set in the Polish city of Łodz, and covers the period from the early years of the nineteenth century until 1919. It is about the gradual taking over of the textile industry in the city by Jewish entrepreneurs, and its eventual collapse. In the last part, when we reach the third generation of the Ashkenazi family, Max is the brilliant student, his brother Jacob the hedonist. Yet the latter dies for the former when their enterprise is destroyed by the advent of war and by Polish anti-Semitism. Like all Singer's work, the novel is replete with sordid description and depictions of terrible events, yet the British novelist J. D. Beresford, reviewing it in the *Manchester Guardian*, wrote that despite there being "scarcely a figure in the book . . . that is admirable or even attractive. . . . we can never question the truth and sincerity." The novel is monumental because, its economic and lucid style apart, it tells of a whole way of life that has vanished, and because, as Leon Crystal wrote in the *Saturday Review of Literature*, Singer "does not lionize the enterprising resourceful industrialist . . . his fellow-Jews do not fare with him any better than do the Russians, Poles, or Germans." Singer, with this novel, established himself as the greatest of those Yiddish novelists who felt the full impact of the naturalist movement. But, as in Zola's and the other naturalists' fiction, good actions and intentions are inevitably canceled out by historical events over which human beings have no control.

As a dramatist Singer had a greater success with adaptations of his novels than with his few original plays. His dramatic version of *The Family Karnovsky*, made in the year before his sudden and unexpected death from a heart attack, was well received. Schwartz's adaptation of *The Brothers Ashkenazi* (1937) was also moderately successful.

One of Israel Joshua Singer's finest and gentlest books, the unfinished memoirs *Fun a velt vos iz nishto mer (Of a World That Is No More)*, appeared in Yiddish in 1946, and was translated (by his son Joseph) in 1970.

PRINCIPAL WORKS IN ENGLISH TRANSLATION: *Novels*—The Sinner (tr. M. Samuel) 1933 (reissued as Yoshe Kolb in 1965); Blood Harvest (tr. M. Kreitman) 1935 (tr. as Steel and Iron by J. Singer 1971); The Brothers Ashkenazi (tr. M. Samuel) 1936; East of Eden (tr. M. Samuel) 1939; the Family Carnovsky (tr. J. Singer) 1969. *Short stories*—The River Breaks Up (tr. M. Samuel) 1938. *Memoirs*—Of a World That Is No More (tr. J. Singer) 1970.

ABOUT: The autobiographical material quoted above was written for Twentieth Century Authors, 1942. Dictionary of American Biography, 1973; Howe, I. and Greenberg, E. (eds. and introducers) A Treasury of Yiddish Stories, 1954; Klein, L. S. (ed.) Encyclopedia of World Literature in the Twentieth Century, 1971–1984; Liptzin, S. The Maturing of Yiddish Literature, 1970; Madison, C. Yiddish Literature: Its Scope and Major Writers, 1968; Norich, A. The Homeless Imagination in the Fiction of Israel Joshua Singer, 1991; Roback, A. A. The Story of Yiddish Literature, 1940; Sinclair, C. The Brothers Singer, 1983; Singer, I. B. In My Father's Court, 1962; Singer, J. B. A Day of Pleasure, 1969; Singer, J. B. *introduction to* Yoshe Kalb, 1965; Singer, I. J. Of a World That Is No More, 1971; Steinbach, A. A. (ed.) Jewish Book Annual 26, 1968. *Periodicals*—Commetary March 1966; Contemporary Literature 22, 1981; Manchester Guardian October 30, 1936; Nation May 10, 1933; August 12, 1938; September 17, 1938; New York Herald Tribune Books, March 26, 1939; New York Times March 12, 1933; March 12, 1939; February 11, 1944; Saturday Review of Literature September 12, 1936; Times Literary Supplement April 15, 1939; April 20, 1983; Wilson Library Bulletin January 1937.

**SINGMASTER, ELSIE** (August 29, 1879–September 30, 1958), American novelist, wrote: "I was born in the Lutheran parsonage at Schuylkill Haven, Pennsylvania. My father, Dr. John Alden Singmaster, was chiefly of Pennsylvania German stock, my mother, Caroline (Hoopes) Singmaster, chiefly English Quaker. When I was four years old, we moved to Macungie, Pennsylvania, where my father was born. We returned there later for  many summers, when we lived in Brooklyn, New York and in Allentown, Pennsylvania. I was graduated from high school in Allentown, then went for a year to the West Chester Normal School, then to Cornell. At the end of my sophomore year, having taken most of the English courses under a far too elective system, I returned home. Five years later I entered Radcliffe, completed my course, and was graduated in 1907.

"When I was about eleven years old, my teacher directed us to write a story. Already I dreamed of becoming an author and I composed a story of a paper doll. The plot was not wholly original; when the story was printed in a teachers' journal my conscience began to trouble.

"In my early acquaintance with the Pennsylvania Germans I was extremely fortunate. The 'local color' buoyed, I suspect, many of my early stories into port, which had not a great deal to recommend them. My father's later connection with the Lutheran Theological Seminary at Gettysburg, which gives Seminary Ridge its name, provided me with material about the battle and the Civil War.

"I married, in 1912, Harold Lewars, a musician, who died in 1915. During this time I lived in Harrisburg, Pennsylvania [then I returned to Gettysburg]. I have no children. I like to raise trees and flowers and I am very fond of music, though I am a very poor musician I still love reading above all other sports."

---

Elsie Singmaster lived for many years in Gettysburg, Pennsylvania. Her attic studio overlooked Seminary Ridge, the site of America's preeminent school for the Lutheran ministry, of which her father had long been president. The importance of home, family, education, her Lutheran religion, and her German pioneer heritage played a prominent role in all of her work, from an introductory biography of Martin Luther written in commemoration of the four hundredth anniversary of the Reformation to her histories and stories of Gettysburg and the Civil War.

Singmaster showed her love of Pennsylvania, and her passion for its early German settlers—known as the Pennsylvania Dutch—by capturing their folkways in many historical novels and children's stories. Most of these stories were set in Millerstown, a thinly disguised Allentown, where, as a

*New York Times* reviewer of her *Bred in the Bone and Other Stories* (1925) wrote, "lives change little with the generations and are almost void of drama and variety." The reviewer went on to call the book "chronicles of wholesome people whose conversation has a piquant flavor and whose customs both tickle our humor and command our respect."

Reviewers praised Singmaster for her first-hand knowledge and sympathetic treatment of her subjects. Her restrained style matched the simple lifestyles and religious beliefs of the Pennsylvania Dutch—and was more convincing (but less satirical) than the work of Helen Reimensnyder Martin, who wrote in the same genre. Singmaster, although adept at creating convincing characters and delving into local lives, was frequently criticized for a stiff, sluggish, and sentimental style that lacked imagination and seemed over-detached. For example, in a *New York Tribune* review of *The Hidden Road* (1923), the story of Phoebe, a young woman from Millerstown whose desire for learning rivals her yearning for a man, F. F. Van de Water wrote that Singmaster "comes little closer to life than to pass it on the other side of the street." The character of Phoebe typifies many of Singmaster's female protagonists, as in *Katy Gaumer* (1915), *Ellen Levis* (1921), and *Keller's Anna Ruth* (1926), novels that portray young Pennsylvania Dutch girls who seek to rise above their provincialism, get an education, fall in love, or find prosperity. For younger readers, Singmaster created Virginia, who, home alone in *Virginia's Bandit* (1929), becomes preoccupied with thoughts of freedom and arranges to rob the local post office, and Nellie Strickhouser, who takes up teaching, falls in love, and ventures into a cave of bootleggers in *You Make Your Own Luck* (1929).

While not entirely devoid of humor, Singmaster created characters that seemed all too appropriate to the pen of a minister's daughter in their portrayal of small-town families with fixed notions of high morality and concerns for traditional values. The eponymous protagonist of *Bennett Malin* (1922) learns the bitter lessons of "selling one's soul" after abandoning his clergyman's vocation to be a writer—a career in which he succeeds only briefly, and then by plagiarizing.

Singmaster's interest in the Civil War, whose most decisive battle was fought near Seminary Ridge, resulted in *Gettysburg: Stories of the Red Harvest and the Aftermath* (1913, reissued in 1993), which recounted the three days of the 1863 battle and the thoughts of the old men who survived to remember its significance. She also wrote two juvenile titles about the battle, one being *Swords of Steel: The Story of a Gettysburg Boy* (1933).

PRINCIPAL WORKS: *Fiction*—Gettyburg: Stories of the Red Harvest and the Aftermath, 1913; Katy Gaumer, 1915; Basil Everman, 1920; Ellen Levis, 1921; Bennett Malin, 1922; The Hidden Road, 1923; Bred in the Bone and Other Stories, 1925; Keller's Anna Ruth, 1926; What Everybody Wanted, 1928; The Magic Mirror, 1934; TheLoving Heart, 1937; A High Wind Rising, 1942; The Isle of Que, 1948. *Juvenile*—When Sarah Saved the Day, 1909; When Sarah Went to School, 1910; Emmeline, 1916; The Long Journey, 1917; John Baring's House, 1920; Virginia's Bandit, 1928; You Make Your Own Luck, 1929; A Little Money Ahead, 1930; The Young Ravenels, 1932; Swords of Steel, 1933; Stories of Pennsylvania, 3 vols., 1937-1938; Rifles for Washington, 1938; Stories to Read at Christmas, 1940; I Heard of a River: The Story of the Germans in Pennsylvania, 1948. *Biography*—Short Life of Martin Luther, 1917; I Speak for Thaddeus Stevens, 1947. *History*—Book of the United States, 1926; Book of the Constitution, 1926; Book of the Colonies, 1927; Pennsylvania's Susquehanna, 1950.

ABOUT: The autobiographical material quoted above was written for Twentieth Century Authors, 1942. Overton, G. The Women Who Make Our Novels, 1977; Warfel, H. R. American Novelists of Today, 1973. *Periodicals*—Bookman February 1931; Ladies' Home Journal March 1925; New York Times November 8, 1925; November 22, 1942; June 8, 1947; October 1, 1958; New York Tribune June 10, 1923; New Yorker May 31, 1947; Publishers Weekly October 27, 1958; Scholastic February 12, 1938; April 4, 1941.

**SITWELL, EDITH** (September 7, 1887–December 9, 1964), English poet, anthologist, and critic, was born in Scarborough, the oldest child and only daughter of Sir George Reresby Sitwell, 4th Baronet, and Lady Sitwell, the former Lady Ida Emily Augusta Denison. She was the sister of Osbert and Sacheverell Sitwell, both writers, with whom she established a collective reputation for their outspokenness toward the accepted modes of all things from poetry to politics.

Sitwell grew up in a world of wealth and leisure, spending much of her early life—until she was twenty-six—at her family's home, Renshaw Hall, or at her grandmother's home in Scarborough. Educated at home, she developed an interest in music and, thanks to her governess Helen Rootham, the French symbolists.

In 1913 Sitwell published her first poem in the *Daily Mirror*. In 1914 she and Rootham moved to London and took a flat together. After the publication of her first collection of poems, *The Mother*, Sitwell became increasingly active in literary circles, at one time becoming an intimate friend with Gertrude Stein. From 1916 to 1921 she edited a yearly anthology of new poetry, *Wheels*. Through the publication, which was a reaction to the conservatism of the Georgian poetry of the time, Sitwell recognized the talent of Wilfred Owen, and in 1919 *Wheels* was the first to publish his work. However, Sitwell's notoriety was not complete until 1923, with her poetry recital, *Facade*, set to music by her friend William Walton. Sitwell spoke from behind a curtain on which was painted the figure of a woman with her eyes closed and her mouth open. Her aim, the author was later quoted as saying, was to challenge the rhythmical flaccidity, the verbal deadness, and the expected patterns of some of the poetry immediately preceding this. She did that through poems such as "Trio for Two Cats and a Trombone," with its exciting rhythms which seem to move the listener (and reader) along in a whirl of sound and meaning:

Long steel grass—
The white soldiers pass—
The light is braying like an ass.
See
The tall Spanish jade
With hair black as nightshade
Worn as a cockade!
Fee
Her eyes glasconade
And her gowns parade
(As stiff as a brigade).
Tee-hee!

That same year she had published *Bucolic Come-dies*, very different in their technique and tone from the more experimental works in *Facade*. These, as in her following collections, *The Sleeping Beauty* and *Troy Park*, were more romantic and el-egiac in tone, calling on images of beauty and na-ture which she had enjoyed as a child. Many reviewers were critical of Sitwell's tendency to fill her work with too many clever or unintelligible im-ages, commenting, as W. R. Benét had in *Outlook*, that "The maze is full of color schemes, but some-times it is a labor to untangle the yarn. What she cares most for are the design and the opportunity for fandango." Others were more generous. Babette Deutsch, in the *Literary Review*, complimented the author, saying: "Magic she has, and lyricism, and color," and in the *Saturday Review of Litera-ture* Louis Untermeyer praised her "pages which sparkled with observations that are both fantastic and exact."

Sitwell changed tone again with her next major work, a poetic satire on contemporary mores, *Gold Coast Customs*. In it the author contrasts the cus-toms of a tribe of cannibals to the life of her present-day England. The book received mixed re-views, being described as anything from brilliantly chequered with bold expressions (*Nation*) to a joke on the British reading public (*New York Evening Post*). Again, the ambiguity of her language was called into question, with the *Saturday Review of Literature* commenting that while "No one wishes her to restrain the richness of her vocabulary . . . her work . . . is most powerful where it is most simple," and the *New York Evening Post* simply stated: "She is so clever that she succeeds in being dull." However, the *New Republic* came to her res-cue, explaining that "by elaborating her imagery to the point of an extraordinary pictorial virtuosity, Miss Sitwell reveals anew her amazing technical re-sources."

During the 1930s Sitwell, who was now living in Paris, wrote little poetry. Her friend and room-mate, Rootham, had been going through an extend-ed illness (she died in 1938), for which Sitwell took on the responsibilities of her care, and much of her writing of this time was produced out of financial need. These works included critical studies (*Alex-ander Pope*), biographies (*Victoria of England, English Eccentrics*), anthologies (*Pleasures of Poet-ry*), and novels (*I Live Under a Black Sun*). These were generally warmly received by the likes of such reviewers as E.M. Forster, Robert Graves, and Katherine Anne Porter.

Sitwell's poetic silence was broken with the out-break of World War II, with the publication of *Street Songs, Green Song, Song of the Cold*, and *The Shadow of Cain*, collections which were more concerned than her earlier works with the atrocities of war and human suffering produced by the mod-ern world. In these, also, she began to show a deep spiritualism and belief in God, which culminated, in 1955, with her acceptance into the Catholic Church. We can see the beginnings of this in her poem about the London air raids of 1940, "Still Falls the Rain":

Still falls the rain—
Dark as the world of man, black as our loss—
Blind as the nineteen hundred and forty nails
Upon the cross

Still falls the rain
With a sound like the pulse of the heart that is changed
to the hammerbeat
In the Potters Field, and the sound of impious feet. . . .

In the works that followed, some critics accused the poet of repeating herself, but her reputation was once again revived with her last collections, *Gar-deners and Astronomers, The Outcasts*, and *Music and Ceremonies*. The volumes, still showing her concern for sound and sound patterns, were praised for their beauty. Still, F. R. Leavis thought that she, along with her brothers Osbert and Sacheverell, be-longed "to the history of publicity, rather than of poetry."

During her life, Sitwell was awarded honorary degrees from Oxford, Leeds, Durham, and Shef-field. In 1933 she was awarded the medal of the Royal Society of Literature. Standing over six feet tall, she dressed in flowing robes of an almost Medi-eval style and was known for the large aquamarine rings she liked to wear, though she insisted that she was no eccentric, just more alive than most people. Her career spanned over fifty years, and traced the development of English poetry from the musical experiments of the post-World War I era to the so-cial concerns after World War II. She was a great lover of the arts, especially painting, and was known for the kindness and support she gave to young artists.

Her autobiography, *Taken Care Of*, was pub-lished in 1965.

PRINCIPAL WORKS: *Poetry*—The Mother and Other Poems, 1915; (with O. Sitwell) Twentieth Century Harlequinade and Other Poems, 1916; Clown's Houses, 1918; The Wooden Pega-sus, 1920; Facade, 1922, new ed. 1950; Bucolic Comedies, 1923; The Sleeping Beauty, 1924; (with O. Sitwell and S. Sit-well) Poor Young People, 1925; Troy Park, 1925; Twelve Po-ems, 1926; Rustic Elegies, 1927; Popular Song, 1928; Five Poems, 1928; Gold Coast Customs, 1929; The Collected Poems of Edith Sitwell, 1930, 1968; In Spring, 1931; Selected Poems, 1936; Poems New and Old, 1940; The Song of the Cold; The Shadow of Cain, 1947, rprt. 1977; The Canticle of the Rose: Selected Poems, 1920–1947, 1949; Facade, 1951; Gardeners and Astronomers: New Poems, 1953; Collected Poems, 1954; Edith Sitwell, 1960; The Outcasts, 1962; Music and Ceremo-nies, 1963; Selected Poems, 1965. *Criticism*—Poetry and Criti-cism, 1926, 1969; Aspects of Modern Poetry, 1934, 1972. *Biography*—Alexander Pope, 1930; rprt. 1972; The English Eccentrics, 1933, rev. 1957, 1960; I Live Under a Black Sun, 1937, 1938, new ed. 1948; English Women, 1942; Fanfare for Elizabeth, 1946, 1989. *As editor*—The Pleasures of Poetry: A Critical Anthology vol. I, 1930; vol. II, 1931; vol. III, 1932; Edith Sitwells Anthology, 1940; Look! The Sun, 1941; The

American Genius, 1951; The Atlantic Book of British and American Poetry, 1958; Swinburne: A Selection, 1960. *As compiler*—Planet and GlowWorm: A Book for the Sleepless, 1944; A Book of the Winter, 1950, 1951; A Book of Flowers, 1952. *Autobiography*—Taken Care of, 1965. *History*—Bath, 1932, 1948, rprt. 1981, 2nd ed. 1984.

ABOUT: Bradford, S., Clerk, H., et al. The Sitwells: And the Arts of the 1920s and 1930s, 1996; Dictionary of National Biography 1961–1970, 1981; Encyclopedia of World Literature in the 20th Century, 1984; Norton Anthology of English Literature, vol. 2, 5th ed. 1986; Seymour-Smith, M. Guide to Modern World Literature, 1986; Who's Who, 1963. *Periodicals*— Literary Review August 23, 1924; Nation and Athenaeum March 2, 1929; New Republic October 30, 1929; New York Evening Post October 12, 1929; New York Times Book Review October 27, 1966; New Yorker April 11, 1964; Outlook December 30, 1925; Saturday Review February 9, 1929; Saturday Review of Literature December 5, 1925.

## SITWELL, (FRANCIS) OSBERT (SACHEVERELL)

(December 6, 1892–May 4, 1969), English satirist, poet, short story writer, and

memoirist, was born in London, the second child and first son of Sir George Reresby Sitwell, 4th Baronet, and Lady Sitwell, the former Lady Ida Denison, daughter of the first Earl of Londesborough. His older sister was the writer Edith Sitwell, and his younger brother was the poet and art critic Sacheverell Sitwell. The family was descended from the Saxons of Northumberland.

Sitwell was first educated at home by tutors and governesses before being sent away, at the age of ten, to a private boarding school. Here the young boy did not do well. Excelling neither at sports nor his studies, he was often bullied by the other boys. He emerged from the school with both his health and his self respect impaired. His next experiences, at Eton (1906–1909), proved happier and gave him the opportunity, as the *Dictionary of National Biography 1961–1970* described it, to read and to educate himself in his own way. In fact he has often been quoted as saying that his education was gotten during the holidays from Eton. Here also he was able to make friends, many of whom he would have for the rest of his life.

Instead of attending university after his graduation from school, he began preparing for a military career, attending a crammer. But he failed his entrance exam to Sandhurst, the British equivalent of West Point. However, due to his father's persistence, the boy was given a commission in 1911 in the Sherwood Rangers and then, in 1912, in the Grenadier Guards, during which time he saw action in France fighting in the battle of Loos. On leave in England in 1916, Sitwell was diagnosed with having blood poisoning as a result of a cut he had gotten in the trenches, and he remained ill for many years. He was released from the army in 1919 with the rank of captain.

During the war, Sitwell's distaste for militarism, nationalism, and the horrors of war increased. One

day, near Ypres, he expressed his feelings in a poem, "Babel." The piece was published in the *Times* (London) in 1916.

He continued to write, authoring a series of satirical war poems printed in the *Nation*, for which he used the pseudonym Miles. With these and other works, such as a collection of verse, *Twentieth Century Harlequinade* (1916), Sitwell began to sharpen not only his distaste for profiteers, scamps, fools, and the selfishly sentimental, but his skill at expressing these feelings with irony and satire. Through his writing the author hoped, according to *Current Biography 1965*, to shock his countrymen out of their intellectual lethargy and to laugh away the pretention and hypocrisy of the postwar newly rich, a desire he shared with his siblings. In 1919 he and his brother mounted an exhibit of controversial modern French art in London, and in 1922 the two collaborated with their sister on her experimental verse sequence, *Facade*, which was set to music by William Walton.

Sitwell's first verse collection, *Argonaut and Juggernaut*, appeared in 1919. The book received mixed reviews, with the author described by the *Nation* as being moved to write by the unbelief in the ideals of other people rather than by the passionate force of ideals of his own. The book was followed by several other collections, including *Out of the Flame, England Reclaimed*, and its companion volume *Wrack at Tidesend*, in which he was able to display lyrical talents which the *Spectator* called admirable.

*The Triple Fugue*, a collection of six short stories, was Sitwell's first published work of prose. The book, which prompted R. Aldington in *The Saturday Review of Literature* to compare the author to Oscar Wilde, Bernard Shaw, and Max Beerbohm, was quickly followed by Sitwell's first novel, *Before the Bombardment*, which was called a remarkable piece of work. Other novels, travel books, essay collections, plays, and criticisms followed. These include his *Discursions on Travel, Art, and Life; All at Sea* (a social tragedy in three acts); *Dumb Animal and Other Stories*; and *Miracle on Sinai*. But perhaps Sitwell is best known for his series of autobiographical novels, the first of which, *Left Hand, Right Hand!*, appeared in 1945. It was followed by *The Scarlet Tree, Great Morning, Laughter in the Next Room, Noble Essences*, and *Tales My Father Taught Me*. The memoirs were all well received by reviewers.

In addition to his novels and collections, Sitwell served as a regular contributor to such publications as the *Times, Spectator, Harper's, New Yorker*, and *Atlantic Monthly*. He also contributed poems to many of the anthologies of the time, and, with Herbert Read, he acted as literary editor of the quarterly *Arts and Letters*.

Sitwell, who never married, succeeded his father in the baronetcy in 1943. In 1946 he received an honorary LL.D. from St. Andrews, and in 1951 he received an honorary D. Litt from Sheffield University. From 1951 to 1958 he was a trustee of the Tate gallery. He was a member of the Society of

Authors, the Royal Society of Literature, and the American Institute of Arts and Letters. Increasingly incapacitated by Parkinson's disease, Sitwell finally died in Italy at Montegufoni, a medieval castle that his father had acquired in 1909.

On the whole, Sitwell is considered to be a writer of notable richness and elegance as well as a keen critic of society. As he was summed up by Evelyn Waugh: "The interest of Sir Osbert's fame is that it rests on a lifetime of uninterrupted development and enrichment. His natural growth . . . continued into late middle age so that his latest book has always been his best. He acquired his reputation first, then seriously settled down to earn it."

PRINCIPAL WORKS: *Poetry*—(with E. Sitwell) Twentieth Century Harlequinade and Other Poems, 1916; Argonaut and Juggernaut, 1919, 1921; At the House of Mrs Kinfoot, 1921; Out of the Flame, 1923; England Reclaimed, 1927, 1949, reprt. 1972; Collected Satires and Poems, 1931; Selected Poems Old & New, 1943; Wrack at Tidesend, 1952; On the Continent, 1958. *Short stories*—Triple Fugue, 1924, 1925, reprt. 1970; Dumb Animal and Other Stories, 1930 (in U.S. 1931); Penny Foolish, 1935, reprt. 1967; A Place of One's Own, 1941, (published as A Place of One's Own and Other Stories, 1961); Alive-Alive Oh!, 1947; Death of a God and Other Stories, 1949; Collected Stories, 1953; Tales My Father Told Me, 1962; Queen Mary and Others, 1974. *Novels*—Before the Bombardment, 1926; The Man who Lost Himself, 1929, 1930; Miracle on Sinai, 1933, 1934, new ed. 1948; Those Were the Days, 1938. *Drama*—(with S. Sitwell) All At Sea: A Social Tragedy in Three Acts for First-Class Passengers Only, 1927, 1928; Gentle Caesar, 1942; The Cindarella Complex, 1960. *Travel*—Discursions on Travel, Art and Life, 1925, reprt. 1970; Writers of Content, 1932 (published as Writers of Content and Other Discursions, 1950); Escape With Me! An Oriental Sketchbook, 1939, 1940, new ed. 1948; The Four Continents, 1954, 1972. *Autobiographies*—Left Hand, Right Hand!, 1944; The Scarlet Tree, 1946; Great Morning!, 1947, reprt. 1972, Laughter in the Next Room, 1948, reprt. 1972; Nobel Essences, 1950, reprt. 1972. *Nonfiction*—The People's Album of London Statues, 1928; The True Story of Dick Whittington, 1945. *Essays*—(with E. Sitwell And S. Sitwell) Trio: Dissertations on Some Aspects of National Genius, 1938, reprt. 1970; Sing High! Sing Low!, 1944; Pound Wise, 1963.

ABOUT: Contemporary Authors vol. 2 1978; Current Biography 1965; Dictionary of National Biography 1961–1970, 1981; Who's Who 1968. *Periodicals*—Athenaeum November 28, 1919; Nation December 6, 1919; January 15, 1949; Nation and Athenaeum October 23, 1926; New York Times May 14, 1944; Saturday Review of Literature August 2, 1924; June 22, 1946; Spectator July 4, 1952.

# SITWELL, SACHEVERELL (November 15, 1897–October 1, 1988), English art critic and poet, was born in Scarborough, the younger son of Sir

George Reresby Sitwell, 4th Baronet, and Lady Ida Sitwell, the former Lady Ida Denison. His older sister was the poet Edith Sitwell, and his brother was the popular satirist, poet, and autobiographer Osbert Sitwell. He was educated at St. Davids, Eton College, and Balliol College, Oxford University, but he claimed mostly to be self-taught.

At the outbreak of World War I, the seventeen-year-old Sitwell joined the Special Reserve of the Grenadier Guard. It was at this time that he began to write poetry. From the start the two older siblings were supportive of their younger brother. A lover of art, especially Italian art of the seventeenth and eighteenth centuries, he published his first work of prose, *Southern Baroque Art: A Study of Painting, Architecture and Music in Italy and Spain in the 17th and 18th Centuries*, in 1924. The volume, which would be the first of many books he would write on the topic of art and art criticism, was well received by reviewers.

As a poet, he was classically minded (unlike his brother and sister, who were more Romantic), and was influenced by the Italian futurist Marinetti and also by the Chinese classical poets. His collections of poetry include such titles as *The Thirteenth Caesar, and Other Poems*, which caused a reviewer in the *Times* (London) to comment that "Mr. Sitwell has spirited us into a nimbler element and reminded us that beauty is a living flame which can always be renewed in poetry," and *Doctor Donne and Gargantua: The First Six Cantos*, which was called lovely poetry by the *Saturday Review of Literature*.

In a *New Yorker* interview, Sitwell was quoted as saying "Thank goodness, I've always had a small income of my own and was able to travel when young. Travel is a great advantage to writers." Sitwell used this advantage well, turning out a number of travel books that were, as his other works, well praised. But probably the youngest Sitwell is best known for his autobiography, *All Summer in a Day*.

As a whole, Sitwell's work, be it poetry, criticism, or travel log, is generally summed up as packed with art and music and picturesque items of history, as the *New York Times* described *Roumanian Journey* in 1938. But, as some critics have asserted, Sitwell's ability is limited. The beauty and poetry with which he fills his pages is overly concerned with method and sometimes artificial. And, as one critic has pointed out, his elegant and assured manner conceals a lack of poetic conviction and self-confidence.

In 1925 Sitwell married Georgia Doble, of Montreal. The two had two sons.

PRINCIPAL WORKS: *Art and music criticism and history*—Southern Baroque Art: A Study of Painting, Architecture and Music in Italy and Spain of the 17th and 18th Centuries, 1924, 1930, reprt. 1971; German Baroque Art, 1927, 1928; The Gothik North: A Study of Medieval Life, Art, and Thought, 1929 (in U.K.: The Gothik North in three volumes: The Visit of the Gypsies, These Sad Ruins, The Fair-Haired Victory); Spanish Baroque Art: With Buildings in Portugal, Mexico, and other Colonies, 1931, reprt. 1971; Mozart, 1932, reprt. 1970; Liszt, 1934, rev. 1956; Conversation Pieces: A Survey of English Domestic Portraits and Their Painters, 1936, 1937; Narrative Pictures: A Survey of English Genre and its Painters, 1937, 1938, reprt. 1972; German Baroque Sculpture, 1938; British Architects and Craftsmen: A Survey of Taste, Design, And Style During Three Centuries, 1600–1830, 1945; Monks, Nuns, and Monasteries, 1965; Baroque and Rococo, 1967; Gothic Europe, 1969. *Poetry*—Doctor Donne and Gargantua: First Canto, 1921, 1930; The Hundred and One Harlequins, 1922; Doctor Donne and Gargantua: Canto the Second, 1923; The Thirteenth Ceaesar, and Other Poems, 1924, 1925; (with E. Sitwell and O. Sitwell) Poor Young People, 1925; Doctor Donne And Gargantua: Canto the Third, 1926; The Cyder

Feast, and Other Poems, 1927; Two Poems, Ten Songs, 1929; Doctor Donne and Gargantua: The First Six Cantos, 1930; Collected Poems, 1936; Selected Poems, 1948. *Travel*—Roumanian Journey, 1938; The Netherlands: A Study of Some Aspects of Art, Costume, and Social Life, 1948, rev. 1974; Spain, 1950, 2nd ed. 1953, 1962; Portugal and Maderia, 1954; Denmark, 1956; Arabesque and Honeycomb, 1957, 1958; (illus. T. A. Jones) Malta, 1958; Bridge of the Brocade Sash: Travels and Observations in Japan, 1959, 1970; (with T. Schneiders) Austria, 1959; Golden Wall and Mirador: From England to Peru, 1961; Great Temples of the East, 1963. *Autobiography*—All Summer in a Day: An Autobiographical Fantasia, 1926.

ABOUT: Contemporary Authors vol. 21–24, 1977; Seymour-Smith, M. Guide to Modern World Literature, 1986; Who's Who, 1968. *Periodicals*—New Republic April 27, 1927; New Statesman March 8, 1924; New York Times August 14, 1938; Saturday Review of Literature August 30, 1930; Spectator April 19, 1924; Times Literary Supplement November 6, 1924, October 28, 1926.

---

**SIWERTZ, SIGFRID** (January 24, 1882–1970), Swedish poet, dramatist, novelist, and theater critic wrote (in English): "I was born in a wing in the

Academy of Arts in Stockholm, and Stockholm has since then been my home and my love. At the University of Upsala I studied philosophy and the history of literature from 1901 to 1905. My literary début took place in 1904 with a book of verse. Since then I have been living the life of an author and have published forty-five works, verse, short stories, travel books, essays, dramas and comedies, of which seven have been played at the Royal Theatre in Stockholm. During the last twenty years, I have traveled much, in 1923 to the Fiji Islands and Sumatra for an ethnographical film, in 1926 with a caravan through Abyssinia, in 1937 all around South America. I have visited the United States three times. In 1932 I was made a member of the Swedish Academy. Most of my novels have been translated into German and French, some into Italian, Dutch, and English. My psychological play, *Ett Brot (A Crime)* was played in all the Scandanavian capitals and in Prague. In sports I prefer yachting and often live in the summer out amongst the 'skerries' of the Swedish coast."

---

Martin Seymour-Smith wrote in his *Guide to World Literature* that the "huge fictional output, much of it topical, of the popular author Sigfrid Siwertz . . . is distinguished by intelligence and consistency of attitude, but two or three books stand out above the rest." Seymour-Smith identifies these as his autobiographical works (untranslated); his two novels, *Selambs* (1920, translated as *Downstream*) and *Det stora varuhuset* (1926, translated as *Goldman's*); and *Jonas och draken* (*Jonas and the Dragon*), a scarifying account of the world of conscienceless journalism.

Siwertz began as a "decadent," somewhat self-consciously pessimistic (and erotic) poet and story writer. His atmospheric tales of Stockholm were in the manner of his great contemporary Hjalmar Söderberg, thirteen years his senior, and clearly a major influence upon him, as upon so many other Scandinavian writers. Siwertz was also influenced by the melancholy Bo Bergman.

In 1907 Siwertz went to Paris, where he attended a series of lectures by the philosopher Henri Bergson. The effect of the Frenchman's optimistic and semi-mystical vitalism brought him into maturity. He abandoned the fin de siècle mannerisms of the early poetry and stories in favor of a more positive and sociological—if still defiantly romantic—approach. His first book of real note was the classic children's adventure story *Mälar-pirater* (The pirates of Lake Mälar, 1911). He abandoned "decadence," and became one of the *tiotalisterna*, the writers of the decade 1910–1920 who created the realistic novel in Sweden. Siwertz was a member of the Swedish Academy, and helped to judge the award of the Nobel Prize for literature from 1932 until his death.

The massive *Downstream*, which reflects Siwertz's reading in French, particularly of the naturalist Zola, relates the story of the Selamb children, left as orphans in their early youth because of the greedy ferocity of their grandfather—an unforgettable portrait of sheer evil. They grow up degenerate and twisted, the result of heredity and a cruel environment. The theme, as an unsympathetic reviewer in the *Dial* stated it, is "the rise of a family to mammonish power by the sale of its soul." C. E. Stork, the translator of Söderberg and an expert in Swedish literature, gave a more informed judgment in the *Literary Review*: "Siwertz has intelligently followed the models of his two older contemporaries, Verner von Heidenstam and Per Hallström [the first a poet and historical novelist who helped to change the course of Swedish prose, the second a short story writer and dramatist]. Without the salient genius of either of these, he is more accessible to the average reader. . . . he is never insipid or obvious. Few better balanced masters of fiction are writing today." The novel reaches its climaxes in terrifying scenes of sexual primitivism, and in the account of the family's war racketeering. Siwertz was always an outspoken critic of the capitalist system, and never became reconciled to it.

*Goldman's* is a series of linked stories set in a department store in Stockholm. It opens with two penniless lovers who enter the store, are accidentally locked in for the night, and spend their bridal night in the store's finest and most expensive bed. The *New York Times* reviewer felt that this was always "warm and loving," and gave a "record of real people . . . It is vastly different from any Scandinavian literature that has to date found its way into English translation." This last observation, though, may have reflected the unusual excellence of the translation, rather than its uniqueness in Swedish fiction: the *Times Literary Supplement* reviewer wrote of the "excellent English" of E. G. Nash's translation, justifiably commenting on the inferiority of so many other English versions from the Swedish.

Critics found the post-*Downstream* Siwertz to be at his best in the short story. He dealt with both artistic and more robust types with humor and sensitivity.

Siwertz was no more than a minor poet, his most successful book having been *Taklagssölet* (1923, Rooftree ale), a dramatic piece written for the dedication of the new Town Hall for Stockholm. As a dramatist he was superficial by comparison with Hedberg, Hallström, or Ernst Didring, but he was skilled—and was never trite. Most of his plays, none of which have been translated, were produced in the 1930's, and deal with contemporary issues.

PRINCIPAL WORKS IN ENGLISH TRANSLATION: Downstream (tr. E. Classen) 1922; Goldman's (tr. E. G. Nash) 1929. Stories *in* Stork, C. W. (ed. and tr.) Modern Swedish Masterpieces, 1923; Larsen, H. A. (ed.) Sweden's Best Stories, 1928.

ABOUT: The autobiographical material quoted above was written for Twentieth Century Authors, 1942. Bach, G. The History of the Scandinavian Literatures, 1938; Columbia Dictionary of European Literature, 1947; Gustafson, A. A History of Swedish Literature, 1961; Seymour-Smith, M. Macmillan Guide to Modern World Literature, 1986. *Periodicals*—Dial August 1923; Literary Review March 24, 1923; New York Times March 23, 1930; Times Literary Supplement October 10, 1929.

## SKINNER, CONSTANCE LINDSAY (1877?–March 27, 1939), American novelist, historian, and poet, was born on an isolated fur trading post on the

Peace River in British Columbia, Canada, the daughter of Robert James Skinner, a factor, and Annie (Lindsay) Skinner. Her education consisted primarily of reading from her parents' well-stocked library, although she received some formal instruction from tutors and private schools in Vancouver, to which her family moved when she was fourteen. A precocious writer, she began composing short stories before she was ten, wrote a children's operetta at fourteen, and by sixteen—when she went to live with an aunt in California—had already published short stories and written for British Columbia newspapers. By the age of eighteen, she was writing drama and music criticism, as well as a variety of occasional pieces, for the *Los Angeles Times* and the *Los Angeles Examiner*.

Her early novel "*Good-Morning, Rosamond!*" was followed by historical studies, *Pioneers of the Old Southwest* and *Adventurers of Oregon*, both published as part of the Yale University Press Chronicles of America series.

Most of Skinner's novels are historical adventures written for young people. These tales are set in disparate locales—from Kentucky (*Becky Landers*) to Central America (*The Tiger Who Walks Alone*)—but Skinner's favorite literary terrain was her native northwestern Canada, the setting of such juvenile novels as *Roselle of the North* and *Red Man's Luck*. *Red Willows*, which Skinner considered the best of her novels, is an adult tale of adventure that examines pioneer life in northwestern Canada. Reviewing it in the *New York Herald Tribune Books*, Horace Gregory lauded her "accurate interpretation of the Northwest," noting, "It would be well to remember . . . that Miss Skinner is a poet of unusual distinction and that the quality of her prose has given her story the attributes of conviction and steadily growing power."

*Beaver, Kings and Cabins*, perhaps her best known book, is a vivid account of the North American fur trade from colonial times to the 1930s. Praising it in the *Saturday Review of Literature*, Henry Steele Commager wrote, "[her] history has all the flavor of a personal chronicle, and it is written out of a rich background of experience and of understanding." At the time of her death, she was the editor of Farrar and Rinehart's Rivers of America series, of which she oversaw the first six volumes. In 1940 the Women's National Book Association instituted an award in Skinner's name, presented annually to a woman who has made outstanding contributions to the world of books. Though only a minor writer, Skinner retains significance as a chronicler of late-nineteenth-century pioneer life in Canada.

PRINCIPAL WORKS: *Novels*—Good-Morning, Rosamond!, 1917; The Search for Relentless, 1925; Red Willows, 1929. *Poetry*—Songs of the Coast Dwellers, 1930. *History*—Pioneers of the Old Southwest: A Chronicle of the Dark and Bloody Ground, 1919; Adventurers of Oregon: A Chronicle of the Fur Trade, 1920; (with C. Wissler and W. Wood) Adventurers in the Wilderness (vol. 1 of The Yale Pageant of America series) 1925; Beaver, Kings and Cabins, 1933. *Juvenile*—Silent Scott, Frontier Scout, 1925; Becky Landers: Frontier Warrior, 1926; The White Leader, 1926; The Tiger Who Walks Alone, 1927 (in U. K.: The Jaguar of San Cristobal); Roselle of the North, 1927; The Ranch of the Golden Flowers, 1928; Andy Breaks Trail, 1928; Red Man's Luck, 1930; Debby Barnes, Trader, 1932; Rob Roy: The Frontier Twins, 1934. *As editor*—Rivers of America vols. 1–6, 1937–1939.

ABOUT: Eastman, A. (and others) Constance Lindsay Skinner, Author and Editor: Sketches of Her Life and Character, with a Checklist of Her Writings, 1980; Dictionary of Literary Biography vol. 92, 1990; Fuller, M. (ed.) More Junior Authors, 1963. *Periodicals*—Library Journal April 15, 1939; New York Herald Tribune Books November 10, 1929; New York Times March 28, 1939; Poetry August 1930; Saturday Review of Literature September 30, 1933; Wilson Library Bulletin May 1939.

## SKINNER, CORNELIA OTIS (May 30, 1901–July 9, 1979), American author, actress, and monologist, was born in Chicago, Illinois, the only child of a theatrical couple,

Otis Skinner and Maud (Durbin) Skinner. Maud Skinner pursued her professional acting career until shortly after her marriage, but Otis Skinner, who had played with Edwin Booth in the 1880s, went on to become one of the best known actors of his generation; he

also wrote a number of books on the theater. Cornelia Skinner spent much of her early childhood on the road, with her father's touring companies. Her parents bought a house in Bryn Mawr, Pennsylvania, and there she attended the Baldwin School and Bryn Mawr College. Leaving college after her sophomore year, she sailed for Paris, where she took classes at the Sorbonne and studied acting—classical drama under Émile Dehelly of the Comédie Française and modern methods with Jacques Copeau.

She made her professional acting debut with a small role in *Blood and Sand*, the bullfighting play based on Ibañez's novel in which her father starred. It opened in Buffalo, New York, in August 1921 and moved to Broadway the following month. Recognition as an actress came slowly. In a 1951 *New Yorker* essay, she recalled her early difficulties on the stage: "Thanks to my father's name, managers would see me once, but they seldom looked at me twice. Grotesquely thin and gawky, I did my best to disguise a chronic shyness with an appearance of world-weariness." Her first leading role came in 1935, when she played Candida Morell in George Bernard Shaw's *Candida*. Later, during the 1940s and 1950s, she won plaudits for her leading role in *Theatre, The Searching Wind, Lady Windermere's Fan,* and *Major Barbara*.

Although Skinner's career as an actress in the legitimate theater progressed somewhat fitfully, she achieved success as a writer and monologist while still in her twenties. *Captain Fury*, a play she wrote for her father, was produced in 1925. In the late 1920s, inspired by the monologues of Ruth Draper, Skinner began writing and performing her own "monodramas," witty and satirical character sketches based on the lives of historical subjects. These included *The Wives of Henry VIII, The Empress Eugénie,* and *The Loves of Charles II.*

Skinner took her solo performances all over the United States and to London, where she appeared for the first time in 1929. She adapted Margaret Ayer Barnes's best-selling novel *Edna, His Wife* into a series of monologues, which she presented to London audiences in 1937, and to those in America the following year. For her one-woman musical revue *Paris '90*, which premiered in New York in 1952, Skinner created and played fourteen characters associated with fin-de-siècle France.

By the 1930s, Skinner had gained widespread popularity for her humorous personal essays, which appeared in the *New Yorker, Ladies' Home Journal, Harper's Bazaar,* and other periodicals. Her early essay collections, including *Dithers and Jitters* and *Soap Behind the Ears*, were anthologized in *That's Me All Over.* Her best known book, *Our Hearts Were Young and Gay*, is a memoir of her European adventures in the early 1920s, written in collaboration with her Bryn Mawr friend Emily Kimbrough. Well-received by critics, it quickly became a best-seller and inspired a 1944 Paramount film of the same title. *Family Circle*, an affectionate chronicle of her parents' lives and of her own early years, was also a success. *New York Times* (1948) reviewer G. W. Gabriel observed that the book "probably could have been composed only by someone with Miss Skinner's dual authority as an actress and authoress."

Skinner's collections of humorous essays continued to enjoy popular success during the 1950s. In a *Christian Science Monitor* review of one of these volumes, *The Ape in Me*, Pamela Marsh noted, "Miss Skinner writes like a jet-propelled butterfly—an impression of light, funny, tossed-off absent-mindedness masking her disciplined prose." Skinner had success on Broadway with *The Pleasure of His Company*, a two-act comedy of manners she wrote with Samuel Albert Taylor. With Skinner in a crucial supporting role—that of the ex-wife of a footloose playboy who utterly disrupts his daughter's wedding—the play opened at New York's Longacre Theatre in October 1958, and was later taken on tour.

Later in life, Skinner undertook more ambitious writing projects. Her book *Elegant Wits and Grand Horizontals*, an examination of Parisian society during the "belle époque," grew out of the research she had done for her revue *Paris '90. Madame Sarah*, her biographical study of the French actress Sarah Bernhardt, elicited a more mixed response from reviewers. In a front-page *New York Times Book Review* (1967) notice, André Maurois wrote, "Cornelia Otis Skinner has written the life of Sarah Bernhardt as it must be written, with love and devotion." Skinner's last book, *Life With Lindsay and Crouse*, is a biography of the American playwrights Howard Lindsay and Russel Crouse.

In addition to her various theatrical and literary activities, Skinner wrote scripts for the radio serial "William and Mary," and was a frequent guest on the radio program "Information Please." In 1928 she married Alden Blodget, with whom she had one son and raised two adopted children.

PRINCIPAL WORKS: *Humor and essays*—Tiny Garments, 1932; Excuse It, Please, 1936; Dithers and Jitters, 1938; Soap Behind the Ears, 1941; Popcorn, 1943 (in U.K. only); That's Me All Over: All the Favorite Absurdities from Dithers and Jitters, Soap Behind the Ears, and Excuse It, Please! along with Tiny Garments, 1948; Nuts in May, 1950; Bottoms Up! 1955; The Ape in Me, 1959. *Memoirs*—(with E. Kimbrough) Our Hearts Were Young and Gay, 1942; Family Circle, 1948 (in U.K.: Happy Family). *Drama*—(with S. A. Taylor) The Pleasure of His Company, 1959. *History*—Elegant Wits and Grand Horizontals: A Sparkling Panorama of "La Belle Epoque," Its Gilded Society, Irrepressible Wits and Splendid Courtesans, 1962. *Biography*—Madame Sarah, 1966; Life with Lindsay and Crouse, 1976.

ABOUT: American Women Writers vol. 4 1982; Contemporary Authors Vols. 17–20, 1976; Current Biography 1942; 1964; 1979; Robinson, A., Roberts, V., and Barranger, M. (eds.) Notable Women in the American Theatre, 1989; Who's Who 1979–1980. *Periodicals*—Christian Science Monitor September 17, 1959; New York Times September 5, 1948; July 10, 1979; New York Times Book Review September 24, 1950; January 8, 1967; New Yorker October 27, 1951; Times (London) July 10, 1979.

**SKLAR, GEORGE** (June 1, 1908–May 16, 1988), American novelist and playwright, wrote: "I was born in Meriden, Connecticut, within sound of a munitions plant, where my father worked as a gun assembler. . . .

"At Meriden High School, after I had won an essay contest on the subject of the Child Labor Amendment, I added writing to the imposing list of careers which were the shifting subjects of my

Algeresque fantasies. I also fancied myself as a budding young movie critic, and the publication of some half dozen letters—very technical disquisitions on the then silent art—in Richard Watts' movie column in the *New York Herald Tribune* seemed to confirm a definite leaning toward writing.

"Even at that optimistic age, I was aware that it wasn't a very practical way of earning a living. Being very realistic, I decided I'd teach—of all things,  Latin—and devote spare time and summers to writing. So I majored in the classics at Yale and wrote one-act plays on the side. One of them, an expressionistic piece called *Pity* was produced by the Yale Dramat and received with such enthusiastic applause by a very undiscriminating Derby Day audience that I was then and there lost to the teaching profession. That, plus the fact that I graduated with the Class of '29 into a depression economy which would have none of teachers, nor, it seemed, anything else.

"So, having tried the practical and found it to be highly impractical, I switched horses. I enrolled in Professor George Pierce Baker's famous 47 Workshop in playwriting at the Yale department of drama. While there, in collaboration with Albert Maltz, I wrote a play called *Merry Go Round*. It was produced simultaneously at the University Theatre and on Broadway. Five other plays followed, all produced between the years 1932–1939. I then signed a writing contract with Columbia Pictures and sweated out a four-year stretch, which, aside from salary, I regretted.

"In 1945, I turned to the writing of novels, a medium which I increasingly prefer. *The Two Worlds of Johnny Truro* appeared in 1947; *The Promising Young Men* in 1951; and *The Housewarming* in 1953. I am now at work on my fourth.

"My work would probably be described as of the realistic school. I believe that a writer should reflect the times and society in which he lives and, more importantly, the aspirations of the human heart. I live in Los Angeles with my wife and three children; work six days a week, on a regular schedule, slowly and painfully."

---

George Sklar's early plays were written in collaboration with Albert Maltz and Paul Peters, and were produced during the 1930s by the nonprofit group Theatre Union. They were fairly typical examples of the proletarian drama of that period. The best known was *Stevedore*, a crude but effective three-act drama about black dockworkers in New Orleans and their white bosses. The *New York Herald Tribune Books* wrote, "*Stevedore* is frankly propaganda, but doesn't forget to be theatrical. It is crude, one-sided, blatant, but swift, passionate and melodramatic, driving a hard fist with proletarian passion."

The novels that Sklar began writing after anti-communist blacklisting made theatrical work increasingly difficult for him were more sophisticated than his plays, but they rarely received good reviews. His first novel, *The Two Worlds of Johnny Truro*, was the story of a love affair between a teenage boy and an older married woman. In it, wrote the *Saturday Review of Literature*, "Sklar has set himself the difficult and delicate task of making such a relationship understandable and acceptable. I do not think he has quite succeeded; not because the situation itself is impossible, but because the two people involved, Johnny, aged seventeen, and Helen Borden, thirty-one, are inconsistent and unreal." The last of his four novels, *The Identity of Dr. Frazier*, the story of a successful physician who reveals racist and anti-Semitic impulses when drunk, elicited similarly ambivalent responses. Anthony Boucher wrote of it in the *New York Times Book Review*, "Sklar poses an absorbingly provocative question here, which causes the reader to follow his story with intense fascination—and an exasperated sense of frustration when the author finally manages to round everything out without ever really coming to grips with his problem. In the light of its significant theme, it's a disappointingly superficial novel . . . but it's a hard story to stop reading."

Sklar returned to playwriting in the 1960s and 1970s with two socially conscious dramas that harkened back to his earliest work: *And People All Around*, which concerned the murders of three civil rights workers, and *Brown Pelican*, a drama on the theme of environmental degradation.

PRINCIPAL WORKS: *Drama*—(with A. Maltz) Peace on Earth: An Anti-War Play in Three Acts, 1934; (with P. Peters) Stevedore: A Play in Three Acts, 1934; Life and Death of an American, 1942; (with V. Caspary) Laura: A Play in Three Acts, 1945; And People All Around, 1967; Brown Pelican, 1974. *Novels*—The Two Worlds of Johnny Truro, 1947; The Promising Young Men, 1951; The Housewarming, 1953; The Identity of Dr. Frazier, 1961.

ABOUT: The autobiographical material quoted above was written for Twentieth Century Authors First Supplement, 1955. Contemporary Authors Vols. 1–4, 1967. *Periodicals*—Nation May 2, 1934; New York Herald Tribune Books July 15, 1934; New York Times May 18, 1988; New York Times Book Review September 3, 1961; Saturday Review of Literature May 10, 1947.

**SLADE, CAROLINE (BEACH)** (October 7, 1886–June 25, 1975), American novelist, was born in Minneapolis, the daughter of William G. McCormick and his wife. At the age of seven she moved with her family to Saratoga Springs, New York, where she lived for the rest of her life. She attended Skidmore College, married John A. Slade, a lawyer and lecturer at Skidmore, and began a career as a social worker. She became the  first executive director of the Saratoga County Board of Child Welfare, but retired in 1933 to devote herself to writing. The six novels that followed were based on her social-work experience.

Slade's subject was the social dynamics of urban poverty, and in deference to that subject many reviewers willingly overlooked her fairly obvious shortcomings as a novelist: her "failure to employ a rigid economy of means as well as her flat projection of character and rudimentary sense of pace," as George Mayberry described them in the *New Republic*. Yet even Mayberry was won over by the documentary-life force of Slade's work. Of *Lilly Crackell*, the story of an impoverished mother who fights the welfare bureau for the right to keep her legitimate and illegitimate children, Mayberry wrote, "This long episodic novel, Dickensian both in its sympathy with all forms of suffering and in its unashamed melodrama, is a staggering account of the underside of American life. . . . In spite of its weaknesses it is worth a dozen of the shapely, shrewd and at bottom sterile novels that the more fluent writers annually deposit."

Slade's most fervent champion was probably James T. Farrell, whose own naturalistic novels, including the *Studs Lonigan* trilogy, had affinities with hers. Farrell thought her works "major social indictments, and they deal with the most vital problem which faces American people today." Writing in the *Saturday Review of Literature*, Farrell maintained that from such a novel as *Job's House*, the story of an elderly couple forced to give up their one possession—their house—and move into a slum, "we can learn more of the social character of good and evil, of hope and despair, of beauty and ugliness than we can in all the vague and abstract moral preachments of the critics who are so concerned with some abstracted soul of man that they see, in honest pictures of human souls, only ugliness and wallowing misery."

Several of Slade's novels were used as texts in college social work courses, and in more recent years feminist critics have praised them—especially *Sterile Sun*, *Margaret*, and *Mrs. Party's House*, three novels about prostitution—for their frank depiction of the oppression of women.

PRINCIPAL WORKS: *Novels*—Sterile Sun, 1936; The Triumph of Willie Pond, 1940 (in U.K.: Poor Relief); Job's House, 1941; Lilly Crackell, 1943; Margaret, 1946; Mrs. Party's House, 1948.

ABOUT: American Women Writers, 1982; Blair, V. and others (eds.) The Feminist Companion to Literature in English, 1990; Warfel, H. R. American Novelists of Today, 1951. *Periodicals*—New Republic June 7, 1943; New York Times June 29, 1975; Saturday Review of Literature April 12, 1941.

**SLATER, HUMPHREY** (1906–September 1, 1958), English novelist, journalist, left-wing activist, and artist, was educated at Sedbergh and Tonbridge schools. He studied painting at the Slade School of Art, London, where he was awarded scholarships and prizes.

Slater's devotion to art was sidetracked by the rise of fascism in Europe. At the age of twenty-four he had traveled to Soviet Russia, where he became a convert to communism. In 1932, just before Hitler's takeover, he was actively involved in anti-Nazi rallies in Berlin. He traveled in France and Spain

as a political journalist, and then fought against Franco. He was appointed Chief of Operations in the International Brigade (1936–1938). He also edited a short-lived, leftist magazine, *Polemic*.

Slater was active in the Second World War. He initiated the training of the Home Guard, then he served as a gunner in the R.A.F. before joining the army. An instructor in tactics, he had reached the rank of major when he was invalided out of the service in 1944. From then onwards his health was always poor. For the remaining twelve years of his life he devoted himself (as his *Times* obituarist and fellow-toper John Davenport made  clear) to drinking, good conversation, playing chess, "talking away books," and, occasionally, to the writing of fiction (and a political book, in which he made a final official farewell to his earlier Stalinism, *Who Rules Russia?*).

Slater's first novel, *The Heretics*, was reprinted in 1991. This is a two-part tale, in which the lives of three children who take part in the Children's Crusade are seen in parallel with those of three Cambridge students who become involved in the Spanish civil war. This passionately anti-war (and anti-Catholic and anti-communist) book might have lasted better had Slater been able to take more trouble with it. Reviewing it in the *Nation*, Diana Trilling aptly summed up its virtues and defects: "Unfortunately Mr. Slater's good sense and taste, while they save him from the common pitfalls of current political fiction, seem also to put a strong brake on his novelistic energy. *The Heretics* is lamentably underwritten in point of character development and drama. It is only the suggestion of the fine novel it might have been, a seed rather than a full growth." Other reviewers pointed out the historical howlers in it. All seemed to agree that it was a good novel marred by poor research and hasty writing.

Slater's later novels are of less interest and were less discussed, although *Conspirator* attracted some attention because it was filmed (indifferently, by Victor Saville), with Robert Taylor and Elizabeth Taylor (1949); but one verdict on it pronounced the "story better than the stars." Once again reviewers praised the original conception, of an army officer, also a Soviet spy, who marries a loyal English girl; and once again they faulted Slater for his careless and hasty writing, his melodrama, and his implausibility. *The Calypso*, the story of a poet and his love, attracted much the same kind of criticism.

When Slater died in Spain he had an autobiography half-completed. Davenport in the *Times* lamented that this had died with him: "He had an unusually rich and full life, and it is the literary form above all others that might have enabled him to express himself with ease and freedom." Davenport went on to record Slater's "egocentricity," his eccentricity, his habit of drinking straight from the bottle, and his inability to submit to "any formal academic discipline." "Each of his novels has uniquely original touches, although he was not a natural novelist. His real interests lay in the field of philosophy, philosophy pure and, as it were, applied."

PRINCIPAL WORKS: *Politics*—Who Rules Russia?, 1955; (with C. Barnett) The Channel Tunnel, 1957. *Novels*—The Heretics, 1946; Conspirator, 1948; Calypso, 1953; The Malefactor, 1958; Three Among Mountains, 1959.

ABOUT: *Periodicals*—Christian Century October 8, 1947; Nation October 25, 1947; New York Times October 5, 1947; Times (London) September 1, 1958.

**SLAUERHOFF, JAN JACOB** (September 15, 1898–October 5, 1936), Dutch poet, novelist, dramatist, and translator, was born at Leeuwarden in the extreme north west of the Netherlands. Although a presence in the Dutch literature of his time, and one to whom an entire number of the periodical *Groot-Netherland* was devoted at his premature death, serious and prolonged interest in him was not aroused until some time after his death—in fact when the Dutch critic C. J. Kelk published his fascinating and acute study of him, *Het Leven von Slauerhoff* (The life of Slauerhoff) in 1959; he revised it twelve years later. Slauerhoff's work is better known in France than in English speaking countries.

Slauerhoff was always a rebel, not only against the middle-class society from which he originated but also, to a certain extent, even against the critics and poets who took his work up. His earliest poetry was published in 1921 in the then leading modernist literary magazine, *Het getij* (The Tide). At that time the romantic phase of Dutch poetry was just coming to a close, although the Yeats-influenced Adriaan Roland Holst was still read and admired. Slauerhoff's poetry never really quite fit into any category, and, although it was praised for its indifference to tradition, it was also much criticized for its informality. Slauerhoff was, with his strange manner, at once lyrical and sneering, struggling to discover his own voice, a lonely and in many ways tergiversating one; but he was also plain careless—heedless to advice—and undecided about whether he really wanted to pursue a literary career. Slauerhoff's *Archipel* (Archipelago), his first book of verse, gave the lie to those who had derided his technique, but received little attention on account of what his detractors described as his excessive romanticism. But Slauerhoff, who had qualified as a doctor at medical school in Amsterdam (1923), went his own way. It is only now perhaps, when the polemics of those post-World-War-I days have long passed, that his achievement (and the flaws in it) may be clearly seen.

He may now be classified, with confidence, as a modernist romantic, and as one whose own mood was "decadent" long after what is called decadence (it was never "a movement") had ceased. He is in many ways nearer to such an anticipator of modernism as the cynical, world-weary French poet Tristan (really Édouard-Joachim) Corbère, whose work he read and admired. In France Slauerhoff is usually introduced as Holland's "poète maudit."

From the time of his qualification in medicine in 1923, Slauerhoff, who was known for his anti-social and often deliberately boorish behavior, worked as a ship's doctor. In that capacity he travelled all over the world: to Java; to the Far East, where he picked up (notably from China) philosophical ideas which he expressed in his novels and several other books, including the posthumous *Een Bezoek aan Makallah* (1975, A visit to Makallah) Africa; and South America. At some time he married Darja Collin, but there are few details of this marriage except that it ended in divorce.

Slauerhoff published two of his earlier collections of poetry, *Clair obscur* (1927) and *Ost-Azi* (1928), under the name of John Ravenswood. These were collected along with most of the rest of his works (but five more, including a diary, were issued later) in the eight volumes of his *Verzamelde werken* (1940–1958, Collected works) and with his last characteristically entitled collection, published under his own name, *Een eelijk zeemansgraf* (1936, Tomb of an honest seafaring man). This poetry was disfigured by lapses into sentimentality—the obverse of Slauerhoff's cynicism—and by a maladroit carelessness. But at its best it could be extremely concentrated, beautiful and "metaphysical."

Slauerhoff's themes in his death-haunted prose were unusual in the context of their times: he treated the exotic, the foreign, the unfamiliar. His great novel *Het verboden rijk* (1932, The forbidden kingdom) is a tour de force: the life of the epic Portuguese poet Luis Vaz de Camoes (author of the Lusiads) is counterpointed with that of the antihero, a ship's radio operator, a self-portrait. Under the spell of Zen philosophy, this man's strange affinity with the sixteenth-century poet, allows him to shed his own hated personality.

The central character of *Het leven op aarde* (1934, Life on earth) is also a radio operator (significantly, a man cut off from civilization, but connected to it in a mysterious manner); this novel, distinguished by the uniquely "hoarse, shy" tone to which a Dutch critic drew attention, explores the world to which Slauerhoff gained entrance by his use of opium. These novels were the first of a projected trilogy, but death interrupted the author's plans.

Slauerhoff, one of the most original writers of his time in any language, also wrote a play, *Jan Pietersz Coen* (1931), and did several translations from the Spanish and the Portuguese. So far there is nothing detailed about him in English, but, for those who have no Dutch, the French study by L. J. E. Fessard, *Jan Slauerhoff, l'homme et l'oeuvre* (1964), is useful and interesting. Both Eddy du Perron, a leading light in Dutch literature, and the major novelist Simon Vestdijk wrote about him with affection and regard.

ABOUT: Columbia Dictionary of Modern European Literature, 1980; Kelk, C. J. Het Leven van Slauerhoff, 1971 (in Dutch); Encyclopedia of World Literature in the Twentieth Century, 1983; Meijer, R. P. The Literature of the Low Countries, 1978; Seymour-Smith, M. Macmillan Guide to Modern World Literature, 1986.

**SLAUGHTER, FRANK G(ILL) (pseudonym "C. V. TERRY")** (February 25, 1908– ), American novelist, wrote: "I was born in Washington, D.C., but when I was about five years old, my family moved to the old home on a farm about twelve miles north of Oxford, North Carolina, in the Piedmont section, where we raised tobacco and corn. My father was a rural mail carrier, operating several farms, a sawmill, and some other enterprises. Since I was rather small to walk three miles each way to a country school, my mother taught me until I was ready for the sixth grade, which I entered at the age of nine. I was always studious and an omnivorous reader, traits which have stood me in very good stead as a writer of historical novels, where much research is necessary. Even today, I find that I enjoy the research for my novels more than any other part of my work.

"At fourteen I graduated as valedictorian from the Oxford High School and at eighteen *magna cum laude* from Duke University, being a member of Phi Beta Kappa at seventeen. At twenty-two, I received my M.D. from John Hopkins Medical School and spent four years in surgical training at the Jefferson Hospital, Roanoke, Virginia. There I met Jane Mundy. We were married in June 1933 and have two sons, Frank, Jr., and Randolph  Mundy. In 1934 I came to Florida to practice surgery and was associated with a group clinic until I entered the army as major M.C. in July 1942. Promoted to lieutenant colonel in March 1944, I served at Camp Kilmer, New Jersey and on a hospital ship out of Los Angeles. In 1938 I became a Fellow of the American College of Surgeons and in 1940 was certified as a Specialist in Surgery by the American Board of Surgery.

"I began writing as a hobby in 1935 and wrote 250,000 words a year for five years, earning $12, roughly five cents a week. My first novel, *That None Should Die*, was published in 1941 and has been translated into ten foreign languages, as have most of my other books. . . .

"Writing, I think, is one of the most satisfying occupations one could have. Through it I reach millions of people, since many of my books have a larger sale in foreign countries than they do in America. I now have ten foreign publishers in addition to my American publishers."

---

Frank G. Slaughter's long list of best selling novels fall into three categories: medical, biblical, and historical. He has achieved great success in all three categories, but never with critics. "No one, I suppose, will ever accuse Dr. Slaughter of writing 'literature' but, on the other hand, I doubt that many will deny he is a whale of a spinner of tales," wrote a reviewer for the *Chicago Sunday Tribune*. Reviewers have tended to think Slaughter's medical novels have a clinical authenticity deriving from Slaughter's own experience as a physician. For example, a critic in the *New York Times Book Review* wrote of *Epidemic!*, a thriller about an imagined outbreak of bubonic plague in New York, "While the dozen or so characters in the novel are never very thoroughly explored, the sequence of events does allow Dr. Slaughter to delve into areas where he feels most at home. The book is a kind of eminently readable medical text, in which the author guides us through a brain operation, an autopsy, heart repair, and a visceral search to find a bullet."

The praise or blame of critics has made little difference to Slaughter or to his millions of faithful readers; indeed, he is proudest of the fact that none of his books have ever lost a publisher money, and he has always avoided taking on subjects he considers insufficiently "profitable." Slaughter's *Transplant* was published in his seventy-ninth year.

PRINCIPAL WORKS: *Novels*—That None Should Die, 1941; Spencer Brade, M.D., 1942; Air Surgeon, 1943; Battle Surgeon, 1944; A Touch of Glory, 1945; In a Dark Garden, 1946; The Golden Isle, 1947; Sangaree, 1948; Divine Mistress, 1949; The Stubborn Heart, 1950; Fort Everglades, 1951; The Road to Bithynia: A Novel of Luke, the Beloved Physician, 1951; East Side General, 1952; Storm Haven, 1953; The Galileans: A Novel of Mary Magdalene, 1953;(as "C. V. Terry") Buccaneer Surgeon, 1954 (in U.K.: Buccaneer Doctor); The Song of Ruth, 1954; (as "C. V. Terry") Darien Venture, 1955; The Healer, 1955; (as "C. V. Terry") The Golden Ones, 1955; Flight from Natchez, 1955; The Scarlet Cord: A Novel of the Woman of Jericho, 1956; The Warrior, 1956 (in U.K.: The Flaming Frontier); The Mapmaker: A Novel of the Days of Prince Henry, the Navigator, 1957; Sword and Scalpel, 1957; Daybreak, 1958; (as "C. V. Terry") The Deadly Lady of Madagascar, 1959; (as "G. Arnold Haygood") Deep Is the Shadow, 1959; The Crown and the Cross: The Life of Christ, 1959; The Thorn of Arimathea, 1959; Lorena, 1960; Pilgrims in Paradise, 1960 (in U.K.: Puritans in Paradise); Epidemic! 1961; The Curse of Jezebel: A Novel of the Biblical Queen of Evil, 1961 (in U.K.: Queen of Evil); Tomorrow's Miracle, 1962; Devil's Harvest, 1963; Upon this Rock: A Novel of Simon Peter, Prince of the Apostles, 1963; A Savage Place, 1964; Constantine: The Miracle of the Flaming Cross, 1965; The Purple Quest: A Novel of Seafaring Adventure in the Ancient World, 1965; Surgeon, U.S.A., 1966, 1967 (in U.K.: War Surgeon); Doctors' Wives, 1967; God's Warrior, 1967; The Sins of Herod: A Novel of Rome and the Early Church, 1968; Surgeon's Choice: A Novel of Medicine Tomorrow, 1969; Countdown, 1970; Code Five, 1971; Convention, M.D.: A Novel of Medical In-Fighting, 1972; Women in White, 1974 (in U.K.: Lifeblood); Stonewall Brigade, 1975; Plague Ship, 1976; Devil's Gamble, 1977; The Passionate Rebel, 1979; Gospel Fever: A Novel about America's Most Beloved TV Evangelist, 1980; Doctors' Daughters, 1981; Doctors at Risk, 1983; No Greater Love, 1985; Transplant, 1987. *Medical*—The New Science of Surgery, 1946 (revised as Science and Surgery, 1956); Medicine for Moderns: The New Science of Psychosomatic Medicine, 1947 (reissued as The New Way to Mental and Physical Health, 1949). *Biography*—Immortal Magyar: Semmelweis, Conqueror of Childbed Fever, 1950 (reissued as Semmelweis, the Conqueror of Childbed Fever, 1961); David, Warrior and King: A Biblical Biography, 1962. *Juvenile*—Apalachee Gold: The Fabulous Adventures of Cabeza de Vaca, 1954. *Other*—The Land and the Promise: The Greatest Stories from the Bible, 1961.

ABOUT: The autobiographical material quoted above was written for Twentieth Century Authors First Supplement, 1955. Contemporary Authors New Revision Series 5, 1982; Contemporary Literary Criticism Vol. 29, 1984; Current Biography 1942; Twentieth Century Romance and Historical Writers, 2nd ed., 1990. *Periodicals*—Chicago Sunday Tribune June 25, 1950; New York Times Book Review January 8, 1961; Satur-

day Review January 10, 1953; Saturday Review of Literature
July 29, 1950.

**SLESINGER, TESS** (July 16, 1905–February 21,
1945), American short story writer, screenwriter,
and novelist, was born in New York City, the

daughter of Anthony and
Augusta (Singer) Sles-
inger. In a life cut short in
her fortieth year by can-
cer, Slesinger had pro-
duced twenty-one short
stories, one novel, and
eight Hollywood screen-
plays. Her notebooks in-
dicated that she was
planning to get back to
"serious" fiction writing,
including a novel about her experiences in Hollywood. While her works were moderate critical and
popular successes at the time, she was largely neglected until "rediscovered" in the 1970s by editors
who were revisiting the social and political trends
of the 1930s, especially by women writers.

Slesinger's childhood was comfortable. She once
remarked that "I was born with the curse of intelligent parents, a happy childhood and nothing valid
to rebel against, so I rebelled against telling the
truth. I told whoppers at three, tall stories at four,
a home-run at five; from six to sixteen I wrote them
into a diary." Her parents encouraged her to develop her imagination and lively story-telling ability
from an early age, and had the means to send
young Slesinger to the Ethical Culture Society
School in New York, to Swarthmore College in
Pennsylvania, and to Columbia University, where
she received her B.Litt. in 1927.

In 1928, Slesinger married Herbert Solow, a
member of New York's Jewish intellectual community with leftist leanings. A disciple of Elliot Cohen,
he was one of the editors of the *Menorah Journal*
and one of the founders of *Commentary* magazine.
Through her husband, Slesinger met Clifton Fadiman, Lionel Trilling, and others active in New
York's political and publishing circles. Trilling, who
attended their wedding, remembered Slesinger in
these terms: "Her natural charm was of a daughter-
ly or youngsterly kind, and in some considerable
part consisted of her expectation of being loved, indulged, forgiven, of having permission to be spirited and even naughty." Indeed, Slesinger was to
explore the role of women from the vantage point
of the "second" lost generation—not the disillusioned Fitzgeraldesque types who fled to Europe in
the 1920s, but the Village intellectuals who turned
their disillusion into political activity and the over-
turning of traditional social codes during the de-
pression-ridden 1930s. *Mother to Dinner*,
Slesinger's first published story, in the *Menorah
Journal*, described a newlywed torn with conflicting loyalties between husband and mother. Slesinger continued to publish stories in small
magazines, most notably the *American Mercury*,
and joined the creative-writing faculty of Briarcliff
Manor, a girl's finishing school in the northern suburbs of New York City.

In 1932, around the time her marriage was dissolved by a Reno divorce, she met the "magnetic"
Maxwell Perkins, with whom she later acknowledged having an affair. Not long afterwards, she
began writing her first novel, published in 1934 as
*The Unpossessed*, sending the first fifty pages to
Fadiman at Simon and Schuster. Of the novel's
characters, Fadiman recalled: "They were unpossessed people who wanted to be possessed by something . . . and weren't." She wrote the book as a
"psychological" investigation of a Greenwich Village set—intellectuals and pseudo-intellectuals—
caught between hedonism and the demands of
strict conscience. It employs irony and a stream-of-
consciousness format to delineate the main character, Margaret Flinders, in her struggle for personal
identity. The *Nation* went so far as to describe the
theme of this "brilliant and cutting first novel" as
"on the one hand a sort of D. H. Lawrence critique
of sexual integrity, and on the other redemption by
social action."

*The Unpossessed* was a moderate critical and
commercial success. Reviewing it for the *New Republic*, T. S. Matthews wrote: "Miss Slesinger's is a
first novel of such extraordinary promise. . . . The
subject is neither fresh nor savory, but Miss Slesinger has whipped it into a very lively semblance. . . . Its conscious sentimentality, its
conscious self-mockery, in its fundamental unwillingness to be content with either, this novel is au-
thentically of our day." When Quadrangle
reprinted some of her later work in the 1970s, the
publisher wrote: "What must have been equally obvious to *The Unpossessed* 's first readers was that its
author, at twenty-nine, was the real thing, an authentic writer. Although the novel is not without its
flaws as a work of art, that it is the work of an artist
is unmistakable . . . hers is a unique voice, one
that captures its readers right off. It is, those who
read further will find, a wholly feminine voice—
compelling, shooting off insights, sure of its tone,
searching after the feeling behind appearances,
and everywhere finding it." But the high claims
made for her failed to establish her as a major talent.

Slesinger's second book, published a year later,
was *Time: The Present*, reprinted in 1971 and afterwards with the title *On Being Told that Her Second Husband Has Taken his First Lover and Other
Stories* (the title of the closing story in the 1935
book). This work carried forward the theme of her
earlier novel in stories that explored depression-era
disillusionment, America's racial conflicts, the
changing role of women, and the gap between proletarian idealism and bourgeois conformity. In this
collection, Slesinger paid special attention to the
changing role of women in society. Reviewers on
both sides of the Atlantic were again excited about
the potential of this budding writer, with the *Times
Literary Supplement* writing that "if all the eleven
tales in Miss Tess Slesinger's [book] were as good as
the three or four best, there would be no option but
to term it frankly one of the most striking first short
story volumes which has come from America in recent years." After a *New York Times* reviewer

wrote that "Miss Slesinger would appear to be standing in line for Dorothy Parker's shoes," Slesinger's quick reply was: "I am not conscious of dropping epigrams as she does." The two women soon became friends and political allies.

About this time, MGM offered her $1,000 a week to write screenplays, and she joined the ranks of many "Eastern" writers who moved to Hollywood in the 1930s. In Mexico in 1936 she married Frank Davis, with whom she collaborated on a number of screenplays, including the one for Betty Smith's novel *A Tree Grows in Brooklyn*, which opened in New York just a week after Slesinger's death in 1945.

During the years in Hollywood, the former Village intellectual continued her progressive activities and was instrumental with Donald Ogden Stewart and others in the formation of the Screen Writers Guild, much to the dismay of the studios, notably MGM's Irving Thalberg, who had hired her. She also joined with Dorothy Parker and others in the formation of the Anti-Nazi League, accused of Communist party ties in the early 1940s.

The later revival of interest in Slesinger's work was partly stimulated by the publication of Annie Gottlieb's favorable commentary in "Woman Writer Before Woman Writers," a 1974 piece for the *New York Times Book Review*. In it, Gottlieb praised her "fresh-minted, sassy, and insightful short stories" while regretting that her screenplays did not live up to the 'rough promise' of her novel" and "the more finished brilliance of her short stories." Gottlieb added that "Like all good writers she is ultimately an androgyne and knows it" and points to the "decidedly female" characteristics of the male protagonist of the story, "A Life in the Day of a Writer," who exhibits an overt "female" hysteria when under stress. That story was selected by Martha Foley for inclusion in her *Fifty Best American Short Stories, 1915–1965*.

Sixty years after they were written, in an age in which marriage was still the expected norm for women, the stories of Tess Slesinger retain their freshness and ability to speak to issues of sexual and social politics. But she wrote too little to be made the subject of a major revival.

PRINCIPAL WORKS: Fiction—The Unpossessed, 1934; Time: The Present (short story collection), 1935 (reprinted in 1971 and 1990 as On Being Told that Her Second Husband Has Taken his First Lover and Other Stories).

ABOUT: Mainiero, L. (ed.) American Women Writers, 1982; Wald, A. M. The Rise and Decline of the Anti-Stalinist Left: From the 1930s to the 1980s, 1987. *Periodicals*—Antioch Review Spring/Summer 1977; New York Times February 22, 1945; October 13, 1974; Publishers Weekly March 10, 1945; The Review of Politics Fall 1991.

**SLICHTER, SUMNER HUBER** (January 8, 1892–September 27, 1959), American economist, was born in Madison, Wisconsin, the son of Charles Sumner Slichter and Mary Louise (Byrne) Slichter. His father was a professor of mathematics and later dean of the University of Wisconsin Graduate School. After spending a year at the University in Munich in 1909, Sumner entered his father's university, taking a bachelor's degree in economics in

1913 and a master's the following year. He received his Ph.D. from the University of Chicago in 1918.

After teaching at Princeton and Cornell, he joined the faculty of Harvard University in 1930, a position he kept until his death. A specialist in labor-management rela-tions, Slichter set up a program of fellowships for trade-union leaders at Harvard, and wrote about the role of labor and the public sector in the American economy, in addition to serving as an advisor to government agencies, as well as private groups. He is credited with having coined the term "creeping inflation," which he held as necessary for growth—a concept considered controversial at the time, but which was later accepted by economists in the post-World War II period.

Although his views were generally liberal, Slichter was not an advocate of an unchecked labor movement. In 1947, he was instrumental in the passage of a Massachusetts law that permitted the state to seize and operate industries where a work stoppage would endanger public health or safety. While the law did not apply to the nation as a whole, the philosophy it embodied helped President Truman justify his seizure of the American steel industry during a strike in 1952. Slichter's testimony before Congressional committees in the late 1940s helped establish the principles of compulsory arbitration that were embodied in the landmark Taft-Hartley Act of 1952, which defined labor-management relations for a generation of American life.

An advocate of neither Keynesian experimentation nor doctrinaire orthodoxy, Slichter told *Time* magazine that he was "a Wisconsin liberal—a conservative liberal that does not go off half-cocked." Slichter maintained a lifelong bond with the Wisconsin of his youth, which was shaped by the progressive politics of LaFollette and the heady academic life at the University, which then included Frederick Jackson Turner, Charles Van Hise, and John R. Commons among its notable faculty members.

Slichter wrote more than a dozen books during his career, beginning with *The Turnover of Factory Labor* in 1918. Other books, some of which were chosen as textbooks, established his reputation as one of the profession's foremost experts on collective bargaining. Notable among these were *Modern Economic Society*, published in 1931, and *Union Policies and Industrial Management*, in 1941, the year he served as president of the American Economic Association. To depression-era reviewers, both books were welcomed for their cogent analysis of an economy in the midst of catastrophe. Carter Goodrich wrote of the former text in *New Republic* that "If the serious layman wishes to see what professional economists have, and have not, to contribute to the solution of the world's economic difficulties, and if he must test his case by a single book, let him by all means choose and read *Modern Economic Society*. In it he will find the main stream of American economics at its current best."

Even before the end of World War II, Slichter foresaw the problems of conversion to a peacetime economy that had not known relative prosperity since the 1920s. In 1944, he addressed the issue in a brief monograph entitled *Present Savings and Postwar Markets*. The book was not favorably received by his professional colleagues. Writing in the *American Economic Review*, Milton Gilbert said "While Professor Slichter's work is very suggestive and penetrating in many of its details, it is rather disappointing as a whole. Primarily this is because the conceptual framework behind the quantitative models presented is neither well-knit nor adequate. Furthermore, the handling of some of the statistics is superficial."

Some of Slichter's positions were vindicated over the next few years, however. His evaluation of consumer demand formed the basis for his accurate predictions that the economy could convert quickly from a wartime to a peacetime footing without large-scale unemployment. By 1947, he was held in sufficiently high regard to be appointed associate chair of a citizens' advisory council of the U.S. Senate, whose mission was to advise legislators on social security policy.

However, in a field dominated by Keynesians, Slichter remained wedded to a generally laissez-faire approach. In a 1945 article in *Fortune* magazine, he opposed President Truman's proposed Full Employment Bill, arguing that government deficit spending would be harmful and that a guarantee of full employment would offer disincentives to quality performance. He also urged the temporary continuation of OPA price controls at a time when most economists and politicians were arguing for their abolition in the heady period of postwar optimism.

Although he differed with the Truman administration on these issues, he generally supported Democratic politics on lower tariffs, in the belief that foreign exports would prove a stimulus to the economy.

During the 1950s, Slichter chaired the research advisory committee of the Committee for Economic Development and joined the conservative think-tank, the Brookings Institution.

PRINCIPAL WORKS: The Turnover of Factory Labor, 1919; Modern Economic Society, 1931; Towards Stability, 1934; Union Policies and Industrial Management, 1941; Economic Factors Affecting Industrial Relations Policy in National Defense, 1941; Social Security After the War, 1943; Present Savings and Postwar Markets, 1943; Trade Unions in a Free Society, 1947; The Challenge of Industrial Relations, 1947; The American Economy: Its Problems and Prospects, 1948; What's Ahead for American Business, 1951; Collected Writings, 1959.

ABOUT: Dunlop, J. T., (ed.) Potentials of the American Economy, 1961; Ingram, M. H., Charles Sumner Slichter: The Golden Vector. Periodicals—Business Week, October 25, 1952; Current Biography 1947; Newsweek, October 12, 1959; New York Times, September 29, 1959; Time, October 12, 1959.

**SMART, CHARLES ALLEN** (November 30, 1904–March 11, 1967), American novelist and essayist, wrote: "I was born in Cleveland, Ohio, and moved to New York in 1917. I was educated in the public schools of Cleveland and New York, and at Harvard, B.A. *cum laude*, 1926. In college I was secretary of the *Harvard Advocate* and class poet, God save the mark. After brief periods with a printing firm and the Viking Press, I  worked for three years in the trade editorial department of Doubleday, Page and its successor, Doubleday, Doran. I resigned to do freelance editing, ghost-writing, and advertising copy-writing. My first novel was published in 1931 and had fair luck. I spent most of that year and the next in Europe, wandering and loafing. In 1932 I became an instructor in English at the Choate School, Wallingford, Conn. My second novel was published in 1933 and died at birth. I spent that summer in France. The following June I resigned my teaching job and undertook the operation of a small farm I inherited in southern Ohio, and the management of another. In 1935 I married Margaret Warren Hussey, of Plymouth, Massachusetts. My *R.F.D.*, an account of farming as experienced by city-bred people, had good luck. Since then I have learned a bit more about farming, and, on the literary side, have been studying Utopian Socialism and writing personal essays. . . .

"Just before the [Second World] War, with rising prices, I increased my farming operations largely and actually made money. In May 1942 I enlisted as an apprentice seaman, USNR, and became a signalman, then quartermaster, serving entirely in the LST's, including the New Guinea, Normandy, and Okinawa campaigns. I was commissioned a lieutenant (junior grade) then made lieutenant being released as such in September 1945. During the war I had to sell our larger farm and all our livestock. When I returned, prices were very high for going back into farming, more machinery was necessary, and I was a bit tired. In February 1946 I became writer-in-residence at Ohio University, Athens, Ohio, sixty miles east of my home, and held this position until February 1953. . . . "

Charles Allen Smart was the son of George Smart, an editor, and the former Lucy Allen. The personal essays collected in *Wild Geese and How to Chase Them* discussed "life in terms of the fun that can be made out of it." But "fun" was Smart's flippant term for the Good Life, and most of his books were about various notions of that desirable thing. It is agonized over by the callow young graduates in his first novel, *New England Holiday*, and dreamed of in terms of a utopian farming community in *Rosscommon*.

In 1934, as he records, Smart himself inherited

a sixty-acre farm near Chillicothe, Ohio. He and his new wife, both city-bred intellectuals, continued their pursuit of the good life there, learning as best they could to work the farm, and to understand their animals, their neighbors, and each other. Their first three years at Oak Hill were the subject of Smart's best-known book, *R.F.D.* ("Rural Free Delivery"). Like most of his writings, it had a mixed reception. Jonathan Daniels wondered "if this stout, humorous, and moving book is not as important to this America as what Thoreau wrote" was to his (*Saturday Review of Literature*). But Philip Burnham in *Commonweal* damned its publisher "for promoting in this way the decline of the American town and country." The positive view prevailed, and *R.F.D.* was a Book of the Month Club Choice, and a best-seller.

Before World War II, Smart produced plays at the Chillicothe Little Theatre, and after it wrote a historical play of his own, *The Green Adventure*, celebrating Ohio University's Sesquicentennial in 1954. *The Long Watch* was a memoir of his wartime experiences. Beginning in 1953, Smart and his wife divided their time between Oak Hill and the Mexican village of San Miguel de Allende. There Smart pursued his avocation as a painter, and yet another notion of the good life, dispassionately evoked in *At Home in Mexico*.

Smart was an unexceptional stylist, sometimes a clumsy one. It was his ideas and his sincerity that attracted readers.

PRINCIPAL WORKS: *Novels*—New England Holiday, 1931; The Brass Cannon, 1933; Rosscommon, 1940; Sassafras Hill, 1947. *Essays*—R.F.D., 1938 (in U.K.: The Adventures of an American Farmer); Wild Geese and How to Chase Them: An Informal Discussion of Living as an Art, 1941; At Home in Mexico, 1957. *Drama*—The Green Adventure, 1954. *Other*—Viva Juarez!, 1963 (biography); The Long Watch, 1968 (memoirs). *As editor*—(with R. P. Elmer) The Book of the Long Bow, 1929.

ABOUT: The autobiographical material quoted above was written for Twentieth Century Authors, 1942 and Twentieth Century Authors First Supplement, 1955. Smart, C. A. R.F.D., 1938; Smart, C. A. At Home in Mexico, 1957; Smart, C. A. The Long Watch, 1968. *Periodicals*—Best Sellers June 1, 1968; Commonweal April 8, 1938; New York Times March 13, 1967; Saturday Review of Literature February 26, 1938.

# SMART, ELIZABETH (December 27, 1913–March 4, 1986), Canadian novelist, poet, and diarist, was born into affluent circumstances in Ottawa, Ontario, Canada. She was the daughter of a successful barrister, Russel Smart, and his wife Emma (Parr). She was educated at private schools. She finished her education by taking no fewer than twenty-one transatlantic trips—as well as travels to Sweden, Norway, Germany, New York, Mexico, and California—before she reached twenty-one years of age.

Elizabeth Smart worked for the *Ottawa Journal* in her early twenties, but soon became disillusioned with her country's (and her parents') provincialism and puritanical attitudes. She fled to England, and then to Monterey, California. Much more of her early life was revealed when Alice Van Wart (a colleague of Smart's at the University of Alberta in 1982 and appointed by her as executor) published

an edited and much abridged version of *Necessary Secrets: The Journals of Elizabeth Smart* in 1990; this consisted of thirty-four notebooks kept by Smart between 1924 and 1941, when she ceased to keep a journal. But Smart's "secrets" were in fact fairly banal, as Joyce Carol Oates suggested in her *Times Literary Supplement* review of it: "*Necessary Secrets* is an ironic title for a book that—like its author—is so bent on keeping nothing secret. . . . It is inevitably uneven, but gathers momentum. . . . Smart often transcribed rapt interior states without noting where these states were occurring, or why." What was most interesting about this publication was the revelation that parts of *By Grand Central Station I Sat Down and Wept*, Smart's single book of real account, had been "stitched together, like an elaborate quilt, out of journal entries, some transcribed verbatim into the novel" (Oates).

In 1940 Smart met the married English poet George Barker, well known in England from the early 1930s until his death in 1990, but still hardly read in America. They had a long and, initially, very unhappy affair. In the 1940s she had four children by him. She lived with him on and off in London until her death; but he did not marry her. The "on" periods, however, often struck visitors as consisting of perfectly normal domestic harmony. Barker's own impressions of the affair are contained in his novel *The Dead Seagull* (1950). At one time in the 1950s this novel was much read, regarded, and discussed, but it is now more or less forgotten. *By Grand Central Station I Sat Down and Wept* (1945) has, by contrast, survived as a "cult book," and has been the subject of much discussion.

*By Grand Central* is a remarkable although not quite, by general critical consensus, a major work. It is a passionate love-poem in prose, taking as its model the *Song of Solomon*. Feminists have called it "masochistic," but it is quite the contrary: not only does it express emotions over which the author had no control, but also it is clear that she took no enjoyment at all from her experience—she was just very unhappy and very much, and very complainingly, in love. The circumstances of the beginning of Smart's affair with Barker were traumatic for her. They were wandering about America, usually without money (Barker's pennilessness was proverbial), and were even arrested in Arizona under suspicion of being Nazi spies. Her ultra-respectable parents had disowned her, and she found herself pregnant by the unreliable married man who (she discovered, as she put it in her diary) had lied to her about his attitude to his wife: "O the fact, the unalterable fact: It is she he is with: He is with her: He is not with me because he is sleeping with her."

Joyce Carol Oates, when she was discussing the diaries, has delivered what is probably the most balanced judgment on the novel. "If there is a primary fault . . . it lies in the work's static conception, the hyperbolic sensibility that seeks an epiphany in every line, forever straining to outdo itself. . . . Had George Barker been allowed a voice in Smart's novel (as, in his own hand, he intruded in her journal, in a dialogue with her entries), the work might have been more dramatically engaging." But as a lament for love only half requited—for all that it is over-strained and often too rhetorical—it hardly has a parallel in modern English-language fiction for its candor.

Smart's parents went to some lengths to prevent *By Grand Central* from appearing in Canada. By using Russel Smart's influence with the then prime minister, MacKenzie King, they were able to ban its importation into the country, and it was not officially seen there until 1966. This of course drew attention to it in just the way that Mr. and Mrs. Smart wished to avoid: many copies were smuggled into Canada throughout the 1950s.

Smart, like Barker, became a character in the public houses of Soho and Fitzrovia, near where she lived in London, until she moved to Suffolk. She was acquainted with most of the poets and many of the painters of her day. She was not much like her wild legend (of which too much was made), but was, rather, gentle, moderate, helpful and generally well-liked. Her and Barker's son Sebastian became a fairly well-known poet; but there was tragedy when they lost one of their daughters to drug addiction.

Smart's own later output was sparse: a novel, received with respect but with not great enthusiasm, *The Assumption of the Rogues and Rascals*, and a couple of volumes of surprisingly simple, modest poems. But it is for her first work (and perhaps, too, for the diaries which cast so much light on it) that she will be chiefly remembered.

Smart went back to Canada only twice: once, briefly, in 1970; and then again in 1982 as writer-in-residence at the University of Alberta. When she needed to support her family (Barker's contributions being sporadic, although substantial at times) she worked in advertising and journalism.

PRINCIPAL WORKS: *Fiction*—By Grand Central Station I Sat Down and Wept, 1945; The Assumption of the Rogues and Rascals, 1978. *Poetry*—A Bonus, 1977; Eleven Poems, 1982. *Poetry and prose*—In the Meantime, 1984.

ABOUT: Ousby, I. (ed.) Cambridge Guide to Literature in English, 1988. *Periodicals*—Globe and Mail (Toronto) March 6, 1986; Times (London) March 6, 1986; Times Literary Supplement February 8, 1991; Toronto Star March 5, 1986.

**SMEDLEY, AGNES** (1894–May 6, 1950), American novelist, journalist, and commentator on Chinese issues, was born in Oklahoma and reared in the coal-mining town of Trinidad, Colorado. She was the second of five children born to Charles H. Smedley, a hardscrabble itinerant laborer, and Sarah (Ralls) Smedley, a washerwoman. None of the Smedley children completed high school, and, as did her parents, Agnes began working full time in early adolescence. Little is known about her early years. "One strain—my mother's—was of a hard-working, gentle, and devout folk," Smedley wrote. "The other consisted of rebels, wanderers, tellers of tall tales . . . the two family strains, meeting in me, made my spirit a battlefield across which a civil war raged endlessly."

After her mother's death in 1910, Smedley left home. She spent a brief period as a schoolteacher in a remote region of New Mexico. In 1911, she enrolled for a year at the Tempe Normal School in Arizona, then attended a summer session at the University of California at Berkeley. She was briefly married to Ernest Brundin, an undergraduate there, but within a year they were divorced, and in 1918 Smedley moved to New York City.

She was immediately attracted to the cause supporting the liberation of India, helping to obtain the release of Hindu activists imprisoned on charges of political conspiracy. Ironically, Smedley was arrested and sent to the Tombs Prison in New York, on grounds that her political activities "jeopardized U.S. neutrality" during World War I. Soon after the Armistice, Smedley was released (her case was dismissed for lack of evidence).

She left for Berlin in 1919, and established the first birth-control clinic in Germany. Smedley also taught English to university students there.

In 1927, she wrote her best-known work, the semi-autobiographical novel *Daughter of Earth*. She described the writing process as a "desperate attempt" to re-orient her life. The book was eventually published in 1929 as a narrative account of the life of Marie Rogers, a woman who grew up on a desolate Wisconsin farmstead "with a dissipated half-Indian father, a weary drudge for a mother, and an ever-increasing brood of younger brothers and sisters."

Smedley embarked on her career as a journalist in 1928, when she secured a position in China as correspondent to the *Frankfurter Zeitung*. The abject poverty and high illiteracy rate in the country immediately made a profound, lasting impression on her already radical politics. The first account of these conditions appeared in her 1933 book, *Chinese Destinies*.

Smedley spent 1933 in the Soviet Union, during which time she wrote *China's Red Army Marches*, a chronicle of its establishment and expansion between 1927 and 1931, and its remarkable defense in formidable encounters with Kuomingtang forces. Smedley's role in the now mythic "long march" of the 8th Route Army was far from that of distant observer. She walked, rode horseback, and even traveled by stretcher with a badly sprained back in the course of recording the historic military campaign. Her eyewitness accounts of the floods, famines, and massive carnage along the march were included in *Battle Hymn of China*, a book documenting the years 1929 to 1941.

In a 1938 review of her book *China Fights Back*, the *New York Times* suggested that Smedley's insights, notwithstanding strong partisanship, contained a critical element of perspicacity. "Being . . . passionately devoted to the Chinese cause, Miss Smedley is not a military specialist nor an objective observer, and does not pretend to be.

She does write superbly of what she saw, experienced, and was told." The more descriptive features of her reportage redeemed much of her work from collapsing altogether into party-line dogmatism. *Battle Hymn of China*, a collection of stories culled from Smedley's years of engagement in China's revolutionary struggle and transition, did not present anything approaching blind, bland socialist realism.

"Her book is not pleasant," wrote Clifton Fadiman in a September 1943 *New Yorker* review. "It is full of horrors, tortures, betrayals, and poverty, poverty, poverty . . . her tone is harsh and sometimes raucous. I think, however, that for all her violences and prejudices, she is worth listening to."

From 1938 to 1941, Smedley worked as a publicist and field worker for the Chinese Red Cross Medical Corps. Late in December 1941, she left China and was subsequently unable to return. In lectures and radio appearances in the United States and England, Smedley tenaciously sought to bring the free world's attention to the plight of the Chinese. Her last years were difficult, principally because of her finally unwavering support for the Chinese Communist party in the face of mounting hostility to communism in postwar America. In February 1949, a lengthy intelligence report prepared by Gen. MacArthur's staff identified Smedley as a Soviet operative. Smedley vehemently denounced the allegation, prompting the secretary of defense to withdraw the formal charges. By this time, Smedley felt like a stranger in her native country, and so, failing an opportunity to create an adequate life for herself in the United States, she left for England in November, 1949. There, she continued work on a biography of General Chu Teh, commander-in-chief of the Communist military forces in China, but died several months later.

*The Great Road: The Life and Times of Chu Teh* was published posthumously. Her remains were interred in the National Revolutionary Martyrs Memorial Park in Beijing (the only other Westerner buried there was Smedley's friend Edgar Snow). The inscription placed near her grave reads, simply, "Agnes Smedley, revolutionary writer and friend of the Chinese people."

PRINCIPAL WORKS: Daughter of Earth, 1929; Chinese Destinies, 1933; China's Red Army Marches, 1934; (later edition as Red Flood Over China); China Fights Back, 1938; Battle Hymn of China, 1943; The Great Road: The Life and Times of Chu Teh, 1956.

ABOUT: Periodicals—Current Biography 1944; Christian Century March 2, 1949; Nation February 19, 1948; New Republic May 29, 1950; New Statesman and Nation May 20, 1950; New York Times May 9, 1950; Newsweek May 28, 1951; Publishers Weekly May 5, 1949.

## SMITH, ALFRED ALOYSIUS. See HORN, A. A.

## SMITH, ARTHUR COSSLETT (January 19, 1852–May 22, 1926), American short story writer, was the son of James Cosslett Smith, a justice of the New York Supreme Court, and Emily Ward (Adams) Smith. He attended Hobart College in Geneva, New York, graduating with an M. A. in 1875.

He gained his law degree from Columbia Law School. From 1879 until the turn of the century he practiced law in Rochester, New York. Smith seems to have thought of writing as a diversion from his legal and business careers, and he published only two collections of short stories and a few uncollected pieces in *Scribner's*. He gave up writing altogether soon after the publication of *The Monk and the Dancer* in 1900 and *The Turquoise Cup and The Desert* in 1903, and slipped into obscurity long before his death.

Nevertheless, Smith's deliberately artificial, *fin-de-siècle* manner found favor with such marginal critics as Henry Wysham Lanier, who wrote of Smith in the *Golden Book*, "He seems to have found the chief expression of an unusually sensitive, cultivated, beautyloving nature in producing this handful of exquisitely wrought stories. There is something about Arthur Cosslett Smith, and the polished finish of his two slim volumes of short stories, that makes him beloved of reading folk. . . . Many will not cease to remember this lawyer of Rochester, New York, whose pen was so quiet, so exquisite, so delightful." Vincent Starrett believed that Smith was a "very considerable artist," neglected, perhaps, because of his own indifference. "His style is not nasal and it is obviously his theory that literature need not uplift anybody to be very good literature indeed," wrote Starrett. "His characters have not 'brave, honest hearts,' of the adult Horatio Alger, Jr., variety, and they talk perhaps more as people should talk than as people do talk. . . . Essentially, he is a writer of *contes* in the veritable French manner, and there is a delicate Gallic wit and malice in his lines." In particular, Starrett thought "The Monk and the Dancer," the story of a monk who is nearly undone by his infatuation for a dancing girl, "a masterpiece of short fiction if any has been written in this country."

A man of independent means, Smith belonged to a small circle of Rochester intellectuals and, according to a correspondent in the *Saturday Review of Literature*, "worked only desultorily at the law and literature."

PRINCIPAL WORKS: Short stories—The Monk and the Dancer, 1900; The Turquoise Cup and The Desert, 1903.

ABOUT: Starrett, V. Buried Caesars: Essays in Literary Appreciation, 1923. Periodicals—Golden Book June 1928; New York Times May 23, 1926; Saturday Review of Literature May 18, 1946.

## SMITH, A(RTHUR) J(AMES) M(AR-SHALL) (November 8, 1902–1980), American poet, critic, and editor born in Canada, wrote: "I was born in Montreal and educated at McGill University and at Edinburgh University, where I worked under Sir Herbert Grierson, receiving a Ph.D. degree for a thesis on the metaphysical poets of the Anglican church in the seventeenth century.

As an undergraduate at McGill I was one of the founders and editors of the *McGill Fortnightly Review* (1926–1927), which introduced the new poets  of the 'Montreal School' who were instrumental in bringing modern cosmopolitan poetry into Canada, and I contributed verse and criticism to the *Canadian Forum*, the *Nation* and the *Dial*. Since 1929 I have been a college teacher of English and after various brief excursions into Indiana, Nebraska, and South Dakota, I became a member of the English department at Michigan State College, where I am now a professor. I continued to contribute verse to such magazines as *Hound and Horn*, the *Adelphi*, *New Verse*, *Twentieth Century Verse*, and *Poetry*, receiving *Poetry*'s Harriet Monroe Memorial Prize in 1941. A volume of poems, *News of the Phoenix*, was published in 1943 and was awarded the Governor General's Medal for the best Canadian book of verse of the year. I traveled across Canada in 1941 and '42 on a Guggenheim fellowship and prepared a critical and historical anthology of Canadian poetry, *The Book of Canadian Poetry*, which was published in 1943. A new and enlarged edition was brought out in 1948. At the present time I am preparing a larger collection of Canadian prose literature, much of the initial work having been made possible by grants from the Rockefeller Foundation. I spend some part of each year in Canada. In 1946 I delivered the Founders' Day Address at the University of New Brunswick and since then have taught in the summer schools at the University of Toronto and Queens University, Kingston. I have also taught in the summer at the University of Washington. I have published two anthologies of poetry outside the Canadian field: *Seven Centuries of Verse*, a collection of poems for college students, which surprised me by selling nearly fifteen thousand copies, and *The Worldly Muse*, an anthology of 'serious light verse' compiled for fun, which, though the *Nation* called it 'an altogether delightful anthology,' is not nearly so well known as I could wish."

---

A. J. M. Smith, who became a naturalized American citizen in 1941, is probably best remembered for his still standard, trend-setting anthologies of Canadian poetry. "If," wrote George Woodcock in *Commonwealth Literature*, they "are not unquestioningly accepted as the definitive statements on the development of poetry in Canada, they have greatly influenced trends in literary history and critical evaluation alike." Smith's criticism and poetry are also still the subject of debate in Canada, and his place in its literature is fairly secure.

Smith remained throughout his life a very influential figure in Canadian letters. Of his *Collected Poems* Stanley Kunitz wrote, in the *New York*

*Times Book Review*, that "although a more selective offering than this collection of 100 poems . . . would have been to Smith's advantage," nonetheless, the "best . . . are notably fine and sinewy . . . 'The Two Birds' [is] a fierce lyric with a metaphysical clang." This "metaphysical" voice of Smith's is to the fore in the eloquent "The Plot Against Proteus," which begins:

This is a theme for muted coronets
To dangle from debilitated heads
Of navigation, kings or riverbeds
That rot or rise what time the seamew sets
Her course by starts among the smoky tides
Entangled.

Smith, wrote Woodcock, was an artist "whose self-criticism has been almost fanatical. His four volumes of highly metaphysical poetry . . . are rigorously chosen . . . the *Collected Poems* honed down the canon to a hundred pieces, all that Smith wished to keep from more that thirty years of writing poetry." This is poetry for a literary palate rather than for those who yearn after ordinary speech-rhythms, or after the colloquial:

This is a beauty
of dissonance
this resonance
of stony strand
this smoky cry
curled over a black pine
like a broken
and wind-battered branch
when the wind
bends the tops of pines
and curdles the sky
from the north.

Smith's most important book of criticism is *Towards a View of Canadian Letters: Selected Critical Essays 1928–1972*. In it Smith insisted that "to be mature in a creative sense," Canadian literature required a critical tradition. He, his friend and colleague F. R. Scott, together with Northrop Frye—and later the Englishman George Woodcock—went a long way towards providing this. Smith and Scott compiled an influential anthology, *New Provinces* (1936), in which they gave a selection from the work of the few modernist poets then working in Canada, and thus gave the culture itself a lift which it badly needed. Smith's anthologies of Canadian poetry, eventually culminating in *The Oxford Book of Canadian Verse: In English and French* (1960, revised 1965), completed the task, and for the first time gave Canadian poets the chance to see, in a single volume, their own roots.

Smith also provided critical commentary on the poetry of Anne Wilkinson (which he also edited) and on one of Canada's pioneer poets, E. J. Pratt. His *Seven Centuries of Verse* is highly valued as a general anthology.

PRINCIPAL WORKS: *Poetry*—News of the Phoenix, 1943; A Sort of Ecstasy, 1954; Collected Poems, 1962; Poems: New and Collected, 1967; The Classic Shades: Selected Poems, 1978. *Criticism*—The Poetry of Robert Bridges, 1943; (with M. L. Rosenthal) Exploring Poetry, 1955, rev. ed. 1973; Some Poems of E. J. Pratt: Aspects of Imagery and Theme, 1969; Towards of View of Canadian Letters: Selected Essays 1928–1972, 1973; Of Poetry and Poets: Selected Essays, 1977. *As editor*—(with F. R. Scott) New Provinces: Poems of Several Authors, 1936; The Book of Canadian Poetry, 1943, 2nd rev. ed. 1957;

Seven Centries of Verse, 1947, 2nd rev. ed. 1967; The Worldly Muse: An Anthology of Serious Light Verse, 1951; (with F. R. Scott) The Blasted Pine: An Anthology of Satire, Invective and Disrespectful Verse, Chiefly by Canadian Writers, 1957, rev. ed. 1967; The Oxford Book of Canadian Verse: In English and French, 1960, rev. ed. 1965; The Book of Canadian Prose, 2 vols. 1965–1973; 100 Poems: Chaucer to Dylan Thomas, 1965; Modern Canadian Verse: In English and French, 1967; The Collected Poems of Anne Wilkinson and a Prose Memoir, 1968; The Canadian Experience, 1974.

ABOUT: The autobiographical material quoted above was written for Twentieth Century Authors First Supplement, 1955. Commonwealth Writers, 1979; Contemporary Poets, 1980; Ferns, J. A. J. M. Smith, 1979; Klinck, C. F. (ed.) Literary History of Canada, 1969; Pacey, D. Ten Canadian Poets, 1958; Percival, W. P. (ed.)Leading Canadian Poets, 1948; Stevens, P. (ed.) The McGill Movement: Smith, F. R. Scott and Leo Kennedy, 1969; Woodcock, G. Odysseus Ever Returning, 1970. Bibliography—Darling, M. E., A.J.M. Smith: An Annotated Bibliography, 1981. Periodicals—Book Week November 7, 1943; Canadian Forum February 1963; Canadian Literature Winter 1963; New Republic May 8, 1944; New York Times Book Review November 27, 1960; July 21, 1963; New Yorker February 26, 1961.

**SMITH, BETTY (WEHNER)** (December 15, 1904?–January 17, 1972), American novelist and playwright, was born in the Williamsburg section of Brooklyn, New York, the daughter of John C. Smith, an actor, and Catherine Hummel Wehner. She wrote four novels and dozens of one-act plays, and compiled several drama anthologies, but only one of her works, A Tree Grows in Brooklyn, is remembered.

Smith ended her formal schooling after the eighth grade but participated in amateur dance and dramatics classes at a settlement house and at  the local YMCA. She later attended the University of Michigan as a special student (1927–1930) and the Yale University Drama School (1930–1934). At Michigan, she began to write one-act plays and feature articles for a Detroit newspaper. After her stint at Yale, she became associated with the Federal Theater and accepted a Rockefeller fellowship to study playwriting at the University of North Carolina. Many of the plays she wrote during this period were one-acters in collaboration with others; some of them were used as texts for classroom study.

At the time of its publication in 1943, A Tree Grows in Brooklyn became an immediate best seller. The novel told the story of young Francine Nolan, a girl who watched a common ailanthus tree grow in her tenement airshaft "which would be considered beautiful except that there are too many of it, for it grows lushly, but only in the tenement districts." At the time of Smith's death in 1972, the book had gone through thirty-seven printings in hard cover and been published in sixteen languages. It was made into a motion picture, and Smith herself collaborated with George Abbott on an adaptation for Broadway, which opened in 1951.

In 1943, though, Smith told Current Biography that Brooklyn was only tenuously connected to the novel. Only "some of the book is me," she said. "Every character in it is a composite of a hundred characters I've met—in Michigan, North Carolina, everywhere I've been. The dialogue, though, is Brooklyn, and I've put in things that could only happen in Brooklyn. . . . It is not the story of my life." Reading Thomas Wolfe's Of Time and the River was the propulsive force behind her own book, the thing that "made it all come back then, like a flood. All of Brooklyn."

A Tree Grows in Brooklyn won almost unanimous praise from reviewers. The New Yorker called it a "remarkably good first novel. . . . The author sees the misery, squalor, and cruelty of slum life but sees them with understanding, pity, and sometimes with hilarious humor." Yet other critics were clear to point out that this was a "popular novel." Diana Trilling noted in the Nation, "Surely popular taste should be allowed to find its emotional level without being encouraged to believe that a 'heart-warming' experience is a serious literary experience."

The year that A Tree was published, Smith began a mail correspondence with Joe Jones, who had been an assistant editor of the Chapel Hill Weekly; they had been introduced by mutual friends. After his induction into the Army, they met in person and were married two days later. Smith's first marriage had been in 1924 to George H. E. Smith; they were divorced in 1938. Her marriage to Jones also ended in divorce, in 1951. In 1957 she married Robert Finch, who died in 1959. She had two children by her first marriage.

Smith's next two novels—Tomorrow Will be Better (1948) and Maggie-Now (1958)—were also set in Brooklyn but never achieved the fame of A Tree. These and her final novel, Joy in the Morning (1963)—a fictionalized account of her personal angst after her first marriage while a student at the University of Michigan—have been reprinted. Smith's New York Times obituarist wrote of her novels that "all possessed the same strong autobiographical overtones of precocity among poverty and enduring optimism amid oppression and travail."

PRINCIPAL WORKS: Novels—A Tree Grows in Brooklyn, 1943 (in U.K.: The Tree in the Yard); Tomorrow Will be Better' 1948 (in U.K.: Streets of Little Promise), 1948; Maggie-Now, 1958; Joy in the Morning, 1963. Dramas—Murder in the Snow, 1938; Lawyer Lincoln, 1939; Room for a King, 1940; 25 Non-Royalty One-Act Plays for All-Girl Casts, 1942; 20 Prize-Winning Non-Royalty One-Act Plays, 1943.

ABOUT: Current Biography 1943. Periodicals—Good Housekeeping January 1958; Nation September 4, 1943; New York Times Book Review August 22, 1948; Newsweek February 24, 1958.

**SMITH, CECIL BLANCHE WOODHAM-.**
See **WOODHAM-SMITH, CECIL BLANCHE**

**SMITH, CHARD POWERS** (November 1, 1894–October 31, 1977), American poet and novelist, wrote: "I was born in Watertown, New York, the son of Edward North Smith and Alice Lamon (Powers) Smith. Most of my ancestors were Yankees, dating back to the beginning, just solid folk, with a pretty pervasive love of learning. Educated at Pawling School, Yale (B.A. 1916), Harvard (LL.B. 1921), miscellaneous studies without degrees at Columbia and Oxford. Practiced law one year, then in 1922 inherited a small competence and went to writing poetry. Was assisted in this enterprise by my first wife, Olive Cary Macdonald, whom I married in 1921, and who died in Naples in 1924. After her death I took part in the typical life of 'self-expression' of the intellectuals of the time, my two foci being the popular expatriate cafes on the left bank of the Seine and, in America, the MacDowell Colony at Peterborough, New Hampshire. Also lived a good deal in New York, and spent a summer in Nebraska as a hand on a little expedition of the American Museum of Natural History, my object being to get material for my epic of evolution *Prelude to Man*, which was the big job which gave my life continuity at this time. Visited Panama in order to collect jungle copy. Also worked with expedition in the Dordogne region in France, and in various parts of Kent in England. During this period my only real interest was in myself and in my sensual and mystical desires. Edwin Arlington Robinson was my god and my friend, his encouragement being probably responsible for keeping me at work during a period when the publishers and the public were not clamoring for my work.

"In the autumn of 1929 I returned to the United States and married Marion Antoinette Chester [they were divorced in 1957], proposing to settle

down to respectable matrimony, which I more or less proceeded to do. Meanwhile I had outgrown the expatriate contempt for my country and had discovered a deep affection for her. I began to study the civilization represented by my two Yankee grandfathers. I came to realize that whatever strength I possessed came from it, and that what of me was empty and futile came from the industrial snobbish pseudo-civilization of my own early environment.

"I got mixed up in the Distributist Movement, along with Ralph Borsodi on the one hand, and the Southern Agrarians on the other. The attempted alliance didn't jell, and we scattered in a series of little schisms, but the Decentralist idea is still the center of my political convictions. For a year I wrote the editorials in the magazine, *Free America*.

"I brought out my epic of evolution by subscription — a successful form of publication for poetry, by the way. This ended my self-centered, poetic phase. I began to do the research for my first book,

*Artillery of Time*. This book got the best press of any book of mine, the implication being that fiction was my chief talent. I don't know whether this is true or not.

"The three literary influences in my life have been my first wife, E. A. Robinson, and Maxwell Perkins. I have known most of my contemporary writers, but I have always walked by myself, having no gang, hating all extremes, despising the self-indulgent aesthetes and the Radicals just as much as the Republicans and the Democrats. It is possible that the spectacle of the outer world may awaken us to our terrible responsibility of maintaining the ideal of individualism against the savages pressing Westward across the Rhine. The problem is to orient political expediency to the meaning of America. It may be possible to do it in time. It just may be. . . . "

In 1955, Smith wrote: "My *Ladies Day*, like *Artillery of Time* (1939), had a fine press, but, unlike *Artillery of Time* it was not a best-seller. In 1943 I published two small war novels, one of merely current interest, and the other, *Turn of the Dial*, a valuable book for the long run but a failure in immediate sales. It may have been too strong medicine, for it showed with some precision how Hitler's methods were learned from American advertising. In 1946 I moved out of fictionized history a little closer to real history with *The Housatonic* in the Rivers of America series, again a critical success and again a bestseller. It did me the great service of introducing me to the history of New England, especially to the Puritans who have been so absurdly villified by debunking historians, especially Charles Beard and James Truslow Adams. Since 1946 I have had two aims, which I retain. One is to finish the three-generation trilogy which *Artillery of Time* introduced (Civil War generation), *Ladies Day* continued (the 80s and 90s) and which needs finishing with the story of my—the Lost—generation. I have made two starts at this novel, and each has been unsatisfactory, perhaps through the conscious proximity of my other aim. This is to write a real history of New England culture, from the Atlantic to the Pacific, and from 1620 to date. It has never been done, and it is the story of the only two true cultures this country has produced, the other being that of the Old South. In pursuance of this aim, I took an M.A. at Columbia and have been doing some teaching.

"Meanwhile, I have become a professing Christian, combining two approaches that are not as incompatible as is sometimes supposed. Emotionally and ecclesiastically, I have become a Quaker. [Smith was a trustee of the Friends Seminary and the Brooklyn Friends School, both in New York.] But intellectually, I am a Calvinist. I am of those who believe that America's only hope is in a great Christian awakening, not only emotionally but intellectually as well."

---

Chard Powers Smith did not accomplish the first of the two aims he had expressed in 1946, to complete his three-generation trilogy of American life.

The first volume, *Artillery of Time,* published in 1939, was a lengthy epic about the Civil War era as told through the lives of a family in upstate New York. The *Nation* praised its "rich, sympathetic characterization, breadth of scope, and easy mastery of style," which raised the book "far above the rank and file of Civil War novels." Indeed, as Smith's *New York Times* obituarist pointed out, the novel was even viewed in some circles as a "Northern *Gone With the Wind.*" The second novel in the series, *Ladies Day,* carried the saga forward to the 1884–1900 period; it was also generally well received by reviewers and the reading public, at a time when American historical "family sagas" were in vogue. In 1946, Smith drew on his knowledge of geology, history, and local color to produce *The Housatonic: Puritan River* for the popular Rivers of America series.

But Smith did achieve his "other aim" with the 1954 publication of *Yankees and God,* a lush historical overview of New England culture from the Puritans onward. The book was described by the *Christian Science Monitor* as "a rambunctious, opinionated, idiosyncratic, difficult, and delightful book. Mr. Smith is a passionate Puritan rising to the defense of a stout-hearted Puritan culture." This popular history, written after his "conversion" to a Quaker-Calvinist worldview—or, more accurately, after his "rediscovery" of his own ancestral heritage—appealed to educated readers of the 1950s who were seeking a reaffirmation of American idealism after a tumultuous two decades of economic depression, world war, and the emergence of the nation as a cold-war superpower. The book was published in the middle of a decade that marked the zenith of mainstream Protestantism in America, in the very year that "under God" was added to the pledge of allegiance; its thesis paralleled Smith's own inner journey toward a kind of "civic" Christianity and underscored his belief that religious institutions played a vital cementing role in society.

Smith attempted to write in many genres over his career, and produced, at best, minor popular works. The several books of lyrical verse and experimental poetic drama that he published in the 1920s and 1930s were not taken seriously. Critics thought the work too ambitious for one of Smith's talents, and he soon abandoned the lyric form altogether. But before leaving it behind, he wrote two books—neither of them in the mainstream of criticism at the time—that attempted to apply scientific and psychological methodology to poetry: *Pattern and Variation in Poetry* (1932) examined 2,000 poems in English in an attempt to deduce a "law" of subject matter and form; *Annals of the Poets: Their Private Lives and Personalities* (1935) was a collection of anecdotes and trivia — much of it admittedly drawn from secondary sources — that was described by William Rose Benét in the *Saturday Review of Literature* as a "good anecdotal book" but one that necessarily forced the "lives of all the poets . . . [into] very condensed form, like concentrated beef cubes."

Smith's greatest contribution to American literary history was through his association with the "crepuscular" poet Edward Arlington Robinson, whom Smith got to know at the MacDowell Colony in the 1920s. In the same way that Boswell observed Johnson and Traubel Whitman, Smith saw Robinson almost daily for long periods of time, and his detailed observations and analysis of the older man offer an intimate portrait of a poet who had been temporarily eclipsed by the modernists and the New Criticism. It is clear that Smith took a worshipful attitude toward his subject, variously described as a "literary father," a "mentor," an "avatar," and a "god." When he met Robinson, Smith had just returned, disillusioned, from Europe, with the body of his dead wife on board ship. It is obvious that the younger man found spiritual sustenance and regeneration at the feet of his newfound mentor.

Published in 1965 as *Where the Light Falls,* Smith's memoir of Robinson was described by Granville Hicks in the *Saturday Review* as "the best book on Robinson we have." Smith himself saw it as a "partial biography" that would be useful for the "ultimate, definitive biographer" of the future. *Where the Light Falls* presented an intimately revealing narrative of his own interaction with Robinson, attempted to evaluate Robinson's place in American letters, and tried to offer a psychological explanation for the source of Robinson's angst (Smith suggested it was Robinson's "true love," Emma).

Two years after the publication of *Where the Light Falls,* Smith produced *Poets of the Twenties,* an anthology with a foreword by Peter Viereck. Published decades after modernism had left its solid imprint on American letters, this book was Smith's "last gasp" at offering his own idiosyncratic view on behalf of "neoromantic" poetry. It included works by Robinson, and by Mark Van Doren, Elinor Wylie, the Benéts, and Robinson Jeffers, among others. In his preface, Smith expresses his disdain for the then-prevailing orthodoxy: "Since the ascendance of the New Criticism in the late thirties, one of the fallacies it has imposed upon the English curricula in the colleges has been the dating of Modern American Poetry from the appearance of Eliot's *The Waste Land* in 1922. . . . Of permanent importance was the neo-romantic movement whose principal work is the subject of this book and whose revolt, beginning in the 1890s, against late nineteenth-century pseudo-romanticism, was the real beginning of modern American poetry."

He tried to ally himself in the end with those universalist thinkers who sought a spiritual regeneration of culture. He wrote in his introduction to *Poets of the Twenties,* for example, of his hopes for a reconciliation of "the ancient and always absurd controversy between science and religion," casting his lot with "all affirmative contemporary theologians, from Tillich through Bonhoeffer, Bultmann, the others mentioned in Bishop Robinson's *Honest to God,* and above all Teilhard de Chardin, who are working toward a new Christian symbolism which will retain unaltered the fundamental, transcendental Christian symbolism, while implementing them in a new mythology acceptable to science, a mythology, for example, based in the latest timetables of paleontology or the last developments of Jungian psychology."

PRINCIPAL WORKS: *Poetry*—Along the Wind, 1925; Lost Address, 1928; The Quest of Pan, 1930; Hamilton: A Poetic Drama, 1930; Prelude to Man, 1935. *Criticism*—Pattern and Variation in Poetry, 1932; Annals of the Poets, 1935; Poets of the Twenties, 1967. *Novels*—Artillery of Time, 1939; Ladies Day, 1941; Turn of the Dial, 1943. *Prose*—He's in the Artillery Now, 1944; The Housatonic, Puritan River, 1946; Where the Light Falls, 1965.

ABOUT: The autobiographical material quoted above was written for Twentieth Century Authors, 1942 and Twentieth Century Authors First Supplement, 1955. *Periodicals*—New York Times November 3, 1977; Saturday Review of Literature October 14, 1939; Scribner's Magazine May 1936.

## SMITH, ELEANOR FURNEAUX (1902–October 20, 1945), English novelist, wrote: "My father's family had gypsy blood, and on my mother's

side I am Cornish, of French descent. I love music, ballet, swimming, and riding. I am also fond of skiing, but dislike most games. I like Schiaparelli's clothes, Patou's 'Joie' scent, and circuses. I like circuses now as a recreation, although a few years ago they were my living, for I not only wrote novels and stories about them, but I worked in the publicity department of one for some months. I have, on occasion, myself ridden in the ring. I hate noise—motorcycles in particular—society snobs, roast beef, whiskey, air-raid sirens, and people who mistreat children. I like traveling, champagne, bread-and-cheese, and playing darts."

Lady Eleanor Furneaux Smith was the elder daughter of the barrister F. E. Smith, later the first Earl of Birkenhead (where she was born). She specialized in writing vivacious gypsy romances, inspired by the knowledge that she had a small amount of gypsy blood in her (from her paternal great-grandmother), and by her precocious readings of George Borrow. Brought up partly in London and partly in Charlton, Oxfordshire, she was educated by French governesses, and later attended schools in France and Belgium. Immediately after World War I she embarked on a career as a journalist, obtaining positions as society reporter and film critic on various London papers.

She claimed to have written her first novel, *Red Wagon*, at the age of twenty, while still working as a journalist, although it was not published until 1930. Of this first book, V. S. Pritchett wrote, in the *Spectator* (1930), "Lady Eleanor Smith's knowledge of circus life is immense," but added, "Yet there remains a general impression of monotony." This was partly due to the author's inclination to be what the *Times Literary Supplement* (1930) called "a trifle over-lavish with the details of professional life." Indeed, the novel had the unusual distinction of possessing a glossary.

*Flamenco*, her second novel, was set in the early nineteenth century. Like many of her books—for all the sincere partisanship—the overall effect is a bolstering of gypsy stereotypes. A reviewer in *Christian Century* wrote that the whole story is built "around an unjust estimate of the gypsies as thieves, kidnappers and cut-throats, and an untenable view of heredity which makes the wildness of the gypsy a matter of physical rather than social inclination."

In *Ballerina*, the third novel, Lady Eleanor, because she was not writing about gypsies or the circus, did not feel the same need to digress and philosophize or educate, but was able to concentrate on the plot. For this reason, it is one of her better books. The stories in *Christmas Tree*, on the other hand, are whimsically sentimental. Graham Greene, reviewing the collection for the *Spectator* (1933), wrote, "The atmosphere has the terrible timeliness of wooden robins, kind hearts and synthetic snow." Peter Quennell, in the *New Statesman*, asked of the author, "Is her facility more apparent than genuine aptitude?"

*Satan's Circus*, another collection of short stories, confirmed that whatever aptitude the author possessed it was more suited to the form of the novel, and the rest of Lady Eleanor's publications were all full-length romantic tales of the type that could justifiably be characterized as "harmless, well-patterned flummery" (the *New Yorker*). One of her last books, *Magic Lantern*, was well summed-up by a writer of similar disposition, Taylor Caldwell, who wrote in *Book Week*: "It is not 'important.' It is no 'document.' It has no 'message,' and there isn't the slightest taint of 'social consciousness' in all its 276 pages. . . . The book tells a turbulent tale, but joyously points no moral."

Lady Eleanor Smith, never having married, died in London at the early age of forty-two. Her brother, the biographer F. W. Birkenhead, wrote a short memoir of his sister, published in 1953, and some of her writing about British circus life was edited and published posthumously in an illustrated edition.

PRINCIPAL WORKS: Red Wagon, 1930; Flamenco, 1931; Ballerina, 1932; Christmas Tree, 1933; Satan's Circus, 1934; Tzigane, 1935 (in U.S.: Romany); Portrait of a Lady, 1936; The Spanish House, 1938; Life's a Circus, 1939; Lovers' Meeting, 1940; The Man in Grey, 1941; Caravan, 1943; Magic Lantern, 1944; British Circus Life, 1948.

ABOUT: The autobiographical material quoted above was written for Twentieth Century Authors, 1942 and Twentieth Century Authors First Supplement, 1955. Birkenhead, F. W. Lady Eleanor Smith: A Memoir, 1953; Vinson, J. (ed.) Twentieth Century Romance And Gothic Writers, 1982; Who's Who 1945. *Periodicals*—Book Week April 29, 1945; Christian Century May 6, 1931; New Statesman December 2, 1933; New York Times October 21, 1945; New Yorker July 27, 1940; Spectator March 8, 1930; December 29, 1933; Times (London) October 22, 1945; Times Literary Supplement February 27, 1930.

## SMITH, ERNEST BRAMAH. See BRAMAH, ERNEST

**SMITH, H(ARRY) ALLEN** (December 19, 1906–February 24, 1976), American humorist who published under the name H. Allen Smith, wrote: "I am an Egyptian in the sense that I was born in that part of Illinois known as 'Egypt' [in the town of McLeansboro]. I have expended a good many units of energy explaining to people that the H. stands for Harry. One of nine children, I grew up in Illinois, Ohio, and Indiana. On finishing the eighth grade I went to work as a chicken picker in a poultry house (hens, 2½ cents, roosters, 3 cents) then became a shoeshine boy and sweeper-up of used hair in a barber shop. At this period of my life I despised Horatio Alger, Jr.

"From the barber shop I moved to my first newspaper job as proofreader. Soon I became a reporter and later an itinerant newspaperman in Indiana,

Kentucky, Florida, Oklahoma, Colorado, and, in 1929, New York. I worked five years for the United Press and five years for the *World-Telegram*. In 1939 I wrote a book and in 1940 I wrote another. Their publication led me to seek employment as a crossing guard for a railroad. Before I could make such a connection, a man asked me to put together some flippant newspaper reminiscences and these were published under the title *Low Man on a Totem Pole*. People lost their heads. They bought it. I quit newspapering and wrote another one, *Life in a Putty Knife Factory*. Madness seized the populace. They bought it. . . .

"I am generally referred to as a humorist although a good many people think of me as a suppuration, or worse. There appears to be nothing I can do about this latter crowd. I don't believe, if it came right down to it, that I would push them off cliffs. Yet I feel that they are entitled to the sleep that is eternal, starting right away. . . .

"I have been married to the same party since 1927 and have a grown son who is a chemical engineer and a daughter who is married. I have two major hobbies: my grandson, born in 1952, and playing low-brow, i.e., popular, music on the Hammond organ. I am a baseball fan, a Mark Twain fan, a James Thurber fan, a Mencken fan and a Bertrand Russell fan. I believe that the human race will shortly blow itself up and I am already at work weaving the handbasket which shall serve as my transportation into the after-world."

---

In his introduction to *Low Man on a Totem Pole*—the book whose title transformed that expression into an American idiom—the comedian Fred Allen dubbed Smith "the screwball's Boswell." That collection of humorous interviews and reminiscences was a tremendous popular success, and Smith's work was rarely absent from the best-seller lists for the remainder of the 1940s. Between 1941 and 1946, he reportedly sold some 1.4 million books. *Low Man* was followed by two books in a similar vein, *Life in a Putty Knife Factory* and *Lost in the Horse Latitudes*, the latter volume consisting primarily of sardonic observations on Hollywood.

A speedy and prolific writer, Smith published nearly forty books, as well as innumerable newspaper and magazine features. His best work generally follows the pattern of his early hits: humorous, irreverent essays inspired by incidents in his own life. In *Larks in the Popcorn* and *Let the Crabgrass Grow*, he lampooned the folkways of suburban life in affluent Mount Kisco, New York, where he made his home from 1945 to 1967. His travels in the United States and abroad are chronicled in such works as *We Went Thataway* (about a trip through the American West), *Smith's London Journal, The Pig in the Barber Shop* (concerning a Mexican sojourn), and *Waikiki Beachnik. Rhubarb*, the most popular of his several novels, is a satirical tale about a cat who inherits millions of dollars and a professional baseball team. In his autobiography, *To Hell in a Handbasket*, Smith recounts his early life in the Midwest and his years as an itinerant reporter.

In his introduction to his anthology *The World, the Flesh, and H. Allen Smith*, Bergen Evans placed Smith in the tradition of such Midwestern-bred humorists as Mark Twain, Ring Lardner, and James Thurber. Smith is notable, according to Evans, for his honesty, his perceptiveness, and his "sympathy with the defeated, the frustrated and the hopeless. Nobility and absurdity are often intertwined and the pathetic and the ludicrous are freqently inseparable." Like his friend and mentor H. L. Mencken, Smith was something of a curmudgeon. In 1967 he left suburban Westchester and relocated to the remote community of Alpine, Texas. "Pollution is the reason I moved," he remarked. "Air pollution and people pollution." Although his popularity had already begun to decline by the late 1950s, and many of his later books received relatively little notice, Smith continued to produce a steady stream of books and articles during the last decade of his life. His papers are at the University of Southern Illinois.

PRINCIPAL WORKS: *Humor*—Low Man on a Totem Pole, 1941; Life in a Putty Knife Factory, 1943; Lost in the Horse Latitudes, 1944; Lo, the Former Egyptian!, 1947; Larks in the Popcorn, 1948; We Went Thataway, 1949; (with I. L. Smith) Low and Inside: A Book of Baseball Anecdotes, Oddities, and Curiosities, 1949; People Named Smith, 1950; (with I. L. Smith) Three Men on Third: A Second Book of Baseball Anecdotes, Oddities, and Curiosities, 1951; Smith's London Journal: Now First Published from the Original Manuscript, 1952; The Compleat Practical Joker, 1953; The Rebel Yell, Being a Carpetbagger's Attempt to Establish the Truth Concerning the Screech of the Confederate Soldier Plus Lesser Matters Appertaining to the Peculiar Habits of the South, 1954; Write Me a Poem, Baby, 1956; The Pig in the Barber Shop, 1958; Don't Get Personal with a Chicken, 1959; Waikiki Beachnik, 1960; Let the Crabgrass Grow: H. Allen Smith's Suburban Almanac, 1960; How to Write Without Knowing Nothing: A Book Largely Concerned with the Use and Misuse of the Language at Home and Abroad, 1961; A Short History of Fingers and Other State Papers, 1963; Two-Thirds of a Coconut Tree, 1963; Poor H. Allen Smith's Almanac: A Compendium Loaded with Wisdom and Laughter, Together with a Generous Lagniappe of Questionable Natural History, All Done Up in Style, 1965; Buskin' with H. Allen Smith, 1968; The Great Chili Confrontation: A Dramatic History of the Decade's Most Impassioned Culinary Embroilment, with Recipes, 1969; Low

Man Rides Again, 1973. *Biography*—Robert Gair: A Study, 1939; The Life and Legend of Gene Fowler, 1977. *Autobiography*—To Hell in a Handbasket, 1962. *Novels*—Mr. Klein's Kampf; or, His Life as Hitler's Double, 1939; Rhubarb, 1946; Mr. Zip, 1952; The Age of the Tail, 1955; Son of Rhubarb, 1967; The View from Chivo, 1971; Return of the Virginian, 1974. *As editor*—Desert Island Decameron, 1945; (with G. Fowler) Lady Scatterly's Lovers, 1973. *Collections*—3 Smiths in the Wind: Low Man on a Totem Pole; Life in a Putty Knife Factory; Lost in the Horse Latitudes, 1946; The World, the Flesh, and H. Allen Smith (ed. B. Evans) 1954; The Best of H. Allen Smith, 1972.

ABOUT: The autobiographical material quoted above was written for Twentieth Century Authors First Supplement, 1955. Authors in the News vol. 2 1976; Contemporary Authors New Revision Series 5 1982; Current Biography 1942; 1976; Dictionary of American Biography, Suppl. 10 1976–1980, 1995; Dictionary of Literary Biography vol. 11 1982; vol. 29 1984. *Periodicals*—New York Times February 25, 1976; Texas Monthly February 1976.

**SMITH, JUSTIN HARVEY** (January 13, 1857–March 21, 1930), American historian, was born at Boscawen, New Hampshire, the youngest son of the Rev. Ambrose Smith, a Congregationalist minister, and Cynthia Maria (Egerton) Smith. He and his family lived in Pembroke, New Hampshire, when he was a boy and later in Norwich, Vermont. Justin graduated from Portsmouth in 1887.

From 1879 to 1881 Smith attended the Union Theological Seminary, New York, spending some time at the Paris Exposition as private secretary of John D. Philbrick, who was in charge of the American educational exhibit. He then worked in publishing for Charles Scribner's Sons, and Ginn & Co., where he was in charge of the editorial department from 1890 to 1898. He was professor of modern history at Dartmouth (1899–1908). He resigned to dedicate himself to historical reseach, writing and travel.

His first work, *Troubadours at Home: Their Lives and Personalities, Their Songs and Their World* (1899), was the result of his travels to Provence in 1895 and 1898 to study the Provençal poets of the tenth and early eleventh centuries. He wrote in the preface that his purpose "is to place the literature of the troubadours as it originally appeared, to show their world and to explore the forest of chalcedony."

Two other early historical works concentrated on revolutionary times. In 1903 he reprinted Benedict Arnold's Journal and included it with a critical study of Arnold's march from Cambridge to Quebec. The book was reprinted in 1970 and again in 1989.

*Our Struggle for the Fourteenth Colony: Canada and the American Revolution* (1907) focused on how the American colonies tried to force independence on Lower Canada. *The New York Times* wrote that the book "will appeal primarily to the specialist in American history, for few general readers of history would care to digest some twelve hundred pages to gain even a thorough understanding of a failure." *Outlook* wrote that Smith's "obvious passion for research induces him to include much petty detail that obscures rather than illuminates." Despite the lack of editing, the study

was considered a definitive account of this aspect of the American Revolution involving Canada from 1775 to 1783. It was reissued in 1974.

Smith then turned to Texas, to produce a painstaking history in *The Annexation of Texas* (1911). E. C. Barker in *American History Review* mentioned Smith's "occasional lack of perspective which is sometimes merely amusing, but which at other times leads to inconsistency, and still others to questionable conclusions." *English History Review* wrote that, "upon the whole the effect of Mr. Smith's investigations is to put the conduct of the United States in a more favourable light than has been the prevailing impression."

In 1920 Smith received the Pulitzer Prize for history for his two-volume *The War With Mexico* (1919), a follow-up to his Texas study. This exhaustive study of American expansion and the war period of 1846–1848 is still consulted, and was reprinted in 1971.

PRINCIPAL WORKS: Troubadours at Home: Their Lives and Personalities, Their Songs and Their World, 1899; Arnold's March From Cambridge to Quebec: A Critical Study: Together with a Reprint of Arnold's Journal, 1903; Our Struggle for the Fourteenth Colony: Canada and the American Revolution, 1907; The Annexation of Texas, 1911; The War With Mexico, 1919. *As editor*—The Historie Booke, 1903; Letters of Santa Anna, 1919.

ABOUT: Smith, J. H. *preface to* Troubadours at Home, 1899. *Periodicals*—American History Review April 1912; English History Review July 1912; New York Times September 7, 1907; June 6, 1920, March 24, April 24, 1930; Outlook October 12, 1907; June 2, 1920.

**SMITH, LILLIAN (EUGENIA)** (December 12, 1897–September 28, 1966), American novelist and social critic, wrote: "I was born in Jasper, Florida. There were nine of us who grew up in a big old rambling house set under great oaks heavy with Spanish moss, in a small Florida town just across the Georgia line. My mother's people were rice planters near St. Mary's; my father's family were pioneer folk who settled southwest Georgia and helped drive the Seminoles into Florida. Both families had had slaves; both thought slavery wrong.

"I began writing 'books' about the time I learned to read them. . . . Asking questions which no one would answer, perhaps because they could not. 'Where did I come from? . . . where was I going? . . . what is eternity?' I must have been a nuisance of large dimensions for I remember my Sunday School teacher firmly laying down the law that never must I ask about eternity again in Sunday School. So I tried to find my answers in our  library. I read Shakespeare one day, *Elsie Dinsmore* the next, *Pilgrim's Progress* the next. I had read all of Shakespeare's plays by the time I was ten or eleven years old. And though I had not found the answers to my questions I had found something very wonderful that made me know that magic of words and poetry at an age when it almost got into my bloodstream.

"And then one day I discovered music. Every one in my family played or sang. I was used to music; but one day, it became something for me. And though I continued my love for books, music was my ardent passion for the next twelve years. . . .

"In between times, I went to college, to Peabody Conservatory in Baltimore; I taught music for three years in Huchow, China; I came home and was secretary to a city manager of a south Florida city and played the organ in a church. Then I took over my father's summer camp for girls which happened to be the first private camp to open in Georgia. It was in the mountains close to North Carolina, and I still live on top of the mountain at the old camp site. I directed it for twenty-four summers. It became a camp known for its creative activities; music, sculpture, the children's theatre; and for the success it often had in dealing with the emotional problems of its children.

"While I had this camp, I also edited and published a magazine (for ten years) called South Today. This psychically rewarding and financially impoverishing venture began with twelve pages and twenty-five subscribers and ended as a hundred-page magazine with 10,000 subscribers. But I abandoned the project in 1946 to give all of my time to writing.

"My first two novels were never published. One was about missionaries in China; the other was a family chronicle. My third novel was Strange Fruit, published in 1944. It was turned down by seven publishers all of whom said it was interesting but not 'salable.' The eighth publisher accepted it immediately. . . .

"In 1949, Killers of the Dream was published. This book was an experiment in the joint autobiography of a person and her region: a searching out of the creative and destructive forces at work in a culture and in the lives of the children who grow up in it. . . . "

---

Despite her desire to be recognized as a literary artist, Lillian Smith believed that fiction should have a strongly social character. Strange Fruit, therefore, the novel by which she is chiefly remembered, reads more like an intelligent and courageous tract than a "literary" effort. It tells the story of the secret and ultimately tragic love affair in a small Southern town in the 1920s between Nonnie Anderson, a young, educated black woman, and Tracy Deen, a white man of high social standing. Tracy's betrayal of Nonnie, and the cycle of violence that swiftly ensues once the affair becomes public, served as an emblem for the spiritual sickness that Smith saw as the central fact of Southern life. Given the shock value of its subject matter and its comparative sexual frankness, Strange Fruit was (almost inevitably) destined for commercial success. The clumsy attempt by the United States Postal Service to ban it from the mails (the intercession of Eleanor Roosevelt caused the ban to be quickly

revoked) only added to its notoriety and sales. The book received largely favorable reviews. Malcolm Cowley wrote of it in the New Republic, "Miss Smith seems to lack the specifically literary gifts of William Faulkner, let us say, or Carson McCullers; and it is possible that her talents will lead her eventually into some other field than the novel. But she has done something in this book that nobody did before her; she has shown that a lynching was intimately connected with the life of a whole community; that it explains and condemns a whole social order. Her book is not a promise but an achievement."

Cowley's guess that Smith's talents might lead her into fields other than the novel proved to be accurate. Her only other novel, One Hour, the story of a respected scientist falsely accused of raping an eight-year-old girl, was an ambitious but not wholly convincing attempt to capture the mood of mass hysteria that characterized McCarthyism. While he admired the novel's "reach," Edmund Fuller, writing in the Saturday Review of Literature, felt that "Smith's effort to encompass all the sins and sorrows of man, to create a microcosm to end all microcosms, to be liberal, just, righteous, and realistic, to be social caseworker, spiritual counselor, and clinical psychologist, all at once, falls by the weight of its over-elaboration."

Apart from Strange Fruit, Smith's most important books were probably Killers of the Dream and The Journey, two intensely personal reflections on her experience of Southern racism. In Killers of the Dream, wrote Fred Hobson, "her thesis was familiar: the South was a sick society, plagued by sin and guilt, tormented by racial segregation." This was not a thesis calculated to win friends in the South; in her last years she received more than one death threat—and in 1955 arsonists set fire to her house in Georgia, destroying her most valuable papers and manuscripts. Smith mistakenly came to feel that more moderate Southern liberals, such as Hodding Carter and Ralph McGill, conspired to "smother" the expression of her views.

A less polemical work than Killers of the Dream, the spiritual autobiography The Journey testified, as did virtually everything Smith wrote, to the soul-destroying effects of racism and segregation. Indeed, all of her work, wrote Hobson, was "so devoted to her particular truth that she sometimes lost sight of all others. That single truth . . . was the destructive power of segregation by race and sex. . . . Ironically, Smith came to see the South in a manner not unlike that in which her greatest adversaries, the staunchest segregationalists, saw it in the 1950s: the Southern way of life was segregation and it seemed to be little else. Such a belief caused Smith to miss much of what else the South was and had been."

Smith's commitment to racial justice extended beyond the written word. She was on the advisory board of the Congress of Racial Equality (though she resigned in 1966 over CORE's gradual movement toward violence and black militancy) and made many appearances on radio and television decrying the injustice of Southern society. She kept up these and other obligations (periodic lecturing appearances, a year as a writer-in-residence at Vassar College) in spite of the debilitating cancer for which she underwent surgery in 1953 and which eventually killed her. She was buried on Old Screamer, the mountain in northern Georgia where she had lived with Paula Snelling, her companion of many years. Smith was undoubtedly years ahead of the moderate white liberals whom she scorned, but, as Anne C. Loveland wrote, "her philosophical thinking was generally derivative and superficial and her literary effort unexceptional. Her primary significance lies in the role she played in the southern civil rights movement of the 1940s, 1950s, and 1960s."

The Lillian Smith Collection is at the University of Georgia in Atlanta.

PRINCIPAL WORKS: Novels—Strange Fruit, 1944; One Hour, 1959. Social criticism and autobiography—Killers of the Dream, 1949, rev. ed. 1961; The Journey, 1954; Now Is the Time, 1955; Memory of a Large Christmas, 1962; Our Faces, Our Words, 1964. Correspondence—How Am I to Be Heard? Letters of Lillian Smith (ed. M. R. Gladney) 1933. Other—The Winner Names the Age: A Collection of Writings by Lillian Smith (ed. M. Cliff) 1978.

ABOUT: The autobiographical material quoted above was written for Twentieth Century Authors First Supplement, 1955. Blackwell, L. and Clay, F. Lillian Smith, 1971; , Current Biography 1944; Dictionary of American Biography, Suppl. 8, 1988; Hobson, F. Tell about the South: The Southern Rage to Explain, 1983; Loveland, A. C. Lillian Smith: A Southerner Confronting the South: A Biography, 1986; Notable American Women: The Modern Period: A Biographical Dictionary, 1980. Periodicals—New Republic March 6, 1944; New York Times September 29, 1966; Saturday Review of Literature October 3, 1959.

## SMITH, LOGAN PEARSALL (October 18, 1865–March 2, 1946), Anglo-American lexicographer and essayist, was born in Millville, New Jersey.

His Quaker family could be traced back to James Logan, secretary to William Penn, and both his paternal grandfather and uncle had served as librarian of Philadelphia. For a time Logan's parents became roaming evangelical revivalists. When their enthusiasm waned they resettled in Germantown, Pennsylvania, where Logan went to school. He attended Haverford College and spent one year at Harvard, after which he joined the family bottle-making business. Soon discovering that this was not to his liking, he settled for a handsome annuity, and moved to England, where he spent the rest of his life as a typical rich American expatriate of the time. He became a British citizen in 1913.

Smith entered Balliol College, Oxford, and, after obtaining his degree, spent some time in Paris. His first book, The Youth of Parnassus, consisted of short stories in the Maupassant manner. On returning to England he produced, with his sister, a short-lived review, The Golden Urn, in which he began printing the gnomic, aphoristic observations on which his reputation rests. These he assembled in

a privately-printed collection titled Trivia in 1902. The book did not attract much attention until it was enlarged and revised in 1917, when its popular success prompted a quick sequel, More Trivia (1922) and, in due course, a third installment, Afterthoughts. All three titles were published in compendium form as All Trivia (containing a new section, "Last Words") in 1933. The individual pieces, scarcely more than a page in length and often, especially in Afterthoughts, consisting of just a few lines, were unique. The Boston Transcript described them as "dainty little paragraphs of gilded whim," and R. P. Blackmur, reviewing All Trivia for the Nation, wrote, "Mr. Smith's literary aphorisms are in the line of La Rochefoucauld, only less malicious, and of La Bruyère, only less organic; he has less knowledge of the world than either, and therefore, perhaps, less sympathy with himself. But thus, on the other hand, his wit is freer and its flights more delightfully irrelevant."

Smith was the embodiment of one of his own observations—"Hearts that are delicate and kind and tongues that are neither—these make the finest company in the world." Robert Gathorne-Hardy's book about his friendship with Smith (which had sprung from their mutual interest in the work of Jeremy Taylor), Recollections of Logan Pearsall Smith, gives an unflattering view of the older man's declining years, in which the tendency towards verbal malice hardened into flashes of illogical and paranoid cruelty. The closing picture in this book—of a bloated and selfish man—needs balancing by Smith's own account of his earlier life, published as Unforgotten Years, and containing brief anecdotes about many of the distinguished personalities known to him in his childhood and youth, such as Walt Whitman, Edith Wharton, and James Whistler. The book, which Edmund Wilson (who wrote about Smith in The Bit Between My Teeth) thought "one of the best things he has done," was written in the same limpid and ironical style as his aphorisms. "Every sentence is shapely and lucid," wrote the Times Literary Supplement. "But the chuckles in passing and the recurrent little flushes of pleasure are but so many invitations to go back to the beginning and this time (and as many other times as can be contrived) to take it all slowly."

Apart from several volumes of popular philology—in the Preface to Words and Idioms Smith claimed that he was a lexicographer and not a philologist, interested in semantics rather than the forms of words—he published the Life and Letters of Sir Henry Wotton, On Reading Shakespeare and Milton and His Modern Critics, the last of these a brief but lively defense of his subject against the criticisms of Eliot and Pound.

With Robert Bridges, Smith was one of the founding members of the Society for Pure English. Apart from his relationship with Gathorne-Hardy, he was on friendly terms with Cyril Connolly and corresponded with the likes of Sir Kenneth Clark and Hugh Trevor-Roper (an edition of Smith's letters was published in 1984), but he lived essentially for reading. Michael Shelden, reviewing an anthology of Smith's work in the Times Literary Supple-

*ment*, wrote: "His witty remarks and thoughtful observations have a cold, artificial quality to them because they have so little bearing on the world outside their author's consciousness. There is art in his work, but not much life." However, many of Smith's titles went into several editions, and at any one time there have always been some Logan Pearsall Smith books in print.

PRINCIPAL WORKS: The Youth of Parnassus and Other Stories, 1895; Trivia, 1902 (rev. 1917); The Life and Letters of Sir Henry Wotton 2 vols., 1907; The English Language, 1912; More Trivia, 1921; Afterthoughts, 1931; All Trivia, 1933; On Reading Shakespeare, 1933; Reperusals and Re-Collections, 1936; Unforgotten Years, 1938; Milton and His Modern Critics, 1940. *As editor and compiler*—Donne's Sermons, 1919; A Treasury of English Prose, 1919; Words and Idioms, 1925; A Treasury of English Aphorisms, 1928; The Golden Grove, Selected Passages From the Sermons and Writings of Jeremy Taylor, 1930; The Golden Shakespeare, 1949; A Religious Rebel 1949 (in U.S.: Philadelphia Quaker, The Letters of Hanna Whitall Smith).

ABOUT: Dictionary of American Biography, 1946–1950; Dictionary of Literary Biography vol. 98 1990; Parker, R. A. The Transatlantic Smiths, 1959; Smith, L. P. Unforgotten Years, 1938; Tribble, E. (ed.) A Chime of Words, The Letters of Logan Pearsall Smith, 1984; Who's Who 1946: Wilson, E. The Bit Between My Teeth, 1965. *Periodicals*—Boston Transcript October 20, 1917; Nation June 6, 1934; London Times March 4, 1946; New Republic January 25, 1939; New York Times Mar 3, 1946; Times Literary Supplement October 8, 1938, January 5, 1991.

## SMITH, MARY PRUDENCE (WELLS): (July 23, 1840–December 17, 1930), American writer of children's books, was born in Attica, New York, the daughter of Dr. Noah S. and Esther Nims (Coleman) Wells. Her family was of New England stock, and when she was nine they moved to Greenfield, Massachusetts. Mary Wells was educated in the local schools and then attended Miss Draper's Female Seminary in Hartford, Connecticut. After teaching for a brief period in the Greenfield high school she went to work in a local bank, filling a position made vacant because the young men of the town had gone to fight the Civil War. She thus became the first woman employee of a Massachusetts bank. At the end of eight years, as assistant to the treasurer, she asked for the same pay a man in her position would have earned, and resigned when the bank management refused to meet her "equal pay for equal work" request. She then went to Philadelphia and studied art for two years; in 1875 she married Judge Fayette Smith of Cincinnati, and lived in that city for the next twenty-one years. Most of Smith's books were written for her daughter, Agnes Mary (who died at the age of fourteen) and for her three stepchildren.

In the year of her marriage Mary Wells Smith, using the pseudonym "P. Thorne," wrote her first book, *Jolly Good Times; or, Child-Life on a Farm.* It was the first of the very popular Jolly Good Time series, and was followed by *Jolly Good Times at School,* one of her biggest favorites among children. Other series followed. There was the Summer Vacation series, the last volume of which, *Five in a Ford* (written when the author was seventy-eight years old), brings her characters into the automobile age. The books in the Young Puritan series and

the Old Deerfield series were based on New England colonial history; both detailed and lively, they recreate life in western Massachusetts from the time of King Philip's War to the Deerfield Massacre and the revolutionary period. Among the titles are *The Boy Captive of Old Deerfield* (which remained in print for some fifty years); *The Boy Captive in Canada,* which completes the story of Stephen Williams (1603–1782), captured by the Indians in 1704; *Boys of the Border,* about events in the Deerfield region during the French and Indian Wars; and *Boys and Girls of Seventy-Seven,* a story of a Massachusetts family during the Revolutionary War. Many of Smith's books remained popular into the 1920s and 1930s; several have been reprinted as recently as 1990 and 1991. The writer died in her home in Greenfield.

PRINCIPAL WORKS: *Fiction*—(as "P. Thorne") Jolly Good Times; or, Child-Life on a Farm, 1875; (as "P. Thorne") Jolly Good Times at School: Also Some Times Not Quite so Jolly, 1877; The Browns, 1884; Their Canoe Trip, 1889; Jolly Good Times at Hackmatack, 1891; More Good Times at Hackmatack, 1892; Jolly Good Times To-Day, 1894; A Jolly Good Summer, 1895; The Young Puritans of Old Hadley (illus. L. J. Bridgman) 1897; The Young Puritans in King Philip's War (illus. L. J. Bridgman) 1898; The Young Puritans in Captivity (illus. J. W. Smith) 1899; The Young and Old Puritans of Hatfield (illus. B. C. Day) 1900; Four on a Farm (illus. E. McConnell) 1901; The Boy Captive of Old Deerfield (illus. L. J. Bridgman) 1904; The Boy Captive in Canada (illus. A. E. Becher) 1905; Boys of the Border (illus. C. Grünwald) 1907; Boys and Girls of Seventy-Seven (illus. C. Grünwald) 1909; Two in a Bungalow (illus. J. Goss) 1914; Three in a Camp (illus. J. Goss) 1916; Five in a Ford (illus. J. Goss) 1918. *Nonfiction*—Miss [Sarah] Ellis's Mission, 1886.

ABOUT: *Periodical*—New York Times December 18, 1930.

## SMITH, NAOMI ROYDE-. See ROYDE-SMITH, NAOMI

## SMITH, SHELIA KAYE-. See KAYE-SMITH, SHEILA

## SMITH, S. S.          See WILLIAMSON, THAMES ROSS

## SMITH, THORNE (March 27, 1891?–June 21, 1934), American novelist and humorist, was born James Thorne Smith, Jr., at the United States Naval Academy, Annapolis, Maryland, the son of Commodore James Thorne Smith. (Accounts of his birth date vary.) He attended Locust Dale Academy in Virginia; St. Luke's School in Wayne, Pennsylvania; and completed his formal education at Dartmouth College. After graduation he went to work for an advertising agency; during World War I he enlisted in the Navy, in which he reached the rank of boatswain's mate; he edited the Naval Reserve journal *Broadside,* to which he also contributed a humorous series of stories about a hapless naval recruit. These were later collected in 1918 and 1919 as *Biltmore Oswald* and *Out o'Luck.*

After the war Smith returned to advertising. In 1926 he published *Topper,* his first successful novel, about a prim and proper banker—"The Toppers' house was not one of mirth"—who is haunted by the ghosts of a recently deceased society couple. The goal of the ghostly, playful Kerbys is to liven up Cosmo Topper's staid life, usually resulting in embarrassing moments from which Topper must extricate himself. The popularity of *Topper* led to a sequel, *Topper Takes a Trip*, as well as several movies and a television sitcom. Smith's string of best-sellers allowed him to leave advertising for a writing career, which included a brief stint in Hollywood writing dialogue for Metro-Goldwyn-Mayer in 1933.

In his day, however, Smith was popular with the public for what the *New York Times* called his "humorous extravaganzas." In *Turnabout* he describes  the adventures of a lively young suburban couple who switch bodies, but not personalities, under the influence of an idol which possesses unsuspected powers. *The Bishop's Jaegers* concerns an embarrassed cleric set down in the midst of a nudist colony. Of *Skin and Bones*, the story of a photographer who turns into a skeleton at the worst moments, the *Chicago Daily Tribune* declared that the "reader reels with amazement and laughter through 306 hilarious but utterly mad pages."

Smith wrote at a time when verbal wit and visual farce were merging to usher in the period of the "screwball comedy." The blend of slapstick and wit proved perfect for the screen comedies of his era.

Smith left an unfinished novel, *The Passionate Witch*, which was completed by another American fantasist, Norman Matson.

PRINCIPAL WORKS: *Novels*—Topper: An Improbable Adventure, 1926 (reissued as Topper: A Ribald Adventure, 1933); Dream's End, 1927; The Stray Lamb, 1929; Did She Fall?, 1930; The Night Life of the Gods, 1931; Turnabout, 1931; The Bishop's Jaegers, 1932; Topper Takes a Trip, 1932; Rain in the Doorway, 1933; Skin and Bones, 1933; The Glorious Pool, 1934; (with N. Matson) The Passionate Witch, 1941. *Short stories*—Biltmore Oswald: The Diary of a Hapless Recruit, 1918; Out o'Luck: Biltmore Oswald Very Much at Sea, 1919. *Poetry*—Haunts and By-Paths and Other Poems, 1919. *Juvenile*—Lazy Bear Lane, 1931.

ABOUT: Bleiler, E. G. (ed.) Supernatural Fiction Writers: Fantasy and Horror, 1985; Gale, S. H. (ed.) Encyclopedia of American Humorists, 1988; Van Doren, C. The American Novel: 1789–1939, 1940. *Periodicals*—Chicago Daily Tribune December 30, 1933; New York Times June 22, 1934.

## SMITH, WALLACE (1888?–January 31, 1937),

American journalist, illustrator, novelist, and short story writer, was a native of Chicago, where he became well known as a newspaper artist and reporter before launching a career of adventure in Mexico. He was a veteran of four Mexican campaigns, two of them with Pancho Villa.

Smith was a master of the realistic pen-and-ink drawing. In 1922 he executed illustrations and page-borders for Ben Hecht's privately printed erotic horror novel, *Frantazius Mallare*, which was published in Chicago (and deemed obscene by authorities). Smith was briefly jailed on obscenity charges for his contribution to the venture. He then turned his talents toward establishing a career in fiction writing.

"There is a saying," Smith wrote, "that once the dust of Mexico has settled on your heart there can be no rest for you in any other land." It is not surprising that his first book was titled *The Little Tigress: Tales Out of the Dust of Mexico*. The *Boston Transcript* found the stories "brief, romantic, tragic, full of color, and song, and cruelty and death. Their fascination is brutal but inescapable." The book remains in print, as does *Are You Decent?*, his second published collection of short stories, which recounts the lives of a troupe of vaudeville players living in Mrs. Emily Fisher's boarding house. Smith's most successful novel, *The Captain Hates the Sea*, might be described as a *Grand Hotel* on water. It records the voyage of an ocean liner from San Francisco to New York via the Panama Canal with a colorful assortment of cast and crew on board, including a disgruntled captain who does indeed hate the sea.

In 1929, when silent movies were beginning to give way to the talkies, Smith went to Hollywood, where he became a successful screenwriter. One of his credits included the screenplay for his novel *The Captain Hates the Sea*, which was filmed with a cast that included Victor McLaglen, John Gilbert, and the Three Stooges.

PRINCIPAL WORKS: *Short stories*—The Little Tigress: Tales Out of the Dust of Mexico, 1923; Are You Decent?, 1927. *Novels*—Tiger's Mate, 1928; The Captain Hates the Sea, 1933; Bessie Cotter, 1934; The Happy Alienist: A Viennese Caprice, 1936. *Nonfiction*—On the Trail in Yellowstone, 1924; Oregon Sketches, 1925.

ABOUT: Maltin, L. TV Movies & Video Guide, 1988; Sullivan, J. (ed.) The Penguin Encyclopedia of Horror and Supernatural, 1986. *Periodicals*—Boston Transcript September 26, 1923; New York Times February 1, 1937.

## SMITTER, WESSEL (1894–November 7, 1951),

American novelist, was born near Grand Rapids, Michigan, and was educated at Calvin College and at the University of Michigan. After graduation he received what he called a "sort of scholarship" from one of the big automobile manufacturers in Detroit, and for two years learned the business "from the ground up," eventually taking a position in the company's advertising department. The result was not what the manufacturer intended; instead of devoting his life to automobiles, Smitter grew to detest the factory and to consider industry a monster which crushed the lives of those it overwhelmed. He fled abruptly to Hollywood, where he made his living selling and transplanting trees for homeowners.

Smitter published only two novels. *F.O.B. Detroit* tells the story of a lumberjack who tries and fails to fit into the world of the automobile factory. It is autobiographical in spirit though not in story, and reflects the yearning for escape from mechanized industry which drove its author from Detroit. Critical reaction was positive; Louis Adamic, of the *Saturday Review of Literature*, thought that Smitter "writes from the inside with powerful feeling. Machines and workers are vividly described in a simply told, restrained, but intensely moving narrative." Smitter's second novel, *Another Morning*, concerns modern pioneers in Alaska and garnered only mixed notices. The *Boston Transcript* reviewer, the novelist Wallace Stegner, found parts of the novel didactic and wrote that the "chronicle of the

actual breaking of the soil . . . is the stale chronicle of all pioneer novels." But Stegner also went on to declare the novel "important because it transplants the typical frontier virtues from a dead past to a living present and future, and shows us an America trying to remake itself on a different and more enduring pattern."

Wessel Smitter was in northern California gathering material for a new novel when he died of a heart attack while chopping redwoods.

PRINCIPAL WORKS: *Novels*—F.O.B. Detroit, 1938; Another Morning, 1941.

ABOUT: *Periodicals*—Boston Transcript April 26, 1941; New York Times November 6, 1951; Saturday Review of Literature November 5, 1938.

## SNAITH, JOHN COLLIS (1876–December 3, 1936), English novelist, was born in Nottingham, the oldest of four children of Joseph Dawes Snaith,

owner of a wholesale paper business, and Elizabeth (Walker) Snaith. He received a commercial education at High Pavement School in Nottingham, but was sent at the age of thirteen to work as a clerk in the offices of the Midland Railway. He compensated for his interrupted schooling by wide reading in the library of the Nottingham Mechanics' Institute, earning the reputation of being something of a loner.

According to Sir Charles Tennyson in *Life's All a Fragment*, it was Snaith's grandmother, to whom he regularly read aloud, who encouraged him to write a story of his own; his first attempt, written in his early teens, was published in a Nottingham newspaper. Tennyson also stated that as early as a year or two after Snaith left school he had begun his first novel. Certainly, after he broke his leg playing football in 1894, he devoted solid time to writing. Two years later *Mistress Dorothy Marvin* was published. A lengthy historical romance about England in the time of James II, it is the work of a young literary enthusiast with little experience of real life, crammed with exciting incidents and excessively overwritten. The London critics for the most part praised it, but the *Athenaeum* reviewer thought it rambling and verbose and too much influenced by the style of Robert Louis Stevenson.

Snaith then fell under the influence of George Meredith and began work on another historical novel, *Fierceheart, the Soldier*, a lively yarn about the rebellion led by the Young Pretender in 1745.

This work, too, received good reviews in the London papers, and even more attention in the United States. On the strength of this success Snaith resigned from the railway company, and in 1897–1898 enrolled at University College, Nottingham.

A year later he was back at writing. He produced a potboiler, *Lady Barbarity*, a romantic comedy about the Jacobite rebellion of 1745. It became a best-seller, and was subsequently dramatized in New York. His fourth novel, *Willow the King*, about a Midlands family devoted to the game, was described as "the best cricket story ever written." Snaith's first attempt at a contemporary subject, it told a lively story with fairly successful characterizations. His next book about the Stuart dynasty, *Patricia at the Inn*, spins a story of Charles II in flight and narrowly escaping capture after the Battle of Worcester. Tennyson thought this the most effective of Snaith's historical romances.

With *Broke of Covenden* he began writing in another mode. This is a forceful story of an old family threatened by the pressures of modern industrial life. Arthur Conan Doyle, in his *Through the Open Door*, wrote: "I do not say that the book is a classic, and I should not like to be positive that it is not, but I am perfectly sure that the man who wrote it has the possibility of a classic within him."

*William Jordan, Junior* concerns a frail, unworldly boy, brought up a bookish recluse by his father but forced to make his way in the commercial world. The novel has obvious autobiographical overtones; Snaith's own reclusive nature had earned him the nickname "the gloomy scribe" among his cricketing friends. While working on the book he had a psychotic episode and was hospitalized for some months. What few reviews the novel received were negative; the *Times* of London, for example, dismissed it as "so bizarre, so grotesque, so mysterious . . . as to afford little pleasure." His next novel, *Araminta*, was a distinct turnabout: a comedy of manners done in eighteenth-century style. His most financially rewarding book, it was staged in London in 1921. Snaith's imaginative powers broke out again in two more bizarrely plotted novels about the young man of odd powers facing a hostile world. *The Sailor* tells of an illiterate boy who overcomes his years of terror at sea to become a novelist. *The Coming* attempts a satire on modern society with a Christ-like hero who is eventually committed to an asylum as a dangerous pacifist, and there writes a play that wins him, posthumously, the Nobel Peace Prize. While a few reviewers praised its delicacy and sincerity, most deplored it as overwrought, unconvincing, and finally, absurd.

From then on Snaith's writing was a kaleidoscope of moods, modes, and settings: novels of contemporary realism, historical romances, futuristic fantasies; thrillers, comedies of manners, political satires. *The Principal Girl* concerns American politics; *There Is a Tide* tells of a girl from the American Midwest trying to make a go of life in London. Reviewers were puzzled by his shifts of style, and applied the label "potboiler" frequently. Nevertheless, he sold well (even more in America than in Britain) and died a wealthy man.

PRINCIPAL WORKS: *Fiction*—Mistress Dorothy Marvin: Being Excerpts from the Memoirs of Sir Edward Armstrong . . . Edited into Modern English by J. C. Snaith, 1896 (in U.S.: Mistress Dorothy Marvin: A Seventeenth Century Romance of England, 1906); Fierceheart, the Soldier, 1897 (in U.S.: Fierceheart the Soldier: A Story of the Days of 1745 in England, 1906); Lady Barbarity: A Romantic Comedy, 1899; Willow the King: The Story of a Cricket Match (illus. L. Davis) 1899; Patricia at the Inn, 1901; Love's Itinerary, 1902; The Wayfarers (illus. F. H. Townsend) 1902; Broke of Covenden, 1904 (rewritten 1914); Henry Northcote, 1906; William Jordan, Junior, 1907; Araminta, 1909; Fortune, 1910; Mrs. Fitz, 1910; The Principal Girl, 1912; An Affair of State, 1913; Anne Feversham, 1914 (in U.K.: The Great Age); The Sailor, 1916; The Coming, 1917; Mary Plantagenet: An Improbable Story, 1918; The Time Spirit: A Romantic Tale, 1918; Love Lane, 1919; The Undefeated, 1919; The Adventurous Lady, 1920; The Unforeseen, 1920; The Council of Seven, 1921; The Van Roon, 1922; There Is a Tide, 1924; Time and Tide, 1924; Thus Far, 1925; What Is to Be, 1926; The Hoop, 1927; Surrender, 1928; Cousin Beryl, 1929; Indian Summer, 1931; But Even So, 1935; Curiouser and Curiouser, 1935 (in U.S.: Lord Cobleigh Disappears). *Drama*—(with H. A. Vachell) The Hour and the Man: A Play, 1921.

ABOUT: Conan Doyle, A. Through the Open Door; Tennyson, Sir C. Life's All a Fragment, 1953. *Periodicals*—New York Times December 10, 1936; Times (London) November 15, 1907; December 10, 1936.

## SNOW, EDGAR PARKS (July 19, 1905–February 15, 1972), American journalist, wrote:

"On my mother's side I am descended from Irish and German families. On my father's side there is Irish and English. The Snow clan claims connection with that capacious tub, the *Mayflower*. My own father grew up on a farm, and after college went to Kansas City, Missouri, where I was born. We were a middle-class family, with more respectability than money, though we had enough to eat and wear always, and a comfortable home. When I first took an interest in how we lived my father was editing a business paper and operating a printing shop. In summer vacations I worked for him as printer's devil. There I learned to set type and feed a press and to like the smell of ink and freshly cut paper. When I was in high school I edited a paper of my own and wrote all the copy and set and printed and mailed it. Once I set up and printed a book of my own verse, but the only person who saw it was the girl to whom I dedicated it. Despite such ominous signs my parents took no precautions. Before I entered college I had determined to be a writer.

"In 1923–1924 I attended junior college in Kansas City; then I went to the school of journalism at the University of Missouri. Later I studied at Columbia—a few courses in Extension. With this inadequate preparation I became a newspaper man. I got my first newspaper job, in fact, while at the university, with the *Kansas City Star*, which eventually gave me the sack. My second newspaper job was with the *New York Sun*.

"In 1928, in New York, I decided I needed adventure and the experience of travel and I started off to see the world. I have been a newspaper correspondent ever since. During the past thirteen years I have traveled thousands of miles in the Orient and visited practically every country from Baluchistan to Siberia. Most of my time has been in China, but the Philippines was my headquarters for nearly two years, and off and on I spent many months in Japan, Manchuria, India, the Dutch Indies, etc. From 1933 to 1937 I made my home in Peking, and while there I studied the Chinese language, in which I have a fair fluency.

"In 1929 I was correspondent for the *Chicago Tribune*, and from 1930 to 1938 for the *New York Sun*. In 1933 I was also appointed staff correspondent for the *London Daily Herald*, and in 1937 I became that paper's chief correspondent in the Far East. I began to write for the *Saturday Evening Post* in 1938, and have contributed to it every year since then. In 1936 I entered what was then Soviet China, and traveled with the Chinese Red Army for five months. I was able to bring out the first eyewitness account of that 'lost country' and break a news blockade of nine years. The strangest moment of my life occurred when I returned from Red China and read my own obituary in the American papers.

"Once I wrote a book called *Impressions of the Northwest*, but it was published only in Chinese. My wife, whose pen name is 'Nym Wales,' has published three books in Chinese, none of which had appeared in English. She is an American; we were married in Tokyo in 1932. Her latest book, *China Builds for Democracy*, is the story of the Chinese Industrial Co-operatives, which she originally conceived, and helped to plan with myself and Rewi Alley.

"We returned to American in 1941. It is good to be back. There is no other country on earth like this: none with such treasure, culturally and materially, none with such possibilities in an age of science. Most important of all, this is no other land which offers the facilities and the freedom essential to a fearless search for truth. To preserve that freedom and those facilities and to help continue that search—surely these are the minimum conditions on which honest journalists can support any régime today."

———

During and after the Second World War, Snow covered most of the important events around the world for the *Saturday Evening Post* and wrote a number of books as well as articles for the *Nation*, the *New Republic*, and *Life*. But it is for his writings on China that he will be remembered. "Snow's career was remarkable," the London *Times* wrote, "not simply for being the first serious journalist to explore and describe the Chinese Communist movement at the moment when it consolidated itself under Mao Tse-tung's leadership in Northwest China in 1936, but in being one of the tiny handful of Westerners who established a personal and lasting contact with Mao Tse-tung himself." In 1937 Snow published what became his best known book, *Red Star Over China*, an insider's account of the tumultuous Chinese revolution that the author witnessed first hand. *Yale Review* critic Owen Lattimore called it the "biggest journalistic scoop in years," and went on to state that "with one book Edgar Snow has become one of the greatest authorities in the world on the struggle for liberty of four hundred million people."

In 1960 the Chinese Communist government granted Snow permission to travel thousands of miles around the country. The resulting impressions were recorded in the book *The Other Side of the River*, but this time Snow was accused of biased reporting. "This reviewer found it hard to believe everything could be as good, helpful, or progressive as Mr. Snow portrays it," remarked H. S. Hayward of the *Christian Science Monitor*. *Commonweal*'s H. C. Hinton went so far as to warn that the book was "so biased and naive as to constitute a public danger."

It is not surprising that during the anti-Communist fervor of the McCarthy era Snow was viewed with suspicion in certain circles. Alden Whitman, writing Snow's obituary in *New York Times*, pointed out that the fact he was offered unique access to the country "did not signify that Mr. Snow agreed with Chinese doctrines, but rather that the Chinese thought him a fair and sensitive recorder of Mainland moods and events." John Maxwell Hamilton, in his biography *Edgar Snow*, found Snow a journalist unafraid to voice skepticism. When presented with dubious production figures by a Chinese steel plant official, Snow snapped, "Figures don't lie, but liars figure." Hamilton believes Snow's humanism was at the core of his remarkable rapport with, and insights into, the people of China. But more recent views have also faulted Snow for his uncritical view of Mao's China. Jonathan Mirsky, in his review for the *Times Literary Supplement* of S. Bernard Thomas's book *Season of High Adventure: Edgar Snow in China*, wrote that "The plain truth is that Edgar Snow, the energetic and probing reporter who in the 1920s and 1930s looked under every stone in Chiang Kai-Shek's China, stopped looking when he succumbed to Mao's seduction. . . . It is disgraceful and unprofessional to go to Snow's lengths to avoid serious consideration of China's 1959–61 famine—probably the worst in the history of the world—in which 20 to 30 million people died: 'I saw no starving people in China, nothing that looked like an old-style famine . . . malnutrition undoubtedly existed. Mass starvation? No.' How did Snow arrive at this conclusion. It was simply that his friends in Peking—including Zhou Enlai—told him so. Was there any real reporter's investigation? No."

Snow was an early critic of the United States' involvement in Vietnam, and his personal relationships with the Chinese Communist leadership continued to the end of his life. As Snow was dying of cancer in Eysins, Switzerland, where he made his home, he was invited by Premier Chou En-lai to come to Peking for treatment, and a Chinese medical team was dispatched to help him make the journey. "The Chinese act of concern for Snow was extraordinary," Hamilton notes. "China certainly would not have reached beyond its borders in such a way for any other American." Snow declined the offer. He did request, though, that some of his cremated remains be buried in China, where in fact they are interred on the campus of Peking University.

PRINCIPAL WORKS: *Nonfiction*—Far Eastern Front, 1933; Red Star Over China, 1937, rev. ed. 1968; The Battle for Asia, 1941 (in U.K.: Scorched Earth); (with E. Taylor and E. Janeway) Smash Hitler's International: The Strategy of a Political Offensive Against the Axis, 1941; People On Our Side, 1944 (in U.K.: Glory and Bondage); The Pattern of Soviet Power, 1945; Stalin Must Have Peace, 1947; Random Notes on Red China (1936–1945), 1957; Journey to the Beginning, 1958; The Other Side of the River: Red China Today, 1962 (rev. as Red China Today, 1971); The Long Revolution, 1972; Edgar Snow's China: A Personal Account of the Chinese Revolution, compiled by Lois Wheeler Snow, 1983. As editor—Living China: Modern Chinese Short Stories, 1936.

ABOUT: The autobiographical material quoted above was written for Twentieth Century Authors, 1942. Current Biography 1941; Farnsworth, R. M. (ed.) Edgar Snow's Journey South of the Clouds, 1991; Hamilton, J. M. Edgar Snow, 1988; Snow, L. W. A Death With Dignity: When the Chinese Came, 1975; Thomas, S. B. Season of High Adventure: Edgar Snow in China, 1996. *Periodicals*—Christian Science Monitor November 30, 1962; Commonweal January 11, 1963; New York Times February 16, 1972; Times (London) February 16, 1972; Times (London) Literary Supplement, October 25, 1996; Yale Review Summer 1938.

**SOBY, JAMES THRALL** (December 14, 1906–January 29, 1979), American art critic, wrote: "I was born and grew up in Hartford, Connecticut. Attended Williams College, where I became interested in illustrated books, particularly those done by the leading Parisian artists—Picasso, Matisse, Bonnard, Rouault, etc. After two years I decided to leave college for Paris and there, in the late 1920s, began to collect contemporary paintings.  Returned to Hartford and became a partner in the bookshop of Edwin Valentine Mitchell and took part in various staff capacities in the activities of Hartford's remarkable art museum, the Wadsworth Atheneum. I continued to collect modern paintings and sculptures, both European and American, and began to write articles about living artists and, presently, some books about the latter. Gravitated more and more toward New York City. Was on the staff of the Museum of Modern Art for several years, beginning in 1942, and have since continued to serve on various of the museum's committees. Since 1946 have been art critic for *Saturday Review of Literature* and have continued to write articles and books on art, past and present; at present am chairman of the editorial board of the *Magazine of Art*. I live in New York City, which seems to me an extraodinarily vital art center.

"I am more and more convinced what we all think of as 'modern' art is of vast and enduring importance, though only in its fine examples, since no work of art is automatically valid because of the era to which it belongs. Also, I've always believed that an understanding of contemporary art must be accompanied by devotion to the art of the past. Hence I've tried to spend as much time on art-historical research as on the modern field. My one serious complaint about the state of the arts in America is that too many professional critics, myself included, tend to become over-involved in executive art tasks of one kind and another, thus not allowing themselves enough time for the tiring but I think inescapable chore of trying to write about painting, sculpture and the graphic arts."

---

Despite his self-proclaimed over-involvement "in executive art tasks of one kind and another," James Thrall Soby produced an impressive number of books. Soby was quoted in the *New York Times* as stating that "criticism is the art of affection. I like to write only about people whom I admire enormously, and say why I think they are good." This philosophy is apparent in his 1959 book about the Catalan painter *Joán Miró*. The *New Yorker* (1959) found that it "suffers a bit from what might be called total acceptance. All is praise, and . . . the unvarying adulation tends, paradoxically, to obscure the value of Miró's many real masterpieces." However, the reviewer went on to praise Soby's impeccable scholarship: "The book benefits . . . from the author's intimate acquaintance with Miró's work and his deep understanding of the whole Surrealist phase of contemporary art, and a number of his observations are penetrating indeed." Among the other subjects of Soby's books and monographs are Giorgio de Chirico, Salvador Dali, Georges Rouault, and Juan Gris. In its review of *Contemporary Painters*, the *New Yorker* (1948) called him "one of the most discerning writers on modern art."

Soby's father Charles made his fortune in the tobacco business and also helped pioneer the pay telephone. This financial security made it possible for his son to accumulate his impressive collection of art. After James Soby's death in Norwalk, Connecticut, many of his pieces were willed to the Museum of Modern Art, where he had served in various capacities. William Rubin, the Museum's director of painting and sulptor, declared in the *New York Times* that "Jim Soby was the complete museum man. He was curator, scholar, critic, trustee and collector, all rolled into one. In every one of those capacities, he was the most selfless and self-effacing of men."

PRINCIPAL WORKS: *Nonfiction*—After Picasso, 1935; The Early Chirico, 1941 (rev. as Giorgio de Chirico, 1955); Eugene Berman: Catalogue of the Retrospective Exhibition of His Paintings, Drawings, Illustrations and Designs, Organized by the Institute of Modern Art, Boston, 1941; Paintings, Drawings, Prints: Salvador Dali, 1941 (rev. as Salvador Dali, 1946); (with D. C. Miller) Romantic Painting in America, 1943; The Prints of Paul Klee, 1945; Ben Shahn, 1947; Sculpture by Houdon, 1947; Contemporary Painters, 1948; Paintings, Drawings, and Prints by Paul Klee from the Klee Foundation, Berne, Switzerland, 1949; (with A. H. Barr, Jr.) Twentieth-Century Italian Art, 1949; Modigliani: Paintings, Drawings, Sculpture, 1951, rev. ed. 1963; Yves Tanguy: Exhibition and Catalogue, 1955; Balthus, 1956; Paintings from the Museum of Modern Art: Series II: Expressionism, Impressionism, Surrealism, 1956; Ben

Shahn: His Graphic Art, 1957; Modern Art and the New Past, 1957; Juan Gris, 1958; Joán Miró, 1959; The James Thrall Soby Collection of Works of Art . . . Exhibited . . . New York, Feb. 1 to Feb. 25, 1961; Ben Shahn: Paintings, 1963; (with J. Elliott and M. Wheeler) Bonnard and His Environment, 1965; René Magritte, 1965. *As editor*—The Booklover's Diary, 1930; Georges Rouault: Paintings and Prints, 1947; Arp, 1958.

ABOUT: The autobiographical material quoted above was written for Twentieth Century Authors First Supplement, 1955. Contemporary Authors vol. 103 1981. *Periodicals*—New York Times January 30, 1979; New Yorker December 18, 1948; November 28, 1959.

## "SOLOGUB, FYODOR (KUZMICH)" (pseudonym of FYODOR KUZMICH TETERNIKOV)

(March 1, 1863–December 6, 1927), Russian playwright, novelist, and translator, was born in St. Petersburg, the son of a shoemaker. After the death of his father, his mother was forced to become a servant. By dint of hard work, and no other advantages except that his mother's enlightened employers made proper provision for his education, he was able to graduate, at the age of twenty-one, from the Teachers' Institute in St. Petersburg. Until 1907 he led a life he found miserable: first as a teacher of (mostly) mathematics in small provincial towns, and then as an inspector of schools in St. Petersburg.

Sologub started to publish in the 1880s in magazines, and was known as a loose associate of the symbolist poets—in whose activities, however, he did not participate. As Andrew Field wrote, Sologub was the possessor of one of the subtlest senses of humor of all the early European modernists; part of this lay in the fact that, as a pessimist, he was "never seen to smile." Mirsky called him "the greatest and most refined of the first generation of the Symbolists." Sologub was a profoundly original writer—a major poet, a major novelist and story-writer, and an important dramatist.

Sologub made pessimism a special, yet ironic, feature of his work. He was by no means a total pessimist, however. On the contrary: behind his frequently contorted, and always exceedingly subtle and humorous, rejection of *poshlost*—the Russian word for "vulgarity" or "awfulness"—lay a vision of serene beauty.

Sologub's reputation as a "decadent" stemmed at first less from his poetry than from such early prose works as the story collection *Teni* (Shadows, 1896) and the novel *Tyazhelye sny* (1896; translated as *Bad Dreams*). In the year 1896 he also published the first book of his poetry, called simply *Stikhi* (Poems). In the stories Sologub depicted the children he taught as gifted but helpless dreamers and fantasists unwilling to face a vile reality. In his symbolic system the sun (also shown as a dragon or serpent) represented the horrors of vulgar life, of *poshlost*; children were opposed to life; and death was the great deliverer. The antihero of his first novel, *Shadows*, tormented by the stagnation around him, was modeled directly on Huysman's notorious Des Esseintes (of *A Rebours*). The poems conjured up, with meticulous and often incantatory technique, a gnostic world—created by an evil demiurge—in which evil is the norm. Yet not all is lost:

What are our poor villages,
What is time and space!
The father has many mansions
But we do not know their names.
Yet I can sense a paradise with joys:
It's life that's the dream.
I relinquish the old lies
And the torturings of time.

Decadence offered, for Sologub and for the others who like him then sympathized with the revolutionaries, a convenient means of expressing dissatisfaction. Sologub regarded Aleksandr Dobrolyubov (1873–1944) and his verse collection of 1895, *Natura naturans, Natura naturata*, as paradigmatically decadent; it influenced Sologub's production after the mid-nineties.

Sologub's *Melki bes* (translated as *The Little Demon* and later as *The Petty Demon*) was serialized in a periodical between 1905 and 1907, appearing as a book in the latter year. D. S. Mirsky called it the most "perfect Russian novel since Dostoievsky." It is a portrait, as the title implies, of a petty monster, first and foremost a satirically ironic one of Sologub himself; Peredonov was drawn, as a type, from Gogol; he also has affinities with Karamazov senior. But Sologub was extending past models, not borrowing: he was digging into the depths of his being to express his disgust at what his own petty bourgeois life had been. When the book appeared in the Cournos-Aldington translation in 1916, a perceptive reviewer in the *Times Literary Supplement* wrote: "The quality of this book . . . is not merely a matter of the novelist's art, nor by any means only to be found in the episodical story of Liudmilla and Pilnikov. Sologub so tells the tale of Peredonov, his cousin and his mistress Varvara, and his stupid and vicious friends, as to let the reader feel that there is another kind of life." It is this "other kind of life"—the gnostic alternative to a life on an earth created by a malicious demiurge—that haunts all Sologub's work. Yet his portrait of Peredonov's provincial town is simultaneously strictly realistic, a sort of prophetic anticipation of life under Stalin.

In 1908 Sologub's life changed. Having left his post as inspector of schools and found fame with *The Petty Demon*, he published some of his finest works at this time: the almost naturalistic story *V tolpe* (In the crowd, 1907), is based on the incident in which many people were crushed to death at the coronation of Nicholas II (1896); *Plammennyi krug* (Circle of fire, 1908) is the greatest single collection of poetry from his first period; *Pobeda smerti* (The conquest of death, 1908; translated as *The Triumph of Death*), a symbolist pageant-drama set in medieval times, is perhaps his best play. Sologub also married the playwright Anastasiya Chebotareskaya (1908), a witty, tempestuous and ironic woman who "preached the union of all futurists." This led Sologub into a sort of humorous flirtation with the futurists, although he was rather more substantial than any of these.

This lighter-hearted time for Sologub ended abruptly with the Revolution. During it he wrote more poems and plays, and his *Sobranie sochinenii* (Collected works) appeared in twenty volumes between 1913 and 1916. One of these, *Ocharovaniya zemli* (Charms of the earth), contained ironic triolets celebrating his associations with the futurists.

His trilogy of novels *Tvorimaya legenda* (translated as *The Created Legend*) was written between 1908 and 1912, and published in full as the conclusion to the *Collected Works*. When Cournos's incomplete translation appeared, the *Times Literary Supplement* reviewer summarized it admirably: "There is more magic in Sologub's touch, perhaps, than in that of any of the modern Russian novelists whose work is becoming known in England. If this novel sometimes hurts with deliberate brutality it does more than heal the injuries." A new, more accurate and complete translation was published in the late 1970s.

In 1921 Chebotareskaya drowned herself in the River Neva—on the day before the couple was given permission to leave Russia. The devastated Sologub then asked permission to leave the Soviet Union, but could no longer obtain it. Nor could his books after 1923 be published as he wrote them, since they were decreed to be "too advanced"; there were revivals only after his death. As the author of *The Petty Demon* who had not been altogether against revolution, he was allowed to exercise some nominal influence, as chairman of the Leningrad Union of Writers. Mention of him was not encouraged, yet he managed to write his finest poetry. His work merits further discussion—both in his own country and outside it.

PRINCIPAL WORKS IN ENGLISH TRANSLATION: *Poetry*—Markov, V. and Sparks, M. (ed.) *Modern Russian Poetry*, 1967 (pages 90–111). *Short stories*—Sweet Scented Name (tr. S. Graham) 1915; The Old House (tr. J. Cournos) 1916; Little Tales (tr. anon) 1917; The Magic Goblet (tr. anon) 1970; The Kiss of the Unborn (tr. M. Barker) 1977; Bad Dreams (tr. M. Barker) 1978. *Novels*—The Little Demon (tr. J. Cournos and R. Aldington) 1916 (tr. R. Wilks, 1962; tr. A. Field; 1962, tr. S. D. Cioran and M. Barker, 1983); The Created Legend (tr. J. Cournos), 1916 (tr. S. D. Cioran, 3 vol., 1979). *Drama*—The Triumph of Death (tr. J. Cournos) 1916.

ABOUT: Columbia Dictionary of Modern European Literature, 1947, 1980; Greene, D. Insidious Intent: An Interpretation of Sologub's The Petty Demon, 1986; Mirsky, D. S. Contemporary Russian Literature 1881–1925, 1926; Poggioli, R. The Poets of Russia 1890–1930, 1960; Rabinowitz, S. Sologub's Literary Children, 1980; Seymour-Smith, M. Macmillan Guide to Modern World Literature, 1986. *Periodicals*—Russian Review July 1971; Slavic and East European Journal Winter 1989, Spring 1984; Times Literary Supplement March 30, 1916.

## SOMERVILLE, EDITH (ANNA ŒNONE)

(May 2, 1858–October 8, 1949), Irish novelist, short story writer, and essayist, was born on Corfu, where her father, Lieutenant Colonel Thomas Henry Somerville, commanded a battalion of the Third Foot Regiment. Her mother was Adelaide Eliza, daughter of Vice-Admiral Sir Josiah Coghill and granddaughter of Charles Kendal Bushe, Chief Justice of Ireland.

In 1859, Colonel Somerville retired to Drishane House, Castletownshend, in County Cork, where eight generations of his family had lived. He and his wife provided seven siblings for Edith, the eldest. There were six boys, and, Somerville said in *Irish Memories*, "daughters were at a discount," permitted only "to eat of the crumbs that fell from their brothers' tables." This may explain in part why she never had much time for men, in her life or in her books, where women are morally and intellectually the stronger sex.

Nevertheless, growing up at the heart of the Protestant Anglo-Irish ruling class, Edith Somerville joined vigorously in all its pleasures—parties,  picnics, and dancing, tennis, boating and riding—fox-hunting above all. Educated mostly at home, by governesses and by her mother, she also loved reading and music, and had a passion for drawing. In her teens she studied for a term at the South Kensington School of Art, then at art schools in Düsseldorf and Paris. She later had a number of one-woman shows in Dublin, London, and New York.

On January 17, 1886, Edith Somerville met her second cousin Violet Martin ("Martin Ross," her collaborator), whose family had been even longer in Ireland. Somerville described this meeting in *Irish Memories* as "the hinge of my life, the place where my life, and hers, turned over." According to Ann Power in the *Dublin Magazine*, it was an attraction of opposites, Somerville being an optimistic extrovert, Martin reserved and intellectual, inclined to depression. It is generally supposed that she was the stylist in the collaboration, Somerville providing the comic energy.

As far as anyone knows, Somerville never had any kind of romantic relationship with a man. Martin, who had one such, always wrote the love scenes in their books. However, Hilary Robinson, in her book on the cousins, says categorically that Somerville had no orientation towards lesbianism. She "hardly knew that such sexual liberation existed," and was "shocked and horrified" when it was proposed by her friend, the composer Dame Ethel Smyth. Both cousins worked for what was then called the suffragette movement, though they opposed militancy.

Martin was already intent on writing, an occupation considered unsuitable for young ladies. When their unremarkable first novel, *An Irish Cousin*, appeared in 1889, both authors were obliged by family pressure to use *nommes de plume*. Somerville called herself "Geilles Herring," a disguise thereafter discarded, Martin signing herself, as she always would, "Martin Ross."

Their masterpiece was their third novel, *The Real Charlotte*. It tells the story of Charlotte Mullen, the plain daughter of a Protestant farmer in the west of Ireland. Her rough and ready jocularity conceals avid greed and a passion that turns to vengeful jealousy. Charlotte bullies and maneuvers her way up the social ladder, in the process destroying at least three lives, as well as her own. She is the product of a society in flux, its rigid caste system crumbling, along with its moral certainties.

The novel differs from most of the cousins' fictions in the ruthlessness of its realism. It is nevertheless rich in humor and satire, and in striking felicities of style and observation. When Roddy Lambert, Charlotte's perfidious beloved, loses his first wife, he "honeymooned with his grief in the approved fashion"; Lady Dysart (modeled on Somerville's mother) is "constitutionally unable to discern perfectly the subtle grades of Irish vulgarity"; in the "difficult revelry" of her garden party, the ladies sit in "midge-bitten dulness"; "Washerwomen do not, as a rule, assimilate the principles of their trade"; a beggar is "a bundle of rags with a cough in it." The book is equally exact in its evocations of Irish landscapes.

Somerville and Ross were daughters of the Big Houses of the Anglo-Irish Ascendancy, and wrote from an absolute understanding of their own hybrid and declining caste. They were undeniably snobs. Nevertheless, they studied the speech, manners, and customs of their social inferiors—the new middle class, farmers, servants, shopkeepers, beggars—with clinical interest and surprising sympathy. No one has equalled them in their reproduction for the page of Irish dialects—and of what they called in *Some Irish Yesterdays* "the wayward and shrewd and sensitive minds that are at the back of the dialect."

*The Real Charlotte* is a dark and pitiless book, with touches of almost gothic horror. Many of its first reviewers disliked it. In *Writers and Politics*, Conor Cruise O'Brien later commented: "evil has often been more dramatically exhibited, but I do not think it has ever been more convincingly worked out in humdrum action, or brought home with such terrible cumulative effect as an element in everyday life." Over the years, *The Real Charlotte* has earned comparisons with George Eliot, Jane Austen, Maria Edgeworth, Mrs. Gaskell and above all with Balzac's *Cousin Bette* (which the authors had not then read). Serious critics from Andrew Lang to V. S. Pritchett have claimed it as the greatest realist novel to come out of Ireland.

The reading public, however, was much more comfortable with comedy. This was famously provided by Somerville and Ross in their stories about a Resident Magistrate, Major Yeates, and his doomed attempts to impose English laws on an Irish province. Originally published in the *Badminton Magazine*, they were first collected in *Some Experiences of an Irish R.M.* This, like many of their books, was illustrated with Somerville's amusing drawings.

Irresistibly comic—often blackly so—these vignettes of hard-riding Big House life, canny horse-copers and sophisticated horses, were composed largely of dialogues and monologues that range from the extravagant flights and turns of peasant speech to English public school slang. Some critics have complained that the R.M. stories contributed to "stage Irish" stereotypes, but they satirize the gentry as cheerfully as the peasantry. They enjoyed a popularity comparable to that of the James Herriot books fifty years on.

The public wanted more and Somerville and

Ross provided it in *Further Experiences* and *In Mr. Knox's Country*. As F.S.L. Lyons wrote in *Ariel*, "generations of readers, captivated by the vividness, humour and sheer high spirits of the stories, have agreed in establishing them as classics of the hunting-field and in placing the two ladies firmly in the same stable as Surtees, forgetting that the stable was never more than an outlying appendage to the Big House which was their real habitation."

The cousins also had to spend their gifts on other light fictions and pot-boiling sketches for magazines: both women were struggling to maintain their respective estates, and they needed money. In 1903, moreover, Somerville, a superb horsewoman, had become Ireland's first female M.F.H. As Master of the West Carbery Foxhounds, she had the upkeep of horses, men, and sixteen couples of hounds.

Ross died in 1915 of a brain tumor. Somerville consulted a spiritualist and they went on writing together as "Somerville and Ross." In *Wheel-Tracks*, Somerville wrote that "Martin's mind, blended with mine, no less now than in the past, has aided, and made suggestions, taking, as ever, full share . . . in the task in hand." However, *Mount Music*, an interesting novel about a marriage between a Catholic and a Protestant, was marred by stylistic weaknesses that Ross would not have permitted, and there are constructional failures in *The Big House of Inver*. The latter, strongly reminiscent of Maria Edgeworth's *Castle Rackrent*, is about the pathetic end of an old family and a great house. It is widely regarded as a flawed masterpiece.

A witty conversationalist and splendid raconteur, Somerville had an army of friends at every level of society. She knew Yeats and Lady Gregory, but wanted no part in the Irish literary revival. It happened in Dublin, too far from Drishane, the hunters and race horses she bred there, the church choir she ruled as organist for seventy-five years. She lived on at Drishane House throughout the Troubles, refusing to be driven out by the bloodshed and destruction around her. In 1932, Trinity College gave her an honorary doctorate. The following year she was a founder member of the Irish Academy of Letters, whose Gregory Medal she received in 1941. She was finally forced to sell Drishane House in 1946, and spent her last years in a modest house ironically named Tally-Ho.

PRINCIPAL WORKS: With "Martin Ross"—The Hitchcock Edition of Somerville and Ross, 7 vols., 1927. *Fiction*—An Irish Cousin, 1889; Naboth's Vineyard, 1891; The Real Charlotte, 1894; The Silver Fox, 1897; Some Experiences of an Irish R.M., 1899; All On the Irish Shore, 1903; Further Experiences of an Irish R.M., 1908; Dan Russel the Fox, 1911; In Mr. Knox's Country, 1915; Mount Music, 1919; An Enthusiast, 1921; The Big House of Inver, 1925; French Leave, 1928; The Irish R.M. Complete, 1928 (also published as The Irish R.M., His Experiences, 1929); The Smile and the Tear, 1933; Sarah's Youth, 1938. *Memoirs and letters*—Irish Memories, 1917; Wheel-Tracks, 1923; The Selected Letters of Somerville and Ross, 1989. *Other*—Through Connemara in a Governess Cart, 1892; In the Vine Country, 1893; Beggars on Horseback: A Riding Tour in North Wales, 1895; Some Irish Yesterdays, 1906; Stray-Aways, 1920; An Incorruptible Irishman: Being an Account of Chief Justice Charles Kendal Bushe, 1932; The Sweet Cry of Hounds, 1936; Notions in Garrison, 1941; Happy Days! Essays of Sorts, 1946; Maria, and Some Other Dogs, 1949. *By Somerville alone*—Slipper's ABC of Fox Hunting, 1903; The States Through Irish

Eyes, 1930. *As editor*—The Mark Twain Birthday Book, 1885; Notes of the Horn: Hunting Verse, Old and New, 1934. *As compiler*—(with B. T. Somerville) Somerville Family Records: 1174–1940, 1940.

ABOUT: Collis, M. Somerville and Ross, 1968; Corkery, D. Synge and Anglo-Irish Literature, 1965; Cronin, J. Somerville and Ross, 1972; Cummins, G. Dr. E. OE. Somerville, 1952; Dictionary of Literary Biography Vol. 135. 1994; Dictionary of National Biography, 1941–1950, 1959; Gwynn, S. L. Irish Books and Irish People, 1919; Higginson, A. H. British and American Sporting Authors, 1949; Lewis, G. Somerville and Ross: The World of the Irish R.M., 1985; O'Brien, C. C. Writers and Politics, 1965; Peppin, B. and Micklethwait, L. Book Illustrators of the Twentieth Century, 1984; Powell, V. G. The Irish Cousins, 1970; Pritchett, V. S. The Living Novel, 1967; Quiller-Couch, A. The Poet as Citizen, 1935; Robinson, H. Somerville and Ross: A Critical Appreciation, 1980; Schlueter, P. and J (eds.) Encyclopedia of British Women Writers, 1988; Todd, J. M. (ed.) British Women Writers, 1989; Weekes, A. O. Irish Women Writers, 1990. *Bibliography*—Hudson, E. Bibliography of the First Editions of E. OE. Somerville and Martin Ross, 1942. *Periodicals*—Ariel July 1970; Commonweal October 3, 1947; Dublin Magazine Spring 1964; Economist August 26, 1989; English Literature in Transition 30 1 1987; New Statesman May 24, 1968; August 4, 1989; New York Times October 10, 1949; Quarterly Review July 1913; Times (London) October 10, 1949.

**SORENSEN, VIRGINIA (EGGERTSEN)** (February 17, 1912–December 24, 1991), American novelist, wrote: "My great-grandparents all came West with the Mormon pioneers, the Danish half of them directly from conversion in Denmark. I was born in Provo, Utah, to Helen (Blackett) and Claude E. Eggertsen. Provo is dominated by two great things—the memory of Brigham Young, after whom the Mormon University there is named, and by Mount Timpanogas, one of the highest peaks of the Wasatch Range of the Rocky Mountains. Both of these have been of increasing importance in my life and my writings, although during the last twenty years I have lived in California, Colorado, Indiana, Michigan, Alabama, and Pennsylvania. About history I have a curious feeling of presentness, perhaps because in Utah 'long ago' is no more than yesterday. In my childhood I actually heard stories of the long trek and of the settlement of our town from people who had experienced it all.

"I was educated in public schools in Utah and graduated from Brigham Young University. By then I had spent one year away from the mountains, studying writing at the University of Missouri. Returning to Brigham Young to graduate was the first of many returns, and I do not speak of journeys away and back again, but of constant returns in my stories. Whether in Utah or not, I find myself at my desk constantly living in her climate and with her history and her people. The chief meaning of my other homes, I believe, has been complementary—they serve for comparison, to complete with what I believe to be the virtue of objectivity my particular view of the people to whom I belong.

"While still an undergraduate I was married in the Salt Lake Temple to Frederick Sorensen of Mendon, Utah. I received my diploma and my baby daughter Elizabeth during the same week in June, 1934. For the next five years my husband taught and studied at Stanford University, in Palo Alto, California, and our son, Frederick Walter, was born there in 1936. Taking care of the two babies and a typical graduate-student apartment took up my days, but I wrote a good deal at night and managed to audit one evening course in poetry writing. . . .

"Before we left Stanford . . . we had decided to live in as many places as possible. . . . Our first two stops were both in the Midwest, close to the beginnings of Mormonism. Visiting the early homes of our wandering grandfathers in Illinois and Missouri and Ohio, we found of special fascination the old city of Nauvoo, Illinois, on the Mississippi, and I soon was at work on a novel about a lady who lived and died there as the city itself lived and died. It was published under the title of *A Little Lower than the Angels*.

"My next three novels were about Mormons in the West and all traced the relationships of men and environment, of generation and generation. The problems of rootlessness entered somehow into every story. In 1946 I had my first real years of freedom for study and writing, receiving a Guggenheim fellowship. Intending to complete a study of a Mormon apostate who had cut an important figure in the Gold Rush and lived for many years in Sonora, Mexico, I went to Guaymas and to the Yaqui Indian villages beyond. There I found my hero much belittled by the wonderful people he had tried to exploit. At first only curious, I was presently fascinated by the Yaquis, and wrote their story into a novel called *The Proper Gods*. This novel, like all the others, was concerned with roots and rebellion, with age and youth, for I had begun to see these as the universal themes they are. . . ."

---

Virginia Sorensen wrote both fictional chronicles of Mormon life and children's books. *A Little Lower Than the Angels*, her first published novel, is set during a crucial period in the history of the Church of Jesus Christ of Latter-Day Saints—around the time of church founder Joseph Smith's death (he was killed by an anti-Mormon mob in 1844) and the accession of Brigham Young. It received a warm reception, especially for its treatment of such sensitive issues as polygamy and women's lives in the Mormon community. "For all the sophistication and polish of her prose," Wallace Stegner—perhaps the leading interpreter of the Mormons of his time—wrote in a *Saturday Review of Literature* notice of the novel, "she looks through no literary glass. She sees with her own eyes, thinks with her own head." Her novel *The Proper Gods*, which examines a Yaqui Indian's struggle to reacquaint himself with the traditions of his forbears, won similar praise.

Sorensen's juvenile fiction, which began to appear in the early 1950s, was written primarily for pre-teen girls. *Plain Girl*, about the travails of a nine-year-old Pennsylvania Amish girl, won the Annual Children's Book Award of the Child Study Association of America in 1955. In *Miracles on Maple Hill*, her best-known juvenile novel, a man recently released from prisoner-of-war camp moves to a Pennsylvania farm with his wife and two children. It was awarded the John Newberry Medal in 1957. Sorensen spent her second Guggenheim Fellowship (1954–1955) in Denmark, the setting of her adult historical novel *Kingdom Come. Where Nothing Is Long Ago* is a collection of ten autobiographical short stories. After divorcing her first husband, Sorensen married the novelist and travel writer Alec Waugh in 1969.

PRINCIPAL WORKS: *Novels*—A Little Lower Than the Angels, 1942; On This Star, 1946; The Neighbors, 1947; The Evening and the Morning, 1949; The Proper Gods, 1951; Many Heavens, 1954; Kingdom Come, 1960; The Man with the Key, 1974. *Short stories*—Where Nothing Is Long Ago: Memories of a Mormon Childhood, 1963. *Juvenile*—Curious Missie, 1953; The House Next Door, 1954; Plain Girl, 1955; Miracles on Maple Hill, 1956; Lotte's Locket, 1964; Around the Corner, 1971; Friends of the Road, 1978.

ABOUT: The autobiographical material quoted above was written for Twentieth Century Authors First Supplement, 1955. Contemporary Authors vol. 139, 1993; Contemporary Authors New Revision Series 22, 1988; Current Biography 1950; Who's Who in America 1990–1991. *Periodicals*—Library Journal March 15, 1957; Publishers Weekly January 27, 1992; Saturday Review of Literature May 9, 1942.

**SORELY, CHARLES HAMILTON** (May 19, 1895–October 13, 1915), English poet, was born in Old Aberdeen, Scotland, the elder of twin sons born to William Ritchie Sorley, then Professor of Moral Philosophy at the University of Aberdeen, and Janet (formerly Smith) Sorley. He was a Scot on both sides of his family. For one who published so little—killed in World War I before his twenty-first birthday—  Sorley's long-lasting reputation is remarkable. It was achieved because of the unusually certain promise of his poetry and because, in his famous letters, the chief flower of his still budding genius, he discerned the true nature of war. Even the poet who was initially the idol of English World War poets, Rupert Brooke, had been unable to discern or to express this before his own death. Sorley, it may safely be stated, was one of this century's greatest losses to war.

In 1900 Sorley's father achieved the prestigious post of Knightsbridge Professor of Philosophy at Cambridge University. Charles's childhood was therefore spent in England, divided between King's College Choir School (1900–1905) and Marlborough (1905–1913), in Wiltshire, one of Britain's leading public schools. He gained a scholarship to University College, Oxford—but was, of course, never able to take this up. His literary promise was shown in the poems he contributed to his school's magazine, the *Marlburian*. These are among the most promising of all known juvenilia. In his single posthumous collection, *Marlborough*, the earlier poems are printed in the back; outstanding among them is "The River," a juvenile poem, sometimes clumsily rhymed, but one which has an edge and somberness that only a true poet could achieve. Apparently about a suicide, it may at some deeper level express his premonition of early death: "It was so black. There was no wind / Its patience to defy. / It was not that the man had sinned, / Or that he wished to die. / Only the wide and silent tide / Went slowly sweeping by."

Sorely's achievement and status were summed up by Vivian de Sola Pinto in *Crisis in English Poetry 1880–1940:* "I. A. Richards remarked that Rupert Brooke's poetry had no inside; Sorley had made the 'voyage within' and his poems have a solidity that contrasts with the hollowness of the smooth verses of the Georgians. These poems embody attitudes to the war which are quite different. . . . One of these attitudes is a sense of aimlessness and frustration, of being part of a huge machine that functions in an inhuman and incomprehensible way." Sorley's most famous poem is the sonnet which might well have been the last poem he wrote:

> When you see millions of the mouthless dead
> Across your dreams in pale battalions go,
> Say not soft things as other men have said,
> That you'll remember. For you need not so.
> Give them not praise. For, deaf, how should they know
> It is not curses heaped on each gashed head?
> Nor tears. Their blind eyes see not your tears flow.
> Nor honor. It is easy to be dead
> Say only this, "They are dead." Then add thereto,
> "Yet many a better one has died before."
> Then, scanning all the o'ercrowded mass, should you
> Perceive one face that you loved heretofore,
> It is a spook. None wears the face you knew.
> Great death has made all his for evermore.

Of Sorley's *Letters*, a selection of which was published—edited by his parents—in 1919, John Middleton Murry said in the *Athenaeum:* "We do not receive many such gifts as this wonderful book: the authentic voice of those lost legions is seldom heard." The *New Republic* commented: "One approaches them prepared to find little beyond promise—a hint of something fine cut down before fulfillment; they turn out to be very much more than mere promise; they are in themselves achievement, the expression of a rarely independent mind, humorous, rich and wise far beyond its years."

PRINCIPAL WORKS: *Anthology*—The Poems and Selected Letters of Charles Hamilton Sorley (ed. H. D. Spear) 1978. *Poetry*—Marlborough, 1916; The Collected Poems of Charles Hamilton Sorley, 1985. *Letters*—The Collected Letters of Charles Hamilton Sorley (ed. J. M. Wilson) 1990; Letters from Germany and from the Army (ed. W. R. Sorley) 1916; The Letters of Charles Sorley with a Chapter of Biography (eds. W. R. and J. Sorley) 1919.

ABOUT: Lehmann, J. English Poets of the First World War, 1982; Pinto, V. de S. Crisis in English Poetry 1880–1940, 1951; Press, J. Poets of World War I, 1983; Swann, T. B. Ungirt Runner: Charles Hamilton Sorley, Poet of World War I, 1965. *Periodicals*—Athenaeum January 30, 1920; Friends' Quarterly Examiner October 1937; New Republic July 21, 1920; Saturday Review March 20, 1920.

**\*SOROKIN, PITIRIM ALEXANDROVICH** (January 21, 1889–February 10, 1968), Russian-born American sociologist, wrote: "Eventfulness has possibly been the most significant feature of my life-adventure. In a span of sixty-three years I have passed through several cultural atmospheres: pastoral-hunter's culture of the Komi, agricultural and then urban culture of Russia and Europe, and finally, the megalopolitan technological culture  of the United States. Starting my life as a son of a poor itinerant artisan and peasant mother, subsequently I have been a farmhand, itinerant artisan, factory worker, clerk, teacher, conductor of a choir, revolutionary, political prisoner, journalist, student, editor of a metropolitan paper, member of Kerensky's cabinet, an exile, professor at Russian, Czech, and American universities, and a scholar of an international reputation. No less eventful has been the range of my life-experience: joy and sorrows, successes and failures of normal human life. I fully tasted six imprisonments—three under the Czarist and three under the Communist regimes; the unforgettable experience of a man condemned to death and daily during six weeks, expecting his execution by the Communist firing squad. I know what it means to be damned and praised, to be banished or to lose one's brothers and friends in a political struggle, and, in a modest degree, I have experienced also the blissful grace of creative work.

"These life-experiences have taught me more than innumerable books I have read and lectures I listened to.

"Born and reared among the Komi, Ugro-Finnish people in the North of Russia, up to the eleventh year of my life, I did not see even a small town. Incidentally I learned to read and write, incidentally became a pupil of a 'normal school,' and at age of ten, father and mother dead, I became 'independent,' penniless, but free to chart my life-course. Earning my living, subsequently I was a student of a teachers' college, arrested and imprisoned four months before graduation for my political activites in 1906. Then a starving and hunted revolutionary, student of a night school, of the Psycho-Neurological Institute, and of the University of St. Petersburg. Two more imprisonments gave me a first-hand experience in criminology and penology—the field of my graduate study and then of my first professorship. Besides several papers, in my junior year I published my first volume: *Crime and Punishment, Service and Reward* (1913). In 1916 I received a masters degree in criminal law; in 1922, the degree of Doctor of Sociology from the University of St. Petersburg. With the explosion of the Russian Revolution I became one of the founders of the Russian Peasant Soviet (dispersed by the Communists), editor of a metropolitan paper, the *Will of the People*, member of the Council of the Russian Republic, a secretary to Prime Minister Ke-

\*SAW ruh kin

rensky, and a leading member of the Russian Constituent Assembly (dispersed by the Communist government). From the beginning of the revolution I vigorously fought Lenin, Trotsky, Kamenev and other Communist leaders. For this reason I was arrested on January 3, 1918, and imprisoned for four months in the Russian 'bastille,' fortress of Peter and Paul. Released, I resumed my struggle with the Communists and was one of the group which engineered the overthrow of the Communist government in Archangel in 1918. In October 1918, I was again arrested and condemned to death by the Communist government of Vologda province. After six weeks of waiting to be shot, by Lenin's order [Lenin had commented favorably on his work in *Pravda*] I was freed and returned to my academic activity at the University of St. Petersburg. There I became the founder, first professor, and chairman of the department of sociology. During the years 1920–1922 I published five volumes in law and sociology. In 1922 I was again arrested and, finally, banished by the Soviet government. A few days after my arrival in Berlin, my good friend President Masaryk invited me to be a guest of Czechoslovakia. I stayed there for some nine months. Having received an invitation from the Universities of Illinois and Wisconsin to lecture there on the Russian Revolution, in November 1923 I came to the United States, and in 1924 was offered a professorship by the University of Minnesota. After six years of happy work there, I was invited to be the first professor and chairman of the sociology department at Harvard. Since 1930 I have been living and working in this great university.

"In 1948 Mr. Eli Lilly and the Lilly Endowment by their own initiative kindly offered $120,000 for my studies of how to make human beings less selfish and more creative. This generous offer led to the establishment of the Harvard Research Center in Creative Altruism in 1949, which I am directing now. In 1930 I became a naturalized American citizen.

"During the years of my being in America, honorary memberships in several academies of science and arts, presidency of the International Institute of Sociology, honorary doctorates and similar distinctions have been granted to me. During the same years I have published, besides many scientific papers, some twenty-one substantial volumes. All in all, so far, I have twenty-nine translations of my published volumes . . . the translations go on *crescendo*. Rapidly grows also the already considerable literature about my theories. In recent years books began to be published and Ph.D. theses written about my books.

"In 1917 I was happily married and have two sons. . . . My main recreations are now: my professional creative work, enjoyment of great music, my azalea-rhodo-lilac-rose garden, grown by my and my family's labor, and each spring enjoyed by several thousands of visitors, and various forms of outdoor recreation: camping, mountain-climbing, fishing, etc.

"I have also been lucky in having a warm friendship with many a simple and eminent person. If I have had many a sorry and trying experience, I have also had a full measure of the purest and most meaningful happiness. Both have made my life worth living."

———

It was not until towards the end of Pitirim Sorokin's life, in the mid-sixties, that some American sociologists began to pay serious tribute to him; by that time he had changed from a truly scientific sociologist—he had been one of the earliest in America—into a full blown utopian prophet, of increasingly apocalyptic proportions. The greater part of his reputation as a sociologist depends mainly on the work he did in the 1920s and 1930s.

Sorokin's three major books are *Social Mobility* (1927, reissued and augmented as *Social and Cultural Mobility*, 1959), *Contemporary Sociological Theories* (1928), and the massive, four-volume *Social and Cultural Dynamics: A Study of Change in Major Systems of Art, Truth, Ethics, Law and Social Relationships* (1937–1941). This last work was published in a single-volumed revised and abridged edition in 1957. A more popular, briefer version of the same material appeared in a shorter book of 1941: *The Crisis of Our Age: The Social and Cultural Outlook*.

Sorokin, although his main contribution was to scientific sociology, was always eclectic by inclination. By the time he was forced out of Russia in his mid-thirties he had written no fewer than ten works; one of them was on Tolstoy as a philosopher; another was a piece of science fiction. *Golod kak Factor* (1921) was, he claimed, "destroyed by the Soviet government"; a version of it was published, posthumously, in a translation by his widow, as *Hunger as a Factor in World Affairs*.

When Sorokin arrived in America he found that the Chicago School of Sociology, under Robert Park, was beginning to flourish. That school produced what J. H. Abraham called, in his *Origins and Growth of Sociology*, one of the three "breakthroughs" "into real sociological understanding" of the time—W. I. Thomas and F. Znaniecki's *The Polish Peasant in Europe and America* (1918–1920), H. and R. Lynd's studies of "Middletown," and Sorokin's *Social Mobility*. Abraham wrote, "Sorokin was *the* scholar in American sociology at a time when this discipline, let alone a broad philosophical training, was not rated high or not rated at all." He adds that it "is not surprising . . . that Sorokin, for almost one generation, was totally ignored. But with the optimism that characterized his outlook, he made no concession to current fashion, refused to be beguiled by spurious . . . research and never ceased to proclaim the . . . proper goals of sociology. . . . In this respect he may be said to have been the gadfly of American sociology . . . leading it back to the right path." Sorokin, during his long tenure at Harvard, built up the sociology department there in an exemplary manner, always insisting on properly scientific investigations. Kingsley Davis, in his magisterial survey *Human Society* (1949), observed that *Social Mobility*, written "when Sorokin was still content to be a scien-

tist . . . is a classic of the sociological literature."
Giddings wrote (of *Social Mobility*) in the *Saturday
Review of Literature* that it was "for three reasons
a work of first rate importance. . . . it is a study
of an important process in human society which has
never before been examined in a thoroughgoing
way . . . its method is scientific . . . the material
brought to light and presented in orderly arrangement is surprisingly extensive and valuable."

The successor volume to *Social Mobility*, entitled
Contemporary Sociological Theories, provided the
earliest and most thoroughgoing critical analysis of
the state of a field which at the time was confused
and lacking in methodology. Sorokin, concentrating on interaction as the main factor to be analyzed,
isolated nine basic theories in a logical, "focused,"
and scientific fashion.

Sorokin's *magnum opus* was his *Social and Cultural Dynamics*. Although written in a quaint and
often pontifical manner, which alienated many
readers, it was based on a solid and formidable
foundation of fact. R. M. MacIver, reviewing it in
the *American Economic Review*, wrote: "Thrice
happy Mr Sorokin! We admire his labors and we
would not disturb his peace. . . . We are impressed with his vast Spenglerian antitheses, his
more than Spenglerian erudition, and his utterly
un-Spenglerian massing of statistics. We envy his
short way with critics. . . . We genuinely applaud
his vindication of the integrity of knowledge, his
vehement polemic against positivists and pragmatists, neo-realists and mechanists. If we still cavil at
the Dynamics, it may only be because the inner
light that guides the author has not been vouch-
safed to such critics as the present reviewer."

Sorokin, an authoritarian, was also an idealist; his
theory of "sensate," "ideational" and "idealistic" su-
persystems was idiosyncratic by comparison with
Pareto's more clear-cut theory of a circulation of
elites.

Sorokin saw societies, or what he called super-
systems, as either *sensate*, that is ruled by the senses,
or *ideational*, that is ruled by the notion (reminiscent of Plato if not actually Platonic) that behind
sense impressions there lies a deeper truth. When
these two kinds of thinking and feeling combine, a
third type of society eventuates: this is *idealistic*
when the two approaches are combined harmoniously, but *mixed* if they are merely juxtaposed. A
sensate society, in which sensory impressions are
foremost, was one in which science was primary; it
also eventually became sexually (in Sorokin's eyes)
decadent. An ideational society, in which rationality is dominant, was one focused upon God, faith,
mystical experience, and authority. The history of
world society, he contended, has been one of cyclic
oscillation between sensate and ideational—with
various sorts of mixtures in between. Medieval Europe, in Sorokinian terms, was a highly ideational
culture; Western culture was (and, to Sorokinians,
still is) a sensate one, and on the very verge of disintegration to boot. Only rarely in history is an idealistic balance, in which the supersensory or intuitive
is dominant, achieved. But it could be reached if
Sorokin's program were followed. Thus, Sorokin

was pessimistic about the situation, but optimistic
about its outcome.

His program was one of Altruistic Love, or "creative altruism": if it could be fulfilled, then the
spontaneous emanations of what Sorokin called the
"Infinite Manifold" would be heeded. Although
Sorokin was himself Greek Orthodox, he appealed
to enlightened people to turn to eastern philosophies for help and guidance. His work was taken up
and published in India, and became associated in
particular with Darshana-Yoga, a type of salvation-
yoga which is concerned with contemplation and
with the precise stages of spiritual growth. Sorokinians were recommended to cease to identify with
their activities and at the same time to practice
specified restraints and exercises.

Sorokin's writings, as he built upon the foundation of the *Social and Cultural Dynamics*, became
less and less sociological and more and more exhort-
atory and prophetic. His is a full-blown religious
philosophy.

One reason for Sorokin's failure to make a larger
or more widespread impression lies in his failure
ever to develop a coherent psychological approach.
Yet in its own discomforting way, *Social and Cultural Dynamics* contains much wisdom and good
sense, and, above all, it contains sets of social statistics taken from various periods of history which
cannot be found elsewhere, and which are of great
interest and importance. The clearest introduction
to Sorokin's *Social and Cultural Dynamics* is Frank
R. Cowell's exposition.

PRINCIPAL WORKS: *Society and sociology*—The Sociology of
Revolution, 1925; Social Mobility, 1927 (augmented ed. as Social and Cultural Mobility, 1959); Contemporary Sociological
Theories, 1928; (with C. C. Zimmerman) Principles of Rural-
Urban Sociology, 1929; Social and Cultural Dynamics, 1937–
1941 (abridged ed. 1957); Time-Budgets of Human Behaviour, 1939; The Crisis of Our Age: The Social and Cultural
Outlook, 1941; Man and Society in Calamity: The Effects of
War, Revolution, Famine, Pestilence upon Human Mind, Behavior, Social Organization and Cultural Life, 1942; Sociocul-
tural Causality, Space, Time: A Study of Referential Principles
of Sociology and Social Science, 19043; Russia and the United
States, 1944; Society, Culture and Personality: Their Structure
and Dynamics: A System of General Sociology, 1947; The Reconstruction of Humanity, 1948; Altruistic Love: A Study of
American "Good Neighbours" and Christian Saints, 1950; Social Philosophies in an Age of Crisis, 1952 (reissued as Modern
Historical and Social Philosophies, 1963); S.O.S.: The Meaning
of Our Crisis, 1951; The Ways and Power of Love: Types, Factors and Techniques of Moral Transformation, 1954; Fads and
Foibles in Modern Sociology and Related Sciences, 1956; The
American Sex Revolution, 1956 (published as Sane Sex Order,
1961); (with W. A. Lunden) Power and Morality: Who Shall
Guard the Guardians?, 1959; The Basic Trends of Our Times,
1964; Sociological Theories of Today, 1966; Sociology of Yesterday, Today, and Tomorrow, 1969. *Other*—Leaves from a
Russian Diary, 1925 (augmented as Leaves from a Russian Diary: and Thirty Years After, 1950); A Long Journey; The Auto-
biography of Pitirim A. Sorokin, 1963. *As editor*—(with C. C.
Zimmerman and C. A. Galpin) A Systematic Source Book in
Rural Sociology, 1930–1932; Explorations in Altruistic Love
and Behavior, 1950; Forms and Techniques of Altrustic and
Spiritual Growth, 1954.

ABOUT: The autobiographical material quoted above was writ-
ten for Twentieth Century Authors First Supplement, 1955.
Abrahams, J. H. Origins and Growth of Sociology, 1973; Allen,
P. (ed.) Pitirim A. Sorokin in Review, 1963; Bochenski, I. M.
Contemporary European Philosophy, 1966; Bottomore, T. So-

ciology, 1962; Brinton, C. A. History of Western Morals, 1959; Cowell, F. R. History, Civilization and Culture: An Introduction to the Historical and Social Philosophy of Pitirim A. Sorokin, 1952; Current Biography 1968; Davis, K. Human Society, 1949; Delfgaauw, B. Twentieth Century Philosophy, 1969; Hallen, G. C. and Prasad, R. (eds.) Sorokin and Sociology, 1972; Maquet, J. (ed.) The Sociology of Knowledge: Essays in Honor of Pitirim A. Sorokin, 1963; Sorokin, P. Leaves from a Russian Diary, 1925; Sorokin, P. A. A Long Journey, 1963; Tiryakian, E. (ed.) Sociological Theory, Values and Sociological Changes: Essays in Honor of Pitirim A. Sorokin, 1967; Unnithan, T.K.N. (ed.) Sociological Theories of Pitirim A. Sorokin, Sociology January 1969. *Bibliography—in* Tiryakian, E. (ed.) Sociological Theory, Values and Sociological Changes, 1967. *Periodicals*—American Economic Review December 1941; Annals of the American Academy September 1928; British Journal of Sociology January 1969; New York Times February 11, 1968; Newsweek February 19, 1968; Russian Review July 1968; Saturday Review of Literature August 6, 1927; Time February 16, 1968; Times (London) February 19, 1968; Washington Post February 12, 1968.

**SOULE, GEORGE HENRY** (June 11, 1887–April 14, 1970), American economist, wrote: "I was born in Stamford Connecticut, of a New England family extending back on both sides to the 'Mayflower.' Though I am a namesake of a signer of the Mayflower Compact, had one ancestor in the Boston Tea Party and several in the American Revolution, my most prized progenitor was Robert Calef, who wrote a book satirizing cotton Mather and the Salem witchcraft persecutions—a book banned by the conservatives of the time and sold from under the counter in Cambridge, Massachusetts.

"Educated at Stamford High School and Yale, from which I was graduated in 1908, I early developed an interest in writing, being editor of my school paper and later of the *Yale Literary Magazine*. Aside from English, my major study in college was economics. After graduation my first work was in book publishing; until 1914 I was connected with the house of Frederick A. Stokes Co., where I also became editor of the first cooperative book announcement of the publishers—an attempt to present bonafide news of new books without praise of them. But my interest in the success of the aesthetically meritorious books came into constant collision with exploitation of so-called popular taste, and I began to believe that something better than a commercial civilization was necessary if cultural values were to be well served.

"An opportunity for activity in a broader sphere came with an invitation to join the staff of the *New Republic* in 1914—the year of its foundation. There I performed many duties—from makeup and proof-reading to editing of musical articles and art criticism and writing of my own. Gradually, however, my major interest veered to public affairs. In the early months of our participation in the First World War, I was stationed in Washington as special writer on the war organization, where I helped both to explain it and to stimulate changes in desirable directions.

"Entering the army in May 1918, I was assigned to the Coast Artillery Corps, where, after serving in the ranks and as corporal, I was assigned to anti-submarine devices and achieved the rare military grade of 'First Class Listener.' Appointed then to the artillery school at Fort Monroe, I went through a stiff cramming in engineering, and after three months of struggle with logarithms emerged as a Second Lieutenant just as the Armistice was declared. I was immediately demobilized.

"The war stirred many minds. It not only reinforced the conviction of this one that a reformed social and economic order was desirable, but brought the belief that it could not be pulled out of a hat. Careful and practical work to build it on a scientific basis would be necessary. Therefore, I joined with Stuart Chase and others to found the Labor Bureau, Inc.—a body to do technical and professional work for labor and cooperative organizations. There I did a great deal of economic research relevant to labor arbitrations and attained scientific recognition with papers read before the American Economic Association and other learned societies.

"In 1923 I was invited to become an editor of the *New Republic*, a position which I have held ever since. In addition to weekly writing and editorial duties, I have acted as a director and at one time chairman of the National Bureau of Economic Research, as chairman of the National Economics and Social Planning Association, as a member of the Columbia University Commission on Economic Reconstruction. I have taught at the Yale Law School and at Columbia.

"I am married to Dr. Flander Dunbar, a member of the staff of Presbyterian-Columbia Medical Center, of the Faculty of the College of Physicians and Surgeons, and managing editor of *Psychosomatic Medicine*."

———

"Anyone who reads Mr. Soule puts himself in touch with one of the sanest and most civilized minds now at work on man and his problems," Yale law and political scientist H. D. Lasswell was quoted as saying in Soule's *New York Times* obituary. Soule was the first person to introduce case methods into industrial economics. He was a prolific author of books and articles on socio-economic subjects, including his nine-volume *Economic History of the United States*. One of the most enduring titles in that series is volume eight, *Prosperity Decade; from War to Depression: 1917–1929.* "A prodigious collection of facts has been organized into a smooth-running narrative, and it would be difficult to cite any major omissions," wrote the *Nation* reviewer.

In 1936 Soule published *The Future of Liberty* and explained: "My bias is democratic and liberal. I believe in the right of the individual to seek his own fulfillment, in equality of status, in the attempt of man to control his own destiny . . . I believe in the legitimacy of revolution; not merely the revolution that my forefathers helped to make in the 18th century, but any new revolution that may be justified by the interest and reason of the common man." *New York Times* (1936) critic Henry Hazlitt felt that here Soule "greatly exaggerates the obstacles to a system of free competition," and "fails almost completely to recognize the enormous problems raised by the system of complete socialism that he advocates." Henry Mussey, of *New York Herald Tribune Books*, however, found merit: "I wish that every thoughtful person in the United States might be induced to read Mr. Soule's little book. The danger of violence in impending social changes might conceivably thereby be slightly lessened, since it is a plea for understanding and for intelligent choice between true alternatives."

Soule put in a brief stint on the editorial staff of the *New York Evening Post* in 1919, and was called in as an expert investigator for the Inter-Church World Movement Commission of the great steel strike that same year. In 1927 he was special advisor to the Secretary of the Interior on reclamation and rural development in the South, and from 1948 to 1957 a consultant to the Twentieth Century Fund. He had left the *New Republic* in 1936 to devote himself to writing and to teaching at various colleges and universities as a visiting professor of economics; from 1947 to 1957 he served on the faculty of Bennington College.

When Soule died, Professor Carl Beck claimed in the *New York Times* that Soule belonged "with those Socialists of the Norman Thomas brand who believe that it is necessary to socialize the means of production, but differ from the Communists in believing that the means of production can be socialized by peaceful democratic procedure."

PRINCIPAL WORKS: Nonfiction—(with J. M. Budish) The New Unionism in the Clothing Industry, 1920; The Intellectual and the Labor Movement, 1923; The Accumulation of Capital: Social vs. Personal Savings, 1924; Wage Arbitration: Selected Cases 1920–1924, 1928; (with E. D. Howard, R. E. Heilman, et. al.) Society Tomorrow, 1929; (with L. Fischer and E. A. Filene) Can We Have National Planning Without a Revolution?: New York Luncheon Discussion, 1932; The Idea of Planning, 1932; A Planned Society, 1932; The Coming American Revolution, 1934; Does Socialism Work?: Three Articles on Soviet Russia, 1936; The Future of Liberty, 1936; (with F. L. Schuman) America Looks Abroad, 1938; An Economic Constitution for Democracy, 1939; Sidney Hillman: Labor Statesman, 1939; The Strength of Nations: A Study in Social Theory, 1942; America's Stake in Britain's Future, 1945; (with D. Efron, N. T. Ness, and A. H. Hansen) Latin America in the Future World, 1945; Prosperity Decade; From War to Depression: 1917–1929, 1947 (also published as Prosperity Decade: A Chapter from American Economic History 1917–1929, 1947); Introduction to Economic Science, 1948 (rev. as The New Science of Economics: An Introduction, 1964); The Costs of Health Insurance, 1949; (with M. W. Thornburg) Turkey: An Economic Appraisal, 1949; Compilation Showing Progress and Status of the Defense Minerals Production Program, 1952; Economic Forces in American History, 1952 (rev. ed. with V. P. Carosso as American Economic History, 1957); Gypsum: Information Concerning Gypsum and a New All-Purpose Building Material, 1952; Ideas of the Great Economists, 1952; Economics for Living, 1954, rev. ed. 1961; Men, Wages and Employment in the Modern U.S. Economy, 1954; Time for Living, 1955; What Automation Does To Human Beings, 1956; Longer Life, 1958; The Shape of Tomorrow, 1958; (with L. E. Traywick and F. C. Boddy) Economics: Measurement, Theories, Case Studies, 1961; Planning: U.S.A., 1967.

ABOUT: The autobiographical material quoted above was writ-ten for Twentieth Century Authors, 1942. Contemporary Authors, 1994; Current Biography 1945. *Periodicals*—Nation January 24, 1948; New York Herald Tribune Books November 22, 1936; New York Times November 29, 1936; April 15, 1970.

**SOUTHERN, R. W.** (February 8, 1912– ), English historian, was born Richard William Southern in Newcastle upon Tyne, England, the son of Matthew Henry Southern, a merchant, and Eleanor (Sharp) Southern. He was educated at Royal Grammar School, Newcastle upon Tyne, and Balliol College, Oxford. A Junior Research Fellow at Exeter College, Oxford (1933–1937), and fellow and tutor of Balliol (1937–1961), he joined the army in 1940 and became a major, serving in the Political Intelligence Department of the Foreign Office. From 1959 to 1960 he was Birkbeck Lecturer in Ecclesiastical History at Trinity College, Cambridge. He became Chichele professor of Modern History at Oxford in 1961, holding this appointment until 1969, when he became president of St. John's College, where he served until 1981, when he became an Honorary Fellow. Southern published scholarly articles in such journals as *English Historical Review* and *Medieval and Renaissance Studies*. His chief field of study lay in the Middle Ages. His first and most widely read book, *The Making of the Middle Ages*, was highly influential in a whole generation of students, many of whom formed their view of the period from its pages. Of special interest to him is the life of Anselm, eleventh-century Archbishop of Canterbury. In 1963 he published his Birkbeck Lectures under the title *St. Anselm and His Biographer*, a study of both the Archbishop and his biographer Eadmer. On a broader scale, as the book's subtitle indicates, it is a "study of monastic life and thought" in the years 1059 to 1130. "The scholarship behind it is sound and creative," W. R. Cannon wrote in the *Journal of Religion*. "The style is clear and in places even epigrammatic. The advanced student of medieval history will find the study of this book both interesting and rewarding."

Twenty-eight years later Southern published *Saint Anselm: A Portrait in a Landscape*, which in the *Times Literary Supplement*, the historian Christopher Brooke, described as a "masterpiece." "The supreme quality of this new book is that it unfolds, with extraordinary care, lucidity and precision, the message of Anselm's own writings— prayers, meditations, treatises and letters," Brooke wrote. "With their help we are taken step by step through the progress of Anselm's mind and attitudes and interests."

In 1962 Southern collected three of his Harvard lectures under the title *Western Views of Islam in the Middle Ages*. In his opening lecture he states that "we have reached a point in the study of medieval history at which it is very important that attention should be directed to communities outside western Europe, and especially to those that exercised an influence on the development of the West. This, of course, is not a new idea. But it is one that has to struggle against the conservatism of academic routine." He goes on to provide a survey of the cultural confrontations between Islam and Christianity, conflicts which spanned over eight centuries and which continue to exert a strong influence on modern world affairs.

PRINCIPAL WORKS: *Nonfiction*—The Making of the Middle Ages, 1953; The Shape and Substance of Academic History: An Inaugural Lecture Delivered Before the University of Oxford, 1961; Western Views of Islam in the Middle Ages, 1962; Saint Anselm and His Biographer: A Study of Monastic Life and Thought, 1059–c. 1130, 1963; Medieval Humanism, 1970; Western Society and the Church in the Middle Ages, 1970; Robert Grosseteste: The Growth of an English Mind in Medieval Europe, 1986; Saint Anselm: A Portrait in a Landscape, 1990; The Rise of Scholastic Humanism: Aims, Methods, and Places, 1994. *As editor*—Eadmer, The Life of St. Anselm, 1962; Essays in Medieval History: Selected from the Transactions of the Royal Historical Society on the Occasion of Its Centenary, 1968; Memorials of St. Anselm, 1969.

ABOUT: Contemporary Authors vols. 9–12, 1974; Who's Who 1995. *Periodicals*—Journal of Religion April 1964; Times (London) February 1, 1991.

## SOUTHWOLD, STEPHEN (pseudonyms "NEIL BELL" and "PAUL MARTENS")

(1887–1964), English novelist and children's writer, was born in Southwold, Suffolk. Described as lazy and insubordinate as a schoolboy at Saint Mark's College in Chelsea, he went on to attempt to be an artist, traveling through Europe but not achieving much success; he later worked as a drawing teacher. During World War I he was grouped with the "soldier poets," a misrepresentation which he himself deflated as "a double lie, for I was neither."

Abandoning teaching and an attempt at freelance journalism, in 1928 Southwold married an Irish girl and settled, penniless, in Cornwall. Here

they had three children, and he began a hugely prolific but patchily successful writing career. His first novel was *Precious Porcelain* (1931), a mystery tale on a modern Jekyll and Hyde theme, set in an English cathedral town. It was greeted with warmth, critics recognizing an exuberant new talent which, while undisciplined, promised great things. "If Mr. Bell could catch himself in one of his quieter moments, and take himself into a corner, and work out what it was that he wanted to do, there is every probability that he would succeed in doing it," said the English dramatist Harold Harwood.

His second novel, *Life and Andrew Otway* (1931), likened by the author and critics to H. G. Wells's *Tono-Bungay*, was deemed a flop by some, but was considered by others as a fine piece of escapism. In the face of contradictory reviews whose only agreement was that this was a writer of verve and imagination, Southwold continued to write at a furious pace. He was a gifted storyteller, but while his greatest strength was in creating realistic characters, he often sacrificed emotional depth for effect. *Lord of Life* was a fantasy about nineteen stranded survivors of a world holocaust, of which only one was female and on to whom the burden

fell of repopulating the earth. Graham Greene considered that "the manner is better than the matter," while V. S. Pritchett commented, "Mr. Bell has a good deal of ingenuity, but he is apt to be so dazzled by his original ideas that he can do nothing with them."

Southwold's works were varied in theme, setting, and period, and included fictionalized biography, such as *So Perish the Roses*, about Mary and Charles Lamb; he wrote countless stories for children, as in *Listen, Children!*, a collection of over fifty tales. He also wrote a play for youngsters, *The Wonderful Ingredient* (1935).

PRINCIPAL WORKS: *Juvenile*—In Between Stories, 1923; Twilight Tales, 1925; (as editor) Old Gold: A Book of Fables and Parables, 1926; Listen, Children!' 1926; Once Upon a Time Stories, 1927; Ten-Minute Tales, 1927; The Children's Play Hour Books, 1927–1930; Listen Again, Children!, 1928; Yesterday and Long Ago, 1928; Man's Great Adventure, 1929; Happy Families, 1929; Fiddlededee: A Medley of Stories, 1930; Hey Diddle Diddle, 1930; The Hunted One and Other Stories, 1930; The Jumpers, 1930; The Last Bus and Other Stories, 1930; The Welsh Rabbit and Other Stories, 1930; Tick Tock Tales, 1930; True Tales of an Old Shellback, 1930; The Sea Horses and Other Stories, 1930; Tales of Forest Folk and Other Stories, 1930; Three by Candlelight and Other Stories 1930; The Old Brown Book, 1931; Fairy Tales, 1931; Once Upon a Time, 1931; The Wonderful Ingredient, 1935 (play); Forty More Tales, 1935; More Animal Stories, 1935; Tell Me Another, 1938; Now For a Story, 1938; Now For More Stories!, 1938. *As "Neil Bell"*—Precious Porcelain, 1931; Life and Andrew Otway, 1931; The Marriage of Simon Harper, 1932; The Disturbing Affair of Noel Blake, 1932; The Lord of Life, 1933; Bredon and Sons, 1934; Winding Road, 1934; Mixed Pickles: Short Stories, 1935; The Days Dividing, 1935; The Son of Richard Carden, 1935; Crocus, 1936; Strange Melody, 1936; Pinkney's Garden, 1937; The Testament of Stephen Fane, 1937; One Came Back, 1938; Smallways Rub Along, 1938; Abbot's Heel, 1939; Love and Julian Farne, 1939; Not A Sparrow Falls, 1939; So Perish the Roses, 1940; Desperate Pursuit, 1941; Spice of Life 1941 (short stories); Tower of Darkness, 1942. *As Paul Martens*—Death Rocks the Cradle, 1933; The Truth About My Father, 1934.

ABOUT: My Writing Life (S. Southwold as Neil Bell, 1955). *Periodical*—Boston Evening Transcript September 14, 1935.

## SOUZA, ERNEST. See SCOTT, EVELYN

## SPADE, MARKE. See BALCHIN, NIGEL MARLIN

## SPAETH, SIGMUND GOTTFRIED (April 10, 1885–November 11, 1965), American musicologist, wrote: "Music has always been my hobby, and I am fortunate in having been able to turn this hobby into a profession through the unique development of the Tune Detective idea. This simple habit of tracing tunes to their source has provided material for a number of books and magazine articles, eight short motion pictures, innumerable broadcasts and lectures, and now frequently brings me into court as an expert in musical plagiarism and infringement suits. I have used the tracing of tunes as a simple way of getting people to listen to music, removing the inferiority complex from the average listener, and generally eliminating the curses of snobbery, highbrowism, and hypocrisy from America's musical life. Six of my books have gone into the reprint stage, which is rather unusual for works on music. *The Art of Enjoying Music* is used as a

textbook by many schools and colleges. *Great Symphonies* is used by teachers and also by adult radio listeners. *Barber Shop Ballads* is the official songbook of the Society for the Preservation and Encouragement of Barber Shop Quartet Singing in America. *Read 'Em and Weep* has become the chief source of musical Americana.

"I was in YMCA uniform in the First World War and did a lot of entertaining and song-leading in the Second, besides editing *A Guide for Army Song Leaders. . . .*"

———

Sigmund Spaeth was born in Philadelphia, Pennsylvania, the son of Reverend Adolph Spaeth, a Lutheran minister who had emigrated from Germany, and Harriett Reynolds (Krauth) Spaeth, a writer and editor on music subjects. He took his B.A. and his M.A. from Haverford College, Philadelphia (1905, 1906), and taught German at Princeton University (1906–1908), where he earned his Ph.D. He taught music at the Asheville School for Boys in North Carolina.

In 1912 Spaeth went to New York City to take up a part-time position as assistant editor with the G. Schirmer music publishing house. He was music critic for the *Evening Mail* throughout the war years. When he left the *Mail* to do war work he was succeeded as music critic by his wife, Katharine Lane. She was so successful in the job that he had to seek new employment for himself. He went to the *New York Times* as sports and occasional music commentator.

Spaeth was director, then promotion manager, for the American Piano Company (1920–1927); his promotion of an electric instrument called the Ampico brought him into contact with many of the great composers and musicians of his day.

Spaeth's goal in life was to instill a love and understanding of music in everyone. To quote the *New York Times*, the "contention that brought Dr. Spaeth to fame was that behind the tune of each popular song were roots reaching back to folk music and the classics." As such, Spaeth became an expert witness in cases of alleged musical plagiarism. On one occasion, in the words of the *New York Times*, Spaeth "demonstrated by singing and tapping his feet that parts of [the song "Yes, We Have No Bananas"] could be found in the great chorus of Handel's *Messiah* and in Michael Balfe's *Bohemian Girl*, several Wagner operas, *My Bonnie Lies Over the Ocean, I Dreamt I Dwelt in Marble Halls*, and *Aunt Dinah's Quilting Party*."

Spaeth was active in radio, television, film, and the stage, and served as music editor of several national magazines, including the original *Life, Esquire, McCall's*, and the *Literary Digest*. He was involved in a number of radio and television shows,

both as host and guest, his two best known radio programs being *The Tune Detective* and *The Song Sleuth*. In another popular radio program he gave piano lessons.

Spaeth was much in demand as a lecturer; the forums for his programs included colleges and universities, New York's Town Hall, Carnegie Hall, Radio City Music Hall, the White House, and even the vaudeville stage, upon which he appeared in Sherlock Holmes garb. He used his "Tune Detective" approach in a series of short films produced by major movie studios. Another of his passions was barbershop singing.

In his memoir *Fifty Years with Music* Spaeth declared that "though radio and television are obviously the most far-reaching media of communication . . . I never underestimated the power of the printed word, even in connection with a largely abstract art." In addition to his articles, columns, opera guide books, and program notes, Spaeth was a prolific writer and editor of music books, including appreciations, histories, and song collections. In a review of the 1933 *Art of Enjoying Music*, the *Christian Century* claimed that "no one who has had the luck to hear 'the tune detector' over the radio will need to be told that Sigmund Spaeth has the gift to clarify and charm in the popular presentation of music. But those light and chatty programs conveyed no more than a hint of the vast amount of musical scholarship that lay behind them. In this volume he comes as near as any man can to telling all about music."

Sigmund Spaeth was dean of the Wurlitzer School of Music; president of The Songmart, a "clearinghouse for new authors and composers whose works are subject to helpful criticism"; and president of the Louis Braille Music Institute.

PRINCIPAL WORKS: *Nonfiction*—Milton's Knowledge of Music: Its Source and Its Significance in His Works, 1913; Offenbach's Tales of Hoffmann: Concise Guide to the Words and the Music, 1913; Saint Saëns Samson and Delilah: Concise Guide to the Words and Music, 1913; Verdi's Il Trovatore: Concise Guide to the Words and Music, 1913; Wagner's Lohengrin: Concise Guide to the Words and Music, 1913; The Common Sense of Music, 1924; (with J. T. Howard) The Ampico in Music Study, 1925; The Musical Adventures of Jack and Jill, 1926; Read 'em and Weep: The Songs You Forgot to Remember, 1926 (rev. as Read Ēm and Weep: A Treasury of American Songs: The Songs You Forgot to Remember, Some Sad, More Merry, Some Sentimental: With a Wealth of Amiable Anecdotes, Comment and Fascinating Folklore, a Flavorful Feast of Melodious Music, 1945); Words & Music: A Book of Burlesques, 1926; (with R. H. Schauffler) Music as a Social Force in America and the Science of Practices, 1927; Weep Some More, My Lady, 1927; (with D. Paskman) "Gentlemen Be Seated!": A Parade of the Old-Time Minstrels, 1928; They Still Sing of Love, 1929; "Sing a Song of Contract": The Bidding and Playing Fundamentals of Contract Bridge (Regardless of Systems) in Thirty-One Verses, 1931; The Art of Enjoying Music, 1933; The Facts of Life in Popular Song, 1934; Music for Everybody, 1934; Great Symphonies: How to Recognize and Remember Them, 1936; Stories Behind the World's Great Music, 1937; (with R. Bruce) The Fundamentals of Popular Songwriting, 1939–  ; Music for Fun, 1939; Great Program Music: How to Enjoy and Remember It, 1940; Fun with Music, 1941; A Guide to Great Orchestral Music, 1943; At Home with Music, 1945; A History of Popular Music in America, 1948; Dedication: The Love Story of Clara and Robert Schumann, 1950; Opportunities in Music, 1950, rev. ed. 1958 (rev. as Opportunities in Music Careers, 1966); How

To Play the Hohner Harmonica: New Easy Method for Beginners, 1957; The Importance of Music, 1963. *Juvenile*—Maxims to Music: Traditional Proverbs, Mottoes and Maxims of the World Fitted to Music for the Well-Tempered Piano-Child, 1939; Music, a Priceless Heritage, 1945. *Memoirs*—Fifty Years with Music, 1959. *As editor*—Barber Shop Ballads: A Book of Close Harmony, 1925 (rev. ed. as Barber Shop Ballads and How To Sing Them, 1940); American Mountain Songs, 1927; The International Who Is Who in Music, 1927– ; Who Is Who in Music: Biographical Reviews, Pictorial and Other Features of Interest To and Concerning Persons in the World of Music, 1927– ; "Let's Sing and Be Merry—:" Songs for a Good Time, 1937; (with D. Paskman) Operetta Merry-Go-Round: A Musical Review, 1937; Barber Shop Harmony: A Collection of New and Old Favorites for Male Quartets, 1942; (with C. O. Thompson) 55 Art Songs, 1943 (rev. ed. as Favourite Art Songs, 1947); More Barber Shop Harmony: A Collection of New and Old Favorites for Male Quartets, 1945; Barber Shop Classics, 1946– ; (with J. I. Krug) Fifty Favorite Operatic Arias, 1947; Music and Dance in New York State, 1951; Music and Dance in the New England States, 1953; Music and Dance in Pennsylvania, New Jersey, and Delaware, 1954.

ABOUT: The autobiographical material quoted above was written for Twentieth Century Authors, 1942 and Twentieth Century Authors First Supplement, 1955. Contemporary Authors Vols. 5–8, 1970; Current Biography 1942; Dictionary of American Biography, Supplement 7, 1981. *Periodicals*—Christian Century November 22, 1933; New York Times November 13, 1965.

## SPEARMAN, FRANK HAMILTON (September 6, 1859–December 29, 1937), American novelist and short story writer, was born in Buffalo, New

York, the son of Simon Spearman and Emmaline E. (Dunning) Spearman. He was educated in public and private schools, and at Lawrence College, Appleton, Wisconsin. His plans to become a doctor were ruined when poor health—and probably a degree of disinclination—forced him to abandon study.

Spearman was a traveling salesman at the age of twenty, a bank cashier at twenty-seven, and a bank president at twenty-nine. Although some of his best-known stories are about railroad life and adventure, he was never employed by a railroad: his acquaintance with railworkers derived solely from his contact with them as a banker. William A. Titus, in *Wisconsin Writers*, points out that Spearman "had the opportunity to listen to the stories told by the veteran trainmen while they were 'held for orders;' and thus absorbed a wealth of railroad lore which he used to advantage when he turned to writing as a profession."

Spearman made an intensive study of McCook, Nebraska, a division point on the Burlington Railroad, at which he spent a number of years as a bank employee. In 1904 he published *The Strategy of Great Railroads* which, according to Catherine M. Neale of *Catholic Authors*, "became a standard reference for students of economics, being a critical study of the major period of development of transportation by rail in the United States."

Spearman was best known for his western and

railroad stories. His most famous work is *Whispering Smith*, a novel concerning a dismissed foreman of bridges who joins a band of outlaws and robs and pillages the railroads until the hero, Whispering Smith, captures the gang. According to Spearman's son the novel was written after two weeks spent in Cheyenne, Wyoming, and the central character was said to be a composite study of Timothy T. Keliher, a special agent of the Union Pacific stationed in Cheyenne, and Joe La Fors, U.S. Deputy-Marshal, a gun-handler never equaled in that country. "The characters are railroad men and cattle-ranchers, and the action rapid and adventurous in a way that holds the attention from start to finish," was the *Bookman's* assessment of this 1906 bestseller. *Whispering Smith* was filmed three times, in 1915, 1926 and 1948 (with Alan Ladd as the detective) and was the first of several Spearman stories to be adapted for the screen.

A popular Spearman short story was titled "Second Seventy-Seven" and was published in *The Nerve of Foley, and Other Railroad Stories*. Here a brakeman named Ben Buckley is the hero for averting a terrible collision between a passenger train and a train carrying stock by throwing a switch at the last possible moment. It was "breathless" stuff, and Spearman was expert at it. He spent his last years in Hollywood writing several movie serials.

PRINCIPAL WORKS: *Novels*—Doctor Bryson, 1902; The Daughter of a Magnate, 1903; The Close of the Day, 1904; Whispering Smith, 1906; Robert Kimberly, 1911; The Mounted Divide, 1912; Merrilie Dawes, 1913; Nan of Music Mountain, 1916; Laramie Holds the Range, 1921; The Marriage Verdict, 1923; Selwood of Sleepy Cat, 1925; Flambeau Jim, 1927; Spanish Lover, 1930; Hell's Desert, 1933; Gunlock Ranch, 1935; Carmen of the Rancho, 1937. *Short stories*—The Nerve of Foley, and Other Railroad Stories, 1900; Held for Orders: Being Stories of Railroad Life, 1901; (with H. Martin, F. S. Palmer, W. Drysdale, et. al.) Adventures in Field and Forest, 1909; (with V. T. Sutphen, P. Bigelow, et. al.) Making Good: Stories of Golf and Other Outdoor Sports, 1910. *Nonfiction*—The Strategy of Great Railroads, 1904.

ABOUT: The autobiographical material quoted above was written for Twentieth Century Authors First Supplement, 1955. Hoehn, M. (ed.) Catholic Authors: Contemporary Biographical Sketches: 1930–1947, 1948; Titus, A. Wisconsin Writers, 1930. *Periodicals*—Bookman October 1906; New York Times December 31, 1937.

## SPENCE, LEWIS (November 25, 1874–March 3, 1955), Scottish authority on mythology and folklore, critic, and poet, was born at Broughty Ferry, near Dundee. He was educated at the local collegiate school, before completing his studies at Edinburgh University, where his paternal grandfather had been professor of surgery. Spence took a course in dentistry but abandoned it in favor of earning his living by writing.

In 1899 he joined the staff of the *Scotsman*, became editor of the *Edinburgh Magazine* in 1904, and news editor of the *British Weekly* in London in 1906. Speaking of his return to Edinburgh, Spence wrote:

"Leaving London in 1909, I returned to Edinburgh to take up the career of a freelance and soon established a firm footing, contributing articles to many newspapers and journals of importance.

Apart from journalistc work, my efforts have been directed into two distinct channels: the writing of verse, both in English and Scots, and research into  the mythology and antiquities of ancient Central America. As regards the first, I resolved . . . to 'rescue' the Scottish tongue from the sadly degenerate condition into which it has fallen. This I sought to achieve by composing verses in its dialect strengthened and embellished by the addition of words and phrases taken from the old Court Scots. . . . "

Spence's two best-known poems are the widely anthologized "The Prows o'Reekie" (a brief and pugnacious defense of Edinburgh) and "Great Tay of the Waves" (about the powers of early impressions): "Deep in the saul the early scene— / Ah, let him play wi' suns wha can, / The cradle's pented on the een, / The native air resolves the man!" He published three books of poetry—in 1910, 1913, and 1926 (*Collected Poems* appeared in 1953)—but his other work as a freelance writer, primarily the study of mythology, meant that his project of rescuing the Scottish tongue was left to a younger generation—led by Hugh Macdiarmid (Christopher Murray Grieve) —which took Spence's synthetic Scots several stages further. Like Macdiarmid, Spence was one of the founding members of the National party of Scotland and was the first member of the party to stand (unsuccessfully) as a Parliamentary candidate.

Although prevented from traveling by indifferent health and lack of finance, Spence resolved, from his Edinburgh base, to focus his mythology studies on Central America, and labored for more than twenty years on his major work, *The Gods of Mexico*, described in the *New Statesman* as "the first attempt in English to restore the Mexican pantheon in intelligible form, along the scientific lines employed in the reconstruction of more venerable religions." But it was the wider-ranging studies which he produced for the general reader and folklore enthusiast that proved to be his most enduring contribution as a writer. Many people between the wars learned their mythology from Spence, and his *An Encyclopedia of Occultism*, although first published in 1920, continues to be available and widely consulted in inexpensive, modern editions. (There is also a revised, scholarly edition, *Encyclopedia of Occultism and Parapsychology*, edited by Nandor Fodor and published in 1983.) A serious scholar, Spence was awarded a royal pension for his services to literature in 1951. But he did have his eccentric side, which found expression in a series of studies on the lost continents of Atlantis and Lemuria; he was not afraid to propound personal theories in the hope that evidence might one day turn up to support them.

Many of his titles have been continuously in print since his death.

PRINCIPAL WORKS: The Mythologies of Ancient Mexico and Peru, 1907; The Civilization of Ancient Mexico, 1912; A Dictionary of Medieval Romance and Romance Writers, 1913; The Myths of Mexico and Peru, 1913; The Myths of the North American Indians, 1914; Heros Tales and Legends of the Rhine, 1915; Myths and Legends of Ancient Egypt, 1915; Myths and Legends, Babylonia and Syria, 1916; Legends and Romances of Britanny, 1917; Mexico of the Mexicans, 1917; An Encyclopedia of Occultism, 1920; (rev. ed. published an Encyclopedia of Occultism and Parapsychology ed. N. Fodor 1983); Legends and Romances of Spain, 1920; Cornelius Agrippa, 1921; An Introduction to Mythology, 1921; The Gods of Mexico, 1922; The Problem of Atlantis, 1924; Atlantis in America, 1925; The History of Atlantis, 1926; The Mysteries of Britain, 1928; The Mysteries of Egypt, 1929; The Magic and Mysteries of Mexico, 1930; The Problem of Lemuria, 1932; Boadices, 1937; Legendary London, 1937; The Occult Causes of the Present War, 1940; The Occult Sciences in Atlantis, 1943; The Outlines of Mythology, 1944; The Magic Arts in Celtic Britain, 1945; The Religion of Ancient Mexico, 1945; British Fairy Origins, 1946; Myth and Ritual in Dance, Game, and Rhyme, 1947; The Fairy Tradition in Britain, 1948; The Minor Traditions of British Mythology, 1948; The History and Origins of Druidism, 1949; Second Sight, Its History and Origins, 1951. *Poetry*—Le Roi d'Y's, 1910; Songs Satanic and Celestial, 1913; Plumes of Time, 1926; Weirds and Vanities, 1927; Collected Poems, 1953.

ABOUT: The autobiographical material quoted above was written for Twentieth Century Authors First Supplement, 1955. Contemporary Authors Vol. 115; Hamilton, I. (ed.) The Oxford Companion to Twentieth-Century Poetry, 1994; Who's Who 1955. *Periodicals*—New Statesman June 30, 1923; New York Times March 4, 1955; Times (London) March 4, 1955.

**SPENCER, CLAIRE** (April 20, 1899–    ), Scottish-American novelist, was born in Glasgow, Scotland, the daughter of William Stephens Spencer and Jessie Janet Jones (MacGlashan) Spencer. She was educated at the Paisley Grammar School in Scotland and the Bournemouth Art School in England. She emigrated to the United States in 1917 and became a naturalized American citizen two years later. Her marriage to Harrison Smith, a  New York City publisher, began in 1920 and ended in divorce in 1933; that same year she married novelist John Ganson Evans—of West Brooksville Maine—a son of the literary diarist Mabel Dodge Luhan.

*Gallows' Orchard* was Claire Spencer's first and best-known novel. It tells the story of Effie Gallows, a gallant, wayward girl in a Scottish village, her several lovers—especially the village school master, who tells the tale—and the suspicious puritanical villagers who resent her and eventually stone her to death for protecting the identity of a murderer. Effie's dying words are, "Flatten my hands upward to the sky, stretch my arms like leafless trees. Take the words from my dying throat! I am tired of people and their ways!" V. S. Pritchett, in a *Spectator* (1930) review, had some concerns with the novel's plot development, but still declared it a "flashing and tragic piece of romantic fiction with undeniable moments of greatness."

Claire Spencer's second novel, *The Quick and*

the Dead, disappointed critics. The Saturday Review of Literature found this character study of a man ruined by his mother's hatred of him "cruel, morbid, powerful, surgically adept, with occasional flashes of hysteria." Spencer's last novel, The Island, is set on a Scottish island and concerns twin brothers who love the same young woman with tragic results. The New York Herald Tribune called it a "dour and wind-swept book," but found "it has in it something of that eerie poetry, that Scottish integrity which made Gallows' Orchard so memorable a novel." A review in the Spectator (1936) offered a description that fits all three of Spencer's novels: "strong meat and cold comfort." Spencer was, like the far better known and remembered Mary Webb, of the school satirized in Stella Gibbon's Cold Comfort Farm.

PRINCIPAL WORKS: Novels—Gallows' Orchard, 1930; The Quick and the Dead, 1932; The Island, 1935.

ABOUT: Periodicals—New York Herald Tribune April 15, 1935; Saturday Review of Literature May 14, 1932; Spectator April 26, 1930; January 3, 1936.

**SPENCER, ELIZABETH** (July 19, 1921–    ), American novelist, wrote: "The events of my life are completely unremarkable. It seems to me there

must be somebody exactly like me living in every small Mississippi town perhaps in every Southern town. However: I was born in Carrollton, Mississippi, a town of 500 people, but with, I believe, more than normal share of history and legend, or perhaps more than the usual number of old people around to remember it. As a young child, I was sick a good deal and was read to. Later I disliked everything but Edgar Rice Burroughs and never read with much pleasure until I finished college. But I cannot remember a time when I did not make up stories and from the time I was nine I was writing them down with intense pleasure. This impulse was not suggested to me by my family, though they always praised and encouraged me. Both my parents came of farming families who had lived in Carroll County, Mississippi, since the early 1830s. My father's family has, in later generations, combined business with farming; my mother's family, the McCains, have tended to select military careers. I have one brother, a doctor now serving with the Navy.

"I was sent to a small denominational school, Belhaven College, in Jackson, Mississippi, and upon graduation there was awarded a scholarship to Vanderbilt University in Nashville, Tennesse. Here it was my good fortune to study with Donald Davidson [one of the original Fugitive group and an ex-editor of The Fugitive ], a great teacher, whose encouragement and help have meant more to me and to others of his students than any of us are qualified to say.

"My study at Vanderbilt (1942–1943) was fol-

lowed by some lean years. I had got my B.A. degree in English and my M.A. degree in English: there was nothing to do but teach. I taught one year at a junior college in Senatobia, Mississippi; another at Ward-Belmont School in Nashville. Then, dissatisfied, I resigned to work as a newspaper reporter on the Nashville Tennessean. This kind of writing was still not what I wanted. I had earlier, during my senior year in college, started a novel, never titled, never finished, and mercifully never published. Poor and inept as it was, certain characters from it did not forsake me. I at last shut my eyes and jumped: resigned from the paper, cleaned my portable, and bought a ream of paper. I had been sending out short stories which met with complimentary notes but no takers. I was determined to try another novel. The old characters, and some new ones, took their places in a new plan. A year later, at Donald Davidson's suggestion, an editor from Dodd, Mead, David M. Clay, asked to look at my work in progress. What little I could show him received favorable attention; he asked that more be sent when it was ready. I sent a second section in due time and received a contract in return. This novel, Fire in the Morning, was published in 1948 and was accorded wide praise—perhaps too much, a mixed blessing.

"In 1948 I joined the faculty of the University of Mississippi where [1953] I am still employed in half-time teaching—one class in creative writing. In 1952 my second novel, This Crooked Way, was published. In the interim I have written a few short stories, one published in the Virginia Quarterly Review in Summer 1950, titled 'Pilgrimage.' It was listed by Matha Foley as one of the year's best. Last Spring (1952) I was awarded $1000 by the National Institute of Arts and Letters.

". . . . I do not feel that my work to this date has anything tremendous to offer. Older writers whom I admire have generously accorded me such encouragement, especially Eudora Welty and Robert Penn Warren. It is always the next thing I am writing that I hope will be the fine one."

_____

Not long after she wrote the sketch above, Elizabeth Spencer, who left her native South in 1953 for what turned out to be a long period of time, married (on September 26, 1956) John Arthur Blackwood Rusher, a British businessman. From 1976 until 1981 she was a visiting professor at Concordia University in Montreal. From 1981 she combined her teaching in Canada (until 1986, when she gave this up) with a visiting professorship at the University of South Carolina, Chapel Hill. She held the latter position until 1992.

By 1995 Spencer had completed nine novels as well as collections of stories and a play. Although her essentially "southern sensibility" is invariably mentioned by critics of her work, Spencer's experiences of life "in exile" in Italy, and then in Canada, have been especially noted as both shaping it and giving it a wider range.

In an interview with Publishers Weekly Spencer explained that her five years in Italy (1951–1955) had given her freedom from what she had previously thought would be a lifelong encasement in "the Southern social patterns and lineage and tradition." For a time her works were not very widely discussed. George Core, a noted critic, bibliographer, and historian of Southern literature, declared in the *Washington Post* (1988), that she "has worked in the shadow of William Faulkner, Eudora Welty and other leading Southern authors. Now, by dint of long persistence and considerable accomplishment, she may be coming into her own so far as critical recognition is concerned."

Spencer's first three novels were all based in the South. *Fire in the Morning* had the blessing of Eudora Welty, who announced on its jacket that the author was already "completely at home in the world of the novel." This world is that of a Mississippi town in which a feud between two families leads to violence and tragedy. It was generally noted that Spencer was, at this stage, overinfluenced by Welty herself, by McCullers, and by Capote; but that, as Hubert Creekmore put it in the *New York Times* (1948), it was still a "fine picture—evenly balanced, perceptive and barely tinged with romanticism—of life in the Eighteen Hundreds." Its successor, the simpler *This Crooked Way*, less technically ambitious, is about a farm boy, Amos Dudley, who has "both religion and a mean streak." Harvey Swados (prematurely, as it turned out) in the *Nation* (1952) called the author a "talented and skillful member of the Southern regional group" but "perfectly content to work within the confines of a strictly Faulknerian scene, a faithful disciple of the master."

By 1956 she had cast off the more obvious influences on her writing, and had made a considerable advance. The significantly entitled *The Voice at the Back Door*, often referred to as the most powerful of her novels, is still "Faulknerian." But already the novelist is doing something that Faulkner—as a man—could not have done: namely, record with a new accuracy and panache something of the feminine attitude towards "southern violence." The truculent but honest Duncan Harper is made Sheriff of Winfield County, Mississippi, on the "macho" strength of his prowess as a football player. But he gives the bigoted inhabitants something they had not expected: equal justice to white and black alike. Although openly liberal and democratic in its sentiments, the book was seen by most critics to work well—and not to have manipulated events to suit its thesis: "No two ways about it," Brendan Gill wrote in the *New Yorker* (1956), "[it] is a practically perfect novel. Miss Spencer has a thrilling story to tell and she tells it quickly and modestly, never raising her voice and never slurring a syllable." The novel is a chilling study of corruption in the person of lawyer Kerney Woolbright—one of the author's most memorable characterizations—who sacrifices his sense of decency and justice for the sake of political advancement. Many have felt that, although Spencer has done perhaps as well in later novels, some of them not set in the South, she has hardly bettered this stark tale of corruption, in which the female characters are knowingly counterpointed with their various male counterparts.

Spencer told *Publishers Weekly* in 1988 she had "got to thinking that the Southerner has a certain mentality, especially Southern women—you can no more change Southern woman than you can a French woman. . . . So I thought that really nothing was going to happen to me as far as my essential personality was concerned . . . from the standpoint of my characters . . . the Southern approach was going to be valued no matter where they found themselves. . . . you could be Southern anywhere, in Florence, in Paris, or anywhere you found yourself."

In 1961 Spencer published what has become her best-known book—in part, no doubt, because it was the subject of an unusually sensitive movie, although its own merits are considerable—a novella about Americans in Florence called *The Light in the Piazza*. Part of it appeared in the *New Yorker* prior to publication in book form. Here Spencer genuinely widened her range. Faulkner is never evoked at all: the author's master is an even more ubiquitous one, Henry James. Clara, the child of Margaret Johnson, is in her twenties, but, because of an accident, has the mental age of a child of ten. She is courted by a young Italian called Fabrizio. Margaret at first takes her away to Rome, but she is unhappy; finally—although Fabrizio's father raises the price—Margaret allows her to marry him.

All reviewers commended *The Light in the Piazza*, but were divided about its true merits. Was it an ultimately insensitive pastiche of James, as Elizabeth Janeway implied in her review of it in the *New York Times* (1961), or did it transcend this influence, as Granville Hicks, reviewing it in the *Saturday Review* (1961) believed? George Steiner, discussing it in the *Yale Review*, thought the author "so gifted" that he complained of "the genteel facility of this little romance: she never takes us inside Clara's bruised consciousness." Hicks, though, was certain that it "combined great artistry" with "moral intelligence," and that it was a work "as strong as it is delicate."

Its successor *Knights and Dragons* is also set in Italy. But for *No Place for an Angel* Spencer turned to New York, Dallas, Key West, Washington, and New England for settings, depicting Rome and Sicily only briefly.

In 1968 Spencer published her first short-story collection, *Ship Island*, to sharply divided critical reaction. Her second collection, *The Stories of Elizabeth Spencer*, appeared in 1981. This was a collection of thirty-three tales including the contents of *Ship Island*. Reviewing it for the *New York Times* (1981), the novelist Reynolds Price, a long-standing admirer, thought that she was on the whole better when dealing with the South: even if her "impressive observatory continues to register extraordinary reports . . . once abroad her characters . . . levitate unpredictably and sometimes dangerously."

*The Salt Line*, a novel, set on the Mississippi Gulf Coast in the aftermath of Hurricane Camille, tells of one-time 1960s activist and ex-college professor Arnie Carrington's attempt to rediscover himself as he becomes compassionately involved in storm-wrecked real estate. Christopher Porterfield in *Time* (1984) saw it as Spencer's *Tempest*, with Arnie as an "eccentric but passionate Prospero"; but, he was a little suspicious of the author's "too conscious" "high skill and intelligence." As Elaine Kendall wrote in the *Los Angeles Times*, of her later work, her "vision penetrates the blanket of homogeneity that blurs the American landscape."

Concordia awarded her an honorary doctorate of law in 1988, and she gained the same honor from the University of the South in 1992. In 1968 Southwestern University at Memphis had awarded her an honorary doctorate of letters. She has won several prestigious prizes, including the first McGraw-Hill Fiction Award (1960), an Award of Merit Medal for the Short Story (1983), and the Dos Passos Award for Fiction (1992).

PRINCIPAL WORKS: *Novels*—Fire in the Morning, 1948; This Crooked Way, 1952; The Voice at the Backdoor, 1956; The Light in the Piazza, 1960; Knights and Dragons, 1965; No Place for an Angel, 1967; The Snare, 1972; Marilee, 1981; The Salt Line, 1984. *Short stories*—Ship Island, 1968; The Stories of Elizabeth Spencer, 1981; Jack of Diamonds, 1988. *Drama*—For Lease or Sale, 1989.

ABOUT: The autobiographical material quoted above was written for Twentieth Century Authors First Supplement, 1955. Contemporary Literary Criticism vol. 22, 1982; Dictionary of Literary Biography vol. 6, 1980; French, W. (ed.) The Fifties: Fiction, Poetry, Drama, 1970; Prenshaw, P. W. *in* Women Writers of the Contemporary South, 1984; Prenshaw, P. W. Elizabeth Spencer, [Twayne] 1985; Prenshaw, P. W. Conversations with Elizabeth Spencer, 1991; Roberts, T. Self and Community in the Fiction of Elizabeth Spencer, 1994; Vinson, J. (ed.) Contemporary Novelists, 1982; Who's Who in America 1995. *Periodicals*—Los Angeles Times September 16, 1988; Mississippi Quarterly Winter 1992–1993, Spring 1994 (checklist); Nation June 7, 1952; November 18, 1968; New Republic June 26, 1965; New York Herald Tribune Book Review October 28, 1956; New York Times September 12, 1948; October 27, 1967; March 1, 1981; New Yorker March 22, 1952; December 15, 1956; Paris Review Summer 1989; Publishers Weekly September 9, 1988; Saturday Review November 26, 1961; October 7, 1967; Southern Review January 1982; Time October 7, 1967; February 13, 1984; Village Voice September 20, 1984; Washington Post August 9, 1988; Yale Review March 1961.

**SPENCER, THEODORE** (July 4, 1902–January 18, 1949), American poet and scholar of Elizabethan literature, was born in Villanova, Pennsylva-

nia. His father, the vice-president and general manager of Bell Telephone Company, died in 1905, and Spencer and his sister were brought up in Haverford by their mother, Helena Carroll Frazier. He was educated at Haverford Academy, and at Princeton before going to the University of Cambridge in England to take a B.A. (1925), returning to Harvard to take his Ph.D. in 1928 on the subject of Elizabethan tragedy.

Spencer became a tutor and then assistant professor at Harvard. In 1939 he was appointed permanent lecturer in English at the University of Cambridge in England, the first American ever of-

fered this post, but because of the outbreak of World War II he was unable to take up his position. Instead, he stayed at Harvard, and in 1946 became Boyleston Professor of Rhetoric and Oratory there.

He was distinguished on two counts: first as an academic whose analysis of Shakespearean England and the works of this age were remarkable for their sense of period, and secondly as a minor poet, his lyricism and metaphysical approach much influenced by W. B. Yeats and T. S. Eliot. As a scholar, in *Death and Elizabethan Tragedy* he highlighted the tension between the medieval religious outlook that coexisted in Shakespeare's era with that of a growing Renaissance humanistic philosophy. *Shakespeare and the Nature of Man* drew considerable praise.

As a poet, Spencer attracted mixed reviews. His first collection, *The Paradox in the Circle*, was described by Harold Rosenberg in *Poetry* as tending "towards the cerebral compression of the riddle, posing dichotomies concerning man and woman, youth and age, seeking and finding, beginning and ending." Later works such as *Act of Life* were less well received, some discerning a mismatch between Spencer's intellectual concerns and his lyrical abilities. "He is at his best when he is creating the sense of search, not of moral certainty," said Elizabeth Drew in *Weekly Book Review*. His last, posthumous collection, *Acre in the Seed*, however, drew warmer comments, perhaps because of his untimely death, perhaps because he had relaxed and was more keen to impart what he felt than to demonstrate literary pyrotechnics. The best poems are still read and respected.

Spencer had one son by his first marriage to Anna Murray; he died only a year after his second marriage, to Eloise Bergland Worcester. Shortly afterwards, F. O. Matthiessen wrote this tribute to his friend and colleague: DdHis stylish clothes and bright bow ties, the lifelong fondness for playing the piano as a delight to himself and his friends, the eager knowledge of birds which can be seen also in his poems, the verve with which he read Shakespeare aloud, the capacity for throwing himself into each new enthusiasm—all these things had seemed to keep him younger than middle age."

PRINCIPAL WORKS: Garland for John Donne, 1932; Death and Elizabethan Tragedy, 1936; (with M. Van Doren), Studies in Metaphysical Poetry 1939; Shakespeare and the Nature of Man, 1942: Selected Essays (ed. A. C. Purves), 1967. *Poetry*—The Paradox in the Circle, 1941; An Act of Life, 1944; Poems, 1940–1947, 1948; An Acre in the Seed, 1949.

ABOUT: Matthiessen, F. O. Theodore Spencer, 1902–1949 *in* Responsibilities of the Critic, 1952. *Periodicals*—New York Herald Tribune Books april 3, 1932; January 10, 1943; New York times January 27, 1949; Poetry August 1941; Publishers Weekly February 5, 1949; Weekly Book Review April 9, 1944.

**SPENDER, STEPHEN (HAROLD)** (February 28, 1909–July 16, 1995), English poet and critic, was born in London, the second son and third of four children of Violet Hilda (Schuster) and Edward Harold Spender. Spender had a materially comfortable and intellectually stimulating Edwardian childhood. His father was a journalist and author of a biography of David Lloyd George; his uncle, J. A. Spender, was the editor of the *Westminster Gazette*. However, it was a childhood that had its own pressures and miseries, as is made apparent  in Spender's autobiography *World Within World* (1951) and, in a different way, in the poem 'My Parents Kept Me From Children Who Were Rough.' His adolescence was significantly affected by the death of his mother when he was twelve, after which his maternal grandmother,      Hilda Schuster, a cosmopolitan widow, featured strongly during his years of adolescence. He attended University College School, Hampstead, and then went to University College, Oxford. Prior to this he had set up his own miniature printing press, using it to earn money printing chemists' labels. It was on this press that he printed his first pamphlet of poems, *Nine Experiments, Being Poems Written At The Age Of Nineteen*. Auctioned at Christie's in New York in October 1995, a copy of this flimsy rarity was listed in the catalogue with an estimated price of $35,000.

At Oxford he mixed with W. H. Auden, Louis MacNeice (with whom he edited *Oxford Poetry* in 1929) and Christopher Isherwood. Spender printed Auden's first collection *Poems* (1928) on his hand press. The group, which included others, but was predominantly led by Auden, quickly became known as the 'Oxford poets,' and were brought to public attention in Michael Roberts's 1932 anthology *New Signatures*. Spender had left Oxford the previous year to spend some time in Germany, having already brought out a second individual collection of his student poems, *Twenty Poems* (1930), but it was his third collection, *Poems*, published by Faber in 1933, that was the first to be properly reviewed. The reviewers welcomed Spender's gentle lyricism in contrast to Auden's more acerbic and aggressive style. Many critics have noted that Spender gave too much of his energies to commentary and criticism, editorial work, and committee-sitting, and that his best poetry remains the earliest. It was Spender's talent as a prose commentator, as much as his ability as a poet, that contributed to this view. (G. S. Fraser said that Spender was the nearest thing in Britain to a continental intellectual.) *The Destructive Element* (1935) was described in his London *Times* obituary as "one of the few volumes of 'committed' Thirties literary criticism which is still worth reading." And *Forward From Liberalism*, published the following year, appeared to confirm his radical credentials, but several reviewers pointed to its soft and sensible center. *The Economist* commented: "This is an interesting and curious book by a young intellectual and poet who wants to call himself a communist. It is a curious book because it makes quite clear that Mr. Spender is in fact a liberal." After the book's publication Spender was invited to join the British Communist party, but his membership quickly lapsed.

During the Spanish Civil War Spender managed to get himself into Spain and serve as a delegate to the International Writers' Conference at Barcelona in 1937. The collection *The Still Centre* (1939) contained several of his Spanish war poems and his journalism from this time (some of it collected in *The Thirties And After*) shows how his experiences in Spain strengthened his pacifism. Writing in the *New Statesman*, he said: "The dead in wars are not heroes: they are freezing or rotting lumps of isolated insanity. . . . It may be true that at certain times the lives of individuals are unimportant in relation to the whole of future history . . . But to say that those who happen to be killed are heroes is a wicked attempt to identify the dead with the abstract ideas which have brought them to the Front. . . ."

During this period, Spender experimented with verse forms. "Vienna," a long narrative poem published in 1935, had been seen at the time as a sign that he was increasing his range as a poet, and *Trial of a Judge*, a full five-act poetic drama published in 1938, was further evidence of his claim to be seen as more than a writer of short poems. Despite Nevill Coghill's enthusiasm in *The Spectator*—he spoke of "This extraordinary performance, which I consider the finest English poetic drama written since Otway's *Venice Preserv'd*—it received a cool critical reception.

At the start of World War II in 1939, Spender was living alone in a London flat, his first wife having left him to marry the poet Charles Madge. The vacuum in Spender's personal life was filled by *Horizon*, the magazine he helped Cyril Connolly to launch, offering his flat as the publishing headquarters. In 1941 he joined the fire service. In the same year he married Natasha Litvin, a concert pianist, and moved to Hampstead. Spender's two main poetry collections of the 1940s, *Ruins and Visions* (1942) and *Poems of Dedication* (1947) saw a return to more personal subject-matter. However, several reviewers remarked upon the shift in mood since his early work—an increased hesitancy and uncertainty, together with a growing pessimism. Louis Untermeyer, reviewing the 1942 collection in the *Saturday Review of Literature*, summed up Spender's strengths and weaknesses as a poet: "The limitations are obvious: the frequent failure of the head to impose its wisdom upon the heart, the heavily burdened and sometimes inchoate line, the lack of self-discipline, and the total absence of humor. But, underneath the blemishes, there is the clear voice of something dearly held and deeply felt as true. Here blending tradition and experiment, is a voice of courage and—there is no lesser word for it—nobility."

A good example of Spender at his best from this period is the poem written about the death of his sister-in-law, "Elegy For Margaret." This is heartfelt and sympathetic—in part written to console his brother—but never sentimental:

The deprived fanatic lover,
Naked in the desert
Of all except his heart,
In his abandon must cover

With wild lips and torn hands,
With blankets made from his own hair,
With comfort made from his despair,
The sexless body in the sands.

'Tom's a-Cold' is one of Spender's jauntier comments on his own loss of idealism: "Preachers said 'Life ascends, like a plant,'/But to me things seemed all aslant,

*World Within World*, a memoir published in 1951, is considered one of the classic accounts of the period. Peter Porter, writing Spender's obituary in the *Independent*, has called this book: "One of the 20th century's great biographies: in it Spender's endearing Boswellian honesty about himself and his motives enables him to present a portrait of a generation and a country unrivalled even in the works of such great truth-tellers as Orwell and Koestler." In the early 1950s Spender founded the journal *Encounter*, and was its co-editor from 1953 until 1967, when he resigned following an American report that the financial backers of the magazine had received funds from the Central Intelligence Agency. The story of his relationships with co-editors and with the Congress for Cultural Freedom (the Paris-based organization that helped to fund *Encounter*) will present a challenge for future biographers.

Spender published a first *Collected Poems* in 1955 ("The young poet wrote better than the middle-aged one, and that's saddening," observed Randall Jarrell in the *Yale Review*), and a further distillation thirty years later, *Collected Poems 1928-1985*. Nine years later, to mark his eighty-fifth birthday, he published his final new collection. To produce the poems in *Dolphins* he had relied heavily on his notebooks and journals. Some were not new poems at all, but final versions of poems he had been working on for years. Nevertheless, there was a distinct note of valedictory and grandfatherly gentleness in the slim volume. Indeed, he wrote movingly of what it is like to grow old, and see younger generations usurping the active roles. At the end of a family reunion "We ourselves / Though ancient, not yet ghosts, feel two-dimensional. . . . "

Near the end of his life, Spender became embroiled in a legalistic dispute with the American novelist David Leavitt. Leavitt was accused of plagiarism in basing the central relationship in his novel *While England Sleeps* on Spender's *World Within World*. The book was withdrawn in the United Kingdom, but Spender was unable to prevent its continued sale in other countries. On the occasion of this dispute, Ian Hamilton contributed a long article to the *New Yorker* magazine, discussing Spender's reputation as a poet and his feelings about homosexual relationships. Spender spoke for himself in the *New York Times Book Review*, defending his suit for copyright infringement. An accomplished editor and translator, Spender became professor of English at University College London 1970-1977. He was appointed a Commander of the British Empire in 1962 and given a knighthood in 1983. In 1988 he authorized publication of a revised novel, *The Temple*, the main character of which was a bisexual youth.

PRINCIPAL WORKS: *Poetry*—Nine Experiments, 1928; Twenty Poems, 1930; Poems, 1933; Vienna, 1934; At Night, 1935; The Still Centre, 1939; Selected Poems, 1940; Ruins and Visions, 1942; Spiritual Exercises, 1943; Poems of Dedication, 1946; Returning to Vienna, 1947; The Edge of Being, 1949; Collected Poems 1928–1953, 1955; Selected Poems, 1964; The Generous Days, 1969; Art Student, 1970; Recent Poems, 1978; Collected Poems 1928–1985, 1985. *Drama*—Trial of a Judge, 1938; To the Island, 1951; Mary Stuart, 1959; Rasputin's End, 1963. *Fiction*—The Burning Cactus, 1936; The Backward Son, 1940; Engaged in Writing, 1958; The Temple, 1988. *Nonfiction*—The Destructive Element: A Study of Modern Writers and Beliefs, 1935; Forward and Liberalism, 1937; The New Realism, 1939; Life and the Poet, 1942; Citizens in War—And After, 1945; Botticelli, 1945; European Witness, 1946; Poetry Since 1939, 1946; World within World, 1951; Shelley, 1952; The Creative Element, 1953; The Making of a Poem, 1955; The Struggle of the Modern, 1963; The Year of the Young Rebels, 1969; Love-Hate Relations: A Study of Anglo-American Sensibilities, 1974; Eliot, 1975; Cyril Connolly: A Memoir, 1978; The Thirties and After, 1978; Letters to Christopher (ed. L. Bartlett) 1980; China Diary (with D. Hockney) 1982; Journals 1939–1983 (ed. D. Finn) 1985.

ABOUT: Current Biography 1977; David, H. Stephen Spender 1992; Kulkarni, H. B. Spender, Poet in Crisis, 1970; Smith E. The Angry Young Men of the Thirties, 1975; Pandey S. Spender A Study in Poetic Growth, 1982. *Periodicals*—Economist February 13, 1937; Guardian July 17, 1995; Independent July 18, 1995; New Statesman May 1, 1937; New Yorker February 28, 1994; New York Times Book Review September 4, 1994; Partisan Review Winter 1988; Saturday Review of Literature September 26, 1942; Spectator March 18, 1938; Sunday Times July 23, 1995; Time July 31, 1995; Times (London) July 18, 1995; October 18, 1995; Yale Review Autumn 1955.

**SPENGLER, OSWALD (ARNOLD GOTTFRIED)** (May 29, 1880–May 8, 1936), German philosopher of history, was born, the son of a post office official, at Blankenburg am Hars, in the Harz Mountains, Prussia. His *Der Untergang des Abendlandes* (*The Decline of the West*) is the most eloquent, and the most initially persuasive, of all the grand-scale expressions of the spirit of pessimism and "decadence"  that swept over Europe between 1890 and the end of World War I. Despite its distortions and oversimplifications, the book was enormously popular in the 1920s and 1930s, and has to be reckoned a significant force in the history of Western popular thought. Spengler's dreamy, fantastic version of history seems to recall Nietzsche; but, while it echoes Nietzsche's aphoristic style, it lacked his psychological insight. Initially Spengler was not attracted by the grandiose: he tried to write poetry. But he very soon failed dismally. So he changed his perspective. The stifled poet became a grand prophet. His gloomy synthesis of decadence and grandeur, attractively oversimplified and yet apparently erudite, appealed to readers of the 1920s and 1930s.

After attending the Halle Latin School, Spengler went to the universities of Munich, Berlin, and Halle, where his main study was in mathematics, at which he attained a reasonable proficiency. He also studied philosophy, history, and art. His doctoral dissertation at Berlin was on the Greek pre-Socratic philosopher Heraclitus (1904). His qualifying thesis for the teaching profession was on the subject of "The development of the organ of sight in the chief stages of animal life." The greatest of his general debts was undoubtedly to Wilhelm Dilthey (1833–1911), who—indebted in his turn to Kant—was one of the first modern philosophers to emphasize that the history of the world must essentially be the history of the manner in which human beings experience, perceive, and interpret it.

Spengler at twenty-eight became a schoolmaster in Hamburg, teaching science and math. But this did not satisfy his aspirations, and in 1911 he went to Munich, where he lived in poverty, in an unheated and bare room, to work on the first volume of his *magnum opus.* This was not only an analysis of the state to which Western civilization had come by the time of World War I, but also a confident prophecy of the direction it would take. The opening volume, *Gestalt und Wirklicheit* (Form and actuality), a draft of which was completed in 1914, for long failed to find a publisher; eventually it was issued by Braumüller of Vienna, in 1917. It took the German-speaking world by storm, and was reissued in Munich in the following year.

In 1922 the second volume, *Welthistorische Perspektiven* (Perspectives of world history) appeared, together with an ambitious revision of the first volume. The whole was soon translated into English (and many other languages), in two volumes, as *The Decline of the West* (1922–1926).

Spengler used the analogy of a plant to describe his view of civilization: It is born and grows ("Blute"), it matures and flowers ("Reife"), then it must decline ("Verfall") and eventually die. Each great philosophy or religous system is an expression and product of its own world, and only of that world. In Spengler's view, the Apollonian world, which preceded our own, was "finite": confined to the strictly local space of the *polis*, the city state. The idea, the essence, of the classical world—each of the civilizations has its special driving idea—was one of *delimitation*: its aim was to cut nature—always terrifying—down to size, thus making it less threatening. By contrast, Spengler described the essence of Western civilization, already at the stage of its final decline, as "Faustian," characterized by an outwards, thrusting spirit, a striving for *infinitude*, as expressed by its baroque poetry, and the soaring buttresses of its great cathedrals. In this light, Western civilization had now become degenerate, sentimental, rootless, and chaotic. Modern art and culture, in particular the atonal music of Arnold Schönberg, and the androgynous night clubs of Berlin, showed its decay.

Nazi ideologists, welcomed the ideas of Spengler, with his call for a "beast of prey," an "irrational man," a hero who might after all save at least the Germans from the fate of oblivion. A nationalist, a Prussian German, a disciplinarian, he invented, but out of a perfectly well established tradition, a "new" mystical "Prussian socialism." The Nazis had already developed their own idea of "socialism"—the "national" one. It looked very much like the solution Hitler was just proposing, and Spengler himself, in speeches and essays, called for new leaders—and gave his approval to parts of the Nazi program. His *Der Mensch und die Technik* (1931, *Man and Technics*) warned of the dangers of technology: this would, Spengler insisted (just as Heidegger did at the same time), overwhelm humanity.

But Spengler, when it came to it, found Hitler vulgar. Germany didn't want—he famously said—a "heroic tenor but a real hero." He made critical remarks about the Nazis, and, all his critics have conceded, would have been genuinely aghast had he lived to see the "full flowering" of Nazidom. He had a public quarrel with one of the chief Nazi theoreticians, Albert Rosenberg. His *Jahre der Entscheidung* (1933; translated as *The Year of Decision* in 1934), somewhat critical of the Nazis, had a huge German sale—and was eventually proscribed; nor could it be mentioned on the radio. Like Jünger at the time, Heidegger later, Spengler grew distressed at the new government.

Spengler's system is seductive because so much in it—the dangers of technology, the loss of religious faith, the violence endemic in modern society, the dishonesty and ineptness of politicians—is so clearly relevant to the modern world. Its appeal lies in the vague poetry of despair and sense of helplessness with which it is imbued. The English popular philosopher C.E.M. Joad, in the *Spectator* summed up *The Decline of the West* thus: "One has the sensation of ascending a lofty tower from which all the kingdoms of history are seen, and, becoming visible, become also intelligible. The process is an exhilarating one, and the impressionable reader is apt to lose his head. For Spengler's work, impressive as it undoubtedly is, suffers from two defects. The first is inaccurary . . . The second defect is obscurity . . . I cannot avoid the suspicion that factual inaccuracies, tricks of reasoning and an obscurity which at times seems almost deliberate, have played no small part in building up the impressive structure of Spengler's world history. It may well be that without them it would fall to the ground."

Interest in Spengler's thought was rekindled briefly in the 1960s with the publication of an abridged English version of *The Decline of the West* (1962) and the *Letters of Oswald Spengler, 1913–1936* (1966). The former book was prepared by Arthur Helps from the translation by Charles Francis Atkinson. The letters were translated and edited by Helps himself. Critical reception was mixed: John Lukacs in *The New York Times* called the work "insubstantial" and "an editorial failure in many ways; Franz Schoenberner, in the *Saturday Review* thought it a "loose collection of notes and very often meaningless letters." The book was welcomed more for its insights into German thinking between the world wars than for any into Spengler's philosophy.

PRINCIPAL WORKS IN ENGLISH TRANSLATION: The Decline of the West, 2 vols. (tr. C. F. Atkinson) 1926–1928; Man and Technics (tr. C. F. Atkinson) 1932; The Hour of Decision (tr. C. F. Atkinson) 1934; Today and Destiny (abridged edition of Atkinson's translation), 1940; The Decline of the West (abridged edition of Atkinson's translation), 1962. Selected Essays (ed. And tr. H. Kornhardt) 1967. Aphorisms (ed. and tr. H. Kornhardt) 1967. *Letters*—Letters of Oswald Spengler, 1913–1936 (abr., ed. and tr. by A. Helps) 1966.

ABOUT: Fennelly , J. F. (ed.) Twilight of the European Lands—Oswald Spengler a Half Century Later, 1972; Fischer K. P. History and Prophecy: Oswald Spengler and the Decline of the West, 1989; Hughes, H. S. Oswald Spengler: A Critical Estimate, 1952; Oswald Spengler, 1992; Lewis, W. Time and Western Man, 1927; Makers of Modern Culture, 1981; Russell B. History of Western Philosophy, 1946; Steiner, R. Oswald Spengler: Prophet of World Chaos (trs. N. Macbeth and F. E. Dawson) 1949; Thinkers of the Twentith Century, 1985; Wistrich, R. (Ed.) Who's Who in Nazi Germany, 1982. *Periodicals*—Antiquity September 1927; Book Week March 20, 1966; Clio Fall 1989, Summer 1990; German Quaterly Summer 1985; Journal of the History of Ideas July–September 1991; New York Times May 9, 1936; New York Times Book Review March 6, 1966; Saturday Review March 19, 1966; Spectator January 12, 1929; Times Higher Educational Supplement August 19, 1980; Times (London) Literary Supplement, March 31, 1966.

## SPEWACK, BELLA (COHEN) (March 25, 1899–April 27, 1990) and SPEWACK, SAMUEL

(September 16, 1899–October 14, 1971), American playwrights who collaborated on all their works, supplied the following statements: "Bella Spewack, born Bella Cohen in New York [some sources list her place of birth as Bucharest, Romania, or Hungary]. Educated in Washington Irving High School, was reporter on *Brown Home News, Yorkville Home News*; feature writer on *New York Call, Socialist Daily* for several years. Became literary editor of *New York Evening Mail*. Was publicity director of Girl Scouts [she has been credited with originating the Girl Scout cookie sale] and Campfire Girls. During this period she wrote many short stories, some of which were republished in O'Brien's *Best Short Story* anthologies. In 1923 she was correspondent in Berlin for the *New York Evening World*. Began writing for the theater in 1927 in collaboration with Samuel Spewack. From 1930 until the present day 1942, several months each year are spent writing pictures for Hollywood."

"Samuel Spewack, born in New York [some sources say Ukraine], educated at Columbia University. Worked on the *New York World* from 1918 to 1926, during which time he was a reporter in New York and for four years correspondent in Moscow and Berlin. Wrote short stories and articles, then plays and pictures."

————

Bella and Samuel Spewack were well known for the string of "wacky" Broadway comedies and films they wrote together. As a writing team they were so closely knit that it was impossible to say which part of a play was Bella Spewack's and which part was her husband's. According to the *New York Times* (1990) "their comedy was almost always madcap, verging on the slapstick and knock-about farce. It was often peopled by the harassed, the rattle-brained, the blunder-prone and the pompous, among other cartoon-like characters."

In 1931 the Spewacks had their first major success with *Clear all Wires!*, a farcical melodrama

based on their experiences as correspondents in Moscow; six years later it was revived under the title *Leave It to Me*, with a score by Cole Porter. Another Spewack hit was the 1935 *Boy Meets Girl*, a farce about a pair of Hollywood zanies who make a star out of an infant *in utero*. Writing in *Anatomy of a Hit*, Abe Laufe called it a "clever satire on the motion picture industry with an undertone of criticism, a humorous indictment of the follies of Hollywood. . . . At times the humor is obvious and contrived but, nonetheless hilarious." The Spewacks themselves wrote the script for the film version.

Their most famous hit was the Tony Award winning *Kiss Me Kate*, a sparkling musical with another Cole Porter score, which ran on Broadway from 1949 to 1950 and continues to flourish in revivals. The plot concerns a vain actor and his temperamental ex-wife who are performing in a Baltimore production of Shakespeare's *The Taming of the Shrew*. Noting that the comedy was grounded in character and in a keen appreciation of backstage life, Brooks Atkinson declared that "Bella and Samuel Spewack have contrived an authentic book which is funny without the interpolation of gags." (*New York Times*, 1948). *Kiss Me Kate* was also made into a very successful film.

*My Three Angels*, the Spewacks adaptation of Albert Husson's *La Cuisine des Anges*, was one of the comedy hits of the 1953 season. Set in French Guiana, the story concerns a trio of escaped convicts who save a general store from going bankrupt.

"The Spewacks had their share of flops," the *New York Times* (1990) reported. "But, in 1955, on the night after a play called *Festival* received a chilly reception from the critics, Mrs. Spewack—a tiny, round woman—fought back. She marched onto the stage during curtain calls and appealed to the audience to go tell their friends if they had liked the show." She repeated her appeal on radio and television programs, but only managed to buy *Festival* a few more weeks of life.

Among the Spewacks' many film credits were *The Nuisance, Three Loves Has Nancy, The Cat and the Fiddle, Rendevous, Weekend at the Waldorf, My Favorite Wife*, and *Move Over Darling*. During World War II, Samuel Spewack also compiled and wrote a grim documentary, *The World at War*, for the U.S. Office of War Information.

PRINCIPAL WORKS: *Drama*—Pincus, 1927 (also titled Hizzoner, 1927, and Poppa, 1929); Clear All Wires!, 1932 (rev. as Leave It to Me, 1938); The Solitaire Man, 1934; Spring Song, 1934; Boy Meets Girl, 1937; Vogues of 1938, 1937; Miss Swan Expects, 1939; Trousers to Match, 1941; Woman Bites Dog, 1947; Kiss Me Kate, 1951; My Three Angels, 1953; The Festival, 1955 (also titled Play It By Ear, 1955).

ABOUT: The autobiographical material quoted above was written for Twentieth Century Authors, 1942. Contemporary Authors 1994; Gould, J. Modern American Playwrights, 1966; Laufe, A. Anatomy of a Hit, 1966. *Periodicals*—New York Times December 31, 1948; April 29, 1990; Times (London) May 1, 1990.

**SPEWACK, SAMUEL.** See **SPEWACK, BEL-LA**

**\*SPEYER, LEONORA (VON STOSCH)** (November 7, 1872–February 10, 1956), American poet, wrote: "Having played the violin since my early youth, it seemed but another expression, perhaps a more subtle one, of the same art to find myself writing, studying, deep in the metrics of musical words. I think my friendship with Amy Lowell and being so personally and vigorously brought into immediate contact with the writing of the Imagist poets with whom she was so identified, is as comprehensive an explanation as any, of this change of expression. 'There,' she said, dumping the little olive-colored paper-bound books into my lap, "Don't blame me if you don't like them. You asked for them.' And she added, 'But you go on playing the violin. There are plenty of us to write poetry.' And I did like them, no one was to blame; and I did not go on playing the violin. By the time I was healed of an acute neuritis I was not thinking of much else but verse. I was writing wildly, prolifically, and wholly happily.

"I published too soon and too much. (Harriet Monroe and Robert Bridges are partly responsible for that—and I am not ungrateful.) I sometimes am confronted with one of those early bits of juvenilia—infantilia is perhaps the better word—and I look the other way, pretending not to hear, hoping no one does. I studied, I read, I pondered; I sought my fellow-poet and listened to wise and kindly (or unkindly) criticism. I wrote less, I wrote better. 'Two words are not as good as one,' sang the anonymous poet, several centuries ago of 'the written word.' It is as true today. I can hardly remember a time that the violin was not under my chin, since that chin was firm enough to hold it, until the sense of poetry and the wonder of poetry came to push it from its place.

"The last few years I have taught at Columbia University. . . . 'What , can you *teach* poetry?' I am sometimes asked with a fine irony. And the answer, if there be one, as well as I can express it, is: there is no teaching a student to acquire talent; no amount of study may contrive a gift. That is God's affair. But the actual process of poetry-writing, the color and harmony of words, can be, surely must be learned. The instrument must be mastered like any other instrument. Coming from the unplumbed depths of the subconscious, it is perhaps the most controlled of the arts. It is unpremeditated only to the lark."

———

Leonora Speyer was born in Washington, D.C., the daughter of Count Ferdinand von Stosch, who had fought with the Union Army in the Civil War. Her mother, Julia (Thompson) von Stosch, was an

\*SPY er

American. As the poet noted: "I can hardly remember a time that the violin was not under my chin . . . until," she went on, "poetry came to push it from its place." She studied music at the Brussels Conservatory, where she took a first prize at the age of sixteen. As a concert violinist she toured Europe and the United States, making a debut appearance with the Boston Symphony Orchestra in 1890. Speyer, who was married twice, had four daughters. After her divorce from her first husband she married (in 1902) the English banker and patron of the arts Sir Edgar Speyer, a founder of London's Whitechapel Art Gallery. The Speyers lived in Europe until coming to New York in 1915.

After giving up music, Leonora Speyer wrote lyric and narrative verse that appeared regularly in periodicals such as *Poetry* and the *Nation*. Five collections were issued, beginning with *A Canopic Jar*, published when she was forty-nine years old. Her second collection, *Fiddler's Farewell*, received the Pulitzer Prize for poetry in 1927. The Irish poet and critic Padraic Colum was a notable admirer: he noted her "unusual power of dramatic narrative" (*Saturday Review of Literature*); other critics praised her ability at "word-music" and a certain psychological penetration in her love sonnets. But G. Campbell, writing in *Poetry* (July 1940), objected that these were not truly lyric poems: "They seem so only because of [her] virtuosity in creating melodious and rhythmical sound effects." As for her images, they were not appropriate to the context either in mood or logic. Reviewing *Naked Heel*, Stanley Kunitz flatly stated—and posterity has endorsed him—that "despite the ardent testimonials on the jacket, Leonora Speyer remains a mediocre poet, manifesting states of heightened emotions without corresponding states of heightened consciousness" (*Poetry*, November 1932). He, too, thought her least pallid efforts her narrative poems, in which she displayed her knack for ironic humor—as in "Ballad of Old Doc Higgins" and "Monk and Lady."

For several years, from 1937 on, Speyer taught poetry at Columbia University. She was active in the Poetry Society of America (president from 1934 to 1936), which awarded her its Gold Medal for Distinguished Achievement in 1955.

PRINCIPAL WORKS: A Canopic Jar, 1921; Fiddler's Farewell, 1926; Naked Heel, 1931; Slow Wall, Poems New and Selected, 1939; The Slow Wall: Poems, together with Nor without Music, 1946. As compiler—American Poets, an Anthology of Contemporary Verse, 1923.

ABOUT: The autobiographical material quoted above was written for Twentieth Century Authors, 1942. New York Times May 12, 1946, February 11, 1956; Poetry November 1932, July 1940; Saturday Review of Literature February 4, 1939.

**SPINGARN, JOEL ELIAS** (May 17, 1875–July 26, 1939), American critic and political activist, was born in New York City, the oldest of four sons of Elias Spingarn, a tobacco wholesaler born in Austria, and Sarah Barnett Spingarn, born in England. Young Spingarn attended Dr. Julius Sachs' Collegiate Institute and took his bachelor's degree from Columbia College in 1895; after a year at Harvard, he returned to Columbia for his Ph.D. in 1899. In that year, he married Amy Einstein, whose family was later to help underwrite some of her husband's projects on behalf of racial justice. Spingarn was de-

scribed by admirers as a "Renaissance" man, a "scholar-activist" who introduced the critical theories of Benedetto Croce to America, who got involved in progressive politics and the fight for racial justice in the early days of the NAACP, and who lived the life of a gentleman farmer on his country estate as one of the horticultural world's expert cultivators of the clematis flower, which attracted his attention during a visit to England in 1927.

Spingarn's early academic career was spent at Columbia, in George E. Woodberry's Department of Comparative Literature, where he rose to the rank of full professor by 1909 and succeeded his mentor as department head. His first published work, *A History of Literary Criticism in the Renaissance* (1899), was translated into Italian, with an introduction by Croce, in 1905 and reprinted in an expanded English edition in 1908 His other works on literary theory, *The New Criticism* (1911) and *Creative Criticism* (1917) were well-received by scholars (he also edited a collection, published in 1908, of *Critical Essays of the Seventeenth Century*). George Saintsbury, while disagreeing with some of his ideas, acknowledged Spingarn's contributions to the field in his own *History of Criticism*. His 1911 book bore traces of influence by Matthew Arnold and Walter Pater, as well as Croce. *Creative Criticism* includes the text of the 1911 book augmented by three additional essays, plus a reply to John Galsworthy's criticism of the first essay. Of this book, the *Times Literary Supplement* wrote: "He demolishes more decayed and genteel traditions than the Victorians can justly be taxed with; and in the face of new realities his enthusiasm is so keen and clear-sighted that we wish that he would give us a few examples of the art besides this spirited defence of it." An expanded edition of this book was published in 1931

During his tenure at Columbia, Spingarn became involved in progressive politics in New York City, and was an unsuccessful candidate for the state legislature from Manhattan in 1908. He took on the role of a crusader against racial injustice and personally advocated the cause of Negroes who were trying to secure equal access to public accommodations in the years immediately following *Plessy v. Ferguson*'s juridical legitimation of segregation. A dispute with Columbia's president, Nicholas Murray Butler, over the restructuring of academic departments led to Spingarn's dismissal from the faculty in 1911. The incident only seemed to whet his appetite for political combat, however, and the thirty-six-year-old ex-professor eagerly took on the role of scholar-activist. He involved himself even more deeply in the progressive causes

espoused by Theodore Roosevelt's Bull Moose Party, and served as a delegate to that group's national conventions in 1912 and 1916 (he had first been inspired by a speech Roosevelt made at Columbia in 1899). Spingarn also bought a small newspaper, the *Amenia Times* near his country estate in rural New York State and, in 1919, was one of the founders of Harcourt, Brace and Company. He maintained his scholarly pursuits by teaching occasionally at the New School for Social Research.

Spingarn's dismissal from Columbia came at about the time of the formation of the National Association for the Advancement of Colored People (NAACP), and that organization responded eagerly when the scholar-activist made contributions on behalf of a black man the association was defending against charges he had murdered his white landlord. Oscar Garrison Villiard and W. E. B. DuBois succeeded in persuading Spingarn to join the NAACP's executive committee, and he also served as an officer of the group's New York Vigilance Committee, which took direct legal action against theater managers who maintained a 'whites-only' seating policy. He quickly rose in the ranks of the organization and, in 1913, established the Spingarn Medal still awarded annually to "the man or women of African descent and American citizenship who has made the highest achievement during the preceding year in any honorable field." (Several weeks before Spingarn's death in 1939, it was presented to singer Marian Anderson by Eleanor Roosevelt.) Spingarn, although not "colored," took a pro-active conciliatory role in focusing the energies of rival factors in the fervent atmosphere of race-based activism during the Progressive Era. In 1915, upon the death of Booker T. Washington, Spingarn invited feuding activists to his country estate at Troutbeck to attract Washington's followers to the NAACP and to plan the association's future strategy, which he helped redirect toward a more aggressive stance against Jim Crow legislation in the South and against the "white supremacist" ideology of the recently released film *Birth of a Nation*. His efforts at creating the national New Abolition campaign in 1913, and his support of training programs for Negro officers in World War I—Spingarn held the rank of major in the infantry—were rewarded in 1919 when he became the NAACP's treasurer. He later served as the group's national president during the troubled depression years, from 1930 until his death in 1939, when he was succeeded by his brother Arthur B. Spingarn. In his 1972 book, *J. E. Spingarn and the Rise of the NAACP 1911–1939*, B. Joyce Ross calls Spingarn the "most flamboyant of the twentieth-century Abolitionists," "describing him as an intellectual prodded into activism by the "economic plutocracy" of the era.

During the 1920s, Spingarn and his wife became directly involved in philanthropic activities on behalf of Langston Hughes. Ann Douglas, in her 1995 monograph *Terrible Honesty: Mongrel Manhattan in the 1920s*, wrote that it was Amy Spingarn who financed Hughes's first semester at Lincoln College in 1926 and that "with her husband, Joel, and her brother-in-law Arthur, she contributed a good deal of money and intelligently informed support to the Harlem Renaissance, and Hughes was genuinely devoted to her." Douglas stated elsewhere in the same book that "Jewish money, particularly that of the Spingarns and Julius Rosenwald, the Sears, Roebuck potentate, funded many of the Harlem Renaissance political organizations, publications, and prizes."

When Spingarn died on the eve of World War II, many tributes were paid. Lewis Mumford, in his "Scholar and Gentleman" article in the *Saturday Review*, wrote that "No one else in his literary generation had produced so decisive an effect with such a fine economy of means." He acknowledged Spingarn's critical studies, which, he rightly claimed, foreshadowed the New Criticism of later years. Recalling his 1911 dispute with the Columbia administration, Mumford said that Spingarn's academic activism had paved the way for the concept of an "autonomous faculty" at American institutions of higher learning.

Oswald Garrison Villiard, of the NAACP, paid similar respects to his colleague in an essay in the *Nation*, entitled "Issues and Men." In it, he spoke of him as a "great lover of peace, this quiet, gentle scholar—gentle until aroused by his keen sense of wrong and injustice." He reminded his readers of the "Renaissance" aspects of Spingarn's life expressed in his country estate, Troutbeck, where he cultivated his clematis and created a garden that John Burroughs called the "loveliest farm in America" and that Sinclair Lewis called "a grass-grown cathedral."

PRINCIPAL WORKS: A History of Literary Criticism in the Renaissance, 1899; The New Criticism, 1911; The New Hesperides and Other Poems, 1911; Creative Criticism, 1917; Poems, 1924; Poetry: A Religion, 1924; Creative Criticism and Other Essays, 1931. As editor—Critical Essays of the Seventeenth Century, 1908–1909; Temple's Essays, 1909; Goethe's Literary Essays, 1921; Criticism in America, 1924; European Library, 1925; Troutbeck Leaflets, 1924–1926.

ABOUT: Dictionary of American Biography, 1940; Douglas, A. Terrible Honesty: Mongrel Manhattan in the 1920's, 1995; Ross, B. J. J. E. Spingarn and the Rise of the NAACP, 1911–1939, 1972; Van Deusen, M. J. E. Spingarn, 1971; Whitman, A., American Reformers, 1986. Periodicals—Living Age September 1939; Nation August 12, 1939; New York Times July 27, 1939; Publishers Weekly August 5, 1939; Saturday Review of Literature August 5, 1939; Survey August 1939; Time August 7, 1939.

## SPITTELER, CARL (FREDERICK GEORG)

(April 24, 1845–December 24, 1924), Swiss-German poet, novelist, short story writer, and essayist, was born in Liestal (Canton Basel-Land), the son of a high-ranking civil servant, Carl Spitteler, and his wife Anna Brodbeck. In 1849 the father was appointed treasurer of the new Swiss confederation at Bern, to which the family then moved. The young Carl, however, was left behind in the care of an aunt, to attend junior school in Basel.

Spitteler studied theology and law at the Obergymnasium of Basel, where he was first inspired to be a painter by the eminent art historian Jacob Burckhardt (1818–1897). Burckhardt, and other teachers, gave the boy a taste for the Renaissance epic,

especially for Ariosto. Between 1863 and 1870 he studied law and theology at Zurich; then he turned to theology alone, at Heidelberg and Basel (again), in preparation for a career as a Protestant minister. But in 1867 he began to lose his faith. By 1870 he felt that he must decline the offer of a pastorate in Austria. He now wished to devote himself to a writing career, but as yet had no means of supporting himself.

Through a military friend of his father's he managed to obtain a post as tutor to the family of a Russian general in St. Petersburg. He lived there for eight years (1871–1879). He made a few excursions to (the then Russian) Finland, but spent most of his spare time composing his first epic, which he had already conceived while still a student at Basel. He published it at his own expense but it was not a commercial success, so in 1879 he moved back  to Switzerland. Two years later, he became a schoolteacher in Neuveille. He taught there for three years, in the meantime (1883) marrying one of his ex-pupils, a Dutch woman named Marie op der Hoff, by whom he had two daughters. In 1885 he took up journalism, first on a paper in Basel (1885–1856) and then later (1890–1892) in Zurich, on the *Neue Zürcher Zeitung*, on which he worked as a temporary literary editor. When, in 1892, his wife inherited from her wealthy parents, he became financially independent. The family moved to Lucerne, where he lived in relative seclusion for the rest of his life.

Spitteler was among the earliest readers of Friedrich Nietzsche, whom he met at Basel while the latter was teaching there (1869–1879). (His old mentor Jacob Burckhardt had a reserved, but nonetheless genuine, admiration for Nietzsche.) Spitteler's first work, the epic *Prometheus und Epimetheus* (1881, *Prometheus and Epimetheus*) was deeply influenced by the books Nietzsche had published. Published by Spitteler himself under the pseudonym of Carl Felix Tandem, it was a commercial failure. However, its theme is not without interest in the context of Spitteler's later and better books. The Nietzschean Prometheus, the high-souled man, a sort of "overman" or *übermensch* (often misleadingly translated as "superman"), is contrasted with his brother King Epimetheus, who is drab, dull, and conventional.

At the end of his life Spitteler recast this epic into rhyming iambic hexameters, as *Prometheus der Dulder* (Prometheus the long-suffering, 1924). He then presented the Prometheus figure more critically, as one who must painfully renounce his subjectivism. Of Muirhead's version of the original the *New Statesman* commented: "One can only surmise that this 'prose epic,' the first considerable literary publication of the late Carl Spitteler, possessed in the original German some more vigorous quality than appears in this translation, the conventional lifeless language of which renders it all but unreadable." Alas, much the same does have to be said of the original German. However, the *Times Literary Supplement* was a little more positive, remarking that some of it was "very fine indeed."

In 1889 Spitteler published a volume of shorter, more lyrical, and more accessible poems, *Schmetterlinge* (Butterflies). A few of these are included in the English-language *Selected Poems* (1929), translated by Muirhead and Mayne. The *Nation* reviewer praised Muirhead's renderings, but described (all too accurately) Ethel Colbert Mayne's, which are unfortunately in the majority, as "mangling" the author "beyond recognition." The review called Spitteler "a minor Heine" who "blew faintly on the dying embers of the classical romances."

Spitteler's first creative book of real note is his long story *Conrad der Leutnant* (Conrad the lieutenant, 1898). This was followed in 1907 by another story, *Gerold und Hansli: Die Mädchenfeinde* (translated as *Two Little Misogynists*). Spitteler collected satirical and other essays in a book published at Jena in 1898: *Lechende Wahreiten.* This was eventually translated (by his English champion Muirhead) as *Laughing Truths* in 1927. Most of the essays are on writers and literature, but there are others on composers (Schubert in particular), gardening, and even on public amusements. The *New Statesman* reviewer described the essays on music as "enclosed in the turgid, demoded imagery of nineteenth-century musical criticism." Richard Church was more generous: "Spitteler's unpretentious sureness acts like a tonic mountain air on the reader whose senses have been dulled by the enervating valleys, fat with culture, where he spends his tired life." There is real learning in the essays and some penetrating wit—and the one on Schubert, as the *Statesman* itself conceded, "shows a real appreciation of music." The best essays in *Laughing Truths* concern Nietzsche.

Spitteler produced yet another enormous epic in *Der Olympische Frühling* (1900–1904, *Olympic Spring*; revised edition, 1909). This, in four volumes, is a strange Homeric-style epic of the twentieth century, in which men populate Olympus and the gods become Swiss citizens. Its humor, like the rest of it, has a very heavy touch. But it did gain Spitteler the attention he thought that he ought to command, if only temporarily. The conductor Felix Weingartner wrote an essay commending it, and so did several others only a little less eminent. The vision of *Olympic Spring*, often genuinely modern, is vitiated by the old-fashioned and lumbering form it is given. But, as Marianne Burkhard noted, Spitteler deserves recognition not only for his more obviously accomplished prose but also for his "final bold attempt to adapt the old epic form."

Spitteler's most important book is the novel *Imago* (1906), about a sexually obsessed man, Viktor, who finally succeeds in sublimating his love into a devotion to art. The beloved, Theuda, is split into two distinct parts: her false married self, called Pseuda, and her true inspirational self, called Imago. Spitteler took as much from Nietzsche on the subject of sublimation as he did from Freud, but the main thrust of the book is clearly based upon psychoanalytic insights. Freud and Jung discussed the work at length between themselves. Hans Sachs and Otto Rank, two non-medical followers of Freud, named their celebrated psychoanalytic magazine *Imago* (1912–1924, revived in Boston in 1939) after Spitteler's novel.

When World War I broke out, Spitteler took a stand against a "racial alliance" of the Swiss with the Germans. He came out strongly for Swiss neutrality, which probably helped him gain the Nobel Prize for literature in 1919. Spitteler's autobiographical *Meine frühesten Erlebnisse* (My earliest experiences, 1914), is a still fascinating reminiscence that explains his use of mythological and psychoanalytic themes.

Spitteler died in Lucerne in 1924. Upon his death, Romain Rolland expressed the esteem in which he was held by his contemporaries, particularly the French, by calling him "our Homer, the greatest German poet since Goethe, the only master of the epic since Milton died three centuries ago, but a more solitary figure amid the art of his day than either the one or the other of these."

PRINCIPAL WORKS IN ENGLISH TRANSLATION: *Verse*—Selected Poems (ed. and tr. J. F. Muirhead, with translations by Muirhead and E. C. Mayne) 1929; Prometheus and Epimetheus (tr. J. F. Muirhead) 1931. *Essays*—Laughing Truths (tr. J. F. Muirhead) 1927. *Short stories*—Two Little Misogynists (tr. J. F. Muirhead) 1922.

ABOUT: Butler, E. M. The Tyranny of Greece over Germany, 1935; Columbia Dictionary of Modern European Literature, 1947 and 1980; Closs, A. Twentieth Century German Literature, 1969; Fleischmann, W. B. (ed.) Encyclopedia of World Literature in the Twentieth Century (1967–1982); Transactions of the Royal Society of Literature of the United Kingdom 10 1931; Wasson, T. (ed.) Nobel Prize Winners, 1987. *Periodicals*—German Life and Letters 31, 1977; Nation February 6, 1929; New Statesman June 4, 1929; April 4, 1931; New York Times December 30, 1924; Spectator August 13, 1927; Times Literary Supplement April 30, 1931.

**SPRIGG, CHRISTOPHER ST. JOHN (pseudonym "CHRISTOPHER CAUDWELL")** (October 20, 1907–March 5, 1937), English critic, novelist, and poet, was born in Putney. He attended school in Ealing, but left at an early age to become a reporter on the *Yorkshire Observer*, where his father was literary editor. Two years later he joined his brother in London, and together they founded an aeronautical publishing com-pany. His interest in poetry developed alongside his expertise in aviation and aerodynamics, a subject which he popularized in a number of books aimed at boys. He also published, while still in his twenties, a series of thrillers (featuring the detectives Charles Venables and Inspector Bray) which appeared under his own name. Sprigg's pseudonym was reserved for his more serious work—the psychological novel *This My Hand*; poetry; and, most important of all, the books of criticism (all of which were published posthumously).

In the thirties he became a staunch Marxist, and was a Communist activist in the East End, serving as secretary of the Poplar branch. After a day working at the typewriter, he would go and sell the *Daily Worker* at the corner of Crisp Street market, or speak at a branch meeting. In December 1936 he joined the International Brigade, and permitted himself to be called "Spriggy" by his fellow men-at-arms. Two months later, in his first taste of action, he was killed at the Battle of Jarama.

His reputation rests mainly on his critical work, especially *Illusion and Reality, A Study of the Sources of Poetry*, which certainly transcends the narrow Marxism that was only apparently its source of inspiration. In his own poems (in manner and diction he was heavily influenced by the Metaphysicals, especially John Donne) Sprigg was occasionally capable of working a conceit to an effect consistent with his political and intellectual position. However, the general view is that the poetry is too uneven in tone, and insufficiently individual in expression. Another problem is that it does not neatly fit the legend of the politically activist thirties writer, killed in Spain. Only a poem or two have survived, and those in Marxist or historical anthologies.

The critical writing does, however, survive. *Illusion and Reality*, best appreciated by the like-minded (E. M. Forster said, in a *New Statesman* review, "He ought not to be read outside the fold"—but this was ironic, meaning the human and not just the narrowly Marxist "fold"), is a lengthy anti-bourgeois treatise, redeemed by its naive earnestness and optimistic view of the future of literature in a new social order. The argument in this book was not a barren one, even outside the bounds of Marxist theory: it was, essentially, that literary language had become, in the likes of Joyce and Proust, too esoteric, and poetry, in particular, had taken on a vocabulary that no longer spoke to a wide audience. Seeking to separate itself from the common and the vulgar, "[i]t did not take their vulgarised values and outraged instincts and soothe both in an ideal wish-fulfilment world like that of religion, jazz or the detective novel. It quietly excluded all those vulgarised values, but in doing so, it step by step excluded more and more of concrete living, and it was this process that called into being the world of art for art's sake, of otherness and illusion, the towering heaven of dream which ultimately became completely private and turned into an abyss of nightmare and submarine twilight."

*Studies in a Dying Culture* and *Further Studies in a Dying Culture* collected his essays on, among other subjects, Freud, Shaw, and pacifism. *Poems* (1939) was a posthumous selection edited by Sprigg's friend, Paul Beard. The more recent *Collected Poems*, edited by Alan Young, although incomplete, contains a greater range of work.

PRINCIPAL WORKS: *Poetry*—Poems, 1939; Ccollected Poems 1924–1936, 1986. *Nonfiction*—The Airship, 1931; Fly With Me, 1932; British Airways, 1934; Great Flights, 1935; Illusion and Reality, 1937; Let's Learn to Fly, 1937; Studies in a Dying Culture, 1938; The Crisis in Physics, 1939; Further Studies in a Dying Culture, 1949; The Concept of Freedom, 1965; Romance and Realism, 1970. *Fiction*—Crime in Kensington,

1933; Pass the Body, 1933; Death of an Airman, 1934; The Perfect Alibi, 1934; The Corpse with the Sunburned Face, 1935; Death of a Queen, 1935; This My Hand, 1936; The Six Queer Things, 1937.

ABOUT: Contemporary Authors Vol. 120, 1994; Cunningham V. British Writers of the Thirties, 1988; Daiches, D. (ed.) The Penguin Companion to British and Commonwealth Literature, 1971; Hamilton, I. (ed.) The Oxford Companion to Twentieth Century Poetry. *Periodicals*—New Statesman December 10, 1938; Times (London) March 11, 1937.

**SPRIGGE, ELIZABETH** (June 19, 1900–February 4, 1974), English novelist and biographer, was born in London. Her father, Sir Squire Sprigge, was an editor of the *Lancet*. She was educated at St. Paul's Girls' School, London, and at Havergal College, Toronto (her maternal grandfather had been a chief justice of Ontario). She returned to England to study at Bedford College, University of London. In her early twenties, after her mar-

riage to Mark Napier, she spent several years living in Sweden and began, in collaboration with her father-in-law, to translate works from Scandinavian into English, developing a special interest in August Strindberg, who was eventually to be the subject of her first biography. Her marriage was dissolved in 1946.

She started publishing in her own right as a novelist. From 1929 to 1940 she wrote half a dozen adult novels, most of them light romances that received mixed reviews. Graham Greene, commenting in the *Spectator* on *The Old Man Dies*, her third book, wrote: "The style is irritatingly chatty; for the first hundred pages the characters discuss at great length for the benefit of the reader what they themselves know already . . . Miss Sprigge's problem depends on dialogue, and dialogue is just what she is least able to write." Her last novel was a fictional biography of the empress Elizabeth of Austria, wife of Franz Josef, about whom she also wrote a play, *Elizabeth of Austria*, with her sister-in-law, Katriona Sprigge. It was produced at the Garrick Theater in 1938. In this same period she published three children's books, including *Pony Tracks*.

During the war years she worked at the Ministry of Information as an expert in Swedish affairs, and then, for a short period, pursued her interest in the theater, becoming a director of a notable experimental theater club, the Watergate, which put on many versions of plays by Ibsen and Strindberg. Apart from her continuing translations of Strindberg, her postwar literary production turned to biography. *The Strange Life of August Strindberg* was an analysis of the character rather than of the writer. Walter Allen, in the *New Statesman*, for example, spoke of it as "wholly uncritical." Her second biography, *Gertrude Stein*, was the first of its kind about the American author. Lightly written, with generous quotations from Stein's own work, the book failed to place its subject in a social or literary context. The same criticism was directed at *Jean Cocteau*, which Sprigge wrote with Jean-Jacques Kihm, and—but to a lesser degree—at her portrait of Ivy Compton-Burnett, who had been a personal friend. The book read very much as a friend's memoir. As biography, it has since been superseded by Hilary Spurling's two-volume treatment.

Sprigge's work as a translator (concentrating on Strindberg) continued, and in 1960 there was a production of her version of Bjornsterne Bjornson's *Mary Stuart in Scotland* at the Edinburgh Festival.

PRINCIPAL WORKS: *Novels*—A Shadowy Third, 1929; Faint Amorist, 1930; The Old Man Dies, 1933; Castle in Andalusia, 1935; The Son of the House, 1937; The Raven's Wing, 1940. *Juvenile*—Children Alone, 1935; Pony Tracks, 1936; Two Lost on Dartmoor, 1940; (with E. Muntz) The Dolphin Bottle. *Biography*—The Strange Life of August Strindberg, 1949; Gertrude Stein: Her Life and Work, 1957; (with J. J. Kihm) Jean Cocteau: The Man and the Mirror, 1968; Sybil Thorndike Casson, 1971; The Life of Ivy Compton Burnett, 1973.

ABOUT: Contemporary Authors vols. 13–16; Who's Who 1974. *Periodicals*—New Statesman January 22, 1949; March 2, 1973; Newsweek April 23, 1973; Spectator July 14, 1933; Times (London) February 11, 1974; Times Literary Supplement February 8, 1957.

**SPRING, (ROBERT) HOWARD** (February 10, 1889–May 3, 1965), English novelist, wrote: "I was born at Cardiff in South Wales. My mother was an

Englishwoman and my father an Irishman. The family was very poor. My father was a casual laborer in gardens. He was often out of work. Nine children were born of the marriage, and I grew up as the middle child. My father died when I was eleven years old. Almost at once, I left for school for good, to help my elder brother and sister and my mother with the task of bringing up the younger members of the family. The elder girls became domestic servants. My brother and I became messenger boys in a newspaper office. Mrs. Essex, in my *My Son, My Son!* and Mrs. Ryerson in *Fame Is the Spur* may both be taken as containing substantial characteristics of my mother.

"The younger children continued their school courses to the end; I and the others had to educate ourselves. The two elder girls turned themselves into district nurses; my elder brother, worn out by excess of study, died in his early twenties; my younger brother was killed in action at Arras in 1917. I am the sole surviving male member of the family.

"I became a reporter on the *South Wales Daily News*, in Cardiff; left to take up a similar appointment on the *Yorkshire Observer*, in Bradford, in 1911; and when the war came I was reporting for the *Manchester Guardian* I served with the British army in France throughout the war, being attached for most of the time to the Intelligence Service.

"I returned to the *Guardian* after the war. In

1920 I married Marion Ursula Pye. We have two sons.

"I remained with the *Guardian* till 1931, when Lord Beaverbrook invited me to join the staff of his paper, the *Evening Standard*, in London. I became literary critic of the paper soon afterwards, and examples of the work done in this connection are collected in the volume *Book Parade*.

"I was rather late beginning as a novelist. *Darkie & Co.*, a book written to amuse my two small sons, was all I had published when *Shabby Tiger*, my first novel, came in 1934. This was successful enough in England, and so was its successor and sequel, *Rachel Rosing*, but neither of these hinted at the world-success that was to come with my next book, called in English *O Absalom!* and in America *My Son, My Son!* Within a short time of its publication, it had been translated into French, German, Italian, Danish, Norwegian, Swedish, Finnish, Polish, Spanish, Dutch, and Portuguese; and in at least two of these languages—German and Italian—as well as in the British and American editions, it was a 'best-seller' in the outstanding sense of the word. This success permitted me to retire from newspaper work, and to buy a home where I had long desired to be: on the sea's edge in Cornwall.

"The outbreak of the Second World War in 1939 found me half-way through the writing of *Fame Is the Spur*, a book a more ambitious scale than any I had yet attempted. It was finished at the end of January, 1940, and published the following summer."

In 1955, he wrote: "Cornwall is the background to much of Mr. Spring's recent writing. He has lived in that county, in the port of Falmouth, since leaving London. During the troubles which broke out after the 1914 war, he was a special correspondent of the *Manchester Guardian* in Ireland, and what he saw there was effectively used in *My Son, My Son!* which, like his later novel *Fame is the Spur*, was made into a motion picture. His English, he says, he owes largely to Cobbett's *Grammar*. In his teens he attended night classes with a view to matriculation at London University, but he never sat the examination. The deepest literary influence upon his work would appear to be that of Dickens, his favorite novelist since childhood. His recently published novel *The Houses in Between* (1951), was a choice of the Book-of-the-Month Club in America. In 1941 when Mr. Winston Churchill crossed the Atlantic to meet President Roosevelt off the Newfoundland coast, Spring was one of the two English writers chosen to accompany him."

---

Howard Spring remained with the *Guardian* until 1931, when a piece about one of Lord Beaverbrook's election speeches with the headline "Peddler of Dreams" so impressed the subject that he offered Spring a job on the *London Evening Standard*. Initially appointed as a feature writer with star billing, Spring was soon made chief reviewer of books, a role previously filled by Arnold Bennett and J. B. Priestley, and one which he undertook—though not quite able to equal the eminence of such predecessors—with characteristic conscientiousness. Working at home, and having to read a great number of works of fiction each week, as well as select the "*Evening Standard* Book of the Month," he began to consider writing a novel himself.

His first effort was a book for children—*Darkie and Co.*—written for his two sons; but in 1934, already into his mid-forties, he published his first adult novel, *Shabby Tiger*, the opening sentence of which was vivid and arresting: "The woman flamed along the road like a macaw." Elsewhere, however, the style was floridly overblown: "With diminishing beats of his pinions he subsided, till he was rocking over the broken image of his own majesty." Neither this book, nor its sequel, *Rachel Rosing*—both set in the Manchester he had left behind—gave Spring any inkling that he might be able to earn his living as a novelist.

Success came with his third adult novel, the best-selling *My Son, My Son!* (originally published in England as *O Absalom!*, but retitled in America to avoid confusion with Faulkner's recently published *Absalom, Absalom!*). Again set in Manchester, it told the story of two boyhood friends who rise from the slums—one making a fortune as a furniture manufacturer, the other becoming a famous novelist—only to be disillusioned by what fate holds in store for their sons. In the middle volume of his autobiography, *In the Meantime*, Spring described how the idea for this novel came to him while traveling on the Cornish Riviera Express, and how his first hurried notes were scribbled onto the reviewing slip of a book he was reading. Able only to work in the evenings, Spring took fourteen months to complete the book. Its success enabled him to give up journalism and become a full-time writer. It also meant that he could achieve a long-nurtured desire: to move his family to the west country. He bought a house near Falmouth, Cornwall.

Both *My Son, My Son!* and Spring's next novel *Fame Is the Spur*, (which tells the story of a Labour politician's social and political rise, and which reviewers thought superior), were conventionally structured sagas—"Built along solid Victorian lines, well-timbered and four square," a reviewer in the *New York Times* (1938) commented on the former. Because of his characterization, depiction of metropolitan life, and sentimental streak, he was repeatedly portrayed as writing in the tradition of Dickens. *Fame Is the Spur*, which was successfully filmed, told the story of a man who started as a radical but later turned—out of conviction—to the political center. Many felt that its story aptly paralleled the rise and fall of Ramsay MacDonald.

The character of Spring's work changed somewhat after his move to Cornwall, which became the setting of much later fiction, such as *There Is No Armour* and *Sunset Touch*. These books did not match the success of *My Son, My Son!* but Spring remained a very popular, if unfashionable, writer throughout the 1950s and 1960s and his books were much in demand on library shelves.

*And Another Thing*, the third installment (even-tually all three parts were published in a single volume) of his autobiography, written during the last year of World War II, was discursively philosophical about cats and Christianity, and contained a call for the Church to take an unequivocally pacifist stance. Spring wrote as a humanist who had recently rediscovered God, and in the epilogue criticized the dropping of the atomic bomb on Hiroshima. His wife's memoir, *Memories and Gardens*, quotes extensively from her husband's books, and adds only domestic detail to the story of their life together. Spring continued to review regularly (latterly for *Country Life*) and in between his novels, for relaxation, wrote play-scripts for a local amateur dramatics society.

PRINCIPAL WORKS: *Fiction*—Darkie and Co., 1932; Shabby Tiger, 1934; Sampson's Circus, 1936; Rachel Rosing, 1935; My Son, My Son! (orig. British title: O Absalom!) 1938; Tumbledown Dick, 1939; Fame Is the Spur, 1940; Hard Facts, 1944; Dunkerley's 1946; There Is No Armour, 1948; The Houses in Between, 1951; A Sunset Touch, 1953; These Lovers Fled Away, 1955; Time and the Hour, 1957; All the Day Long, 1959; I Met a Lady, 1961; Winds of the Day, 1964; Eleven Stories and a Beginning, 1973. *Nonfiction*—Book Parade, 1938; Heaven Lies About Us, 1939; All They Like Sheep, 1940; In the Meantime, 1942; And Another Thing, 1946; Three Plays, 1953; The Autobiography of Howard Spring, 1972.

ABOUT: The autobiographical material quoted above was written for Twentieth Century Authors, 1942 and Twentieth Century Authors, First Supplement, 1955. Current Biography 1941; Dictionary of National Biography, 1961–1970, 1981; Spring H. The Autobiography of Howard Spring, 1956; Spring, M. H. Memories and Gardens, 1964; Who's Who 1965. *Periodicals*—Illustrated London News May 15, 1965; New York Times May 15, 1938; May 4, 1965; Times (London) May 4, 1965.

**SQUIRE, JOHN COLLINGS** (April 2, 1884–December 20, 1958), English editor, poet, critic, anthologist, biographer, parodist, and man of letters, was born in Plymouth, Devonshire, the only son of Jonas Squire, a veterinary surgeon, and his wife the former Elizabeth Rowe Collings. He was educated in a Plymouth Corporation school, and then at Blundell's, Tiverton, Devon (John Ridd's school in R. D. Blackmore's famous romance *Lorna Doone*). He went up to St. John's College, Cambridge, as a scholar, and received what was regarded as a "good second" in history (1905). In 1908 Squire married Eileen Harriet Anstruther, a vicar's daughter. They had three sons and a daughter. His youngest son died in World War II in 1943.

Squire was an active member of the Fabian Society, but his first passion was always for poetry. His initial collection of poems, *Poems and Baudelaire Flowers* (1909), made no impression. He had to be content to work in journalism, in Plymouth and then in London— sometimes contributing to the *Observer*, where his name began to be noticed—until 1913, when his first real chance came: the literary editorship of the newly founded Labour weekly, the *New Statesman*. (Squire remained interested enough in politics to stand as parliamentary candidate twice: for Labour in 1918, and for the Liberals in 1924. He failed on both occasions.) Much of his criticism in the *New Statesman* appeared under the pseudonym of "Solomon Eagle," though everyone knew his identity. Four collections of this criticism appeared under the titles *Books in General* (1918–21) and *Essays at Large* (1922).

Bad eyesight had kept him, to his regret, out of the war and in 1917, he was made acting editor of the *Statesman*. In 1919 Squire founded what Edmund Blunden in his memorial in the *Dictionary of National Biography* called the "nobly printed" *London Mercury*. He presided over it until 1934. The magazine, which satisfied an uncritical readership, was spoiled for some of its readers not only by Squire's "unbusinesslike methods" (he drank and did not always pay his authors or his printers on time), but also, more seriously, by its aggressive anti-modernism.

In the clash between "Georgian" and "modernist" poetics that enlivened British criticism after World War I, Squire appointed himself "nononsense" leader of the conservative traditionalists, much to his eventual detriment as a critic and editor. He made a poor critic: one who had already made up his mind. Squire wielded, as Robert H. Ross claims in *The Georgian Revolt*, "vast power" on the postwar scene. Harold Monro wrote, in *Some Contemporary Poets*, that "such young poets as are not blessed with his favour need not fear to be snubbed, drubbed or neglected by the press." So Squire blinded himself to the gifts of many original poets in order to concentrate on certain signally ungifted and now deservedly forgotten ones as Edward Shanks, John Freeman and J. D. C. Pellow. As "Solomon Eagle" he castigated such movements as "Futurism" without discerning what really was new about them, or the spirit they were trying to express. Thus the *London Mercury*, although it could count for a time on the talents of such hungry young poets as Robert Graves (who had been represented in *Georgian Poetry* but who was no Georgian), became a coterie magazine, soon distinguished by the kind of "slop" (Squire's own word for what he disliked) that its editor so uncritically favored. Eliot and his readers had nothing but contempt for the magazine. By the mid-1930s with Eliot's moving into the limelight and the advent of Auden, MacNeice, and Spender, Squire's power was gone. As Blunden put it, Squire, feeling himself eclipsed, now became "increasingly disorganized: he had left home and was dependent on the care of friends and the stimulus or sedative of alcohol."

Squire was actually a generous and gifted man who became over-identified with his role as bluff literary reactionary. His own "serious" poetry was better, more accomplished, more skilful, more felt, than the general run of the sort of average "Georgian" verse that he favored in the Mercury. Above all, he was a very gifted parodist: as Mick Imlah wrote in the *Oxford Companion to Twentieth Century Poetry*, his parodies "may oddly capture more of his own character than his poems do." His parodies were gathered together in 1921 and gained him many appreciative readers.

But even among his more serious poems there are exceptions, a few of them notable. He had already published, in 1916, a volume called *The Survival of the Fittest*, and, as Blunden noted, it "calls for mention as being perhaps the earliest poetic protest against the war to win much attention in England." Soon afterwards it was eclipsed by the (then) unknown poetry of Wilfred Owen and others; but it was reprinted several times. "The Rugger Match" might be limited in its appeal, but is probably (as Blunden believed) the first "noteworthy poem in English on football." It is certainly done with skill and aplomb. "The Stockyard" is a powerful poem of disgust written after a visit to the Chicago slaughterhouses. Even the poems that Imlah criticized as seeming too "easy to write" have technical skill. "Discovery," is a still famous and much anthologized poem; "Winter Nightfall" is, as Imlah claimed, "a surprisingly tough elegy for a retired colonel," and, he could have added, beautifully done: "The old yellow stucco/Of the time of the Regent/Is flaking and peeling:/The rows of square windows/In the straight yellow building/Are empty and still. . . . " He possessed, as Blunden claimed, "Squire's private tune." His long poem of 1917 "The Lily of Malud" has been singled out as remarkable for its time. Sovereign amongst Squire's poems, however, is surely "Under," a dream-poem in which the dreamer fishes beneath the floorboards.

Squire wrote several plays, the most successful of which was his (and John L. Balderstone's) adaptation of Henry James's *The Sense of the Past* as *Berkeley Square* (1926). Squire was also a keen cricketer, who founded his own "literary" team, The Invaders. An account of this team, and of Squire, is to be found in A. G. Macdonell's famous cricketing novel *England Their England* (1933). He was knighted in 1933 for his services to literature. His numerous anthologies were influential and useful, and sent many a young reader scurrying to poetry. In the last twenty-five years of his life Squire wrote weekly book reviews for the *Illustrated London News*. He had also been editor of the *English Men Heritage* series, and edited and introduced the *Collected Poems* of James Elroy Fletcher, a modern poet after his own heart. In the year after his death in the village of Rushlake Green in East Sussex, his *Collected Poems* were published, with a sympathetic introduction by John Betjeman. The title of Patrick Howarth's biography of him, *Squire: Most Generous of Men*, is apt: his Times obituarist described him as "staunch, difficult and greatly beloved."

PRINCIPAL WORKS: *Poetry*—Poems and Baudelaire Flowers, 1909; The Three Hills, 1913; The Survival of the Fittest, 1916; Twelve Poems, 1916; The Lily of Malud, 1917; Poems first series, 1918; The Birds, 1919; The Moon, 1920; Poems second series, 1912; The Rugger match, 1922; American Poems, 1923; Poems in One Volume, 1916; A Face in Candlelight, 1932; Poems of Two Wars, 1940; Collected Poems, 1959. *Essays and studies*—Socialism and Art, 1907; The Gold Tree, 1917; (as "Solomon Eagle") Books in General, three volumes, 1918,

1920, 1921; Life and Letters, 1920; Books Reviewed, 1922; (as "Solomon Eagle") Essays at Large, 1922; Essays on Poetry, 1923; Life at the Mermaid, 1927; Sunday Mornings, 1930; Reflections and memories, 1935; Weepings and Wailings, 1935; Shakespeare as Dramatist, 1935; The Way to a Horse, 1936; Water Music, 1939. *Autobiography*—The Honeysuckle and the Bee, 1937. *Short stories*—The Grub Street Nights Entertainments, 1924; Outside Eden, 1933. *Drama*—The Clown of Stratford, 1922; (with J. L. Balderstone) Berkeley Square, 1928; (with J. R. Young) Robin Hood, 1928; (with E. H. Squire) Pride and Prejudice (from Austen's novel). *Parodies*—Imaginary Speeches, 1912; Steps to Parnassus, 1913; Tricks of the Trade, 1917; Collected Parodies, 1921. *Biography*—William the Silent, 1912. *Anthologies*—A Book of Women's Verse, 1921; Selections from Modern Poets, 1921, 1924, in a single volume, 1930; The Comic Muse, 1925; The Cambridge Book of Lesser Poets, 1927; Apes and Parrots, 1930.

ABOUT: Hamilton, I (ed.) Oxford Companion to Twentieth Century Poetry, 1994; Howarth, P. Squire: Most Generous of Men, 1963; Monro, H. Some Contemporary Poets, 1920; Ross, R. H. The Georgian Revolt: Rise and Fall of a Poetic Ideal, 1965; Squire J. C. The Honeysuckle and the Bee, 1937; Swinnerton, F. The Georgian Literary Scene, 1951. *Periodicals*—Illustrated London News January 3, 1959; Times (London) December 22, 1958.

---

**STAFFORD, JEAN** (January 1, 1915– March 26, 1979), American novelist and short story writer, was born at Covina, California, the daughter of  Mary McKillop Stafford and John Richard Stafford, a reporter and Western writer who wrote his stories under the pseudonym, Jack Wonder. Her early years were spent in Covina and later, Boulder, Colorado, where she attended the State Preparatory School. In 1936, she took both her B.A. and M.A. at the University of Colorado, Boulder. That same year, Stafford traveled to Germany to study. However, the German state under Hitler soon repelled her and she returned to the United States. She taught the following year as an instructor at Stephens College in Missouri, but found teaching distasteful. "There's something inimical to me in an academic atmosphere," she said, "I can't work at all."

In 1940 Stafford moved to Tennessee, where she took a job as a secretary at the *Southern Review*. Here she began work on the first of several novels, all of which she later discarded. This was her apprenticeship period—a difficult time for the young writer, who was always severely critical of her own work. Her painstakingly crafted writing would later draw this comment from the *Saturday Review of Literature* on Stafford's short story collection, *Children Are Bored on Sunday*. "There is no sentence . . . which doesn't not have its clean, premise line. Difficult ideas are stated with effortless ease, the difficulty of the idea not being a metaphysical difficulty but a difficulty of conveying to the reader the impression made upon some problematical personality by a particular human situation." Stafford herself once said in an interview: "I am a rather slow person, in that experience has to sink in for years before I can use it . . . I have to let impressions and experience age within me."

It was during this period that Stafford moved to Boston, where she finished *Boston Adventure*, a novel four years in the writing and, finally, a popular and critical success. Her career was launched. The *New York Times* commented that: "*Boston Adventure* was a remarkable achievement for a first book, a bold foray into the double-tiered society of Boston, done with a sureness of touch, a control of literary material that bespoke the born writer. The writing was mandarin and embroidered, yet it conveyed with claustrophobic exactness the ingrown, hothouse atmosphere in which the event of the novel took place."

*Boston Adventure* is the story of Sonia Marburg, daughter of a chambermaid who works in a summer hotel for the rich, and of her mentor, the Bostonian Miss Pride, who employs Sonia and introduces her to Boston society. The reviews were not unanimous in their approval. "Stafford may indeed be a 'unique, vigorous and remarkable artist,' as a distinguished critic has stated. But to the novel readers west of Massachusetts Ave. and south of Boylston St., desirous of understanding the quaint customs of the Brahmins, this reviewer would recommend Henry James's *The Bostonians*, Santayana's *The Last Puritan*, or even thinner works of John Marquand, rather than Miss Stafford's highly stylized and romanticized literary adventure," wrote Mina Curtiss (*Boston Globe*).

Stafford won *Mademoiselle* magazine's Merit award for *Boston Adventure*. A year later she received a Guggenheim fellowship and a thousand-dollar prize from the American Academy and National Institute of Arts and Letters. Stafford's next novel *The Mountain Lion* drew wider praise and fewer detractors. The book contrasted starkly from its predecessor in its style. An allegory set in the Colorado mountain country, it is the story of a brother and sister and their years of bitterness between childhood and adolescence. "This is an even finer novel than *Boston Adventure*, though less brilliant," wrote *Commonweal*. "It does not have the dazzling wealth of anecdote which Jean Stafford offered in her first novel; but it has a deeper richness of child-myth and childlore—charms against the adult-world, rhymes, ritualistic 'dialogues' and shared 'jokes,' intimations of mortality—and the statement it makes of good and evil, innocence and experience, is tantalizing in its possibilities of extension."

"Stafford writes with brilliance," wrote C. M. Brown in the *Saturday Review*. "Scene after scene is told with unforgettable care and tenuous entanglements are treated with wise subtlety. She creates a splendid sense of time, of the unending afternoons of youth, and of the actual color of noon and of night. Refinement of evil, denial of drama only make the underlying truth more terrible."

In addition to her novels Jean Stafford wrote numerous short stories which appeared in the *New Yorker*, *Harper's Magazine*, *Atlantic Monthly*, and many other leading periodicals, such as *Partisan*, and *Mademoiselle*. Her collection *Children Are Bored on Sunday* contained ten of these stories, which *Time* called "ten small monuments to minor tragedy." The reviews were mixed, however. Paul Pickerel wrote in the *Yale Review*, "The pieces are overwrought both in an emotional sense and in the sense that they are decked out in too much verbal embroidery." William Peden, in the *New York Times*, was more generous. "She is always the artist working painstakingly in prose of admirable texture and variety."

In 1970, Stafford won the Pulitzer Prize for her *Collected Stories*. Pete Axthelm in *Newsweek* wrote, "This collection will undoubtedly become a textbook for many students of short fiction. Jean Stafford can teach almost anything one could want to know about swiftly and deftly developing characters, balancing them in delicate counterpoint or wrenching conflict, and probing their thoughts and emotions." Axthelm was not without his reservations, however. " Stories that stood alone with a precise and delicate beauty totter precariously when piled together in a unit of 30. . . . Taken individually, many of these stories show how much can be accomplished in a few pages; taken together, they unfortunately dramatize some of the limitations of Miss Stafford's genre."

Stafford ventured into journalism with her book *A Mother in History*, based on a three-day interview with Marguerite Oswald, the mother of Lee Harvey Oswald, the alleged assassin of President John F. Kennedy. The reviews were not unanimously favorable.

Stafford's first husband was the poet, Robert Lowell. They divorced in 1948. She married *Life* magazine editor, Oliver Jensen in 1950. This marriage ended in divorce in 1953 and Stafford married A. J. Liebling, a *New Yorker* columnist that same year. After Liebling died, ten years later, Stafford often referred to herself as "The Widow Liebling."

PRINCIPAL WORKS: *Novels*—Boston Adventure, 1944; The Mountain Lion, 1947; The Catherine Wheel, 1952. *Short stories*—Children Are Bored on Sunday, 1953; Bad Characters, 1964, Collected Stories, 1969. *As editor*—The Arabian Nights: The Lion and The Carpenter and other Tales, 1963. *Nonfiction*—A Mother in History, 1966. *Juvenile*—The Cat with the High I.Q., 1962.

ABOUT: Breit, H. (ed.) The Writer Observed, 1956; Contemporary Literary Criticism, volume IV 1975, vol. VII, 1977; Current Biography 1951, 1979; Encyclopedia of World Literature in the Twentieth Century, 1967; Goodman, C. M. Jean Stafford: the Savage Heart, 1990; Hulbert, A. the Interior Castle: the Art and Life of Jean Stafford, 1992; Magill, F. N. Great Women Writers, 1994; Roberts, D. Jean Stafford. *Periodicals*—Bookweek October 11, 1964; New York Times Book Review October 11, 1964, February 16, 1969; New Republic October 31, 1964; New York Times March 28, 1979; South Atlantic Quarterly Spring 1986; Virginia Quarterly Review Spring 1986; Kenyon Review Spring 1987; Southwest Review Summer 1987; Newsweek August 22, 1988; New York Times Book Review August 28, 1988; American Scholar Summer 1988; Sewanee Review Summer 1990; Southern Review Winter 1993.

**STALLINGS, LAURENCE** (November 25, 1894–February 28, 1968), American playwright, screenwriter, editor, and novelist, was born in Macon, Georgia, the son of Larkin Tucker Stallings, a wholesale chemist, and Aurora Brooks Stallings.

As a boy he imbibed highly romanticized ver-

sions of Southern history and became fascinated by the events and Confederate heroes of the Civil War. After studying biology and the classics at Wake Forest College, where he completed his studies in 1915, Stallings joined the *Atlanta Constitution* as a reporter. When the United States entered World War I in April 1917, Stallings, like thousands of young men, quit his job to go to war. He joined the Marine Corps and by October  was commissioned a second lieutenant in the Fifth Marine Regiment. In the early 1918 the regiment sailed for France and the Western Front.

The Fifth Marines, part of the U.S. 2nd Division, soon saw its first action at the battles of Château-Thierry and Belleau Wood where they were ordered to counterattack the German Aisne offensive. On June 26, 1918, Stallings was seriously wounded in his right knee. He spent the next eight months in a French hospital, undergoing several operations to save his leg. In February 1919 he returned to America, a captain, recipient of the Croix de Guerre, and badly crippled. By now he had shed his earlier romantic views of warfare and heroism, and at some point during his recuperation must have decided to set about portraying the war in the light of his own harrowing experience.

He married Helen Poteat, the daughter of the president of Wake Forest, and the couple lived for a while in Washington, D.C., while Stallings underwent further surgery at Walter Reed Hospital. After a trip to Europe they settled in New York City, and Stallings resumed newspaper work, joining the *New York World*, where he soon became the book reviewer. Among his colleagues at the newspaper were Franklin P. Adams, Heywood Broun, and an aspiring playwright, Maxwell Anderson.

Based on some of the stories about the war that Stallings frequently told, Anderson developed a script for a play, which Stallings rewrote to make it more realistic. The collaboration, sometimes conducted on a bench at the New York Public Library, turned out to be fruitful, and on September 25, 1924, *What Price Glory?* opened on Broadway at the Plymouth Theater. With its harsh language and grim details of men in war, the play shocked some but clearly suited the sensibilities of the postwar age, becoming a great hit and running for 299 performances. (It was released as a film in 1926, starring Victor McLagen, Edmund Lowe, and Dolores Del Rio.) Stallings and Anderson renewed their collaboration in two more plays, *First Flight* and *The Buccaneer*, both produced in 1925, but neither came close to the success of their first venture, and the two writers never worked together again.

Meanwhile, Stallings's first and only novel, *Plumes*, written while he recuperated in Washington, D.C., was published in 1924. Autobiographical, angry, and no doubt cathartic for its author, *Plumes* is the story of Lieutenant Richard Plume, a member of a family that has supplied soldiers for every one of America's wars. Badly wounded in France, Plume returns home, crippled in body and spirit, to protest the crime and futility of war. For the most part, reviewers agreed that the clarity and power of the book's antiwar message outweighed its deficiencies as a novel. Robert Littell in the *New Republic* wrote "if *Plumes*, by reason of its narrowness, its singleness of suffering is not an interesting book, nor its characters very real, except in that core of themselves which feels and suffers really deeply, it is far harder to forget than many a more interesting book. *Plumes*, since it is an almost undiluted record of personal anguish so absorbing and terrible as easily to affect the reader, is the kind of book that makes wars permanently less interesting." *Plumes* sold better than its reviews suggested—some 20,000 copies, more than Fitzgerald's *The Great Gatsby*, which was published the next year—probably on the strength of the Broadway success of *What Price Glory?*

With success came money and opportunities. While his two plays with Anderson failed, as did his own *Deep River* in 1926, Stallings now turned his talent to writing screenplays for Hollywood. His very first effort was the immensely successful antiwar film, *The Big Parade* (1925), which starred John Gilbert and was directed by King Vidor and produced by Irving Thalberg. It was praised as the best war film since *The Birth of a Nation*. Over the years, he wrote or contributed to screenplays for many films, among them *Old Ironsides* (1925); *Show People* (1928); *So Red the Rose* (1935), starring Randolph Scott; *After Hours* (1935), starring Clark Gable and Constance Bennett; *Too Hot To Handle* (1938), starring Gable and Myrna Loy; *Northwest Passage* (1940), an adaptation of the Kenneth Roberts novel, and *The Jungle Book* (1942).

At the same time, Stallings kept his hand in the theater by collaborating with Oscar Hammerstein II is writing the musical comedy *Rainbow*, which was a success on Broadway. In 1932 he adapted Ernest Hemingway's *A Farewell to Arms* for the stage, but this was not successful. Stallings also wrote a number of short stories and nonfiction pieces for magazines like the *Saturday Evening Post*, *Esquire*, and *Cosmopolitan*. One of his short stories, "Vale of Tears," was included in Ernest Hemingway's 1942 anthology *Men at War*. Stallings also edited a photographic history, *The First World War* (1933), which, like *Plumes* and *What Price Glory?*, delivered a vivid antiwar message through its captions and often horrifying pictures. Writing in the *New York Times*, R. L. Duffus said, "As one looks at these photographs one realizes that the strategy, diplomacy and final outcome were not mainly what mattered. What mattered was that human life in Europe was for four years reduced to the level here depicted. Civilization was in reverse gear, and destruction and butchery had become its objectives. What difference did it make who was the slayer and who the slain?"

In August 1935, under the sponsorship of the *New York Times*, the North American Newspaper Alliance, and Fox Movietone News, Stallings led a team of photographers to Ethiopia to observe and record the events leading up to the impending Italian invasion. Returning to the United States in 1936, Stallings divorced his wife and married Louise St. Leger Vance. The couple settled in Santa Barbara, California, and Stallings resumed his screenwriting.

Stallings's medical problems continued throughout his life. In 1922 he had a bad fall that resulted in the amputation of his war-damaged leg, and thereafter he walked on an artificial limb with the aid of a cane. Nevertheless, when the United States entered World War II, Stallings returned to active duty, this time with the Army Air Corps, first as a liaison officer stationed at the Pentagon and later as a public relations advisor, in which position he was sent to Africa, Europe, and England. He retired from the military in 1943 with the rank of lieutenant-colonel and returned to California and screenwriting. Among his postwar scripts were those for *Miracles Can Happen* and *She Wore a Yellow Ribbon*, the John Ford film that starred John Wayne.

In 1963 Stallings lost his remaining leg and also published his last book, *The Doughboys*, an account of America's military role in World War I, illustrated with photographs. The book was well received as a popular chronicle, but some reviewers, including the British military historian Alistair Horne, felt that the book was too much a collection of vivid vignettes and anecdotes, while lacking a coherent narrative that readers unacquainted with the events of the war could follow. Nevertheless, the *New York Times* chief book reviewer, Charles Poore, gave it very high praise when he called it "a book to stand beside Miss [Barbara] Tuchman's masterpiece, *The Guns of August*."

PRINCIPAL WORKS: *Novel*—Plumes, 1924. *Drama*—Three American Plays (What Price Glory?, First Flight, The Buccaneer), 1926. *Nonfiction*—The Doughboys: The Story of the A. E.F., 1917–1918, 1963. *As editor*—The First World War: A Photographic History, 1933 (issued as The World War in Photographs, 1934).

ABOUT: Brittain, J. T. Laurence Stallings, 1975; Dictionary of American Biography, Supp. 8; Dictionary of Literary Biography vol. 44. *Periodical*—New York Times February 29, 1968.

**STANDISH, BURT L.** See **PATTEN, GILBERT**

**STANTON, SCHUYLER.** See **BAUM, F. L.**

**STAPLEDON, WILLIAM OLAF** (May 10, 1886–September 5, 1950), English philosopher and novelist who signed his works Olaf Stapledon, wrote: "I was born in the Wirral, across the water from Liverpool. The Wirral has nearly always been my headquarters. I now live at the opposite corner of the peninsula, across the water from Wales. Most of my childhood, however, was spent on the Suez Canal, which in a way still seems my home. Subsequently I was educated at Abbotsholme School and Balliol College, Oxford. Then, for a year, with much nerve strain and little success, I taught at the Manchester Grammar School. Next I entered a shipping office in Liverpool, to deal ineffectively with manifestoes and bills of lading. A short period in a shipping agency at Port Said concluded my business career. I then lectured to tutorial classes for the Workers Educational Association, under the University of Liverpool, imparting my vague knowledge of history and English literature to a few of the workers of Northwestern England. For the three last years of the first great war I was with the Friends Ambulance Unit, in a motor convoy attached to a division of the French Army. After the war I married Agnes Miller, an Australian. Thus was sealed an intermittent romance of twelve years standing. We have a daughter and a son.

"Having returned to Workers Educational Association work, I also began to study philosophy and psychology at Liverpool, and took a Ph.D. Hence-forth these were my lecturing subjects, both outside the university and for a short time within. I wrote a technical philosophical book, and purposed an academic career. But I also wrote my *Last and First Men*, which was a success. I therefore, relying on unearned increment, rashly gave up my university post, determining to pull my weight by writing. Well, well! I have written mostly fantastic fiction of a semiphilosophical kind, and occasionally I have ventured into sociological fields.

"I find it difficult to summarize the main interests and influences in my life. Philosophy, in spite of a late attack, has always taken a high place. Formerly English literature dominated. Science, though I lacked scientific training, was first a sort of gospel and later something the fundamental principles of which must be carefully criticized. It took me long to realize both its true value and its mischief. In politics I accept the label Socialist, though all labels are misleading. My chief recreations have been foreign travel, and rough walking with a very small spot of rock climbing. I am addicted to swimming, and I like the arduous and brainless side of gardening."

---

William Olaf Stapledon is best remembered as what E.V. Rieu called a writer of cosmic "histories of the future." A history of the future, as Rieu termed it, is a science fiction based upon the raw material of present day reality and forecasting future existence as it can be drawn from society's present state. George Orwell's *1984* is perhaps the most acclaimed example of this brand of fiction. Stapledon never hit the literary heights achieved by Orwell but the few novels that he wrote were well respected for their penetrating social insight. Stapledon's novels are an intricate blend of "social commentary . . . scientific speculation . . . warning . . . and revelation." His first novel, *Last and First Men: A Story of the Near and Far Future* (1930) was his most acclaimed and best received

work, allowing him to quit teaching at the University of Liverpool and write full time. In this first work, Stapledon traces the future of humanity from the present time until its extinction two million years in the future.

The work was considered to be intellectually challenging, employing present day awarenesses of both the physical sciences and biochemistry, thereby establishing a firm link between the present reality and a future projection of that reality. Perhaps this reliance on scientific or technical data prompted reviewers to describe *Last and First Men* as somewhat dispassionate or detached, and rather grave. Yet, Stapledon's subject matter was regarded as interesting in itself, regardless of the style in which what it was conveyed. As the *Saturday Review of Literature* remarked the novel is not told with great artistry but the sheer effect of the material is tremendous. Elmer Davis noted that while fiction is a tool Stapledon uses awkwardly the sheer nature of the content of *Last and First Men* is compelling enough to create perhaps the boldest and most intelligently imaginative book of our times.

Yet such high praise could not sustain the works status throughout the years, and while *Last and First Men* enjoyed high sales and tremendous popularity for a time it never achieved true classic status. In addition to *Last and First Men*, Stapledon wrote several other science-fiction novels as well as a few philosophical treatises. His philosophical writings, which include *Modern Theory of Ethics: A Study of the Relations of Ethics and Psychology*, were regarded as significant and scholarly and as relatively important contributions. His last work, *The Opening of the Eyes*, completed and edited by his wife from notes, is a mystical conclusion to his search for singular philosophical truth. In 1953, a posthumous collection of his science-fiction was published as *To The End of Time* and contained an introduction by Basil Davenport.

PRINCIPAL WORKS: *Novels*—Last and First Men, 1931; The Last Men in London, 1932; Waking World, 1934; Odd John, 1935; Star Maker, 1937; Darkness and Light, 1942; Sirius; a Fantasy of Love and Discord, 1944; Youth and Tomorrow, 1946; Flames, a Fantasy, 1947; Man Divided, 1950; The Opening of the Eyes, 1951; To the End of Time: The Best of Olaf Stapledon, 1953.

ABOUT: Stapledon, O. The Opening of the Eyes; To the End of Time, *Periodicals*—New York Times, September 8, 1950; Times (London) September 8, 1950.

**STARK, FREYA MADELEINE** (January 31, 1893–May 9, 1993), English travel writer, historian, and autobiographer, was born in Paris, the elder daughter of the sculptor Robert Stark and the painter Flora Stark. She was brought up in Devon, on the edge of Dartmoor and manifested the first intimations of her future career at the age of four, when, with a mackintosh and a penny she tried to leave home for Plymouth to find a ship and go to sea. In 1901 her parents separated, her father moving to Canada, her volatile mother taking her and her sister Vera to Asolo in Italy, near the Dolomites, where they lived on very little money. Later they moved to Dronero. It was not an entirely happy time, Flora Stark preferring to give her attention to an overbearing suitor (who later married Vera instead), rather than to her daughters. During this period Freya learned independence and a certain sense of moral superiority that never left her; nor did an ambivalent but very close attachment to her mother, to whom she wrote almost daily for over forty years once she had left home.

Quickly fluent in Italian and teaching herself French and German as a teenager—she and Vera had little formal education—Freya went to Bed-ford College, London University, in 1912 to read history; but on the outbreak of World War I trained as a nurse and served with the George Trevelyan Ambulance Unit near Gorizia, Italy, thus witnessing the famous retreat of the Italians at Caporetto. After the war, Freya discovered a passion for mountaineering, fostered by her great friend and mentor, the Scottish critic W. P. Ker. Following the war, she felt dogged by a sense of failure for being a spinster, and was not helped by a crippling shyness that followed a teenage accident, when part of her scalp was ripped off, leaving her face slightly lopsided. Frequently unwell, Freya Stark used one long period of invalidity to learn Arabic, already forming the idea of traveling to the east. This she did in 1927, the year after her sister's death, traveling first to Lebanon and then on to Jerusalem and Cairo. Out of this came *Letters from Syria*. In 1930–1931 she returned, going on to Baghdad and braving the censure of the ultra-conservative colonials there, who objected to her bohemian lifestyle. Despite being a fervent royalist and believer in the Empire, Freya Stark also treated all those she met on her travels with courtesy and respect, longing to get to know the people she was among. This is one of the qualities which distinguishes her writing. From 1932–1933 she worked on the *Baghdad Times*, and the following year published what is her best known work. *The Valleys of the Assassins*, widely applauded by critics and described by V. S. Pritchett as "serious, vivid and delicate, her sympathy with the people could hardly be closer, and she draws really fine pictures of them." She also became a skilled photographer.

Further travels at this time produced a crop of titles such as *The Southern Gates of Arabia*, as she penetrated areas of the Arab world hitherto rarely reached by Westerners. "I always travel alone and I am not frightened," she later said. "I used to walk on ahead of my miserable guide because even a bandit would stop and ask questions before shooting when he saw a European woman strolling alone, hatless."

During World War II Freya Stark worked for British Intelligence, attempting to counteract Axis propaganda with her own pro-British information. Always an independent thinker, she approached this task by showing British films to harems, whose favorite turned out to be *Ordinary Life in Edin-*

*burgh*. Her most critical contribution was the foundation in Cairo of the Brotherhood of Freedom, a group of small gatherings who disseminated anti-fascist beliefs and prepared the Arabs for future freedom. After she left, the movement continued to flourish.

In 1941 she inherited a house in Asolo from the aritist Herbert Young, which was to become her base between travels for a large part of her life. In 1942 she was awarded the Royal Geographical Society's Founder's Medal, one of many honors she was to receive throughout her career.

After World War II she worked for a time for Lady Wavell, Vicereine of India in Delhi, the last 'proper' post she was to hold. In 1947 she married her old friend the diplomat and orientalist Stewart Perowne, a marriage which failed within five years, leaving Stark feeling, as she had written on her mother's death (1940), "as if no one in all the world belongs to me and it is rather like being in a room far too big for one." Her great consolation always came from traveling, which she continued intrepidly into her eighties, sometimes taking along younger protégés who arranged details and did the donkey work.

During her life, Freya Stark ceaselessly wrote letters, instructing their receivers not to destroy them. In late life she recalled these, which served as the basis for her autobiographies as well as for a seven-volume collection of letters that vividly capture the place, mood and history of the regions she reached.

A forceful, charming, frequently unscrupulous and sometimes ruthless woman, Freya Stark inspired great devotion among her friends and contributed some of the most personal, evocative and intelligent travel commentaries ever written about the Middle East. An original, at times eccentric woman who loved to discuss ideas, she also had a passion for expensive and flamboyant clothes. In his autobiography, Peter Coats commented of her time in Delhi that her "poke bonnets, aprons and a hat with a clock-face on the crown were second only to Gandhi's fast as a topic of conversation." Starting out as a Victorian-style adventurer, she became renowned as a political figure whose ideas of policy and diplomacy were welcomed by those in British government. She died at the age of 100 with twenty-five travel books and many other writings to her name. Her many awards included becoming a Dame of the British Empire in 1972, the Royal Scottish Geographical Society Medal, the Mungo Park Medal an honorary L.L.D. from the University of Glasgow in 1951, and an honorary D.Litt. from the University of Durham in 1971. Her exact achievements have become the subject of controversy. As Izzard's biography has shown, she was a great liar as well as a great traveler.

PRINCIPAL WORKS: Baghdad Sketches, 1933; The Valleys of the Assassins, 1934; The Southern Gates of Arabia, 1936; Seen in the Hadhramant, 1938; A Winter in Arabia, 1940; Letters from Syria, 1942; Arab Island, the Middle East, 1939–1943, 1945 (in U.K.: East Is West), Perseus in the Wind, 1948; Traveller's Prelude, 1950; Beyond Euphrates, 1951; The Freya Stark Story, 3 vols., 1953; Ionia: A Quest, 1955; The Letters of Freya Stark, 7 vols., 1974–1982.

ABOUT: Izzard, M. Freya Stark: A Biography, 1993; The Letters of Freya Stark, 7 vols., 1974–1982; Moorehead, C. Freya Stark, 1985; Over the Rim of the World: Selected Letters, 1988; Ruthven, M. Traveller Through Time: A Photographic Journey with Freya Stark, 1986; Ruthven, M. and Stark, F. Freya Stark in Iraq and Kuwait, 1994; Freya Stark in Persia, 1994; Freya Stark in the Levant, 1994; Stark, F. Perseus in the Wind, 1948; The Freya Stark Story, 3 vols., 1953; Dust in the Lion's Paw, 1962; Steffoff, R. Women of the World: Women Travelers and Explorers, 1994. Periodicals—Christian Science Monitor July 11, 1934; Saturday Review of Literature, November 30, 1940.

**STARKEY, JAMES SULLIVAN (pseudonym "SEUMAS O'SULLIVAN")** (1879–March 24, 1958), Irish poet and editor, wrote: "James Starkey  was born in Dublin. His father, William Starkey, M.D., was the author of *Poems and Translations* (1875) and a contributor to the *Dublin University Magazine*. His own first published poems appeared in the *United Irishman* and the *Irish Homestead*, 1902. He was one of the original members of W. G. Fay's Irish National Dramatic Company (later the Irish National Theatre Society), and acted with these companies on many occasions between 1902 and 1905, when he resigned membership and founded, with Seumas O'Kelly, F. Morrow, and others, the Theatre of Ireland. On two occasions he visited London with the Irish National Theatre Society, when they gave successful performances at the Queen's Hall, Kensington, and the Royalty Theatre. On the foundation of the Irish Academy of Letters he was one of the first to be elected, and was, for some years, a member of the Council. In 1939, Trinity College, Dublin, conferred on him the Doctorate of Literature. He has been a frequent contributor to the leading Irish journals. He has edited the Tower Press Booklets, twelve volumes (1906-1908), and in 1938, with Austin Clarke as co-editor, published a third series of the booklets in six volumes. In 1923 he founded the *Dublin Magazine*, which is now in its sixteenth volume, and which he edits."

James Sullivan Starkey—or Seumas O'Sullivan, as he was known—whose father was a pharmacist, was a minor poet of the Celtic Twilight school. His first collection, in 1905, was entitled *The Twilight People*—enjoying, for many years, a considerable reputation in Dublin circles. His friend, James Stephens, playfully pronounced him to be "better than Joyce." The university, when awarding him his doctorate, over-extravagantly described him as "the most notable poet of Ireland since the death of W. B. Yeats" (who had died earlier in the same year). Some of his most popular poems—"The Lamplighter" for example—have endured. O'Sullivan did have the ability to write movingly of town life. Quoting from the once-popular "Nelson Street" in his book *Modern Irish Poetry*, Robert F. Garratt ob-

serves: "In what are supposed to be poetic observations from *The Diary of a Dublin Man*, the title of which creates expectations of urban poetry, we see the mode of rural Celtic Twilight engulfing urban subject matter."

Starkey had his foot in several different Dublin coteries. A passionate supporter of Sinn Fein, he was on friendly terms with many of the leaders of the 1916 rebellion; he belonged to the Sunday afternoon group that met with "Æ" (George Russell) for weekly literary and political discussion; and he was, with James Joyce, among the frequenters of the Old Martello Tower in Sandycove, which figures so famously in Joyce's fictions.

His influence increased in 1923, when he became founder-editor of the *Dublin Magazine*, a publication that grew into a widely influential quarterly. A prose contributor to his own magazine, and to other journals, his essays were collected in book form in later life. A year before his death he was awarded the prestigious Lady Gregory Medal. His Dublin home was filled with a library of 20,000 books, many of them rare editions. His love of fine books was reflected in the fact that many of his own verses were published in limited, numbered editions. Starkey was married to Estella Solomons, an artist.

PRINCIPAL WORKS: Poetry—The Twilight People, 1905; Verses Sacred and Profane, 1908; The Earth-lover and Other Verses, 1909; Poems, 1912; An Epilogue to the Praise of Angus and Other Poems, 1914; Mud and Purple, Pages from the Diary of a Dublin Man, 1917; Requiem and Other Poems, 1917; The Rosses and Other Poems, 1918; The Lamplighter and Other Poems, 1929; Twenty-Five Lyrics, 1933; At Christmas, 1934; Personal Talk, 1936; Poems 1930–1938, 1938; Collected Poems, 1940; The Ballad of the Fiddler, 1942; This is the House and Other Verses, 1942; Dublin Poems, 1946; Translations and Transcriptions, 1950. Essays—Essays and Recollections, 1942; The Rose and Bottle and Other Essays, 1946.

ABOUT: The autobiographical material quoted above was written for Twentieth Century Authors, 1942. Garratt, R. Modern Irish Poetry, 1986; Miller, L. (ed.) Retrospect: The Work of Seumas O'Sullivan and Estella F. Solomons, 1973; Russell, J. James Starkey/Seumas O'Sullivan, 1987; Who's Who 1958. Periodicals—New York Times March 26, 1958; Times (London) March 26, 1958.

**STARKIE, ENID** (1901/2?–April 12, 1970), Irish biographer, critic, and academic was born in Dublin, the daughter of W. J. M. Starkie, a classical scholar who was also the last Minister of Education under the British rule of Ireland, and his wife the former May Caroline Walsh. Her brother was the writer Walter Starkie.

Enid Starkie was educated in Dublin, at Alexandra College, and then at the Royal Irish Academy of Music. She went up to Somerville College, Oxford—with which she was closely associated for most of the rest of her life—in 1918, and graduated from there three years later with first-class honors in modern languages. Instead of immediately seeking the academic appointment that could have been hers for the asking, she went to Paris in order to be a close-at-hand student of French letters. She lived there in poverty until forced by a lack of funds to take up an appointment as assistant lecturer at the University of Exeter. Her doctoral dissertation was on the Belgian poet Emil Verhaeren; and he was the subject of her first book, published in Paris in French in 1928. This gave her a doctorate from the Sorbonne and a small prize from the French Academy. Later (1967) her services to French literature were to gain her the award of the Légion d'Honneur.

Starkie returned to Somerville (lecturer, 1929–1935, fellow and tutor, 1935–1946, reader, 1946–1965, honorary fellow, 1965–1970) in 1929. Her greatest work was done in teaching, and she made lifelong friends of many of her distinguished pupils.

Her first book was a biography of Charles Baudelaire. Ernest Boyd in his *Saturday Review of Literature* notice wrote that Starkie's "book has little

original value, except in so far as it brings between two covers, in a more or less consecutive narrative, what we have learned in various volumes elsewhere. . . . Two things that make the book exasperating reading are that Miss Starkie has no literary style and that she feels obliged to defend Baudelaire at every turn from charges which have long since been exploded or forgotten." This is in part just, but Boyd failed to recognize that Starkie's book was not written for the enlightened like himself, but for English prudes who could not appreciate Baudelaire because they believed an "immoral" man could not write well. This educative work had to be done, and Starkie, if without much literary elegance, did it well. The *Times Literary Supplement* (1933) made just that important point. But Starkie's account of Baudelaire's influence on English literature in her *From Gautier to Eliot* remains useful. Of the later version of this book, the Baudelaire scholar Margaret Gillman, in the *Nation*, had this to say: "Except for minor errors . . . the book is . . . the most thorough and generally reliable biography."

Starkie's work on Rimbaud undoubtedly led many English readers into a fruitful acquaintance with her subject. Her only challenger is perhaps Wallace Fowlie's shorter *Arthur Rimbaud* (1965).

Regarding Starkie's biography of Rimbaud (which she revised in 1947 and again in 1962), Babette Deutsch, like other critics, pointed to the inadequacy of Starkie's style, but, in *New York Herald Tribune Books*, welcomed the biography as "almost uniformly interesting. Her subject takes care of that." W. M. Frohock, who later composed his own study, wrote in *Commonweal* (1939): "This is a fuller, more nearly definitive biography. . . . the ultimate in physical and moral misery . . . Starkie . . . has done us the service of sparing no detail." Lloyd Morris, in the *New York Herald Tribune Weekly Book Review*, commenting on the 1947 edition, praised Starkie's "brilliant interpretation" of Rimbaud noting that although Starkie portrayed Rimbaud's life as "a tragic example of

ultimate waste," in her words, she elucidated his poetry so that "its sources, its philosophy and its real meaning are now clear."

In certain respects Starkie's biography of the eccentric Petrus Borel, the self-styled "lycanthrope," was her most lively book. If Borel was a minor figure, Starkie was herself much fascinated by the kind of crooked and gifted eccentricity he exhibited. The *Times Literary Supplement* (1954) pointed out that Borel's story was "well worth telling and Dr. Starkie has told it very well."

Starkie's two-volume biography of Flaubert was written under the pressure of severe illness. V. S. Pritchett in the *New Statesman* (1971) termed the second volume superior to the first and remarked that in addition to being "the most sympathetic, best written modern account in English, or in French, of Flaubert's complete later career," the biography is "a worthy monument to the great novelist and to his indomitable biographer."

PRINCIPAL WORKS: *Biography and criticism*—Baudelaire, 1933; Arthur Rimbaud in Abyssinia, 1937; Arthur Rimbaud, 1939 (rev. eds. 1947, 1962); André Gide, 1954 Petrus Borel, 1955; From Gautier to Eliot, 1960; Flaubert: The Making of the Master, 1967; Flaubert, the Master: A Critical and Biographical Study, 1971. *Autobiography*—A Lady's Child. 1941. *As editor*—Baudelaire's Les Fleurs du Mal, 1942; The French Mind: Studies in Honor of Gustave Rudler, 1952; Arthur Rimbaud, 1854–1954.

ABOUT: Richardson, J. Enid Starkie, 1974. *Periodicals*—New York Herald Tribune Books; Commonweal October 13, 1939; Nation June 7, 1958; New Statesman July 22, 1933; January 8, 1928; September 17, 1939; December 24, 1971; New York Times February 13, 1938; Saturday Review of Literature August 19, 1933; Spectator October 31, 1947; Times (London) April 23, 1970; Times Literary Supplement June 15, 1933; June 4, 1954.

## STARKIE, WALTER FITZWILLIAM (August 9, 1894–November 2, 1976), Irish scholar and traveler, wrote: "I was born in Dublin, of parents who

came from Cork and Kerry but who are proud to be Anglo-Irish in blood. I was educated in Dublin and at Shrewsbury School in England and I finished my education at Trinity College, Dublin, and abroad. My education was not only humanistic, but also musical, for I studied violin-playing at

the Royal Irish Academy of Music. During the war of 1914–1918, I served abroad with the British Expeditionary Force in Italy, and after demobilization I trekked on foot through the whole of South Italy and Sicily, living with gypsies. In 1924 I was appointed Life Fellow of Trinity College, and in 1926 Professor of Spanish Studies and lecturer on Italian Literature at the same college. In 1927 I was appointed by W. B. Yeats and Lady Gregory a director of the Irish National (Abbey) Theatre. [Of interest in this regard is the fact that Starkie was, according to Hugh Hunt, in *The Abbey, Ireland's National Theatre 1904–1978*, the only director to support Sean O'Casey on initial submission of *The Silver Tassie*.]

"It has been my custom ever since 1919 to consort annually during my long vacation (university terms do not take up more than twenty-four terms in the year) with gypsies abroad, with the object of collecting language, folk-lore, and folk-music, and generally living the life of the open road. In 1923–24 I trekked through Spain and during the next ten yearsI had wandered on foot through all Spain, north to south, including Morocco. In 1925–26, I trekked through Dalmatia and part of Albania, and also went as visiting professor to the University of Upsala in Sweden. In 1929 I went on foot all through Hungary, Transylvania, and Romania, as far as the Black Sea, collecting tunes, stories, and living with nomads, and earning my living, as I have always done on my trips, by playing in street, cafe, or camp.

"I have been on four lecture tours to the United States, and in 1930 I was visiting professor in Romance languages at the Uninversity of Chicago. I trekked through New Mexico and Arizona as far as California, and was present at the Indian festivals in Santa Fé.

"In 1931 I was present in Madrid after the declaration of the Republic, and was a member from 1925 to 1936 of many of the principal literary tertulias [circles] of Madrid, including those of Ramón Valle Inclán, Benavente (whose biography I wrote), the brothers Machado, Azorin, Blasco Ibáñez, etc. From 1936 to 1939 I visited Spanish friends on three occasions. In 1940 I accepted from the British Council the post of first director and founder of the British Institute in Madrid."

---

Starkie was brought up in a distinguished and scholarly milieu, which included figures such as James Stephens and Dr. Mahaffey, the latter being Starkie's own godfather. His father, William Joseph Myles Starkie, became a Commissioner of National Education in Ireland, and his mother, Mary Caroline (Walsh), herself a scholar, supported her son in his desire, after being presented with his first violin in 1906, to have formal music lessons. He was enrolled at the Royal Irish Academy of Music, where he acquired a proficiency in the instrument which he was able to put to use while on the road during the long, vagabonding vacations enjoyed throughout his twenty-year tenure of the professorship at Trinity College. Between 1940 and 1954, after making his home in Spain, Starkie was an offical representative for the British Council in Madrid.

His first book appeared in 1925, a year after he had been awarded his doctorate, and a year before his appointment as professor of Spanish and Italian literature. *Jacinto Benavente* (Benavente was the Spanish playwright who won the Nobel Prize for literature) bore the hallmarks of academic ambition. It was a critical rather than biographical study: on the dull side, jam-packed with quotations, plot-summaries, and references to a host of other critics and commentators. His next book, *Luigi Pirandello*, the first English-language study of the Italian playwright, was similarly conscientious. (This book was thought sufficiently highly of to re-

quire a second, revised edition in 1937, and a third in 1965. It is still widely used by students of Italian literature as an introduction, although in terms of serious criticism it has long been superseded.) If Starkie's critical approach was overly objective, synthetic and unadventurous, his travel writing was of a quite different hue.

The first of Starkie's accounts of his adventures with his fiddle—*Raggle-taggle* (1933)—was so highly-colored that some readers suspected a good deal of embellishment in the retelling. A reviewer of the next book, *Spanish Raggle-taggle*, made so bold as to suggest in the *Spectator*, "The proverbs, aphorisms and scraps of folklore with which his conversations are larded bear every evidence of having been garnered from written sources, and the folk tunes which he prints are all taken from the collections of Olmeda, Chavarri etc."

During the thirties Starkie—like the subject of his first book, Benavente—was a supporter of Franco. In *The Waveless Plain*, subtitled "An Italian Biography," he endorsed Mussolini and fascism. He went further in his support than a polite expatriate resident, with an Italian wife, need have. V. S. Pritchett, writing about this book in the *Christian Science Monitor*, said of Starkie, "Sympathy is his strong card; but one cannnot be romantic about tyranny and dismiss standards because they embarrass friendship. So that while this is often a rich and entertaining book, its politics are mainly rhetoric and, presented in Professor Starkie's disarming way, insidious rhetoric."

After his retirement from academic life, he continued to publish volumes of travel, gypsy life, musicianship, and autobiography, concentrating on the latter in *Scholars and Gypsies*, the story of his early life. Starkie published a not very lively translation of *Don Quixote*, in both abriged (1954) and full versions (1964). In addition to his full-length works, Starkie contributed to a number of reference books, including *Grove's Dictionary of Music* and *Encyclopaedia Britannica*. Enid Starkie, an eminent and influential specialist in French literature, was his sister.

PRINCIPAL WORKS: Jacinto Benavente, 1924; Luigi Pirandello, 1926; Raggle-taggle, Adventures with a Fiddle in Hungary and Roumania, 1933; Spanish Raggle-taggle, Adventures with a Fiddle in North Spain, 1934; Don Gypsy, Adventures with a Fiddle in Southern Spain and Barbary, 1936; The Waveless Plain, an Italian Autobiography, 1938; Grand Inquisitor, 1940; In Sara's Tents, 1953; The Road to Santiago, Pilgrims of St. James, 1957; Scholars and Gypsies, an Autobiography, 1953.

ABOUT: The autobiographical material quoted above was written for Twentieth Century Authors, 1942. Contemporary Authors vols. 69–72, 1978; vols. 77–80, 1979; Current Biography 1964; Starkie, W. Scholars And Gypsies, 1963; Who's Who 1976. Periodicals—Christian Science Monitor June 29, 1938; New York Times November 9, 1976; Specator November 30, December 7, 1934; Times (London) November 8, 1976.

**STARRETT, VINCENT** (October 26, 1886– January 5, 1974), American novelist, short story writer, and essayist, sent this biographical sketch written by Ben Abramson: "By heritage, inclination, appearance, baptism, and temperament Vincent Starrett was destined to be a bookman. By that is meant not one who deals in books or necessarily one who writes them, but rather a man who lives by them. As Samuel Johnson was a bookman so Vincent Starrett is one.

"Charles Vincent Emerson Starrett, to muster all his names at once, was born in Toronto of Scotch-Irish parentage. His maternal grandfather was John  Young, a famous Canadian publisher and bookseller. He was brought to Chicago while still a child, and received his schooling from the public schools, his education from the newspaper offices of that city. His newspaper career began with the *Chicago Inter-Ocean* in 1906. Then for ten years he was on the staff of the *Chicago Daily News*, covering assignments in all parts of the continent. During 1914–1915 he served as war correspondent in Mexico, and was wounded in the leg at the unrecorded battle of Xochimilco.

"Mr. Starrett's earliest ambition was to be an illustrator, but he took to writing stanzas and stories instead. His course was determined suddenly when he received a check for $75 from *Collier's Weekly* for a mystery story. In that exciting moment, for better or for worse, he put his Rubicon of journalism behind him and became a 'writing man.' His first published book was a monograph on Arthur Machen, the Welsh novelist, whom he introduced to America. He founded and edited the *Wave*, a literary miscellany issued monthly, which died, however, in its second year. Several of his mystery stories have appeared as motion pictures. He is also the author of the standard bibliographies of Stephen Crane and Ambrose Bierce, has written innumerable critical monographs, and has edited the uncollected works of Stevenson, Crane, Gissing, Machen, and other writers beloved of collectors.

"Two of his greatest enthusiasms are Conan Doyle's immortal detective, and the fellowship of books. He is one of the founders (with Christopher Morley) of the Baker Street Irregulars, and a member of the Sherlock Holmes Society of England. He is a former president of the Society of Midland Authors, and was at one time an instructor in short story writing (which he believes 'cannot be taught') at Northwestern University. He has traveled extensively and has lived at one time or another in most of the important capitals of the world, including Peiping (Peking). He is married and lives in Chicago, his home for forty years.

"'Even if Mr. Starrett had decided to become something else,' it has been written of him, 'his appearance and his manner would have determined his career. In an Inverness cape he looks like a composite of half the writers and artists of *fin de siècle* London. His classic profile, his piercing eyes, his aristocratic bearing, and a speech that has the perfection of Stevenson's prose, make him that rare combination—a man of letters who looks like one.'"

On the occasion of Vincent Starrett's eighty-first birthday, Peter Ruber published *The Last Bookman*, a tribute of anecdotes, reminiscences, and poetry composed by Starrett's friends and fellow writers. In his foreword Ruber wrote: "Vincent Starrett is something more than a man of very conspicuous creative and critical gifts and talents— poet, writer of ingenious and imaginative prose fiction, critic, bibliophile, connoisseur of the caviar of belle-lettres, scholar, lexicographer, historian, essayist, epigrammatist, and columnist; he is something that perhaps you have not suspected: he is a teacher, an educator, in the finest sense of those two words."

Starrett's most long-lasting work is *The Private Life of Sherlock Holmes*, a classic miscellany of Holmesian lore. In its original review the *New York Times* (1933) noted that the "material, gathered from many sources, is presented in a way to make the most fascinating story of what the private life of Sherlock Holmes might have been had he had any life at all except in the brain of his creator."

Likewise, Starrett's bibliography, *Ambrose Bierce*, has remained in print, as have literary essays collected in *Bookman's Holiday* and *Buried Caesars*. *Books Alive*, takes its title from Starrett's column in the Sunday edition of the *Chicago Tribune*. In his foreword Starrett stated: "This is not a history of literature; it is a book of gossip. . . . [It is a] chronicle of literary endeavor and literary misdemeanor." The *Atlantic Monthly* urged readers to "savor his flow of spicy anecdote, of odd things he has picked up about plagiarism, theft, and literary hoax."

Starrett was also a well known mystery writer and received the first Mystery Writers of America Edgar Award; however, only *The Case Book of Jimmie Lavender*, featuring the short story adventures of a detective of the same name, has remained in print.

PRINCIPAL WORKS: *Nonfiction*—Arthur Machen: A Novelist of Ecstasy and Sin, 1918; Ambrose Bierce, 1920; (with T. Kennedy, G. Seymour, and B. Thompson) Estrays, 1920; Self Portrait, 1920; A Student of Catalogues, 1921; Buried Caesars: Essays in Literary Appreciation, 1923; Persons from Porlock, 1923; Stephen Crane: A Bibliography, 1923; Flame and Dust, 1924; One Who Knew Poe, 1927; Seaports in the Moon: A Fantasia on Romantic Themes, 1928; Penny Wise and Book Foolish, 1929; All About Mother Goose, 1930; The Private Life of Sherlock Holmes, 1933, rev. ed. 1960; Oriental Encounters: Two Essays in Bad Taste, 1938; An Essay on Limited Editions, 1939; Books Alive: A Profane Chronicle of Literary Endeavor and Literary Misdemeanor, 1940; First Editions: A Note for Beginners on the Proud and Profitable Hobby of Book Collecting, 1940; Bookman's Holiday: The Private Satisfactions of an Incurable Collector, 1942; Books and Bipeds, 1947; (with A. W. Williams) Stephen Crane: A Bibliography, 1948; Best Loved Books of the Twentieth Century, 1955; Book Column, 1958; Monologue in Baker Street, 1960; Late, Later and Possibly Last: Essays, 1973; An Essay on Limited Editions, 1982. *Novels*—Murder on "B" Deck, 1929; Dead Man Inside, 1931; The End of Mr. Garment, 1932; Recipe for Murder, 1934; The Great Hotel Murder, 1935; Midnight and Percy Jones, 1936; Murder in Peking, 1946. *Short stories*—The Escape of Alice: A Christmas Fantasy, 1919; The Unique Hamlet: A Hitherto Unchronicled Adventure of Mr. Sherlock Holmes, 1920; Coffins for Two, 1924; The Blue Door: Murder—Mystery— Detection in Ten Thrill-Packed Novelettes, 1930; Snow for Christmas, 1935; Two Short Stories [The Dreamer; The Ghost],

1941; The Case Book of Jimmie Lavender, 1944; The Quick and the Dead, 1965. *Poetry*—Rhymes for Collectors, 1921; Ebony Flame, 1922; Banners in the Dawn: Sixty-Four Sonnets, 1923; Fifteen More Poems, 1927; Autolycus in Limbo, 1943; Sonnets and Other Verses, 1949. *Juvenile*—The Great All Star Animal League Ball Game, 1957. *As editor*—In Praise of Stevenson: An Anthology, 1919; Men, Women and Boats, by Stephen Crane, 1921; The Shining Pyramid, by Arthur Machen, 1923; Et Cetera: A Collector's Scrap-book, 1924; The Glorious Mystery, by Arthur Machen, 1924; Fourteen Great Detective Stories, 1928, rev. ed. (with H. Haycraft) 1949; Three Poems, by Lionel Johnson, 1928; Two Poems, by Lionel Johnson, 1929; (with G. R. Gissing) Brownie, 1931; Maggie: A Girl of the Streets and Other Short Stories, by Stephen Crane, 1933; A Modern Book of Wonders: Amazing Facts in a Remarkable World, 1938; 221 B: Studies in Sherlock Holmes, 1940; The Mystery of Edwin Drood, by Charles Dickens, 1941; Three Great Documents on Human Liberties: Magna Charta, Declaration of Independence, Constitution of the United States, 1942; World's Great Spy Stories, 1944. *Memoirs*—Born in a Bookshop, 1965.

ABOUT: The biographical material quoted above was written for Twentieth Century Authors, 1942. Contemporary Authors 1994; Ruber, Peter A. The Last Bookman: A Journey Into the Life and Times of Vincent Starrett, Author, Journalist, Bibliophile, 1968; Twentieth-Century Crime and Mystery Writers, 1985. *Periodicals*—Atlantic Monthly November 1940; New York Times October 29, 1933; January 6, 1974.

## STAUFFER, DONALD A(LFRED) (July 4, 1902–August 8, 1952), American literary critic and novelist, was born in Denver, Colorado, the son of

Alfred Vincent Stauffer, a salesman, and Carrie Ella (Macdonald) Stauffer. He attended Princeton University, where he graduated as class valedictorian in 1923 and where he obtained an M.A. in 1924. As a Rhodes scholar, he continued his studies at Merton College, Oxford University, receiving a Ph.D. in 1928. Stauffer was appointed to an instructorship in the English department at Princeton in 1927. At the time of his death in 1952 he had been chairman of the English department for some years; the previous April he had been appointed to the Woodrow Wilson Professorship of Literature.

Stauffer began his career with two studies of biography as a literary genre, *English Biography before 1700* and *The Art of Biography in Eighteenth Century England.* "The story which Dr. Stauffer tells with faithful weaving of a great many threads . . . is the growth of biography into recognition and practice as a literary art," wrote a reviewer in the *Times Literary Supplement* of the first, while Edgar Johnson wrote of its successor in the *New Republic*, "The riches of this book lie not in life organized but in life in all its primitive and chaotic variety. Professor Stauffer seizes unerringly on the best critical comments of the eighteenth-century biographers, but he is less a critic himself than a journalist-antiquary with a lively nose for news and an enjoyment of human nature."

Stauffer's third critical monograph, *The Nature of Poetry*, is, as a reviewer in the *New Yorker* de-

scribed it, "a critical examination of the structure, texture, and meaning of English poetry, with examples running from Spenser to Yeats." This was certainly an ambitious undertaking, and the same *New Yorker* critic found in Stauffer's performance "a tendency to formalize and over-simplify." On the other hand, G. F. Whicher, writing in the *New York Herald Tribune Weekly Book Review*, considered *The Nature of Poetry* "a model of careful, highly competent and infectious presentation. . . . The book can be summarized in one sentence: Poetry is exact, intense, significant, concrete, complex, rhythmical and formal. But the value of the book lies in the crisp, assured illustration of these seven topics."

Stauffer's last two books were *The Golden Nightingale: Essays on Some Principles of Poetry in the Lyrics of William Butler Yeats* and *Shakespeare's World of Images: The Development of His Moral Ideas*, both published in 1949. The Shakespeare volume was the longer and more ambitious of the two, and it received favorable but guarded reviews. "Intelligent and 'thematic' as it is," wrote Howard Nemerov, "this work is another tour through Shakespeare, and subject not only to individual faults but to some of the loathsome requirements of its kind, such as the one that demands the author sustain an interest in all the plays though his best efforts be called forth by but a few."

In addition to his five major works of criticism, Stauffer was the author of *The Saint and the Hunchback*, a droll and erudite novel about two seventh-century monks who set out from Scotland in a floating stone coffin to convert the European heathens to Christianity.

PRINCIPAL WORKS: *Criticism*—English Biography before 1700, 1930; The Air of Biography in Eighteenth Century England, 1941; The Nature of Poetry, 1946; The Golden Nightingale: Essays on some Principles of Poetry in the Lyrics of William Butler Yeats, 1949; Shakespeare's World of Images: The Development of His Moral Ideas, 1949. *Novel*—The Saint and the Hunchback, 1946. *As editor*—The Intent of the Critic, 1941; (with H. K. Russell and W. Wells) Literature in English, 1948.

ABOUT: National Cyclopaedia of American Biography vol. 42, 1958; Nemerov, H. Poetry and Fiction: Essays, 1963. *Periodicals*—New Republic May 26, 1941; New York Herald Tribune Weekly Book Review June 15, 1946; New York Times August 9, 1952; New Yorker May 4, 1946; Times Literary Supplement December 11, 1930.

## STEAD, CHRISTINA ELLEN (July 17, 1902–March 31, 1983), Australian novelist, short story writer and translator, wrote: "Both my parents

were Australian-born, children of youthful English immigrants of poor origins. My mother died in my babyhood, my father soon remarried and I became the eldest of a large family. My father was an early twentieth-century Rationalist Press Association Rationalist, Fabian Socialist, by profession a naturalist in the Government Fisheries

Department; later he formed and managed the New South Wales Government State Trawling Industry. My childhood was—fish, natural history, Spencer, Darwin, Huxley, love of the sea (from dinghies and trawlers to the American Navy of 1908 and the British Navy), and the advancement of man (from the British Association for the Advancement of Science to the Smithsonian Institution). Eldest, and a girl, I had plenty of work with the young children, but was attached to them, and whenever I could, told them stories, partly from Grimm and Anderson, partly invented.

"I went to Teachers' College, but did not like teaching and took a business course at night, so that I could travel while working. It took me some years to save up the money, but in 1928 I went to London, to look for a job, and hoped later to get a job in Paris somehow. By pure accident this worked out and I was in Paris in the spring of 1929 and working there for some years. Before leaving Sydney, while still at Teachers' College, I wrote a collection of tales of imagination, turned down by a local publisher because he could not distribute more than 500 of such a book, but later incorporated in part in *The Salzbury Tales*.

"At thirteen I began to learn French and soon became an impassioned adept of Guy de Maupassant, whom I regarded as a master of style; later I followed Chateaubriand, Huysmans, Balzac (for expression), Hugo and Zola (for viewpoint), and am influenced by modern French authors, for example, Louis Gilloux in his brilliant *Le Sang Noir* (*Black Blood*). In English and American letters my favorites were Thoreau, Melville, Ambrose Bierce, Poe, along with Bacon (for pithiness alone). Shelley, Shakespeare, and many others, of course. I dislike polite letters, self-conscious classicism, pseudo-philosophers (among writers), and the monosyllabic mucker-pose (for example: Pater, Lamb, Emerson, Wordsworth, and a local, present tendency). The essence of style in literature, for me, is experiment, invention, 'creative error' (Jules Romains), and change; and of its content, the presentation of 'man alive' (Ralph Fox), I am not puritan nor party, like to know every sort of person; nor political, but on the side of those who have suffered oppression, injustice, coercion, prejudice, and have been harried from birth."

---

Christina Ellen Stead was born in Rockdale, Sydney, Australia, the daughter of David George Stead, a naturalist, and his wife, Ellen Butters. The unlikely manager of the firm of grain merchants with whom she found work on her arrival in England was an American communist, William Blake, who also wrote romantic and historical novels. Stead lived with him from 1928 until his death from cancer in 1968 at the age of seventy-three—they married in 1952 when he was able to get a divorce. Blake was still Wilhelm Blech when Stead met him (he was the son of German and Latvian parents). To him and to his memory Stead was always grateful, and it is clear that his death was a great blow to her. It was he, she reckoned, that had made her creative life possible.

Stead had an impressive degree of critical success (except, curiously, for her most famous novel, which, when it appeared in 1940 was virtually ignored). But her books did not begin to attract the attention of the general public until the 1960s, when the now famous *The Man Who Loved Children* (1940), by consensus her masterpiece, was reissued with an influential preface by the American poet Randall Jarrell.

Stead's first book was *The Salzburg Tales* (1934), Gothic tales overwritten and deliberately excessive, but also exuberant and, it turns out, original for their time and place. An admirer of these stories was Angela Carter, who was influenced by them. More important, though, was the massive *House of All Nations*, about the collapse of a Swiss banking house. Although Stead was at that time a communist, the novel transcends categories, and was of course written with an intimate knowledge (supplied by Blake) of its subject. Nor are the satiric details it gives of financial manipulation much outdated. R. G. Geering, in his study of the novelist deemed this her highest intellectual achievement. Elaine Feinstein, reviewing a reprint of it in the *New Statesman*, found it similarly fascinating, for all its flaws and length.

Next came *The Man Who Loved Children*, in which she treated her main theme of the damaging effects of egotism. To a certain extent the study of the monstrously self-centered Sam Pollit had been anticipated in that of Jules Bertillon in the preceding novel. In *The Man Who Loved Children* the author sees the family as a symbol for the world of capitalism depicted in her *House of All Nations*. Sam Pollit is, as she happily conceded, a portrait of her father, whose children by his second wife Christina had helped to bring up. But it is not really an autobiographical novel, as it has occasionally been taken to be: rather, it employs autobiographical material.

Jarrell, when he arranged for its republication in 1965, judiciously wrote in his introduction that it seemed to him "as plainly good as *Crime and Punishment* and *Remembrance of Things Past* and *War and Peace* are plainly great. I call it a good book, but it is a better book, I think, than most of the novels people call great; perhaps it would be fairer to call it great. It has one quality that, ordinarily, only a great book has: it makes you part of one family's immediate existence as no other book quite does. One reads the book, with an almost ecstatic pulse of recognition. You get used to saying: 'Yes, that's the way it is!'; and you say many times, but can never get used to saying, I didn't know anybody knew that. Henny, Sam, Louie, and the children are entirely real to the reader, and reality is rare in novels."

Stead published two other remarkable novels, *The Dark Places of the Heart* (in U.K.: as *Cotter's England*) and *I'm Dying Laughing*, which was pieced together after her death. But probably the best of her novels after *The Man Who Loved Children* is the one that followed it: *For Love Alone*. This, more autobiographical, tells the story of Teresa Hawkins, an idealistic girl who follows a detestable man, Jonathan Crow, with whom she had fallen in love (just as Stead did back in the 1930s before she met Blake), to England. Blake appears here as Theresa's savior, James Quick—and the English communist writer Ralph Fox, with whom Stead did have a short affair, as Harry Girton.

Stead's obituarist in the *Times* (London) seems to have made a just summing-up: "in the end Stead did achieve a fame almost commensurate with her towering and always human achievement. She was one of the great originals, by whom it was almost impossible to be influenced."

PRINCIPAL WORKS: *Selection*—Read, J. R. (ed.) A Christina Stead Reader, 1981. *Novels*—Seven Poor Men of Sydney, 1935; The Beauties and Furies, 1936; House of All Nations, 1938; The Man Who Loved Children, 1940; For Love Alone, 1944; Letty Fox: Her luck, 1946; A Little Tea, A Little Chat, 1948; The People With the Dogs, 1952; Dark Places of the Heart, 1966 (in U.K.: Cotter's England); The Little Hotel, 1973; Miss Herbert, 1976; I'm Dying Laughing, 1987. *Short stories*—The Salzburg Tales, 1934; The Puzzleheaded Girl: Four Novellas, 1968; Ocean of Story: The Uncollected Stories, 1986. *Letters*—Talking into the Typewriter: Selected Letters, 1992; A Web of Friendship: Selected Letters, 1992.

ABOUT: The autobiographical material quoted above was written written for Twentieth Century Authors, 1942. Brydon, D. Christina Stead, 1987; Gardiner, J. L. Rhys, Stead, Lessing and the Politics of Empathy, 1989; Geering, R. E. Christina Stead, 1969; Gribble, J. Christina Stead, 1994; Jarrell, R. The Third Book of Criticism, 1969; Lidoff, J. Christina Stead, 1983; Rowley, H. Christina Stead: A Biography, 1993.

## STEARNS, HAROLD E(DMUND) (May 7, 1891–August 13, 1943), American editor and critic, wrote: "I was born in Barre, Massachusetts, and ed-

ucated at the Malden (Massachusetts) High School and at Harvard (B.A. *cum laude in philosophia*, 1912 as of 1913). My first work after being graduated was as editorial writer on the *New York Sun*. Then I became a writer on the theatre, first for the old *New York Dramatic Mirror* and later for the *New York Press*. In the summer of 1914 I made my first trip to Europe, and was in Paris when war was declared. I returned home in the autumn and did free-lance writing in New York, with regular work, chiefly book reviewing, on the early *New Republic*. (By 'regular,' I mean on a salary.) In the winter of 1917 and on in 1918 to July, I edited the old *Dial* in Chicago, then I brought it to New York, where it underwent changes and later, after the war, was bought by my classmate, Scofield Thayer, and converted into an aesthetic monthly called *Reconstruction Dial*—for a short time on the war's ending, I worked on the *New Freeman* as a contributor, but pretty regularly, and started *Civilization in the United States*.

"Meanwhile, I married Alice Macdougal. She died in 1919 in childbirth; our son was adopted by her father and took the name of Macdougal. On the completion of *Civilization* (July 4, 1921), I sailed the same day for Europe, where I remained (with only one trip home to California for a few weeks

to see my son) for eleven years. The first five years I spent in Paris, I was correspondent of the *Baltimore Sun* and *Town and Country* (New York), and worked also on the *New York Herald* (Paris Edition). In my last years abroad I was racing editor first for the *Chicago Tribune* and later on for the London *Daily Mail* (Continental Edition). Illness forced me finally home in 1932. . . . "

Harold E. Stearns's first book, *Liberalism in America*, argued that the liberal credo of "respect for the individual and his freedom of conscience and opinion" had been dealt a severe blow by the chauvinism and mass hysteria that characterized American society during and after World War I. Stearns's rhetoric was intemperate, but most critics took his argument seriously. "It is no engaging picture of our American war mind that Mr. Stearns paints, and twenty months ago it would have been hotly resented by the great majority of our people," wrote a *Survey* reviewer. "That the average man of intelligence is likely to find himself mainly in agreement with it now . . . is the best evidence that the picture is essentially true."

Stearns stepped up the attack in his next book, *America and the Young Intellectual*, in which he maintained that American society had become so poisoned by puritanism, hypocrisy, and greed that a meaningful intellectual life was no longer possible there. According to Hugh Ford, Stearns brought "a lucid and cogent intelligence to the work," but *America and the Young Intellectual* had considerably less public impact than the nearly six-hundred-page volume he edited the following year, *Civilization in the United States*. For this work Stearns solicited contributions from such writers as H. L. Mencken, Van Wyck Brooks, and George Jean Nathan, all of whom discussed the manifold shortcomings of American culture, though none so over-corrosively as Stearns in his introduction. Whether the book was taken as "the cry of the American young, the fierce slogan of the intelligentsia" (*New Statesman*) or "thirty gloomy young persons standing arm in arm and making faces at the United States" (*New York Evening Post Literary Review*), *Civilization in the United States* was intended to provoke controversy, and it did. Furthermore, Stearns took the dramatic and well-publicized step of acting on his principles. On July 4, 1921, only hours after finishing the introduction to *Civilization in the United States*, he boarded a ship for Europe, where, as he had written, "life can still be lived."

The life that Stearns lived in Paris during the next eleven years was surely not what he, or the legions of young Americans who followed in his wake, had in mind. Beginning his European sojourn as a would-be glamorous member of the Left Bank expatriate community and as a foreign correspondent for H. L. Mencken's *Baltimore Sun*, he ended it as a seedy, alcoholic hack writer covering the horse races for the Paris edition of the *Chicago Tribune*. (Hemingway portrayed him as the sodden drunk Harvey Stone in *The Sun Also Rises*.) To his surprise, wrote Hugh Ford, Stearns soon discovered that "exile could destroy as well as liberate" and that "being in Paris has strengthened his weaknesses and eroded his strengths." Finally, near physical collapse and utterly destitute, he was given the return fare to the United States by the American Aid Society and arrived in New York early in 1932.

In the course of putting his life back together, Stearns discovered that the America he had abjured now had much to offer and perhaps hadn't been quite so spiritually impoverished as he once imagined. In *Rediscovering America*, his first book in a dozen years, he rather drastically revised his opinions about American life, prompting Carl Van Doren to write in the *Nation* (1934), "Mr. Stearns's discoveries will seem to the Americans who stayed at home possibly commonplace. Some of these things were true in 1922, although he then failed to see them. He needed thirteen years and a long exile to become aware of the obvious America." Of its companion volume, *America: A Re-Appraisal*, R. L. Duffus wrote in the *New York Times Book Review*, "The truth about Mr. Stearns seems to be that he can do nothing by halves. When he ceased to approve of the United States he couldn't even stand them. Now that he again approves of them he draws a picture of a country and people which is certainly recognizable but isn't quite what one sees—at least not what this reviewer sees—when he goes for a stroll."

Probably the most successful book of Stearns's later, and perhaps of his entire, career was *The Street I Know*, a frank and at times painful memoir that, in the words of Hugh Ford, "could be subtitled 'The Autobiography of a Failure.' As a recantation of his once spirited defense of exile, the work reveals the depths of humiliation and disillusionment. He admits that his 'revolt' had failed, that the dream existence in Paris had often been useless and silly, and that only the drug of self-deception had made his life there bearable." In his review of *The Street I Know*, Carl Van Doren wrote in the *Nation* (1935), "Mr. Stearns's autobiography is at many points a touching and revealing book . . . .I have never met Harold Stearns and should not know him if I saw him. All I know is the legend and the autobiography. But I have read his book with interest in a real human being as well as curiosity about an age that has already come to seem unreal."

In 1937 Stearns married a wealthy and cultivated divorced woman named Elizabeth Chapin and moved with her to her estate in Locust Valley, Long Island. "As a symbol of expatriation," wrote Hugh Ford, "Harold Stearns holds primarily a literary interest. The progression of his life, however, from denial, to exile, to repatriation, to acceptance and affirmation . . . remains part of the social pattern of our time. 'For better or worse,' Stearns the repatriate confessed, 'I am an American after all.'"

PRINCIPAL WORKS: *Criticism and essays*—Liberalism in America: Its Origins, Its Temporary Collapse, Its Future, 1919; America and the Young Intellectual, 1921; Rediscovering America, 1934; America: A Re-Appraisal, 1937. *Autobiography*—The Street I Know, 1935. *As editor*—Civilization in the United States: An Inquiry by Thirty Americans, 1922; America Now: An Inquiry into Civilization in the United States by Thirty-Six Americans, 1938.

ABOUT: The autobiographical material quoted above was written for Twentieth Century Authors, 1942. Dictionary of American Biography, Suppl. 3, 1973; Dictionary of Literary Biography Vol. 4, 1980; Ford, H. Four Lives in Paris, 1987. *Periodicals*—Nation May 2, 1934; November 13, 1935; New Statesman June 3, 1922; New York Evening Post Literary Review February 11, 1922; New York Times August 14, 1943; New York Times Book Review February 7, 1937; Survey May 29, 1920.

**STEED, HENRY WICKHAM** (October 10, 1871–January 13, 1956), English foreign correspondent and editor of the London *Times*, was born at Long Melford, Suffolk, and educated at Sudbury Grammar School. Two sprained wrists sustained in a bicycle accident rendered him unfit to sit the civil service entrance examination, as intended, and instead he joined the city office of Sir Cuthbert Quilter, M.P. for South-West Suffolk. He had no  thought of becoming a journalist until the age of twenty when, having been aroused by a lecture at Toynbee Hall on the subject of old-age pensions, he submitted a report to the *Pall Mall Gazette*. It was accepted and he determined, "on a warm evening in June 1892," (according to his autobiography) to leave the city and pursue his education at first a German and then a French university (the Sorbonne).

During his time abroad, he posted reports to news agencies. In 1895 an interview on the subject of the French president's resignation, which he contributed to the *Westminster Gazette*, so impressed the editor of the *New York World* that Steed was appointed its Paris correspondent. The following year he was made acting *Times* correspondent in Berlin, and in 1897 took on a similar role in Rome, where he stayed until 1902, when he transferred to Vienna. This last position he held for more than a decade, the experience and knowledge gained in that time finding outlet in his first book, *The Hapsburg Monarchy*, published on his return to England.

Back in London, he was put in charge of the *Times*'s foreign news department on the strength of his understanding of German foreign policy. When, at the end of the First World War, Northcliffe fell out with his editor, Geoffrey Dawson, Steed took over. In bearing—he was a tall slim man, with a pointed beard—Steed always gave the impression of being a senior diplomat rather than a journalist, and he now used his office to influence the course of events on both the world and domestic stage. In particular, he saw to it that the paper did everything it could to help the Conservatives return to power in the 1922 general election. In a period of just three months Steed personally wrote some 100 leading articles. Shortly afterwards he was dismissed by the new owners.

He then became owner and editor of the *Review of Reviews* and wrote a two-volume autobiography,

*Through Thirty Years 1892–1922*. On the appearance of these memoirs, the *Saturday Review of Literature* commented, "Wickham Steed is one of the few journalists who have definitely affected the international relations of Europe. By his persistent labor in Europe, mainly for the *Times*, he unquestionably made himself an international figure, and his influence upon the course of European history can never be overlooked." In his autobiography he set out his journalistic creed, looking on his role as "a chance to help things forward on the road I thought right, a quest taxing to the point of exhaustion every energy of heart and brain but having in it what I hold to be the secret of happiness—constant striving towards ends which, even if they recede upon approach, yet reveal themselves, in receding, as worthy of approach."

Steed could also write fluently in French and German, and published a number of books in those languages. During the 1930s he was one of the first to warn of the dangers of Hitler and the Nazis, and was an outspoken opponent of appeasement. His 1934 book, *Hitler: Whence and Whither*, originally delivered as a course of lectures at King's College, London, was criticized at the time—notably by Kingsley Martin in the *New Statesman*—for not acknowledging that Hitler's opportunities had been created by mistakes of the Allies.

When war did break out, Steed joined the BBC and continued broadcasting on world affairs until 1947.

PRINCIPAL WORKS: The Hapsburg Monarchy, 1913; Through Thirty Years 1892–1922, 1924; The Real Stanley Baldwin, 1930; The Antecedents of Post-War Europe, 1932; Hitler: Whence and Whither, 1934; Vital Peace, 1936; The Press, 1938; Our War Aims, 1939; The Fifth Arm, 1940; That Bad Man, 1942; Words on the Air, 1946.

ABOUT: Dictionary of National Biography, 1951–1960; Steed, H. W. Through Thirty Years, 1924; Who's Who 1955. *Periodicals*—Illustrated London News January 21, 1956: New Statesman January 27, 1934; New York Times January 14, 1956; Saturday Review of Literature December 27, 1924; Times (London) January 14, 1956.

## STEEGMULLER, FRANCIS (pseudonyms "DAVID KEITH" and "BYRON STEEL")

(July 3, 1906–October 21, 1994), American biographer, editor, translator,  and novelist, wrote: "I was born in New Haven of Connecticut parents and attended the public schools of Greenwich. My first two books were written [under the pseudonym "Bryon Steel"] while I was a student at Columbia College,[B.A. 1927; M.A. 1928] and soon thereafter I began to contribute to the *New Yorker*. Some of my stories still appear in that magazine, and for a time [1934–1935] I was a member of its staff, writing 'Talk of the Town.'

"Two of my principle interests are the psychology of the creative process, and the art and nature of painting. The first is evidenced in my books on

Flaubert and Maupassant, the second in my biography of James Jackson Jarves, a fascinating, little-known nineteenth century American art critic and collector whose collection of Italian primitives hangs in the Yale University art gallery.

"After trying my hand at various kinds of novels, including a series of mysteries [under the pseudonym "David Keith"] I finally wrote *States of Grace*. It discusses, rather lightly, uncharitable behavior in supposedly religious circles, and it achieved the distinction of receiving two reviews in the same issue of a Roman Catholic newspaper—one for and one against.

"In 1935 I married the painter Beatrice Stein. We live in an apartment in New York but spend part of our time in France."

---

Francis Steegmuller was the son of Joseph F. Steegmuller, a businessman, and Bertha (Tierney) Steegmuller, a former schoolteacher. Raised as a Roman Catholic, with an uncle who was bishop of Hartford, he was expected to enter a seminary but "nothing was further from my mind" (as he told a *Wilson Library Bulletin* interviewer in 1992).

Steegmuller attended Dartmouth College for a year (1923–1924) before going to Columbia, where a course in biography and an introduction to modern French painting were influential. His first trips to France and Italy, just after college, were paid for by writing travel articles for White Star Line's publicity magazine. After getting his M.A. he taught American Civilization at the University of Wisconsin, then spent two years as a copy editor for the *Encyclopedia of the Social Sciences*. From 1935 to 1942 he wrote light, humorous stories and articles for the *New Yorker*; some of these were published in *French Follies and Other Follies* and *Stories and True Stories*. During World War II Steegmuller was a writer for the Office of Strategic Services, in Washington, D.C., and in France.

His abiding involvement—as biographer and translator—with Gustave Flaubert began in 1930 when he read Flaubert's letters to his niece, in which the novelist talks of his struggles with writing. Steegmuller was having his own troubles, too, at the time. Flaubert, he stated, "gave me courage." *Flaubert and Madame Bovary: A Double Portrait* is an account of the inception and development of the writer's great novel; Steegmuller's "clever and provocative portrait of Flaubert depends in a large degree on his translations from the letters and journals of Flaubert and his friends which have not been available in English before" (P. M. Jack, *Yale Review*). Steegmuller's best-known work is probably *Flaubert in Egypt: A Sensibility on Tour*. Translations of Flaubert's travel notes and letters home are woven together with a "lucid and subtle" accompanying narrative that provides necessary background information. The subtitle, Germaine Bree noted, "underscores the principle that shaped . . . an urbanely presented book [that] makes delightful reading" (*New York Times*).

In his review of Steegmuller's edition of *The Se-*

lected Letters of Gustave Flaubert, the Roman Catholic critic Martin Turnell praised the lively and authoritative translations and the judicious selection of representative examples that afford "a unique view of the artist engaged in the composition of his book" (*Commonweal*). A two-volume edition of *The Letters of Gustave Flaubert* eventually replaced *The Selected Letters*. Robert Alter, reviewing Volume 1 (1830–1857), praised Steegmuller's succinct notes, which provide needed identifications, and his "short narrative bridges . . . between one group of letters and the next, so that we know what is happening in the novelist's life in the midst of his constant correspondence" (*New Republic*). Volume 2 (1857–1880) reveals Flaubert's thoughts and character in the years between the completion of *Madame Bovary* and his death, and includes some of his splendid letters to George Sand. Later, with the collaboration of Barbara Bray, Steegmuller edited and translated a volume of the Flaubert-Sand correspondence. Julian Barnes, in the *New York Review of Books*, commented on the "precise, elegant, and wise interpolations of Francis Steegmuller, our premier Flaubertian"; John Bayley, in the *Yale Review*, called "the understanding of the text and the rendering of it into a supple and responsive English . . . beyond compare."

Biographies of other French writers include *Maupassant, a Lion in the Path*, which includes translations of four short stories never before put into English; and *Apollinaire: A Poet among the Painters*, a life of the poet and innovator. Translations of Apollinaire's verse "[keep] the reader's attention firmly fixed on [his] identity as a serious and accomplished writer, acting as a brake against some of the more extravagant anecdotes" (Hilton Kramer, *Reporter*). Steegmuller's life of one of Apollinaire's early associates, Jean Cocteau, is an even-handed picture of a complex genius and his literary and artistic milieus, which manages to separate myth from reality and explore the central issue: Cocteau's creative processes as writer and artist. *Cocteau, a Biography* won a National Book Award in 1971, and the author himself considered it his most solid work.

Steegmuller used memoirs and letters to tell the story of three other subjects, representative of widely different eras and concerns: the memoirist Anne Marie Louise d'Orleans, Duchess of Montpensier and cousin of Louis XIV (*The Grand Mademoiselle*); the modern dancer Isadora Duncan and her lover Gordon Craig ("*Your Isadora*"); and the eighteenth-century Parisian bluestocking Madame d'Epinay and her friend the Neapolitan Abbé Ferdinando Galiani—subjects of Steegmuller's last biography, *A Woman, a Man, and Two Kingdoms*. As the critic Benedetta Craveri remarked, his renderings of their correspondence and his connecting narrative are a "skillful work of literary marquetry" that enables him to "create an elegant period piece and give plausible characterizations" (*New York Review of Books*).

Steegmuller's first wife died in 1961 and in 1963 he married the Australian-born novelist and *New Yorker* writer Shirley Hazzard. They divided their time between homes in New York, Capri, and Naples, where Steegmuller died. He was a member of the American Academy and Institute of Arts and Letters (recipient of its Gold Medal in 1982), and a Chevalier of the French Legion of Honor.

PRINCIPAL WORKS: *Fiction*—(as "Byron Steel") Java-Java, 1928; The Musicale, 1930; (as "David Keith") A Matter of Iodine, 1940; (as "David Keith") A Matter of Accent, 1943; French Follies and Other Follies: Twenty Stories from The New Yorker, 1946; States of Grace, a Novel, 1946; (as "David Keith") Blue Harpsichord, 1949 ; The Christening Party, 1960; Stories and True Stories,1972;Silence at Salerno: A Comedy of Intrigue, 1978. *Nonfiction*—(as "Byron Steel") O Rare Ben Jonson, 1927; (as "Byron Steel") Sir Francis Bacon: The First Modern Mind, 1930; (with M. D. Lane) America on Relief 1938; Flaubert and Madame Bovary, a Double Portrait, 1939 (2nd rev. ed. 1950; rev. ed. 1977); Maupassant, a Lion in the Path, 1949 (in U.K.: Maupassant); The Two Lives of James Jackson Jarves, 1951; The Grand Mademoiselle, 1956 (in U.K.: La Grande Mademoiselle); Apollinaire, Poet among the Painters (with tr. by William Meredith and Francis Steegmuller) 1963; Jacques Villon, Master Printmaker, 1964; Cocteau, a Biography, 1970; Stories and True Stories, 1972; A Woman, a Man, and Two Kingdoms: The Story of Madame d'Epinay and the Abbé Galiani, 1991; Jean Cocteau: The Mirror and the Mask, a Photo-Biography (ed. and comp. J. Saul) 1992. *As editor*—Flaubert, G. November (tr. F. Jellinek) 1967. *As translator*—Venturi, L. Modern Painters, vol. 2: Impressionists and Symbolists, 1950; Flaubert, G. Madame Bovary: Patterns of Provincial Life, 1957 (2nd ed. with new introd. 1982; reissued 1992). *As editor and translator*—The Selected Letters of Gustave Flaubert, 1953 (Great Letters Ser.); (with N. Guterman) Sainte-Beuve, C. A. Selected Essays, 1963; Flaubert in Egypt: A Sensibility on Tour, a Narrative Drawn from Flaubert's Travel Notes and Letters, 1972; "Your Isadora": The Love Story of Isadora Duncan and Gordon Craig, 1974; The Letters of Gustave Flaubert, 2 vols., 1980–1982 (Vol. 1: 1830–1857; Vol. 2: 1857–1880); (with B. Bray) Flaubert-Sand: The Correspondence, 1993.

ABOUT: The autobiographical material quoted above was written for Twentieth Century Authors First Supplement, 1955. Dictionary of Literary Biography Vol. 111, 1991. *Periodicals*—Commonweal November 19, 1954; New Republic February 3, 1980; New York Review of Books December 17, 1992; June 10, 1993; New York Times February 27, 1972; April 29, 1973; October 22, 1994; New Yorker July 2, 1973; April 21, 1986; November 14, 1994; Reporter January 2, 1964; Wilson Library Bulletin January 1992; Yale Review 1939; October 1993.

## STEEL, BYRON. See STEEGMULLER, FRANCIS

## STEEL, FLORA ANNIE

**STEEL, FLORA ANNIE** (April 2, 1847–April 12, 1929), English author and educator, was born at Sudbury Park, near Harrow. Much of her childhood was spent in Scotland. Her father, George Webster, was made sheriff-clerk of Forfarshire, and the family set up home at Burnside. Holidays were spent in the West of Argyll, with Flora's maternal grandmother. After an erratic education, mainly self-administered but including a short spell at a private school in Brussels, where her uncle was living, she was married at the age of twenty, to Henry William Steel of the Indian civil service, and spent the next twenty years in India, where she became tirelessly active in a range of community projects. Although she exhibited many of the colonial attitudes of her period, she did display genuine sympathy and concern for the plight of Indian women, gaining access to aspects of their lives from which men were debarred.

After one stillbirth, a daughter was born in 1870. The Steels settled in Kasur, in the district of Lahore, and in 1874 Flora Steel set up a school for small

girls and became a strong advocate of education for Indian women. This proved to be a protracted campaign, which bore fruit in 1884, when, not without controversy, she was made the first inspector of girls' schools in the district and served as a member of the Provincial Education Board (alongside John Lockwood Kipling, the father of Rudyard Kipling). At the same time she published her first book, a collection of Indian folktales for young readers, *Wide-a-Wake Stories*. Towards the end of her stay in India (Henry Steel retired from the civil service in 1889) she, in collaboration with a friend, Grace Gardiner, published *The Complete Indian Housekeeper and Cook*. This book, dedicated to "The English Girls to whom fate may assign the task of being House-Mothers in Our Eastern Empire," became an essential primer for an entire generation of colonial wives and is still said by cooks to be full of good recipes.

But Flora Annie Steel's real work as a writer did not begin until her own role as "House-Mother" was at an end. During the early years of the 1890s she carried out research (involving return visits to India) into the background of the novel for which she is best known. *On the Face of the Waters*, a heavily documented reconstruction of the Indian Mutiny—narrated by an English major's wife, Kate Erlton—brought the author considerable celebrity. Her biographer, Violet Powell commented: "She accepted praise for the fidelity of her Indian background, her interpretation of Indian character and her grasp of miltary history, with the knowledge that it was the not unmerited acclaim of hard work and sympathy for her subject."

In 1897, she made her final journey to India, visiting Lucknow to collect background material for the book that was to become *Voices in the Night*. There she experienced a total eclipse of the sun, and simultaneously contracted a malarial fever. She was looked after by her friends the Nicholsons—Mrs. Nicholson being "Laurence Hope," the author of "Pale hands I love beside the Shalimar"—and was given a medicinal dose of hashish. This, she says in her autobiography, reduced her, for the first time in her life, to "smiling placidity." Although she considered that *Voices in the Night* contained her best work, especially in its depiction of Jan-ali-shan, its commercial reception was disappointing.

At the turn of the century the Steels settled in Wales. Flora embarked on the life of a professional author. Continuing to write mainly about India, although she produced some work with a different setting, her concern about the woman of India developed into a broader interest in the position of women in general. A critic of purdah, and of the consequent preoccupation with their sexual lives

which isolation induced in Indian women of the townships, Flora began to read everything she could about the sexual impulse and an obsession with what she came to refer to as the "Curse of Eve" occupied her last years. She used the phrase for the title of her last novel, in which sex is seen as the root of all evil. This theme was also explored in a pamphlet which she published at her own expense, *The Fruit of the Tree*.

In Britain she supported women's suffrage, and marched alongside the other suffragists in 1910. Although recent readings of her Indian books have been at pains to underscore the view that her essential attitudes differed little from the other colonialists, her autobiography does exhibit a degree of self-scrutiny concerning the meeting of two cultures which was ahead of her time.

PRINCIPAL WORKS: Wide-a-Wake Stories, 1884 (republished as Tales From the Punjab, 1894); The Complete Indian Housekeeper and Cook, 1887; Miss Stuart's Legacy, 1893; From the Five Rivers, 1893; The Flower of Forgiveness, 1894; The Potters Thumb, 1894; Red Rowans, 1895; On the Face of the Waters, 1896; In the Permanent Way, 1897; The Hosts of the Lord, 1899; Voices in the Night, 1900; In the Guardianship of God, 1903; A Book of Mortals, 1906; A Sovereign Remedy, 1906; India Through the Ages, 1908; A Prince of Dreamers, 1908; The Gift of the Gods, 1911; King Errant, 1912; The Adventures of Akbar, 1913; The Mercy of the Lord, 1914; Marmaduke, 1917; Mistress of Men, 1917; English Fairy Tales, 1918; Tales of the Tides, 1923; the Law of the Threshold, 1924; The Builder, 1928; The Curse of Eve, 1929; The Garden of Fidelity (autobiography) 1929; Indian Scene, Collected Short Stories, 1933.

ABOUT: Blain, V., et. al (eds.) The Feminist Companion to Literature in English, 1990; Dictionary of National Biography, 1922–1930, 1937; Powell, V. Flora Annie Steel, Novelist of India, 1981; Steel, F. A. The Garden of Fidelity, 1929; Schlueter, P. and J. (eds.) An Encyclopedia of British Women Writers; Todd, J. (ed.) British Women Writers, 1989; Who's Who, 1928. *Periodicals*—New York Times April 15, 1929; Times (London) April 15, 1929.

**STEELE, WILBUR DANIEL** (March 17, 1886– May 26, 1970), American short story writer and novelist, was born in Greensboro, North Carolina, also the birthplace of O.

Henry. He was the son of W. Fletcher Steele and the former Rose Wood. His father's work as a Methodist Episcopal minister took the family to Germany in the late 1880s, and Steele began his education at a kindergarten in Berlin (1889–1892). Over the next ten years he attended various schools in Colorado, and in 1903 entered the University of Denver, where his father had become professor of Biblical Literature. He graduated with a B.A. in 1907. Male members of the family were traditionally ministers, but Steele initially wanted a career as a painter. After studies in 1907–1908 at the Museum School of Fine Arts in Boston, he spent a year at the Académie Julien in Paris, then two at the Art Students' League in New York City, before joining the artists' colony in Provincetown, Massachusetts.

Steele seems to have had little success as a painter. He turned to fiction with a story set on Cape Cod, "A White Horse Winter." This was published in 1912 in the *Atlantic Monthly*, and much praised. It appeared, along with other stories set on the bleak coasts of New England, in *Land's End, and Other Stories*. In his introduction, Edward J. O'Brien wrote that these stories, "almost without exception . . . , represent the best that is being accomplished in America to-day by literary artists." There were similar encomia for subsequent collections. These drew on Steele's travels in the West Indies (1916–1917), his experiences as a naval correspondent in Britain and Europe during World War I, a year in Bermuda (1919–1920), and other journeys to Africa and the Middle East.

In 1919 Steele received the first of four O. Henry Awards. Two years later the Society of Arts and Sciences gave him a special award for maintaining over a three-year period the highest level of merit among writers of short stories in America. Steele published nearly two hundred stories. The best of them include "How Beautiful With Shoes,"about the emotional awakening of a young Appalachian woman kidnapped by a psychotic, and "The Man Who Saw Through Heaven," an O. Henry first prize winner: a missionary, seeking to understand "all space and time," takes a "cosmic flight" back to humanity's beginnings. "Footfalls" centers on a blind cobbler who waits nine years to revenge himself on the man who had destroyed his honor and his son. According to Thomas A. Gullason in *The American Short Story*, "Steele demonstrated that the traditions of Edgar Allan Poe and O. Henry, along with that of the well-made story, were . . . very much alive. Steele had the master's touch, with all the plot formulas at his command; the subtleties and intricacies of plotting were far more important to him than any moral theme. . . . As a 'romantic realist,' he was often attracted by the primitive, the exotic, and the remote."

Steele published a number of novels, though most critics agree that he was not at home in the longer form. One writer in *Saturday Review* discussing *Their Town*, said that Steele "tends to sprawl, and the narrative force with which he builds individual scenes is vitiated by his failure to supply inevitable connections." He also tried his hand as a dramatist with the Provincetown Players, and had some success with the two-act comedy *Post Road*. It was written in collaboration with Norma Mitchell Talbot, an actress and dramatist whom Steele married in 1932, his first wife having died a year earlier. They lived in Lyme, Connecticut. Interviewed by Harvey Breit in *The Writer Observed*, Steele said that, for him, "to put a sentence together is like climbing a mountain range," but "it's the only God's way I can make a living."

Throughout most of the 1920s, Steele was the acknowledged master of the popular short story in America. However, the vogue for neat plots and surprise endings was passing, superseded by the poetic realism of Sherwood Anderson and Hemingway, both superior writers. Steele recognized in his interview with Breit that he was "the last gasp of an epoch." He published no new collection of short stories after 1929, though there were more novels, most set in the American West. His *Best Stories* were nevertheless still in print in 1994, and some continue to appear in anthologies.

PRINCIPAL WORKS: *Short stories*—A Devil of a Fellow, and The Yellow Cat, 1918; Land's End and Other Stories, 1918; The Shame Dance and Other Stories, 1923; Urkey Island, 1926; The Man Who Saw Through Heaven and Other Stories, 1927; Tower of Sand and Other Stories, 1929; The Best Stories of Wilbur Daniel Steele, 1946; Full Cargo: More Stories, 1951. *Novels*—Storm, 1914; Isles of the Blest, 1924; Taboo, 1925; Meat, 1928; Undertow: A Thrilling Romantic Tale of Love and Sacrifice, 1930; The Sound of Rowlocks, 1938; That Girl from Memphis, 1945; Diamond Wedding, 1950; Their Town, 1952; The Way to the Gold, 1955. *Drama*—The Giant's Stair, 1924; The Terrible Woman and Other One-Act Plays, 1925; (with N. Mitchell) Post Road, 1935.

ABOUT: Breit, H. The Writer Observed, 1956; Bucco, M. Wilbur Daniel Steele, 1972; Contemporary Authors vol. 109, 1983; Dictionary of Literary Biography vol. 86, 1989; National Cyclopedia Of American Biography, 1946; Stevick, P. (ed.) The American Short Story, 1900–1945, 1984; Twentieth Century American Literature, 1980; Warfel, H. R. American Novelists of Today, 1951; Williams, B. C. Our Short Story Writers, 1925. *Periodicals*—Books Abroad Spring 1971; New York Herald Tribune Book Review July 23, 1950; New York Times May 27, 1970; New York Times Book Review August 6, 1950; Saturday Review August 23, 1952; Washington Post May 28, 1970.

## STEEN, MARGUERITE (pseudonyms "LENNOX DRYDEN" and "JANE NICHOLSON")

(May 12, 1894–August 4, 1975), English novelist, wrote: "Up to the last few years, when writing became a full-time occupation for me, I have combined never less than two or three simultaneous careers! Writing is not a lucrative profession for the beginner. I have been in turn a kindergarten teacher (I managed in some moment to get a  Froebel certificate, more through oversight on the part of the examiners than by personal effort), dancer, actress, accmompanist, lecturer, dramatic producer, private governess, and 'helper' in a sandwich bar; I have had the interesting and educative experience of being *quite* penniless, and there have been a few bright patches of something near opulence. After the First World War, I was so much out of sympathy with the general trend of thought and opinion in England that I spent as much time as possible abroad; at first in Paris, and later in Spain, which came to be the country of my adoption.

"Born in the Victorian twilight (I can just remember being lifted out of my cot to listen to the cheering over the relief of Ladysmith), the rich prodigality of the Edwardian reign, the dark drama of the war years, the post-war complications with leaping income tax and 'servant problem'—all left their various impressions upon my work. They are wonderful years for a novelist to have lived through: I am grateful for the experience they have taught me. The best one can wish for is an utterly full life. Now I look forward to *the next thing*; I wonder what it will be?

In 1955, she wrote: "The war destroyed her London home and after five wandering years (principal sport, bomb-dodging), she bought the eighteenth century cottage in Berkshire—from which nothing would induce her to return to London. Her recreations are traveling—so far as a British travel allowance permits—the collection of all-white china and porcelain, Negro literature, and making a new home. Elected a Fellow of the Royal Society of Literature, 1951."

---

Marguerite Steen was born in Liverpool, the daughter of a British army officer, Captain George Conolly Benson, and Margaret (Jones) Benson, and adopted daughter of Joseph and Margaret Steen.

Educated privately, she exhibited an interest in writing from a young age. For the duration of World War I she reluctantly became a kindergarten teacher in a private school, but gave this up in 1919 to become a classical dancing and eurythmics teacher in Halifax. It was a well-paid job, but she tired of it after three years, and, following her girlhood passion, went on stage with the Fred Terry-Julia Neilson Company, with which she toured Britain and the U.S. In the process she became good friends with the actress Ellen Terry who, when Steen was enduring a six-month period of unemployment, encouraged her to write a novel. The result was *The Gilt Cage*, published in 1927. A society novel gleaning its characterisation from the people Steen had met and worked with in the theater, *The Gilt Cage* received a mild reception, but was the start of an intense writing career. Further novels followed, but popularity were not achieved until the publication of *Unicorn* in 1932. The story of a Bavarian Archduchess evicted with her family in a revolution, it was admired for its atmosphere, and established Steen as a vivid storyteller. Of her later titles, the most successful was *The Sun Is My Undoing*, a melodramatic and epic-length novel about the slave trade. Set in England and the West Indies, it revealed her passion for history, intricate plots and emotional characterization.

A vivacious writer, increasingly given to lavishness of prose and romance, Steen plumbed some unusual and juicy subjects for her fiction—*Bell Timson* (in Britain, *Rose Timson*), for example, has a masseuse-abortionist for a heroine, while *The Spider* revolves around a power-seeking widow who feeds off her dead husband's fame. Steen elicited decidedly mixed reviews. She took little notice of reviews, and continued to write prolifically.

As well as novels, she wrote two candid autobiographies, *Looking Glass* and *Pier Glass*. The latter covered her relationship with the painter Sir William Nicholson, and was described by *The Observer Review* as revealing Steen as "the genuine article, a great emotive partisan, an unrepentant hater, a fairly outrageous snob and, even if she does cosset her poetic streak, a writer of natural vigour and style." She also wrote two plays, of which *Matador* and *French for Love* which were produced in London in 1936 an 1939. Her only volume of literary criticism was a work on Hugh Walpole.

PRINCIOAL WORKS: *Fiction*—The Gilt Cage, 1927; Duel in the Dark, 1928; The Reluctant Madonna, 1929; They That Go Down in Ships, 1930 (in U.K.: They That Go Down); Where the Wind Blows, 1931; Unicorn, 1931; The Stallion, 1931; The Wise and the Foolish Virgins, 1932; Matador, 1934; The Tavern, 1935; The One-Eyed Moon, 1935; Who Would Have Daughters?, 1937; The Marriage Will Not Take Place, 1938; Family Ties, 1939; The Sun is My Undoing, 1941; Bell Timson, 1946 (in U.K.: Rose Timson); Twilight on the Floods, 1949; Granada Window, 1949; The Swan, 1951; Jehovah Blues, 1952; Anna Fitzalan, 1953; The Bulls of Parral, 1954; A Candle in the Sun, 1964. *Drama*—Oakfield Plays, 1932 (for Juvenile), 1933 Peepshow (for Juvenile); (with Matheson Land) Matador, 1936; (with D. Patmore) French for Love, 1939. *Nonfiction*—Hugh Walpole: A Study, 1933; The Lost One: A Biography of Mrs. Mary (Perdita) Robinson, 1937; William Nicholson, 1943; Looking Glass, 1966; Pier Glass, 1968; (with A. John, L. Lee, and others) Paintings and Drawings of the Gypsies of Granada 1969.

ABOUT: The autobiographical material quoted above was written for Twentieth Century Authors, 1942. Current Biography 1941; Steen, M. Looking Glass, 1966; Steen, M. Pier Glass, 1968; Vinson J. Twentieth-Century Romance and Gothic Writers, 1982. *Periodicals*—New Republic September 1, 1941; New York Times Book Review August 17, 1941; August 6, 1975; Observer Review March 24, 1968.

**STEFÁNSSON, VILHJALMUR** (November 3, 1879–August 26, 1962), Arctic explorer, geographer, and writer, was born at Arnes, Northern Manitoba, Canada, of Icelandic parents, Johann and Ingibjorg Stefánsson, who were among the 1887 pioneer settlers there. He was christened William Stephenson, but changed this back to the Icelandic form of the name when he came of age. Stefánsson's greatest achievement as explorer  and geographer arose from his investigations of the Beaufort Sea area (1915–1917), which was previously virtually unknown. His explorations there, wrote his (London) *Times* obituarist, "in boldness of concept, in endurance, and in the range of the journeys undertaken, resemble the great expeditions of Nansen and Peary" (the former almost reached the North Pole in 1893, the latter did so in 1909). He was also an expert on the Eskimo peoples, although, as his *Times* obiturarist mentioned, his "somewhat irritating suggestion of superiority in his disdain of conventional ideas of Arctic travel . . . did not make for universal popularity." His notion of the "friendly Arctic" caused much controversy.

Stefánsson's childhood and youth were exceptionally hard. When he was less than two years old his parents were forced, after struggles with famine and the loss of two of their children from floods, to move to a farm near the hamlet of Mountain, in Pembina County, North Dakota. Here he grew up. At fourteen his father died; he became a cowboy, even trying, with some other young men, to manage a ranch. When this failed he decided that he wanted to be a poet—and that he would put himself through college in the manner in which so many other determined young Scandinavians did in those days. He succeeded, although not before he had been expelled from the University of North Dakota for reasons that are not now clear: it was claimed that he had encouraged fellow students to revolt, but, in his posthumous autobiography, *Discovery*, he denied this: "the faculty thought I was the spark most likely to start a blaze," he wrote. Certainly he was a fearless and confident promoter of himself: after his escapade, he coolly ran for the position of state superintendent of education on a Democratic ticket (he was not elected). He graduated from the State University of Iowa (summer 1903) after a special one-year course (which took into account his work at North Dakota), and then, owing to his decision to become a Unitarian minister, entered Harvard University's Divinity School (fall 1903). He sponsors, William Wallace Fenn and Samuel Eliot, had allowed him to study theology from an "anthropological perspective," and in 1904 he abandoned the former entirely, in favor of anthropology. The University of Iowa, proud that he had studied there, held the Centennial Symposium on him in 1979.

He now began to attract attention. In 1904 he visited Iceland, and in the following year was sent there as a member of the archeological expedition sponsored by the Peabody Museum of Harvard University. He began to write articles for *Harper's*. One of these reached Ernest de Koven Leffingwell, who was preparing an expedition to the Beaufort Sea, the purpose of which was to study Eskimo life; early in 1906 he invited Stefánsson to join it as ethnologist.

But Stefánsson failed, through no fault of his own, to join it: its boat was wrecked, and he was stranded. Instead of getting help, he decided to live in an Eskimo village near the mouth of the Mackenzie River as (he later wrote) "combination guest, student, and pauper." This "field work" was of course no more scientific (in the modern sense) than any other anthropological investigation of the period. But Stefánsson's report of it (*My Life with the Eskimo*, 1913), and his later abridgements, elaborations of, and additions to it, while often controversial, were universally respected, and are still widely quoted. During World War II the American government retained him as a valued Arctic consultant.

In his investigations into the Eskimo peoples Stefánsson mastered their language (a group of dialects which form the northernmost branch of Amerindian), and adopted their ways of living, which included hunting. Over-didactically and hyperbolically, and much to the annoyance of those who knew far less than he did of the matter, he maintained that the Arctic was "friendly," and that "adventures" were simply a matter of personal inefficiency. Since he had many "adventures" himself, his attitude, maintained with an amused vehemence, was taken far too seriously: he had a case— that the Arctic was less unfriendly than had been supposed—and his way of stating it was to overstate it. He was temporarily lost in a gale in 1913, off the coast of Alaska; in 1914–1915 he disappeared from view for a time (and had his obituary printed) while crossing—with two companions, a sledge, and six dogs—the pack-ice of the Beaufort Sea to Banks Land; then in 1918 while on Herschel Island he developed pneumonia and typhoid, but continued to work. Of course such endeavors were hazardous, and, equally, Stefánsson's calm insistence that the "accidents" that befell other explorers were a result of their lack of properly "scientific" preparation and even "incompetence" caused extreme exasperation. But for all that, he was himself as scientific as he could be, and he was often right, as when he sought to change the old view of the Arctic regions as "lifeless."

Dislike of his brashness came to a head after he had retired from active exploration. He had decided to devote himself to writing and to continuing what he called his "campaign of education with regard to the Arctic regions," in the early 1920s, over the Wrangel Island affair.

He now put himself squarely behind what he considered to be the British Empire's claim to Wrangel Island, off the coast of Siberia, which he regarded as an important potential air and submarine base. Neither the British nor the Canadian government would act decisively, and so he took the matter into his own hands by sending four young men (and an Eskimo seamstress) to the island (September 1921); the small expedition was financed by funds raised by himself. Three years later Harold Noice went out to discuss the matter with the men there, but a year later, at the head of a rescue party, he found the four men dead (the Eskimo was still alive). He wrote a book, *With Stefánsson in the Arctic*, making charges—almost all unfounded—that Stefánsson had allowed the expedition to go out ill-equipped and unprepared.

Now the many who disliked Stefánsson and resented his fame and eminence, had the opportunity, despite all the honors he had received for his work, to attack him on other scores. And attack him they did. His own book, *The Adventure of Wrangel Island*, was an attack on Noice—which gained a partial retraction by the latter—but, more important, it was in the words of one of its reviewers, Raymond Holden of the *Saturday Review of Literature* (1925), "one of the most interesting and tragic documents of Arctic history."

But he had so disturbed some members of the "Arctic establishment" by his "friendly Arctic" thesis—or, rather, by the manner of his advancement of it—that the Wrangel affair spurred on his enemies, the most eminent of whom was Roald Amundsen, who had been the first to reach the South Pole and had also sailed the entire Northwest Passage in a single voyage. Amundsen wrote in his autobiography that the "friendly Arctic" thesis was "not only nonsense but even harmful and dangerous nonsense." Soon afterwards the Wilkins expedition showed that it was, indeed, largely as Stefánsson had claimed it was: the polar seas were warmer than had been supposed, and planes could be landed on the ice. Since the British had shown such a small inclination to spend money on taking Wrangel Island under the colonial flag, the Soviets had moved in and claimed it. They now took advantage of several of Stefánsson's earlier proposals.

In the latter part of his life Stefánsson did little more of a practical nature, with the notable exception of spending one year—under the auspices of the Russell Sage Institute of Pathology—living (1928) on an all-meat diet (something he had done before in the Arctic, when he lived on bear-meat). He claimed no more than that he had demonstrated the soundness of the human body: "you can be healthy on meat without vegetables, on vegetables without meat, or on a mixed diet."

His books were many and varied, and, while they lacked elegance, they were vivid, readable, lucidly expressed, well organized and packed with information. For example, *The Mountain of Jade*—written in collaboration with Violet Irwin—for juveniles, attracted this comment from the *Saturday Review of Literature* (1926): "Here is a story that instructs while it entertains. . . . a worthwile juvenile indeed!" The more seriously intended but lightly expressed *The Standardization of Error*, written to show how error contributed to scientific progress, was thus praised by the *New York Times* (1928): "The famous conqueror of Arctic regions appears in this volume in a new role. For he shows himself to be the possessor of a devastating sardonic humor and a master of the satiric essay." The *Geographic Review* said, about his *Iceland: the First American Republic*, that, like "all his writings" it combined a "fresh and lively style, scholarship and the depth, perspective and direction that result from a distinctive viewpoint and philosophy." When, in the year before his death, he published *Cancer: Disease of Civilization*, it was greeted as a serious and useful contribution to the problems set by the disease. Edward Weyer in the *Geographical Review* reminded readers that it had been Stefánsson, "not a medical scientist," who "in 1906 indicated the possible existence of trichinosis, the 'pork disease,' in the Arctic, far from the nearest pigs." This new book, Weyer noted, was "eminently well written, and the reader . . . can scarcely brush aside the carefully marshalled data it presents." Stefánsson's argument was that cancer was "rare or non-existent among primitive peoples untouched by civilization . . . the white man's diet may be the major cause."

Stefánsson's swan song, his autobiography, issued two years after his death, was reviewed by his old friend Jim Lotz in the *New York Times* (1964): "Perhaps he should have published his autobiography earlier. For this book too often sounds like the ramblings of an angry and embittered old man. This Stef certainly was not. . . . Whenever men talk of the Arctic, Stef will be remembered." And Benjamin deMott in *Harper's* felt that "for a living likeness of a scientist in process of freshening his soul by contact with elemental reality, *My Life with the Eskimo* remains the best book of Stefánsson's to read." But this book, obviously the product of old age, did little to detract from the high reputation of a man who is still regarded an authority on what he knew best, the Arctic and the Eskimo.

In 1941 Stefánsson married the former Evelyn Schwartz Bland. They had no children. He lived in New York until 1951, when he moved to a farm in Vermont. He died suddenly, after suffering a stroke while at a dinner in honor of a Danish diplomat. Among his many honors were Founder's Medal of the Royal Geographical Society.

PRINCIPAL WORKS: My Life with the Eskimo, 1913; The Friendly Arctic, 1921; The Northward Course of Empire, 1922; Hunters of the Great North, 1922; The Adventure of Wrangel Island, 1925; The Standardization of Error, 1927; Adventure in Error, 1937; Three Voyages of Martin Frobisher, 1938; Unsolved Mysteries of the Arctic, 1938; Iceland: The First American Republic, 1939; The Problem of Meighan Island, 1939; Ultima Thule, 1940; Greenland, 1942; Arctic Manual, 1944; Compass of the World, 1944; The Arctic in Fact and Fable, 1945; Not By Bread Alone, 1946; Great Adventure and Explorations, 1947; New Compass of the World, 1949.

ABOUT: Baker, D. Explorers and Discoverers of the World, 1993; Best, A. Mr. Arctic: An Account of Vilhjálmur Stefánsson, 1966; Current Biography 1962; Dictionary of American Biography, 1961–1965, 1967; Duibaldo, R. Stefánsson and the Canadian Arctic, 1973; Folk, E. (ed.) Vilhjálmur Stefánsson Centennial Symposium (1979; University of Iowa) 1984; Gregor, A. D. Vilhjálmur Stefánsson and the Arctic, 1977; Hansen, E. P. Stefánsson: Prophet of the North, 1941; Hunt, W. R. Stef: A Biography, 1986; Le Bourdais, D. M. Stefánsson: Ambassador of the North, 1963; McKinlay, W. L. Karluk: The Great Untold Story of Arctic Exploration, 1976; Myers, H. and Burnett, R. Vilhjálmur Stefánsson: Young Arctic Explorer, 1966 (juvenile); Taylor, R. L. Doctor, Lawyer, Merchant, Chief, 1948; Parkman, N. R. High Adventurers, 1931; Service, E. R. The Hunters, 1966. *Bibliography*—Matilla, R. W. A Chronological Bibliography 1879–1962, 1978. *Periodicals*—Coronet September 1959; Geographical Review October 1961; Harper March 1940, June 1964; New Yorker February 12, 1949; August 27, 1962; September 13, 1964; Pacific Historical Review May 1992; Saturday Review of Literature May 30, 1925; November 26, 1926; Science July 1949; Time September 7, 1962; Times (London) August 27, 1962; Travel June 1939.

**STEFFENS, LINCOLN** (April 6, 1866–August 9, 1936), American journalist and political writer, was born Joseph Lincoln Steffens in San Francisco, the son of Joseph Steffens, a successful business man, and Elizabeth Louisa (Symes) Steffens. He spent his childhood on a ranch near Sacramento where the family moved in 1870. He seemed an indifferent student, so his father sent him to St. Matthew's Hall, a military academy in San Mateo; although he did not distinguish himself there he was editor of the school's literary journal and published verse in the *Sacramento Record-Union*. After leaving St. Matthew's Steffens failed the entrance exam at the University of California, Berkeley. He attended private school in San Francisco and also received tutoring which enabled him to enter Berkeley in the fall of 1885. He took his degree in 1889.

After declining his father's offer to enter the business world, Steffens went to Europe where he studied in Berlin, Heidelberg, Leipzig, Paris, and London. By the time he returned to New York his father's patience had run out, and he was forced to find a job.

In 1892 he started as a reporter for the *New York Evening Post*; he followed this with a tenure as city editor for the *New York Commerical Advertiser* from 1897 until 1901 when he became managing editor of *McClure's Magazine*. During the next decade his career blossomed. He had already met Theodore Roosevelt and Jacob Riis and had become interested in social concerns. In his book *Lincoln Steffens* Robert Stinson writes of Roosevelt's rise to the Presidency and states that "Steffens kept up with him in a dialogue of growing intimacy concerning public policy." Stinson goes on to describe the years before and after Steffens's move to *McClure's*: "In the previous decade he had published skillful vignettes of city life which were buried on the back pages of newspapers or obscure magazines. But in the next ten years Steffens published long, well-considered articles in national monthlies and saw them collected in three successive books." This publishing established him as one of the leading "muckrakers" of his day. "Muckrakers" was the name given to journalists bent on investigating and exposing business and governmental corruption. But Stinson describes Steffens's muckraking pieces as "more purposive than descriptive, and he composed them more with the reformer's sense of argument than the feature writer's more neutral aim of evoking a slice of life."

Published in 1904, *The Shame of the Cities*, a collection of seven of his *McClure's* essays, offers an exposé of big city governmental corruption. Next Steffens went after corruption at a higher level in an evaluation of the governments of six states in *The Struggle for Self-Government*. As Steffens stated in his autobiography: "The State Machine . . . would back the city machine; a corrupted State would defend the graft of a corrupted city." *The Upbuilders*, which appeared in 1909, offers character studies of five state and local reform-minded politicians.

In 1906 Steffens left *McClure's* to become co-owner of *American Magazine*, but sold his share the following year to free-lance and to join the editorial board of *Everybody's Magazine*. When the public's appetite for muckraking waned, Steffens became interested in revolutions; his views began to take a decidedly radical turn. Traveling to Mexico in 1914, and to Russia in 1917, he studied the revolutions there; after interviewing Lenin he wrote in a letter, "I have seen the future; and it works." He later interviewed Benito Mussolini, however, and was just as impressed by what he called the Duce's efforts to combine the "government of business and the business of government." The *New York Times* commented that "at the end Mr. Steffens faced the world with what he described as 'my optimistic grin,' seeing Russia and America, each in a different fashion, approaching the goal of a state of society in which "not the cunning, grasping possessors of things but the generous, industrious producers and the brave imaginative leaders of the race shall be fit to survive."

In 1931 Steffens published his much praised two-volume autobiography, considered his best book, which the *Forum* compared favorably to *The Edu-*cation of Henry Adams*: "It has not the literary quality of Adams' record, but what it reveals is of comparable importance. . . . It is a book to study and ponder. Especially should it be studied by young men, for the wisdom of Steffens at sixty-five should be in the possession of every young man of twenty who faces the world today." This proved to be somewhat of an exaggeration.

Steffens continued to be a much sought-after lecturer. From 1928 until his death he contributed a column to the local publications *Controversy*, the *Pacific Weekly*, and the *Carmelite*. This commentary was collected the year of his death in *Lincoln Steffens Speaking*. At his death the *San Francisco Chronicle* declared: "No other journalist of our time has exerted so great an influence upon the public mind. No other journalist of our time has used his power with more consistent devotion to the principles of human justice."

The papers of Lincoln Steffens are housed in the Bancroft Library, University of California, and in the Columbia University Library.

PRINCIPAL WORKS: *Nonfiction*—The Shame of the Cities, 1904; The Struggle for Self-Government: Being an Attempt to Trace American Political Corruption to Its Sources in Six States of the United States, 1906; The Upbuilders, 1909; Moses in Red: The Revolt of Israel as a Typical Revolution, 1926; Lincoln Steffens Speaking, 1936. *Memoirs*—The Autobiography of Lincoln Steffens, 1931.

ABOUT: Aaron, D. Writers on the Left, 1961; Cook, F. J. Muckrakers, 1972; Filler, L. The Muckrakers: Crusaders for American Liberalism, 1968; Horton, R. M. Lincoln Steffens, 1974; Kaplan, J. Lincoln Steffens: A Biography, 1974; Madison, C. A. Critics and Crusaders: A Century of American Protest, 1947; May, H. The End of American Innocence: A Study of the First Years of Our Own Times: 1912–1917, 1959; Palermo, P. F. Lincoln Steffens, 1978; Reiger, C. C. The Era of the Muckrakers, 1936; Stinson, Robert. Lincoln Steffens, 1979; Sullivan, M. The Education of an American, 1938; Whitman, A. (ed.) American Reformers, 1985; Wilson, H. McClure's Magazine and the Muckrakers, 1970; Winter, E. And Not To Yield: An Autobiography, 1963; Winter, E. and Hicks, G. (eds.) The Letters of Lincoln Steffens, 1938; Winter, E. and Shapiro, H. (eds.) The World of Lincoln Steffens, 1962. *Periodicals*—Forum May 1931; New York Times August 10, 1936; San Francisco Chronicle August 10, 1936.

**STEGNER, WALLACE (EARLE)** (February 18, 1909–April 13, 1993), American novelist, wrote: "My life has been neither eventful nor dull. Born on my grandfather's farm near Lake Mills, Iowa, I was traveling most of the time from then on. We lived successively in Iowa, North Dakota, Washington, Saskatchewan, Montana, Utah, Nevada, and California, with stops of some years in both Saskatchewan and Utah. Conse-

quently Eastend, Saskatchewan, and Salt Lake City are the closest things to 'home' in my life, the only places where I put down any roots. Because my father had the pioneering itch in his bones, my childhood was spent on almost the last frontier. From 1914 to 1919, in Saskatchewan, I had plenty of chance to observe the odd collection of bad men and drifters and cockneys and Texas cowboys at close range. I think those five years in a really tough and unregenerate frontier hamlet are more important to me than any five years of my life. And living in the country has given me an apparently permanent distaste for cities and city ways. It has made me a bad joiner and a worse 'belonger.'

"For the rest, I went through high school and college in Salt Lake, graduating from the state university in 1930. A few years of graduate work at California and Iowa gave me two other degrees, and I began teaching. My teaching experience seems to follow the peripatetic patterns of my childhood; I have taught at Augustana College, the Universities of Iowa, Utah, and Wisconsin, and at Harvard, where I am currently a Briggs-Copeland Instructor in English Composition. In 1934 I was married to Mary Page; we have one son.

"I got into writing, I suppose, by not being able to keep my hands off a typewriter. My M.A. thesis at Iowa was a group of short stories, and after I finished my doctorate I turned by preference away from scholarship and back to fiction. I had published a couple of stories when in 1937 *Remembering Laughter* won the Little, Brown novelette contest. Since then I have published three other short novels and short stories in various magazines. I am working on a long novel on the general theme of what happens to the pioneer virtues and the pioneer type of family when the frontiers are gone and the opportunities all used up. It will be, in some of its aspects, a fairly close parallel to the experiences of my own family between 1907 and 1930.

"I left Harvard in 1945 to become professor of English and director of the Creative Writing Center at Stanford University. My present home is Los Altos, California, in the hills behind Stanford.

"*One Nation* won the Houghton Mifflin Life-in-America award and shared the *Saturday Review*'s Anisfield-Wolfe award in 1945. Three of my short stories have won O. Henry prizes, the latest one being 'The Blue Winged Teal,' which won first prize in 1950. In 1950 and again in 1952 I have held Guggenheim fellowships, and in 1950–1951 my wife and I were sent around the world on a literary reconnaissance of Asia by the Rockefeller Foundation and Stanford University. At present I am completing a biography of Major John Wesley Powell, the explorer of the Colorado River and the founder of many of Washington's government bureaus. Since 1945 I have been West Coast editor for Houghton Mifflin Company, in addition to my teaching at Stanford."

---

Wallace Stegner taught at Stanford University from 1945 until his retirement in 1971. To aid in his research he was awarded Guggenheim fellowships in 1950 and 1959; he received many other grants and honors. In his last two years at Stanford he was Jackson Eli Reynolds Professor of the Humanities. In 1972 he won a senior fellowship from the National Endowment for the Humanities. Stegner wrote a number of books relating to education and the teaching of creative writing.

Although Stegner always managed to combine a career as teacher and writer, it is for his fictional, historical, and biographical works about the American west that he will be remembered. *Remembering Laughter*, his first short novel, wryly presented an adulterous love triangle set in austere Iowa farm country. His ability to suggest the complexity of human motive and action with concision drew strong critical praise. His next short novel, *The Potter's House*, dealt with a deaf mute seeking social acceptance. The human need for community was central to the theme of his third short novel, *On a Darkling Plain*, where an embittered veteran returns to Saskatchewan; he gives up his self-imposed isolation in an act of renewal when he aids his fellow prairie dwellers during an influenza epidemic. *Fire and Ice*, another short novel, treated social and economic panaceas, and their appeal to young radicals. Stegner's first full-length novel, was *The Big Rock Candy Mountain*, a family chronicle from pioneering days through the early twentieth century. In the book he presented characters trapped by outdated beliefs in material success as the vanishing frontier changed to the modern realities of the west. Howard Mumford Jones, writing in the *Saturday Review of Literature* in 1943, called the novel "a vast living untidy book" with a special "quality of vitality, of generous strength."

In his next book, *Second Growth*, Stegner turned to New England for his setting. *The Preacher and the Slave* is a fictionalized biography about Joe Hill, radical labor leader and—with his martyr's death—an American legend. Stegner's next two books of fiction were collections of short stories: *The Women on the Wall* and *The City of the Living*. In *A Shooting Star* he traces the disillusionment of a young woman whose infidelity leads her to question not only her marriage but the romantic affair as well. Most reviewers praised the author's fully realized characterizations. On the other hand, *All the Little Live Things*, which won a Commonwealth Club Gold Medal in 1968, seemed a bit too schematic for several critics. Its narrator, a retired literary agent, becomes involved with the lives of a hippie and a young mother, and is forced to make an uneasy truce with life. It was followed by what most critics now consider his finest work, *Angle of Repose*, the story of a historian who, in writing of his grandparents' seemingly exemplary life in the west in the late 1800s, discovers the flaws in their bond and is thus better able to understand the problems in his own relationship with his own family. William Abraham, writing in the *Atlantic* in 1971, praised the novel's "amplitude of scale and richness of detail altogether uncommon in contemporary fiction." The book was awarded the Pulitzer Prize for fiction in 1972. *The Spectator Bird* reintroduced the protagonist of *All the Little Live Things*; and *Recapitulation* continued the story begun in *The Big Rock Candy Mountain* nearly fifty years earlier.

Stegner's nonfictional works include two books about the Mormons, biographies of John Wesley Powell and Bernard De Voto, and a number of volumes focusing on the west's natural environment and the need for strong and urgent conservation measures to preserve it. In collaboration with the editors of *Look* magazine Stegner wrote the text for a photographic study of the effects of racial and ethnic prejudice in America entitled *One Nation.* Stegner's essays were collected in two volumes, and he published two books of reminiscences, *Wolf Willow* and *The Bluebird Sings to the Lemonade Springs.*

A regional writer in the fullest sense, Stegner declared that his work was characterized by "a respect for the heroic virtues—fortitude, resolution, magnanimity." To this should be added his pragmatism and his fidelity to the truth, both responsible for his avoidance of the tendency to glorify and mythicize the west. His characters were drawn honestly and yet remain, perhaps because of their heroic virtues, somewhat larger than life. "As Americans," Stegner remarked, "we are expected to make the whole pilgrimage of civilization in a single lifetime. That's a hell of a thing to ask of anybody. It seems to me an extra hardship. It may also be an extra challenge, and it may be good for us."

PRINCIPAL WORKS: *Fiction*—Remembering Laughter, 1937; The Potter's House, 1938; On a Darkling Plain, 1940; Fire and Ice, 1941; The Big Rock Candy Mountain, 1943; Second Growth, 1947; The Preacher and the Slave, 1950 (reissued as Joe Hill: A Biographical Novel, 1969); The Women on the Wall, 1950 (stories); The City of the Living, 1956 (stories); A Shooting Star, 1961; All the Little Live Things, 1967; Angle of Repose, 1971; The Spectator Bird, 1976; Recapitulation, 1979; Crossing to Safety, 1987; Collected Stories, 1990. *Nonfiction*—Mormon Country, 1942; (with editors of Look magazine) One Nation, 1945; The Writer in America, 1951 (lectures); Beyond the Hundredth Meridian, 1954 (biography of John Wesley Powell); The Gathering of Zion: The Story of the Mormon Trail, 1964; Teaching the Short Story, 1965; The Sound of Mountain Water, 1969 (essays); Variations on a Theme of Discontent, 1972; Robert Frost and Bernard De Voto, 1974; The Uneasy Chair, 1974 (biography of Bernard De Voto); *foreword to* Images (by A. Adams) 1974; (with P. Stegner and E. Porter) American Places, 1981; One Way to Spell Man, 1982 (essays); (with R. Etulain) Conversations with Wallace Stegner on Western History and Literature, 1983, rev. ed. 1990; The American West as Living Space, 1987 (with E. C. Lathem) On the Teaching of Creative Writing, 1988; Wilderness at the Edge, 1990. *Autobiography*—Wolf Willow, 1962; Where the Bluebird Sings to the Lemonade Springs, 1992. *As editor*—(with others) An Exposition Workshop, 1939; (with others) Readings for a Citizen at War, 1941; (with R. Scowcroft and B. Ilyin) The Writer's Art, 1950; This Is Dinosaur, 1955; The Exploration of the Colorado River of the West (by J. W. Powell) 1957; (with M. Stegner) Great American Short Stories, 1957; Selected American Prose, 1841–1900, 1958; Adventures of Huckleberry Finn (by Mark Twain) 1960; The Outcasts of Poker Flat (by B. Harte) 1961; Report on the Lands of the Arid Region of the United States (by J. W. Powell) 1962; (with others) Modern Composition, 1964; The American Novel, 1965; The Big Sky (by A. B. Guthrie, Jr.) 1965; (with others) Twenty Years of Stanford Short Stories, 1966; Twice-Told Tales (by N. Hawthorne) 1967; The Letters of Bernard De Voto, 1975.

ABOUT: The autobiographical material quoted above was written for Twentieth Century Authors, 1942 and Twentieth Century Authors First Supplement, 1955. Arthur, A. (ed.) Critical Essays on Wallace Stegner, 1982; Lewis, M. and Lewis, L. Wallace Stegner, 1972; Robinson, F. G. and Robinson, M. C. Wallace Stegner, 1977. *Bibliography*—Colberg, N. Wallace Stegner: A Descriptive Bibliography, 1990. *Periodicals*—American Heritage August/September 1985; American West April 1988; Atlantic November 1943, April 1971, June 1976; Audubon September 1987; Esquire December 1988; Life February 1991; New York Times September 26, 1943; July 27, 1967; March 24, 1971; February 24, 1979; New York Times Book Review October 28, 1962; February 10, 1974; May 30, 1982; New York Times Magazine December 27, 1981; Paris Review Summer 1990; Saturday Review September 11, 1954; May 20, 1961; December 1, 1962; January 16, 1965; March 20, 1971; May 15, 1976; Saturday Review of Literature October 2, 1943; August 17, 1946; Sewanee Review Winter 1962; Smithsonian April 1990; Southern Review Autumn 1973; Time July 12, 1976; Virginia Quarterly Review Spring 1991; Western Review Autumn 1955; Wilderness Spring 1983; Spring 1985; Fall 1987; Yale Review Winter 1944; Spring 1968.

**STEIN, GERTRUDE** (February 3, 1874–July 27, 1946), American experimental writer in many genres, and patron of the arts, who lived most of her life in France, was born in Allegheny, Pennsylvania. She was the youngest of five children of Daniel Stein, a traction-company executive, of German Jewish descent, and Emilia (Keyser) Stein. When she was less than a year old her father's business took him to Europe, and she and

her two brothers, Michael and Leo, spent the next four years in Vienna and Paris. In 1879 the family returned to America, settling first in Oakland, California, later in San Francisco. After an erratic education, with governesses and at local schools, she followed her brother Leo to Harvard University, entering Harvard Annex (later renamed Radcliffe College) in 1893. She studied psychology with William James, and two of her papers on brain psychology were published in the *Harvard Psychological Review*, in 1896 and 1898. One of the many stories that make up the Stein "legend" is of her joking to Professor James on one occasion: "I am so sorry but I do not feel a bit like an examination paper . . . today." Stein nevertheless finished the course with the highest mark in the class.

Stein went on to study at the Johns Hopkins University medical school in 1897, but, declaring herself "bored" with medicine, failed her examinations. (some biographers believe there were other, emotional, reasons). In any case she left (1910) without taking a degree. After a period in London, studying Elizabethan literature, she joined her brothers in Paris in 1903. Leo had established a studio there, and he and Michael had begun to collect art. Influenced by them, Gertrude Stein's own interest in contemporary painting was kindled, and she and Leo purchased a Cézanne portrait from the dealer Ambrose Vollard. It was the start of a world-renowned collection of modern art, (based almost exclusively on Leo's rather than her judgment) established in the apartment they shared at 27, rue de Fleurus, near the Luxembourg Gardens, which became a gathering place for the pre-war School of Paris artists and their writer colleagues. Leo's next purchase, in 1905, was the Matisse *Woman with the Green Hat*; their support of Matisse helped to establish his reputation. Similarly, they were among the first collectors of Picasso's work. The Spanish artist's seated portrait of

Gertrude Stein (1905–06, now in the Metropolitan Museum of Art)—has become famous. Stein responded with the 1909 "word-portrait" of her friend, and went on in 1938 to write *Picasso*, a study of his development. The monograph, originally written in French and published first in Paris, was then translated into English by Alice B. Toklas; its style is "easy and affable . . . rather remote from her usual stern mood of grammatical Calvinism, with its unshakable faith in original syntax"— according to Clifton Fadiman (*New Yorker*). The two pieces were reprinted in 1971, together with unpublished material relating to the painter excerpted from Stein's notebooks, in *Gertrude Stein on Picasso*, a Museum of Modern Art publication. "Small doses" of her observations and anecdotes can, according to Hugh Kenner in his review of the latter, "exhilarate"; much is "pseudo-Delphic" and the whole "a chunk of history as mute and in its way as authentic as a fossil" (*New Republic*). In 1913, as a result of a bitter argument with Gertrude—who objected to his attempts to dominate her—Leo Stein moved; they never spoke to one another again.

In the meantime she had been introduced to Alice Toklas, a fellow San Franciscan, who came to live with her in 1910. As their first meeting is recalled (in Stein's words), in *The Autobiography of Alice B. Toklas*: "I was impressed by the coral brooch she wore and by her voice. I may say that only three times in my life have I met a genius and each time a bell within me rang. . . . The three geniuses of whom I wish to speak are Gertrude Stein, Pablo Picasso and Alfred Whitehead. . . . In this way my new full life began." Stein and Toklas lived together for the next thirty-six years. Only once, in 1934 when she came on a lecture tour, did Stein return to America. "Paris was the place," she once wrote, "that suited us who were to create the twentieth century art and literature."

On her arrival there she had begun to write. Her first published work, *Three Lives: Stories of the Good Anna, Melanchtha, and the Gentle Lena*, reflects her psychological training under James. As Edmund Wilson remarked in *Axel's Castle*, these stories of two German servant-girls and a young American mulatto seem "to have caught the very rhythms and accents of their mind. . . ." Further, different from ordinary realistic fiction, "Miss Stein is interested in her subjects, not from the point of view of their social conditions . . . but as three fundamental types of women. . . ." The story of "passionate and complex Melanchtha, who 'was always losing what she had in wanting all the things she saw,'" and her ill-fated affair with a doctor, is usually considered Stein's most substantial work. One of the first attempts at a sympathetic, subjective treatment of black life, it is also a reworking of an earlier, autobiographical, story of an unhappy lesbian love affair, titled "Q.E.D." Because of its subject "Q.E.D." remained unpublished until after Stein's death, appearing first in *Things as They Are*, later in the collection titled *Fernhurst, Q.E.D. and Other Early Writings*. All of these, Diana Loercher suggested, "share a quaintness . . . that recalls Jane Austen, a convolution of style that recalls Henry James, and a liturgical cadence that recalls the Bible, all of which characterize her later work in more extreme forms. . . . " (*Christian Science Monitor*). All these earlier works have a complicated chronological history, and efforts to establish Stein's bibliography have been further complicated by the fact that individual pieces were often included in several different compilations.

Between 1906 and 1908 she wrote *The Making of Americans*, a novel based on her own family history, which becomes in the course of its 925 pages a history of the whole of humanity. It marks the beginning of Stein's full-fledged "experimental" style—a label she herself would not have used, because "artists do not experiment. Experiment is what scientists do. . . . An artist puts down what he knows and at every moment it is what he knows at that moment." Richard Kostalanetz called the novel the "first giant step beyond nineteenth-century fiction," coming as it did before the work of Joyce or Faulkner. Ford Madox Ford finally serialized it in 1924–25 in *Transatlantic review*. Conrad Aiken found it "a complete esthetic miscalculation" (*New Republic*). Her new style, as it evolved in an effort to show "things as they are," not as they are assumed to be, included: abandonment of conventional plot and dialogue; elimination of punctuation and capitalization; repetition of simple words, or phrases, generally employed without regard to literal meaning but to create incantatory sound patterns. For this reason, Stein's work is often more effective read aloud; for several years a New York art gallery invited the public to New Year's celebrations with a two-day-long marathon reading of *The Making of Americans*. As Malcolm Cowley wrote (in a review of a later book, *Brewsie and Willie*): "She writes conversation pieces, and if one merely reads them . . . listens to the words, there is a very definite meaning" (*Weekly Book Review*). Her use of words as autonomous objects to create an effect or an image has also been compared to cubist (or collage) painting. Whether or not this is a wholly correct comparison, her writing is certainly process-oriented in its attempt to reproduce thought processes without intermediation; her narrative evokes what she termed a "continuous present" rather than proceeding in linear, time-oriented fashion. To quote the author herself (writing in the third person), defining her method and purpose: "Gertrude Stein in her work has always been possessed by an intellectual passion for exactitude of inner and outer reality. She has produced a simplification by this concentration, as a result the destruction of associative emotion in poetry and prose."

For the next forty years critics and public, with few exceptions, attacked or lampooned her work, or simply admitted their uncomprehending boredom. Even such contemporary admirers as Wilson or her friend and collaborator the American composer Virgil Thomson were often puzzled. Thomson, in a 1971 *New York Review of Books* essay, described some of her fiction (*Lucy Church Amiably, ida*, and *Mrs. Reynolds*) as "simply dense" works that "have long discouraged readers." The consensus was that she was incomprehensible but somehow "interesting," and certainly "one of the most brilliant women of her time." With the publication in the 1950s of Van Vechten's Yale Edition of the *Unpublished Writings of Gertrude Stein* and its scholarly introductions, more sophisticated critical analysis and understanding of her objectives has developed, but it has never found complete acceptance.

Stein's forging of a new technique has meant that conventional classification of her work is often arbitrary; plays, poems, novels, even "nonfictional" essays are virtually undifferentiable. *Tender Buttons*, the first of her works to attract attention, is ostensibly a poem and so defined in her *Lectures in America*, where she announced that: "Language as a real thing is not imitation either of sound or colors or emotions it is an intellectual secretion. . . . And so for me the problem of poetry was and it began with *Tender Buttons* to constantly realize the thing anything so that I could recreate that thing."

The best known of all Stein's works, and most easily understood, is *The Autobiography of Alice B. Toklas*, really her own story but perhaps a joint venture, and—as scholars now believe—based on Toklas's clipped, laconic speech. Edmund Wilson hoped it would cause the general public to recognize her charm and originality (*New Republic*). They did; it was a *Literary Guide* selection in 1933. The usually dry and humorless Samuel Chew (*Yale Review*) found it an appealing mix of naive wisdom and profound sophistication, and subtle malice—as in this remark about Ezra Pound who "came home to dinner with us and he stayed and he talked about japanese prints among other things. Gertrude Stein liked him but did not find him amusing. She said he was a village explainer, excellent if you were a village, but if you were not, not." This and other witty and malicious characterizations of the people who gathered at the rue de Fleurus form a vivid picture of an extraordinary period in the world of the arts. It was as a result of the *Autobiography* that Stein was invited to lecture in the United States. During her six-month stay she attended the New York staging of her opera *Four Saints in Three Acts*, had tea at the White House, was entertained and interviewed extensively. *Everybody's Autobiography*, the sequel to the Toklas "autobiography," is a rambling, "intensely readable and funny" (Iris Barry, *Books*) account of this celebrity junket.

Besides several plays (some of them staged, as was *Yes Is for a Very Young Man*), Stein wrote the librettos for two operas by Virgil Thomson. *Four Saints*, which she called "a perfectly simple description of the Spanish landscape" and is, actually, about *two* saints—Teresa of Avila and Ignatius—was produced at the Wadsworth Athenaeum in Hartford, Connecticut, before moving to New York. It is a timeless sequence of tableaux and arias; the often (and derisively) quoted line "Pigeons on the grass alas" occurs in a third-act aria and refers to St. Ignatius's vision of the Holy Ghost. It was the composer who noted that, as with Stein's other dramatic works, the seemingly nonsensical text some-

how "works," comes alive, when spoken or sung (*New York Review of Books*, April 13, 1989). The premiere of their other collaboration, *The Mother of Us All*—about Susan B. Anthony, was given at Columbia University in 1947, the year after her death.

All these years Stein and Toklas had lived in moderate luxury in Paris, and in summer at their seventeenth-century villa near Bilignin, with Stein customarily writing at night, after their guests had been entertained. Toklas typed the manuscripts, read proofs, and negotiated with publishers. During World War I they distributed medical supplies for the American Fund for the French Wounded and were awarded the Reconnaissance Française medal. After World War I the expatriate writers of the "lost generation" (her phrase) flocked to their salons—notably Ernest Hemingway, Scott Fitzgerald, Thornton Wilder, and Carl Van Van Vechten. Stein's influence on their careers been noted by literary historians, and the story of her strained relationship with Hemingway given much attention. Despite his publishing efforts on behalf of *The Making of Americans*, he and Stein quarreled in 1933. Infuriated by her comments on him in the *Autobiography*, he retaliated with a scathing attack on his erstwhile patron in his memoir *A Moveable Feast* (1946). In 1938 Toklas and Stein were forced to leave their flat for one in the rue Christine, but spent all of World War II in a house in Culoz, in occupied France, living under harsh conditions. The journal of her thoughts and experiences during that time (written illegibly enough to escape scrutiny by the enemy authorities) was eventually published as *Wars I Have Seen*. "Nobody else, among all the writers who have told us about life in occupied France, has made the story so intimate, homely, immediate. . . . For the first time since 'Three Lives,' . . . she has an intelligible and important subject outside of Gertrude Stein. . . ." Malcolm Cowley commented (*New York Times*). Edmund Wilson once again came to her defense, emphasizing that although she started out in "her more tiresome vein" the "alternation of comments on history with anecdotes of daily life . . . gradually becomes exciting and, finally, exhilarating" (*New Yorker*).

After the Liberation she and Toklas returned to Paris, where Stein continued to write and enjoyed her role as mentor of a new circle: American G.I.s who flocked around her and who renewed her never-renounced ties with America. Her book *Brewsie and Willie* is an affectionate tribute to them and records, in Stein fashion, their talk about what Stein might face on returning home. The characteristic repetitions here "have the justification of appropriateness to the endless repetitions of soldier conversation and the stultifying monotony of soldier life. . . ." (Edmund Wilson, *New Yorker*).

Stein died of cancer soon afterwards; she was buried in Père-Lachaise Cemetery in Paris, as was Alice B. Toklas, who survived her by twenty-one years.

Stein's art collection, bitterly fought over by her family, was dispersed among private collections and museums in the United States. Her papers were bequeathed to the Beinecke Library at Yale University, the major repository of her manuscripts, correspondence, and unpublished notebooks. There are, as well, significant collections at the Bancroft Library of the University of California at Berkeley, and at the University of Texas in Austin. The bibliography below is a selective listing both of her own writings—to which is added the two volumes in the Library of America—and of the enormous number of works about her that have accumulated over the course of eight decades.

PRINCIPAL WORKS: *Fiction*—Three Lives: Stories of the Good Anna, Melanctha, and the Gentle Lena, 1909; The Making of Americans: Being a History of a Family's Progress, 1925 (in U.S.: The Making of Americans: The Hersland Family; A Novel of Romantic Beauty and Nature and Which Looks Like an Engraving: Lucy Church Amiably, 1930 (also issued as Lucy Church Amiably; ida, a novel, 1941; Four in America (introd. Thornton Wilder) 1947 Things as They Are, a Novel in Three Parts, 1950; Mrs. Reynolds, and Five Earlier Novelettes (forword L. Frankenberg) 1952 (The Yale Edition of the Unpublished Writings of Gertrude Stein, vol. 2); As Fine as Melanchta, 1914–1930 (foreword Natalie Clifford Barney) 1954 (Yale Edition 4); A Novel of Thank You (introd. Carl Van Vechten) 1958 (Yale Edition 8); Fernhurst, Q.E.D., and Other Early Writings (introd. L. Katz) 1971 Blood on the Dining-Room Floor, 1985 (Virago Press). *Nonfiction*—Composition as Explanation, 1926 (The Hogarth Essays 2nd ser., 1); How to Write, 1931 (repr. 1975 with new pref. and introd. by P. Meyerowitz; The Autobiography of Alice B. Toklas, 1933; Portraits and Prayers, 1934; Lectures in America, 1935; Narration: Four Lectures (introd. Thornton Wilder) 1935; The Geographical History of America; Or; The Relation of Human Nature to the Human Mind (introd. Thornton Wilder) 1936 (repr.1973 with new introd. by W. H. Gass); Everybody's Autobiography, 1937 Picasso, 1938 (tr. Alice B. Toklas) 1938; Paris France, 1940 (repr. 1971 as Paris, France: Personal Recollections); What Are Masterpieces, 1940; Wars I Have seen, 1945; Brewsie and Willie, 1946; Two: Gertrude Stein and Her Brother, and Other Early Portraits, 1908–12 (foreword Janet Flanner) 1951 (Yale Edition 1); Motor Automatism (with L. M. Solomons) 1969 (repr. from Psychological Review Sept. 1896 and May 1898); Gertrude Stein on Picasso (ed. E. Bruns; afterword L. Katz and E. Burns) 1970 (Museum of Modern Art); How Writing Is Written (ed. R. B. Haas) 1974 (The Previously Uncollected Writings of Gertrude Stein, vol. 2); Dear Sammy: Letters from Gertrude Stein and Alice B. Toklas (ed. with memoir by Samuel M. Steward) 1977; The Letters of Gertrude Stein and Carl Van Vechten, 1913–1946, 2 vols. (ed. E. Burns) 1986. *Poetry*—Tender Buttons: Objects, Food, Rooms, 1914; Stanzas in Mediation, and Other Poems, 1929–1933 (pref. D. Sutherland) 1956 (Yale Edition); Alphabets and Birthdays (introd. D. Gallup) 1957 (Yale Edition 7); Lifting Belly (ed. R. Mark) 1989. *Drama*—A Village, Are You Ready Yet Not Yet: A Play in Four Acts, 1928; Opera to be Sung, 1932 (with Virgil Thomson) Four Saints in Three Atcs: An Opera to Be sung, 1933; In Savoy; or, Yes Is for a Very Young Man, a Play of the Resistance in France, 1947; (with Virgil Thomson) The Mother of Us All, 1947; Last Operas and Plays (ed. and with introd. by Carl Van Vechten) 1949; In a Garden, an Opera in One Act, 1951; Selected Operas and Plays of Gertrude Stein (ed. and with introd. by John Malcolm Brinnin; Bibliog. comp. D. Gallup) 1970. *Miscellaneous*—Georgraphy and Plays, 1922 (repr. 1968 with foreword by S. Anderson); Matisse, Picasso and Gertrude Stein, with Two Shorter Stories, 1932; Selected Writings of Gertrude Stein (ed. with introd. and notes by Carl Van Vechten) 1946 (repr. 1972 with Essay on Gertrude Stein by F. W. Dupee; The Yale Edition of Unpublished writings by Gertrude Stein (general ed. Carl Van Vechten) 8 vols., 1951–58; Bee Time Vine, and Other Pieces, 1913–1927 (pref. and notes Virgil Thomson) 1953 (Yale Edition 3); Painted Lace, and Other Pieces, 1914–1937 (introd. Daniel-Henry Kahnweiler) 1955 (Yale Edition 5); Gertrude Stein's America (ed. G. A. Harrison) 1965; Writings and Lectures

1911–1945 (ed. P. Meyerowitz; introd. E. Springge) 1967 (also issued as Look at Me Now and Here I Am: Writings and Lectures 1909–1945, 1971); A Primer for the Gradual Understanding of Grutrude Stein (ed. R. B. Haas) 1971; Sherwood Anderson/Gertrude Stein: Correspondence and Personal Essays (ed. R. L. White) 1972; The Yale Gertrude Stein: Selections (ed. R. Kostelanetz) 1980; Really Reading Gertrude Stein: A Selected Anthology with Essays by Judy Grahn, 1989.

ABOUT: Bridgman, R. The Colloquial Style in America, 1966; Bridgman, R. Gertrude Stein in Pieces, 1970; Brinnin, J. M. The Third Rose: Gertrude Stein and Her World, 1987; Copeland, C. F. Language and Time and Gertrude Stein, 1975; DeKoven, M. A Different Language: Gertrude Stein's Experimental Writing, 1983; Dictionary of American Biography Suppl. 4, 1946–1950, 1974; Doane, J. L. Silence and Narrative: The Early Novels of Gertrude Stein, 1986; Dubnick, R. K. The Structure of Obscurity: Gertrude Stein, Language, and Cubism, 1984; Firmage, G. J. A Check-List of the Published Writings of Gertrude Stein, 1977; Flanner, J. "Memory Is All," New Yorker December 15, 1975; Four Americans in Paris: The Collections of Gertrude Stein and Her Family, 1970 (Museum of Modern Art exhibn. catalogue); Gallup, D. C. (ed.) The Flowers of Friendship: Letters Written to Gertrude Stein, 1953; Gaunt, W. The March of the Moderns, 1949; Hobhouse, J. Everybody Who Was Anybody: A Biography of Gertrude Stein, 1975, 1986; Keller, R. (ed.) A Gertrude Stein Companion: Content with the Example, 1988; Knapp B. L. Gertrude Stein, 1990; Kostelanetz, R. (ed.) Gertrude Stein Advanced: An Anthology of Criticism, 1990; Liston, M. R. Gertrude Stein: An Annotated Critical Bibliography, 1979; Mellow, J. R. Charmed Circle: Gertrude Stein and Company, 1991; Newman, S. S. (with I. B. Nadel, eds.) Gertrude Stein and the Making of Literature, 1988; Rewald, John. Cézanne, the Steins and Their Circle, 1987; Rogers, W. G. When This You See Remember Me: Gertrude Stein in Person, 1948, 1964; Rule, J. Lesbian Images, 1975; Ryan, B. A. Gertrude Stein's Theatre of the Absolute, 1984; Saarinen, A. The Proud Possessors, 1958; Sawyer, J. Gertrude Stein: A Bibliography, 1977; Secor, C. "The Question of Gertrude Stein," *in* American Novelist Revisited: Essays in Feminist Criticism (ed. F. Fleischmann) 1982; Showalter, E. (with others, eds.) Modern American Women Writers, 1991; Simon, L. The Biography of Alice B. Toklas, 1977; Souhami, D. Gertrude and Alice, 1991; Sprigge, E. Gertrude Stein: Her Life and Work. 1957; Stein, G. The Autobiography of Alice B. Toklas, 1933; Stein, G. Dear Sammy: Letters from Gertrude Stein and Alice B. Toklas (ed. with memoir by Samuel M. Steward) 1977; Stein, G. The Letters of Gertrude Stein and Carl Van Vechten, 1913–1946 (ed., E. Burns,) 2 vols., 1986; Stein, G. Sherwood Anderson/Gertrude Stein: Correspondence and Personal Essays (ed. R. L. White 1972; Stein, G. Two: Gertrude Stein and Her Brother . . . 1951; Stein G. Wars I Have Seen, 1945; Steiner, W. Exact Resemblance to Exact Resemblance: The Literary Portraiture of Gertrude Stein, 1978; Sutherland, D. Gertrude Stein: A Biography of Her Work, 1951, 1971; Twentieth-Century Literary Criticism vol. 1, 1978, vol. 6, 1982, vol. 28 1988; Walker, J. L. The Making of a Modrnist: Gertrude Stein from Three Lives to Tender Buttons, 1984; Wells, W. Gertrude Stein and a Companion: A Play, 1986; White, R. L. Gertrude Stein and Alice B. Toklas: A Reference Guide, 1984; Wilder, T. *introduction to* Stein, G. Four in America, 1947; Wilson, E. Axel's Castle: A Study in the Imaginative Literature of 1870–1930, 1945. *Periodicals*—Chicago Daily Tribune February 10, 1934; Christian Science Monitor October 7, 1971; Harper's December 1947; New Republic October 11, 1933, April 4, 1934, January 16, 1971; New York Herald Tribune Book December 12, 1937 New York Review of Books April 8, 1971, April 13, 1989; New York Times March 11, 1945, July 28, 1946; New Yorker March 17, 1945, June 15, 1946, August 10, 1946; Times (London) July 29, 1946; Weekly Book Review July 21, 1946; Yale Review Winter 1934, Summer 1988.

## STEIN, LEO (DANIEL)

**STEIN, LEO (DANIEL)** (May 11, 1872–July 29, 1947), American art critic, brother of Gertrude Stein, was born in Allegheny, Pennsylvania. He was

the son of Daniel Stein, and the former Amelia Keyser. The Steins had agreed to have five children and, by 1871, had done so. Then two of the children died, so they produced two more. These were Leo and his younger sister Gertrude, both of them sometimes troubled by the thought that they owed their lives to their siblings' deaths.

Daniel Stein was an impatient and aggressive man. In 1874 he fell out with his brother and their business partnership was dissolved. For several years after that the family lived in Vienna, then for another year in Paris. Stein was often away on business, and his wife was an ineffectual mother. The children were raised mostly by nursemaids and governesses, and by each other. Leo and Gertrude, both of them precocious and bookish, were very close, with Leo as his sister's mentor. As a child, Leo read Gibbon and, deciding to be a historian, set himself to memorize long lists of dates and dynasties.

In 1879 the family moved back to the United States. They settled briefly in Baltimore, then in East Oakland, California, across the Bay from San Francisco, where Daniel Stein was involved with street railways, cable cars, mines and the stock market. Leo Stein, by contrast, had become interested in esthetics, at fourteen wrestling with theories of composition and "significant form." Mrs. Stein died of cancer in 1888, after a prolonged illness. Daniel Stein died suddenly in 1891, his body being found one morning by Leo.

The following year, Leo went off to study history at Harvard, where he also became a student and admirer of William James. Losing respect for history, he tried a year at Harvard Law School, disliked that, and took a trip around the world. Finding biology at Johns Hopkins (1897) no more to his taste, he went to Europe to research a book on Andrea Mantegna, but decided to become a painter himself, in Paris. Gertrude joined him there in 1903 and they took a two-story studio flat at 27 rue de Fleurus. Leo was then thirty-one.

From the outset, the Steins attracted a good deal of attention in Paris. Both dressed invariably in brown corduroy and wore sandals (described by Apollinaire as "Bacchic") which denied them entry to the Café de la Paix. Leo tried painting, but was not satisfied with the results. Instead, having bought his first painting in England in 1902, he began to think of himself as an esthetic theorist and a collector, like Bernard Berenson. Stein could find nothing of interest in the Paris salon art of the time. It was Berenson himself who, although he thought Stein a bore, suggested that he should visit the dealer Ambrose Vollard and look at his Cézannes. Leo was converted at once, and began to buy.

By that time, Leo's eldest brother Michael had quit the business world and arrived in Paris with his wife Sarah. The Steins began to tour the avant-garde galleries *en famille*. Although they received comfortable incomes from San Francisco properties, they were not rich; but the new art was cheap. The leader of these expeditions was Leo, a connoisseur of extraordinary discernment. His mournful face smothered in the rabbinical beard he affected at that time, he would sprawl in an armchair in Vollard's gallery, his feet high up on a bookcase to relieve his indigestion. From Cézanne, the Steins moved on to Matisse, whose "La Femme au Chapeau" they bought for $100, then to Picasso, who did a famous portrait of Gertrude. Soon there were Renoirs and Gauguins and Braques.

Most of these painters and many others attended the Steins' Saturday evenings at rue de Fleurus. They came at first for the buffet food and wine, then to eye one another's work in a great and growing collection. Matisse and Picasso first met there. Aline Saarinen in *The Proud Possessors* wrote: "The Saturday night salons were an international pre-café society—Russians, Poles, Scandinavians and Germans along with English, Americans, Spaniards and French were there. The Steins' salon was the artists' showcase and press conference. It was the crossroads and the vortex. Perhaps no other collection was ever so effective a stimulant and catalyst."

Both Steins were profoundly neurotic, but, whereas Gertrude celebrated her neuroses in her writings, which Leo despised, he was incapacitated by his. His main problems, he decided, were an inferiority complex, a pariah complex, and a castration complex. Dealing with this formidable triumvirate occupied all of his creative energies. In 1919 he returned permanently to Settignano and in 1921, twelve years after he met her, he married Nina Auzias. She was a former artist's model, warm and sympathetic, whose adviser he had been on the conduct of her many love affairs.

According to Aline Saarinen, Leo "never 'enjoyed' a painting. He struggled to discover why he felt it has power. Once acquired, a picture became like a microscopic slide to a scientist. . . . Dispassionate thoroughness was Leo's hallmark. Cerebrally, relentlessly, he pursued whatever subject hooked his questing mind." This was his approach in his first book, *The A.B.C. of Aesthetics*, finally published in 1927. It was not a success. One approving reviewer in *Theatre Arts Monthly* called it "a general study of first principles rather than a particular statement. He describes the processes by which a work of art is understood—assimilated—and defines the aesthetic experience; he analyzes emotions and feeling, and discusses distortion, composition and pictorial seeing in a way that illuminates the approach of a modern painter to his art." Most critics, however, shared the opinion of Edgar Johnson, who wrote: "Even greater intellectual merits than this volume holds could not excuse its intolerably flat, muddy and needless verbiage" (*New York Herald Tribune Books*).

Over the next twenty years, Leo Stein continued his self-analysis and his thinking about art, though he had to sell most of his paintings to provide an income. He and Nina spent World War II at their villa in Settignano, and were liberated by the American army. In 1947, ill with cancer, he sold one of his last treasures, a Picasso drawing, to pay for radium treatments. His second book, much better than the first, appeared in June 1947, a month before his death at seventy-five. *Appreciation: Painting, Poetry and Prose* was a volume of essays full of warm and often witty reminiscences of the painters and writers Leo Stein had known, and trenchant analysis of their work. An esthetic testament, it was also an attempt to counter Gertrude Stein's account of their years at rue de Fleurus in her hugely successful *Autobiography of Alice B. Toklas* (which Leo called a "romance")—to offer a competing version of the truth. Anthony Bower, in the *Nation*, wrote that "without the least trace of snobbery or obscurantism, he has stated the bases of his appreciation with a lucidity and directness which should disarm the most ardent of philistines and inform the most erudite of pundits. . . . Certainly it is a fact that he had obviously integrated his own appreciations so thoroughly into his life and culture that makes this such a charming, informative, and human book."

In 1950, Edmund Fuller edited Leo Stein's letters and other papers into an autobiography, *Journey Into the Self*. "Thanks to Stein's own frankness and the sensibility of the editing," wrote J. J. Sweeney, "we see the gradual working out of the critical approach on which he felt his pictorial taste was based. We witness his life-long struggle with deep-seated neuroses, which were only conquered in his last years and which only then allowed him any real confidence, or any pleasure or ease in self-expression. The result is a volume that sums up an unusual individual, his contribution and his tragedy" (*New York Times*, 1950). And Lloyd Morris, in the *New York Herald Tribune Review*, called it "a genuinely important book, and an extremely fascinating one," which "contemporary readers are likely to find as exciting a discovery as, thirty years ago, their predecessors found *The Education of Henry Adams*."

PRINCIPAL WORKS: The A.B.C. of Aesthetics, 1927; Appreciation: Painting, Poetry and Prose, 1947; Journey Into the Self: Letters, Papers and Journals (ed. E. Fuller) 1950.

ABOUT: Brinnin, J. M. The Third Rose: Gertrude Stein and Her World, 1952; Brooks, V. W. The Confident Years: 1885–1915, 1952; Dictionary of American Biography 1946–1950, 1974; Dictionary of Literary Biography, vol. 4 1980; Rewald, J. Cézanne, the Steins, and Their Circle, 1987; Saarinen, A. The Proud Possessors, 1958; Stein, G. Two: Gertrude Stein and Her Brother, and Other Early Portraits, 1908–1912, 1951; Stein, L. Appreciation, 1947; Stein, L. Journey Into the Self, 1950; Wickes, G. Americans in Paris, 1969. *Periodicals*—American Scholar Autumn 1958; Apollo September 1976; Art News April 1987; Life April 23, 1971; Nation September 13, 1947; New York Herald Tribune Book Review July 2, 1950; New York Herald Tribune Books November 13, 1927; New York Times July 31, 1947; July 2, 1950; Newsweek December 14, 1970; Theatre Arts Monthly May 28, 1928.

**STEINBECK, JOHN (ERNST)** (February 27, 1902–December 20, 1968), American novelist, playwright, and journalist, was born in Salinas, California, one of four children of John Ernst Steinbeck, a county treasurer, and Olive (Hamilton) Steinbeck, a former schoolteacher. Steinbeck's childhood was both emotionally and financially secure; his mother encouraged his avid reading, and well before he entered Stan-

ford University in 1919 he had decided to become a writer. Steinbeck spent seven years at Stanford, alternating an eccentric course of study with long leaves of absence as a manual laborer. Leaving without a degree in 1925, he went to New York to work—with little success—as a newspaper reporter. In 1926 he got a job as a caretaker at a resort on Lake Tahoe, and it was here in the following months that he wrote his first book, *Cup of Gold*. This romantic novel about the seventeenth-century buccaneer Henry Morgan hardly presaged *The Grapes of Wrath*, and though his next two books, *The Pastures of Heaven* and *To a God Unknown*, worked closer to the vein of socially conscious realism that was his greatest strength, neither work received enough attention to establish him as a writer of particular promise. That situation changed in 1935 with the publication of *Tortilla Flat*, an episodic novel about a community of Mexican-American laborers living in self-respecting poverty in Monterey, California. Though *Tortilla Flat* ends tragically, it has passages of exuberant humor and is comparatively free of the didacticism and sentimentality that mar much of Steinbeck's subsequent work. It received excellent reviews and, with *Of Mice and Men*, *The Grapes of Wrath*, and *Cannery Row*, is still considered one of his three or four most enduring works. "*Tortilla Flat* is a tour de force," wrote Jackson J. Benson in his biography of Steinbeck. "It is the kind of book, deceptively simple, that is invariably underestimated. . . . It took Steinbeck fifteen years of practice to make a book look that easy, and behind that relaxed manner is a world of experience with sympathy for his subject."

*In Dubious Battle*, the work that followed, gave evidence of Steinbeck's increasing concern with economic and political injustice in the midst of the Great Depression. This novel about the violent suppression of a strike called by exploited migrant workers in the apple orchards of the Torgas Valley was praised at the time, but is undoubtedly flawed by the clumsy manner in which Steinbeck subjects his characters to the biological determinism that he had adapted from his friend, the marine biologist Edward F. Ricketts. "*In Dubious Battle* is now certainly a period piece, and is of more interest to social historians than to literary critics," wrote Harold Bloom in 1987. On the other hand, *Of Mice and Men*, published one year after *In Dubious Battle*, retains its interest for literary critics and common readers alike. The popularity of this simple, tragic tale of the physically powerful but mentally "wanting" ranch hand Lennie and his friend and protector George was greatly enhanced by a dramatic adaptation written by Steinbeck with the help of George S. Kaufman in 1937 and by the first film version in 1941. Indeed, many critics rank the modestly scaled *Of Mice and Men* above the far more ambitious (and lengthy) *Grapes of Wrath*. R.W.B. Lewis writing in the collection *The Young Rebel in American Literature* called *Of Mice and Men* "probably the only one of Steinbeck's works which is satisfying as a whole," and added, "the entire action of the story moves to its own rhythm, rescued and redeemed by a sort of wistful toughness, a sense not of realism but of reality. The end is an authentic purgation of feeling, pity if not terror, and the end crowns the whole."

*The Long Valley*, a volume of short stories containing "The Red Pony" and several other distinguished pieces, was published in 1938 and became Steinbeck's fourth best-selling book in as many years. Two years earlier he had spent several weeks with California farm laborers, reporting on the appalling conditions of their employment in a seven-part series commissioned by the *San Francisco News*. In 1939, after two more trips to the laboring camps, he returned to the subject in an enormous, biblical narrative about one Oklahoma family making the cross-country trip from the depleted "dust bowl" of the Midwest to the illusory promised land of California, where, with thousands of other migrant workers, they are systematically abused and exploited by the owners and overseers of the agricultural laboring camps. *The Grapes of Wrath*, as Steinbeck called the novel, won the Pulitzer Prize in 1939 and brought its modest, unpretentious author far more attention than he liked. (Steinbeck reacted to the attendent furor by retreating in 1940 to the Gulf of California with Edward Ricketts in a quasi-scientific expedition that resulted in his best work of nonfiction, *Sea of Cortez*.) If *The Grapes of Wrath* is Steinbeck's masterpiece, it is a problematic one; as Brad Leithauser wrote in the *New Yorker*, it "contains in profusion the strengths commonly associated with Steinbeck (sympathy for the disenfranchised, moral urgency, narrative propulsion) and also the weaknesses (repetitiveness, simplistic politics, sentimentality)." Critical opinion, as distinct from popular approval, remains divided over *The Grapes of Wrath*, as over Steinbeck generally, yet many would agree with Leithauser that "the chief wonder of the novel is that it's as good as it is. Steinbeck was a writer of such variable strengths and such uncertain instincts that any attempt at an epic novel would seem destined for failure. What probably saved *The Grapes of Wrath* was his reservoir of rage. . . . The book is a call to arms, and it manages, in the enormity of the iniquity it exposes, to render irrelevant many of the aesthetic qualifications it raises along the way."

Partly under the strain of his unwished-for fame, Steinbeck's twelve-year marriage to Carol Henning, who had been his best critic, dissolved in 1942; the following year he married Gwyndolyn Conger, a singer who became the mother of his two children; but it was not a happy marriage and they were divorced in 1948. Although most have argued that Steinbeck's decline began immediately after *The Grapes of Wrath*, he did produce several popular works in the 1940s, notably *Sea of Cortez*, a collaboration with Ricketts containing a fascinating account of their travel and research along with some muddy philosophizing, and *Cannery Row*, an almost plotless novel about a varied group of characters living amid the sardine canneries of Monterey before the Second World War. *Cannery Row* has sometimes been dismissed as an exercise in nostalgia, but some critics consider it Steinbeck's last successful work. In *Western American Literature* Stanley Alexander compared it favorably to the somewhat similar *Tortilla Flat*, observing that "the differences are owing to a superior conception of style and its appropriateness to content rather than to any basic change in the intensity of [Steinbeck's] hatred of artificiality in society.

Such relative successes of the 1940s as *Sea of Cortez*, *Cannery Row*, and perhaps *The Pearl* were not enough to stave off the decline of Steinbeck's reputation that set in after *The Grapes of Wrath*. These works appeared amid a string of unequivocal failures—*The Moon Is Down, Bombs Away, The Wayward Bus, Burning Bright*—that only hardened the critical animus against him. Nor did Steinbeck help his case with the publication in 1952 of *East of Eden*, a Bible-tortured epic of rival California families in the early part of the century. He himself saw this as his crowning achievement. Instead, it was regarded as an almost unmitigated disaster and even now is remembered more for the performance of James Dean in the film version (1955) than for whatever literary merit it may possess. The critical onslaught against Steinbeck, continuing apace throughout the 1950s, reached unusually rancorous heights when, to the surprise of everyone, including the author, he was awarded the Nobel Prize for Literature in 1962. Steinbeck bore the attacks as stoically as he could, but he wrote no more fiction after winning the Nobel, and it is no doubt true, as John Sutherland wrote in the *London Review of Books*, that "America's treatment of Steinbeck was spiteful during the man's life and remains graceless." Unfortunately, Steinbeck's books of the 1950s and 1960s—*Sweet Thursday, The Short Reign of Pippin IV, The Winter of Our Discontent, Travels with Charley*—were difficult to defend, and his hawkish support of the Vietnam War disillusioned many who remembered him as a champion of social justice in the 1930s. One of his last projects was a retelling of Malory's *Morte d'Arthur*, a revered book of his childhood. Though he abandoned the project, it might have been one of his better works. Reviewing the posthumously published sections in the *New York Times Book Review*, John Gardner wrote, "The fact that he lacked the heart to finish the book, or even put what he did complete into one style and tone, is exactly the kind of petty modern tragedy he hated. The idea was magnificent—so is much of the writing."

After the mid-1940s Steinbeck lived in New York City and in Sag Harbor, Long Island. This change from the California that had nurtured him and provided the setting for most of his work, wrote Warren French, "was accompanied by an undeniable deterioration in his imaginative power." His third marriage, to Elaine Scott, was a contented one, and despite his creative disappointments, he never lapsed into the alcoholism or depression that claimed some of his more esteemed rivals. In spite of recent attempts by his biographers to elevate him to the front ranks of American literature, Steinbeck, as Harold Bloom has claimed, "is not one of the inescapable American novelists of our century; he cannot be judged in close relation to Cather, Dreiser, and Faulkner. . . . Yet there are no canonical standards worthy of human respect that could exclude *The Grapes of Wrath* from a serious reader's esteem. Compassionate narrative that addresses itself so directly to the great social questions of its era is simply too substantial a human achievement to be dismissed."

Steinbeck's papers are in the libraries of Stanford University, San Jose State University, the University of California at Berkeley, the University of Texas at Austin, and the John Steinbeck Library in Salinas, California.

PRINCIPAL WORKS: *Novels*—Cup of Gold: A Life of Henry Morgan, Buccaneer, 1929; The Pastures of Heaven, 1932; To a God Unknown, 1933; Tortilla Flat, 1935; In Dubious Battle, 1936; Of Mice and Men, 1937; The Red Pony, 1937; The Grapes of Wrath, 1939; The Moon Is Down, 1942; Cannery Row, 1945; The Wayward Bus, 1947; The Pearl, 1947; Burning Bright: A Play in Story Form, 1950; East of Eden, 1952; Sweet Thursday, 1954; The Short Reign of Pippin IV: A Fabrication, 1957; The Winter of Our Discontent, 1961. *Short stories*—The Long Valley, 1947. *Drama*—Of Mice and Men: A Play in Three Acts, 1937; The Moon Is Down: A Play in Two Parts, 1942; Burning Bright: A Play in Three Acts, 1951. *Adaptation*—The Acts of King Arthur and His Noble Knights: From the Winchester Manuscripts of Thomas Malory and Other Sources (ed. C. Horton) 1976. *Nonfiction*—(with E. F. Ricketts) Sea of Cortez: A Leisurely Journal of Travel and Research, 1941; Bombs Away: The Story of a Bomber Team, 1942; A Russian Journal, 1948; Once There Was a War, 1948; (with E. F. Ricketts) The Log from the Sea of Cortez: The Narrative Portion of the Book "The Sea of Cortez," 1951; Travels with Charley: In Search of America, 1962; America and Americans, 1966. *Journals and correspondence*—Journal of a Novel: The East of Eden Letters, 1969; Steinbeck: A Life in Letters (ed. E. Steinbeck and R. Wallsten) 1975; Working Days: The Journals of The Grapes of Wrath, 1938–1941 (ed. R DeMott) 1988. *Anthologies*—The Portable Steinbeck (ed. P. Covici) 1946, rev. ed. 1971; The Short Novels of John Steinbeck, 1981.

ABOUT: Astro, R. John Steinbeck and Edward F. Ricketts: The Shaping of a Novelist, 1973; Astro, R. and Hayashi, T. (eds.) John Steinbeck: The Man and His Work, 1971; Benson, J. J. Looking for Steinbeck's Ghost, 1988; Benson, J. J. (ed.) The Short Novels of John Steinbeck: Critical Essays with a Checklist to Steinbeck Criticism, 1990; Benson, J. J. The True Adventures of John Steinbeck, Writer, 1984; Bode, C. (ed.) The Young Rebel in American Literature, 1959; Coers, D. V. John Steinbeck as Propagandist: The Moon Is Down Goes to War, 1991; Davis, R. M. (ed.) Steinbeck: A Collection of Critical Essays, 1972; Davis, R. M. (ed.) Twentieth Century Interpretations: The Grapes of Wrath, 1982; Ditsky, J. (ed.) Critical Essays on Steinbeck's The Grapes of Wrath, 1989; Enea, S. and Lynch, A. With Steinbeck in the Sea of Cortez, 1991; Fensch, T. (ed.) Conversations with John Steinbeck, 1988; Fensch, T. Steinbeck and Covici: The Story of a Friendship, 1979; Ferrell, K. John Steinbeck: The Voice of the Land, 1986; Fontenrose, J. John Steinbeck: An Introduction and Interpretation, 1963;

French, W. John Steinbeck, 1961, 2nd ed. 1975; Hayashi, T. John Steinbeck: A Dictionary of His Fictional Characters, 1976; Hayashi, T. John Steinbeck: The Years of Greatness, 1936–1939, 1993; Hughes, R. S. John Steinbeck: A Study of the Short Fiction, 1989; Ito, T. John Steinbeck, 1994; Knox, M. and Rodriguez, M. Steinbeck's Street: Cannery Row, 1989; Levant, H. The Novels of John Steinbeck: A Critical Study, 1974; Lewis, C. and Britch, C. Rediscovering Steinbeck: Revisionist Views of His Art, Politics, and Intellect, 1989; McCarthy P. John Steinbeck, 1980; Millichap, J. R. Steinbeck and Film, 1983; Moore, H. T. The Novels of John Steinbeck: A First Critical Study, 1939; Owens, L. John Steinbeck's Re-Vision of America, 1985; Parini, J. John Steinbeck: A Biography, 1994; Tedlock, E. W. and Wickers, C. V. (eds.) Steinbeck and His Critics: A Record of Twenty-Five Years, 1957; Timmerman, J. H. John Steinbeck's Fiction: The Aesthetics of the Road Taken, 1986; Valjean, N. John Steinbeck, the Errant Knight: An Intimate Biography of His California Years, 1975; Watt, F. W. John Steinbeck, 1962; Williams, S. John Steinbeck, 1991; Wyatt, D (ed.) New Essays on The Grapes of Wrath, 1990; Writers at Work: The Paris Review Interviews, Fourth Series, 1976. *Bibliography*—De Mott, R. Steinbeck's Reading: A Catalogue of Books Owned and Borrowed, 1984; Hayashi, T. A New Steinbeck Bibliography, 1929–1971, 1973; Hayashi, T. A New Steinbeck Bibliography, 1971–1981, 1983. *Periodicals*—London Review of Books May 12, 1994; New York Times December 21, 1968; New York Times Book Review October 24, 1976; Steinbeck Quarterly 1969– ; Western American Literature 2, 1968.

**STEKEL, WILHELM** (1868–June 25, 1942), Austrian psychoanalyst and writer, was born in Bukovina, Romania, then part of the Austrian empire. His father was an orthodox Jew who became a freethinker. Both parents were easy-going, and Stekel recorded his debt to his "bookish" mother, in particular, for teaching him the "value of training by love."

Stekel was one of the analysts closest to Sigmund Freud, the founder of psychoanalysis, in its early days. At one time Freud valued him highly. Stekel made a special study of the role symbolism played in the formation of dreams. This is still recognized by the historians of psychoanalysis.

Stekel, after a slow start at school—he wrote poetry and composed music—gained his medical qualifications from the University of Vienna. He started work, after military service, in the Krafft-Ebing clinic. Krafft-Ebing was not a Freudian, but he was an enlightened clinician, under whom Stekel gained useful experience.

In order to marry, Stekel went into practice as a general physician. (His first marriage, which produced a son and a daughter, ended in divorce.) Ernest Jones, Freud's biographer, wrote:

"He began to practise psychoanalysis in 1903, and was the only member of the [Vienna Psycho-Analytical] Society [previously the Psychological Wednesday Evening Society] who referred to Freud by his surname instead of Herr Professor. The fourth of these earliest followers [the first two were Kahane and Reitler] was Alfred Adler. . . . Stekel may be accorded the honour, together with Freud, of having founded the first psycho-analytic society." Stekel became editor of the Society's journal, the *Zentralblatt*.

In 1910 both Stekel and Adler—and to a lesser extent the other Viennese analysts—"angrily opposed" (Jones continued) "the nomination of Swiss analysts [Jung and Honegger] to the position of President and Secretary, their own long and faithful service being ignored." On this occasion Freud managed to calm Stekel down, and the latter agreed to the appointment of Jung; but two years later the final break came. Jones wrote: "The trouble Stekel gave Freud was of quite a different nature from that provided by Adler. Stekel had none of Adler's heaviness, and far from being engrossed in theory alone, he had very little interest in it." Jones and others referred to Stekel at this time as empirical, "above all practical" and with ready access to the unconscious motivations of his patients. Freud "freely admitted" that Stekel was more gifted than he himself was in the matter of making symbolic interpretations.

Yet Stekel lacked the faculty of self-criticism. When in 1911 he published *Die Sprach des Traums* (translated in 1917 as *The Technique of Dream Interpretation*), Freud was, in Jones's word, "mortified" "in spite of the new contributions it makes." As Jones (whose account is supported elsewhere) wrote: Stekel was "a born journalist in the pejorative sense." He enjoyed lying, thought it a great joke to do so, and made no bones about it. He also, for all his verve, lacked the conscience of a scientist. The "verities communicated," as Jones quaintly put it, were for him secondary. Yet, despite his carelessness, his fellow-analysts at first liked him. Freud told a friend: "He's only a trumpeter, but still I'm fond of him." Stekel's arrogance—"I'm here to make new discoveries; other people can prove them, just as they like!"—seemed more innocent than actually roguish. Once Stekel wrote an interesting paper about the psychological significance of names, in which he went through a list of patients whose names had profoundly affected their lives. Freud asked him how he could possibly consider publishing the actual names. Stekel responded: "I made them all up!" Freud forbade him to publish the paper in any journal connected with the Vienna society. Stekel, quite unabashed, and not to be put down, issued it elsewhere.

The final break came when Stekel began to believe that he had surpassed Freud. The former had been neglecting the reviewing side of the *Zentralblatt*, and Freud proposed to appoint an analyst Stekel greatly disliked, Viktor Tausk, to supervise this department. Stekel said that he would not allow Tausk to have anything to do with "his" journal. . . . Freud at last defied his old friend, and in a huff Stekel resigned from the Vienna Society. Freud then called him an "unbearable fellow," and later even described him as a "case of moral insanity."

This is sadly illustrative of the difficulties Stekel made for himself, owing to lack of self-control and indifference to the impression he made on others. He thereafter frequently exaggerated his contribution to Freud's own thinking, declaring that he had first thought of the "death instinct"—and that Freud refused to give him credit for his discoveries. Yet, as Frank J. Sulloway wrote, Freud did indeed credit Stekel with having brought dream-symbolism to his attention (he added the acknowledgment to a new edition of his *Interpretation of Dreams* in 1925).

More pertinently, Stekel assimilated some of Adler's concepts. He came to regard the unconscious as over-emphasized by Freud, and interpreted many instances of "total repression" along Adlerian lines, utilizing the concept of "the blind eye": the patient, in his "life-lie" (another and perhaps more accurate name for Adler's "life-line" or "life-style") *chooses* to ignore his failures—they are not repressed beyond consciousness, but just wilfully "tucked away."

Stekel made a second marriage (he trained his wife to be an analyst), and worked in a Vienna hospital throughout World War I as psychiatrist and neurologist. His new method, with a drastically shortened treatment period, he officially described as "Active Analytic Therapy." He was often successful with patients, and many well-known people (the socio-political commentator and novelist John Gunther was the most notable) consulted him.

Stekel came to the United States in 1921 to lecture to the Neurological Society of Chicago. He made a reputation there, and not only in analytic circles. Reviewing his *Nervöse Angstzustände und ihre Behandlung* (1912, *Conditions of Nervous Anxiety and Their Treatment* in 1923), the reliable and informed Millais Culpin wrote, in *Nature*, that it was a "mixture of useful information with rash dogma." Many of the "case histories" drawn on for it were invented, or were conflations of several cases. Other books by Stekel, some on such subjects as homosexuality, sadism and masochism, and "perversions," were for "strictly restricted audiences": said to be "on sale to the medical profession only," but actually available in what is now called "adult" bookstores. Serious as the books tried to be, Stekel was well aware of their commercial value and was frowned upon by some for taking advantage of the laws then in vogue in the U.S. and Great Britain.

Stekel's technique is still remembered, and has had some influence. David Stafford-Clark (a celebrated psychiatrist, and author of the widely read and respected *What Freud Really Said*) described it thus: the "technique embraces the enterprising innovation of announcing beforehand that the treatment is to be limited in time to a certain fixed period . . . no matter what the outcome. Thereafter, whatever resistance is encountered, interpretation of that resistance is made at once, and in this way the patient is constantly thrown back upon the necessity for facing reasons for evading the issues involved, or dreading the feelings when they arise."

Stekel stated the case thus: "Day by day I attack the patient's system by storm, showing that he will get well . . . if only he will discard his fictive aims." The chief problem with this technique he also (perhaps unwittingly) stated: "my system requires the skill of a physician, a detective, and a diplomat rolled into one." As J.A.C. Brown ironically commented, "not all analysts are as clever or 'intuitive' as Stekel."

He returned to Austria in the early 1920s, and became director of the Medical School at the University of Vienna—the most stable period of his life. He was there until the *Anschluss*, when as a Jew, he had to escape to London. He was not (as a long declared antifascist) treated fairly by the immigration authorities, was in no position to turn to English Freudians for help, and was in any case by now seriously ill. In 1942, depressed, believing that he would soon become helpless, he checked into a London hotel and took his own life.

Stekel's autobiography, which for all its inaccuracies is his most interesting book, appeared in English in 1950. Bruno Bettleheim wrote of it, in the *American Journal of Sociology*, that it "sheds light on the personalities of the men who formed the first psychoanalytic society" and "characterizes the life of the educated classes in Vienna, particularly of Jewish physicians."

PRINCIPAL WORKS IN ENGLISH TRANSLATION: *Psychoanalytical subjects*—The Technique of Dream Interpretation (tr. J. E. Lind) 1917; The Beloved Ego: The Foundations of the New Study of the Psyche (tr. R. Gabler) 1921; The Depths of the Soul (tr. S. A. Tannenbaum) 1921; Bi-Sexual Love: The Homosexual Neurosis (tr. J. S. Van Teslaar) 1922; Twelve Essays on Sex and Psychoanalysis (ed. and tr. S. A. Tannenbaum) 1922; Sex and Dreams (tr. J. S. Van Teslaar) 1922; Disguises of Love (tr. R. Gabler) 1922; Conditions of Nervous Anxiety and Their Treatment (tr. R. Gabler) 1922; Peculiarities of Behaviour: Wandering Mania, Dipsomania, Cleptomania [sic], Pyromania and Other Impulsive Acts (tr. J. S. Van Teslaar) 1924; Sexual Aberrations: The Phenomenon of Fetishism in Sex (tr. S. Parker) 1930; A Primer for Mothers (tr. F. Ilmer) 1931; Marriage at the Crossroads (tr. A. D. Garman) 1931; Psychoanalysis and Suggestion Therapy (tr. J. S. Van Teslaar) 1932; Sadism and Masochism: The Psychology of Hatred (tr. L. Brink) 1935; Technique of Analytical Psychotherapy (tr. E. and C. Paul) 1939; The Meaning and Psychology of Dreams (tr. E. and C. Paul) 1943; Auto-Erotism: A Psychiatric Study of Onanism and Neurosis (tr. J. S. Van Teslaar) 1950; Patterns of Psychosexual Infantilism (ed. E. A. Gutheil) 1952; Impotence in the Male (tr. O. H. Boltz) 1959; Frigidity in Women (tr. J. S. Van Teslaar) 1962; Compulsion and Doubt (tr. E. A. Gutheil) 1962. *Autobiography*—Autobiography: The Life-Story of a Pioneer Psychoanalyst (ed. E. A. Gutheil) 1959.

ABOUT: Brown, J.A.C. Freud and the Post-Freudians, 1961; Hendrick, I. Facts and Theories of Psychoanalysis, 1954 (rev. ed. 1958); Jones, E. The Life and Work of Sigmund Freud, 1953–1957; Stafford-Clark, D. Psychiatry Today, 1952 (rev. ed. 1963); Stekel, W. Autobiography, 1959; Sulloway, F. J. Freud: Biologist of the Mind, 1979. *Periodicals*—American Journal of Sociology November 1950; Nature July 21, 1923.

**STEPHENS, JAMES** (February 1880?–December 26, 1950), Irish novelist and poet, was born in Dublin in obscure circumstances. It may even be that his father was not called Stephens. James Joyce said that, if he should die before finishing *Finnegans Wake*, then only James Stephens would be able to complete it. This was a profound tribute.

Stephens's own prose masterpiece *The Crock of Gold* has not yet been given the critical examination it deserves, and his other works in prose are still undervalued. Oliver St. John Gogarty claimed he was the "most cantative poet of his time." Writing

in *The Oxford Companion to Twentieth-Century Poetry*, Martin Seymour-Smith called him "a neglected figure" and remarked that his work "cries out for judicious selection, only partly fulfilled in *Collected Poems* (incomplete; 1954), or in *James Stephens: A Selection* (London, 1962; ed. Lloyd Frankenberg)."

Stephens may have known little about himself, since his father probably died when he was only two years old. He seems to have lived with his mother in various Dublin slums until he was about six. Then she married, or took up with another man, and he himself was shunted into the Meath Protestant Industrial School for Boys. This place was not quite an advertisement for Christianity. What is vital here is, of course, the effect on  the boy of being sent away by a mother who suddenly did not want him. By all accounts, he lost touch with her. She is a pervasive presence in all his work, in which he was unusually generous and positive toward her. Stephens's lies about himself were always charming and gentle; he desired to be known, publicly, for his literary achievements and for nothing else.

At some time he ran away from the Meath institution, and, according to one of his patrons, the fourth Earl Grey (quoted by Oliver St. John Gogarty in the *Dictionary of National Biography*) he had "been hungry for weeks as a boy," had "slept in the parks . . . fought with swans for a piece of bread (a good example of Stephens's poetic inventiveness) . . . tramped the roads . . . lived on the kindness of poor people who liked the queer little boy and [grew up with] the most independent spirit and with tireless energy, humour, inquisitiveness"; he was, continued Grey, "a born Bohemian, small in stature not more, even with elevators in his shoes, than four and a half feet high but quite big inside, large and roomy."

Stephens has been much criticized, even by those who recognize the extent of his achievement, for "playing the leprechaun." However, he did seem to be like a leprechaun. Leprechauns meant as much to Stephens as Blake's visions meant to him. As Gogarty, who knew him well, explained, his "large eyes and full throat, due to a goitre, prevented anyone from thinking of him as a dwarf although they often thought of him as a leprechaun and sometimes as a changeling. His eyes were those of genius . . . . His lack of inches gave him one advantage. He could cast off the conventions which bound ordinary people and become a gleeman, the most lyrical spirit of his time."

From about 1896 Stephens, who must have put himself through a peculiarly hard literary apprenticeship (as George Moore affirmed in *Hail and Farewell*, no one ever discovered how he had acquired his learning, but all wondered about it) was working in Dublin solicitors' offices as a clerk. In the period 1903–1913 he worked for Messrs Thomas Tighe, McCready, and Son, solicitors, of Merrion Square, as scrivener. A testimonial to "his industrious work in filing and indexing, as well as typing and shorthand," "mainly at correspondence," is now in the National Library of Ireland. He was "unestablished Registrar of the National Gallery of Ireland," from August 5, 1918, until January 18, 1925, when he resigned; but he was working at the National Gallery from 1915. By the good offices of Mary and Padraic Colum he made his first lecture-tour of America, where he was a great success, in 1925. He went there almost annually until 1937.

Stephens had endured such appalling hardships as a boy—as well as having been cruelly abandoned by his mother, a traumatic experience in itself—that he could never be quite well physically, or, in one sense mentally, for the rest of his life. From 1920 Stephens was troubled by severe gastric ulcers, for which he had to receive surgery on a number of occasions. In the words of Alan Denson, the editor of the letters of Stephens's chief mentor George Russell ("Æ"), the "surgical operations exasperated his tense nervous system, and his later years were marred by occasional unprovoked emotional storms, and physical weakness." He was looked after by many friends, who understood and cherished his genius and the great warmth of his heart (of which his books are so redolent); chief among these friends, aside from Æ ("What a door was opened to him when he met Æ!" wrote George Moore) were the editor Arthur Griffith, who published Stephens's first story in 1905 in his The United Irishman (this became Sinn Fein in 1906), and Dr. and Mrs. Thomas Bodkin (with whom he felt safe), who often took him in when he was troubled and afraid.

On December 19, 1908 Æ wrote to his friend the poet and hostess Katherine Tynan: "I have discovered a new young poet in a young fellow called James Stephens who has a real original note in him. He has had the devil of a time poor fellow. Works about fourteen hours a day for twenty shillings and is glad to get it. Was out of work for a year once and went hungry and homeless and was saved from starving by a woman who sold fruit from a stall. Good education for the soul sometimes but bad for the body."

The generous Æ, introduced Stephens to all the Irish writers he knew: Yeats, George Moore himself, Lady Gregory and others. They were delighted with him. His first novel, The Charwoman's Daughter, was published in 1912, after appearing serially in The Irish Review, as Mary, Mary, in 1911. The Crock of Gold followed in 1913, and The Demi-Gods in 1914. Indeed, most of Stephens's important work in prose was done before 1920. The Insurrection in Dublin in his (now neglected) account of the Easter Rising; Green Branches is an elegy on the same subject. His poems began to appear in The United Irishman; he had published eight collections by 1918. The later poetry, now neglected and almost unexamined or even read, is more evidently concerned with mystical subjects than the earlier.

In November 1918, in St. Bride's Ward in London, Stephens married Millicent Josephine (Gardiner) Kavanagh, by then a widow, the "Cynthia" of his writings. She had been deserted by her husband—a company director who had been by trade a master upholsterer—a decade earlier than this, and Stephens (who had previously been taken in by the married couple) set up house with her as early as 1908. Millicent Stephens had two daughters by her previous marriage; with Stephens she had a son, James Naoise, born in about 1912, who was tragically killed when he stepped on a live rail at a railway station near London on Christmas Eve, 1937; he, too is said to have been a "gifted writer." Mrs. Stephens died on December 18, 1960. The death of his son shattered Stephens and caused a further deterioration in his delicate health.

In America, wrote Denson, Stephens, under the stress of his illnesses, "could not be preserved from some lionizing whilst on tour. He could be wheedled into excessive boozing, became inflated and quarrelsome with his friends, and afterwards crushed by remorse instead of a hangover." With his closer friends, however, he was "always companionable." Until 1939 he had been an ardent Irish nationalist, and had learned Gaelic; but when World War II came he wrote to the London Times to distance himself from Irish neutrality, and specifically (as he would explain to friends) from De Valera's undying hatred for England. He was granted a Civil List pension in 1942.

He began writing, Patricia McFate observed on his own premise that "the art of prose-writing does not really need a murder to carry it." This conviction he acquired from a study of Wilde's A House of Pomegranates. He wrote the mock-novel Mary, Mary, which became The Charwoman's Daughter, with the notion that he might be "doing something which I conceived Wilde has tried, and perhaps failed to do." It is a fairy tale in which two Dublin characters, the Makebelieves, achieve happiness in accordance with the standards of the nineteenth-century-novel-with-the-happy-ending. This type of novel Stephens parodies. Also in this book are affectionate and accurately fanciful portraits of Yeats, Æ, and other Irish notables. The huge policeman who terrifies the indomitable old charwoman is none other than Blake's Nobodaddy, the moralistic and puritanical pseudo-God set up by unhappy, pleasure-fearing human beings in place of the real God (who, in their reading of the universe, partakes of much that is conventionally called "evil"). The Blakean nature of the enterprise is made obvious by one of the sayings in it: "Next to good the most valuable factor in life is evil."

The Crock of Gold used to be taken as a delightful but zanily incoherent fantasy. Thus, its admirer Walter de la Mare wrote, in a preface to a 1953 paperback reissue: "It is not a book at all, but a crazy patchwork, stitched zigzag loosely together—a kind of motley overall in which one may sit in one's bones on the verge of time and space and contemplate everything and nothing, the high gods, the ninety-six Graces and Man and Pan and Innocence . . . ." But Barton Friedman (in Eire-Ireland), Hilary Pyle, Patricia McFate, John Cronin and other critics demonstrated that the work is based on Blakean "theology." Hilary Pyle has quoted from an article Stephens published in the *Irish Review* in the year that *The Crock of Gold* appeared, in which he said that Blake did not "postulate a Trinity but a quarternity, in his Republic. His battlefield is the human body; the protagonists under the titles of Urizen, Luvah, Tharmas and Urthona, are Powers, Intellect, Love, Spirit and Matter."

Stephens put Blake's gnosticism to a uniquely comic and contemporary use, taking the innocent viewpoint of the child (as Blake himself did) to look at the world. The main subject is simple enough: the God Angus Og, with the help of the Thin Woman of Inis Magrath, wins the peasant girl Caitlin from Pan, her ravisher. The crock of gold of the title is what the leprechauns have collected from the clippings of money they have stolen from houses: any leprechaun who is captured by menfolk has to have a crock of gold, in order to ransom himself. That this represents Stephens's view of the predicament of the artist, or poet, or mystic, goes without saying. It is the Philosopher (significantly in Stephens's world-view) who gives away the secret of where the crock of gold is hidden, to Meehawl MacMurrachu; the latter steals it, thus setting off all the trouble, and in particular causing Caitlin to become susceptible to the lures of Pan.

The last two of Stephens's major prose works (*The Demi-Gods* is the fairy-tale version of *The Charwoman's Daughter*, which had parodied the realistic novel), *Deirdre* and *In the Land of Youth*, were to have formed a series of five books in which Stephens would construct a modern mythology. But his health was not up to it. However, those tales in the two books he did manage to write were justly compared to both Homer and to the stories in the *Mabinogion*, the Welsh epic.

Stephens as a poet could, on occasions, be guilty of the "rough versification" of which Moore accused him in *Hail and Farewell*. However, at his best he could resemble Blake without ever being in danger of imitating him. Other particular influences were Wordsworth and Emerson. A poem such as "The Snare," which Stephens dedicated to Æ, demonstrates Stephens's poetic gifts at their best. This poignant poem begins "I hear a sudden cry of pain! / There is a rabbit in a snare: / Now I hear the cry again, / But I cannot tell from where" and ends: "And I cannot find the place / where his paw is in the snare: / Little one! Oh, little one! / I am searching everywhere." The Stephens of the later poetry, much of which is to be found in the 1954 *Collected Poems*, and in *Strict Joy* (1931) and in the depressed but often grand and mysterious *Kings and the Moon* (1938) has not yet, owing to its too unfamiliar subject-matter, been fully or thoroughly assessed.

Recordings of all Stephen's famous BBC radio talks (he was also among the first writers to be televised in Great Britain, from Alexandra Palace in 1937) have been preserved, and some have been issued commercially in America. Some of them are in *Uncollected Prose*. The portrait in oils of him by

Patrick J. Tuohy (National Gallery of Ireland) was believed by his widow and by Padraic Colum to be the most faithful to life; Æ, Max Beerbohm (a caricature), Sir William Rothenstein and Julietta Huxley all left drawings of him. Æ wrote of him (in a letter to John Quinn of May 26, 1912), that he was one of the "most vivid, vital and delightful" persons known to him, "bigger in himself than Synge," and "charged with endless grit and fire."

PRINCIPAL WORKS: *Collections and selections*—James Stephens: A Selection, 1962 (ed. L. Frankenberg) (in U.S.: A James Stephens Reader) James, Seumas and Jacques: Unpublished Writings; 1964. *Novels*—The Charwoman's Daughter 1912 (in U.S.: Mary, Mary); The Crock of Gold, 1913; The Demi-Gods, 1914; (as James Esse) Hunger: A Dublin Story, 1918; Deirdre, 1923; In the Land of Youth, 1924. *Short stories*—Here are Ladies, 1913; Etched in Moonlight, 1928; How St. Patrick Saves the Irish, 1931. *Other*—The Insurrection in Dublin, 1916; Arthur Griffith: Journalist and Statesman, 1922; Little Things, 1924; On Prose and Verse: Two Essays, 1928; Dublin Letters, 1928; Optimist, 1929; Uncollected Prose, (ed. P. McFate) 1983. *Poetry*—Insurrections, 1909; The Lonely God, 1909; The Hill of Vision, 1912; Five New Poems, 1913; The Adventures of Seumas Begg: The Rocky Road to Dublin, 1915; Songs from the Clay, 1915; Green Branches, 1916; Reincarnations, 1918 (adaptations from Gaelic poets); A Poetry Recital, 1925; Collected Poems, 1926 (rev. and expanded 1954); The Outcast, 1929; Theme and Variation, 1930; Strict Joy, 1931; Kings and the Moon, 193. *Drama*—Julia Elizabeth: A Comedy in One Act, 1929. *As editor*—Irish Fairy Tales, 1920. *Letters*—Letters, (ed. R. J. Finneran) 1974; Some Unpublished Letters from Æ to James Stephens, 1979.

ABOUT: Æ (George Russell) Imaginations and Reveries, 1915; Bramsbäck, B. James Stephens: A Literary and Bibliographical Study, 1959; Colum, P. On James Stephens, 1977; Cronin, J. Irish Fiction 1919–1940, 1992; Denson, A. (ed.) Letters from Æ, 1961, Dictionary of National Biography 1941–1950, 1959; Finneran, R. J. The Olympian and the Leprechaun: W. B. Yeats and James Stephens, 1978; O'Connor, F. A Short History of Irish Literature, 1967; Hamilton, I. (ed.) Oxford Companion to Twentieth-Century Literature, 1994; Hogan, R. (ed.) Macmillan Dictionary of Irish Literature, 1979; Martin, A. James Stephens, 1977; McFate, P. The Writings of James Stephens: Variations on a Theme of Love, 1979; Moore, G. Hail and Farewell, 1911; Pyle, H. James Stephens: His Work and an Account of his Life, 1965; Robinson, L. (ed.) Lady Gregory's Journals 1916–1930, 1947; Seymour-Smith, M. Macmillan Guide to Modern World Literature, 1986; Swinnerton, F. The Georgian Literary Scene, 1951. *Periodicals*—Atlantic Monthly April 1958; Eire-Ireland I, 3, 1966; Forum January 1915; Irish Writing March 1951; New York Times December 27, 1950; Studies in Anglo-Irish Literature, 1982; Times (London) December 27, 1950.

**STEPHENS, ROBERT NEILSON** (July 22, 1867–January 20, 1906), American dramatist and novelist, was born in New Bloomfield, Pennsylvania, was the son of James Andrew Stephens, a teacher who died when Stephens was nine, and Rebecca (Neilson) Stephens, also a teacher. Soon after graduating, Stephens worked as a stenographer for the Pennsylvania Railroad in Philadelphia and then joined the staff of the  *Philadelphia Press*, which he called "a cradle of authors," and where he soon became the drama critic.

In 1893 he began writing melodramas, the first

being a five-act comedy-drama produced at New York's Lyceum Theatre (January 1895) entitled *On the Bowery*, an account of Steve Brodie, a real-life heroic bridge jumper and swimmer who had jumped from the Brooklyn Bridge.

Stephens's passion for history and romance became even more apparent a year later with the drama *An Enemy to the King*, based on the recently discovered memoirs of the Sieur de la Tournoire, which recounted the adventures of a young French nobleman at the court of Henry III. Stephens set *The Continental Dragoon* (1898) in the American Revolution in an estate north of New York City; he turned it into the play *Miss Elizabeth's Prisoner*.

*A Gentleman Player* (1899) introduced Shakespeare in person—and sold well enough to allow Stephens to travel to England for several months of intensive study for subsequent novels, including *Philip Winwood* (1900), a sketch of the domestic history of an American captain in the Revolution told by his enemy, Herbert Russell; and *Captain Ravenshaw* (1901) a romance of Elizabethan London. In his preface to this work, Stephens wrote: "The characters are every-day people of the London of the time, and the scenes in which they move are the street, the tavern, the citizen's house and garden, the shop, the river, the public resort—such places as the ordinary reader would see if a miracle turned backed time and transported him to London in the closing part of Elizabeth's reign. The atmosphere of that place and time, as one may find it best in the less known and more realistic comedies of Shakespeare's contemporaries, in prose narratives and anecdotes, and in the records left of actual transactions, strikes us of the twentieth century as a little strange, somewhat of a world which we can hardly take to be real."

The *New York Times* called the stories in *Tales from Bohemia*, "vivid bits of the kaleidoscopic life of New York," adding, "There is little plot in any of them. They derive their interest from their air of truthfulness and from the author's method of bringing out their psychological and dramatic values."

PRINCIPAL WORKS: The Life and Adventures of Steve Brodie, 1894; An Enemy to the King, 1897; The Continental Dragoon, 1898; The Road to Paris, 1898; A Gentleman Player, 1899; Philip Winwood, 1900; Captain Ravenshaw, 1901; The Mystery of Murray Davenport, 1903; The Bright Face of Danger, 1904; The Flight of Georgiana, 1905; (with G. H. Westley) Clementina's Highway, 1907; Tales from Bohemia, 1908; A Soldier of Valley Forge (unfinished, completed by G. E. Theodore Roberts) 1911.

ABOUT: Starrett, V. Buried Caesars; Stephens, R. N. *Preface to Captain Ravenshaw*, 1901. *Periodicals*—Independent May 11, 1911; New York Times January 21, 1906; October 26, 1907; November 14, 1908; Outlook September 30, 1905; Saturday Review of Literature January 31, 1948.

## STEPTOE, LYDIA. See BARNES, DJUNA

## STERLING, GEORGE (December 1, 1869–November 17, 1926), American poet, was born in Sag Harbor, Long Island, the oldest of the nine children of a wealthy physician, Dr. George Ansel Sterling, and the former Mary Parker Havens. His father was descended from early English settlers; his mother was the daughter of a Sag Harbor whaling captain. Dr. Sterling became a convert to Roman Catholicism when the boy was seventeen. The family followed suit and George Sterling was sent to a Catholic college, St. Charles, in Ellicott City, Maryland. His father hoped that he would become a priest, but he had no vocation for that or, it seemed, for anything else. Restless and rebellious, he renounced the church and the college in 1890. The family despatched him to work as personal secretary to his mother's brother, a real estate magnate in Oakland, California.

Sterling took at once to the Bohemian style of the San Francisco Bay area, and lived there for most of the rest of his life. He spent his days reluctantly in his uncle's office, his eve-nings in the company of artists and writers, generally in the convivial circle around the poet Joaquin Miller, famously generous with his homemade liquor. Under these influences, Sterling began to write poetry of his own. In 1892 he met Ambrose Bierce, whose work he admired. Bierce reciprocated, and became the young poet's mentor. Until Bierce disappeared into Mexico in 1913, Sterling submitted to him virtually every poem he wrote, for better or worse accepting all or most of the master's revisions and suggestions. Sterling was married in 1896 to Caroline Rand, a stenographer in his uncle's office.

A first collection, *The Testimony of the Suns*, was published in 1903 in San Francisco. It had a respectful reception, but Sterling's reputation was a local one until, in 1907, his long poem "A Wine of Wizardry" appeared in *Cosmopolitan*. It evokes the journey of Fancy, personified as a winged female figure, through a macabre fantasy world. Bierce provided an extraordinary preface, which compared the poem to Milton's *Comus*, and introduced Sterling as "a very great poet—incomparably the greatest that we have on this side of the Atlantic." Critics who demurred were subjected to Bierce's savage wit. Such excessive claims were a mixed blessing, but won Sterling notoriety at least. His poems began to appear in journals as various as the *Smart Set* and *Poetry*, though he found no eastern publisher for his books until 1923.

In 1908, "freedom money" from his aunt enabled Sterling to leave her husband's employment. He bought land at Carmel, where an artists' colony was growing up, built a cabin, and thereafter devoted himself to writing, drink, and sex. Tall, slim, and handsome, with a marked, resemblance to Dante, of which he made the most, Sterling was generous and gentle, romantic and witty, with a great talent for friendship. He was called "the King of Bohemia" and (by Bierce) its "High Panjandrum." H. L. Mencken, Robinson Jeffers (of whom he wrote a biography), and Upton Sinclair were all among his friends. When Bierce's work as a Hearst journalist took him off to Washington, Sterling transferred his allegiance to Jack London, with whom he toured the bars, brothels, and burlesque houses of the Barbary Coast. It was too much, in the end, for his wife to bear. She divorced him in 1915. Sterling lived for a time in the East, but returned to California in 1918, after his wife's suicide.

His reputation at this time was quite high. During the last part of his life he lived at the Bohemian Club in San Francisco. The Club conducted an annual "High Jinks" at "The Grove," its summer encampment on the Russian River. Sterling wrote several of the "Grove Plays" produced on these occasions. He also wrote two "dramatic poems." One of these, *Lilith*, about the destructive power of sexual desire, was admired by Theodore Dreiser and others. But as his work began to go out of fashion, his drinking grew ever heavier, and induced acute gastric pain. In 1926, shortly before his fifty-seventh birthday, Sterling took cyanide and died at the Bohemian Club.

Sterling was a lyric poet combining old-fashioned poetic diction with extravagant imagery and a "decadent" nihilism. The effect is reminiscent less of Poe or Baudelaire, than of their *fin de siècle* imitators. He was probably at his best in short poems that concentrated his thinking, especially in his sonnets, of which the most famous is "The Black Vulture."

In *Americans and the California Dream*, Kevin Starr has discussed Sterling specifically as "the laureate of California." He attributes Sterling's failure not to Bierce but to California's escapist poetic tradition of "defensive aetheticism." According to Starr, Sterling sought "emotional solace in poetry, the magic of word-music and the elusive quest for Beauty, capitalized and Neoplatonic. . . . In the long run his poetry would turn out to be tragically passé, and in provincial gratitude Californians overrated it scandalously; but for a brief moment, in his own time, before the verdict of history was in, George Sterling held his own. Singlehandedly, he revived poetry in California, opening it up to new ranges of consideration."

Charles Angott edited *A Centenary Memoir-Anthology* in 1969, and Sterling's *Selected Poems* and the posthumous *Sonnets to Craig* were reprinted in the 1970s.

PRINCIPAL WORKS: *Poetry*—The Testimony of the Suns, 1903; A Wine of Wizardry, 1907; The House of Orchids, 1911; Beyond the Breakers, 1914; The Evanescent City, 1915; The Caged Eagle, 1916; The Binding of the Beast, and Other War Poems, 1917; Thirty-Five Sonnets, 1917; Sails and Mirage, 1921; Selected Poems, 1923; Sonnets to Craig, 1928; Poems to Vera, 1938; After Sunset, 1939. *Drama*—The Triumph of Bohemia, 1907; The Twilight of the Kings, 1918; Lilith, 1919 (dramatic poem); Rosamund, 1920 (dramatic poem); Truth, 1923. *Other*—Robinson Jeffers, 1926 (biography); George Sterling: A Centenary Memoir-Anthology (ed. C. Angoff) 1969. *As translator*—The Play of Everyman (new version by Hugo von Hofmannsthal) 1917. *As editor*—(with others) Continent's End: An Anthology of Contemporary California Poets, 1925.

ABOUT: Austin, M. Earth Horizon, 1932; Benediktsson, T. E. George Sterling, 1980; Bierce, A. Letters (ed. B. C. Pope) 1921; De Ford, M. A. They Were San Franciscans, 1941; Dickson, S. San Francisco Is Your Home, 1947; Dictionary of American Biography, 1935; Dictionary of Literary Biography Vol. 54, 1987; Everson, W. Archtype West, 1976; Gregory, H. and Za-

turenska, M. History of American Poetry, 1900–1940, 1946; Holliday, R. C. Literary Lanes and Other Byeways, 1925; Noel, J. Footloose in Arcadia: A Personal Record of Jack London, George Sterling, and Ambrose Bierce, 1940; Sinclair, U. Money Writes!, 1927; Starr, K. American and the California Dream: 1850–1915, 1973; Sterling, G. A Centenary Memoir-Anthology (ed. C. Angoff) 1969; Untermeyer, L. American Poetry Since 1900, 1924. *Bibliography*—Johnson, C. A Bibliography of the Writings of George Sterling, 1931; Longtin, R.C. Three Writers of the Far West, 1980. *Periodicals*—American Book Collector November–December 1973; American Mercury May 1927; Bookman September 1927; California Historical Society Quarterly June 1961; September 1967; Literary Digest December 11, 1926; Literary Review Winter 1971–72; Markham Review May 1968, Winter 1979; New York Times November 18, 1926; Overland Monthly November and December 1927; Poetry March 1916, January 1927; Romanticist 1 1977, 3 1979, 4–5 1982; San Francisco Chronicle November 18, 1926; San Francisco Review November 1926, December 1926; Saturday Review of Literature July 27, 1929; August 10, 1929.

**STERN, G(LADYS) B(RONWYN)** (June 17, 1890–September 19, 1973), English novelist, short story writer, and memoirist, was born in London, the second daughter of Albert Stern, who was in the jewel trade, and Elizabeth (Schwabacher) Stern. When she was fourteen her parents lost much of their money in a South African diamond venture and were forced to sell their home. Two years later Stern left Notting Hill High School to  travel with her family to Europe; she finished her schooling in Wiesbaden, Germany, and Montreux, Switzerland. Back in London, she studied for two years at the Academy of Dramatic Art, in the meantime writing short stories and working as a free-lance journalist. Stern had, in fact, been writing since childhood; her first play, written at the age of seven, was put on (with herself as star) in the billiard room of her home. Her first published novel, *Pantomime*, was written in her early twenties; her third novel, *Two and Threes*, established her reputation as a writer of witty and vivacious if not profound fiction, laced with ironic humor. Under the bright, clever comedy of *Children of No Man's Land* (published in the United States as *Debatable Ground*) there is, however, a serious theme: the dilemmas of an English-Jewish family during World War I forced to confront their German origin. The novel was the prelude to a five-volume semiautobiographical family saga that properly begins in *Tents of Israel* (*The Matriarch* in its American edition). A novel in the *Forsyte Saga* vein, it was, appropriately, dedicated to John Galsworthy. The series deals with the turbulent affairs of the interrelated Rakonitz and Czelovar families, a large, cosmopolitan, Jewish clan, of Viennese origin, with branches in Paris and London. As Stern explained: "Maximilian Rakonitz was the name I gave one of my three uncles in those family chronicles, half truth, half invention, which I have written round the personality of my great-aunt, the Matriarch," in real life Anastasia Schwabacher, who lived to be ninety years old. "I was not very deeply attached to the Matriarch. She was too despotic." In 1929 Mrs. Patrick Campbell played in *The Matriarch*, Stern's dramatization of *Children of No Man's Land* and *Tents of Israel*. The others in the series are *A Deputy Was King*, *Mosaic, Shining and Free*, and *The Young Matriarch*, in which last Toni Rakonitz (thought to be a self-portrait of the author) takes over the family. As a whole, the work, with its kaleidoscopic activity and enormous cast of complex, highly articulate characters (each vividly drawn), demonstrates Stern's creative energy. The Matriarch novels remain her best-known fiction, well received by contemporary readers and reviewers (despite some objections to their loquaciousness), and of interest to later feminist critics for their portrayals of women who manage to take control of their own circumstances. Both *The Matriarch* and *A Deputy Was King* have been reprinted in the Virago series of works by women novelists.

It has been pointed out that all Stern's fiction adhered to old-fashioned narrative techniques. As Rebecca West put it: "Miss Stern has one of the queerest talents among contemporary novelists, for she lives by choice on a mental desert rich in natural beauties but unvisited by culture. She simply does not care for any of the literary conventions of to-day" (*New Statesman*). But the author's rejoinder was that she preferred to examine life on a (relatively) small, intimate scale, where one could more easily see what was going on. Whatever her scale, her output—in fiction alone—was large, with an infinite variety of plots and characters. Besides the Rakonitz novels, a large number of her other books dealt with family life and relationships. Among this subgenre were *Long-Lost Father*, which was made into a film in the United States in 1934, and *The Reasonable Shores*, set in World War II England and a good example of Stern's delight in family give-and-take. *The Back Seat, The Donkey Shoe*, and *For All We Know* are specifically about theater families. Stern's output includes a mystery story, *The Shortest Night*—an ingenious thriller despite a somewhat banal houseparty setting—and two novels about dogs. *The Dark Gentleman* and *The Ugly Dachshund*, with their whiff of satire directed at the Legs (humans), almost manage to avoid sentimentality and whimsy. The latter, about a Great Dane puppy, a misfit in a family of dachshunds, was the basis for a 1965 Walt Disney movie. Critics have agreed that as Stern went on (and she wrote her last novel, *Promise Not to Tell*, in her seventies), her stories became more determinedly bright and amusing, more contrived and inconsequential—as in *Little Red Horses* (*The Rueful Mating* in America), about two child prodigies in love; or *The Woman in the Hall*, a potentially serious story of a con artist, which Stern was content to present simply as entertainment. The latter was filmed in England in 1941.

Stern's many passions included good food and wine (*Bouquet* describes a wine-tasting tour in France), boating and swimming, gardening, stimulating conversation, and the work of Jane Austen

and Robert Louis Stevenson. In *No Son of Mine* she wrote a fictionalized biography, for young readers, of the Scottish writer, from the point of view of a man posing as his son.

Interspersed throughout all Stern's writing were her volumes of memoirs, books full of engaging chat about her life in city and country, in Italy, in New York and Hollywood. They are as much "commonplace books" recording travels, good company, and talk as they are conventional autobiography (Elizabeth Janeway, *New York Times*). Two of the volumes are devoted specifically to her conversion to Roman Catholicism in 1947; *All in Good Time* and *The Way It Turned Out* are musings about her experience, neither ecstatic in tone, nor proselytizing.

In 1919 G. B. Stern was married to Geoffrey Lisle Holdsworth, a New Zealand journalist who had made her acquaintance through their friend Noël Coward. (Stern helped Coward select the period songs for his 1931 play *Cavalcade*.) They were subsequently divorced. During the blitz in 1941 the author's London flat and library were destroyed and she moved to the country. Later she took up permanent residence in a cottage in Wallingford, Berkshire.

PRINCIPAL WORKS: *Fiction*—Pantomine, a Novel, 1914; See-Saw, 1914; Twos and Threes, 1916; Grand Chain, 1917; A Marrying Man, 1918; Children of No Man's Land, 1919 (in U.S.: Debatable Ground); Larry Munro, 1920 (in U.S.: The China Shop); The Room, 1922; The Back Seat, 1923; Smoke Rings, 1923 (stories); Tents of Israel, a Chronicle, 1924 (in U.S.: The Matriarch, a Chronicle); Thunderstorm, 1925; A Deputy Was King, 1926; The Dark Gentleman, 1927; Jack a'Manory, 1927; Debonair: The Story of Persephone, 1928; Modesta, 1929; Petruchio, 1929; The Slower Judas, 1929 (stories); Mosaic, 1930; The Shortest Night, 1931; Little Red Horses, 1932 (in U.S.: The Rueful Mating); Long-Lost Father, a Comedy, 1932; The Rakonitz Chronicles, 1932 [Children of No Man's Land, Tents of Israel, A Deputy Was King, Mosaic]; The Augs, an Exaggeration, 1933 (in U.S.: Summer's Play: An Exaggeration); Pelican Walking: Short Stories, 1934; Shining and Free: A Day in the Life of the Matriarch, 1935; The Matriarch Chronicles (with new pref. by au.) 1936 [The Matriarch, A Deputy Was King, Mosaic, Shining and Free]; Oleander River, 1937; The Ugly Dachshund (illus. K. F. Barker) 1938; Long Story Short: A Collection, 1939; The Woman in the Hall, 1939; A Lion in the Garden, 1940; Dogs in an Omnibus (illus. K. F. Barker) 1942 [The Dark Gentleman, Toes Unmasked, The Ugly Dachshund]; The Young Matriarch, 1942; The Reasonable Shores, 1946; No Son of Mine, 1948; A Duck to Water, 1949; Ten Days of Christmas, 1950; Unless I Marry, 1950; The Donkey Shoe, 1952; Johnny Forsaken, 1954; For All We Know, 1955; Seventy Times Seven, a Novel, 1957; The Patience of a Saint, or Example Is Better than Precept: Being A Faithful Account of the Almost Incredible Happenings at the Millenary of St. Cedric in the Ruins of Hallowbrige Abbey, 1958; Dolphin Cottage, 1962; Promise Not to Tell, 1964. *Nonfiction*—Bouquet, 1927; Monogram, 1936; Another Part of the Forest, 1941; (with S. Kay-Smith) Talking of Jane Austen, 1943 (in U.S.: Speaking of Jane Austen); Trumpet Voluntary, 1944; Benefits Forgot, 1949; (with S. Kaye-Smith) More about Jane Austen, 1949 (in U.S.: More Talk of Jane Austen); A Name to Conjure With, 1953; All in Good Time, 1954; He Wrote Treasure Island: The Story of Robert Louis Stevenson, 1954 (juvenile; in U.S.: Robert Louis Stevenson, The Man Who Wrote "Treasure Island"); The Way It Worked Out, 1956;  . . . and Did He Stop and Speak to You?, 1957 (essays); Bernadette (illus. D. Brookshaw) 1960; One Is Only Human, 1960 (essays); The Personality of Jesus, 1961 (juvenile; The Catholic Know-Your-Bible Program). *Drama*—The Man Who Pays the Piper: A Play in a Prologue and Three Acts, 1931; The Matriarch: A Play in a

Prologue and Three Acts, 1931; Gala Night at "The Willows":
(with R. Croft-Cooke) A Comedy in One Act, 1950; Raffle for
a Bedspread [A One-Act Play for Women Only] 1953. *As edi-*
*tor*—R.L.S.: An Omnibus, 1950; Selected Poems of Robert
Louis Stevenson, 1950; Tales and Essays of Robert Louis Stevenson, 1950.

ABOUT: Shattock, J. (ed.) The Oxford Guide to British Women
Writers, 1993; Stern, G. B. Monogram, 1936; Stern, G. B. An-
other Part of the Forest, 1941; Stern, G. B. Trumpet Volun-
tary, 1944; Stern, G. B. Benefits Forgot, 1949; Stern, G. B. A
Name to Conjure With, 1953; Stern, G. B. All in Good Time,
1954; Stern, G. B. The Way It Worked Out, 1956; Stern, G.
B. One Is Only Human, 1960; Todd, J. M. (ed.) British Women
Writers: A Critical Reference Guide, 1989. *Periodicals*—New
Statesman April 1, 1922; New York Times June 21, 1953; Sep-
tember 20, 1973; Times (London) September 20, 1973; Yale
Review Autumn 1944.

## STERN, PHILIP VAN DOREN (September 19,
1900–July 31, 1984), American novelist, historian,
and anthologist, wrote: "I was born in Wyalusing,

Pennsylvania, a little village on the Susquehanna
River, but grew up in
New Jersey, where I was
graduated from Rutgers
in 1924. (In 1940 the university gave me an hon-
orary doctorate for my
work on Lincoln.) I had
been interested in sci-
ence, particularly chem-
istry, during my pre-
college days, but a summer in a chemical
laboratory cured me of that. I turned to the liberal
arts and at graduation was offered an instructorship
in English. I refused it and went into advertising
during the pioneer days of radio. I made a lot of
money, but chucked the job in 1926 and went to
Europe. During my advertising work I had become
increasingly interested in printing and wrote a book
on typography. On the strength of it, I got a job as
designer for Alfred A. Knopf and then Simon and
Schuster. Once in the publishing business, where I
had always wanted to be, I began to write.

"I edited the papers of Thomas De Quincey, did
a mystery under the name 'Peter Storme,' and then
wrote my first historical work, *The Man Who
Killed Lincoln*, which was taken by the Literary
Guild. I thought I could earn a living from writing,
so I resigned from Simon and Schuster and edited
*The Life and Writings of Abraham Lincoln*. Then
I began work on a long historical novel of the Abolition period, *The Drums of Morning*. I ran out of
money before I finished it and returned to publishing on a part-time basis with Pocket Books, Inc. I
edited half a dozen anthologies for them, one of
which sold more than a million copies. When the
war came, I left there to join the Office of War Information, where I was editor and then on the planning board. In 1943 I became general manager for
Editions for the Armed Services, a non-profit organization that issued 122,000,000 paperbound books
for the troops overseas.

"In 1944 a short story I had written as a Christmas booklet for distribution to my friends, under
the title 'The Greatest Gift,' was bought by the

movies and made into Frank Capra's first post-war
picture, *It's a Wonderful Life*. After the war, I returned to Pocket Books, where I became vice-
president in charge of editorial work and printing
production. In 1946, I again had a chance to try to
earn a living from writing when a motion picture
company offered me a fabulous option for a novel
about Lola Montez. I left Pocket Books and began
work, but by the time the book was finished, the
bottom had dropped out of Hollywood, so I returned to publishing, this time in the printing
end. . . . Recently I have become fascinated by
boats and boating, as a result of which I invented
a new almanac."

---

Most Americans associate actor Jimmy Stewart
and director Frank Capra—rather than Stern—
with the film version of *It's a Wonderful Life*,
which has become an American Christmas classic—rivaling even Dickens's *A Christmas Carol* as
a parable of the season. However, Stern's contribution to American letters was in the field of historical
scholarship. His *New York Times* obituary noted
that he was "widely respected by scholars for his
authoritative books on the Civil War," which
ranged from historical novels written under the
pseudonym of Peter Storme to narratives of the war
seen from the viewpoint of the ordinary Union and
Confederate troops (*Soldier Life in the Union and
Confederate Armies*), of spies (*Secret Missions of
the Civil War*), to pictorial histories (*They Were
There: The Civil War in Action as Seen by its Combat Artists; The Confederate Navy: A Pictorial History*), and biographies of war leaders (*Robert E.
Lee: The Man and the Soldier*). The above is only
a partial listing of Stern's many Civil War monographs, which pleased scholars as well as general
readers.

The historian Henry Steel Commager, in reviewing *An End to Valor: The Last Days of the Civil
War* for the *New York Times* (April 13, 1958), admitted that Stern's account did not have the poetry
or the intensity of several earlier histories. However, Commager thought that "what Mr. Stern does,
and with great skill, is to weave the whole story together, the North and the South, the military and
the civilian, the portentous and the trivial, into a coherent pattern, and to present it all with the impartiality of an artist."

Stern's epic novel *The Drums of Morning* chronicles the abolitionist movement in one boy's struggles and adventures through the end of the Civil
War. *The Man Who Killed Lincoln* combines fact
and fiction to recreate the shooting of Abraham
Lincoln and the subsequent escape of John Wilkes
Booth. "The tangled story of Lincoln's assassination
has been told, usually badly, many times," stated
Clifton Fadiman in the *New Yorker*, who added "it
has never, as far as I know, been told by anyone
combining a respect for the facts of history with an
intense interest in the psychology of Booth.
Now . . . the gap is filled."

Some of Stern's other works, written for a popular audience, were more sensationalistic in tone.

*Breathless Moment*, his depression-era compendium (with Herbert Asbury) of "the world's most sensational news photos" was, as its title implies, a Grand-Guignolish display of images for a public just becoming fascinated with the new genre of on-the-spot news photography. Critics felt it their duty to warn squeamish readers of the book's contents. Seven years later, Stern published *Midnight Reader: Great Stories of Haunting and Horror*, which included stories by Oliver Onions, Sir Hugh Walpole, Kipling, Poe, Edith Wharton, Henry James, and other writers.

In later years, he wrote several books of "general" history with wide sweep, such as *Prehistoric Europe: From Stone Age Man to the Early Greeks* and *The Beginning of Art*. In 1964, he published, an extensive annotation of Stowe's *Uncle Tom's Cabin*, and in 1970 an annotation of Thoreau's *Walden*.

Stern continued work well into his seventies. His *Portable Poe* was published in 1977.

PRINCIPAL WORKS: *Nonfiction*—An Introduction to Typography, 1932; The Man Who Killed Lincoln: The Story of John Wilkes Booth and His Part in the Assassination, 1939; (as "Peter Storme," with P. Stryfe) How to Torture Your Friends, 1941; Our Constitution: Presented in Modern Everyday Language, 1953; A Pictorial History of the Automobile, as Seen in Motor Magazine 1903–1953, 1953; Tin Lizzie: The Story of the Fabulous Model T Ford, 1955; An End to Valor: The Last Days of the Civil War, 1958; Secret Missions of the Civil War: First-Hand Accounts by Men and Women Who Risked Their Lives in Underground Activities for the North and the South, Woven into a Continuous Narrative, 1959; They Were There: The Civil War in Action as Seen by Its Combat Artists, 1959; The Confederate Navy: A Pictorial History, 1962; Robert E. Lee: The Man and the Soldier: A Pictorial Biography, 1963; When the Guns Roared: World Aspects of the American Civil War, 1965; (with L. Stern) Beyond Paris: A Touring Guide, 1967; Prehistoric Europe: From Stone Age Man to the Early Greeks, 1969; Henry David Thoreau: Writer and Rebel, 1972; The Beginnings of Art, 1973. *Novels*—(as "Peter Storme") The Thing in The Brook, 1937; The Drums of Morning, 1942; Lola: A Love Story, 1949; Love Is the One with Wings, 1951. *Short stories*—The Greatest Gift: A Christmas Tale, 1943. *As editor*—The Breathless Moment: The World's Most Sensational News Photos, 1935; Selected Writings of Thomas De Quincey, 1937; The Life and Writings of Abraham Lincoln, 1940; The Pocket Reader, 1941; The Midnight Reader: Great Stories of Haunting and Horror, 1942; The Pocket Book of America, 1942, rev. ed. 1975; The Pocket Companion, 1942; Great Tales of Fantasy and Imagination, 1943; The Moonlight Traveler: Great Tales of Fantasy and Imagination, 1943; The Pocket Book of Modern American Short Stories, 1943; Edgar Allan Poe, 1945; The Pocket Book of Adventure Stories, 1945; (with B. Smith) The Holiday Reader, 1947; The Pocket Book of Ghost Stories, 1947; Travelers in Time: Strange Tales of Man's Journeyings into the Past and the Future, 1947; Tales of Horror and the Supernatural, 1948; The Pocket Week-End Book, 1949; The Civil War Christmas Album, 1961; Prologue to Sumter: The Beginnings of the Civil War from the John Brown Raid to the Surrender of Fort Sumter, Woven into a Continuous Narrative, 1961; Soldier Life in the Union and Confederate Armies, 1961; The Annotated Uncle Tom's Cabin, 1964; Strange Beasts and Unnatural Monsters, 1968; The Other Side of the Clock: Stories Out of Time, Out of Place, 1969; The Annotated Walden: Walden; or Life in the Woods, 1970; The Portable Edgar Allan Poe, 1977. *Juvenile*—Edgar Allan Poe: Visitor from the Night of Time, 1973.

ABOUT: The autobiographical material quoted above was written for Twentieth Century Authors First Supplement, 1955. *Periodicals*—Chicago Sunday Tribune April 27, 1958; New York Times April 13, 1958; August 1, 1984; New Yorker February 4, 1939.

**STERNE, EMMA (GELDERS)** (May 13, 1894–August 29, 1971), American historical novelist and writer for children, wrote: "I was born and grew up in Birmingham, Alabama, in the days when it was still young enough to feel some surprise in being a city at all. The first two years of my life were spent in the Opera House Hotel, connected with the town's only theatre; my first memory was of being held up for a sight of a corner of the stage.  Then we moved out to the edge of the city, almost to the top of Red Mountain, where I picked blackberries and rode horseback with my father. I was always a voracious reader and soon learned to read my way through the stacks of the public library, from which (on the top floor of the City Hall) I could see the city jail. I have a strong interest in the problems of social welfare; I was an ardent suffrage worker, and my first job was a column in a Birmingham paper conducted to advance the interest of women in politics. I started a school for delinquent children under the just-created juvenile court in 1917; it has long been incorporated into the regular system of the state. I married a few months after graduating from Smith College, in 1916, and a year later my husband, Roy M. Sterne, our infant daughter, and I moved to New York City, where my husband is now general counsel of a large drug company.

"I had always intended to write, and had served in an editorial capacity on the literary magazines both in high school and at Smith College. When my second daughter was born we moved to Pelham, New York. I came in occasionally to Columbia and took a few graduate courses in English and philosophy. I began making my first garden and sold my first story in the same week in May 1923. From that time on the pattern of my life has been pretty steadily the same. I garden and write children's books and dive sporadically into civic reform. I write now for a variety of ages in a variety of form, but almost always on subjects of historical background, and always looking through the windows of research on some bright far-off corner of the scene of action. I also write children's plays, one of which won a $500 prize in 1931. I still think I am a better critic than I am a writer, and as a critic I don't think much of my writing. But I love to do research, and in an unscholarly, essentially feminine sort of way I am pretty good at it. We have now moved to Wilton, Connecticut, and have turned farmers.

"In politics I am a left-wing New Dealer and internationalist. That is, my radical friends call me (sneeringly) a liberal, and my conservative relations and friends, including my publishers, think I wear a red shirt. I am working now on a book based on the Amistad case of 1840."

In 1955, Sterne wrote: "The war years were spent in Cambridge, Massachusetts, writing pamphlets for the Office of War Information and later for the United Nations left little time for creative work. But I did manage to do two more books, *We Live to Be Free*, a study of the rise of democratic thought, and *Incident in Yorkville*, a wartime novel for teenagers, before the stress of those eventful years engulfed my writing entirely.

"My husband and I returned for a brief span to our country home in Connecticut, and for five years I taught at the Thomas School in Rowayton, Connecticut. My path back to writing lay through textbook editing. For the first group of the American Heritage Series, published by Aladdin Books, I wrote *Printer's Devil*. I am now editing the American Heritage Series and have had the pleasure of guiding through the press my story of the Amistad captives, *The Long Black Schooner*, finished after ten years of interruption! I am now living and working in New York City. Grandchildren—five of them—fill hours and thought that gardens once held in a busy life."

---

Opinion was divided on Emma Sterne's work, which consisted largely of stories for children and young adults. Her first story, *White Swallow*, the tale of an Indian boy who drifted away from his home along America's eastern shore to find a hermit with whom he spent the winter, then to be led home by a white swallow which had nested near the family teepee, drew this comment from the *Saturday Review of Literature*: "'White Swallow,' though designed for children under ten, in its simplicity approaches inanity—a sweetish mixture of canoes, papoose, and fairies with a little vague woodcraft and a Prince Charming to top it off." Sterne's next effort, *Loud Sing Cuckoo*, fared better. This historical romance set in Chaucerian England with Richard II, Chaucer, Wat Tyler, and the priest, John Ball, filling out the background, drew this comment from the *New York Times*. "*Loud Sing Cuckoo* is like a tapestry woven in clear, unfaded colors to show us one scene after another in fourteenth century England. . . ."

In the 1930s, Sterne began writing a trilogy of novels on the American South during the Civil War and Reconstruction eras. In 1933, she published *No Surrender*, the tale of Manthy, a woman struggling against all odds, with virtually nothing to sustain her, to hold on to the family plantation near the end of the war.

In her later years, Sterne wrote a series of nonfiction books on African-American heritage and heroes, including W.E.B. DuBois and Mary McLeod Bethune. In 1965, when the nation's attention was focused on the movement for desegregation and civil rights, Knopf published her *I Have a Dream*, a history of the movement for racial justice and equality that included many lesser-known figures as well as the more celebrated ones such as Marian Anderson, A. Phillip Randolph, Thurgood Marshall, and James Farmer. The title was based on the famous speech delivered by Martin Luther King at the Lincoln Memorial in 1963. Despite the timeliness of this work, some reviewers thought Sterne's style and technique were antiquated.

PRINCIPAL WORKS: *Fiction*—White Swallow, 1928; Blue Pigeons, 1929; Loud Sing Cuckoo, 1930; No Surrender, 1931; Amarantha Gay, M.D., 1932; Calico Ball, 1933; Drums of Monmouth, 1935; Miranda Was a Princess, 1936; Far Town Road, 1937; Some Plant Olive Trees, 1937; European Summer, 1938; Pirate of Chatham Square, 1939; America Was Like This, 1940; We Live to Be Free, 1942; Incident in Yorkville, 1943; Printer's Devil, 1951; Long Black Schooner, 1953; Let the Moon Go By, 1954; (as editor) Moby Dick, 1954; (as editor) Little Women, 1957; Blood Brothers, 1958; (with B. Lindsay) The Sea, 1958; (with B. Lindsay) King Arthur and the Knight of the Round Table, 1962. *Nonfiction*—Mary McLeod Bethune, 1956; I Have a Dream, 1965; Benito Juarez: Builder of a Nation 1967, (biography); They Took Their Stand, 1968; His Was the Voice: The Life of W.E.B. Dubois, 1971.

ABOUT: The autobiographical material quoted above was written for Twentieth Century Authors, 1942 and Twentieth Century Authors First Supplement, 1955.

**STEVENS, JAMES FLOYD** (November 25, 1892–December 29, 1971), American writer of folk stories, wrote: "This life of mine appeared with the customary gulp and howl, to add to the gayety of a rocky rented farm in Monroe County, Iowa. There it grew on lean sustenance for four years. Its one important adventure, said its elders, was a runaway that ended in a pigsty and a nick-of-time rescue from the jaws of a brood sow. Brothers and  sisters it had none. There was a gypsy father who felt free to go a-roving to far places, and did so. A mother who worked as a hired girl for $12 a month. A grandmother with a widow's pension of $8 a month. On this joint income the three moved to a little town in Appanoose County, and there they lived for six more years.

"This life, in the shape of a ten-year-old boy, was then sent out alone to relatives in Idaho. For the most of five more years it grew on a dry-land homestead, learning to handle horses and cattle, learning a little from books in school. At fifteen it struck out on a man's way in the world.

"The West was a great country those times, for a willing worker, and these hands were willing and not unskilled. For nine years they did hard work on many jobs throughout the states west of the Mississippi, mostly in handling horses and mules on construction projects of large scale, and in the forest industry. Then it was war, and a year and a half in France as a sergeant of infantry for this one. Back to the woods, to the camps and mills, and to much study of books in off-hours and much thinking of books and the writing of them, when on the job.

"In November 1923, Mr. Mencken of Baltimore received a letter from an admirer of long standing. The writer described himself as a Western hobo laborer with wistful literary yearnings. Mr. Mencken's reply was three bombshells: (1) 'You write well.' (2) 'Your experiences must have filled you with capital material.' (3) 'Why not try an article for the *American Mercury*?' The article was tried, successfully. Another was invited. A story on Paul Bunyan, mythical giant of the big timber, was attempted. It followed the method of Homer, who translated the folklore of his land and time into literary terms, and it rejected the method of the professors who demand stenographic transcriptions of folklore. The story became a book of stories which has sold more than 75,000 copies. So the hobo laborer became an author. A life designed for other pursuits had to toil hard to produce with words. It has pounded and sweated out five more books, and another, *American Psalm*, is in preparation. . . . "At present I am public relations man for the West Coast Lumbermen's Association, in Seattle. I much prefer this to producing literary trade goods as a means of making a living. I was married to Theresa Seitz Fitzgerald in 1929. We have no children, but my wife's niece makes her home with us. No enthusiast on anything, I do approve America and the Democratic Party. My favorite people are foresters. I am glad of all my life, and I like the present part of it best of all.

"Now I am an associate member of the Society of American Foresters and an honorary life member of the College of Forestry, University of Washington, Alumni Association. I am a member of Plymouth Congregational Church, Seattle, of Seattle Post No. 1 of the American Legion, and of the public relations committee of the Seattle Chamber of Commerce. A trustee of the Washington State Forestry Conference and of the Keep Washington Green Association, Inc., I still wear the Democratic Party label, but I have become the most Republican-voting Democrat extant."

---

James Floyd Stevens carved out a name for himself in American letters chiefly through his Paul Bunyan stories. The poet Percy Mackaye, eminent in his time, reviewing *Paul Bunyan* in the *Bookman* when it first appeared, thought that Stevens well merited "to be known as the prose Homer of that American mythology which has sprung gigantically into being from the campfires of our vast timberland during the past half century." J. F. Dobie, in the *Nation* sounded a more cautious note: "*Paul Bunyan* is the apotheosis of American tall tale-telling, but sheer exaggeration, even if it is 'real American,' becomes at length tiresome." But Dobie did add that Stevens's account of the Black Duck Dinner was "unique in American literature."

The semi-autobiographical *Brawny-man* also received excellent reviews. H. L. Stuart wrote in the *New York Times* that he thought it "important . . . among the human documents that are interpreting life to us as it is lived." It was, he declared, a "frank exposition of life as a hefty young pagan feels it and tastes it." P. C. Kennedy, commenting on it from across the Atlantic, in the *New Statesman*, found this candor "ragged" but, he added, "one feels oneself to be getting the genuine record . . . not the pseudo-primitiveness of lust and violence as seen so often and so pervertedly through the sentimental appreciations of the over-civilized."

Stevens resigned from his public relations job in 1957, to live out his retirement in Seattle, to which he had moved in the mid-1930s.

PRINCIPAL WORKS: *Fiction and folklore*—Paul Bunyan, 1925 (pub. with an additional story, 1948); Brawny-man, 1926; Mattock, 1927; Homer in the Sagebrush, 1928; The Saginaw Paul Bunyan, 1932; Paul Bunyan's Bears, 1947; Big Jim Turner, 1948; Tree Treasure, 1950; Farthest West in the Timber—Grays Harbour Country of Washington State, 1955. *Other*—Timber! The Way of Life in the Lumber Camps, 1942; Green Power: The Story of Public Law 273, 1958.

ABOUT: The autobiographical material quoted above was written for Twentieth Century Authors, 1942 and Twentieth Century Authors First Supplement 1955. Magill, F. N. (ed.) Cyclopaedia of World Authors, 1958; Montgomery, E. R. The Story Behind Modern Books, 1949; Warfel, H. R. American Novelists of Today, 1951. *Periodicals*—Bookman January 1925; Nation August 26, 1925; New Statesman September 26, 1926; New York Times June 13, 1926; January 1, 1972.

**STEVENS, WALLACE** (October 2, 1879–August 2, 1955), American poet, was born in Reading, Pennsylvania, the second of five children of Garrett Barcalow Stevens, a prosperous country lawyer, and Margaretha Catharine (Zeller) Stevens. He attended the Reading Boys' High School, where the curriculum was rigorous (Latin, Greek, mathematics, the English classics, and ancient history) and where he excelled in oratory and composition. Mindful of the advice of his severely practical father to "make something" of himself, he enrolled at Harvard College in 1893 as a "special student" and completed his course of study in three years. While there he applied himself with greater diligence than his more gentlemanly classmates, and the fluent, conventional verse he began writing for the *Harvard Advocate* earned the approbation of George Santayana (then on the faculty), who replied to a sonnet by Stevens with one of his own. In his last year at Harvard he edited the *Advocate* and resolved on a career in journalism as a practical route to a literary life.

After leaving Harvard without a degree in 1900, Stevens moved to New York, where he got a job as a reporter for the *New York Tribune*. Finding journalism to be neither fulfilling nor remunerative, he capitulated to his father's wishes in 1901 and entered New York Law School, graduating two years later. Admitted to the bar in 1904, he struggled in various unsuccessful ventures before securing a promising position with the American Bonding Company in 1908. The following year he married Elsie Kachel Moll, a hometown girl six years his junior whom he had been courting for the previous five years. Despite the ardor and tenderness apparent in Stevens's love letters to Elsie, theirs was not a happy marriage; among Elsie's grievances was the fact of her husband's poetry. According to Joan Richardson, when "Stevens's identity as a poet began to be recognized in the real world, Elsie became enraged. She resented his sharing what she thought belonged only to her and began objecting to his indulging in poetry at all."

Whatever Stevens's domestic disappointments in the early years of his marriage, he found the intellectual stimulation he needed in the circle of his Harvard classmate Walter Arensberg, whose Manhattan salon he began frequenting around 1912. Sometime during the next year he resumed writing poetry and shared the results with William Carlos

Williams, Marianne Moore, Alfred Kreymborg, and other friends of Arensberg. These poems, heavily influenced by imagism and French symbolism, were very different from the decorous sonnets he had written as an undergraduate. His breakthrough, most critics agree, was "Sunday Morning," written in 1914, followed soon after by the equally distinctive "Peter Quince at the Clavier." In the following decade he published in a smattering of little magazines "The Snow Man," "Thirteen Ways of Looking at a Blackbird," "The Emperor of Ice Cream," and the other quirky masterpieces that would comprise his first (and best) collection, *Harmonium*.

Published to mostly hostile or uncomprehending reviews in 1923, *Harmonium* is now generally regarded as one of the great works of modern American poetry. But Stevens still has his detractors and for them the author of *Harmonium* is, in Harold Bloom's words, "a rather luxurious and Frenchified exquisite, a kind of upper-middle-class mock-Platonist who represents at best an American Aestheticism, replete with tropical fruits and aroma-laden invitations to the voyage." Yet the characteristic themes of *Harmonium* are not only, or even primarily, the narrow epistemological ones concerning the relationship between language and reality that these critics find in the volume. *Harmonium*'s hallmarks, wrote James Longenbach, are "the latent but ever-present threat of death, and the inability of Christian belief to account for it; the reduction of the gods themselves to beings 'humanly near'; the imagination's moonlight transforming the 'wearier end' of bare reality." Some of the most affecting poems in *Harmonium* are the most intensely personal, though Stevens was careful to disguise their autobiographical origins with mocking titles like "The Man Whose Pharynx Was Bad" and "Le Monocle de Mon Oncle." Indeed, it is not too much to see the latter poem as centrally concerned with the failure of Stevens's marriage, as in these lines from the eighth stanza:

Our bloom is gone. We are the fruit thereof.
Two golden gourds distended on our vines,
Into the autumn weather, splashed with frost,
Distorted by hale fatness, turned grotesque.

Seven years previous to the publication of *Harmonium* Stevens had moved to Connecticut to accept a position as head of the claims department of the Hartford Accident and Indemnity Company. His "double life" as corporate lawyer and lyric poet was thus firmly established by the time he was named a vice president of the Hartford in 1934; but if there was anything odd in this combination of roles, it was not apparent to Stevens, who, in later years, wrote Milton J. Bates, "would neglect few opportunities to *épater le bohème* with his business-like manner and verbal assaults upon the stereotype of the poet as a loafer and man of 'no account.'" Clearly, Stevens's business life did not impede his creativity (he generally composed in the evening or while walking to and from work), yet there was a six-or seven-year period after the publication of *Harmonium* when particularly burdensome professional responsibilities as well as the birth of his

daughter Holly in 1924 combined to prevent any serious attempt at writing poetry. This was, however, a period of gestation as well as fallowness, and the poems he began writing again in the early 1930s were in some ways deeper and richer, though undeniably less brilliant, than those of *Harmonium*. These were the poems of Stevens's second collection, *Ideas of Order*, a collection that contains, according to A. Walton Litz, Stevens's "fullest and most satisfying treatments of our common experience, cast in a language which is both traditional and distinctive." Although the magnificent *ars poetica* "The Idea of Order at Key West" is the most frequently anthologized piece from the collection, a more intimate lyric such as "A Postcard from the Volcano" perhaps gives a better sense of the human concerns that characterize the work as a whole. In this poem, wrote Helen Vendler, "Stevens' continuing wish to write with the utmost simplicity, and to reach us, his posterity, with his spirit still storming on the blank pages of his book is nowhere clearer than in this parable of pastness."

Although *Ideas of Order* received more sympathetic reviews than *Harmonium* had, Stevens was stung by accusations of dandyism—and of indifference to social and political reality. In response, he brought out *Owl's Clover* (1936), a slim volume of somewhat forced meditations on art and politics which he omitted from his *Collected Poems*. In fact, Stevens was neither the apolitical aesthete nor the reactionary burgher that some critics have taken him to be. Though capable of deliberately outrageous utterances in support of Italian fascism and suchlike monstrosities, he thought of himself as a moderate liberal, and his poetry was hardly uninformed by such events as the depression and the Spanish civil war. "Unlike many other American intellectuals and poets," wrote James Longenbach, "Stevens did not retreat from political concerns when the ideals of [the 1930s] began to seem tarnished; his refusal of utopian seductions saved him from apocalyptic despair. And the great long poems of the early 1940s ('Notes toward a Supreme Fiction' and 'Esthétique du Mal') were born of Stevens's continuing engagement with the realities of the Second World War." But the charge of a certain cold indifference to suffering has remained, and has never been fully refuted.

Political ideas were not absent from Stevens's next collection, *The Man with the Blue Guitar and Other Poems*, though these were only one part in the larger orchestration of themes. In the packed couplets of the title poem Stevens considered the role of the artist in a chaotic world, affirming that

Poetry
Exceeding music must take the place
Of empty heaven and its hymns.

Accomplished as "The Man with the Blue Guitar" is, many critics consider it something of a prologue to the immensely ambitious poem that followed, "Notes toward a Supreme Fiction." In three sections of seventy tercets each, Stevens attempted to elaborate a totalizing theory of the imagination that would supplant the exhausted mythology of Christianity. Discursive, abstract, and formidably difficult, "Notes toward a Supreme Fiction" remains somewhat controversial. To M. L. Rosenthal and Sally M. Gall, the poem "suggests a mind so swaddled in its ponderings that the poetic instinct mummifies out of sheer empathy with its surroundings," while to Helen Vendler, "the flawless energy of 'Notes' is matched by an unusual forthrightness, so that the poem feels at once both liberated and restrained: liberated in its fancifulness, its fables, its many manners, but restrained in its soberer forms of assertion and its more varied resolutions." Its peculiar mix of the tentative and the transcendent is nowhere more apparent than in the conclusion, at once a summing up and a circling back:

> They will get it straight one day at the Sorbonne.
> We shall return at twilight from the lecture
> Pleased that the irrational is rational,
>
> Until flicked by feeling, in a gildered street,
> I call you by name, my green, my fluent mundo.
> You will have stopped revolving except in crystal.

By the time "Notes toward a Supreme Fiction" was published in 1942, Stevens was held in high esteem by fellow poets like William Carlos Williams and Marianne Moore and by critics like R. P. Blackmur, and as he entered a period of extraordinary creativity that continued undiminished until his death thirteen years later, his reputation rose accordingly. Not only did his longer poems, such as "The Auroras of Autumn" and "An Ordinary Evening in New Haven," become ever more magisterial, but his lyrics moved toward a greater simplicity and purity. In "The Planet on the Table," occasioned by the ordering of his Collected Poems, he was able to write his own epitaph, giving himself, as Helen Vendler noted, "the name appropriate to his ethereal soul and call[ing] himself Ariel, the airy spirit trapped in an earthly prison":

> Ariel was glad he had written his poems.
> They were of a remembered time
> Or of something seen that he liked.
>
> It was not important that they survive.
> What mattered was that they should bear
> Some lineament or character,
>
> Some affluence, if only half-perceived,
> In the poverty of their words,
> Of the planet of which they were part.

Harold Bloom regarded Stevens's last phase (1950–1955) as his best. "No single poem written after he turned seventy has the scope and ambition of his three masterpieces, 'Notes,' 'The Auroras,' 'An Ordinary Evening,'" wrote Bloom. "But 'The Rock,' the elegy 'To an Old Philosopher in Rome,' and some twenty-five shorter poems have an uncanny intensity and originality that surpass nearly all his previous work at middle length or shorter." Stevens had the satisfaction in these years of achieving the public recognition that had long been his due. In 1946 he was elected to the National Institute of Arts and Letters, in 1950 he received the Bollingen Prize in Poetry, and in 1955 he was awarded (shortly before his death) both the Pulitzer

Prize and the National Book Award for his Collected Poems. He was also much in demand for readings and lectures. The Necessary Angel, an important collection of theoretical essays originally delivered at various universities, had been published to exemplary reviews in 1951, and in 1954 he was offered the Charles Eliot Norton lectureship at Harvard, an invitation that his corporate responsibilities (as well as temperament) forced him to decline. Moreover, he seemed to relax his famous aloofness as he approached old age. He reestablished warm relations with his family in Pennsylvania, he grew closer to his daughter Holly and her young son Peter, and he wrote bantering, affectionate letters to old friends like Marianne Moore and William Carlos Williams and to newer ones like Richard Eberhart and José Rodríguez Feo. "As he drew closer to the ultimate cause of the pathos of the human condition," wrote Joan Richardson, "he could not hide from his feelings; he no longer turned away from what in his youth would have bathed him in tears. The poet would not die a stranger on the earth."

After several months of illness, Stevens died of cancer in St. Francis Hospital in Hartford. The deathbed conversion to Roman Catholicism that has been attributed to him is unlikely, given the lack of corroborating evidence and Stevens's lifelong commitment to the secular imagination as the greatest good. Although some readers will always find his poetry remote and abstract, the opinion that holds Stevens as a major poet continues to gain force. In his best work, wrote Helen Vendler in the New York Review of Books, "Profound feeling, sustained intelligence, whimsical self-derision, and a discipline of aesthetic outline coexist."

The Wallace Stevens Collection in the Huntington Library, San Marino, California, is the largest repository of the poet's manuscripts.

PRINCIPAL WORKS: Poetry—Harmonium, 1923, rev. ed. 1931; Ideas of Order, 1935; Owl's Clover, 1936; The Man with the Blue Guitar, and Other Poems, 1937; Parts of a World, 1942; Notes toward a Supreme Fiction, 1942; Esthétique du Mal, 1945; Transport to Summer, 1947; The Auroras of Autumn, 1950; Selected Poems, 1952; The Collected Poems of Wallace Stevens, 1954; Opus Posthumous (ed. S. F. Morse) 1957 (rev. ed. by M. J. Bates, 1989); The Palm at the End of the Mind: Selected Poems and a Play (ed. H. Stevens) 1971. Essays—The Necessary Angel: Essays on Reality and the Imagination, 1951. Correspondence—Letters of Wallace Stevens (ed. H. Stevens) 1966; Secretaries of the Moon: The Letters of Wallace Stevens and José Rodríguez Feo (eds. B. Coyle and A. Filreis) 1986. Other—Souvenirs and Prophecies: The Young Wallace Stevens (ed. H. Stevens) 1977; Sur Plusieurs Beaux Sujects: Wallace Stevens' Commonplace Book (ed. M. J. Bates) 1989.

ABOUT: Axelrod, S. G. (ed.) Critical Essays on Wallace Stevens, 1988; Baird, J. The Dome and the Rock: Structure in the Poetry of Wallace Stevens, 1968; Bates, M. J. Wallace Stevens: A Mythology of Self, 1985; Beckett, L. Wallace Stevens, 1974; Benamou, M. Wallace Stevens and the Symbolist Imagination, 1972; Berger, C. Forms of Farewell: The Late Poetry of Wallace Stevens, 1985; Bevis, W. W. Mind of Winter: Wallace Stevens, Meditation, and Literature, 1988; Bloom, H. Wallace Stevens: The Poems of Our Climate, 1977; Bloom, H. (ed.) Wallace Stevens, 1985; Borroff, M. (ed.) Wallace Stevens: A Collection of Critical Essays, 1963; Brazeau, P. Parts of a World: Wallace Stevens Remembered, 1983; Brogan, J. V. Stevens and Simile: A Theory of Language, 1986; Brown, A. and Haller, R. S. (eds.) The Achievement of Wallace Stevens, 1962;

Brown, M. E. Wallace Stevens: The Poem as Act, 1970; Burney, W. Wallace Stevens, 1968; Buttell, R. Wallace Stevens: The Making of Harmonium, 1967; Carroll, J. Wallace Stevens' Supreme Fiction: A New Romanticism, 1987; Cook, E. Poetry, Word-Play, and Word-War in Wallace Stevens, 1988; Dictionary of American Biography, Suppl. 5, 1977; Doggett, F. Wallace Stevens' Poetry of Thought, 1966; Doggett, F. Wallace Stevens: The Making of the Poem, 1980; Doggett, F. and Buttel, R. (eds.) Wallace Stevens: A Celebration, 1980; Doyle, C. (ed.) Wallace Stevens: The Critical Heritage, 1985; Ehrenpries, I. (ed.) Wallace Stevens: A Critical Anthology, 1972; Enck, J. J. Wallace Stevens: Images and Judgements, 1964; Filreis, A. Wallace Stevens and the Actual World, 1991; Fisher, B. M. Wallace Stevens: The Intensest Rendezvous, 1990; Gelpi, A. (ed.) Wallace Stevens: The Poetics of Modernism, 1985; Grey, T. C. The Wallace Stevens Case: Law and the Practice of Poetry, 1991; Halliday, M. Stevens and the Interpersonal, 1991; Hines, T. J. The Later Poetry of Wallace Stevens: Phenomenological Parallels with Husserl and Heidegger, 1976; Holmes, B. The Decomposer's Art: Ideas of Music in the Poetry of Wallace Stevens, 1990; Jarraway, D. R. Wallace Stevens and the Question of Belief: A Metaphysician in the Dark, 1993; Kermode, F. Wallace Stevens, 1960; Kessler, E. Images of Wallace Stevens, 1971; LaGuardia, D. M. Advance on Chaos: The Sanctifying Imagination of Wallace Stevens, 1983; Leggett, B. J. Early Stevens: The Nietzschean Intertext, 1992; Leggett, B. J. Wallace Stevens and Poetic Theory: Conceiving the Supreme Fiction, 1987; Lensing, G. Wallace Stevens: A Poet's Growth, 1986; Leonard, J. S. and Wharton, C. E. The Fluent Mundo: Wallace Stevens and the Structure of Reality, 1988; Litz, A. W. Introspective Voyager: The Poetic Development of Wallace Stevens, 1972; Longenbach, J. Wallace Stevens: The Plain Sense of Things, 1991; MacLeod, G. G. Wallace Stevens and Company: The Harmonium Years, 1913–1923, 1983; MacLeod, G. G. Wallace Stevens and Modern Art: From the Armory Show to Abstract Expressionism, 1993; McMahon, W. E. The Higher Humanism of Wallace Stevens, 1990; McNamara, P. L. (ed.) Critics on Wallace Stevens, 1972; Morris, A. K. Wallace Stevens: Imagination and Faith, 1974; Morse, S. F. Wallace Stevens: Poetry as Life, 1970; Nasser, E. P. Wallace Steven: An Anatomy of Figuration, 1965; Newcomb, J. T. Wallace Stevens and Literary Canons, 1992; O'Connor, W. V. The Shaping Spirit: A Study of Wallace Stevens, 1950; Pack, R. Wallace Stevens: An Approach to His Poetry and Thought, 1958; Patke, R. S. The Long Poems of Wallace Stevens: An Interpretive Study, 1985; Pearce, R. H. and Miller, J. H. (eds.) The Act of the Mind: Essays on the Poetry of Wallace Stevens, 1963; Penso, K. Wallace Stevens, Harmonium, and the Whole of Harmonium, 1991; Perlis, A. Wallace Stevens: A World of Transforming Shapes, 1976; Peterson, M. Wallace Stevens and the Idealist Tradition, 1983; Rehder, R. The Poetry of Wallace Stevens, 1988; Richardson, J. Wallace Stevens: The Later Years, 1923–1955, 1988; Riddel, J. N. The Clairvoyant Eye: The Poetry and Poetics of Wallace Stevens, 1965; Rosenthal, M. L. and Gall, S. M. The Modern Poetic Sequence: The Genius of Modern Poetry, 1983; Sawaya, R. N. The Scepticism and Animal Faith of Wallace Stevens, 1987; Schaum, M. Wallace Stevens and the Critical Schools, 1988; Schaum, M. (ed.) Wallace Stevens and the Feminine, 1993; Schwarz, D. R. Narrative and Representation in the Poetry of Wallace Stevens, 1993; Serio, J. N. and Leggett, B. J. Teaching Wallace Stevens: Practical Essays, 1994; Sexson, M. The Quest of Self in the Collected Poems of Wallace Stevens, 1981; Stern, H. J. Wallace Stevens: Art of Uncertainty, 1966; Sukenick, R. Wallace Stevens: Musing the Obscure, 1967; Vendler, H. On Extended Wings: Wallace Stevens' Longer Poems, 1969; Vendler, H. Wallace Stevens: Words Chosen out of Desire, 1984; Wells, H. W. introduction to Wallace Stevens, 1964; Weston S. B. Wallace Stevens: An Introduction to the Poetry, 1977; Willard, A. F. (ed.) Wallace Stevens: The Poet and His Critics, 1978; Woodman, L. B. Stanza My Stone: Wallace Stevens and the Hermetic Tradition, 1983. Bibliography—Edelstein, J. M. Wallace Stevens: A Descriptive Bibliography, 1973; Serio, J. N. Wallace Stevens: An Annotated Secondary Bibliography, 1993. Periodicals—New York Review of Books November 20, 1986; Wallace Stevens Journal Spring 1977– .

**STEVENSON, BURTON EGBERT** (November 9, 1872–May 13, 1962), American librarian, anthologist, and novelist wrote: "Born at Chillicothe, Ohio; went through high school there. Carried newspapers as a boy and set up own printing office at age of twelve, starting a monthly amateur paper, and continued publishing it until departure for Princeton in 1890. At Princeton paid own way first by setting type in a local printing office and afterwards as correspondent for the *New York Tribune* and the United Press. Was on the board of the *Tiger*, the college humorous weekly. Never did anything but write and never wanted to. While back in Chillicothe at close of junior year was offered a newspaper position and accepted it, not returning to college. Married Elizabeth Shepherd Butler in 1895.

"In 1899 Stevenson was elected librarian of the local library, and has held the position ever since, with long leaves of absence from time to time. For the first time had the leisure to do some serious literary work, and first book published in 1900. One or two every year after that. Many times abroad. He was at Monte Carlo when the present war broke out, but managed to catch the last boat home. Several of his novels use the Riviera as a background.

"In the spring of 1917, the government began to build Camp Sherman just on the outskirts of Chillicothe, and Stevenson made a state-wide appeal for books and set up libraries in all the recreation huts. In the fall the American Library Association took over the work and appointed Stevenson camp librarian. Many of the librarians assigned to other camps were detailed for a training course at Camp Sherman. Called to Washington to manage the publicity campaign for the nation-wide appeal for books and then sent to Paris to act as European director for the Library War Service. Remained in charge until 1920, during which time over two million books and countless thousands of magazines were circulated. In 1918 established the American Library in Paris, to act as center of information about the United States. Returned to Chillicothe in 1920 but was called back to Paris in 1926 to act as director of the library, holding this position until 1930, doubling the library's collections and tripling its resources.

"Since 1937 has been engaged in the compilation of a dictionary of proverbs and proverbial phrases.

In 1955, he wrote: "Returned from a long vacation at Monte Carlo in late August 1939 and settled down to a compilation which he determined should be as scholarly, accurate and comprehensive as he could make it, *The Home Book of Proverbs, Maxims and Familiar Phrases*. He spent nearly ten years at this task, checking every quotation with the original, using in every case the original language as well as the English translation (except of course such languages as Chinese and Arabic), and carefully dating every quotation in order that the development of the proverb in question, from its first vague form to its final finished one, could be clearly seen. This book, a tome of over 2800 double-column pages, was published in 1948.

"To round out the series, Mr. Stevenson then turned to the Bible, and in 1949 published *The Home Book of Bible Quotations*, a hefty double-columned volume of 650 pages. There seemed to be no more worlds to conquer, but he finally decided to do his Shakespeare over again from the beginning. He had never been satisfied with the original book, into which he had crammed so much extraneous detail that its chief appeal was to Shakespeare students and reference libraries, rather than to the general public.

"So he went to work, again, reading Shakespeare very carefully from the first page to the last, and managed to put together a book equally comprehensive but in more compact form, which could also be printed in less expensive textbook form for school use. As soon as it is finished, he plans to go to Monte Carlo again for a long stay, and perhaps write a book about the Littoral with special reference to his experiences in the Casino over the past thirty years, or perhaps another mystery story, of which several of his older ones were laid in this locale. Or perhaps he will call it a day and lay aside his pen for good. He was eighty years old last [November 1952], and the idea has occurred to him occasionally that it is about time to quit.

"Mr. Stevenson is still librarian of the Chillicothe Public Library, having completed his fifty-third year in that position last September, which is perhaps a record. It is worth remarking that the library, which was established in 1848, has had only three librarians, all of them men (another record?). He is a member of the National Institute of Arts and Letters and of the Century Club in New York. He has lived for more than fifty years in a rambling old house on a hill overlooking Chillicothe and the Scioto valley. From spring to fall he spends a part of his days, like Candide, cultivating his garden and looking after his vines and hundred fruit trees growing on the three acres surrounding his home. He is found of mystery stories, reads one almost every night, and thinks on the whole that the English writers in this genre are better and more literate than their American confreres. He works only a few hours a day, but remarks, 'It is astonishing how much one can get done in fifty years, working only an hour or two a day.' His forty novels, mystery stories, children's stories and what not, added to the 15,000 pages or so of his compilations seen to prove that this is true."

---

Burton Egbert Stevenson's "Home Books" were standard reference tools in libraries everywhere; his *Home Book of Proverbs, Maxims and Familiar Phrases*, has gone through many editions and continues to be widely used by librarians and general reader. When it was first published in 1948, the *New York Times* remarked that "if a reader has oc-

casion to explain such a proverbial phrase as 'hoist on his own petard,' he can find a proverbial gloss for it in 'caught in his own trap,' or 'dose of his own medicine'—all under the subject of 'retribution.' All this constitutes a superb work of reference."

Stevenson was also a popular mystery writer: His best known whodunit was *The Mystery of the Boule Cabinet*, in which a New York sleuth is pitted against a cunning French villain over a Louis XIV cabinet. It was filmed four times and adapted as a play. Stevenson also wrote historical novels, travel and children's books.

At his death the *New York Times* (1962) called him a "man of boundless industry who packed his long life with solid literary achievement," and offered this anecdote: "Mr. Stevenson's scholarship was exhaustive. When he first tackled the problem of who originated the expression about the world beating a pathway to the door of a man who would build a better mousetrap, Ralph Waldo Emerson's authorship was in serious doubt. Mr. Stevenson successfully blasted the claims of others and, in fact, pinpointed the exact month in which Emerson had used the expression—April, 1871, in a lecture at either San Francisco or Oakland."

PRINCIPAL WORKS: *As editor*—Stories of the Colleges: Being Tales of Life at the Great American Universities Told by Noted Graduates, 1901; Mr. Waddy's Return, by Theodore Winthrop, 1904; Poems of American History, 1908; The Home Book of Verse, American and English, 1580–1912, 1912, rev. ed. 1918 under the title The Home Book of Verse, American and English, 1580–1918; rev. ed. 1922 under the title The Home Book of Verse, American and English, 1580–1920; later eds. under the title The Home Book of Verse, American and English); The Home Book of Modern Verse: An Extension of The Home Book of Verse: Being a Selection from American and English Poetry of the Twentieth Century, 1925; Great Americans as seen by the poets, 1933; The Home Book of Quotations, Classical and Modern, 1934 (7th rev. ed. 1964; also published under the title Stevenson's Book of Quotations, Classical and Modern, 1936 and 1946); The Home Book of Shakespeare Quotations: Being Also a Concordance and a Glossary of the Unique Words and Phrases in the Plays and Poems, 1937; The Home Book of Proverbs, Maxims and Familiar Phrases, 1948 (later eds. under the title The Macmillan Book of Proverbs, Maxims and Famous Phrases; in U.K.: Book of Proverbs, Maxims and Familiar Phrases); The Home Book of Bible Quotations, 1949; The Standard Book of Shakespeare Quotations, 1953 (in U.K.: Stevenson's Book of Shakespeare Quotations). *Novels*—At Odds with the Regent: A Story of the Cellamare Conspiracy, 1901; A Soldier of Virginia: A Tale of Colonel Washington and Braddock's Defeat, 1901; The Heritage: A Story of Defeat and Victory, 1902; The Holladay Case, 1903; The Marathon Mystery: A Story of Manhattan, 1904; Affairs of State: Being an Account of Certain Suprising Adventures which Befell an American Family in the Land of Windmills, 1906; The Girl with the Blue Sailor, 1906; That Affair at Elizabeth, 1907; The Quest for the Rose of Sharon, 1909; The Path of Honor: A Tale of the War in the Bocage, 1910; The Mystery of the Boule Cabinet: A Detective Story, 1912; The Destroyer: A Tale of International Intrigue, 1913; Little Comrade: A Tale of the Great War, 1915 (reissued as The Girl fron Alsace, 1915, and Little Comrade: The Romance of a Lady Spy in the Great War, 1917); A King in Babylon, 1917; The Kingmakers, 1922; The Storm-Center: A Romance, 1924; The Coast of Enchantment, 1926; The House Next Door: A Detective Story, 1932; Villa Aurelia: A Riviera Interlude, 1932; The Red Carnation, 1939. *Short stories*—Cadets of Gascony: Two Stories of Old France, 1904. *Nonfiction*—A List of All the Most Important and Interesting Poems Relating to the History of America from Its Discovery Down to the Present Day, 1908; The Spell of Holland: The Story of a Pilgrimage to the Land of Dykes and Windmills, 1911; American Men of Mind, 1913; The Charm of Ireland, 1914; Famous Single Poems and the Controversies Which Have Raged Around Them, 1923. *Juvenile*—Tommy Remington's Battle, 1902; The Young Section-Hand, 1905; (with E. B. Stevenson) Days and Deeds: A Book of Verse for Children's Reading and Speaking, 1906 (3rd rev. ed. 1939); The Young Train Dispatcher, 1907; A Child's Guide to Biography: American—Men of Action, 1909 (reissued as A Guide to Biography for Young Readers: American—Men of Action, 1910); The Young Train Master, 1909; A Guide to Biography for Young Readers: American—Men of Mind, 1910; The Young Apprentice; or, Allan West's Chum, 1912; The Home Book of Verse for Young Folks, 1915 (2nd rev. ed. 1958); American History in Verse for Boys and Girls, 1932; My Country: Poems of History for Young Americans, 1932.

ABOUT: The autobiographical material quoted above was written for Twentieth Century Authors, 1942 and Twentieth Century Authors First Supplement, 1955. *Periodicals*—New York Times November 7, 1948; May 15, 1962.

## STEVENSON, D(OROTHY) E(MILY) (1892–

December 30, 1973), Scottish novelist, wrote: "I was born at Edinburgh and brought up in that city and at North Berwick. My father, David Alan Stevenson, was civil engineer to the Northern Lighthouse Board and a first cousin of Robert Louis Stevenson. My mother was a first cousin of Earl Roberts of Kandahar. I learned to play golf at North Berwick at the age of four and afterwards took part in various championships. I started my literary career at the age of six, but, as my family did not approve of my 'wasting my time writing stories,' I was obliged to hide in an attic when I wanted to write. Naturally, this circumstance whetted my interest and encouraged me to further flights of fancy. I have always been deeply interested in the historical associations of Edinburgh, but even more interested in the lives of the people in bygone years.

"In 1916 I married Major James R. Peploe of the Highland Light Infantry. My family consists of two sons and one daughter. My elder son is a Captain in the Royal Artillery and my daughter is serving in the War Relief Nursing Service. I followed the drum for years and gained a good deal of valuable experience meeting people of all kinds.

"I am now settled at Moffat, a small town in beautiful Annandale in the county of Dumfries. It is a peaceful spot and a marvellous place for writing. I enjoy a good walk over the hills with my spaniel, and then come home to find tea waiting, spread on a table before a bright log fire.

"My favorite author is Jane Austen. My favorite occupations are reading, writing and talking to my friends. I am fond of golf, skating, swimming, and fishing. I dislike proof-reading and housekeeping.

"My books are all novels, as it is the human element which interests me most in life: some of my books are light and amusing and others are serious studies of character, but they are all human and carefully thought out, and perhaps it is for these

two reasons that my public is so diverse, and ranges from university professors to old ladies and small boys! My books are published in all English-speaking countries and have been translated into several foreign languages. I have done a good deal of lecturing—chiefly on literary subjects. I am a member of the R.L.S. Club, and of several literary societies in the United States. . . ."

D. E. Stevenson's most popular novels were those that concerned two recurring characters, Miss Buncle, a writer of modest ambitions who achieves unexpected success when her book about the English village where she lives becomes a best-seller, and Mrs. Tim, the plucky and resourceful wife of an English army officer during World War II. *The Two Mrs. Abbotts*, which takes up Miss Buncle (now Mrs. Abbott) in married life during World War II, is representative of the series about her. A critic in the *New York Times Book Review* thought the novel "delightful" and added, "The whole rambling story keeps the reader continuously interested in the minor incidents of village life and at the same time gives a very English—and mildly satirical—picture of the way the English upper middle class carries on in wartime."

The Mrs. Tim books, with their more direct backgrounding in World War II, were somewhat less frothy than the Miss Buncle series, but they too offered pleasing doses of whimsy and measured sentimentality. Of *Mrs. Tim Carries On: Leaves from the Diary of an Officer's Wife in the Year 1940*, a reviewer in the *Christian Science Monitor* wrote, "It is true that Mrs. Tim's observations are not profound, but they may be nearer the truth for not being arrived at elaborately. She finds enjoyment in the feeling of kinship which unites the whole population of London into one vast family . . . and in this feeling she finds an aid to courage and the explanation of many a brave deed. This is pretty obvious, but it is expressed with freshness and a good deal of conviction."

Stevenson's many other novels were not very different from the Miss Buncle and Mrs. Tim books. "Served up in a very gracious prose . . . as virtuous as a vicar [and] as comfortable as an old shoe," as a *San Francisco Chronicle* reviewer described one of them, they were extremely popular in their time and more than a dozen remain in print.

A collection of Stevenson's papers is at the library of Boston University.

PRINCIPAL WORKS: *Novels*—Peter West, 1923; Mrs. Tim of the Regiment: Leaves from the Diary of an Officer's Wife, 1932; Miss Buncle's Book, 1934; Golden Days, 1934; Divorced from Reality, 1935 (in U.S.: Miss Dean's Dilemma); Miss Buncle, Married, 1936; Smouldering Fire, 1936; The Empty World: A Romance of the Future, 1936 (in U.S.: A World in Spell); The Story of Rosabelle Shaw, 1937; Miss Bunn, the Baker's Daughter 1938 (in U.S.: The Baker's Daughter); The Green Money, 1939; The English Air, 1940; Rochester's Wife, 1940; Spring Magic, 1941; Mrs. Tim Carries On: Leaves from the Diary of an Officer's Wife in the Year 1940, 1941; Crooked Adam, 1942; Celia's House, 1943; The Two Mrs. Abbotts: A New Buncle Book, 1943; Listening Valley, 1944; The Four Graces, 1946; Kate Hardy, 1947; Mrs. Tim Gets a Job, 1947; Young Mrs. Savage, 1948; Vittoria Cottage, 1949; Music in the Hills,

1950; Winter and Rough Weather, 1951 (in U.S.: Shoulder the Sky); Mrs. Tim Flies Home: Leaves from the Diary of a Grass-Window, 1952; Five Windows, 1953; Charlotte Fairlie, 1954 (in U.S.: Blow the Wind Southerly); Amberwell, 1955; Summerhills, 1956; The Tall Stranger, 1957; Anna and Her Daughters, 1958; Still Glides the Stream, 1959; The Musgraves, 1960; Bel Lamington, 1961; Fletchers End, 1962; The Blue Sapphire, 1963; Katherine Wentworth, 1964; Katherine's Marriage, 1965 (in U.S.: The Marriage of Katherine); The House on the Cliff, 1966; Sarah Morris Remembers, 1967; Sarah's Cottage, 1968; Gerald and Elizabeth, 1969; The House of the Deer, 1970. Poetry—Meadow-Flowers, 1915; The Starry Mantle, 1926. Juvenile—Alister and Co. 1940.

ABOUT: The autobiographical material quoted above was written for Twentieth Century Authors, 1942. Contemporary Authors Permanent Series 1 1975; Twentieth Century Romance and Historical Writers, 3rd ed., 1994. Periodicals—Christian Science Monitor August 2, 1941; New York Times Book Review January 9, 1944; San Francisco Chronicle November 23, 1947; Saturday Review of Literature January 15, 1944.

## STEWART, ALFRED WALTER (pseudonym "J. J. CONNINGTON") (1880–July 1, 1947),

English university professor and writer of detective fiction, was the youngest son of Professor William Stewart, former Dean of Faculties in Glasgow University. He was educated at the Universities of Glasgow and Marburg and at University College, London. He was a Mackay-Smith Scholar in 1901 at Queen's University, Belfast, where he was also 1851 Exhibition Scholar from 1903 to 1905 and Carnegie Research Fellow from 1905 to 1908. He became a lecturer on organic chemistry there in 1909, after already publishing two chemistry texts. He returned to the University of Glasgow in 1914 to lecture on physical chemistry and radioactivity until 1919, when he returned, as a professor of chemistry, to Queen's College, where he later served as chairman of the chemistry department until his retirement in 1944.

Tapping into his knowledge of chemistry and science, Stewart began using his pseudonym J. J. Connington by writing a book of science fiction, Nordenholt's Million, in which a millionaire schemes to save the masses from a sudden plague in London with the help of atomic energy. His details of future science are poor, according to Jacques Barzun and W. H. Taylor in A Catalogue of Crime, and perhaps led him to abandon the genre for mysteries, of which he wrote approximately two dozen from 1926 to 1944. There his scientific expertise was put to better use, in adding credibility and detail regarding medical considerations involved in crime, such as poisons and blood tests. He was also adept at painting a realistic and thorough portrait of upper-middle class life in the English countryside between the wars. He wrote in a quintessential British mystery style popular in his day.

Stewart, writing as Connington, was best known, however, for his later creation, the detective team of Chief Constable Sir Clinton Driffield and Squire Wendover, who worked together in several thrillers and were one of the first detective pairs who, unlike Holmes and Watson, frequently disagreed and competed with each other over who was the real detective.

Murder in the Maze (1927), concerning the dou-ble murder of twin brothers, is considered one of the best Driffield/Wendover books.

As an explanatory sequel to his mysteries, Stewart wrote twelve essays on crime-writing in Alias J. J. Connington. The subjects ranged from ether-drinking to the nature of evidence, from Sherlock Holmes to Gilles de Rais, and they show erudition, critical prowess and more humor than he allowed to come through in his stories, at least according to Barzen and Taylor.

PRINCIPAL WORKS: Stereochemistry, 1907; Recent Advances in Organic Chemistry, 1908; Chemistry and Its Borderland, 1914; Recent Advances in Physical and Organic Chemistry, 1919; Some Physico-Chemical Themes, 1922; Alias J. J. Connington, 1947 (essays). As "J. J. Connington"—Nordenholt's Million, 1923; Almighty Gold, 1924; Death at Swaythling Court, 1926; The Dangerfield Talisman, 1927; Tragedy at Ravensthorpe, 1927; Murder in the Maze, 1927; Mystery at Lynden Sands, 1928; The Case With Nine Solutions, 1928; Grim Vengence, 1929; Nemesis at Raynham Parva, 1929; The Eye in the Museum, 1929; The Two Ticket Puzzle, 1930; The Boathouse Riddle, 1931; The Sweepstake Murders, 1931; The Castleford Conundrum, 1932; Tom Tiddler's Island, 1933 (in U.S.: Gold Brick Island); The HaHa Case, 1934 (in U.S.: The Brandon Case) In Whose Dim Shadow, 1935 (in U.S.: The Tau Cross Mystery); A Minor Operation, 1937; For Murder Will Speak, 1938 (in U.S.: Murder Will Speak) Truth Comes Limping, 1938; The Counsellor, 1939; The Four Defences, 1940; The Twenty-One Clues, 1941; No Past Is Dead, 1942; Jack-in-the-Box, 1944; Common Sense Is All You Need, 1947.

ABOUT: Barzun, J. and Taylor, W. H. A Catalogue of Crime, 1971; Stewart, A. W. Alias J. J. Connington, 1947; Twentieth Century Crime and Mystery Writers; Who's Who 1946. Periodicals—Manchester Guardian August 13, 1940; New Statesman April 9, 1927; New York Times February 20, 1927, January 24, 1932; Spectator December 28, 1929; Times (London) December 17, 1931; May 23, 1942; July 3, 1947.

## STEWART, DONALD OGDEN (November 30, 1894–August 2, 1980),

American screenwriter, humorist, playwright, and actor, was born in Columbus, Ohio, the son of Gilbert Holland Stewart and Clara Landon (Ogden) Stewart. He attended Phillips Exeter Academy and went to Yale, graduating in 1916. He served in the Navy for two years during World War I, and worked in banking in Columbus and the bond business in Dayton, Ohio. He also worked for American Telephone and Telegraph Company in various U. S. cities, including Minneapolis, where he met F. Scott Fitzgerald, who introduced him to Vanity Fair editor Edmund Wilson, who published Stewart's first parodies of famous writers.

In the 1920s he associated with the Algonquin Round Table, joined many writers and artists as an expatriate in Europe, living in Paris, Vienna, Budapest, and Capri, and wrote social parodies as well as acted and wrote for the theater.

His reputation as a humorist started with his first book, A Parody Outline of History (1921), a spoof that hit a national funny bone, according to the New York Times, and mocks the styles of H. G. Wells, Ring Lardner, Sinclair Lewis, Edith Wharton, Eugene O'Neill, Harold Bell Wright, and others. His style, full of nonsense and non sequitur, became known as crazy humor.

He continued down the parody path, tackling Emily Post and etiquette in Perfect Behavior

(1922), a guide for ladies and gentlemen in all social crises. Stewart turned his satire toward religious, middle-class values in *Aunt Polly's Story of Mankind* (1923), in which a

successful banker's socialite wife shares her narrowness with her nieces and nephews in telling them her version of the history of the world. Stewart later told the *New York Times* this was the book he was proudest of, for it had more bite than mere drawing room humor. He continued in the same satiric vein, taking an average Midwestern family, from Legion, Ohio, to Europe in *Mr. and Mrs. Haddock Abroad* (1924). W. R. Benét in the *Saturday Review of Literature* called the novel excruciatingly funny.

Stewart's bright and lighthearted dialogue, combined with his keen and witty observations, lent itself well to the movies and proved far more profitable than writing for publishers. Following many of his contemporaries, he went to Hollywood, and in 1932 was hired by Irving Thalberg to write screenplays for MGM, where he thrived, according to Ronald Brownstein in *The Power and the Glitter* (1990). "Since his days at Exeter, Stewart, the outsider from a middle-class family in Ohio, had longed for the social approval of the wealthy and well-connected . . . In Hollywood, for the first time, he earned enough money to feel he truly belonged in that company. He spent money as stylishly as he earned it. Through the most bitter years of the Depression, he appeared entirely comfortable manufacturing witty scripts for MGM, enjoying the sun at his Bel Air home, and drinking until he passed out at parties," Brownstein wrote.

Stewart's greatest Hollywood notoriety came when he won an Academy Award in 1940 for best screenplay for his adaptation of Philip Barry's play, *The Philadelphia Story*. He worked with Dalton Trumbo on the critically acclaimed *Kitty Foyle* (1940), and also wrote or collaborated on such hits as *The Barretts of Wimpole Street* (1934), *Love Affair* (1939), *Keeper of the Flame* (1942), and *Life With Father* (1947).

In the 1930s, while he was one of the highest paid screenwriters in Hollywood, Stewart began to feel that life lacked meaning. His political consciousness was stirred in the early 1930s when, while researching for a character in a play, he read tracts by the British left-wing polemicist John Strachey and underwent an apparently searing midlife conversion He took up the anti-Fascist cause and became a spokesperson for civil liberties and other labor and liberal causes. Stewart was a member of the Communist Party briefly, before quitting over the Hitler-Stalin pact in 1939. He served as president of the League of American Writers from 1937 to 1941. His autobiography, *By a Stroke of Luck!* is a careless but still informative record of his interests. Called to testify before the House Un-American Activities Committee during its investigation of al-

leged Communist influence in Hollywood, he refused to implicate himself or anyone else. As a result, he was blacklisted and lost his job at MGM. With his second wife, Ella Winter, the political journalist, radical activist, and the widow of Lincoln Steffens, he moved to England, living in London for the rest of his life.

PRINCIPAL WORKS: A Parody Outline of History, 1921; Perfect Behavior, 1922; Aunt Polly's Story of Mankind, 1923; Mr. and Mrs. Haddock Abroad, 1924; The Crazy Fool, 1925; Mr. and Mrs. Haddock in Paris, 1926; Father William, 1929; as editor Fighting Words, 1940; By A Stroke of Luck!, 1975 (autobiography) Plays Rebound, 1928; Fine and Dandy, 1930; How I Wonder, 1947; The Kidders, 1957; Honor Bright, 1958. Screenplays Laughter, 1930; (with J. Balderston) Smiling Through, 1933; White Sister, 1933; Going Hollywood, 1933; (with E. Vajda and C. West) The Barretts of Wimpole Street, 1934; (with H. J. Mankiewicz) Another Language, 1935; (with H. Jackson) No More Ladies, 1935; (with B. and W. Root) Prisoner of Zenda, 1938; (with S. Buchman) Holiday, 1938; (with E. Vajda and C. West) Marie Antoinette, 1938; Night of Nights, 1939; (with D. Davis) Love Affair, 1939; (with D. Trumbo) Kitty Foyle, 1940; The Philadelphia Story, 1940; That Uncertain Feeling, 1941; (with E. Paul) A Woman's Face, 1941; Keeper of the Flame, 1942; Without Love, 1945; Life With Father, 1947; (with S. Levien) Cass Timberlane, 1947; Edward My Son, 1949; Malaya, 1950.

ABOUT: Brownstein, R. The Power and the Glitter; Current Biography 1941, 1980; Stewart, D. O. By A Stroke of Luck!, 19? *Periodicals*—Library Journal December 15, 1975; Nation November 29, 1922; New York Times November 16, 1924; September 12, 1926; August 3, 1980; New Yorker January 5, 1976; Saturday Review of Literature December 6, 1924; Times (London) August 5, 1980.

**STEWART, ELEANOR.** See **PORTER, E. H.**

**STEWART, GEORGE R(IPPEY)** (May 31, 1895–August 22, 1980), American novelist and non-fiction writer, wrote: "My family goes back chiefly to Scotch-Irish origins, though with strong English and some French and Dutch strains. I was born in Sewickley, Pennsylvania. My boyhood was spent in the small town of Indiana, Pennsylvania. My family moved to California in 1908. I graduated from Pasadena High School in 1913, and in the same year entered Princeton, the traditional college of my mother's family. I graduated in 1917, with a major in English, fairly near the head of the class scholastically but not otherwise distinguished.

"In May 1917, I enlisted in the U.S. Army Ambulance Service. I never got overseas, but the Army taught me a lot.

"In March 1919, I was discharged from the Army, and that fall I began graduate work in the English department at the University of California. For the next fifteen years I was definitely academic. I took an M.A. (California, 1920), and a Ph.D. (Columbia, 1922). I was an instructor at the University of Michigan (1922–1923), and then went to the English department at Berkeley as an instructor.

"During the next decade and more I lived a pleasantly academic life. I was married (Theodosia Burton, 1924), and the father of two children (Jill, 1925, and John Harris, 1928). I published a book *The Technique of English Verse*, and many scholarly articles, such as 'The Meaning of *Bacheler* in Middle English.'

"My first book on a 'general' list was my life of

Bret Harte. In the next few years the universities were caught in the depression, and advancement was slow and the situation discouraging. Partly for these reasons I turned to nonacademic writing with *Ordeal by Hunger*, a thoroughly historical, nonfictional book, but meant for the general reader. Its good reception encouraged me to take the next step and write a historical novel—*East of the Giants.*

"From that time on, I have lived a rather complicated life, being all at once a professor, a novelist, and a writer of nonfiction. As might be expected

from my background, however, my novels have had a strongly authentic basis, and *Storm* and *Fire* have been used as reading in university courses on meteorology and forestry. On the other hand, *Man* was a selection of the Non-Fiction Book Club, even though it makes use of many fictional devices. I consider *Names on the Land* my most important contribution to scholarship, and it is, I think, my own favorite among my books. *Storm* and *Fire*, however, remain the most popular, and have been widely translated. . . . "

George R. Stewart taught in the English department at Berkeley for almost forty years, but he published few works of literary scholarship. He was known to the public, instead, as a novelist and miscellaneous writer—and one of unpredictable inclinations. Indeed, as a reviewer in the *Nation* remarked apropos of *Names on the Land*, a history of American place-names, "One can never tell what George R. Stewart is going to write about next, but one can always be certain it will make lively reading." In the 1930s alone Stewart published popular biographies of the humorists Bret Harte and George H. Derby (*Bret Harte, Argonaut and Exile, John Phoenix, Esq., the Veritable Squibob*); a history of a disastrous migration to California by a group of settlers in the winter of 1847 (*Ordeal by Hunger*); a historical novel about a pioneering woman in early California (*East of the Giants*); and a novel of manners about academic life (*Doctor's Oral*).

Successful—and relatively superficial—as most of these books were, they were surpassed by *Storm*, a 1941 novel about an invented storm named "Maria" that destroys a good swath of California in the few short days of its life. The Book of the Month Club chose *Storm* as a main selection, and although many critics felt its human characters lacked much depth, it was a commercial success, and received good reviews. J. H. Bradley wrote of it, in the *Atlantic*, "In writing the biography of one hypothetical storm Mr. Stewart . . . tells all that needs to be told about storms in general, and he tells it with a significance which neither meteorologists nor common men have ever before achieved. . . . Mr. Stewart's style is rather febrile and blown up, but

so was Maria's. His distaste for understatement can be forgiven him in view of the originality of his theme and the imagination of its treatment." Equally good, in the opinion of most critics, was the 1948 novel *Fire*, which did for the phenomenon of its title what the earlier book had done for storms. Reviewing *Fire* in the *Christian Science Monitor*, Horace Reynolds wrote, "The writing is superb—hard, lean, expressive prose. . . . It's an exciting story, all told, and so real it's hard to believe that the Spitcat never existed, never burnt a tree, so magnificently has Stewart imagined and circumstantially created it."

Between *Storm* and *Fire* Stewart wrote *Man*, an anthropological account of the human race in which, most critics felt, he overreached the limits of his knowledge, and *Names on the Land*, a much more circumscribed and successful study of American place names. "This book," wrote Eudora Welty in the *New York Times Book Review*, "is a labor of love, such as few people would have had the energies, much less the abilities, or the pure courage, to undertake—and finish. The whole is written with a grace and engaging humor belying the work behind it. The nation from Seldom Seen to Possum Glory, Hog Eye to Bug Tustle, does owe Mr. Stewart a debt of gratitude for getting the tremendous material here between the covers of a book." Stewart returned to the subject of onomastics twenty-five years later with *American Place-Names*, a dictionary that was considered an exemplary reference work in every respect.

Stewart's later books encompassed an equally broad variety of subjects and forms: a science-fiction fantasy about a band of survivors at the end of the world (*Earth Abides*); a defense of academic freedom during the McCarthy era (*The Year of the Oath*); a philosophical novel about a poet's meditation of the human and geological past (*Sheep Rock*); travel books about life along the transcontinental highways of North America (*U.S. 40, N.A. 1*); an informal anthropological study of various American customs (*American Ways of Life*); and a polemic about the environmental consequences of proliferating waste (*Not So Rich As You Think*). Again, most of these books received good reviews, and one, *Earth Abides*, is regarded by some as something of a classic in its field ("it is a novel told with explicit deliberation, an excellent eye for the right detail, and a cumulative effect of power and faith in man's destiny," wrote the *Saturday Review of Literature*).

Perhaps the most praised of all Stewart's latter books was *The Years of the City*, a novel that conceived of the rise and fall of a fictitious colonial Greek city named Phrax. "This is a book built out of many knowledges and wide scholarship," wrote Wallace Stegner in the *San Francisco Chronicle*, "but the effect is single and powerful, for the imagination behind all the facts is large. Phrax is not an historical reconstruction, but a real city: we would know it even from its ruins."

Before retiring from Berkeley in 1962 Stewart taught for brief periods at Duke and Princeton Universities. In the 1952–1953 academic year he was

Fulbright Professor of American Literature and Civilization at the University of Athens.

PRINCIPAL WORKS: *Novels*—East of the Giants, 1938; Doctor's Oral, 1939, Storm, 1941; Fire, 1948; Earth Abides, 1949; Sheep Rock, 1951; The Years of the City, 1955. *Nonfiction*—The Technique of English Verse, 1930; Bret Harte, Argonaut and Exile, 1931; Ordeal by Hunger: The Story of the Donner Party, 1936; English Composition: A Laboratory Course, 2 vols., 1936; John Phoenix, Esq., the Veritable Squibob: A Life of Captain George H. Derby, 1937; Take Your Bible in One Hand: The Life of William Henry Thomes, 1939; Names on the Land, 1945, 3rd ed. 1967; Man: An Autobiography, 1946; (with others) The Year of the Oath: The Fight for Academic Freedom at the University of California, 1950; U.S. 40: Cross Section of the United States of America, 1953; American Ways of Life, 1954; N.A. 1: The North-South Continental Highway, 2 vols., 1957; Pickett's Charge: A Microhistory of the Final Attack at Gettysburg, 1959; Donner Pass and Those Who Crossed it, 1960; The California Trail: An Epic with Many Heroes, 1962; Committee of Vigilance: Revolution in San Francisco, 1851, 1964; Good Lives, 1967; Not So Rich As You Think, 1968; American Place-Names: A Concise and Selective Dictionary for the Continental United States of America, 1970; Names on the Globe, 1975; American Given Names: Their Origin and History in the Context of the English Language, 1979. *Juvenile*—To California by Covered Wagon, 1954. *As editor*—The Luck of the Roaring Camp and Selected Stories and Poems (by B. Harte) 1928; The Opening of the California Trail: The Story of the Stevens Party from the Reminiscences of Moses Schallenberger, 1953.

ABOUT: The autobiographical material quoted above was written for Twentieth Century Authors First Supplement, 1955. Caldwell, J. George R. Stewart, 1981; Contemporary Authors New Revision Series 3, 1981; Current Biography 1942; Dictionary of Literary Biography vol. 8 1981; Twentieth Century Science Fiction Writers, 3rd ed., 1991. *Periodicals*—Atlantic January 1942; Christian Science Monitor April 22, 1948; Nation July 7, 1945; New York Times August 26, 1980; New York Times Book Review May 6, 1945; San Francisco Chronicle August 28, 1955; Saturday Review of Literature November 26, 1949.

## STEWART, J(OHN) I(NNES) M(ACKINTOSH) (pseudonym "MICHAEL INNES")

(September 30, 1906–November 12, 1994), Scottish

novelist, critic, and detective story writer, wrote: "I was born just outside Edinburgh and almost within the shadow of the centenary monument to the author of *Waverley*. Edinburgh Academy, where I went to school, had Scott as one of its founders, and Robert Louis Stevenson was a pupil there for a short time. My headmaster told me that one day I might write *Kidnapped* or a *Treasure Island*; I remember his tone as one of mild censure and suppose he didn't greatly care for romances. I devoured them and no doubt they colored my mind. But the books that chiefly impressed me as a boy were Christian de Wet's *Three Years' War*, Swinburne's *Atalanta in Calydon*, and the plays and prefaces of Bernard Shaw. Since then I have come to realize that Homer, Dante, and Shakespeare are the world's most satisfactory writers. But I don't get from them quite the electrical effect of those early books.

"At Oxford I had a great Elizabethan scholar as my tutor; he got me a first class in English and then I went to Vienna for a year to recover. After that I had the good luck to fall in with Francis Meynell, and for him I edited the Nonesuch Edition of Florio's *Montaigne*; this in turn got me a job as a lecturer in the University of Leeds. I was recommended to two excellent lodgings by the professors who appointed me; in the one there was already a lodger, a young woman; in the other not. I made the natural choice and a year later the young woman and I married. My wife [the former Margaret Harwick who died in 1979, and who bore Stewart five children] is a doctor and although we have three small sons still finds time for infant welfare work.

"Leeds lasted five years and then, when I had sold all my Nonesuch books and was rather wondering about the rent, I was invited to become professor of English at Adelaide University. It was on the way out that I wrote my first mystery story. For nine months of the year, and between six and eight o'clock in the morning, the South Australian climate is just right for authorship of this sort, so I have written a good many similar stories since. I would describe some of them as on the frontier between the detective story and fantasy; they have a somewhat 'literary' flavor but their values remain those of melodrama and not of fiction proper. Sometimes I lie on the beach in the sun and wonder if I mightn't some day write something else."

---

J. I. M. Stewart had three distinct reputations: as the detective story writer "Michael Innes"; as a critic (and university teacher); and, from 1954 as "straight" novelist. An industrious writer, he found time to conduct a busy teaching career, write forty-five books as "Michael Innes," twenty-six works of fiction as himself, an autobiography—*Myself and Michael Innes* (1987)—and some dozen works of criticism.

His father, John Stewart, was Director of Education in the city of Edinburgh; his mother was the former Eliza Jane Clark. The atmosphere in which he moved as a boy and young man was extremely cultivated. He was a brilliant scholar, although never a particularly original one. When after gaining his First he went to Vienna he took the opportunity to study Freudian psychoanalysis. After holding appointments at the Universities of Leeds, Adelaide and Queen's (Belfast), Stewart became Student at Christ Church, Oxford, where he remained until 1973; for the last four years of his tenure he was University Reader. A man mild in manner, his politeness was much appreciated by his colleagues and his students.

He began writing detective fiction while teaching at the University of Adelaide—where he profoundly disliked what he saw as Australian roughness. It is mainly by means of his skill in this light genre that his memory will be perpetuated. *Death at the President's Lodging* (*Seven Suspects* in America), urbane and civilized, was greeted with great approval and pleasure.

Stewart's detective stories were treasured by the cultivated. It was *Hamlet, Revenge!*, his second mystery, that confirmed his reputation. Will Cuppy in *New York Herald Books* thought it "quite the worthiest baffler . . . in some time." The reviewer for the *Times Literary Supplement* (1937) wrote: "*Hamlet, Revenge!* confirms the fact that became clear in his first book, that Mr. Michael Innes is in a class by himself among writers of detective fiction." *The Spider Strikes* (in U.K.: *Stop Press*) elicited from Will Cuppy, again in *Books* (1939), even richer praise: "pretty sure to go down as one of those mystery milestones." But it did demonstrate Stewart's powers to entertain and puzzle: "not a book for those mystery fans who demand a murder in the first chapter," explained the *New York Times*, "but it has a fascination all its own." Some reviewers, such as the one for the *New Yorker*, complained of its "almost vulgar display of book-learning"; but Stewart of course wrote exclusively for the "book-learned." The *Saturday Review of Literature* (1939) gave a more balanced description: "*The Spider Strikes* is long, leisurely, packed to the gunwales with learned conversations, not free from dull and ponderous pages, and yet with more real wit, sparkle and zest than about any other detective story of the year. Distinctly a 'literate' mystery, and assuredly caviare to the general reader, but the caviare is the very best grade, with every bead a pearl."

Stewart's chief detective was Inspector John Appleby, a gentleman turned policeman who rises in the course of the books from inspector to knighted commissioner. Sometimes, however, Stewart dispensed with a detective altogether; on other occasions he replaced Appleby with the somewhat more conventional Inspector Cadover. If he had a model for his more adventurous yarns, then this was surely his fellow-Scot John Buchan. This is particularly apparent in *From London Far* (in America as *The Unsuspected Chasm*), which has a long and (most readers thought) thrilling chase sequence—"utterly unbelievable," thought the *Saturday Review of Literature* (1946), "and ditto delightful."

As a "serious novelist," Stewart was far less successful. As his *Times* obituarist put it, his works in this field "always promised . . . fiction of a high order" but "somehow never quite" delivered it. The first "serious" book was *Mark Lambert's Supper*, an essay in the style of Henry James (and depending much upon his *The Aspern Papers*); like its successors, it "never really shook off the influence of its great inspirer, either in point of style or content, and remained a work to be appraised with interest rather than admired."

Stewart's attempt to emulate the great masters of the *roman fleuve* was even more disastrous, since he chose as his model C. P. Snow. As Stewart's *Times* obituarist argued, "the absence of a genuine creative spark in Snow made him a bad master—especially for a writer of such natural grace and refinement as Stewart." The "quintet" *A Staircase in Surrey* (1974–1979), with Duncan Patullo as its central figure, attempted to make the University of Oxford its main subject; but it ultimately amounted to no more than an only mildly readable "campus" sequence, "too bloodless, too insubstantial" (H. M.

Klein). Of *The Gaudy*, the first in the sequence, the *Times Literary Supplement* reviewer wrote: "The present reviewer . . . hopes to be spared the next four instalments. One feels that Mr. Stewart would have written better if he had known Christ Church, Oxford, less well."

As a critic Stewart was sound, scholarly, useful, and conventional. It is perhaps significant that the major critical biographers of such figures as Conrad, Kipling, and Hardy—upon all of whom he wrote books—find little or nothing to say of his views in their own discussions. He was chary, in his over-refined way, of using biographical information about his subjects, yet unclear about his own position with regard to this much vexed matter. When he entitled his 1971 book on Thomas Hardy, *Thomas Hardy: A Critical Biography* a (1972) reviewer asked in exasperation, "Whatever led Mr. Stewart to subtitle his book [thus]? It is nothing of the sort." John Bayley, though, in the *New Statesman* (1973), called the chapter on the "Private Life" "a masterpiece of sceptical lucidity." Jacques Berthoud, in his Penguin edition of Conrad's *The Shadow Line*, wrote of Stewart's book on Conrad: a "depressing example of English common sense in action." Of his book on Kipling, the *Economist* (1966) stated: " [it] does not push the doors of perception very much further apart." The fact is that, although Stewart's criticism was perhaps rather more friendly and useful than comment upon it might imply, he was too good mannered to be sufficiently critical.

*Eight Modern Writers* formed—to the surprise of many, since writers other than Hardy, James, Shaw, Conrad, Yeats, Joyce, and Lawrence were deemed hardly to exist in any significant manner—the last volume of the *Oxford History of English Literature*. Writers then living were excluded, and the first chapter, on the literary scene from 1880 to 1940, was barely adequate. "For whom it is the book meant?" asked the *Economist* (1964), and, granted that many of Stewart's critical remarks were "acute and witty," went on to draw attention to the "misgivings . . . aroused by the consistently urbane tone. . . . accents of slightly amused condescension are quite unmistakable." Frank Kermode in the *New Statesman* (1963) pointed out that "to qualify for treatment in this book a writer must be British or Irish and dead. Since this rule excludes Eliot and Pound it must be called an absurdity. . . . This huge book is, then, as part of a literary history, quite simply a non-starter. . . . Since the essays have none of that personal urgency which might have excused so wide a departure from the original plan, the prospect of pleasure seems bleak." However, he was inclined to compliment Stewart for this "independence of mind" which (he thought) largely redeemed the book.

PRINCIPAL WORKS: *Crime novels (as "Michael Innes")*—Death at the President's Lodging, 1936 (in U.S.: Seven Suspects); Hamlet, Revenge!, 1937 Lament for a Maker, 1938; Stop Press, 1939 (in U.S.: The Spider Strikes) The Secret Vanguard, 1940; There Came Both Mist and Snow, 1941 (in U.S.: A Comedy of Terrors); Appleby on Ararat, 1941; The Daffodil Affair, 1942; The Weight of the Evidence, 1943; Appleby's End, 1945; From London Far, 1946 (in U.S.: The Unsuspected

Chasm); What Happened at Hazelwood, 1946; A Night of Errors, 1947; The Journeying Boy, 1947 (in U.S.: The Case of the Journeying Boy); Operation Pax, 1948 (in U.S.: The Paper Thunderbolt); A Private View, 1952 (in U.S.: One Man-Show, and as Murder Is an Art); Christmas at Candleshoe, 1953; The Man from the Sea, 1955 (in U.S.: Death by Moonlight); Old Hall, New Hall, 1956 (in U.S.: A Question of Queens); Appleby by Plays Chicken, 1957 (in U.S.: Death on a Quiet Day); The Long Farewell, 1958; Hare Sitting Up, 1959; The New Sonia Wayward, 1960 (in U.S.: The Case of Sonia Wayward,) and as The Last of Sonia Wayward; Silence Observed, 1961; A Connoisseur's Case, 1962 (in U.S.: The Crabtree Affair); Money from Holme, 1964; The Bloody Wood, 1966; A Change of Heir, 1966; Appleby at Allington, 1968 (in U.S.: Death by Water); A Family Affair, 1969 (in U.S.: Picture of Guilt); Death at the Chase, 1970; An Awkward Lie, 1971; The Open House, 1972; Appleby's Answer, 1972; Appleby's Other Story, 1974; The Mysterious Commission, 1974; The Gay Phoenix, 1976; Honeybath's Haven, 1977; The Ampersand Papers, 1978; Going It Alone, 1980; Lord Mullion's Secret, 1981; Sheiks and Adders, 1982; Appleby and Honeybath, 1983; Carson's Conspiracy, 1984; Appleby and the Ospreys, 1986. *Short stories* (as "Michael Innes")—(with R. Heppenstall) Three Tales of Hamlet, 1950; Appleby Talking, 1954 (in U.S.: Dead Man's Shoes); Appleby Talks Again, 1956; The Appleby File, 1976. *Novels* (as *J.I.M. Stewart*)—Mark Lambert's Supper, 1954; The Guardians, 1955; A Use of Riches, 1957; The Man Who Won the Pools, 1961; The Last Tresilians, 1963; An Acre of Grass, 1965; The Aylwins, 1966; Vanderlyn's Kingdom, 1967; Avery's Mission, 1971; A Palace of Art, 1972; Mungo's Dream, 1973; A Staircase in Surrey: The Gaudy, 1974, Young Pattulo, 1975, A Memorial Service, 1976, The Madonna of the Astrolable, 1976, Full Term, 1978; Andrew and Tobias, 1981; A Villa in France, 1982; An Open Prison, 1984; The Naylors, 1985. *Short stories*—The Man Who Wrote Detective Stories, 1959; Cucumber Sandwiches, 1969; Our England Is a Garden, 1979; The Bridge at Arta, 1981; My Aunt Christina, 1983; Parlour 4. *Autobiography*—Myself and Michael Innes, 1987. *Criticism*—Educating the Emotions, 1944; Character and Motive in Shakespeare, 1949; James Joyce, 1957 (rev. ed. 1960); Thomas Love Peacock, 1963; Eight Modern Writers, 1963; Rudyard Kipling, 1966; Joseph Conrad, 1968; Thomas Hardy: A Critical Biography, 1968; Shakespeare's Lofty Scene, 1971. *As editor*—Montaigne's Essays: John Florio's Translation, 1931; The Moonstone by Wilkie Collins, 1966; Vanity Fair by Thackeray, 1968.

ABOUT: The autobiographical material quoted above was written for Twentieth Century Authors, 1942. Stewart, J.I.M. Myself and Michael Innes, 1987. *Periodicals*—Economist August 16, 1963; December 3, 1966; January 15, 1972; New Statesman August 2, 1963; September 24, 1971; New York Herald Tribune Books August 29, 1937; New York Times November 192, 1939; New Yorker December 2, 1939; Saturday Review of Literature November 11, 1939; March 9, 1946; Times (London) November 16, 1994; Times Literary Supplement July 3, 1937, October 25, 1974.

**STICKNEY, (JOSEPH) TRUMBULL** (June 20, 1874–October 11, 1904), American poet, was born in Geneva Switzerland, the third of the four children of Austin Stickney, a former classics professor at Trinity College in Hartford, Connecticut, and Harriet Champion Trumbull, a descendent of Jonathan Trumbull, a colonial governor of Connecticut. A great part of Stickney's childhood was spent traveling in Europe with his family. He spent a year at school in Clevedon, England and another at Dr. Cutler's school in New York. Other than that, his father was his only teacher until Stickney entered Harvard, from which he earned a B.A. in 1895. In his first year at Harvard he was elected to the editorial board of the *Harvard Monthly*—the first freshman ever to win that honor. But Stickney's first published poem "Elizabethan Lyrics: A

Villanelle" appeared in 1892 in a rival student publication, the *Harvard Advocate*, and a *Harvard Crimson* reviewer likened the poet's brightness of fancy to that of Robert Herrick. While at Harvard Stickney became good friends with George Cabot Lodge and William Vaughn Moody—both of whom he met through the *Monthly*. Stickney had a deep admiration for the classics, which had affected his ideas about poetry. While an undergraduate he published several essays about classical authors such as Pliny and Euripides, in whose work he found a vitality of expression that was in direct conflict with what he felt to be the stagnant and repressive characteristics of nineteenth-century poetry. After graduation Stickney went to Paris to attend the Sorbonne, where he studied Greek and Sanskrit, and, after nearly eight years, he became the first American to receive that school's *doctorate ès lettres* (in 1903). These studies affected Stickney's perception of Western thought and poetic expression. He became more attracted to the elements of Eastern philosophy. He and his Sanskrit instructor Sylvain Lévy translated the *Bhagavad Gita*, (published in 1938 by Lévy's widow). After graduation from the Sorbonne Stickney spent three months in Greece before returning to Harvard to take a position as an instructor in Greek.

Stickney had been writing and publishing (in the *Monthly*) steadily during this time, the results of which were collected and published as *Dramatic Verses* in 1902. The volume includes stylistically varied selections beginning with some of his earliest work such as several romantic sonnets written while still an undergraduate at Harvard and addressed to F.L.P. and the romantic ballads "In the Past" and "Age in Youth." Also included in *Dramatic Verse* is the Eride sequence—twenty-seven poems following the development of a love affair from euphoria to disillusionment to pain—and his blank-verse drama *Prometheus Pyrphoros*. Though not widely reviewed, it was well-liked by those who read it. The *New York Times Book Review* likened it to the work of Dante Gabriel Rossetti, and the *Dial* commented that Stickney had a certain power to grip the imagination and excite the nobler emotions.

During the second semester of the 1903-1904 year Stickney began to suffer from severe headaches and periods of partial blindness. His writing now was turning more toward the dramatic verse of *Prometheus* and other earlier attempts at verse drama such as his The Cardinal Play (1897), Oneiropolos (1897), and Requiescam (1900). Despite deteriorating health, Stickney continued to work on the book through the summer of 1904, while staying with his parents in New Hampshire. Returning to Boston, totally blind, he continued to work on his poetry until his death of a brain tumor. Typical of these late fragments of verse are the lines: "Sir, say no more./Within me is as if/The green and climbing eyesight of a cat/Crawled near my mind's poor birds."

Following his death, his work was collected by his friends Lodge and Moody for a memorial volume, *The Poems of Trumbull Stickney*. The book did little to enhance the poet's reputation with the general public, though the list of writers and poets who have subsequently acknowledged admiration for him and included his work in their anthologies is impressive. Among these are Conrad Aiken, William Rose Benét, Louis Untermeyer, Allen Tate, Mark Van Doren, W. H. Auden, and Oscar Williams.

With the exception of only a few poems, Stickney published exclusively in the *Harvard Monthly*, expressing a distaste for the commercial publications of that time. However, in 1929 Conrad Aiken began to take an interest in the poet's work, as did Edmond Wilson in 1940. But it was not until the 1960s and 1970s that Stickney's work began to get some of the recognition that it deserved. In 1972 a second *The Poems of Trumbull Stickney*, based largely on the 1905 *Poems*, was brought out. It remains in print today along with the original *Dramatic Verses*.

After his death, his family destroyed or removed passages from any of his letters they felt to be incriminating with respect to Stickney's various love affairs, as well as letters in which the poet asked his family for money (which his younger brother though to be undignified). Many of Stickney's other papers are housed in the Houghton Library at Harvard.

PRINCIPAL WORKS: Dramatic Verses, 1902; (ed. G. C. Lodge, J. E. Lodge, and W. V. Moody) The Poems of Trumbull Stickney, 1905.

ABOUT: Dictionary of Literary Biography American Poets 1880-1945, 1987; The Fright of Time: Joseph Trumbull Stickney, 1874-1904, 1970. *Periodicals*—Dial July 16, 1903, New York Times Book Review March 3, 1903.

**STILL, JAMES** (July 16, 1906–   ), American poet, novelist, short story writer, and children's author, wrote: "I was born at Double Creek, among Alabama's red hills, one of ten children. The Stills came from England; my mother's people, the Lindseys, were Scotch-Irish. My ancestors fought in the American Revolution and in the War of 1812; my grandfathers were Confederate soldiers. My father is a veterinarian. As a boy I expected to follow him in this profession, often sitting up all night in barn lots attending sick horses. At seventeen I went away to a mountain school near Cumberland Gap, Tennessee. I worked in a rock quarry to pay expenses. Later I attended Vanderbuilt University (M.A.) and the University of Illinois Library School (B.S. in L.S.). For six years I was librarian of the Hindman Settlement School at the forks of Troublesome Creek in the Kentucky Mountains. Along with other duties I conducted a library-on-foot, delivering books in a carton on my shoulder to one-room schools, walking fifteen to eighteen miles a day.

"My first poem appeared in the *Virginia Quarterly Review* in 1935, my first short story in the *Atlantic Monthly* the next year. Taking time off to complete my first novel, I went to live two miles from a highway in an old log house on Dead Mare Branch of Little Carr Creek [Ky.]. I completed the novel, but didn't return to the Settlement. The log house is now my home. I cultivate a garden, a vineyard; I farm a bit; I can play a few ballads on the dulcimer."

James Still has devoted his entire literary career to describing the people and places of the Cumberland Mountains of eastern Kentucky, where he has lived since the early 1930s. He was recognized as a leading regional voice with the publication of his first book, a collection of verse, *Hounds on the Mountain*. The novel *River of Earth* chronicles two years in the lives of a Kentucky family that has fallen on hard times with the closing of the local coal mines. Like John Steinbeck's *The Grapes of Wrath*, which appeared just one year earlier, *River of Earth* is a novel about a desperate search for work and sustenance during the Great Depression. But Still's characters, unlike Steinbeck's, travel only short distances, and their hardships, seen through the eyes of a young boy, are not punctuated with social and political commentary.

Still has often been praised for his skillful portrayal of Appalachian dialect. Reviewing *River of Earth* in the *New York Times Book Review*, Rose Feld noted, "To call the novel homespun is not enough. Still's language and native idiom, joyfully wedded, give it special excellence as a regional document." In his foreword to a 1978 reissue of the novel, Dean Cadle observed, "Still's 'secret' lies in his ability to use language so that it per-forms the functions of both music and painters' pigments." Discussing Still's work in the *Yale Review*, Cadle earlier insisted, "Certainly no one has written more effective prose about the Appalachian South."

Despite his early critical success—*River of Earth* shared the 1940 Southern Authors Award with Thomas Wolfe's *You Can't Go Home Again*—Still published no books between 1941 and 1974. He did, however, continue to publish verse and short fiction in various periodicals. He served in Africa and the Middle East with the U.S. Army Air Force during World War II, after which he returned to rural Kentucky to work as a librarian for the Hindman Settlement School. From 1962 to 1971, he taught English at Kentucky's Morehead State University, and has since lectured at other colleges.

Several of Still's later works are for juvenile readers, including *The Wolfpen Rusties*, a collection of Appalachian riddles and folktales, and the novel *Sporty Creek*. The 1970s and 1980s saw a revival of interest in Still's short fiction and poetry. "What one notices at once is the language used in these stories," Cleanth Brooks wrote in a foreword to *The Run for the Elbertas*. "It is idiomatic, highly concrete, richly metaphoric, and has the true lilt of oral speech." Reviewing *The Wolfpen Poems* in the *Los Angeles Times Book Review*, James Dickey hailed Still as "the truest and most remarkable poet that the mountain culture has produced. . . . The poems are quiet, imaginative and sincere, and the poet's terrible grief over the loss of a way of life . . . registers with double effect because of the modesty of statement."

In 1991 Still published *The Wolfpen Notebooks*, a collection of Appalachian folklore, expressions, and yarns, in order to preserve what he considers the unique mountain culture. As he noted in an interview published in that volume, "Now and then I still hear remnants of the language spoken by Chaucer and the Elizabethans, such as 'sass' for vegetables. . . . People here are more likely to express themselves in an original manner than any place I know. I think it is something to celebrate." In recent years Still has made his home in the town of Hindman. Although he is the recipient of numerous awards and honors, including two Guggenheim fellowships, he remains little known to the general public and has always eschewed publicity of any sort.

PRINCIPAL WORKS: *Poetry*—Hounds on the Mountain, 1937; River of Earth: The Poem and Other Poems, 1982–1983; The Wolfpen Poems, 1986. *Novel*—River of Earth, 1940. *Short stories*—On Troublesome Creek, 1941; Pattern of a Man and Other Stories, 1976; The Run for the Elbertas, 1980. *Notebooks*—The Man in the Bushes: The Notebooks of James Still, 1935–1987, 1988; The Wolfpen Notebooks: A Record of Appalachian Life, 1991. *Juvenile*—Way Down Yonder on Troublesome Creek: Appalachian Riddles and Rusties, 1974; The Wolfpen Rusties: Appalachian Riddles and GeeHaw Whimmy-Diddles, 1975 (reissued, with Way Down Yonder on Troublesome Creek, as Rusties and Riddles and Gee-Haw Whimmy-Diddles, 1989); Jack and the Wonder Beans, 1977; Sporty Creek: A Novel about an Appalachian Boyhood, 1977.

ABOUT: The autobiographical material quoted above was written for Twentieth Century Authors, 1942. Contemporary Authors vols, 65–68, 1977; Contemporary Authors New Revision Series 26, 1989; Contemporary Literary Criticism vol. 49 1988; Cyclopedia of World Authors vol. 3 rev. ed. 1974; Dictionary of Literary Biography vol. 9 1981. *Periodicals*—Los Angeles Times Book Review December 7, 1986; New York Times Book Review February 4, 1940; Yale Review December 1967.

**ST. JOHN ERVINE. See ERVINE, ST. JOHN GREER**

**ST. JOHN GOGARTY. See GOGARTY, OLIVER ST. JOHN**

**ST.-J. PERSE. See LÉGER, ALEXIS SAINT-LÉGER**

**ST. -JOHN PERSE.  See LÉGER, ALEXIS SAINT-LÉGER**

**STOKER, BRAM** (November 1847–April 20, 1912), Irish novelist and short story writer, was born Abraham Stoker in Dublin. He was named for his father, a civil servant in the Chief Secretary's Office at Dublin Castle. His mother was the former Charlotte Thornley, twenty years younger than her husband. A Sligo woman, she told her children vivid tales of the dreadful cruelties inspired by panic during the cholera epidemic of 1832. She and her family had themselves came near to being burned alive by a mob that believed they carried the infection. Charlotte Stoker was also a feminist and a reformer, and campaigned against the sexual exploitation of young women in the Dublin workhouses.

The third of seven children, Bram Stoker was sickly, prone to every ailment and bedridden from his third to his seventh year. He recovered to grow tall, burly, and exceptionally strong, though he was always bookish and "a bit of a scribbler." Stoker attended a Protestant day school and then Trinity College, Dublin's university, where he excelled at everything he attempted. He became Trinity's athletics champion and president of both the philosophical and historical societies. He won prizes for history, English and oratory, and graduated in about 1868 with honors in mathematics.

Stoker followed his father into the Irish Civil Service, in which he spent ten drab years, ending as Inspector of Petty Sessions (1877–1878). Stoker wrote his first book on the duties of clerks to such courts, while dreaming of an altogether more glamorous literary career. He loved the theater, and idolized the English actor Henry Irving. In 1871 he became the unpaid drama critic of the *Dublin Mail*, initially so that he could do something to redress Ireland's neglect of Irving. He was soon contributing articles to other journals.

Then he wrote some sensational serials, his first published fiction. In 1873 he became part-time editor of a short-lived Dublin newspaper. He was also studying for his Trinity M.A. and giving private lessons to boost his income. Then in his mid-twenties, Stoker was six foot two inches tall, with a rich auburn beard. Personable, confident, and articulate, he began to find a welcome in the upper reaches of Dublin society, including the circle around Sir William and Lady Wilde, parents of Oscar.

When Henry Irving played Dublin in 1876, Stoker's reviews so pleased him that he asked for a meeting, beginning a friendship important to both of them. After years of rejection, Irving's mannered and mesmeric style of acting had finally gained acceptance. In 1878 he took over the Lyceum Theatre in London. He needed a business manager and offered the job to Stoker, who promptly accepted and resigned from the civil service. In the same year Stoker married Florence Balcombe (previously playfully courted by Oscar Wilde). They set up house in Cheyne Walk, Chelsea, where guests at their Sunday evenings included Wilde, Whistler, and many other luminaries.

At the Lyceum, with Ellen Terry as his leading lady, Irving began a twenty-year reign as the principal Shakespearean actor-manager of his day. Stoker served him devotedly at the Lyceum, and on tours of America and Europe, for the rest of Irving's life. He was not only "the Chief's" friend and business manager, but front-of-house manager, press agent, private secretary, and unofficial social secretary to Ellen Terry. In his *Personal Reminiscences of Henry Irving*, Stoker estimated that he had written half a million letters on Irving's behalf. He also ruefully quoted an American journalist who spitefully wrote of Irving's retinue, that among them, he, Stoker, "seems to occupy some anomalous position between secretary and valet. Whose manifest duties are to see that there is mustard in the sandwiches and to take the dogs out for a run."

Overworked though he was in Irving's service, Stoker had not abandoned his literary ambitions. *Under the Sunset*, his first collection of short stories, was published in 1882—mostly dreamy fantasies typical of the period. The darkest piece was "The Invisible Giant," based on his mother's memories of the cholera epidemic. The book made little money but was generally well received, as was Stoker's first novel, *The Snake's Pass*, an adventure story set on the west coast of Ireland. More tales followed, including the notable horror story "The Squaw," and then, in 1897, *Dracula*.

Stoker's most famous novel begins with the journey of a young English lawyer, Jonathan Harker, to the Transylvanian castle of Count Dracula. He is to arrange the Count's purchase of an estate in England. Harker discovers that Dracula is a vampire, and the master of three predatory female vampires. The Count imprisons Harker in the castle and leaves for England, which he intends to colonize with vampires. Some weeks later, a Russian schooner runs ashore at Whitby, in Yorkshire. It is deserted and empty except for the corpse of the captain, lashed to the wheel, and fifty coffins. Dracula escapes from his coffin and attacks Lucy Westenra, friend of Harker's fiancée Mina. The scene shifts to Victorian London, where Lucy becomes a vampire also, despite the efforts of Dr. Van Helsing, an expert in the supernatural. The same fate threatens Mina. Escaping from the castle, Harker joins Van Helsing and his companions in the hunting down of the vampire.

The vampire was a familiar figure in Gothic fiction, from Polidori's "The Vampyre" to Sheridan Le Fanu's *Carmilla*. The real historic Dracula was Voivode Dracula, fifteenth-century ruler of Walachia, a warrior and alchemist notorious for hideous cruelties. Stoker claimed that the germ of his story came to him in a dream, as *Frankenstein's* did to Mary Shelley. Like *Frankenstein*, *Dracula* is an epistolary novel.

A popular success from the outset, *Dracula* has never been out of print. Hamilton Deane's stage version ran for eighteen years. The first screen adaptation, Murnau's *Nosferatu*, appeared in 1922, and was followed in 1931 by Tod Browning's *Dracula* for Universal, which made a star of Bela Lugosi. There have been innumerable other adaptations, serious and otherwise, in every medium, all over the world.

The first reviewers of the book, unaware that they were dealing with so potent a text, assessed it simply as a horror story, comparing it favorably (or otherwise) with Poe and Wilkie Collins. Influenced by Freud's theory that dread of the uncanny signifies repressed sexuality, later critics saw this as the source of the novel's power. Maurice Richardson found in it "a sort of homicidal lunatic's brothel in

a crypt, where religious and psychopathological motives intermingle." Feminist critics have taken the argument further. Phyllis A. Roth wrote that the novel's "great appeal derives from its hostility toward female sexuality." She argued that the book conceals a deep identification with the ostensibly hated Dracula, who "acts out the repressed fantasies" of the other men, notably "a fantasy of matricide" (*Literature and Psychology*).

It is an indication of the complex energies of *Dracula* that it has also been discussed in both religious and political terms, and as a novel of alienation. Few, however, have ever regarded it as a great book, or even a particularly good one. A contemporary reviewer in the *Athenaeum* found it "highly sensational, but . . . wanting in the constructive art as well as in the higher literary sense." Apart from the demonic Count himself, who has touches both of nobility and vulnerability, and the strange "zoophagous maniac" Renfield, the characterization is perfunctory. Stoker's later fictions, lacking the psychosexual intensity of *Dracula*, are of no literary interest.

By the time *Dracula* appeared, Henry Irving's health was failing, and so was The Lyceum. Box office disasters were compounded by Irving's legendary extravagance, and by a fire that destroyed all of the theater's stored scenery and properties. There were further American tours and other desperate rescue attempts, but The Lyceum closed in 1902. Irving died in 1905. Stoker, heartbroken, had a stroke that left his vision impaired. Long afflicted with gout, he now contracted Bright's disease. He nevertheless went on writing until his death.

Stoker left less than £5,000. His *Times* obituary prophesied that "his chief literary memorial" would be his laudatory reminiscences of Irving. It scarcely mentioned *Dracula*, soon to become one of the most popular books ever published.

PRINCIPAL WORKS: *Fiction*—Under the Sunset, 1882 (short stories); The Snake's Pass, 1890; The Watter's Mou', 1894; Crooken Sands, 1894; The Shoulder of Shasta, 1895; Dracula, 1897; Miss Betty, 1898; The Mystery of the Sea, 1902; The Jewel of Seven Stars, 1903; The Man, 1905; Lady Athlyne, 1908; The Gates of Life, 1908; Snowbound: The Record of a Theatrical Touring Party, 1908; The Lady of the Shroud, 1909; The Lair of the White Worm, 1911; Dracula's Guest, 1937 (short stories); Shades of Dracula: Bram Stoker's Uncollected Stories (ed. P. Haining) 1982; The Dualitists; or, The Death Doom of the Double Born, 1986. *Nonfiction*—The Duties of Clerks of Petty Sessions in Ireland, 1879; A Glimpse of America, 1886; Personal Reminiscences of Henry Irving, 1906; Famous Impostors, 1910.

ABOUT: Carter, M. L. (ed.) Dracula: The Vampire and the Critics, 1988; Dictionary of Literary Biography vol. 36 1985; vol. 70 1988; Farson, D. The Man Who Wrote Dracula, 1975; Irving, L. Henry Irving, 1951; Kline, S. J. The Degeneration of Women: Dracula as Allegorical Criticism of the Fin de Siecle, 1992; Leatherdale, C. Dracula: The Novel and the Legend, 1993; Ludlam, H. Biography of Dracula: The Life of Bram Stoker, 1962; McNally, R. T. and Florescu, R. Dracula: A True History of Dracula and Vampire Legends, 1972; Ronay, G. The Truth About Dracula, 1972; Roth, P. Bram Stoker, 1982; Schick, A. and J. Bram Stoker's Dracula, 1980; Senf, C. A. (ed.) The Critical Response to Bram Stoker, 1993; Skal, D. J. Hollywood Gothic: Dracula from Novel to Stage to Screen, 1990; Stoker, B. Personal Reminiscences of Henry Irving, 1906; Terry, E. The Story of My Life, 1908; Who's Who 1911; Wolf, L. The Essential Dracula, 1993. *Bibliography*—Dalby, R. (ed.)

Bram Stoker: A Bibliography of First Editions, 1983; Riccardo, M. V. (ed.) Vampires Unearthed: The Complete Multi-Media Vampire and Dracula Bibliography, 1983. *Periodicals*— American Imago Summer 1972; Athenaeum June 26, 1897; History Today July 1982; Literature and Psychology 3 1977; Midwest Folklore Spring 1956; Midwest Quarterly July 1977; New York Times April 23, 1912; Times (London) April 22, 1912; Twentieth Century December 1959; Victorian Newsletter Fall 1972.

## STONE, GRACE ZARING (pseudonym "ETHEL VANCE")

(January 9, 1891–September 29, 1991), American novelist, wrote: "Born in New

York City. Educated under private tutors, and at the Sacred Heart Convents of Paris and New York. Traveled extensively in Europe, Asia, and the South Seas. In the Great War, served with the British Red Cross in England. In 1917, I married Ellis S. Stone, an officer in the United States Navy, now with the rank of captain and serving as the American Naval Attaché in Paris [February 1940]. First book was written after two years in the West Indies; the second was the result of years in China. Numerous short stories in magazines. Have one daughter, now baroness Perényi, of Budapest. My principal interest, apart from writing, is music. Since the beginning of the present war, am volunteer worker of American Hospital, Paris. It might be of interest to add that my great-grandfather was Robert Owen."

---

Grace Zaring Stone, the author of twelve novels, was the daughter of Charles Wesley Zaring, a lawyer, and Grace (Owen) Zaring, who died giving birth to her. She began keeping a diary at an early age, a habit she picked up from her Owen relations. As the wife of a naval officer, she lived all over the world, and her intimate knowledge of a variety of exotic locales is reflected in her fiction.

In later life Stone rarely acknowledged her first novel, *Letters to a Djinn*, a fictional travelogue in the form of letters by a young American woman journeying from Australia to Singapore. The novel she often referred to as her first, *The Heaven and Earth of Doña Elena*, is a historical romance about a seventeenth-century Spanish nun, and was compared at the time to Thornton Wilder's *The Bridge of San Luis Rey*. Stone came to prominence with the publication of her third novel, *The Bitter Tea of General Yen*, in which an American missionary woman in Shanghai is captured by a seductive and enigmatic anti-Communist warlord. The popular 1932 film version starred Barbara Stanwyck, and was the first movie shown in New York's Radio City Music Hall.

*The Cold Journey*, a historical novel about a French and Indian assault upon a Massachusetts village in 1704, prompted the *New York Herald Tribune Books* to hail Stone as "the most distinguished

of the younger American women writers." Although Stone's work could by no means justify such a claim, it was recognized as high-quality popular fiction, which seemed to satisfy the author. As Stone told a *New York Times Book Review* (1942) interviewer, "I don't try to imitate genius. . . . I work terribly hard to tell a story effectively, and do a good, tight construction job, because I can do that much, I can be a craftsman."

Her most famous novel, *Escape*, is the story of a German actress who returns to her homeland after a long absence, runs afoul of the Nazi authorities, and is sentenced to death. Adapted for the screen in 1940, the novel won considerable popular praise; but, as Philip Burnham noted in *Commonweal*, "*Escape* stays closer to the 'mystery' than the 'big novel' classification first of all because that appears obviously the author's intention." In order to protect her husband, then stationed in France as a naval attaché, and her daughter, who was living in occupied Czechoslovakia, Stone chose to publish *Escape* pseudonymously, as Ethel Vance. The identity of "Ethel Vance" was revealed in 1942, but Stone continued to use that pseudonym for the duration of World War II and for several years thereafter.

Stone's novel *Reprisal*, about life in a Nazi-occupied Breton village, was a major bestseller. *Winter Meeting*, another Vance novel, recounts a brief love affair between an American woman and a war hero. It was the third and last of her novels to be filmed, providing a vehicle for Bette Davis in 1948. A *Times Literary Supplement* reviewer thought that *The Secret Thread*, the last of her Vance novels, was "a competent but unexciting thriller," and Stone's later novels (all published under her real name) received little attention.

Stone and her husband continued to travel widely after his retirement from the navy. She was affiliated with the Council of the Authors League and the Committee for Cultural Freedom, was made a fellow of the Royal Society of Literature, and maintained an informal literary salon in Rome and New York that attracted the likes of Mary McCarthy and Gore Vidal. A long-time resident of Stonington, Connecticut, she died in a nursing home in nearby Mystic at the age of 100.

PRINCIPAL WORKS: *Novels*—Letters to a Djinn, 1922; The Heaven and Earth of Donà Elena, 1929; The Bitter Tea of General Yen (in U.K.: Bitter Tea) 1930; The Almond Tree, 1931; The Cold Journey, 1934; (as "E. Vance") Escape, 1939; (as "E. Vance") Reprisal, 1942; (as "E. Vance") Winter Meeting, 1946; (as "E. Vance") The Secret Thread, 1948; The Grotto, 1951; Althea, 1962; Dear Deadly Cara, 1968.

ABOUT: The autobiographical material quoted above was written for Twentieth Century Authors, 1942. The Annual Obituary 1991 (ed. D. Andrews) 1992; Contemporary Authors, vol. 135, 1992; Contemporary Authors Permanent Series, vol. 2, 1978; Halliwell's Film Guide, 8th ed. (ed. J. Walker) 1991. *Periodicals*—Commonweal October 6, 1939; New York Herald Tribune Books September 16, 1934; New York Times October 1, 1991; New York Times Book Review May 3, 1942; Times Literary Supplement September 4, 1948.

## STONE, IRVING (July 14, 1903–August 26, 1989), American biographer, wrote:

"I was born in San Francisco, the son of Charles and Pauline (Rosenberg) Tennenbaum. I worked my way through high school selling newspapers, driving a delivery wagon for a vegetable market, and as an errand boy and stock-boy in leather goods and men's clothing stores. I worked my way through the University of California by playing a saxophone for dances, by working during summers on the fruit ranches, in a meat-packing plant, a powerhouse, as a hotel clerk, and a salesman in such diverse stores as a diary and sporting goods house. At the university I majored in political science, fought on the boxing team, and argued for the debating societies. I graduated in 1923 with honors, and had the distinction of being the first undergraduate to be permitted to conduct classes in economics. In 1924 I taught economics at the University of Southern California and took a Master's degree, returning to the University of California to teach economics for two more years and became a candidate for a Ph.D.

"I had always been a hopeless bookworm; from the age of six I had known that I wanted to be a writer. At the age of twenty-three, after having written short stories and one-act plays for several years, I quit the teaching profession altogether and jumped with both hands and feet into the writing game. I lived in New York for ten years, where I wrote eighteen full-length plays; two of them were produced, with no startling success. While in Europe in 1930 I encountered the life and works of Vincent Van Gogh; three years later *Lust for Life* emerged, and I suddenly found myself a biographer. . . .

"I think that the main influences on both my writing and thinking have been European. However, what little I know about writing I can also attribute to the books of such Americans as Hemingway, Sherwood Anderson, Jack London. My main professional ambition for the next few years is to revitalize and reshape the biographical form, much as I have tried to do in *Lust for Life* and *Sailor on Horseback*, to make the biography as dramatic and deeply moving as any novel or play, and at the same time make it a clear and penetrating portrait of how the world came into its present state. . . .

"In 1943 I published *They Also Ran*, which was the story of all the men who were defeated for the presidency, starting with Henry Clay and coming down through the chapter on Thomas E. Dewey. During the second half of the writing of the book, which took me a full two years, I made myself literally ill with apprehension that the theme was in much too minor a key to attract serious attention. I was therefore delighted when upon publication I received the best press I had had since *Lust for Life* and found that the book was taking a permanent place for itself not only on the shelves of university libraries but on city editor desks as well, and was being used as almost an object lesson in practicing political circles.

"In 1944 I published *Immortal Wife*, a biographical novel about Jessie Benton Fremont with whom I had fallen in love in 1924 while a student at the University of California. I had read about her over a period of twenty years and had always hoped someone would write a novel about her. However, when I saw that no one else would, and finally managed to convince myself that I could write a book about a woman, I undertook the task myself. *Immortal Wife* proved to be my most successful book, remaining in the top five on the best-seller lists for some fifteen months and earning me a much wider public among American readers than I had ever enjoyed before.

"In 1947 *Adversary in the House*, a biographical novel about Eugene V. Debs, was published. In 1949 I published *Passionate Journey*, a biographical novel about John Noble, an American painter, unknown, who lived one of the most interesting lives of any of our contemporary artists. In 1950 I published *We Speak for Ourselves, a Self-Portrait of America*, including excerpts from outstanding autobiographies of over sixty Americans, representing every time, class, and professional level in our history.

"At the present time [December 1952] I am in the middle of a biographical novel about Mary Todd Lincoln and Abraham Lincoln [published in 1954 as *Love Is Eternal*]. This book, along with *The President's Lady* [a novel about Rachel and Andrew Jackson, made into a motion picture in 1953] and *Immortal Wife*, concludes a trilogy of great American women I've had in mind and in work for the past ten years."

———

Irving Stone has been credited, by some, for inventing what he called the "biographical novel," a combination of biography and fiction in which he attempted to create historical portraits that were at once informative and entertaining to a general readership.

An exhibition at Paris's Rosenberg Galleries, where Stone saw the paintings of Vincent Van Gogh, led to an epiphany: "It was the single most compelling emotional experience of my life," he was quoted as saying in *Current Biography*. "When I got out I knew that I had to find out more about Van Gogh." Stone's research took him to four countries and by 1931 he had a manuscript which was rejected by seventeen publishers over a three-year period. During that time he did manage to publish *Pageant of Youth*, a novel about life at the University of California. According to Stone it was a "very bad novel indeed," but it led to a connection with a publisher for his Van Gogh manuscript. *Lust for Life*, based on the painter's letters to his brother Theo, appeared in 1934 and became a best seller. In the introduction to *The Irving Stone Reader* Joseph Henry Jackson points out that *Lust for Life* provided the spark that would fire Stone's imagination for years and best sellers to come: "That spark was character ready-made, the story of someone who had lived, whose acts could be found in the record and whose motives might be traced by patient, careful, sympathetic investigation, with due balance and interpretation to follow. And, with Stone, what fanned this spark into flame was any suspicion that such a character had been misunderstood, perhaps even misrepresented through historical accident or through an early biographer's prejudice."

Over a fifty-year period Stone applied his technique to Jack London, Sigmund Freud, Henry and Sophia Schliemann, Charles Darwin, and Camille Pissarro. In 1961 he published his best known work, *The Agony and the Ecstasy: A Novel of Michelangelo*. It became a monumental best seller and, in 1965, was released as a movie starring Charlton Heston, one of four of Stone's books to be adapted to film. Stone also wrote biographies of Clarence Darrow and Earl Warren.

Readers have been sharply divided on the worth of Stone's work: reviewers tended to like them, critics to despise them. There were those who found his portraits compelling; others accused him, with justice, of treating historical facts loosely. In his review of *Those Who Love: A Biographical Novel of Abigail and John Adams*, the Historian of American literature Marcus Cunliffe presented both sides of the argument (*New York Times Book Review*). At first Cunliffe is ready to place the book among the "legion of bad historical novels," but he comments: "It struck me at the beginning as laboriously undistinguished, a tedious assembly of sheer information. . . . I had the queer sense of reading a ghost novel—the doings of a famous family 'told to' the author—or maybe a better comparison would be with an old painting, well-meaning but excessively 'restored.'" But Cunliffe's reservations gradually gave way to "qualified admiration": "In balance Mr. Stone's novel stands as a solid effort. It should please those members of the public who like to have their history—in the phrase of John Adams which the author employs as an epigraph, possibly with unconscious ambiguity—'a little embellished with fiction.'"

PRINCIPAL WORKS: *Biography*—Lust for Life: A Novel of Vincent Van Gogh, 1934; Sailor on Horseback: The Biography of Jack London, 1938 (also published as Jack London: Sailor on Horseback: A Biographical Novel, 1938); Immortal Wife: The Biographical Novel of Jessie Benton Fremont, 1944; Adversary in the House, 1947; The Passionate Journey, 1949; The President's Lady: A Novel About Rachel and Andrew Jackson, 1951; Love Is Eternal: A Novel About Mary Todd Lincoln and Abraham Lincoln, 1954; The Agony and the Ecstasy: A Novel of Michaelangelo, 1961; Those Who Love: A Biographical Novel of Abigail and John Adams, 1965; The Passions of the Mind: A Novel of Sigmund Freud, 1971; The Greek Treasure: A Biographical Novel of Henry and Sophia Schliemann, 1975; The Origin, 1980; Depths of Glory, 1985. *Novels*—Pageant of Youth, 1933; False Witness, 1940. *Nonfiction*—Clarence Darrow for the Defense, 1941, abridged ed. 1958; They Also Ran: The Story of the Men Who Were Defeated for the Presidency, 1943; Dewey Also Ran, 1945; Earl Warren: A Great American Story, 1948; Men To Match My Mountain: The Opening of the Far West: 1840–1900, 1956; The Irving Stone Reader, 1963; The Story of Michelangelo's Pietà, 1964; Three Views of the Novel: Lectures by Irving Stone, John O'Hara, and MacKinley

Kantor, 1957; The Science and the Art of Biography, 1986. *Drama*—The White Life: A Play in One Act Based on the Life of Baruch Spinoza, 1932?. *Juvenile*—The Great Adventure of Michelangelo, 1965. *As editor*—(with J. Stone) Dear Theo: The Autobiography of Vincent Van Gogh, 1946; (with R. Kennedy) We Speak for Ourselves: A Self Portrait of America, 1950; (with J. Stone) I, Michelangelo, Sculptor: An Autobiography Through Letters, 1962; (with A. Nevins) Lincoln: A Contemporary Portrait, 1962; There was Light: Autobiography of a University: Berkeley, 1868–1968, 1970.

ABOUT: The autobiographical material quoted above was written for Twentieth Century Authors, 1942 and Twentieth Century Authors First Supplement, 1955. Contemporary Authors 1994; Contemporary Novelists, 1986; Current Biography 1967, Newquist, R. Counterpoint, 1964. *Periodicals*—New York Times August 28, 1989; New York Times Book Review November 7, 1965; Times (London) August 29, 1989.

## STONE, ROSETTA. See GEISEL, THEODOR SEUSS

## STONG, PHIL(IP DUFFIELD) (January 27, 1899–April 26, 1957), American novelist and children's author, was born near Keosauqua, Iowa, the son of Benjamin J. Stong, a store owner and postmaster, and Evesta (Duffield) Stong. He attended Keosauqua public schools and earned a B.A. in journalism from Drake University in 1919. After teaching school for one year in Biwabik, Minnesota, he enrolled in the graduate English program at Columbia University, but left in 1921 without a degree. It was while he was a schoolteacher in Neodesha, Kansas (1921–1923), that he began to publish short fiction in *Midland* magazine. In 1924 he returned to Iowa to teach journalism and debate at Drake University. He soon became a regular contributor to the *Des Moines Register* and decided to pursue a career in writing. In *If School Keeps*, a memoir of his early years, he credits *Register* editor Harvey Ingham with helping him to "peel the more florid terms and locutions" out of his writing.

Stong held a succession of editorial positions in New York City (1925–1932) before he achieved instant fame, for his novel, *State Fair*—his thirteenth, but first published, effort. Thereafter he was able to devote the rest of his life to writing.

*State Fair*, the story of a farm family's week-long visit to the Iowa State Fair, became a Literary Guild selection and was filmed three times, most notably in 1933, with Will Rogers. Although Stong went on to publish forty more books—novels, nonfiction, and children's stories—he is best remembered as the author of *State Fair*.

From 1934 on, Stong lived and wrote in Washington, Connecticut, but his literary imagination remained firmly rooted in Iowa, the setting of most of his novels. Many of these—*State Fair, Stranger's Return, Village Tale, Career, The Rebellion of Lenny Barlow, The Long Lane, The Princess, One Destiny, Return in August*, and *Blizzard*—are set, during various times in the first half of the twentieth century, in and around the town of Pittsville, a fictional place that bears a striking resemblance to Stong's hometown of Keosauqua. *Buckskin Breeches*, a historical novel about pioneer life in Iowa, was inspired by the journals of George Duffield, Stong's maternal grandfather, and one of the first white settlers in the Keosauqua region. *Ivanhoe Keeler* and *Forty Pounds of Gold*, two of his subsequent historical novels, are set partly in frontier Iowa.

Unlike such better Iowa writers as Hamlin Garland, Stong usually depicted small town and farm life in a positive, sometimes idealized, light. As

Clarence Andrews noted in *A Literary History of Iowa*, "Although Stong's farm novels were written during the depression years of the thirties, they ignore the problems . . . facing the farmers of those years. . . . Stong's novels belong in the 'bless the farm' group." Still, at least one of the "Pittsville" novels, *Village Tale*, presents a starker, more violent, side of rural life. *Nation* reviewer Carl Van Doren praised that novel's "many thrusts of wit," but *New York Times Book Review* (1934) critic Louis Kronenberger described Stong as "slick," noting, "At bottom Stong has a certain feeling for reality, but he refuses to honor it."

Stong's non-Iowa novels include *Week-End*, about a Connecticut house party attended by ostensibly sophisticated New Yorkers, and *Marta of Muscovy*, a fictionalized biography of Russian empress Catherine I. Although Stong and his wife, the novelist Virginia Maude Swain, had no children, a number of his children's books—particularly *The Hired Man's Elephant*, winner of the 1939 *New York Herald Tribune* prize for juvenile fiction—were widely admired. There are collections of his papers in the libraries of the University of Iowa and Drake University.

PRINCIPAL WORKS: *Novels*—State Fair, 1932; Stranger's Return, 1933; Village Tale, 1934; Week-End, 1935; The Farmer in the Dell, 1935; Career, 1936; Buckskin Breeches, 1937; The Rebellion of Lennie Barlow, 1937; Ivanhoe Keeler, 1939; The Long Lane, 1939; The Princess, 1941; One Destiny, 1942; The Iron Mountain, 1942; Marta of Muscovy: The Fabulous Life of Russia's First Empress, 1945; Jessamy John, 1947; Forty Pounds of Gold, 1951; Return in August, 1953; Blizzard, 1955; The Adventure of "Horse" Barnsby, 1956. *Juvenile*—Farm Boy: A Hunt for Indian Treasure, 1934; Honk: The Moose, 1935; No-Stitch: The Hound, 1936; High Water, 1937; Edgar: The 7:58, 1938; Young Settler, 1938; The Hired Man's Elephant, 1939; Cowhand Goes to Town, 1939; Captain Kidd's Cow, 1941; Way Down Cellar, 1942; Missouri Canary, 1943; Censored, the Goat, 1945; Positive Pete!, 1947; The Prince and the Porker, 1950; Hirum, the Hillbilly, 1951; Mississippi Pilot: With Mark Twain on the Great River, 1954; A Beast Called an Elephant, 1955; Mike, the Story of a Young Circus Acrobat, 1957; Phil Stong's Big Book: Farm Boy, High Water [and] No-Stitch, the Hound, 1961. *Nonfiction*—(with V. Elliott) Shake 'Em Up! A Practical Handbook of Polite Drinking, 1930; County Fair (photos by J. von Miklos and others) 1938; Horses and Americans, 1939; Hawkeyes: A Biography of the State of Iowa, 1940; Gold in Them Hills: Being an Irreverent History of the Great 1849 Gold Rush, 1957. *Memoirs*—If School Keeps, 1940. *As editor*—The Other Worlds: 25 Modern Stories of Mystery and Imagination, 1941.

ABOUT: Andrews, C. A Literary History of Iowa, 1972; Cyclopedia of World Authors, rev. ed., vol. 3 1974; Dictionary of American Biography, Suppl. 6, 1956–1960, 1980; Paluka, F. Iowa Authors: A Bio-Bibliography of Sixty Native Writers, 1967; Something About the Author vol. 32 1983. *Periodicals*—Nation March 14, 1934; New York Times April 27, 1957; New York Times Book Review March 11, 1934; Palimpsest December 1957.

**STOUT, REX (TODHUNTER)** (December 1, 1886–October 27, 1975), American detective story writer, wrote: "My father, John Wallace Stout, and my mother, Lucetta Elizabeth Todhunter, were

both birthright Quakers, so I am too. I was born at Noblesville, Indiana, but was still a baby when we moved West, so my early environment was Kansas. . . . I attended a little country school in Shawnee County, and then the Topeka public schools through high school. At thirteen years of age I was the state spelling champion. . . . At eighteen I joined the Navy, became a yeoman, and after two years of it purchased my discharge with the intention of becoming a lawyer in order to be in a good strategic position for abolishing all injustice everywhere. My attention was distracted from that design by the receipt of a check for fourteen dollars from *Smart Set* in payment for a poem. They bought two more, but the fourth was rejected, so I got a job as a clerk in a cigar store.

"My twentieth to twenty-fourth years were spent at a dozen different jobs in ten cities in six states, though I was only once a fugitive. From my twenty-fifth to thirtieth years I wrote stories for magazines, investigated the woman question, went to plays, operas and symphonies, and continued to read books. In 1916 I married Fay Kennedy of Topeka, Kansas, and invented a school banking system and proceeded to install it in four hundred towns and cities from coast to coast. That filled ten years. In 1927, at the age of forty, having made some money, I quit business, went to Paris, and wrote a psychological novel. The economic disillusionment starting in 1929 took most of my money, and caused me to switch to mystery stories. . . .

"In 1933 I was divorced, and that same year married Pola Hoffman of Vienna. We have two daughters, Barbara and Rebecca. . . . I love books, food, music, sleep, people who work, heated arguments, the United States of America, and my wife and children. I dislike politicians, preachers, genteel persons, people who do not work or are on vacation, closed minds, movies, loud noises, and oiliness. I hate Adolf Hitler. This is 1939."

———

Rex Stout, the creator of the detective Nero Wolfe, was a colorful character in his own right. He claimed to have left Indiana with his family—he was one of nine children—at the age of one because he was already "fed up with Indiana politics." As a youngster he was something of a prodigy: he had read the Bible twice by the time he was four and soon learned to add up long columns of figures in his head. He devoured his father's library, well over a thousand volumes, but his formal education ended abruptly at the University of Kansas, which he left after two weeks. Making his way to the East coast, he joined the Navy. "I was assigned to Teddy Roosevelt's yacht, *Mayflower*, as pay-yeoman. I saw a lot of the Caribbean and became a good whist player." After two years, in 1908, Stout purchased his release from the Navy and began four years of wandering.

During this time he studied law and was employed in a succession of jobs as cook, clerk, bellhop, plumber, cigar salesman, stablehand, tourist guide, and hotel manager. His writing career began in 1912, when he sold for $200 an article about palmistry, of which he knew nothing, using President William Howard Taft's palm prints as examples. He went on to sell articles and stories to a variety of magazines, although he spent as much as he earned. He achieved financial security shortly after his marriage to Fay Kennedy in 1916, when he developed a school savings-account system that proved to be both popular and lucrative.

After ten years Stout was able to retire from the business and travel to Paris, where he began to write in earnest. His first book, published in 1929, was a well-received psychological study called *How Like a God* (1929). Three novels followed, winning compliments but only modest sales, and Stout reassessed his talents. "I was a good storyteller but would never make a great novelist, so I decided to write detective stories."

In 1933, upon his return to the U.S., he divorced his first wife and that same year married Pola Hoffman. Stout's first detective novel, *Fer-de-lance*, appeared as a serial in the *Saturday Evening Post* and in book form in 1934. It introduced the 286-pound detective Nero Wolfe and his confidential assistant Archie Goodwin. The book was an instant success, as was its follow-up, *The League of Frightened Men* (1935). Reviewing the latter for the *New York Times*, Isaac Anderson wrote, "The story has everything a good detective story should have," and readers obviously agreed.

During the course of his career Rex Stout mastered a variety of literary forms, including the short story, the novel, science fiction, and propaganda. But nothing he wrote could compare to the immensely popular and highly literate mystery novels featuring Nero Wolfe. To detective story fans, Wolfe's Manhattan brownstone has become almost as well known as the lodgings of Sherlock Holmes at 221B Baker Street; readers have become intimately acquainted with the layout of Wolfe's home, his eccentricities (which are many), and his antagonistic yet affectionate relationship with his assistant, Archie Goodwin. A diamond in the rough, Goodwin is the "legs" of the detective operation, pursuing leads and gathering evidence while Wolfe remains at home, seemingly torpid. In the security of his brownstone he eats elaborate meals prepared by his personal chef, tends his precious orchids, and, in the end, deftly unravels the mystery.

Politically, Stout belonged to the non-communist left. He espoused many liberal causes both before and after World War II. During the war, he cut back on his detective writing to contribute to the war effort. He wrote propaganda, joined the Fight for Freedom organization, and was master of ceremonies on the radio program "Speaking of Liberty" in 1941. After the war Stout resumed his Nero Wolfe novels, and took up the role of gentleman farmer on his estate at High Meadow in Brewster, some fifty miles north of New York City. He attributed the success of his books to human nature: "You know goddam well why, of all kinds of stories, the detective story is the most popular. It supports, more than any other kind of story, man's favorite myth, that he's *Homo sapien*, the rational animal. And of course the poor son-of-a-bitch isn't a rational animal at all—I think the most important function of the brain is thinking up reasons for the decisions his emotions have made. Detective stories support that myth."

Stout's Nero Wolfe books have appeared in twenty-two languages and sold more than forty-five million copies. He served as President of the Authors Guild and of the Mystery Writers of America, and received from the latter organization a Grand Master award in 1959.

PRINCIPAL WORKS: *Nero Wolf Mysters*—Fer-de-Lance, 1934; The League of Frightened Men, 1935; The Rubber Band, 1936; The Red Box, 1937; Too Many Cooks, 1938; Some Buried Caesar, 1939; Over My Dead Body, 1940; Black Orchids, 1942; Not Quite Dead Enough, 1944; The Silent Speaker, 1946; Too Many Women, 1947; And Be a Villain, 1948; Trouble in Triplicate, 1949; The Second Confession, 1949; Three Doors to Death, 1950; In the Best Families, 1950; Murder by the Book, 1951; Curtains for Three, 1951; Triple Jeopardy, 1952; Prisoner's Base, 1952; The Golden Spiders, 1953; The Black Mountain, 1954; Three Men Out, 1954; Before Midnight, 1955; Three Witnesses, 1956; Three for the Chair, 1957; Champagne for One, 1958; And Four to Go, 1958; Plot It Yourself, 1959; Crime and Again, 1959; Murder in Style, 1960; Three at Wolfe's Door, 1960; Too Many Clients, 1960; The Final Deduction, 1961; Gambit, 1962; Homicide Trinity, 1962; The Mother Hunt, 1963; Trio for Blunt Instruments, 1964; A Right to Die, 1964; The Doorbell Rang, 1965; Death of a Doxy, 1966; The Father Hunt, 1968; Death of a Dude, 1969; Please Pass the Guilt, 1973; A Family Affair, 1975. Collections—Full House, 1955; All Aces, 1958; Five of a Kind, 1961; Royal Flush, 1965; Kings Full of Aces, 1969; Three Trumps, 1973; Triple Zeck, 1974; The First Rex Stout Omnibus, 1976. Other novels—How Like a God, 1939; Seed on the Wind, 1930; Golden Remedy, 1931; Forest Fire, 1933; O Careless Love!, 1935; The Hand in the Glove: A Dol Bonner Mystery, 1937; Mr. Cinderella, 1938; Double for Death: A Tecumseh Fox Mystery, 1939; Mountain Cat: A Mystery Novel, 1939; Red Threads, 1939 (an Inspector Cramer Mystery); Bad for Business, 1940 (A Tecumseh For Myster), 1940; The Broken Vase: A Tecumseh Fox Mystery, 1941; Alphabet Hicks: A Mystery, 1941; The President Vanishes, 1967. As editor—The Illustrious Dunderheads, 1942; (with L. Greenfield, 1946); Rue Morque No. 1.

ABOUT: The autobiographical material quoted above was written for Twentieth Century Authors, 1942. Contemporary Authors vols. 61–64, 1976; Current Biography 1946; Encyclopedia Mysteriosa, 1994; Encyclopedia of Mystery and Detection, 1976; Anderson, D. Rex Stout, 1984; Baring-Gould, W. S. Nero Wolfe of West Thirty-Fifth Street: The Life and Times of America's Largest Detective, 1969; McAleer, J. J. Rex Stout: A Biography, 1977. Periodicals—Journal of Popular Culture Summer 1993; New York Times August 18, 1935; October 29, 1974; New York Times Book Review November 15, 1953; New Yorker July 16 and July 23, 1949; Newsweek March 22, 1971.

**STOWE, LELAND** (November 10, 1899–January 16, 1994), American journalist, was born in Southbury, Connecticut, the son of Frank Philip  Stowe, a lumberman, and Eva Sarah (Noe) Stowe. He attended Wesleyan University, where he worked as campus correspondent for the *Springfield Republican*, and took his B.A. in 1921. He then became a cub reporter for the *Worcester Telegram* in July of 1921, before leaving for New York City the following November. There he went to work on the *New York Herald*, remaining with the paper after it merged to become the *New York Herald Tribune*. In 1924 he became the news editor of *Pathé News*, a newsreel company, but returned to the *Herald Tribune* in 1926, joining the paper's Paris bureau. What followed was a distinguished career as correspondent and commentator covering five continents in war and peace for the *Herald Tribune*, Chicago Daily News, ABC Radio, the *New York Post* syndicate, and the Mutual Broadcasting System.

Stowe quickly gained a reputation as an authority on international affairs. In 1930 he won the Pulitzer Prize for his reports on the four-month Young Reparations Conference in Paris. In 1933 he published *Nazi Means War*, reporting firsthand on Germany's growing militarization and other preparations for aggression.

When his predictions came true and Hitler invaded Poland, Stowe asked the *Herald Tribune* to assign him to cover the conflict, only to be denied on the grounds that he was too old. He was thirty-nine. But Stowe was destined to do some of his finest writing reporting the war, and the *Chicago Daily News* gave him his chance. During two long tours of duty for that paper he was often in the thick of the action. A dispatch sent from Finland on January 3, 1940, reflects the tragedy of war as reported by an unusually sensitive journalist: "In this vast solitude lie the dead: Uncounted thousands of Russian dead. They lie as they fell—twisted, gesticulating and tortured. But they lie beneath a kindly mask of fallen snow. Now they are one with the cold, white shapes of the illimitable pine and spruce trees. An unknown legion of the fallen, they have been sacrificed by winter's hands and covered over with winter's spotless sheet. They will not go back to the earth now for many months."

One of Stowe's major scoops was recounted by John Hohenberg in his book *Foreign Correspondence: The Great Reporters and Their Times*. Hohenberg relates that Stowe "scored over all others as the Nazi blitz spread to Norway. On April 16, a week after the invasion of Oslo, he reached Stockholm with the story of how the traitor Vidkun Quisling had helped the Nazis take Norway. With Edmund Stevens of the *Christian Science Monitor* and Warren Irvin of NBC, Stowe was an eyewitness—and got over the border first with the news."

At college Stowe earned a letter as a cross-country runner. This training served him well when he and a photographer made a harrowing ten-mile hike, through mud and snow in mountainous terrain, to get from Norway to Sweden, where he issued an exclusive report on the British military's tragic Norwegian debacle. As Hohenberg pointed out, "this exploit was all the sweeter" for a man once deemed too old to report from the front. In 1941 Stowe published *No Other Road to Freedom*, a memoir of his war years. Mill Lampell wrote in a *New Republic* review that "it isn't exactly fair to expect a war correspondent to be what his publishers try to make him—a sort of Lord Byron out of Charles and Mary Beard. Leland Stowe is sensitive and emotional, a good writer who sometimes works harder at his prose style than at getting all the facts. But he writes it the way he sees it, and he saw plenty."

After the war Stowe worked as a free-lance reporter, writer, and lecturer. He was foreign editor of the *Reporter* magazine from 1949 to 1950 and director of Radio Free Europe's news service, Munich, from 1952 to 1954. In 1956 he joined the University of Michigan as professor of journalism while working as roving editor and writer for the *Readers' Digest*. He also continued to published books, some recounting his experiences in journalism laced with commentary, others warning of the dangers of the United States military build-up and Soviet aggression.

Stowe retired from teaching in 1969. Writing in the *New York Herald Tribune*, Joseph Barnes had (1941) called him one of the "most legitimately distinguished foreign correspondents of his generation."

The papers of Leland Stowe are housed in the Mass Communications History Center in Madison, Wisconsin.

PRINCIPAL WORKS: Nonfiction—Nazi Germany Means War, 1933; Target You, 1949; Conquest by Terror: The Story of Satellite Europe, 1952; Crusoe of Lonesome Lake, 1957; The Last Great Frontiersman: The Remarkable Adventures of Tom Lamb, 1984. *Memoirs*—No Other Road to Freedom, 1941; They Shall Not Sleep, 1944; While Time Remains, 1946.

ABOUT: Contemporary Authors, 1994; Current Biography 1940; Dictionary of Literary Biography vol. 29 1984; Hohenberg, J. Foreign Correspondence: The Great Reporters and Their Times, 1964. *Periodicals*—New Republic September 29, 1941; New York Herald Tribune September 7, 1941; New York Times January 18, 1994.

**\*STRACHEY, (EVELYN) JOHN (ST. LOE)** (October 21, 1901–July 15, 1963), English writer on politics and economics, and Labour minister, was born at Newlands Corner—one of his family's three houses—near Guildford, in Surrey. He was the youngest of the three children of John St. Loe Strachey, owner and editor of the *Spectator*, an influential Conservative journal of opinion. His mother was the former Amy Simpson, granddaughter of the political economist Nassau Senior. The Stracheys were an old and distinguished family. The iconoclastic biographer Lytton Strachey was John Strachey's second cousin.

In 1915 Strachey went to Eton, which he hated, and in 1920 up to Magdalen College, Oxford. He
°STRAY chee

was an aesthete as well as an athlete at Magdalen, writing poems and plays, acting in some, outraging the conventional by batting for his college in a  straw hat with pink ribbons. All the same, like his father, he was a Conservative at Oxford. He was prominent in the Canning Club and, with his lifelong friend Robert (later Lord) Boothby, edited the Conservative *Oxford Forthnightly Review*. Strachey's elder brother had died of pneumonia at Oxford. When Strachey contracted peritonitis in 1922, his parents feared another such loss and readily agreed when he proposed to leave Oxford without a degree.

At first, Strachey worked for his father on the *Spectator*, writing editorials and reviews. However, his political views were changing. Raised in the Church of England, "the Tory Party at prayer," he lost his religious faith at Oxford, and with it his belief in the whole structure of Tory ideology. He had also been influenced by his love affairs with a radical French intellectual, Yvette Fouquet, and with Elizabeth Ponsonby, daughter of a Labour politician. The latter had introduced him to Fenner Brockway of the Independent Labour Party, which Strachey joined around the end of 1923. A year later, aged twenty-three, he stood unsuccessfully as an ILP candidate for Parliament.

Strachey put his journalistic skills at the service of socialism, as editor first of the ILP's *Socialist Review*, then of *The Miner*, official organ of the Miners' Federation. He did much to popularize the miners' cause during the General Strike of 1926. By this time Strachey was under the influence of Oswald Mosley, who then seemed (if only to some) to be the best hope for Labourites frustrated by the conservatism of their leaders. Strachey's first book, *Revolution by Reason*, was an account of Mosley's economic thinking, which was much influenced by that of another ex-socialist, Benito Mussolini; Mosley adopted its title as his campaign slogan.

In the Labour landslide of 1929, Strachey was elected Member of Parliament for the Aston division of Birmingham. He became Mosley's parliamentary private secretary and his chief lieutenant. In 1931, when Mosley left the Labour party to form his own New party, Strachey went with him. But he became increasingly disillusioned with Mosley's arrogance, and with his growing hostility towards the Soviet Union. Strachey left the New party after six months and was an independent M.P. until he was ousted from Parliament in the 1931 general election.

Strachey had found a new hero in Aneurin Bevan, who turned him towards left-wing socialism as Mosley turned towards fascism. Strachey was no more communist than Bevan, but throughout most of the 1930s was Marxist socialism's most powerful ideologist in Britain. On this account he was twice arrested in the United States by the immigration authorities.

*The Coming Struggle for Power* was a Marxist analysis of the origins, growth, and inevitable decay of capitalism. The book was of course condemned by most anticommunists, but Frank Pakenham, in the senior Strachey's *Spectator*, described John Strachey as a "gentleman-Marxist" of "probably unique sophistication," whose book "is far the best restatement of the Marxian-Leninist gospel . . . which has any application to the England of today." Others praised the author's learning, wit, and eloquence. There was equal enthusiasm for the more technical analysis in *The Nature of the Capitalist Crisis*. Strachey's prophetic *The Menace of Fascism* had a cooler reception, its warnings against the dangers of that movement being dismissed as "hysterical" by some contemporary reviewers.

During these years, Strachey worked on H. N. Brailsford's *New Leader*, and in 1936 helped in the founding of Victor Gollancz's Left Book Club, which became in effect a political movement. Strachey wrote for its monthly *Left News*, spoke at its meetings, and was the author of two of its Book Club choices, *The Theory and Practice of Socialism* and *What Are We To Do?* Both examined the development of labor movements in general in search of contemporary and local solutions. The latter condemned Fabian "evolutionary socialism" and called for a Popular Front. Strachey's pamphlet *Why You Should Be a Socialist* sold over 300,000 copies.

The Nazi-Soviet pact of 1939 disillusioned Strachey. *A Programme for Progress* showed him turning away from Marxist economics under the influence of John Maynard Keynes, whom he had previously bitterly criticized. The book strongly influenced economic thinking in the Labour party. Strachey publicly broke with all-out Marxism in 1940. At that time he was serving as an air raid warden in London. His experiences of the Blitz were published in *Post D*, in which the *New York Times* (1941) found "information and descriptive clarity, human drama, insight, wit, and profound and reticent eloquence." There was similar praise for Strachey's *A Faith to Fight For*, which maintained that Hitler's empire, built on lies and hatred, would fail as surely as the Roman Empire had.

In 1941 Strachey volunteered for the Royal Air Force. He served for a time as adjutant of a fighter squadron, then as public relations officer with a bomber group. Strachey subsequently joined the directorate of bomber operations at the Air Ministry, and began the BBC radio commentaries on the war in the air which made his a household name. He left the R.A.F. with the rank of wing commander and, once again a member of the Labour party, was returned to Parliament in 1945 as a Member for Dundee.

Strachey was effective as Under-Secretary of State for Air in Atlee's postwar government, and in 1946 was given the sensitive post of Minister of Food. Continuing food shortages and the peacetime rationing of bread brought him savage but usually unfair criticism, especially from the Conservative Beaverbrook press. In 1949 he was much ridiculed for the expensive failure of a plan to increase oil supplies by growing peanuts in Tanganyika. The following year, now Secretary of State for War, Strachey was confronted with a new crisis. In the fever of anxiety caused by the arrest of the atomic spy Dr. Fuchs, the *Evening Standard* pilloried the war minister with the accusation that he had never renounced communism."But Strachey remained in the government until its defeat in 1951.

During the 1950s, Strachey wrote a series of books seeking a democratic socialist approach to world problems. The most lucid of these was *The End of Empire*, about modern imperialism in general and the future of postwar Britain in particular. A.P. Thornton called it "a strikingly argued and vigorous book that in style and matter could not have come from his radical pen twenty-five years ago" (*Nation*, 1960). *On the Prevention of War* showed that Strachey, almost alone among his British contemporaries, had mastered the thinking of American experts on the strategy of nuclear deterrence. Strachey also published an attractive volume of essays, *The Strangled Cry*, and a novel, *The Frontiers*.

Strachey was first married in 1929 to an American, Esther Murphy, who divorced him in 1933. The same year he married Celia Simpson, They had a son and a daughter, to whom Strachey dedicated *A Faith to Fight For*. He died suddenly after a spinal operation. Noel Thompson, in his biography of Strachey, concludes that "his life was an intellectual odyssey, a quest for understanding both as a good in itself and as a means of transforming the world for the better."

PRINCIPAL WORKS: *Economics and politics*—Revolution by Reason, 1925; The Coming Struggle for Power, 1932; The Menace of Fascism, 1933; Literature and Dialectical Materialism, 1934; The Nature of Capitalist Crisis, 1935; The Theory and Practice of Socialism, 1936 (revised and abridged as How Socialism Works, 1939); What Are We To Do?, 1938; Hope in America, 1938; Why You Should Be a Socialist, 1938; A Programme for Progress, 1940; Federalism or Socialism?, 1940; A Faith to Fight For, 1941; Socialism Looks Forward, 1954; Contemporary Capitalism, 1956; The End of Empire, 1959; On the Prevention of War, 1962. *Other*—Post D, 1941 (in U.S.: Digging for Mrs. Miller); The Frontiers, 1952 (novel); The Strangled Cry, and Other Unparliamentary Papers, 1962.

ABOUT: Barker, R. Political Ideas in Modern Britain, 1978; Branson, N. History of the Communist Party of Great Britain, 1985; Brockway, F. Inside the Left, 1942; Current Biography 1946; Dictionary of National Biography, 1961–1970, 1981; Dowse, R. Left in the Centre: The Independent Labour Party, 1966; Lewis, J. The Left Book Club, 1970; Morgan, K. Labour in Power, 1985; Newman, M. John Strachey, 1989; Oxbury, H. F. Great Britons, 1985; Sanders, C. R. The Strachey Family, 1968; Strachey, J. Digging for Mrs. Miller, 1941; Strachey, J. The Strangled Cry, 1962; Thomas, H. John Strachey, 1973; Thompson, N. John Strachey: An Intellectual Biography, 1993; Who's Who 1963; Wood, N. Communism and British Intellectuals, 1959; Wright, A. British Socialism, 1983. *Periodicals*—Commentary February 1957; Encounter September 1963; Nation August 13, 1938; March 5, 1960; New York Times July 27, 1941; July 15, 1963; New York Times Magazine September 30, 1973; New Statesman July 19, 1963; Political Quarterly July-September 1960; Spectator November 11, 1932; Times (London) July 16, 1963; Tribune June 15, 1962.

**\*STRACHEY, (GILES) LYTTON** (March 1, 1880–January 21, 1932), English biographer, essayist, and critic, a member of the Bloomsbury Group,

introduced the "new" biography, characterized by an urbane, witty iconoclasm and modern psychological insights. According to his biographer, Michael Holroyd, Strachey's influence on the genre "matched that of Plutarch and Boswell." Born in London, into a family that on both sides had been distinguished in public affairs and letters since the sixteenth century, Lytton Strachey was the eleventh of the thirteen children of Lieutenant-General Sir Richard Strachey, a respected army man and director of Public Works in India, and Jane Maria (Grant) Strachey. Many of his siblings went on to distinguished careers in the army, education, or letters. His sister, Dorothy Bussy, translated Gide's novels (and was Gide's mistress); his youngest brother, James—to whom he was particularly attached—studied with Sigmund Freud and, with his wife, Alix, was the translator and editor of the standard English edition of Freud's works. Lady Strachey, a domineering presence, encouraged her eleventh child's precocious writing talent (he began writing poetry at five) and encouraged his enthusiasm for French literature. At the age of nine he was sent to school in Dorset; three years later he left to go on a sea voyage to South Africa with one of his older sisters. In 1893 Strachey was briefly enrolled at Abbotsholme School, in Derbyshire, but was unable to keep up with the school's required farm work. From there he went to Leamington College (1894–1896) and in 1897 entered University College, Liverpool, studying under the well-known teacher Sir Walter Raleigh.

In 1899 Strachey matriculated at Trinity College, Cambridge, where he read history and established lifelong friendships with Leonard Woolf, Clive Bell, Thoby Stephen (brother of Vanessa Bell and Virginia Woolf), Desmond MacCarthy, and John Maynard Keynes—the nucleus of the Bloomsbury Group to-be. In 1901 he was elected to the prestigious Conversazione Society (better known as the "Apostles"), and shortly afterward received the Chancellor's Medal for English Verse for his poem "Ely: An Ode."

Apart from his prize, Strachey's academic career was disappointing. He achieved only second-class honors in the history tripos, and twice (in 1904 and 1905) failed to win a coveted fellowship at Trinity with a dissertation in defense of the controversial eighteenth-century governor of India, Warren Hastings. Nor was his almost as lengthy essay "English Letter Writers" successful in a bid for the Le Bas Prize in 1905.

In the fall of that year Strachey returned to his parents' home in London and began work as a journalist. He began also—with his other Cambridge friends—to visit the Gordon Square home of

Thoby, Vanessa, and Virginia Stephen; their Thursday nights were the first Bloomsbury gatherings. And in 1905 Strachey and the painter Duncan Grant (a cousin) became lovers; the first of Strachey's three most significant relationships, the affair lasted until 1908, when Grant left him for Maynard Keynes. Since 1903 Strachey had been writing reviews and literary criticism for the *Independent Review* and for the *Spectator*, the weekly journal edited by another cousin, the right-wing St. Loe Strachey. In 1907 he was invited to join the staff, and although he declined his cousin's offer of editorship, continued to contribute weekly reviews of French and English literature, and did drama criticism for the next seven years. Thirty-five of these reviews were published in *Spectatorial Essays*, one of several posthumous collections of his writings edited by his brother James. Through Virginia Stephen—to whom he rashly proposed marriage in 1909, only to withdraw his offer almost immediately—Strachey met the historian H.A.L. Fisher, who had been impressed by his command of French literature.

In 1910 Fisher invited Strachey to write a survey of French literature for the Home University Library series. *Landmarks in French Literature* was finished the following year, by which time Strachey had become a member of Lady Ottoline Morrell's famous set of intellectuals and artists, and had fallen in love with another artist, Henry Lamb. (It was Lamb who painted the best-known portrait of Strachey—a wraith-like, red-bearded figure in carpet slippers—which hangs in the Tate Gallery.) *Landmarks* was much praised as a sound, concise introductory study, although MacCarthy referred to it as "a little textbook of enthusiastical critical clichés." Later critics were also dismissive: Leon Edel, for example, termed it a "potboiler" and John Ferns called Strachey's approach rhetorical, "impressionistic," and imbalanced in favor of his favorite eighteenth-century writers (Voltaire especially) while scanting Hugo and Zola. But it does have the merit of arousing enthusiasm and interest in its readers.

After its publication he began *A Son of Heaven*, a four-act melodrama, set in China during the Boxer Rebellion. Two performances of the play were given in London in 1925, and it was revived in 1949, but has never been published. Strachey also tried his hand at fiction, writing the novella *Ermyntrude and Esmeralda* in 1913 for Lamb's amusement and Bloomsbury's titillation. This story of the sexual awakening of two adolescents was finally published in 1969, by which time its flaunting of Edwardian proprieties seemed to modern readers only moderately enjoyable.

In 1914 Strachey began writing a biographical sketch of Cardinal Henry Manning, the first of the four vignettes that became his most famous book, *Eminent Victorians*. Portraits of Florence Nightingale, Dr. Arnold (headmaster of Rugby), and General Gordon—all singularly obsessed people of action—followed. The writer now met another of the influential figures in his life, the painter Dora Carrington. With her and her lover (and later, husband), Ralph Partridge, Strachey lived in a ménage à trois at the Mill House, Tidmarsh, Berkshire, from 1917 to 1924—the happiest and most productive years of his life. World War I did not interrupt his work, for after writing a manifesto declaring his objections to war service, he was, in any case, exempted from the draft on medical grounds. Published at the end of the war, *Eminent Victorians* had (as Edel points out) "one of the greatest literary successes of the century," and brought its author international fame. An expression of postwar disillusion with the certainties of the older generation, it was the right book at the right time, and is still regarded as a landmark work that "debunked" certain idols of the past and exposed Victorian hypocrisy. The exposure caused some outrage; even Max Beerbohm, in his otherwise warm tribute to Strachey as "a delicately effulgent master . . . of English prose," felt obliged to note that the Arnold portrait was sheer mockery, the only one in the book that "does not seek . . . does not penetrate, and is definitely unfair." The writing style was, and still is, much admired: the concision learned from classical French literature, the Voltairean wit and skepticism, the mix of irony and innuendo. Strachey's ability to deflate a reputation is illustrated in his dry comment on the event that removed a major obstacle to Manning's later career in the Roman Catholic church: "When Mrs. Manning [he was then a married Church of England rector] prematurely died, he was at first inconsolable. . . . How could he have guessed that one day he would come to remember that loss among 'God's special mercies'?" The preface to the book is often quoted as a statement of what biography should be. "Those two fat volumes, with which it is our custom to commemorate the dead" are to be replaced with works written with "a brevity which excludes everything that is redundant and nothing that is significant" and with "freedom of spirit." Strachey's approach also included an effort to understand the subconscious motivations of his subjects, drawing upon the Freudian psychology to which his brother had introduced him. Modern critics have directed the same insights back to the author, to understand what drew him to his subjects, especially to women of unusual power: Nightingale, then (in his next book) Queen Victoria, and finally Elizabeth I. The consensus is that they were reflections of his mother.

Of *Queen Victoria* it is often said that Strachey came to criticize but ended in admiration of her ability; as the *Times* of London obituary noted, he "criticize[d] like an eighteenth-century rationalist and admire[d] like a nineteenth-century romantic." It is a much mellower book than its predecessor (humor replacing satire), and at the same time conventionally scholarly, with abundant footnote annotations. (*Eminent Victorians* provided only brief bibliographies.) Particularly moving is the final paragraph, frequently anthologized, that imagines Victoria on her death bed, her "fading mind call[ing] up once more the shadows of the past to float before it." As Ferns points out, Strachey here seems to borrow Virginia Woolf's stream-of-consciousness technique; significantly, the book was dedicated to her. Three years after its publication Strachey moved, alone, to Ham Spray House, near Hungerford, Berkshire; and in 1926 he began another affair, with the much younger Roger Senhouse (later a director of Secker and Warburg publishers). Their stormy relationship is paralleled in the content of Strachey's next biography, *Elizabeth and Essex*, which he presented as a "tragic history." (As he wrote to one of his sisters, in 1927: "I lead a dog's life, between Queen Elizabeth's love affairs and my own.") Unlike the spare, distilled style of his earlier writing, the prose here is denser, more colorful and poetic. Freudian psychology is evident in his speculations ("essentially guesswork," Beerbohm objected) on the divided nature of his protagonists, their destructive mother-son relationship, the reasons for Elizabeth's sexual repression. On these "speculations" Freud—in a letter to Strachey indicating he had read all his books with pleasure—commends the author for having shown that "you are steeped in the spirit of psycho-analysis. . . . it is very possible that you have succeeded in making a correct reconstruction of what actually occurred." While most contemporary reviewers praised the book, Edmund Wilson, referring to the "high-voiced catty malice" of the author, termed its effect "slightly disgusting" (*New Republic*). Virginia Woolf, questioning his "fictive facts," concluded that *Elizabeth and Essex* was Strachey's weakest book, but stated "because it was the result of a daring experiment carried out with magnificent skill, it leads the way . . . in which others may advance." Maxwell Anderson acknowledged that this "colorful rendering of history" inspired his play *Elizabeth the Queen*; and the book served as the basis of William Plomer's libretto for Benjamin Britten's opera *Gloriana* (1953).

For the last four years of his life the biographer devoted himself to research for notes and commentaries to be contributed to an eight-volume edition of the memoirs of the nineteenth-century government official Charles Greville. After an illness of several months Strachey died of cancer, at Ham Spray House, in his fifty-second year. Two months later the grieving Carrington committed suicide. In 1948 an edition of his *Collected Works* appeared in six volumes, two of which were new compilations of his widely scattered journal articles, *Biographical Essays* and *Literary Essays*, selected by his brother. There is as yet, however, no complete edition of his work, nor a complete edition of his voluminous correspondence. Letters exchanged with Virginia Woolf between 1906 and 1913 are available in a selection issued by Leonard Woolf and James Strachey. "The fencing and the shocking, so typical of Bloomsbury, are marked. . . . Gay, sharp-tongued, wilful and very visual the letters are," V. S. Pritchett commented (*New Statesman and Nation*). Strachey kept no continuous journal but from time to time—beginning with his childhood voyage to Africa—jotted down notes of events and travels. A collection of these, published as *Lytton Strachey by Himself: A Self-Portrait*, was edited by Michael Holroyd. *The Really Interesting Question*, edited by Paul Levy, is a gathering of pa-

pers read at meetings of the Apostles, letters to his brother, and some "ephemeral" writing described by the publishers as "ambitious failures" and by the *Times Literary Supplement* reviewer as "written with a giggle . . . read with a yawn." A useful introduction to his work is provided by *The Shorter Strachey*, selected and edited by Holroyd and Levy, who after the death of James and Alix Strachey, became his literary executors.

Indispensable to any study of the writer is Holroyd's two-volume *Lytton Strachey: A Critical Biography. Lytton Strachey: The New Biography* is a substantially revised version, providing newly discovered material and personal disclosures heretofore not publishable.

PRINCIPAL WORKS: *Fiction*—Ermyntrude and Esmeralda: An Entertainment (introd. M. Holroyd; illus. Erté) 1969. *Nonfiction*—Landmarks in French Literature, 1912 (Home Univ. Library of Modern Knowledge); Eminent Victorians, 1918 (repr. 1989 with foreword by Frances Partridge); Queen Victoria, 1921; Books and Characters, French and English, 1922 (essays); Pope, 1925 (Leslie Stephen Lecture, 1925); Elizabeth and Essex: A Tragic History, 1928; Portraits in Miniature, and Other Essays, 1931; Characters and Commentaries, 1933 (essays); The Collected Works of Lytton Strachey 6 vols., 1948; Letters: Virginia Woolf and Lytton Strachey (ed. L. Woolf and J. Strachey) 1964; Lytton Strachey by Himself: A Self-Portrait (ed. and introd. by M. Holroyd) 1971; The Really Interesting Question, and Other Papers (ed. P. Levy) 1972; The Shorter Strachey (comps. M. Holroyd and P. Levy) 1980. *Poetry*—Euphrosyne: A Collection of Verse, 1905. *As editor*—(with R. Fulford) The Greville Memoirs, 1814–1860, 8 vols., 1938.

ABOUT: Beerbohm, M. Lytton Strachey, 1943 (The Rede Lecture); Bell, C. Old Friends: Personal Recollections, 1957; Bell, Q. Virginia Woolf: A Biography, 2 vols., 1972; Clemens, C. Lytton Strachey (foreword A. Maurois) 1975; Dictionary of Literary Biography Documentary Series: An Illustrated Chronicle, vol. 10, 1992; Dictionary of National Biography, 1931–1940, 1949; Edel, L. Bloomsbury: A House of Lions, 1979; Encyclopedia of World Literature in the Twentieth Century, rev. ed., vol. 4, 1984; Ferns, J. Lytton Strachey, 1988 (Twayne); Garnett, D. Great Friends, 1980; Holroyd, M. Lytton Strachey: A Critical Biography, vol. I: The Unknown Years 1880–1910, vol. II: The Years of Achievement 1910–1932, 1967–1968 (rev. ed. 1971 pub. as Lytton Strachey: A Biography and Lytton Strachey and the Bloomsbury Group: His Work, Their Influence; rev. ed. 1995 pub. as Lytton Strachey: The New Biography); Johnstone, J. K. The Bloomsbury Group: A Study of E. M. Forster, Lytton Strachey, Virginia Woolf, and Their Circle, 1963; Kallich, M. The Psychological Milieu of Lytton Strachey, 1961; MacCarthy, D. Memories, 1953; Maurois, A. Points of View, 1968; Partridge, F. Everything to Lose: Diaries, 1945–1960, 1985; Partridge, F. Love in Bloomsbury: Memories, 1981; Sanders, C. R. Lytton Strachey: His Mind and Art, 1957; Sanders, C. R. The Strachey Family 1588–1932: Their Writings and Literary Associations, 1953; Scott-James, R. A. Lytton Strachey, 1955 (Bibliog. Ser. of Suppls. to British Book News); Seymour-Smith, M. Who's Who in Twentieth Century Literature, 1976; Spurr, B. A Literary-Critical Analysis of the Complete Prose Works of Lytton Strachey (1880–1932): A Re-Assessment of His Achievement and Career, 1994; Strachey, L. Lytton Strachey by Himself: A Self-Portrait (ed. and introd. by M. Holroyd) 1971; Strachey, L. The Really Interesting Question and Other Papers (ed. P. Levy) 1973; Swinnerton, F. A. Georgian Literary Scene, rev. ed. 1969; Trevor-Roper, H. R. Men and Events, 1957; Twentieth Century Literary Criticism vol. 12, 1984; Woolf, L. Sowing: An Autobiography of the Years 1880–1904, 1960; Woolf, V. The Art of Biography *in* The Death of the Moth and Other Essays, 1942; Woolf, V. Letters: Virginia Woolf and Lytton Strachey (eds. L. Woolf and J. Strachey) 1956; Yu, M.M.S. Two Masters of Irony: Annotations on Three Essays by Oscar Wilde and Lytton Strachey, with Special Reference to Their Manner of Writing, 1978. *Bibliography*—Edmonds, M. Lytton Strachey, a Bibliography, 1981 (Garland Ref. Lib. of the Humanities). *Periodicals*—American Scholar Winter 1995; Commonweal May 10, 1968; Encounter January 1971; New Republic September 21, 1932; New Statesman and Nation November 17, 1956; Sewanee Review Summer 1992; Times (London) January 22, 1932; Times Literary Supplement December 8, 1972.

**STRAMM, AUGUST** (July 29, 1874–September 1, 1915), German poet and playwright, was born in Munster (Westphalia), the son of an authoritarian railway official, a Protestant who had ambitions for his son to do better than he had, and who believed that the only way that this could be achieved was for him to become a civil servant. His mother, on the other hand, was a Roman Catholic who pressed the boy hard to become a priest.

August was educated at the gymnasiums at Eupen and at Aachen. Eventually he did as his father had insisted. After studying philosophy and economics at the Universities of Berlin and Halle, he entered the postal division of the civil service. In 1909 he obtained a doctorate for a thesis on the unification of European postal rates. Stramm served as a postal inspector at Bremen and in Berlin, and was then promoted to a post at the ministry. As a captain in the army reserve, however, he was called up to serve in 1914. He was killed at Horodec (Gorodenka) on the Russian front.

For twenty years Stramm labored at his writing in vain: no publisher would take it, and few even looked at it. However, in 1912 he suddenly began to write seriously. This was the direct result of his reading of the declarations of the Italian futurist Filippo Tommaso Marinetti. Then very early in 1913 Marinetti himself came to Berlin to read his manifesto, and its *Supplement*, at the Choralion Hall. The excited Stramm destroyed all his previous compositions and began to follow the recommendations of the Italian. Stramm's poems are best rendered in English in Patrick Bridgwater's *Twenty-Two Poems* (1969).

In 1913 Walden published Stramm's drama *Sancta Susanna* (translated, 1914, as *Sancta Susanna: The Song of a May Night*). After the impact of Marinetti had slightly worn off, he had turned to the brusque if still naturalistic one-act plays of Arno Holz, and then to Maurice Maeterlinck. *Sancta Susanna*, about a nun stoned by other nuns after she has stripped herself naked and kissed a figure of Christ, which reciprocates by coming to life, shows all these influences. Paul Hindemith chose to use it as the libretto for his third (1922) opera, which created a scandal; he later repudiated it. Although Stramm's "scream-plays" have a place in literary history, they have not survived except as part of the record. Stramm was dismissed by many of the later expressionists, and more or less ignored by its chief theorists Kurt Hiller and Kurt Pinthus. Bridgwater, the sympathetic biographer and interpreter of Georg Heym, is balanced in his summary of Stramm's achievement when he writes that his intention was to convey an "inner vision without reference to anything else."

Stramm's poems written at the front, posthumously published, do more or less adhere to his principles—and are his most poignant in the circumstances. An example is "Patrouille" ("Patrol"):

Stones hostile
Window grins betrayal
Branches strangle
Mountain shrubs like rustling pages
Scream Death.

Stramm described his fascinatingly meticulous method of composition in letters to Walden which were later published. His work was finally collected and edited in 1963, by René Radizzani, as *Das Werk*.

PRINCIPAL WORKS IN ENGLISH TRANSLATION: *Drama*—Two plays, Sancta Susanna and The Bride of the Moor (translated by E. O'Brien) in Poet Lore, XXI, VI, 1914; Awakening *in* Ritchie, J. M. and Garten, H. F. (ed. and tr.) Seven Expressionist Plays, 1968. *Poetry*—Twenty-Two Poems (translated by P. Bridgwater), 1969.

ABOUT: Seymour-Smith, M. Macmillan Guide to Modern World Literature, 1986; Columbia Dictionary of Modern European Literature, 1947, 1980; Cyclopedia of Literature in the Twentieth Century, 1982; Hamburger, M. and Middleton, C. (eds. and trs.) Modern German Poetry 1900–1960, 1962. *Periodical*—Journal of European Studies 15 1985.

**STREET, CECIL JOHN CHARLES (pseudonyms "JOHN RHODE" and "MILES BURTON")** (1884–1964), was an English political writer and author of detective novels featuring a grouchy but likeable mathematician, Dr. Priestley. Of these books—all the best known were written under the "John Rhode" pseudonym—H. Haycraft wrote in *Murder for Pleasure*: "At their best, they are good examples of the British routine, fair-play school. But too frequently, one regrets to say, they oscillate between impossible drama and deadly dullness . . . They have, nevertheless, been influential in the widening popularity of the detective story."

Street avoided all personal publicity, with the result that little is known about him, other than that he was a major. His books about international political themes were published under his own name, as was his biography of Lord Reading, Viceroy of India, which garnered some very negative reviews.

Apart from a translation of a French biography of Captain Cook, Street published only one more book of nonfiction—a biography of the Czechoslovakian President, Thomas Masaryk— concentrating the rest of his career upon his slowly and meticulously developed works of detection, which he produced at a prolific rate, not infrequently publishing half a dozen titles in a single year. His productivity was disguised for a time,  with his use of a second pseudonym, "Miles Burton," under which name he developed the characters Inspector Arnold and Desmond Merrion.

Street was a member of the London Detection Club, and included in the 1940 anthology, *Line-Up*, which he edited, an account of the club's history and its activities.

PRINCIPAL WORKS: As *"John Rhode"*—The Double Florin, 1924; A.S.F. The Story of a Great Conspiracy, 1925; The Alarm, 1925; Dr. Priestley's Quest, 1926; The White Menace, 1926; The Ellerby Case, 1927; Mademoiselle from Armentières, 1927; The Case of Constance Kent, 1928; The Murders in Praed Street, 1928; Tragedy at the Unicorn, 1928; The Davidson Case, 1929 (in U.S.: Murder at Bratton Grange); The House on Tollard Ridge, 1929; Dr. Priestley Investigates, 1930; Peril at Cranbury Hall, 1930; Pinehurst, 1930; The Hanging Woman, 1931; Dead Men at the Folly, 1932; Mystery at Greycombe Farm, 1932 (in U.S.: Fire at Greycombe Farm); Tragedy on the Line, 1932; The Claverton Affair, 1933; Dr. Priestley Lays a Trap, 1933; The Motor Rally Mystery, 1933; The Venner Crime, 1933; The Paddington Mystery, 1934; Poison for One, 1934; The Robthorne Mystery, 1934; Shot at Dawn, 1934; The Corpse in the Car, 1935; Hendon's First Case, 1935; Mystery at Olympia, 1935; Death at Breakfast, 1936; The Clue of the Silver Brush, 1936; In Face of the Verdict, 1936; Murder at the Motor Show, 1936; The Clue of the Silver Cellar, 1937; Death on the Board, 1937; Death in the Hop Fields, 1937; Proceed with Caution, 1937; The Bloody Tower, 1938; Body Unidentified, 1938; Invisible Weapons, 1938; Death on a Sunday, 1939; Death Pays a Dividend, 1939; The Elm Tree Murder, 1939; (with John Dickson Carr pseud. *"Carter Dickson"*) Fatal Descent, 1939; Death on the Boat Train, 1940; (as ed.) Line-Up, 1940; Murder at Lilac Cottage, 1940; Death at the Helm, 1941; Signal for Death, 1941; Dead of the Night, 1942; The Fourth Bomb, 1942; Night Exercise, 1942; Dead on the Track, 1943; Men Die at Cyprus Lodge, 1943; Death Invades the Meeting, 1944; Vegetable Duck, 1944; Bricklayer's Arms, 1945; Shadow of a Crime, 1945; Too Many Suspects, 1945; Accidents do Happen, 1946; Death in Harley Street, 1946; The Lake House, 1946; The Clue of the Fourteen Keys, 1947; Death of an Author, 1947; Experiment in Crime, 1947; Nothing But the Truth, 1947; The Links in the Chain, 1948; The Paper Bag, 1948; Shadow of an Alibi, 1948; The Telephone Call, 1948; Blackthorn House, 1949; Up the Garden Path, 1949 (in U.S.: The Fatal Garden); Double Identities, 1950; Family Affairs, 1950; The Two Graphs, 1950; The Affair of the Substitute Doctor, 1951; Dr. Goodwood's Locum, 1951; The Last Suspect, 1951; The Secret Meeting, 1951; Death at the Dance, 1952; Death in Wellington Road, 1952; By Registered Post, 1953; Death at the Inn, 1953; The Mysterious Suspect, 1953; The Case of the Forty Thieves, 1954; Death on the Lawn, 1954; The Dovebury Murders, 1954; Death of a Godmother, 1955; The Domestic Agency, 1955 (in U.S.: Grave Matters); Death of a Godmother, 1955 (in U.S.: Delayed Payment); An Artist Dies, 1956; Open Verdict, 1956; Death of a Bridegroom, 1957; Robbery with Violence, 1957; Death Takes a Partner, 1958; Licensed for Murder, 1958; Murder at Derivale, 1958; Three Cousins Die, 1959; The Fatal Pool, 1960; Twice Dead, 1960; The Vanishing Diary, 1961. As *"Miles Burton"*—The Hardway Diamonds Mystery, 1930; The Secret of High Eldersham, 1930; The Menace on the Downs, 1931; The Three Crimes, 1931; Death of Mr. Gantley, 1932; Tragedy at the Thirteenth Hole, 1933; The Charabanc Mystery, 1934; Murder at the Moorings, 1934; To Catch a Thief, 1934; The Devereux Court Mystery, 1935; The Milk-Churn Murder, 1935; Dark Is the Tunnel, 1936; Death in the Tunnel, 1936; Murder of a Chemist, 1936; Where Is Barbara Prentice?, 1936; Death at the Club, 1937; The Man with the Tattooed Face, 1937; Murder in Crown Passage, 1937; The Platinum Cat, 1938; Death Takes a Flat, 1940; Mr. Westerby Missing, 1940; Murder in the Coalhole, 1940; Written in Dust, 1940; Death of Two Brothers, 1941; Death Visits Downspring, 1941; Vacancy with Corpse, 1941; This Undesirable Residence, 1942 (in U.S.: Death at Ash House); Dead Stop, 1943; Murder M.D. 1943; Four-ply Yarn, 1944 (in U.S.: The Shadow on the Cliff); Early Morning Murder, 1945 (in U.S.: Accidents Do Happen); Not a Leg to Stand On, 1945; Situation Vacant, 1946; Heir to Lucifer, 1947; A Will in the Way, 1947; Devil's Reckoning, 1948; Death Takes the Living, 1949; The Disappearing Parson, 1949; Look Alive, 1949; Beware Your Neighbour, 1951; Murder on Duty, 1952; Heir to Murder, 1953; Something to Hide, 1953; Murder in Absence, 1954; Unwanted Corpse, 1954; A Crime in Time, 1955; Murder Unrecognized, 1955; Death in a Duffle Coat, 1956; Found Drowned, 1956; The Moth-Watch Murder, 1957; Return from the Dead, 1959; A Smell of Smoke,

1959. *Other*—The Administration of Ireland, 1921; Ireland in 1921, 1922; Hungary and Democracy, 1923; Rhineland and Ruhr, 1923; East of Prague, 1924; The Treachery of France, 1924; Lord Reading, 1928; Slovakia Past and Present, 1928; President Masaryk, 1930.

ABOUT: Haycraft, H. Murder for Pleasure, 1941; Reilly, J. M. (ed.) Twentieth Century Crime and Mystery Writers, 1985. *Periodicals*—New Statesman August 4, 1928; Saturday Review of Literature March 15, 1947; Spectator June 23, 1928.

**STREET, JAMES** (October 15, 1903–September 28, 1954), American historical and regional novelist, was born in Lumberton, Mississippi. He was educated at Laurel High School, and at the Massey Military School in Pulaski, Tennessee. During his teenage years he dallied in both journalism (at the age of fourteen he became a part-time reporter on the *Laurel Leader*) and theological study (he attended the Southwestern Theological Seminary and a Baptist seminary in Fort Worth, Texas). In 1923 he was married and, at the age of nineteen, became the youngest Baptist minister in America. He was pastor of churches in St. Charles, Missouri, Lucedale, Mississippi, and Boyles, Alabama. Discovering that he was unfitted, emotionally and religiously, for the ministry, he returned to journalism in 1925, joining the *Pensacola Journal* as news editor. He remained a journalist for the next thirteen years and, after a spell on the *Arkansas Gazette*, became a correspondent and feature writer for the Associated Press, in which capacity he worked in all the southern states. In 1933 he went to New York, where he spent the next five years establishing himself as an author.

Street's first book was a collection of unorthodox sketches about southern life. *Look Away! A Dixie Notebook* was a collection of material handed down by his father, a black nurse, and his Aunt Mattie. Street turned next to fiction and sold a short story, "Nothing Sacred," to Hollywood. The screenplay was worked on by Ben Hecht, the film starred Carole Lombard, and it became one of the comedy hits of the year, on the strength of which Street was able to give up newspaper work. His first published novel was a different affair. *Oh, Promised Land* was a long historical epic, written as rousing romance, about the southern frontier, and featuring the Dabney family, which was to become the linking dynasty in a series of best-selling historical sagas. The other Dabney books included *Tap Roots* (also turned into a film, 1948), set in the period of abolition, and *Tomorrow We Reap* (written in collaboration with his friend James Childers), which brought the Dabney story to the close of the nineteenth century.

*The Gauntlet*, one of the more compact and small-scale of Street's adult novels, was based on his youthful experience as a preacher. The central character was a Protestant minister named London Wingo. Six years later Street published a sequel,

*The High Calling*, which took Wingo's story forward twenty years.

Street was also the author of popular dog stories, the best known of these being *The Biscuit Eater*, another of his books adapted for film. Other work included two lightweight, debunking histories— one on the Civil War, the other on the Revolution. Street's *Look Away! A Dixie Notebook* has been consulted by those studying race relations in the South and by students of William Faulkner looking for possible source material.

PRINCIPAL WORKS: *Fiction*—Oh, Promised Land, 1940; The Biscuit Eater, 1941; In My Father's House, 1941; Tap Roots, 1942; By Valour and Arms, 1944; The Gauntlet, 1945; Short Stories, 1945; Tomorrow We Reap, 1949; Mingo Dabney, 1950; The High Calling, 1951; The Velvet Doublet, 1953; Goodbye My Lady, 1954; (with Don Tracy) Pride of Possession, 1960. *Nonfiction*—Look Away! A Dixie Notebook, 1936; The Civil War, 1953; The Revolutionary War, 1954; James Street's South (ed. J. Street, Jr.) 1955.

ABOUT: Current Biography 1946; Who's Who in America 1946–1947. *Periodicals*—New York Times September 29, 1954; Times (London) September 20, 1954.

## STREET, JEAN. See BAZIN, RENÉ

## STREET, JULIAN LEONARD (April 18, 1879–February 19, 1947), American novelist, essayist, and writer on gastronomy, was born in Chicago and educated at Ridley College Preparatory, St. Catharines, Ontario, Canada. He began as a reporter on the *New York Mail and Express* in 1899, serving as drama editor from 1900 to 1901.

He later spent a number of years living on the Riviera, where he established a lifelong friendship with the novelist Booth Tarkington. In 1921 the two men collaborated on a comedy in four acts called *The Country Cousin*.

Street was best known for his articles and books on food, wine, and restaurants. The government of France awarded Street the Chevalier's Cross of the Legion of Honor in gratitude for his work in popularizing knowledge of French wines and cooking.

As a writer of fiction Street produced a number of "light and agreeable" novels, such as *Rita Coventry*, in which a beautiful opera star gives a vain Wall Street businessman his comeuppance. He was also a skilled writer of commercial stories: *Mr. Bisbee's Princess* tied for first-place honors in the 1926 O. Henry Memorial Prize competition. This fantasy about a jeweler who meets a princess was made into a movie starring W. C. Fields.

Early in the century Street and the artist Wallace Morgan journeyed across the United States, recording their impressions with pen and drawing, and publishing the results under the title *Abroad at Home*. The *New York Times* (December 20, 1914) called it the "most engaging, the most American, the most amusing and satisfactory and interesting record of a joyful pilgrimage imaginable." The two men continued their travels and, in 1917, brought out *American Adventures*.

PRINCIPAL WORKS: *Novels*—After Thirty, 1919; Sunbeams, Inc., 1920; Rita Coventry, 1922; (with A. Street) Tides, 1926. *Short stories*—The Need of Change, 1909; Ship-Bored, 1912; Cross-Sections, 1923; Mr. Bisbee's Princess, and Other Stories, 1925. *Nonfiction*—My Enemy the Motor: A Tale in Eight Honks and One Crash, 1908; Paris a la Carte, 1911; Welcome to Our City, 1913; Abroad at Home: American Ramblings, Observations, and Adventure, 1914; The Most Interesting American, 1915; American Adventures: A Second Trip "Abroad at Home," 1917; Mysterious Japan, 1921; Where Paris Dines, with Information about Restaurants of All Kinds, Costly and Cheap, Dignified and Gay, Known and Little Known, and How to Enjoy Them, 1929; Civilized Drinking, 1933; Wines: Their Selection, Care and Service, with a Chart of Vintage Years, and Observations on Harmonies Between Certain Wines and Certain Foods, and On Wineglasses, Cradles, Corkscrews and Kindred Matters, 1933, rev. ed. 1948, 3rd ed. by A.I.M.S. Street 1960; Men, Machines and Morals, 1942; Table Topics, 1959. *Drama*—(with B. Tarkington) The Country Cousin, 1921. *Juvenile*—The Goldfish: A Christmas Story for Children Between Six and Sixty, 1912; (with M. S. Whitten) Lyrics for Lads and Lasses, 1927. *As editor*—A Woman's Wartime Journal: An Account of the Passage Over a Georgia Plantation of Sherman's Army on the March to the Sea, as Recorded in the Diary of Dolly Sumner Lunt (Mrs. Thomas Burge) 1927.

ABOUT: *Periodicals*—New York Times December 20, 1914; February 20, 1947; Saturday Review of Literature July 25, 1925.

## STREET, CLARENCE KIRSHMAN (January 21, 1896–July 6, 1986), American journalist and publicist, wrote: "Clarence Streit was born in the little town of California, Missouri. On his mother's side he is a Missourian three generations deep. His father, Josiah Streit, was a fiddling farmer who composed a number of tunes he played at country dances around Streit's Ford, Missouri. Clarence Streit's first experience with the press began as editor of the eighth grade paper. When he was fifteen his family moved to Missoula, Montana. There he founded the high school paper. Majoring in journalism at the State University of Montana, he was editor of its student paper. He worked his way through high school and university mainly by surveying in the Rocky Mountains, the Bad Lands, and Alaska. In 1917 he volunteered. In that capacity he was given a confidential post with the American Peace Commission at the Versailles Conference, and at one time was a bodyguard of President Wilson. He did some studying at the Sorbonne.

"Demobilized, he worked as a reporter in Missoula, but soon returned to Europe as a Rhodes Scholar at University College, Oxford. During vacations he got his first job as a foreign correspondent in 1920, in Paris on the *Philadelphia Public Ledger*. After covering the Greco-Turkish War, he resigned his scholarship to marry Jeanne Defrance of Paris and take a permanent post with the *Ledger* as its Rome correspondent. He began at  Genoa, was assigned to Constantinople, and then transferred to Paris. In 1925 he began his career on the *New York Times* as ghost writer on Count de Prorok's expedition to excavate the ruins of ancient Carthage. He then covered the Riff War in Morocco. He was next stationed in Vienna, with the Balkans for beat, and was expelled from Rumania, but has since been invited to return. He was shifted back to New York where he served on the telegraph and cable desk and did special reporting assignments. In 1929 he was sent by the *Times* to cover the League of Nations at Geneva, remaining until transferred in 1938 to the *Times* Washington Bureau.

"During the last five years of his stay in Geneva he was engaged in writing *Union Now*. After its publication he resigned from the *Times* to devote all his time to bringing about the Federal Union of democracies his book proposed. The book was also published in London, Paris and Stockholm, and Streit crossed the United States three times on speaking tours. He is the president of the InterDemocracy Federal Unionists.

"Unlike most other correspondents, Streit in his books does not tell so much about his own experiences as what he has learned from them. He has written an adaptation of the Persian poet Hafiz in rubaiyat, and a report, *How to Combat False News*, made in 1932 for the Council of the League of Nations as President of the International Association of Journalists Accredited to the League. His favorite sport is skiing. He and his wife, son, and two daughters now make their home in Washington, D.C."

---

The publication of *Union Now* (1939) marked the turning point in Clarence Kirshman Streit's career. The book led him away from reporting for the *New York Times* to the role of crusader for his concept of a federal union of democracies. Rather than a culmination, *Union Now* proved to be a mere building block for an idea to which Streit devoted the remainder of his life. He persisted in his advocacy by writing more books, editing a monthly magazine, delivering lectures, and forming organizations that promoted his dream.

Streit's plan called for a government comprised of the major democracies of the world, in which member-countries function similarly to states, handling their own domestic affairs; and the federal union manages the common defense, currency, trade and communications of a common citizenship.

The idea held some relevance during and immediately following World War II. When *Union Now* was first published, Streit became chairman of the Inter-Democracy Federal Unionists (I.F.U.), an association formed as a natural outgrowth of the book. He embarked on a nationwide lecture tour in 1940 to explain the proposal and to claim that such a union was a challenge similar to the one faced by the framers of the U.S. Constitution in the late 1700s. Union Now chapters were organized in more than 100 communities throughout the United States and England, and a Gallup poll in 1940 indicated that two million American voters would support such a federation in order to maintain world peace.

All Streit's subsequent publicatons were devoted to this theme. He wrote *The Need for Union Now* (1940), *Union Now With Britain* (1941), and a post-war edition of the original *Union Now* (1949), which was introduced by Tennessee Senator Estes Kefauver, one of Streit's leading supporters. This new edition included five new chapters covering events since the original publication, and took into account the formation of the North Atlantic Treaty Organization that year. Streit now revised his plan, calling it the Atlantic Union—and urging that it include the NATO member countries.

Largely due to Kefauver's support, Streit and several of his associates and supporters testified in 1950 before a Senate Foreign Affairs Committee on the North Atlantic Treaty, and Kefauver introduced into the Senate a resolution calling for the United States to invite other Western nations to pursue the road to federal union.

But the plan received little support from legislators and editors who had influence. After a decade of promotion by its author, *Time* speculated that "a majority of U.S. citizens have never heard of it, and many who have read of it in the inside pages have long since forgotten its details." Those in power, who may have had more familiarity with Streit's arguments, were equally unmoved. Reaction from European officials "ranged from a slight interest . . . to suspicion and outright hostility. British statesmen listened to the scheme with the look of deliberate patience reserved for small children and the harmlessly insane," and the response from official Washington was "just as discouraging."

This negativity failed to dissuade Streit, who wrote two sequels: *Freedom Against Itself* in 1954 and *Freedom's Frontier: Atlantic Union Now* in 1961, and served as editor of *Freedom and Union*, a monthly magazine that he called "the journal of the World Republic that does not yet exist." Published in Washington, D.C., from 1946 until 1975, it was the mouthpiece of Federal Union, Inc., an organization, along with the International Movement for the Atlantic Union, that Streit founded and for which he served as president.

Streit continued his advocacy even after the magazine ceased publication, and several times was nominated for the Nobel Peace Prize, most recently in 1985, one year before his death. Besides the Nobel nominations, Streit's dedication to his union plan made him the first recipient of the Estes Kefauver Union of the Free Award in 1968.

PRINCIPAL WORKS: Where Iron Is, There Is the Fatherland, 1920; Hafiz—The Tongue of the Hidden, 1928 (rev. as Hafiz in Quatrains, 1946); Union Now, 1939; The Need for Union Now, 1940; Union Now With Britain, 1941; Not Again in Vain, 1942; Union Now (rev. and enlarged) 1949; (as ed., with others) The New Federalist, 1950; Freedom Against Itself, 1954; Freedom's Frontier—Atlantic Union Now, 1960.

ABOUT: The autobiographical material quoted above was written for Twentieth Century Authors, 1942. Current Biography 1940; 1950; 1986; International Authors and Writers Who's Who 1982; The International Who Who's 1984; International Who Who's in Poetry 1982; National Cyclopedia of American Biography 1952. *Periodicals*—Fortune April 1939; New York Times July 8, 1986; Newsweek September 30, 1946; Pittsburgh Press July 9, 1986; Saturday Review of Literature February 19, 1940; Time June 17, 1940; March 17, 1941; September 23, 1946; March 27, 1950.

## "STRIBLING, T(HOMAS) S(IGISMUND)" (pseudonym of THOMAS HUGHES STRIBLING) (March 4, 1881–July 8, 1965), American

novelist, was born in Clifton, Tennessee, the son of Christopher Columbus Stribling and the former Amelia Annie Waits. His parents ran, together, a small weekly newspaper in Clifton, so that writing of some kind was always in his blood and at the forefront of his interests. When he was four years old they shut the paper and opened a general store on the same premises; he remembered hating being set to work there handing out groceries—and how he would retreat under the counter to compose his earliest fiction.

Stribling is today most widely known for *The Store*, because it won the Pulitzer Prize. This novel is the middle part of a trilogy (*The Forge, The Store, The Unfinished Cathedral*), which is in no wise inferior to it as a whole. Thirty years after Stribling's death the entire trilogy was still in print, as were three more of his titles.

Stribling spent his youthful summers with an aunt in the northern part of Alabama. For a brief period in 1900 he was editor of the *Clifton News*, all the contents of which he wrote himself. He published a couple of stories in a Kentucky magazine. At Normal College, Florence, at his father's insistence, he trained for two years as a teacher, graduating in 1903. After one year of teaching mathematics at Tuscaloosa, Alabama, he went on to study at the Law School of the University of Alabama, and graduated with an LI.B. degree from there at the age of twenty-four. His eight-month stint in the governor's law office was not a success. He drifted back to Nashville, in his native state, to become (1906) a kind of office boy on the *Taylor-Trotwood* magazine. Of liberal convictions, disturbed and angered by the political and racist complexion of the South, not at all successful—or much interested—in the professions he had attempted, Stribling, fired from the *Taylor-Trotwood*, turned to hack writing, sheerly for cash: most of it, he later declared, had been "moral adventure stories for the Sunday School magazines."

By composing stuff for more straightforward adventure magazines, pulps such as *Youth's Companion* and *American Boy*, he earned enough to travel to Europe and South America. He lived in Caracas, Venezuela, for six months, trying to research a novel. In 1917, the same year he took a job as reporter on the *Chattanooga News*, he published what has been described as the "last of his juvenile books."

Stribling now began to develop more serious aspirations. He felt himself to be ignorant of literature, but nonetheless the possessor of a well-developed conscience and with something important to say. He took temporary work as a stenographer for the Federal Aviation Bureau in Washington, D.C., as his contribution to the war effort, and wrote pulps at night, now exclusively for *Adventure Magazine*. In 1919, the war over, Stribling returned to Clifton intent on producing his first "literary" novel. *Birthright* was serialized in *Century Magazine* during 1921–1922, and then published as a book in the latter year. The story of a mulatto Harvard graduate, Peter Siner, who returns to his native Tennessee hill town, Hooker's Bend, quickly to recognize how powerless he is to change his society, it attracted wide attention, not always of a positive nature. Thus a "W.S.B." of the *Boston Transcript* (1922) pronounced, "This novel shows a very bad moral standard; it shows an infinitely worse artistic standard." *Birthright* is undoubtedly the work of a man so angered by injustice that it is almost, if not quite, hopelessly distorted. The book's humane and literary impulses are all but submerged beneath raw journalistic intent.

Stribling's next serious novel, *Teeftallow*, made his name. The vileness of the people in the Tennessee mountain town, the exploitation of which enables the confidence trickster and small-time politician Railroad Jones to achieve prosperity and power, is authentic; so is the corrosive bitterness of the whole enterprise. H. L. Stuart, reviewing the book in the *New York Times*, admitted that it would "strengthen Mr. Stribling's reputation," and that he possessed "objective honesty and clarity"; but he added that in one respect he had not "paid his debt to truth": his failure to show the "kindliness and gentleness which is an inseparable part of the nature of these folk."

Before embarking on the trilogy for which he is now best remembered, Stribling wrote a potboiler, *Clues of the Caribbees, Being Certain Criminal Investigations of Henry Poggioli, Ph.D.* Will Cuppy in the *New York Herald Tribune* thought that Stribling's sleuth, the psychologist Poggioli, "appears to be a real master mind." These intriguing and readable adventures are still maintained in print.

After two slighter efforts, Stribling published the first of his trilogy, *The Forge*. The trilogy as a whole deals with the fortunes of the Vaidens, a middle-class family of Alabama, from just prior to the Civil War to the 1930s. Jimmy Vaiden rises from "poor white trash," but then falls into the clutches of a storekeeper, Handback. His son Miltiades (colonel, Klan leader), who becomes a cotton planter and landowner on a grand scale, outwits Handback by attrition and dishonesty. He becomes bank president, and in a final folly begins to build a cathedral to his own memory; he ends crushed to death by it when it is bombed by the son of a man he had cheated.

Andrew Lytle reviewing the first volume in the *New Republic*, noted that, while the narrative moved "with vigor," the author gave "no evidence that he has made any study" of the Civil war. Yet the veteran novelist Robert Herrick wrote in the *Saturday Review of Literature* that *The Forge* was "honest" and "altogether intelligent"—even if it was more a "study" than the "informed commentary of a benevolent observer."

Stribling's last two books, satires on greed, education, and politics, were set in the north. He continued to write detective stories for *Ellery Queen* until 1955. He married the former Lou Ella Kloss in 1930; they had no children. His papers are kept in Clifton, together with a taped interview from 1964. He died in a rest home in Florence.

PRINCIPAL WORKS: *Novels*—The Cruise of the Dry Dock, 1917; Birthright, 1922; Fombombo, 1923; Red Sand, 1924; Teeftallow, 1926; Bright Metal, 1928; East Is East, 1928; Strange Moon, 1929; The Backwater, 1930; The Forge, 1931; The Store, 1932; Unfinished Cathedral, 1934; The Sound Wagon, 1935; These Bars of Flesh, 1938. *Short stories*—Clues of the Caribbees: Being Certain Criminal Investigations of Henry Poggioli, Ph.D. *Letters*—Piacentino, E.J. (ed.) Selected Letters of T. S. Stribling 1910–1934 *in* Mississippi Quarterly Fall 1985.

ABOUT: Baldwin, C. C. The Men Who Make Our Novels, 1924; Cross, R. and McMillan, J. T, Laughing Stock: The Posthumous Autobiography of T. S. Stribling; Eckley, W. T. S. Stribling, 1975; Piacentini, E. J. T. S. Stribling: Pioneer Realist in Modern Southern Literature, 1988; Reilly, J. M. Twentieth Century Crime and Mystery Writers, 1985; Seymour-Smith, M. Macmillan Guide to Modern world Literature, 1986; Zabel, M. D. (ed.) Literary Opinion in America, 1937. *Periodicals*—American Review February 1934; Boston Transcript April 19, 1922; September 29, 1928; English Journal February 1925; Literary Review April 22, 1922; Nation June 20, 1934; New Republic June 3, 1931; New York Call April 16, 1922; New York Times March 14, 1926; July 9, 1965; Saturday Review of Literature April 4, 1931; Southern Literary Journal Fall 1990; Survey August 25, 1922.

## STRIBLING, THOMAS HUGHES. See STRIBLING T. S.

## STRINDBERG, (JOHAN) AUGUST (January 22, 1849–May 14, 1912), Swedish dramatist, poet, novelist, short story writer, occult "scientist," journalist, painter, photographer, and essayist, was born in Ridderholm, near Stockholm, the son of a steamship agent, Carl Oscar Strindberg, and Ulrike Norling, whom Carl Strindberg married (September 1847) after they had already had two sons (Axel and Oscar). After August the couple had nine more children. The family was musical and cultured. In 1862 August's mother died, and his father married his housekeeper, whom Strindberg grew to hate as a stepmother.

At eighteen Strindberg went to the University of Uppsala to study medicine. He failed an examination, left, and tried to take up acting at the Royal

Theater, but did not achieve success. He took up studies in political science at Uppsala, and, more seriously, began a career as a left-wing journalist and supporter of the French Communes. He worked as editor of an insurance company's magazine for a spell. In December 1874 he obtained a post at the Royal Library, serving until his resignation in 1882.

Meanwhile, after several torrid love-affairs, Strindberg became involved (1875) with the former Sigrid ("Siri") von Essen, the wife of Baron Carl Gustaf Wrangel. She had ambitions to become an actress, and Strindberg told her that he would "create a theater" for her, that his "fire was the greatest in Sweden" and that he would "set fire to the entire miserable hole"—"if you want me to." They were married, after her divorce, on December 30, 1877. Siri was by that time seven months pregnant; the child was entrusted to a midwife and died two days later. The couple later had three more children, one of whom, Kristin, wrote an account of her parents' stormy life together.

The best years of Strindberg's first and longest marriage were the first five, when the couple lived together in Stockholm. Later they lived abroad, in France, Austria, Switzerland, Denmark, and Germany. The most vivid account of their life together (and apart) is to be found in the Swedish biographer Olof Lagercrantz's *August Strindberg*. These were difficult years for the Strindbergs: It was at this time that Strindberg began to show symptoms of emotional disturbance seriously complicated by chronic heavy drinking (he indulged in absinthe) and feelings of persecution. Indeed, one of his chief works, written in French in 1883 and then later published in Swedish, is called *Le Plaidoyer d'un fou* (1887, published in a pruned version in French in 1895 and then in Swedish as *En dresfarsvarstal* after his death): *A Madman's Defence*. He and Siri, whom he physically assaulted on one occasion, were divorced in 1892. Within a year, he married an Austrian journalist, Maria Uhl (known as Frida Uhl). With Frida, he had one daughter, Kerstin.

This fraught second marriage ended in divorce in 1897, and Strindberg entered into his third and final marriage, to an actress, Harriet Bosse, in 1901; they were divorced in 1904, after they had had a daughter, Anne-Marie. In many ways this was the least unsatisfactory of his marriages. After the divorce they remained friends—and were even for a time, occasionally, and despite Strindberg's reservations, lovers.

Strindberg's work may be divided into four categories: journalism, drama, fiction, and verse. His works were collected together in fifty-five volumes soon after his death.

Strindberg's earlier work is sometimes naturalistic in the strictly literary sense of "giving the raw facts without fear or favour," according to Martin Seymour-Smith; it is also "occult" (the Swedish visionary Swedenborg, whom he discovered properly in the 1890s, was the chief influence in this respect).

Strindberg wrote (and in many cases revised) over fifty plays, many novels, and other important but unclassifiable works. He made his first real mark in fiction with *Röda rummet* (1879, translated as *The Red Room*), a novel in which he balances two themes: satire of Swedish society from a radical viewpoint, and presentation of a highly principled hero—based on one of his many views of himself—called Arvid Falk. The satire in this book possesses a hyperbolic humor not yet seen in Scandinavian writing. *The Red Room*, a hit from the day it reached the bookstalls, November 14, 1879, automatically put Strindberg at the head of a socialist group.

Other substantial prose works are the naturalistic *Hemsborna* (1887, *The Natives of Hemsö*), tales of the natives of the Stockholm archipelago, which remains his most popular book in Scandinavia, and the similarly set novel *I havsbandet* (1890, translated as *By the Open Sea*), which tackles the Nietzschean theme of the "overman" in the person of Inspector Axel Borg. Mary Sandbach, the author of the best translation (1984), argued persuasively for John Stuart Mill's *Autobiography* as a stronger influence here than Nietzsche, although she underplayed the autobiographical element in the novel itself. The presence of Goethe, the unconventional scientist, is also evident. A key passage (in terms of all Strindberg's work as well as in this novel) is contained in what Borg tells a preacher in Chapter XIV:

> Do you know what God is? He is the fixed point outside ourselves. . . . He is the imaginary magnet inside the earth. . . . He is the ether that must be discovered so that the vacuum may be filled. . . . Give me a few more hypotheses, above all the fixed point outside myself, for I am quite adrift.

The 1987 publication of *The Silver Lake With His The Roofing Ceremony*, two short stories, led Raymond Lindgren in *Library Journal* to comment: "Just preceding the frenzied writing that came at the end of Strindberg's life, these stories reflect his dark thoughts at that time: thoughts on mysticism and tension, death and its meaning, the bitter past. In *The Roofing Ceremony* death is treated with disdain, women with contempt, and man with sarcasm."

Strindberg's chief impact was on the drama, and it was in his plays that he reached the height of his achievement. With his first major play, *Master Olof*, he scandalized society. The play was written about 1873 but was refused production until 1881 because of its recognizable portrayal of important national figures.

Among Strindberg's most important plays are the 1887–1888 group, *Fardren* (1887, *The Father*), *Fröken Julie* (1888, *Miss Julie*), and *Fordringsgare* (1888, *Creditors*). These realist, naturalist plays were influenced by the conflicts of his first marriage and depict psychological warfare between men and women. In *Fardren* (1887, *The Father*), a woman torments her husband by implying that his daughter is not his and causing others to believe he is insane. The husband is finally driven to actual madness. The real reason the wife torments the husband, though, is the wife's having been denied a right to a life of her own. This play moves from a naturalist to an expressionist mode as the characters gradually lose their individuality and turn into shrieking masks. To Arnold Weinstein, writing in *Scandinavian Studies*, the play "revolves around the power struggle as to who will finally control the fate of the child . . . leaving little doubt as to the central issues of the text: ownership, control."

In *Miss Julie* the daughter of a count is forced to suicide when she, trained to believe in her own aris-

tocratic primacy and imperviousness, finds herself seducing a footman, Jean, a man on the rise. The play's power in the theater resides in the hypnotic atmosphere it can evoke in good productions, and in its convincing demonstration that sexual desire can be destructive of lives. In *Creditors* a painter, Adolf, is stripped of his illusions by his wife, Tekla, and her first husband, who is assuming a false name.

In 1892 Strindberg gave up writing for the theater for a time, and concentrated on his "occult" studies. He became, in Berlin, a part of a group centering on the Polish dramatist and novelist Stanislaw Przybyszewski. The years in Paris from 1894 have been called those of the "Inferno" crisis. "If," wrote Seymour-Smith, "expressionism is rightly characterized as a shriek (alluding to Edvard Munch's famous painting of that name), then Strindberg was one of the first to open his mouth."

The trilogy *Till Damaskus* (1898–1901, *To Damascus*), *Päsk* (1900, *Easter*), and the famous *Ett drömspel* (1901, *A Dream Play* ) contain more expressionistic and symbolic modes. In the *Damascus* trilogy, in which Strindberg made use of details of his second marriage, he becomes a self-conscious symbolist. His philosophy, upon emerging from his *Inferno* period, had now become one of compassion, stoical resignation, and even renunciation. The protagonist of the three plays is called, simply, the "Stranger" or "The Unknown One." He is purportedly Everyman, a man on a penitential journey to discover his fate.

The theme "everything comes back," a sort of Swedenborgian notion of karma, is perhaps even more effectively expressed in the shorter *Easter*. In the play, a woman lives with her son; his fiancée; her daughter, an escapee from a mental hospital; and a young lodger. Her husband is in prison for embezzlement. They live in fear of the coming of the creditor, who, in fact, brings reconciliation and the remission of debt. Michael Meyer, one of Strindberg's principal modern translators and interpreters, in a *Times Literary Supplement* review of a 1995 production of *Easter* quoted Charles Morgan's 1928 explication of Strindberg's aim in the play: "We die continually that we may have continual resurrection. This is Strindberg's answer. . . . The truth seems to be that Strindberg's desperate swerving towards orthodoxy yielded him an answer that was still no answer for him."

In *A Dream Play* Strindberg tried, he wrote, "to imitate the disconnected but apparently logical form of a dream. . . . One consciousness remains above the characters: the dreamer's." Göran Stockenström, in an article in *Comparative Drama* entitled "Strindberg's Cosmos in *A Dream Play*: Medieval or Modern," posits the view that Strindberg's modernity is paradoxically derived from a world view that embraces the idea of the Great Chain of Being and the cosmic elements of earth, water, air, and fire. "Love as a flower, death through fire and death through water, the hierarchy of the four elements. . . . In the canonical play of dramatic modernism ancient conceptions recur with renewed vitality," Stockenström quotes

Sven Delblanc as saying. The modernism of the play, according to Stockenström, lies in Strindberg's "conscious manipulation of time, space, and properties on the stage. . . . Characters appear and vanish along with the settings . . . to produce a surreal montage by the technique of juxtaposition." The central protagonist is known as The Daughter or Agnes. She is the daughter of the god Indra, who descends to Earth, "the dark and heavy world the moon lights up," in order to teach the ways of God to men, principally by engaging dialectically with the Poet, her disciple.

Strindberg, particularly in the period after 1899, when he settled in Stockholm again, wrote a series of history plays directly influenced by Shakespeare's similar sequence. It is remarkable that they do stand the comparison—and no such similar series in recent world literature could be claimed to come up to its standard; all it lacks is Shakespeare's poetry. Strindberg's own verse, of which he wrote much, sometimes descends to badly rhymed doggerel; at its best it has been neglected outside Scandinavia. There is no substantial translation into English (except for a somewhat pedestrian, if nevertheless useful, version of *Sleepwalking Nights*); Lagerkrantz's biography contains some well translated and sometimes intriguing examples.

As a dramatist Strindberg was a source of inspiration to the German expressionists, and to Eugene O'Neill, Eugène Ionesco, and Tennessee Williams. O'Neill—who won the Nobel Prize that Strindberg coveted but never received—wrote of him, "Strindberg still remains among the most modern of moderns . . . he knew and suffered with our struggle years before many of us were born. . . . All that is enduring in what we loosely call 'Expressionism'—all that is artistically valid and sound theater—can be clearly traced back through Wedekind to Strindberg's *The Dream Play, There Are Crimes and Crimes, The Ghost Sonata.*"

The bibliography that has collected around Strindberg is enormous; what follows gives, where available, the more modern translations.

PRINCIPAL WORKS IN ENGLISH TRANSLATION: *Novels*—The Son of a Servant (tr. C. Field) 1913; Inferno and From an Occult Diary (tr. M. Sandbach) 1962; The Red Room (tr. E. Sprigge) 1967; By the Open Sea (tr. M. Sandbach) 1984. *Short stories*—The People of Hemsö (tr. E. H. Schubert) 1959; The Silver Lake With His The Roofing Ceremony, 1987. *Essays*—Zones of the Spirit: A Book of Thoughts (tr. C. Field) 1913. *Drama*—The Plays (tr. M. Meyer) 2 vols., 1964; The Road to Damascus (tr. G. Rawson) 1958; The Chamber Plays (tr. E. Sprinchorn and others) 1962; Eight Famous Plays (tr. E. Borkman and N. Erichsen, 1979. *Letters*—Letters of Strindberg to Harriet Bosse (tr. A. Paulson) 1959; Open Letters to the Intimate Theater (tr. W. Johnson) 1959; Strindberg's Letters (ed. and tr. M. Robinson) 1992.

ABOUT: Bellquist, J. E. Strindberg as a Modern Poet, 1986; Borlund, H. Nietzsche's Influence on Swedish Literature, 1956; Brustein, R. The Theater of Revolt, 1964; Campbell, G. A. Strindberg, 1933; Dahlstrm, C. E. W. L. Strindberg's Dramatic Expressionism, 1930; Jaspers, K. Strindberg and Van Gogh, 1977; Johanneson, E. The Novels of August Strindberg, 1968; Klaf, F. S. Strindberg: The Origin of Psychology in Modern Drama, 1963; Lagerkrantz, O.G.H. August Strindberg (tr. A. Hollo) 1984; Lagerkvist, P. Modern Theatre, 1966; Lamm, M. August Strindberg, 1971; McGill, V. L. Strindberg: The Bedevilled Viking, 1930; Meyer, M. Strindberg, 1985; Morgan, M. M. August Strindberg, 1985; Mortenson, B. W. and Downs, B. W. Strindberg: An Introduction to His Life and Work, 1949; Robinson, M. Strindberg and Autobiography, 1986; Sprinchorn, E. Strindberg as Dramatist 1982; Sprigg, E. The Strange Life of August Strindberg, 1949; Steene, B. The Greatest Fire: A Study of August Strindberg, 1973; Tornqvist, E. Strindbergian Drama: Themes and Structure, 1982; Valency, M. The Flower and the Castle, 1963; Waal, C. Harriet Bosse: Strindberg's Muse and Interpreter, 1990; Ward, J. The Social and Religious Plays of August Strindberg, 1980. *Bibliography*—Gustafson, A. A History of Swedish Literature, 1961. *Periodicals*—Comparative Drama Spring 1996; Library Journal November 15, 1987; Scandinavian Studies Summer 1994; Times Literary Supplement August 28, 1992; February 18, 1995.

**STRINGER, ARTHUR JOHN ARBUTHNOT** (February 26, 1874–September 14, 1950), Canadian-American poet and popular novelist, was born in Chatham, Ontario. His father was the captain of a boat that sailed the Great Lakes; his mother was Irish and an amateur poet. Stringer was educated at the Universities of Toronto and Oxford, where he developed an interest in Shakespeare.

On his return from England, Stringer worked as a reporter, first for the *Montreal Herald*, and then for the American Press Association. He tried a variety of other occupations—railway office clerk, fruit farming—but his major endeavors were always literary. By the 1920s he was living in America, and working as a screenwriter. He adopted U.S. citizenship in 1937. However, he located most of his action novels in the northern Canadian territories. Notable among these wilderness novels was the trilogy *The Prairie Wife, The Prairie Mother,* and *The Prairie Child.* They told, in diary form, the story of Chaddy McKail and her troubled marriage to "Dinky-Dunk" Duncan McKail. The final volume, prepared initially for serialization in a women's magazine, succumbed to the sentimentality that was barely kept at bay in the earlier volumes.

While a good deal of his fiction was set in the imagined landscape of his childhood, Stringer did take pride in the authenticity of his regional color, when compared with the misconceptions found in the work of Jack London and others who wrote of the northern lands. His now largely unread verse found inspiration in his ancestral Ireland.

PRINCIPAL WORKS: *Poetry*—Watchers of Twilight, 1894; Pauline and Other Poems, 1895; Hephaestus, 1903; The Woman in the Rain, 1907; Irish Poems, 1911; Open Water, 1914; A Woman at Dusk, 1928; Dark Soil, 1933; The Old Woman Remembers, 1938; The King Who Loved Old Clothes, 1941; Shadowed Victory, 1943; New York Nocturnes, 1948. *Fiction*—The Silver Poppy, 1903; Lonely O'Malley, 1905; The Wire Tappers, 1906; The Loom of Destiny, 1907; Phantom Wires, 1907; The Under Groove, 1908; The Gun Runner, 1909; The Shadow, 1913 (also published as Never Fail Blake); The Hand of Peril, 1915; The Prairie Wife, 1915; The Door of Dread, 1916; The House of Intrigue, 1918; The Man Who Couldn't Sleep, 1919; The Prairie Mother, 1920; Twin Tales, 1921; The Wine of Life, 1921; The Prairie Child, 1922; The City of Peril, 1923;

The Diamond Thieves, 1923; Empty Hands, 1924; Power, 1925; In Bad With Sinbad, 1926; Night Hawk, 1926; White Hands, 1927; The Wolf Woman, 1928; Cristina and I, 1929; The Woman Who Couldn't Die, 1929; A Lady quite Lost, 1931; The Mud Lark, 1932; Marriage by Capture, 1933; Man Lost, 1934; The Wife Traders; Heather of the High Hand, 1937; The Lamp in the Valley, 1938; The Dark Wing, 1939; The Ghost Plane, 1940; Intruders in Eden, 1942; Star in a Mist, 1943; The Devastator, 1944. *Nonfiction*—A Study in King Lear, 1897; Red Wine of Youth, A Life of Rupert Brooke, 1948.

ABOUT: Lauriston, V. Arthur Stringer, Son of The North, 1941; Percival W. P. (ed.) Leading Canadian Poets, 1948; Thomas C. Canadian Novelists 1920–1945, 1946. *Periodicals*—Boston Transcript January 16, 1915; Dial January 1, 1915; New York Times August 18, 1948, September 15, 1950; Times September 25, 1950; Saturday Review of Literature June 6, 1925.

**STRODE, HUDSON** (October 31, 1892–September 22, 1976), American biographer and travel writer, wrote: "Hudson Strode, son of Thom-

as Fuller Strode and Hoper (Hudson) Strode, was born on Halloween. It was only by chance that the birthplace was Cairo, Illinois, for his people were all Southerners. His ancestors settled in Virginia in 1640, and his maternal grandfather was a Confederate colonel from Georgia. He was brought up in the South, in Demopolis, Alabama. During his freshman year at the University of Alabama, the bank containing all the money impounded for his education failed, and he is probably the first college student in the state ever to make his way to graduation by selling subscriptions for magazines. He was graduated after three and a half years' attendance, taking a half-year off to work on a farm in Kentucky. While doing graduate study at Columbia University, Mr. Strode had a variety of jobs, the most exciting being a 'walk-on' engagement with Sir Johnston Forbes-Robertson.

"For two years he was instructor in English at Syracuse University. At the age of twenty-four he was made Associate Professor of English at the University of Alabama, declining an offer at Yale the same week. While at Syracuse he did dramatic criticism and book reviewing. In 1917 *Forum* published his first magazine story. In 1924 he was upped to a professorship, and in the same year he married Thérèse Cory.

"Besides teaching Shakespeare and three other courses in English, Mr. Strode was for several years the entire Department of Speech, the debate coach, and the director of Blackfriars, the dramatic organization that went on tour each season. In spare time he was giving out-of-town lectures and writing or reviewing for American and British periodicals. In 1929 a one-act play called *The End of the Dance* (which he wrote in bed during a spell of influenza) was produced at the Waldorf Theatre, New York, and won first place in the National Little Theatre Contest. In 1929 he was very ill and was let out on leave to recuperate. So he and his wife

went to Bermuda. The process of recuperation took three and a half years. He raised vegetables and wrote articles, and his wife was secretary to a member of Parliament.

"In 1933 he and his wife weathered the revolution in Cuba, and in 1935 they spent a summer flying all over South America. *Immortal Lyrics*, published in 1938, is an anthology of English lyric poetry, but interpretation of foreign countries remains his métier. In 1939 the university granted him a year's leave of absence to study the Scandinavian and Finnish way of life.

"Strode is a liberal in politics and deeply interested in the plight of the farmer and progress in the South. He is a warm admirer of the Scandinavian way of life. He dislikes automobiles and radios and has never owned either. His favorite hobby after travel is gardening."

In 1955, Strode wrote: "At the University of Alabama Strode lectures on Shakespeare and gives a nationally famous course in advanced fiction writing. In the past twelve years students from his class have published more than twenty-five novels and also numerous short stories, several of them being national prize-winners.

"Strode lectures extensively and gives dramatic readings of Shakespeare's tragedies. He has lectured from Amherst to San Antonio and from Richmond to San Francisco, and in Sweden, Italy, and Brazil. In the spring of 1941 he bought twenty acres of woodland five miles from Tuscaloosa and built a Swedish modern house with a separate studio. He and his wife are devoted gardeners and interested in metaphysics. The Strodes have never owned a radio, and they are still driving their first car, a 1941 Olds-hydramatic.

"At present Strode is at work on a biography of Jefferson Davis, president of the Confederacy. At Commencement in 1952 the University of Alabama conferred upon Strode an honorary degree of Doctor of Letters."

———

Hudson Strode's travel books combined personal accounts with history and interpretation. Reviewing *The Pageant of Cuba* for the *New York Post*, Herschel Brickell found it "unusually well-written and as readable as history can be." Especially popular was *South by Thunderbird*, an impressionistic account of Strode's flight around South America with his wife.

Strode's two books on Mexico were equally well-received—Mildred Adams described *Now in Mexico* as being "provocative, amusing and filled with useful information, vividly conveyed" (*New York Times*, 1947). Strode's particular passion, however, was Scandinavia, and his enthusiasm shines through in works such as *Finland Forever*.

Strode's three-volume biography of the Confederate President Jefferson Davis remains his most substantial achievement. As a Southerner, Strode set out to counter the accumulated effects of what he saw as unjust assaults on the rebel leader's reputation. Hardly surprisingly, however, Strode's objectivity was called into question. In a review for the *New York Times Book Review* (1959), J. K. Bettersworth suggested that "in rescuing the bones of the Confederate President from the infidels he may, indeed, be guilty of an indefensible defensiveness." David Donald concluded, "If Mr. Strode's trilogy is not truly a great biography, it is much superior to all previously published lives of Jefferson Davis" (*New York Times Book Review*, 1964). The second volume won the 1960 Award of the American Academy of Public Affairs.

Strode's creative writing course at the University of Alabama became quite well known, launching many young writers on successful careers. As well as lecturing widely, Strode gave dramatic readings of Shakespeare's tragedies. He was made a Knight of the Royal Order of the North Star by King Gustaf Adolf of Sweden in 1961.

PRINCIPAL WORKS: *Travel*—The Story of Bermuda, 1932; The Pageant of Cuba, 1934; South by Thunderbird, 1937 rev. ed. 1945; Finland Forever, 1941; Timeless Mexico: A History, 1944; Now in Mexico; A Book of Travel, 1947; Sweden: Model for a World, 1949; Denmark Is a Lovely Land, 1951; Ultimates in the Far East; Travels in the Orient and India, 1970. *As editor*—Immortal Lyrics; An Anthology of English Lyric Poetry, 1938; Spring Harvest: A Collection of Short Stories from Alabama, 1944; Jefferson Davis; Private Letters, 1823–1889, 1966. *Biography*—Jefferson Davis: Confederate President, 1959; Jefferson Davis: Tragic Hero, 1964. *Autobiography*—The Eleventh House: Memoirs, 1975. *Drama*—(with L. Hornthal) The Dance Below, 1928; The End of the Dance, 1929.

ABOUT: The autobiographical material quoted above was written for Twentieth Century Authors, 1942 and Twentieth Century Authors First Supplement, 1955. Herzberg, M. J. The Reader's Encyclopedia of American Literature, 1962; Strode, H. The Eleventh House: Memoirs, 1975. *Periodicals*—Atlantic June 1956; American Historical Review January, 1956; New York Times October 10, 1937; March 16, 1941; November 16, 1947; October 21, 1951; September 23, 1976; New York Times Book Review October 18, 1959; September 27, 1964; New York Post November 3, 1934; March 20, 1950; New York October 22, 1938; Newsweek May 13, 1940; Saturday Review October 31, 1959; Time July 30, 1945; October 16, 1964; Washington Post September 24, 1976; Wilson Library Bulletin February 1939.

**STRONG, ANNA LOUISE (pseudonym "ANISE")** (November 24, 1885–March 29, 1970), American writer and journalist, was born in Friend,

Nebraska. She was the eldest of the three children of the Reverend Sydney Strong, a Congregationalist minister who managed to combine fundamentalism and Darwinism, and who gave her a devoutly religious upbringing. Her mother was the former Ruth Maria Tracy. One of the first generation of women to receive a college education, Mrs. Strong became president of the Women's Home Missionary Union of Ohio and Illinois.

The family moved about as Sydney Strong became pastor at different churches. Anna Louise attended a private school in Cincinnati. Her first poems and stories appeared in *Youth's Companion*. Too young for university, she studied languages in

Germany and Switzerland. In 1903 she entered Bryn Mawr. Strong moved to Oberlin in 1904, when she also published a precocious first collection of poems.

Her first job was as associate editor of a fundamentalist Christian weekly, the *Advance*. She subsequently enrolled in a philosophy program at the University of Chicago. In 1908, Strong became the youngest student ever to receive a Ph.D. there, with a thesis published as *A Consideration of Prayer from the Standpoint of Social Psychology*. She was obliged to defend it before the theological and philosophical faculties combined.

Strong had developed an interest in reform work. She rejoined her father, who by then had a church in Seattle, Washington, and worked with him in 1909–1910, organizing a "Know Your City" civic improvement program there and in other northwestern cities. This led in 1911 to a post as assistant director of the New York Child Welfare Exhibit.

Before long, Strong embraced socialism, as well as her father's pacifism. In 1916 she joined Crystal Eastman's Truth About Preparedness campaign, organizing antiwar rallies in the midwest. Later that year she returned to Seattle and ran for the state legislature. Unsuccessful in this, she instead won election to the Seattle school board. After America entered World War I, Strong began to write against war capitalism in the socialist *Seattle Daily Call*. Her articles were anonymous, but her public involvement in pacifist activities led to her recall from the school board in March 1918. From then until 1921, Strong was features editor of a labor daily, the *Seattle Union Record*, contributing editorials and militant verses under the pseudonym "Anise." Her 1919 editorial, "No One Knows Where," is credited with launching the Seattle General Strike, which she described in a pamphlet published the same year.

The *Record* collapsed during the depression of 1920–1921. In the latter year Strong secured a post with the American Friends Service Committee. She went first to Poland to work with famine victims, then on to investigate famine conditions in Bolshevik Russia.

In 1922, Strong returned to Russia as Moscow correspondent for Hearst's International News Service. She greatly admired Trotsky, to whom she reportedly taught English, and raised money to establish the John Reed Children's Colony for victims of the Volga famine. *Children of Revolution* told the story of the Colony, while *The First Time in History*, which had an introduction by Trotsky, was a defense of Lenin's economic policies. A reviewer in *Survey* said that, "after two years in the very thick of Russian ferment, Miss Strong writes with all the vigor and dramatic quality which flash from contact with stirring events. Vivid picture and concrete incident follow each other in rapid succession, fresh from the notebook of a quick and keen reporter."

Seeking support for the American Educational Workshops in Moscow, Strong returned to the United States in 1925. For the next ten years, she alternated periods of work in Russia with fund-raising lecture tours in America. In 1930 she founded *The Moscow News*, an English-language newspaper under Soviet government sponsorship, serving as managing editor, then feature writer. Strong entered into a common law marriage in 1932 with a Russian agronomist, Joel Shubin, editor of the *Peasant's Gazette*.

During the 1920s and 1930s, Strong published a stream of books about the Soviet Union—its industry, agriculture, politics, and society. *Road to the High Pamir* was an account of her hazardous journey on horseback in a desolate region of Soviet Central Asia, and the political changes there. It was reviewed by Ernestine Evans in *New York Herald Tribune Books*: "Miss Strong always wrote clearly and with force. She has a fine eye for social direction, for communicating the rush of life in a revolutionary period. Each new book now has the added charm of ease and humor . . . as she piles up the incidents and vast panoramas that, as one of the foremost journalists in the world, she has taken in her stride." *The Soviets Conquer Wheat*, about the imposition of collective farming in 1929–1930, was received with equal enthusiasm. "More than any other of our writers on Russia," wrote Simeon Strunsky in the *New York Times* (1931), "Miss Strong has the gift of vivid authentic detail. The individual Russian, as distinguished from the statistical Russian, stands out vividly on her page. . . . The fervor, the fanaticism, the confusion, the clamor, the vast churning up process now under way in Russia's fields are excellently suggested."

Strong's 1935 autobiography, *I Change Worlds*, gave most attention to her years in Russia. C. G. Stillman in the *Nation* called it "one of the most remarkable and exciting autobiographies of our generation. . . . The author admits you fully into this strange adventure of an individual soul trying to become collectivized. For she is a mystic, and for all its objective truth this is a soul drama."

Editorial differences at *The Moscow News* led to Strong's resignation in 1936. She went off to cover the Spanish civil war (*Spain in Arms*), then settled for a time in California, separated from her husband, who died in 1942. At the suggestion of Eleanor Roosevelt, with whom she corresponded for several years, Strong traveled about the United States in an old automobile, interviewing workers and others about the New Deal and its effects. *My Native Land* is a moving piece of reportage, marred for some by its extreme anti-capitalism.

Strong's later books about Russia did not escape criticism. Some reviewers thought they painted too rosy a picture of the Soviet experiment—that they were either naive or deliberately propagandist. Such charges grew more frequent during the 1940s, as Strong continued to eulogize Stalin and his policies in the face of mounting evidence of his catastrophic errors and atrocities. By that time, she had found a new revolution to report and support.

The author had gone to China in 1927, and described what she saw in *China's Millions*. A later visit produced *One Fifth of Mankind*. In 1946–1947, Strong lived at Communist Chinese headquarters at Yenan. She had a new hero in Mao Tsetung. A famous interview with Mao, in which he coined the term "paper tiger," was published in *Amerasia* (April 1947) and then in Mao's "little red book." More books appeared—*Tomorrow's China*, *The Chinese Conquer China*. They were as partisan about Mao's China as earlier works had been about the Soviet Union, and this new enthusiasm was not welcomed in Russia. In 1949, on her way back to China, Strong was arrested in Moscow on trumped-up espionage charges, and deported. She returned to the United States, where party members shunned her until the Soviet authorities exonerated her some years later.

In 1958, Strong took up permanent residence in Beijing, where in 1962 she began the publication of a regular newsletter for Western readers, *Letter from China*. It survived until 1969, and was one of the few reliable sources of information about life there. Anna Louise Strong was a revered figure in Beijing, regularly visited by high officials, invited to banquets and literary salons, provided with an automobile and a secretary.

In her late seventies, Strong continued to travel, covering the revolutionary regimes in Tibet, Laos, and North Vietnam. She was honored by Mao with a party on her eightieth birthday, and made an honorary member of the Red Guards. Some of her closest Chinese friends were arrested as deviationists during the Cultural Revolution. There were reports that Strong planned to return to America to campaign against the Vietnam War, but in the last issue of *Letter from China* she said that she would stay, since in China, unlike America, "they respect old age." She was still in Beijing in 1970, when she died of a heart attack. She was buried there, in the National Memorial Cemetery of Revolutionary Martyrs. The *New York Times* (1970) described her as "a large woman of powerful frame, with white hair and piercing blue eyes." It quotes a former American consul in China as saying "She sold Communism to the world and the Communists rightly loved her for it."

PRINCIPAL WORKS: *Politics, history, and reportage*—On the Eve of Home Rule: Snapshots of Ireland, 1914; History of the Seattle General Strike, 1919; The First Time in History: Two Years of Russia's New Life, 1924; Children of Revolution: Story of the John Reed's Children's Colony on the Volga, 1925; Marriage and Morals in Soviet Russia, 1927; China's Millions, 1928; Red Star in Samarkand, 1928; The Road to the Grey Pamir, 1931; The Soviets Conquer Wheat, 1931; From Stalingrad to Kuzbas, 1932; This Soviet World, 1936; The New Soviet Constitution, 1937; Spain in Arms, 1937; One-Fifth of Mankind, 1938 (in U.K.: China Fights for Freedom); My Native Land, 1940; The Soviets Expected It, 1941; The New Lithuania, 1941; The Russians Are People, 1943; The People of the U.S.S.R., 1944; I Saw the New Poland, 1946; Tomorrow's China, 1948; The Chinese Conquer China, 1949; The Stalin Era, 1956; Tibetan Interviews, 1959; The Rise of the Chinese People's Communes, 1959 (enlarged version, 1964); When Serfs Stood Up in Tibet, 1960; Cash and Violence in Laos, 1961; Selected Works on China's Revolution (Peking), 1965– . *Poetry*—Storm Songs and Fables, 1904; The Songs of the City, 1906; Ragged Verse by Anise, 1918; God and the Millionaires, 1951. *Other*—The King's Palace, 1908 (play); A Consideration of Prayer from the Standpoint of Social Psychology, 1908 (republished as The Psychology of Prayer, 1909); Boys and Girls of the Bible, 1911 (juvenile); Child Welfare Exhibits: Types and Preparation, 1915; I Change Worlds: The Remaking of an American, 1935 (autobiography); Wild River, 1944 (novel).

ABOUT: American Reformers, 1985; American Women Writers, 1983; Blain, V. and others (eds.) Feminist Companion to Literature in English, 1990; Chen, P. China Called Me, 1979; Conway, J. K. (ed.) Written by Herself: Autobiographies of American Women: An Anthology, 1992; Current Biography 1950; Gayle, H. American Women Civil Rights Activists, 1993; Gitlow, B. The Whole of Their Lives, 1948; Milton, D. and N. D. The Wind Will Not Survive, 1976; Nies, J. Seven Women, 1977; Notable American Women: The Modern Period, 1980; Sale, R. Seattle: Past to Present, 1976; Strong, A. L. I Change Worlds, 1935; Strong, A. L. My Native Land, 1940; Strong, T. B. and Keyssar, H. Right in Her Soul: The Life of Anna Louise Strong, 1983. Periodicals—Beijing Review July 15, 1985; December 16, 1985; March 26, 1990; April 9, 1990; China Quarterly September 1985; Christian Science Monitor Magazine September 28, 1940; Eastern Horizon 9, Nos. 2 and 3, 1970; Nation May 1, 1935; New Republic March 19, 1984; New York Herald Tribune March 27–April 1, 1949; New York Herald Tribune Books May 8, 1931; New York Times September 6, 1931; March 30, 1970; New York Times Book Review March 11, 1984; Reporter April 7, 1955; Survey May 15, 1924; Time March 7, 1949; April 4, 1949; Times (London) March 30, 1970; Washington Post March 30, 1970.

## STRONG, L(EONARD) A(LFRED) G(EORGE) (March 8, 1896–August 17, 1958), English poet and novelist, was born in Plymouth. Both his

parents had Irish blood, and summers were spent with the maternal grandparents, who lived on the Dublin to Dalkey road, near Sandycove Station. These holiday experiences were later used by L. A. G. Strong in his novels; and his poetry certainly possesses a marked Irish character. His early education was undertaken by governesses and tutors. Later, at the Hoe preparatory school, he was inspired to a love of literature by his teacher of English and drama, Miss Cherrill. In 1910 he earned himself a scholarship place at Brighton College, where he spent five years—and developed the idiosyncrasy of setting his watch twenty-five minutes adrift of Greenwich, so that he could keep "Irish time."

Strong was afflicted with a low-grade spinal disability during adolescence, and at one period was confined to bed for three months and had to spend a further six months away from school. In his posthumously published autobiography, Green Memory, he writes of the illness that, "It damaged my self-confidence, it interrupted my school life, it stamped me with an inhibiting sense of guilt." The disability disappeared in adulthood, but it kept him out of active service during the war and, in the view of several critics, lay behind his inclination as a novelist to dwell on themes of brutality and violence.

From Brighton Strong went up to Wadham College, Oxford, in 1915. He graduated in 1920, after an interruption of two years standing in for a schoolmaster at Summer Fields, a prep school near Oxford. During his final year at the University,

Strong was publishing his poetry widely enough to be parodied (by Louis Golding) for his West Country and Irish allusions: "O it's dimpsey on the water!/If yer wants brand new effects/—Dublin, Devon, it don't matter—/Just combine the dialects." He also became acquainted with Yeats and interested in psychic research.

After graduation he returned to Summer Fields and worked as a schoolmaster there for the next ten years. Among his pupils were the sons of Harold Nicolson and Vita Sackville-West. Initially his literary efforts remained concentrated on poetry. During his twenties he published two full-length and several shorter collections, and was also invited by his publisher, Basil Blackwell, to edit anthologies. Marriage in 1926—to Sylvia Brinton, the daughter of an Eton housemaster—determined him to turn his pen to more productive effect, and he set about writing his first novel. Dewer Rides, published in 1929, about a Dartmoor farm laborer, sold well, and Strong felt emboldened to give up teaching.

His second novel—which appeared after a volume of short stories featuring dialect-speaking fishermen and rustics—was autobiographical. The Garden drew on memories of his childhood holidays in Ireland and was written in a style which was both delicate and simple. It won strong praise from V. S. Pritchett, in the Christian Science Monitor, who called it "one of the sanest and most beautiful books we have read for a long time. It will assure him a high place in English literature and, we fancy, a permanent one." The Spectator (1931) spoke about an "unqualified triumph . . . written about a people, a scene, a life which Mr. Strong understands with his blood." The third novel, The Brothers, a Cain and Abel story, was more unsettling. Some readers were repelled by scenes of violence which were presented in a strangely neutral manner, rather than in the context of a human tragedy.

L.A.G. Strong's subsequent fiction, both short stories and novels, continued to be written in what the New York Times called a "grave and lovely prose" and exhibited—as William Plomer, in the Spectator (1934), put it—"a true nobility of sentiment." But the highest expectations were not realized. A deficiency in narrative construction rendered the short fiction commonplace, and muddled the novels. Relying on autobiographical material sometimes had the effect of contributing to the fragmentary impression. Strong, seeming to recognize his failings as a writer of fiction, began to branch out from the mid-thirties onwards. He produced biographies of Thomas Moore and John McCormack. He wrote a good book about boxing in Shake Hands and Come Out Fighting, and another passable one about James Joyce in The Sacred River. He lectured and spoke on the radio; taught at the Central School of Speech and Drama; was an adjudicator in amateur dramatics; published a book about public speaking, A Tongue in Your Head; and, late in his career, developed a line of detective fiction.

Strong's poetry, written in a concise epigrammatic minor vein, and collected in The Body's Imperfection (1957 edition), is considered the aspect of his work most worthy of preservation—a judgment with which he would not have argued. The summarizing paragraph of his short book on Joyce carries a note of implied self-criticism: "With a literary gift that could have been turned to money-making, with a singing voice that would have made him wealthy, Joyce preferred the drudgery of ill-paid teaching to a misuse of his powers."

PRINCIPAL WORKS: *Poetry*—Dublin Days, 1921; Says The Muse to Me, Says She, 1922; The Lowery Road, 1923; Difficult Love, 1927; At Glenan Cross: A Sequence, 1928; Northern Light, 1930; Selected Poems, 1931; March Evening and Other Verses, 1932; Call to the Swan, 1936; The Body's Imperfection, 1948, 1957; The Magnolia Tree, 1953. *Fiction*—Doyle's Rock and Other Stories, 1925; The English Captain and Other Stories, 1929; Dewer Rides, 1929; The Jealous Ghost, 1930; The Garden, 1931; The Brothers, 1932; Don Juan and the Wheelbarrow, 1932; Sea Wall, 1933; Corporal Tune, 1934; Mr. Sheridan's Umbrella, 1935; The Seven Arms, 1935; Tuesday Afternoon and Other Stories, 1935; The Last Enemy, 1936; The Swift Shadow, 1937; The Open Sky, 1939; Sun on the Water and Other Stories, 1940; The Bay, 1941; Slocombe Dies, 1942; The Unpractised Heart, 1942; All Fall Down, 1944; The Director, 1944; Murder Plays an Ugly Scene, 1945; Othello's Occupation, 1945; Travellers, 1945; Trevannion, 1948; Which I Never, 1950; Darling Tom and Other Stories, 1952; The Hill of Howth, 1953; Deliverance, 1955; Light Above the Lake, 1958; Treason in the Egg, 1958. *Drama*—The Absentee, 1939; Trial and Error, 1939. *Nonfiction*—Common Sense About Poetry, 1931; Common Sense About Drama, 1937; The Man Who Asked Questions, 1937; The Minstrel Boy, 1937; Shake Hands and Come Out Fighting, 1938; English For Pleasure, 1941; John McCormack, 1941; Authorship, 1944; An Informal English Grammar, 1944; A Tongue in Your Head, 1945; Maud Cherrill, 1949; The Sacred River, An Approach to James Joyce, 1949; Personal Remarks, 1953; The Writer's Trade, 1953; The Story of Sugar, 1954; Dr. Quicksilver, 1955; English Novelists Today, 1955; Flying Angel, 1956; The Rolling Road, 1956; Instructions to Young Writers, 1958; Green Memory, 1961. *Juvenile*—Patricia Come Home, 1929; The Old Argo, 1931; (with M. Redlich) Life in English Literature, 1932; King Richard's Land, 1933; The Westward Rock, 1934; The Fifth of November, 1937; Henry of Agincourt, 1937; House in Disorder, 1941.

ABOUT: Dictionary of National Biography, 1951–1960; Strong L.A.G. Green Memory, 1961; Who's Who 1958. *Periodicals*—Christian Science Monitor February 28, 1931; Illustrated London News August 23, 1958; New York Times August 12, 1934; August 19, 1958; Spectator February 14, 1931; June 22, 1934; Times (London) August 19, 1958.

**STRUNSKY, SIMEON** (July 23, 1879–February 5, 1948), American journalist, essayist, and novelist, was born in Vitebsk, Russia. He was next to the  youngest of the seven children of Isadore Strunsky, a grain and lumber merchant, and the former Pearl Weinstein. The family emigrated to the United States when Strunsky was seven, living on New York's Lower East Side. An exceptional student, he received one of the first Pulitzer scholarships to the Horace Mann High School, and another scholarship to Columbia University. There, with Henry Sydnor Harrison and others, he made the Columbia *Monthly* an almost professional publication.

Graduating A.B. in 1900, Strunsky was for six years a departmental editor of the *New International Encyclopedia*, and subsequently an outside contributor. In this way he gained a wide knowledge of literature and history. He was married in 1905 to Rebecca Slobodkin of Philadelphia. She died only a year later, leaving Strunsky to raise their son alone until, in 1910, he married Manya Gordon. They had a daughter.

Strunsky had meanwhile begun to write for various newspapers and magazines, and in 1906 he joined the staff of Oswald Garrison Villard's *New York Evening Post*. As "The Patient Observer," Strunsky contributed increasingly popular miniature essays on current events, fads and fashions. Many of these "Post-Impressions" were reprinted in the *Nation*, also owned by Villard, and subsequently in book form. Reviewers of the first such collection, *The Patient Observer and His Friends*, were variously, and possibly over-enthusiastically, reminded of Hazlitt, Charles Lamb, and Chesterton. A critic in the *Nation* (1911) wrote: "The merit of Mr. Strunsky's sketches is somewhat unequal, occasionally the brush is roughly applied, the humor deciduous. But a considerable body of work remains which is of more than passing interest—work informed with the fresh observation of the journalist and subtilized by the finer sympathy and humor of the elder essayist."

Memorable among the "Post-Impressions" was the series called "Through the Outlooking Glass," about Theodore Roosevelt's attempt in 1912 to re-enter the White House for a third term. The victim himself, "Theodore the Red Knight," was said to have enjoyed this Lewis Carroll pastiche. At about the same time, Strunsky contributed to the *Atlantic Monthly* a set of essays on life in an uptown New York apartment house. These were published as *Belshazzar Court*, and warmly praised for their gentle humor.

During World War I, as the *Evening Post's* authority on foreign affairs, Strunsky firmly supported the Allies. *Little Journeys Towards Paris* collected his satirical essays on the Kaiser's unavailing efforts to reach the French capital. At the end of the war Strunsky reported on the Paris Peace Conference and the Washington Disarmament Conference. His second wife, Russian-born like himself, had been an associate of Alexander Kerensky in the Social Revolutionary party. Strunsky was at that time also a moderate socialist, opposing Bolshevism and supporting the Mensheviks.

In 1920 Strunsky became the *Evening Post's* chief editorial writer, championing an internationalist policy and the League of Nations. He left the paper in 1924, when it was sold to an ultraconservative, and joined the *New York Times*. There he remained for the rest of his life, writing editorials and a weekly book column and, beginning in 1932, a series of essays, similar to "Post-Impressions," called "Topics of the Times." A colleague recalled his delight in knowledge, the hours he spent in the paper's library where, researching one topic, he would often stumble upon some irrelevant but irresistible fact that would grow into his column for another day (*New York Times*, February 6, 1948.)

Strunsky's picaresque first novel, *Professor Latimer's Progress*, was written and set during the First World War. Worn down by the conflict, the professor is ordered off by his doctor on a month-long ramble in the country. Latimer's encounters with a cross-section of the population, from an efficiency expert to a movie queen, convince him that America will somehow win through, and "will bring together and hold together" a world gone mad. Some reviewers found it overly whimsical—the commonest complaint against Strunsky's work. Most, like one in the *Nation* (1918), admired "its sanative masculine blend of deep feeling, fluid intelligence, and heart-easing mirth." Several later novels used historical situations and characters to comment on contemporary problems. In *King Akhnaton*, for example, the royal martyr of Ancient Egypt is made to bear a strong resemblance to Woodrow Wilson in his commitment to the League of Nations. Again there was a generally enthusiastic response, muted in the case of the *Times Literary Supplement*: "The author has a talent for portraiture, and is readable even when he writes hastily and defies grammar."

In later years, reacting against the seduction of many American intellectuals by Soviet communism, Strunsky moved to the right in his politics, describing himself as a "Tory." Apart from his novels, he published *The Rediscovery of Jones*, a collection of essays defending the ordinary American against the derision of writers like Sinclair Lewis, and *The Living Tradition*, a survey of economic, social, and political conditions in the United States seeking to illustrate the survival of traditional American ideals. Henry Hazlitt in the *New York Times* (1939) found the latter "encyclopedic in range and substance, familiar in tone, and as witty as it is wise. Its great service is to assert the claims of common experience at a time when fanaticism and the doctrinaires are running wild." There was similar praise for *No Mean City*, a volume of essays in praise of New York.

A stocky bald man, with thick spectacles, Strunsky was a witty and epigrammatic conversationalist. A member of the National Institute of Arts and Letters, he served on the editorial board and the editorial council of the *New York Times*. When he died of cancer, an editorial in that paper said of Strunsky: "His style, like his personality (and indeed it was his personality), was a perfected instrument, but it was also the whole man—honest, sincere and benevolent."

PRINCIPAL WORKS: *Essays*—The Patient Observer and His Friends, 1911; Post-Impressions, 1914; Belshazzar Court; or, Village Life in New York City, 1914; The Rediscovery of Jones, 1931; No Mean City, 1944; Simeon Strunsky's America: "Topics of the Times," 1933–1947 (ed. H. P. Stokes) 1956. *Fiction*—Professor Latimer's Progress, 1918; Little Journeys Towards Paris, 1918; Sinbad and His Friends, 1921; King Akhnaton, 1928; Two Came to Town, 1947. *Other*—The Living Tradition: Change and America, 1918.

ABOUT: Berger, M. The Story of the New York Times, 1951; Dictionary of American Biography, 1946–1950, 1974; Morley, C. Modern Essays: First Series, 1921. *Periodicals*—Commentary March 1957; Nation May 4, 1911; May 11, 1918; New York Times November 1, 1931; January 17, 1932; November 19, 1939; February 6, 1948; February 9, 1948; February 13, 1948; February 14, 1948; February 21, 1948; Saturday Review of Literature February 21, 1948; Time February 16, 1948; Times Literary Supplement October 18, 1928.

**STRUTHER, JAN** (June 6, 1901–July 20, 1953), English poet, humorist, essayist, hymnwriter, and creator of *Mrs. Miniver*, was born Joyce Anstruther.

Her parents were Henry Torrens Anstruther and the former Eva Sudeley, daughter of the fourth Baron Sudeley. The Honorable Eva was made a Dame of the British Empire for her work during World War I as Director of the Camps Library, which sent millions of books to British troops overseas. Dame Eva was also a writer, using the pseudonym her daughter inherited, Eva "Struther."

Jan Struther, educated privately in London, published her first poems and stories when she was sixteen. In 1923 she married Anthony Maxtone Graham, an insurance broker from an old Scottish family. They had two sons and a daughter. She continued to write, contributing poems, essays and short stories to such journals as the *London Mercury*, the *Spectator*, the *New Statesman*, and the London *Times*. Some of her magazine verse, much of it evoking the pangs and pleasures of domesticity and parenthood, was collected in her first published book, *Betsinda Dances*.

An entertaining versifier, Jan Struther possessed a talent for rhyme and meter that equipped her also as a hymn writer. The popular *Songs of Praise*, in its enlarged edition of 1932, contained twelve of her hymns. The same year came *Sycamore Square*, containing poems first published in *Punch* and illustrated by Ernest H. Shepard, best known for his contributions to A. A. Milne's Christopher Robin books. "Sycamore Square" is really Wellington Square, Chelsea, where the Maxtone Grahams lived. "With delicate strokes and an irresistible sense of humor," wrote A. T. Eaton, "the author makes Sycamore Square very real and its inhabitants very much alive—pigeons, flower women, street musicians, muffin man and pavement artist, including the 'Cycling Club,' whose small members ride about triumphantly on scooter, tricycles and bicycles" (*New York Times*, 1932). There followed two verse collections for children and then *Try Anything Twice*, a volume of urbanely humorous essays and sketches.

In 1937 meanwhile, noting the success of *Sycamore Square*, the London *Times* had invited Jan Struther to contribute to its Court page a series of similar vignettes in prose. Hence "Mrs. Miniver," who delighted *Times* readers with her amused accounts of the small vicissitudes of middle-class family life—coping with three children and four servants, shopping, holidays and festivities, visiting the dentist. Some of these sketches were published in book form in October 1939, just after the outbreak of World War II, and in the United States during the Blitz of 1940. For many, *Mrs. Miniver* seemed an embodiment of the decent and civilized values of an England now in mortal danger. A best-seller on both sides of the Atlantic and a Book of the Month Club choice, it is still in print.

But Clifton Fadiman in the *New Yorker* recognized "a certain oversweet gentility about Mrs. Miniver, a too comfortable delight in the prospect of a good tea, complete with 'honey sandwiches, brandy-snaps, and small ratafia biscuits.' But underneath this domestic sentiment, this ladies' home journalism, lie perceptions, not at all original, but deeply humane and humorous. Mrs. Miniver, like Charles Lamb, will place a gentle hand on your elbow and bid you stop to observe something insignificant, and lo! it is not insignificant at all." This was the general view, especially in America; some English reviewers, including E. M. Forster and Rosamond Lehmann, responded less warmly, finding Mrs. Miniver insufferable in her cozy and well-heeled complacency. Jan Struther, it must be said, came to share the latter view; when a newspaper offered a prize for the best parody of *Mrs. Miniver*, she competed under a pseudonym, and won. She gave her first-prize money to "an organization for distressed gentlewomen." Part of her disaffection stemmed from the fact that her own family became inextricably confused in the public mind with Mrs. Miniver's; her husband had to inure himself to being addressed as "Clem" at his club.

In 1940, Jan Struther brought her two younger children away from the Blitz to New York City. Warm and witty, she became a popular lecturer in America, raising funds for British War Relief. She was also a frequent guest on "Information Please" and other radio programs. In 1942 came William Wyler's hugely successful film version of *Mrs. Miniver*, carrying the story forward into the war. Deeply sentimental, it has the Minivers (Greer Garson and Walter Pidgeon) stiffening their upper lips against rationing, bombs, Dunkirk, and death. It carried off five Oscars, and as propaganda was much admired by Joseph Goebbels. By that time Jan Struther's own husband, an officer in the Scots Guards, had been taken prisoner in Libya.

The Maxtone Grahams were divorced in 1947. Jan Struther settled in New York and in 1948 married Adolf Kurtz Placzek, a librarian at Columbia University. *A Pocketful of Pebbles*, collecting essays, lectures, fables and poems, was her last book.

PRINCIPAL WORKS: *Fiction*—Mrs. Miniver, 1939. *Poetry*—Betsinda Dances and Other Poems, 1931; Sycamore Square and Other Verses, 1932; The Modern Struwwelpeter, 1936 (juvenile); When Grandmamma Was Small (adapted from the Swedish of Ingrid Smith) 1937; The Glassblower and Other Poems, 1940. *Other*—Try Anything Twice, 1938 (essays and sketches); (as ed.) Women of Britain: Letters from England, 1941; A Pocketful of Pebbles, 1946 (essays, lectures, poems).

ABOUT: Blain, V. and others (eds.) The Feminist Companion to Literature in English, 1990; Current Biography 1941; Schlueter, P. and J. (eds.) An Encyclopedia of British Women Writers, 1988; Van Gelder, R. Writers and Writing, 1946; Who's Who 1953. *Periodicals*—New York Herald Tribune July 25, 1940; New York Herald Tribune Book Review August 2, 1953; New York Times November 20, 1932; July 21, 1953; New York Times Book Review August 25, 1940; New Yorker July 27, 1940; Spectator July 24, 1953; Times (London) July 22, 1953.

**STUART, (HENRY) FRANCIS (MONTGOMERY)** (April 29, 1902– ), Irish novelist, playwright, and poet, wrote: "Born in Australia of North of Ireland parents. Returned to Ireland at an early age. Educated at Rugby. Instead of entering the University took part in Irish civil war and spent fifteen months in internment camp at Curragh 1922–1923. Married Iseult Gonne, adopted daughter of Maud Gonne McBride [Iseult Gonne was the natural daughter of Maud Gonne and the French deputy Lucien Millevoye—she adopted her] whose husband Major McBride, was executed after the 1916 Rebellion. Have two children, a son and a daughter. First published work was a small volume of poems, *We Have Kept the Faith*, which was awarded a prize by the Royal Irish Academy [and another from Harriet Monroe's *Poetry Chicago*]. . . . Two plays produced: *Glory* (dramatized from novel) by the Arts Theatre, London, *Men Crowd Me Round* by the Abbey Theatre, Dublin. Have travelled in many European countries, lectured through Germany and at Berlin University. A member of the Irish Academy of Letters. Live in County Wicklow, in the mountains. Recreations: golf and horse-racing.

"Among favorite contemporary authors are: W. B. Yeats, Proust, Rilke, Thomas Wolfe, Franz Kafka. Among actually living writers: Thomas Mann, Somerset Maugham, J. B. Priestley.

"I believe that the novel has not yet been developed to anything like the degree of which this form is capable. My ambition is to go on experimenting in this medium."

---

Francis Stuart was the son of Henry Irwin Stuart, a prosperous sheep rancher who had emigrated to Australia from County Antrim, Ireland, and Elizabeth Montgomery. Before he was a year old, his father died and his mother brought him back with her to Ireland.

When, in 1940, Francis Stuart accepted a post as lecturer in English and Irish literature at the University of Berlin, he was, wrote J. H. Natterstad, "troubled by a declining career as well as by lingering financial and marital problems." Leaving his wife Iseult in Ireland, he remained in Berlin (except for a few months in Luxembourg) until the German defeat. During that time, between 1942 and 1944, he gave weekly broadcasts from Berlin in which he urged the Irish government to stay neutral, and expressed support for the Irish Republican Army. As a result of this, which made him unpopular with some sections of Irish as well as with British opinion, he was arrested by French occupation forces, and imprisoned. But no charges could be brought against him (he was an Irish citizen), and he was released in July 1946.

In 1953 his first wife died, and he married

Gertrud Meissner, whom he had met at the university and with whom he was imprisoned. He lived in Germany, Paris, and from 1951, London.

Since it has long been established that Stuart was neither a Nazi nor an anti-Semite, his support for the Nazi cause was forgiven him by British critics; but his decision to stay on in Germany (he could have left) still puzzles many. It has been put down to his hatred of the British. Stuart in 1958 returned to Ireland, first to County Meath; he ended up (1971) in Windy Arbour, a section of Dublin. In the latter part of his long life, he was best known as the author of *Black List, Section H* (1971).

Stuart's poetry, perfervid, highly romantic, youthful, and uneven, gained the Irish Academy Award and (later) the award from *Poetry Chicago* because of its unusual ardor. This may have been just what W. B. Yeats, who presided over the committee that awarded the Academy Prize, meant when he declared: "If luck comes to his aid he will be our great writer." So far as poetry was concerned, Stuart's promise came to little. He himself in an interview of 1976 (published in the *Journal of Irish Literature*) said that in the 1930s he came to recognize that his "real interests were far more in certain experiences—very often personal experiences, human relationships, human activities—which are certainly not best communicated through poetry." He continued to write it for a bit, gradually abandoned it, and then took it up again in his old age.

Stuart's first novel was a failure, but the second and third, *Pigeon Irish* and *The Coloured Dome*, attracted the attention of Yeats, who told Olivia Shakespear in a letter that he found the latter "strange and exciting in theme and perhaps more personally and beautifully written than any book of our generation." L. A. G. Strong, in the *Spectator*, thought it "most original and beautiful": it gave him a "rare kind of delight."

Both novels are mystical and Catholic, and neither they nor the remaining eight that Stuart published in the 1930s are, according to Natterstad, of "compelling importance." Gerald Sykes wrote in the *Nation* that the praise Stuart had received for *Pigeon Irish* and for *The Coloured Dome* was "likely to prove embarrassing to him and perhaps injurious. . . . His novel *The Coloured Dome* . . . remaining derivatively and thinly in the ether of ideas, is no more than a spiritual slumming party, a well-bred peep into the lower depths."

Stuart published eight more novels after the end of World War II, before in 1971 *Black List, Section H*, (the "H" stands for the unused Henry in his name) appeared in America. It took four more years for it to be taken up in Great Britain. This, although certainly fiction, is autobiographical. It covers his life from the time of his first marriage until the end of his imprisonment. The well mitigated response of R. J. Thompson in *Best Sellers* typified that of those who could not really like the book: Stuart, wrote Thompson, "moves through most of the book with all the conviction and speed of a tree sloth. He is a kind of literary Victor Ma-

ture. . . . One finishes the book wondering what it is that H has been doing for the last twenty-five years. . . . " However, he concluded that the book "is motivated by moral force and a genuine sense of what it means to try to be an artist. It is a book which one respects even while noticing its lapses." Diana Fortune in the *Saturday Review* thought that "Stuart seems monstrously detached from human values." But Harry T. Moore, who contributed a preface and a postscript to the original edition, believed it to be "one of the imaginative masterpieces of modern Ireland." The book was given its greatest fillip, however, by Lawrence Durrell, who reviewed it in the *New York Times* (1972) and called it "a book of the finest imaginative distinction." As Natterstad wrote, *Black List, Section H* "presents the clearest expression of Stuart's thoughts about the artist and society, a subject that has long obsessed him." Many have read this novel for the amusing and potentially valuable portraits, in its first part, of such Irish writers as Liam O'Flaherty and Yeats.

Other novels by Stuart regarded as notable are the two he wrote immediately after the end of the war: *The Pillar of Cloud* and *Redemption*. *The Pillar of Cloud*, set in postwar Germany, traces the spiritual pilgrimage of a poet, Dominic Malone. *Redemption* has as its central character Ezra Arrigho, a sort of Irish D. H. Lawrence.

Stuart's five plays (all unpublished) have not received much attention even from those critics who are convinced of his major status. But the two plays produced at the Abbey, *Men Crowd Me Round* and *Strange Guest*, did attract some attention from theatergoers at the time.

Stuart's philosophy, which combines a fervent nationalism with an equally fervent Catholic mysticism, is best inferred from *Black List, Section H*— and, in particular perhaps, from the agonized predicament of the poet Dominic Malone in *The Pillar of Cloud*, who finds solace in a "selfless love." This frame of mind may be criticized for its lack of precision and for its unoriginality, but Stuart leaves us in no doubt that is deeply felt.

PRINCIPAL WORKS: *Novels*—Women and God, 1931; Pigeon Irish, 1932; The Coloured Dome, 1933; Try the Sky, 1933; Glory, 1933; In Search of Love, 1935; The Angel of Pity, 1935; The White Hare, 1936; The Bridge, 1937; Julie, 1938; The Great Squire, 1939; The Pillar of Cloud, 1948; Redemption, 1949; The Flowering Cross, 1950; Good Friday's Daughter, 1952; The Chariot, 1953; The Pilgrimage, 1955; Victors and Vanquished, 1958; Angels of Providence, 1959; Black List, Section H, 1971; Memorial, 1973; A Hole in the Head, 1977; The High Consistory, 1980. *Verse*—We Have Kept the Faith, 1923, (for 1924), revised with new poems as We Have Kept the Faith: New and Selected Poems, 1982; (with P. Durcan) Ark of the North, 1982; Night Pilot, 1988.

ABOUT: The autobiographical material quoted above was written for Twentieth Century Authors, 1942. Vinson, J. (ed.) Contemporary Novelists, 1982. McCormack, W. J. (ed.) A Festschrift for Francis Stuart on His Seventieth Birthday, 1971; Natterstad, J. W. Francis Stuart, 1974. *Periodicals*—Best Sellers February 1, 1972; Eire-Ireland Autumn 1974; Envoy July 1951; Journal of Irish Literature January 1976; Nation February 15, 1933; New York Times April 9, 1972; Saturday Review January 1, 1972; Spectator, February 6, 1932; Times Literary Supplement January 16, 1981; June 29, 1984; January 17, 1986.

**STUART, HENRY LONGAN** (1875–August 26, 1928), Anglo-American critic, journalist, translator, and novelist, was born in London and educated at Ratcliffe College. As a young man he worked as a journalist in London before coming to the United States to ranch in Colorado for two years.

*Weeping Cross*, his historical novel, was partly written during this period and was finished in Florence and London, where he later lived and worked in journalism. During World War I he served as a captain in the Royal Field Artillery, and was attached to the Italian army as liaison officer in 1917 and 1918. Later he was attached to the Military Mission at Paris.

Stuart returned to America in 1919 and joined the news staff of the *Boston Herald*; later he took charge of the wire from the *New York Times'* of-

fices to the *Herald*. In 1924 he became associate editor on the newly founded Catholic weekly *Commonweal*, a position he held until his death. He also became a frequent book reviewer for the *New York Times Book Review*, the *New York Sun*, and the *Herald Tribune*, and was a contributor to the *Freeman*.

*Weeping Cross: An Unworldly Story*, which derives the first two words of its title from Montaigne, drew little attention when it was published in the United States in 1908. Nevertheless, as Paul Cuneo asserts in his foreword to the 1954 edition, "competent critics" compared it to *The Scarlet Letter*, and it attracted a "small group of admirers who would not let it be completely forgotten." Set in 1652, the story deals with a young English officer, an erstwhile Jesuit, who is sent by Cromwell for ten years' servitude among the New England Puritans of Boston; there he attracts the love of Agnes Bartlett, his master's widowed daughter. According to a review in the *Outlook*, the "conflict between religion and passion that follows is analyzed with extreme keenness, but is hardly edifying in its bold realism, and is agonizing in its relation of mental and physical suffering."

PRINCIPAL WORKS: *Novels*—Weeping Cross: An Unworldly Story, 1908; Fenella, 1911. *As translator*—The Gardens of Omar (by H. Bordeaux) 1924; Sutter's Gold (by B. Cendrars) 1926; The Crimson Handkerchief, and Other Stories (by J. A. Gobineau) 1927; Letters to a Doubter (by P. Claudel) 1927; The Closed Garden (by J. Green) 1928; The Emperor Falls in Love: The Romance of Josephine and Napoleon (by O. Aubry) 1928; Who Is Then This Man? (by M. Marnas) 1929; (with M. Bishop) Beatrice Cenci (by C. Ricci) 1933; Adrienne Mesurat (by J. Green) 1991.

ABOUT: Undset, S. Men, Women and Places, 1939. *Periodicals*—Catholic World December 1928; New York Times August 27, 1928; Outlook September 19, 1908.

**STUART, JESSE** (August 8, 1907–February 17, 1984), American novelist and short story writer, wrote: "In World War II, I was in the Navy. I did boot-training at Great Lakes Naval Training Station where I was made seaman 2d class. Later I was commissioned lt. j.g., and served during the war in the United States Naval Reserve. I have traveled over the United States and have lectured at colleges, university and teacher groups—

Harvard, Columbia, Vanderbilt, Peabody College for Teachers, the universities of Illinois, Kentucky, West Virginia, Florida, etc. . . .

"In addition to my books I have had many short stories, poems, and articles published. Halsey P. Taylor, graduate student at the University of Southern California, did his thesis on my short stories. He listed 190 stories from 1934 to 1951. One of my collections, *Men of the Mountains*, won the Academy of Arts and Sciences Award of $500. Then I have had numerous articles published and many, many poems. Also, I have the most triple-starred stories in the late Edward J. O'Brien's collections of the *Best Short Stories*. One year, 1939 I believe it was, I had eighteen triple-starred stories. At present I have twenty-three short stories in secondary and college English textbooks, which is almost a record for an American author, living or dead.

"We live here, my wife Naomi, our daughter Jane, on the land where I was born in W-Hollow. We live in the house where I lived as a child when my parents rented this farm. Lived here when I was nine and left when I was twelve. Later I bought this place and we used the house for housing cattle, corn and hay, for barnroom was scarce at that time with 500 sheep, 60 head of cattle, and 3 mule teams. But in the meantime I got married and my wife loved the old house, so we put the cattle out and went to work. It is our home today. We have 723 acres of land here now, most of it in timber. We farm, raise corn, hay, and tobacco, but we no longer have sheep, and we don't have as many cattle as we once had here."

———

"Poet, novelist, short story writer, educator, and social philosopher, Jesse Stuart is considered by many critics to be one of the most dynamic and original figures in contemporary American literature," Everetta Love Blair wrote in her 1967 book *Jesse Stuart: His Life and Works*. "These critics hold that Stuart's strongly personalized writing has in it such deep insight into the basic character of mankind, such truth applicable to the general experience of all men living, that he must be placed in the realm of those writers considered universal . . . and must be looked upon as a strong contender for a lasting place in world literature." But, as Blair continues, other critics (most, in fact) have relegated Stuart to the ranks of the regional writers: the source and inspiration of most of his work are the environs and people in and around his beloved W-Hollow, Kentucky. Today he is best remembered for his memoir *The Thread that Runs So True*, and only a few of his other books remain in print.

Stuart wrote much verse; his work appeared in books and in such publications as *International Poetry Magazine*, *The American Poet*, and *Poetry Quarterly*. In his monograph *Jesse Stuart*, Ruel E. Foster quotes from a letter Stuart wrote to him on August 17, 1962: "When I write a poem or poems, I am moved by a mood which is often tied up with an incident. If I have the mood and don't have the incident, I will find one. If I have the incident and not the mood I don't write the poem or poems." Blair describes Stuart's poetry as a "great, compulsive flow of words, with scant attention to form, characterized by a strong subjectiveness, lyrical quality, and intensity of emotion."

Foster places *Man with a Bull-Tongue Plow* at the apex of Stuart's poetic output. Mark Van Doren, in a *New York Herald Tribune* review, called Stuart a "modern Robert Burns." Malcolm Cowley, a critic whose praise many writers coveted, wrote that "at their best, his poems have the springtime freshness of medieval ballads. Their worst fault is that they are written without effort or economy." The book consists of 703 sonnets of an autobiographical nature, divided into four sections corresponding to the seasons.

Stuart also wrote many short stories. They are peopled with rural Kentuckians with names like Snort Pratt, Zeke Hammertight, and Birdneck Sweetbird and, even as he wrote about them, they were clearly part of a vanishing world. Broad humor, authentic dialect, and an empathy with simple, hard-working people, were some of the ingredients that made Stuart so popular.

Stuart's novels were extensions of his short stories. Foster called him the "Grandma Moses of the novel. That is, he is a kind of a 'primitive' also. He uses strong, stark scenes clearly and sharply delineated. His style is simple and direct to the point of crudity." Stuart's best known novel, *Taps for Private Tussie*, began as a short story. It opens with the burial of Kim Tussie, a soldier who has been killed in World War II. His poverty-stricken family receives $10,000 in insurance money, and proceeds to raise its standard of living by moving into and redecorating a big house, only to be brought low again by excess and swarms of free-loading relatives. In the end it turns out that Private Tussie isn't dead after all. Behind the extravagant humor and "hillbilly" caricatures lies a satire of abuses in "relief" programs like the one which precipitates the Tussies' rise and fall. As one relative says to Kim: "I thought about everything we had, even to the clothes I wore, had come from money that we got for your dust."

*The Thread that Runs So True* is Stuart's account of his experiences as a teacher in Kentucky and Ohio over a period of twenty years. The *New York Times* (September 25, 1949) reviewer, the novelist Harriette Arnow, found that Stuart "speaks elo-

quently of the many injustices in educational opportunity that arise from poverty, both in the individual and the unit of government under which he lives." The National Education Association selected it as the "most important book of 1949," and it was widely used in schools of education around the country.

In 1954 Stuart was named the poet laureate of Kentucky. He was a visiting professor at the University of Nevada, Reno; American University, Cairo; and Eastern Kentucky University. He was also a popular speaker.

Jesse Stuart died in an Ironton, Ohio nursing home. In her book *Jesse Stuart's Kentucky*, Mary Washington Clarke wrote: "Some regional writers have attempted the folkways and dialects of their subjects and have failed because theirs has been imitation, the self-conscious and too-often patronizing effort to depict what one sees and hears but does not *know*. Stuart expresses the hill man's deep feelings about God, man, and the seasons because these are his own feelings."

PRINCIPAL WORKS: *Poetry*—Harvest of Youth, 1920; Man with a Bull-Tongue Plow, 1934; Album of Destiny, 1944; Kentucky Is My Land, 1952; Hold April: New Poems, 1962; The World of Jesse Stuart: Selected Poems, 1975; The Seasons of Jesse Stuart: An Autobiography in Poetry 1907–1976, 1976. *Short stories*—Head o' W-Hollow, 1936; Tim: A Story, 1939; Men of the Mountains, 1941; Foretaste of Glory, 1946; Tales from the Plum Grove Hills, 1946; Clearing in the Sky, and Other Stories, 1950; Plowshare in Heaven: Stories, 1958; A Jesse Stuart Reader: Stories and Poems Selected and Introduced by Jesse Stuart, 1963; A Jesse Stuart Harvest, 1965; My Land Has a Voice, 1966; Come Gentle Spring, 1969; Come Back to the Farm, 1971; Dawn of Remembered Spring, 1972; 32 Votes Before Breakfast: Politics at the Grass Roots, as Seen in Short Stories by Jesse Stuart, 1974; The Best Loved Short Stories of Jesse Stuart, 1982; Cradle of the Copperheads, 1988. *Novels*—Trees of Heaven, 1940; Taps for Private Tussie, 1943; Hie to the Hunters, 1950; The Good Spirit of Laurel Ridge, 1953; Daughter of the Legend, 1965; Mr. Gallion's School, 1967; The Land Beyond the River, 1973. *Nonfiction*—Beyond Dark Hills: A Personal Story, 1938; The Thread that Runs So True, 1949; The Year of My Rebirth, 1956; God's Oddling: The Story of Mick Stuart, My Father, 1960; To Teach, To Love, 1970; My World: Jesse Stuart's Kentucky, 1975; Dandelion on the Acropolis: A Journal of Greece, 1978; The Kingdom Within, 1979. *Juvenile*—Mongrel Mettle: The Autobiography of a Dog, 1944; The Beatinest Boy, 1953; A Penny's Worth of Character, 1954; Red Mule, 1955; Huey, the Engineer, 1960; The Rightful Owner, 1960; Andy Finds a Way, 1961; A Ride with Huey, the Engineer, 1966; Old Ben, 1970; Come to My Tomorrowland, 1971.

ABOUT: The autobiographical material quoted above was written for Twentieth Century Authors, 1942 and Twentieth Century Authors First Supplement, 1955. Blair, E. L. Jesse Stuart: His Life and Works, 1967; Clarke, M. W. Jesse Stuart's Kentucky, 1968; Contemporary Literary Criticism Vol. 34, 1985; Current Biography 1940; Foster, R. E. Jesse Stuart, 1968; LeMaster, J. R. Jesse Stuart: A Reference Guide, 1979; LeMaster, J. R. and Clarke, M. W. Jesse Stuart: Essays on His Work, 1977; LeMaster, J. R. Jesse Stuart: Kentucky's Chronicler—Poet, 1980; LeMaster, J. R. Jesse Stuart on Education, 1992; LeMaster, J. R. Jesse Stuart: Selected Criticism, 1978; Pennington, L. The Dark Hills of Jesse Stuart, 1967; Perry, D. Reflections of Jesse Stuart on a Land of Many Moods, 1971; Richardson, H. E. Jesse! The Biography of an American Writer—Jesse Hilton Stuart, 1984; Spurlock, J. H. He Sings for Us: A Socio-linguistic Analysis of the Appalachian Subculture and of Jesse Stuart as a Major American Author, 1979. *Bibliography*—Woodbridge, H. C. Jesse Stuart: A Bibliography, 1960. *Periodicals*—Los Angeles Times Book Review June 12, 1988;

New Republic October 31, 1934; New York Herald Tribune June 12, 1934; New York Times September 25, 1949; February 19, 1984; Saturday Review of Literature November 27, 1943.

**STUBBS, J. F. A. HEATH-.** See HEATH-STUBBS, JOHN FRANCIS ALEXANDER

**STURE-VASA, MARY O'HARA ALSOP.** See O'HARA, MARY

**STURGIS, HOWARD OVERING** (1855–1920), American novelist, was the youngest of the three sons of Russell Sturgis, a Boston lawyer who came to England as a partner in Barings Banks in 1851. The family lived in considerable style at their town house in Carlton House Terrace and their country seat in Surrey. Russell Sturgis was a cultured man, and distinguished writers like Henry James were often among his guests.

Howard Sturgis was the pet of his mother, from whom he acquired a precocious skill at embroidery. He was educated at Eton, having been preceded there by his brother Julian, an acclaimed school athlete. Howard, often did not play games, and his sense of being overshadowed by Julian (who also became a novelist) is evident in Belchamber.

From Eton, Sturgis went to Trinity College, Cambridge University. He was active in university theatricals, and also discovered a talent for drawing. After graduating in 1878, Sturgis rejoined his mother at Carlton House Terrace and helped her to nurse his father, who had begun to suffer from seizures. For a time he took art classes at the Slade. Russell Sturgis died in 1887, his wife a year later. Only then, at the age of thirty-three, did Howard Sturgis begin a life of his own.

He first visited America, where he met numerous relations, among them his cousin the philosopher George Santayana, and began his friendship with Edith Wharton. Having inherited his parents' large fortune, he bought a house, Queen's Acre, on the edge of Windsor Park. There he was close to Eton friends like A. C. Ainger, who had been his tutor, and A. C. Benson, a young teacher at the school who was himself a former pupil of Ainger's.

Sturgis enjoyed giving hospitality as much as his parents had, and this seems to have been his principal activity at Qu' Acre, as the house was called by initiates. He was a splendid host and an excellent conversationalist. George Santayana was among his guests and described to Alan Harris how Sturgis would sit "at the head of his sparkling table dressed in sky-blue silk, surrounded by young dandies and distinguished elderly dames," or would drive "his wagonette and high-stepping pair skilfully and festively, holding high the reins in his white-gloved hands, as if he were dancing a minuet." Sturgis virtually adopted a handsome young Etonian cousin, William Haynes Smith, known as "the Babe," who helped to run his household, and became his lifelong companion.

In 1891 came Tim, a Story of School Life which, according to the dedication, had been written for Sturgis's mother: "On the shrine of her deathless memory I lay my little book." Tim is a physically frail little boy at Eton, as his author had been. The novel tells the story of his consuming love for a handsome school athlete, Carol. This survives Carol's kindly incomprehension, and Tim's father's attempts to end the relationship. However, when Carol goes to Cambridge and falls in love with a young woman, Tim has no recourse but noble renunciation and a welcome death. Wholly Victorian in its pathos and sentimentality, its homosexual content apparently unremarked, Tim enjoyed considerable popularity.

It is for his third, best, and last novel, Belchamber, that Sturgis is remembered. Lord Belchamber, known as "Sainty," is the reluctant heir to a great estate, a shy and sickly idealist with radical sympathies and no taste for hunting and fishing. Such pursuits are the province of Sainty's younger brother Arthur, an athletic vulgarian who had outclassed him at Eton and since. Saintly is actually relieved when he is crippled in a riding accident, since he is thus released from his gentlemanly duties and can look forward to an early death, upon which Arthur will inherit the role he was born for. However, Arthur is trapped into marrying a music-hall actress and it becomes Sainty's task to prevent her from becoming the lady of the manor by himself marrying. He finds a woman who seems to love him, but it turns out, when they are married, that she loves only his fortune. This she spends lavishly on a fast and loose life style in the corrupt London smart set. When she has a baby by another man, Sainty adopts it as his own, finding his only happiness in his love for the boy. But the child dies in infancy and Sainty and his wife live on, locked together in mutual distaste.

As Alan Harris writes, Belchamber is "a fine satirical picture of Vanity Fair, a trifle conventional in its handling of some of the minor figures, maybe, but always sharply observed in detail and treated with an urbane irony which rises to something fiercer at the appropriate moments." The book was generally well reviewed, and Wharton herself, in the Bookman (1905), wrote that it has "at once the faults and the freshness of the novelist who has told little but observed much: faults of construction and perspective . . . and freshness of sensation and perception."

Not so Henry James. Sturgis had shown him the book in installments. James, at first encouraging, grew increasingly critical. (He told A. C. Benson that "it is a mere passage, a mere antechamber and leads to nothing.") In the end Sturgis had to be dissuaded from withdrawing the book, and he published no more. Benson suggests that he may subsequently have written a few short stories, and among his manuscripts is a fantasy parodying the criticism of Henry James, which drives one of his victims to suicide.

Sturgis lived on at Queen's Acre, which had become dilapidated. But the food was still good, and the conversation, and he was still regularly visited by Wharton and James and others. Wharton recalled him there in A Backward Glance. For a time during the First World War, Sturgis did some work for the Red Cross. He had an operation for cancer in 1914, but recovered and lived on with William Smith for the rest of his life.

PRINCIPAL WORKS: *Novels*—Tim, a Story of School Life, 1891; All That Was Possible: Being a Record of a Summer in the Life of Mrs. Sibyl Crofts, Comedian: Extracted from Her Correspondence, 1895; Belchamber, 1904.

ABOUT: Benson A. C. Memories and Friends, 1924; Forster, E. M. Abinger Harvest, 1936; Harrris, A. *introduction to* Belchamber, 1965; Readers's Companion to the Twentieth Century Novel, 1994; Wharton, E. A Backward Glance, 1934. *Periodicals*—Bookman May 1905; April 1906; Modern Philology May 1961; Raritan Winter 1991.

**\*SUCKOW, RUTH** (August 6, 1892–January 23, 1960), American novelist and short story writer, wrote: "I was born in Hawarden, Iowa, a quite recently settled town on the western border of the state. My father was a Congregational minister, and we lived in a variety of towns and cities in Iowa. Both my father's and mother's parents were born in Germany, the former coming from Mecklenburg and the latter from the small province of Lippe-Detmold. The one grandfather was a farmer, the other a minister. I attended college for three years at Grinnell, Iowa, spent some time at the Curry Dramatic School in Boston, and received degrees of B.A. and M.A. for work at Denver University, where I also taught literature for one year. I was given a degree of M.A. from Grinnell College in 1931. While in Colorado I became interested in bee-keeping as a way of earning a living, and spent a summer as an apprentice in a beeyard thirty miles from Denver. For six years I operated an apiary at Earlville, Iowa, which with some small earnings from writing gave me a living during this time. I spent some winters in New York City and later lived there for a number of years.

"My first work published was short stories in the *Midland*, then edited by John T. Frederick in Iowa City. At Mr. Frederick's suggestion I sent a group  of stories to the *Smart Set*, at that time edited by H. L. Mencken and G. J. Nathan, which were accepted. Thereafter I owed a great deal professionally to the aid and encouragement of Mr. Mencken. My first published novel was *Century People*, printed serially in the *Century*, then edited by Carl Van Doren.

"In 1929 I married Ferner Nuhn, also an Iowan, and have lived since that year for varying periods in California, New Mexico, Vermont, New York City, Iowa, and Washington, D.C. Since 1937 my home has been in Cedar Falls, Iowa."

---

Although she was not quite the militant social critic that H. L. Mencken and Sinclair Lewis, in their different ways, took her to be, Ruth Suckow, in her eight novels and four collections of short stories, depicted her native Iowa with a scrupulous realism that was sometimes construed as, in Herbert

°SOO koh

Asbury's words, "a brilliantly cruel picture of the utter futility of a life which is bounded on one side by a row of corn and on all others by intolerance and stupidity" (*New York Herald Tribune Books*). Her first book, *Country People*, was a chronicle of three generations of a German-American farming family, the Kaetterhenrys, who rise from near poverty in 1859 to relative prosperity in 1922. The simple, plain storytelling and the lack of dramatic event were taken as sheer monotony by some critics, but others saw the design in Suckow's simplicity. A reviewer in the *Boston Transcript* wrote of the novel, "we find it little short of remarkable that Ruth Suckow has been able to make it all so vivid and so interesting when not once has she deviated from her plan, from her faithful protrayal of the life of these country people of the Iowa farmlands. Only a very high degree of talent could have accomplished the unforgettable vividness of this picture from the materials with which she works."

Suckow's next four novels—*The Odyssey of a Nice Girl*, *The Bonney Family*, *Cora*, and *The Kramer Girls*—continued her exploration of the inner lives of ordinary Midwesterners, particularly those of young women forced to endure the circumscribed roles of housewife and mother. These earlier novels led up to her most ambitious and characteristic work, *The Folks*, a seven-hundred-page family chronicle published in 1934. This story of the Ferguson family's outwardly unremarkable passage through three decades of Iowan history was, like most of Suckow's work, short on plot and long on atmosphere. Although criticized for its excessive length and somewhat confused orchestration of characters and themes, *The Folks* was regarded as a significant contribution to the tradition of American realism. Lewis Gannett wrote of it in the *New York Herald Tribune*, "Miss Suckow reports American speech as accurately as Sinclair Lewis; but she has none of the bitterness of his satire. She has the insight of Sherwood Anderson, with none of his restless anger. She has something of Willa Cather's sense of the sun on the soil, and none either of her glamour or her homesick retreat into the past. She is as honest as a mirror."

*New Hope* and *The John Wood Case*, the two novels Suckow wrote after *The Folks*, were notably sunnier than their predecessors and perhaps for that reason struck some reviewers as less than convincing. In any case, she published at much longer intervals in the last two decades of her life and came to be almost forgotten. However, her last collection of short stories, *Some Others and Myself*, was one of her best and lent credence to the opinion that she had always been a master of the short form. In her short fiction, wrote Margaret Stewart Omrcanin, Suckow's "feeling for the concrete which overloads the longer fiction gives fullness to the limited scene of the short story. . . . The confinements of the short narrative enable Ruth Suckow to concentrate her pictorial and narrative talents upon a single situation, character and mood. And in these stories, her tenderness and compassion attain their consummate expression."

Suckow was perhaps not a writer of the first

rank, but her reputation has risen somewhat in recent years; Elizabeth Hardwick, notably, helped bring several of her books back into print.

PRINCIPAL WORKS: *Novels*—Country People, 1924; The Odyssey of a Nice Girl, 1925; The Bonney Family, 1928; Cora, 1929; The Kramer Girles, 1930; The Folks, 1934; New Hope, 1942; The John Wood Case, 1959. *Short stories and collections*—Iowa Interiors, 1926; Children and Older People, 1931; Carry-Over, 1936; Some Others and Myself: Seven Stories and a Memoir, 1952; A Ruth Suckow Omnibus, 1988.

ABOUT: The autobiographical material quoted above was written for Twentieth Century Authors, 1942. American Women Writers, 1981; Dictionary of Literary Biography vol. 9 1981; vol. 102 1991; Hamblen, A. A. Ruth Suckow, 1978; Kissane, L. M. Ruth Suckow, 1969; Notable American Women: The Modern Period, 1980; Omrcanin, M. S. Ruth Suckow: A Critical Study of Her Fiction, 1972. *Periodicals*—Boston Transcript June 1, 1924; New York Herald Tribune October 1, 1934; New York Herald Tribune Books October 3, 1926; New York Times January 24, 1960.

**SUDERMANN, HERMANN** (September 30, 1857–November 22, 1928), German dramatist and novelist, was born in Matziken, a village in East

Prussia, close to the Russian border, where German, Russian, and Lithuanian cultures coexisted. In his autobiography, *Das Bilderbuch meiner Jugend* (1922, *The Book of My Youth*), Sudermann depicts himself as a shy, sensitive, and lonely child with a deep sense of inferiority. He found what solace he could in books and fantasy.

Sudermann's father was a brewer, a stern and reserved man of Dutch Mennonite stock. He had little talent for the business and the family was often in acute financial difficulty. Sudermann was much closer to his gentle and affectionate mother, daughter of a ship's captain. With his two younger brothers, Sudermann attended a school run by a clergyman's wife. There, as at home, he was imbued with a strict Puritan morality and an ardent devotion to the Prussian monarchy. The latter was dispelled when, at nine or ten, he discovered some old copies of an antimonarchist magazine, the *Gartenlaube*, and became, as he wrote in his autobiography, "a wild-eyed barricade fighter."

At fourteen, Sudermann was apprenticed to an apothecary. He disliked the work and, with his mother's encouragement, resumed his education at the Tilsit gymnasium. From there he went on to the University of Königsberg (1875–1877), studying philology, and joining the fencing club, acquiring the dueling scars then considered *de rigueur*. During this time, he also wrote his first stories and plays.

Sudermann continued his education at the University of Berlin, in which city he spent the rest of his life. A socialist by the time he was twenty, he became increasingly impatient with the conservatism of the educational system. One day he walked out of his class and never returned. He lived in a

garret on bread and cheese, went on with his writing and grew his enormous beard—"the envy and also the joke of my contemporaries," as he says in his autobiography. From time to time he found work as a private tutor and he was briefly editor of and principal contributor to a liberal political journal, *Das Deutsches Reichsblatt* (1881–1882).

Sudermann's first collection of short stories was published in 1886 and was followed by two novels. None of these made much impression until he was swept to fame with his play *Die Ehre (Honor)*, staged at the Berlin Lessing Theatre in 1889. Set in the Berlin home of a wealthy Junker businessman, the play contrasts the life and mores of the rich family in the *Vorderhaus*—the front part of the house—with those of his poor employees in the *Hinterhaus* behind. The poor man's son Robert returns from abroad, freed from the values of his class, to find that his sister has been seduced by her employer's son. Although Robert's family is quite willing to be bribed off, he challenges the seducer to a duel. The challenge is refused, on account of Robert's inferior social status. Leaving the house, he is joined by the rich man's daughter, who loves him. This spirited gesture earns them a fortune, supplied by an avuncular *deus ex machina*, Count von Trast. He tidily sums up the play's message: "Each caste has its own honor. Unhappy the man who has broken with his caste without having the courage to break with his conscience too."

*Die Ehre* was the first great triumph of the new naturalistic drama in Germany. It appeared in the same year as Gerhart Hauptmann's *Vor Sonnenaufgang*, but, although inferior, was then far more successful. At first Sudermann was even placed with or above Hauptmann as a master of the Ibsenite problem play. His second piece, *Sodoms Ende* (1890, *The Man and His Picture*), was about an idealistic artist corrupted by his association with the frivolous society of the Berlin *nouveaux riches*. That it was labeled immoral, and for a time suspended, only added to Sudermann's fame. He had his greatest success with *Heimat* (1893, *Magda*), which initially won comparison with Ibsen's *A Doll's House*. The meaty central role attracted such stars as Sarah Bernhardt, Eleanora Duse, and Mrs. Patrick Campbell, ensuring the play's international popularity.

By the turn of the century Sudermann's reputation had gone into rapid decline. The critics—and especially Hauptmann's champion, Alfred Kerr—had decided that Sudermann was not a genuine social critic, but merely a clever and opportunistic entertainer. This view has persisted, and is summarized by H. F. Garten in *Modern German Drama*: "Sudermann's technique derived from the French *pièce à thèse* of Dumas and Sardou. All the well-worn devices—soliloquies, asides, the *coup de théâtre*—are there. His plots are artificially contrived with the sole object of theatrical effect; his characters are the stock-types of the sentimental domestic play. But these devices he skilfully infused with the ideas and problems of the new drama—a fusion which for some time deceived both critics and public." The final blow to Sudermann's reputation came with his play *De Sturmgeselle Sokrates* (Socrates, companion in storm, 1903), satirizing the political idealism which inspired the *Volkerfruhling*, the liberal uprising of 1848. Outraged, the public joined the critics in their contempt for Sudermann's theater and his career as a dramatist was in effect ended.

After that, it was the received wisdom that Suderman should be remembered, if at all, not for his plays but for his fiction—especially for his closely autobiographical early novel *Frau Sorge* (1887, *Dame Care*) and for *Litauische Geschichten* (1917, *The Excursion to Tilsit*). This collection of four long stories about Lithuanian peasant life in the area around Matziken, reminiscent of Maupassant in their economy and observation of character, was regarded for a time as Sudermann's masterpiece.

Paul K. Whitaker has argued that Sudermann's defense of individual freedom against social convention, seen in *Heimat* and elsewhere, was far from opportunistic. Whitaker believes that it was for Suderman an obsession that grew out of his repressed childhood and pervaded his work. Sudermann's insistence upon "unhampered development of the personality and free expression of the inner self" was crucial in his own behavior, not least in the nature of his marriage in 1891 to Clara Schulz Lauckner, herself a writer. Sudermann believed that a conventional marriage would set up irreconcilable conflict between his duty to family and his duty to self and art. The marriage was entered into on the understanding that it would be dissolved after a year. In fact it survived through many difficulties until Clara's death in 1924 and, Whitaker says, "she was indeed his true happiness, a source of strength, aid, and encouragement."

As William Maitland asserts in *German Men of Letters*, Sudermann was "egocentric, opinionated, ebullient, and weak"; but he adds, "this is not the full picture of Sudermann." He was also "a deliberate craftsman, aware of the demands of his art, and of his own shortcomings." He was, in other words, a worthy and serious entertainer whose drama and fiction have not stood the test of time.

PRINCIPAL WORKS IN ENGLISH TRANSLATION: *Drama*—Magda (tr. C. E. A. Winslow) 1896 (also translated by E. b. Ginty as Argument of Magda, 1896); The Three Heron's Feathers, 1900; The Joy of Living (tr. E. Wharton) 1902; The Man and His Picture, 1903; Fires of St. John (tr. C. Swickard) 1904 (also translated by C. and H. C. Porter as St. John's Fire, 1905); John the Baptist (tr. B. Marshall) 1909; The Roses: Four One-Act Plays (tr. G. Frank) 1909; Morturi: Three One-Act Plays (tr. A. Alexander) 1910; The Battle of the Butterflies (tr. A. Greeven and J. T. Grein) 1914; A Good Reputation, 1915; The Vale of Content (tr. W. E. Leonard) 1915; Honor (tr. H. R. Baukhage) 1915. *Novel*—Dame Care (tr. B. Overbeck) 1891; The Wish (tr. L. Henkel) 1894; Regine (tr. H. E. Miller) 1894 (also translated by B. Marshall as Regina, 1898); The Undying Past (tr. B. Marshall) 1906; The Song of Songs (tr. T. Seltzer) 1909; The Mad Professor (tr. I. Leighton and O.P. Schinnerer) 1928; The Wife of Steffen Tromholt (tr. E. and C. Paul) 1929; The Dance of Youth (tr. E. and C. Paul) 1930. *Other*—The Indian Lily and Other Stories (tr. L. Lewisohn) 1912; Iolanthe's Wedding (tr. A. S. Seltzer) 1918 (short stories); The Excursion to Tilsit (tr. L. Galantiere) 1930. *Autobiography*—The Book of My Youth (tr. W. Harding) 1923.

ABOUT: Bauland, P. The Hooded Eagle: Modern German Drama on the New York Stage, 1968; Columbia Dictionary of Modern European Literature, 1980; Dictionary of Literary Biography vol. 118, 1992; Garten, H. F. Modern German Drama, 1959; Heller, O. Studies in Modern German Literature, 1905; International Dictionary of the Theatre, vol. 2, 1994; Lewisohn, L. The Modern Drama, 1911; Natan, A. (ed.) German Men of Letters, vol. 2, 1963; Nicoll, A. World Drama, 1950; Sudermann, H. The Book of My Youth, 1923. *Periodicals*—Bookman August 1906; Monatshefte January 1948, February 1956; New York Times November 22, 1928.

**SUGIMOTO, ETSU (INAGAKI)** (1874–June 20, 1950), Japanese autobiographer and novelist, wrote: "My native province is Echigo, a Northern district conspicuously noted for its deep snow and long winters. As my father was the First Karo, Chief Counsellor in the daimiate for which he and his forefathers had served, the fall of feudalism six years before my birth meant to our family an utter come-down. Education for girls in my  girlhood days was very different from what it is now. My people, especially, were even more conservative than most families. According to the custom of the day, I was betrothed when I was a mere little girl. My fiancé was a Japanese merchant living in Cincinnati, in the United States. I was sent to a Methodist girls' school in Tokyo to prepare for my destined home in the far, strange land. Here in this school I became a Christian. In 1898 I sailed for the United States. I claim Cincinnati as my American home. There I was married, to that city I owe my happy bridehood, and motherhood of two daughters. There I met my life-long friend, Miss Florence Mills Wilson, without whose friendship my widowhood might have been a most sorrowing life.

"In the meantime I brought my daughters to Japan for their Japanese education, spending six years in Tokyo with my mother and Miss Wilson. Then our little family returned to Cincinnati and later moved to New York. In this city, with the support and encouragement of Miss Wilson, I made my first start in literary work. It was a tedious, long way. At last a modest success was reached. Just about this time I was asked by the Columbia University Extension Department to conduct classes in elementary Japanese and Japanese history and culture. I was connected with the university from 1920 to 1927. Occasionally I contributed to New York and Philadelphia papers and to the *Bookman*. My first book, *A Daughter of the Samurai*, ran in *Asia* before it was published in book form."

Etsu Sugimoto, like Pearl Buck, enjoyed widespread popularity in the United States during the 1930s for the glimpses into Asian life her works provided. She is still remembered primarily for her first book, *A Daughter of the Samurai*, a good-natured memoir written in English about her Japanese childhood and her life in the United States in

the early years of the twentieth century. It was
warmly received by American readers and critics,
including the *New York Times*, which noted, "The
book does not plead any 'cause' or discuss vexing
questions. Instead it contains miniature stories . . .
that delight by their delicacy of feeling." Several
years after the memoir was published, its publisher
called it "the most enormously successful book of
nonfiction on the Doubleday-Doran list." Reissued
several times, it remains in print in the United
States. In her second book, *With Taro and Hana in
Japan*, Sugimoto recounts a summer visit to Japan
with her two young American-born daughters.

Sugimoto's fiction focuses on the lives of Japanese women. The heroine of her first novel, *A
Daughter of the Narikin*, is a shy Japanese girl who
submits unhappily to a marriage arranged by her
stepmother. *A Daughter of the Nohfu*, set in a Japanese village, examines a family in which the children, drawn to the ways of the modern world, rebel
against their tradition-bound father. Praising the
novel in the *New York Times Book Review* (1935),
Alfred Kazin wrote, "It may be reckoned a model
of what an unpretentious, good-mannered novel
should be . . . though the artistry has been confined to understatement, the final pleasure is not
unlike the kind one receives from looking at birds
in a Japanese print—seemingly so fixed upon a single field and yet able to suggest continual and full-
bodied movement." *Grandmother O Kyo*, her last
novel, is another story of family life in Japan. Although it is set against the backdrop of Japan's war
with China in the 1930s, Sugimoto refers only
obliquely to that conflict. "Very delicately, very
tactfully," wrote the *New York Times Book Review*
(1940), "Sugimoto supplements the headlines—
shows one the daily life of her people as they
plunge proudly and loyally into what they feel is
a righteous war."

Sugimoto returned to Japan after her two daughters were grown up, spent the entirety of World
War II there, and died in Tokyo.

PRINCIPAL WORKS: *Memoirs*—A Daughter of the Samurai: How
a Daughter of Feudal Japan, Living Hundreds of Years in One
Generation, Became a Modern American, 1925 (in U. K.: Sam-
urai Daughter in America, 1963): (with N. V. Austen) With
Taro and Hana in Japan, 1926. *Novels*—A Daughter of the
Narikin, 1932; A Daughter of the Nohfu, 1935; Grandmother
O Kyo, 1940.

ABOUT: The autobiographical material quoted above was written for Twentieth Century Authors, 1942. Ferris, H. (ed.)
When I Was a Girl: The Stories of Five Famous Women as
Told by Themselves, 1930. *Periodicals*—Bookman January
1926; New York Herald Tribune Books May 12, 1940; New
York Times June 22, 1950; New York Times Book Review December 1, 1935; May 12, 1940; New York Tribune November
22, 1925; Wilson Library Bulletin September 1950.

\*SUGRUE, THOMAS (JOSEPH) (May 7,
1907–January 6, 1953), American journalist, biographer, and novelist, was born in Naugatuck, Connecticut, the son of Michael Patrick Sugrue, a Post
Office employee, and Mary Ann (Doolan) Sugrue.
After graduating from Naugatuck High School in
1924, Sugrue worked in a bank for two years—long
enough for him to determine never to have anything to do with commerce or business again. He

°shuh GROO

then entered Washington and Lee University in
Lexington, Virginia, where he studied English literature and journalism and edited the campus literary magazine. After
receiving his B.A. in 1929
and his M.A. a year later,
he embarked on a career
in journalism. His first job
was with the *Naugatuck
Daily News*; in 1931 he
moved to the *New York
Herald Tribune* and later
in the decade he joined
the staff of the *American
Magazine*. Throughout
his career he free-lanced for such publications as
the *New York Times* and the *Saturday Review of
Literature*; but in the 1940s he began to turn most
of his attention to the writing of books.

Sugrue's first significant book was *Such Is the
Kingdom*, an autobiographical novel based on his
childhood in the Irish Catholic community of Naugatuck. It received generally favorable reviews and
was compared by some critics to the work of James
T. Farrell, but Sugrue was essentially a journalist,
not a novelist, and he never attempted another
work of fiction. His next book, *There Is a River*, was
a biography of the clairvoyant and psychic healer
Edgar Cayce, whom Sugrue had known since 1927.
Although a devout Roman Catholic, Sugrue was
also a mystic of sorts, and in the biography he made
no secret of his belief in Cayce's clairvoyant powers
and beneficent personality. If the book failed to
win many converts, it nevertheless made the best
possible case for Cayce and in the judgment of
many critics was judiciously and eloquently written. "Whatever else may be said about the story,"
wrote R. L. Duffus in the *New York Times Book
Review*, "one is convinced in reading it that Mr.
Cayce is not a charlatan, and that Mr. Sugrue . . .
has written what he honestly believes to be the
truth." This remains the standard work on Cayce.

Sugrue lent his talents to Edmund William Starling, a former Secret Service agent who had guarded five presidents, and Eddie Condon, the jazz
guitarist, in two "as told to" books of 1946 and 1947,
*Starling of the White House* and *We Called It Music*. These were certainly successful books of their
kind, but Sugrue's spiritual autobiography of 1948,
*Stranger in the Earth*, was a much more ambitious
undertaking. For the most part, critics applauded
this unusual mixture of confession and philosophical rumination. J. W. Chase in the *Saturday Review
of Literature* wrote of it, "This is one of the most
perplexing, at times confusing, books to appear in
some time; also, it is one of the most interesting. . . . It is possible that this book, with all its frequent charm of writing and challenge to action,
will leave certain readers unsatisfied. . . . But despite these and other possible blemishes, it is this reviewer's opinion that if the reader will only meet
Mr. Sugrue with the charity and sympathy that lie
in the author's heart, he will discover a rich and often stimulating mind."

Sugrue's last two books were *Watch for the*

*Morning*, an account of the founding of modern Israel, and *A Catholic Speaks His Mind*, a brief polemic against religious sectarianism and the more rigid orthodoxies of the Catholic Church. Sugrue managed to write these books in a fairly advanced state of the meningitis and arthritis from which he had suffered since 1937, and which finally killed him.

PRINCIPAL WORKS: *Satire*—(with J. Lardner) The Crowning of Technocracy, 1933. *Novel*—Such Is the Kingdom, 1940. *Biography, criticism, and other*—There Is a River: The Story of Edgar Cayce, 1942; (with E. W. Starling) Starling of the White House: The Story of the Man Whose Secret Service Detail Guarded Five Presidents from Woodrow Wilson to Franklin D. Roosevelt, 1946; (with E. Condon) We Called It Music: A Generation of Jazz; Watch for the Morning: The Story of Palestine's Jewish Pioneers and Their Battle for the Birth of Israel, 1950; A Catholic Speaks His Mind on American's Religious Conflict, 1952. *Autobiography*—Stranger in the Earth: The Story of a Search, 1948.

ABOUT: Current Biography 1948; Hartzell, H. A Seer out of Season: The Life of Edgar Cayce, 1989. *Periodicals*—New York Times January 7, 1953; New York Times Book Review March 14, 1943; Saturday Review of Literature May 22, 1948.

**SULLIVAN, FRANK** (September 22, 1892–February 19, 1976), American humorist and journalist, was born Francis John Sullivan in Saratoga

Springs, New York, the son of Dennis Sullivan and Catherine (Shea) Sullivan. After graduating from Cornell in 1914, he returned to his hometown and worked as a reporter for the *Saratogian*, where he had begun his journalistic career while still in high school. Drafted into the U.S. Army in 1917, he served until 1919, at which point he moved to New York City, where he wrote for the *Herald* and the *Evening Sun* before landing a job with the *New York World* in 1922. At the *World*, his colleagues included Walter Lippmann, Alexander Woollcott, and Heywood Broun. Originally hired as a news reporter and features writer, Sullivan discovered his talent for humor while writing a column on the 1924 Democratic Convention in New York. Finding himself short of copy, he added a paragraph about a certain Aunt Sarah Gallup, an elderly upstate New York resident—Sullivan gave her age as 104—who has scrimped and saved to attend the convention to support Al Smith. Although Aunt Sarah was strictly a product of Sullivan's imagination, his account was so convincing that reporters from other papers tried to track her down.

Noting Sullivan's gift for beguiling fabrication, his editor, Bayard Swope, transferred him out of the news department and gave him a humor column. By 1925 Sullivan was earning the then princely sum of $190 a week for this thrice-weekly column, which appeared in the *World* until that paper's demise in 1931. During those early years in New York, Sullivan was a member of the Algonquin Round Table, that informal group of writers renowned for their witty table talk—Dorothy Parker, Edna Ferber, and Robert Benchley among them—who met regularly for lunch and literary conversation at the Algonquin Hotel. In 1925 Sullivan began contributing to Harold Ross's recently launched *New Yorker*. Throughout his long career, Sullivan was a free-lance contributor to a variety of publications, including *PM*, the *New York American*, *Harper's Bazaar*, *Good Housekeeping*, and *Vanity Fair*, but was most closely associated with the *New Yorker*. His annual "Christmas Greeting" poem, published from 1932 to 1974, became an institution in the magazine. Sullivan also wrote satirical opera librettos, but these were never produced.

Sullivan was at his creative and popular peak from the mid-1920s to the early 1950s, during which time he published a number of well-received humor books, most of them consisting of previously published magazine and newspaper pieces. His gently mocking humor, took aim at a broad range of topics—contemporary manners, modern inventions, literary trends, and especially the absurdities of city life as seen from the point of view of an exasperated Everyman. Some of his best work appeared in the Depression-era collection *In One Ear*, of which *New York Times* (1933) critic C. G. Poore noted, "Mr. Sullivan is a master of unmildewed humor in a world forlorn. . . . He touches nothing that he does not adorn with fresh insanities." One of the pieces in that collection, "Yo Ho Ho and a Bon Voyage," written from the point of view of a stay-at-home travel expert, ridicules the pretensions of travel writers, one of Sullivan's favorite targets; Sullivan himself was notoriously travelphobic, and rarely went anywhere. Sullivan's literary satire can be sampled in "Life is a Bowl of Eugene O'Neills" and "One Year Later," a mock epilogue to D. H. Lawrence's novel *Lady Chatterley's Lover*. Sullivan's most popular and enduring fictional character, the cliché expert Mr. Arbuthnot, with whom he conducted a series of mock interviews, appeared first in the *New Yorker* around 1934 and was featured in *A Pearl in Every Oyster*, *Sullivan at Bay*, and other collections.

Sullivan became increasingly disenchanted with urban life, and after 1935 spent most of his time in Saratoga Springs, where he later became known as the Sage of Saratoga. The title essay of his last notable work, *The Night Old Nostalgia Burned Down*, is both a parody of the nostalgia-laden personal reminiscence and a heartfelt retrospective on his own life and career. In a brief self-portrait that appeared in the *New York Herald Tribune Book Review* around the time of that collection's publication, Sullivan summed up his literary perspective: "Since I reached voting age I have survived three wars (two hot, one cold, none ended) and one depression (hot) and am still here, on guard with my little wooden sword against whatever lies around the corner." Sullivan's work was admired by such disparate talents as P. G. Wodehouse and Groucho Marx, but demand for his brand of humor had declined by the 1960s. Several years before Sullivan's death, George Oppenheimer published the collection *Frank Sullivan Through the Looking*

*Glass*, a compilation of his best-loved essays and poems, as well as selections from his voluminous correspondence.

PRINCIPAL WORKS: *Humor*—The Life and Times of Martha Hepplethwaite, 1926; The Adventures of an Oaf, 1927; Innocent Bystanding, 1928; Broccoli and Old Lace, 1931; In One Ear. . . . 1933; A Pearl in Every Oyster, 1938; Sullivan at Bay, 1939 (in U.K. only); A Rock in Every Snowball, 1946; The Night Old Nostalgia Burned Down, 1953; Sullivan Bites News: Perverse News Items, 1954; A Moose in the House, 1959; Frank Sullivan Through the Looking Glass: A Collection of His Letters and Pieces (ed. G. Oppenheimer) 1970 (reissued as Well, There's No Harm in Laughing, 1972). *As editor*—The Sergeant Says (by J. Cannon) 1943.

ABOUT: Contemporary Authors vols. 65–68, 1977; Dictionary of Literary Biography vol. 11 1982; Kramer, D. Ross and the New Yorker, 1951. *Periodicals*—New York Herald Tribune Book Review October 11, 1953; New York Times May 21, 1933; February 20, 1976; Times (London) March 15, 1976.

## SULLIVAN, HARRY STACK (February 21, 1892–January 14, 1949), American Neo-Freudian psychiatrist and social scientist best known for his theory of interpersonal relations, was born in Norwich, New York, the son of Timothy J. Sullivan and Ellen M. (Stack) Sullivan.

A lonely, intelligent Irish-Catholic farmboy in a largely Yankee-Protestant community, Sullivan at age eight became friends with Clarence Bellinger, a local boy five years older, and the two were close until Bellinger left town for medical school. Both were outcasts, both became psychiatrists and neither ever married. "The 'quiet miracle' of having Clarence as a friend in the early years was of crucial importance in rescuing Sullivan from spending his life in a mental hospital, or as a rural eccentric," wrote Helen Swick Perry in *Psychiatrist of America: The Life of Harry Stack Sullivan* (1982). Biographers differ as to the level of intimacy in the relationship, but all agree that it played a major role in Sullivan's adolescent struggles, which in turn influenced greatly his novel theories on schizophrenia.

At sixteen, Sullivan graduated at the head of his high school class in Smyrna, New York, and was awarded a scholarship to go to Cornell University. He intended to major in physics but was suspended due to poor performance after failing all his second semester courses. "No matter what led to the failure—and there has been considerable speculation by biographers, from too much sex to too little sex to a brush with the law—the result had to be a loss of self-esteem," wrote Irving E. Alexander in *Personology* (1990). In psychological distress, Sullivan disappeared for two years and his whereabouts at that time remain unknown. Perry wrote that he may have been in the psychiatric ward of New York's Bellevue Hospital under the care of pioneering psychoanalyst A. A. Brill for part of the period. Sullivan's later work and writings on young male schizophrenics emphasized the need for sympathetic assistants to help reduce the patients' fear and panic of homosexual impulses.

Sullivan reemerged to enter the Chicago College of Medicine and Surgery in 1911, but left school in 1915 with no degree. He worked for half a year as an assistant surgeon for the Illinois Steel Company in its Chicago-area hospitals, then disappeared again for four months. In 1916 he joined the Illinois National Guard as a sergeant in a medical unit stationed near San Antonio, but "his tenure was ended abruptly and under cloudy circumstances," wrote Alexander. The following winter Sullivan was in crisis, and some believe he was hospitalized.

Without returning to classes or serving an internship, Sullivan mysteriously received his medical degree in 1917. Perry wrote that the story is "as puzzling and as complex as many stories in his life," and that "it seems quite likely that Sullivan himself was persuasive and determined to overcome the irregularities of his record." Alexander wrote that the degree might have been fraudulently acquired with the help of an authorized school official or even forged. Sullivan did not join the American Medical Association until 1930, and the degree did not show up in his effects until after his death.

Sullivan went on to serve in the Army Medical Corps and then in the rehabilitation section of the Federal Board for Vocational Education, where he drafted policies for dealing with men with psychiatric disabilities. This work led to his appointment in 1922 as the United States Veteran's Service liaison officer at St. Elizabeth's Hospital in Washington, D.C., the federal hospital for the mentally ill that was under the direction of William Alanson White, one of the most prominent psychiatrists in America and an early advocate of psychoanalysis in the United States. White became a professional father figure to Sullivan, and in 1933 Sullivan set up the William Alanson White Psychiatric Foundation. It paid for the establishment of both the Washington School of Psychiatry, which Sullivan helped form with anthropologist Edward Sapir and political scientist Harold Laswell, and the journal *Psychiatry*, which Sullivan founded and for which he served as editor.

In 1923, Sullivan left St. Elizabeth's for Sheppard and Enoch Pratt Hospital, a private facility near Baltimore, where in 1929 he began operation of a special schizophrenia ward for male patients that gained national recognition as a place that cured schizophrenia. It became a famous training center which attracted therapists for decades. At Sheppard, Sullivan became acquainted with leading social scientists and with another young psychiatrist, Clara Thompson, who became an important friend who later analyzed Sullivan. At Sheppard he also began to formulate his interpersonal theory of psychiatry, which concentrated on viewing mental illness in terms of human interaction. "Sullivan wanted psychiatry to emphasize man's humanness, the fact that man's feelings, motives, thoughts and values are uniquely human and have no counterpart at the animal level," wrote David Elkind in the *New York Times*.

In 1927 Sullivan established a relationship with a patient, James "Jimmie" Inscoe, age fifteen, who, according to Alexander, was in severe psychological distress. He became a permanent member of the Sullivan household, serving as Sullivan's secretary and becoming known as James I. Sullivan, although there is no record of a legal adoption.

Sullivan practiced psychiatry in New York from 1931 until 1937. In 1939 he moved to Bethesda, Maryland, where he lived until his death. He was a consultant at the White House during World War II, setting standards for psychiatric examination of draftees for the Selective Service System and as a participant in the 1948 UNESCO study of tensions that cause wars. Besides teaching and training, he continued to make *Psychiatry* a respected journal. In the late 1930s he worked with Afro-American sociologists Charles S. Johnson and E. Franklin Frazier in studies of black youth in the rural South and Midwest.

Besides articles in professional journals and editorials in *Psychiatry*, a single monograph was published in his lifetime, *Conceptions of Modern Psychiatry* (1947), a compilation of highly condensed lectures, which was originally published in *Psychiatry* in 1940 and was republished in 1953. The poet Lloyd Frankenberg, who knew Sullivan, praised the work in the *New York Times*, calling Sullivan "one of the least widely known of great men." His review in large part "first brought Sullivan's ideas to the attention of a wide audience," wrote Perry.

Sullivan died in the Ritz Hotel in Paris of a meningeal hemorrhage, on his way home from a meeting in Amsterdam of the World Federation of Mental Health. After his death, his students and colleagues created a number of volumes from his recorded lectures and notes, including *Interpersonal Theory of Psychiatry* (1953), "certainly the most original systematic contribution to come so far from an American-born psychiatrist," according to Rollo May in *Saturday Review*.

Upon publication of *The Fusion of Psychiatry and Social Science* (1964), a compilation of Sullivan's writings that complements *Schizophrenia as a Human Process* (1962), Patrick Mullahy wrote in the *New York Times* that "Sullivan stands second only to Freud in psychiatry." He praised the book for offering insights not only to psychiatrists but to students of culture and social scientists. He criticized Sullivan's theory, however, for being "too rigidly deterministic. Perhaps because of his work with patients, he underestimates the normal person's capacity for free choice—a failing that seems to be almost universal in psychiatry and psychology."

In the *New York Times* in 1972, Elkin wrote that Sullivan, "like most inventors . . . was considerably ahead of his time. Only today are his concern for the dignity of blacks, his demand that professionals care for and about the people to whom they minister, his emphasis on the humanness of mental disorder and his criticism of sexual taboos coming to be part of the value structure of the society at large."

PRINCIPAL WORKS: Conceptions of Modern Psychiatry, 1947; The Interpersonal Theory of Psychiatry, 1953; Psychiatric Interview, 1954; Clinical Studies in Psychiatry, 1956; Schizophrenia as a Human Process, 1962; The Fusion of Psychiatry and Social Science, 1964; Collected Works, 1965; Personal Psychopathology, 1972.

ABOUT: Alexander, I. E. Personology; Chapman, A. H. Harry Stack Sullivan: His Life and His Work; Chatelaine, K. Harry Stack Sullivan: The Formative Years; Current Biography 1942, 1949; Dictionary of American Biography 1974; Perry, H. S. Psychiatrist of America: The Life of Harry Stack Sullivan. *Periodicals*—New York Times August 3, 1947, January 16, 1949, May 30, 1965, September 24, 1972; Saturday Review August 15, 1953.

**SULLIVAN, JOHN WILLIAM NAVIN** (January 22, 1886–August 12, 1937), English writer on scientific subjects, was born in London, the son of John William Sullivan, an official of a Protestant mission, and Caroline (Navin) Sullivan, a teacher. At the age of fourteen, he went to work for a manufacturer of underwater cables, which paid for his secondary education at the North London Polytechnic School, where he received a solid grounding in mathematics and science. From 1908 until 1909 he studied science at University College, London.

From 1910 to 1913, he lived in the United States, working first for an electrical company, and later as a freelance science journalist. Upon returning to England, he held a succession of temporary positions, including journalistic work, and served briefly in the ambulance corps during World War I. Invalided home, he secured a post with the Censorship Department, where he became a protégé of the well-established editor and critic John Middleton Murry, husband of Katherine Mansfield. He was a regular contributor to *Nature, Athenaeum*, the *Times Literary Supplement*, and the other publications.

After publishing an unsuccessful novel, *An Attempt at Life*, he found his métier as a popularizer and explicator of science, particularly physics. His widely praised *Aspects of Science* was followed by *Atoms and Electrons* and *The History of Mathematics in Europe*. He gave a valued exposition of Einstein's theory of relativity to the public in *Three Men Discuss Relativity*, a book inspired by his conversations with Aldous Huxley and with Einstein himself. A *New York Times Book Review* critic of that work noted approvingly, " . . . Sullivan is never so abstruse or so abstract that he fails in what he has set out to do. He reveals a genial, enviable clarity of mind and transmits this successfully to the printed page." In a *New Republic Review* of *Aspects of Science: Second Series*, Edmund Wilson wrote, "with the exception of Bertrand Russell, he is probably, from the literary point of view, the most accomplished and brilliant popularizer of modern scientific theory."

Sullivan was a gifted critic of classical music, and a competent pianist. In the celebrated and still read *Beethoven: His Spiritual Development*, he analyzes the emotional and intellectual appeal of the music. In his autobiographical novel *But for the Grace of God*, Sullivan traces his own spiritual and intellectual development in the character of one Julian

Shaughnessy. "One cannot help regretting the novelist who has been lost to mathematics," Graham Greene wrote in a *Spectator* (1932) review of the fictional memoir. "The unhappy bewildered love story with which the book ends is described so sensitively, with such unpretentious insight, that no living novelist could have bettered it."

In his later work, Sullivan was interested above all in exploring the inherent restrictions of the scientific method and of scientific investigation in general. He presented these problems most cogently in *The Limitations of Science*, one of his best known and most controversial books. In the *Nation* William Gruen regretted Sullivan's resort to subjectivity and "religious interpretation," noting, "Science is what we know of reality; it is not what we experience." A *Spectator* (1933) critic, however, lauded the book as "the most lucid of its kind that has recently appeared. . . . while insisting on the complete autonomy of science, he approaches it as an artist."

Sullivan's last book, the biographical study *Isaac Newton*, appeared posthumously.

PRINCIPAL WORKS: *Science and mathematics*—Aspects of Science 1923; Atoms and Electrons, 1923; The History of Mathematics in Europe, from the Fall of Greek Science to the Rise of the Conception of Mathematical Rigours, 1924; Three Men Discuss Relativity, 1925; Aspects of Science; Second Series, 1926; Gallio; or, The Tyranny of Science, 1927; The Bases of Modern Science, 1928; The Physical Nature of the Universe, 1932; The Limitations of Science, 1933; Contemporary Mind: Some Modern Answers, 1934; Science: A New Outline, 1935; Living Things, 1938. *Novels*—An Attempt at Life, 1917; But for the Grace of God, 1932; A Holiday Task, 1936. *Biography*—Beethoven: His Spiritual Development, 1927; Isaac Newton, 1742–1727, 1938. *Juvenile*—Present-Day Astronomy, 1930; How Things Behave: A Child's Introduction to Physics, 1932.

ABOUT: Who's Who 1937. *Periodicals*—Nation November 8, 1933; New Public January 26, 1927; New York Times Book Review May 9, 1926; Spectator April 2, 1932; October 13, 1933; Times (London) August 13, 1937.

**SULLIVAN, MARK** (September 10, 1874–August 13, 1952), American journalist and social historian, was born in Avondale, Pennsylvania,

where he grew up on a fifty-two-acre farm owned by his parents, originally Irish immigrants. His rural childhood is described at length in the autobiographical *The Education of an American*. Sullivan's formal education—he attended neighborhood schools, in East Grove and West Grove, from the age of eight, and then (from 1888 to 1892) West Chester Normal school, where students were trained to be teachers—culminated in his failure, on medical grounds, to be admitted to West Point. From an early age he had been fascinated by newspapers, and he read avidly the two local papers delivered to the farmhouse, the *West Chester Village Record* and the *Kennett Advance*. In his autobiography he wrote: "I could hardly have been ten when I conceived

and began to carry out a project which I never heard of any other boy attempting. I undertook to collect issues of every newspaper in the world."

In 1896, when he was twenty-two, Sullivan decided to pursue a college education, and entered Harvard. Graduating in 1900, he relinquished his business interest in the Phoenixville paper, and joined the staff of the *North American* in Philadelphia. The association was shortlived. He found the work he was asked to do—acquiring photographs under false pretenses—sordid, and before the year was out had returned to Harvard to enter the law school, helping to finance these three years of study with contributions to the *Boston Transcript*. But he contributed his most striking piece to date, "The Ills of Pennsylvania," to the *Atlantic Monthly*. This critical piece about corrupt practices was written in the muckraking style which came to typify the greater part of his, and others', journalism during the Progressive era.

Sullivan never practiced law. An exposé of fraudulent claims in the patent medicine industry, written in installments for the *Ladies' Home Journal*, led to a job on *McClure's* and then, in 1906, on *Collier's Weekly*, where he stayed until 1919, acting as editor from 1914 to 1917. After leaving *Collier's*, Sullivan worked for four years as the Washington correspondent of the *New York Evening Post*. After he left that paper in 1923, although he continued to write syndicated columns, the greater part of his energies went into the writing of *Our Times*, a six-volume popular social history covering the years 1900 to 1925. The first volume states the aim of the series: "The purpose of this narrative is to follow an average American through this quarter-century of his country's history, to recreate the flow of the days as he saw them, to picture events in terms of their influence on him, his daily life and ultimate destiny." To do this Sullivan adopted a montage style, including liberal use of newspaper headlines and examples of advertising, which the *New York Times* called "gathering together the raw material of a period." Each successive volume was enthusiastically received. "He is making a sort of exalted, detached, objective Pepys diary of the American Republic," wrote the *Saturday Review of Literature*.

Sullivan was a friend of President Hoover, joining him for early morning exercise on the White House lawn, and during the Roosevelt presidency remained staunchly Republican, denouncing what he considered to be New Deal radicalism.

PRINCIPAL WORKS: The Great Adventure at Washington, The Story of the Conference, 1922; Our Times—The United States, 1900–1925, 6 vols., 1923–1935; The Education of an American, 1938.

ABOUT: Dictionary of American Biography, 1951–1955; Graham, O. L. An Encore for Reform, 1967; Sullivan, M. The Education of an American, 1938. *Periodicals*—New York Times March 21, 1926; August 15, 1952; Saturday Review of Literature December 13, 1930; Time August 25, 1952.

**SULLIVAN, RICHARD** (November 29, 1908–
September 13, 1981), American novelist and short
story writer, was born in Kenosha, Wisconsin,

where he was educated at
a local high school. When
he enrolled as a freshman
at Notre Dame, intend-
ing to study fine art, a
mistake was made and he
found himself entered for
a course in the liberal
arts. He went along with
this; but, still wishing to
become a painter, attend-
ed the Art Institute of
Chicago during his summer vacations. After marriage in 1932, a short trip to Europe, and a realization that he would never be a good painter, Sullivan
returned to Kenosha, where he worked in his father's retail business and began to write—radio
plays, childrens's thrillers, and a few serious stories.

In 1936 he returned to Notre Dame to take up
an appointment in the English department, which
was to be his professional home for the next forty
years. From that point onwards, Sullivan's writing
was always an adjunct to his academic life. He was
a prolific reviewer, mainly working for the *New
York Times Book Review* and the *Chicago Tribune*.
His most substantial, and some consider his best,
book was *Notre Dame: The Story of a Great University*.

His first novel, *Summer After Summer*, published in 1942, told the story of a young lower-
middle-class couple awaiting the birth of their second child. The *Saturday Review of Literature* said,
"The merciless employment of exact detail makes
the book a clinical study." Cool objectivity became
the hallmark of his writing about the small-town
Midwest—seen to best effect in *The World of Idella May*. Sullivan's shorter fiction, mainly about ordinary people living ordinary lives, is considered
well-written but ultimately too placid and mellow
for the period in which it was written and set.

In his portrait of Notre Dame University, Sullivan succeeds in injecting both an autobiographical
warmth and sense of humor eschewed by conscious
design in his fiction. He retired from the university
in 1976, and spent his last years as a freelance journalist, mainly writing reviews.

PRINCIPAL WORKS: *Fiction*—Summer After Summer, 1942; The
Dark Continent, 1943; The World of Idella May, 1946; First
Citizen, 1948; The Fresh and Open Sky and Other stories,
1950; 311 Congress Court, 1953. *Drama*—Our Lady's Tum-
bler, 1940. *Nonfiction*—Notre Dame, 1951.

ABOUT: Contemporary Authors vol. 104 1982; Hoehn, M. (ed.)
Catholic Authors, 1948; Twentieth Century Authors, 1942. *Periodicals*—New York Times September 15, 1981; Saturday Review of Literature October 5, 1942.

**SUMMERS,   (ALPHONSUS   JOSEPH-
MARY AUGUSTUS) MONTAGUE** (April 10,
1880–August 8, 1948), English priest and writer on
Restoration drama and occultism, wrote: "I was
born at Clifton Down, Bristol, the son of Augustus
William Summers, J.P. I was educated at Clifton
College and at Trinity College, Oxford, reading
chiefly classics and (in private) English. I came under the influence of Robinson Ellis, Corpus Professor of Latin, whose genius and enthusiasm notably
increased and fostered my early love for Latin literature, especially for the later Latin writers of the
Italian Renaissance. Other great influences on me
at the time were John Addington Symonds and
Hartwell de la Grande Grissell, Chamberlain of
Honour to three Popes. I gave several years of concentrated study to theology, and after ordination
worked for some time in the slums of London, and
also on more than one country mission.

"For health's sake I resided abroad during considerable periods, mainly in Italy and the South of
France. There is no place dearer to me than Venice.

"Even when a mere lad at school I had always
been writing essays, stories, poems, plays; but with
the exception of a few verses and theological studies
contributed anonymously
to magazines, and one
book of poems, I did not
publish any work until
1914, when the great
Elizabethan scholar, Ar-
thur   Henry   Bullen,
pressed me to edit Buck-
ingham's *The Rehearsal*
and the works of Mrs.
Aphra Behn. I had always
especially loved the Res-

toration period and literature, from the age of
twelve when I began to prowl around bookshops for
old plays. My first work as editor brought me the
friendship of Sir Edmund Gosse, to whose kindness
and criticism I owe much. In 1916 I was elected a
Fellow of the Royal Society of Literature.

"For many years I had urged that the real test of
the worth of dramatic literature is performance in
the theatre. In 1916 the London Stage Society suggested that I make the experiment I advocated. The
result was the revival, after more than a century
and a half, of Congreve's *The Double Dealer*. In
1919 there was founded The Phoenix, a society
formed for the adequate presentation of the plays
of the older dramatists. Until 1924, during which
time I was director and chairman, it produced
twenty-one plays, and 'created a revolution in English taste.' In 1925 I acted as advisor to the Renaissance Theatre, and also organized one special
performance of Congreve's *The Mourning Bride*. I
have edited the plays of Congreve, Wycherley, Otway, and Dryden.

"My *History of Witchcraft and Demonology*
caused a sensation and was a 'best seller.' It was
written from what people are pleased to call a 'medieval' standpoint, an absolute and complete belief
in the supernatural, and hence in witchcraft.

"After a residence of some years at Hove, Sussex,

I moved to Oxford in order to work at the Bodleian Library, where I am engaged in daily research.

"I have great dislike of and contempt for that superficial charlatanry in literature which now seems to pervade the world of letters. I find modernity frankly detestable. I like old books, old china, old wine, old houses, tranquillity, reverence, and respect. My chief recreations are travel, staying in unknown monasteries and villages in Italy, pilgrimages to famous shrines, investigations of occult phenomena, research in hagiology, liturgies, and mysticism, and talking to intelligent dogs—that is, all dogs.

"Above all, I hate the skeptic and modernist in religion, the Atheist, the Agnostic, the Communist, and all Socialism in whatever guise or masquerade."

---

In common with others he gave, this written account of his life given by Montague Summers to *Twentieth Century Authors* was incorrect in many details. He was born in Bristol as Augustus Montague Summers, where he attended school at Clifton College. He then attended Trinity College, Oxford, where he came to know Robinson Ellis and other noted teachers of the time. Ordained a priest in the Church of England in the first decade of the twentieth century, he was deacon, and then curate in a Bristol parish. He did good pastoral work, but all this came to an end when he was accused of "pederasty," a charge he evaded by fleeing abroad (to Italy). He did convert to Catholicism, and he did wear the vestments of a priest (from 1913), but there is no record of his ordination.

Summers re-established himself, and became well known as a cofounder of The Phoenix dramatic society. He was also elected a Fellow of the Royal Society of Literature (as he claimed) in 1916. His work on the Restoration drama was unscholarly, but he was a moving spirit in its revival, and certain plays would not have been put on had it not been for his enthusiasm.

Summers's other claim to fame is far less substantial. A few of his books on witchcraft are still kept in print, but the scholarly verdict of these books is unanimously negative. S. Foster Damon, the scholar of Blake and of witchcraft, wrote of Summers's *The Geography of Witchcraft* in the *Saturday Review of Literature*: "To the charge of prejudice we must add that of ignorance of his subject." Another very eminent scholar of the subject, Lynn Thorndike, wrote thus of *The History of Witchcraft and Demonology* in the *Nation* : "Except for a few useful titles in the bibliography, it does not appear that any serious historical use can be made of this farrago from literature of witchcraft, while it is to be hoped that it may not come to prurient and superstitious ears, though they, too, would probably be disappointed in it."

Summers's line was that of a credulous "medieval" Roman Catholic who was warning the world of the horrors of witchcraft. But their only merit may be that they amount to fascinating anthologies

of similar credulities. His still-read *Supernatural Omnibus* is a useful anthology of out-of-the-way occult tales by such as Le Fanu, and remains in print. His "editions" of such playwrights as Shadwell and Wycherley gave students and readers what was often their only opportunity to read those authors in full.

PRINCIPAL WORKS: *Verse*—Antinous and Other Poems, 1907. *Drama*—William Henry, 1939; Edward II, 1940. *Fiction*—Horrid Mysteries, 1927; The Grimoire and Other Ghostly Tales, 1936; Six Ghost Stories, 1937; The Sins of the Fathers, Supernatural Tales, 1947. *As editor*—Works of Mrs. Aphra Behn, 1915; Complete Works of Congreve, 1923; Complete Works of Wycherley, 1924; The Complete Works of Thomas Shadwell, 1927; Covent Garden Drollery, 1927; Sinistrati's Demoniality, 1927; The Compendium Maleficorum of Francesco Guazzo, 1929; Victorian Ghost Stories, 1933; The Complete Works of Otway, 1936; Supernatural Omnibus, 1935. *Witchcraft and demonology*—The History of Witchcraft, 1926; The Geography of Witchcraft, 1927; The Necromancer of the Black Forest, 1927; The Discovery of Witchcraft, 1928; The Vampire, His Kith and Kin, 1928; The Vampire in Europe, 1929; The Werewolf, 1933; Witchcraft and Black Magic, 1946; The Physical Phenomena of Mysticism, 1947. *Literary criticism and other*—St. Catherine of Siena, 1903; Lourdes, 1904; A Great Mistress of Romance: Ann Radcliffe, 1917; Jane Austen, 1919; St. Antonio-Maria Zaccaria, 1919; Architecture and the Gothic Novel, 1931; The Restoration Theatre, Vol. I (further volumes never appeared) 1934; Essays in Petto, 1933; The Playhouse of Pepys, 1935.

ABOUT: The autobiographical material quoted above was written for Twentieth Century Authors, 1942. Frank, F. S. (ed.) Montague Summers: A Bibliography Portrait, 1988; Joseph, J. Montague Summers, 1965; Sewell, B. The Galanty Show, 1980. *Bibliography*—A Bibliography of the Restoration Drama, 1934; A Gothic Bibliography, 1941; D'Arch Smith, T. Montague Summers: A Bibliography, 1983. *Periodicals*—Nation January 12, 1927; Saturday Review of Literature August 13, 1927; Times (London) August 11, 1948.

**SUTRO, ALFRED** (August 7, 1863–September 11, 1933), English playwright and translator, was born in London, the youngest of the three sons of Sigismund Sutro, a physician and noted authority on European hydropathy. Details about his mother are unknown. Alfred attended the City of London School at Cheapside, whose headmaster at the time was the scholar and writer E. A. Abbott, who encouraged the boy in his literary interests. Sutro finished off his education in Brussels, where he first became interested in Belgian writing.

He was still in his teens when he started to train as a clerk in the city; at the age of twenty he went into partnership with his elder brother Leopold, as a wholesale merchant in glucose, from which he made enough money to retire after fourteen years in it. In 1894, he married the former Esther Stella Isaacs, the daughter of a London fruit importer and the sister of Rufus Isaacs, the politician who became Marquess of Reading. She was an artist who later wrote books on art (including *Nicolas Poussin*, 1923). They went to Paris, where they met many writers, including the Belgian Maurice Maeterlinck—then still a symbolist—with whom they became very friendly. Maeterlinck liked and appreciated Sutro so much that he dedicated to him his celebrated *La Vie des abeilles* (1901). Sutro, who had already rendered a play and two of Maeterlinck's minor works into English then translated this as *The Life of Bees* (1901). From then onwards he was considered by the Belgian as the more or less official English translator of his prose, although the plays were for the most part left to other hands.

Sutro's first produced play, *The Chili Widow*, was written in collaboration with Arthur Bourchier, an actor and man of the London theater. It was a very free adaptation of a French play, *Monsieur le Directeur*, by Alexandre Bisson. Put on at the Royalty, it was not successful. He then started to collaborate with George Meredith on a stage adaptation of the former's novel *The Egoist*, but this never got off the ground.

Sutro was a very fashionable dramatist in Edwardian times. His first great hit was *The Walls of Jericho* (1904). Produced by Bourchier at the Garrick Theatre in October 1904, it dealt with the return of an "upright man," an Australian backwoodsman who has made a fortune, and who sets an example to a corrupt society.

Sutro for long wrote (with the exception of the war years) a play for every season after this success. *Mollentrave on Women* did well, and so did the sentimental *The Perfect Lover. John Glayde's Honour*, perhaps his best play, was about a man who discovers that his wife has taken an artist as a lover. *Living Together* was his last play to be produced. T. H. Dickinson, in *The Contemporary Drama of England*, called Sutro "the last survivor of the well-made era of Grundy and Pinero," a master of stage high society, who "dealt with the comedy of artifice, with the 'serious' situations that always had more of the flavour of the footlights than of real experience." However, while critics are unanimous in this verdict, Sutro himself defined a good play as "one that succeeds."

During World War I Sutro joined the Artists Rifles and other organizations fitted for middle-aged men who wanted to "do their bit." Owing to his commercial experience, he eventually joined the War Trade Intelligence Department, for his work in which he received the Order of the British Empire. A popular clubman (he was a member of the Garrick and Beefsteak Clubs) and a genial friend to many authors—such as Thomas Hardy, whom he used to visit at his home at Max Gate—he lived at Regents Park in London, and at a country home. His cheerful autobiography, *Celebrities and Simple Souls*, was issued only a few days after his death, of pneumonia. His *Times* obituarist said that "there was something half-wilfully sharp in the flavour of his comments on men and women and things, which only added zest to the true kindliness and friendliness of him."

PRINCIPAL WORKS: *Autobiography*—Celebrities and Simple Souls, 1933. *Drama*—The Cave of Illusion, 1900; Women in Love: Eight Studies in Sentiment, 1902; The Foolish Virgins, 1904; A Marriage Has Been Arranged, 1904; Mollentrave on Women, 1905; John Glayde's Honour, 1906; The Price of Money, 1906; The Walls of Jericho, 1906; The Fascinating Mr. Vandervelt, 1907; The Builder of Bridges, 1909; The Man in the Stalls, 1911; The Firescreen, 1912; Five Little Plays, 1912; The Perplexed Husband, 1913; The Two Virtues, 1913; Freedom, 1914; The Marriage . . . Will Not Take Place, 1914; The Choice, 1918; Uncle Anyhow, 1919; The Laughing Lady, 1922; The Great Well, 1923; Far Above Rubies, 1924; A Man with a Heart, 1924; The Desperate Lovers, 1926; Living Together, 1929. *Translations from Maeterlinck*—Aglavaine and Selysette, 1897; The Treasure of the Humble, 1897; Wisdom and Destiny, 1898; Alladine and Palomides, 1899; The Life of the Bee, 1901; Buried Temple, 1902; Ancient Egypt, 1925; The Life of the White Ant, 1927; The Magic of the Stars, 1930. *Other*—About Women, 1931; Which: Lord Byron of Lord Byron: A Bet, 1932.

ABOUT: Dictionary of National Biography, 1931–1940, 1949; Millet, F. B., Manly, J. M., and Rickert, E. Contemporary British Literature, 1935; Sutro, A. Celebrities and Simple Souls, 1933; Vines, S. A Hundred Years of English Literature, 1950. *Periodicals*—Nation February 27, 1913; New York Times September 9, 1933; Times (London) September 11, 1933.

**SUZUKI, DAISETSU TEITARO** (October 18, 1870–July 12, 1966), was born in Kanazawa, Japan, one of several sons of Ryojun and Masu (Kojima) Suzuki. Suzuki's ancestors were physicians belonging to the samurai class. Soon after the Meiji Emperor Mutsuhito assumed the throne in 1867, he abolished all privileges enjoyed by the samurai. Teitaro was subsequently unable to complete his medical training after his father died, instead setting off to become a teacher in a fishing village shortly upon finishing secondary school.

Suzuki left his teaching post in the early 1890s, departing for Tokyo where he took courses sporadically at the Imperial University. Gradually, he began spending more time at a Zen monastery in nearby Kamakura, undergoing the disciplines of a novice monk. His Zen master, Soyen Shaku, noticing his student's promise, recommended Suzuki for a position in the United States as a translator at Open Court Publishing Company in La Salle, Illinois. Suzuki secured this position in 1897, and for the next eleven years he worked as a proofreader, translator, and editor.

Suzuki left Open Court in 1908, departing for Europe, where he would spend the balance of the year translating the work of Swedish philosopher Emanuel Swedenborg from English into Japanese, and served as a vice president of the International Swedenborg Congress in London in 1911. An English version of some of Suzuki's works on the Swedish philosopher, translated by Andrew Bernstein, was published in 1996 as *Swedenborg: Buddha of the North*. In his introduction, Bernstein notes that "[Suzuki] is not interested in portraying Swedenborg as an historical individual, but as a timeless mystic whose perception of truth differs from that of Buddhism in form, but not substance." Winthrop Sargeant noted in a profile of Suzuki for the *New Yorker* (August 31, 1957), that "already he was assuming the peculiar role of interpreter of Eastern religious ideas for the West and Western religious ideas for the East that he has played ever since."

Upon his return to Tokyo in 1909, Suzuki became a professor of English at the Imperial University and later became a full-time member of the faculty at Otani University in Kyoto, where he continued to teach English and Buddhist philosophy. In 1911, he married Beatrice Erskine Lane, an American teacher, who died in 1938; they had one son. During the thirty years following his return to Japan, Suzuki wrote his first important works on Zen, including *An Introduction to Zen Buddhism* and the three-volume *Essays in Zen Buddhism*. By the 1930s he began to attract attention outside of Japan through his translation from the original Sanskrit of *The Lankavatara Sutra* and for his book *Zen and Its Influence on Japanese Culture*.

During World War II, Suzuki drew considerable criticism from colleagues and fellow countrymen for his steadfast opposition to Japanese militarism. Naturally, his pacifism generated suspicion from the government, which placed him under police surveillance for the duration of the conflict. After the war, Suzuki's analyses and interpretations of Zen philosophy began to enjoy prominence among Western students of Far Eastern religion and culture.

Suzuki moved back to the United States shortly after the war, teaching and lecturing at various institutions, most notably at Columbia University. In 1957, two volumes by Suzuki were published in America, *Zen Buddhism*, edited by William Barrett, and *Mysticism, Christian and Buddhist*, edited by Ruth Nanda Anshen (Harper). They were described as "sprightly" by Daniel J. Bronstein in the *Saturday Review*. His *Essays in Zen Buddhism* were reprinted at this time as well, prompting Gerald Heard to comment in the *New York Times* on the value of the volumes as "windows on Eastern thought, a clear introduction to the subject."

The Zen philosophy was perceived as inimical to conventional Western thought precisely because its conventions emphasized the living fact over the "mere idea." Suzuki, however, did not confine Zen to an impenetrable, diffuse sector beyond occidental apprehension. He strongly suggested that Zen could not be known or even adequately approached using traditional theories or conceptual resources. "Zen never explains but indicates . . . it always deals with facts, concrete and tangible . . . It does not challenge logic, it simply walks its path of facts, leaving all the rest to their own fates. As in everything else, but most particularly in Zen, all its outward manifestations or demonstrations must never be regarded as final. They just indicate the way where to look for the facts," he wrote in his *Essays on Zen Buddhism*.

Suzuki's long-standing interest in Western culture was in evidence in his prominent volume on comparative religion, *Mysticism: Christian and Buddhist*. In marking the differences and similarities between the religions, Suzuki focused on Zen Buddhism for the East and the gnostical reflections of Johannes Eckhardt for Christianity and the West.

In a preface to a chapter in *Zen Buddhism*, Suzuki reflects, "as a tentative experiment . . . I hope I have worked towards removing some of the difficulties usually besetting us in the mastery of Zen thought." He acknowledged that Western students would be mistaken in assuming that Zen could be meaningfully understood from a critical socio-philosophical description but, "this ought not to mean that Zen is not to be intelligently approached or to be made somewhat accessible by our ordinary means of reasoning." This effort at creating an innovative, imaginative perspective to an historically baffling subject distinguished Suzuki's intellectual endeavors.

PRINCIPAL WORKS: *Novels*—Outlines of Mahayana Buddhism, 1907; Zen and Its Influence on Japanese Culture, 1938; An Introduction to Zen Buddhism, 1948; Essays in Zen Buddhism (three vols.) 1949–50; A Manual of Zen Buddhism, 1950; An Introduction to Zen Buddhism (foreword by C. G. Jung), 1950; Studies in Zen, 1955; Zen Buddhism, 1957; Mysticism, Christian and Buddhist, 1957; Swedenborg: Buddha of the North (tr. A. Bernstein), 1996. *As translator*—Awakening of Faith, 1900; (with P. Carus) Tao Te Ching, 1909; The Lankavatara Sutra, 1932.

ABOUT: Current Biography 1966. *Periodicals*—New Yorker August 31, 1957; New York Times July 12, 1966.

## "SVEVO, ITALO" (pseudonym of SCHMITZ, ARON HECTOR, or ETTORE)

(December 19, 1861–September 13, 1928), Italian novelist, short story writer, diarist, and playwright, was born in Trieste, then a part of the Austro-Hungarian empire, but from 1919 a part of Italy. The pseudonym Svevo eventually adopted, "Italo the Swabian," was chosen to reflect his mixed descent and his self-identification as an Italian, not Austrian writer. He was one of the seven sons of Francesco and Allegra (Moravia) Schmitz. His father was the son of an Austrian customs official—his family hailed from the Rhineland—who was posted to Treviso, near Venice. His mother was of Italian (Triestine) descent. The family, which respected but did not strictly observe Jewish customs, had to a large extent Italianized itself: Ettore (he was called by this Italianized form of Hector) was brought up to speak, at home, the Triestine dialect of Italian. But his father insisted that to be successful in business his son would need to know German well. From 1874 until 1878, therefore, after an initial schooling in Trieste, he attended the Brüssel Institute, a well-known college of commerce for the sons of Jewish businessmen at Segnitz-am-Main, near Würzburg, in Bavaria. There he became devoted to literature, and was able to gain a wider cultural background than he could have received back in Trieste. The already precocious Svevo read Schiller, Goethe and Schopenhauer (an especially powerful influence), as well as Shakespeare and the great Russian writers of the time.

When he returned to Trieste, Svevo attended a commercial institute there—the Instituto Superiore Revoltella. In 1880 Francesco went bankrupt, and collapsed. Ettore was obliged, in October of that year, to find work in a bank, as a correspondence clerk; he remained there for nineteen years.

He now began to study Italian and French literature. He read Machiavelli and other Italian classics, including the then still-living Carducci, using for guidance the great critic Frederico de Sanctis's invaluable *Storia della letteratura italiana* (this was translated into English as *History of Italian Litera-*

ture in 1931). He also eagerly devoured the novels of Flaubert and Zola.

Meanwhile he began to write a regular theater column under the pseudonym E. Samigli for the Trieste newspaper *L'Indipendente*, which, as its ti-tle indicated, advocated Triestine independence, as he himself did. His first story, "L'assassinio di via Belpoggio" ("The Murder in the Via Belpoggio"), appeared in its columns in 1892. In that same year, with the false date of 1893, he published, at his own expense, the novel *Una vita* (*A Life*), using his pseudonym of Italo Svevo for the first time.

*Una vita* is about Alfonso Nitti, an inept man who, as Svevo did, works at a bank. Alfonso, unlike his creator, comes from the country and is badly educated. He is an awkward young man, who in a few but unmistakable respects, resembles Dostoyevski's Myshkin, "the idiot." He also has more than a passing resemblance to Flaubert's Frédéric Moreau of *A Sentimental Education*—with which *A Life* has been compared. Alfonso Nitti turns everything that comes to him as luck into ill fortune: his romance with his boss's daughter Annetta—who has to seduce him, since he is too feeble to seduce her—ends in failure when he flees from her to his mother. Ultimately he faces death at the hands of Annetta's brother, and so kills himself.

This is, above all, a comi-tragic novel written by a supreme ironist and humorist. Yet the novel also shows him to be a deeply serious artist. *A Life* met with no interest, and, apart from a few local mentions, not single critic saw any sign of genius in it. Yet today, with its successor *Senilità*, it is seen to form a triptych, of which *Zeno* is the central panel.

For six years Svevo worked at *Senilità* (1898, eventually translated, though its Italian title means "Senility," as *As a Man Grows Older*). Its protagonist's Emilio Brentani, a man in his thirties who has aged, become withered, before his time. Emilio has an affair with a street-wise working-class girl, Angiolina Zarri with whom, for all his awareness of her true nature, he becomes obsessed. Svevo became bitterly, if also humorously, discouraged at the lack of response to this work. He wrote: "This incomprehension baffles me. It demonstrates that they just don't follow me. It is pointless for me to write, let alone publish." Reviewing the 1949 translation in the *New Statesman* V. S. Pritchett wrote: "The scenes of action are brilliant, freshly observed and as real as anything in Madame Bovary and a good deal better natured. . . . Svevo's scenes of illness are among the most dramatic in any literature."

In 1896 Svevo married his cousin Livia Veneziani. Her family was fiercely Catholic, and, together with Livia, pressured Svevo himself to convert, much to his distress, for he saw himself as an agnos-

tic. He did so, however, though the conversion was never more than merely a gesture, and there is much about the inner tribulations it caused him in his letters. But his wife's family, for which he began to work in 1899, were also prosperous manufacturers of marine paint. He traveled much on business and even set up a branch of the firm in England. With the outbreak of war in 1914, Svevo and the firm became even richer—a further irony inasmuch as Svevo was an outspoken opponent of all war.

Svevo, a gifted linguist, had begun to teach, part-time, a course in French and German correspondence at the Institute Revoltella (after 1918 the University of Trieste) in 1893. In 1907, though, as a consequence of his business in England, he needed to improve his English and became the pupil of James Joyce, the Irish writer who had just arrived in Trieste to teach English at the Berlitz School there. Svevo and Livia became his pupils. Joyce—who came, through Svevo, to teach at the Revoltella in 1912—read and praised *As a Man Grows Older*, and Svevo read and praised the early drafts of Joyce's *Portrait of the Artist as a Young Man*. In what became one of the most important literary friendships of the century, the two men encouraged each other to a remarkable degree, although Svevo's praise of Joyce was the more decisive. Richard Ellmann, in *James Joyce*, said Svevo had, "concealed his talent under amiability. . . . he turned his rather wistful cleverness against himself to the entertainment of . . . company." It has been declared that Joyce's Leopold Bloom, the Jewish central figure in *Ulysses*, was "modeled to a large extent on Svevo," and Ellmann has been cited in support of this contention.

Svevo began to write *La conscienza di Zeno* in 1919, and published in 1923. It has always been translated as *The Confessions of Zeno* (1930), although "conscienza" means "conscience; scruple; consciousness." He had been reading Freud since 1912, and had even (in 1918) started a translation of *The Interpretation of Dreams* in collaboration with a nephew, a doctor. Freud is the main overt influence upon—but also butt of—this tragedy cast as ironic comedy, since its protagonist, Zeno Cosini, is writing the history of his life at the instigation of the psychoanalyst, "Dr. S," to whom he has gone for a cure for his smoking habit. After this, there follow six sections, the first about Zeno Cosini's contemplation of his "last cigarette" (more poignant than all the others); others about how in his own estimation he killed his father, about his marriage, and about a business partnership. The novel ends apocalyptically. The poet and critic Eugenio Montale thought *Zeno* "the poem of our complex modern madness."

During Svevo's last years he lectured on his own work in France, began to write a sequel to *Zeno*, and issued a few more stories. In September 1928 he had a car accident at Motta di Livenza, near Treviso. He broke his femur, and died a few days later from the shock that was aggravated by a heart condition he had suffered for many years.

PRINCIPAL WORKS IN ENGLISH TRANSLATION: *Fiction*—A Life (tr. A.

Colquhoun) 1963; As A Man Grows Older (tr. B. de Zoete), 1932; Confessions of Zeno (tr. B. de Zoete), 1930; Further Confessions of Zeno (tr. B. Johnson and P. N. Furbank; contains plays) 1969. *Short stories*—The Hoax (tr. B. de Zoete) 1930; The Nice Old Man and the Pretty Girl and Other Stories (tr. L. Collinson Morley, with note by Montale) 1930; Short Sentimental Journal and Other Stories (tr. B. de Zoete, L. Collinson-Morley, B. Johnson; contains plays) 1980. *Criticism*—James Joyce (tr. S. Joyce) 1950.

ABOUT: Biasin, G-P. Literary Diseases: Theme and Metaphor in the Italian Novel, 1975; Columbia Dictionary of Modern European Literature, 1947 and 1980; Ellman, R. James Joyce, 1965; Furbank, P. N. Italo Svevo: The Man and the Writer, 1966; Hays, P. L. The Limping Hero: Grotesques in Literature, 1971; Lebowitz, N. Italo Svevo, 1978; Moloney B. Italo Svevo: A Critical Introduction, 1974, Pacifici, S. From Verisimo to Experimentalism: Essays on the Modern Italian Novel, 1969; Poggioli, R. The Spirit of the Letter: Essays in European Literature, 1965; Russell, C. Italo Svevo, the Writer from Trieste, 1978; Seymour-Smith, M. Who's Who in Twentieth Century Literature, 1976, Fifty European Novels, 1979, Guide to Modern World Literature, 1986; Svevo, L. V. Memoir of Italo Svevo (tr. B. Johnson), 1990; Weiss, B. Italo Svevo, 1987; Wisse, R. R. The Schlemiel as Modern Hero, 1971. *Bibliography*—Weiss, B. An Annotated Bibliography on the Theatre of Italo Svevo, 1974. *Periodicals*—Italian Quarterly Summer, 1959; Italian Studies 1976; James Joyce Quarterly Summer, 1964; Modern Fiction Studies Spring, 1972; Modern Language Notes February 1953; March 1956; January 1962; January 1975; New Republic November 2, 1963; New York Times Book Review January 21, 1968; New Yorker June 3, 1967; Studies in Short Fiction Summer, 1971; Times Literary Supplement March 30, 1962; May 13, 1988.

**SWANSON, NEILL HARMON** (June 30, 1896–February 5, 1983), American novelist and journalist, was born on a farm near Minneapolis,

Minnesota. He enrolled at the University of Minnesota to study English but soon left to work for the *Minneapolis Journal.* He volunteered for the military service at the outbreak of World War I and served as a company commander in France. After the war, he returned to the *Journal* for two more years before moving on to other papers, including the *Baltimore Sun, Evening Sun* and *Sunday Sun.*

He wrote carefully researched but lightly handled historical fiction, much of it (including his first book, *The Judas Tree*) inspired by stories of Missouri told to him by his father, a Swedish settler. *The First Rebel* was illustrated by old prints and documents and presented as a "true narrative." It carried enough credibility to win a commendation from the historian H. S. Commager, who wrote in the *New York Herald Tribune Books*: "*The First Rebel* is no imaginative recreation of Indian captivities and border warfare; it is a carefully documented historical biography based on sources, substantiated by footnote references, and bolstered with appendices."

The best-remembered of Swanson's books, largely because of a Cecil B. De Mille film version, starring Gary Cooper, is *Unconquered*, a novel about the Pontiac uprising. As well as specializing in the

Wild West, Swanson became something of an expert on the War of 1812. One of his later books, written with Anne Sherbourne (whom he later married), and marketed as a teenage novel, was *The Star-Spangled Banner*, the story of a fourteen-year-old boy's exploits during one phase of that war.

As an editor Swanson was eccentric and flamboyant, but with a recognized talent for the content and format of newspapers. He was married four times and retired from active newspaper work in 1973.

PRINCIPAL WORKS: The Judas Tree, 1933; The Flag Is Still There, 1933; The Phantom Emperor, 1934; The First Rebel, 1937; The Forbidden Ground, 1938; The Silent Drum, 1940; The Perilous Fight, 1945; Unconquered, 1947; (with A. Sherbourne) The Star Spangled Banner, 1958.

ABOUT: Contemporary Authors, vol. 109 1985. *Periodicals*—Boston Transcript, January 11, 1941; New York Herald Tribune Books July 18, 1937; New York Times February 7, 1983; Washington Post February 7, 1983.

**SWEENEY, JAMES JOHNSON** (May 30, 1900–April 14, 1986), American art critic and museum director, was born in Brooklyn, New York,

the son of Patrick M. Sweeney, founder of a textile firm, and his wife Mary. He received his B.A. from Georgetown University in 1922 and spent the following years studying at Jesus College, Cambridge, the Sorbonne and the University of Siena. At Cambridge he became interested in

Matisse and Picasso, and was introduced to the leading British art critic Roger Fry. He began to contribute essays on modern art to the *Irish Statesman* and the *New York Times* and subsequently became art correspondent for the *Chicago Evening Post.* He also published verse and later, in his capacity as associate editor of the Parisian literary magazine *transition* in the mid-1930s, gave help to James Joyce in his final editing of *Finnegans Wake.*

In 1933–1934 Sweeney directed an exhibition of twentieth-century painting and sculpture for the University of Chicago. In 1935, after spending some months in Europe collecting materials, he organized an exhibit of African art for the Museum of Modern Art, New York. In the 1940s he wrote the first analysis of Jackson Pollock in a catalogue for the Art of the Century Gallery (1943) and directed exhibitions of Miró, Alexander Calder and Mondrian for the Museum of Modern Art. In 1945 he was appointed to the position of director of the same museum's department of painting and sculpture, but he left the post the next year after a conflict over administrative responsibilities. He went on to organize a Picasso exhibition in Toronto in 1949 and the Calder exhibition for the United States Pavilion at the Biennial Exposition in Paris in 1952. In October 1952 he was appointed director of the Solomon R. Guggenheim Museum in New York. This museum had specialized in "nonobjective" abstract art, but Sweeney made it a major showcase for all forms of modern art. The Frank Lloyd Wright exhibition (1953) and the controversial "Younger American Painters" (1954) were especially notable. Sweeney left the Guggenheim in 1959 after another disagreement over policy and in 1961 became director of the Museum of Fine Arts in Houston. His tenure was remembered among other things for his bringing to the museum a sixteen-ton Olmec head that he had found in a Mexican jungle. In the early 1970s he was chairman of the executive committee of the Israel Museum in Jerusalem.

In addition to his catalogue essays and numerous articles, Sweeney was the author of an apologia for modernism in art, *Plastic Redirections in Twentieth Century Painting*, and books on the architect Gaudi and the sculptor Chillida. A man of enormous energy, he was "a demanding and innovative" curator and director, in the words of his *New York Times* obituarist Grace Glueck, and from first to last "a forceful spokesman for the new and the experimental."

PRINCIPAL WORKS: Plastic Redirections in Twentieth Century Painting, 1934; Joan Miró, 1941; Alexander Calder, 1943; Stuart Davis, 1945 (reprinted in Three American Modernist Painters, 1970); Piet Mondrian, 1945; Marc Chagall, 1946; Henry Moore, 1947; Modern Art and Tradition *in* Three Lectures on Modern Art, 1949; (with J. L. Sert) Antoni Gaudi, 1953; Burri, 1955; The Miró Atmosphere, 1959; Irish Illuminated Manuscripts of the Early Christian Period, 1965; Vision and Image; A Way of Seeing, 1968; Five American Sculptors: Calder, Lipchitz, Flanagan, Lachaise, Nadelman, 1971; Contemporary Spanish Painters: Miró and After, 1975; (with P. Seltz) Chillida, 1986. *As editor*—African Negro Art, 1935; Three Young Rats, and Other Rhymes, drawings by Alexander Calder, 1944; (with P. Radin) African Folk Tales and Sculpture, 1952 (Sweeney's contribution reprinted as African Sculpture, 1970).

ABOUT: Ashton, D. Life and Times of the New York School, 1972; Current Biography 1955; Guilbaut, S. How New York Stole the Idea of Modern Art, 1983; Hoehn, M. (ed.) Catholic Authors II, 1952; Lynes, R. Good Old Modern: An Intimate Portrait of the Museum of Modern Art, 1973. *Periodicals*—Apollo March 1981, September 1986; Art Digest November 1, 1952; Art in America November 1963; Artforum June 1962; New York Times April 15, 1986; Newsweek February 12, 1945; January 23, 1961; Progressive Architecture September 1960; Studio September 1963; Time August 1, 1960.

## SWIFT, ANTHONY. See FARJEON, J. J.

## SWING, RAYMOND (March 25, 1887–December 22, 1968), American radio news commentator, foreign correspondent, and author, was heard by millions all over the world during the war years of the 1930s and 1940s. After years of newspaper bylines for his coverage of World War I, he won the Du Pont and Peabody awards for his radio work during World War II, and wrote books warning of the dangers of American demagogues and the atomic bomb, as well as a memoir recapping his vast experiences abroad on the foreign desks of various American newspapers and at home over the airwaves.

Born in Cortland, New York, the son of the Reverend Albert Temple Swing and Alice Edwards (Mead) Swing, he was sent to Oberlin College and Conservatory of Music, where his father taught religious history. Raymond was suspended for misbe-

havior after his freshman year.

After stints as a cashier, clothing-store clerk, and an organist for an evangelist, he found his niche in news, working as office boy, reporter, and then editor for newspapers in Ohio and Indiana for eight years. Then he suffered from nervous exhaustion brought on by heavy drinking, had an appendectomy, and was offered a year abroad in 1912 by a wealthy uncle.

While visiting Berlin, Swing began a notable career as a foreign correspondent, first for the *Chicago Daily News*, then for the *New York Herald*. Later, he directed foreign coverage for the *Wall Street Journal* and headed the London bureau of the *Philadelphia Public Ledger* and *New York Evening Post*. During World War I, he cut his teeth as an international journalist, evading German censors and scooping the story on the mysterious large-bore gun responsible for shelling Liège.

Returning stateside in 1934, Swing joined the board of editors of the *Nation*. A year later he made his radio debut as a commentator on American affairs for the British Broadcasting Corporation and commented on foreign affairs for the School of the Air, a venture of Columbia Broadcasting System (CBS). In Great Britain the broadcast was known as "American Commentary," and it was avidly followed. Later, Alastair Cooke would take it over.

At the same time, Swing wrote *Forerunners of American Fascism* (1935), an analysis of the demagoguery of five American leaders: U.S. senators Theodore Bilbo and Huey Long, Father Charles Coughlin, William Randolph Hearst, and Dr. Francis E. Townsend. "Everything about this book from his choice of title to his last words is good. The biographical method and the way Mr. Swing has handled his material make what he has written as interesting as it is socially important," wrote Norman Thomas in the *Nation*. Despite favorable reviews, "the book-reading public at that time was not much interested in fascism or disturbed by its demagogues," Swing later wrote.

Swing worked for the Mutual Broadcasting System (1936–1945), and for the American Broadcasting Company (1942–1948), becoming one of the best known American radio commentators in a crowded field. He became known outside America as the "radio Uncle Sam" during the height of World War II. With his steady, soft-spoken sobriety and his thoroughly researched analysis, he attracted many fans, including Roosevelt, Winston Churchill, King George VI, General George Marshall, Supreme Court Justice Felix Frankfurter, and Tallulah Bankhead, among some thirty-seven million other listeners around the world.

Swing grew powerful enough to dictate his own terms to commercial sponsors. Famously, he opposed a commercial for While Owl cigars when it came in the middle of his broadcast. The General Cigar Company agreed to eliminate the obtrusive spot. After 1945, however, with the war over, Swing's popularity began to decline. This may have been due in part to his being harassed by the U.S. House of Representatives' Committee on Un-American Activities for his liberal views.

In 1946 he wrote *In the Name of Sanity*, "a survey of the political aspects and the potentialities of the atomic bomb, which . . . the author considers to be something like the Apocalypse" (*New Yorker*). George Soule in the *New Republic* called the book "vivid, logical, forceful."

Two other books were collections of his radio broadcasts. *How War Came* (1939) covered six months of European crisis in 1939, including the fourteen days in August and September directly before Britain formally declared war. The other broadcast collection, *Preview of History* (1943), included an introduction on postwar problems, the Munich crisis of 1938, war broadcasts from 1941 to 1943, and eight of his speeches. "At his worst, the author can be positively Coolidgean, but this book contains a good percentage of his more acute writings, too," wrote the *New Yorker*.

Swing rounded out his career as a news commentator for station WOR in 1948 and then for the Liberty Network. He served as political commentator for Voice of America from 1951 to 1953, and again from 1959 to 1964.

"Raymond Swing belonged to the era of the elite. His book explains better than I have ever seen it done elsewhere the origins, the influence, the professional pride and the personal importance of the 'foreign correspondents' in that era of American journalism which, I suppose, opened with Richard Harding Davis and closes with Raymond Swing," wrote Joseph C. Harsch in the *Christian Science Monitor*.

PRINCIPAL WORKS: Forerunners of American Fascism, 1935; How War Came, 1939; Preview of History, 1943; In the Name of Sanity, 1946. *As editor*—This I Believe vol. 2, 1954; Good Evening!, 1964.

ABOUT: Current Biography 1940; 1969; Fang, I. E. Those Radio Commentators; Fisher, D. F. American Portraits; Heald, M. Transatlantic Vistas; Murrow, E. R. *in* This I Believe (ed. R. Swing) vol. 2, 1954; Swing R. Good Evening!, 1964. *Periodicals*—Atlantic Monthly July 1945; Christian Science Monitor March 26, 1964; Library Journal April 1, 1964; Nation May 8, 1935; November 4, 1939; January 24, 1948; New Republic April 15, 1946; New York Times October 29, 1939; December 24, 1968; New Yorker September 18, 1943; March 16, 1946; Newsweek September 23, 1963; January 6, 1969; Time January 3, 1969.

**SWINNERTON, FRANK (ARTHUR)** (August 12, 1884–November 6, 1982), English novelist and critic, wrote: "I was born in a London suburb, Wood Green. My father's family was Midland English, my mother's Scottish. I taught myself to read by the time I was four, and have been reading ever since. Severe illness (first diphtheria, followed by paralysis, and then scarlet fever) changed a healthy child into a boy subject to illness, and a period of starvation did not help, either. But at the age of fourteen, having determined to be a journalist, I

went as office boy in the firm of some Scottish newspaper proprietors named Hay, Nisbet & Co., and two years later, having a little shifted ground, so that I wanted to write books as well as newspapers, I went into the office of J. M. Dent & Co., the publishers of the Temple Shakespeare and, later, Everyman's Library. I was with Dent's for six years, and left to be a proof-reader and assistant with another firm of book publishers, Chatto & Windus. I was then twenty-two, and when I was twenty-three I wrote my first novel. It was a failure, but was much liked; and I was offered the post of reader, or editor, to the firm. This I held for sixteen years, and during that period the firm had some resounding successes, which included *The Young Visitors*, for the publication of which I was responsible.

"Meanwhile, having continued to write books, I produced, in 1917, a short novel, *Nocturne*, which made a lucky hit all over the world. It was praised in England by Arnold Bennett and H. G. Wells, both of whom had become my friends, though they were greatly senior to me; and I wish to state that all the success I have had dates from, and arises from, the friendship of these two men. I married Mary Dorothy Bennett in 1924, and have one daughter.

"I am in politics a Liberal, slightly to the left of orthodox Liberalism; and I think the only hope for peace and happiness in the world is not materialism but love between human beings. I dislike Communism for its materialism, and Fascism for its brutality, but both because they subordinate the individual to dogmatic and fanatic beliefs.

"As a novelist I owe a lot to my childhood love of Louisa Alcott's books and the immense admiration I have always felt for Henry James' technique—not his nambypambiness. I am temperamentally cheerful, cold (and therefore kind through a sort of indifference), and easily moved to liveliness of speech by congenial company. My marriage has been happy, and so has my life. My best books, in my own opinion, are *Harvest Comedy* and *The Georgian Literary Scene*, but I do not regard either one as of lasting importance. *Nocturne* has been included in the series of World Classics issued by the Oxford University Press. I live in the country, am very lazy, work unwillingly very hard, and have few intolerances."

Frank Swinnerton was the younger of the two sons of Charles Swinnerton, a copperplate engraver, and the former Rose Cottam, known in the family as O.M.—"the Old Ma." Both grandfathers were master craftsmen, one a steel engraver, the other a glass cutter. Engraving was being supplanted by modern printing methods, and for Charles Swinnerton it was ever harder to find work. The family was a close and happy one, but often went hungry. In his *Autobiography* (the source of all the Swinnerton quotations in this profile), Swinnerton said that they "regarded themselves as being altogether outside class; they were Swinnertons or Cottams, craftsmen, ironists, characters." Frank Swinnerton followed this tradition.

During his years of childhood illness, Swinnerton played for hours on end with the small wooden pieces from a board game, giving them paper costumes, names, characters, careers, romances, and wars. This game, he said, together with his delight in the stories of Louisa M. Alcott, prepared him for his career as a novelist: "Ever since . . . I have been composing, and trying to tell with an appearance of naturalness, stories about invented human beings who behave as they do because of the forces of character and the influences of environment."

As the family's fortune waxed and (more often) waned, they moved from one London house or flat to another. When his health permitted, Swinnerton attended an assortment of schools until he was fourteen. Thereafter he took what menial jobs he could get until he found his niche in publishing, initially as clerk and receptionist to Joseph Mallaby Dent. Swinnerton's education proceeded informally through his contacts with Dent's writers and artists, through visits to the theater and the Promenade Concerts and lectures by the likes of Shaw and Chesterton, and through discussion with serious-minded young friends and endless reading. By the time he was sixteen, he knew many plays and books by heart, and had read all of Ibsen then available in translation.

In 1907, when he was twenty-two, Swinnerton moved on to Chatto & Windus. They published his first novel, *The Merry Heart*, centering on an unshakably optimistic young clerk. An apprentice piece, sometimes labored, it was praised for its characterization and atmosphere, but was financially unsuccessful. So was its successor, *The Young Idea*, about a group of young friends and lovers in London before World War I.

Swinnerton sent a copy of the latter to Arnold Bennett, whose novels he had just discovered. Bennett responded enthusiastically, initiating what eventually became a close friendship. This move was not typical of Swinnerton. He confessed to a "reserve," a "frigidity of heart," that disqualified him for what is nowadays called "networking"; "Unless a man took the trouble to approach me . . . , I missed knowing him altogether." In the course of his long life, Swinnerton was nevertheless to accumulate many literary friends. One of these was H. G. Wells, whose warm praise of Swinnerton's first work of criticism, a study of George Gissing, was followed by an invitation to a Sunday soirée at Wells's house in Hampstead.

Most of Swinnerton's novels are set in London or its suburbs. As Walter Allen wrote in *The English Novel*, they can be seen as late contributions to the "Cockney school" of realist fiction, whose exponents included Arthur Morrison, W. W. Jacobs, and others who "aimed at describing the everyday reali-

ty of the lower middle-class and working-class London scene." Praised in particular for his portrayal of women, Swinnerton generally worked with a small cast of characters, and was more interested in observing their behavior than in plot.

Swinnerton's best novel was his seventh, written at the invitation of his friend, the publisher Martin Secker. Appearing in 1917 as *In the Night*, it coincided with another book of that title. It was reissued the same year as *Nocturne*, a title suggested by the historical novelist Rafael Sabatini. In England, *Nocturne* was not much noticed. The American edition, however, appeared with an adulatory introduction by H. G. Wells. This, echoed in the reviews, made the book a best-seller. There followed a reappraisal in Britain and translations into several languages. Swinnerton found himself placed for a while in or near the front rank of contemporary British novelists. Wells wrote that Swinnerton "sees life and renders it with a steadiness and detachment and patience quite foreign to my disposition. He has no underlying motive. He sees and tells. His aim is the attainment of that beauty which comes with exquisite presentation. . . . This is a book that will not die. It is perfect, authentic, and alive." Others praised the novel's compassionate understanding of stunted lives, its good plain prose and almost flawless structure.

With characteristic modesty and honesty, Swinnerton always insisted that he was a minor novelist. He called *Nocturne* a "stunt" because it was conceived "in terms of a time-table." And he quoted a letter from George Bernard Shaw, who found *Nocturne* "a damned dismal book about people who ought not to exist. . . . I get dreams like that when I am run down."

In 1918 Swinnerton became Bertrand Russell's lodger in Bury Street, Bloomsbury. The following year he began a brief, unhappy marriage to Helen Dircks, a poet. By then a reviewer for the *Manchester Guardian* and drama critic for *The Nation*, as well as an established novelist, Swinnerton "began to know almost everyone in literary London." This helped him to build a formidable list as reader and editor at Chatto & Windus. During his years there, he was responsible for the commissioning or discovery not only of Daisy Ashford's *The Young Visiters*, but of Constance Garnett's translations of Chekhov, Lytton Strachey's *Eminent Victorians*, Aldous Huxley's *Limbo*, and Barbellion's *The Journal of a Disappointed Man*, among other notable books.

Swinnerton made a lecture tour of the United States in 1923, meeting many eminent writers. *Young Felix*, one of his most successful novels, appeared the same year. Largely autobiographical, it resembled *The Merry Heart* in its account of a young man dogged by misfortune but immune to it, buoyed up by an indomitable mother. In 1924, by then divorced, Swinnerton married his Chatto colleague Mary Dorothy Bennett. They settled in the Surrey village of Old Tokefield, and had two daughters, one of whom died in infancy. Swinnerton left Chatto in 1926 to become a full-time writer and critic.

Apart from *Nocturne*, Swinnerton's best known book was *The Georgian Literary Scene*. This is a large gossipy volume of essays, not without malice, on some seventy-five writers, most of whom he had known, from Wells and Bennett to Edgar Wallace and P. G. Wodehouse. Lewis Gannett called it "the kind of criticism most worth reading: personal, informed, honest and prejudiced" (*New York Herald Tribune*). There was more of the same in Swinnerton's generous and unaffected *Autobiography*, and in such later works as *Background with Chorus* and *Figures in the Foreground*.

Swinnerton was literary critic of the *London Evening News* in 1929–1932, fiction reviewer for the *Observer* in 1937–1943, and a columnist as "John O'London" for *John O'London's Weekly* in 1949–1954. He was president of the Royal Literary Fund in 1962–1966, and an Honorary Life Member of the Reform Club. His novels continued to appear—more than forty in all, the last published when the author was ninety-two. By then his critics had accepted Swinnerton's own verdict on his work—that his work was not of the top rank, but that he was a good craftsman.

A small man with a neat beard, "Swinny" retained to the end of his life a great capacity for friendship, a fondness for cats, and a talent for storytelling and mimicry. His wife died in 1980. Swinnerton lived on in his ancient cottage in Old Tokefield, still working his beloved garden, writing in his minute and elegant hand, and entertaining admirers and researchers from all over the world.

PRINCIPAL WORKS: *Novels*—The Merry Heart, 1909; The Young Idea, 1910; The Casement, 1911; The Happy Family, 1912; On the Staircase, 1914; The Chaste Wife, 1916; In the Night, 1917 (republished the same year as Nocturne); Shops and Houses, 1918; September, 1919; Coquette, 1921; The Three Lovers, 1922; Young Felix, 1923; The Elder Sister, 1925; Summer Storm, 1926; A Brood of Ducklings, 1928; Sketch of a Sinner, 1929; The Georgian House: A Tale in Four Parts, 1932; Elizabeth, 1934; Harvest Comedy, 1937; The Two Wives, 1939; The Fortunate Lady, 1941; Thankless Child, 1942; A Women in Sunshine, 1944; English Maiden, 1946; The Cats and Rosemary, 1948 (juvenile); Faithful Company, 1948; The Doctor's Wife Comes to Stay, 1949; A Flower for Catherine, 1950; Master Jim Probity, 1952 (in U.S.: An Affair of Love); A Month in Gordon Square, 1953; The Summer Intrigue, 1955; The Woman for Sicily, 1957; A Tigress in Prothero, 1959 (in U.S.: Tigress in the Village); The Grace Divorce, 1960; Death of a Highbrow, 1961; Quadrille, 1965; Sanctuary, 1966; The Bright Lights, 1968; On the Shady Side, 1970; Nor All Thy Tears, 1972; Rosalind Passes, 1973; Some Achieve Greatness, 1976. *Others*—George Gissing: A Critical Study, 1912; Robert Louis Stevenson: A Critical Study, 1914; Women, 1918; Tokefield Papers, 1927 (enlarged as Tokefield Papers, Old and New, 1949); A London Bookman, 1928; Authors and the Book Trade, 1932; The Georgian Literary Scene, 1910–1935, 1935 (in U.S.: The Georgian Scene: A Literary Panorama); Swinnerton: An Autobiography, 1936; The Reviewing and Criticism of Books, 1939 (Dent Memorial Lecture); Arnold Bennett, 1950; The Bookman's London, 1951; Londoner's Post: Letters to Gog and Magog (Selections from John O'London's Weekly), 1952; Authors I Never Met, 1956; The Adventures of a Manuscript, Being the Story of "The Ragged-Trousered Philanthropist," 1956; Background with Chorus: A Footnote to Changes in English Literary Fashion Between 1901 and 1927, 1956; Figures in the Foreground: Literary Reminiscences, 1917–1940, 1963; A Galaxy of Fathers, 1966; Reflections from a Village, 1969; Arnold Bennett: A Last Word, 1978. *As editor*—An Anthology of Modern Fiction, 1937; The Journals of Arnold Bennett, 1954.

ABOUT: The autobiographical material quoted above was written for Twentieth Century Authors, 1942. Allen, W. The English Novel, 1958; Bennett, A., Wells, H. G., and Overton, G. M. Frank Swinnerton: Personal Sketches, 1920; Church, R. British Authors, 1948; Contemporary Novelists, 1982; Dictionary of Literary Biography vol. 34 1985; Dictionary of National Biography, 1981–1985, 1990; McKay, R. C. George Gissing and His Critic, Frank Swinnerton, 1933; Swinnerton, F. Autobiography, 1936; Swinnerton, F. Tokefield Papers, Old and New, 1949; Swinnerton, F. Background with Chorus, 1956; Swinnerton, F. Figures in the Foreground, 1963; Swinnerton, F. Reflections from a Village, 1969; Who's Who 1982–1983. *Periodicals*—New York Herald Tribune November 26, 1934; New York Times November 10, 1982; Times (London) November 10, 1982.

**SYKES, CHRISTOPHER** (November 17, 1907– December 8, 1986), English novelist and biographer, was born in Menethorpe, Yorkshire. His father, Sir Mark Sykes, was an adviser to Lloyd George on Oriental affairs. After attending the Roman Catholic school, Downside, the young Sykes studied unsuccessfully at the Sorbonne and at Christ Church, Oxford, failing to obtain a degree. In 1928 he was made an attaché to the British Em-bassy in Berlin, and the following year joined a diplomatic legation in Teheran, where he worked as private secretary to Sir Robert Clive. Deciding he did not wish to dedicate his life to the diplomatic service, he made a serious study of oriental affairs and travelled widely in Persia (now Iran) and Afghanistan, reporting occasionally as a correspondent for the London *Times*, before writing more sustained and thoughtful journalism for *The Spectator* and *The Observer*. His first book, *Wassmuss*, was published in 1936. It was the biography of a German consul who, at the outbreak of World War I, had attempted to fan the flames of anti-British feeling in southern Persia. This ambitious and extremely complex subject was handled with considerable skill, and the *New York Times* found in it "a Homeric quality." Sykes's next two books were written in collaboration with Robert Byron. Travel accounts by Englishmen abroad, they were much slighter than *Wassmuss*.

Sykes served most of World War II in the Green Howards, a Yorkshire regiment. He was mainly occupied with diplomatic duties in Teheran and Cairo, but towards the end of the war he joined the SAS and was parachuted into France behind enemy lines, where his fluent French and diplomatic instinct proved invaluable. After the war he returned to Persia, wrote about the Azerbaijan campaign for the *Daily Mail*, and then joined the BBC, where he produced radio programs until 1968. It was work which, in those days of the broadcasting service, allowed Sykes time to write. The book that he published immediately after the war—*Four Studies In Loyalty*—is considered by many to be his best. It consists of four long biographical essays, including one about Sykes's great-uncle, who had been a friend of Edward VII, and another about Robert Byron, with whom Sykes had collaborated on the earlier travel books. But the most gripping portrait is one of a Persian who sacrifices comforts and pleasures rather than betray the country (England) to which he is romantically devoted. This book was followed by a first novel, *Answer To Question 33*, in which the theme of betrayal is once again explored. The main character in the book is called to sit before a committee at the House of Commons to give evidence against an Italian woman who had been broadcasting anti-British propaganda from Moscow. Walter Allen, reviewing the novel in the *New Statesman*, remarked: "One has the sense of being in the company of a man at ease with life, an amateur of more than one art, who has seen many countries and enjoyed rich experiences."

Apart from a collection of short stories, *Character And Situation*, all about Englishmen in embarrassing situations abroad, and two slight novels during the 1950's, Sykes concentrated on nonfiction and increasingly on biography. *Two Studies In Virtue* contained a pair of extended biographical essays—one about Richard Sibthorp, a Victorian clergyman vacillating between Anglicanism and Roman Catholicism, and the other mainly about his father, Mark Sykes. Most of his later books were full-length biographies, beginning with *Orde Wingate* in 1959, a detailed and thoroughly researched treatment of a complex military man. The book's frankness unsettled family survivors and gave rise to heated debates in literary journals. *Nancy*, Sykes's biography of Nancy Astor, was written at the request of her literary executors. Claud Cockburn, in the *New Statesman*, commented, "It is by no means pejorative to say that Sykes's book is biased by affectionate admiration." The same type of comment was applicable to Sykes's biography of his friend Evelyn Waugh. Auberon Waugh, writing in *The Literary Review* about the biographies of his father, said: "The first, by his old crony Christopher Sykes, was spoiled by Sykes's failing powers of concentration, as well as by an unexpected element of professional jealousy which surfaces from time to time." However, although Sykes's obituarist in the London Times conceded that it "should not, perhaps, have been the official biography. It is more a memoir based upon intimate friendship," the piece continues: " . . . It is a book whose merits no younger writer could have matched."

PRINCIPAL WORKS: Wassmuss, 1936; Innocence and Design (with R. Byron), 1936; Stranger Wonders, 1937; High-Minded Murder, 1944; Four Studies in Loyalty, 1946; Answer to Question 33, 1948; Character and Situation, 1949; Two Studies in Virtue, 1953; A Song of a Shirt, 1953; Dates and Parties, 1955; Orde Wingate, 1959; Cross Roads to Israel, 1965; Troubled Loyalty: A Biography of Adam von Trott, 1968; Nancy, the Life of Lady Astor, 1972; Evelyn Waugh, 1975.

ABOUT: Who's Who 1986. *Periodicals*—Literary Review May 1996; New Statesman, June 5, 1948; October 6, 1972; New York Times August 16, 1936; Times (London) December 10, 1986.

**SYKES, GERALD** (1903–July 15, 1984), American novelist, playwright, and critic, was born in Peterborough. Ontario, but grew up in Covington, Kentucky. He was educated at the University of Cincinnati; later he studied at Columbia University and the Sorbonne. For a time he worked as a reporter for the *Kentucky Post*; by the 1930s he had moved to New York, where he joined the Alfred Stieglitz-Georgia O'Keeffe circle, and  wrote plays for the Group Theater. During World War II he served with the State Department and the Office of War Information. Throughout most of his career Sykes supported himself as a lecturer at Columbia University and the New School for Social Research, and as free-lance reviewer and critic for such publications as the *New York Times Book Review*, the *New Republic*, and *Harper's*.

Sykes published three novels in the 1950s; but thereafter turned to philosophy and social commentary. Both his fiction and his nonfiction were marked by their intellectuality, but his ideas often provoked strong disagreement.

His first book, *The Nice American*, concerned the existential plight of a young American colonel stationed in Algeria at the end of the Second World War. Although a *New Yorker* critic complained that "Mr. Sykes uses the English language as though he disliked it but were determined to contend with it," certain reviewers of the time admired the novel's intellectual ambitions—if nothing else. Frederic Morton wrote of it in the *New York Herald Tribune Book Review*, "This could have been a good story if only its execution were on a level with its aim. It is a novel of praiseworthy ideas and implausible people."

Sykes's second novel, *The Center of the Stage*, showed some advance in novelistic technique. A reviewer in *Time* magazine considered this story of a brilliant, middle-aged actress and the people surrounding her in a Long Island summer house "a quiet and thoughtful novel. . . . Sykes has an enviable gift for writing cultivated dialogue and intelligent reflection; his book, even in its limp spots, reveals the controlling presence of a grown-up mind."

Sykes's last novel was *The Children of Light*. This ambitious account of an American diplomat returning home to find his son immersed in a vicious campaign for elective office was "marred not only by its climatic ambiguity but also by minor inconsistencies and loose ends," wrote Granville Hicks in the *New York Times Book Review*. Hicks went on to say that Sykes was "one of our most intelligent and therefore one of our most interesting novelists, but his intelligence sometimes outruns either his talent or his patience. Here it is patience that seems to be lacking."

In 1962 Sykes published his first work of nonfiction, *The Hidden Remnant*, a critique of Freud,

Jung, Adler, and other psychoanalytic thinkers. His belief in a "hidden remnant" of superior beings who might achieve true self knowledge and thereby renovate the political and social order was not original, and did not sit well with reviewers. The ideas that he expounded in his other works of nonfiction were similarly controversial. For example, Melvin Maddocks took exception to Sykes's derogatory characterization of modern art in *The Perennial Avantgarde*, writing in the *Christian Science Monitor*, "Pollution of the arts is a difficult problem, to which 'Back to the cottage industry' is not the answer. . . . The nearest [Sykes] can come to a solution is to imply that maybe the artist should drop out of the overorganized, regimenting avantgarde just as he once dropped out of the rest of overorganized, regimenting society to found the avantgarde in the first place."

Sykes's last book, published in 1975, was *Foresights: Self-Evolution and Survival*, an extension of the arguments of *The Hidden Remnant*. He died in New York City, mourned by his friend Isaac Bashevis Singer (quoted in Sykes's obituary in the *New York Times*) as "a man of great taste in literature and an important critic and teacher."

PRINCIPAL WORKS: *Novels*—The Nice American, 1951; The Center of the Stage, 1952; The Children of Light, 1955. *Criticism and philosophy*—The Hidden Remnant, 1962; The Cool Millennium, 1967; The Perennial Avantgarde, 1971; Foresights: Self-Evolution and Survival, 1975. *As editor*—Alienation: The Cultural Climate of Our Time (2 vols.) 1964.

ABOUT: *Periodicals*—Christian Science Monitor January 28, 1971; Commonweal September 22, 1967; New York Herald Tribune Book Review March 4, 1951; New York Times July 16, 1984; New York Times Book Review February 20, 1955; New Yorker March 17, 1951; Time September 29, 1952.

**SYLVESTER, HARRY** (January 19, 1908–September 26, 1963), American novelist and short story writer, wrote: "The real landmarks in anyone's life lie within. A  man's birthplace and travels are meaningful only in that they may have helped shape and mark him. That I was born in Brooklyn, worked for newspapers and traveled and lived in many parts of the hemisphere seem less to me than that I was raised as a Roman Catholic.

"To begin an autobiographical note with a reference to religion may seem gauche but since the Catholic Church has been the central theme of almost all of my serious writing, I cannot write of myself as a writer without making clear my relation to that Church, past and present. I wrote three serious novels about the Church in the United States because I was emotionally and intellectually committed to it and felt it to be the highest and best authenticated 'Way.' A concern with a society operating within the framework of the Catholic Church and deeply affected by its precepts is not one common to writers in the United States. It is a

concern common to French writers and as much as I consciously patterned myself on anyone in the early days, I did so on Georges Bernanos.

"My first and third novels have been called anti-clerical, which should have surprised no one as they were intended to be anti-clerical. The second novel is more affirmative and represents a final venture into writing of religious mysticism. For years I considered myself to be a Catholic troubled by the corruption within the Church although not by its central ideas.

"In 1947 I was asked to deliver a lecture at a school in Chicago on 'Problems of the Catholic Writer.' I agreed to try to do so and in writing my lecture began a process that brought into consciousness doubts more serious than those engendered merely by an occasional androgynous cardinal. The lecture was well-received at this school sponsored by a liberal bishop. Only a few local protests were heard until some weeks later the lecture was published in the *Atlantic Monthly*. The many letters, the numerous angry, astonished and occasionally vicious replies in the Catholic press to what I had thought of only as a somewhat weary statement of problems with which I had lived and under whose pressures done my writing for fifteen years, forced me to consider the possibility that between myself and my variously excited critics, one of us was not a Catholic and that it might be me. Other letters, including some of the friendly ones, suggested that I was already out of the Church or on the way out.

"I discovered this to be true. Not everyone, like Paul, has the moment of his conversion or disconversion marked for him. I do not know exactly when I left the Catholic Church although I know that I am out of it permanently and irrevocably. For those interested in such details, I last 'attended Sacraments' in a church whose name I have forgotten in a suburb of Lima, Peru. The month was March, 1949, the disconversion intellectual. I cannot accept the Church's teaching on such basic matters as transubstantiation, the assumption of the Virgin, or the infallibility of the Pope. I do believe that great aboriginal truths lie at the roots of Christianity but that in its formative decades some dreadful error involving misinterpretation or expediency, like a mistake made early in a long algebraic equation, conditioned and invalidated all that followed. There is no other explanation for a church finding its way from the Sermon on the Mount to the four hundred thousand dead of the Inquisition.

"There might have been more books, better written, if there had not been an almost constant financial pressure requiring me to sell over the years about 150 short stories, most of which I would rather not have written, in order to raise my children and find occasional free months in which to accomplish the novels. Recently, I have returned to journalism as a more honorable and less debilitating way of supporting them.

"The sense of freedom and release which has steadily grown since leaving the Church is worth whatever I may have paid for it. I do not know the course of books I have yet to write for they will flow from different wells than those already written."

———

"Mr. Sylvester's first three novels present a comprehensive treatment of the Roman Catholic Church in the United States," Harry R. Warfel rather optimistically wrote in *American Novelists of Today*. "Strong elements of anti-clericalism mark his serious work, but his central and pervading theme has been that of growth, spiritual and intellectual, and the various ways and events by which he feels it is sometimes achieved." *Moon Gaffney*, Sylvester's best known novel, tells the story of a young Catholic whose political activities bring him into conflict with a political machine and with his church. A *Canadian Forum* review noted that "it took courage to write this book. If the writing seems self-conscious now and then, it is because Mr. Sylvester's technique doesn't quite reach the heights of his ambitious project."

Sylvester took his B.A. degree at the University of Notre Dame in 1930. He spent three years writing for the *New York Herald Tribune*, the *New York Post*, and the *Brooklyn Daily Eagle*, before turning to freelance work. He contributed short stories to magazines such as *Commonweal, Collier's, Cosmopolitan, Esquire*, and *Good Housekeeping*. From 1951 to 1971 he served as a writer and a spokesman for the United States Information Agency and was stationed in New York, Washington, and Mexico City. Half of the fourteen stories included in the 1948 *All Your Idols* use Mexico as a backdrop. A reviewer in the *Saturday Review of Literature* asserted that the stories showed Sylvester to be a "craftsman of considerable facility, certainly above the run-of-the-mill magazine writer. . . . But all too often there is something missing, something that technique alone cannot cover up, the lack of poignant verifiable truth, an emotion and discovery which last long after the story has been put aside."

Sylvester lived in Peru for a time. He set his last novel, *A Golden Girl*, in Lima.

PRINCIPAL WORKS: *Novels*—Big Football Man, 1933; Dearly Beloved, 1942; Dayspring, 1945; Moon Gaffney, 1947; A Golden Girl, 1950. *Short stories*—All Your Idols, 1948.

ABOUT: The autobiographical material quoted above was written for Twentieth Century Authors First Supplement, 1955. Hoehn, M. (ed.) Catholic Authors, 1948; Warfel, H. R. American Novelists of Today, 1951. *Periodicals*—Canadian Forum September 1947; Library Journal April 1, 1950; New York Times September 30, 1993; Saturday Review of Literature September 18, 1948.

## SYMONS, ALPHONSE JAMES ALBERT

(1900–August 26, 1941), English biographer and bibliographer, was the son of Morris Albert Symons and Minnie (Bull) Symons, Russian immigrants. While growing up in a London suburb, Symons's family endured financial difficulties and he became an apprentice to a fur dealer. After his apprenticeship, he worked for the First Edition Club of London as a secretary and director. There, he was also a bibliographer.

Symons never became a prolific, accomplished writer. However, he is remembered for his biography *The Quest for Corvo* and the invaluable encouragement and support he consistently gave to his younger brother and now well-regarded mystery writer and biographer, Julian Symons.

Between 1928 and 1934 Symons was a somewhat active writer. In 1933 he published a brief biography of the African explorer H. M. Stanley. The book was regarded as "well written" but "not very lively or vivid." Next came *The Quest for Corvo: An Experiment in Biography*. This book, about Frederick Rolfe, who called himself 'Baron Corvo,' departs from the restrictive boundaries of traditional biography by its account of Symons'  own process of gathering the necessary information—a procedure followed in more recent times by Ian Hamilton in his attempt to write a biography of J. D. Salinger. Thus *The Quest for Corvo* is a biography about not only an historical figure but also of the process of writing a biography.

*The Quest for Corvo* elicited a range of reactions. John Langdon-Davies, writing in *Books*, remarked that "the method of this biography with its emphasis on the sometimes not very interesting ways in which Mr. Symons got his knowledge, rather than on the knowledge itself, is unjustifiable." But Burton Rascoe, also reviewing for *Books*, stated that *The Quest for Corvo* is "an experiment in biographical writing and a distinctively successful one." *The Quest for Corvo* has remained in print and is universally regarded as a wholly original approach to biography.

In 1950, nine years after Symons's early death, Julian Symons published a biography of his brother entitled *Symons: His Life and Speculations*, which was reprinted in 1986.

PRINCIPAL WORKS: Emin, Governor of Equatoria, 1928; H. M. Stanley, 1933; The Quest for Corvo, 1934.

ABOUT: Symons, J. A.J.A. Symons: His Life and Speculations.

## SYMONS, ARTHUR (WILLIAM) (February

28, 1865–January 22, 1945), English poet, critic, and editor, was born at Milford Haven, Wales, the second child and only son of Mark Symons, a Wesleyan Methodist minister, and Lydia Pascoe. Both parents came from old Cornish families, and Symons always felt, especially in the company of his many Irish friends, that he was a full-blooded Celt. In the first twenty years of Arthur's life his  father was given charge of nine different circuits. Symons later wrote: "I have never known what it is to have a home, as most children know it; a home that has been warmed through and through by the same flesh. . . . If I have been a vagabond and have never been able to root myself in any one place in the world, it is because I have no early memories of any one sky or soil. It has freed me from many prejudices in giving me its own unresting kind of freedom."

Until he was sixteen Symons was educated in schools in Devonshire; he was even then an introspective, slightly morbid boy, determined to pursue a literary career, and the author of hundreds of mostly melancholy poems.

In 1884, at the age of nineteen, Symons met Richard Garnett of the British Museum, who introduced him to the eccentric scholar F. J. Furnivall, who gave him a job as overseer of the Bernard Quaritch reprints of the Shakespeare Quartos (this was scarcely a task of "editing" in the modern sense, but it encouraged Symons, who wrote confident prefaces). In 1886 he began a career as a literary critic, and his first book, *An Introduction to the Study of Browning*, appeared in that year.

Symons did not have to look back: his Browning study was reviewed very favorably by Walter Pater, doyen of aesthetes and "decadence," in the *Manchester Guardian*. Pater was the decisive influence upon Symons, who ever after tried to re-create, for the reader, the impressions made by whatever he had read or seen. He got to know Pater, and was introduced by him to many of the leading writers of the day. He published his first collection of poetry, *Days and Nights*, in 1889. He rapidly became what Thornton called a "trendsetter": he contributed to the *Yellow Book*, edited such magazines as the *Savoy* (which he produced with Aubrey Beardsley), and became a regular and much heeded contributor to all the leading literary reviews, including the *Athenaeum* and the *Fortnightly Review*. He went to France in 1889—and often thereafter—and there met the leading symbolist poets, including Mallarmé and Verlaine. Thus he became the leading British authority on the French symbolist movement. He had made himself fluent in French and Italian.

Symons also became friend to W. B. Yeats. The Rhymer's Club met with such as Ernest Rhys, Ernest Dowson, and John Davidson in attendance. Joseph Hone in his biography of Yeats wrote that "the talk owed its chief distinction to Symons, who knew Paris and its excellencies." He was, Hone continued, "the channel . . . between the French influences and English literature. It was through Symons that Yeats made his acquaintance with the literary decadentism of France, recognizable in much of the poetry of the Symbolists as an aspect of their reaction against positivism and the scientific movement to which the Rhymers drank 'confusion.'"

Later, in 1896, Yeats lived for some months in the chambers that, Hone related, "opened into those of Arthur Symons." Symons, as always, held the Patersque view that both art and life were but a "series of impressions," and this had discouraged Yeats; later, however, "Yeats discovered in Symons the sympathetic intelligence of a woman. . . . He was the first man with whom Yeats formed a real intimacy, and their thoughts flowed side by side for many years."

In 1906 Symons bought a beautiful twelfth-century cottage, Island Cottage, at Wittersham, Kent, where he spent the rest of his days. In 1907 Desmond MacCarthy paid him perhaps the most generous tribute he had yet received, in the *Albany Review*: he was, declared MacCarthy, "one of the subtlest critics now writing, here or abroad . . . remarkable for wide sensibilities, for connoisseurship in music and painting and acting, as well as in literature. . . . He can also transmit the emotions which a work of art has stirred in him, and he writes of these things like one possessed of the idea that the beauty which artists create and discover is as important as anything in the world."

In 1908, while walking on a street in Naples, Italy, Symons lost his reason completely. He was picked up by policemen, who maltreated him; it was some time before his wife could arrange for his hospitalization in a mental institution. He remained mentally ill for two more years, when at last, upon recovery from an attack of pneumonia, he found himself sane but shattered in mind and body. In Symons's account of the affair in his *Confessions: A Study in Pathology* (1930), he wrote that he had experienced the "fatal initiation of madness."

Symons had been exceedingly active in those years just preceding his tragic collapse: he wrote plays and had them performed, he published books about his travels, he edited anthologies (some of them still invaluable), he edited plays by the Jacobean dramatists for the Mermaid series—and he wrote poetry and did numerous translations. The pressure of work, which included much literary journalism, must have contributed to the severity of his illness. He had experienced fits of amnesia before this, but nothing as intense.

After his recovery in 1910 he was unable to develop his ideas. His last published book was, significantly, a study of Pater (1932). He wrote sporadically in the last dozen years of his life, but published nothing more. He more or less cut himself off from the society of his literary friends from the time of his illness. A projected edition of his collected works, begun in 1924, reached its ninth volume, but then petered out.

Symons will be remembered for his influence on other writers. His *The Symbolist Movement in Literature* (1898) is a key work, and the one that led T. S. Eliot to discover Laforgue and the other French symbolists. The best of his poetry is largely unknown except for the much anthologized "White Heliotrope"). And there are a handful of *fin de siècle* poems—besides "White Heliotrope"—that are distinguished. His technique is sure and elegant. The first stanza of his "Prologue," from the second edition of his *London Nights* (1897), serves as a fitting epitaph: "My life is like a music-hall. / Where, in the impotence of rage. / Chained by enchantment to my stall, / I see myself on the stage, / Dance to amuse a music-hall." He was all his life, wrote Lhombréaud, "an artist, contemptuous of success, perceptive, and scrupulous. His work was constructed on his own exacting faith in the eternal value of art. . . . He wrote an exquisite sensitive prose which perfectly conveyed his personal judgments on an eclectic field of art."

PRINCIPAL WORKS: Collections—Poems, 2 vols., 1902; Collected Works, 9 vols. (incomplete; includes his tragedies and most of his poems) 1924. Critical and biographical studies—An Introduction to the Study of Browning, 1886; Studies in Two Literatures, 1897; Aubrey Beardsley, 1898; The Symbolist Movement in Literature, 1899; Plays, Acting and Music, 1903; Studies in Prose and Verse, 1904; Studies in Seven Arts, 1906; Great Acting in English, 1907; William Blake, 1907; The Romantic Movement in English Poetry, 1909; Dante Gabriel Rossetti, 1910; Figures of Several Centuries, 1916; Studies in the Elizabethan Drama, 1920; Charles Baudelaire, 1920; Dramatis Personae, 1923; The Café Royal and Other Essays, 1924; Notes on Joseph Conrad with Some Unpublished Letters, 1925; Studies on Modern Painters, 1925; Eleanora Duse, 1926; A Study of Thomas Hardy, 1926; From Toulouse Lautrec to Rodin with Some Personal Impressions, 1929; Studies in Strange Souls, 1929; A Study of Oscar Wilde, 1930; A Study of Walter Pater, 1932. Poetry—Days and Nights, 1889; Silhouettes, 1892; London Nights, 1895 (augmented 1897); Amoris Victima, 1897; Images of Good and Evil, 1899; The Loom of Dreams, 1901; Poems, 1902; Lyrics, 1903; A Book of Twenty Songs, 1905; The Fool of the World, 1906; On Craig Dhu, 1909; Wanderer's Song, 1909; Knave of Hearts, Poems 1894–1909, 1913; Songs for a Medium Voice, 1919; Lesbia, 1920; Love's Cruelty, 1923; Jezebel Mort, 1931. Belles lettres and memoirs—Parisian Nights, 1926; Mes Souvenirs, 1929; Confession: A Study in Pathology, 1930. Travel—Cities, 1903; Cities of Italy, 1907; London: A Book of Aspects, 1908; Cities and Sea-coasts and Islands, 1918; Wanderings, 1931. Sketches—Spiritual Adventures, 1905; Colour Studies in Paris, 1918. Drama—Tragedies, 1916; Tristan and Iseult, 1917; The Toy Cart, 1919. Letters—Beckson, K. (ed.) Selected Letters, 1989.

ABOUT: Beckson, K. (ed.) Memoirs of Arthur Symons: Life and Art in the 1890s, 1977, Arthur Symons: A Life, 1987; Denson, A. (ed.) Letters from Æ, 1961; Dictionary of National Biography, 1941–1950, 1959; Hone, J. W. B. Yeats, 1943; Lhombréaud, R. Arthur Symons: His Life and Letters, 1962, Arthur Symons: A Critical Biography, 1963; Munro, J. M. Arthur Symons, 1969; Thornton (ed.), R.K.R. Poetry of the Nineties, 1970; Welby, T. E. Arthur Symons: A Critical Study, 1925. Periodicals—Albany Review May 1907; Journal of Aesthetics June 1951; Review of English Studies May 1968; Thought 23 1948; Times (London) January 26, 1945; Times Literary Supplement February 3, 1945.

## SYMONS, JULIAN (May 30, 1912–November 19, 1994), British crime writer, biographer, social historian, essayist, radio playwright, literary critic, and poet, was born in

London, into a family of Russian-born immigrants. His Jewish father was Morris Albert Symons, an auctioneer, his gentile mother the former Minnie Bull. His elder brother was A.J.M. Symons, bibliophile and author of the famous The Quest for Corvo. Julian, who suffered from so severe a stammer that he was sent to a school for backward children, owed much to A.J.M.'s encouragement, and later wrote a biography of him. He left school at fourteen to go to work as a shorthand typist in an office. Later he became a secretary in an engineering firm.

In 1937 Symons, having educated himself impressively in all aspects of literature, decided to found and edit a poetry magazine, Twentieth Century Verse. He managed to keep the little magazine going until the outbreak of war: the final number was the eighteenth. It was not as well known or as widely circulated as its rival, Geoffrey Grigson's New Verse, but it did champion the cause of the then unpopular P. Wyndham Lewis (to whom it devoted a double number), and it introduced a number of until then unread American poets to Great Britain; these included Theodore Roethke, John Berryman, Allen Tate, and Wallace Stevens. Symons himself produced a volume so deeply influenced by his lifelong idol, W. H. Auden, that it was hard to see the real author. This, too, applied to his next collection, The Second Man. Thereafter Symons virtually gave poetry up until his old age, when he produced graceful minor poems, including some moving ones in memory of his daughter Sarah Louise, who had died tragically young.

In 1942 Symons entered the Royal Armoured Corps; after a troubled time he was invalided out (1944), and went into advertising. He had in 1941 married the former Kathleen Clark, by whom he had two children, Sarah, and a son, Marcus (Mark). From 1947 he was able to live by his prolific pen. Although his first three crime stories did quite well, he was never satisfied with them. His real beginning, as he claimed and as most critics agree, was with The Thirty-First of February, possibly the finest of all his crime novels. This is a psychological study of an advertising man who is driven by the police into insanity by their harassment of him over his wife's possible murder, of which he is not guilty. What the Times Literary Supplement reviewer (1950) wrote about The Thirty-First of February perhaps best sums up both Symons's chief virtues and faults as a purveyor of high-class entertainment for intelligent readers: "The solution is. . . . both improbable and unsatisfactory," wrote the reviewer, "yet the author's compelling narrative gift cannot be denied; and this book, in spite of its curious lapses from credibility, is a definite step towards the evolution of the psychological mystery without bloodshed, at which Mr. Symons is obviously aiming."

Besides this one, the most highly regarded of his twenty-nine crime novels include The Colour of Murder, The Progress of a Crime, The End of Solomon Grundy—and perhaps some of the books he wrote set in Victorian times. Symons's popular biographies and social histories, while engagingly written, do not go into their subjects deeply enough to survive as more than lively, intelligent but essentially minor contributions. The End of Solomon Grundy, set in suburbia with the unpleasant Grundy a suspect in the murder of a playgirl, is again mainly satirical: the characters, wrote the reviewer in the Times Literary Supplement (1964), squirm "under his pen. . . . This is a good book, yet properly orthodox in its crime writing, nicely observed in its manners." Yet in a sense it was just this admirable "orthodoxy" that stymied Symons in his attempt to become a novelist. Valentine Cunningham, devoting a Times Literary Supplement article to Symons at eighty, asked why "given his unashamed espousal of unfashionable elitist critical views" he should have had a "career devoted in generous measure to crime fiction?" Cunningham answers thus: "Any answer must . . . look to the Thirties. . . . Trying to make money through the detective and crime genres that were acknowledged to be inferior to the higher and less popular modes was a common resort of serious 1930s writers, in particular, leftists such as Cecil Day Lewis "Nicholas Blake", G.D.H. Cole . . . Graham Greene. . . . Certainly, by writing in this *engagé* way, Symons has made his crime novels superior to the run of the Christie-Sayers mill."

Symons' three novels set in the Victorian or Edwardian era were *The Blackheath Poisonings, Sweet Adelaide*, and *The Detling Secret*. His own favorite was the first of these, which was televised not long before his death of cancer. Like its two companions, it was deservedly well received by viewers of crime fiction. It remains to be said that, among crime writers, Symons was often the firm favorite of those whose reading was not confined to the genre. He reached eminence in this field, first as Chairman of the Crime Writers Association (1958–1959), and then as President of the Detectives Club. *The Colour of Murder* received the Crime Writers Associations Crossed Herrings Award for the best crime story of its year (1957), and *The Progress of a Crime* received the Edgar Allan Poe Award (1961).

Symons wrote some excellent popular biographies—notably those of his brother and of the outrageous Horatio Bottomley—and social histories, such as a vivid one about the British General Strike. His most sheerly valuable book, for which he did more research than he could usually manage (one year in the British Museum Library trawling through obscure detective stories), was *Mortal Consequences* (1972), which was throughly revised in 1985. A history of the detective story through to its modern counterpart, the crime novel, it has high status as a guide, and has recommended hitherto unknown crime books to many readers. His *Critical Occasions* is an impressive and readable collection of essays on figures as diverse as Robert Graves, Laura Riding, Wyndham Lewis, and James Branch Cabell. Never critically profound, it compensates for by its lack of depth by its good sense, fairness, and what Cunningham well calls its "ungrudging affection for literary merit wherever it crops up."

PRINCIPAL WORKS: *Omnibus*—The Julian Symons Crime Omnibus (The Thirty-First of February, The Progress of a Crime, and The End of Solomon Grundy), 1966. *Crime novels*—The Inmaterial Murder Case, 1945; A Man Called Jones, 1947; Bland Beginning, 1949; The Thirty-First of February, 1950; The Broken Penny, 1952; The Narrowing Circle, 1954; The Paper Chase, 1956 (in U.S.: Bogues Fortune); The Colour of Murder, 1957; The Gigantic Shadow, 1958 (in U.S.: The Pipe Dream); The Progress of a Crime, 1960; The Killing of Francie Lake, 1962 (in U.S.: The Plain Man); The End of Solomon Grundy, 1964; The Belting Inheritance, 1965; The Man Who Killed Himself, 1967; The Man Whose Dreams Came True, 1968; The Man Who Lost His Wife, 1970; The Players and the Game, 1972; The Plot Against Roger Rider, 1973; A Three-Pipe Problem, 1975; The Blackheath Poisonings: A Victorian Murder Mystery, 1978; Sweet Adelaide: A Victorian Puzzle Solved, 1980; The Detling Murders, 1982; (in U.S.: The De-tling Secret); The Name of Annabel Lee, 1983; The Criminal Comedy of the Contented Couple, 1985 (in U.S.: A Criminal Comedy); The Kentish Manor Murders, 1988; Death's Darkest Face, 1991; Something Like a Love Affair, 1994; Playing Happy Families, 1995. *Short stories*—Francis Quarles Investigates, 1965; The Tigers of Subtopia, 1982. *Verse*—Confusions About X, 1939; The Second Man, 1943; A Reflection on Auden, 1973; The Object of an Affair, 1974; Seven Poems for Sarah, 1979. *Biography*—A.J.A Symons: His Life and Speculations, 1950; Charles Dickens, 1951; Thomas Carlyle, 1952; Horatio Bottomley, 1955; The Tell Tale Heart: The Life and Works of Edgar Allan Poe, 1978; Portrait of an Artist: Conan Doyle, 1980; Dashiell Hammett, 1985. *Social history, history, and social commentary*—The General Strike: A Historical Portrait, 1957; The Thirties: A Dream Resolved, 1960, rev. ed. 1975; Bullers Campaign, 1963; England's Pride: The Story of the Gordon Relief Expedition, 1965; Notes From Another Country, 1972. *On crime*—A Reasonable Doubt: Some Criminal Cases Re-examined, 1960; Crime and Detection: An Illustrated History from 1940, 1966 (in U.S.: A Pictorial History of Crime); Mortal Consequences: A History—From the Detective Story to the Crime Novel, 1972, (rev. as Bloody Murder, 1985); Great Detectives: Seven Original Detectives, 1981; Crime and Detection Quiz, 1983. *Literary criticism*—Critical Occasions 1966, (essays); Critical Observations, 1981; Makers of the News: The Revolution of Literature, 1987. *As editor*—An Anthology of War Poetry, 1942; Selected Writings of Samuel Johnson, 1949; Selected Works of Thomas Carlyle, 1956; Verdict of Thirteen: A Detection Club Anthology, 1979; The Essential Wyndham Lewis: An Introduction to His Work, 1989.

ABOUT: Contemporary Authors Autobiography Series vol. 3, 1986; Dictionary of Literary Biography, vol. 87: British Mystery and Thriller Writers since 1940, 1989; Scarfe, F. Auden and After, 1942. *Periodicals*—Armchair Detective January 1979; New Republic August 26, 1978; September 2, 1978; Manchester Guardian July 5, 1957; New Statesman August 3, 1957; December 23, 1966; October 20, 1978; New York Herald Tribune September 25, 1960; New York Times October 23, 1949; November 9, 1952; November 6, 1987; November 23, 1994; Publishers Weekly July 2, 1982; Time, February 24, 1986; Times (London) February 14, 1981; May 13, 1982; September 22, 1983; November 22, 1994; Times Literary Supplement August 4, 1950; September 24, 1964; April 8, 1965; February 1, 1975; March 17, 1989.

**SYNGE, (EDMUND) JOHN MILLINGTON** (April 16, 1871–March 24, 1909), Irish dramatist, poet and descriptive writer, was born in Rathfarnham, now a Dublin suburb, the youngest of the five children of John Hatch Synge, a barrister, and Kathleen Traill, the daughter of a Protestant clergyman. Synge is considered modern Ireland's first great playwright.

Sickly from birth, he was reared by his mother in the strict evangelical tradition. His father had died when he was only a year old, and she had been obliged to move to Rathgar, also near Dublin and also now a suburb. To her great sorrow, Synge early announced that he was not a nonconformist. It had been his reading of Darwin at fourteen that led him away from the family pietism. He entered Trinity College, Dublin, at the age of seventeen, and first studied natural science there. Then he became interested in music, and began to study it.

His studies at the university were so perfunctory

that he was only able to gain a pass—then called a "gentleman's degree"—when he left in 1892. However, he fared better at the Royal Irish Academy of Music, at which he had enrolled in 1889, and he gained scholarships in both harmony and counterpoint. In 1893 a member of his family, a cousin to his mother, Mary Synge, offered to take him to Coblenz, Germany, to carry on with his musical studies. In January 1894 he went on from there to Wurzburg, where he studied the violin, the piano, and composition. By then he had started to write poetry and articles for magazines. By June 1894, when he returned to Dublin, he seemed set on a literary rather than a musical career. He later explained his state of mind at the time: "I wanted to be at once Shakespeare, Beethoven and Darwin; my ambition was boundless and amounted to a real torture in my life." At that time he began in earnest to prepare himself for the role of writer.

After applying himself to the study of Hebrew and Irish antiquities (and winning prizes for both), starting a play in the German language, and writing a long poem, he settled in Paris in 1895. The next seven years he spent between there and his mother's house in Ireland, conducting an unhappy love affair, and making important Irish contacts. The vital one was with W. B. Yeats, whom he met in December 1896. Eighteen months later he took Yeats's advice, which was to abandon his decadent pursuits and to go to the Aran islands to seek authentic experience. "Live there as if you were one of the people themselves," Yeats suggested; "express a life that has never found expression." And his work, which had been artificial and immature, suddenly flowered into maturity. By 1901, he had completed his book *The Aran Islands*, installments of which appeared in the *New Ireland Review*, although the whole book was not published until 1907. Synge had less than a decade left. But in it he wrote the plays upon which his enormous reputation now rests: *The Riders to the Sea* (1902), *In the Shadow of the Glen* (1902), *The Well of the Saints* (1905), and then his masterpiece *The Playboy of the Western World* (1907). He had not put the final touches to *Deirdre of the Sorrows* before he died, although it was performed in 1910. *Riders to the Sea*, arguably the best one-act play ever written, was described as "the most significant play of the last two hundred years" by George Moore, a critic not much given to praise.

*The Playboy of the Western World*, essentially a tragicomedy, dramatizes what Synge, now free of fin de siècle affectations, felt about the tragic life of the Aran islanders: "the mood of beings who feel their isolation in the face of a universe that wars on them with winds and seas." It depicts the loss to a woman of her sons by drowning; but the genius is in the elegiac language, for Synge was a poet above all. The chief character is a liar, Christy Mahon, who boasts of killing his father. The father turns up and beats his deceitful son. Interrupted by protesters who thought the play an "insult to Irishmen," its first performance could not be completed. It may now clearly be seen, however, that all Synge did, with his miraculous use of folk language, was to

"depict the follies of mankind." Synge himself simply said, "We shall have to establish a society for the preservation of Irish humor."

Denis Johnston wrote that Synge "had heard all the words he uses" in *Playboy*, "but not necessarily in the same order"—and he quoted Synge's own famous comment: "In a good play every speech should be as fully flavored as a nut or an apple . . . Those of us who wish to write, start (in Ireland) with a chance that is not given to writers in places where the spring time of local life has been forgotten, and the harvest is a memory only, and the straw has been turned into bricks."

Synge, although he had a strong constitution, was gravely ill in his last years. He suffered from asthma, and also from Hodgkins' disease, which eventually killed him. But he gained comfort from the girl who had played the part of Pegeen in his greatest play, Maire O'Neill, and he was able to write good-humoredly:

> I've thirty months, and that's my pride,
> Before my age's a double score,
> Though many lively men have died
> At twenty-nine or little more.

PRINCIPAL WORKS: *Drama*—When the Moon Has Set, unpublished, 1901; Riders to the Sea, 1903; In the Shadow of the Glen, 1904; The Well of the Saints, 1905; The Playboy of the Western World, 1907; The Tinker's Wedding, 1908; Deirdre of the Sorrows, 1910. *Poetry*—Poems and Translations, 1909. *Nonfiction*—The Aran Islands, 1907. *Collections*—Works of John Millington Synge, 4 vols., 1910; Plays by John Millington Synge, 1932; Collected Works, 4 vols., 1962–68. *Letters*—Letters to Molly: John Millington Synge to Maire O'Neill, 1971; Some Letters of John Millington Synge to Lady Gregory and W. B. Yeats, 1971.

ABOUT: Bushrui, S. B. Sunshine and the Moon's Delight: A Centenary Tribute to John Millington Synge, 1972; Greene, D. H. and Stephens, E. M. J. M. Synge 1871–1909, 1959; Gregory, I. A. Our Irish Theatre, 1913; Harmon, M. (ed.) J. M. Synge Centenary Papers, 1971; Howarth, H. The Irish Writers 1880–1940, 1958; Johnston, D. John Millington Synge, 1965; Kilroy, J. The Playboy Riots, 1971; Price, A. Synge and Anglo-Irish Drama, 1961; Saddlemeyer, A. J. M. Synge and Modern Irish Drama, 1968; Skelton, R. J. M. Synge and His World, 1971; The Writings of J. M. Synge, 1971; Yeats, W. B. Autobiographies, 1955.

**SZCZUCKA, ZOFIA KOSSAK-.** See **KOSSAK-SZCZUCKA, ZOFIA**

**TABORI, GEORGE** (May 24, 1914–   ), Hungarian-British novelist, playwright, screenwriter, and theatrical director, was born in Budapest, Hungary, the son of Kornel Tabori, a well-known newspaper reporter and writer on the occult (he died in Auschwitz), and his wife, the former Elsa Ziffer. He received his education from Zrinyl Gymnasium. His Jewish parents, wishing him to avoid the journalistic or literary professions, encouraged him to go into the hotel business. He did his apprenticeship in this trade at the famous Hotel Adlon, in Berlin, where he was, successively, cleaner, assistant cook, and waiter. He then graduated to "captain" at a smaller hotel and cafe, a popular meeting-place for artists and intellectuals, on the Kurfürstendamm. But the advent of the Nazis forced Tabori's return to Budapest, where he worked as desk clerk at the Ritz. He then took a job with a travel agency conducting deluxe tours around Europe. In 1935, wishing to devote himself to writing, he asked his father to find him a place on a magazine, which the latter reluctantly did.

Two years later, foreseeing the storm clouds ahead, Tabori repaired to England. He perfected his grasp of the language, which he had already learned, and adopted it as the one in which he would write. He pointed out to incredulous enquirers that this was, in one important sense at least, an advantage: "You don't write in clichés, because you don't know them."

Tabori worked as a journalist in London and, on the outbreak of World War II, joined the staff of a Hungarian newspaper operating from the British capital. From 1941 until 1943 he was in the British Army, given the rank of lieutenant as a BBC wartime broadcaster from Cairo and from various cities in Palestine.

Throughout the war Tabori was working on a novel, which appeared as *Beneath the Stone* (in England as *Beneath the Stone the Scorpion*) in 1945. Constructed like a play, and tersely written, it is set in the Balkans during World War II and deals with a German major, a captured English parachutist, and a Gestapo man who wants to kill the prisoner. The accomplished thriller-writer and poet Kenneth Fearing, discussing the novel in the *New York Times* (1945), commented that the book was "one of the most moving, convincing, poignant between-the-lines and in-back-of-the-line novels to come out of the war." Orville Prescott wrote in the *Yale Review* that, while "Mr. Tabori has nothing very new to say" he said it "with such bravura, such subtle perception, and such dramatic power that the book is engrossing."

Tabori's next novel, *Companions of the Left Hand*, was published in the following year. Hugh Ianson Fausset, in the *Manchester Guardian* wrote that Tabori's writing was distinguished by "dramatic suspense" and a "Latin clarity." But this ironic tale of a man who tries to remain aloof from politics, and achieves the status of a left-wing political martyr, did not quite live up to the promise offered by its predecessor.

There were four more novels after this. One of them, *The Journey*, set in Budapest in 1956, served as the basis of the screenplay for the film of that title made by Anatole Litvak in 1959. The most arresting was perhaps *The Caravan Passes* (1951), the story of the inhabitants of an unnamed Eastern port rising against their colonial oppressors. The main character, Vargas, is—like the hero in *Companions of the Left Hand*—a man trying to evade his responsibilities; and, once again, he causes disaster. "A rich and violent book," wrote Vance Bourjaily in the *Saturday Review of Literature*, "a book of trenchant ideas . . . [Tabori] has the indispensable gift which makes a novelist good: everyone on

whom his writing touches, be it only for a paragraph, comes to life."

After this, and his 1954 marriage to the Swedish actress Viveca Lindfors, Tabori, began to concentrate on filmwriting and theater. His first play, *Flight into Egypt*, about a Hungarian family on their way to America who decided to return to help rebuild their country, produced on Broadway in 1952, attracted favorable notices.

Tabori learned much about the theater by directing a number of plays, most of which he had a hand in himself. He adapted Strindberg's *Miss Julie* for the Phoenix Theatre (New York) in 1956, and Brecht's *The Guns of Carrar* for the Theatre de Lys (New York) in 1968; his adapted version of Brecht's *The Resistible Rise of Arturo Ui* played successfully on Broadway (1963) and in the West End of London (1972); and his adaptation of Max Frisch's *Andorra* was produced on Broadway in 1963. He also directed a version of Euripides' *Trojan Women* in Bremen in 1976. His own most notable original play, *The Cannibals*, was produced Off Broadway at the American Place Theatre in 1967, with him as director. This is a tragi-farcical account of prisoners in a Nazi concentration camp.

Tabori also had a distinguished career in films. Alfred Hitchcock chose him (and William Archibald) to write the screenplay for *I Confess* (1953), which featured Montgomery Clift as a priest who receives a confession of murder and who is then suspected as the murderer: it is generally regarded as "lesser Hitchcock," but has its adherents. Tabori's unpublished play "The Prince" was turned by him into a script for John Boorman's *Leo the Last* (1970), about a decayed prince who becomes involved with the denizens of his block. The script for *Secret Ceremony* was also Tabori's.

Robert Graves, Tabori's friend of the late 1940s, believed that a potentially major novelist might have been lost to the interest of first-rate and intelligent entertainment. If Tabori failed to ascend to the top flights of the theater, this may well have been because his message was such a bleak one.

PRINCIPAL WORKS: *Novels*—Beneath the Stone, 1945 (in U.K.: Beneath the Stone the Scorpion); Companions of the Left Hand, 1946; Original Sin, 1947; The Caravan Passes, 1951; The Journey: A Confession, 1958; The Good One, 1960. *Drama*—Flight Into Egypt, 1953; The Emperor's Clothes, 1953; The Cannibals, 1973.

ABOUT: Frick, J. W. and Vallillo, S. M. (eds.) Theatrical Directors, 1994; Vinson, J. (ed.) Contemporary Dramatists, Third Edition, 1982. *Periodicals*—Manchester Guardian March 29, 1946; New York Times August 26, 1945; June 30 1946; New York Times Magazine March 9, 1952; Saturday Review of Literature March 17, 1951; Yale Review Autumn 1945.

**TAGGARD, GENEVIEVE** (November 28, 1894–November 8, 1948), American poet and biographer, wrote: "I was born on an apple farm in Waitsburg, Washington. My parents were schoolteachers, Alta Gale (Arnold) Taggard and James Nelson Taggard. Both my grandfathers fought for the Union under Grant. Both were farmers, Scotch-Irish on one side, Huguenot French and Scotch on the other. I was raised on stories of the Ozarks and Lincoln. When I was two years old my parents went to the Hawaiian Islands to teach in the public schools. At first we lived on a sugar plantation; then my father was given a school (Kalihi-waena) near

Honolulu. I grew up with and knew intimately the Hawaiian, Chinese, Portuguese, and Japanese children who were the pupils in the school my parents were building. Outside the family I knew almost no white people until I was sent to Punahou School, a private school founded by the first missionaries. When my father's health failed we returned twice to Waitsburg, but found the adjustment to the small town too difficult for all of us.

"My parents were devoted Disciples of the Christian Church, and they started a mission in our community. The Bible and hymns were my chief background. I remember telling my mother that I disliked poetry because it was insincere, and about this time I became a bookworm, but read only prose.

"When I was about thirteen I began to write imitations of a few favorite poets, which were very bad, awkward, and meaningless. Keats was my first big passion; I began to see what poetry does when I read him. His luxury suited the Island radiance. I did not love any stern or bare speech for many years. The Greek myths were discouraged when I was little because they were pagan; in school they were too school-bookish my taste. I was never excited by Greek culture until I saw the Black Sea in 1936. I think I understand and like Asia and the dark peoples better than Europe. The Bible was always a great Oriental story book for me.

"In 1914 some friends gave me a small scholarship and my family bought tickets for San Francisco. We had a pretty desperate time of it for the next five years. My father was too ill to do much; my mother ran a boarding-house for students at the University of California and I earned what I could while going to college. Finally I became editor of the *Occident*, the college literary magazine, which paid a small salary. But it took five years.

"At the end of college I called myself a Socialist in a rather vague way. Since then I have always been to the left of center. In those days Frank Norris and Jack London were still heard of as friends of friends. The great city of San Francisco taught me a good deal that I needed to know.

"My first published poem was in *Harper's* magazine. When I came to New York in 1920 I worked in the publishing house of B. W. Huebsch, who had just started the *Freeman*. Van Wyck Brooks very kindly gave me a few books of poetry to review. That year I joined a group of young writers to get out a little poetry magazine called the *Measure*. I married Robert Wolf and in 1921 my daughter was born.

"Since 1921 I have published thirteen books

(some of them anthologies); written many stories, articles, and book reviews. I taught literature at Mt. Holyoke College before I was awarded a Guggenheim Fellowship in 1931; returned to the opening of the new Bennington (Vermont) College, and since 1934 have taught at Sarah Lawrence College in Bronxville, New York. In 1934 I was divorced and in 1935 married Kenneth Durant. In the summer we live on a boat, going up the Hudson each summer to Lake Champlain. I have learned to fish.

"In 1931 on a Guggenheim Fellowship my daughter and sister and I lived in Capri and Mallorca. Part of *The Life and Mind of Emily Dickinson* was written in southern France. I have lived in Spain and England and for one long summer in the Soviet Union on the Black Sea, and later in Tiflis (now Tiblisi), where I fell in love with that city.

"When I face the fact that my poetry is not very much read in my own country I console myself by the fact that my work has been translated into many foreign languages. My poems have also been set to music by William Schuman, Aaron Copland, Roy Harris, and Henry Leland Clarke. In 1939 a song set by Mr. Schuman was sung at Carnegie Hall and in stadium concerts by a chorus of two hundred school children.

"I am a member of the Teacher's Union, and an elected member of the Executive Council of the League of American Writers. I helped start the League School for young writers, which has been a success. I have given several readings from the works of Whitman, Emily Dickinson, and Shakespeare over the radio. I am now writing a prose book about the life of my parents in the islands. It will be very slow in the writing.

"Being a teacher, a poet, and a student, I am not very much impressed by the present standards that measure our culture. To speak bluntly I think most of the intellectuals are provincial. I think I can foresee an American literature and especially an American poetry that make most of what we have now look pretty stuffy. Even those who are called our best critics are ignorant of two things: excellence in world literature, and the life and talents of the American people."

———

Genevieve Taggard's earliest work showed evidence of an ability to introduce political consciousness into poetry without undermining its literary value. Barbara Antonina Clarke Mossberg said that Taggard's first collection, *For Eager Lovers* (1922), "established her unique idiom as a metaphysical Marxist, a lyric intellectual who incorporates Hawaiian exotica into poems about revolution and a woman's experience in love. Even such Marxist visions of doomed decadence as 'Twentieth Century Slave-Gang' eschew rhetoric and combine modern directness ('the ants are hurried') with extraordinary images: 'oaks bend knotted knees in labor, a pond is wrinkled with velvet oil, wasps carry spider-spoil to where crude honey hangs in mud." Mossberg adds that, "While this volume commemorates a first year of marriage, and Taggard occasionally speaks as an 'eager lover,' she insists on the necessary independence—even defiance—of soul, voice, whole being, especially in the potentially compromising love relationship. Her resolute quest for freedom (personal, artistic, social, and political) is the dominant theme of Taggard's poetry; here the tone is 'caged arrogance' as the voice celebrates its emancipation."

Taggard was also one of the principal biographers of Emily Dickinson at a time when the poet from Amherst was beginning to be taken seriously as an American writer. When her *The Life and Mind of Emily Dickinson* was published in 1930, Percy Hutchison wrote in *The New York Times Book Review* that it was " . . . a book distinguished both for its penetration and its sympathy . . . It is an indispensable completion of the books that have gone before. . . . " Other reviewers acknowledged how Taggard had recognized the important role of Dickinson's domineering father in her life and writing.

Taggard's papers are collected variously at the Dartmouth College Library, the New York Public Library, and the Lockwood Memorial Library, Buffalo, New York.

PRINCIPAL WORKS: *Poetry*—For Eager Lovers, 1922; Hawaiian Hilltop, 1923: Words for the Chisel, 1926; Traveling Standing Still, 1928; Remembering Vaughn in New England, 1933; Not Mine to Finish, 1934; Calling Western Union, 1936; Collected Poems: 1918–1938, 1938; Long View, 1942; Falcon, 1942; A Part of Vermont, 1945; Slow Music, 1946; Origin: Hawaii, 1947; Collected Poems, Charles Erskine Scott Wood (co-editor) 1949. *Biography*—The Life and Mind of Emily Dickinson, 1930.

ABOUT: The autobiographical material quoted above was written for Twentieth Cenutry Authors, 1942. Aaron, D. Writers on the Left, 1961; Lins, K. L. An Interpretive Study of Selected Poetry by Genevieve Taggard, 1956; Mossberg, B. A. and Mossberg, C. L. Genevieve Taggard. *Periodicals*—Bennington College Alumnae Quarterly, 1949; Nation, December 11, 1948; New York Times Book Review; New York World; Sarah Lawrence Alumnae Magazine Fall 1948; Saturday Review of Literature December 14, 1946; November 20, 1948.

## TAGORE, RABINDRANATH (May 6 or 7 1861–August 7, 1941) Indian poet, songwriter, playwright, short story writer, philosopher, musician and essayist, winner of the Nobel Prize for literature, has been described as one of the architects of modern India.

He was born in Calcutta into a wealthy Brahmin family, the fourteenth of fifteen children. His father was Maharishi Debendranath Tagore, a reli-gious reformer and scholar, his mother Sarada Devi. His grandfather, Dwarkanath Tagore, was known as Prince Dwarkanath, having established a huge financial empire for himself, and used much of his money funding public projects, such as the Calcutta Medical College. Rabindranath Tagore's father was a more spiritual and philosophical man than his grandfather, and was described by Rabindranath as "one of the deepest

influences on my life." It was with his father that he first visited the Himalayas, which were to play a significant role in the young boy's spiritual development.

Tagore's mother died of tuberculosis when he was thirteen. He was largely educated by tutors at home, having rebelled against school, which he found intolerable. Gifted from an early age, he started writing poetry as a boy, and read widely, including the English classics. In 1879, at the age of seventeen, he went to University College, London, to study law, but spent only a year there, returning to India without a degree. At this point he took up writing. In 1883, when he was twenty-three, he married the ten-year-old Mrinalini Devi Raichaudhuri, with whom he was to have two sons and three daughters. In 1890 he was put in charge of the family estate at Shelaidaha on the Ganges in East Bengal, where he drew inspiration for his work from the rural life of the Bengali peasantry. His time here was to prove "the most productive period of my literary life." Work from this time, which is among his most romantic and lush, includes several poetry collections, such as *Sonar Tari* (The golden boat). From this period came his rather misleading epitaph "The Bengal Shelley."

In 1901 he moved to family land at Santiniketan, near Calcutta, where he founded a school, Visva-Bharati, which became a university in 1921. This was one of Tagore's dearest projects, to which he gave his Nobel Prize money and all earnings from his lectures. He had a strong social conscience, and was instrumental in founding several institutions, including a weaving school and an agricultural cooperative bank.

A hugely prolific writer, whose work spans almost every genre, Tagore was to prove an immense influence on the growth of Bengali literature, and his work—especially his songs—quickly became an integral part of Bengali culture. He was pleased to comment, late in his life, that his songs were so famous that he himself had become invisible. His roots in his native country, however, have generally been ignored by Western critics.

Tagore's meteoric—if short-lived—success in the West happened largely by chance. Following the death of his wife in 1902, he wrote a somber collection of devotional songs. The following year, 1903, one of his daughters died, then his father and another son in 1905 and 1907. Although, according to his elder son, Tagore remained calm despite these bereavements, he attempted to regain inner peace through his poems; their theme was that God can be found through personal purity and service to others. While in England in 1912 on his way to take his son to a university in America, he showed some of his own translations of these poems to a British friend, the painter William Rothenstein. As a result, they came to the attention of writers such as W.B. Yeats and Ezra Pound, and were published as *Gitanjali: Song Offerings*. Yeats described them as "the work of supreme culture," and Pound likened them to Dante's *Paradiso*. On the strength of their popularity Tagore was nominated to the Nobel Prize committee, and won the Nobel Prize for literature in 1913. In his presentation speech, Harald Hjarne of the Swedish Academy described Tagore's poems as "by no means exotic but truly universally human in character."

Partly a product of his Hindu revivalist upbringing—he was undeviatingly loyal to the precepts of Rammohan Roy throughout his life—Tagore was also a free thinker who rejected many current attitudes. Eager to emphasize the concept of a deity who can be known through love. He took much of his ideology from the teaching of the *Upanishads* and from his own belief in the unity of nature and spirit. He stressed the need for East and West to unite, and longed for all world religions to come together and recognize their common roots.

For a while, he represented the mystical face of the East for the Western world, and was looked to as a seer, which he never claimed to be. He was instead a profoundly humanitarian figure who challenged oppression and inequality, a spiritual man who strove constantly to understand the world and, at the same time, improve it. His popularity abroad declined when he gave a controversial lecture in Japan in 1916 against Nationalism, and when in 1919 he returned his knighthood (awarded in 1915) to Britain following the massacre of 400 Indian demonstrators by British troops at Amritsar.

Politically active in India, he was a supporter of Gandhi—it was he who gave Gandhi the title Mahatma—and Indian Nationalism; but was unable to accept either Gandhi's non-cooperation movement or the Nationalist movement's adoption of violent tactics. For these views he was for a time shunned, and he retreated into relative solitude.

Tagore's literary legacy is enormous. He produced over sixty volumes of poetry, over forty plays, fourteen novels, and about two hundred short stories. He was inventive and deliberately experimental in each form, which drew some criticism from conservative Bengali critics, particularly for his use of colloquialisms, but which has immensely enriched Bengali literature. He was the first Indian to bring an element of psychological realism to his novels. It is in his short stories, however, that he has perhaps had the most literary impact within India. One critic believed that "the modern short story is Rabindranath Tagore's gift to Indian Literature." Tagore once commented that: "If I do nothing but write short stories I am happy, and I make a few readers happy." The best of these are published in four English collections: *The Glimpses of Bengal Life, The Hungry Stones and Other Stories, Mashi and Other Stories* and *Broken Ties and Other Stories.*

Tagore's literary reputation in the West is based predominantly on his poetry, and is now relatively dim. This stems largely from the fact that many of Tagore's poems are actually songs, and are inseparable from their music. Any attempt to translate them results in a bland or trite imitation, even when translated by the author himself. It is in his songs, however, that his greatest genius is apparent, and where he comes closest to the culture of his country.

Between the years 1916 and 1934, Tagore trav-eled extensively, at times driving himself close to exhaustion as he attempted to spread the ideal of uniting East and West. He was himself aware of the difficulties of this taken seriously. "I know what a risk one runs from the vigorously athletic crowds in being styled an idealist these days, when thrones have lost their dignity and prophets have become an anachronism, when the sound that drowns all voices is the noise of the market-place," yet he remained optimistic that "after the forgetfulness of his own divinity, man will remember again that heaven is always in touch with his world, which can never be abandoned for good to the hounding wolves of the modern era."

He was awarded honorary degrees from four Indian universities, and an honorary doctorate from Oxford. At the age of sixty-eight, he took up art, expressing a darker side of himself in this form, and exhibiting widely—Munich, Berlin, New York, Moscow, Paris, Birmingham.

Tagore worked right up to the day of his death when, only hours before he died, he dictated his last poem. His biographer Krishna Kripalani concluded that "Tagore's main significance lies in the impulse and direction he gave to the course of India's cultural and intellectual development. . . . He gave his people faith in their own language and in their cultural and moral heritage." On his seventieth birthday, Tagore admitted that, "Looking back, the only thing of which I feel certain is that I am a poet."

PRINCIPAL WORKS: *Novels*—The Home and the World (tr. R. Tagore) 1919; The Wreck (tr. J. G. Drummond) 1921; Gora (tr. R. Tagore) 1924. *Short stories*—The Hungry Stones and Other Stories, 1916; Mashi and Other Stories, 1918; Stories from Tagore, 1918; Glimpses of Bengal, 1921; Broken Ties and Other Stories, 1925. *Poetry*—Song Offerings (tr. R. Tagore) 1912; The Crescent Moon (tr. R. Tagore) 1913; Poems, 1923; Rabindranath Tagore: Twenty-Two poems (tr. E. J. Thompson) 1925; Sheaves, Poems and Songs (tr. N. Gupta) 1932; Collected Poems and Plays, 1936; Rabindranath Tagore: Selected Poems (tr. W. Radice) 1985. *Drama*—Chitra (tr. R. Tagore) 1913; The King of the Dark Chamber (tr. R. Tagore) 1914; The Post Office, 1914; The Cycle of Spring (tr. R. Tagore) 1917; Sacrifice, and Other Plays, 1917; Red Oleander, 1924; Collected Poems and Plays, 1936. *Nonfiction*—Sadhana: The Realization of Life, 1914; My Reminiscence, 1917; Nationalism, 1917; Personality, 1917; Greater India (tr. S. Ganesan) 1921; Creative Unity, 1922; Letters from Abroad, 1924; Letters to a Friend, 1928; The Religion of Man, 1930.

ABOUT: Anand, M. R. The Humanism of Rabindranath Tagore, 1979; Atkinson, D. W. Gandhi and Tagore: Visionaries of Modern India, 1989; Basak, K. Rabindranath Tagore, a Humanist, 1991; Bhattacharya, V. R. Tagore's Vision of a Global Family, 1987; Bhattacharya, V. R. Relevance of Tagore, 1979; Chakrabarti, M. Tagore and Education for Social Change, 1993; Chakravorty, B. C. Rabindranath Tagore: His Mind and Art, 1971; Chattopadhyay, S. The Universal Man, Tagore's Vision of the Religion of Humanity, 1987; Ghose, S. Rabindranath Tagore, 1986; Lago, M. and W. R. Rabindranath Tagore, 1989; Mitra, H. Tagore Without Illusions, 1983; Mool, C. Nationalism and Internationalism of Gandhi, Nehru, and Tagore, 1989; Naravene, V. S. An Introduction to Rabindranath Tagore, 1977; Raj. G. V. Tagore, The Novelist, 1983; Ramaswami Sastri, K. S. Sir Rabindranath Tagore: His Life, Personality and Genius, 1988; Robinson, A. The Art of Rabindranath Tagore, 1989; Roy, B. K. Rabindranath Tagore, The Man and His Poetry, 1978; Radice, W. Rabindranath Tagore: Selected Poems, 1985; Tagore, R. My Reminiscences, 1917; Thompson, E. J. Rabindranath Tagore, Poet and Dramatist, 1991; Visva-Bharati, Rabindranath Tagore in Perspective, 1989.

## TAINE, JOHN. See BELL, ERIC TEMPLE

**TALLANT, ROBERT** (April 20, 1909–April 2, 1957), American novelist, wrote: "I was born in New Orleans, the son of James Robb Tallant and Lucy Texada (Magruder) Tallant. My father died when I was sixteen. After high school I went to work in a bank as a 'runner,' from which position it was assumed by my relatives I would rise rapidly to vice-president. Although I did not like bank work much, I did have some fun, for I used to play hookey between runs and go to movies, so that I probably made the slowest runs of any bank runner then extant. However, for some reason, I was soon promoted and became a teller—it may have been only that they thought it best to put me in a cage— where I remained for some years, during which time the only fun I had was when I was once held up by bank robbers. I got out of the cage and out of work when the banks crashed. After that I was a young man caught by the Great Depression, with no profession and no training that could be useful in making a living during times so difficult. I once estimated that I had nineteen jobs in five years during this period, none of which I could tolerate.

"Yet I didn't decide to become a writer until 1937, when I was already twenty-eight, an advanced age at which some writers are today publishing their memoirs and  making farewell appearances. Until now I don't know the reason for my decision to be an author, except that I had always been highly imaginative, was an avid reader, and had always thought a man who had a book published was superior to all other human beings. Anyway, I bought a writer's magazine, discovered that manuscripts should be submitted typed on one side of the page only, doublespaced, and then I went out and bought a secondhand typewriter for five dollars, which was truly possible in those days. Since my mother was born on a plantation, and there were a lot of family stories, I started writing a novel about a southern plantation. It seemed to end in a few chapters, so I threw it away, and I've never written about a southern plantation since. Then I began writing short stories, and after selling the first one I wrote (for six dollars) I was definitely encouraged. During the next five years I wrote around five hundred, of which I sold, or gave away to 'little' magazines and university quarterlies, about sixty.

"In 1940, needing a job, for the stories were not earning me a real living, I managed to attach myself to the Louisiana Writers' Project as an editor. The late Lyle Saxon, then the dean of Louisiana writers, was its state director, and I had met him casually a few times before he became my boss. In fact he was the first book writer I ever met, and at that first meeting I trembled visibly with sheer awe. Later, after we became close friends, he told me that he had been under the impression that I was ill.

"During the months I spent on the project I did the final writing of *Gumbo Ya-Ya, A Collection of Louisiana Folk Tales*, from data that had been collected by scores of project research workers. This was edited by Saxon and Edward Dreyer for publication, but was not published until 1945 because of the coming of World War II.

"When the war came I went to work in the New Orleans Office of Censorship. Rejected by the draft, I remained there until late in 1945, when wartime censorship ended, and by which time I was a department head. During this period I wrote *Voodoo in New Orleans*, working at night and on Sundays, and began my first novel, *Mrs. Candy and Saturday Night*. In October 1945 I was transferred by the government from the closing censorship office to the Social Security Office. In November, on a Sunday, Lyle Saxon telephoned me and suggested we go to New York that night. We went, and when I returned I resigned from the Social Security Office. Since then I have devoted all my time to writing books. . . .

"I write fast when I work, and never do a complete second draft although I sometimes re-do pages. Somehow I also manage to loaf a good deal, but always am afflicted with an acute sense of guilt when I do, which at times can be almost painful physically. All my books have been about life in the South, and almost all have in some way concerned New Orleans. . . .

"I am unmarried. Politically I am a liberal Democrat. I was reared a Methodist, but am not now a church member. I do not care much about traveling, but like to stay here in New Orleans, although I realize it would be better for me to get around more. I hate sports and games, including parlor games. I like parties, and eating and drinking. I don't like historical novels much, but prefer modern ones, usually those of a humorous and/or satirical sort. For sheer escape and wonderment I dote on science fiction, but I've never attempted to write it. I will not do any public speaking, and radio and television appearances terrify me when I am coerced into making them. If my writing has been influenced by anyone it is probably by such diverse authors as Norman Douglas, Evelyn Waugh, Somerset Maugham, William March, and by the conversation of Lyle Saxon."

———

Considered the "novel-laureate of New Orleans" at the peak of his career in the late 1940s and early 1950s, Robert Tallant spent his entire life in the Crescent City. For nearly twenty years he explored the city's rich history, elaborate customs and particular social fabric to produce a body of work that ranged from novels and histories to juveniles and crime reports, ghost stories, and a guide book.

While his work took many different forms, Tallant's subjects, like the writer himself, never ventured far from New Orleans or Louisiana. As Tallant himself admitted, the South teemed with a

TAPPAN

plethora of writers, and he believed writing was one of the region's natural resources, comparing it to turpentine. Pine trees down south, like the writers there, "have a longer oozing period," he said. Despite mixed reviews of much of his output, Tallant was frequently praised for creating realistic dialogue in his novels; the *Chicago Sun* said he captured "much of the color, the drama and the flamboyance of a truly great city."

In his fiction, Tallant delved into French Quarter rooming houses and the city's predators and parties, class struggles and social mores. His most famous fictional creation was that of Mrs. Eustacia Candy Petit, commonly referred to as Mrs. Candy, a widow who was the heroine of three Tallant novels. He introduced her in 1947 in *Mrs. Candy and Saturday Night*, in which he took his readers to a Saturday night party in her rooming house in a poor quarter of New Orleans in the 1940s, where characters talk "as tangy as shrimp jambalaya," said the *New York Times*. Mrs. Candy reappeared in *Love and Mrs. Candy* in 1953, and again the following year in *Mrs. Candy Strikes It Rich*, which the *Chicago Sunday Tribune* called "ideal summer fare." But in this third installment, Mrs. Candy had inherited her husband's money and moved to the Garden District, where "her parties lack[ed] the spontaneity of the ones she gave downtown," according to *Kirkus*, which went on to say, "we almost hope the well runs dry before her next adventure."

Contemporary New Orleans life was also the grist of two other novels: *Angel in the Wardrobe* and *Mr. Preen's Salon*. The former concentrated on the city's changing societal rules, and in it Tallant created characters that "are enchantingly alive," according to the *San Francisco Chronicle*. The latter was a light treatment on the life of a widower and his tenants in a French Quarter apartment house, "viewed with indulgence and described in relaxed, nimble and slightly bawdy fashion," said the *New York Herald Tribune Weekly Book Review*.

Outside the New Orleans city limits, Tallant concentrated on life and prejudices in a small southern town in *State in Mimosa*. In *Southern Territory* he told the story of a traveling salesman in the South, which was praised for its convincing conversations and its evocation of dreary hotel rooms and the lonely depression of travelers.

His last work of fiction was *Voodoo Queen*, a novel based on the life of Marie Laveau (1794–1881), whom the author called "the last great American witch." Tallant had written an account of Laveau in a section of an earlier nonfiction work, *Voodoo in New Orleans*, which presented the cult of voodooism in all of its manifestations, from its first known appearances in New Orleans more than 200 years ago.

Tallant turned from voodoo to Mardi Gras, giving similar treatment to the great New Orleans carnival in *Mardi Gras*, published in 1948 and reissued in 1989 as *Mardi Gras—As It Was*.

Other nonfiction works include *The Romantic New Orleanians*, an anecdotal history of the city

and its famous families, and a true crime volume, *Ready to Hang*, originally published in 1952 and reissued a year later as *Murder in New Orleans: Seven Famous Trials*. The book consisted of accounts of seven famous New Orleans murders from 1883 to 1933; these were considered by reviewers to be excellent narratives and important additions to murder collections.

Tallant wrote three works of regional history for juvenile readers. *Pirate Lafitte and the Battle of New Orleans* is an account in fiction form of the famous pirate Jean Lafitte, who took the American side in the Battle of New Orleans. *Saturday Review* called the book "an authentic and well-written account of one of the most colorful episodes in our history," and it won a 1951 award from the Louisiana Library Association. It was followed by *The Louisiana Purchase* and *Evangeline and the Acadians*, which traced the Acadians from their settlement in Nova Scotia to their eventual arrival in Louisiana.

PRINCIPAL WORKS: *Novels*—Mrs. Candy and Saturday Night, 1947; Angel in the Wardrobe, 1948; Mr. Preen's Salon, 1949; A State in Mimosa, 1950; Southern Territory, 1951; Love and Mrs. Candy, 1953; Mrs. Candy Strikes It Rich, 1954; The Voodoo Queen, 1956, 1983. *Nonfiction*—Gumbo Ya-Ya, A Collection of Louisiana Folk Tales (ed. L. Saxon and E. Dreyer) 1945, 1984; Voodoo in New Orleans, 1946, 1983; Mardi Gras, 1948 (reissued as Mardi Gras—As It Was, 1989); The Romantic New Orleanians, 1950; The Pirate Lafitte and the Battle of New Orleans, 1951, 1994; Ready to Hang, 1952 (reissued as Murder in New Orleans: Seven Famous Trials, 1953); The Louisiana Purchase, 1952; Evangeline and the Acadians, 1957, 1995.

ABOUT: The autobiographical material quoted above was written for Twentieth Century Authors First Supplement, 1955. Current Biography 1953; Warfel, H. R. American Novelists of Today 1951. *Periodicals*—New York Times Book Review December 10, 1950.

**TAPPAN, EVA MARCH** (December 26, 1854–January 30, 1930), American writer for children, spent nearly forty years both studying and teaching English before writing her first book. She eventually wrote, edited, or compiled more than fifty different books for children and students.

Tappan was born in Blackstone, Massachusetts, the daughter of Edmund March and Lucretia (Logee) Tappan. Her father, a graduate of Dartmouth College and pastor of the Free Baptist Church, died when she was six, and she spent much of her childhood in seminaries where her mother taught. She remained her mother's devoted companion until her death in 1911.

In the 1870s, Tappan was accepted as a student at the newly established Vassar College, where she studied in the department of English language and literature, receiving an A.B. degree in 1875. After graduating from Vassar, Tappan taught school, spending five years at Wheaton Seminary, Norton, Massachusetts, and then serving as associate principal at Raymond Academy, Camden, New Jersey, from 1884 to 1894.

She received her master's degree in 1895 and a Ph.D. a year later, both from the University of Pennsylvania, where she was one of the first women to be admitted to the new graduate program in the philosophy department.

Her formal education completed, Tappan returned to teaching in 1897, beginning a seven-year tenure as head of the English department in the Worcester English High School in Worcester, Massachusetts. Here she began to write and was also an active advocate for the teaching of English literature in the secondary school.

Her first book was *Charles Lamb: The Man and the Author*, published in 1896. Seven years later she gave up teaching to write full time. In the meantime she had started to write the first of her many popular books. All of these were intended to serve as a springboard to spur young people on to further reading and study.

Tappan was often praised for her clearly written accounts and sensibly chosen and edited anthologies. Of *A Short History of England's Literature*, published in 1905, *Outlook* said, "to write a short history of a vast subject in the form of an animated story is so difficult a task that its successful achievement is specially commendable. Miss Tappan has done this skillfully."

With her *In The Days Of . . .* books, Tappan enriched the historical periods of Alfred the Great, William the Conqueror, and Queens Victoria and

Elizabeth by providing additional social and political context. She encouraged children to do future biographical study by writing about a wide range of heroes, both Old World and American, and she provided students with early exposure to both English and American literature, both in short historical overviews and in works devoted to individual authors. Besides *Charles Lamb*, she produced *Emerson, Selected Poems and Essays* (1898), and retold twelve stories in the *Canterbury Tales* in the prose of the day in *The Chaucer Story Book* (1908). She recounted her own girlhood experiences in *Ella, A Little Schoolgirl of the Sixties*, in 1923.

One of Tappan's most ambitious works was as compiler of a ten-volume collection of children's literature, *The Children's Hour* (1907), devoted to poetry, fairy tales, legends, essays and informative material about animals, birds, flowers, earth and sky, and books about pictures, music and song. It included an accompanying guide for parents, in which Tappan wrote that she believed her purpose was not to merely provide good reading to young people, but to "point out the way to more good reading. To read and think about what one has read is a most excellent groundwork for all education." In 1916, an additional five volumes of *The Children's Hour* were published, and in 1929 a new edition of the first ten volumes were published.

Tappan never married, rarely traveled, and other than an occasional year in which she took time off to care for her mother, she spent most of her time writing and reading at her home in Worcester.

(Upon her death, her estate went to Vassar to establish the Eva March Tappan scholarship for young women.)

PRINCIPAL WORKS: Charles Lamb: The Man and the Author, 1896; In The Days of Alfred the Great, 1900; In the Days of William the Conqueror, 1901; England's Story, 1901; Old Ballads in Prose, 1901; Old World Hero Stories, 1901; In the Days of Queen Elizabeth, 1902; Our Country's Story, 1902; In the Days of Queen Victoria, 1903; The Christ Story, 1903; Robin Hood: His Book, 1903; A Short History of England's Literature, 1905; A Short History of America's Literature, 1906; The Chaucer Story Book, 1908; The Story of the Greek People, 1908; Dixie Kitten, 1910; The Story of the Roman People, 1910; When Knights Were Bold, 1911; The House With the Silver Door, 1913; The Industrial Readers, 1916; Our European Ancestors, 1918; The Story of Our Constitution, 1922; Ella: A Little Schoolgirl of the Sixties, 1923. *As compiler and editor*—Emerson, Selected Poems and Essays, 1898; American Hero Stories, 1906; Letters from Colonial Children, 1907; The Children's Hour, 10 vols., 1907; A Friend in the Library, 12 vols., 1909; European Hero Stories, 1909; Heroes of the Middle Ages, 1911; The World's Story: A History of the World in Story, Song and Art, 14 vols., 1914; Hero Stories of France, 1920; Heroes of Progress, 1921; American History Stories for Very Young Readers, 1924; Andrew Carnegie's Own Story for Boys and Girls, 1930.

ABOUT: Junior Book of Authors; American Women vol. 3, 1971. *Periodicals*—English Journal December 1986; New York Times January 31, 1930.

**TARBELL, IDA MINERVA** (November 5, 1857–January 6, 1944), American journalist and biographer, is best known as the muckraker whose extensive and relentless expose led to the breakup of John D. Rockefeller's Standard Oil Company. Her work stands as one of the best examples of the Progressive-era investigative journalism that revealed widespread corruption in business, labor and politics just after the turn of the century.

Born on a farm in Hatch Hollow, Erie County, Pennsylvania, she was the eldest child of Franklin Sumner Tarbell and Esther Ann (McCullough) Tarbell. Her father, who became an independent oil prospector and driller, moved the family to Titusville, Pennsylvania, near where oil was discovered in 1859 and where he established the first shop for the production of wooden oil storage tanks. Tarbell attended public school in Titusville

and went on to Allegheny College in Meadville, Pennsylvania, the only woman in her freshman class. After studying biology and graduating with an A.B. degree in 1880, she taught for two years at Poland Union Seminary in Poland, Ohio. She returned to Meadville, receiving her M.A. degree in 1883, and worked for eight years as an editor for the *Chautauquan*, a monthly magazine produced by the Chautauqua Literary and Scientific Circle, an adult education movement.

In 1891, restless in her native western Pennsylvania, Tarbell ambitiously went to Paris as a freelance writer, primarily to research the life of Madame Marie Jeanne Roland, a prominent figure in the French revolution. Tarbell studied at the Sorbonne and the Collège de France for three years, living in relative poverty, her only proceeds coming from contributing articles to American publications.

Her finances began to improve when publisher S. S. McClure of McClure's Syndicate visited her in Paris and asked if she would contribute special articles to his new magazine venture. She agreed, returned to the states in 1894, and wrote an eight-part series on Napolean Bonaparte, "an early prototype of the Tarbell hero—entirely self-made, born in squalor and risen to power on the world stage," wrote Kathleen Brady in the biography, *Ida Tarbell Portrait of a Muckraker* (1984). Her articles, which were published as a book, gained her national recognition and helped to dramatically increase the new magazine's circulation.

The next subject of her scholarly approach to biography was Abraham Lincoln, whom she revered and would return to write about throughout her career. Her extensively researched twenty-two part series was a popular fixture in *McClure's* from 1895 to 1898 and was published as the two-part *The Life of Abraham Lincoln* (1900), which remained standard until 1947, when Lincoln papers were finally released to scholars.

Tarbell's greatest impact came when she took on John D. Rockefeller, whom she claimed to be the embodiment of the evil arrogance of big business that threatened democracy. This was the plum assignment of her career, which only Upton Sinclair's *The Jungle* would rival in muckraking notoriety. Her five years of research and writing culminated in nineteen *McClure's* articles and the two-volume *The History of the Standard Oil Company* (1904). This work was one of the factors that prompted Congress to establish a Department of Commerce and speed up antitrust prosecution of Standard Oil. The Supreme Court decided in 1911 to break up the monopoly. At the pinnacle of her career, Tarbell had become an international celebrity "as eminent in the journalism of her day as were Woodward and Bernstein in theirs," wrote Boylan.

By 1906, the *McClure's* staff was disgruntled. Editor John S. Phillips, Baker, Steffens and Tarbell quit working for the erratic McClure and joined with Finley Peter Dunne and William Allen White to take control of the *American Magazine*, a McClurian spin-off that Tarbell continued to serve as business historian. She launched a major series on the history of the protective tariff, published as *The Tariff in Our Time* (1911), in which she attacked these tariffs as another means of fostering the interests of trusts, while sacrificing worker and consumer interests. President Woodrow Wilson offered her an appointment to the new Federal Tariff Commission in 1916, but she refused it and continued with journalism.

An unmarried career woman, Tarbell paradoxically remained lukewarm to women's suffrage, finding it a threat to family and stability in society. She believed, contrary to the way she lived, that a woman belonged at home and not in the work place. "Her political ideas were progressive, but her ideas on women were hackneyed," wrote Brady.

"In terms of woman's advancement, she was a weather vane, not an engine of change." Tarbell wrote three works on women's issues: a history of the women's movement in the United States, "The American Woman," a seven-part series in the *American Magazine* in 1909 and 1910; *The Business of Being a Woman* (1912), in which she concentrated on applying methods of industrial efficiency to housework; and *The Ways of Woman* (1915), originally serialized in *Ladies' Home Journal.*

Her involvement with the *American Magazine* ended in 1915. Thereafter she remained an active freelance writer, lecturer and teacher of biography for two decades. She served on several government commissions, including the Woman's Committee of the U.S. Council of National Defense during World War I, President Wilson's Industrial Conference in 1919, and President Harding's Conference on Unemployment in 1921.

She surprised many when she wrote pro-business biographies on Elbert H. Gary, who founded the United States Steel Corporation, and on Owen D. Young, chairman of the board of the General Electric Company, who was considered a likely candidate to run against Franklin D. Roosevelt for the presidential nomination.

Tarbell's autobiography, *All in the Day's Work* (1939), reissued in 1985, is a restrained account of a woman married to her work, with little time or inclination for introspection. R. L. Duffus wrote in the *New York Times* that old-fashioned words described her best: "intelligence, simplicity, unselfishness, utter lack of vanity, energy, conscientiousness, kindness, imagination . . . Taken together, they add up to a truly American species of genius."

PRINCIPAL WORKS: A Short Life of Napolean Bonaparte, 1895; Madame Roland, 1896; The Early Life of Abraham Lincoln, 1896; The Life of Abraham Lincoln, 1900; The History of the Standard Oil Company, 1904 (reprinted, 1993); He Knew Lincoln, 1907; The Tariff in Our Times, 1911; The Business of Being a Woman, 1912; The Ways of Woman, 1915; New Ideals in Business: An Account of Their Practice and Their Effects upon Men and Profits, 1916; The Rising of the Tide: The Story of Sabinsport, 1919; In Lincoln's Chair, 1920; Boy Scouts' Life of Lincoln, 1921; He Knew Lincoln, and Other Billy Brown Stories, 1922; Peacemakers—Blessed and Otherwise, 1922; In the Footsteps of the Lincolns, 1924; The Life of Elbert H. Gary, 1925; A Reporter for Lincoln: Story of Henry E. Wing, Soldier and Newspaperman, 1927; Owen D. Young: A New Type of Industrial Leader, 1932; The Nationalizing of Business, 1878–1898, 1936; All in the Day's Work, 1939.

ABOUT: Brady, K. Ida Tarbell Portrait of a Muckraker; Chalmers, D. M. The Social and Political Ideas of the Muckrakes; James, E. T. (ed.) Dictionary of American Biography 1941–1945; Kochersberger, R. C. More Than a Muckraker: Ida Tarbell's Lifetime in Journalism; McKerns, J. (ed.) Biographical Dictionary of American Journalism; Mainiero, L. (ed.) American Women Writers; Tomkins, M. E. Ida M. Tarbell; Twentieth Century Literary Criticism vol. 40; Whitman, A. (ed.) American Reformers. Periodicals—Columbia Journalism Review March/April 1985; Nation January 5, 1905; New York Times April 23, 1939, January 7, 1944.

**TARDIVEAU, RENÉ MARIE AUGUSTE.** See BOYLESVE, RENÉ

**TARKINGTON, BOOTH** (July 29, 1869–May 19, 1946), American novelist, wrote: "This writer was born in a quiet, lovely little city, Indianapolis, Indiana, and began to talk when he was seven months old by calling the family dog. That small city, the Indianapolis where I was born, exists no more than Carthage existed after the Romans had driven ploughs over the ground where it had stood. Progress swept all the old life away. I still live in Indianapolis, though, and am glad I do. I've lived in other places; in Exeter, New Hampshire, where I went to prep school; in Lafayette, Indiana, when I went to Purdue University for a year; and in Princeton, New Jersey, when I was in the university there, in the class of 1893. Since then I've lived a while in New York and Paris and Rome, and for a little time on the island of Capri; and for many years now I have been spending long seasons [year-long, and what to others would seem a permanent residence] in Kennebunkport, Maine, on the sea. But I always speak and think of Indianapolis as home. Almost all Hoosiers are that way about where they grew up.

"During my boyhood I wanted to be an artist, a painter, or at least an illustrator. I tried persistently to draw pictures after I found it was hopeless for me  to think of painting them. But at last I found out that my hand would never do what my mind wanted it to do; and so, since my hand could make nothing better than symbols (written words, that is), I discovered that I was a writer. As a matter of fact, I always had been a writer, but didn't realize it because like a great many other people, I pined to do what I couldn't.

About five years after I began being a writer seriously and professionally, a magazine editor accepted the manuscript of a long novel of mine, and since then a great many other novels and stories of mine have been published, and something over a score of plays I have written have been put upon the stage. All this means millions of words scribbled and crossed out and rewritten, and, as every old-fashioned autobiography should end with a summing-up, I conclude these memories by saying it seems to me that judging by what I know of my character I wouldn't have done all this work if I hadn't liked doing it."

---

Booth Tarkington was the younger of two children born to John Stevenson Tarkington, a judge, and Elizabeth (Booth) Tarkington, the descendant of a prominent New England family. Christened Newton Booth Tarkington, he dropped the use of his first name early on. After graduating from Phillips Exeter in New Hampshire, he attended Purdue University for a year, then transferred to Princeton as a non-degree student from 1891 to 1893. He returned to his native Indianapolis, where he spent the next six years writing prolifically, unfazed by a steady steam of rejection notices. His career as a novelist was launched when *McClure's* editor, the novelist Hamlin Garland, accepted *The Gentleman from Indiana*, which was an immediate best-seller.

Intent upon commercial success as well as artistic recognition, Tarkington had made a careful study of the literary marketplace. Having rejected the tenets of naturalism, he gravitated toward historical romance, a tendency plainly visible in his second published novel, *Monsieur Beaucaire*, set in eighteenth-century England. Despite his own penchant for romanticism, Tarkington admired and made friends with the novelist, critic, and editor William Dean Howells, then America's foremost champion of realism. Howells's influence is especially evident in Tarkington's mature novels, in which romance is tempered by careful social observation.

Soon after marrying Louisa Fletcher in June of 1902, Tarkington learned that he had been nominated as a Republican candidate for the Indiana state legislature. He was elected to that body and served as a state representative in 1903 and 1904, but was forced to abandon his political career after contracting a near-fatal case of typhoid fever. His reflections on political life are contained in his short story collection *In the Arena*, which won praise in print from Theodore Roosevelt.

By 1905, the year in which he began a long association with the *Saturday Evening Post*, Tarkington's serial publications were in great demand, and he was earning high sums. Although now best remembered as a novelist and short story writer, he devoted considerable effort (particularly between 1905 and 1911) to theatrical productions, and wrote (or cowrote) some two dozen plays in the course of his career. Some of these, including *The Man from Home*, *The Country Cousin*, and *Clarence*, were quite successful, and provided stage roles for actors who later became well known.

Tarkington was at the height of his powers between 1914 and 1924. In 1922 he was voted the greatest living American writer in a *Literary Digest* survey, and a *New York Times* poll of the same year placed him on the list of the ten greatest contemporary Americans. His most memorable novels, those written in the 1910s and early 1920s, fall into two basic categories: humorous stories of boyhood and adolescence exemplified by his *Penrod* trilogy (*Penrod*, *Penrod and Sam*, and *Penrod Jashber*) and the novel *Seventeen*; and socially observant chronicles of upper- and middle-class life that trace the transformation of America from a rural, agricultural society to one in the throes of urbanization and industrialization. Works belonging to the second category include *The Turmoil*, *The Magnificent Ambersons*, and *The Midlander* (later reissued as the *Growth* trilogy), as well as *Alice Adams*. Literary critics have by far preferred the books in the first category.

Set in a rapidly industrializing Midwestern city in the early 1900s, *The Turmoil* focuses on the vicissitudes of the Sheridan family. James Sheridan, owner of the Sheridan Pump Works, is a wealthy first-generation entrepreneur. His son, Bibbs Sheridan, is a sickly, dreamy youth more interested in literature and art than in high finance. By the end of the novel, however, Bibbs has joined the family business, renounced his artistic ambitions, and become, like his father, a devotee of "Bigness." *The Turmoil* is similar, in some respects, to William Dean Howells's 1885 novel *The Rise of Silas Lapham*; both portray American tycoons beset by domestic problems.

While *The Turmoil*, like the other novels in *Growth*, offers a gently satiric perspective on the foibles of the American business class, Tarkington was, on the whole, a supporter of big business and industrial expansion. He saw the growth of business as a sign of progress (if not an entirely unmixed blessing), and for him the transformation of Bibbs Sheridan from artist manqué to business executive was hardly a tragedy—though many of his readers differed.

*The Magnificent Ambersons* (famously filmed in 1942 by Orson Welles) charts the decline, over three generations, of a once-illustrious Midwestern family. "Major Amberson had 'made a fortune' in 1873, when other people were losing fortunes, and the magnificence of the Ambersons began there," it begins. The Major's only grandson, George Amberson Minafer, an insolent and overprivileged youth who assumes it is his destiny to live as a gentleman, must, and does, receive his "come-uppance": he survives to witness the decline of the Ambersons' fortune and prestige. Tarkington is by no means wholly critical of the Ambersons, but he faults them above all for their attachment to the past, and their fear of new technologies. The hidebound George is contrasted with the dynamic entrepreneurship of Eugene Morgan, a pioneer automobile manufacturer who captures perfectly the spirit of the emerging age.

Well received by critics—a 1918 review in *The Nation* hailed it as "a fascinating picture of a national phase already past"—*The Magnificent Ambersons* was awarded the Pulitzer Prize for literature in 1919.

Tarkington won a second Pulitzer Prize for *Alice Adams*. It is a sensitive and realistic portrait of a young urban woman struggling to overcome her greatest liability—a lack of money and good family connections. One of many reviewers to praise the novel was Carl Van Doren, who wrote in the *Nation* (1921), "[Tarkington] attempts no detours and permits himself no superfluities. It is packed with piercing observation." *The Midlander*, the final installment of the *Growth* trilogy, recounts the rise and fall of a Midwestern real estate developer. Notices of the novel were mixed, portending Tarkington's popular decline. A *Dial* reviewer thought it "somewhat epic in intention, but slightly commonplace in execution"; and *Nation* (1924) critic J. W. Krutch complained that "Tarkington attempts to write an epic around a central character who never

rises above the level of the enthusiastic realtor." *The Midlander*, like his later satirical novel *The Plutocrat*, illustrates a pressing dilemma at the heart of Tarkington's fictional enterprise: how to write probingly and critically about a business class whose fundamental philosophy he shares.

In 1945, the year before his death, Tarkington received the Howells Medal of the American Academy of Arts and Letters. Although rendered nearly blind by cataracts in his sixties, Tarkington remained steadily productive until his final two-month-long illness. He lived through the financial panic of the 1890s, the Great Depression, and two world wars, but, unlike so many other writers of his generation, he died with his optimism largely intact. While most of his more than fifty books are now regarded as inconsequential, Tarkington retains historical importance as a chronicler of America's march toward urban industrialization and, above all, as the still admired creator of "Penrod."

There is a large collection of his manuscripts, letters, and other materials in the Princeton University Library.

PRINCIPAL WORKS: *Novels*—The Gentleman from Indiana, 1899; Monsieur Beaucaire, 1900; The Two Vanrevels, 1902; Cherry, 1903; The Beautiful Lady, 1905; The Conquest of Canaan, 1905; His Own People, 1907; The Guest of Quesnay, 1908; Beasley's Christmas Party, 1909; Beauty and the Jacobin: An Interlude of the French Revolution, 1912; The Flirt, 1913; Penrod, 1914; The Turmoil, 1915; Seventeen: A Tale of Youth and Summer Time and the Baxter Family, Especially William, 1916; Penrod and Sam, 1916; The Magnificent Ambersons, 1918; Ramsey Milholland, 1919; Alice Adams, 1921; Gentle Julia, 1922; The Midlander, 1924; Women, 1925; The Plutocrat, 1927; Claire Ambler, 1928; Young Mrs. Greeley, 1929; Penrod Jashber, 1929 (also published as The New Penrod Book: Penrod Jashber, 1929); Mirthful Haven, 1930; Mary's Neck, 1932; Wanton Mally, 1932 (in U.K.: Wanton Mally: A Romance of England in the Days of Charles II); Presenting Lily Mars, 1933; Little Orvie, 1934; The Lorenzo Bunch, 1936; Rumbin Galleries, 1937; The Fighting Littles, 1941; The Heritage of Hatcher Ide, 1941; Kate Fennigate, 1943; Image of Josephine, 1945; The Show Piece, 1947; Three Selected Short Novels, 1947. *Collected novels*—Monsieur Beaucaire, The Beautiful Lady, His Own People, 1915; Growth, 1927; Penrod, His Complete Story, 1931. *Short stories*—In the Arena: Stories of Political Life, 1905; Harlequin and Columbine, and Other Stories, 1918; The Fascinating Stranger, and Other Stories, 1923; Strack Selections from Booth Tarkington's Stories (ed. L. Strack) 1926; Mr. White, The Red Barn, Hell, and Bridewater, 1935. *Drama*—(with H. Wilson) The Man from Home, 1908; (with J. Street) The Ohio Lady, 1916; (with H. Wilson) The Gibson Upright, 1919; Clarence: A Comedy in Four Acts, 1921; (with J. Street) The Country Cousin, 1921; The Intimate Strangers: A Comedy in Three Acts, 1921; The Ghost Story: A One-Act Play for Persons of No Great Age, 1922; The Wren: A Comedy in Three Acts, 1922; The Trysting Place, a Farce in One Act, 1923; Bimbo, the Pirate: A Comedy in One Act, 1924; (with H. Wilson) Tweedles, a Comedy, 1924; Mister Antonio: A Play in Four Acts, 1925; Station YYYY, 1927; The Travelers: A One-Act Play, 1927; (with H. Wilson) How's Your Health?, 1930; The Help Each Other Club, 1934; Lady Hamilton and Her Nelson, 1945. *Nonfiction*—(with K. Roberts and H. Kahler) The Collector's Whatnot: A Compendium, Manual, and Syllabus of Information and Advice on All Subjects Appertaining to the Collection of Antiques, Both Ancient and Not So Ancient, 1923; Looking Forward and Others, 1926; Some Old Portraits: A Book About Art and Human Beings, 1939; As I Seem to Me, 1941. *Autobiography*—The World Does Move, 1928. *Correspondence*—Your Amiable Uncle: Letters to His Nephews by Booth Tarkington, 1949; On Plays, Playwrights, and Playgoers: Selections from the Letters of Booth Tarkington to George C.

Tyler and John Peter Toohey, 1918–1925 (ed. A. Downer) 1959. *Collected works*—The Works of Booth Tarkington, 27 vols., 1922–1932; The Gentleman from Indianapolis: A Treasury of Booth Tarkington (ed. J. Beecroft), 1957.

ABOUT: The autobiographical material quoted above was written for Twentieth Century Authors, 1942. Dictionary of American Biography, Suppl. 4: 1946–1950, 1974; Fennimore, K. Booth Tarkington, 1974; Who's Who 1945; Woodress, J. Booth Tarkington: Gentleman from Indiana, 1955. *Bibliography*—Russo, D. and Sullivan, T. Bibliography of Booth Tarkington, 1869–1946, 1949. *Periodicals*—American Scholastic May 10, 1950; Boston Transcript February 13, 1915; Dial March 1924; Nation November 16, 1918; August 3, 1921; March 19, 1924; New York Times May 20, 1946; New Yorker February 25, 1985; Times (London) May 21, 1946; World's Work January 1929.

**TATE, (JOHN ORLEY) ALLEN** (November 19, 1899–February 9, 1979), American poet, novelist, historical biographer, and critic, wrote: "I was

born at Winchester, Clark County, Kentucky, in the Kentucky Blue Grass. My early education was entirely at home; when at the age of nine I entered a private school in Louisville. I remember that I astonished the teacher by reciting 'The Chambered Nautilus' and Poe's 'To Helen.'

When I was twelve my mother said to me one day, 'Put that book down and go out and play. You mustn't strain your mind; it isn't very strong.' (As a boy of four or five I had a big bulging head; my elders, who discussed children in those days as if they were inanimate objects, used to say, 'Do you think he has water on the brain?') The family belief that I was an imbecile redoubled my secret efforts to prove them wrong: secret efforts, because outwardly until I was through college I was trying to appear to be just like other boys—a role in which I was not successful. Then, after I had left Vanderbilt, my brother gave me a job in his coal office in Eastern Kentucky; in one day I lost the company $700, by shipping some coal to Duluth that should have gone to Cleveland; and my business career was over.

"I have been asked many times why I became a writer. I simply could not put my mind on anything else. As far back as I can remember I was wondering why the people and families I knew—my own family particularly—had got to be what they were, and what their experience had been. This problem, greatly extended, continues to absorb all my study and speculation, and is the substance of my novel, *The Father*."

---

Allen Tate, the son of John Orley and Nellie (Varnell) Tate, was at Vanderbilt University from 1918 to 1923. (A threat of tuberculosis sent him away in 1922 to a California mountain resort, but he graduated *magna cum laude* the following year as part of the Class of '22.) As a promising student he was associated with the founding of the bi-

monthly "little magazine" *The Fugitive* and with the famous group that formed around it. The leader of the "Fugitives", and the leader, too, of the "Southern Renaissance" movement in American letters, was the poet, critic and Vanderbilt professor John Crowe Ransom. The ambitious and gifted young Tate trod in his footsteps, and those of Robert Penn Warren and Donald Davidson. The "southern agrarian" theories upon which the Fugitive Group based their literary practice were "traditionalist but modernist": T. S. Eliot was something of an influence, but they were as interested in Robert Graves, who became a contributor to the magazine. Their political theory was highly conservative, ignored social issues in the segregated South altogether, and was essentially utopian—the Fugitives wanted culture to take the place of politics in a non-industrialized South.

After Vanderbilt, Tate worked in New York City for a year as an editorial assistant before marrying the novelist Caroline Gordon in 1924. The two had one daughter. From 1928 to 1929, Tate went to Paris on a Guggenheim fellowship. He published two workmanlike biographies, of Stonewall Jackson and Jefferson Davis, in these years.

His first poetry collection, *Mr. Pope and Other Poems* (1928), contained what became by far his most famous poem, the "Ode to the Confederate Dead." It did not reach its final form until 1936. The poem was widely anthologized and widely quoted and admired. It was, in Tate's own words, "the objective frame for the tension between the two theses, 'active faith' which has decayed, and the 'fragmentary cosmos' that surrounds us." Tate was trying to do, in a shorter compass, and for the South, what Eliot had done in *The Waste Land*; he almost succeeded, but today the poem has lost some of its high status.

Tate's one novel, *The Fathers*, although now not much read, is perhaps a greater single achievement than anything he did in verse. Called a "beautifully written and profoundly searching story" by the *New York Times*, it is set in the old South, just prior to the outbreak of the Civil War. Its narrator is an old man, and the central character is his son, Major Buchan, a federal gentleman and an antisecessionist who is without defense against the commercial North. His son-in-law, George Posey, represents man uprooted from tradition. Tate's South may be idealized, but he imbues it with a robustness of feeling absent from much of his poetry. George Hemphill, in his study of Tate, called Major Lewis Buchan "surely one of the sweetest products of the American imagination."

Tate's criticism, respected in its time, has not stood up as well as it might have done. His best known term, "tension," for the strain set up between the abstract and the concrete, the denoted and the connoted, is not much used, and perhaps lacked powerful explanatory potential. Yet Mark Van Doren (*Books*) was hardly wrong in calling *Reactionary Essays on Poetry and Ideas* "contemporary criticism at its best"—it was thoughtful, well reasoned, well written and provocative.

Tate taught at Memphis in Tennessee (1934–1936) and at Princeton (1939–1942), where he was poet-in-residence. In 1950 he converted to Roman Catholicism. After many years with his wife Caroline Gordon, who portrayed him rather unfavorably in her novel *The Malefactors*, Tate left her to marry the poet Isabella Stewart Gardner (1959); later (1967) he married Helen Heinz. Most of his papers are at Princeton and Columbia.

PRINCIPAL WORKS: *Poetry*—(with R. Wills) The Golden Man, 1923; Mr. Pope and Others Poems, 1923; Ode to the Confederate Dead (in Mr. Pope, rev. 1930, rev. 1936 in The Mediterranean); Selected Poems, 1937; Sonnets at Christmas, 1941; The Winter Sea, 1944; Poems 1922–1947, 1948; Poems, 1960; The Swimmers, 1970; Collected Poems 1919–1976, 1977. *Fiction*—The Fathers, 1938. *Biography*—Stonewall Jackson, 1928; Jefferson Davis: His Rise and Fall, 1929. *Criticism*—Reactionary Essays on Poetry and Ideas, 1936; Reason in Madness, 1941; On the Limits of Poetry, 1948; The Hovering Fly, 1949; The Forlorn Demon, 1953; The Man of Letters in the Modern World, 1955; Essays of Four Decades, 1968; Brown, A. and Cheney, F. N. (ed.) The Poetry Reviews of Allen Tate, 1983. *Letters*—Fain, J. T. and T. D. Young (ed.)The Literary Correspondence of Donald Davidson and Allen Tate, 1974; T. D. Young and Hindle, J. J. (ed.) The Republic of Letters in America: The Correspondence of John Peale Bishop and Allen Tate, 1981; T. D. Young and Sarcone, E. (ed.) The Tate-Lytle Letters, 1987; J. M. Dunaway and Maritain, J. (ed.) The Letters of Jacques and Raissa Maritain, Allen Tate, and Caroline Gordon, 1992.

ABOUT: The autobiographical material quoted above was written for Twentieth Century Authors, 1942. *Bibliography*—Fallwell, M. Allen Tate; A Bibliography, 1969. Arnold, W. B. The Social Ideas of Allen Tate, 1955; Bishop, F. Allen Tate, 1967; Bradbury, J. M. The Fugitives, 1958; Cowan, L. The Fugitive Group, 1959; Doreski, W. The Years of Our Friendship: Robert Lowell and Allen Tate, 1990; Dupree, R. S. Allen Tate and the Augustinian Imagination, 1983; Pratt, W. (ed.) The Fugitive Poets, 1965; Squires, J. R. Allen Tate: A Literary Biography, 1971; Sullivan, W. Allen Tate: A Recollection, 1988; Stewart, J. L. The Burden of Time, 1969. *Periodicals*—Books April 12, 1936; Nation September 5, 1936; New York Times May 4, 1996.

**TAWNEY, RICHARD** (November 30, 1880–January 16, 1962), English economic historian, was born in Calcutta, where his father, Charles Henry

Tawney, a Sanskrit scholar, was head of Presidency College. His mother was Constance Catherine (Fox) Tawney. He was sent to England to be educated at Rugby School and Balliol College, Oxford, at which he read classics. In 1905 he took his degree, and despite having received second-class honors was elected a Fellow of Balliol in 1918–1921 and an Honorary Fellow in 1938. After leaving Oxford, Tawney did social work in the Toynbee Hall University Settlement in London's East End; his experiences in the slums helped to shape his lifelong liberal social and political convictions, especially his belief in education as the most effective means of social reform. He soon joined the newly formed Worker's Educational Association (WEA) and remained a member until 1947, serving as president from 1928 to 1944. In 1906 Tawney joined

the Fabian Society (he was a member of the executive board from 1921 to 1933). He was subsequently a lecturer in political economy at the University of Glasgow. In 1908–14, he was a teacher for the Oxford University Tutorial Classes Committee sponsored by the WEA, working with adult students in industrial towns such as Rochdale, Lancashire, and Longton, in the so-called Potteries area of Great Britain.

Tawney joined the Independent Labour party in 1909. He soon became an influential spokesman for the then growing socialist movement. For many years his idealistic, egalitarian Christian principles served as a guide for Labour party programs; nor has his influence entirely faded away.

In 1909, Tawney married Annette Jeanie Beveridge, sister of his close college friend William Beveridge. Soon after their marriage the Tawneys settled in Manchester, where they lived until 1914. His first book published was *The Agrarian Problem in the Sixteenth Century*. It is still considered a pioneering historical study of the impact of the first land enclosures and the rise of capitalism on the old agricultural society. As with all his writing, his concern here was with the shifts in attitudes and in social and economic relationships rather than with the presentation of dry statistical information (of which, however, he had a firm grip). It was also the first of his several studies of the economic history of England between 1540 and 1640 (which colleagues affectionately dubbed "Tawney's Century") and the causes of the civil war.

From 1912 to 1931 Tawney was a member of the Consultative Committee of the (then) Board of Education; in 1913–1914 he served as director of the Ratan Tata Foundation for the study of poverty—for which he wrote two directives on the establishment of minimum wages in the iron chain-making and tailoring industries. Throughout his life he continued to combine writing and teaching with an active role in labor and social affairs. In 1915 Tawney enlisted as a private in the 22nd Manchester Regiment, having refused a commission, as he was years later to refuse a peerage. Badly wounded on the Somme in 1916, he was invalided home, served briefly in the Ministry of Reconstruction, and in 1917 was appointed a lecturer in economic history at the London School of Economics (LSE). In 1923 he became a reader, and in 1931 a full professor, retiring as a professor emeritus in 1949.

In 1918, and again in 1922 and 1924, Tawney unsuccessfully stood for Parliament as a Labour candidate. Meanwhile, in 1919, he was appointed to the Coal Industry Commission. His pamphlet *The Nationalization of the Coal Industry* was published under Labour party auspices. Another pamphlet, *The Sickness of the Acquisitive Society*, written for the Fabians, served as the basis for a book titled *The Acquisitive Society*, one of his most impassioned and influential works. It argues that the acquisitiveness encouraged by the capitalist system is morally wrong, that in a capitalist society work is performed not for its own ends but solely as a means of acquiring something else, and thus is deprived of its inherent value. Contemporary reviewers praised his temperate condemnation of capitalism and appeal for a return to the economic principles of pre-industrial Britain—an argument based on logic and illustrated by historical precedents.

As a spokesman for Ramsay MacDonald's first Labour government, Tawney participated in the 1924 conference held at Williams College, in Massachusetts, under the auspices of the Institute for Politics. *The British Labour Movement*, which was based on his lectures, gives an historical survey of the party from 1815 to 1914, and in scholarly, objective fashion explains the new government's aims and programs. Two years later Tawney helped found the Economic History Society, and he was a coeditor of its journal, the *Economic History Review*, from 1927 to 1934. Meanwhile he wrote his best-known and most influential work, *Religion and the Rise of Capitalism*. According to the *Times* of London, no other economic historian "has combined economic study with moral purpose and the analysis of ideas to quite the same illuminating effect as Tawney in [this] classic volume." Based on lectures given at the LSE, it deals with the relationships between sixteenth- and seventeenth-century religious changes—the Reformation, the establishment of the Anglican Church, Puritanism—and economic behavior; and it to some extent modifies the theory of the German sociologist Max Weber that Calvinism fostered capitalism.

In Tawney's next book, *Equality*, he denounces the inequities fostered by the British class system and advocates a number of practical reform programs, illustrating his argument "with a wealth of pertinent figures and eloquent comment upon them, proceeding impressively from . . . ethical premises to . . . political conclusion. . . . " (*Spectator*).

Asa Briggs, in his *Dictionary of National Biography* essay, points out that equality "served as a driving force behind many of the policies of the Labour Government after 1945," and calls Tawney one of the principal architects of the postwar "welfare state" (though Tawney himself disliked the term).

The last substantial work published during Tawney's lifetime, *Business and Politics under James I: Lionel Cranfield as Merchant and Minister*, deals with social change·in the half century preceding the civil war, as a result of a new financial system— exemplified in the activities of the cloth exporter, later Lord Treasurer Cranfield. Tawney, with his "habitual eloquence and . . . feeling for significant incident" gives a "picture of an age—a dynasty, a political system, a method of government—on the way to its doom" (*Times Literary Supplement*) in the approaching Puritan revolution.

At the start of World War II Tawney wrote a letter explaining "Why the British People Fight," published in the *New York Times* in 1940; it was expanded into a book titled *Why Britain Fights* the next year. Briefly, in 1941–1942, Tawney served as attaché at the British Embassy in Washington, D.C., advising on labor problems. He was for the next five years a member of the University Grants Committee, advocating the expansion of opportunities for higher education. *The Attack, and Other Papers* makes available a number of Tawney's essays on social problems written between 1916 and 1950: on Beatrice and Sidney Webb (founders of the Fabian Society), as well as on personal matters—the title essay being a description of the battle in which he was wounded. "His gentle reflections evoke a vision of society which is neither utopian nor doctrinaire . . . founded on common sense and knowledge of how human beings can reasonably be expected to behave" (Noel Annan, *Manchester Guardian*). The *Radical Tradition*, a posthumous collection, includes twelve of Tawney's previously published essays on politics, education, and literature. Most reviewers were struck with the freshness of his ideas and the moral vision that inspired them. The right-wing philosopher Alasdair MacIntyre, however, writing in the *New York Review of Books*, alleged that Tawney was guilty of "insularity" and a "lack of political intelligence and imagination" about the postwar role of the Labour government.

Tawney, a Fellow of the British Academy since 1935 and the recipient of many honorary degrees, was honored on the occasion of his eightieth birthday by a dinner given in the House of Commons, attended by educators, politicians, historians, and trade unionists. A festschrift, *R. H. Tawney, a Portrait by Several Hands*, marked the occasion. At the memorial service after his death, the Labour party leader Hugh Gaitskell praised him as "the democratic socialist *par excellence*," a verdict that endures.

PRINCIPAL WORKS: The Agrarian Problem in the Sixteenth Century, 1912; The Establishment of Minimum Rates in the Chain Making Industry under the Trade Boards Act of 1909, 1914 (Studies in the Minimum Wage, no. 1); The Establishment of Minimum Rates in the Tailoring Industry under the Trade Boards Act of 1909, 1915 (Studies on the Minimum Wage, no. 2); The Nationalization of the Coal Industry, 1919?; The Sickness of an Acquisitive Society, 1920; The Acquisitive Society, 1920; Education: The Socialist Policy (pref. C. Trevelyan) 1924; The British Labor Movement, 1925 (The Inst. of Politics Pubs., Williams College, Williamstown, Mass.); Religion and Rise of Capitalism, a Historical Study, 1926 (Holland Memorial Lectures, 1922; Foreword to Max Weber, The Protestant Ethic and the Spirit of Capitalism (tr. T. Parsons) 1930; Equality, 1931 (Halley Stewart Lectures, 1929; 4th rev. ed. 1952; reissued 1964 with a new introd. by R. M. Titmuss); A Memorandum on Agriculture and Industry in China, 1931 (Inst. of Pacific Relations papers); Land and Labour in China, 1932 (reissued 1955); Some Thoughts on the Economy of Public Education, 1938 (L. T. Hobhouse Memorial Trust Lectures, no. 8); Why Britain Fights, 1941 (Macmillan War Pamphlets no. 13); The Problem of the Public Schools, 1944; Beatrice Webb, 1858–1943, 1945 (Proceedings of the British Academy vol. 29); Social History and Literature, 1950 (National Book League Annual Lecture, 7; new rev. ed. 1958); The Attack, and Other Papers, 1953; The Webbs in Perspective, 1953 (Webb Memorial Lecture, 1952); Business and Politics under James I: Lionel Cranfield as Merchant and Minister, 1958; The Radical Tradition: Twelve Essays on Politics, Education, and Literature (ed. R. Hinden) 1964 (in U.S.: ed. Hugh Gaitskell); The Assessment of Wages in England by the Justices of the Peace in Wage Regulation in Pre-Industrial England . . . (ed. W. E. Minchinton) 1972; R. H. Tawney's Commonplace Book (ed. and introd. J. M. Winter and D. M. Joslin) 1972 (Economic History Review, Suppl. 5); History and Society: Essays (ed. J. M. Winter) 1978; R. H. Tawney: The American Labour Movement and Other Essays (ed. J. M. Winter) 1979. *As editor—*

Secondary Education for All: A Policy for Labour, 1922; (with E. Power) Tudor Economic Documents: Being Select Documents Illustrating the Economic and Social History of Tudor England, 3 vols., 1924 (University of London Historical Ser., no. 4); A Discourse upon Usury . . . 1572 by Thomas Wilson (with historical intro.) 1925; Studies in Economic History: The Collected Papers of George Urwin (with introd. memoir) 1927; Economic History Review, 1927–1934; (with others) English Economic History: Select Documents, 1937.

ABOUT: Ausubel, H. (ed., with others) Some Modern Historians of Britain, 1951; Dictionary of National Biography 1961–1970, 1981; Fisher, F. J. Tawney's Century in Essays in the Economic and Social History of Tudor and Stuart England in Honour of R. H. Tawney (F. J. Fisher, ed.) 1961; Hinden, R. (ed.) The Radical Tradition: Twelve Essays on Politics, Education, and Literature, 1964 (in U.S.: ed. Hugh Gaitskell); International Encyclopedia of the Social Sciences vol. 15, 1968; Ormrod, D. (ed.) Fellowship, Freedom, and Equality: Lectures in Memory of R. H. Tawney, 1990; Reisman, D. Tawney, Galbraith and Adam Smith: State and Welfare, 1982; Tawney, R. H. The Attack, and Other Papers, 1953; Tawney, R. H. R. H. Tawney's Commonplace Book (ed. and introd. J. M. Winter and D. M. Joslin) 1972 (Economic History Review, Suppl. 5); Terrill R. R. H. Tawney and His Times: Socialism as Fellowship, 1973; Turner, R. (ed.) Thinkers of the Twentieth Century, 2nd ed, 1987; Williams, J. R. (and others) R. H. Tawney, a Portrait by Several Hands, 1960; Winter, J. M. Tawney the Historian in History and Society: Essays by R. H. Tawney (ed. J. M. Winter) 1978; Wright, A. R. H. Tawney, 1987 (Lives of the Left). Periodicals—American Economic Review June 1933; American Sociological Review December 1962; British Academy Proceedings vol. 48; Journal of Economic Issues June 1982; Manchester Guardian January 30, 1953, January 17, 1962; Nation and Athenaeum April 17, 1926; New Statesman September 7, 1984; New York Review of Books July 30, 1964; New York Times January 17, 1962; Spectator February 28, 1931; Times (London) January 17, 1962; Times Literary Supplement December 22, 1932; December 26, 1958.

## TAYLOR, BERT LESTON (November 13, 1866–March 19, 1921), American newspaper columnist, was best known for his daily column "A Line-o'-Type or Two," written in the early 1900s for the Chicago Tribune and signed "B.L.T."

Born in the hill town of Goshen, Massachusetts, the son of A. O. and Katherine (White) Taylor, he attended the College of the City of New York. He

 began his career in journalism in New England in the 1890s as a reporter for newspapers in small New England towns such as Plainfield, New Hampshire, and Montpelier, Vermont. After marrying Emma Bonner of Providence, Rhode Island, in 1895, he became an editorial writer for the News-Tribune in Duluth, Minnesota. He went to Chicago in 1899 to join the Chicago Journal. Two years later he moved to the Tribune, where his famous column originated.

Taylor's humorous but kindly column was rooted in a rural consciousness that was celebrated in the small-town press that nurtured him as a young reporter, but it held its own in the tradition of a Chicago press that also produced Eugene Field's "Sharps and Flats" and George Ade's "Stories of the Streets and of the Town." While Taylor avoided using dialect, phonetic spelling, and homely anec-

dotes—the staples of the "homespun" genre—he did draw his inspiration from rural life and the rural press and included his original poetry. A reviewer in the Springfield Republican wrote: "Tho the most widely read newspaper columnist of our sophisticated day, he remained essentially true to the small town."

"A Line-o'-Type or Two" appeared six days a week as a full column on the Tribune's editorial page. In writing it, Taylor included comments submitted from many readers—comments that were said to have reached him from all parts of the globe addressed simply "B.L.T." Even established writers considered it an honor to have met Taylor's standards and "make the Line." One such contribution was from "F.P.A.," a Chicago youth named Franklin Pierce Adams, who later acknowledged Taylor as his mentor.

In 1903, Taylor left Chicago for a six-year stint in New York City. He wrote for the New York Telegraph and worked as an assistant editor on Punch, a humor publication. He returned to Chicago and the Tribune in 1909, resumed his column and stayed with the paper until his death.

Taylor's bibliography also included several books, most of them derived from his column. Some were published posthumously. A collection of Taylor's light verses was published in 1913 under the title Motley Measures, reprinted in 1927 with a foreword by Ring Lardner. A Penny Whistle (1921) is a collection of his own selections from eight years of columns. The So-Called Human Race, including prose and verse and published posthumously the following year, is the second volume in the collected edition of his works. A Line o Gowf or Two (1923), an anthology of Taylor's golf quips, includes a preface by golfer Charles "Chick" Evans. B.L.T. was an avid golfer, and the volume was considered by the New York Times to be "one of the most whimsical and yet serious-minded books on golf that has been published for a long time."

A more serious, reflective Taylor is evident in the essays that make up The East Window, and The Car Window (1924). Brief essays in "The East Window"—meditations on literature, poetry, nature, music, and life. In "The Car Window," Taylor takes a look at the American and Canadian scene. "The essays are like tiny bottles of an exquisite and potent essence," said Bookmark. And H. J. Mankiewicz wrote in the New York Times that "Taylor shows himself an expert at a form of writing rarely attempted in America—the construction and the execution of feuilletons."

On Taylor's death the Chicago Tribune paid him perhaps the highest compliment when it wrote: "Newspaper people are disciplined in one thing which is good for the ego. None is indispensable. The paper would look the same no matter who became a dropout. That was not true of Mr. Taylor. It is not true now. It was a rare genius which broke down the rule of destiny for newspaper folk."

PRINCIPAL WORKS: Under Three Flags: A Story of Mystery (with A. T. Thoits), 1896; Line-o-Type Lyrics, 1902; The Well in the Wood, 1904; (with A. H. Folwell and J. K. Bangs) Monsieur den Brochette, 1905; (with W. C. Gibson) The Log of the Water Wagon, 1905; Extra Dry, 1906; The Charlatans, 1906; A Line-o'-Verse or Two, 1911; The Pipesmoke Carry, 1912; Motley Measures, 1913; A Penny Whistle, 1921; The So-Called Human Race, 1922; A Line o Gowf or Two, 1923; The East Window, and The Car Window, 1924.

ABOUT: Atlantics Bookshelf June 1922; Dictionary of Literary Biography vol. 25; National Cyclopaedia of American Biography, vol. 24; Rascoe, B. Before I Forget. *Periodicals*—Bookmark July 1924; Chicago Sunday Tribune March 20, 1921; Everybody's Magazine October 1920; Literary Digest April 9, 1921; New York Evening Post March 1921; New York Times November 17, 1906; March 20, 1921; April 8, 1923; May 4, 1924; Poetry May 1921.

**TAYLOR, DEEMS** (December 22, 1885–July 3, 1966), American composer, music critic, and radio commentator, was born in New York, the son of Jo-

seph and Katharine (Johnson) Taylor. He attended the Ethical Culture School in New York and received a B.A. from New York University in 1906. While an undergraduate he wrote the music for several campus shows; one of them was heard by Victor Herbert, who advised Taylor to study music theory. Accordingly, between 1908 and 1911 he took lessons in harmony and counterpoint—the only formal musical training he received other than piano lessons as a child.

After college Taylor began work as a reference book editor (including a stint on the *Encyclopædia Britannica*), and from 1912 to 1916 was associate editor of the *Western Electric News*. In 1916 he became assistant Sunday editor of the *New York Tribune* and spent a year in France as a war correspondent. From 1917 to 1919 Taylor was an associate editor of *Colliers Weekly*. During all this time he had continued writing music. Although a musical comedy, *The Echo* (1910) was unsuccessful, his tone poem *The Siren Song* (1913) won the orchestral prize of the National Federation of Music Clubs. *The Highwayman* (1914), inspired by Alfred Noyes's ballad, was commissioned by the MacDowell Festival in Peterborough, New Hampshire. From then on, Taylor's best-known pieces were connected with more significant literary works. *Through the Looking Glass*, an orchestral suite based on *Alice in Wonderland*, was first performed in 1918; *Jurgen*, composed in 1925 for the New York Symphony Orchestra led by Walter Damrosch, was inspired by James Branch Cabell's fantasy. *The King's Henchman* (1927), an opera commissioned by the Metropolitan Opera Company, with a libretto written by Edna St. Vincent Millay, ran for three consecutive seasons (fourteen performances in all). His second opera, *Peter Ibbetson* (1931), was based on the George Du Maurier novel; it incorporated a number of French folk songs to good effect and, with the soprano Lucrezia Bori as the heroine, the Duchess of Towers, was a great popular (if not critical) success. Between 1931 and 1935 sixteen performances were given at the Metropolitan—the longest run of any opera by an

American composer up to then. His third, and last, opera, *Ramuntcho*, staged by the Philadelphia Opera Company in 1942, has Pierre Loti's story as libretto. Taylor's other music included incidental pieces for plays, orchestral works, and vocal scores. His body of work (about 150 pieces in all) is considered to have been deftly constructed; though derivative, it is a skillful blend of European influences.

Deems Taylor's work as a critic began in 1921 when he started writing for the *New York World*; he resigned four years later to compose his first opera. From 1927 to 1929 he edited *Musical America*; and in 1931–1932 he was music critic of the *New York American*. Taylor's connection with radio began in 1936 when (until 1943) he was consultant on music for the Columbia Broadcasting System and gave talks during the intermissions of its Sunday afternoon broadcasts of the New York Philharmonic. His persuasive, informal but informed commentaries were a popular feature and helped introduce a wide audience to serious music. These talks—together with a selection of his reviews and articles in magazines such as the *Saturday Evening Post*, the *New Yorker*, and *Vanity Fair*—were collected in two books: *Of Men and Music* and *The Well Tempered Listener*. A later collection of his radio commentaries was published under the title *Music to My Ears*. Taylor was also a commentator during Metropolitan Opera broadcasts, delivering witty, urbane observations on the performances being aired. In addition to appearing regularly on these musical programs, he took his place as a panelist (along with the pianist Oscar Levant, the critic Clifton Fadiman, and the newspaper writers Franklin Pierce Adams and John Kieran) on the quiz show "Information Please."

Like his radio talks, Taylor's books *A Pictorial History of the Movies* (devoted mostly to American films) and *Some Enchanted Evenings*, "not a biography, but a story" of Richard Rodgers and Oscar Hammerstein 2d, were light in tone, meant to appeal to the general reader. His text for what amounted to a souvenir program of Walt Disney's *Fantasia*—with notes on the musical selections—helped popularize this now classic film (Taylor appeared in the film as narrator).

On the more serious side, reverting to his early reference book work, Taylor coedited revised texts of *The Biographical Dictionary of Musicians* and *Music Lovers Encyclopedia*, both originally compiled by the biographer Rupert Hughes. Taylor also translated and edited *The One-Track Mind*, a selection of French love poetry of the seventeenth and eighteenth centuries.

The recipient of several honorary degrees in music (from his alma mater in 1927, from the Cincinnati Conservatory in 1941, among others), Deems Taylor was for many years a member of the board of the American Society of Composers, Authors, and Publishers (ASCAP), and president from 1942 to 1948. In 1967 the society established its annual ASCAP-Deems Taylor Award for outstanding books and articles on music.

PRINCIPAL WORKS: Of Men and Music, 1937; Walt Disneys Fantasia (foreword by Leopold Stokowski) 1940; The Well Tempered Listener, 1940; (with others) A Pictorial History of the Movies, 4th rev. ed. 1951; Music to My Ears, 1949; Some Enchanted Evenings: The Story of Rodgers and Hammerstein, 1953. *As editor*—The Biographical Dictionary of Musicians, Originally Composed by Rupert Hughes, Completely Revised and Newly Edited by Deems Taylor and Russell Kerr, 1940; A Treasury of Gilbert and Sullivan (illus. L. Corcos; arr. A. Sirmay) 1941; Music Lovers Encyclopedia . . . Completely Revised and Newly Edited by Deems Taylor and Russell Kerr, 1954. *As editor and translator*—The One-Track Mind: Love Poems of XVIIth and XVIIIth Century France, 1953.

ABOUT: The ASCAP Biographical Dictionary of Composers, Authors, and Publishers, 1966; Current Biography 1940; Ewen, D. (ed.) Composers since 1900, 1962; Ewen, D. World of Twentieth Century Music, 1968; Goss, M. Modern Musicmakers, 1952; The New Grove Dictionary of Music and Musicians Vol. 18, 1980. *Periodicals*—New York Times July 5, 1966; Times (London) July 5, 1966.

## TAYLOR, ELIZABETH (COLES) (July 3, 1912–November 19, 1975), English novelist and short story writer, wrote:

"Born in Reading, Berkshire, England. Educated at the Abbey School, Reading—a school which carries on the name of an eighteenth-century school, run by French refugees, at which Mrs. Sherwood, Mrs Mitford, and Jane Austen were pupils. As a young child I began to write stories and always wanted to be a novelist; but I earned nothing from writing until after I was thirty. When I left school, worked as a governess and, later, in a library—and continued to write in my spare time. I learnt so much from these jobs and have never regretted the time I spent at them. I married when I was twenty-four, John William Kendal Taylor; and we have a son, Renny and a daughter, Joanna. Living, during the war, a lonely life in the country, while my husband was in the Royal Air Force, I wrote the first of my published novels—*At Mrs. Lippincote's*. My short stories have been printed, for the most part in the *New Yorker*; but also in *Harper's Bazaar* and *Harper's* magazine. A study of the novels of I. Compton-Burnett appeared in the English *Vogue*.

"I live in the country, in the village of Penn, Buckinghamshire. I dislike traveling, I love London; but not to live in. Village-life, with its wider differences—in every social sense—seems a better background for a woman novelist, and certainly more congenial to me. In towns, one tends to select one's friends. In the country, they are chosen for one—and oneself, so much the better; so much the richer.

"I suppose that I have no hobbies, although I am interested in painting. I like to have a house full of children to cook for; and as many cats sitting in front of the fire as possible. I love England and it would be painful to me to consider living in any other place. I find so beautiful, harmonious, and evocative, its landscape, style, tradition, even its climate. I should like to feel that the people in my books are essentially English and set down against a truly English background."

Elizabeth Taylor was the daughter of Oliver Coles, an insurance agent, and Elsie (Fewtrell) Coles. According to Elizabeth Jane Howard, "Her life was a quiet one, centered upon her marriage and her grandchildren." She did not publish her first book until she was thirty-four. However, she wrote steadily thereafter, ultimately producing twelve novels and four collections of short stories that won her wide esteem and a modest place in the modern hierarchy of British novelists.

Her mature work was of a uniformly high quality, seldom straying from the domestic, middle-class milieus that she described with (in Howard's words) "her own unique blend of humanity and razor-sharp observation that enabled her to be sardonic, devastating, wry and sly but mysteriously without malice."

A fairly representative novel, and one that Howard singled out for Taylor's "capacity for romantic feelings and situation that never spills over into sentiment," is *A Game of Hide and Seek*, the story of a reasonably contented married woman who, inconveniently for both of them, encounters the man she had loved passionately years before as an adolescent. This was precisely the sort of humdrum situation that led some critics to dismiss Taylor as a safe, middlebrow writer ("She seems to me almost impenetrably cosy," Walter Allen wrote of her in the *New Statesman*); others found a much tougher book beneath its placid surface. Florence Leclercq described *A Game of Hide and Seek* as "a pessimistic novel which explores Taylor's growing concern for wasted existences. Relentlessly, Taylor describes how human beings fail themselves and others through a series of wrong choices. It is a dispiriting notion, one that Taylor will explore again in her later novels."

No Taylor novel stands out as her magnum opus, but among the highest regarded are *The Sleeping Beauty*, the story of a well-meaning middle-aged man who contracts a bigamous marriage with a fragile young beauty in a small seaside town; *Angel*, the story of an untalented and romantic novelist who craves the admiration of people who can never give it to her; and *In a Summer Season*, the story of an intelligent and attractive widow who, to the consternation of her friends and family, remarries a charming but feckless Irishman ten years her junior. Like most of her books, they received generally favorable reviews, sold respectably but not spectacularly, and have been reprinted in recent years. "*The Sleeping Beauty* is a solid, articulate pattern of nicely contrasted and very sharply observed people," wrote Arthur Mizener in the *New Republic* (1953). "It is a world, and a complete one." Of *Angel* and its heroine, Angelica Deverell, Paul Bailey wrote, "To write about a purveyor of twaddle and yet render her preposterousness human is a challenging task. . . . Elizabeth Taylor reveals Angelica's feet of clay from the very start of *Angel* and because she does so she solicits an unlikely pity for the deluded creature later in the narrative. Angelica is drawn with a sharpness that never becomes derisive or satirical, and as a consequence she remains real." Reviewing a reprint of *In a Summer Season* in the *Times Literary Supplement*, Joy Grant asked, "Has any other woman described women's sexual feeling with such easy frankness, exactitude, and lyrical intensity? Indeed, there is a poetic quality in much of Taylor's writing, finding its fullest expression when she touches on the English weather or natural scene. The title—*In a Summer Season*—hints at what we find: passages of prose-poetry dovetailing smoothly with the narrative."

Grant maintained that Taylor's greatest shortcoming was "her difficulty in organizing a long fictional work." Following Taylor's avowed preference for writing "in scenes" to writing "in narrative," some critics favor her short stories over her novels. Florence Leclercq wrote that "besides her discreet yet vital reliance upon details, what makes Taylor's stories so fascinating to read may well be her cyrstallization of one particular 'moment of being'. . . . She manages to capture brief moments of awareness, loaded with significance . . . her characters, she implies, will never be the same again. Yet the turmoil of emotions which they often experience in Taylor's stories are mostly described quietly." But even in her novels, according to Susannah Clapp, "There is nothing clammy or precious in her presentation of life as a series of random, vivid moments: she investigates people's sense of themselves with her sense of humor. There is nothing cosy either. Most people's lives are laid waste not by one fell blow, but by a daily piling-up of small losses or small lies."

PRINCIPAL WORKS: *Novels*—At Mrs. Lippincote's, 1945; Palladian, 1946; A View of the Harbour, 1947; A Wreath of Roses, 1949; A Game of Hide-and-Seek, 1951; The Sleeping Beauty, 1953; Angel, 1957; In a Summer Season, 1961; The Soul of Kindness, 1964; The Wedding Group, 1968; Mrs. Palfrey at the Claremont, 1971; Blaming, 1976. *Short stories*—Hester Lilly and Twelve Short Stories, 1954; The Blush and Other Stories, 1958; A Dedicated Man and Other Stories, 1965; The Devastating Boys and Other Stories, 1972. *Juvenile*—Mossy Trotter, 1967.

ABOUT: The autobiographical material quoted above was written for Twentieth Century Authors First Supplement, 1955. Bailey, P. introduction to Angel (by E. Taylor) 1983; Clapp, S. introduction to The Sleeping Beauty (by E, Taylor) 1983; Contemporary Literary Criticism vol. 2, 1974; vol. 4, 1975; vol. 29, 1984; Current Biography 1948; Dictionary of Literary Biography vol. 139, 1994; Howard, E. J. introduction to A Game of Hide-and-Seek (by E. Taylor) 1986; Leclercq, F. Elizabeth Taylor, 1985; Schlueter P. and J. Schlueter (eds.) Encyclopedia of British Women Writers, 1988; Twentieth Century British Literature vol. 5 1987. *Periodicals*—New Republic November 2, 1953; March 26, 1984; New Statesman December 20, 1958; Times (London) November 21, 1975; Times Literary Supplement July 1, 1983.

**TAYLOR, PETER** (January 8, 1917–November 2, 1994), American short story writer and novelist, was born in Trenton, Tennessee, the son of Matthew Hillsman Taylor, a lawyer, and Katherine Baird (Taylor) Taylor. The family moved to Nashville, Tennessee, when he was seven, and two years later to St. Louis, Missouri. From 1932 until 1937 they lived in Memphis, Tennessee. The frequent moves gave Taylor the opportunity to observe at first hand the effects of urbanization and industri-

alization on the lives of middle-class families transplanted from small rural southern towns. This clash of cultural and social values is a recurrent theme in his fiction.

He enrolled at Vanderbilt University in 1936 to study literature and creative writing with the poet and critic John Crowe Ransom. The school was the base of a group of writers known as the Fugitives, who were attempting to bring about a southern literary and political renaissance. They included Ransom, Allen Tate, and Robert Penn Warren, Much of their original work was published in the *Fugitive* literary journal between 1922 and 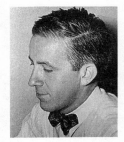 1925. Essentially conservative, they were committed to traditional "agrarian" ideals. With Cleanth Brooks they helped to establish the New Criticism, a movement which focused on the text of literary work, rather than on its social or cultural context.

Taylor transferred to Southwestern College in Memphis, where Tate was on the faculty, for a year—and then to Kenyon College, where Ransom was teaching. One of his poems was published in the *Kenyon Review*. Among Taylor's fellow students were the poets Randall Jarrell and Robert Lowell. Taylor received his B.A. degree from Kenyon in 1940.

Taylor's first stories were published in 1940, in the *Southern Review*. Over the years he contributed short fiction to many publications, and became best known for his stories in the *New Yorker*. He married the poet Eleanor Lilly Ross in 1943. During World War II he served in the army and was stationed in England. After the war he joined the faculty of the University of North Carolina at Greensboro, where he taught intermittently until 1967. In that year he became professor of English and director of the creative writing program at the University of Virginia.

Taylor's first book was a collection of stories entitled *A Long Fourth*. Marjorie Brace noted in the *Saturday Review of Literature* in 1948 that Taylor "writes with limpid sobriety of undramatic incidents. . . . What [he] is really doing, with honesty and sureness and beauty, is to experiment, both technically and psychologically, with very difficult approaches to extremely difficult definitions. . . . He is a thoroughly unpretentious and original talent." The book that many critics regard as his finest work is the novella *A Woman of Means*. Set in St. Louis in the 1920s, it is an adolescent boy's account of the disintegration of his widowed father's second marriage and of his loving but troubled stepmother's descent into madness. The book makes use of the narrative skills that mark Taylor's best work: gentle irony, a sense of things seen and heard but now lost, and a narrator whose credibility is in doubt owing to his prejudiced involvement.

Taylor's next three books were all collections of

stories—*The Widows of Thornton, Happy Families Are All Alike*, and *Miss Leonora When Last Seen*. The story "Venus, Cupid, Folly and Time," which won an O. Henry Memorial Award in 1959, was included in the third of these collections. It was about two people unable to escape from the past. The past in Taylor's world always intrudes into the present, often in ways that are neither pleasant nor helpful.

In 1969 Farrar, Straus brought out *The Collected Stories of Peter Taylor*. After this he began experimenting with free-verse narratives, which he described as "broken-line prose." They were more intense and created a greater intimacy with the narrator and the process of storytelling; but they met with less than universal praise. Stories using this style appeared in his collection called *In the Miro District*.

Taylor's most recent volume of short fiction was *The Old Forest*. The judges of PEN voted it the best work of fiction in 1985. His second novel, *A Summons to Memphis*, was about a middle-aged editor's odyssey into his past, related with both humor and pathos. It was given the $50,000 Ritz-Hemingway Award as well as the Pulitzer Prize for fiction in 1987.

Taylor was also the author of several experimental one-act plays. *A Stand in the Mountains*, published in the *Kenyon Review* in 1965, was produced at the Barter Theater in Abingdon, Virginia, in 1971. With Robert Lowell and Robert Penn Warren, Taylor edited *Randall Jarrell, 1914–1965*, a volume of essays and reminiscences published two years after the poet's death. Taylor's honors and awards include a Guggenheim Fellowship (1950), a Fulbright Fellowship (1955), a Ford Foundation Fellowship (1960), and a Rockefeller Foundation Grant (1966). He received the Gold Medal for Literature from the National Institute and American Academy of Arts and Letters (of both of which he is a member) in 1979. He has been a visiting lecturer at a number of universities, including Indiana and Oxford.

PRINCIPAL WORKS: *Collected stories*—A Long Fourth, 1948; The Widows of Thornton, 1954; Happy Families Are All Alike, 1959; Miss Leonora When Last Seen, 1963; Collected Stories, 1969; In the Miro District, 1977; The Old Forest, 1985. *Novels*—A Woman of Means, 1950; A Summons to Memphis, 1986. *Drama*—Death of a Kinsman, 1954; Tennessee Day in St. Louis, 1959; Presences: Seven Dramatic Pieces, 1973. *As editor*—(with R. Lowell and R. P. Warren) Randall Jarrell, 1914–1965, 1967; The Road and Other Modern Stories, 1979.

ABOUT: Eisinger, C. E. Fiction in the Forties, 1963; Griffith, A. J. Peter Taylor, 1970; Rubin, L. D. Jr., and Jacobs, R. D. South: Modern Southern Literature in Its Cultural Setting, 1966. *Periodicals*—New York Times May 7, 1986; Saturday Review May 14, 1977; Saturday Review of Literature March 27, 1948; Sewanee Review Autumn 1962; Shenandoah Winter 1977; Virginia Quarterly Review Spring 1978.

## TAYLOR, PHOEBE ATWOOD (May 18, 1909–January 9, 1976), American crime novelist, creator of the detectives Asey Mayo and Leonidas Witherall, was born in Boston, Massachusetts, and educated at Columbia University. She published her first detective book, *The Cape Cod Mystery* (1931), a year after graduation. Introducing Asey Mayo and his assistant, Miss Prudence Whitsby, the

book was notable for its sense of humor and lively handling of local color. Of a later Asey Mayo mystery, *Figure Away* (1937), the *New York Times* wrote: "Phoebe Atwood Taylor can get more fun into a detective story than any writer at present producing books of this sort." Amusement, as much as bafflement or excitement, was the key to the entertainment value of her books. The *New York Times*, in its review of *Octagon House*, the next book after *Figure Away*, observed, "half the fun in reading her stories lies in the talk and actions of her characters. There is mystery to be sure, but it is the author's keen sense of humor that is the chief attraction."

Having published under her own name during most of the thirties, Miss Taylor adopted a pseudonym, "Alice Tilton," for *The Cut Direct* (1938), in which Leonidas Witherall made his first appearance. In this and the succeeding "Tilton" books, Taylor became increasingly frivolous. Some readers found the atmosphere too farcical for mystery fiction—reviewers dubbed the books "manic," "wacky," and "mad."

Taylor is said to have given herself a three-week deadline in which to complete each of her books, writing between midnight and three in the morning. She continued producing new titles into the fifties, and when her publisher, W. W. Norton, reissued much of her older work during the sixties, she enjoyed a continuing popularity. A large number of her Cape Cod titles have been continuously available in paperback.

PRINCIPAL WORKS: *Fiction*—The Cape Cod Mystery, 1931; Death Lights a Candle, 1932; The Mystery of the Cape Cod Players, 1933; The Mystery of the Cape Cod Tavern, 1934; Sandbar Sinister, 1934; Deathblow Hill, 1935; The Tinkling Symbol, 1935; The Crimson Patch, 1936; Out of Order, 1936; Beginning with a Bash, 1937; Octagon House, 1937; Figure Away, 1937; The Amulet of Gilt, 1938; Banbury Bog, 1938; The Cut Direct, 1938; Cold Steal, 1939; Spring Harrowing, 1939; The Criminal C.O.D. 1940; The Deadly Sunshade, 1940; The Left Leg, 1940; The Hollow Chest, 1941; The Perennial Border, 1941; The Six Iron Spiders, 1942; File For Record, 1943; Going, Going, Gone, 1943; Dead Ernest, 1944; Proof of the Pudding, 1945; The Asey Mayo Trio, 1946; Punch with Care, 1946; The Iron Clew, 1947; Diplomatic Corpse, 1951.

ABOUT: Reilly J. M. (ed.) Twentieth Century Crime and Mystery Writers. *Periodicals*—New York Times June 5, 1932; January 17, 1937; August 29, 1937; January 12, 1976.

## TAYLOR, RACHEL (ANNAND) (1876–1960), Scottish poet and historian, the daughter of John Wilson Annand and Clarinda (Dinnie) Annand, was born in Peterhead. She was educated at school in Aberdeen, and was one of the first female students at the university there. She attracted the notice of one of her tutors, the great Donne scholar, Herbert Grierson. Impressed by her talent, he sent some of her poems and prose to the editor of the *British Weekly*, which published them. In 1904 her first collection of poems was issued by John Lane.

In 1901 she married Alexander Cameron Taylor, with whom she lived for several years in Dundee. His poor health, however, led to her taking up a literary career in London.  She was helped in this by the support of friends such as Sir Patrick Geddes, who joined together to publish a second collection, *Rose and Vine*, in 1909. This book was described by the classical historian and translator Gilbert Murray as "poetry of intense imagination and exquisite craftmanship, never simple, never commonplace, never easy, defiantly and mockingly anti-modern."

Encouraged by Murray, Taylor turned to history, producing several passionate works, the first of which was *Aspects of the Italian Renaissance*, later expanded and revised as *Invitation to Renaissance Italy*. As an exercise in lyricism and adjectival breadth these were successful, leaving critics reeling from the purple prose but nevertheless impressed by grasp of the period. Her second historical work was a biography of Leonardo da Vinci, *Leonardo the Florentine*.

Both her Renaissance histories and her biography of Leonardo were successful in America, but although she was thought well of by, among others, G. K. Chesterton and Hilaire Belloc, the minor reputation she achieved during her lifetime has now completely faded. In 1943, as part of the celebrations marking its granting of full membership to women, Aberdeen University conferred an honorary LL.D. upon Taylor.

PRINCIPAL WORKS: Poems, 1904; Rose and Vine, 1909; The Hours of Flammetta: A Sonnet Sequence, 1910; Aspects of the Italian Renaissance, 1923; The End of Flammetta, 1923; Leonardo the Florentine: A Study in Personality, 1927; Invitation to Renaissance Italy, 1930; William Dunbar: The Poet and His Period, 1931; Renaissance France, 1939.

ABOUT: Lawrence, D. H. Eight Letters to Rachel Annand Taylor, 1956; Murray, G. Introduction to Leonardo the Florentine, 1927.

**TEALE, EDWIN WAY** (June 2, 1899–October 18, 1980), American nature writer, was born in Joliet, Illinois, the son of Oliver Cromwell Teale and  Clara Louise (Way) Teale. Christened Edwin Alfred Teale, he changed his name at age twelve, believing that his mother's maiden name was more befitting an author. He won the Pulitzer Prize for general non-fiction in 1966 for *Wandering Through Winter* and received frequent praise for combining a poet's sensitivity with a photographer's keen eye, a scientist's accuracy and a teacher's ability to stimulate. His favorite book was *Walden*, his favorite author was W. H. Hudson,

and he was often grouped with Roger Tory Peterson and William Beebe as America's preeminent twentieth century naturalists.

In his books, Teale wrote and photographed mayflies and monarchs, bee hives and birds' nests, grassy meadows in Connecticut and redwood forests in California, and presented a panorama of the four seasons throughout North America, rarely receiving a bad notice. He also wrote guide books for younger readers, edited many volumes by other nature authors, and penned innumerable magazine and newspaper articles, working as a staff writer for *Popular Science* magazine for thirteen years and as a contributing editor to *Audubon* magazine for nearly forty years.

His love for nature started as a young boy when he got away from the railroad yards of Joliet, "the kind of neighborhood where boys put rocks in their snowballs," to spend each summer at his maternal grandparents' farm, Lone Oak, in the dune country of northern Indiana. Here he began to take notes on "wild creatures" and "all the moods of Nature," he wrote in *Dune Boy* (1943), his Tom Sawyer-like recollections of this formative life period. He continued: "In a way, during the evenings of those golden summer days, my passionate love of the out-of-doors and my interest in the world of books found a common meeting-ground. I even dreamed of some glorious, far-off future—shrouded in a sort of glowing mist—when I, too, would write a book."

Teale met his wife, Nellie, while attending Earlham College in Richmond, Indiana, and she served as travel companion and researcher over the years. His early interest was insects, and his first nature book, *Grassroot Jungles* (1937), focused on the habits of those backyard denizens and led to his being compared to French entomologist Jean Henri Fabre. Its publication marked the first time the *New York Times Book Review* put a praying mantis on its front cover. Teale was praised by the *Saturday Review of Literature* for the "technical perfection and informative character" of his 130 insect photographs, which accompanied text that was described as pithy, enthusiastic, and eloquent.

*Near Horizons* (1942) explained the origin and uses of the author's insect garden on Long Island, which he called "a banquet hall for the six-legged." Then Teale broadened his scope with *The Lost Woods* (1945), offering snippets of information, philosophy and photographs on a variety of outdoor subjects, from the oddities seen while flying through the heart of a cloud to the beauties of individual snowflakes. *Days Without Time* (1948) followed in the same meandering vein.

Teale began his four-volume series on the American seasons with his *North With the Spring* (1951), for which he and his wife made a 17,000-mile journey following the early stages of spring from the Florida Everglades to the Canadian border. He took to the road with Nellie again for *Autumn Across America* (1956), for which the two traveled 20,000 miles from Cape Cod to the California coast, focusing largely on the autumnal splendor around four major flyways of migrating birds.

For the third volume, *Journey Into Summer* (1960), the Teales set out from Franconia Notch, New Hampshire, and ended atop Pike's Peak in Colorado, for a trip that resulted in "a rediscovery of America and a plea for conservation of American wilderness, forests, swamps and rivers," wrote Raymond Holden in the *New York Times Book Review*. Lewis Gannett in the *New York Herald Tribune Book Review* wrote that Teale "belongs in a class with John Bartram and John James Audubon and, in a way, is entitled to even more credit than those early travelers. They, after all, found it much easier to present their readers with things which had never been seen or imagined," wrote Lewis Gannett in the *New York Herald Tribune Book Review*. The series, which was reissued in the 1980s, culminated in the Pulitzer Prize-winning *Wandering Through Winter* (1965). Roger Tory Peterson wrote in the *New York Times*, "There is something of all the great nature writers in Teale."

As editor, Teale brought back to print the writings of two great naturalists with the anthologies *The Insect World of J. Henri Fabre* (1949) and *The Wilderness World of John Muir* (1955). He enriched Thoreau's *Walden* (1946) with new photographs and commentary, and Hudson's *Green Mansions* (1949) with new illustrations and an introduction. He also compiled a sampling of the classics in *Green Treasury* (1952). His edition of Audubon's *Wildlife* (1965) marked the first time that reproductions of Audubon's birds and animals were combined in a single book.

Among his many honors, Teale was awarded the John Burroughs Medal for distinguished writing in 1943, the Christopher Medal in 1957, and honorary degrees from Earlham College in 1957 and from Indiana University in 1978.

PRINCIPAL WORKS: The Book of Gliders, 1930; Grassroot Jungles, 1937; The Junior Book of Insects, 1939; The Boys' Book of Photography, 1939; The Golden Throng, 1940; Byways to Adventure, 1942; Near Horizons, 1942; Dune Boy, 1943; The Lost Woods, 1945; (ed.) Walden, 1946; Days Without Time, 1948; (ed.) The Insect World of J. Henri Fabre, 1949; (ed.) Green Mansions, 1949; North With the Spring, 1951; (ed.) Green Treasury, 1952; The Circle of the Seasons, 1953; (ed.) The Wilderness World of John Muir, 1954; Insect Friends, 1955; Autumn Across America, 1956; Adventures in Nature, 1959; Journey Into Summer, 1960; The Lost Dog, 1961; The Strange Lives of Familiar Insects, 1962; (ed.) The Thoughts of Thoreau, 1962; Wandering Through Winter, 1965; (ed.) Audubon's Wildlife, 1964; The American Seasons, 1966; Springtime in Britain, 1970; Photographs of American Nature, 1972; A Naturalist Buys an Old Farm, 1974; A Walk Through the Year, 1978; A Conscious Stillness (with Zwinger, A.) 1982.

ABOUT: Current Biography 1961; Dodd, E. H. Of Nature, Time and Teale; Teale, E. W. Dune Boy. *Periodicals*—Audubon Magazine May 1952, May 1962, May 1965, November 1969, January 1981; Book Week, October 17, 1965; Collier's February 26, 1949; Conservationist April 1974; Newsweek November 3, 1980; New York Herald Tribune Book Review October 7, 1951; December 2, 1951; October 30, 1960; New York Times October 30, 1960; October 24, 1965; October 21, 1980; July 22, 1990; Time November 3, 1980.

**TEASDALE, SARA** (August 8, 1884–January 29, 1933), American poet, was born in St. Louis, Missouri, the daughter of John Warren Teasdale and Mary Elizabeth (Willard) Teasdale. A delicate child, she was educated at a private school. Throughout her life she showed an almost neurotic attachment to (yet discontent with) her family, a concern for her health that came near to hypochondria, and an inability to adjust herself to the  demands of maturity. She was torn between the desire to experience life and the need to seclude herself from it. She first started writing in school, influenced strongly by the verse of Christina Rossetti. For a few years after leaving school she and some friends edited a monthly journal called *Potter's Wheel*. Her first appearance as a poet was with "Guenevere," a blank verse monologue that was published in *Reedy's Mirror* in 1907. This was followed by her first book of verse, *Sonnets to Duse and Other Poems*, which included poems about well-known women—Helen, Sappho, Beatrice—as well as the famous Italian actress.

Teasdale lived with her parents in St. Louis until 1914. During these years she did not have to worry about money and was able to travel; in 1905 she made her first trip to Europe and the Near East. Her most frequent refuge from her home was Chicago, where she became attached, if only loosely, to the group of writers forming that city's literary renaissance. There she met the poet Vachel Lindsay, with whom she developed a close emotional bond; but she refused to marry him. Instead, in 1914, she suddenly married a St. Louis businessman, Ernst B. Filsinger. For a number of years the marriage afforded her security, privacy, and the opportunity to write; but she became increasingly reclusive, and eventually divorced her husband in 1929.

Teasdale's next volumes of verse—*Rivers to the Sea, Love Songs* (which was given the Pulitzer Prize for poetry in 1918, as well as a Poetry Society award), and *Flame and Shadow*—revealed a certain artistic maturity, but she avoided any modernist experimentation in subject or technique, instead concentrating her impressions into simple lyrics with regular rhymes. Reviewing *Dark of the Moon*, her next book of poems, in the *New Republic* in 1926, Babette Deutsch observed: "The tempo is slower throughout than that to which she has accustomed us, to fit the more sombre thought. But the clear melody, the reverberant simplicity of statement are the same."

Teasdale spent her later years in New York City. She edited two volumes of verse: *The Answering Voice*, a collection of love poems by women, and *Rainbow Gold*, containing poems for a juvenile audience. She also wrote a book of her own poems, *Stars Tonight*, for young readers. Vachel Lindsay's suicide in 1931 shocked and depressed her. Despite increasing poor health, she journeyed to London in 1932 to do initial research for a biography of Christina Rossetti. There she contracted pneumonia and returned to New York, where her recovery was slow. She was found drowned in the bathtub of her Fifth Avenue apartment after taking an overdose of sleeping pills, almost certainly deliberate. Her last volume of verse, *Strange Victory*, on which she had been working, was published posthumously. It contained, as Harriet Monroe wrote in *Poetry* in November 1933, "poems of farewell—farewell to life and love, to the sea and the stars, to two or three persons unnamed. These lyric farewells, deeply colored with tragic emotion, are on the whole not tragic. Indeed, they are almost joyous—the finale of a life completely lived and ready for the end."

PRINCIPAL WORKS: *Poetry*—Sonnets to Duse and Other Poems, 1907; Helen of Troy and Other Poems, 1911; Rivers to the Sea, 1915; Love Songs, 1917; Flame and Shadow, 1920; Dark of the Moon, 1926; Stars Tonight, 1930 (juvenile); Strange Victory, 1933; Collected Poems, 1937. *Collection*—Mirror of the Heart (ed. W. Drake) 1984. *As editor*—The Answering Voice, 1917, enlarged ed. 1928; Rainbow Gold, 1922 (juvenile).

ABOUT: Carpenter, M. H. Sara Teasdale, 1960; Drake, W. Sara Teasdale, 1979; Gould, J. American Women Poets, 1980; Monroe, H. Poets and Their Art, 1926; Schoen, C. Sara Teasdale, 1986; Sprague, R. Imaginary Gardens, 1969; Untermeyer, L. From Another World, 1939. *Periodicals*—Commonweal February 15, 1933; New Republic December 1, 1926; February 15, 1933; New York Times January 30–31, 1933; New York Times Book Review August 26, 1984; Poetry April 1933, November 1933, December 1937; Saturday Review of Literature February 11, 1933.

**TEIRLINCK, HERMAN** (February 24, 1879–February 4, 1967), Belgian (Flemish) playwright, novelist, editor, essayist, short story writer, cultural official and poet, was born in Sint Jans Molenbeeka, a suburb of Brussels, the only son of the well-known linguist and folklorist Isidore Teirlinck (1851–1934). The elder Teirlinck instilled into his son his nationalism and particular love of the Brabant countryside and of its folklore.

Herman Teirlinck chose to write in his own Flemish tongue rather than in French, like other contemporary Flemings such as Maeterlinck, Verhaeren, and de Ghelderode. He knew that in so doing he was limiting his audience but felt, no doubt rightly, that he could do justice to his genius only in the Flemish language. He was influenced from the 1890s by a group of liberal, internationalist Flemish writers who produced the periodical *Van Nu en Straks* (Today and Tomorrow).

He went to school in Brussels, taught literature and art there, and eventually co-founded (1946) the leading magazine *Nieuw vlaams tijdschrift*. He advised three Belgian kings on cultural matters relating to the Flemish language, and was a tutor to one of them. He also ran the experimental section of the National Theatre for a time after World War II. He was himself a bold experimentalist, in both the play and the novel. In 1956 he received the Prize for Dutch Letters, awarded by the combined governments of Belgium and Holland.

Teirlinck's earlier books were, in a sense false starts. From his first volume, *Verzen* (1900, Poems), he learned that verse was not his natural mode of expression. His early regional fiction, such as the three tales contained in *De wonderbare wereld* (1902, The wondrous world), and the novel *De doolage* (1905, The swamp), was stylistically efficient in its description of peasants, but artificial in the light of the later standards he set.

The two books that gave Teirlinck his first fame were *Mijnheer J. B. Serjanszoon, orator didacticus* (1908) and *Het ivoren aapje* (1909, The ivory monkey). *Mijnheer Serjanszoon*, a tour de force, is the story of an eighteenth-century hedonist, epicure, and dilettante whose narcissism gets the better of him. The novel might have been directed at, if not exactly against, the Dutch novelist Louis Couperus, who had put on a similar dandy-like mask. Like that of some of Couperus's own later works, the essential message of *Mijnheer J. B. Serjanszoon* is that decadence, the cult of death and decay, however dazzling, eventually corrupts—and can never really help to dispel the fear of death, or be a help in self-tormenting solitude.

*Het ivoren aapje* is possibly even more successful because it is set in the city of Brussels, about which Teirlinck, to his regret, always wrote better than he could about the country. In both novels—the second is set in the Belle Époque (around the turn of the century)—Teirlinck is setting out to destroy, or at least to examine and challenge, his own "decadent" tendencies.

Teirlinck did write some more novels during this initial period of his literary activity, including the relatively straightforward *Johan Doxa* (1917), as well as an unfinished epistolary novel, written (1915) in collaboration with his friend Karel van de Woestijne, *Leemen torens* (Clay towers). From 1922, for the time being dissatisfied with his fiction, Teirlinck gave up novel-writing for eighteen years in pursuit of a scheme to build a genuinely Flemish theater. In this endeavor, Teirlinck single-handedly introduced expressionist techniques into the Belgian theater. His first play, *Der Vertraagde Film* (1922, Movie in slow motion), drew not only from the work of German expressionist dramatists such as Kaiser, but also from the silent cinema. This account of a couple rescued from a love suicide by drowning has a second act that takes place under water.

Other experimental plays followed; the more conventional *De ekster op de galg* (1937, The crow on the gallows), featuring simultaneous sets, was a tragedy about an old man who, feeling that he has not lived his life to the full, tries to have one last sexual fling. Teirlinck owed much in the technique of this play, probably his best, to that of Luigi Pirandello. At this time, too, he made strikingly effective adaptations of Sophocles and Aeschylus, and of medieval plays, pageants, and farces. His was a leading presence in the Flemish theater. He summed up all that he had learned, and all that he wished to teach, about the theatre in a well-regarded survey of dramatic art, which has not yet been translated.

Teirlinck was deeply affected by the Nazi occupation of his country and by the fact that some nationalistic Flemings welcomed the invasion. He returned to the novel, producing what many critics believe are the most original of all his works. *Maria Speermalie*, about a passionate and polyandrous woman who rises to the aristocracy, and *Griseldis*, a retelling of the "patient Griselda" story, are each in their different ways tributes to the strength and sexuality of women. *Het Gevecht met de engel* (1952, The battle with the angel) ranges over six centuries, and its energy never flags. They have not yet been translated into English. They have much in common with the writing of both Knut Hamsun and D. H. Lawrence (but "Lawrentian figures pale beside the ebullient primitives of Teirlinck," wrote E. M. Beekman in the *Encyclopedia of Twentieth-Century Literature*, who noted that Teirlinck shared the interest or obsession with many modernist writers in both "sexual passion and perversion."

Teirlinck's last novel, and undisputed masterpiece, *Zelfportret of het galgemaal* (1955) has been translated by James Brockway, as *Man in the Mirror*. In it, essentially, the author makes an autobiographical statement—and rewrites and infinitely improves upon his earlier tour de force, *Mijnheer J. B. Serjanszoon*. The buffoonish and clown-like protagonist, Henri M., a middle-class businessman who addresses himself throughout in the second person—this is perhaps the most convincing use of the technique ever made— is like J. B. Serjanszoon in that he is motivated by selfish lust and narcissism, but in the course of this more mature book, he gradually peels off each of his masks.

Although Teirlinck has been faulted by some for allegedly lacking in political motivation, he is seen by his admirers as a realist of the tormented modern psyche as well as a realist of the inner life. His extreme vitalism may be less "hedonistic" than simply essential to his vision.

Teirlinck's collected works, *Verzameld Werk*, were published, in nine volumes, between 1955 and 1973. A few of his plays exist in English, in versions made for the amateur stage; but these are in typescript and difficult to find.

PRINCIPAL WORK IN ENGLSIH TRANSLATION: *Fiction*—The Man in the Mirror (tr. J. Brockway) 1963.

ABOUT: Columbia Dictionary of Modern European Literature, 1947, 1980; Encyclopedia of Literature in the Twentieth Century, 1983; Lilar, S. The Belgian Theatre Since 1890, 1962; Meijer R. P. The Literature of the Low Countries, 1978; Seymour-Smith, M. Macmillan Guide to Modern World Literature, 1986.

**TERHUNE, ALBERT PAYSON** (December 21, 1872–February 18, 1942), American journalist, novelist, and writer of animal stories, wrote: "I was six years old when I teased a puppy by swinging it by its ears. My father appeared and without a word did the same to me. When I stopped bawling I began to think. Since that day I have never been able to see any fun in hurting anyone or anything which had neither the power nor the right to resent it. More—since that day I have always tried to understand the thoughts and impulses and natures of animals. It became a hobby with me then and there. We like to talk and to write about the things which interest us most. That is why I always craved to write about animals; chiefly about dogs. And I have

had the same desire to write about every phase of outdoor nature.

"My father was a clergyman, the Rev. Dr. Edward Payson Terhune. My mother was a writer, who used the pen-name of 'Marion Harland' (Mary Virginia [Hawes] Terhune). It was she who taught me to love writing. I was born in Newark, New Jersey, in the parsonage of my father's church. While I was still a child the whole family went to Europe to live for several years, and it was there—at Paris and Geneva—that my education began. We came back to America and I was graduated from Columbia University in 1893. Many years afterwards, I had the good luck to receive the Columbia Medal of Excellence, as 'explorer, man of letters, and true interpreter of Nature.'

"After I finished college, I went back to Europe for a while; and thence to the Near East, where I wandered through Egypt and Syria, living for a short time as a member of a desert Bedouin tribe, which wanted to adopt me. I also did a little unimportant exploring. Back in America, I took up newspaper work. I hated it. I wanted to be a writer, and not a reporter or an editor. So in my spare time late at night I used to write stories for magazines. It was slow and grindingly hard work until I began to write about dogs and the outdoors. After that it was much smoother sailing; and soon I was able to give up the drudgery of newspaper toil and devote my whole time to my books and stories and articles. And I was able to move out to Sunnybank, near Pompton Lakes, New Jersey. . . . Here I am surrounded by my pack of collie dogs, and can tramp the hills with them and fish and hunt."

———

Primarily known for writing scores of collie stories, the most famous being *Lad: A Dog* (1919), Albert Payson Terhune struggled as a newspaperman and part-time writer of short stories, serials, and mediocre melodrama until he brought his true passion to the page—his dogs.

Once he started writing these heartwarming stories, he achieved phenomenal success. He had an especially great effect on young readers, although he said he did not intend his books for young audiences and was astonished to find they constituted more than half of his readership. Many of his books are still in print.

Born in Newark, New Jersey, Terhune grew up in Springfield, Massachusetts, and Brooklyn, New York, where his father, a Presbyterian minister, held pastorates. Terhune spent his summers at his parents' country home, Sunnybank, in Pompton Lakes, New Jersey. It was a beloved place to the young Terhune; when he became successful he purchased Sunnybank and spent his adult life there, raising collies in his kennels and using the estate as the setting for many of his books.

Terhune fell in love with writing at an early age thanks largely to his mother, who under the pen name Marion Harland wrote best-selling romantic novels and a manual on home economics, *Common Sense in the Household*, which sold nearly half a million copies when it was published in 1871. Her subsequent cookbooks became Victorian household standards. Terhune wrote his first novel, *Dr. Dale* (1910), in collaboration with her.

Terhune subsequently took a reporter's post at the *New York Evening World*, eventually becoming a feature writer and editor. He worked there for twenty years. But he found little reward in newspaper work—he called it drudgery—and he developed the habits of a relentless workaholic, spending his evening and late night hours at home, writing magazine articles and serials, short stories, and motion-picture serials in hopes of becoming a financially independent writer.

During this period, he wrote *Caleb Conover, Railroader* (1907), about a corrupt political boss; a series of stories for *Smart Set* from 1913 to 1915; *The Fighter* (1909), which he considered his best novel; and *Dad* (1914), which included a contribution by Sinclair Lewis.

*Lad: A Dog* was an instant success; these collected stories that chart the adventures of this brave and loyal collie saw thirty-eight printings in ten years and sold an untold number of copies. Terhune reinforced his reputation by writing more than twenty other dog books in the next two decades.

Besides animal story books, Terhune found time to produce some adult novels, three screenplays, and two autobiographical volumes: *Now That I'm Fifty* (1925) and *To The Best of My Memory* (1930), in which he recounted his more colorful life experiences, including his days at Columbia University when he was an expert swordsman and boxer.

Terhune served as a park commissioner for the State of New Jersey from 1925 to 1942. His legacy continued after his death: his second wife, Anice Terhune, a composer and writer whom he had married in 1901 after the death of his first wife, wrote *Across The Line*, a book based on her husband's notes speculating on eternal life. Anice Terhune wrote that her husband still maintained communication with her after his death, and claimed she was able to take dictation from him, "a celestial being," who, through electrical impulse, manipulated her pencil.

Sunnybank was sold after Anice Terhune died in 1964. The Albert Payson Terhune Foundation, a charitable organization, remained, as did efforts of collie lovers to turn the dilapidated Sunnybank into a shrine, according to a 1968 report in *Sports Illustrated*, which added that "some of what Terhune wrote is outdated or flimsy cardboard, but much still has a magic."

PRINCIPAL WORKS: Syria From the Saddle, 1896; Columbia Stories, 1897; (with "Marion Harland") Dr. Dale, 1900; Caleb Conover, Railroader, 1907; The New Mayor, 1907; The World's Great Events, 1908; The Fighter, 1909; The New Mayor, 1910; The Woman, 1912; Around the World in Thirty Days, 1914; Dad, 1914; Dollars and Cents, 1914; The Locust

Years, 1915; Superwomen, 1916; Fortune, 1918; Wonder Women in History, 1918; Lad: A Dog, 1919; Bruce, 1920; The Pest, 1920; Buff: A Collie, 1921; The Man in the Dark, 1921; Black Caesar's Clan, 1922; Black Gold, 1922; Further Adventures of Lad, 1922; His Dog, 1922; The Amateur Inn, 1923; Lochinvar Luck, 1923; Dogs of the High Sierras, 1924; Wolf, 1924; Treve, 1924; The Tiger's Claw, 1924; Najib, 1925; Now That I'm Fifty, 1925 (autobiography); The Runaway Bag, 1925; The Heart of a Dog, 1925; Treasure, 1926; My Friend the Dog, 1926; Blundell's Last Guest: A Detective Story, 1927; Bumps, 1927; Gray Dawn, 1927; The Luck of the Laird, 1927; Lad of Sunnybank, 1928; Black Wings, 1928; Water!, 1928; Proving Nothing, 1929; The Secret of Sea-Dream House, 1929; To the Best of My Memory, 1930 (autobiography); A Dog Named Chips, 1931; The Son of God, 1932; The Way of a Dog, 1932; Letters of Marque, 1934; The Book of Sunnybank, 1934; Real Tales of Real Dogs, 1935; The Critter and Other Dogs, 1936; True Dog Stories, 1936; Unseen!, 1936; A Book of Famous Dogs, 1937; Dog Stories Every Child Should Know, 1937; The Terhune Omnibus, 1937; Grudge Mountain, 1939; Collie to the Rescue, 1940; Dogs, 1940; Loot!, 1940; Famous Hussies of History, 1943.

ABOUT: The autobiographical material quoted above was written for Twentieth Century Authors, 1942. Commire, A. (ed.) Something About the Author vol. 15; Dictionary of Literary Biography vol. 9; Dodd, L. H. Celebrities at Our Hearthside; Junior Book of Authors; Litvig, I. The Master of Sunnybank, A Biography of Albert Payson Terhune; Terhune, A.M.S. The Bert Terhune I Knew, Across The Line; National Cyclopedia of America Biography, 1948; Unkelbach, K. Albert Payson Terhune; Ward, M. E. and Marquardt, D. A. Authors of Books for Young People. *Periodicals*—Good Housekeeping April 1939; Junior Bookshelf December 1978; New York Herald Tribune February 19, 1942; New York Times February 19, 1942; New York Times Book Review March 27, 1983; Saturday Evening Post March 28, 1925; Sports Illustrated January 15, 1968.

**TETERNIKOV, FEDOR KUZMICH.** See SOLOGUB, FYODOR

**TEY, JOSEPHINE.** See MacKINTOSH, ELIZABETH

**THARAUD, JÉROME** (May 18, 1874–January 28, 1953) and **THARAUD, JEAN** (May 9, 1877– April 9, 1952), French journalists and novelists. The brothers were born in the village of Saint-Junien in the Haute-Vienne, Limousin, but for economic reasons the family moved to Angouleme, in western France, where they attended elementary school. At the age of eleven, Jérome went to Paris, where he attended the Sainte-Barbe school and then the Lycée Louis-Le-Grand. While at the Lycée, he also won prizes for French, history, and geography— though he had only learned to read after the age of ten. In school he continued to win prizes, in the end earning for himself two baccalaureates.

With the support and encouragement of his friend and schoolmate Charles Péguy, Jérome then began to prepare for entrance into L'École Normale, studying hard and winning the Concours Générale for his composition, "Letters from Voltaire to Diderot." Jérome entered L'École Normale in 1895, where he remained for four years.

In the meantime Jean had come to Paris, studying mathematics at the École Sainte-Geneviève from 1895 to 1896 before preparing to enter the École Militaire de Saint-Cyr at the Lycée Saint-Louis, which he attended from 1897 to 1898. He failed to pass his oral examinations, and had to return to Angouleme for a year of military service. He then returned to Paris, where, throwing himself into his studies, he earned a *licence* in philosophy from the faculty of the Sorbonne in 1901, a diploma from the École des Sciences Politiques, and a law degree from the Faculté de Droit in 1902.

By this time Jérome had taken a position teaching French language and literature at Joseph Eotvos College in Budapest. Never having learned to

read Hungarian, he asked his students to translate for him the works of their native writers such as Mor Jokai and Miksath. These he collected, revised, edited, and published in 1903. It was also at this time that Jérome often wandered throughout Budapest's Jewish ghettos, beginning to develop the profound understanding of Jewish psychology and culture that he would display in his later works. During his vacations he traveled in Russia, Germany, Rumania, Bulgaria, and Turkey, often taking Jean along. It was with their journal recording these journeys, "Les Deux Pigeons" (The Two Pigeons), that the two brothers began their life-long collaboration. Their first work, *Le Coltineur Debile*, was published in 1898 by Charles Péguy. It was followed by *Lumière* in 1900.

The Tharauds were soon advised by their friend and teacher Joseph Bedier to study material "more sober" and more simple in style. The results of their

studies were stories such as those found in their *La Legende de la Vièrge* (1902) and *Contes de la Vièrge* (1904). Before writing these fictional works, Jérome had tried, unsuccessfully, to become a war correspondent at the outbreak of the Transvaal War. Through photographs and postcards he was able to reconstruct a narrative of the campaign which, after their return to Paris, the brothers worked into the manuscript for *Dingley* (1902). Though the book readily found an admiring public, it was completely revised and rewritten by the authors, and in 1906 won the Goncourt Prize. Their extreme meticulousness would pay off in other instances, too. *La Maîtresse Servante* had appeared in sketchy form in periodicals as early as 1908, but did not appear in book form until 1911—and in such complete form that even the harsh critics, such as the novelist and essayist Barrès, for whom the brothers worked as secretaries for seven years, called it "a somber little masterpiece."

In 1912 the Tharauds covered the Balkan War, from which resulted their well-received *La Bataille à Scutari d'Albaine*. Their impressionistic observations of World War I again brought them recogni-

tion when the French Academy awarded them the Grand Prix for *Une Réléve* (1919). Following publication of *The Shadow of the Cross* (1917) the Tharauds won praises for their characterization of the Jewish ghetto of Budapest. Morris Bishop of *Literature Review* remarked of the book: "The reader is astonished by the minuteness of the author's documentation; it seems incredible that any non-Jew could have assembled such a mass of information upon Jewish law, ceremonial and superstition." They were given similar recognition for *Next Year in Jerusalem*, *Chosen People*, and *When Israel is King*, though they were often criticized for their "antagonism toward young Zionist pioneers" (*New York Tribune*), and their sincerity regarding their feelings toward their subject matter was sometimes called into question. However, the Tharauds continued to make a respectable reputation for themselves, writing books about distant people and places, striving to depict details of landscape, culture, and psychology. Among these works are *Long Walk of Samba Diouf*, about life among the Senegalese, *Spain in the Riff*, about the 1925 campaign of France and Spain against the Berbers, and *Vienne La Rouge*, *Le Passant d'Ethiopie*, and *Cruelle Espagne*, about the Austrian, Ethiopian, and Spanish crises.

In 1938 the French Academy wished to honor both brothers, who were often referred to as "Jéromejean." In the end, it was decided that the one available seat would go to Jérome because he was the older. Jean was awarded a place in 1946.

PRINCIPAL WORKS IN ENGLISH TRANSLATION: The Shadow of the Cross, 1917; The Long Walk of Samba Diouf, 1924; When Israel Is King, 1924; Next Year in Jerusalem, 1925; Spain and the Riff, 1926; The Chosen People, 1929.

ABOUT: Authors Today and Yesterday, 1933; Columbia Dictionary of Modern European Literature, 1980; Encyclopedia of World Literature in the 20th Century, 1982; International Who's Who, 1951. *Periodicals*—Literature Review; May 3, 1924; New York Times April 10, 1952; January 29, 1953; New York Tribune July 26, 1925; New York World March 24, 1929; Times (London) April 10, 1952; January 30, 1953.

**THAYER, TIFFANY ELLSWORTH** (March 1, 1902–August 23, 1959), American novelist, wrote: "Tiffany Thayer was born in show business, to Sybil Farrar (soubrette) and Elmer Ellsworth Thayer (comedian). One grandfather was a G.A.R. chaplain (Methodist), the other a ne'er-do-well inventor. Freeport, Ill., was the scene from 1902 until 1910, then Rockford, 1910 to 1916. His parents were divorced when he was five. In 1916 he ran

from his father, joined his mother, quit high school (middle of third year), was apprenticed to a commercial artist in Chicago. In 1917 he was a copyboy on the Chicago *Examiner*; went to the United Press and then into dramatic stock at Oak Park and hence into road shows (one night stands) through 1918 to 1922, with intervals of newspaper reporting between theatrical seasons. From 1922 to 1926 he alternated theatrical work with old-and-rare book store clerking; became store manager and worked in that capacity in Chicago, Detroit, and Cleveland.

"In 1926 Thayer went to New York intending to re-enter the show business on the big time. Savings were exhausted before he could find a part and he was forced against his will to write for a living; became advertising copy-writer in 1927, partner in the agency in 1928. He wrote *Thirteen Men* evenings and week-ends through 1928 and 1929. It was published in May 1930. A week after publication he sailed to France and Spain, returning in the fall to find himself the notorious author of a best-seller. Since 1930 he has published nineteen volumes—his own favorite being Rabelais rewritten for children. From 1930 to 1932 he was advertising manager of the Literary Guild. In 1931 he founded the Fortean Society, to honor the late Charles Fort and to combat the stultifying influence of orthodox science. He is permanent secretary of this organization. From 1932 to 1936 he was in Hollywood. He did stretches on all the major lots and finally heard his own dialogue on the screen through Walter Wanger. From 1936 to date [written in 1940] back in advertising in New York, in the radio department of a big agency.

"His first novel (unpublished) was written at the age of eleven. He rolls his own cigarettes, draws and paints for mental relaxation, fences (foils) for exercise. He would rather act than write and in Hollywood made an abortive effort to return to that work, appearing in one bad motion picture and on the stage in a revival of *Whistling in the Dark*, of which performance the local papers said he 'scored a personal triumph.' He is an atheist, an anarchist—in philosophy a Pyrrhonean—and regrets the legitimacy of his birth. He likes to think of hmself as a gypsy—but he has a library of rare books (about 3,000 volumes) which keeps him off the open road. He writes articles and short stories but rarely. He has never had a serial published in a popular magazine. Most of his books concern feminine psychology, a sort of specialty. He writes under various pseudonyms as well as under his own name. Five feet, seven inches; 148 pounds; fair; green eyes. Marital status throughout life—nobody's business."

---

Tiffany Ellsworth Thayer was born in Freeport, Illinois. He attended Illinois public school until quitting in his junior year of high school, preferring to follow the theatrical path of his actor parents. After taking odd jobs and acting in stock companies, the aspiring actor thought he was ready for New York City. No one else in the theater seemed to think so, so he was "forced to write for a living," he said.

While he was working as advertising manager for the Literary Guild in New York, his first published novel, *Thirteen Men* (1930), became a best-seller. Thayer subsequently wrote nineteen novels under his own name and numerous others under pseudonyms that included Elmer Ellsworth and John Doe.

*Thirteen Men* is the story of Frank Miller, a young intellectual who murders thirty-eight persons before giving himself up, saying his motive is the desire to rid the world of a number of stupid people and also, since life bores him, to provide himself with a novel method of suicide. *Books* called it "smart and smutty," and *Outlook* said, "This curious book is full of a macabre sort of gaiety and has somewhat the effect of a rain of machine gun bullets on the reader. At least interest does not languish for lack of good red blood which flows freely." *Bookmark* said "it will shock the simple and bore the sophisticated."

With a successful first novel under his belt, the early 1930s became active and prolific years for Thayer. In 1931 he founded the Fortean Society to combat what he considered to be he stultifying influence of orthodox science, in honor of the late Charles Fort, a critic of science. Thayer was permanent secretary of the society as well as the editor of *Doubt*, the group's quarterly literary magazine. Other members of the society included Alexander Woollcott, John Cowper Powys, and Ben Hecht.

He returned to New York in 1936 and worked as a radio advertising writer for the J. Walter Thompson advertising agency until 1948, when he went to another advertising firm, Sullivan, Stauffer, Colwell, and Bayles. He worked the first six months of each year in the agency's New York office and spent the rest of the year writing in Nantucket, an annual pattern that would continue until his death.

PRINCIPAL WORKS: Thirteen Men, 1930; The Illustrious Corpse, 1930; Call Her Savage, 1931; Eye-witness!, 1931; The Greek, 1931; Thirteen Women, 1932; Three-Sheet, 1932; An American Girl, 1933; One Woman, 1933; Doctor Arnoldi, 1934; Kings and Numbers, 1934; Cluck Abroad, 1935; The Old Goat, 1937; One-Man Show, 1937; Little Dog Lost, 1938; Rabelais for Boys and Girls, 1939; Tiffany Thayer's Three Musketeers, 1939. *As editor*—33 Sardonics I Can't Forget, 1946; "Said" 800 Ways, 1946; Adults' Companion, 1948; Mona Lisa: The Prince of Taranto, 1956.

ABOUT: The autobiographical material quoted above was written for Twentieth Century Authors, 1942. de Rachewiltz, M. Discretions 1971; Hall, D. Remembering Poets 1978; Heymann C. D. Ezra Pound: The Last Rower 1976; Twentieth Century Authors (1st supp.) 1955. *Periodicals*—Advertising Age August 31, 1959; Bookman December 1930; New York Herald Tribune Book Review June 10, 1956; New York Times August 24, 1959; New York Times Book Review June 10, 1956; Newsweek June 11, 1956; Saturday Review June 9, 1956; Time June 11, 1956; August 31, 1959.

## THAYER, WILLIAM ROSCOE (January 16, 1859–September 7, 1923), American historian, biographer, and editor, was born in Boston, Massachusetts, the son of Frederick William Thayer. He attended St. Paul's School in Concord, New Hampshire, after which he was taken to Europe, where he was tutored privately. A year in Siena inspired a lasting fascination with Italian history and culture.

After graduating from Harvard in 1881, he worked briefly for the *Boston Sunday Budget*, then spent four years writing literary, theater, and music reviews for the *Philadelphia Evening Bulletin*. An inheritance from his mother enabled him to quit newspaper work and attend the Harvard Graduate

School, where he earned a master's degree in 1886. He taught English at Harvard during the 1888–1889 academic year, and although that appoint-

ment was not renewed, Thayer maintained a life-long affiliation with the university. He was editor of the *Harvard Graduates' Magazine* from 1892 to 1915, was twice elected to the university's board of overseers, and was responsible for the founding of the Harvard Union. In 1893 he married Elizabeth Hastings Ware, the daughter of a Cambridge family that had produced numerous scholars and clerics.

Thayer dabbled in fiction and poetry, and contributed articles on a variety of subjects to both popular and scholarly journals. His major intellectual preoccupation, however, was Italian history; in later life he wrote biographies of seminal American figures. His early work *The Dawn of Italian Independence* was followed by *A Short History of Venice*, which examines the city from the fifth century through the eighteenth. *The Life and Times of Cavour*, his most ambitious work, is a two-volume study of the statesman most responsible for the unification of Italy under King Victor Emmanuel II. In an American Academy of Arts and Letters tribute to Thayer, the historian James Ford Rhodes remarked, "Thayer's successful *Life and Times of Cavour* was made more so by his knowledge of European affairs. As one reads the story, one is amazed at his varied information and the charm he has thrown upon the setting of his subject." In recognition of Thayer's efforts, the Italian government presented him with its highest civic honor, the rank of *Commendatore* in the Order of Saints Maurizio and Lazzaro.

While writing the Cavour biography, Thayer was plagued by a severe chronic nervous disorder, which delayed publication of the work for several years. His next book, *The Life and Letters of John Hay*, received an extremely enthusiastic critical reception and reinforced Thayer's reputation as a major biographer. By the time he finished writing the book, he was blind in his right eye. He went on, however, to complete full-length biographies of Theodore Roosevelt, whom he considered a friend, —John Hay served as his Secretary of State—and George Washington. In 1918–1919 he served as president of the American Historical Association. Thayer was staunchly critical of Germany's role in World War I. His thoughts on the war are contained in such pamphlets as *Germany vs. Civilization* and *The Collapse of Superman*, as well as the essay *Collection Volleys from a Non-Combatant.*

PRINCIPAL WORKS: *History*—An Historical Sketch of Harvard University, from Its Foundation to May 1890, 1890; The Dawn of Italian Independence: Italy from the Congress of Vienna, 1814, to the Fall of Venice, 1849, 2 vols., 1892; A Short History of Venice, 1905; Italica: Studies in Italian Life and Letters, 1908; Germany vs. Civilization: Notes of the Atrocious War, 1916; (with C. D. Hazen and R. H. Lord) Three Peace Confer-

ences of the Nineteenth Century, 1917; The Collapse of Superman, 1918; Democracy: Discipline: Peace, 1919; Volleys from a Non-Combatant, 1919; The New American Historians, 1920. *Biography*—The Influence of Emerson, 1886; Throne-Makers, 1899; Sons of the Puritans: A Group of Brief Biographies, 1908; The Life and Times of Cavour, 2 vols., 1911; The Life and Letters of John Hay, 2 vols., 1915 (also published as John Hay, vols. 36 and 37 of the American Statesmen series); Theodore Roosevelt: An Intimate Biography, 1919; The Art of Biography, 1920; George Washington, 1922. *Fiction*—In the Meshes; or, A Drop of Boston Blue Blood, 1881. *Poetry*—(as "Paul Hermes") The Confessions of Hermes, 1884; Hesper: An American Drama, 1888; Halid: An Eastern Poem, 1889; Poems, New and Old, 1894; Retrospect of War: Ode Delivered Before the Phi Beta Kappa Society of Tufts College, May 12, 1920, 1920. *Correspondence*—The Letters of William Roscoe Thayer (ed. C. D. Hazen) 1926. *As editor*—Our French Visitors: Documents of Extra-Ordinary Interest Relating to Their Magnificent Reception in Boston and Delightful tour (by C. A. Coolidge) 1882; The Best Elizabethan Plays, 1890; (with J. L. Chamberlain and others) Universities and Their Sons: History, Influence and Characteristics of American Universities, with Biographical Sketches and Portraits of Alumni and Recipients of Honorary Degrees, 1898–1900; (with J. L. Chamberlain and others) Harvard University: Its Influence, Equipment and Characteristics, with Biographical Sketches and Portraits of Founders, Benefactors, Officers and Alumni, 1900; Letters of John Holmes to James Russell Lowell and Others, 1917.

ABOUT: Commemorative Tributes of the American Academy of Arts and Letters, 1905–1941, 1942; Dictionary of American Biography vol. 18 1936; Howe, M.A.D. Later Years of the Saturday Club, 1870–1920, 1927; Russell, F. Mount Olive Biographies, 1953. *Periodical*—New York Times September 8, 1923.

**THEVENIN, DENIS.** See **DUHAMEL, GEORGES**

**\*THIESS, FRANK** (March 13, 1890–December 22, 1977), German novelist and essayist, was born in Eluisenstein, near Uexküll, then part of Russian Livonia; he was of German descent on his mother's side. The family moved to Germany when he was a young boy, and Thiess was educated in Berlin and Tübingen. He served briefly with the German army on the Eastern front during World War I, after which he spent several years as a journalist and sub-editor for the *Berliner Tageblatt*. He worked as a playwright in Stuttgart in 1920, then wrote theater criticism for two years in Hanover. He had his first success with the novel *Die Verdammten* (The damned, 1922). He was in Austria from 1933 until 1952. He experienced difficulties with the Nazis, but refused to emigrate.

In his early novels, which were popular and solidly written, Thiess was concerned chiefly with the depiction of psychological problems in German so-

ciety. The novels in his ambitious tetralogy *Jugend* (Youth) focus on the lives of young people in post-World War I Germany. One of these, *The Gateway to Life*, the first of Thiess's novels to be translated into English, examines the passions and conflicts of a group of high school boys in southern Germany. *Farewell to Paradise*, another volume of the tetralogy, is a story of adolescent love

\*TEES

set in a resort hotel in the German countryside. Like *The Gateway to Life*, the novel was generally well received by American critics, although a *Nation* reviewer deemed it "largely Wedekind *rechauffé*," noting that Thiess added little to the insights on adolescent psychology already found in the novels and dramas of Frank Wedekind.

Historical themes dominate much of Thiess's later work, both fiction and nonfiction. *The Voyage of Forgotten Men*, a novel set during the Russo-Japanese War of 1904–1905, is a fictional account, from the Russian point of view, of the battle of Tsushima, in which the Russian fleet was destroyed by Admiral Togo's navy. *Neapolitan Legend*, the last of Thiess's works to be translated into English, is a fictional biography of opera singer Enrico Caruso. *Das Reich der Dämonen* (Empire of the demons), about the ancient and medieval world, and *Die griechischen Kaiser* (The Greek emperor), about the Byzantine Empire, are historical narratives that combine rather haphazard research and philosophical speculation on the nature of epochal transformation.

A prolific author, Thiess continued to publish novels, criticism, and historical essays in the years after World War II. None of his later work was translated into English. He published several volumes of personal reminiscences, including the 1963 *Verbrannte Erde* (Scorched earth). Seven volumes of his *Gesammelte Werke* (Collected works) appeared between 1956 and 1963.

PRINCIPAL WORKS IN ENGLISH TRANSLATION: *Novels*—The Gateway to Life (tr. H. T. Lowe-Porter) 1927; The Devil's Shadow (tr. H. T. Lowe-Porter) 1928; Farewell to Paradise (tr. H. T. Lowe-Porter) 1929; Interlude (Frauenraub) (tr. C. Fredrick) 1929; The Voyage of Forgotten Men (Tsushima) (tr. F. Sallagar) 1937; Neapolitan Legend (tr. B. Pritchard) 1949.

ABOUT: Closs, A (ed.) Twentieth Century German Literature, 1969. Garland, H. and M. (eds.) The Oxford Guide to German Literature, 2nd edition, 1986; Literatur Lexicon, Vol. 11, 1991. *Periodicals*—Nation December 4, 1929; New Statesman and Nation March 16, 1946.

**THIRKELL, ANGELA** (January 30, 1890–January 29, 1961), English novelist, was born in London and grew up in Kensington, where she was

educated privately and at the Froebel Institute, before being numbered among the first class at St. Paul's School for Girls. Her father, J. W. Mackail, was a classical scholar and the author of a still-read biography of William Morris. Eventually he became professor of poetry at Oxford. Her mother was the daughter of Edward Burne-Jones, the painter. Angela's childhood memories are recounted in her first book, *Three Houses*, in which the importance and influence of her grandparents, particularly her grandfather, on her life is apparent. The three houses referred to were her own home in Kensington and the two Burne-Jones residences—The Grange, in Fulham, London, and a seaside home, North End House, in Rottingdean, near Brighton.

Her first husband, James Campbell McInnes, whom she married in 1911, was a singer and alcoholic. The marriage failed within six years and she obtained a divorce on grounds of adultery and cruelty, by which time two sons, Graham and Colin, had been born. Colin, when grown up and established as the author Colin MacInnes, declared that he had never liked his mother; their mutual ill-feeling towards one another eventually led to a complete estrangement.

In 1918 she remarried. Her new husband, George Thirkell, was an engineer. Together they sailed for Australia and settled in a Melbourne suburb, where a third son, Lance, was born. After twelve years, during which time she began to write short articles and submit them to magazines, she walked out on her husband, having failed to persuade him to return to England. Together with her youngest son she moved back into her parents' house and committed herself, belatedly, to earning a living as a writer.

After *Three Houses*, she turned to fiction and, for the rest of her career, produced, at the rate of one a year, a series of novels about a mode of life that was, as she wrote, in the process of being dismantled and replaced by by a new order. The novels of the 1930s were well-crafted comedies, their breezy gaiety ruffled only by occasional outbreaks of sentiment. The general reception, both critical and popular, in the pre-war years was positive. H. C. White, writing of *The Brandons* (1939) in *Commonweal*, observed, "She knows how, in the turn of a sentence, to remind one of a whole tribe of too human human-beings and to give the precise definition of the generic absurdity. To do that takes intelligence and artistry of a very unusual order."

After the war, disenchantment with the political turn of events, and some personal unhappiness, infused her novels with a new acidity. They might well have benefited from a sharper sense of satire, but the new tone was confined to the expression of personal prejudices, particularly her loathing for the new Labour government. In addition, the climate of taste and of reviewing turned against her. Philip Toynbee in the *New Statesman* said dismissively of *Marling Hall* (1942), "She writes untruthfully about unreal and uninteresting people."

Still, the books kept coming, and a certain readership remained loyal, assisted by the fact that she had adopted the topography of Trollope, setting her books in the fictional landscape of Barsetshire. *The Three Houses* and one or two of the early novels remain of interest (many of them have still remained in print), if only from the point of view of social history, and because of her autobiographical references to Burne-Jones and to Kipling, who was a cousin of her mother. A last novel, left unfinished at her death, was completed by C. A. Lejeune.

PRINCIPAL WORKS: *Fiction*—Ankle Deep, 1933; High Rising, 1933; (as "Leslie Parker") Trooper to the Southern Cross, 1934; Wild Strawberries, 1934; The Demond in the House, 1935; O, These Man, These Men! 1935; August Folly, 1936; Coronation Summer, 1937; Summer Half, 1937; Pomfret Towers, 1938;

Before Lunch, 1939; The Brandons, 1939 Cheerfulness Breaks In, 1940; Northbridge Rectory, 1941; Marling Hall, 1942; Growing Up, 1943; The Headmistress, 1944; Miss Bunting, 1945; Peace Breaks Out, 1946; Private Enterprise, 1947; Love Among the Ruins, 1948; The Old Bank House, 1949; County Chronicle, 1950; The Dukes's Daughter, 1951; Happy Returns, 1952; Jutland Cottage, 1953; What Did It Mean?, 1954; Enter Sir Robert, 1955; Never Too Late, 1956; A Double Affair, 1957; Close Quarters, 1958; Love At All Ages, 1959; (completed by C. A. Lejeune) Three Score and Ten, 1961. *Nonfiction*—Three Houses, 1931; The Fortunes of Harriette, 1936 (in U.S.: Tribute for Harriette).

ABOUT: Contemporary Authors Vol. 140, 1993; Dictionary of National Biography, 1961-1970, 1981; McInnes G. Road to Gundagai, 1965; Shattock, J. Oxford Guide to British Women Writers, 1993; Schlueter, P. and J. An Encyclopaedia of British Women Writers, 1988; Strickland, M. Angela Thirkell, 1977; Todd, J. M. British Women Writers, 1989; Who's Who 1961. *Periodicals*—Commonweal July 28, 1939; Illustrated London News February 4, 1961; New Statesman October 31, 1942; New York Times January 30, 1961; Spectator June 29, 1934; Times (London) January 30, 1961; Times Literary Supplement September 12, 1942.

**THOBY-MARCELIN, PHILIPPE** (December 11, 1904–August 17, 1975) and **MARCELIN, PIERRE** (August 6, 1908–    ), Haitian novelists

and brothers, were coauthors of a number of novels on life in their native land. In 1955, Philippe wrote: "Born in Port-au-Prince, to a family of political and literary tradition. One of his ancestors, Boisrond-Tonnerre, was the author of the Act of Independence (January 1, 1804) and for this fundamental text, as well as his *Memoirs*, is considered the "initiator of Haitian literature." His maternal grandfather, Armand Thoby (1841–1899), besides being an important statesman, attained eminence as a writer. So did Frédéric Marcelin (1848–1917), a cousin on the paternal side and the creator of the Haitian realistic novel. His father, too, Émile Marcelin (1874–1936), in addition to having a political career which culminated in the post of Minister of Finance, was a novelist and literary critic.

"Although he hasn't followed his elders in the political field, Philippe Thoby-Marcelin has devoted himself to writing. His first medium was poetry, of which he produced five volumes: *Lago-Lago* (1924-1930), *La Négresse Adolescente* (1928-1931), *Le jour et la nuit* (1932-1941), *Dialogue avec la femme endormie* (1940), *A fonds perdu* (1943-1948).

"He was also active as a critic and has borne the responsibilty for much of Haiti's renaissance in the arts and was a leader in the *avant-garde* literary movement there. A member of the group which centered around *La revue indigène*, he took a strong stand against the imitation of French writing which has been the custom of most of his forebears. The tenets of this circle were frankly nationalistic and stemmed from the belief that their cultural heritage was the strongest weapon against any dele-

terious influences from abroad. By writing as Haitians, speaking the languages of their own people and their own times, they stove to encourage a respect for values native to their country.

"It was not until his late thirties that, in collaboration with his brother Pierre, Philippe Thoby-Marcelin started to write a series of three novels which made them known abroad, mainly in the United States, Latin America, Great Britain, France—and the first Haitian novelists to be translated into English and Spanish. Their first novel, *Canapé-Vert*, was awarded the prize in the second Latin-American contest (1943) by John Dos Passos, Ernesto Montenegro, and Blair Niles. In 1951 they were each granted a fellowship by the Guggenheim Foundation."

———

The Marcelins grew up in a household that welcomed as guests many of the distinguished literary and political figures of Haiti. Educated privately in Catholic schools, they both studied law at the University of Haiti and became public officials in Haiti in the Ministry of Public Works. Philippe, the better known of the two, was initially a poet, who began, to write verse while at the university. Following Haitian custom, he prefixed his mother's maiden name to his own. During the 1920s he was a leader in the *avant-garde* literary movement in Haiti, playing an important part in the renaissance in Haitian arts.

In their mid to late thirties the Marcelin brothers collaborated on a series of novels on Haitian life that made them famous at home and abroad. Their first novel, *Canape Vert* (translated under that name) about life in a Haitian village, described the voodoo culture in some detail. Rendered into English by Edward Larocque Tinker, it was the first piece of Haitian fiction so translated. Edmund Wilson wrote that this novel demonstrated the existence of a Haitian literary culture "which is serious and not at all a mere aping of the French . . . it gives us an inside picture of the Negro population of Haiti, which so far as I know, is unique and which will be of special interest to anyone with an appetite for finding out how other kinds of human beings live." (*New Yorker*).

Another collaboration, *The Beast of the Haitian Hills*, was praised by Arna Bontemps as "a poetically conceived account" in which "the skill, grace, and spice of the storytelling are art from a distant and neglected world" (*New York Times Book Review*). The Marcelin brothers drew on their knowledge of Haitian folklore and anthropology for the background of their novels, illustrating the contrast between the voodoo-influenced life of the peasants and that of the urban middle class. Other important issues they address are the conflict between the practitioners of voodoo and the Catholic Church and corruption in Haitian politics. Although social comment is implicit in the novels, the brothers have been criticized for their aloof stance and lack of ideology.

Philippe Thoby-Marcelin moved to the United States in 1949 to work as a translator for the Pan

American Union in Washington, D. C., and remained in the United States until his death. Pierre Marcelin remained in Haiti.

PRINCIPAL WORKS: *Philippe Thoby-Marcelin and Pierre Marcelin*—Canapé-Vert (tr. E. Larocque Tinker) 1944; The Beast of the Haitian Hills (tr. P. C. Rhodes) 1964; The Pencil of God (tr. L. Thomas) 1951; The Singing Turtle and Other Tales from Haiti (tr. E. Thoby-Marcelin) 1970. *Philippe Thoby-Marcelin*—Lago-Lago, 1943; La negresse adolescente, 1932; Le jour et la nuit 1932–1941; Dialogue avec la femme endormie, 1941; A fonds perdu, 1953; Haiti, 1959.

ABOUT: Wilson, E. *preface to* The Pencil of God. *Periodicals*—New York Times August 17, 1975; New York Times Book Review November 24, 1946; New York February 26, 1944; Saturday Review March 3, 1951.

**THOMAS, AUGUSTUS** (January 8, 1857–August 12, 1934), American playwright, was born in what has become the outskirts of St. Louis, Missouri, the son of Dr. Elihu Baldwin Thomas and Imogene (Garrettson) Thomas. Although he was president of the Society of American Dramatists from 1906 to 1914, and subsequently came to be known as the "dean of American playwrights" in the early part of the twentieth century, his plays about American life have since fallen into obscurity.

Until he discovered his vocation, Thomas occupied a variety of positions, including newspaper reporter, illustrator, railroad brakeman, messenger, law student, and labor leader. During the Civil War, his father, Dr. Elihu Baldwin Thomas, managed the St. Charles Theater in New Orleans. When the war ended, the Thomas family returned to Missouri and, in the winter of 1868, young Augustus became a page boy in the Missouri House of Representatives. He later worked as a railroad brakeman in St. Louis. There he was a member of the Knights of Labor, eventually becoming chief spokesman for Missouri Central, Local 9. Yet Thomas was never able to stray too far from the theater, and throughout the time he worked for the railroad he also participated in the local theater group, and even toured with the Vokes Company for two summers.

Asked to give advice to young playwrights, he replied: "First, the study of good modern plays, both on the stage and printed; second, acting professionally for a while; third, reporting on a metropolitan newspaper." Thomas followed his own advice. After working for the railroad, he drew cartoons for the *St. Louis World* and toured the state for Joseph Pulitzer's *New York World*, observing reactions to the inauguration of women's suffrage. His career as reporter culminated when he became the editor and proprietor of the now defunct *Kansas City Mirror*.

While working as a reporter, Thomas dramatized Frances Hodgson Burnett's novel *Editha's Burglar* as a one-act play. By 1889 he had expanded this into a four-act play entitled *The Burglar*. Soon thereafter, Thomas moved to New York where he managed the Madison Square Theater, where his 1891 play *Alabama* was soon produced. This, coupled with the 1893 production of his *In Mizzoura*, established Thomas as a writer of theatrically effective melodramas.

Thomas's plays, which centered on typical scenes from everyday American life, were generally well liked and received favorable reviews. The *New York Times*, in a review of Thomas's *As A Man Thinks* (1911), remarked that while Augustus Thomas "cannot be regarded as a leader of thought," there can be no doubt that "he is exceptionally clever in seizing upon subjects which have become pretty common property for discussion." His plays were drawn largely from his experiences as a reporter, in 1934, and his *New York Times* obituary noted that "Mr. Thomas knew his subjects well; had lived there and seen the people of whom he built the characters."

Thomas, who was married to Mrs. Lisle Colby, a sister of Woodrow Wilson's Secretary of State, was vehemently opposed to the censorship of drama. "Censorship," he said, "is wrong in principle. . . . It is a sectarian, Puritanical idea, and it grows out of fanaticism." In sum, Thomas, as his obituary notes, was a "guide, philosopher and friend" to the theater community. He believed in uninhibited dramatic expression, and as he planned the establishment of both a national theater and a national conservatory, he strove to convey that belief to the entire country.

His pleasant, melodramatic style of drama is of an outmoded school and has largely been forgotten by all but theater archaeologists. Thomas was the recipient of an M.A. degree from Williams College, a Litt.D. from Columbia (1921), and LL.D. from the University of Missouri (1923). From 1906 to 1914 he was president of the Society of American Dramatists.

PRINCIPAL WORKS: *Drama*—Alabama, 1891; In Mizzoura, 1893; Arizona, 1898; Oliver Goldsmith, 1900; Champagne Charley, 1901; The Earl of Pawtucket, 1903; Mrs. Leffingwell's Boots, 1905; The Embassy Ball, 1905; The Witching Hour, 1907; The Harvest Moon, 1909; As a Man Thinks, 1911; The Nightingale, 1914; Rio Grande, 1916; The Copperhead, 1917; Palmy Days, 1920; Nemesis, 1921. *Autobiography*—The Print of My Remembrance, 1922.

ABOUT: Thomas, A. The Print of My Remembrance, 1922; Winter, W. The Wallet of Time, 1913; Woollcott, A. Shouts and Murmurs, 1922. *Periodical*—New York Times August 13, 14, 16, 19, 1934.

**THOMAS, DYLAN** (October 27, 1914–November 9, 1953), Welsh poet, was born in Swansea and had a middle-class upbringing in the home of his parents, Florence Hannah (Williams) and David John Thomas, an English master at Swansea Grammar School, which Thomas himself attended. He began keeping notebooks and writing poems at an early age but did not do well academically. When he left school he worked as a reporter on the South Wales *Daily Post*, but left the paper when he was eighteen. From then onwards he scraped a living from his wit and his pen, ever dependent on the generosity of family and friends.

He had had poems published in the school magazine, but his first official success came in September 1933 when the Sunday *Referee* printed a sample of  his work. His first book of poems, *18 Poems*, published in 1934, met with a mixed reception. It included the poem "The force that through the green fuse drives the flower," about which Bruce Kellner has written: "It suffers from a number of youthful indiscretions: too rich and complex an imagery; a faulty parallelism in structure; an erratic accentual pattern; enjambments anticipating double readings that lead to obscurity instead of ambiguity. Nevertheless, it is a quintessential Thomas poem, crucial in tracing his development and in charting the juxtaposition of themes that preoccupied him in nearly everything he wrote. . . ."

The poems as a whole, though appearing irrational and indecipherable, were expressed in a language that demanded attention. H. G. Porteus called the work "an unconducted tour of bedlam," but it had its champions, not the least of which was Edith Sitwell, who reviewed Thomas's second collection, *Twenty-five Poems* (nearly all of them written at the same time as the ones in the first volume), in the Sunday *Times*. She praised the beauty of the verse, both visual and oral, but also sought to interpret lines that others had mocked as gibberish. "The atlas-eater with a jaw for news,/Bit out the mandrake with to-morrow's scream," from the sonnet sequence "Altarwise by owl-light," she thought referred to "the violent speed and the sensation-loving, horror-loving craze of modern life."

The poems in both these early volumes defied classification. Although they were hard to interpret, they were not surreal in the modern sense. They were clearly not the work of the Auden-Spender school. Nor were they traditional, though they carried echoes of Gerard Manley Hopkins, the Metaphysical poets, and certain Elizabethans. There were identifiable themes—creation, desire, death, and religion. (To these Thomas's later work adds only the themes of childhood and memory.)

After an abortive, mainly epistolary relationship with the poet and novelist Pamela Hansford-Johnson, Thomas married Caitlin Macnamara, an out-of-work dancer, in 1937, already having established his boozy, bohemian reputation. They had three children—two sons and a daughter. *The Map Of Love* was published in 1939. It contained sixteen poems and seven stories. Commercially it was a failure, and critically it fared little better; the general view remains that it does not contain many examples of Thomas's writing at its best. An exception is "After the funeral," written after the death of his aunt, Ann Jones, whose farm is later celebrated in the superior "Fern Hill."

*Portrait of the Artist as a Young Dog*, published the following year, was a volume of stories, described by Thomas while he was writing them as "pot-boiling . . . semi- autobiographical." Those who found Thomas's poetry maddeningly baffling could at least understand these childhood stories. The reviews were mainly pleasant, although the *Times Literary Supplement* rather sniffily complained: "The atmosphere of schoolboy smut and practical jokes and poetry is evoked with lingering accuracy but with nothing more: the boys themselves are mere phantoms." The book did nothing spectacular at the time of publication, but has since proved to be one of Thomas's best-selling works.

There is some debate as to whether Thomas avoided active service in the war by fair means or foul. He was exempted on medical grounds, but his wife later claimed (among, it has to be said, many vengeful remarks about her dead husband) that he purposefully misled the examining medical officer by carefully scheduled heavy drinking. The result, whatever the truth, was that he was employed during the war years in the BBC's documentary department. This had the advantage of providing him with a steady income for the first time since his marriage.

His next volume of poetry, *Deaths and Entrances*, did not appear until after the war, and it made his reputation. Containing many of the poems that have come to be associated with Thomas's name— "Poem in October," "The Hunchback in the Park," "Fern Hill," "A Refusal to Mourn the Death, by Fire, of a child in London," and "A Winter's Tale."—*Deaths and Entrances* had to be reprinted a month after publication. Although less compressed than Thomas's early work, the poems were still constructed in verse-forms that adhered to a stringent syllabic design. In many cases Thomas worked in traditional forms, for example the villanelle; at other times he created his own template. His notebooks reveal the number of revisions required to make each poem fit the desired pattern.

Thomas, already a legend in the pubs and bars of London and Laugharne, was now a celebrity. His work at the BBC, where he was used extensively as an actor and reader as well as a writer, brought him further to the attention of the public. Nevertheless, he was constantly short of money. His American tours—the first was in 1950—were undertaken as money-making expeditions. Thomas did not like traveling, and although he was a brilliant performer, he did not like reading his own work. He prepared an account of one of these tours in the radio talk "Visit To America." To coincide with one of his visits, the collection *In Country Sleep* appeared in the United States, though not in Britain, where the poems it contained were included in *Collected Poems 1934-1952*, a volume that contained all that Thomas wished to preserve at that date. He wrote the poem "Author's Prologue" as an introduction.

Thomas's fourth tour to the United States, in the autumn of 1953, was his last. He took part in a presentation of *Under Milk Wood* on October 24 in New York, and then, after a series of binges, died of alcoholic poisoning while still in New York. The burst of inspiration that he had experienced during 1944 and 1945 had not been sustained. His death was tragic, from many points of view, but there were few signs that he had been about to add to the legacy of his work.

Dylan Thomas is considered variously as brilliant bard or intellectual fake, as inspired genius or drinking demon. His poetry remains enormously popular, goes on selling, and—along with the work of John Betjeman—stands as a curious anomaly in the history of twentieth-century British poetry.

PRINCIPAL WORKS: *Poetry*—18 Poems, 1934; Twenty-Five Poems, 1936; The Map of Love, 1939; New Poems, 1943; Deaths and Entrances, 1946; Twenty-Six Poems, 1950; In Country Sleep and Other Poems, 1952; Collected Poems 1934-1952, 1952; The Notebook Poems 1930-1934, 1989. *Fiction*-Portrait of the Artist as a Young Dog, 1940; A Prospect of The Sea and Other Stories, 1955; Adventures in the Skin Trade and Other Stories, 1955; Rebecca's Daughters, 1965; Two Tales, 1968; The Collected Stories, 1984. *Drama*—The Doctor and the Devils (film-script), 1953 Under Milk Wood, 1954. *Miscellaneous*—Quite Early One Morning, 1954; Conversations about Christmas, 1954; Letters to Vernon Watkins, 1957; Miscellany, 1963; The Colour of Saying, 1963; (ed.) FitzGibbon C. Selected Letters of Dylan Thomas 1966; Miscellany Two, 1966; The Notebooks, 1967; Early Prose Writings, 1971; Miscellany Three, 1978; (ed. Feris, P.) The Collected Letters, 1985.

ABOUT Ackerman, J. A Dylan Thomas Companion; Brinnin, J. M. Dylan Thomas in America 1956; Contemporary Authors v. 120; Davies, J. A. Dylan Thomas's Places; Dictionary of National Biography 1951-1960; Ferris P. Dylan Thomas A Biography 1977; FitzGibbon C. The Life of Dylan Thomas 1965; Olson E. The Poetry of Dylan Thomas, 1954; Thomas C. Life With Dylan Thomas, 1987; Tindall W. Y. A Reader's Guide to Dylan Thomas, 1962; Tremlett, G. Dylan Thomas in the Mercy of His Means, 1992; Who's Who 1952. *Periodicals*—New Republic June 10, 1967; New York Times November 11, 1953; Spectator November 13, 1953, November 29, 1957; Times (London) November 10 1953; Voice Literary Supplement March 1992.

**THOMAS, EDWARD** (March 3, 1878–April 9, 1917), English poet, nature writer, essayist and reviewer, was born in Lambeth, south London. He was educated at St. Paul's School and at Lincoln College, Oxford where, in 1900, he gained a second class degree in history.

Inspired by frequent visits to his Welsh relatives (on his mother's side of the family) and by the books of his favorite author, Richard Jefferies,  Thomas began by writing nature essays. When he was fifteen he started to record his walks in the country, in the style of a Victorian naturalist, and a collection of nature essays, *The Woodland Life*, appeared in print when he was eighteen. Thomas had been encouraged to complete this book by the critic, John Ashcroft Noble, and in 1899 he married Noble's daughter, Helen, who was expecting their first child.

After graduation from Oxford, Thomas began to earn his living as a literary hack. Exhausted by the need to be constantly at work (between 1910 and 1912 he produced twelve books), and inclined to a melancholy which was probably exacerbated, in the early years of his marriage, by his use of opium,

Thomas often appeared cold and distracted as a husband and father (the Thomases eventually had three children). The family was always short of money, and there were frequent enforced moves from one country cottage to another. Of the books that Thomas produced in this period of his life, the most notable were the critical and biographical studies *Richard Jefferies, His Life And Work* (1909), a breezy and evocative biography that communicates well the character of the countryside in southern England (a subject he looked at separately in *The South Country*, published the same year); *Swinburne* (1912); and *Walter Pater* (1913). None of these, however, won him much recognition.

The turning point in Thomas's life came in 1913 when he met the American poet, Robert Frost, who was in England. After their initial introduction (Thomas had a short time previously written an appreciative review of Frost's first collection) the two spent a considerable amount of time together and Frost encouraged his colleague to turn to writing poetry. He did not do so immediately, but when he began in December 1914 it was, in the words of his friend Eleanor Farjeon, as if a "living stream was undammed." By the time of his death twenty-eight months later he had produced 143 poems.

Thomas's verse was certainly influenced by Frost—he had been impressed by the American's lack of exaggeration and rhetoric and his reliance on the speaking voice—but it is unmistakably the work of an Englishman. It has characteristics in common with the Georgians (although it is too conversational and the meter is too loose to be properly classified as such). By virtue of the time and conditions in which it was written, it has much in common with the group of World War I poets that included Wilfrid Owen, Siegfried Sassoon, and Ivor Gurney, but the work is too preoccupied with the eternal elements of nature as opposed to the precise circumstances of human conflict to be properly bracketed as war poetry. Nor is it simply "nature" poetry in the sense of verse that deals with its subject in a purely descriptive or celebratory way. His poetry explores a solitude which was becoming increasingly difficult, in southern England, to achieve. Martin Seymour-Smith has described Thomas's poetry as "The last body of work to seek to define a rural concept of beauty that was finally invalidated by the First World War."

Thomas is now valued as an important figure in a line of especially English pastoral poets. His poems were thus described by Andrew Motion, the biographer of Philip Larkin: "For all their occasional lapses (they were written hurriedly) and traces of an earlier idiom (inverted syntax, sweetly sentimental ruralism), they are now clearly and rightly established as part of the tradition of English pastoral lyricism which runs forward from Wordsworth through Hardy and Housman to Larkin himself." Thomas's poetry is always meditative, concerned with self-discovery in the purest sense. Daniel Huws, writing in the *Times Literary Supplement* about the Edward Thomas Collection at the University of Wales College, Cardiff, and other manuscripts held by the National Library of Wales, observed: "In Thomas's spartan later life and constant writing . . . there is something religious; private writing as prayer, the object a *dea abscondita*." Many of his poems were about annihilation and death. This is from "Rain," written in 1916:

Rain, midnight rain, nothing but wild rain
On this bleak hut, and solitude, and me
Remembering again that I shall die
And neither hear the rain nor give it thanks
For washing me cleaner than I have been
Since I was born into this solitude.

Having enlisted in July 1915, Thomas was sent overseas in 1917. He was killed during the first hour of the Battle of Arras, on Easter Sunday, 1917.

PRINCIPAL WORKS: *Poetry*—Poems (as "Edward Eastaway"), 1917; Last Poems, 1918; The Collected Poems of Edward Thomas, 1920 (new edition 1974) *Prose*—The Woodland Life, 1897; Horae Solitariae, 1902; Oxford, 1903; Rose Acre Papers, 1904; Beautiful Wales, 1905; The Heart of England, 1906; Richard Jefferies: His Life and Work, 1909; The South Country, 1909; The Isle of Wight, 1911; Light and Twilight, 1911; The Tenth Muse, 1911; Algernon Cahrles Swinburne: A Critical Study, 1912; George Borrow: The Man and His Books, 1912; The Icknield Way, 1913; The Country, 1913; Walter Pater: A Critical Study, 1913; The Life of the Duke of Marlborough, 1915; Keats, 1916; Cloud Castle and Other Papers, 1922; The Last Sheaf, 1928; Letters to Gordon Bottomley (ed. R. G. Thomas), 1968.

ABOUT: Cooke, W. Edward Thomas a Critical Biography, 1970; Coombes, H. Edward Thomas 1956; Dictionary of National Biography 1912–1931; Eckert, R. P. Edward Thomas: A Biography and a Bibliography, 1937; Farjeon, E. Edward Thomas the Last Four Years, 1958; Kirkham, M. The Imagination of Edward Thomas, 1986; Marsh, J. Edward Thomas a Poet for His Country, 1978; Motion, A. The Poetry of Edward Thomas, 1980; Scannell, V. Edward Thomas, 1963; Smith, S. Edward Thomas 1986; Thomas, E. The Childhood of Edward Thomas: A Fragment of Autobiography, 1938; Thomas, H. As It Was, 1926; Thomas, H. World Without End, 1931; Who's Who 1916. *Periodicals*—Country Life September 22, 1977; New York Review of Books October 23, 1986; Times Literary Supplement March 20, 1992.

**THOMAS, LOWELL JACKSON** (April 6, 1892–August 29, 1981), American journalist, radio and television broadcaster, author, and world traveler, was born in Wood-

ington, Ohio, the son of Harry Thomas and Harriet (Wagner) Thomas. When Thomas was a boy, his father established a medical practice in Cripple Creek, Colorado, the famous gold-mining camp in the Rocky Mountains. Thomas moved back to Ohio at age fifteen and graduated from high school there, then attended the University of Northern Indiana, now Valparaiso University, where he obtained a B.S. in two years. He returned to Cripple Creek, working briefly in the mines and as a newspaper reporter and editor. After spending a year at the University of Denver, receiving his B.A. and M.A., he moved to Chicago and worked as a reporter for the *Chicago Journal* while attending Kent College of Law, where he later became a professor.

In 1914, he received an M.A. in English literature from Princeton University, where he served as a part-time instructor of public speaking. While at Princeton, he showed movies and gave lectures on a trip he had made to the Klondike region of Alaska; the popular reception he received convinced him that he had a gift for showmanship. Soon afterwards, the Wilson administration—Woodrow Wilson had been president of Princeton before his election to the White House—unofficially commissioned him to go to Europe as an unpaid reporter on the Great War for the American people. He raised funds for the venture from a group of Chicago meatpacking millionaires and, with photographer Harry Chase, toured the Western front and the Middle East. In Jerusalem he met Thomas Edward Lawrence—"Lawrence of Arabia"— who helped liberate Arabia from the Turks. Thomas followed Lawrence through the Arabian Desert and got an exclusive story and photographs of the famous revolt that gained him world recognition. He turned his experiences with Lawrence into two successful ventures: *The Last Crusade*, a theatrical travelogue show that toured Britain and then the world, and *With Lawrence in Arabia* (1924), the first and one of the most well-known books of his career.

Simeon Strunsky in the *New York Times* called the book "an admirably well-poised history in which full credit is given to everybody concerned without detracting from the extraordinary dramatic values of his central figure." Some Lawrence specialists, however, believed that Lawrence "fed Mr. Thomas outlandish stories and had willingly posed for pictures, and that Mr. Thomas had swallowed them whole. Thomas was loathe to concede that he might have been gulled and that he, in turn, had misconstrued history for others," wrote the *New York Times*.

When the war was over, Thomas went to Germany, which was still under Allied blockade, and produced an eyewitness account of the German revolution. He continued traveling the world, visiting India, Antarctica, Burma, Malaya and Afghanistan, among other places. He took his film shows to Paris, London, and the United States, earning a reputation as a leading popularizer of exotic locales until, after giving more than three thousand such shows, he realized it was easier to write about his adventures.

Thomas had already made a million dollars and would go on to earn an even larger fortune. For four years (1919–1923), he served as associate editor of *Asia*, then founded and edited the *Commentator*, which was later combined with *Scribner's*. Among his contributions to these periodicals were a report of the first flight around the world in 1924, a prototype of subsequent articles and books in which he made clear his love of courage and adventure. Subjects of his biographies over the next few decades include Count Luckner, the "Sea Devil" of World War I, American frontier wilderness surveyor George Rogers Clark, World War I hero Dan Edwards, Arctic explorer Sir Hubert Wilkins, and World War II general Jimmy Doolittle. In writing *Raiders of the Deep* (1928), he obtained first-hand stories of undersea warfare from survivors of German U-boat crews; for a motion picture and book *India: Land of the Black Pagoda* (1930), he recorded a two-year journey through the Indian subcontinent. For readers and moviegoers seeking relief from news of economic depression at home, the energetic reporter provided vicarious witness to wars and revolutions, visited pygmies in Southeast Asia and cannibals in New Guinea, and provided footage of exotic spots previously unseen by many people in the Western world.

Lowell Thomas's radio career began in 1930 by happenstance, when someone at Columbia Broadcasting System remembered his strong and exciting voice from hearing one of his shows. He was called to New York, auditioned with William S. Paley and sponsors, and was hired on the spot, according to the *New York Times*. He remained with CBS until 1932, switching to the National Broadcasting Company until 1947, when he returned to CBS until 1976. His was the longest unbroken career of any radio newscaster; it was estimated that Thomas had been heard by more than seventy billion people over nearly half a century. "No other journalist or world figure, with the possible exception of Winston Churchill, has remained in the public spotlight for so long," wrote Norman R. Bowen in *Lowell Thomas: The Stranger Everyone Knows* (1968). His broadcast formula never varied, and he did not consider himself a journalist but an entertainer, comparing himself to Bob Hope and Bing Crosby.

Al Hirshberg wrote (*Argosy*) that Thomas had "the itchiest feet in the world," and "He has traveled by every known means of locomotion, from perambulator to pinto pony, from horseless carriage to helicopter, from rickshaw to roller coaster, from jitney to jet pursuit plane." Along the way he developed a worldwide network of prominent friends, including kings, queens, premiers, generals, explorers and many U. S. presidents. Herbert C. Hoover wrote that if he were to be reincarnated, he would prefer it to be as Lowell Thomas. Franklin D. Roosevelt managed a softball team, the Roosevelt Packers, that annually battled Thomas's team of "Nine Old Men" (a reference to FDR's characterization of a recalcitrant Supreme Court). Harry S Truman called him "the Methuselah of radio broadcasts." Lyndon B. Johnson wrote, "Long before airliners had shrunk the world, Lowell Thomas had it in his pocket. He is one of those persons who has been everywhere—twice." Richard M. Nixon played on his golf course; Gerald R. Ford awarded him the Presidential Medal of Freedom and, along with then vice-president George Bush, attended his funeral, which was presided over by Rev. Dr. Norman Vincent Peale.

Thomas was also "the grandfather of Cinerama," the three-dimensional film process he produced in 1952, after it had remained dormant in a laboratory for fourteen years. He served as chairman of the board of the Cinerama Company and produced *This Is Cinerama*, *Search for Paradise*, and other Cinerama shows, including *The Seven Wonders of the World*, which was also published as a book in 1956.

*History As You Heard It*, a collection of brief excerpts from twenty-five years of his radio broadcasts, was published in 1957, but Thomas's career and expeditions were far from over. At age sixty-five he set out for the North Pole, New Guinea, the Sahara, Nepal, and the desert of northern Australia while preparing for a monthly CBS television series, *High Adventure with Lowell Thomas*. "Like all his adventures, Thomas's TV series is a triumph of seemingly amateur enthusiasm over the techniques of usually sophisticated, high-style professions," wrote *Newsweek*.

After his nightly radio news program was taken off the air by CBS in 1976, he began a thirty-nine-week television series, *Lowell Thomas Remembers*, that ran for three years on the Public Broadcasting Service and included profiles of many outstanding figures in history. The first of his two-part autobiography, *Good Evening, Everybody* (his radio sign on), was published in 1977, and the second volume, *So Long Until Tomorrow*, his radio tag line, was published a year later. In 1979 he began a daily syndicated radio series, *The Best Years*, about the accomplishments of famous people in their later years. Known by his friends as Tommy, he received more than twenty honorary degrees.

PRINCIPAL WORKS: With Lawrence in Arabia, 1924; The First World Flight, 1925; Beyond Khyber Pass, 1925; Count Luckner, The Sea Devil, 1927; European Skyways, 1927; The Boy's Life of Colonel Lawrence, 1927; Adventures in Afghanistan for Boys, 1928; Raiders of the Deep, 1928; The Sea Devil's Fo'c'sle, 1929; Woodfill of the Regulars, 1929; The Hero of Vincennes, 1929; The Wreck of the Dumaru, 1930; Lauterbach of the China Sea, 1930; India—Land of the Black Pagoda, 1930; Rolling Stone, 1931; Tall Stories, 1931; Kabluk of the Eskimo, 1932; This Side of Hell, 1932; Old Gimlet Eye: The Adventures of General Smedley Butler, 1933; Born to Raise Hell, 1933; The Untold Story of Exploration, 1935; Fan Mail, 1935; A Trip to New York With Bobby and Betty, 1936; Men of Danger, 1936; Kipling Stories and a Life of Kipling, 1936; Seeing Canada With Lowell Thomas, 1936; Seeing India With Lowell Thomas, 1936; Seeing Japan With Lowell Thomas, 1937; Seeing Mexico With Lowell Thomas, 1937; Adventures Among the Immortals, 1937; Hungry Waters, 1937; Wings Over Asia, 1937; Magic Dials, 1939; In New Brunswick We'll Find It, 1939; Soft Ball! So What?, 1940; How To Keep Mentally Fit, 1940; Stand Fast for Freedom, 1940; Pageant of Adventure, 1940; Pageant of Life, 1941; Pageant of Romance, 1943; These Men Shall Never Die, 1943; Back to Mandaley, 1951; Great True Adventures, 1955; The Story of the New York Thruway, 1955; Seven Wonders of the World, 1956; History As You Heard It, 1957; The Story of the St. Lawrence Seaway, 1957; The Vital Spark, 1959; Sire Hubert Wilkins, A Biography, 1961; More Great True Adventures, 1963; Book of the High Mountains, 1964; Famous First Flights That Changed History, 1968; Burma Jack, 1971; Doolittle: A Biography, 1976; Good Evening Everybody: From Cripple Creek to Samarkand, 1976; So Long Until Tomorrow, 1977.

ABOUT: Bowen, N. R. (ed.) Lowell Thomas: The Stranger Everyone Knows; Contemporary Authors vol. 104; Current Biography 1940; 1952; Who's Who 1979. *Periodicals*—Argosy August 1958; New York Times October 12, 1924; March 6, 1932; August 30, 1981; September 3, 1981; Newsweek November 25, 1957; San Francisco Chronicle November 16, 1956; Times (London) August 31, 1981.

# THOMASON, JOHN WILLIAM (February 28, 1893–March 12, 1944), American military officer, short story writer, and artist, was born in Huntsville, Texas, the oldest of nine children in a family that revered the Confederate veterans in its lineage. His father was a physician, but Thomason's

interests lay in another direction. He briefly attended three colleges, including the University of Texas, where he drew for the college monthly magazine. For a short stint, he was the principal of a small school, but in 1913, he headed for New York City to spend two years at the Art Students' League. After his funds ran out he returned home, where after a time he found a job as a cub reporter on the *Houston Chronicle*.

When the U.S. entered the First World War in 1917, Thomason joined the Marine Corps, receiving a second lieutenant's commission. He served in  France with the 1st Battalion of the 5th Marine Regiment, part of the 2nd U.S. Division. Thomason saw heavy fighting at Belleau Wood, Soisson, Blanc Mont, and the Meuse-Argonne. For heroism in action, he received both the Navy Cross and the Silver Star. Robert Leckie wrote: "Such experiences were to provide Thomason with the first great lump of raw material on which his writer's mind and his artist's eye—in short, his creative spirit—were to work. He had found his metier at last."

In finding the beginnings of a successful career in the military, Thomason also found a second career as a writer-illustrator. In 1925, at the urging of his friend and fellow Marine Lawrence Stallings, coauthor with Maxwell Anderson of the hit Broadway play *What Price Glory?*, Captain Thomason offered to Charles Scribner's Sons a group of short stories with illustrations based on his war experiences. The collection was published in early 1926 under the title *Fix Bayonets!* Critical acclaim for both stories and artwork was widespread, led by reviewers like James Norman Hall, who ranked him as a war writer with Barbusse, Masefield, and Stallings. From London the *Times Literary Supplement* said: "No book which we can recall that has for subject the actual fighting man in the Great War, has appeared to us to equal this. The drawings match the prose. This book, it may be, falls short of the highest work of its kind in its lack of that restraint which most great writers force upon themselves. . . . And yet it has the elements of life in it to a greater degree than almost all the long series of war books one has encountered."

Thomason's postwar military service gave him a variety of assignments, including an expedition to Cuba, a posting with the Horse Marines in Beijing, service in Central America and at sea, and command of a rifle battalion. It also provided him with fresh material for his second career. With the great success of *Fix Bayonets!*, his stories and illustrations—paintings in oil and watercolors, sketches in charcoal, pencil, and pen and ink—now began to appear often, and for large fees, in popular magazines like *Scribner's* and *Saturday Evening Post*.

Dealing with swaggering, colorful characters in exotic settings, Thomason's stories—appearing as they did in large-circulation magazines—served to introduce the Marine Corps, the smallest of the military services, to the American public, which responded with enthusiasm. For this reason, his stories have been compared with Kipling's tales of the British Army in the late Victorian age and with Remington's paintings of the U.S. Army during the era of the Indian wars. Leckie observed: "Everything that he wrote either was about something that had happened to him or someone he knew or was based on some sea story told him by one of those salty sergeants or old China hands who are the bards of the Marine Corps."

After their initial appearance in magazines, many of Thomason's stories were collected along with new ones and published in several volumes, *Red Pants and Other Stories*, *Marines and Others*, *Salt Winds and Gobi Dust*, and *And a Few Marines*. Amid the press of military duties and magazine deadlines, he also found the time to write nonfiction articles on various topics, two novels, and a biography of the Confederate cavalry leader J.E.B. ("Jeb") Stuart. Reviews of *Jeb Stuart* were enthusiastic, most of them noting the strong affinity of the author for his subject. A reviewer for the *Christian Science Monitor* wrote: "Captain Thomason neglects none of the little touches that so clearly reveal the human and lovable side of Jeb Stuart. At the same time he retells, in unforgettable language, the story of the Confederate cavalry's part in the fighting done by the Army of Northern Virginia."

When the United States entered the Second World War, Thomason was a full colonel. Assigned to the amphibious training command of the Pacific Fleet in 1943, he hoped for another opportunity to lead Marines in combat, but ill health intervened, and he died in the Naval Hospital at San Diego, California.

*Jeb Stuart* and *Fix Bayonets!* have remained in print since their original publication, the latter especially popular with Marines and former Marines.

PRINCIPAL WORKS: *Novels*—Gone to Texas, 1937; Lone Star Preacher, 1941. *Biography*—Jeb Stuart, 1930. *Short stories*—Fix Bayonets!, 1926 (reissued in an expanded edition, 1970); Red Pants and Other Stories, 1927; Marines and Others, 1929; Salt Winds and Gobi Dust, 1934; And a Few Marines, 1943. *As editor and illustrator*—Adventures of General Marbot, 1935.

ABOUT: Encyclopedia of Frontier and Western Fiction, 1983; Leckie, R. *introduction to* Fix Bayonets!, 1970; Lee, J. W. Classics of Texas Fiction, 1987; National Cyclopedia of American Biography vol. 33 1947; Norwood, W. D. John W. Thomason (Southern Writers Series No 25) 1969; Turner, M. A. World of Colonel John W. Thomason, U.S.M.C., 1984; Willock, R. Lone Star Marine, 1961. *Periodicals*—Christian Science Monitor 1930; New York Times March 13, 1944; Saturday Evening Post November 14, 1936; Saturday Review of Literature, March 18, 1944; Times Literary Supplement May 20, 1926.

**THOMPSON, DOROTHY** (July 9, 1893–January 30, 1961), American journalist, was born in Lancaster, New York, the eldest of three children of Peter Thompson, a Methodist minister, and Margaret Grierson Thompson. Her mother died when Dorothy was eight, and two years later her father, to whom she was extremely close, married his church organist, a dour and disapproving middle-aged woman whose dislike for her spirited step-daughter was reciprocated.

When the tension became unbearable, Dorothy was sent to Chicago to live with relatives. There she attended the Lewis Institute and compiled an out-standing scholastic record, which made possible her admission to Syracuse University as a transfer student in 1912. Although her self-confidence scared off potential suitors, she flourished socially and intellectually at Syracuse. Upon graduating in 1914 she went to work as a publicist and organizer for the New York State Woman Suffrage Party in Buffalo.

In 1917 she moved to Greenwich Village. For the next several years she dabbled in journalism while working as the publicity director for the National Social Unit Organization, a progressive social-work agency. Partly to distance herself from the Social Unit's married director, with whom she had had an unhappy affair, she resigned from the organization in 1920 and sailed (with a female friend) to Europe. Onboard ship she made the acquaintance (flirting "outrageously," she said) with a group of rabbis and Jewish propagandists on their way to London for a conference on Zionism; she seized the opportunity to transform herself into a journalist. According to Peter Kurth, "By the time she got to London she had an article in her head and the beginnings of a legend on her hands—the legend of a fresh-faced girl from the American heartland, 'an amiable, blue-eyed tornado' who roared through Europe stirring up trouble and making news happen wherever she went." She sold the story on the Zionist conferees to the International News Service and in the following months parlayed several "scoops" into headline stories for the INS syndicate.

In 1921, while stationed in Vienna, she began writing for the *Philadelphia Public Ledger*, and though as yet unsalaried, she was soon promoted to permanent European correspondent and in 1924 became the Central European bureau chief for both the *Public Ledger* and the *New York Evening Post*. She resigned from these positions in 1928, soon after marrying Sinclair Lewis, whom she had met at a party in Berlin the year before. The marriage to Lewis, which produced one child, Michael, and ended in divorce in 1942, proved to be even more miserable than had her previous one to Joseph Bard, a philandering Hungarian writer of little talent whom she had married in 1922 and divorced in 1927. Given Lewis's alcoholism and self-pity, it is small wonder that Thompson, who had been attracted to women since her college days, found refuge in an intense friendship with Christa Winsloe, a Hungarian countess whose novel *The Child Manuela* formed the basis for the lesbian cult film *Mädchen in Uniform*. Thompson was, however, an ambisexual with a strong disposition toward men; her third marriage, to a minor Austrian emigré painter named Maxim Kopf, was happy.

Thompson was aware that the force of her personality and the drama of her life risked overshadowing her work, and her complaint to an editor that "it seems to be my fate always to be judged as a conscience and a character rather than as a mind and a writer" is a judgment that posterity has, on the whole, endorsed. All of the eight books published in her lifetime were collections or reworkings of her newspaper writings and radio broadcasts (which she began making in 1937), and not one is in print. Her career, wrote Naomi Bliven in the *New Yorker*, "illustrates one reason that even great journalists may be forgotten: the issues that inflamed them disappear." Some of her books were hardly more than pamphlets. For example, *I Saw Hitler!* was a thirty-six-page account of her 1931 interview with the Nazi-party chief in which she made the unfortunate prediction that this man of "startling insignificance" would never rise to power in Germany. After realizing her mistake, she argued insistently thereafter, according to Geoffrey C. Ward in the *New York Review of Books*, that "Adolf Hitler meant precisely what he said in *Mein Kampf* and [that] the future of civilization depended upon stopping him in his tracks."

Many of Thompson's most astute political judgment were brought together in three collections from the late 1930s and early 1940s, *Dorothy Thompson's Political Guide*, *Let the Record Speak*, and *Listen, Hans*. As the subtitle to *Dorothy Thompson's Political Guide* had it, her great subject was "American Liberalism and Its Relationship to Modern Totalitarian States," and after the war she never quite found an issue to match her passion for the cause of intervention. In the late 1940s and 1950s she rallied to the defense of Palestinian Arabs, but her pro-Arab stance alienated many Jewish readers, and the *New York Post*, which had carried her "On the Record" column since 1941, after it was dropped by the *Herald Tribune*, dropped her in 1947. Aside from her forays into Middle Eastern politics, her writings from the 1950s, many of which appeared in the *Saturday Evening Post* and the *Ladies' Home Journal*, took on an increasingly domestic and conservative cast. By the end, wrote Kenneth S. Lynn in *Commentary*, the woman who had once rivaled Eleanor Roosevelt in popular influence could "assert disingenuously that she had 'an ever-increasing respect for women who stick to their knitting.' Even more nauseating was the assurance she offered to homemakers that 'It is never futile to grow sweet peas, or arrange roses in a bowl.'"

Thompson's last significant piece of writing was a profile of Sinclair Lewis for the *Atlantic* in 1960. After giving up her magazine column in 1958, she intended to write her memoirs, but her health and high spirits declined rapidly after the death of Maxim Kopf, and she never got past a nostalgic account of her childhood. She died of a heart attack at the age of sixty-seven while visiting her grandchildren in Portugal. Her books do not survive, but "as a journalist," wrote Naomi Bliven, "she was an abstract and brief chronicle of her time. She was also, I think, an exemplary figure—a woman who represented her era as well as reported it."

Thompson's papers are at the George Arents Research Library at Syracuse University.

PRINCIPAL WORKS: *Reportage and opinion*—The New Russia, 1928; I Saw Hitler!, 1932; Dorothy Thompson's Political Guide: A Study of American Liberalism and Its Relationship to Modern Totalitarian States, 1938; Refugees: Anarchy or Organization?, 1938; Let the Record Speak, 1939; Listen, Hans, 1942; The Courage to Be Happy, 1957. *Juvenile*—Once on Christmas, 1938. *Correspondence*—Dorothy Thompson and Rose Wilder Lane: Forty Years of Friendship: Letters 1921–1960 (ed. W. Holtz) 1991.

ABOUT: Current Biography 1940; Dictionary of American Biography Suppl. 7 1981; Dictionary of Literary Biography vol. 29 1984; Kurth, P. American Cassandra: The Life of Dorothy Thompson, 1990; McKerns, J. P. (ed.) Biographical Dictionary of American Journalism, 1989; Notable American Women, the Modern Period: A Biographical Dictionary, 1980; Sanders, M. K. Dorothy Thompson: A Legend in Her Time, 1973; Sheean, V. Dorothy and Red, 1963. *Periodicals*—Commentary October 1990; New York Review of Books August 16, 1990; New York Times February 1, 1961; New Yorker September 17, 1990; Times (London) February 1, 1961.

**THOMPSON, EDWARD JOHN** (April 9, 1886–April 28, 1946), English novelist, playwright, writer of verse, and translator—he is remembered  as an authority on India—was born in Stockport, England, the eldest son of the Reverend John Moses Thompson and his wife, both Wesleyan ministers. After studying at Kingswood School, Bath, he received his M.A. from Oxford University; he gained a Ph.D. from London University in 1909. By this time he had already begun his literary career as a poet, publishing his first book of verse, *The Knight Mystic* in 1907. In 1910 Thompson was ordained as a Wesleyan minister and went to India, where he taught English literature at Bankura College in Bengal. While there he studied the Bengali language and culture, eventually coming to have a deep understanding and admiration of it, though Rabindranath Tagore said his Bengali was not good. Thompson would later translate several volumes of Tagore's work, as well as work by other Indian writers, and publish *Rabindranath Tagore: His Life and Work* (1921) and *Tagore: Poet and Dramatist* (1925). Unfortunately, Tagore hated and disapproved of both Thompson's criticism of and translations from his work. It has lately been adjudged by William Rudice that he was right—but somewhat ungracious. The grounds for Tagore's dissatisfaction lay in the undoubted fact that Thompson thought of him—quite wrongly, for he was a Bengali modernist—as an English poet of the style of Swinburne or Tennyson and "translated" him accordingly.

During World War I Thompson served as a chaplain in Mesopotamia from 1916 to 1917. In 1918 he was transferred to Palestine, where he met and, in 1919, married Theodosia Jessup, the daughter of an American missionary in Lebanon and a nurse in a Jerusalem hospital. She later collaborated with him on several of his dramatic works, including *Three Eastern Plays* (1927) and *Last Voyage* (1934), a play about the death of Sir Walter Raleigh.

In 1922 Thompson retired from Bankura College, where he had been made acting principal in 1920, and returned to England. He also resigned from the Wesleyan ministry. Shortly after his return he became lecturer in Bengali at the University of Oxford, and in 1925 he was admitted to Oriel College, where he was appointed research fellow in Indian history from 1936 to 1946. In 1945 he published *100 Poems*, a compilation spanning the length of his career. The reviews were fair: Thompson was not an impressive poet, but he was sincere and competent. Thus the reviewer for the *Times Literary Supplement* described the volume as a "sensitive reflection of varied experience, both outward and inward."

At first an imperialist, Thompson became in time devoted to the idea of Indian self-determination; he produced many books devoted to the relationship between India and England. *The Other Side of the Medal* (1925), which chronicled English atrocities during the Indian mutiny of 1857, was the first of many books to deal with this subject. Painfully truthful, it received reviews ranging from what Howard Swiggett writing in the *Saturday Review of Literature* called "awkward and uninspired" to what *Nation and Athenaeum* called "the most important contribution in recent years to the criticism of the British dominion in India." *Reconstructing India* (1930), *Rise and Fulfillment of British Rule in India* (1935), and *Making of the Indian Princes* (1943) followed; all received good reviews and were praised for their truthfulness and honesty.

Of the handful of novels written by Thompson, most are set in India, where the author, as in *An Indian Day* (1927), draws upon his love for the country The book was compared to E. M. Forster's *A Passage to India*, though some reviewers felt that it was "rather heavily written" and "not an easy book to read" (*New Statesman*, 1927). This semi-autobiographical story of an Englishman who comes to understand the Indian way of life was followed by *Farewell to India* (1931), in which the hero, an educational missionary in Bengal, considers some of the political and social problems facing India as he prepares to leave his post after twenty years. The final part to the trilogy, *An End of the Hours*, was published in 1938.

In addition to his writing, Thompson was an active lecturer, and in 1929 he came to the United States where he lectured at Vassar for a year. Thompson also took up journalism for a time, serving as special correspondent for the *Manchester Guardian* in India in 1932.

PRINCIPAL WORKS: *Poetry*—The Knight Mystic, 1907; John in Prison, 1212; Ennerdale Bridge and Other Poems, 1914; Waltham Thickets, 1917; Mesopotamian Verses, 1918; Via Triumphalis, 1922; Poems, 1902–1925, 1926; The Thracian Stranger, 1928; Collected Poems, 1930; New Recessional, and Other Poems, 1942; 100 Poems, 1944. *Drama*—Krishna Kumari, 1924; Atonement, 1924; (with T. Thompson) Three Eastern Plays, 1927; Plays and Pageants, 1931; (with T. Thompson) Last Voyage, 1934; Essex and Elizabeth: A Play in Four Acts, 1943.

*Nonfiction*—The Leicestershires Beyond Bagdad, 1919; Rabindranath Tagore: His Life and Work, 1921; The Other Side of the Metal, 1925; Tagore: Poet and Dramatist, 1926; A History of India, 1927; Crusader's Coast, 1928; Suttee, 1928; Reconstruction of India, 1930 (in U.S.: Reconstructing India); (with G. T. Garratt) Rise and Fulfillment of British Rule in India, 1934; Sir Walter Raleigh, 1935; Lord Metcalfe, 1937 (in U.S.: The Life of Charles, Lord Metcalfe); You Have Lived Through All This: An Anatomy of the Age, 1939; Enlist India for Freedom!, 1940; Ethical Ideas in India Today, 1924; Making of the Indian Princes, 1943; Robert Bridges, 1844–1930, 1944. *Fiction*—An Indian Day, 1927; These Men Thy Friends, 1927; Night Falls on Siva's Hill, 1928; In Araby Orion, 1928; A Farewell to India, 1931; Lament for Adonis, 1933 (in U.S.: Damascus Lies North); So Poor a Ghost, 1933; Introducing the Arnisons, 1935; Burmese Silver, 1937; The Youngest Disciple, 1938; An End of the Hours, 1938; John Arnison, 1939. *As editor*—(with H. Wolfe) The Augustan Books of English Poetry, 1935. *As translator*—(with A. M. Spencer) Bengali Religious Lyrics, 1923; The Curse of Farewell (by R. Tagore) 1924; Rabindranath Tagore (by R. Tagore) 1925; Rabindranath Tagore: Twenty-Two Poems (by R. Tagore) 1925; The Brothers (by T. Ganguli) 1928.

ABOUT: Dictionary of National Biography 1941–1950, 1959; Radice, W. *preface to* Rabindranath Tagore: Selected Poems, 1985; Who's Who 1946. *Periodicals*—Nation and Athenaeum January 2, 1926; New Statesman June 4, 1927; May 4, 1946; New York Times April 29, 1946; Saturday Review of Literature May 15, 1926; Times (London) April 29, 1946; Times Literary Supplement August 12, 1944.

## THOMPSON, J(AMES) M(ATTHEW) (September 27, 1878–October 10, 1956), English historian and theologian, was born in Gloucestershire, the eldest son of Catherine (Paget) Thompson and the Reverend Henry Lewis Thompson, then the Rector of Iron Acton. He was educated at the Dragon School, Oxford. After winning a scholarship he attended Winchester and Christ Church, Oxford. In 1902 Thompson obtained second-class honors in theology, and, following two terms at Cuddeson theological college, was ordained deacon in 1903. He was a Fellow of Magdalen College, Oxford (1904–1938) specializing in modern French history; from 1906–1925 he was also Dean of Divinity, and Vice President (1935–1937).

Thompson retired from the college in 1938. He edited the *Oxford Magazine* (1945–1947) but was forced to give up owing to poor health. Thompson also served as a temporary Master at Eton College (1914–18).

He began his literary career with the publication of theological works, including *An Annotated Psalter* (1907), *Jesus According to St. Mark* (1909), *Miracles in the New Testament* (1911), and *Through Facts to Faith* (1912). But because of his nonmiraculous view of Christianity, seemingly heavily influenced by both the Catholic Modernist school and the methods of modern biblical criticism, he soon fell into disfavor with his church and so was transferred to the History School.

At this point, Thompson began to publish the historical studies for which he is now best known. Most of them dealt with the French Revolution or its aftermath, the Napoleonic era. *Leaders of the French Revolution* (1929), a collection of eleven biographical sketches of the men who had played prominent parts in the revolution, was his first attempt at examining this period. *Napoleon I: Emperor of the*

*French* (1934) was a compilation of three hundred letters written by Napoleon between 1784, when he was a fifteen-year-old military student, and one month after the battle of Waterloo in 1815. The book was followed by *Robespierre* (1935), a biography Thompson had written after years of intensive research in France. It received warm but mixed reviews, being described by Leonard Woolf (*New Statesman and Nation*) as, "the best book about Robespierre in the English language"; however, Woolf added that "Mr. Thompson's attempt to explain Robespierre's psychology is the only unsatisfactory part of the book." Albert Guerard, Jr., wrote in *New York Herald Tribune Books*: "The biography of Robespierre remains to be written: but this is a valuable contribution."

In 1945 Thompson published his chief work, *The French Revolution*. In this almost-six-hundred-page volume, which remains in print as a standard book, the author examines letters and other previously ignored records to explain the economic and political background of the revolution. Generations of history students formed their first views of the Revolution from this book.

Thompson's other historical works include *Napoleon Bonaparte* (1951), *Robespierre and the French Revolution* (1952), and *Louis Napoleon and the Second Empire* (1954).

Thompson married Mary Meredyth, the daughter of the Reverend David Jones, Vicar of Penmaenmawr, in 1913. The couple had one son.

PRINCIPAL WORKS: An Annotated Psalter, 1907; Jesus According to Saint Mark, 1909; Miracles in the New Testament, 1912; Through Facts to Faith, 1912; Lectures of Foreign History 1494–1789, 1926; Historical Geography of Europe 800–1789, 1929; Leaders of the French Revolution, 1929; Notes on the French Revolution, 1934; Robespierre, 1935; The French Revolution, 1943; Napoleon Bonaparte: His Rise and Fall, 1951, rev. ed. 1990; Robespierre and the French Revolution, 1952; Louis Napoleon and the Second Empire, 1954. *Poetry*—Collected Verse, 1939–1946, 1947; Spider's Web: A Philosophical Essay in Verse, 1949. *As editor*—The French Revolution: Documents 1789–1794; English Witnesses of the French Revolution, 1938.

ABOUT: Dictionary of National Biography, 1951–1960, 1971; Who's Who 1956. *Periodicals*—American Hisotry Review October 1953; Canadian Forum December 1952; Christian Science Monitor January 29, 1944; Nation April 21, 1945; New Statesman and Nation January 4, 1936; New York Herald Tribune Books June 14, 1936; Times (London) October 10, 1956.

## THOMPSON, SYLVIA (September 4, 1902–April 27, 1968), English novelist, was born in Scotland, Thompson grew up in Hampshire, and was educated at various schools, including Cheltenham, and at Somerville College, Oxford. Her marriage, in 1926, to Theodore Luling, an American artist, introduced the new dimension of American characters and manners to her fiction, which up to that point had been exclusively English.

*Rough Crossing* (1921), a charming and innocuous personal history of a 'flapper,' was appealingly unassuming and revealed a precocious narrative talent. There was little in this, or any subsequent Thompson novel, for the more demanding reader, and the thirty-year-old Rebecca West, writing in the *New Statesman* declared herself amazed that

the author "can actually think that this sort of thing is worth writing about." In her third and most successful novel, *The Hounds of Spring*—a story about an upper-class girl whose fiancée goes "missing, probably killed" in the First World War, only to be declared alive and well four years later, by which time the heroine has undergone a marriage of convenience—Thompson did attempt to add weight to her story with what the *New York Herald Tribune* reviewer described as "long Wellsian dissertations," but the book was very well received and enjoyed for its high-minded idealism.

*Battle of the Horizons* was the first book Thompson produced after her marriage; in it she reversed her own situation to tell the story of an American girl who marries into an English family. Although she brought no new insights to this theme, the cinematic pace of the telling ensured that readers of the previous book were well-satisfied with the new offering. *Chariot Wheels* confirmed her as a novelist with few aspirations beyond entertainment. V. S. Pritchett, writing in the *Spectator*, considered that she had fallen victim to her own dexterity. "One must admire her delightful technical subtlety and resourcefulness, but I am not sure they have not made her too successful in avoiding direct conflicts."

Of her other books, *Breakfast in Bed* was something of a departure. Its narrative, confined to a single day, concerned the interlocking lives of characters from different classes and households and was her first attempt to delve into the working-class psyche. She remained, in essence, a lightweight chronicler of a privileged and self-centered generation, content to draw what she described as "the inconsequent and attractively rhythmic pattern of modern life."

She wrote one play, with Victor Cunard. *Golden Arrow* (1935), in which Laurence Olivier and Greer Garson starred, had a run at the Whitehall Theatre, in London's West End.

PRINCIPAL WORKS: The Rough Crossing, 1921; A Lady in Green Gloves, 1924; The Hounds of Spring, 1926; The Battle of the Horizons, 1928; Chariot Wheels, 1929; Portrait By Caroline, 1931; Winter Comedy, 1931; Summer's Night, 1932; Unfinished Symphony, 1933; Breakfast in Bed, 1934; A Silver Rattle, 1935; Third Act in Venice, 1936; Recapture the Moon, 1937; The Adventure of Christopher Columin, 1939; The Gulls Fly Inland, 1941; The People Opposite, 1948; The Candle's Glory, 1953. *Drama*—(with V. Cunard) Golden Arrow, 1935.

ABOUT: Who's Who 1968. *Periodicals*—Boston Transcript February 13, 1932; New Statesman May 28, 1921; New York Herald Tribune February 28, 1926; Spectator October 19, 1929; Times (London) April 29, 1968.

# THOMSON, EDWARD WILLIAM (February 12, 1849–March 5, 1924), Canadian journalist, editor, poet, and author of short stories for boys, was born on his family's farm in Peel County, Ontario, just outside Toronto, the son of William Thomson,

a banker, and his wife, Margaret Hamilton (Foley) Thomson. He was educated in public schools and Trinity College School, Weston, Ontario. His family's roots were in the United States; they had been Loyalists who came to Canada after the American Revolution.

Thomson seemed to have felt these ties strongly, for at the age of fifteen, after a chance meeting with Abraham Lincoln while visiting an uncle in Philadelphia, he ran off to fight in the American Civil War. He served with the Pennsylvania Cavalry in the Virginia campaigns of 1864 and 1865, before parental intervention caused him to return home. He continued his military career in Canada, and became a member of the Queen's  Own Rifles in 1866 and fighting during the Fenian raids. From 1868 to 1879 he worked as a civil engineer and land surveyor, working on the construction of the Carilon Canal around the rapids of the Ottawa River.

His literary career began in 1878, when he became chief editorial writer for the *Toronto Globe*, where he soon developed a reputation for soundness. He resigned in 1891 after a disagreement with its policy of supporting "unrestricted reciprocity" in trade between Canada and the United States. He took a position in Boston as an associate editor of the *Youth's Companion*, a magazine for boys. From 1902 until he retired from journalism in 1922, Thomson lived in Canada, working as a Canadian correspondent for the *Boston Evening Transcript*, for which he traveled extensively across the country.

His exposure to a variety of people during this time obviously affected his fiction, which, in one instance, was described in the *New York Times* as "stories from Canada, not from any one class or of any one ancestry," which "cover a wide range of time and circumstance."

Thomson was a follower of the liberal Canadian leader Sir Wilfred Laurier. As such, he advocated Canadian independence from Great Britain, and pleaded for this in his nonfiction. In 1909, for the Lincoln centennial, he published *When Lincoln Died and Other Poems* (published as *The Many Mansioned House and Other Poems* in Canada). This tribute to the president—not so poor as most such efforts have been—of whom Thomson was a great admirer (a sentiment perhaps strengthened by the fact that the two shared a birthday), was described—although a little absurdly—by the *A.L.A. Booklist* as "a pleasing collection. . . . Having sufficient merit to warrant comparison with Lowell's and Whitman's classics."

Thomson is best known, however, as a story writer. Many of his tales appeared in newspapers and magazines in both Canada and the United States, and were collected in several different volumes.

The best-known of these collections is *Old Man Savarin and Other Stories* (1895), still in print today. The collection contains three types of stories: those set in various Canadian villages and lumbering camps; those of war; and those set in Boston. In each Thomson makes use of regional attitudes, dialects, and customs to give life to his characters and their situations.

For his achievements in journalism, fiction, and poetry, Thomson was made a fellow of the Royal Society of Literature in 1909; he was elected to the Royal Society of Canada in 1910. He died in Boston. His wife, the writer Adelaide (St. Denis) Thomson, whom he had married in 1873, predeceased him. Their only son, Bernard, worked for several years on the editorial staff of the *New York Times*.

PRINCIPAL WORKS: *Short stories*—Great Godfrey's Lament, 1892; Old Man Savarin and Other Stories, 1895; Walter Gibb: The Young Boss, 1896; Smokey Days, 1896; Between Earth and Sky, 1897; Selected Stories of E. W. Thomson, 1973. *Poetry*—Peter Ottawa, 1908; When Lincoln Died and Other Poems 1909 (in Canada: The Many Mansioned House and Other Poems).

ABOUT: Creative in Canada vol. II, 1972; Dictionary of Literary Biography vol. 92, 1990; Who's Who 1924. *Periodicals*—A. L.A. Booklist December 1909; New York Times March 7, 1924; Times (London) March 10, 1924.

## THOMSON, GEORGE DERWENT (August 19, 1903–February 3, 1987), English classical scholar, educator, and translator, was the son of William

Henry and Minnie Thomson. Thomson's parents sent the boy to Dulwich College, London, and King's College, Cambridge where he was a fellow from 1927 to 1933 and again from 1934 to 1936. He began his teaching career at University College, Galway. In 1937 he took a position at the University of Birmingham where he remained until 1970. An authority on Greek language and literature, Thomson wrote several books on the origins of classical drama and poetry. His *Aeschylus and Athens: A Study in the Origins of Drama*, prompted the *Classical Review* to note how its author denied "the possibility of objective truth or historical impartiality." He also wrote *Greek Lyric Metre*, and *The Prehistoric Agean*, volume I of the series "Studies in Ancient Greek Society."

Thomson described this effort as his attempt to "reinterpret the legacy of Greece in the light of Marxism." For this and other works he was likened to the poet and Marxist critic Christopher Cauldwell who, like him, saw the origin of poetry in collective primitive rituals such as the harvest. Stanley Edgar Hyman noted that Thomson approached his subject using both an anthropological and a Marxist analysis.

Thomson also edited and translated versions of *Prometheus Bound* and *Orestia* and knew enough of the Irish language to translate, with Moya Llew-

wlyn Davies, *Twenty Years A-Growing*, the autobiography of the Irish writer Muiris O Suileabhain (M. O'Sullivan).

In 1947 Thomson became a member of the executive committee of the Communist party in Great Britain, and continued to expound his political theories through books like *Marxism and Poetry, From Marx to Mao Tse-Tung*, and *Capitalism and After*. Thomson married Katharine Fraser Stewart in 1934. They had two daughters.

PRINCIPAL WORKS: Greek Lyric Metre, 1929; Aeschylus and Athens, 1941; Marxism and Poetry, 1945; The Prehistoric Agean, 1949; The First Philosophers, 1955 (new ed. 1973); The Greek Language, 1960 (new ed. 1966); A Manual of Modern Greek, 1966; From Marx to Mao Tse-Tung, 1971; Capitalism and After, 1973.

ABOUT: Contemporary Authors vol. 121 1987; Who's Who 1984. *Periodical*—Times (London) February 7, 1987.

## THOMSON, JOHN ARTHUR (July 8, 1861– February 12, 1933), Scottish biologist and writer on sociological topics, was born in Pilmuir Manse, East

Lothian, Scotland, the son of the Reverend Arthur Thomson and Isabella (Landsborough) Thomson. He was educated in the local schools and at the universities of Edinburgh, Jena, and Berlin, where he specialized in zoology. Upon completing his studies abroad, Thomson re-

turned to Scotland and began, but never finished, divinity classes at the New School, opting instead to lecture on zoology and biology at the Edinburgh School of Medicine. Through these speaking tours in the larger Scottish cities, Thomson gained a reputation of being able to convey vast amounts of knowledge with charm and ease. In 1899 he was appointed regius professor of Natural History at the University of Aberdeen, where he remained until his retirement in 1930, when he was knighted.

While lecturing in Edinburgh, Thomson became associated with the biologist and sociologist Sir Patrick Geddes. Together they wrote several books, the first being *The Evolution of Sex* (1889). Their works were well received for their facility in presenting complex subject matter in a form easily comprehensible to the lay reader. Undoubtedly, Geddes, who continuously strove to relate biological knowledge to civil welfare through town planning, influenced and molded Thomson's style in relaying, through the written and spoken word, an immense amount of data in an appealing and often "entrancing" manner.

As Geddes related science to daily life, so Thomson attempted to reconcile science with religion. His mission was to promote a widespread interest in and devotion to scientific method and inquiry in an era characterized by strident conflict with religious thought. In a letter written to aid Clarence Darrow's defense of Tennessee schoolteacher John Scopes in the famous "monkey" trial in 1925, Thomson called Darwin's theory of evolution a "child of vast" understandings (i.e., creationism) and a "parent of the future." In this way, Thomson recognized science and religion as springing from desparate world-views, yet ultimately reconciled in a continuum of thought that represents progress in human understanding.

The London *Times* obituary correctly notes, "It cannot be claimed [that he] made any notable additions to zoology or biology by original work," but Thomson was nonetheless an immensely successful and well-known "scholarly popularizer" of the natural sciences and of Darwin's theory of evolution. His prolific output included books entitled *Heredity* (1908), *Darwinism and Human Life* (1910), *Problems of Sex* (1913), *Secrets of Animal Life* (1919), and *New Natural History* (1925). The latter work, a three-volume encyclopedic work, prompted an overenthusiastic reviewer in the *New York World* to exclaim "Prof. Thomson . . . is without doubt the most brilliant, the most gifted, and the most sympathetic writer of natural history that has ever lived." Less perfervidly, *The New York Times* wrote of his *Riddles of Science* (1932): "It has been his particular mission to take the curse off the word 'popular' . . . and to show that such [scientific] writing can be done with scientific authoritativeness, literary dignity and fascinating readibility."

Thomson was named professor emeritus of Natural History at the University of Aberdeen. He was survived by his wife, Lady Thomson, a well-known translator, and his four children, all of whom became published authors.

PRINCIPAL WORKS: (with P. Geddes) The Evolution of Sex, 1889; Zoology, 1892; The Study of Animal Life, 1892; The Natural History of the Year: For Young People, 1896; The Science of Life: An Outline of the History of Biology and Its Recent Advances, 1899; Progress of Science in the Century, 1906; Herbert Spencer, 1906; Heredity, 1908; The Bible of Nature, 1908; Darwinism and Human Life, 1910; The Biology of the Seasons, 1911; Introduction to Science, 1911; (with P. Geddes) Problems of Sex, 1912; The Wonder of Life, 1914; The Study of Animal Life, 1917; Secrets of Animal Life, 1919; Natural History Studies, 1920; (with others) The Control of Parenthood, 1920; The System of Animate Nature, 1920; Nature All the Year Round, 1921; The Control of Life, 1921; The Haunts of Life, 1921; The Outline of Science, 1922; The Bible of Nature, 1923; The Biology of Birds, 1923; What Is Man?, 1923; Everday Biology, 1923; Science Old and New, 1924; Science and Religion, 1925; Man in the Light of Evolution, 1926; Ways of Living: Nature and Man, 1926; The Wonder of Life, 1927; Towards Health, 1927; The Minds of Animals, 1927; Modern Science: A General Introduction, 1929; The Outline of Natural History, 1931; (with P. Geddes) Life: Outline of General Biology, 1931; Scientific Riddles, 1932 (in U.S.: Riddles of Science); The Great Biologists, 1932; Biology for Everyman, 1934; The Ways of Birds, 1935: The Ways of Insects, 1935.

ABOUT: Bridges, T. C. and Tiltman, H. H. Master Minds of Modern Science; East Lothian Antiquarian and Field Naturalists' Society Transactions: vol. 2. *Periodicals*—Christian Century Feburary 13, 1933; Review of Reviews March 1933; Scottish Geographical Magazine March 1933; Nature March 4, 1933; New York Times February 13, 1933; Times (London) Feburary 13, 1933.

## THOMSON, VIRGIL (GARNETT) (November 25, 1896–September 30, 1989), American composer, conductor, musician, and music critic, was born in Kansas City, Missouri, the son of Quincy Alfred Thomson and Clara May (Gaines) Thomson.

He studied piano from the age of five, attended Central High School in Kansas City, enlisted in the National Guard at the onset of World War I and studied radiotelephony at Columbia University and aviation at the University of Texas. He received overseas orders in September 1918, but the Armistice was signed before his troop was to embark for France.

After attending the Junior College of Kansas City, he entered Harvard in 1919, which had a profound impact on his life. He studied with two French-trained musicians, Edward Burlingame Hill and Archibald Davison, and with S. Foster Damon, a poet, Blake scholar, and composer, who introduced Thomson to the piano works of Erik Satie and to Gertrude Stein's *Tender Buttons*. Satie would be the most influential composer on  Thomson's music, and Stein would become his most important collaborator. As an occasional conductor of Davison's Harvard Glee Club, Thomson traveled to Europe and remained in Paris for a year on a John Knowles Paine Traveling Fellowship. He studied organ and counterpoint with Nadia Boulanger, who went on to teach several generations of American composers, from Aaron Copland to Philip Glass. In Paris he got to know Copland, Jean Cocteau, Darius Milhaud and Francis Poulenc.

He returned to Harvard in 1922 to complete his bachelor's degree. He served as organist and choirmaster of King's Chapel in Boston for a year. In 1924 he began writing about music in magazines. For H. L. Mencken's *American Mercury* he wrote a piece defining jazz, and he also contributed pieces to *Vanity Fair*, the *New Republic*, and the *Boston Transcript*.

Thomson returned to Paris in 1925, remaining there until 1940 except for brief visits to the States. Despite his many years abroad, he never scorned America, as did many expatriates, but instead thrived on putting his heritage into his music. Ned Rorem, writing in the *Times* (London) in 1989, described Thomson: "American he utterly was despite, or maybe because, of the removal from his homeland which gave him a new slant towards his roots. For it was he who first legitimized the use of home-grown fodder for urban palates. He confected his own folk-song by filtering the hymns of his youth through a chic Gallic prism. This was the 'American Sound' of wide-open prairies and Appalachian springs, soon borrowed and popularized by others." Rorem worked for Thomson as his in-house copyist in the mid-1940s and recalled in his memoirs, *Knowing When to Stop* (1994), how Thomson, usually in bed and wearing orange pajamas, "rules the world" with his telephone and legal pads.

But in the mid-1920s Thomson was still maturing his musical style, writing a chamber score, four organ pieces based on Baptist hymns, and a symphony. Among his acquaintances in Paris were

Joyce, Pound, Stravinsky, and Picasso. Composer George Antheil introduced him to Gertrude Stein in 1926, and the two "got along like Harvard men," he said (according to Rorem.) Thomson had already set her poem "Susie Asado" before they met, and shortly afterward composed music for her "Preciosilla" and "Capital Capitals". They began work on the opera "Four Saints in Three Acts," with Stein writing every word of the libretto and stage direction, which was completed in 1928. "Originally a plotless effusion by celestial Spanish saints, full of whimsical questions and paradoxical mystical visions, the opera was pruned by Mr. Thomson," according to the New York Times, and fit into a pageant-like scenario created by Thomson's longtime companion, painter Maurice Grosser. Thomson decided it should be performed by an all-black cast, and it caused a considerable sensation when it premiered in Hartford, Connecticut, in 1934, presented by the Friends and Enemies of Modern Music. It also travelled to New York and Chicago and was revived in New York to much critical praise in 1952. It "was then and perhaps remains the most viable opera by any American," wrote Rorem in the London Times. Thomson also collaborated with Stein on her last completed work, another opera, The Mother of Us All (1947), a quirky pageant about Susan B. Anthony and women's suffrage.

Still in Paris, Thomson composed a body of instrumental works, mostly for string instruments, and wrote a series of musical portraits, mostly for piano, capturing his friends and acquaintances in sound. He wrote two still famous film scores, The Plough That Broke the Plains (1936) and The River (1937) for documentary filmmaker Pare Lorentz and wrote the ballad "Filling Station" for Lincoln Kirstein's Ballet Caravan.

After the Nazi occupation of France, he returned to New York in 1940 and settled at the Chelsea Hotel "where his grand apartment, awash with artistic memorabilia, became a cultural landmark," wrote the New York Times. "Manhattan during the war and up through the early 1950s was governed by Aaron Copland and Virgil Thomson, the father and mother of American music. Young composers joined one faction or the other, there was no third," wrote Rorem in his memoirs.

In 1940 Thomson became chief music critic of the New York Herald Tribune, "where his criticism infuriated precisely the people it should have, while setting standards for newspaper criticism that have yet to be matched. By standing outside of the musical power structure, he could regard it all with a seigneurial detachment tinged with an air of disfranchisement, which gave his criticism precisely the right mixture of disinterestedness and passion," wrote Edward Rothstein in the New Republic (1988). For fourteen years, Thomson served as a composers' advocate against the world of musical commerce. Rothstein recalled that he "came onstage ready for a fight . . . He referred to the 'silk-underwear music' of Heifetz . . . and the 'dull and brutal' playing of the New York Philharmonic. He attacked the management network in New York and the meretricious claims of Germanic musical taste."

Thomson's first book on modern music, The State of Music (1939), was considered "one of the best volumes of criticism we shall have for many a day," according to John Erskine in Books, who wrote that Thomson's "style is so brilliant and on most pages he is so amusing that we may at first overlook the solidity of his contribution."

Several dozen reviews and Sunday articles on opera and orchestras, composers and conductors were collected in Musical Scene (1945) and a companion book, The Art of Judging Music (1948). "Paste-up collections of old reviews usually make dreary reading, but Mr. Thomson's book is an exception, because he can discuss even the most ephemeral musical event in relation to the whole art. He is also, of course, a very witty and astringent writer," wrote the New Yorker. The Art of Judging Music was reissued in 1969.

On Thomson's tenth anniversary at the Herald Tribune, he published Music Right and Left (1951), which includes a three-page prelude that the composer Roger Sessions in the New York Times described as "a statement of critical principles difficult to improve on." In it Thomson explained his belief "that a musician's account of a musical event has legitimate interest for readers. Personal tastes I consider it fair to state, because by admitting one's prejudices and predilections one helps the reader to discount these. I do not consider them otherwise interesting nor ask for agreement regarding them. Description and analysis, however, I have tried to make convincing and, as far as possible, objective, even when sympathy is present. My own sympathies, frankly, are normally with the artist. I try to explain him, not to protect the public against him, though preserving a status quo or protecting anybody's career is not my intention either. Neither do I think myself entitled to make out report cards. I do not give an examination; I take one. I write a theme about an occasion."

When Thomson left the Herald Tribune in 1954 his career as a composer and performer floundered for a time. Nevertheless he continued composing, most notably, the opera Lord Byron (1972). He also wrote criticism, mainly for The New York Review of Books, remained a power within musical and arts circles, and more than a decade later was famous enough to title his autobiography Virgil Thomson (1966). The book was not the sensational tell-all some expected. Harold Clurman in the Nation called it "most discreet," and wrote that more of Thomson's personality came out in his criticism than in this memoir. Rorem's Paris Diary, published only a few months before Thomson's work, eclipsed it in frankness, with Rorem making plain his own homosexuality. Thomson in turn deleted any reference to Rorem in his book "for fear of being compromised," according to Rorem, who called Thomson's autobiography "an otherwise unique document on the economic history of the arts in contemporary America" with a faint but common stench, not just because he doesn't mention what Gide called la chose, but because, hypocritically, he does mention his passions for various women." Thomson's autobiography was reprinted in 1977, and an anthology of his writing, *A Virgil Thomson Reader*, won the National Book Critics Circle Award for criticism in 1981.

Thomson donated his letters to Yale, and in 1988 the *Selected Letters of Virgil Thomson*, was published, edited by Tim and Vanessa Weeks Page. Among his many awards were sixteen honorary doctorates, the Kennedy Center Award for Lifetime Achievement, and membership in the National Institute of Arts and Letters and in the French Legion of Honor.

PRINCIPAL WORKS: The State of Music, 1939; The Musical Scene, 1945; The Art of Judging Music, 1948; Music, Right and Left, 1951; Music Reviewed, 1940–1954, 1967; American Music Since 1910, 1971; A Virgil Thomson Reader (anthology), 1982; Selected Letters of Virgil Thomson (T. and V. W. Page, eds.) 1988; Music with Words: A Composer's View, 1989. *Autobiography*—Virgil Thomson, 1966.

ABOUT: Current Biography 1940; 1966; 1989; Hoover, K. O. and Cage, J. Virgil Thomson: His Life and Music; Rorem, N. Knowing When to Stop; Thomson, V. Prelude to Music Right and Left, Virgil Thomson. *Periodicals*—Books November 19, 1939; Nation October 24, 1966; New Republic March 25, 1940, June 20, 1988; New York Times March 21, 1951; October 9, 1966, October 1, 1989; New Yorker February 21, 1948; December 25, 1971; Times (London) October 2, 1989; December 22-28, 1989.

## THORNDIKE, ASHLEY HORACE (December 26, 1871–April 17, 1933), American literary historian, Shakespeare scholar—he was the first president of the Shakespeare Society of America—was born at Houlton, Maine, the son of Edward R. Thorndike and his wife the former Abby B. Ladd. He obtained his B. A. degree from Wesleyan (1893), and, before becoming professor of English at Columbia (1906), was principal of Smith Academy, and instructor at Harvard and at Western Reserve, and professor at Northwestern. He gained his master's and Ph.D. degrees from Harvard (1896, 1898). He is now hardly remembered, and his name seldom turns up in discussions of Shakespeare or even in notes to the texts of the plays. He edited with William A. Neilson *The Tudor Shakespeare*, published in forty volumes between 1911 and 1913, and wrote one of the first books trying seriously to establish the facts about Shakespeare's life: *The Facts About Shakespeare*. This was soon superseded by Chamber's magisterial two-volumed reference work, *Shakespeare: A Study of the Facts and Problems*. Thorndike's two very distinguished (and better remembered) brothers also taught at Columbia: Edward L. Thorndike, psychologist, and Lynn Thorndike, the celebrated historian of magic.

The *Tudor Shakespeare* was among the first trustworthy collected editions of Shakespeare and, although it was soon superseded by the *Yale Shakespeare* and others, it did play a very small part in the establishment of a reliable modernized text. Thorndike's most important book, *Shakespeare's Theater*, although again superseded, was among the first to try to place the plays in their context. The *Times Literary Supplement* thought at the time that it was the product of a mind that was "cautious, pliable, judicial." It is seldom consulted now since (once again) it has been thoroughly superseded. O. J. Campbell's *A Shakespeare Encyclo-*

*pedia*, although it contains a brief entry on Thorndike, cites no work by him in its extensive bibliography. *The Outlook for Literature*, Thorndike's final substantial work, made little impact.

It was as a teacher that Thorndike made his real mark. He became much loved at Columbia, by pupils and colleagues alike; in 1930 he was appointed University Orator. He did useful if plodding work as editor of Warner's *Library of the World's Best Literature*, of Scribner's *Modern Reader* series, and of Longman's *English Classics*.

PRINCIPAL WORKS: The Influence of Beaumont and Fletcher on Shakespeare, 1901; The Elements of Rhetoric and Composition, 1905 (rev. with K. Morse, 1918); Tragedy, 1908; Everyday English, 1913; The Facts About Shakespeare, 1915; (with B. Matthews) Shakespearian Studies, 1916; Shakespeare's Theater, 1916; Literature in a Changing Age, 1920; A History of English Literature, 1920; Shakespeare in America, 1927; English Comedy, 1929; The Outlook of Literature, 1931; The Minor Elizabethan Drama, 1933. *As editor*—(with W. A. Neilson) The Tudor Shakespeare, 40 vols., 1911–1913.

ABOUT: Campbell, O. J. (ed.) A Shakespeare Encyclopaedia, 1966. *Periodicals*—New York Times April 18, 19, 20, 1933; Times Literary Supplement June 1, 1916.

## THORNDIKE, (EVERETT) LYNN (July 24, 1882–December 29, 1965), American scholar and historian, wrote: "I was born in Lynn, Massachusetts, and was named after that city, where my father [Edward R. Thorndike] was pastor of the Boston Street Methodist Church. [His mother was the former Abby B. Ladd.] But the members of his previous congregation at near-by Everett insisted on that name also, although—I mention this for the astrologically inclined—I had not even been conceived there, the family having moved to Lynn more than a year before. In thus christening me Everett Lynn, my parents, both of whom originally came from Maine, overlooked the fact that one of my two older brothers, later a distinguished psychologist, already had the initials, E. L. [His brothers were Edward Lee Thorndike, educator and psychologist, compiler of the *Thorndike Century Dictionary*, and Ashley Horace Thorndike, literary historian.] When in 1902 I came as a graduate student in history (Ph.D., 1905) to Columbia University, where E. L. was already a professor, and especially when I became chief clerk under Fred Keppel, then secretary of the University, in 1905–06, this gave rise to endless confusion, so that I dropped my first name and have been simply Lynn Thorndike ever since.7

"The itinerant system of the Methodist ministry involved change of residence to Lowell and Roxbury, Massachusetts, Providence, Rhode Island, Lynn again, Springfield, Massachusetts, and Lynn, *noch einmal*, whence I left home for college at Wesleyan in Middletown, Connecticut. There I was a member of the Phi Nu Theta fraternity, and also achieved Phi Beta Kappa, and an A.B. *magna cum laude*. I had not been outside of New

England until, shortly before graduation, I paid a preliminary visit to New York.

"The most dramatic incident of my boyhood occurred when in the seventh grade of grammar school in Springfield. The class, of which I was the youngest member, had not been doing well, and the principal, Elias Brookings, a burly Civil War veteran with side whiskers who on occasion wielded a wicked strap, came in to give us a scare. After a talk with that intent, he stood in front of the last row and asked anyone in that row who thought that he would be promoted, if he did not do better, to stand up. I should explain that members of the class were re-seated each month in order of their standing in their studies. Two girls and I had been vying for the three top seats in the first row. This month Dell Rogers headed the class, I was next, and Ada Rosenberg sat at the desk immediately behind me. Since those at the bottom of the class were not likely to be promoted, no one in that row ventured to stand up. But neither did anyone in the next file or the next.

"'What nonsense!' I thought, 'they always promote at least four-fifths of a class.' And I looked hopefully for some or all of those in the four remaining rows to rise. But even Ada and Dell failed to do so; I was the only one to stand up. Psychiatrists will tell you that this made me aloof from, not to say, scornful of my fellowmen. It certainly did not make me popular with my classmates. However, not only at the end of the school year did I receive a double promotion into the ninth grade, skipping the eighth, but so did seven or eight of the modest cowards who had kept their seats.

"Although I played baseball with the older boys in vacant lots, reading and writing were my chief pastimes. At college I failed to make the literary monthly, but Caleb T. Winchester, professor of English literature, heartened me greatly by saying that I had a style of my own, and I took several essay prizes. As a graduate student I earned my way for two years by tutoring and the third year had a fellowship to live on.

"In 1906–07 I taught at the University School, Cleveland, and, after two years at Northwestern University in Evanston, Illinois, returned to Cleveland for fifteen years at Western Reserve University. Whenever I felt a little blue, all I needed to put me in the best spirits again was to walk past the grim buildings of the University School and remind myself that I was no longer connected with it. In 1924 I was called to Columbia and gave graduate courses in intellectual history there until I became professor emeritus in 1950.

"At Northwestern I became associated with a faculty group—Locy, Crew, and Libby—interested in the history of science, and also played the card game, 'skat,' with them. At Cleveland I continued to play 'skat,' and when the American Historical Association met there in 1920, organized the first session devoted to the history of science in this country. Next year the American Association for the Advancement of Science followed suit, and soon afterwards the History of Science Society was founded. I served as its president in 1928-29. I was one of the founding fellows of the Mediaeval Academy of America, and of l'Academie Internationale d'Histoire des Sciences; and am a member of the American Philosophical Society and a corresponding member of l'Academie des Inscriptions et Belles-Lettres. In 1930 Wesleyan awarded me the honorary degree of Doctor of Humane Letters.

"Upon graduation from college I weighed only 130 pounds. Fifteen or twenty years later, when I could afford to dine at university clubs instead of boarding houses, my weight slowly but steadily increased to a trifle over 200.

"My first trip to Europe was in the summer of 1909, when I landed in Glasgow and made the grand tour through southern Scotland, England, Rouen and Paris, Switzerland, down the Italian peninsula to Naples and back, Germany and Holland. I have been there nineteen times since, sometimes for a half year, and have worked in many libraries and especially with medieval Latin manuscripts, although of late the investigation of magic and experimental science in the sixteenth century has called chiefly for reading of printed books. In addition to the following list of books, I have contributed more than two hundred articles and seventy reviews to over sixty periodicals representing varied fields of learning and human interest."

---

Thorndike's groundbreaking and exhaustive studies of pre-Renaissance thought earned him a deserved reputation as one of the world's foremost medievalists. A specialist in the history of scientific thought, he devoted nearly six decades to exhaustive studies that ranged from inquiries into magic, alchemy, astrology, and other 'pseudo-scientific' spheres that he believed were earlier manifestations of modern scientific method. His doctoral dissertation in 1905 was entitled 'The Place of Magic in the Intellectual History of Europe'; his last book, *Michael Scot*, written some sixty years later, was an analysis of alchemical and astrological references in the writings of the twelfth-century scientist.

For more than half a century, he assiduously studied codices, incunabula, journals, church documents, and other historical records of the late Middle Ages to compile his most comprehensive work, *A History of Magic and Experimental* Science, published in eight volumes between 1923 and 1958. Thorndike also influenced a generation of scholars through his lectures at Columbia University and the two popular college textbooks he wrote: *The History of Medieval Europe* and *A Short History of Civilization*.

First published in 1917 and revised in 1949, *The History of Medieval Europe* served as an introduction to the period for thousands of college students in the United States. It was one of the first books of its kind to look at medieval Europe as an entity, putting less emphasis on the histories of individual countries and peoples, and to downplay the purely military and political in favor of a greater emphasis on social, economic, and culture factors. But the eight-volume *A History of Magic and Experimen-*

*tal Science* remains Thorndike's most enduring work of scholarship. He was encouraged to begin the work, he said, by James Harvey Robinson, one of his professors at Harvard. Thorndike explained his aims in his preface to the first volume, published in 1923: "The book aims to treat the history of magic and experimental science and their relation to Christian thought during the first thirteen centuries of our era, with especial emphasis upon the twelfth and thirteenth centuries . . . Magic is here understood in the broadest sense of the word, as including all occult arts and sciences, superstitions and folklore . . . My idea is that magic and experimental science have been connected in their development; that magicians were perhaps the first to experiment; and that the history of both magic and experimental science can be better understood by studying them together."

In these earlier volumes, Thorndike also researched Babylonian, Chaldean, and Arabic sources, as well as classical writers like Galen and Pliny and modern scholars like James Frazer (*The Golden Bough*) to establish the historical roots of 'magical' thought. At the end of the fourth volume (1935), he writes: "Read it and smile or read it and weep, as you please. We would not credit it the history of human thought with the least particle of modern science that does not belong to it, nor would we deprive it of any of that magic which constitutes in no small measure its peculiar charm."

The fifth and sixth volumes (1941), carried Thorndike's odyssey through to the time of Kepler and Galileo in the sixteenth and seventeenth centuries. By this time Thorndike was being hailed by popular reviewers as one of America's experts on his subject. The *Journal of Philosophy* wrote: "Thorndike's is certainly the most important single contribution to the intellectual history of the sixteenth century made in some years. All students of the period willl greatly appreciate his achievement and constantly use his book as an invaluable guide and reference." And the *New Republic* thought it "a monumental, erudite, and informative work . . . Primarily a work for the specialist, it is so clearly written that the general reader interested in its subject matter will turn to it with confidence and delight." But more academic critics were not so generous in the pages of *Isis*, the journal of the history of science. George Sarton, the publication's founder, wrote, in 1924, a review of the first two volumes that called into question some of Thorndike's assumptions about the nature of experimental science. In 1942, when the fifth and sixth volumes were published, Dana B. Durand reexamined Sarton's essay in a review of his own. Durand wrote "Any comprehensive judgment must start with the recognition that *Magic and Experimental Science* is not a complete work. Thorndike himself says so explicitly. The magnitude of his task imposed a principle of economy, the deliberate avoidance of repeating work satisfactorily accomplished by other scholars . . . Though this principle of economy has undoubtedly saved effort to the author, and has cut down the already considerable bulk of the work itself, it is also one of the chief rea-sons why *Magic and Experimental Science* failed to achieve a rounded synthesis." Throughout his work, Thorndike defended alchemists and astrologers of the Middle Ages against their detractors, who he believed erroneously considered them "magicians" or "charlatans" when they should have been considered "pre-scientists" since they were seeking for truth. "Call them wizards and magicians if you please," he wrote, "but essentially they were scientists, for the magic of the Middle Ages has developed into the science of today. . . . Alchemy and astrology, they are both science and magic. They are on that borderline where we find the preternatural—strange unknown things that seem above the ordinary course of nature." Thorndike's work also illuminated the role the medieval church played in the development of science by pointing out that it was a much more complex role than is generally supposed thanks to the 'popular' image of Galileo and the Inquisition. He examines in depth the thought of Albertus Magnus ("the dominant figure in . . . learning and natural science of the thirteenth century") and of Thomas Aquinas, its preeminent theologian, whom Thorndike saw as "somewhat of a scientist" when he declared alchemy "a true, though difficult art." According to Thorndike, it was an oversimplification to conclude that science was merely the handmaiden of religion during the medieval period. He also published many texts and translations from Latin that were previously unavailable to modern scholars.

His first work, *The Herbal of Rufinus*, was a comprehensive source of knowledge about plants, originally compiled by the thirteenth-century botanist. He disseminated invaluable information about medicine and surgery in that period with his 1928 translation of *Opuscula medica*, a fifteenth-century autopsy by Bernard Tornius. With the publication of *The Sphere of Sacrobosco* and Its Commentators and *Latin Treatises on Comets Between 1238 and 1368 A.D.* he devoted his considerable research abilities to interpreting medieval treatises on astronomy and meteorology.

His *University Records and Life in the Middle Ages* provided a comprehensive and authoritative overview of what forms higher learning took in the earliest European universities.

PRINCIPAL WORKS: The Place of Magic in the Intellectual History of Europe, 1905; The History of Medieval Europe, 1917; Galen: The Man and His Times, 1922; A History of Magic and Experimental Science, vols. 1-2, 1923; vols. 3-4, 1935, vols. 56, 1941, vols. 7-8, 1958; A Short History of Civilization, 1926; Science and Thought in the Fifteenth Century, 1929; Vatican Latin Manuscripts in the History of Science and Medicine, 1929; A Catalog of *Incipits* of Medieval Scientific Writings in Latin, 1937; University Records and Life in the Middle Ages, 1944. *As translator*—A Fifteenth Century Autopsy by Bernard Tornius, 1928; The Herbal of Rufinus, 1945; (ed. & tr.); Translation of Works of Galen from the Greek, 1946; The Sphere of Sacrobosco and Its Commentators, 1949; (ed.) Latin Treatises on Comets Between 1238 and 1368 A.D., 1950.

ABOUT: The autobiographical material quoted above was written for Twentieth Century Authors First Supplement, 1955. *Bibliography*—Bibliography of Lynn Thorndike, 1931; Isis, 1942; Spring 1966. *Periodicals*—Newsweek January 10, 1966; New York Times December 29, 1965. Time January 7, 1966.

**THORNE, P.** See **SMITH, M. P. W.**

**THURBER, JAMES (GROVER)** (December 8, 1894–November 2, 1961), American humorist, was born in Columbus, Ohio, the second of three sons of Charles L. Thurber and Mary (Fisher) Thurber. Charles Thurber worked as a clerk for the local and state Republican party; he went through many periods of unemployment and barely managed to keep his family in middle-class respectability. Though Thurber later portrayed his family and their relatives as a collection of lovable or at least colorful eccentrics, they were strangely detached from each other, and he grew up a shy, repressed, and unathletic child, blind in one eye and only partially sighted in the other—the result of an accident with bows and arrows at the age of six. He was, however, a good student and might have attended a university more challenging than Columbus's own Ohio State had he or his family thought more highly of his abilities. He languished throughout most of his protracted undergraduate years, until taken up by Elliott Nugent, a popular and talented younger student who got Thurber admitted into the "right" fraternity and with him edited the campus humor and literary magazine, the *Sundial.* In 1918, when he was twenty-three and still well short of the necessary credits for graduation, Thurber joined the State Department as an apprentice code clerk. This wartime appointment took him to Paris for a year and a half, and he returned to Columbus in 1920 intending to become a newspaper reporter. He might have been content to remain on the *Columbus Dispatch* for the rest of his days if not for the pressure exerted on him by Althea Adams, the socially and intellectually ambitious hometown girl he married in 1922. The marriage was a mismatch from the start but Althea goaded her husband into becoming something more than the promising local journalist he was from 1920 to 1923. At her urging they moved to Paris in 1924, where Thurber worked as a correspondent for the *Chicago Tribune,* and in 1926 they moved to New York, where he worked for the *New York Evening Post.* After twenty rejections, a short humorous piece was accepted by the *New Yorker,* and in 1927 he was asked to join the staff. At the *New Yorker* he shared a cramped office with E. B. White, under whose influence Thurber's prose arrived at the sheen and precision for which it became famous.

Though still trapped in a loveless marriage and given to excessive drinking, Thurber produced much of his finest work in his early years at the *New Yorker.* With White, he published his first book, *Is Sex Necessary?,* a parody of psychological sex books of the day that, to the surprise of both authors, became a best-seller in 1929. Burton Bernstein wrote that despite its occasional repetitiveness and slowness of pace, *Is*  *Sex Necessary?* "will live in American humorous literature as a tour de force by virtue of its originality, exuberance, and dazzling display of promise. As in all good parody, there are truths lurking in the madness, and it should be stated that the book is one of the few satires of sex and sex literature ever written that is not in the least bit dirty."

At the insistence of White, *Is Sex Necessary?* contained an additional feature that their editors at Harper could scarcely credit at first: Thurber's illustrations. Utterly devoid of artistic propriety, these squiggly cartoons delighted most reviewers and accounted for a good part of the book's success. Though Thurber thought little enough of his draftsmanship, his "nonmastery of line came out magically close to Matisse," wrote Wilfrid Sheed, and he accommodated his admirers by including a generous sampling of his artwork in his second book and first independent collection, *The Owl in the Attic and Other Perplexities,* and by issuing as his third book a selection of eighty-five captioned drawings titled *The Seal in the Bedroom and Other Predicaments.* Both of these works were highly successful, but they were surpassed by his next book, *My Life and Hard Times,* the work that most consider his masterpiece. This brief memoir of family eccentricities in Ohio was an obvious attempt at exorcising the ghosts of his childhood, and a subtle anxiety underlay its most comic episodes. How much rage and repression should be read into Thurber's comedy has always been a controversial question; Robert Emmet Long wrote that in much of Thurber's work an "acute sense of threat to the self, of violation of integrity . . . arises from the depths of some unheard-of innocence . . . creat[ing] an alienation so profound that it cannot be ameliorated." Yet whatever depths Thurber may or may not have sounded in *My Life and Hard Times,* the surface itself was a brilliant achievement. "The book is the definitive image of Thurber's special comic world," wrote Charles S. Holmes. "Here the eccentric characters, comic situations, and the strange blend of the realistic and the fantastic . . . are present in their purest and most concentrated form. It mines one of his richest veins of subject matter . . . and out of these autobiographical materials he creates a mad comic world in which the normal order of things is constantly exploding into chaos and confusion."

In 1935 Thurber divorced Althea Adams and married Helen Wismer, a magazine editor—though he was persistently unfaithful to her—who brought a measure of comfort and stability into his life. After 1936 they lived primarily in northwestern Connecticut, where they were occasionally visited by Thurber's daughter from his first marriage, and where their neighbors included Malcolm Cowley and Mark Van Doren. Helen saw her husband through one of his most creative periods in the early years of their marriage, as well as through a nervous breakdown in 1942, the progressive loss of his vision culminating in total blindness by the early 1950s, and any number of drunken rages. She was emphatically not the castrating virago who appeared repeatedly in Thurber's next collection, *The Middle-Aged Man on the Flying Trapeze,* and again in his most famous story, "The Secret Life of Walter Mitty," published in the *New Yorker* in 1939. The question of Thurber's misogyny continues to roil many critics; for some, his prejudice against women is palpable and unambiguous. For others, such as Wilfrid Sheed, "his feeling for women is usually more complicated than that. . . . Thurber's women may be illogical, but they are seldom stupid—and there is always a sense that they are probably right. . . . Furthermore, in emphasizing his alleged hatred of women, commentators have overlooked his equal and similar hatred of men."

Beginning in the 1940s the most characteristic vehicle for Thurber's imagination became the comic fable or fairy tale. To a degree, these works represented a turning away from a contemporary world that increasingly filled him with digust and indignation; more simply, they were the results of his blindness. Thurber stopped drawing in 1947 and began dictating his stories, a method that, in his case (as in that of his favorite writer, Henry James), lent itself to verbal elaboration. For example, *The White Deer*, wrote Burton Bernstein, "is a thicket of puns, spoonerisms, anagrams, iambic couplets, backward spellings, and private allusions. . . . Thurber played with words in this medieval fantasy for the sheer fun of it, most of the fun reaching the reader by a kind of joyful osmosis." Despite the comparative success of such fables as *The 13 Clocks* and *The Wonderful O*, Thurber by the 1950s had passed his peak, and in such late works as *Further Fables for Our Time* and the posthumous *Credos and Curios*, the humor had turned sour. The latter collection, wrote John Updike in the *New York Times Book Review*, displayed "an irritation with the present state of things so inclusive as to be pointless. . . . The writer who had produced *Fables for Our Time* and *The Last Flower* out of the thirties had become, by the end of the fifties, one more indignant senior citizen penning complaints about the universal decay of virtue."

Though Thurber bore his hardships with fortitude, his last years were decidedly grim, plagued as they were by blindness, alcoholism, creative sterility, and outbursts of rage that alienated most of his friends. Nevertheless, he was cheered by the continuing popularity of his books and by such tributes as a 1958 luncheon in his honor given by the editors of *Punch* magazine—the first American to be so honored since Mark Twain. In 1960 he fulfilled his lifelong dream of performing on stage by appearing in eighty-eight performances of *A Thurber Carnival*, an Off-Broadway revue based on his writings. When the revue closed he sank back into depression and died in New York the following year of a blood clot on the brain. He was sixty-six. Despite the accusations of misogyny, Thurber's reputation as the greatest American humorist since Mark Twain remains intact. His best work, wrote John Updike, evokes "a fluid chaos where communication is limited to wild, flitting gestures and where humans revolve and collide like glowing planets, lit solely from within, against a cosmic backdrop of gathering dark. Thurber's genius was to make of our despair a humorous fable."

The James Thurber Collection is in the Ohio State University Library.

PRINCIPAL WORKS: *Fiction and humor*—(with E. B. White) Is Sex Necessary?, or, Why You Feel the Way You Do, 1929; The Owl in the Attic and Other Perplexities, 1931; The Seal in the Bedroom and Other Predicaments, 1932; My Life and Hard Times, 1933; The Middle-Aged Man on the Flying Trapeze: A Collection of Short Pieces, 1935; Let Your Mind Alone! and Other More or Less Inspirational Pieces, 1937; Cream of Thurber, 1939; The Last Flower: A Parable in Pictures, 1939; Fables for Our Time and Famous Poems Illustrated, 1940; My World—and Welcome to It, 1943; Many Moons, 1943; Thurber's Men, Women and Dogs: A Book of Drawings, 1943; The Great Quillow, 1944; The Thurber Carnival, 1945; The Beast in Me and Other Animals: A New Collection of Pieces and Drawings about Human Beings and Less Alarming Creatures, 1948; The 13 Clocks, 1950; The Thurber Album: A New Collection of Pieces about People, 1950; Thurber Country: A New Collection of Pieces about Males and Females, Mainly of Our Own Species, 1953; Thurber's Dogs: A Collection of the Master's Dogs, Written and Drawn, Real and Imaginary, Living and Long Ago, 1955; Further Fables for Our Times, 1956; The Wonderful O, 1957; Alarms and Diversions, 1957; Lanterns and Lances, 1961; Credos and Curios, 1962; Vintage Thurber: A Collection in Two Volumes of the Best Writings and Drawings of James Thurber, 1963; Thurber and Company, 1966; Collecting Himself: James Thurber on Writing and Writers, Humor and Himself (ed. M. J. Rosen) 1989. *Drama*—(with E. Nugent) The Male Animal, 1940; A Thurber Carnival, 1962. *Biography*—The Years with Ross, 1959. *Correspondence*—Selected Letters of James Thurber (eds. H. Thurber and E. Weeks) 1981.

ABOUT: Bernstein, B. Thurber: A Biography, 1975; Black, S. James Thurber: His Masquerades, 1970; Contemporary Authors New Revision Series 17, 1986; Dictionary of American Biography, Suppl. 7, 1981; Dictionary of Literary Biography vol. 4 1980; vol. 11 1982; vol. 22 1983; vol. 102 1991; Fensch, T. (ed.) Conversations with James Thurber, 1989; Holmes, C. S. The Clocks of Columbus: The Literary Career of James Thurber, 1972; Kenney, C. M. Thurber's Anatomy of Confusion, 1984; Long, R. E. James Thurber, 1988; Morsberger, R. E. James Thurber, 1964; Sheed, W. The Good Word and Other Words, 1978; Tobias, R. C. The Art of James Thurber, 1969; Twentieth Century American Literature: The Chelsea House Library of Literary Criticism vol. 7 1988; Writers at Work: The Paris Review Interviews, First Series, 1959. *Bibliography*—Toombs, S. E. James Thurber: An Annotated Bibliography of Criticism, 1987. *Periodicals*—New York Times November 3, 1961; New York Times Book Review November 25, 1962.

**THURSTON, ERNEST TEMPLE** (September 23, 1879–March 19, 1933), English novelist and playwright, began his career as a poet, publishing two adolescent volumes when aged sixteen. Two years later, having been told by his father that he must earn his own living, he wrote his first novel, *The Apple of Eden*. The book which had to wait until 1905 to be published, was, for its time, an audaciously frank treatment of a Roman  Catholic priest's struggle to maintain his vows of celibacy.

Thurston married the Irish novelist, Katherine Cecil Madden (when he was twenty-two and she was four years older) and adapted for the stage her novel of impersonation, *John Chilcote, M.P.* He continued to write for the theater, the most well-known of his plays being *The Wandering Jew* (1920); but his more sustained energies went into the writing of novels characterized on the one hand by a harsh naturalism and on the other hand by a penchant for sentimental melodrama. In the early books the first of these characteristics was dominant; as his career progressed, the second proclivity became more pronounced. It could be argued that Thurston simply responded to criticisms of his early work. His second novel, *Traffic*, was severely panned, *Outlook* saying that its "plain-speaking in describing coarse viciousness exceeds good taste and sound literary judgement." However, he did write, as early as 1911, in *The Patchwork Papers*, a book of whimsical sketches and essays, "In all my early work until, in fact, I wrote *Sally Bishop*, I was inclined to find the world ugly enough in all conscience. But now beauty does seem inevitable and, what is more, the only reality we have."

In his trilogy about Richard Furlong, a country boy who comes to London to make his fortune as an artist, Thurston made a conscious effort to construct an optimistic fable. The *Catholic World*, a publication that was consistently hostile to Thurston's work, found the final volume, *Achievement* (1914), "pagan and immoral to the core," and it is true to say that Thurston's peculiar brand of honesty stood between him and the creation of work of truly popular sentiment—although not sufficiently to protect him from over-sentimentality, as shown in *The World of Wonderful Reality* (1919), one of his more fanciful novels.

Thurston was a keen golfer and water-colorist. An exhibition of his paintings was mounted at a small London gallery in 1930. Three years later, while still in his early fifties, he developed pneumonia after a round of golf at Rye. He had been married three times. His obituary in the *Times* said of his qualities as a playwright, "He had an intuitive knowledge of how to lend emotional color to particular scenes; he had an eye for the stage that greatly assisted him in giving theatrical vitality to such spectacular pieces as *The Wandering Jew*; and, even in the midst of much that seemed to be aimed too directly at the gallery, a shrewd irony or an unexpected and gratifying plainness would appear now and then to proclaim that the dramatist was less deceived than many supposed by his own facility."

PRINCIPAL WORKS: *Fiction*—The Apple of Eden, 1905; Traffic, 1906; The Evolution of Katherine, 1907 (in U.S.: Katherine, A Novel); Mirage, 1908; Sally Bishop, 1908; The City of Beautiful Nonsense, 1909; The Greatest Wish in the World, 1910; The Garden of Resurrection, 1911; The Antagonists, 1912; Thirteen, 1912; The Open Window, 1913; Richard Furlong, 1913; Achievement, 1914; The Passionate Crime, 1915; Tares, 1915; The Five-Barred Gate, 1916; Enchantment, 1917; Over the Hill, 1917; David & Jonathan, 1918; The Nature of the Beast, 1919; The Forest Fire and Other Stories, 1919; Sheepskins and Grey Russett, 1919; The World of Wonderful Reality, 1919; The Green Bough, 1921; The Eye of the Wift, 1922; The Miracle, 1922; May Eve, 1923; Mr. Bottleby Does Something, 1925; The Goose-feather Bed, 1926; Jane Carroll, 1927; The Rosetti and Other Tales, 1927; Millenium, 1929; Portrait of a Spy, 1929; Man in a Black Hat, 1930; The Rosicrucian, 1930; The Broken Heart, 1932; The Diamond Pendant, 1932;

A Hank of Hair, 1932. *Drama*—The Cost, 1914; Driven, 1914; The Wandering Jew, 1920; Judas Iscariot, 1923; A Roof and Four Walls, 1923; The Blue Peter, 1924; Charmeuse, 1924; Snobs, 1925. *Nonfiction*—The Flower of Gloster. *Miscellaneous*—The Patchwork Papers, 1911; Summer 1917 and Other Verses, 1917; Poems 1918–1923, 1923.

ABOUT: Who's Who 1933. *Periodicals*—Catholic World February 1915, August 1917; New York Times March 20, 1933; Outlook November 9, 1906; Times (London) March 20, 1933.

## THURSTON, KATHERINE CECIL (MADDEN) (April 18, 1875–September 5, 1911), Irish novelist, was born at Wood's Gift, County Cork. She was the only child of Paul Madden and the former Catherine Barry. Her father, a wealthy man, chairman and director of the Ulster and Leinster Bank, and one-time mayor of Cork, campaigned on behalf of his close friend, the Irish Nationalist Parnell.

Katherine Thurston was privately educated. A vivacious, energetic child, she spent a happy girlhood enjoying the pleasures of her class: dancing, riding, and swimming. In 1901, at the age of twenty-six, she married the English novelist and dramatist E. Temple Thurston, and embarked upon her own literary career.

Thurston's first publication was an undistinguished novel entitled *The Circle*. It received little critical attention, and was quickly followed by her best known and most accomplished work, the melodramatic *John Chilcote, MP*. This revolves around an opium-addicted member of Parliament, and Loder, a poor young writer. A chance meeting reveals that Loder is Chilcote's double, and so he agrees to assume many of the  MP's duties. As Chilcote becomes increasingly incapacitated, so Loder achieves ever greater heights of success, both politically and in terms of his relationship with Chilcote's wife. At length John Chilcote dies, and Loder is free to carry his name to the grave.

Despite the improbable plot, the novel's ingenuity and skill made it extremely popular. *John Chilcote, MP*, published in the U.S. as the *The Masquerader*, was one of the most successful books of its decade. A best-seller in Britain and America, with sales running over 150,000, it was dramatized by the author's husband in 1905, and then twice filmed.

None of the subsequent novels was as popular, although Thurston's fluent style and her gift for sound construction and character development saved her from literary obscurity in her own time. *The Gambler* focuses on an Irish girl who is rescued from a life of fashionable dissipation by a respectable young suitor. Although one reviewer remarked upon the "defects of Miss Thurston's literary style and the crudity of her methods" (*Independent*), most shared the opinion of the *New York Times* critic, who admired the book for the "vitality of its characters, the cohesion of its plot, the fidelity of both to possibility and its literary art" (1905).

Thurston was an uneven writer. Response to *Mystics*, a tale of greed and revenge, was unambiguously damning. Indeed, a reviewer for the *Literary Digest* felt that "the wild improbability of the plot and the essentially childish nature of the story make barren as a subject for criticism."

Thurston's sixth novel was her last. *Max* was a romance, more successful with the public, in which a Russian princess falls in love with a Parisian artist. "The story is virtually a fairy tale rather than an exposition of real life," said the *Athenaeum* (1910), "but it is none the less pleasing for that." In 1910 Katherine Thurston was granted a divorce from her husband.

PRINCIPAL WORKS: *Novels*—The Circle, 1903; John Chilcote, MP, 1904 (in U.S.: The Masquerader); The Gambler, 1906; Mystics, 1907; The Fly on the Wheel, 1908; Max, 1910.

ABOUT: Boylan, H. (ed.) A Dictionary of Irish Biography 2nd ed., 1988; AM. and Cleeve, B. A Biographical Dictionary of Irish Writers, 1985; Dictionary of Nautical Biography 1901–1911, 1927; Who's Who 1910. *Periodicals*—Athenaeum March 28, 1908; October 15, 1910; September 9, 1911; Current Literature April 1905; Harper's Weekly September 16, 1911; Independent October 12, 1905; Literary Digest May 11, 1907; New York Times October 7, 1905; September 7, 1911; Putnam's August 1907; Times (London) April 8, 1910; September 7, 1911.

**THWAITES, REUBEN GOLD** (May 15, 1853– October 22, 1913), American librarian, historian, editor, and journalist, was born at Dorchester, Massachusetts. His parents, William George Thwaites and the former Sarah Bibbos, moved there from Yorkshire, England, shortly before his birth.

After attending school in Massachusetts, Thwaites set off, at the age of thirteen, for Wisconsin to work on a farm while he completed a college course. Thus equipped, he embarked on a journalistic career as a reporter on the *Oshkosh Times*.

In 1874 Thwaites gained a place at Yale to study history and economics. Two years later he became managing editor of a leading Republican newspaper, the *Wisconsin State Journal*. The ten years he spent with the *Journal* provided him with a lively style and a thorough knowledge of the state of Wisconsin, which was to become the focus of his own work. Thwaites's interest in the history of Wisconsin brought him into regular contact with the State Historical Society. He became its secretary in 1887, and did much to make the society an important center for historical research, augmenting its manuscript collection, and moving the library to larger premises on the university campus. He was president of the American Library Association in 1900.

An energetic man, Thwaites also lectured and worked on his own publications. He edited many historical volumes, including the journals of the Lewis and Clark Expedition and *Jesuit Relations and Allied Documents*—the latter a comprehensive collection, well translated and annotated, that confirmed his reputation as a historical scholar. *Early Western Travels* constituted thirty-one annotated volumes of reprints of rare manuscripts. Frederick Jackson Turner described it as an "excellent series" (*Dial*). Thwaites also compiled *The Revolution on the Upper Ohio* and *Frontier Defense on the Upper Ohio* from the historical society's Draper manuscripts, and edited the society's *Proceedings* and *Collections*.

Thwaites's original, writing included several books on the history of Wisconsin, the most significant of which was *Wisconsin: The Americanization of a French Settlement*. It was described as "an account of his state that is as entertaining as it is scholarly" (*Outlook* 1909). Thwaites also wrote biographies of Father Marquette and Daniel Boone, a study entitled *France in America*, and a *History of the Untied States for Grammar Schools*.

No desk-bound scholar, Thwaites enjoyed outdoor pursuits, and gave entertaining accounts of his ventures in *Our Cycling Tour in England* and *Afloat on the Ohio*. He married Jessie Inwood Turville in 1881, and they had one son.

PRINCIPAL WORKS: Historical Sketch of the Public Schools in Madison, Wisconsin, 1886; Historic Waterways, 1888 (published as Down Historic Waterway 1902) The Story of Wisconsin, 1890; The Colonies, 1891; Our Cycling Tour in England, 1892; Afloat on the Ohio, 1892 (published as On the Storied Ohio, 1975); The State Historical Society of Wisconsin, 1898; Stories of the Badger State, 1900; Father Marquette, 1902; Daniel Boone, 1902; How George Rogers Clark Won the Northwest, and Other Essays in Western History, 1903; A Brief History of Rocky Mountain Exploration, 1904; France in America, 1905; State and Local Historical Societies, 1906; The Romances of Mississippi Valley History, 1907; Wisconsin: The Americanization of a French Settlement, 1908; The Ohio Valley Press Before the War of 1813–1815, 1909; (with C. N. Kendall) A History of the United States for Grammar Schools, 1912; Lyman Copeland Draper—A Memoir, 1928. *As editor*—Reminiscences of Morgan L. Martin, 1888; Jesuit Relations and Allied Documents, 73 vols., 1896–1901; The University of Wisconsin 1634–1760, 1900–1908; Hennepin, L. New Discovery, 2 vols., 1903; Original Journals of the Lewis and Clark Expedition, 8 vols. 1904–1905; Early Western Travels, 32 vols., 1904–1907; Lahontan, Baron de. New Voyages, 2 vols., 1905; Documentary History of Dunmore's War, 1905; Travels in the Far Northwest 1893–1846, 1906; The Revolution on the Upper Ohio, 1908; Frontier Defense on the Upper Ohio, 1912.

ABOUT: Concise Dictionary of American Biography, 1964; Dictionary of American Biography Vol. 18, 1936; Dictionary of American Library Biography, 1978; Dictionary of Literary Biography Vol. 47, 1986; Dictionary of Wisconsin Biography, 1960; Marshall, J. D. (ed.) American Library History Reader, 1961. *Periodicals*—Dial July 1, 1906; Library Journal March 15, 1951; New York Times November 23, 1913; Review of Reviews December, 1913; Wisconsin State Journal October 23, 1923.

**TIAN HAN** (March 12, 1898–December 10, 1968), Chinese dramatist and poet, was born Tian Shou-chang into a peasant family living in Changsha County, Hunan Province. His father, Tian Yuqin, loved school but was forced to discontinue his education at eighteen for financial reasons. His mother, Yi Keqin, though an uneducated housewife, was determined to put Tian through school after seeing that the young boy loved books even more intensely than his father did. Although he was removed from school several times due to financial difficulties, Tian was such a hard-working and gifted learner that some of his teachers helped him financially, including Xu Teli, the head master at Changsha Teacher's School and one of the initiators of the 1911 Revolution.

In 1916, Tian, with help from his uncle, went to Japan and studied at the Japan Teacher's Higher Institute. While in Japan, he began writing poetry. Initially fascinated by Walt Whitman, he soon became an avid reader of Goethe, Schiller, Heine, Shakespeare, Poe, and Wilde. During this time, he also produced his earliest plays, claiming ambitiously that he would be "a budding Ibsen in China." His earliest plays include *Huaièlin Yu Qiangwei* (The violin and the rose), *Lingguang* (Enlightenment) and *Kafeidian Zhi Yi Ye* (A night at a cafe). When *Lingguang* was staged in Japan, it was considered the first Chinese production to reach the international stage. These were the first in a series of sentimental one-act plays designed to reveal the dark side of the old society, in particular the sufferings of young Chinese intellectuals. In 1920, Tian became acquainted with Guo Moruo, who was also studying in Japan, and the two maintained a lengthy correspondence. Guo wrote to Tian: "I have been anxious to meet you ever since I read your article about Whitman and your bold and unconstrained free verses." Guo and Tian were among the co-founders, in 1921, of the Creation Society (*Chuangzao She*), an avant-garde literary group.

After returning to China in 1922, however, Tian soon broke off with the Creation Society due to differences of opinions. In 1923, together with his wife, Yi Shuyu, he established a literary journal called *Nanguo Banyue Kan* (Southern biweekly). In 1926 he founded the Southern Motion Picture Society and attempted to produce several films. He failed in both endeavors, but that only stirred his determination to devote himself to education in the theatrical arts.

In the fall of 1927, Tian became chair of the literature program at Shanghai University of Art, and soon was elected its president. He soon made the university a center for Shanghai's literary and artistic circles. With Ouyang Yuqian and Zhou Xinfang, he also successfully organized the *Yishu Yulong Hui* performing arts festival, which opened up a new path for modern Chinese theater. The University was dissolved soon afterwards, and he founded the Southern Society and Southern Institute of Art to continue these endeavors.

From 1922 to 1930, Tian Han published some sixteen plays in which the romantic undertone of his early work gave way to serious realism. *Jiangcun Xiaojing* (The riverside village) and *Suzhou Yehua* (Night stories from Suxzhou) described the calamitous life ordinary people suffered in wartorn China; *Sun Zhongshan zhi se* (Death of Sun Yat-sen), a historical drama, is aimed at the rightwing Nationalists who betrayed the Revolution. In 1930, Tian Han joined the Leftist Writers' Coalition (*Zuolian*) and founded the Leftist Dramatists' Coalition (*Zuoyi Xijijia Lanmeng*).

After the 1931 Japanese invasion and occupation of Manchuria, Tian wrote several plays deploring the Nationalist government's nonresistance policy with the aim of inspiring the people to fight the invaders. The following six years were prolific for Tian. He produced more than twenty plays and many movie scripts, including *Fengyun Ernu* (Children of the storm). Two heartening songs in this film, "Biyege" (Graduation song) and "Yiyongju Jinxingqu" (March of the volunteers), became known throughout the entire country and were often sung on the battlefields; the latter was officially designated as the Chinese National Anthem after 1949.

In 1935, Tian was arrested on a charge of leading the leftist cultural movement and of being anti-Japanese, but was released on bail. During the Sino-Japanese War (1937–1945), he devoted himself to the National Salvation Movement and continued to write patriotic and protest dramas.

In 1944, Tian and Ouyang Yuqian organized the South-West Theatrical Exhibition (*Xinan Xiju Zhanlanhui*), an event that lasted three months and involved more than thirty theatrical companies and nine hundred performers. Also during the war, he completed a dozen or so Beijing operas, based on historical subjects analogous to the contemporary situation, and a few movie scripts, such as *Shengli Jinxinggu* (March of victory). He also wrote numerous poems both in traditional style and in free verse.

During the Civil War (1946–1949), Tian wrote three plays, the best being *Liren Xing* (Story of three women), three Beijing operas, two movie scripts, and a number of poems. After the establishment of the People's Republic in 1949, Tian was given a number of key cultural posts in the new government, including the chairmanship of the National Writers' Association. He was also elected to be a deputy to the First and Second National People's Congress.

From 1949 to 1958, Tian continued to write historical dramas and hortatory polemics as well as two Beijing operas and more poems. *Guan Hangin* is considered the best of his dramatic works. It is based on an incident in the life of a thirteenth-century dramatist who risked his life by writing a play *Dou'e Yuan*, (Injustice to Dou'e) that exposed corrupt officials. Guan rebuked his would-be censors with the words: "the jade can be broken, but its color cannot be changed; the bamboo can be burned, but its integrity cannot be destroyed."

In the early 1960's Tian began to losing his political influence as Jian Qing, the wife of Mao Zedong, began gradually to gain power. Tian wrote for two more years and produced a few more major pieces. His play *Xie Yaohuan*, about a Tang Dynasty protagonist who was executed after asking the Empress for political reforms, implicated Tian in 1966 when the Cultural Revolution (1966–1976) began. Tian was detained, and subjected to cruel political persecution and endless physical and mental torture. On December 10, 1968, Tian Han died in prison of septicemia. His family was not informed of his death until six years later; his remains were never recovered.

PRINCIPAL WORKS IN ENGLISH TRANSLATION: The White Snake: A Beijing Opera, 1957; Poems in Twentieth Century Chinese Poetry, 1964; Twentieth Century Chinese Drama Anthology, 1983.

ABOUT: Haringova, J. "The development of T'ien Han's dramatic writings during the years 1920–1937," in Studies in Modern Chinese Literature, 1964; Kaplan, R. "Images of Subjugation and Defiance: Female Characters in the Early Dramas of Tian Han," in Modern Chinese Literature, 1988; Larson, W. Literary Authority and the Modern Chinese Writer, 1991; Seymour-Smith, M. Macmillan Guide to Modern World Literature, 1985; Wagoner, R. The Contemporary Chinese Historical Drama, 1990.

*TIETJENS, EUNICE (STRONG HAMMOND) (July 29, 1884–September 6, 1944), American poet and novelist, wrote: "I was born in  Chicago, the daughter of William A. Hammond and Idea (Strong) Hammond, and educated mostly in Europe—in Switzerland, Germany, and France, with courses at the Université de Genève and the Collège de France. Having been born under a wandering star, I have been traveling off and on ever since, having lived for long enough to keep house, in addition to the countries mentioned, in Italy, Tunisia, Japan, China, and the island of Moorea in the Society Islands of the South Seas, and having visited many other countries. In 1904 I married Paul Tietjens, composer of music; divorced 1914. One daughter, and one grandchild (very proud of this last). In 1920 I married Cloyd Head, playwright, theatrical director, and publisher of medical books. He founded a community theatre in Miami, Florida, called the Miami Players. We have one son.

"For the last year of the First World War I was correspondent for the Chicago Daily News in France. I have been on the staff of Poetry: A Magazine of Verse, in one capacity for more than twenty-five years. . . . For two academic years, 1933–1935, I was lecturer in Oriental poetry at the University of Miami. I spent the summer of 1939 in Scandinavia, being in Finland when World War II broke out. . . ."

———

Eunice Tietjens, herself a very minor poet, played a role in the emergence of one of America's most important literary magazines, Poetry: A Magazine of Verse, founded by Harriet Monroe in Chicago in 1912. In her autobiography, The World at My Shoulder, Tietjens states that she was "reborn" at the age of twenty-seven, when she met Monroe. Tietjens joined the staff of the magazine in 1913, and was associated with its various editorial capacities, including brief stints as editor, until the end of her life. She developed a close personal friendship with Harriet Monroe, and with Carl Sandburg, Edgar Lee Masters, and other leading lights of the

°TEE jens

Chicago Renaissance, a movement that was spearheaded by Poetry.

A cosmopolitan woman who spoke several Romance languages fluently, Tietjens devoted her life to two passions: literature and travel. Tietjens's later verse elicited mixed reviews. Jake, her only novel, was received with no great enthusiasm, and Arabesque, a play written in collaboration with her husband, Cloyd Head, was a flop on Broadway in 1925. She did, however, win some praise as editor of the anthology Poetry of the Orient. A number of Tietjens's children's books, including Boy of the Desert and Boy of the South Seas, were inspired by her sojourns to exotic locales.

Tietjens's most interesting work was her autobiography, The World at My Shoulder, which Poetry reviewer Edgar Lee Masters thought "a very honest book, and of fascinating interest." In it, Tietjens recounts her eventful life and her numerous literary friendships. She was the oldest of four siblings, all of whom gained recognition in various fields. One of her sisters, Louise Hammond, was a noted missionary in China, while her brother, Laurens Hammond, was the inventor of the Hammond electronic organ. There is a collection of Tietjens's papers at the Newberry Library in Chicago.

PRINCIPAL WORKS: Poetry—Profiles from China, Sketches in Verse of People and Things Seen in the Interior, 1917; Body and Raiment, 1919; Profiles from Home: Sketches in Free Verse of People and Things Seen in the United States, 1925; Leaves in Windy Weather, 1929. Novel—Jake, 1921. Travel—Japan, Korea and Formosa, 1924; (with L. S. Hammond) China, 1930. Juvenile—Boy of the Desert, 1928; The Romance of Antar, 1929; (with J. Tietjens) The Jaw-Breaker's Alphabet, 1930; Boy of the South Seas, 1931; The Gingerbread Boy, 1932. Autobiography—The World at My Shoulder, 1938. As editor—Poetry of the Orient: An Anthology of the Classic Secular Poetry of the Major Eastern Nations, 1928; An Adventure in Friendship, 1936.

ABOUT: The autobiographical material quoted above was written for Twentieth Century Authors, 1942. Dictionary of Literary Biography vol. 54 1987. Periodicals—Masses August 1917; New York Times September 7, 1944; Poetry September 1938.

**TIKHONOV, VALENTIN. See PAYNE, P.S.R.**

**TILLICH, PAUL JOHANNES** (August 20, 1886–October 22, 1965), German-born theologian, was the son of a Lutheran pastor, Johannes Tillich, and Mathilde (Dürselen) Tillich. He was born in Starzeddel kreis Guben, Prussia, and was educated at gymnasium in Schonfliess, a small community east of the Elbe, where his father served as a minister and diocesan superintendent in the Prussian Territorial Church. He studied theology at the Universities of Berlin, Tübingen and Halle, and received his Ph.D. from the University of Breslau and the Licentiate in Theology from Halle, with his thesis for both degrees on the subject of Schelling's philosophy of religion. In 1932 Tillich was ordained a minister of the Evangelical Lutheran Church. During World War I he was a chaplain with the German forces. He was bitterly opposed to the war itself and when hostilities ended, he took an active part in the establishment of a German republic. Meanwhile he began teaching theology at the University of Berlin, 1911–1924, and at the Universities of Marburg, Dresden, Leipzig, and finally at Frankfurt-am-Main. His liberal, humanitarian views brought him into sharp conflict with the rising Nazi regime, and in 1933 he lost his professorship at Frankfurt. "I had the great honor and luck," he said, "to be about the first non-Jewish professor dismissed from a German university."

Tillich came to the United States in 1933 and became a naturalized citizen in 1940. From 1933 to 1954 he was on the faculty of the Union Theological Seminary in New York. During this period he traveled widely, in the United States and abroad, on lecture tours. In 1953 he went to Edinburgh to deliver the Gifford lectures on theology, and in 1948 and again in 1951 he returned to Germany to lecture. After the end of World War II his teachings became popular in Germany and many of his English writings were translated and published there. In 1954 he was appointed to the faculty of the Divinity School of Harvard University, and in 1962 to the faculty of the University of Chicago. He was married to Hannah Werner. They had a son and a daughter.

One of the greatest of contemporary Protestant theologians, Paul Tillich sought to clarify the meaning of Christianity in the light of the needs and dilemmas of modern life. His writings blended politics, arts, sociology, philosophy, and psychology. Some of his books, in particular *The Courage To Be* (1952) and *Dynamics Of Faith* (1957), reached a large public audience not usually concerned with religious matters. The three-volume *Systematic Theology* (1951-63) was his major life's work, employing current philosophical and psychological concepts and relating them to sociological and scientific theories. *Systematic Theology's* primary thesis held that Protestant theology can "without losing its Christian foundations, incorporate strictly scientific methods, a critical philosophy, a realistic understanding of man and society and powerful ethical principles and motives." He believed that any division between philosophy and theology would be impossible, "for, whatever the relation of God, world, and man may be, it lies in the frame of being; and any interpretation of the meaning and structure of being as being unavoidably such has consequences for the interpretation of God, man and the world in their interrelations."

Tillich was a pure philosophical theologian. He saw the phenomenon of the Christian faith expressed in religious symbols that have always required continuous reinterpretation. "The way in which this event can be understood and received changes with changing conditions in all periods of history," he wrote. For the modern person "the traditional language has become irrelevant," and the meaning of Christian symbols has become increasingly problematic. The "meaning," the ultimate message of the Christian faith, must be interpreted with the language and conceptual tools of our own culture. He saw the tradition task of philosophical theology to resuppose some common ground between the questions our own culture is asking, or should be asking, and the answers found in Christian symbols, properly interpreted. Tillich found this common ground in the fact that, while the questions must be formulated in modern language and concepts, the questions themselves are part of the universal human situation. It is precisely these eternal questions, Tillich proclaims, to which the Christian message and symbols have always given an answer.

Tillich's legacy evolves, writes Rev. James R. Lyons, from his claim than our modern culture is no longer directed, as were past cultures, to a God "up there," as expressed by Bishop John Robinson and Harvey Cox. Our own culture strives for self-sufficiency, without any religious expression at all. Tillich's conviction was that all cultural forms should be seen as expressions of our human "ultimate concern." In Tillich's own technical language, our culture had ceased to be heteronomous— deriving its law from on high. It is at the moment trying to be autonomous—finding its law in itself. He went on to argue that it should endeavor to become theonomous—to find its law in its genuine "ultimate concern, the divine."

In the end, for Tillich, "the most intimate motions within the depths of our souls are not completely our own. For they belong also to our friends, to mankind, to the universe, and to the Ground of being, the aim of our life. Nothing can be hidden ultimately. It is always reflected in the mirror in which nothing can be concealed."

PRINCIPAL WORKS IN ENGLISH TRANSLATION: The Interpretation of History, 1936; The Protestant Era, 1948; Shaking the Foundations, 1948; The Courage to Be, 1952; Love, Power, and Justic, 1954; The New Being, 1955; Dynamica of Faith, 1957; Systematic Theology, I, II, III, 1951, 1957, 1963.

ABOUT: Adams, James Luther, Pauck, Wilhelm, Shinn, Roger L. (eds.) Kegly, C. W. & Bretall, R. W. (eds.) The Theology of Paul Tillich; The Thought of Paul Tillich; Lyons, Jame R. (ed.) The Intellectual Legacy of Paul Tillich; Taylor, Mark Kline Paul Tillich, Theologian of the Boundaries.

**TILLYARD, E(USTACE) M(ANDEVILLE) W(ETENHALL)** (1889–May 24, 1962), English scholar critic, wrote: "Born in Cambridge, grew up with University in background. Attended Perse School and learnt Latin and Greek by Rouse's 'direct method.' Head of school and captain of hockey and cricket. Classical scholar of Jesus College, Cambridge, first classes in Classical Tripos. B.A. 1911 and studentship to British School of Archaeology, Athens; travel in Greece and Turkey. 1912 got access to Hope Collection of Greek antiques, long closed to students; began cataloguing vases there. College elects me Fellow. 1914 War catches me with catalogue unfinished. Volunteer,

serve first with infantry France, surviving nine months trench warfare. Transfer to Salonika Force because of languages, spend rest of war there on Intelligence. Captain, with military O.B.E., Greek Military Cross. Return Cambridge University 1919, transfer from Classics to recently created English Tripos, then becoming University Lecturer in English. Helped by wife (college girl who drove ambulance in France and Salonika) finish vase catalogue. But real tastes literary. Helped build up English School at Cambridge along with I. A. Richards and others. Began critical writing with anthology of Lamb's criticism. Turned to early love, Milton, and wrote the book on him that gave me standing as scholar-critic. From Milton turned to epic general on which am still engaged, other business having intervened. Demand from Sorbonne for lecture on Shakespeare diverted me to him; also found Shakespeare's history plays were epic in spirit and had to be dealt with before could write on English epic proper. Three books on Shakespeare and two on English Renaissance. Second World War found me too old for service except in Home Guard and created shortage of college administrators. Became Senior Tutor of Jesus College, Cambridge and in 1945 Master.

"I address most of my books to educated reader not to professional scholar; deplore growing gap between scholar and public.

"I like travel and have been east as far as the river Euphrates and west as far as Vancouver. Gave Alexander Memorial Lectures at Toronto University and Turnbull Memorial Lectures at the Johns Hopkins University. Civil honours include degree of Litt.D. at Cambridge, honorary membership of Modern Language Association of America, and Fellowship of British Academy.

"I like open air and exercise and intend to continue to walk and cycle till stopped by infirmity.

"I vote Liberal when there is a candidate, but my only active intervention in politics has been on behalf of Federal Union and United Europe."

———

E.M.W. Tillyard was the son of Alfred Isaac Tillyard, a former Mayor of Cambridge, and his wife, the former Catherine Wetenhall. His elder brother, Henry Julius Wetenhall Tillyard, was a distinguished classicist. Eustace, too, began as a classicist, a brilliant one. He went to Athens in 1911 to study at the British School of Archaeology there; this led to his first book, on the Hope Vases. In 1919 he married Phyllis, the daughter of Henry M. Cook. They had a son and two daughters.

The energy he expended in establishing the English School at Cambridge was largely instrumental in its foundation, although he himself was not one of the actual founders. He built up a huge and grateful following among students. His Times obituarist wrote: "Others may have won more widespread celebrity as scholars or as critics, Richards and Leavis among them, but everyone in Cambridge knew that Tillyard, because of his selfless and unremitting thought and care for the good of

the School, was its chief mainstay." He retired from the Mastership of Jesus College in 1959.

His *Milton* was considered a major contribution to its subject. It is an enthusiastic defense of Milton from a man who, although a classicist with great sympathy for Puritanism (he had been brought up in a Puritan atmosphere) was also markedly humane. F. A. Patterson (a noted Milton scholar, and the editor of the best edition of his complete poetry) remarked of Tillyard's *Milton*, in the *New York Herald Tribune Books*: "He has tried rather to explain Milton the thinker and artist through a study of inner motives as revealed by known facts, and by obscure hints given in his writings. The total result is satisfactory: Milton stands out as incomparably the greatest English poet of his century and of succeeding centuries—but that he has always been; he is further felt to be the greatest man and practical thinker of his age. The large conclusions, one feels, are sound; in parts, however, the study is weak." Milton was at that time under some attack, from Ezra Pound, T. S. Eliot, and F. R. Leavis.

Tillyard also has some importance, if smaller, in Shakespearean criticism, as one of the comparatively early pioneers of what is usually called "historical criticism." This was the movement, propelled by A. C. Bradley's seminal *Shakespearean Tragedy* (1904), that sought to place Shakespeare in his time and to see his work as expressions of the beliefs of his time. Tillyard made his contribution in *The Elizabethan World Picture* (1943), read by scholars and laymen alike as a useful exposition of the universe as Tillyard believed the Elizabethans saw it. As the *New York Times* put it, "This short book introduces the general reader to the orthodox religio-cosmic background. . . . It attempts to clarify and systematize an exceedingly complex subject: the great universal synthesis inherited from mediaeval scholasticism, built up through centuries from various elements of Christian, Classical and Eastern philosophy, science, religion, folklore, magic and superstition. The author coordinates material not before collected in one book—and seeks to show that the vast majority of Europeans . . . accepted the mediaeval cosmos uncritically." Wrong though Tillyard may inevitably have been in certain matters of emphasis and detail, *The Elizabethan World Picture* was Tillyard's most influential and important book.

In 1944 Tillyard published his learned *Shakespeare's History Plays*. The *Manchester Guardian* complained that it "conscientiously and compendiously examines Shakespeare's History Plays as if they were solemn documents drafted as a deliberate expression of their author's analysis of the political forces and principles (and their theological implications) which explain the history of England. Such a use of poetic material is hazardous." And the American critic Samuel Chew, in the *Weekly Book Review*, thought that Tillyard's "ingenuity" led him "at times to press the evidence pretty far."

Tillyard tended to believe that great or important poetry was more the product of the beliefs of the time in which it was written than that of the individual poet. In *Five Poems: 1470–1870*, he discusses Henryson's "The Testament of Cresseid," Sir John Davies's "Orchestra," Dryden's "Ode on Anne Killigrew," Coleridge's "Ancient Mariner" and Swinburne's "Hertha," with special concern about their relationship to their historical context.

Tillyard was an avid traveler abroad, especially to the French Alps. He loved both to bicycle and to walk. As a man, wrote his *Times* obituarist, he was "at once frank and reserved, simple and weighty."

PRINCIPAL WORKS: The Hope Vases, 1923; Lamb's Criticism, 1923; The Poetry of Sir Thomas Wyatt: a Selection and a Study, 1929; Milton, 1930; Milton's Correspondence and Academic Exercises, 1932; Poetry Direct and Oblique, 1934, rev. ed. 1945; Shakespeare's Last Plays, 1938; The Miltonic Setting, 1938; (with C. S. Lewis) The Personal Heresy, 1939; The Elizabethan World Picture, 1943; Shakespeare's History Plays, 1944; Five Poems 1470–1870, 1948; Shakespeare's Problem Plays, 1950; Studies in Milton, 1951; The English Renaissance, Fact or Fiction, 1952; The English Epic and its Background, 1954; The Metaphysicals and Milton, 1956; The Epic Strain in the English Novel, 1958; The Muse Unchained, 1958; Some Mythical Elements in English Literature, 1961.

ABOUT: The autobiographical material quoted above was written for Twentieth Century Authors First Supplement 1955. Campbell, O. J. and Quinn, E. G. (eds.) A Shakespeare Encyclopaedia, 1966. Proceedings of the British Academy, Vol. 49, 1964. *Periodicals*—Illustrated London News June 2, 1962; Manchester Guardian February 28, 1945; New Statesman August 21, 1948; New York Herald Tribune Books October 26, 1930; New York Times April 2, 1944; Saturday Review of Literature August 21, 1948; Spectator May 3, 1930; Times (London) May 26, 1962; Weekly Book Review March 10, 1946.

## TILTON, ALICE. See TAYLOR, P. A.

## TIMMERMANS, FELIX (July 5, 1886–January 24, 1947), Belgian (Flemish) fiction writer, children's writer, draftsman and painter, dramatist and poet, was born in the town of Lier, where he would live for almost the whole of his life. His father was a traveling salesman of lace. A thirteenth child, he was superstitiously called "Felix," but he was always, in fact, known as a melancholy man, most of whose humor and good nature went into his writing. Felix left the local school at the age of fourteen, and later sporadically attended some classes at the art institute in his native town. Otherwise he had no formal education, a fact often noted by critics when explaining the difficulties offered by his style.

Timmermans's first success came with *Pallieter* (1916, translated under that title), a series of lyrical sketches centering on a miller who takes all he can out of every instant of his existence, and who gave a word to the Flemish language ("joy of life"). With its portrait of a robust and life-affirming young man, the book appealed to Catholic readers in Europe after the disillusionment brought by World War I, even though the book can also be seen as celebratory of pagan hedonism. When C. B. Bodde's translation appeared in America in 1924 reviewers welcomed it, the *Boston Transcript*, for example, exclaiming: "here we have a story so full of joy and of the gratitude for the mere gift of living that it seems to move to unseen music."

In *Boerenspsalm* (1935, Peasant hymn), nineteen years later, Timmermans tried to repeat this success

in the form of a longer and more sustained novel about a peasant called Wortel, similar in temperament to the miller Pallieter. A few critics have claimed it as deeper and more significant than the earlier book; but it has not yet attracted an English translator (there is a French version, *Psaume Paysan*, 1942).

Timmermans had more success outside Belgium with his *Het Kindeke Jezus in Vlaanderen* (1917, translated as *The Christ Child in Flanders*; and with his novel about the painter Peter Bruegel, *Pieter Bruegel* (1928, translated as *Droll Peter*). *The Christ Child in Flanders* was meant for children, although it was read by adults, and was not translated (and only then from a German version) into English until 1960. The illustrations were by Timmermans himself. In many ways the most charming and characteristic of all his many books, it deservedly became a European classic; it tells the story of Christ in a deliberately anachronistic manner: through the paintings of the Flemish masters, and against a medieval background. *The New York Times* (1960) reviewer was not unusual in finding that reading the book was like "looking at one of the pictures by those Flemish artists who obviously inspired the author, in which the very anachronisms of costume and background emphasize the timelessness of the story. And the homely, earthy aspects of peasant life . . . make it, infused with the author's love and devotion, all the more poignant." *The Christ Child in Flanders*, filmed in 1928 by the Flemish theatre, will undoubtedly live on, as an enchanting and enchanted account of the life of Jesus.

An ardent Flemish nationalist, a Flamingant, he was essentially a naive man, however—he was friendly to the Nazis when they invaded Belgium in World War II, truly believing that they were friendly to the Flemings, and would grant them autonomy. He did not perform any treasonable acts, but, like Hamsun in Norway, lost much of his popularity after 1945. Accusations of collaboration made against him distressed him considerably.

Timmermans was married, and his daughter Lia wrote an illuminating, affectionate and useful book about him, *Mijn vader* (1951). Much of his graphic work may be seen at Lier.

PRINCIPAL WORKS IN ENGLISH TRANSLATION: Fiction—Pallieter (tr. C. B. Bodde,) 1924; Droll Peter (tr. M. C. Darnton and W. J. Paul) 1930; The Triptych of the Three Kings (tr. H. Ripperger) 1936; The Christ Child in Flanders (tr. E. C. Briefs) 1960. Other—The Harp of St. Francis (tr. M. Bird) 1949; The Perfect Joy of St. Francis (tr. R. Brown) 1952; A Gift from St. Nicholas (tr. C. Kismaric) 1988.

ABOUT: Columbia Dictionary of Modern European Literature, 1947, 1980; Backer, F. de Contemporary Flemish Literature, 1934; Encyclopedia of Literature in the Twentieth Century, 1983; Greshoff, J. Belgian Literature in the Dutch Language, 1945; Mallinson, V. Belgian Literature, 1966; Meijer, R. P. The Literature of the Low Countries, 1978; Seymour-Smith, M. Macmillan Guide to Modern World Literature, 1986. *Periodicals*—Boston Transcript October 11, 1924; Literary Review October 4, 1924; New York Times January 26, 1947; December 4, 1960; Times Literary Supplement December 4, 1924.

**TINDALL, WILLIAM YORK** (March 7, 1903–September 8, 1981), American critic and literary historian, wrote: "I was born in Williamstown, Vermont. My father, a country doctor, complete with horse and buggy, was a Vermont Democrat; My mother a former New York City school teacher, came from Kutna Hora, in what is now Czechoslovakia. Her desire for New York accounts for my middle name. I attended the public schools of Montpelier, Vermont, until 1918 when, upon removal of the family to New York City, I entered a high school in Hell's Kitchen. Later, in Columbia College, where the pressures were less intense, I was moved by the lectures of John Erskine to specialize in literature rather than in journalism as I had intended. By the aid of the Proudfit fellowship I added a year of graduate work in English. My teaching career began at Washington Square College in 1926. Tom Wolfe was a colleague there; and Greenwich Village provided an even more liberal education than Hell's Kitchen or Morningside Heights.

"In 1931 I became an instructor in the Graduate School at Columbia. My full professorship came in 1950. In 1932 I went to the British Museum for a

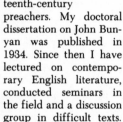

year on a Cutting fellowship to study seventeenth-century preachers. My doctoral dissertation on John Bunyan was published in 1934. Since then I have lectured on contemporary English literature, conducted seminars in the field and a discussion group in difficult texts.

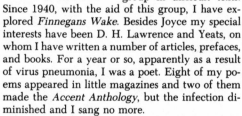

Since 1940, with the aid of this group, I have explored *Finnegans Wake*. Besides Joyce my special interests have been D. H. Lawrence and Yeats, on whom I have written a number of articles, prefaces, and books. For a year or so, apparently as a result of virus pneumonia, I was a poet. Eight of my poems appeared in little magazines and two of them made the *Accent Anthology*, but the infection diminished and I sang no more.

"In 1937 I married Cecilia Kramer of Ohio. We have one daughter, Elizabeth, and she has a cocker spaniel. As for politics, I voted for Coolidge, but since that time I have been a Democrat. For a year I served Tammany Hall as a county committeeman, but the voters of my district denied me a second term."

---

Best known for his scholarly analyses of the writings of James Joyce, William York Tindall made Joyce's *Ulysses* required readings in his classes at New York University in the late 1920s, while the book was still officially banned in the United States as "obscene." Tindall considered it the "greatest novel of the twentieth century, including Proust and everyone else."

A professor, scholar, critic, and literary historian, Tindall wrote four books on Joyce, as well as books

on W. B. Yeats, Wallace Stevens, D. H. Lawrence, Dylan Thomas, and Samuel Beckett, whom he nominated for the Nobel Prize.

Tindall came under Joyce's spell in 1925 while he was in Paris, the first stop of his post-college tour of Europe. He bought a copy of *Ulysses*, thinking it was a dirty book, on June 16, the day known to Joyceans as Bloomsday because of Leopold Bloom's adventures in the novel. Tindall said he finished the novel straightway and found it fascinating rather than smutty.

Tindall began teaching at Columbia in 1931, where he once again experienced a Joycean coincidence. His office number was 616 Philosophy Hall—the number marked the sixth month, the sixteenth day—Bloomsday all over again.

Tindall's first book on Joyce, *James Joyce: His Way of Interpreting the Modern World* (1950), concentrated on *Ulysses* and *Finnegans Wake*, and was praised for its insight, clarity and brevity. Nathan Halper wrote in the *New Republic* that Tindall extended known horizons on Joyce; the *New Yorker* remarked that Tindall wrote for nonspecialists, provided handy notes on all those who had an influence on Joyce and made *Finnegans Wake* sound as if it would be fun to read.

Tindall continued to identify Joyce's purposes, themes and methods in another Joyce handbook, *A Readers Guide to James Joyce* (1960), which concentrated more extensively on *Ulysses*. The handbook approach was criticized by the *Times Literary Supplement*: Tindall, the reviewer wrote, "takes it too far. It is really a way of reducing the whole thing *Ulysses* to allegory." Writing in the *Guardian*, Douglas Hewitt recommended the book, but said Tindall "weakens the effect of his useful guide by subordinating discrimination too readily to explanation." He also wrote of how Tindall enjoyed solving Joycean puzzles, but that he "might more often heed Joyce's transformation of the appellation Shem the Penman into the injunction Shun the Punman."

Tindal produced a similar manual, *A Reader's Guide to Finnegans Wake* (1969), which he said was not intended to be read through but to be held in one hand with the *Wake* in the other, "while the eye, as at a tennis match, moves to and fro." A page-by-page analysis of Joyce's puns, allusions, and word plays, the book was favorably reviewed, especially in comparison to the similar earlier guide *The Skeleton Key to Finnegans Wake* (1944) by Joseph Campbell and Henry Morton Robinson. Vivian Mercier in *Book World* wrote that Tindall's book, unlike *Skeleton Key*, does not try to paraphrase Joyce but instead offers commentary on the text. He acknowledged Tindall's expertise on his subject, pointing out that he had been reading the *Wake* "in committee or with seminars of Columbia graduate students since 1940," and said Tindall was right in insisting that the *Wake* "is by and large a very funny book."

Christopher Lehmann-Haupt in the *New York Times* (1969) praised Tindall for not oversimplifying Joyce's language and for offering "fresh perspectives for anyone who has felt the obsession" of *Finnegans Wake*, mentioning that the book "rests securely as a love object to the band of men who, seduced by it long ago, have been pursuing its protean images ever since," with Tindall one of the first in the chase. He also credited Tindall for paying attention to the bawdiness in the *Wake.* "This is necessary not only because the book is riotously bawdy—enough so that it 'would have detained the censor in 1939 had he been able to read it'—but because the *Wake* as well as being about the rise and fall and rise of all civilization, is also about the intimate relations of a couple during a single night. The macrocosm in the microcosm."

Tindall focused on other writers besides Joyce. For his doctoral dissertation and first published work, *John Bunyan, Mechanick Preacher* (1934), Tindall wrote a historical study—"not just another biography," he said—on several aspects of the work of the author of *Pilgrim's Progress.* Paul Crowley the *Catholic Weekly* in *Commonweal* praised it as "an unusually good, representative sample of the work being done by younger American scholars."

Tindall then turned his attentions to D. H. Lawrence with *D. H. Lawrence and Susan His Cow* (1939), in which he concluded that Susan, the cow in Lawrence's Taos, New Mexico, backyard who "claimed the respect and love of her master" provided a means of salvation for Lawrence. For Tindall Susan served as a convenient starting-point to trace Lawrence's ideas to their sources. Lorine Pruette in *New York Herald Tribune Books* said the book is "uneasy reading, often clever but at times too hellbent in pursuit of cleverness," but E. V. Wyatt in *Commonweal* called it "a super-smart commentary," and H. T. Moore in *Saturday Review of Literature* said it is "the most valuable book on the informational side that has yet been written about Lawrence." Tindall also edited *The Later D. H. Lawrence* (1952).

*A Reader's Guide to Dylan Thomas* (1962), analyzed the work of the Welsh poet. Of it, *Kirkus* wrote that "Tindall expertly and elegantly wanders the Thomistic labyrinth, solving almost all the extravagant riddles," and that, eight years after his death, Thomas had found in Tindall a "most enthusiastic champion."

In *The Literary Symbol* (1955), Tindall presented his definition and history of the symbol in literature, gave a comprehensive account of the symbolist novel, analyzed symbolic parts, and concluded with a discussion of form as a symbol, illustrating his analysis and impressions with passages from such contemporary writers as Proust, Joyce, Yeats, Thomas, and Faulkner. Edzia Weisberg in *New Republic* wrote: "It is pleasant to read good criticism written well."

Besides his forty-year career as professor at Columbia, Tindall was president of the James Joyce Society for several years, served as a visiting lecturer at various colleges and universities, and was a frequent guest on the CBS radio program "Invitation to Learning." He was awarded a Guggenheim Fellowship in 1954 and an honorary degrees for Columbia in 1978 and from Iona College.

PRINCIPAL WORKS: John Bunyan, Mechanick Preacher, 1934; D. H. Lawrence and Susan His Cow, 1939; Forces in Modern British Literature, 1947; James Joyce: His Way of Interpreting the Modern World, 1950; (as ed.) The Later D. H. Lawrence, 1952; (as ed.) James Joyce, Chamber Music, 1954; The Literary Symbol, 1955; A Reader's Guide to James Joyce, 1960; The Joyce Country, 1960; Wallace Stevens, 1961; A Reader's Guide to Dylan Thomas, 1962; Samuel Beckett, 1964; W. B. Yeats, 1966; A Reader's Guide to Finnegans Wake, 1969; (as ed.) The Poems of W. B. Yeats, 1970.

ABOUT: The autobiographical material quoted above was written for Twentieth Century Authors First Supplement, 1955. *Periodicals*—Book World March 2, 1969; Commonweal January 25, 1935; November 3, 1939; Guardian March 4, 1960; Kirkus January 15, 1962; New York Herald Tribune Books November 26, 1939; New Republic March 27, 1950; January 2, 1956; New York Times March 15, 1969; September 9, 1981; New Yorker March 18, 1950; Saturday Review of Literature October 28, 1939; Times Literary Supplement June 3, 1960.

**TINKER, CHAUNCEY BREWSTER** (October 22, 1876–March 16, 1963), American university professor, literary historian and critic, and book collector, was born in Auburn, Maine, the son of Reverend Anson Phelps Tinker and Martha Jane (White) Tinker. He grew up in Colorado, where his parents, both of whom suffered from tuberculosis, had gone to improve their health. He graduated from East Denver High School and received his university training at Yale (B.A. in English literature, 1899, and Ph.D., in 1902).

After teaching at Bryn Mawr College for one year, he joined the English faculty at Yale in 1903. With the exception of his brief duty as an intelligence officer during World War I, and two visiting professorships at Harvard, Tinker spent his entire career at Yale. His tenure there coincided with the rising eminence of the university's English department. From 1924 until his retirement in 1945, he was Sterling Professor of English Literature. The most celebrated authority on James Boswell, Samuel Johnson, and the eighteenth-century English literary scene, Tinker also taught classes on nineteenth-century English poetry, and was for many years one of Yale's most popular and revered professors. Many of his students went on to become leading scholars, while others—including Sinclair Lewis, Archibald MacLeish, Thornton Wilder, and Stephen Vincent Benét—achieved recognition as creative writers. "I shall be remembered for my students," Tinker insisted. "They are my jewels."

Tinker began his academic career by publishing his own translation of *Beowulf* and a critical bibliographic survey entitled *The Translations of Beowulf.* He is best known, however, for his contributions to the study of "The Age of Johnson" (as he called his famous graduate seminar at Yale), and particularly for having revived the reputation of, and spurred scholarly interest in, James Boswell, Johnson's biographer. His *Young Boswell* is a biographical and critical study consisting of eleven essays examining various aspects of the early career of the Scottish diarist and man of letters. Based in large part on Boswell material that was then new, the volume generated considerable excitement among scholars and critics. A *Spectator* reviewer praised Tinker for having "completely vindicated the artist in the biographer," and a *New York Times* (1922) critic praised "his penetrating interpretations, his many sagacious comments, and the delightful style in which he has presented the results of a fine and thorough scholarship." With the publication of the two-volume *Letters of James Boswell* soon thereafter, Tinker became, as Mary Hyde has noted in *Modern Philology*, "the doyen of Boswell studies."

Not long after the appearance of the *Letters*, Tinker learned of the existence—previously only rumored—of a substantial collection of unexamined Boswell manuscripts in Ireland. In the course of researching his two books on Boswell, Tinker had placed an advertisement in the *Times Literary Supplement* requesting any information concerning papers Boswell had allegedly deposited in an ebony cabinet. Based on an anonymous response, he learned that the cabinet and the Boswell papers did indeed exist, in Castle Malahide, near Dublin, the home of Lord Talbot de Malahide, one of Boswell's descendants. In 1925 Tinker traveled to Ireland to meet with Lord Talbot, but the latter refused to sell the papers, and even denied Tinker's request to inspect them. In 1927 Lord Talbot sold most of the Boswell papers in his possession to Ralph Isham, an English collector. However, a series of lawsuits kept the bulk of those papers—which included original manuscripts of Boswell's *The Life of Samuel Johnson* and *The Journal of a Tour to the Hebrides*—out of the hands of scholars until 1949, when the Yale University Library purchased the collection for $450,000.

Although Tinker received credit for uncovering the existence of the Boswell papers at Castle Malahide, the whole affair was a source of frustration for him. His own studies of Boswell, so widely commended for the new material they presented, could not longer be considered definitive; what was perhaps worse, Tinker never got an opportunity to edit the largest trove of manuscripts by Boswell, the author whose work has been the central focus of his career. During the 1930s and beyond, he turned increasingly to the study of nineteenth-century English poetry, and devoted much of his energy to overseeing the rare book collection at Yale. From 1931 until his retirement, he was in charge of Yale's Rare Book Room, and over the years he donated many of the rare books in his personal collection, as well as his extensive correspondence with various collectors, to the university. He presented the Charles Eliot Norton lectures at Harvard in 1937–1938; these were later published as *Painter and Poet*, a consideration of the influence of English poetry on the works of seven English painters. He collaborated with Howard Foster Lowry in writing *The Poetry of Matthew Arnold*, a critical companion volume to *The Poetical Works of Matthew Arnold*, which he edited with Lowry. Tinker's lack of enthusiasm for twentieth-century poetry was noted

by H. E. Woodbridge, in a *Yale Review* notice of *Essays in Retrospect*: "He makes no concessions to the 'moderns,' except that he has a good word for the later work of T. S. Eliot."

After Tinker's retirement from Yale, a group of his former students paid tribute to him with the essay collection *The Age of Johnson*. Yale presented him with an honorary doctorate in 1946, and awarded him the Alumni Medal in 1955. A lifelong bachelor, Tinker spent his last years living with his sister in Wethersfield, Connecticut. There is a Tinker Collection in the Beinecke Rare Book and Manuscript Library at Yale.

PRINCIPAL WORKS: *As translator*—Beowulf: Translated Out of the Old English, 1902. *Literary criticism*—The Salon and English Letters: Chapters on the Interrelations of Literature and Society in the Age of Johnson, 1915; Nature's Simple Plan: A Phase of Radical Thought in the MidEighteenth Century, 1922; Rasselas in the New World, 1925; The Wedgewood Medallion of Samuel Johnson: A Study in Iconography, 1926; The Good Estate of Poetry, 1929; (with C. P. Rollins) Addresses Commemorating the One Hundredth Anniversary of the Birth of William Morris Delivered Before the Yale Library Associated in the Sterling Memorial Library, 1935; Painter and Poet: Studies in the Literary Relations of English Painting: The Charles Eliot Norton Lectures for 1937–1938, 1938; (with H. F. Lowry) The Poetry of Matthew Arnold: A Commentary, 1940; Essays in Retrospect: Collected Articles and Addresses, 1948. *Biography*—Young Boswell: Chapters on James Boswell, the Biographer, Based on Largely New Material, 1922; (with F. A. Pottle) A New Portrait of James Boswell, 1927. *As editor*—(with A. S. Cook) Select Translations from Old English Poetry, 1902, rev. ed. 1926; (with A. S. Cook) Select Translations from Old English Prose, 1908; Selections from the Works of John Ruskin, 1908; Dr. Johnson and Fanny Burney: Being the Johnsonian Passages from the Works of Mme. D'Arblay, 1911; The Tempest (by W. Shakespeare) 1918; Letters of James Boswell, 2 vols., 1924; (with H. F. Lowry) The Poetical Works of Matthew Arnold, 1950. *Other*—The University Library: An Address on Alumni Day, 1925.

ABOUT: Dictionary of Literary Biography Vol. 140, 1994; Hilles, F. W. (ed.) The Age of Johnson: Essays Presented to Chauncey Brewster Tinker, 1949; Metzdorf, R. F. (comp.) The Tinker Library: A Bibliographic Catalogue of the Books and Manuscripts Collected by Chauncey Brewster Tinker, 1959; Who's Who 1963. *Bibliography*—The Translations of Beowulf: A Critical Bibliography, 1903; Catalogue of an Exhibition of Manuscripts, First Editions, Early Engravings and Various Literature Relating to Samuel Johnson, 1709–1784, 1909. *Periodicals*—Modern Philology May 1988; New York Times April 9, 1922; March 19, 1963; Newsweek March 7, 1955; Spectator October 14, 1922; Time March 28, 1949; Times (London) March 19, 1963; Yale Review Summer 1948.

**TINKER, EDWARD** (September 12, 1881–July 6, 1968), American novelist, biographer, and historian, wrote: "Edward Larocque Tinker was born in New York City. He went to Browning Boys School and received his B.A. from Columbia University in 1902, LL.B. 1905 [from New York University]. In 1905 he was admitted to the bar, and after one year with the Legal Aid Society was appointed assistant to William Travers Jerome,  then district attorney of the city of New York, where he served three years. For five years he lived in Texas, where he installed a Railroad Safety Organization, the first west of Chicago, went as observer on Pancho Villa's train at the battle of Celaya, and was with General Alvaro Obregon before he became the President of Mexico. In 1916 he married Frances McKee of New Orleans and took up the career of writing for a living. Mrs. Tinker collaborated with him in the four novelettes called *Old New Orleans*, for the Old Cities Series.

"*Les Écrits de Langue Francaise en Louisiane au XIX Siècle (Writings in the French Language in Louisiana in the Nineteenth Century)* was his thesis for a doctorate at the Sorbonne. It was crowned by the French Academy and given the Gold Medal in 1934. He received the Academy's Gold medal again in 1937 for *Gombo: The Creole Dialect of Louisiana and French Newspapers and Periodicals*, which appeared originally in the *Proceedings* of the American Antiquarian Society. In 1936 he was put in charge of a department of the New York *Times Book Review*, called 'New Editions Fine and Otherwise,' where for many years he contributed a weekly page, reviewing reprints of books of permanent value.

"In 1933 he was decorated by the government of France with the *Palme d'Académie*, in 1939 was made a Chevalier of the Legion of Honor, and in the same year was given a medal by Columbia. . . .

"He was one of the chancellors of the American Antiquarian Society, to which he gave his collection of French Imprints of Louisiana, probably the most complete yet made; and he presented to the Houghton Library of Harvard the letters, manuscripts, and association copies of Lafcadio Hearn upon which he based his biography of that author. His library on the history and Creole dialect of Haiti enabled him to translate *Canapé Vert*, a novel of the peasant life of that country written by Pierre Marcelin and Philippe Thoby-Marcelin.

"In 1943 the Carnegie Endowment for International Peace sent Mr. Tinker to Mexico to give a course on American literature at the National University, which later conferred on him the degree of Professor Extraordinario. Two years later he went to Uruguay and Argentina as exchange lecturer under the auspices of the Department of State. While in South America he made an important collection of books on the gaucho and published a monograph on *The Cult of the Gaucho and the Birth of a Literature*, and followed it with *Los Jinetes de las Américas y la Literatura por Ellos Inspirada* (1951), a comparative study of the gaucho, vaquero, and cowboy, accompanied by a long bibliography, published in Buenos Aires. An English version followed in 1953 under the title *The Horsemen of the Americas and the Literature They inspired*. In the same year *Creole City* appeared, an informal history of New Orleans and various facets of its life.

"Mr. Tinker was a trustee of the Museum of the City of New York and of the French Institute of New York, a member of the Council on Foreign Relations and of the Society of American Historians, as well as a corresponding member of the Hispanic Society. He has an LL.D. from Middlebury College."

———

Fascination with charros and cowboys, Latin America and Louisiana, took Edward Larocque Tinker far from his comfortable childhood homes in New York City and Long Island to railroad boxcars in the Arizona desert, to remote attics in outpost bayou parishes in Louisiana, to Mexico with Pancho Villa,3 and to the old bookstores of New Orleans Vieux Carré. His journeys and research resulted in a number of histories and novels, ranging from an account of Lafcadio Hearn's Cincinnati period to histories of eighteenth-century New Orleans to a study of the different horsemen of the Americas.

The son of Henry Champlin Tinker and Louise (Larocque) Tinker, he became interested in Mexico at age eleven, after his parents, returning from a visit there, bought him a chamois leather charro suit, a saddle, a bridle, and a pony. But first he finished his education, receiving an A.B. degree from Columbia University in 1902 and a law degree three years later from New York University. He served as a Navy lieutenant in World War I and spent four years in the legal profession before he would get back to his riding gear.

Tinker became an assistant attorney general in New York, but resigned that post and practiced halfheartedly in his grandfather's law firm for a year before taking off to work as a railroader, settling in El Paso, Texas, "which in 1912 as a most exciting place," he wrote in his memoirs, *New Yorker Unlimited* (1970). "It was right on the border, the Mexican Revolution was in full swing and the town swarmed with spies, gunrunners, racing touts, adventurers and Secret Service men."

But Tinker went farther than El Paso and the Arizona desert, where he supervised a crew laying railroad track. He crossed into Mexico at every opportunity and got to know General Alfar Obregon during the Sonora campaign. He also traveled as an observer in Pancho Villa's train at the battle of Celaya. Throughout his life, Tinker wore many other hats beside a sombrero: he worked as a banker, a realty company president, an expert printer who owned his own press, a wood engraver—and a writer.

The young adventurer was called back to the States as his father approached death, and met Frances McKee Dodge, a native of New Orleans. They were married in 1916 and established a winter home on St. Charles Street. It was there that Tinker became acquainted with the writings of Lafcadio Hearn. His first book, *Lafcadio Hearns American Days* (1924), was considered a frank yet not unsympathetic portrait of the journalist's life in the three cities—Cincinnati, New Orleans, and New York—where he spent two decades before his departure for Japan in 1890. *The Independent* called Tinker's account "a truly fascinating story of the strangest years in the life of this strange, timid, passionate outcast."

Tinker, it turned out, was merely getting his feet wet in nineteenth-century New Orleans history when he focused on the years Hearn spent there (1877 to 1887). His second book, a novel entitled *Toucoutou*, was published in 1928; it told the story of race prejudice in New Orleans in the 1850s. The title character is raised as a white child by a black woman and goes to marry a young patrician, learning later that the black woman is really her mother. The humiliation of the young couple is intensified by the cruel treatment of their former friends, and unable to endure it, they flee from New Orleans. Writing in *Bookmark*, Herschel Brickel made special mention of the books interesting forenote on the word Creole and its good brief glossary of creole words and phrases, and wrote that *Taucoutou* "brings vividly to life a period in the fascinating history of New Orleans that now seems as remote as ancient Chaldea." However, while praised for being a revealing and intensive study of a neglected period, the novel was criticized for its defective, stilted characterizations.

Tinker was by this time a devotee of Louisiana history. "The longer I stayed in New Orleans," he wrote in his memoirs, "the deeper grew my interest in the city's Creole background and history. I began to haunt the old bookstores in the Vieux Carré, trying to collect everything published in French in the state—books, broadsheets, poetry, and newspapers, and would come home at night, happy and dirty as a chimney sweep with a few tattered pamphlets under my arms." His collection of Louisiana imprints in French, approximately 5,000 items, many of which he found in the cellars and attics of publishers descendants' in New Orleans and rural Louisiana, were left to the American Antiquarian Society at Worcester, Massachusetts.

Collaborating with his wife, he published in 1930 a four-volume set of romances modeled after the Edith Wharton series *Old New York*. They were, aptly, entitled *Old New Orleans*. Portrayed in the volumes, respectively, were Creole life during the Civil War in the 1860s, the carpetbaggers of the 1870s, improverished aristocrats of the 1880s, and, in the final volume, *Mardi Gras*, New Orleans "in its holiday attire," said E.R. Richardson in *Bookmark*. *Old New Orleans* contained reproductions of sketches of the old quarter by Joseph Pennell, one of the author's close friends and a subject of a later Tinker book, *The Pennells* (1951).

Tinker populated several other volumes with the rich and fascinating characters he found in the region, such as the man who, born in New Orleans, first brought the craps game to America; and the notorious madam of a Basin Street brothel. He also wrote a book on the African-American poetry of Louisiana and a bibliography of the French-language periodical press there. In 1953, he published *Creole City: Its Past and Its People*, an anecdotal history of New Orleans from the eighteenth century through the 1950s. The *Chicago Tribune* pronounced it the source of "a charming, factual account of how the city acquired its never fading cloak of glamor." But, in the *New York Times*, fellow Louisiana writer Robert Tallant thought that "much of it is composed of old pieces written long ago and here put together without careful editing."

*The Cult of the Gaucho and the Creation of a Literature* (1947) reflected Tinker's other passion—cowboys. He followed up with *The Horsemen of the Americas and the Literature They Inspired* (1953), a brief illustrated history of the caballeros of Argentina, Mexico, and the United States, with emphasis on the gauchos of Argentina. Tinker was struck by the fact that "the gaucho of Argentina, the huaso of Chile, the lanero of Venezuela, and the cowboy of North America were as much alike as Fords off the assembly line." He therefore decided that the nations producing men so similar should be bridges to better understanding, so he founded and served as president of the Tinker Foundation to promote the idea, to which he remained dedicated until his death. As he was completing his memoirs at age eighty-six, he wrote, "I am more firmly convinced than ever that the future, freedom, and prosperity of all the peoples of the Americas depend upon their mutual trust, friendship, and cooperation."

Tinker's large collection of Latin American Art is housed at the University of Texas at Austin, in the Hall of the Horsemen of the Americas. He also left an extensive collection of Lafcadio Hearn material to Harvard University.

PRINCIPAL WORKS: Lafcadio Hearn's American Days, 1924; Toucoutou, 1928 (novel); (with F. McK. Tinker) Old New Orleans, 1930; Les Cenelles (The Haws): Afro-American Poetry in Louisiana, 1930; Les Ecrits de la Langue Française en Louisiane au XIX Siècle, 1932; The Palingenesis of Craps, 1933; Bibliography of the French Newspapers and Periodicals of Louisiana, 1933; Gombo: The Creole Dialect of Louisiana, 1936; The Cult of the Gaucho and the Creation of a Literature, 1947; The Pennells, 1951; Creole City: Its Past and Its People, 1953; The Horsemen of the Americas and the Literature They Inspired, 1953; The Life and Literature of the Pampas, 1961; Corridos and Calaveras, 1961; Centaurs of Many Lands, 1964; The Splendid Spectacle of Portuguese Bull Fighting, 1967; The Machiavellian Madam of Basin Street & Other Tales of New Orleans, 1969; New Yorker Unlimited; the Memoirs of Edward Larocque Tinker, 1970.

ABOUT: The autobiographical material quoted above was written for Twentieth Century Authors, 1942 and Twentieth Century Authors First Supplement, 1955. Antiquarian Bookman May 10, 1952. Periodicals—Bookmark March 1931; Boston Transcript September 1, 1934; Chicago Tribune September 13, 1953; New York Times September 20, 1953; July 7, 1968; Publishers Weekly July 22, 1968.

**TODD, MABEL LOOMIS** (November 10, 1856–October 14, 1932), American editor and writer of travel and natural history books, was born in Cambridge, Massachusetts, the daughter of Eben Jenks Loomis, an astronomer and mathematician, and Mary Alden (Wilder) Loomis. Her family was descended from the original Puritan settlers, and her father had been an acquaintance of Thoreau, Whitman, and Burroughs. She was educated in private schools in Washington, D.C., and Boston, and after a year of social life in the nation's capital she married David Peck Todd in 1879. Two years later her husband was appointed professor of astronomy and director of the observatory at Amherst College in Massachusetts. Over the next few decades they traveled around the world to study eclipses of the sun and other phenomena. Todd's first-hand accounts of solar eclipses, as well as of the local cultures of Japan, Africa, Russia, and Chile were published in the leading American magazines. On her first trip to Japan she climbed Mount Fuji (the first woman to do so). The experience and knowledge acquired in this manner were embodied in her own books on astronomy (*Total Eclipses of the Sun* and *A Cycle of Sunsets*) and travel (*Corona and Coronet* and *Tripoli the Mysterious*) which sold well, and led to her being much in demand as a lecturer.

In Amherst Mabel Todd taught at private schools for young women, participated in church events, and helped to organize civic groups, notably the Amherst Historical Society and the local chapter of the Daughters of the American Revolution. She opened her house to those who cared for art, music, and literature, and established the Boston Authors' Club in her home. Among her friends who shared these cultural interests was William Austin Dickinson, the college's treasurer. Publicly she worked with him to develop and preserve the town's graceful natural environment; privately they carried on a thirteen-year love affair while remaining married to their spouses (who clearly knew of the relationship). At times they were aided by Austin's sister Lavinia. After Austin's death his wife Susan successfully challenged his will, which left a major bequest to Mabel.

Of greater importance is Mabel Todd's relationship to Austin's other sister, Emily. When Emily Dickinson died in 1886, over 1700 manuscript poems were discovered in her house. Some had been previously copied over for friends, but the vast bulk of them—written on scraps of paper and often sewn together in little packets—had remained largely unknown during the poet's life. Mabel Todd began the arduous task of deciphering the handwriting, collating the variants, arranging the poems chronologically, and transcribing them for publication. She worked carefully to establish the accurate text of each poem, but in general was obliged to give in to coeditor Thomas Wentworth Higginson's desire to "correct" Dickinson's idiosyncratic punctuation and syntax, notably her characteristic use of capital letters and dashes. With Higginson she published two series of Dickinson's poems in 1890 and 1891, and on her own a third series in 1896. In addition she edited a selection from the poet's letters. Mabel Todd was responsible for bringing the first volumes of Emily Dickinson's verse to the reading public, but her estrangement from the Dickinson family following Austin's death in 1895 forced her to postpone work on the remaining poems. Her daughter Millicent Todd Bingham drew upon her editorial work when she published her own edition of Dickinson's poems, *Bolts of Melody*, over a decade later.

In 1913 Todd became partially paralyzed, but in the last nineteen years of her life she continued to be culturally and socially active in Miami, Florida, where she wintered. Her papers are in the Boston Public Library.

PRINCIPAL WORKS: *Fiction*—Footprints, 1883. *Nonfiction*—

Total Eclipses of the Sun, 1894; Corona and Coronet, 1898; Witchcraft in New England, 1906 (address); A Cycle of Sunsets, 1910; Tripoli the Mysterious, 1912; The Thoreau Family Two Generations Ago (ed. M. T. Bingham) 1958. *As editor*—(with T. W. Higginson) Poems of Emily Dickinson, 1890, 1891, and 1896; Letters of Emily Dickinson, 1894, enlarged ed. 1931; A Cycle of Sonnets (by C. E. H. Whitton-Stone) 1896; Popular Astronomy (by J. D. Steele) 1899; (with M. T. Bingham) Bolts of Melody (by E. Dickinson) 1945. *Correspondence*—Austin and Mabel: The Amherst Affair and Love Letters of Austin Dickinson and Mabel Loomis Todd (ed. P. Longworth) 1984.

ABOUT: Walsh, J. E. This Brief Tragedy: Unraveling the Todd-Dickinson Affair, 1991. *Periodicals*—Harper's March 1930; New Republic April 23, 1984; New York Times October 15, 1932; New York Times Book Review March 4, 1984; Saturday Review of Literature November 19, 1932.

**\*TODD, RUTHVEN** (June 14, 1914–1978), British-born poet, editor, novelist, and essayist, wrote: "I was born in Edinburgh, Scotland, the eldest of ten children of W. J. W. Todd, A.R.S.A., architect, and Christian (Craik) Todd. My ancestry is mixed, Scottish, English, Irish, Spanish and French. Literary ancestors on my father's side include Sir Walter Scott, and Henry Mackenzie, 'The Man of Feeling,' and on my mother's side the Scottish man of letters, George Lillie Craik, whose son married Dinah Mulock, author of *The Little Lame Prince* and *John Halifax, Gentleman* and Sir Henry Craik, the educator and politician, who wrote a history of English literature, a life of Jonathan Swift, and other books.

"This literary background had, I fear, little influence on me as a child. I wanted to paint and it was assumed that I would follow my father as an architect. At Fettes College, Edinburgh, I succeeded in winning the school prize for painting, and also contributed verse to the *Fettesian*; during several vacations I worked in my father's office, but found little to attract me in architecture, so, at the age of sixteen, I entered the Edinburgh College of  Art, studying painting. I quickly discovered that I had technical facility but no originality and gave up painting to work as a farm-laborer on the Isle of Mull, off the West of Scotland. During the two years I spent there I devoted my spare time, such as it was, to writing poems, and my first poems were published in the *Bookman*, having been sent there by Mr. Geoffrey Grigson, the editor of *New Verse*. I next spent a short time in Edinburgh, as assistant editor of the *Scottish Bookman*, and then went to London. During the Thirties I wrote many poems, publishing them in such papers as *New Verse*, the *Listener*, *Poetry*, etc. As a method of staying alive I did anything that came along, working in art galleries (including the First International Surrealist Exhibition in 1936, and a gallery that specialized in pottery), as a tutor, as John Lehmann's secretary in the Hogarth Press, as a publisher's reader and so on.

"At the outbreak of war I worked for a short time

°RIV en

on the embryonic *Horizon*, and then joined the Civil Defense, from which I was ejected as unfit for service in 1942. After that I worked for a while in a bookstore, Zwemmer's, in the Charing Cross Road, and, after a flying-bomb damaged my London flat, retired to live in a farm house in Essex. There I lived by writing extremely poor detective novels, at terrific speed, under the pseudonym of 'R. T. Campbell.' All this time I had been working on William Blake and his paintings, and, with the aid of a Pilgrim Trust grant, I visited the United States in 1947; for a short while I worked, teaching creative writing at Iowa State University, a thing I had no right to do on a visitor's visa, so I left the United States for six weeks, returning as a permanent resident in 1948. In 1952 I married."

---

Ruthven Todd, poet, novelist, and critic, is now remembered as an engaging personality and man of letters as well as a graceful and much-liked minor poet of the 1930s and 1940s; his most important book, *Tracks in the Snow*, critical essays, is still consulted—and, perhaps more important, enjoyed. As a novelist he has sunk without trace. Some of his later poems, written in his last years in America, are lacking, as Trevor Tolley writes in the *Oxford Companion to Twentieth-Century Poetry*, in any sense of "emotional involvement." In his final years, in the Balearic island of Mallorca he wrote nothing substantial; possibly his heavy drinking helped to shorten the span of his life, since he was subject to bouts of pneumonia—the last of which killed him.

But Todd, for all his life was somewhat difficult and disorderly at times—always in need of money—and for all that his mental faculties ultimately went to pieces so far as serious work was concerned, was a born scholar, a marvelous talker about literature and poetry—of which he had an enormous fund of intelligent knowledge—and a genial and good friend to other writers. There were not a few young poets who, during World War II while he was working in Zwemmer's famous and poetry-rich bookshop in central London, were eternally grateful to him for kindly guidance as to what to buy and what not to buy. Added to this, Todd did play a small but significant part in the British poetry scene throughout the 1930s and World War II.

At first, from 1948, his career seemed to pick up in America, when he was running the tiny Weekend Press (1950–1954) in New York; as late as 1972 he spent a year at the State University of New York at Buffalo, when he was appointed Visiting Professor there; but this was not very productive. He wrote nothing of significance after that.

Todd told *Contemporary Poets* that he had "printed rather more than I should have done in the way of weak, derivative and just simply bad poems." He added, with modest humor but significance, "what could have been expected from a Gemini whose given name, although spelled Ruthven, is pronounced 'Riven?' The Shorter Oxford English Dictionary defines that as 'Split, cloven, rent, torn asunder.'" He is seen at his best in *Garland for the Winter Solstice: Selected Poems*, which

gives a generous choice of poetry written between the later 1930s and the mid-1950s. The back of the jacket carries praise from three notable judges of poetry. Richard Wilbur wrote: "These poems have . . . erudition, heart, and a casual eloquence." W. H. Auden wrote: "I always think of . . . Todd as a Nineteenth Century Country Clergyman who has mysteriously managed to get born and to survive in this hectic age. . . . As a 'nature' poet, he is almost the only one today who is a real naturalist and can tell one bird or flower from another—his erudition in these matters makes me very jealous. It is pleasant, too, in reading a selection . . . to find a poet who has grown steadily better, more himself, with each succeeding year." (It is salutary to recollect, apropos of Auden's tribute to Todd as "nature poet," that in 1954 he received, from the National Institute of Art and Letters, a citation for his "loving devotion to natural history.") But perhaps the most impressive of all the endorsements of Todd's poetic gifts—and the one for which he was most grateful—was Marianne Moore's comment: that he was a "poet both in words and with the brush, uniquely skilled as an observer, indeed a true Renaissance figure of many proficiencies." This very early (1936) poem, "Sometimes Ghosts," is perhaps as evocative of Todd's quality as a poet than any other:

Sometimes I watch the ghosts walking,
Tall shapes that I know to expect now;
Sometimes, after midnight, I hear them working,
Mower and tractor against scythe and plough.

Sometimes I am dead when they visit me
Carrying presents to place upon my bed;
I am the other side of time, in a country
Where the owl talks and the mouse leads.

Sometimes I call a ghost by name,
He will not answer; he does not know my voice.
I meet them, neatly clothed in purple flame;
Sometimes I am afraid of their egg-smooth faces.

Sometimes I know I am a ghost myself
But not one of them, a second-hand spirit
That is no longer useful, is left upon the shelf.
Sometimes I think I am a talking ferret.

Todd's three "serious" novels—apart from the crime ones written as by "R. T. Campbell"—were *Over the Mountain*, *The Lost Traveller*, and *Loser's Choice*. As the *Times Literary Supplement* wrote of the first: "the theme a too signally Kafkaesque one, in which the hero is transported to another land has already been tackled so superbly i.e. by Kafka that it is hazardous for a new writer to embark upon it, and Mr. Todd has not been particularly successful in his attempt." *Loser's Choice*, which came twelve years later, and was on a similar type of theme, was not better received. The second of these novels, *The Lost Traveller*, was reprinted as an example of science fiction in 1968, but did not do any better then than it had in 1944.

Todd's most distinguished book of prose was the collection of four related essays entitled *Tracks in the Snow*. They explore the effects that the awakenings of modern science had upon certain mystic poets and painters of the eighteenth–nineteenth century, in particular William Blake and Henry Fuseli. Mark Schorer, in the *New York Herald Tribune Weekly Book Review*, called Todd "a gifted exemplar of the British tradition of amateur scholarship." Each essay, he thought, was "rich in tangential suggestion, as sinuously vernacular as a poem." The *Spectator* believed that the essays did "shed some light on Blake's mythology." Most students of Blake would still agree that they are essential reading—and most have particularly enjoyed the pleasantly ambulatory fashion in which Todd conducted his exploration of his theme.

Todd also wrote a number of pleasing juvenile items, some of them in collaboration with the artist Paul Galdone. He edited Gilchrist's *Life of William Blake* and Christopher Smart's *A Song to David*—at a time when Smart had hardly been rediscovered.

PRINCIPAL WORKS: *Poetry*—(with others) Poems, 1938; (with others) Poets of Tomorrow, 1939; Ten Poems, 1940; Until Now, 1942; Poems for a Penny, 1942; The Acreage of the Heart, 1943; The Planet in My Hand, 1946; In Other Worlds, 1951; A Mantelpiece of Shells, 1954; Garland for the Winter Solstice: Selected Poems, 1961. *Novels*—Over the Mountain, 1939; The Lost Traveller, 1942; Loser's Choice, 1953. As "R. T. Campbell"—Unholy Dying, 1945; Take Thee a Sharp Knife, 1946; Adventure with a Goat: Two Stories, 1946; Bodies in a Bookshop, 1946; Death for Madame, 1946; The Death Cap, 1946; Swing Low, Swing Death, 1946. *Juvenile*—First Animal Book, 1946; Space Cat, 1952; Trucks, Tractors and Trailer, 1954; Space Cat Visits Venus, 1955; Space Cat Meets Mars, 1957; Space Cat and the Kittens, 1958; Tan's Fish, 1958. *Other*—The Laughing Mulatto: The Story of Alexandre Dumas, 1940; Tracks in the Snow, 1946; The Tropical Fish Book, 1953; William Blake the Artist, 1971. As *editor*—Gilchrist's Life of Blake, 1942, rev. 1945; Smart's Song to David, with other poems, 1947; William Blake, Songs of Innocence and Experience, 1947; Blake: Selected Poetry, 1960; Blake's Dante Plates, 1968.

ABOUT: The autobiographical material quoted above was written for Twentieth Century Authors First Supplement, 1955. Fuller, M. (ed.) More Junior Authors, 1963; Hamilton, I. (ed.) Oxford Companion to Twentieth-Century Poetry, 1994; Vinson, J. (ed.) Contemporary Poets, 1975. *Periodicals*—New York Herald Tribune Weekly Book Review July 6, 1947; Spectator January 17, 1947; Times Literary Supplement March 18, 1939.

**TOLLER, ERNST** (December 1, 1893–May 22, 1939), German playwright, autobiographer, prose and speech writer, and poet, was born in Samotschin, Posen, East Prussia (now Szamocin, Poland), the son of a Jewish merchant who died when the boy was sixteen.

Toller had a lonely childhood. Educated at the Bromberg Gymnasium, he began, soon after his father died, wandering in Denmark and France. He

attended a few desultory courses at the Universities of Heidelberg and Munich, but, sensitive to the extreme anti-Semitism at those institutions, he preferred to go to Grenoble (where he read law). When World War I began, feeling intensely patriotic, he instantly returned from Lyons in France to join up. He saw over a year's service in

the trenches before having a breakdown, and being discharged as unfit. By that time he was as disillusioned with war as were his counterparts from France and Great Britain: such men as Barbusse, Duhamel, Sorley, Sassoon, and Graves. He went back to Heidelberg and Munich to complete his courses, now with more seriousness of purpose. At Heidelberg he helped form a Students' League for Peace, and thus drew the attention of the police. He fled to Munich, where he fell in with the socialist and political journalist Kurt Eisner, who had in 1917 gone over into active opposition to the Kaiser's government. He joined Eisner's USPD (Independent Social Democratic Party) and played a major part in the organization of students, for which he was imprisoned for a few months in 1918. When Eisner formed his short-lived Bavarian Socialist Republic he played a leading role in it. After Eisner was murdered, an act which led to the formation of the Bavarian Soviet Republic (*Bayerische Räterepublik*), Toller became Chairman of the Social Council and Commander of the Red Army (officers and men were to address one another with the familiar "Du," he ordered). The Republic was soon violently suppressed, and Toller was tried for high treason—and, despite respected character witnesses such as Thomas Mann and the sociologist Max Weber, sentenced to five years in prison, all of which time he served. Toller was fortunate, however. He had originally been sentenced to death—only the appointed firing squad would not cooperate!

Toller had already written his first play to be produced: *Die Wandlung* (translated as *Transfiguration*). This is in thirteen *Stationen*, or tableaux, and is a fairly crude and rhetorical affair, although it is said to have played well in its time, and to have been effective. Here Toller combined realism with expressionist techniques, such as the portrayal of what is going on in the mind of the protagonist—a middle-class or bourgeois Jewish patriot, Friedrich, who is transformed into a sensitive socialist by his experiences of war. The play, like all Toller's dramatic work, is strident throughout— he has been much criticized for this; yet his best plays survive. *Transfiguration* was good enough that Mann (as his diary shows) wrote a testimonial for it.

In prison Toller wrote both plays and poetry, in particular the sequence *Das Schwalbenbuch* (1924, *The Swallow Book*), inspired by the attempts of swallows to build nests in his prison cell—and claimed by a few as the most lasting of all his works. *Masse Mensch* (1921; translated as *Man and the Masses*) depicts the Munich uprising, and shows that Toller was no simple-minded Marxist. It was produced with great success in Berlin in 1921. When it appeared in the translation by Louis Untermeyer in 1924 the *Times Literary Supplement* (1924) wrote that his play proved "that his writing is not a mere 'war reaction,' that his art is not mere war propaganda." D. J. Enright commented retrospectively, again in the *Times Literary Supplement* (1991) that it suffered "from the typical inexpressiveness of expressionism." Most critics, however, considered it a masterpiece of expressionist theater.

The story of the torment and death of the protagonist, simply named "Woman," works well within the expressionistic parameters.

*Die Maschinenstürmer* (1922; translated as *The Machine-Wreckers*), which just preceded *Man and the Masses* in its translated form, is set in 1815 Nottingham, among the English Luddites, the group famous for wrecking industrial machinery because they believed it would put them out of work. In the play, a prophetic leader arises who condemns them as stupid, but the group kills him. This is at the least a magnificent spectacle, and the *Times Literary Supplement* (1923) once again commended it, pointing out that Toller handled his characters with a masterly hand, using them in numbers to produce an orchestral effect: "its claim to attention as a work of art is strong enough to stand alone."

What may very well be his best play, *Hinkemann* (1924; translated as *Brokenbow*), is somewhat of an exception in his drama. Dealing with a similar basic theme to that treated by Hemingway in *The Sun Also Rises* (or *Fiesta*), that of a veteran emasculated in battle who cannot satisfy his wif and who takes a lowly job as a sacrifice to her, it is more realistic. Toller also wrote comedies, such as his prophetic exposure of the young Hitler as a rabble-rousing barber in *Der entfesselte Wotan* (The raging Wotan, 1923), but these are hardly known.

When Hitler came to power Toller was in Switzerland, which may have saved his life, since Goebbels was quick to number him as a major "public enemy." In the last six years of his life he gave, his biographer Richard Dove writes, more than two hundred speeches, lectures and broadcasts on Nazism and its menace. He was in England for two-and-a-half of these years, and there he made friends with many notable people, including Harold Laski and Edward Crankshaw. He worked hard for the Spanish Republic, by organizing food relief. By the time he reached New York his marriage to an actress much younger than himself had broken up and he was suffering from depression and insomnia. He committed suicide by hanging himself in New York's Mayflower Hotel. Thomas Mann called him a "martyr of his age" and referred to the news in his diary as "terrible"—he had been asked to speak at the funeral, but was unable to get there. Toller also wrote comedies, such as his prophetic exposure of the young Hitler as a rabble-rousing barber in *Der entfesselte Wotan* (The raging Wotan, 1923), but these are still hardly known.

Toller left a superb set of letters from prison, *Briefe aus dem Gefängis* (1935; translated as *Look Through the Bars*), and an early, poignant and invaluable biography, *Eine jugend in Deutschland* (1933, translated as *I Was a German*). Its introduction is dated as "the day my books were burned in Germany." It tells his story up to his release from prison in 1924, and, wrote M. L. Becker in *New York Herald Tribune Books*, was "furiously timely and exciting." To the *Nation* it cried "out on every page" "because it is never formally drawn up." It is still in print in its English translation, as a part of a series devoted to "studies in fascism."

PRINCIPAL WORKS IN ENGLISH TRANSLATION: *Drama*—Seven Plays (tr. by others: Transfiguration, Man and the Masses, The Machine-Wreckers, Brokenbow, Hoppla! Such is Life!, The Blind Goddess, Draw the Fires!, and Mary Baker Eddy) 1935. *Autobiography*—I Was a German (tr. E. Crankshaw) 1934. *Letters*—Look Through the Bars: Letters from Prison (tr. R. E. Roberts) 1937. *Poetry*—The Swallow Book (tr. A. Dukes) 1974. ABOUT: Benson, R. German Expressionist Drama, 1984; Bullivant, K. (ed.) Culture and Society in the Weimar Republic, 1978; Columbia Dictionary of Modern European Literature, 1980; Dove, R. Revolutionary Socialism in the Work of Ernst Toller, 1986; Dove, R. He Was a German: A Biography of Ernst Toller, 1991; Kane, M. Weimar Germany and the Limits of Political Art, 1987; Ossar, M. Anarchism in the Dramas of Ernst Toller, 1980; Pittock, M. Ernst Toller, 1979; Sokel, W. The Writer in Extremis, 1959; Spalek, J. M. Ernst Toller and His Critics, 1968; Willibrand, W. A. Ernst Toller: Product of Two Revolutions, 1941. *Periodicals*—Nation April 4, 1934; New York Herald Tribune Books April 8, 1934; Times (London) May 3,1939; Times Literary Supplement March 28, 1923; January 10, 1924; February 1, 1991.

**TOLSTOY, ALEXEY NIKOLAEVICH** (December 22, 1882 [January 9, 1883 new style]– February 22, 1945), Russian novelist, playwright, essayist, publicist, and poet, was born in Nikolaevsk (now Pugachyov), Samara, into a family of Volga gentry. He was distantly related to the poet Aleksey Tolstoy (1817–1875) and, through his mother, to Turgenev. An extremely able, if often facile and superficial writer, Tol-  stoy made several volte-faces, from liberal nobleman to anti-Bolshevik to influential about-faces apologist for Stalin. At his death Tolstoy was mourned by the Soviet state as a great loss to its letters. Much attention—almost all of this irrelevant to literary merit—was lavished upon him by the Soviets, and he received many state prizes.

As a student at the St. Petersburg Technological Institute Tolstoy thought of himself as a poet and member of the symbolist movement. He began to publish his work at the age of twenty-three. His poetry is skillfully imitative of various symbolists (Balmont and Ivanov in particular, later Sologub). His prose, however, is well known for its litheness and vitality, if not for its profundity. By 1917 Tolstoy had written seven bright plays, mainly comedies, and a number of novels and tales. Among the prose works were *Sorochi skazki* (Magpie stories, 1910), retold folktales, and the fine and memorable *Khromoy barin* (The lame prince, 1912), which has been called "Homeric" and perhaps deserves such an epithet.

During part of World War I Tolstoy was a war correspondent. In 1918–1919 he served in the White Army, in the propaganda department, a job that involved denouncing the Reds. Then he went into exile, first to Paris and later to Berlin. While in exile he wrote the first of his major books, *Destvo Nikity* (1919–1922, translated as *Nikita's Childhood*), "one of the great pictures of childhood in Russian literature," in the words of Janko Lavrin.

Tolstoy set most of his prose tales in his own native Volga region, which Marc Slonim aptly described as "a kind of Russian Arkansas," and delighted in portraying eccentric types and grotesques. The poet and critic Alexander Blok wrote that he admired Tolstoy's "blood, and fat, and lust, and . . . snobbery" but he objected to his "hooliganism, his immature approach to life." Slonim thought it was this "immaturity" that was responsible for Tolstoy's "literary and political mutations": he followed his impulses rather than his reason. The great poet and critic Mikhail Kuzmin had early referred to Tolstoy's "superficiality and excessive concern with the extrinsic and with chance." Thus, there might be a sense in which this gifted writer never really quite grew up.

Tolstoy had been a liberal before the Revolution. After turning against the Bolsheviks and living in Paris as a notedly ferocious anti-Bolshevik, he grew homesick. He felt he needed to be in Russia to work properly. Under the influence of the Berlin "Changing the Landmarks" movement (exiles who had changed their minds), he obtained permission to return to Russia. He had serious enemies, but his rise was rapid. The astuter Bolsheviks saw in him a man who could put things in an acceptable way. He was never original, but he was a highly capable journalist. With his science-fiction tales of that time (based ingeniously in H. G. Wells), such as *Aelita* (1923), about an attempt to colonize Mars, he gained an increasingly wide Soviet audience. This, ingratiating to the Soviets, is also an undeniably enjoyable yarn. Zamyatin wrote of it: "Tolstoy attempted to transfer from the mail train to the airplane of the fantastic, but all he managed was to jump up and plop back on the ground with awkwardly spread wings, like a fledgling jackdaw that has fallen out of its nest (daily life). Tolstoy's Mars is no further than some forty versts from Ryazan; there is even a shepherd there, in the standard red shirt . . . . The only figure in the novel that is alive . . . is the Red Army soldier Gusev. He alone speaks, all the others recite." Two more science-fiction novels, and several potboilers, followed this. Tolstoy made the right friends in the right places, watched how politics developed, but did not join in the Communist party. A *bon viveur* and lover of drink and women, he was, as Slonim wrote, "crafty," but he was also not without a certain reckless courage—for these were dangerous times for everyone.

While in exile Tolstoy had written the first part of the trilogy that became *Khozhdenie po mukam* (1921–1941, translated as *The Road to Calvary*): *Syostry* (Sisters). This was a work of great journalistic brilliance and value. The first volume deals with the sort of people Tolstoy mixed with when he was young: "decadents," Old Believers, aesthetes; the second, *1918*, with the collapse of 1917–1918; and the third, *Murky Dawn*, with the beginning of the Soviet paradise. This work a highly readable, clever and intelligent narrative, written in a style that had already been established before the Bolshevik Revolution. In it, history itself, Janko Lavrin suggested, is "treated in a manner transcending the peripeties of a mere class struggle."

In his unfinished historical trilogy *Pyotr Pervy* (1929–1945, translated as *Peter the Great* and *Peter the First*) lies whatever claims to international literary importance Tolstoy may have. Both Marxists and anti-Communists have praised it lavishly. The portrait of Peter, based on careful research, is—at least initially—enthrallingly vivid. Yet the book is plotless, or, more to the point, without design of any kind; it is, too, a glorification of Lenin and above all of Stalin (as Peter). Seeming to be a great work while it is being read, it is perhaps, in light of reflection, a less truly impressive one.

Tolstoy's plays were cleverly written and appealing to audiences, but in them he was less ambiguous than in his novels, even in the dramatizations of his historical works. They were written to please officials. It will be interesting to see what the critics of post-Soviet Russia will finally make of this talented, prolific, and versatile writer. Will they agree with Zamyatin, who wrote of the first part of *the Road to Calvary*, which he certainly deprecated in part, that it was "the last old Russian novel, the last fruit of realism, of the real Tolstoy—Lev . . . true, the wineskin is old, but it is filled with good wine. Gulping down some of the pages, the reader becomes intoxicated. . . . " Or will they agree with Martin Seymour-Smith, who summed him up by writing that "for the Soviets, who were touchy, he symbolized a reconciliation between culture and communism."

PRINCIPAL WORKS IN ENGLISH TRANSLATION: The Road to Calvary (tr. R. H. Townsend) 1923 (Sisters); Imperial Majesty (tr. H. C. Matheson) 1932 (tr. by E. Bone and E. Burns as Peter the Great, 1936); Darkness and Dawn (tr. E. Bone and E. Burns) 1936 (tr. in 1945 as The Road to Calvary); The Death Box (tr. B. G. Guerney) 1936; Fox Fables (tr. G. Hanna) 1936; Bread (tr. S. Garry) 1938; Daredevils (tr. L. Fromberg) 1942; Russian Tales for Children (tr. E. Shimnskaya) 1944; Nikita's Childhood (adapted by F. Y. Vladimirsky and V. A. Zaitsev) 1953 (tr. V. L. Dutt, 1945); The Golden Key (tr. E. Hartley) 1947; Selected Stories, 1949; Ordeal (tr. I. and T. Litvinov) 1953 (The Road to Calvary complete); Aelita (tr. L. Flaxman) 1954; The Garin Death Ray (tr. G. Hanna) 1957.

ABOUT: Columbia Dictionary of Modern European Literature, 1947, 1980; Field, A. The Complection of Russian Literature, 1971; Gasiorowska, X. The Image of Peter the Great in Russian Fiction, 1979; Lavrin, J. A Panorama of Russian Literature, 1973; Seymour-Smith, M. Macmillan Guide to Modern World Literature, 1986; Slonim, M. Soviet Russian Literature, 1977; Zamyatin, E. A Soviet Heretic (tr. M. Ginsburg) 1970. *Periodicals*—New York Times February 24, 1945; New York Times Book Review February 2, 1986; Times (London) February 26, 1945.

**TOMLINSON, HENRY MAJOR** (June 21, 1873–February 5, 1958), English travel writer, essayist, and novelist, was born in Poplar. His father, who was a foreman at the West India Docks, died in 1888, soon after losing the family savings in a foolhardy speculation. As a result, young Henry's formal education ended at an early age, his uncle finding him a position as a clerk in a shipping firm. He disliked the environment of the office, but spent much time wandering the docks, which he later said formed his university. Encouraged by his mother, he embarked on a course of independent study, specializing in geology, botany, and navigation, in which he was so successful that in 1895 he was considered as a member of the Jackson-Harmsworth Polar Expedition. To his bitter regret, medical opinion advised against his taking part.

Tomlinson stuck it out in the shipping office until 1904, when he joined the staff of the *Morning Leader*, to which he was already a contributor. One  of his assignments was to spend several weeks, in midwinter, living with a fleet of trawlers fishing off Dogger Bank; but his first major adventure was an expedition that took him up the Amazon and Madeira rivers, in the first English steamer to make such a journey. He traveled as the ship's purser, and the experience led to the publication of his first book, *The Sea and the Jungle* (1912).

War interrupted his progress as a writer. Between 1915 and 1917 he was an official correspondent for the *Daily News* (with which paper the *Morning Leader* had been amalgamated in 1912) and the *Times*, at the General H.Q. of the British Armies in France. After 1917 he became literary editor of the *Nation*—until 1923, when he was able to turn free-lance. There, he established a reputation for reflectively descriptive travel writing (he was once called, in the *Manchester Guardian*, "the greatest living master of tersely comprehensive description") that owed much to his reading of and admiration for Melville, Thoreau, and Emerson. *Old Junk* collected articles and sketches written between 1907 and 1918; *London River* was a rhapsody to his beloved docklands, a theme returned to in *Below London Bridge*, a picture-book in which the text was accompanied by photographs taken by Tomlinson's son; *Tidemarks* took him further afield again, on a voyage through the Suez Canal to the islands of the Malay archipelago, a journey that also inspired his first novel.

*Gallions Reach* appeared in 1927 and told the story of a clerk, Jim Colet, who, having struck his employer dead, escapes justice by sailing for the tropics. The book was awarded the Femina Vie Heureuse prize. Reviewers admired the style and the scope of the narrative but found it flawed as a novel, a verdict which was passed on all Tomlinson's fiction. William Plomer, reviewing (for the *Spectator*) *The Snows of Helicon*, a strange visionary adventure in which an English architect sets out to save a Greek temple from destruction, wrote: "Tomlinson makes considerable demands upon the reader, and it is doubtful whether the reader, though careful and hopeful, is adequately rewarded for his efforts to cope with an episodic story, nebulous characters, a moral of no great originality, and prose which tends to be jerky and mannered."

Tomlinson's nonfiction became increasingly concerned with the subject of war. In *Mars His Idiot*, which the *Times Literary Supplement* described as "a long grumble written in a mood of vivacious impatience," he published a series of essays denouncing war and, when war did break out, he wrote a

series of monthly articles for the *Atlantic*, published in book form as *Wind Is Rising*. Further wartime writings appered in *Turn of the Tide*; his last novel *The Trumpet Shall Sound*, published a year before his death, when he was well into his eighties, looked back at the Blitz and its effects on different types of character.

Tomlinson, who had married in 1899, spent his last years in Dorsetshire, and was buried at Abbotsbury. The odd-man-out among his books is a brief study of Norman Douglas.

PRINCIPAL WORKS: *Nonfiction*—The Sea and the Jungle, 1912; Old Junk, 1918; London River, 1921; Waiting for Daylight, 1922; Tidemarks, 1924; Under the Red Ensign, 1926; Gifts of Fortune, 1926; Out of Soundings, 1931; Norman Douglas, 1931; South to Cadiz, 1934; Below London Bridge, 1934; Mars His Idiot, 1935; The Wind Is Rising, 1941; The Turn of the Tide, 1945; The Face of the Earth, 1950; A Mingled Yarn, 1953. *Fiction*—Gallions Reach, 1927; All Our Yesterdays, 1930; The Snows of Helicon, 1933; Pipe All Hands, 1937; The Day Before, 1940; Morning Light, 1946; The Trumpet Shall Sound, 1957.

ABOUT: Contemporary Authors vol. 118 1986; Dictionary of National Biography 1951–1960; Who's Who 1958. *Periodicals*—Manchester Guardian January 30, 1940; New York Times February 6, 1958; Spectator September 15, 1933; Times (London) February 6, 1958; Times Literary Supplement November 30, 1935.

**TONSON, JACOB.** See **BENNETT, ARNOLD**

**TORRE, LILLIAN DE LA.** See **DE LA TORRE, LILLIAN**

**TORRENCE, FREDERIC RIDGELY** (November 27, 1874–December 25, 1950), American poet and playwright, wrote: "Ridgely Torrence comes of a stock now in its fourth century of settlement in this country. He was born in Xenia, Ohio, a place which has been described as more Southern than any other north of the Mason and Dixon Line. He spent two of his boyhood years, largely on horseback, in Santa Ana, California. For two years he attended Miami University, then entered Princeton as a junior. There he was on the editorial boards of the *Nassau Literary Magazine* and the *Princeton Tiger*. From Princeton he came to New York, where for six years he was a librarian in the New York Public Library. Later he was an editor of the *Cosmopolitan*, and from 1920 to 1933 was poetry editor of the *New Republic*. Soon after coming to New York, he published his first book of verse, became linked in poetic activity with his friends William Vaughn Moody and Edwin Arlington Robinson and with the former made a grand tour of Europe and North Africa.

"At the same time his natural inclination was leading him toward the theatre. Believing then as now that the state 'cries out for poetry,' he cast his first two published plays in verse. But after these experiments he turned reluctantly to a medium of greater immediacy, the poetry of idiom and of folkways. For his source he turned to the American Negro, whose possibilities had never been taken seriously in the theatre. His first Play for a Negro Theatre, *Granny Maumee*, was produced by the New York Stage Society in 1914, but with a white cast. It was produced in 1917 at the Garden and Garrick Theatres, and a Negro cast was collected with great difficulty. There were no serious Negro  actors, for there had been no such plays. With the *Plays for a Negro Theatre* the racial group was launched into an artistic milieu in whch it has flourished ever since, thus opening the way to such plays as *The Emperor Jones*, *Porgy*, *The Green Pastures*, and *Mamba's Daughters*, all of which included actors trained in the Torrence plays.

"But at no period in his career has Torrence been diverted from his lifelong absorption in poetry itself and all through these years he was writing his own poetry. At intervals he has given readings and talks on poetry, chiefly at colleges. In 1938 he was Poet in Residence at Antioch College. In 1939 he began, for the Rockefeller Foundation, a National Survey of the Negro Theatre, and to this end spend the winter working with the Karamu Theatre, Cleveland, the oldest Negro theatre in the country. In 1940 he edited the *Selected Letters* of Edwin Arlington Robinson, and in 1941 he brought out a volume of his own, entitled *Poems*. In the latter year he was appointed Fellow of Creative Literature at Miami University, Oxford, Ohio."

Although Ridgely Torrence was praised during his lifetime, he did not achieve lasting popularity and is now better remembered for his close friendships with Robert Frost, Edwin Markham, William Vaughn Moody, and Edwin Arlington Robinson than for his verse. It was his work as an editor, above all, especially on the *New Republic* that brought him into contact with such eminent writers. In this capacity, too, he helped introduced both Wallace Stevens and Hart Crane to American readers.

Torrence had once been considered a promising poet, but he was never able to establish himself as a major voice, and is now hardly read. His first collection, *The House of a Hundred Lights* (1899), consisted of a twenty-seven-page poem written in the style of *The Rubaiyat of Omar Khayyam*. His next book, *Hesperides*, did not appear until 1925. In the title poem a young man dreams of a better world and has a vision that the golden apples of Hesperus's daughters are within his reach. However, he finds the apples bitter and returns to reality only to realize that a better world is a possibility. "So his vision had brought one thing from the waves he had passed, / For his eyes held fast to the fire-like seed of his gleam; / He had brought that back for the fruit of a better dream." In the *Saturday Review of Literature* (1925) Louis Untermeyer said that the poem held the "mysterious ichor which preserves a few poems beyond their generations." But Torrence failed to make a real impression with

such vague poetry. However, Robert Frost dedicated *A Passing Glimpse*, a new poem, "To Ridgely Torrence / On Last Looking into His 'Hesperides.'" Despite positive comments from personal friends Torrence did not publish another book of lyric poetry for sixteen years; when *Poems* finally appeared in 1941 it contained only fourteen new poems— along with the verse previously published in *Hesperides*. Writing in the *Saturday Review of Literature* (1941) Louis Untermeyer admitted that Torrence was a real puzzle; he believed that the new volume "presents a continuing problem, a conflict without solution. . . . there is the question of power withheld or diminished, the creative energy dissipated, the expectation unfulfilled." Despite his bafflement, however, Untermeyer went on to write that the "very restraint which limits the expression of a lifetime to thirty-four poems emphasizes the tensity of 'The Bird and the Tree,' the unforgettable poem of a lynching; 'The Singers in a Cloud,' one of the finest lyrical poems of the period; 'Eye Witness,' an evocation of the second coming of Christ seen through the eyes of a tramp; and 'The Son,' which packs a life tragedy in sixteen lyrical lines." Although critical praise was again forthcoming—a 1942 Shelley Memorial Award; the title of Poet of the Year from the National Poetry Center that same year; and a $5,000 fellowship from the Academy of American Poets in 1947 and election to its Board of Chancellors three years later— Torrence would complete only two more poems during the final nine years of his life. These were included in a reprint of *Poems* published posthumously.

"Perhaps the aspect of Torrence's career for which he will be most remembered is his important contribution to the role of the Negro in American literature," Clum writes in his monograph. "Before Torrence's three Negro plays, there has been no *serious* drama about the Negro in America. Negroes were presented either as faithful, if stupid, servants, or as comic characters. Torrence presented the Negro not only as a viable dramatic character but also as a serious actor in the legitimate theater." Torrence's interest in the African-American experience had its roots in his childhood. His home town, Xenia, Ohio, was a stop on the underground railroad and became home to many blacks after the Civil War. African-American children were among his childhood playmates. Torrence's *Plays for a Negro Theater* succeeded at the box office and led the way for both white and black playwrights to turn "to the Negro as a rich source of dramatic material." *Granny Maumee* tells the story of an African-American woman, blinded in a futile effort to save her son from being burned alive by a white mob, who now discovers that her granddaughter has given birth to a child who is half white, the father being the grandson of one of her son's murderers. "This was the first time that a New York audience was presented with a picture of a Negro's bitterness toward the white man, much less a depiction as powerful as *Granny Maumee*," Clum writes. "Granny's horror that the blood of her race would be tainted with white blood must have had a great deal of dramatic impact in 1917." *The Rider of Dreams* concerns an African-American man who, wants "room to dream my dreams an' make my own music." *Simon the Cyrenian*, a Biblical drama in verse, recounts the incident of Simon being forced to carry Christ's cross on the day of his crucifixion. "That Jesus' cross bearer was black man," as the early painters represented him, is a fact that holds a certain suggestion bearing upon a phase of modern society," Torrence commented.

On the whole, Torrence was more important to American poetry as a friend to poets and a discerning editor than as a poet himself.

PRINCIPAL WORKS: *Poetry*—The House of a Hundred Lights, 1899; Hesperides, 1925; Poems, by Ridgely Torrence, 1941, rev. ed. 1952. *Drama*—El Dorado: A Tragedy, 1903; Abelard and Heloise, 1907; Granny Maumee, The Rider of Dreams, Simon the Cyrenian: Plays for a Negro Theater, 1917. *Biography*—The Story of John Hope, 1948. *Juvenile*—The Story of Glo, from the Heike Monogatari, 1935. *As editor*—Selected Letters of Edwin Arlington Robinson, 1941; The Last Poems of Anna Hempstead Branch, 1944.

ABOUT: The autobiographical material quoted above was written for Twentieth Century Authors, 1942. Clum, J. M. Ridgely Torrence, 1972; Dictionary of American Biography Suppl. 4, 19xx; Dictionary of Literary Biography vol. 54 1987; Dunbar, O. A House in Chicago, 1947; Hagedorn, H. Edwin Arlington Robinson, 1938; Isaacs, E. J. R. The Negro in the American Theater, 1947; Mason, D. G. Music in My Time and Other Reminiscences, 1938; Moody, W. V. Letters to Harriet, 1935; Rittenhouse, J. B. The Younger American Poets, 1904; Smith, C. P. Where the Light Falls: A Portrait of Edwin Arlington Robinson, 1965. *Periodicals*—New York Times December 26, 1950; Saturday Review of Literature May 16, 1925; July 19, 1941.

**TOVEY, DONALD FRANCIS** (July 17, 1875–July 10, 1940), English musician and writer, created a knight in 1935, was born at Eton, where his father  (later becoming rector at Worplesdon, Surrey) was then a master at the public school. Neither the Rev. Duncan Tovey nor his wife was musical, but the young Donald quickly revealed a marked aptitude for singing and composition. He did not receive a traditional schooling; instead his musical upbringing, up to the age of nineteen, was put in the hands of Sophie Weisse. At her initiative Tovey was tutored by, among others, Walter Parratt and Charles Parry. His piano playing was extraordinarily accomplished and his public performances included a concert with the famous violinist Joseph Joachim, whom he had first met in Berlin when aged nine.

Tovey was the first recipient of the Lewis Nettleship memorial scholarship in 1894, when he went to Balliol College, Oxford, from which he graduated in 1898. During the next few years he performed a number of chamber music concerts, mostly arranged and promoted by Sophie Weisse. It was while engaged as an active concert performer that Tovey was invited to prepare articles for the eleventh edition of *Encyclopaedia Britannica*, pub-

lished in 1910. The commission changed the focus of his career and, in 1914, he was made Reid professor of music at Edinburgh University, where he founded the Reid Orchestra. The program-notes he prepared for recitals given by the Orchestra—which he conducted himself—were eventually gathered together and printed in six volumes. "Nobody else," Richard Aldrich wrote, in the *New York Times*, when the first two volumes were published in 1935, "writes program notes so learned, so comprehensive, so full of meat and information conveyed not at all in a dry-as-dust manner but brilliantly and often with an unexpected glancing humor."

Although he composed a number of works, including an opera, *The Bride Of Dionysus*, and a cello concerto for Pablo Casals, Tovey was known—to his own dissatisfaction—chiefly as a musicologist. However, he never produced the single, concentrated volume which many presumed would eventually come from his pen. His forte was the program note, the encyclopedia entry, and the short essay. In addition to the six volumes of his Reid essays, a number of collections were published posthumously. In 1945 all of his *Britannica* articles, which he had revised for the fourteenth edition, were printed together in a volume entitled *Musical Articles From The Encyclopaedia Britannica*. The closest Tovey had come to producing a full written work was also published posthumously. *Beethoven*, dictated towards the end of his life, conveyed the tenor of his musical mind and the book's reviewer in the *New Republic* wrote: "It has its advantages in grasping the warm informality of a man who moved leisurely and, in turn, passionately through the realm of essential musical ideas, and made so much effort, even at the risk of being verbose in his metaphors, to convey his very keen experience to non-professional musicians."

PRINCIPAL WORKS: Beethoven's Ninth Symphony, 1922; A Companion to Beethoven's Pianoforte Sonatas, 1931; Essays in Musical Analysis (6 vol.), 1935–39; A Musician Talks, 1941; Beethoven, 1944; Musical Articles From The Encyclopaedia Britannica (The Forms of Music), 1945; Essays and Lectures on Music (in U.S.: The Main Stream of Music and Other Essays), 1949.

ABOUT: Grierson, M. Donald Francis Tovey, 1970; Dictionary of National Biography 1931–1940. *Periodicals*—New New Republic January 7, 1946; New York Times July 7, 1935, July 12, 1940; Times (London) July 12, 1940.

**TOWNE, CHARLES HANSON** (February 2, 1877–February 28, 1949), American writer and editor, called by the *New York Times* (1949) at the time of his death "New York's most invited out bachelor," was born in Louisville, Kentucky, the youngest of the six children of Paul A. Towne, a mathematician, and Mary Stuart (Campbell) Towne. When he was three, the family moved to New York City, where he attended public school and received some private tuition. He then spent a year at the College of the City of New York.

From childhood, Towne had dreamed of writing and editing; he said that he could "not remember a time when [he] did not love the smell of printer's ink." At the age of eleven he began his career by typing his own paper, the *Unique Monthly*, illustrated by his friend Harry Pray. The periodical appeared in a single copy—rented out for five cents per reading!

In 1907 Theodore Dreiser, then editor of the women's magazine *The Delineator*, hired Towne as fiction editor. Three years later he was appointed editor of *Designer*, and in 1915 became managing editor of *McClure's* magazine. A founding memeber of the Vigilantes, a group of writers and editors dedicated to the production of pro-war and pro-Allied propaganda, Towne helped to transform *McClure's* into an outspoken supporter of American involvement in World War I. During this time he published *For France* (1917), a compilation of stories, poems, and songs by American authors, painters, musicians, sculptors, and actors in show of their sympathy to and support of France, and *Shaking Hands with England* (1918), a collection of impressions of England, Scotland, and France during the latter years of the war. These efforts won him the admiration of Theodore Roosevelt, in whose honor he later published *Roosevelt as the Poets Saw Him* (1923), a memorial volume containing more than one hundred fifty poems from both American and British writers, including Edith Wharton and Edgar Lee Masters.

In 1920 Towne left *McClure's* to concentrate more fully on his own literary career. His works of verse, such as *Manhattan: A Poem* (1909) and *Youth and Other Poems* (1911), are now forgotten, but his novels were less shallow.

Towne was a traditionalist. Most of his novels took the conflict between a somewhat over-romanticized past, and a present he disliked, as their theme. They received the same kind of reviews, ranging from "a fairly interesting narrative, spoiled by some very poor writing" (*Literary Review*) to, simply, "an amusing novel" (*International Book Review*). His later attempts at fiction, such as *Good Old Yesterday* (1935) about a young family in the 1880s relocated to New York City from a small southern village, and *The Shop of Dreams* (1939), which told the story of a young man from the midwest who opens a book shop in New York, fared a little better with reviewers.

In 1926 Towne returned to publishing, taking an editorial position at *Harper's Bazaar*, where he remained for three years. From 1931 to 1937 he contributed a weekly column of insights and opinion to William Randolph Hearst's *American*; in 1940 he toured in the road-company production of Howard Lindsay's dramatization of Clarence Day's famous account of a New York family, *Life With Father* (1935). In addition, he published a book of etiquette, *Gentlemen Behave* (1939) and collaborated as a songwriter with Amy Woodforde-Finde and Deems Taylor.

Always popular, Towne was remembered as a man "whose urbanity, wit and conversational sparkle made him dinner guest par excellence" with a "list of friends, particularly in the field of letters which read like a Who's Who" who had a "flaming passion for Manhattan—a love affair with New York [which] had been going on sixty-eight years" (*New York Times*, 1949).

PRINCIPAL WORKS: *Poetry*—Ave Maria, 1898; The Quiet Singer and Other Poems, 1908; Manhattan: A Poem, 1909; Youth and Other Poems, 1911; (with H. Mayer) The Tumble Man, 1912; Beyond the Stars and Other Poems, 1914; Today and Tomorrow and Other Poems, 1916; A World of Windows and Other Poems, 1919; Selected Poems, 1925; Two Singers, 1929; An April Song: New Poems, 1937; Testament of Love: A Sonnet Sequence, 1945. *Novels*—The Bad Man: A Novel, 1921; The Chain, 1922; The Gay Ones, 1924; (with C. Maude) Actor in Room 931, 1926; Good Old Yesterday, 1935; The Shop of Dreams, 1939; Pretty Girls Get There, 1941. *Nonfiction*—Autumn Loiterers, 1917; The Rise and Fall of Prohibition, 1920; Loafing Down Long Island, 1922; Ambling Through Acadia, 1923; W. Somerset Maugham: Novelist, Essayist, Dramatist, 1925; Adventures in Editing, 1926; This New York of Mine, 1931; Jogging Around New England, 1939; Gentlemen Behave: Charles Hanson Towne's Book of Etiquette for Men, 1939; So Far So Good, 1945. *As editor*—Today and Tomorrow, 1916; For France, 1917; The Balfour Visit, 1917; (with C. T. Hillman) Roosevelt as the Poets Saw Him, 1923; Lichfield School, 1935. *Poetry*—Ave Maria, 1898; The Quiet Singer and Other Poems, 1908; Manhattan: A Poem, 1909; Youth and other Poems, 1911; (with H. Mayer) The Tumble Man, 1912; Beyond the Stars and Other Poems, 1914; World of Windows and Other Poems, 1919; Selected Poems, 1925; Two Singers, 1929; An April Song: New Poems, 1937; Testament of Love: A Sonnet Sequence, 1945. *Drama*—Bird of Passage: A Comedy in Three Acts, 1938.

ABOUT: Dictionary of American Biography 1946–1950, Supplement 4, 1974; Who's Who in America 1948–1949. *Periodicals*—Bookman September, 1925; Independent March 21, 1912; International Book Review June 1926; Literary Review June 4, 1921; October 12, 1922; New York Herald Tribune Books March 24, 1935; New York Times May 6, 1923; March 1 1949; New Yorker August 11, 1945; Outlook May 2, 1923; Times Literary Supplement April 25, 1935.

## TOYNBEE, ARNOLD JOSEPH (April 14, 1889–October 22, 1975), English philosopher of history best known for his twelve-volume survey of the rise and fall of civilizations, *A Study of History*, was born in London, the eldest of the three children of Harry Volpey Toynbee, a social worker, and Sarah Edith (Marshall) Toynbee. An uncle, the economist Arnold Toynbee, founded Toynbee Hall, a London settlement house; one of his

sisters was Jocelyn Toynbee, professor of classical archaeology at Cambridge University.

Arnold J. Toynbee attended Winchester College and Balliol College, Oxford—both on scholarships—and received his university degree in 1911 with first-class honors in classics. It was in the course of a year (1911–1912) of further study at the British School of Archaeology in Athens that he became interested in international affairs and the relationship between ancient civilizations and modern times—concerns that he dealt with in his subsequent public and academic careers.

On his return from Greece, Toynbee became a fellow and tutor in Greek and Roman history at Balliol (1912–1915). In 1913 he married Rosalind Murray, daughter of the classical scholar Gilbert Murray; they had three sons. His early books, *Nationality and the War* and *The New Europe*, published in the first years of World War I, were reprintings of his articles in the London *Nation*. Both set forth his suggestions for postwar reconstruction, which were judged lucid and stimulating if not particularly original. During the war Toynbee was engaged in government work, and in 1918 he joined the Political Intelligence Department of the British Foreign Office. In the following year he served as a member of the Middle East section of the British delegation to the Paris Peace Conference (as he did again in 1945, after the World War II). In 1919 he was appointed Koraes Professor of Byzantine and Modern Greek Language, Literature and History at the University of London, serving until 1924.

From 1925 to 1955, when he retired as professor emeritus, Toynbee was research professor of international history at the university. In the course of his teaching career he was also a visiting lecturer at the Institute for Advanced Studies at Princeton, among many other institutions in the United States and Europe. In 1921–1922, during the Greco-Turkish conflict, Toynbee acted as a correspondent for the *Manchester Guardian*; his observations were the basis for his books *The Western Question in Greece and Turkey* and *Turkey*. In addition to writing regularly for the *Guardian*, the *Observer*, and *Asia*, he contributed a weekly column to the *Economist* from 1930 to 1939. Beginning in 1924 he was also served as director of studies at the Royal Institute of International Affairs (RIIA) in London, and from 1925 to 1956 (interrupted by service in World War II as director of the Foreign Research and Press Service of the Foreign Office) he edited the annual RIIA *Survey of International Affairs*. These volumes—many of them written by Toynbee himself—were prepared with the collaboration of his second wife. From the appearance of the first volume, covering events of 1920–1923, the series was generally regarded as a useful work of reference.

Talking of the genesis of *A Study of History*, Toynbee recalled that the sight of present-day Bulgarian peasants wearing caps that were similar to the headgear of Xerxes's troops, as described by Herodotus, awoke him to the idea of historical continuities. The idea stayed with him, and in 1921 he began to draft notes for his monumental attempt to show how civilizations arise in response to creative leadership and how, when this source of inspiration ceases, they fall victim to nationalism, militarism, and tyranny. Scholars, among them the Harvard historian Crane Brinton (whose essay in the *Yale Review* praised the "accuracy and authoritativeness" of Toynbee's), compared the *Study* to Oswald Spengler's *The Decline of the West*, by which it was considerably influenced. Twelve years after

starting his text, the first three volumes—dealing with the genesis and growth of the twenty-six civilizations he chose to study—were published. The eminent American historian Charles A. Beard was not impressed with Toynbee's comparative method (*American Historical Review*, 1934). Five years later, when volumes IV–VI—dealing with the breakdown of civilizations—appeared, Beard acknowledged Toynbee's immense erudition, but noted that his overall design seemed elusive and unlikely to get clearer as the work progressed (*American Historical Review*, 1939–1940). Leonard Woolf, who earlier had been impressed by the grace and wit with which Toynbee applied his learning (*New Statesman and Nation*, 1934), now sounded the note of disenchantment that most critics would later take: viewed as a whole this "large-scale historical speculation" was fascinating, Woolf said, but on reconsideration "the more doubtful one becomes of the legitimacy of [Toynbee's] general method and the soundness of his general conclusions" (*New Statesman and Nation*, 1939). A reviewer of the last volume (Christopher Hall, writing in the *Spectator*) echoed this: "One feels increasingly that [Toynbee] tried to master a volume of knowledge which is beyond the capacity of one man, and that only a team could cope with his subject."

In his own defense Toynbee reflected that rather than becoming a specialist in any one field of history his aim had been to be a "student of human affairs . . . as a whole." As time went on, scholars began to detect errors in factual details and to criticize the writer's oracular tone and use of myth and aphorism to make his points. There was also controversy over his belief—advanced more explicitly from volume VII on—that spiritual rather than material forces control history, that history, in fact, is "God revealing Himself in action." (This belief is detailed in *An Historian's Approach to Religion*, a book based on lectures given at the University of Edinburgh in 1952–1953.) In 1948 another line of criticism developed, with the ethnologist Paul Radin commenting (in a *Kenyon Review* essay on the *Study*) that Toynbee's scholarship had deserted him in his treatment of Jewish history. Thereafter, the charge of anti-Semitism—exacerbated by Toynbee's stance on Zionism (which he equated with Nazism) and on the nation-state of Israel vis-à-vis the Arabs—shadowed his reputation. The statesman Abba Eban, in an address at Yeshiva University in New York in 1955, drew attention to the professor's "fossil theory," his denial of any viable post-Biblical Jewish culture. Eliezer Berkovits, in his *Judaism, Fossil or Ferment?*, contested at length Toynbee's contention that the Judaism of the Diaspora (after 70 A.D.) was merely a "fossilized survival." The most outspoken critic of Toynbee's "monument of wasted erudition," however, has always been Hugh Trevor-Roper, who in a famous *New York Review of Books* article (October 12, 1989) attacked his fellow historian's obscurantist theories and arbitrary conclusions, which he called the product of a "grotesque egotism" fed by the adulation of *Time* publisher Henry Luce and the

American press. Much earlier, in 1954, Trevor-Roper had stated: "Conjuring with his twenty-one 'civilisations,' and helping out his conjuring tricks with imperfect light, distracting noises and a certain amount of intellectual hanky-panky, he pretends that he has proved what he has merely stated. This seems to me, in so learned a man, a terrible perversion of history" (*Sunday Times*).

Almost forty years after he had begun his work Toynbee issued the final volume, *Reconsiderations* in which he acknowledged and discussed all the charges that had been leveled against the *Study*, and indicated his willingness to amend some of his conclusions. Critics such as H. S. Hughes found this "one of the strangest literary endeavors of our time," a masochistic exercise "to be read primarily for its psychological interest" (New York *Herald Tribune*). Toynbee was, though—according to Christopher Hill—"utterly impenitent" about the charge raised almost universally against him, to the effect that "what began as an attempt at scientific history ends as a theological treatise and spiritual autobiography" (*Spectator*).

With Toynbee's collaboration, an abridged— and much easier to read—version of volumes I–VI of the *Study* was prepared by D. C. Somervell and published in 1947. An article in *Time* magazine praised it as the "most provocative work of historical theory written in English since Karl Marx's *Capital*." Toynbee "had found history Ptolemaic and left it Copernican." This led to *A Study of History*'s rise to best-sellerdom in America; the one-volume abridgment was a Book of the Month Club selection. Somervell's shortened version of volumes VII–X (again in one volume) followed. Three years before his death Toynbee did his own one-volume condensation of the entire twelve volumes, in collaboration with Jane Caplan, with revisions and illustrations. It was universally judged superior to Somervell's work and even easier to read; but the latter remains in print while the Toynbee-Caplan edition does not. In any case, Toynbee's enormous opus and the passions it inspired were largely forgotten by the 1970s.

However, Toynbee displayed better scholarship in his specialized studies. Among these are the earlier *Greek Civilisation and Character* and the much later *Hannibal's Legacy: The Hannibalic War's Effects on Roman Life, Constantine Porphyrogenitus and His World*, and *The Greeks and Their Heritages*. His last book, *Mankind and Mother Earth*, aimed to "give a comprehensive bird's eye view of . . . history in narrational form." Though Toynbee's "whimsical if not grotesque" choice of events and characters to stress—and failure to include references to fascism, for example—struck the *Christian Science Monitor* reviewer, J. G. Harrison, as "intellectually puckish and historically ridiculous," he concluded that Toynbee was one of those historians "who can be read for broader knowledge, a more inspiring view of mankind's course, and for sheer pleasure."

Toward the end of his career Toynbee's musings about mortality, the world to come, and human survival were the subject of books such as *Change and Habit: The Challenge of Our Times*; *Cities on the Move*, which envisions a world united in one global city, "Ecumenopolis"; *Surviving the Future*; *Choose Life*, later titled *The Toynbee-Ikeda Dialogue*, a conversation with a Japanese Buddhist leader; and *An Historian's Conscience*, which reprints his correspondence with Columba Cary-Elwes, an English Benedictine monk. In a lighter vein, recondite historical lore is mixed with vignettes of people and scenery in Toynbee's accounts of his worldwide travels, beginning with *A Journey to China*. Toynbee left no full memoir of his own history, but *Acquaintances* talks about the great public figures he had known; and its sequel, *Experiences*, sheds some light on his personal development—amid soliloquies on his familiar themes: fear of modern science; yearning for world unity; and attacks on "colonialist powers," the United States and Israel especially.

Arnold J. Toynbee was a fellow of the British Academy and was named a Companion of Honour by the Queen in 1956. In 1968 he was made an associate member of the Institut de France, taking the place of Sir Winston Churchill. And in the same year a Toynbee Society was founded in Japan, where there was much interest in his work and recognition of his non-Eurocentric view of the world. Most of his papers are housed in the Bodleian Library at Oxford.

PRINCIPAL WORKS: Armenian Atrocities, the Murder of a Nation, 1915 (2nd ed. 1975; Nationality and the War, 1915; The New Europe: Some Essays in Reconstruction, 1916; The German Terror in Belgium, 1917; The German Terror in France, 1917; The Western Question in Greece and Turkey: A Study in the Contact of Civilisation, 1922; The World after the Peace Conference, Being an Epilogue to the "History of the Peace Conference of Paris" and a Prologue to the "Survey of International Affairs, 1920–1923," 1925; (with K. P. Kirkwood) Turkey, 1926 (The Modern World: A Survey of Historical Forces, vol. 6; repr. 1976); The Islamic World since the Peace Settlement, 1927 (Survey of International Affairs, 1925, vol. 1); The Conduct of British Empire Foreign Relations since the Peace Settlement, 1928; A Journey to China; or, Things Which Are Seen, 1931; A Study of History, 12 vols., 1934–1961; (with V. M. Boulter) International Repercussions of the War in Spain (1926–1937) 1938 (Survey of International Affairs, 1937, vol. 1); A Study of History: Abridgement of volumes I–X by D. C. Somervell, 2 vols., 1947–1957 (Royal Institute of International Affairs); Can We Know the Pattern of the Past? Discussion between Pieter Geyl . . . and Arnold J. Toynbee . . . Concerning Toynbee's Book A Study of History, 1948; Civilization on Trial, 1948; The Prospects of Western Civilization, 1949 (Bampton Foundation Lectures, 1, Columbia Univ.); War and Civilization, Selected by A.V. Fowler from A Study of History, 1950; The World and the West, 1953 (BBC Reith Lectures, 1952); An Historian's Approach to Religion: Based on Gifford Lectures Delivered in the University of Edinburgh in the Years 1952 and 1953, 1956 (2nd. ed. 1979); Christianity among the Religions of the World, 1957 (Hewett Lectures, 1956); East to West: A Journey round the World, 1958; Hellenism: The History of a Civilization, 1959 (Home Univ. Library of Modern Knowledge, 238); (with E. D. Myers) Historical Atlas and Gazetteer, 1959 (A Study of History, vol. 11) (Royal Institute of International Affairs); Between Oxus and Jumna, 1961; Reconsiderations, 1961 (A Study of History, vol. 12) (Royal Institute of International Affairs); America and the World Revolution, and Other Lectures, 1962; Comparing Notes: A Dialogue across a Generation [by] Arnold and Philip Toynbee, 1963; Between Niger and Nile, 1965; Hannibal's Legacy: The Hannibalic War's Effects on Roman Life, 2 vols., 1965; Change and Habit: The Challenge of Our Time, 1966; Acquaintances, 1967; Between Maule and Amazon, 1967; (with others) Man's Concern with Death, 1968; Some Problems of Greek History, 1969; Cities on the Move, 1970; An Ekistical Study of the Hellenistic City-State, 1971 (Anicent Greek Cities, 1); (with Kei Wakaizumi) Surviving the Future, 1971; (with J. Caplan) A Study of History, new ed., rev. and abr., 1972; Constantine Porphyrogenitus and His World, 1973; Toynbee on Toynbee: A Conversation between Arnold J. Toynbee and G. R. Urban, 1974 (12 radio discussions, 1972–1973, Radio Free Europe); Choose Life: A Dialogue/ Arnold Toynbee and Daisaku Ikeda (ed. R. L. Gage) 1976 (in U.S.: The Toynbee-Ikeda Dialogue: Man Himself Must Choose); Life after Death/Arnold Toynbee, Arthur Koestler, and Others, 1976; Mankind and Mother Earth: A Narrative History of the World, 1976; Arnold Toynbee, a Selection from His Works (ed. E.W.F. Tomlin) 1978; The Greeks and Their Heritages, 1981; An Historian's Conscience: The Correspondence of Arnold J. Toynbee and Columba Cary-Elwes, Monk of Ampleforth (ed. C. B. Peper) 1986. As editor—The Treatment of Armenians in the Ottoman Empire, 1915–1916 . . . , 1916 (Great Britain. Foreign Office. Miscellaneous Report no. 31, 1916); (with V. M. Toynbee and others) Survey of International Affairs, 1924–1958 (Royal Institute of International Affairs); (with J.A.K. Thompson) Essays in Honour of Gilbert Murray, 1936; (with others) Cities of Destiny, 1967; The Crucible of Christianity: Judaism, Hellenism and the Historical Background to the Christian Faith, 1969; Half the World: The History and Culture of China and Japan, 1973. As editor and translator—Greek Civilisation and Character: The Self-Revelation of Ancient Greek Society, 1924 (The Library of Greek Thought); Greek Historical Thought from Homer to the Age of Heraclius . . . 1924 (The Library of Greek Thought); Twelve Men of Action in Graeco-Roman History, 1952.

ABOUT: Ashley-Montagu, M. F. (ed.) Toynbee and History: Critical Essays and Reviews, 1956 (An Extending Horizons Book); Baker, J. The Superhistorians: Makers of Our Past, 1982; Berkovits, E. Judaism, Fossil or Ferment?, 1956; Current Biography 1947; Dictionary of National Biography, 1971–1980, 1986; Eban, A. The Toynbee Theory, 1955 (address to Israel Inst., Yeshiva Univ. Jan. 18, 1955); Gargan, E. T. (ed.) The Intent of Toynbee's History: A Cooperative Appraisal (pref. A. J. Toynbee) 1961; McNeill W. H. Arnold J. Toynbee, a Life, 1989; McNeill, W. H. Toynbee Revisited, 1993; Peper, C. B. (ed.) An Historian's Conscience: The Correspondence of Arnold J. Toynbee and Columba Cary-Elwes, Monk of Ampleforth, 1986; Perry, M. Arnold Toynbee and the Crisis of the West, 1982; Perry, M. Arnold Toynbee and the Western Tradition, 1995; Smith, P. The Historian and History, 1964; Smurr, J. W. Toynbee at Home, 1990; Stromberg, R. N. Arnold J. Toynbee, Historian for an Age in Crisis (pref. H. T. Moore) 1972; Thinkers of the Twentieth Century: A Biographical, Bibliographical and Critical Dictionary, 1983; Thompson, K. W. Toynbee's Philosophy of World History and Politics, 1985;Toynbee, A. J. Acquaintances, 1967; Toynbee, A. J. Experiences, 1969; Toynbee, A. J. Toynbee on Toynbee: A Conversation between Arnold J. Toynbee and G. R. Urban, 1974; Trevor-Roper, H. Arnold Toynbee's Millennium in Encounters (ed. S. Spender and others) 1963; Walsh, W. H. An Introduction to the Philosophy of History, 1967; Winetrout, K. After One Is Dead, Arnold Toynbee as Prophet: Essays in Honor of Toynbee's Centennial, 1989. Bibliography—Morton, S. F. A Bibliography of Arnold J. Toynbee (foreword V. M. Toynbee) 1979. Periodicals—American Historical Review vol. 40, 1934; vol. 45, 1939–1940; Book World April 27, 1969; Christian Science Monitor August 15, 1934; August 17, 1976; Harper's February 1947; International Affairs January 1976; Journal of Modern History March 1986; Kenyon Review vol. 9, 1948; New Republic August 7–14, 1989; New Statesman and Nation August 18, 1934; September 23, 1939; New York Herald Tribune July 23, 1961; New York Herald Tribune Books October 28, 1934; New York Review of Books June 1, 1989; October 12, 1989; New York Times October 23, 1975, December 29, 1985; New York Times Magazine April 5, 1967; Saturday Review of Literature April 5, 1969; Spectator May 12, 1961; Time March 17, 1947; Times (London) October 17, 1954; October 23, 1975; Yale Review Spring 1940.

**TOYNBEE, PHILIP** (June 25, 1916–June 15, 1981), English novelist and journalist, son of the historian Arnold Toynbee, and grandson (on his mother's side) of Gilbert Murray, was born at Oxford, where he grew up in an atmosphere of scholarship. In an adolescent act of rebellion he ran away from Rugby School and declared himself a Communist. Nevertheless, he won a scholarship to Christ Church College, Oxford,  and entered the university in 1935, at the same time formalizing his membership of the Communist party. His time at Oxford was largely spent in political activity, and he became the first Communist president of the Oxford Union Society. On leaving university Toynbee spent a year editing the Birmingham Town Crier, and then, on the outbreak of war, served in the Intelligence Corps and the Ministry of Economic Warfare, having by then ended his Communist affiliations.

Spending most of the war years in Britain, he became friendly with Cyril Connolly and contributed regularly to Horizon. Toynbee's first three novels were conventionally naturalistic. The Savage Days had been published in 1937, while he was still at Oxford. He quickly disowned it as a naively autobiographical performance. School in Private and The Barricades were both concerned with teacher-pupil relationships, but where the first of these was actually set in a prep school (some consider it an extremely vivid evocation of school life), the second is about breaking loose into the outside world. The main character, Michael Rawlins, is a schoolmaster who quits the classroom for a life of adventure, and the pupil, David Markham, runs away to fight in Spain. V. S. Pritchett, reviewing this book for the New Statesman, wrote: "Mr. Toynbee is an intellectual: supple minded, sensitive, witty, brilliant—too brilliant, one might say, for all his characters except the schoolboy, who is admirably drawn. The end of the novel is rather lame. Mr. Toynbee is too clever for the other people, and the fact is that Rawlins is not the man to bring out their real story. He is too convenient a projection of the author and does not—perhaps dare not—give the other characters a chance. They are impressions not protagonists." Elsewhere Toynbee's early novels (only the third had been published in America) were more summarily dismissed as smart displays of shallow brilliance.

Dissatisfied with the conventions of formal narrative, Toynbee's fourth novel, Tea with Mrs. Goodman (published as Prothalamium in America), was an experimentally impressionistic description of a tea party. It remains his most considered work. He later wrote, in the autobiographical Part of a Journey, "Ever since I began to plan Tea with Mrs. Goodman . . . I've seen that for me the only way of writing is to string together a necklace of sharp occasions and to conceal as best I can any narrative or explanatory thread." Reviewers' response to this change of style was, in the main, to add to their "too clever by half" comments snide references to the influence of James Joyce and Virginia Woolf, and Toynbee's continuing preference for experiment—culminating in the failed, multi-part, unfinished free-verse novel *Pantaloon*—never achieved any degree of reader-acceptance. Even the widely praised *Garden to the Sea*, a psychological and allegorical novel in which the hero, Adam, converses with three interior voices, failed to find many readers. Toynbee was an alcoholic, and there is a view that, but for this, he could have been a major novelist. But since both his early conventional work and his later experiments were seriously marred—the former by a failure of characterization, the latter by pretentiousness—it is a view difficult to sustain. The downfall of *Pantaloon* (he was unable to persuade anyone to publish the later parts) is principally due to the fact that Toynbee was not a poet. Initially it was poets who were prepared to receive the work politely. Donald Davie, reviewing the first installment in the *New Statesman*, wrote: "The verse is attractive; there is just enough vivacity and invention in the words to match the similarly unambitious but mildly interesting manipulations of rhythm." But after the three subsequent volumes had appeared there were few who would have maintained this line.

Toynbee's life, both personal and professional, was severely affected by alcoholism and depression. Twice married—the first time in 1939, the second in 1950—he was prone to making sudden shifts in his living arrangements and, notoriously, during the 1970s, turned his home into a commune. Towards the end of his life he embraced Christianity, in the manner of one testing out another enthusiasm. But this enthusiasm he held to the end, and with apparent sincerity. As a journalist he was a good professional, and for many years wrote as the chief reviewer for the *Observer*. It was in his nonfiction that he achieved his most fluent style and amongst his more interesting and successful titles are *Friends Apart* (his memoir of friends Esmond Romilly and Jasper Ridley), *Comparing Notes* (a dialogue conducted with his father, Arnold Toynbee) and the two volumes of autobiographical journal, *Part of a Journey* and *End of a Journey*.

PRINCIPAL WORKS: *Fiction*—The Savage Days, 1937; A School in Private, 1941; Tea with Mrs. Goodman 1947 (in U.S.: Prothalamium), The Barricades, 1944; Garden to the Sea, 1953; Pantaloon; or The Valediction, 1961; Two Brothers or The Fifth Day of the Valediction of Pantaloon, 1964; A Learned City, The Sixth Day of the Valediction of Pantaloon, 1966; Views from the Lake, The Seventh Day of The Valediction of Pantaloon, 1968. *Nonfiction*—Friends Apart, 1954; The Fearful Choice, 1958; (as ed.) Underdogs, 1961; (with A. Toynbee) Comparing Notes, a Dialogue Across a Generation, 1963; Towards the Holy Spirit, 1973; The Distant Drum, 1976; Part of a Journey, 1981; End of a Journey, 1988.

ABOUT: Mitford, J. Faces of Philip, 1984; Parker, P. ed. The Reader's Companion to Twentieth Century Writers, 1995; Who's Who 1980. *Periodicals*—New Statesman December 18, 1943; October 27, 1961; Sunday Times February 28, 1988; Times Literary Supplement July 24, 1953; May 13, 1988.

**TOZZI, FEDERIGO** (January 1, 1883–March 21, 1920), Italian novelist, story writer, and poet, was born in Tuscan city of Siena, the only one of his parents' seven children to survive birth. His mother, an epileptic subject to severe depression, died when he was twelve, leaving him in the care of a brutal father. He failed at school and was expelled at least once for unruly behavior. To escape his father's beatings, he went to work as a clerk for a railway. When his father died in 1908 he inherited two farms. In the same year he married. As poor a student as he had been, he early on developed a passion for literature in which he immersed himself, perhaps as a form of escape, and began writing in 1908. His first substantial book was an anthology of old Sienese writers.

By 1910 Tozzi had written his first notable prose work, *Ricordi di un impegiato* (translated in 1964 as *Journal of a Clerk* in *Six Italian Novellas*). His first poetry collection, *La zampogna verdi* (The green bagpipe) was published in 1911; a second *La Città della vergine* (1913, The city of the virgin), reveals his enthusiasm for d'Annunzio. His most important works are the novels *Eyes Shut*, about a young man who wills himself to fall in love with a young woman in order to avoid the meaninglessness of his life; *Three Crosses*, which concerns three destructive brothers; and the untranslated *Il Podere*, about a railway clerk who inherits a farm from his father.

Initially Tozzi had been an enthusiastic socialist. His meeting and subsequent close friendship with the fervent theological polemicist and Tuscan nationalist, the Florentine Domenico Giuliotti (1877–1956) profoundly influenced him, and led him into a somewhat confused, but, for him, fruitful and mystical phase. Giuliotti, who had once been interested in theosophy, and whose intellectual roots lay in a perfervid medievalism and a devotion to primitive Tuscany, introduced Tozzi to some of the literary figures he most admired: Villon, Jacoponi da Todi, and others. In 1913, the two authors founded a short-lived fortnightly, *La Torre* (The tower), seen as reactionary by its readers.

In 1914, he had to sell his second farm, Pecorile. He then went to Rome, and through World War I worked at the Red Cross office. He was to spend the rest of his life in the capital. Only in 1917 did he begin to publish his greatest books: the autobiographical *Bestie* appeared in 1917, when Borghese drew the attention of the Milan publisher Treve to his work. In 1918, he published his book about Caterina Benicases, *Santa Caterina*, by whom he had early become fascinated, and whose influence upon him was eventually crucial.

Tozzi's early works were not always readily available in his own country. Two months after his death, *Ricordi di un impregiato* was published in a "mutilated" version in 1920 by Borghese, his literary executor, in an effort to comfort his widow. It was this version that was reprinted in book form in 1927. Only in 1960, did Vallecchi, the publishers of Tozzi's collected works, issue Tozzi's own text, in a faithful edition by his son Glauco. Tozzi was thus for nearly forty years a badly misread writer, one who was judged as a realist-naturalist. Like Kafka, Tozzi seemed a bit pathological to some of those sympathetic to him, but he was not so much "mad" as intensely "modern"—intensely alienated, intensely puzzled. Leopoldo Gradi, the chief character in *Ricordi di un impiegato*, seems to parallel Kafka's Samsa in being a very part of the absurdities of the railway system for which he works. There is a profound and mystical irony here, born of rage at his lot, but suffused, too, with "socialist" passion.

Tozzi's masterpieces are *Eyes Shut*, *Three Crosses*, and *Il Podere*. In the first Pietro wills himself to fall in love with Ghisola, in order to escape from meaninglessness. In this book, too, occurs a key passage in Tozzi: that in which Pietro witnesses, with stunned horror, all the male animals on the farm being castrated indiscriminately, at his father's behest. *Three Crosses* is an ostensibly naturalist novel about three self-destructive Sienese brothers Gambi, booksellers and antique dealers who have forged a promissory note and who are, all three, overtaken by exposure and then death. In *Il Podere*, Remiglio Selmi, like Tozzi himself, leaves his job as a railway clerk to run the farm he inherits from his father. Again in relentlessly naturalist form, Tozzi demonstrates how Remiglio destroys the farm, his reputation, and himself in order to triumph over his father.

Alberto Moravia ranked Tozzi highly among Italian novelists of his period, which includes Manzoni, Verga, and Svevo. Giacomo Debenedetti found in Tozzi's work an important nonrealist dimension that puts him closer to Kafka. Debenedetti wrote, "blindness to life . . . is Tozzi's central myth, the open or secret connecting theme that runs through all his most important fiction." And he added, " . . . his novels are irresistibly dramatic; they are concerned with the origin and development of that mortal illness, the inability to live, or, rather, to adapt to life. . . . The contemporary novel, such as Tozzi wrote before its time, has a nocturnal point of view; it operates in a zone where there are no worldly explanations, no cut-and-dried solutions, in the true realm of the psyche, whose chance cannot be abolished by the throw of the dice."

PRINCIPAL WORKS IN ENGLISH TRANSLATION: Three Crosses (tr. R. Capellero) 1921; Ghisola (tr. J. J. Wilhelm) 1924 (tr. as Eyes Shut by K. Cox in 1990); Journal of a Clerk in Six Italian Novellas (ed. W. Arrowsmith) 1964; Christmas Eve (story) *in* Modern Language Notes January 1990.

ABOUT: Columbia Dictionary of Modern European Literature, 1947, 1980; Debenedetti, G. *in* Pacifici, S. (ed.) From Verisimo to Experimentalism, 1969, The Modern Novel from Capuana to Tozzi, 1973; Seymour-Smith, M. Macmillan Guide to Modern World Literature, 1986; Ulivi. F. Federigo Tozzi (in Italian) 1962; Vittorini, D. The Modern Italian Novel, 1930. *Periodicals*—Italica, 60, 1983; Modern Language Notes January 1993, January 1994; Newsletter of the Istituto Italiano di Cultura, 28, 1970.

**TRACY, HENRY CHESTER** (August 26, 1876–December 19, 1958), American essayist, wrote: "Henry Chester Tracy, second son of Charles C. Tracy who founded Anatolia College, was born in Athens, Pennsylvania, and spent an impressionable childhood in Merzifun, Turkey, in Asia; there formed a taste for outdoor life and study of a fascinating fauna and flora. Sent at fourteen to America for his schooling, he resumed the study of birds and plants in Pennsylvania and Ohio, majoring in the nature sciences when in college at Oberlin, and believing that he had a vocation in that field. His literary work while in college, however, attracted notice, and under the influence of the late Dr. C. H. A. Wager he came to feel that he might some time do something in letters. Teaching biology for two years after graduation (in Oberlin Academy, since closed), he began to know the sterilizing effects of an academic life and broke away to join the group of college men who went in 1905 to Montana to build the trails in Glacier National Park. Followed four years of nomadic existence, during which he worked in lumber mills, surveyors' camps, apiaries, and the like; was principal of a high school, wrote editorials for a newspaper, homesteaded in Utah, taught school in Idaho, and thence, having married Miriam Lee of the Whitman College (Washington) faculty, went to Berkeley, California, as assistant in zoology at the University of California. Acquiring a master's degree while there, he next joined the faculty of the Hollywood High School, where he remained for fifteen years, drowning his literary aspirations in laboratory and field routine, but breaking the shackling restraint toward the end with tentative ventures in prose and (1924) a rounded book which was accepted by the Yale Press as *belles lettres*. About that time he began to contribute papers to the *Adelphi*, London, in a happy relation with the staff and other contributors which lasted nearly a decade. Meanwhile he was writing *Towards the Open* and *English as Experience* as protests against over-specialization at the cost of human values and powers of appreciation. Attracted by the merit of the work of John Laurence Seymour, he wrote librettos for that composer, one of whose operas (*The Pasha's Garden*) was produced by the Metropolitan Opera Company. From 1931 on, he has been occupied chiefly with reviewing for periodicals in New York and London, and in editing his own bulletin—this last having merged into a system of monthly book talks for gatherings of the Readers' Book Groups under his direction. The purpose of these groups is to combat 'best-settlerism' and promote selection of the best books that appear each month, avoiding those written either for a commercial notive or as propaganda; and to promote the amateur spirit in literature."

In 1955, Tracy added: "In 1942 I was made head of the book department in *Common Ground*, program of the Common Council for American Unity, New York City, concerned with promoting better relations among the many national and racial groups in the United States. I held this position for six years, and at the same time continued my work with the book groups. The excessive reading and reviewing required, and the confinement involved, injured my eyes and health to such an extent that

although I resigned the position, I soon after lost my eyesight completely. This might seem to end my career as a writer and critic. However, since recovering a degree of health and some progress in touch typing, I have begun to do some creative writing and am also at work on a series of studies of birds, including a now completed monograph on the 'Great Birds of Asia Minor.'"

Of Henry Chester Tracy's works, all received appreciative reviews. His *Island in Time* (1924), recounts the events in the life of the son of a rich Armenian merchant as he matures from a child to a young adult. The book was described by the *Saturday Review of Literature* as "worthy of note as revealing a new writer of strong and yet delicate prose, with almost defiant disregard of the lesser conventions that make book weak and sometimes popular." *Towards the Open* (1922) explores Tracy's ideas on scientific humanism, explaining that "The Open towards which we are moving, is a more natural and a freer life in which a man's responsibility is measured by his real relation to his social-natural environment, and his value is measured by his real capacity, discovered under treatment to which he is entitled as a man" (*Book Review Digest*, 1927). Zona Gale, who reviewed it for *New York Herald Tribune Books* (June 26, 1927) called *Towards the Open* "A delightful book, written with 'the gift of language'."

Henry Chester Tracy died in Hollywood, California. He and his wife had two sons.

PRINCIPAL WORKS: *Fiction*—An Island in time, 1924; The Shadow of Eros, 1927. *Nonfiction*—Towards the Open, 1927; English as Experience, 1928; American Naturalists, 1930; The Amateur Writer, 1935.

ABOUT: The autobiographical material quoted above was written for Twentieth Century Authors, 1942 and Twentieth Century Authors First Supplement, 1955. Who Was Who in America vol. III 1951–1960. *Periodicals*—New York Herald Tribune Books June 26, 1927; Saturday Review of Literature September 27, 1924.

**TRADER HORN. See HORN, A. A.**

**TRAIN, ARTHUR CHENEY** (September 6, 1875–December 22, 1945) American novelist and short story writer, was born in Boston, Massachusetts, the son of Charles Russell Train and Sarah M. (Cheney) Train. Train, born while his father was Attorney General for Massachussets (1873–1890), took his law degree from Harvard in 1899. After practicing in Boston and being admitted to the Massachussets bar, he spent several bored, impatient, and unhappy months in a New York City law firm. In 1901 he joined the New York District At-

torney's office and served as an Assistant District Attorney under the well-known William Travers Jerome. At the New York City Criminal Courts Building, Train began to see every case as a tragedy; every trial as a detective story; his interractions with clients, together with his experiences in the courtroom, provided the material for the more than 250 short stories and novels he would write during his lifetime. As his *New York Times* obituarist noted, it was not as a lawyer but as a writer of fiction that he became famous in his time. From 1904 to 1905, Train published seven short stories, based on his experiences in the legal profession, in both *Scribners* and the *Saturday Evening Post*. These were collected and reprinted as *McAllister and his Double*. Fame came to Train in 1919 when his character Ephraim Tutt made his appearance in *The Saturday Evening Post*. Mr. Tutt (not to be confused with his law partner Tutt) became an immensely popular hero/lawyer devoted to protecting the poor and friendless against the stupidities and brutalities of the law and some of those who practice it. His adventures, a recounting of the events that led to either the acquittal or conviction of his client were more than simple crime stories; they provided commentary on the philosophy of the law and justice. Mr. Tutt was, as a *Saturday Review of Literature* critic wrote, "a genuine creation, a human being whom Mr. Train has given to us as a friend and companion." Tutt's characterization was so convincing that he was often regarded as a real person and was even the object of a legal embroilment when his presence was demanded by an angered lawyer. Perhaps this was because of the close parallels between the experiences of the fictional Mr. Tutt and of Train, his creator, as revealed in *Yankee Lawyer: The Autobiography of Ephraim Tutt*. Tutt was always shrewd enough to find a law to fit the necessities of the oppressed innocent, and his tricks and schemes never lost their appeal over the quarter century of his existence. *Mr. Tutt as his Best, Tutt & Mr. Tutt*, and *Yankee Lawyer: The Autobiography of Ephraim Tutt* were reprinted in 1975.

Train was a prolific writer, though none of his other works attained the popularity of the Mr. Tutt series. His novels of manners and society life generally received mediocre reviews. The best known of these, *Ambition* (1928), was most appreciated for the scenes of legal life it included. In contrast Train's *Manhattan Murder* was seen as lurid and melodramatic, and, in a similar vein, his *Jacob's Ladder* was described by one reviewer

as "superficial . . . and too long." Train's work is worth reading for the sheer entertainment value of Tutt's schemes and the keen insights into the legal workings of the time.

Train was a founding member of the Authors League of America, which promoted copyright reform and improved author contracts. He was presdident of the American Institute of Arts and Letters at the time of his death, from cancer, in New York City.

PRINCIPAL WORKS: McAllister and His Double, 1905; The Prisoner at the Bar, 1906; True Stories of Crime, 1908; The Butlers Story, 1909; Mortmain, 1909; Confessions of Artemus Quibble, 1909; C.Q.; or, In the Witches House, 1910; Courts, Criminals, and the Camorra, 1911; The Goldfish, 1914; The Man Who Rocked the Earth (with R. W. Wood) 1915; The World and Thomas Kelly, 1917; The Earthquake, 1918; Tutt and Mr. Tutt, 1920; By Advice of Counsel, 1921; The Hermit of Turkey Hollow, 1921; As It Was in the Beginning, 1921; Tut, Tut, Mr. Tutt!, 1923; His Childrens Children, 1923; The Needles Eye, 1924; On the Trail of the Bad Men, 1925; The Lost Gospel, 1925; Page Mr. Tutt, 1926; The Blind Goddess, 1926; When Tutt Meets Tutt, 1927; Ambition, 1928; The Horns of Ramadan, 1928; Illusion, 1929; Paper Profits, 1930; The Adventures of Ephraim Tutt, 1930; The Strange Attacks on Herbert Hoover, 1932; No Matter Where, 1933; Tutt for Tutt, 1934; Jacob's Ladder, 1935; Manhattan Murder, 1936; Mr. Tutt's Case Book, 1937; Old Man Tutt, 1938; My Day in Court, 1939; From The District Attorney's Office, 1939; Tassles on Her Boots, 1940; Mr. Tutt Comes Home, 1941; Yankee Lawyer: the Autobiography of Ephraim Tutt, 1943; Mr. Tutt Finds a Way, 1945.

ABOUT: Newsweek September 13, 1943; Time September 20, 1943; Saturday Evening Post April 8, 1944; Publishers Weekly May 27, 1944; New York Times December 23, 1945.

**TRAUBEL, HORACE L(EGO)** (December 19, 1858–September 8, 1919), American editor, essayist, and amanuensis to Walt Whitman, was born in

Camden, New Jersey, the fifth of seven children of Maurice Henry Traubel, a printer, engraver, and lithographer, and Katherine (Grunder) Traubel. His father was German-born, of Jewish heritage but a freethinker who had revolted against the strict Talmudic codes of his parents; his mother was a Christian whose family, of Scottish heritage, had settled in Philadelphia. The young Horace would later describe himself in these terms: "I am a half breed. Huxley says a half breed is a man who inherits the vices of both parents and the virtues of neither." Traubel, who advocated utopian and socialist principles throughout his life, said he went back and forth between being "half Christian" and "half Jewish" whenever justice demanded it— "brave with Jesus . . . afraid with Pilate," as he once put it.

Gay Wilson Allen, one of Whitman's biographers, reported that the young Traubel "grew up in a home in which Goethe, Heine, Schiller, and the great German authors were known and respected." Maurice Traubel hoped that his son would become a portrait painter—the Philadelphia area was then a center of much serious American painting—but young Horace took his first jobs in several occupations, including newsboy, printer's devil, paymaster, and bank clerk, where he sometimes found himself at odds with his employers because of his outspoken criticism of the capitalist system.

An advocate of the ideas of Henry George as well as other utopian socialists, Traubel began writing on social and economic matters for small publications, such as Unity, an organ of liberal Unitarianism.

In 1890 he founded a monthly periodical called The Conservator, which served as a bully pulpit for his liberal economic and social ideas as well for the cult of Whitman that he so assiduously promoted for the rest of his life.

Simultaneously, from 1903 to 1907 he was, with Will Price and Hawley McLanahan, editor of the Artsman, the organ of the Rose Valley movement, a utopian society influenced by the arts-and-crafts ideals of William Morris and others. Located on an eighty-acre farm near Philadelphia, Rose Valley endeavored to nurture the production of beautiful crafts by giving their crafters a beautiful place to live. "The Rose Valley shops are temples," he wrote. "Here men pray in their work."

Traubel met Whitman after the poet took up residence in Camden in 1873, and soon became a trusted confidant of the older man, assisting him in personal and business matters and, later, seeing to it that Whitman's medical needs were taken care of. Traubel recorded nearly every scrap of information and utterance of the poet in his With Walt Whitman in Camden journals that began on March 28, 1888 and ended with the poet's death four years later. Traubel himself edited and published three volumes of them during his lifetime; three more were published many decades later. The 1940 Dictionary of American Biography concluded that this record of Whitman's daily life "is neither dull nor unimportant, but it exasperates at times by its merciless record of Whitman's every remark, however casual or commonplace."

When Traubel died, he left in manuscript form three unpublished volumes. The fourth volume was not published until 1953, under the editorial supervision of Sculley Bradley and with the aid of Charles E. Feinberg, a Whitman collector.

The fifth volume was published in 1964, edited by Gertrude Traubel, who noted in the preface that hers was the first of them to appear in print "without the benefit of a final reading by the author." A sixth volume, edited by her and William White, appeared in 1982. A seventh volume, which covers the period from July 7, 1890 to February 10, 1891, was published in 1992, the centenary year of Whitman's death, edited by Jeanne Chapman and Robert MacIsaac.

On Whitman's seventy-second birthday, in 1891, Traubel was married to Anne Montgomerie; the couple had one daughter. After Whitman died, Traubel presided over meetings of the Walt Whitman Fellowship and other events designed to immortalize the memory of the poet, who had in Traubel what might be called the first publicity agent in American literary history.

A year and a half after Whitman's death, Traubel wrote a retrospective essay "Walt Whitman: Artistic Atheism" published in Poet Lore (October, 1893). Its tone is replete with late nineteenth-century chiliasm and sentimentality: "Like the orbs, this book has gravitation. Like man it has organs, continuity, mystery, measureless reach. . . . As to the exact degree of his success, men may differ; but that he has caught the flavor of evolution, and immortality, and of that eternal music which stirs the soul from resident torpors to spring-tide, making it reliant and holy in self. . . . "

Traubel organized a special tribute in May of 1919 for the centenary of Whitman's birth. It had a political as well as a literary tone: The names of Eugene V. Debs and Emma Goldman were invoked, and the blind and deaf Helen Keller, a Whitman admirer, spoke, describing Traubel as "the chiefest of his lovers."

Although Traubel wrote much during his lifetime, only the Whitman material is of lasting literary value. The comment that Traubel was the "platitudinizer of the American Socialist movement" approaches the truth. In the quarter-century left him after Whitman's death, Traubel published several books of his own, but they are today regarded as little more than literary curiosities. In 1904, he published *Chants Communal*, a paean to (or diatribe on) universal brotherhood, written as a stream of epigrams, at once pithy and bombastic. The *Chants* are remembered today more as a snapshot of turn-of-the-century innocent idealism than for any stylistic grace. Like many progressive intellectuals, Traubel was deeply disappointed at the outbreak of World War I, though he made it clear that he looked favorably on socialist revolutions in Germany and Russia and the 1916 Easter Rising in Dublin.

Traubel died in the literary colony of Bon Echo, Ontario. A "hail-and-farewell" service was scheduled to take place at the Community Church on Park Avenue in New York City on September 11, 1919. (Traubel was not an adherent of organized religion but he admired the church's pastor, John Haynes Holmes, a clergyman who preached the 'Social Gospel' during the Progressive Era.) Just as the service was to begin, a fire broke out in the organ loft, wrecking the entire interior. Traubel's body was removed to the Rand School of Social Science, a socialist organization downtown, where a hastily improvised memorial took place.

PRINCIPAL WORKS: (as editor, with M. Bucke and T. Harned) In Re Walt Whitman 1893; The Dollar or the Man?, 1900; Chants Communal, 1904; The Master of Money Is Dead, 1913; Optimos, 1914; With Walt Whitman in Camden, 3 vols. 1906–1914 (vol. 4, ed. by S. Bradley, published in 1953; vol. 5, ed. by G. Traubel, published in 1964; vol. 6, ed. by G. Traubel and W. White, published in 1982; vol. 7, ed. by J. Chapman and R. MacIsaac, published in 1992).

ABOUT: Allen, G. W. Solitary Singer; Bain, M. Horace Traubel, 1913; Homer, W. I. Letters Between Marsden Hartley and Horace Traubel 1906–1915, 1982; Traubel, H. With Walt Whitman in Camden 1906–1914, 1953, 1964, 1982, 1992; Walling, W. E. Whitman and Traubel. *Periodicals*—The Artman 1903–1907; The Conservator 1890–1919; Forum December, 1913.

**TRAVEN, B.** (February 23, 1882?–March 26, 1969), novelist and short story writer, has been described by Paul Theroux as "the greatest literary mystery of this century." Many books and articles have been devoted to speculation about his identity. This article draws mainly on the two most authoritative works on him: Will Wyatt's *The Secret of the Sierra Madre: The Man Who Was B. Traven*, and Karl S. Guthke's *B. Traven: The Life Behind the Legends*.

It has been conjectured that B. Traven was the son of an American farmer or of a German theater impresario, that he was a bastard of Kaiser Wilhelm II, that he was black or a woman or a whole team of writers, a convict from Devil's Island or a Stalinist spy or the president of Mexico or a leper. From time to time, Traven himself issued statements, at least partially false, about his identity and his life. When it was suggested that Jack London did not commit suicide in 1916 but went to Mexico and became B. Traven, the latter did not disparage the theory.

The theory now most widely held (though not by Guthke) is the one developed by Will Wyatt: that Traven was born in 1882 in Schwiebus, Pomerania, and christened Hermann Albert Otto Macksymilian Wienecke. He was the illegitimate son of Hormina Wienecke, a textile worker, and Adolf Rudolf Feige, a potter. His parents were married soon after his birth, and he became Otto Feige. In 1896 he was apprenticed to a locksmith in Schwiebus and worked with the same firm until 1902. In 1902–1904 he did military service in Bückeburg, then rejoined his parents, who had moved to Wallensen, Lower Saxony. Formerly interested in theology, he was by then a political activist, an anarchist. In about 1904 Otto Feige disappeared. His family heard from him only once more, after World War I, when he reported that the British authorities were about to expel him from England.

This is very different from the version Traven gave his Mexican wife many years later. She said that Traven never spoke of his father, or of any other relative except his mother. He claimed that she was an actress or a singer, often on tour. He traveled a great deal with her as a child, but rebeled against her strictness.

Guthke found some evidence to suggest that Traven had been a seaman, and he could have been during 1904 and 1907, In 1907 a little certainty begins. Records show that in that year a young actor and director named Ret Marut joined the Essen Municipal Theatre. It is now beyond dispute that this man became Traven. He was already an anarchist, and already at pains to conceal his identity—"Marut" was itself a pseudonym.

In 1907, Ret Marut was working in Essen. The following year, he was playing "youthful heroes and lovers" in various small-town theaters. In 1911–1912 Marut was with the Danzig Municipal Theatre, and in 1912–1915 with the Dusseldorf Schauspielhaus, usually taking minor roles. Applying for the latter job, Marut claimed to be an English national, then an American, born in San Francisco in 1882.

Little is known of Marut's private life during those years, except that he had an affair with an actress named Elfriede Zielke. Her daughter Irene, born in 1912, was probably Marut's (though later he denied this). The end of this relationship in 1914 inspired the novella translated many years later as *To the Honorable Miss S . . . .*

In 1915, Marut left the Schauspielhaus and went to Munich, probably to pursue a full-time career as a writer. Beginning in 1912, his stories and sketches had been appearing frequently in Dusseldorf papers. According to Guthke, "Marut's prose rarely rises above the level of the popular literature of the time," though his themes closely resemble those of Traven's maturity, as several researchers have shown. In *To the Honorable Miss S . . .*, Marut's most substantial published work, the young officer who dies in action and is praised for heroism is revealed in his diaries to be an unhappy lover and a suicide.

The novella was published in 1916. It appears to have been the sole publication of a Munich press set up by Irene Mermet, with whom Marut had begun a relationship that lasted ten years. She is believed to have assisted him with *Der Ziegelbrenner* (The brickburner), the anarchist-pacifist magazine he launched in Munich in 1917. Brick red and brick-shaped, its affirmed intention was to provide "building blocks for a better postwar Germany," and to create a "community of selves." In fact, in its strident and messianic polemics against the status quo, it more resembled a brick through the window of German society.

Marut, who had meanwhile been charged with treason, but had escaped, continued to publish *Der Ziegelbrenner* until December 1921. There is some evidence that Marut and Irene Mermet spent time in Berlin and in Cologne. In 1923, with help from fellow revolutionaries, Marut escaped to England, where he was imprisoned for violating alien-registration regulations. Released after three months, he made his way by unknown means to revolutionary Mexico. He spent the rest of his life there.

Shortly after his arrival in Mexico, he wrote in his notebook: "The Bavarian of Munich is dead." Thereafter, he generally presented himself as an American of Scandinavian extraction. He became B. Traven, sometimes Traven Torsvan, later Hal Croves.

Traven first surfaced in June 1924 in the oil town of Tampico, on the Gulf of Mexico. The following month, he rented a dilapidated cabin, on stilts in bush country some thirty-five miles out of town. The cabin completely isolated, had no electricity and little water. It was plagued by mosquitoes, visited by jaguars and hurricanes, infested with scorpions, tarantulas, and rattlesnakes. Traven lived there for six or seven years, writing his first stories and novels under his new name. In humid weather, the mosquitoes were so bad that he worked with his hands and head wrapped in towels. Irene Mermet was with him when he first went to Mexico, though it is not clear how this was managed. She lived close

enough to type his manuscripts. Before long she moved to the United States. Their interests diverged, but correspondence continued until 1928, when she married an American.

At first, Traven had to earn his living as a day laborer on nearby cotton and fruit plantations or oil camps. Probably, as he claimed, he also worked as a "drover, hunter, and trader among the wild Indian tribes." Many of these experiences went into his stories and articles. Armed with a German-English dictionary, he wrote in both languages, bombarding editors in both countries. He had no success in America, but his stories began to appear in German newspapers and magazines as early as 1925, most of them sketches of Mexican or Indian life seen with the fresh and wondering eye of a newcomer. The narrator is usually a *gringo*. Often he is named Gales, regarded by critics as a persona of the author. Gales is the protagonist of Traven's novel *Das Totenschiff (The Death Ship)*. It appeared in Germany in 1926, and was an immediate and lasting success.

After that, Traven could afford to abandon casual employment and devote himself to writing. He had been moving in leftist circles in Tampico, then a center for the anarchist-syndicalist "Wobblies" (Industrial Workers of the World). After 1926 he was able to spend an increasing amount of time in Mexico City. There he joined the circle around the muralists Diego Rivera and David Alfaro Siqueiros, who were Communists, and began to take courses at the university in Spanish, and in Mexican archeology, folklore, literature, art, history, and politics.

In 1926 Traven was able to join a government-sponsored scientific expedition to Chiapas, in the southwest. He went along as a photographer, taking the pictures that subsequently illustrated a travel book published in Germany, and finding material for his later novels. Traven also became fascinated by the region's rich archeological and ethnological heritage, subjects that absorbed him for the rest of his life. He returned to Chiapas several times, traveling on horseback with an Indian guide, and spending months at a time in the jungles of the south. Traven visited pre-Columbian sites, stayed both with landowners and his "soul mates," the region's Indians, and researched the exploitation of the latter by the former.

Meanwhile, the German success of *The Death Ship* in 1926 had released in Traven a flood of creativity. Another novel, *Der Wobbly (The Cotton Pickers)* appeared the same year, *Der Schatz der Sierra Madre (The Treasure of the Sierra Madre)* in 1927, then the three novellas collected in *Der Busch* (1928). *Die Brücke im Dschungel (The Bridge in the Jungle)* followed in 1929, *Die weisse Rose (The White Rose)* the same year. By 1930, their mysterious author was a household name, and not only in Germany. His work had been or was being translated into a dozen languages, though not yet into English, which Traven insisted was his native tongue.

In 1930, Traven moved into a small house, El Parque Cachu, set in an orchard just outside Acapulco. He lived there for twenty-five years, though he was frequently away for weeks or months on end, visiting Mexico City, Chiapas, and elsewhere. El Parque belonged to María de las Luz Martínez, a Mexican of Indian descent who ran a restaurant there. According to one account, she and Traven were married, though there is little evidence of this.

Several of Traven's books appeared in 1933 on the Nazi's first blacklist of undesirable works. Guthke quotes his response, in a letter to his German publisher: "I therefore now wish to ban from Germany also those books that those jerks have not banned and that they are apparently hoping to use for some purpose or other. . . . In matters like this I prefer clarity to profit." This was a courageous decision, cutting off Traven's principal source of royalties at a time when his finances were very precarious. He had apparently seen little of the money due to him from the sales of translations, and in spite of his international fame was living on rice and beans.

It was at this point that Traven turned his attention to the market in the United States, which he had previously scorned for its intrusive publicity methods. In 1933 he authorized the publication of his own English version of *The Death Ship*. Both in vocabulary and syntax, it was so Germanic as to be virtually unreadable. With the author's permission, it was revised by Bernard Smith, who retained a good deal of its dated or inaccurate American slang.

*The Death Ship* is narrated in this humorous and hyperbolic style by Gales, an American sailor who loses his identity papers in Antwerp. This being a world in which bureaucracy is "fate," a man without papers no longer qualifies as a human being. In scenes equally reminiscent of Kafka and Chaplin, Gales is shuffled across one European border after another until he reaches Cadiz. There, willy-nilly, he signs on as a stoker aboard the death ship *Yorikke*, a decaying freighter soon to be sunk in an insurance fraud. Only the officers have lifeboats. Gales and the others who toil and suffer in the Dantean stokehold will die. Indeed, since they are all without papers, all outcasts with false names, they are already "dead men." But Gales comes to embrace his namelessness as an expression of his existential freedom, even coming to love the no-man's-land of the *Yorikke*. And Gales survives, perhaps, drifting alone on a raft in a hallucinatory state.

Traven's version, revised by Bernard Smith, appeared in the United States in 1934. Eric Sutton's translation from the German came out in England the same year. Both were warmly received. Mark Van Doren in the *Nation* (1934) wrote: "If the *Yorikke* is intended to represent the modern world in little, then we have here the bitterest indictment of that world—an indictment all the bitterer, too, because its language is so spirited, so opulent, and even in its ghastly fashion so gay." James Hanley called it "the finest modern sea story I have ever read" (*Spectator*). Most critics regard it as Traven's masterpiece.

*The Treasure of the Sierra Madre* followed, translated in England by Basil Creighton, in the United States again in Traven's own English version. It tells the story of three down-and-out Americans in Mexico who go prospecting. They find gold dust, and protect it from bandits until they are ready to carry it down from the mountains. Then the tensions that have been mounting between them, fanned by greed, erupt into treachery. Dobbs, escaping with all the gold, is ambushed by thieves and beheaded. The thieves, supposing that the gold dust is sand, let it blow away in the wind. The oldest and wisest of the prospectors, Howard, bellows with anarchic laughter as he watches it go. Howard finds serenity in the end. He becomes a sort of doctor in an Indian village, where the people know that happiness comes, not from gold, but from living at one with nature.

Of Traven's other novels, the most admired is *The Bridge in the Jungle*. Gales returns as narrator, hunting alligators in jungle country infested with foreign-owned oilfields. He is staying in an Indian village when a little boy is reported missing. Gales witnesses the mother's increasingly desperate search and the intolerable discovery of the boy's death by drowning. Her anguish through a whole night of mourning is shared by the entire village.

Traven had placed strict limitations on the style and amount of advertising his novels should receive. Perhaps for this reason, American sales were modest. After the publication there of *The Bridge in the Jungle* in 1938, there were no further translations for fourteen years. Traven was in financial difficulties throughout the 1930s. The outbreak of World War II, cutting off foreign royalties, exacerbated the situation. Traven went on working, between 1931 and 1940 publishing the six interrelated novels of the Mahogany or jungle cycle. The novels are *Der Karren* (*The Carreta*), *Regierung* (*Government*), *Der Marsch ins Reich der Caoba* (*March to the Montería*), *Die Troza* (*The Troza*), *Die Rebellion der Gehenkten* (*The Rebellion of the Hanged*), and *Ein General kommt aus dem Dschungel* (*General from the Jungle*).

The cycle forms an epic history of the events in southern Mexico leading up to the revolution of 1910. It centers on the brutal exploitation of the Indians by Spanish landowners and their hirelings in the infamous *monterías* (logging camps) of Chiapas. Traven identified the Indians with the oppressed and misused underclass in every society. His account of what he called the "Indian-proletarian struggle for liberation" was recognized to be as much an indictment of Hitler's Reich, say, as of the Diaz dictatorship. However, whereas in earlier novels like *The Death Ship*, Traven's white proletarians are disabled by their alienated individual psyches, the Indians in the jungle cycle share a collective psyche. From this they draw humane values, shared motivations and actions that, for Traven, could be the basis for a post-capitalist utopia of small agrarian communes.

It was not until 1948, with the release of the first Traven film, that his star began to rise again. *The Treasure of the Sierra Madre* established John Huston as a director of the first rank, and provided major roles for Humphrey Bogart (Dobbs) and the director's father, Walter Huston (Howard). It was a popular as well as a critical success, and revived interest in Traven (who served as technical advisor, masquerading as Traven's "representative," Hal Croves).

Traven wrote little after 1940. *BT News* had to counter rumors that he was dead or insane. He was neither. In 1953, when "Hal Croves" was working on the screenplay of *The Rebellion of the Hanged*, he was introduced to Rosa Elena Luján, who was to make the Spanish translation. She subsequently translated most of the Traven books not yet available in Spanish, and became his trusted representative in all things. Rosa Elena Luján and "Traven Torsvan" were married in 1957. He was perhaps seventy-five (sixty-seven according to some accounts); she was forty-two. Thereafter, until his death, they were never separated for a single day.

The Torsvans had custody of Rosa Elena's two teen-aged daughters by an earlier marriage. The family moved to Mexico City, where Señora Torsvan established the Literary Agency R. E. Luján. It existed to manage all of Traven's literary, financial, and legal affairs while preserving his anonymity. In 1963 they moved into an elegant house on Calle Mississippi, where Traven spent the rest of his life.

By this time, Traven was, thanks partly to his wife's management of his affairs, rich. Nevertheless, he lived simply. He went to the opera and concerts, but liked nothing better than endless explorations on foot of "his" city, or evenings of conversation or play-reading with "his" daughters. In his last years, when both his hearing and sight were failing, he was pursued by journalists from all over the world, all seeking to unravel the Traven mystery. Several he entertained, at home or in favorite restaurants. He was always Hal Croves or Traven Torsvan; he was certainly not B. Traven.

"Just before he died," his wife said, "he told me that I could reveal to the world that he was Ret Marut the Bavarian anarchist." After elaborate ceremonies in Mexico City, his ashes were flown to Chiapas and scattered over the Río Jataté. Later there was a kind of wake, with music and fireworks, in the nearby Tzeltal Indian village of Ocosingo, henceforth Ocosingo de Traven.

PRINCIPAL WORKS IN ENGLISH TRANSLATION: *Fiction*—The Death Ship: The Story of an American Sailor (in U.S.: tr. by author; in U.K.: tr. E. Sutton) 1934; The Treasure of the Sierra Madre (in U.K.: tr. B. Creighton, 1934; in U.S.: tr. by author); The Carreta (in U.K.: tr. B. Creighton, 1935; in U.S.: tr. by author, 1970); Government (tr. B. Creighton) 1935; The Bridge in the Jungle (tr. by author) 1938; The Rebellion of the Hanged (tr. C. Duff) 1952; General from the Jungle (tr. D. Vesey) 1954; The Cotton-Pickers (in U.K.: tr. E. Brockett, 1956; in U.S.: tr. by author, 1969); March to Caobaland, 1960 (also published as March to the Monteria, 1963); Aslan Norval, 1960; Stories by the Man Nobody Knows: Nine Tales, 1961; The White Rose (tr. by author) 1965; The Night Visitor and Other Stories, 1966; The Creation of the Sun and the Moon, 1968; Macario (tr. R. E. Luján) 1971 (tr. *in* The Night Visitors and Other Stories); The Kidnapped Saint and Other Stories, 1975; To the Honourable Miss S . . . , and Other Stories (tr. P. Silcock) 1981; The Troza, 1994.

ABOUT: Baumann, M. B. Traven, 1976; Chankin, D. D. Anonymity and Death: The Fiction of B. Traven, 1975; Dictionary of Literary Biography vol. 9 1981; Guthke, K. S. B. Traven: The Life Behind the Legends, 1991; Mezo, R. E. A Study of B. Traven's Fiction, 1993; Raskin, J. My Search for B. Traven, 1980; Schürer, E. and Jenkins, P. B. Traven: Life and Work, 1987; Stone, J. The Mystery of B. Traven, 1977; Wyatt, W. The Secret of the Sierra Madre: The Man Who Was B. Traven, 1980; Zogsbaum, H. B. Traven: A Vision of Mexico, 1992. *Periodicals*—Bibliographical Society of America 53 1 1959; German Quarterly November 1963; Literature/Film Quarterly 27 4 1989; Nation May 16, 1934; August 6, 1938; New Republic March 24, 1947; February 28, 1981; New York Herald Tribune June 10, 1935; New York Times March 27, 1969; New York Times Book Review April 17, 1966; November 20, 1966; November 10, 1985; New Yorker July 22, 1967; Smithsonian March 1983; Spectator January 26, 1934; Times (London) March 28, 1969.

**TRAVERS, P. L.** (1906–April 23, 1996), British poet and juvenile author, wrote: "I was born in the tropics of Australia [North Queensland], of Irish parents her mother was Scottish, and feel myself and my work to be Irish rather than Australian. I lived in Australia during my childhood and then came to live in Ireland and later in England. I have a nine-hundred-year-old house [in Mayfield, Sussex], mentioned in the Doomsday Book, and live in it for most of the year. I began to write when I was seventeen and first became known, if I may put it that way, as a poet. It was George Russell, the great Irish poet and economist, known more popularly as Æ, who first published my work in his paper, *The Irish Statesman*, and who, since we became great friends, in a way presided over it until his death some years ago. I think I may say that my poetry is known in America; it has appeared in periodicals and anthologies there over a number of years. I have published only three books as yet, but am now working on two more which I hope the war will not hold up too long."

———

P. L. Travers is most celebrated for her Mary Poppins books—and the more so through the 1964 Walt Disney movie, made from her original story, which starred Julie Andrews and Dick Van Dyke.

She began as a poet, and her work appeared in many anthologies in both Great Britain and, to a greater extent, in America. Since she grew up listening to folk tales told to her by her parents, and since her interest in the poetic was one chief source of her best-known work, the poetry she wrote is significant in her development. She never, however, issued a collection of her poetry. Earlier examples show the influence of Russell, but also a  strong element of the folkloric which was all her own. She was also gifted with a genuinely singing line, as these two-and-a-half stanzas from "The Dark Heart" demonstrate (the poem originally appeared in Alida Monro's anthology *Recent Poetry* in 1933):

> The exquinoxes pass
> With banners and are gone
> She sits among the seasons
> Stiller than stone.

Immutable and bowed
Beneath the wheeling spheres—
Lord, how can you get in
That dark heart of hers
That has for its business
The root and the seed?

While she was working as a journalist, dancer, and actress in Australia and England in her early life, Travers's main ambition was to become a poet—and that was why she traveled to Dublin when she was in her twenties, to become acquainted with the poet, editor, and self-proclaimed "student of esoteric wisdom" George Russell, known as Æ. He had a profound influence upon her. This influence was probably, with that of Russell's friend A. R. Orage, an important factor in her decision to become a follower of the quasi-gnostic system synthesized by Gurdjieff. As might be expected from a Gurdjieffian, she remained largely silent about her religious beliefs—and also stated that she sought no recognition for her work.

Travers initially invented Mary Poppins for her own amusement, although she showed some early Poppins stories to Russell, who encouraged her to go on with them. In the early 1930s Travers was writing film and drama—and some literary—criticism for the New English Weekly. In 1933 she fell ill, and it was while she was recovering at her old cottage at Mayfield, in East Sussex, that she wrote the first stories in the saga. Later a friend suggested that she make the tales into a book, and the result was Mary Poppins. It and its successors have been best-sellers ever since. The New York Times (1934) did not like it: "not very convincing . . . Mary Poppins' doings lack the logic of true nonsense . . . the book is spun out to too great a length." But others very strongly disagreed: "We'll bet the ghost of Jean Ingelow wishes she had thought of Mary Poppins!" exclaimed the Saturday Review of Literature critic in 1934.

Mary Poppins is an improbable, and surprisingly ill-humored, nursemaid who appears at a household in a high wind—but floats away when the wind changes. Travers built up her creation over a series of seven more books. Since then, serious investigations of Mary Poppins's origins and significance have proliferated.

Travers was economical in her continuation of her Poppins saga, as a poet who wanted to preserve the sources of her inspiration. As a Times Literary Supplement critic observed, Mary Poppins is "the embodiment of authority, protection, and cynical common sense; her powers are magical. Basically, she is the Good Fairy, whom we are all seeking, but in priggish human guise." She thus does, as Æ insisted long ago, "come straight from myth."

Travers's single essay in popular journalism, written just after the first Poppins book, showed sharpness and wit. This was Moscow Excursion, a series of letters written home from a tour of Russia, in which the author is much irritated by the interferences into her trip by Intourist, but at the same time relaxed about what most of her readers regarded as the depths of horror: the Russian Revolu-

tion. The Saturday Review thought it a "cheap caricature" of Soviet Russia, but others were delighted: the Times Literary Supplement stated that "The Russian Revolution has been regarded with such horror by its opponents and such reverence by its exponents that the humorous aspects of everyday life have been overlooked. In this book the author, who is neither the one nor the other, treats it with complete irreverence and gives an admirable picture of a specially conducted tour." Reprinted in the light of the collapse of Soviet Russia, this amusing book might seem less frivolous than it did in 1934.

As a modest but profound mythographer, Travers acted for many years as consultant to Parabola: The Magazine of Myth and Tradition, to which she herself made a few important contributions. The most revealing book about her is Jonathan Cott's extended interview, Pipers at the Gates of Dawn, the title of which recalls her own characteristically modest early poem, "The Poet":

Mine is a still small cry
a pipe with one stop,
one and calling
like a lost girl
in a wood of fauns.

Friend Monkey, ostensibly set in Victorian times, is really a subtle and memorable examination of the myth of the Indian God Hanuman, from the Ramayana. Travers for long issued small private publications at Christmas time. Having lived for some time in the United States, where she did war work in World War II, she returned to Chelsea in London to pass the years of her old age.

PRINCIPAL WORKS: Collections—Stories From Mary Poppins, 1952 (selected and abridged); Mary Poppins from A to Z, 1962. Fiction—Mary Poppins, 1934; Happy Ever After, 1940; I Go By Sea, I Go By Land, 1941; Mary Poppins Opens the Door, 1943; Mr. Wiggs Birthday Party, 1952; The Gingerbread Shop, 1952; The Magic Compass, 1953; Mary Poppins Comes Back, 1937; Mary Poppins in the Park, 1952; The Fox at the Manger, 1962; Friend Monkey, 1971; Two Pairs of Shoes, 1980; Mary Poppins in Delacorte Lane, 1982. Private publications—Aunt Sass, 1941; Ah Wong, 1943; Johnny Delaney, 1944. Other—Moscow Excursion, 1934; George Ivanovitch Gurdjieff, 1973; (with M. Moore-Betty) Mary Poppins in the Kitchen, 1975; About the Sleeping Beauty, 1975; What the Bee Knows: Reflections on Myth, Symbol and Story, 1994.

ABOUT: The autobiographical material quoted above was written for Twentieth Century Authors, 1942. Bergsten, S. Mary Poppins and Myth, 1978; Cott, J. Pipers at the Gate of Dawn, 1983; Denson, A. (ed.) Letters from Æ, 1961; Doyle, B. (ed.) Who's Who of Childrens Literature, 1963; Guppy, S. Looking Back, 1992; Montgomery, E. R. The Story behind Modern Books, 1949. Periodicals—New York Times December 9, 1934; December 19, 1982; New Yorker October 20, 1962; Paris Review Winter 1982; Saturday Review of Literature December 8, 1934; August 17, 1935; Times Literary Supplement June 28, 1934; November 28, 1952; July 23, 1982.

**TREADWELL, SOPHIE** (October 3, 1890–February 20, 1970), American playwright, journalist, and novelist, was born in Stockton, California, the daughter of Alfred Benjamin Treadwell and Nettie (Fairchild) Treadwell. She graduated from the Girls' High School in San Francisco in 1902, then attended the University of California (1902–1906) studying liberal arts. While there she wrote one-act plays, comic sketches, and songs. After graduation she intended to pursue a stage career, but, first decided to study journalism, in case she should fail. She wrote her first full-length play, *Le Grand Prix*, while contributing feature articles to the *San Francisco Sunday Chronicle*.

In 1907 Treadwell (and her mother) went to Los Angeles, where she worked as an extra and a vaudeville performer. She began newspaper work in 1908, covering police beats, sports, and theater for the *San Francisco Bulletin*. She met and married a fellow-reporter, W. O. McGeehan. By then a feminist, she retained her maiden name. Treadwell covered the Carranza revolution in Mexico for the *New York Tribune*, and interviewed both Obregon and Pancho Villa.

Her play *Sympathy* was produced in San Francisco in 1915. Then she was off to cover World War I, returning to New York in 1918. *Gringo*, a melodrama based on her experiences in Mexico, opened in New York in 1922 to mixed reviews, and had only a short run. Helen Hayes played the lead in *Loney Lue*, in 1923 in Atlantic City. Unable to find a producer in New York, Treadwell produced *Loney Lue* herself under the title *Oh Nightingale*.

Treadwell's greatest success, and the one for which she is remembered today, is the expressionist *Machinal* (1928). It was loosely based on the Ruth Snyder murder case in which a stenographer and her boyfriend kill the former's husband, and are eventually both executed. The original New York production in 1928 starred Zita Johann, with Clark Gable as the lover. It ran for ninety-one performances on Broadway and toured in London, Paris, Moscow, and the Soviet provinces. It was revived at New York's Public Theater in 1990 and at London's Royal National Theater in 1993.

*Machinal* (in French, "mechanical") is written in nine scenes with no intermission. Reviewing the 1990 New York revival of the tragedy, Edith Oliver (*New Yorker*, 1990) assessed it thus: "This script is earnest and humorless and deeply condescending toward working people and toward its heroine as victim. The point of view expressed in the title was a standard left-wing cliché until, seven years later, Clifford Odets' *Awake and Sing!* broke the mold of 'social protest' and cleared the air."

Writing of the 1993 London production, featuring the versatile Fiona Shaw, John Lahr wrote (*New Yorker*, 1993) that Treadwell "seems to have reflected, as well as chronicled, the era's restless obsession with productivity. In *Machinal*, the heroine is not a corporate highflier but a young, poorly educated stenographer who is swept up in the slipstream of the century's velocity, where she cannot find 'any place, any peace' . . . Miss A. is a model of alienated labor, a victim of economic necessity, whose life factors out neatly in a Marxist equation, which explains the long and successful run of *Machinal* in the U.S.S.R. The murderous energies of capitalism, in which all life is dedicated to 'making a killing,' are transmuted into a numbed female heart."

Lahr added that the London revival "gives the production a significance that the text, finally, can't

bear . . . There are good plays that are not important, and important plays that are not good. *Machinal* falls into the latter category. Even this outstanding revival will not put *Machinal* in the canon of American dramatic literature. The failure is not due to sexual politics but to writing. *Machinal* provides no substantial character development for its heroine and only one dimension for the subsidiary characters, who remain stick figures."

A string of failures followed *Machinal*. *Ladies Leave*, a seriocomic, psychoanalytical approach to adultery, ran for only fifteen performances in 1929. She had to produce her next play, *Lone Valley*, then she sank into depression over its lack of success and over the death of her husband in 1933. Three other plays written in the early 1930s were never produced.

Finally in 1936, Treadwell came to see her lifelong passion for Edgar Allan Poe take the stage at last: in her *Plumes in the Dust*, which featured Henry Hull. But it ran for only eleven performances on Broadway. Treadwell had started writing it in 1922, and had always wanted John Barrymore to play Poe. Barrymore did read the play, and liked it, unfortunately, however, Barrymore's wife wrote a vehicle for her husband about Poe. Treadwell, under foolish advice, sued. A two-year legal battle prevented the production of both plays; the case confirmed her reputation as a difficult author.

*Hope for a Harvest*, adapted from her own novel, was produced in 1941, with Frederic March and his wife, Florence Eldridge in the leads. After a successful tour, the play ran for only thirty-eight performances on Broadway, thus once again dashing her hopes. She had little further success. Her volatile personality was of no help to her career as a playwright: apart from the innovative nature of her subject matter, she had small skill as a writer of dialogue, and less as an arranger of stage business.

Treadwell's papers are housed at the University of Arizona Library.

PRINCIPAL WORKS: Sympathy, 1915; Madame Bluff, 1918; Gringo, 1922; Loney Lue (produced as Oh Nightingale), 1923; Machinal, 1928; Ladies Leave, 1929; Lusita, 1931 (novel); Lone Valley, 1933; Plumes in the Dust, 1936; Hope for a Harvest, 1938 (novel and play); One Fierce Hour and Sweet, 1959 (novel); Poe, 1962 (novel).

ABOUT: Robinson, A. M., et. al. (eds.) Notable Women in the American Theatre, 1989; Ross, I. Ladies of the Press, 1974. *Periodicals*—New York Times March 14, 1970; New Yorker October 29, 1990, November 22, 1993.

**TREECE, HENRY** (December 22, 1911–June 10, 1966), English poet, author of historical novels for adults and children, essayist, and editor, wrote: "I was born in the West Midlands of England, of Welsh extraction originally. I went to school at Wednesbury Grammar School in Staffordshire, where I won the science prize for two years in the senior school. Then followed a scholarship to Birmingham University, where I took a poor degree in 1933, and where I played hockey for the third eleven and boxed for the university as a welterweight. I was captain of university boxing in 1932. At the same time I acted, in occasional small and violent parts, with the university dramatic society; but in the main was more interested in the unacademic, mundane things—like weight-lifting and playing the piano in various small dance-bands. We played anywhere, from country clubs to Saturday night dives, where gangs of hooligans sometimes began fights in the middle of the floor.

"At this time my attitude to life was robust rather than aesthetic, and I spent most weekends on the River Severn in Shropshire, with roaming unliterary strong-arm friends, expending surplus energy brawling and swimming over weirs.

"In 1933 I spent a period in Spain and there became flamenco-conscious. My musical taste switched from blues to Scarlatti and de Falla, and I found as much to admire in a matador as in a world heavyweight champion.

"Back home I accepted a post as officer at a Home Office School for delinquents in Leicestershire, where I learned how to make adolescents wash but not how to stop them reading comic papers in church.

"With great relief I then found a post as English master at Cleobury Mortimer College in the most beautiful area of Shropshire, a Tudor school with a love for the old traditions. There, one summer afternoon in 1934, looking down from Titterstone Clee Hill across the patchwork fields that lead to Wales, I first realized that I was perhaps a poet, and began to write seriously. There too I met Mary Woodman, whom I married in 1939.

"In 1935 I became English master at Tynemouth School, a public school in Northumberland, at which time I came to know the late Michael Roberts, a fine poet and critic. Now my verse began to appear in the little magazines and in 1938 I first became acquainted with Dylan Thomas, about whom I later published a critical estimate, which did neither of us much good!

"In the same year I met J. F. Hendry, a Scots philosopher and poet, with whom—and with the encouragement of Sir Herbert Read—I helped to found a Romantic literary movement which was known as the 'New Apocalypse' and which attracted many of our poet-contemporaries. In the three anthologies which we published (*The New Apocalypse; The White Horseman; The Crown and the Sickle*) we made a stand against all forms of totalitarianism—an unusual literary attitude at that time—asserted man's right to free expression and the express the age we lived in.

"When the war broke out, Henry and I joined the armed forces and this group lost its coherence. I served with the Royal Air Force for five years, largely as an intelligence officer in Bomber Command. Then, in the early war years, and largely through the agency of Sir Herbert Read, I met Stefan Schimanski—then personal secretary to Lord Wedgewood—and there began a literary partnership which lasted until Schimanski was killed in an air-crash in 1950 on his way to a journalistic assignment on the war-front in Korea.

"With Schimanski I edited first a magazine, *Kingdom Come*, and later a literary bi-yearly, *Transformation*, the 'party line' of which was Personalism (i.e. man's right to attain to and express the dignity of which God had made him the custodian). About this time, 1942, T. S. Eliot began to take an interest in and to publish my poetry; while the late George Orwell, who was working with the B.B.C., introduced me to broadcasting. I was also working now at short stories and began to find them appearing in various publications in Britain and the U.S.A.

"After my demobilisation in 1946 I turned more seriously to radio, and when I had served some apprenticeship at writing talks, stories and topographical features, wrote verse dramas for radio. These allowed me to express myself more broadly, and to use the elements of narrative and character which straight poetry precluded. During these years I completed the radio trilogy, *The Dark Island, The End of a World* and *The Tragedy of Tristram*, all based on archetypal Celtic themes. . . .

"The inevitable development then followed: having learned by poetry and the short story to manipulate words, and by drama to construct forms, I turned to the novel, using the title of my earlier radio play, *The Dark Island*, for my first novel. . . .

"I find the novel a most satisfying literary form: it allows the poet to exercise his talent with as much license as he wished, and the dramatist to employ as big a cast and as many changes of scene as he needs. It lets the writer create the film he would love to see, but which no director could afford to make. It has this advantage over radio that a book is durable, whereas the word once spoken, however exciting while the vibration lasts, soon passes from the memory. I ask only that my novels should entertain; my evangelical days are now so far away that I would not wish to persuade anyone of anything, except perhaps the multiplicity of man's mind.

"As senior English master at Barton-on-Humber Grammar School, and as the father of a boy and a girl, I am naturally interested in children and have . . . written radio plays and stories for them, usually based on historical themes. . . .

"In the winter of 1950, I spent five weeks in the United States covering New York theatre for the *Manchester Guardian*, and lecturing at the Poetry Center and at the University of Buffalo.

"Although I am a strong monarchist and inflexible European, I regard the United States as my second spiritual home. I shall never forget that a press in Illinois published my first book of poems; that a New York publisher first brought out my *Collected Poems* and that another has so enthusiastically received me . . . as a novelist. I can never forget, or adequately repay, the heart-warming hospitality which I received on my first visit to the United States. Both as writer and as person, these things are of the greatest importance to me."

Henry Treece was born in Wednesbury, Staffordshire, the son of Richard Treece and the former Mary Mason. A grandfather who possessed a rusting old sword and a great fund of memories fired his historical imagination. Poetry he discovered himself in second-hand bookshops in Manchester.

The poetic movement called the New Apocalypse, launched at a meeting in Leeds in August 1938, flourished for only a very few years before and during the Second World War. Treece and J. F. Hendry, who founded it (with Dorian Cooke), edited three Apocalyptic anthologies, *The New Apocalypse* (1940), *The White Horseman* (1944), and *The Crown and the Sickle* (1944). Their most prominent contributors, apart from the founders themselves, were G. S. Fraser, Norman MacCaig, Nicholas Moore, Tom Scott, and Vernon Watkins. *The New Apocalypse* developed in romantic reaction against the urban, political, and colloquial poetry of the 1930s. It wanted something wilder and stranger, and looked to surrealism, the writings of Sir Herbert Read, and the poetry of Dylan Thomas and George Barker. In his introduction to *The Crown and the Sickle*, Treece wrote that the anthologies were designed to illustrate "a new Romantic tendency, whose most obvious elements are love, death, and adherence to myth and an awareness of war."

Treece's own poetry includes narratives invoking Celtic culture, Roman Britain, Arthurian legend. G. S. Fraser in *The White Horseman* was reminded of Spenser by this "rich, elaborate world, in which you can lose yourself." Babette Deutsch remarked that Treece "is content to celebrate the rural scene or to lament man's fate in his own gaudily fanciful, rhetorical fashion" (*Weekly Book Review*). Treece was no critic, and this was evident in his muddled book on Dylan Thomas.

The New Apocalypse gave way to "the New Romanticism," itself soon silenced by postwar skepticism. Treece himself wrote little verse after about 1950. Instead he put his bardic gift to work in historical novels. The majority of these were written for children, though all can be enjoyed by adults. They were usually set at historical "crossroads," when migration or invasion produce a conflict, then a mingling, of different cultures. There are two Viking trilogies: *Viking's Dawn*, *The Road to Miklagard*, and *Viking's Sunset* follow the travels and adventures of Harald Sigurdson from youth to death; the second trilogy has disparate heroes: *Horned Helmet*, *The Last of the Vikings*, *Splintered Sword*. Four books center upon the Iceni queen Boudicca and her rising against the Romans: *The Bronze Sword*, *The Queen's Brooch*, *The Centurion*, and the adult novel *Red Queen, White Queen*. Three more adult novels deal with figures of Greek mythology: *Jason*, *Electra*, and *Oedipus*. Treece's obituarist in the *New York Times* said that he was "a severe trial to literary critics. They were practically unanimous in their concessions to his formidable learning in history, anthropology, and archeology. But they were often convinced that they were being led down a misty, spirit-ridden path in Mr. Treece's historical novels, in which the author was the only one able to make out the guideposts."

Treece was a scrupulous researcher and a prolific storyteller of steadily increasing skill. He had told stories in his poems, used stories in teaching, and developed his command of narrative and dialogue in the verse dramas and plays for schools he had written for radio. Treece often dictated his novels into a tape recorder to check rhythm of his sentences, feeling that in this sense he was literally "telling" his stories. According to Margery Fisher, Treece's "early fiction, for whatever readership, showed the fault of superfluity. He had to learn to discipline his delight in a pictorial past, to select from an overplus of material, to let action speak for itself. . . . Under the influence of the Norse sagas he came more and more to believe that action should be the basis of his story and he worked to achieve a concise style . . . in which every descriptive word, every spoken word should count." Treece's characters "are not deeply analysed as individuals," according to Fisher: "Often they represent a stage in the development of a tribe or a movement."

Like his Apocalyptic poems, Treece's novels show "love, death . . . and an awareness of war." Also "an adherence to myth," especially the Earth Mother-Corn King myths. However, Treece also enjoyed demythologization—in *The Eagles Have Flown*, King Arthur (Count Artorius) is presented as a half-Barbaric Celt who had learned military skills from the Romans. Although he said (in a letter) "I abhor violence, and distrust victory," Treece the college boxer nevertheless had a romantic admiration for brave fighting men. And even in his books for children, he showed the brutality of the past with an explicitness and apparent relish that often troubled reviewers. A number of the books end with the young hero finding a father figure—a theme that has been attributed to Treece's grief at the death in infancy of his own first child.

Treece wrote a number of amusing mystery stories for young adults, all with contemporary settings. These were of no great importance but, as Margery Fisher says, Treece's historical novels for children got better and better. One of the best was *Man with a Sword* (1962), about Hereward the Wake and his complex relationship with William the Conqueror. A reviewer in the *Horn Book* called this "a masculine, robust telling . . . accentuated with dry, understated humor: constantly changing scenes permit glimpses into several warring kingdoms and give an over-all view of the times. For perceptive readers, there are acute observations on the ways and weaknesses of men and a poetic prose that rings with the haunting voices of the troubled past."

An even better book was *The Dream-Time*, published posthumously. Set in a neolithic society, it tells the story of Crookleg, an artist in a violent world, a boy who would rather create than fight. The *Times Literary Supplement* found it a "strangly haunting fable. . . . the kind of dream one would expect from a poet, a lover of history and a lover of man. It is simple in language and thought, and its simplicity seems to reflect that uncomplicated wisdom we sometimes attain between sleep and waking." In her introduction to *The Golden Strangers*, another novel of prehistory, Rosemary Sutcliff wrote of Treece: "He had an intuitive feeling for what it must have been like to be a man in a time when awareness of one's own individuality—or possession of a human soul—was still a comparatively new and a very frightening thing. He understood better than any other writer I have ever read, the appalling intricacy of life in a primitive society."

Treece taught at Barton-on-Humber Grammar School until his retirement in 1959 after a heart attack. He remained in the small Lincolnshire market town, and was a member of the Barton Cricket Club and president of the Drama Club. He was a popular lecturer, especially delighting young audiences, and appeared often on radio and television. Though he was an immensely productive writer, publishing about four books a year, he was always ready to leave his work to answer requests for information or advise on a school essay.

PRINCIPAL WORKS: *Poetry*—Thirty-Eight Poems, 1940; Towards a Personal Armageddon, 1940; Invitation and Warning, 1942; The Black Seasons, 1945; Collected Poems, 1946; The Haunted Garden, 1947; The Exiles, 1952. *History*—The Dark Island, 1952 (in U.S.: The Savage Warriors); The Rebels, 1953; The Golden Strangers, 1956 (in U.S.: The Invaders); The Great Captains, 1956; Red Queen, White Queen, 1958 (in U.S.: The Master of Badger's Hall); Jason, 1961; Electra, 1963 (in U.S.: The Amber Princess); Oedipus, 1964 (in U.S.: The Eagle King); The Green Man, 1966. *Historical nonfiction*—Castles and Kings, 1959; The True Book About Castles, 1960; The Crusades, 1962 (published as Known About the Crusades for children, 1963); (with R. E. Oakeshott) Fighting Men, 1963. *Other*—How I See Apocalypse, 1946; I Cannot Go Hunting Tomorrow, 1946 (short stories); Dylan Thomas: Dog Among the Fairies, 1949; Carnival King, 1955 (play). *Juvenile*—Legions of the Eagle, 1954; The Eagles Have Flown, 1954; Viking's Dawn, 1955; Hounds of the King, 1955; The Road to Miklagard, 1957; Men of the Hills, 1957; The Children's Crusade, 1958 (in U.S.: Perilous Pilgrimage); The Return of Robinson Crusoe, 1958 (in U.S.: The Further Adventures of Robinson Crusoe); Wickham and the Armada, 1959; The Bombard, 1959 (in U.S.: Ride into Danger); Red Settlement, 1960; Viking's Sunset, 1961; The Jet Beads, 1961 (contemporary novel); The Golden One, 1961; War Dog, 1962; Man with a Sword, 1962; Horned Helmet, 1963; The Burning of Njal, 1963; The Last of the Vikings, 1964 (in U.S.: The Last Viking); Splintered Sword, 1965; The Bronze Sword, 1965 (in U.S.: The Centurion); The Queen's Brooch, 1966; Swords from the North, 1967; Vinland the Good, 1967 (in U.S.: Westward to Vinland); The Dream-Time, 1967; The Windswept City, 1967; The Invaders: Three Stories, 1972; The Magic Wood, 1992 (poetry). *Mysteries for young adults*—Desperate Journey, 1954; Ask for King Billy, 1955; Hunter Hunted, 1957; Don't Expect Any Mercy, 1958; Killer in Dark Glasses, 1965; Bang, You're Dead!, 1965. *As editor*—(with J. F. Hendry) The New Apocalypse, 1939; (with J. F. Hendry) The White Horseman, 1941; (with J. F. Hendry) The Crown and the Sickle, 1943; (with S. Schimanski) Wartime Harvest, 1943; (with S. Schimanski) Transformation, 1943; (with S. Schimanski) Transformation Two, 1944; Herbert Read: An Introduction, 1944; (with J. Pudney) Air Force Poetry, 1944; (with S. Schimanski) Transformation Three, 1945; (with S. Schimanski) A Map of Hearts, 1945; (with S. Schimanski) Transformation Four, 1947; (with S. Schimanski) Leaves in the Storm: A Book of Diaries, 1947; (with S. Schimanski) A New Romantic Anthology, 1949.

ABOUT: The autobiographical material quoted above was written for Twentieth Century Authors First Supplement, 1955. Fisher, M. Henry Treece *in* Three Bodley Head Monographs (ed. K. Lines) 1969; Fraser, G. S. The Modern Writer and His World, 1964; Fraser, G. S. and Treece, H. The White Horseman, 1941; Fraser, G. S. and Treece, H. The Crown and the Sickle, 1943; Fuller, M. (ed.) More Junior Authors, 1963; Press, J. A Map of Modern English Verse, 1969; Salmon, A. E. Poets of the Apocalypse, 1983; Scarfe, F. Auden and After, 1942; Twentieth Century Children's Writers, 1978; Ward, M. E. and Marquardt, D. A. Authors of Books for Young People, 1964. *Periodicals*—Horn Book October 1964; New York Times June 11, 1966; Times (London) June 11, 1966; Times Literary Supplement November 30, 1967; Weekly Book Review September 8, 1946.

**TRENCH, (FREDERICK) HERBERT** (November 26, 1865–June 11, 1923), British poet and dramatist was born at Avoncore, County Cork, in Ireland. He was the eldest son of William Wallace Trench and the former Elizabeth French Allin, and a great-nephew of Richard Chenevix Trench, Archbishop of Dublin.

Trench was sent at fifteen to Haileybury, an English public school, where he wrote some dreamy verses. In 1884, with an exhibition (scholarship) in modern history, he went up to Keble College, Oxford. He was a handsome young man, with deep-set black eyes, and a heavy black mustache. Handicapped at first by ill-health, he nevertheless graduated in 1888 with first- class honors in modern history, then traveled for a time, sailing up the Nile and visiting Russia, Austria and Spain. Back in Oxford in 1889, he was elected a Fellow of All Souls College.

In 1891, Trench entered the civil service as an examiner with the Board of Education. The same year he married Lillian Isabel Fox. They had two sons and three daughters. In 1900, the Board appointed him senior examiner and assistant director of special inquiries. He remained so until his early retirement in 1909. According to his friend Harley Granville-Barker, Trench "was temperamentally unsuited to administrative work. When the burden of routine at the Board of Education was much increased after the Education Act of 1902, it was probably with feelings of mutual relief that his retirement was arranged" (*Dictionary of National Biography*).

All the same, Trench's work left him a good deal of leisure, in which he traveled, collected pictures and sculpture, and wrote verse. His first mature collection, *Deirdre Wed*, showed him to be a philosophical poet, more interested in ideas and ideals than in the individual or the particular. The title poem is a long blank verse narrative spoken by three ghostly figures, and making skillful use of a variety of different styles and meters. It draws upon a tragic Irish legend that also engaged at least four poets of the "Celtic Twilight," including Yeats. However, Harold Williams, in his introduction to the *Collected Works*, wrote that, although "Herbert Trench has been described as a mystical poet," he had no sympathy "with emotional and hazy thinking. The Celtic Twilight he regarded as sentimental mystery mongering. . . . His thought and writing move on the plane where intellect and spirit meet."

"Apollo and the Seaman," a "philosophic ballad," an allegory in which immortality is represented by a ship, was praised by W. M. Payne for a "Meredithian glow and opulence," a "Meredithian swiftness of intellectual motion" (*Dial*). Others, however, thought that the vigor of the opening was not sustained —that, like most of Trench's longer poems, it lacked intellectual coherence, and declined into empty grandiosity. A *Spectator* reviewer concluded that "the cumulative effect of the long poems is like that of a prolonged and colorless piano solo, played by a school girl intent on 'expression.'" For many critics, Trench came closest to achieving a proper tension between thought and emotion in less ambitious lyrics like "Come, let us make love deathless, thou and I."

Trench had demonstrated some feeling for the theater with his translation of a Russian play, *The Death of the Gods*, by the symbolist Dmitri Merezhkovsky (the only one of Trench's works to have remained in print). He went from the Board of Education to the Haymarket Theatre in London's West End, where he served for two years as artistic director. Arnold Bennett in his *Journals* recorded a 1909 lunch at which Trench described "his airy plans for a high-class theatre." This skepticism increased noticeably when Trench, having commissioned a comedy from Bennett, demanded radical changes—and finally rejected the piece. Trench made mistakes at the Haymarket, but did remarkably well for a complete newcomer to the commercial theater. He alternated popular with more experimental plays, and had major hits with productions of Maeterlinck's *The Blue Bird* and of *King Lear*. Trench was also prepared to take chances on young and unknown writers, and to employ composers and painters who had not previously worked in theater.

Trench himself tried his hand as a dramatist, and had considerable success with an unwieldy but passionately argued four-act *Napoleon*. It was produced by the Stage Society in 1919 with a cast led by Sybil Thorndike and Leon Quartermaine. A prose play that rises in one crucial scene to blank verse, it is a debate between egotism and a transcendent humanism. The underlying theme of this, as of several of the later poems, is an exalted notion of the family. The family is seen as the "chalice" of a spiritual development that will lead humanity from a barren individualism, through "spirals of creation," to oneness with a universal consciousness. Mark Van Doren thought Trench's play "worth all of his poems twice over" (*Nation*).

In about 1912, meanwhile, Trench bought the Villa Viviani at Settignano, near Florence. He lived there almost a year, installing in the great entrance hall his Greek bronze of Apollo. Never robust, Trench's health was declining. He worked when he could, nevertheless, and in Florence established the

Instituto Britannico, to foster better understanding between Britain and Italy. Harold Williams described Trench as "high-spirited, eager, delighted in the beauty of art and nature, at times intellectually assertive," but "friendly and simple." He set himself, Williams said, "never to write a line that is not more beautiful than silence," and discarded anything which, in his opinion, failed to meet this criterion.

Trench never fully recovered from a serious accident in 1919. He fell ill on a journey to England and died in a Boulogne hospital. He left uncompleted a play about Talleyrand.

PRINCIPAL WORKS: Collected works, 3 vols., 1924. *Poems*—Haileybury Verses, 1882; Deidre Wed and Other Poems, 1900; New Poems, 1902 (republished as Apollo and the Seaman, 1907); Lyric and Narrative Poems, 1911; Ode from Italy in Time of War, 1915; Poems, with Fables in Prose, 1918; Selected Poems of Herbert Trench, 1924. *Drama*—Napoleon, 1919. *As translator*—The Death of the Gods (by D. Merezhkovsky) 1901; The Romance of Leonardo da Vinci (by D. Merezhkovsky) 1924.

ABOUT: Bennett, A. The Journals of Arnold Bennett: 1896–1910, 1932; Dictionary of National Biography, 1922–1930, 1937; Trench, H. Collected Works (intro. by H. Williams), 1924. *Periodicals*—Contemporary Review July 1924; Dial August 16, 1909; London Mercury June 1924; London Times June 14, 1923; Nation March 29, 1920; Spectator November 23, 1918.

**TRENT, GREGORY.** See **WILLIAMSON, THAMES ROSS**

**TRENT, WILLIAM PETERFIELD** (November 10, 1862–September 7, 1939), American academic, critic, and scholar of Milton and Defoe, was born in Richmond, Virginia, the son of Peterfield Trent, a physician, and Lucy (Burwell) Trent. A promising scholar from the beginning, he graduated from the University of Virginia (1884). After reading law (1885–1887) in Richmond, he enrolled for a year of postgraduate study at the Johns Hopkins University. Here he came under the influence of distinguished teachers, among them Herbert B. Adams, who became his virtual mentor, and Woodrow Wilson. In 1888 he joined the faculty at the University of the South, Sewanee; he became dean of the academic department there in 1894. He shifted decisively from history to literature when he went to Columbia as a professor of English literature in 1900, where he remained until a stroke, suffered in Paris in 1927, left him unable to teach.

Trent had made his mark, as a leader of southern liberal historical thought, long before receiving his final Columbia appointment (this he owed, at least in part, to the fact that his 1892 biography of the lawyer and novelist William Gilmore Simms had pleased Theodore Roosevelt as well as Brander Matthews and the president of Columbia himself, Seth Low). He established historical societies for the proper and scholarly investiga-

tion of southern historical facts. He founded the *Sewanee Review* in 1892; for seven years he also edited it, striving through its pages to arouse the south from what he angrily—and, in the end, influentially—denounced as its fatal reactionary torpor. His *Southern Statesmen of the Old Regime* (1897) helped to establish sound lines of research. While at Sewanee he also wrote, besides this and the crucial Simms study, biographies of Benjamin Franklin, Robert E. Lee, and John Milton—of whose complete works he would later become the first really scholarly co-editor. He also wrote other books—and found time to edit no fewer than sixty-seven texts.

The Simms biography was his first important book. Besides convincingly explaining the mixed achievements of its subject, whom it dismisses as a largely mediocre talent who attracted more than due attention because of the absence of much other talent at the time, it violently upset southern conservatives by its incidental claims that the Civil War had come about because of slavery (rather than states' rights). It became a standard work, and even now provides (if sometimes only at second or third hand) at least a starting point for any investigation into Simms. The influence of Trent, whether negative or positive, is clear in the important criticism of Simms later undertaken by C. Hugh Holman, John C. Guilds (the editor of Simms's writing) and, in particular, Donald Davidson. It was, Paul Buck observed in *The Road to Reunion* (1937), "the most devastating indictment of the intellectual life of the old South ever written by an informed scholar."

At Columbia Trent's teaching was, from the start, mainly at graduate level. Carl Van Doren, one of his pupils, and later a collaborator, wrote of him: "William P. Trent, my favorite teacher and the noblest man I ever knew, was by temper a philosophical statesman as much as a scholar of the most exacting erudition . . . . [he was] a kind, fierce, gray Virginian lion" and a man of "noble" and "witty" rages. Trent's and Van Doren's jointly edited *Cambridge History of American Literature* (with Stuart Sherman and John Erskine) was one of the first such surveys, and it demonstrated Trent's own persistent view that specialist studies such as philosophy and even criticism should be subordinated to that of actual literary appreciation.

Trent's greatest achievement was doubtless his enormous eighteen-volume *Complete Works* (1931–1938) of John Milton, the concept of which he suggested in 1908. He himself had to give up the editorship-in-chief of this work in 1925. Although now in the gradual process of being superseded by the Yale edition of the prose, it is still (in the edition overseen by F. A. Patterson) the most complete, and it helped to lay the foundations of Miltonic studies.

The most dramatic event in Trent's personal life arose as a result of the outbreak of World War I. Always an anti-imperialist—he had already protested at the time of the American-Spanish conflict in 1901, with his book *War and Civilization*—he formed the view that the Americans ought not to enter the war, which he regarded as a mere extension of British imperialism, on the allied side. He even published, in 1915, a poem in enthusiastic support of the Germans. This caused breaches with many Columbia colleagues who otherwise admired or even revered him. Athough "courteous and sympathetic" and of "penetrating intelligence" Trent was obstinate in his views, and could easily become angry. His sympathetic apologist Carl Van Doren wrote that he "suffered everything a prophet can suffer when the pack turns against him."

Although he published a short book on the English novelist Daniel Defoe in 1916, the fruit of Trent's two decades of work on him, a massive manuscript deposited (by his wishes) at Yale, remained unpublished. Its ten volumes were, reportedly, being edited by Harry C. Hutchins, during the years of World War II. Since Trent's death two or three scholarly biographies of Defoe have appeared.

Trent wrote several general books on literature, a few of which, such as *Greatness in Literature*, remained for long in print. His main achievment, however (as well as his work on Milton), was in his influential attacks on the intellectual quality of the old South.

PRINCIPAL WORKS: English Culture in Virginia, 1889 (rev. 1973); William Gilmore Simms, 1892 rev. 1969; Southern Statesmen of the Old Régime, 1897; The Authority of Criticism, and Essays, 1899; John Milton: A Short Study of His Life and Works, 1899, 4th rev. ed. 1978; Robert E. Lee, 1899, rev. ed. 1972; Verses, 1899, rev. ed. 1977; (with B. W. Wells) Colonial Prose and Poetry, 1901, rev. ed. 1970; Progress of the United States of America in the Century, 1901; War and Civilization, 1901; A History of American Literature: 1607–1865, 1903, rev. ed. 1978 Greatness in Literature, and Other Papers, 1905, rev. ed. 1967; Southern Writers, 1905, rev. ed. 1980; Longfellow and Other Essays, 1910, rev. ed. 1967; Great (with J. Eskine) Writers of America, 1912, 2nd rev. ed. 1992; Defoe: How to Know Him 1916, 2nd rev. eds. 1992; (with J. E. S. P. Sherman and C. Van Doren) The Cambridge History of American Literature, 1945, rev. ed. 1961.

ABOUT: Buck, P. H. The Road to Reunion 1937; Van Doren, C. Three Worlds 1936; George Peabody College for Teachers, 1943. *Periodicals*—American Historian Review April 1940; American Notes & Queries July 1941; Journal of Southern History May 1949; New York Times December 8, 1939; School and Society December 16, 1939.

## TREVELYAN, G(EORGE) M(ACAULAY)

(February 16, 1876–July 21, 1962), English historian, was born at Welcombe, his mother's house near Stratford-on-Avon, and spent much of his youth on his parents' Northumberland estate. The scion of an ancient, wealthy, and accomplished family, he was the third son and youngest child of George Otto Trevelyan, a historian, Whig politician, and government official, and Caroline  (Philips) Trevelyan, the daughter of a prominent Manchester merchant and politician. His grandfather, Charles Edward Trevelyan, was a colonial official who played a critical role in the creation of the modern British Civil Service. His great-uncle was the noted Whig politician and historian Thomas Babington Macaulay. As David Cannadine noted in *G. M. Trevelyan*, "Trevelyan, like his youthful friend and near contemporary Bertrand Russell, belonged to two separate but overlapping aristocracies of late-nineteenth-century Britain: the aristocracy of privileged birth, and the aristocracy of exceptional talent." Although his popularity began to wane even before his death, from the 1920s through the 1950s G. M. Trevelyan was one of the most famous, the most honored, and the most widely read historians of his generation.

Trevelyan was educated at Harrow and Trinity College, Cambridge University, where he studied under the liberal historian Lord Acton, and was elected to the Apostles, an exclusive debating society. His major intellectual influences seem to have been his great-uncle Macaulay, Thomas Carlyle, and the English poet, novelist, and critic George Meredith. His first book, *England in the Age of Wycliffe*, a study of the great fourteenth-century religious reformer, was a revision of his Trinity fellowship dissertation. Trevelyan remained in Cambridge as a lecturer in history until 1903, when he moved to London to pursue a career as an independent writer and lecturer.

In 1904 Trevelyan married Janet Penrose Ward, a writer and social worker with an impressive pedigree of her own: she was the daughter of the novelist Mrs. Humphry Ward, and a niece of poet and critic Matthew Arnold. In London, Trevelyan was a frequent lecturer at the Working Men's College in Bloomsbury, and a cofounder and editor of the liberal journal *Independent Review*. His second book, *England Under the Stuarts*, appeared to widespread critical and popular acclaim. Trevelyan believed that the primary role of the historian was that of public educator; hence, his book on the Stuarts, like most of his subsequent work, was written for the intelligent layperson as well as the university scholar.

The title essay of Trevelyan's collection *Clio, a Muse* is a passionate defense of literary history, or the traditional narrative approach to writing history, which Trevelyan viewed as being under siege with the rise, especially in the academy, of so-called "scientific" history, largely inspired by German scholarly methods. Trevelyan, who had been deeply influenced by Carlyle's *On Heroes, Hero-Worship, and the Heroic in History*, cemented his reputation as a historian with a three-volume biography of the Italian patriot and Risorgimento leader Giuseppe Garibaldi. His father had been an ardent Garibaldi supporter, and Trevelyan himself retraced many of the routes of Garibaldi's campaigns during extended walking and bicycle tours of the Italian countryside. Although some reviewers chided Trevelyan for his quasi-devotional stance toward the Italian hero—a prejudice the author made no attempt to disguise—the critical response to the trilogy was favorable, making Trevelyan a respected historian on both sides of the Atlantic.

During World War I, Trevelyan headed a British Red Cross ambulance unit on the Italian front. The war dealt a severe blow to his sanguine liberal internationalism and his Whiggish certainty that progress and improvement were the inevitable lot of mankind. As he noted in *An Autobiography and Other Essays*, "I had been too bookish an historian. Moreover, the war had helped to free me from some party prejudices and from too easy an historical optimism." In the years following World War I, he published most of the books for which he is now best known, and became one of the most widely-read living historians in the world.

*Scenes from Italy's War* and *Lord Grey of the Reform Bill*, both published in the immediate aftermath of World War I, were followed by two books that secured his reputation as a "national historian": *British History in the Nineteenth Century* and *History of England*. The latter is a one-volume survey covering more than 2,000 years—from the invasions of the Iberians and Celts to the 1920s. J. R. Green's immensely popular *Short History of the English People*, first published in the 1870s, had been the last comparable one-volume effort, and most critics welcomed Trevelyan's book. *Nation and Athenaeum* reviewer Leonard Woolf lauded Trevelyan's *History* as "complex and kaleidoscopic," and commended the author for having written "a book which will be useful to many generations of young and old who want the facts about English history compressed within a single volume." In 1944, the *History* was used as a textbook by eighteen-year-old Princess Elizabeth; it had been chosen for her because Trevelyan was regarded as an exponent of Britain's democratic heritage, which the future monarch was sworn to uphold.

In 1927 Trevelyan was made the Regius Professor of Modern History at Cambridge University. Several years later there appeared his three-volume study *England Under Queen Anne*, which Trevelyan conceived as a continuation of his great-uncle Macaulay's most famous work, *History of England from the Accession of James the Second*. *England Under Queen Anne* was—along with the biography of Garibaldi—the work Trevelyan himself was proudest of, and it is probably his finest achievement, both as scholarship and prose narrative. Reviewing *Ramillies and the Union with Scotland*, the work's second volume, a *Times Literary Supplement* critic remarked, "Among the minor delights of Mr. Trevelyan's writing are its continual surprises—asides, epigrams, excursions, vignettes, such as might be the property . . . of a writer who had the discernment to use them." Others, however, found his digressions irritating and unscholarly.

From 1940 to 1951, Trevelyan served as Master of Trinity College, a post for which he was recommended by the then prime minister, Winston Churchill, a man he respected but with whom he often disagreed. *English Social History*, his most commercially successful book, appeared during World War II. (It was published first in the United States due to a wartime paper shortage in England.) In it, he traces the growth of England as a national community by examining daily life from the time of Chaucer to the reign of Queen Victoria. It is both a celebration of the uniqueness of English character and institutions, and (at least implicitly) a critique of the depredations of industrialism. When Trevelyan wrote, "social history" hardly existed as a subject for serious inquiry, and while his book seems, at first glance, to bear little resemblance to more modern "social histories"—it is determinedly nonpolitical, and largely ignores such factors as economics and class struggle—it was, in many respects, a groundbreaking work, particularly as a chronicle of the victims of the Industrial Revolution. It was favorably reviewed in the American press, but in the years after its publication was openly disparaged by many of Trevelyan's younger British colleagues. Sir Geoffrey Elton, who succeeded Trevelyan as the Regius Professor of Modern History at Cambridge, deplored the author's "smooth sentimentalities," and concluded that *English Social History* was a book that "sired nothing."

In *An Autobiography and Other Essays*, Trevelyan wrote, "I have been not an original but a traditional kind of historian. The best that can be said of me is that I tried to keep up to date a family tradition as to the relation of history to literature, in a period when the current was running strongly in the other direction towards history exclusively 'scientific.'" Trevelyan's literary bent, his disdain for historical theory, and his commitment to writing for the general public all mark him as a traditionalist. Nonetheless, he was a wide-ranging writer, "neither the crude Whig nor the superficial amateur that his more extravagant critics have caricatured him as having been," David Cannadine claimed in *G. M. Trevelyan*. "But there is more substance to the claim that he was, as he himself admitted, a 'traditional' historian. Having formed his mind on the great staples of late-nineteenth-century liberal education, he did not feel any urge to keep up with new, or newly fashionable writing." Trevelyan was concerned above all with accurate, detailed historical chronicles, and was not a consistent thinker. He professed agnosticism, but his ethics and his concept of good and evil were clearly derived from Christianity. Although he displayed a decided preference for stories with happy endings, he was not a thoroughgoing optimist; he despaired, especially in later life, of the ways in which encroaching urbanization and industrialization had ravaged the English countryside. (An inveterate walker and nature lover, he devoted much attention to the preservation projects of the National Trust.) He was an English nationalist, certainly, but a stern critic of imperialism as well.

Trevelyan was the recipient of myriad awards and honors, including the Order of Merit (1930), and from 1950 to 1958 served as the chancellor of Durham University. While his reputation has declined, most of his major books remain in print. There are collections of Trevelyan's letters and manuscripts in many locations, including Trinity College, Cambridge.

PRINCIPAL WORKS: *History and biography*—England in the Age of Wycliffe, 1899; England Under the Stuarts, 1904; Garibaldi's Defence of the Roman Republic, 1907; Garibaldi and the Thousand, 1909; Garibaldi and the Making of Italy, 1911 (reissued, with "Garibaldi's Defence" and "Garibaldi and the Thousand" in 1 vol., as Garibaldi, 1933); The Life of John

Bright, 1913; Clio, a Muse, and Other Essays Literary and Pedestrian, 1913, rev. ed. 1930 ; Scenes from Italy's War, 1919; The Recreations of an Historian, 1919; Lord Grey of the Reform Bill: Being the Life of Charles, Second Earl of Grey, 1920; The War and the European Revolution in Relation to History, 1920; British History in the Nineteenth Century, 1922 (revised and reissued as British History in the Nineteenth Century and After, 1937); Manin and the Venetian Revolution of 1848, 1923; History of England, 1926, 3rd ed. 1945 (reissued as A Shortened History of England, 1942, and as Illustrated History of England, 1956); England Under Queen Anne, 3 vols. [Blenheim; Ramillies and the Union with Scotland]; The Peace and the Protestant Succession 1930–1934; Grey of Fallodon: The Life and Letters of Sir Edward Grey, Afterwards Viscount Grey of Fallodon, 1937; The English Revolution, 1688–89, 1938; Trinity College: An Historical Sketch, 1943; English Social History: A Survey of Six Centuries, Chaucer to Queen Victoria, 1942 (reissued as Illustrated English Social History, 4 vols. 1949–1952). *Literary criticism*—The Poetry and Philosophy of George Meredith, 1906; A Layman's Love of Letters, 1954. *Memoirs*—Sir George Otto Trevelyan, a Memoir by His Son, 1932. *Autobiography*—An Autobiography and Other Essays, 1949. *Nature*—Walking, 1928; Must England's Beauty Perish? A Plea on Behalf of the National Trust for Places of Historic Interest or Natural Beauty, 1929. *As editor*—(with E. Powell) The Peasants' Rising and the Lollards: A Collection of Unpublished Documents Forming an Appendix to "England in the Age of Wycliffe," 1899; English Songs of Italian Freedom, 1911; Letters and Recollections of Mazzini (by H. King) 1912; Macaulay's Lays of Ancient Rome and Other Historical Poems (by T. B. Macaulay) 1928; Select Documents from Queen Anne's Reign Down to the Union with Scotland, 1702–1707, 1929; Bolingbroke's Defense of the Treaty of Utrecht, 1932; The Seven Years of William IV: A Reign Cartooned by J. Doyle, 1952; Carlyle: an Anthology, 1953; Selected Poetical Works of George Meredith, 1955.

ABOUT: Cannadine, D. G. M. Trevelyan: A Life in History, 1992; Contemporary Authors vols. 89–92, 1980; Dictionary of National Biography, 1961–1970, 1981; Moorman, M. George Macaulay Trevelyan: A Memoir by His Daughter, 1980; Plumb, J. H. G. M. Trevelyan, 1951; Who's Who 1962. *Periodicals*—Midwest Quarterly October 1976; Nation and Athenaeum July 10, 1926; New York Review of Books July 5, 1993; New York Times July 22, 1962; New York Times Book Review May 30, 1933; Times (London) July 23, 1962; Times Literary Supplement October 6, 1932.

**TREVOR-ROPER, HUGH REDWALD (LORD DACRE)** (January 15, 1914– ), English historian, was born in Glanton, Northumberland, and was educated at Charterhouse and Christ Church, Oxford, where, as an undergraduate, he studied classics and modern history. From 1937 to 1939 he was a research fellow at Merton College, working on an M.A. that resulted in his first and, in conventional terms, most substantial book, *Archbishop Laud, 1573–1645*.  After the war he was sent as a British Intelligence Officer to investigage the death of Hitler. *The Last Days of Hitler* (1947), established Trevor-Roper as the most exciting historian of his generation, with an ability to construct a readable narrative from the details of research. Arthur Schlesinger Jr., writing in the *Nation*, pronounced the book "a brilliant professional performance," and Alan Bullock, in the *Spectator*, found that "Mr. Trevor-Roper's ability in combining the many scraps of evidence into a continuous account is matched by the skill and lucidity with which he tells the story." The book was a commercial success and has never been out of print.

His third book, *The Gentry, 1540–1640*, in which he returned to the Elizabethan period, seemingly established this as his field of special interest, and helped to enhance a reputation that led, in 1957, to his being made Regius Professor of Modern History. His attack on Arnold Toynbee—now generally accepted as a cantankerous expression of the truth—published in a 1954 *Sunday Times* review of Toynbee's *A Study of History*, was considered by some to be so personal as to put his selection in jeopardy. Others thought that the position should have been given to A.J.P. Taylor, Trevor-Roper's Oxford rival. (The two held opposing views on Hitler, Trevor-Roper contending that the war was the direct result of the Nazi leader's evil genius, and Taylor believing that Hitler's original objectives were limited and that the war resulted from diplomatic bungling.)

In 1964 he courted controversy again when, having spent three months in Los Angeles studying the twenty-six volumes of the Warren Commission's Kennedy assassination report, he declared, in the *Times*, that he was skeptical of the report's theory of a lone assassin. (Another note of controversy occurred in 1983 when he too quickly pronounced genuine a recently "discovered" set of Hitler's "diaries," which were soon found to be fakes.) His two principal books of the 1960s—*The Rise of Christian Europe* and *Religion, The Reformation and Social Change* (published in America as *The Crisis of the Seventeenth Century*)—were both collections of essays and lectures, rather than self-contained studies. In the words of G. R. Elton, writing for the *New York Times Book Review*, they established Trevor-Roper's predilection for "the long essay on some major topic, embodying vast reading rather than detailed research, and concerned to establish interpretative schemes which seize upon the imagination and stimulate thought." Lawrence Stone, reviewing *From Counter-Reformation to Glorious Revolution* in the *Times Literary Supplement*, and dubbing Trevor-Roper "an old Whig," called the collection "the most brilliant and perceptive set of essays written by any historian of our time," but prefaced this remark by saying, "It is hard not to feel a sense of regret that not for half a century has Trevor-Roper written a major work of history, but has contented himself with producing dozens of essays, many of which could and should have formed the framework for a major study."

Created a life peer—Baron Dacre of Glanton—in 1979, he gave up his Regius professorship the following year and moved to Cambridge to become master of Peterhouse College. In 1995, to tie in with the fiftieth anniversary of the ending of the Second World War, Lord Dacre wrote a new preface for the seventh edition of *The Last Days of Hitler*. He also updated a retrospective written a few years previously for *Encounter*, a reconsideration of an over-positive interpretation of Albert Speer. But he stood by his portrait of Himmler as a crackpot governed by masseurs and astrologers.

As for his depiction of Hitler, when interviewed by Ron Rosenbaum as part of a long article entitled *Explaining Hitler* and printed in the *New Yorker*, in May 1995, Trevor-Roper defended himself robustly against the idea that *The Last Days of Hitler* had been, in large part, responsible for creating an image of Hitler that amounted to a form of fictional characterization. The argument was most cogently delivered by Professor Alvin Rosenfeld's *Imagining Hitler* (1985), which argued that, in attempting to describe Hitler's spell, Trevor-Roper had fallen under it and "the fiction writer within the scholar seemed to come alive." To Trevor-Roper it has always been those who attempt to demythologize Hitler—among them Alan Bullock and A.J.P. Taylor—who have been promulgating fiction.

PRINCIPAL WORKS: Archbishop Laud 1573–1645, 1940; The Last Days of Hitler, 1947 (7th ed. 1995); Christ Church, Oxford, 1950; The Gentry 1540–1640, 1953; Historical Essays, 1957 (in U.S.: Men And Events); Essays in British History, 1964; The Rise of Christian Europe, 1965; George Buchanan and the Ancient Scottish Constitution, 1966; Religion, The Reformation and Social Change, 1967 (in U.S.: The Crisis of the Seventeenth Century); The Philby Affair, 1968; The Plunder of the Arts in the Seventeenth Century, 1970; Hermit of Peking: The Hidden Life of Sir Edmund Backhouse, 1976; Catholics, Anglicans and Puritans, 1988; From Counter Reformation to Glorious Revolution, 1992.

ABOUT: Contemporary Authors vol. 101; Current Biography 1983; Lloyd-Jones and Pearl V. (eds.) History & Imagination, Essays in Honor of H. R. Trevor-Roper, 1981. *Periodicals*—Encounter December 1988; Nation September 20, 1947; New York Times Book Review March 31, 1968; New Yorker May 1, 1995; Spectator March 21, 1947; Times December 13, 1964; Times Literary Supplement June 5, 1992.

**TRILLING, LIONEL** (July 4, 1905–November 5, 1975), American critic and scholar, wrote: "Lionel Trilling was born in New York City, the son of David W. and Fannie (Cohen) Trilling. He attended the public schools of the city and in 1925 was graduated from Columbia College. In 1926 he took his Master of Arts degree in English literature at Columbia University and taught for a year at the University of Wisconsin. After re-  turning to New York he taught at Hunter College until his appointment as instructor of English at Columbia in 1932. He took his doctorate at the university in 1938, his dissertation being his first published book, *Matthew Arnold*. He passed through the usual academic grades (assistant professor 1939, associate professor 1945) and since 1948 he has been professor of English, giving courses in the literature of England and America in Columbia College and in the Faculty of Philosophy.

"Mr. Trilling's first published work, a short story, appeared in 1925 in the *Menorah Journal*, to which he subsequently contributed other stories as well as essays and reviews. He was one of the group of young writers who reviewed extensively with terrifying authority for the literary section of the *New York Evening Post* when it was under the generous editorship of Harry Dounce. His later critical writing has appeared in the *Nation*, the *New Republic*, the *Times Book Review*, *Partisan Review* and the *Kenyon Review*. He is a member of the advisory boards of the two latter periodicals. With John Crowe Ransom and F. O. Matthiessen, he was one of the organizers of the Kenyon School of Letters at Kenyon College, and he has continued to serve as one of the Senior Fellows of the School, which has now become the School of Letters—Indiana University.

"In 1943 Mr. Trilling published *E. M. Forster*, a critical study of the British novelist which had its part in making Forster's work known in this country. His novel, *The Middle of the Journey*, appeared in 1947, and a collection of his critical essays, *The Liberal Imagination*, in 1950. He has published a few short stories, of which two, 'Of This Time, of That Place,' and 'The Other Margaret,' have become especially well known and have been frequently reprinted.

"Mr. Trilling is married to Diana Trilling who is known for her critical writing. They have one son and they live in New York."

---

As his (London) *Times* obituarist wrote in 1975, Lionel Trilling had been "one of the three or four finest American literary critics of his time." This judgment has merit. Like the wider-ranging Edmund Wilson, Trilling was a scholar who could write lucid prose, accessible to academic and nonacademic alike—a too-rare combination. What he had to say about the literary works he discussed invariably illuminated them; agreement with his point of view was always a secondary factor.

As Thomas Lask, who had written about Trilling on previous occasions, wrote in his obituary of him in the *New York Times*, in his hands "criticism became not merely a consideration of a work of literature but also of the ideas it embodied and what those ideas said of the society that gave them birth. Criticism was a moral function, a search for those qualities by which every age in its turn measured the virtuous man and the virtuous society."

Trilling's inspiration throughout his life was Matthew Arnold, about whom he wrote his first book, originally a doctoral dissertation. He explained in his preface that he wanted "to show the thought of Matthew Arnold in its complex unity and to relate it to the historical intellectual events of his time." It was, he asserted, "a biography of Arnold's mind. . . . I have made clear what . . . Arnold as poet and critic of literature, politics and religion actually said and meant." G. F. Whicher in *New York Herald Tribune Books* thought that the biography "alters the picture of the man Arnold in several respects." The book's reception was in general excellent, although C. F. Harold in *Modern Philology* did put his finger on a lack in Trilling: while applauding the "sane judgment" and "wise comprehension" of the book, he pointed out that it was not "the last word on Arnold's mind." Harold

might have written that it did not provide enough information about Arnold's "heart." It was not "the last word" because Trilling, despite his fascination with and admiration of Sigmund Freud, tended to intellectual rather than emotional evaluations of his subjects. This tendency was to vitiate his own attempts at creative writing.

Trilling had much in common with Arnold, not the least a keen and overriding intelligence and breadth of vision. In his book *Matthew Arnold and American Culture*, J. H. Ralegh suggested that certain critics had assumed that, for Trilling, Arnold had become a model. "What he had tried to do as a whole . . . is to perform in twentieth-century America two roles that . . . Arnold performed in nineteenth-century England: the conservor of what was valuable from the past and the proponent of the free play of the critical intelligence on the present." Irving Howe summed up his career thus in the *New Republic* (1976): "Trilling, while performing superbly as an interpreter of texts, was not read primarily for literary guidance. His influence has to do with that shaded area between literature and social opinion, literature and morality; he kept returning to 'our' cultural values, 'our' premises of conduct, for he was intent upon a subtle campaign to transform the dominant liberalism of the American cultivated classes into something richer, more quizzical and troubled than it had become. . . . He sought to melt ideological posture into personal sensibility."

Trilling followed his study of Arnold with one of E. M. Forster. This was a less important book, but one that helped Americans come to terms with a novelist whom they had never quite been able to take to heart. It was widely recommended by reviewers and critics, G. F. Whicher for example praising it in the *Weekly Book Review* as "mature and vibrant" and a useful counterbalance to T. S. Eliot's "sad spiritual fascism."

Trilling's next important nonfiction book—still the work upon which he is most frequently judged—was the collection of essays called *The Liberal Imagination: Essays on Literature and Society*. In this book, Trilling fully committed himself to what may be described as his "right-wing liberalism." Trilling's argument was that liberalism must be saved from its own idealistic excesses. Trilling's own humane liberalism was not questioned, but he was seen as, and to an extent was, an enemy of the left, which was exemplified by such anti-Stalinist but still leftist critics as the editor of the *Partisan Review*, the critic Philip Rahv. Indeed, Trilling was, in Rahv's famous paleface/redskin distinction, the paradigmatic paleface: the exclusive intellectual, scourge of such writers as Sherwood Anderson and Theodore Dreiser. Trilling stated that these writers espoused a shallow democratic optimism "that despises the variety of modulations of the human story." Against them Trilling opposed not Matthew Arnold but the other great idol of his life, Sigmund Freud. Freud, according to Trilling, was much more of a realist in his pessimism, and possessed much more flexibility of mind.

Trilling became markedly more pessimistic in

his later critical work, since he had started with the essentially Arnoldian view that art could "prevent" (as he put it in his essay "Manners, Morals, and the Novel") "our being seduced by the godhead of disintegration." He was genuinely horrified when such ex-pupils of his as Allen Ginsberg were taken seriously by critics. In one of the essays collected in *Beyond Culture*, Trilling, a man notably opposed to extremes, made one of his more extreme pronouncements, about "adversary culture," his own term for the capacity of poets and novelists to "disturb complacency:" "we can say of it . . . that it has developed . . . habitual response to the stimuli of its environment. It is not without power . . . it seeks to aggrandize and perpetuate itself." Trilling then went on to write, to the dismay and surprise of many of his fellow liberals: "art does not always tell the truth and does not always point out the right way . . . it can even generate falsehood . . . it might well be subject . . . to the scrutiny of the rational intellect." And he spoke of the error of attributing to literature "virtually angelic powers."

In *Sincerity and Authenticity* he argues passionately against the irrational nature of the notion of "authenticity," scoring many excellent points—especially against the notion that "madness" was "the only sanity"—but never quite being able to deal with the question of the nature of creativity. Thus L. D. Lerner, discussing the book in the *New Statesman*, found Trilling at "his best and worst" in his argument that "the 19th-century Englishman found himself through integration into his society, in contrast to the American. This leads to some admirable insights, though the whole point could have been made without bringing in 'sincerity' at all."

Trilling's own novel, *The Middle of the Journey*, has been much praised mainly by his colleagues at Columbia. But it has not caught the imagination of readers of fiction in the way in which Dreiser's or Anderson's best stories and novels continue to do. The novel is a portrait of a man who goes to rural Connecticut to recover from serious illness and runs into difficulties owing to his having been a fellow-traveler of the Communist Party. *Time*—calling Trilling an author of "neat books"—found that a "good deal of the book frays out in thin, earnest psychologizing, a weakness which Trilling's clear grey style has not enough impetus to overcome." The problems are the ones with which Trilling himself struggled, from his too optimistic left-wing beginnings: how to maintain his relations with his old friends, how to deal with his fear of the irrational, how to guard himself against his own tendency to reactionary conservatism.

Trilling discussed the writings of others with unusual and highly intelligent lucidity. Thus it hardly matters whether he is "right" or "wrong" when he discusses such texts as Wordsworth's *Immortality Ode*, or the novels of E. M. Forster, or the career of Robert Graves—the value of his work lies in the illuminations it always lends to its subjects and in how it stimulates the reader.

PRINCIPAL WORKS: *Biography and criticism*—Matthew Arnold, 1939, rev. ed. 1949; E. M. Forster, 1943, rev. ed. 1965; The Liberal Imagination: Essays on Literature and Society, 1950; The Opposing Self: Nine Essays in Criticism, 1955; Freud and the Crisis of Our Culture, 1955; A Gathering of Fugitives: Essays, 1956; Beyond Culture: Essays on Literature and Learning, 1965; Sincerity and Authenticity, 1972; Mind in the Modern World: Thomas Jefferson Lectures in the Humanities, 1973; The Last Decade: Essays and Reviews 1965–1975 (ed. D. Trilling) 1979. *Fiction*—The Middle of the Journey, 1947; Of This Time, Of This Place, and Other Stories (ed. D. Trilling) 1979.

ABOUT: The autobiographical material quoted above was written for Twentieth Century Authors First Supplement, 1955. Anderson, Q., Donadio, S. and Marcus, S. (eds.) Essays in Honour of Lionel Trilling, 1977; Blackmur, R. The Lion and the Honeycomb, 1955; Boyers, R. Lionel Trilling: Negative Capability and the Wisdom of Avoidance, 1977; Chace, W. M. (ed.) Lionel Trilling: Criticism and Politics, 1980; Eisinger, C. E. Fiction of the Forties, 1963; Fraiburg, L. B. Psychoanalysis and American Literary Criticism, 1960; Frank, J. The Widening Gyre: Crisis and Mastery in Modern Literature, 1963; Hart, J. Acts of Recovery, 1989; Krupnick, M. Lionel Trilling and the Fate of Cultural Criticism, 1986; Milne, G. The American Political Novel, 1966; O'Hara, D. Lionel Trilling: The Work of Liberation, 1988; Ralegh, J. H. Matthew Arnold and American Culture, 1957; Scott, N. A. Three American Moralists: Mailer, Bellow, Trilling, 1973; Seymour-Smith, M. Macmillan Guide to Modern World of Literature, 1986; Shoben, E. J. Lionel Trilling, 1981; Simpson, L. Air With Armed Men, 1972; Tanner, S. L. Lionel Trilling, 1988; Trilling, D. The Beginning of the Journey, 1993; Wald, A. M. The New York Intellectuals: The Rise and Decline of the Anti-Stalinist Left, 1987; Zabel, M. D. Craft and Character: Texts, Method and Vocation in Modern Fiction, 1957. *Bibliography*—Leitch, T. L. Lionel Trilling: An Annotated Bibliography, 1993. *Periodicals*—American Scholar Winter 1978; Atlantic June 1950; September 1988; Commentary February 1982; November 1986; Modern Philology November 1939; New Republic October 13, 1947; March 13, 1976; New Statesman October 20, 1972; November 14, 1975; New York Times November 7, 1975; October 24, 1993; New Yorker September 13, 1993; Partisan Review Winter 1987; Salmagundi Spring 1978; Saturday Review of Literature February 14, 1948; Time October 20, 1947; Times (London) November 10, 1975; Times Literary Supplement March 11, 1939; August 23, 1955; August 21, 1981; Weekly Book Review September 5, 1943.

**TRIOLET, ELSA. See ARAGON, LOUIS**

**TROUBETZKOY, AMELIE (RIVES)** (August 23, 1863– June 15, 1945), wrote: "I was born in Richmond, Virginia, of old Virginia families on both sides. My French Christian name came from Queen Amelia, wife of Louis Philippe, who was my grandmother's friend when my grandfather was Minister Plenipotentiary to France. I was taken as a baby to the estate of Castle Hill, Virginia, which belonged to my Rives grandparents, and brought up there in its lovely surroundings. I learned early to bridle, saddle, and harness my pony, and had my first ride on horseback when I was two years old. As I grew older, the country life charmed me more and more. All my long life . . . I have loved the country far more than any town.

"My father was a colonel in the Confederate Army. I was taught at home by my mother and later by tutors and governesses. I cannot remember when I did not want to 'make up stories' or spin queer rhymes. As soon as I could write I began to set them down on paper. When my grandmother disapproved and quietly took the paper from me, I began to write on the wide hems of my starched white petticoats!

"I really haven't much to say about my writing in later years. Some of it, I suppose, was good, and some I know was bad. The book of mine that I like best is a drama in blank verse called *Augustine the Man*, which was published in England. . . .

"In 1888, my first marriage, to John Armstrong Chanler, took place. In 1895, after a long separation, I obtained a divorce. In 1896 I married Prince

Pierre Troubetzkoy, the portait painter. We had nearly forty-one years of great happiness together. He died suddenly in 1936. His mother was an American. Until the winter of 1941, I did not know that all those who married foreigners before 1922 lost their American citizenship. I shall soon take steps to regain mine. To me democracy is a religion, a great faith, which like all religions has to be ever renewed; and the democracy of the United States of America is a living, growing thing. I hope to grow with it until I die. I also hope that before I die there will be a union of all English-speaking democracies throughout the world."

---

Amelie Rives, Princess Troubetzkoy, did not live to see her dream of an English-speaking union fulfilled. She died in Charlottesville, Virginia, in the closing months of World War II, after the surrender of the Axis powers in Europe. Despite her firm affirmation of democracy in her final years, she rarely commented on political affairs in her novels, which generally featured the exploits of strong heroines in the Old South.

Amelie Rives first came to the public's attention in 1888 as the author of *The Quick or the Dead?*. Fred Lewis Pattee, once an influential critic, placed *The Quick or the Dead?* first on a list of four novels "all of them by women that were marked 'unsafe,' even 'scandalous' and 'immoral,' and thus despite their feebleness, were elevated into the ranks of the best sellers." The others, he wrote, were *Eros* by Laura Daintry, *Miss Middleton's Lover* by Laura Jean Libby, and *What Dreams May Come* by Gertrude Atherton. Pattee prefaced his remark by noting that these four "feminine" novels had scandalized readers by 1888, "a whole decade before Crane's *Maggie: A Girl of the Streets.*" One of the major criticisms of *The Quick or the Dead?* was that it gave "permission" for widows to debate about remarrying just a few months into their widowhood, and that it scandalously allowed its heroine to request a kiss from a suitor.

Oscar Wilde, playing Cupid, introduced Rives to her future husband, Prince Pierre Troubetzkoy, at a garden party. Rives married Prince Troubetzkoy after a "South Dakota divorce" (in those days, that state had the most liberal divorce laws). At the time, a young freelancer named Willa Cather wrote in *The Nebraska State Journal:* "So Amelie Rives is married again and to a Russian Prince. Princess

Troubetzkoy, that will look well under the title of her next promotional novel."

Princess Troubetzkoy also tried her hand at playwriting: a closet drama, *The Fear Market*, had a run of 118 performances at the Booth Theater in 1918; *Allegiance*, another play that exploited the anti-German sentiment of the period, was thought to have be cowritten by her husband, the Prince. She also wrote *The Fear Market* (later made into a film) and a stage adaptation of Mark Twain's *The Prince and the Pauper*. Her obsession with youth and beauty may have been the inspiration for *Young Elizabeth*, a play she wrote but never published on the early life of the sixteenth-century monarch. It was, however, given a production by the Little Theater of St. Louis in 1938.

Anne Newman summarized her career: "Troubetzkoy has been called a realist, a fine local colorist, and an important social historian; she has also been called a semierotic, a sensationalist, a romantic who revels in morbid scenes and hysterical passions."

PRINCIPAL WORKS: The Quick or the Dead?, 1888; A Brother to Dragons (short stories) 1888; Virginia of Virginia, 1889; According to St. John, 1890; Athelwold (drama in blank verse) 1891; A Faithful Lover, 1892; Selene (poem), 1905; Augustine the Man, 1906; The Golden Rose, 1908; Trix and Over the Moon, 1909; Pan's Mountain, 1910; Hidden House, 1911; World's End, 1913; Shadows of Flames, 1915; The Ghost Garden, 1918; As the Wind Blew (poems), 1922; The Sea Woman's Cloak (play), 1923; The Queerness of Celia, 1926; Love-in-a-Mist (play), 1927; Firedamp, 1930.

ABOUT: The autobiographical material quoted above was written for Twentieth Century Authors, 1942. American Women Writers, 1982; Clark, E. Innocence Abroad, 1931; Longest, G. Three Virginia Writers: Mary Johnston, Thomas Nelson Page, and Amelie Rives Troubetzkoy: A Reference Guide, 1978; Mott, F. L. Golden Multitudes, 1947; Pattee, F. L. The New American Literature, 193; Taylor, W. Amelies Rives (Princess Troubetzkoy) 1973.

**TRUMBO, DALTON** (December 9, 1905–September 10, 1976), American screenwriter and novelist, was born in Montrose, Colorado, the son of Orus Bonham and Maud (Tillery) Trumbo. He attended the University of Colorado (1924–1925), what was then the Southern Branch, University of California, now the University of California, Los Angeles (1926), and the University of Southern California (1928–1930). In 1932 he

began contributing to the film magazine, the *Hollywood Spectator*.

His first published novel, *Eclipse* (1935), tells the story of John Abbott, the most respected businessman in Shale City, Colorado, who finds his fortunes reversed as he faces the depression alone and ultimately ends up dying in a fire in a department store he once owned. "A kind of *Babbitt*-in-reverse," wrote Trumbo's biographer Bruce Cook. The novel was published in England after being rejected by nineteen publishers in the United States.

From an early age Trumbo was determined to be a novelist, but he backed into screenwriting, signing a contract with Warner Brothers in 1935, considering it a temporary solution to financial problems. Trumbo wrote twenty-one screenplays in the next six years, many of them low-budget remakes for the B-picture units at Warner's, Columbia and RKO. His adaptation of Christopher Morley's *Kitty Foyle*, however, garnered him an Oscar nomination. During the same period he wrote three more novels.

The inspiration for *Johnny Got His Gun* (1939) came when Trumbo read an article about a British officer who was horribly disfigured during World War I. Throughout this stream-of-consciousness novel, this living dead man lies in a hospital bed—without arms, legs, face, sight, or hearing—and becomes an educational exhibit on the realities of war. Harold Strauss wrote in the *New York Times*, "There can be no question of the the effectiveness of this book, nor that it tells a story such as has never before been told." Bruce Cook, exaggerating, pleaded that this novel should be considered one of the finest written by an American in the 1930s: one "that has spoken more directly than any other to the Vietnam generation." A National Book Award winner, it was reprinted twice, in the 1960s and 1970s, and Trumbo adapted it into a screenplay for a 1971 movie of the same name. This received the International Critics Award at the Cannes Film Festival.

The early forties brought Trumbo success as a screenwriter. His credits, which included *A Bill of Divorcement*, *A Guy Named Joe*, *Thirty Seconds Over Tokyo*, and *Our Vines Have Tender Grapes* made him a famous name. Until his blacklisting in 1947—as a result of the "anti-communist" witch-hunt—he had been according to the *New York Times* "one of the highest-paid screen writers in the film capital, earning as much as $4,000 a week while assigned to a script."

Trumbo faced trouble when he, along with nine other prominent directors and screenwriters—the so-called Hollywood Ten—were subpoenaed to appear before the House Un-American Affairs Committee, which was investigating alleged Communist infiltration of the motion-picture industry. All ten refused to testify whether they had ever been a member of the Communist party, and all ten were eventually jailed and fined for contempt of Congress. Trumbo was fined $1,000 and spent ten months in 1950 in a federal prison.

Blacklisted, for the next thirteen years he was unable to find work in the United States. He sold his California ranch and moved his family to Mexico, living with a colony of other blacklistees. But he did not stop working. Cook wrote that "Even during the blacklist period he continued to work in the so-called black market, writing screenplays at cut-rate prices." Written under various pseudonyms, the scripts were mostly low quality for low budget films, but in 1957 the Academy Award for best screenplay went to "Robert Rich" for *The Brave One*. Some were embarrassed to discover that Rich was Trumbo as they continued to fear political reprisals.

In 1960, with the help of director Otto Preminger, Trumbo broke the blacklist, and was hired to write the screenplay for *Exodus*. As Hollywood finally put behind it the hysteria of searching for Communists, Trumbo racked up more screenwriting credits in the 1960s for *Spartacus*, *Lonely Are The Brave*, *The Sandpiper*, *Hawaii*, *Papillon*, and *The Fixer*.

When a book of his letters was published in 1970, Trumbo spoke to the *New York Times* of his Communist involvement with his characteristic humor: "I joined the Communist Party in 1943 and left it in 1948 on the ground that in the future I should be far too busy to attend its meetings, which were, in any event, dull beyond description, about as revolutionary in purpose as Wednesday evening testimonial services in the Christian Science Church." The *New York Times*, also quoted him as saying that "I never considered the working class anything other than something to get out of."

Trumbo was rewarded by finally being presented the Oscar for *The Brave One* in 1975. But he had already died from cancer when the Academy of Motion Picture Arts and Sciences in 1977 retroactively awarded him the 1953 Oscar for Best Motion Picture Story for *Roman Holiday*. Ian McLellan Hunter had been awarded an Oscar for the film in 1953, but refused to pick it up out of respect for Trumbo.

PRINCIPAL WORKS: *Novels*—Eclipse, 1935; Washington Jitters, 1936 (dramatized by J. Boroff and W. Hart, 1938); Johnny Got His Gun, 1939; The Remarkable Andrew, 1940; Night of the Aurochs (ed. Robert Kirsch) 1979. *Screenplays*—Kitty Foyle (adaptation of the book by C. Morley) 1940; A Bill of Divorcement, 1940; A Guy Named Joe, 1943; Thirty Seconds Over Tokyo, 1944; Our Vines Have Tender Grapes (adaptation of the book by G. V. Martin) 1945; (as "Robert Rich") The Brave One 1957; Exodus (adaptation of the book by L. Uris) 1960; Spartacus (based on the novel by H. Fast) 1960; Lonely Are the Brave (based on The Brave Cowboy by E. Abbey) 1962; The Sandpiper, 1965; Hawaii (adaptation of the book by J. A. Michener) 1966; The Fixer (adaptation of the book by B. Malamud) 1968; Johnny Got His Gun, 1971; (with L. Semple, Jr.) Papillion (based on the book by H. Charriere) 1973. *Drama*—The Biggest Thief in Town, 1949.

ABOUT: Cook, B. Dalton Trumbo 1977; Dick, B. F. Radical Innocence, 1989; Hamilton, I. Writers in Hollywood, 1990; Krisch, R. (ed.) Trumbo, D. Night of the Aurochs, 1979; Trumbo, D. Additional Dialogue: Letters of Dalton Trumbo 1942–1962, 1970. *Periodicals*—Nation February 8, 1941; New Republic December 15, 1979; New York Times September 27, 1936; September 10, 1939; June 10, 1950; September 11, 1976; Newsweek November 9, 1970; People Weekly May 17, 1993; Saturday Review of Literature September 9, 1939; Time February 3, 1941; Washington Post September 11, 1976; November 27, 1979.

# TUCKER, BENJAMIN RICKETSON

**TUCKER, BENJAMIN RICKETSON** (July 2, 1864–June 22, 1939), American political philosopher, was born in New Bedford, Massachusetts, the only child of Abner Ricketson and Caroline Tucker. His father, a successful wholesale grocer and ship-supply merchant, was a Quaker of colonial New England lineage; his mother was a Unitarian. Young Tucker received his formal education at the Boston Friends Academy and the Massachusetts Institute of Technology, intending to make civil engineering his profession. After two years at college, Tucker opted to go to France in place of a third academic term in Boston. In Paris he first encountered P. J. Proudhon's writings on anarchism. During his year abroad, he developed a profound respect and admiration for the political anarchist thought associated with Kropotkin and Bakunin.

Soon after returning to the United States, Tucker launched a biweekly journal, *Liberty*, which he continued to edit and publish until 1908. *Liberty* quickly evolved into the most important organ for the propagation of Tucker's philosophical anarchism. Over the course of thirty years, its pages showcased the writings of leading radical thinkers, including George Bernard Shaw and Herbert Spencer.

In 1882, Tucker openly advertised and sold Whitman's *Leaves of Grass*, which had recently been censored in the United States. Prior to establishing *Liberty*, Tucker  had for several years worked on the editorial staff of *The Boston Globe*, but his responsibilities there were confined to the rewriting and editing of news items and reports. He also translated two of Proudhon's major works into English: *What is Property?* and *A System of Economic Contradictions*. Tucker went on to become a well-known translator from the French. Over his career, he produced translations of Bakunin, Tolstoy, Tchenchewsky, Victor Hugo, Zola, and Claude Tiller.

In 1910, fire destroyed the offices of *Liberty* in New York. Since Tucker had not—as a matter of principle—insured his printing shop and equipment, he chose to return to Europe. He remained in France and Monaco for the rest of his life, practicing the "gospel of simple living and higher thinking." He continued to write and publish as an emigré, developing a magazine, *Transatlantic*, and authoring several books, chief among them being *Individual Liberty* in 1927.

Tucker's philosophical anarchism was steadfastly pacifistic, rejecting all forms of governmental coercion as immoral. His beliefs held that the gradual abolition of the state through nonviolent means would radically reduce, if not end, the conditions of poverty and injustice extant under a traditional capitalist economy. He thus regarded the issues of his period as being principally economic rather than political. Tucker consequently focused much of his scorn upon four monopolies: land, money and banking, patents and copyrights, and trade. To dispense with these, he thought, would result in the emancipation of individuals from the tyranny of government and their many forms of interference. The subject who wanted real liberty, Tucker reasoned, would refrain from casting ballots for any candidate for public office. Voting in state elections transferred power into the hands of politicians who sustained and invigorated the monopolies. Their legislative privilege, he believed, was directly responsible for unemployment and abject poverty.

Tucker's following was never large, and his personal life was, in the words of Michael Williams, " . . . almost monastic." Marriage was one of the legal institutions of the state that he opposed, although he lived for almost fifty years with his companion, Pearl Johnson, and had one child with her. Pieces of Tucker's Quaker heritage were found later in his militant pacifism and unwavering devotion to the idea of human goodness. His philosophical anarchism was among the last clear residue of traditional American radical thought, heavily influenced by Thoreau and Emerson. Tucker committed his life to bringing about economic justice and economic opportunity through clear, trenchant writing. As a writer, editor, and translator, he brought ideas to the attention of many American radical thinkers. He died in Monaco several weeks before the outbreak of the Second World War.

PRINCIPAL WORKS: Instead of a Book: By a Man Too Busy to Write One, 1893; Individual Liberty, 1927.

ABOUT: Eltzbacher, P. Anarchism; MacDonald, G. E. Fifty Years of Free Thought; Sprading, C. T. Liberty and the Great Libertarians; Whitman, A. American Reformers. *Periodicals*—American Journal of Sociology January 1936; Commonweal July 7, 1939.

## TUNIS, JOHN ROBERTS (December 7, 1889–February 4, 1975), American sportswriter, wrote:

"John R. Tunis was born in a log cabin on the sunny side of Beacon Street, Boston, just before the turn of the century and just before Beacon turns in to Commonwealth Avenue. The R in his name stands for 'Amateur-Lover.' He rose to greet me, a clean-limbed young American with a chest like a beetle. 'Tunis?' I asked. 'Tunis in on  station WEAF,' he replied, for he has a pawky Gaelic wit though he is often sober. There was something in his whimsical smirk which made me realize that I was in the presence of the man who revolutionized tennis by making the balls round, instead of oblong as they were in the days of Big Dough and Little Dough. Asked to reminisce, Tunis—for he prefers to be called Tunis—said:

"'It was during the blizzard of Naughty-Seven. I happened to be captain of the Harvard eleven. I was also captain of the Yale team and more than once saved the game for the Crimson by tackling myself on my own six-inch line. We were playing Princeton, and the score stood 116 to 115 for the Bengals. There was less than an hour to play—we played from 8 A.M. to 6 P.M. in those days—and the situation was desperate. I passed to Trumbull who fumbled and Poe fell on the ball, but Longfellow got it away from him with a crotch and cross buttocks hold. The spheroid dribbled into the Wellesley cheering section where I fell on the ball, and then like a flash of molasses passed to P. Withington who passed to T. Withington, who passed to Kelley who passed out. Mrs. Simpson, who was playing for Princeton that year under the name of Louisa May Alcott, got home a snappy signet ring to my chin, but I was not daunted. I scooped up the ball and dropping back to Harvard Square booted it clean as a whistle over the Charles and through the goal posts, as cheer on cheer like volleyed thunder echoed to the sky. It was on the strength of that play that I got a flattering offer from Vassar, which because of the many little hungry mouths depending on me I could not refuse. I would have made the Daisy Chain had I not refused to shave my sideburns.

"'I am not ashamed,' Tunis thundered, 'of the part I played in the War of the Roses. I never took a dollar from sport, where I could get two.'

"Tunis went to the door, shot a couple of amateurs, and returned, calmer. Asked what he was doing at present, he thought several weeks and then replied: 'It is a secret that I am telling nobody but the A.P., the U.P., and Universal Service. I am training Eddie Cantor to lift the Davis Cup. He tried to lift it last year but could only raise it a few inches. If he follows my system I believe he will he able to raise it to his lips.'"

In 1955 he added: "Death, imminent unless I sell something soon because I carry so damn much insurance. Uneducated at Harvard, degree A.B. That means At Bat, and refers to my record in books, which is, to date, nine, no hits, no runs, and a good many errors. Been writing sports and other things too numerous to mention since 1920. Married a Vassar girl in 1918, same wife, same home, same mortgage, right this minute."

---

Though Tunis was called "the paragon of boys' sports novelists" by the New York Times, he said that he did not write his novels specifically for boys. A generation of young sports fans in the 1940s and 1950s were nonetheless delighted to read a Tunis novel, which not only described the action of an exciting game but hit home the importance of sportsmanship, teamwork, discipline and perseverance.

Born in Boston, the son of a Unitarian minister who died when Tunis was seven, and Caroline Roberts Tunis, a cook and a teacher, he took to sports at an early age, learning to read the sports pages and going to National League baseball games with his grandfather. He developed a particular passion for tennis, which he played at Harvard, where he graduated in 1911.

After serving in the Army in France during World War I, Tunis wrote on sports for the New York Evening Post from 1925 to 1932. In 1932 he moved to radio, announcing tennis for the National Broadcasting Company, and in 1934 was the first to broadcast the Wimbledon tennis tournament to the United States. He then became one of the country's most successful free-lance writers, with articles appearing in Collier's, Harper's, Esquire, The New Yorker, and The Saturday Evening Post, among other magazines. Many selections from his twenty years of freelancing were compiled in This Writing Game (1941).

The turning point in Tunis's career came when Iron Duke, a novel about team sports at Harvard, was published in 1938 and, much to the chagrin of Tunis, was marketed as a juvenile. Although he said he had not written the book for young people, it sold more than 60,000 copies and was still bringing in respectable royalties twenty-five years after its publication. The author, at age forty-nine, finally had reached success as a writer of books for boys, which "took him off the free-lancer's financial treadmill," wrote Epstein, who added that prior to that, Tunis was "turning out as many as two books a year, picking up magazine pieces where he could, covering European tennis tournaments in the summers for American newspapers, knocking out roughly 2,000 words a day six days a week." His messages tended to be those of the old-style liberal, the hater of snobbery and prejudice." A good example is All-American (1942), the story of an upper class high school football quarterback who transfers from a prep school called the Academy to the public Abraham Lincoln High, where he leads his team and school in not succumbing to a neighboring school's demand that their star end, an Afro-American, be left off the team. Saturday Review of Literature called it "the outstanding young people's novel of 1942," and E. L. Buell wrote in the New York Times, "No one writing for boys today can describe a touch-down or a home run with more photographic clarity than John Tunis."

After racism, Tunis took on anti-Semitism. In Keystone Kids (1943) he tells the story of Jocko Klein, a rookie catcher for the Dodgers who is taunted by fellow teammates and the opposing teams for being a Jew.

Tunis used the Keystone Kids as the basis for more novels. The Dodgers came from tenth place to have a chance at the pennant in Rookie of the Year (1944), which was "made of thinner stuff than its predecessors," wrote the New York Times. Teamwork was also at the forefront of Highpockets (1948), in which a naive young fielder from the bush leagues becomes an unpopular member of the Dodgers because of his selfish attitude—until an automobile accident straightens him out.

Tunis was equally proficient in writing about basketball. Yea! Wildcats! (1944) tells how a young basketball coach gets his Indiana high school team to the state finals, interwoven with the more important story of how he refuses to participate in the unfair practice of parceling out valued tickets to the tournament games, which costs him dearly with the folks back home. The New York Times reviewer wrote: "Tunis assumes that is important for young people to realize their personal stake in democracy, and he relates Don Henderson's struggle for decency in town as well as school affairs to America's war against nazism. Yea! Wildcats! has the usual brilliant Tunis sports writing—varied, vivid, swiftly paced."

Tunis used his knowledge of sport to write guidebooks. Sport For the Fun of It (1940), which was updated and reissued in 1950, describes twenty indoor and outdoor games, with brief historical information, lists of equipment and official rules; and

*Lawn Games* (1943) covers the rules on outdoor sports from archery to volleyball.

Tunis wrote a different kind of survey in *Was College Worth While?* (1936). On the twenty-fifth anniversary of his graduating from Harvard, he surveyed the records of the 541 members of the Class of 1911 and wrote about their earning power, professions, religious beliefs, politics, hobbies, and families. The result was "a strong attack on the hidebound nature of most Harvard men," Epstein wrote. Tunis concluded that his class was "practically barren of leaders of public life," that only "a small minority . . . appear to have done any original thinking in their field," and that the overwhelming ambition of most members was "to vote the Republican ticket, to keep out of the bread line, and to break 100 at golf."

Much of Tunis's adult nonfiction is critical analyses of the business of sports. In *$port$; Heroics and Hysterics* (1928), he attacked the rising commercialism of amateur sports. *Democracy and Sport* (1941) presented sports as the testing ground for a constructive society, and in *The American Way in Sport* (1958) he again criticized the profit motive in sports and the overemphasis on competitiveness rather than scholarship.

Tunis continued bemoaning the death of sportsmanship in his autobiography, *A Measure of Independence* (1964). "Why is being a winner more important in the United States than being a loser, good or bad? In short, why do Americans always have to win?" he wrote. With sportsmanship on the wane and winning at all costs on the rise, Tunis had become "an often bitter critic of the sports he had always loved," wrote the *New York Times*.

PRINCIPAL WORKS: $port$: Heroics and Hysterics, 1928; American Girl, 1930; Was College Worth While?, 1936; Choosing a College, 1940; Sport for the Fun of It, 1940; Democracy and Sport, 1941; This Writing Game, 1941; World Series, 1941; Lawn Games, 1943; The American Way in Sport, 1958; A Measure of Independence, 1964. Juveniles: The Iron Duke, 1938; The Duke Decides 1939; Champion's Choice, 1940; The Kid from Tomkinsville, 1940; Million-Miler: The Story of an Air Pilot, 1942; All-American 1942; Keystone Kids, 1943; Rookie of the Year, 1944; Yea! Wildcats!, 1944; A City for Lincoln, 1945; The Kid Comes Back, 1946; Highpockets, 1948; Son of the Valley, 1949; Young Razzle, 1949; The Other Side of the Fence, 1953; Go, Team, Go!, 1954; Buddy and the Old Pro, 1955; Schoolboy Johnson, 1958; Silence Over Dunkerque, 1962; His Enemy, His Friend, 1967; Two by Tunis: Highpockets and Go, Team, Go!, 1972; Grand National, 1973.

ABOUT: The autobiographical material quoted above was written for Twentieth Century Authors, 1942 and First Supplement, 1955. Tunis, J. R. A Measure of Independence. *Periodicals*—Advertising Age May 2, 1985; Booklist April 15, 1944; Commentary December 1987; New Yorker May 18, 1940; New York Times November 1, 1942; April 23, 1944; November 12, 1944; February 5, 1975; April 6, 1986; Publishers' Weekly April 30, 1938; Saturday Review June 19, 1954; January 17, 1959; Saturday Review of Literature December 5, 1942; Scholastic September 17, 1938; Weekly Book Review September 5, 1943.

## TURNBULL, AGNES (SLIGH)

**TURNBULL, AGNES (SLIGH)** (October 14, 1888–January 31, 1982), American novelist and short story writer, wrote: "I was born in the little village of New Alexandria, Pennsylvania. My father was Alexander Halliday Sligh, from Berwick-on-Tweed, Scotland; my mother, Lucinda Hannah

McConnell, was a native of this country of Scotch-Irish pioneer descent. I attended the village school, then Washington (Pennsylvania) Seminary, and was graduated from Indiana (Pennsylvania) Teachers' College in 1910. Following this I went to the University of Chicago for a year's work in English, and taught for some years in high schools in Pennsylvania. In 1918 I was married to James Lyall Turnbull, of Hebburn-on-Tyne, England. We came then to live in Maplewood, New Jersey, where we have been ever since. We have one adopted daughter.

"I was always interested in writing and sold my first story to the *American Magazine* in 1920. For ten years I worked exclusively with the short story, developing one field which was somewhat unusual: namely, fiction based on Biblical material. In 1936 my first novel was published. Since then I have become interested in the western Pennsylvania scene as material for books.

"I am a Presbyterian and a Republican. I am one of the last remaining writers who do not use the typewriter."

———

A popular and prolific author, Agnes (Sligh) Turnbull published fifteen novels as well as numerous short stories and books for children. Her most characteristic fiction examines the lives, during various periods in American history, of Scotch-Irish Presbyterians in western Pennsylvania. Her first novel, *The Rolling Years*, is set primarily during the last decades of the nineteenth century and the first decade of the twentieth, and chronicles three generations of a family. Turnbull highlights the experiences and perspectives of the family's women, for whom religious practice is an integral aspect of daily life. *Boston Transcript* critic Richard Doughton conceded that some readers might find the novel overly sentimental, but insisted, "it is not mawkish; it is not maudlin; it is that rare sentiment which is of the richness of the full life." A less sympathetic reviewer from the *Times Literary Supplement* noted simply, "Will be liked by unsophisticated readers."

In *The Day Must Dawn*, set during the era of the American Revolution, settlers—again in a rural western Pennsylvania community—try to eke sustenance from the frontier while living in constant fear of Indian attacks. As in *The Rolling Years*, women's experiences are the central focus of the novel's narrative. *The Gown of Glory*, another of her Pennsylvania novels, centers on the life of a small-town minister in the early years of the twentieth century. "Taken together," Mary Jean DeMarr wrote in a *Journal of Popular Culture* essay analyzing these works, "these four novels give a varied and truthful picture of the Ulster Scotch and their descendants, its coherence being strengthened by the fact that all four are set in western Pennsylvania, where the Scotch-Irish early penetrated and where their influence was long lasting."

Not surprisingly, clerical figures play a prominent role in a number of Turnbull's novels, including her bestseller *The Bishop's Mantle*, and her last novel, *The Two Bishops*, published when she was over ninety years old. Turnbull was a self-proclaimed optimist, and outlined her personal and religious philosophy in *Dear Me*, a selection of her diary entries, and in her essay collection *Out of My Heart*.

PRINCIPAL WORKS: *Novels*—The Rolling Years, 1936; Remember the End, 1938; The Day Must Dawn, 1942; The Bishop's Mantle, 1947; The Gown of Glory, 1952; The Golden Journey, 1955; The Nightingale, a Romance, 1960; The King's Orchard, 1963; The Wedding Bargain, 1966; Many a Green Isle, 1968; Whistle and I'll Come to You: An Idyll, 1970; The Flowering, 1972; The Richlands, 1974; The Winds of Love, 1977; The Two Bishops, 1980. *Short stories*—Far Above Rubies, 1926; The Four Marys, 1932; The Colt that Carried a King, 1933; Old Home Town, 1933; This Spring of Love, 1934; Once to Shout, 1943; Little Christmas, 1964. *Religion*—In the Garden: A Story of the First Easter, 1929. *Juvenile*—Elijah, the Tishbite, 1940; Jed, the Shepherd's Dog, 1957; George, 1965; The White Lark, 1968. *Diary*—Dear Me: Leaves from the Diary of Agnes Sligh Turnbull, 1941. *Essays*—Out of My Heart, 1958.

ABOUT: The autobiographical material quoted above was written for Twentieth Century Authors, 1942. Contemporary Authors vol. 105 1981; Contemporary Authors New Revision Series 2 1982; Warfel, H. American Novelists of Today, 1951. *Periodicals*—Boston Transcript February 8, 1936; Journal of Popular Culture Spring 1986; New York Times November 27, 1938; February 2, 1982; Times Literary Supplement October 3, 1936.

# TURNER, FREDERICK JACKSON (November 14, 1861– March 14, 1932), American historian, known primarily for his "frontier thesis," was born

in Portage, Wisconsin, the son of Andrew Jackson Turner, a newspaper editor, and Mary (Hanford) Turner. In 1888 he enrolled in the doctoral program at John Hopkins University in Baltimore; one of his instructors there was the young Woodrow Wilson. Turner's dissertation, for which he was awarded a Ph. D. in 1890, was an expansion of his master's thesis titled (and published as) *The Character and Influence of the Indian Trade in Wisconsin: a Study of the Trading Post as an Institution*. Returning to the University of Wisconsin in 1889 as assistant professor, Turner set about reorganizing the Department of History on more modern lines. He began to work out a theory of American history very different from that of his professors at Johns Hopkins, who had been concerned primarily with the social development of New England as it evolved from northern European prototypes. His first salvo against this Teutonic School, as it was called, was his article "The Significance of History" (1891), in which he stated that "each age writes the history of the past anew with

reference to the conditions uppermost in its own time," and implicitly rebuked the nostalgic conservatism of his mentors.

But Turner's first really outspoken attack on the eastern bias and covert snobbery then dominant in American historiography was the lecture he delivered at the 1893 Columbian Exposition in Chicago: "The Significance of the Frontier in American History." It was hardly noticed at the time, but Turner's strenuous promotion of its ideas gradually gave the thirty-page essay the reputation it has maintained ever since, according to John Mack Faragher "the single most influential piece of writing in the history of American history."

Turner's thesis—"The existence of an area of free land, its continuous recession, and the advance of American settlement westward, explain American development"—has been endlessly debated, with acceptance and rejection seeming to come in generational cycles. In the 1990s with the dominance of a multicultural historiography of the West, the frontier thesis was more rejected than accepted. There are many arguments against Turner's theses: that he never adequately defined the frontier in the first place; that he was wrong about its "closing" in the 1890s; that he excluded from serious consideration women, Native Americans, and other dispossessed groups, for whom the experience of "westering" was hardly the triumph he believed it to be; that his myth of frontier individualism simply substituted one type of nostalgia (western) for another (eastern). But, despite a barrage of attacks from the 1930s to the 1990s, Turner's thesis refused to lie down and die. Indeed, some scholars have claimed Turner as a precursor to the *Annales* school of French historiography, and others have argued that, with all the biases and blindness, he was far more sensitive to such issues as environmental degradation and economic exploitation than commonly believed. His legacy, wrote John Lauritz Larson in *Journal of the Early Republic*, "continues to stimulate reiteration, refutation, and recognition. It cannot be because he 'got it right': too many solid studies reveal serious flaws in the substance of Turner's history. . . . It must be because of Turner's wild, sweeping, reckless vision, grasping for the key to 'explain American development,' set a goal, laid down an objective that historians still find worth pursuing—to explain the significance of things gone by, that we might understand what has come to pass."

For a historian of such influence, Turner wrote remarkably little. Much of his professional life was taken up with pedagogic and administrative duties—and there was always the temptation to go fishing, his passion from childhood. "The Significance of the Frontier in American History" was not published in book form until 1920 (in the collection *The Frontier in American History*). The other essay for which he is best known, "The Significance of the Section in American History," in which he argued that the interaction of geographically distinct regions made of America a uniquely "composite" nation, was not published in book form until the year of his death, in the collection *The Significance of Sections in American History.* The only other major book published in his lifetime was *Rise of the New West, 1819–1829.* He died before finishing what he hoped would be the capstone of his career, *The United States, 1830–1850: The Nation and Its Sections.*

"In having a major reputation and a memorable leading idea but only a minor body of work," Richard Hofstadter wrote of him, "he is perhaps the most reminiscent of Lord Acton. . . . But the writing of full-length works of history . . . bored and oppressed him." His few works, however, continue to exert an influence.

An inspired if erratic lecturer, Turner influenced a generation of future historians (among them Carl Becker and Samuel F. Bemis) who studied with him at the University of Wisconsin from 1886 to 1910 and at Harvard University, where he was a professor of history from 1910 to 1924. Turner was also president of the American Historical Association in 1910, a member of the editorial board of the *American Historical Review* and a contributor to the *Encyclopedia Britannica* and such other popular magazines as the *Atlantic Monthly* and the *Nation.* After retiring from Harvard, where he had never felt entirely at home, he returned to Wisconsin. Ill health and hard winters compelled him to move to southern California in 1926. There he accepted a position as a research associate at the Huntington Library in San Marino and worked intermittently on *The United States, 1830–1850.*

Although the debate about Turner's interpretation of western expansion is not over, most contemporary historians would probably agree with Faragher that Turner "read back into the past both the assurance and the arrogance of the victors in a centuries-long campaign of conquest. Turner made that victory seem inevitable, but the history of the American West now being written serves to remind us that there was nothing smooth about it at all— that the victory of one people was usually at the expense of another." If Turner's "version of western history has lost much of its explanatory power and punch," what endures, wrote Faragher, "is Turner's commitment to history as contemporary knowledge, his understanding that debates about the past are always simultaneously debates about the present. It marks him as America's first truly modern historian."

Turner's manuscripts are at the Huntington Library.

PRINCIPAL WORKS: *History*—The Character and the Influence of the Indian Trade in Wisconsin: A Study of the Trading Post as an Institution, 1891; Rise of the New West, 1819–1829, 1906; (with others) Guide to the Study and Reading of American History, 1912; Reuben Gold Thwaites: A Memorial Address, 1914; The Frontier in American History, 1932; The United States, 1830–1850: The Nation and Its Sections (ed. M. Y. Crissey and others) 1935; The Early Writings of Frederick Jackson Turner, with a List of All His Works (ed. E. E. Edwards) 1938; Frontier and Section: Selected Essays (ed. R. A. Billington) 1961; Frederick Jackson Turner's Legacy: Unpublished Writings in American History (ed. W. R. Jacobs) 1965; Rereading Frederick Jackson Turner: "The Significance of the Frontier in American History" and Other Essays, 1944. *As editor*—Correspondence of the French Ministers to the United States, 1791–1797, 1904; List of References on the History of the West, 1915. *Correspondence*—"Dear Lady:" The Letters of Frederick Jackson Turner and Alice Forbes Perkins Hooper, 1910–1932 (ed. R. A. Billington) 1970.

ABOUT: Bennett, J. D. Frederick Jackson Turner, 1975; Billington, R. A. Frederick Jackson Turner: Historian, Scholar, Teacher, 1973; Carpenter, R. H. The Eloquence of Frederick Jackson Turner, 1983; Dictionary of American Biography vol. 19, 1936; Dictionary of Literary Biography vol. 17, 1983; Faragher, J. M. *introduction and afterword to* Rereading Frederick Jackson Turner: "The Significance of the Frontier in American History" and Other Essays (by F. J. Turner) 1994; Hofstadter, R. The Progressive Historians: Turner, Beard, Parrington, 1968; Jacobs, W. R. On Turner's Trail: One Hundred Years of Writing Western History, 1994; Thinkers of the Twentieth Century, 2nd ed. (ed. R. Turner) 1987. *Bibliography*—Mattson, V. E. and Marion, W. E. Frederick Jackson Turner: A Reference Guide, 1985. *Periodicals*—Journal of the Early Republic Summer 1993; New York Times March 16, 1932.

**TURNER, W(ALTER) J(AMES)** (October 13, 1889–November 18, 1946), British poet, novelist, dramatist, editor, and music critic, wrote: "It is reputed—and I would like to believe—that I was born in Melbourne, Australia, by the side of the sea, on the 13th October, 1890: [it was in 1889] but it may have been that I was born in Shanghai a year earlier. My father was organist at St. Paul's Protestant Cathedral, Melbourne, and also oc-

cupied simultaneously (which I believe is unique) the position of music director of the Jewish Synagogue. This, I understand, was owing to his personal friendship with the Chief Rabbi.

"I was educated at Scotch College, Melbourne, and was sent with my brother to learn carpentry at the Working Men's College, as my father believed that everyone should have some mechanical training. Although both my parents were professional musicians, I am totally devoid of musical talent and was given up at an early age by both my parents as being musically hopeless. My father having died, I was taken from Scotch College and sent to the School of Mines to be trained as a mining engineer. I stayed there a year, and then, at the age of seventeen, came to London, where my mother was living, and after a few months there went to Germany, where I studied at Munich and Vienna. I then spent six months in Marseilles and served in the war of 1914–18, first in the 28th London Battalion and later in the Royal Garrison Artillery, in the anti-aircraft section [he ended with the rank of captain].

"I have no political convictions, except that I think it is impossible to have a really civilized society unless every member of it is assured, without work, of his livelihood. I dislike almost everything and have hardly any likes. There are no public figures known to me for whom I have any respect—except, perhaps, Dr. Weizmann, Zionist leader, whose belief in Zionism, however, fills me with derision. If I were a dictator, I would solve the Jewish problem by forbidding marriage between the Jews.

This, incidentally, would enormously improve the so-called Aryan stock.

"Among contemporary writers, those I admire chiefly are Virginia Woolf, Walter de la Mare, Ralph Hodgson, Dorothy Wellesley, and William Faulkner, and there are naturally many others whose writings I enjoy. I should like very much to live in America—if I could discover an agreeable place. As for work in progress—this is the only piece of work I have undertaken for some time."

---

W. J. Turner remains one of the more interesting of the poets originally classified as "Georgian." When W. B. Yeats included a comparatively large number of poems by Turner (while excluding Wilfred Owen and John Davidson) in the *Oxford Book of Modern Verse* (1936) he was much criticized for it, but Turner has always had his admirers, and some of them, such as Kathleen Raine and, with reservations, Robert Graves, have been eminent. Yeats wrote that he was "lost in admiration and astonishment" at Turner's "majestic song."

Turner's interests included Plato, the European symbolists, and Kierkegaard—all reflected in his poetry. Turner refused to have his poems appear in the fifth and final *Georgian Poetry*, telling Marsh that "a blind devil" rose up in him "Which is too strong even for my admiration and liking for you." The unconventional and unusual manner in which Turner dealt with those aspects of culture that led to modernism are of great interest.

Turner's mother, was a gifted musician, and the pianist Noel Mewton-Wood was his nephew. In 1918 he married Delphine Marguerite Dubuis. Turner received a very severe blow in his childhood when his younger brother died. This is reflected in some of his earlier poetry, and particularly in "Romance," about how he was "stolen away" as a child by the exotic names of the places Chimborazo and Cotopaxi; the second stanza reads "My father died, my brother too / They passed like fleeting dreams, / I stood where Popocatapetl / In the sunlight gleams." In other related poems Turner worked out quite an elaborate mythology based upon this incident.

Turner was, as his friend Jacquetta Hawkes conceded in her portrait of him for the *Dictionary of National Biography*, "cussed" by nature. She draws attention to his two autobiographical volumes (classified as fiction), *Blow for Balloons* and *Henry Airbubble*, as evidence of this—and of his "wit, poetic penetration" and gift for "fantasy." She also implied what most critics who have studied his poetry have concluded: that much of it is spoiled by "concessions to the spirit of the time" and too great richness in "imagery and sound." Turner's poetry was, Hawkes thought, "too lyrical, too sensuous and unintellectual" to appeal to poetry readers of the between-wars period in Great Britain. It was as "idiosyncratic as his nature."

Harold Monro, who published some of Turner's earlier poetry at the Poetry Bookshop, believed Turner to have "suffered from the disadvantages of learning the 'tricks of the trade in the neo-Georgian school" and had "the habit of applying them with a certain craftiness to the particular subject at hand." But he found him "rich in beauty": "he seems able to step aside from himself, and his idiom and measure become at such moments unaffected and delightful." Monro was saying in essence that Turner too often wrote just for the sake of writing, but that when he did not, he was curiously original.

Robert H. Ross, the American scholar of the Georgians, writing in *The Georgian Revolt*, quotes from Turner's poetry to make a point about his "bloodless" verse, and "essentially unreal, remote and fervorless" post-war poetry. Still, Turner could find his own voice in poems like "Talking with Soldiers:"

The mind of the people is like mud,
From which arise strange and beautiful things,
But mud is none the less mud,
Though it bear orchids and prophesying Kings,
Dreams, trees, and water's bright babblings.

This poem ends

The mind of the people is like mud:
Where are the imperishable things,
The ghosts that flicker in the brain—
Silent women, orchids, and prophesying Kings,
Dreams, trees, and water's bright babbling!

Turner's posthumous collection, *Fossils of a Future Time?* is a selection from the poetry he wrote in his final decade. Richard Church summed up the general critical attitude towards Turner's poetry: "Turner was a genius rather than a talented artist. As a craftsman I have always found him capricious, and much at the mercy of willful ideas, so that poetry of the purest water, some of the most original in our language, is to be found juxtaposed to wild statements and often comic associations of ideas" (*Spectator*, 1947). This would command complete agreement except that Church, who was a traditionalist, never had any time for free verse; some of Turner's is in fact not without interest in its search for a kind of music.

Turner left a surprisingly vivid mark on music criticism. His books on Mozart and Beethoven in particular show a poetic, perhaps unique, appreciation of those composers. The *New York Times* called *Beethoven: The Search for Reality* an "intelligent and well-organized summary of the master's life." Of his study of Mozart the *Christian Science Monitor* wrote: "it was a happy idea to let Mozart himself take a hand in destroying his sweetly pretty picture." The musicologist Cecil Gray wrote, in the *New Statesman*: "Turner has written an admirable book. Those who have occasionally felt in some of his former writings a certain dilettantism, a certain lack of solidity in his scholarship, will not find these defects in the present book. In addition to the critical acumen and poetic intuition which invariably characterizes his work, however violently one may disagree with his judgements on occasion, one finds here on every page the evidence of painstaking research into every aspect of his subject."

Turner's exceedingly dogmatic but readable book on *Wagner*, a forthright attack on the man and on his music, has delighted every Wagner-hater, but scandalized every Wagner-lover, to whose consternation it has been kept in print as (possibly) one of the most vehement of all criticisms of him.

Turner not only wrote poetry, music criticism, and fictional autobiography; he also contributed to the drama. *The Man Who Ate the Popomack*, which was produced in London in 1923, is a highly original play and something of a *tour de force*. It is on the theme of a man who eats a strange fruit which causes him to smell abominably—but it is not quite a comedy. Another play, *Smaragda's Lover*, was not so successful.

Turner made much of his living from his weekly music criticism in the *New Statesman* (1916–1940) and the *Daily Express.* He was literary editor of the *Daily Herald* (1920–1923) and of the *Spectator* (1942 until his death). He also wrote well-regarded drama criticism for the *London Mercury*, the magazine edited and owned by his friend and champion Sir John Squire. His association with Yeats's friend the poet Dorothy Wellesley led to the launching of the wartime *Britain in Pictures* series, of which he was general editor.

PRINCIPAL WORKS: *Poetry*—The Hunter, 1916; The Dark Fire, 1918; The Dark Wind, 1920; In Time Like Glass, 1921; Paris and Helen, 1921; Landscape of Cytherea, 1924; The Seven Days of the Sun, 1925; Marigold, 1926; New Poems, 1928; A Trip to New York, 1929; Miss America, Altiora in the Sierra Nevada, 1930; The Pursuit of Psyche, 1931; Jack and Jill, 1934; Songs and Incantations, 1936; Selected Poems, 1939; Poems of Peace and War, 1945; Fossils of a Future Time?, 1946; W. J. Turner: Selected Poetry (ed. W. McKenna) 1990. *Fiction*—Blow for Balloons, 1935; Henry Airbubble, 1936; The Duchess of Popacatapetl, 1939. *Drama*—The Man Who Ate the Popmack, 1922; Smaragda's Lover, 1924. *Music*—Music and Life, 1921; Variations on the Theme of Music, 1924; Orpheus; or, the Music of the Future, 1926; Beethoven, the Search for Reality, 1927; Musical Meanderings, 1928; Music, a Short History, 1932; Facing the Music, Reflections of a Music Critic, 1933; Wagner, 1933; Berlioz, the Man and his Work, 1934; Mozart, 1938. *Criticism*—The Aesthetes, 1927; Plots, Parables and Fables, 1944.

ABOUT: The autobiographical material quoted above was written for Twentieth Century Authors, 1942. Dictionary of National Biography, 1941–1950, 1959; Hamilton, I.(ed.) Oxford Companion to Twentieth-Century Poetry, 1944; McKenna, W. W. J. Turner, Poet and Music Critic; Monro, H. Some Contemporary Poets, 1920; Ross, R. H. The Georgian Revolt, 1965; Seymour-Smith, M. Macmillian Guide to Modern World Literature, 1986. *Periodicals*—English Studies 40 and 41, August 1959, August 1950; New Statesman March 12, 1938; New York Times January 1, 1928; Spectator November 22, 1946; January 18, 1947; Times (London) November 20, 1946.

**TUVE, ROSEMOND** (November 27, 1903–December 20, 1964), American scholar wrote: "I was born in a small South Dakota town between the Big Sioux and the prairies. My father was a mathematician, president of a small Lutheran college (Augustana) then located at Canton, and my mother taught music at the same college. My four grandparents had severally come from Norway as pioneers, escaping from rigors of one sort or another, a too dominating state church or a sea-captain's hard life or too much family, and we children were taught to think that America was synonymous with freedom, and that each man's own mind and spirit was the measure of his excellence. . . .

"Since the only kind of books I write, or will write, are those which concern what other men have written, and I would gladly keep myself out of them if I could, the details of my own life have the less relevance. But why people write at all, or keep on once they start, is always a puzzle, and in my case probably the only interesting one. I suppose one persists in writing my kind of books because one becomes curious when very young, and cannot stay away from certain authors and kinds of problems and pleasures. As the third child among four I chiefly did what my three brothers thought was important, such as learning the morse code to take down their wireless messages, and playing in neighborhood gangs, but I learned without noticing it before I was ten to care about most of the things I have since thought or written about—and no doubt was equally inescapably made ready to miss the rest. . . .

"We had less and less money but thought nothing of it; but when I was fifteen, some months after my father died, we hurriedly picked up the household in mid-year and moved to Minneapolis to put safely into the University of Minnesota my next oldest brother, now a physicist with the Carnegie Institution, to prevent him from saving the family fortunes by going on the boards with a Chicago opera company; in another year I went on like my two elder brothers into the university, paying for it mostly by a job in which I put three trees into three holes in a Christmas card of which inexplicable thousands were needed to satisfy the demands of the country. I stopped off after my sophomore year to teach 4th and 5th grades in a tiny prairie town, returned with joy and (having become enamored of medieval literature) gave up the Christmas cards and addressographs to be a student assistant to Friedrich Klaeber, who taught me to respect philology, then to Thomas Raysor, who tempered the ideas I had got about Romantic poets from reading Babbitt; I took my B.A. in 1924, and acting on the family principle and with their reckless advice borrowed a thousand dollars to go to Bryn Mawr for graduate work, first as Scholar and then as Fellow. When I was given a Bryn Mawr European fellowship I took out two years to pay my debts, teaching at Goucher and going to Johns Hopkins; then adding an A.A.U.W. fellowship went into residence at Somerville College, Oxford. There I swam among the Bodleian manuscripts—a sort of imrama for anyone working as I was on medieval subjects—and did the B.Litt. courses and viva, but being unable to complete my residence returned to teach three years at Vassar, finish the Bryn Mawr Ph.D., and teach three more summers at the Bryn Mawr School for Women Workers in Industry, an experience which left me forever (I hope) left of center, at least of where this country has taken to placing the center.

"I then returned in 1932, to France to see a book through to the press in Paris, and to work and write in Oxford, London and Ireland; after a second year living mostly with friends in a village in Somerset, I came to Connecticut College in 1934. On various leaves I have gone back to England to work or Italy and France to sit and stare, taught refugees in a Quaker seminar at Black Mountain, held a visiting lectureship in Renaissance literature at the University of Minnesota. Three divorces that have become accepted in modern American intellectual life I have been unable to accede to because of the faith of those I lived among when I as young: that between scholarship and criticism, that between research or writing and teaching (these I saw unified too often to believe them inimical), and most important that between science and the humanities. I first read Milton and Eliot through aloud in a laboratory, and the philosophy to which I was introduced in a scientific household filled with the arguing friends of three brothers in mechanical engineering, physics, and chemistry, was not naturalistic positivism. Among dozens of scientific friends I leaned to expect one combination (whose recurrence finally led me to relate it to the nature of their discipline): music, humility, and intellectual courage (except, alas, in politics). These are what I pay allegiance to in poetry; what they leave out—the poet's eye for truth in figure—I see as threatened rather by those more potent enemies who despise all four; I only write so that the poets may be heard better, being more potent than the enemies, if we do not bind them while they sleep. I suppose everyone who does this brings his own cord to it, to be cut by the next."

---

Rosemond Tuve did indeed make the metaphysical and Elizabethan poets heard better, working always to answer her question, "what kind of readers do we make, whom circumstances have invented to make ignorant of what every literate man once knew?"

After publishing her dissertation *Seasons and Months: Studies in a Tradition of Middle English Poetry* in France in 1933, Tuve returned to the United States where, in 1947, she published *Elizabethan and Metaphysical Imagery* which "confirmed her as the foremost American literary scholar of the Renaissance," according to *Notable American Women*. "The most comprehensive effort of traditional historical criticism to answer the ahistorical premises of the New Criticism," at the time, the study focused on the poetry of Donne, Drayton, Herrick, King, and Spenser, among others. It was described by Kenneth Young in the *Spectator* (1947) as "not an easy book to read, but it must be considered for the new perspective in which it sets the Elizabethan and the so-called Metaphysical poets." *U.S Quarterly Book List* commented that "the volume is rich in suggestion for all who are interested in the poetic imagery of any era, and it can give hints on method . . . to attain an adequate appreciation of its art."

Throughout her career Tuve remained concerned with the proper understanding of poetic images in the light of historical scholarship. In her *A Reading of George Herbert* (1952) the author, who, in the claim of her contemporary the medievalist Dorothy Bethurum, "rescued Herbert from the Freudian critics," explores the symbolic tradition, as well as the liturgical and iconographic, that would have been familiar to the seventeenth-century poet. Tuve had dismissed as inadequate an earlier critique of Herbert's work by her fellow scholar William Empson. The result was an "array of illustrations chosen from old devotional books, stained glass windows and other 'iconographical' legacies. . . . By which she means to make her conclusions concerning what Herbert had in his mind still more persuasive," as the *Times Literary Supplement* described it. And the *Manchester Guardian* called it "a vital scholarship . . . combined with critical insight, a pithy style, and some fascinating illustrations." *Images and Themes in Five Poems by Milton* (1957) continues her exploration of Renaissance imagery. The book received mixed reviews, with the London *Times* commenting that "if, as one lays the book down, dissatisfaction mingles with one's admiration and humility, it is because Miss Tuve . . . shows so little consideration to her readers." The *Yale Review* describes the work as creating the impression that Milton was "working within a highly deterministic universe of symbols with his creative powers severely controlled, as well as inspired by tradition," and going on to say that, "Within this limitation, Miss Tuve's interpretations exert great force." In Tuve's last study, *Allegorical Imagery* (1966), the author "examined the uses, pleasures and apparent meaning of 'allegory' in certain available medieval texts," as she explained in the foreword of the volume. To do this, Tuve drew primarily upon the poetry of Spenser. The *Times Literary Supplement* commented that *Allegorical Imagery* was "characteristic of its author," and it "demands attentive reading by its involved manner . . . and its width of reference."

Tuve also published numerous articles, reviews, and essays, some of which were collected, edited, and published by Roche in 1970 under the title *Essays by Rosemond Tuve*. The volume also containes a bibliography of all the author's articles and reviews, and all but one of her books, *Allegorical Images*.

Tuve remained on the faculty of Connecticut College until 1962, when she left to become professor of English at the University of Pennsylvania in Philadelphia, from 1963 to 1964. In 1952 she was visiting lecturer in English at the University of Minnesota, at Harvard University from 1956 to 1957, NATO visiting professor of English at Aarhus University, Denmark, in 1960, and visiting professor at Princeton University in 1961. She was a member of the American Academy of Arts and Sciences, and the executive board of the Modern Language Association of America, and Phi Beta Kappa. She was awarded the Rosemary Crawshaw Prize for English Literature of British Academy for *Elizabethan and Metaphysical Imagery* in 1949, the Achievement Award of the American Association of University Women in 1955, and the American Council of Learned Societies award in 1960.

PRINCIPAL WORKS: Seasons and Months: Studies in a Tradition of Middle English Poetry, 1933; Survey's of Scholarship in the Field of the Renaissance, 1943; Elizabethan and Metaphysical Imagery, 1947; A Reading of George Herbert, 1952, 1982; Images and Themes in Five Poems by Milton, 1957; Allegorical Imagery, 1966; Essays by Rosemond Tuve, 1970.

ABOUT: The autobiographical material quoted above was written for Twentieth Century Authors First Supplement, 1955. American Women 1935–1940, 1981; American Women Writers, 1982; Contemporary Authors vol. 9–19, 1964; Contemporary Authors Permenant Series vol. 1 1975; Notable American Women: The Modern Period, 1980; Who's Who in America 1964–1965. Periodicals—Choice October 1966; Manchester Guardian September 2, 1952; New York Times December 22, 1964; Spectator November 28, 1947; Times Literary Supplement August 22, 1952; April 18, 1958; September 8, 1966; U.S. Quarterly Book List September 1947; Yale Review December 1957.

**TWEEDSMUIR, BARON.** See **BUCHAN, JOHN**

**TYLER, PARKER** (March 6, 1907–July 24, 1974), American poet and critic, wrote: "As to life, Thomas Z. Tyler and Eva (Parker) Tyler gave it to me. The place was New Orleans. The reason was love. And I can never cease being as grateful for all the particular facts of it as I am critical of all the general. For life imposes on us with primal desire and its endless satisfactions, the strange and cleansing negative of criticism. My maternal grandfather was a newspaper editor who achieved public prominence in Louisiana. His spirited daughter, who was to be my mother married a member of an old South Carolina family with impressive forebears. Our little family (with one other child, Phyllis) soon became nomadic. Urban and suburban America unfolded for our innocence like one of the original prairies or forests here.

"Our fortunes were uneven. Revelation of the daily was certainly novel and often interesting—especially (for me) those dusky theatres where living pictures unrolled on a  flat screen. I vacillated between the work of books and the image of the film screen. Extraordinarily self-fixated, I turned on myself a pitiless criticism and imbued myself with a steely ambition to do something with life besides live it. That is, I meant to contribute to the things of the world. My adolescence, in retrospect, seems to have been unusually painful—perhaps because my family was so inward and so complacent in a tight moral sense. I suddenly became an actor in a little theatre, the Cleveland Playhouse. Before that, I had put certain lyrical daydreams into verse. And I had abandoned, in Chicago, my formal education in the very middle. Only one thing seemed to face me: New York with all its mysteries and glory.

"Today it is merely factual for me to say that I rushed at everything in New York and therefore had to turn back on many things before I could say I had profited by experiencing them. My oldest friend, Charles Henri Ford, provided the first little magazine of those that soon represented for me the literary heights. But I had already contributed precocious book reviews to weeklies and even read manuscripts for a publisher. As an advance-guard poet, I took Ezra Pound, William Carlos Williams, E. E. Cummings for my masters, and attained print in transition. I was published and encouraged even by the conservative organ, Poetry, where now I am one of the active 'old contributors.' With nods from Eliot and Pound, I issued my own anthology of modern verse. If I have a venial sin, it was and is impatience.

"Then came Ford's internationally inflected View (1940–47) and I was given carte blanche to write almost anything. The dance, painting, literature, the movies, all appeared as grist for aesthetic-philosophic speculation, and I wrote on them all. Out of this came the fruit of my childhood initiation in the movie-house: my first book on the cinema; and also, analogously, my first full-length poem showing the influence of the movies on my imagination. Friends deep and light, dangerous and hale, had come, stayed, gone, returned. Life seemed only practice for expression in my chosen media. Of course, public appreciation had a good deal to do with my main pursuit of film criticism. I was delighted to become, in Kenyon Review, an interpreter of film to an elite interested primarily in literature.

"One day, lately, I realized that I have concentrated so much on work, to the slighting of social activity, that I could tell a poet I had lost sight of for years that I am virtually a recluse. Well, not quite. The basic spiritual gesture is what counts, then criticism, with its myriad lights, can only help show the way through the purlieus of the common soul that both engulfs and separates men from each other . . . in life as in books. But love and creation remain the torch-bearers."

———

Determined to write poetry, Harrison Parker Tyler at age twenty took his flamboyant theatrical manner to New York and quickly become a star attraction of Greenwich Village speakeasy poetry readings and a prominent fixture of the gay subculture of the city. He was named for two of his ancestors, U. S. presidents William Henry Harrison and John Tyler.

Tyler refused to enter college, preferring to learn about life and literature by immersing himself in the bohemian subculture of New York. He particuarly appreciated the modernist sensibility of such writers as Ezra Pound, Marianne Moore, Jean Cocteau, and e.e. cummings, and by James Frazer's writings on the evolution of religion and ritual. "Tyler believed that as a poet he could understand—intuit—without any of the crutches scholars and politicians required," wrote May Natalie Tabak in a 1977 article in Christopher Street. He wrote Marxian essays without reading much Marx and wrote an essay on Mallarmé without being able to read French. "Having absolute faith in himself as a poet, Parker used a vocabulary and images of his own choice," Tabak added.

Tyler began a friendship and professional collaboration with poet Charles Henri Ford through the mail, contributing to Ford's *Blues* magazine and writing candid letters, many of which are alluded to in George Chauncey's *Gay New York*, that described the homosexual subculture in the city before the Depression. Tyler's tales whetted Ford's appetite to come to New York in 1930, where the two co-authored *The Young and Evil* (1933). The novel is a frank, first-hand account of the randy adventures and bohemian lifestyles of Tyler, Ford, and their friends in Greenwich Village. Far from being a literary masterpiece, the novel is remembered today as breaking new ground for gay American literature. "While not the first American novel to present homosexual characters on its pages . . . it is the first American novel to take its characters' sexuality for granted," wrote Steven Watson in the introduction to the 1988 edition.

When the novel was finished, Ford left Tyler in a cold-water flat on the Lower East Side and went to Paris to get it published. "On the recommendation of Gertrude Stein and Djuna Barnes, the book was put out in 1933 by the radical Obelisk Press, Henry Miller's publisher. Banned and burned, it was destined to travel the underground circuit only," wrote Tyler's biographer Catrina Neiman in her introduction to Ford's *View: Parade of the Avant-Garde*.

Gertrude Stein declared on the novel's original dust jacket: "*The Young and Evil* creates this generation as *This Side of Paradise* by Fitzgerald created his generation." American readers did not encounter the novel until 1960, when it was reissued by Olympia Press, for which Tyler adapted Stein's words to re-introduce it as "the novel that beat the beat generation by a generation." In 1975, the novel was part of the "Documents in Homosexuality" series published by The New York Times Company, and it was reissued again in 1988 by Gay Presses of New York.

Tyler later served as associate editor and art director for Ford's avante-garde magazine *View*, published in the 1940s. On his own, Tyler published poetry filled with surrealist dream imagery. His *Metaphor in the Jungle* (1940) meshed the styles of Eliot, Joyce, and Auden and showed a Freudian slant that would shape all of his later work. "It may be said of surrealism that if you get what it is about, it has failed . . . One of its avowed intentions is to mystify. Judged by such a standard, Parker Tyler's poems are not quite surrealist. They are obscure, yes, but it is the conscious obscurity of an argot or of a neo-argot," wrote Lloyd Frankenburg in *Books*.

The "zenith of Tyler's poetry career," according to Watson, is the epic poem, *The Granite Butterfly* (1945); the poem was reprinted in full with more than thirty undated short poems in the collection, *The Will of Eros: Selected Poems 1930–1970* (1972).

Tyler also made a minor mark as a commentator on film. Watson credits him for engaging in "depth criticism, a Freudian unveiling of screen iconography." Despite his often arcane evaluations and haughty attitude, Tyler's extensive references and thorough psychological treatments left little doubt about his intimate knowledge of film and his passion for analyzing its mythical implications. "His ability to read the encoded messages of the screen was certainly sharpened by his experience of the semiotic charade of homosexual life. While contemporaries like James Agee and Otis Ferguson described the surface of the film, Tyler attempted to unveil the film," Watson concluded. *The Hollywood Hallucination* (1944) was the first of several books Tyler wrote on film criticism. It was followed by its sequel *Magic and Myth of the Movies* (1947), prompting Eric Bentley to remark that Tyler was "one of the most interesting writers on the movies in America today." Later books on the subject included *Underground Film: A Critical History* (1969) and *Screening the Sexes: Homosexuality in the Movies* (1972). In the latter book, Tyler defined his task in these words: "to read aright the signs of sexual style in the movies"—from Mae West as "a Mother Superior of the Faggots" to the range of gay mannerisms displayed in *The Boys in the Band*—in order to "descry the true, the actual, the varied features of the whole repertory of human sexuality."

Tyler himself was fictionalized in Gore Vidal's *Myra Breckinridge* (1968) as "the great film critic Parker Tyler," the obsession of Myra, who considered him "our age's central thinker," and his vision as "perhaps the only important critical insight this century has produced." Vidal's novel inspired the re-publication of several of Tyler's early works, and prompted Vidal to say, "I did for Parker Tyler what Edward Albee did for Virginia Woolf."

Many of Tyler's letters are housed at the Parker Tyler Archive in the Harry Ransom Humanities Center at the University of Texas at Austin.

PRINCIPAL WORKS: *Poetry*—Vision: A Poem Preceded by an Argument (1934); Three Examples of Love Poetry (1936); The Metaphor in the Jungle, 1940; Yesterday's Children, 1944; The Granite Butterfly, 1945; The Will of Eros: Selected Poems, 1930–1970, 1972. *Prose*—(with C. H. Ford) The Young and Evil, 1933; The Hollywood Hallucination, 1944; Magic and Myth of the Movies, 1947; Chaplin: Last of the Clowns, 1948; The Three Faces of the Film, 1960; Classics of the Foreign Film, 1962; Florine Stettheimer, 1963; Every Artist His Own Scandal, 1964; The Divine Comedy of Pavel Tchelitchew, 1967; Cezanne/Gauguin, 1969; Degas/Lautrec, 1969; Renoir, 1969; Sex, Psyche, Etcetera in the Film, 1969; Underground Film: A Critical History, 1969; Van Gogh, 1969; Screening the Sexes: Homosexuality in the Movies, 1972; The Shadow of an Airplane Climbs the Empire State Building: A World Theory of Film, 1972; Carl Pickhardt, 1972; A Pictorial History of Sex in Films, 1974.

ABOUT: The autobiographical material quoted above was written for Twentieth Century Authors First Supplement, 1955. Chauncey, G. Gay New York; Neiman, C. Introduction to C. H. Ford's View: Parade of the Avant-Garde; Hoffman, F. J. (and others) The Little Magazine; Miller, H. Sunday After the War; Murray, E. Nine American Film Critics; Tyler, P. The Granite Butterfly, The Young and Evil, Screening the Sexes; Vidal, G. Myra Breckinridge; Watson, S. Introduction to C. H. Ford's and P. Tyler's The Young and Evil, 1988 edition. *Periodicals*—Books October 19, 1941; Book Week May 21, 1944; Choice March 1973; Christopher Street February 1977; Harper's January 1964; New York Herald Tribune July 25, 1948; New York Times May 18, 1947, July 26, 1974; Out December 1973; Village Voice July 1, 1986.

**TYNAN, KATHARINE** (January 21 [or 23], 1861–April 2, 1931), Irish poet, novelist, essayist, and memoirist, was born in Dublin, the fourth

daughter of Andrew Cullen Tynan, a dealer in cattle, and Elizabeth O'Reilly, a puritanical invalid who forbade dances, the theater, and even the reading of novels. Andrew Tynan was active in the Irish Nationalist cause. When Katharine was seven she moved with her father to Whitehall, Clondalkin (also in County Dublin). She lived, and from 1880 acted as her father's hostess, at this "hospitable farm" until 1893, the year of her marriage to the barrister and classical scholar Henry Albert Hinkson (she became for a time known and published under the name of "Katharine Tynan Hinkson").

Tynan received her only formal education (1869–1875) from the school of St. Catherine of Drogheda (the "Sienna convent"). During her childhood she suffered badly from ulcerated eyes, as an aftermath to an attack of measles. She was eventually cured of this, but was left with a permanent near-sightedness, and at the end of her life became virtually blind. During the period before her marriage she was, like her father, a strong supporter of Parnell, but she later confessed that she had not much enjoyed being a member of the Ladies' Land League. For all of this time she enjoyed the reputation of a gracious, gifted, charming, and well-read hostess.

In the 1880s Whitehall had something of the character of a literary salon, and Katharine came to know, in her capacity as hostess, W. B. Yeats, who became a close friend and an encourager of her poetic talents. She was the youngest contributor to Poems and Ballads of Young Ireland, which, published in Dublin in 1888, was the first fruit of what is usually called the Irish Literary Revival.

Tynan's first collection and first book, Louise de la Vallière (published in 1885 with financial support from her father) established her as one of the most promising young poets of the Irish Renaissance. In his Some Contemporary Poets of 1920 the poet and editor Harold Monro listed her name, along with those of several others, and then commented: "It may be remarked of some of the above that they seem like people whose eyes, ears, and brains are closed in respect of our general Humanity, or who behave as if they thought Parnassus had been enclosed within the walls of some landed proprietor." Thus had her reputation become eclipsed by the time she reached sixty.

M. Kelly Lynch asserted, in the Dictionary of Irish Literature, that the young Tynan was a "master of the lyric," and that her decline began only af-

ter the "deft metrics" of The Wind in the Trees and Innocencies (1905), which latter collection Lynch described as "a Freudian celebration of the eros of motherhood." Tynan's somewhat perfervid early poetry, whose inspiration is Roman Catholic, was well executed in the context of the poetical fashions of its time, and was not undeserving of the temporary success it achieved. Yeats believed that her once famous lyric "Sheep and Lambs" (better known, however, by its first line: "All in the April morning") found beauty in the "most hackneyed symbols." He also compared her to Christina Rossetti, and wrote of her: "[She]is happiest when she puts emotions that have the innocence of childhood into symbols and metaphors from the green world about her. She has . . . a devout tenderness like that of St. Francis for weak instinctive things." George Russell, in his introduction to her Collected Poems (1930), remembered her affectionately, and said that she was "happy in religion, friendship, children."

Upon Tynan's marriage to Hinkson (who became a convert to Roman Catholicism) in 1893 she went to live in London, where she knew and helped scores of writers, both minor and major. She was a friend of both Thomas Hardy and of Florence Dugdale, who became his second wife. But she herself became overprolific. In London she published the first of her 117 books of fiction (only two of these are listed below, since all have vanished without discernible trace). This fiction, of mild and well-meant social protest (it dealt with such themes as the plight of unmarried mothers and the poor conditions of work of factory—and shop-girls), was journalistic by intention; it won her a wide following, but proved ephemeral.

When her husband died in 1919, and she was unable to live in Ireland owing to her political sympathies. She had to write in order to live, and her last decade showed, as Lynch remarked, "an astonishing output." This, too, including much journalism written in Europe when she was almost blind, did not last.

Tynan lost her appeal for Irish readers because she and her husband identified themselves with the British cause. Hinkson (who also wrote fiction), by whom Tynan had three children, was appointed Resident Magistrate for County Mayo in 1911, and as such was pleased to represent British interests. For her the Rising was simply a rebellion.

The best of her work is contained in her five volumes of memoirs: Twenty-Five Years, The Middle Years, The Wandering Years, The Years of the Shadow, and Memories. Although sometimes too bitter because her pro-British stance had lost her so many friends, those volumes are full of useful information about such figures as Yeats, Alice and Wilfred Meynell, Francis Thompson, and Lionel Johnson. Her daughter, Pamela Hinkson, who helped her in her last years, was also a novelist. Both of Tynan's two sons fought in World War I. Of Tynan's true place in the Irish Renaissance Herbert Gorman, in her New York Times obituary, probably wrote most precisely: "She is one of the lesser figures of the Irish Renaissance, a thin, cool voice like the faraway whistle of a blackbird . . . . The pulse beats feebly, however."

PRINCIPAL WORKS: *Poetry*—Louise de la Vallière, 1885; Shamrocks, 1887; Ballads and Lyrics, 1891; Innocencies, 1905; Collected Poems, 1930; Poems of Katherine Tynan, 1963. *Novels*—The Way of a Maid, 1895; Her Father's Daughter, 1930. *Memoirs*—Twenty-Five Years, 1913; The Middle Years, 1916; The Wandering Years, 1922; The Years of the Shadow, 1919; Memories, 1924.

ABOUT: Boyd, E. Ireland's Literary Renaissance, 1916; Dictionary of National Biography, 1931–1940, 1949; Gibbon, M. *in* Poems of Katharine Tynan, 1963; Hogan, R. (ed.) Dictionary of Irish Literature, 1979; Hone, J. W. B. Yeats, 1943; Rose M. G. Katharine Tynan, 1973; Russell, G. Æ foreword to Collected Poems 1930; Yeats, W. B. Autobiographies, 1926, Yeats, W. B. Letters to Katharine Tynan (ed. R. McHugh) 1953. *Periodicals*—Bookman 72 June 1931; Ireland America Review 4 1940; New York Times April 3, 1931.

## TYNE, CLAUDE HALSTEAD VAN. See VAN TYNE, CLAYDE HALSTEAD

**TYRRELL, GEORGE** (February 6, 1861–July 15, 1909), English theologian, and Roman Catholic priest, was born in Dublin, Ireland, the youngest and posthumous son of William Henry Tyrrell, a journalist, and his second wife, Mary (Chamney) Tyrrell. An unpromising student with a strong imagination and a mistrust of authority, he attended Rathmines School, near Dublin. At the age of eighteen, Tyrrell became a Roman Catholic. In 1882 he took his first vows as a Jesuit, and in September, 1891, he was ordained a priest. For a time he busied himself with mission work at Oxford, Preston, and St. Helen's before becoming a lecturer of philosophy at St. Mary's Hall, Stonyhurst. In 1896 Tyrrell was transferred to the literary staff of his order, in London, where he began his writing career. His first publications, *Nova et Vetera: Informal Meditations* (1897, 3rd ed. 1900), *Hard Sayings: A Selection of Meditations and Studies* (1898), and *External Religion: Its Use and Abuse* (1899) were quite orthodox with regard to the views of the church at the time. It was not until the publication of an article on hell, "A Perverted Devotion" which he contributed to the *Weekly Register* in December of 1899 that Tyrrell showed signs of broadening his views on religion. It was such a change that prompted his removal to a mission house at Richmond, Yorkshire, where he continued to live until 1906 when he was dismissed from the order.

While in seclusion Tyrrell completed several works, including *Oil and Wine* (1902, new ed. 1907), *Lex Orandi* (1903) which originally ap-

peared as a pamphlet entitled "Religion as a Factor of Life" under the pseudonym Dr. Ernest Engels, and its sequel, *Lex Credendi* (1906). The last was described by *Catholic World* (1906) as "an altogether worthy continuation of the previous work published with full theological censorship and ecclesiastical sanction." It was at this time

that Tyrrell also published a translation of "The Church and the Future," a quite liberal essay he himself had written in French under the pseudonym Hilaire Bourdon. The true identity of the author was not known until after his death.

Tyrrell's break with the church came with the publication of his privately printed *Letter to a Professsor of Anthropology*, in which Tyrrell directed his attention to what he considered were the defects of the Catholic Church and takes up the question of the relation between faith and culture, all the while attempting to convince a university professor not to give up his religion. Enraged, his superiors dismissed Tyrrell from the Society of Jesus in 1906, claiming that it was not possible for him to reconcile the views he had put forth in *Letter* with those of his order. In an effort to further explain himself, Tyrrell published *The Much Abused Letter* (1906), a heavily annotated version of his *Letter to a Professor of Anthropology*. The effect on his superiors was minimal, and only served to complete his estrangement from the church.

After his dismissal, Tyrrell tried unsuccessfully to gain Episcopal recognition. He spent the remainder of his days in Storrington, Sussex, immersed in his literary work, much of which was published after his death. Though alienated from the leaders of his church, he seems never to have lost his love for and devotion to the faith itself. In 1909 he published *Christianity at the Crossroads*, an examination of the Modernist movement in both the Catholic and the Protestant churches. It was praised by the *Spectator* (1909) as being a book "which must be read and pondered, and reckoned with." The reviewer went on to say that, "England in our time has not produced Tyrrell's equal for depth, breadth, subtlety, honesty, and courage in theological matters." Tyrrell's *Essays on Faith and Morality* was collected from notebooks and journals and published in 1914 by his literary executrix, Maude D. Petre, who later published a collection of his letters (*Letters*, 1920). Petre also published *The Autobiography and Life of George Tyrrell* (1912), which appeared in two volumes, and was well received by reviewers, though, as one reviewer for *Atheneum* (1912) put it, "not because of anything specially remarkable in his life, or character, or opinions, but because he, more than any other Irishman (or Englishman) of his day, represents that special phase of thought in religion with which the twentieth century was inaugurated." Before his death, he had given his last confession, and was granted absolution, but because he did not recant, he was denied burial in Catholic ground. He was buried in the parish cemetary at Storrington, Sussex.

PRINCIPAL WORKS: Nova et Vetera, 1897; Hard Sayings, 1898; External Religion, 1899; The Faith of the Millions, 1901–1902; Lex Orandi, 1903; Another Handful of Myrrh, 1905; A Much Abused Letter, 1906; Lex Credendi, 1906; Oil and Wine, 1907; Through Scylla and Charybdis, 1907; Medievalism, A Reply to Cardinal Mercier, 1908; Christianity at the Cross—Roads, 1909; The Church and the Future, 1910; Autobiography and Life of George Tyrell, 1912; Essays of faith and Immortality, 1914.

ABOUT: Dictionary of National Biography 1901–1911. *Periodi-*

cals—Atheneum Novermber 2, 1912; Catholic World July 6, 1906; Spectator Novermber 6, 1909; Times (London) July 16, 1909.

## ULLMAN, JAMES RAMSEY (November 24, 1907–June 20, 1971), American novelist, and writer on mountaineering and travel, wrote:

"A New Yorker to begin with (and probably to end with), I was born on West 90th Street and such roots as I have are anchored firmly in Central Park. Attended Ethical Culture School, Andover and Princeton, emerging from the last in 1929 with the usual B.A. My senior thesis, *Mad Shelley*, won a prize and was subsequently published—which encouraged me in my hope for a writing career—and after graduation I took off for Paris, with the twin purposes of getting a job as foreign correspondent and writing the Great American Novel. Neither materialized, however, and I returned to New York, arriving on the day of the 1929 stock market crash.

"After much pavement-pounding I found a reporter's job on the now defunct Brooklyn *Standard Union* and held it for two years. On the side I tried my hand at play-writing. Two of my efforts were tried out in summer theatres, but none (just as well, no doubt) reached Broadway. In the process, however, I made many theatrical contacts, and in 1933, to my considerable surprise, found myself no longer a newspaperman but a producer of plays. During the next few years I had a hand in ten New York productions. One of them, *Men in White*, won the Pulitzer prize for 1934; two, *The Milky Way* and *Blind Alley*, were modest successes; the rest are best forgotten. After demobilizing myself from the commercial theatre I spent two hysterical but fascinating years as an executive of the WPA's Federal Theatre Project. And at last in 1939, I got back to what I had always wanted to do (and should have been doing): i.e., writing.

"I had already, in off hours, done a travel book, *The Other Side of the Mountain*, based on a trip I had made across the Andes and down the Amazon. Now, as a full-time author, I wrote short stories and articles for the magazines and a history of mountaineering called *High Conquest*. Came 1941, Pearl Harbor—and an interruption. The army wanting no part of me (near-sightedness), I joined the American Field Service as an ambulance driver. Served for eighteen months with the British Eighth Army in Africa—from El Alamein through to Tunisia.

"Returning home, and to writing, I concentrated on the novel and produced, over the next several years, *The White Tower*, *River of the Sun* and *Windom's Way*, all three of which were lucky enough to be book-club selections.

"Over the years I have managed to escape occasionally from the desk and lead something of a double life as a traveler and mountaineer, venturing as far afield as Brazil and Hawaii, Russia and South Africa, the Alps and the Andes. And, inevitably, my love of far and high places has strongly influenced my writing. As far back as I can remember, my fondest dream has been to have a try at Mount Everest; but, at the age of forty-five, I am afraid it will remain just that. . . . "

Although he was born and raised in comfortable circumstances in New York City, James Ramsey Ullman's major writings, both fiction and nonfiction, focus on remote, often inhospitable, and decidedly nonurban places. "Though I've been to more cocktail parties in New York than I care to remember," he told a *New York Times Book Review* (1951) interviewer, "my talent doesn't seem to me to be in dealing with the small social habits and mores of city people."

Ullman's best known and most widely acclaimed books concern mountaineering, a sport he first engaged in as a sophomore at Princeton, when he traveled to Switzerland and climbed the Matterhorn and Jungfrau. He later scaled many high peaks around the world, including Mount Kilimanjaro, Mount Olympus, and Popocateptl. Writing in the *New Yorker* (1941), Clifton Fadiman said of his history of mountaineering, *High Conquest*, "I put it down among the finest popular histories (at least in English) of its subject that I am familiar with and as a sound job of narrative in its own right." In a *Saturday Review* notice of *The Age of Mountaineering* (as the second edition of *High Conquest* was retitled), Supreme Court justice William O. Douglas—himself a climbing enthusiast—wrote, "Ullman puts the grandeur, the severity, the terror of mountains into beautiful English." Ullman's first novel, *The White Tower*, in which six people ascend an arduous peak in the Swiss Alps, was a best-seller, a Book of the Month Club choice and won numerous critical plaudits for its realistic depiction of mountaineering, although some reviewers found its philosophical and psychological ruminations less than satisfying. As Hamilton Basso noted in the *New Yorker* (1945), "The part of the book devoted to climbing is excellent. . . . But, while he's a good man with a piton, the thin, high air of philosophy and mysticism does strange things to him."

Ullman achieved a considerable degree of popular success as a novelist. Most of his fiction features Americans or Europeans in exotic, far-flung locales, most of which Ullman had visited himself during his many travels. The protagonist of *Windom's Way* is an American doctor practicing in a tiny village in southern Asia. In *The Sands of Karakorum*, a foreign correspondent follows American missionaries through the wilds of China. *The Day on Fire* is based on the life of the French poet Arthur Rimbaud, who, after a remarkably precocious and brief literary career, wandered through Europe and North Africa as a merchant and gun-runner. Perhaps Ullman's most highly-praised novel was the one he wrote for younger readers, *Banner in the Sky*, about a sixteen-year-old Swiss boy on an expedition to a climb a daunting Alpine peak—the story based in part on the tragic first ascent of the Matterhorn in 1865. A *Horn Book* reviewer hailed it as "a masterpiece of adventure-writing," and Walt Disney studios filmed it as *Third Man on the Mountain.*

Ullman helped the Sherpa climber Tenzing Norkay, who climbed Mount Everest with Sir Edmund Hillary in 1953, to write his autobiography, published in the United States as *Tiger of the Snows.* Ullman never did get an opportunity to climb Mount Everest, the world's highest mountain, but he was an official member of the 1963 American Mount Everest Expedition. Then in his mid-fifties, and suffering from a circulation disorder, Ullman traveled as far as Katmandu, Nepal, where he maintained radio contact with the climbing team. The story of that expedition is contained in his best-selling book *Americans on Everest*, written in collaboration with other members of the team.

Many of Ullman's books were as popular in Great Britain as they were in the United States, and many were translated into European languages. For his ambulance-driving work with the British Eighth Army, the British government awarded him the Star of Africa in 1945. In 1965 he participated in a civil rights march from Selma to Montgomery, Alabama. Twice divorced, he was survived by his third wife, Marian (Blinn) McCown. His papers are housed in the Princeton University Library.

PRINCIPAL WORKS: *Literary criticism*—Mad Shelley, 1930. *Drama*—(with A. Scheuer, Jr.) Is Nothing Sacred? A "Success Story" in Three Acts, 1934. *Novels*—The White Tower, 1945; River of the Sun, 1950; Windom's Way, 1952; The Sands of Karakorum, 1953; The Day on Fire: A Novel Suggested by the Life of Arthur Rimbaud, 1958; Fia Fia: A Novel of the South Pacific, 1962 (in U.K.: Island Below the Wind); And Not to Yield, 1970. *Short stories*—Island of the Blue Macaws, and Sixteen Other Stories, 1953 (in U.K.: The Silver Cloud, and Other Stories). *Mountaineering*—High Conquest: The Story of Mountaineering, 1941; The Age of Mountaineering, 1954, rev. ed. 1964; (with others) Americans on Everest: The Official Account of the Ascent Led by Norman G. Dyhrenfurth, 1964. *Travel*—The Other Side of the Mountain: An Escape to the Amazon, 1938; Where the Bong Tree Grows: The Log of One Man's Journey in the South Pacific, 1963; (with A. Dinhofer) Caribbean Here and Now: The Complete Vacation Guide to 52 Sunny Islands in the Caribbean Sea, 1968, 3rd rev. ed. 1970. *Juvenile*—Banner in the Sky, 1954 (reissued as Third Man on the Mountain, 1954); Down the Colorado with Major Powell, 1960. *Autobiography*—(with T. Norgay) Tiger of the Snows: The Autobiography of Tenzing of Everest, Written in Collaboration with James Ramsey Ullman, 1955 (in U.K.: Man of Everest: The Autobiography of Tenzing, Told to James Ramsy Ullman; in U.S.: Tenzing: Tiger of Everest). *Biography*—Straight Up: The Life and Death of John Harlin, 1968. *As editor*—Kingdom of Adventure: Everest, a Chronicle of Man's Assault on the Earth's Highest Mountain, 1947.

ABOUT: The autobiographical material quoted above was written for Twentieth Century Authors First Supplement, 1955. Contemporary Authors New Revision Series 3 1981; Current Biography 1945, 1971. National Cyclopedia of American Biography vol. 56 1975. *Periodicals*—Horn Book October 1954; New York Times June 21, 1971; New York Times Book Review January 21, 1951; New Yorker October 18, 1941; September 29, 1945; Saturday Review November 13, 1954; Times (London) June 22, 1971.

**UNAMUNO (Y JUGO), MIGUEL DE** (September 29, 1864–December 31, 1936), Spanish philosopher, novelist, dramatist, poet, and educator, was born in Bilbao, the  third of six children of Félix Unamuno and his wife Salomé de Jugo, who was also his niece; both parents were of Basque ancestry. His father, a proprietor of a bakery shop, died when Miguel was six, and he was brought up by an uncle. Félix Unamuno, though not university educated, left an extensive book collection in philosophy, history, and social and natural science—augmented by the uncle's private library. Unamuno's life encompassed an especially turbulent period of Spanish history. As a boy he witnessed the bombardment of his native city in the havoc of the last Carlist War (recalled in his first novel *Paz en la guerra* (1897, *Peace and War*); his emergence into literary prominence coincided with the final collapse of Spain's colonial empire; he lived through several violent changes of government, culminating with the civil war instigated by Francisco Franco, which broke out several months before his death. This atmosphere of unrest helps to account for the sceptical outlook that pervades his writing, his penchant for enigma and paradox, and particularly the oscillations of his academic situation and political position.

Unamuno's enduring reputation as a nonconformist had early roots. He chafed at the traditional curriculum imposed on him at the Instituto Viscaíno, which he entered at the age of eleven. While a student of classical literature in the School of Philosophy at the University of Madrid, he immersed himself in the more heterodox and radical writings of the time—the higher criticism of the Bible, the positivism of Auguste Comte, and the economics of Karl Marx (recapitulated in the education of young Pachico Zabalbide in *Peace and War*). His doctoral dissertation controverted the received tradition that the Basques were the first Iberians, a possible reason why his applications for chairs in Basque and philosophy at the Instituto Viscaíno were rejected by the supervisors.

After several years of struggle as a private tutor and free-lance journalist, Unamuno won appointment as professor of Greek language at the University of Salamanca in 1891, through the influence of the scholar Menéndez y Pelayo, his mentor at the University of Madrid, then president of the Royal Spanish Academy. In this same year he married his childhood sweetheart Concepción Lizáraga, a union which produced eight children. Following publication of *Paz en la guerra* he became associated with a circle of discontented young writers dubbed "the Generation of 1898"—among whose leading lights besides Azorín, who coined the term, were the poet Antonio Machado and the novelists Pio Baroja and Ramón del Valle-Inclán. With Spain humiliated in the Spanish-American War, Unamuno and his colleagues sought to bring their country out of its slump through a regeneration of its culture. His elevation to the post of rector of the University of Salamanca in 1900 made him the preeminent figure in the new movement. His voice reached wide, holding forth at *tertulias* (gatherings) in the cafes of the Plaza Mayor, stimulating generations of students with his unorthodox teaching methods, stirring up the reading public with his provocative books in a variety of genres, attacking traditional institutions, and urging rethinking of old religious dogmas.

Unamuno's seminal book is *Del sentimiento trágico de la vida en los hombres y en los pueblos* (1913, translated as *The Tragic Sense of Life*), the first of his books to be translated into English (1921), a plangent meditation on the human condition distilling his wide reading in theological writers, notably Kierkegaard. Like the Danish existentialist (whom he read in Danish), Unamuno argues that man "philosophizes not with the reason only, but with the will, with the feelings, with the flesh, and with the bones, with the whole soul and the whole body." The "tragedy" of humanity lies in the unresolved conflict between the soul with its intuitive belief in immortality, and the reason which confutes it. For the way out of this abyss, Unamuno turns to Cervantes's great hero who had been transformed in his earlier *Vida de don Quijote y Sancho* (1905, *The Life of Don Quixote and Sancho*) into a secular Christ ("The Knight of Faith, he whose madness makes us sane").

Unamuno's fictional works, with their willful characters, are most fruitfully read as parables vitalizing his tragic sense of life. To signalize their bare-boned nature—spare settings, telescoping of time and space—he coined the term *nivolas* for his best known tales, distinguishing them from his more fully developed *novelas.* Augusto Pérez, the effete hero of the appropriately named *Niebla* (1914, *Mist*) the first of his *nivolas* to be translated into English (1928), wanders about in what he thinks of as a dream world, torn between two women, one who appeals to his imagination and one to his heart; he eventually loses both, and contemplates suicide. However, Unamuno teases the reader by allowing Augusto to confront the author, arguing that he has a right to determine his own fate. This so-called "farcical tragedy" thus becomes at once a paradigm of the struggle between man and God and an extension of Unamuno's concept, introduced in *The Life of Don Quixote and Sancho*, of the autonomous character. Ultimately the author decides that because he is mortal, the creature of his mind must die, but in a final twist Augusto returns in a dream to reassert his independent identity.

As a thinker, Unamuno was preoccupied with what he called "intra-history," extracting what was essential and timeless from the ephemeral events of the past for the edification of mankind. By analogy, in his imaginary works he extrapolated universal human symbols from the Bible and literature. He was drawn in particular to the figure of Cain, both from the Creation story and the Byron's epic poem,

incarnated notably in Joaquín (Yo-Cain) Monegro in *Abel Sánchez, una historia de pasión* (1917, *Abel Sánchez, a History of Passion*). Joaquín's consuming envy of the successful artist Abel, leading him eventually to cause his friend's death, bears generally on the divisiveness in the human soul, and specifically on the fratricidal history of Spain beset with recurrent civil wars.

The figures who dominate *Tres novelas ejemplares y un prólogo* (1920, *Three Exemplary Novels*) personify "the anxiety to perpetuate our name and fame, to grasp at least a shadow of immortality," a leading motif of *The Tragic Sense of Life.* The devious schemes of the ruthless matriarchs of "The Marquess of Lumbría" and "Two Mothers" recall the biblical Rachel and Rebecca. The upstart hero of the most powerful of the tales, "Nothing Less than a Man" (which was subsequently dramatized) pursues his Don Juan complex to disastrous consequences. The heroine of *La Tía Tula* (Aunt Tulce, 1921) carries her devotion to the ideal of the virgin mother to self-sacrificing extremes. All of these stories represent the decadence of such Spanish traditions as family pride, honor, and the Catholic faith.

Called the Salamancan Socrates, Unamuno was associated with Spain's oldest seat of learning, which he helped to revitalize, until the end of his life, but his career there was broken up by dismissals and reinstatements reflecting the viscissitudes of Spanish politics. Opposed to autocracy in any form, his outspoken attacks on King Alfonso XIII led to his dismissal as rector in 1914, although he was allowed to retain his professorship. A prison sentence imposed on him at the time was revoked by royal pardon as a result of protest by scholars throughout Europe. In 1920 he was given a new appointment as vice-rector, but a clash with the dictator Primo de Rivera, whose coup d'état occurred in 1923, led to his exile, first to Fuerteventura, one of the Canary Islands. His subsequent escape to Paris, arranged by the newspaper *Quotidien*, made him an international celebrity. Although, as it happened, he was accorded amnesty by Rivera on the very day of his escape, Unamuno chose not to return to Spain or even to remain in Paris, but moved to Hendaye near the Spanish border where he remained in self-imposed exile for the next five years. His principal publication in exile was *The Agony of Christianity*, first printed in French (1925), a sequel to *The Tragic Sense of Life*, expounding on the baroque conception of Jesus as a suffering human being, introduced in his long poem *El Cristo de Velázquez* (1920, *The Christ of Velázquez*). During these years translation of some of his principal works in America (e.g., *Essays and Soliloquies, The Life of Don Quixote, Mist*) brought him recognition by such influential critics as Mark Van Doren, Eliseo Vivas, and Ernest Boyd.

Shortly after the fall of Primo de Rivera early in 1930, Unamuno ended his exile, and was welcomed back to his native land by the succeeding Berenguer government. The following year, with the inauguration of the Republic under Admiral Juan Aznar, he was reappointed rector of the University of Salamanca, and entered public life as a deputy in the parliament. *The Agony of Christianity* had its first Spanish publication at this time (*La agonía del cristianismo*, 1931). Its imaginative counterpart in Unamuno's last major work *San Manuel Bueno, martír* (1933) centered on a priest who faithfully serves his pastoral ministry and performs acts of charity and consolation even though, unknown to his flock, he has lost his faith. Generally regarded as Unamuno's greatest work of fiction (certainly his most heartfelt), it has been taken as his apology to his public for having vexed and perplexed them, mingled with a note of nostalgia for a lost time of simple faith.

Unamuno's last years were marked both by honor and humiliation. In 1934 he retired as a professor and was named lifetime rector of Salamanca. The following year the Ministry of Public Education supported his candidacy (unsuccessful) for a Nobel Prize. Early in 1936 he received an honorary doctorate from Oxford, and later that year was honored at the University of Grenoble. Not long afterwards his lifetime post was rescinded when he expressed admiration for the Franco rebellion. This most controversial of his political actions has since been accounted for as the effect of his disenchantment with the republic which he came to see as Communist-dominated, and riddled with factionalism. Subsequently, shortly before his death, came another turnabout when he repudiated his pro-Franco stand out of revulsion at the Falangist takeover of Spain. On December 31, 1936, he died of a brain clot at the age of seventy-two, isolated and embittered. He was buried next to his wife who had predeceased him by two and a half years. One of his last poems concludes:

I am not, but my song lives after me
And carries round the world
The shadow of my shadow
Sad non-existence.
("For After My Death," tr. Eleanor Turnbull)

"It cannot be denied that the sheer bulk of Unamuno's work is threatening, that his thought is meandering, incongruent, asystematic, as much the outcroppings of his irresponsible daemons, as of ratiocination," in the judgment of Martin Nozick, one of America's foremost Unamunmists. He seems best summed up as the eternal gadfly suggested by the title of one of his volumes of essays, *Contra esto y aquello* (Against this and that, 1912), a paradoxical combination of Spanish Shaw and Spanish Sartre. To the poet William Jay Smith he represented "the embodiment of his country," incarnating its conflicts and contradictions as it struggled into the twentieth century. As a literary figure he can be considered a proto-modern with his intellectual gamesmanship, ambivalent characters, and open endings; he even anticipates current reader response theory. Although the most Europeanized of Spanish writers—his private library contained books in twenty languages—he never achieved the world-wide readership he sought. However, since the posthumous publication of his *Obras completas* (1959–1964), he has been the subject of numerous studies and continually commemorated at confer-

ences by Hispanicists on both sides of the ocean. His house in Salamanca is now maintained as a museum.

PRINCIPAL WORKS IN ENGLISH TRANSLATION: *Fiction*—The Life of Don Quixote and Sancho According to Miguel de Cervantes Saavedra (tr. H. P. Earle) 1927 (ed. and tr. as Our Lord Don Quixote. The Life of Don Quixote and Sancho with Related Essays By A. Kerrigan, 1967); Mist (tr. W. Fite) 1928; Three Exemplary Novels and a Prologue (tr. A. Flores) 1930; Abel Sánchez, 1947 (tr. as Abel Sanchez and Other Stories by A. Kerrigan, 1956); San Manuel Bueno, mártir (tr. F. de Segovia and J. Pérez) 1957; Ficciones: Four Stories and a Play (ed. and tr. by A. Kerrigan) 1976; Peace in War (tr. A. Lacy, M. Nozick, and A. Kerrigan) 1983; Love and Pedagogy (tr. M. Vande Berg) 1993. *Poetry*—The Christ of Velázquez (tr. E. L. Turnbull) 1951; Poems (tr. E. L. Turnbull) 1952; The Last Poems of Miguel de Unamuno (tr. E. Mas-López) 1974. *Nonfiction*—The Tragic Sense of Life in Men and in Peoples (tr. J.E.C. Flitch) 1921 (tr. as The Tragic Sense of Life in Men and Nations by A. Kerrigan, with M. Nozick, 1972); Essays and Soliloquies (tr. J.E.C. Flitch) 1925; The Agony of Christianity (tr. from French by P. Loving) 1928 (ed. and tr. as The Agony of Christianity and Essays on Faith by A. Kerrigan, 1974); Perplexities and Paradoxes (tr. S. Gross) 1945; Novela/Nivola (ed. and tr. A. Kerrigan) 1976; The Private World: Selections from the Diario intimo and Selected Letters 1890–1936 (eds. and tr. A. Kerrigan, A. Lacy, and M. Nozick) 1984.

ABOUT: Barea, A. Unamuno, 1952; Basdekis, D. Unamuno in Spanish Literature, 1967; Choi, J-S. Greene and Unamuno; Two Pilgrims to la Mancha, 1990; Del Rio, A. *introduction to* Three Exemplary Novels, 1956; Earle, P. Unamuno and English Literature, 1960; Ellis, R. The Tragic Pursuit of Being: Unamuno and Sartre, 1988; Eoff, S. The Modern Spanish Novel, 1961; Ferrater Mora, J. Unamuno, a Philosophy of Tragedy (tr. P. Silver) 1962; Ilie, P. Unamuno: An Existential View of Self and Society, 1967; Jurkevich, G. The Elusive Self, 1991; Madariaga, S. de. *introduction to* The Tragic Sense of Life, 1921; Nozick, M. Miguel de Unamuno, 1972 (republished 1982 as Miguel de Unamuno, the Agony of Unbelief); Rudd, M. The Lone Heretic, 1963. *Bibliography*—Larson, E. E. Miguel de Unamuno: A Bibliography, 1986. *Periodicals*—Hispania July 1941; Modern Language Notes March 1987; Modern Language Association Publications October 1990; New York Times January 2, 1937; Times (London) January 4, 1937.

**UNDERHILL, EVELYN** (December 6, 1875– June 15, 1941) English religious writer and novelist, was born at Wolverhampton, and educated at home until the age of thirteen, when she was sent away to Sandgate House, a boarding-school in Folkestone. She then read history and botany at King's College, London. Her first publication was a book of light verse, *A Bar-Lamb's Ballad Book* (1902), in which she had some playful fun at  the expense of the law. (Her father, Arthur Underhill, was a barrister.) Two years later Underhill published the first of three early novels, having already had some supernatural stories published in *Horlicks* magazine. In *The Grey World* a child from the slums is reincarnated into the household of a successful tradesman. Her second novel, *The Lost Word*, about an architect commissioned to design and erect a church on a friend's estate, shared the first book's atmosphere of weird morbidity. After her marriage in 1907 to Hubert Stuart Moore a barrister, and her conversion to the Christian faith in the same year, Underhill produced only one more novel. *The Column of Dust* (1909) is considered the best of the three, but Underhill's reputation is based upon her religious writing, the first significant title being *Mysticism* (1911), a book considered essential reading for anyone interested in the subject. It owes its success to its thematic, psychological approach; to its fund of biographical information about some hitherto little-known figures, such as the East Anglian mystic, Margery Kempe; and to an extensive bibliography. In 1915 she published a short biographical book about the fourteenth-century Flemish mystic, Jan van Ruysbroeck, again seeking to put before the public a figure little known. Her next biography, about the rather better-known Jacapone da Todi, Italian author of the 'Stabat Mater,' was reviewed by Marianne Moore in the *Dial*: "The biographer's comprehension of the worldly accomplishments of her subject and her equal insight into his spiritual attainments, is strikingly the counterpart of that two-sidedness which she emphasizes in the man himself."

Before her conversion, Underhill had been attracted to the occult and was, for a short period, involved with the Golden Dawn. Initially, and at the time of her conversion in 1907, she was drawn to Catholicism, and soon after the publication of *Mysticism* adopted Friedrich von Hügel, the unorthodox Roman Catholic scholar, as her spiritual teacher. But in the end the high value she placed on intellectual independence led her, in 1921, to Anglicanism (although she remained von Hügel's pupil until his death in 1925), and the book she published that year, a collection of essays entitled *Essentials of Mysticism*, formed a kind of compendium of her thinking about both the theory and practice of the spiritual life.

In *Practical Mysticism* (1914) she articulated a theme which was the basis of her teaching—that the mystical life is available to everybody, but requires nurturing. The books's subtitle is *A Little Book for Normal People*. The ideal religious life should contain a balance of piety and service to others. The retreats which she led from the 1920s onwards were designed to provide opportunities for Anglican clergy and laymembers to enrich their spiritual life. Several of her later books—*Mixed Pasture* is an example—began as retreat addresses, but *Worship*, published in 1936, was a major historical study of liturgy, and became as standard a work as her earlier *Mysticism*.

During World War I, Underhill was a declared pacifist, having joined APF—the Anglican Pacifist Fellowship—and written for them a pamphlet, *The Church and War*, which became a key manifesto.

While Underhill's learning and knowledge impressed lay readers, theological scholars found that occasional inaccuracies, and a rather deadpan style of writing, were sometimes at odds with her mystical subject matter. Immediately after her death there was a rush of posthumous publications, including a collection of letters. *Light of Christ*

(1944)—previously unpublished retreat addresses—contained a short memoir by Lucy Menzies, who also edited one of Underhill's early travel diaries, published as *Shrines and Cities of France and Italy*. More recently, Dana Greene, who had written extensively about Underhill, edited the notebooks, published as *Fragments From an Inner Life* (1993).

PRINCIPAL WORKS: *Poetry*—A Bar-Lamb's Ballad Book, 1902; Immanence, 1912; Theophanies, 1919; The Gray World, 1904. *Novels*—The Lost Word, 1907; The Column of Dust, 1909. *Nonfiction*—Mysticism, 1911; The Path of The Eternal Wisdom, 1911; The Spiral Way, 1912; The Mystic Way, 1913; Practical Mysticism, 1914; Ruysbroeck, 1915; Jacapone da Todi, 1919; The Essentials of Mysticism and Other Essays, 1920; The Life of the Spirit and The Life of Today, 1922; The Mystics of the Church, 1925; Concerning the Inner Life, 1926; Man and the Supernatural, 1927; The House of the Soul, 1929; The Golden Sequence, 1932; Mixed Pasture, 1933; The School of Charity, 1934; Worship, 1936; The Spiritual Life, 1937; The Mystery of Sacrifice, 1938; Abba, Meditations on The Lord's Prayer, 1940; The Fruits of the Spirit, 1942; The Letters of Evelyn Underhill (ed. C. Williams) 1943; Light of Christ, 1944; Collected Papers of Evelyn Underhill, 1946; The Church and War, 1947; Meditations and Prayers, 1949; Shrines and Cities of France and Italy, 1949; Fragments from an Inner Life, 1993.

ABOUT: Armstrong, C. Evelyn Underhill, 1975; Cropper, M. Evelyn Underhill, 1958; Dictionary of National Biography, 1941–1950, 1959; Greene, D. Evelyn Hill, 1990; Menzies, L. in Light of Christ, 1944; Schlueter, P. and J. An Encyclopaedia of Women Writers, 1988; Who's Who, 1941. *Periodicals*—Commonweal March 22, 1991; Dial January 1921; Times (London) June 18, 1941.

**UNDSET, SIGRID** (May 20, 1882–June 10, 1949), Norwegian historical novelist, playwright, and essayist, was born in Kalundborg, Denmark, the eldest of the three daughters of Ingvald Martin Undset, a distinguished archeologist, and his Danish wife Anna Charlotte—towards whom, as Undset tells the reader in her autobiographical novel, she developed a great bitterness. The fact seems to have been that, although Anna was intelligent and enlightened, she was too much so for her daughter, who throughout her own life opposed what she perceived as her mother's rationalism. Yet she owed much to her, and to her attempts to instill a sense of reality into her dreamy child at a young age. When Sigrid was two years old the family moved back to Oslo (then Christiania). Her father, whose health had been undermined by malaria, died when she was eleven, but not before he had given his extremely precocious and unusually observant daughter the run of his very extensive library.

Ingvald Undset's death, which indelibly marked both the life and the oeuvre of his eldest daughter, left the family quite impoverished, and Sigrid, after education at the enlightened Ragna Nelson School, sacrificed her chance of enrolling at the University in order to earn money as a secretary: she chose at only fifteen to attend secretarial college; at sixteen she gained a certificate of competence. For ten years she worked for the German Electric Company; in her free time, initially most interested in the welfare of the working girls whom she knew so well, she began to write.

She tried her hand at a historical novel, only to be told by the Oslo publishers Glydendal that she ought to turn her attention to contemporary life. The result was *Fur Mart Julie* (1907, Mrs Mart Julie). She quickly wrote more, similarly contemporary novels. All three of these books were well enough received for her to be able (1908) to leave her job and set out on a career as a novelist and author. She told the story of these years in her novel *Elev. aar* (1934, translated as *The Longest Years*); this is faithful to the events of her life at that stage, and her feelings about them.

Undset then received a travel grant from the government, with which she went to Rome. There she met a painter, Anders Svarstad, with whom she had three children, one of whom, Maren, was born retarded and only survived until her twenty-fourth year; in 1924 they were divorced (after she had been, despite her Lutheran upbringing, received into the Roman Catholic Church). While in Rome Undset published *Jenny* (1911, translated under that title in 1921), her first really successful book. The story of a young artist who is driven to suicide by her unfulfilled quest for love, and who has a baby by her fiance's father, caused a stir in Oslo, particularly in feminist circles. Of her novels of contemporary life, it is generally judged to be the best; but a few prefer the story-collection *Fattige skjoebner* (1912, Humble existences).

Undset's real strength, however, lay in the historical novel. In 1909, inspired by her father's example, she had already written and published *Fortellingen om Viga-Ljot og Vigdis* (translated as *Gunnar's Daughter*), little more than a pastiche of an Icelandic saga, of which the *New Republic* reviewer wrote, "It is full of dark violence and relieved but little by the humanity of understanding that Sigrid Undset brings to her later work."

Her first historical novel of serious account is also by far her most famous work, and the one for which she received the Nobel Prize: the trilogy *Kristin Lavransdatter* (1920–22, translated as *The Bridal Wreath*, *The Mistress of Husaby*, and *The Cross*). The first part is set in Norway at the beginning of the fourteenth century. It tells of the aristocratic Lavrans Bjorgulfsson and his daughter: first, of their idyllic relationship when she is a girl, then of the clash of wills between them when she defies him to marry the man she loves, Erlend Nikolausson. In the second part the unhappy marriage is described: here Kristin's own selfishness, deceptions, and pettiness are seen as in part responsible for her sad lot. Of this volume the *New York Times* critic wrote: "The second part of the story . . . confirms the impression left by the first; that here is a very remarkable piece of work, a story of mediaeval times told as naturally and with as little apparent strain as if it were a tale of today. The wealth of learning which must have been necessary to produce such a book is never paraded; the clothes and

customs, the manners and . . . points of view of the time appear only as they are needed for the carrying on of the chronicle. *The Mistress of Husaby* is interesting, dramatic, and very far indeed out of the ordinary." The final part, *The Cross*, the novelist Ruth Sukow remarked in *Books*, showed a "decline in lyric passion" but a deepening of "emotional power." In this tragic section Kristin is shown stripped of her great estate (Erlend had already retreated to a shack in the mountains) and ending as a commoner. She dies in a convent of the Black Death. As in almost all Undset's books, there is a painful conflict between the public and the private sphere; but Undset seems to have felt that the attainment of love was an impossibility. Undset was never able to equal the genuine grandeur of the narrative of *Kristin Lavransdatter*. In that work, the chief technical triumph is achieved in the brilliant and convincing juxtaposition of the spiritual and material worlds as they lay themselves open to the young Kristin's vital attentions. The first part, above all, is an example of a reconstruction of medieval life seldom equaled.

Undset's next historical cycle, *Olav Audunsson i Hestviken* (1928–30, translated as *The Master of Hestviken* in four volumes), is, although impressive—and deserving of the adjective usually applied to it, "monumental"—not as successful. Set in a period (late thirteenth-century to early fourteenth-century) very slightly earlier than its predecessor, it gives even greater emphasis to the themes of guilt and concealed sin. It is a work more obviously inspired by Roman Catholicism than *Kristin Lavransdatter*. Undset did gain a great deal of publicity (perhaps not unduly sought) from her conversion, which she had made mainly as a result of her conviction that only the Catholic Church could offer a true bastion against materialism. The "moral" of the whole saga, that vengeance belongs to God alone, is rather heavily asserted; on the other hand, the medieval world of the novel is evoked quite as powerfully as it was in the earlier trilogy. It is the psychological detail that is weaker.

Undset was one of the first well-known Norwegians to draw attention to the Nazi menace. She remained in Lillehammer until 1940; in that year her eldest son, Anders, was killed defending his country when the Germans invaded. She was now left with her only surviving son, Hans, with whom she fled through Sweden to Russia, and from Russia to the United States via Japan. She was very active throughout World War II as lecturer and propagandist for Norway and its plight. She returned to Norway as soon as the war ended, and was honored for her services. She died at her home in Lillehammer. Her last fiction, *Madame Dorthea* (1939, translated under that title), was left incomplete. It is far better than the tendentious *Gymnadenia* (1929, translated as *The Wild Orchid*) and its sequel *Den braedenden busk* (1930, translated as *The Burning Bush*), of the first part of which the reviewer in *Books* (1931) wrote: "In all respects one may admit the genius . . . yet regret that so great a writer should twist and turn a man's character into a groove channeled for him not by necessity but by the intention and almost caprice of religious . . . invention." Set in Norway during the eighteenth century, it is about the attempts of a woman to discover the reasons for her husband's inexplicable disappearance.

Undset was not a feminist, but she was always a humanist. Her essays may be read in the two volumes of *Etapper* (1929, 1933, translated as *Stages on the Road*) and in *Selvpotretter og landskapsbilleder* (1938, translated as *Men, Women and Places*).

PRINCIPAL WORKS IN ENGLISH TRANSLATION: Kristin Lavransdatter: The Bridal Wreath (tr. C. Archer and J. S. Scott), 1920, *Novels*—Jenny (tr. W. Emme), 1921; The Mistress of Husaby (tr. C. Archer) 1923, The Cross (tr. C. Archer), 1927, in one volume, 1929; Olav Audunsson: The Axe (tr. A. W. Chater), 1928, The Snake Pit (tr. A. W. Chater), 1929, In the Wilderness (tr. A. W. Chater), 1929, The Son Avenger (tr. A. W. Chater), 1930; The Wild Orchid (tr. A. W. Chater), 1931; The Burning Bush (tr. A. W. Chater), 1932; Ida Elizabeth (tr. A. W. Chater), 1933; The Faithful Wife (tr. A. W. Chater), 1936. Gunnar's Daughter (tr. A. W. Chater), 1936; Madame Dorthea (tr. A. W. Chater), 1940. *Short stories*—Images in a Mirror (tr. A. W. Chater), 1938; *Essays and miscellaneous*—Stages on the Road (tr. A. W. Chater), 1934; The Longest Years (tr. A. W. Chater), 1939; Four Stories (tr. N. Walford), 1959.

ABOUT: Bayerschmidt, C. Sigrid Undset, 1970; Beach, J. W. The Twentieth Century Novel: Studies in Technique, 1932; Columbia Dictionary of Modern European Literature, 1947, 1980; Gustafson, Six Scandinavian Novelists, 1940; McFarlane, J. Ibsen and the Temper of Norwegian Literature, 1960; Monroe, N. The Novel and Society, 1941; Vinde, V. Sigrid Undset: A Nordic Moralist (tr. B. Hughes and G. Hughes), 1930; Winsnes, A. H. Sigrid Undset: A Study in Christian Realism (tr. P.G. Foote), 1953. *Periodicals*—Books March 20, 1927, September 27, 1931; Nation August 10, 1940; New Republic August 12, 1936; New York Times May 17, 1925.

**UNRUH, FRITZ VON** (May 10, 1885–November 28, 1970), Austrian playwright, novelist, and poet, was born at Coblenz, the son of a Prussian general who was governor of East Prussia and a close friend of Hindenberg. (His younger brother Friedrich Franz Unruh, born in 1893, also became a writer, mainly of stories, and a pacifist.) Fritz von Unruh, a leading expressionist of the 1920s, was best known both immediately before World War I and then in the interwar period. After World War II he continued to write, but, although respected as an honored and fearless opponent of the Nazis—and praised by Albert Einstein and Thomas Mann as such—he never recovered his old prestige.

Unruh was educated at the military school at Plön, Schleswig-Holstein, which the Emperor's sons attended. After serving one of the princes as his page, and then adjutant, he joined the cavalry. However, feeling that artistic values could not really be mixed with Prussian military life, he resigned his commission in 1912. The first of his plays, *Offiziere* (Officers, 1911), in its skillful production by Max Reinhardt (on December 15, 1912), was one of the great hits of its time. Inspired mainly by Heinrich von Kleist, Unruh's first romantic and patriotic model (of whose influence he gradually purged himself), it depicted—in language that anticipated expressionism, the conflict between the idealism of youth and the cold, in part sadistic, formalism of duty (in the notorious Prussian sense). *Officers* was not wholly expressionistic, however; nor was its more lyrical successor *Louis Ferdinand*

*Prinz von Preussen* (Louis Ferdinand Prince of Prussia, 1913), about the reforming and womanizing nephew of Frederick the Great, who associated with romantic poets, wrote music, patronized painters, and who died in battle in 1806. This too—in it blind duty is, once again, seen to undermine good judgment and humanity—was produced by Reinhardt, and gained Unruh an even larger following. *Louis Ferdinand King of Prussia* was banned from performance, as lending support to a defeatist attitude; but Unruh was awarded the Kleist Prize in the year of its publication.

In 1914 Unruh joined a lancer regiment (Ulan) and saw much active service as a captain. He was awarded the Iron Cross twice for his bravery. In his new works his style changed with some abruptness, although the tendency to shrillness remained. What was very sharply tempered, by the war horrors he witnessed, was his romanticism. He became, almost overnight, an aristocratic member of the expressionist left. Three important works followed: the prose narrative *Opfergang* (translated as *Way of Sacrifice*, actually written in 1916 near Verdun—the catastrophic retreat it dealt with—and published in 1918), and two plays, *Ein Geschlecht* (A family, 1916) and its sequel *Platz* (Town square, 1920). The later and less effective *Dietrich* (1936) made up a trilogy.

In 1914 Unruh had written the declamatory dramatic poem, *Vor der Entscheidung* (Before the Decision), one of the first of all the German anti-war tracts. With the sternly graphic and ironic diary *Way of Sacrifice* Unruh encountered serious censorship problems. The theologian Reinhold Niebuhr wrote in *Christian Century*, (1928) of the translation: "Von Unruh belongs to Germany's military aristocracy. But he has the mind of a poet and a clairvoyant insight. He reveals the horror of war as it appears on the surface. But he also senses the inner tragedy." Some reviewers of a more conservative cast of mind were shocked at what they felt was Unruh's disrespectful attitude towards authority. But Gerhart Hauptman nominated Unruh for the Schiller Prize on the strength of this narrative as well as his two plays. The horrified Prussian Minister of Culture immediately turned the nomination down: Unruh, although a hero to young leftwing writers, was for the establishment a traitor to his family and his class. However, things had relaxed enough for him to be awarded the Schiller Prize seven years later: he received it in 1927, along with Franz Werfel and the novelist and painter Hermann Burte.

Unruh's major achievement is reckoned to be *A Family*. By the time he came to write it his technique had become expressionist, so that the characters are presented as types, and realism is foregone in the interests of what may be called a somewhat obvious symbolism. These plays, written in a verse that is for the most part an equivalent to a declamatory prose, trace the history of a family through the war and the leftist revolution which almost immediately followed it. In the first play the action takes place at the entrance to a graveyard where a mother is burying one of her sons, just slain in the war.

It is said to have been highly effective on stage, and even to have had an "Aeschylean intensity." Mother, Youngest Son, and Daughter are at loggerheads with one another (and the son even wishes to rape his sister), and they wrangle in front of the gate to the cemetery. In the sequel—implicitly a criticism of the revolution—set in a Town Square, the Youngest Son (Dietrich) of the earlier play seeks the regeneration of mankind."

Unruh entered the Reichstag as a supporter of Walther Rathenau, who was highly unpopular amongst nationalists owing to his policy of compliance with the allies' demands for reparations. When Rathenau was murdered (1922) Unruh, also of the Realism Party, made a dithyrambic speech in the Reichstag as an obituary. He threw himself wholeheartedly into the pacifist cause, publishing his speeches and other appeals for peace. *Heinrich von Andernach*, a festival play of 1925, fervently appealed for peace and understanding amongst men. *Bonaparte*, about the trial an execution of the Duc d'Enghien (the real protagonist, despite the title) was an appeal to his countrymen to be on the alert for a takeover of power. But when in 1929 it appeared in an English translation by Edwin Björkman it was very badly received. The *Times Literary Supplement* remarked that Unruh's Napoleon was "more like a peevish old gentleman bordering on his second childhood than the youthful figure of the First Consul. . . . the central and most arresting figure appears to be, not the petulant First Consul, but the unfortunate Duc d'Enghien." The reviewer missed the point (although Hitler was, after all, petulant), but the *New York Times* (1928), too, found the piece difficult: it was certainly "dramatic," but it was "so crowded with personages . . . as to be . . . bewildering." The *New Statesman*, conceding that the German original might have a "certain violent effectiveness," simply stated that the "English version" was "no good at all."

In 1932 Unruh emigrated. The Nazis, when they came to power, offered to make him the "modern Schiller" if he would return. He refused, so they deprived him of his citizenship and burned his works. He lived in Italy and France, an activist in behalf of the anti-Nazi cause. When war broke out the French put him into a concentration camp; but in 1940 he managed to escape to the United States. From that time onwards he devoted the major part of his time writing novels. Of these the epic *The End Is Not Yet*—"a Hitler novel"—is certainly the most notable. It was denounced by conservatives and by the *Catholic World*. Its alleged flaws—"vague analysis" and "exhortative moralizing," accordingly to the *New Republic*—were widely noticed; still, the same *New Republic* reviewer, John Farrelly, also praised it, writing that it contained "magnificent dramatic scenes." The *New York Times* (1947) praised it even more thoroughly: "Nine-tenths of Unruh's poetry comes across, and since he writes German as if it were Attic Greek, this gives the story pace and forward drive. Its ethical greatness is attested by the absence of bitterness." "Ethical greatness," it may be noted, is a quality that Unruh even at this most tedious or declamatory always possessed in abundance. This novel did not appear in German (*Die nie verlor*) until two years after its English translation.

Unruh returned to Germany in 1952, settling at Diez on the Lahn, having been exhorted to come back by letters from thousands of students. Three years later he returned to the United States, but was unfortunate enough to lose all his possessions in a flood (1962), whereupon he returned to Diez. His most notable work after *The End Is Not Yet* was an extraordinary novel about Catherine of Siena, *Die Heilige* (*The Saint*, 1950). It shocked a few by its technique of paralleling the intensely religious with the intensely erotic. "Sister Julie," reviewing the translation for the Catholic *Commonweal*, called it "flamboyant," "a magnificent failure": Unruh, she claimed, did not understand the nature of St. Catherine's love. However, Gouverneur Paulding of the *New York Tribune Book Review* thought that Unruh's portrait of Catherine rang "true": a "sustained lyricism helps him vastly but his brain helps him even more. On the one hand he knows that the Christian mystic does not float about in confused sentimentality, that such a saint as Catherine thinks clearly . . . he knows, on the other hand, something equally important to know: that the enemy of Christ thinks clearly too and can define the object of his hatred. . . . Fritz von Unruh has found words adequate to the importance of what he has to say."

The fullest and most incisive English study of Unruh is by W. F. Mainland in *German Men of Letters, III*. Unruh's informative novel-autobiographies *Der Sohn des Generals* (1957) and *Im Haus der Prinzen* (1967), in which he figures as "Uhle," unfortunately remain untranslated.

PRINCIPAL WORKS IN ENGLISH TRANSLATION: *Novels*—Way of Sacrifice (tr. C. A. Macartney) 1928; The End Is Not Yet (tr. anon) 1947; The Saint (tr. W. R. Trask) 1950. *Drama*—Bonaparte (tr. E. Björkman) 1928.

ABOUT: Kronacher, A. Fritz von Unruh (tr. J. R. Stiller) 1946; Natan, A. (ed.) German Men of Letters, III, 1964; Seymour-Smith, M. Macmillan Guide to Modern World Literature, 1986; Sokel, W. H. The Writer in Extremis, 1959. *Periodicals*—Books Abroad Summer 1951, Spring 1955; Catholic World June 1947; Christian Century June 7, 1928; Commonweal November 17, 1950; New Republic June 2, 1947; New York Herald Book Review October 15, 1950; New York Times December 30, 1928; May 4, 1947; Newsweek December 14, 1970; Time December 14, 1970; Times Literary Supplement March 21, 1929.

**UNTERMEYER, LOUIS** (October 1, 1885–December 18, 1977), American anthologist, poet, and editor, was born in New York City, the son of Emanuel Untermeyer, a jewelry manufacturer, and Julia (Michael) Untermeyer. Finding little to interest him in his school work, Untermeyer dropped out of high school and entered his father's jewelry company, where he worked until 1923. His true passions, however, were music and the theater. He also began to write verse, which, although he achieved nothing memorable in that line, led him to become the most useful and celebrated anthologist of his era—althought by no means did everyone disagree with E. E. Cummings's famous four-liner: "Mr. U. will not be missed/Who as an anthologist/Sold the many on the few/Not excluding Mr. U."

In 1911 he published his first book of "serious verse" with a vanity press and his father's financing. It was titled *First Love*, and Untermeyer de-

scribed it as managing to "draw a long sigh through seventy-two lyrics plus a sweetly swooning envoy." As the serious poet he so wished to be, he decisively failed. But he was establishing himself as a leading editor. He was a contributing editor for the socialistic *Masses*, and—with Robert Frost

and Van Wyck Brooks—advised the short-lived magazine *The Seven Arts*, which, with James Oppenheim, he had founded. In the mid-1930s he was poetry editor of the *American Mercury*.

Meanwhile, Untermeyer's love of burlesque, parody, and lampoon had developed. Collections of his light verse include "*—and Other Poets*," *Including Horace*, and *Heavens*. Amy Lowell declared him "simply a genius when it comes to parody." Parody was undoubtedly his only real literary gift.

In *Bygones*, his autobiography of 1965, Untermeyer comments on his love of food, particularly smorgasbord, "that lavish range of appetizers—which, of course, is what an anthology is or should be. It was, therefore, only natural that one of the happiest episodes in my life was tasting, testing, and spreading out my first anthology, *Modern American Poetry*, in 1919." Although he considered it a "tentative, experimental, and uneven affair," the *Yale Review* viewed it in a different light: "This book is a delightful one to read; it has a distinctive individuality, and if Mr. Untermeyer, in avoiding the beaten track, does not always publish the finest work of his poets, he recovers many a line that has been undeservedly forgotten." *Modern American Poetry* went through many editions and was greatly enlarged along the way; it became standard reading in schools and colleges and, over the years, was joined on the shelf by many other Untermeyer anthologies. This volume, together with *Modern British Poetry*—for long the best anthology of English poetry in America—forms his chief contribution to letters. In their study, *A History of American Poetry: 1900–1940*, Horace Gregory and Marya Zaturenska made the point that Untermeyer was the "first to recognize the importance of the anthology in voicing a critical survey of his chosen field."

In addition to anthologies and poetry, Untermeyer published biographies, children's books, travel reminiscences, literary essays, translations, and one novel. He held many important literary positions. During World War II he served as senior editor of publications in the Office of War Information and later as editor for Armed Services Editions. After the war, he became cultural director at Decca Records, where he worked on the production of literary recordings until 1956. During the

1950s he was accused of "radicalism" (he was a moderate liberal) by the right wing, and was subsequently dismissed from his spot as a panelist on the popular television program "What's My Line?" From 1961 to 1963 Untermeyer was poetry consultant to the Library of Congress. He knew many of the major literary figures of his day, although he was close to few; his acquaintances included Amy Lowell, Edward Arlington Robinson, Ezra Pound, D. H. Lawrence, H. L. Mencken, Carl Sandburg, and Robert Frost.

The *New York Times* obituary, called him a "minor poet and a major anthologizer. . . . Louis Untermeyer was once described by a student as 'an entire semester of required reading.'" He wrote under various pseudonyms, including those of "Michael Lewis" and "Joseph Lauren." He was married, first to the poet Jean Starr Untermeyer, and then in 1947, to his collaborator in juvenile books, Boyna Ivens.

PRINCIPAL WORKS: *As editor*—Modern American Poetry, 1919, 8th rev. ed. 1969; Modern British Poetry, 1920, 6th rev. ed. 1969; Modern American and British Poetry, 1922, 4th rev. ed. 1962; American Poetry Since 1900, 1923; Yesterday and Today: A Comparative Anthology of Poetry, 1926; Conrad Aiken, 1927; Emily Dickinson, 1927; American Poetry from the Beginning to Whitman, 1931; Come In, and Other Poems by Robert Frost, 1943 (rev. ed. as The Road Not Taken: An Introduction to Robert Frost, 1951); The Poems of John Greenleaf Whittier, 1945; The Poems of Ralph Waldo Emerson, 1945; The Poems of William Cullen Bryant, 1947; The Best Humor Annual, 1949/50–. *Juvenile*—This Singing World: An Anthology of Modern Poetry for Young People, 1923; This Singing World for Younger Children: Modern Poems, 1926; All the French Fairy Tales by Charles Perrault, 1946; More French Fairy Tales by Charles Perrault, 1946; The Golden Treasury of Poetry, 1959; (with B. Untermeyer) Big and Little Creatures, 1961; (with B. Untermeyer) Beloved Tales, 1962; (with B. Untermeyer) Fun and Fancy, 1962; Legendary Animals, 1963; (with B. Untermeyer) Tall Tales, 1963; The Golden Book of Fun and Nonsense, 1970; Plants of the Bible, 1970; The Golden Book of Poems for the Very Young, 1971; The Golden Treasury of Animal Stories and Poems, 1971. *Poetry and parodies*—First Love: A Lyric Sequence, 1911; The Younger Quire, 1911; Challenge, 1914; "—and Other Poets," 1916; These Times, 1917; Including Horace, 1919; The New Adam, 1920; Heavens, 1922; Roast Leviathan, 1923; Collected Parodies, 1926; Burning Bush, 1928; Adirondack Cycle, 1929; Food and Drink, 1932; First Words Before Spring, 1933; Selected Poems and Parodies of Louis Untermeyer, 1935; Long Feud: Selected Poems, 1962; Labyrinth of Love, 1965. *Nonfiction*—The New Era in American Poetry, 1919; The Forms of Poetry: A Pocket Dictionary of Verse, 1926, 2nd rev. ed. 1967; Blue Rhine, Black Forest: A Hand- and Day-Book, 1930; The Donkey of God, 1932; The Last Pirate: Tales from the Gilbert and Sullivan Operas, 1934; Heinrich Heine: Paradox and Poet, 1937; Play in Poetry: The Henry Ward Beecher Lectures Delivered at Amherst College, 1938; A Century of Candymaking 1847–1947: The Story of the Origin and Growth of New England Confectionary Company Which Parallels That of the Candy Industry in America, 1947; Makers of the Modern World: The Lives of Ninety-Two Writers, Artists, Scientists, Statesmen, Inventors, Philosophers, Composers, and Other Creators Who Formed the Pattern of Our Century, 1955; Lives of the Poets: The Story of One Thousand Years of English and American Poetry, 1959; Robert Frost: A Backward Look, 1964; The Pursuit of Poetry: A Guide To Its Understanding and Appreciation with an Explanation of Its Forms and a Dictionary of Poetic Terms, 1969; James Branch Cabell: The Man and His Masks, 1970; 50 Modern American and British Poets 1920–1970, 1973. *Novel*—Moses, 1928. *As translator*—Poems of Heinrich Heine, 1917; Man and the Masses (Masse Mensch): A Play of the Social Revolution in Seven Scenes (by

E. Toller) 1924; The Fat of the Cat, and Other Stories (by G. Keller) 1925; Hymn of the Soviet Union (The New Russian National Anthem; by A. V. Aleksandrov) 1944; Cyrano de Bergerac (by E. Rostand) 1954. *Memoirs*—From Another World: The Autobiography of Louis Untermeyer, 1939; Bygones: The Recollections of Louis Untermeyer, 1965. *Limericks*—Lots of Limericks, 1961.

ABOUT: Current Biography 1967; Frost, R. Letters of Robert Frost to Louis Untermeyer, 1963; Gregory, H. and Zaturenska, M. A History of American Poetry: 1900–1940, 1946; Pound, E. EP to LU: Nine Letters Written to Louis Untermeyer, 1963; Something About the Author vol. 26 1982. *Periodicals*—Christian Century April 1, 1936; Christian Science Monitor June 28, 1962; New York Evening Post July 7, 1928; New York Times December 29, 1946; December 20, 1977; Springfield Republican October 6, 1935; Yale Review October 1920.

**UPFIELD, ARTHUR WILLIAM** (September 1, 1888–February 13, 1964), Australian crime and adventure novelist, was born in Gosport, near Portsmouth, England. His

parents, Annie (Barmore) and James Upfield, a draper, sent him to live for a time with his grandmother and her two sisters. These three ladies insisted the young boy adhere strictly to a Victorian regime, one of the conditions of which was that he should not speak until after his afternoon tea. On moving back to live with his parents he was imbued with a love of the past by an Uncle William, in whose company he visited all the historical sites in and around Portsmouth, including the home of Dickens and the bedroom where Nelson last slept on land. These rambles left a more vivid impression than the formal education he received at the Blenheim House, a small public school in Fareham, where he came top of his class in history and geography and bottom in every other subject.

On leaving school he was articled to a firm of surveyors, but at the end of his apprenticeship failed all three of his exams, largely because he spent his time working on three unpublished novels. At his father's instigation Upfield was put on a boat to Australia, to seek his fortune.

He worked for three years as a cowhand and boundary rider and during World War I served in Gallipoli, Egypt, and France with the Australian Imperial Forces. At the end of hostilities he returned to England to work for a time as a private secretary to an army officer. But he had been bitten by the bug of the outback and went back to Australia for good in 1921. Looking back, at the age of sixty, on the life that followed his second departure from England, Upfield wrote: "For the next sixteen years of my life was influenced by the sheep, cattle, riding camel, women, gold, opals, delirium tremens, and, fortunately, Mary.

"Mary was a genuine colonial pioneer, the wife of a man who owned 60,000 acres and 10,000 sheep, etc. She drilled it into me that I was going nowhere of importance very fast, that I was industriously building a mountain of regrets, and that

my salvation might lie in the exercise of the only talent she could observe.

"It was due to Mary that I began writing with ambition to make something of the rest of my life. I sent an article on trapping for fur to the *Wide World* magazine, and received a cheque and a commission to write a series of articles. I wrote a thriller the theme of which was a home for murderers run by a millionaire murderer. This was accepted by Hutchinson & Co. London, and the contract required three optionals. I raced to the great mining town of Broken Hill where I was drunk for a solid month and was rescued by Mary's husband and put to work by Mary on the optionals.

"There came a half-caste horse breaker who had gone to a university from high school, and who, as though inevitably, had been reclaimed by the bush. He liked James Joyce: I liked Edgar Wallace. He loved poetry: I loved brandy. His greatest attribute was patience, never more greatly exercised than with me. He taught me to read the Book of the Bush. He revealed the eternal war within himself, as example for me. He did not know, nor did I, the influence he was to exert on my career as a writer.

"Now for twenty-five years I have earned my living solely with the pen. Running books is infinitely better as a gamble than running horses. Writing is easier work than riding a horse all day in the sun, or gouging for opals, and to-day I am what I am through and because of the influence of women on my life. Which is why I never been able to portray an evil feminine character."

Upfield's novels were slow-moving and somewhat clumsily written, but they proved popular when eventually published in England and America. Their stumbling pace was a change from the usual style of hardboiled crime fiction; the vividly described Australian background was an appealing feature; and, in Napoleon Bonaparte (known in the books familiarly as 'Bony'), Upfield created a unique detective, loquacious with aboriginal "wisdom." Based on the half-caste horse-breaker Upfield had met in the bush, Bonaparte made his first appearance in *The Barrakee Mystery*, and featured in all but four of Upfield's novels.

*The Barrakee Mystery* was one title which did not appear in America until after Upfield's death. Its publication (with a new title, *The Lure of the Bush*) drew the following comment from Anthony Boucher (an admirer of the later Upfield books), writing in 1965 for the *New York Times Book Review*: "This book is, in many respects, a pretty bad book. It is phenomenally long and slow, the prose seem somewhat antiquated even for 1928; and the treatment of interracial relations would meet with no objections in South Africa or Mississippi. But the germ of Upfield's later magnificence is here: as the new title indicates, the uncivilized parts of Australia (in this case, the Western Division of new South Wales) already cast their spell, and Bony, on his first appearance, is already completely himself—and by his existence contradicting all that the novel asserts about racial mixtures."

Upfield married a nurse in 1915, and they had

one son. His last book, which had been left unfinished, was published in 1966, the manuscript having been completed and revised by J. L. Price and Dorothy Strange.

PRINCIPAL WORKS: The Barrakee Mystery, 1929 (published as The Lure of the Bush, 1965); The House of Cain, 1929; The Sands of Windee, 1931; A Royal Abduction, 1932; Mr Jelly's Business, 1937 (in U.S.: Murder Down Under); Winds of Evil, 1937; The Bone is Pointed, 1938; Bushranger of the Skies, 1940; Wings Above Diamantia, 1940 (in U.S.: Wings Above the Claypan); The Mystery of the Swordfish Reef, 1943; No Footprints in the Bush, 1944; Death of a Swagman, 1945; The Devil's Steps, 1946; An Author Bites the Dust, 1948; The Mountains Have a Secret, 1948; The Bachelors of Broken Hill, 1950; The Widows of Broome, 1950; The New Shoe, 1951; Venom House, 1952; Murder Must Wait, 1953; Death of a Lake, 1954; Sinister Stones, 1954; Cake in the Hatbox, 1955; The Man of Two Tribes, 1956; Bony Buys a Woman, 1957; The Bushman Who Came Back, 1957; Bony and the Black Virgin, 1959; Bony and the Mouse, 1959; Journey to the Hangman, 1959; Bony and the Kelley Gang, 1960; The Battling Prophet, 1961; Bony and the White Savage, 1961; Winds of Evil, 1961; The Will of the Tribe, 1962; Madman's Bend, 1963 (in U.S.: The Body at Madman's Bend); The Lake Frome Monster, 1966.

ABOUT: The autobiographical material quoted above was written for Twentieth Century Authors First Supplement, 1955. Browne, R. B. The Spirit of Australia, The Crime Fiction of Arthur W. Upfield, 1988; Contemporary Authors vol. 114 1985; Current Biography 1948; Hawke, J. Follow My Dust! A Biography of Authur Upfield, 1957; Reilly, J. M. (ed.) Twentieth Century Crime and Mystery Writers, 1985. Periodicals—New York Times February 14, 1964; New York Times Book Review June 20, 1965; Times (London) February 14, 1964.

## UPWARD, EDWARD (FALAISE) (September 9, 1903– ), English novelist, short story writer, and essayist, was born in Romford, Essex, the son of Harold Arthur Upward, a doctor, and Isa Jones. He was educated at Repton School (1917–1921), where he met Christopher Isherwood, later famous as a novelist.

Upward appears as "Chalmers" in Isherwood's autobiographical Lions and Shadows: "Chalmers was a pale, small, silent boy, a year older than myself, strikingly handsome, with dark hair and dark blue eyes. On the rare occasions when he got excited and began to talk, his face became flushed; he spoke so quickly and indistinctly . . . that it was very difficult to understand what he was saying. His nervous energy made him extremely good at football. . . . People in his house liked him but didn't altogether understand him. He was rather isolated there and had no intimate friends." Isherwood was strongly attracted to "Chalmers," who wrote poetry, and "determined to get to know him well. . . . He was a natural anarchist, a born romantic revolutionary. . . . Above all things, Chalmers loathed the school, which he invariably referred to as 'Hell.'"

In 1922 Upward went with a scholarship to Corpus Cristi College, Cambridge University, to read history. Isherwood joined him there the following year; their friendship continued. The developed a kind of private language in which they improvised a bizarre "Other Town," both menacing and satirical. It was a way of escaping and revenging themselves upon all that they found threatening or tedious in university life—its prescribed codes of conduct, the rich or aristocratic "Poshocracy," obsequious and sinister servants and shopkeepers: all part of a malevolent "Combine." This anti-Cambridge, with its Rats' Hostel and loathsome dons, drew upon children's stories, writers as diverse as Poe and Sir Thomas Browne, and images in the three Dürer engravings in Upward's room.

Later this imagined town was translated into an equally grotesque English village, Mortmere. In Mortmere, conventional moral and social values are turned upside down. The Rector, the Reverend Welken, is engaged in the breeding of angels. He has as his best friend a lying alcoholic, Ronald Gunball, who lives in a ghoulish world of delirium tremens. Parts of the Mortmere saga were written down as short stories and eventually published in 1994. Upward, who had continued to write poetry, and had won the Chancellor's Medal for Verse with a long poem called "Buddha," now found himself unable to "write a single line that isn't strange."

Graduating in 1924, Upward at first worked as a private tutor in various parts of England. He planned a novel and wrote a final long Mortmere story, "The Railway Accident." Hearn, the narrator, escapes a horrific train crash only to become involved in Rector Welken's ridiculous Treasure Hunt, which ends in a serious shooting accident. These and other fantastic events, many of them involving violence or humiliation, are described in a plain, dispassionate style, ironic in its effect, which, according to Isherwood, Upward modeled on E. M. Forster's:

> The express had taken the points. Booster-fitted, excessively rolling, the racing mogul engine rounded the curve, bounded into the rear of the carriage we had left. Coaches mounted like viciously copulating bulls, telescoped like ventilator hatches. Nostril gaps in a tunnel clogged with wreckage instantly flamed. A faint jet of blood sprayed from a vacant window. Frog-sprawling bodies fumed in blazing reeds. The architrave of the tunnel crested with daffodils fell compact as hinged scenery. Tall rag-feathered birds with corrugated red wattles limped from holes among the rocks.

What distinguished "The Railway Accident" from the earlier Mortmere stories is that all of its horrors and grotesqueries are shown to be imaginary, the products of Hearn's own fears and morbid fantasies—of a disorientation accelerating towards insanity. Hearn is not shocked by what he sees or thinks he sees because he is beyond normal moral responses. The story can be seen as a preliminary sketch for Upward's first novel, Journey to the Border, but with an important difference.

Isherwood was finished with Mortmere but, he wrote in Lions and Shadows, Upward "was to spend three years in desperate and bitter struggle to relate Mortmere to the real world of the jobs and lodging-houses; to find the formula which would transform our private fancies and amusing freaks and bogies into valid symbols of the ills of society and the toils and aspirations of our daily lives. For the formula did, after all exist. And Chalmers did at last find it . . . quite clearly set down, for everybody to read, in the pages of Lenin and of Marx."

In 1928 Upward began work as a schoolmaster.

He remained so all his life, until his retirement in 1962. In the early 1930s, as Isherwood implied, Upward also became a Marxist. This changed his approach to fiction in ways implicit in his essay "Sketch for a Marxist Interpretation of Literature," in *The Mind in Chains*, edited by Cecil Day Lewis. Here he denounced fantasy as "a retreat from the real world into the world of imagination," and declared: "no modern book can be true to life unless it recognizes, more or less clearly, both the decadence of present-day society and the inevitability of revolution." For better or (mostly, as every critic has agreed) worse, this recognition underlies everything Upward wrote thereafter, including his first novel, finally published in 1938.

*Journey to the Border* has as its unnamed hero a young man working as tutor to the son of a wealthy family. The Parkins are merely conventional members of their class but the tutor, as radically disorientated as Hearn in "The Railway Accident," perceives them as monsters, physically diseased and spiritually corrupt. He fears that they will infect and destroy him. In the course of a day that includes a visit to the races, the tutor tries in various ways to solve "the problem of how to live in this house." A deliberate attempt to idealize his situation fails, and a series of encounters at the racetrack sparks off fantasies or hallucinations in which he is repeatedly humiliated as a coward and a fake. These hallucinations become increasingly political in content, reflecting the imminent victory of fascism.

The tutor is in despair, paralyzed by fear and hopelessness, on the borderline between sanity and insanity. Utterly impotent, he can no longer silence the voice he has been suppressing all day. This alter ego tells him that neither his mind nor his heart can resolve his problems; they must be "dealt with in the external world" and through practical action—action in the cause of the workers. And then at last the tutor can see, with Marxist clarity, people and things as they really are. He goes off to join the movement.

Some contemporary reviewers saw the influence of Kafka in both the style and content of the novel. Others regarded its dark irrationality as surrealist, and it has been claimed as the most nearly successful surrealist fiction produced by an English writer. But the majority of critics shared the reservations expressed by Wilfred Sellers in his introduction to *The Railway Accident and Other Stories*. He points out that *Journey to the Border* meets Upward's own criteria for the modern novel: that it should recognize "both the decadence of present-day society and the inevitability of revolution." Sellers goes on: "Aesthetically, however, the novel founders before the end: after depicting brilliantly a mind journeying towards madness, it suffers from a jolting and bathetic descent from subtle fiction into *Tendenzpoesie*. The alter ego's lengthy Marxist discourse resembles too much an extended footnote that Upward affixed to his obliquely political psychological novel to make absolutely sure that the reader did not miss the point. . . . Political necessity drove Upward into blatancy and prevented him

from finding the new literary form that would permit a truly satisfactory union of his Mortmere gift and his Marxist faith."

Much the same is true of everything that Upward wrote thereafter. After *Journey to the Border*, he published nothing for twenty-five years. A new and very different novel, *In the Thirties*, appeared in 1962. Clearly autobiographical, it is narrated by Alan Sebrill, a young poet for whom the "poetic life" is only possible in a just and humane society. Seeking a system of belief—a "church"—that might bring such a society into being, he finds it in Marxism. Sebrill's story is continued in *The Rotten Elements and No Home But the Struggle*, and the trilogy was collected in one volume as *The Spiral Ascent*. Having joined the British Communist party in the 1930s, Sebrill leaves it in the 1940s (as Upward did), believing that it had betrayed Marxism-Leninism by aligning itself with the Labour party. Perhaps he and his wife will find a new "church" in the Campaign for Nuclear Disarmament.

For the most part, *The Spiral Ascent*, though of political and historical interest, is prosaic and humorless. Fantasy is replaced by documentary realism and Marxist dogma. It is as if Upward had deliberately sacrificed his imaginative gifts to a Marxist puritanism. Only the third volume, *No Home But the Struggle*, which flashes back to Sebrill's childhood and youth, has touches of brilliance and exuberance, especially in its account of his friendship with Richard Marple (Isherwood) and their creation of the "Other Town" and Mortmere.

Upward was married in 1936 to Hilda Maude Percival. He served on the editorial board of *The Ploughshare* in 1936–1939. Upward lived on the Isle of Wight, where he was a student of the island's botany and geology.

Although his output is relatively small and mostly flawed, Upward remains an almost legendary figure in the literary history of England in this century. His early writings influenced W. H. Auden in *The Orators*, and Auden often quoted Upward in lectures. Isherwood said in 1961 that "he's the final judge, as far as I'm concerned; I always send everything to him" (*London Magazine*). Stephen Spender, writing in the *Times Literary Supplement* in 1993, said: "Of the writers of the 1930s 'Oxbridge' generation . . . he is the one whose life has been most in keeping with his principles and ideals, the most deserving, as such, of being honoured. . . . The case history of his unremittingly autobiographical writings is one of the most interesting in this century's literature." For John Lehmann, Upward gave "evidence of an imaginative gift . . . the fate of which one will never cease to mourn, slowly killed in the Iron Maiden of Marxist dogma" (*The Whispering Gallery*).

PRINCIPAL WORKS: *Fiction*—Journey to the Border, 1938; In the Thirties, 1962; The Railway Accident and Other Stories (includes Journey to the Border) 1969; The Rotten Elements, 1969; The Spiral Ascent; A Trilogy of Novels (In the Thirties, The Rotten Elements, No Home But the Struggle), 1977; The Night Walk and Other Stories, 1987; An Unmentionable Man, 1994; (with C. Isherwood) The Mortmere Stories, 1994. *Other*—Buddha, 1924 (poetry); (with others) The Mind Chains:

Socialism and the Cultural Revolution (ed. C. Day Lewis) 1937.

ABOUT: Contemporary Authors vols. 1977–1980, 1979; Hyman, S. The Armed Vision, 1948; Hynes, S. The Auden Generation, 1976; Isherwood, C. Lions and Shadows, 1938; Lehmann, J. The Whispering Gallery, 1954; Seymour-Smith, M. (ed.) Guide to Modern World Literature, 1986; Twentieth-Century Fiction, 1983; Upward, E. The Railway Accident (intro. W. H. Sellers; foreword C. Isherwood) 1969. *Periodicals*—London Magazine June 1961, June 1969; New Statesman August 1, 1969; Spectator July 26, 1969; Times Literary Supplement July 31, 1969; September 10, 1993.

**USSHER, ARLAND PERCIVAL** (September 9, 1899–December 24, 1980) Irish philosopher and critic, wrote: "I grew up on my grandfather's estate of Cappagh in West Waterford, where—unlike W. B. Yeats' Sligo of a half a century earlier—the Gaelic was still a spoken tongue; and the old-style storyteller, with his courtly pre-Christian sagas, could still be met with. I quickly picked up the language, to the uncomprehending amazement of 'County neighbours;' though it was not, alas, till many years later—and when much had perished beyond recall—that I put together my two volumes of Gaelic colloquialisms. I may thus claim to have been present at the death of an old culture: an experience of some interest today, when we are likely to see the extinction of many another culture but, for the same reason, not to be taken too tragically.

"My parents were liberal intellectuals, who always felt themselves, unquestionably, to be a part of the British ruling class in an enlightened era; so  that an act of injustice anywhere in the world—a massacre of Armenians, a pogrom in Russia—affected them with a sense of almost personal responsibility. A cabinet minister should be spoken to about it, a committee formed, and so forth. I have inherited, I believe, their sense of responsibility without their optimism. I have always felt that, simply by being born one has 'joined the racket' and taken on oneself the burden of the world's guilt. And as I believe neither in Heaven nor in Utopia, I see redemption and finality only in a possible esthetic view of life and history. As a philosopher, I should define the human problem in these terms: to see the world in order to stop it, and to stop it by seeing it.

"In my English school at Abbotsholme, Derbyshire, I learnt a little; but the headmaster, Cecil Reddie, a student of German metaphysics and also of the mystics, gave a powerful prod to my intelligence. Upon leaving, I was sent to Trinity College, Dublin, and afterwards to St. John's, Cambridge; but about this time a friend happened to lend me an unpublished (now lost) work of D. H. Lawrence, and its impact on me was such as totally to preclude my working for a degree in either university. Since then I have lived on a small income in Waterford and Dublin—with intervals abroad—trying to

hammer out a new *esthetic* philosophy, which should carry on the work of our great Irish thinker, George Berkeley.

"I have published (privately) two volumes of philosophical essays, which are little known. My books on more popular topics, on the other hand, have had fair success; but they are not the works which contain my more personal—or if one wish eccentric—speculations.

"Philosophy today, it seems to me, stands where the art of painting did a century ago: it has become an academy-monopoly, and has not as yet got its Impressionist movement—though I see hope in Existentialism. Philosophers (for I scarcely count the Pragamists as such) have not yet learned that 'the Absolute is dead.' The classical philosophies, it might be suggested, set up a single Absolute Truth like a lamp-stand in a room, and tried to explain all things by its light; for us that lamp-stand is smashed, and we must rediscover the contents of our world gropingly like a man in a dark house striking one match after another. Thus the short essay and aphorism (like the repeated spurt of the match) seem to me a better method in philosophy than the old-fashioned 'system' and more appropriate to the 'faceted' modern way of seeing. My hope is for a revival of the essay, which at present suffers under the aspersion of bellelettrism and literary trifling."

———

Arland Ussher's *The Face and Mind of Ireland*, on the subject of his own people, remains his best known book. *Three Great Irishmen* on Shaw, Yeats, and Joyce, was regarded as his best and most stimulating work. Both of these books, and *The Magic People*, on the Jews (much admired at the time of its appearance by Robert Graves) remain in print. Ussher's work on such esoteric subjects as the Tarot, and his interpretations of the fairy tales of the Brothers Grimm, have fared less well.

Ussher knew Gaelic thoroughly, and his translation of the eighteenth-century poem *The Midnight Court*, by Brian Merriman, was praised when it was published in 1926 with a preface by W. B. Yeats.

James Stern, reviewing *The Face and Mind of Ireland* in the *New York Times*, put it alongside the recently published *The Irish* of Sean O' Faolain and called it: "profound, provocative, even wittier . . . admirable for its freshness, objectivity and wisdom."

*The Magic People*, a kind of well-informed ramble on the subject of the Jews and their history, led C. E. M. Joad to write in the *New Statesman* that it was "gay and vigorous," mixing "delight with enlightenment." However, the *Times Literary Supplement* reviewer put a finger on one of Ussher's weaknesses by suggesting that a "cautious reader will pause now and then and wonder whether it would not have been just as true to say the exact opposite." This was indeed one of the dangers of Ussher's aphoristic method.

The reviewer of *Three Great Irishmen* for the *Catholic World* insisted that the book was "brilliant" but "not definitive." Padraic Colum discussed *Three Great Irishmen* for the *Saturday Review*, commenting: "It is literary criticism on the level of philosophical discussion which, through the use of dialectic, becomes something of a symposium. . . ."

Patrick Kavanagh in the *Spectator* went so far as to state that Ussher although "very readable," adds "nothing to our understanding. . . . His philosophy is a coarse substitute for poetic perception." Readers may not have been encouraged by Ussher's stated preference, in this book, for the Rosie of Maugham's *Cakes and Ale* over the Molly Bloom of Joyce's *Ulysses*—a gaffe that in its time, earned him ridicule throughout literary Ireland.

*Journey Through Dread* got Ussher into waters for which he was not, at least by training, fit to navigate. About the philosophy of Kierkegaard, Heidegger, and Sartre, it led Alfred Duhrssen to declare, in *Ethics*, that Ussher was a "literary man" who played "fast and loose with philosophic concepts." Abraham Edel was more generous in the *Nation*: Ussher's reflections were "interesting" even if they were not "systematic." *Journey Through Dread*, lively and amusingly eccentric though it is, goes largely unheeded as a guide to its subjects.

Ussher was rightly respected for his unusual and interesting mind. Those who care to study this might read one or two of his less well-known books, the ones he himself most valued: *Alphabet of Aphorisms*, the autobiographical *Spanish Mercy*, and the journal he called *From a Dark Lantern*. He was a member of the Irish Academy of Letters, and was awarded its Gregory Medal.

PRINCIPAL WORKS: Postscript on Existentialism, 1946; The Twilight of the Ideas, 1948; The Face and Mind of Ireland, 1950; The Magic People, 1952; Three Great Irishmen: Shaw, Yeats, Joyce, 1953; Alphabet of Aphorisms, 1953, Journey Through Dread: Kierkegaard, Heidegger and Sartre, 1955; (with C. von Metzradt) Enter These Enchanted Woods: Grimm Fairy Tales, 1955; The Twenty-Two Keys of the Tarot, 1957; Spanish Mercy, 1960; Sages and Schoolmen, 1965; Eros and Psyche, 1977; From a Dark Lantern: A Journal, 1978; The Juggler, 1980. As translator—The Midnight Court and the Adventures of a Luckless Fellow (by B. Merriman), 1926.

ABOUT: The autobiographical material quoted above was written for Twentieth Century Authors First Supplement, 1955. *Periodicals*—Catholic World October 1953; Ethics April 1956; Nation March 1956; New Statesman December 23, 1950; New York Times July 30, 1950; Spectator August 15, 1952; Times Literary Supplement December 22, 1950.

---

**VACHELL, HORACE ANNESLEY** (October 30, 1861–January 10, 1955), English novelist and playwright, wrote: "I was born about the time when the Prince Consort died, born (I hope) of well-to-do and honest parents. My *cacoethes scribendi* may have come from my great grandfather, George, Lord Lyttleton, the historian, to whom Fielding dedicated *Tom Jones*. Now I live in the house where Fielding wrote all or part of his famous novel. I was self-educated at Harrow, where

I was very happy. I adventured in Sandhurst, our Royal Military College, where I became an under-officer. The late Field Marshal, Lord Allenby, was another under-officer at the time, and also the late Egerton Castle, famous swordsman and novelist. I had to wait eighteen months for my commission in the Rifle Brigade. Meanwhile I visited California. I resigned my commission in 1883, because I had fallen in love with the Golden State, which I regarded as a sort of Tom Tiddler's Ground. I married a Daughter of the Golden West, planted out orchards and a vineyard, and became a cowpuncher.

"I made many dollars and lost them during three years of drought. I returned to England in 1899, happily able to support myself with my pen. My wife had died in 1895, leaving me with two children. My son went to Harrow and Sandhurst, and was killed in 1915, during the Great War. My daughter, who married her cousin, another Vachell, lives with me.

"In my seventy-ninth year, I can look back upon an eventful and on the whole happy life. I like (in moderation) good food, good wine, and good company. The last is not the least of this Trinity in Unity. I have played many games with diminishing zest for them. I have hunted and shot and fished with ardor. All my experiences, particularly in California, were fish to my net as a dramatist and novelist.

"I cling to life, because I am so curious to see what the immediate future holds for the democracies. The golden age of leisure is at an end. Hitler has already broken the backbone of England, the squirearchy. I do not think that the fate of Humpty Dumpty awaits the British Empire. San Francisco survived the earthquake and fire. England, I confidently believe, will survive this war; and for the many it may be merrier than it was in the days of Queen Elizabeth."

---

Horace Annesley Vachell was born at Sydenham, in Essex, the eldest of the three sons of Richard Tanfield Vachell and Georgina Annesley. He told a good story, his characters are never unconvincing; yet he lacked psychological depth or linguistic genius. Of all his books, of which there were exactly one hundred, only *Bunch-Grass: A Chronicle of Life on a Cattle Ranch* (1912), a collection of stories based on memories of his experiences in California, remains in print.

Vachell is today mainly remembered, by historians of the novel, for two achievements: his story of Harrow School, *The Hill*, and his creation of an antique dealer called Quinney. His plays, although very popular in their time, are now forgotten.

He came to writing almost by accident, at the age of twenty-nine: more for amusement than for anything else, he tried his hand at some stories. One of these was accepted by the magazine the *Pall Mall Gazette*. By 1895—the year in which his American wife, the former Lydia Phillips, died in giving birth to their daughter—he had published his first novel, *The Romance of Judge Ketchum*, for which he drew on his own experiences, first of aristocratic life in England and then of ranching in California. Judge Ketchum, a rough-and-ready Yankee, turns out to be the heir to an English peerage. This did not sell well, and Vachell (with others) tried his hand at plays. These were not successful either; but then he wrote *John Charity* (1900), a romance set in the Alta California of the fourth decade of the nineteenth century. This competent historical novel helped to establish him. When he followed it with *Brothers: The True History of a Fight Against Odds* (1904), he found real success. This was a sentimental, well written tale of two brothers (educated at Harrow), who grow up different: one is bold, successful and empty, the other is a good and gifted man who sacrifices all for his brother. Archibald the bold one gets the girl, but after their marriage she discovers that she really loves his stammering brother.

Vachell turned to the theater, gaining success with such plays as *Jelf's*, produced in London in 1912. But the most successful of all his plays came from his best novel: *Quinney's*, a light-hearted account of how an antique dealer's wife and daughter save him from the temptation of faking. *Quinney's* owed much to Arnold Bennett's innovative *The Card*. The *New York Times* reviewer wrote: "Vachell finds this dealer in antiques and his career both amusing and appealing, and the reader is entirely in accord with him." Vachell wrote more books about Quinney, delighting thousands of readers.

*Fellow-Travellers*, *Distant Fields*, and *Methuselah's Diary* are pleasantly anecdotal and racy autobiographies. Vachell wrote "honestly and carefully, and his work illumines, with shrewdness and good humour, the beliefs, customs, and circumstances of English upper-middle-class life over a long period," according to L.A.G. Strong, writing in the *Dictionary of National Biography*.

For many years Vachell lived in Bath, in a house with a beautiful garden famous among his friends. Later he moved to a smaller house in Sherborne, Dorset.

PRINCIPAL WORKS: *Novels*—The Romance of Judge Ketchum, 1894; The Model of Christian Gray, 1895; The Quicksands of Pactolus, 1896; A Drama in Sunshine, 1898; The Procession of Life, 1899; John Charity, 1900; The Shadow Third, 1902; The Pinch of Prosperity, 1903; Brothers, 1904; The Hill, 1905; The Face of Clay, 1906; Her Son, 1907; The Waters of Jordan, 1908; An Impending Sword, 1909; The Paladin, 1909; The Other Side, 1910; John Verney, 1911; Blinds Down, 1912; Quinney's, 1914; Spragge's Canyob, 1914; The Triumph of Tim, 1916; Fishpingle, 1917; The Soul of Susan Yellam, 1918; The Fourth Dimension, 1920; Whitewash, 1920; Blinkers, 1921; Change Partners, 1922; Quinney's Adventures, 1924; Watlings for Worth, 1925; A Woman in Exile, 1926; Miss Torrobin's Experiment, 1927; The Actor, 1928; Virgin, 1929; Out of Great Tribulation, 1930; Into the Land of Nod, 1931; The Fifth Commandment, 1932; Vicar's Walk, 1933; The Old Guard Surrenders, 1934; When Sorrows Come, 1935; Moonhills, 1935; The Golden House, 1937; Lord Samarkand, 1938; Phoebe's Guest House, 1939; Great Chameleon, 1940; The Black Squire, 1941; Gift from God, 1942; The Wheel Stood Still, 1943; Hilary Trent, 1944; Averil, 1944; Farewell Yesterday, 1945; Now Came Still Evening On, 1946; Rebels, 1946; Eve's Apples, 1946; Quiet Corner, 1947; Twilight Grey, 1949;

Children of the Soil, 1948; In Sober Livery, 1949; Quest, 1954. *Mysteries*—The Yard, 1923; (with A. Marshall) Mr. Allen, 1926; The Disappearance of Martha Penny, 1934. *Short stories*—Bunch Grass, 1912; Loot from the Temple, 1913; Some Happenings, 1918; Leaves from Arcady, 1924; Dew of the Sea, 1927; The Enchanted Garden, 1929; At the Sign of the Grid, 1931; Experiences of a Bond Street Jeweller, 1932; Joe Quinney's Jodie, 1936; Quinney's for Quality, 1938. *Drama*—Her Son, 1907; Jelf's 1912; Who Is He?, 1915; Searchlights, 1915; Quinney's, 1915; The Case of Lady Camber, 1915; Fishpingle, 1916; Humpty Dumpty, 1917; (with T. Cobb) Mrs. Pomeroy's Reputation, 1918; The House of Peril, 1919; (with H. Simpson) Plus Fours, 1923. *Nonfiction*—Life and Sport on the Pacific Slope, 1900; Pepper and Salt, 1900; The Best of England, 1930; Arising Out of That, 1935; My Vagabondage, 1936; Where Fancy Beckons, 1938; Little Tyrannies, 1940. *Autobiography and reminiscence*—Fellow-Travellers, 1923; Distant Fields, 1937; Methuselah's Diary, 1950; More From Methuselah, 1951.

ABOUT: The autobiographical material quoted above was written for Twentieth Century Authors, 1942. Dictionary of National Biography, 1951–1960, 1971; Vachell, H. A. Fellow-Travellers, 1923; Vachell, H. A. Distant Fields, 1937; Vachell, H. A. Methuselah's Diary, 1950; Vachell, H. A. More From Methuselah. *Periodicals*—Illustrated London News January 15, 1955; New York Times November 1, 1914; Times (London) January 11, 1955.

**VALÉRY, (AMBROISE) PAUL (TOUSSAINT JULES)** (October 30, 1871–August 20, 1945), French poet, dramatist, and essayist, was born in Cette (now Sette), the son of a Corsican customs officer, Barthelmy Valéry (his seafaring family's name had originally been Valerj), and Fanny Grassi, an Italian descended from Venetian nobility.

Valéry was educated in Sette and then, when his family moved there (1884), at the lycée at Montpellier, whose strictness he disliked. Already at the age of ten he had decided to "make an island of his mind": a "secret garden," as he later put it, where he could cultivate his own images. He wanted to join the navy, but, ironically (in view of his later preoccupations), was too bad at mathematics even to think of it.

He read law at the University of Montpellier, not because he was interested in it, but because that was what his elder brother, Jules, had done. He was already deeply absorbed in his studies of painting, architecture, mathematics, and philosophy, though he said that he did not take poetry seriously before he was twenty. He suddenly discovered Wagner, Edgar Allen Poe (a giant in France such as he never quite was elsewhere), Parnassian poets such as Herodia—and then Rimbaud, the symbolists, Huysmans's "decadent" novel *A Rebours* (a bible to him until 1892)—and, above all, the poetry of Mallarmé, who was to become his first master. He also started to write poetry, some of which he published in Montpellier magazines.

He met the writer Pierre Louys while he was performing his compulsory military service, in May 1890, and, through him André Gide, who was to become his lifelong friend, with whom he would have an extensive correspondence—edited by Robert Mallet in 1955. When Gide looked over Valéry's letters to him of 1890 and 1891 (in 1950) he exclaimed to Mallet: "What style! What precociousness! What intelligence!" As Mallet wrote, it was through the rather precious and unreliable dreamer, Louys, that Gide (and thus many others) was introduced to the "grandeur of an adolescent mind."

When Valéry went to Paris for a short visit in 1891 Louys introduced him to Mallarmé; the next year he settled in Paris, and became a regular, and soon well-known, attendant at Mallarmé's "Tuesday evenings." Much happened to him in this year of 1892. His poetry, notably the famous "Narcisse parle," (Naricissus speaks), was published in an influential anthology, Poètes d'aujourd'hui. This poem, made him famous beyond his immediate literary circle. The title "Narcisse parle" was in a sense appropriate, for he would become known as a "cerebral narcissist." His first small collection, Premiers Poèmes was published. But twenty-six years was to elapse before the next volume appeared—and a period of almost twenty years of literary silence.

It was also in 1891 that Valéry experienced a passionate but "ludicrous" attraction for a young Spanish girl; indeed, as Mallet wrote, in that year "the chips were very nearly down" for him: he decided, in short, to "refuse" an erotic and "decadent" life. Essentially, he announced a withdrawal from the powerfully sensual part of his nature, which he feared.

Valery experienced the famous "night of Genoa," when, during an autumn thunderstorm of 1892, he "felt himself enlightened by the convictions he had held up to that point but never put into practice," according to Mallet. This Nuit de Genes has considerable symbolic importance. It caused Valery to renounce a literary career: the very act of writing, he decided, was one of vanity; the creative act was an empty one. He kept poetic silence, and instead published two prose works, Introduction de la méthode de Léonard da Vinci (1894) and the story La Soirée avec Monsieur Teste (1896), the first of the Teste cycle, in which Monsieur Teste represents consciousness in a pure form. In 1894 he began his 250 Cahiers (notebooks), which he would get up at five o'clock in the morning to work at; and which became his most "public" utterances. They were eventually published in facsmile, almost as if they were as important as his poetry.

Valéry was dedicated—impossibly, as it turned out to purity of thought. "Writing," he declared in the preface to Monsieur Teste, "always exacts a certain amount of intellectual sacrifice." This strategic position led him into many misjudgments, and deliberately incomplete readings of other writers. It has also been recognised that Valéry was "backing into the limelight." Everyone begged him to divulge his "secrets." And in the end he did. Yet Valéry tried to strike to the heart of a paradox that has troubled all major modernist writers: as long as a writer bears an audience in mind, he wrote in the Cahiers, "there are always reserves, a concealed in-

tention in which a whole stock of charlatanism exists . . . every literary product is an impure product." He said in Ebauche d'un serpent: " . . . l'univers n'est qu'un défaut / Dans la pureté du Non-Etre!" (the universe is only a defect in the purity of non-being).

Valéry seemed (to many of his readers) politically naive, to say the least. He was a quiet but persistent anti-Dreyfusard. He was friend to and an admirer of Pétain, and he was fascinated by power and by dictators (as his poem "Caesar" demonstrates). However, he withheld sympathy from the Nazis (because they wished to "destroy thought"), and was a supporter of De Gaulle.

Valéry obtained employment (1897) at the Ministry of War (on the suggestion of Huysmans). In 1900 he married the former Jeannie Gobillard (niece to the painter Berthe Morisot, and close friend to Mallarmé's daughter), with whom he had three children. In that year Valéry also obtained the semi-sinecure which he retained until 1922: as private secretary to Edouard Lebey, a senior executive of the news agency Havas.

In both the Da Vinci study and the Teste series Valéry dealt with the problems presented by his attempts to attain "pure thought." In the Da Vinci piece he wrestled with a means of (almost) sacralizing the intellect; Teste, on the other hand, is a fictional genius, a "monster of the intellect," a witness, an "abstraction that could not exist in the concrete," horribly austere and self-absorbed, offering no concessions whatever to convention, and saying neither good-morning nor good evening. The figure of Teste is conceived humorously. Teste "is himself, seeing himself." This is echoed later in a phrase in the poem La Jeune Parque: "Je me voyais me voir" ("I saw myself seeing myself").

In 1912 Gide, on behalf of the publisher Gallimard, tempted Valéry out of his poetic silence by requesting him to collect and revise all his early poems. The result, eight years later, was Album de vers anciens (Album of old poems). But the very act of revision forced Valéry into a new outburst of poetry. In 1917 he published La Jeune Parque (The young fate) this immediately elevated him into one of France's supreme poets. In it Valéry, for the most part, transcended the painful confusions of his thinking. As Martin Seymour-Smith noted, with La Jeune Parque the poet regained his powers and abandoned "the shadowless death of thought for the disturbing uncertainties of life":

Something of disquiet is a holy gift:
Hope, which in your eyes lights up dark alleyways,
Does not arise from a more settled earth;
All your splendours spring from mysteries.

Valéry renounces death and affirms life, and pehaps also obliquely criticizes himself for his scornful austerity:

The most profound, not self-understood,
From certain night derive their riches,
And the pure objects of their noble love.

Valéry most famous poem, published in Charmes Le Cimetière marin (The Graveyard Is by the Sea). Le Cimetière marin perfectly illustrates Valéry's dictum that sound and sense cannot be disassociated in a successful poem. The poet meditates as he looks at the cemetery by the sea at Sette where his parents—and himself ultimately—are buried. He initially feels that he loves and envies the stillness of death, in which the earth warms up the dead, so that they lie easy; but he comes, after all, to affirm life, in the famous lines: "Le vent se lève! . . . Il faut tenter de vivre!" ("The wind rises! . . . We must try to live!").

After the success of *Charmes* Valéry became France's official man of letters. He was made Grand Officier of the Légion d'Honneur (1931), and on Anatole France's death was admitted to the Academy. After that happened (1925), he broke precedent (in 1927) by boldly attacking Anatole France.

An exchange which Gide recorded in his diary for 1938 reveals the artificiality and provocativeness of Valéry's stance. The two were about to give a broadcast when Valéry leaned over to Gide and whispered: "Do you know anything more boring than the *Iliad*?" Gide, who of course thought that the *Iliad* was perpetually enthralling, found it "more friendly" not to "protest," and forced Valéry to "agree" by replying: "Yes, the *Chanson de Roland*."

When Valéry died he was given a state funeral. The street in which he had lived was named after him. He had, from 1938, been Professor of Poetry at the Collège de France. One of the best studies of this writer whose work is still being quarried for what he called, in *Le Cimetière marin*, the "depths beyond" his reach, remains A. Berne-Joffroi's *Paul Valéry* (1960). His bibliography is already vast: that given below is a selection from the best translations and the best introductions to him.

PRINCIPAL WORKS IN ENGLSIH TRANSLATION: *Collections*—The Collected Works of Paul Valéry, 15 vols., 1956–1975: (tr. J. Matthews, D. Paul, R. Fitzgerald, W. M. Stewart, O. Nadal, D. Folliot, M. Cowley, J. R. Lawler, H. Corke, R. Shattuck, F. Brown, R. Manheim, and M. Matthews). *Selections*—Lawler, J. (ed) Selected Writings. 1950, Paul Valéry: An Anthology, 1977. *Poetry*—Charms (tr. J. L. Brown) 1983; The Graveyard by the Sea (tr. C. Day-Lewis) 1946, tr. by G. D. Martin under the same title, 1976; Sketch of a Serpent and Other Poems (tr. L. Hoggard) 1986. *Prose*—Epaulinos (tr. W. M. Stewart) 1932, other trs. by D. Bussy, as Dance and the Soul, 1951, and by V. J. Daniel, 1967. *Correspondence*—Mallet, R. (tr. and abridged by J. Guicharnaud) Self-Portraits: The Gide/Valéry Letters 1890–1942, 1966.

ABOUT: Berne-Joffroi, Paul Valéry, 1960 (in French), 1960; Burnshaw, S. (ed.) The Poem Itself, 1960; Crow, C. M. Paul Valéry: Consciousness of Nature, 1972, Paul Valéry and the Poetry of Voice, 1982; Derrida, J. (tr. A. Bass) The Margins of Philosophy, 1982; Grigson, G. (ed.) Concise Encyclopedia of Modern World Literature, 1963; Harari, J. V. (ed.) Textual Strategies, 1979; Hartman, G. The Unmediated Vision: An Interpretation of Wordsworth, Hopkins, Rilke and Valéry, 1954; Ince, W. N. The Poetic Theory of Valéry, 1961; Lawler, J. The Poet as Analyst: Essays on Paul Valéry, 1974; Mackay, A. The Universal Self: A Study of Paul Valéry, 1961; Mallet, R. (ed.) Self-Portraits (above); Maurois, A. From Proust to Camus, 1966; Nash, S. Paul Valéry's Album de vers anciens: A Past Transfigured, 1983; Sewell, E. Paul Valéry, 1961; Seymour-Smith, Macmillan Guide to Modern World Literature, 1986; Suckling, N. Paul Valéry and the Civilized Mind, 1954; Thompson, A. W. Paul Valéry, 1965; Vines, L. Valéry and Poe: A Literary Legacy, 1992; Whiting, C. G. Paul Valéry, 1978.

*Periodicals*—French Review February 1946; New York Times July 21, 1945; Times (London) July 21, 1945.

## "VALLE-INCLÁN, RAMÓN (MARÍA DEL)" (pseudonym of RAMÓN DEL VALLE Y PETA) (October 28, 1886–January 3, 1936), Span-

ish novelist, dramatist, and poet, was born in Villanueva de Arosa, in the Galician province of Pontevedra, into an aristocratic but impoverished family. He was one of the leading figures in the Generation of 1898, the movement associated with Miguel de Unamuno, Pio Baroja, and Azorín, in which the intellectual leaders of Spain determined both to come to terms with their country true identity and its place in Europe.

Valle-Inclán, always both extravagant and a rebel, in the end rebelled against the Generation of '98, too. A bohemian figure in the literary circles Madrid, he created a scandal in 1907 by marrying an actress, raising a large family with her, and then, later, leaving her and taking the children. He lost an arm in a cafe brawl (1889) with a critic, Manuel Bueno (who later became a fascist). With his one arm, long hair, straggling beard and pebble-thick glasses, he became the best-known of all the figures on the Spanish literary scene.

Valle-Inclán began as a conservative, embracing the *modernismo* of Rubén Darío. He ended up on the non-communist left. But sometimes he hardly believed in the efficacy of the experiments he was carrying out. José Ortega y Gasset admired him, but accused him of an unnecessary precocity and falsity in his style; instead of being at the "height" of his own times, Ortega thought, he was a "Renaissance man" who indulged himself in needless mannerisms. Much of Valle-Inclán's work is based in the folk traditions of his native Galicia, of which he possessed a unique understanding. His best-known collection of poems is *La Pipa de Kif* (1919, The hashish pipe), but the collection is undermined by its labored medievalism. The poems of *El pasajero* (1920, The wanderer) draw on Pythagorean and gnostic themes, but again, they are somewhat mannered.

His fiction developed over time. *Sonatas* (1902, translated as *The Pleasant Memoirs of the Marquis of Brandon*), the adventures of himself in a grotesque fictional guise, partook too much of French "satanism" and of D'Annunzio at his most feverish. This does, however, anticipate the more mature *Tirano Banderas* of 1926 (*The Tyrant Banderas*). The sonatas (there is one for each season of the year) have in them almost all of the ingredients of a masterpiece: irony, subtlety, and ingenuity. In all his earlier stories Valle-Inclán had been working slowly up to this: in *Femeninas* (1895), his first book, in *Jardín umbrío* (1903, Shaded garden) and the "shocking" *Flor de santidad* (1904, Flower of sanctity), in which a country girl seduced by a wanderer pathetically believes that she has been made pregnant by Jesus Christ.

In about 1905 Valle-Inclán began to experiment with the dramatic form. His dramatic experiments were intimately connected with his fictional ones; therefore the term "dialogued novels" is probably appropriate for his plays. However, whether they are plays or novels, Valle-Inclán's twenty-six "plays" anticipate the Theater of the Absurd, more remarkably than any other writer's of that time. He saw the theater as a spectacle, and as a symbol for the entire process of art. Like Pirandello, but earlier, he tried the resources of the stage to their uttermost limit. His stage directions are complex and novelistic. It was in the decade before the outbreak of World War I that he developed his notions, first, of "savage comedy" (*comedia barbara*) and then of the all-important *esperpento*. *Esperpento* is a "deformation of style" intended, wrote Valle-Inclán, to "transform, with the mathematics of a concave mirror, the classic norms." The word in Spanish means "funhouse distorting mirror."

*Divinas palabras* (1920, *Divine Words*) is a typical play, first written in 1913, which was characterized by its author as both a barbaric comedy and an *esperpento*. This "tragi-comedy of village life" is set in Valle-Inclán's native Galicia; its preposterously savage plot is enacted in an idyllic, pastoral setting. Although Valle-Inclán was imprisoned under the dictatorship of Primo de Rivera, the play was able to be produced in 1933, just a few years before Spain was plunged into the barbaric darkness of Franco; the writer was fully aware of the forces that threatened Spain. Other notable plays by Valle-Inclán include *Luces de Bohemia* (1920, *Bohemian Lights*) and such "melodramas for marionettes" as *La rosa de papel* (1924, The paper rose).

Among his novels, Valle-Inclán's masterpiece is *The Tyrant Banderos* is set in "Tierra Caliente." A satire of an imaginary Latin American dictatorship tells of the tyrant Banderos and of his enemy Colonel Gandarita. The novel influenced a whole flood of South-American "dictator novels." *The Tyrant Banderos* may be termed an *esperpento* of a novel.

At first Valle-Inclán was considered a nonrealist; but interest in the grotesque means by which he pursued the real has increased since his death, and he is now regarded as a classic avant-gardist whose work has yet to be fully appreciated outside Spain and Latin America. His plays continue to be produced by avant-garde groups. There have been two editions of his complete works in Spanish.

PRINCIPAL WORKS IN ENGLISH TRANSLATION: *Fiction*—The Pleasant Memories of the Marquis de Bradomin (tr. M. H. Broun and T. Walsh), 1924; The Tyrant Banderos: A Novel of Warm Lands (tr. M. Pavitt), 1929. *Drama*—The Dragon's Head (tr. M. H. Broun), 1919; Divine Words (tr. A. Zahareas in Modern Spanish Theater, 1968; The Lights of Bohemia (tr. A. Zahareas and G. Gillespie), 1969; Three Plays (tr. R. Lima) 1993. *Other*—Autobiography, Aesthetics and Aphorisms (tr. R. Lima), 1966.

ABOUT: Greenfield, S. M. Valle-Inclán, 1972 (in Spanish); Gullon, R. Valle-Inclán Centennial Studies, 1968; Lyon, J. The Theater of Valle-Inclan, 1984; Seymour-Smith, M. Guide to Modern World Literature, 1986; Zahareas, A. (ed.) Ramón del Valle-Inclán: An Appraisal of His Life and Works, 1968.

**VALLENTIN, ANTONINA** (1893–1957), Polish-born biographer and political journalist, was born into a wealthy upper-class family, and privately educated. Fluent in English, German, French, and Italian, she was a cosmopolitan intellectual. During the Weimar Republic, she worked as a political journalist in Berlin, where her brilliant salon attracted many of the literary and political leaders of the day. Among her close  friends was the German statesman Gustav Stresemann, whom she served as unofficial press secretary. With her marriage to Julien Luchaire, she moved to Paris. Her husband, an official of the French Ministry of Education, was well known as the author of books on Italian intellectual history, and as a dramatist and novelist. He wrote both a biography of Boccaccio and a play about his life.

In Paris Antonina Vallentin continued her work as a correspondent for various major newspapers. Her articles admired for the verve of her style, the breadth of her knowledge, and the thoroughness of her research. Her interests ranged from the position of women in the labor market to the dangers of totalitarianism in Germany and Italy. She also embarked on a new career as a biographer. Redhaired, energetic, and enthusiastic, she managed, according to Benjamin Huebsch in *Publishers Weekly* to "roam up and down Europe, working in libraries and museums," while at the same time being "an efficient mother, housekeeper, and coworker of her husband."

Vallentin's first biography was of her friend Gustav Stresemann, once described as "the greatest German statesman since Bismarck." Incorporating a summary history of German politics since the end of World War I, it concentrated on the last six years of Stresemann's life (1923–1929) when, as Foreign Minister, and in spite of grave illness, he worked heroically in the cause of European peace. Lewis Gannett wrote in *New York Herald Tribune Books* that Vallentin "writes of Stresemann with intimacy and devotion—sometimes with a loyalty of defense that is not wholly convincing, but always with a color and understanding that gives one faith that this is the authentic Stresemann as his closest friends knew him."

The book appeared with a foreword by Albert Einstein, whose family Vallentin knew well for many years, and who was the subject of a later loving tribute. Apart from these two relatively personal *hommages*, Vallentin's biographies were sympathetic but more objective studies of crucial figures in European history—statesmen like Mirabeau, writes as different as Heinrich Heine and H. G. Wells, artists from da Vinci to Picasso.

Writing usually in French, sometimes in German, Vallentin was a "psychological" biographer in the tradition associated with Stefan Zweig. A typical response to her work was Malcolm Cowley's review in the *New Republic* of her biography of Leonardo da Vinci, a Book of the Month Club choice. Cowley called it "simply the best we have in English and the clearest approach to his work. She has not discovered many new sources nor examined many manuscripts, apparently, except those of Leonardo himself, but these she has studied with great care. Merely by setting facts in their proper context, she throws new light on what he was trying to do." Vallentin's ability to organize her material for maximum clarity was the aspect of her biographies most often commended by reviewers; the commonest criticism was that this clarity was sometimes overwhelmed by a plethora of detail.

A collection of documents and statements on German atrocities in Vallentin's native Poland was published in France in 1940, but not translated. The author died in Paris in 1957.

PRINCIPAL WORKS IN ENGLISH TRANSLATION: Stresemann (tr. E. Sutton) 1931 (published as Frustration; or, Stresemann's Race with Death, 1935); Poet in Exile: The Life of Heinrich Heine (tr. H. Brown) 1934 (published as Heine: Poet in Exile, 1956); Leonardo da Vinci: The Tragic Pursuit of Perfection (tr. E. W. Dickes) 1938; Mirabeau: Voice of the Revolution, 1948; This I Saw: The Life and Times of Goya (tr. K. Woods) 1949; H. G. Wells: Prophet of Our Day (tr. D. Woodward) 1950; The Drama of Albert Einstein (tr. M. Budberg) 1954 (in U.K.: tr. as Einstein, a Biography); El Greco (tr. A. Revai and R. Chancellor) 1954; Picasso (ed. consultant K. Woods) 1963.

ABOUT: *Periodicals*—Bookman August 1931; New Republic January 4, 1939; New York Herald Tribune Books May 31, 1931; Publishers Weekly September 30, 1957; Wilson Library Bulletin December 1957.

**VALTIN, JAN** (December 17, 1905–January 1, 1951), German political writer who became a U.S. citizen in 1947, was born Richard Julius Herman

Krebs. He wrote: "I was born in the German Rhineland. Since my father was a German sea captain, the family traveled with the skipper to China, Singapore, South Seas, Dutch East Indies. At the outbreak of World War I the family was in Genoa, and when Italy declared war on Germany, we fled across Switzerland into Germany. After a childhood absence of ten years, I entered the 'Fatherland' at the age of eleven.

"I left home at the age of fifteen, immediately after the 'Peace of Versailles,' to go to sea and sailed four years on windjammers and tramp steamers. I returned again to Germany in 1923, when the country was in the throes of a wild and uncontrolled inflation. In 1923, I joined the German Communists and fought on the barricades of the Hamburg insurrection during the autumn of the year. The revolutionists were defeated and I fled the 'Fatherland' for the U.S.

"I served under the American flag in 1924 and 1925 and went to Hawaii and a number of Latin American countries. I returned to Germany, where things had quieted down, and then visited Russia. After the Russian visit I traveled to the Far East as a courier of the Communist International. In Shanghai (1926) I embarked for the United States, as a stowaway, and arrived in San Francisco. Three months later I was in San Quentin Prison, Calif., convicted for assault. This period of life formed the subject matter of my book, *Bend in the River*.

"I was released in 1929 and returned to Germany. There Hitler and his Nazis were struggling bloodily toward power. I joined the most militant and violent anti-Hitler group, the Communist Party of Germany (1930). My travels as a revolutionist took me to France, Scandinavia, and other countries, during 1931 and 1932. I was in Germany when Hitler came to power. When the Reichstag burned and the German horror began, I went underground. In November 1933 I was arrested by the Gestapo for treason against the Hitler regime. I was sentenced to thirteen years' imprisonment in 1934. After four years spent in various concentration camps, I escaped. My wife, also imprisoned as an anti-Nazi, died. I fled to Copenhagen, where Russian secret service agents insisted that I should work for them. I refused. I had enough of politics; I thought it was time to look for a home. As a result, Nazi police hunted me as a Communist, and Russian police hunted me as a Nazi.

"In March 1938, I came to America again as a sailor aboard a British ship. I jumped ship, ill and penniless, in Norfolk, Virginia, and made my way to Manhattan. The next two years I worked at manual labor in New York. Again I began to write—a personal account of life under totalitarian rule. In 1940 I moved into a tent, and then into a garage in a New England wood, and there I finished my first book. I called it *Out of the Night*.

"Since 1941 it has sold a million copies in a dozen languages. It was published in Yiddish and it was published in China. It was fought over, acclaimed, attacked, and it was outlawed in Germany, Italy and Russia. Goebbels broadcast against it over Radio Berlin, and Moscow campaigned against it viciously. American Communists launched a campaign to have me deported from the U.S. to Germany and death. I lectured all over the U.S. during 1942, sold war bonds, and volunteered for the Army at the ripe old age of thirty-eight. In November 1942, through a Communist trick, I was arrested and placed on Ellis Island among captured Nazis and Japanese—and it took me six months to bring the matter to the attention of the Attorney General of the U.S., who then ordered my release.

"From 1943 to 1945 I served in the U.S. Army. I fought in New Guinea and in the Philippines with the 24th Infantry Division (Leyte, Mindanao, Corregidor, etc.) and graduated from rifleman to combat reporter and several medals, among them the Bronze Star for heroism in action. While overseas, I wrote the book *Children of Yesterday*, a day-by-day account of tropical warfare. In 1946, I wrote my first novel, entitled *Castle in the Sand*.

"Other activities since the war include: winning my U.S. citizenship in 1947 after an incessant nine-year struggle, on the basis of my war record. Conducted a search all over defeated Germany for my lost son (lost in 1937, when I escaped from Germany, at which time Hitler's police seized the child, then four, as a hostage)—and found him, skinny, ragged, but in good spirits; I brought him to the U.S. for a very personal job of 're-education.'"

*Out of the Night* (1940) exposed Valtin's activities as an agent for both the Communists and the Nazis. It was one of the most highly publicized books of the early 1940s, and its author was the first of a string of former Communists who profited from books that told of their experiences and disillusionment. But many critics questioned whether the "strong raw meat," as W. H. Chamberlin called it in the *Atlantic*, of his long and startling story was authentic.

Few events in the book could be verified, and Communists called it a complete fraud; but as additional information became known about Communist and Nazi methods, many felt that the harrowing acts Valtin described were possible, even if all of them did not happen to just one man. Valtin admitted he included others' experiences in order to paint a more complete picture of totalitarianism.

B. D. Wolfe, believing in the book's truthfulness, wrote in the *New Republic* that he found it "as vast in background, as moving, illuminating and humanly significant as a great novel. *Time* wrote: "the ultimate horror in reading it is less its portrait of violence, of crimes, of vague or too real terrors, than the sense it gives of the soft, slow collapse of civilized men into total depravity."

None of Valtin's subsequent works matched the power or popularity of *Out of the Night*, although Valtin returned to its themes, depicting the same kind of misery and struggle in later semi-autobiographical novels, and showed similar reporting skill in a volume of non-fiction about war in the Pacific.

With the success of *Out of the Night*, Valtin a year later published *Bend in the River and Other Stories* (1942), which he wrote while serving time in San Quentin in the late 1920s and originally published in the prison's bulletin. Valtin had been sentenced there for assaulting a Los Angeles businessman. After he became known as the author of *Out of the Night*, California governor Olson granted him a full pardon, at the urging of William Allen White and others.

PRINCIPAL WORKS: Out of the Night, 1941; Bend in the River, and Other Stories, 1942; Children of Yesterday, 1946; Castle in the Sand, 1947; Wintertime, 1950.

ABOUT: Current Biography 1941; Gitlow, B. Whole of Their Lives; Valtin, J. Out of the Night; Van Gelder, R. Writers and Writing. *Periodicals*—Atlantic February 1941; Boston Globe May 6, 1942; New York Herald Tribune May 14, 1950; New Republic January 27, 1941; September 9, 1946; New York Times May 10, 1942, November 9, 1947; January 3, 1951; Newsweek January 15, 1951; New Yorker November 29, 1947; Saturday Evening Post February 3, 1951; Saturday Review of Literature January 18, 1941, November 8, 1947; Time January 20, 1941.

**VANCE, ETHEL.** See **STONE, GRACE ZARING**

**VANCE, LOUIS JOSEPH** (September 19, 1879–December 16, 1933), American novelist and short story writer, was born in Washington, D.C., the only child of Wilson Vance, a Civil War veteran, and Lillie (Beall) Vance. He wrote prolifically about both high society and the underworld, created the popular thief-hero The Lone Wolf, and saw many of his romance and adventure novels become magazine and radio serials as well as motion pictures. He was not, however, of any intrinsic literary importance. he attended the Brooklyn Polytechnic Institute and studied drawing at night at the Art Students League in Manhattan, intending to be an illustrator. Instead he married an artist, Nance Elizabeth Hodges, and went to work for a public service corporation during the day and wrote short stories at night.

After a slow start in which he experienced either rejections or low pay for his stories, Vance sold a serial to *Munsey's Magazine* for $500, quit his job, and became a dedicated writer. "Day and night my typewriter roared and sang, producing some of the most awful stuff that has ever been printed. Every time I wrote a short story I learned something about what it should not have been," he said. Vance turned out books quick-

ly—100,000 words in two months—and finally had a best seller with *The Brass Bowl* (1907). The popular mystery novel concerned a young woman in New York who assumes the role of a burglar to bring comfort to her grief-stricken father. Complications ensue as a real burglar enters the picture as well as a young millionaire who resembles him. Reviewers praised it for its rapid action, well-written dialogue and ingenious plot. "A reader may protest, may resent the undue strain upon his sense of probability, but he will be tolerably sure to follow the story to its end," wrote the *New York Times*.

Vance knew a winning formula and continued with the same kind of action and romance in *The Black Bag* (1908), in which a young English heiress and her black bag of jewels cause considerable stir, and *The Bronze Bell* (1909), where a young American on a duck hunt in Long Island is mistaken for a rajah. Both books were popular successes with no literary pretensions.

After a trio of adventure novels, Vance found even more success when he created Michael Lanyard, or *The Lone Wolf* (1914). Lanyard spent his childhood stealing from Paris hotels to stay alive. A more experienced crook taught him in his teens that to be successful at thievery he must avoid friendships, especially with women, hence his moniker. But, alas, the underworld and the right woman prove dangerous. Vance brought back The Lone Wolf in six more novels.

Besides The Lone Wolf, Vance also created some popular female characters in a number of rags-to-riches romance novels, including *Joan Thursday* (1913), in which the title character is a shop girl who makes it to Broadway but not without a price; Miss Sally Manvers, an impoverished shop girl who, after many a strange incident, ends up with her own apartment on New York's Riverside Drive in *Nobody* (1915).

According to the *New York Times*, Vance declared that he had no illusions about his ability to write anything except adventure books and short stories, but in so doing, he wrote many a snappy yarn that kept readers awake. He also once told an interviewer that his ultimate ambition was "to be so rich that I may lie in bed and smoke forever." He was in fact found dead in his New York apartment, slumped in a blazing upholstered armchair next to a coffee table full of cigarette butts.

PRINCIPAL WORKS: Terence O'Rourke, Gentleman Adventurer, 1905; The Private War, 1906; The Brass Bowl, 1907; The Black Bag, 1908; The Bronze Bell, 1909; The Pool of Flame, 1909; No Man's Land, 1910; The Fortune Hunter, 1910; Cynthia-of-the-Minute, 1911; The Destroying Angel, 1912; The Bandbox, 1912; The Destroying Angel, 1912; The Day of Days, 1913; Joan Thursday, 1913; The Lone Wolf, 1914; The Trey O'Hearts: A Motion Picture Melodrama, 1914; Nobody, 1915; Sheep's Clothing, 1915; The False Faces, 1918; The Dark Mirror, 1920; Alias the Lone Wolf, 1921; Red Masquerade, 1921; Linda Lee, Incorporated, 1922; Baroque, 1923; The Lone Wolf Returns, 1923; The Road to Endor, 1923; Mrs. Paramor, 1924; The Dead Ride Hard, 1926; White Fire, 1926; They Call it Love, 1927; The Woman in the Shadow, 1930; Speaking of Women, 1930; The Lone Wolf's Son, 1931; The Trembling Flame, 1931; Detective, 1932; Encore the Lone Wolf, 1933; The Lone Wolf's Last Prowl, 1934; The Street of Strange Faces, 1934.

ABOUT: Dictionary of American Biography vol. XXI; Reilly, J. M. (ed.) Twentieth-Century Crime and Mystery Writers. *Periodicals*—New York Times April 6, 1907; December 17, 1933; February 25, 1934; Saturday Review of Literature May 5, 1926; Times (London) December 18, 1933.

**VANCE, ETHEL.** See **STONE, G. Z.**

**VANCURA, VLADISLAV** (June 23, 1891–June 1, 1942), Czech novelist, short story writer, and playwright, was born in Háj, near Opava (then in Austria). During World War I he served in the medical corps of the Austrian army; he qualified as a doctor in Prague in 1921, practiced for a few years in nearby Zbraslav, and then gave it up to dedicate himself to authorship. The rest of his life, apart from writing, was spent in devotion to left-wing causes. He was intellectually vague about his political beliefs; a member of the Czech Communist Party (1921) from its beginning, he was, owing to internecine quarrels, expelled from it in 1929; however, he was working for the communist underground when he was picked up by the Gestapo as a "reprisal" for the assassination of Reinhold Heydrich and murdered, together with many others.

He began with two collections of stories, but began to develop his his own voice with the 1924 novel *Pekawr Jan Marhoul* (Baker Jan Marhoul). This, is a rhapsodic celebration of a modern Don Quixote. It mixes Czech-style lyricism, the influence of Dostoyevski's *Idiot*, dada, and Christian humility.

The more mature saga *Pole orná a válecná* (1925, Fields for work and war), is his description of the dissolution of the hated Hapsburg tyranny during the course of World War I. It is a novel that reveals the unbearable horrors of war. In this savagely conceived record, intended to shock, Vancura stepped, emotionally, far beyond the boundaries of Marxist theory. The most sharply ironic of all Vancura's novels also became his most popular: the satirical *Rozmarné léto* (1926, Freakish summer) is cast as a romance, in which the antics of the bourgeoisie are counterpointed with a religiously ceremonial style that it has led more than a few critics to suppose that its attitude towards its victims is "immensely" affectionate.

Of especial interest in this prolific writer's work, in view of the split, in the early 1990s, of Czechoslovakia into two independent republics, is the novel *Utek do Budina* (1932, The flight to Budapest), about a falling-out between a husband and his aristocratic wife. One is Czech, the other Slovak. Here the language is somewhat subdued in the interests of portraying the psychological differences between the two, most of which are seen as deriving from their origins; the differences are explored by Vancura, and not without humor.

*Konec starych casu* (1934, translated as *The End of the Old Times*) is in appearance a picaresque adventure novel based on Munchausen's Baron Prasil tale. The author (with a bow of relish to Munchausen) alters his story whenever he feels like it "in the interests of the reader," particularly any "bourgeois" reader who likes a "good story."

Vancura's brilliant and deeply felt final work was political—the Germans made many Czechs feel intensely "political." It was done in collaboration with historians, and in the face of the Nazis: it was *Obrazy z dejin národa ceskeho* (1939–40, Images of the history of the Czech nation): it goes back to legend and Przemysl dynasty to make its point, and its sad humor (added by Vancura himself) is considerable.

Vancura's theatre, consisting mostly of literary tragedies such as *Joseffna* (1941), has not aroused much interest. His collected works, *Spisy*, appeared in fifteen volumes during the 1950s. The most innovative and productive Czech writer between the wars, he has been the subject of many studies. Milan Kundera, notably, has written of him at length in his *Umeni romanu* (1960, The art of the novel).

PRINCIPAL WORK IN ENGLISH TRANSLATION: The End of the Old Times (translated anon), 1965.

ABOUT: Columbia Dictionary of Modern European Literature, 1947, 1980; Dolewzel, L. Narrative Modes in Czech Literature, 1975; Rechcigl, M. Jr. (ed.) The Czechoslovak Contribution to World Literature, 1964; Seymour-Smith, M. Macmillan Guide to Modern World Literature, 1986; Sturm, R. Czechoslovakia: A Bibliographic Guide, 1968.

**VAN DER MEERSCH, MAXENCE** (1907–January 14, 1951), French novelist, was born in Roubaix, an industrial town in northern France. He studied in Roubaix, in nearby Tourcoing, and finally at the University of Lille, where he took degrees in law and literature. His father not only encouraged his literary pursuits, but predicted his success and served as his secretary, promoter, and literary agent. Van der Meersch wrote, "Without him I would never have written a word, much less published anything." Van der Meersch listed Molière, La Fontaine, Rousseau of the *Confessions*, Balzac, Flaubert, Zola, Dickens, Dostoyevski, and Mauriac as literary influences, but most of all Tolstoy. "I have read *War and Peace* more than twenty times and I never tire of it," he said.

Van der Meersch's first novel, *La Maison Dans la Dune* (1938, *The House in the Dunes*), attracted wide attention at the time of its publication, espe-

cially among working-class audiences. Indeed, he is characterised in French dictionaries as having "repudiated his bourgeois origins" in order to "paint passionate pictures of working-class life" (*Dictionaire des littératures*). The setting of *The House in the Dunes* is that of most of his other works, the Franco-Belgian frontier, and the chief subject of the plot is tobacco smuggling. The first of the novels to be translated into English was *Quand les Sirènes se Taisent* (1934, *When the Looms Are Silent*), the story of the strike and struggles of textile workers in Roubaix. Critical reaction among English-language reviewers was mixed. As the *New York Times* pointed out in Van der Meersch's obituary, readers in "this country were more often than not overwhelmed by the exhaustive nature of his researching and the complexities of his narrative," which is to say that he wrote in the naturalist tradition.

In 1937 Van der Meersch's pacifist novel *Invasion 14* was translated and published in the United States under the title *Invasion*. The plot deals with the people of German-occupied French territory during World War I. Mary Colum wrote in *Forum* that "*Invasion* is a fine, even a powerful book, not in the sense of being a fine, well-told story but powerful in the originality of its attempt to deal with war. It is the effort of a sensitive and thoughtful mind to fathom the mystery of evil, the insanity of man's inhumanity to man, of which war is only one manifestation."

In 1937 *L'Empreinte du Dieu* (translated as *Hath Not the Potter*) also appeared in the United States. It is a character study of a writer and the two women who love him, his wife and her young niece. The *New York Times* commented that "although the intricate love story wobbles badly in parts, descriptions of the Low Countries are superb."

The London *Times* obituary noted that Van der Meersch's "work was marked by the sort of realism which is often associated with the Flemish school of art, and there was evidence in it of his nonreligious upbringing. In his later years, however, partly through the influence of a priest he met during an investigation into prison life, he drew nearer

to Christianity." *Pêcheurs d'Hommes* (1947, *Fishers of Men*) is a documentary novel recounting a worker's conversion to the cause of the Young Christian Workers, a French youth organization active in bringing social change and Catholicism to the working class. Van der Meersch wrote to the Young Christian Workers and declared: "I am proud to have been chosen by God to write of you, living witness to Christ. In fact I consider it the greatest work of my career and my existence."

Van der Meersch stirred up controversy in the medical profession with *Corps et Âmes* (1948, *Bodies and Souls*), his best known novel outside France. The *New Yorker* found it an "impressive work" which leads the reader "through a practically continuous succession of hospital wards and operating rooms, madhouses, tuberculosis sanatoriums," and went on to claim that it "constantly reminds us of the universality of suffering and the almost infinite corruptibility of the flesh. . . . Yet all this merely a counterpoint to his theme, which is the pandemic spiritual disorder of bourgeois society."

PRINCIPAL WORKS IN ENGLISH TRANSLATION: *Novels*—When the Loomis Are Silent (tr. F. A. Blossom) 1934 (in U.K.: The Looms Are Silent); Hath Not The Potter (tr. G. Hopkins) 1937; Invasion (tr. G. Hopkins) 1937 (in U. K.: Invasion' 14); The House in the Dunes (tr. A. Glendinning) 1938; Fishers of Men, 1947; Bodies and Souls (tr. E. Wilkins) 1948; The Poor Girl (tr. E. Wilkins) 1949; The Bellringer's Wife (tr. E. Wilkins) 1951; The Dynamite Factory, 1953; The Hour of Love (tr. E. Fitzgerald) 1956; They Know Not What They Do (tr. E. Fitzgerald) 1958; Mask of Flesh (tr. M. Savill) 1960.

ABOUT: *Periodicals*—Forum March 1937; New York Times January 16, 1951; New Yorker March 13, 1948; Times (London) January 16, 1951.

## VAN DE WATER, FREDERIC FRANKLYN

(September 30, 1890–September 16, 1968), American novelist, memoirist, and essayist, wrote: "An instinct for imitation and a monumental incomprehension of mathematics were the major forces that thrust me into the writing profession. My maternal grandmother, Mary Virginia Terhune, wrote for seventy-odd years under the pen name of 'Marion Harland.' Her three chil-

dren: Christine Terhune Herrick, Virginia Terhune Van de Water, and Albert Payson Terhune all were successful authors. Their example must have influenced me. Certainly, I inherited their inability to accomplish anything but the simplest process of arithmetic.

"I was born in Pompton, New Jersey, the son of Frederic Franklyn and Virginia (Terhune) Van de Water. Though years of residence in Vermont have not eradicated native belief that my surname is indicative of foreign birth, my earliest Van de Water ancestor came to New Amsterdam almost a century before the first permanent dwelling was raised on Vermont soil.

"Public schools in New Jersey and New York

City gave me my preparatory education. In 1912, when, conforming to my Terhune inheritance, I had acquired all the mathematics conditions available at New York University, Columbia providentially established its School of Journalism which required no knowledge of geometry or calculus. I was graduated from the school in 1914, worked briefly thereafter as a reporter on the *New York American* from 1915 to 1922, led a protean existence on the *New York Tribune*, serving at one time or another as reporter, special writer, night city editor, columnist and pinch-hitting now and then as literary or theatrical critic.

"Meanwhile, I had married Eleanor Gay of New York, October 4th, 1916, and our son, also Frederic Franklyn, had been born. Some ambition and more economic pressure impelled me in my spare time to edit a state police magazine and write a book that my psychiatrist-employer signed. In 1921, my own first volume was published: *Grey Riders*, a history of the New York State Police, an organization in which I still hold the rank of honorary-sergeant.

"In 1922, I left full-time employment on the *Tribune* and began a disheveled but generally rewarding career as a free lance writer, running a book column on the *Tribune* and later on the *Evening Post*, undertaking assignments for a number of magazines and selling to these and others on my own initiative a rather appalling number of serials, short stories, articles and verses. Possibly I am most distinguished in my profession by the fact that though I have written mysteries, novels, histories, biographies and a number of books that can be most accurately listed as essays, I am one working-author who at no time in his creative life ever has even attempted to write a play.

"Since 1934, when we left Manhattan with brief and non-recurrent regret, my wife and I have lived on a Vermont hillside farm that still shows every indication of being our permanent home. Most of my work that has been done here has concerned itself, directly or indirectly, with my adopted state. Though in the eyes of my native neighbors I continue to be 'city folks,' Vermont has been kind to us; its charity being best exemplified by the degree of Doctor of Humane Letters conferred on me by Middlebury College in 1952."

---

By the time he had reached his early thirties, as Frederic Franklyn Van de Water related, he had done every job on a newspaper except that of type-setter. So he quit to become a writer himself.

His first book, *Grey Riders*, was a history of the New York state troopers, a competent journalistic survey. He followed this with a series of detective stories, all trooper-related. From that genre he turned to the American West, and wrote what was considered at the time to be the definitive biography of General George Custer. Then he moved his family and literary focus eastward, to Vermont, specializing in histories and novels relating to the Green Mountain state.

Throughout his career he published more than twenty books, including light essays on topics ranging from moving to the country to going fishing and traveling across the United States by automobile. He was often praised for his wit and powers of observation in capturing Vermont rural life, and for his thoroughness and accuracy in certain histories—some of them were reissued in the 1970s and 1980s.

With *Grey Riders* (1922), Van de Water captured the spirit of the New York state troopers "freshly and vigorously," according to the *New York Times*. Murders and lawmen continued to be the chief subject of other thrillers he wrote in the 1920s: *Horsemen of the Law* (1926), *The Eye of Lucifer* (1927), *Hurrying Feet* (1928), *Still Waters* (1929), and *Alibi* (1930). None of these early efforts made "any notable stir," according to C.J. Finger in the *New York Herald Tribune Books*.

Van de Water took a break from the troopers and headed to the highways himself, taking his family on vacation and writing a travel journal, *The Family Flivvers to Frisco* (1927), which first appeared serially in *Ladies' Home Journal*; it told of how he, his wife and son set forth from New York in a Ford touring car, and traveled 4,500 miles in thirty-seven days via Yellowstone and the Columbia River to San Francisco. The *New York Times* wrote that Van de Water gave the book "a literary touch and real significance that have been lacking in most other accounts" of car-touring summer vacations, a burgeoning American activity in the 1920s.

The author went West again in writing *Thunder Shield* (1933), an historical novel praised for its authenticity in portraying "the ruthless decimation of the Indian tribes, and their struggle for survival" during America's Westward expansion, the *New York Times* critic wrote. The book ended with the last stand of General Custer, who was the subject of Van de Water's 1934 biography *Glory Hunter*, which Stuart Rose in *New York Herald Tribune Books* called "the Custer book to end all Custer book's." W. R. Benét commented in *Saturday Review of Literature* that the biography "says the final word," painting Custer as a cruel, egotistical power hungry "tangle of contradictions," a far different portrait than that written by Custer's widow, who "enshrined her husband in the folklore of America." Van de Water's account was reissued in 1988.

Vermont beckoned Van de Water during the depression, when he and his wife had grown apprehensive of living in New York City and "wanted something more substantial than could be kept in a safe-deposit box." Their house hunting and exodus to the country was the crux of *A Home in the Country* (1937), subtitled "an adventure in serenity." The *New York Times* found it wise and witty: "A good many books have been written on the subject of a home in the country, as discovered by city dwellers here and in England. This is one of the best of them all."

A sequel, *We're Still in the Country*, and *The Circling Year* (1940), comprised of twelve essays, one for each month, describe the pleasures of country living and serve as an intimate chronicle of the Van de Water's daily life. As war progressed in Europe, Van de Water had found more peaceful pastures, writing: "Men cry that the world plunges toward doom. We look out upon our small patch of earth and disbelieve." E. F. Allen wrote in the *New York Times*, "The author wears the shirt of a happy man, and in *The Circling Year* he takes off and gives it to the reader."

Besides stories of his own life and times, Van de Water wrote histories of the founding days of the state and fictionalized accounts of its colonial period. The first was *Rudyard Kipling's Vermont Feud* (1937), a detailed account of the feud between Rudyard Kipling and his brother-in-law, which ended in the departure of the Kiplings from Vermont and from America. *The Reluctant Republic* (1941) is a narrative history published on the 150th anniversary of Vermont statehood that focused on the pioneer founders of the state and was favorably received by most reviewers as authentic and lively.

Van de Water went on to write a tetralogy of historical novels on Vermont during the American Revolution: *Reluctant Rebel* (1948), a romance that culminates with Ethan Allen and his Green Mountain Boys capturing Fort Ticonderoga in 1775; *Catch A Falling Star* (1949), a further re-evaluation of Ethan Allen and his brother Ira; *Wings of the Morning* (1955), another love story set amidst the fight for freedom; and *Day of Battle* (1938), "an inspiring footnote to our American history," and "a fine tribute to stouthearted Vermont character," according to Bennett Epstein in the *New York Herald Tribune Book Review.*

Three of Van de Water's novels are set in contemporary Vermont: *Mrs. Applegate's Affair* (1944), about a marriage going stale; *Fool's Errand* (1945) regarding an artist who leaves New York for Vermont but cannot adapt; and *The Sooner to Sleep* (1946), which pictures the women left behind in a village during World War II. But his deep affection for Vermont was perhaps best expressed in *In Defense of Worms, and Other Angling Heresies* (1949), a collection of contemplative essays on the joys of fishing in which Van de Water wrote, "What I bring back from my Vermont fishing is likely to lie longer in my mind than in my stomach."

PRINCIPAL WORKS: *Fiction*—Horsemen of the Law, 1926; The Eye of Lucifer, 1927; Elmer 'n' Edwina, 1928; Hurrying Feet, 1928; Still Waters, 1929; Alibi, 1930; Havoc, 1931; Plunder, 1933; Thunder Shield, 1935; Hidden Ways, 1935; Death in the Dark, 1937; Mrs. Applegate's Affair, 1944; Fool's Errand, 1945; The Sooner to Sleep, 1946; Reluctant Rebel, 1948; Catch a Falling Star, 1949; Wings of the Morning, 1955; This Day's Madness, 1957; Day of Battle, 1958. *History*—Grey Riders, 1922; (with M. Van Rennsekaer) The Social Ladder, 1924; The Reluctant Republic; Vermont, 1724–1791, 1941; Lake Champlain and Lake George, 1946; The Captain Called it Mutiny, 1954. *Biography*—The Real McCoy, 1931; Glory Hunter: A Life of General Custer, 1934; Rudyard Kipling's Vermont Feud, 1937. *Essays*—A Home in the Country, 1937; We're Still in the Country, 1938; Fathers Are Funny, 1939; The Circling Year, 1940; Members of the Family, 1942; In Defense of Worms, 1949. *Travel*—The Family Flivvers to Frisco, 1927.

ABOUT: The autobiographical material quoted above was written for Twentieth Century Authors First Supplement, 1955. Warfel, H. R. American Novelists of Today. *Periodicals*—Library Journal September 1, 1949; New York Herald Tribune Books October 29, 1933; November 18, 1934; New York Herald Tribune Book Review May 11, 1958; New York Times August 20, 1922; April 10, 1927; May 23, 1937; August 4, 1940; September 17, 1968; Publishers Weekly September 30, 1968; Saturday Review of Literature December 1, 1934; August 2, 1941.

**VAN DINE, S. S.** See **WRIGHT, WILLARD HUNTINGTON**

**VAN DOREN, CARL (CLINTON)** (September 19, 1885–July 18, 1950), American critic and biographer, was born in Hope, Illinois, the son of Charles Lucius Van Doren, a physician, and Dora Anne (Butz) Van Doren. In 1900 the family moved to Urbana where the elder Van Doren took up farming and business. Carl was educated at Thronburn High School and the University of Illinois, where he took his B.A. in 1907. He did graduate work at Columbia and earned his Ph.D. there in 1911; his soon to be published biography, *The Life of Thomas Love Peacock*, was his dissertation. From 1911 to 1930 he taught English at Columbia on a full-and part-time basis. He was also headmaster of the Brearley School from 1916 to 1919.

Van Doren's first wife, Irita Bradford, was editor of the book section of the *New York Herald Tribune.* Van Doren himself rose to prominence as literary editor of the *Nation* from 1919 to 1922, a time when the revitalized journal was at the center of new writing. Van Doren became a supporter of struggling writers; in his memoir *Three Worlds* he states that "almost at once young writers turned to the *Nation* as a critical friend." James Branch  Cabell, Sinclair Lewis, and Elinor Wylie were among those who benefitted from Van Doren's early recognition. In a *Nation* review of Van Doren's second book, *The American Novel*, H. L. Mencken's specific praise can be used to describe Van Doren's overall strengths as a critic and scholar: "He is intelligent; he is persuasive; he is readable; most of all, he is quite remarkably learned. Here we have something far above and beyond the usual scholastic compilation, by a tutor out of a row of textbooks. The man has read the novels themselves."

During his 1922 to 1925 tenure as literary editor of the *Century Magazine*, Van Doren wrote a column titled *The Roving Critic*, and his first collection of literary essays and reviews was published under that title in 1923. "The measure of the creator is the amount of life he puts into his work," he wrote. "The measure of the critic is the amount of life he finds there." The following year Van Doren published a second collection titled *Many Minds.* The *New York Times* (April 6, 1924), found "something disarming about Van Doren's impersonality—disarming and cool but seldom cold," and went on to note that an "Emersonian note often creeps into his sentences. If there is no overwhelming enthusiasm in them, there is never any venom. He is virtually never lyrical, but when he begins to finger the wealth of a talent the pulse of his writing quickens. But he never passes dross for gold. His touch for the counterfeit is as unerring as a banker's is said to be. He is never cruel because he is never personal." In one of the essays included in *Many Minds* Van Doren described himself: "That he is little perturbed by his limitations, that he does not greatly care to rise to passion or to descend to prejudice, means, in part, that he is more willful in his behavior than sometimes appears. It means, also, that criticism has never been with him a major aim. What really interests him is human character, whether met in books or out of them, and it is always human character which he studies."

Although Van Doren's brief foray into fiction writing proved disappointing, his biographies and histories were highly praised. Of his Pulitzer Prize-winning biography, *Benjamin Franklin*, Van Doren wrote the "chief aim of this book is to restore to Franklin, so often remembered piecemeal in this or that of his diverse aspects, his magnificent central unity as a great and wise man moving through great and troubling events."

From 1917 to 1921 Carl Van Doren was managing editor of the *Cambridge History of American Literature*. He was also a founder of the Literary Guild and from 1926 to 1934 served as its editor-in-chief.

PRINCIPAL WORKS: *Nonfiction*—The Life of Thomas Love Peacock, 1911; The American Novel, 1921 (rev. ed. as The American Novel: 1789–1939, 1940); Contemporary American Novelists: 1900–1920, 1922; The Roving Critic, 1923; Many Minds, 1924; (with M. Van Doren) American and British Literature Since 1800, 1925, rev. ed. 1939; James Branch Cabell, 1925, rev. ed. 1932; Other Provinces, 1925; Swift, 1930; American Literature: An Introduction, 1933 (reissued as What Is American Literature?, 1935); Sinclair Lewis: A Biographical Sketch, 1933; Benjamin Franklin, 1938; Secret History of the American Revolution: An Account of the Conspiracies of Benedict Arnold and Numerous Others, Drawn from the Secret Service Papers of the British Headquarters in North America, Now For the First Time Examined and Made Public, 1941; Mutiny in January: The Story of a Crisis in the Continental Army Now for the First Time Fully Told from Many Hitherto Unknown or Neglected Sources, Both American and British, 1943; Carl Van Doren: Selected By Himself, 1945 (reissued as The Indispensable Carl Van Doren: Selected By Himself, 1951); (with C. Carmer) American Scriptures, 1946; The Great Rehearsal: The Story of the Making and Ratifying of the Constitution of the United States, 1948; Jane Mecom: The Favorite Sister of Benjamin Franklin: Her Life Here First Fully Narrated from Their Entire Surviving Correspondence, 1950. *Novel*—The Ninth Wave, 1926. *Memoirs*—Three Worlds, 1936. *As editor*—Benjamin Franklin and Jonathan Edwards: Selections from Their Writings, 1920; Seven Stories by Nathaniel Hawthorne, 1920; Selections from the Writings of Thomas Paine, 1922; (with W. P. Trent, J. Erskine, and S. P. Sherman) A Short History of American Literature Based Upon the Cambridge History of American Literature, 1923; Tales by Washington Irving, 1928; The Travels of Baron Munchausen, 1929; Modern American Prose, 1934; An Anthology of World Prose, 1935; The Borzoi Reader, 1936; Cato's Moral Distichs, 1939; Twenty Stories, by Stephen Crane, 1940; (with W. P. Trent, J. Erskine, and S. P. Sherman) The Cambridge History of American Literature, 1945; Benjamin Franklin: The Autobiography with Sayings of Poor Richard, Hoaxes, Bagatelles, Essays and Letters, 1940; The Literary Works of Abraham Lincoln, 1942; Letters and Papers of Benjamin Franklin and Richard Jackson: 1753–1785, 1947; The Letters of Benjamin Franklin & Jane Mecom, 1950. *As translator*—Judith: A Tragedy in Five Acts (by F. Hebbel) 1914.

ABOUT: Twentieth-Century Literary Criticism 18, 1985. *Periodicals*—Nation July 6, 1921; New York Times April 6, 1924; July 19, 1950; New York Times Book Review September 20, 1936; October 9, 1938; Times (London) July 19, 1950.

**VAN DOREN, MARK** (June 13, 1894–December 10, 1972), American critic, editor, and poet, was born in Hope, Illinois, one of five sons of Charles Lucius Van Doren, a physician and farmer, and Dora Anne (Butz) Van Doren. He was six when his family moved to Urbana, Illinois, where he attended public schools and then the University of Illinois, taking his B.A. in 1914 and M.A. in 1915. He then moved to New York  to study at Columbia. In 1916 Houghton Mifflin published his master's thesis titled *Henry David Thoreau: A Critical Study*.

Van Doren's studies at Columbia were interrupted by World War I; for two years he served stateside in the infantry. After his discharge he and Joseph Wood Krutch toured Europe together on traveling scholarships from Columbia. In 1920 Columbia awarded him his Ph.D.; that same year his doctoral thesis, *The Poetry of John Dryden*, was published. A review in the *Times Literary Supplement* stated that the "consideration is so thorough, the matter so compact, the appreciation is so just, temperate and enthusiastic and . . . the suggestion of acutely placed facts leads our thoughts so far—that it is a book every practitioner of verse should study." The review was anonymous, as was then the custom at the *Times*, but the reviewer is known to have been T. S. Eliot. The book became a staple on college campuses and has remained in print through the years.

Also in 1920, Van Doren became an instructor in Columbia's English department; from 1924 to 1942 he served as assistant and then associate professor. In 1942 he was appointed professor of English, a post he held until his retirement in 1959. According to the *New York Times* (1972), he "exhibited an uncanny sensitivity to literature that fascinated Columbia students for nearly four decades. John Berryman, Clifton Fadiman, Thomas Merton, Lionel Trilling, Herbert Gold, Louis Simpson and Jack Kerouac were among the diverse writers who came under his spell as students." Among Van Doren's most praised literary studies were *Shakespeare* and *Nathaniel Hawthorne*. Of the former, the *New York Times* (November 12, 1939) commented that for "any one who has read Shakespeare or is about to read Shakespeare this is by far the best modern commentary." In praise of the latter, *Commonweal* wrote: "This brief critical biography maintains an admirable balance between narrative and comment and is a model of its kind." Among Van Doren's many collections as editor was the 1928 *Anthology of World Poetry*; it was such a success that he and his wife were able to buy a house in the city with the money it earned.

Van Doren was a graduate student when he published his first poem, a semisatirical sonnet about a woman student, in H. L. Mencken's *Smart Set*. *Spring Thunder*, his first collection of poems, appeared in 1924; in *The Autobiography of Mark Van Doren*, he called them poems of the "utmost simplicity," and said that "people called them country poems, and doubtless this was fair even when it implied a limitation." In 1923 the Van Dorens had bought a 150-acre farm in Falls Village, Connecticut, as a retreat, and rural images would provide expanding themes throughout his long career as a poet.

In 1940 Van Doren was awarded a Pulitzer Prize for his *Collected Poems*. S. I. Hayakawa wrote in *Poetry* that "he has mastered his devices (or they have mastered him) so well that he has fallen into the fatal trap of being able to continue writing extremely plausible verses even after his subject matter has been used up." However Allen Tate, in a 1963 *New York Herald Tribune Book Week* review defended his old friend gracefully: "If he seems to publish too much of what he has done, we must remember once more what kind of poet he is. He is a formalist who is not trying in every poem to write a masterpiece; he is day by day the whole man who submits the whole range of his awareness to the forms that he has elected to use."

Although known primarily as a critic, editor, and reviewer, Van Doren also wrote novels, short stories, and plays. From 1924 to 1928 he was literary editor of the *Nation*, having succeeded his brother Carl, and from 1935 to 1938 he served as its movie critic. He was married to Dorothy Graffe, also a writer; his son Charles became notorious when he became involved in a famous 1959 television-quiz-show scandal.

Mark Van Doren's greatest achievement lay, not in his writings, but in his inspirational reading. Many writers owed their beginnings to him.

PRINCIPAL WORKS: *Nonfiction*—Henry David Thoreau: A Critical Study, 1916; The Poetry of John Dryden, 1920, rev. ed. 1931 (reissued as John Dryden: A Study of His Poetry, 1946); Edwin Arlington Robinson, 1927; (with T. Spencer) Studies in Metaphysical Poetry, 1939; The Private Reader: Selected Articles and Reviews, 1942; Liberal Education, 1943; The Noble Voice: A Study of Ten Great Poems, 1946 (reissued as Mark Van Doren on Great Poems of Western Literature, 1962; On Great Poems of Western Literature, 1962; and as Great Poems of Western Literature, 1966); Nathaniel Hawthorne, 1949; Man's Right to Knowledge and the Free Use Thereof, 1954?; Walt Whitman: Man, Poet, Philosopher: Three Lectures, 1955; Don Quixote's Profession, 1958; The Happy Critic and Other Essays, 1961; The Dialogues of Archibald MacLeish and Mark Van Doren, 1964; (with A. Jewett, O. Achtenhagen, and M. Early) Insights Into Literature, 1965; Introduction to Poetry: Commentaries on Thirty Poems, 1966; (with others) Insights Into Literature, 1968; Carl Sandburg, 1969; (with M. Samuel) In the Beginning, Love: Dialogues on the Bible, 1973; (with M. Samuel) The Book of Praise: Dialogues on the Psalms, 1975. *Poetry*—Spring Thunder and Other Poems, 1924; 7 P.M. and Other Poems, 1926; Now the Sky and Other Poems, 1928; Jonathan Gentry, 1931; A Winter Diary and Other Poems, 1935; The Last Look and Other Poems, 1937; Collected Poems: 1922–1938, 1939; The Mayfield Deer, 1941; Our Lady Peace and Other War Poems, 1942; The Seven Sleepers and Other Poems, 1944; The Country Year, 1946; The Careless Clock: Poems About Children in the Family, 1947; New Poems, 1948; Humanity Unlimited: Twelve Sonnets, 1950; In That Far Land, 1951; Mortal Summer, 1953; Spring Birth and Other Poems, 1953; Selected Poems, 1954; Morning Worship and Other Poems, 1960; Collected and New Poems: 1924–1963, 1963; Narrative Poems, 1964; Mark Van Doren: 100 Poems Selected by the Author, 1967; That Shining Place: New Poems, 1969; Good Morning: Last Poems, 1973. *As editor*—A History of the Life and Death, Virtues & Exploits of General George Washington, by Mason Weems, 1927; Samuel Sewall's Diary, 1927; An Anthology of World Poetry, 1928, rev. ed. 1936; A Journey to the Land of Eden and Other Papers by William Byrd, 1928; An Autobiography of America, 1929; Correspondence of Aaron Burr and His Daughter Theodos, 1929; (with G. M. Lapolla) A Junior Anthology of World Poetry, 1929; The Life of Sir William Phips, by Cotton Mather, 1929; (with G. M. Lapolla) The World's Best Poems, 1929; American Poets 1630–1930, 1932 (reissued as Masterpieces of American Poets, 1936); The Oxford Book of American Prose, 1932; (with C. Van Doren) American and British Literature Since 1890, 1939; Shakespeare, 1939; (with J. W. Cunliffe and K. Young) Century Readings in English Literature, 1940; The Travels of William Bartram, 1940; (with H. Cairns and A. Tate) Invitation to Learning, 1942; The Voice of America, 1942; The Night of the Summer Solstice and Other Stories of the Russian War, 1943; Walt Whitman: Selected and With Notes, 1945; The Portable Emerson, 1946; Selected Poetry (by W. Wordsworth) 1950; Introduction to Poetry, 1951 (also published as Enjoying Poetry, 1951); (with M. Moore and R. Eberhart) Riverside Poetry 2: 48 New Poems by 27 Poets, 1956. *Novels*—The Transients, 1935; Windless Cabins, 1940; Tilda, 1943. *Short stories*—Short Stories, 1950; Nobody Said a Word and Other Stories, 1953; Home with Hazel and Other Stories, 1957; Collected Stories, 1962–1968. *Drama*—The Last Days of Lincoln: A Play in Six Scenes, 1959; Three Plays, 1966. *Juvenile*—Dick and Tom: Tales of Two Ponies, 1931; Dick and Tom in Town, 1932; The Transparent Tree, 1940; The Witch of Ramoth and Other Tales, 1950; Somebody Came, 1966. *Memoirs*—The Autobiography of Mark Van Doren, 1958.

ABOUT: Claire, W. (ed.) The Essays of Mark Van Doren (1924–1972) 1980; Current Biography 1940; Hendrick, G. (ed.) The Selected Letters of Mark Van Doren, 1987; Merton, T. The Seven Storey Mountain, 1948; Newquist, R. Counterpoint, 1964. *Periodicals*—Commonweal May 13, 1949; Nation October 15, 1973; New York Herald Tribune Book Week September 29, 1963; New York Times November 12, 1939; December 12, 1972; Poetry June 1939; Prairie Schooner Summer 1974; Times Literary Supplement June 9, 1921; Western Humanities Review Summer 1974.

## VAN DRUTEN, JOHN WILLIAM (June 1, 1901–December 19, 1957), English dramatist

wrote: "John William Van Druten was born in London, the son of a Dutch father, Wilhelmus Van Druten, a banker, and an English mother. He was educated at University College School, London, where he showed an enthusiasm, rather than a talent, for writing. On leaving school he studied for the law, serving his Articles of Clerkship with  a City firm of solicitors, and attending lectures and classes at the Law Society's School. In 1923 he was qualified with honors in the Solicitors' Examination and was admitted as a Solicitor of the Supreme Court of Judicature. He also took the degree of L. L.B. at London University. The practice of the law, however, was not to his liking, which turned more towards the academic side of his profession. (The profession itself, by the way, was his father's choice rather than his own.) He therefore applied for and obtained a post, which he held from 1923 to 1926, as Special Lecturer in English Law and Legal History at the University College of Wales, Aberystwyth.

"During these years his interest in writing had continued. A large flow of poems and short stories had come back from magazines; a few of them had found homes, particularly in *Punch*. In 1923 a three-act play entitled *The Return Half* was produced by the Ex-Students' Club of the Royal Academy of Dramatic Art. The names of the author and the leading actor were equally unknown: they were John Van Druten and John Gielgud. The play received encouraging reviews, and in the following year Mr. Van Druten's play *Young Woodley* was written, and bought by an English and an American manager for production in London and on Broadway. The London production, however, was forbidden by the censor on the ground that the piece constituted an attack on the English Public School System, a ban which was later reversed after the successful New York production in 1925 and a private performance by the London Stage Society in 1927. Eventually produced at the Savoy Theatre in London early in 1928, it ran for the rest of that year.

"In 1926 M. Van Druten gave up the law as a career and came to America, where he went on lecture tours of the principal cities. . . . "

---

Well known as a dramatist in both his native England and his adopted United States, John Van Druten wrote almost thirty plays. His biggest stage successes came from a string of drawing-room comedies—two of the most notable being *The Voice of the Turtle*, produced in 1943, and *Bell, Book and Candle*, produced in 1954—as well as from his creative adaptations of already popular material: *I Remember Mama*, from Kathryn Forbes's book of stories called *Mama's Bank Account*, and *I Am a Camera*, based on Christopher Isherwood's *Berlin Stories*.

Besides writing plays, Van Druten worked as a stage director, directing all of his own plays after 1942, and staging the classic Rogers and Hammerstein musical *The King and I*. He also wrote four novels, several screenplays—including a number of adaptations of his own plays for the screen—an autobiography of his early years, a guide to playwriting, and later in life, a chronicle of reminiscences in which he discussed his spiritual adventures and his farming activities on a California ranch that, along with New York City, was his home after he became a naturalized American citizen in 1944.

Many critics praised his plays for being well constructed, amusing and filled with natural dialogue. They were, almost paradigmatically, "well made plays." But many reviewers said they would not last, and that, though skillful, they were excessively genteel and sentimental. Many of them had successful Broadway runs and screen adaptations, and were kept alive by little theaters and stock companies.

Van Druten witnessed early success with *Young Woodley*, a drama of adolescent anguish and sexual experience. Written when he was only twenty-three while serving as a university lecturer in Wales, the play was first a victim of the Lord Chamberlain's ban. It was published as a novel in 1928.

The central character of *Young Woodley*, a young poet and idealist, is a pupil in an English public school where he falls in love with his headmaster's wife. In a review of the novel, the *Times Literary Supplement* commented, "The dialogue, which was so effective on the stage is equally here, and the descriptive passages which have to take the place of direct representation are well written and well managed."

With this play, Van Druten established himself as a professional playwright, and so hit the lecture trail throughout the United States. He later told the *New York Times* that "a too-big, too-soon success is a bad thing. It happened to me. It calls too much attention to the author. Too many people can't wait until he comes crashing down. A false standard is set up, which is dreadful."

Later in his career, Van Druten was often credited more as a director than a writer (he developed four of the 1951–1952 Broadway season's top performances.

*The Voice of the Turtle*, was the most successful of all his plays. A three-character comedy whose title is from the Song of Solomon, the play focuses on a soldier spending a weekend in New York and a young actress from Missouri who is rebounding from a failed romance. After receiving favorable reviews, it had a long run on Broadway starring Margaret Sullavan and Elliott Nugent, had a nationwide tour, and was later filmed.

A lifelong bachelor, Van Druten frequently chose women as his protagonists. It served him well in *The Distaff Side* (1933), about which W. P. Eaton in the *New York Herald Tribune Books* wrote that "John Van Druten seems to be a born dramatist. He gives the impression of doing little more than setting a number of assorted people, mostly females, on the stage and letting them talk. A story wanders in and gets itself told, somehow . . . and it all looks so easy! Well, it isn't."

Van Druten went on to idolize motherhood in his play *I Remember Mama* (1945), the story of a Norwegian-American family living at the foot of a San Francisco hill in the early 1900s. But perhaps his most remembered female characterization is that of Sally Bowles in *I Am a Camera*, taken from Isherwood's autobiographical stories of life in pre-Nazi Berlin, which won the Drama Critics Award of 1951. J. M. Brown in *Saturday Review of Literature* wrote, "Whatever its faults may be, the play is never dull. Its best scenes are fresh and sensitive and have a fine honesty. Few characters I can remember have been drawn as candidly as Sally Bowles. Part of her validity is that she is left unresolved and that her inconsistency is shown as her chief consistency."

In his early fifties Van Druten became a theater

fixture and, "looks about the way a professional playwright should. He is what thoughtful toastmistresses would call suave," wrote Lewis Nichols in the *New York Times* in 1953. He was elected to the (American) National Institute of Arts and Letters. He also wrote *Playwright at Work*, which "discusses the varied problems of writing plays and the methods which (Van Druten) had adopted to meet these problems . . . not so much a manual with formulas for constructing the perfect play as a history of how the author himself works." Van Druten told *The New York Times* that he wrote the book "because I was told to write it. I had been wandering around lecturing, speaking most of it to my friends. Perhaps for too long a time. They said that, as a favor, maybe I would write it out, and then stop talking."

Van Druten's 1957 play, *The Widening Circle*, was based on his spiritual adventures and life on his California ranch. Of the play, he wrote: "There is always the conflict between the instinct to 'grab while the grabbing is good,' to embark on the journey to hell on a roller coaster, and the deeper awareness, felt even here in the city, though muffled by its noises, that the old, the Bible texts are still true. The eternal question of 'What shall it profit a man if he shall gain the whole world, and lose his own soul?' has still power to disturb. I make no claim that the play answers the big question or that it even attempts to do so. I still think that question too large to be answerable so easily, but it seems to me that the play may start on an avenue at the end of which the answer can ultimately be found." In reviewing *The Widening Circle*, the *New Yorker* wrote that "although the author calls this book 'a personal search,' it is a curiously impersonal work, for there is a fastidious untouchability about Mr. Van Druten. But even though he delves into some of his inner conflicts and perplexities, as well as into his inner perceptions and religious searchings, he writes like a man looking at himself through the wrong end of a pair of binoculars."

PRINCIPAL WORKS: *Drama*—The Return Half, 1924; Chance Acquaintances, 1927; Young Woodley, 1928; Return of the Soldier, 1928; Diversion, 1928; After All, 1929; London Wall, 1931; There's Always Juliet, 1931; (with B. W. Levy) Hollywood Holiday, 1931; Somebody Knows, 1932; Behold, We Live!, 1932; The Distaff Side, 1933; Flowers of the Forest, 1936; Most of the Game, 1936; Gertie Maude, 1937; Leave Her to Heaven, 1940; Old Acquaintance, 1941; (with L. R. Morris) The Damask Cheek, 1943; The Voice of the Turtle, 1944; I Remember Mama, 1945; The Mermaids Singing, 1946; The Druid Circle, 1948; Make Way for Lucia (based on novels of E. F. Benson) 1949; Bell, Book and Candle, 1951; I Am a Camera, 1952; I've Got Sixpence, 1953. *Novels*—Young Woodley, 1929; A Woman on Her Way, 1930; And Then You Wish, 1936; The Vicarious Years, 1955.

ABOUT: Current Biography 1944. *Autobiography*—The Way to the Present (autobiography) 1938. *Other*—Playwright at Work, 1953; The Widening Circle, 1957; Morris, L. R. Postscript to Yesterday; Van Druten, J. Playwright at Work, 1953; Van Druten, J. The Way to the Present, 1938. *Periodicals*—Literary Digest January 26, 1935; Newsweek December 30, 1957; New York Herald Tribune Books November 18, 1934; New York Herald Tribune Magazine September 20, 1931; New York Times January 25, 1953; December 20, 1957; New Yorker October 5, 1957; Saturday Review of Literature December 22, 1951; Times Literary Supplement February 21, 1929; Time December 30, 1957.

**VAN DYKE, HENRY** (November 10, 1852–April 10, 1933), American clergyman, fiction writer, essayist, and diplomat, was born in Germantown, Pennsylvania, the son of Henry Jackson Van Dyke, the pastor of the First Presbyterian Church there, and Henrietta (Ashmead) Van Dyke. He was raised in Brooklyn, New York, where he attended Brooklyn Polytechnic High School. He studied at Princeton University  and at Princeton Theological Seminary and did graduate work abroad, chiefly in Germany. Ordained to the ministry, his first pastorate was at the United Congregational Church in Newport, Rhode Island (1879–1883). He next went to the Brick Presbyterian Church in New York City (1883–1899), where his pulpit skills and literary productivity began to grow. From 1899 to 1923 he held the James O. Murray Chair of English Literature at Princeton University, a chair named for his predecessor at Brick Church and at Princeton, except for three years spent as Woodrow Wilson's ambassador to the Netherlands and Luxembourg (1913–1916).

Van Dyke's core beliefs in God's grace and human freedom were tested by the deaths of two infant sons, one older boy, and one daughter in childbirth. Two older brothers of his had also died in infancy, perhaps forming uncommonly strong bonds between surviving children and parents in his family, forcing a constant awareness of "natural evils" and prompting a joy and zest for living to the fullest. Early in his career, Van Dyke paid a visit of hommage to Tennyson, on whose work he published his most significant literary criticism. He ranked Tennyson with Robert Browning in importance, though acknowledging the widely varied level of quality in the poet laureate's work. Van Dyke's sympathy for the genteel tradition and its combination of moral and spiritual commitments in art, is seen in statements such as this one from *The Man Behind the Book*: " . . . the highest function of the novel: to enlarge life for us by bringing us acquaintance with men and women worthy to be loved." Van Dyke shared with Tennyson the ability to bring landscape to life. His own preference for rhyme and meter (though generally in shorter lines and poems than Tennyson used) keeps his verse in a traditional mode. At its weaker moments, it is simply allegory in rhymed prose, always clear and graceful but over-mannered commonsense observation. As in his sermons, Van Dyke would try to restate basic truths regularly, but found it difficult to manage new insight and inspiration each time. Van Dyke's many nature idylls spoke to a public experiencing industrialization and urbanization at an unprecedented scale. His sure feel for American culture and politics can be seen in his French lectures, which display his own adventurer's emphasis on "self-reliance," "fair play," "energy" and "sentiment for common order."

While pastor of Brick Church in New York, Van Dyke published some of his most famous works. *The Story of the Other Wise Man* and *The First Christmas Tree* were originally given in the form of sermons, and were soon widely published and translated into all European languages. *The Story of the Other Wise Man* is still frequently reprinted at Christmastime in the United States; it tells the story of a late-arriving Magi who misses the Christ Child but searches for him for thirty-three years, continually taken off course by people in need, on whom he uses up all his gifts. This story, originally published in 1896, sold more than 800,000 copies in his lifetime. Another widely known Van Dyke work, *The Blue Flower*, was really a translation from the German of a work by Novalis, who used the figure to symbolize poetry. In it, Van Dyke evidenced some affinities for Goethe's views about the spiritual effects of poetry and art. Van Dyke considered his most important work, however, to be his *The Book of Common Worship*, a book of liturgies and prayers for the Presbyterian Church, used extensively throughout that denomination in the twentieth century. The fourth edition, published in 1993, retains sections that reflect Van Dyke's deep faith and sure ear and feel for the canons of biblical and English literature. He chaired the committee that produced this book and its first revision, writing or editing much of the text.

As a pastor, Van Dyke combined writing and publication with energetic participation in public activities. Although he is today rarely identified with the more activist ministers of the progressive era, like Rauschenbusch and Norman Thomas, Van Dyke embraced many of their causes, denouncing slum conditions in New York and corruption in city government, opposing prohibition, championing conservation and the national parks, favoring independence for the Philippines, and American participation in the League of Nations. He also took a strong stand in favor of copyright protection for European authors, whose works were pirated freely by American publishers until 1891. Van Dyke's much reprinted sermon "The National Sin of Literary Piracy" (1888), had much to do with the initial success of this legislation.

Van Dyke's involvement in public issues were initially formed in the struggles over creedal and liturgical revision in the Presbyterian Church, where he was a progressive force for change and openness to scientific discoveries. Van Dyke styled himself an "adventurous conservative," but this was partly a public stratagem. Certainly his constant efforts to liberalize the Presbyterian Church on doctrines such as predestination, and in opposing biblical literalism and fundamentalism, were inspired in part by loyalty to his father, who was a man of principle, orthodox but tolerant, and willing to fight for reconciliation between North and South after the Civil War. His father had served as Moderator of the Northern Presbyterian General Assembly in 1876, and Van Dyke himself served in that office in 1902, after a successful preaching campaign on behalf of the new "Brief Statement of Faith," his elegantly rewritten recasting of the Westminister Confession

that was intended to stress God's love over God's judgment. In the theological struggles of that period, he challenged his church to provide "the bread of truth rather than the stone of controversy." A controversial aspect of Van Dyke's method is hinted at in a seminary dialogue he wrote contrasting John Milton with Johann Goethe. In it, he stressed how Milton was the tireless poet, pamphleteer, and rebel, while Goethe was a more private aesthete who shied away from public issues in Germany. Van Dyke's own son Tertius, in writing his father's biography, thought that he had taken a too personalistic approach toward public issues.

Princeton University considered Van Dyke as a candidate for its presidency, an ambition that he disavowed, though his two threats to resign over matters of curriculum and student life showed his willingness to use his considerable influence at the school. He generally got his way. After his retirement from the University in 1923, he continued to give a well-attended public lecture series until 1930.

In 1913, fellow Presbyterian Woodrow Wilson, who had just been elected President of the United States after serving as president of Princeton University and governor of New Jersey, appointed Van Dyke Ambassador to the Netherlands. In his service at The Hague, Van Dyke was a great success, but he eventually returned to Princeton in frustration, taking too personally the immorality of German preparation for war. After his resignation, he began to write and speak out more forcefully for American resistance to this aggression. With typical flair, he asked for—and received, at age 62—a position as naval chaplain usually restricted to men under 35. After World War I, he argued even more strongly for international cooperation.

His son, Tertius Van Dyke, articulated his father's literary creed in these words: "The highest element in the best art is always moral, and fitted to make men and women better as well as happier . . . Immoral art is one of the most evil influences in the world. . . . Virtue may be adorned and made attractive by a pure art. Truth and goodness are not complete until beauty is added to the trinity of excellence." In retrospect, Van Dyke was poised culturally at the point when art was replacing religion in the "piety" of many well-to-do Americans. For him, art and worship were one.

In his 1963 study of the clergyman-author, Roland Frye noted a democratic impulse in Van Dyke's allegiance to the "genteel" tradition. He was a popularizer as well as one who tried to elevate public taste and virtue. This might be called "participatory elitism"; there is no question, despite his extroverted love of common people, that, after his years as a pastor, his close companions were few in number, except as guides on Canadian fishing trips. Frye describes Van Dyke and others like him in these terms: "Their mark is eccentricity. Their aim is the visible separation of people from the common herd. His favorite poet must be one who is caviar to the vulgar. . . . He must know more than anyone else about the things that are not worth knowing, and care very passionately for the things that are not usually considered worth caring about. He must believe that Homer and Dante and Milton and the Bible have been very much overrated, and carefully guard himself, as Oscar Wilde did in the presence of the ocean, from giving away to sentiments of vulgar admiration. . . . He must . . . find his chief joy in the consciousness that his tastes, his opinions, and his aspirations are unlike those of common people."

Ever an opponent of censorship, he would have insisted on toleration of the decidely unpopular. Ironically, now, several of his themes are back in fashion. One of his story poems on labor, *The Toiling of Felix*, is built on a verse from the rediscovered Gnostic Gospel of Thomas; his celebration of strong male friendships and positive experiences of fatherhood and sonship, as well as the "rugged" outdoors is reflected in the men's movement popularized by Robert Bly and others.

PRINCIPAL WORKS: The Reality of Religion, 1884; The Poetry of Tennyson, 1889 (completely revised as Studies in Tennyson, 1920); Little Rivers, 1895; The Story of the Other Wise Man, 1896; The First Christmas Tree, 1897; Fisherman's Luck, 1899; The Ruling Passion, 1901; The Blue Flower, 1902; The Book of Common Worship, 1906 (rev. ed., 1923, 1993); Days Off, 1907; Out of Doors in the Holy Land, 1908; Poems, 1911; The Unknown Quantity, 1912; The Red Flower, Fighting for Peace, 1917; The Valley of Vision, 1919; Studies in Tennyson (complete revision of The Poetry of Tennyson, 1889), 1920; Poems (rev. ed.), 1920; Camp Fires and Guide Posts, 1921; Companionable Books, 1922; Half Told Tales, 1925; The Man Behind the Book, 1929; Gratitude, 1930; A Creelful of Fishing Stories, 1932.

ABOUT: Frye, R. M. "Henry Van Dyke—Many Sided Litterateur" in Kerr, H. (ed.) Sons of the Prophets, 1963; Van Dyke, T. Henry Van Dyke: A Biography, 1935; The Van Dyke Book, 1905 (rev. ed. 1920). *Periodicals*—New New York Times April 11, 1933; Princeton Alumni Weekly May 5, 19, July 3, 1933; Suburban Life May 1908; Times (London) April 11, 1933.

## VAN DYNE, EDITH. See BAUM, L. FRANK

**VANE, SUTTON** (November 9, 1888–June 15, 1963) English dramatist, was the son of Sutton Vane, a writer of Victorian melodramas. After education at Radley, young Vane became an actor. Eagerly enlisting for service in World War I, he was soon sent home with shell shock. When he was well enough to return to France, it was as the member of the cast in productions staged for the troops' entertainment.

Vane's first two plays were of little note. *Very Much Married*, a farce, was performed at the Little Theater in Ascot Week, 1912, and *The Blow* had a short run in 1915. *Out-*

*ward Bound* (1923) was initially turned down by every company to which it was offered. In the end, at his own expense, Vane hired the small Everyman Theatre, in Hampstead, London, designed the set himself, and hired a cast willing to work for a cut of whatever profits accrued. His first wife, Diana Hamilton, took a leading part. The play was an immediate success

and was soon given a full West End production at the Garrick. It was revived in 1926 and 1928 and produced intermittently throughout the 1930s.

The play is about a group of passengers on an ocean liner (all three acts are set in the ship's bar) who gradually make the discovery that they are dead and sailing for the "port of judgment." The theme found special favor in the United States, where it was produced at the Ritz Theatre early in 1924, with Leslie Howard and Alfred Lunt. Howard also appeared in the first movie version of the play, produced in 1930. *Variety* commented that the film seemed "to lack the essentials of mass entertainment," and when, during World War II, it was remade as *Between Two Worlds* the cinema again failed to convey the atmosphere of pathos and humor achieved in the theater.

Vane wrote sparingly. Two more plays in the 1930s—*Time, Gentlemen, Please* and *Marine Parade*—like *Outward Bound*, had just one setting, but neither made any mark. He also turned *Outward Bound* into a novel, published (1930) under the same title. The *New York Times* commented: "The author has handled his subject with the same restraint that marked the play. It is not a pretentious work; it is for the most part subdued; but it is thoroughly worth reading." As a play, *Outward Bound* continues to be a popular production with student and amateur theater groups.

PRINCIPAL WORKS: Drama—Outward Bound, 1923; Falling Leaves, 1924; Overture, 1925. *Fiction*—Outward Bound, 1930.

ABOUT: *Periodicals*—New York Post December 17, 1938; New York Times June 18, 1963; Outlook March 5, 1924.

**VAN GULIK, ROBERT HANS** (August 9, 1910–September 27, 1967), Dutch mystery writer, translator, Orientalist, and diplomat, was born in Zutphen in the Dutch province of Gelderland. He was the son of a medical officer of the Netherlands army of Indonesia, where he lived as a colonial in early boyhood.

He returned with his family to Holland in 1922 and was educated at Nijmegen and at the University of Leyden, where he studied Chinese, Japanese, and other Asian languages and literatures. He received his doctorate in Oriental languages at Utrecht University in 1935, the same year he joined the Dutch foreign service, which took him to Tokyo. In Japan, Van Gulik, an accomplished calligrapher, translated a Chinese text by Mi Fu about calligraphers' "ink stones". He played the ancient Chinese lute and wrote two scholarly books on the instrument based on Chinese sources. He also studied Chinese popular literature, especially detective and courtroom stories. Considering modern Western thrillers to be inferior to ancient Chinese mystery stories, he translated what he considered to be the best of the Chinese stories and adapted them for modern readers, starting in 1940 with *Dee Goong An*, an anonymous eighteenth-century Chinese detective novel. He translated it into English and in 1949 introduced the Western world to Judge Dee, "the Sherlock Holmes of China" and the sleuth-hero of a successful series of novels that Van Gulik wrote in the 1950s and 1960s for which he received his greatest popular reputation.

During World War II, Van Gulik was sent to Chungking as secretary of the Netherlands mission to China. There he married a Chinese woman, Shui Shih-fang, in 1943, and in 1944 he published an edition of a rare Chinese work about the Ch'an master Tung-kao, a Buddhist monk who was loyal to the Ming cause in the days of its defeat. He remained in China until 1945, when he returned to The Hague until 1947. He then became attached to the Dutch Embassy in Washington, D.C.

Returning to Tokyo in 1949 for a four-year tour of duty, he began to meld his worlds of scholarship, diplomacy and art into the Judge Dee novels. With no previous experience at writing fiction, he began writing in English, a second language, with the intent to publish works in Japanese and Chinese. His first effort was *The Chinese Bell Murders*, written in Tokyo in 1950, followed by *The Chinese Nail Murders*, written in Beirut in 1956. Van Gulik ordinarily chose his plots and characters while relaxing from official duties, and it usually took him six weeks to write one of the novels, according to Donald F. Lach in the introduction to the 1977 reprint of Van Gulik's *The Chinese Nail Murders*. Judge Dee lived during the Tang dynasty from A.D. 630 to A.D. 700 and served as a direct magistrate in the province and as an important statesman, holding high office in the capital, Van Gulik claimed in his postcript to *The Monkey and the Tiger* (1965).

The five earliest Judge Dee novels, including *The Chinese Bell Murders* (1958) and *The Chinese Nail Murders* (1961) are closer to the originals than later novels, according to Lach. Except for *The Chinese Bell Murders*, Van Gulik supplied all the themes and plots. Anthony Boucher, writing in the *New York Times*, considered *The Chinese Nail Murders*, a trio of cases in the year 676, "one of the very best of the wondrous Dee books, with fine complexity of plots, and more personal involvement of the Judge." Boucher also took note of Van Gulik's two novelettes published as *The Monkey and the Tiger* (1965). In *The Monkey*, Dee's gibbon draws his attention to the murder of an old tramp and the judge proceeds to solve the case in only one day and with only two clues. In *The Tiger*, Dee's investigative prowess stands up to solving the murder of a young girl—with only one clue. Boucher wrote that both novelettes are "excellent at evoking an ancient civilization by means of first-rate modern puzzle-entertainment."

Van Gulik also took interest in Chinese erotic literature and art with a focus on the Ming dynasty and published in Tokyo in 1961 a private edition of fifty copies of erotic color prints of the Ming era along with a handwritten essay on the history of Chinese sex life from 206 B.C. to A.D. 1644. "Through a number of works Van Gulik showed that although the gentlemen of traditional China often gave lip-service to high moral standards, they displayed in their personal lives the moral weakness of people everywhere," Lach wrote.

Van Gulik was director of research with the Ministry of Foreign Affairs in The Hague from 1962 to 1965, when he returned to Tokyo as the Netherlands Ambassador to Japan and the Republic of Korea. He lectured on ancient Chinese history at the University of Malaya in 1960–1961.

All of the Judge Dee series were translated into Dutch, and the earlier stories were translated into French, Swedish, Spanish, Finnish, Yugoslavian, Japanese, Italian, and German. Many were reprinted in English in the 1990s by the University of Chicago Press.

PRINCIPAL WORKS: (translator) Dee Goong An, 1949; The Chinese Bell Murders, 1958; The Chinese Gold Murders, 1959; The Chinese Lake Murders, 1960; The Chinese Nail Murders, 1961; The Red Pavilion, 1961; The Haunted Monastery, 1962; The Lacquer Screen, 1962; The Emperor's Pearl, 1963; The Willow Pattern, 1965; The Monkey and the Tiger, 1965; The Phantom of the Temple, 1966; Murder in Canton, 1966; Judge Dee at Work, 1967; Necklace and Calabash, 1967; Poets and Murder, 1968. Nonfiction—The Lore of the Chinese Lute, 1940; Sexual Life in Ancient China, 1961; The Gibbon in China, 1967.

ABOUT: Lach, D. F. Introduction to 1977 edition The Chinese Bell Murders; Van Gulik, R. H. Postscript, The Monkey and theTiger. Periodicals—New York Times October 14, 1962; April 24, 1966; September 29, 1967; Times (London) September 27, 1967.

**VAN LOAN, CHARLES EMMET** (June 29, 1876–March 3, 1919), American short story and sports writer, was born in San Jose, California, the son of Richard and Emma J. (Blodgett) Van Loan.

Van Loan, whose only education came from the San Jose public schools, worked in the mercantile business until 1903. His writing career began when he became a sports editor in Los Angeles. Shortly afterward, he moved to New York City, where he sold his first piece of fiction, "The Drug Store Derby," to *All-Story Weekly* in 1909. A number of his stories also appeared in such magazines as *Collier's Weekly, Popular, Metropolitan,* and *Munsey's* magazines.

A *New York Times* reviewer praised Van Loan's first book, *The Big League* (1911), writing: "Mr. Van Loan knows baseball from backstop to field fence, and he has the breezy newspaper style which is necessary to make baseball reading worth while."

Those in the boxing game often gave Van Loan's third book, *Inside the Ropes* (1913)—a collection of stories about boxing—to newly appointed boxing commissioners because of its precision and details. The *New York Times* wrote of it: "all of the tales are better done told with more dash and go and with better art as well, than were the baseball stories."

A few months prior to his death, the delayed results of a car accident of 1914, Van Loan became associate editor of the *Saturday Evening Post.*

"During the years between 1909 and 1919 he had made himself the *prose* laureate of the golf course, the prize ring, the diamond, and the race track," wrote Robert H. Davis after Van Loan's death. "He possessed the peculiar gift of characterization developed to a high degree and could cover a baseball game, a horse race, a prize fight, or any sport event with fine grace and distinction."

PRINCIPAL WORKS: The Big League, 1911; The Ten-Thousand-Dollar Arm, 1912; Inside the Ropes, 1913; The Lucky Seventh, 1913; Buck Parvin and the Movies, 1915; Old Man Curry, 1917; Fore!, 1918; Score By Innings, 1919; Taking the Count, 1919.

ABOUT: Periodicals—The New York Times August 6, 1911; July 27, 1913; American Magazine December 1918; Bookman May 1919; Outing November 1919.

*VAN LOON, HENDRIK WILLEM (January 14, 1882–March 10, 1944), Dutch-American historian, wrote: "I was born in Rotterdam, just around

the corner from the birthplace of Erasmus, the son of a rich father who lived in a realm a million miles away from his child and never made the slightest effort to construct a bridge across that chasm. And so I escaped entirely into the past, and revaluated all the adventures of my own existence into terms of a bygone era. Even today I know the seventeenth century better than the twentieth.

"We were sent to school at an astonishingly young age. I do not know when I first learned to read and write. I cannot remember any time during the many years that I have spent upon this planet when I was not in direct and immediate touch with both the past and the future. I lived in a world in which the ideals of the eighteenth century were still the aim of the spiritual realm. The book which taught me English was Henry Esmond. I still read that magnificent opus regularly once every year. Because English is a tongue which I had to acquire when I was already full grown, and with which I shall have to struggle until the end of my days, I love and revere it with a personal passion which few of those who were born in English-speaking countries will ever be able to share.

"My work would not be my work without those endless little pictures, to draw which I had to fight from early childhood, for nobody at home really approved of them. I believe that I can honestly state that I write entirely by ear. I am one of those few and highly fortunate people who can write under any and all circumstances. When I am in a hurry with a drawing job I find that music is absolutely indispensable. I will draw with anything that comes handy and within reach.

"The older I grow the more I agree with Spinoza and Frederick the Great and Goethe that Chance plays a tremendously important role in our lives. If I had not lost my mother when I was seventeen I never would have left my own country, and would undoubtedly have tried to do there what is really the object of my life, the humanization and popularization of history, and I would have failed most

°van LONE

miserably. For nobody in my native land would have felt the slightest sympathy with what I was trying to do, and with the rather melancholic natural tendencies in my mental make-up, I would have drifted into a hopeless state of despair which would have meant an end to all further creative efforts; whereas in my adopted country I have enjoyed just enough opposition to be encouraged to work still harder and write something that shall be better yet.

"I claim that reason and intelligence and a scientific acceptance of all the facts related to life will eventually turn this world of ours into a truly decent place of residence for civilized human beings. Of happiness in the usual sense of the word I probably have not had a great deal. But I have had my work, and that is the greatest good that can come to any man born with a sense of a creative duty."

———

Hendrik Willem Van Loon was the son of Hendrik Willem Van Loon, a prosperous jeweler, and Elisabeth Johanna (Hanken) Van Loon. He left Holland for the United States in 1903 and, after a year at Harvard took his B.A. at Cornell. He then joined the Associated Press in Washington, D.C., and was dispatched to Russia to cover the revolution. He was later assigned to Warsaw, but resigned to enter the University of Munich where he earned a Ph.D. in history in 1911. Returning to Washington in that same year Van Loon became a correspondent for the Amsterdam Handelsblad and published his first book, The Fall of the Dutch Republic, based on his doctoral thesis. The summer of 1914 found him lecturing at the University of Wisconsin. During World War I he returned to Europe as a free-lance journalist.

Van Loon was back in the United States for the publication of his second book, The Rise of the Dutch Kingdom, in 1915. He then spent a year as a history lecturer at Cornell and published several more histories. These included his children's book, History of a Match: Being an Account of the Earliest Navigators and the Discovery of America, which Van Loon himself illustrated by drawing with a match dipped in ink. Another self-illustrated children's book, Ancient Man, was published in 1920. In 1919 he became a United States citizen.

Meanwhile in England H. G. Wells published his two-volume Outline of History, which proved hugely successful in the United States. This, plus the encouraging sales of Ancient Man, led Van Loon's publisher to suggest that Van Loon write and illustrate a history of the world for children. Published in 1921 The Story of Mankind was a major best-seller. Carl Van Doren described it this way: "It looked like a book for children and was that too. It was sparkling with pictures . . . pictures that at first appeared scratchy and casual and then suddenly were seen to illuminate the text and to reinforce the meaning of the historian. . . . The American public called for thirty-two printings in five years. . . . It has been translated into so many languages that only Upton Sinclair can count them. At least outside Russia it has become the chief historical primer of the age." It also won Van Loon the first John Newbery Medal from the American Library Association.

In 1922 Van Loon spent a year teaching at Antioch College in Ohio followed by a year on the *Baltimore Sun* editorial staff. He went on to write and illustrate a string of best-selling histories for adults and children.

Van Loon was not a historian's historian. His aim was to produce popular, not scholarly works, and as such he wrote in a "folksy" anecdotal style that was not above humor and generalizations. Van Loon's *New York Times* obituary quotes critic John Chamberlain as stating that "when Hendrik Willem Van Loon writes history, you can be certain of getting both plenty of history and plenty of Van Loon." In his 1942 *Van Loon's Lives* the author offered unusual portraits of forty personages from history, using the device of bringing them back from Heaven or Hell to a dinner, where they come to life. "To readers familiar with Mr. Van Loon's previous profitable ventures in the dilution of history no comment on this volume is necessary," the *American Historical Review* declared. "This contribution is perhaps more Van Loony than any previous one. The tip-off is the title. As a delicate compliment the author and publisher recall the fact the Plutarch once did something along the same lines. The *mise en scène* is simple and clever."

Van Loon, who had an acquaintance with many eminent people, was a popular lecturer, as well as a radio personality on the National Broadcasting System. Forty of his radio speeches were collected in 1935 under the title *Air-Storming*. During World War II Van Loon organized a short-wave radio program originating in Boston and aimed at the Nazi-occupied Netherlands, broadcasting as "Uncle Hank." For his efforts he was awarded the Order of Knight of the Netherlands Lion by Queen Wilhelmina.

PRINCIPAL WORKS: *Nonfiction*—The Fall of the Dutch Republic, 1913; The Rise of the Dutch Kingdom, 1795–1813: A Short Account of the Early Development of the Modern Kingdom of the Netherlands, 1915; The Story of Rabelais and Voltaire, 1925; The Story of Wilbur the Hat: Being a True Account of the Strange Things Which Sometimes Happen In a Part of the World Which Does Not Exist, 1925; Tolerance, 1925 (in U.K.: The Liberation of Mankind: The Story of Man's Struggle for the Right to Think); America, 1927 (reissued as The Story of America, 1942); Life and Times of Pieter Stuyvesant, 1928; R. v. R.: Being an Account of the Last Years and the Death of One Rembrandt Harmenszoon van Rijn . . . Who Was Attended in His Afflictions by One Joannis Van Loon, Doctor Medicinae and Chirurgion in Extraordinary . . . Who During a Most Busy Life Yet Found Time to Write Down These Personal Recollections of the Greatest of His Fellow-Citizens and Which Are Now for the First Time Presented (Provided with as Few Notes, Emendations and Critical Observations as Possible) by His Great, Great Grandson, Nine Times Removed, Hendrik Willem Van Loon, 1930 (reissued as Life and Times of Rembrandt, R. v. R., 1930); Van Loon's Geography: The Story of the World We Live In, 1932 (in U.K.: The Home of Mankind: The Story of the World We Live In); An Indiscreet Itinerary; or, How the Unconventional Traveler Should See Holland, by One Who Was Actually Born There and Whose Name is Hendrik Willem Van Loon, 1933, rev. ed. 1939; Re: An Elephant up a Tree: This Is the True Story of Sir John; or Why the Elephants Decided to Remain Elephants, As Told By One of Them, 1933; Ships and How They Sailed the Seven Seas (5000 B.C.–A.D. 1935) 1934; Air-Storming: A Collection of 40

Radio Talks, 1935; A World Divided Is a World Lost, 1935; The Arts, 1937 (in U.K.: The Arts of Mankind); (with G. Castagnetta) Christmas Carols, Illustrated and Done Into Simple Music, 1937; Observations On the Mystery of Print and the Work of Johann Gutenberg, 1937; How To Look at Pictures: A Short History of Painting, 1938; Our Battle, by Hendrik Willem Van Loon: Being One Man's Answer To My Battle, by Adolph Hitler, 1938; (with G. Castagnetta) The Last of the Troubadours, Carl Michael Bellman, 1740–1795, His Life and His Music, 1939; The Life of Napoleon Bonaparte, 1939; (with E. B. White, K. Roberts, et. al.) Our Cornell, 1939; (with G. Castagnetta) The Songs America Sings, 1939; Invasion: Being the Personal Recollections of What Happened to Our Family and to Some of Our Friends During the First Forty-Eight Hours of the Terrible Incident in Our History Which Is Now Known as the Great Invasion and How We Escaped with Our Lives and the Strange Adventures Which Befell Us Before the Nazis Were Driven from Our Territories, 1940; The Life and Times of Johann Sebastian Bach, Described and Depicted by Hendrik Willem Van Loon, 1940; The Story of the Pacific, 1940; (with G. Castagnetta) Good Tidings, 1941; (with G. Castagnetta) Christmas Songs, 1942; Van Loon's Lives: Being a True and Faithful Account of a Number of Highly Interesting Meetings With Certain Historical Personages From Confuscius and Plato to Voltaire and Thomas Jefferson, About Whom We Had Always Felt a Great Deal of Curiosity and Who Came to Us as Our Dinner Guests In a Bygone Year, 1942; The Life and Times of Simon Bolivar: This Is the Story of Simon Bolivar, Liberator of Venezuela, the Man Who First of All Had a Vision of a United States for the Whole of the American Continent, 1943 (reissued as Fighters For Freedom: Jefferson and Bolivar, 1962, and in U.K.: Jefferson and Bolivar: New World Fighters For Freedom); Thomas Jefferson: The Serene Citizen from Monticello Who Gave Us an American Way of Thinking and Who Gained World-Wide Renown by His Noble Understanding of That Most Difficult of All the Arts, the Art of Living, As He Felt That It Should Be Practiced In the Republic of Which He Was One of the Founders, 1943 (reissued as Fighters For Freedom: Jefferson and Bolivar, 1962, and in U.K.: Jefferson and Bolivar: New World Fighters For Freedom); Adventures and Escapes of Gustavus Vasa and How They Carried Him from His Rather Obsure Origin to the Throne of Sweden, 1945; (with G. Castagnetta) The Message of the Bells; or, What Happened to Us One Christmas Eve, 1949. *Juvenile*—The Golden Book of the Dutch Navigators, 1916; History with a Match: Being an Account of the Earliest Navigators and the Discovery of America, 1917 (also published as The Romance of Discovery, 1917); Ancient Man: The Beginning of Civilizations, 1920; The Story of Mankind, 1921, rev. ed. 1936; The Story of the Bible, 1923; Man, the Miracle Maker, 1928 (reissued as The Story of Inventions: Man, the Miracle Maker, 1928, and in U.K.: Multiplex Man, or, The Story of Survival Through Invention); How To Do It: A Book for Children, 1933; Around the World With the Alphabet and Hendrik Willem Van Loon: To Teach Little Children Their Letters and at the Same Time Give Their Papas and Mamas Something To Think About, 1935; (with G. Castagnetta) The Songs We Sing, 1936. *As editor*—(with G. Castagnetta) Folk Songs of Many Lands, 1938. *Memoirs*—Report To Saint Peter, Upon the Kind of World In Which Hendrik Willem Van Loon Spent the First Years of His Life, 1947.

ABOUT: The autobiographical material quoted above was written for Twentieth Century Authors, 1942. Brooks, V. W. Days of the Phoenix, 1957; Contemporary Authors vol. 117, 1986; Dictionary of American Biography Suppl. 3; Kunitz, S. (ed.) Living Authors, 1931; Miller, B. E. and Field, E. W. (eds.) Newbery Medal Books: 1922–1955, 1955; Something About the Author Vol. 18, 1980; Van Loon, G. W. The Story of Hendrik Willem Van Loon, 1972; Ward, M. E. and Marquardt, D. A. Authors of Books for Young People, 1964; Widdemer, M. Golden Friends I Had, 1964. *Periodicals*—American Historical Review January 1943; Choice November 1972; New York Times March 12, 1944.

**VAN PAASSEN, PIERRE** (February 7, 1895–January 8, 1968), Dutch-American journalist, was born in Gorcum, the Netherlands, and educated at

the local Calvinist Athenaeum. His family moved to Toronto in 1911, and between 1914 and 1916 he studied for the ministry at Victoria College. He was appointed assistant pastor to a Methodist Mission in Alberta. He enlisted in the armed forces and served with the Canadian Expeditionary Force in France. At the end of the war he did not return to the ministry, but studied in Paris and became a foreign correspondent for, successively, the *Toronto Globe*, the *Atlanta Constitution*, the *New York Evening World*, and the *Toronto Star*. For these papers, Van Paassen covered nearly every important foreign news story during the 1920s and early 1930s.

In the wake of assignments to Palestine, Van Paassen became an advocate of the Jewish state, and was even described as "probably the only Gentile Zionist alive." His first book was titled *Israel and the Vision of Humanity*. His second was an edition (co-edited with J. W. Wise) of writings about Nazism. Published in 1934, the year in which he was given more than one opportunity of personally interviewing Hitler, it established Van Paassen as one of Nazism's sternest opponents. Because of his outspokenness he was expelled from Germany, Italy, and France.

His name became more widely known with the publication of *Days of Our Years*, an autobiography that combined accounts of his journalistic exploits with humanitarian sermonizing. The *New Yorker* commented: "It is the special quality of this book that beneath all its complex unravelling of political and social forces and its masses of reporting, one feels what one can only call a spiritual base." Van Paassen wrote with passion, but was often inaccurate in detail. Of a later autobiography, *Earth Could Be Fair*, which recollected impressions and personalities from his hometown in Holland, the *New Yorker* referred to "a slipshod attitude towards facts, which makes him probably the most creative nonfiction writer at work today." His angriest book was *Forgotten Ally*, published in 1943, an indictment of Allied betrayal of the Jews.

Also in 1943, Van Paassen became an American citizen and was ordained as a Unitarian minister. He already had a degree in theology from the Faculté Libré Protestante, and was now made an Honorary Doctor of Divinity by the University of London and a Doctor of Hebrew Letters by the Jewish Institute of Religion. After a single attempt at writing a novel—*Tower of Terzel*—the majority of Van Paassen's later books were explicitly religious in theme. *Why Jesus Died* used the apocryphal gospels to explore the historical facts behind the crucifixion, in a manner which attempted to explain why the Jews had been blamed in versions promulgated by the early church. One of his last books, *A Crown of Fire*, was an admiring biography of the Dominican, Savonarola.

PRINCIPAL WORKS: (as ed. with J. W. Wise) Nazism, An Assault on Civilisation, 1934; Days of Our Years, 1939; The Battle for Jerusalem, 1941; That Day Alone, 1941; The Time Is Now!, 1941; The Forgotten Ally, 1943; Earth Could Be Fair, 1946; The Tower of Terzel, 1948 (novel); Why Jesus Died, 1949; Jerusalem Calling!, 1950; Visions Rise and Change, 1955; A Pilgrim's Vow, 1956; A Crown of Fire, the Life and Times of Girolamo Savonarola, 1960; To Number Our Days, 1964.

ABOUT: Current Biography 1968. *Periodicals*—New Yorker February 4, 1939; May 11, 1946; Publishers Weekly January 22, 1968; Time January 21, 1946; March 17, 1947.

**VAN TYNE, CLAUDE HALSTEAD** (October 16, 1869–March 21, 1930), American historian, was born in Tecumseh, Michigan, the son of Lawrence M. Van Tyne and Helen (Rosecrans) Van Tyne. He received his B.A. from the University of Michigan in 1896 and a Ph.D. from the University of Pennsylvania in 1900. While studying abroad at Heidelberg, Leipzig, and Paris, from 1897 to 1898, Van Tyne took many trips down the

Danube with his wife, Bell Joslyn, whom he married in 1896, and with whom he had three sons and a daughter.

Van Tyne began teaching American history at the University of Michigan in 1903. He was made full professor in 1906, and in 1911 was appointed head of the department of history, a position he held until just before his death.

Van Tyne's main body of work, beginning with his first book, *The Loyalists in the American Revolution* (1902), dealt with the topic of the American Revolution. He also worked consistently as a contributor to several encyclopedias and history books, as well as to such periodicals as *Atlantic Monthly* and *American History Review* (of which Van Tyne was a member of the board of editors from 1916 to 1921). In 1921 Van Tyne published *The Causes of the War of Independence*, which many reviewers, such as one writing for the *Boston Transcript*, considered "lucid enough and provok[ing] such interest that the everyday reader can enjoy every word." The second volume, *The War of Independence: American Phase* (1929) was given equally good reviews, being called by E. E. Curtis "not only good history but good reading" (*American History Review*); it received the Pulitzer Prize in 1930.

In 1921–1922 Van Tyne spent five months in India. From his first-hand study of the political situation there, which included talks with Mahatma Gandhi, he produced *India in Ferment* (1923). Unlike his previous work, this book was not well liked by reviewers and was criticized for being too one-sided; as one reviewer for the *New York Tribune* wrote, "Professor Van Tyne's British sympathies are so evident and indeed so frankly admitted in the preface as somewhat to rob the succeeding chapters of the suspense proper to a good argument."

In 1927 Van Tyne lectured at Cambridge University, England. These lectures were published in 1927 as *England and America: Rivals in the American Revolution.*

PRINCIPAL WORKS: *Nonfiction*—The Loyalists in the American Revolution, 1902; (with W. G. Leland) Guide to the Archives of the Government of the United States in Washington, 1904; Washington, First in War, First in Peace, 1904; The American Revolution: 1776–1783, 1905; (with A. C. McLaughlin) School History of the United States, 1911; Influence of the Clergy, and of Religious Sectarian Forces, on the American Revolution, 1913; Democracy's Educational Problem, 1918; The Causes of the War of Independence, 1922; India in Ferment, 1923; England and America: Rivals in the American Revolution, 1927; The War of Independence: American Phase, 1929. *As editor*—The letters of Daniel Webster, 1902.

ABOUT: Dictionary of American Biography vol. X, 1936; Who's Who in America 1928–1929. *Periodicals*—American History Review April 1930; Boston Transcript September 20, 1922; New York Tribune November 4, 1923; New York Times March 22, 1930.

**VAN VECHTEN, CARL** (June 17, 1880–December 21, 1964), American novelist, composer, journalist, music and dance critic, and photographer, was born in Cedar Rapids, Iowa, the son of Charles Duane Van Vechten, a banker and insurance man, and the former Ada Amanda Fitch.

Carl Van Vechten, after an education at Cedar Rapids High School, entered the University of Chicago in 1899. Among his professors there were the  novelist Robert Herrick and the poet and dramatist William Vaughn Moody. He graduated in 1903 with a Ph.B. He then joined the *Chicago American* as general factotum. His first break came in 1906 when, having moved to New York, he was spotted by Theodore Dreiser, the editor of *Broadway*, who commissioned him to write an article on Richard Strauss's opera *Salome.* The article was in its turn spotted by Richard Aldrich, music editor of the *New York Times*, who took on Van Vechten as his assistant. In June 1907, in London, Van Vechten married an old friend from Cedar Rapids, Anna Elizabeth Snyder. They were divorced five years later. In 1914 he married the actress Fania Marinoff. He later described this union as "a mutual admiration society."

Van Vechten, a sympathic, generous, tender, and appreciative man—and one who in many respects anticipated, in his person and his writings, the contemporary sense of the word "camp"—was an authority on so-called "decadents" of all kinds, from the American Edgar Saltus to the English Ronald Firbank. Although a journalist who deliberately wrote in journalistic style—rather than as a learned critic—Van Vechten acquired an unusually wide and deep knowledge of modern music, art, and literature, particularly of the avant garde, to which he was always attracted. He wrote many

books about modern music; and he was forever advancing the causes of those in whose work he believed. He was one of the earliest to discern the genius of Erik Satie, of Stravinsky, and of Schoenberg. And while Melville's *Moby Dick* was still neglected and thought of, even by college professors, as the work of an eccentric and unbalanced minor writer, he championed it. Although he generously and vigorously took the part of many trivial talents, often just to encourage them on their difficult way as human beings, his judgment in general was highly perceptive. As Bruce Kellner has written, a "partial list of his discoveries is staggering. As a newspaper critic he endorsed the first performances in America of Isadora Duncan, Anna Pavlova, Mary Garden, Feodor Chaliapin and Serge Rachmaninov . . . Firbank and Arthur Machen owe their American reputations to him. . . . Van Vechten's tireless efforts on behalf of Gertrude Stein are well known; he was instrumental in placing the first books of Wallace Stevens and Langston Hughes; he fostered the careers of George Gershwin, Ethel Waters, Paul Robeson amongst musicians, and James Purdy amongst writers." Stein made Van Vechten her literary executor, and after her death he published not only a still unsurpassed *Selected Writings* (1946) but also her *Last Operas and Plays* (1949) and the indispensable *Unpublished Writings* in eight volumes (1951–1958).

Van Vechten's musical and other criticism is still readable and relevant. It directs the reader to the works of the subjects of discussion rather than to the critic himself. *Excavations: A Book of Advocacies* deals with composers and writers. In it Van Vechten praises the virtues of, among others, Ouida, Melville, Saltus, Henry Blake Fuller, M. P. Sheil, Machen, and Firbank. Of his short piece on Oscar Hammerstein the *Nation* (1926) wrote that it was beautiful "because simply written": it was "valuable as biography and moving as characterization."

Van Vechten's witty, learned, and elegant *Tiger in the House* (1920) remains one of the most outstanding of all the tens of thousands of books about cats. Likewise, the anthology of thirteen cat stories with the title *Lords of the Housetops* is, for most cat-lovers who are also serious readers, one of the best.

Van Vechten's major writings are his seven novels. The last of the novels appeared in 1930, after which Van Vechten slowed down the pace of all his writing in order to devote himself to photography. This had long been a recreation, but at that time he wished to document his century with unretouched portraits of those who typified it. In this capacity he founded the James Weldon Johnson Memorial Collection of Negro Arts and Letters, at Yale, and the George Gershwin Memorial Collection of Music and Musical Literature, at Fisk. The first showing of his photographs was held at Bergdorf Goodman, in New York City, in 1935, as a part of the Leica Exhibition.

During this long final period Van Vechten wrote little more than the *Fragments from an Unwritten Autobiography*, which he published in 1955—and various essays. His *With Formality and Elegance*, on photography itself, did not appear until 1977.

As Bruce Kellner noted, two or three of the seven novels achieve what no other novels achieve: no novel better conveys the atmosphere of New York and Paris before World War I than *Peter Whiffle*, nor any that of Harlem in the 1920s than *Nigger Heaven*.

His first novel *Peter Whiffle: His Life and Works* is a mock biography. (The name "Whiffle" was originally given by Tobias Smollett to a homosexual type he satirized in *Ferdinand, Count Fathom*.) Reviewers were immediately reminded of Van Vechten's friends, James Branch Cabell; critic James Huneker, author of the "perverse" or "outrageous" novel *Painted Veils* (1921); and Arthur Machen, whose disciple the biographee Peter Whiffle himself aspired to be. The book is often described today as "semi-autobiographical," but it is rather an elaborate exercise in self-mockery. It is a *roman à clef* which also incorporates real characters—and it does not take itself at all seriously. It is, however, serious.

*Nigger Heaven* is undoubtedly the most celebrated of Van Vechten's novels. As Marcus Cunliffe pointed out, this title (it is an old slang term for the topmost balcony seats in the theater) was "more ironic . . . than was recognized by the public," which simply was not ready for such a novel from a white writer. One of the characters, Mary Love, has an almost "fanatic faith in her race, a love for her people in themselves"; "the Negroes never premeditate murder. . . . There had never been, her information assured her, a Negro poisoner. Negroes use the instruments that deal death swiftly: knives, razors, revolvers." All such thinking, on the part of all the races, are here thus ironically exposed. Carl Van Doren, discussing *Nigger Heaven* in the *Nation* (1922), wrote that Van Vechten was "full of allusions, of pungencies, of learning in his times. He knows how to laugh, he scorns solemnity, he has filled the book with wit and erudition. He is a civilised writer." And the *New York Times* called it as "delightful fare after the solemn dishes of our solemn realists." The *New York World* believed it to be "at least as good as Huxley's *Chrome Yellow*" and added that no one in that age could achieve such "perfection" except Max Beerbohm.

In the case of *The Tattooed Countess* Van Vechten depicts small-town life around 1900; in those of *The Blind Bow-Boy*, *Firecrackers*, and *Parties* it is the "drunken twenties."

The argument against Van Vechten's importance as a writer has been stated by Darryl Pinckney, writing in the *New York Review of Books* in 1988: "[he] churned out a series . . . mostly inspired by the paganism of the nineties. For all the chatter in them about culture, these . . . were limited, unworldly and narrowly autobiographical." Pinckney went on to write that *Nigger Heaven* was a "best-seller thanks to the author's reputation for knowing the Harlem Renaissance and the book's local color," and adds that "many black critics ridiculed" *Nigger Heaven*. However, it is also true that black critics such as Langston Hughes did praise it. As Henry Blake Fuller wrote in the *Saturday Review of Literature*, of *Firecrackers*: "The artist, true, may have been born beyond its [the city's] bounds, yet he is best nourished within them. Mr. Van Vechten will doubtless leave any metropolitan epic to other pens, but his own seems equal to turning the peculiar lyrics that the 'time' and the 'place'—to borrow the language of the playbill—alike call for."

Other reviewers find the fiction worthy of survival because of its, in Kellner's words, "slinky elegance and wit." Van Vechten, a novelist of great intelligence and stylistic brilliance, cannot be left out of any account of modern American fiction. He surfaces not only in the best of James Purdy's fiction, in particular in the poignant *Malcolm*, but also in most good American fiction concerned with homosexuality. Although somewhat flamboyant, as a writer he was humane, tolerant, and intelligent.

PRINCIPAL WORKS: *Fiction*—Peter Whiffle: His Life and Works, 1922; The Blind Bow-Boy, 1923; The Tattooed Countess, 1924; Firecrackers, 1925; Nigger Heaven, 1926; Spider Boy: A Scenario for a Moving Picture, 1928; Parties: Scenes from Contemporary New York Life, n.d. *Criticism and autobiography*—Music after the Great War, 1915; Music and Bad Manners, 1916; Interpreters and Interpretations, 1917 (revised as Interpreters, 1920); The Merry-Go-Round, 1918; The Music of Spain, 1918; In the Garret, 1920; The tiger in the House, 1920; Red: Papers on Musical Subjects, 1925; Excavations: A Book of Advocacies, 1926; Fathers, 1930; Sacred and Profane Memories, 1932; Fragments from an Unwritten Autobiography, 1955; With Formality and Elegance, 1977. *As editor*—Lords of the Housetops: Thirteen Cat Tales, 1921: My Musical Life by N. Rimsky Korsakoff (in a tr. by J. A. Joffe) 1923, rev. ed. 1942; Gertrude Stein: Selected Writings, 1946; Gertrude Stein's Last Operas and Plays, 1949; Unpublished Writings of Gertrude Stein, 8 vols. 1951–1958. *Letters*—The Letters of Gertrude Stein and Carl Van Vechten; 2 vols., 1913–1946 (ed. E. Burns) 1986; The Letters of Carl Van Vechten (ed. B. Kellner) 1987. *Photographs*—The James Weldon Johnson Memorial Collection of Arts and Letters (ed. R.P. Byrd), 1933.

ABOUT: Bender, T. New York Intellect: A History of Intellectual Life in New York City from 1750 to the Beginnings of Our Own Times, 1987; Cunliffe, M. The Literature of the United States, 1954 rev. ed. 1986; Dictionary of American Biography, 1961–1965; Dynes, W.A. (ed.) Encyclopaedia of Homosexuality, 2 vols. 1990; Hughes, L. The Big Sea, 1940; Kellner, B. Van Vechten and the Irrelevant Decades, 1968; Leuders, E. Van Vechten and the Twenties, 1955; Leuders, E. Van Vechten, 1965; Padgett, P. The Dance Photography of Carl Van Vechten, 1981; Seymour-Smith, M. Macmillan Guide to Modern World Literature, 1986; Van Vechten, C. Sacred and Profane Memories, 1932; Van Vechten, C. Fragments from an Unwritten Autobiography, 1955. *Bibliography*—Cunningham, S. A Bibliography of the Writings of Carl Van Vechten, 1977; Kellner, B. A Bibliography of the Work of Carl Van Vechten, 1980. *Periodicals*—Nation May 10, 1922; August 11, 1926; New York Review of Books August 18, 1988; New York Times July 2, 1922; December 22, 1964; New York World May 6, 1922; Saturday Review of Literature August 15, 1925; Yale Review Summer 1988.

**VAN VOGT, A(LFRED) E(LTON)** (April 26, 1912–   ), Canadian-American science fiction writer, wrote: "I was born a Canadian. My origin is Dutch, my great grandfather on my father's side having settled near what is now Portland, Oregon, about 1860, although his family moved to the province of Manitoba in Canada. As a child I lived in the prairie province of Saskatchewan, and it was there that I first ran into the very curious assumption that the world around me was full of common people. This was never said in so many words. It was just understood that greatness or extra value as a human being existed only among the dead, or else it was an attribute of someone far away, whom one never met. I grew up  feeling the full weight of my insignificance, and slowly, slowly, began to build up my ego. Receiving no help from the environment, I withdrew from it into a world of imagination which was particularly illuminated by science fiction stories which I read in the British *Chum* magazine, and later in *Amazing Stories*, when it was edited by Hugo Gernsback, its founder.

"Looking back I would not exchange my countryside childhood for a city existence at that time but as I grew older, there was no place in the country to hide. The first feel of the big city streets filled what was then an undefinable need in me, to be swallowed up by bigness. I felt safer in the city, but presently this environment also got too close to me, and again I pulled back out of sight behind a solid phalanx of fiction—not only science fiction. From this comparatively secure environment, I began a creative writing activity based upon a certainty that I was a writer; that no one had ever thought to deny, they not understanding the enormous egotism of it. I didn't understand it either. But I knew I was a writer; other people simply didn't have enough data to know differently, so it was taken for granted.

"I moved innocently and unhindered along this open channel, and presently at the age of twenty sold the first short story I ever completed, a confession-type story which was purchased by the *True Story* group of magazines. I sold a few more stories of this type, and then wrote some radio plays, and then some love stories, and then became a business paper representative for western Canada, and then in January 1939 grew interested again in science fiction (after an eight-year absence from the field even as a reader). I wrote and sold a science fiction novelette, *Black Destroyer*, the first of a series which a couple of years ago I revised into a novel, *The Voyage of the Space Beagle*.

"A characteristic, much-commented on in many of my stories, has been: a man who does not know who he is goes in search of himself. The question of identity is never more than partially answered. The most interesting example of such a search is *The World of A*, where the philosophic-logic system of General Semantics, as developed by Alfred Korzybski, is presented in story form. The book has been my bestseller, it having gone to about fifteen thousand copies to date.

"At one time, my science fiction protagonists were human mutations (outstanding example: *Slan*), but I no longer consider such physical alterations necessary, being convinced that human beings need only be freed from false assumptions in order to achieve the highest goals. . . . "

———

In the 1940s and 1950s A. E. Van Vogt—with Robert A. Heinlein, Isaac Asimov, and Theodore Sturgeon—was one of the four leading writers in what some considered the "Golden Age" of American science fiction. He established his reputation among aficionados with his regular contributions to *Astounding Science Fiction*, the chief organ of the movement. Like many of his subsequent novels, his first, *Slan*, originally appeared as a series of stories in that magazine. Still his best-known and perhaps most original work, *Slan* is the story of a mutant persecuted by humans because of his superior intellectual and physical powers. Despite its important place in the annals of science, or speculative fiction, *Slan* has been condemned as much as it has been extolled. The controversy surrounding it indeed reflects the failure of the author—along with the genre itself—to achieve literary respectability. Calling Van Vogt "the first science fiction author with the courage to explore the sociological implications of the superhuman race living in and among humans," Sam Moskowitz wrote of *Slan*, "The moving and dramatic detail with which Van Vogt relates the perpetual persecutions of the slans by the 'normal' people . . . lift[s] this novel a big step above ordinary action adventure. The story is convincingly told from the viewpoint of the superman or 'slan,' which helps to give an air of believability unmatched by its predecessors." On the other hand, Robert Scholes and Eric S. Rabkin—critics more oriented towards the literary end of the spectrum—maintained that, after a vivid opening, "the novel falls apart. Young Jommy Cross wanders through buildings, caves, cities, and worlds that are so riddled with internal inconsistencies that we must either forget the past with each new episode or get lost trying to understand how this world functions. In his lust for adventure Van Vogt neglects to construct a world which will make adventures intelligible and believable."

The immediate successors to *Slan*—*The Weapon Makers, The World of A, The Voyage of the Space Beagle*—were among Van Vogt's most successful books, but the controversy continued, and was especially heated regarding *The World of A* (republished as *The World of Null-A*), a novel written expressly to illustrate the "General Semantics," a system advocating separation between the word and the object, of Count Alfred Korzybski. The superman in this story is again subject to interplanetary persecution but dies to be reborn into the higher consciousness of non-Aristotelian thought. John W. Campbell, the influential editor of *Astounding Science Fiction*, called *The World of A* "one of the truly great stories of science fiction," but in a notorious retort Damon Knight described it as "one of the worst allegedly-adult science fiction stories ever published," and said of Van Vogt generally, "his reputation rests largely on what he does not say rather than on what he says. It is his habit to introduce a monster, or a gadget, or an extraterrestrial culture, simply by naming it, without any explanation of its nature. . . . By this means, and by means of his writing style, which is discursive and hard to follow, Van Vogt also obscures his plot to such an extent that when it falls to pieces at the end . . . the event passes without remark."

Although Van Vogt brought out nine or ten novels in the 1950s, these books represented work he had published years earlier in *Astounding Science Fiction* and other magazines. In fact, he wrote almost nothing between 1950 and 1962, devoting his time instead to running the Los Angeles branch of "Dianetics," a cultish system of psychology built up by L. Ron Hubbard from a few words in Gurdjieff's *Hill and Everything*. During these years, wrote Moskowitz, "Van Vogt unflaggingly dedicated all his energies to the teaching and promotion of a 'science' that has been exposed as without foundation in a dozen or more periodicals, and which even Hubbard, its originator, has deserted for the more 'advanced concept' he terms 'Scientology.'" Van Vogt returned to writing in 1962 with *The Violent Man*, a novel about mass psychology and the psychogenesis of violence that remains his only full-scale attempt to break out of the science fiction genre. After its critical and commercial failure, he returned to the science fiction formulas that he had mastered, but he never reclaimed the popularity he enjoyed in the 1940s.

"Van Vogt is a test case" wrote Leslie Fielder in the collection *Coordinates*, "since any apology for or analysis of science fiction which fails to come to terms with his appeal and major importance, defends or defines the genre by falsifying it. . . . Any bright high school sophomore can identify all the things that are *wrong* about Van Vogt, whose clumsiness is equaled only by his stupidity. But the challenge to criticism which pretends to do justice to science fiction is to say what is *right* about him: to identify his mythopoeic power, his ability to evoke primordial images, his gift for redeeming the marvelous in a world in which technology has preempted the provinces of magic and God is dead."

Following the death of his first wife and sometime collaborator Edna Mayne Hull in 1975, Van Vogt married Lydia Brayman, a linguist with whom he shared a passion for language study. (He founded an organization called the 200 Language Club in 1974.) He won the Jules Verne Award in 1983 and has an honorary degree from Golden Gate University in San Francisco.

PRINCIPAL WORKS: *Novels*—Slan, 1946; The Weapon Makers, 1947 (reissued as One against Eternity, 1955); The Book of Ptath, 1947 (reissued as Two Hundred Million A. D., 1964); The World of A, 1948 (reissued as The World of Null-A, 1969); The Voyage of the Space Beagle, 1950 (reissued as Mission: Interplanetary, 1952); The House That Stood Still, 1950 (reissued as The Mating Cry, 1960); The Weapon Shops of Isher, 1951; The Mixed Men, 1952 (reissued as Mission to the Stars, 1955); The Universe Maker, 1953; (with E. M. Hull) Planets for Sale, 1954; The Pawns of Null-A, 1956 (reissued as The Players of Null-A, 1966); Empire of the Atom, 1957; The Mind Cage, 1957; The War against the Rull, 1959; Seige of the Unseen, 1959; The Violent Man, 1962; The Wizard of Linn, 1962; The Beast, 1963 (in U.K.: Moonbeast); Rouge Ship, 1965; (with E. M. Hull) The Winged Man, 1966; The Silkie, 1969; Quest for the Future, 1970; Children of Tomorrow, 1970; The Battle of Forever, 1971; The Darkness on Diamondia, 1972; Future Glitter, 1973 (in U.K.: Tyranopolis); The Secret Galactics, 1974 (reissued as Earth Factor X, 1976); The Man with a Thousand Names, 1975; The Anarchistic Colossus, 1977; Supermind, 1977; Renaissance, 1979; Cosmic Encounter, 1980; Computer-world, 1983 (reissued as Computer Eye, 1985); Null-A Three, 1985. *Short stories*—(with E. M. Hull) Out of the Unknown, 1948 (in U.K.: The Sea Thing and Other Stories); Masters of Time, 1950 (reissued as Earth's Last Fortress, 1960); Away and Beyond, 1952; Destination: Universe!, 1952; The Twisted Men, 1964; Monsters, 1965 (reissued as The Blal, 1976); The Far-Out Worlds of A. E. Van Vogt, 1974; More than Superhuman, 1971; M33 in Andromeda, 1971; The Book of Van Vogt, 1972 (reissued as Lost: Fifty Suns, 1980); The Best of A. E. Van Vogt, 1974; Gryb, 1976; Pendulum, 1978. *Nonfiction*—(with C. E. Cooke) The Hypnotism Handbook, 1956; The Money Personality, 1972 (reissued as Unlock Your Money Personality, 1983). *Autobiography*—Reflections of A. E. Van Vogt: The Autobiography of a Science Fiction Giant, 1975.

ABOUT: The autobiographical material quoted above was written for Twentieth Century Authors First Supplement 1955. Contemporary Authors New Revision Series 28, 1989; Dictionary of Literary Biography vol. 8 1981; Knight, D. In Search of Wonder: Essays on Modern Science Fiction, rev. ed. 1967; Moskowitz, S. Seekers of Tomorrow: Masters of Modern Science Fiction, 1966; Scholes, R. and E. S. Rabkin, Science Fiction: History, Science, Vision, 1977; Slusser, G. E. and others (ed.) Coordinates: Placing Science Fiction and Fantasy, 1983; Twentieth Century Science Fiction Writers, 3rd ed., 1991.

**VASA, MARY O'HARA ALSOP STURE-.** See O'HARA, MARY

**VAUGHAN, HILDA** (1892–November 4, 1985), Welsh novelist, was born in her ancestral family home at Builth Breconshire, Wales; she was a collateral descendant of the seventeenth-century poet Henry Vaughan. She was educated privately and was not allowed by her family to read newspapers or modern novels, to which she attributed her love for quiet and leisurely writing. Vaughan started writing during World War I while serving in a Red Cross hospital and then as organizing secretary for the Woman's Land Army. In 1922 she went to London to attend lectures at Bedford College, and there met the novelist Charles Morgan, whom she married the following year.

Vaughan's first five novels concerned the country and people she knew as a child, the part of Wales on the borders of Breconshire and Radnorshire. *The Battle to the Weak* focused on a feud between Welsh peasant farmers and the love between a man and a woman in the warring families. The *New York Times* noted that a "tensely wrought narrative brings Wales once more into fiction and introduces to American  readers a new writer of promise and achievement." Ten years later Vaughan published *The Curtain Rises*, a novel tracing a young unsophisticated Welsh girl's journey to London where she achieves some success as a playwright, only to fall in love with a worthless actor. This novel failed to impress reviewers. The *Times Literary Supplement* found that Vaughan "does not altogether lose her sense of character in this novel, nor does she abandon her habit of restraint in matters of sentiment, but the story she has chosen to tell is so little credible that she has thrown away all opportunity to reveal her talent."

In 1942, with *Fair Woman*, Vaughan attempted a different kind of novel, focusing on the character of an old Welsh harpist to recount the story of Owain, a musician who gives up his harp to take on the life of a farmer, thereby losing his wife. Vaughan drew more positive reaction in 1943 for *Pardon and Peace*, a story of Welsh lovers separated and united twenty years later. The *Saturday Review of Literature* praised the "vitality in Miss Vaughan's country people," while *New York Herald Tribune Books* declared that the "book would be worth reading if only for its minor figures and glimpses of the Welsh character. . . . And there is the countryside itself which Miss Vaughan describes with a feeling that is part of her heritage." Of her Welsh settings and characters Vaughan once said: "I know this life more intimately than any other, and I am anxious to record the old ways and types which are fast vanishing before the levelling influences of universal education, easy transportation, and wireless."

During the early years of World War II, Vaughan spent two years in the United States with her more famous husband. In addition to novels Vaughan collaborated with Laurier Lister on stage plays that ran on London's West End and later on British television.

PRINCIPAL WORKS: *Novels*—The Battle to the Weak, 1925; Here Are Lovers, 1926; The Invader: A Tale of Adventure and Passion, 1928; Her Father's House: Here Is Eleanor, Daughter of Gethin Tretower, Gentleman of the Hafod, in the County of Radnor: Wife of Evan Harris: Shepherdess, Maidservant, Exile, and Wayfarer: She Loved Her Father's House, 1930; The Soldier and the Gentlewoman, 1932; A Thing of Nought, 1934; The Curtain Rises, 1935; Harvest Home, 1936; The Fair Woman, 1942; Pardon and Peace, 1943; Iron and Gold, 1948; The Candle and the Light, 1954. *Drama*—(with L. Lister) She Was Too Young, 1938.

ABOUT: *Periodicals*—New York Herald Tribune Books July 11, 1942; February 7, 1943; New York Times February 21, 1926; Saturday Review of Literature February 20, 1943; Times (London) November 19, 1985; Times Literary Supplement July 11, 1935.

## VEBLEN, THORSTEIN (BUNDE) (July 30, 1857–August 3, 1929), American economist and social critic, was born in Cato, Wisconsin, the sixth of

the twelve children of Thomas Anderson and Kari (Bunde) Veblen, prosperous Norwegian immigrant farmers. His oldest brother, Andrew, became a professor of physics; his nephew Oscar Veblen was a noted mathematician. Like his siblings Veblen was bilingual, and he studied Old Norse in college, which explains his ability to make a translation, sometime in the 1880s, of the Icelandic Laxdaela Saga; it remained unpublished, however, until after he retired from teaching.

In 1865 the family moved to a farm in Wheeling Township, Rice County, Minnesota. Veblen attended a Norwegian Lutheran parochial school, then, like his brothers and sisters, was sent to Northfield,

Minnesota, to Carleton College Academy, preparatory to entering Carleton College. There he majored in philosophy and received his undergraduate degree in 1880. For a year after this he taught at Monona Academy, a Lutheran school in Madison, Wisconsin, before starting graduate work at Johns Hopkins University. Failing to obtain a scholarship, he left before the first semester ended and transferred to Yale University. Veblen received his Ph.D. in philosophy there in 1884 with a dissertation on "Ethical Grounds of a Doctrine of Retribution." Because of his professed agnosticism he was barred from study courses. In 1888 he married Ellen Rolfe (niece of the president of Carleton College) and settled in Staceyville, Iowa. In the course of these years he turned from philosophy to economics, and in 1891 applied to Cornell University for further study in that field.

The following year the University of Chicago was founded, and Veblen secured a fellowship in the economics department, where he taught a course in the history of socialism and assisted in editing the newly established *Journal of Political Economics*—for which he also wrote many review articles. A colleague of scholars such as Franz Boas and John Dewey, Veblen began to explore the related fields of anthropology and sociology. He was a reader in political economy from 1893 to 1896, served as an instructor from 1896 to 1900, and was then appointed an assistant professor. It was at Chicago that he started to lecture on economic factors in civilization, a course he developed throughout his academic career and for which he was best known. Veblen never really cared for teaching, though, and was far from an inspiring lecturer, lolling at a table, cheek on hand, mumbling to his class in low monotone. For this reason, and because of his notorious extra-marital affairs (his marriage was going badly), he was invited to leave the university in 1906.

While at Chicago Veblen wrote his first major work, *The Theory of the Leisure Class: An Economic Study in the Evolution of Institutions*, the book for which he is best known and which introduced the terms "conspicuous waste" and "conspicuous consumption" into the language. The work is based on his own observations of everyday life, and is an indictment of social and economic institutions of the Gilded Age, in particular the wasteful consumption that was a symbol of upper-class status. Basic to Veblen's argument here, as in all his books, is the idea that modern industrial society is characterized by a conflict between "pecuniary employment" and "industrial employment"—that is, between those who make money and those who make goods. In connection with this, Veblen discusses the way business interests "sabotage" (hold back) productivity in order to keep prices high. Many other concepts are advanced in the course of his long, complex text. According to him, humanity has evolved from a "savage state" to the "predatory society" of historic times, which in turn can be divided into a time of barbarism (as in the Middle Ages) and modern "pecuniary times." Veblen distinguishes between human instincts (which are good) and social institutions and habits (which are evil): the instinct for parenting, for "workmanship," and for "idle curiosity," as distinct from nationalism and militarism, drives that are bound up with the capitalist system. And Veblen devotes a section to the business values which have permeated such areas of American life as higher education, where "captains of erudition" run the universities.

*The Theory of the Leisure Class* is notoriously difficult to read, often ambiguous because of the idiosyncratic twist given to certain words, and because of Veblen's pervasive irony, the mark of his moral fervor. According to the social critic Max Lerner, Veblen's mordant wit was the self-defense of "a man whose sense of reality was so shattering . . . he had to . . . fashion for himself a mask of mockery and indirection." The economist John K. Galbraith, in his introduction to a recent edition of the classic, states that despite this indirection no one has looked as perceptively as Veblen at the way the pursuit of money makes people behave. The book had a modest success when it first came out, and was the subject of an admiring essay by William Dean Howells. Veblen's suggestion that American democracy was evolving an absentee leisure class with patrician aspirations to live in Europe, even marry into European aristocracy, is, Howells proposes, "by far the most dramatic social fact of our time, and if some man of creative imagination were to seize upon it, he would find in it the material of that great American novel which . . . has not yet seen the light."

Veblen's next book, *The Theory of Business Enterprise*, dealt with modern business financing and the quest of profit, with business seen as being in thrall to the predatory habits of barbaric culture. The work's difficult style is enlivened by satiric thrusts at the less than savory aspects of American industrialism—in response to which a *Nation* reviewer protested that "such a theory as is here set forth may impress the readers of sensational magazines: but it is a travesty of economics and an unjust aspersion on our business morality."

Veblen taught at Stanford University (1906–1909), but was abruptly forced to resign for the same reasons as at Chicago. His much-quoted self-defense: "What is one to do if the woman moves in on you?" failed to help. He was divorced in 1912 and in 1914 married Anne Fessenden Bradley, who died in 1920. A teaching post opened to him next at the University of Missouri in 1911. From 1914 on he wrote the majority of his books, starting with *The Instinct of Workmanship, and the State of the Industrial Arts*. This enlargement on one of the themes of his first book was considered by the author his most important work. It proclaims technology as the source of human welfare and views economic history as a cyclic battle between obsolete, "imbecile" institutions and the instinct for creativity. Most critics accepted it as a stimulating analysis of the psychology and sociology of work. *Imperial Germany and the Industrial Revolution*, published early in World War I, argued that that nation had learned modern industrial techniques from Great Britain but had combined them with

old feudal-military institutions. Although reviewers did not hesitate to recommend Veblen's admittedly cumbersome text to the general public, the U.S. postal authorities decided the book was subversive, and for a time held up delivery of copies. At the beginning of World War II some of Veblen's admirers succeeded in getting a new edition published; according to Eli Ginzberg, this book "written a quarter of a century ago . . . remained the best guide" to the new German menace (*Saturday Review of Literature*).

Veblen remained at Missouri until 1918, when he left for Washington, D. C., to serve in the Food Administration, advising on government price fixing. With the war almost over, his ideas for mobilizing the American economy went unnoticed (for example, his proposal that the government step into the place of middlemen and supply farmers with necessities directly in return for their products). Later, his plans submitted to the House Inquiry on the Peace were also turned down. Within five months he left for New York to become a member of the editorial board of the *Dial*. Among Veblen's outspoken articles (vitriol now tending to replace irony) was a series on the discrepancy between business (pecuniary interests) and industry, enlarged on in his book *The Vested Interests and the State of the Industrial Arts*. Another series discussed the way these pecuniary interests thwart technical efficiency, and urge engineers/technicians to unite and take over the economy. The latter series, which was reprinted in *The Engineers and the Price System*, inspired the short-lived Technocracy movement.

In 1919 Veblen was invited to teach at the New School for Social Research in New York; he lectured there occasionally until 1923, when his last book was published. *Absentee Ownership and Business Enterprise in Recent Times* is, according to Max Lerner, his most mature analysis of the American business system and how it controls industry.

In 1926 Veblen left New York and moved back to Cedro, near Palo Alto, where he lived in a mountain cabin with his stepdaughter, Rebecca Veblen, in relative obscurity and semi-poverty. *Essays in Our Changing Order*, posthumously edited by his friend and coworker Leon Ardzrooni, is a collection of essays written over a thirty-year period. Notable among them is "The Intellectual Pre-Eminence of Jews in Modern Europe" (published in the *Political Science Quarterly* of March 1919), dealing with the role of the outsider in society, and which Veblen scholars agree has particular autobiographical significance.

Thorstein Veblen received no formal honors for his work other than election as vice president of the Institut International de Sociologie in 1916; he had been a member since a trip to Europe in 1904. He turned down the presidency of the American Economic Association in 1925, however, declaring that it had not been offered to him when he really expected it.

Although Veblen has come to have almost cult

status as an American original and radical reformer; he was too individualistic ever to be formally allied with any political group. His suggestion that government controls were necessary to keep big business from wrecking the economy did influence New Deal reforms, if only indirectly. In the same way, while he founded no school of economic thought, he influenced the institutional school which, in opposition to abstract neoclassical economics, is concerned with how social institutions influence economic behavior. Several books popular in the 1930s reflected Veblenian ideas on the impact of technology, among them Stuart Chase's *The Economy of Abundance* and Lewis Mumford's *Technics and Civilization* (both 1934). Following Lerner's introduction to *The Portable Veblen* (1948) and the 1953 monograph by the sociologist and literary critic David Riesman (the first full-length critical study), reappraisals continued to appear. Joseph Dorfman's biographical study, *Thorstein Veblen and His America*, is still considered an indispensable source.

The last word on Veblen should go perhaps to Veblen's old colleague at Chicago, the pragmatist philosopher John Dewey: Veblen's phrases such as "the leisure class," he wrote, have been better remembered than the concepts he elaborated."

PRINCIPAL WORKS: The Theory of the Leisure Class: An Economic Study in the Evolution of Institutions, 1899 (new ed. 1912; Modern Library ed. 1934 with foreword by Stuart Chase; New American Library ed. 1953 with introd. by C. Wright Mills; 1965 repr. with add. off review by William Dean Howells; 1967 ed with introd. by Robert Lekachman; 1973 ed. with introd. by John K. Galbraith); The Theory of Business Enterprise, 1904; The Instinct of Workmanship, and the State of the Industrial Arts, 1914 (repr. 1964 with introd. by Joseph Dorfman; Imperial Germany and the Industrial Revolution, 1915; An Inquiry into the Nature of Peace and the Terms of Its Perpetuation, 1917; The Higher Learning in America: A Memorandum on the Conduct of Universities by Business Men, 1918 (repr. 1954 with introd. by David Riesman); The Place of Science in Modern Civilisation and Other Essays, 1919 (1969 ed. titled: Veblen on Marx, Race, Science and Economics . . . ); The Vested Interests and the State of the Industrial Arts, 1919 (1920 ed. titled: The Vested Interests and the Common Man); The Engineers and the Price System, 1921 (1963 ed. with new introd. by Daniel Bell); Absentee Ownership and Business Enterprise in Recent Times: The Case of America, 1923 (1967 ed. with introd. by Robert Lekachman); Essays in Our Changing Order (ed. L. Ardzrooni) 1934; What Veblen Taught: Selected Writings of Thorstein Veblen (ed. W. C. Mitchell) 1936; The Portable Veblen (ed. with introd. by Max Lerner) 1948 (new ed. 1965) (The Viking Portable Library); Thorstein Veblen selections from his work (ed. with introd. by B. Rosenberg) 1963 (Major Contributors to Social Science Ser.); Essays, Reviews, and Reports: Previously Uncollected Writings (ed. with introd., "New Light on Veblen," by Joseph Dorfman) 1973; A Veblen Treasury: From Leisure Class to War, Peace, and Capitalism (ed. R. Tilman) 1993. As translator—The Science of Finance (by G. Cohn); Science and the Workingmen (by F. J. G. Lessell) 1900; The Lacdaela Sage, tr. from the Icelandic (with introd.) 1925.

ABOUT: Arestis, P and Sawyer, M.C. (eds.) A Biographical Dictionary of Dissenting Economists, 1991; Blaug, M. Great Economists before Keynes: An Introduction to the Lives and Works of One Hundred Great Economists of the Past, 1989; Blaug, M. (ed.) Thorstein Veblen (1859-1929) 1992; Daugert, S. M. The Philosophy of Thorstein Veblen, 1950; Davis, A. K. Thorstein Veblen and the Culture of Capitalism in Goldberg, H. (ed.) American Radicals, 1957; Davis, A. K. Thorstein Veblen's Social Theory, 1980; Dente, L. A. Veblen's Theory of Social Change, 1977; Devine E. (ed.) Thinkers of the Twentieth Century: A Biographical, Bibliographical and Critical Dictionary, 1983; Dictionary of American Biography vol. 10 1936; Diggins, J. P. The Bard of Savagery: Thorstein Veblen and Modern Social Theory, 1978; Dorfman J. New Light on Veblen in Veblen, T. Essays, Reviews, and Reports: Previously Uncollected writings, 1972; Dorfman, J. Thorstein Veblen and His America, 1934, rev. ed. 1964; Dowd, D. F. Thorstein Veblen, 1964 (Great American Thinkers); Dowd, D. F. (ed.) Thorstein Veblen, a Critical Reappraisal: Lectures and Essays Commemorating the One Hundredth Anniversary of Veblen's Birth, 1977; Duffus, R. L. Innocents at Cedro: A Memoir of Thorstein Veblen and Some Others, 1972 (Reprints of Economic Classics); Galbraith, J. K. introduction to The Theory of the Leisure Class, 1994; Griffin, R. A. Thorstein Veblen, Seer of American Socialism, 1982; Hobson, J. A. Veblen, 1971; (Reprints of Economic Classics); Howells, W. D. An Opportunity for American Fiction in Literature: An International Gazette of Criticism, First Paper April 28, 1899, Second Paper May 5, 1899; International Encyclopedia of the Social Sciences Vol. 16, 1968; Lerner, M. introduction to The Portable Veblen, 1948; Madison, C. A. Critics and Crusaders: A Century of American Protest, 1959; Marshall, H. D. Great Economists, 1967; Mencken, H. L. Prejudices, ser. 1 1919; Mitchell, W. C. introduction to What Veblen Taught, 1936; Mumford, L. Thorstein Veblen in Faces of Five Decades, 1964; Qualey, C. C. (ed.) Thorstein Veblen: The Carleton College Veblen Seminar Essays, 1968; Riesman, D. Thorstein Veblen: A Critical Interpretation, 1953; (repr. Rosenberg, B. The Values of Veblen, 1956; Schneider, L. The Freudian Psychology and Veblen's Social Theory, 1948, 1974; Seckler, D. W. Thorstein Veblen and the Institutionalists: A Study in the Social Philosophy of Economics, 1975; Simich, J. L. (with R. Tilman) Thorstein Veblen: A Reference Guide, 1985; Tilman, R. Thorstein Veblen and His Critics, 1891-1963: Conservative, Liberal, and Radical Perspective, 1992; Whitman, A. (ed.) American Reformers, 1985; Who's Who in Economics: A Biographical Dictionary of Major Economists, 1700-1981, 1983; Wood, J. C. (ed.) Thorstein Veblen: Critical Assessments, 3 vols., 1993. Periodicals—American Journal of Economics and Sociology April 1984; American Quarterly Fall 1959; Antioch Review September 1947; Journal of Economic Issues December 1989, September 1993; Monthly Review: An Independent Socialist Magazine July-August 1957 (Thorstein Veblen issue); Nation July 13, 1905; New York Times August 6, 1929; Partisan Review vol. 21 1954; Saturday Review of Literature July 15, 1939; Science and Society vol. 21 1957; Social Science Quarterly December 1979; Springfield Republic June 2, 1917.

**VECHTEN, CARL VAN.** See **VAN VECHTEN, CARL**

**VEILLER, BAYARD** (January 2, 1869–June 16, 1943), American playwright, was born in Brooklyn, New York, the son of Philip Bayard Veiller, a broker and banker, and Elizabeth (Dupuy) Veiller. Bayard Veiller was educated in New York, Chicago, and Boston, and briefly attended the College of the City of New York. An avid theatergoer from an early age, he wrote his first play while still in his teens. He sent it to the theatrical manager Augustin Daly, who rejected it—but found it worthwhile to provide a detailed critique of its faults.

Veiller spent more than a decade as a newspaperman, first in New York City, and later in Chicago, Seattle, and San Francisco. In 1902 he left newspaper work to become the press agent for an actor, James K. Hackett; subsequently he served as press agent for various other actors. He became active in the production of plays, and was the first American producer to stage the dramas of W. B. Yeats. The productions of Veiller's early plays attracted little attention, and had scant success. His melodrama *Within the Law* ran for more than a year on Broadway, but Veiller hardly shared in the profits. The play had opened in Chicago, but its

lackluster reception there prompted the debt-ridden Veiller to sell his share of the royalty rights to Edgar Selwyn and others. In 1912 *Within the Law* opened at the newly-built Eltinge Theatre in New York, where it quickly became a huge popular success. Veiller wrote and staged several more plays, none successful, before having his second hit in 1916, *The Thirteenth Chair*, in which a spiritual medium unmasks a murderer during a seance. It was twice filmed by Metro-Goldwyn-Mayer, in 1929 and again in 1936. The first film version, like the stage production, starred Veiller's second wife, Margaret Wycherly.

His third and last hit, *The Trial of Mary Dugan*, a three-act court-room melodrama, appeared on the stage in 1927. Translated into Spanish, French, and Dutch, it was also filmed twice. Veiller cowrote and directed the 1929 MGM film version, which was that studio's first all-talking motion picture. Much of his later career was spent in Hollywood, where he wrote screenplays for MGM and Paramount. His autobiography, *The Fun I've Had*, is an informal recounting of his life in journalism, the theatre, and Hollywood. He was survived by his third wife, Marguerite Smith, who, under the pen name Martin Vale, collaborated with Veiller on several later plays, including his last, *Courtesan in Green*.

PRINCIPAL WORK: *Drama*—Within the Law: A Melodrama in Four Acts, 1912; The Thirteenth Chair: A Play in Three Acts, 1922; The Trial of Mary Dugan: A Melodrama of New York Life, in Three Acts, 1928; Bait for a Tiger, 1941. *Autobiography*—The Fun I've Had, 1941.

ABOUT: Current Biography 1943; Halliwell's Film Guide, 8th ed. 1991; The National Cyclopaedia of American Biography Vol. 33, 1947. *Periodicals*—New York Times June 17, 1943; Times (London) June 17, 1943.

**\*VENTURI, LIONELLO** (1885–August 14, 1961), Italian art historian and critic, wrote: "Born in Modena, studied in Rome and became Ph.D.,

1907. Traveled in Europe from Spain to Russia before 1914. Was appointed assistant director and then director of the galleries of Venice, Rome, and Urbino. At the beginning of 1915 he became professor of art history at Turin University. His lecturing there was not regular before 1918 because he participated in the war, was permanently wounded and got a silver medal of military merit. From 1918 to 1931 he built up in Turin a successful school of art historians on the following principles.

°vayn TOO ree

He realized that the method prevailing in teaching art history was unilateral and faulty. The erudition was very great, the progress in the knowledge of details was amazing, but the interpretation of a work of art as art was lacking everywhere. In art history, history had slowly annihilated art. To modify this condition of things he based his teaching on three principles: 1) art history must be identified with art criticism in order to harmonize the exposition of historical facts with esthetic judgment; 2) the history of ancient art must become a consciousness of actual taste, by judging the works of art of the past through the experience of the art in the making, the contemporary art; 3) the principles of art criticism must be drawn not from the last esthetic theory but from the knowledge of the whole history of esthetics and art criticism.

"While writing books and articles to support these principles, he was required, like all Italian professors, by the government of an oath of faithfulness to Fascism. He refused, was dismissed and left Italy to settle in Paris from 1932 to 1939 and in New York from 1939 to 1945. While in France he dedicated himself to the study of Cézanne and other French painters of the Impressionistic and Symbolistic periods, and generally of the nineteenth century. His attention in the painting of the twentieth century was focused on Rouault and Chagall.

"In America he was visiting professor at the Johns Hopkins University, Baltimore (1940), at the University of California, Berkely (1941), Mexico University, Mexico City (1942) and Ecole Libre des Hautes Etudes, New School for Social Research, New York (1943–1944).

"In 1945 he was recalled by the democratic government of Italy and appointed professor of history of modern art at Rome University."

———

Son of the renowned Italian art historian Adolfo Venturi (1856–1941), Lionello Venturi was himself a distinguished art critic and historian who gained an international reputation as author and lecturer. He is still best known, at least in the English-speaking world, for his *History of Art Criticism*, an examination of aesthetic theories from the time of the ancient Greeks to the nineteenth century. In that volume Venturi insisted, "The essential condition of the artistic judgement is to have a universal idea of art, and at the same time to recognize it in the personality of the artist to be judged." According to Venturi, the "eternal value" of a work of art does not depend on its adherence to the "rules of art," which, he noted, "have a contingent and ephemeral character." Rather, "It is the personality of the artist which impresses eternal character upon the elements of taste, the so-called 'rules of art.'"

*Art Criticism Now*, based on a series of lectures delivered at Johns Hopkins in 1941, derides the sloppy thinking and inconsistency of contemporary theory-dominated criticism, which, Venturi contended, obliterated the subjective and emotional appreciation of art. Praising it in the *New York Times* (1942), Dino Ferrari noted, "Once in a blue moon a book like the present one is published, a book which affords the reviewer both a fresh intellectual experience and an esthetic pleasure."

In a *New York Times* (1947) review of the first volume of Venturi's *Modern Painters*, Clement Greenberg wrote, "Lionello Venturi is one of the few serious and informed art critics now alive, and nothing he says on art can go unheeded." In a *Kenyon Review* notice of the same volume, Jerome Mellquist commented, "Here, in a mere nine essays on selected painters, Signor Venturi catches the soar and fire of the 19th Century. . . . Almost every page can be underlined for a quotation, for Lionello Venturi writes with the thought-gristle of some 18th Century *philosophe*." Venturi also earned widespread praise—and from properly qualified critics—for *Impressionists and Symbolists*, the second volume of *Modern Painters*, and for *Italian Painting*, a three-volume work written in collaboration with his daughter, Rosabianca Skira-Venturi.

Venturi wrote a number of critical biographies—on Piero della Francesca, Marc Chagall, and Georges Rouault—as part of the Skira publishing house's "The Taste of Our Time" series. From 1945 until his retirement in 1955, he was a professor of art history and aesthetics at the University of Rome, and took an active part in the intellectual and artistic ferment in postwar Italy. He served on the visual arts commissions of the first two postwar biennial exhibitions in Venice (1948 and 1950), and wrote numerous essays defending abstract art. As Marcia E. Vetrocq remembered, in an *Art History* essay on the post-World War II Italian art scene, "Several brief but revealing essays of the 1950s convey what would become the signature axioms of the Venturian position: nationalism produces provincialism in art, which is antithetical to aesthetic quality; individual expression and aesthetic quality flourish only in a climate free from sectarian pressure; and the new internationalism in art and its *lingua franca*, abstraction, constitute the only valid direction in contemporary art."

PRINCIPAL WORKS IN ENGLISH AND ENGLISH TRANSLATION: *Art history and art criticism*—Italian Paintings in America, 3 vols., (tr. V. Heuval and C. Marriott) 1933; History of Art Criticism (tr. C. Mariott) 1936, rev. ed. 1964; Cézanne's Art and Oeuvre: A Catalogue Raisonné, 2 vols., 1936; Botticelli, 1937; Art Criticism Now: Lectures Delivered . . . at the John Hopkins University, 1941; Paul Cézanne Water Colours, 1943; Painting and Painters: How to Look at a Picture, from Giotto to Chagall, 1945; Modern Painters: Goya, Constable, David, Ingres, Delacroix, Corot, Daumier, Courbet, 1947; Impressionists and Symbolists: Manet, Degas, Monet, Pissarro, Sisley, Renoir, Cézanne, Seurat, Gaugin, Van Gogh [and Toulouse-Lautrec,] 1950 (published as vol. 2 of Modern Painters); (with R. Skira-Venturi) Italian Painting, 3 vols., [The Creators of the Renaissance]; The Renaissance: From Caravaggio to Modigliani (tr. S. Gilbert) 1950–1952; Four Steps Toward Modern Art: Giorgione, Caravaggio, Manet, Cézanne, 1956; The Sixteenth Century, from Leonardo to El Greco (tr. S. Gilbert) 1956; (with A. Maiuri and others) Painting in Italy, from the Origins to the Thirteenth Century (tr. J. Emmons) 1959; Italian Painters of Today (tr. D. Cater) 1959; Italian Sculptors of Today (tr. D. Cater) 1960. *Biography*—Georges Rouault, 1940; Marc Chagall, 1945; Piero della Francesca: Biographical and Critical Studies (tr. J. Emmons) 1954; Chagall: Biographical and Critical Study (trs. S.J.C. Harrison and J. Emmons) 1956; Rouault: Biographical and Critical Study (tr. J. Emmons) 1959. *As edi-*

*tor*—(with S. F. Kimball) Great Paintings in America: One Hundred and One Masterpieces in Color, 1948.

ABOUT: The autobiographical material quoted above was written for Twentieth Century Authors First Supplement, 1955. *Periodicals*—Art History December 1989; Kenyon Review Spring 1948; New York Times March 28, 1942; November 9, 1947; August 16, 1961; Time (London) August 17, 1961.

**\*VERCEL, ROGER** (1894–February 26, 1957), French novelist, biographer, and essayist, was born Roger Crétin in Le Mans, the son of a career military man. His university studies in Caen were interrupted by the outbreak of World War I, during which he served as an officer in France and the Balkan Peninsula. After the war, he completed his doctorate in literature at the University of Caen; his two theses, examining the work of

the seventeenth-century playwrights Corneille and Racine, were awarded the Prix Saintour of the French Academy. He then settled in Brittany, in the coastal town of Dinan, where he taught literature at the local collège for many years.

His first novel, *Notre Père Trajan* (Our father Trajan), set in the post-World War I Balkans, appeared in 1930. Like all his subsequent literary work, both fiction and nonfiction, it was published under the pseudonym Roger Vercel. English translations of Vercel's books began appearing in the mid-1930s. The first, his novel *In Sight of Eden*, a tale of conflict among Breton cod fishermen plying their trade in the frigid waters off the coast of Greenland, was greeted with some enthusiasm, and was described as "an extremely pertinent piece of literary achievement," by *New York Times* (1934) reviewer Percy Hutchinson.

Seafaring men and, to a lesser extent, soldiers were Vercel's principal protagonists, and his novels were sometimes compared to those of Pierre Loti and Joseph Conrad. His novel *Captain Conan*, which won the Prix Goncourt in 1934, is the story of a roguish French officer serving in the Balkans in the immediate aftermath of World War I. A former merchant from a small Breton town, *Captain Conan* becomes, by the war's end, the leader of a marauding band of storm troopers. Reviewing it in the *New Statesman and Nation*, Peter Quennell wrote, "Captain Conan deserves to be read, not only as an extraordinary vivid account of life with the French army in the Balkans, but as the study of a type that . . . grows daily more difficult to understand." *Salvage* focuses on the life of a French tugboat captain in Brest, and portrays both his hazardous professional duties and his heart-rending marital problems. Critics praised the novel's stirring depiction of maritime life, but found its account of the middle-aged protagonist's domestic difficulties less convincing. As V. S. Pritchett remarked in a *Christian Science Monitor* review, "Beside the genuine *tour de force* of the storm writing, the rest of M. Vercel's story, though interesting in itself, is smaller and more rigid stuff." *Remorques*, the 1941 film version of the novel (with a screenplay by Jacques Prévert), was released in the United States as *Stormy Waters*.

*Tides of Mont St.-Michel*, one of Vercel's most popular novels in the United States, concerns neither sailors nor soldiers, but rather the unhappy marriage and spiritual yearnings of a man employed as a tour guide at the famous abbey-fortress just off the coast of Brittany. *New York Herald Tribune Books* critic Alfred Kazin gave the novel a mixed review, noting, "Vercel lacks the sharp touch, the quick feeling for the flow of human character, that can give such a novel depth and space. . . . Yet [his] work has a quality that is unusual, a loving, pulsating sense of the Mont and its human horizons."

Vercel is now remembered primarily as a writer of sea stories, and most of his novels of the 1940s and 1950s do, indeed, focus on some aspect of nautical life. *The Easter Fleet* examines life in a Breton fishing village, and *Ride Out the Storm* (a translation of his trilogy *La Fosse aux Vents*, and the last of his works to appear in English), chronicles the career of a French merchant captain in the years prior to World War I. In a *New York Herald Tribune Book Review* (1953) notice of the novel, James Hilton commended its "authentic detail," but noted, "Since M. Vercel is no Conrad, the insight is rational rather than mystical."

Much of Vercel's fiction—that which deals with soldiering and the lives of Breton fishermen—sprang from personal experience or observation. But his tales of adventure on the high seas were strictly the product of his imagination. While many reviewers praised his realistic portray of shipboard life, it is probable that realism, strictly speaking, was not Vercel's major concern; the sea, like war provided an arduous arena in which he could examine the psychological make-up of his characters, and test the limits of their heroic potential. Vercel published two nonfiction books on polar exploration—*A'lassaut des poles* (1938) and *Pole Nord* (1947)—and edited a collection of sea stories, *L'Homme devant l'océan* (1949).

PRINCIPAL WORKS IN ENGLISH TRANSLATION: *Novels*—In Sight of Eden (tr. A. Bessie) 1934 (in U.K.: Jealous Waters); Captain Conan (tr. W. Wells) 1935; Salvage (tr. W. Wells) 1936 (in U.K.: Tug-Boat); Lena (tr. W. Wells) 1937; Tides of Mont St-Michel (tr. W. Well) 1938 (in U.K.: St. Michael Puts His Foot Down); Troubled Waters (tr. W. Wells) 1940; Madman's Memory (tr. W. Wells) 1947; Northern Lights (tr. K. Woods) 1948; The Easter Fleet (tr. K. Woods) 1950; Ride Out the Storm (tr. K. Woods) 1953. *Biography*—Bertrand of Brittany: A Biography of Messire due Guesclin (tr. M. Saunders) 1934.

ABOUT: Dictionnaire des Littératures de la Langue Française, 1994; Halliwell's Film Guide, 8th ed. 1991. *Periodicals*—Christian Science Monitor July 22, 1936; New Statesman and Nation June 29, 1935; New York Herald Tribune Book Review June 14, 1953; New York Herald Tribune Books September 4, 1938; New York Times March 25, 1934; February 27, 1957; Time (London) February 27, 1957.

## "VERCORS" (pseudonyn of JEAN BRULLER)

(February 26, 1902–June 1991), French novelist, essayist, playwright, translator, and graphic artist, was born in Paris of parents both of whom had emigrated from Hungary. He had two distinct careers. One, in which he achieved success early, was as an artist and illustrator under his own name. The other was as a novelist, writing under the resistance pseudonym of "Vercors." The name

was taken from the Alpine Vercors range in which he found himself with his unit, wounded, in June 1940—it also became the name of a celebrated Resistance group, betrayed to the Nazis in 1944.

It is for his first novel, *Le Silence de la Mar* (1942; translated into English as *Put Out the Light* and as *The Silence of the Sea*), published by the clandestine Editions de Minuit (which he had co-founded with Pierre de Lescure, in occupied France, in 1941), that Vercors is most famous. Copies were dropped, by the R.A.F., all over France. *The Silence of the Sea*, which sold more than a million copies in seventeen languages, is the story of a "good" German billeted on a French family, and of the latter's silent but obdurate resistance to his claim that the Nazis mean well. Its message was that any kind of collaboration with the Nazis, even "good" ones, was ethically impossible. The translation, when it first appeared in England and America, was read widely and avidly, and curiosity as to its author reached fever pitch, with, among others, André Gide, Louis Aragon, and François Mauriac being put forward as candidates. "Its beauty, its stark simplicity, its stillness—these one cannot forget," wrote the *Christian Science Monitor*. Vercors followed it with many more novels, but, although almost all of these were translated, and fairly well received, none achieved the same kind of success.

Bruller, who was a pacifist until the outbreak of the war, first studied to be an electrical engineer at the École Alsacienne. He soon abandoned this to work as an engraver. His whimsical and blackly humorous book of colored drawings, *21 Recettes de Mort Violente* (1926, translated as *21 Delightful Ways of Committing Suicide for the Use of Persons Who are Discouraged or Disgusted With Life for Reasons Which Do Not Concern Us*), when it was published in America in 1930, was found by W. R. Brooks, writing in *Outlook*, to be "extremely clever" and "tremendously funny"; but, he added, "the effects of strangulation, immersion and decomposition are . . . rather difficult to make pictorially amusing." Bruller continued to produce artwork, almost all of it of a scathingly ironic and pacifist nature. A typical title is *Visions intimes et rassurants de la guerre* (Intimate and comforting visions of war, 1936).

After the French surrender of 1940 Bruller took on several simultaneous identities: the carpenter quietly working outside Paris was the clandestine writer Vercors, the publisher Desvignes, and the printer Drieu (a thumbed nose at the novelist Drieu La Rochelle, who was collaborating with the Nazis). His most important book, after the novel which made him so famous, is his account of those years: *La Bataille du Silence: Souvenirs de Minuit* (1967, *The Battle of Silence*). Reviewing the translation in 1969, the *Times Literary Supplement* found that Vercors's modesty prevented his narrative from "coming fully to life"—and it was critical of the "over-literal" translation by Rita Barisse, the author's second wife (from 1957). Others were less grudging: the story it told, thought H. T. Anderson in *Best Sellers*, was "at once personal, engrossing, and universal" and the translation was "admirable."

After the war Bruller took to signing his art books "J. Bruller Vercors" and his novels and political nonfiction simply "Vercors." An industrious man, he found time to invent a highly effective way of reproducing paintings, and to write several more novels and political, historical, and general works. These latter include a cookbook, a book for children, illustrations for children's classics such as Kipling, an original play, and adaptations of *Hamlet* and Sophocles's *Oedipus*. Many of these were translated by his wife. But he never, in fiction, managed to reach the heights of *The Silence of the Sea*. However, one novel has been highly commended by some critics. This is *Sylva* (1961, translated under that title), the strange tale of a fox, Sylva, who, discovered in a field by an English squire, who is having an affair with a drug addict named Dorothy—turns into a woman. The author admitted that he had made a deliberate reversal of David Garnett's theme in *Lady Into Fox*. As Dorothy Nyren wrote in the *Library Journal*, "the story counterpoints Sylva's gradual humanization with Dorothy's dehumanization"; she thought it "fascinating entertainment . . . a relatively serious study of just what humanity is." Others, such as Albert Guerard in the *New York Herald Tribune* (1962), were less convinced, finding the material "trivial": "a *conte philosophique* becomes increasingly prurient fantasy." But *Sylva* is one of the few books by Vercors, aside from *The Silence of the Sea*, that is still read and admired by critics. However, as the obituarist of the London *Times* remarked, Vercors "never sought the mantle of a great author. His wartime experiences had taught him one profound truth, that the battle against evil is never over." The verdict of the majority of critics is that *The Silence of the Sea* is not only a key text of wartime heroism but also a profound and lasting work in its own right.

PRINCIPAL WORKS IN ENGLISH TRANSLATION: *Fiction*—Put Out the Light (tr. C. Connolly) 1944 (in U.S.: The Silence of the Sea); Guiding Star (tr. E. Sutton) 1946; Three Short Novels (tr. E. Sutton, H. M. Chevalier) 1947; You Shall Know Them (tr. R. Barisse) 1953 (tr. as Borderline, 1954, and as The Murder of the Missing Link, 1958); The Insurgents (tr. R. Barisse) 1956; Freedom in December (tr. R. Barisse) 1961 (in U.S.: Paths of Love); Sylva (tr. R. Barisse) 1962; Quota (tr. R. Barisse) 1966; The Raft of the Medusa (tr. A. C. Foote) 1971. *Drama*—Zoo, or the Philanthropic Assassin (tr. J. Clancy) 1968. *Other*—21 Delightful Ways of Committing Suicide for the Use of Persons Who are Discouraged or Disgusted With Life for Reasons Which Do Not Concern Us, 1930; For the Time Being (tr. J. Griffin) 1960; The Battle of Silence (tr. R. Barisse) 1968.

ABOUT: Brown, J. W. The Silence of the Sea: A Novel of French Resistance During World War II, 1991; Columbia Dictionary of Modern European Literature, 1947 and 1980; Pearson, M. Tears of Glory: The Heroes of Vercors 1944, 1979. *Periodicals*—Christian Science Monitor April 29, 1944; Library Journal December 16, 1961; New Literary History Spring 1985; New Yorker March 9, 1946; New York Herald Tribune June 28, 1953; January 14, 1962; New York Times June 13, 1991; Outlook February 12, 1930; Partisan Review vol 14, no 4, 1947; Saturday Review June 20, 1953; Times (London) June 13, 1991; Times Literary Supplement January 9, 1969.

**VERGA, GIOVANNI** (September 2, 1840–January 27, 1922), Italian (Sicilian) novelist, short story writer, and dramatist, was born in Catania (possibly in Vixen), in Sicily, the son of Giovanni Battista Verga, a landowner, and his wife the former Caterina Di Mauro. He studied law at Catania University, and then spent four years—which he found unpleasant—in the National Guard. His father eventually agreed to buy him  out, and he was able to devote himself to writing. Because Sicily was primitive and isolated, Verga went to Florence. In 1872 he went on to Milan, where he lived until 1893. He then returned to Catania for the rest of his life.

Verga began as a journalist and conventional novelist. It was another Sicilian, his close friend Luigi Capuana (1839–1915), who first imported the ideas of French naturalism, as practiced by Zola and others, into Italian fiction; naturalism became known there as verismo. But it was Verga, with the help of Capuana and of the critic Francesco de Sanctis, who consolidated verismo—and much else.

Verga's creative life had two phases. The fiction of the first, usually referred to as his first manner, attained popularity but is of little account; it was in his mature manner that he practiced truth to nature.

The best book from his early period is the epistolary novel *Storia di una capinera* (1871, *Story of a Blackcap*), which gave him fame. This melodramatically tells of a nun driven to madness by unrequited love.

Verga, who saw the possibilities inherent in his own work, was not satisfied with it. He turned from the invention of plots about unrequited love to write of his native Sicily and of the harsh and peculiar conditions there. His reputation is based on his novellas and short stories, and on two majestic novels, *I Malavoglia* (1881, translated as *The House by the Medlar Tree*) and *Mastro-Don Gesualdo* (1888, translated under that title). These were to form parts of a massive series of five novels with the general title of I Vinti (The Conquered), which were to deal with the "flood of human progress" (as Verga ironically called it) at all levels: "a phantasmagoria," he wrote in a letter, "of life's struggle, extending from the ragpicker to the minister of state and the artist, assuming all forms from ambition to avidity of profit, and lending itself to a thousand representations of the great, grotesque play of mankind, the providential struggle guiding humanity through all appetites, high and low, to its conquest of truth." But he only managed to get two of the books written, and to begin a third (dealing with the aristocratic side): he spent the last twenty years of his life in an almost unrelieved depression.

The first of the Sicilian stories was "Nedda" about a young peasant girl who goes off to try to make money, becomes pregnant, and loses, in turn, her lover (to malaria) and her baby (by starvation): a grim study of the hardness of Sicilian life and of the attitudes of those who suffer it. Verga followed this up with *Primavera*, a collection of stories set partly in Milan but also partly in the Sicilian countryside. In *Vita dei campi* (1880, Tales of the fields) he pushed further, now going beyond French techniques. *Cavalleria rusticana* became famous when the composer Mascagni took it as a basis for his famous short opera. Later Verga adapted it himself, as a play, with which he had a great success—perhaps because Eleanora Duse starred in it in Turin, where it was first performed. But, although he was successful, too, with other plays, he had no real ear for the stage.

Work on the tales naturally led him to his first novel, *I Malavoglia* (1881), which deals with the life of fishermen. Here, in a triumph of technique, he reflected the chance nature of life by making sudden changes of scene. He went as far as any writer had done in creating an apparent "invisibility of the author." The narrator is simply an unidentified inhabitant of the pre-industrial society of Aci Trezza, which provides the setting. *Novelle rusticane* (1883, translated as *Little Novels of Sicily*) depicts a society ruled by greed, by the desire to acquire and hang on to property at all costs.

The second novel was *Mastro-Don Gesualdo*, in which a humble builder is tryies to build himself up into an aristocrat by acquiring property and marrying into the nobility. Although he succeeds financially, he also fails by always betraying his origins, so that even servants despise him. Verga was himself a conservative landowner; but he was those things because he was what was called a pessimist, even more so than the English writer who shared his year of birth, Thomas Hardy. He himself said, " I am thought of as being an artistic revolutionary, but in politics I'm irremediably old-fashioned."

From the start William Dean Howells admired him, and so, after his fashion, did D. H. Lawrence. The best introductory book about him is by Thomas Bergin; the book by Alfred Alexander is useful to the intitiated. Verga had several "scandalous" affairs, but did not marry. He was named a Senator in the Italian parliament before his death, but it was an honor that did not really much appeal to him.

PRINCIPAL WORKS IN ENGLISH TRANSLATION: The Sea Wolf and Other Stories (tr. G. Cecchetti), 1973; The House by the Medlar Tree (tr. R. Rosenthal), 1983; Mastro-Don Gesualdo (tr. G. Cecchetti), 1979; Cavalleria Rusticana and Other Tales of Sicilian Peasant Life (tr. A. Strettell) 1983; Short Sicilian Novels (tr. D. H. Lawrence), 1984 (a reprint of Lawrence's earlier Little Novels of Sicily).

ABOUT: Alexander, A. Giovanni Verga, 1972; Bergin, T. Verga, 1931; Columbia Dictionary of Modern European Literature, 1947, 1980; Cecchetti, G. Giovanni Verga, 1978; Lucente, G. L. The Narrative of Realism and Myth: Verga, Lawrence, Faulkner, Pavese, 1981; Pacifici, S. The Modern Italian Novel, 3 vols, 1967–69; Ragusa, O. Verga's Milanese Tales, 1964; Seymour-Smith, M. Guide to Modern World Literature, 1986; Woolf, D. The Art of Verga, 1977.

**VERHAEREN, ÉMILE (ADOLPHE GUSTAVE)** (May 21, 1855–November 27, 1916), Belgian poet, dramatist, and short story writer, who wrote in French, was born in the Flemish town of Saint-Amand-Lez-Puers, near Antwerp. His father, Gustave Verhaeren, a retired cloth merchant, was from Brussels; his mother was Flemish—and he himself, as the Belgian critic Robert Frickx has pointed out in the *Columbia Dictionary* (1980), was typical of "those poets of Flemish origin who dominated Belgian literature from 1880 to 1920."

Verhaeren was a sickly child who spent his earliest years dreaming on the banks of the River Scheldt, or watching the ships pass up and down it from the upstairs window of the large old house in which his parents lived. Part of this house was given over to a general store run by his mother and her sister Marie; his maternal uncle (also Gustave) ran a small adjoining coleseed-oil factory. The idea was that when the boy could "give proof of accountancy" the concern would be passed to him. He already had other ideas. However, the family initially prevailed. He tried, because only French was spoken at home, to get lessons in Flemish from a local schoolmaster; that effort was knocked on the head. His mother wanted him to become a priest, and he was sent first to the Catholic College of Saint Louis at Brussels and then to the Jesuit College of Saint Barbe at Gand. He rebelled, and became known as disruptive and awkward, a betrayer of his promise.

But then he decided, with the extreme fervor that was to distinguish him until his dying day, that he was in a state of grace. Although he later lost that kind of faith, he never really forgot the experience, just as he never ceased, for all his pantheism, to believe in God. He maintained mystical faith in the possibility of achieving a state of grace through recognition of the fact that "Il faut admirer tout s'exalter soi-même" ("one must admire everything in order to achieve exaltation").

In 1874, at nineteen, his school education completed, he persuaded his parents that he was neither for the priesthood nor the factory: he must, he insisted, read law. So he went to the university at Louvain to study it. But what he did there was only just sufficient to pass examinations; otherwise he devoted himself to drink and tobacco, to sexual exploits usual to young men, and to the writing of poetry.

When Verhaeren left Louvain with his diploma in law (1881), he got himself articled, in Brussels, to Edmond Picard (nicknamed "The Admiral"), an eminent lawyer and also editor of *L'Art Moderne*. This magazine, together with *La Jeune Belgique* (edited by Max Waller), was at the center of the newest movement in Belgian letters, itself called *La Jeune Belgique*. This was a group of young men, with the naturalistic novelist and art critic Camille Lemonnier at their head, determined to get Belgian literature accorded the recognition in Paris that it deserved.

These men of "Young Belgium," or most of them, had been brought up, like Verhaeren himself, in francophone households. They struggled to incorporate the Flemish element into a French that seemed too elegant for them.

Verhaeren read his new poems to Lemonnier, and there then appeared in Brussels, in February 1883, *Les Flamandes* (The Flemish women), in an edition of 500 copies. Verhaeren's book astonished his readers. He has "burst like an abscess," commented a polite reviewer. His parents were horrified and grieved, and the vicaire of Saint-Amand reproved him. But discerning readers recognized this new poet as distinctively Flemish. The "abscess" that took everyone by storm consisted of a blend of sexual energy, Zolaesque naturalism, deliberate excess, and, above all, an original genius for transforming both Flemish landscape itself, and the Flemish painters' representations of it, into evocative words. "Nothing," wrote Mansell-Jones, "can conceal the fact that a personality of singular vehemence had gate-crashed . . . into the devitalized coteries of the Parnasse."

Unfortunately Verhaeren's next volume, one of his least vital, was written as the result of a "rescue": the poet went home and did his best to pretend that he had returned to Catholicism. He even went on retreat to a Trappist monastery. *Les Moines* (The monks, 1886, but written for the most part in 1883) is full of artificial Parnassian verse, beautifully wrought, but dutiful and inert. Verhaeren himself admitted that he did not possess a "sufficiently Gothic brain to adore the Lord," by which he meant only that he could not stomach the pious Catholicism of his family.

His next three collections were the result of a mental collapse tantamount to madness. The "trilogy of gloom" consisted of *Les Soirs* (1887, *Evenings*), *Les Débacles* (The debâcles, 1888), and *Les Flambeaux noirs* (The black torches, 1890). In these volumes under the influence of both French symbolist poetry and the fatigued and subtle ironies of Jules Laforgue, the poet is the alternately terrified and ecstatic victim of "the Decadence." The key line here is "Les maux du coeur qu'on exaspère, on les commande" ("By tormenting the heart's anguish one may command it"). This welter of intensive adjectives, hyperbole often verging on the absurd, and whirling verbs is subdued by a sense that some intellectual self-analysis is taking place.

His great neurasthenic tryptych almost completed, Verhaeren met Marthe Massin, a teacher of drawing. Eventually (1891) he married her. Characteristically, he made his love for her into a kind

of public religion (his letters to her were published in 1937). Characteristically again, he for some time felt that he was "not a suitable candidate for marriage." Just at this time, now a leading citizen of his country, he became interested in international socialism: he visited European capitals, including London, gave support to his friend the politician Emile Vandervelde, helped to edit a socialist magazine, and lectured.

After writing a series of transitional works, Verhaeren burst upon the European scene once more. His marriage "resolved his psychological difficulties," and he contructed an edifice of "an idyllic married life," lived famously in two houses, one at Saint-Cloud and the other, smaller, at Hainaut, and became in effect a "cured poet." It was, by Verhaeren's standards, a false position. Mansell-Jones (who knew him) remarked, of one of the volumes containing the poetry of this period, that its "vision lacks intimacy": it has the air of a "deserted concentration camp."

In the new poems, written in a strongly accentuated free verse, the voice was that of a dazed, appalled countryman reacting with horror and a sort of reluctant admiration to the new great cities and the giant machines. The advances of science are revered—but revered just as falsely as Verhaeren "believed in" conventional mores. The poems of *Les Campagnes hallucinées* (The hallucinated countrysides, 1893) and *Les Villes tentaculaires* (The tentacular cities, 1895) only just fail to make a virtue of their confusion. As Verhaeren would write later, for him "Une tendresse énorme emplit l'apre savoir" ("a huge tenderness floods the harshness of science").

Verhaeren's poetry anticipated the French "unanimism" of only a few years later—the idea, embraced by Romains, Duhamel, and others, that there is a sense in which communities, from the few inhabitants of a block of flats to the masses of citizens of a large country, have an authentic voice.

Before World War I, Verhaeren wrote many love poems dedicated to his wife. These were collected in *Les Heures claires* (1898, *The Sunlit Hours*), *Les Heures d'après-midi* (1905, *Afternoon*), and *Les Heures du soir* (1911, *The Evening Hours*). The war led him into relentless propaganda activity. He and his wife were received as refugees in England in 1914, and he toured England and Wales extensively. Then, at Rouen on November 27, 1916, he slipped and was crushed by the train he was about to board to return to Paris.

Verhaeren's plays, though full of intense and sometimes exciting language, have dated. In *Les Aubes* (1898, *The Dawn*), conflicting views of rural and urban life are finally reconciled, as he accepts the energy of the city. His art and literary criticism, such as his studies of Rembrandt (1904) and Paul Verlaine (not published until 1928), remains fascinating.

PRINCIPAL WORKS IN ENGLISH TRANSLATION: *Poetry*—Poems, 1899; The Sunlit Hours (tr. F. S. Flint) 1916; Afternoon (tr. F. S. Flint) 1917; The Evening Hours (tr. F. S. Flint), 1916; Evenings (tr. J. Murphy), 1918. *Prose*—Belgium's Agony (tr. M. Sadleir) 1915. *Fiction*—Five Tales (tr. K. Wallis) 1924. *Dra*-

ma—The Dawn (tr. by A. Symons), 1898; Helen of Sparta (tr. J. Bithell), 1916; Philip II (tr. F. S. Flint) 1916; The Cloister (tr. O. Edwards) 1918.

ABOUT: Columbia Dictionary of Modern European Literature, 1947, 1980; Hellens, F. Verhaeren (in French), 1951; Mansell-Jones, P. Verhaeren, 1957; Sadleir, M. Things Past, 1945; Seymour-Smith, M. Macmillan Guide to Modern World Literature, 1986; Thum, R. H. The City: Baudelaire, Rimbaud, Verhaeren, 1984; Zweig, S. Verhaeren (tr. J. Bithell) 1970. *Periodicals*—Books Abroad Summer 1955; Modern Language Notes April 1947.

## VESTAL, STANLEY (pseudonym of WALTER STANLEY CAMPBELL)

(August 15, 1887–December 26, 1957), American college professor and writer on the American West, wrote: "

[He] was born of parents of old American stock (Massachusetts and Virginia) near Sevry, Kansas, son of Walter Mallory Vestal and Isabella Louise (Wood) Vestal. His father died soon after, and his mother became a teacher, a profession which she followed with enthusiasm for considerable portions of her life. He was educated at the public schools in Fredonia, Kansas; Guthrie, Oklahoma; and at Southwestern State Normal School, Weatherford, Oklahoma, of which his stepfather, J. R. Campbell, was first president. In 1908 he went to Oxford University, as the first Rhodes Scholar from the new state of Oklahoma. There he became a member of Merton College, and read . . . English language and literature, taking his B.A. in 1911, M.A. in 1915. During boyhood he had been led to read good literature, and had become acquainted with the Cheyenne Indians and acquired a keen interest in their ways and history. His stepfather had been one of Bancroft's men, and the history of the West was a familiar subject in the family. On returning to the states from Oxford, these interests persisted. His work was teaching: first in the Male High School, Louisville, Kentucky; later at the University of Oklahoma. When the United States entered the World War, he enlisted in the first Officers' Training Camp, Fort Logan H. Roots, and three months later, on his birthday, 1917, was commissioned a captain of field artillery. After graduating from the School of Fire (First War Class), Fort Sill, he rejoined his regiment and served until March 1919 (six months in France). He found the war a stimulating experience, but the army rather a bore.

"Back in the states, he pursued his hobbies, read widely, traveled during his summer vacations over most of the plains and Rocky Mountain states, and began to feel the inconvenience of living on a region which, though possessing a colorful past, had comparatively little literature of its own. He decided to try to create something to satisfy this craving. His first attempts were published in the *American Mercury*, the *Southwest Review*, and *Poetry*, and led to the publication of a book, *Fandango: Ballads of the Old West*. Since that time he has published twelve more books, edited three, and appeared in various magazines, his work including poetry, biography, history, juvenile and adult fiction, a murder mystery, and two textbooks. . . .

"He was at Yaddo, 1927; Fellow, Guggenheim Memorial Foundation, 1930. Member of Authors' Club (London), Association of University Professors, Phi Beta Kappa, Author's League of America."

Stanley Vestal was a rugged outdoorsman who became a leading authority on the old Southwest and its native Americans. His writings include ballads, a novel, a mystery, biography, and history, all of it factual in background. He began teaching at the University of Oklahoma in 1915 and in 1939 became director of courses in professional writing. His historically based works reflect a sympathetic view of native Americans, for which he was sometimes criticized. He was regularly praised by reviewers for his careful use of sources and his ability to place the reader directly in the scene. Less appreciated were his writing style and, in his fiction, his plotting and characterization. His books on writing, published under the name of Campbell and used in his teaching, were sometimes faulted for overemphasis on the need to publish. In the *Writer* Campbell expressed his belief that overall symmetrical form was central: "architecture is the only guarantee of success."

In the *New Republic* Allan Nevins joined other reviewers in praise of *Kit Carson*, calling it "condensed, swift and vivid . . . a character sketch of the famous scout, a study of the life of the mountain men and buffalo hunters." *Sitting Bull*, a biography stripped of the legends and falsehoods about the Sioux chieftain, was called "a splendid biography," by Stanley Walker, writing in *New York Herald Tribune Books*. Robert L. Duffus, writing in the *New York Times* (1932), said the book was "not only the story of an individual Indian, but, in a way, the whole story of the plains Indians during the middle and latter parts of the nineteenth century." Companion books on the Sioux were *New Sources of Indian History* and *Warpath*. Horace Reynolds of the *New York Times* (1939) said that in *The Old Santa Fe Trail* Vestal's "enthusiasm makes his knowledge infectious." Bernard de Voto, writing in *Weekly Book Reveiw*, called *Jim Bridges* "sketchy" and faulted its use of detail from earlier, untrustworthy, biographies. In the *San Francisco Chronicle* noted Western authority William H. Hutchinson proclaimed *Joe Meek* "the best" of Campbell's eighteen published books and praised his "reportorial sense." In the *New York Times* (1952) Reynolds reviewed *Queen of Cowtowns*, about Dodge City, which Campbell called "the wickedest little city in America"; Reynolds said it was "both a dime novel and a document in our social history." Using his real name Campbell also produced editions of such important works as Francis Parkman's *The Oregon Trail* and Lewis H. Garrard's *Wah-to-yah and the Taos Trail*.

PRINCIPAL WORKS: As *"Stanley Vestal"*—Fandango: Ballads of

the Old West, 1927; Kit Carson, the Happy Warrior of the Old West: A Biography, 1928; Happy Hunting Grounds, 1928; 'Dobe Walls: A Story of Kit Carson's Southwest, 1929; Sitting Bull, Champion of the Sioux: A Biography, 1932; Warpath: The True Story of the Fighting Sioux Told in a Biography of Chief White Bull, 1934; New Sources of Indian History, 1934; The Wine Room Murder (mystery novel) 1935; Mountain Men (novel) 1936; Revolt on the Border, 1938; The Old Santa Fe Trail, 1939; King of the Fur Traders: The Deeds and Deviltry of Pierre Esprit Radisson, 1940; Short Grass Country, 1941; Bigfoot Wallace: A Biography, 1942; The Missouri, 1945; Jim Bridges, Mountain Man: A Biography, 1947; Warpath and Council Fire: The Plains Indians' Struggle for Survival in War and in Diplomacy, 1948; Queen of Cowtowns, Dodge City, 1872–1886, 1952; Joe Meek, the Merry Mountain Man: A Biography, 1952; Book Lover's Southwest, 1955. As "Walter Stanley Campbell"—Professional Writing, 1938; Writing Magazine Fiction, 1940; Writing Nonfiction, 1944; Writing: Advice and Devices, 1950.

ABOUT: The autobiographical material quoted above was written for Twentieth Century Authors, 1942. Oxford Companion to American Literature, 1983. Periodicals—New Republic May 16, 1928; New York Herald Tribune Books October 2, 1932; New York Times October 2, 1932; September 3, 1939; February 10, 1952; December 26, 1957; Rotarian November 1940; San Francisco Chronicle June 25, 1952; Weekly Book Review October 6, 1946; Writer January 1941.

## VIAUD, JULIEN. See LOTI, PIERRE

*VIDAL, GORE (October 3, 1925– ), American novelist, playright, and essayist wrote: "I was born at the United States Military Academy, West Point, New York, where my father was instructor in aeronautics. Shortly after my birth he left the army to pioneer two national airlines and to serve as Roosevelt's Director of Air Commerce. My childhood was spent in Washington, D.C., much of the time in the house of my maternal grandfather, the blind senator, T. P. Gore, a scholarly, witty man who represented Oklahoma from statehood (1907) to 1937. He had a vast library and he was read to constantly by his family and secretaries. I was pressed into service at seven, not only as reader but as guide: I would lead him onto the floor of the Senate, on one occasion barefoot, to the delight of the Capitol guards who were quite informal in the summer days of twenty years ago.

"I graduated from the Phillips Exeter Academy, New Hampshire, in 1943, enlisting that same year in the army where I served without distinction until

1946. A number of obscure convolutions turned me into a warrant officer and, as such, I was first mate aboard an army freight-supply ship in the Aleutians. While making the dreary run from Chernowski Bay to Dutch Harbor week after week, I composed, slowly, in longhand, in a gray ledger marked Accounts, Williwaw. I was then nineteen.

"Williwaw was published after my discharge in 1946. It did not receive any dispraise which is of course a spoiling thing for a young man. The next book, rapidly written, was as well received and I

*vee DAHL

found myself hailed as one of the ornaments of a brave new generation. Wisely, I left the country for Guatemala. There, in the ruins of a monastery, I composed my third and fourth books, not leaving Central America until 1947, after a nearly fatal attack of hepatitis.

"The third novel was a wicked popular novel called The City and the Pillar. Despite some stunning bad writing, it had a rude power and honesty which has kept it alive for some years now. I was just twenty-one when I finished it and I earnestly believed that truth without artifice would prevail. The publication of this novel fortunately relieved me of the 'spokesman for his generation' label: I could now revel, if I chose, in a wild Byronism for I was every-where attacked as vicious, decadent, un-American, the author of the worst novel ever written.

"Somewhat bemused, I left the country again, traveling this time to Europe and North Africa. I was gone two years and I was happiest in Italy (the Vidals were a Venetian family who came to the United States in the 1860s). I wrote, read, thought; I met strangers and some venerable men, among them Santayana and Gide. Gradually, reluctantly, I realized that the manner of my early books was not adequate to support a vision of any but the meaner sort, and I flattered myself that I had something of curious importance to communicate. Until 1948 I wrote in what I call 'the national manner': a flat, precise realism derived from Crane and Hemingway. With The City and the Pillar I attempted to do something of my own, and failed. Not until A Search for the King and The Judgment of Paris was the voice suddenly my own, for better or worse: I was able at last to project with it the themes which most concerned me, those elusive richer variations which cannot, one might say, be whistled.

"I have been called a war writer, a Southern writer, a decadent writer. I am, I suggest, none of these. I have led a bookish life and the influences upon me are more ancient than modern. I am not one of those who see in a recently dead writer, no matter how noble, the proud shape of a final art. I have been a student of Petronius and Apuleius, Peacock and Meredith, as well as of that grand but unpopular line which amuses itself with ideas and wit, with an irreverence for whatever 'truth and verities' are currently regnant. I detest dogma. I believe it possible, mandatory, to function without absolutes: to realize simultaneously that though life is human relationships, splendid in human terms, all our games, nonetheless, are essentially irrelevant in the impersonal universe. I suspect it is this double sense which I have tried most to communicate: the 'yes' at the center of the 'no.' In art one orders reality while existing in a universe whose order, if any, is inscrutable. To convey a private small vision of this large paradox is the reason for my writing, for the main work which is just beginning, or so I like to think."

In the light of his subsequent career, Gore Vidal's judgment that he found his voice with A Search of the King and *The Judgment of Paris* must be considered premature. In fact, most critics believe that Vidal had an unusually long literary apprenticeship, ending only with *Julian* in 1964. The eight novels published before then, though "workmanlike enough," according to Gerald Clarke in the *Atlantic*, "are curiously flat and undefined, without any of the zest and bitchy vitality Vidal shows in even the most ordinary conversation." The best of them, *Williwaw* and *The City and the Pillar*, stand out as much for extra-literary as literary reasons: *Williwaw*, a taut, Hemingwayesque tale of survival and endurance at sea, for being the work of a nineteen-year-old, and *The City and the Pillar*, the story of a young man's lasting attachment to a married man with whom he had once had an affair, for dealing so openly with the subject of homosexuality.

Perhaps *The City and the Pillar* dealt *too* openly with its subject; the furor it aroused may, as Vidal maintains, have damaged his standing with the homophobic literary establishment of the time and guaranteed the harsh dismissals of his next several novels.

Whatever the literary politics involved, the five books that followed *The City and the Pillar* were critical and commercial failures, and the three pseudonymous mystery novels he wrote concurrent with them were only slightly more successful. Increasingly unable to support himself as a novelist, or at least to live in the patrician style to which he was accustomed, Vidal temporarily abandoned his estate on the Hudson River in 1954 to make a more remunerative living as a scriptwriter in Hollywood. He chose a good time to go, for television was then it its "Golden Age," and the new medium accorded an unusual degree of deference to writers like Vidal and Paddy Chayefsky. Among the many successful scripts Vidal produced in the middle 1950s, one, *Visit to a Small Planet*, was later expanded into a full-length comedy that ran for over three hundred performances on Broadway in 1957. Although Vidal regarded playwriting as a secondary activity, the success of this pointed farce concerning an extraterrestrial's bemused observations of the planet Earth was more than matched by that of *The Best Man*, a drama about presidential politics that was a hit of the 1960 Broadway season. Vidal himself wrote the screenplay for the remarkably faithful film version of 1964, but generally speaking the movies have been less hospitable to his talents than has television. Although he made a good deal of money in the late 1950s contributing to the scripts of such films as *Ben Hur*, *The Scapegoat*, and *Suddenly, Last Summer*, he has also described the process by which his carefully crafted screenplays were destroyed by megalomaniacal producers and directors.

Returning to New York in 1960, he ran for Congress on a platform that advocated massive increases in taxes for the rich and the re-financing of public education. Given the heavily Republican makeup of the district, his respectable second-place finish surprised nearly everyone.

In the next several years Vidal traveled in Europe and the Near East, wrote essays for *Esquire* and *Partisan Review*, and undertook exhaustive research for *Julian*, a novel about the fourth-century Roman emperor known for his renunciation of Christianity. *Julian* did not receive uniformly favorable reviews—no book by Vidal, one of the leading controversialists of the age, ever achieved that feat—but many critics recognized it as a significant breakthrough. In the *New York Times Book Review* (1964) Walter Allen wrote that *Julian* "brings together and dramatizes more effectively and with much greater authority than ever before preoccupations that have been present in his fiction almost from its beginnings. . . . It is the index of Vidal's achievement that he makes us understand how Christianity could appear to a learned, sophisticated, Poltinus-inspired religious pagan as a barbarous regression into the illiberal and the absurd, a return to deathworship."

Although published seventeen years later and concerning a much earlier period of the ancient world, *Creation* is usually regarded as a companion piece to *Julian*. The protagonist, Cyrus Spitama, a half-Greek, half-Persian diplomat in the court of the emperor Darius, is fictitious, but his diplomatic errands bring him into contact with the Buddha, Confucius, Pericles, Xerxes, and other great figures of the fifth century B.C. A more uneven novel than *Julian*, *Creation*, wrote Robert F. Kiernan, seems "not so much a narrative as a gallery hung with several serious portraits, a number of caricatures, and a great many genre studies, with almost all of the hangings superior to the overarching gallery itself."

Immediately after *Julian* Vidal turned to a historical subject closer to home: the American political scene from 1937 to 1952. *Washington, D.C.*, a novel that unfolds a story of backroom senatorial politics between these years, initiated the literary specialty for which Vidal is probably best known: that of historical novelist of his own country. In the series of six novels that followed, *Washington, D.C.* occupies a position in time nearest the present but functions as something of a prologue to the more ambitious and daring narratives that precede it in historical sequence. Of these, *Burr*, and *Lincoln*, which took as their subjects the myth-encrusted figures of the Founding Fathers and Abraham Lincoln, probably received the most praise. The Aaron Burr of the first book, far from being the Machiavellian traitor of legend, is seen as a disappointed pragmatist, while his rivals—Washington, Jefferson, Hamilton, and others—are seen as incompetents, hypocrites, and social climbers. Admittedly, Burr himself, in a memoir discovered by his (fictional) illegitimate son, Charlie Schuyler, does much of the seeing, and Vidal plays different historical perspectives against each other, but as Robert F. Kiernan wrote, "*Burr* is absorbing precisely because it debunks the Founding Fathers so gloriously." John Leonard, writing in the *New York Times Book Review* (1973), called *Burr* "Mr. Vidal's witty revenge on an America he doesn't like very much." It may or may not have been good history, but as Leonard added, "there aren't many writers around today who can put together sentences as craftily as Gore Vidal, who promise a story and deliver it as well, for whom wit is not a mechanical toy that explodes in the face of the reader but a feather that tickles the bare feet of the imagination. Not to read *Burr* is to cheat yourself of considerable charm, intelligence, and provocation."

Given Vidal's jaundiced view of American history, his portrait of the sixteenth president in *Lincoln* surprised many readers. Despite his emphasis on Lincoln's apparent disregard for the Constitution or the fate of the slaves, "it is a well-founded, complex, very nearly heroic portrait of Lincoln that Mr. Vidal presents in his lengthy chronicle," wrote Christopher Lehmann-Haupt in the *New York Times*. Indeed, some critics thought *Lincoln* Vidal's finest historical novel, perhaps his finest novel.

Harold Bloom observed in the *New York Review of Books*, "it was a little difficult to see just how the author of *Julian* was one with the creator of *Myra*," but to some critics the authentic Vidal is not the author of scholarly historical novels like *Julian* or *Lincoln* but the creator of outrageous satirical fantasies like *Myra Breckinridge* and *Myron*. *Myra Breckinridge*, the story of a transexual drama instructor besotted by old Hollywood movies and determined to realign the sexes, belongs to the genre that Brigid Brophy defined in the *Listener* as "the high baroque comedy of bad taste" and as such it "is a masterpiece: the funniest event since *Some Like It Hot* (and some can't recommend more hotly than that)." "The polemic of *Myra*," wrote Bloom, "remains the best embodiment of Vidal's most useful insistence as a moralist, which is that we ought to cease speaking of homosexuals and heterosexuals. There are only women and men, some of whom prefer their own sex, some the other, and some both. This is the burden of *Myra Breckinridge*, but a burden borne with lightness, wildness, abandon, joy, skill." The sequel, *Myron*, in which the irrepressible Myra does battle against her rigidly conservative, heterosexual alter-ego Myron and American culture generally, surpassed its predecessor in sheer outrageousness and struck some critics as an even better book than *Myra*. Reviewing it in the *Times Literary Supplement*, Francis Wyndham wrote, "Just as *Burr* consolidated the qualities of his earlier historical novels and made a considerable advance on them, so the basic joke established by *Myra Breckinridge* is used in *Myron* as a launching-pad for increasingly dazzling and outrageous elaborations. These twin exercises in cerebral fantasy are unlike anything else in literature, except perhaps the two *Alices* . . . *Myron* may not measure up to some purists' idea of a novel, but its originality is undeniable. So too is the hermetic shapeliness of its construction, which is elegant without being precious. It is also very funny."

To yet a third group of readers, the essential Vidal is neither the satirical fantasist nor the historical novelist but the critical essayist. As R.W.B. Lewis suggested, Vidal writes faster than most people read, and the essays on literature, politics, cinema, and sex that he has contributed over the years to the *Nation*, the *New York Review of Books*, and other publications, comprise nine full-length volumes. "It is not that Vidal's essays are better than his novels,"

wrote Gerald Clarke in the *Atlantic*. "It is rather that his essays are more consistently good and that those qualities that limit him as a novelist are precisely those that a good essayist needs: a forceful intelligence, a cool detachment, an unpretentious, graceful style, and a sense of perspective." On the other hand, Vidal's criticism has been criticized for not going very far or deep. Reviewing the collection *Homage to Daniel Shays* in the *New York Times Book Review* (1972), Roger Sales wrote that we should think of Vidal as a writer "who, in his own eloquent words, seeks to make 'the gossip of his day our day's gospel.' " It seems to me a not very lofty aim, but if one is convinced that the time is truly artless and that literature is a declining kingdom, then it may seem aim enough. It is certainly true that for those who can find the gospel of their days in their gossip, Vidal has rightfully secured an important place."

There is also the matter of Vidal's political judgment, which may be taken as the bracing warnings of an acute social critic or as the unrealistic prescriptions of an aristocratic radical utterly detached from contemporary American life. Certainly he has played the role of political gadfly and on one famous occasion on national television drew the response from the normally unflappable William F. Buckley, Jr., "Now listen, you queer. Stop calling me a crypto-Nazi or I'll sock you in your goddamn face." In 1982 he ran for office a second time, and though he lost, as expected, the nomination for Democratic Senator from California, he used the campaign to advocate the taxing of church income, the nationalization of natural resources, and other measures the public was not quite ready for.

Since the 1960s Vidal has lived primarily in Italy, sharing an apartment in Rome and a villa in Ravello with his longtime companion, Howard Austen. According to Robert F. Kiernan, "Vidal is a very private person at the same time that he is a self-confessed exhibitionist." Certainly he is one of the most famous writers in the world, even if that fame depends as much on his always-entertaining television talk show appearances as on his best-selling novels. It may be, as Kiernan speculated, that "the Vidalian persona, *con brio*, is the ultimate achievement of Vidal's art," but purely as a writer, wrote Harold Bloom, he "has the capacity to confound our expectations. Such a capacity, in so bad a time for the republic, both of letters and of politics, scarcely can be overpraised."

Vidal's manuscripts are at the University of Wisconsin, Madison.

PRINCIPAL WORKS: *Novels*—Williwaw, 1946; In a Yellow Wood, 1947; The City and the Pillar, 1948, rev. ed. 1965; The Season of Comfort, 1949; Dark Green, Bright Red, 1950; A Search for the King: A Twelfth Century Legend, 1950; The Judgment of Paris, 1952, rev. ed. 1965; Messiah, 1955, rev. ed. 1965; Julian, 1964; Washington, D.C., 1967; Myra Breckinridge, 1968; Two Sisters: A Memoir in the Form of a Novel, 1970; Burr, 1973; Myron, 1974; 1876, 1976; Kalki, 1978; Creation, 1981; Duluth, 1983; Lincoln, 1984; Empire, 1987; Hollywood, 1990; Live from Golgotha, 1992. *Mysteries*—(as "Edgar Box") Death in the Fifth Position, 1952; Death before Bedtime, 1953; Death Likes It Hot, 1954. *Short stories*—A Thirsty Evil: Seven Short Stories, 1956. *Drama*—Visit to a Small Planet and Other Television Plays, 1956; The Best Man: A Play about Politics, 1960;

Romulus: A New Comedy, 1962; Weekend: A Comedy in Two Acts, 1968; An Evening with Richard Nixon, 1972. *Criticism and essays*—Rocking the Boat, 1962; Sex, Death, and Money, 1968; Reflections on a Sinking Ship, 1969; Homage to Daniel Shays: Collected Essays, 1952–1972, 1972 (in U.K.: Collected Essays, 1952–1972); Matters of Fact and Fiction: Essays, 1973–1976, 1977; The Second American Revolution and Other Essays, 1976–1982, 1982 (in U.K.: Pink Triangle and Yellow Star and Other Essays); At Home: Essays, 1983–1987, 1988 (in U.K.: Armageddon?); The Decline and Fall of the American Empire, 1992; Screening History, 1992; United States: Essays, 1952–1992, 1993. *As editor*—Best Television Plays, 1956.

ABOUT: The autobiographical material quoted above was written for Twentieth Century Authors First Supplement, 1955. Bloom, H. (ed.) Twentieth Century American Literature: The Chelsea House Library of Literary Criticism, vol. 7 1988; Contemporary Authors New Revision Series 13, 1984; Contemporary Novelists, 5th ed., 1991; Current Biography 1983; Dick, B. F. The Apostate Angel: A Critical Study of Gore Vidal, 1974; Dictionary of Literary Biography vol. 6 1980; Kiernan, R. F. Gore Vidal, 1982; Stanton, R. J. (ed.) Views from a Window: Conversations with Gore Vidal, 1980; White, R. L. Gore Vidal, 1968. *Bibliography*—Stanton, R. J. Gore Vidal: A Primary and Secondary Bibliography, 1978. *Periodicals*—Atlantic March 1972; Listener September 26, 1968; New York Review of Books July 19, 1984; New York Times May 30, 1984; New York Times Book Review July 30, 1964; December 31, 1972; October 28, 1973; Times Literary Supplement April 11, 1975.

## "VIÉLÉ-GRIFFIN, FRANCIS" (pseudonym of EGBERT LUDOVICUS VIÉLÉ)

(May 26, 1863–November 12, 1937), American-French symbolist poet, was born in Norfolk, Virginia. His engineer father, General E. L. Viélé, a Federal military governor of Virginia during the Civil War, came from a Huguenot family who, although citizens of the United States for eight generations (the Viélés had originally emigrated in the last decade of the seventeenth century), had always preserved great pride in their French identity. In accordance with this spirit, and because his parents had just divorced, the boy Francis was taken by his mother, the former Teresa Griffin, to France in 1872.

He never returned; he wrote always in French, and became to all intents and purposes a Frenchman; yet he never renounced his American citizenship (he wrote a threnody to President Lincoln in 1908), and so could not be elected to the French Academy, which—so successful was he in his career as poet—would have liked to thus honor him. He was, however, elected a member of the Belgian Academy, which was less strict in its rules. France awarded him with the Legion of Honor in 1913.

Viélé-Griffin was educated at the Collège Stanislas, in Paris, and then at the Sorbonne, where he studied law and art history. At first he wanted to be a painter, but by the time he had reached the age of twenty-two he decided he would have more success as a poet. His first volume, *Cueille d'avril* (April gathering), influenced by the "decadence" of Jules Laforgue, but mostly by Verlaine, was published in 1886. He had met such poets as Laforgue

and Henri de Regnier early in his life, as well as Whistler and the regular frequenters of the bohemian cabaret Le Chat-Noir. Later he married Marie Louis Brocklé de Grangeneueve, a Frenchwoman, by whom he had four daughters—all of whom married Frenchmen. Of independent means, he divided his time between Paris—where he knew every poet and writer of note—and Touraine, the landscape of which figures much in what are probably his best poems.

Viélé-Griffin's early poetry, at first written in traditional forms, was slightly world-weary and exquisitely bored in tone, as befitted a young man under the influence of decadents—decadence in any case being the initial cradle of symbolism in France. He soon turned to the latter. He had already translated not only Swinburne but also his compatriot Whitman. With Henri de Regnier, Paul Adam, and Bernard Lazare, he founded the review *Entretiens politiques et litéraraires* (1890–1892). By now of strongly anarchistic leanings, he published in it both the Russian anarchist Bakunin and the young Paul Valéry, Émile Verhaeren and André Gide. He argued in its pages for a new "emancipated" versification: like other symbolists, he wanted to achieve more *fluidité* (combining the English senses of "smoothness" and "fluidity") for French verse, so that poets could introduce a sense of their own individuality. The influence of Walt Whitman upon French *vers libre* is a much disputed matter; but assuredly Viélé-Griffin was not the first French poet to employ it. But Viélé-Griffin—who certainly himself learned from Whitman—was undoubtedly a genuine pioneer, and his own poetry was remarkably successful in its use of the technique. He devoted his last years to the personal exposition and explanation of symbolism, upon which movement he eventually became the leading authority. Yet he published little after World War I. He was respected not merely by Valéry and his contemporaries, but also by younger poets such as Paul Éluard and André Breton—for whom he illuminated the way by giving them a clear sense of what the symbolist movement had meant.

His main achievement was to write verse in speech rhythms, so that his poems—however emotionally flaccid and commonplace they may seem to modern readers—did seem almost amazingly natural to their first readers. His *La Chevauchée d'Yeldis* (1894), published with other poems, is one of the first long narrative poems to be written in a genuinely free verse. If it does partake too much of the craze in the 1890s for all things medieval, it is hardly readable today; but it is still interesting as being typical of the symbolist method, and it is admirably accomplished.

There is no selection of Viélé-Griffin in English.

ABOUT: Columbia Dictionary of Modern European Literature, 1947; Kuhn, R. The Return to Reality: A Study of Viélé-Griffin, 1962; Seymour-Smith, M. Macmillan Guide to Modern World Literature, 1986.

**\*VIERECK, GEORGE SYLVESTER** (December 31, 1884–March 19, 1962), German-American novelist, poet, and polemicist, wrote: "I have been called 'the stormy petrel of American literature.' I am. My life has always been stormy. At my birth, in Munich, the shot of a late reveler landed in the bed in which I was born.

"Always ahead of my time, I arrived two months before I was expected. My mother was born in San Francisco. She was my father's first cousin. Her fa-ther, Wilhelm Viereck, a contemporary of Carl Schurz, came to the U.S. in 1849, aided by my paternal grandmother, Edwina Viereck, who was said to be the 'most beautiful actress Berlin had seen in one hundred years.' Her bust in the Royal Playhouse was destroyed in World War II by precision bombers.

"I was eleven when my father, also a stormy petrel, decided to emigrate to the U.S. At one time in his career, he was a Socialist member of the German Diet. Incarcerated with Bebel, the chief of the party, for one year, he discovered that he did not believe in 'the dictatorship of the proletariat,' and quit. I was astonished to find his picture and the exchange of his letters with Marx in the Marx-Engels Museum in Moscow. Engels . . . was a witness at the wedding of my parents in London.

"We are a literary family, breeding books like rabbits. My father, Louis Viereck, was the author of several scholarly volumes. My wife edited several educational books. Genius is hereditary in our family. My son, George Sylvester II, who fell at Anzio in defense of the U.S., published a symposium, *Before America Decides*, at Harvard. My son, Peter Viereck, historian and poet, received the Pulitzer prize for his verse.

"At the age of twelve, I wrote a theosophical essay, based, no doubt, on my reading of esoteric books. At fourteen I dashed off in a school notebook 'Eleanor, the Autobiography of a Degenerate,' in German. The book, dedicated to Emile Zola, and fortunately unpublished, now reposes in the archives of Professor Alfred Kinsey.

"My first little sheath of verse containing a baker's dozen of German poems, with a preface by Ludwig Lewisohn, created a stir. I was hailed as a 'wonder child.' When the distinguished playwright, Ludwig Fulda, came to the U.S., he carried back with him all my German verse and persuaded Goethe's publisher, Cotta, to issue the book. That was in 1906.

"My first book of English verse, out one year later, *Nineveh and Other Poems*, created a furor. I was hailed as America's poet of passion and the liberator of American poetry from the shackles of Puritanism. A conceited brat, I decided to become an American classic. The literary supplement of the *New York Times* devoted two successive front

\*VEER ek

pages to the youthful prodigy (1907). Poe, Whitman, Swinburne, Rossetti, Wilde, Lord Alfred Douglas, Heine and a now almost completely forgotten woman poet, Marie Madeleine, were my poetic progenitors.

"While I was still a college boy, my friend and advisor, James Huneker, secured a publisher for my *Game at Love and Other Plays*. These rather sophisticated dramulets were not intended for the stage. Nevertheless one of them was produced in Japan. The College of the City of New York granted me the indulgences latterly reserved only for athletes. I won my B.A. in 1906, in spite of my lamentable failure in chemistry, physics and mathematics. The president of the college, John F. Finley, procured for me a job on the editorial staff of *Current Literature*. I was associate editor of that magazine for nearly ten years. I also edited a magazine of my own, *The International*, which did spade work in introducing divers daring European authors to the American public. I was literary editor of a German-language magazine *Der Deutsche Vorkaempfer*, published by my father.

"It was always my ambition to be a living link between the country of my birth and the country of my adoption. Like two great men who gave me their confidence and their friendship, Theodore Roosevelt and Emperor Wilhelm II, I held that the future of Western civilization rested upon the cooperation of the three countries to which I owed most, the United States, England and Germany. Two World Wars thwarted my efforts and almost wrecked me.

"One week after the first World War broke out, newsstands blazoned forth my magazine, *The Fatherland*, advocating fair play for the Central Powers. It became a powerful organ of public opinion and within a few months achieved a circulation of 100,000. When the U.S. broke with Germany, it became the *American Monthly*.

"In spite of my staunch support of the American war effort, I was decried as an isolationist and a pro-German. I was boycotted by the war party. Five celebrated authors banded themselves together under the slogan, 'Never Again Viereck.' My verse was dropped from anthologies and my name from *Who's Who in America*. I was expelled from the Poetry Society of America which owed its existence largely to my efforts and from the Authors' League. I was now a poet without a license.

"My English friends, Wells, Zangwill, Chesterton, Douglas, Shaw, Le Gallienne, Frank Harris, and others remained unaffected by war hysteria. I was almost lynched but not jailed in World War I, in spite of rumors to the contrary.

"I remained in the dog house for almost ten years. It was only then that my name was restored to *Who's Who*. Much to my surprise I found myself riding on the crest of the wave. I became an interviewer de luxe for such publications as the *Saturday Evening Post*, the Hearst papers, and *Liberty*. I was advisory editor of *Liberty* for nearly ten years. With Paul Eldridge, I wrote the Wandering Jew series (1928, 1931, 1932) which proved a best seller over many years and is still being republished both in this country and in England. The German edition was burned by the Nazis in their first auto-dafé.

"I interviewed many of my greatest contemporaries, Foch, Joffre, Hindenburg, Clemenceau, Shaw, Hauptmann, Einstein, Henry Ford, Schnitzler, Freud, Hitler, Mussolini, etc. Wilhelm II, then in exile in Doorn, became my friend. I collaborated with him on many articles published under his name throughout the world. I exploited my World War experiences in a book on propaganda, *Spreading Germs of Hate*. My friendship with Freud bore fruit both in my novels and in *My Flesh and Blood, A Lyric Autobiography with Indiscreet Annotations*. My correspondence with Wilhelm II was acquired by Harvard University. Yale has added to her collection my letters from Colonel House, and microfilms of my letters from the 'Columbus of the Unconscious' are preserved in the Freud Archives in the custody of the Library of Congress.

"World War II brewed more trouble for me. I made every attempt to keep my country, America, out of the war. The atrocity stories that were beginning to seep in, seemed to me mere repetitions of similar tales with which propaganda regaled us in World War I. I had no hesitation to act as literary advisor to the German Library of Information. The world had forgotten that a great British statesman, Lloyd George, after a visit to the Fuehrer in 1936, called him 'the German George Washington.' Churchill praised him 'as a bulwark against Bolshevism.' He said in 1938 that he wished England would find a Hitler to lead her back to power if she ever were defeated in war. Is it surprising that I did not evaluate the pathological aspect of Hitler's genius? I first interviewed him in 1923 when he was still comparatively obscure, I wrote 'This man, if he lives, will make history for better or for worse.' He did both. I called him 'the overcompensation of Germany's inferiority complex.'

"Under the influence of war psychosis, I was indicted and eventually sent to prison under an obscure clause of an act of Congress that had to be rewritten after my trial to make it intelligible. After my release, G.B.S. wrote in one of his characteristic notes, 'I say, G.S.V., they have let you out after five years. You seem to have stood it with extraordinary spirit. Most martyrs are duds.' I do not claim to be a martyr. My incarceration has broadened the circle of my experience. I can well say with Terence, 'I am a man; nothing human is alien to me.' My contact with murderers, thugs, thieves, etc. on terms of complete social equality inspired my novel, *All Things Human*, published under the pen name of 'Stuart Benton' in the United States and under my own name in England. *Men Into Beasts*, recently published under my own name, candidly reflects the tensions of prison life. After my conviction I was ousted once more from *Who's Who* and most periodicals remain closed to me. Having been buried before, I calmly await my second resurrection. [Viereck went to prison for not declaring himself to be the agent of a foreign power.]

"I have been discussed in many books and periodicals too numerous to cite. I figure as Forrest Quadratt in four volumes of Upton Sinclair's 'Lanny Budd' series, and as Strathcona, a decadent poet in Sinclair's *Metropolis*, published a generation ago. In T. Everett Harre's *Behold the Woman*, I am the poet Almachus. Various writers, including John Roy Carlson, author of *Under Cover*, have found me a convenient target. I figure quite innocently in *The Great Beast*, a recent biography of Aleister Crowley, who once edited *The Internatinal* for me. Professor Tansill in *Back Door to War* deals with me in a scholarly and impartial manner."

———

Although George Sylvester Viereck's son Peter has a claim to distinction, his father, by now, is remembered for little more than the eccentric part he played in the history of American immigration from Germany. His verse was "decadent" in its style and content, and greatly reminiscent, in its personal aspects, of that of Ernest Dowson, and in its public, of Alfred Lord Tennyson. His (and Paul Eldridge's) now dated *Wandering Jew* has been kept in print by a small press interested in preserving historical documents. There is also a biography of him, *Odyssey of a Barbarian* (his own description of himself in a book published in 1910). His first poetry was in German, and *Gedichte* (Poems, 1904) was his first collection; *Nineveh* (1907) was in English.

A sensational, and at his best, shrewd journalist, Viereck believed was given to strange opinions, such as that he would have been regarded as a great poet "in any other age," and that he had modeled himself on an extraordinary triumvirate consisting of Jesus Christ, Napoleon—and Oscar Wilde. Hitler he never ceased to admire, and for many years he kept a portrait of him, "the man of dynamic power," along with that of others he worshipped: Einstein, Freud, Kaiser Wilhelm, and Joseph Goebbels. It is possible that Viereck was in fact the grandson, through his father Louis (who came to the U.S. in 1896), of Kaiser Wilhelm I, politely described as his "cousin."

Viereck was a highly readable journalist, known for his newspaper profiles of famous people. He was intrusive in his conducting of interviews, which gave his pieces shock value. His arrogance was, in part, simply facetious—but as time went by he came to believe in the claims he made for his own greatness and for the infallibility of his opinions. He was not in any serious way a traitor to his adopted country, but he had only his own arrogance to blame for his prison sentence. He had been, after all, taking the Nazis' money for spreading good news about them. Yet his book about the years he spent in prison, *Men into Beasts* (1952) is probably his best: it deals with humorous frankness sensitively" with his experiences in prison.

*My First Two Thousand Years: The Autobiography of the Wandering Jew*, which he wrote with Paul Eldridge, is written in the voice of Isaac Laquedem, who tells his story in the twentieth century under hypnosis. The narrative is supposed to be an "erotic interpretation of history"; Laquedem has experienced everything, and has triumphed in all aspects of sex—except that he has been unable to seduce Salome. This volume, for all that it impressed a few reviewers, is not likely to be revived as a neglected masterpiece, for, as the reviewer for the *Nation* wrote, its "halfpenny cynicism . . . is of the type which results from protracted adolescence. The greatest mystery of it all is that the authors, if not the book, come commended, however guardedly, by no less persons than Sigmund Freud, George Bernard Shaw, and Havelock Ellis." *My First Two Thousand Years* was burned by the cultural officers of the Third Reich.

The novels he wrote after he left prison were not successful. His wife, Margaret Edith Hein, became ashamed of him after his conviction, and left him. He spent his final years in South Hadley, Massachusetts, in the generous care of his surviving son. Although a dupe and often a fool, Viereck was not himself the kind of cruel person who is generally attracted to fascism.

PRINCIPAL WORKS: *Verse*—Nineveh, 1907; Songs of Armageddon, 1916; My Flesh and Blood, 1931. *Fiction*—The House of the Vampire, 1908; All Things Human, 1949; The Nude in the Mirror, 1949; Gloria, 1952. *Nonfiction*—Confessions of a Barbarian, 1910; The Viereck-Chesterton Debate, 1915; Roosevelt: A Study in Ambivalence, 1919; (as George Four Corners) Rejuvenation, 1923; An Empress in Exile, 1928; Glimpses of the Great, 1930; Spreading Germs of Hate, 1931; The Strangest Friendship in History: Woodrow Wilson and Col. House, 1932; The Temptation of Jonathan, 1938; Seven Against Man, 1941; Men into Beasts, 1952. *Drama*—A Game at Love, 1906; (with "Paul Eldridge")—My First Two Thousand Years, 1928.

ABOUT: The autobiographical material quoted above was written for Twentieth Century Authors First Supplement 1955. Dictionary of American Biography 1961–1965, 1981; Gertz, E. Odyssey of a Barbarian: The Biography of George Sylvester Viereck, 1976; Keller, P. States of Belonging: American Intellectuals and the First World War, 1979. *Periodicals*—Nation June 23, 1910; New York Times March 20, 1962.

## VIERECK, PETER ROBERT EDWIN (August 5, 1916– ), American political writer and poet, was born in New York City, the son of Margaret

Edith (Hein) and George Sylvester Viereck, who had gained notariety during both World War I and II for his proGerman writings. The younger Viereck did not support his father's political views. Viereck attended public schools in New York City before enrolling at the Horace Mann School for Boys, from which he graduated in 1933. In 1937 he graduated *summa cum laude* with a B.S. and a Phi Beta Kappa key from Harvard. He was also one of the seven Americans to win the Henry fellowship for study at Oxford University from 1937–1938. After Oxford he returned to Harvard, receiving his M.A. in 1939 and his Ph.D. in 1942. His time at the University was certainly rewarding: he was one of the founding editors of the *Harvard Guardian*, for which he served as a foreign correspondent during his travels in central Europe

in 1937. He also won several prizes for his literary work, including the Bowdoin Prize Medal for best prose with an essay on Romanticism, and the Garrison Prize Medal for best poetry—the first student in Harvard's history to hold both prizes simultaneously.

Viereck's first book, *Metapolitics, from the Romantics to Hitler*, was published in 1941. It was described by the *Saturday Review of Literature* as "the best account of the intellectual origins of Nazism available to the general reader" and was praised by Thomas Mann as a work of "profound historical and psychological insight." His next book, *Conservativism Revisited: The Revolt Against Revolt*, an examination of the political ideas of the Austrian statesman and extreme conservative Count Metternich recieved similar praise, being called "a penetrating, paradoxical, and highly provacative book" (Geoffrey Brunn *Saturday Review of Literature*) and "well worth the attention of all students of current politics" by Arthur Schlesinger, Jr. (*New York Times*).

Viereck's other political books, often described as "thoughtful" and "well documented" (*Kirkus*) generally fared as well with the critics as these first efforts. For example, his *Shame and Glory of the Intellectuals*, in which the author takes up the fight against totalitarianism *Unadjusted Man*, reflections on the differences between conforming to the norms of a group or organization and conservativism (as the author sees it) were generally described as a "marriage of liberal sentiment with conservative truth" (*New York Times*) and "breathless and stimulating" (*Atlantic*).

In 1949 Viereck won the Pulitzer Prize for poetry for *Terror and Decorum: Poems 1949–1950*, his first collection of poetry. It was described by Selden Rodman in the *New York Times* as "rich in experimental vigor, so full of new poetic attitudes toward civilization and its discontents, so fresh and earthy in its reanimation of the American spirit, that it seems to offer endless possibilities for development." Unfortunately, some critics felt—especially by the time of the publication of his third book of verse, *First Morning*—that Viereck had not "developed" his possibilities as a poet. Anne Fremantle writing in *Commonweal* was one of these, commenting that "Dr. Viereck is staying young too long. His 'new poems' are still full of promise; but by now, in his thirties, he should have backed them up with performance . . . . Too many of the poems are marred by Dr. Viereck's combined will to preach and to be pert, which is, frankly, a pity." The feeling was the same for Viereck's next collection, *Persimmon Tree*, and Selden Rodman, who had spoken so highly of Viereck's earlier work, stated: "I find his new book diffuse, sentimental, academic, boring, and (with the exception of one poem) disapointing" (*Saturday Review of Literature*). But the reviews, though not good, were not entirely discouraging for the poet. *Persimmon Tree*, according to the *Atlantic* "displays a more mellow mood than in his former volumes of verse. His technical virtuosity is still here . . . Gone is that vague unease . . . that haunted his earlier work."

Nearly a decade later Viereck was praised by Lewis Turco in the *Saturday Review of Literature* for the "incredible range, and abundance of techniques" that he displayed in *New and Selected Poems 1932–1967*.

During World War II Viereck served as a sergeant in Africa and Italy and was decorated with two battle stars. In 1945 he became an instructor in the U.S. Army University at Florence. In that same year he married Anya de Markov. The couple had two children, a boy and a girl, before divorcing in 1970. In 1972 Viereck married Betty Martin Falkenberg. From 1947 to 1948 he was assistant professor of history at Smith College. In 1948 Viereck went to Mount Holyoke College as associate professor of modern European and Russian history, and from 1955 as professor.

In the course of his career Viereck served as visiting lecturer at several universities and colleges, including the University of California at Berkeley and the City University of New York. As historian, political philosopher, and poet, Viereck maintained a reputation for being one of the leading spokesmen for New Conservatism. When asked by an interviewer about his relations with his father, he replied: "I disagree with him politically. But when we do have dinner together we stay away from politics. We talk about Goethe and the German poets. (Oh, why couldn't the Germans have stuck to poetry!) But to get me to attack him as a man is an impossibility. George Sylvester Viereck is my father."

PRINCIPAL WORKS: *History*—Metapolitics: From the the Romantics to Hitler, 1941 (new ed. 1982); Conservatism Revisited: the Revolt against Revolt 1815–1949, 1949 (repr. 1978); Shame and Glory of the Intellectuals: Babbit, Jr. Versus the Rediscovery of Values, 1953 (repr. 1978); The Unadjusted Man: A New Hero for Americans: Reflections on the Distinction between Conserving and Conforming, 1956 (repr. 1973); Conservatism: From John Adams to Churchill, 1956 (repr. 1978); Inner Liberty: The Stubborn Grit in the Machine, 1957; Conservatism from Burke and John Adams till 1982: A History and an Anthology, 1982. *Poetry*—Terror and Decorum: Poems 1940–1948, 1948 (repr. 1972); Strike Through the Mask: New Lyrical Poems, 1950 (repr. 1972); The First Morning: New Poems, 1952 (repr. 1972); Dream and Responsibility: The Tension between Poetry and Society, 1953 (repr. 1972); The Persimmon Tree, 1956; The Tree Witch: A Poem and a Play, 1961 (repr. 1973); New And Selected Poems, 1932–1967, 1967 (repr. 1980); Archer in the Marrow: The Applewood Cycles of 1967–1987, 1987.

ABOUT: Contemporary Authors New Revision Series Vol 47, 1995; Current Biography Yearbook, 1943; Who's Who in America 1995 vol. 2 1994. *Periodicals*—Atlantic October 1956, June 1957; Commonweal October 24, 1952; Kirkus September 1, 1949, February 1, 1953; New York Times October 23, 1949; Saturday Review of Literature October 4, 1941; October 9, 1948; October 15, 1949, October 14, 1967; Times Literary Supplement March 8, 1957.

## VIETH VON, GOLSSENAU ARNOLD FRIEDRICH. See RENN, LUDWIG

## VILLA, JOSÉ GARCÍA (August 5, 1914– ),
American poet, wrote: "Born in Manila, Philippines, of Philippine parentage. His father was a doctor and was chief of staff for General Aguinaldo in the Philippine revolution against Spain. Villa came to the United States in 1930 and attended the University of New Mexico, from which he graduat-

ed. He did post-graduate work at Columbia University. He is now a permanent resident of the United States.

"While an undergraduate at New Mexico he wrote short stories and edited a little magazine *Clay*, which published the early work of Saroyan, Caldwell, William March, David Cornel DeJong, etc. Edward J. O'Brien, the short story critic, was his first literary encourager and reprinted several of his stories in *The Best Short Stories* annuals, dedicating the 1932 volume to Villa. Scribner's later published a collections of these stories.

"Although the short story form was his first literary interest, Villa felt that later that it was not his proper métier, as he was not interested in outward events and his tendency was toward more and more concision. He therefore undertook the study of poetry seriously and from 1933 onwards he delved intesively into English and American poetry. He wrote a great deal but did not publish anything until 1942, when his book of poems *Have Come, Am Here* appeared. It recieved warm recognition and later Villa was awarded a Guggenheim fellowship and the $1,000 poetry award of the American of Arts and Letters.

"Villa has always been interested in technical experiment and in *Have Come, Am Here* he introduced a new rhyming method which he calls 'reversed consonance'. In his next book, *Volume Two*, he introduced the 'comma poems' where the comma is employed as a modulator of line movement. Both experiments are explained in notes to be found in books.

"Recently someone remarked to Villa that he found Villa's poetry 'abstract,' contrary to the general feeling for detail and particularity that characterizes most contemporary poetry. Villa comments: 'I realize now that this is true; I had not thought of my work in that light before. The reason for it must be that I am not at all interested in description or outward appearance, nor in the contemporary scene, but in *essence*. A single motive underlies all my work and defines my intention as a serious artist: The search for the metaphysical meaning of man's life in the Universe—the finding of man's selfhood and identity in the mystery of Creation. I use the term *metaphysical* to denote the ethic-philosophic force behind all essential living. The development and unification of the human personality I consider the highest achievement a man can do."

Villa's poetry was praised by many eminent writers and critics, including Edith Sitwell, Horace Gregory, Louise Bogan, Cyril Connolly, Marianne Moore, David Daiches, E.E. Cummings, Mark Van Doren, Richard Eberhart and others. Cyril Connolly made him known in Great Britain when he published, in his widely read magazine *Horizon*, Villa's strange and powerful poem "Inviting a Tiger for the Weekend." Martin Seymour-Smith commented: "He is a genuine eccentric . . . and he may have disfigured some of his poetry by over-ingenious tricks"

Villa's "reversed consonance" As in the case of a discreetly practiced syllable-count (as done by Marianne Moore in particular, and less often by Robert Graves), it can supply a poet with a set of intimate parameters, beyond the normal ones of rhyme and rhythm. Also famous were Villa's "comma poems." The poet's experimentation grew from his desire to fashion a whole, probably esoteric, system of thought. His own remark about "essence" will recall, for students of such systems, the ideas of Plato, of Boehme, and (nearer to our own times) of Rudolph Steiner, and of Gurdjieff. Villa has explained that his two technical innovations—which he never recommended for the use of other poets—were originally inspired by his study of faceted jewels. His other main interest was cubist painting.

Villa's position vis-à-vis the poetry of his native country is, again, an odd one. In the early 1930s Villa became a role-model for Filipinos who aspired to acceptance abroad; later he was represented as one who had denied his heritage. This had more to do with politics than with poetry. Leonard Casper, explained that, although Villa's interests were "peripheral to the community service traditional in the Philippines," he still received (1973) the Republic Cultural Heritage Award and was designated National Artist, with a lifelong pension.

"Villa's poems," Edith Sitwell wrote in her preface to her anthology *The American Genius*, "are of great beauty . . . His poetry springs with a wild force, straight from the poet's being, from his blood, from his spirit, as a fire breaks from wood, or as a flower grows from its soil . . . 'All absolute sensation is religious,' wrote Novalis. And this absolute sensation is known by Mr. Villa . . . this luminosity, this darkness, bears a resemblance to that in the work of Blake and of Boehme. 'Sir, there's a tower of fire in me!' cries the poet . . . and . . . 'O the brightness of my dark.'"

Marianne Moore wrote of Villa: "He is not a destroyer, his work is reverent. Final wisdom is encountered in poem after poem."

Villa and his wife were divorced in 1954; there were two sons of the marriage. In 1994 his own Bravo Press (which publishes some books in Tagalog), from which his selection from his own poetry, *Appassionata* (1979), is still available, published *Parlement of Giraffes: Poems for the World's Children*.

PRINCIPAL WORKS: *Collections*—The Portable Villa, with Critical Essays by David Daiches and Others, 1962; The Essential Villa, 1965. *Short stories*—Footnote to Youth, 1933; Selected Stories, 1962. *Poetry*—Many Voices, 1939; Have Come, Am Here, 1942; Volume Two, 1949; Selected Poems and New, 1958; Poems in Praise of Love, 1962; Poems 55: the Best Poems of Jose Garcia Villa as Chosen by Himself, 1962; Appassionata, 1979; Parlement of Giraffes: Poems for the World's Children, 1994. *As editor*—Philippine Short Stories, 1929; A Celebration of Edith Sitwell, 1946. *As doveglion*—Poems by Doveglion, 1941; A Doveglion Book of Philippine Poetry, 1962; The New Doveglion Book of Philippine Poetry, 1975.

ABOUT: The autobiographical material quoted above was written for Twentieth Century Authors First Supplement, 1955. Birney, E. The Creative Writer, 1966; Casper, L. New Writing from the Philippines, 1966; Contemporary Poets, 1985; Deutsch, B. Poetry in Our Time, 1963; Lopez, S.P. Literature and Society, 1940; Manuud, A. (ed.) Brown Heritage, 1967; Raiziss, S. The Metaphysical Passion, 1952; Seymour-Smith, M. Macmillan Guide to Modern World Literature, 1986; Sitwell, E. The American Genius, 1952; Van Doren, M. Autobiography, 1958; Villa, J.G. The Portable Villa, 1962. *Periodicals*—Melus Summer 1988; New Republic October 19, 1942; New York Herald Tribune Book Review January 6, 1950; Scholastic February 17, 1947; Sunday Times May 20, 1973; Yale Review Winter 1950.

**VILLARD, OSWALD GARRISON** (March 13, 1872–October 1, 1949), American editor, author, and reformer, was born in Wiesbaden, Germany. His German-born father, Henry Villard (originally Ferdinand Heinrich Gustav Hilgard), had arrived in the United States virtually penniless in 1853, proceeded to establish himself as a successful journalist, and eventually amassed a substantial fortune as a railroad magnate, financier, and newspaper owner. His mother, Helen Francis "Fanny" (Garrison) Villard, was the daughter of the renowned abolitionist William Lloyd Garrison. Villard revered both of his parents, and his beliefs were shaped by his father's liberal capitalism, and particularly by his mother's uncompromising sense of moral duty, which would guide him through so many crusades for pacifism and civil rights. He grew up primarily in New York City, where he attended the private Rogers Morse Preparatory School. He studied in Germany from 1884 to 1886, and, after returning to New York to complete his secondary education, enrolled in Harvard, earning a B.A. there in 1893. Despite his mediocre academic record, he returned to Harvard in 1894 as a graduate teaching assistant in history, and was awarded an M.A. in that subject in 1896.

In late 1896, having grown bored with the staid conventions of academic life, he took a ten-dollar-a-week job as a reporter with the *Philadelphia Press*, a Republican journal he later disdained as a "journalist harlot" because of its unfailing servility to advertisers and powerful interests. He left the *Press* after only six months, and in 1897 joined the editorial staff of the *New York Evening Post*, a paper his father had owned since 1881. Villard had been reluctant to work for his father, but decided to do so after a number of the *Post*'s top writers defected to another New York daily. The reform-minded Edwin L. Godkin, a man for whom Villard had enormous respect, was then editor-in-chief of the *Post*. Villard found himself swept up in the paper's crusade against the American war with Spain in Cuba and the Philippines, and was soon writing scathing editorials denouncing President William McKinley. Although pacifism would remain the defining aspect of Villard's political identity, he was, in the course of his long journalistic career, the champion of numerous other liberal causes.

In 1900, upon the death of his father, Villard inherited ownership of the *Post*. After his 1903 marriage to Julia Breckenridge Sandford of Kentucky, he became increasingly interested in the plight of Southern blacks, and in 1909 was among the founders of the National Association for the Advancement of Colored People. He was also active in the suffragist movement, and in 1911 helped to found the Men's League for Women Suffrage. He used the *Post* to espouse these and other liberal causes, but his unrelenting moral ardor sometimes made him a difficult man to work for. As he later admitted in his memoir, *Fighting Years*, "I have never been able to work happily with men or women who are incapable of hot indignation at something or other—whether small or big, whether it stirred me personally or not, if only it was *something*."

Villard was an enthusiastic supporter of the early presidency of Woodrow Wilson, and sometimes acted as the president's advisor on race relations. With the outbreak of World War I in 1914, and especially after the sinking of the Lusitania in 1915—when Villard became the *Post*'s chief Washington correspondent—most of his energy was devoted to promoting American neutrality, and he grew increasingly critical of Wilson. When American troops entered the war in 1917, Villard broke with Wilson for good. Meanwhile, the circulation of the *Post* had declined drastically, largely due to its stridently antiwar editorial policy. In 1918 Villard was forced to sell the paper to Thomas Lamont.

Villard retained ownership, however, of the *Nation*, which until that time had served as the *Post*'s weekly literary supplement. He was editor in chief of the *Nation* from 1918 to 1932, during which time he completely revamped the magazine, hiring new editors and correspondents, and significantly increasing coverage of both international and domestic political affairs. Villard himself covered the post-World War I Paris Peace Conference and the Second (or Socialist) International in Berne. Defying an Allied travel ban, he filed dispatches from inside Germany. By 1920 the *Nation* had become the most widely read liberal weekly in the United States, with a circulation exceeding that of the *New Republic*, its main competitor.

Villard published more than a dozen books, most of them during the 1920s and 1930s, the two decades when his influence and productivity were at their peak. *Some Newspapers and Newspaper-Men* is a critical examination of various metropolitan dailies. *Prophets True and False*, praised in a *Nation* (1928) review by H. L. Mencken as a book "packed with the fruits of his experience," is a collection of biographical portraits of American business and political leaders. *The German Phoenix*, published shortly after Hitler's rise to power, is a history of the Weimar Republic, and reiterates many of Villard's previous criticism of the Treaty of Versailles. His memoir, *Fighting Years*, although widely admired at the time of its appearance, was deemed a "disappointment" by biographer Michael Wreszin, who noted, "It was written at a time when

he was under great emotional strain and suffering from an overriding bitterness and despair."

Villard's later life was indeed filled with frustrations, both personal and political. He sold the *Nation* in 1935, but remained actively associated with the magazine through his weekly column "Issues and Men," which appeared from 1933 to 1940. Although Villard had always been something of a political outsider (and was scorned as a dangerous radical by many), by the late 1930s he found himself estranged even from many of his former liberal allies, largely because of his stalwart pacifism. He greeted Franklin Roosevelt's early New Deal programs with tempered optimism, but—just as he had done with Woodrow Wilson—became progressively disenchanted as Roosevelt moved the country toward involvement in World War II. In 1940, when the editors of the *Nation* endorsed military aid to Britain, Villard decided to dissociate himself from the journal, and penned a stinging final column entitled "Valedictory."

Throughout World War II, and for the rest of his life, Villard was increasingly a marginal figure. Pacifism was the subject of much of his later journalistic work, which appeared in such small liberal magazines as *Christian Century* and the *Progressive*, but was also published in *Harper's* and the *Atlantic Monthly*. While Villard never renounced the liberal causes he had espoused as a younger man, his uncompromising opposition to foreign military entanglements and to the growth of an all-powerful (and potentially warlike) state led him to make common cause with many conservatives, and he was an occasional contributor to the right-wing journal *Human Events*. His liberalism was still evident, however, in *The Disappearing Daily*, in which he decried the decline of independent daily papers, and the increasing subservience of the press to business interests. His last book, *Free Trade, Free World*, was an attack on the tariff system.

If, as *Nation* editor Max Lerner claimed, Villard was a "crusader for lost causes," he was also, as biographer D. Joy Humes insisted, "one of the few outspoken, crusading liberals of his time." In his study *Oswald Garrison Villard: Pacifist at War*, Michael Wreszin called Villard "a representative figure of his time," and noted, "One is tempted to dismiss him as a stubborn old crank. . . . And yet in the present day world of garrison states . . . Villard's vision of man's potential and his fears for the future have meaning." Villard's papers are in the Houghton Library, Harvard University.

PRINCIPAL WORKS: *History, politics, and foreign affairs*—The Early History of Wall Street: 1653–1789, 1897; Germany Embattled: An American Interpretation, 1915; Russia from a Car Window, 1929; The German Phoenix: The Story of the Republic, 1933; Our Military Chaos: The Truth about Defense, 1939; Within Germany: with an Epilogue, England at War, 1940 (in U.K.: Inside Germany); Free Trade, Free World, 1947. *Biography*—John Brown, 1800–1859: A Biography Fifty Years After, 1910; Prophets True and False, 1928; Henry Villard: A True Fairy Tale, 1931. *Journalism and press criticism*—Some Newspapers and Newspaper-Men, 1923, rev. ed. 1971; The Press Today, 1930; The Disappearing Daily: Chapters in American Newspaper Evolution, 1944. *Memoirs*—Fighting Years: Memoirs of a Liberal Editor, 1939. *As editor*—(with H. G. Villard) Lincoln on the Eve of '61: A Journalist's Story (by

H. Villard) 1941; The Early History of Transportation in Oregon (by H. Villard) 1944.

ABOUT: Contemporary Authors vol. 113 1984; Current Biography 1940; 1949; Dictionary of American Biography, Supplement 4: 1946–1950, 1974; Dictionary of Literary Biography vol. 25 1984; vol. 91 1990; Humes, D. Oswald Garrison Villard: Liberal of the 1920s, 1960; McGuire, W. and Wheeler, L. (eds.) American Social Leaders, 1993; McKerns, J. (ed.) Biographical Dictionary of American Journalism, 1989; Radosh, R. Prophets on the Right: Profiles of Conservative Critics of American Globalism, 1975; Who's Who 1949; Wreszin, M. Oswald Garrison Villard: Pacifist at War, 1965. *Periodicals—* Antioch Review Summer 1963; Nation July 25, 1928; February 14, 1959; New York Times October 2, 1949; Times (London) October 6, 1949.

## VILLARS, GABRIELLE CLAUDINE GAUTHIER-. See COLETTE

**VILLIERS, ALAN JOHN** (September 23, 1903–March 3, 1982), Australian sea writer, wrote: "Alan Villiers was born in Melbourne. Educated at state schools and at the Essendon High School, Melbourne, he went to sea at the age of fifteen as cadet in the barque *Rothesay Bay*. He sailed for five years in various square-rigged ships in the Cape Horn trade. In 1923 and 1924 he was a member of the Norwegian, Carl Anton Larsen's pioneer modern whaling expedition to the Ross Sea. After this he was employed in journalism, on the Hobart (Tasmania) *Mercury*, for three years, leaving this to return to the sea in the Finish four-masted barque *Herzogin Cecilie*. Later he served in the Finnish full-rigged ship *Grace Harwar*, and in conjunction with the Aland Islander, Captain Ruben de Cloux, bought the famous four-masted barque *Parma*. This ship he sailed successfully in the Australian grain trade for several years after 1930, winning the grain race for surviving windjammers two years in succession, in 1932 and 1933, with passages of 103 and 83 days from South Australia to the English Channel. In 1934, selling out of the *Parma*, he bought the full-rigged ship *Georg Stage* from the Danish Government at Copenhagen. Renaming her the *Joseph Conrad*, he sailed her from Ipswich, England, 60,000 miles around the world with a crew largely consisting of young cadets. This was in 1934–1936. The *Joseph Conrad* was sold to American registry at the conclusion of this voyage, and later became a schoolship for the American merchant service.

"In 1938, Alan Villiers went to Arabia to sail with the Arabs in their deep-sea dhows, in order to learn at first hand about these ancient vessels and old methods of navigation. During 1938 and 1939 he sailed in the Red Sea and down to Tanganyika and Zanzibar, afterwards spending a season pearling in the Persian Gulf. . . .

"Mr. Villiers was awarded the Portuguese Camões Prize for Literature for 1952 for his book *The Quest of the Schooner Argus*. He is a governor of the *Cutty Sark* Preservation Society, trustee of the National Maritime Museum, chairman of the Records Committee of the Society for Nautical Research and member of the Council. He is a Commander of the Portuguese Order of St. James of the Sword and holds the British Distinguished Service Cross for his work at the Normandy landings. Since the end of the war, he has commanded the sail training-ship Warspite for the Outward Bound Sea School, made a dory-fishing voyage to the Grand Banks and Greenland fishing grounds, sailed the bark Sagres. . . . "

---

The second of six children, Alan Villiers was the son of Leon Joseph Villiers, a poet, and Anastasia (Hayes) Villiers. He went to sea soon after the death of his father, and, in a writing career that spanned half a century, published more than thirty books, all of them about some aspect of nautical life. Villiers was particularly devoted to sailing in and writing about what he considered "real" ships, that is, full-rigged, wind-driven ocean-going vessels, whose widespread commercial use was already in serious decline when he embarked on his career as a seaman. His early book *Falmouth for Orders* chronicles a three-month-long clipper ship race from Australia to England. In a *New Republic* review, the sea-novelist William McFee described the book as "belonging to the highest class of marine literature," and noted that Villiers exhibited a "comparatively rare" combination of talents, being "not only an able seaman but an able writer." An able photographer, too, Villiers illustrated many of his books, including *The Sea in Ships*, *Last of the Wind Ships*, and *The Making of a Sailor*, with his own photographs.

*Sons of Sinbad*, Villiers's firsthand account of life among modern Arab merchant seamen, was reissued more than twenty-five years after its original appearance, prompting *New York Times Book Review* (1969) critic E. B. Garside to hail it as "a landmark in the literature of ships, a work even likely to last and gain status with time's passage." Villiers published several volumes in conjunction with the McGraw (later McGraw-Hill) "Oceans of the World" series: *The Coral Sea*, *Monsoon Seas*, a history of the Indian Ocean, and *Wild Ocean*, a study of the North Atlantic.

Villiers published his autobiographical *The Set of the Sails* at a time when "much of his life and achievements [were] still before him," as Keith K. Howell observed in an obituary notice in *Oceans*, a journal to which Villiers was a frequent contributor. His *Camões* Prize-winning book *The Quest for the Schooner Argus* recounts his voyage to Greenland and Newfoundland in the company of Portuguese deep-sea fisherman. In 1957 Villiers sailed the Mayflower II, a replica of the ship used by the Pilgrims in 1620, from England to Plymouth, Massachusetts. Details of that voyage are contained in *Give Me a Ship to Sail*, and in his children's book *The New Mayflower*. Villiers published a number of popular nonfiction books for juveniles, including *Stormalong*, the story of a boy's around-the-world sailing adventure, and *Joey Goes to Sea*, about a shipboard cat. He was a regular contributor to *National Geographic*, and in the 1950s and 1960s acted as the nautical consultant for such films as *Moby Dick* and *Hawaii*.

PRINCIPAL WORKS: *Sailing and nautical life*—Whaling in the Frozen South: Being the Story of the 1923–1924 Norwegian Whaling Expedition to the Antarctic, 1925; The Wind Ship, 1928; Falmouth for Orders: The Story of the Last Clipper Ship Race Around Cape Horn, 1929; By Way of Cape Horn, 1930, rev. ed. 1952; Vanished Fleets: Ships and Men of Old Van Diemen's Land, 1931 (reissued as Convict Ships and Sailors, 1936); Sea Dogs of To-Day, 1931; The Sea in Ships, the Story of a Sailing Ship's Voyage Round Cape Horn, 1932; Grain Race, 1933 (in U.K.: Voyage of the "Parma": The Great Grain Race of 1932); Last of the Wind Ships, 1934; Cruise of the Conrad: A Journal of a Voyage Round the World, Undertaken and Carried Out in the Ship Joseph Conrad, 212 Tons, in the Years 1934, 1935, and 1936 by Way of Good Hope, and the South Seas, the East Indies, and Cape Horn, 1937, rev. ed. 1952; The Making of a Sailor: The Photographic Story of Schoolships Under Sail, 1938; Sons of Sinbad: An Account of Sailing with the Arabs in Their Dhows, in the Red Sea, Around the Coasts of Arabia, and to Zanzibar and Tankganyika; Pearling in the Persian Gulf; and the Life of the Shipmasters, the Mariners and Merchants of Kuwait, 1940; The Coral Sea, 1949; The Quest for the Schooner Argus: A Voyage to the Banks and Greenland, 1951; Monsoon Seas: The Story of the Indian Ocean, 1952 (in U.K.: The Indian Ocean); The Cutty Sark: Last of a Glorious Era, 1953; The Way of a Ship, 1953; Sailing Eagle: The Story of the Coast Guard's Squarerigger, 1955; Posted Missing: The Story of Ships Lost Without a Trace in Recent Years, 1956; Pioneers of the Seven Seas, 1956; Wild Ocean: The Story of the North Atlantic and the Men Who Sailed It, 1957 (in U.K.: The Western Ocean: The Story of the North Atlantic); The Navigators and the Merchant Navy, 1957; Give Me a Ship to Sail, 1958; (with others) Men, Ships, and the Sea, 1962; The Ocean: Man's Conquest of the Sea, 1963 (in U.K.: Oceans of the World: Man's Conquest of the Sea); The Deep Sea Fishermen, 1970; The War with Cape Horn, 1971; (with H. Picard) The Bounty Ships of France: The Story of the French Cape Horn Sailing Ships, 1972; (with O. Hasslöf) Problems of Ship Management and Operation, 1870–1900, 1972; Voyaging with the Wind: An Introduction to Sailing Large Square-Rigged Ships, 1975; (with B. Bathe) The Visual Encyclopedia of Nautical Terms Under Sail, 1978. *Autobiography*—The Set of the Sails: The Story of a Cape Horn Seaman, 1949. *Biography*—Captain James Cook, 1967 (in U.K.: Captain Cook, the Seamen's Seaman: A Study of the Great Discoverer). *Juvenile*—Whalers of the Midnight Sun: A Story of Modern Whaling in the Antarctic, 1934; Stormalong: The Story of a Boy's Voyage Round the World in a Full-Rigged Ship, 1937; Joey Goes to Sea, 1939; And Not to Yield: A Story of the Outward Bound School of Adventure, 1953; Pilot Pete, 1954; The New Mayflower, 1958; The Battle of Trafalgar: Lord Nelson Sweeps the Sea, 1965. *As editor*—Great Sea Stories, 1959; Of Ships and Men, a Personal Anthology, 1962; My Favourite Sea Stories, 1972.

ABOUT: The autobiographical material quoted above was written for Twentieth Century Authors, 1942 and Twentieth Century Authors First Supplement, 1955. Contemporary Authors New Revision Series 1, 1981; Something About the Author Vol. 10, 1976; Who's Who 1982. *Periodicals*—New Republic April 24, 1929; New York Times Book Review May 8, 1949; November 9, 1969; Oceans July–August 1982.

**\*VITTORINI, ELIO** (July 23, 1908–February 14, 1966), Italian novelist, translator, critic, and cultural entrepreneur, wrote: "I was born at Sircusa, Sicily. My father was a railroad employee, and we used to live most of the time in small railway stations, with grilled windows, surrounded by desert country. In one of these stations I read the very first book that ever made a deep impression on me: *Robinson Crusoe*. I didn't have much schooling: five years of

°veet toh REE nee

primary schools, and three years at an accountants' school. At seventeen, however, after several previous attempts, I left school, and, six months afterwards, found myself working on road building. In 1927 I helped build a bridge near Udine.

"I had also started, however, to write some stories. I sent one of these to a small review: they published it. Later, I became a steady contributor to a small Florentine magazine, *Solaria*, which was published by our cooperative financial and literary efforts. There I published almost all the short stories which later on, in 1931, were collected to form my first book, *Piccola Borghesia*.

"I was then living in Florence (since 1930), having left my work with the road company, and correcting, instead, proofs at a Florentine daily, called *La Nazione*. It was then that I got to learn English: an old typographer, who had been abroad, taught me.

"In 1934 an Italian publisher printed, translated by me, a novel by D. H. Lawrence. Soon afterwards, I fell ill, with a severe lead-intoxication, and I was forced to leave my job at the paper. However, I had discovered that I could live by doing translations, and from then on, up to 1941, I made a living by translating Lawrence, Poe, Faulkner, Defoe, and many stories by Hemingway, Saroyan. These I used to publish in various papers and magazines, with short critical introductions. At that time, I also introduced several English and American poets to Italy: T. S. Eliot, W. H. Auden, Louis MacNeice.

"In 1936 I had started *In Sicily*: it was published, in installments, by a new Florentine magazine, *Letteratura*, which had taken the place of *Solaria*. I finished the book two years later, in the autumn of 1938. A first edition of 300 copies had good critical notices, but caused me no trouble. Then a commercial publisher risked a 5,000 copies' edition: it was sold out in a month: a second one, again of 5,000, went at once; but at this stage the same papers that had praised my book in their review section, started to attack it bitterly in their front page articles. In 1942 I was summoned by cable to the headquarters of the [Fascist] Party in Milan: they threatened to throw me out of the party because I had written a book; when at last, my turn to speak came up, I pointed out that I couldn't possibly be thrown out, since I wasn't a member of the party. Incredible as it may seem, they apologized, and let me go.

"The book went through six clandestine editions, and was translated into German (in Switzerland) and into French. Finally, in 1943, the party caught up with me, and I was arrested: from the windows of my cell I saw Milan burning after the bombardments. In September 1943 the prison commander set us all free again before the Germans walked in. But our files were not destroyed, and I had to go into hiding. The life we led during the German Occupation would deserve to be told: it had the same importance, for me, as that first reading of *Robinson Crusoe*. However, I came out of the fight for liberty without knowing how to pull a trigger.

"I didn't know when I went underground, and, as time passed, I got more and more ashamed of admitting my ignorance. In July 1945 I published my second novel *Uomini e No*, which I had written during the lulls of the 'Liberation' war. It was translated into French, German, and into other minor languages, but not into English, and not into Russian.

"At the beginning of 1947 my third book came out, *Il Sempione Strizza l'Occhio al Frejus* (*The Twilight of the Elephant*): there are a good many translations of this, too. In 1948 I published an older book, written in 1933–1935: *The Red Carnation*, which has been translated into more languages than any other one of my books, except *In Sicily*. In 1949 I published what, so far, is my latest novel *Le Donne di Messina*. I am rewriting this at present [1953], and no foreign translations are therefore available."

---

Elio Vittorini, one of the most influential writers in Italy in the decades after World War I, only came to the attention of English-language readers after World War II, when some of his works began to be translated. When the antifascist journal *Solaria* was closed down by the Mussolini government in 1934, one reason was its serialization of Vittorini's *The Red Carnation*, a novel about adolescent sexuality and political revolution, themes the authorities considered to work "against morals and good conduct." The plot, involving a young man who falls in love with a prostitute and who then is led into the fascist movement, depicts the considerable allure that facism had for the younger generation. The novel was not published in Italy in book form until 1948. When it appeared in an English translation in 1952, Irving Howe, reviewing it in the *New Republic*, wrote that it was "depressingly precise, perhaps even a bit more so than Vittorini intended. . . . Still, it would be absurd to blame Vittorini for having been what he was: he could not help growing up in, and being twisted by, Mussolini's Italy. We need only insist on certain standards: between a novel like this one, for all its talent, and a novel like *Bread and Wine* by Vittorini's fellow-Italian and antifascist, Ignazio Silone, there is a moral chasm." Other reviewers criticized the book for being "glib," "pretentious" and suffering from "seamy sentimentality," but several noted that it came as a disappointment after the 1949 translation of Vitorini's later-written (1938) novel *In Sicily*. The latter, with an introduction by Ernest Hemingway and a rave from Stephen Spender, was widely praised, and Robert Penn Warren called it "a remarkable, quite beautiful, and original little book." Still in print in the *Vittorini Omnibus*, it deals with the visit to his mother in Sicily by a long-absent son and is an account of a dark night of the soul and of the human rottenness that turned Italy toward fascism.

At the end of World War II, Vittorini was Italy's leading novelist-editor-critic. In 1959 he and Italo Calvino founded the avant garde journal *Il Menarò*, which during its brief life (1959–1965) published the work of writers like Jean Genêt, Maurice Blanchot, Uwë Johnson, and Roland Barthes.

While *In Sicily* is regarded as his masterpiece, other of Vittorini's fiction was translated into English and published in the United States to mixed, respectful, and occasionally enthusiastic reviews. Of *The Twilight of the Elephant* (1951), which was published in Italy in 1949, the *New York Times* said it was "Important for an understanding of the Italian scene, both social and literary," but "an artistic failure . . . particularly to American readers who need most to understand the insight it affords."

Of *The Dark and the Light*, which comprised two novellas, "Erica" and "La Garabaldina" (the English edition added a third, "Woman of the Road"), Anthony West wrote in the *New Yorker* that "La Garabaldina" was "as good as anything [the author] has ever done," but that "Erica" was "an untypical example of his work and it is too bad that its leaden weight has been tied to the flying feet of the joyous Garabaldina." Several reviewers noted similarities between Vittorini's style and Hemingway's.

*Women of Messina*, translated in 1973, was an attempt to recreate the scene of devastated postwar Sicily through the experiences of a group of men and women rebuilding their lives and village. Reviews were favorable, with Bernard Weinstein, in *Bestseller*, ranking Vittorini with "Moravia and Pavese, among the great realists of twentieth-century Italian fiction."

As a critic Vittorini's development was predictable enough. Initially he embraced the concept of "pure literature"; this was followed by a theory of "commitment" which began as "left-wing fascism," was transformed into communism, and ended as a very leftist brand of democratic socialism. His Marxism, even at its most intense, was more humane than theoretical; and his creative work, the most essential aim of which was to bring what he called "poetry" (which he discovered he could not write) into fiction, takes precedence.

In the last years before his early death, Vittorini published *Diario in public* (1957, Public diary) and *Le due tensione* (1967, The two tensions), neither so far translated. Of *Men and Not Men*, a translation of *Uomini e no* published in 1956; J. M. Potter said that it read like a bad pastiche of Hemingway and of his own *In Sicily*.

PRINCIPAL WORKS IN ENGLISH TRANSLATION: *Collections*—The Dark and the Light (tr. F. Keene) 1960 (in U.K.: Women of the Road, which edition adds B. Wall's tr. of the title story, 1961); A Vittorini Omnibus (contains In Sicily, The Twilight of the Elephant, and La Garibaldina) 1973. *Novels*—In Sicily (tr. W. David) 1949 (in U.K.: Conversation in Sicily); The Twilight of the Elephant (tr. C. Brescia) 1951 (in U.K.: tr. by E. Mosbacher as Tune for an Elephant, 1955); Women of Messina (trs. F. Keene and F. Fresnaye) 1973; The Red Carnation (tr. A. Bower) 1952; Men and Not Men (tr. S. Henry) 1986.

ABOUT: The autobiographical material quoted above was written for Twentieth Century Authors First Supplement, 1955. Columbia Dictionary of Modern European Literature, 1980;

Heiney, D. Three Italian Novelists: Moravia, Pavese, Vittorini, 1968 (part of the section of Vittorini is reprinted in Pacifici, S. ed., From Verismo to Experimentalism, 1970); Pacifici, S. A Guide to Contemporary Italian Literature, 1962; Potter, J. M. Elio Vittorini, 1979; Seymour-Smith, M. Macmillan Guide to Modern World Literature, 1956. *Periodicals*—College English 17 May 1966; Italian Quarterly I, 1958; IV, 15, 1960, 39–40, 1967; Modern Language Notes 90 1975; Nation December 3, 1939; New Republic August 4, 1953; New Yorker August 26, 1961; Wisconsin Studies in Contemporary Literature III, 1962.

**VIZETELLY, FRANK** (April 2, 1864–December 20, 1938), Anglo-American lexicographer and editor, was born in Kensington, London. His father, Henry Vizetelly, was

posted to France as a correspondent for the *Illustrated London News*, when Frank was one year old. He received his early education, in France, at Christian Brothers schools in Brittany and at the Lycée Baudard, Nogent-sur-Marne. His mother died when he was ten and he returned to England where he underwent an eye operation (his sight in one eye was always poor) and continued his schooling in Brighton (the Lansdowne School) and Eastbourne (Arnold College). By the time of his adolescence, his father had given up journalism in favor of printing, for which there was a long family tradition, and Frank went to work in the newly-established publishing firm of Vizetelly & Company. But when prosecution on charges of obscenity, for publication of works by Emile Zola, ruined the senior Vizetelly (he was imprisoned and the business went into liquidation), Frank decided to emigrate to America.

He arrived in New York in 1891 and, after a period of job-hunting, landed a position with the firm of Funk & Wagnalls, where he worked as an increasingly senior and influential editor. His first job was assisting Dr. Isaac Funk in the compilation of *A Standard Dictionary of the English Language*, and later on he took charge of the revisions which led to the *New Standard Dictionary* (1913).

Vizetelly had the journalist's hunger to communicate and ran a weekly question and answer column, called "The Lexicographer's Easy Chair," in the in-house *Literary Digest*, until the publication's demise in 1937. He was also a regular radio broadcaster. A man of wide interests, his principal concern was orthoepy, and the majority of his own titles were guides to the correct usage and pronunciation of words, an example being *Desk-Book of Twenty-Five Thousand Words Frequently Mispronounced*.

He was closely involved in the preparation of some valuable reference works, including the forty-volume *Columbia Cyclopaedia* (1897–1899), the twelve-volume *The Jewish Encyclopaedia* (1901–1906) and the small-format, twenty-five-volume *Funk & Wagnalls New Standard Encyclopaedia of Universal Knowledge* (1931).

Having become an American citizen in 1926,

Vizetelly set up home in the Bronx, New York. On his death, at the age of seventy-four, the *New York Times*, for whom he had regularly contributed, accorded him an obituary which filled two columns. He was described as a "unique international figure," and an "etymological Sherlock Holmes."

PRINCIPAL WORKS: The Preparation of Manuscripts for the Printer, 1905; A Desk-Book of Errors in English, 1906; Essentials of English Speech and Literature, 1915; A Desk-Book of Twenty-Five Thousand Words Frequently Mispronounced, 1917; The Soldiers Service Dictionary of English and French Terms, 1917; Mend Your Speech, 1920; Who? When? Where? What?, 1920; Punctuation and Capitalization, 1921; Words We Misspell in Business, 1921; A Desk-Book of Idioms and Idiomatic Phrases in English Speech and Literature, 1923; How to Use English, 1932; How to Speak Effectively, 1933; Foreign Phrases in Daily Use, 1933.

ABOUT: Dictionary of American Biography; Who Was Who in America, 1942; Who's Who 1938. *Periodicals*—New York Times December 19, 1925; December 22, 1938; Publishers Weekly December 31, 1938; Times (London) December 22, 1938.

**VOGT, ALFRED ELTON VAN.** See VAN VOGT, ALFRED ELTON

**VOLLMER, LULA** (1898–May 2, 1955), American dramatist, scriptwriter, and short story writer, was born in Keyser, near Southern Pines, North Carolina, the daughter of an itinerant lumberjack. From the age of eight, she was sent to boarding school and, in her teenage years at the Normal Collegiate Institute, a strict religious school (later Asheville College), began to write one-act plays for performance by her friends. She was eighteen, and on a family holiday in New Orleans, before she was taken to the professional theater for the first time. Afterwards she resolved to spend the rest of her life writing plays.

On the strength of a few hundred dollars saved from a brief spell as a local reporter, she moved to New York. There she wrote *Sun-up*—a melodramatic three-act play—in the space of a week, but had to return home after a year, her money gone, and the play not taken up. She was supported and encouraged by her mother to persevere and, returning to New York, where she worked in the box office of the Theater Guild, she wrote new

plays and at the same time continued submitting *Sun-up* to producers. It was eventually performed at the Provincetown Theatre in 1923, before having a run on Broadway. On the strength of admiring reviews the play was eventually produced in Chicago, London and Amsterdam. Royalties amounting to more than $40,000 were given by Vollmer as a donation towards an educational initiative amongst the hillbilly communities she knew so well.

Other plays—including *The Shame Woman*, *The Dunce Boy* and *Trigger*—were produced, but she never had a stage success to match that of *Sun-up*. In the thirties she wrote serials for radio, broadcast by the NBC. These included *Moonshine and Honeysuckle* (a stage version was produced at the Hollis Street Theatre, Boston) and *Grits and Gravy*. Her main activity in her last years was writing short stories for publication in the *Saturday Evening Post* and *Collier's*.

PRINCIPAL WORKS: The Shame Woman, 1923; Sun-up, 1923; The Dunce Boy, 1925; Moonshine and Honeysuckle, 1933; In a Nutshell, 1937; The Hill Between, 1938; Dearly Beloved, 1946 (rewritten as She Put Out to Go).

ABOUT: Boardman, G. The Oxford Companion to American Theatre, 1922. *Periodical*—New York Times May 3, 1955.

## VON HAGEN, VICTOR WOLFGANG (February 29, 1908–    ), American naturalist, biographer, and explorer, wrote: "I was born in St. Louis,

Missouri, descendant of noble German émigrés who came to America and St. Louis in 1844. My father being a paper-chemist with a papermill I was brought up in a paper-world, which influence was to provide me with the stimulus for my second expedition—a paper search in Mexico for primitive paper-making and eventually my most important book (*The Aztec and Maya Papermakers*, 1943). After an education, mostly between literature and science, between the active life of an explorer and the contemplative life of a writer, I read widely and voraciously. But my second expedition—this time to Mexico (1931–1933) at the age of twenty-three—and my research into the origins and technics of primitive Mexican paper-making gave me the direction I needed, and henceforth I devoted all my explorations and all my books and articles to the subject of the Americas. An expedition to Ecuador and the Galapagos Islands (1934–1936) gave me the material for my first book. *Off With Their Heads* (1937) dealt with the headhunters; it was supposed to be worldly and ironic; it apparently was neither for one critic said of it 'There is no substitute for good writing.'

"The need for craftsmanship in writing now assailed me and on my fourth expedition, this time to capture in Honduras (1937–1938) the legendary Quetzal Bird, I availed myself of the critics; and did a little better on the new books. But still I was writing panoramic travel books with an overlay of science. So it was that my *South America Called Them* (1945), a biography of four famous naturalist-explorers of South America, opened up the world that I wanted. I had found, at last, the large canvas that I needed to bridge the conflict of my own world: literature and science. Through my explorations of the Americas from Mexico to Chile I would cover all the historical ground of the explorer-naturalists and I would recast their own experiences and discoveries and so do a new history, a different history of the Americas. This I am now doing. Of the projected eight volumes, three have been published and a fourth, the life of the American explorer-archeologist E. G. Squier (with

the aid of a Guggenheim grant), is about ready. The other four are in various stages of completion. But I am happily thrown off occasionally from this by such as the intrusion of Manuela Saenz, the fiery mistress of Simon Bolívar, of whom I did a biography as *The Four Seasons of Manuela*; and I am going nicely astray by translating and editing the memoirs of J. B. Boussingault, a now little-known but fascinating nineteenth century chemist-explorer in South America. In the main whoever sets foot in the Americas and represents the *zeitgeist* becomes grist for my literary mill. In the main I seem to lean toward men of action rather than men of contemplation and that is why I have not written the biography of William Prescott—as I should.

"The adventure of and within the Americas; the impression that this continent left on the myriad of travelers, explorers, scientists; the books that came out of this and which shaped our American history ( I use America in its full continental sense), is the fundamental animating theme of my interests—my published books and my projected books. I dare say it will keep me occupied for a little while. Since I cannot yet be said to write literature it would be a mis-use of the term to speak of my 'literary influences'; influences however have been many: irony from the French, seriousness from the German, stimulation from the Spanish, and as would be natural, direction from personal friendships. A long friendship (only through correspondence) with George Santayana from 1930 until his death led me to a broad reading in philosophy much helped by his suggestions; a personal friendship with Van Wyck Brooks—in whose house I briefly lived— brought about another change of interest and through his urging the authoring of two books in which there was much about the North American scene and which forced me to read deeply into epochs I knew only dimly.

"I am now (1953–1955) leading an expedition in Peru for the American Geographical Society in an attempt to rediscover the Inca Highways, and that should keep me out of publishers' circles long enough not to hear them say 'You publish too much.'"

* * *

The *Saturday Review's* Carleton Beals was one critic who would not have accused Victor Von Hagen of publishing too much. In describing the explorer's publishing history Beals wrote: "his books are technical, for he is a geographer and naturalist with a wide knowledge of anthropology and archaeology, but all are careful, honest books, mostly well written and interesting. He emerges as our best scholar and best writer in the field he has chosen."

Dr. Von Hagen was known for combining scientific fact with first-person accounts of journeys to exotic regions. In 1952, for example, he published *Highway of the Sun*, an account of a 1952 National Geographic Society expedition to trace the Inca roads of western South America. *Kirkus* declared that "though we detect notes of overdramatization and high regard for personal accomplishment, the account is frankly and excitingly written and takes the armchair archaeologist right into the mountains, the jungle and the desert."

Von Hagen also received positive critical comment when he ventured into biography. He collaborted with his first wife Christine on the first biography of Manuela Sáenz and her long love affair with Simón Bolívar. "As Mr. Von Hagen tells her story she emerges not only as one of the most appealing women South America has ever known but as one of the fascinating mistresses of history": thus the *New York Times* praised *The Four Seasons of Manuela*. "Indeed, one might be tempted to think the author had embroidered on facts to create this dynamic personality were his book not so impressively documented."

Through the years Von Hagen continued to explore the world, writing about his findings and experiences. He succeeded in shipping "legendary Quetzal Birds" to the London and Bronx Zoos; "discovered" the Jicaque, a tribe of Indians descended from the Mayas, and thought extinct; and won praise for "compiling the first complete study of the Great Tortoise of the Galápagos Islands." Collections of his artifacts can be found at the American Museum of Natural History and the British Museum. He served as Research Associate at the Museum of the American Indian, Director of the American Geographical Society, and consultant to the United Nations. In addition to his books Dr. Von Hagen contributed to such publications as the *New York Times, Travel, Science Digest*, and *Scientific Monthly*.

PRINCIPAL WORKS: *Nonfiction*—Off With Their Heads, 1937; (with Q. Hawkins) Quetzal Quest: The Story of the Capture of the Quetzal, the Sacred Bird of the Aztecs and the Mayas, 1939; Ecuador, the Unknown: Two and Half Years' Travels in the Republic of Ecuador and Galápagos Islands, 1939; The Tsátchela Indians of Western Ecuador, 1939; Jungle in the Clouds, 1940; (with Q. Hawkins) Treasure of the Tortoise Island, 1940; Riches of South America, 1941; The Aztec and Maya Papermakers, 1943; The Jicaque (Torrupan) Indians of Honduras, 1943; South America Called Them: Explorations of the Great Naturalists: La Condamine, Humboldt, Darwin, Spruce, 1945; South American Zoo, 1946; Maya Explorer: John Lloyd Stephens and the Lost Cities of Central America and Yucatan, 1947; Ecuador and the Galápagos Islands, 1949; A Guide to Cusco, 1949; A Guide to Lima, the Capital of Peru, 1949; A Guide to Machu Picchu, 1949; A Guide to Sacsahuaman, the Fortress of Cusco, 1949; Frederick Catherwood, Archt., 1950; A Guide to Guayaquil, 1950; A Guide to St. Vincent, 1950; Huancayo and Ayacucho, 1950; (with C. Von Hagen) The Four Seasons of Manuela: A Biography: The Love Story of Manuela Sáenz and Simón Bolívar, 1952; Highway of the Sun, 1955; Realm of the Incas, 1957; rev. ed. 1961; The Aztec: Man and Tribe, 1958; World of the Maya, 1960; The Ancient Sun Kingdoms of the Americas: Aztec, Maya, Inca, 1961; The Desert Kingdoms of Peru, 1964; The Roads That Led to Rome, 1967; Search for the Maya: The Story of Stephens and Catherwood, 1973; The Golden Man: A Quest for El Dorado, 1974; The Germanic People in America, 1976; The Royal Road of the Inca, 1976; The Persian Realms, 1977. *As editor*—The Encantadas, or Enchanted Isles, by Herman Melville, 1940; The Green World of the Naturalists: A Treasury of Five Centuries of Natural History in South America, 1948 (in U.K.: South America, Green World of the Naturalists: Five Centuries of Natural History in South America); Incidents of Travel in Egypt, Arabia, Petraea, and the Holy Land, 1970. *Juvenile*—Miskito Boy, 1943; The Sun Kingdom of the Aztecs, 1958; Maya, Land of the Turkey and the Deer, 1969; The Incas: People of the Sun, 1961; Roman Roads, 1966.

ABOUT: The autobiographical material quoted above was written for Twentieth Century Authors First Supplement, 1955. Current Biography 1942. *Periodicals*—Kirkus September 15, 1955; New York Times May 11, 1952; Saturday Review June 7, 1952.

**VON HAYEK, FRIEDRICH AUGUST.** See **HAYEK, FRIEDRICH**

**VON HEIDENSTAM, VERNER.** See **HEIDENSTAM, VERNER VON**

**VON HOFMANNSTHAL, HUGO.** See **HOFMANNSTHAL, HUGO VON**

**VON HORVÁTH, ODÖN.** See **HORVÁTH, ODÖN VON**

**VON KEYSERLING, HERMANN.** See **KEYSERLING, HERMANN VON**

**VON UNRUH, FRITZ.** See **UNRUH, FRITZ VON**

**VON GOLSSENAU, ARNOLD FRIEDRICH VIETH.** See **RENN, LUDWIG**

**VORSE, MARY MARVIN (HEATON)** (October 9, 1874–June 14, 1966) American novelist and labor journalist, wrote: "Mary Heaton Vorse was educated abroad. She began as an art student, but her interest swerved to writing. She married Albert White Vorse, editor, writer, and music critic; married (2) Joseph O'Brien, newspaper man and author. She has three children. In 1915 she was a war correspondent, covering the effect of war on civil populations for various magazines. Did pamphlets on the rights of small nations—Poland, Czecho-Slovakia, Jugo-Slavia—for Committee of Public Information. Overseas member of the Red Cross in 1918 and 1919. Served in France, Italy, and the Balkan Commission. In 1919 she was briefly with the American Relief Administration, writing on the condition of children under blockade in Central Europe. She has written widely on European affairs; contributed articles to *Harper's Magazine* on post-war conditions in Europe, reported Russian famine in 1921 and 1922 for the Hearst papers. She has done much work as foreign correspondent for various magazines, varying in interest from a series of articles for *Harper's* on North Africa, and a series of articles on the Montessori Method, to the London Economic Conference. She covered the first phases of the Hitler régime in 1933. She wrote a series of pre-war articles for syndicates and magazines, and covered the first phases of the present war. She has held several government publicity positions, including those in wartime and for the Committee of Public Information, and was for a year and a half in the Indian Bureau, Department of the Interior. . . . She . . . specialized in the situation of labor and . . . reported labor conditions for various magazines and periodicals."

———

Mary Heaton Vorse was born in New York City, the daughter of Hiram Heaton and Ellen (Blackman) Heaton. The family spent its summers in Amherst, Massachusetts, and usually wintered in Europe, where Mary studied art in Paris at the age of sixteen. In 1898 she married Albert White Vorse.

Vorse's literary career began with occasional book reviews in the *Criterion*. She published more than 190 routine short stories in such magazines as  the *Woman's Home Companion*, and, later, the *New Yorker*. Her first book, *The Breaking In of a Yachtsman's Wife*, was a compilation of pieces first published in the *Atlantic Monthly*; it features an overbearing husband who convinces his landlubber bride to help him with his new boat. The wife, however, becomes a skilled sailor, thereby bruising her husband's male ego. There were autobiographical elements in the book: the Vorses had recently purchased a boat, and Mary's early success together with the continuing failure of Albert's created tension in their marriage. By 1906 Mary was supporting the family with her pen; four years later Albert died of a cerebral hemorrhage.

Vorse moved her family back to New York's Greenwich Village and continued to sell stories. Dee Garrison claimed: "three intense emotional experiences of that period increased her awareness of the lives of poor women and inspired her lasting commitment to radical politics. Vorse outgrew the last vestiges of habit and thought that characterized the often-indulged daughter of a privileged family." The first of these "emotional experiences" was a crusade she joined to protest New York City's high infant mortality rate; the second was the death of 146 workers in the infamous 1911 Triangle Shirtwaist Company fire (which she witnessed); the third resulted from her reportage for *Harper's* of the Lawrence, Massachusetts, textile strike of 1912. According to Garrison "for thirty years after Lawrence, the by-line of Mary Heaton Vorse would represent the work of one of the earliest and most important of the new labor reporters." In her memoir *Footnote to Folly*, Vorse recorded: "I wanted to see wages go up and the babies' death rate go down. There must be thousands like my self who were not indifferent, but only ignorant. I went away from Lawerence with a resolve that I would write about these things always."

Vorse was as good as her word; but her activism was not limited to the written page: she was frequently in the thick of the conflict. In 1937, while covering a strike at Youngstown's Republic Steel Corporation, a bullet fired by company thugs grazed her forehead. In the resulting story she wrote: "at the hospital where I go to get my head sewed up, the wounded are arriving by carloads." Her commitment to labor causes continued throughout her life, although her liberal outlook did not prevent her from attacking corrupt unions. In 1962 she was awarded the United Auto Workers'

Social Justice Award. Near the end of her life she protested nuclear waste dumping and the Vietnam War and supported enviromental causes.

In addition to journal articles Vorse expressed her social concerns in such books as *The Passaic Textile Strike: 1926–1927*, *Men and Steel*, and *Labor's New Millions*. Her 1930 novel *Strike!* tells the story of Southern textile workers struggling for better working conditions. Vorse, however, continued writing lighter fiction for money; she called these tales her "lollypops." Like *I've Come to Stay*, a love story, they are of little account in literary history; she is now remembered, not as a novelist, but as a courageous reporter and activist.

Vorse married Joseph O'Brien, whom she had met on the picket line in Lawrence, in 1912; but she continued to write under her first married name. After O'Brien's death she married radical artist and writer Robert Minor; this ended in divorce.

Many of Mary Heaton Vorse's papers are housed at the Archives of Labor History and Urban Affairs, Wayne State University, Detroit.

PRINCIPAL WORKS: *Nonfiction*—The Very Little Person, 1911; Men and Steel, 1920; The Passaic Textile Strike: 1926–1927, 1927; Labor's New Millions, 1938. *Novels*—The Breaking In of a Yachtsman's Wife, 1908; (with W. D. Howells, M.E.W. Freeman, et.al) The Whole Family: A Novel By Twelve Authors, 1908; The Heart's Country, 1914; I've Come to Stay: A Love Comedy of Bohemia, 1918; The Prestons, 1918; Growing Up, 1920; The Ninth Man, 1920; Second Cabin, 1928; Strike!, 1930. *Short stories*—Fraycar's Fist, 1924. *Drama*—(with C. C. Clements) Wreckage: A Play In One Act, 1924. *Memoirs*—Autobiography of an Elderly Woman, 1911; A Footnote to Folly: Reminiscences of Mary Heaton Vorse, 1935; Time and the Town: A Provincetown Chronicle, 1942; The Reminiscences of Mary H. Vorse, 1957.

ABOUT: The autobiographical material quoted above was written for Twentieth Century Authors, 1942. Dictionary of American Biography, 1981; Garrison, D. Mary Heaton Vorse: The Life of an American Insurgent, 1989; Garrison, D. Rebel Pen: The Writings of Mary Heaton Vorse, 1985; Sternsher, B. and Sealander, J. (eds.) Women of Valor: The Struggle Against the Depression as Told in Their Own Life Stories, 1990; Whitman, A. American Reformers, 1985. *Periodicals*—Boston Transcript July 5, 1919; Forum February 1936; New York Times June 14, 1966.

## VOTO, BERNARD DE. See DE VOTO, BERNARD

## WADDELL, HELEN

(May 31, 1889–March 5, 1965), English novelist and translator of medieval Latin verse, was born in Tokyo. Her inclination to portray the scholarly vagabonds of her books in the manner of Chinese sages was probably due to the influence of her father, Rev. Hugh Waddell, an Oriental scholar, who was working at the Imperial University of Japan at the time of her birth. Of Ausonius she says: "He reminds one of half-a-dozen provincial governors in the *Dictionary of Chinese Biography*: of Han Yü, whose friends washed their hands in rose water before opening the manuscript of his poems. . . . of Po Chu-I, sitting on the terrace under the peach trees in blossom." Her translations undoubtedly have something of the atmosphere of translations from the Chinese, and her first book was *Lyrics from the Chinese* (1913), verse renderings from the fine prose translations by the Chinese scholar and translator of the *I Ching*, Dr. James Legge.

Both Waddell's parents came from Northern Ireland; Helen, who was the youngest of a family of eight, was educated in Belfast, at Victoria College,  and Queens University, where she obtained her M.A. Her mother died when she was two, and her father when she was ten. She remained in Belfast until the death of her stepmother, Martha Waddell, in 1919. During these years she worked alongside her brother Samuel, whose plays (under the pseudonym of Rutherford Mayne) were regularly performed by the Ulster Literary (later Group) Theatre. *The Spoiled Buddha*, written jointly, was performed in 1915, and published four years later.

After teaching Latin for two years at Somerville College, Oxford, and then lecturing for a year at Bedford College, London, she was awarded a Susette Taylor Fellowship from Lady Margaret Hall, Oxford, on the recommendation of Professor George Saintsbury, and used it to help fund two years of research in Paris. *The Wandering Scholars*, published in 1927, was the result.

The book began as an introductory essay to an intended volume of translations from Latin lyrics. The *Times Literary Supplement* wrote: "She has produced not merely the best but the only book on the subject for English readers. We believe that it will be welcomed alike by the professional medievalist and by the lover of classical Latin who is curious to know something of the later history of that literature and language which lasted a thousand years after they should, in the opinion of some old-fashioned scholars, have been dead and decently interred." It was an immediate success, and went into three editions in the year of publication. Five years later, for the sixth edition, Waddell revised and enlarged the text, adding also to the invaluable bibliography. Despite more recent theories about the origins of, for instance, the *Carmina Burana* anthology, the book remains an indispensable introduction to its subject.

Helen Waddell's other major work was the novel *Peter Abelard*, depicting the love affair between Abelard and Heloise. Of this book V. S. Pritchett wrote in the *New Statesman*, "The style is serious, subtle and poetic, and carries a pleasingly robust humour. Sometimes her allusiveness is distracting, but it stipples and breaks up her learning. One might complain that Abelard himself is a series of fugitive impressions rather than a man four-square upon the page. But the nature of her approach justifies her." American reviewers compared the book, as literature, less favorably with George Moore's *Heloise and Abelard*, but acknowledged that it was an ideal vehicle for raising awareness of the medieval world.

Waddell was a popular lecturer during the 1930s. She became assistant editor of *The Nineteenth Century* and was the recipient of a number of honorary degrees. Her other publications included an anthology of *Medieval Latin Lyrics* and *The Desert Fathers*, a treatment, through translation of Rosweyd's *Vitae Patrum*, of the ascetic tradition.

After the war her mental powers went into decline. *Poetry in the Dark Ages* (1948), a record of her W. P. Ker Lecture at Glasgow University, and *Stories from Holy Writ* (1949) were her final publications. Monica Blackett's *The Mark of the Maker* (1973) includes extracts from the voluminous correspondence between Helen and her sister Margaret Waddell. Felicitas Corrigan published a more formal biography in 1986.

PRINCIPAL WORKS: Lyrics from the Chinese, 1913; The Spoiled Buddha, 1919 (play); The Wandering Scholars, 1927; Medieval Latin Lyrics, 1929; A Book of Medieval Latin for Schools, 1931; Peter Abelard, 1933 (novel); The Abbè Prévost, 1933 (play); Beast and Saints, 1934; The Desert Fathers, 1936; Poetry in the Dark Ages, 1948.

ABOUT: Blackett, M. The Mark of the Maker, 1973; Corrigan, F. Helen Waddell, 1986; Contemporary Authors Vol. 102; Dictionary of National Biography, 1961–1970, 1981; Schlueter, P. and J. (eds.) An Encyclopaedia of British Women Writers, 1988; Who's Who 1965. *Periodicals*—New Statesman May 27, 1933; Times (London) March 6, 1965; Times Literary Supplement May 26, 1927.

## *WAGENKNECHT, EDWARD CHARLES

(March 28, 1900–   ), American critic, biographer, and anthologist, wrote: "I was born in Chicago and grew up on the West Side. I decided to be a writer when I first read *The Wizard of Oz* ; I was about six years old at the time. Nobody greatly encouraged this insane idea until I got my fourth grade teacher, Miss Mary Dwyer, at the Plamondon School. Miss Dwyer made me promise to send her a copy of my first book, a promise which was kept.

"When I was halfway through high school, we moved to Oak Park, where both Oak Park High School and the Oak Park Public Library became important factors in my development. I became locally famous as a public speaker and graduated in 1917 as valedictorian of my class, which was also Ernest Hemingway's class.

"So far as scholarship goes, I consider myself essentially a product of the University of Chicago, in the days when John M. Manly was head of the department of English. From the University of Chicago I received both the Ph.B. and the M.A. degree. (My Ph.D. I took at the University of Washington, while I was teaching there.) The greatest single influence upon me at Chicago was that of Edith Rickert, the only person I have ever  encountered whom I could honestly describe as both a great scholar and a great teacher. Besides the

*WAHG en ekt

universities already mentioned, I have taught at Illinois Institute of Technology and at Boston University, where I have been professor of English since 1947. In 1932 I married Dorothy Arnold, of Seattle. We have three sons.

"During my high school days I became greatly interested in essays and criticism, and particularly in the work of Agnes Repplier and Samuel McChord Crothers. Dr. Crothers influenced my career when he advised me to try to break in first as a book reviewer. I followed his advice literally and was reviewing for the *Atlantic Monthly* and the *Yale Review* when I was in my early twenties. I have since reviewed for nearly all the important American book-reviewing media. Since 1944 I have been a featured reviewer for the *Chicago Sunday Tribune Magazine of Books.*

"More important than this, however, was my association with Gamaliel Bradford, through whom I acquired a method. I used the Bradford psychography in my books on Dickens, Mark Twain, and Jenny Lind. My preoccupation, in later years, with the history of the novel has taken me away from psychography, but I intended to return to it in a series of books in which I hope to make use of the rich literary deposits in the Boston area, relating to New England writers.

"Because I was distressed by the amount of time it took me to write the history of the English and American novel, I determined to try to keep on the market by editing anthologies. The result was that I produced fourteen of them, the most successful of which was *The Fireside Book of Christmas Stories.* I have enough ideas in mind now to keep me busy until I am a hundred, but I shall probably not be able to carry them all out.

"I have no theories about writing except that I think people should write about what they care for. I compose directly upon the typewriter, and what I can do at all, I can do at any time and under any circumstances. I would much rather write than eat. I believe that waiting upon 'inspiration' is a lazy man's excuse and that 'writers' conferences' are for people who do not want to write but prefer to talk about writing. All my work has long roots in my own experience: I wrote about Jenny Lind, for example, because she was a family tradition from the time my grandfather heard her sing. I try to steep myself in my material; I take copious notes, but much of what finally reaches the printed page was not in my notes at all. I have never begun a book or an article with a preconceived theory, and I do not consider myself to have much control over the final end product."

———

Wagenknecht's method was also based on that of Sainte-Beuve. In his 1954 study *Preface to Literature* Wagenknecht declares that a "book is the product of the man who writes it. It is also the product of its age. It is a product of the civilization which produced it because that civilization also produced the author."

During his long career Wagenknecht produced an impressive list of useful biographies, as well as literary critiques and histories. *Cavalcade of the English Novel* and *Cavalcade of the American Novel,* to name two of his books, were widely used in colleges and universities. In a review of *William Dean Howells: The Friendly Eye, American Literature* critic E. H. Cady commented: "[The author's] 'psychographs' have been accumulating toward the substance of one man's history of American literature. By design the books are personal in method, revisionist in perspective, thoroughly independent, and prepared to irritate vested critical interests if only by ignoring them."

In 1965 Boston University named Edward Wagenknecht professor emeritus.

PRINCIPAL WORKS: *Nonfiction*—Lillian Gish: An Interpretation, 1927; Values in Literature, 1928; Geraldine Farrar: An Authorized Record of Her Career, 1929; A Guide to Bernard Shaw, 1929; The Man Charles Dickens: A Victorian Portrait, 1929, rev. ed. 1966; Utopian Americana, 1929; Jenny Lind, 1931; Mark Twain: The Man and His Work, 1935, rev. eds. 1961, and 1967 as Mark Twain: The Man and His Work: With a Commentary on Mark Twain Criticism and Scholarship Since 1960; Cavalcade of the English Novel, from Elizabeth to George IV, 1943; Shakespeare, a Man of This World, 1947; Cavalcade of the American Novel, from the Birth of the Nation to the Middle of the Twentieth Century, 1952; A Preface to Literature, 1954; The Unknown Longfellow, 1954; Longfellow: A Full Length Portrait, 1955, rev. as Henry Wadsworth Longfellow: Portrait of an American Humorist, 1966; The Seven Worlds of Theodore Roosevelt, 1958; Nathaniel Hawthorne: Man and Writer, 1961; The Movies in the Age of Innocence, 1962; Washington Irving: Moderation Displayed, 1962; Edgar Allan Poe: The Man Behind the Legend, 1963; Chicago, 1964; Seven Daughters of the Theater: Jenny Lind, Sarah Bernhardt, Ellen Terry, Julia Marlowe, Isadora Duncan, Mary Garden, Marilyn Monroe, 1964; Dickens and the Scandalmongers: Essays in Criticism, 1965; Harriet Beecher Stowe: The Known and the Unknown, 1965; Merely Players, 1966; John Greenleaf Whittier: A Portrait in Paradox, 1967; The Personality of Chaucer, 1968; William Dean Howells: The Friendly Eye, 1969; The Personality of Milton, 1970; James Russell Lowell: Portrait of a Many-Sided Man, 1971; Ambassadors for Christ: Seven American Preachers, 1972; The Personality of Shakespeare, 1972; Ralph Waldo Emerson: Portrait of a Balanced Soul, 1974; (with A. Slide) The Films of D.W. Griffith, 1975; A Pictorial History of New England, 1976; Eve and Henry James: Portraits of Women and Girls in His Fiction, 1978; James Branch Cabell: 1879–1979, 1979; (with A. Slide) Fifty Great American Silent Films: A Pictorial Survey, 1980; Henry David Thoreau: What Manner of Man?, 1981; American Profile: 1900–1909, 1982; Gamaliel Bradford, 1982; Daughters of the Covenant: Portraits of Six Jewish Women, 1983; The Novels of Henry James, 1983; Henry Wadsworth Longfellow: His Poetry and Prose, 1986; Stars of the Silents, 1987; Sir Walter Scott, 1990. *As editor*—Six Novels of the Supernatural, 1944; The Fireside Book of Christmas Stories, 1945; The Story of Jews in the World's Literature, 1946; When I Was a Child: An Anthology, 1946; Abraham Lincoln: His Life, Work, and Character: An Anthology of History and Biography, Fiction, Poetry, Drama, and Belles-Lettres, 1947; The Fireside Book of Ghost Stories, 1947; The Fireside Book of Romances, 1947; The Fireside Book of Yuletide Tales, 1948; Joan of Arc: An Anthology of History and Literature, 1948; Murder By Gaslight: Victorian Tales, 1949; An Introduction to Dickens, 1952; Mrs. Longfellow: Selected Letters and Journals, 1956; Chaucer: Modern Essays in Criticism, 1959; Stories of Christ and Christmas, 1963; Marilyn Monroe: A Composite View, 1969; The Letters of James Branch Cabell, 1974; The Stories and Fables of Ambrose Bierce, 1977; Washington Irving: Tales of the Supernatural, 1982. *Novels*—(as Julian Forrest) Nine Before Fotheringhay: A Novel About Mary Queen of Scots, 1966; (as Julian Forrest) The Glory of the Lillies: A Novel About Joan of Arc, 1969. *Memoirs*—As Far As Yesterday: Memories and Reflections, 1968.

ABOUT: The autobiographical material quoted above was written for Twentieth Century Authors first Supplement, 1955. Contemporary Authors, 1994; Dictionary of Literary Biography Vol. 103, 1991; Who's Who 1996. *Periodical*—American Literature March 1970.

## WAITE, ARTHUR EDWARDS (October 2, 1857–May 19, 1942), Anglo-American writer on religious cults, wrote:

"I was born at Brooklyn, New

York. My father Charles Frederick Waite, came out of unmixed Connecticut stock and was himself born at Lyme. He was descended in a direct line from the regicide John Wayte. Some or many who bore the name fled at the Restoration and found haven in New England. My father as a boy probably ran away to sea. In any case, he was later in command of sailing ships, some of which were also passenger boats. When I was less than a year old he died and was buried at sea. My sister was a posthumous child.

"My mother had been Emma Lovell, an Englishwoman. The loss of her husband, who left next to nothing, took my mother to Lyme. But Lyme was impossible for a still young and educated Englishwoman of the upper-middle class; and she made a last voyage to England accompanied by two babes. My first days in England abide in a cloud of unknowing. My mother, a Church-going woman of the Anglican type, became a Roman. Presently we drifted northward from Kentish Town and at Highgate I served at the altar, which gave me my first love of all that belongs to rites. As days went on, I had been for brief periods at three small private day-schools, where I learned nothing. I was probably thirteen when my mother moved to Bayswater and sent me for three years to St. Charles College, where I learned Latin and Greek and forgot most of the French she had taught me.

"When my schooling came to an end, I accepted a clerical appointment, with supposed prospects, but for me it proved narrow and dull. Between the nameless misery of this external plight and dejection at the death of my sister; it was a dark night indeed about me, till a sudden change came when on a certain red-letter day I found that I could write verses. A sleeping soul awakened then within me; a hunger and thirst after glory in the craft of song possessed my whole being. For months upon months I read nothing but poems and the lives of the poets. For some subsequent years there was a fever of verse upon me. Now, I know in my heart that the poet's vocation was that for which I was meant.

"At nineteen the halter of clerical work had long since removed its yoke. I began to see my way. The first path which I entered was that of physical research. It must not be supposed that I became convinced Spiritist, having no qualifications at that period to be assured of anything. Intellectually speaking, I had no faculty of easy belief. But I had

a living interest and curiosity that centered in the claims of so-called occult sciences. And at twenty-one the British Museum opened the doors of its reading room, with the gift of a reading ticket for the rest of my natural life.

"I have now reached that point when my books must speak for themselves and my memoirs must take care of external things. Those who need may learn in their pages of my two marriages; of the growth of my poet's mind in the world of verse; of my experience in Secret Orders, including the great Masonic complex in all its rites and degrees. They may learn above all what is meant in the plenary sense by Sacramental Mysticism and its external distinction from the speculations and experiments of the pseudo-occult arts.

"Setting aside early efforts, translations, and things belonging to the passing moment, my books are all the work of a mystic and of one who *in spiritu humilitatis* has sought as such to find new paths therein. His work in this direction is by no means finished, and even at this great age he prays to be spared, that he may add to his studies of the Secret Tradition in Christian times one further memorial."

---

Arthur Edward Waite's autobiographical resumé gives the flavor of the man and of his generation of "occult" thinkers. His autobiography, *Shadows of Life and Thought*, is couched in just such terms (although, naturally, at a greater length), and is historically valuable for the light it casts upon not only Waite but on the nonorthodox, "esoteric" religious beliefs of his time.

Waite was known among lay readers for many years as a deeply learned scholar of that most mysterious and complex of Judaic phenomena, Kabbalah (or, Cabala), which in Hebrew simply means "tradition." Furthermore, his works on the Tarot—an even more esoteric phenomenon, whose exact origins are forever lost, although they do lie (in part) in the Cabala—are still extant, and still sell in large quantities. Yet they go unmentioned by such scholars of the Tarot as Stuart Kaplan.

Waite's poetry meant much to him, but was written in a tradition in which such poets as Ernest Dowson were genuine masters; it is mellifluous and sincere, but lacks the gift of inspired language.

As a would-be scholar Waite was for many years widely read, and his books were in much demand. *The Holy Kabbalah* (1929) received respectful reviews even from such journals as the *Times Literary Supplement*, whose reviewer wrote that Waite had "given a remarkably true picture of the Kabbalistic movement." This was not quite the case. Even the reader of the time might have warned, had he read S. B. Freehof's review of the same book in the *Journal of Religion*: "Mr. Waite . . . should have confined himself to this subject and not have dealt with the difficult problems of text criticism. To judge texts one must have an intimate knowledge of original sources. That Mr. Waite lacks this knowledge strikes the reader at once." But even

Freehof thought the work "erudite" and "informative" on the subject of mysticism. Waite, as the *New Statesman* wrote of his *The Secret Tradition of Freemasonry* (1937), undertook "stupendous" amounts of research into the arcane. But he appears to have taken no heed of the really scholarly work that was then being done, on the matters about which he wrote, such as the history of freemasonry, the life and works of Paracelsus, alchemy, or Raymond Lully.

Yet, for all that, Gershom Scholem wrote of him, in his great *Major Trends in Jewish Mysticism* (third revised edition, 1954) "It is a pity that the fine philosophical intuition and natural grasp of such students [as Waite and others] lost their edge because they lacked all critical sense as to the historical and philological data in this field, and therefore failed completely when they had to handle problems bearing on facts." Elsewhere in his book, Scholem described Waite's *The Secret Doctrine in Israel* (this earlier book is incorporated in *The Holy Kabbalah*) as representing "a serious attempt to analyze the symbolism of the Zohar [the Cabalistic book written in Spain in the thirteenth century by Moses de Leon or another]. His work . . . is distinguished by a real insight into the world of Kabbalism; it is all the more regrettable that it is marred by an uncritical attitude to matters of history and philology, to which it must be added that he has frequently been led astray by [a] faulty and inadequate translation of the Zohar, which, owing to his own ignorance of Hebrew and Aramaic, he was compelled to accept as authoritative."

Waite's books have now been read by scholars, their insights garnered: thus he is now important only historically. Yet, as Scholem conceded, he possessed genuine insights, even if these were hampered by his ignorance of texts. He was thus amongst the most distinguished of the largely amateur scholars of the arcane of his time and place.

Waite was married twice: first, to the former Enid Lakeman, a woman of Irish and Greek extraction whom he called "Lucasta," and by whom he had a daughter; second, after her death in 1924, to Mary Broadbent Schofield. Waite lived for many years near Canterbury, in Kent, where he died, at work until the last.

PRINCIPAL WORKS: *Mysticism and secret/esoteric doctrine*—The Magical Writings of Thomas Vaughan, 1888; Hermetic and Alchemical Writings of Paracelsus, 2 vols., 1894; Devil Worship in France, 1896; Thomas Vaughan's Lumen de Lumine, 1910; The Works of Thomas Vaughan, 1919; The Holy Kabbalah, 1929; A Mystagogical Quintology, 1935; Encyclopaedia of Freemasonry, enlarged and transformed, 2 vols., 1937; Raymond Lully, 1939. *Verse*—Elfin Music, 1888. *Autobiography*—Shadows of Life and Thought in the Form of Memoirs, 1938.

ABOUT: The autobiographical material quoted above was written for Twentieth Century Authors, 1942. Scholem, G. Major Trends in Jewish Mysticism, 1954; Waite, A. E. Shadows of Life, 1938. *Periodicals*—Journal of Religion April 1930; New Statesman August 14, 1937; Times Literary Supplement December 12, 1929.

**WAKEMAN, FREDERIC** (December 26, 1909– ), American novelist, was born in Scranton, Kansas, the son of Don Conklin Wakeman, a newspaperman, politician and civil servant, and Myrtle (Evans) Wakeman.

Following in his father's footsteps and under the influence of fellow Kansas journalist William Allen White, Wakeman started out in journalism, editing the college paper and literary magazine at Park College at Parksville, Missouri, from which he graduated in 1933. Wakeman eventually moved to New York, where he became an advertising copywriter and agency account executive.

Wakeman joined the Navy in 1942, in which he saw active duty in the Pacific. From his naval experience he derived the basis for his first novel, *Shore Leave* (1944), which pictured five war-weary Naval officers in San Francisco on leave from the South Pacific. In the *Nation*, Diana Trilling called it "a first report on our newest lost generation; it can be read as the spiritual parallel from this war, to Ernest Hemingway's version of  World War I." F.J. Bell wrote in the *New York Times* that the novel "is a harbinger of post-war literature that will combine the early frustration of a Woolfe with the belligerent intensity of a young Hemingway." Other reviewers, however, faulted Wakeman for not writing, but merely reporting, and for not bringing out deeper significance in his characters and for crowding too much superfluous information into the book. A few also called the novel "cheap" and "vulgar."

After medical discharge from the Navy, Wakeman returned to advertising. In 1945, he accepted a scriptwriting job with M.G.M. in Hollywood; but his health forced him to move to Cuernavaca, Mexico, where in two months, he wrote *The Hucksters*, about an advertising man who discovers the difference between infatuation and love while working on a major soap company account. Wakeman tapped into his own experience in handling major corporate advertising for Westinghouse, American Can, Ford Motor, Campbell's Soup, Lucky Strike cigarettes and RKO pictures to paint a realistic picture of those who work to sell products over the airwaves. The advertising world was astir trying to get advance copies of the book, whose characters so strikingly resembled real people in the industry. The *New York Herald Tribune* reported that "whatever the nation may be reading, every other person you meet along Broadway is carrying with him a copy of *The Hucksters*."

The novel climbed up the best-seller list, became a Book of the Month Club selection, a *Reader's Digest* condensed book and an M.G.M. motion picture. Russel Maloney wrote in the *New York Times* that only Dickens could have done justice to the character of Evan Llewelyn Evans and his soap business: "Quite a book, quite a book!" Many other critics gave praise for Wakeman's shrewd observations and satirical and savage portrayal of a business filled with excesses and eccentricities. Others, however, mentioned how he was less proficient in writing the accompanying love story woven into the book. George Mayberry commented in *New Republic* that "Wakeman is just a copywriter at heart;" and Wolcott Gibbs in the *New Yorker* called *The Hucksters* "a remarkably silly book."

Wakeman failed to match the success of *The Hucksters* with the novels that followed it, in which characters were in troubled marriages, on European vacations or involved in international motion pictures. *Saxon Charm* (1947), the story of a playwright, his wife, his mistresses and his producer, received largely negative reviews, although it, too, was made into a motion picture. *The Wastrel* (1949), in which a wealthy and cynical American fights to save himself and his son after a boating accident, was called "heavy-hearted moralizing" by the *New Yorker*, which went on to say that the main character "is about as uninteresting as it is possible for a man to be."

Critics were harsh in their assessment of a string of novels Wakeman wrote during the 1950s. Not until *A Free Agent* (1963) did Wakeman manage to garner significant praise again. This is the story of an adopted son of a Kansas City doctor who ponders his identity and raison d'être as he fights in World War II, buries his father, serves as an intelligence agent and then falls in love with a Greek woman with Communist roots. "Wakeman has succeeded in writing exactly the kind of thoughtful, readable *au courant* novel he has intended to write for a long time. It is impressive beyond anything he has done before. It fulfills an obligation to entertain without by-passing the mind or overlooking chances to kick sacred cows when they stray onto the path," according to James Kelly in the *New York Times*. Yet Haskel Frankel wrote in *Saturday Review* that Wakeman was still riding on the laurels of his fame from *The Hucksters*, commenting that "an established name will sell anything."

PRINCIPAL WORKS: Shore Leave, 1944; The Hucksters, 1946; The Saxon Charm, 1947; The Wastrel, 1949; Mandrake Root, 1953; The Fabulous Train, 1955; Deluxe Tour, 1956; The Fault of the Apple, 1960; A Free Agent, 1963; The Flute Across the Pond, 1966.

ABOUT: Warfel, H. R. American Novelists of Today; Current Biography 1946. *Periodicals*—Nation April 1, 1944; New Republic June 9, 1946; New Yorker June 1, 1946; February 19, 1949; New York Times March 12, 1944; May 26, 1946; August 4, 1946; September 7, 1947; April 14, 1963; PM Magazine August 25, 1946; Saturday Review March 23, 1963.

**WALEY, ARTHUR** (August 11, 1889–June 27, 1966), English writer and translator of classical Far Eastern poetry and prose, was born at Tunbridge Wells, Kent. He was the second of three sons born to David Frederick Schloss, an economist and Fabian socialist, and his wife Rachel, the daughter of political economist Jacob Waley, whose surname was adopted by the family in 1914.

Waley was brought up in Wimbledon and attended school at Rugby (1903–1906). His aptitude as a student of classical Greek and Latin earned

him an open scholarship at King's College shortly before his seventeenth birthday.

Prior to entering the university, Waley spent a year traveling through France gathering a knowledge of the French language. He received a first class in part 1 of his final examinations for classical languages, but in 1910 was forced to abandon his final year after suffering from severe eye trouble, which left his sight permanently diminished.

In 1911 Waley set out again for the Continent, in an attempt to rest and to restore his eyesight. While traveling through Spain and Germany, he quickly learned the languages.

In June 1913 Waley was appointed to the British Museum's newly formed sub-department of Asian prints and drawings under Laurence Binyon, scholar, poet, and translator of Dante. Waley's chief responsibility involved compiling a rational index of Sino-Japanese painters represented in the museum's collection. He spent several years there cataloging a series of Buddhist paintings. His principal duties consisted of reading and interpreting the complex, often incomplete, inscriptions on the paintings and identifying the subjects illustrated. In 1920–1921 Waley submitted a total of eight translations of classical Chinese art critiques to *Burlington Magazine*. The sensitivity with which he rendered the original texts into English was quickly recognized as demonstrating an unusual understanding of classical Chinese nuance and feeling.

On his application form for the museum post Waley indicated that he was already conversant in Italian, Dutch, Portuguese, French, German, and Spanish. Oswald Sickert, brother of the painter, remarked upon Waley's "exceptional intelligence and originality. . . . the quickness of his interest and his capacity for making something of his own out of everything he observes seem to be extraordinary." Waley's proficiency in Far Eastern classical languages enabled him to issue a steady stream of translations, beginning in 1916 with a series of published works of pre-T'ang poetry that appeared in The *New Statesman*, the *Little Review* (1919), and elsewhere. In 1921 he issued a version of a set of Japanese Noh plays. As with his translations from the Chinese, Waley treated classical Japanese poetry and prose in a limpid, eloquent fashion that brought forth brilliant shadings and descriptions hitherto thought to be untranslatable into English. He was never as adept at translating Japanese poetry as he was in Chinese, but the Noh plays were influential—upon, for example, Yeats and Pound.

Waley translated from classical Asian literature for the rest of his life, often devoting large amounts of time and energy to learning obscure, obsolescent languages such as Ainu or Mongol.

Waley often remarked that he could translate "nothing that did not excite, grip, or haunt the imagination." He would, if necessary, fly to Paris in order to discover the meaning of a single word. Poetry contained musical resonances and textures for Waley. He likened the translator's role to that of a musician's: "His (poet's) role is rather like that of the executant in music, as contrasted with the composer, he must start with a certain degree of sensibility to words and rhythm." His poetic imagination and intuition appeared effortless, though he would spend many hours laboring over a single text. The difficulty in translating from a Far Eastern language is considerable. Aside from the virtual absence of word-for-word equivalents in English, the translator of Chinese poetry must find meaning and intention in often as few as five syllables per verse line.

It is hence important that the translator have a deep understanding of the emotional emphasis suggested in the original text if it is to be rendered meaningfully into English. Waley remarked, "There do exist texts in which only logical meaning, and not feeling is expressed . . . but, particularly in the Far East, they are exceedingly rare." He firmly believed that the translator must always "feel" the subject of the translation in much the same way the author of the original text wanted his audience to respond. He stressed the importance of voice in his translating methods: "When translating prose dialogue one ought to make the characters say things that people talking English could conceivably say. One ought to hear them talking." Waley reasoned that "ordinary" English people enjoyed his translations in *A Hundred and Seventy Chinese Poems* because they dealt with particular subjects and situations, "with things one can touch and see . . . and not with abstract conceptions such as Beauty and Love."

Waley maintained a large circle of friends, although he was close to only a few. He lived in Bloomsbury for over forty years, but remained at a distance from the established "set." He occasionally gave seminars at the University of London or the School of Oriental Studies, but when asked if he would accept the Chair in Chinese at Cambridge, he murmured, "I would rather be dead." He was later elected an honorary fellow at King's College (1953), although his disdain for institutional approaches to Far Eastern literature and scholarship was no secret.

Waley was married for over forty years to Beryl de Zoete, an anthropologist and renowned interpreter of Eastern dance forms. She died in 1962 from Huntington's Chorea. Her painful death saw him at his best: a friend observed "a tenderness" in Waley, "a courage in grief and adversity, which my circumscribed encounters with him had not revealed."

Waley was known for his periods of silence in the midst of casual conversations and formal receptions. He spoke only when he felt that something needed to be said. This particular trait often created awkward first encounters which gradually developed into substantial friendships—but only after people adjusted to the long and difficult periods of silence.

Undoubtedly, one of the oddest features of Waley's life was his refusal to visit the Far East despite invitations from friends, foundations, and universities. He did not want to confront contemporary Sino-Japanese political cultures, although known to

be an outspoken critic of Western chauvinism toward Asia. Nor did he ever learn to speak an Asian language fluently. His scholarly focus remained fixed entirely upon ancient cultures. When he met with visitors from the Far East, he often had to communicate with them by writing Chinese characters on slips of paper.

Although he never traveled east of Turkey, Waley carried his own images of China and Japan around within himself. He moved with "the smooth grace of a skier, his gesture courtly in salutation." His comportment, though unmannered, reminded friends of an almost Eastern sensibility. Waley never strayed from a state of humble refinement even as honors accrued around him. In 1945 he was elected to the British Academy, and following that he received the Queen's Medal for Poetry (1953), as well as honorary doctorates from Aberdeen and Oxford universities.

After the death of his first wife in 1962, Waley left his modest flat in Bloomsbury and moved to Highgate. He lived with Alison Grant Robinson, a longtime friend whom he married just a month before his death of spinal cancer.

In 1970, Ivan Morris edited a collection of writings by and about Waley entitled *Madly Singing in the Mountains*. The title of the tribute was borrowed from a poem of the same name by the ninth-century poet Po Chu-i, first translated by Waley in 1917:

> And often, when I have finished a new poem,
> Alone I climb the road to the Eastern Rock.
> I lean my body on the banks of white stone.
> I pull down with my hands a green cassia branch.
> My mad singing startles the valleys and hills:
> The apes and birds all come to peep.
> Fearing to become a laughing-stock to the world,
> I choose a place that is unfrequented by men.

As Asian studies began to diversify into sub-disciplines, Waley's distinct methods of intuitive interpretation and rigorous scholarship applied to Far East Asia as a whole became an anachronism; it was seen that of those aspects of Asian culture that had not attracted him, he had artfully ignored. But his influence on English poetry endures. Poets who were influenced in one way or another include Edwin Muir, James Reeves, Roy Fuller, and Philip Larkin.

PRINCIPAL WORKS: An Introduction to the Study of Chinese Painting, reprinted; Travels of an Alchemist, the Journey of the Taoist Ch'ang-ch'un from China to the Hindukush at the Summons of Chingiz Khan (Illus.); Three Ways of Thought in Ancient China, 1939; The Poetry and Career of Li Po, 1951; Yuan Mei: Eighteenth Century Chinese Poet, 1956. The Opium War Through Chinese Eyes, 1958; The Noh Plays of Japan, 1976; The Originality of Japanese Civilization, 1980. *As translator*—The Books of Songs: The Ancient Chinese Classic of Poetry, 1987; The Temple and Other Poems, Adventures of the Monkey God, 1987; The No Plays of Japan, 1988; The Analects of Confucius, 1989; (with E. Conze, I. B. Horner, and D. L. Snellgrove) Buddist Texts Through the Ages, 1990; The Tale of Genji (S. Murasaki) 1993; Monkey (Wu-Cheng-en) 1994.

ABOUT: Oxbury, H. F. Great Britons, 1985; Waley, A. A Half of Two Lives, 1983. *Bibliography*—Johns, F. A. A Bibliography of Arthur Waley, 1988.

**WALKER, MILDRED** (May 2, 1905– ), American novelist, attended Germantown High School in Philadelphia, where her father was a Baptist minister. She then went to Wells College in New York State, graduating in 1926. She first decided she was a writer when aged twelve, having won a fifteen dollar prize for an essay about fire prevention. Continuing to write, she was sued for libel while at Wells by a character described too obviously from life. After gaining her degree she went back to Philadelphia, to work in Wanamaker's department store, soon becoming a copywriter in the advertising department. This career was short-lived. In 1927 she married Ferdinand Schemm, a surgeon, and went with him to a Michigan lumbering village, on the edge of Lake Superior. The next few years were spent having children and setting up home.

Although Walker continued to write, most of the results were consigned to the fire. An opportunity to continue her education arose when her husband

accepted a teaching post at the University of Michigan's Medical School. She enrolled in the English department and worked for her master's degree while writing *Fireweed*, a novel based on her experience in the lumber town. It won an Avery Hopwood award (administered by the University of Michigan) and was published as her first book in 1934.

In summarizing a response to *Fireweed*, the reviewer in the *Saturday Review of Literature* might have been describing any of Mildred Walker's later books: "The characters are fully rounded, thought out from depths of actual experience, and the incidents of a disarmingly unpretentious story, not without some pleasing passages of sentiment, are carefully chosen for the light they shed on these people."

Walker's third book, published in 1938 after the Schemm family had moved to Montana, was her most ambitious. *Dr. Norton's Wife* tackled disturbing subject matter, in a web of married love, incurable disease and medical ethics. *Unless the Wind Turns*, a suspense story about a group of characters trapped by a forest fire, demonstrated Walker's ability to develop action and character simultaneously, although the development of character was always her main interest. Both *Winter Wheat* (set in Montana) and *The Quarry* (about life in a Vermont village between the Civil War and World War I) are regional novels in which character and place are more important than plot.

Her work was increasingly seen as competent but unexciting, criticized for being old-fashioned and lacking humor. The *Library Journal* tellingly recommended *The Southwest Corner* (1951) for "clients in their middle years and older." In the 1990s the University of Nebraska Press undertook to reprint her work.

After her husband's death in 1955, Walker returned to Wells College, Aurora, as an English professor, and spent the academic year 1959–1960 as a Fulbright lecturer in Japan, at Kyoto.

PRINCIPAL WORKS: Fireweed, 1934; Light from Arcturus, 1935; Dr. Norton's Wife, 1938; The Brewers' Big Horses, 1940; Unless the Wind Turns, 1941; Winter Wheat, 1944; The Quarry, 1947; Medical Meeting, 1949; The Southwest Corner, 1951; The Curlew's Cry, 1955; The Body of a Young Man, 1960; If a Lion Could Talk, 1970; A Piece of the World, 1972.

ABOUT: Current Biography 1947. *Periodicals*—Library Journal May 1, 1951; Nation March 19, 1955; New York Times February 9, 1947; Saturday Review of Literature February 17, 1934; January 22, 1944.

**WALKLEY, ARTHUR BINGHAM** (December 17, 1855–October 8, 1926), English drama critic and essayist, was born in Bedminster, Bristol, the only child of Arthur Hickman Walkley, a book-seller, and Caroline Charlotte (Bingham) Walkley. He attended Warminster School, entered Balliol College, Oxford, and was admitted as a scholar of Corpus Christi College in January of 1873. In 1877, Walkley was appointed third-class clerk in the secretary's office of the General Post Office. By 1899, he had risen to the rank of principal clerk and in 1911 he was made assistant secretary in charge of the Post Office telegraph branch.

As Walkley climbed the ranks of the civil service, he became interested in the drama criticisms of his friend, the playwright and translator of Ibsen, William Archer. Having read Archer's *English Dramatists of Today* (1882), Walkley began to focus on the theater, and in 1888, under the name of "Spectator," became the drama critic for the newly formed *Star* evening newspaper. Following this tenure at the *Star* he became in 1890 drama critic for the *Speaker*. In 1892 many of his articles written for the *Speaker* and other periodicals were published as a volume entitled *Playhouse Impressions*. In 1899, he was appointed drama critic of the *Times*, where, as his obituary notes, he became a critic "so sensitive, so fearless, so acute . . . that his work was the creative art of letters, not the writing of news." His first article for the *Times* was a review of Herbert Beerbohm Tree's production of *King John*. Walkley also contributed to the *Times'* weekly publication, *Literature*, as well as to the *Times Literary Supplement* upon its formation in 1902. While writing for The *Times*, Walkley became an accomplished essayist. His miscellaneous essays, printed on Wednesdays, were collected and published in three volumes entitled *Pastiche and Prejudice* (1921), *More Prejudice* (1923), and *Still More Prejudice* (1925). All three volumes were generally praised for their stimulating and entertaining insights into the theater world.

Walkley, whose criticism was sound rather than in any sense deep, often described himself as an "impressionist" critic who came fresh and unprejudiced to each book and play he reviewed. Calling drama "a pleasure of the senses" in his *Dramatic Criticism*, he based his critical approach not on a drama's adherence to convention or rule, but rather to the emotion and sensation the production aroused. Owing to this critical approach, Walkley (influenced here by Archer) praised Ibsen's plays and thereby countered the contempt and misunderstanding to which they were initially subjected by English audiences. Later in life, however, Walkley, who was conventional at heart, favored light French comedies. He became highly critical of the newly emerging "drama of ideas" as written, most notably, by Bernard Shaw.

Walkley so far as he is remembered at all, is remembered as "A great reader, a greater lover of letters, and at the same time a man of the world" (*Time*). He was widely read not only in England but in America and France as well. Fruit-growing and rock gardening at his country home in Brightlingsea, Essex, were his favorite hobbies. In 1881, he married Frances Eldridge; they had one daughter.

PRINCIPAL WORKS: Playhouse Impressions, 1892; Frames of Minds, 1899; Dramatic Criticism, 1903; Drama and Life, 1907; Pastiche and Prejudice, 1921; More Prejudice, 1923; Still More Prejudice, 1925.

ABOUT: Child, H. H. The Post Victorians; Dictionary of National Biography, 1922–1930; London Mercury November 1926; New Statesman October 16, 1926; Times (London) October 9, 1926.

**WALLACE, EDGAR** (April 1, 1875–February 10, 1932), English novelist, dramatist, balladeer, and journalist, was born in Greenwich, the illegiti-

mate son of Marie (known as Polly) Richards, an actress, and Richard Marriott. Wallace was brought up by George Freeman, a Billingsgate fishporter, and his wife, and was known, for much of his early life, as Dick Freeman. He was educated at St. Peter's School, in Thames Street, and, after the Freemans moved to Camberwell, at a Board School in Reddin's Road. Of the education he and other poor children received, Wallace was later dismissive, saying in his *Autobiography*, "the system is as wrong as it can be, and hour after hour of time is wasted in inculcating into a class of fifty, knowledge which is of no interest whatever except to possibly two or three."

His formal schooling officially ended at the age of twelve, but before this he had been a regular truant, selling newspapers at Ludgate Circus, very close to where a bronze plaque commemorating him would later be placed. Between the ages of twelve and eighteen, Wallace worked in various occupations, including spells in a shoe shop, a mackintosh factory, and as the assistant to a milkman. An avid reader, he obtained his favorite authors (Rider Haggard, J. J. Jerome) from the circulating library. Increasingly frustrated by the limited horizons pro-

vided by working-class employment, he joined the Royal West Kent Regiment as a seven year enlistee. Transferred to the Medical Staff Corps at his own request, he was drafted to South Africa.

His early writing consisted of Kiplingesque cockney ballads, which he sold to various publications, both in South Africa and London, for ten shillings or a guinea. His most notable poem—"Welcome to Kipling," written to coincide with the imminent arrival in South Africa of Rudyard Kipling, whom Wallace was invited to meet at a City Club dinner—was printed in the *Cape Times*, in January 1898. Four collections of his verse were published, among them *The Mission that Failed* and *Writ in Barracks*. Purchasing his discharge from the army in 1899, Wallace became a Reuters correspondent, covering the Boer War, then contributor to the *Daily Mail*, before becoming the first editor of the South African *Rand Daily Mail*, founded in 1902. Wallace had been married the previous year to Ivy Waldecott, and feeling prosperous for the first time in his life began to develop the extravagant habits and luxurious tastes that were to force him to maintain that prodigious productivity that was his hallmark as a thriller-writer.

His first novel, *The Four Just Men*, about a group who take the law into their own hands, was published in 1905. By this time his short South African editorship was at an end, and he was back in England, working in the first instance for the *Daily Mail*, where he had been given a job as a staff reporter, later taking over from Walter J. Evans as editor of the *Evening News*. *The Four Just Men* was written while his wife and child were on holiday in South Africa, and in their absence Wallace thought up a grandiose scheme of self-publication and self-publicity, the crowning touch of which was the announcement of prizes for readers coming up with the most ingenious solutions to the mystery. The novel's profits were eaten up by the administration of prizes and other advertising, and although its sales ultimately convinced Wallace of his marketing acumen, Margaret Lane shows in her biography how close the episode brought him to nervous collapse.

Outwardly lethargic, with a distaste for any form of exercise, Wallace did much of his work in a dressing-gown, chain-smoking (from expensive cigarette holders, to keep the smoke out of his eyes) and drinking copious amount of weak, sweetened tea, which he had freshly brewed every thirty minutes. Once he had gone earnestly into the production of thrillers—by the 1920s and 1930s it was claimed that a quarter of all books read had been written by Wallace—he established a routine of starting work very early in the morning, getting two or three hours done before breakfast. Most of his novels were spoken into a dictaphone, typed up by his wife or a secretary, and then rapidly and not too painstakingly corrected.

Wallace was an imaginative, and at times bizarre, creator of plots. If his characterization was two-dimensional, this was compensated for by narratives so intricate and sensational that they bordered on the surreal. Writing in 1928, Arnold

Bennett said, "Edgar Wallace has a very great defect. . . . He is content with society as it is. He parades no subversive opinions. He is 'correct.'" However, Martin Seymour-Smith, in *Who's Who in Twentieth Century Literature*, commented that "*The Fellowship of the Frog (1925)* . . . is in fact a superb—if illiterate—surrealist novel; it is magnificently imagined and, if only in a socioanthropological sense, critical of society." *The Four Just Men*, Seymour-Smith also observed, was "founded on an essentially subversive and antiestablishment concept."

As stated in the *New York Times* obituary, Wallace's "actual output was declared to be beyond accurate computation." It is estimated that he wrote between one hundred-fifty and two hundred novels. Although he never forgave his mother for abandoning him, and refused to have anything to do with her when she eventually made contact with him, he was always conscious that the theater was in his blood, and towards the end of his life his work as a playwright assumed, in his own estimation, more importance than his work as a writer of stories, and he confided to his publisher, "If I can only get my plays to go, I will give up writing books." Wallace had his first play, *The Ringer*, produced in 1926. It was largely the success of the plays—*The Calendar* (1929), *On the Spot* (1930), and *The Case of the Frightened Lady* (1931)—which led to his being invited to Hollywood to work as a scriptwriter. (He was already on the Board of the British Lion Film Corporation, which had made silent movies out of several Wallace stories, one of which, *Red Aces*, he had directed himself, and was to direct the company's first 'talkie,' a production of his own *The Squeaker* (1930).

Despite his success, Wallace was attracted to Hollywood by the lure of money. He had backed his own plays and kept them running longer than was commercially viable. His ownership of racehorses and attendant gambling were only one aspect of an expensive lifestyle. Just before departing for the United States he stood as an unsuccessful Liberal candidate in Blackpool. He sailed in November 1931, leaving behind his second wife, Ethel Violet (King), known as 'Jim,' who was twenty-three years younger than himself. In February of the new year he was taken suddenly ill, his constitution weakened by nervous exhaustion and (undiagnosed) diabetes; double pneumonia set in, and news of his death reached England just as 'Jim' was preparing to sail out to his bedside.

His journalistic career had continued alongside his phenomenal literary output. He had been a racing editor of several papers, including *The Week-End Racing Supplement*, and founded two racing broadsheets of his own—*Bibury's* and *R.E. Walton's Weekly*. He was a drama critic for the *Morning Post* and contributed on an occasional basis to the *Birmingham Post*. During World War I he served in the Lincoln's Inn branch of the Special Constabulary and as one of the civilian debriefing interviewers employed by the War Office to assess enemy treatment of invalided soldiers.

PRINCIPAL WORKS: *Fiction*—The Four Just Men, 1905; The Council of Justice, 1908; Sanders of the River, 1911; Bones, 1915; The Clue of the Twisted Candle, 1916; The Just Men of Cordova, 1917; The Man Who Knew, 1919; The Daffodil Mystery, 1920; The Angel of Terror, 1922; The Crimson Circle, 1922; The Clue of the New Pin, 1923; Room 13, 1924; The Fellowship of the Frog, 1925; The Mind of Mr. J. G. Reeder, 1925; The Black Abbot, 1926; The Man from Morocco, 1926; The Forger, 1927; Terror Keep, 1927; The Double, 1928; The Flying Squad, 1928; The Cat Burglar, 1929; Red Aces, 1929; The India Rubber Men, 1929; Green Ribbon, 1930; The Frightened Lady, 1932. *Poetry*—The Mission that Failed, 1898; Writ in Barracks, 1900. *Drama*—The Squeaker, 1927; The Ringer, 1929; On the Spot, 1931. *Autobiography*—People, 1926.

ABOUT: Dictionary of National Biography, 1931–1940, 1949; Lane, M. Edgar Wallace: The Biography of a Phenomenon, 1938; Reilly, J. M. (ed.) Twentieth Century Crime and Mystery Writers, 1985; Seymour-Smith, M. Who's Who in Twentieth Century Literature, 1976; Wallace, E. People, 1926; Who's Who 1932. *Bibliographies*—Lofts, O.G. and Adley, D. The British Bibliography of Wallace, 1969. *Periodicals*—New York Times February 11, 1932; Times (London) February 10, 1932.

**WALLAS, GRAHAM** (May 31, 1858–August 19, 1932), English political psychologist and educator, was born in Monkwearmouth, Sunderland, the son of Gilbert Innes Wallas, a vicar, and Frances Talbot (Peacock) Wallas. Graham was educated at Shrewsbury, and then went on as a scholar, to Corpus Christi College, Oxford (1877–1881). Later he was to have misgivings about Great Britains's public school system. In 1881 Wallas  became a teacher of classics at Highgate School; but he resigned in 1885 "on a question of religious conformity." From 1890 until 1895 he was a university extension lecturer. In 1895 he was appointed lecturer in political science at the London School of Economics and Political Science (LSE), the school he helped to create; he held (1914–1923) the political science chair at London University of which the LSE was part. He lectured in the United States four times between 1890 and 1928, delivering the Lowell lectures at Boston in 1914 and the Dodge lectures at Yale University in 1919.

Wallas's keen interest in education prompted him to serve in a number of academic posts in and around London, but he said he desired to be known best by his books—which, according to Gilbert Murray, demonstrate that Wallas was "one of the keenest and subtlest critics of the Victorian age in thought, in convention, in education, in methods of government . . . one of the most original minds of his generation."

In 1896 Wallas, as a confirmed socialist, joined the Fabian Society, a group formed by George Bernard Shaw and Sidney and Beatrice Webb. In 1889 he contributed to *Fabian Essays on Socialism*. He resigned from the society in 1904, disapproving of some of its dominant members' support for Joseph Chamberlain's "Empire preferential" tariff policy. He was really too original a thinker for the Fabians, and dissented in particular from their rather muddled educational policies. He was less of a Marxist than, as Terrence H. Qualter put it, morally "outraged" at the whole notion of Capitalism. Although his formal ties with the society were severed, he remained sympathetic to the Fabian concept of socialism throughout his life, and continued to promote notions of social and political intervention. He freely criticized British leadership in World War I on both the civil and military fronts, fruitlessly, and argued that politics should be more rationalized and scientific.

For his first book, *The Life Of Francis Place* (1898), Wallas researched the records of the British labor movement pioneer who helped to initiate wholesale social legislation in England. "Few people had heard of Francis Place till Wallas discovered him," wrote Gilbert Murray; but by the time an American edition was published in 1920, H. J. Laski wrote in the *Dial* that, "It is almost idle to praise it now, for it has taken its place among the accepted masterpieces of English political biography."

Wallas's *Human Nature in Politics* (1908), was considered an innovative book, warning of excessive intellectualization in political thinking. In it Wallas pleaded for a closer association between psychological and political studies and warned that without such ties, democracy would be in greater peril. Wallas "has not simply applied already worked out psychological doctrines to a new subject matter: he has enlarged and enriched psychology itself by his interpretation," wrote Ernest Talbert in *Psychology Bulletin.* The *Saturday Review* credited Wallas for "some profound reflections," but wrote that many of the book's earlier chapters are "a repetition, in a less lucid form, of Walter Bagehot's *Physics and Politics.*" Yet the book was hardly representative of the central thrust of Wallas's work, which was directed, mainly, at the dangers of irrational thinking, of which he was much more afraid. He wanted to teach people to think more clearly.

In his treatise on social psychology, *The Great Society* (1914), Wallas stressed the need for humanizing modern large-scale life. He aimed to bring psychological knowledge into the realm of political thought. "Arriving at many significant conclusions about human nature in our modern environment, the author is led into a startlingly clear criticism not only of the classic moralists and economists, but also of the dogmatists of conservatism, socialism, and syndicalism. These criticisms give the book its principal value," wrote the *New York Times.* "It was the work of a close observer, a clear thinker, and a real humanitarian," according to *Outlook.*

With *Our Social Heritage* (1921), Wallas wrote a political analysis of the different elements of the social tradition that helped to create the individual of that time. *Literary Review* wrote that the book explained politics "as a force shaped in part by influence of individual heredity, and in part by that of an inherited environment." H. E. Barnes in the *American Political Science Review* claimed that the book "is probably as progressive and constructive a work as one can look for within the camp of liberal orthodoxy in social and political theory."

Wallas next wrote a description of the creative thinking process in *The Art of Thought* (1926), in which he presented four stages of an individual's scientific growth. It was praised for being stimulating, unconventional and engagingly intimate. "Unlike most psychologists Professor Wallas knows how to write. He has known, moreover, most of the distinguished and interesting men of his day, who seem to have asked nothing better than to favour him with private information about their intellectual methods with exact particulars of how and when they wrote and thought. As a consequence, his book is unusually full of anecdote and illustration," commented C. E. M. Joad in *Spectator.*

Only half finished at his death, and edited by his daughter, May Wallas, *Social Judgment* (1934) used history and psychology as a base for concentrating on "the nature, history and possible improvement of the judgment process" and "the institutions through which judgement influences social action." The *Times Literary Supplement* wrote, "Incomplete though it is, it reveals the qualities which made its author so stimulating and so lovable a teacher—the close contact of his thought with the life around him, the richness and integrity of his mind, his curious, demure deadliness in criticism."

Published posthumously, *Men and Ideas* (1940) is a collection of Wallas's lectures and articles on social and political science and education as well as biographical sketches he wrote of relevant leaders in these fields with whom he agreed, including Bentham, Froebel, and Ruskin.

In a prefatory character sketch of Wallas, Gilbert Murray commented that Wallas was "free from fixed orthodoxies, prejudices, partisan feelings. His eyes used positively to sparkle when he came to the conclusion that some former view of his own was wrong and he could effectively set to work disproving it."

PRINCIPAL WORKS: *As contributor*—Fabian Essay on Property Under Socialism, 1889; The Life of Francis Place, 1898; Human Nature in Politics, 1908; The Great Society, 1914; Our Social Heritage, 1921; The Art of Thought, 1926; Social Judgment, 1934; Men and Ideas, 1940.

ABOUT: Barnes, H. E. *introduction* to the History of Sociology; Dictionary of National Biography, 1931–1940; Qualter, T. H. Graham Wallas and the Great Society, 1980. Wallas, G. Men and Ideas (preface by G. Muray); Wiener, M. J. Between Two Words, 1971. *Periodicals*—New York Times July 19, 1914, August 11, 1932; Outlook September 9, 1914; Psychology Bulletin December 15, 1909; Saturday Review January 9, 1909; Spectator August 14, 1926; Times (London) August 11, 1932; Times Literary Supplement January 3, 1935.

**WALLER, MARY ELLA** (March 1, 1855–June 15, 1938), American novelist and essayist, was born in Boston, the daughter of David Waller of Vermont and Mary Doane (Hallet) Waller of Cape Cod; she was twelve when her father and her only brother died. She then toured Europe for four years with her mother. On her return to Boston, she began teaching at Mrs. Shaw's finishing school; and later held a similar position at the Brearley School in New York. She later founded Miss Waller's School for Girls in Chicago, but retired after five years due to poor health.

Before beginning her writing career, Waller translated many German poems. She described herself as a "quite old-fashioned person" and a disciple of Louisa May Alcott. Her early novels were written in Vermont. *A Daughter of the Rich* (1903), a favorite among young readers, told the story of the daughter of a wealthy father who has to leave New York due to illness. *The Wood-Carver of 'Lympus'* (1904) is the story of a family living in a small settlement in the Green Mountains in the 1890s; this went through twenty-eight editions.

When Waller's focus moved away from her native New England, it was often toward Europe. She wrote for example, an intimate sketch of Holland and the Dutch people in *Through the Gates of the Netherlands* (1906), narrated by an architect's wife during a sojourn with her husband.

Nanette, a Parisian waif who learns the secret of happiness and shares it with a world-weary artist, was the heroine of *My Ragpicker* (1911). The *New York Times*, with an indulgence typical of the period, wrote that the "charming novelette shows no abatement of that artistic touch and fine, sweet insight into the nobilities of human nature that have distinguished [Waller's] previous works and given them a remarkable vogue."

In *From an Island Outpost* (1914), part diary and part journal, Waller recorded days spent on an island off the Massachusetts coast, probably Nantucket, where she had moved in 1910. "In every page Miss Waller has written a striking autobiography of her mind," wrote the *Boston Transcript*. "Jottings and reflections on whatsoever crops up in the daily life of her island home . . . strung together loosely as a necklace of seashell," wrote he *New York Times*, adding "there is nothing too trivial to start Miss Waller's facile pen, nothing too humble for her contemplation."

Waller set *Deep in the Hearts of Men* (1924) in the mountains of New Hampshire, West Virginia, and the central Alleghenies of Pennsylvania, where a coal miner searches for spirituality. "This book will appeal strongly to those readers who still have some faith in old-fashioned goodness, idealism, and even in romantic love as distinguished from the sometimes clinical 'realism' of the more modern schools of fiction," wrote H. L. Pangborn in *Literary Review*. *Outlook* called Waller "a yearning sentimentalist," who "has a large following among readers who like a rich frosting on their spongecake."

Waller's final book, *The Windmill on the Dune* (1931), written when she was over seventy-five, tells the story of an artist from Cape Cod who, deserted by his young wife, moves to France, studies painting in Paris, and finally goes to the coast of Brittany to paint and find new happiness. Considered overly sentimental by discerning critics, the book was praised by *Chum* for its picturesque descriptions of both the Cape Cod and Brittany coasts.

PRINCIPAL WORKS: The Little Citizen, 1902; A Daughter of the Rich, 1903; The Wood-Carver of 'Lympus,' 1904; Sanna, 1905; Through the Gates of the Netherlands, 1906; Our Benny, 1909; A Year Out of Life, 1909; Flamsted Quarries, 1910; My Ragpicker, 1911; A Cry in the Wilderness, 1912; Aunt Dorcas'

Change of Heart, 1913; From an Island Outpost, 1914; Out of the Silences, 1918; Deep in the Hearts of Men, 1924; The Windmill on the Dune, 1931.

ABOUT: Waller, M. E. *introduction to* The Wood-Carver of 'Lympus,' 1929. *Periodicals*—Boston Transcript April 8, 1914; Literary Review August 2, 1924; Outlook October 1924; New York Times June 21, 1914; June 15, 1938; Publishers Weekly July 2, 1938.

**WALLING, ROBERT ALFRED JOHN** (January 11, 1869–September 4, 1948), English journalist and mystery and travel writer, was born in Exeter. His father was a journalist and he followed the same path, serving as a newspaperman in Plymouth for fifty years. In America he was known primarily for his mystery stories, many of which featured the detective Philip Tolefree, whom Walling first introduced in *The Fatal Five Minutes* (1932).

The praise continued throughout the 1930s and 1940s for both the writer and his fictional investigator. "Tolefree, of all detectives of fiction, is one of the most likeable—free from mannerism and affectation, charitable to friends whose perceptions fail to equal his, but with insatiable curiosity and boundless energy when once on the trail of a crime. Tolefree is a welcome relief after one has been in the presence of those uppity sleuths who 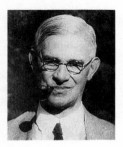 drop their g's and smoke esoteric fags," wrote the *Boston Transcript* critic.

Walling was equally adept at writing about travel and history, focusing on regions he knew and loved, including *The Charm of Brittany* (1933), *The West Country* (1935); an anecdotal guidebook to Devon and Cornwall, which was considered "a better guide than anything else in print to the south-western countries," by the *Spectator*, and *The Green Hills of England* (1938), in which he recounted for fellow travelers his walks through the hill districts of southern England.

Walling's visit to the United States in 1928 as part of a group of British journalists who were guests of the Carnegie Foundation for international peace resulted in the book *Adventures of a Rubberneck* (1929).

PRINCIPAL WORKS: *Mysteries*—The Strong Room, 1926; The Dinner at Bardolph's, 1928; Murder at the Keyhole, 1929; The Man with the Squeaky Voice, 1930; Stroke of One, 1931; The Fatal Five Minutes, 1932; Murder at Midnight, 1932; In Time for Murder, 1933; The Tolliver Case (in U.S.: Prove It, Mr. Tolefree!) 1933; The Bachelor Flat Mystery, 1934; Legacy of Death, 1934; Behind the Yellow Blind, 1935; Follow the Blue Car, 1935; The Cat and the Corpse, 1935; The Corpse in the Green Pajamas, 1935; The Corpse in the Crimson Slippers, 1936; The Corpse with the Dirty Face, 1936; The Corpse with the Floating Foot, 1936; The Five Suspects, 1936; Mr. Tolefree's Reluctant Witnesses (in U.S.: The Corpse in the Coppice) 1936; Bury Him Deeper, 1937; Marooned with Murder, 1937; The Mystery of Mr. Mock, 1937; The Coroner Doubts (in U.S.: The Corpse with the Blue Cravat) 1938; The Corpse with the Grimy Glove, 1938; Dust in the Vault, 1939; The Corpse with the Blistered Hand, 1939; The Corpse with the Red-Headed Friend, 1939; The Spider and the Fly, 1940; Why

Did Trethewy Die?, 1940; By Hook or Crook, 1941; The Corpse with the Eerie Eye, 1942; A Corpse By Any Other Name, 1943; The Corpse without a Clue, 1944; The Late Unlamented, 1948; The Corpse with the Missing Watch, 1949. Nonfiction—A Sea Dog of Devon: A Life of Sir John Hawkins, 1907; George Borrow: The Man and His Work, 1908; On the British Front, 1919; Adventures of a Rubberneck, 1929; The Diaries of John Bright (ed.) 1931; The Charm of Brittany, 1933; The West Country, 1935; The Green Hills of England, 1938; The Story of Plymouth, 1950.

ABOUT: Haycraft, H. Murder for Pleasure: The Life and Times of the Detective Story; Who's Who 1949. Periodicals—Books July 1, 1934, January 5, 1936; Boston Transcript February 4, 1933; New York Herald Tribune Weekly Book Review August 22, 1948; New York Times January 26, 1930; July 17, 1932; September 18, 1949; Publishers' Weekly October 8, 1949; Saturday Review of Literature October 16, 1937; Spectator June 21, 1935; Times (London) March 18, 1939; September 6, 1949; November 24, 1950; Weekly Book Review March 28, 1943.

**WALMSLEY, LEO** (September 29, 1892–June, 1966) English novelist, wrote: "My published works bear a close relation to my own life. That is, my first

book *Flying and Sport in East Africa*, is a record of my war service, 1914–18. Two boys' books of African adventure were drawn from my war experiences in Africa and from post-war expeditions to Central Africa. The 'thrillers' followed, but they were not good. I did, however, write some nature stories that appeared in *Adventure* that I'm not ashamed of. But I hope as a writer to wipe out all these early books from the record, which begins after a three-year fallow period (during which I actually earned my way as an inshore fisherman on the Yorkshire coast), with the four novels starting with *Three Fevers*. Storm Jameson, then Sir Arthur Quiller-Couch and Edward Garnett, were the first to acclaim these books, but none of them made 'sold,' although *Three Fevers* made fame (but little money) in its film version, *Turn of the Tide*. Some of these novels are referred to in my autobiographical novel, *Love in the Sun*, my first popular success in England and the United States. It was the English Book Society choice for the August before the outbreak of the present war.

"I make no bid for laurels as a literary bloke. I think I can describe myself as a *story teller*, and to me the main thing is to have the experience, digest it, and recreate it as a story, to be told in the simplest language, but with absolute sincerity. I have been accused of 'journalism,' but journalism is an art form I accept provided I am licensed to reject the literal truth for the aesthetic one. Philosophically I am humanist, and prefer to look for the good in people. I hate war, of course, but not so much as I hate Nazism. And I believe the highest hope for the world is in a Federal Union of all the English-speaking peoples."

---

Leo Walmsley was born at Shipley, Yorkshire. His father, J. U. Walmsley, was an artist. One of

Leo Walmsley's first jobs was as curator of the Marine Biological Station at Robin Hood's Bay, which he later fictionalized as the seacoast village of Bramblewick, notably in *Three Fevers* and *Sally Lunn*, which describe a feud between two fishing families. Walmsley considered the Bramblewick books as marking the real beginning of his career as a novelist. There had been earlier books. An account of his war service—he was a flying officer in East Africa, received the Military Cross and was mentioned in dispatches four times—*Flying and Sport in East Africa*, was followed by two books for boys and three thrillers.

Most of Walmsley's books were autobiographical. He had actually worked as an inshore fisherman before writing the Bramblewick books. *Love in the Sun*, a best-seller, describes how he and his first wife went about building themselves a house and a boat in Cornwall.

The London *Times*, in its obituary, commented, "The great charm of Leo Walmsley's writing sprang from its absolute honesty, simplicity and eager affection. He was warmly and keenly interested in all he saw." He continued his fictional autobiography in *The Golden Waterwheel* (1954) and in *The Happy Ending* (1957). *So Many Loves* (1944), published in America as *Turn of the Tide*, was his formal autobiography.

Walmsley was divorced in 1955. He continued to live in Cornwall with his second wife, at Fowey, calling his house "Bramblewick." His nonfiction work included a book on petroleum, a study of fishermen at war, and a short guide to Lancashire and Yorkshire.

A new edition of *So Many Loves*, with an introduction by his second wife, Stephanie Walmsley, was published in 1969.

PRINCIPAL WORKS: Fiction—Toro of the Little People, 1926; Three Fevers, 1932; Phantom Lobster, 1933; Sally Lunn, 1937; Love in the Sun, 1939; Foreigners,1944; Master Mariner, 1948; The Golden Waterwheel, 1954; The Happy Ending, 1957; Sound of the Sea, 1959. Nonfiction—Flying and Sport in East Africa, 1920; Fishermen At War, 1941; British Ports and Harbours, 1942; So Many Loves, 1944 (in U.S.: Turn of The Tide); Lancashire and Yorkshire, 1951; Invisible Cargo, 1952; Angler's Moon, 1965.

ABOUT: Twentieth Century Authors, 1942; Walsmley, L. So Many Loves, 1944 and 1969; Who's Who 1966. Periodicals—New York Times July 24, 1932; Times (London) June 13, 1966; Times Literary Supplement January 20, 1945.

**WALN, NORA** (June 4, 1895–September 27, 1964), American journalist and writer on China and Germany, was born in Grampaign, Pennsylvania, the daughter of Thomas Lincoln Waln, a descendent of some of the first Philadelphians, and Lillia (Quest) Waln, one of whose forefathers was a signer of the Declaration of Independence. At the age of nine she came upon several 1805 issues of the *United States Gazette* in her grandmother's attic. Her interest was immediately sparked by the mention of an ancestor, J. S. Waln, in conjunction with several brigs, schooners and sloops, all of which were headed for China. She began reading Chinese philosophy, memorizing Confucius, collecting maps, log books, and old letters, and even wrote what was called a sad ballad about the emperor. Waln entered Swarthmore College with the class of 1919, but did not graduate, staying only until her junior year, when the United States entered World War I. (The college later awarded her an honorary M.A. in 1940.) Moving to Washington DC, she took a job as editor of a newspaper page called Women's Work in the War and from 1917 to 1919 she worked as publicity director for the Near East Relief Committee in New York City. She held the position for two years. In 1920 Waln set sail for China in search of the Lin family of Hopei Province. The Lins, who lived in their family homestead "The House of Exile" were descendants of those with whom the early Walns—who Nora Waln had read about in her childhood—had a history of trade and friendship. Waln lived with the family for two years. On one of her visits to America during this time she met George Edward Osland-Hill, an Englishman in the foreign service in Peking. The two were married in 1922 in Shanghai, but only after the Dean of the Cathedral of the Church of England in Shanghai could be persuaded to perform the service since Waln, a Quaker, had never been baptized. The two had one daughter, Marie. The rise of nationalism in China made anti-western feelings almost unbearable for the couple, and, in the fall of 1926 Waln went to England and then to Italy where her husband had told her to remain until conditions in China became more friendly. Unable to wait, she returned to China, settling in Tientsin for two years. While there, Waln returned to the Lins once more, this time bearing the manuscript she had written based on her stay at The House of Exile. She allowed the family to read it before its submission to the publisher, but their reaction was less than enthusiastic. The ninety-six-year-old Kuei-Tzu remarked: Scholarship is useless to a woman. All she needs to know is how to handle men, which any woman can do if she is a good cook. In contrast to the Lins' feelings, reviews of *House of Exile*, which was published in 1933, were good. The *Saturday Review of Literature* (1933) critic called it undoubtedly one of the most delightful books of personal experience that has yet been written about China, and *New Republic* reviewer commented that "by shrewd selection and narrative skill this material is made very interesting." *House of Exile* was reprinted in 1992 with five chapters of a previously unpublished sequel, which the author had written in 1947.

In June 1934 Waln went to Germany with her husband, who had since retired from the foreign service and was now interested in studying music. At first the two were accepted warmly by the German government—Hitler had actually bought thirty-five copies of *House of Exile*. Things changed, however, when it was learned that Waln was writing a book based on her impressions of Nazism. She

and her husband prepared to leave Germany, and, as a precaution, she mailed each of the three copies of her manuscript out of the country, each from different post offices. None were ever delivered, and the author was forced to rewrite the book from her notes and from memory. *Reaching for the Stars* was published in 1939. According to the *New York Times* (September 27, 1964) Waln had sent a copy of the published book, along with an inscription, to Himmler, Hitler's SS and police chief. In reaction, Humbler tracked down and seized seven children, all of whom had been mentioned in *Reaching for the Stars*, though their names had been disguised in the book. Entering Germany secretly for a meeting with Himmler, Waln offered herself as a hostage in place of the children. He agreed on the condition that she write nothing further about Germany. The author declined saying, "if you make a bargain like that, God takes away the power to write. If you don't tell the truth you lose your talent." Elsewhere *Reaching for the Stars* received good reviews. The *Atlantic* (1939) called it "a human document of gripping intensity," and R.C. Feld for *Books* (1939) commented: "To every intelligent person who wants to know what the German people are thinking while they are acting according to the rule, *Reaching for the Stars* is mandatory reading." In 1993 a new edition of the book was printed under the title *The Approaching Storm: One Woman's Story of Germany 1934–1938.*

In London, where Waln and her husband had settled after leaving Germany, she began doing war work, becoming a member of several relief organizations including the American Outpost in Britain and the China Convoy Committee of Friends Ambulance Unit, and her college sorority established the Nora Waln Fund for Refugee Children, for which she distributed the funds. After the war, Waln traveled extensively throughout Europe as a correspondent for the *Atlantic Monthly*. In 1946 she returned to the United States for the first time in more than twenty years, where the *Atlantic Monthly* published a chapter of her unfinished book on the Quaker, Rufus Jones. From 1947 to 1951 she was Tokyo correspondent for the *Saturday Evening Post* and was attached to General MacArthur's headquarters, spending six months on the Korean battlefield. Waln died in Spain at the home of a friend. She lived the last three years of her life in Rincón de la Victoria, near Malaga, in Southern Spain.

PRINCIPAL WORKS: Street of Precious Pearls, 1921; House of Exile, 1933 (rpt. 1992); Reaching for the Stars, 1939 (rpt. as The Approaching Storm: One Womans Story of Germany 1934–1938, 1993).

ABOUT: Contemporary Authors vol. 89-92, 1980; Current Biography Yearbook 1940, 1964; Who Was Who in America vol. IV 1961–1968, 1968; Who's Who 1964. *Periodicals*—Atlantic April 1939; Books March 5, 1939; New Republic May 31, 1933; New York Times September 27, 1964; Saturday Review of Literature April 22, 1933.

**WALPOLE, HUGH** (March 13 1884–June 1, 1941) English novelist, was born in Auckland, New Zealand, where his father, Rev. George Somerset  Walpole (later Bishop of Edinburgh), was then serving as canon of St. Mary's, Parnell. In 1890 the Walpole family moved to New York, where Somerset Walpole had been appointed Chair of Systematic Theology at a theological seminary. Hugh was taught by a governess, but in 1893, when he was nine years old, was sent home to England to attend the tiny Newhan House school in Truro, Cornwall. A year later he transferred to a school at Marlow, where he endured two years of misery. He was little happier at the King's School, Canterbury, and when his father was made principal of Bede training college, Durham, Walpole moved north to live with his family, attending Durham School as a day student.

In 1906 Walpole left Emmanuel College, Cambridge, having gained a disappointing third in the historical tripos. After two months of tutoring he spent six months at the Mission to Seamen, in Liverpool, an occupation for which he was entirely unsuited, and in a decisive moment beside the Mersey he determined that he would not take holy orders, as his father hoped, but would become a novelist. Thinking that schoolmastering would be congenial to this ambition, Walpole took up a post at Epsom College, and started work on what was to be his first published novel, *The Wooden Horse*. Deciding, after all, that teaching and writing did not mix, Walpole left the school at the end of 1908 and, moving to London, set about earning his living as a novelist, supported by free-lance work for the Curtis Brown agency (an arrangement which was short-lived), reviewing for the *Standard*, and a capacity for making the right contacts. He enjoyed a close and influential relationship with Henry James, a more adversarial one with Arnold Bennett, and corresponded with a host of literary figures, including reviewers of his own novels.

Walpole was an admirer of Trollope and derided what he called, in a letter to Arnold Bennett, the "tight little right little novels done on the Flaubert model." But he was much more intrigued with the portrayal of evil than Trollope and had been influenced by a teenage reading of *The Scarlet Letter*. Rupert Hart-Davis, in his 1952 biography, quoted from an unpublished essay on Hawthorne in which Walpole identified polarities in the American author that applied equally to himself—"the normal and the abnormal, the law-abiding, slightly priggish, amiable citizen, and the rebel, the necromancer, the solitary outcast."

The "abnormal" presented itself in Walpole's third (most consider it his best) novel, *Mr. Perrin and Mr. Thrail*, the first of his books which sold well. Based on his experiences at Epsom College, its psychologically morbid treatment of the relation-ship between an older and a younger schoolmaster represents Walpole writing at the height of his powers. But thereafter his reputation as a serious novelist was repeatedly undermined by uneven output, as he fell victim to his own facility. "My hatred of revision and my twist towards abnormality spoil much of my work," he confided to his diary, when aged forty and in the middle of his career. *Portrait of a Man with Red Hair*, which Walpole described to Frank Swinnerton as a "simple shocker" certainly shocked many readers with its depiction of sadism.

Excused from active service during World War I on the grounds of his near-sightedness, Walpole—determined to be involved—served with the Russian Red Cross. Both *The Dark Forest* and *The Secret City* draw on his experiences in Petrograd. Walpole was at his weakest when, ceasing to rely on personal experience and denying his homosexuality, he wrote self-consciously in the vein of Trollope. *The Cathedral*, set in the Barchester-equivalent Polchester (a fictional cathedral-town based on Truro), Walpole's novel at least had the virtue of drawing on details gleaned from his father's background. The book sold well, and Walpole went on to produce three sequels—*Judith Paris*, *The Fortress*, and *Vanessa*.

*John Cornelius*, a long mock-biography of an imaginary Edwardian author, received particularly hostile treatment. V. S. Pritchett wrote, in the *New Statesman* that "no other living novelist puts so many Baedeker stars and pointers to good passages." And Louis Kronenberger, the *New York Times* reviewer, found the book "stained, smeared, vitiated with second-rateness."

Caricatured in Somerset Maugham's *Cakes and Ale* as Alroy Kear, Walpole became increasingly irritated by the realization that he was considered a hack. His self-justifying replies to hostile reviewers became notorious; but he failed to channel his sense of indignation into the creation of a late novel that might shore up his reputation.

Walpole wrote two critical studies—of Conrad and Trollope—and was a regular reviewer. He was chairman of the Society of Bookmen (before it became the National Book League) and was financially generous to several struggling young writers. Knighted in 1937, his portrait was painted by Augustus John and Walter Sickert and a bronze bust was sculpted by Jacob Epstein. Walpole, a collector of first and fine editions, bequeathed his library to the Fitzwilliam Museum, the Bodleian, the King's School, Canterbury, and the National Library of Scotland.

PRINCIPAL WORKS: The Wooden Horse, 1909; Maradick at Forty, 1910; Mr. Perrin and Mr. Traill, 1911 (in U.S.: The Gods and Mr. Perrin); The Prelude to Adventure, 1912; Fortitude, 1913; The Dutchess of Wrexe, 1914; The Golden Scarecrow, 1915 (stories); The Dark Forest, 1916; The Green Mirror, 1917; The Secret City, 1919; The Captives, 1920; The Thirteen Travellers, 1921 (stories); The Young Enchanted, 1921; The Cathedral, 1922; The Old Ladies, 1924; Portrait of a Man with Red Hair, 1925; Harmer John, 1926; The Silver Thorn, 1928 (stories); Wintersmoon, 1928; (with J. B. Priestly) Farthing Hall, 1929; Hans Frost, 1929; Rogue Harrier, 1930; Above the Dark Circus, 1931 (in U.S.: Above The Dark Tumult); Judith

Paris, 1931; The Fortress, 1932; All Soul's Night, 1933 (stories); Vanessa, 1933; Captain Nicholas, 1934; The Inquisitor, 1935; A Prayer for My Son, 1936: John Cornelius, 1937; Head in Green Bronze, 1938 (stories); The Joyful Delaneys, 1938; The Sea Tower, 1939; The Bright Pavilions, 1940; Roman Fountain, 1940; The Blind Man's House, 1941; The Killer and the Slain, 1942; Katherine Christian, 1943; Mr. Huffam, 1948 (stories). Nonfiction—Joseph Conrad, 1916; Reading, 1926; Anthony Trollope, 1928; My Religious Experience, 1928. Autobiography—The Crystal Box, 1924; The Apple Trees, 1932. Drama—The Haxtons, 1939. Juvenile—Jeremy, 1919; Jeremy and Hamlet, 1923; Jeremy at Crale, 1927.

ABOUT: Dictionary of National Biography, 1941–1950, 1959; Hart-Davis, R. Hugh Walpole, 1952; Seymour-Smith M. Guide to Modern World Literature, 1985; Steele, E. Walpole, 1972; Who's Who 1941. Periodicals—New Statesman September 11, 1937; New York Times September 26, 1937; June 2, 1941; Spectator September 22, 1939; Time May 13, 1940; August 18, 1952; Times (London) June 2, 1941.

**WALSH, MAURICE** (May 2, 1879–February 18, 1964), Irish novelist and short story writer, wrote: "Where was I born a good half century ago? Kerry.

Kerry is that most mountainous county in the far South and West of Ireland. I was the son and the grandson and the great-grandson of farmers and rebels, but we could take our genealogy back to the sixteenth century, when our forefather was hanged for piracy on the high seas. I lived close to the soil well into my teens and learned to use a Queen Anne duck gun eight feet long to the danger of bird, beast, and any British subject. I once killed 95 curlew at one shot, sold them for what you would call $20, and bought beer for the community. My father had a fine library and was a powerful authority on blood horses. I began trying my hand at writing short stories, and the Weekly Freeman, a Dublin paper, used to give me an occasional two guineas. I wrote about Australian bush-ranging, and Klondike gold-digging, and the Boer War, and other subjects with which I was closely acquainted at a distance. Also I wrote a long historical romance, blood and love on every page, and I couldn't tell you which was hotter and which redder. I used some of that material later on in Blackcock's Feather.

"I never saw the walls of a city until the end of last century when, a growing lad, I went to Dublin at the request of my mother to stand a Civil Service examination. I didn't want to pass. I wanted to go out and fight for the Boers, but had a loyalty to my mother. I did that exam so recklessly, so debonairely, that I was in the first fifty of two thousand, and the next thing I knew I was pitchforked into the Customs Excise Service. With a couple hundred youngsters like myself I wandered up and down in Ireland, Scotland, Wales, and England. I was drawn back again and again and yet again to the Highlands of Scotland. She had red hair and a temperament also. She married me at long last, and though her hair is not now quite so red I will say nothing about her temperament. During the war I

was on War Service on the coast, sword unbloody and head unbowed. And after the Irish Treaty I volunteered to serve my own country.

"Up to then I had scarcely written a thing—too busy living. But here in Dublin during the Civil War, my family still in Scotland, and night-sniping the national pastime, I had to stay largely indoors of nights, and I got tired of reading. So I tried to recapture in the written word some of the scenes and characters and stories that I had known in Scotland. The result of that scribbling was The Key Above the Door, and that thing has sold some hundred thousand copies. Somehow, like a damn fool, I couldn't stop after that, but my pace was never fast. So here I am living outside Dublin within sound of the sea and sight of the hills. We intend to move out into the wilds when the bombing planes come over. Meantime I write a little, shoot a little, fish a little, garden a lot, and go on talking. We have three sons, one a doctor, one a banker, and one a medical student. We have two grandsons and I will now write you sixteen pages on the ways of grandsons. But no. . . . "

———

Maurice Walsh was born in County Kerry, the son of Elizabeth (Buckley) and John Walsh, a farmer and land-leaguer. Educated at Lisselton, Ballybunion and St. Michael's College, Listowel, Walsh entered the Customs Excise Service, and did not become a full-time writer until 1934.

Walsh's stories and novels were routinely described by reviewers as "wholesome" and "contagiously healthy." The Key above the Door, set in the Highlands, packed with outdoor pursuits, and with a couple of episodes of hand-to-hand combat, set the pattern for Walsh's subsequent novels. It was an immediate success, and elicited a congratulatory letter from Sir James Barrie. The setting and period would sometimes change—Blackcock's Feather, based on his adolescent attempt at romance writing, was set in sixteenth-century Ireland—but the emphasis was always on entertainment. Although the Saturday Review of Literature forecast that "to some children of our realistic age [Walsh's work] may appear sugary in its romantic attitudes," it was not until the end of his career that his brand of romance began to pall. The New York Times Book Review, in its notice of Tomasheen James Gets His Hair Cut, a posthumous collection of short stories, pronounced the book "suitable fare only for those . . . who still think of Ireland as a place where everybody is Barry Fitzgerald on a coy day."

Barry Fitzgerald was the actor who played the part of Michaeleen Flynn in the movie version of The Quiet Man, Walsh's best-known story, about a boxer who returns to his native Irish village. The film, which was directed by John Ford, scripted by his son-in-law Frank Nugent, and starring Maureen O'Hara and John Wayne, does more than justice to the original story. Of the novels, no single title stands out, although his third, The Small Dark Man, serves well enough as a representative title, particularly as Walsh's obsession with red-haired, freckle-faced Highland beauty is, in this book, made the focal point for the romantic quest embarked upon by the hero, Hugh Forbes. Books in which characters exclaim "Crikes!" and "Blazes!" are very much of their period. But Walsh had a talent for bringing gloomy glens and braes to bright life, and an idiosyncratic style in dialogue humor. Sometimes compared with Buchan and Neil M. Gunn (mainly because Walsh's readers tended to be Buchan and Gunn readers too), there is really very little similarity between the three, other than the Scottish setting.

Walsh established his family home at Blackrock, on the foothills of the Dublin Mountains, where, after the death of his wife in 1941, he was looked after by a housekeeper and his grandchildren.

PRINCIPAL WORKS: The Key above the Door, 1927; While Rivers Run, 1928; The Small Dark Man, 1929; Blackcock's Feather, 1932; The Road to Nowhere, 1934; Green Rushes, 1935; And No Quarter (in U.S.: The Dark Rose) 1937; Sons of the Swordmaker, 1938; The Hill Is Mine, 1940; Thomasheen James, 1941; The Spanish Lady, 1943; Nine Strings to Your Bow, 1945; The Man in Brown, 1946; Castle Gillian, 1948; The Damsel Debonair, 1948; Trouble in the Glen, 1950; Son of a Tinker, 1951; Take Your Choice, 1954 (in U.S.: The Honest Fisherman and Other Stories); A Strange Woman's Daughter, 1954; Danger under the Moon, 1956; The Smart Fellow, 1964; Thomasheen James Gets His Hair Cut, 1964.

ABOUT: Contemporary Authors vol. 133 1991; Twentieth Century Authors, 1942. Who's Who 1964. Periodicals—New York Times Book Review November 15, 1964; Saturday Review of Literature February 26, 1927; Times (London) February 19, 1964; Times Literary Supplement August 16, 1928.

**\*WALTARI, MIKA (TOIMI)** (September 19, 1908–August 26, 1979), Finnish novelist, poet, and dramatist, wrote: "I was born in Helsinki. My father

was a clergyman and idealist: among the offices he held was that of prison chaplain in Helsinki. He died early, when I was five. We were poor at home. My mother brought up and schooled her three sons on her small pay as civil service clerk. The most deeply stamped memories I retain from childhood are of the first World War, the Finnish civil war of 1918 and the ensuing famine.

"I passed the university matriculation examination in 1916 and first studied theology. However, my literary career had started the same year I entered school and in 1929 I passed the candidate of philosophy (Master of Arts) examination. My first literary efforts were poems and a collection of stories, published when I was seventeen.

"After that I traveled for a while, studied in Paris, worked in a publishing company, translated books, reviewed books, edited an illustrated weekly and even wrote some movie scenarios. All that time I kept publishing one or two books a year, novels, short stories, plays and some poetry. My greatest artistic success before the wars was due to my novel Vieras mies tuli taloon (A Stranger Came to the Farm) which won first prize in a competition in 1937 and afterwards was translated into eleven Eu-

*VAHL tah ri, MEE kuh

ropean languages. In October 1952 it appeared also in the United States. In 1938 I started living entirely by my pen, but during the Finnish Winter War (1939–1940) and in the following war of 1941–1944 I was doing military service at the governmental information center. . . . My principal work . . . The Egyptian, was written in 1945 and published in the United States in 1949. It has also been translated into ten languages (Swedish, Norwegian, Danish, German, French, English, Spanish, Dutch, Japanese, Portuguese, and Italian). In a certain sense I consider this novel as the sum of my literary efforts and experiences. The research work for it took more than ten years.

"I have knocked about in most of the countries of Europe. The cities dearest to me are Helsinki, Paris, and Istanbul. Spiritually I feel a European as much as a Finn. I am happiest when allowed to work in peace. I have separated myself from all social intercourse. In wintertime I live in Helsinki or travel. The summers I spend in the country writing.

"Of my family I may mention that I married at twenty-two, which was the most sensible act of my life. In addition to my wife [the former Mariatta Luukkonen] our family consists of one daughter, who recently passed her matriculation examination and published her first novel Cafe Mabillon. . . .

"That would be my life in a few words: I am neither a preacher nor a fighter by nature. But if there is any program or tendency to be found between the lines in the books I write nowadays, it is: individual liberty, humaneness, tolerance."

---

Mika Waltari was the son of Toimi Armes Waltari, a pastor and schoolmaster, and Olga Maria Johansson. He was precocious and published a collection of stories while he was still at school. He also wrote two mystery novels and continued to produce these from time to time, although under pseudonyms. He left school at eighteen and entered Helsinki University, initially as a student of theology. But he soon rebelled against his parents' wishes, and turned to the study of philosophy. Even in this early period he blended a virtuosic technical brilliance of expression, a rather superficial and mannered pessimism (learned in Paris, which he visited in 1927), and an extreme conservatism. At only twenty-one he published, and attracted great critical interest in, his first novel, Suuri illusioni (The great illusion, 1928). This, a description of youthful and rebellious bohemian life in the Helsinki of the time, was quickly translated into Swedish, Norwegian, and Estonian. Like the other books (poems, folk tales, plays, more novels) he wrote at that time, it dealt with more or less "post-decadent" themes. He was, it was said by a Finnish critic, "in almost revolutionary disagreement with his background"—which was somewhat severe. His prose style was elegant and amusing, and clearly came from him without much effort.

Waltari was associated at this time with Finland's newest literary movement, Tulenkantajat, "The Torchbearers," a left or liberal-leaning group, some of whose members tried (rather belatedly in their case) to introduce the influence of Russian and Italian futurism into Finnish literature. Waltari wrote fashionable, futurist-tinged verse, but he also soon became the best-known writer of prose in this new movement.

Waltari's writing dealt throughout with the same kind of person: a young—or if not young then sweetly naive—man, who is an idealist who suffers from the presence of wickedness in the world, and who is always made to suffer by women. This central character usually finds that he is incapable of effecting any change to his environment. Waltari was criticized for his capricious, wily, and frequently calculatingly evil female characters; other females in his books tend to be sentimentalized.

In the 1930s the Torchbearer Group came to seem somewhat old-fashioned, and was supplanted by a new and more resolutely left-wing group, consisting of poets, critics, and some prose writers: *Kiila*, "The Wedge." Waltari now became an ultra-conservative, and flirted with the extreme right-wing elements then dominating Finland. He took to satirizing the kind of liberal, bohemian Finnish society of which he had only a few years earlier been an enthusiastic member, in smart and clever (and highly amusing) stage comedies such as *Kuriton sukuppolvi* (1937, Undisciplined generation), which was successful at the time of its production. He had already drawn attention to himself in 1936, by denouncing two leading liberal critics as "communists," which brought the wrath of the left on his head. In that year he became editor of Finland's leading illustrated weekly.

He won the National Literary Prize in 1934 for his novel of the previous year, *Appelsiininsiemen* (Orange seed), his first full-scale attack on "decadence." Next came his first "blockbuster," a novel which delighted the middle classes at whom he would, for the rest of his life, aim all his accomplished and vivid writings: *Vieras mies tuli* (this means "From father to son" but was translated in 1952 as *A Stranger Came to the Farm*). Most markedly influenced by Knut Hamsun, and skillfully transferring Hamsun's Norwegian landscapes to spectacular Finnish ones, the novel deals with the stranger Aaltonen—yet another of Waltari's stoical idealists—and his mistress, the farmer's wife. Reviewing the translation in the *New York Times* (1952), James Macbride called it a "Perelman take-off on Eugene O'Neill" and praised Naomi Walford's rendering as perfectly reflecting the "diabetic solemnity of the original." Others were less critical, and found it impressive.

A readable work that might have found greater acceptance and unanimity among English-language reviewers, Waltari's trilogy of novels about the growth of Helsinki seen through the eyes of a single family (1933–1935), published in its entirety as *Isästä poikkaan*, Fathers and sons, in 1942), has remained untranslated.

At this time Waltari started extensive research into ancient Egypt: essentially, he wanted a vehicle to express his view of the contemporary political situation, which he saw as disastrous. The first result

was his play *Akhnaton*, which was very successfully produced at the National Theatre of Helsinki in 1938. Akhnaton was represented as the prophet of a "single just god" to replace a corrupt priesthood (stand-ins for Finland's governors tainted by dangerously communist-appeasing liberal elements). A novel, *Sinuhe, egyptiläinen* (translated as *The Egyptian*), set in the same period, followed in 1945. Naomi Walford's translation (which reduced the length of the original by about a third) headed the American best-seller list for many weeks.

The novel received mixed reviews. The *Catholic World* pronounced it, simply, "not a good book." *Library Journal*, however, called it "powerful" but with "rather a gamy flavor; detailed to the point of surfeit." It was made into a lavish movie of which the film critic Bosley Crowther remarked "All of it is big." Although praised at the time for its historical authenticity, the book is full, as Gladys Schmitt asserted in her *New York Times* (1949) review, of improbabilities: "many of the incidents are sensational and at best the characters are types."

*The Egyptian* had many successors in Waltari's works, all based in various eras of history. What they had in common was that in each there was a hero who saw the outline of the future, but who could do little about it except express his resignation and his pessimism. Finnish critics and those with some knowledge of Finnish literature have preferred his stories, such as are to be found in *Kuun maisema* (1953, translated as *Moonscape*). Charles Lee in the *New York Times* (1954) found that these ended "raggedly, in a smother of resignation to the transiency and meaninglessness of life. . . . like truncated novels, dwarfed by their own dreariness, chilling even to their creator."

PRINCIPAL WORKS IN ENGLISH TRANSLATION: *Novels*—The Egyptian (tr. and abridged by N. Walford) 1949 (in U.K.: Sinuhe the Egyptian); The Adventurer (tr. N. Walford) 1950 (in U.K.: Michael the Finn); The Wanderer (tr. N. Walford) 1951; A Stranger Came to the Farm (tr. N. Walford) 1952; The Dark Angel (tr. N. Walford) 1953; The Etruscan (tr. L. Leino) 1956 (also tr., from the Swedish version, by E. Ramsden, published in U.K. under the same title, 1957); The Tongue of Fire (tr. A. Blair) 1958; The Secret of the Kingdom (tr. N. Walford) 1959; The Roman (tr. J. Tate) 1966. *Short stories*—Moonscape (tr. N. Walford) 1954; The Tree of Dreams (tr. L. Leino, A. Beesley, and P. Sjoeblom) 1965. *Travel*—Greetings from Finland, 1961.

ABOUT: The autobiographical material quoted above was written for Twentieth Century Authors First Supplement, 1955. Current Biography 1950; Ungar, L. (ed.) Encyclopaedia of World Literature in the Twentieth Century, 1967; Seymour-Smith, M. Macmillan Guide to Modern World Literature, 1986. *Periodicals*—Books Abroad Spring 1956; Catholic World November 1949; Library Journal August 1949; Newsweek September 25, 1950; New York Times September 3, 1949; October 19, 1952; September 19, 1954; August 28, 1979.

**WARBURG, JAMES P(AUL)** (August 18, 1896–June 3, 1969), American writer on politics and economics, wrote: "Although being the seventh generation in a family of bankers and therefore, predestined to that career, I have wanted to be a writer ever since I can remember.

"The Warburgs lived in Hamburg, Germany, ever since they moved to that Hanseatic city from the little Westphalian town of Warburg, some time in the sixteenth century. My mother was a native New Yorker and I have always held it against her that she allowed me to be born in Germany before she persuaded my father to move to this country and become an American citizen.

"However, the transatlantic nature of my early childhood had certain advantages, such as growing up multilingually and establishing a feeling of world citizenship at an early age. It also had the disadvantage of going to school here but spending every summer vacation until I was seventeen in Europe. These annual family migrations were due to my father's maintenance of his European business affiliations, especially with the century-old family firm of M. M. Warburg & Co., until 1914, when he was appointed to the first Federal Reserve Board by President Wilson.

"After the war, in which I served as a naval aviator, I entered the banking business and this, again, caused me to make at least one trip a year to Europe, until after my father's death in 1932, [when] I made up my mind to leave the banking profession. The immediate cause of the break was my being drafted by President Roosevelt as one of his financial advisers during the early part of the New Deal. This did not last long, because, while in basic sympathy with the New Deal, I became an outspoken critic of the Roosevelt monetary policies.

"From 1935 to the present—except for service during World War II—I have been a student of international affairs. During World War II, I had charge of American propaganda policy in the European Theatre.

"The first writing venture that I can remember was an essay on Lincoln, written when I was attending grammar school in New York. This effort won some sort of minor prize in a *New York Times* competition. At Middlesex School, in Concord, Massachusetts, I became editor of the *Anvil* and at Harvard I was one of the editors of the *Crimson*. My one and only scientific piece was published during World War I by the U.S. Navy. This, a dissertation on compass navigation, resulted from my more or less accidentally inventing a new type of compass for use in aircraft.

"During my fifteen years as banker, I wrote a number of books and pamphlets dealing with financial matters and industry. I also wrote verse, some of which was published in magazines and in two slender volumes. Writing poetry has been a lifelong avocation. During the same period I wrote some extremely bad plays, none of which ever saw the light of day, but as a lyric-writer for popular songs I did achieve a modest success. A few of my lyrics still occasionally haunt me on the radio, particularly one very uninspired song, called 'Fine and Dandy.'

"My recent life has been devoted almost entirely to international affairs. I have worked as a free-lance reporter and commentator, with a large part of each year spent in informing myself abroad and writing and lecturing at home. My work has been mostly of a pamphleteering nature, directed toward the development of a more creative American foreign policy.

"Although much more in sympathy with the post-war Republican opposition, a long series of books and pamphlets, as well as magazine articles, have expressed a growing dissent from a foreign policy which has seemed to me too negatively preoccupied with Russia, too unimaginative and too inflexible. I have been particularly concerned with our policy as to Germany, which has seemed to me a tragic series of blunders.

"Wherever I have expressed criticism, I have tried to present concrete alternatives which seemed to me more likely to lead to enduring peace. I have frequently been called an idealist and accused of making impractical suggestions. This has not troubled me, because I believe that, in the world of today, foreign policy must concern itself with *what should be* as well as with *what is.* . . . "

---

The son of Paul Moritz Warburg and Nina Loeb Warburg, James P. Warburg was one of the most brilliant and restless members of the Warburg and Loeb Jewish-German banking dynasties. However, his rebellious temperament led him away from the traditional banking career—in which, as a young man, he had amassed a fortune—into a position as a free-lance writer specializing in foreign policy analysis from a liberal, Democratic perspective. His early association with Franklin Roosevelt, though unsettling enough to the conservative Republican Warburgs, was something of an anomaly: he began as a supporter of the president, switched to the opposition in two virulently anti-Roosevelt books (*Hell Bent for Election* and *Still Hell Bent*), and ended by campaigning for Roosevelt's re-election during World War II.

After the war Warburg became increasingly dovish and internationalist as the cold war wore on. Until his death in 1969 he produced almost annually books and pamphlets on such subjects as the Marshall Plan, the role of NATO, and the possibilities for disarmament. Although briefly courted by the Kennedy administration, Warburg was "a professional maverick, not a Washington insider," (Ron Chernow). In the opinion of a *Christian Century* critic, his books betrayed "an incredibly naive belief in rational discussions and international organizations" and certainly they had little concrete influence on government policy. Nevertheless, they were widely read within their field, and respectfully reviewed by such establishment figures as John Kenneth Galbraith, Reinhold Niebuhr, and Arthur Schlesinger, Jr.

One of Warburg's particular interests was the rebuilding of Germany after World War II. In such books as *Germany: Bridge or Battleground* and *Germany: Key to Peace* he argued for a middle course between punishment and appeasement, and upbraided the United States for reacting excessively to Soviet policy rather than evolving a considered and coherent German policy of its own. A critic in the *Times Literary Supplement* wrote that the former book "discusses in a reticent and conscientious spirit the nature of the quarrel between the occupying Powers, and throws valuable light on the sometimes wayward course of official American thought about Germany." A *San Francisco Chronicle* reviewer wrote of the latter book, "*Germany: Key to Peace* is the best book Mr. Warburg has written, and probably the best anyone has written on the problems facing the United States in its new role as an adult, if not a 'pater familias,' in the family of nations. It asks some infernally embarrassing questions, and then goes on to suggest lucid answers."

Another key preoccupation of Warburg was the threat posed by the Soviet Union or, more insidiously, the threat the United States posed to itself in its obsession with communism. In *The United States in a Changing World, The United States in the Postwar World*, and other works, Warburg carefully distinguished between real and imagined dangers. He decided that the enemy within posed a greater threat than the enemy without. In common with other critics, Arthur Henderson felt that Warburg overemphasized the failures of the West, especially the United States, in regard to the Soviet bloc; but in reviewing *The West in Crisis* in the *Saturday Review* he wrote, "Mr. Warburg has marshaled his case clearly and succinctly in a survey that is large in range and scope. . . . He is positive and constructive, and he puts forward a series of concrete proposals for resolving the major problems facing the Anglo-American alliance in Europe, the Middle East, and the Far East. . . . Mr. Warburg's book is both a challenge and an inspiration to all those who are concerned to create a better and more peaceful world."

Warburg's last book was *Crosscurrents in the Middle East*, an examination of the role of the West in the Arab-Israeli conflict that was extremely sympathetic to the plight of the Arabs. It may be, as Ron Chernow suggested, that Warburg never quite came to terms with his own Judaism: "By no accident had he married three non-Jewish women and moved to the WASP enclave of Greenwich, Connecticut, when it wasn't hospitable to Jews." In any event, "Jimmy" Warburg was a complex man, "extremely handsome, loaded with brains and charm," who had "excelled at everything" at Harvard and in later life "could indulge his preferred maverick role of producing unsparing, irreverent opinions that would provoke and even scandalize Washington." Eventually, wrote Chernow, "He became a freelance crusader, a wandering troubadour of Democratic liberalism, an 'itinerant preacher' of a new foreign policy." Friend to George Gershwin, Adlai Stevenson, and countless other luminaries, he moved with patrician ease between his estates in Greenwich and Florida and his townhouse in Manhattan, supporting himself, his seven children, and his wives and ex-wives with a series of shrewd business investments that he made almost casually. "He remained a brilliant, uncompromising iconoclast until the end," wrote Chernow.

PRINCIPAL WORKS: *Political and economic*—The Money Muddle, 1934; It's Up to Us, 1934; Hell Bent for Election, 1935; Still Hell Bent, 1936; Peace in Our Time?, 1940; Our War and Our Peace, 1941; The Isolationist Illusion and World Peace, 1941; Foreign Policy Begins at Home, 1944; Unwritten Treaty, 1946; Germany: Bridge or Battleground, 1947; Put Yourself in Marshall's Place, 1948; Last Call for Common Sense, 1949; Faith, Purpose, and Power: A Plea for a Positive Policy, 1950; Victory without War, 1951; How to Co-Exist without Playing the Kremlin's Game, 1952; Germany: Key to Peace, 1953; The United States in a Changing World: An Historical Analysis of American Foreign Policy, 1954; Turning Point toward Peace, 1956; Danger and Opportunity, 1956; Agenda for Action: Toward Peace through Disengagement, 1957; The West in Crisis, 1959; Reveille for Rebels: A Book for Americans of Prevoting Age, 1960; Disarmament: The Challenge of the Nineteen Sixties, 1961; Toward a Strategy of Peace: An Election Year Guide for Responsible Citizens, 1964; The United States in the Postwar World: What We Have Done, What We Have Left Undone, and What We Can and Must Do, 1966; Western Intruders: America's Role in the Far East, 1967; Crosscurrents in the Middle East: A Primer for the General Reader, 1969. *Poetry*—(as "Paul James") And Then What?, 1931; (as "Paul James") Shoes and Ships and Sealing Wax, 1932; Man's Enemy and Man, 1942. *Autobiography*—The Long Road Home: The Autobiography of a Maverick.

ABOUT: The autobiographical material quoted above was written for Twentieth Century Authors First Supplement, 1955. Chernow, R. The Warburgs: The Twentieth-Century Odyssey of a Remarkable Jewish Family, 1993; Current Biography 1948; Dictionary of American Biography, Suppl. 8, 1988. *Periodicals*—Christian Century December 9, 1959; New York Times June 4, 1969; San Francisco Chronicle November 22, 1953; Saturday Review August 1, 1959; Times Literary Supplement November 29, 1947.

**WARD, ARTHUR HENRY (SARSFIELD).** See **ROHMER, SAX**

**WARD, BARBARA** (May 23, 1914–May 31, 1981), British economist and writer on geopolitics, was born in Yorkshire and brought up in the nearby Suffolk town of Felixstowe. She was the oldest daughter of Walter Ward, a lawyer for the Port of Ipswich, and Teresa Mary Ward. Her father's interest in Quaker precepts informed her lifelong commitment to social justice and peace, although her mother's devout Roman Catholicism became Ward's professed faith. She began her formal education at the Jesus and Mary Convent School before departing England at age 15 to attend the Lycée Molière and the Sorbonne in Paris.

In 1932, Ward returned to England to enter Somerville College at Oxford University. She displayed initial enthusiasm for a musical career, joining the operatic society and madrigals group, as well as participating in fencing and equestrian activities. She later migrated to political science, graduating with highest honors in philosophy, politics, and economics in 1935. Shortly upon leaving Oxford, Ward accepted a post-graduate Vernon Harcourt fellowship enabling her to spend the following three summers abroad studying economic and political climates in Austria, Italy, and several other European countries. During the winters, she taught university extension courses to workers' groups at Cambridge University.

Ward's first book, an examination of colonial problems entitled *The International Share-Out*, was published in 1938. Her trenchant analysis and understanding of the issues that mattered in historical relations between colonies and empires attracted the attention of Geoffrey Cowther, editor of *The Economist*. Cowther invited Ward to contribute articles on international affairs, work that subsequently led to an assistant editorial position in 1939. The following year she was appointed to the foreign editor's desk where she would remain a valued correspondent for the next decade. In addition to her work for *The Economist*, Ward also began an association with the BBC in 1943 when she became well known as a panelist on "Brains Trust," a popular news discussion program. During the war years Ward frequently participated in lecture tours that took her to America, Sweden, and British military bases in Europe. She quickly earned a reputation as a brilliant speaker who could make complex issues intelligible to the general public.

Ward's range of concerns in the years immediately following World War II were concentrated on European reunification and the new sets of challenges facing devastated regional infrastructures and economies. Ward expanded upon postwar socio-political issues in a prolific series of books including, *The Defense of the West, The West at Bay, Policy for the West, Britain's Interest in Atlantic Union*, and *Interplay of East and West*. Her books found a receptive audience among Americans as the United States emerged from World War II encountering new responsibilities as a global power and protector of the non-Communist world. Ward advocated non-violent methods of containing Communist expansionism—at one time urging the establishment of, "a unified free-trade area from Scandinavia to the Pyrenees," as a basis of economic and ideological resistance to Communist expansion.

In 1950 Ward married Sir Robert Gillman Jackson, an Australian-born international civil servant and economic development expert who enjoyed a successful career with the United Nations. Ward lived for six years in Ghana during her husband's time of service on the Volta River project. This period provided her with opportunities to witness the abject poverty and rotting infrastructures unregarded by developed countries in the Western world. She was henceforth inspired to explore practical means of ameliorating the deplorable conditions existent in developing nations.

Ward entered academia in 1957, spending winters as a visiting scholar and Carnegie fellow at Harvard University, where she remained for the next nine years. She frequently conducted seminars on problems related to economic development in poorer countries, emphasizing the critical need for Western aid to bolster ravaged economies. At the request of United Nations Secretary General U Thant, Ward anonymously wrote a mid-term report on the first UN Development Decade. Ward exerted some influence on key American policy makers in the Kennedy and Johnson administra-

tions. *Time* magazine noted that she had become, "an influential if unofficial adviser," to the Johnson administration.

On December 16, 1967 Ward became the first woman appointed to the Albert Schweitzer Chair of International Economic Development at Columbia University. She grew increasingly concerned with the explosive growth of urban poverty in developing regions and the associated conflict between economic development and environmental regulations. "As we enter the global phase of human evolution, it becomes obvious that each man has two countries, his own and the planet Earth," Ward writes in her 1973 book, cowritten with René Dubos, entitled *Only One Earth*. This book was a seminal work in environmental ethics, an exploration of ecological matters from a global perspective that brought social, economic, and political dimensions into the "green" discourse. Ward examined blatant threats to the environment, e.g. carbon emissions, as well as less obvious hazards and currents including unchecked population growth, misuses of natural resources, and drastically uneven development and global migration patterns.

Ward's incisive, pioneering work in environmental ethics helped construct the conceptual foundations for successive advances in disciplines as ostensibly varied as political economics and deep ecology. She perceived points of intersection and common cause in the conditions which contributed to global poverty. In his 1993 book, *Preparing for the Twenty-First Century*, political scientist Paul Kennedy echoes one of Ward's chief concerns, specifically the emphasis developing countries place upon short-term economic growth at the expense of long-term threats to public health and safety. "Why should rich countries care about the fate of far-off poor peoples?" Kennedy muses, "It is that economic activities in the developing world, whether the work of billions of peasant farmers or of emerging factory enterprises, are adding to the damage to the world's ecosystem."

The intellectual framework for Kennedy's responses to environmental crises beyond our borders has its antecedents in Barbara Ward's perspectives, most of which are treated at length in her published works. In *Faith and Freedom*, Ward strongly advocated substantial increases in aid to developing nations, a theme she would frequently bring into discussions on global affairs. She never wavered from a refined position of advocacy for poorer people. *The Rich and the Poor Nations*, issued in 1962, is a vivid restatement of Ward's pleas for more cohesive, intensified efforts to build international channels for economic and trade assistance to the Third World. The *New York Times* lauded *Rich Nations* as, "wondrously lucid . . . and trenchantly argued, tough-minded but never failing to assume that intelligence and will can move human society forward."

*Spaceship Earth*, published in 1966, addressed the ways of introducing Western advances in science and technology into less developed regions. Ward's belief in emerging conditions of interdependence among the entire global population was tempered by a practical understanding of particular nationalisms and cultural politics resistant to Western ideas and technologies. She stressed the importance of cooperation in matters of environmental maintenance and humanitarian aid because her conception of Earth excluded boundaries and political systems. However optimistic her metaphor of the planet as spaceship might appear today, the principles behind it remain powerfully salient.

Ward remained friendly with the Johnson administration, but as early as 1966 she made appeals for the de-escalation of the Vietnam War. At a gathering of Washington officials in March 1967, Ward declared that American bombing in Vietnam was, "an inflexible instrument," that, "your allies would like to see—even if you don't—stopped." Ward's Catholicism was deeply rooted in a commitment to social justice and peace. At a World Congress of Roman Catholic lay people in October 1967 she assisted in crafting a controversial resolution recommending an end to the Vatican's policy banning birth control. Ward was never reconciled to this position but her profound concerns about massive population migrations and explosions weighed in her decision to support control measures. "The balance of our community living," she wrote, had evolved into, "a major theme in the life of Western man."

Her final completed work, *The Home of Man*, was a comprehensive assessment of modern urban-environmental problems originally presented in a series of seminars given at a June 1976 United Nations Conference on Human Settlement. Ward called for a halt to nuclear proliferation, enhanced attention to solar energy and other safe sources of power, and a pressing need for development of clean water supplies for poorer countries. The *New York Times* regarded *Home of Man* as, "a virtuoso display of familiarity with both history and contemporary evolvements all the way from Tokyo to Massachusetts."

In her final years, she served as acting president of the International Institute for Environment and Development. In 1976 she was made a life peer with the title Baroness Jackson of Lodsworth. At the time of her death, she was working on a book with environmentalist, Erik Eckholm, on social justice and the state of the Earth. Ward concluded *Only One Earth* on a note of cautious optimism that speaks to her broader vision of a graceful future for our planet and its people, "Alone in space, alone in its life-supporting systems, powered by inconceivable energies . . . is this not a precious home for all of us earthlings? Is it not worth our love?"

PRINCIPAL WORKS: Nationalism and Ideology (Carleton University Ottawa. The Plaunt Lectures); The Lopsided World, 1965; Only One Earth: The Care and Maintenance of a Small Planet; The Home of Man (intro. by Enrique Penalosa) 1976; Progress for a Small Planet (foreward by Mostafa K. Tolba), 1979; The Rich and Poor Nations, 1962; Five Ideas That Change the World, 1984.

ABOUT: An Encyclopedia of British Women Writers, 1988.

**WARD, MARY AUGUSTA (ARNOLD)** (June 11, 1851–March 24, 1920), English novelist who published under the name Mrs. Humphry Ward, was born at Hobart Town, Tasmania, Australia. Her father, Thomas Arnold, second son and namesake of Dr. Thomas Arnold of Rugby and brother of the poet and critic Matthew Arnold, had been appointed an inspector of schools in Tasmania. There he met and married Julia Sorrell,

a descendant of Spanish Protestants who had come to England in search of religious freedom and later emigrated to Australia. In 1856 Thomas Arnold had the first of what were to be several extraordinary religious experiences: he converted to Roman Catholicism. The decision forced his resignation from his government post and his return to England with his wife and three small children, of whom Mary was the eldest. With the assistance of John Henry Newman, Thomas Arnold found work as a teacher of English first at Catholic University in Dublin, then at Newman's Oratory School in Birmingham. Following the custom in religiously mixed marriages, his sons were reared in their father's faith as Catholics and Mary as a Protestant. She spent her early years in the Arnold family home, Fox How, in the Lake District of England and attended boarding schools where, by her own account, she received very little education. At fourteen, however, her fortunes and those of her family improved considerably when, in another profound religious crisis, Thomas Arnold left the Roman Church to return to the Church of England and received an appointment as a tutor at Oxford University. (He reconverted to Catholicism in 1876, sacrificing an Oxford professorship, and remained Catholic until his death in 1900.)

For the young Mary Arnold, hungry for learning and painfully conscious of the inadequacies of her education, Oxford was "a great voyage of discovery," where as she recalled in her memoir *A Writer's Recollections*, she attended lectures, read independently in the Bodleian Library, and mingled with distinguished scholars like Benjamin Jowett, Mark Pattison, and Walter Pater. She acquired such mastery of Spanish literature that a few years later she was able to contribute more than two hundred entries to the *Dictionary of Christian Biography*, edited by Sir William Smith and Dean Henry Wace (1877–1887). In 1872 she married a young scholar of Brasenose College, Thomas Humphry Ward. Struggling but managing on a meager academic income, they settled down to domesticity. In addition to bearing and raising children—Dorothy (b. 1874), Arnold (b. 1876), and Janet (b. 1879)—she published a pamphlet on infant feeding, organized education programs for poor women, and helped raise money for the establishment of a women's college at Oxford (Somerville, opened in 1879). She also assisted her husband in the editing of his four-volume anthology *The English Poets*, published by Macmillan (1880). In 1881 Humphry Ward joined the staff of the London *Times* as a leader writer, and, later, art critic. The family took a house in Russell Square where they entertained some of the leading figures of London literary and artistic life, including Henry James who became a devoted family friend. Mary supplemented the family income with book reviews for *Macmillan's* magazine, a translation from the French of the *Journal Intime* by the Swiss philosopher Frédéric Amiel, a children's book, *Milly and Olly*, and a novel, *Miss Bretherton*, suggested by the successful career in England of the American actress Mary Robinson.

The peculiar circumstances of her early life and education in Oxford, the center of theological debate in the nineteenth century, had made Mary Ward acutely sensitive to the religious controversies raging in post-Darwinian England. As an Arnold—a family heritage she always prized—she had inherited a tradition of liberalism that combined a distaste for evangelical Christianity with a profound yearning for religious certainty. When therefore in 1881 she heard a lecture at Oxford by the Reverend (later Bishop) John Wordsworth, a grandnephew of the poet, attacking liberal Christians for arrogance and unbelief, she responded immediately and indignantly with a pamphlet, "Unbelief and Sin." Not until 1888, however, did she publish her full and exhaustive answer in the form of a three-volume novel, *Robert Elsmere*. It is today difficult to account for the enormous success of the weighty, slow-moving story of a young Oxford-educated clergyman whose gradual alienation from the Church, based on his reading of *The Origin of Species* and many other works of history, theology, and philosophy, causes a crisis in his private life. Within a year of its publication in February 1888, *Robert Elsmere* sold close to 40,000 copies in England and made its author rich and famous. The novel was even more of a best-seller in the United States (an estimated 100,000 copies sold by November 1888) although, because it was published three years before passage of the American Copyright Act of 1891, Mrs. Ward received no royalties and only £100 for the American rights.

Contributing to the success of *Robert Elsmere* was its notoriety. The shock and indignation of many of the clergy and, especially, a rebuttal in a lengthy essay defending revealed religion by the former prime minister William Ewart Gladstone, published in the *Nineteenth Century* (May 1888), helped to publicize the book and promote its sales. If its more sophisticated readers found *Elsmere* didactic and tedious (in a direct reference to her uncle Matthew Arnold, Oscar Wilde called it *Literature and Dogma* without the literature), a far wider public relished its sweetly sentimental love story and its lyrical prose descriptions of the English Lake Country where much of the story is set. Indeed, *Robert Elsmere* established the pattern for the more than twenty novels that Mary Ward was to publish in the next three decades. None of these matched its dazzling success, but most of them sold well.

By instinct probably more than calculation, Ward understood precisely the needs and tastes of the English reading public. The most perceptive tribute paid her came from an American contemporary who disliked her work intensely, William Lyon Phelps: "She has a well-furnished and highly developed intellect; she is deeply read; she makes her readers think that they are thinking." Hers was a largely self-educated and aspiring readership, middle- and working-class men and women eager to learn about the major religious, political, and social issues of their times but equally curious about the manners and morals of the upper classes. All this information she supplied in ample detail—with the added spice of romance and melodrama. Her novels took their readers into stately English country manors and slum hovels, to the houses of Parliament and the cottages of miners and farm workers. Such readers gladly absorbed long passages of exposition because these were woven into plots that often verged on the sensational, with jealousy, adultery, murder or violent death, tragically misguided idealism, noble renunciations and self-sacrifice. Nevertheless, Ward never violated decorum and never insulted her readers with slipshod writing, taking great pains to work up her background material and polish her prose.

Mary Ward's biographer John Sutherland writes that by 1905 she "could plausibly claim to be the most famous living novelist in the world." She was able to maintain her family in grand style with foreign boarding schools for her daughters, Eton and Oxford for her son, a large old country house in Herfordshire, Stocks, and a fine townhouse in London, many servants, and frequent travel abroad. In 1908 she traveled to the United States and Canada, lecturing to large audiences on "The Peasant in Literature" and raising money for several of her favorite charities. She was entertained at the White House by President Theodore Roosevelt and by the Canadian governor-general and prime minister in Ottawa. Her only disappointment was her failure to have any sustained success with dramatizations of her novels and with her one original play *Agatha*. In both England and America, productions of her plays received polite reviews but had short runs and poor box-office receipts.

Increasingly Ward assumed the role of social polemicist and political activist. Despite frequent bouts of ill health and fatigue from her demanding writing schedule, she organized and raised funds for a settlement house in London, named for the philanthropist J. Passmore Edwards. Completed in 1897, the building housed programs of adult education, a day care center for children of working mothers, and a school for sick and crippled children. (Now known as Mary Ward House, the building still stands in Tavistock Place, Bloomsbury.) Ironically, however, much of her social activism was directed toward losing or at best questionable causes. Alarmed by the iconoclasm and rebellion of the younger generation of the 1890s—the New Woman and aesthetic movements in particular—she heartily endorsed the prosecution of Oscar Wilde in 1895, exerting pressure on publishers to "purge" what she regarded as the corrupting influences of "Yellow Bookery." She was zealous in her support of the British Empire in the Boer War and during World War I campaigned tirelessly to bring the United States into combat. Though aging and ailing, she went to the battlefront several times and wrote three books—*England's Effort, Towards the Goal,* and *Fields of Victory*—that mix war reporting with fervent war propaganda. In 1920, only two months before her death, her public service was recognized with an appointment by the Lord Chancellor as one of the first women magistrates in England.

On no issue was Ward's political conservatism more striking than in her fierce opposition to the women's suffrage movement. Like George Eliot and a surprising number of other talented and professionally successful women who advocated higher education and greater personal freedom for women while opposing female suffrage, she believed that active participation in politics was degrading to "the special moral qualities of women." In 1908 she founded the Women's National Anti-Suffrage League, an organization "for bringing the views of women to bear on the legislature without the aid of the vote." She portrayed a suffragette leader as neurotic and destructive in her novel *Delia Blanchflower,* where she wrote that "women everywhere" were destroying all the old values and traditions by demanding "self-realization."

Notwithstanding the liberalism of her religious views, by the late 1890s the image of Ward as an aloof, humorless icon of Establishment conservatism made her the target of the satirical barbs of the younger generation of writers—Lytton Strachey, H. G. Wells, Rebecca West, Arnold Bennett. Max Beerbohm sketched a solemn little Mary Augusta looking up at her bemused famous uncle and saying, "Why, Uncle Matthew, oh, why will not you be always wholly serious?" Virginia Woolf said that reading Ward was like catching the flu. Even her young nephew Aldous Huxley satirized her in an early short story in *Limbo* (1920). Sadly too she lived to see the decline in her readership. The highest paid English woman novelist of her time, she outlived her time which was eminently the nineteenth century. Not until well past the middle of the twentieth century was any attempt made to reevaluate her fiction. Although her opposition to women's suffrage has not endeared her to modern feminist readers, she has enjoyed something of a modest revival. As of 1990 at least six of her novels were in print. These included *Robert Elsmere,* respected today as a register of the profound ideological dilemmas that confronted the Victorians. In the current re-evaluation several other novels are notable. *The History of David Grieve* is a portrait of a self-educated Scotsman spiced with lurid glimpses into "Bohemian" life among Paris artists and prostitutes; *Marcella* has a captivating and headstrong heroine who dabbles dangerously in politics (it includes a character inspired by Charles Stewart Parnell whose political career was ruined by scandal in 1890). The novel that current readers regard as her best work is *Helbeck of Bannisdale,* like *Robert El-*

*smere* a novel about religious doubt and conflict. Her hero here, however, undergoes no test of faith. He is a devout Catholic, sensitive, intelligent, almost monastic in his lonely life as the master of an old Tudor house in the ruggedly beautiful Westmoreland countryside. His crisis comes when he falls in love with a beautiful young woman as firm in her free-thinking skepticism and contempt for ritual and dogma as he in his faith. She returns his love but cannot reconcile herself to conversion to Catholicism. Both characters are drawn with genuine compassion, and Ward acknowledged that they were inspired by her father's troubled religious history and the terrible demands it made upon her Protestant mother.

In only one other novel did Ward draw so closely on her private life. This is *The Coryston Family,* in which an aristocratic matriarch is bitterly disappointed in the political careers and personal lives of her sons. The Wards' only son, Arnold, elected to a seat in the House of Commons in 1910 with his mother's hearty endorsement, had a brief but undistinguished political career. He also incurred large gambling debts that his parents felt honor bound to settle. Mary Ward was obliged to sell most of her fiction copyrights and remortgage her country estate to pay his creditors. Soaring tax rates during World War I and the shrinking sales of her books forced her to continue writing almost up to her death in London. At her funeral Dean Inge eulogized her as "perhaps the greatest Englishwoman of our time," and King George V and Queen Mary sent a message of condolence honoring her "distinguished literary achievements, her philanthropic activities, and her successful organisations to promote the health and recreation of children." She was survived by Humphry Ward, who died in 1926, her son Arnold, and her daughters Dorothy and Janet, the latter the wife of the historian G. M. Trevelyan and author of a biography of her mother published in 1923.

PRINCIPAL WORKS: *Novels*—Miss Bretherton, 1884; Robert Elsmere, 1888; The History of David Grieve, 1892; Marcella, 1894; The Story of Bessie Costrell, 1895; Sir George Tressady, 1896; Helbeck of Bannisdale, 1898; Eleanor, 1900; Lady Rose's Daughter, 1903; The Marriage of William Ashe, 1905; Fenwick's Career, 1906; The Testing of Diana Mallory, 1908; Daphne: Or, Marriage a la Mode; Canadian Born, 1910; The Case of Richard Meynell, 1911; The Mating of Lydia, 1913; The Coryston Family, 1913; Delia Blanchflower, 1915; Eltham House, 1915; A Great Success, 1916; Lady Connie, 1916; Missing, 1917; The War and Elizabeth, 1918; Cousin Philip, 1919; Harvest, 1920. *Drama*—(with L. N. Parker) Agatha, 1903. *Nonfiction*—England's Effort, 1916; Towards the Goal, 1917; A Writer's Recollections, 1918; Fields of Victory, 1919. *As translator*—Amiel's Journal, 1885. *Juvenile*—Milly and Olly: Or, A Holiday Among the Mountains, 1881.

ABOUT: A. M. Mrs. Humphry Ward: A Study in Late Victorian Feminine Consciousness and Creative Expression, 1985; Colby, V. The Singular Anomaly: Women Novelists of the Nineteenth Century, 1970; Dictionary of Literary Biography, Vol. 18, 1983; Gwynn, S. Mrs. Humphry Ward, 1917; Jones, E. H. Mrs. Humphry Ward, 1973; Peterson, W. S. Victorian Heretics: Mrs. Humphry Ward and Robert Elsmere, 1976; Phelps, W. L. Essays on Modern Novelists, 1910; Sutherland, J. Mrs. Humphry Ward: Eminent Victorian, Pre-Eminent Edwardian, 1990; Trevelyan, J. P. The Life of Mrs. Humphry Ward, 1923; Ward, Mrs. Humphry, A Writer's Recollection, 1918. *Bibliography*—Thesing, W. B. and S. Pulsford. Mrs. Humphry

Ward, Victorian Research Guide XIII, 1987. *Periodicals*—Clio Spring 1990; Fortnightly Review June 1920; London Review of Books September 13, 1990; New York Review of Books February 14, 1991; New York Times March 25, 1920; New York Times Book Review November 18, 1990; North American Review June 1920; Prose Studies December 1985; Quarterly Review July 1920; Times (London) March 25, 1920; Times Literary Supplement November 9, 1990.

## WARD, MARY JANE (August 27, 1905– ),

American novelist wrote: "I was born in Fairmount, Indiana. My parents Marion Lockridge and Claude

Arthur Ward, brought my sister and me to Evanston, Illinois, in 1915. After graduating from the Evanston High School, I attended Northwestern University for two years. Then I studied art and worked briefly at a variety of jobs. I took piano lessons for some ten years and although I can't play now as I did in my early teens when I won a year's scholarship at a Chicago conservatory, I find playing the piano a pleasant relaxation.

"In 1928 I married Edward Quayle, a statistician whose avocation is painting. Except for a period of four years divided between New York City and a farm forty miles west of Chicago, our headquarters have been in Evanston.

"I didn't settle down to serious writing until after my marriage. I've had a dozen short stories and articles published, have done book reviews and a little reporting of lectures and musical events, but my chief interest is in the field of the novel.

"*The Snake Pit* was a dual selection of the Book of the Month Club for April 1946, and it has had sixteen foreign translations. The motion picture based on this novel received the Robert Meltzer and the Screen Writers Guild awards for 1948. In 1949, I received an Achievement Award from the Women's National Press Club, 'for outstanding accomplishment in Mental Health.'

"I am a member of the Unitarian church, the Society of Midland Authors, the National Association for Mental Health and the Illinois Society for Mental Health. Recently I have been doing some speaking for groups especially interested in mental illness problems.

"I keep to a fairly regular writing schedule but whenever there's a chance, we go fishing."

---

Before the success of *The Snake Pit* in 1946, Mary Jane Ward personified the struggling writer. She began her literary career placing occasional short stories in such publications as the midweek magazine of *Chicago Daily News*. In 1937 she was book reviewer, editor of a short story feature, and sometime reporter of concerts and lectures for the *Evanston News-Index*. "For years we lived on pork and spaghetti," she reported, "and for a while our home was on top of a garage where we didn't have to pay rent."

Ward's first two novels received some positive critical notice, but did not achieve commercial success. The episodic *Tree Has Roots* focuses on the lives of a university community's support staff— the superintendent of buildings, a handyman, waitresses, secretaries, etc. The *New York Times* found it an "unusually even work and very moving," but also stated, "To repeat, however, that her book is solely a portfolio of first-rate portraits is to praise and to damn it at the same time." Ward's second novel, *The Wax Apple*, tells the story of two lower-middle-class families who have lived for twenty years in the same Chicago duplex.

In 1939 Ward and her husband moved to New York City's Greenwich Village; there she wrote for three years with little financial reward. Finally, in 1941, Ward suffered a nervous breakdown and was confined for nine months in a mental hospital. This unfortunate period in her life provided the inspiration for *The Snake Pit*. The title refers to the medieval practice of lowering the mentally ill into snake pits in the hopes of shocking sanity back into them. Ward tells the story of a young woman's fight to regain her sanity in a mental institution: "A new voice interrupted. It was a shrill voice. No water, deep or shallow. It was a sharp knife that cut you away from the sun. The creeping fear returned. Like cold wet sheets it wound around and around your body and made you its prisoner." Parallels with the author's own life were obvious and Ward did admit that the "novel was based on personal experience and observation." However, she also made it clear that it was a work of fiction, not autobiography: "There was no attempt to write any sort of factual report. . . . Juniper Hill, from tubs to tunnel, was built and peopled by a mind that was on vacation." Psychiatrists confirmed the novel's authenticity, and reviewers praised it. "Charm and humor are strange words to describe a novel of life in an insane asylum," the *New Yorker* wrote, "but they apply to this record of the year spent by a patient in a state hospital." The review continued: "Chronicled so quietly and unemphatically, the horrors of asylum life became infinitely more poignant than they appear in the hands of grimmer writers who are out to shock."

In 1946 Ward and her husband bought a dairy farm thirty miles west of Chicago, where she continued to write. Although her later novels failed to match the success of *The Snake Pit*, they were well received by reviewers and public alike. Her fiction continued to feature meticulous character sketches, especially of women, and sensitive subjects. *The Professor's Umbrella* is the story of an English instructor who faces anti-Semitism in a Midwest college town. In *A Little Night Music* a forty-year-old woman re-evaluates the love she feels for her deceased father. *It's Different for a Woman*, is a study of a middle-aged wife and mother who has doubts about her future and her past. "Mary Jane Ward has already staked out her own claim . . . on material which superficially might be considered unpalatable as popular fiction," the *Saturday Review* declared. "*It's Different for a Woman* is in very much lighter vein and never harrowing but in its own way displays equally well the author's sensitive and compassionate insight into feminine psychology."

PRINCIPAL WORKS: *Novels*—The Tree Has Roots, 1937; The Wax Apple, 1938; The Snake Pit, 1946; The Professor's Umbrella, 1948; A Little Night Music, 1951; It's Different for a Woman, 1952; Counterclockwise, 1969; The Other Caroline, 1970.

ABOUT: The autobiographical material quoted above was written for Twentieth Century Authors First Supplement, 1955. Current Biography 1946; Warfel, H. R. American Novelists of Today, 1951. *Periodicals*—New York Herald Tribune Books January 16, 1938; New York Times April 25, 1937; New Yorker April 6, 1946; Saturday Review November 22, 1952.

## WARD, WILFRID PHILIP (January 2, 1856– April 9, 1916), English biographer and Roman Catholic religious writer, was born at Old Hall

House, Ware, Hertfordshire, the son of William George Ward, ("Ideal" Ward, of the Oxford movement) and Frances (Wingfield) Ward. He was raised in an ultramontanist household and was encouraged to consider a religious vocation by his father. One of his father's friends was Alfred, Lord Tennyson, and a close bond developed between young Wilfrid and the poet. In an introductory study prefacing her husband's *Last Lectures*, Mrs. Wilfrid Ward writes: "I believe it was a deep satisfaction to Tennyson that a 'papist' boy, son of an Ultramontane of the deepest dye, studied and learnt and made his own the poet's thoughts on the philosophy of religion. It was one of the earliest and most unconscious signs of a vocation—he was already beginning to be, as Dr. Sadler wrote of him after his death, a 'liaison' officer between the historic Church and religious thinkers outside of it."

Wilfrid Ward did begin studies for the priesthood at the Gregorian University in Rome, but left after nine months to attended Ushaw College, Durham. He returned to Ushaw in 1890 to lecture on philosophy, and over the next decade was an examiner in mental and moral science at the Royal University of Ireland, and a member of the royal commission on Irish university education. In 1906 he became an editor of the *Dublin Review*. He also toured the United States and delivered a Lowell Lecture at Harvard in 1915.

In 1886 Ward published *The Clothes of Religion*, a "reply to popular positivism," but it was in the field of biography that he made his mark. In 1889 he published the first volume of a biography of his father, *William George Ward and the Oxford Movement*; the second volume appeared in 1893. His *Life and Times of Cardinal Wiseman*, undertaken at the request of Cardinal Vaughan, required five years of work and was published in 1897. A small memoir of the Irish poet Aubrey de Vere followed in 1904. But his major work was *The Life of Cardinal Newman* (1912), which wove a thousand letters by the Cardinal into its 1,300 pages and took seven years to complete.

Shane Leslie said of Ward that "more than any single man he held the balance and kept comparative peace among the thinkers of English Catholicism." As Mrs. Ward stated: "There were indeed deep underlying forces at work in as well as outside the Catholic Church, which occupied a great part of Wilfrid Ward's intellectual life. . . . he and some of his friends were greatly preoccupied with the work of reconciling modern thought and religious faith, of acquiring greater liberty for thought within the Church by sanction of authority and not by revolutionary methods."

PRINCIPAL WORKS: *Nonfiction*—The Clothes of Religion, 1886; William George Ward and the Oxford Movement, 1889; William George Ward and the Catholic Revival, 1893; Witness to the Unseen, 1893; The Life and Times of Cardinal Wiseman, 1897; Aubrey de Vere: Memoir, 1904; Problems and Persons, 1905; Ten Personal Studies, 1908; The Life of Cardinal Newman, 1912; Men and Matters, 1914; Last Lectures, 1918.

ABOUT: Dictionary of National Biography 1912–1921; Ward, M. Wilfrid Ward and the Transition, 1934. *Periodical*— Dublin Review July 1916.

## WARNER, REX (March 9, 1905–June 24 1986), English poet, novelist, and translator, was born in Birmingham, the son of a vicar. He was educated

at St. George's, Harpenden, and Wadham College, Oxford, where he mixed with the C. Day Lewis/Stephen Spender set. After Oxford he spent some years as a schoolmaster, both in England and in Egypt, where he began work on a novel, *The Wild Goose Chase*, a satirical allegory about

three brothers and their quest for freedom and happiness. In this and his next two novels Warner's attempt to make his narrative represent ideas, as well as plot, encouraged some to compare the tone of his books with that found in Kafka's fiction— they were, indeed, too close imitations of Kafka. But reviewers found Warner's technical accomplishment wanting. Christopher Isherwood, writing in the *New Republic* about Warner's second novel, *The Professor*—which recounts the last week in the life of a liberal confronted with his own powerlessness in the face of totalitarianism, said: "The characters cease to be characters, and fade into anonymous members of a debating society."

Warner's third novel, *The Aerodrome*, published in 1941, was an elaborately allegorical fantasy about a rural idyll, the cosiness of which is unsettled by the arrival of a military airbase, run by a fascist Air Vice Marshal. Bernard Bergonzi, in his overview of wartime literature, *Wartime And Aftermath* (1993), said of *The Aerodrome*: "Insofar as it retains a thematic interest, it works not so much as an exposure of fascism as a parable of the destruction of a traditional rural order by advancing modernity."

Warner's fourth novel, *Why Was I Killed?* (published in America as *Return of the Traveller*), a piece of philosophical fantasy rather than allegory, formed a bridge between the three early allegorical novels and the more straightforward, classically-inspired later work. In *The Cult of Power*, he tackled the conflict between freedom and authority in a series of essays. After the war he became director of the British Institute in Athens, where he stayed till 1947, refreshing his love of the classics, which he had studied at Oxford, and forming a friendship with the diplomat and poet George Seferis. Increasingly, he turned his literary energies to translation and by the mid-fifties had translated several works by Euripedes, Aeschylus, Xenophon, and Thucydides.

In 1958 he published *The Young Caesar*, a biographical novel which Robert Graves (resenting, no doubt, an intruder on territory pioneered by his own *I, Claudius*) dismissed, in the *New Republic*, with the assertion that Warner "does not know his stuff, and writes unconvincingly." Neither Warner's follow-up novel, *Imperial Caesar*, nor *Pericles The Athenian*—despite being competent and reliable expositions of their source material—created any kind of novelistic life. Christopher Ricks, reviewing *Pericles The Athenian* for the *New Statesman*, wrote: "The style is so bland that it seems urged on by a passion not so much for the past as for the pastiche."

Much of the poetry Warner wrote in the thirties consists of undistinguished political verse. A good deal of this was removed from the revised edition of *Poems* (1937), published as *Poems and Contradictions* in 1945. Most consider him at his best when writing about nature, particularly birds, of which he was a keen watcher. He published a children's book about birds. For eleven years, from 1963, Warner was professor of English at the University of Connecticut.

PRINCIPAL WORKS: *Fiction*—The Wild Goose Chase, 1937; The Professor, 1938; The Aerodrome, 1941; Why Was I Killed? (in U.S.: Return Of The Traveller), 1944; Men Of Stones, 1949; The Young Caesar, 1958; Imperial Caesar, 1960; Pericles The Athenian, 1963; The Converts, 1967. *Nonfiction*—English Public Schools, 1945; The Cult Of Power, 1946; John Milton, 1949; E. M. Forster, 1950; Men And Gods, 1950; Greeks And Trojans, 1951; Eternal Greece, 1953; The Vengeance Of The Gods, 1954; Athens, 1956; The Greek Philosophers, 1958; The Stories Of The Greeks, 1967; Athens At War, 1970; Men Of Athens, 1972. *Poetry*—Poems, 1937.

ABOUT: Contemporary Authors v. 119; Contemporary Poets, 1985; ed. McLeod, A. L. A Garland For Warner, 1985; Reeve, N. H. The Novels Of Rex Warner, 1989; Who's Who 1986–1987. *Periodicals*—New Republic March 8, 1939; New Statesman February 8, 1963; New York Times July 17, 1986; Times (London) June 27, 1986.

**WARNER, SYLVIA TOWNSEND** (December 6, 1893–May 1, 1978) English novelist, short story writer and poet was born in Harrow-on-the-Hill, Middlesex, England to George Townsend and Eleanor Mary (Hudleston) Warner. After working in a munitions factory during World War I, she pursued her interest in music and became a member of the editorial board which produced the 10 volume set, *Tudor Church Music*. Despite her eventual fame as a novelist, she never lost interest in music, and, later in life, became a contributor to *Grove's Dictionary of Music*, being considered an authority on 15th to

16th century music. However, she is best remembered for creating a very individual brand of both fantastic and socially penetrating fiction. Both in her short stories and novels she wrote of eccentric characters in an admirably spare and elegant prose and provided insight into "states of mind" always striving to uncover new, and often overlooked, corners of the human condition.

While indulging her early interest in music, she began to write poetry. Her first publication, a collection of poetry entitled *The Espalier*, was published in 1925. It is a book of simple, yet often ironic, poetry in which the salient qualities of Warner's prose—craftmanship, restraint and clarity—were given birth. Critics, as they would for many years after, praised her as an "intricate craftsman" who wrote with a "fine clarity" and "honesty of treatment" most reminiscent of "Wordsworth's earliest and best."

Although *The Espalier* was Warner's first publication, it was reviewed after Warner's second publication, the novel—*Lolly Willowes* (1926) was released. *Lolly Willowes* was the first *Book of the Month* selection and it earned Warner an immediate following. The novels tells of a spinster's long overdue escape from her restrictive family and her subsequent bargain with the Devil to insure her independence and separation from that family. Warner's prose in *Lolly Willowes* was immediately praised as "beautiful . . . not fantastic, but of a delicate precision which is all too rare in contemporary letters." Critics also noted her "crisp and restrained English" and her "spare . . . but emotionally rich [outline]." In addition to her engaging, polished style, Warner was able to fill the novel with "refreshing wisdom about life and folks of all kinds."

The provision of such insight would, in tandem with the quality of her prose, endear her to countless readers and propel her though a prolific career of some 35 books of fiction, nonfiction, and poetry. It is probable that Warner gained much of the precision and restraint that distinguishes her prose from her initial interest in music. As she once stated, "I began as a musician. I think musical considerations—form, modulation, tempi and so on—have always been an influence on my work."

In her next novel, *Mr. Fortune's Maggot* (1927), Warner departed from the fantastic and devised a story about a homosexual English missionary, Reverend Timothy Fortune, and his attempts to convert and seduce a young native of the island of Fanua. Eventually the Reverend Timothy's efforts become futile and he returns home "slightly heathenized" and with a deeper insight into genuine human emotion. Once again, Warner's work was received with praise as critics noted her "careful craftsmanship" and "meticulous and graceful phrasing." Yet beyond praising her prose, critics, such as Edwin Clark from the *New York Times* also noted that Warner had departed from the fantastic concerns of *Lolly Willowes* and instilled a realism into her work that allowed her to say "many wise things about the human adventure." Masked behind the the charm and wit so inherent to the relaying of Rev. Timothy's disillusionment lies a "subtle social criticism" in which one can read "an attack on foreign missions and conventional religion" or a "skit on the Church's methods of salvation." As her obituary noted, "Miss Warner's move from fantasy to realism to subtle social criticism could be found between the lines" and within the events that affected her characters.

Warner continued her ventures into realism in her 1928 novel—*True Heart*. In comparison to "Lolly Willowes," Victoria Sackville-West noted, "*True Heart* is a great advance . . . for those who prefer the realistic to the fantastic." In *True Heart*, Warner employs a typically refined prose to tell of a young woman's escape from a life of farm drudgery so that she can seek out her true love. Told in a manner that blends "humor . . . and lyric tenderness" *True Heart* marks the last of Warner's purely fictional novels, as the substantial portion of her remaining output became increasingly related to historical and social realities.

As her writing commenced a deeper engagement with realism, Warner herself, in both her public and private lives, underwent a similar process. Shortly after the publication of *True Heart*, Warner moved to the country with Valentine Ackland, the woman who would be her companion for the next forty years. Together, Warner and Ackland wrote a well-reviewed book of poetry entitled *Whether a Dove or a Seagull*. In 1935, Warner joined the Communist party, eventually serving in the Spanish Civil War, with Ackland, as a Red-Cross volunteer in Barcelona, Spain.

During this period, Warner wrote what has recently become her most heavily discussed work—*Summer Will Show* (1936). *Summer Will Show* has been called a "novel of social protest—feminist and economic" and concerns an aristocratic English woman, Sophia Willoughby, during the Paris Revolution of 1848. After the death of her children to smallpox, Sophia travels to Paris to find her husband and, becoming embroiled in the Revolution, finds a reason for her existence. Clear feminist undertones, which have been seized upon by present day critics, are evidenced when, at the climax of the novel, the heroines sit down together and read the *Communist Manifesto*.

*Summer Will Show*, as with most of her previous novels, was nearly universally praised as much for its "clear and elegant prose" as for the use of a new "factualness in [Warner's] subject matter." Warner's engagement with social reality were further praised as a reviewer from *The Nation* called *Summer Will Show* the "most triumphal single moment in revolution fiction" and "the most sure-footed, sensitive, witty piece of prose yet to have been colored by left-wing ideology." Given these criticisms, it is not surprising that recent feminist critics with a basis in Marxist ideology have renewed critical interest in *Summer Will Show*, publishing articles such as "Dream Made Flesh: Sexual Diffference and Narratives of Revolution in Sylvia Townsend Warner's *Summer Will Show*."

Inspiration from Warner's time in Spain resulted in her writing of *After the Death of Don Juan* (1938). Here, she blends thematic concerns of class conflict and individual liberty with the Don Juan legend. The "stilted grace" of Warner's "extremely effective style" was praised, as was typical, but the novel was not considered among her best. Many critics felt it to be an overly personal, parabalic expression of "willfullness," while others did not "succeed in blending the pleasant irony of her dramatic sequel to Don Giovanni with her perfectly serious picture of a downtrodden people attempting to better their conditions."

Warner went on to write two other semi-historical novels—*The Corner that Held Them* (1948) and *The Flint Anchor* (1954). *The Corner that Held Them* retells the daily happenings of a group of cloistered nuns at the Convent of Oby in 14th century England. The novel received good reviews and Warner was praised for her ability to "deepen our sense of the common human lot, its limits and possibilities." Such delving within the "common lot" is, in fact, a consistent thread which links all of her works. This ability to trod withing typically overlooked aspects of the "human fabric" is seen again in Warner's *The Flint Anchor*. Here, Warner gives an account of fifty years of an aristocratic English family dominated by a tyrant father. Warner mantaned the usual restraint of prose that is characteristic of her style and provided a narrative whose events and characters transcend time, such that it becomes "a novel of people of any period."

Warner's creative output was not limited to the novel format. She wrote detailed biographies of Jane Austen and T. H. White and translated Proust's *By Way of Saint-Beuve* which was published as *Marcel Proust on Art and Literature, 1896–1919*. In addition, since her emergence, and subsequent culling of a large readership, she published more than 140 short stories in the *New Yorker* which have been consistently reprinted in a variety of collections that include *Salutation* (1932) and *American Life: Dream and Reality* (1954). When examined panoramically, one can see the wide breadth of eccentricities within characters whose tales are told with an everpresent "subtlety and finesse." These stories relay a universe in which "human beings are dangerous, incalculable and extraordinary."

In 1996 *Sylvia and David*, a compilation of the letters of Warner and David Garnett, was issued. Their shared interests of "cats, cookery, and the English countryside" are discussed, according to the *Choice* reviewer. Frank Kermode in the *London Review of Books* called the correspondents "distinguished inhabitants of the same distinguished literary parish," sharers of the same culture.

Warner has been compared to Jane Austen and

Katherine Mansfield. Her diaries were posthumously released as *The Diaries of Sylvia Townsend Warner* (1996). Warner remains one of the finest examples of a writer who has mastered the craft of writing and subsequently used that talent to explore the hidden niches of the society and culture. She may not have provided her reader with startling insight or new and profound truth, but she succeeded in consistently entertaining that reader through an individual style that breathed life and soul into all the thematic concerns it portrayed. As her obituary noted, "Warner was one of the most stylish, one of the most civilized and cultivated of writers. Idea and word worked together like engaged gears." In 1968, she was awarded the Prix Menton and she was a member of the Royal Society of Literature, the American Academy of Arts and Letters and a sponsor of the Rachel Carson Trust.

PRINCIPAL WORKS: Lolly Willowes, 1926; Mr. Fortune's Maggot, 1927; True Heart, 1928; Summer Will Show 1936; After the Death of Don Juan, 1939; The Corner That Held Them, 1948; Flint Anchor, 1954. *Poetry*—L'Espalier, 1925; Time Importuned, 1928; Opus 7, 1931; Whether a Dove or a Seagull, 1933; King Duffus and Other Poems, 1968. *Short stories*—Salutation, 1932; The Cat's Cradle Book, 1940; A Garland of Straw, 1943; Winter in the Air and Other Stories, 1955. *Biography*—Jane Austen, 1775–1817, 1957; T. H. White: A Biography, 1967.

ABOUT: The autobiographical material quoted above was written for Twentieth Century Authors, 1942. Ackland, V. For Sylvia: An Honest Account, 1986; Harman, C. Sylvia Townsend Warner, 1991; Harman C. (ed.) The Diaries of Sylvia Townsend Warner, 1996; Maxwell, W. (ed.) Letters of Sylvia Warner, 1982; Warner, S. T. Scenes of Childhood, 1982; Warner, S. T. and Garnett, D. Sylvia and David: The Townsend-Warner/Garnett Letters, 1994. *Periodicals*—Choice March 1995; Guardian, January 5, 1977; London Review of Books July 21, 1995; New Yorker May 30, 1983; New York Review of Books July 1985; New York Times May 10, 1978; Time May 22, 1978; Times (London) May 2, 1978.

**WARREN, AUSTIN** (July 4, 1899–August 20, 1986), American scholar and educator, wrote: "I was born in Waltham, Mass., ten miles from Boston,

where my city-born father tried variously to earn a living. As I was entering high school, he yielded to his steady desire-about which there was nothing Utopian or doctrinaire: only an indistinctive fondness for animals and an archaic versatility-and moved his family to a country village north of Concord.

"The Stow high school, with a male principal and two women assistants, gave me a sound education in Latin and German. The two centers of my life, however-neither of them shared by my parents-were music and religion. I taught myself to play the piano; then had the instruction of an excellent teacher who paid a weekly visit to Stow. Ecclesiastically the village was divided between the Unitarians and the Evangelicals, to which later I adhered.

"College was—by my grandmother's choice—Wesleyan, in Connecticut. Our admirable German-trained professors had assembled an admirable library. In my years (1916–20), alas, they were all nearing retirement and too old and remote for concern with teaching the few students desirous of education. Partly taught by an older student, I chiefly taught myself by systematically reading through the alcoves of the almost unfrequented library. I remember discovering Emily Dickinson and Jane Austen, Swedenborg, and Albrecht Durer.

"For the next six years, I alternated teaching and studying—the 'studying' at Harvard and at Princeton. My one great 'official' teacher was Irving Babbitt; but I had, during those years, two unofficial teachers—philosopher-theologians; and then, as always, I learned from all my contemporary friends whatever they lovingly knew: French poetry, for example, from Wallace Fowlie; contemporary American poetry from John Wheelwright and Howard Blake.

"Since taking my doctorate at Princeton in 1926, I have taught in universities, for the last fifteen years chiefly graduate students in age between twenty and thirty; but all through my professional life I have been primarily a teacher—a 'coach' of creative writers and critics rather than of academic scholars.

"It is difficult to earn an honest livelihood as a teacher and still write; but in our competitive world there is, it would seem, no easy and honest way to live while writing. My chief resource is my steady conviction that I can't be an honest teacher without managing time for writing: a New England justification for what I would do anyway had I independent means.

"I have been a copious writer. During my twenties I wrote and published theology. In the next ten years I disciplined myself to scholarly research, on the specious ground that, having proved to scholars that I was a scholar, I would then be at liberty to be a critic. The last ten years have gone to literary criticism and literary theory. I trust to live to publish an autobiography, a novel, a thin book of rich and meticulous poems, and a 'philosophy of religion.'"

Austin Warren taught at a number of different universities, but spent most of his time at the University of Iowa, where he was a full professor from 1939 to 1948, and then the University of Michigan, where he spent the next twenty years. He contributed regularly to quarterlies such as the *Kenyon Review* and the *Partisan Review*, and his books of literary criticism reflected a strong personal interest in philosophy and religious thought. His first book was originally published as his doctoral thesis; his second was a biography of the Swedenborgian father of Henry and William James, an extraordinary figure in his own right. *The Elder Henry James* was well-received and Warren was praised for paying close attention to James's own writings. *Richard Crashaw*, his second book, was less biographical than critical, and analyzed Crashaw's poetry from a well-informed Catholic perspective.

In the essays collected in *Rage for Order* (all previously published, with the exception of an excellent one on Hawthorne), Warren demonstrated a versatility of approach, a lucidity of style and an enhanced view of literary criticism (involving the analysis of constructions and systems) which have ensured that his work is still referred to in universities. The preface to this book states: "The critic has his own rage for order, a passionate desire to discover, by analysis and comparison, the systematic vision of the world which is the poet's construction, his equivalent of a philosphical or other conceptual system."

The encyclopedic *Theory of Literature*, produced in collaboration with Rene Wellek, was described in the *New York Times* as "the most ordered, ranging and purposeful attempt that has been made in some time toward keeping the study of literature at once intelligent and liberal." The *Times Literary Supplement* was less impressed, observing that the book's main themes "will be found unexceptionable by those familiar with modern critical thought." Nevertheless, it is still, and deservedly, much consulted because of its all-inclusiveness; it has given many more colorful critics their impeccable starting-point.

Warren's two books on New England—*New England Saints* and *The New England Conscience*—are both meditations on the Yankee sense of duty; demonstrated by means of individual case histories. The theme and legacy of Bostonian puritanism is pursued more personally in the posthumously-published *Becoming What One Is*.

PRINCIPAL WORKS: Alexander Pope as Critic and Humanist, 1929; The Elder Henry James, 1934; Richard Crashaw: A Study In Baroque Sensibility, 1939; Rage for Order: Essays in Criticism, 1948; (with R. Wellek) Theory of Literature, 1949; New England Saints, 1957; The New England Conscience, 1966; Connections, 1971; Becoming What One Is, 1995.

ABOUT: Twentieth Century Authors First Supplement, 1955; Warren, A. Becoming What One Is, 1995. *Periodicals*—New York Times Janaury 30, 1949; August 22, 1986; Sewanee Review 94 Fall 1986; Times Literary Supplement February 24, 1950.

## WARREN, CHARLES

**WARREN, CHARLES** (March 9, 1868–August 16, 1954), American legal historian, was born in Boston, Massachusetts, the son of Winslow Warren

and Mary Lincoln Tinkham Warren. He took his B.A. from Harvard in 1889, taught for a year, and then earned his M.A. at Harvard Law School in 1892. He was admitted to the Massachusetts bar in 1897 and began practice in Boston. In 1893 he became the private secretary of Massachusetts Governor William E. Russell, and then his law partner. After unsuccessful runs for the state senate in 1894 and 1895, Warren chaired the Massachusetts State Civil Service Commission from 1905 to 1911. As a reform-minded commissioner he ran afoul of those who enjoyed the power of political patronage, and was not reappointed.

In 1914 President Woodrow Wilson appointed Warren assistant attorney general of the United States, a position he held until 1918. During World War I Warren became an influential expert in affairs of international law and neutrality. Over the years his expertise was sought by the State Department, Congress, the Supreme Court, and others; his articles in such journals as *Foreign Affairs* were widely read. During World War II Warren served on the War Relief Control Board, but after the war he retired from public service.

In addition to articles Warren published a number of books that have remained in print. His best known, the three-volume *Supreme Court in United States History*, won the Pulitzer Prize in history for 1923. *The Making of the Constitution*, another durable title "measures up to every demand of authoritative history, alike in its scholarly research, its liberal humanitarianism and its smoothly flowing style," according to the *New York Times* (November 25, 1928). Of *Jacobin and Junto* the *Harvard Law Review* wrote: "Using the little-known diary of Nathaniel Ames, Jr., of Dedham, Massachusetts, a physician, a farmer, a minor public official, and editor of his father's almanac, Mr. Warren has drawn, with the aid of newspapers and letters of the day, a vivid portrayal of the tumultuous struggle over the political control of the doubtful experiment in representative government which the victorious American rebels began in 1789."

The Library of Congress manuscript division houses some of Warren's papers.

PRINCIPAL WORKS: *Nonfiction*—History of the Harvard Law School and Early Legal Conditions in America, 1908; A History of the American Bar, 1911; The Supreme Court in United States History, 1922, rev. ed. 1926; The Supreme Court and Sovereign States, 1924; Congress, the Constitution, and the Supreme Court, 1925, rev. ed. 1935; The Making of the Constitution, 1928; Jacobin and Junto; or, Early American Politics as Viewed in the Diary of Dr. Nathaniel Ames, 1758–1822, 1931; Congress as Santa Claus, or, National Donations and the General Welfare Clause of the Constitution, 1932; (with A. Zimmren, W. E. Dodd, et. al.) Bankruptcy in the United States History, 1935; Neutrality and Collective Security, 1936; Odd Byways in American History, 1942. *Novel*—The Girl and the Governor, 1900. *As editor*—The Story-Marshall Correspondence (1819–1831) 1942.

ABOUT: Dictionary of American Biography Suppl. 5, 1981. *Periodicals*—American Historical Review January 1955; American Journal of International Law January 1955; Harvard Law Review 1931; New York Times November 25, 1928; August 17, 1954.

## WARREN, ROBERT PENN

**WARREN, ROBERT PENN** (April 24, 1905–September 15, 1989), American novelist, poet, critic, editor, and dramatist, wrote: "I was born in Todd, County, Kentucky, in the section which provides the background for *Night Rider*. I attended the school at Guthrie, Kentucky until my fifteenth year, when I went to Clarksville, Tenn. In 1921 I entered Vanderbilt University, where I remained for four years. From 1925 until 1927 I was a teaching fellow at the University of California, taking an M.A. After another year of graduate work at Yale, where I held a fellowship, I went to Oxford as a Rhodes Scholar. I received the B.Litt degree in 1930 and returned to this country to teach. For one winter I was at Memphis, Tenn., as assistant professor at Southwestern College. From 1931 to 1934 I was at Vanderbilt and in 1934 I came to Louisiana State University, where I am now associate professor in the department of English, and, with Cleanth Brooks, managing editor of the *Southern Review*. In 1930 I married Emma Brescia.

"My early boyhood was spent in Southern Kentucky and in Tennessee, the winters in town at school and the summers in the country. I read rather widely, a great mixture of stuff, whatever happened to come to hand—the usual nineteenth century novelists, the Boy Scout books, Buckle's *History of Civilization*, Darwin, thrillers, detective stories, a lot of poetry, Macaulay and Gibbon, and a good deal of American history. I entered college with the idea of studying science, but circumstances quickly altered that: on the negative side, a freshman course in chemistry, and on the positive side, the influence of Donald Davidson and John Crowe Ransom. In my second year in college I began to spend a good deal of time writing poetry. In this connection my association with the Fugitive Group was extremely important to me; my first poetry was to be published in the *Fugitive*.

"Editing the *Southern Review* is pretty grim work, with some hundreds of manuscripts to handle every month, and teaching, in addition, three quarters of a full schedule. The general principle, especially for fiction and poetry, has been to hunt for new writers—for that seems to us to be the true function of a magazine of our type—and to use work by established writers only when we have a genuine enthusiasm for it. For a person who wants to write, the advantages of teaching, I believe, outweigh the disadvantages; a teacher is forced to clarify—or to try to clarify—his own mind on certain questions which are necessarily involved in the business of writing.

"I received a Guggenheim Award in 1940, and am at work on my next novel, which will deal with the period from 1920 to 1930. Meanwhile I am also in the middle of a play, mixed verse and prose, on a contemporary Southern project. It now seems that my next book to be published will be a collection of poems, new ones and some of the pieces included in *XXXVI Poems*.

"I am sympathetic with the objectives of the New Deal but feel that the administration has never clarified its basic philosophy. And I believe that unless ownership and control can be more widely diffused American democracy is a goner."

---

Warren, known affectionately as "Red" Warren because of his red hair, was highly distinguished in three genres: criticism, poetry, and the novel. Of the so-called "new critics" he was one of the most useful. He did not possess the originality of his friend John Crowe Ransom, but he wrote (with Cle-

anth Brooks) one of the most valuable of all critical textbook/anthologies, *Understanding Poetry*, then *Understanding Fiction*, and several other books. *Understanding Poetry*, and then its successors, revolutionized the way in which poetry was taught in America. Equally vital as a textbook was his and Brooks's *Fundamentals of Good Writing*. Many college students owed a debt to Warren, who provided practical experience and good sense and instilled a love of literature.

Warren's poetic style was, at the beginning, tightly controlled in form and ended with looser forms, often in free verse. Although he expressed with reservations his interest in the Fugitives' program of "Southern Agrarianism," he remained well to the "left" of his friends and colleagues in the group.

Irony was from the beginning his main means of self-expression. Less personally unhappy with himself, or tortured by religious certainties and uncertainties, than Allen Tate (with whom he once roomed), he was a far more robust writer, more toughly empiricist and realistic, with a straightforwardly humane attitude. He did not suffer from a bad conscience, even if he agonized about the shortcomings of intellectuals. He considered that the problems of the South could not be cured by socialistic means, but he was, he declared in *Segregation: The Inner Conflict in the South* (1956), "unequivocally against the philosophy of the adman, the morality of the Kinsey Report, and the gospel of the bitch-goddess." He was one of the earliest critics to discern that William Faulkner's work went far beyond politics and saw that Faulkner's power derived in part from his nonintellectual stance.

Warren's large output of poetry is a body of always interesting and often striking work. His themes are powerfully expressed in the novel-inverse, the *Tale in Verse*, *Voices*, and *Brother to Dragons*, in lines such as

> . . . the sad child's play
> An old charade where man puts down the bad and then
> feels good.
> It is the sadistic farce by which the world is cleansed, for
> in the deep
> Hovel of the heart that Thing lies
> That will never unkennel himself to the contemptible
> steel.

In his fiction, his respect for the dignity of the individual is most passionately clear. *Night Rider*, his first novel, dealt with the Kentucky tobacco wars of 1905–08, but was not intended as strictly historical. Perse Munn, the central character—a kind of a study for the Willie Stark of *All the King's Men*—is a man for whom power is both irresistible and fatal. As his assertiveness succeeds, so does his self-destructiveness set in. *Night Rider* is a violent book, containing within it all the themes with which Warren would be concerned: will, identity, time, power, evasion, guilt, and violence itself, but it fails to cohere. The Jacobean-style melodrama finally plunges it out of control.

After *At Heaven's Gate*, another highly readable and intelligent novel, Warren published his masterpiece, *All the King's Men*, a study of power in the process of corruptors. It was always assumed that Warren's Stark, the demagogue of this book, "was" Louisiana's Huey Long. Some have even accused Warren of being disingenuous in his careful denials. While his finally enlightened narrator, Jack Burden, is ultimately unconvincing (perhaps because he is too intellectually conceived), Warren's portrait of the state that "made" the monster Stark, is quite unforgettable.

Warren's marriage to Emma Brescia (1930) ended in divorce in 1950. He married the novelist Eleanor Clark in 1952; with her he had a son and a daughter. Throughout his life he was an academic: he taught at the universities at Memphis and Vanderbilt, then Baton Rouge (where he learned about Louisiana at first hand, 1924–42), and Minnesota. He received many honors, including the Bollingen Prize for poetry (1967), the Pulitzer for *All the King's Men* (1947), and many honorary degrees. He edited many much-used anthologies.

PRINCIPAL WORKS: *Collection*—Erskine, A. (ed.) A Robert Penn Warren Reader, 1987. *Novels*—Night Rider, 1939; At Heaven's Gate, 1943; All the King's Men, 1946; World Enough and Time: A Romantic Novel, 1950; Band of Angels, 1955; The Cave, 1959; Wilderness: A Novel of the Civil War, 1961; Flood: A Romance of Our Times, 1964; Meet Me in the Green Glen, 1971; A Place to Come To, 1977. *Short stories*—Blackberry Winter, 1946;The Circus in the Attic, 1947. *Poetry*—Thirty-Six Poems, 1935; Eleven Poems on the Same Theme, 1942; Selected Poems 1923–1943, 1944; Brother to Dragons, 1953; You, Emperors and Others: Poems 1953–1960, 1960; Selected Poems: New and Old, 1966; Incarnations, 1968; Audubon: A Vision, 1969; Or Else; Poem/Poems 1968–1974, 1974; Now and Then, 1978; Being Here, 1980; Rumor Verified, 1981; Chief Joseph of the Nez Percé, 1983; New and Selected Poems, 1985. *Nonfiction*—John Brown, the Making of a Martyr, 1929; A Poem of Pure Imagination, 1946; Segregation: The Inner Conflict in the South, 1956; Remember the Alamo!, 1958; Selected Essays, 1958; The Gods of Mount Olympus, 1959; Who Speaks for the Negro?, 1965; Homage to Theodore Dreiser, 1971; Democracy and Poetry, 1975; New and Selected Essays, 1989. (with Brooks, C.) Understanding Poetry, 1938 (rev. 1960); Understanding Fiction, 1943 (rev. 1959); Modern Rhetoric 1949 (rev. 1958).

ABOUT: The autobiographical material quoted above was written for Twentieth-Century Authors, 1942. Bedient, C. In the Heart's Last Kingdom; Robert Penn Warren's Major Poetry, 1984; Bohner, C. H. Robert Penn Warren, 1964; Caspar, L. Warren: The Dark and Bloody Ground, 1960; Guttenberg, B. The Novels of Warren, 1975; Justus, J. H. The Achievement of Robert Penn Warren, 1981; Longley, J. L. (ed.) Warren: A Collection of Critical Essays, 1965; Strandberg, V. A Colder Fire: The Poetry of Warren, 1965, The Poetic Vision of Warren, 1977; West, P. Robert Penn Warren, 1964.

# WASSERMANN, (KARL) JACOB (March 10, 1873–January 1, 1934), German novelist, short story writer, essayist, and autobiographer, was born in Fürth, near Nuremberg, the son of a poor Jewish trader.

As a Jew who was influentially critical of Jews, and who wrote about his own experiences of being a Jew in hostile contexts, he is still quoted, and he still has historical importance. The qualities that made Wassermann popular were a clear style, bold characterization, effective dialogue, and skillful plots. He was also blessed with competent translators.

His autobiography *Mein Weg als Deutsche und*

*Jude* (1921, translated, with an extra section about the rise of Hitler, as *My Life as German and Jew*, 1933) offers vivid testimony of his times, which were for Jews dreadful ones. The *New York Times* reviewer commented on the story: "It is told with simplicity, sincerity, and the rare faculty of self-revelation. As for his analysis of the artistic imagination, casual though it is, there are passages that might have come from that still unsurpassed book by John Livingston Lowes, *The Road to Xanadu.* Here Wassermann holds out a beacon of faith and humility . . . that shines brilliantly from the tortured probings of his book."

Wassermann's early years were unhappy. His reaction to his mother's death when he was nine, and then to a pathological stepmother, was to create his own fantasy world. Yet he was persistent as well as precocious, publishing a novel in a local newspaper when he was only thirteen. He was taunted during his army service because he was Jewish. After that he led for some years a wretched existence, feeling himself unjustly shunned, but determined to assert himself. At last his work was taken up by the comic magazine *Simplicissimus*. Wassermann's first novel to make a mark, *Die Juden von Zirndorf* (1897; translated as *The Jews of Zirndorf*, and as *The Dark Pilgrimage*), is concerned with injustice, the place of women in society, and, above all, the isolation of Jews. The novel is divided into two parts, the first set in the seventeenth century and the second in the nineteenth. The village of Zirndorf is settled by Jews in search of a messiah who turns out to be false. Then, two hundred years later, a man appears who seems to be able to work miracles. In this book the author took a rationalistic view, which he equated with a humane one. He would reverse this only in his final novel.

Wassermann, now well established, wrote many more novels and stories, most of which were translated. In *Caspar Hauser; oder Die Trägheit des Herzens* (1908; translated as *Caspar Hauser* in 1928 and again in 1985), he chose a subject especially fascinating to the expressionists: Caspar Hauser was the young man found, in 1828, in a wild state in a cellar. The case of Hauser raised questions hardly yet resolved in Germany and elsewhere: questions of what makes one human; how much abuse is it possible to survive; and what is the nature and value of education. Wassermann researched the affair, and then skillfully fictionalized it.

In the novel *Christian Wahnschaff*, published in Germany in two volumes in 1919, and translated as *The World's Illusion* in the following year, the eponymous hero is born into a world of aristocratic idlers and philistine magnates. He gives up his wealth, studies medicine, and eventually disappears into the lower depths of society, in which (it is very clearly implied) he performs quasi-miraculous good works. The novel—"penny-dreadful stuff" (as the *Boston Transcript* reviewer put it)—contains many powerful profiles of corrupt and perverse idlers, bizarre usurers, and the like. H. L. Mencken in the *Nation* appreciated the grotesque elements in the novel and its "ironical quality," but he thought that too many of the characters were "pathological cases."

Wassermann wrote many *novellen*, which were less encumbered with the grandiosity that tended to flaw his "big" novels. *Der unbekannte Gast* (1927, translated as *The World's End*) contains five of his tales. Ruth Suckow, reviewing the volume in the *New York World*, thought them "exceedingly imperfect": the author stood in front of his characters, "declaiming."

When Hitler took power, Wassermann, along with Heinrich and Thomas Mann and many others, was expelled from the writers' section of the Prussian Academy. As a Jew it was necessary for him to flee to Austria, where after a short period he died very suddenly. His final Andergast trilogy of novels, more simply written, is undoubtedly his best work in fiction. Skillfully cast in the form of a crime story, the first volume—*Der Fall Maurizius* (translated as *The Maurizius Case*)—tells of the condemnation of an art historian, Leonhart Maurizius, for the murder of his wife. When after eighteen years he is finally cleared and released, owing to inquiries made by the chief prosecutor's young son Etzel Andergast, he can make no sense of his life, and so he kills himself. In the sequel, *Etzel Andergast* (translated as *Doctor Kerkhoven*), Joseph Kerkhoven, a psychiatrist to a dying man, undergoes a change of nature and becomes alienated from his wife Marie; she takes Etzel Andergast as a lover. In the posthumous (and uncorrected) *Joseph Kerkovens dritte Existenz* (*Kerkhoven's Third Existence*), Kerkhoven is reunited with Marie, undergoes psychoanalysis, and finally discovers peace in religious faith. The work as a whole could be said to trace Wassermann's own progress from hopeful rationalist to despairing mystic. The *New Statesman* thought *The Maurizius Case* to be a "great book." Other reviewers, however, made the familiar charges of sensationalism. The one book by him which did not attract such criticism was Wassermann's *My Life as German and Jew.*

PRINCIPAL WORKS IN ENGLISH TRANSLATION: *Novels*—World's Illusion (tr. L. Lewisohn) 1920; The Goose-Man (tr. A. W. Porterfield) 1922; Gold (tr. L. C. Willcox) 1924; Faber; or, The Lost Years (tr. H. Hansen) 1925; Oberlin's Three Stages (tr. A. W. Porterfield) 1926; The Triumph of Youth (tr. O. P. Schinnerer) 1927; Wedlock (tr. L. Lewisohn) 1927; Caspar Hauser (tr. C. Newton) 1928 (tr. by M. Hulse under the same title, 1985); The Maurizius Case (tr. C. Newton) 1929; Dr. Kerkhoven (tr. C. Brooks; in U.K. tr. as Etzel Andergast) 1930; The Dark Pilgrimage (tr. by C. Brooks) 1933; Kerkhoven's Third Existence (tr. E. and C. Paul) 1934; Alexander in Babylon (tr. anon.) 1949. *Short stories*—Worlds' Ends (tr. L. Galantière) 1928. *Biography*—Columbus: Don Quixote of the Seas (tr. E. Sutton) 1930; Bula Matari: Stanley, Conqueror of a Continent (tr. E. and C. Paul) 1933. *Autobiography*—My Life as German and Jew (tr. S. N. Brainin) 1933. *Letters*—The Letters of Jacob Wassermann to Frau Julie Wassermann (trs. P. and T. Blewitt) 1935.

ABOUT: Blankenagel, J. The Writings of Jacob Wassermann, 1942; Columbia Dictionary of Modern European Literature, 1947, 1980; Garrin, S. Jacob Wassermann's Andergast Trilogy and the Concept of Justice, 1979; Mann, T. Dairies 1918–1939 (trs. R. and C. Winston) 1983; More, H. T. Twentieth-Century German Literature, 19?; Seymour-Smith, M. Macmillan Guide to Modern World Literature, 1986. *Periodicals*—Boston Transcript December 4, 1920; German Quarterly January 1954; Nation December 8, 1920; New Statesman March 8, 1930; New York Times November 26, 1933; New York World January 1, 1928.

**WAST, HUGO.** See **MARTINEZ ZUVIRIA, GUSTAVO**

**WATER, FREDERIC FRANKLYN VAN DE.** See **VAN DE WATER, FREDERIC FRANKLYN**

**WATKIN, LAWRENCE EDWARD** (December 9, 1901– ), American novelist and screenwriter wrote "Born in Camden, New York. Education in public school. My father died while I was in my early teens, leaving the family with too much land. (I was born in a section of town called Watkin's Addition.) Lack of cash should have precluded college education, but my mother's driving energy sent me to Syracuse University, forty miles away, where I read largely and associated with a small, hardbitten literary group of boys who scorned fraternities, athletics, activities, and formal education. The only activity I ever went out for was the *Phoenix*, the college literary publication. As one of the editors, I submitted verse and satire and for month after month read a novel a day to supply book reviews. I don't remember doing much studying, but I did follow up tips about books from professors. Because of my limited interests I might have become a literary snob, but was saved from that by association with the essentially good, humble people I met while doing odd jobs after school hours and during vacations to help pay for my education. I still think the cook, waiter, window-washer, janitor, factory hand, farmer or lumberjack who, with love of personal liberty, rolls his own, is a better man than the middle-class fellow who burns whatever brands of cigarettes, books, or witches his bullying betters tell him to.

"Further education included a year of graduate work at Harvard and a few summers at Columbia. In 1926 I taught English at Syracuse, since then at Washington & Lee University, Lexington, Virginia, where composing plays for the college players I coached revived my interest in writing. I have done a few magazine articles besides my books. My interest in writing will always embrace the independence of Americans—and I don't mean the D.A.R. Daughters of the American Revolution."

---

The revival of Lawrence Edward Watkin's "interest in writing" led to a varied career as a novelist (both children's and adult), screenwriter, magazine writer, and producer. In addition he was, for most of his life, a professor of English and composition at both Washington & Lee and California State University, Fullerton. Both his novels and screenplays, while neither particularly insightful or profound, held appeal.

While a professor at Washington & Lee, Watkin published his first novel, *On Borrowed Time* (1937). Full of "charm and native breeziness," the novel recounts a grandfather's relationship with his grandson. *On Borrowed Time*, a fantasy on the theme of death, possessed everything but originality, and was quite popular in its day. After being promoted to associate professor at Washington & Lee, Watkin wrote *Geese in the Forum* (1940) and a children's novel entitled *Thomas Jones and his Nine Lives* (1941). With *Geese in the Forum*, Watkin departed from the fantastic to write a humorous story of academic life in a small southern college.

Hints of his later career as a screenwriter for Disney are evident in both Watkin's *Thomas Jones and His Nine Lives* and *Marty Markham*. In the former novel, Watkin writes an "engagingly droll little story" concerning a cat, Thomas Jones, and his five-year-old owner. In *Marty Markham*, Watkins conveys the "essentials of boy-nature" as he tells of a spoiled city-boy's reform and enlightenment on a dude ranch in Virginia. *Marty Markham* was praised as having "genuine appeal," and it became the basis for the later "Spin and Marty" television series.

Soon after the publication of *Thomas Jones and his Nine Lives*, Watkin joined the naval reserve as a lieutenant commander. There, he wrote "sense manuals" with a group of other popular novelists of the day, including Roark Bradford, John Faulkner, and Jesse Stuart. Watkin commented that it was the "most unmilitary group ever gathered together in one room." Yet, being with such writers allowed him to maintain the creative momentum he had built up prior to enlisting. Upon leaving the Navy in 1945, he continued to pursue his interest in children's writing by moving to Hollywood and learning the screenwriter's trade "in brief assignments at Goldwyn's, Columbia, and Warner Brothers." Following his brief screenwriting education, Watkin took both this interest in screenwriting and children's literature to Walt Disney where he became the screenwriter for several major juvenile motion pictures.

From 1947 to 1965, Watkin received sole screenwriting credit for several productions that have since been regarded as classic of the Disney canon. These include *Treasure Island* (1950), and *The Story of Robin Hood and his Merrie Men* (1952). In 1965 Watkin returned to academia as a full professor of English at California State University, Fullerton. In 1970 he returned to Walt Disney to work as a screenwriter.

PRINCIPAL WORKS: On Borrowed Time, 1937; Geese in the Form, 1940; Thomas Jones and His Nine Lives, 1941 (juvenile); Marty Markham 1942 (juvenile). *Screenplays*—Beaver Valley, 1950; Treasure Island, 1950; The Story of Robin Hood and His Merrie Men, 1952; The Sword and the Rose, 1953; Rob Roy, the Highland Rogue, 1954; The Great Locomotive Chase, 1956; The Light in the Forest (based on the novel by Conrad Richter) 1958; The Biscuit Eater, 1970.

ABOUT: The autobiographical material quoted above was written for Twentieth Century Authors, 1942.

**WATKINS, VERNON PHILLIPS** (June 27, 1906–October 8, 1967), the son of Welsh parents, William Watkins and Sarah (Phillips) Watkins, spent nearly his entire life in his native Wales, living in Swansea on the Gower Peninsula and serving as cashier at a local branch of Lloyds Bank until his retirement in 1960. Although he could not speak Welsh, Watkins clung to Welsh themes, myths, and landscapes in many of his poems and called himself a Welsh poet writing in English. "I am, like Dylan Thomas, entirely Welsh by birth, and I believe that my verse is characteristically Welsh in the same way that the verse of Yeats is characteristically Irish," he said in 1967 at a reading at Gregynog, Wales.

While the influence of W. B. Yeats (whom Watkins visited in Ireland) was apparent in his early work, Watkins is more closely associated with Thomas, who was his friend, and whose fame overshadowed his own work as a neo-romantic poet. That situation was exacerbated when Watkins publicized the friendship after Thomas's death in 1953 by publishing *Dylan Thomas: Letters to Vernon Watkins* (1957). Thomas is also the subject of hundreds of Watkins's poems, and his fixation continued until his own death. Dylan was for him a kind of alter ego, a poet who had taken the chance that he himself had balked at, wrote Watkins's wife, Gwen Watkins, in *Portrait of a Friend* (1983).

"We became close friends almost immediately, from an affinity . . . that was particularly clear when we talked about poetry or read it aloud; yet our approach to it and our way of working presented a complete contrast. Dylan worked upon a symmetrical abstract with tactile delicacy . . . I worked from music and cadence towards the density of physical shape. He disliked the sociological poetry of the thirties. My own themes were really closer to his; we were both religious poets, and neither of us had any aptitude for political reform . . . his poems spoke to me with the voice of metaphysical truth; if we disagreed it was on a metaphysical issue, for natural observation in poetry meant nothing to us without the support of metaphysical truth," Watkins wrote in his introduction to the letters.

Gwen Watkins wrote of the similarities between her husband and Thomas: Vernon's mask was a different one, but it concealed the same guilt and immaturity, the same inability or unwillingness to cope with practical matters, the same dependence on other people to take care of him. She claimed that both her husband and Thomas were terrified by the possibility of death and both were hapless to adapt their lives in any way to prevent it; and both of them wrote poems about death to fortify themselves against the fear.

The theme of death, a merging of the past and present, where the living have supernatural communication with the dead, shows up in many of Watkins's ballads, bespeaking his constant preoccupation with the central question of time. It is central to his *Ballad of the Mari Lwyd* (1941), the first of eight volumes of poetry published in his lifetime. Based on the Welsh tradition where singers and poets carry a horse's skull from door to door on New Year's Eve in a rhyming contest, it was praised—and published by—T. S. Eliot, and was followed by *The Lamp and the Veil* (1945). American readers were introduced to his work through *Selected Poems* (1948), selections from the first two books. *The New Yorker* noted his melodious and colorful lyrics and images and the obvious influence of Yeats; and Richard Eberhart wrote in the *New York Times* of powerful instances of verbal and conceptual splendor.

The fifty-one poems in *Cypress and Acacia* (1959) are notable in showing that Watkins held tight to his Christian principles and romantic reflections at a time when a younger generation of modern poets were skeptical, even hostile, to such traditions. Louis Bogan wrote in the *New Yorker* that his poetry at times seemed distinctly nineteenth-century.

*Affinities* (1963) included two memorial poems to Dylan Thomas as well as tributes to Wordsworth, Eliot, Browning, Heine and Holderlin, too many of which have an air of commissioned obituaries, owing to Watkins's cold ornateness, thought D. J. Enright in the *New Statesman*.

Contrary to legend, Watkins was no mild and gentle creature, but a passionate and often angry man, who demanded the highest standards from those around him and was intolerant when they failed. He played hockey, cricket, and tennis with utter seriousness and dedication, finding the same sort of satisfaction from a good forehand drive as he did from a good line or image. But he entirely lacked humor, and deeply resented the fact that he, a poet, should have to work in a bank.

In 1966 Watkins became the first Calouste Gulbenkian Fellow in Poetry at University College, Swansea. He died a year later while playing tennis in Seattle, where he was Visiting Professor of Poetry at the University of Washington.

Among his many honors was election as Fellow of the Royal Society of Literature in 1951. He won the first Guinness Prize for Poetry in 1957, was twice awarded the Travelling Fellowship of the Society of Authors, in 1952 and 1956, and was awarded an honorary doctorate in literature by the University of Wales in 1966.

After Watkins's death, his widow issued new volumes of his previously published poetry. The neglect into which he fell was in part because of his neurotic attitude, according to his biographers, adding that Watkins believed his audience was intelligent enough to understand his poetry without the help of scholars, critics and other guides. But this expectation was all the more forlorn when we consider that the background of Celtic myth, folklore, and hermetic symbolism out of which he wrote is now quite alien to the majority of his readers. His status as a minor poet is secure, but he failed to reach the heights to which he aspired.

PRINCIPAL WORKS: The Ballad of the Mari Lwyd and Other Poems, 1941; The Lamp and the Veil, 1945; The Lady With the Unicorn, 1948; Selected Poems, 1948; The North Sea (trans. from H. Heine) 1951; The Death Bell: Poems and Ballads, 1954; Cypress and Acacia, 1959; Affinities, 1962; Selected Poems 1930–1960, 1967; Fidelities, 1968; Uncollected Poems, 1969; I That Was Born in Wales, 1976; The Breaking of the Wave, 1979; The Ballad of the Outer Dark and Other Poems, 1979; Unity of the Stream: Selected Poems, 1983; The Collected Poems of Vernon Watkins, 1986.

ABOUT: Ferris, P. Dylan Thomas; Mathias, R. Vernon Watkins; Norris, L. Vernon Watkins 1906–1967; Polk, D. Vernon Watkins and the Spring of Vision; Raine, K. Defending Ancient Springs; Tremlett, G. Dylan Thomas; Watkins, G. Portrait of a Friend; Watkins, V. Introduction to Dylan Thomas: Letters to Vernon Watkins. *Periodicals*—Choice January 1984; London Times October 10, 1967; New Statesman January 4, 1963; December 13, 1968; New York Times August 8, 1948; March 27, 1960; New Yorker September 4, 1948; March 26, 1960; Poetry March 1970.

**WATSON, JOHN** (August 2, 1858–August 12, 1935), English poet and critic, was born at Burley-in-Wharfedale, Yorkshire, the son of John Watson, a merchant who soon moved his family to Liverpool, and Dorothy (Robinson) Watson. Though he had little formal schooling because of ill health, Watson developed a precocious passion for poetry, reportedly memorizing *Paradise Lost* at the age of ten, and determining on a literary  career before he was out of his teens. At his father's expense he had printed in 1880 *The Prince's Quest*, a pseudo-medieval romance in heroic couplets. Though a work of juvenilia, it presaged virtually all of the poetry that Watson would ever write: fluent, mellifluous—and, obstinately dedicated to a dead aesthetic.

If Watson's poetry was conservative, his criticism was belligerent. He seemed to take any deviation from the Miltonic, Tennysonian tradition—as he construed it—as a personal affront. "The fact that as a critic Watson could praise without reservation the poetic effusions of Madame Darmesteter and Graham R. Tomson's (i.e. Rosamund Tomson's) 'The Ballad of the Bird-Bride,' but condemn in the harshest terms poets such as Donne, Browning, and Whitman is, to say the least, hardly reassuring," wrote James G. Nelson. Naturally, the opinions so violently expressed in such works as *Excursions in Criticism* and *Pencraft: A Plea for the Older Ways* made him enemies, but at least in the 1890s his reputation continued to rise, perhaps owing to his persistence. Indeed, it was an 1891 review by the popular novelist Grant Allen in the *Fortnightly Review* that could be said to have made his name.

Praising Watson's third volume, *Wordsworth's Grave and Other Poems*, for its reassuring orthodoxy, Allen wrote, "There have been bards unintelligible, bards hysterical, bards nympholeptic . . . but for the most part there has been a want in our era of good sound common-sense married to good sound poetry, clear, terse, and polished. Mr. Watson has come in the nick of time to fill this aching void in our contemporary Helicon." Though today's readers are unlikely to be impressed by such lines from the title poem as "Poet who sleepest by this wandering wave! / When thou wast born, what birth-gift hadst thou?," a significantly powerful few thought highly of Watson's gifts, and he was considered a leading candidate for the laureateship after the death of Tennyson. Watson campaigned actively for the honor, and it is thought that his anxiety to attain it helped to unhinge his mind in 1892; when he spent some time in a mental asylum.

Watson recovered and wrote much more verse, in the next five or six years. Much of his poetry was political, as in the sonnets of *The Purple East*, a hectoring denunciation of British foreign policy regarding the conflict between Turkey and Armenia. He also turned to religious and philosophical matters in *The Hope of the World and Other Poems*, a melancholy expression of late Victorian agnosticism that shocked his more pious readers.

The florid "Coronation Ode," which enjoyed a temporary vogue, was Watson's last great success. He lost some good will with the anti-Boer War poems he published in 1903 as *For England*, and was roundly attacked six years later for writing "The Woman with the Serpent's Tongue," a viciously satirical poem denouncing the wife of Prime Minister Asquith. (For an apparently trivial insult regarding a previous prime minister, she was described as one "Who slights the worthiest in the land, / Sneers at the just, contemns the brave, / And blackens goodness in its grave.") As the Asquith affair revealed, Watson's personality was not an asset in the literary politics he played so assiduously. His "arrogant conceit of himself was painful," wrote a contemporary (quoted in J. M. Wilson's biography of Watson), and the laureateship he so ardently desired might have been his had he alienated fewer people But it was not primarily for such extrinsic factors that Watson's popularity declined so precipitously soon after the turn of the century. There was simply no place for his platitudes and poeticisms, even in the age of the Georgians, and all he could do was rail against the decline of standards and taste.

Watson was knighted in 1917, but though he took comfort from his marriage and two daughters, his last years were bitter and creatively sterile. He and his family were kept from poverty by the largesse of a few wealthy admirers and a subscription provided by George Bernard Shaw, Rudyard Kipling, A. E. Housman, and other men of letters.

When he died, wrote Nelson, "many were shocked to learn that the poet had lived on for so many years. Lacking the genius to create poetry of the highest kind, wholly dependent upon his extraordinary memory and its ability to combine in poems of 'fancy the echoes, images, and rhythms

of the great poets of the Miltonic tradition, Watson had lost his vitality when that from which he derived his strength and inspiration failed to appeal to the mind and imagination of the modern world."

The Sir William Watson Collection is at Yale University, New Haven, Connecticut.

PRINCIPAL WORKS: *Poetry*—The Prince's Quest and Other Poems, 1880; Epigrams of Art, Life and Nature, 1884; Wordsworth's Grave and Other Poems, 1890; Poems, 1892; Lachrymae Musarum and Other Poems, 1892; The Poems of William Watson, 1893; The Eloping Angels: A Caprice, 1893; Odes and Other Poems, 1894; The Father of the Forest and Other Poems, 1895; The Purple East: A Series of Sonnets on England's Desertion of Armenia, 1896; The Year of Shame: Sonnets and Other Poems on Public Affairs, 1896; The Hope of the World and Other Poems, 1898; The Collected Poems of William Watson, 1898; Ode on the Day of the Coronation of King Edward VII, 1902; For England: Poems Written during the Estrangement, 1903; The Poems of William Watson (ed. J. A. Spender) 1905; New Poems, 1909; Sable and Purple with Other Poems, 1910; The Muse in Exile: Poems, 1913; Retrogression and Other Poems, 1917; The Man Who Saw and Other Poems Arising Out of the War, 1917; The Superhuman Antagonists and Other Poems, 1919; Ireland Unfreed: Poems and Verses Written in the Early Months of 1921, 1921; A Hundred Poems, 1922; Poems Brief and New, 1925; Selected Poems, 1928; The Poems of Sir William Watson, 1878–1935, 1936; I Was an English Poet (ed. M. P. Watson) 1941. *Criticism and essays*—Excursions in Criticism: Being Some Prose Recreations of a Rhymer, 1893; Pencraft: A Plea for the Older Ways, 1916; Ireland Arisen, 1921. *Drama*—The Heralds of the Dawn: A Play in Eight Scenes, 1912.

ABOUT: Dictionary of National Biography, 1931–1940, 1949; Nelson, J. G. Sir William Watson, 1966; Wilson, J. M. I Was an English Poet: A Critical Biography of Sir William Watson, 1981. *Periodicals*—Fortnightly Review August 1891; New York Times August 14, 1935; Times (London) December 14, 1892; August 14, 1935.

**WATTS , MARY (STANBERY)** (November 4, 1868–1961), American novelist, was born on a farm in Delaware County, Ohio, the daughter of John Rathbone Stanbery and Anna (Martin) Stanbery. She attended Cincinnati's Convent of the Sacred Heart from 1881 to 1884, married Miles Taylor Watts in 1891 and continued to live in Cincinnati. She wrote in 1910: "Nobody ever had a duller time of it living, or a more commonplace life."

She published her first novel, *The Tenants* (1908), at the age of forty, following it two years later with her best-known book, *Nathan Burke* (1910), an historical novel set in her native Scioto River country during the Mexican War. So authentic was this portrayal that some readers thought the backwoods Lincolnesque title character was a real person.

The Thackerayan style of Watts's second novel ran through the remainder of her novels, which were usually set in puritanical small-town Ohio. Watts was often criticized for her flippant, hurried, and verbose style, and for her reliance on a not always authentic slang. The *New York Times* (1911) wrote that, although Watts showed "the artist's sense of proportion and sureness of touch" in *The Legacy*, she was not simply influenced, but actually controlled by Thackeray— and that anyone who had read *Vanity Fair* could skip this book.

While the poet Joyce Kilmer wrote in the *New York Times* (1913) that "it seems a pity that such firmly drawn characters should live between the covers of but one novel," and called Watts "one of the very few writers now living who creates people

in whom the reader can feel a deep personal interest," other reviewers took a different view, of, for example, *The Rudder* (1916), which they found filled with repetition and feeble irony. The author's superior, detached attitude toward her characters also resulted in mixed reviews for *The Boardman Family* (1918), in which an Ohio society girl escapes convention in New York, where she becomes a famous dancer until the sinking of the *Lusitania* and other events make her marry the boy back home.

For the rest of her literary career, Watts continued to write regional novels that captured realistically the life and times of wealthy Midwestern families.

In a selection Watts contributed to Grant Overton's book, *The Women Who Make Our Novels*, she wrote "that the thing to do was not to muddle around with romance, ancient or modern, but to write about people and to 'lie like the truth.' I remember reading Thackeray, and being struck with the profitable use of the conversational style, as conversation is carried on between persons in good society." She concluded, "Re-reading Thackeray more carefully, with side excursions into Swift and Thomas Hardy, it seemed to me that I have succeeded once or twice by the fact that nobody will believe that I have invented a single person or incident."

PRINCIPAL WORKS: The Tenants, 1908; Nathan Burke, 1910; The Legacy, 1911; Van Cleve: His Friends and His Family, 1913; The Rise of Jennie Cushing, 1914; The Rudder, 1916; Three Short Plays, 1917; The Boardman Family, 1918; From Father to Son, 1919; The Noon Mark, 1920; The House of Rimmon, 1922; Luther Nichols, 1923; The Fabric of the Loom, 1924.

ABOUT: Overton, G. M. The Women Who Make Our Novels. *Periodicals*—Bookman July 1910; Literary Review April 15, 1922; Mentor August 15, 1919; Nation November 20, 1913; New York Times May 14, 1911; October 19, 1913; New York Tribune October 14, 1923.

**WAUGH, ALEC** (July 8, 1898–September 3, 1981), English novelist and travel writer, was born Alexander Raban Waugh in Hampstead, London. His father, Arthur Waugh, was a writer of literary memoirs, and the managing director of the Chapman and Hall publishing firm. His younger brother was the writer Evelyn Waugh.

Alec was the favored child of his parents. He attended Sherborne School where, in his fourth year, he was thrown out for homosexual involvement with another student. He thereupon joined the army and "with the energy of a man who knows that he might be dead in two months" (according to Martin Stannard) completed in seven and a half weeks an autobiographical novel based on his experiences at Sherborne. *The Loom of Youth* was pub-

lished a year and a half later, when Waugh was a nineteen-year-old officer en route to France, soon to be captured by the Germans and imprisoned in Mainz. It reads tamely now, but created a a sensation on its publication. In 1917, homosexuality in the schools was a subject discussed only in smoking-rooms; the book's comparative candor scandalized older readers. But it made the author, wrote Stannard, "the champion of rebel-

lious youth, the hero of those critical of the public school spirit in which the war was being fought."

*The Loom of Youth* was certainly a remarkable achievement for a seventeen-year-old, and Waugh was not to have a comparable success for another forty years. During that interim he was married, divorced, and remarried, had three children and a great many mistresses, worked briefly for his father's publishing company, re-enlisted in the army as an intelligence officer upon the outbreak of World War II, traveled to the South Seas, the Caribbean, and the United States, and wrote over thirty books, most of them indifferently received by reviewers and critics alike but popular enough to bring him an income.

Waugh was probably a better travel writer than a novelist, and the personality he conveyed in such works as *Love and the Caribbean* (an anthology of his previous travel writings) was, as a *New Yorker* critic wrote, "cheerful, inquisitive, and both acute and sympathetic in its observation of strangers and their habits. Whether this personality—the personality of a good traveling companion—belongs to Mr. Waugh or is the reflection in his mind of the island life he revels in hardly matters. What does matter is that his book is delightful." On the other hand, reviewers often felt there was something strangely lacking in Waugh's novels, which did not begin to compare to the satirical masterpieces his brother was writing through much of this period. (Although Alec took the decline in his literary fortunes and the rise in Evelyn's with good grace, the brothers were not close.) A reviewer in the *Times Literary Supplement* complained of *Jill Somerset*, a novel of English manners published in 1936, "Mr. Waugh's method is too familiar to need any comment. He sees his people clearly enough and is content to describe what he sees. The result is a readable story with credible actions and conversations, characters that do the acceptable thing we should expect of them but do not greatly stir our imagination or enthusiasm." Similar things had been said about Waugh's novels for so long that it came as a great surprise when *Island in the Sun*, a lurid story of political, sexual, and racial intrigue set on a fictional island in the British West Indies, became one of the best sellers of 1956 and made more money for the author than all his previous books combined. It is still regarded as Waugh's best work of fiction.

Waugh once described himself as "a very minor writer," and his career bore out that description. The novels and travel books continued, but none achieved that acclaim or the popularity of *Island in the Sun* or the earlier *Loom of Youth*. Probably the most successful works of his later years were the autobiographical volumes *The Early Years of Alec Waugh* and *My Brother Evelyn and Other Profiles*. Reviewing the latter in the *Saturday Review*, Walter Guzzardi wrote, "Waugh clearly found his métier as a diarist, a chronicler, and an observer of contemporary literary life, his prose style direct and unaffected, his tone of voice intimate and gossipy, his ear for anecdote just about perfect. . . . Many of the figures whom Waugh introduces are minor, or less. . . . But never mind; they are so tellingly described, so chattily discussed, and so engagingly characterized that their own accomplishments are of secondary importance."

PRINCIPAL WORKS: *Novels*—The Loom of Youth, 1917; Pleasure, 1921; The Lonely Unicorn, 1922; Roland Whately, 1922; Card Castle, 1924; Kept, 1925; Love in These days, 1926; Nor Many Waters, 1928 (in U.S.: Portrait of a Celibate); Three Score and ten, 1929; "Sir!" She Said, 1930; So Lovers Dream, 1931 (in U.S.: That American Woman); No Quarter, 1932 (in U.S.: Tropic Seed); Leap Before You Look, 1932; Wheels within Wheels, 1933 (in U.S.: The Golden Ripple); Playing with Fire, 1933; The Balliols, 1934; Jill Somerset, 1936; Going Their Own Way, 1938; No Truce with Time, 1941; Unclouded Summer, 1948; Guy Renton, 1952; Island in the Sun, 1956; Fuel for the Flame, 1960; The Mule on the Minaret, 1965; A Spy in the Family, 1970; The Fatal Gift, 1973; Brief Encounter, 1975; Married to a Spy, 1976. *Short stories*—The Last Chukka: Stories of East and West, 1928; Pages in a Woman's Life, 1934; Eight Short Stories, 1937; My Place in the Bazaar, 1961. *Travel and history*—The Coloured Countries, 1930 (in U.S.: Hot Countries); Most Women, 1931; The Sunlit Caribbean, 1948; The Sugar Islands: A Caribbean Travelogue, 1949; Where the Clock Strikes Twice, 1951 (in U.K.: Where the Clock Chimes Twice); Love and the Caribbean: Tales, Characters, and Scenes of the West Indies, 1958; A Family of Islands: A History of the West Indies from 1492 to 1898, 1964; Bangkok: The Story of a City, 1970. *Memoirs*—The Prisoners of Mainz, 1919; Myself When Young: Confessions, 1924; Thirteen Such Years, 1932; His Second War, 1944; The Early Years of Alec Waugh, 1962; My Brother Evelyn and Other Profiles, 1967 (in U.S.: My Brother Evelyn and Other Portraits); A Year to Remember: A Reminiscene of 1931, 1975; The Best Wine Last: An Autobiography through the Years 1932–1969, 1978. *Poetry*—Resentment, 1918. *Biography*—The Lipton Story: A Centennial Biography, 1950. *Other*—Public School Life: Boys, Parents, Masters, 1922; On Doing What One Likes, 1926; Merchants of Wine: Being a Centenary Account of the Fortunes of the House of Gilbey, 1957; In Praise of Wine, 1959 (in U.S.: In Praise of Wine and Certain Noble Spirits); Wine and Spirits, 1968. *As editor*—These Would I Choose: A Personal Anthology, 1948.

ABOUT: Bloom, H. (ed.) Twentieth Century British Literature: The Chelsea House Library of Literary Criticism Vol. 5, 1987; Contemporary Authors New Revisions Series 22, 1988; Harris, M. Outsiders and Insiders: Perspectives of Third World Culture in British and Post-Colonial Fiction, 1922; Stannard, M. Evelyn Waugh: The Early Years, 1903–1939, 1986. *Periodicals*—New York Times September 4, 1981; New Yorker April 4, 1959; Saturday Review January 20, 1968; Times (London) September 5, 1981; Times Literary Supplement October 31, 1936.

**WAUGH, ARTHUR** (August 24, 1866–June 26, 1943), English publisher and critic—most famous as the father of Evelyn and Alec Waugh—was born at Midsomer Norton, Somerset, the son of Alexander Waugh, a physician, and Annie (Morgan) Waugh. After writing a prize-winning poem at Oxford University and graduating with a B.A. in 1889, he went to London, and, with the useful help of his cousin, Edmund Gosse, secured a position

with the publishing firm of John W. Lovell. In this capacity he met Rudyard Kipling. Although the firm went bankrupt in 1893, Waugh had by then established a name for himself with a biography of Tennyson, rushed into print only eight days after the poet's death in 1892. The success of the Tennyson biography—in fact sketchy and unsatisfactory—led to various freelancing opportunities, and to an editorial position at the *New Review*.

Waugh might have prospered as a freelance editor and critic, but his marriage to Catherine Raban in 1893 caused him to accept a more financially secure position with the publishing firm of Kegan Paul in 1896 and, six years later, the managing directorship of Chapman and Hall.

Although he continued to write book reviews for the *Daily Telegraph*, and brought out two collections of essays in 1915, and 1919 (*Reticence in Literature* and *Tradition and Change*, respectively), his work after joining Kegan Paul, wrote Martin Stannard, "was primarily concerned with the business rather than the writing of books. . . . He realised that the acceptance of the managerial post represented the death of any serious artistic aspiration." Moreover, such writing as he produced was not of the highest order. He had "the fatal facility of the second-rate," according to Selena Hastings, and his dismissal of T. S. Eliot, Ezra Pound, and the entire modernist movement bespoke a fundamentally uninteresting critical mind. He was, however, a discerning and able publisher, one who turned around the dwindling fortunes of Chapman and Hall and had the sagacity to sign on such writers as H. G. Wells, Arnold Bennett, and Somerset Maugham.

Neither his achievements as a publisher nor his more modest ones as a writer sufficed to secure a place for Waugh in literary history; it was the birth of son Evelyn in 1903 that did that. Their relationship was a vexed one. Arthur preferred Evelyn's older brother Alec, who was indeed a less neurotic and pleasanter man than his famously disturbed younger brother, and Evelyn preferred his mother. According to Martin Stannard, "It had been in reaction to Arthur's timidity, 'masculinity' and respectability that Evelyn had gravitated towards arrogance, homosexuality and bohemianism." Because it deals with Evelyn at some length—but also because of its remarks about Kipling and other literary contemporaries—Waugh's autobiography,

*One Man's Road*, has lasting interest. Selena Hastings described it as "Engaging, discursive, nostalgic and slightly fatuous."

PRINCIPAL WORKS: *Criticism, biography, and other*—Alfred Lord Tennyson: A Study of His Life and Work, 1892; Robert Browning, 1900; Reticence in Literature, and Other Papers, 1915; Tradition and Change: Studies in Contemporary Literature, 1919; A Hundred Years of Publishing: Being the Story of Chapman and Hall, 1930. *Autobiography*—One Man's Road: Being a Picture of Life in a Passing Generation, 1931.

ABOUT: Hastings, S. Evelyn Waugh: A Biography, 1994; Stannard, M. Evelyn Waugh: The Early Years, 1903–1939, 1986; Stannard, M. Evelyn Waugh: The Later Years, 1939–1966, 1992. *Periodical*—Times (London) June 28, 1943.

**WAUGH, EVELYN** (October 28, 1903–April 10, 1966), English novelist, biographer, travel writer, and diarist, was born in Hampstead, London.

Waugh's father, Arthur, about whom there is a long and characteristically clinical chapter in *A Little Learning*, a volume of autobiography, worked full-time for the publisher Chapman & Hall, and also wrote reviews, essays, and verse. The chapter makes it clear that as a child and young man Waugh viewed his father as decrepit and uninspiring. Alec, Waugh's older brother by five years, was forced to leave Sherborne school in disgrace. As a consequence Evelyn, to his eternal resentment, was educated at the supposedly "inferior" Lancing College, in Sussex. From there he won a scholarship to Hertford College, Oxford, where he read history, acquired a third class degree and the spur to a lifelong vendetta against his tutor, C. Cruttwell, whose name Waugh used for a number of unsavory characters in his fiction. "The only serious regret of my Oxford life," Waugh wrote, "is the amount of time I wasted on my books in my last term."

Initially more interested in fine art than literature, after Oxford Waugh apprenticed himself to James Guthrie, a printmaker; the arrangement lasted a day. In January 1925 he took up his first post as schoolmaster, at Arnold House, Llanddulas. This was the start of a period in which teaching formed a somewhat tiresome backdrop to his private life and to his growing resolve to become a writer.

Waugh's first book, *Rossetti*, contained a number of examples of his pedagogical method in the schoolroom. One of his ploys was to show the boys a particularly intricate pre-Raphaelite print, remove it, and then ask them to write down as many details as they remembered. Such ingenuities were well-received, and Waugh was popular with the pupils. His next post was at Aston Clinton, in Buckinghamshire. By this time he was writing short stories, one of which—'The Balance'—appeared in *Georgian Stories*, an annual collection published by his father's firm, and in that year (1926) edited by his brother, Alec.

In January 1927 Waugh was dismissed by the headmaster of Aston Clinton, for drunken and ungentlemanly conduct. He worked for a few weeks on the *Daily Express*, spent the summer writing his biography of Rossetti, and in the autumn began a comic novel based on his experiences at the Welsh school. Both *Rossetti* and *Decline and Fall* were published in 1928. The biography was generally well-received, though on its own would not have made much of a stir. Most notably, its anonymous reviewer in the *Times Literary Supplement*—according to a footnote in Selena Hastings's biography of Waugh this was the poet T. Sturge Moore—misconstrued the sex of the author, referring to "Miss Waugh," a matter which Waugh was able to make mileage out of in the letters column the following week.

*Decline and Fall*, which had been rejected by Duckworth, the publisher of *Rossetti*, and taken up by Waugh's father's firm, Chapman & Hall, is a satirical comedy in which the innocent hero, Paul Pennyfeather, is continuously ambushed by the vagaries of experience. Stylistically it was indebted to Ronald Firbank and Ernest Hemingway, and in certain aspects borrowed its tone from Lewis Carroll and Kenneth Grahame. Waugh, who had married Evelyn Gardner two months before publication, knew that its reception was critical. The book's humor was not enjoyed by all reviewers, particularly in America, where it was found tasteless and juvenile. But Cyril Connolly spoke for many when, in the *New Statesman*, he wrote: "The humour throughout is of that subtle metallic kind which, more than anything else, seems a product of this generation."

*Vile Bodies*, Waugh's second novel (during the writing of which his marriage broke down), was even more attuned to the mood of his generation. As a caricature of the life of the metropolitan Bright Young People of the twenties, it stands as a trenchant counterpart to the novels of F. Scott Fitzgerald. Edmund Wilson said of these early Waugh novels that they were "the only things written in England that are comparable to Fitzgerald and Hemingway. They are not so poetic; they are perhaps less intense; they belong to a more classical tradition." The hilariously far-fetched and apocalyptically bleak conclusion to *Vile Bodies* was certainly influenced by difficulties in his private life, and on the whole was not so well constructed as the first novel but, as Waugh himself explained in a *Paris Review* interview (conducted in 1962, printed in *Writers at Work* in 1967), "I popularized a fashionable language, like the beatnik writers today, and the book caught on." Published in January, 1930, it had to be reprinted eleven times by the end of the year.

Although unimpressed in younger life with his father's role as "man of letters," Waugh quickly realized—the success of *Vile Bodies* notwithstanding—that novel writing would have to be supplemented with work of a journalistic nature. Travel writing served this purpose. While his journeys are of interest for the influence they had on his fiction, the general consensus is that Waugh was a dull and uninspiring travel writer, too intent on conveying a sense of his own ennui, and fussy about the inevitable discomforts of tourism. The exception is *Remote People* (published in America as *They Were Still Dancing*), about an expedition to Abyssinia, in which the boredom is comically exaggerated. This book's fictional companion is *Black Mischief*, a satirical comment on the west's naive attempts to 'civilize' Africa.

*A Handful of Dust* (originally to be "A Handful of Ashes") was published in 1934, by which time Waugh had been accepted into the Roman Catholic Church. This book was more serious in tone. Even the names of the characters were studiedly ordinary. The hero is called Tony Last. Waugh himself knew that he had achieved something in this book of a different order compared with his earlier novels. He told Diana Cooper, "What I have done is *excellent*. I don't think it could be better. Very gruesome. Rather like Webster in modern idiom." The ending was criticized by Waugh's friend Henry Yorke (Henry Green), for being too fantastic, and he did write an alternative conclusion for publication in *Harper's Bazaar*, about which Selina Hastings comments: "In this version Waugh in a sense parts company with himself. The Tony Last of *A Handful of Dust* is a man with whom Waugh identifies, recognizing that men such as he and Last, when betrayed by their wives, are doomed to end up dying among savages. The Tony Last of the short story is the personification of the man Waugh would like to be, the betrayed husband who can shrug off his betrayal, remain invulnerable to his wife, and take a flat in Mayfair in which to conduct his affairs." Angus Wilson, in his review of Christopher Sykes's biography of Waugh for the *Times Literary Supplement*, wrote: "The only hero whose painful predicament, especially because of its terrible, ludicrous climax, seems truly to touch one's heart is Tony Last, the hero of *A Handful of Dust*, and it is this which makes me place that novel above Waugh's others as a work of art."

A decade passed between this book and Waugh's next substantial novel. The intervening years were filled with more travel writing, a biography of Edmund Campion, for which he won the Hawthornden Prize, some short fiction, and two satirical novels, *Scoop* and *Put Out More Flags*. During the early part of the war he served in the Middle East as personal assistant to Robert Laycock. Later he accompanied Randolph Churchill on a mission into Yugoslavia, and both were injured when their plane caught fire on landing.

About *Brideshead Revisited*, published at the end of the war, there are conflicting opinions. Some consider it Waugh's major achievement, others a stylistic freak produced when the artistic defenses were down. Waugh gave credence to the latter view when he later revised the book in an attempt to minimize the lushness of its prose. It is the most explicitly Catholic of his books (Edmund Wilson called it, in his *New Yorker* review, "a Catholic tract"). As Angus Wilson observed, again in his *Times Literary Supplement* review of the Sykes biography, "[The] social-religious flavour is no longer, as it was, a relevant eccentricity, but rather an irrelevant one."

*Brideshead Revisited* is essentially a family saga, chronicling twenty years in the lives of an upper-class family of English Catholics, the Marchmains. The narrator, Captain Charles Ryder, is an outsider. Waugh himself explained his change of style with reference to the bleakness and deprivation of wartime. "In consequence," he wrote in the preface to the revised edition, "the book is infused with a kind of gluttony for food and wine, for the splendors of the recent past, and for rhetorical language, which now with a full stomach I find distasteful." Bernard Bergonzi, a writer consistently critical of this novel, has summarized his view in *Wartime and Aftermath* (1993): "Waugh was attempting something new in his writing, but it was surely unwise of him to abandon so completely the satiric edge and the comic sense that are his principal strengths as a novelist. Much of *Brideshead Revisited* is weak in conception, and indulgent to the point of absurdity in writing and attitudes." However, the book was Waugh's biggest commerical success, and was given a new lease on life when dramatized for television, in a production which took the original more opulent text as its guide, in 1981.

Between *The Loved One* (1947), a satire on Hollywood death-rites, and *The Ordeal of Gilbert Pinfold* (1957), Waugh embarked on a series of wartime novels over-ambitiously modelled on Ford Madox Ford's *Parade's End*. *Men at Arms*, the first installment, traces the adventures of Guy Crouchback, deserted by his wife and filled with religious gloom, from his enrollment in the Royal Corps of Halberdiers up to 1940. Essentially a satire on military inefficiency, it was malice applied with a new mellowness rather than the familiar brand.

The 1950s was not a good decade for Waugh. His health was bad and he relied increasingly on narcotics for a sound night's sleep. He also had his first failure. *Love Among the Ruins*, described by Selina Hastings as "a nasty little tale set in a dystopia of the near future," was turned down by American publishers. *Officers and Gentlemen*, the sequel to *Men at Arms*, was published in 1955, to a muted reception. One of the difficulties the novel presents to readers, as the story of Guy Crouchback continues, is that, in comparison with the comically drawn minor characters, Guy himself comes across as a crashing bore. The trilogy (Waugh had initially envisaged four or five novels) drew to a close with *Unconditional Surrender* (1961), and was then issued in one volume under the composite title *Sword Of Honour*. If, as is generally agreed, the sequence of novels fails in it intentions, and contains some of Waugh's flattest writing, the explanation is to be found in the splendidly dotty *The Ordeal of Gilbert Pinfold*, an autobiographical account of a midlife mental breakdown induced, at least in part, by bromide poisoning.

Much of the description used to define Pinfold was equally apt for Waugh himself. "In England he was rather constant and rather romantic in his affections. Since marriage he had been faithful to his wife. He had, since his acceptance of the laws of the Church, developed what approximated to a virtuous disposition; a reluctance to commit deliberate grave sins, which was independent of the fear of Hell; he had assumed a personality to which such specifically forbidden actions were inappropriate." However, a "virtuous disposition" was not a description which many of Waugh's own contemporaries would have applied to him, especially at this late period in his life, when his behaviour became increasingly eccentric and contrived. Ever a dandy, his choice of tailoring became more buffoon-like. One of his favorite suits was made of a large checked cloth which made him look like a circus clown. He exaggerated the ailments of middle age, pretending to a greater severity of deafness than he really suffered, in order that he could use an oversized ear trumpet. He was fiercely opposed to every aspect of modern life, refusing to speak on the telephone, and was refreshingly tight-lipped in rarely-given interviews.

Waugh had remarried in 1937 and established country homes first at Piers Court in Gloucestershire, and later at Combe Florey in Somerset, subsequently occupied by one of his six children, the journalist Auberon Waugh. It was there that he died in 1966, on Easter Sunday, after attending Mass in the village of Wiveliscombe. He is valued especially for the energy and economy of a style which Anthony Burgess in *The Novel Now* (1967) described as the result of a "cool, patrician, Augustan craftsmanship." Editions of his diaries and letters have been published posthumously. In the diaries he could be venomous, but the letters reveal a chummier and more playful side to his character, especially when writing to his children. One explanation has been that he wrote the letters in the mornings when sober, and the diaries at night, when drunk.

The greater part of Waugh's archive was sold by his wife to the University of Texas and is listed in a catalogue by Robert Murray Davis (1981).

PRINCIPAL WORKS: Fiction—Decline and Fall, 1928; Vile Bodies, 1930; Black Mischief, 1932; A Handful of Dust, 1934; Mr. Loveday's Outing and Other Sad Stories, 1936; Scoop, 1938; Put Out More Flags, 1942; Brideshead Revisited, 1945; The Loved One, 1948; Scott-King's Modern Europe, 1949; Helena, 1950; Men at Arms, 1952; Love Among the Ruins, 1953; Tactical Exercise, 1954; Officers and Gentlemen, 1955; The Ordeal of Gilbert Pinfold, 1957; Unconditional Surrender, 1961; Basil Seal Rides Again, 1963; Sword of Honor, 1966. Nonfiction—Rossetti, 1928; Labels, 1930; Remote People, 1932 (in U.S.: A Bachelor Abroad), Ninety-Two Days, 1934; Edmund Campion, 1935; Waugh in Abyssinia, 1936; Robbery Under Law, 1939 (in U.S.: Mexico: An Object Lesson); When The Going Was Good, 1947; The Holy Places, 1953; Monsignor Ronald Knox, 1959; Tourist in Africa, 1960; A Little Learning, 1964; The Diaries of Evelyn Waugh (ed. M. Davie) 1976; The Letters of Evelyn Waugh (ed. M. Amory) 1980; The Essays, Articles and Reviews of Evelyn Waugh (ed. D. Gallagher) 1984.

ABOUT: Bradbury, M. Evelyn Waugh, 1964; Carpenter, H. The Brideshead Generation, 1989; Dictionary of National Biography, 1961–1970; Gale, I. Waugh's World, 1990; Hastings, S. Evelyn Waugh, 1994; Hollis, C. Evelyn Waugh, 1954; Lodge, D. Evelyn Waugh, 1971; Phillips, G. Evelyn Waugh's Officers, Gentlemen and Rogues, 1975; Plimpton, G. Writers at Work, 1967; Stannard, M. Evelyn Waugh 2 vols., 1987, 1992; Sykes, C. Evelyn Waugh, 1975; Waugh A. My Brother Evelyn, 1967; Waugh E. A Little Learning 1964; Who's Who 1966. Bibliography—Doyle, P. A Bibliography of Evelyn Waugh, 1986. Periodicals—London Review of Books May 14, 1922; New Statesman November 3, 1928; September 15, 1934; April 24, 1992; New York Times August 11, 1957; April 11, 1966; New Yorker January 5, 1946; Times (London) April 11, 1966; Times Literary Supplement October 3, 1975; September 8, 1989; April 24, 1992.

**WAY, ARTHUR SANDERS** (February 13, 1847–September 25, 1930), English translator of classsics, and educator, was born in Dorking, England, the second son of Reverend William Way, a Wesleyan minister, and his wife Matilda (Francis) Way. He was educated at Kingswood School, Bath, and later became a fellow at Queen's College, Melbourne, Australia, where he also served as classical lecturer for a time. After returning to Kingswood School as vice-master from 1876 to 1881, he was appointed as headmaster of Wesley College in Melbourne, where he stayed with his wife, Rubena Blanche (Barnicotte) and their daughter, until shrinking enrollment and salary cuts forced him to resign in 1892. Way then returned to England to serve as examiner in Latin to the Central Welsh Board of Secondary Education from 1897 to 1904, and then to be acting headmaster of Mill Hill High School in 1913. In England, he regularly continued to publish his classical translations, occasionally using the pseudonym "Avia."

A flexible and accurate translator whose vocabulary was sometimes quaint and stilted in the manner of his times—which he failed to transcend—Way tackled a diverse number of Greek and Latin authors, ranging from Sappho and Pindar to Sophocles and Virgil. His work was always respected, as his obituarist in the London *Times* commented: "It is difficult to think of any translator who approaches Dr. Way in fertility, and, it may be added, in versatility, in view of the wide difference between the authors whose works he rendered. But epic, lyric, and dramatic—all were congenial to him." In 1929 Way published *Sons of the Violet-Crowned*, a work of fiction.

PRINCIPAL WORKS: The Odes of Horace, 1876; The Odyssey of Homer in English Verse, 1880; The Illiad, 1886–1889; Tragedies of Euripides in English Verse, 1894–1898; Epodes of Horace in English Verse, 1898; The Letters of St. Paul to Seven Churches and Three Friends, 1901; Aeschylus in English Verse, 1906–1908; Sophocles in English Verse, 1909–1914; The Nibelungenlied in English Verse, 1911; The Cyclops of Euripides, 1912; Le Chanson de Roland in English Verse, 1913; Virgil's Georgics in English Verse, 1912; Theocritus, Bion, and Moschus in English Verse, 1913; Virgil's Aeneid in English Verse, 1916–1924; Sappho and the Vigil of Venus, 1921; Pindar, 1921; Greek Through English, 1926; Aristophanes in English Verse, 1927; Psalms: A Verse Translation, 1929; Sons of the Violet-Crowned, 1929; (with W. R. Robert) Longinus on the Sublime, 1979; Letters of Paul and the Book of Psalms, 1981.

ABOUT: Australian Dictionary of Biography vol. 6: 1851–1890, 1976; Who's Who 1929. Periodical—Times (London) September 26, 1930.

**WEAVER, JOHN VAN ALSTYN** (July 17, 1893–June 14, 1938) American poet and novelist, was born in Charlotte, North Carolina, the son of John Van Alstyn Weaver and Anne Randolph (Tate) Weaver. He received his B.A. from Hamilton College, Clinton, New York in 1914. He put in a year at Harvard before taking a job as an assistant to the book editor at the *Chicago Daily News*. Weaver left the *News* in 1917 to enlist in the Army as a second lieutenant. In 1919 he returned to the *Chicago Daily News* for a short period before going to the *Brooklyn Daily Eagle*, where he remained as literary editor until 1924.

Weaver published his first collection of what the *New York Times* called "shirtsleeve poetry" in 1921. *In American*, so titled for the language in

which it was written— the language of the "thousands and thousands who make America what she is and who do not know what the inside of a drawing-room is like," as the *Boston Transcript* explained—received favorable reviews. *Finders: More Poems in American*, Weaver's second collection of poetry, appeared in 1923. The volume, a continuation of the style and theme of *In American*, received more mixed reviews than its predecessor. One reviewer, writing in *Bookman* (1923), remarked that the author had "an unusual faculty for choosing a common incident in life, giving it an original twist, then clothing it with the sure sentiment of the common people." But others were less impressed with Weaver's language, including one who commented that "Mr. Weaver . . . relies on his one divine invention: that of trying to compensate for his sentimentality by couching said sentimentality in bad English" (*Dial*)." H. S. Gorman, in *International Book Review* mildly condemned the volume: "distorted language does not make poetry." A third collection, *More in American*, was published in 1925 to similar reviews.

Weaver produced two more collections, *To Youth* (1927) and *The Turning Point* (1930) before publishing *Trial Balance: A Sentimental Inventory* (1930). In *Trial Balance*, a series of autobiographical poems, Weaver abandoned the "man-on-the-street" style that had become his trademark, and the *New York Times* called it "simple and natural."

Weaver's first novel, *Margie Wins the Game* (1922), about a pretty young girl who must save herself from becoming a wall-flower, suffered the same criticism as his poetry. The *New York Times* (May, 1922) described it as "a badly written short-story dragged out to undue length. The slang vernacular in which it is written suggests nothing more than a High School sophomore." The *Boston Transcript* also panned the book, suggesting that the author go "to school and learn to write, not the balderdash that he calls 'American,' but the English language." Weaver's second novel, *Her Knight Comes Riding* (1928), although equally sentimental, was better written, and better received.

Beginning in 1928, Weaver began writing for Hollywood. His work included original dialogue for such stars as Clara Bow, and a screen adaptation of Mark Twain's *Tom Sawyer* for David O. Selznick was released just before Weaver's death. During this period, he gained material for his third novel, *Joy Girl* (1932), a bitter satire of Hollywood and the

film industry. The book was given a lukewarm review by the *New York Times* (June, 1932), which commented that the "fearful roasting" of the movie industry was "robbed of full comic effectiveness by the maudlin banality of the love story." In addition to his film credits, Weaver wrote one play, *Love 'Em and Leave 'Em*, in collaboration with George Abbot. This was produced in 1926 and ran for a few weeks in New York.

PRINCIPAL WORKS: *Poetry*—In American, 1921; Finders, 1923; More in American, 1925; To Youth, 1927; The Turning Point, 1930; Trial Balance: An Emotional Inventory, 1932; In American: Collected Poems, 1939. *Novels*—Margie Wins the Game, 1922; Her Knight Comes Riding, 1928; Joy Girl, 1932. ABOUT: Who's Who in America 1936–1937. *Periodicals*— Bookman March 1923; February 1926; Boston Transcript May 1922; Dial March 1923; International Book Review June 1923; New Republic September 1928; New York Times May 1922; March 1932; June 1932; Saturday Review of Literature August 1928.

**WEAVER, WARD.** See **MASON, V. W.**

**WEBB, BEATRICE (POTTER)** (January 22, 1858–April 30, 1943) and **WEBB, SIDNEY,** (July 13, 1858–October 13, 1947), English social researchers and reformers who, after their marriage in 1892, became a husband-and-wife industry devoted first to the Fabian cause, and then to the Labour party. Although they have been the subjects of much satire (notably in H. G. Wells's *The New Machiavelli*), their influence on left-wing thinking and policy in Britain during the first half of the twentieth century was immense. They founded the *New Statesman*, helped to establish the London School of Economics, were instrumental in drafting "Clause 4" of the Labour party manifesto (relating to public ownership), and published a number of methodical sociological studies, both jointly and individually. Sidney was M. P. for the Seaham Harbour constituency of Durham from 1922 to 1929. His peerage was an expedient plot to allow him to continue serving in the Cabinet after 1929.

Beatrice Webb, who refused to share in the title, was the youngest daughter of Richard Potter, a railway magnate. She was educated at home, Standish House, near Gloucester, by governesses and was influenced by Herbert Spencer, a family friend. When she was sixteen she spent a short time in a private school in Bournemouth, and was presented at court in the 1876 season. Despite possessing fine looks, she had no interest in making her  mark in society. Her mother died in 1882 and she joined Charles Booth's team of social investigators. The next few years she devoted to the collection of data in the East End and to a tentative affair with Joseph Chamberlain (who was almost her political opposite). Her first writing was printed in the *Pall Mall Gazette* in 1886, under the title "A Lady's View Of The Unemployed," and the following year she had a more serious article, "Dock Life," printed in *Nineteenth Century*.

Sidney Webb's background was lower middle-class. His father, Charles Webb, was a process clerk, but the family was supported principally from the proceeds of his mother's hairdressing business. Sidney attended the City of London school, where he won several academic prizes. He left at age sixteen and, performing impressively in various civil service exams, worked in the War Office, the Inland Revenue and the Colonial Office. He remained in the civil service until 1891, the year before his marriage to Beatrice, whom he met through mutual membership of the Fabian society. Sidney was the author of numerous Fabian tracts, including *Facts for Socialists* (1887) and *Facts for Londoners* (1889). A proportion of the adverse comment, much of it vulgar, made about the two of them derived from the apparent incongruity in their match. She was tall, graceful, and from a wealthy background; he was short, ugly and a hairdresser's son. But they thought and wrote as one, and they often did so formidably—for all their joint lack of a sense of humor.

Beatrice called herself the "investigator" and Sidney the "executant" in "the firm of Webb." The "firm" went into instant operation, with their honeymoon spent investigating trade societies in Ireland and attending the Trades Union Congress in Glasgow. Their debut as joint authors appeared in 1894. *The History of Trade Unionism*, the first serious study of its subject, went into several editions and remains essential reading for students of trade union history. Their next book was *Industrial Democracy* (1897).

The Webbs' domestic routine followed a strict regime, which permitted Sidney initially, but in due course both of them, to become involved in committees and politics. Sidney, from the outset, was a busy politician, having been elected onto the London County Council in the year of his marriage. He devoted much of his energy as a councillor to the issue of education. In 1905 Beatrice was appointed as a member of the Royal Commission on the Poor Laws, and won a reputation as a brilliant cross-examiner. She published her own Minority Report in 1909.

By this time the Webbs had established themselves in the socialist movement as gradualists and centralists, proponents of deliberate planning, and evangelists in the cause of minimum wage. They founded the *New Statesman* in 1913, both as a means of raising the profile of the new science of social investigation, and of providing an arena for Fabian debate.

At the end of the war both of the Webbs launched themselves into the 1919 General Election campaign, and so successful were they that the Seaham Harbour constituency, which Sidney was contesting, became a safe seat for Labour. Beatrice established the practice of composing open newsletters to the constituents. In the first of these she described the household routine: "My husband and I live a very regular life. Every morning at 8 o'clock punctually we have each one cup of coffee and bread and butter on a tray in our workroom . . . and then we go to work, and work steadily until our midday meal at 1 o'clock. When Parliament is sitting my husband has to be in the House of Commons at 2:20 to late night."

Sidney was chairman of the Labour Party Conference in 1923 and the conclusion of his presidential address voiced a Fabian and not a Marxist philosophy: "We shall not achieve much, whatever changes we can bring about, unless what we do is done in the spirit of fellowship. For we must always remember that the founder of British Socialism was not Karl Marx but Robert Owen and that Robert Owen preached not 'class war' but the ancient doctrine of human brotherhood—the hope, the faith, the living fact of human fellowship." Sidney's obituary in the London *Times* justly claimed that he had helped to convert "British Socialism from a propaganda of social revolution to a programme for the working class movement, and more than any other led the Labour Party to accept the Fabian interpretation of Socialism." He became President of the Board of Trade on the first Labour administration.

Neither of the Webbs supported the General Strike of 1926, both of them believing that universal suffrage had removed the excuse for mass direct action. Their stance did not make them popular in Seaham Harbour, and Sidney decided to resign his seat at the next election. (It was taken on by the party leader, Ramsay MacDonald.) Involvement in national politics had not been allowed to get in the way of their other work. In addition to revising their history of trade unions, their joint publications during the 1920s included *English Prisons* (1922), and *English Poor Law History* (1927–1929). In addition, Beatrice published a first volume of her autobiography, *My Apprenticeship*. Based on the diaries which she kept from the age of fifteen, its warm and confessional tone surprised those who had come to equate the name Webb with gloomy and exacting social science. The story was continued in *Our Partnership*, published posthumously, and there are those who think that her name will be remembered for the diaries rather than the sociology. Extracts from the diaries appeared in the fifties (two volumes), and work on a full scholarly edition was carried out by Norman and Jeanne MacKenzie in the 1980s.

The Webbs moved out of London to Hampshire in 1929 and for his peerage Sidney took the title Baron Passfield. They became increasingly detached from the mainstream of socialist thought and their principal publication during the thirties, *Soviet Communism: A New Civilisation?*, revealed a blinkered, uncritical admiration for centralized power which brought them much criticism. Their last years were blighted by ill health. Sidney outlasted Beatrice, but was an invalid at the time of her death.

G. B. Shaw, in the introduction to *My Apprenticeship*, wrote of the Webbs' partnership: "The collaboration is so perfect that her part in it is inextricable. I, who have been behind the scenes of it, cannot lay my hand on a single sentence and say this is Sidney or that is Beatrice."

PRINCIPAL WORKS: *Beatrice and Sidney Webb*—The History of Trade Unionism, 1894; Industrial Democracy, 1897; Problems of Modern Industry, 1898; History of Liquor Licensing, 1903; Bibliography of Road Making and Maintenance in Great Britain, 1906; English Local Government, 1906–1922; English Poor Law Policy, 1910; The State and the Doctor, 1910; The Prevention of Destitution, 1911; A Constitution for the Socialist Commonwealth of Great Britain, 1920; The Consumers' Co-operative Movement, 1921; The Decay of Capitalist Civilization, 1923; English Poor Law History, 1927–1930; Methods of Social Study, 1932; Is Soviet Communism a New Civilization?, 1935; The Truth About Soviet Russia, 1942; Visit to New Zealand in 1898 (ed. D. A. Hamer) 1959; The Diary of Beatrice Webb (eds. N. and J. MacKenzie) 4 vols., 1982–1985; Indian Diary (ed. N. G. Jayal) 1987. *Beatrice Webb*—The Cooperative Movement in Great Britain, 1891; Women and the Factory Acts, 1896; Health of Working Girls, 1917; The Abolition of the Poor Law, 1918; Men's and Women's Wages: Should They Be Equal?, 1919; My Apprenticeship, 1926; Our Partnership, 1948; Diaries, 4 vols., 1982–1985. *Sidney Webb*—Facts for Londoners, 1889; Socialism in England, 1889; Facts for Socialists, 1890; Socialism in England, 1890; The Eight Hours' Day, 1891; The London Programme, 1891; Labour in the Longest Reign, 1897; London Education, 1904; The Decline in the Birthrate, 1907; The Basis and Policy of Socialism, 1909; Grants in Aid, 1911; Towards Social Democracy?, 1916; The Restoration of Trade Union Conditions, 1917; The Works Manager Today, 1917; Story of the Durham Miners, 1921.

ABOUT: Cole, M. Beatrice Webb, 1946; The Webbs and Their Work, 1974; Dictionary of National Biography, 1941–1950, 1959; MacKenzie, J. A Victorian Courtship, 1979; Muggeridge, K. and Adam, R. Beatrice Webb: A Life, 1967; Nord, D. The Apprenticeship of Beatrice Webb, 1985; Radice, L. Beatrice and Sidney Webb, 1984; Schlueter, P. and J. (eds.) An Encyclopaedia of British Women Writers, 1988; Seymour-Jones, C. Beatrice Webb, 1992; Who's Who 1943. *Periodicals*—History Today May 1987; Horizon Summer 1973; New Statesman October 18, 1947; New Republic March 19, 1984; New York Times October 14, 1947; Nineteenth Century October 1887; Pall Mall Gazette February 18, 1886; Saturday Review of Literature November 1, 1947; Times (London) October 14, 1947.

# WEBB, MARY (GLADYS) (March 25, 1881–October 8, 1927), English novelist, poet, and essayist, was born Mary Gladys Meredith at Leighton-

under-the-Wrekin, in Shropshire. The oldest of five children of George Edward Meredith, a schoolmaster and occasional farmer, and Sarah Alice (Scott) Meredith, Mary was educated primarily at home. She early imbibed from her father a love of nature and a deep attachment to the Shropshire countryside. At the age of twenty she was struck by Graves' disease, a recurring hyperthyroid condition that left her with a goiter and eventually caused her early death. The first attack confined her to bed for three years, but it was during her recovery that she began writing poetry and essays. Although not published until 1917 as *The Spring of Joy*, these early writings, though neither mature nor of interest, heralded the themes of her later work, defined by her tendentious biographer Michèle Barale as follows: "Earth's gospel, the superiority of the quiet watcher to the active person, the adventures of the soul versus those of the powerful body, the greater satisfaction found in spiritual comprehension contrasted to physical mastery of the natural world."

*The Spring of Joy* was Webb's second published book. It had been preceded the year before by her first novel, *The Golden Arrow*. (By then she had married Henry Webb, a Cambridge-educated schoolmaster who then shared her literary and spiritual inclinations.) Neither this nor the remaining four novels published during her lifetime sold more than a few thousand copies, but they were respectfully reviewed, and initially earned the qualified approval of such writers as Rebecca West and G. K. Chesterton—and especially of the politician (and prime minister), Stanley Baldwin. This helped her sales.

All of Webb's novels may be described as pastoral romances. *The Golden Arrow* concerns a shepherd's daughter who falls in love with a former minister; it is, Glen Cavaliero has claimed, notable for "a certain terseness and vigour in the writing which Mary Webb was never to recapture." Nevertheless, most of her readers have preferred, like Baldwin, its more famous successor, *Gone to Earth*, the story of an unconventional country girl driven to her death by her inability to choose between two unsatisfactory suitors. The *Nation* reviewer felt at the time that it was "compelling" but that "its faults" were plain to see: "Hazel is innocent beyond belief, Reddin physical beyond belief, Marston spiritual beyond belief, the plot itself beyond belief in every way. And yet, at its core is something all too believable: a vision of the relentlessness of human cruelty."

Webb's next two novels, *The House in Dormer Forest* and *Seven for a Secret*, were again set in Shropshire and Welsh borderland and again concerned the spiritual and romantic crises of country people. Essentially, they re-work the material of *Gone to Earth*. Patricia Beer wrote in the *Times Literary Supplement*, "The reason Mary Webb's novels are little regarded today is that they are not very good, and no amount of drawing attention to them or talking of neglected talent will make them so."

Largely because of Stanley Baldwin's admiration, *Precious Bane* was awarded the Prix Femina Vie Heureuse. This, her last finished novel, brought Webb a measure of the popular recognition she had so long desired. She was, however, by then too ill and dispirited to enjoy it. Dissatisfied with her last novel, the unfinished *Armour Wherein He Trusted*, and despondent over the fact that Henry Webb had left her, she died while on a journey. It is sadly ironic that the real measure of her achievement should be found in the hilarious satire of which her humorless and over-intense prose was one of the main targets: *Cold Comfort Farm*.

PRINCIPAL WORKS: *Novels*—The Golden Arrow, 1916; Gone to Earth, 1917; The House in Dormer Forest, 1920; Seven for a Secret: A Love Story, 1922; Precious Bane, 1924; Armour Wherein He Trusted: a Novel and Some Stories, 1929. *Essays, poetry, and collections*—The Spring of Joy, 1917; Poems and The Spring of Joy, 1928; A Mary Webb Anthology (ed. H.L.B. Webb) 1940; Fifty-One Poems, 1946; The Essential Mary Webb (ed. M. Armstrong) 1949; Collected Poems and Prose (ed. G. M. Coles) 1977; Selected Poems, 1981.

ABOUT: Barale, M. A. Daughters and Lovers: The Life and Writings of Mary Webb, 1986; Barale, M. A. *introduction to Seven for a Secret* (by M. Webb) 1982; Cavaliero, G. The Rural Tradition in the English Novel, 1900–1939, 1977; Coles, G. M. The Flower of Light: A Biography of Mary Webb, 1978; Dictionary of National Biography, 1922–1930, 1937. *Periodicals*—Nation September 25, 1982; Times Literary Supplement September 22, 1978.

**WEBB, SIDNEY.** See **WEBB, BEATRICE**

**\*WEBER, (KARL EMIL) MAX(IMILIAN)** (April 21, 1864–June 14, 1920), German economist and social historian, was born in Erfurt, the oldest of eight children of Max Weber, Sr., and Helene (Fallenstein) Weber. His father was active in National Liberal party politics during the Bismarck era and was for many years a member of the Reichstag; his mother, highly educated and deeply religious, was active in social welfare. In 1869 the family moved to Berlin, and Weber grew up in a household where political and intellectual figures of the day were frequently entertained. He attended a Gymnasium in Berlin and in 1882 entered the University of Heidelberg, where he studied jurisprudence. The following year he did his first round of required military service (in Strasbourg) and in 1884 resumed his studies in law and legal history— first at the University of Berlin and then in Göttingen in 1885–1886. He returned to Berlin in 1886 and received a doctorate in 1889, with a dissertation on medieval trading companies. His postdoctoral degree was received in 1891, with a thesis on Roman agrarian history and its importance for state and civil law. In the meantime he had been commissioned by the Verein für Sozialpolitik (Union for Social Policy) to study the problems created by the employment of seasonal Polish labor on farms along the German border; Weber's solution recommended the termination of the traditional large-estate economy. In 1892 he began to lecture at the University of Berlin on commercial law and Roman legal history, and to work as a lawyer. A year later he married his cousin Marianne Schnitger, who had been one of his students and who later became a leader of the German women's movement and, in 1919, the first woman delegate to a state legislature (the Baden Landtag).

As Weber's thinking developed he became convinced that law, generally regarded as the ultimate authority in a society, is actually itself dependent

upon economic and technological factors. His appointment in 1894 as a full professor of political economy at the University of Freiburg marks this change in intellectual direction. After two years he went on to Heidelberg and taught there until a nervous breakdown, in 1898, made it impossible for him to lecture or meet writing deadlines. (Nevertheless, he did continue to publish articles every year, except 1901, up to the time of his death.)

*VAY ber

Granted a leave of absence, he spent the next five years traveling or in sanatoriums to regain his health.

Dirk Räsler and Raymond Collins are among the scholars who point out that an understanding of the genesis of his illness (or, as Collins phrases it, the "Freudian skeleton in Max Weber's emotional closet") is essential to evaluation of his book. For many years there had been tension between Weber's parents, and he had generally sided with his mother and her social idealism rather than with his pragmatic, domineering father—as happened again during a violent family quarrel in 1897. The elder Weber died suddenly after this; his son's breakdown seems to have been precipitated by guilt and by ongoing ambivalence about his parental loyalties. Sexual frustration in his marriage may also have been a contributing factor. It is a fact that after his recovery he began having affairs, notably (beginning in 1907) with Else von Richthofen, a member of the German avant-garde and sister of Frieda von Richthofen (later D. H. Lawrence's wife). In 1903 Weber formally resigned his chair at Heidelberg, and did not resume regular teaching until after World War I. Essentially an independent scholar for many years, he lived on in Heidelberg, where his home became a center for a circle of intellectuals, including some of Freud's early followers.

Weber now began to work on a study of the origins of modern, or rational (that is, ordered, bureaucratized) Western capitalism; the study would become his best-known book, translated into English as *The Protestant Ethic and the Spirit of Capitalism*. In 1904 he traveled to the United States, gave some lectures, and did research on his new work at Columbia University. It first appeared in 1904–1905 as a series of essays in the *Archiv für Sozialwissenschaft und Sozialpolitik* (Archives of social science and social policy), of which Weber was cofounder and coeditor from 1903 on, and in which he published most of his writing. Later the text was incorporated into Volume 1 of the *Gesammelte Aufsätze zure Religionssoziologie* (*Collected Essays on the Sociology of Religion*), assembled and edited by his wife in 1920. What Weber proposed "stood Marx on his head" (as the American sociologist Talcott Parsons put it), for he ascribed the rise of the capitalist system not to changes in technology and class relations but to an ideology, specifically, Calvinist doctrine. Calvinist belief in predestination—that some have been foreordained to be among the Elect—encouraged a devotion to steady, unremitting, hard work as a way of showing worthiness of God's grace. In time, Weber argued, the "light cloak" of such asceticism became the "iron cage" of the market forces and bureaucratic structures of modern economic life, which determine the social conditions of those born into it. He does not solve the fundamental paradox here, that despite Protestant condemnation of acquisitiveness, many adherents to the "Protestant work ethic" have managed to lay up an abundance of worldly goods. According to Collins, Weber's own family afforded him an example of the connection between "puritanical normalism and the nature of hardworking capitalism." As the *Protestant Ethic* essays began to appear in the *Archiv* they aroused intense debate, much of it carried on between the author and his readers in the pages of the journal. The work became available in English in 1930, when Parsons translated it, with a foreword by the English economic historian R. H. Tawney. The latter's book, *Religion and the Rise of Capitalism* (1926), served as a gloss on Weber and somewhat reversed his thesis with respect to England. (Tawney suggests that a capitalist system began to develop there even before the Reformation, and thus favored the growth of Protestantism.) Debate on Weber's *Protestant Ethic* continues, with other modifications and outright rebuttals; it remains a classic text.

Broadening his study of the cultural contexts in which capitalism was either encouraged or discouraged, Weber went on to write three studies of Eastern religions. These were published originally in the *Archiv* in 1915–1916 and then in his collected essays on the sociology of religion. *The Religion of China: Confucianism and Taoism*, and *The Religion of India: The Sociology of Hinduism and Buddhism* attempt to show that where these creeds have been dominant, capitalism did not develop, despite economic factors that might have made it possible. In *Ancient Judaism*, however, he discusses Jewish "inner-worldly asceticism" (the opposite of otherwordly mysticism) as contributing to the eventual rise of capitalistic endeavor. Weber projected—but did not live to write—three more volumes, on early and medieval Christianity and on Islam, that would complete his survey of different religious world views and demonstrate why modern capitalism developed in Western Europe and not elsewhere. He also proposed a work that would sum up all the forces (social institutions and historical conditions in addition to religion) that contributed to the rise of this system.

About 1902 Weber had begun to write articles (published in the *Archiv*) on methodology in the social sciences. In an essay on objectivity (1904, *The "Objectivity" of Social and Socio-Political Thought*), he first presented his concepts of value freedom and the ideal-type. Value-free social science implies teaching without expressing one's own social or political views. An ideal-type is an abstraction, established by comparison of historical evidence, that may exaggerate or simplify a concept but can be used to clarify the "infinite manifold" of reality; it is a method of analysis that Weber used throughout his own work.

In 1909 Weber agreed to do a new edition of a handbook on political economy and to contribute to it a study of the social behavior of groups as revealed by their economic activity; in effect, this would be a comprehensive treatise on sociology. His work, interrupted by the war and left unfinished at his sudden death, was essentially a series of essays and hypotheses that look at problems from several angles. The fragmented text was collected by his widow and published as *Wirtschaft und Gesellschaft* (1922, *Economy and Society*).

Written in his always tortuous style, with a mind-boggling array of historical example, it has presented difficulties of interpretation and translation. From 1922 to 1947 fewer than 2,000 copies of the work were sold in Germany; it is now recognized, however, as Weber's greatest contribution to his subject. And yet, according to Collins, "we are very far from having made the fullest use of his theories in order to develop our own sociology to the fullest extent." An introductory section of definitions and principles of sociology, kinds of economic behavior, and types of authority (charismatic, traditional, or legal) constitutes Part I of *Wirtschaft un Gesellschaft*, and was translated by Parsons and A. M. Henderson as *The Theory of Social and Economic Organization*. In the much longer, more discursive second part, Weber works out a sociology of law, state, and bureaucracy, and deals with the organizing of social groups and their struggles for political power.

At the outbreak of the war Weber served briefly as an administrator of military hospitals (which gave him an insight into the workings of bureaucracy); in 1915–1916 he was active in efforts to bring about a negotiated peace. At the end of the war he was a delegate to the Versailles peace conference and served on the committee that prepared the first draft of a new German constitution. And now, after twenty years, he began to teach again, first at the University of Vienna, then in 1919–1920 at the University of Munich until his death from pneumonia. The lectures he gave that last year, in which he enlarged on his idea of the dominant role of rationality in all phases of social life, were published in 1923 and translated four years later as *General Economic History*.

In *Ancient Judaism*, Weber remarks that "the possibility of questioning the meaning of the world presupposes the capacity to be *astonished* about the course of events." His own capacity for astonishment was vast, measured in the flow of observations and theories that have made his writing, especially *Economy and Society*, a quarry of suggestive ideas now pervasive throughout the social sciences. Yet because these writings lack a central idea or focus, Weber established no formal school of economics or sociology. International interest in his work began to develop after World War II, and a complete edition of his writings, in German, was begun in Munich in 1976.

PRINCIPAL WORKS IN ENGLISH TRANSLATION: General Economic History (tr. F. H. Knight) 1927 (Adelphi Economic Ser.); The Protestant Ethic and the Spirit of Capitalism (tr. T. Parsons: foreword by R. H. Tawney) 1930 (2nd ed., introd. by A. Giddens, 1976); The "Objectivity" of Social and Socio-Political Knowledge (tr. W. J. Goode) 1941?; From Max Weber: Essays in Sociology (tr., ed., and with introd. by H. H. Gerth and C. W. Mills) 1946 (International; new ed. with pref. by B. S. Turner, 1991); The Theory of Social and Economic Organization (tr. A. M. Henderson and T. Parsons; ed. with introd. by T. Parsons) 1947 (Wirtschaft und Gesellschaft, Pt. I); Max Weber on the Methodology of the Social Sciences (tr. E. A. Shils and H. A. Finch; foreword by E. A. Shils) 1949; The Hindu Social System (trs. ed. H. Gerth and D. Martindale) 1950 (U. of Minnesota Sociology Club Bull. no. 1, Historical Ser. vol. 1); The Religion of China: Confucianism and Taoism (tr. and ed. H. H. Gerth) 1951 (His Religions of the East); Ancient Judaism (trs. H. H. Gerth and D. Marindale) 1952 (His Religions of the East); Max Weber on Law in Economy and Society (trs. E.

Shils and M. Rheinstein; ed. with introd. by M. Rheinstein) 1954 (20th Century Legal Philosophy Ser. vol. 6) (from Wirtschaft un Gesellschaft Pt. I, selected passages); The City (tr. and ed. D. Martindale and G. Neuwirth) 1958; The Rational and Social Foundation of Music (tr. and ed. D. Martindale, with others) 1958; The Religion of India: The Sociology of Hinduism and Buddhism (tr. and ed. H. H. Gerth and D. Martindale) 1958; Basic Concepts in Sociology (tr. with introd. by H. P. Secher) 1962; Max Weber selections from his work, with introd. by S. M. Miller 1963 (Major Contributors to Social Science Ser.); The Sociology of Religion (tr. E. Fischoff; introd. T. Parsons) 1963 (reissued 1993) (Wirtschaft und Gesellschaft Pt. II, chap. 4); Politics as a Vocation lecture (tr. H. Gerth and C. W. Mills) 1965; Economy and Society (tr. E. Fischoff, with others; ed. G. Roth and C. Wittick) 3 vols., 1968 (Wirtschaft und Gesellschaft, Pts. I and II); Max Weber on Charisma and Institution Building: Selected Papers (ed. and introd. by S. N. Eisenstadt) 1968 (The Heritage of Sociology); Max Weber: The Interpretation of Social Reality (ed. and introd. by J. E. T. Eldridge) 1970; Max Weber on Universities: The Power of the State and the Dignity of the Academic Calling in Imperial Germany (tr., ed., and introd. by E. Shils) 1974; Roscher and Knies: the Logical Problems of Historical Economics (tr. and introd. by G. Oakes) 1975; The Agrarian Sociology of Ancient Civilizations (tr. R. I. Frank) 1976 (Foundations of History Library); Max Weber: Selections in Translation (tr. E. Matthews; ed. W. G. Runciman) 1978; Max Weber on Capitalism, Bureaucracy, and Religion: A Selection of Texts (tr. and ed. s. Andreski) 1983; A Weber-Marx Dialogue (eds. R. J. Antonio and R. M. Glassman) 1985; Max Weber's "Science as a vocation" (with others eds. P. Lassman) 1989 [lecture]; Sociological Writings (ed. W. V. Heydebrand), 1994; Weber: Political Writings (eds. P. Lassman and R. Speirs) 1994.

ABOUT: Abraham, G. A. Max Weber and the Jewish Question: A Study of the Social Outlook of His Sociology, 1992; Albrow, M. Max Weber's Construction of Social Theory, 1990; Andreski, S. Max Weber's Insights and Errors, 1984; Beetham, D. Max Weber and the Theory of Modern Politics, 2nd ed., 1985; Bendix, R. Max Weber: An Intellectual Portrait, 1960 (new ed., with introd. by G. Roth, 1977); Bendix, R. and Roth, G. (eds.) Scholarship and Partisanship: Essays on Max Weber, 1971; Blaug, M. Great Economists before Keynes: An Introduction to the Lives and Works of One Hundred Great Economists of the Past, 1989; Bologh, R. W. Love or Greatness: Max Weber and Masculine Thinking—a Feminist Inquiry, 1990; Ebubaker, R. The Limits of Rationality: An Essay on the Social and Moral Thought of Max Weber, 1984; Collins, R. Max Weber: A Skeleton Key, 1986 (in U.K.: Weberian Sociological Thought, 1977; Dronberger, I. Political Thought of Max Weber: In Quest of Statesmanship, 1971; Ferrarotti, F. Max Weber and the Crisis of Western Civilization, 1987; Ferrarotti, F. Max Weber and the Destiny of Reason, 1982; Fischoff, E. The Protestant Ethic and the Spirit of Capitalism: The History of a Controversy, in Social Research vol. 11, 1944; Gerth, H. H. and Mills, C. W. introduction to From Max Weber: Essays in Sociology (tr., ed., and with introd. by H. H. Gerth and C. W. Mills) 1946 (International Library of Sociology and Social Reconstruction); Giddens, A. Politics and Sociology in the Thought of Max Weber, 1972; Glassman, R. M. and Murvar, V. (eds.) Max Weber's Political Sociology: A Pessimistic Vision of a Rationalized World, 1984; Green, B. S. Literary Methods and Sociological Theory: Case Studies of Simmel and Weber, 1988; Green, M. The Von Richthofen Sisters: The Triumphant and the Tragic Modes of Love: Else and Frieda von Richthofen, Otto Gross, Max Weber, and D. H. Lawrence, in the Years 1870–1970, 1974; Hamilton, P. Max Weber, Critical Assessment, 1991; Hennis, W. Max Weber: Essays in Reconstruction, 1988; Holton, R. J. and Turner, B. S. Max Weber on Economy and Society, 1989; Honigsheim, P. On Max Weber (tr. J. Rytina) 1968; Huff, T. E. Max Weber and the Methodology of the Social Sciences, 1984; Internationsl Encyclopedia of the Social Sciences, vol. 16, 1968; Jaspers, K. Karl Jaspers on Max Weber (tr. R. J. Whelan; ed. J. Dreijmanis) 1989; Karlberg, S. Max Weber's Comparative Historical Sociology, 1994; Kasler, D. Max Weber: An Introduction to His Life and Work, 1988; Kivisto, P. and Swatos, W. H. Max Weber: A Bio-Bibliography, 1988; Kronman, A. T. Max Weber, 1983 (Juris-

tis: Profiles in Legal Theory); Lachmann, L. M. Legacy of Max Weber: Three Essays, 1971; Lehman, H. and Roth, G. (eds.) Webers' Protestant Ethic: Origins, Evidence, Contexts, 1993; Lessnoff, M. H. The Spirit of Capitalism and the Protestant Ethic: An Enquiry into the Weber Thesis, 1994; Lowith, K. Max Weber and Karl Marx (eds. T. B. Bottomore and W. Outhwaite) 1982; Macrae, D. C. Max Weber, 1974; Marshall, G. In Search of the Spirit of Capitalism: An Essay on Max Weber's Protestant Ethic Thesis, 1982; Max Weber, 1864–1964 in Sociological Quarterly 5, 1964 (100-page article with comprehensive bibliog.); Mayer, J. P. Max Weber and German Politics: A Study in Political Sociology, 2nd rev. ed., 1956; Mitzman, A. The Iron Cage: An Historical Interpretation of Max Weber, 1970; Mommsen, W. J. Max Weber and German Politics, 1890–1920, 1985; Mommsen, W. J. and Osterhammel, W. (eds.) Max Weber and His Contemporaries, 1987; Mommsen, W. J. The Political and Social Theory of Max Weber: Collected Essays, 1989; Murvar, V. Max Weber Today, an Introduction to a Living Legacy: Selected Bibliography, 1983 (Max Weber Colloguia and Symposia at the University of Wisconsin); Parkin, F. Max Weber, 1982; Parsons, T. introduction to The Theory of Social and Economic Organization (trs. A. M. Henderson and T. Parsons; ed. with introd. by T. Parsons) 1947 (Wirtschaft und Gesellschaft, Pt. I); Parsons, T. The Structure of Social Action: A Study in Social Theory with Special Reference to a Group of Recent European Writers, 1937; Poggi, G. Calvinism and the Capitalist Spirit: Max Weber's Personality, 1986; Roth, G. and Schluchter, W. Max Weber's Vision of History, Ethics and Methods, 1984; Sayer, D. Capitalism and Modernity: An Excursus on Marx and Weber, 1991; Scaff, L. A. Fleeing the Iron Cage: Culture, Politics, and Modernity in the Thought of Max Weber, 1989; Schluchter, W. Rationalism, Religion, and Domination: A Weberian Perspective, 1985; Segady, T. W. Values, Neo-Kantianism, and the Development of Weberian Methodology, 1987; Sica, A. Weber, Irrationality, and Social Order, 1988; Thinkers of the Twentieth Century: A Biographical, Bibliographical and Critical Dictionary (ed. E. Devine) 1983; Tribe K. (ed.) Reading Weber, 1989; Turner, B. S. Max Weber: From History to Modernity, 1992; Turner, S. P. and Factor, R. A. Max Weber: The Lawyer as Social Thinker, 1994; Turner, S. P. and Factor, R. A. Max Weber and the Dispute over Reason and Value: A Study in Philosophy, Ethics, and Politics, 1984; Wallace, W. L. A Weberian Theory of Human Society: Structure and Evolution, 1994; Weber, Marianne. Max Weber: A Biography (tr. and ed. H. Zohn) 1975; Who's Who in Economics: A Biographical Dictionary of Major Economists, 1700–1981, 1983; Wiley, N. (ed.) The Marx-Weber Debate, 1987; Wrong, D. (ed.) Max Weber, 1970 (Makers of Modern Social Science). Periodicals— American Journal of Sociology July 1982; American Sociological Review April 1965; British Journal of Sociology September 1976, June 1982, June 1985, June 1988; History and Theory vol. 30, 1991; New York Review of Books February 12, 1992; Sociological Review February 1985, February 1988.

## WEBSTER, ELIZABETH CHARLOTTE

(1914–1946), Scottish novelist, was born in Edinburgh. Because of her ongoing battle with bronchial asthma, she was confined to her bedroom for most of her childhood. Her illness kept her, for the most part, from attending school with any regularity, and she once remarked that her total days in attendance could not have been more than five. But  these extreme circumstances did not stop the young Webster from reading, an activity she took to almost automatically, and, being a naturally wise and witty girl, she was often surrounded by friends and relatives who sought her advice on many matters, particularly those of the heart.

For health reasons Webster moved with her sister and close companion, Mary Morison Webster, to Johannesburg, South Africa, whose mild climate contrasted greatly with that of Edinburgh. It was here that she completed her four novels. She was relatively unknown until the last, *Ceremony of Innocence* (1949), which was published three years after her death. The novel, praised as a "boldly original morality tale . . . aimed at the shams of professional holiness" (C. J. Rolo, *Atlantic*), tells the story of life in a South African convent inhabited by a clairvoyant novice, Sybil.

Webster spent two years writing *Cermony of Innocence*. Three days after its completion she was struck down with pneumonia and died less than a week later. "It is with deep regret that one learns that Elizabeth Charlotte Webster died . . . and that one recommends[*Ceremony of Innocence*] knowing that nothing more will follow from her pen. . . . If you can imagine a first-rate novelist of social manners—urbane, witty, a fine stylist, an acutely satiric but sympathetic observer of social behavior—who at the same time is concerned to hypothecate man's ultimate fate, you perhaps have some notion of Miss Webster's unusual gift," wrote Diana Trilling in the *Nation*.

Webster's other works include *High Altitude: A Frolic* (1949), which she wrote with her sister.

PRINCIPAL WORKS: Pot Holes: An Adventure of the Diamond Fields, 1928; Bullion, 1933; Expiring Frog, 1946; Ceremony of Innocence, 1949; (with M. M. Webster) High Altitude: A Frolic, 1949.

ABOUT: *Periodicals*—Atlantic April 1949; Library Journal February 1, 1949; Nation March 12, 1949; New York Herald Tribune Weekly Book Review February 13, 1949; Saturday Review of Literature February 12, 1949.

**WEBSTER, HENRY KITCHELL** (September 7, 1875–December 9, 1932), American novelist, was born and spent his life in Evanston, Illinois, a

Chicago suburb where for many years he maintained a "fiction factory" writing studio where, at rapid speed, he dictated to a stenographer bestselling mysteries and popular magazine serials, as well as some more seriously intended novels, such as *Mary Wollaston* (1920), in which he pushed Victorian mores to the limit with portraits of contemporary women. The son of Towner Keeney Webster and Emma J. (Kitchell) Webster, he attended Alexander Woollcott's alma mater, Hamilton College, where he changed his career course from law to literature.

When editors' rejections began coming his way, Webster turned to writing magazine articles—pot boilers for pulp magazines—written under five different pen names, or anonymously. Webster's work between 1908 and 1912 shows the early signs of his interest in more serious plots and his attempt to write realistic novels to which he would be proud to attach his real name: *The Whispering Man* (1908), about an amateur detective who knows by instinct when he is looking at a criminal; *A King in Khaki* (1909), an adventure of a former New York newspaperman who takes charge of an industrial enterprise on a little island in the West Indies; *The Sky Man* (1910), another adventure, in which a young man accused of a crime he did not commit flies away with a pair of giant wings powered by his own muscular strength; and *The Girl in the Other Seat* (1911), a romance set in the world of automobile racing.

In 1913 *The Saturday Evening Post* ran Webster's novel *The Butterfly* as a serial, and he said he felt he had gotten past the pot-boiler point of his career and was on to more serious work. *The Butterfly* was published as a book in 1914 and told the story of a world-famous sensational dancer whose three-night engagement in a small midwestern college town rocks the sleepy local drama league and causes the usually staid and respected young drama professor to partake of a series of amazing adventures including spending time in a hen house. *Nation* called it "a most entertaining mixture of mystery, fantasy, and farce."

When *The Real Adventure* was published as a magazine serial in *Everybody's* in 1915 and as a book in 1916, "Webster began to take on stature among editors and readers, a novelist capable of creating character and commenting upon the world rather than of merely telling a light romance or swiftly moving mystery tale," wrote the *Newberry Library Bulletin* reviewer. The story of Rose and Rodney Aldrich, *The Real Adventure* presented one woman's attempt to find satisfaction in marriage. E. E. Hale wrote in *Dial* that "Webster certainly does one thing worth doing: he takes the real woman's view."

Webster was frequently credited for his understanding of women, and although many critics of his time considered him conservative, many of his readers and magazine editors saw him as "part of 1920s revolt against certain Victorian sex-taboos that still hung over fiction," according to the *Newberry Library Bulletin*. In reviewing *The Thoroughbred* (1917), E.P. Wyckoff wrote in *Publishers Weekly*, "Webster certainly understands the ways of women, which is another way of saying that he understands human nature."

With *Mary Wollaston*, Webster created a heroine in a young woman engaged in war work in New York, who has a casual love affair with a young soldier bound overseas. *Booklist* wrote, "This will be pronounced immoral by some readers. The analysis of women's thoughts and emotions is illuminating." W. L. Phelps in *The New York Times* called it "accurately contemporary."

The last of his novels published in his lifetime was *Who Is The Next?* (1931), which presented greed and murder among the landed gentry of the Midwest through the story of two brutal murders on an estate on the outskirts of Chicago. "Webster already has several good mystery stories to his credit, and this new one is additional proof of his skill," wrote Isaac Anderson in *The New York Times*. It was reissued in 1976 as part of the series *Fifty Classics of Crime Fiction 1900-1950*. At his death, he left unfinished a mystery novel, *The Alleged Great Aunt*, which was published in 1935 after it had been completed by two of his closest friends, Janet Ayer Fairbank and Margaret Ayer Barnes, whom Webster had long ago encouraged to take up writing careers. "The point where the collaboration began is our little mystery," the Ayer sisters wrote in the preface.

Webster's best tale was probably *Calumet K* (1901) which was reprinted in 1993. This he wrote with Samuel Merwin, who may have been responsible for its narrative skill. It is a vivid story of a business conflict.

PRINCIPAL WORKS: The Banker and the Bear, 1900, 1968; Roger Drake: Captain of Industry, 1902; The Duke of Cameron Avenue, 1904; Traitor and Loyalist, 1904; The Whispering Man, 1908; A King in Khaki, 1909; The Sky Man, 1910; The Girl in the Other Seat, 1911; The Ghost Girl, 1913; The Butterfly, 1914; The Real Adventure, 1915; The Painted Scene, 1916; The Thoroughbred, 1917; An American Family, 1918; Hugh Corbett's Wife, 1919; Mary Wollaston, 1920; Real Life, 1921; Joseph Greer and his Daughter, 1922; The Other Story, and Other Stories, 1923; The Innocents, 1924; The Corbin Necklace, 1926; The Beginners, 1927; Philopena, 1927; The Sealed Trunk, 1927; The Clock Strikes Two, 1928; The Quartz Eye, 1928; The Man with the Scarred Hand, 1931; Who is the Next? 1931, 1976, 1981; The Alleged Great-Aunt (completed by J.A. Fairbank and M.A. Barnes), 1935. *With Samuel Merwin*—The Short Line War, 1899, 1967; Calumet K, 1901, 1993; Comrade John, 1907.

ABOUT: *Periodicals*— New York Times December 10, 1932; Newberry Library Bulletin December 1946.

**WEBSTER, JANE** (July 24, 1876–June 11, 1916), American novelist and short story writer, was born Alice Jane Chandler Webster in Fredonia, New  York, the eldest child and only daughter of Charles Luther Webster and Annie (Moffett) Webster. Webster's interest in writing was awakened early by her childhood environment: her maternal grandmother was Mark Twain's older sister, and her father was his partner and publisher; Webster herself was named for Twain's mother, Jane Clemens.

She attended public school in Fredonia, and then prepared for college at the Lady Jane Grey school in Binghamton, New York. She then attended Vassar, majoring in English and economics (B.A. 1901). While still an undergraduate she contributed a weekly column to the *Poughkeepsie Sunday Courier* and published many pieces in her college paper, the *Vassar Miscellany*. Many of these stories, whose main character is believed to be modeled after Webster's friend and classmate the once-fashionable poet Adelaide Crapsey, were collected in 1903 and published as *When Patty Went To College*. The author continued the "Patty" stories—as

they came to be known—in *Just Patty* (1911), which chronicled the adventures of the popular heroine as a young schoolgirl.

While a guest in a convent in the Sabine mountains in Italy, Webster wrote *The Wheat Princess* (1905), the story of an American girl and her philanthropist aunt and uncle just outside Rome during a wheat famine. *Jerry, Junior* (1907) the love story of two Americans staying at an out-of-the-way Italian resort, was also written during this time. Both books received similar comment, such as "a delightful bit of nonsense" (*New York Times* 1907), and "an entertaining and well written story along novel lines" (*Outlook*).

After taking a world tour from 1906 to 1907 Webster returned to New York, settling in Greenwich Village. Here, in addition to continuing her writing, which included *The Four Pools Mystery* (1908), published anonymously, and *Much Ado about Peter* (1909), she served on several committees for prison reform, becoming a familiar figure at Sing Sing state prison, in Ossining, New York, where she worked with convicts, some of whom became her life-long friends. But as a humanitarian her main devotion was to the welfare of underprivileged children and the improvement of orphanages, an interest she developed in college after visiting institutions for the delinquent and destitute as part of an assignment. Her belief that underprivileged children could succeed in life if only given a chance was expressed in the most famous of all her novels, *Daddy-Long-Legs* (1912), about Jerusha Abbott, a seventeen-year-old orphan sent to college by an anonymous trustee. The book, a series of letters from Jerusha to her benefactor (who she has named Daddy-Long-Legs), was well liked by critics, and was called "full of quaint charm and rippling with humor that is partly girlish spirits and partly a delightful sense of drollery" (*New York Times* 1912). In 1919 the book was made into a silent film starring Mary Pickford (who bought the film rights in 1918). Since then the movie has been remade twice, once in 1931 and then again in 1955, when it featured Leslie Caron and Fred Astaire. In 1914 it was adapted for the stage by the author and enjoyed an extensive run at New York's Gaiety Theater. The book itself has never been out of print since it first appeared.

In its many forms, *Daddy-Long-Legs*, with its portrayal of the dull and limited training provided by custodial facilities, succeeded in stirring the conscience of many people. And, as a result, a committee of the New York State Charities Aid Association organized auxiliary groups in colleges, each responsible for the education of an orphan.

*Dear Enemy*, a sequel to *Daddy-Long-Legs* also in the form of a series of letters, this time between Jerusha Abbott and the new superintendent of the orphanage where she was raised, was published in 1914 and also received warm reviews. The *New York Times* (1915) said of it: "The real achievement of Miss Webster in this book, as in [*Daddy-Long-Legs*] is her combination of serious social modernity with the other modernity of gaiety and humor. . . . it is a delightful little story, with a sane philosophy."

In 1915 Webster married Glenn Ford McKinney, a lawyer. She died soon after giving birth to their daughter, Jean Webster McKinney.

PRINCIPAL WORKS: Novels—When Patty Went to College, 1903; The Wheat Princess, 1905; Jerry Junior, 1907; The Four Pools Mystery, 1908; Much Ado about Peter, 1909; Just Patty, 1911; Daddy-Long-Legs, 1912; Dear Enemy, 1914.

ABOUT: Contemporary Authors vol. 116, 1986; Dictionary of American Biography vol. X, 1936; Notable American Women 1607–1950 Vol. III, 1971; Something about the Author vol. 17 1979; Who's Who in America 1916–1917. Periodicals—New York Times June 16, 1907; October 26, 1912; October 31, 1915; June 12, 1916; Outlook November 18, 1905.

**WECTER, DIXON** (January 12, 1906–June 24, 1950), American historian, was born in Houston, Texas, the son of John Joseph Wecter, an employee of the Southern Pacific Railroad, and Eugenia (Dixon) Wecter.

Wecter attended Baylor University in Waco, Texas, receiving his B.A. in 1925. A year later he earned an M.A. from Yale University at which he held a Sterling Junior Research fellowship (1927–1928). He was a Rhodes Scholar at Oxford (1928–1930), and was awarded a B.Litt.

Returning to the U.S. in 1933, Wecter taught for a year at the University of Denver before joining the faculty at the University of Colorado. He later

became professor of English at the University of California at Los Angeles; he also taught at the California Institute of Technology. In 1945 he became the first professor to teach American history in Australia as a visiting professor at the University of Sydney. From 1946 to 1949 he served as chairman of research at the Huntington Library at San Marino, California. In 1949 Wecter went to Berkeley to take the Margaret Byrne Chair of United States History, which he held until his death the following year.

In 1939 Wecter published *Edmund Burke and His Kinsmen: A Study of the Statesman's Financial Integrity and Private Relationships.* The *Times Literary Supplement* called this interesting and still consulted examination of Burke's probity an "admirable monograph." In 1941 he published *Hero in America: A Chronicle of Hero Worship,* a history of the United States told through a series of biographical sketches of some of America's best-known heroes, including such men as Captain John Smith, George Washington, Thomas Jefferson, Daniel Boone, The Unknown Soldier, Thomas Edison, and Franklin Roosevelt. The book, an admirable blend of the accessible and the scholarly, received generally good reviews, such as that in the *Yale Review:* "surprising well-proportioned book, which comes close to justifying completely its compromise between the demands of historical scholarship and the desires of the desultory reader." Arthur M. Schlesinger, Jr., remarked of the author that "his well stocked and cultivated mind gives the study a

breadth of allusion which vastly enriches the book" (*New England Quarterly*).

Wecter next turned his attention to the study of the American serviceman, publishing *Our Soldiers Speak* in 1943 and *When Johnny Comes Marching Home* in 1944. As with his earlier work, Wecter approached his subject not as a dry list of historical facts, but in the light of human experience. Both books drew heavily upon first-person accounts from diaries and letters of the American servicemen who had taken part in the American Revolution, the Civil War, and World War I. *Our Soldiers Speak*, written with William Matthews, was described by S. T. Williamson of the *New York Times* (1943) as producing "a picture seldom found in formal histories. . . . Whereas history records and reconstructs the past, these soldier letters and diaries briefed by Messrs Matthews and Wecter rub readers' shoulders with the past." Others, such as B. I. Wiley of the *American History Review* were not so enthusiastic about the authors's format, commenting that they had drawn "almost exclusively on printed material," and that "in so doing they withhold from the reader some of the most vivid and most human of soldier testimony."

*When Johnny Comes Marching Home* examined the problems often faced by servicemen returning home after their tours of duty. With an eye to the demobilization of troops after World War II, Wecter looked to the past for both examples and solutions. As with *Our Soldiers Speak*, he relied heavily upon the diaries and letters of the men who had served in the three previous wars. Bernard De Voto, writing for *Weekly Book Review*, described the book as "distinguished, timely . . . and, though absorbing reading . . . not in the least frivolous or superficial."

With *The Age of the Great Depression, 1929–1941* (1947) Wecter looked to that period of American history. The book, which remains in print was praised by *New York Times* (1948) as "fair and complete." Joseph Kraft of the *Nation* described it as "clearly, if not brilliantly written," but went on to suggest that "what it lacks is depth of historical perspective and philosophical insight."

In 1949 Wecter won the editorship of the Mark Twain Estate after publishing a chapter on the author in *The Literary History of the United States*, for which he was an associate editor in 1948. In 1952 his *Sam Clemens of Hannibal* was published posthumously. The work, which followed Twain only to the age of nineteen, was only the first installment of what was to be a definitive biography of Twain. Yet a reviewer for the *New York Times* (1952) believed, possibly hyperbolically, that it "render[ed] obsolete all previous accounts of [Mark Twain's] formative years."

In December of 1937 Wecter married Elizabeth Farrar, who had been a student in one of his English classes at the University of Colorado. The couple had no children.

Wecter's work was aptly summed up by the historian James Truslow Adams as "excellent examples of the newest school of historical writing which stresses synthesis and interpretation rather than the piling up of facts. . . . "

PRINCIPAL WORKS: Saga of America Society, 1937; Edmund Burke and His Kinsmen, 1939; The Hero in America, 1941; (with W. Matthews) Our Soldiers Speak, 1775–1918, 1943; When Johnny Comes Marching Home, 1944; (with others) The Age of the Great Depression, 1948; Mark Twain in Three Moods, 1948; The Love Letters of Mark Twain, 1949; Changing Patterns in America Civilization, 1949; Sam Clemens of Hannibal, 1952; The American Character, 1993.

ABOUT: Current Biography 1944; 1950. Periodicals—American History Review October 1942; Nation July 24, 1948; New England Quarterly September 1941; New Republic October 2, 1944; New York Times March 14, 1943; July 18, 1948; June 26, 1950; August 31, 1952; Times Literary Supplement July 8, 1939; Weekly Book Review September 17, 1944; Yale Review Summer 1941.

## WEDEKIND, BENJAMIN FRANKLIN (July 24, 1864–March 9, 1918), German dramatist, journalist, poet, actor, and short story writer, was born

in Hanover, the second of the six children born of a physician, Friedrich Wedekind, who was dedicated to the ideals of liberal democracy and in particular to George Washington; and a former actress, Emilie Kammerer. After serving for a decade as physician to the Sultan of Turkey, Friedrich had participated in the 1848 Revolution and had escaped to America, where his marriage took place (he was twenty-three years older than Emilie).

The couple were able to purchase a castle in Switzerland, Lenzburg in Aarau; it was here that Frank grew up. He was educated in Zurich, and attended the University there for a short while, studying law. Then he took a brief job as a publicity agent. But he was soon able to settle safely in Germany: his father died in 1888 and left him independent. Initially he was in advertising there; then he became secretary to a circus, the Herzog. After this (1888) he turned to literature and the theater, to acting in both plays and cabaret, and to producing and eventually writing plays.

Easily aroused to hatred and scorn, he fell out with the young Gerhart Hauptmann and even wrote a short play satirizing Hauptmann's theatrical naturalism, which he considered "photographic." His first play of any account, and his first full-length one, was Fuhrlings Erwachen (1892, Spring's Awakening). This was the start, in Germany, of the drama of social satire with an absurdist tinge about it. Still performed, the play deals with adolescent passion, with the absurdities of German education at that time, and with the hypocrisy of society in general. It is deliberately crass, but also brilliantly constructed in a series of short and explosive scenes.

One of Wedekind's models was the Friedrich von Shchlegel of the sexually candid 1799 epistolary novel Lucinde. But the writer who affected him most profoundly was Strindberg. Another strong influence was the just then recently rediscovered dramatist Georg Bruchner (1813–37), from whose Woyzeck he derived so much of his own method. Like many writers of the time, Wedekind was also influenced by his reading of the popular philosophy of Edoard von Hartmann.

Wedekind's fiction is still interesting. Der Erdgeist and its sequel Die Busch der Pandora (Earth Spirit and Pandora's Box, both translated in Five Tragedies of Sex) combine social satire with a morbid but enormously energetic dissection of femininity. Alban Berg made his unfinished opera Lulu out of them. Wedekind wrote the two parts as a whole, but was forced by the censors to divide it. The stage is peopled by crooks, whores, and perverts, in whom Wedekind, who often celebrated outcasts and criminals, took an especial interest; at the center is Lulu—according to her creator, the archetypal woman.

Karl Kraus wrote of Wedekind that in his work "the gutter poetry becomes the true poetry of the gutter." He did not fail to be imprisoned: cofounder of the famous satirical magazine Simplicissimus, he spent six months there for a satire (not by him) which he published (1899). He married Tilly Newes, an actress, in 1906. His plays were banned by the Nazis, as he would have expected.

PRINCIPAL WORKS IN ENGLISH TRANSLATION: Drama—Plays, I, 1993. Pandora's Box (tr. S. A. Eliot), 1914; Earth Spirit (tr. S. A. Eliot), 1914; Spring's Awakening (tr. T. Osborn), 1969; The Lulu Plays and Other Sex Tragedies (tr. S. Spender), 1972. Short stories—Princess Russalka (tr. anon) 1919. Other—Diary of an Erotic Life (tr. G. Hay ) 1990.

ABOUT: Barnes, P. The Frontiers of Farce, 1977; Best, A. Frank Wedekind, 1975; Boa, E. The Sexual Circus: Frank Wedekind's Theater of Subversion, 1987; Brouner, S. E. and Kellner, D. Passion and Rebellion, 1983; Columbia Dictionary of Modern European Literature, 1947, 1980; Gittleman, S. Frank Wedekind, 1969; Kaiser, R. and Grimm, R. Frank Wedekind, 1992; Seymour-Smith, M. Guide to Modern World Literature, 1986; Skrine, P. N. Hauptmann, Wedekind and Schnitzler, 1989.

## WEEKLEY, ERNEST (1865–May 7, 1954) English etymologist, was born at Hampstead, London. He studied at universities in Berne, Paris (the Sorbonne and the École des Hautes Études), Freiburg-im-Breisgau (where he was a lecturer in English) and Cambridge (where he was a Major Scholar and Prizeman at Trinity College). He took an M.A. in French and German at the university of London and, after spending a few years as

schoolmaster and private tutor, he became, in 1898, professor of French at University College, Nottingham, where he stayed for forty years, for much of that time being head of the Modern Language Department. He produced a number of widely-used French grammar textbooks and courses. From this academic base he pursued his interest in etymology, publishing a number of successful, popularizing titles, beginning with The Romance of Words

(1912), which concerned the migratory behavior of words from one language to another.

*The Romance of Names* and *Surnames* staked out his particular territory as an etymologist—the belief that the part played by personal names in the creation of vocabulary was not given due emphasis by other workers in the field. These two books established something of a devoted following and in 1918 the *Times Literary Supplement* declared, "We simply cannot help reading him." Although he frequently differed from the views of the *Oxford English Dictionary*, he was used as an adviser. His own *Etymological Dictionary of Modern English* (1921—a 'concise' version was produced in 1924), although never rivaling Oxford or Webster's, was authoritative and has remained in print.

Weekley's most popular book was *Words Ancient and Modern*, in which he treated words as characters with interesting pasts, investing them with a sense of narrative adventure. This was followed by *More Words Ancient and Modern* and *Words and Names*, in which he returned to his hobby-horse. There was little stuffiness about Weekley and he had no qualms confessing in the Preface to *Words and Names* that he was "acutely conscious of [this book's] scrappy and unsystematic nature."

Weekley is also famous, if only unintentionally, for having been the husband of Frieda Von Richthoven, who later married D. H. Lawrence.

PRINCIPAL WORKS: The Romance of Words, 1911; The Romance of Names, 1914; Surnames, 1916; An Etymological Dictionary of Modern English, 1921; A Concise Etymological Dictionary of Modern English, 1924; Words Ancient and Modern, 1926; More Words Ancient and Modern, 1927; The English Language, 1928; Adjectives and Other Words, 1930; Cruelty to Words, 1931; Words and Names, 1932; Something About Words, 1935; Jack and Jill, 1939.

ABOUT: Who's Who 1954. *Periodicals*—Times (London) May 8, 1954; Times Literary Supplement November 16, 1916.

## WEEKS, AGNES RUSSELL. See PRYDE, ANTHONY

## WEEKS, EDWARD (AUGUSTUS) (February 19, 1898–March 11, 1989), American editor and essayist, was born in Elizabeth, New Jersey, the eldest son of Edward Augustus Weeks, a cotton merchant, and Frederica (Suydam) Weeks. He entered Cornell University in 1915 as an engineering student, but dropped out in 1917 to drive an ambulance for the French army during World War I. Returning to the United States in 1919—with a Volunteers' Medal and the Croix de Guerre—he entered Harvard University on scholarship and graduated in 1922 with a concentration in English literature. There followed a year's fellowship at Trinity College, Cambridge University, and, upon returning from England in 1923, six months as a manuscript reader and book salesman for the publishing firm of Horace Liveright in New York. In 1924 he began working as an associate editor for the *Atlantic Monthly* in Boston; four years later he was appointed editor of the *Atlantic*'s book publishing division, the Atlantic Monthly Press.

Weeks succeeded in turning the *Atlantic Monthly*, whose editorship he took over in 1938 from El-

lery Sedgwick, into a more issue-oriented, socially aware magazine. "Colonialism, race relations, the future of science and technology, the lack of American awareness of the challenges posed by different cultures—these subjects . . . were hallmarks of Weeks's years as editor," wrote his *Atlantic* obituarist. Weeks officially resigned his editorship in 1966, but, as the same writer pointed out, "he continued to edit books for nearly twenty years."

Week's career as an author was distinctly secondary to his career as an editor, but he did publish several volumes of memoirs and general reflections. His first book, *This Trade of Writing*, proffered advice to would-be writers from his perspective as editor of Atlantic Monthly Press.

Of Weeks's books of reminiscence perhaps *Writers and Friends*, which recounts his friendships with Walter Lippmann, Vladimir Nabokov, Edith Sitwell, and others is the most interesting. "In this book," wrote the *New York Times Book Review*, "Mr. Weeks comes across as a sort of model *Atlantic* reader, who shared rather than shaped the tastes and concerns of his generation. . . . Throughout the book, Mr. Weeks is free-roving, quick to deal and dispatch, able to leap from the death of Dylan Thomas to the management recruitment methods of Standard Oil. But this is not to say that he is led from topic to topic through whim or happenstance. His personality, with its dry humor and evident modesty, becomes a continuous and reassuring presence."

Weeks was well known to the public for his book review column in the *Atlantic Monthly* and his lectures and radio broadcasts on literary and other subjects. A man of "gaiety and grace," according to the *Atlantic* obituarist, Weeks was twice married, and had two children.

PRINCIPAL WORKS: *Essays and other*—This Trade of Writing, 1935; The Open Heart, 1955; In Friendly Candor, 1959; Breaking into Print: An Editor's Advice on Writing, 1962; The Lowells and Their Institute, 1966; Fresh Waters, 1968. *Memoirs*—My Green Age, 1973; Writers and Friends, 1981. *As editor*—Great Short Novels: An Anthology, 1941; The Pocket Atlantic, 1946; (with E. Flint) Jubilee: One Hundred Years of the Atlantic, 1957 (in U.K.: New England Oracle: A Choice Selection of One Hundred Years of the Atlantic Monthly, 1958); (with H. Thurber) Selected Letters of James Thurber, 1981.

ABOUT: Contemporary Authors New Revision Series 36 1992; Current Biography 1947; Dictionary of Literary Biography vol. 137 1994. *Periodicals*—Atlantic May 1989; New York Herald Tribune Book Review November 22, 1959; New York Times March 14, 1989; New York Times Book Review March 21, 1982; Saturday Review of Literature December 7, 1935; Times (London) March 16, 1989.

## *WEIDMAN, JEROME (April 4, 1913– ), American novelist, playwright, and short story writer, was born in New York City, the son of Joseph Weidman, a tailor, and Annie Falkovitz Weidman, Jewish immigrants from Eastern Eu-

°WIDE muhn

rope. Jerome was an able student. He worked his way through high school, City College, and New York University. In 1934 he entered New York University Law School. After three years he dropped out and started to try to establish himself as a writer.

Weidman had already published short stories in the *New Yorker, Scribner's,* and the *American Mercury,* and in 1937, at the age of twenty-four, his first novel made a stir. Unhappily he was not to be able to follow this success through.

*I Can Get It for You Wholesale,* the story of a scheming garment industry clerk's rise to power, is still Weidman's best-known work. Although its re-lentless cynicism dismayed some polite reviewers, this is precisely the quality that makes the novel so memorable. "There has been no more scathing portrait of an obnoxious wise guy than Mr. Weidman's hero in some time," wrote the *New York Times Book Review.* "In any poll of characters you would like to garrot, Harry Bogen would be a favorite. Yet Mr. Weidman's novel about him is racy, fresh, and continuously interesting. Its language could hardly be racier, as a matter of fact, or its hero more loathsomely fresh."

The sequel, *What's in It for Me?,* which depicted Harry Bogen's inevitable fall, is no less seamy or compelling, but adds nothing in psychological depth to its predecessor. *New York Herald Tribune Books* commented: "Harry is an individualist, no longer rugged, ragged and sinking in mud. His story can't be a pretty one. Mr. Weidman writes it well, mercilessly, with great skill and speed and hardness. That's what it needs."

In the course of Weidman's prolific career he has explored the lives of many more Jewish-American characters; but none of his other books seized the public imagination as did the first two novels. However, a few of the later novels stand out. One such is *The Enemy Camp,* a 1958 study of a Jewish man living in the gentile world of suburban Connecticut. Writing in the *Saturday Review* (1958), Edmund Fuller called *The Enemy Camp* "the best of Jerome Weidman's many excellent novels in depth, scope, and in human sympathy. . . . It deals honestly with some tragedy-producing characteristics of the human creature, mingling with its seriousness a wealth of sharp laughter at behavior from the East Side to Suburbia and within family walls." Another of his better novels was the semi-autobiographical *Fourth Street East,* about Weidman's childhood on the Lower East Side. Terming it a "nostalgic ramble," the *New York Times Book Review* (1971) critic wrote, "Not every kid can claim, with Benny, that his elocution contest was rigged by the Mafia. Or know a Fourth Street blacksmith who turned out to be the star in a multiple crime of passion. . . . Mr. Weidman's reprise of his past vividly reconstructs a yesterday when

lifestyles were not elective but were determined by life."

These novels aside, Weidman could produce novels such as *Other People's Money,* which read, according to the *Saturday Review* (1967), "like a novice's attempt to write a reverse-English Great American Novel with the help of one of those One Hundred Sure-Selling Plot manuals." The judgment of another *Saturday Review* critic concerning *The Price Is Right,* a 1949 novel about a brutally ambitious newspaper man, was more polite but perhaps more damning: "The story is deftly, wittily told. Each chapter ends with a cliff-hanging touch of suspense. The scenes are handled with a playwright's skill. But *The Price Is Right* is not much of a novel. Weidman is clever about people without being really wise about them. The emotional penetration and the understanding of the sources of human ethics are essentially superficial."

In addition to his twenty-two novels and five collections of short stories, Weidman was the co-author of the Pultizer Prize-winning musical *Fiorello!* and a memoirist whose autobiography *Praying for Rain,* according to the *New Yorker,* "reads like one of his novels, which are neat, old-fashioned, realistic, canny, comic, moralistic, and full of narrative pull." "Everything I've written is autobiographical, but *everything,*" he told *Publishers Weekly* in 1986. "I've lived through it all."

Weidman's son John was the author of the musical *Pacific Overtures.*

PRINCIPAL WORKS: *Novels*—I Can Get It for You Wholesale, 1937; What's in It for Me?, 1938; I'll Never Go There Anymore, 1941; The Lights around the Shore, 1943; Too Early to Tell, 1946; The Price Is Right, 1949; The Hand of the Hunter, 1951; Give Me Your Love, 1952; The Third Angel, 1953; Your Daughter Iris, 1955; The Enemy Camp, 1958; Before You Go, 1960; The Sound of Bow Bells, 1962; Word of Mouth, 1964; Other People's Money, 1967; The Center of the Action, 1969; Fourth Street East: A Novel of How It Was, 1970; Last Respects, 1972; Tiffany Street, 1974; The Temple, 1975; A Family Fortune, 1978; Counselors-at-Law, 1980. *Short stories*—The Horse That Could Whistle Dixie and Other Stories, 1939; The Captain's Tiger, 1947; A Dime a Throw, 1957; My Father Sits in the Dark and Other Selected Stories, 1963; The Death of Dickie Draper and Nine Other Stories, 1965. *Drama*—(with G. Abbott) Fiorello!, 1960; (with G. Abbott) Tenderloin, 1961; I Can Get It for You Wholesale, 1962; (with J. Yaffe) Ivory Tower: A Play in Three Acts, 1969; Asterik! A Comedy of Terrors, 1969. *Travel*—Letter of Credit, 1940. *Essays*—Back Talk, 1963. *Autobiography*—Praying for Rain: An Autobiography, 1986. *As editor*—The W. Somerset Maugham Sampler, 1943 (reissued as The Somerset Maugham Pocket Book, 1944); Traveler's Cheque, 1954; (with others) The First College Bowl Question Book, 1961.

ABOUT: Contemporary Authors New Revision Series 1, 1980; Contemporary Literary Criticism vol. 7 1977; Current Biography 1942; Dictionary of Literary Biography vol. 28 1974; Twentieth Century Novelists, 5th ed., 1991. *Periodicals*—New York Herald Tribune Books October 30, 1938; New York Times Book Review May 16, 1937; January 3, 1971; New Yorker December 8, 1986; Publishers Weekly September 12, 1986; Saturday Review February 19, 1949; June 28, 1958; May 20, 1967.

**WEIGALL, ARTHUR EDWARD PEARSE BROME** (November 20, 1880–January 2, 1934), English Egyptologist and writer, was the son of Major A.A.D. Weigall and  Alice (Cowan) Weigall; he attended Hillside School in Malvern, and then Wellington College. He matriculated at New College, Oxford, in 1900, but soon left when he was offered the chance to become an assistant to the eminent Professor Flinders Petrie, on the staff of the Egyptian Exploration Fund.

Weigall was appointed Inspector General of Antiquities for the Egyptian government in 1905, serving in that capacity until 1914. In Luxor he discovered the tomb of Queen Tiy, which also contained the tomb of Akhnaton (Tutankhamen's father-in-law) and his grandparents.

Akhnaton was the subject of Weigall's first popular success, *The Life of Akhnaton: Pharaoh of Egypt* (1910), which was revised and reissued in 1922, the year of the "King Tut craze." Weigall witnessed the opening of Tutankhamen's tomb, and his *Tutankhamen and Other Essays* (1924) recounted the recent excavations and discoveries in the Valley of the Tombs of the Kings, and also contained informative chapters on Egyptian history. Weigall "builds up an elaborate but very convincing thesis concerning the identity of this king, the most important conclusion being that Tutankhamen was none other than the former Tutu, court chamberlain to Pharaoh Akhnaton, and that he became the Pharaoh of the Exodus" (*Literary Review*).

Even during this intensive period, Weigall was able to put aside his more serious archeological studies to write three desert romance novels largely modeled on E. M. Hull's popular success *The Sheik*. Weigall also wrote lyrics for some of the songs in *Charlot's Revue*, in which his sister-in-law, Beatrice Lillie, made the first of many successful stage appearances in the United States.

Weigall wrote numerous books on Egyptian travel, archeology, and history, including a two-volume history of the pharaohs, an outline of more contemporary Egyptian politics (proved wrong by posterity on almost every count), travel guides to the desert and excavation sites, essays on archeology, and *Laura Was My Camel* (1933), a collection of slight humorous stories about a number of animal friends he met throughout his years in Egypt. He also wrote pot-boiling biographies of ancient figures, such as Cleopatra, Nero, Marc Antony, Sappho of Lesbos, and Alexander the Great. *Personalities of Antiquity* (1928) imparted the allegedly scandalous doings of some thirty famous persons of the past, including Julius Caesar, the Empress Theodora, Boadicea, and St. Anthony.

In *The Life and Times of Cleopatra: Queen of Egypt* (1914) Weigall set out to present an objective portrayal of "the events of her troubled life." But his efforts were not well received by serious reviewers. The *Nation* criticized him for his disregard "for careful historical method," and the *Spectator* agreed, writing that Weigall "pursues a hobby and thinks he is a historian." Nonetheless, the book was sensational enough to sell well, and was reissued in 1924. Weigall took a similar approach in writing about Nero, trying to rescue his reputation, claiming his faults were the result of hereditary taints and a corrupt social environment. "Nero cannot be whitewashed," wrote the *Times Literary Supplement*.

Weigall's superficial biographies were geared for general readership, not scholars. Reviewing *Sappho of Lesbos: Her Life and Times* (1932), the *Saturday Review of Literature* commented that "Mr. Weigall knows his sources, but he combines a broad scholarship with a remarkable lack of discrimination." While most critics questioned his precision, President Theodore Roosevelt, according to the *New York Times*, called Weigall "a true scholar, not merely accurate, but truthful, with the truth that comes only from insight."

Weigall supervised the reproduction of the tomb of Tutankhamen for the British Empire Exhibition at Wembley; his archeological work resulted in decorations from four countries. His death, which occurred in London after a long illness, could not be explained, according to the *New York Times*. The London *Daily Mail* reported that he may have fallen victim to the legend of Tutankhamen's curse, which malady comes to those who violate the pharaoh's tomb. Similar and persistent speculation had arisen in 1923 upon the death of the Earl of Carnarvon, who sponsored the work that led to the discovery and opening of Tutankhamen's tomb by the American Howard Carter.

PRINCIPAL WORKS: A Report on the Antiquities of Lower Nubia, 1907; A Catalogue of the Weights and Balances in the Cairo Museum, 1908; Travels in the Upper Egyptian Deserts, 1909; A Guide to the Antiquities of Upper Egypt, 1910; The Life of Akhnaton: Pharaoh of Egypt, 1910; The Treasury of Ancient Egypt, 1911; (with A. H. Gardiner) A Topographical Catalogue of the Tomb of Thebes, 1913; The Life of Cleopatra: Queen of Egypt, 1914; Egypt from 1798 to 1914, 1915; Madeline of the Desert, 1920; The Dweller in the Desert, 1921 (in U.S.: Burning Sands); Bedouin Love, 1922; The Glory of the Pharaohs, 1923; The Garden of Paradise, 1923; Tutankhamen and Other Essays, 1923; Ancient Egyptian Works of Art, 1924; The Way of the East, 1924; A History of the Pharaohs, 1925-26; The Not Impossible She, 1926; Wanderings in Roman Britain, 1926; Wanderings in Anglo-Saxon Britain, 1927; The Grand Tour of Norman England, 1927; Saturnalia in Room 23, 1927; Flights into Antiquity, 1928; The Paganism in our Christianity, 1928; Personalities of Antiquity, 1928; The King Who Preferred Moonlight, 1928; Nero, 1930; Life of Marc Antony, 1931; Sappho of Lesbos, 1932; Alexander the Great, 1933; Laura Was My Camel, 1933.

ABOUT: Who's Who 1934. Periodicals—Literary Review May 3, 1924; Nation October 29, 1914; Nature January 13, 1934; New York Times January 28, 1923; December 12, 1930; January 3, 1934; Saturday Review of Literature October 29, 1932; Spector November 21, 1914; Times (London) October 2, 1930; January 1934.

**WEIL, SIMONE (ADOLPHINE)** (February 3, 1909–August 24, 1943), French essayist, philosophical thinker, poet, political activist, and mystic, was  born in Paris, the daughter of a well-to-do Jewish family originally from Alsace, all of whose members were freethinkers and agnostics. Her father was a doctor. Like her elder brother André, who became a leading mathematician, she was exceedingly precocious. Throughout her life, in addition to her grasp of the humanities, she had an equally certain understanding of concepts both mathematical and scientific. At the age of six she could quote long passages from Racine. She was adept at acquiring foreign languages.

Weil received the privileged education her scholastic brilliance deserved, first at the Lycée Henri IV and then, along with Jean-Paul Sartre, Paul Nizan, Simone de Beauvoir, and others who were to become illustrious, at the École Normale Superièure.

Weil cannot really be called a "philosopher," although she could have been one—or almost anything else, even a tragic poet (she wrote poetry, as well as a tragedy called *Venise sauvé*, in three acts, which was published in France in 1955). One thing is certain: she was one of the most intensely serious and dedicated persons of the twentieth century. As a small child she refused to eat sugar at home because there was none for the soldiers fighting on the front; nor would she put on warm stockings, since there were poor people who had none to wear.

At the age of thirty-four, Weil could not be persuaded to save herself from the ravages of tuberculosis, for which she was being treated in a hospital at Ashford, Kent, by eating more than she believed her compatriots (in France) were getting. So very convincing—as well as, no doubt, exasperating—was she in her pursuit of the living meaning of virtue that an insensitive English doctor's verdict of "suicide" is still widely regarded as having been an impertinence. Yet, too, she has been severely taken to task, particularly by her fellow Jews, for ignoring the Holocaust in her voluminous works and, in general, for regarding Jewishness as an irrelevance. General de Gaulle, for whose Free French Movement she was working at the time of her death, pronounced, simply: "The woman was mad." But others have seen her, and her death, as Christ-like. "We should prefer hell to a paradise which is a product of mere fantasy," she insisted.

Weil's thinking is, in essence, an elaboration, even an existential exploration, of the sixteenth-century catalist Isaac Luria's concept of contraction: that God, in order to bring about creation, withdrew from "him"-self to "make room for the world"—and that therefore human beings were obliged to "bring him back to himself." This paradox, of God's shrinking ever more deeply into himself in order to create outside of himself, is central to Weil's theology. As George Steiner interpreted it in a *Times Literary Supplement* article, the "personal self [for Weil] can only be redeemed if we offer it to God for annihilation." For Weil all action was inevitably tainted by egoism: the offer to annihilate the ego might "allow the recuperation of the creation within the perfect oneness of the Creator." When God withdrew from himself in order to effect creation, God (for her) also effaced himself from that which he had made. "We have to believe" (she wrote) "in a God who is like the true God in everything except that he does not exist, for we have not yet reached the point at which God exists."

Two of Weil's teachers were Emile Chartier, more famous as the fiercely left-wing and humanitarian aphorist "Alain," and René Le Senne, whose anti-positivist stance, and postulation of a bio-psychological "given," a permanent "essence" which grants a small measure of freedom to individuals provided they recognize and thus transcend their limitations, must also have left its mark upon her. She was also much influenced by Marx, in particular by his analysis of the psychological effects of capitalist exploitation on workers. But her use of Marx was very much her own, and was not in line with that of the more conventional Marxists. Nor did she, in any way, idealize workers: she regarded the proper destiny of all human beings to be work. She did think and feel in an especially French-Catholic tradition (also to be found in such French writers as Bloy and Bernanos) that the poor, just because they were wretched, were "closer to God." But as workers they needed, if they were to achieve true dignity, to become "celestial."

After passing her *agrégation* (1931) Weil taught in *lycées* at Le Puy, Auxerre, and elsewhere. From 1934 until 1935 she also worked in industrial plants, and then (1935–1937) on a farm. She also worked for a time for the anarchist trade union La Révolution Prolétarienne, for whose periodical she wrote essays and articles. She was not at all effective in "worker" roles: she caught the tip of her thumb in a mailing machine, tried to drive a plough and overturned it—and then later, in Spain (where she joined the anti-Franco forces), was a danger to her fellow soldiers during rifle practice—they were relieved when she trod in a pan of boiling cooking-oil and had to be rushed to a hospital.

Yet she was effective, and much more so than her compatriots in general, when she early saw through not only Hitler, but also Stalin. She wrote *Oppression et liberté*, still one of the most memorable critiques of totalitarianism, as early as 1934, although it was not published until after her death (translated as *Oppression and Liberty*). She had seen the rise of Nazism at first hand in 1932 on a visit she made to Germany.

Soon after, she considered joining the Communist party (she could not bring herself to sign the membership form), but initially found herself in more immediate sympathy with the Trotskyites. She had Trotsky himself to stay at her parents' home, and goaded him with arguments against his beliefs so insistently that he asked her why she was putting him up: "Are you the Salvation Army?" Dialectic by nature, whatever attracted her, she needed also to repel. Soon after this she reached the point of describing politics as a "sinister farce," and drew attention to the fact that neither Lenin nor Trotsky had ever set foot in a factory and knew nothing about conditions there.

Weil's interest in Roman Catholicism began in earnest after she had spent some time in 1938 in retreat at Solesmes monastery. But she would never finally embrace that tradition because it was "too Jewish" and had too many associations with the Old Testament and its God; for her, as a gnostic attached to the historical Cathars, the Old Testament God was an evil demiurge, and the Catholic Church had invented the Inquisition in order to rid itself of the gnostic heresy. It was just after this that she had a series of mystical experiences, and for a time adhered to a pacifist program. When she called herself a "Catholic by right but not in fact" she was clearly implying that the Church had taken a wrong turn when it decided to end the harmonious equilibrium that (or so she asserted) it had achieved with the Cathars. That civilization, she declared, had come close to a Utopia.

Her true Church would have been an absolutely nonsecular one which married Catholicism with its greatest heresy. She persisted, often in a manner which was for a true scholar extremely forced and awkward, in her beliefs that Greek lyric poetry and drama prefigured the Christianity of the Gospels. Her essay on the *Iliad*, the most directly Marx-influenced of her works, is, however, classic—not for the light it casts on Homer, but for its use of his poem in order to illuminate and elaborate her thesis that "might makes people into things." Her celebrated pessimism is apparent, since she argues that deliverance comes only through total destruction.

Weil lived with her family in Marseilles for two years after the Nazi occupation of June 1940. Then she accompanied them to New York. But this safety did not satisfy her, and she went to England, to work for De Gaulle. She collapsed in April 1943 and was found to be suffering from tuberculosis.

A veritable Weil industry arose after her death. A definitive collected works (in French) is in process. The most accessible of her writings to the general reader remains the two-volume *The Notebooks*, translated into English in 1956, together with *First and Last Notebooks*, translated in 1970—and considerably augmented in French, as *Cahiers* (1970–1974). An unusually well balanced view is to be gleaned from G. A. White's *Simone Weil: Interpretations of a Life* (1980), and from Dorothy Tuck McFarland's critical biography (1983). The most complete life is that by Pétrement.

PRINCIPAL WORKS IN ENGLISH TRANSLATION: *Selections*—Selected Essays 1934–1943, 1962; Gateway to God (ed., tr., and sel. D. Raper) 1974; A Simone Weil Reader (ed. G. A. Panichas) 1977; Simone Weil: An Anthology (ed. S. Miles) 1986; Waiting for God [in some editions Waiting on God] (tr. E. Craufurd) 1951; Gravity and Grace (tr. A. Wills) 1951 (also tr. by E. Craufurd, 1951); The Iliad or the Poem of Force (tr. M. McCarthy) 1952; The Need for Roots (tr. A. Wills) 1952; Letter to a Priest (tr. A. Wills) 1953; The Notebooks, 2 vol. (tr. A. Wills) 1956; Intimations of Christianity Amongst the Ancient Greeks (tr. A.

Wills) 1957; Oppression and Liberty (tr. A. Wills and J. Petrie) 1958; Seventy Letters (ed. and tr. R. Rees) 1965; On Science, Necessity and the Love of God (tr. R. Rees) 1968; First and Last Notebooks (tr. R. Rees) 1970; Lectures on Philosophy (tr. anon) 1978; McFarland, D. T. and Van Ness, W. (ed. and tr.) Formative Writings 1929–1941, 1987.

ABOUT: Abnosch, H. Simone Weil: An Introduction, 1994; Allen, D. Three Outsiders: Pascal, Kierkegaard, Simone Weil, 1994; Bell, R. H. (ed.) Simone Weil's Philosophy of Culture, 1993; Blum, L. and Seidler, V. J. A Truer Liberty: Simone Weil and Marxism, 1989; Brueck, K. The Redemption of Tragedy: The Literary Vision of Simone Weil, 1995; Cabaud, J. Simone Weil: A Fellowship in Love, 1964; Columbia Dictionary of Modern European Literature, 1980; Dietz, M. G. Between the Human and the Divine: The Political Thought of Simone Weil, 1988; Dunaway, J. M. Simone Weil, 1984; Fiori, G. Simone Weil: An Intellectual Biography, 1989; Hellman, J. Simone Weil: An Introduction to Her Thought, 1984; Indopolos, T. A. (ed.) Mysticism, Nihilism, Feminism: New Critical Essays on the Theology of Simone Weil, 1984; McFarland, D. T. Simone Weil, 1983; McLane-Iles, B. Uprooting and Integration in the Writings of Simone Weil, 1987; McClellan, D. Utopian Pessimist: The Life and Thought of Simone Weil, 1990; Nevin, T. R. Simone Weil: Portrait of a Self-Exiled Jew, 1991; Perrin, J. M. and Thibon, G. Simone Weil as We Knew Her, 1953; Pétrement, S. (tr. R. Rosenthal) Simone Weil: A Life, 1976; Rees, R. Simone Weil: A Sketch for a Portrait, 1966; Tomlin, E.W.F. Simone Weil, 1954; White, G. A. (ed.) Simone Weil: Interpretations of a Life, 1981; Winch, P. Simone Weil: The Just Balance, 1989; Zimmerman, D. W. (ed.) French Woman Writers, 1991. *Periodicals*—Christian Century August 22, 1990; Commentary January 1951; Harper's November 1990; New Statesman September 13, 1968; New York Times October 11, 1975; New Yorker March 2, 1992; Times Literary Supplement July 13, 1990; June 4, 1993; Yale Review Winter 1984.

**WEINER, HENRI.** See **LONGSTREET, STEPHEN**

**WEINSTEIN, NATHAN WALLENSTEIN.** See **WEST, NATHANAEL**

**WEISKOPF, FRANZ CARL** (1900–1955), Czechoslovakian novelist, poet, essayist, and editor, was born in Prague, then a provincial capital of the Hapsburg empire. He served in World War I in 1917 with a Hungarian regiment of the Imperial and Royal Army, then studied history, literature, and philosophy at the University of Prague, where he wrote a play, *Foehn*, and received his doctorate in 1923, the same year his first book, a volume of poetry, was published. Several of Weiskopf's early works were burned by the Nazis, and in 1939 the author moved to the United States. *Dawn Breaks* (1942), his first novel in English translation, told of the sabotage efforts of Slovakian peasants in warding off a German invasion. It was praised for its realistic picture of the Slav people and their heroic quest for survival.

Weiskopf edited *Hundred Towers* (1944), a collection of stories, short essays, and poems by twenty-four Czechoslovakian writers, which was considered a worthy introduction to Czech literature for American readers. "The fact that many of the authors have died before Nazi firing squads or in concentration camps gives . . . poignancy to the anthology," wrote the *New Yorker* reviewer.

The novel *Twilight on the Danube* (1946) tells the story of the wealthy Reither family of Prague as they witness the slow demise of the Austrian monarchy and the beginning of World War I. It was criticized for lacking the emotional restraint and realism of his earlier novel, *The Firing Squad* (1944), which recounted Nazi atrocities in World War II.

*Children of Their Time* (1948) continued the Reither family's saga, following them through the beginning of Czech nationalism and the first onslaught of the Russians. The trilogy was interrupted by the author's death.

Weiskopf returned to Czechoslovakia in 1949 and was named Ambassador to Sweden, then Minister Plenipotentiary for the Czech Embassy in Washington, D.C., and finally Ambassador to Communist China. Many of his books were translated into several languages, but without much success; some were reissued in the 1960s and 1970s.

PRINCIPAL WORKS IN ENGLISH TRANSLATION: Land without Unemployment (ed. with E. Glaeser) 1931; Dawn Breaks (tr. H. and R. Norden) 1942; The Firing Squad (tr. J. A. Galston) 1944; Hundred Towers (ed.) 1945; Twilight on the Danube (tr. O. Marx) 1946; Children of Their Time (tr. H. Norden and I. R. Sues) 1948.

ABOUT: *Periodicals*—New York Times March 4, 1945; New Yorker March 3, 1945.

**WELLES, SUMNER** (October 14, 1892–September 24, 1961), American diplomat and author, was the architect of the "Good Neighbor Policy" with Latin America during the Roosevelt years. In his twenty year career as a diplomat, he served in many world capitals and made significant contributions toward the planning and early development of the United Nations. After his retirement, he wrote a number of much heeded books on foreign affairs.

Born in New York City, the son of Benjamin Welles and Frances (Swan) Welles, and a grandnephew of the celebrated U.S. Senator Charles

Sumner of Massachusetts, he graduated from Groton School in 1910 and from Harvard in 1914. At the suggestion of Franklin D. Roosevelt, a family friend, then assistant secretary of the Navy, Welles entered the Foreign Service in 1915 as a secretary in the Tokyo embassy. Two years later he went to the embassy in Buenos Aires. There he became proficient in Spanish and studied Latin American history and literature.

Returning to Washington in 1920, he became, at the age of twenty-eight, the youngest man to head the State Department's Latin American Affairs division, but discouraged by the limitations of career service, he resigned his post in 1922, only to be called back to service by Secretary of State Charles Evans Hughes, who appointed him commissioner to the Dominican Republic. In that capacity he devised plans for the withdrawal of American troops and the military government and oversaw the inau-

guration of a new independent Dominican government. Welles also assisted the Dominicans with some of the problems they faced after independence. He was dismissed by President Calvin Coolidge in 1925, although he had served him as personal representative in mediating the Honduras Revolution in that same year.

Besides relying on his own diplomatic experience, Welles studied hitherto unpublished State Department archives and gathered information from local political leaders to write *Naboth's Vineyard—Eighty Years of Dominican History* (1928). This was not only a historical survey but also an outline of how Welles believed relations to be between nations the Western Hemisphere. He used the metaphor of the Biblical story in which Jezebel (the United States) instigates the murder of Naboth to obtain his vineyard (Dominican Republic) to make the point that America needed to be more cooperative with Latin America.

In 1929 he made an official visit to the Dominican Republic, after which he became even more critical of America's patronizing attitude toward its Latin American neighbors. His liberal thinking then developed into what became known as the Good Neighbor Policy. It had a profound effect on Roosevelt, who chose him as his principal advisor on Latin American affairs; in 1933 he named him Assistant Secretary of State and Ambassador to Cuba. There, somewhat ill-advisedly, he worked to force the leftists out of power.

At that time Cordell Hull was Secretary of State, and "for the next ten years, the names Cordell Hull and Sumner Welles were linked—though not always in agreement—whenever United States foreign policy was discussed," the London *Times* critic wrote, adding that while rumors had it that the two men differed on policy, "other reports . . . had it that there was a clash of personality between them. Supporters of Hull said that Welles was a difficult subordinate; critics of Hull said that while the Secretary of State had the power, it was the Under-Secretary who had the ideas."

Despite this friction with Hull, Welles continued in Roosevelt's confidence. He persuaded the President to hold a special inter-American peace conference at Buenos Aires in 1936, where Welles was instrumental in gathering support for the principle of collective consultation in the event of war.

Welles was promoted to Undersecretary of State in 1937. In 1940 he was sent to European capitals to confer with Hitler, Mussolini, Daladier, and Chamberlain to determine whether any chance of peace remained before Germany's expected spring offensive.

Hull, who was often ill, was increasingly annoyed with Welles's closeness with the President. Eventually he was able to convince Roosevelt that Welles should resign, claiming that he had knowledge of a homosexual incident involving his bitter rival. On September 25, 1943, giving his wife's poor health as an excuse, Welles ended his official career.

After leaving the administration, Welles recapped his diplomatic missions and presented his views on the international situation and his blueprint for the postwar world in the best-selling *The Time for Decision* (1944). V. M. Dean wrote in *Saturday Review of Literature* that while Welles "does not command the literary skill of Walter Lippmann," his book "is crammed with mature and stimulating comment on this country's foreign policy . . . comment offered by a man versed in the pitfalls of practical politics who does not hesitate to speak his mind on controversial questions—notably Spain and Argentina."

Welles then edited *The Intelligent American's Guide to the Peace* (1945), which provided an encyclopedic snapshot of every nation of the world, discussing geography, people, modern history, economic and different countries' roles in the world's future. Written in a compact, textbook style, it was criticized for being oversimplified and nonobjective.

*Where Are We Heading?* (1946), Welles's analysis of U.S. foreign policy and diplomatic trends during the final period of World War II and the initial peacemaking that followed it, was called "inclusive, global, lucid and logical" by C. L. Sulzberger in the *New York Times*. A. M. Schlesinger, Jr., wrote in the *Nation* that it "is the most important book published in some time on the subject of United States foreign policy."

In *We Need Not Fail* (1948), Welles focused on Palestine and its potential as a crisis point for the future of the United Nations, an organization he helped formulate under Roosevelt. Richard Watts in the *New Republic* called it "a short, angry and impressive book . . . valuable for its complete survey of the issue it contemplates, and it is particularly useful for the average reader in its account of the background of the Zionist case."

With *Seven Decisions that Shaped History* (1951), Welles wrote a personal account of the war years and a critical summary of foreign policy mistakes after Roosevelt. Samuel Grafton wrote in the *New Republic* that the book's importance came from its support of Roosevelt and that "it carries more force than many a stereotyped tribute from others in the Roosevelt political family." J.P.C. Casey in the *Survey* praised Welles's "knowledge of history, languages, diplomacy, and world problems, and especially of Latin America," and wrote that Welles's policy recommendations "reaffirms one's belief that somehow means must be found for Mr. Welles once more to serve his country from 1949 to 1953."

After a severe heart atttack in 1948, Wells served as editor of the American Foreign Policy Library, a series of books published by Harvard University Press.

Welles's personal papers are in the Franklin D. Roosevelt Library at Hyde Park, New York, and his official activities are in the records of the Department of State in the National Archives, Washington, D.C.

PRINCIPAL WORKS: Naboth's Vineyard, 1928; United States and the World Crisis, 1941; The World of the Four Freedoms, 1943; The Time for Decision, 1944; (as ed.) Intelligent American's Guide to the Peace, 1945; Where Are We Heading?, 1946; Cooperation Between Canada and the United States in the Search for World Peace, 1947; We Need Not Fail, 1948; Seven Decisions That Shaped History, 1951.

ABOUT: Current Biography 1940; Dictionary of American Biography, 1961–1965; Gellman, Irwin F. Secret Affairs: Franklin Roosevelt, Cordell Hull, Sumner Welles; Graff, F. W. Strategy of Involvement: A Diplomatic Biography of Sumner Welles; Karsh, Y. Faces of Destiny. *Periodicals*—Nation November 16, 1946; New Republic June 14, 1948; August 13, 1951; New York Herald Tribune Book Review October 7, 1951; New York Times October 13, 1946; September 25, 1961; Saturday Review of Literature July 29, 1944; June 12, 1948; Survey May 1951; Time January 3, 1946; Times (London) September 25, 1961.

**WELLMAN, PAUL ISELIN** (October 14, 1898– September 16, 1966), American novelist and historian wrote: "A somewhat unusual childhood left no very great impress on me, unless it had something to do with cultivating my imagination. I was born in Enid, Oklahoma, my parents Dr. Frederick C. Wellman, and Lydia (Isely) Wellman, having moved to the newly opened Cherokee Strip soon after their marriage. My father, a physician  with a brilliant mind, who became noted in both scientific and artistic fields, came from an old American family, the progenitors of which settled in Jamestown from Devonshire England about 1627, moving west through Virginia, Kentucky and Missouri with the frontier. My mother was of Swiss stock, with musical and literary tastes and profound religious convictions. These factors combined to send my parents to Africa when I was less than a year old, my father to become expert in tropical medicine, my mother to do mission work among the Bantu natives of Angola. I spent my first ten years in West Africa, save for brief 'furloughs' in England and once in the United States, and spoke the native tongue, Umbundu, before I spoke English.

"Returning to this country with a younger brother to go to school, I lived three years with my aunt, Miss M. Alice Isely, then a teacher in a non-Mormon school in Utah. It might be supposed that out of the African experiences, which were rich in episode and color, I might have used something in my writings, but save for one brief section in *The Iron Mistress* nothing of this kind has ever appeared. I sometimes question myself as to why the early part of my life seems to have been lived by someone other than myself. Emotional trouble, growing out of the incompatability of my parents, may be the explanation. In any case the whole African part of my life, though I have the clearest memories of it, seems almost shut out of my mind as creative source material.

"Not so my life in America, every part of which has contributed to my interests and authorship. With my aunt I lived successively in Salt Lake, Provo, and Vernal, Utah—the latter town just then emerging from the primitive frontier stage. For a year I was in Washington, D.C., where my father was connected with the Smithsonian Institution. After the break-up of our family, I went with my mother, two younger brothers and a sister, to Cimarron, a small hamlet in western Kansas, an area just beginning to turn from the cowboy to the plowman, and worked on farms and cattle ranches. There I knew some of the verterans of the Indian fighting and trail-driving West, who still were living.

"This period was the genesis of my three historical works, *Death on the Prairie, Death in the Desert*, and *The Trampling Herd*, and also "The Spanish Southwest" on which I am now [1952] engaged. Such novels as *Jubal Troop*, and *Broncho Apache* also had their beginnings in the interests started in those days.

"I graduated from the University of Wichita in 1918, and went into the army, the First World War being then in progress serving in 1918 and 1919. After the war I devoted the next twenty-five years of my life to the newspaper field, an ideal career because it is an eventfully episodic one in which to gather a vast fund of experience and material for writing.

"Though I found newspaper work interesting, and did my best to excel in it, I always desired to do more important writing. While holding down full-time jobs as city editor and later editorial writer on various newspapers, including writer on various newspapers, including the Kansas City *Star*, I wrote and published my first seven books. Inevitably this dual career of intensive work on the newspaper by day, followed by equally intensive work on authorship at night, brought about a physical breakdown. The doctors told me I must give up either journalism or authorship. I did not find the choice difficult, and in 1944 resigned from the Kansas City *Star* and went to Los Angeles with my wife—I had married Miss Laura Mae Bruner in 1923—and our son, Paul I. Wellman Jr.

"After two years of screenplay writing at Warner Brothers and Metro-Goldwyn-Mayer, I settled down at last to writing of novels and historical works without any other deviating demands on my time and thought. Such books as *The Walls of Jerico, The Chain* and *The Bowl of Brass* came out of my newspaper experience, and my historical interests resulted in *The Iron Mistress, The Comancheros, Angel with Spurs*, and *Female*.

"For the history and background of this country, its varied peoples, and its uniquely magnificent characteristics I have an almost spiritual reverence, and these are my central interest. Mrs. Wellman is of immense help to me, particularly with suggestions in handling feminine characters in my novels. My viewpoints are liberal and tolerant in most matters. I concede the right to others to have their own opinions, but I also maintain my right to my own. By religion I am an Episcopalian, by politics a Democrat. My recreations are a cattle ranch in Oregon, in which I have a partnership; fishing when I can get to it; and extensive reading.

"I work in the mornings, starting early and writing until after luncheon, seven days a week. My theory is that style should be clear, simple, yet varied enough to be interesting, and I have no sympathy with self-concious ornamentations or obscurities in writing which are sometimes affected, and which only serve to confuse the reader. In every book I seek to add something of interest, perhaps even of value, to my reader's knowledge of his country."

———

Wellman knew the plains and prairies, and continued his prolific output of histories, folklore, and fiction about Native Americans, outlaws and other legendary figures of bygone America. His style and drama made much of his fiction perfect fodder for motion pictures. *The Iron Mistress* (1951), a historical novel based on the life of James Bowie, was made into a movie in 1952. His Indian novel *Broncho Apache* (1936) became the basis for the 1954 film *Apache; The Comancheros* (1952) also became a film.

After spending 25 years writing and editing for Kansas newspapers in Wichita and Kansas City, Wellman harvested his knowledge of wheat-belt people and places to write a tetralogy of novels based in the fictional town of Jericho, Kansas, beginning with *The Bowl of Brass* (1944), which was called an authentic portrait of western Kansas life in the late 1880s. "The counterparts of his unlovely characters really existed; indeed, they were the sort who gave western Kansas a reputation for hypocrisy, snide dealing and all-around cheapness which all the winds of decades have not entirely erased," wrote the critic of the *Weekly Book Review*. In The *Walls of Jericho* (1947) he "caught the authentic accents of an especial era in American history, an era of abundant vitality, crass provincialisms and rich vulgarity . . . which was one of the main fountainheads of our national character," according to the *Chicago Sun Book Week*. "They are already building its sets in Hollywood," the *Saturday Review of Literature* critic noted. *The Chain* (1949) focuses on an Episcopalian minister in Jericho who encounters the consternation of his country-club congregation when he tries to open the church doors to the poor population of nearby Jugtown. The tetralogy ends with *Jericho's Daughters* (1956), a contemporary story of the heirs of the town's virtues and evils. "A dramatic array of small-town and big-town types are engaged in its lively plot, which belies any theory that life is uneventful under the broad skies of Kansas," according to the *New York Herald Tribune Book Review*.

A *Dynasty of Western Outlaws* (1961), presented Wellman's theory that the organized gangs of outlaws who roamed the American frontier from the 1860s to the 1930s had their roots in a common school of crime, which has a "contagious nature" and was founded after the Civil War by the Confederate guerrilla turned compulsive killer Quantrill—and ended with the F. B. I. killing of Pretty Boy Floyd. "At first blush it would appear that this book is based on a gimmick . . . that it is possible to draw a genealogical chart to illustrate Midwestern outlawry—a sort of ruffian's family tree. But, surprisingly, Wellman's thesis does hold water," wrote R. H. Dillon in the *San Francisco Chronicle*. The book was reissued in 1986. In *Spawn of Evil* (1964), Wellman went down a similar path, telling the story of the criminal empire that existed along the Ohio and Mississippi rivers and through the South and Midwest from 1707 to 1845.

Away from the West, Wellman wrote a story of Justinian's wife, Theodora, who became an empress of the Roman Empire in sixth century Constantinople in *The Female* (1953), a historical novel that "carried off the bare-flesh prize of the season," according to the *Saturday Review*.

PRINCIPAL WORKS: Nonfiction—Death on the Prairie, 1934; Death in the Desert, 1935; The Trampling Herd, 1939; Glory, God, and Gold, 1954; The Blazing Southwest, 1954; Portage Bay, 1957; Stuart Symington, 1960; A Dynasty of Western Outlaws, 1961; Spawn of Evil, 1964; The Devil's Disciples, 1964; The House Divides, 1966. Fiction—Broncho Apache, 1936; Jubal Troop, 1939; Angel With Spurs, 1942; The Bowl of Brass, 1944; The Walls of Jericho, 1947; The Chain, 1949; The Iron Mistress, 1951; The Comancheros, 1952; The Female, 1953; Jericho's Daughters, 1956; Ride the Red Earth, 1958; The Fiery Flower, 1959; Magnificent Destiny, 1962; The Buckstones, 1967. Juveniles—Gold in California, 1958; Indian Wars and Warriors, East, 1959; Indian Wars and Warriors, West, 1959; Race to the Golden Spike, 1961; The Greatest Cattle Drive, 1964.

ABOUT: The autobiographical material quoted above was written for Twentieth Century Authors First Supplement, 1955. Warfel, H. R. American Novelists of Today; Contemporary Authors 1985; Current Biography 1949. Periodicals—Chicago Sun Book Week February 9, 1947; Chicago Sunday Tribune March 9, 1958; Kirkus October 15, 1958; Library Journal January 15, 1960, August 1962; New York Herald Tribune Book Review October 7, 1956; New York Times February 16, 1947; May 26, 1957; September 19, 1966; San Francisco Chronicle March 12, 1961; Saturday Review October 3, 1953, February 12, 1966; Saturday Review of Literature March 29, 1947; March 19, 1949; Weekly Book Review April 2, 1944.

**WELLS, CAROLYN** (June 18, 1869–March 26, 1942), American anthologist and mystery writer wrote more than 170 books, mostly detective stories, humorous verse and juveniles.

Born in Rahway, New Jersey, the daughter of William E. Wells and Anna (Woodruff) Wells, she could read fluently from books and magazines by

age three, was afflicted with deafness from scarlet fever at age six, and after an informal education during which she studied everything from botany to Shakespeare, she began writing jingles and parodies that were published in popular humor magazines of the day such as *Punch*, *Puck*, and Gelett Burgess's *The Lark*. One of her best known anthologies was *The Nonsense Anthology* (1902). Books of parodies and satire followed, and then she went off on a "whimsey," which she defined as "a whim, a freak, a capricious notion, an odd device," and included nearly 300 selections from old and

new poets in *A Whimsey Anthology* (1906). "Here we have famous wheezes touching the eccentricities of the English language, typographical frenzies in which the compositor shapes the poem as nearly as possible like the object it treats of . . . alphabetical nonsense . . . acrostics and lipograms, alliterative efforts, enigmas and charades, macaronic poetry, travesties, certomes . . . and palindromes . . . in rich profusion," wrote the *New York Times*.

One example of Wells's wit was a parody of *Main Street* called *Ptomaine Street* (1921), which featured Dr. Bill Petticoat, a ptomaine specialist, and his wife, Warble, who believes in the virtues of childishness as distinct from art and more serious adult endeavors. Some of her anthologies were reprinted in the 1950s, 1960s, and 1970s.

Busy with her humor and juveniles, Wells claimed she was not familiar with mystery stories until she read one of Anna Katharine Green's stories and was captivated by it. She proceeded to write more than seventy-five mystery and detective stories, creating the detective Fleming Stone, whose investigations came out on a regular schedule of three books per year. Some readers became addicted to his jigsaw prowess, yet discerning critics faulted both Wells's writing weaknesses and Stone's investigative methods. "Without skill in plot, incident, or wording," Dashiell Hammett observed in the *Saturday Review of Literature* in reviewing *All At Sea* (1927). "He (Stone) never produces the vital clues until he is ready to spring the solution. There is no chance for the reader to do any detecting on his own account," Isaac Anderson remarked in the *New York Times* about *Roll-Top Desk Mystery* (1932).

In 1932 Wells became confined to bed with a heart ailment and wrote a magazine article on what it was like to have only two years to live. She recovered and continued writing for another decade, including an autobiography, *The Rest of My Life* (1937), whose focus was what she had not yet accomplished.

PRINCIPAL WORKS: At the Sign of the Sphinx, 1896; Patty Fairfield, 1901; A Nonsense Anthology, 1902; A Parody Anthology, 1904; A Satire Anthology, 1905; A Whimsey Anthology, 1906; Patty in Paris, 1907; The Clue, 1909; A Chain of Evidence, 1912; The Technique of the Mystery Story, 1913; The Curved Blades, 1916; The Book of Humorous Verse, 1920; Ptomaine Street, 1921; The Affair at Flower Acres, 1923; The Outline of Humor, 1923; The Book of American Limericks, 1926; All At Sea, 1927; The Book of Charades, 1927; Fleming Stone Omnibus, 1931; Roll-Top Desk Mystery, 1932; Broken O, 1933; Visiting Villain, 1934; Beautiful Derelict, 1935; The Cat in Verse, 1935; The Radio Story Murder, 1937; The Rest of My Life, 1937; Who Killed Caldwell?, 1942; Murder Will In, 1942.

ABOUT: Contemporary Authors Volume 113; Honce, C. A. Sherlock Holmes Birthday; Haycraft, H. Murder for Pleasure: The Life and Times of the Detective Story; Masson, J. L. Our American Humorists; Twentieth Century Crime and Mystery Writers; Overton, G. M. When Winter Comes to Main Street; Wells, C. The Rest of My Life. Periodicals—Books October 31, 1937; New York Herald Tribune March 27, 1942; New York Times September 22, 1906; December 12, 1920; May 29, 1932; March 27, 1942; Publishers' Weekly July 22, 1939; Saturday Review of Literature May 21, 1927.

**WELLS, H(ERBERT) G(EORGE)** (September 21, 1866–August 13, 1946), English novelist and writer of speculative fiction and prophetic nonfiction, produced a hundred and twenty books.

He was born at Atlas House, the dismal family home in the High Street of Bromley, Kent. Now a suburb of London, Bromley was then a small town

a few miles south of the city. Wells was the son of Joe Wells and the former Sarah Neal. The father was intelligent and imaginative, a genial and irresponsible man, and sometimes irritable. Wells in his autobiography wrote that "his was a mind of inappeasable freshness, in the strangest contrast to my mother's." A lover of nature, originally a gardener, Joe Wells ran a chronically unsuccessful shop on the ground floor of Atlas House, selling a mixture of chinaware and cricket goods. He was himself a cricketer of exceptional ability, and coached and played professionally during the season. In this way he could escape from his wife while earning enough to stave off bankruptcy.

Sarah Wells was over forty when "Bertie" was born, her fourth child and third son. Formerly a lady's maid, she was a snobbish and deeply pious drudge, disappointed in her marriage but a devoted mother. Both parents were better educated than most of their class. Joe in particular loved reading, and brought books home from the Bromley Literary Institute.

Bertie learned to read at a local dame school when he was five. Two years later his leg was accidentally broken by the son of a High Street innkeeper. The boy's mother atoned by plying the Wells household with expensive delicacies, and the immobilized Bertie with books, including Wood's *Natural History*. This was an important influence, as in a different way were the Bible and *The Pilgrim's Progress*. His mother's fundamentalist belief in a hell-fire God induced guilt and fear in the boy. He was troubled by terrible nightmares, some of them later shaped into stories.

At eight, Wells was enrolled at Mr. Thomas Morley's Commercial Academy for Young Gentlemen. Here, some thirty sons of lower-middle-class parents were crammed into one room to study for the examinations of the College of Preceptors and prepare to be genteel clerks or shop workers. There was great antipathy—sometimes pitched battles—between the young gentlemen and the working-class boys at the National School. Wells never lost the fear and distrust of the working class he learned at Morley's—there are virtually no manual workers in his books. On the other hand, he was not a candidate for the establishment. The stories he wrote at school, liberally illustrated with sketches and caricatures, already showed a marked irreverence towards authority. When he graduated at thirteen, he and one other Morley boy were "first in all England" in bookkeeping.

Meanwhile, Joe Wells had broken his leg, which ended his cricketing career, and its vital income. The shop struggled on for a few more years, but the home was broken up. Sarah Wells returned to her former employer. Bertie, whose elder brothers were both journeymen drapers, was briefly a probationary apprentice with a drapery firm in Windsor. At fourteen he went as pupil-teacher to a village school in Wookey, Somerset, just taken over by a distant relative. That post disappeared when it emerged that "Uncle" Williams's teaching credentials were forged. Wells then spent some months as assistant to a pharmacist in Midhurst, Sussex, who purveyed a "universal cure"—certainly the origin of *Tono-Bungay*.

There followed a formative few weeks "below stairs" at Up Park, the beautiful Sussex mansion where Sarah Wells was now installed as housekeeper. It appears as "Bladesover" in *Tono-Bungay*. Wells came to believe that country houses like Up Park were the cradle of free inquiry, leisurely thought, artistic patronage—of a peculiarly English civilization. He studied the stars through a Gregorian telescope, made free use of the library, and was deeply impressed by Plato's *Republic*. Then Wells was seriously hurt in a school football match. The local doctor diagnosed a crushed kidney and tuberculosis. This assessment has been questioned, but for the rest of his life Wells was liable to pulmonary hemorrhages when under stress, as well as recurrent kidney ailments.

At Up Park, then at a friend's house near Stoke-on-Trent, Wells gradually recovered. He was increasingly drawn to a literary career, and spent his time reading and writing poetry and fiction. In the summer of 1888, he was well enough for a fresh assault on London. When he arrived, he owned some worn clothes, a cheap cane, an eraser, and five pounds provided by his mother. Soon he began to earn a little by inventing (and answering) questions about science for the new penny weeklies. He moved in again with Aunt Mary and his cousin Isabel, to whom he became engaged. In 1889 came another teaching post, at Henley House School in London. This was an excellent private academy run by the father of A. A. Milne, who was one of Wells's pupils there. He began to think of teaching as an acceptable career.

Wells had been studying for a B.Sc. He received it in 1890 from London University, with first-class honors in zoology. This brought him a well-paid post at a tutorial college in the Strand. In a letter, one of his students there described Wells at twenty-three as "plain and unvarnished" in speech, dress and manner, "abrupt and direct, with a somewhat cynical and outspoken scorn of the easy luxurious life," but kindly and "extremely painstaking."

By 1891, Wells could afford to marry Isabel and install her in a rented house. The marriage was not a success. Wells, before long, seduced or was seduced by one of her friends, greatly enjoyed himself, and embarked on a lifelong series of love affairs.

Wells began his career as a writer with essays and

sketches for the *Pall Mall Gazette* and other such journals, then proliferating in response to increased literacy. He wrote amusingly on everything from "Angels" to "The Art of Being Photographed," and was soon making a living. Wells had been conducting a serious affair with a former student, Amy Catherine Robbins, an attractive and intelligent "New Woman." This led in December 1893 to the break-up of his two-year-old marriage. He and Robbins moved into cheap lodgings in London.

Over the next year, now writing with great confidence and fluency, Wells published not only articles but several short stories with scientific themes. In 1895, W. E. Henley launched the *New Review* with a new version of "The Chronic Argonauts," a serialized version of Wells's "The Time Traveller's Story." It convinced the *Review of Reviews* that "H. G. Wells is a man of genius."

In that year, Frank Harris at the *Saturday Review* took Wells on as a fiction reviewer, and the *Pall Mall Gazette* made him a theater critic, although he had seen only two plays in his life. He received some helpful advice from a young Irish critic who was to be important in his life, George Bernard Shaw. Then Wells's health deteriorated again. He resigned from the *Gazette* and he and his partner—now rechristened Jane—moved to a house in the country, at Woking in Surrey. They were married before the end of 1895, which also saw the publication of no less than four books, one of them a masterpiece.

*Select Conversations with an Uncle* was a collection of humorous essays, reprinted from magazines, involving an amiable rogue modeled on Wells's disreputable "Uncle" Williams. It appeared in June 1895, followed a day later by *The Time Machine*—a further revision of "The Time Traveller's Story." The story involves a scientist who constructs a machine utilizing the concept of time as a fourth dimension. In it he travels forward to A.D. 802701, landing amid great ruins in the Thames Valley. The place is populated by the Eloi, frail and gentle hedonists four feet tall, living an apparently peaceful, idyllic life. However, the scientist discovers that these graceful vegetarians of the Upper World are preyed upon by the "bleached, obscene, nocturnal" Morlocks, carnivorous denizens of a dark underworld. Following a journey millions of years into a desolate unpeopled future, the earth moribund under a dying sun, the scientist returns, shattered, to the present, where he describes his adventures to friends gathered for a dinner party.

This short novel was an instant success, selling six thousand copies in its first months. It has never been out of print, and is now universally recognized as a pioneering classic of science fiction. Wells fully intended that it should make his reputation and, repeatedly revised, it was much more carefully written than most of his books. Some read it simply as a gripping adventure story, the work of an "English Jules Verne." However, *The Time Machine*, like all of Wells's speculative fiction, has increasingly been seen as an allegory—in this case a darkly satirical warning that human progress is not inevitable, that our universe itself is doomed. It is also a parody of English class divisions, with effete Elois "upstairs," brutalized Morlocks "downstairs." David Lodge, in *The Language of Fiction*, called it "one of the most desolating myths in modern literature."

A volume of short stories followed, *The Stolen Bacillus and Other Incidents*. It included memorable stories such as "The Diamond Maker," which demonstrated Wells's debt to Poe, and "Aepyornia Island," in which a shipwrecked explorer hatches out of the egg of a prehistoric bird.

Wells's fourth book of 1895 was another novel, *The Wonderful Visit*, slighter and less well accomplished than the first, though well received at the time. A wounded angel falls into an English village and, being an outsider, is persecuted. His principal tormentor is the village doctor. Dr. Crump wants to improve the angel's "degenerate" physique by surgery, like a boy pulling the wings off a fly. The novel is a satire, directed against the crass brutality of people in general, against positivist science in particular. It nevertheless gives a vivid and affectionate account of English village life and village characters. There is more of the same in *The Wheels of Chance*, an amiable, picaresque novel about a draper on a bicycling holiday.

*The Island of Doctor Moreau*, which followed, was the first of Wells's books to arouse controversy. Another shipwrecked traveler, Edward Prendick, is marooned on a Pacific island. Its inhabitants are Moreau and his drunken assistant, and the Beast Folk. These apparently human creatures are actually animals transformed by Moreau through agonizing surgery. The Beast Folk have developed a travesty of human civilization, with their own primitive religion and laws. But they still have "the souls of beasts," and have to struggle constantly against their evil animal natures. When Prendick escapes back to England, he can see little difference between his fellow countrymen and the Beast Folk.

This Swiftean satire was greeted with distaste at its cruelties and outrage over what the *Guardian* saw as an attempt "to parody the work of the Creator of the human race, and cast contempt upon the dealings of God with his creatures." But *The Invisible Man* thrust Wells back into public favor. One wintry day, a stranger arrives in a Sussex village, his face swathed in bandages, hands gloved. This is Griffin, a scientist who has made himself invisible. Having thus tampered with nature in pursuit of superhuman powers, Griffin degenerates into murderous madness. He becomes a fugitive, forced to go naked so that his pursuers cannot see him, cold, hungry and alone. In an ending that rises close to tragedy, this Faustian outcast is hunted down and beaten to death.

In *The Time Traveller*, their biography of Wells, Norman and Jeanne Mackenzie suggest that "the symbolic power" of his stories derived from his ability to dig "into himself to uncover buried feelings and even archetypal patterns of thought. . . . He had found a knack of writing that was similar to the process of dreaming, in which powerful and primitive emotions were translated into visual images." Wells himself, in his introduction to *The Country* of the Blind, said he had found that, "taking almost anything as a starting point and letting my thoughts play about with it, there would presently come out of the darkness, in a manner quite inexplicable, some absurd or vivid little nucleus. . . . I would discover I was peering into remote and mysterious worlds ruled by an order logical indeed but other than our common sanity."

Wells was still living in Woking when he wrote The War of the Worlds, a novel of an invasion of Martians who land in that quiet Surrey town, causing a panic evacuation and the eventual destruction of civilization, though in the end, the Martians are annihilated by earthly diseases to which they have no immunity. In October 1938, Orson Welles adapted the story for his Mercury Theater on radio, transferring the locale to Grover's Mill, New Jersey and setting off a panic by credulous American listeners.

In 1900, Wells built Spade House, near Folkestone, with Charles Voysey as his architect. Prosperous at last, on the way to wealth, he could begin to enjoy his success. His health had improved, and he was able to cycle about the Kent countryside, and to travel abroad with Jane. Their two sons were born in 1901 and 1903. Convivial and hospitable, the Wellses entertained freely, enlisting their guests in charades and new games of H. G.'s own devising.

The scientific romances continued to appear, but Wells also wanted success as a "real" novelist. The Wheels of Chance was a lighthearted first attempt; the second appeared in 1900 after long gestation. Love and Mr. Lewisham was based on Wells's own experiences at Midhurst Grammar School and the Normal School of Science. It ends with young Mr. Lewisham, who might have become an education reformer, succumbing to the financial and emotional problems of an unwise marriage. In this way it introduces a theme recurrent in Wells's subsequent work—the conflict between intellectual ambition and sexual passion. Carefully written and much revised, Love and Mr. Lewisham was generally well received, but with reservations. It was thought that Wells had not distanced himself sufficiently from his material, so that the Speaker found "a disproportionate realism that almost amounted to vulgarity."

Several more scientific fantasies followed, including one of the finest in the literature, The First Men on the Moon. Rich in humor and in satire, it was also uncannily prophetic in its account of the methodology and the experience of space flight, with a splendidly lyrical description of a lunar dawn.

Wells's first major success as a realistic novelist came in 1905 with Kipps. The "simple soul" Arthur Kipps is one of H. G.'s many partial self-portraits. Raised by his aunt and uncle, Artie is apprenticed to a draper. Learning that he has been left a fortune, he becomes engaged to Helen, an upper-class young woman who grooms him to enter Folkestone society. At a dinner party, he finds that one of the servants is Ann, his first love. After their elopement, it emerges that Kipps's fortune has been embezzled by Helen's brother. They settle cheerfully in Hythe and open a bookshop.

Kipps had been conceived as early as 1898 as a "great novel on the Dickens plan." Unlike Love and Mr. Lewisham, which had been carefully mapped out, Wells had deliberately given himself scope in Kipps to sprawl, digress and theorize at will. Touching and funny, with some memorable characters, the novel also contains sharp social criticism of a society which denied a role to the likes of Kipps, the half-educated genteel poor. Although the last part of the book deteriorates into political propaganda, its largely autobiographical account of Kipps's life in a "middle-class academy" and as a draper's apprentice is masterly. Arnold Bennett complained in a letter about Wells's "ferocious hostility to about five sixths of the characters," but Henry James was "prostrate with admiration" at the novel's "brilliancy of true truth."

Success, fame, and his improved health had eroded Wells's pessimism and released a messianic streak. The cosmos was ultimately doomed, but humanity, he believed, might meanwhile make something of itself. During the late 1890s, he began to adumbrate a secular version of his mother's salvationism. His first manifesto was Anticipations, published at the beginning of a new century and a new reign in 1901. It made inspired guesses about population trends, social changes, the rise of the automobile, and much else, and sought to extrapolate a history of the future as a basis for wise decisions. Democracy had failed and was drifting towards a catastrophic war. From the ashes would rise a "new mass of capable men"—mostly scientists and engineers—who would create a utopian world state. This elite of "New Republicans" would "check the procreation of base and servile types," and would not "hesitate to kill" troublesome members of the underclass.

Anticipations had great popular success, and established Wells as a prophet in his own time. Graham Wallas brought him into that upper-class socialist think-tank, the Fabian Society. It was then dominated by Shaw and the Webbs, all of whom admired Anticipations. The Webbs introduced H. G. to Lady Elcho's brilliant salon, where his exuberance and tumbling ideas captivated earls and cabinet ministers.

In 1906, Wells visited the United States, where he was lionized, and gathered material for The Future in America. At the same time, in a bid for leadership, he was campaigning to radicalize the gradualist Fabians. Beatrice Webb commented in her diary on Wells's "conceit as to his ability to settle all social and economic questions in general, and to run the Fabian Society in particular."

After such pride, came a fall. Emotionally claustrophobic, Wells feared domestic imprisonment, and was incapable of sexual commitment to any one woman, including his second wife. Jane was his devoted secretary, business manager, housekeeper, and hostess. She gave stability and order to his undisciplined life, and made possible his gargantuan labors. However reluctantly, she also gave him freedom to indulge a compulsive sexual wanderlust. Wells sought to justify this arrangement in *A Modern Utopia* and many subsequent books. In the former, unfaithful wives are punished because they have failed in their duty to their children. However, "a reciprocal restraint on the part of the husband is clearly of no importance whatever," so long as the wife is complaisant.

This remarkable prescription was not much noticed. However, the science fiction fantasy *In the Days of the Comet*, notable for a loving portrait of Sarah Wells, advocated what was later called wife-swapping. If property is theft, Wells said in effect, so is "proprietary" love. This was going too far. Excoriated in the press, thundered against from the pulpit, the novel failed. Shaken and angry, Wells returned to his attacks on the Fabian "Old Gang." They valued him, but were puzzled by his ungentlemanly vehemence. Bernard Shaw did all he could to avert a crisis and, when Wells persisted, outmaneuvered and crushed him in a crowded meeting. Wells remained a force in the Society, but gradually lost interest.

After *The War in the Air*, an odd hybrid that places a Kipps-like Cockney hero in the context of a catastrophic aerial war, came *Tono-Bungay*, regarded by many as Wells's greatest novel.

In *Ann Veronica*, the young heroine suggests to her married science tutor that she should become his mistress. They run off together, turning "life into a glorious adventure." Once again, Wells has used literature to justify life—his own inveterate promiscuity. Famous as a writer and a thinker, a daring rebel against convention, Wells had the charisma of success. Only Shaw had captured so successfully the excitement of release from Victorian values. The liberated young women of the Fabian Society idolized H. G., and he was ready to help them turn "life into a glorious adventure." There was a series of more or less scandalous affairs. These were patiently borne by Jane Wells who, when Amber Reeves, a brilliant young Fabian, had a child by H. G., went out and bought the baby clothes. Wells almost left Jane for Reeves, but could never quite bring himself to relinquish the stability his wife represented. Rebecca West, who met H. G. after attacking the theories expressed in the 1912 novel *Marriage*, also had a child by him, the writer Anthony Panther West. Throughout Wells's work there is a conflict between reason and romanticism, between the intellectual rigor of the socialist reformer, and a sentimental nostalgia for a vanished England, a pastoral dream. *The History of Mr. Polly*, Wells's best-loved work, is an ode to that imaginary paradise. A novel on a much smaller scale than *Tono-Bungay*, it is also a more perfect work of art.

In 1909 Wells sold Spade House. After three years in Hampstead, he bought Easton Glebe, near Dunmow, in Essex, where he lived until Jane's death in 1927. Wells had long prophesied a disastrous world war. After its outbreak in 1914, he became obsessed with the need for world peace and unification. He was passionately involved in the development of the League of Nations, and in book after book argued for a global approach to disarmament, the conservation of natural resources, transport planning, and political and educational reform.

Wells believed that human history should be taught on a world, not national, basis, and showed how this might be done in *The Outline of History*. Clearly opinionated and full of errors, it is remembered more for its narrative sweep than for its value as a historical text. But it outsold all of his other works combined. Most of his other nonfictional works, overtaken by events, are forgotten.

Wells traveled a great deal between the wars, and spent his winters in France, where he found another young companion and built a house, Lou Pidou, near Nice. After 1914, he disclaimed literary ambition and described himself as a journalist. He nevertheless continued to produce fiction—mostly novels.

Restless and impatient, Wells had seldom allowed himself time to shape and polish his books. "I fail to see how I can be other than a lax, undisciplined storyteller," he wrote in *Tono-Bungay*. "I must sprawl and flounder, comment and theorise, if I am to get the thing out I have in mind." All of his novels, including those that have achieved the status of classics, were tracts for their times. Most of the later ones have not survived those times. A reassessment is underway, with large claims being made for such novels as *Mr. Britling Sees It Through, Mr. Blettsworthy on Rampole Island* and *The Bulpington of Blup*, more surprisingly for *The Croquet Player* and *Apropos of Dolores*.

Beginning in 1933, Wells lived at various addresses in London, in 1937 settling in a Nash house near Regents Park. Many of his books were filmed, some of them more than once, and during the 1930s he himself wrote scenarios for *Things to Come* and *Man Who Could Work Miracles*. H. G. survived World War II, refusing to let the blitz drive him out of London, but became increasingly frail and ill because of diabetes, the ravages of which he had been able to fend off for a long time. He had not lost his taste for combat, however, and as late as 1943 published a polemic against the Roman Catholic Church as an enemy of change. He published in 1945 both *Mind at the End of Its Tether*, a declaration of almost hopeless pessimism, and the serene volume of essays, *The Happy Turning: A Dream of Life*.

PRINCIPAL WORKS: The Works of H. G. Wells, 28 volumes, 1924-1927; The Essex Thin-Paper Edition of the Works of H. G. Wells, 24 volumes, 1926–1927; Early Writings in Science and Science Fiction (ed. R. M. Philmus and D. Y. Hughes) 1975; The H. G. Wells Papers at the University of Illinois (ed. G. N. Ray) 1958. *Novels*—The Time Machine, 1895; The Wonderful Visit, 1895; The Wheels of Chance: A Holiday Adventure, 1896; The Island of Doctor Moreau: A Possibility, 1896; The Invisible Man, 1897; The War of the Worlds, 1898; When the Sleeper Wakes: A Story of the Years to Come, 1899; Love and Mr. Lewisham, 1900; The First Men in the Moon, 1901; The Sea Lady, 1902; The Food of the Gods, and How It Came to Earth, 1904; A Modern Utopia, 1905; Kipps: The Story of a Simple Soul, 1905; In the Days of the Comet, 1906; The War in the Air, 1908; Tono-Bungay, 1909; Ann Veronica: A Modern Love Story, 1909; The History of Mr. Polly, 1910; The New Machiavelli, 1911; Marriage, 1912; The Passionate Friends, 1913; The Wife of Sir Isaac Harman, 1914; The

World Set Free, 1914; Bealby: A Holiday, 1915; Boon, The Mind of the Race, The Wild Asses of the Devil, and The Last Trump: Being a Selection from the Literary Remains of George Boon (originally published as by "Reginald Bliss"), 1915; The Research Magnificent, 1915; Mr. Britling Sees It Through, 1916: The Soul of a Bishop, 1917; Joan and Peter: The Story of an Education, 1918; The Undying Fire, 1919; The Secret Places of the Heart, 1922; Men Like Gods, 1923; The Dream, 1924; Christina Alberta's Father, 1925; The World of William Clissold: A Novel at a New Angle, 1926; Meanwhile: The Picture of a Lady, 1927; Mr. Blettsworthy on Rampole Island, 1928; The King Who Was a King: The Book of a Film, 1929; The Autocracy of Mr. Parham, 1930; The Bulpington of Blup: Adventures, Poses, Stresses, Conflicts, and Disaster in a Contemporary Brain, 1932; The Shape of Things to Come 1933; Seven Famous Novels by H. G. Wells, 1934; The Croquet Player, 1936; Star-Begotten: A Biological Fantasia, 1937; Brynhild; or, The Show of Things, 1937; The Camford Visitation, 1937; Apropos of Dolores, 1938; The Brothers, 1938; The Holy Terror, 1939; Babes in the Darkling Wood, 1940; All Aboard for Ararat, 1940; You Can't Be Too Careful: A Sample of Life, 1901–1951, 1941; The Wealth of Mr. Waddy (early draft of Kipps, ed. H. Wilson) 1969. *Short stories*—The Stolen Bacillus and Other Incidents, 1895; Thirty Strange Stories, 1897; The Plattner Story, and Others, 1897; Tales of Space and Time, 1899; Twelve Stories and a Dream, 1903; The Door in the Wall and Other Stories, 1911; The Country of the Blind, and Other Stories, 1911; Tales of the Unexpected, 1922; Tales of Life and Adventure, 1924; The Complete Short Stories of H. G. Wells, 1927; The Adventures of Tommy 1929; Tales of Wonder, 1930; The Favourite Short Stories of H. G. Wells, 1937; (for children) The Famous Short Stories of H. G. Wells, 1938; The Empire of the Ants, 1943; The Desert Daisy, 1957 (for children); Selected Short Stories, 1960; The Inexperienced Ghost, and Nine Other Stories, 1965; Best Science Fiction Stories of H. G. Wells, 1966; The Man with a Nose: And the Other Uncollected Short Stories of H. G. Wells (ed. J. R. Hammond) 1984. *History and the future, sociology and politics*—Anticipations of the Reaction of Mechanical and Scientific Progress upon Human Life and Thought, 1901; The Discovery of the Future, 1902; Mankind in the Making, 1903; The Future in America, 1906; Socialism and the Family, 1906; This Misery of Boots, 1907; New Worlds for Old, 1908; An Englishman Looks at the World, 1914 (in U.S.: Social Forces in England and America), The War That Will End War 1914; (essays), The War and Socialism, 1915; What Is Coming, 1916; The Elements of Reconstruction (newspaper articles), 1916; War and the Future 1919; (in U.S.: Italy, France, and Britain at War), In the Fourth Year: Anticipations of a World Peace, 1918; (with others) The Idea of a League of Nations: Prolegomena to the Study of World-Organization, 1919; (with others) The Way to the League of Nations, 1919; The Outline of History: Being a Plain History of Life and Mankind, 1920 (The New and Revised Outline of History, 1931; The Enlarged and Revised Outline of History, 1940; revised by Raymond Postgate under original title, 1949) Russia in the Shadows, 1920; The Salvaging of Civilization: The Probable Future of Mankind, 1921; A Short History of the World, 1922; Washington and the Hope of Peace 1922 (in U.S.: Washington and the Riddle of Peace); A Year of Prophesying; 1924 (essays and articles), Mr. Belloc Objects to "The Outline of History," 1926; Wells's Social Anticipations (ed. H. W. Laidler) 1927; The Way the World Is Going: Guesses and Forecasts of the Years Ahead, 1928; The Open Conspiracy: Blue Prints for a World Revolution, 1928 (revised as What Are We to Do with Our Lives?, 1931); (with others) Points of View: A Series of Broadcast Addresses, 1930; (with others) The New Russia: Eight Talks Broadcast, 1931; The Work, Wealth, and Happiness of Mankind, 1931 (as the Outline of Man's Work and Wealth, 1936); After Democracy: Addresses and Papers, 1932; The New America, 1935; World Brain, 1938; (articles and lectures), The Fate of Homo Sapiens, 1939; (in U.S.: The Fate of Man), The New World Order, 1939; Travels of a Republican Radical in Search of Hot Water, 1939; The Common Sense of War and Peace, 1940; The Rights of Man; or, What Are We Fighting For?, 1940; Guide to the New World: A Handbook of Constructive World Revolution, 1941; The Pocket History

of the World, 1941; The Outlook for Homo Sapiens, 1942; (amalgamating and revising The Fate of Homo Sapiens and The New World Order), Phoenix: A Summary of the Inescapable Conditions of World Reorganisation, 1942; '42 to '44: A Contemporary Memoir upon Human Behaviour, 1944; (with J. Stalin) Marxism vs. Liberalism: An Interview, 1945; Journalism and Prophecy, 1893–1946 (ed. W. W. Wagar) 1964. *Science*—Text-Book of Biology (two volumes) 1892–1893; (with R. A. Gregory) Honours Physiology, 1893; (with J. S. Huxley and G. P. Wells) The Science of Life, 1930; (with J. S. Huxley and J. S. Haldane) Reshaping Man's Heritage: Biology in the Service of Man, 1944. *Autobiography and letters*—Certain Personal Matters: a Collection of Material, Mainly Autobiographical, 1898; First and Last Things: A Confession of Faith and Rule of Life, 1908 (replaced by The Conquest of Time, 1942); Experiment in Autobiography: Discoveries and Conclusions of a Very Ordinary Brain (Since 1866) 1934; Mind at the End of Its Tether, 1945; The Happy Turning: A Dream of Life, 1945; Henry James and H. G. Wells: A Record of Their Friendship, Their Debate on the Art of Fiction, and Their Quarrel (letters, ed. L. Edel and G. N. Ray) 1958; Arnold Bennett and H. G. Wells: A Record of a Personal and a Literary Friendship (letters, ed, H. Wilson) 19; George Gissing and H. G. Wells: Their Friendship and Correspondence (ed. R. A. Gettmann) 1961; H. G. Wells in Love: Postscript to An Experiment in Autobiography (ed. G. P. Wells) 1984; Bernard Shaw and H. G. Wells: Selected Correspondence (ed. J. P. Smith) 1995. *Other*—Select Conversations with an Uncle, 1895; Floor Games 1911; (for children), Little Wars: A Game for Boys, 1913; God, the Invisible King, 1917; (with A. Bennett and G. Overton) Frank Swinnerton: Personal Sketches, 1920; The Story of a Great Schoolmaster; Sanderson of Oundle 1924; (with Bertrand Russell and others) Divorce As I See It, 1930; Selections from the Early Prose Works of H. G. Wells, 1931; Things to Come 1935; (film script), Man Who Could Work Miracles 1936; (film script), The Anatomy of Frustration: a Modern Synthesis, 1936; Crux Ansata: An Indictment of the Roman Catholic Church, 1943; Hoopdriver's Holiday, 1964; (dramatization of The Wheels of Chance, ed. M. Timko), H. G. Wells's Literary Criticism (eds. P. Parrinder and R.M. Philmus), 1980; Treasury of H. G. Wells, 1985. *As editor*—The Book of Catherine Wells, 1928.

ABOUT: Bergonzi, B. The Early H.G. Wells, 1961; Bergonzi, B. (ed.) H. G. Wells: A Collection of Critical Essays, 1976; Bloom, R. Anatomies of Egotism: A Reading of the Last Novels of H. G. Wells, 1977; Brooks, V. W. The World of H. G. Wells, 1915; Dickson, L. H. G. Wells: His Turbulent Life and Times, 1969; Dictionary of Literary Biography Vol. 34, 1985; Dictionary of National Biography, 1941–1950, 1959; Hammond, J. R. Herbert George Wells: An Annotated Bibliography, 1977; Hammond, J. R. An H. G. Wells Companion, 1979; Hammond, J. R. H. G. Wells and the Modern Novel, 1988; Hillegas, M. R. The Future as Nightmare: H. G. Wells and the Anti-Utopians, 1967; Lodge, D. The Language of Fiction, 1966; McConnell, F. The Science Fiction of H. G. Wells, 1981; Mackenzie, N. and J. The Time Traveller: The Life of H. G. Wells, 1973; Parrinder, P. H.G. Wells, 1972; Parrinder, P. (ed.) H. G. Wells: The Critical Heritage, 1972; Parrinder, P. and Rolfe, C. (eds.) Proceedings of the International H. G. Wells Symposium, 1986; Scheick, W. J. The Critical Response to H. G. Wells, 1995; Scheick, W. J. and Cox, J. R. H. G. Wells: A Reference Guide, 1988; Smith, D. C. H. G. Wells: Desperately Mortal, 1986; Wagar, W. W. H. G. Wells and the World State, 1961; H.G. Wells Society H.G. Wells: A Comprehensive Bibliography, 1966; West, G. H. G. Wells: A Sketch for a Portrait, 1930. *Periodicals*—Daily Telegraph February 10, 1909; Encounter July/August 1985; English Literature in Transition, 1880–1920, Special Series, No. 3, 1985; Extrapolation Summer 1982; Futurist August 1983; Guardian June 3, 1896; Horizon Winter 1966; Journal of Commonwealth Literature 18 1 1983; Journal of Popular Culture Fall 1976; New Criterion November 1986; New Statesman August 17, 1946; New York Times August 14, 1946; New York Times Book Review September 2, 1973; October 13, 1974; New York Times Magazine August 21, 1966; Nineteenth-Century Fiction June 1966; Review of Reviews March 1895; Saturday Review January 1898; January 1, 1972; Science-Fiction Studies July 1976; Slavonic and East European

Review July 1966; Speaker June 16, 1900, Times (London) August 14, 1946.

## WELTY, EUDORA (ALICE) (April 13, 1909– ), American short story writer and novelist,

was born in Jackson, Mississippi, the eldest of three children, of Christian Webb Welty, an insurance company president, and Mary Chestina (Andrews) Welty, a former schoolteacher. Although most of Welty's fiction is set in and around Mississippi, her father was from Ohio and her mother from West Virginia. Both were loving and devoted parents, but the Weltys did not have deep roots in the region, a factor frequently cited in accounting for Eudora's affectionate but detached stance towards the South.

After the happy but sheltered childhood so well evoked in her memoir, *One Writer's Beginnings*, she entered Mississippi State College for Women in 1926, transferred after two years to the more challenging University of Wisconsin, and received her B.A. in 1929. By then she knew she wanted to write, but heeding her father's advice to combine literature with something more remunerative, in 1930 she enrolled in the Graduate School of Business at Columbia University in New York to study advertising.

She returned to Jackson upon her father's sudden death in 1931, and, while comforting her grieving mother, began writing for a local newspaper and radio station. (Advertising, she later said, was "too much like sticking pins into people to make them buy things they didn't need," and was soon abandoned.) In 1933 she was hired by the Works Progress Administration (a New Deal program) to travel throughout the state, interviewing and photographing depression-era Mississippians, many of them black and most of them poor. This invaluable three-year experience not only supplied a wealth of material for her writing but resulted in the accomplished photographs exhibited in the Lugene Gallery in New York City in 1936 and published in the 1971 volume, *One Time, One Place: Mississippi in the Depression, a Snapshot Album*.

1936 was also the year in which her first achieved short story, "Death of a Traveling Salesman," was published (in the little magazine *Manuscript*). In the next two years other important stories—"A Memory," "A Piece of News," "A Curtain of Green," "Petrified Man"—were published in the *Southern Review*, the influential journal coedited by Robert Penn Warren, who became, with his fellow Southerner Katherine Anne Porter, one of Welty's earliest champions. These stories and a dozen others were brought together in her first book, *A Curtain of Green*, published with an introduction by Porter ("In all of these stories . . . I find nothing false or labored, no diffusion of interest, no wavering of mood") in 1941. Some reviewers dis-

liked the more grotesque characters and situations, but the collection was too various and original to be labeled simply "Southern Gothic," and as many critics have remarked, Welty has never fitted comfortably into any critical pigeon-hole. "All of the stories in *A Curtain of Green* bear the impress of Miss Welty's individual talent," wrote Warren, "but there is a great variety among them in subject matter and method and, more particularly, mood. . . . The material of many of the stories was sad, or violent, or warped, and even the comedy and wit were not straight, but if read from one point of view, if read as performance, the book was exhilarating, even gay."

Resisting commercial pressure to write a full-length, realistic novel, Welty next published *The Robber Bridegroom*, a novella-length romance "about the Natchez Trace and beautiful planters' daughters, and Indians and bayonets and so on," as she described it. Again, the fantastic elements of the story irked a few reviewers, and Lionel Trilling suggested in the *Nation* that Miss Welty's was "prose whose eyes are a little too childishly wide; it is a little too conscious of doing something daring and difficult." Alfred Kazin, however, writing in the *New York Herald Tribune Books*, found in it "what so many have been trying to capture by dint of will and bibliography alone—the lost fabulous innocence of our departed frontier, the easy carelessness, the fond bragging and colossal buckskin strut. And Miss Welty can capture it only because she is not trying to produce historical chromos at all, only because she is writing out of a joy in the world she has restored, and with an eye toward the comedy and poetry embedded in it."

Welty never again wrote anything quite so far-fetched as *The Robber Bridegroom*, but her next book, *The Wide Net*, a series of linked tales set on the old frontier road of the Natchez Trace, was characterized (according to Ruth M. Vande Kieft) by a "tendency to fantasy and the depiction of dream life." Among the eight well-known stories in this collection, "A Still Moment," which concerns the potentially murderous encounter of three solitary obsessives (one of whom is John James Audubon) on the Natchez Trace in 1811, may be considered representative. Linking it with the later and similarly haunting "The Burning," Harold Bloom wrote, "I do not propose to count [their] virtues. . . . Both narratives are as thoroughly written through, fully composed, as the best poems of Wallace Stevens or of Hart Crane, or the strongest of Hemingway's stories, or Faulkner's *As I Lay Dying*."

In 1946 Welty published her first full-length novel, *Delta Wedding*, and proved to the satisfaction of most readers that her mastery of fictional technique was not confined to the short story. This story of the Fairchild family's preparation for the wedding of one of its eight daughters to a plantation overseer contained "a few distressing lapses into an over-precious style," wrote the *Sewanee Review*, but its "depiction of the Delta society and its structure, of the family as the typical unit of that society, is studiedly accurate, right, always in substance and . . . nearly always in tone." Among the novel's technical resources was a mythical framework in which the marriage of Dabney Fairchild and Troy Flavin alluded to the union of Persephone and Pluto, and George Fairchild, who rescues his niece from an oncoming train, was seen as a modern Saint George. Welty further explored mythic parallels in her next book, *The Golden Apples*, a collection of seven interdependent short stories set in the fictional town of Morgana, Mississippi, in the 1930s and 1940s. The myths that governed this work were the astronomical ones of Perseus, Orion, and Cassiopeia and the Celtic legend of Aengus, whose quest for "the golden apples of the sun" gave the book its title. For all its mythological allusiveness, *The Golden Apples* hardly treated its schoolteachers, night watchmen, department store clerks, and rebellious teenagers in a remote or abstract way.

In Welty's next book, the more sheerly comic novella *The Ponder Heart*, she returned to the riotous first-person vernacular she had earlier used in such stories as "Why I Live at the P.O." and "Petrified Man." In a one-hundred-fifty-page monologue, Edna Earle Ponder, a spinsterish hotel keeper in Clay, Mississippi, tells the story of her Uncle Daniel's outrageous and catastrophic marriage to a seventeen-year-old girl far below his station. *The Ponder Heart* was undoubtedly, as V. S. Pritchett wrote in the *New York Times Book Review* (1954), "one of Miss Welty's lighter works, but there is not a mistake in it." Pritchett thought Edna Earle's narrative "remarkable for its headlong garrulity and also for its preposterous silences and changes of subject at the crises of the tale. . . . Her breathless, backhanded, first-person singular has been caught, word by awful word, in all its affectionate self-importance, by a writer with a wonderful ear."

By the 1950s Welty had won a Guggenheim Fellowship and been elected to the National Institute of Arts and Letters. Her 1955 collection, *The Bride of Innisfallen*, which contained three stories set, atypically, in Europe, further enhanced her reputation. It was with considerable anticipation, therefore, that readers awaited her next book, *Losing Battles*, a novel published after a fifteen-year interval in 1970. During that time Welty had received more honors (the William Dean Howells Medal of the American Academy of Arts and Sciences, an Honorary Consultancy from the Library of Congress) and lectured at numerous colleges but also endured the deaths of her two brothers and nursed her mother through her old age and final illness. In any event, *Losing Battles* disappointed some critics ("It does not seem to me as successful a novel as *Delta Wedding*, nor is it as warmly comic and appealing as *The Ponder Heart*," wrote Joyce Carol Oates in the *Atlantic*). At 436 pages, this story of a large family reunion taking place on a hot August Sunday in northeast Mississippi in the 1930s was almost twice as long as anything she had yet written. Though less exuberant than *The Ponder Heart*, *Losing Battles*, wrote Louis D. Rubin, Jr. in the *Hollins Critic*, "is not, as it moves along its way, a somber book. It is alive in humor and merriment . . .

filled with almost constant humor and diversion. But there are no shortcuts. It demands that the reader invest time and attention without stint. . . . What it requires is sentence-by-sentence participation. What it proves, for those willing to take part, is delight ending in wisdom."

The special demands of Welty's fiction precluded the attainment of mass popularity, but with her short, Pulitzer Prize-winning novel of 1972, *The Optimist's Daughter*, she reached more readers than before. The autobiographical elements in this story of a middle-aged daughter grieving over the recent death of her father lent greater accessiblity to the work, and there was little dispute regarding its general excellence. Reviewing it in the *New York Times Book Review* (1972), the *New Yorker*'s poetry editor Howard Moss called it "a miracle of compression, the kind of book, small in scope but profound in its implications, that rewards a lifetime of work. . . . Its story has all those qualities peculiar to the finest short novels: a theme that vibrates with overtones, suspense and classical inevitability. . . . The best book Eudora Welty has ever written is a long goodbye in a very short space not only to the dead but to delusion and to sentiment as well."

Welty brought out her *Collected Stories* in 1980 and a graceful memoir, *One Writer's Beginnings*, in 1984. *The Optimist's Daughter* was her last sustained imaginative effort. She lived in her family's house in Jackson since 1931 and became something of an institution in that city. Invariably described as gentle, kind, and unassuming, she is also, in the judgment of Walter Clemons (*Newsweek*), "one of the most ambitious romancers, in Hawthorne's sense, in the history of American writing. Her *Collected Stories* give ample pleasure, but they inspire awe: she is bigger, and stranger, than we have supposed."

Her novels and short stories in translation have been very popular in France. In 1987 the French government knighted her a Chevalier. In 1996 she received France's highest civilian honor, The Legion of Honor.

Most of Welty's papers are in the Mississippi Department of Archives and History in Jackson and at the University of Texas in Austin.

PRINCIPAL WORKS: *Short stories*—A Curtain of Green, 1941; The Wide Net, and Other Stories, 1943; The Golden Apples, 1949; The Bride of Innisfallen, and Other Stories, 1955; The Collected Stories of Eudora Welty, 1980. *Novels*—The Robber Bridegroom, 1942; Delta Wedding, 1946; The Ponder Heart, 1954; Losing Battles, 1970; The Optimist's Daughter, 1972. *Juvenile*—The Shoe Bird, 1964. *Photography*—One Time, One Place: Mississippi in the Depression, a Snapshot Album, 1971; Photographs, 1989. *Criticism*—The Eye of the Story: Selected Essays and Reviews, 1978; A Writer's Eye: Collected Book Reviews (ed. P. A. McHaney) 1994. *Memoirs*—One Writer's Beginnings, 1984. *As editor*—(with R. A. Sharp) The Norton Book of Friendship, 1991.

ABOUT: Appel, A., Jr. A Season of Dreams: The Fiction of Eudora Welty, 1965; Binding, P. The Still Moment: Eudora Welty, Portrait of a Writer, 1994; Bloom, H. (ed.) Eudora Welty, 1986; Bryant, J. A., Jr. Eudora Welty, 1968; Champion, L. (ed.) The Critical Response of Eudora Welty's Fiction, 1994; Current Biography 1975; Desmond, J. F. (ed.) A Still Moment: Essays on the Art of Eudora Welty, 1978; Devlin, A. J. (ed.)

Welty: A Life in Literature, 1987; Devlin, A. J. Eudora Welty's Chronicle: A Story of Mississippi Life, 1983; Vol. 143; 1994; Dollarhide, L. and Abadie A. J. (eds.) Eudora Welty: A Form of Thanks, 1979; Evans, E. Eudora Welty, 1981; Gretlund, J. N. Eudora Welty's Aesthetics of Place, 1994; Gygax, F. Serious Daring from Within: Female Narrative Strategies in Eudora Welty's Novels, 1990; Howard, Z. T. The Rhetoric of Eudora Welty's Short Stories, 1973; Kreyling, M. Author and Agent: Eudora Welty and Diarmuid Russell, 1991; Kreyling, M. Eudora Welty's Achievement of Order, 1980; Manning, C. S. With Ears Opening Like Morning Glories: Eudora Welty and the Love of Storytelling, 1985; Manz-Kung, M. A. Eudora Welty: Aspects of Reality in Her Fiction, 1971; Mark, R. The Dragon's Blood: Feminist Intertextuality in Eudora Welty's The Golden Apples, 1994; Porter, K. A. introduction to A Curtain of Green (by E. Welty) 1941; Prenshaw, P. W. (ed.) Conversations with Eudora Welty, 1984; Prenshaw, P. W. (ed.) Eudora Welty: Critical Essays, 1979; Schmidt, P. The Heart of the Story: Eudora Welty's Short Fiction, 1991; Trouard, D. (ed.) Eudora Welty: Eye of the Storyteller, 1990; Turner, W. C. and Harding, L. E. (eds.) Critical Essays on Eudora Welty, 1989; Vande Kieft, R. M. Eudora Welty, rev. ed. 1987; Warren, R. P. Selected Essays, 1958; Writers at Work: The Paris Review Interviews, Fourth Series 1976. *Bibliographies*—Polk, N. Eudora Welty: A Bibliography of Her Work, 1994; Swearingen, B. C. Eudora Welty: A Critical Bibliography, 1936–1958, 1984; Thompson, V. H. Eudora Welty: A Reference Guide, 1976. *Periodicals*—Atlantic April 1970; Hollins Critic June 1970; Nation December 19, 1942; New York Herald Tribune Books October 25, 1942; New York Times August 10, 1995; New York Times Book Review January 10, 1954; May 21, 1972; Newsweek November 3, 1980; Sewanee Review Summer 1952.

**WENDELL, BARRETT** (August 23, 1855–February 8, 1921), American educator, essayist, and literary historian, was born in Boston, the eldest

of the four sons of Jacob Wendell and Mary Bertodi (Barrett) Wendell. Shortly after graduating from Harvard University in 1877, Wendell spent three unhappy years studying law, culminating in his failure of the 1880 Boston bar examinations. Soon thereafter, Wendell married Edith Greenough, and they had two sons and two daughters. In 1880, Wendell returned to Harvard and commenced what was to become a life-long devotion to the university. Beginning as an instructor, he became an assistant professor in 1888, and by 1908, he was a full professor of English. Throughout his tenure at Harvard, he was an immensely popular professor.

As a scholar, Wendell was the first American to give regular lectures on English literature at an English university. These lectures were given at Cambridge University in 1902–1903, and were focussed on the age of Dryden. Eventually they were collected and published as *Temper of the 17th century in English Literature.*

As Wendell felt that "Americans know little of the literary traditions of our ancestral Europe," his primary scholarly concern rested with the interrelationship between the histories, societies, and politics of England and America. *A Literary History of America* (1908) sets out to demonstrate this interre-

lationship but was regarded as having an overly narrow breadth and as being intolerant in its tone. Wendell's interpretative works, however, which include *Cotton Mather: The Puritan Priest* and *William Shakespeare: A Study in Elizabethan Literature*, were regarded as useful and well-rounded texts.

Wendell is best remembered for the works derived from his lectures at Harvard University. *Traditions of European Literature*, which was taken from his lectures in a comparative literature course, was popularly known as *A Romp through Ages With Barrett Wendell* and was praised by the *New York Times* as being "worthy in theme, comprehensive in conception, shapely in plan and skillful in execution."

PRINCIPAL WORKS: The Duchess Emilia: A Romance, 1885; Rankell's Remains: An American Novel, 1887; Cotton Mather: The Puritan Priest, 1891; Stelligeri and Other Essays Concerning America, 1893; William Shakespeare: A Study in Elizabethan Literature, 1894; A Literary History of America, 1900; Raleigh in Guiana, 1902; The France of To-Day, 1908; The Mystery of Education, 1909; The Traditions of European Literature, 1920.

ABOUT: Castle, W. R., Jr. Barrett Wendell—Teacher in Essays in Memory of Barrett Wendell By His Assistants; Edgett, E. F. I Speak for Myself; Howe, M. A. D. W. Barrett Wendell and His Letters; Phelps, W. L. Autobiography. *Periodicals*—New York Times February 9, 1921.

**WENDT, GERALD (LOUIS)** (March 3, 1891–December 22, 1973), American scientist, wrote: "I was born in Davenport, Iowa, then still a distinctively German town. I

had no great love for the agricultural environment, nor was I much attracted by the rather unusual literary group that then thrived there, but I was entranced by the excellent science then being taught in the schools. By the time I reached Harvard, in 1909, human affairs seemed incomprehensible and I embraced the study of science in a spirit that was quite monastic. When I received the Ph.D. degree at Harvard in 1916, I was wholly immersed in atoms and interested in nothing but their structure and their reactions. In 1914 I went to Paris to work in radium and X-rays, and in this field of research I was immured from the world. As a young instructor in chemistry I went to the Rice Institute, then almost at once to the University of Chicago. I had served briefly in the United States Bureau of Mines, and also for six months of 1918 was a captain in the Chemical Warfare Service of the army, stationed in Washington. But the students at the university proved increasingly interesting and my education in terms of humanity at last began.

"In 1921 my health collapsed and I gave up my research on atoms. Upon recovery I took charge of scientific research for a large oil company. This proved so meaningless to me that in 1925 I accepted an appointment as dean of the School of Chemistry and Physics at Pennsylvania State College. Here

I hoped to undertake research once more, but actually by 1929 I had become assistant to the president, in charge of the college research program.

"Then came an absorption in patents and the creation of new economic values by research, which led, in 1930, to my organizing a corporation to develop some of my new knowledge in an old industry. In 1935 I became director of research for the General Printing Ink Corporation in New York. During this period I awoke fully to social problems and to the tragic neglect by America of the values inherent in science. In 1936, therefore, I also became director of the American Institute of the City of New York. It was my hope through the Institute to develop a better understanding of science as a social force.

"In 1938 I joined the staff of the New York World's Fair as Director of Science, to which was later added the post of Director of Education.

"In 1942 I became science editor of Time, Inc., thus counsellor in science for the editors of *Time, Life, Fortune,* and *The March of Time,* but left in 1946 to assist the McGraw-Hill Publishing Company in launching the new monthly *Science Illustrated,* as editorial director. It was the first major American effort to establish a popular magazine of science above the adolescent level and attained a monthly circulation of 650,000 within three years but failed for lack of adequate advertising support. By this time my experience with the media of popular education in science and my devotion to the cause were sufficient to lead me to accept an invitation from the United Nations Educational, Scientific and Cultural Organization in Paris to take charge of the Division of Teaching and Dissemination in the Department of Natural Sciences. This involves the improvement of science instruction in schools and colleges throughout the world, the incorporation of science into elementary and 'fundamental' education, popular education by means of exhibits, films and radio, the organization in many countries of science clubs for youth, the dissemination of science news by the diverse media of mass communication, and the study and wide discussion of the social consequences of science.

"It is my growing conviction that the age of science is not yet here and that no amount of gadgets, inventions, or technology will bring it. Much more important are the research method of investigation and the fuller realization that science not only studies the enviroment in which we live, but alters it so completely that our institutions and traditions are, for the most part, in full conflict with the actual conditions of modern life. Until human society is regarded with a scientific attitude as the product of people, to be arranged and managed for the benefit of people, until it is studied by the realistic detached methods of science, and until a new faith and culture emerge which are based on science and not merely on all our yesterdays, science cannot achieve its major purpose and humanity cannot achieve happiness. . . . "

A teacher, lecturer, editor, researcher, adminis-

trator, and energetic proselytizer for science, Gerald Wendt was also a writer of merit. His half dozen books were intended for lay readers as much as for scientists, and were generally welcomed by the press for their usefulness. One of his most successful books, *Science for the World of Tomorrow,* grew out of his work for the New York World's Fair from 1938 to 1940 and took as its subject "those elements in the life of today that are to build the world of tomorrow." While the *New Republic* thought that Wendt's forecasts "show little understanding of the social forces at work," the *New York Herald Tribune* wrote, "Dr. Wendt never loses sight of humanity, and never abandons his scientific attitude."

*You and the Atom,* an explanation of nuclear energy and its uses, grew out of Wendt's work for UNESCO, and although it too may have shown "little understanding of the social forces at work," it was praised for its lucid presentation of scientific concepts.

Wendt was also the editor of a six-volume survey of the sciences, of which his own contribution, *Chemistry,* was successful in its time. He wrote in the preface: "It embodies a selection of the principles that are most important and far-reaching, of the topics that play the greatest part of modern life. It is intended for the student, whether in college or not, who will some day be a business man, a teacher, a banker, a journalist or statesman, a housewife or head of a family—in short for all citizens of a democracy in an age of science."

In 1955 Wendt established the UNESCO Publications Center, which he directed until his retirement in 1967. In addition, he was chairman of the North American Commission of the International Humanist and Ethical Union from 1956 to 1967.

PRINCIPAL WORKS: *Scientific*—(with O. F. Smith) Matter and Energy: An Introduction by Way of Chemsitry and Physics to the Material Basis of Modern Civilization, 1930; Science for the World of Tomorrow, 1939; Chemistry, 1942; Atomic Energy and the Hydrogen Bomb, 1950; You and the Atom, 1955; The Prospects of Nuclear Power and Technology, 1957. As editor—(with D. Geddes) The Atomic Age Opens, 1945.

ABOUT: The autobiographical material quoted above was written for Twentieth Century Authors, 1942 and Twentieth Century Authors First Supplement, 1955. Current Biography 1940; National Cyclopaedia of American Biography, vol. 58 1979. *Periodicals*—New Republic December 29, 1939; New York Herald Tribune Books December 10, 1939; 1939; New York Times December 24, 1973; New York Times Book Review January 15, 1956; Springfield Republican April 29, 1942.

## "WENTWORTH, PATRICIA (DELTA)" (pseudonym of DORA TURNBULL) (1878– January 28, 1961), English writer of detective and historical novels wrote: "Patricia Wentworth comes of an old army family. Her father was a distinguished general, and she is married to a soldier. She began her literary career by writing historical novels, with the first of which, a romance of the French Revolution, she won a prize for the best first novel. It scored an immediate success, and has been used as a textbook for students. Later she turned to the romantic thriller, her first book in this style, *The Astonishing Adventure of Jane Smith,* being hailed as quite a new departure in detective fiction. Her books are in continuous demand at the libraries and

attract a widening public. It is her aim to portray ordinary, convincing human characters in extraordinary circumstances, and in this she has been told that she succeeds. Miss Silver, who knits her way through one mystery after another and flavours detection with moral maxims, is quite unlike any one else in this field and has become a favorite."

---

Patricia Wentworth was born Dora Amy Elles in Mussoorie, India, the daughter of Lieutenant-General Sir Edmund Roche Elles. Educated privately, and at Blackheath High School, she returned to India when she married Lieutenant-Colonel George Dillon. Dillon, who had three sons by an earlier marriage, died in 1906. Widowed at twenty-eight, Wentworth entered the first-novel competition with *Marriage Under the Terror*.

This book, like Wentworth's other early thrillers, was originally published under the pseudonym "Delta." It tells the story of a convent-reared young  aristocrat pursued by a bestial follower of Marat, finally snatched from the guillotine by the death of Robespierre. Reviewers found it amateurish in style, but well plotted and suspenseful, and grimly realistic in its account of the Terror. Five more novels followed, most of them also historical romances.

Wentworth made a second marriage in 1920 to Lieutenant-Colonel George Oliver Turnbull, D. S. O. They had one daughter. In 1923, Wentworth took up her pen again with her first thriller. *The Astonishing Adventure of Jane Smith*. Set mostly in an isolated house by the sea, well provided with trapdoors and secret passages, it has a melodramatic plot about anarchists eager to blow up the world, a likable young heroine, and a judicious admixture of romance. Warmly received by reviewers and public alike, it was followed by many similar stories, appearing at the rate of one or two a year. There were haunted houses, evil foreigners, secret weapons, eccentric wills, blackmail stories, amnesia stories—every kind of well-tried plot, always leavened with a substantial love story and touches of humor. The heroines and heroes were stock figures, but often there would be an eccentric minor character of some originality.

It was when Patricia Wentworth put such a character at the center of her stories that her work began to be seen as something more than "light, fluffy and harmless" (Will Cuppy in *New York Herald Tribune Books*). Miss Maud Silver made her first appearance in 1928 in *Grey Mask*, and in virtually all of Wentworth's novels after 1941—thirty-two in all, most of them still in print, and consumed for the most part by older readers.

Miss Silver is an elderly retired governess who knits little garments and runs a private detective agency from her drawing room. She delivers moral homilies to her clients as once she had to the children in her care, and laces her conversation with quotations from her beloved Tennyson. Miss Silver's harmless appearance and gentility are deceptive; she is a "sleuthess" of inexorable intelligence, and rich in Christian charity. Her cases usually involve agreeable young people of good family, falsely accused of crime, generally murder. Miss Silver knits her way through to the truth and presents it gently to the baffled police. Her innocent clients are free to marry and live happily ever after. The real culprits are punished, and in the time of the death penalty in England, often that meant hanging.

Patricia Wentworth lived a quieter life than Maud Silver. She shunned publicity, and spent her days at Camberley working, reading, gardening, and listening to music.

PRINCIPAL WORKS: *Novels*—A Marriage Under the Terror, 1910; A Little More Than Kin, 1911 (in U.S.: More Than Kin); The Devil's Wind, 1912; The Fire Within, 1913; Simon Heriot, 1914; Queen Anne Is Dead, 1915. *Mystery novels*—The Astonishing Adventure of Jane Smith, 1923; The Red Lacquer Case, 1924; The Annam Jewel, 1924; The Black Cabinet, 1925; The Dower House Mystery, 1925; The Amazing Chance, 1926; Anne Belinda, 1927; Hue and Cry, 1927; Will-o'-the-Wisp, 1928; Fool Errant, 1929; Beggar's Choice, 1930; The Coldstone, 1930; Kingdom Lost, 1930; Danger Calling, 1931; Nothing Venture, 1932; Red Danger, 1932 (in U.S.: Red Shadow); Seven Green Stones, 1933 (in U.S.: Outrageous Fortune); Walk with Care, 1933; Fear by Night, 1934; Devil-in-the-Dark, 1934 (in U.S.: Touch and Go); Blindfold, 1935; Red Stefan, 1935; Hole and Corner, 1936; Dead or Alive, 1936; Down Under, 1937; Mr. Zero, 1938; Run!, 1938; The Blind Side, 1939; Who Pays the Piper?, 1940 (in U.S.: Account Rendered); Rolling Stone, 1940; Unlawful Occasions, 1941 (in U.S.: Weekend with Death); Pursuit of a Parcel, 1942; Silence in Court, 1945. *The Miss Silver mysteries*—Grey Man, 1928; The Case Is Closed, 1937; Lonesome Road, 1939; Danger Point, 1942 (in U.S.: In the Balance); The Chinese Shawl, 1943; Miss Silver Intervenes, 1944 (in U.S.: Miss Silver Deals with Death); The Key, 1944; The Clock Strikes Twelve, 1944; The Traveller Returns, 1948 (in U.S.: She Came Back); Pilgrim's Rest, 1946 (in U.S.: Dark Threat 1950); Latter End, 1947; Spotlight, 1949 (in U. S.: Uncle); The Case of William Smith, 1948; Eternity Ring, 1948; Miss Silver Comes to Stay, 1949; The Catherine Wheel, 1949; The Brading Collection, 1950; Through the Wall, 1950; Anna, Where Are You?, 1951 (in U.S.: Death at Deep End); The Ivory Dagger, 1951; The Watersplash, 1951; Ladies' Bane, 1952; Vanishing Point, 1953; Out of the Past, 1953; The Benevent Treasure, 1954; The Silent Pool 19454; Poison in the Pen, 1955; The Listening Eye, 1955; The Gazebo, 1956 (in U.S.: The Summerhouse); The Fingerprint, 1956; The Alington Inheritance, 1958; The Girl in the Cellar, 1961. *Poetry*—A Child's Rhyme Book, 1910; Beneath the Hunter's Moon, 1945; The Pool of Dreams, 1953. *Other*—Earl or Chieftain? The Romance of Hugh O'Neill, 1919.

ABOUT: The autobiographical material quoted above was written for Twentieth Century Authors first Supplement, 1955. Blain, V. and others (eds.) Feminist Companion to Literature in English, 1990; Craig, P. and Cadogan, M. The Lady Investigates, 1986; Dictionary of Literary Biography vol. 77 1988; Twentieth Century Crime and Mystery writers, 1985; Who's Who 1961. *Periodicals*—New York Herald Tribune Books July 31, 1938; New York Times May 12, 1912; October 11, 1953; February 1, 1961; Times (London) January 31, 1961.

**WERFEL, FRANZ** (September 10, 1890–August 26, 1945), Czech poet, novelist, dramatist, and essayist (who wrote in German), was born in Prague, the son of a Jewish manufacturer. Werfel converted to Catholicism and became famous for the popular novel *Das Lied von Bernadette* (1941, *The Song of Bernadette*), the inspirational story of St. Bernadette of Lourdes. Werfel's achievements in litera-

ture came early in his life. His popularity prompted the Austrian novelist Robert Musil to exclaim, in 1930, "what business have I in a world in which Werfel has interpreters?" Yet he was, as a *Times Literary Supplement* critic remarked, "an all too vulnerable individual, one lacking the fibre to resist being inwardly torn by history, and between faiths, ideologies and individuals."

Werfel's early poems in *Das Weldfreund* (1911, Friend of mankind) created a sensation. He had served for a year as a volunteer in the Austrian army and entered the civil service. He was then called up to regular war service, and served on the Russian front in World War I. The experience, according to *Current Biography*, "had a shattering effect on him . . . as he had seen in actual crystallized form all the evil of which the premonition had always haunted him." After the end of World War I, Werfel became an active social revolutionary, and his fantastic expressionist play *Spiegelmensch* (1920, *Mirror Man*) was put on, to great praise—but also with dissent from Karl Kraus, who parodied it. Influenced by the Faust legend, it presents a Faust-like figure, Thaumal, a monk who grows tired of the contemplative life. He releases his evil counterpart by shooting at him in a mirror, and then abets him in the murder of his father and in the tyrannical oppression of a country that he himself had freed. He then brings himself to trial and condemns himself to death by poison. One reason that Kraus parodied this play was that it contained satire directed at him, as well as his archenemy Sigmund Freud.

Werfel had another sensational success with *Bockgesang* (1921, *Goat Song*). According to *Current Biography*, the "hidden thesis" of this symbolic drama is that "natural impulses held down by traditional shackles of shame grow evil and eventually destroy their jailers."

In Werfel's atypical comedy, *Jacobowski und der Obertst* (1944, *Jacobowsky and the Colonel*), Saint Francis and Ahasuerus appear together. Its self-mocking spontaneity makes it delightful.

As a novelist Werfel produced huge volumes with world-wide sales. In all of them the prevailing theme is that of world brotherhood. The best is *Verdi* (1924), which has as its subject the challenge set up to the traditional Italian opera by the Wagnerian Musikdrama.

Werfel's next great popular success was with *Die viertzig Tage des Musa Dagh* (1933, *The Forty Days of Musa Dagh*), which deals with the Armenian struggle against the Turks during World War I. In this novel he expressed his hope that the day would come when moderns could be "no longer condemned to hypercritical materialism but could at last take our place without supercilious mental reservations in an ordered universe, in a radiant cosmic system reaching from the skies above to the earth beneath."

Driven out of Vienna by the German-Austrian Anschluss in which Hitler had annexed Austria in 1938, Werfel and his well-known wife Alma, who was the widow of Gustave Mahler and Walter Gropius, went to Switzerland, to France, and then to America. There, having converted to Roman Catholicism, he produced *The Song of Bernadette*, the most popular of all his works. Throughout his life, he had been possessed by a sense of "personal responsibility for all of mankind's shortcomings."

PRINCIPAL WORKS IN ENGLISH TRANSLATION: *Fiction*—Verdi (tr. H. Jessiman), 1925; The Pascarella Family (tr. D. F. Tait), 1932; The Forty Days of Musa Dagh (tr. G. Dunlop), 1934; Embezzled Heaven (tr. M. Firth), 1940; The Song of Bernadette (tr. L. Lewisohn), 1942. *Short Stories*—The Class Reunion (tr. W. Chambers) 1929. *Plays*—Goat Song (tr. R. Laugner) 1926; Mirror Man (tr, anon) 1925; Jacobowski and the Colonel (adapted S. N. Berhman) 1942. *Poetry*—Poems (tr. E. Snow) 1945.

ABOUT: Columbia Dictionary of Modern European Literature 1947, 1980; Current Biography Yearbook, 1940; George, E. Franz Werfel: A Gambler in Life and Art, 1991; Huber, L. (ed.) Franz Werfel, 1989; Jungk, P. Franz Werfel, 1990; Keegan, S. The bride of the Wind: The Life and Times of Alma Mahler-Werfel, 1992; Michaels, J. E. Franz Werfel and the Critics, 1994; Seymour-Smith, M. Guide to Modern World Literature, 1986. *Periodical*—Times Literary Supplement October 9, 1987.

**WERTHAM, FREDRIC** (1895–November 18, 1980), German-born American psychologist, wrote: "Since adolescence I have been a voracious reader and interested in literature. I think it was literature that led me to psychiatry. And psychiatry led me back to literature.

"I was born in Germany and educated there and in England. My training in medicine was also partly in Germany, partly in England. My post-

graduate studies in neurology and psychiatry were in Munich, Vienna, Paris, and London. In 1921 I came to the United States to work under Professor Adolf Meyer at Johns Hopkins, where I stayed for seven years, teaching and doing research. I was the first American psychiatrist to be awarded a research fellowship by the National Research Council (Washington, D.C.). In 1932 I organized and directed the first psychiatric clinic in a major court where all convicted felons got a psychiatric examination about which a report was made to the judges. Since then my main psychiatric interest has been the practice and organization of psychotherapy in mental hygiene clinics. I have become acquainted with the personal, sexual, social and bureaucratic difficulties of innumerable people. And I plan to write about that some day. My interest in psychoanalysis started through my personal acquaintance with Freud after the First World War; my training in it came from Dr. Horace Westlake Frink, whom Freud regarded as his best American pupil. I have been director of some of the largest clinics in the country, the mental hygiene clinic of Bellevue Hospital and that of the Queens Hospital Center. I also organized two free clinics on my own, the Quaker Emergency Service Readjustment Center, devoted entirely to the psychotherapy of sexual difficulties (most of which were homosexual), and the Lafargue Clinic. I started that in 1946 in the heart of a slum area in Harlem. The Lafargue Clinic fulfilled such a need that from the day it opened we were swamped with patients. However, we have never been able to get any endowment from any individual or any oranization and are still dependent upon very small contributions from well-wishers all over the country. None of the staff gets paid. Aside from these clinics, I have been practicing psychiatry and psychoanalysis in New York for some twenty years.

"My first book, The Brain as an Organ, is entirely technical, being a textbook of neuropathology. Dark Legend, which appeared first in 1941, is a factual story in literary form. It deals with a seventeen-year-old boy who committed matricide. I found that no psychiatric nor psychoanalytic study of such a case had been made before and was impressed by the fact that this untutored boy of the slums used expressions paralleling those of Orestes and Hamlet in high tragedy. The British edition had censorship trouble and could not be published for a few years. My next book, The Show of Violence, also is a factual description. In it I present the details of a few of the many murderers I have psychiatrically studied and discuss the whole question of murder and insanity. The main point of that book is that we could prevent violence if we wanted to. My latest book deals with the same subject in another field. It is called Seduction of the Innocent and is the first complete independent study of a type of literature that has become the greatest publishing success in all history, the comic book. A condensation of this book appeared in the Ladies' Home Journal for November 1953.

"I wrote a study of Ezra Pound called The Road to Rapallo. In The World Within, an anthology of short stories with psychiatric subjects edited by Mary Louise Aswell, I wrote an introduction, on 'Psychiatry and Literature,' and an analytic comment on each story. A type of of literature—for that is what I think it should be—much neglected at present is the book review. The essay-review is one field where literature and social criticism can help to reestablish the often-broken link between life and literature. I have written book reviews for the New Republic, psychiatric and legal journals, Saturday Review, etc. My essay on Tolstoy has elicited so much comment that is has reinforced my opinion that the prevention of violence is on many people's minds."

———

Many of the violence-related topics Fredric Wertham wrote about in the 1950s and 1960s con-

tinue to concern Americans. Wertham's books on juvenile crime offer insights that seem even more on target thirty years later, especially in terms of the necessity for adults to take a collective societal responsibility for violent youths.

Wertham used a series of case studies in The Show of Violence (1949) to draw attention to his belief that murderers do not have to be sick people; rather, he saw murder as preventable crime, an indicator of a greater social ill: a callous disregard for human dignity and life. "Some of Dr. Wertham's more controversial views might suggest that he has an axe to grind. Actually, he has none. He is, above all, a humanist whose sincerity shines through every ringing sentence of his book. The weakness of his position . . . lies in the fact that, in holding up such high expectations for the individual and society, he is ahead of his time," wrote Dr. W. M. Hitzig in the Saturday Review of Literature.

While Wertham's earlier works received praise, his study on the effect of comic books on the minds and behavior of children, Seduction of the Innocent (1954), resulted in his sometimes being considered more of an anti-comic campaigner than an objective, well-rounded scholar of the psychology of crime. Wolcott Gibbs wrote in the New Yorker that "Wertham provided enemies of the comics with some of their most potent ammunition," although he found the book to be "frequently absurd and alarmful . . . full of examples of the psychiatrist's peculiar gift for referring all abnormal behavior to one special stimulus." Reuel Denney wrote in the New Republic of the scant apparatus of criticism in Wertham's presentation of his interview materials, faulted his apparent lack of interest in broader cultural themes, and considered his argument that juvenile crimes seemed to increase proportionately with the rise in crime comic books largely unjustifiable.

Circle of Guilt (1956) followed the case-study format. This time, Wertham chose the headline-grabbing story of Frank Santana, a young man who shot another in the Bronx in 1955, to exemplify larger issues of juvenile delinquency, especially what he saw as the muddled thinking of professionals, the media, and the general public and the lack of any collaboration between various disciplines in solving the problem. Wertham once again pointed his finger of blame at the usual media and comic culprits.

In A Sign for Cain (1966), an exploration of human violence, Wertham postulates that no crime is ever an isolated event, but is always linked by a thousand threads to the fabric of our social and institutional life. He traces many roots and fostering factors of violence, including a commercial disrespect for human life that he discerns in cigarette and alcohol advertising. In his section on juvenile violence, Tired of Home, Sick of School, and Bored With Life, he wrote that youths themselves are not to blame for the vast amount of juvenile crime in the United States. Instead, it is "a direct reflection of adult life . . . The attitude toward violence within adult society is what makes the violence of children possible.

His final book, *The World of Fanzines* (1974), is a guide to small-circulation, noncommercial magazines that deal primarily with fantasy, literature, and art. He covered many aspects of this area of publishing, including circulation, content, and style, but *Choice* considered the book "repetitious . . . limited and shallow, particularly in his effort to place fanzines in historical perspective."

PRINCIPAL WORKS: The Brain As an Organ, 1934; Dark Legend, 1941; The Show of Violence, 1949; The Road to Rapallo, 1949; Seduction of the Innocent, 1954; The Circle of Guilt, 1956; A Sign for Cain, 1966; The World of Fanzines, 1974.

ABOUT: The autobiographical material quoted above was written for Twentieth Century Authors First Supplement, 1955. Contemporary Authors, 1982; Current Biography 1949; Wertham, F. A Sign for Cain, 1966. *Periodicals*—America September 24, 1966; Choice April 1974; New Republic May 3, 1954; January 14, 1957; New York Times February 1, 1981; New Yorker September 27, 1941; May 8, 1954; Saturday Review October 20, 1956; Saturday Review of Literature May 7, 1949.

**WESCOTT, GLENWAY** (April 11, 1901– February 22, 1987), American novelist and poet, wrote: "My birthplace was a poor farm in Wisconsin. I sought education at the University of Chicago and there I began to write poetry, but only so that I could belong to the Poetry Club, with ambition instead of inspiration. I pretended to be a genius, you might say, in order to get on in the world; and ever since, it has been as some god had heard me and somehow condemned me to the uneasy fulfillment of that juvenile bluff and boast. I have had good luck in every respect but one; my talent has not seemed equal to my opportunities or proportionate to my ideas and ideals. Lately I have been glad of that too; for while I so painfully labor to compose exact sentences and easy paragraphs and pages in good narrative order, I find time to recall emotion as well as experience, and to include my second thoughts.

"I left the university half way through my sophomore year, in mediocre health and melancholy. My real education was in the sixteenth or seventeenth century way, by the grand tour of the continent of Europe. I matured by fits and starts and, as long as I felt young, wrote with some facility: four volumes (or three and a half) about Wisconsin. For nine years I resided on the Riviera and in Paris, which in the twenties was a great fools' paradise, the perfect time and place to study human nature: nothing else seemed more important or urgent. When in the thirties everything else developed an urgency of hell and damnation, I returned to America. In the spring of 1939 I suddenly felt at home where I belong: then my youthful promise seemed to me fulfillable: my ability, such as it may be, began to get its stride. Naturally everyone gave me bad marks for my failure to publish anything to speak of during the thirties. Now I hope to show how much I learned about the art of narration by unceasing,

fruitless endeavor all the while. I also invented and accumulated a series of characters and plots.

"Having been born with the twentieth century I realize that I am now approximately middle-aged. But I feel excited, cheerful, and indeed youthful about it. World-war or world-revolution raging again, reminds us for one thing to hurry up with our literary art and the like. If I were to die now I should die ashamed and cursing. For, as it seems to be, my circumstances and adventures always have been practically ideal for a novelist: and they still are. I am in excellent health; and I still have a family-farmhouse in New Jersey to live in, and part of a New York apartment to see life from. In my teens I once worked for a firm of mass-production tailors: and one year I attended an aged millionaire art-collector who was going blind. But as a rule, thanks to a book-loving family and generous friends, I have not been obliged or expected to do anything except write.

"Also my twenty grown-up years have provided me with the several sorts of experience I want to write about. I saw a brotherhood of penitents flagellate to an accompaniment of flutes during a snowstorm in the Rockies. I sat up all one night with the glorious beheaded body of Isadora Duncan. After Rathenau was murdered I watched a mob remurder him in effigy. The old man who first turned these base metals to gold and got the Nobel Prize for it, presented me with a fine jewel which he made by a similar process. But, I must admit, the bulk of my subject matter is not so sensational. Roughly speaking, it is the private life: the education of the young, the religion of the old, love-affairs, death-beds. My recently published pint-size novel, *The Pilgrim Hawk*, is characteristic.

"I have been thinking, for fun, what books and authors have had a decisive influence on my writing, to date. They are the *Oz* books; Hall Caine; Owen Johnson's *The Salamanders*; Henry James: D.H. Lawrence's *Sons and Lovers*; Chateaubriand; W. Somerset Maugham. There is more in this list than meets the eye: it is not what I admire most. E.M. Forster, I think, is the greatest living master of English prose. Yeats was the greatest English poet since Blake or perhaps Pope. The other Lawrence, Colonel T.E. Lawrence, is an immortal, I believe, although he was not a lovable man. Mr. Maugham's *Christmas Holiday* seems to me the finest novel of this decade; far and aware the most significant socially and historically. Younger writers whose work I love are Katherine Anne Porter, Richard Hughes, W.H. Auden.

"I believe, as doubtless a majority of Americans believe, in our American power and prosperity and those luxuries of the spirit, fine art and education, free speech, free publication, and free faith, which today depend to a great extent upon power and prosperity. I hope for a continuous evolution leftward in the spheres of economics and politics; but I am not a Marxist. I do not believe in falsification of facts for any purpose whatsoever; nor in the least infringement of individual morality today for the sake of general benefit tomorrow."

In 1955, Wescott added: "Perhaps I should speak of myself with a sharper sense of humor, a turn of phrase less melancholy, than in 1942. On the other hand, my prognosis of further production of volumes of fiction is less optimistic or less ambitious. Evidently I felt then that I had mastered the narrative art, so that it would be easy for me to call myself a man of letters rather than a novelist. In the past decade I have produced only one novel, *Apartment in Athens*, a Book-of-the-Month Club selection in the spring of 1945.

"Having been found ineligible for the selective service, I wanted some other part in the tragic necessity of the war. Living in Germany in 1921–1922, and traveling there from time to time after that, I had made friends with Germans of all sorts; and it seemed to me that I had an understanding of certain mysteries of the German mentality and Central European history out of which Nazism developed, and that in the form of a novel this might serve a useful national and international purpose. So many Americans were having to fight and to sacrifice in ignorance. I first attempted a tale of the fall of France, but I found that unwritable, perhaps because the French spirit seemed to fluctuate too much, and my imagination likewise; and in what information came to me I could not see the wood for the trees. Then I happened to meet a hero of the Greek underground who was visiting this country on a secret mission, and although I had never been to Greece even as a tourist, I was inspired by his account of the German occupation of Athens to begin all over again, with Greek everyman and everywoman and everychild instead of my familiar, too familiar, French.

"Since the war I have published nothing in book form except two fairly important critical studies, introductions to *The Maugham Reader* (1950) and to *Short Novels of Colette* (1951). I am now at work on a novel of remembrances of Europe, especially Paris in the twenties, to be entitled "A Hundred Affections." I have also undertaken one other ambitious volume, "The Small World," an account of my education and foreign travel, famous friends and worldly influences. Two further volumes, nonfiction, I keep still about. I am an incorrigibly copious letter writer, and doubtless I have wasted time in that way and in more or less parallel ways."

---

Glenway Wescott is described in his *New York Times* obituary as "one of the last of the major expatriate American writers." Yet, as his biographer William H. Rueckert notes, he "has fallen into near obscurity" and today, if he is remembered, it is as an accomplished stylist and a friend of such literary greats as Katherine Anne Porter, Somerset Maugham, and Thornton Wilder. No doubt Wescott's fall into "near obscurity" is a result of his highly sporadic and infrequent creative output, coupled with a nearly unbroken fifty-year term of silence. From 1932 to his death in 1987, he published only one work of any merit.

Wescott published his first novel, *Apple of the Eye*, at the age of 23. While the novel, said reviewers, exhibited "many of the shortcomings of youthful first works," it is nonetheless "a first novel of real distinction," portraying Wescott's own development in the Wisconsin countryside that serves as setting for most of his work. It centers around a young man's quest to extricate himself from his strong moral, nearly puritanical, upbringing, with its narrow conception of sexuality. In this sense, the novel is based upon the conflict between pagan and religious conceptions of morality.

Literary acclaim came to Westcott three years later with the publication of what most consider his most endearing novel—*Grandmothers: A Family Portrait* (1927). As the Harper Prize Novel for 1927, *Grandmothers* prompted comparisons to such classics as *The Spoon River Anthology* and *Winesburg, Ohio*. Focusing upon early Wisconsin pioneer life and, like *Winesburg, Ohio*, composed of interwoven short sketches, *Grandmothers* is framed by the narrator's nostalgic perusal of an old family album. Written in Wescott's typically high and intricate "Flaubert-like" style, *Grandmothers* marked a creative highpoint to which Wescott would return but once.

In Wescott's collection of stories *Good-Bye, Wisconsin*, he offers the reasons why he finds the Middle West and America a place that in countless ways prevents the development of the self. Lionel Trilling remarked that the stories contained in this work slip away . . . [and] refuse to be memorable, but they anticipate, Wescott's own growing disillusion with American life. These misgivings are explored in *Babe's Bed*, in which he states America "is not a rich country, not in real values, not yet."

Wescott's perception of America as stifling prompted his departure for Europe shortly before the publication of *Good-bye Wisconsin*. By the time *Babe's Bed* was published, he had been living in Paris for over five years. Yet, Wescott's disillusionment with America may have only been a mask for a loss of faith in his own skills as a novelist. His biographer, William Rueckert, noted that in *Babe's Bed*, Wescott expresses for the first time his self-doubts about himself as a fiction writer.

From this point forward his creative output, became entirely sporadic and infrequent, and his reputation as a novelist commenced an irreparable decline. He did not publish any fiction for the next eight years, writing only two nonfiction works—*Fear and Trembling* (1932) and *A Calendar of Saints for Unbelievers* (1933).

Returning to New York City in 1934, Wescott regained critical acclaim with the publication of *The Pilgrim Hawk* in 1940. *Pilgrim Hawk*, a novelette of a little over 100 pages, recounts a single afternoon involving an aged bachelor (an expatriate novelist) and a married couple. Its central image, a pet falcon, is emblematic of the bachelor's feeling towards marriage. A London *Times* reviewer described it as a haunting, poetic, compressed story of love and art, freedom and captivity. An intriguing tale, *The Pilgrim Hawk* stands as the "culmination of his career as a fiction writer and, arguably, as his one authentic masterpiece."

*Apartment in Athens* (1945), the account of a Greek family forced to house a German soldier during World War II, did not fare quite as well. After the publication of *Apartment in Athens*, Wescott stopped writing novels, opting for an unbroken forty-year silence. Rueckert wrote that "Any explanation of Wescott's diminishing career is probably psychological and personal" and we are led to conclude that the answer ultimately lay only within the novelist himself. Most critics believe Wescott wrote at least two other novels that he never published. He did write essays about his association with figures such as Katherine Anne Porter, Somerset Maugham, and Colette, published in *Images of Truth: Remembrances and Criticism* (1962). Although *Grandmothers* was reprinted in 1986, Wescott did not create a sustained body of work and thus occupies a "minor place in the literary history of our time."

PRINCIPAL WORKS: Apple of the Eye, 1924; Grandmothers, 1927; Good-bye Wisconsin, 1928; Babe's Bed, 1931; Calendar of Saints for Unbelievers, 1933; Fear and Trembling, 1932; The Pilgrim Hawk, 1940; Apartment in Athens, 1945; Images of Truth, 1972.

ABOUT: The autobiographical material quoted above was written for Twentieth Century Authors 1942, and Twentieth Century Authors First Supplement 1955; Johnson, I. Glenway Wescott: The Paradox of Voice, 1971; Rueckert, W. H. Glenway Wescott, 1965. *Periodicals*—Atlantic October 1927; Books September 23, 1928; Commonweal 1962; New York Times February 24, 1987.

## WEST, ANTHONY (PANTHER) (August 5, 1914–December 27, 1987), English novelist, critic and biographer, was born in Hunstanton, Norfolk, the son of two writers, H. G. Wells and Rebecca West. His book about his father, *H. G. Wells: Aspects of a Life*, is also a partial biography of his mother. (This is the source of all the quotations in this profile, except those otherwise attributed.)

H. G. Wells's meetings with Rebecca West were elaborately and almost farcically discreet. When she became pregnant and refused an abortion, he

installed her in rented rooms in the bleak seaside resort of Hunstanton, where she was unlikely to meet anyone they knew. From time to time, he visited her there. Jane Wells, H. G.'s wife, knew of the affair and the pregnancy, but accepted H. G.'s assurance that this was no more than one episode among many such.

Soon after the birth, Wells moved his mistress to an isolated hamlet not far from his own home. A series of unsatisfactory moves followed until Rebecca West settled herself and her son into a house at Leigh-on-Sea in Essex.

Anthony West was educated at Stowe School, in Buckinghamshire, where he was an undistinguished student. He makes only a few references to himself in his biography of his father. In one of these, he recalls himself at fourteen, staying with

Wells and his current mistress Odette Keun at Lou Pidou, their house near Nice. He was shy and "very uncertain of my sexual identity." At about the same time, in 1928, West was formally adopted by his mother—a move which he believed deprived him of a paternal "pedigree." Soon after, he became ill with tuberculosis. He makes much of the fact that, while his mother prophesied doom, Wells came to the rescue, giving him hope and energy in their "first moment of man-to-man complicity." West was packed off to a sanitarium in Norfolk, where he recovered. He had a breakdown at eighteen, and underwent psychoanalysis with Hanns Sachs, a colleague of Freud's.

Hoping to be a painter, West studied for a time at the Central School of Arts and Crafts in London. Finding no success in that field, he spent some years traveling around the world. He was married in 1936 to Katharine Church, an artist, with whom he had a son and a daughter before they divorced. In 1937 he began to review for the *New Statesman and Nation*, becoming the magazine's regular reviewer of new fiction. It was about this time that there began "an era of frankness and plain speaking" between West and his father "in which I learned a great deal about him that led me to love and respect him." Disqualified from military service by his history of tuberculosis, West joined the British Broadcasting Corporation. He worked as an editor on the Far Eastern Desk in 1943–1945, and with the Japanese Service in 1945–1947. Jane Wells had died in 1927, and by that time H. G., himself ill with cancer and diabetes, was living alone in an elegant house overlooking Regent's Park. This was around the corner from Broadcasting House, and West moved into the flat at the end of his father's back garden.

Wells died soon afterwards. Not long after that, West decided that he must write his own account of Wells's life, to keep the record straight "of what my father had been." Many years were to pass before he completed that task, though much of what he wrote in the interim was marked by his preoccupation with his parents.

Encouraged by his friend Graham Greene, West left the BBC in 1947 to work on his first novel, *On a Dark Night*, called in America *The Vintage*. It centers on an English lawyer, a liberal humanist softened by privilege, who commits suicide after taking part in the Nuremberg trials. Arriving in the next world, he finds that he is sharing it with the Nazi war criminal whom he had helped to condemn to death. Flashbacks to the earlier lives of both men lead to the conclusion, as one reviewer wrote in the *Times Literary Supplement*, "that hell is made up merely of human falsehoods and evasions; and that heaven may be gained by the acceptance of moral responsibility." Not everyone accepted the equating of the Nazi's terrible and premeditated crimes with the lawyer's sins of selfishness and hedonism, but the book was generally well received on both sides of the Atlantic as a "sensitive and interesting first novel" (*Commonweal*). It brought West a Houghton Mifflin literary fellowship.

A cooler reception greeted *Another Kind*, which examined the tangled affairs of its architect hero and took a gloomy view of a future Britain in which social breakdown is followed by civil war. A critic in the *New Republic* termed it "a silly and irritating book," but softened the opprobrium by noting that "West has talent, originality and brains."

The book appeared in 1951, as did a study of D. H. Lawrence. A year before West had emigrated to the United States, where he joined the staff of the *New Yorker*, which had published much of his mother's reportage from around the world. In 1952 he married Lily Dulany Emmet.

West's third novel, the autobiographical *Heritage*, is about Richard Savage, an illegitimate boy who grows up to be a happy man, in spite of a childhood divided between famous and self-absorbed parents, one an actress, the other a writer. The protagonist's name evoked Richard Savage, the eighteenth-century poet who had claimed to be the bastard son of the Countess of Macclesfield. Critics praised its maturity and balance, its avoidance of self-pity. The *Chicago Sunday Tribune* reviewer found it "a penetrating, amusing, often satirical, often affectionate picture of highly individualistic human beings." The novel appeared in 1955, but only in the United States. Rebecca West threatened to sue anyone who published it in England. She died in 1983, and *Heritage* came out in England the following year, with an introduction by Anthony West which expressed his resentment toward her.

*The Trend Is Up*, West's only novel with an American setting, tells the story of the ambitious son of a Boston banking family who sets himself to make a million and does so, but at dreadful emotional cost to himself, his wife, and his children. Its reception was mixed but generally negative. The *Commonweal* reviewer called it "stuffed with 'fact,' crammed with money and sex" and seeking "to overwhelm with an abundance of machine-tooled 'authenticity.'"

*David Rees, Among Others*, an autobiographical sequence of related stories, some originally published in the *New Yorker* is set in England during World War I and the next two decades. It follows its young hero through a childhood troubled by the mystery of his illegitimate birth, unhappy days at boarding school, and an attack of tuberculosis, to his first love affair.

Some of West's *New Yorker* reviews and essays were collected in *Principles and Persuasions*. J. W. Aldridge in the *New York Times* (1957) was reminded of Edmund Wilson by these vigorous essays—"just about the only survivors we have in the genre of the literate long review done regularly by an educated critic." *Mortal Wounds* assembles psychological studies of "three tormented women," all "mortally wounded" in childhood by the denial of love: Madame de Staël, Madame de Charrière and George Sand.

West retired from the *New Yorker* in 1972, thereafter concentrating mainly on *H. G. Wells: Aspects of a Life*. It appeared in 1984, the year after his mother's death. Many reviewers commented on West's obvious hatred of her. This spoiled his account for some; others, though, found it witty and convincing. The *Los Angeles Times* reviewer concluded that "at seventy, Anthony West never has got over his parents. The pain and allure of their relationship to each other—and their lack of a relationship to him—have overshadowed his life."

PRINCIPAL WORKS: *Fiction*—On a Dark Night, 1949 (in U.S.: The Vintage); Another Kind, 1951; Heritage, 1955; The Trend Is Up, 1960; David Rees, Among Others, 1970. *Biography and criticism*—D. H. Lawrence, 1951; Principles and Persuasions, 1957 (essays and reviews); Mortal Wounds: The Lives of Three Tormented Women, 1973; John Piper, 1979; H. G. Wells: Aspects of a Life, 1984. *Other*—Gloucestershire, 1939; The Crusades, 1955 (juvenile); Elizabethan England, 1965. *As editor*—The Galsworthy Reader, 1968.

ABOUT: about Anthony West.) Contemporary Authors New Revision Series 19, 1987; Dictionary of Literary Biography vol. 15 1983; West, A. H. G. Wells, 1984; Who's Who 1984. *Periodicals*—Chicago Sunday Tribune October 2, 1955; Commonweal February 10, 1950; Los Angeles Times May 9, 1984; New Republic May 26, 1952; New York Review of Books March 1, 1984; New York Times March 31, 1957; December 28, 1987; Observer October 2, 1955; Publishers Weekly April 20, 1984; Saturday Review of Literature January 14, 1950.

**WEST, EDWARD SACKVILLE-.** See **SACKVILLE-WEST, EDWARD**

**WEST, (MARY) JESSAMYN** (July 18, 1902–February 23, 1984), American novelist, short story writer, librettist, essayist, playwright, and poet, was born near Mt. Vernon, Indiana, the oldest of four children of Eldo Ray and Grace Anna (Milhous) West. She grew up on a lemon grove in Yorba Linda, Orange County, California, operated by her father. (Through her mother, she was a cousin of President Nixon, born in Yorba Linda.) An avid reader and thoughtful child who even in early adolescence kept a notebook of story ideas, West was greatly influenced by her mother's Quaker family.

She attended school in nearby Fullerton and Whittier College. Immediately after graduation she married Harry Maxwell McPherson, also a Quaker, who later became a professor of education at the University of California and a superintendent of schools. For one year, West taught in a one-room schoolhouse; then she served as society editor for the *Yorba Linda Star*. After spending the summer of 1929 at Oxford University, she returned to the University of California, Berkeley, to pursue a Ph.D. in English literature. As the completion of her program neared, she suffered a hemorrhage and was diagnosed with advanced tuberculosis, a condition which at the time was almost always fatal. After two years in a sanatorium she was discharged to her family's care.

According to West, her mother saved her by caring for her both physically and spiritually, plying her with food and amusing her with tales of her

own life as a child in a close-knit Quaker community. The Quaker beliefs, her mother's lovely and
lively stories of an earlier time, and her long illness
were the pivotal influences on her early writing;
she drew inspiration and information from the former two and opportunity from the latter. She began
to write and embellish some of her mother's tales
and was encouraged by her husband to submit
them. Immediately, these first stories were accepted by the *Atlantic Monthly*, *Harper's*, and other
magazines.

These gentle, pastoral tales, which wove a rich,
bright tapestry of rural life, revolved around the
lives of Jess and Eliza Birdwell. They were collected in *The Friendly Persuasion*, which was widely
praised. Hailed for the grace and subtlety of her
prose, West sold the screen rights to Frank Capra,
and set to work on her first novel, *The Witch Diggers*. Here she demonstrated her vigor and versatility. Few writers of the early fifties empowered
female characters to take action in their own lives,
and recognize the disaster that ensues if they make
the incorrect decision—as Cate Conboy does in *The
Witch Diggers*. Eudora Welty called *The Witch
Diggers* "a physical panorama concerned morally
with man's infatuation with plans and calculations,
from the noblest of them to the maddest" (*New
York Times Book Review*).

Next, West turned to the essay form in *Love Is
Not What You Think* to explore the idea that the
heart does not answer to logic or expedience. The
novel *South of the Angels*, considered by the *Atlantic* to be "of Chaucerian dimension," received
mixed reviews. Set in the familiar territory of farm
life in California, the book explores the human connection among a large cast of characters.

Despite her initial reputation as a writer of
charming, light stories, West tackled many of the
problematic issues of modern life, including abortion, infidelity, homosexuality, and murder. In *A
Matter of Time*, West explored a topic she was to
revisit in both fiction and nonfiction, the morality
of assisted suicide. In the book, two sisters, one of
whom is dying of cancer, review their lives in the
process of planning a death. *A Matter of Time*, like
most of West's fiction, is based on familial events,
in this case the terminal illness and death of her sister, Carmen Clara West.

In West's final novel, *The State of Stony Lonesome*, she examines the psychology of a woman between adolescence and maturity, the period in
which self-assessment is forged into self-
knowledge.

PRINCIPAL WORKS: *Nonfiction*—To See the Dream, 1957; Love
Is Not What You Think, 1959 (in U.K.: A Woman's Love),
1960. *Drama*—A Mirror for the Sky, 1948. *Novels*—The
Witch Diggers, 1951; Little Men, 1954 (republished as The
Chile Kings, 1967; South of the Angels, 1960; A Matter of
Time, 1966; Leafy Rivers, 1967) The Massacre at Fall Creek,
1975; The Life I Really Loved, 1979; The State of Stony Lone-
some, 1984. *Short stories*—The Friendly Persuasion, 1982;
Cress Delahanty, 1953; Except for Me and Thee: A Compan-
ion to "The Friendly Persuasion" Crimson Ramblers of the
World, Farewell, 1970; The Collected Stories of Jessamyn
West, 1986.

ABOUT: Gleasner, D. Breakthrough; Women in Writing, 1959;

Muir, J. Famous Modern American Women Writers, 1959.
Shivers, A. S. Jessamyn West 1972. *Periodicals*—Atlantic July
1960; Critic Winter 1976; New York Times Book Review April
27, 1975; Publishers Weekly April 28, 1969.

**WEST, NATHANAEL** (October 17, 1902–
December 22, 1940), American novelist and screenplay writer, was born Nathan Weinstein in New
York City, the son of Max Weinstein, a construction
contractor, and Anna (Wallenstein) Weinstein. In
hopes that his son would enter the successful family
business, West's father gave him several popular
Horatio Alger novels to read as a young boy—a way
to wealth that he later parodied in *A Cool Million*.

As a young man West showed little ambition. He
dropped out of high school but applied to Tufts
University (which he attended briefly in 1921) using falsified academic records. He used the same
trick successfully to gain admission to Brown University. There he discovered literature and began
writing short surrealistic sketches which he later
collected as the novel *The Dream Life of Balso
Snell*. He also gained a reputation as a wit, spending
far more time socializing than studying and attending classes. Nevertheless, he graduated from Brown
with a Ph.B. degree in 1924.

During the 1920s West worked occasionally for
his father's business. In 1926 he changed his name
legally. In the following year his father funded a
trip to France, where for a few months he mixed
with expatriate writers in Paris. When he returned
to New York City he gained employment (again
through family connections) managing residence
hotels: Kenmore Hall from 1927 to 1930 and the
Sutton Club Hotel from 1930 to 1933. In these jobs
West was able to assist other writers—such as Dashiell Hammett, Lillian Hellman, Erskine Caldwell,
and Edmund Wilson—by quietly offering them
free housing. With the publication of his own first
novel, *The Dream Life of Balso Snell*, a fantasy
about western civilization set in the innards of the
Trojan horse, West also benefited from exchanges
of ideas and encouragement from other artists. Hotel life provided him with numerous anecdotes, often vivid and bizarre.

In sporadic residence at one hotel was the satirist
S. J. Perelman, who married West's sister. Perelman introduced West to a newspaper advice columnist, who showed the two men a collection of
letters in the hope that Perelman would write a
stage comedy based on them. Instead, West was inspired to begin *Miss Lonelyhearts*, a novel whose
columnist protagonist becomes emotionally and
spiritually entangled in the lives of the people to
whom he gives advice. Mixing savage satire and
bleak humor, West memorably presented the modern results of an attempt to live by compassionate
ideals. The advice columnist is the therapist, priest,
and messiah to those alienated and in pain, but is
overwhelmed by the misery he encounters in the
numerous daily letters "stamped from the dough of
suffering with a heart-shaped cookie knife." The
world about him is marked by violence, decay, and
emptiness:

. . . the gray sky looked as if it had been rubbed with

a soiled eraser. It held no angels, flaming crosses, olive-bearing doves, wheels within wheels. Only a newspaper struggled in the air like a kite with a broken spine.

Moreover, in his own life he is unable to believe in and live by the help and hope that he offers others.

> The walls were bare except for an ivory Christ that hung opposite the foot of the bed. He had removed the figure from the cross to which it had been fastened and had nailed it to the wall with large spikes. But the desired effect had not been obtained. Instead of writhing, the Christ remained calmly decorative.

Despite generally encouraging reviews, the book sold poorly, and led the author to doubt his ability as an artist and as a self-sustaining writer. It later came to be considered a classic.

In the early 1930s West was also involved with a pair of literary magazines which did not thrive. When Columbia Pictures offered him work as a screenplay writer in 1933 he moved to Hollywood, but within a year was unemployed. His third novel, *A Cool Million*, was an attack on the optimistic rags-to-riches themes of the American dream. The reviews were mixed, and the reading public showed little interest in the book. But when the film rights to the novel were purchased in 1935, West returned to California to attempt to find work again as a script writer. In the year before he found employment he eked out a precarious life, often supported by Perelman. West lived among the riff-raff and outcasts of Los Angeles and put together a collection of their slang. Finally he got work at Republic Pictures, a low-budget studio which made formula films. The assignments there, and later at RKO and Universal, were unimaginative but also unexacting, giving West the time, energy, and money to continue as a writer of fiction. *The Day of the Locust*, his fourth, last, and greatest novel, captured the Hollywood of second-rate actors, technicians, laborers, and hack designers and writers, not that of the glamorous stars, directors, and producers. It is the story of Tod Hackett, who comes to California in hopes of a career as a scenic artist but soon joins (as West had done) those living on the fringes of the film industry. Tod's work on a film called "The Burning of Los Angeles" turns prophetic: the disenchanted and dispossessed men and women around him assuage their frustration and despair in an apocalyptic orgy of violence. The critics were mostly enthusiastic about the novel but it, too, failed commercially.

Despite such recurring setbacks to his sense of identity and achievement as a writer, West was, by the late 1930s, doing relatively well working on scripts for mostly minor films. In April 1940 he married Eileen McKenney, the subject of Ruth McKenney's popular book *My Sister Eileen*, and bought a house in the Hollywood hills. In December of that year the two were killed in a car accident near El Centro, when West failed to notice a stoplight. His fiction did not develop a following or attract serious literary investigation until some years after his death. Even though he focused on issues distinctly modern and inherently American, the macabre irony and brutal hopelessness that permeate his writing tended to discourage readers. As Leslie Fiedler noted, however, this is his very strength as a writer: "Putting down a book by West, a reader is not sure whether he has been presented with a nightmare endowed with the conviction of actuality or with actuality distorted into the semblance of a nightmare; but in either case, he has the sense that he has been presented with a view of a world in which, incredibly, he lives."

PRINCIPAL WORKS: *Novels*—The Dream Life of Balso Snell, 1931; Miss Lonelyhearts, 1933; A Cool Million, 1934; The Day of the Locust, 1939. *Drama*—(with J. Schrank) Good Hunting, 1938. *Collection*—The Complete Works of Nathanael West, 1978. *Screenplays*—(with J. Natteford) Ticket to Paradise, 1936; (with L. Cole and S. Ornitz) Follow Your Heart, 1936; (with L. Cole) The President's Mystery, 1936; Rhythm in the Clouds, 1937; (with S. Ornitz) It Could Happen to You, 1937; Born to Be Wild, 1938; (with J. Cady and D. Trumbo) Five Came Back, 1939; I Stole a Million, 1939; (with W. Bolton) The Spirit of Culver, 1939; Men Against the Sky, 1940; Let's Make Music, 1940.

ABOUT: Bloom, H. (ed.) Nathanael West: Modern Critical Views, 1986; Bloom, H. (ed.) Nathanael West's Miss Lonelyhearts, 1987; Comerchero, V. Nathanael West, 1964; Dardis, T. Some Time in the Sun, 1981; Fiedler, L. Love and Death in the American Novel, 1966; Hamilton, I. Writers in Hollywood, 1990; Hyman, S. E. Nathanael West, 1962; Light, J. F. Nathanael West, rev. ed., 1971; Long, R. E. Nathanael West, 1985; Madden, D. (ed.) Nathanael West: The Cheaters and the Cheated: A Collection of Critical Essays, 1973; Malin, I. Nathanael West's Novels, 1972; Martin, J. Nathanael West, 1970; Martin, J. (ed.) Nathanael West: A Collection of Critical Essays, 1971; Reid, R. The Fiction of Nathanael West, 1967; Widmer, K. Nathanael West, 1982; Wisker, A. The Writings of Nathanael West, 1990. *Bibliography*—White, W. Nathanael West: A Comprehensive Bibliography, 1975. *Periodicals*—Atlantic September 1950, October 1970; CLA Journal March 1991; College Literature Fall 1989; Hudson Review Winter 1951; Journal of American Culture Fall 1986; Kenyon Review Autumn 1961; Massachusetts Review Winter/Spring 1965; MELUS Winter 1988; Modern Fiction Studies Summer 1974, Summer 1990; New York Times December 23, 1940; New York Times Book Review May 12, 1957; December 23, 1990; New York Times Magazine June 2, 1974; Newsweek September 4, 1950; May 13, 1957; June 29, 1970; Saturday Review May 11, 1957; June 27, 1970; South Atlantic Quarterly Summer 1984; Studies in Short Fiction Winter 1992; Theatre Arts August 1951; Time June 17, 1957; August 17, 1970.

## "WEST, REBECCA" (pseudonym of CECILY ISABEL FAIRFIELD)

(December 21, 1892–March 15, 1983), English novelist and journalist, was born in Paddington, London, the youngest of three sisters. Her father, Charles Fairfield, was Irish and her mother, Isabella Mackenzie, a Scot. West's early childhood was spent in Streatham, south London. Fairfield, a journalist who wrote for the *Melbourne Argus* and the *Glasgow Herald*, was frequently away from home. In 1901, due to declining prospects, he gave up journalism, abandoned his family, and sailed to Sierre Leone to set up a pharmaceuticals factory. In consequence, the rest of Rebecca West's growing-up took place in Edinburgh, where she attended George Watson's Ladies' College. Her father's West African speculation came to nothing and he quickly returned to England, but never rejoined his family.

At the age of seventeen West (still known as Cecily Fairfield), together with her mother and sisters, left Edinburgh and moved back to London. She attended the Academy of Dramatic Art in Gower Street, but did not last the course, although she did work for a short time as an actress, being cast in summer productions on the south coast. By this time she had already shown a talent for writing, having won a Best Essay prize at school. In 1911 she  began writing, initially using her own name, for the *Freewoman*, a suffragist weekly edited by Dora Marsden. She adopted her pseudonym (from Ibsen's *Rosmersholm*) the following year, when she also began contributing to the socialist *Clarion* and, in a less political vein, to the *English Review*. West gave notice of her combative style in her first article for the *Freewoman*, a review of a book about the position of women in India, which opened with the arresting sentence: "There are two kinds of imperialists—imperialists and bloody imperialists." In subsequent articles she took on such stalwarts as the anti-suffrage novelist Mrs. Humphry Ward, and was nicknamed "Shaw in skirts" for her pains.

In September 1912 she wrote a stinging review of *Marriage* by H. G. Wells. She described his charm, as manifested in *Kipps*, as "slow and spinsterish." In the new book he was revealed as "the old maid among novelists; even the sex obsession that lay clotted on *Ann Veronica* and *The New Machiavelli* like cold white sauce was merely old maids' mania, the reaction towards the flesh of a mind too long absorbed in airships and colloids." This aspersion had far-reaching consequences, for it prompted the middle-aged Wells to seek out and seduce the young journalist. Their affair lasted several years and, early in its course, West gave birth to a son, named Anthony Panther West (the boy's middle name being taken from the amused term of endearment used by Wells for Rebecca).

First dispatched to have the child in secret on the Suffolk coast, and then set up in a furnished house in Hertfordshire, she continued to work as a journalist but also completed her first full-length book, a critical study of Henry James, published in 1916, the year of his death. The following year she moved to Leigh-on-Sea in Essex, but was frequently in London, trysting with Wells at their Pimlico lovenest. Her first (and shortest) novel, *The Return of the Soldier* (1918), exploited the new theme of shell-shock induced amnesia.

*The Judge*, her second novel, was longer and less carefully crafted. Its epigraph, "Every mother is a judge who sentences the children for the sins of the father" (invented by West herself), indicates the dour tone, influenced at least in part by the fact that the book was written while her affair with Wells was disintegrating.

Her third novel, *Sunflower*, was loosely based on her relationship with the man who replaced Wells—the Canadian press baron Lord Beaverbrook (fictionalized as Francis Pitt); it was left unfinished, although published posthumously.

Her next book was nonfiction. H. G. Wells was one of the first to criticize *The Strange Necessity*, writing to her: "You are ambitious and pretentious and you do not know the measure and quality of your power." The book is certainly rambling, self-questioning and histrionic. The *Times Literary Supplement*, while praising the author's intellect and vivacity, admitted that "she plunges frequently into obscurity."

Her next novel, *Harriet Hume*, her own favorite, was difficult to follow, according to L. P. Hartley, writing in the *Saturday Review*, and V. S. Pritchett, in the *Spectator*, said, "But for [West's] wit and the warm flashes of beauty in her intricate, slow-moving style, one might easily run aground halfway through her book and give up the struggle with its psychological shallows."

In 1930 West married Henry Andrews, a banker, and with him established a more settled routine at their home, Ibstone House, near High Wycombe. A short popular biography, *St. Augustine* (1933), was indicative of the new tenor in her life. Crisply written, the book applied a modern psychological manner to its spiritual subject matter. West explained Augustine's belief in predestination in terms of a parental rejection in infancy: Evelyn Underhill, reviewing the book in the *Spectator*, commented that West "lays bare [Augustine's] psychology with precision and wit; but leaves on one side the spirituality by which that difficult psychology was transformed."

*The Thinking Reed*, West's subsequent novel, is described by her biographer Victoria Glendinning as "the only funny novel she ever wrote." Dedicated to her husband, and written during the first five years of their marriage—the happiest time of her life, according to a statement she made in old age—it is a novel about a rich, calculating widow who marries for convenience and then falls in love with another. Soon after completing this novel West was sent to the Balkans by the British Council, on a lecture tour. She came back determined to write a book about Yugoslavia. The result was *Black Lamb and Grey Falcon*, and the timing of its publication (1941) matched the scale on which it was conceived. A book which defies summary, Diana Trilling called it in her *New York Times* obituary of West "surely one of the very greatest books of the last 50 years."

After this, the greater part of West's literary effort went into journalism, both long and short. Her next full-length book was *The Meaning of Treason* (revised as *The New Meaning of Treason* in 1964); written after attendance at the closing sessions of the Nuremberg trials. In it West sought to explain the motives that led men who, in certain aspects of their private lives, to be caring and humane, to behave in the public sphere like inhumane beasts. She found the reason in the decline of religion. "Those who have discarded the idea of a super-personal God and still desire an enduring friendship must look for it in those fields of life farthest removed from ordinary personal relationship, because human personality lacks endurance in any form of love." This bleak view reflected her own experience of personal affairs. The physical relationship between her and her husband had come to an end in the mid-thirties, and her son by Wells, Anthony, now felt an extreme animosity towards his mother. Anthony West wrote in *Heritage*: "The truth of how things were between my mother and myself was that from the time that I reached the age of puberty, and she came to the point of a final rupture with my father, she was minded to do me what hurt she could, and that she remained set in that determination as long as there was breath in her body to sustain her malice." Many readers were convinced that Anthony West did have good reason to complain.

In *The Fountain Overflows*, written about the same time as *Heritage*, Rebecca West produced a commercially successful and warmly Dickensian portrait of family life, based on her own relationship with her sisters. *The Birds Fall Down*, reflecting her continuing interest in treason, is also successful at the "good commercial" level.

West was made a Dame of the British Empire in 1959, and continued to play a prominent part in British letters during the sixties and seventies. She was a Booker Prize judge in its first and second years, and a lead reviewer for the *Sunday Telegraph*. Indeed, many feel that it is as a literary critic that West's intellect found best expression. *The Courts and the Castle*, a book of literary essays, remains one of her most stimulating titles. In her last years—the late seventies and early eighties—she enjoyed a revival of interest in her earlier work, when the novels were reprinted by the Virago Press. *The Young Rebecca*, edited by Jane Marcus in close collaboration with West, reprinted much of her youthful journalism. *This Real Night* and *Cousin Rosamund*, fragmentary sequels to *The Fountain Overflows*, were published in 1984 and 1985, respectively. An annotated bibliography by Jean Garrett Packer was published in 1991.

Carl Rollyson's 1996 biography *Rebecca West: A Life*, details her bitter relationship with her son, Anthony, who revealed their contentiousness in his 1984 biography of Wells, his father. Walter Kendrick, reviewing Rollyson's book in *The New York Times Book Review*, judged it a balanced account: "He provides enough evidence, pro and con, for his readers to make up their own minds. In the end, posterity's equivocal verdict on West seems exactly appropriate," he wrote.

PRINCIPAL WORKS: *Fiction*—The Return of the Soldier, 1918; The Judge, 1922; Harriet Hume, 1929; The Harsh Voice, 1935; The Thinking Reed, 1936; The Fountain Overflows, 1956; The Birds Fall Down, 1966; This Real Night, 1984; Cousin Rosamund, 1985; Sunflower, 1986. *Nonfiction*—Henry James, 1916; The Strange Necessity, 1928; Ending in Earnest, 1931; St. Augustine, 1933; Black Lamb and Grey Falcon, 1941; The Meaning of Treason, 1947 (rev. ed. The New Meaning of Treason, 1964); A Train of Powder, 1955; The Court and the Castle, 1958.

ABOUT: Contemporary Authors, vol. 109 1983; Deakin, M. F. Rebecca West; Glendinning, V. Rebecca West, A Life; Ray, G. N. H. G. Wells and Rebecca West, 1974; Rollyson, C. Rebecca West: A Life, 1996; Schlueter, P. and J. An Encyclopaedia of British Women Writers, 1988; Todd, J. M. British Women Writers, 1989; West, A. P. H. G. Wells: Aspects of a Life, 1984; West R. Family Memoirs, 1988; Who's Who 1983–1984. *Periodicals*—Freewoman September 19, 1912; The New Republic October 19, 1987; New Statesman August 11, 1928; New York Times March 16, 1983; New York Times Book Review, October 27, 1966; Saturday Review of Literature November 10, 1928; Scotsman October 16, 1907; Spectator February 10, 1933; Times Literary Supplement August 2, 1928; December 21, 1973.

**WEST, VICTORIA SACKVILLE-.** See **SACKVILLE-WEST, VICTORIA**

**WESTERMARCK, EDVARD ALEXANDER** (November 20, 1862–September 3, 1939), Finnish sociologist, social analyst, and anthropologist, was born in Helsingfors (Helsinki), the son of Nils Christian Westermarck, who taught Latin at the University of Finland, and the former Constance Blomqvist, daughter of the university librarian. He was educated at the Swedish lyceum and then at the university, where he gained his degrees in philosophy. He taught at the University of Finland (1984) and at the University of Abo in Helsinki (1894–1935). His interest in the institution of marriage, which he made it his life's work to investigate, and upon which subject he produced his massive (continually revised, and widely translated) *The History of Human Marriage*, began early. He was able to visit England in 1887 to study at the British Museum, and as a result wrote his dissertation *The Origins of Human Marriage*. He was married, and had a son, but the details and dates, evidently by his own wish, are scant. He managed, to the envy of many of his colleagues, to hold down two simultaneous jobs: Professor of Sociology at the University of London (1907–19), and an equivalent position in the University at Helsinki. He lived for much of his time in Surrey, where he was well acquainted with English men of letters such as Edmund Gosse. He lived in Morocco from 1898 until 1902, where he observed marriage customs.

Widely celebrated as an expert on marriage, Westermarck is now considered of historical interest only. Martin Seymour-Smith, in *Sex and Society*, gave him credit for having helped to "render untenable" the "evolutionary view" taken, in the work of Lewis Henry Morgan and J. F. MacLennan, that society "progressed" from a state of "universal promiscuity" to "matriarchy." Seymour-Smith maintained that *The History of Human Marriage* is a "landmark" because it helped to demonstrate that the "matriarchate was not a stage of human development and that universal promiscuity was a myth." However, Seymour-Smith also pointed out that, while Westermarck's view of the incest taboo—that "familiarity breeds contempt"—fails to account for all the facts, it is "not without merit." As a philosopher trying to replace conventional ethics with what was once called "ethical subjectivism" (or "relativism"), Westermarck could be said to have anticipated a later and more scientific approach. His work, too, was thorough and exhaustive in its treatment of facts. He wrote in both English and Finnish.

PRINCIPAL WORKS: *Sociology and philosophy*—The Origin of Human Marriage, 1889; The History of Human Marriage, 1891, rev. ed. 1921; The Origin and Development of the Moral Idea, 1906–1908; Marriage Cermonies in Morocco, 1914; The Origins of Sexual Modesy, 1921; Ritual and Belief in Morocco,

1926; A Short History of Marriage, 1926 (abridged as Marriage, 1929); The Goodness of Gods, 1926; Wit and Wisdom in Morocco: A Study of Native Proverbs, 1930; Ethical Relativity, 1932; Early Beliefs and Their Social Influence, 1932; Pagan Survivals in Mohammedan Civilisation, 1933; Three Essays on Sex and Marriage, 1934; The Future of Marriage in Western Civilisation, 1936; Christianity and Morals, 1939. Autobiography—Memories of My Life (tr. A. Barwell) 1929.

ABOUT: Seymour-Smith, M. Sex and Society, 1976; Devine, E., Vinson, J., Held, M., and Walsh, G. (eds.) Thinkers of the Twentieth Century, 1985. Periodicals—Acta Sociological Vol. 25, 1982; British Journal of Sociology Summer 1984.

## WESTMACOTT, MARY. See CHRISTIE, AGATHA

## WESTON, CHRISTINE (GOUTIERE) (August 31, 1904–May 3, 1989), Anglo-American novelist and short story writer, wrote: "I was born in Unao, in the United Provinces of India. There were five of us—three boys and two girls. My parents [Georges and Alicia (Wintle) Goutiere] were born in India; my father's people were French indigo-planters, my mother the daughter of an English army officer. For many years my father, who had become a naturalised Englishman, was an officer in the Indian Imperial Police. Later he went to London, where he retired from the Police and studied for the bar. He returned to India and practised as a barrister until his death in 1921. Except for brief visits to England as a child I lived in India until my marriage in 1923. The country of one's childhood is always predominant in one's memory: India is a beautiful, brown, kindly land, and notwithstanding all the perils of life in the tropics, it is a fine country for any child to grow up in. I was fortunate, too, in my parents, whose attitude towards the natives was quite different from the attitude of most English people.

"The war of 1914 intervened between me and the customary English education. My oldest brother was already in school in England: I was destined

for a convent in Bruges, Belgium, my younger brother for Douai College. We were to have sailed from India on the S.S. Persia, which was sunk by the Germans, I think early in 1915. My parents sent me to a convent school in the hills. It was a school run by English, German, and Irish nuns. My father, whose radical spirit had long since revolted against official discipline, apparently retained vestiges of his French Catholic upbringing. He hoped that his oldest daughter would acquire certain of the gentle and lady-like arts, amongst which he classed music and beautiful needle-work. I acquired neither. In fact I acquired absolutely nothing except the Catholic ritual and a desperate loathing for my teachers and most of my classmates. My aversion to convent life became chronic, and I kept running away until my parents withdrew me. I had been a peripatetic boarder for almost four years. I had learned to read at the age of

four and was writing stories and poems at four and a half. I marvel, now, at the almost anarchic freedom of those days. However, when much later my father discovered my taste for penny thrillers he offered me the use of his professional library, which included a whole series of famous English trials. I think this was during one of my legal winter holidays from the convent. I must have been about twelve. There are two books whose color, weight, shape and content are forever fixed in my memory: Plutarch's Lives and The Trial of Eugene Aram.

"As I grew up I helped my father in his law work. Our house was always filled with odds and ends of humanity. One might suppose that in a country so large and a society so diverse the net impression would be confused and blurred. On the contrary, every face and every personality emerged vivid in that strong light. I can still see the long, shady, pillared verandah outside my father's study. Rows of jutas (native shoes) left outside, like boats tied up to a wharf. In India people remove their shoes, not their hats, when they enter a house. From inside the great airy room came the chant of voices and the click of a typewriter where the Mohammedan clerk was taking down dispositions."

"In 1923 I married an American [Robert Weston] and came to the United States. I've lived in Maine ever since."

———

Christine Weston's best-known novel, Indigo drew comparisons from its first reviewers with E. M. Forster's A Passage to India. Set in India, it concerns four young friends from different backgrounds and nationalities. At the core of the plot is the issue of white bigotry and savagery as experienced by one of the four, the son of a Hindu lawyer. "Mrs. Weston has written a book that casts a spell—a mature and melancholy book that clarifies and explains the emotions, prejudices, and animosities that underlie the Indian crisis," Orville Prescott wrote in the Yale Review. "But, although Indigo is enlightening, it is burdened with fate, defeat, frustration, and tragedy; it is sad with the sorrow of all the ages, weary and profoundly pessimistic."

In 1947 Weston published There and Then, a collection of short stories set in India. Her next book, the novel The World Is a Bridge, takes place in India at the very end of the British occupation and records the tumultuous effect of withdrawal upon Hindu and Moslem alike. E. M. Forster himself reviewed this novel for the New York Times (March 26, 1950): "Mrs. Weston writes seriously, carefully, compassionately; she is not interested in the glamorous East or in the boosting of this or that political creed; she writes for those who are already emotionally involved in the country and who love it."

Most of Weston's short stories first appeared in the New Yorker magazine. In 1940 she was awarded a Guggenheim Fellowship.

PRINCIPAL WORKS: Novels—Be Thou the Bride, 1940; The Devil's Foot, 1942; Indigo, 1943; The Dark Wood, 1946; The World Is a Bridge, 1950; The Wise Children, 1957; The Hoopoe, 1970. Short stories—There and Then, 1947. Juvenile—

Bhimsa, the Dancing Bear, 1945; Ceylon, 1960; Afghanistan, 1962.

ABOUT: The autobiographical material quoted above was written for Twentieth Century Authors First Supplement, 1955. *Periodicals*—New York Times March 26, 1950; May 6 1989; Yale Review Winter 1944.

**WEYER, MAURICE CONSTANTIN-.** See CONSTANTIN-WEYER, MAURICE

**WEYGANDT, CORNELIUS** (December 13, 1871–July 31, 1957), American regionalist, essayist, and critic, wrote: "Cornelius Weygandt has found the material of his writing, half of it in the study, half of it on the road in back country places. Born in Germantown, Pennsylvania, then a country town with stores in which you could buy everything from a needle to an anchor, he fell in young boyhood into the hands of older boys who knew birds. His mother had been born on a farm in Chester County, Pennsylvania, and his uncles and aunts told him much of the phases of life on that hill farm with its great barn and grist mill. All his life he has continued the studies of the countryside begun in childhood. The names of all country things have always fascinated him, Sheldon pears and undershot water wheels, Dominique hens and merino sheep, springhouses and covered wooden bridges and the like.

"His father's books and his grandfather's, Carlyle and Thackeray, Wordsworth and Ossian, were at hand always. He saw Longfellow's brother and

Whitman daily on the streets of Germantown, and writing about the Pennsylvania countryside became the purpose of his life while he was a boy at college. He graduated from the University of Pennsylvania in 1891 Ph.D., 1901. He had newspaper experience [on the Philadelphia *Record* and *Evening Telegraph*] from 1892 to 1897. Since the latter year he has been a teacher at Pennsylvania. He is now Professor of English literature.

"He married Sara Matlack Roberts in 1900. They have a son and a daughter. He lives in Philadelphia with a summer home in the White Mountains. His books on the American scene are concerned with folklore and objects of art and passing phases of American civilization."

---

Cornelius Weygandt continued to teach at the University of Pennsylvania, in 1908 becoming professor of English literature there. Four years later he was in Dublin, researching the book published in 1913 as *Irish Plays and Playwrights*. It was a thorough account of the Irish literary renaissance and its effects on the theater, the first by an American. There were critical-biographical chapters on Yeats, Lady Gregory, Synge and others prominent in the movement, and detailed accounts of their plays. Joyce Kilmer wrote that Weygandt "had three qualifications for writing about the present generation of Irish dramatists—he is informed, he is enthusiastic, and he is not Irish" (*New York Times*, 1913). This still useful book was last republished as recently as 1979.

Another work, *A Century of the English Novel*, contained Weygandt's sometimes unorthodox essays on writers from the heyday of Scott to the death of Conrad. It was found both entertaining and illuminating, though some critics thought it dealt too briefly with too many authors. Books on Tennyson and Yeats were less accomplished.

Although his writings on literature were all well received, Weygandt reached a larger audience with the dozen books he published about his native Pennsylvania and New Hampshire, where he spent his summers. *The Red Hills*, the first of these, centers on the lives and customs of the Pennsylvania Dutch, focusing on the region's pottery, of which Weygandt was a collector. In *Wissahickon Hills* he lovingly evokes the people, birds, and flowers of the valley of the Wissahickon, north of Philadelphia, where he had wandered from childhood. A reviewer in the *New York Times* (1931) wrote that "Weygandt's narrative flows along, with ease and simplicity, but with wide horizoned curiosity and love, in rich mellow English."

In *The White Hills*, Weygandt turned for the first time to New Hampshire, in chapters each dedicated to a friend or relation. "He loves the White Mountains," wrote Lewis Gannett, "particularly the Sandwich country, the quaint ways of local speech, the bear stories of the old men, the gray houses, the stone wall, the local names, the old people, their Puritan tradition. If his book is sometimes sentimental, it is with a persuasive, communicated sentiment" (*New York Herald Tribune*).

Shamelessly nostalgic, and written in a leisurely old-fashioned prose, Weygandt's bucolic essays were not for all tastes. Henry Tetlow, discussing *The Dutch Country* in *Commonweal*, said: "It is definitely not my book. Partly because I stomach Weygandt's writing only with the greatest difficulty, but mainly because I am getting a little tired of the Pennsylvania Dutch cult." A *New Yorker* reviewer of *Heart of New Hampshire* was similarly unenthusiastic about Weygandt's style, which he felt suggested "a badly mixed concoction made up of one part Thoreau, one part E. B. White, and one part county archivist, with a dash of Robert Frost."

In spite of such criticisms, Weygandt had a devoted following among older readers. He retired in 1942 as professor emeritus, with honorary doctorates from Franklin and Marshall College and Susquehanna University, as well as his own. In his autobiography, *On the Edge of Evening*, he concluded: "I have had enough of many things in life, of the city, the theater, of lecturing. I have not had enough of writing, of listening to music, of country contentments. I hope I am privileged to live on the Wissahickon Hills to the end. I could not be happy where there are houses just across the street and lack of elbow room about the house. The little things, as all my life long, are still the most of life to me."

PRINCIPAL WORKS: *Literary criticism*—Irish Plays and Playwrights, 1913; A Century of the English Novel, 1925; Tuesdays at Ten, 1928 (essays and lectures); The Time of Tennyson: English Victorian Poetry as It Affected America, 1936; The Time of Yeats, 1937. *Americana*—The Red Hills, 1928; The Wissahickon Hills: Memories of Leisure Hours Out of Doors, 1930; A Passing America, 1932; The White Hills, 1934; The Blue Hills, 1936; New Hampshire Neighbors, 1937; Philadelphia Folks, 1938; The Dutch Country, 1939; Down Jersey, 1940; November Rowen, 1941; The Plenty of Pennsylvania, 1942; Heart of New Hampshire, 1944. *Autobiography*—On the Edge of Evening, 1946.

ABOUT: The autobiographical material quoted above was written for Twentieth Century Authors, 1942. Weygandt, C. On the Edge of Evening, 1946. *Periodicals*—Commonweal December 1, 1939; New York Herald Tribune May 26, 1934; New York Times March 2, 1913; February 22, 1931; August 2, 1957; New York July 1, 1944; Saturday Review of Literature August 3, 1946.

## *WEYMAN, STANLEY J(OHN) (August 7, 1855–April 10, 1928), English historical novelist, was born at Ludlow in Shropshire, the second son

of Thomas Weyman, a lawyer, and his wife, the former Mary Maria Black. He was educated at Shrewsbury School and at Christ Church, Oxford (1874–1877), where he gained second-class honors in Modern History. Once a very popular historical romancer, his *Collected Works* of 1911 took up twenty-one volumes, and he wrote five more books after that.

As a historical novelist, his characterization is rudimentary, even though he did have an occasional knack for evoking the atmosphere of a period or a place. His chief claim to fame is probably that Oscar Wilde, while in Reading Gaol, generously wanted to procure copies of his books, which he believed suitable, not for himself, but for his fellow inmates.

Weyman became a barrister, but was so indolent, nervous, and awkward in court—that he earned hardly anything. Then he picked up Henry White's *Massacre of St. Bartholomew*, and thought he would have a try at the genre. He wrote three books without success; then *A Gentleman of France*, after a poor start, suddenly came into demand owing to Andrew Lang's recommendation of it in a public speech. *Under the Red Robe*, an adventure set in the times of Cardinal Richlieu, was the most successful of all Weyman's books; it was both dramatized and filmed. The best, however, and his own favorite, was *Chippinge Borough*, set against the background of the passing of the First Reform Bill of 1832. The atmosphere is conjured up with some skill, and the melodrama is, for once, lacking. Yet the *New York Times* complained that it was too long, and that the "temptation to skip" was "overpowering."

PRINCIPAL WORKS: *Collected edition*—The Novels of Stanley Weyman, 21 vols., 1911. *Novels*—The House of the Wolf, 1890; The New Rector, 1891; The Story of Francis Cludde, 1891; A Gentleman of France, 1893; The Man in Black, 1894;

°WY mun

My Lady Rotha, 1894; Under the Red Robe, 1894; From the Memoirs of a Minister of France, 1895; The Red Cockade, 1894; The Castle Inn, 1898; Shrewsbury, 1898; Sophia, 1900; Count Hannibal, 1901; The Long Night, 1903; The Abbess of Vlaye, 1904; Starvecrow Farm, 1905; Chippinge Borough, 1906; The Wild Geese, 1908; The Great House, 1919; Ovington's Bank, 1922; The Traveller in the Fur Coat, 1924; Queen's Folly, 1925; The Lively Peggy, 1928. *Short stories*—In Kings' Byways, 1902; Laid Up in Lavender, 1907.

ABOUT: Baker, E. A. and Packman, J. A Guide to the Best Fiction, 1932; Dictionary of National Biography, 1922–1930, 1937; Feiling, K. In Christ Church Hall, 1960. *Periodicals*—New York Times December 1, 1906; Times (London) April 12, 1928.

## WHARTON, EDITH (NEWBOLD) (January 24, 1862–August 11, 1937), American novelist and short story writer, was born Edith Newbold Jones in New York, daughter of

George Frederic Jones and Lucretia Stevens Rhinelander Jones. The family moved in high society, and was well off, owing to its holdings in real estate. Young Edith was educated at home in the "proper" manner, and found this (she later wrote) "safe, guarded, monotonous." In her childhood, she spent a substantial number of years in Europe: in Italy, Spain, Germany, France, and England. She had wanted to be a writer from early on, and found much solace in her father's well-stocked library of the classics. Her mother paid for her youthful verses to be published, and the novelist and critic William Dean Howells published one of them in the *Atlantic*.

Wharton never, owing to the social position of which she was so bitterly satirical in her major novels, had to struggle much for recognition both as a novelist and as a woman. Wharton learned much from her friend Henry James, and he, for his part, did much to encourage her to express her femininity.

Wharton "came out" into society at the age of seventeen. In 1885 she married Edward (Teddy) Wharton, a man who was by no means of her type; he was a wealthy sportsman, selfish and neurotic, with little or no interest in his gifted wife; the marriage drove Edith into physical and mental torpor, fits of nausea, and depression. In the mid-nineties she broke down altogether, and had at one point to enter a sanatorium. The creative urge in her was frustrated, and she felt her specifically feminine genius to be stifled. She compensated by writing, with the architect Ogden Codman, a book on the innocuous subject of house decoration. In 1899 Scribners published her first fiction: a collection of stories called *The Greater Inclination*.

By this time neither wealth nor travel were enough to distract Wharton from the unhappiness of her marriage, and she was advised to ease her nervous tension by writing. She began publishing fiction that started to skirt around zones of experience that were supposed to be "forbidden" to women. She listened to the sage advice of Henry James:

"Don't pass it by—the immediate, the real, the only, the yours." She also recognized that James was right in dissuading her from continuing in the vein of the historical novel, which she had tried, with poor artistic results, in *The Valley of Decision*. She made a beginning on her first major novel: *The House of Mirth*.

James helped her to start to write with more confidence, and to make the difficult decision to break, mentally, with the male-centered assumptions of her past. Lily Bart, the New Yorker who is at the center of *The House of Mirth*, is torn between her moral sense and her delicacy, and the love of wealth and luxury. She triumphs and retains her morality and self-dignity—but declines into poverty and eventual death. She is ruined by the very society whose values—as she believed them to be—she strove to uphold. In reality, she is destroyed by its vulgarity and its hypocritical contempt for morality.

In 1906 Wharton settled permanently in France, selling her Lenox, Massachusetts home, "The Mount." Here, she met some of James's French literary friends; she also met a London *Times* correspondent, Morton Fullerton, and with him began a passionate affair that lasted for two years.

In 1911 Wharton published *Ethan Frome*, her most unusual novel. The story of an embittered farmer and his gothically miserable household of two complaining women, *Ethan Frome* contains a surprise, when the reader learns that things are not what they seem and that the crippled Frome and the invalid woman were once lovers about to run away from the shrewish wife who must now tend the broken body of her rival. Her next novel, *The Reef*, was perhaps the closest she ever came to the "Jamesian" novel. This was followed by *The Custom of the Country*, a somewhat allegorical study of the breakdown, morally and aesthetically, and the destruction by greed, of the New York society of Wharton's youth.

Wharton divorced Edward, now sunk into alcoholism, in 1912. He had, among other things, been embezzling her money to pay off his debts. World War I aroused her feelings, and she remained in Paris doing relief work. France awarded her its Cross of the Legion of Honour for this. Later she became the first woman to receive an honorary D. Litt. from Yale—and the Gold Medal of the National Institute of Arts and Letters. She published *Fighting France: from Dunkerque to Belfort* in 1915; *A Son at the Front*, not issued until 1923, was also on a war theme.

With the end of the war there also came a change, as with many writers of the time, in Wharton's focus and tone. Her divorce, too, had brought her a certain amount of creative freedom, as did her later love affairs. With these came an awareness of subsurface passion in her characters. In *The Age of Innocence* she illustrated these passions in conflict with societal codes, adding something new to the theme she had visited in *The House of Mirth*. The effort won her the Pulitzer Prize in 1921, and the distinction of being the first woman so honored.

(She would later win the prize for drama with her "The Old Maid" from the collection *Old New York*.) After this Wharton continued to publish both novels and short stories. Among these are such titles as *The Mother's Recompense* (1925), *The Glimpses of the Moon* (1922), and *The Children* (1928). Her final novel was left unfinished, but was completed by Marion Mainwaring. Hoping to make the transition as seamless as possible, Mainwaring was said to have copied over several of Wharton's original chapters in longhand in order to get a feel for the flow of words. The result was *The Buccaneers*, published in 1994. The story of four American girls, shunned by American society because their money is "too new" (a major stumbling block at the time), the book takes up the question again of what happens when societal duties and expectations are in direct conflict with personal preference, as was the case with Newland Archer and Ellen Olenska in *The Age of Innocence*. In *The Buccaneers*, however, Wharton seems to view the unspoken rules and regulations of society as much less dangerous to cross than she had in previous novels. The choosing of happiness over conformity results not in disaster but triumph. Several of Wharton's novels and stories, including *The Age of Innocence*, were adapted and dramatized for film.

As far as her short stories are concerned, Wharton's tales are carefully crafted and psychologically insightful. Perhaps her best known collection is *Old New York* (1924), four stories of four successive decades (the 1840s to the 1870s) in New York society, which are, aside from entertaining, useful as historical studies. She was also quite good at writing ghost stories, some of which are collected in *Ghosts* (1937).

In 1934 Wharton published her autobiography, *A Backward Glance*. The memoir was reissued in 1965 with an introduction by Louis Auchincloss. In it the author not only shares the stories of her childhood and other experiences, but also her views on American, English, and European society, as well as insights into the characters of many of her literary acquaintances.

Wharton continued to write up until the time of her death, at her villa in France. There is a collection of her papers at Yale University, and several volumes of her letters, as well as a few very good biographies, have been published.

PRINCIPAL WORKS: *Collections*—Collected Short Stories (ed. R. W. B. Lewis), 2 vols, 1967. *Fiction*—The Greater Inclination, 1899 (stories); The Touchstone, 1900 (long story); Crucial Instances, 1901 (stories); The Valley of Decision, 1902; Sanctuary, 1903; The Descent of Man, 1904 (stories); The House of Mirth, 1905; Madame de Teymes, 1907; The Fruit of the Tree, 1907; The Hermit and the Wild Woman, 1908 (stories); Tales of Men and Ghosts, 1910 (stories); Ethan Frome, 1911; The Reef, 1912; The Custom of the Country, 1913; Xingu, 1916 (stories); The Marne, 1918; The Age of Innocence, 1920; The Glimpses of the Moon, 1922; A Son at the Front, 1923; Old New York, 1924 (four stories); The Mother's Recompense, 1925; Here and Beyond, 1926 (stories); Twilight Sleep, 1927; The Children, 1928; Hudson River Bracketed. 1919; Certain People, 1930 (stories); The Gods Arrive, 1932; Human Nature, 1933 (stories); The World Over, 1936 (stories; The Buccaneers, 1938 (unfinished). *Poetry*—Verses, 1878; Artemis to Actaeon, 1909; Twelve Poems, 1926, *Other*—(with O. Codman) The

Decoration of Houses, 1897; Italian Gardens and Their Gardens, 1904; Italian Backgrounds, 1905; A Motor-Flight Through France, 1908; Fighting France, 1915; French Ways and Their Meaning, 1919; In Morocco, 1920; The Writing of Fiction, 1925; A Backward Glance, 1934. *Letters*—The Letters (ed. N. and R. W. B. Lewis), 1988; Henry James and Edith Wharton: Letters 1910–1915 (ed. L. H. Powers) 1990.

ABOUT: Ammons, E. Edith Wharton's Argument with America, 1980; Auchincloss, L. Edith Wharton, 1961; Bendixen, A. (ed.) Edith Wharton: New Critical Essays, 1992; Bloom, H. (ed.) Edith Wharton, 1986; Erlich, G. C. The Sexual Education of Edith Wharton, 1992; Ford, F. M. The March of Literature from Confucius to Modern Times, 1938; Howe, I. (ed.) Edith Wharton: A Collection of Critical Essays, 1963; James, H. Notes on Novelists, 1914; Lewis, R. W. B. Edith Wharton, 1975; Lubbock, P. A Portrait of Edith Wharton, 1947; Raphael, L. Edith Wharton's Prisoners of Shame, 1991; Saunders, C. E. Writing the Margins: Edith Wharton, Ellen Glasgow, and the Literary Tradition of the Ruined Woman, 1987; Showalter, E. (ed.) Modern American Writers, 1991; Walton, G. Edith Wharton: A Critical Interpretation, 1982; Vita-Finzi, P. Edith Wharton and the Art of Fiction, 1990; Wolff, C. G. A Feat of Words: The triumph of Edith Wharton. *Bibliography*—Garrison, S. Edith Wharton: A Descriptive Bibliography, 1990.

## WHEELER, WILLIAM MORTON (March 19, 1865–April 19, 1937), American entomologist and university professor, was born in Milwaukee, Wis-

consin, the son of Julius Morton Wheeler and Caroline Georgiana (Anderson) Wheeler. After completing his studies at the German-American Normal College, he was hired by Henry Augustus Ward's Natural Science Establishment in Rochester, New York. There he met and became friends with Carl Akeley, the "father" of modern taxidermy.

In 1890, while Wheeler was working with Akeley at the Milwaukee Public Museum, he became fellow and assistant in morphology at Clark University, where he studied and received his Ph.D in 1892 upon the completion of his thesis, "A Contribution to Insect Embryology." Shortly thereafter, he became an instructor at the University of Chicago. In 1899, he left Chicago to become a professor of zoology at the University of Texas, where he wrote nearly fifty papers on his principal subject—ants. His most notable publication of this period is *Ants: Their Structure, Development and Behavior* (1910). Critics at the time praised this work as one of the "most important contributions to etymology," being interesting to both naturalists and to the average reader. From this point on Wheeler's scientific pursuits were devoted almost entirely to the study of ants and their hierarchies.

In 1903 Wheeler became the curator of Invertebrate Zoology for the Museum of Natural History in New York City. His most important appointment came in 1908 when the Bussey Institution of Harvard University offered him a Professorship of Economic Entomology. From 1915 to 1929, Wheeler served as dean of the faculty of the Bussey Institution. He continued his research at Harvard until his death.

Wheeler's writings transcend mere biological analysis and deal with a wide variety of topics, including evolution, ecology, philosophy and behavior. While his books on entomology are not noted for the liveliness of their prose, he was able to convince his readership of his enthusiasm. Although Wheeler has more than 450 titles to his credit, his findings and conclusions failed to set any sort of precedent for research and scholarship.

Wheeler received four honorary doctorates as well as the Elliot Medal of the National Academy of Sciences and the Leidy Medal of the Philadelphia Academy of Natural Sciences.

PRINCIPAL WORKS: Ants; Their Structure, Development, and Behavior, 1910; Social Life Among the Insects, 1923; Foibles of Insects and Men, 1928; The Social Insects, Their Origin and Evolution, 1928; (with H. W. T. Barbour) The Lamarck Manuscripts at Harvard 1993.

ABOUT: National Academy of Sciences; Biographical Memoirs, 1938; Dictionary of American Biography, Suppl. 2, 1940. riodical—New York Times April 20, 1937.

## WHEELOCK, JOHN HALL (September 9, 1886—March 22, 1978), American poet and editor, wrote: "John Hall Wheelock was born at Far Rock-

away, Long Island, N.Y., the son of William Efner and Emily (Hall) Wheelock. His mother's father was a Presbyterian minister from Dublin; on his father's side his ancestry goes back to Ralph Wheelock, a classmate of Milton's at Cambridge, and the first Wheelock to come to America. Among his ancestors is Eleazar Wheelock, the founder of Dartmouth College.

"John Hall Wheelock began writing verse at an early age. At Harvard, from which he graduated in 1908, he became a friend of Van Wyck Brooks, with whom he published anonymously, during their freshman year, a pamphlet entitled *Verses by Two Undergraduates*. He edited the *Harvard Monthly*, and was Class Poet at graduation. He spent two years in study for a Ph.D. degree at universities in Germany, and wrote a great deal of verse during that period. In 1910 he returned to America, and shortly thereafter became associated with Charles Scribner's Sons. In 1932 he became a director, and was later elected secretary of the corporation.

"His volume of collected poems, in 1936, was awarded the Golden Rose by the New England Poetry Society, as the most distinguished contribution to American poetry of that year. His poem, 'Affirmation,' was read before the Phi Beta Kappa Society at Harvard University in 1927.

"Wheelock lives in New York and spends his vacations on the south shore of Long Island. He is a great lover of the sea, and his principal recreations are swimming and walking along the shore."

He added in 1955: "I have written poems that would fall in the first two categories—none that I know of that woould answer to the third—but they form a very small proportion of my work, which is in the main metaphysical and concerned, to use the words of one critic, with 'the mystery, the beauty, the sadness and the unity of life'—especially the last. . . . Seeger's work is entirely opposite in method and point of view from mine. . . . My first book was published in 1905, some fifty years ago, and it is true that I belong to the generation preceding the one which has since made poetic history. At the time that my first books appeared they were distinctly in the contemporary movement, and certainly the range of my poems, both in subject matter and form, has been far from narrow."

The Human Fantasy, Wheelock's first individual collection, was published in 1911. New volumes appeared regularly until the 1920s. In 1936 his first collected poems—Collected Poems 1911–1936—was issued, and from that point onwards most of his books combined old work alongside new. That Wheelock's verse has a metaphysical message to convey cannot be denied, but it is also true to say that this message is, indeed, frequently conveyed via poems about lost love, loneliness and nostalgia. Readers haphazardly making their way from poem to poem in any of the collected editions will be struck by the number with autumn, evening, or deserted beaches as their theme. The opening verse of "September by the Sea" captures the typical Wheelock tone:

The melancholy mood of bleak September
Chills the forsaken beach here by the sea—
The gray pavilion stares out wearily,
The old, wretched seats and railings half remember
Their summer gayety

In spite of his own resistance, the consensus is that the modern move towards colloquialness in verse affected Wheelock's later work for the good. Thomas Lask, in Wheelock's New York Times obituary, after quoting from "The Mask," a late poem, observed: "Critics did find a difference in the later work, a longer view, a more sustained line and a wisdom that only oncoming age could provide." And, according to Allen Tate, "Like Hardy and Yeats [Wheelock] has done his best work in old age."

He was active in various arts and literary societies, including the Academy of American Poets and the Poetry Society of America, the latter organization awarding him a Gold Medal in 1972. Louis Simpson, reviewing What Is Poetry, a prose collection, and complaining of Wheelock's "predilection for the language of stars, waves, beauty, et cetera, which is not, in my opinion, the language of poetry in our time—the time that matters," also went on to say, "The personality that emerges is noble. He has written and read a great deal of poetry for poetry's sake, and has done more—especially through his publications in the Scribner's 'Poets of Today' series—to encourage poetry in this country, than anyone else I can think of. His views of poetry are large and serious."

PRINCIPAL WORKS: Poetry—The Human Fantasy, 1911; The Beloved Adventure, 1912; Love and Liberation, 1913; Dust and Light, 1919; The Black Panther, 1922; The Bright Doom, 1927; Collected Poems 1911–1936, 1936; Poems Old and New, 1956; The Gardener and Other Poems, 1961; Dear Men and Women, 1966; By Daylight and in Dream, 1970; In love and Song. 1971. Other—Alan Seeger: Poet of the Foreign Legion, 1918; A Bibliography of Theodore Roosevelt, 1920; (as ed.) Editor to Author: The Letters of Maxwell E. Perkins, 1950; What Is Poetry?, 1963.

ABOUT: Oxford Companion to American Literature 4th ed., 1965; Oxford Companion to Twentieth Century Poetry, 1994; Rood, K. (ed.) American Literary Almanac, 1988. Periodicals—Book Week October 27, 1963; New York Times March 23, 1978; New York Times Book Review November 15, 1970; Newsweek September 14, 1959; Paris Review Fall 1976.

**WHETHAM, WILLIAM CECIL DAMPIER.** See **DAMPIER, WILLIAM CECIL DAMPIER**

**WHIBLEY, CHARLES** (December 9, 1859–March 4, 1930), English critic, was born in Sittingbourne, Kent. He was the eldest son of Ambrose Whibley, a merchant, and the former Mary Jenn Davey. Whibley went with a scholarship from Bristol Grammar School to Jesus College, Cambridge. Graduating in 1883 with first class honors in the classical tripos, he worked for a time with the publishing house of Cassell, and Company. He then joined the staff of the Scots Observer, which moved to London and became the National Observer. Whibley shared rooms, and became friendly with, the magazine's editor, the poet W. E. Henley, whose imperialist and High Tory views he shared.

Whibley attacked all forms of liberal thinking, and all that seemed to him "flabby" or "pretentious" in literature and criticism, in particular the estheticism of Ruskin. He wrote effectively, but was far too sweeping and unsubtle for his purely literary criticism to have any permanent value.

Whibley also followed Henley in making a special feature of the "Englishness" of English literature, which he celebrated in his introductions to the versions of Elizabethan and Jacobean prose that he and Henley published in the 1890s as Tudor Translations. These introductions have not been influential, but the series made important work available to the reading public.

When Henley retired in 1893, Whibley moved on to Harry Cust's Pall Mall Gazette, the most influential of the London evening newspapers. He also contributed to the New Review. In 1894 Cust sent him to Paris, where he joined the circle around the painter Whistler, and became acquainted with Mallarmé and his young disciple Valéry. In 1896 he married Whistler's sister-in-law, Ethel Birlie Philip, and returned to England.  For over a quarter of a century he contributed a characteristically controversial column, "Musings Without Method," to Blackwoods. He became celebrated as the denouncer of all the dominant opinions of the age, and politicians of all parties.

Among Whibley's publications are several volumes of critical essays. *Studies in Frankness* dealt knowledgeably with such authors as Petronius, Laurence Sterne, and Poe. Railing against "the censure of the puritan" in his introduction, Whibley outlined his view that "the past at any rate holds a treasury of masterpieces, open and unashamed, which need no concealment for their dignity or their courage." *Literary Portraits* includes essays on Rabelais, Holland, and Montaigne, among others.

Whibley's *Political Portraits*, which includes studies of Wolsey, Shakespeare, Peel, and Napoleon is, according to the Tory *Spectator*, "too often biased by his inveterate Toryism." However, it fared better in America.

In 1912 Whibley was elected an honorary fellow of Jesus College, with which he had maintained contact over the years. He received honorary degrees from Edinburgh University and St. Andrews. His first wife having died in 1920, in 1927 he married Phillipa, daughter of his friend Sir Walter Raleigh, professor of English at Oxford University. They lived in the country house Whibley had built at Bletchley, Buckinghamshire, though in later years he spent much of the year in rooms at Jesus College.

T. S. Eliot praised Whibley as "a master of invective." Eliot concluded: "He has the first requisite of a critic: interest in his subject, and ability to communicate an interest in it."

Whibley could be fierce in defense of the high standards he set the world, and was not without prejudice. He was, however, an excellent companion, capable of enormous wit and warmth. "He was intolerant of fools and humbugs," said his obituarist in the London *Times*, "and did not conceal his opinions . . . but we may be glad that there was at least one of his sort among us."

PRINCIPAL WORKS: The Cathedrals of England and Wales, 1888; A Book of Scoundrels, 1897; Studies in Frankness, 1898; The Pageantry of Life, 1900; William Makepeace Thackeray, 1903; Literary Portraits, 1904; William Pitt, 1906; American Sketches, 1908; The Letters of an Englishman, 1911; Essays in Biography, 1913; Call to Arms, 1916; Jonathan Swift, 1917; Political Portraits, 1917; (2nd series, 1923); Literary Studies, 1919; Lord John Manners and His Friends, 1925. *As editor*—In Cap and Gown; Three Centuries of Cambridge Wit, 1889; (with W. E. Henley) A Book of English Prose, Character and Incident 1387–1649, 1894; Wyndham, George Essays in Romantic Literature, 1919; Collected Essays of W. P. Ker, 1925.

ABOUT: Dictionary of National Biography 1922–1930, 1937; Eliot, T. S. The Sacred Wood, 1920; Charles Whibley; A Memoir, 1931; Ward, A. C. Longman Companion to Twentieth Century Literature 3rd ed., 1981; Who's Who 1930. *Periodicals*—Blackwood Magazine April 1930; New York Times April 1, 1905; March 5, 1930; Saturday Review January 17, 1920; Spectator December 15, 1917; Times (London) March 5, 1930.

**WHITE, EDWARD LUCAS** (May 18, 1866– March 30, 1934), American novelist and short story writer, was born in Bergen, New Jersey, the son of Thomas Hurley White and Kate Butler (Lucas) White. At the age of eleven he moved with his parents to Baltimore, where he lived for the rest of his life. After earning a B.A. from John Hopkins University in 1888 he began three years of graduate study in the classics. Thus qualified, he embarked on a career as a teacher of Latin and Greek at vari-

ous private schools in Baltimore. His last such position was at the University School for Boys, where he himself had been educated and where he taught for a decade until the school closed in 1930.

Except for the fact that it was written in verse, White's first book, *Narrative Lyrics*, resembled much of his later prose fiction in its interest in the ancient world and classical mythology. His first novel, however, was set in nineteenth century Paraguay. *El Supremo: A Romance of the Great Dictator of Paraguay* was the story of an American adventurer entangled in the regime of José Gaspar Rodríquez de Francia, the half-mad dictator who ruled Paraguay from 1813 to 1840.

White's next novel, *The Unwilling Vestal*, was the story of the daughter of a Roman patrician consecrated, against her will, to serving thirty years as a priestess of Vesta. *Andivius Hedulio*, another story set in Roman times is the tale of a young man exiled from the court of the Emperor Commodus on a false charge of treason.

Critics were impressed by White's ability to combine a scholar's knowledge of Roman history, language, and customs with the excitements of popular fiction.

White's two volumes of short stories, *The Song of the Sirens* and *Lukundoo*, were more fantastic and macabre than his novels. "Lukundoo," for example, depicted a white man suffering from the curse of an African witch doctor in which tiny, hostile creatures erupt from the victim's body. Indeed, it is probably for this grotesque and disquieting story that White is most remembered.

His last book was *Matrimony*, an autobiography written in memory of his wife, who had died in 1927. He was found dead, apparently by suicide, in his Baltimore home.

PRINCIPAL WORKS: Poetry—Narrative Lyrics, 1908. *Novels*—El Supremo: A Romance of the Great Dictator of Paraguay, 1916; The Unwilling Vestal: A Tale of Rome under the Caesars, 1918; Andivius Hedulio: Adventures of a Roman Nobleman in the Days of the Empire, 1921; Helen: The Story of the Romance of Helen of Troy, 1925. *Short stories*—The Song of the Sirens and Other Stories, 1921; Lukundoo and Other Stories, 1927. *History*—Why Rome Fell, 1927. *Autobiography*—Matrimony, 1932.

ABOUT: National Cyclopedia of American Biography Vol. 18, 1922; Sullivan, J. (ed.) Penguin Encyclopedia of Horror and the Supernatural, (J. Sullivan, ed.) 1986. *Periodicals*—Bookman December 1927; Dial November 30, 1916; New York Times Book Review November 13, 1921.

**WHITE, E(LWYN) B(ROOKS)** (July 11, 1899– October 1, 1985), American essayist, humorist, and children's writer, was born in Mount Vernon, New York, the youngest of six children of Samuel White, a prosperous piano manufacturer, and Jessie (Hart) White. As a child, White once wrote of himself, he was "frightened but not unhappy. I lacked for nothing except confidence. I suffered nothing except the routine terrors of childhood." This timid boy blossomed at Cornell University, which he entered in 1917, into a popular fraternity man and the editor of the campus newspaper. He also met William Strunk, an English professor whose pithy book, *The Elements of Style*, White would revise and expand many years later into an invaluable brief guide to English usage, still frequently consulted.

Graduating in 1921 with a B.A. and the determination to become a writer, he began working as a reporter, first for the United Press in New York,

 then for the *Seattle Times* in Washington. White had little aptitude for daily journalism, however, and in 1923 he returned home and found work as an advertising copywriter in New York. Equally unhappy with this, he gave it up after a year or two, moved to Greenwich Village, and began publishing comic poems and short pieces in the *New York World*—and in a then-fledgling magazine called the *New Yorker*.

White's contributions to the *New Yorker* so impressed its editor-in-chief, Harold Ross, and Ross's assistant, Katherine Angell (White's future wife), that he was hired as a full-time member of the staff (1926). He was immediately put to work writing "Talk of the Town" pieces: humorous squibs, parodies, and cartoon captions. His wit, elegance, and simplicity helped to define the famous *New Yorker* style.

Not the least of his achievements at the magazine was in helping to refine the comic sensibility of his colleague James Thurber, who collaborated with him on *Is Sex Necessary?*, a highly successful parody of 1920s sexspeak that included, at White's insistence, Thurber's own hilariously un-Raphaelesque drawings. Burton Bernstein wrote that *Is Sex Necessary?* "will live in American humorous literature as a tour de force by virtue of its originality, exuberance, and dazzling display of promise"; but White was not, like Thurber, primarily a humorist, and the longer essays he began writing for the *New Yorker* in the 1930s became his true metier. Many of the essays were about life on his farm in North Brooklin, Maine, to which he had moved in 1938.

By 1954 the philosopher Irwin Edman, in the *New York Times Book Review*, could reasonably call White "the finest essayist in the United States. He says wise things gracefully; he is the master of an idiom at once exact and suggestive, distinguished yet familiar. His style is crisp and tender, and incomparably his own." Reviewing *The Essays of E. B. White* in the *New Review of Books*, Nigel Dennis wrote, "Though only an essayist, he makes definite assertions and says shortly what others say at length. He will never win the Nobel Prize and will certainly never approach a Great Work; but he will always make sense, which is an achievement too."

White also wrote one of the most popular children's books of the last half century, *Charlotte's Web*. His first children's book, *Stuart Little*, was a charming story of an independent and adventurous mouse born into a human family, but the parts were greater than the whole; and his third and last children's book, *The Trumpet of the Swan*, failed to come fully to life even in parts. *Charlotte's Web*, though, "is full, sustained, serene, a *book* in ways that perhaps only the great Potters and [Kipling's] *Kim* rival or exceed" (Roger Sale). This story of the friendship between a young pig and the spider who craftily saves him from the butcher's knife only to die quietly and alone toward the book's end, has been translated into more than twenty languages and is still regarded as one of the most sensitive treatments of death in children's literature. "The delight of E. B. White's story, the elegance of his prose, the clarity of his vision, the brightness of his wit, and the beauty of the world he reveals to us are not likely to be matched any time soon," wrote the *New Yorker* (1991).

White continued to publish essays in the *New Yorker* into the 1970s, and the retrospective collections of essays, letters, poems, and sketches he brought out in that decade and after received enthusiastic reviews. However, the death in 1977 of Katherine White, the formidable fiction editor of the *New Yorker*, who had been his wife for forty-eight years, deprived him of his greatest source of strength, and his increasing fraility made writing, not to mention farming, an ever more onerous task. "He never wished his readers to think him deeper or wiser than he found himself to be," wrote his stepson Roger Angell in the *New Yorker* (1985). "Relieved of that frightful burden, he got more of himself onto paper in a lifetime than most writers come close to doing."

White's manuscripts are in the E. B. White Collection at Cornell University, Ithaca, New York.

PRINCIPAL WORKS: *Poetry*—The Lady Is Cold: Poems, 1929; The Fox of Peapack and Other Poems, 1938; Poems and Sketches of E. B. White, 1981. *Humor*—(with J. Thurber) Is Sex Necessary?, or, Why You Feel the Way You Do, 1929; Ho Hum: Newsbreaks from the New Yorker, 1931; Another Ho Hum: More Newsbreaks from the New Yorker, 1932; Quo Vadimus? or, The Case for the Bicycle, 1939. *Essays*—One Man's Meat, 1942, rev. ed. 1944; The Wild Flag: Editorials from the New Yorker on Federal World Government and Other Matters, 1946; Here Is New York, 1949; The Second Tree from the Corner, 1954; The Points of My Compass: Letters from the East, the West, the North, the South, 1962; Essays of E. B. White, 1977. *Correspondence*—Letters of E. B. White (ed. D. L. Guth) 1976. *Anthologies*—An E. B. White Reader (ed. W. W. Watt and R. W. Bradford) 1966; Writings from the New Yorker, 1925–1976 (ed. R. M. Dale) 1990. *Juvenile*—Stuart Little, 1945; Charlotte's Web, 1952; The Trumpet of the Swan, 1970. *As editor*—(with K. S. White) A Subtreasury of American Humor, 1941. *Other*—(with W. Strunk, Jr.) The Elements of Style, 1959, rev. ed. 1979.

ABOUT: Bernstein, B. Thurber: A Biography, 1975; Current Biography 1960; Dicitonary of Literary Biography vol. 11 1982; Vol. 22, 1983; Elledge, S. E. B. White: A Biography, 1984; Root, R. L. (ed.) Critical Essays on E. B. White, 1994; Sale, R. Fairy Tales and After: From Snow White to E. B. White, 1978; Sampson, E. C. E. B. White, 1974. *Periodicals*—New York Review of Books October 27, 1977; New York Times October 2, 1985; New York Times Book Review January 17, 1954; New Yorker October 14, 1985; November 25, 1991; Saturday Review August 20, 1977.

**WHITE, HELEN CONSTANCE** (November 26, 1896–June 7, 1967), American scholar and novelist, took part in the women's suffrage movement  in Massachusetts as a young girl. By the time the Nineteenth Amendment was passed in 1919, she was an instructor of English at the University of Wisconsin, where in 1924 she received her Ph.D. Her dissertation was published as *The Mysticism of William Blake* (1927). In 1936 she joined the small number of women in the country who then had full professorships. White studied the English religious literature of the early seventeenth century at Oxford as a Guggenheim Fellow in 1928–1929 and published *English Devotional Literature: Prose 1600–1640* in 1931. Seventeenth-century thought was also the theme of *Metaphysical Poets: A Study in Religious Experience* (1936), in which White concentrated on English writers including John Donne, George Herbert, Richard Crashaw, Henry Vaughan, and Thomas Traherne. *Catholic World* praised White for "her scholarship, her spiritual insight, her critical acumen" but thought her style "characterized by a kind of metaphysical obscurity rather than by the forthright clarity for which the metaphysicals strove and for the most part achieved."

Other scholarly writings included *Social Criticism in Popular Religious Literature of the Sixteenth Century* (1944), a treatise that examines popular literature of the time to determine how religion affected social revolt and stabilization. White was self-effacing about her fiction, saying that "as a novelist I could barely be admitted to the sophomore class." A Roman Catholic, she brought a strong religious nature to her historical novels. *Watch in the Night* (1933) is based on the life of the thirteenth-century Umbrian lawyer and poet Jacopone da Todi, who, upon the death of his wife, renounced his worldly career and joined the Franciscans to help the poor.

White wrote a story of the French Revolution told from the viewpoint of a priest in *To the End of the World* (1939), which L. B. Salomon in the *Nation* called "an ambitious, many-faceted chronicle . . . without any of the usual clichés of that breed." In *Dust on the King's Highway* (1947) she turned her attention to the struggle of the Spanish missionary priests who worked among the Indians of California and Mexico in the colonial period.

White served as a visiting professor at Barnard College and Columbia University and was a member of many educational, religious, and social organizations, including the United States Commission for UNESCO, the American Council on Education, and the American Association of University Women, for which she served as president from 1941 to 1947. She was the recipient of many academic awards and honorary degrees.

PRINCIPAL WORKS: The Mysticism of William Blake, 1927; Victorian Prose (ed. with F. Foster) 1930; English Devotional Literature: Prose 1600–1640, 1931; The Metaphysical Poets: A Study in Religious Experience, 1936; Social Criticism in Popular Religious Literature of the Sixteenth Century, 1944; Tudor Books of Private Devotion, 1951; (ed., with others) Seventeenth Century Verse and Prose, vol. I, 1951, vol. II, 1952; Prayer and Poetry, 1960; Changing Styles in Literary Studies, 1963; Tudor Books of Saints and Martyrs, 1963. Fiction: A Watch in the Night, 1933; Not Built with Hands, 1935; To the End of the World, 1939; Dust on the King's Highway, 1947; The Four Rivers of Paradise, 1955; Bird of Fire, 1958.

ABOUT: Hoehn, M. (ed.) Catholic Authors; Warfel, H. R. American Novelists of Today; Current Biography 1945; Notable American Women: The Modern Period. *Periodicals*—Catholic World May 1937; Chicago Sunday Tribune September 28, 1958; Commonweal April 19, 1933, May 24, 1935; Nation January 20, 1940; New York Herald Tribune Book Review April 20, 1947, November 16, 1958; New York Times June 2, 1935; Saturday Review June 25, 1955; Women's Studies Quarterly Spring/Summer 1994.

**WHITE, NELIA GARDNER** (November 1, 1894–June 12, 1957), American novelist, wrote: "I can think of no better training for the life of a writer than that of living in a Methodist parsonage in the early part of this century. Andrews Settlement, Little Genesee, Ceres, Pulteney, Cameron, Canaseraga, Knoxville—all were little towns, so small that you could see their pattern clearly, if you would, could know all the peo-  ple, see their relationship to the whole. Ministers' children are unafraid of change, yet aware of the value of roots. They are used to making homes in all sorts of houses, with other people's furniture. They are not afraid of society because they have always felt secure even inside what would nowadays be called poverty, but which never seemed like poverty then because there was always a margin for books, for friendships, for music and hospitality. No matter how limited the materials with which we worked, we clung to an ideal. This is a security far beyond any offered by money. Nearly all ministers' children I know have rebelled against orthodoxy. This rebellion seems to me normal and good, coupled as it nearly always is with a never-lost idealism. No writer can ever be worth his salt if he is not a questioner, a doubter. This does not mean he can have no standards by which to live, but only that his approach to life must forever be a question. The how and the what and the why of living are his business.

"Out of this background, plus two years at Syracuse University and two more at Emma Willard Kindergarten School, I began to write. First I wrote stories for kindergarten-age children and articles on how to bring up children for a kindergarten journal. Then I knew how very well to bring up children. When I had two of my own I made a few changes in my approach to the matter. But I have been writing ever since, countless short stories and novelettes, books for children, books for adults. I started out in a green, blind way, with no agent, no real knowledge of writing, but my youth had made me ambitious and unafraid and I was pleased but not too surprised when I sold what I wrote. I know now that I was lucky, and that the gift of words that came to me from my father and mother was a greater gift than I realized then. I know, too, that there is no end to learning how to write and that your living is tied inexorably to your writing. I know now how immeasurably richer my life has been because I blindly chose this work. The discipline, the ever-widening interests entailed, the joy of creating characters that seem like flesh and blood people—all these are gifts the business of writing gives the writer. I have heard a number of writers say they hate writing. I do not hate it; I love it. It is hard work, calls for tremendous concentration, involves endless disappointments, and there is always the knowledge that your vision exceeds your grasp, but these things are part of the challenge, the excitement of writing. I raise my brows in doubt when writers say they hate to write.

"It would be futile to discuss all my books. Some are not worth discussing. *Daughter of Time*, a fictionalized biography of Katherine Mansfield, was a labor of love. It involved a long journey to England and the continent for material, made some wonderful friends for me. *No Trumpet Before Him* won the Westminster prize and was perhaps responsible for my receiving the Arents award for literature from Syracuse University. During the last war I was in England with several other writers observing England in wartime, afterwards writing various stories that grew out of this experience. Now, in an old farmhouse on a back road in western Connecticut, we again begin to put down roots. Our son, with the same heritage of questioning and idealism, studies Polynesian culture in Tahiti. Up in the old schoolhouse at the corner our daughter has established a thriving library, for which she begged books, and neighbors built shelves and painted walls. My husband interests himself in civic affairs. It is a long way back to parsonage days but my security comes still from the same things, love of family, books, music, work."

———

Born in Andrews Settlement, Pennsylvania, Nelia Gardner White was one of five children of John Adrian Gardner a Methodist minister, and Anna (Jones) Gardner. She married Ralph Leon White, a lawyer, in 1917.

After her start writing articles for a kindergarten journal, she went on to write children's stories and books as well as articles for *Ladies' Home Journal*, *Saturday Evening Post*, *Harper's Bazaar*, and other popular magazines. According to the *New York Times*, her novels, which usually focused on American country life, were filled with characters that were "plain, ordinary American citizens of good, sound stock." Many of these were strong or searching women, which helped account for her appeal to female readers. For example, *Jen Culliton* (1927) is the story of a big, brusque woman who works a farm alone after her husband's death and her children's departure; Mary Goodspeed in *Fam-*

*ily Affair* (1934) faces the problems of keeping peace in a complex extended family.

Katherine Mansfield was one of White's favorite authors, and her life was the basis for *Daughter of Time* (1942), a convincing fictional biography. White tapped into her own childhood experiences of growing up in parsonages for the background of her most successful novel, *No Trumpet Before Him* (1948), winner of the 1947 Westminster Press Fiction Award. Called "a richly satisfying novel" by the *New York Times*, the book describes the difficulties of a young, inexperienced country minister who is assigned to a wealthy and worldly congregation. "Mrs. White has complete mastery of the formula novel," wrote Jane Voiles in the *San Francisco Chronicle*. "She holds your interest even though you know, more or less, what is going to happen."

PRINCIPAL WORKS: Jen Culliton, 1927; David Strange, 1928; Tune in the Tree, 1929; Hathaway House, 1931; Mrs. Green's Daughter-in-law, 1932; This, My House, 1933; A Family Affair, 1934; The Fields of Gomorrah, 1935; A Daughter of Time, 1942; Brook Willow, 1944; No Trumpet Before Him, 1948; The Pink House, 1950; The Woman at the Window, 1951; The Merry Month of May, 1952; The Spare Room, 1954; The Thorn Tree, 1955; A Little More than Kin, 1956; The Gift and the Giver, 1957. *Juveniles*—Mary, 1925; Marge, 1926; And Michael, 1927; Joanna Gray, 1928; Kristin, 1929; Toni of Grand Isle, 1930; Boy of Scott's Corners, 1938;

ABOUT: The autobiographical material quoted above was written for Twentieth Century Authors First Supplement, 1955. Current Biography 1950. *Periodicals*—Kirkus July 15, 1957; New York Times March 29, 1942, November 26, 1944, March 21, 1948, March 5, 1950, June 13, 1957; Publishers' Weekly June 24, 1957; San Francisco Chronicle April 4, 1948.

**WHITE, PATRICK** (May 28, 1912-September 30, 1990), Australian novelist, wrote: "Although fourth-generation Australian, I was born by chance in London [while his parents, Victor Martindale White and Ruth (Withycombe) White were on vacation]. At the age of six months I was taken to Sydney, and proceeded to spend my childhood in Australia, mainly in the country. Whatever has come since, I feel that the influences and impressions of this strange, dead landscape of Australia predominate.

"My boyhood I spent at an English public school, learning very little, except from my own private reading, and detesting everything connected with this educational system. Even holidays abroad, in France, Belgium, and Scandinavia, were never free from the prospect of returning to prison. These four years were largely unpleasant.

"I escaped early from school and returned to Australia, where I found I had become a stranger. I had acquired too much European veneer, and was too young and inexperienced to practice tolerance. During three years I lived in the country, working on two sheep stations in New South Wales, writing immature novels, discontented with my own isolation, though aspects of this existence, with its droughts, floods and fires, and of course the landscapes, were impressive.

"From 1932 to 1935, I made up for time lost, intellectually, reading Modern Languages at King's College, Cambridge, and for the first time, making human contacts. I also continued writing. Two inferior comedies, *Bread and Butter Women* and *The School for Friends*, were produced at Bryants' Playhouse, a small basement theatre in Sydney. Verses and a story appeared in the *London Mercury*.

"Coming down from Cambridge, I set up in London, writing plays that nobody produced, travelling much in France and Germany, but only taking root at Hanover and St. Jean-de-Luz.

"*Happy Valley*, my first success, was published in London, 1939. This novel appeared in New York the following year, and won the Australian Literature Society's Gold Medal. A second novel, *The Living and the Dead*, came out both in New York and London in 1941.

"Much of 1939 and 1940 was spent wandering in the United States, with a period of several months in New York, a city both stimulating and repellent, sympathetic and antipathetic, to which I shall always hope to return.

"In August 1940 I left New York for England, and since then have served with the R.A.F. in the Sudanese and Egyptian Deserts.

"Since the war my life has been practically uneventful. I returned to Australia, to a small property at Castle Hill, about twenty-five miles from Sydney, where I breed Schnauzers, Saanen goats, cultivate olives and citrus fruit, grow vegetables, and live more or less off my own produce.

"A novel, *The Aunt's Story*, was published in New York and London in 1948. A French translation of *Happy Valley* and an Italian one of *The Aunt's Story* have appeared. French translations of the latter and *The Living and the Dead* are in preparation. Some time after the war a play, *Return to Abyssinia*, was produced in London.

"For the last three years I have been working on a novel and expect I shall take several more years to finish it on account of the great amount of other work that has to be done."

---

White was sent to Cheltenham College in 1925, an English boarding school, after having previously attended Australian schools. He did his best to be a joiner. In his last year he became a House prefect and, despite his asthma, ran on the athletics team. He won a French essay prize and spent the summer of 1929 in a Dieppe school to extend his ability with the language. Nevertheless, he spent three years trying to get the hated regime out of his system by working on various Australian sheep stations; as a result, he was already twenty when he arrived at King's College, Cambridge. *Happy Valley*, the first of White's novels to be published, was the fourth he had written. As with his next two novels, it was written in a style much influenced by Joyce and other experimentalists of the period. Although his style would become more straightforward, this first published novel was characteristic of much of White's later work in its character development. The protagonists of *Happy Valley*, a novel of small-town life in Australia, are developed in terms of their petty interrelationships. From the beginning White was at pains to avoid sentimentality in his depiction of everyday existence, with the result that the epithet "sordid" is frequently applied in early reviews, particularly in response to his second novel, *The Living and the Dead*, a story set in pre-World War II Bloomsbury, depicting the degrading liaisons indulged in by three unfulfilled characters. This book was published in 1941, by which time White was serving as an intelligence officer in the Royal Air Force, stationed in Sudan and Egypt. There he met Manoly Lascaris, who became his lifelong companion.

It was seven years before his third novel appeared, *The Aunt's Story*. This has a narrower focus than many of White's books. It is a character study of a plain woman who, following the death of her mother, undertakes a journey of discovery, traveling from Australia to the French Riviera and then to the United States. Following publication of this book, White brought the itinerant phase of his own life to a close, returning to Australia and settling (with Lascaris) on six acres of farmland in Castle Hill, New South Wales. White's obituarist in the London Times observed: "Without doubt *The Tree of Man*, *Voss* and *The Solid Mandala* are among the most important novels of the century in any language; and as a whole his tormented oeuvre is that of a great and essentially modern writer."

*The Tree of Man*, published in 1955, was White's longest book to date, in a style closer to poetic drama than conventional fiction (Ted Hughes once described White as "the most exciting poet Australia has yet produced"). It portrayed the struggles of a pioneering couple, Stan and Amy Parker, at the turn of the century. Although it was downbeat, and as unflinching in its unsentimentality as the earlier novels, reviewers were less inclined to focus on the sordid realities of the story and more willing to emphasize its redeeming qualities. In the *New York Times* James Stern wrote: "In it is all the sorrow and senselessness of living, the profound loneliness of mortal man, his cowardice, his cruelty, as well as his dignity, his indomitable courage, and the comedy, the fun his imagination is able to create." *Voss* (1957) was set in an earlier period. Loosely based on the accounts of the German explorer Ludwig Leichardt, it is the story of a German adventurer who sets out to discover uncharted parts of Australia. Reviewing this book for the *New Statesman*, Walter Allen wrote: "It is a work of brilliant virtuosity, and I suggest it is much more than that: I suppose it would need an Australian to gauge its full significance for, as it seems to me, Mr. White is attempting to create an Australian myth." In fact, as became increasingly apparent with each new novel, White, although the Australian background was decidedly important to him, was dealing with universal, rather than purely national themes. In *Voss* itself the principle themes are divine mission and spiritual quest. The exploration of physical terrain becomes a metaphor for spiritual discovery. White was later to acknowledge (in 1969, in conversation with Craig McGregor) that religion lay behind all of his books. "What I am interested in is the relationship between the blundering human being and God. I belong to no church; but I have a religious faith; it's an attempt to express that, among other things, that I try to do."

*Riders in the Chariot*, another very long novel, is directly mystical in theme. Set in postwar Australia, in an imaginary suburb called Sarsaparilla (used also in other works), it concerns a collection of misfits—Mary Hare, a spinster and heir to a decaying estate; Mordecai Himmelfarb, a Jewish refugee; Mrs. Godbold, a washerwoman; and a half-caste aborigine raised by missionaries—all seeking enlightenment. Martin Seymour-Smith has said of this book: "White achieves on a major level, with alienated freaks, what Carson McCullers could only hint at."

In the early 1960s White concentrated on the theater and confined his fictional output to the short story. The collection *The Burnt Ones*, containing pieces set in Australia and Greece, served to illustrate White's need of the broad canvas to achieve his effects. *The Solid Mandala*, a novel once again set in small-minded Sarsaparilla, was White's own favorite book. An updated Cain and Abel story, it recounts, over a fifty-year period, the lives of the twin brothers Waldo and Arthur, the latter an innocent collector of marbles who sees a mandala design in a book and decides that the markings of his favorite marble constitute a solid mandala and the embodiment of the universe. *The Vivisector*, White's eighth novel, is set in a big city, Sydney. White described his aim in his memoir, *Flaws in the Glass*: "setting out to portray a convincing artist, I wanted at the same time to paint a portrait of my city: wet, boiling, superficial, brash, beautiful, ugly Sydney." Hurtle Duffield, the main character and son of a laundress, is adopted (sold for 500 pounds) by rich Australians. After action in World War I he becomes an artist, painting his way to fame and fortune, but forever obsessed by the "Mad Eye," a vision of his childhood. The painter is depicted as seer and destroyer, with the metaphor of vivisection sustained throughout the novel, which is considered by many to be White's most powerful. Three years after its appearance White was awarded the Nobel Prize for Literature. *The Eye of the Storm* and *A Fringe of Leaves* were both more accessible than White's more difficult novels, and in the wake of his Nobel prize received wider attention from reviewers.

His next novel, *The Twyborn Affair*, is his most explicitly autobiographical. It takes the theme of quest into the area of gender, with Eddie Twyburn becoming in turn the wife of a wealthy Greek, a World War I hero, and lastly the madame of a London brothel. White was expecting an outcry on its appearance, but it was published in a permissive and understanding age, and there was little furor.

White dedicated much of his own energy in his last years to various protest campaigns. However, he would play no part in the gay-rights movement.

He famously said to someone who asked him why he was not joining a march, "I may be homosexual, but I am certainly not gay." Although notoriously cantankerous and irascible, White's correspondence (published in 1995) is a testimony to his dedication as an artist and to his compassion. He died from lung complications connected with chronic asthma and emphysema. Both his plays and his early poetry (much of which David Marr quotes in his detailed biography of White), while not successful in themselves, are of significance in relation to the fiction.

PRINCIPAL WORKS: *Fiction*—Happy Valley, 1939; The Living and the Dead, 1941; The Aunt's Story, 1948; The Tree of Man, 1955; Voss, 1957; Riders in the Chariot, 1961; The Burnt Ones, 1964; The Solid Mandala, 1966; The Vivisector, 1970; The Eye of the Storm, 1974; The Cockatoos, 1975; A Fringe of Leaves, 1977; The Twyborn Affair, 1980; Memoirs of Many in One, by Alex Xenophon Demirjian Gray, 1986; Three Uneasy Pieces, 1988. *Drama*—Return To Abyssynia, 1947; Four Plays, 1965. *Poetry*—(as "Patrick Victor Martindale") Thirteen Poems, 1930; The Ploughman and Other Poems, 1935; Poems, 1974. *Autobiography*—Flaws in the Glass, 1981.

ABOUT: Beatson, P. The Eye in the Mandala, 1976; Bjoerksten, I. Patrick White, 1976; (ed.) Joyce, C. Patrick White: A Tribute, 1991; Marr, D. Patrick White, A Life, 1991; Walsh, W. Patrick White's Fiction, 1977; Who's Who 1990; (ed.) Wolfe, P. Critical Essays on Patrick White, 1990; Wolfe, P. Laden Choirs the Fiction of Patrick White, 1983. *Periodicals*—New Statesman December 7, 1957; London Review of Books August 15, 1991; New York Times August 14, 1955; September 30, 1990; New York Times Book Review August 18, 1957; February 7, 1982; Observer January 15, 1995; Times (London) October 1, 1990; January 15, 1995; Times Literary Supplement August 9 1991.

**WHITE, STEWART EDWARD** (March 12, 1873–September 18, 1946), American novelist, regional and travel writer, and in later life a writer on spiritualism, was born in Grand Rapids, Michigan. He was the eldest of the five sons of Thomas Stewart White, a millionaire lumberman, and the former Mary Eliza Daniell. The family was of English and Scottish descent. Thomas White had lumber interests both in northern Michigan and in  California, and traveled a great deal to visit them. As a child, Stewart White was allowed to go with him, developing a lifelong love of the outdoors. During his early teens he lived and worked on a California ranch. His formal schooling did not begin until he was sixteen.

White entered Grand Rapids Central High School in the third year. He graduated at eighteen, president of his class and holder of the five-mile running record. For two years after that, White lived in the Michigan woods, studying bird life and writing articles and a monograph published by the Ornithologists' Union. He entered the University of Michigan in 1891, graduating in 1895 with a Ph.B.; his M. A. followed in 1903. During summer vacations, White cruised on the Great Lakes in a sailing boat. After an unsuccessful stint as a gold prospector in the Black Hills of South Dakota, he resumed his education at Columbia University Law School (1896–1897).

At Columbia, White took an English course taught by Brander Matthews, professor of literature. Matthews encouraged him to seek a publisher for a short story based on his experiences as a prospector. "A Man and His Dog" sold to *Short Story* for $15 and White became a writer. Leaving Columbia, he worked briefly in a Chicago bookstore, then set out for the wilderness. Lumberjacking in Michigan, then trapping in the Hudson Bay area, he wrote his first novel, *The Westerners*, about frontier life in South Dakota.

White's first major success was his third novel, *The Blazed Trail*. Packed with action, it describes the Herculean labors of a young lumberjack, Harry Thorpe. There is rather more to the book than a standard American success story—an almost mystical sense of Harry Thorpe's growing oneness with the natural world, harsh as that seems to be.

*The Blazed Trail* was a best seller and established White as a member of the "red-blooded school" of realist writers, whose mentors included Bret Harte, Jack London, and Owen Wister. Over the next forty years, White produced nearly thirty more works of fiction—novels or collections of short stories about cowboys and rustlers, miners and prospectors. Many deal with the frontier past, like the trilogy forming a history of the growth of California: *Gold, The Gray Dawn*, and *The Rose Dawn*. White's characterization was elementary and his style no more than "breezy," but he provided plenty of action, drama or melodrama, and romance. The reviewers were, on the whole, not impressed. A typical response was J. M. Crawford's to *Skookum Chuck*, a novel set in British Columbia. In the *New York World* Crawford said: "White dresses his story in somewhat grandiose language, and produces carefully detailed thrills. The hairbreadth escapes, the girl, and the fresh outdoor life combine to awaken [the hero's] interest in life, but not the reader's interest in the book."

Ironically, it was one of White's rare urban novels that fared best with the reviewers, a comic morality tale called *The Glory Hole*. In a booming midwestern town at the turn of the century, a family is almost destroyed by a huge inheritance until the dominated husband asserts himself and brings his ambitious wife to order. There were comparisons with Sinclair Lewis's *Babbitt*, and H. L. Pangborn wrote that "The book holds the interest, inexorably, simply as a story. It is by far the best thing Mr. White has ever done, quite out of the class of his earlier work in conception and in execution" (*Literary Review*).

White was married in 1904 to Elizabeth Calvert Grant of Newport, Rhode Island—the *Billy* to whom he dedicated many of his books. They settled in Santa Barbara, California, later moving to Burlingame. Stewart White did his research at Stanford University or the University of California. The Whites had no children, and often traveled, camped and hunted together. White served during the First World War as an artillery major.

During the 1920's, Elizabeth White began to experiment with a ouija board, coming to believe that she had psychic powers. White became a convert, and *The Betty Book* was a compilation of the messages his wife had received from "the invisibles." After her death in 1939, he communicated with her daily through a medium. Several of the later books record the results of these "meetings," or offer his own thoughts on spiritualism and life in general. A few of his books remain in print.

PRINCIPAL WORKS: *Fiction*—The Westerners, 1901; The Claim Jumpers, 1901; The Blazed Trail, 1902; Conjuror's House, 1903 (dramatized in "narrative form" as The Call of the North, 1903); The Magic Forest, 1903; The Silent Places, 1904; Blazed Trail Stories, and Stories of Wild Life, 1904; (with S. H. Adams) The Mystery, 1907; Arizona Nights, 1907; The Riverman, 1908; The Rules of the Game, 1909; The Adventures of Bobby Orde, 1911 (juvenile); The Sign at Six, 1912; Gold, 1913; The Gray Dawn, 1915; The Leopard Woman, 1916; The Works of Stewart White, 10 vols. 1916; Simba, 1918; White Magic, and Other Tales, 1918; The Killer, 1919; The Rose Dawn, 1920; On Tiptoe, 1922; The Glory Hole, 1924; Skookum Chuck, 1925; Secret Harbour, 1925; Back of Beyond, 1927; The Shepper-Newfounder, 1931; The Long Rifle, 1932; Ranchero, 1933; Folded Hills, 1934; (with H. DeVighne) Pole Star, 1935; Wild Geese Calling, 1940; Stampede, 1942; The Saga of Andy Burnett (contains The Long Rifle, Ranchero, Folded Hills, Stampede), 1947. *Travel*—The Forest, 1903; The Mountains, 1904; The Pass, 1906; Camp and Trail, 1907; The Cabin, 1910; The Land of Footprints, 1912; African Camp Fires, 1913; The Rediscovered Country, 1915; Lions in the Path, 1926. *Spiritualism*—The Betty Book: Excursions into the World of Other-Consciousness, Made by Betty (Elizabeth Calvert White) Between 1919 and 1936, 1937; (with H. White) Across the Unknown, 1939; The Unobstructed Universe, 1940; The Road I Know, 1942; The Stars Are Still There, 1946; With Folded Wings, 1947; The Job of Living, 1948. *Other*—The Forty-Niners, 1918; (with C. K. Field) The Cremation of Care, 1921 (play with music for the Bohemian Club of San Francisco); Daniel Boone, 1922; Credo, 1925; Why Be a Mud Turtle?, 1928 (essays); Dog Days, 1930; (autobiography); Anchors to Winward, 1943; Speaking for Myself, 1943 (essays and reminiscences).

ABOUT: Current Biography 1947; Dictionary of American Biography, 1941–1945, 1973; Fadala, S. Great Shooters of the World, 1990; Overton, G. M. When Winter Comes to Main Street, 1922; Saxton, E. F. Stewart Edward White, 1947; Underwood, J. C. Literature and Insurgency, 1914; White, S. E. Dog Days, 1930; White S. E. Speaking for Myself, 1943. *Periodicals*—Bookman August 1921; Literary Review November 29, 1924; New York Times September 19, 1946; New York World October 18, 1925.

**WHITE, TERENCE HANBURY** (May 29, 1906–January 17, 1964), English novelist remembered principally for his treatment of Arthurian legend in *The Once and Future King*, was born in Bombay, India. His childhood was made acutely unhappy by his parents' arguments and, from the age of six, White spent much of his time at the home of his maternal grandparents. In 1920 his parents divorced, and White was  sent to Cheltenham College, where he was made equally miserable by the rough discipline. As an undergraduate at Queen's College, Cambridge, he was much happier. It was there that he began to write, his first publications being two small volumes of verses. His first novel was composed during a period of convalescence in Italy, where he had been sent to recover from tuberculosis, halfway through his time at Queen's. *They Winter Abroad* was finally published in 1932 (by which time White was working as a schoolmaster) under the pseudonym James Aston—Aston being the name of his mother's family.

White worked as head of the English department at Stowe school, Buckinghamshire, until 1936, continuing to write novels in the school holidays. With his third book, a detective story, and a change of publisher, he reverted to his real name. *Farewell Victoria* was a rural panorama, in the manner of Noel Coward's *Cavalcade*, and *Earth Stopped, or, Mr. Marx's Sporting Tour* was an anti-Socialist curiosity.

White wrote that "At the age of thirty, I realized that if I stayed (at Stowe) any longer I should remain a schoolmaster forever, so I resigned . . . , on a capital of £100 which I have saved, and went to live in a labourer's cottage in the middle of the wood, at a rental of five shillings a week." Abandoning regular employment was also made possible by the commercial success of *England Have My Bones*, a diary recounting his outdoor experiences as hunter, ornithologist, and fisherman, and revealing his loathing of suburbia.

*The Sword in the Stone*, published in England in 1938, became a Book-of-the-Month Club selection in America the following year. A high-spirited account of Arthur "Wart"'s boyhood under the tutelage of Merlin (who turns the future king into various animals), it combines erudite lore with satire and bumptious humor, and soon attracted a cult following. One reviewer of the book, in the *Christian Science Monitor*, described White's imagination as "a mixture of Walt Disney, P. G. Wodehouse, Sir Thomas Malory, and the authors of schoolboy howlers."

White quickly followed this success with a sequel, *The Witch in the Wood*, in which Arthur, now crowned, is at war with rebellious kings of the north. *The Ill-Made Knight*, which introduces Lancelot, followed on its heels. White came to regret the speed with which he had produced these two sequels, and in the omnibus edition, *The Once and Future King* (1957), he considerably reworked those books and added new material in the form of a fourth part, *The Candle in the Wind*. Much of the rewriting was undertaken in response to suggestions from David Garnett, who had been an epistolary friend since writing a review of White's first novel. (*The White/Garnett Letters* was published in 1968.)

White's modernization of Malory, unlike Tennyson's *Idylls of the King*, retained the element of incest. At the end of Part II, now retitled "The Queen of Air and Darkness," he makes it plain why this aspect of the narrative is essential. "That is why we have to take note of the parentage of Arthur's son Mordred, and to remember, when the time comes, that the king has slept with his own sister. He did

not know that he was doing so, and perhaps it may have been due to her, but it seems, in tragedy, that innocence is not enough." *The Once and Future King* inspired the Broadway musical *Camelot*, and was then taken up by Disney (*The Sword in the Stone*).

*Mistress Masham's Repose*, written in an attempt to make money, is about a professor, a ten-year-old girl, and a colony of Lilliputians. The novel starts well but whimsy takes over. The review in the *New York Times* was representative: "The story has neither the charm nor the simplicity to enchant children, nor the maturity which will be expected of it by adult readers." But it was again a Book-of-the-Month Club selection, and brought White renewed financial security at the end of World War II, which he had spent in Ireland.

White lived alone with only a series of red setters for company. His last years were dominated by involvement in the production of *Camelot* and an increasing resort to alcohol. He died while sailing home from a lecture tour in America. *The Book of Merlyn*, a concluding fifth part to *The Once and Future King*, was not published until 1977.

PRINCIPAL WORKS: *Poetry*—Loved Helen and Other Poems, 1929; The Green Bay Tree, 1929; Song Through Space and Other Poems, 1935; Verses, 1962; A Joy Proposed, 1983. *Fiction*—(as "James Aston") They Winter Abroad, 1932; First Lesson, 1932; (as "T. H. White") Darkness at Pemberly, 1932; Farewell Victoria, 1933; Earth Stopped; or, Mr. Marx's Sporting Tour, 1934; Gone to Ground, 1935; The Sword in the Stone, 1938; The Witch in the Wood, 1939; The Ill Made Knight, 1940; Mistress Masham's Repose, 1946; The Elephant and the Kangaroo, 1947; The Scandalmonger, 1952; The Master, 1957; The Once and Future King, 1958; The Book of Merlyn, 1977. *Nonfiction*—England Have My Bones, 1936; Burke's Steerage, 1938; The Age of Scandal, 1950; The Goshawk, 1951; The Book of Beasts, 1954; The Godstone and the Blackymor, 1959; America at Last: The American Journal of T. H. White, 1965; The White/Garnett Letters (ed. D. Garnett) 1968; Letters to a Friend: The Correspondence Between T. H. White and L. J. Potts (ed. F. Gallix) 1982.

ABOUT: Contemporary Authors Vol. 37, 1992; Doyle B. (ed.) Who's Who of Children's Literature, 1968; Garnett, D. *foreword to* The White/Garnett Letters, 1986; Warner, S. T. H. White, a Biography, 1967; White T. H. America at Last, 1965; Who's Who 1964. *Bibliography*—Gallix, F. The Annotated Bibliography, 1986. *Periodicals*—Illustrated London News January 25, 1964; New York Times September 29, 1946; January 18, 1964; Times (London) January 18, 1964.

## WHITE, WALTER FRANCIS (July 1, 1893–March 21, 1955), African-American civil rights leader and novelist, wrote: "Walter White, executive secretary of the National Association for the Advancement of Colored People, was born in Atlanta, Georgia, and lived in the south to 1918 when he became an executive officer of the NAACP. He is a graduate of Atlanta University, and has also done post-graduate work in economics and  sociology in the College of the City of New York. . . . As an official of the NAACP, he has made investigations of forty-one lynchings and

eight race riots; has traveled more than 400,000 miles in the United States and Europe. . . .

"His first novel, *Fire in the Flint*, was published in England, France, Germany, Russia, Norway, Denmark, and Japan. . . .

"Upon the retirement of Mr. James Weldon Johnson in 1931 as secretary of the NAACP, Mr. White was elected as his successor. He was appointed by President Roosevelt as a member of the Advisory Council for the Government of the Virgin Islands in March 1934. . . .

"He has taken a prominent part in the fight against lynching and for enactment of federal legislation against this evil, especially in the marshaling of public opinion on behalf of the Costigan-Wagner anti-lynching bill in the 74th Congress, and he led the forces which succeeded in bringing to passage the Gavagan anti-lynching bill in the 75th Congress.

"In 1937 he was awarded the Spingarn Medal for his personal investigation of lynching and race riots and for his 'remarkable tact, skill and persuasiveness' in lobbying for a federal anti-lynching bill."

---

Walter White's autobiography, *A Man Called White*, opens with these words: "I am a Negro. My skin is white, my eyes are blue, my hair is blond. The traits of my race are nowhere visible upon me." His parents, George W. White, a postal worker, and Madeline (Harrison) White, a schoolteacher, were both extremely fair-skinned. The week-long Atlanta riot of 1906, during which roving white mobs beat, tortured, and killed blacks, made White acutely aware of his racial heritage. The riot was sparked by the appearance of an inflammatory (and false) newspaper story about black rapists preying on white women. Along with his father and brother, the thirteen-year-old White took up arms to defend the family home from an approaching mob, which turned back only when shots were fired from a nearby house. "I knew then who I was." White wrote in his autobiography. "I was a Negro, a human being with an invisible pigmentation which marked me as a person to be hunted, hanged, abused, discriminated against, [and] kept in poverty and ignorance."

White turned to fiction-writing at the instigation of H. L. Mencken, who had asked him to review T. S. Stribling's novel *Birthright*. When White replied that he found Stribling's treatment of educated black Americans to be wholly inadequate, Mencken suggested "Why don't you do the right kind of novel?" The result, written in just two weeks, was *The Fire in the Flint*, the story of Kenneth Harper, a young black doctor who returns to his Georgia hometown to practice medicine shortly after World War I. Harper arrives in Georgia a starry-eyed idealist, but a series of ugly racial incidents transforms him into a zealous civil-rights organizer. Resentful local whites retaliate by raping his sister; his brother, who has killed several of the malefactors, commits suicide rather than face the inevitable lynch mob. In the end, Harper himself is killed by a white mob that has lured him to the home of an allegedly ailing white girl. Reviewers, even while conceding its many artistic flaws, praised *The Fire in the Flint* as an honest book. Writing in the NAACP journal *Crisis*, W.E.B. DuBois called it "a good, stirring story and a strong bit of propaganda against the white Klansman and the black pussyfoot." Du Bois did not deny the novel's shortcomings—its characters, he wrote, are "like labeled figures on a chess board"—but noted, "Perhaps most significant . . . is the fact that a book like this can at last be printed."

In later years, during the 1930s and 1940s, White and Dubois were often at odds over the political direction of the NAACP (which Du Bois had co-founded) and the journal *Crisis* (which Du Bois edited for many years). Both men agreed that blacks should strive for absolute political and social equality with whites, although DuBois thought they might best do so by pursuing economic self-sufficiency through voluntary racial separation, a position that was unacceptable to White, a convinced integrationist.

White's second novel, *Flight*, examines the phenomenon of "passing," or pretending to be white. The protagonist, a light-skinned, New Orleans-born "Negro-Creole" named Mimi Daquin, moves from one city to another, eventually settling in the white world of Manhattan.

Despite significance and timeliness of White's themes, his novels are now generally regarded as lacking in literary distinction. As Edward Waldron remarked in his book *Walter White and the Harlem Renaissance*, "The two novels that Walter White produced were not to survive as models of excellence from the Harlem Renaissance. . . . The most important contribution White was to make to the Harlem Renaissance . . . was not his writing, but his aid to artists who were at the core of that movement: Claude McKay, Rudolph Fisher, Langston Hughes, and Countee Cullen."

Awarded a Guggenheim Fellowship in 1927, White went to France to begin another novel, but instead wrote the nonfiction book *Rope and Faggot*, which is both a documentary history of racial lynching in the United States and a psychosocial analysis of lynchers. Reviewers praised the documentary aspects of the book as invaluable. However, several took strong exception to portions of White's analysis, in particular his contention that lynching was not only sanctioned but often encouraged by the two dominant Christian sects of the American South—Methodists and Baptists. In a *Nation* review, the anthropologist Melville Herskovits praised White for providing "a mine of factual material," but considered his theorizing concerning the religious roots of lynching "too simplistic to be acceptable." On the other hand, the renowned defense attorney Clarence Darrow wrote in a glowing *New York Herald Tribune Books* (1929) review, "I am convinced that he has been a good student of anthropology and knows what he is talking about."

White's last book, *How Far the Promised Land?*, completed just before his death, assesses the progress made by the civil rights movement during his lifetime. In a *New York Herald Tribune Book Review* (1955) notice of that volume, the South African novelist Alan Paton wrote, "Of his own leadership during the closing days of this long journey through the wilderness he says hardly a word. He has praise for the courage of others, but his own courage one must discover for oneself."

White was one of his generation's most important and capable civil rights leaders. Nevertheless, as executive secretary of the NAACP, a post he held from 1931 until his death, he was often seen as overly autocratic. Toward the end of his tenure at the NAACP, internecine disputes multiplied, particularly around the question of how much autonomy the local branches could have. After 1949—when he divorced his first wife, Leah Gladys Powell, a black woman, and married Poppy Cannon, a white editor and writer—his real power in the NAACP declined. Cannon commemorated White in her memoir *A Gentle Knight: My Husband, Walter White*. There is a collection of White's papers in the James Weldon Johnson Collection at the Beinecke Library, Yale University. Material pertaining to White's leadership of the NAACP is housed in the Manuscript Division of the Library of Congress in Washington, D.C.

PRINCIPAL WORKS: *Novels*—The Fire in the Flint, 1924; Flight, 1926. *Race relations*—The American Negro and His Problems: A Comprehensive Picture of a Serious and Pressing Problem, 1927 (pamphlet); The Negro's Contribution to American Culture: The Sudden Flowering of a Genius-Laden Artistic Movement 1928 (pamphlet); Rope and Faggot: A Biography of Judge Lynch, 1929; (with T. Marshall) What Caused the Detroit Riot?, 1943; A Rising Wind, 1945; How Far the Promised Land?, 1955. *Autobiography*—A Man Called White: The Autobiography of Walter White, 1948.

ABOUT: The autobiographical material quoted above was written for Twentieth Century Authors, 1942. Bone, R. The Negro Novel in America, rev. ed. 1965; Cannon, P. A Gentle Knight: My Husband, Walter White, 1958; Current Biography 1942; Dictionary of American Biography, Supplement 5: 1951–1955, 1977; Dictionary of Literary Biography vol. 51 1987; Du Bois, W.E.B. Collected Published Works of W.E.B. Du Bois: Book Reviews, 1977; Fraser, J. Walter White: Civil Rights Leader, 1991: Jakoubek, R. Walter White and the Power of Organized Protest, 1994; Singh, A. The Novels of the Harlem Renaissance: Twelve Black Writers, 1923–1933, 1976; Twentieth-Century Literary Criticism vol. 15 1985; Waldron, E. Walter White and the Harlem Renaissance, 1978. *Periodicals*—American Mercury July 1929; Nation May 15, 1929; New York Herald Tribune Book Review December 11, 1955; New York Herald Tribune Books April 21, 1929; New York Times March 22, 1955; March 25, 1955; New Yorker September 4, 1948; Phylon September 1978; Times (London) March 23, 1955.

**WHITE, WILLIAM ALLEN** (February 10, 1868–January 29, 1944), American journalist, wrote: "I was born in Emporia, Kansas. My father, Dr. Allen White, was from Ohio and his father and mother were from New England, where the family had lived since the 1630s. My mother, Mary Hatton, was pure-bred Irish. Her parents came from Ireland three months before she was born. I grew up in El Dorado, Kansas, sixty miles south of Emporia, and was graduated from high school in 1884. I came to Emporia to go to the College of Emporia that year, and later quit to learn the printer's trade.

I was a reporter going to school at the Kansas State University from 1886 to January 1890. I did not graduate; I quit to take a job on the El Dorado *Republican* as business manager. Later I was editorial writer on the Kansas City *Star* from 1892 to 1895; and in 1895 I bought the Emporia *Gazette*, which I have owned and edited ever since.

"In 1896 I published a book of short stories called *The Real Issue*. Since then, I have published four books of short stories, three novels, three biographies, and five books of political essays.

"I was married in 1893 to Sallie Lindsay Watts. Two children have been born to us, William Lindsay (a syndicated newspaper correspondent and novelist) and Mary Kathrine, who died in 1921. I have held no public office except Regent of the State University. I have served on one or two traveling commissions of no great importance. I have honorary doctor's degrees from Baker University, Washburn College, Beloit College, Knox College,  Oberlin College, Columbia University, Brown University, and Harvard University. I have worked most of my life within a thousand feet of my birthplace. I have been to Europe six times, once to Russia, once to the Orient. That's the story."

One of the last American practitioners of a personal, grass-roots journalism full of local boosterism, William Allen White, from his roll-top desk in Emporia, became one of the nation's leading liberal voices in the early decades of the century.

Considered the epitome of the Midwest common man, White, "the sage of Emporia," gained the respect of several U. S. presidents. His writings were published by many of the most important newspapers and magazines in America. Yet White turned down editorships at more powerful Eastern media and resisted the siren song of public office—except for an unsuccessful run for governor of Kansas as an independent opposing the Ku Klux Klan in 1924—remaining loyal to his hometown newspaper.

White's first taste of national attention came in 1896, when his raging anti-Populist editorial, "What's the Matter with Kansas?," was reprinted in newspapers and distributed in Republican pamphlets across the United States. Though he later regretted its conservative narrowness, the editorial helped him launch his first book of fiction, *The Real Issue* (1896), a collection of stories on Kansas life inspired by James Whitcomb Riley. By the turn of the century White was a supporter of Theodore Roosevelt, who returned the admiration, and for years handed foreign diplomats a copy of White's *Stratagems and Spoils* (1901), which Roosevelt considered the best picture of American politics.

Theodore Roosevelt was, to White, a more invigorating figure than McKinley, who, as White wrote in his *Autobiography*, "had buttoned himself up, and had become almost unconsciously the figure that stands now in Canton not far from his door— William McKinley in bronze." White saw in Roosevelt "something extraordinary, some unusual power . . . which made him a man of destiny. So I followed his train," he wrote. The train led White into more progressive territory. He built an anti-railroad wing of the Republican party in Kansas, helped found the National Progressive Republican League in 1911, gave early support to Robert M. La Follette for president, and followed Roosevelt into the Bull Moose Party in 1912.

His newly acquired liberalism was reflected in his articles for *American* and *Collier's* magazines, and in *A Certain Rich Man* (1909), his attempt at the definitive American novel—tracing the evolution of fictional Sycamore Ridge, Kansas, through the story of a barefoot boy who becomes a greedy multi-millionaire.

Having proved that he could write an epic as well as an editorial or short story, White painted another broad picture, a semi-autobiographical novel of a prodigal son from a small Kansas town, *In the Heart of a Fool* (1918). Some reviewers faulted White for too much morality and sentimentality, but others praised his humor and friendliness.

Although his early writings were primarily Kansan in content, his political activism frequently took him far from Emporia. The American Red Cross sent him, with a colleague, Henry Allen, to France in 1917 as an activities observer. The result was *The Martial Adventures of Henry and Me* (1918), "a trivial book . . . the story of two fat middle-aged men who went to war without their wives," he wrote in his *Autobiography*. White covered the Paris Peace Conference in 1918, and in 1919 was an American delegate to the Russian conference at Prinkip. Throughout the nineteen-teens he was an advocate for the League of Nations.

By the 1920s, White was politically alienated, unhappy in a decade he considered filled with corruption, social privilege, and reaction, epitomized by the rise and fall of Warren G. Harding. "I believe now that the death of Theodore Roosevelt and the rout of his phalanx of reform, together with the collapse of Wilsonian liberalism when America rejected the League of Nations, the eclipse of the elder La Follette's leadership, all created in my heart a climax of defeat. Indeed, the whole liberal movement . . . was tired," he wrote in his *Autobiography*.

He and his wife, Sallie, experienced their own personal tragedy in 1921 when their 16-year-old daughter, Mary, was fatally injured in a horse-riding accident. His editorial, "Mary White," became well-known.

White's biography, *Woodrow Wilson: The Man, His Times, and His Task* (1924), was well-received and marked the start of his career as political biographer. Through portraits of major political players from Grover Cleveland to Alfred E. Smith—whom White bitterly opposed in his 1928 bid for the presidency due to Smith's stance against Prohibition— White sketched fifty years of American political history in *Masks in a Pageant* (1928).

The 1930s saw White still actively editing his newspaper, covering political conventions, writing editorials, articles, and books, and playing a part in public service. In 1930 he went to Haiti as a member of President Herbert Hoover's Commission for Conciliation. Hoover appointed him in 1931 to the Organization for Unemployment Relief. He was elected president of the American Society of Newspaper Editors in 1938, and in 1940 he founded the Committee to Defend America by Aiding the Allies, which was dubbed the William Allen White Committee. He also pushed for developing Palestine for large-scale colonization of Jewish refugees and denounced discrimination against black defense workers.

White himself seemed to know that his political and literary longevity were questionable when he predicted, in his unfinished *Autobiography*, which was completed by his son, William Lindsay White, "Probably if anything I have written in these long, happy years . . . survives more than a decade beyond my life's span, it will be the thousand words or so that I hammered out on my typewriter that bright May morning under the shadow and in the agony of Mary's death." The *Autobiography* was awarded a Pulitzer Prize in 1946 and revised, abridged, and reprinted in 1990.

PRINCIPAL WORKS: *Short stories*—The Real Issue, 1896; The Court of Boyville, 1899; Stratagems and Spoils, 1901; In Our Town, 1906; God's Puppets, 1916; *Boys*—Then and Now, 1926. *Novels*—A Certain Rich Man, 1909; In the Heart of a Fool, 1918. *Biography and essays*—The Old Order Changeth, 1910; The Martial Adventures of Henry and Me, 1918; Woodrow Wilson: The Man, the Times, and His Task, 1924; Politics: The Citizen's Business, 1924; The Editor and His People, 1924; Some Cycles of Cathay, 1925; Calvin Coolidge: The Man Who is President, 1925; Conflicts in American Public Opinion (with W. E. Meyer) 1925; Masks in a Pageant, 1928; What's It All About, 1936; Forty Years on Main Street, 1937; A Puritan in Babylon, 1938; The Changing West, 1939; (ed.) Defense for America, 1940; Autobiography, 1946; Selected Letters, 1899–1943 (ed. by W. Johnson) 1947; Letters of William Allen White and a Young Man (with G. B. Wilson) 1948.

ABOUT: Clough, F. C. William Allen White of Emporia; Current Biography 1940, 1944; Dictionary of American Biography, 1941–1945; Griffith, S. F. Home Town News: William Allen White and the Emporia Gazette; Hinshaw, D. Man From Kansas; Jernigan, E. J. William Allen White; Johnson, W. William Allen White's America; Lippmann, W. Public Persons; McKee, J. D. William Allen White: Maverick on Main Street; McKerns, J. P. (ed.) Biographical Dictionary of American Journalism; Mencken, H. L. Prejudices: First Series; Rich, E. William Allen White: The Man from Emporia; White, W. A. Autobiography. *Periodicals*—Atlantic February 1939; Nation July 27, 1918, April 24, 1937; New York Times November 10, 1918; June 1, 1924; April 25, 1937; January 30, 1944; Times (London) January 31, 1944.

## WHITE, WILLIAM ANTHONY PARKER. See BOUCHER, ANTHONY

## WHITE, WILLIAM LINDSAY (June 17, 1900– July 26, 1973), American journalist and author, was born in Emporia, Kansas, the only son of the celebrated journalist William Allen White, and Sallie (Lindsay) White. While his father worked all his

life near his birthplace, "Young Bill," as he was called to distinguish him from his famous father, spent much time out of Kansas. His first taste of journalism came just after he had graduated from Emporia High School at age eighteen, when he accompanied his father to the Versailles Peace Conference.

He came back to Kansas and attended Kansas State University from 1918 to 1920 and then went on to Harvard University, from which he graduated in 1924. He went to work as a reporter at his father's newspaper, the *Emporia Gazette*, in 1914 and worked in various positions there and for other media until he became editor and publisher of the *Gazette* in 1944, when his father died.

He served in the Kansas legislature in 1931–32 and was on the staff of the *Washington Post* for three months in 1935, but was dismissed. He then

spent two years working on his novel *What People Said* (1938), a chronicle of the mythical Midwestern town of Athena in the era of World War I. The book was criticized for its lack of organization and artistic deficiencies but praised for its social analysis of small town America, which "has rarely been surpassed in American literature," according to Harold Strauss in the *New York Times*.

White moved to New York and joined the staff of *Fortune* in 1937. He was European correspondent for the *New York Post* in 1939–40, and for the Columbia Broadcasting System in 1939. His Christmas broadcast from the Mannerheim Line in Finland received first prize from the National Headliners Club as best European broadcast of the year, and was the inspiration for Robert Sherwood's play *There Shall Be No Night*.

While in London during World War II, White wrote *Journey for Margaret* (1941), recounting the air raids of the winter of 1940–41 and his adoption of a three-year-old English orphan. Nym Wales in *Saturday Review of Literature* called it "a charming and unusual human-interest story." It became an MGM motion picture in 1942. White's next two books focused on World War II combat. *They Were Expendable* (1942) is written as a booklength interview with four young American naval officers of a Motor Torpedo Squadron in the Philippines, and was called "a short, grim, glorious book" by Clifton Fadiman in the *New Yorker*. It, too, became a motion picture. In *Queens Die Proudly* (1943), White let the crew of The Swoose, one of the American Army Air Force's flying fortresses, tell their story of fighter plane action over the Pacific.

White also wrote two books relating to the Korean conflict. *Back Down the Ridge* (1953), the story of twelve wounded men, was described by the *New York Times* as "a short, choppy book that nevertheless conveys something of the horrors of front-line

combat and of the magnificent work of the Army's medical teams." *Captives of Korea* (1957) was an unofficial white paper dealing with prisoner-of-war problems.

PRINCIPAL WORKS: What People Said, 1938; Journey for Margaret, 1941; They Were Expendable, 1942; Queens Die Proudly, 1943; Report on the Russians, 1945; Report on the Germans, 1947; Lost Boundaries, 1948; Land of Milk and Honey, 1949; Bernard Baruch, Portrait of a Citizen, 1950; Back Down the Ridge, 1953; The Captives of Korea, 1957; The Little Toy Dog, 1962; Report on the Asians, 1969.

ABOUT: Contemporary Authors 1981; Current Biography 1943; Van Gelder, R. Writers and Writing. *Periodicals—* Commonweal May 21, 1948; Library Journal January 1, 1969; New Republic June 14, 1943; Newsweek August 6, 1973; New York Times April 10, 1938; February 15, 1953; May 19, 1957; July 27, 1973; New Yorker September 26, 1942; March 17, 1945; October 7, 1950; Time August 6, 1973; Saturday Review of Literature January 17, 1942; Times (London) July 28, 1973.

**WHITEHEAD, ALFRED NORTH** (February 15, 1861–December 30, 1947), British mathematician, philosopher, and educational reformer, was born at Ramsgate, in the Isle of Thanet, East Kent, the son of the Rev. Alfred Whitehead, and his wife, Maria Sarah Buckmaster. Whitehead's childhood years were important to him because, as the philosopher Dorothy M. Emmet wrote in the *Concise Encyclopedia of Philosophy and Philosophers*,  "his boyhood, spent first in Ramsgate and then in the country . . . gave him a strong sense of the continuity of the life of a society over the generations, and of religion as intimately bound up with its way of life."

After having been taught by his father at home for nine years, on account of his supposed frailty, Whitehead was sent to Sherborne School in Somerset, at which he learned what Emmet described as the "Whig" view of history and of the classics: everything was studiously compared to modern institutions and events. Whitehead never lost this Whig habit of seeing everything in terms of a final result, and it may be said to have contributed to his final and most profound metaphysical notion, of "process." As John Passmore put it, from the start Whitehead displayed a "passion for arriving at the most extensive of generalizations." Yet, as Passmore concedes, he at the same time showed more "concreteness" than most of his philosophical contemporaries, in that he wanted to "interpret his generalizations as theories of physics, or education, or of art." At his school Whitehead was equally distinguished at work and games, particularly rugby football; he was head prefect and captain of games. Accounts of his boyhood appear in his *Essays in Science and Philosophy*.

In 1880 Whitehead went to Trinity College, Cambridge, where he would remain for thirty years. In the mathematical tripos of 1883 he was bracketed fourth wrangler, and in the following year was elected a fellow of his college. He became an assistant lecturer at Trinity just afterwards. Thus he entered upon the first of the three main phases of his life.

His first book was *A Treatise on Universal Algebra*. This was early recognized as highly original in its investigation of systems of symbolic logic and Boolean algebra; it gained Whitehead election to the Royal Society in 1903.

Bertrand Russell, then a young scholar of Trinity, became Whitehead's leading pupil and, temporarily, his ardent disciple. Russell would later say, long after their paths had diverged, that Whitehead "inspired a very real and lasting affection." Whereas Russell went on to be influenced by Wittgenstein, and to regard logical (and mathematical) truths as tautologies, Whitehead took a Platonic path; he would call Russell "simplistic" in philosophical matters, even while retaining his admiration for him as "the greatest logician since Aristotle."

In 1900 Whitehead took Russell with him to Paris to attend the First International Congress of Philosophy. While there Russell learned more about the work of an Italian logician, Giuseppe Peano, who had recently invented a new set of symbols for use in symbolic logic. Russell wrote, on his own, but in consultation with Whitehead, his *First Principles of Mathematics* (1901).

The pupil was now beginning to influence his mentor. With their knowledge of the work done in Germany by Gottlob Frege, the true founding father of modern logic, the two men were led to work for ten years on a method by which they might settle the question of the foundations of mathematics. Their monumental three-volumed *Principia Mathematica* (1910–1913) is an attempt to prove that "mathematics is a part of logic"—this had been the thesis of Russell's own book—an ambitious endeavor which seeks to undermine Kant's view that all mathematical proofs are *a priori*. This "colossal" book is, naturally, extremely technical; while it has not commanded universal agreement, and despite later reservations by such logicians as Gödel and by Russell himself, it is still recognized as a major landmark in the history of logic. After some earlier misguided attempts to argue that it was mostly Russell's work, it has finally been shown, in particular by Victor Lowe, that it was a true collaboration, as Russell himself always insisted. Russell was deferred to on matters of logical theory, Whitehead on those of mathematics. The later fourth volume that was to be (by agreement) by Whitehead alone, on geometry, was never finished, since the latter's interests changed and widened.

The experience with Russell—whose pioneering book on Leibniz (1900) had also influenced him—led Whitehead to make a revealing statement: in September 1941 he said in conversation, according to Lucien Price, that he had first observed while working with Russell that "people compose in one or the other of two ways": "He loved words, and words . . . satisfied his craving for expression. . . . But people compose either in words directly . . . or they compose in concepts and then

try to find words. . . . I may add that my own method is the second."

In 1910 Whitehead left Cambridge for London. He became reader in geometry at University College (1912); then, in 1914, he was elected to the chair of applied mathematics at the Imperial College of Science of Technology. He remained there until 1924. It was in this period that he entered into his second phase, in inward terms largely prompted by the death in action of his second son Eric in March 1918. He found it hard at the time to continue with his public work. His elder son and first child, Thomas, served throughout World War I.

During and just after the war, Whitehead was active in educational reform. As a member of the university Senate he helped run the University of London. His address to the Mathematical Association of 1916 was titled "The Aims of Education: A Plea for Reform," and in it he protested the habit of imparting "inert ideas" and argued for, instead, "receptiveness to beauty and humane feeling."

In philosophy Whitehead now took the direction that was already being followed by certain metaphysicians, notably Henri Bergson (whose influence upon Whitehead, has, however, been exaggerated) and Samuel Alexander (author of *Space, Time and Deity*). He had originally been content to describe the universe in Newtonian terms: as consisting of particles of matter and points of space. But from 1906 (in the paper "On Mathematical Concepts of the Material World") on, he began to depart from this view, and thus to sever his connections with what was then classical physics. This was under the impact of Einstein's 1904 formulation of the special theory of relativity, which Whitehead was among the first to discern could open up the way to a new philosophy of Nature itself. He was, as has often been said, one of the very few philosophers able to discuss relativity on "something like equal terms" with Einstein (Dr. T. E. Burke, in *Makers of Modern Culture*). As Passmore writes, Whitehead's books *An Enquiry Concerning the Principles of Natural Knowledge* and *The Concept of Nature* are regarded by many as "the highwater mark of his philosophical achievement."

The germ of Whitehead's philosophy in these works of his middle period lies in his assertion that the perceiver of the universe is a natural organism reacting to it. Space and time, for him, are abstractions from qualities of nature: *spatiality* and *temporality*. Matter itself, and all the properties of matter, are also abstractions from "events" in nature—they are not elements in it. "There is only one nature which is before us in perception"; nature is a "processive flow of occurrences" (many of Whitehead's readers were reminded, here, of Heraclitus). Finally, there is a "special sort of event" in nature, "the mind's foothold in nature." Whitehead boldly stated that this happened in "great Poetry."

Whitehead was now elaborating on what William James had called "stream of consciousness," and on what Bergson had called *la durée*, duration: our experience cannot be explained unless in terms of what he called "events." It was "the fallacy of misplaced concreteness" to suppose that because science genuinely needed discrete "instants" ("moments"), such instants form a real part of our experience. He did not assert that an "instant" is a "fiction" or even an "as if" "event": he defined instants, instead, as a "class of sets of durations with certain extensive relations to one another." And his newly found Platonism came out in his distinction between "objects" and "events." The events were "the final real things of which the world is made up." The link here with Plato's forms is obvious. Whitehead's God, as he finally saw the matter, is neither omnipotent nor a "Christian" God of any kind: it is a non-temporal but necessary entity. Instead of omnipotence, there was a "cosmic urge towards harmony."

In 1924, when he was sixty-three, Whitehead accepted an invitation from Harvard to become professor of philosophy. He accepted and lived in America until his death. There, with an audience more receptive to the type of work he was doing, he began his last phase, typified by the formidable *Process and Reality* (1929). This is an attempt to erect a metaphysical "cosmology" in the grand tradition of Spinoza or Leibniz. The system of the latter, as mediated by Russell—though Whitehead eventually came to sympathize more with Leibniz than with his critic—greatly influenced it; but in Whitehead's system Leibniz's "windowless Monads" acquire windows: everything stands in relation to everything else.

*Process and Reality*, although the least accessible of Whitehead's books, is his masterwork. When he first presented the kernel of it, in the Gifford Lectures given at Edinburgh in June 1928, he failed: because, wrote Lowe, "of its complexity, and the new terminology that the system required, the lectures were a fiasco, but their publication in 1930 under the title of *Process and Reality* was an important event in the history of metaphysics." An added ingredient in this work was Whitehead's new exposure to the American pragmatists, who, in their own way, were also "process philosophers"—in that they took the notion of "becoming" in the world as an even more immediately real one than "substance" or "being."

In December 1890, while still at Cambridge University, Whitehead married Evelyn Willoughby Wade, described by Victor Lowe as "vivacious, unacademic . . . a 'sofa lady' with heart trouble who lived to be ninety-five." She was a woman of intense likes and dislikes—hardly in this resembling her husband, who was, at least until his old age, uncritical of others almost to a fault. They had two sons and a daughter. "She always had the energy to rule the family . . . and shield her husband from financial anxiety," wrote Lowe. She is very much a presence, and not always a useful one in philosophical terms, in the journalist Lucien Price's *Dialogues of Alfred North Whitehead*: Whitehead tended to defer to her in public conversation. But she played a decisive part in his life, and he fully and warmly acknowledged this. Until shortly before he married her Whitehead, under the personal influence of Cardinal Newman, had considered joining the Roman Catholic Church. But he decided to sell all his theological books instead. The uneasy agnosticism he then embraced did not survive the loss of his son Eric. For a tolerant man, he was unusually acrid about all kinds of churches, and, although in effect the founding father of American Process Theology, never joined any sect.

In 1945 Whitehead was awarded the Order of Merit. In his old age, he became a celebrated conversationalist, entertaining his Harvard students at home on Sunday nights, "well-attended occasions . . . skillfully managed by Mrs. Whitehead." He asked her to destroy all his unpublished manuscripts and correspondence, and this, upon his death, she did. Of the scores of books on him, the best introduction is either the one by Mays, or, even better, his own *Adventures of Ideas*.

PRINCIPAL WORKS: *Selections*—The Wit and Wisdom of Alfred North Whitehead (ed. A. J. Johnson), 1947; Dialogues of Alfred North Whitehead, as recorded by Lucien Price, 1954. A Treatise on Universal Algebra, 1898; The Axioms of Projective Geometry, 1906; The Axioms of Descriptive Geometry, 1907; (with B. Russell) Principia Mathematica, 3 vols., 1910–1913; The Organization of Thought, Educational and Scientific, 1917; An Enquiry Concerning the Principles of Natural Knowledge, 1919; The Concept of Nature, 1920; The Principle of Relativity and Applications to Natural Science, 1922; Science and the Modern World, 1925; Religion in the making, 1926; Symbolism: Its Meaning and Effect, 1927; The Aims of Education and Other Essays, 1929; The Function of Reason, 1929; Process and Reality: An Essay in Cosmology, 1929 ("corrected edition," 1978); Adventures of Ideas, 1933; Nature and Life, 1934; Modes of Thought, 1938; Essays in Science and Philosophy, 1947.

ABOUT: Brumbaugh, R. S. Whitehead, Process Theology, and Education, 1922; Christian, W. A. An Interpretation of Whiteheads Metaphysics, 1959; Emmet, D. M. Whitehead's Philosophy of Organism, 1932, rev. ed., 1981; Hammerschmidt, W. W. Whitehead's Philosophy of Time, 1947; Hartshorne, C. (With A. H. Johnson and V. Lowe) Whitehead and the Modern World, 1950; Hartshorne, C. Aquinas to Whitehead, 1970; Hartshorne, C. Whitehead's Philosophy: Selected Essays 1935–1970, 1972; Hartshorne, C. (with C. Peden) Whitehead's View of Reality, 1981; Johnson, A. H. Whitehead and His Philosophy, 1983; Lawrence, N. M. Alfred North Whitehead, 1974; Leclerk, I. Whitehead's Metaphysics, 1958; Lowe, V. Alfred North Whitehead, 1941; Lowe, V. Understanding Whitehead, 1962; Lowe, V. Alfred North Whitehead: The Man and His Work, 2 vols., 1990; Lucas, G. R. The Rehabilitation of Whitehead, 1989; Mason, D. R. Time and Providence: An Essay based on an Analysis of Time in Whitehead and Heidegger, 1982; Mays, W. The Philosophy of Whitehead, 1959; McHenry, L. B. Whitehead and Bradley: A Comparative Analysis, 1992; Miller, D. L. and Gentry, G. The Philosophy of A. N. Whitehead, 1938; Odin, S. Process Metaphysics and Hua-Yen Buddhism, 1982; Russell, B. Portraits from Memory, 1952; Russell, B. My Philosophical Development, 1959; Sarker, A. K. Buddhism and Whitehead's Process Theology, 1991; Shahan, E. P. Whiteheads Philosophy of Experience, 1950; Schilpp, P. A. (ed.) The Philosophy of Alfred North Whitehead, 1941; Urmson, J. O. (ed.) Concise Encyclopedia of Philosophy and Philosophers, 1960; Weisenbeck, J. D. Whitehead's Philosophy of Values, 1969; Wintle, J. (ed.) Makers of Modern Culture, 1981; Wood, F. Whiteheadian Thought as a Basis for a Philosophy of Religion, 1986. *Periodicals*—Humanist May/June 1995; Journal of Religion April 1986; Mind, April 1948 (Whitehead number); New York Review of Books December 15, 1985; Philosophy Today Fall 1984; Theological Studies March 1985; Time January 12, 1948; May 3, 1954; Yale Review Summer 1987; Zygon June 1985.

**WHITEING, RICHARD** (July 27, 1840–June 29, 1928), English novelist and journalist, was born in London, the son of William Whiteing, holder of "a

modest place in the Inland Revenue Office at Somerset House," and the former Mary Lander, who died soon after his birth. Richard lived with his father in Norfolk Street, off London's Strand, when, as he put it in his autobiography, *My Harvest*, it consisted of "a double line of Georgian houses and was the classic land of the London lodging house."

Whiteing, by virtue of his novels *The Island* and *No 5 John Street*, is associated with the "English realist novelists." These writers—the chief ones are Arthur Morrison, Edwin Pugh, W. Pett Ridge, and Whiteing himself—were, along with the more substantial George Gissing and George Moore, the leading English novelists influenced by the French naturalist school of Émile Zola. All of the minor realist novelists concentrated on the seamy side of London life, and all of them had in varying degrees both a sound knowledge of it and an unusual skill in evoking its atmosphere and its hopelessness.

Whiteing was first a journalist. After living with foster parents in St. Johns Wood, Whiteing was for seven years an apprentice to an engraver. He attended art classes and heard John Ruskin lecture. Then he began to contribute small sketches to the newspapers. The first result of this was a collection called *Mr. Sprouts—His Opinions*, typical of books hopefully imitating Dickens. He obtained work as a foreign correspondent for various papers and visited France and America in that capacity. He was for thirteen years on the staff of the *London Daily News*. He married Helen Harris, the daughter of an American minister to Japan, in 1869.

Whiteing's first novel of note, *The Island: An Adventure of a Person of Quality*, appeared in 1888. In it, an English lord, nauseated by the tone of modern society, abandons the world. To his surprise, he then discovers that, on an island in the Pacific, a community of Englishmen, originally shipwrecked, have contrived to form a peaceful and happy society.

Its sequel, *No 5 John Street*, followed more than a decade later. Its plot is simple: a friend of the lord who was the protagonist of *The Island*, the narrator, himself a baronet, decides to investigate conditions in a London slum by assuming a false identity and himself living in one. He discovers—and the way Whiteing deals with this revelation is effective—a whole new set of values. When the narrator alarmedly tells a friend that there is a "murder going on," the friend simply replies, "Dessay. It's Saturday night." As Vincent Brome wrote in his brief discussion of the novel, "It juxtaposes long descriptions of slum life with a return to luxury living and interlards these again with 'reports to the Governor of what the narrator has found in that black hell be-

yond Shoreditch." Brome also found Whiteing ironical: "We cannot give better than we have, and we must search our hearts deeply to feel sure that we are equal to the high mission of putting others to death for their own good."

Although Whiteing tried to repeat this success with *The Yellow Van* and *Ring in the New*—about an untrained girl setting out to obtain work—as well as two other novels, his ironies fell flat and his plots were weak. His *Times* obituarist maintained that he "detested the power, the influence, even the manners and speech, of the rich, who, in his eyes, were all stupid or vicious idlers." In 1910 he was granted a Civil List pension. His two books on Paris were considered among the best written about that city.

PRINCIPAL WORKS: *Novels*—Mr. Sprouts—His Opinions, 1867; The Democracy, 1876; The Island, 1888; No 5 John Street, 1899; The Yellow Van, 1903; Ring in the New, 1906; All Moonshine, 1907; Little People, 1908. *Travel and essays*—Wonderful Escapes, 1870; The Life of Paris, 1900; Paris of Today, 1900; A Little Book About London, 1911; Drawing From Delight, 1912. *Autobiography*—My Harvest, 1915.

ABOUT: Brome, V. Four Realist Novelists, 1965; Dictionary of National Biography, 1937; Whiteing, R. My Harvest, 1915. *Periodical*—Times (London) June 30, 1928.

**WHITLOCK, BRAND** (March 4, 1969–May 24, 1934), American reformer, diplomat, and novelist, was born in Urbana, Ohio, the son of Dr. Elias

Whitlock, a Methodist minister, and his wife, Mallie Brand. The founder of the family, Thomas Whitlock, had arrived in America from Wiltshire, England, in 1640. Brand Whitlock was educated at Toledo High School, but refused to attend Ohio Wesleyan to study law as his parents had

wished him to do. Instead he went to work as a reporter for the *Toledo Blade* (1887–1890). From there he graduated to the *Chicago Herald*, a newspaper which, with George Ade and F. P. Dunne ("Mr. Dooley") on its staff, had something of a comic literary tradition. But Whitlock was not to take the path of a comic writer; on the contrary, he transformed himself into a political activist and a grimly realistic depictor of the social ills of his country.

As a reforming lawyer and diplomat, Whitlock had a long and varied career. As clerk in the office of the Illinois secretary of state (1893–1897) he was instrumental in securing the state governor's pardons—which he wrote anonymously—for the last three prisoners unjustly detained in connection with the 1886 Haymarket riots. Meanwhile he was studying law. He was admitted to the Illinois bar in 1895 and to the Ohio bar in 1897. He practiced as a lawyer in Toledo, and in 1905 became its reformist mayor. He held this post for four successive terms, but declined a fifth to become U.S. Minister to Belgium. The decision to accept President Wilson's offer—one of many he made to writers and

WICKENDEN

intellectuals—was the result of Whitlock's desire to get on with and to improve the quality of his seriously intended fiction (he had already published five novels). Instead, he soon found himself in the thick of the German invasion of Belgium. The relief commission he organized was credited with saving some ten million Belgians from starvation. All this Whitlock wrote about in *Belgium: A Personal Record*, of which the *New York Times* (1919) remarked "it is history, and history written with a richness, a color, a vitality and a truth which time and changes in public opinion can never make less valuable."

Whitlock's most illuminating book is the autobiography *Forty Years of It*, which the *Boston Transcript* described as "an intensely graphic portrayal of American life and its social upheaval as viewed by a sturdy man who is not afraid to speak and write as he thinks." This book still has its place in the history of the development of American politics, and was reprinted in 1970.

As a novelist, Whitlock has a minor place in the advent of American realism, and his intentions were appreciated by such writers as Upton Sinclair and Jack London. His first novel, *The Thirteenth District*, deals with the corruption of a congressman. Like several of his other novels, it is set in Macochee, an evocation of his own native town of Urbana, Ohio. It was reprinted in the author's revised edition in 1968.

The next two novels, *The Happy Average* and *Her Infinite Variety*, were shorter. The first was semi-autobiographical, the second a distinctly light-hearted treatment of the involvements of suffragists in politics.

In *The Turn of the Balance* he made his nearest approach to a good novel, and it was included in E. A. Baker and James Packman's 1932 list of *The Best Fiction*. These critics called it: "A determined exposure of the legal and other delinquencies of the American social system. . . . Unjust treatment of criminals and victims of legal injustice—both alike presented with much of the angel in their composition—the debasing effects of Mammon-worship and hypocritical laws; all illustrated with abundance of sensations." It "deeply stirred" Jack London, and Upton Sinclair was moved to describe it as greater than Tolstoy's *Resurrection*. One of its more interesting aspects is Whitlock's use of slang—a special glossary was provided for readers. It was reprinted, in Whitlock's own revised version of 1924, in 1970. Judged solely as a public-service novel—in the tradition of Upton Sinclair—it deserves its status.

Only one more of Whitlock's novels possessed anything like the same power: *Big Matt*, a study of a machine politician. Robert Penn Warren, author of *All the King's Men*, profited from his reading of *Big Matt*. *J. Hardin & Son*, a novel of small-town life, was called "a little plodding" by Whitlock's friend Allan Nevins, who edited his posthumous *Letters and Journal*; but it was found worthy of a 1982 reprint in the author's revised edition.

Of Whitlock's biography of Lafayette the London *Times* commented: "Mr. Whitlock continues his straightforward narrative, not eloquent, but concise, good-humoured, shrewd, magnanimous to his hero, able to smile at his foibles . . . Whitlock's geniality, his liberalism and his talent as a writer take command anew."

PRINCIPAL WORKS: *Fiction*—The Thirteenth District, 1902 rev. ed. 1968; The Happy Average, 1904; Her Infinite Variety, 1904: The Turn of the Balance, 1907 rev. ed., 1970; The Fall Guy, 1912; J. Hardin & Son, 1923 rev. ed., 1982; Uprooted, 1926; Transplanted, 1927; Big Matt, 1928; The Little Green Shutter, 1931; Narcissus: A Belgian Legend of Van Dyke, 1931; The Stranger on the Island, 1933. *Nonfiction*—Abraham Lincoln, 1909; The Gold Brick, 1910; On the Enforcement of Cities, 1910; Forty Years of It, 1914 2nd rev. ed., 1970; Belgium: A Personal Record, 1919; La Fayette, 1929; Little Lion: Mieke, 1931; Letters and Journal, (ed. A. Nevins) 1936.

ABOUT: Anderson, D. Brand Whitlock, 1968; Baker E. A. and Packman, J. The Best Fiction, 1932; Crunden, R. Hero in Spite of Himself, 1969; Dictionary of American Biography, 1939; Findling, J. E. Dictionary of American Diplomatic History, 1989; Nevins, A. *in* Letters and Journals 1936; Tager, J. The Intellectual as Urban Reformer, 1968; Whitlock, B. *in* Forty Years of It, 1914. *Periodicals*—Boston Transcript March 7, 1914; New York Times May 11, 1919, May 27, 1934; Survey June 1934; Times (London) November 21, 1929.

**WICKENDEN, DAN** (March 24, 1913–October 27, 1989), American novelist, wrote: "I'm a first-generation American, born [Leonard Daniel Wickenden] of English parents, in Tyrone, Pennsylvania, where my father had a position as chemist with the West Virginia Pulp & Paper Company. Later he became laboratory chief of the New York Office, and my earliest memories are mostly of Long Island, at a time when  Flushing ran off at the edges into a wonderful country of farms and fields and great tracts of swampy woodland.

"Those early years were sharply divided from all the rest by a voyage to England that followed the end of my elementary schooling. By the time we came home I had turned fourteen, and we moved out to Manhasset, where I started high school. I'd always wanted to write and had always written; but now I sometimes wrote middles and ends as well as beginnings, and began to bother magazines with manuscripts. This habit became ingrained during four years at Amherst College, where I majored in English, played character parts with the Masquers, and spent a good deal of my spare time roaming about the countryside—I've always liked weathers and landscapes.

"In the fall after graduation in 1935, I sold a one-act play and a short story, in rapid succession, to magazines that have since gone out of existence, and tried to believe that I had become an author. For some eighteen months I was also a commuter and an employee of the Columbia Broadcasting System; but after the acceptance, in 1937, of my second serious attempt at a novel, I began trying to support myself by writing alone.

"For a few years I succeeded, after a fashion, and in the summer of 1940 set out on a 15,000-mile journey through much of the United States and Mexico. This confirmed a passion for scenery on the grand scale and aroused an interest in the Indians of the Americas that has continued ever since. Poverty began to pinch, though, and early in 1942 I went to Michigan and became a reporter for the *Grand Rapids Press.* This job, too, lasted for about eighteen months, and it was a good and stimulating experience; but I wasn't writing any fiction, so toward the end of 1943 I cut loose again and returned to the East and to free-lancing.

"A period of prosperity made possible two long sojourns in Guatemala, with which I became infatuated, but where I got no writing done. Since 1945, home base has been Westport, Connecticut, where there are neither mountains nor Indians, but which has its advantages and isn't completely suburban yet.

"In 1951 I was married to Hermione Hillman of Grand Rapids, and a son named David was born in 1952. Wife and child are far more important than the six published novels behind me, and most of the time I still don't really feel like an author; but I continue to hope that I may someday write a book which will seem good to me even after it is in print."

----

In 1953 Dan Wickenden joined the staff of the book publisher Harcourt Brace Jovanovich as an associate editor; he was senior editor when he retired in 1978, although he continued with the firm as a freelance editor and consultant.

Wickenden's powers as a novelist were modest but, at his best, he proved, as the *New York Times* (1948) commented, "that it is possible to be warmhearted without being mawkish and wholesome without being insipid." This comes from a review of *Tobias Brandywine*, a Depression-era family story. Wickenden's subject matter was usually, as in this case, contemporary American family life, recorded faithfully, sympathetically, and in an unpretentious and unobtrusive style.

His first novel, *The Running of the Deer*, was a story of Long Island suburban life; reviewers were quick to note its promise. The novelist and editor William Maxwell in the *Saturday Review of Literature* noted a "special excitement" all through the novel and found "evidence on every page, or practically every page, that its author has far more up his literary sleeve than he knows what to do with." There was praise for his second novel, *Walk Like a Mortal*, too. This gave an account of a seventeen-year-old boy trying to cope with the breakup of his parent's marriage. Appreciation continued with Wickendon's third novel, *The Wayfarers*, which chronicled a grieving widower's revaluation of himself and his relationships with his children.

Wickenden chose an exotic setting for his 1950 novel *The Dry Season*. The story concerned a troubled young man who journeys to Guatemala, where he takes up with a colony of writers and artists. Although Wickenden was again praised for his thoughtful, intelligent prose, some reviewers felt he had lost something in the way of power and charm. Wickenden's last adult novel, *The Red Carpet*, chronicled a small-town boy's experiences with New York bohemian life in 1937.

PRINCIPAL WORKS: *Novels*—The Running of the Deer, 1937; Walk Like a Mortal, 1940; The Wayfarers, 1945; Tobias Brandywine, 1948; The Dry Season, 1950; The Red Carpet, 1952. *Juvenile*—The Amazing Vacation, 1956.

ABOUT: The autobiographical material quoted above was written for Twentieth Century Authors First Supplement, 1955. *Periodicals*—New York Herald Tribune Book Review June 8, 1952; New York Times May 2, 1948; October 29, 1989; Saturday Review of Literature October 16, 1937.

**"WICKHAM, ANNA" (pseudonym of EDITH HEPBURN)** (1884–April 30, 1947), English poet, was born Edith Alice Mary Harper at Sutton, Surrey, on the southern outskirts of London. She was the daughter of Geoffrey Harper, a piano tuner who kept a music shop, and Alice Whelan, an eccentric piano teacher. At the age of six Edith Harper was taken to Australia, where she completed her education at Sydney High School. She took her pseudonym from one of her father's Australian addresses, Wickham Terrace, in Brisbane: it was there, at the age of ten, that she first decided that she would be a poet. She was encouraged in her writing by both parents, who had two of her juvenile works—*The Seasons* and *Wonder Eyes*—privately printed.

At the age of twenty she returned to Europe alone, now determined to become a singer. She studied under Jean de Reske in London, and then in Paris; but she fell victim to the apparent charms of Patrick Hepburn, a solicitor and amateur astronomer, whom she married in 1905. She bore him four sons; but he "had no intention of allowing his wife to be a poet," and, after she had defied him by lecturing on motherhood and women's rights, and publishing, with the Women's Printing Society in 1911, *Songs of John Oland*, had her cast into a private "lunatic asylum" for six weeks. Later (1926) Hepburn was to obtain a "judicial separation" from her. They were reunited in 1928; he was killed in a climbing accident in the following year. The opening of her poem "Nervous Prostration," sums up what she thought of Patrick Hepburn:

I married a man of the Croydon class
When I was twenty-two.
And I vex him, and he bores me
Till we don't know what to do!
It isn't good form in the Croydon class
To say you love your wife,
So I spend my days with the tradesmen's books
And pray for the end of life.

What set Anna Wickham off in wholeheartedly determined pursuit of her individuality was the sudden death of her third son in 1922. Before that her children had been some consolation to her in her constant battles with her husband. She went to Paris and there met the rich American lesbian writer Natalie Barney, who encouraged her, gave her both financial and moral support, and introduced her to various writers.

More fruitfully for her, her gift had long been

recognized by Harold Monro of the Poetry Bookshop, who from 1914 had seen to it that her work was published in his various periodicals. Monro issued her first proper collection, *The Contemplative Quarry*, in 1915. Her second, *The Man with a Hammer*, he persuaded Grant Richards to publish. The Poetry Bookshop then published a further volume, *The Little Old House*.

It was Monro who told the American anthologist Louis Untermeyer about Wickham. Untermeyer anthologized her poems in his *50 Modern American and British Poets* and in *British Poetry*—and introduced an American edition of her poetry, a conflation of *The Contemplative Quarry* and *The Man with a Hammer*. He linked her with English "feminist" writers such as Virginia Woolf and Mary Sinclair and described her as "a magnificent gypsy of a woman, wayward, ironic, spontaneous. . . . gnarled in her own nervous protest." D. H. Lawrence heard of her from Monro, and thought highly of a few of her poems.

After Monro's death in 1932, Wickham had few real supporters in England. She herself became increasingly eccentric. No one noticed her among the modernist poets of the 1930s. Poetry-readers' attention shifted to the work of the relatively newly discovered Emily Dickinson, to Edith Sitwell, or, a little later, to the young Kathleen Raine. She was briefly taken up by the erratic and little heeded anti-modernist John Gawsworth who edited a selection of her poems (1936). Her house on Parliament Hill in Hampstead was hit by a German incendiary bomb in 1943, causing the loss of much valuable manuscript material. She gradually fell into a depression. Then, in 1947, she hanged herself. She left behind nearly 1,500 poems, and one or two prose pieces, such as one about D. H. Lawrence, "The Spirit of the D. H. Lawrence Women." David Garnett made a selection from her poems in 1971, but little attention was directed towards her until the publication in 1984 of *The Writings of Anna Wickham, Free Woman and Poet*. Monro in his *Some Contemporary Poets* called her "a brilliant writer of psychological gossip," with "frank sensuality . . . no sharp differentiation between lust and love." The poet Carol Rumens in the *Oxford Companion to Twentieth Century Poetry* wrote that "though her distinctive, forthright voice is always audible, what she called her free rhythms can sound rather inert and unsure."

Wickham's verse is, as has been claimed in the *Feminist Companion*, "sardonic, experimental . . . and charged with exuberant feminist consciousness." She is remembered for her struggle against her husband's attempts to make her into an object, her few epigrammatic successes, her "Fragment of Autobiography" (unpublished until 1984), and the poignancy of her last year.

PRINCIPAL WORKS: *Selections*—Smith R. D. (ed.) Anna Wickham: Poet and Free Woman, 1984. *Poetry*—(as "John Oland") Songs of John Oland, 1911; The Contemplative Quarry, 1915; The Man with a Hammer, 1916; The Little Old House, 1921; The Contemplative Quarry and The Man with the Hammer, 1921; Gawsworth, J. (ed.) Richards Selection from Edwardian Poets: Anna Wickham, 1936; Garnett, D. (ed.) Selected Poems, 1971.

ABOUT: Blain, V., Clements, P., and Grundy, I. (eds.) The Feminist Companion to Literature in English, 1990; Hamilton, I. (ed.) Companion to Twentieth Century Poetry, 1994; Monro, H. Some Contemporary Poets, 1920; Seymour-Smith, M. Macmillan Guide to Modern World Literature, 1986; Shattock, J. (ed.) British Women Writers, 1993; Stark, M. Four Decades of Poetry, 1978. *Periodicals*—New Statesman August 31, 1984; Southern Review 14, 1978; Times Literary Supplement August 10, 1984; Times (London) May 2, 1947.

**WIDDEMER, MARGARET** (September 30, 1884–July 14, 1978), American poet and novelist, wrote: "I was born in Doylestown, Pennsylvania of parents who came of the old colonial stock. My father was a minister. My education was what is called 'private,' given by my grandmother and my father. I had written since my fourth or fifth year, dictating till I could write for myself. It was always in the air that I was to grow up to be a writer, if I didn't sing. At ten I began to publish poems in the *St. Nicholas* league. I took library training at the Drexel Institute of Arts and Sciences, and worked for a year with Dr. A. W. Rosenbach, cataloging his rare books; then at the University of Pennsylvania, where they discharged me for inaccuracy in copying catalogue cards. I was completely crushed by the ruin of a career in youth. I had been writing poems (I suppose to the detriment of cataloguing) during and after hours; I went on with these and short stories. Soon I was making more money than I had at the library. I began to publish novels and poems before I was out of my teens. I have been doing it ever since; lecturing on poetry and the novel, and doing short stories and essays whenever the novels gave me a breathing spell.

"My first novel was a best seller, and I have received a number of awards for poetry. In 1919 I married Robert Haven Schauffler, the poet; the marriage was not of long duration. From 1923 to 1933 I lived in New York. In 1931 Bucknell University awarded me an honorary Litt.D.; in 1933 Middlebury College gave me an honorary M.A. From 1928 to 1932 I lectured at the Middlebury Writers' Conference at Breadloaf; in 1933 at the  University of Colorado Writers' Conference. In 1936 I broadcast a series of talks over the N.B.C. Blue Network, called 'Do You Want to Write?' I live now at Larchmont Manor, New York, and spend my summers in the Adirondacks where I swim and canoe. I am also interested in imaginative sculpture, modeling miniature groups in plasticine, some of which I have exhibited.

"My aesthetic bias has always been toward the classic and conservative; curiously mingled with a deep interest in social problems, which has given my poetry conservative form and modern content in many cases. I am strongly against specialization in art or life, and have continued to do work in as many literary mediums as I could find possible."

Margaret Widdemer considered poetry to be her most important medium of expression. *The Factories*, her first collection, was praised by reviewers in particular for its sincere title poem, a condemnation of labor exploitation. In 1926 she published *The Singing Wood*, a verse play, which the *New York Herald Tribune* called a "compromise between poetry and childishness. Those who are acquainted with Miss Widdemer's work know the two different poets under the same name: the commercial magazine poet and the melancholy artist."

Widdemer also wrote novels, light romances, for the most part. Her best selling first novel, *The Rose-Garden Husband*, tells the story of a poor librarian who marries a wealthy but gravely ill young man and nurses him back to health.

In 1964 Widdemer published *Golden Friends I Had: Unrevised Memories*, recounting her years in the New York literary scene and her acquaintanceship with such writers as Elinor Wylie, Edwin Arlington Robinson, Edna St. Vincent Millay, Ezra Pound, Thornton Wilder, and Amy Lowell.

PRINCIPAL WORKS: *Poetry*—The Factories, with Other Lyrics, 1915; The Old Road to Paradise, 1918; Cross-Currents, 1921; A Tree with a Bird in It: A Symposium of Contemporary American Poets on Being Shown a Pear-Tree on Which Sat a Grackle, 1922; Ballads and Lyrics, 1925; The Singing Wood, 1926; Collected Poems, 1928; The Road to Downderry and Other Poems, 1932; Hill Garden: New Poems, 1936; The Dark Cavalier: The Collected Poems, 1958. *Novels*—The Rose-Garden Husband, 1915; Why Not?, 1915; The Wishing-Ring Man, 1917; You're Only Young Once, 1918; I've Married Marjorie, 1920; The Year of Delight, 1921; Graven Image, 1923; Charis Sees It Through, 1924; Gallant Lady, 1926; More Than Wife, 1927; Rhinestones: A Romance, 1929; All the King's Horses, 1930; Loyal Lover, 1930; The Truth About Lovers, 1931; Pre-War Lady, 1932; Golden Rain, 1933; The Years of Love, 1933; Back to Virtue, 1934; The Other Lovers, 1934; Eve's Orchard, 1935; Marriage Is Possible, 1936; This Isn't the End, 1936; Hand on Her Shoulder, 1938; She Knew Three Brothers, 1939; Someday I'll Find You, 1940; Let Me Have Wings, 1941; Lover's Alibi, 1941; Angela Comes Home, 1942; Constancia Herself, 1944; Lani, 1948; Red Cloak Flying, 1950; Lady of the Mohawks, 1951; The Golden Wildcat, 1954; Buckskin Baronet, 1960; The Red Castle Women, 1968. *Short stories*—The Boardwalk, 1920; A Minister of Grace, 1922; Ladies Go Masked, 1929. *Nonfiction*—Basic Principles of Fiction Writing, 1953; Do You Want to Write?, 1937. *Juvenile*—Little Girl and Boy Land: Poems for Children, 1924; Winona of the Camp Fire, 1915; Winona of Camp Karonya, 1917; Winona's War Farm, 1918; Winona's Way: A Story of Reconstruction, 1919; Winona on Her Own, 1922; Binkie and the Bell Dolls, 1923; Winona's Dreams Come True, 1923; Marcia's Farmhouse, 1939; Prince in Buckskin: A Story of Joseph Brant at Lake George, 1952; The Great Pine's Son: A Story of the Pontiac War, 1954. *As editor*—The Haunted Hour: An Anthology, 1920; The Best American Love Stories of the Year, 1932. *Memoirs*—Golden Friends I Had: Unrevised Memories, 1964 (reissued in part as Summers at the Colony, 1964).

ABOUT: The autobiographical material quoted above was written for Twentieth Century Authors, 1942. *Periodicals*—Christian Science Monitor September 16, 1964; New York Herald Tribune September 5, 1926; New York Times March 7, 1915; July 15, 1978; New York Times Book Review September 6, 1964.

**WIECHERT, ERNST** (May 18, 1887–August 24, 1950), German novelist, short story writer, autobiographer, and essayist, was born in the remote woodlands of East Prussia. His father was a chief forester. In *Walder und Menschen* (Forests and

people)—and later again, but more briefly, in *Jahre und Zeiten* (translated as *Tidings*)—he gives an account of how he grew up in this area of natural wildness and beauty and of how close he felt to nature. His mother, depressed and pathologically sensitive, lived only on the edge of sanity; her melancholy, the tales in the Bible upon which he was brought up, and the bizarre folklore of the lonely region all blended

together to influence him towards a resolutely gloomy pessimism. When at eleven he went to school in Konigsberg—later he attended the University there— and started to read such Russians as Dostoyevski and such Scandinavians as Hamsun, the grimness of these authors confirmed him in his dark view of life.

Wiechert's first novel, written while he was unhappily employed as a teacher in secondary schools, was *Die Flucht* (The flight); it was not published until 1916. It is a "suicide novel," such as were fairly common at that time. In *Die Flucht* the protagonist kills himself, in effect discovering that nothing civilization offers can possibly match the beauties of the Masurian forests.

Wiechert served as an officer in World War I, first on the Eastern front and then in France, where he was wounded. In 1918 he returned to teaching. His best novel from this period is *Jerdermann* (Everyman), about the sufferings caused by the war. He retired to Bavaria in order to devote himself to writing in 1933, the year the Nazis came to power. *Der Wald* (The forest) and *Der Totenwolf* (The death wolf) with their heavy prose, their cult of brutality, and their hatred of the spirit of the age came very close to the *Blut und Boden* (blood and soil) style that the Nazis would take up as their model, and are almost comic in their gloom.

Wiechert, despite his affinities with the *Blut und Boden* school, was no Nazi. He followed up those two novels with *Der Knecht Gottes Andreas Nyland* (God's servant, Andreas Nyland), an account of how Andreas Nyland tries to imitate Christ but is forced to retreat to the forests, which have not been corrupted by civilization.

After the advent of the Nazis, Wiechert was a supporter of Pastor Martin Niemoller, the anti-Nazi Protestant theologian. Weichert's courageous lectures to young people, and in particular the speech "Der Dichter und die Zeit" (The poet and his time), delivered at the University of Munich, caused Himmler in person to order his detention in Buchenwald concentration camp for five months in 1938. He continued to write after his release, but was forbidden to publish, and was carefully watched by the Gestapo until the end of the war. He was then expected to become a leading moral spokesman for his defeated country—but he was not up to it, and died, a still embittered man, in Orikon, Switzerland. The volume *Tidings* is mainly devoted to his own account of his years under the Nazis. The concentration camp experiences are recounted in *Der Totenwald* (*The Forest of the Dead*).

Wiechert became famous throughout Europe and the United States for two novels: *Die Magd des Jürgen Doscozil* (translated as *The Girl and the Ferryman*) and *Die Marjorin* (*The Baroness*), a variation on a well-worn theme: the return of the soldier who has been thought killed in action. Wiechert's protagonist, Michael, is a dead spirit in a living body. Reviewers tended to respond negatively to it: Lionel Trilling in the *New Republic* (1936) thought it written in a "fake biblical-symbolic style, full of lyrical and disgusting *simplesse*," and the *New Statesman* called it "an uneven specimen of its kind" and "one of those irritating books about the soil." William Plomer, however, wrote in the *Spectator* that the story was "told with a grave simplicity that lends it the air of a parable."

*The Girl and the Ferryman* was as widely read, but suffered from an over-melodramatic plot. More representative of Wiechert's powers was a shorter story of 1935, *Hirtennovelle* (The Shepherd's Novella) in which a boy leads the people of his village to safety when they are attacked, and dies when he tries to help a stray lamb.

Wiechert was respected for his courage in opposing the Nazis and for his modestly third-person account of what happened to him just before and during World War II, *The Forest of the Dead*. Margaret Marshall in the *Nation*, praised the book as "impressive," but criticized Wiechert's "simple religious approach" as "a bit archaic." Alfred Werner in the *New York Herald Tribune Weekly Book Review* wrote, "Since VE Day unredeemed Nazis have been smashing the windows on the poet's villa on Lake Starnberg, Bavaria; anonymous letters have threatened the life of this traitor. But we must not be too discouraged. . . . We in this country should read his book with a feeling of hope."

Wiechert's *Rede an die deutsche Jugend* (translated as *The Poet and His Time*, and including the text of the lecture which got him sent to Buchenwald) was little noted. His collected works were published in ten volumes in Germany in 1957.

PRINCIPAL WORKS IN ENGLISH TRANSLATION: *Novels*—The Baroness (tr. P. And T. Blewitt), 1936; The Girl and the Ferryman (tr. E. Wilkins and E. Kaiser) 1947; The Earth Is Our Heritage (tr. R. Maxwell) 1953; The Simple Life (tr. M. Heynemann) 1954. *Autobiography*—The Forest of the Dead (tr. U. Stechow) 1947; Tidings (trs. M. Heynemann and M. B. Ledward) 1959. *Political*—The Poet and His Time: Three Addresses (tr. I. Tauber) 1948.

ABOUT: Columbia Dictionary of Modern European Literature, 1947, 1980. *Periodicals*—Books Abroad Summer, 1950; Commentary August 1951; Nation June 28, 1947; New Republic April 15, 1936; New Statesman May 16, 1936; New York Herald Tribune Weekly Book Review June 22, 1947; New York Times August 16, 1950; Spectator May 8, 1936; Times (London) September 5, 1950.

**WIGGIN, KATE DOUGLAS (SMITH)** (September 28, 1856–August 24, 1923), American writer of children's books, was born in Philadelphia, the oldest daughter of Robert Noah Smith, a lawyer who died when she was three years old, and Helen Elizabeth (Dyer) Smith. Shortly after her husband's death, Wiggin's mother moved the family to Portland, Maine, and remarried. Young Kate's new stepfather, Dr. Albion Bradbury, became a major influence in her life. The family then settled at the doctor's home in Hollis, Maine, where Wiggin spent her childhood. Later in her life, she would buy "Quillcote," the farmhouse in which she had grown up. Much of her writing was done there during summer visits, and she ultimately retired there. A voracious reader, Wiggin was especially fond of Dickens, with whom, in fact, she once shared a train journey during which he discussed with her his feelings about writing. Wiggin held this as one of her most cherished childhood experiences, according to her sister.

Wiggin and her sister were schooled at home for a time by their stepfather but later attended the district school and several private schools. Wiggin also studied at the Abbott Academy, a finishing school at Andover, Massachusetts. Several years later, Dr. Bradbury moved the family to Santa Barbara, California. Wiggin left for Los Angeles the following year to study kindergarten training in a new program. A year later, as her family was suffering through serious financial straits as a result of bad real estate investments her stepfather had made, Wiggin opened the first free kindergarten west of the Rocky Mountains on Silver Street in San Francisco. Then, in 1880 with her sister (and later collaborator in teaching and writing), she founded the California Kindergarten Training School. The two sisters would ultimately write or edit fifteen books together, including *The Story Hour, Children's Rights*, and *The Republic of Childhood*. Her marriage to Samuel Bradley Wiggin, a Boston lawyer, in December 1881, brought an end to her kindergarten work in San Francisco. After moving to New York City in 1884, she continued to travel the country, visiting all of the major kindergarten centers. To raise money for her kindergarten projects, she published, in 1883, *The Story of Patsy*, which advocated the Rousseauian method of education; and later, *The Birds' Christmas Carol*. The success of these efforts persuaded Wiggin to commit herself both to writing and to education.

When her husband died suddenly in 1899, Wiggin made the first of what proved to be many annual trips to Europe, for it was on board ship on her maiden voyage that she met George Christopher Riggs, the man who was to become her second husband. Riggs was a linen importer with good British connections. Wiggin's "Penelope" books would be based on these annual visits to Europe, a period that proved prolific for her.

But the demands of a grueling schedule of readings adversely affected Wiggin's health: it was during one of her hospital stays that the character Rebecca appeared to her, full-blown, as a dark-eyed child with braids and a name: Rebecca Rowena Randall. While recovering, Wiggin began work on what would become the *Rebecca of Sunnybrook Farm* stories. Rebecca, dubbed by Thomas Bailey Aldrich "the nicest child in American literature," was based on Wordsworth's ideal of childhood. Wiggin drew on her own childhood experiences and those of family, friends, and relatives to flesh out the Rebecca character, still enjoyed by contemporary readers. In eleven stories—disseminated as books, magazine serials, plays, and movies—Rebecca grows from a ten-year-old girl to young adulthood. The stories were financially profitable for Wiggin, and in their day were immensely popular. Even Mark Twain called *Rebecca* "that beautiful book." Despite changing tastes after World War I, Wiggin maintained her earlier vision and continued to draw on the past for inspiration.

*Rebecca of Sunnybrook Farm*, according to a recent critic, "reveals the autobiographical character of her work as a whole. . . . In it . . . there appear the same fresh, natural simplicity of style, the same lack of interest in plot as such, the same faithful transcription of a warmhearted, impulsive nature dramatizing its own objective experiences."

PRINCIPAL WORKS: *Novels*—The Village Watch-Tower, 1895; Marm Lisa, 1896; (with others) The Affair at the Inn, 1904; (with others) Robinetta, 1911; The Story of Waitstill Baxter, 1913; Ladies in Waiting, 1919; The Quilt of Happiness, 1923; Love by Express: A Novel of California, 1924. *Juvenile*—The Story of Patsy: A Reminiscence, 1883; The Birds' Christmas Carol, 1887; A Summer in a Canon: A California Story, 1889; (with N. A. Smith) The Story Hour: A Book for the Home and the Kindergarten, 1890; Timothy's Quest: A Story for Anybody, 1890; Polly Oliver's Problem: A Story for Girls, 1893; A Cathedral Courtship, and Penelope's English Experiences, 1893; Penelope's Progress, 1898; Penelope's English Experiences, 1900; Penelope's Irish Experiences, 1901; The Diary of a Goose Girl, 1902; Half-a-Dozen Housekeepers; A Story for Girls, In Half-a-Dozen Chapters, 1903; Rebecca of Sunnybrook Farm, 1903; A Village Stradivarius, 1904; Rose o' the River, 1905; New Chronicles of Rebecca, 1907; The Flag-Raising, 1907; Finding a Home, 1907; The Old Peabody Pew: A Christmas Romance of a Country Church, 1907; Susanna and Sue, 1909; Homespun Tales: Rose o' the River, The Old Peabody Pew, and Susanna and Sue, 1909; Mother Carey's Chickens, 1911; A Child's Journey with Dickens, 1912; Penelope's Postscripts: Switzerland, Venice, Wales, Devon, Home, 1915; The Romance of a Christmas Card, 1916; The Spirit of Christmas, 1927. *Drama*—(With Charlotte Thompson) A State o' Maine Play, 1932; (with H. Ingersoll) The Birds' Christmas Carol, 1914; Bluebeard: A Musical Fantasy, 1914; The Old Peabody Pew, 1917; (with Rachel Crothers) Mother Carey's Chickens, 1925; A Thorn in the Flesh: A Monologue, 1925. *Nonfiction*—The Relation of the Kindergarten to the Public School, 1891; Children's Rights: A Book of Nursery Logic, 1892; (with N. A. Smith) The Republic of Childhood The Kindergarten, 1893; 1895–1896; Nine Love Songs and a Carol, 1896; The Girl and the Kingdom: Learning to Teach, 1915; The Writings of Kate Douglas Wiggin, 1917; My Garden of Memory: An Autobiography, 1923; Creeping Jenny and Other New England Stories, 1924; A Thanksgiving Retrospect; or, Simplicity of Life in Old New England, 1928. *As editor*—(with N. A. Smith) Hymns for Kindergartners, 1881; Kindergarten Chimes: A Collection of songs and Games Composed and Arranged for Kingergarten, 1885; Golden Numbers: A Book of Verse for Youth, 1902; The Posey Ring: A Book of Verse for Children, 1903, published as Fairy Stories Every

Child Should Know, 1942; Baby's Friend and Nursery Heroes and Heroines, 1907; Magic Casements: A Second Fairy Book, 1907; Pinafore Palace: A Book of Rhymes for the Nursery, 1907, published as Pinafore Palace: A Book of Dorcas Dishes: Family Recipes Contributed by the Dorcas Society of Hollis and Buxton 1911; Baby's Friend and Nursery Heroes and Heroines, 1923; Tales of Laughter: A Third Fairy Book, 1908, Arabian Nights: Their Best-Known Tales, 1909; The Talking Beasts: A Book of Fable Wisdom, 1911; An Hour with the Fairies, 1911; Christmas Stories, 1916; Rudyard Kipling, Stories and Poems (by R. Kipling) 1916; Jane Porter, The Scottish Chiefs ( by J. Porter) 1921; Pinafore Palace Series, 1923; Twilight Stories: More Tales for the Story Hour, 1925.

ABOUT: Mason, M. E., Yours with Love, Kate, 1952; Mason, M. E., Kate Douglas Wiggin: The Little Schoolteacher, 1962; The Oxford Companion to American Literature, 4th Ed., 1965; Smith, N. A., Kate Douglas Wiggin as Her Sister Knew Her, 1924; Who's Who of Children's Literature, 1960; Who Was Who in America, vol. I: 1897–1942; Wiggin, K. My Garden of Memory, 1924. *Periodicals*—Current Opinion 1924; Horn Book November 1950; New York Times August 25, 1923.

**WILBUR, RICHARD** (March 1, 1921– ), American poet, wrote: "My father, the artist Lawrence Wilbur, came east from Omaha to New York; my mother, Helen Purdy, came north from Baltimore. I spent the first two years of my life, or so I am told, in what was to be the shadow of the George Washington Bridge; then we moved to New Jersey. My parents rented a pre-Revolutionary stone house in North Caldwell,  in one corner of the large country estate of a retired English manufacturer, and in this pocket of resistance to suburbia (since infiltrated) my brother Lawrence and I grew up among woods, orchards, corn-fields, horses, hogs, cows, and hay-wagons. A friend recently remarked that my poems are unfashionably favorable toward nature, and I must blame this warp on a rural, pleasant and somewhat solitary boyhood.

"I began to write poems very early. Doubtless the fact that my father was an artist encouraged and legitimized this activity, and I suspect that I inherited a facility with words from my mother's family: her father was an editor of the *Baltimore Sun*, and *his* father, an itinerant editor and publisher, had founded some forty Democratic newspapers in his wanderings. My first poem was called 'That's When the Nightingales Wake.' There are, of course, no nightingales in New Jersey, and the poem was a pure verbal and rhythmic exercise, drawing not at all upon my eight years' experience.

"At high school I wrote editorials; at Amherst College I edited the newspaper, and anticipated a career in journalism. The summers were passed in vagrancy; I toured most of the forty-eight states by freight-car. Poetry did not seem a primary occupation, and my poems for the most part continued to be diversions with other people's nightingales. Amherst's excellent instruction in English literature was more likely to produce, immediately, an awakened critical intelligence than an aroused poetic faculty; and it was not until World War II took me to Cassino, Anzio and the Siegfried Line that I began to versify in earnest. One does not use poetry for its major purposes, as a means of organizing oneself and the world, until one's world somehow gets out of hand. A general cataclysm is not required; the disorder must be personal and may be wholly so, but poetry, to be vital, does seem to need a periodic acquaintance with the threat of Chaos.

"I had married Charlotte Ward in 1942, and after the war we went to Cambridge, where I attended Harvard's graduate school, receiving the M.A. in 1947. During the next three years I was a member of the Society of Fellows of Harvard University, and since 1950 have taught in its department of English, living in nearby Lincoln with my wife and three children (Ellen, Christopher, Nathan). In 1946 a friend sent a packet of my poems to Reynal and Hitchcock, and that venturesome house—very much to my surprise—brought out *The Beautiful Changes* in the following year. My second book, *Ceremony*, like the first a collection of lyrics, was published by Harcourt, Brace in 1950. There is hardly space here in which to characterize my work, little of it as there is; as regards technique, a critic has called me one of the 'New Formalists,' and I will accept the label provided it be understood that to try to revive the force of rhyme and other formal devices, by reconciling them with the experimental gains of the past several decades, is itself sufficiently experimental."

---

Richard Wilbur was born in New York City. He attended Amherst College from 1938 to 1942, majoring in English, graduating with a B.A. degree, and taking the school's Rice Prize for the best essay. He began writing poetry seriously while on active duty in the army during World War II. His first collection of poems, *The Beautiful Changes*, was reviewed by Louise Bogan in the *New Yorker* in 1947: "Wilbur is still quite plainly entangled with the technical equipment of his favorite poetic forerunners, specifically Marianne Moore, Eliot, Rilke, and Hopkins, from whose work he has absorbed certain lessons. He has had the wit, however, to point up these influences from time to time with the invisible quotation marks of near parody." But the poems are also characterized by a sensitivity to the surrounding world, an astonishing fluidity of words, and a careful but not insistent use of formal devices.

Wilbur's second book of verse, *Ceremony*, was published three years later. Babette Deutsch, writing in the *New York Times* in 1950, observed that the poems "are charged with responsiveness to the lusters, the tones, of the physical world, and show the poet alert to less apparent matters. The scenes are alive with light." The frequently anthologized poem "The Death of a Toad" appeared in this volume:

> The rare original heartsblood goes,
> Spends on the earthen hide, in the folds
>     and wizenings, flows
> In the gutters of the banked and staring

> eyes. He lies
> As still as if he would return to stone,
>     And soundlessly attending, dies
>         Toward some deep monotone. . . .

During these years Wilbur was a junior fellow (1947–1950) and then assistant professor of English (1950–1954) at Harvard University. He won the Harriet Monroe Prize in 1948 and the Oscar Blumenthal Prize in 1950, both from *Poetry* magazine. A 1952–1953 Guggenheim Fellowship enabled him to travel in New Mexico. In 1954 he was awarded a Prix de Rome Fellowship from the American Academy of Arts and Letters, entitling him to live at the American Academy in Rome for a year. Among the poems reflecting his experience in Italy is the tender and humorous "A Baroque Wall-Fountain in the Villa Sciarra." It was included in his third book of poetry, *Things of This World*, which won both the National Book Award and the Pulitzer Prize in 1957. From 1955 to 1957 Wilbur taught at Wellesley College. He then moved to Wesleyan University where he taught until 1977. From then until 1986 he was writer-in-residence at Smith College.

Wilbur has also gained renown as a translator. In 1955 his version of Molière's comedy *The Misanthrope* was produced in Cambridge, Massachusetts, and a year later in New York City. His translation of *Tartuffe* made him the corecipient of the 1963 Bollingen Prize for translation, and was staged by the Lincoln Center Repertory Theater in New York City in 1965. He has also translated three other plays by Molière (*The School for Wives*, *The Learned Ladies*, and *The School for Husbands*) as well as two by Jean Racine (*Andromache* and *Phaedra*). In 1956 Wilbur was the principal lyricist for a musical version of Voltaire's *Candide*, with music by Leonard Bernstein and book by Lillian Hellman. Wilbur received a Ford Foundation Fellowship for drama in 1960, and another Guggenheim Fellowship in 1963. In 1961 he traveled to Russia under a cultural exchange program sponsored by the State Department, and in 1964 he went to Finland and England.

In his fourth book of poems, *Advice to a Prophet*, Wilbur showed an increasing sensitivity to the pathetic and tragic aspects of the human condition without surrendering his customary wit, technical skill, or joy in nature. In the title poem he asks a prophet come to warn humanity of nuclear annihilation to

> Speak of the world's own change. Though
>     we cannot conceive
> Of an undreamt thing, we know to our cost
> How the dreamt cloud crumbles, the vines
>     are blackened by frost,
> How the view alters. We could believe

> If you told us so, that the white-tailed
>     deer will slip
> Into perfect shade, grown perfectly shy,
> The lark avoid the reaches of our eye. . . .

With Louise Bogan and Archibald MacLeish, Wilbur contributed his literary criticism to *Emily Dickinson: Three Views*. He collected his other prose writings in *Response*. Wilbur wrote a book for children entitled *Loudmouse*, and put together two collections of verse for young readers: *Opposites* and *More Opposites*. He edited (and contributed to) *A Bestiary*, with illustrations by Alexander Calder, and has also been responsible for editions of Poe's poetry and prose, Shakespeare's narrative poems, and Witter Bynner's poetry.

Wilbur later published *Walking to Sleep* (winner of the 1971 Bollingen Prize for poetry) and *The Mind-Reader*. In 1986 he wrote the lyrics for "On Freedom's Ground," a cantata with music by William Schuman to commemorate the centennial of the Statue of Liberty. He was the recipient of the Pulitzer Prize for poetry in 1989 for *New and Collected Poems*. Wilbur's many other honors include the Gold Medal for Poetry from the National Institute and American Academy of Arts and Letters (1991). Wilbur has served as president (1974–1976) and chancellor (1976–1978) of these organizations as well as of the American Academy of Poets. He has received honorary degrees from at least a dozen colleges and universities. In 1987 Wilbur was named Poet Laureate of the United States by the Library of Congress, a post he held for the usual two years.

PRINCIPAL WORKS: *Poetry*—The Beautiful Changes, 1947; Ceremony, 1950; Things of This World, 1956; Advice to a Prophet, 1961; The Poems of Richard Wilbur, 1963; Walking to Sleep, 1969; The Mind-Reader, 1976; New and Collected Poems, 1988. *Nonfiction*—(with L. Bogan and A. MacLeish) Emily Dickinson: Three Views, 1960; Responses: Prose Pieces, 1953–1976, 1976. *Lyrics*—(with others) Candide (by Voltaire) 1957 (music by L. Bernstein; book by L. Hellman). *As translator*—The Misanthrope (by Molière) 1955; Tartuffe (by Molière) 1963; The School for Wives (by Molière) 1971; The Learned Ladies (by Molière) 1978; The Whale and Other Uncollected Translations, 1982; Andromache (by J. Racine) 1982; Phaedra (by J. Racine) 1986; The School for Husbands (by Molière) 1992. *Juvenile*—Loudmouse (illus. D. Almquist) 1963; Opposites, 1973; More Opposites, 1991. *As editor*—(with L. Untermeyer and K. Shapiro) Modern American and Modern British Poetry, rev. ed. 1955; A Bestiary (illus. A. Calder) 1955; Complete Poems of Poe, 1959; (with A. Harbage) Shakespeare's Poems, 1966, rev. ed. 1974; The Narrative of Arthur Gordon Pym (by E. A. Poe) 1974; Selected Poems of Witter Bynner, 1978; Essays and Reviews of Poe, 1984.

ABOUT: The autobiographical material quoted above was written for Twentieth Century Authors First Supplement, 1955. Bixler, F. (ed.) Richard Wilbur: A Reference Guide, 1991; Butts, W. (ed.) Conversations with Richard Wilbur, 1990; Cummins, P. F. Richard Wilbur, 1971; Hill, D. L. Richard Wilbur, 1967; Michelson, B. Wilbur's Poetry, 1991; Salinger, W. (ed.) Richard Wilbur's Creation, 1983. *Periodicals*—American Poetry Review May/June 1991; American Scholar Spring 1991; Contemporary Literature vol. 12 1971; English Literary History vol. 35 1968; Essays in Literature Spring 1989; Mademoiselle August 1953; Massachusetts Review Spring 1982; New Republic March 24, 1982; May 16, 1988; New York Times January 11, 1948; February 11, 1951; May 7, 1954; June 24, 1956; New York Times Book Review October 29, 1961; April 18, 1987; May 29, 1988; New Yorker November 15, 1947; Paris Review Winter 1977; Poetry January 1948, April 1953, September 1956, April 1962; Renascence Fall 1992/Winter 1993; Southern Review Summer 1973, Summer 1979; Time May 9, 1988; Virginia Quarterly Review Summer 1990.

**WILDE, PERCIVAL** (March 1, 1887–September 19, 1953), American playwright and novelist, was born in New York City. He graduated from Columbia University in 1906. For the next five years he worked in a bank, occasionally contributing book reviews to the *New York Times* and the *New York Post*. With the appearance of his first short story in 1912 he was besieged with requests for the dramatic rights, and soon concluded that his

true talent lay in writing for the theater. He thenceforth devoted himself to writing and directing one-act plays for vaudeville, then in its heyday. He quickly became frustrated by the limitations of writing for that genre, but his experience taught him much about how to construct short dramatic pieces pleasing to audiences.

During World War I, Wilde served in the U.S. Navy. Later he spent a brief period in Hollywood and another collaborating on full-length plays, several of which were produced on Broadway. In 1920 he married Nadie Rogers Marckres, with whom he had two sons. Wilde wrote and published scores of one-act dramas; these were performed in Little Theatres throughout the United States and in other parts of the English-speaking world.

Reviewers praised the wit and inventiveness of his work, although some found it too pat and contrived. As a *Nation* reviewer of his early collection *Confessional, and Other American Plays* commented, "All of them would act well, . . . but [they] are too tricky and insincere to have much real dramatic value." A *New York Times* (1922) reviewer of *Eight Comedies for Little Theatres* observed, "Mr. Wilde is always amusing and nearly always clever, but he is in no sense of the word a distinguished literary craftsman." However, a *Theatre Arts Monthly* reviewer of *Ten Plays for Little Theatres* praised Wilde's "undoubted sense of theatre" and his "tried and sure technique." In addition to being a prolific writer of plays, Wilde taught drama as a visiting lecturer at the University of Miami. His *The Craftmanship of the One-Act Play* was for many years a standard text in the field.

Although Wilde continued to write plays until the end of his career—his later works were performed on radio and television, as well as the stage—he devoted increasing attention to fiction from the late 1920s onward. He gained attention in particular for some ephemeral, mystery stories. In a *New Statesman and Nation* review of *Mystery Week-End* Ralph Partridge enthused: "My only complaint about [the novel] is that it seems too short and left me ravenous for more."

PRINCIPAL WORKS: *Drama*—The Line of No Resistance, a Comedy in One Act, 1913; Dawn, with The Noble Lord, The Traitor, A House of Cards, Playing with Fire, The Finger of God: One-Act Plays of Life To-Day, 1915 (reissued as Dawn and Other One-Act Plays of Life To-Day, 1924); Confessional, and Other American Plays, 1916; The Unseen Host, and Other War Plays: The Unseen Host, Mothers of Men, Pawns, In the

Ravine, Valkyrie!, 1917; The Reckoning: A Play in One Act, 1922; A Question of Morality, and Other Plays, 1922; Eight Comedies for Little Theatres, 1922; The Inn of Discontent, and Other Fantastic Plays, 1924; Three-Minute Plays: Innocentia, Musicalia, Immoralia, 1927: Ten Plays for Little Theatres, 1931; The One-Act Plays of Percival Wilde: First Series (ed. J. W. Marriot) 1933; Little Shot: A Comedy in Three Acts, 1935; Comrades in Arms and Other Plays for Little Theatres, 1935; Refund: A Farce in One Act for Seven Males, 1936, rev. ed. 1942; Mr. F., a Comedy in One Act, 1941; Bridge Blackouts . . . (Based on Articles by S. Tupper Bigelow) 1942; The Sportsmen: A War-Time Lancashire One-Act Comedy, 1950; One-Act Plays: New Series (ed. J. W. Marriot) 1953. *Nonfiction*—The Craftmanship of the One-Act Play, 1923, rev. ed. 1951. *Juvenile*—The Toy Shop, 1924; Reverie, 1924; Alias Santa Claus: A Play for Children, 1927. *Short stories*—Rogues in Clover, 1929. *Novels*—The Devils Booth, 1930; There Is a Tide, 1932; Mystery Week-End, 1938; Inquest, 1939; Design for Murder, 1941; Tinsley's Bones, 1942; P. Moran, Operative, 1947. *As editor*—Contemporary One-Act Plays from Nine Countries, 1936; (with others) The Week End Companion, 1941.

About: *Periodicals*—Boston Transcript July 20, 1940; Dial December 6, 1917; Nation December 28, 1916; New Statesman and Nation August 6, 1938; New York Times December 17, 1922; September 20, 1953; Outlook November 26, 1924; Saturday Review of Literature March 10, 1951; Theatre Arts Monthly September 1931.

## WILDER, ROBERT (INGERSOLL) (January 25, 1901–August 22, 1974), American novelist, playwright, and screenwriter, wrote:

"At the age of twelve or thirteen I won a school prize of a dollar for a short story and this seemed such an easy touch that I decided to make a career of writing. Off and on for some forty years, in various fields, I have pursued this goal and, as Somerset Maugham once confessed, I am frequently astonished by the fact that I am a writer and that it never seems to get any easier; the last book being as hard to write as the first.

"I was born of a Spanish mother and a Scotch father in Richmond, Virginia, where at the time my father was working at one of his several careers. He was still going to college after I was born and at different times was a lawyer, a Presbyterian minister, a doctor and, finally, a dentist. Essentially a mechanic at heart he found in dentistry that which appealed to him, returning to his boyhood home, at Daytona Beach, Fla. to open an office and to rear a family. I went through the grade and high schools at Daytona Beach until late in 1917 when, stretching my age a bit, I enlisted in the army for World War I and eventually found myself a member of the S.A.T.C. at Stetson University, in DeLand, Florida. At the conclusion of the war I decided that I was too old to go back to school and went to New York where I found a job behind the soda fountain in a Liggetts drugstore. A year of this made the academic field seem more attractive and I enrolled at Columbia University. I sold a short story then to a magazine, *Telling Tales*, for which I was paid $75. That really cinched the literary life.

"Finishing at Columbia I found a job with a theatrical press agent, Dixie Hines. I remained with him for four years, learning the business and finally branching out on my own, handling the publicity for such stars of the day as Irene Bordoni, Helen Menken, Claudette Colbert, Raquel Meller, and such producers as A. H. Woods, Ray Goetz, the Shuberts, Sam Harris, Charles Wagner and others. At this time I married Sarah Adams Peters, daughter of a well-known illustrator. Theatrical publicity is an uneasy living at best and then the National Broadcasting Company offered me a job, directing the publicity of a nationwide tour which A. H. Rothafel (Roxy) and 'his gang' were making. At the conclusion of this I went with radio station WOR in charge of publicity and remained there for seven years until a change of ownership landed me on the street along with several other executives.

"By the time Sally and I had a son, Robert Wallace Wilder, and I took the first job I could find, rewrite on the lobster trick of the *New York Sun*. I was graduated from this to a daily column of my own, 'On the Sun Deck,' which I wrote for almost nine years. Newspaper work, I decided, was fun if you could afford it. I couldn't. The alternative was to write myself out of it. I wrote two plays, both produced on Broadway, *Sweet Chariot* and *Stardust*, which didn't make much money for anyone concerned. Then I started my first novel, *God Has a Long Face*, which G. P. Putnam's Sons bought on the face of a half-completed manuscript. This was followed by *Out of the Blue*, a reporter's diary, and then I wrote *Flamingo Road*, first as a novel, then as a play for Broadway, produced by Roland Stebbins, and then as a motion picture for Joan Crawford.

"By then I could see daylight and left the *Sun* to work for myself. I went to Hollywood under contract for Metro-Goldwyn, then did a trick of two years for Paramount and later a picture for Warner Brothers. I like pictures and Hollywood but decided that the only way to cope with them was to keep a book ahead. I wrote steadily, publishing nine novels in eleven years. Unfortunately, I don't have a backlog of rejected manuscripts that could be reworked and marketed now.

"I have never written anything which hasn't sold. My writing habits are simple. Once started on a novel I do a thousand words a day; no more and no less. Sometimes they're not always good and I have to re-do them the next day before I start work on the new quota. This, however, works out better for me than saying I'll work so many hours a day. After all, you can sit in front of a typewriter for eight hours and never write a line.

"For the past three years I have made my home in Mexico where, in addition to my other activities, I also serve as correspondent for the Miami *Herald*."

———

An unabashed purveyor of popular fiction, Wilder published more than a dozen novels, several of which were made into successful motion pictures. Most of his fiction was sensationalistic and melodramatic, and reviewers frequently complained of the wild improbability of his plots. For example, in *Flamingo Road*, a young female circus performer stranded in a small Florida town becomes embroiled in the political machinations of the local sheriff. As Bess Jones observed in a *Saturday Review of Literature* notice, "Mr. Wilder's plot becomes almost an extravaganza before he finishes, and he greatly overworks the credibility of the heart-of-gold theme in his heroine." *Written on the Wind*, one of his most popular novels (later made into a movie starring Lauren Bacall and Rock Hudson), examines the degenerate offspring of a North Carolina tobacco baron. Reviewing it in the *New Yorker*, Hamilton Basso commented, "The trouble with this is that it's all made up; every person and incident has simply been too expertly machined to fit into a groove."

Wilder used both contemporary and historical settings. *Wind from the Carolinas*, probably his most popular historical novel, traces six generations of the Cameron family, whose patriarch, a wealthy South Carolina plantation owner, migrates to the Bahamas in the 1790s. Wilder continued to work as a journalist long after establishing himself as a successful novelist, and from 1950 to 1955 served as a *Miami Herald* correspondent in Mexico. He died in La Jolla, California, some months after the publication of his last novel, *The Sound of Drums and Cymbals*.

PRINCIPAL WORKS: *Novels*—God Has a Long Face, 1940 Flamingo Road, 1942; Mr. G. Strings Along, 1944; Written on the Wind, 1946; Bright Feather, 1948; Wait for Tomorrow, 1950, new ed. 1968; And Ride a Tiger, 1951 (also pub. As a Stranger in My Arms); Autumn Thunder, 1952; The Wine of Youth, 1955; The Sun Is My Shadow, 1960; Plough the Sea, 1961; Wind from the Carolinas, 1964; Fruit of the Poppy, 1965; The Sea and the Stars, 1967; An Affair of Honor, 1969; A Handful of Men, 1970; The Sound of Drums and Cymbals, 1974. *Nonfiction*—Out of the Blue: The Informal Diary of a Reporter, 1943.

ABOUT: The autobiographical material quoted above was written for Twentieth Century Authors First Supplement, 1955. Contemporary Authors Permanent Series 2 1978; Warfel, H. American Novelists of Today, 1951. *Periodicals*—Chicago Sunday Tribune March 26, 1950; New York Times October 28, 1951; August 23, 1974; New Yorker January 26, 1946; Saturday Review of Literature June 20, 1942.

**WILDER, THORNTON (NIVEN)** (April 17, 1897–December 7, 1975), American playwright and novelist, was born in Madison, Wisconsin, one  of five children of Amos Parker Wilder, a newspaper editor and diplomat, and Isabella (Niven) Wilder, a cultivated woman who exercised a greater influence over her second son than did her pious, practical husband. When he was nine Thornton was taken to China, where his father was Consul General at Hong Kong and Shanghai, and attended boarding school in Chefoo. After some shuffling back and forth, he returned to the United States in 1912, settling with his mother in Berkeley,

California, and graduating from Berkeley High School three years later. In 1915 he entered Oberlin College in Ohio, where, despite the expectations of his father and the generally conservative nature of the college, he became known as an aesthete, earning mediocre grades but editing the campus literary magazine and cultivating the colorful, gregarious personality for which he was noted. In 1917 he transferred to Yale University, graduating three years later with a B.A. in English and the university's Bradford Brinton Award for *The Trumpet Shall Sound*, a four-act play based on Ben Jonson's *The Alchemist*, which anticipated many of his mature themes and techniques.

With no concrete plans for the future, Wilder went to Rome in 1920, ostensibly to study archaeology at the American Academy, but, more importantly, to absorb European culture and gather material for his first book, *The Cabala*, a novel about a small group of spiritually exhausted Roman aristocrats, and two American students who fall in with them. Wilder wrote most of *The Cabala* while working as a French teacher and housemaster at the Lawrenceville School in New Jersey, a position he accepted reluctantly in 1922—but came eventually to enjoy. He remained at Lawrenceville—with a sabbatical for an M.A. in French literature from Princeton (1926)—until 1928, a year after his second novel, *The Bridge of San Luis Rey*, had won the Pulitzer Prize and made him famous.

Though *The Cabala* was little noticed by the public, it received favorable reviews and is more than a mere precursor to *The Bridge of San Luis Rey*. "The wit and irony, ingenuity of craftsmanship, and bleakness of coloration make it a distinct, if not totally successful, modern novel," wrote David Castronovo. "The excellence of its texture and design—shaped to reveal the failures of a whole class of people—becomes apparent to the reader who is willing to grant Wilder his own artistic terms." Nevertheless, the novel betrayed certain immaturities in structure and characterization that Wilder excised from *The Bridge of San Luis Rey*, an examination of the dovetailing fates of five travelers who, "on Friday noon, July the twentieth, 1714," happen to be crossing "the finest bridge in all Peru" when it breaks and throws them into the gulf below. Edmund Wilson was the first to detect the novel's Proustian patterns of obsessive, enervating love, and though he felt that Wilder sometimes leaned on Proust "a little too heavily," Wilson also wrote that Wilder "has an edge that is peculiar to himself, an edge that is never incompatible with the attainment of a consummate felicity. . . . It is the felicity of a true poet . . . and it makes possible for Thornton Wilder a good many remarkable feats that we should not have expected to see brought off. Mr. Wilder, for example, I understand, has never been to Peru. . . . Yet the author of *The Bridge of San Luis Rey* has been able to give us a Peru that is solid, incandescent, distinct."

Wilder's third novel, *The Woman of Andros*, was published in 1930, the year he began a fruitful and contented six-year teaching stint at the University of Chicago. Though this story of the frustrated love of a worldly Greek courtesan in the years just before the Christian era suffered from an uncharacteristic mawkishness, it did not quite deserve the doctrinaire attack given it by the Communist writer Mike Gold in the *New Republic*. ("Where are the stockbroker suicides, the labor racketeers or the passion and death of the coal miners?" Gold asked in mock outrage.) Nevertheless, the review was much discussed, and though Wilder claimed to be oblivious to critical opinion of his work, his next novel, now regarded by most as his best, *Heaven's My Destination*, was set in a determinedly contemporary Midwest in the worst years of the Great Depression. Far from being a grimly ideological account of class conflict, however, *Heaven's My Destination* is the comic, picaresque story of George Brush, a traveling textbook salesman whose unshakable naiveté and optimism are repeatedly put to the test. The book convinced many detractors that Wilder was no mere mandarin. In it, wrote Rex Burbank, Wilder's "masterly handling of point of view enables him to achieve a vision which affirms much the same values as those in *The Woman of Andros*, but without its sentimentalism, and which satirizes both his hero and his society without lapsing into sarcasm and caricaturism. . . . While one should not miss the deliciously humorous ways Brush exasperates people, it would be a mistake to take the book as a joke. . . . It is as serious as *Candide* and *Huck Finn*." "The comic spirit," Wilder told the *Paris Review*, "is given to us in order that we may analyze, weigh, and clarify things in us which nettle us, or which we are outgrowing or trying to reshape."

Despite his early success as a novelist, Wilder always regarded the theater as the greatest of all art forms, and in 1931 he brought out *The Long Christmas Dinner and Other Plays*, a collection of accomplished and innovative one-act plays that presaged his two Pulitzer Prize-winning dramas, *Our Town* and *The Skin of Our Teeth*. Although *Our Town*, which was produced on Broadway in 1938, seems fated to be misinterpreted as a slice of Norman Rockwell-like Americana, "it is much darker and stranger than it appears to be at first glance," wrote Brendan Gill in the *New Yorker*. An almost plotless series of tableaux, owing much to Pirandello, illustrating the rituals of love, death, and family in the village of Grover's Corners, New Hampshire, *Our Town* straddles a line (somewhat fudged, perhaps, in the third act) between cautious affirmation and the bleakest negation. The drift of Wilder's dramatic argument, wrote Gill, "is not that death is bad because it terminates life but that it is bad because it terminates nothing; it is a mere punctuation mark by which we enter into a new but fundamentally unchanged set of relations, charged with a horror that life mercifully spares us—the horror of continuing forever. Life in *Our Town* has the bittersweetness of a failed opportunity, death in *Our Town* is a nightmare of passive awareness felt through all eternity."

*Our Town* was followed later in the year by *The Merchant of Yonkers*, a four-act farce that furthered Wilder's Pirandellian attack on theatrical illusionism by exaggerating the mustiest conventions of nineteenth-century dramaturgy. It closed in New York after a few weeks, but had a longer run in 1955 in a somewhat tamer version retitled *The Matchmaker*. (In the 1960s *The Matchmaker* was used as the source for the musical *Hello, Dolly!*, with which Wilder had nothing to do except to collect enormous royalty checks.)

In 1942 *The Skin of Our Teeth*, the best of Wilder's full-length plays, was produced on Broadway. A potted history of the human race indebted (perhaps too indebted) equally to Joyce's *Finnegans Wake* and the crisis atmosphere of World War II, *The Skin of Our Teeth* depicts five thousand years in the lives of George and Maggie Antrobus, a suburban New Jersey couple who, with their children Gladys and Henry and their maid Sabina, suffer through cataclysms of flood, famine, ice, and war only to begin the series all over again. There was nothing covert about the borrowings from Joyce, yet Joseph Campbell and Henry Morton Robinson in a *Saturday Review* article of 1942 nonetheless accused Wilder of plagiarism. This criticism provoked a brief furor, but Edmund Wilson answered that "Wilder is a genuine poet with a form and imagination of his own who may find his themes where he pleases without incurring the charge of imitation," and in any case *The Skin of Our Teeth* soon entered the very small repertory of indispensable American plays. "It is astonishing that a play so full of stops, starts, tricks, and dodges should lay a strong grip upon the emotions," wrote Malcolm Goldstein. "It is saved from archness by Wilder's humanity, which expresses itself in this play as in all the others through ordinary speech, though it does so in the midst of many-layered, allusive dialogue and commensurately complex action."

Just prior to the premier of *The Skin of Our Teeth*, Wilder reported for service as a captain in the Army Intelligence Unit. His wartime responsibilities during the next three years included the interrogation of prisoners and the preparation of reports for the Mediterranean Air Headquarters. Wilder enjoyed the enforced discipline of the military and felt somewhat at loose ends after his discharge, but in 1948 he managed to complete *The Ides of March*, a historical novel about Julius Caesar with which he had been long struggling. This complex, epistolary work about the aging emperor's relations with Cleopatra, Catullus, Cicero, and the courtesan Clodia was, in its reliance on the ideas of Sartre and Kierkegaard, too rarefied to attract a large readership, but most critics consider it Wilder's last fully achieved work.

Wilder's life after *The Ides of March* was more a record of traveling, teaching, lecturing, acting (in various productions of *Our Town* and *The Skin of Our Teeth*), accepting awards, and keeping up with his countless friends than of creative activity. Though he berated himself for his lack of discipline, he was unable to resist a good party, and he squandered years in obsessive study of *Finnegans Wake* and the chronology of Lope de Vega's plays. Neither project resulted in a major scholarly work, and even the lectures he delivered as Charles Eliot

Norton Professor at Harvard in 1950 and 1951 never made it into final, publishable form. Doubtless, Wilder was the victim of his own amiability; from Gertrude Stein to Montgomery Clift, he seemed to know everyone, and though he had one or two affairs with younger men, he never allowed a sexual relationship to stand in the way of a friendship and indeed has been described as more asexual than homosexual. Yet more than exterior circumstances were involved in the paucity of Wilder's later creative output. Those works he did bring to completion, the novels *The Eighth Day* and *Theophilus North* and the play *The Alcestiad*, were largely unsuccessful in their various ways, though some critics do regard *The Eighth Day*, a loosely written murder mystery, as a significant summing up of Wilder's thematic preoccupations. The most interesting of Wilder's later works may well be his posthumously published journals, which Daniel Aaron in the *New Republic* (1985) called a "bold and diverting record of intellectual foraging and play, and of fearless self-examination."

Wilder died in his home in Hamden, Connecticut, where he had lived off and on for many years with his devoted sister, secretary, business manager, and literary adviser, Isabel Wilder. His reputation has somewhat declined since his death, but fundamental questions about the nature and scope of his achievement remain. "Wilder knew that there were two major kinds of artists in every generation, and that in his time he was of the tamer, less fevered, less driven and driving breed," wrote R.W.B. Lewis in the *New Republic* (1983). "But there were compensations. 'As I view the work of my contemporaries,' he wrote . . . 'I seem to feel that I am exceptional in one thing—I give (don't I?) the impression of having enormously enjoyed it.' The enjoyment is infectious; and it is no small or transitory thing to be a Thornton Wilder, if you can't be a William Faulkner."

The Beinecke Rare Book and Manuscript Library at Yale University holds most of the important Wilder documents.

PRINCIPAL WORKS: *Novels*—The Cabala, 1926; The Bridge of San Luis Rey, 1927; The Woman of Andros, 1930; Heaven's My Destination, 1934; The Ides of March, 1948; The Eighth Day, 1967; Theophilus North, 1973. *Drama*—The Angel That Troubled the Waters and Other Plays, 1928; The Long Christmas Dinner and Other Plays in One Act, 1931; Our Town: A Play in Three Acts, 1938; The Merchant of Yonkers: A Farce in Four Acts, 1939 (revised as The Matchmaker, 1957); The Skin of Our Teeth: Play in Three Acts, 1942; The Alcestiad; or, A Life in the Sun, 1977. *Essays*—American Characteristics and Other Essays (ed. D. Gallup) 1979. *Journals*—The Journals of Thornton Wilder, 1939–1961 (ed. D. Gallup) 1985.

ABOUT: Bryer, J. R. (ed.) Conversations with Thornton Wilder, 1992; Burbank, R. Thornton Wilder, 1961; Castronovo, D. Thornton Wilder, 1986; Contemporary Authors New Revision Series 40, 1993; Dictionary of Literary Biography Vol. 4, 1980; Vol. 7, 1981; Vol. 9, 1981; Goldstein, M. The Art of Thornton Wilder, 1965; Goldstone, R. H. Thornton Wilder: An Intimate Portrait, 1975; Grebanier, B. Thornton Wilder, 1964; Haberman, D. The Plays of Thornton Wilder, 1967; Harrison, G. A. The Enthusiast: A Life of Thornton Wilder, 1983; Kuner, M. C. Thornton Wilder: The Bright and the Dark, 1972; Simon, L. Thornton Wilder: His World, 1979; Stresau, H. Thornton Wilder, 1971; Twentieth Century American Literature: The Chelsea House Library of Literary Criticism Vol. 7, 1988; Wilder, A. N. Thornton Wilder and His Public, 1980; Williams,

M. E. A Vast Landscape: Time in the Novels of Thornton Wilder, 1979; Wilson, E. The Shores of Light: A Literary Chronicle of the Twenties and Thirties, 1952; Wilson, E. Classics and Commercials, 1950; Writers at Work: The Paris Review Interviews, First Series, 1958. *Bibliography*—Goldstone, R. H. and Anderson, G. Thornton Wilder: An Annotated Bibliography of Works by and about Thornton Wilder, 1982; Walsh, C. Thornton Wilder: A Reference Guide, 1926–1990, 1993. *Periodicals*—New Republic October 22, 1930; December 12, 1983; November 11, 1985; New York Times December 8, 1975; New Yorker December 6, 1969; Saturday Review of Literature December 19, 1942.

**WILENSKI, R(EGINALD) H(OWARD)** (March, 1887–April 19, 1975), English art critic and art historian, wrote: "The basis of my work as an art critic is experience in art schools and practice as a professional portrait painter and draughtsman; I have never used art-critical writings by others. The basis of my work as art-historian is personal study in the museums of various countries; I use other people's art-historical writing to find factual data, never to find art-historical theories. My books and other writings, for good or evil, are thus at any rate my own.

"I was born in London. My father, a naturalised British subject, born in Russian-Poland, was a merchant in the city of London. My mother was English. Neither had artistic interests or talents, though visits to the opera, concerts or the theatre were weekly routine on Saturday evenings. I won a scholarship at St. Paul's School and a special drawing prize for a set of life-sized charcoal portraits when I was sixteen. I went as a Commoner to Balliol College, Oxford, and worked in London art schools in vacations; then came art schools in Munich and Paris and then my own studio in London. I was never much good as an artist but I was good enough to find out that 'modern' art is much more difficult than sheer representational painting and good enough to get hung in reputable exhibitions in London and Paris and efficient enough to make the wherewithal by portrait painting for a tour round Italy. When the Germans began the 1914 war I closed my studio and went into a government office. Between the wars I worked as an art critic on a number of London papers and for a time I was London correspondent for the Paris *L'Amour de l'Art*. I wrote my first art-critical book, *The Modern Movement in Art* in 1925–1927; and my art-historical books *Dutch Painting* and *English Painting* between 1928 and 1933; I worked on *Modern French Painters* from 1935 to 1939. All these were published in London and the U.S.A., and revised editons have appeared in recent years. I have also done some art-historical teaching (Bristol University 1929 and 1930, Manchester University 1933–1939, 1945, and 1946), and written one biography, *John Ruskin*. In the second German war I was seconded from Manchester University to a government department and later to the foreign service of the British Broadcasting Corporation. Since 1946 I have been preparing a book on Flemish Painting (two volumes, 1000 plates); my publishers expect to lose money on it as they have financed my studies, but they hope as I do that it will bring them credit. In these years I have also been general editor of the series of art monographs with colour plates called *Faber Gallery*.

"I married in 1914 a wise and beautiful girl who has written a good novel called *Table Two* [Marjorie Harland Wilenski] and made money in business and attempted unsuccessfully to breed a champion English bulldog. Our recreation formerly was motoring in France, Italy and Spain. Now it is our garden in Berkshire."

———

R. H. Wilenski's major contribution to the study of art was his first full-length book, *The Modern Movement in Art*. He begins: "The idea behind the modern movement in the arts is a return to the architectural or classical ideal." In elaborating on this theme, he provided a comprehensive analysis that had considerable influence in the years to come. Sir John Rothenstein, in his *Modern English Painters*, praised the book as a "closely reasoned introduction to contemporary art."

As a critic, Wilenski worked a broad canvas, and his subjects included painters of several European nationalities, both historical and contemporary. His *Introduction to Dutch Art* was a survey embracing the years 1580 to 1700, described in the *Spectator* as an "acute, stimulating and original book." *A Miniature History of European Art*, an overview of Near Eastern and Western art from the earliest times to the present, was followed by *French Painting*, an account that Thomas Craven considered "The most intelligent history of French painting that has thus far appeared in English" (*New York Herald Tribune Books*).

In *The Meaning of Modern Sculpture*, Wilenski's intention was to dismantle a prevailing, and, as he saw it, questionable, belief in the preeminence of ancient Greek sculpture, and so to promote a more balanced appraisal of modern work. A reviewer for the *Times Literary Supplement* (1932) felt that the author was overly partisan: "Mr. Wilenski has, up to a point, a good case, if he did not spoil it by exaggeration." John Pope-Hennessy detected a similar subjectivity in Wilenski's historical analysis *English Painting*, which appeared in the United States as *Masters of English Painting*. He noted that "[Wilenski's] book has obvious defects. Its attitude is unswervingly romantic," but concluded that an abiding "sense of proportion and selective power make it probable that it will remain the most interesting book on English painting for some time to come" (*New Statesman*).

Wilenski possessed ability to weld close detail to informed generalization. In *An Outline of English Painting*, A. S. Plant found "picturesque detail included in biographical notes in spite of economy of writing" (*Library Journal*). Discussing *Modern French Painters*, a survey of the progression from realism to surrealism, Jan Gordon commented "the

book is packed tight with material" (*Christian Science Monitor*), while Eric Newton felt that "it is of immense value in that it provides a remarkable bird's-eye view of one of the most interesting periods in European art" (*Manchester Guardian*).

*Flemish Painters, 1430–1830*, Wilenski's last full-length work, was his least successful. Chronologically constructed in two volumes, it was an assemblage of facts rather than a developmental study. "A text of this order is self-defeating partly because it is unreadable and partly because it is irrelevant," said a reviewer for the *Times Literary Supplement*. "The reader who requires a coherent account . . . will be forced to look elsewhere" (1960).

For several years Wilenski was general editor of the Faber Gallery series, to which he contributed monographs on his friend and neighbor the painter Stanley Spencer and, among others, Renoir, Bosch, and Picasso. Wilenski was awarded an honorary M.A. by the University of Manchester in 1936, and was elected a Chevalier of the Legion of Honor in 1967.

PRINCIPAL WORKS: The Modern Movement in Art, 1927; An Introduction to Dutch Art, 1929; (with P. G. Konody), Itailain Painting 1929; A Miniature History of European Art, 1930 (in U.S.: as A Miniature History of Art); French Painting, 1931; The Meaning of Modern Sculpture, 1932; An Outline of French Painting, 1932; An Outline of English Painting from the Middle Ages to the Period of the Pre-Raphaelites, 1934; (rev. ed. as An Outline of English Painting, 1969), 1933; English Painting (in U.S.: Masters of English Painting) The Study of Art, 1934; Modern French Painters, 1940; Dutch Painting, 1945; Flemish Painters, 1430–1839, 2 vols., 1960. *Monographs*—Stanley Spencer, 1924; Degas: 1834–1917, 1946; Royal Portraits, 1946; English Outdoor Paintings, 1946; Mantegna and the Paduan School, 1947; Renoir: 1841–1949, 1948; Seurat, 1949; Douanier Rousseau, 1953; Hieronymous Bosch, 1953; Toulouse-Lautrec, 1955; Poussin: 1594–1664, 1958; Picasso (2 vols), 1961. *Biography*—John Ruskin: An Introduction to Further Study of His Life and Work, 1933.

ABOUT: The autobiographical material quoted above was written for Twentieth Century Authors First Supplement, 1955. Chamber's Biographical Dictionary, 1990; Collis, M. Stanley Spencer: A Biography, 1962; Contemporary Authors vol. 57-60, 1976; vols. 61-64' 1976; Pople, K. Stanley Spencer: A Biography, 1991; Who Was Who 1971–1980, 1981. *Periodicals*—A B Bookman's Weekly May 26, 1975; New York Herald Tribune; New Statesman and Nation December 30, 1933; Books January 3, 1932; June 3, 1960; Saturday Review January 2, 1932; Spectator January 26, 1929; Times (London) September 22, 1975; Times Literary Supplement September, 1932.

## WILKINS, MARY ELEANOR. See FREEMAN, M. E. W.

## WILKINS, (WILLIAM) VAUGHAN (March 6, 1890–February, 1959), British novelist, wrote: "I was born in London of stock representing all the races in the British Isles—English, Scottish, Welsh and Irish. When I started life as a journalist I broke away from a family tradition of taking holy orders in the Church of England, or entering the profession of architecture—my great-grandfather, a Royal Academician, built the National Gallery and University College, London, and a distant forebear, Chrysostom Wilkins, was assistant to Sir Christopher Wren in the building of St. Paul's Cathedral.

"I had astonishingly good luck, for when I was

twenty-four years old I was made editor of the *London Daily Call*, creating an age record in Fleet-Street journalism, I believe. Well, I went away to the wars—service in Egypt, Palestine, and France—and when I came back, at the end of 1919, my paper was defunct, and I had to start all over again. I eventually became the assistant editor of the *London Daily Express*—of which the owner, manager, and editor were Canadians!

"In 1936 I sickened of journalism: I told myself that I would write a book. I did. In a lonely house in the Welsh mountains, in a freighter on the Atlantic, in my uncle's home at Lake Charles, Louisiana, at my cousin's ranch in Texas—I have many more relations in America than in England—and in a tall old building in London, overlooking the Thames, with recollections of Samuel Pepys, the diarist, and David Copperfield.

"The book—it was called *And So—Victoria*—became a best seller in America and England and on the Continent; was translated into German, Spanish, Italian, Hungarian, Dutch, Norwegian, and Swedish; and was bought for filming by Metro-Goldwyn-Mayer.

"It was not the first novel that I had written: that was an effort called, 'When and If,' written many years before in my scanty spare time, and so bad that I [use] the back of the manuscript as scribbling paper. It was not even my first book published: that was a monograph on the eighteenth century industrial revolution in England, published in 1925, which I have vaguely regretted since.

"The outbreak of World War II had a serious effect on my output, and it was five years before my next novel appeared. It is extaordinarily difficult to write books in a house shaken by the crash of falling bombs, and in the intervals of military duty with the Home Guard, and of work as a billeting officer for refugees.

"With one single exception all my novels have been historical, ranging roughly over the hundred years 1737–1837. The amount of research involved is very considerable; for the book which I have just completed, *Fanfare for a Witch*, I have had to read twenty specialized works, apart from those I have consulted for confirmatory detail or as a check. It may be that I am getting lazy, but I *should* like to be allowed to write another modern story."

---

Vaughan Wilkins's vigorous popular historical romances earned him wide recognition from reviewers in Britain and the United States, but none was as successful as his first, *And So—Victoria*. It focuses on Christopher Harnish, supposedly the grandson of George III, and his struggle against corrupt Hanoverians at the English court—a struggle that finally clears the way for the accession of the young Queen Victoria. The novel was praised for its strong characterization and skillful construction, although it was marred by what E. F. Edgett called "touches of occasional commonplace" (*Boston Transcript*). "Few first novels have been more facile and technically accomplished than this book," declared the *Saturday Review of Literature*.

*Seven Tempest*, Wilkins's second novel, is the story of the seventh illegitimate son of an unprincipled English financier, and his romance with the niece of King Leopold of Belgium. It makes no claims to literary finesse, but as Wilson Follett pointed out, "The entertainment is, in its escapist kind, unflagging and superb" (*Atlantic*). Equally well-received was *Being Met Together*, a massive volume based very loosely on events in the life of Napoleon Bonaparte. "There is plenty of adventure, suspense and love interest in the book," said *Book Week*. "What distinguishes it from the general run of romantic historical novels is the author's astonishing acquaintance with the period of which he writes."

The novels that followed all combined passable accuracy, pace, and melodramatic invention to good effect, though reviewers were unenthusiastic about *Fanfare for a Witch*, a narrative involving Frederick, Prince of Wales, and a fictitious Moroccan princess. A reviewer for the *Times Literary Supplement* found it "wildly improbable" (1954).

Wilkins also edited an informal history of England, *Endless Prelude*, and wrote two books for younger readers. *After Bath*, a fantasy for children, demonstrated wit and imagination.

Vaughan Wilkins married Mary Isabel Stanistreet Powell in 1930, and the couple had two sons.

PRINCIPAL WORKS: And So—Victoria, 1937; Seven Tempest, 1942; Once Upon a Time, an Adventure, 1949; Crown Without Sceptre, 1952; A King Reluctant, 1952; Fanfare For a Witch, 1954; Valley Beyond Time, 1955; Lady of Paris, 1956; Husband For Victoria, 1958 (in U.S.: as Consort For Victoria, 1959). *Juvenile*—After Bath, 1945; The City of Frozen Fire, 1950. *As editor*—Endless Prelude, 1937. *Other*—Sidelights on Industrial Evolution, 1925; Looking Back to See Straight, 1942.

ABOUT: The autobiographical material quoted above was written for Twentieth Century Authors First Supplement, 1955. Doyle, B. (ed.) Who's Who of Children's Literature, 1968; Ward, A. C. Longman Companion to Twentieth Century Literature, 3rd ed., 1981; Who's Who, 1959. *Periodicals*—Atlantic April 1942; Booklist January 1, 1959; Book Week September 3, 1944; Boston Transcript July 31, 1937; Catholic World May 1951; New York Herald Tribune Book Review February 18, 1951; New York Times October 30, 1949; Publisher's Weekly May 4, 1959; Saturday Review of Literature July 31, 1937; Times (London) February 10, 1959; Times Literary Supplement May 15, 1937; February 18, 1951; Wilson Library Bulletin September, 1959.

**WILKINSON, MARGUERITE OGDEN (BIGELOW)** (November 15, 1883–January 12, 1928), Canadian-American poet and anthologist, was born in Halifax, Nova Scotia, and brought to the United States as a very young child by her parents, Nathan Kellogg Bigelow and Gertrude Zulime (Holmes) Bigelow. A sensitive, imaginative child, she developed into a frail young girl with a passionate love for the outdoors. Educated privately, in the public schools at Evanston, Illinois, and at the Miss-

es Ely's School in New York City, she began to write while attending Northwestern University. In her three years at the college she specialized in English literature and composition, but also studied Greek, biology, and psychology. In 1909 she married James G. Wilkinson, a school principal. Each year the couple took a yearly fishing and camping trip in such places as Oregon and England; in 1922 Ms. Wilkinson published a humorous record of those trips in a book titled *The Dingbats of Arcady*. The *Nation's* Carl Van Doren called it a "naive, pleasant chronicle . . . fresh and sweet."

As a poet Wilkinson produced conventional but technically quite adroit work. In 1923 she published a collection of poems titled *The Great Dream*. The long title work is a paean of visionary hope to the American people. Wilkinson had a special interest in early Christian mystics; of *Citadels*, her last poetry collection, the *Bookman* stated that she had "written a series of religious and mystical poems that have a quality of beauty and originality which we have found previously only in isolated instances of her work." But this opinion has not been subsequently echoed.

In addition to her own verse Wilkinson was a well known commentor on the work of other poets, reviewing poetry in the *New York Times Review* and becoming a popular lecturer on the subject. In 1919 she published *New Voices*, a discussion and anthology of contemporary poetry; the *New York Times* (October 19, 1919) called it "comprehensive, impartial, and tolerant . . . ambitious in scope, but correspondingly thorough and painstaking in treatment." Wilkinson's longest-lasting work as an editor is *Contemporary Poetry* (1923).

PRINCIPAL WORKS: *Poetry*—In Vivid Gardens: Songs of the Woman Spirit, 1911; By a Western Wayside, 1912; Bluestone, 1920; The Great Dream, 1923; Citadels, 1926. *Nonfiction*—New Voices: An Introduction to Contemporary Poetry, 1919, rev. ed. 1921; The Dingbats of Arcady, 1922; The Way of the Makers, 1925; The Poetry of Our Own Times, 1926. *Drama*—The Passing Mars: A Modern Morality Play, 1915. *As editor*—Golden Songs of the Golden State, 1917; Contemporary Poetry, 1923; Yule Fire, 1925; The Radiant Tree, 1927. *Juvenile*—(with L. W. Thacher) The Listening Child: A Selection from the Stores of English Verse Made for the Youngest Readers and Hearers, 1924.

ABOUT: *Periodicals*—Bookman November 1926; Nation October 11, 1922; New York Times October 19, 1919; January 1, 1928.

## WILLARD, JOSIAH FLYNT (January 23, 1869–January 20, 1907), American novelist and memoirist, was born in Appleton, Wisconsin, the son of Oliver Willard, a Chicago newspaper editor, and Mary (Bannister) Willard.

After two years of college in Illinois, he became a farm-hand in Nebraska and eventually made his way in a freight car to Buffalo, New York. He served a year in reform school in Pennsylvania for

stealing a horse and buggy, escaped to tramp through Michigan, eventually finding his way to West Virginia before temporarily settling in Hoboken, New Jersey. But not for long. His patchwork quilt of a life continued overseas as he took a menial job on a boat bound for Bremen.

He met his mother in Berlin and tried briefly to be domestic. Then in Liverpool, instead of sticking with his intended plan to board a ship for Egypt, he fell in love, again briefly, with a con artist of the concert halls—a woman named Alice.

Flynt returned to Germany to study political economy at the University of Berlin in 1890, and his first effort to combine wanderlust and writing happened while traveling through Germany one summer with a Norwegian friend who provided an introduction to Ibsen, who was living in Munich. Flynt sold his story on "The most talked about dramatist in Europe" to a New York newspaper.

In 1896 he found his way to Russia, where he wanted to try his hand at foreign correspondence but realized quickly that "my foreign stuff was not the bread-winning kind," as he wrote in *My Life* (1908). For ten years he worked as a field hand on Tolstoy's farm south of Moscow. Although he found himself fascinated, Flynt admitted in *My Life* that he "honestly did not know what to talk about with the old gentleman."

After a trip to Central Asia in 1897, he returned to the United States and went back to the boxcars, this time working for the Pennsylvania Railroad, policing lines and, taking on undercover tramp status for a month, investigating the riffraff population that had long been infesting American railroads. He wrote about these conditions for *McClure's, Atlantic Monthly, Harper's,* and *Century,* and his articles were the basis of his first

book account of the vagabond life, *Tramping with Tramps* (1899). His purpose, he wrote in the preface, was to take a scientific approach to researching "human parasites." He supplemented his studies and sketches "with incidental reference to causes and occasional suggestion of remedies" and included samples of the international language of tramps. The book was reprinted in 1972 as part of a series in criminology, law enforcement, and social problems.

Befitting a rambler, his writings follow no fixed course and show a mind easily diverted and overly fond of anecdotes that might contain some kernels of significant truth about man and his need to roam. He frequently refers to the concept of *Die Ferne*, the ever-disappearing beyond—and his personal obsession with being "its passionate explorer."

Flynt's novel, *The Little Brother* (1902), was reprinted in 1968 as part of a series of American novels of muckraking, propaganda, and social protest; other works also were reissued in the late 1960s and early 1970s. His articles in McClure's exposing police corruption are among the earliest examples of muckraking, and he is credited for lifting the word "graft" from hobo jargon to common usage when he wrote *The World of Graft* (1901). Flynt best recorded his travels and impressions in the unexpurgated, posthumously published *My Life*, in which he tries to show that there is no such thing as honor among thieves.

Flynt died alone in a hotel room, of pneumonia, brought on by excessive use of stimulants.

PRINCIPAL WORKS: Tramping with Tramps, 1899; The Powers That Prey (with F. Walton) 1900; Notes of an Itinerant Policeman, 1900; The World of Graft, 1901; The Little Brother: A Story of Tramp Life, 1902; The Rise of Ruderick Clowd, 1903; My Life, 1908.

ABOUT: Kerns, J. Biographical Dictionary of American Journalism; Flynt, J. My Life, Tramping with Tramps; Morris, L. Postscript to Yesterday. *Periodical*—New York Times January 22, 1907.

**WILLEY, BASIL** (July 25, 1897–September 3, 1978), British scholar, wrote: "I was born in London, where I lived until I was called up for World

War I [in 1916; he served as lieutenant in the West Yorkshire Regiment]. My father was William Herbert Willey, eldest son of a Cornish Wesleyan minister; my mother was Alice Ann Le Gros, a Jersey woman, through whom I am descended from the old Jersey family of de Carteret. It was in honour of a member of this family, Sir George Carteret, a Royalist admiral in the time of our seventeenth century civil wars, that New Jersey received its name. Carteret had defended the Island of Jersey against the Parliamentary forces, and in return for his services he was granted a piece of land between the Hudson and Delaware Rivers, to be held by him of the Crown as 'Lord Proprietor' at a rent of £5 a year.

"When I was demobilized in 1919, I went up to Cambridge (where I had already won a history scholarship), and I have lived and taught there ever since. My first book, *The Seventeenth Century Background*, was published in 1934, and the following year I became a Fellow of Pembroke College. The second, *The Eighteenth Century Background*, appeared in 1940; the third, *Nineteenth Century Studies*, published in 1949, had previously formed the substance of a course of lectures at Columbia University, where I was visiting professor 1948–1949.

"In 1946 I had succeeded Sir Arthur Quiller-Couch as King Edward VII Professor of English Literature at Cambridge; in 1947 I was elected Fellow of the British Academy, and in 1948 I received from Manchester University the honorary degree of Litt.D. My most recent publication was *Christianity, Past and Present*, which reproduced a series of lectures delivered for the Cambridge Faculty of Divinity in 1950. In 1953 I was privileged to spend

another semester in the United States, this time at Cornell University. While I was there I also lectured at twelve other universities, and afterwards traveled extensively, on holiday, to the Pacific coast and in New England. At other times I have also lectured in France, Ireland, Switzerland and Denmark. Looking back over this outwardly uneventful life, I cannot but think myself singularly fortunate. Happy in my early home, happy again in my marriage [to Zélie Murlis Ricks in 1923], blessed with two sons and two daughters (all of them charming people . . . ), and living for the best part of my life in one of the loveliest cities on earth, I have indeed much to be thankful for. And as if this were not enough, I have the entry into two other worlds: music (in which I am instinctively more at home than in my own chosen field of letters), and the English countryside—of which I am a devoted lover and explorer—particularly the Lake District which I visit constantly for the good of both body and soul."

---

Willey's four books on the seventeenth and succeeding centuries have had a pervasive, although largely unacknowledged, influence. No one who has made a serious study of seventeenth-century writers, in particular, can afford to ignore Willey. He was by no means a profound critic of individual writers—he had little sense of or serious interest in individual psychology—but he was painstaking and illuminating in his explanation of writers' backgrounds, and his work is a landmark in the development of a sensible contextualism.

*The Seventeenth Century Background* was Willey's most important book, demonstrating, for the first time, how both poetry and religion in the seventeenth century were affected by the "climate of opinion." It ends with a postscript—"Wordsworth and the Locke Tradition"—showing how the Romantics attempted to deal with the legacy of seventeenth-century thought. Willey was impressed with the manner in which Wordsworth created his poetry "out of the direct dealings of his mind and heart with the visible universe."

Of *The Eighteenth Century Background* John Hayward wrote, in the *Spectator*: "many people will find that his book is not only useful but also a helpful check on wishful thoughts and feelings. Those who have read [*The Seventeenth Century Background*] will not need to be reminded of the lucidity and grace of his expositions. These admirable and essential qualities are wholly maintained in its sequel."

Readers and scholars were equally impressed with Willey's two volumes on the nineteenth century, *Nineteenth Century Studies* and its successor *More Nineteenth Century Studies*. From the second the *Yale Review* singled out for special praise the pioneer essay on the neglected "Mark Rutherford" (William Hale White), an "honest doubter" with whom Willey had sympathy. V. S. Pritchett, writing about *Nineteenth Century Studies* in the *New Statesman* (1949), summed up most of Willey's virtues when he called him "cool, placid, economical, sensitive and self-effacing"; he also praised him for his "continuous" sympathy: "it is a form of curiosity, so that the great pleasure (and value) of his inquiry is that it really does disclose more and more of his subject."

But for his last book, *Samuel Taylor Coleridge*, Willey did not receive the usual golden reviews. *Choice* even found it "offensive," though the reviewer commended the quality of Willey's analyses of his subject's prose; the *New Statesman* (1972) thought that Willey, in his eagerness to present Coleridge as Christian exegete, had "reduced him as a poet." Willey was stronger, and recognized as such, in his Hibbert Lectures, revised and published as *Darwin and Butler: Two Versions of Evolution*, which a reviewer in the *Times Literary Supplement* (1961) praised as throwing more light on a classic controversy.

Until his elevation to the Edward VII Professorship of English Literature, Willey's London *Times* obituarist wrote, "one thought of Basil Willey as essentially a private person; but when, in his own words, he had recovered from the shock of surprise at his appointment, he quickly recognised that he had public duties." One of these many duties, all of which he performed with peacemaking in mind, was to arrange the prestigious annual Clark Lectures at the University; Willey was not afraid, on one occasion, to invite the eccentric and provocative Robert Graves to deliver them.

In 1958 Willey became President of Pembroke College, Cambridge. He was made Honorary Fellow in 1964. In his retirement he remained active until the final years. He devoted much of his time to two volumes of autobiography. Of the second, *Cambridge and Other Memories 1920–1953*, the *Times Literary Supplement* (1969) wrote: "of course some readers will wish for something grittier. . . . Friends and colleagues appear and are saluted, but they do not come to life. The book is about one man only. . . . The portrait of a Christian academic in a recognised, if weakening English tradition . . . emerges in the sharpest definition. We know from this book not only what Professor Willey has done, but how and by what lights he has lived his life." Willey was a fellow of both the British Academy and the Royal Society of Literature. He and his wife, Zélie Murlis Ricks, had four children.

PRINCIPAL WORKS: *Criticism*—Tendencies in Renaissance Literary Theory, 1922; The Seventeenth Century Background, 1934; The Eighteenth Century Background, 1940; Coleridge on Imagination and Fancy, 1946; Richard Crashaw, 1949; Nineteenth Century Studies: Coleridge to Matthew Arnold, 1949; Christianity, Past and Present, 1952; More Nineteenth Century Studies: A Group of Honest Doubters, 1956; The Religion of Nature, 1957; Darwin and Butler: Two Versions of Evolution, 1960; The English Moralists, 1964; Religion Today, 1969; Samuel Taylor Coleridge, 1972. *Memoirs*—Spots of Time, 1965; Cambridge and Other Memories, 1968.

ABOUT: The autobiographical material quoted above was written for Twentieth Century Authors First Supplement, 1955. *Periodicals*—Choice September, 1972; New Republic April 10, 1950; New Statesman and Nation December 24, 1949; March 17, 1972; Spectator February 9, 1940; Times (London) September 5, 1978; Times Literary Supplement September 9, 1960; February 6, 1969.

**WILLIAMS, BEN AMES** (March 7, 1889–February 4, 1953), American novelist and short story writer, wrote: "I was born in Macon, Mississippi.

My mother, Sarah Marshall (Ames) Williams, was a niece of General James Longstreet of the Confederate Army. My father, Daniel Webster Williams, was an Ohio man, the editor of the *Standard-Journal* in Jackson, Ohio, and at a later period a member of the Ohio State Senate and Consul at Cardiff, Wales. I lived as a boy in Jackson, Ohio; came East in 1904 to attend the Allen School in West Newton, Massachusetts, spent the following year in Cardiff, where my father was then Consul, and entered Dartmouth College in the fall of 1906 (B.A. 1910).

"I went to work as a reporter on the Boston *American* in September 1910, and continued until December 1916. By that time I had sold a few short stories and short serials, principally to the *All-Story Magazine*, which was edited at that time by Robert H. Davis. Since 1916 I have been a professional writer of fiction, and stories of mine have been published in a long list of magazines, to the number of some 382 titles. Most of these have appeared in the *Saturday Evening Post* and *Collier's.*

"My first book, *All the Brothers Were Valiant*, was published in 1919; and since then, more than thirty of my books have appeared. I was married in 1912 to Florence Trafton Talpey of York, Maine, whose father, grandfather, and great-grandfather were all sea captains in the China trade. We have two sons and a daughter. . . . "

———

A prolific writer of efficient formula fiction, Ben Ames Williams was best known for his short stories about rural Maine, and for historical novels about the Revolutionary and Civil wars. The stories about Maine were inspired by his summer vacations in the town of Searsmont (fictionalized as Fraternity), and by his friendship with A. L. McCorrision, a local farmer who served as the model for Bert McAusland, Williams's archetype for the salty, unaffected native of Maine. McAusland and the other regulars of Will Bissell's general store appeared most memorably in the 1949 volume *Fraternity Village*. The *New York Times Book Review* wrote of this: "This collection of sixteen stories about the Maine town Ben Ames Williams calls Fraternity will have a twofold interest. For the fiction reader it presents a community and its people, a simple, solid community and warm, human people. For the writer or student of writing it presents a case-history of a craftsman's short-fiction writing over twenty years."

When Williams turned from short stories to novels, he achieved commercial success with *Leave Her to Heaven* and other books that a *New Yorker* reviewer (1944) described as "quite satisfactory for what is known as summer reading." Williaams's most ambitious novel was *House Divided*, the story of a family of Southern aristocrats during the Civil War. A *New Yorker* reviewer (1947) wrote of this book, which took Williams about fifteen years to research and another four to write, "The novel is frankly written from the Southern viewpoint, but with little of the sentimentality that now colors most accounts of the Civil War. Mr. Williams does not, for example, spare the high-placed politicians (Jefferson Davis is presented as a fool and something of a rogue), hotheads, and profiteers of the Confederacy."

A cheerful and unpretentious man, Williams made no claims for himself as a literary artist. His papers are in the Colby College Library, Waterville, Maine.

PRINCIPAL WORKS: *Novels*—All the Brothers Were Valiant, 1919; The Sea Bride, 1919; The Great Accident, 1920; Evered, 1921; Black Pawl, 1922; Sangsue, 1923; Audacity, 1924; The Rational Hind, 1925; The Silver Forest, 1926; Immortal Longings, 1927; Splendor, 1927; The Dreadful Night, 1928; Death on a Scurvy Street, 1929 (in U.K.: The Bellmer Mystery); Touchstone, 1930; Great Oaks, 1930; An End to Mirth, 1931; Pirate's Purchase, 1931; Honeyflow, 1932; Money Musk, 1932 (reissued as Lady in Peril, 1948); Pascal's Mill, 1933; Mischief, 1933; Hostile Valley, 1934 (reissued as Valley Vixen, 1948); Small Town Girl, 1935; Crucible, 1937; The Strumpet Sea, 1938 (in U.K.: Once aboard the Whaler); Thread of Scarlet, 1939; Come Spring, 1940; Mr. Secretary, 1940; The Strange Woman, 1941; Time of Peace: September 26, 1930–December 7, 1941, 1942; Leave Her to Heaven, 1944; It's a Free County, 1945; House Divided, 1947; Owen Glen, 1950; The Unconquered, 1953. *Short stories*—Thrifty Stock and Other Stories, 1923; The Happy End, 1939; Fraternity Village, 1949. *As editor*—Letters from Fraternity (by A. L. McCorrison) 1931; Amateurs at War: The American Soldier in Action, 1943; A Diary from Dixie (by M. B. Chestnut) 1949.

ABOUT: The autobiographical material quoted above was written for Twentieth Century Authors, 1942. Dictionary of American Biography, Suppl. 5, 1977; Dictionary of Literary Biography vol. 102 1991. *Periodicals*—New York Times February 5, 1953; New York Times Book Review July 10, 1949; New Yorker June 17, 1944; September 13, 1947.

## WILLIAMS, CHARLES (September 20, 1886– May 15, 1945), English novelist, poet, biographer, dramatist, editor, Christian apologist, and literary

journalist, was born in Holloway, London, the only son of Mary (Wall) and Richard W. Stansby Williams. At the age of eight his parents moved out of London. He attended St. Albans School. In 1902 he began a course at University College, London, but, for financial reasons, was forced to leave before taking his degree. He found employment at the Methodist Bookroom, Holborn, and continued his studies in evening classes at the Workingman's College. In 1908 he joined the Oxford University Press, beginning a celebrated association which was to give his career as man of letters a secure foundation. His first book was published in 1912, with the financial help of Wilfrid and Alice Meynell. *The Silver Stair* was a series of

sonnets "now irrecoverably embedded in their own mannerisms," according to his biographer Glen Cavaliero, one of the few to have given William's writing lengthy consideration. Because of poor eyesight, he was unable to continue working for the Oxford University Press during the war, but in 1917, the year in which he also married Florence Conway, the Press published his second collection, *Poems of Conformity*. Third and fourth collections, *Divorce* and *Windows of Night*, quickly followed. They did nothing to secure his reputation, and Martin Seymour-Smith has characterized these early efforts as "a semi-Chestertonian attempt to revive a Victorian style."

His influence grew during the 1920s and 1930s by dint of his increasing seniority at the OUP and his association with T. S. Eliot, W. H. Auden, and C. S. Lewis. (He became a member of the Inklings) or "Oxford Christians," a group of writers and literary dons gathered around Lewis and much interested in allegorical fantasy and science fiction. William's own cosmic thrillers contain visions of ghoulish violence. (According to Valentine Cunningham, in *British Writers of the Thirties*, he was in the habit of threatening his lady admirers with ruler spankings.) He never made inflated claims for his novels. The last two (there were seven in all) are considered the best. *Descent Into Hell* is self-consciously profound. The narrative is about the suburban production of a pastoral in verse by Peter Stanhope, a fictional poet with the eminence of a T. S. Eliot (who wrote an introduction to the American edition of the last novel, *All Hallows' Eve*). Concerning "that great schism in identity which is death," *All Hallows' Eve* follows two young women, Lester and Evelyn, both recently killed in a plane accident, on their separate roads of salvation and damnation. In describing London, transfigured as a city of the dead, Williams produced some of his most effective descriptive writing, and in the character of Simon, sorcerer and magician, he created a simulacrum of the spiritual mastermind identity in which he personally delighted.

He published several works of theology and, with C. S. Lewis, was one of the foremost Christian apologists of his day. *The Descent of the Dove*, a history of the Holy Spirit, is William's finest achievement. In it he stressed, more unambiguously than in the novels, his view of the inclusive nature of Christian belief.

By the 1930s Williams had become a prominent reviewer, writing regularly in *Time and Tide* and the *Dublin Review*. In *The English Poetic Mind* (1932), he wrote about the effect of disillusionment on the work of Shakespeare, Milton, and Wordsworth, and eighteen months later published *Reason and Beauty in the Poetic Mind*. Stephen Spender, writing in the *Spectator*, complained of the second book that "This is the kind of criticism which goes far to explain why so many people detest poetry. It speaks of poets as though they were superior beings incapable of experiencing the feelings of ordinary people; it translates simple and direct poetry, which easily explains itself, into high-flown and indirect language."

As well as biographies (Bacon, James I, Rochester, and others) Williams wrote plays, and achieved a measure of recognition with the production of his *Thomas Cranmer of Canterbury* at the 1936 Canterbury Festival, a year after Eliot's *Murder in the Cathedral*. Williams capitalized on the vogue for religious drama in *Seed of Adam, Judgement at Chelmsford* (written using the pseudonym "Peter Stanhope"), *The House by the Stable, Grab and Grace* and *The House of the Octopus*. Williams always considered himself primarily a poet; in fact some have claimed him as a sort of twentieth-century William Blake. There were two Arthurian series published in his lifetime, *Taliessin through Logres* and *The Region of the Summer Stars*. An unfinished "The Figure of Arthur" was published posthumously in *Arthurian Torso* 1948, which contained a lengthy commentary on William's Arthurian cycle by C. S. Lewis. Apart from this, William's poetry has attracted few commentators, the one exception being John Heath-Stubbs who, in the fifties, wrote *Charles Williams*, a pioneer full-length study, and contributed an introduction to the 1963 edition of the *Collected Plays*.

PRINCIPAL WORKS: *Poetry*—The Silver Stair, 1912; Poems of Conformity, 1917; Divorce, 1920; Windows of the Night, 1924; Taliessin through Logres, 1938; The Region of the Summer Stars, 1944; Arthurian Torso, 1948. *Fiction*—War in Heaven, 1930; Many Dimensions, 1931; The Place of the Lion, 1931; The Greater Trumps, 1932; Shadows of Ecstasy, 1933; Descent into Hell, 1937; All Hallows' Eve, 1944. *Nonfiction*—Heroes and Kings, 1930: Poetry at Present, 1930; The English Poetic Mind, 1932; Bacon, 1933; Reason and Beauty in the Poetic Mind, 1933; James I, 1934; Rochester, 1935; Queen Elizabeth, 1936; Henry VII, 1937; Stories of Great Names, 1937; He Came Down from Heaven, 1938; The Descent of the Dove, 1939; Religion and Love in Dante, 1941; Witchcraft, 1941; The Forgiveness of Sins, 1942; The Figure of Beatrice, 1943; Flecker of Dean Close, 1946; The Image of the City and Other Essays, 1958; Selected Writings, 1961. *Drama*—A Myth of Shakespeare, 1928; Three Plays (The Witch, the Chaste Wanton, The Rite of the Passion) 1931; Thomas Cranmer of Canterbury, 1936; Judgment at Chelmsford, 1939; The House of the Octopus, 1945; Seed of Adam and Other Plays, 1948; Collected Plays, 1963.

ABOUT: Cavaliero, G. Charles Williams, 1983; Carpenter, H. The Inklings, 1979; Contemporary Authors vol. 104 1981; Cunningham, V. British Writers of the Thirties, 1988; Dictionary of Literary Biography vol. 100 1990; Dictionary of National Biography, 1941–1950, 1959; Hadfield, A. H. Charles Williams, 1983; Heath-Stubbs, J. Charles Williams; Sibley, A. M. Charles Williams, 1982; Who's Who 1945. *Periodicals*—Atlantic Monthly November 1949; New York Times May 17, 1945; Spectator December 22, 1933; Times (London) May 17, 1945.

**WILLIAMS, (GEORGE) EMLYN** (November 26, 1905–September 25, 1987), Welsh playwright, actor, and writer, was born near Mostyn, Flintshire, the son of Richard and Mary Williams. Richard Williams was at various times an iron worker, greengrocer, and coal miner, and Emlyn probably would have followed his working-class, Welsh-speaking compatriots into the mines at the age of twelve had it not been for Sarah Grace Cooke, a schoolteacher and social worker from London who perceived his potential. Under Cooke's tutelage, he acquired French, improved his English, and won a scholarship to Holywell County School in Dorsetshire. At seventeen he entered Christ Church Col-

lege, Oxford, on a scholarship, and joined the Oxford University Dramatic Society (the OUDS).

Abandoning the more practical goals of the ministry or scholarship, he embarked on a theatrical career after graduating from Oxford in 1927. In the same year he appeared in London and New York in J. B. Fagan's *And So to Bed*. He had already written parts for himself in apprentice plays at Oxford, and in 1930 had his first commercial success with *A Murder Has Been Arranged*, which he directed. During the following years he  alternated roles in others' plays with roles in his own. In the 1930s and 1940s Williams appeared in several films, usually playing a cunning and unscrupulous scoundrel—a type he imitated to perfection. He did not have another hit as dramatist until 1935, with *Night Must Fall*. This play about a psychopathic bellboy who carries around his landlady's head in a hatbox ran for 435 performances in London and was made into a chilling 1937 movie in which Robert Montgomery starred in the role originated by Williams himself on stage. Apart from *The Corn Is Green*, which appeared three years later, *Night Must Fall* remains Williams's best-known play. Calling it a "minor classic of the macabre," Richard Findlater wrote, "Each curtain in *Night Must Fall* is a perfectly arranged *coup de théâtre*, and the play itself is designed with precise engineering of tension and suspense, presenting Grand Guignol in the semi-realistic trappings of criminal psychology."

In *The Corn Is Green*, about the education of a promising Welsh schoolboy by a driven, spinsterish schoolmistress, Williams turned from the macabre to the nostalgic and autobiographical. Naturally, he played the role of the rebellious adolescent student in the London production; the more pivotal role of Miss Moffat was a triumph, first, for Sybil Thorndike and later, in America, for Ethel Barrymore and Bette Davis. Reviewing the New York production in the *Nation*, Joseph Wood Krutch wrote, "If the play is neither novel nor searching, it is human and sincere, and the fact that it is continuously interesting is probably due less to any single outstanding excellence than to the cumulative effect of various simple virtues in the writing."

As Krutch implied, Williams's plays were of the conventional, "well-made" type, and though he continued to write them into the 1950s, the theatrical innovators of that decade (John Osborne, Harold Pinter, and others) made his work look old-fashioned. He therefore gradually withdrew from playwriting and concentrated instead on acting and his other writing, taking notable roles in such movies as *Ivanhoe* and *The L-Shaped Room*, and in plays by Lillian Hellman, Robert Bolt, and others. His greatest success as an actor was in his impersonation of Charles Dickens, a one-man show based on Dickens's public readings. Williams performed this all over the world from early 1950s to the mid-1980s. *A Boy Growing Up*, his one-man show of readings from the works of his fellow Welshman Dylan Thomas, was similarly praised; but it was not quite the crowd-pleaser the Dickens performance had been.

Williams turned to other forms of writing in later years—a novel (*Headlong*); accounts of actual crimes, one more or less journalistic, about the notorious "Moors murder" (*Beyond Belief*), the other more or less fictional (*Dr. Crippen's Diary*); and two volumes of autobiography (*George*; *Emlyn*). Of these works, the disarmingly frank autobiographies received the kindest reviews. Reviewing the second volume, *Emlyn: An Early Autobiography, 1927–1935*, the radio comedian and humorist Arthur Marshall wrote in the *New Statesman*, "Though the basic material (the ups and downs of a young actor's life and the painful emotional entanglements that accompanied them) is perhaps less rewarding than *George*, this book has the same readability, the same skillful use of words, the same warmth and the same humour. One laughs aloud."

Williams was married to Molly O'Shann and had two sons. He was made a Commander of the Order of the British Empire in 1962.

PRINCIPAL WORKS: *Drama*—A Murder Has Been Arranged: A Ghost Story in Three Acts, 1930; Night Must Fall: A Play in Three Acts, 1935; He Was Born Gay: A Romance in Three Acts, 1937; The Corn Is Green: A Comedy in Three Acts, 1938; The Light of Heart: A Play in Three Acts, 1940; The Morning Star: A Play in Three Acts, 1943; The Druid's Rest: A Comedy in Three Acts, 1944; The Wind of Heaven: A Play in Six Scenes, 1945; Spring, 1600: A Comedy in Three Acts, 1946; Trespass: A Ghost Story in Six Scenes, 1947; Accolade: A Play in Six Scenes, 1950; Someone Waiting: A Play in Three Acts, 1954; Beth: A Play in Four Scenes, 1959; The Collected Plays, 1961. *Adapatations*—The Late Christopher Bean (by R. Fauchois) 1933; A Month in the Country (by I. Turgenev) 1943. *Nonfiction*—Beyond Belief: A Chronicle of Murder and Its Detection, 1947. *Novels*—Headlong, 1981; Dr. Crippen's Diary: An Invention, 1988. *Autobiography*—George: An Early Autobiography, 1961; Emlyn: An Early Autobiography, 1927–1935, 1973.

ABOUT: Current Biography 1952; Dale-Jones, D. Emlyn Williams, 1979; Findlater, R. Emlyn Williams, 1956. *Periodicals*—Nation December 7, 1940; New Statesman October 5, 1973; New York Times September 26, 1987; Times (London) September 26, 1987.

**WILLIAMS, JESSE LYNCH** (August 17, 1871–September 14, 1929), American novelist, dramatist and short story writer, was born in Sterling, Illinois, the son of Meade Creighton Willims and Elizabeth (Riddle) Williams.

He attended Beloit Academy in Wisconsin, and as an undergraduate at Princeton was an editor of the *Nassau Literary Magazine*. With Booth Tarkington and others he founded the Triangle Club, Princeton's well-known amateur acting group. He graduated in 1892 and a year later went to the *New York Sun* as a reporter under Charles Anderson Dana. He received his Master of Arts from Princeton in 1895, the same year he published his first book, *Princeton Stories*, which captured the spirit of undergraduate life and was the first of many college fiction volumes.

After a three-year stint as *Scribner's Magazine*,

Williams returned to Princeton in 1900 as the first editor of the *Princeton Alumni Weekly* until 1903, when he dedicated himself to writing. His journalism experience was the basis of a play, *The Stolen Story* (1899), novelized in 1906 as *The Day-Dreamer* and considered an articulate and entertaining account of the newspaper business.

In *Mr Cleveland: A Personal Impression* (1909), Williams shed an appreciative and different light on President Grover Cleveland, who was his friend and neighbor in Princeton. Williams got beyond Cleveland's rugged honesty and exterior toughness to convey his shyness and soft spots. "It is just such intimate glimpses as this into the private character of public men that are necessary to the proper understanding of their actions and careers," wrote *The New York Times*.

Outside of Princeton and the college scene, Williams was best known for novels and plays that comically analyzed domestic life, beginning with his account of courtship among the leisure class in *My Lost Duchess* (1908), which prompted comparisons to Anthony Hope. The *New York Times*, writing that "Nick, the hero, is as worthy and entertaining a protagonist of the Fifth Avenue phase of New york life as Van Bibber was at his best," commented that Williams was "enough of an idealist to refine the events of daily life without becoming unconvincing."

Williams continued his humorous portraits of marriage with *The Married Life of the Frederic Carrolls* (1910), in which an upper-class couple discover one another on a boring honeymoon at an English country estate and comes back to America to survive financial and other difficulties. The author's spirited and mildly cynical views on wedded bliss reached their zenith and won the first Pulitzer Prize for drama in 1917 when the widely acclaimed Shavian novel, *And So They Were Married* (1914) was staged as the comedy *Why Marry?*, starring the often-married Nat Goodwin. Another amorous comedy, *They Still Fall in Love* (1929), about the capers of a mischievous heiress and an unemotional scientist, was faulted for being too thin on plot and too thick on dialogue, for relying too much on stock characters and allowing too little surprise, but William's common sense, ironic humor and sharp behavioristic reporting filtered through nevertheless.

Known for his meticulousness, Williams rewrote his final work, *She Knew She Was Right* (1930), four time. Published the year after his death, it told of a self-righteous woman of many affairs who is upstaged by the true heroine, her charming secretary. "The story is handled with originality and flavored richly with the observations of a witty, shrewd, laughing mind," wrote Thayer Hobson in *Books*.

Often praised for his genial style, skillful satire

and brilliant characterizations, Williams received his Doctorate of Literature from Princeton in 1919, was elected president of the Authors' League of America in 1921, and received a fellowship in creative art at the University of Michigan in 1925–26.

PRINCIPAL WORKS: Princeton Stories, 1895; The Adventures of a Freshman, 1899; The Stolen Story and other Newspaper Stories, 1899; New York Sketches, 1902; The Girl and the Game and Other College Stories, 1908; My Lost Duchess, 1908; Mr. Cleveland, A Personal Impression, 1909; The Married Life of the Frederic Carrolls, 1910; And So They Were Married, 1914; Remating Time, 1916; Not Wanted, 1923; They Still Fall in Love, 1929; She Knew She Was Right, 1930.

ABOUT: Dictionary of Americn Biography 1936; Egbert, D. D. and Lee, D. M. Princeton Portraits; Leitch, A. Princeton Companion; Princeton College, class of 1892: Quindecennial Report; Quinn, A.H. A History of American Drama. Periodicals—Books June 1, 1930; Boston Transcript July 13, 1929; New York Times March 24, 1906, May 16, 1908, June 13, 1908, April 24, 1909; September 15, 1929; New York World April 14, 1929.

## WILLIAMS, JOEL. See JENNINGS, JOHN EDWARD

## WILLIAMS, MICHAEL (February 5, 1877–October 12, 1950), Canadian-born writer on Roman Catholicism, was born in Halifax, Nova Scotia, the son of Michael Williams, a seafarer, and Anne Colston Williams. He was educated by the Jesuit Fathers in New Brunswick, but his father's death from yellow fever forced him to abandon formal schooling for a job as clerk in a wholesale dry goods warehouse.

In his autobiography, The Book of the High Romance, Williams describes his life at that time as "solitary as a pigeon in a flight of crows." He found solace in reading and in writing tales and poems. At the age of nineteen he was offered the editorship of a little magazine launched by a bookseller friend; work at this more congenial task led to his dismissal from the warehouse. The magazine was short-lived but Williams at least experienced the exhilaration of producing copy.

The "highway" took Williams to Boston, where he worked in a five-and-dime store and lived in poverty. He eventually placed a poem in the Boston Transcript and began to publish stories in the Boston Journal and elsewhere, using the pseudonym "the Quietist." But city life aggravated a lung condition, and he was forced to retreat to North Carolina for eighteen months to regain his health. Upon returning to Boston, he worked for a time as a hack writer for the popular, crude Black Cat magazine, "rewriting short stories, and concocting others; crazy tales of murder and mystery." Soon he "drifted" into journalism, working as a cub reporter for the Boston Post. Later he joined the reporting staff of the New York World and the Evening Telegram. He also wrote for the Sunday Sun and other papers, as well as for McClure's Magazine. He was city edi-

tor of the San Francisco Examiner when the great earthquake of 1906 struck. Six weeks later, following a row with his superiors, he returned to New York and hack writing. He then joined Upton Sinclair's "co-operative home colony," a group of radical and "advanced thinkers" centered at Helicon Hall in Englewood, New Jersey.

Williams's path "among the new cults and religious movements" came to an end when, in 1912, he embraced Roman Catholicism, the religion of his youth. In 1913 he served as an International News Service special correspondent to Mexico. His journalistic career continued until 1915, when he took a job in the publicity department of the Panama-Pacific Exposition, followed by a tenure as organizing secretary of the San Francisco Institute of Art after the Exposition closed. He then worked for United Welfare Organizations and for the National Catholic War Council, later called the Welfare Conference, editing its bulletin and traveling on assignments. In 1921 he published American Catholics in the War. Later he served as president of the American Catholic Historical Association. Williams became president of the Calvert Association, a society devoted to the promotion of religious freedom. In 1924 he founded Commonweal, a weekly Roman Catholic magazine; his editorship, which lasted until 1935, brought high literary standards and a reputation for tolerance and liberality to the publication. Commonweal later stated that its first editior was in the "front rank of those who fought for social justice. He fought with all the charm and exuberance and warm friendliness of his whole personality, but he really fought." In 1929 Williams published Catholicism and the Modern Mind ; in its review the London Times called him a "conversational propagandist," and declared that although he "tells us all about 'Bible Belt bigotries, the Elmer Gantryisms, the prohibitionists, the Lost Angelites, & c., he is sincere and often affecting." In 1932 Williams published a history of anti-Catholicism in America titled The Shadow of the Pope.

As a member of the American Committee on Religious Rights, Williams visited Germany and reported on the persecution of the Jews in a series of articles published in 1933 in the New York Herald Tribune. The New York Times reported that "in a poll of editors of Jewish newspapers he was chosen among the twelve greatest Christian champions of the Jewish people for taking the initiative in creating an international committee for the emigration of German Jews and for combating Nazi denials of the persecution of Jews."

PRINCIPAL WORKS: Nonfiction—(with U. Sinclair) Good Health and How We Won It, 1909; American Catholics in the War, 1921; Little Brother Francis of Assisi, 1926; The Little Flower of Carmel, 1926; Catholicism and the Modern Mind, 1928; The Shadow of the Pope, 1932; The Catholic Church in Action, 1935 (rev. ed. by Z. Aradi, 1958.) Memoirs—The Book of the High Romance, 1918. As editor—The Book of Christian Classics, 1933 (reissued as Anthology of Classic Christian Literature, 1937, and rev. ed. by D. E. Wheeler as They Walked with God, 1957).

ABOUT: Hoehn, M. (ed.) Catholic Authors: Contemporary Biographical Sketches: 1930–1947, 1948. Periodicals—New York Times October 13, 1950; Times (London) January 10, 1929.

**WILLIAMS, OSCAR** (December 29, 1900?–
October 10, 1964), American anthologist and writer
of verse, wrote: "Oscar Williams has spent most of

his life in New York City,
a few years in the West,
and the Depression years
(1931–1936) as an adver-
tising man in the South.
Education, the elementa-
ry schools in Brooklyn,
and never finished high
school. Started writing
poetry when seventeen
years old and continued
until his twentieth year.
In 1921 he stopped writing poetry, and didn't start
again until 1937 in the spring. During this interval
he was in the advertising business in various capacities. In 1923, on the way out of the literary game,
he edited *Rhythmus*, a poetry magazine, for about
a year, and also was the poetry editor for the old
*Forum*."

W. H. Auden affectionately gave Williams's
strange story as follows: "Oscar Williams' poetical
career has been extraordinary. As an undergraduate he wrote and published poetry which he
says 'showed very little promise.' Coming by
chance upon an advertising booklet, he became fascinated by its language, and bluffed his way into
the advertising business, where he forgot all about
poetry and held important and lucrative positions
for sixteen years, though, prompted perhaps by an
unconscious instinct of self-preservation, he took
care to let others write the copy and confined himself to financial organization. A few years ago,
while motoring in the South, he began to feel
strange, so strange that he sought medical advice,
which could diagnose nothing. Suddenly he realized what was the matter: he wanted to write poetry. Obedient, he gave up his job. . . .
Understandably enough under the circumstances,
he feels that the mechanized life is the Devil, and
the subject of many of his poems is just this theme;
while their form and imagery . . . is romantic, violent, and exciting. But, unlike many romantics,
Mr. Williams has lived successfully in the world he
attacks, and believes in its values."

---

A somewhat enigmatic figure who may have
been born in Odessa, Russia, or in Brooklyn, New
York, in 1900 or in 1899, Oscar Williams was more
successful as a somewhat eccentric anthologist than
as a poet. His first volume of poems, *The Golden
Darkness*, was chosen for the Yale Younger Poet series; but then came sixteen years of silence. In 1940
he tried to return to poetry with *The Man Coming
toward You*. Writing in the *Nation*, Morton Dauwen Zabel described it as "a discharge of mixed and
muddled metaphors, a ranting vulgarity of
rhythms, a racket of the massed clichés of tragic
prophecy and moral decay." On the other hand,
Stephen Spender, writing in the *New Statesman
and Nation*, found compensating strengths amid
Williams's weaknesses: "Oscar Williams . . . is dif-

fuse and uncontrolled, but all the same we recognize the world that perplexes us, and we feel that
the writer is aware of the problems of the machine
age. His poetry suffers from the excess of hard visual imagery which spoils much American poetry for
an English reader. But he is worth reading."

Williams's next (and last) new collection, *That's
All That Matters*, was praised and condemned in
similar terms, but by then he had established a
somewhat firmer reputation as an anthologist. The
first of his many anthologies was a round-up of recent British and American verse titled *New Poems,
1940*. This was generally considered a useful collection, as were the three annuals that followed. Williams went on to compile more inclusive
anthologies of British and American poetry, and although he usually included an over-generous sample of his own verse, he was also an effective
evangelist for the work of others, tolerated as such
even by the notoriously intolerant Robert Lowell.

Williams lectured on poetry at numerous
American colleges and taught summer sessions at
New York University. He lived with his wife, a
painter and writer of verse, Gene Derwood, in an
apartment in lower Manhattan.

PRINCIPAL WORKS: *Poetry*—The Golden Darkness, 1921; The
Man Coming toward You, 1940; That's All That Matters, 1945;
Selected Poems, 1947. *As editor*—New Poems, 1940: An An-
thology of British and American Verse, 1941; New Poems,
1942: An Anthology of British and American Verse, 1942; New
Poems, 1943; An Anthology of British and American Verse,
1943; New Poems, 1944, 1944; The War Poets: An Antohlogy
of the War Poetry of the Twentieth Century, 1945; A Little
Treasury of Modern Poetry, English and American, 1946; A
Little Treasury of Great Poetry, English and American, from
Chaucer to the Present Day, 1947; A Little Treasury of
American Poetry The Chief Poets from Colonial Times to the
Present Day, 1948, rev. ed. 1952; A Little Treasury of British
Poetry: The Chief Poets from 1500 to 1900, 1951; Immortal
Poems of the English Language: British and American Poetry
from Chaucer's Time to the Present Day, 1952; The Golden
Treasury of the Best Songs and Lyrical Poems: A Modern Edi-
tion, (by F. T. Palgrave) 1953; The Pocket Book of Modern
Verse: English and American Poetry of the Last Hundred
Years, from Walt Whitman to Dylan Thomas, 1954; The New
Pocket Anthology of American Verse, from Colonial Days to
the Present, 1955; The Silver Treasury of Light Verse, from
Geoffrey Chaucer to Ogden Nash, 1957; (with E. Honig) The
Mentor Book of Major American Poets, from Edward Taylor
and Walt Whitman to Hart Crane and W. H. Auden, 1962;
The Mentor Book of British Poets, from William Blake to Dy-
lan Thomas, 1963; Master Poems of the English Language:
Over One Hundred Poems Together with Introduction by
Leading Poets and Critics of the English-Speaking World,
1966.

ABOUT: The autobiographical material quoted above was written for Twentieth Century Authors, 1942. Contemporary Authors, New Revison Series 6, 1982. *Periodicals*—Nation May
4, 1940; New Statesman and Nation May 11, 1940; New York
Times October 11, 1964; Poetry November 1946; Saturday Review of Literautre September 25, 1948.

**WILLIAMS, TENNESSEE** (March 26, 1911–
February 25, 1983), American playwright, wrote:
"I was born in the Episcopal rectory of Columbus,
Mississippi, an old town on the Tombigbee River
which was so dignified and reserved that there was
a saying, only slightly exaggerated, that you had to
live there a whole year before a neighbor would
smile at you on the street. As my grandfather, with

whom we lived, was the Episcopal clergyman, we were accepted without probation. My father, a man with the formidable name of Cornelius Coffin Wil-

liams, was a man of ancestry that came on one side, the Williams, from pioneer Tennessee stock and on the other from early settlers of Nantucket Island in New England. My mother was descended from Quakers. Roughly there was a combination of Puritan and Cavalier strains in my blood which may be accountable for the conflicting impulses I often represent in the people I write about.

"I was christened Thomas Lanier Williams. It is a nice enough name, perhaps a little too nice. It sounds like it might belong to the sort of writer who turns out sonnet sequences to Spring. As a matter of fact, my first literary award was twenty-five dollars from a woman's club for doing exactly that, three sonnets dedicated to Spring. I hasten to add that I was still pretty young. Under that name I published a good deal of lyric poetry which was a bad imitation of Edna Millay. When I grew up I realized this poetry wasn't much good and I felt the name had been compromised, so I changed it to Tennessee Williams, the justification being mainly that the Williamses had fought the Indians for Tennessee and I had already discovered that the life of a young writer was going to be something similar to the defense of a stockade against a band of savages.

"When I was about twelve, my father, a traveling salesman, was appointed to an office position in St. Louis and so we left the rectory and moved north. It was a tragic move. Neither my sister nor I could adjust ourselves to life in a midwestern city. The schoolchildren made fun of our Southern speech and manners. I remember gangs of kids following me home yelling 'Sissy!' and home was not a very pleasant refuge. It was a perpetually dim little apartment in a wilderness of identical brick and concrete structures with no grass and no trees nearer than the park. In the South we had never been conscious of the fact that we were economically less fortunate than others. We lived as well as anyone else. But in St. Louis we suddenly discovered there were two kinds of people, the rich and the poor, and that we belonged more to the latter. If we walked far enough west we came into a region of fine residences set in beautiful lawns. But where we lived, to which we must always return, were ugly rows of apartment buildings the color of dried blood and mustard. If I had been born to this situation I might not have resented it deeply. But it was forced upon my consciousness at the most sensitive age of childhood. It produced a shock and a rebellion that has grown into an inherent part of my work. It was the beginning of the social-consciousness which I think has marked most of my writing. I am glad that I received this bitter educa-

tion for I don't think any writer has much purpose back of him unless he feels bitterly the inequities of the society he lives in. I have no acquaintance with political and social dialectics. If you ask what my politics are, I am a Humanitarian.

"I entered college during the great American Depression and after a couple of years I couldn't afford to continue but had to drop out and take a clerical job in the shoe company that employed my father. The two years I spent in that corporation were indescribable torment to me as an individual but of immense value to me as a writer for they gave me first-hand knowledge of what it means to be a small wage-earner in a hopelessly routine job. I had been writing since childhood and I continued writing while I was employed by the shoe company. When I came home from work I would tank up on black coffee so I could remain awake most of the night, writing short stories which I could not sell. Gradually my health broke down. One day coming home from work, I collapsed and was removed to the hospital. The doctor said I couldn't go back to the shoe company. Soon as that was settled I recovered and went back South to live with my grandparents in Memphis where they had moved since my grandfather's retirement from the ministry. Then I began to have a little success with my writing. I became self-sufficient. I put myself through two more years of college and got a B.A. degree at the University of Iowa in 1938. Before then and for a couple of years afterwards I did a good deal of traveling around and I held a great number of part-time jobs of great diversity. It is hard to put the story in correct chronology for the last ten years of my life are a dizzy kaleidoscope. I don't quite believe all that has happened to me, it seems it must have happened to five or ten other people.

"My first real recognition came in 1940 when I received a Rockefeller fellowship and wrote *Battle of Angels*, which was produced by the Theatre Guild at the end of that year with Miriam Hopkins in the leading role. It closed in Boston during the try-out run but I have re-written it a couple of times since then and still have faith in it. My health was so impaired that I landed in 4F after a medical examination of about five minutes' duration. My jobs in this period included running an all-night elevator in a big apartment-hotel, waiting on tables and reciting verse in Greenwich Village, working as a teletype operator for the U.S. Engineers in Jacksonville, Florida, waiter and cashier for a small restaurant in New Orleans, ushering at the Strand Theatre on Broadway. All the while I kept on writing, writing, not with any hope of making a living at it but because I found no other means of expressing things that seemed to demand expression. There was never a moment when I did not find life to be immeasurably exciting to experience and to witness, however difficult it was to sustain.

"From a $17 a week job as a movie usher I was suddenly shipped off to Hollywood where M.G.M. paid me $250 a week. I saved enough money out of my six months there to keep me while I wrote *The Glass Menagerie*. I don't think the story, from that point on, requires any detailed consideration.

"If I can be said to have a home, it is in New Orleans where I've lived off and on since 1938 and which has provided me with more material than any other part of the country. I live near the main street of the Quarter which is named Royal. Down this street, running on the same tracks, are two street-cars, one named 'Desire' and the other named 'Cemetery.' Their indiscourageable progress up and down Royal struck me as having some symbolic bearing of a broad nature on the life in the Vieux Carré—and everywhere else for that matter . . . that's how I got the title."

---

Tennessee Williams established himself as one of the leading playwrights in the American theater with *The Glass Menagerie* in 1944. The four-character play focuses on a mother's anxiety over her crippled, unmarried daughter Laura (modeled after Williams's beloved sister Rose, who spent most of her life in mental hospitals and was lobotomized) and the "gentleman caller" brought home by her son. The tightly knit drama is both humorous and poignant as the mother persists in treating her daughter as an eligible Southern belle rather than the emotionally fragile and withdrawn creature she really is. The Broadway production broke box office records, and the play won the New York Drama Critics' Circle Award for 1945, as well as the Donaldson Award and the Sidney Howard Memorial Award. With Donald Windham during the early 1940s Williams dramatized a short story by D. H. Lawrence called *You Touched Me!*, but this optimistic romantic comedy fared poorly on Broadway when it opened in late 1945. By that time Williams was in Mexico at work on another drama called *A Streetcar Named Desire*, set in New Orleans. Technically superb in structure and dialogue as well as poetic and graphic in psychological insight, the play is essentially a complex character study of the disintegration of Blanche DuBois, a penniless Southern woman who clings desperately to illusory mementos of status, refinement, and romance. Assaulted finally by her brutish brother-in-law Stanley Kowalski, she withdraws from reality altogether, her mind shattered, her airs and graces intact. The role of Blanche was created by Jessica Tandy, and the young Marlon Brando rocketed to stardom as Kowalski. The play won the Drama Critics' Circle Award and the Pulitzer Prize for drama in 1948. After a successful Broadway run of more than two years it toured with more than one company.

With *Summer and Smoke*, produced in 1948, Williams again wrote a sensitive study of a repressed Southern woman, mixing realism and symbolism with themes of sex and religion. But most critics and theatergoers found it less trenchant and forceful than *Streetcar*. A revised version, entitled *The Eccentricities of a Nightingale*, was produced in 1964, but neither work gained the stature of Williams's more successful dramas.

Unlike the frustrated heroines of so many of his plays, Serafina Delle Rose of *The Rose Tattoo* is a vigorous and earthy woman. The play, a tragicomedy, opened on Broadway in 1951 and illustrated Williams's ability to deal sympathetically with characters who combined robust sensuality and spirituality.

In a surprising departure from realism he next wrote, under the influence of Thornton Wilder, *Camino Real*, a free verse "cosmic" fantasy full of personal and literary allusions and symbols, peculiar characters such as Kilroy and Lord Byron, and decadent eroticism. The play's disappointing 1953 New York production baffled reviewers and the public alike, but its expressionistic experimentation nevertheless encouraged a number of revivals over the years, with many revised versions by the author.

With *Cat on a Hot Tin Roof* Williams returned to the material his audience expected of him. A drama of passion, greed, and deception, the story takes place at a Mississippi plantation on Big Daddy's birthday. Vital Maggie (his daughter-in-law) desperately struggles to make her unresponsive and alcoholic husband Brick love her and produce an heir to Big Daddy's fortune. She goads Brick with an affair she once had with his best friend. Brooks Atkinson observed in the *New York Times* in 1955 that the play "seems not to have been written. It is the quintessence of life. It is the basic truth." The Broadway production was another big success for Williams, and the play brought him the Pulitzer Prize, the Drama Critics' Circle Award, and the Donaldson Award.

Williams persistently revised his earlier plays. Following *Cat on a Hot Tin Roof* he reworked the 1940 *Battle of Angels*, even though he had already presented other successful dramas on themes of suppressed sexuality. The new version, *Orpheus Descending*, was not a commercial success on Broadway in 1957, although an off-Broadway production two years later fared considerably better. Williams was never one to spare his audience. He treated candidly, sometimes for what seemed to be shock-value alone, subjects that were considered controversial or taboo in the 1940s and 1950s. A mixture of cannibalism and homosexuality underscored the horrifying and suspenseful short drama entitled *Suddenly Last Summer*, which with *Something Unspoken* made up *Garden District*, produced off-Broadway in 1958. The next year he offered another powerful and intense working of the themes of degeneracy and corruption of innocence in *Sweet Bird of Youth*, a smash hit on Broadway for nearly two years. This was followed by a strange "serious comedy" called *Period of Adjustment*, and then in late 1961 by *The Night of the Iguana*. The captured and tormented iguana in the story represents the assortment of lonely and maimed men and women gathered at a sleazy coastal Mexican hotel. But among them is Hannah Jelkes, an indomitable and self-reliant woman, one of Williams's most fascinating characters. *The Night of the Iguana* won the Antoinette Perry ("Tony") Award for 1962, and was the last play by Williams to be a real commercial success.

As an artist Williams mined his personal past and utilized his neurotic present to provide subjects and characters for his plays, stories, and novels. He drew upon his family and their numerous problems, his own feelings of social alienation due to his homosexuality and alcoholism, and, most importantly, his sense of being a romantic in a very unromantic modern world. Like Blanche DuBois he often relied heavily "on the kindness of strangers" as well as those close to him. Highly sensitive to negative reviews (especially after 1961 when his work no longer captivated mainstream theatergoing audiences) he gradually disintegrated. In interviews for magazines in the 1960s he candidly discussed his creative and private difficulties, recognizing their interdependence; but he could not integrate himself. The decade was a difficult one for him. He struggled to write every day, even in the face of illness, including surgery for cancer. He mourned the death of his long-time companion Frank Merlo, and was deeply saddened by the loss of his close friend Carson McCullers. In 1969 he spent two months on a detoxification program, designed to free him from prolonged dependency on alcohol, amphetamines, and barbiturates. Later that year he converted to a nominal Roman Catholicism. Williams traveled frequently, mostly to America and Europe. He had a special fondness for Italy in general, and Venice in particular. He also had homes in Key West, Florida, and New York City.

More than before, he dwelt on the recurrent theme of dying and death in his dramatic work. *The Milk Train Doesn't Stop Here Anymore* moved to Broadway after its première at the Spoleto Festival in 1962 but ran for only a couple of months. Audiences were bewildered by the play's heavy religious symbolism. *Slapstick Tragedy* (containing a pair of one-act plays: *The Mutilated* and *The Gnädiges Fräulein*) failed on Broadway in 1966 and *The Seven Descents of Myrtle* (originally entitled *The Kingdom of Earth*) survived for less than a month in its New York production in 1968. *In the Bar of a Tokyo Hotel* closed after a brief off-Broadway run in 1969 and *Out Cry* (a puzzling play within a play, originally called *The Two Character Play* when it was produced in London in 1967) closed shortly after its New York opening in 1971. The subject matter of these two plays was intensely personal. *In the Bar of a Tokyo Hotel* dealt with the difficulty of creating a work of art, the decline of artistic ability, and death; *Out Cry* grappled with self-doubt, drugs, alcohol, and insanity. By the early 1970s, however, Williams had regained some measure of control in his personal life. His efforts were reflected in *Small Craft Warnings*, a wordy and static drama which enjoyed a limited off-Broadway success. Among his last works for the theater were *The Red Devil Battery Sign*, *Vieux Carré*, and *A Lovely Sunday for Creve Coeur*. The 1980 Broadway production of *Clothes for a Summer Hotel*, directed by José Quintero, was an innovative "ghost play" about Scott and Zelda Fitzgerald, but failed to attract enough theatergoers to make it a success.

Among Williams's several original screenplays the most important was *Baby Doll*, a raw depiction of human depravity, directed by Elia Kazan, who also staged several of the author's Broadway productions. Williams also worked on the film scripts for *The Glass Menagerie*, *A Streetcar Named Desire*, *The Rose Tattoo*, *Suddenly Last Summer*, *The Fugitive Kind* (based on *Orpheus Descending*), and *Boom* (based on *The Milk Train Doesn't Stop Here Anymore*). He produced four volumes of short fiction and a pair of novels. Some of his stories served as narrative drafts for his numerous one-act plays and occasionally for his full-length dramatic works. He also wrote two books of verse (*In the Winter of Cities* and *Androgyne, Mon Amour*) and a collection of essays (*Where I Live*). His *Memoirs* contains frank, thoughtful, and interesting anecdotes of his personal life and his involvement in the theater. Even though his later plays did not receive the accolades that his earlier ones garnered, Williams himself was the recipient of a number of awards during the last years of his life, including the Creative Arts Medal from Brandeis University in 1964 and the Gold Medal from the National Institute of Arts and Letters (of which he was a member) in 1969. He died from choking after a heavy night of drinking. Although in the end he seemed to have outlived his talent, Williams was undoubtedly one of the most significant dramatists of his century. He portrayed highly charged emotional and sexual themes with an honesty that matched their often controversial nature, and his dialogue was more often than not lifted by a poetic beauty that did not sacrifice its inherent realism. Moreover, he created an enduring array of characters who have taken their place in American iconography. His best plays have become part of the standard theater repertory.

Tennessee Williams's papers are in the Humanities Research Center at the University of Texas in Austin.

PRINCIPAL WORKS: *Drama*—Battle of Angels, 1940; The Glass Menagerie, 1944; (with D. Windham) You Touched Me!, 1945; A Streetcar Named Desire, 1947; Summer and Smoke, 1948; The Rose Tattoo, 1950; Camino Real, 1953; Cat on a Hot Tin Roof, 1955; Orpheus Descending, 1957; Suddenly Last Summer, 1958; Sweet Bird of Youth, 1959; Period of Adjustment, 1960; The Night of the Iguana, 1961; The Milk Train Doesn't Stop Here Anymore, 1962; The Eccentricities of a Nightingale, 1964; Kingdom of Earth (The Seven Descents of Myrtle) 1967; Small Craft Warnings, 1972; The Two-Character Play (Out Cry) 1973; The Red Devil Battery Sign, 1976; Vieux Carré, 1977; A Lovely Sunday for Creve Coeur, 1978; Clothes for a Summer Hotel, 1980. *Collections*—27 Wagons Full of Cotton and Other Short Plays, 1982 (plays written and produced in 1946–1980); In the Bar of a Tokyo Hotel and Other Plays, 1981 (plays written and produced in 1951–1978); The Theatre of Tennessee Williams, 8 vols., 1971–1992. *Novels*—The Roman Spring of Mrs. Stone, 1950; Moise and the World of Reason, 1975. *Short stories*—One Arm and Other Stories, 1948; Hard Candy, 1954; The Knightly Quest, 1967; Eight Mortal Ladies Possessed, 1974; Collected Stories, 1985. *Poetry*—In the Winter of Cities, 1956; Androgyne, Mon Amour, 1977. *Nonfiction*—Where I Live: Selected Essays, 1978. *Autobiography*—Memoirs, 1975. *Correspondence*—Tennessee Williams's Letters to Donald Windham, 1977; Five O'Clock Angel: Letters of Tennessee Williams to Maria St. Just, 1990.

ABOUT: The autobiographical material quoted above was written for Twentieth Century Authors First Supplement, 1955. Adler, T. P. A Streetcar Named Desire, 1990; Arnott, C. M.

Tennessee Williams on File, 1985; Bloom, H. (ed.) Tennessee Williams, 1987; Bloom, H. (ed.) Tennessee Williams's The Glass Menagerie, 1988; Bloom, H. (ed.) Tennessee Williams's A Streetcar Named Desire, 1988; Boxill, R. Tennessee Williams, 1987; Choukri, M. Tennessee Williams in Tangier, 1979; Devlin, A. J. (ed.) Conversations with Tennessee Williams, 1986; Donahue, F. The Dramatic World of Tennessee Williams, 1964; Falk, S. Tennessee Williams, rev. ed., 1978; Hirsch, F. A Portrait of the Artist: The Plays of Tennessee Williams, 1979; Kataria, G. R. The Faces of Eve: A Study of Tennessee Williams's Heroines, 1992; Kolin, P.C. Confronting Tennessee Williams's A Streetcar Named Desire, 1993; Leavitt, R. F. (ed.) The World of Tennessee Williams, 1978; Londré, F. H. Tennessee Williams, 1979; Maxwell, G. Tennessee Williams and Friends, 1965; McCann, J. S. (ed.) The Critical Reputation of Tennessee Williams, 1983; Murphy, B. Tennessee Williams and Elia Kazan, 1992; Nelson, B. Tennessee Williams, 1961; Parker, R. B. The Glass Menagerie: A Collection of Critical Essays, 1983; Phillips, G. D. The Films of Tennessee Williams, 1980; Plimpton, G. (ed.) Writers at Work: The Paris Review Interviews, 6th series, 1985; Presley, D. E. The Glass Menagerie, 1990; Rader, D. Tennessee: Cry of the Heart, 1985; Rasky, H. Tennessee Williams, 1986; Savran, D. Communists, Cowboys, and Queers: The Politics of Masculinity in the Work of Arthur Miller and Tennessee Williams, 1992; Smith, B. Costly Performances: Tennessee Williams, the Last Stage, 1990; Spoto, D. The Kindness of Strangers: The Life of Tennessee Williams, 1985; Stanton, S. S. (ed.) Tennessee Williams: A Collection of Critical Essays, 1977; Steen, M. A Look at Tennessee Williams, 1969; Tharpe, J. (ed.) Tennessee Williams: A Tribute, 1977; Thompson, J. J. Tennessee Williams's Plays, 1987; Tischler, N. M. Tennessee Williams, 1961; Vannatta, D. P. Tennessee Williams: A Study of the Short Fiction, 1988; Weales, G. Tennessee Williams, 1965; Williams, D. and Mead, S. Tennessee Williams, 1983; Williams, E. D. and Freeman, L. Remember Me to Tom, 1963; Windham, D. Lost Friendships, 1987; Yacowar, M. Tennessee Williams and Film, 1977. Bibliography—Gunn, D. W. (ed., Tennessee Williams: A Bibliography, rev. ed., 1991. Periodicals—Atlantic November 1970; College English October 1948; Comparative Drama Fall 1988; Esquire November 1969, September 1971, June 1979, December 1983; Harper's July 1948, January 1984, September 1989; Hudson Review Winter 1987; Journal of American Culture Spring 1989; Journal of Modern Literature Spring 1990; Life February 16, 1948; Michigan Quarterly Review Spring 1990; Modern Drama December 1983, September 1984, December 1985, December 1989, September 1990, December 1991, September 1992; New York March 14, 1983; July 25, 1983; New York Review of Books July 13, 1985; July 19, 1990; New York Times March 25, 1955; February 26, 1983; May 30, 1990; New York Times Book Review November 2, 1975; November 20, 1977; May 27, 1990; New York Times Magazine December 7, 1947; New Yorker April 14, 1945; Newsweek April 1, 1957; March 23, 1959; June 27, 1960; March 7, 1983; Partisan Review vol. 45, no. 2 1978; Saturday Review April 29, 1972; November 1, 1975; South Atlantic Quarterly Winter 1989; Southern Literary Journal Spring 1985; Southern Review Spring 1991; Studies in the Literary Imagination Fall 1988; Fall 1991; Theatre Arts February 1946; July 1955; January 1962; Theatre Journal March 1983; October 1986; Time April 23, 1945; April 11, 1960; March 9, 1962; December 24, 1973; December 1, 1975; February 7, 1977; March 7, 1983; Times (London) February 26, 1983; Vogue November 1983; September 1989.

**WILLIAMS, VALENTINE** (October 20, 1883–November 20, 1946), English mystery writer, wrote: "Valentine Williams was a newspaper man before becoming a novelist. As one of the late Northcliffe's principal lieutenants he traveled extensively as special correspondent to the *Daily Mail* [London] and saw fighting in Portugal and the Balkans before the war of 1914 landed him in the army with a commission in the Irish Guards. He was twice wounded, and it was while he was convalesc-

ing from his wounds that he wrote his first novel. Since then he has written some thirty novels of secret service and crime, nearly all of which have been translated into foreign languages, some having been sold to the films. He likes to vary what he calls the monotony of writing fiction by returns to his old love, journalism. Since he gave up his post as cable editor of the *Daily Mail* in 1921 his name has figured in the world's press on many  important assignments. He secured a scoop, legendary in the annals of Anglo-American journalism, at Luxor in 1923 when he was first to announce the discovery of the sarcophagus of King Tutankhamen. He is a well-known visitor to America, having broadcast frequently and lectured in many parts of the United States. He married Alice Crawford, an English star of the theatre, and Australian by birth. When not at war he likes to divide his time between his native country and the United States. He is one of that small band of enthusiasts who play court tennis, and claims that he has never been in a place where there is a tennis court without getting a game. Like most authors, he has not resisted the lure of the screen, and was actually collaborating on *The Lion Has Wings* when he was mobilized in the present war."

———

Valentine Williams was born George Valentine Williams, the son of G. Douglas Williams, chief editor of the Reuter's news bureau, which also employed his uncle and brother. Williams was educated at the Benedictine School of Downside, and privately in Germany. At the age of nineteen he joined Reuter's as a sub-editor; his knowledge of German earned him a position as Berlin correspondent from 1904 to 1909. He spent the next four years working for the *Daily Mail* as Paris correspondent, with assignments in various European locales and Russia.

Williams's first suspense novel, *The Man with the Clubfoot*, was written in Scotland while he was convalescing from wounds suffered at the battle of the Somme: a "shell landed beside me and blew me sky-high. I went up an experienced newspaper man, and came down a budding novelist." Published in 1918, under the name Douglas Valentine, this melodrama was an immediate success. The plot features a villainous, deformed German spy named Dr. Adolph Grundt, or "Clubfoot," who returns in seven later books, matching wits with Desmond Okewood of the British secret service (a recurring character in Williams' novels). In a review of the 1924 *Clubfoot the Avenger*, the *New York Times* (1924) complained that "it would not do to have Dr. Grundt captured or made an end of, and a secret passageway is always provided for his escape down the river, even though half of Scotland Yard may have been sent to surround his rendevous."

Another of Williams's series characters is Detective Sergeant Trevor Dene of Scotland Yard, a sleuth with all too clearly Holmes-like skills. In its review of *Clue of the Rising Moon*, the *New Statesman and Nation* declared that "Williams writes a perfectly adequate 'straight' detective story whenever he chooses." Two other of Williams' characters worthy of mentioning are Baron Alexis De Bahl, or "The Fox," and a tailor/amateur detective named Mr. Treadgold.

PRINCIPAL WORKS: *Novels*—(as "Douglas Valentine") The Man with the Clubfoot, 1918; (as Douglas Valentine) Okewood of the Secret Service, 1919 (in U.K.: The Secret Hand: Some Further Adventures by Desmond Okewood of the British Secret Service); The Yellow Streak, 1922; Island Gold, 1923 (in U.K.: The Return of Clubfoot); The Orange Divan, 1923; Clubfoot the Avenger: Being Some Further Adventures of Desmond Okewood of the Secret Service, 1924; The Three of Clubs, 1924; The Red Mass, 1925; Mr. Ramosi, 1926; The Key Man, 1926 (in U.K.: The Pigeon House); The Eye in Attendance, 1927; The Crouching Beast: A Clubfoot Story, 1928; The Mysterious Miss Morrisot, 1930 (in U.K.: Mannequin); Death Answers the Bell, 1932; The Mystery of the Gold Box: A Clubfoot Story, 1932 (in U.K.: The Gold Comfit Box); The Clock Ticks On, 1933; (with D. R. Sims) Fog, 1933; Masks Off at Midnight, 1934; The Portcullis Room, 1934; The Clue of the Rising Moon, 1935; Dead Man Manor, 1936; The Spider's Touch: A Clubfoot Story, 1936; (with others) Double Death, 1939; Courier to Marrakesh: A Clubfoot Story, 1944; Skeleton Out of the Cupboard, 1946. *Short stories*—The Knife Behind the Curtain: Tales of Crime and the Secret Service, 1930; The Curiosity of Mr. Treadgold, 1937 (in U.K.: Mr. Treadgold Cuts In: Being Some Episodes in the Career of Mr. Treadgold, Tailor and Crime Investigator). *Nonfiction*—With Our Army in Flanders, 1915; (as "Vedette") The Adventures of an Ensign, 1917. *Memoirs*—The World of Action: The Autobiography of Valentine Williams, 1938.

ABOUT: The autobiographical material quoted above was written for Twentieth Century Authors, 1942. Twentieth-Century Crime and Mystery Writers, 1985. *Periodicals*—New Statesman and Nation November 16, 1935; New York Times July 20, 1924; November 21, 1946; Times (London) November 21, 1946.

## WILLIAMS, WILLIAM CARLOS (September 17, 1883–March 4, 1963), American poet and prose writer, also a physician, wrote:

"My origins are obscure, owing to voyages and volcanic action. My English grandmother, named Emily Dickinson, was left an orphan at an early age and adopted by an 'uncle' Godwin who took her to London, where she grew up. Thrown out, as far as I can gather, after her marriage to a certain Mr. Williams. My father, William George, was born to the pair in Birmingham. My grandfather died when Pop was five years old. The old gal, in a fit of temper most likely, took him under her arm and sailed for America, determined to be an actress. She landed in a Brooklyn boarding-house, where she met her second husband, who took her to St. Thomas. It was in St. Thomas that my father grew up. My mother's family on her mother's side came from St. Pierre, Martinique, via Bordeaux, France. The remnants of the family disappeared when Mt. Pelée erupted. They made a good brand of liqueur, I understand. On mother's father's side there was Jewish blood, via some city in Holland. Whether her father was wholly Jew or not it is impossible to say. He was not a practicing Jew. His mother may have been a West Indian.

"My parents moved to New York separately, though they had known each other in the islands, and were married in a Dutch Reformed church in Brooklyn. Mother [Raquel Helene Hoheb] had been bought up a Catholic and father an Episcopalian. They became Unitarians later.

"I was the first child, born in Rutherford Park, New Jersey, where I still live and practice medicine. I married Florence Herman in 1912 and we have two boys. There are a few things in life that one comes to want to do as one grows older, apart from turning over a little cash. I wanted to write, as my mother wanted to paint—and did paint very well. I've been writing, trying to get a few things said, ever since I started to study medicine. One feeds the other, in a manner of speaking. Both seem necessary to me. One gets me out among neighbors, the other permits me to express what I've been turning over in my mind as I go along. I don't know that I'd be any better off if I took all my time to write and made a business of the thing. I wish I could do it, though, now that I'm getting along.

"I wasn't a bad high school pitcher, played a little football (left end) as a kid, and did a little track work, not much. The old pump wouldn't stand up under the strain. I suppose I've always lived a good deal under a strain— physical, financial, moral, but especially emotional. That's one reason I stayed put, too much dynamite inside for me to want to go wandering about wasting time traveling. What the hell is there to see, anyway, compared with what's on the inside? I never saw anything outside equal to what I was going through in my innards.

"I don't play golf, am not a joiner. I vote Democratic, read as much as my eyes will stand, and work at my trade day in and day out. When I can find nothing better to do, I write. Work in progress, if I'm ever able to get at it, should be: my mother's biography; the libretto for an opera on the life of George Washington that has to be rewritten; a new novel on the life of a woikin' goil; a long poem, *Paterson*—boy! how I'd like to get at that one; and some more shorter poems, probably what I most enjoy doing."

———

Williams was educated at public school in Rutherford. In his teenage years he and his brother were taken to Europe, and he attended schools in Switzerland and France. Back in America, after graduating from Horace Mann High School, Williams attended the University of Pennsylvania Medical School, which is where his association began with Ezra Pound and with H. D. (Hilda Doolittle). Another friend was the painter Charles Demuth, who later was inspired by a Williams poem to paint his famous "I Saw the Figure 5 in Gold." After a spell as a hospital intern in New York, and a year studying pediatrics at the University of Leipzig, Williams returned to Rutherford, set himself up in general practice, and married Florence Herman, whom he always called, in his verse as well as in life, Flossie. It was, from the start, a double life, but his medical practice rooted him in one place. As he said in his *Autobiography* (1951): "As a writer I have been a physician and as a physician a writer; and as both writer and physician I have served sixty-eight years of a more or less uneventful existence, not more than half a mile from where I happen to have been born." Linda W. Wagner, in *American Modern: Essays in Fiction and Poetry* (1980), commented: "He worked as a physician so that he might write what he chose, free from any kind of financial or political pressure. From the beginning, in the early 1900s, he understood the trade-offs: he would have less time to write; he would need more physical stamina than people with only one occupation; he would probably demand more from his family."

The matter of Williams's provincialism can be overstated. He traveled regularly into New York City to visit art galleries and to keep himself culturally informed. And he and Flossie were frequently visited by literary friends, some of whom they first met in the 1920s when they spent six months in Europe and mixed with the Hemingway-McAlmon-Stein set.

Williams's first volume, *Poems*, appeared in 1909 (he paid the costs of publication). Excitement at what he saw happening on the avant-garde art scene in New York, particularly the Armory Show of 1913, combined with the influence of his friends (especially Pound and his advocacy of Imagism), and a growing sense of his own American identity, soon encouraged him to experiment. That experiment took the form of a rejection of meter as a means to poetic form. The length of line in a Williams poem came to depend on neither syllables nor accent, but on a measure based on the variable foot—by which he meant the natural rhythmic units (controlled by "breath") of American speech. Gradually this rejection of meter turned into a dogma. He certainly took this aspect of his craft very seriously and contributed several articles to the *Princeton Encyclopaedia of Poetry and Poetics*, as well as covering similar ground in some of his prose writing, for example in the prologue to *Kora in Hell*.

Williams remains a significant poet, who, in poems like "The Red Wheelbarrow" and "This Is Just To Say," woos the reader with irresistible charm and an ability to capture the fleeting moment. In the later "Asphodel, That Greeny Flower" and "The Descent," he does the same with an essential goodness and decency. Those who make larger claims for Williams, and there have been an increasing number, argue that he was a thinking poet capable, especially in *Paterson*, of bringing in large themes.

His second volume of poetry was *The Tempers* (1913), but much more important was a single poem, more than two hundred lines in length, published in the English journal *The Egoist*. This poem—"The Wanderer: A Rococo Study"—was

something of a forerunner to *Paterson*, in that it represented an early manifesto. "How shall I be a mirror to this modernity?" the poet asks. In his third collection, *Al Que Quiere!*, the influence of Imagism was becoming apparent, and from then onwards the distinctive Williams voice became established.

It was next that he wrote the important prologue to *Kora in Hell* (1918), a collection of prose poems or improvisations written during that year's great flu epidemic, in which he was at pains to put some distance between himself and Pound. He went further five years later, in a similar prologue to *Spring and All*, having a go at both Pound and Eliot, calling them "men content with the connotations of their masters." He viewed the success of "The Waste Land" as a catastrophe.

Through the rest of the 1920s and 1930s Williams felt sidelined and unappreciated, except by a few, and it was not until the late 1930s that he found an American publisher who was willing to bring out his work on a regular basis: James Laughlin of New Directions. No sooner was the arrangement secured than Williams began planning *Paterson*, although it was not until 1946 that the first book appeared. There were eventually five books in all, the fifth appearing in 1958.

In *Paterson*, Williams uses the backdrop of the Passaic Falls, the local history of Paterson, and a profusion of documentary material and personal letters (Williams was much criticized in some quarters for not seeking permission to use extracts from his received correspondence) to fix subjects in time and place so that the reader can come to know them intimately. In a statement dated May 31, 1951, Williams explained: "The thing was to use the multiple facets which a city presented as representatives for comparable facets of contemporary thought thus to be able to objectify the man himself as we know him and love him and hate him." Book I, "The Delineaments of the Giants," introduces the landscape of Paterson; Book II, "Sunday in the Park," shows the inhabitants at leisure; Book III, "The Library," is a re-enactment of fire, flood, and tornado; Book IV, "The Run to the Sea," which was to be the concluding part, has a figure that plunges into the river, then emerges from the sea to return inland and begin again. Book V, untitled, is recollective. Between the publication of Book IV and Book V of *Paterson*, Williams published two volumes of poetry, *The Desert Music* (1954) and *Journey to Love* (1955). He had suffered the first of a series of strokes in 1952, and the poetry in these books registers a shift in style and mood. Many of the poems are written in a three-step or "triadic" line, which Williams claimed to have discovered while re-reading the third section of Book II of *Paterson*. (The section in question became the opening poem, "The Descent," in *The Desert Music*.) The form proved ideal for the reflective verse he was inclined to write at the end of his life and influenced those who attended Black Mountain College, where Williams began to be held in high esteem.

*Paterson* can only be fully appreciated within the full context of American literary history. As

Robert Lowell said, in his review of Book II in *The Nation*, "It is an attempt to write the American Poem. It depends on the American myth. . . . For good or for evil, America is something immense, crass, and Roman. We must unavoidably place ourselves in our geography, history, civilization, institutions, and future . . . Paterson is Whitman's America, grown pathetic and tragic, brutalized by inequality, disorganized by industrial chaos, and faced with annihilation."

The "poet-doctor of Rutherford" did write some fiction, aptly described in the *New Yorker* by a reviewer of *In the Money*, as "a kind of radio serial rewritten by a serious artist: a succession of domestic trials, triumphs and tribulations forming the content, but transfigured by Dr. Williams' patient and almost surgically dextrous feeling for the essence of the minutiae of American middle-class life." Williams's other works include *The Knife of the Times and Other Stories* and *Life Along the Passaic River* (two collections of short stories), an experimental novelette, *January*, and *White Mule* (the first of what was to be a trilogy about his wife's family). Williams also completed an autobiography in 1951 and the biography of his mother, *Yes, Mrs. Williams*, in 1959 (Mrs. Williams had lived with the poet and his wife from 1918, when her husband died, until her own death in 1949 at the age of 102). Together, mother and son had collaborated on the translations of several works, including Francisco Quevedo's *The Dog and the Fever*.

Williams was invited to be poetry consultant to the Library of Congress for 1949–1950, but he had to postpone acceptance because of his health. In 1952 he shared with Archibald MacLeish the 1952 Bollingen Prize. Over the next decade, Williams became increasingly debilitated and housebound as a result of his strokes. When he was interviewed a year before his death for the "Writers at Work" series in the *Paris Review*, his wife Flossie had to do much of the talking. He was awarded the Pulitzer Prize for poetry, posthumously, in 1963.

PRINCIPAL WORKS: The Tempers, 1913; Al Que Quiere! 1917; Kora in Hell, 1920; Sour Grapes, 1921; Go Go, 1923; Spring and All, 1923; The Cod Head, 1932; Collected Poems 1921–31, 1934; An Early Martyr and Other Poems, 1935; Adam & Eve & the City, 1936; The Complete Collected Poems, 1906–1938, 1938; The Wedge, 1944; Paterson Book I 1946, Book II 1948, Book III 1949, Book IV 1951, Book V 1958, 1st complete edition 1963; The Clouds, 1948; The Pink Church, 1949; Selected Poems, 1949; The Collected Later Poems, 1950; The Collected Earlier Poems, 1951; The Desert Music and Other Poems, 1954; Journey to Love, 1955; Pictures from Brueghel, 1962. Fiction—The Great American Novel, 1923; A Voyage to Pagany, 1928; The Knife and Other Stories, 1932; A Novelette, 1932; White Mule, 1937; Life on the Passaic River, 1938; In the Money, 1940; The Build-Up, 1952; The Farmer's Daughters: The Collected Stories, 1961; (ed. A. Litz & C. MacGowan) The Collected Poems of William Carlos Williams, 1986. Nonfiction—In the American Grain, 1925; Autobiography, 1951; Selected Essays, 1954; Yes, Mrs. Williams, 1959; I Want to Write a Poem: The Autobiography of the Works of a Poet, 1958; (ed. J. Thirlwall) The Selected Letters of William Carlos Williams, 1985; (ed. E. O'Neill) The Last Word: Letters Between Marcia Nardi and William Carlos Williams, 1994; (ed. H. Witemeyer) Selected Correspondence of Ezra Pound & William Carlos Williams, 1995.

ABOUT: Cushman, C. William Carlos Williams and the Meanings of Measure, 1985; Dictionary of National Biography 1961–1965; Guimond, J. Art of William Carlos Williams 1968; Laughlin, J. Remembering William Carlos Williams, 1995; MacGowan, C. in The Columbia History of American Poetry, 1993; Mariani, P. William Carlos Williams, 1981; Marling, M. William Carlos Williams and the Painters 1909–1923, 1989; Rapp, C. William Carlos Williams and Romantic Idealism, 1984; Tapscott, S. William Carlos Williams and the Modernist Whitman, 1984; (ed.) Terrell, C. William Carlos Williams, 1983; Wagner-Martin, L. William Carlos Williams: A Reference Guide, 1978; Williams W. C. Autobiography 1951. *Periodicals*—Nation June 19, 1948; New York Times January 15, 1950; March 5, 1963; September 18, 1983; New Yorker November 2, 1940; Time March 15, 1963; Times (London) March 5, 1963.

## WILLIAMS-ELLIS, AMABEL (STRACHEY)

(May 10, 1894–August 27, 1984), English novelist, juvenile writer and popularizer of science, was born at Newlands Corner, near Guildford, England, the daughter of J. St. Loe Strachey, the imperialist editor of the *Spectator* (and friend to Rudyard Kipling) and his wife Ann. The politician John Strachey, who became a minister in the 1945–1951 Labour government, was her brother;  Lytton Strachey was her cousin. She was educated at home in a highly cultured household. She traveled widely, especially in Germany and Russia. In 1915 she married Bertram Clough Williams-Ellis, the creator and architect of the Italianate village of Portmeirion in Wales. During the First World War she served as a volunteer auxiliary nurse for five years, which gave her a knowledge of basic science and anatomy, later put to good use in her writing. Reflection on her wartime experiences was also a key factor in her decision in the later 1920s to follow the example of her brother John in becoming a committed socialist.

From 1922–1923 Williams-Ellis worked as the literary editor of the by-then less conservative *Spectator*. Her career as a writer began to develop momentum shortly afterwards. Her novels include *Noah's Ark*, for its period an unusually frank account of the first two years of a marriage; the story of a Labour election campaign, *Wall of Glass*, which the poet and critic Edwin Muir found the "best political novel that has appeared for a long time" (*Nation and Athenaeum*); and a story of big business and science in the 1930s, *The Big Firm*.

Williams-Ellis' forte, however, lay in the writing of useful popularizations of scientific and socioeconomic ideas. She helped found the Left Book Club in the 1930s and turned much of her writing toward socialist educational enterprises. Her interest in Russia is reflected in her translation of *The White Canal (Belmoro)* a cliché-ridden account of a Soviet industrial project by Maxim Gorky and other writers. She was also widely read in biology, and adapted from Darwin's journal an account of his famous voyage to the southern hemisphere on the *Beagle*. She also wrote a perceptive study of John Ruskin. Her own lively memoirs, *All Stracheys*

*Are Cousins*, appeared in her ninetieth year. However, as her London *Times* obiturarist put it, Williams-Ellis's highest achievement was in children's nonfiction. She was the author of the first candid book ever written for young children on biology, *How You Began*: "embryology plus evolution," as she put it in her memoirs. Inspired by the questions asked by her own children and grandchildren, she went onto cover other scientific subjects such as nutrition, oceanography, and the atom. With the historian F. J. Fisher she wrote a history of England for schools that gave due weight to economic, social, and scientific developments, and the life of the common people. She also wrote a series of retellings of legends and fairy tales.

PRINCIPAL WORKS: *Novels*—Noah's Ark; or, The Love Story of a Respectable Young Couple, 1926; The Wall of Glass, 1927; To Tell the Truth, 1933; The Big Firm, 1938; Learn to Love First, 1939. *Short stories*—Volcano, 1931. *Drama*—The Sea-Power of England, 1913. *Nonfiction*—(with C. Williams-Ellis) The Tank Corps, 1919; An Anatomy of Poetry, 1922; (with C. Williams-Ellis) The Pleasures of Architecture, 1924 rev. ed. 1954; The Tragedy of John Ruskin, 1928 (in U.S.: Exquisite Tragedy: An Intimate Life of John Ruskin); (with L. A. Plummer) Why Should I Vote?, 1929; HMS Beagle in South America, 1930 (in U.S.: The Voyage of the Beagle); Women in War Factories, 1943; (with C. Williams-Ellis and children) In and Out of Doors, 1947; The Art of Being a Woman, 1951; (with C. Williams-Ellis) Headlong Down the Years, A Tale of Today, 1951; (with E. S. Cooper-Willis) Laughing Gas and Safety Lamp: The Story of Sir Humphrey Davy, 1951; The Art of Being a Parent, 1952; Darwin's Moon: A Biography of Alfred Russel Wallace, 1966. *Juvenile*—How You Began, 1928 rev. ed. 1929; But We Know Better, 1929 (tales); Men Who Found Out: Stories of Great Scientific Discoverers, 1929; How You Are Made, 1932; What Shall I Be?, 1933; (with F. J. Fisher) A History of English Life, 1936 (in U.S.: The Story of English); Good Citizens, 1938 (in U.S.: Courageous Lives: Stories of Nine Good Citizens); Ottik's Book of Stories, 1939; A Food and People Geography 1951 (in U.S.: The Puzzle of Food and People: A Geography Reader); Changing the World: Further Stories of Great Scientific Discoveries, 1956; Engines, Atoms and Power, 1958; Man and the Good Earth, 1958; Seekers and Finders, 1958; They Wanted the Real Answers, 1958; The Unknown Ocean, 1959; Modern Scientists at Work, 1961; (with W. Stobbs) Life in England, Vol. 1: Early and Medieval Times, 1968; Vol. II: Tudor England, 1968; Vol. III: Seventeenth-Century England, 1968; Vol. IV: Georgian England, 1969; Vol. V: Victorian England, 1969; vol. VI: Modern Times, 1970; Wonder Why Book of Your Body: What You Eat and Where It Goes, 1978. *Fairytales (retold)*—Fairies and Enchanters, 1933; Princesses and Trolls: Twelve Traditional Stories Retold, 1950; The Arabian Nights, 1957; Jacob and Wilhelm Grimm, Fairy Tales, 1959; Fairy Tales from the British Isles, 1960; Round the World Fairy Tales, 1963; (with M. Budberg) Russian Fairy Tales, 1965; Dragons Princes: Fairy Tales from Round the World, 1966; More Fairy Tales, by J. and W. Grimm, 1968; Gypsy Folk Tales, 1971; Fairy Tales from East and West, 1977; Fairy Tales from Everywhere, 1977; Fairy Tales from Here and There, 1977; Fairy Tales from Near and Far, 1977; The Rain-God's Daughter, and Other African Fairy Tales, 1977; The Story Spirits, 1980; The Enchanted World (ed. and illus. Moira Kemp) 1987. *As editor*—(with C. Williams-Ellis) Vision of England, 1946; (with C. Williams-Ellis) Vision of Wales, 1949; (with M. Owen) Out of This World: An Anthology of Science Fiction, 10 vols. (vols. IX and X with M. Pearson), 1960–1973; (with M. Pearson) Tales from the Galaxies, 1973; (with M. Pearson) Strange Universe: An Anthology of Science Fiction, 1974; (with M. Owen and M. Pearson) Strange Orbits: An Anthology of Science Fiction, 1976; (with M. Owen and M. Pearson) Strange Planets: An Anthology of Science Fiction, 1977. *As editor and translator*—The White Canal, by Maxim Gorky and others, 1935 (in U.S.: Belomor).

ABOUT: Contemporary Authors Vol. 105, 1982; Feminist Companion to Literature in English, 1990; Sanders C. R. The Strachey Family 1588–1932: Their Writings and Literary Associations, 1953; Something About the Author Vol. 41, 1985; Williams-Ellis, A. All Stracheys Are Cousins, Memoirs, 1983; Williams-Ellis, C. Architect Errant, 1971. *Periodicals*—Nation and Athenaeum June 4, 1927; New York Herald Tribune Books April 7, 1929; Spectator April 13, 1951; Times (London) August 29, 1984; Times Literary Supplement December 27, 1928.

**WILLIAMSON, ALICE** (1869–September 24, 1933), Anglo-American novelist, was born into a distinguished but not very affluent family in Livingston Manor House, near Poughkeepsie, New York. Of Scottish and Welsh ancestry she was the daughter of Mark Livingston. She was educated privately.

Alice Livingston began to write when she was seven. She had always loved English history and Shakespeare, and in 1893, when she was twenty-four, a small legacy enabled her to go to England. Arriving in London with $500, she found lodgings near Baker Street (because of its association with Sherlock Holmes). With her funds rapidly dwindling, she followed up an introduction to Charles Norris Williamson, an English  journalist and author of a book on Carlyle.

Williamson gave her introductions to several publishers and editors, including Alfred Harmsworth, the newspaper tycoon soon to become Lord Northcliffe. He invited her to try her hand at a magazine serial that would have "plenty of action, but, more important, plenty of love, with a strong curtain for each chapter." All these she could deliver, and began to sell to a variety of newspaper and magazines. Through Williamson she also met Arnold Bennett, George Meredith, Lillie Langtry, the Beerbohm Trees, and a whole gallery of other celebrities.

Charles Williamson proposed but could not afford to marry at once. Alice Livingston went to Harmsworth and persuaded him to let her write six serials simultaneously for $1000. At about the same time, Williamson became editor of a new magazine devoted to European travel. To help him in this work, they invested in an automobile—at a time when such contraptions were "talked about, though seldom used."

They were married in 1895, and, combining their honeymoon with Williamson's new job, toured in France and Italy "in an accident-prone Benz." Almost penniless when they reached Taormina, they found, not the checks they had expected, but news that Williamson's magazine had died at birth. Back in England, they rented an old farmhouse at Cobham, in Surrey, and Alice Williamson published a dozen romantic novels, most of them originally newspaper serials.

Her first real success was also her first collaboration with her husband, *The Lightning Conductor:*

*The Strange Adventures of a Motorcar*, published in 1902. This was a novel in letter form, drawing on the unpublished articles Williamson had written about their honeymoon travels. Its appeal lay in the combination of travelogue and light-hearted romance, and above all in its account of a new and exciting form of transport. *The Lightning Conductor* had a huge success both in England and America, and was followed by a stream of similar collaborations, usually two a year.

Many but not all featured travels by automobile or other means (*The Botor Chaperon* is set on the Dutch waterways; *Lady from the Air* features a Polish aviatrix). Often in these stories, a coldly arrogant English aristocrat is humanized by love of the feisty American heroine. Alternatively, an American "career girl" is rescued for privileged domesticity by love of an English milord.

Fast-paced, romantic, and funny, these frothy concoctions earned the Williamsons a great deal of money. They built a house, La Dragonnière, at Cap Martin on the French Riviera, later sold to Lord Rothermere; then another home at Roquebrune, subsequently owned by Coco Chanel. During World War I Alice Williamson worked with the wounded in French hospitals and raised money to support local families whose men were at the Front. Her 1915 novel *What I Found Out in the House of a German Prince* (by "an English Governess") was a work of anti-German propaganda. The same year she went to New York to write a set of twelve film scenarios about one of her English aristocrats and his adventures in America.

Her autobiography *The Inky Way* was published in 1931. Much of it is devoted to society-page reminiscences of the celebrities, aristocrats and royalty she and her husband so assiduously cultivated, from the Empress Eugénie to Maeterlinck, but there are a few more serious passages. Most surprising is its claim that Alice Williamson alone wrote the novels published as collaborations: "Charlie Williamson could do everything in the world, and do it well—except write stories," she said. "I could do nothing else in particular." She maintained that Charlie planned the travels on which so many of the books were based, and took useful notes on what they saw, but that she alone turned the material into stories.

Her husband's illness and death left her almost penniless, and she had a difficult few years before she began to sell readily again. None of the later novels was a best-seller, but they were generally well received by reviewers, praised as always for their skillful plotting, humor and unflagging pace.

PRINCIPAL WORKS: *Fiction*—The Barn Stormers, 1897; Fortunes Sport, 1898; A Woman in Grey, 1898; Lady Mary of the Dark House, 1898; The House by the Lock, 1899; The Newspaper Girl, 1899; My Lady Cinderella, 1900; Ordered South, 1900; The Adventures of Princess Sylvie, 1900 (in U.S.: The Princess Virginia); Queen Sweetheart, 1901; A Bid for a Coronet, 1901; 'Twixt Devil and Deep Sea, 1901; Papa, 1902; The Silent Battle, 1902; The Woman Who Dared, 1903; The Little White Nun, 1903; The Sea Could Tell, 1904; The Castle of Shadows, 1905; The Girl Who Had Nothing, 1905; (as "Dona Teresa de-Savallo") The House of the Lost Court, 1908; The Underground Syndicate, 1910; (as "Alice Stuyvesant") The Vanity Box, 1911; The Flower Forbidden, 1911; The Girl of the Passion Play, 1911; (as "M. P. Revere") The Brides Hero, 1912; To

M. L. G.; or, He Who Passes, 1912; The Life Mask, 1913; What I Found Out in the House of a German Prince, by an English Governess, 1915; Name the Woman, 1924; The Indian Princess, 1924 (short stories); The Million Dollar Doll, 1924; The Man Himself, 1925; Secret Gold, 1925; Told at Monte Carlo, 1926 (short stories; in U.S.: Black Incense: Tales of Monte Carlo; Publicity for Anne, 1926; Cancelled Love (in U.S.: Golden Butterfly), 1926; Sheikh Bill, 1927 (in U.S.: Bill—The Sheik); Hollywood Love, 1928; Black Sleeves: It Happened in Hollywood, 1928; Children of the Zodiac, 1929; Frozen Slippers, 1930; The Golden Carpet, 1931; Honeymoon Hate, 1931; Bewitched, 1932; Last Years Wife, 1932; Keep This Door Shut, 1933; The Lightning Conductor Comes Back, 1933; The Girl in the Secret, 1934. *Fiction* (with C. N. Williamson)—The Lightning Conductor: The Strange Adventures of a Motor-Car, 1902; the Princess Passes: A Romance of a Motor Car, 1904; My Friend the Chauffeur, 1905; The Car of Destiny, 1906; Lady Betty Across the Water, 1906; Rosemary in Search of a Father, 1906 (republished as Rosemary: A Christmas Story, 1909); The Botor Chaperon, 1907 (in U.S.: The Chauffeur and the Chaperon); The Powers and Maxine, 1907; The Marquis of Loveland, 1908; Love and the Spy, 1908; Scarlet Runner, 1908 (short stories); The Motor Maid, 1909; Set in Silver, 1909; The Golden Silence, 1910; Lord Loveland Discovers America, 1910; The Demon, 1912; The Heather Moon, 1912; The Guests of Hercules, 1912 (republished as Mary at Monte Carlo, 1920); Champion: The Story of a Motor Car, 1913; The Love Pirate, 1913 (in U.S.: The Port of Adventure); The Wedding Day, 1914; A Soldier of the Legion, 1914; It Happened in Egypt, 1914; Secret History, 1915 (in U.S.: Secret History as Revealed by Lady Peggy O'Malley); The Shop-Girl, 1916 (republished as Winnie Childs, The Shop Girl, 1926); (as "Captain Charles de Crespigny") The War Wedding, 1916 (in U.S.: Where the Path Breaks); The Lightning Conductress, 1916 (in U.S.: The Lightning Conductress Discovers America); Angel Unawares: A Story of Christmas Eve, 1916; This Woman to This Man, 1917; the Cowboy Countess, 1917; Tiger Lily, 1917; Lord John in New York, 1918; Crucifix Corner: A Story of Everyman's Land, 1918 (in U.S.: Everyman's Land); The Minx Goes to the Front, 1919 (short stories); Briar Rose, 1919; The Lion's Mouse, 1919; The Second Latchkey, 1920; The Dummy Hand, 1920; Berry Goes to Monte Carlo, 1921 (short stories); Alias Richard Power, 1921; The Great Pearl Secret, 1921; The House of Silence, 1921; The Night of the Wedding, 1921; Vision House, 1921; The Brightener, 1921; The Lady from the Air, 1922; The Fortune Hunters and Others, 1923 (short stories). *Autobiography*—The Inky Way, 1931. *Other*—Queen Alexandra, The Nations Pride, 1902; Princess Mary's Locked Book (published anonymously) 1912; The Bride's Beviary (published anonymously) 1912; The Lure of Monte Carlo, 1924; The Lure of Vienna, 1926; Alice in Movieland, 1927.

ABOUT: Twentieth-Century Romance and Gothic Writers, 1982; Who's Who 1933; Williamson, A. M. The Inky Way, 1931. *Periodicals*—Bookman (London) November 1933; Independent November 15, 1915; New York Times September 26; October 6, 1933; Review of Reviews October 1933.

**WILLIAMSON, CHARLES NORRIS.** See **WILLIAMSON, ALICE**

**WILLIAMSON, HENRY** (December 1, 1895–August 13, 1977), English novelist and nature writer, was born in Brockley, south London, the son of William Williamson, a bank clerk, and Gertrude (Leaver) Williamson. He was educated in London, at Colfe's School, and at the age of eighteen, on the outbreak of World War I, enlisted in the British army. His combat experiences convinced him of the utter futility of armed conflict between nations. He was particularly affected by the Christmas truce of 1914, during which Allied and German soldiers, hours earlier locked in mortal combat, fraternized openly. Williamson returned to England an emotionally shattered young man, surviving for a time on a modest war pension, which he supplemented by writing for various Fleet Street publications.

In that desperate period in the immediate aftermath of World War I, he published *The Beautiful Years*, his first novel and the first installment in his  autobiographical quartet *The Flax of Dream*. In 1921, inspired by the work of the Wiltshire nature writer Richard Jeffries (especially the author's spiritual memoir *The Story of My Heart*), Williamson left London and moved into a cottage in the Devon village of Georgeham. There, he devoted himself increasingly to the study of nature and wildlife, all the while continuing to publish installments of *The Flax of Dream: Dandelion Days, The Dream of Fair Women*, and *The Pathway*. These novels chronicle the early life of William Maddison, Williamson's portrait of himself as a sensitive and idealistic Englishman whose devastating wartime experiences prompt him to retreat to a lonely country house in Devon. Despite the novels' mixed critical reception and indifferent sales, Williamson, always as assiduous rewriter, revised the first three volumes and later published all four together in *The Flax of Dream, a Novel in Four Books*.

Meanwhile, Williamson had come to attention as a more unequivocally gifted writer of animal stories. He achieved international fame with the publication of his children's novel *Tarka the Otter*, the story of two years in the life of an otter dwelling in the Exmoor and Dartmoor rivers. Weighing the novel's weaknesses against its strengths, a *Times Literary Supplement* (1927) reviewer noted, "Mr. Williamson's style is inclined to be precious, and he uses a great number of strange words. . . . But the general effect is remarkably live, and we are won over to forgive extravagances by the vividness of his descriptions." *Tarka* was awarded the 1928 Hawthornden Prize, filmed in the late 1970s, and, like Williamson's later children's novel *Salar the Salmon*, remains a popular classic of animal "biography."

Ten years after World War I, Williamson revisited one of its principal battlegrounds, Ypres, in Belgium. In *The Wet Flanders Plain*, he intermingles impressions garnered on that journey with recollections of his own wartime experiences. Lavishly praised by a number of American critics, it received only a lukewarm response in the British press, many of whom had themselves served in the area and were unmoved by Williamson's recollections. Soon thereafter, he published *The Patriot's Progress*, an ironic and savage World War I novel which examines the "vicissitudes" of an ordinary English soldier. Throughout the 1930s, Williamson published an abundance of essays, sketches, and short stories dealing with English country life, but he gained increasing notoriety for his political

views. He was an ardent admirer of Adolf Hitler and became a follower of the British Fascist Sir Oswald Mosley. After attending the Nuremberg rally in 1936, he concluded that Hitler was presiding over a German rebirth that promised both peace and prosperity. In his introduction to *The Flax of Dream*, he hailed Hitler as "the great man across the Rhine whose life symbol is the happy child." Williamson was briefly imprisoned by British authorities after the outbreak of World War II, but was allowed to return to his Norfolk farm when it was determined he posed no security threat. During World War II, he published *The Story of a Norfolk Farm*, one of his several volumes of autobiography, and *Genius of Friendship*, an appreciation of T. E. Lawrence. Although Williamson was disheartened by World War II, and knew about such things as the Nazi extermination camps, he remained an admirer of Hitler and a Fascist sympathizer until his death. Oddly, he also considered himself a British patriot. Williamson's most ambitious work, but not the one for which he is remembered, is a fifteen-volume *roman fleuve* known collectively as *A Chronicle of Ancient Sunlight*. It was begun some five years after World War II. The first installment, *The Dark Lantern*, opens in 1895 with the birth of the protagonist, Phillip Maddison, a cousin of the central character in *The Flax of Dream* tetralogy (and another self-portrait). Subsequent volumes treat Maddison's childhood, schooling, and World War I combat experiences. The final volume, *The Gale of the World*, is set in the aftermath of World War II, and finds Maddison, like the author, resolving to write a series of novels that will tell the story of his own generation of Englishmen.

While *A Chronicle of Ancient Sunlight* has been praised for its scrupulously detailed portrait of English life in the first half of the twentieth century, much of the work, especially the more tendentious late volumes, received scant critical attention. However, in a judgment based on his reading of the first five volumes—which cover the period from 1895 to 1915—John Middleton Murry concluded, "we have enough to be assured that this will be in its entirety one of the most remarkable English novels of our time. . . . No comparable picture of suburban London in the revolutionary twenty years which changed its southern outskirts from beautiful country to the Greater London that we know has ever been painted. It is amazingly rich in all the living detail of a swiftly changing society." Reviewing Daniel Farson's adulatory biography of Williamson in the *Times Literary Supplement* (1982), Julian Symons thought that *A Chronicle* was Williamson's "principal literary achievement," but found fault with the notion that its neglect was attributable primarily to the author's politics, no matter how repugnant. "[At] best the *Chronicle* can be called no more than a minor achievement," Symons wrote, "flawed by too great an insistence on personal feelings. The nature books show the patient sympathy for animals that Williamson never extended to human beings, but they can hardly be called the work of a great writer."

Williamson was married and divorced twice, and had seven children. Recent years have seen some resurgence of interest in his work, but much less in his autobiographical sagas than in his animal books.

PRINCIPAL WORKS: *Natural History*—The Lone Swallows, 1922, rev. ed. 1933; Midsummer Night, 1924; The Incoming Summer, 1924; The Wild Deer of Exmoor: A Digression on the Logic and Ethics and Economics of Stag-Hunting in England To-Day, 1931; The Linhay on the Downs, and Other Adventures in the Old and New World, 1934. *Nature*—The Peregrine's Saga, and Other Stories of the Country Green, 1923 (in U.S.: Sun Brothers; (reissued as The Peregrine's Saga, and Other Wild Tales, 1934); The Old Stag, Stories, 1926; The Ackymals, 1929. *Juvenile*—Tarka the Otter: His Joyful Water-Life and Death in the Country of the Two Rivers, 1927; Salar the Salmon, 1935; Tales of Moorland and Estuary, 1953; The Scandaroon, 1972. *Country life. Ficiton*—The Village Book, 1930; The Labouring Life 1932; (in U.S.: As the Sun Shines); On Foot in Devon; or, Guidance and Gossip, Being a Monologue in Two Reels, 1933; Devon Holiday, 1935; Life in a Devon Village, 1945; Tales of a Devon Village, 1945; In the Woods, 1960; Village Tales, 1984; Days of Wonder, 1987; From a Country Hilltop, 1988; A Breath of Country Air, 1991; Spring Days in Devon and Other Broadcasts, 1992; Pen and Plough: Further Broadcasts, 1933. *Novels*—The Beautiful Years, 1921, rev. ed. 1929; Dandelion Days, 1922, rev. ed. 1930; The Dream of Fair Women: A Tale of Youth After the Great War, 1924, rev. ed. 1931; The Pathway, 1928; The Flax of Dream, a Novel in Four Books, 1936; The Patriot's Progress: Being the Vicissitudes of Pte. John Bullock, 1930; The Gold Falcon: or, The Haggard of Love, Being the Adventures of Manfred, Airman and Poet of the World War, and Later, Husband and Father, in Search of Freedom and Personal Sunrise in the City of New York, and of the Consummation of His Life, 1933 (revised and reissued as The Gold Falcon; or, The Haggard of Love, 1947); The Star-Born, 1933, rev. ed. 1948; The Sun in the Sands, 1945; The Phasian Bird, 1948; Scribbling Lark, 1949. *A Chronicle of Ancient Sunlight Series*—The Dark Lantern, 1951; Donkey Boy, 1952; Young Phillip Maddison, 1953; How Dear Is Life?, 1954; A Fox Under My Cloak, 1955; The Golden Virgin, 1957, rev. ed. 1963; Love and the Loveless: A Soldier's Tale, 1958; A Test to Destruction, 1960, rev. ed. 1964; The Innocent Moon, 1961; It Was the Nightingale, 1962; The Power of the Dead, 1963, rev. ed. 1966; The Phoenix Generation, 1965; A Solitary War, 1966; Lucifer Before Sunrise, 1967; The Gale of the World, 1969. *Memoirs and autobiography*—The Wet Flanders Plain, 1929; The Children of Shallowford, 1939, rev. ed. 1959; The Story of a Norfolk Farm, 1941; Genius of Friendship, "T. E. Lawrence," 1941; A Clear Water Stream, 1958. *Journal*—Goodbye, West Country, 1937. *Collections*—As the Sun Shines, 1941; The Henry Williamson Animal Saga, 1960; Collected Nature Stories, 1970; Some Notes on "The Flax of Dream" and Other Essays, 1988. *As editor*—An Anthology of Modern Nature Writing, 1936; Hodge and His Masters (by R. Jeffries) 1937; Richard Jeffries: Selections from His Work, with Details of His Life and Circumstances, His Death and Immortality, 1937; Norfolk Life (by L. R. Haggard and H. Williamson) 1943; My Favourite Country Stories, 1966; The Unrelenting Spring (by J. Farrar) 1968.

ABOUT: Contemporary Authors New Revision Series, 36, 1992; Dictionary of National Biography: 1971–1980, 1986; Farson, D. Henry: An Appreciation of Henry Williamson, 1982; Lamplugh, L. A Shadowed Man: Henry Williamson, 1991; Murry, J. M. Katherine Mansfield and Other Literary Studies, 1959; Sewell, B. (ed.) Henry Williamson, the Man, the Writiings: A Symposium, 1980; Who's Who 1977. *Periodicals*—Contemporary Review June 1984, March 1992; New York Herald Tribune Books December 1929; New YorkTimes August 14, 1977; New York Times Book Review September 19, 1948; Times (London) August 15, 1977; Times Literary Supplement November 10, 1927; September 24, 1982.

**WILLIAMSON, THAMES ROSS (pseudonyms "S. S. SMITH," "WALDO FLEMING," and "GREGORY TRENT")** (February 7, 1894–   ), American novelist, was born on the Nez Percé reservation near Genesee, Idaho, the son of Benjamin Franklin Williamson, a trader and a former scout, and Eugenia May (Ross) Williamson. He ran away from home at the age of fourteen and lived the life of a tramp. He then  shipped to Peru on a treasure hunt and later worked on a whaler, which he deserted off the coast of Alaska. He found employment as a railroad worker, a circus roustabout, a cabin boy, a sheepherder in the Sierra Nevada Mountains, and a newspaper reporter in San Francisco. He managed to graduate from high school in Spokane, Washington at sixteen. At twenty he was serving as private secretary to the warden of the Iowa State Prison; he was also a fingerprint and Bertillon expert. Williamson's first encouragement to become a novelist came from a prisoner who criticized a story in the prison magazine, which Williamson edited. Williamson moved to Chicago and joined the staff of Hull House, a settlement house, acting as an interpreter of Italian, Spanish, and modern Greek; he was proficient in ten languages. In 1917 he took his B.A. from the University of Iowa and the following year an M.A. in economics and anthropology at Harvard. From 1920 to 1921 he was an instructor in economics at Simmons College, and from 1921 to 1922 was assistant professor of economics and sociology at Smith College. He wrote a number of textbooks in sociology, and in a few years the income enabled him to quit teaching and begin a long-projected plan to present every aspect of American life in a vast series of novels. After three far from successful volumes in this series, he abandoned the idea.

Nevertheless, he went on to become a prolific novelist. Williamson's 1929 novel *Hunky* is a psychological study of a huge bakery worker, Jencic, whose strength is his only means of self-expression. The novel became a Book-of-the-Month Club selection. Its sequel, *In Krusack's House*, appeared two years later and continues Jencic's story through his unsuccessful marriage to Teena, the bakery girl rescued in *Hunky*. The *Saturday Review of Literature* called it a "mature and perfectly realized piece of work" and stated that the "three main characters are as true as life itself."

Williamson set his fiction in a wide range of locales, including the Lost Mountains of California, the Alaskan tundra, the Ozarks, Pennsylvania Dutch farm country, Germany, the Far East, and Nero's Rome. The latter is the setting for *The Gladiator*, in which a warrior converts to Christianity and eventually flees the burning city. The *New York Times* was of the opinion that the "penetrating portraits of Julius Caesar by Wilder and of

Claudius by Robert Graves show up Mr. Williamson's characters for what they are: foils for the swift paced action of an adventure story wrapped in a toga. But everything contributes expertly to make for light, readable fare."

Williamson made his homes in New England, Canada, France, Mexico, Sweden, and Ashland, Oregon. In 1927 he married his second wife, Sarah Storer Smith, who occasionally collaborated with him—and whose initials and surname he adopted as one of his many pseudonyms.

PRINCIPAL WORKS: *Novels*—Run, Sheep, Run, 1925; Gypsy Down the Lane, 1926; The Man Who Cannot Die, 1926; Stride of Man, 1928; Hunky, 1929; The Earth Told Me, 1930; In Krusack's House, 1931; Sad Indian: A Novel About Mexico, 1931; The Woods Cult: A Novel of the Ozark Hills, 1933; D Is for Dutch: A Last Regional Novel, 1934; Beginning at Dusk: An Interlude, 1935; (as "S. S. Smith") Under the Linden Tree: An Interlude, Christian Roux, 1945; The Gladiator, 1948. *Nonfiction*—Problems in American Democracy, 1922; Introduction to Sociology: With Practical Applications, 1926; Civics at Work: A Textbook in Social and Vocational Citizenship, 1928, rev. ed. by W. A. Hamm as Civics at Work: A Textbook in Elementary Civics, 1934; Introduction to Economics, 1928; (with E. B. Wesley) Principles of Social Science: A Survey of Problems in American Democracy, 1932; Far North Country, 1944. *As editor*—Readings in American Democracy, 1922; Readings in Economics, 1923. *Juvenile*—Opening Davy Jones's Locker 1930; The Flood Fighters, 1931; The Glacier Mystery (as "S. S. Smith"), 1934; The Lost Caravan (as "Waldo Fleming") 1935; The Cave Mystery (as "S. S. Smith") 1935; The Lobster War, 1935; The Falcon Mystery (as "S. S. Smith") 1936; Talking Drums (as "Waldo Fleming")1936; Beyond the Great Wall (as "Edward Dagonet") 1936; In the Stone Age (as "Gregory Trent") 1936; The Last of the Gauchos, 1937; The Spy Mystery (as "S. S. Smith") 1937; A Riddle in Fez (as "Waldo Fleming") 1937; Hunters Long Ago (as "Gregory Trent") 1937; Messengers to the Pharaoh (as "De Wolfe Morgan") 1937; A Tamer of Beasts (as "Gregory Trent") 1938; The Pygmy's Arrow (as "Waldo Fleming") 1938; Saltar the Mongol (as "Edward Dagonet") 1938; Before Homer (as "De Wolfe Morgan") 1938; The Feud Mystery (as "S. S. Smith") 1939; The Island Mystery (as "Waldo Fleming") 1939; The Flint Chipper, 1940.

ABOUT: *Periodicals*—Boston Evening Transcript August 28, 1931; Wilson Library Bulletin January 1932.

## WILLINGHAM, CALDER (BAYNARD) (December 23, 1922–February 19, 1995), American novelist, was born in Atlanta, the son of Calder and

 Eleanor Willingham. Before entering the University of Virginia in 1941, he attended the Darlington School in Rome, Georgia, and the Citadel, the famous—or notorious—South Carolina military academy which gave him a setting for his first and best-known novel, *End As a Man*. In depicting a year in the life of the cadets, Willingham portrayed his Citadel-like institution as a fetid breeding ground of corruption, sadism, and sodomy. This was partly reflected in the well-made movie based on it, which marked the starring debut of Ben Gazzara. Some critics professed surprise that a man in his early twenties could write such a harsh and angry book, and the failed attempt by the New York Society for the Suppression of Vice to prose-

cute Willingham's publisher for obscenity accelerated its sales. Despite certain ritual denunciations, *End As a Man* received a good press. "With all its technical crudities and philosophic immaturity," wrote the *New Yorker*, "this is a novel capable of evoking, even in a seasoned reader, something like cathartic terror."

Willingham's next two novels, *Geraldine Bradshaw* and *Reach to the Stars*, provoked still more outrage by critics offended by his then unfashionably candid depictions of sexuality; however, even sympathetic reviewers considered these linked stories of a libidinous bellhop's sentimental education in Chicago (*Geraldine Bradshaw*) and Los Angeles (*Reach to the Stars*) minor efforts. Similarly, *Natural Child* and *To Eat a Peach*, novels set on the fringes of New York bohemia and in a Georgia summer camp, respectively, received the usual mixed reviews; few reviewers invoked the comparisons to John Dos Passos and Norman Mailer prompted by his far better first novel.

Although it did not fully revive his reputation, Willingham's sixth novel, *Eternal Fire*, impressed some as a wickedly clever parody of "Southern Gothic." This story of a corrupt Southern judge who, for purely mercenary reasons, attempts to prevent the marriage of his ward to a pretty schoolteacher, teems with incest, murder, suicide, rape, and voyeurism in a seeming abstract of all the most lurid elements of the genre. *Washington Book World* (1987) pronounced it "a masterpiece of sorts. . . . It is giant, stem-winding fiction; it is also morbidly funny, erotic, bemused and an unsettling reminder of the callous racism that once was a way of American life."

For financial reasons (the support of one child by his first wife and five by his second, Jane Marie Bennett), Willingham spent much time writing for the movies. Although he took little interest, let alone pride, in his screenwriting, the films he worked on—*Paths of Glory, One-Eyed Jacks* (directed by Marlon Brando), *The Graduate, Little Big Man*—were some of the more interesting of the period. However, only one screenplay truly reflected his sensibility, and this, not surprisingly, was his 1991 adaptation (starring Laura Dern and Robert Duvall) of his own *Rambling Rose*. The original 1972 novel is the story of a nineteen-year-old serving girl whose ripe sexuality and spiritual innocence cause much commotion in the Depression-era Alabama town where she is employed by the Hillyers, a progressive, middle-class family much like Willingham's own.

After some years in New York, Willingham moved with his family in 1953 to New Hampton, New Hampshire, where he was free from the "distractions" of other writers and removed from the critical establishment he so much despised.

PRINCIPAL WORKS: *Novels*—End as a Man, 1947; Geraldine Bradshaw, 1950; Reach to the Stars, 1951; Natural Child, 1952; To Eat a Peach, 1955; Eternal Fire, 1963; Providence Island, 1969; Rambling Rose, 1972; The Big Nickel, 1975; The Building of Venus Four, 1977. *Short stories*—The Gates of Hell, 1951.

ABOUT: Contemporary Literary Criticisms vol. 5 1976; vol. 51

1989; Contemporary Novelists, 5th ed., 1991. *Periodicals*—New York Times February 21, 1995; New Yorker March 8, 1947; Times (London) February 22, 1995; Washington Post Book World October 29, 1972; May 24, 1987.

## WILLISON, GEORGE FINDLAY (July 24, 1896–July 30, 1972), American historian, wrote:

"Born of Scottish parents in Denver, Colorado, I grew up on the outskirts of the city, roaming the neighborhood and the inviting open prairie for miles around even as a small child. City children in those days enjoyed a far-ranging freedom of foot—and with that, a degree of social freedom, and intellectual as well—which the automobile with its whir of death-dealing traffic has destroyed. We did not have to wait for an adult hand to lead us across the street into new adventure.

"Though still desirous of becoming a second Ty Cobb, I did my first serious writing in high school—and never was I more serious. In Latin we were reading Cicero, and I grew so tired of his pomposities, so disgusted with his whining self-righteousness and really dirty digs at Catiline, that I decided to come to the defense with a rousing appeal and silence Cicero forever. It was a long and ambitious work, and not without fruit, leading me to my first acquaintance with the real learning process, seeking sources, weighing evidence, throwing away the second-hand, and with the deep pleasures and high excitements of slowly shaping a creation of one's own. Instead of asking me to read the historic paper to the class, the teacher handed it back a few days later, with scarcely a glance at me as she remarked, 'You seem to have spent a great deal of time on this, which is probably the reason you are not doing so well in what you should be doing.' What I should have been doing, indeed!—which was to toss her to the lions, along with Cicero.

"At the University of Colorado, I 'majored'—as the phrase ran—in Greek, a very rewarding choice. First, for the language and the literature itself, a constant revelation and delight. Second, for the rare spirit that lighted my steps, the late Dr. George Norlin, one of the great Grecians of his day, a humanist in his every fibre.

"As I was usually the only one in the class, we met as we pleased and talked not merely of the text before us, but of everything from Greek games and the cult of Aphrodite to *The Spoon River Anthology* and World War I then raging. A sharp and sensitive critic, a fine writer himself, a wise man of the world, Dr. Norlin was a university in himself, and I know he went to the Elysian Fields to join Aristophanes, Aeschylus, Herodotus, Sappho, and his many old friends there.

"After a stint in the army in 1918, I was named, by good fortune, a Rhodes Scholar and lived abroad for four years—largely in Oxford, London, Paris, and Heidelberg—which opened a new world of both the flesh and the spirit to a still rather naïve youth from the Rockies. Officially, I 'read' history, economics, and political science, but I managed to read as widely in other fields—in English and French literature especially.

"In 1928, after several misguided years in journalism, I went to St. John's College, Annapolis, Maryland, to teach Greek, Latin (but not Cicero), and related subjects. The next year I joined the staff of the experimental Hessian Hills School at Croton on Hudson, New York, remaining there till 1935, when I resigned to get on with my own work. Meantime, I had married Florence Hauser; had a son, Malcolm; and written *Here They Dug the Gold*, a chronicle of gold rush days and early boom towns in Colorado. Just after the book appeared—the Depression had come—the publisher failed, went bankrupt, collapsed, and the book was buried in the debris.

"Removing from Croton to Provincetown, Cape Cod, where living was pleasant and cheap, I completed a study of war as a social and economic institution, which came out in 1936. My luck still held—the publisher collapsed. With all of those who were desperately trying to earn a mere subsistence in the arts and crafts, I welcomed the W.P.A. Federal Arts Program, becoming in 1938 a national editor in the Washington office of the Writers' Project, working chiefly on the American Guide Series, an education in itself. After Pearl Harbor, I transferred to the Civil Aeronautics Administration, as writer-editor, and early in 1944 joined the publicity staff of the Democratic National Committee, remaining there till the summer of 1946.

"In Washington I had continued with my own writing as time from the job allowed. In 1940 appeared *Let's Make a Play* (the publisher didn't collapse) and in 1945, a group biography of the Pilgrims, *Saints and Strangers*, which was well received by the critics and in the bookshops, later chosen as a dividend by the Book-of-the-Month Club. This windfall enabled me to acquire a modest country place in up-state New York, above Albany. . . . [in 1952] I was . . . in Washington, with Senator Estes Kefauver in his campaign for the Democratic presidential nomination.

"In 1946, I revised and added some recently disclosed material to my first book, *Here They Dug the Gold*, which found readers at last, even in Britain, where it became, surprisingly, a book club choice . . . [M]y mature interests are [in] . . . the American people, where they came from, how they got here, and how they have fared along the way in all respects."

---

*Saints and Strangers* was the crowning achievement in George F. Willison's career. Reviewers of the day were quick to praise the author's thorough research and skillful assembling of material. The *New Yorker* remarked that the story had been told before but that "Mr. Willison, by ignoring all the nonsense that has been written about the Pilgrims and by showing that they were not quite the crowd of crape-draped killjoys they are supposed to have been, has told their story in a new, interesting, and highly readable way. He has managed to get some humor into it, too." *Patrick Henry and His World*, however, fared less well. "In this book we learn an inordinate amount about the author's attitudes toward 'the anti-Communist hysteria of the 1940s and 1950s,' the Vietnam war, campus riots, and Lyndon Johnson," the *Journal of American History* commented. "Unfortunately, we learn less about 'Patrick Henry and His World' than we wish."

During the late 1950s and early 1960s Willison was active in public life in various capacities, including a post with the governor of New York's executive chamber staff. In addition to his books he contributed articles to such publications as the *New Yorker, Mademoiselle, Reader's Digest*, and the *Nation*.

PRINCIPAL WORKS: *Nonfiction*—Here They Dug Gold, 1931, rev. ed. 1946; Why Wars Are Declared, 1935; Saints and Strangers: Being the Lives of the Pilgrim Fathers and Their Families, With Their Friends & Foes & an Account of Their Posthumous Wanderings In Limbo, Their Final Resurrection and Rise to Glory, and the Stranger Pilgrimages of Plymouth Rock, 1945, rev. and abridged ed. 1965, 1983 (in U.K.: rev. ed. as Saints and Strangers: The Story of the 'Mayflower' and the Plymouth Colony); Behold Virginia: The Fifth Crown: Being the Trials, Adventures and Disasters of the First Families of Virginia, the Rise of the Grandees and the Eventual Triumph of the Common & Uncommon Sort in the Revolution, 1951; The History of Pittsfield, Massachusetts: 1916–1955, 1957; Patrick Henry and His World, 1969. *As editor*—Let's Make a Play: Twelve Plays by Children, With a Discussion and Explanation of Dramatic Techniques, 1940; The Pilgrim Reader: The Story of the Pilgrims As Told By Themselves and Their Contemporaries, Friendly & Unfriendly, 1953; The Federalist: Notes, Including Bibliographies, Historical Background, Summaries and Commentaries, Review Questions, Selected Bibliography 1971.

ABOUT: The autobiographical material quoted above was written for Twentieth Century Authors First Supplement, 1955. Contemporary Authors 1995; Current Biography 1946. *Periodicals*—Journal of American History September 1969; New Yorker August 11, 1945.

**WILSON, ANGUS** (August 11, 1913–May 31, 1991), English novelist and critic, wrote: "My full name is Angus Frank Johnstone-Wilson. I was born

at Bexhill, Sussex. My father was William Johnstone-Wilson and my mother formerly Miss Maude Caney. She came from Durban, Natal, South Africa, and when the first World War was ended we visited there and I spent three years of my childhood there. On our return I went to Westminster School and subsequently to Merton College, Oxford, where I studied medieval history. After two years in which I did numerous jobs such as tutoring, secretarial work, catering and running a restaurant and acting as social organizer, I went to the Department of Printed Books, British Museum. In the 1939 war I was employed at the Foreign Office and since my return to the British Museum I have first worked on replacing as many as possible of the three hundred thousand books destroyed

here during the bombing, and subsequently as deputy superintendent of the Reading Room.

"It had always been my intention not to write books. I used to say that too many people wrote and I still do. However, during the 1939 war I suffered a nervous breakdown and on my return to London I felt that I could only find satisfaction in life if I gave myself an additional interest. For this reason I began to write short stories, working only at weekends. These stories, luckily for me, turned out successful and formed the first volume which was published in England in 1949 called *The Wrong Set*.

I have continued to be a weekend writer only and have subsequently published another volume of short stories, *Such Darling Dodos*, an examination of the novels of Emile Zola, entitled *Emile Zola*, and last my novel, *Hemlock and After*. Next year I will publish a satirical work on the 1920s entitled *For Whom the Cloche Tolls*. I contribute reviews and literary articles to many of the periodicals here including *Horizon, The Observer, New Statesman and Nation, The Listener*, the *Times Literary Supplement* and the *Sunday Times*. I have also broadcast literary talks on the Third Programme and, recently, a small imaginary autobiographical play.

Although my work has been well received both in England and in the United States, it has been generally criticized for its savage characterization and the unpleasantness of the persons portrayed. In general critics have found it satisfactory to describe the work as satirical. I do not myself feel that this is a satisfactory description except in so far as I like to use irony as my approach. To me the characters do not appear degraded and depraved, but simply realistic accounts of people as they are, and I feel that the general desire that some characters should be faultless is unhealthy and untrue and that to portray characters without saying all that must be said against them is patronage and not praise. I also believe very strongly that if the novel is to recover its strength in the modern world it must, though not returning to the nineteenth century standards, once more acquire that generality which belonged to the great nineteenth century novels and it is for that reason I do not hesitate to mix satire, social realism, farce, melodrama, and tragedy in one work. It has been criticized as an impossible method, but I believe this is only because people are no longer familiar with the wide generalized approach of the last century. Finally I believe that if the novel is to recover from the anemia which has beset it since the 1920s, it must once more cover a wide, social canvas."

———

Wilson had five very much older brothers. His father was a gambler. In 1932 he went to Merton College, Oxford, to study medieval history, supporting himself on a small legacy left by his mother, who had died when he was fifteen. Although Wilson was removed from his position at the British Museum to do decoding work at the famous center at Bletchley Park, which appears to have caused his nervous breakdown, he did, during the time of his psychoanalytic treatment, have a love affair with a young man. After he left the British Museum, he made a living from writing, broadcasting, and lecturing, and he held a position at the then newly formed University of East Anglia.

Although Wilson did not begin to write until 1946, when World War II was already over, by the time *The Wrong Set and Other Stories* was published as a book, he had already achieved a considerable reputation on both sides of the Atlantic. Paul Engle, reviewing it in the Chicago *Sunday Tribune*, called it "the most delightful and disturbing book of stories I've seen in a long time." Edmund Wilson called him "a master of mimicry and parody . . . as funny as anyone can be who never becomes exhilarated." Edmund Wilson also, however, asserted that he saw in Angus "a strain of the harsh Scottish moralist who does not want to let anybody off and does not care if his sarcasm wounds." In his *Paris Review* interview with Michael Millgate, published in the First Series, Wilson showed himself a moralist, declaring, "Most of my characters have a Calvinist conscience . . . ."

*Some Darling Dodos*, Wilson's next book of stories, garnered as much praise as his first. *Hemlock and After*, his first novel, was described in the *Times Literary Supplement* as "a savage exposure of corruption in a disintegrating society." Married, but gay, novelist Bernard Sands, the protagonist, obtains a government grant to set up a retreat for young writers. "As he dominates the grotesques who make up the cast of minor characters, Sands becomes increasingly obsessed with an awareness of evil and his own irresponsibility," according to *Current Biography*. Ernest Jones in the *Nation* endorsed "its brilliant analysis of homosexual society and magnificent portrayal of the British middle class." A later critic, Lorna Sage, reviewing Margaret Drabble's biography of Wilson in the *Times Literary Supplement* (1995), characterized Wilson's writing as fitting into Susan Sontag's definition of "camp," and observed that *Hemlock and After* explores "the corrupting effects of living a closeted life."

Of necessity Wilson had to lead a closeted life because of English law at the time, but some time in the early 1950s he set up housekeeping with a man who was to be his long-term companion. His companion had to leave his job as a probation officer because of scandal, and thus, Wilson's need for money tended to be greater after he had quit his job at the British Museum to write full-time.

Wilson is perhaps best remembered for his second novel, *Anglo-Saxon Attitudes*. Loosely based on the scandal surrounding the discovery that the Piltdown man was a hoax, it has an academic setting. The main character is an archaeologist who has long "suspected that a renowned archaeological discovery of 1912 was a hoax," according to *Current Biography*. "Wilson satirizes various forms of the quest for truth," James Gindin remarked. Arthur Edelstein in *Contemporary British Novelists* compared Wilson to Henry James and commented on "the pervasive thematic and functional influ-

ence of the book's focal event: the discovery . . . of the tomb of Bishop Eorpwald. . . . Suitably . . . the event antedates the time span of the novel . . . But like James's Mrs. Newsome, who never appears in the pages of *The Ambassadors*, it is a looming and potent spectre in the foreground."

*The Middle Age of Mrs. Eliot* is a study in character development. The chief character "uses all forms of art to enhance her own awareness of experience," according to James Gindin.

Although Wilson lauded the value of traditional writing, he did recognize the need for experiment in the revitalization of literature. In *The Old Men at the Zoo*, partly set in an imagined future before the onset of World War III, "reality and myth come together," according to Anthony Burgess, who believed the novel was the best thing Wilson had done. Martin Seymour-Smith, too, characterized the novel as Wilson's best. "We see England invaded by Europe and the Zoo taken over so that the new rulers can throw their opponents to the beasts." The management of animals at the zoo shades into the management of people on earth. "Man can survive . . . only if he recognizes his own animalism but attempts, as intelligently as he can, to govern this brutality rationally and wisely. . . . And . . . the personal control and the professional control are equated," James Gindin noted.

Wilson turned to the family saga, told with experimental twists, in *No Laughing Matter*. Rachel Trickett in the *Yale Review* (1967) compared the novel to three of Virginia Woolf's in its exploration of "the contrast between the external flow of time and the static inner core of personality." Trickett remarked on Wilson's "inclusive view of life" in this novel. Bernard Bergonzi called the sweep of events that overtake the fictional family from 1912 to 1967 in *No Laughing Matter* "a focus for his fictional attempt on the Condition of England question."

In *Setting the World on Fire*, Wilson creates a magical realistic world in London. Palladian architecture and early baroque opera are the motifs by which he explores the nature of art itself. Bernard Bergonzi, writing in the *Times Literary Supplement* (1980), termed the novel "a static or spiralling enactment of the Phaethon myth, turning in and round on itself." Bergonzi deemed the human element as coming off "second-best" in this tale of two brothers attempting to stage *Phaeton*, a never-perfomed Lully opera in a vividly described magically constructed house. Although most reviewers had cavils about the success of the novel, almost all found it filled with "intensity and skill" and "profligate and luxuriant," as did Bergonzi.

Wilson's own life has been characterized as a hectic whirl of "literary tours," travel, parties, broadcasting, speech-making, and other activity. He made friends with many of the important literary figures of his time, including Yukio Mishima and Margaret Drabble. One of his friends was Malcolm Bradbury, who compared him to E.M. Forster: "He measures and judges according to a comic and ironic mode. And one of the functions of irony and comedy in his work is to be directed, as it is in Forster's novels, towards a centre, showing up moral and emotional atrophy, self-deceit and unrecognized failure in the realm of the personal."

Wilson was knighted in 1980 and received many other honors in his lifetime, including the James Tait Black Memorial Prize in 1959 for *The Middle Age of Mrs. Eliot.* The end of his life was a sad one, however. He disapproved of the policies of Prime Minister Margaret Thatcher and moved to France in 1985. His money ran out, and he died in a nursing home back in England.

His friend Jonathan Raban in *The New Review* had written of his novels: "Failure here is dreadfully easy: a small solecism mushrooms into a humiliating disaster: what starts as a polite giggle ends as a shriek. The lights are always on, there are no corners to hide in." Walter Allen had remarked, "One of Wilson's most serious and important qualities is his awareness of the black nightside of life."

PRINCIPAL WORKS: *Fiction*—The Wrong Set and Other Stories, 1949; Such Darling Dodos and Other Stories, 1950; Hemlock and After, 1952; Anglo-Saxon Attitudes, 1956; A Bit Off the Map and Other Stories, 1957; The Middle Age of Mrs. Eliot, 1958; The Old Men at the Zoo, 1961; Late Call, 1964; No Laughing Matter, 1967; Death Dance; Twenty-Five Stories, 1969; As if by Magic, 1973; Setting the World on Fire, 1980. *Drama*—The Mulberry Bush, 1956. *Nonfiction*—Emile Zola, An Introductory Study of His Novels, 1952 (rev. 1965); For Whom the Cloche Tolls: A Scrapbook of The Twenties, 1953; The Wild Garden, 1963; The World of Charles Dickens, 1970; The Naughty Nineties, 1976; The Strange Ride of Rudyard ABOUT: Current Biography 1959; Allen, W. The Modern Novel, 1964; Gindin, J. Postwar British Fiction: New Accents and Attitudes, 1962; Halio, J. Angus Wilson, 1964; Shapiro, C., ed. Contemporary British Novelists, 1965; Wilson, E. The Bit Between My Teeth: A Literary Chronicle 1950–1965, 1965; Gransden, K. W. Angus Wilson, 1969; Contemporary Literary Criticism, 1970; 1975; 1981; Seymour-Smith, M. Guide to Modern World Literature, 1973; Faulkner, P. Wilson: Mimic And Moralist, 1980; Drabble, M. Angus Wilson, A Biography, 1995; (ed.) Parker, P. The Reader's Companion To Twentieth Century Writers, 1995. *Periodicals*—Guardian September 29 1961, May 26 1995; New Statesman August 12 1950, September 29 1961, October 6 1967; New Yorker January 6 1951, April 11 1959; New York Times June 2 1991; Observer June 4 1995; Times (London) June 1, 1991; Times Literary Supplement August 29, 1952; June 9, 1995; Yale Review Spring 1968; Summer 1974.

## WILSON, CHARLES MORROW (June 16, 1905–March 4, 1977), American regionalist, agricultural and social writer, was born in Fayetteville,

Arkansas, the son of Joseph Dickens and Mattie (Morrow) Wilson. After growing up on a small farm in the Ozarks, he graduated from the University of Arkansas (1926). He then worked for the *St. Louis Dispatch* and the *New York Times* for about three years. During this time he made himself known to the public as a frequent contributor of articles to a variety of popular periodicals.

Several social studies and two early novels demonstrate Wilson's intimate knowledge of his Ozark friends and neighbors, whose aspirations in the face of poverty he admired. *Backwoods America* (1935), a collections of articles, most of which appeared in the *Atlantic Monthly*, the *Nation, Commonweal,* and other magazines, surveyed mountain manners, morality, and moonshine, and was considered a notch above most of the other sociological writing of the time.

While Wilson's work never approached the literary prominence or evocative skill of Dos Passos, Steinbeck, and other better-known chroniclers of dust bowl America, it was based on first-hand knowledge. Such closely observed facts were notably harvested in *Roots of America* (1936), a journalistic collage of the depression years which aimed to demonstrate that not all rural dwellers are simple bumpkins. William Allen White wrote in the *Saturday Review of Literature* that "Theodore Roosevelt would have read it with great gusto, bought it in dozen lots to send to his friends." Wilson's report on Maine potato farmers in *Aroostook: Our Last Frontier* (1937) was called "local Americana of real value," by the *New York Times*, and *The Landscape of Rural Poverty: Corn Bread and Creek Water* (1940), his objective report on U. S. farm conditions and agricultural problems, prompted the *Saturday Review of Literature* to claim that "Mr. Wilson is our most gifted country correspondent with a national following."

During World War II, Wilson reported on the social conditions and geography of Central America, beginning with *Challenge and Opportunity: Central America* (1941), an overview of tropical products and trade problems, in which he advocated pan-American cooperation. The *New Yorker* called Wilson "one of our more enterprising social reporters" when he published *Ambassadors in White* (1942), a detailed report on the state of American tropical medicine, health, and sanitation conditions in Central and South America. Twenty years later, with *The Fight Against Hunger* (1969), Wilson, by then an authority on food production and nutrition, tapped into his lifelong reporting experience— from dust-bowl Arkansas and the New Deal days of the 1930s to agricultural solutions available in the 1960s—to find ways to eliminate world hunger. "Opinionated, perceptive, and entertaining, Wilson adds a human element to more scholarly studies of agriculture," wrote *Choice.*

While much of his published output focused on agriculture and Americana, Wilson was a graduate of a generalist school of journalism and took an enthusiastic approach to writing guides for the public on an eclectic array of subjects, including the rubber and banana industries, the development of oil pipelines in America, Liberian history and anthropology, as well as a compendium on plant roots and a survey of the modern barter system. He also wrote biographies of Geronimo, Meriwether Lewis, William Jennings Bryan, and a widely praised juvenile account of the life of the engineer Rudolf Diesel.

PRINCIPAL WORKS: *Fiction*—Acres of Sky, 1930; The Rabble Rouser, 1936; Ginger Blue, 1940 A Man's Reach, 1944. *Nonfiction*—Meriwether Lewis of Lewis and Clark, 1934; Backwoods America, 1935; Roots of America: A Travelogue of American Personalities, 1936; Aroostook: Our Last Frontier, 1937; Country Living Plus and Minus, 1938; Landscape of Rural Poverty: Corn Bread and Creek Water, 1940; Challenge and Opportunity: Central America, 1941; Ambassadors in White: The Story of American Tropical Medicine, 1942; Trees and Test Tubes: The Story of Rubber, 1943; Middle America, 1944. As editor—New Crops for the New World, 1945; Oil Across the World, 1946; Liberia, 1947; Empire in Green and Gold: The Story of the American Banana Trade, 1947: One Half the People: Doctors and the Crisis of World Health, 1949: The Tropics: World of Tomorrow, 1951; Butterscotch and the Happy Barnyard, 1953: Bodacious Ozarks, 1959: Let's Try Barter, 1960; Magnificent Scufflers, 1960; Grass and People, 1961; Common Sense Credit, 1962; Wilderness Explorer: Samuel de Champlain, 1963; Great Turkey Drive, 1964; Green Mountain Toymakers, 1965; Roots: Miracles Below, 1968; The Fight Against Hunger, 1969; The Commoner: William Jennings Bryan, 1970; The Monroe Doctrine, 1971; Liberia: Black Africa in Microcosm, 1971; The Dred Scott Decision, 1973; Geronimo, 1973. Juvenile—(with W. R. Nitske) Rudolf Diesel: Pioneer of the Age of Power, 1965; Crown Point: The Destiny Road, 1965; Commandant Paul and the Founding of Montreal, 1966.

ABOUT: Choice January 1970; New York Herald Tribune June 5, 1960; New York Times October 3, 1937; June 28, 1942; January 1, 1950; March 5, 1977; New Yorker June 27, 1942; Saturday Review of Literature May 2, 1936; November 2, 1940.

**WILSON, EDMUND** (May 8, 1895–June 12, 1972), American critic, literary historian, novelist, and polemicist, was born in Red Bank, New Jersey, the son of Edmund Wilson, a politician, and Helen Mather (Kimball) Wilson. He was educated at Hill School in Pottstown, Pennsylvania, and then at Princeton University. He was on the editorial staff of Nassau Lit and encouraged his fellow student F. Scott Fitzgerald to contribute sketches. Among those who influenced him early and decisively were George Bernard Shaw and H. L. Mencken. Following graduation in 1916 he briefly studied sociology and labor relations at Columbia University and worked as a reporter for the New York Evening Sun. During World War I he served with the army at a hospital unit in France, and then in the intelligence corps. Back in New York City Wilson became the managing editor of Vanity Fair (1920–1921) and collaborated with the poet John Peale Bishop, whom he had known at college, on a book of satirical verse pieces called The Undertaker's Garland. His next book, Discordant Encounters, collected a group of his short plays and dialogues. This was followed by I Thought of Daisy, a novel about the bohemian life of artists and intellectuals in New York City. Reviewers received it more as a bitter critique of contemporary life and literature than as an imaginative piece of fiction. In Poets, Farewell! he further displayed his talent for wit and satire in a variety of lyrics and prose sketches. From 1926 to 1931 Wilson was an associate editor of the New Republic, primarily responsible for writing book reviews.

Axel's Castle established Wilson as a major critic.

In it he examined the writings of W. B. Yeats, Paul Valéry, T. S. Eliot, Marcel Proust, James Joyce, and Gertrude Stein by linking their modernist techniques to the late nineteenth-century French symbolists. For Wilson the six writers "represent[ed] the culmination of a self-conscious and very important literary movement." As in his other works of criticism, Wilson was able to provide lucid interpretations of passages previously regarded as hopelessly obscure. Writing in the Saturday Review of Literature in 1931, Matthew Josephson praised Wilson's studies "for their demure wit, their range of interests, their frequent illumination of modern fetishes and tendencies, and their basic honesty." Literary criticism, Wilson explained in the preface to Axel's Castle, should be "a history of man's ideas and imaginings in the setting of the conditions that shaped them." Throughout his career as a literary critic he adhered to this basic rule of placing the work of art in its social and cultural context. He was the leading major critic to take up a position combining Marxism and Freudianism, although he was not wholly committed to the former. Although he accepted that literature could have a didactic function, Wilson opposed judging it solely by its ideological content. During the early years of the Depression, he showed an increasing interest in political matters. In The American Jitters he reported on current social, economic, and political conditions in the United States. He considered himself Marxist-oriented, but his attitude to Stalinism was negative long before it was exposed as a tyranny. He studied in the Soviet Union in 1935 under a Guggenheim Fellowship and offered his—generally favorable—impressions in Travels in Two Democracies, in which he often satirically and playfully contrasted the Russian scene with the American, to the latter's detriment. Although To the Finland Station, a work of social criticism, garnered mixed reviews, it is considered as important in Wilson's overall work as Axel's Castle. It is a comprehensive study of the European revolutionary tradition from its birth in the early 1800s to its institutionalization in the Soviet Union under Lenin. Wilson's other writings during the 1930s and early 1940s included The Triple Thinkers, a collection of essays on nineteenth-century literature; The Boys in the Back Room, a study of California novelists, notably John Steinbeck; and The Wound and the Bow, in which he employed the myth of Philoctetes—with his stinking wound—to explore the connection between neurosis and artistic creativity. He also continued to write poetry and plays. His huge and influential anthology The Shock of Recognition traced the development of American writing from the romantic era to the present day.

Wilson once said that his own favorite among his books was Memoirs of Hecate County, a group of interrelated first-person stories satirizing the cultural and intellectual elitism of suburbia. A New York court banned the book on grounds of obscenity, which led to increased sales. The Little Blue Light, a play of satire and fantasy, was performed at the ANTA Playhouse in New York City in 1951, and published a few years later with a group of old and new dramatic works. In 1944 Wilson became book reviewer for the *New Yorker*, a position he held until 1948, although he continued to contribute articles to the magazine for the rest of his life. Following World War II he toured Italy, Greece, and England (as a *New Yorker* correspondent) and published his observations in *Europe Without Baedeker*.

A brilliant linguist, Wilson was later drawn to the newly discovered Dead Sea Scrolls; his hostility to orthodox religion conflicted sharply with interpretations by theologians. He regarded the documents as principally socially and culturally significant. In *Red, Black, Blond, and Olive* he provided a comparative investigation of four different cultures— Zuni, Haiti, Soviet Russia, and Israel. *Apologies to the Iroquois* combined a history of Native American tribes in upstate New York (where he lived) with a description of the modern social and economic plight of the Iroquois. In *The American Earthquake* he collected nonliterary articles to provide a portrait of life in the United States in the 1920s and 1930s. As a literary critic he gathered articles and new material for *Classics and Commercials*, a study of writers during the 1940s, and then delved further back with *The Shores of Light*, a study of American writing during the two preceding decades, and *Patriotic Gore*, an in-depth look at the literature of the Civil War era. A few years later he brought his group of "literary chronicles" up-to-date with *The Bit Between My Teeth*, which covered the years between 1950 and 1965.

Of a more personal nature was *Piece of My Mind*, reflective essays written after he had turned sixty. Here he revealed his contentment to live what he deemed to be something of an eighteenth-century existence in the twentieth century, and his desire to investigate all of the major areas of intellectual inquiry and creative endeavor. He covered a wide range of topics, from sex and religion to science and education to war and international affairs. Among his other late nonfictional works were *The Cold War and the Income Tax*, based on his own difficulties with the Internal Revenue Service, but essentially a protest against how the federal government spends tax dollars; *O Canada*, containing *New Yorker* articles on Canadian culture; *A Window on Russia*, a study of that country's literature; and a posthumous collection of critical essays on literature called *The Devils and Canon Barham*. He published his early journals as *A Prelude* and followed them with his recollections of northern New York in *Upstate*. After his death Leon Edel edited Wilson's other journals as *The Twenties*, *The Thirties*, *The Forties*, and *The Fifties*, and Lewis Dabney edited the final volume, *The Sixties*. In these highly readable books Wilson gives a well-rounded account of his personal and public life, including his four marriages (his third wife was the novelist Mary McCarthy), his homes in Talcottville, New York, and Wellfleet on Cape Cod in Massachusetts, and his numerous literary acquaintances. His relations with the writer Vladimir Nabokov, which involved both amity and literary enmity, are detailed in an annotated volume of their correspondence.

Among Wilson's honors were the Gold Medal from the National Institute of Arts and Letters (of which he was a member) in 1955 and the Presidential Medal of Freedom in 1963. Wilson embodied and promoted the ideals of liberal and humanistic learning. In addition to viewing literature as an instrument of pleasure, he saw it as an essential means for bringing humane order to an otherwise chaotic world. Edmund Wilson's papers are at the Beinecke Library at Yale University.

PRINCIPAL WORKS: *Poetry*—(with J. P. Bishop) The Undertaker's Garland, 1922; Poets, Farewell!, 1922; Notebooks of Night, 1942; Night Thoughts, 1961. *Drama*—Discordant Encounters: Plays and Dialogues, 1926; This Room and This Gin and These Sandwiches: Three Plays (The Crime in the Whistler Room; Beppo and Beth; A Winter in Beech Street) 1937; Five Plays (Cyprian's Prayer; The Crime in the Whistler Room; This Room and This Gin and These Sandwiches; Beppo and Beth; The Little Blue Light) 1954; The Duke of Palermo and Other Plays (The Duke of Palermo; Dr. McGrath; Osbert's Career) 1969. *Fiction*—I Thought of Daisy, 1929; Memoirs of Hecate County, 1946, rev. ed., 1958 (stories); Galahad [and] I Thought of Daisy, 1967. *Nonfiction*—Axel's Castle: A Study in the Imaginative Literature of 1870–1930, 1931; The American Jitters: A Year of the Slump, 1932 (in U.K.: Devil Take the Hindmost), Travels in Two Democracies, 1936; The Triple Thinkers: Ten Essays on Literary Subjects, 1938, rev. ed., 1948; To the Finland Station: A Study in the Writing and Acting of History, 1940, rev. ed., 1972; The Boys in the Back Room: Notes on California Novelists, 1941; The Wound and the Bow: Seven Studies in Literature, 1941, rev. ed., 1965; Europe Without Baedeker: Sketches among the Ruins of Italy, Greece, and England, 1947, rev. ed., 1966; Classics and Commercials: A Literary Chronicle of the Forties, 1950; The Shores of Light: A Literary Chronicle of the Twenties and Thirties, 1952; The Scrolls from the Dead Sea, 1955 (rev. as The Dead Sea Scrolls, 1969); A Piece of My Mind: Reflections at Sixty, 1956; Red, Black, Blond, and Olive: Studies in Four Civilizations: Zuni, Haiti, Soviet Russia, Israel, 1956; The American Earthquake: A Documentary of the Twenties and Thirties, 1958; Apologies to the Iroquois, 1960; Patriotic Gore: Studies in the Literature of the American Civil War, 1962; The Cold War and the Income Tax: A Protest, 1963; The Bit Between My Teeth: A Literary Chronicle of 1950–1965, 1965; O Canada: An American's Notes on Canadian Culture, 1965; (with M. Moore) Homage to Henry James, 1971; A Window on Russia for the Use of Foreign Readers, 1972; The Devils and Canon Barham: Ten Essays on Poets, Novelists, and Monsters, 1973. *As editor*—The Shock of Recognition: The Development of Literature in the United States Recorded by the Men Who Made It, 1943, rev. ed., 1955; The Collected Essays of John Peale Bishop, 1948. *Journals*—A Prelude: Landscapes, Characters, and Conversations from the Earlier Years of My Life, 1967; Upstate: Records and Recollections of Northern New York, 1971; The Twenties: From Notebooks and Diaries of the Period (ed. L. Edel) 1975; The Thirties: From Notebooks and Diaries of the Period (ed. L. Edel) 1980; The Forties: From Notebooks and Diaries of the Period (ed. L. Edel) 1983; The Fifties: From Notebooks and Diaries of the Period (ed. L. Edel) 1986; The Sixties: The Last Journal (ed. L. M. Dabney) 1930. *Correspondence*—Letters on Literature and Politics (ed. E. Wilson) 1977; The Nabokov-Wilson Letters: Correspondence between Vladimir Nabokov and Edmund Wilson (ed. S. Karlinsky) 1979. *Collection*—The Portable Edmund Wilson (ed. L. M. Dabney) 1983.

ABOUT: Aaron, D. Writers on the Left, 1961; Berthoff, W. Edmund Wilson, 1968; Castronovo, D. Edmund Wilson, 1984; Costa, R. H. Edmund Wilson, 1980; Douglas, G. H. Edmund Wilson's America, 1983; Frank, C. P. Edmund Wilson, 1970; Goldhurst, W. F. Scott Fitzgerald and His Contemporaries, 1963; Groth, J. Edmund Wilson, 1989; Hyman, S. E. Armed Vision, 1948; Kriegel, L. Edmund Wilson, 1971; Paul, S. Edmund Wilson, 1965; Wain, J. (ed.) Edmund Wilson: The Man and His Work, 1978; Wilson, R. B. Near the Margin: A Memoir of My Father, Edmund Wilson, 1989. *Bibliography*—

Ramsey, R. D. Edmund Wilson: A Bibliography, 1971. Periodicals—American Scholar Spring 1988, Summer 1990, Summer 1992; Atlantic July 1967, March 1974; Commentary January 1978; Commonweal July 8, 1938; May 13, 1960; January 10, 1964; October 27, 1967; July 14, 1972; Comparative Literature Studies March 1978; Esquire December 1983; Georgia Review Spring 1982; Journal of Modern Literature September 1979; Journal of Popular Culture Fall 1981; Nation October 16, 1948; January 27, 1951; January 28, 1978; New Criterion January 1987; New Republic May 9, 1970; November 30, 1974; May 3, 1980; April 4, 1983; New York Herald Tribune Book Review October 12, 1958; November 2, 1952; New York Review of Books July 19, 1979; September 25, 1980; November 10, 1983; New York Times June 13, 1972; New York Times Book Review November 2, 1952; July 2, 1972; October 9, 1977; February 4, 1979; June 10, 1979; May 22, 1983; April 29, 1984; December 10, 1989; New Yorker December 15, 1980; January 5, 1987; Newsweek June 6, 1966; June 26, 1972; May 26, 1975; Paris Review Winter 1985, Summer 1991; Saturday Review May 17, 1975; October 29, 1977; June 23, 1979; Saturday Review of Literature March 7, 1931; Sewanee Review April 1948; Southern Review October 1975; Texas Quarterly Winter 1974; Texas Studies in Language and Literature Spring 1991; Time March 21, 1938; November 13, 1939; October 14, 1940; December 9, 1946; June 26, 1972; April 28, 1975; June 23, 1975; June 18, 1979; Times (London) June 13, 1972; Yale Review Winter 1987, Spring 1987.

**WILSON, FLORENCE ROMA MUIR.** See WILSON, ROMER

**WILSON, (ROBERT) FORREST** (January 20, 1883–May 9, 1942), American biographer, novelist, and historian, was born in Warren, Ohio, the son of James Forrest Wilson and Harriet Rose (Larned) Wilson. He was educated at Allegheny College in Meadville, Pennsylvania. Later he did graduate work at Cambridge University. He began his career as a newspaper reporter in Cleveland. From 1910 to 1916 he worked as a correspondent for the Scripps newspapers in Washington. He traveled throughout South America in 1916. During World War I he served as a captain in the chemical-warfare division. After his military service he worked with the Assistant Secretary of War, Benedict Crowell, in the preparation of *How America Went to War*, a six-volume compilation of data on such subjects as "The Armies of Industry: Our Nation's Manufacture of Munitions for a World of Arms, 1917–1918" and "The Road to France: The Transportation of Troops and Military Supplies, 1917–1918."

Wilson was European correspondent for *McCall's* from 1923 to 1927, during which time he lived in Paris and published an account of that city

(*Paris on Parade*) and an informal history of ancient Egypt (*The Living Pageant of the Nile*). In 1929 he brought out his first and only novel, *Rich Brat*, the story of an innocent American dress buyer making his way through the world of Parisian haute couture. A reviewer in the *Time Literary Supplement* wrote of it, "So circumstantial is the detail accumulated by the author, and so vivid

his rendering of the Parisian atmosphere and of the various characters with whom his hero comes into contact, that its improbabilities are readily condoned in one's enjoyment of an unusually fresh and brightly written novel."

Nothing more was heard of Wilson until 1941, when he published the seven-hundred-page book he had been working on in the intervening years, *Crusader in Crinoline: The Life of Harriet Beecher Stowe*. It won the Pulitzer Prize for biography and constitutes Wilson's only lasting claim to literary significance. Herbert Gorman wrote of it in the *New York Times Book Review*, "Mr. Wilson reveals himself as an astonishingly capable re-creator of period-tissue without obviously dragging in excessive background description. The color of the times is excellently communicated with the development of his subject, and in achieving this art of presentation he has surrounded Mrs. Stowe with all the panoply, emotions and constant stir of the long years through which she lived. She is never in a vacuum, as it were, but always moving, speaking and gesturing through her own times." However, feminism, and more subtle biographical methods, have with time overtaken this pioneer interpretation.

PRINCIPAL WORKS: *History and travel*—(with B. Crowell) How America Went to War, 6 vols., 1921; The Living Pageant of the Nile, 1924; Paris on Parade, 1925; How to Wine and Dine in Paris, 1930. *Novel*—Rich Brat, 1929. *Biography*—Crusader in Crinoline: The Life of Harriet Beecher Stowe, 1941.

ABOUT: Adams, J. R. Harriet Beecher Stowe, rev. ed. 1989. *Periodicals*—New York Times May 11, 1942; New York Times Book Review March 16, 1941; Times Literary Supplement November 14, 1929.

**WILSON, HARRY LEON** (May 1, 1867–June 29, 1939), American comic novelist, playwright, and the creator of *Ruggles of Red Gap*, was one of the most widely read American writers of light fiction in the first two decades of the twentieth century. His popular plays written with Booth Tarkington, and his comic novels featuring such characters as Bunker Bean, Ruggles, Ma Pettengill, and Merton Gill delighted unsophisticated

audiences—and even pleased many intellectuals of the day.

Only twenty years after his death, Wilson had become a quaint, all-but-forgotten relic of a bygone era. Carl Van Doren, in *The American Novel*, claimed that, the eclipse was due only "to short-sighted, low-spirited criticism," but he ignored the datedness of Wilson's style. "Many of the older generation have told me that just to hear Harry Leon Wilson's name again makes them smile in happy recollection," wrote George Kummer, his biographer, in *Harry Leon Wilson* (1963). Many stern critics of the time also enjoyed Wilson's work, including Mencken, W. D. Howells, and even Gertrude Stein.

Wilson was born in Oregon, Illinois, the son of

Samuel and Adeline (Kidder) Wilson. He preferred being a printer's devil at his father's local newspaper to attending school, and at seventeen he forfeited his education for a stenographer's job in the Omaha offices of the Union Pacific Company. Later he served as a secretary at the Bancroft History Company in Denver and in California, helping to collect stories of Western pioneers, work he called "a benign form of literary racketeering." After writing in his spare time for *Puck* for more than five years, he was offered a job by that comic weekly in New York. He served as its editor in 1896 until 1902. In the latter year he wrote a novel, *The Spenders*, the story of a Western family who squandered their mining fortune in Manhattan. Royalties from this provided him with enough money to leave New York, a city that depressed him.

Wilson and his second wife, Rose O'Neill, who, as "O'Neill Latham," illustrated some of his books (and later made a fortune as inventor of the Kewpie doll), moved to a rambling home in the Missouri Ozarks. But three years later, he was off to Capri and Paris to write plays with Tarkington, whom he had met in New York and who was impressed with Wilson's sentimental small-town boyhood tale, *The Boss of Little Arcady* (1905). The pair found more profit in plays than in novels, first collaborating on *The Man from Home* (1908), a sensational moneymaker in which William Hodge, "the Will Rogers of his generation," starred as the rough-hewn Hoosier lawyer who tackles Europe. Although future efforts were not so popular, the Wilson-Tarkington partnership continued to be lucrative, turning out nearly a dozen comedies that were perfect vehicles for the now dormant or demolished stages of rural opera houses and town halls. Settling in the writers' colony of Carmel, California in 1912, Wilson began to produce the best of his work, comic romance novels with memorably innocent characters "who blunder about amusingly in a booby-trapped world," Kummer wrote. H. G. Wells was the inspiration for Wilson's semi-autobiographical *Bunker Bean* (1913). The *New York Times* called it "clever, spontaneous, inimitable." In *Ruggles of Red Gap* (1915) a suave English butler who resembles P. G. Wodehouse's Jeeves but with a bit more depth comes to a Western cattle town as the result of a poker game. In 1922, MGM turned the novel into a silent film starring Edward Everett Horton; and Charles Laughton and Zasu Pitts starred in the memorably funny 1935 Paramount talkie, which is now probably Wilson's chief claim to fame. *Somewhere in Red Gap* (1916) introduced Ma Pettengill, owner of the Arrowhead Ranch, "a cracker-barrel philosopher" and one of the "resolute but motherly old hoydens who had braved the perils of the deserts and mountains, shot catamounts and rattlesnakes, and borne children on the floors of prairie schooners and in lonely ranch houses . . . if their husbands died, they carried on . . . Though some of them smoked, swore and drank whiskey, they were both respectable and respected by men and women in all walks of life," wrote Kummer.

A staple of many of Wilson's novels is the timid character, who after absurd experiences develops assertiveness or finds fulfillment. One of the most notable is Merton Gill of *Merton of the Movies* (1922), a mild-mannered clerk in a village general store who goes to Hollywood and unintentionally becomes a successful comic while trying to be a serious actor. Hildegarde Hawthorne in the *New York Times* called Merton "a triumph, artist, fool, likeable boy, baby, hero, all in one," and Gertrude Stein wrote in *Everybody's Autobiography* (1935) that the novel was "the best book about twentieth-century American youth that has yet been done." It found success on the stage, dramatized by George S. Kaufman and Marc Connelly. Wilson followed the same formula with the hypochondriac Rufus Billop, who finds incentive from a beautiful nurse to leave his sick bed and brave life's dangers in *Oh, Doctor!* (1923).

Having mastered the comic novel, Wilson tried to write a serious novel. *Cousin Jane* (1925), the story of an orphan, came close, but in it Wilson reverted to comedy. *Lone Tree* (1929), the story of a cattle rancher who strikes oil, was also praised for its blend of humor and wisdom, but Wilson, as Kummer wrote, "like his hero, Merton Gill . . . had to reconcile himself to being what God meant him to be—a comedian."

PRINCIPAL WORKS: Zigzag Tales from the East to the West, 1894; The Spenders, 1902; The Lions of the Lord, 1903; The Seeker, 1904; The Boss of Little Arcady, 1905; Ewing's Lady, 1907; (with B. Tarkington) The Man from Home, 1908; Bunker Bean, 1913; Ruggles of Red Gap, 1915; Somewhere in Red Gap, 1916; Ma Pettengill, 1919; The Gibson Upright, 1919; The Wrong Twin, 1921; Merton of the Movies, 1922; So This Is Golf!, 1923; Oh, Doctor!, 1923; Ma Pettengill Talks, 1923; Professor, How Could You!, 1924; (with B. Tarkington) Tweedles, 1924; Cousin Jane, 1925; Lone Tree, 1929; (with B. Tarkington) How's Your Health?, 1930; Two Black Sheep, 1931; When in the Course, 1940.

ABOUT: Dictionary of American Biography, 1958; Kummer, G. Harry Leon Wilson, 1963; Stein, G. Everybody's Autobiography, 1937. *Periodicals*—New York Times February 2, 1913; April 16, 1922; October 5, 1924; June 30, 1939; Times (London) July 1, 1939.

**WILSON, JOHN DOVER** (July 13, 1881–January, 1969), British scholar, editor, educational reformer, and critic, was born in London, the eldest of the six children of Edwin Wilson, an engraver and scientific illustrator, and his wife Elizabeth (Dover) Wilson. Wilson was a brilliant scholar from the first. He won a scholarship from Lancing, a public school situated on the Sussex coast, where his uncle was headmaster. He went up, again on a scholarship, to Gonville and Caius College, Cambridge where he read history. He graduated with second-class honors in both parts of the tripos (1902–1903), and in 1904 won the prestigious Harness Prize for an essay on John Lyly, the author of *Euphues* and an important influence on Shakespeare and his contemporaries. It brought him to the attention of the scholar A. W. Ward, who was just then editing the (still often consulted) *Cambridge History of English Literature*. Ward immediately assigned two chapters to the promising young scholar.

After a year of teaching at Whitgift School in Croydon, Surrey, near London, Wilson went to

Finland to take up the position of English Lektor at Helsingforth (Helsinki) University (1906). While in Finland he came to know Jean Sibelius, Edward Westermarck and other Finnish notables. It was in 1906, too, that he married Dorothy Baldwin, the daughter of a Canon of the Anglican Church. They had three children: a son (who pre-deceased his father) and two daughters.

Wilson was excited by Finland but relinquished his post there in order to take up an appointment (1909) at Goldsmith's College, in London. There he became interested in the cause of educational reform. He also became fast friends with each of the great bibliographical triumvirate of A. W. Pollard, W. W. Greg, and R. B. McKerrow, who laid the foundations of scholarly and scientific texts of Shakespeare and many of his contemporaries. Wilson was not perhaps himself a great bibliographer, although he did contribute much to what we know of the printers who set up the type of the First Folio, but he was undoubtedly a great editor. Dover Wilson and his colleagues prepared most of the ground over which contemporary scholars work. No one could write about Falstaff or Hamlet without referring to his critical work on those characters.

Dover Wilson's obituarist in the *Dictionary of National Biography*, Basil Blackwell, pointed out that when in 1912 his subject was invited to become an inspector for the Board of Education, it "meant that for over twenty years literary scholarship had to accommodate itself to the demands of another career." As an inspector Wilson had for long to do "a perpetual round of evening schools"; in 1921 he wrote the memorandum *Humanism in the Continuation School*, whose very title sums up one of its author's lifelong aspirations. Few did more, in fact, for culture among industrial workers than Wilson. When the scheme for continuation schools was dropped, in the 1918 Education Act, he felt that the nation's youth, and the men just back from First World War, had been cynically betrayed; he remained bitter about this. But he was able to serve on the poet Henry Newbolt's 1919 committee on the teaching of English and to contribute many valuable suggestions. In 1924 he was appointed to the chair of education at King's College, London.

Prompted by disagreements with Greg and Pollard, Dover Wilson became increasingly interested in the problems of Shakespeare's texts, which at the time had received an increasing number of emendations—some of them wholly speculative—from Victorian and Edwardian editors. Pollard had put forward the suggestion that some of the contemporary printed texts of Shakespeare's plays—the Quartos and then the First Folio—may have been much closer to Shakespeare's manuscripts than had previously been supposed. Dover Wilson, becoming, as he put it, "obsessed" with the various texts of *Hamlet*, began to seize on clues contained in the spellings and even in the misprints and mislineations of the texts, as revealing the men who did the printing. In 1919 the Cambridge University Press was looking for a scholar to join Sir Arthur Quiller-Couch in the editing of the *New Cambridge Shakespeare*. This edition (1921–1966), wrote Blackwell, "henceforth dominated his life." Of it, *A Shakespeare Encyclopedia* wrote: "[it] was the first to make use of the discoveries and methodology of scientific bibliographical criticism. . . . The first volume became something of a storm center as a result of the ingenious but often fanciful accounts of the various stages of composition and revision which, according to Wilson, the manuscript of the play had undergone. Many of these reconstructions derived from Wilson's essentially disintegrationist theories. . . . Others resulted in highly original explanations for textual idiosyncrasies. . . . Despite the lack of universal acceptance of his theories, the edition . . . is among the most valuable of the 20th century."

In fact it had been Dover Wilson who restored the reputation of "disintegrationist" theory. The notion that much or even most of Shakespeare's text was not in fact by him, but by other hands, had degenerated by the time of Wilson's youth into a mere craze. J. M. Robertson, for example, by applying wholly subjective "impressions" of Shakespeare's text, came up with the notion that all that he happened to think was "inferior" was by Marlowe, Dekker, or some other contemporary. Robert Greene, for example, had on this view written most of *Two Gentlemen of Verona*.

Wilson set forth a new and more acceptable—if not definitive—disintegrationist theory. He argued that some of the plays were in fact inspired revisions of earlier plays not by Shakespeare. It was under the stimulus and challenge of these arguments that modern views of the authenticity of the canon came into being. Wilson saw the First Folio as in part a patchwork of revisions of older plays (with, of course, exceptions); the accepted view now is that the thirty-six plays in the First Folio are by Shakespeare.

Wilson's 1911 edition of Elizabethan prose, the ever-valuable *Life in Shakespeare's England*, which he revised in 1956, has always been in print. His *What Happens in "Hamlet"* influenced performances of the play, especially those made by the great actor-manager Sir Donald Wolfit. His *The Fortunes of Falstaff* is still arguably a critical classic. He was generous and open-hearted. When, for example, in the immediate wake of his own important *An Introduction to the Sonnets of Shakespeare for the Use of Historians and Others* (1963), a new old-spelling edition of the *Sonnets* appeared, together with glosses on the text that had not been thought suitable for school until then (and which one scholar actively tried to suppress as "obscene"), he welcomed the new edition, praised its young author's candor (not easy for one of his generation), and commented that the modernized spelling that he had himself been forced to employ in the *Cambridge* edition was "only another form of emendation."

Wilson was made a Companion of Honour in 1936 and he received many honorary degrees and accolades. His first wife died in 1961, and two years later he made a second marriage to the former Elizabeth Emma Wintringham. Of the great scholars of his generation, he was the most daring and imaginative.

PRINCIPAL WORKS: *Criticism and bibliography*—John Lyly, 1905; Martin Marprelate and Shakespeare's "Fluellen": A New Theory of the Authorship of the Marprelate Tracts, 1912; Six Tragedies of Shakespeare: An Introduction for the Plain Man, 1929; The Essential Shakespeare: A Biographical Adventure, 1932; The Transmission: An Essay in Critical Bibliography, 1934; What Happened in "Hamlet," 1935, rev. ed. 1951; Leslie Stephen and Matthew Arnold As Critics of Wordsworth, 1939; The Fortunes of Falstaff, 1943; Shakespeare's Happy Comedies, 1962; An Introduction to the Sonnets of Shakespeare for the Use of Historians and Others, 1963. *Autobiography*—Milestones on the Dover Road, 1969. *As editor*—Shakespeare's England, 1911, rev. ed. 1956; The Schools of England, 1928; Various Plays in the Cambridge Shakespeare, 1929–1961; The Poetry of the Age of Wordsworth, 1927. *Other*—The War and Democracy, 1914.

ABOUT: Campbell, O. (ed.) A Shakespeare Encyclopedia, 1966; Oxbury, H. F. (ed.) Great Britains, 1985; Seymour-Smith, M. (ed.) *in* introduction to Shakespeare's Sonnets, 1963; Wilson, J. D. Milestones on the Dover Road, 1969. *Bibliography*—List of His Published Writings Presented to John Dover Wilson on His Eightieth Birthday, 1961. *Periodicals*—Newsweek January 27, 1969; New York Times January 17, 1969; Times (London) January 17, 1969.

**WILSON, MARGARET** (January 16, 1882–October 6, 1973), American novelist, wrote: "I was born in [Traer] Iowa, the most Middle Western of all Middle Westerners. My forebears were in no sense gentlefolk. Being farmers they were not good at keeping up appearances. Indeed, they were too poor to have an appearance to keep up. Yet they could stare reality in the face without batting an eye. They were strong and loving humans. I spent the allotted years in the University of Chicago, where I heard for the first time the venerable Eastern method of pronouncing my native tongue, and upon graduation I proceeded to India as a missionary—why, I am not altogether able to say. Being of a submerging disposition, I sank deeper into that country than the wise do, into Hindustan and Hindustani, into the Punjab and Punjabi, into Curmukha and Curmukhi, all of which are unsettling elements.

"I left India when I did because if I had not I should have died quite futilely of compassion. And when I wrote of India then, I signed myself 'An Elderly Spinster,' because I was at that time the oldest woman in the United States.

"That Oriental interlude had been, I found, an isolating experience. I didn't realize then that the years had absconded with my American point of view, and left me in its place a mongrel attitude. I only knew that Chicago was an excellent place for forgetting any sort of wisdom.

"In this land, if one is to write, one should by all means arrange to be a woman. For is it not true, as the comparatively masculine novelists complain, that a predominance of feminine readers punctures the puffs of masculine gender, while woman's productions can only gain in worth and beauty by the instructive comments of virile critics? I have, moreover, the great advantage of writing consciously for women, and from a point of view entirely feminine, for which—do I apologize?—I do not.

"I was constrained to spend some time in Chicago, and happened to get a chance to teach in a real school, where I taught with delight and satisfaction until I was fired. While I was looking about trying to persuade some other institution to let me amuse myself within it, I happened to hear an American lecturer who lambasted his exotic countrymen in a way so truly diverting that I resolved then and there to write myself a story wholly American. Then the fun began for me. If it continues even mildly for those who read me, I share their gratification."

---

Wilson was first known as a short story writer—publishing in *McClure's, Harper's Weekly*, and the *Atlantic Monthly*—before she became a novelist with a penchant for dialogue and messages. Her first novel, *The Able McLaughlins*, was the Harper Prize Novel for 1923 and took the 1924 Pulitzer Prize. Set on the frontier of the 1860s, the story concerns Wully McLaughlin, who returns from the army to find that his girlfriend is pregnant by her scoundrel cousin. The novel contains two of Wilson's recurring themes: the detrimental effects of religious and moral rigidity, and the subjugation of women.

*The Able McLaughlins* remained her best-known book. She followed it with two more "American" novels. Then she published *Daughters of India*, a novel about an American missionary in India. "So vivid is the narration that the reader can scarcely avoid the conclusion that the imaginary Davida Baillie is a convenient, but rather thin, disguise for the real Margaret Wilson," the London *Times* critic remarked.

Wilson's husband, whom she met in India, eventually became assistant commissioner of prisons for England and Wales, and was at one time the governor of Dartmoor and Wakefield prisons. Influenced by personal observations and her husband's views on prison reform, she published *The Crime of Punishment* in 1931. "The book is at once a history and a critique of methods of punishment . . . by a sensitive, sensible and unsentimental woman who can both think and write with tremendous vigor," the *Christian Century* reviewer wrote.

PRINCIPAL WORKS: *Novels*—The Able McLaughlins, 1923; The Kenworthys, 1925; The Painted Room, 1926; Daughters of India, 1928; Trousers of Taffeta: A Novel of the Child Mothers of India, 1929 (in U.K.: Trousers of Taffeta: A Tale of a Polygamous City); One Came Out, 1932 (in U.K.: The Dark Duty); The Valiant Wife, 1933; The Law and the McLaughlins, 1936. *Nonfiction*—The Crime of Punishment, 1931. *Juvenile*—The Devon Treasure Mystery, 1939.

ABOUT: The autobiographical material quoted above was written for Twentieth Century Authors, 1942. Dictionary of Literary Biography Vol. 9, 1981. *Periodicals*—Christian Century May 6, 1931; New York Evening Post September 12, 1925; Spectator September 28, 1929; Times (London) Literary Supplement May 10, 1928.

**WILSON, P(HILIP) W(HITWELL)** (1875–June 6, 1956), British journalist, biographer, and novelist, was born in Kendal, Westmoreland, the son of I. Whitwell and Annie (Bagster) Wilson. He studied at Clare College, Cambridge, where he was president of the Union Society and editor of *Granta*.

After a two-year stint as editor of the *Railway Herald*, Wilson was elected to Parliament as a Liberal for the constituency of South St. Pancras, Wales, in 1906. He was an MP until 1910. While in the Commons he introduced the first unemployed-worker's compensation bill.

After he lost his seat Wilson moved to the press gallery for twelve years as correspondent for the *London Daily News*. In the early 1920s, he moved to New York City, where he joined the staff of the *New York Times*. He wrote hundreds of Sunday feature articles and book reviews. He also lectured to American audiences on British life.

Many of Wilson's early works were inspired by his religious convictions, and were more evangelical than enlightening. Although no theologian, Wilson chose to draw upon examples from early Christianity to provide encouragement for those of wavering faith. In his preface to *The Church We Forget* (1919), he declared that his objective was to describe the primitive simplicity of Christ's cause to those living in a modern age of change

and upheaval; he believed that the story of the apostles could be seen as particularly relevant. "For what we need today is, after all, a missionary ardour and effort, a passion for the conquest of men's hearts and affections, and impulse towards comfort and rescue and healing and conciliation," he wrote.

This spirituality came to the fore once more in *The Vision We Forget* (1921), and culminated in *Is Christ Possible?* (1932). To Wilson, there was no doubt as to the answer to the question: "For individuals and nations, is life possible without Christ? Christ is not only possible but inevitable. There is none other who meets the need," he wrote.

Wilson wrote enthusiastic biographies, including those of the American merchant and philanthropist Robert C. Ogden, who was the partner of department-store magnate John Wanamaker, and the missionary William Edgar Geil; he also wrote about General Evangeline Booth of the Salvation Army. His biography of William Pitt was a more serious and scholarly effort.

In later years, Wilson turned to futuristic—even utopian—concerns. An authority on the calendar, he was an active proponent of calendar revision. In his amusing *The Romance of the Calendar* (1937), perhaps his most lively book, he surveyed the history of the methods of measuring time in various cultures and advocated a world calendar, a then-popular notion which he considered inevitable.

Soon after World War II began, Wilson, in the fashion of a fireside chat, presented his hopes for a better postwar world in *Newtopia* (1941). Simeon Strunsky wrote of it in the *New York Times* that Wilson's "perspective of the world . . . is much truer than . . . most of the very serious books on the world crisis that refuse to crack a smile. His picture of our human interests is more complete. It is a report on the state of the world grounded in understanding rather than in formula."

His final works, published in the mid-1940s, were three successful mystery stories, praised for their blend of romance, wit, and old-style detective ploys.

PRINCIPAL WORKS: *Nonfiction*—The Unmaking of Europe, 1915; The Christ We Forget, 1917; Two Ancient Red Cross Tales, 1918; The Church We Forget, 1919; The Irish Case Before the Court of Public Opinion, 1920; The Vision We Forget, 1921; A Layman's Confession of Faith, 1924; An Unofficial Statesman: Robert C. Ogden, 1924; Explorer of Changing Horizons: William Edgar Geil, 1927; Simon, the Cross-Bearer, 1929; William Pitt the Younger, 1930; Is Christ Possible?, 1932; General Evangeline Booth, 1935; The Romance of the Calendar, 1937; The Meaning of Moody, 1938; World Calendar Almanac, 1939; Newtopia: The World We Want, 1941. *Fiction*—Bride's Castle, 1944; The Black Tarn, 1945; The Old Mill, 1946.

ABOUT: Who's Who 1956. *Periodicals*—New York Times November 2, 1941; June 7, 1956; Publishers Weekly July 23, 1956; Saturday Review of Literature August 2, 1930; Times (London) June 8, 1956.

**WILSON, "ROMER" (FLORENCE ROMA MUIR WILSON)** (December 16, 1891–January 11, 1930), English novelist wrote: "I lived all my childhood in a dark old manor house on the edge of the moors just outside Sheffield. In this place, formerly the home of Bulsover, who invented electro-plating, and Plimsoll, who instituted the loading mark on ships, I lived from two to sixteen. Every summer we went to a seaside as

wild and cold as could be. Often also, our parents took us on the Continent. When I was fifteen I was suddenly transported to West Heath School, in the soft and luxurious landscape of the Thames Valley. After four years there, I went to Girton College, Cambridge, where I took up law. With considerable boredom I existed at college for three years, passed my examinations with mediocre honors, and through the influence of one of my professors began to imagine half seriously that I might one day write a book.

"I left college in 1914, hoping to have a pleasant social life such as most young women enjoy. The war put an end to these hopes. In the summer of 1915, tired with inactivity, I wrote a draft of *Martin Schüler*. A famous critic saw it by chance and suggested that I should make a novel of it. In three weeks I wrote the first half. Some time during the following year I tore it up and threw it in the wastepaper basket. In my absence a friend fished it out and painstakingly stuck it together. Not until 1917 could I tolerate the sight of it, when in another three weeks I finished it and shortly after had it accepted by a publisher.

"In the meantime, I had taken to war work. I sold potatoes for the Board of Agriculture, and at intervals wrote *If All These Young Men*, a book which no American and very few Englishmen have understood. Immediately after finishing it I wrote a play called *The Social Climbers*. This was followed almost at once by *The Death of Society*, which gained me the Hawthornden Prize in 1921. Shortly after the war I had spent three weeks in Paris, and the result was *The Grand Tour of Alphonse Marichaud*, a *nom de guerre* I had used myself in very early days when writing rubbish for a typewritten private magazine. It was while I was in Italy correcting proof on it that I met Edward J. O'Brien, the American anthologist, whom I married in 1923. Our affection for Portofino, where we had met, was so great that we returned there to live almost directly after our honeymoon, and only left it for Rapallo because there were no houses left in Portofino.

"When I was suddenly commissioned in 1927 to write the life of Emily Brontë, all my latent memories of the old times came back. It is only in this book that I have drawn directly upon what will always be to me a complete life in a country which is no more.

"I cannot, and never shall be able to write what I think people want. I cannot write for the public. I write very rapidly, but I do not scamp or hurry. I always rewrite my books twice, word by word from the beginning, and I have known myself to write a chapter seventeen times."

---

Romer Wilson was the daughter of Arnold Muir Wilson, a Sheffield solicitor, and the former Amy Letitia Dearden. She shared a flat in London with the novelist E. B. C. ("Topsy") Jones, where she became acquainted with Virginia Woolf and other literary luminaries.

It was at this time that she completed her first novel. *Martin Schüler* is a study of the "artistic temperament," exemplified in the life of a young German composer, from childhood in Heidelberg to death in 1914 in the Berlin opera house. He dies at his moment of triumph, during the production of his last opera. Many women had loved him, and he had used and misused them mercilessly to feed his creative energies, his voracious ego. Reviewers recognized this as a first novel of exceptional quality, "un-English" in its rigorous detachment from the mostly unattractive characters it observes. The *Boston Transcript* wrote: "the touch that removes a story from the ordinary brings it very close to greatness. It has a quiet power of analysis, pitiless in certain instances, but which labels it as a creation of art."

*If All These Young Men*, about the heroine's pursuit of love in postwar England, attracted less attention, not so *The Death of Society*. Its young hero,

wandering in Norway, visits an elderly critic and has a transfiguring love affair with his beautiful wife. After a day of ecstasy, the lovers decide to bow to social convention. They part, to wait in patience for a more emancipated world that might come "after the death of society." This was a passionately romantic book, remote from the cool analytic mode of the first novel. It had a very mixed reception. Some reviewers dismissed it as repulsive trash; others responded more favorably. A *New Statesman* critic thought that "its flimsiness, vaguenesses and sillinesses spring from the same stem as the quick, delicate perceptions which also abound in it. She has had the courage of her ignorance, her extravagance, her sense of beauty."

*The Death of Society* received the Hawthornden Prize in 1921. Virginia Woolf had predicted this in her diary for May 3 of that year: "Romer Wilson has brought out a novel—to which [John] Squire will certainly give the Hawthornden prize, thus robbing Katherine [Mansfield] of it; so I have some cause for pleasure. I write this purposely, to shame it out of me." Six days later, having read the novel, she wrote: "Well, but I assure you, when Virginia's old, no one will be talking of Romer Wilson. What a book! What a perfect example of the faux bon: every attitude, scene & word, I should say matched in the old word shop of the minor poets."

Romer Wilson returned to a German setting in *Dragon's Blood*; but it was the Germany of the troubled years after World War I. Friedrich Storm, a pastor's son with proto-Nazi political ambitions, falls in love with a prostitute and murders his rival, a corrupt young aristocrat who had been his idol and ally.

Later novels like *Greenlow*, a *Wuthering Heights* with a happy ending, and novellas like *Latterday Symphony*, were met with skepticism. The latter, which has a young Englishman and a black jazz singer falling in love with the same woman at a Mayfair party, seemed to A. B. Parsons "a nonsense melodrama of the passions done in the approved expressionist manner . . . Miss Wilson's is a real talent that seems to me to have befogged itself in an effort to take short cuts, to lay too violent hands on life, to gain a thing directly that can only be gained by circumlocution" (*New York Herald Tribune Books*).

Like the Brontës, Romer Wilson had grown up on the Yorkshire moors, and she had sometimes reminded readers of the author of *Wuthering Heights*. *All Alone*, her biography of Emily Brontë, is an intensely personal book, damned by some as incoherent and oracular. Clifton Fadiman, however, was impressed: "she admits constantly that her conclusions are the result of feeling and poetic sympathy. She may be totally wrong; but there is no one who can prove it; and there are many who will find her portrait of a greatly misunderstood genius marvelously convincing" (*Nation*). Wilson also wrote a play, *The Social Climbers*, about the decline of a Russian bourgeois family. She edited three anthologies of fairy stories. Her novels were forgotten, as Virginia Woolf had said they would be.

PRINCIPAL WORKS: *Novels*—Martin Schüler, 1918; If All These Young Men, 1919; The Death of Society: A Novel of Tomorrow, 1921; The Grand Tour of Alphonse Marichaud, 1923; Dragon's Blood, 1926; Latterday Symphony, 1927; Greenlow, 1927; The Hill of Cloves, 1929; Tender Advice, 1935. *Other*—The Social Climbers, 1927; (play) All Alone, the Life and Private History of Emily Jane Brontë, 1928 (in U. S. : The Life and Private History of Emily Jane Brontë). *As editor*—Green Magic: A Collection of the World's Best Tales from All Countries, 1928; Silver Magic, 1929; Red Magic, 1930.

ABOUT: The autobiographical material quoted above was written for Twentieth Century Authors, 1942. Blain, V. and others (eds.) Feminist Companion to Literature in English, 1990; Sinclair, M. *introduction to* Martin Schüler, Walpole, H. *introduction to* The Death of Society, 1928; Who's Who 1930; Woolf, V. The Diary, Volume 2: 1920–1924, 1978. *Periodicals*—Boston Transcript April 16, 1919; Living Age January 1931; London Mercury February 1930, August 1930; Nation June 27, 1928; New Statesman July 9, 1921; New York Herald Tribune Books March 13, 1927; Spectator May 26, 1923; Springfield Republican December 5, 1926.

**WINCHELL, WALTER** (April 7, 1897–February 20, 1972), American newspaper columnist and radio broadcaster, was the most famous columnist in the world at the height of his fame in the 1930s and 1940s. A journalistic institution, Winchell reinvented the gossip column and helped to create the American cult of "celebrity."

Born and raised in New York City, he was the son of Jacob Winchel and Janette (Bakst) Winchel (the second "l" was of his own devising: he claimed a careless electrician put it on a marquee sign advertising his short-lived vaudeville career). The stage and the news, his two lifelong venues, were in his blood at an early age. Working as a street corner newsboy and as an usher at the Imperial Theatre in Harlem, he had little time for school and quit in the sixth grade to be in a vaudeville act with George Jessel, Eddie Cantor and others, called the Newsboys' Sextette. After a two-year stint that saw only limited success, he formed the dancing duo of Winchell and Greene, with Rita Greene, whom he married in 1920 and divorced in 1922. He married another dancer, June Magee, in 1923.

In 1919, while on a national tour of second-string vaudeville houses, he began writing a gossip bulletin of the troupe called "Newsense." To many in show business, Winchell remained a nuisance for thirty more years, contributing columns to *Billboard* and then writing the column "Stage Whispers" and selling advertising for The Vaudeville News. He developed a following and by 1924 moved to the *New York Evening Graphic*, a sensational daily tabloid. "The era of the gossip column was born on the day when Walter Winchell was hired by New York's *Evening Graphic*, the sleaziest daily newspaper in the history of American journalism," wrote Milt Machlin in *The Gossip Wars*. Winchell's column there, "Your Broadway and Mine," was credited with providing the newspaper with a hefty portion of its circulation, and not long after he left for the *New York Daily Mirror* in 1929—where he stayed for more than thirty years—the *Evening Graphic* folded.

More popular than the newspaper itself, the self-styled "WW" or "Mrs. Winchell's little boy, Walter," "woke up a dreary phase of American journal-

ism," wrote Alexander Woollcott. In *Winchell: Gossip Power and the Culture of Celebrity*, Neal Gabler credits Winchell with creating the gossip column.

"He used no schooled rhetoric at all. His riffs depended on rhythm, brevity, and mocking parody, in ways reminiscent of song lyrics and vaudeville," wrote Harold Brodkey in *The New Yorker*. This breathless approach worked well on radio, where each week for more than ten years, Winchell turned his column into a Sunday night show that started with his trademark, "Good evening Mr. and Mrs. America—from border to border and coast to coast, and all the ships at sea." Winchell's influence was strongest from 1932 to 1942, when his combined radio and newspaper audience exceeded fifty million. His egotism was evident even in his humility. One dinner companion was reported to have said that his conversation ranged all the way from Walter to Winchell. He relied heavily on press agents he called "field representatives," for submissions, which were then usually written up by secretaries while he stayed home and slept off a night at the Stork Club. Truman Capote, Clifford Odets, Claire Boothe Luce, and Woody Allen submitted items to him, as did George Bernard Shaw and J. Edgar Hoover, the director of the FBI.

Winchell created his own American language, which could be called Winchellingo, as he frequently coupled two words to make one, for example, "Chicagorilla," "debutramp" and "intelligentlemen." In 1933, Wilford Funk cited Winchell as one of the ten most fertile contributors to American argot. However, in a list of Winchellisms that H. L. Mencken compiled for *The American Language*, in the belief that they were destined to become permanent, none can claim to have held more than a temporary vogue, and even "making whoopee" is now no more than passé slang.

Winchell himself said he tried to hide his illiteracy. But Brodkey wrote, "If you consider his sense of conspiracy and of sexual shenanigans, and also his distrust of high style (as British) and his use of a low, invented style, and consider his popularity, you can see that he had great literary impact. Writers who were growing up when Winchell flourished—Thomas Pynchon and Norman Mailer and Don DeLillo—show his influence."

By 1952, decline had set in. Winchell's column virtually disappeared with the death of the *New York Daily Mirror* in 1963. His son, in 1967, committed suicide. In 1968 *Esquire* reported, "Walter Winchell has been replaced. He is through—a has-been. His wife, June, died in 1970. His only book, an autobiography, *Winchell Exclusive: Things That Happened to Me—and Me to Them* (1976), was published posthumously. Wallace Markfield in the *New York Times* called it "a mean, ungenerous, crudely cynical book, boiling and seething with petty spite and prodigious malice—a love letter to himself, a poison-pen letter to the world."

PRINCIPAL WORK: Winchell Exclusive, 1975.

ABOUT: Current Biography 1972; Gabler, N. Walter Winchell, 1994; Herr, M. Walter Winchell: A Novel, 1989; Klurfeld, H.

Winchell: His Life and Times, 1976; Machlin, M. The Gossip Wars, 1981; Mencken, H. L. The American Language, 1936; Mosedale, J. The Men Who Invented Broadway, 1981; Thomas, B. Winchell, 1971. *Periodicals*—American Heritage November 1994; Collier's February 28, 1948; Editor & Publisher February 26, 1972; Esquire August 1968, October 1971; New Republic November 5, 1990; Newsweek October 27, 1947, May 7, 1951, October 14, 1957, May 5, 1958, October 10, 1960, March 6, 1972; New Yorker June 15–July 20, 1940; January 30, 1995; New York Post January 14–19, 1952; New York Times February 21, 1972, November 9, 1975; Publishers Weekly March 30, 1990; Saturday Evening Post September 1976; Time January 21, 1952; June 9, 1958, June 15, 1959, February 3, 1961, April 14, 1961, March 6, 1972, October 10, 1994.

**WINCH, JOHN.** See **LONG. G. M. V. C.**

**WINSLOW, ANNE** (1875–November 25, 1959), American novelist and short story writer, was born in Memphis, Tennessee, the daughter of William W. and Mary Frances (Blythe) Goodwin. Although she branched far from her birthplace during her early career as a writer, she returned to her roots to write her best work, delicate semi-autobiographical stories with a distinctively Southern style.

Winslow had no formal education but was taught at home by her father, an old-fashioned scholar who loved classical languages and literature. She married an  army officer, E. Eveleth Williams, and traveled widely in the United States and abroad, living at times in Switzerland and Italy. It was during her stay in Europe that she began writing poetry, which was collected into a volume, of indifferent verse, *The Long Gallery* (1925).

Nearly twenty years later, following her husband's death (1928), and in an act of "invoking the past for company," she published her memoirs, *The Dwelling Place* (1943), which she wrote after returning to her childhood home in Raleigh, Tennessee. Written as a "year-in-the-life chronicle," this mixed ghosts with real guests, her friends—both black and white, past and present—with peacocks and her Aunt Pauline. Her effort "to give something of the feeling of the life that has gone on about me in this place . . . to throw a little light on one little corner of the American scene" was generally considered humorous, observant and sensible. In a refined style she created a lagoon-like world in which genteel characters fall in love in small Southern towns at the turn of the century—slight stories written with polish and praised for their deftness, understanding and charm. In them, she evoked a warm and sleepy, inherently Southern scene in which personality and philosophy take precedence over plot. Whether on the delta plantation in *Cloudy Trophies* (1946) or in the little village of Cherry Station in *A Quiet Neighborhood* (1947), the most important actions are deep

thought and conversation. "Mrs. Winslow occasionally forgets that she is writing fiction, and in these off moments she is enchanting—reminiscing about her childhood, reflecting with wit and wisdom on the foolishness of the human race, and having her satiric but sympathetic say about the South," wrote a *New Yorker* critic upon the publication of *Winter in Geneva and Other Stories* (1945). In *The Springs* (1949), Winslow looked back to her youth to write of the emotional coming-of-age of a young Southern girl. The *New York Times* praised her "gentle, quicksilver touch, rare naturalness," and "a fresh discernment that is the essence of the true artist."

The author was fond of the work of Isak Dinesen, was herself compared to Katherine Mansfield and, as Diana Trilling observed, was obviously influenced by Henry James. "But I suspect that Mrs. Winslow is less a conscious disciple of the master than a parallel cultural manifestation," wrote Trilling in the *Nation*.

PRINCIPAL WORKS: The Long Gallery, 1925 (poems); The Dwelling Place, 1943 (memoirs); A Winter in Geneva, and Other Stories, 1945; Cloudy Trophies, 1946; A Quiet Neighborhood, 1947; It Was Like This, 1949; The Springs, 1949.

ABOUT: Current Biography 1948; Warfel, H. R. American Novelists of Today, 1973; Winslow, A. The Dwelling Place, 1943. *Periodicals*—Nation February 12, 1949; New York Times January 31, 1926; February 6, 1949; New Yorker March 24, 1945; Yale Review Spring 1949.

**WINSLOW, OLA ELIZABETH** (January 5, 1885–September 27, 1977), American historian and biographer, was born in Grant City, Missouri, the daughter of William De-  los Winslow, a banker, and Hattie Elizabeth (Colby) Winslow. After graduating from Stanford University in 1906, she taught in several preparatory schools in San Francisco until obtaining a position as an English instructor at the College of the Pacific in 1911. She received her Ph.D. from the University of Chicago in 1922 with the dissertation "Low Comedy as a Structural Element in the English Drama from the Beginnings to 1642." She continued to teach both English and American literature at Goucher until 1944.

Having published infrequently, and then with little notice, Winslow brought out in 1940 a Pulitzer Prize-winning biography of the Puritan divine Jonathan Edwards. *Jonathan Edwards, 1703–1758* was almost universally praised as in the *New York Times Book Review*: "chiefly admirable, perhaps, for the justice of its judgments, for the close and sympathetic understanding, never passing into panegyric, which it shows on every page. It is a wise as well as extremely able book."

Winslow moved to the English department at Wellesley College in Massachusetts in 1944 and taught there until her retirement in 1950. The following two and a half decades were the most productive of her life; in her sixties, seventies, and eighties she published four more biographies, including one of John Bunyan, and three studies of the religious and social life of colonial New England. If none of these works had quite the impact of the Jonathan Edwards biography, all were scrupulously researched and received respectful reviews from scholars. For example, a critic in the *Yale Review* wrote of *Meetinghouse Hill, 1630–1783*, "Winslow has succeeded in doing something which sounds nearly impossible: she has written a significant book on New England religious life without more than passing mention of theology. . . . In re-creating the New England meetinghouse and the life it symbolized Miss Winslow writes with sympathetic understanding, yet realistically and with a deal of quiet humor." Similarly praised was *Master Roger Williams*, a biography of the founder of Rhode Island. In the *New York Herald Tribune Book Review*, the historian Perry Miller called it "a deft portrait of the man. . . . Even though for many chapters of his life we possess less factual information than about others in the founding generation of New England, out of his writings emerges the vivid impress of a personality. . . . Winslow presents him with almost motherly affection, contrasts the lights and shadows, and does justice, as it seems to me no previous biographer has done, to the protracted poignance of Williams' long career in the service of [the] ideas of his society."

*Samuel Sewall of Boston*, a life of the jurist who presided over the Salem witch trials, was termed "full of shrewd analyses and insights," by the *American Historical Review* critic. "It makes both delightful and instructive reading, but one lays it aside with the conviction that a fuller study is required to bring Sewall to life for our day and age."

Winslow did much of her writing at her house near Sheepscot, Maine, and most of her research in Boston. Between 1950 and 1962 she served on the faculty of the Radcliffe College Seminars. Her last book, *A Destroying Angel: The Conquest of Smallpox in Colonial Boston*, was published in her ninetieth year. "A prodigious and painstaking worker [who] gently persuaded a whole generation of students to take after her," as *Time* magazine described her, Winslow never married.

PRINCIPAL WORKS: *Criticism*—Low Comedy as a Structural Element in English Drama from the Beginnings to 1642, 1926. *Biography*—Jonathan Edwards, 1703–1758: A Biography, 1940; Master Roger Williams, 1957; John Bunyan, 1961; Samuel Sewall of Boston, 1964; John Eliot: Apostle to the Indians, 1968. *History*—Meetinghouse Hill, 1630–1783, 1952; And Plead for the Rights of All: Old South Church in Boston, 1669–1669, 1970; A Destroying Angel: The Conquest of Smallpox in Colonial Boston, 1974. *Juvenile*—Portsmouth: The Life of a Town, 1966. *As editor and compiler*—Harper's Literary Museum: A Compendium of Instructive, Entertaining, and Amusing Matter, Selected from Early American Writings, 1927; American Broadside Verse from Imprints of the 17th and 18th Centuries, 1930; Basic Writings (by J. Edwards) 1966.

ABOUT: American Women Writers: A Critical Reference Guide from Colonial Times to the Present, 1982; Dictionary of American Biography, Suppl. 10, 1995. *Periodicals*—American Historical Review October 1964; New York Herald Tribune Book Review October 27, 1957; New York Times October 3, 1977; New York Times Book Review March 10, 1940; Time July 3, 1950; Yale Review Winter 1953.

**WINTER, JOHN KEITH** (October 22, 1906–February 17, 1983), English novelist and dramatist who wrote as Keith Winter, wrote: "I was born in a little village called Aber on the North Wales coast. My father was professor of agriculture at the neighboring University of Bangor and ran the university model farm. My early life was spent working and playing on the farm. My favorite occupations were riding—horses, cows and pigs—  and killing hens. When I was twelve, I was sent to school in Berkhamsted. Here I spent one abysmally wretched year, followed by four very happy ones. My first year was chiefly occupied in planning various methods of committing suicide. By the beginning of my second year I had more or less rid myself of an excessive inferiority complex. I represented my school in Rugby football and my house in running and gym. I was probably the worst cricketer in the school, and my detestation of that dreary game remains with me to this day.

"When I left school, aside from a vague inclination for acrobatic dancing, my plans for the future were nebulous, and consequently I found myself installed in a travel agency in London. In the six gloomy months that followed I found time to write a little book of short stories which was subsequently published at my own expense. As far as I know, no copy penetrated beyond the family circle, and so the title of this early masterpiece and its shining contents can be numbered amongst the dark secrets that will accompany me to the grave.

"At the end of six months' well-meaning incompetence in the travel agency, I anticipated my employers by giving notice, and became an assistant master in a preparatory school. In this profession I spent two and a half very happy years. In 1927 I went to Oxford and read history, but not very much. I spent three years there doing nothing, and I must admit they passed very quickly and pleasantly. In my last term, when I should have been assimilating the finer points of political economy, I published *Other Man's Saucer*. What the reviewers were pleased to call the 'outspokenness' of that book [which dealt with school life] brought my scholastic career to an abrupt termination. From that day no headmaster would even consider me as a possible candidate for his staff. A broken knee acquired while playing rugger had finally dispelled my dreams of acrobatic dancing, and so I had no other choice but to take up writing as a profession.

"My dramatized version of *The Rats of Norway* was produced in London, and since then I have written more plays than novels. I am married and live in London."

---

Winter, the son of Thomas Winter and Margaret (Baron) Winter, faded into relative obscurity as a Hollywood contract writer after several of his plays, staged in London in the mid-1930s, failed to excite audiences or critics. He never topped the success of *The Shining Hour* (1934).

Winter's first novel, *Other Man's Saucer* (1930), is adolescent in both tone and content. "A fairly routine piece of youthful highjinks and sophomoric audacity," wrote the *New York Evening Post* reviewer, who called the hero, Shaw Latimer—who has the careless habit of using someone else's saucer as his ashtray at tea time—"a sort of schoolboy version of Nietzsche's superman in a sweater and plus fours."

The self-destructive lemmings of the Norwegian shores inspired the title of Winter's next tale of preparatory school, *The Rats of Norway* (1932). "Mr. Winter has a distinct talent for comedy and apparently a real affection for little boys that scamper about like mice . . . Perhaps later on he will escape from what one of his young friends called the love-trash," wrote the *London Times*. L. A. G. Strong wrote in the *Spectator* that he hesitated recommending the novel or else he "should be overwhelmed with letters from indignant preparatory school headmasters all over the country." Winter dramatized the novel, and Gladys Cooper and Raymond Massey starred in the 1933 London production.

Winter returned to the novel with *Impassioned Pygmies* (1936), the story of an artist's colony on a Mediterranean island, whose characters were supposed to resemble D. H. and Freida Lawrence, Noel Coward, and Sinclair Lewis. Critics noted that Winter obviously wanted to write a successor to Norman Douglas's best selling *South Wind* (1917), but fell short on perspective. "I don't think the author realises that arrogance is an adolescent quality, not a virtue," wrote Cyril Connolly in *New Statesman and Nation*.

Celia Johnson starred in Winter's *Old Music* in 1937, which the *London Times* called "an opulent Victorian period piece" that had more visual than dramatic virtues.

In the 1940s Winter left London for Hollywood, where he worked as a contract writer. He collaborated with Leonard Lee on the screenplay of *The Chocolate Soldier* (1941), wrote the screenplay of *Above Suspicion* (1943), collaborated with Emeric Pressburger on the screenplay of *The Red Shoes* (1948) and worked on several less memorable films as well.

PRINCIPAL WORKS: *Novels*—Other Man's Saucer, 1930; The Rats of Norway, 1932; Impassioned Pygmies, 1936. *Drama*—The Shining Hour, 1934; Worse Things Happen at Sea!, 1935; Ringmaster, 1936; Old Music, 1937; Weights and Measures, 1938; We at the Cross-Roads, 1939; *Screenplays*—The Chocolate Soldier (with L. Lee) 1941; Above Suspicion, 1943; The Red Shoes (with E. Pressburger) 1948.

ABOUT: The autobiographical material quoted above was written for Twentieth Century Authors, 1942. Who's Who 1983. *Periodicals*—Bookmark December 1930; Nation February 28, 1934; New Statesman and Nation March 28, 1936; New York Evening Post November 22, 1930; New York Times March 22, 1936, February 19, 1983; Spectator February 20, 1932; Theatre Arts Monthly June 1934; Times (London) March 17, 1932; March 16, 1983.

**WINTERICH, JOHN TRACY** (May 25, 1891– August 15, 1970), American bibliophile and editor, wrote: "Born Middletown, Connecticut; moved to Providence, Rhode Island, in 1901, and educated at Brown University, graduating with B.A. degree in 1912; continued at Brown as assistant in the English department the following year; joined staff of Springfield, Massachusetts, *Republican* in 1913, and was reporter and  copy-reader until 1917, when I became a private in the United States Army, sailing for France in October, 1917; joined staff of the *Stars and Stripes*, official newspaper of the American Expeditionary Forces, the following February, and served there until May 1919, as reporter and copy-reader; made many trips to the front for the *Stars and Stripes* and am entitled to four battle clasps on Victory Medal; received citation from General Headquarters, A. E.F., for 'exceptionally meritorious and conspicuous services,' which carries with it the award of the Purple Heart medal; on return from France became managing editor of the *Home Sector*, which collided with the memorable printers' strike of the fall of 1919 but survived until the following April, at which time I became managing editor of the *American Legion Weekly* (later *American Legion Monthly*); became editor in 1924, and continued in this position to 1939; on staff of *PM*, 1940; on active duty as major, Officers' Reserve Corps, with Bureau of Public Relations, War Department, since October 1940.

"Served on editorial board of the *Colophon*, book collectors' quarterly, throughout its existence, 1930–1940 . . ."

———

John Tracy Winterich was one of his generation's foremost authorities on book collecting, and was himself the owner of a large collection of first editions. In addition to writing several highly-regarded books on the subject, Winterich contributed introductions to various volumes published by Limited Editions Club and was a versatile literary journalist. From 1938 to 1940, he was on the editorial board of the *Dolphin*, a literary journal, and in 1940 became staff member of the New York newspaper *PM*. During World War II, he served in the U.S. Army in Washington, D.C., as an advisor on censorship with the office of the undersecretary of war; he left the military in 1945 with the rank of colonel.

Soon thereafter, Winterich joined the staff of the *Saturday Review of Literature* (later the *Saturday Review*), first as managing editor, and later as a contributing editor. His column "Bookmarks" appeared in the *Saturday Review* from 1948 to 1956. From 1951 until his retirement in 1970, he wrote the column "Criminal Record," reviewing mystery fiction under the pseudonym Sergeant Cuff (adopted from Collins's detective in *The Moonstone*). These brief, witty reviews were honored by Mystery Writers of America, who in 1966 named Winterich Critic of the Year. In the years after World War II, Winterich was also on the editorial board of the *New Colophon*, and was a regular contributor to the *New Yorker*.

Winterich's most important work was *A Primer of Book Collecting*, which he revised several times, most recently just four years before his death. His valuable volume *Early American Books and Printing*, a standard work, examines the history of book-, magazine-, and newspaper-publishing in America from colonial times to the middle of the nineteenth century. *Twenty-Three Books and the Stories Behind Them*, essays on British and American book lore, was praised by the *New York Times* (1939) as "a book not only of scholarship but also of warmth and wit and taste and individuality."

PRINCIPAL WORKS: *Book collecting, publishing, and book lore*—A Primer of Book Collecting, 1926, 3rd. rev. ed. (with D. Randall) 1966; Collector's Choice, 1928; Books and the Man, 1929 (reissued as The Romance of Great Books and Their Authors, 1937); An American Friend of Dickens, 1933; (pamphlet) Early American Books and Printing, 1935; Twenty-Three Books and the Stories Behind Them, 1938; Three Lantern Slides: Books, the Book Trade, and Some Related Phenomena in America, 1876, 1901 and 1926, 1949; The Grolier Club, 1884–1950; An Informal History, 1950; Writers in America, 1842–1967; An Informal Glance at Some of the Authors Who Have Flourished Since the Establishment of the Davey Company One Hundred and Twenty-Five Years Ago, 1968. *Memoirs*—Another Day, Another Dollar, 1947. *As editor*—Squads Write! A Selection of the Best Things in Prose, Verse and Cartoon from the Stars and Stripes, Official Newspaper of the A.E.F., 1931; Your Literary I.Q., Selected from the Saturday Review, 1968.

ABOUT: The autobiographical material quoted above was written for Twentieth Century Authors, 1942. National Cyclopedia of American Biography, vol. 55 1974. *Periodicals*—New York Times January 15, 1939; August 17, 1970; New York Times Book Review August 31, 1947; Saturday Review June 27, 1970; September 12, 1970.

## WINTERS, (ARTHUR), YVOR (October 17, 1900–Janurary 25, 1968), American critic and poet

wrote: "I was born in Chicago. My father was at the time a free-lance trader or scalper on the Chicago Board of Trade, but a nervous and physical breakdown took him to California before my fourth birthday. He was a real estate agent in Los Angeles for a few years, then went to Seattle as an office manager in 1912, returned to Los Angeles in 1914, and shortly returned to Chicago. I followed my family to Chicago after about a year, spent three years there in high school and four quarters at the University of Chicago, with vacations in California as a milker on my uncle's dairy farm. After my first year in college I contracted tuberculosis and spent three years in bed in Santa Fé, N. M., and two more years as a school teacher (primer class and first, fourth, and fifth grades the first year,

high school English, French, zoology, baseball, basketball, track, and boxing the second year) in the coal camps of Madrid and Cerillos, south of Santa Fé. In 1923 I entered the University of Colorado and in 1925 took my M.A. there in romance languages. From 1925 to 1927 I taught French and Spanish at the University of Idaho; in 1927 I came to Stanford as a graduate student in English, and became an instructor in English there the following year. I took my Ph.D. in English at Stanford in 1934. I am now assistant professor there, teaching American Literature, English poetry, and a little composition. In 1926 I married Janet Lewis, author of *The Invasion*, and we have a son and a daughter.

"My best uncollected critical writing is to be found in the *Hound and Horn* during its last couple of years, and in an article on the English poets of the sixteenth century running in *Poetry*, February to April, 1939. In 1928 and 1929 my wife, Howard Baker, and myself edited a mimeographed journal, the *Gyroscope*, which ran to four numbers. I was also theoretically Western editor of the *Hound and Horn*, actually general advisory editor during its last two years. In this second capacity I laid the foundation for more literary enmities, and for enmities more intense, enduring, and I think I may fairly say unscrupulous, than I should judge have been enjoyed by any other writer of my generation. It was all quite unintentional on my part; I merely took literature seriously, and sought to achieve a precise style in my critical articles. I am at present the owner of a hand-press, on which I intend to publish my own poems [of] the past twenty years, the poems of my wife, and the poems of a few of my friends.

"My early poetry was written under the influence of Ezra Pound, William Carlos Williams, Marianne Moore, and others of their generation. About 1927 I began working in the traditional forms, and have continued to do so since. It is not infrequently said at present that my early work far surpasses my latter, but this opinion appears to me to be largely a part of a general effort to disparage my critical views by indirect suggestion, direct analysis being, it would seem, impracticable. Whatever the virtues of my poetry, past or present, absolutely considered, I think one may reasonably say that the later work surpasses the earlier, and will probably prove, in the long run, of greater value than my criticism."

———

Yvor Winters remained at Stanford until his retirement in 1966, becoming professor in 1948 and Albert Guerard Professor from 1961. The uncollected material he mentions was edited by Francis Murphy in a posthumous volume, *Uncollected Essays and Reviews*, in 1976. His *Collected Poetry* was also edited posthumously (1978) by an English admirer, Donald Davie. This volume in its unrevised form, originally published in 1952, had won a Bollingen Prize— awarded, perhaps, as much for its author's doggedness and determination as for the actual quality of the work (the citation specifically alluded to the "culmination of a poetic discipline").

Winters chose evaluation, rather than illumination of the text, as his primary purpose as a critic. Much of this criticism is marred by its bizarre claims, and by its indiscriminate use of the words "very" and "great." But for all that, the best of it survives because it *does* illuminate texts: by causing us to go back to them, and because it states the case against too thoughtlessly received opinion in a manner at least sufficiently cogent to engage our attention.

Yvor Winters has importance in modern American criticism: his views, highly eccentric—or at least unusual—seldom found acceptance. But they were so trenchantly (indeed, aggressively) argued that they provided a much needed challenge to received opinion. Stanley Edgar Hyman opened his hostile essay on Winters (in *The Armed Vision*) thus: "To the extent that the evaluation of works of art has not become an extinct critical function in our time, credit must be largely due to the redoubtable labors of Yvor Winters . . . Winters is a serious man, and in some respects quite a useful one, and it is regrettable that . . . he has become [to members of a generation younger than himself] largely a comic figure, the man who thinks that Elizabeth Daryush is our foremost living poet and that Edith Wharton is a better writer than Henry James."

His intrinsic importance as a critic is less certain, however, than his historical importance. But Winters was taken seriously, because he was, in Hyman's phrase, "a serious man." What seemed comic about him was his pomposity (as a writer), and his sense of his own rightness. As Hyman suggested, Winters was an insecure man; it is now evident that this insecurity arose, mainly, as a result of his uncertainties about the worth of his own poetry.

Francis Murphy, in his edition of the *Uncollected Essays*, was candid about Winters's serious failings. He wrote "Winters is more astute than most critics in pointing out some of the inanities of Whitman and Emerson, but his refusal to admit that eventually they saw the errors of their ways is willful and uncharitable."

Winters also played an important—if largely negative—role in the examination of the nature of the modernism which he so abhorred. Hating romanticism too much and too narrowly to achieve reasonableness or understanding (he came to distrust and fear it in himself), he nevertheless showed modernism to be more "inescapably romantic" than "Augustan"—as so many had claimed it was. Harold Bloom, who did not share Winters's attitudes, praised him (*Massachusetts Review*) thus: "A man who can tell us accurately and powerfully, what he dislikes, does a greater service than our host of church-wardenly purveyors of historical myths of decline."

Winters, within his limitations, can be helpful to us, even now, in our assessment of a peculiarly, indeed a notoriously, "difficult case" (as William Empson called it) in modern poetry: Hart Crane. The matter of his treatment of Crane is aptly illustrative of his critical methods, and of the degree and the nature of their usefulness. Winters had started his career as a poet partially as a disciple of Pound, imagism (in particular), surrealism—and Hart Crane. Crane's suicide was crucial in Winters's life as in his art. He had known Crane fairly well, although not intimately. Their friendship had come to an end when Winters wrote a careless review of *The Bridge* in *Poetry* (XXXVI, 1930) which has its good and its bad points, but is most notable for ignoring the obligations that most poets would attach to friendship and support for each other. Three years later Winters was emotionally devastated by Crane's suicide. It was this, Donald Davie said of Winters in his obituary in the London *Times*, that was most instrumental in his decision to repudiate modernism in favor of a rational approach based on "just feeling, properly motivated." Winters's critique of Crane is, though marred by its tone (increasingly that of an irascible infallibilist), and severely limited, still useful and relevant. Crane is, Winters rightly insists, the kind of poet who can "easily take possession of us wholly." Winters selected a few poems ("Repose of Rivers," for example, and "For the Marriage of Helen and Faustus," both from *White Buildings*) of Crane as "fine." For Winters the poem (and this defined his own aim in poetry, one attempted with considerable courage) had to make "a defensible rational statement about a given human experience."

He wrote (in *In Defense of Reason*) of Crane as "a poet of great genius, who ruined his life and talent by living and writing as the two greatest religious teachers [Emerson, Whitman] of our nation recommended . . . [he] . . . had not the critical intelligence to see what was wrong with his doctrine." He added that Crane was "worthy of our respect."

Winters's usefulness as a critic lies in his role as what Frank Kermode called, in his *Puzzles and Epiphanies*, "an assailant of temporary orthodoxies." Winters was usually sufficiently formidable, when his attentions were fully engaged, to make the reader think again about what he thought he thought. And some of his own hostile pronouncements may themselves become "orthodoxies."

The general view of Winters's poetry is summed up in what the poet Richard Eberhart wrote of the anthology, *Poets of the Pacific*, which Winters edited from the work of twelve of his one-time pupils: "too much form, too little fire." The translator and poet John Ciardi's *New York Times* (1947) commented on the second issue of the *Collected Poems*: "Read in chronological order, the poems reveal a steady movement from a first flirtation with Imagism (irregular forms, detailed and sparsely stated description, avoidance of any moral) to increasingly orthodox form (the couplet, quatrain, and sonnet predominate), an increasingly abstract diction, and a major emphasis on moral rhetorical statement. Mr. Winters chooses the tradition. Unfortunately, however, he chooses it intellectually, conceptually, scholastically. He is a poet who seems to refuse to enlarge the senses."

PRINCIPAL WORKS: *Poetry*—The Immobile Wind, 1921; The Magpie's Shadow, 1922; The Bare Hills, 1927; The Proof, 1930; The Journey, 1931; Before Disaster, 1934; Poems, 1940;

The Giant Weapon, 1943; To the Holy Spirit, 1947; Collected Poems, 1952, rev. 1960, rev. 1963, rev. as The Collected Poetry (ed. D. Davie) 1978; The Early Poems of Yvor Winters 1920–1928, 1966. *Criticism*—Primitivism and Decadence: A Study of American Experimental Poetry, 1937; Maule's Curse: Seven Studies in the History of American Obscurantism, 1938; The Anatomy of Nonsense, 1943; Edwin Arlington Robinson, 1946, rev. 1971; In Defense of Reason (reprints his first three critical books in rev. form) 1947, rev. 1960; The Function of Criticism, 1957; On Modern Poets, 1959; The Poetry of W. B. Yeats, 1960; The Poetry of J. V. Cunningham, 1961; Forms of Discovery: Critical and Historical Essays on the Forms of the Short Poem in English, 1967; Uncollected Essays and Reviews (ed. F. Murphy) 1976. *Short stories*—The Brink of Darkness, 1932. *As editor*—Twelve Poets of the Pacific, 1937; Selected Poems of Elizabeth Daryush, 1948; Poets of the Pacific Second Series, 1949; (with K. Fields) Quest for Reality: An Anthology of Short Poems in English, 1969.

ABOUT: The autobiographical material quoted above was written for Twentieth Century Authors, 1942. Hyman, S. E. The Armed Vision, 1947; Isaacs, E. An Introduction to the Poetry of Yvor Winters, 1980; Kermode, F. Puzzles and Epiphanies, 1962; McLean, K. The Moral Measure of Literature, 1961; Ransom, J. C. The New Criticism, 1941; Seymour-Smith, M. Macmillan Guide to Modern World Literature, 1986; Sexton, R. The Complex Of Yvor Winters's Criticism, 1974. *Bibliography*—Lohf K. A. and Sheehy, E. P. Yvor Winters: a Bibliography, 1959. *Periodicals*—Essays in Criticism 25, 1975; Massachusetts Review 7 1966; New York Times February 15, 1953; New York Times Book Review August 24, 1947; Quarterly Review of Literature Spring–Summer 1944; Sewanee Review 87 1979; Times (London) February 2, 1968; Times Literary Supplement August 30, 1974; Virginia Quarterly Review 54 1979.

**WINWAR, FRANCES** (May 3, 1900– ), American biographer and novelist, wrote: "I was born as Francesca Vinciguerra at Taormina, Sicily,  a little town that is considered one of the beauty spots of the world. The Vinciguerras trace their ancestry to the eleventh century. As an infant I was baptized in a basilica that was built in the Middle Ages; the Greek Theatre whose marvelously spaced columns frame Aetna and the Ionian Sea was my playground until my eighth year. I remember the tourists of all nations who used to come to Taormina during the 'season.' Perhaps from my exasperation at not understanding the *forestieri* [foreigners] dates my desire to acquire as many languages as possible. My father, a singer, used to take me about with him to the theatre and the hotel salons. By the time I was five I had acquired his repertory, which he was fond of having me repeat before his cronies. Boldly I would oblige with songs that used to be greeted uproariously and rewarded with sweets and sometimes money, which I was never allowed to keep. It was a gay life. Often it would be long past midnight when I was put to bed.

"Then came America, to which my father was drawn by the large promises of a friend. I was sent to the New York public schools, where I soon learned English well enough to compose a poem of eight lines which was published in the school magazine. The fuss that the teachers made over me and

the elation I felt in consequence probably encouraged me in the direction which, in my years of discretion, I decided to follow. Subsequently I attended high school and later college, which I left without taking a degree when life, during the tempestuous years of the war, promised much more than did academic seclusion.

"I do not remember the time when I was not writing something. In my eighteenth year I began sending my efforts to the literary magazines. *The Masses*, then edited by Max Eastman and Floyd Dell, published my first poems, a series of Japanese *tankas*. A year or so later the *Freeman* published an article of mine on Giovanni Verga. The article caught the attention of Laurence Stallings, who was then literary editor of the *New York World* and through his interest I reviewed books for him almost every week for two years. Meanwhile with a number of well-known artists and sculptors I helped found the Leonardo da Vinci Art School, which is still thriving.

"My first novel was autobiographical-of course. It was never published, for in a dramatic moment I re-enacted the first scene of *La Bohème* in my first studio with a fireplace. Free now to write objectively, I began my novel on Francesca da Rimini, which was published as *The Ardent Flame*. There was one condition to its publication: I had to change my high-sounding patronymic. Thus Francesca Vinciguerra became Frances Winwar-which, by the way, is a literal translation of the Italian name.

"In 1925 I married Bernard D. N. Grebanier, professor of English literature at Brooklyn College. We have a son.

"My list of favorite authors would take up too much room, though among my contemporaries I like Thomas Wolfe and Archibald MacLeish. In politics I belong to no particular party or faction, casting my ballot for the candidates who, in my opinion, best understand the meaning of democracy."

———

Winwar's parents were Domenico and Giovanna Vinciguerra; the family moved to America when Francesca was seven years old. Her first novel, *The Ardent Flame*, was a fictional life of Francesca da Rimini, one of Dante's more appealing sinners. *The Golden Round*, also set in thirteenth-century Italy, and *Pagan Interval,* on a modern Mediterranean island, were also novels, but it was with *Poor Splendid Wings* (1933), a narrative biography about the Rossettis and their circle, that Winwar discovered her medium. *Wings* was the first of many such biographies, accurate in the main, but told in a heightened and sentimentalized style. The book won a $5,000 Atlantic Monthly prize, and reviewers admired the author's ability, essentially journalistic, to soak up vast amounts of disparate information and then make intelligent use of it.

*The Romantic Rebels*, published just two years later, interwove the life stories of Byron, Shelley, and Keats, in what one reviewer called a "dovetailed" biography. After returning to fiction for *Gallows Hill*, a novel about witch-hunting in Salem, Winwar produced another group biography set in the Romantic period. In *Farewell the Banner*, about Samuel Taylor Coleridge and William and Dorothy Wordsworth, a tendency to overwrite began to draw negative comment from reviewers. Edgar Johnson, in *New Republic*, commented on "a turgid emotionalism like a seething beneath the surface of a pudding," and the great Wordsworth scholar G. M. Harper, in *Saturday Review of Literature*, said that Winwar "has read too much between the lines. Her book is neither straight fiction nor sound biography. It is excessively sentimental and gives an unfair impression of two great benefactors of mankind. Much of its rhetoric is cheap."

Frances Winwar was able to write more formally when the occasion required, as in her history of Salem, *Puritan City*. This book was also written in a colorful, popular style, but not overdone, and the information was authoritatively conveyed.

During the forties and fifties she continued to produce commercial biographies of reasonably high caliber. Her subjects included Oscar Wilde, Walt Whitman, George Sand, and Joan of Arc. Even in her single-subject biographies she took a "life and times" approach, to permit her to work on the broad canvas she favored. *Immortal Lovers*, her 1950 account of the lives of Robert and Elizabeth Barrett Browning, once again is highly readable, although by this time the vogue for overheated, sentimental biography was beginning to give way to the more solid and academic version of the genre. Newton Arvin, writing in the *New York Times*, summed up Winwar's work when he called her study of Edgar Allan Poe, *Haunted Palace*, "an easy, popular, rather woman's-magazineyish life, dependable enough in its information and often vivid as narrative."

In the later part of her career Frances Winwar began to produce titles for the juvenile market.

Frances Winwar remarried, following a divorce, in 1943, and again in 1949. She had one son by her first husband. Her translations include a Modern Library edition of *The Decameron* and various opera libretti.

PRINCIPAL WORKS: *Fiction*—The Ardent Flame, 1927; The Golden Round, 1928; Pagan Interval, 1929; Gallows Hill, 1937; The Sentimentalist, 1943; The Eagle and the Rock, 1953; The Last Love of Camille, 1954. *Nonfiction*—Poor Splendid Wings, The Rossettis and Their Circle, 1933; The Romantic Rebels, 1935; Farewell the Banner, 1938; Puritan City, the Story of Salem, 1938; Oscar Wilde and the Yellow Nineties, 1940; American Giant, Walt Whitman and His Times, 1941; The Life of the Heart, George Sand and Her Times, 1945; The Saint and the Devil, a Biographical Study of Joan of Arc, 1948; The Immortal Lovers, Elizabeth Barrett and Robert Browning, 1950; The Land of the Italian People, 1951; Napoleon and the Battle of Waterloo, 1953; Queen Elizabeth and the Spanish Armada, 1954; Wings of Fire, a Biography of Gabriele d'Annunzio and Eleanora Duse, 1956; The Haunted Palace, A Life of Edgar Allan Poe, 1959; Jean-Jacques Rousseau, 1961.

ABOUT: The autobiographical material quoted above was written for Twentieth Century Authors, 1942. Contemporary Authors vols. 89–92; Peragallo, O. Italian-American Authors and Their Contribution to American Literature, 1949. *Periodicals*—Boston Transcript August 19, 1933; New Republic October 12, 1938; New Statesman October 7, 1950; New York Times June 4, 1950; January 18, 1959; Saturday Review of Literature October 1, 1938; October 15, 1938.

**WISE, THOMAS JAMES** (October 7, 1859– May 13, 1937), English bibliographer and literary forger, was born in Gravesend, Kent, the eldest of the three children of Thomas Wise, a tobacconist, and the former Julia Victoria Dauncey. His parents were Baptists. Soon after Wise's birth, the family moved to Holloway, north London, where he grew up.

Wise was infinitely reticent about his life and career. The few details he did give out were frequently false. Thus, he claimed variously to have been educated privately and at the City of London School. According to Wilfred Partington in *Thomas J. Wise in the Original Cloth*, he was most likely educated at home on account of his delicate health. Tommy Wise began work in his teens as a junior clerk of Hermann Rubeck, a city merchant  in essential oils. He stayed with Rubeck's becoming an expert in these aromatic oils, which are used in perfumes and flavorings.

At seventeen, Wise began to spend his pocket money on old books. The interest grew rapidly into a passion, and he sometimes walked miles to work to save enough for a special purchase.

Wise had unfounded literary ambitions of his own. At twenty-three, the year after his mother died of tuberculosis, he published privately a collection of sentimental *Verses*. Wise also had both vision and judgment. In his early twenties he saw that Shelley and other great writers of the early nineteenth century, then out of favor, would not remain so—that the demand would come for their first editions. At twenty-five, earning less than four pounds a week, he paid £45 for a fine copy of Shelley's *Adonais* in the Pisa edition, then a record sum. Wise started to seek out surviving descendants of his favored authors or their associates, relieving them of unwanted family letters and diaries.

In 1886 the Browning Society published a facsimile edition of Browning's early poem *Pauline*. Wise, who had suggested the idea, supervised the work. It was done by a respected printing firm, Richard Clay and Sons, skillful and well-equipped. Some copies of this facsimile were "faked up" and sold as originals. Wise had no part in the deception and denounced it in the *Bookman*. But he was already nursing similar plans of his own, and believed that Clay and Sons would be useful to him. They were so almost at once, when Wise began to produce further facsimile editions for the newly formed Shelley Society. In this way, Wise gained typographical expertise and earned the trust of his printers. He needed both. Wise's plan was to produce copies of nineteenth-century pamphlets of poems or letters. They were to bear bogus imprints that seemed to establish them as earlier editions than any previously discovered.

Wise may have begun his forgeries as early as 1886. Early examples included Elizabeth Barrett Browning's *Sonnets*, George Eliot's *Brother and Sister*, and poems by Matthew Arnold, Browning, William Morris, Rossetti, and Swinburne. Having produced them, Wise had to establish them as genuine. He did so by selling a few copies cheaply, often to provincial booksellers, or depositing them at the British Museum. Once they were in circulation, or safely entered in the British Museum Catalogue, he could begin to sell them at prices reflecting their rarity. Along with this enterprise went the more or less legitimate publishing of assorted interesting items, like bowdlerized versions of some of Swinburne's more indiscreetly "festive" letters.

Wise was married in 1890 to Selina Fanny Smith. They moved into a house in north London: 52 Ashley Road. It provided the first home of the Ashley Library, and its name.

In 1893, Wise had been co-compiler of a complete bibliography of the works of John Ruskin—more than complete, since it included some of his own forgeries. It was the first in a long series of much respected bibliographies. The same year he became editor of a regular column in the *Bookman* devoted to "Recent Book Prices." Among the valuable publications he discussed were many of his own. Eventually, the flow of forgeries seems to have ended, though there were a few later cases of literary piracy. Wise, now very well off, began to acquire some of the Ashley Library's greatest treasures, outbidding rich American collectors for first-edition Elizabethan plays and poems, as well as later works.

The first sign of trouble came in 1898, when a correspondence in the *Athenaeum* cast doubt on the authenticity of a couple of Wise's pamphlets. Worse occurred in 1903, when the compilers of a monumental edition of Ruskin's works called in question four pamphlets listed in Wise's Ruskin bibliography, though without accusing him of forgery. The danger passed, and in 1905–1908 Wise published the first catalog of the Ashley Library. Its two volumes listed seven hundred items.

With the death of Swinburne in 1909, Wise bought from his companion and heir Theodore Watts-Dunton the best of the poet's remarkable collection of books and papers, including various unpublished manuscripts. He paid about £3,000. Wise rushed many of the manuscripts into print in pamphlet form, enlisting the critic Sir Edmund Gosse (almost certainly in on the swindle) as "editor." In 1912, Wise sold 700 pamphlets to Herbert Gorfin, an enterprising office boy at Rubeck's who was going into business as a bookseller. Nearly 600 of them were forgeries or piracies—presumably the remains of Wise's stock. The shop closed when Gorfin went off to fight in the First World War, but the deal was to have serious consequences.

There was a vogue for book collecting after the war, especially by Americans, and book prices soared. Wise reduced his buying but saw the value of his collection vastly increase. His fascinating bibliographies, whose annotations were full of "human interest" stories about his authors and their friends,

had brought him international fame. This was further enhanced by his skill in unmasking, with righteous anger, the forgeries and fakes of others.

The Ashley Library, at Wise's house in Health Street, Hampstead, had grown to seven thousand volumes. It included eighty-eight first editions, many unique and most in prime condition (apart from Wise's practice of rebinding almost everything in morocco). There were thousands of autograph letters. Wise's crowning achievement was the second *Ashley Library Catalogue*, published in eleven volumes between 1922 and 1936 and splendidly illustrated. Each volume had a flattering introduction by some famous bookman—among them Gosse, E. V. Lucas, John Drinkwater, Augustine Birrell. Honors followed. In 1922 Wise became president of the Bibliographical Society. Two years later he was made an Honorary Fellow of Worcester College, Oxford, and in 1926 Oxford gave him an honorary M.A.

In October 1933, Wise told Partington, he was visited by a "young man named Pollard, who fired at me a string of questions about some pamphlets." This was Graham Pollard, a young bookseller who, with his colleague John Carter, published in 1934 the most sensational work in the unsensational history of bibliography. It was innocently entitled *An Enquiry into the Nature of Certain Nineteenth Century Pamphlets*. Carter and Pollard had examined the texts, paper, and typography of more than fifty pamphlets. Twenty-nine were found to be forgeries, twenty were suspect, five were pirated. All of these pamphlets had been "discovered" or authenticated by Wise. He was not directly accused, but Carter and Pollard found it "difficult to believe that Mr. Wise cannot now guess the identity of the forger."

Highly technical though it was, the book made headlines even in the popular press. Wise claimed that Carter and Pollard were wrong about many of the pamphlets, but did not say which, or why. Otherwise he pleaded ignorance, pointing out that the forgeries had convinced older and more experienced bookmen than he had been when they came into his hands—mostly, he said, from another collector, a friend now safely dead. Wise suggested that the forgeries were the work of Richard Herne Shepherd, a pioneering bibliographer who had died insane in 1895. He denied that he had ever held stock of them. This was refuted by Herbert Gorfin in the *Times Literary Supplement*, in which a long correspondence ensued. Wise withdrew into silence, claiming ill health. He died three years later, aged seventy-seven. In 1937 the British Museum bought the Ashley Library for an undisclosed sum, and installed it in a room of it own. Some two hundred books entered in the catalog were found to be missing.

PRINCIPAL WORKS: *Catalogues*—The Ashley Library, 1895; The Ashley Library, 2 vols., 1905–1908; The Ashley Library, 11 vols., 1922–1936; A Shelley Library, 1924; A Swinburne Library, 1925; Two Lake Poets: William Wordsworth and Samuel Taylor Coleridge, 1927; A Byron Library, 1928; A Conrad Library, 1928; A Landor Library, 1929; A Brontë Library, 1929; A Browning Library, 1929; A Dryden Library, 1930; A Pope Library, 1931. *Other*—Verses, 1882; Letters of Thomas

J. Wise to John Henry Wrenn (ed. F. E. Ratchford) 1944; Between the Lines: Letters and Memoranda Interchanged Between H. Buxton Forman and Thomas J. Wise (ed. F. E. Ratchford) 1945. *As editor*—A Reference Catalogue of British and Foreign Autographs and Manuscripts, 1893; (with W. R. Nicoll) Literary Anecdotes of the Nineteenth Century, 2 vols., 1895–1896; Catalogue of the Library of the Late John Henry Wrenn, five volumes, 1920; (with J. A. Symington) The Shakespeare Head Bronte, 1931–1938; The Brontës: Their Lives, Friendships, and Correspondence, 1980.

ABOUT: Carter, J. W. Books and Book-Collectors, 1957; Carter, J. and Pollard G. An Enquiry into the Nature of Certain Nineteenth Century Pamphlets, 1934 (2nd, ed. N. Barker and J. Collins, 1983); Carter, J. and Pollard, G. The Firm of Charles Ottley, Landon and Company: Footnote to an Enquiry, 1948; Collins, J. The Two Forgers: A Biography of Harry Buxton Forman and Thomas J. Wise, 1992; Dictionary of National Biography, 1931–1940, 1949; Foxon, D. F. Thomas J. Wise and the Pre-Restoration Drama: A Study in Theft and Sophistication, 1959; Garland, L. The Affair of the Unprincipled Publisher, 1983; Lewis, R. C. Thomas James Wise and the Trial Book Fallacy, 1995; Partington, W. Forging Ahead: The True Story of the Upward Progress of Thomas James Wise, 1939; Partington, W. G. Thomas J. Wise in the Original Cloth, 1947; Ratchford, F. E. Review of Reviews, 1947; Ratchford, F. E. (ed.) Between the Lines: Letters and Memoranda Interchanged Between H. Buxton Forman and Thomas J. Wise, 1945; Todd W. B. (ed.) Thomas J. Wise: Centenary Studied, 1959; Wise, T. J. Letters to John Henry Wrenn, 1944. *Bibliographies*—(with J. P. Smart) John Ruskin, 2 vols., 1891–1893; Robert Browning, 1897; Algernon Charles Swinburne (scarcer works) 1897; Alfred, Lord Tennyson, 2 vols., 1908; Samuel Taylor Coleridge, 1913; George Henry Borrow, 1914; William Wordsworth, 1916; The Members of the Brontë Family, 1917; Elizabeth Barrett Browning, 1918; Coleridgeiana, 1919; (with S. Wheeler) Walter Savage Landor, 1919; Algernon Charles Swinburne, 2 vols., 1919–1920; Joseph Conrad, 1920; George Gordon Noel, Baron Byron, 2 vols., 1932–1933. *Periodicals*—Hobbies August 1951; Modern Language Notes February 1948; New York Public Library Bulletin November 1970; New York Times Book Reveiw July 3, 1949; Papers of the Bibliographical Society of America vol. 77, no. 3 1983; vol. 78, no. 4 1984; Times Literary Supplement October 19, 1956; September 17, 1982.

**WISTER, OWEN** (July 14, 1860–July 21, 1938), American novelist, was born in Philadelphia, the son of Owen Jones Wister, a physician, and Sarah

(Butler) Wister, daughter of the actress Fanny Kemble. Wister grew up in an artistic atmosphere: his mother played the piano, the family took frequent trips abroad, and numerous famous visitors—including Henry James—came to their house in Germantown. After briefly attending schools in Switzerland and England, Wister was sent to St. Paul's School in Concord, New Hampshire, and then enrolled at Harvard University, from which he graduated in music in 1882. An article of his on Beethoven was published in the *Atlantic*. Following graduation he studied music in Paris for another two years. Franz Liszt told his actress grandmother that the young man had a "*talent prononcé*," but loss of interest and poor health led Wister to give up a musical career. On his return to the United States in 1884 he worked for a short time as a bank clerk in New York City. By the summer of

1885 his health was in such serious jeopardy that he was advised by his doctor, as well as by his Harvard classmate Theodore Roosevelt, to spend some time in the West to restore his physical well-being. He lived that summer on a ranch near Buffalo, Wyoming—and returned to the West for many subsequent summers. In the fall of 1885 he entered Harvard Law School, from which he graduated in 1888. He became a member of the Pennsylvania bar and practiced law for two years in his native city.

It was in 1891 that Wister determined to write about the American West. His first story, "Hank's Woman," was eventually joined by three volumes of short fiction—*Red Men and White, Lin McLean,* and *The Jimmyjohn Boss*—whose vivid settings, colorful characters, and dramatic incidents were based on the detailed notebooks that Wister had kept during his summers in Wyoming. Although unrealistic (usually Wister gave way to sentimentality and melodrama), his short stories were a key contribution to the relatively new literary genre of cowboy fiction. However, it was his novel *The Virginian* that had the most significant impact. With a dedication to Theodore Roosevelt and illustrations (in later editions) by Frederic Remington, *The Virginian: A Horseman of the Plains* became a sensational success. Its dramatized version played in New York and on the road for several seasons; it was filmed by Hollywood three times. Although it now seems rather absurd, it did strike, within its genre, a new and bold note, particularly by implying that a hero of American fiction could have a variegated love life, that people in a lawless community would have to find laws for themselves—and that a young woman from New England could be unconventional out West. But above all, the virile and commanding figure of its knightly protagonist impressed the book's audience. A modest man, a quiet man—more comfortable with his horse than with people—the Virginian is nevertheless ready to defend himself and what Wister took to be his inborn sense of decency. His words "When you call me that, *smile* !" became the trademark of the cowboy of fiction and film.

Nothing that Wister wrote after *The Virginian* came anywhere near its influence or popularity. Other fiction included *Philosophy 4*, a story about college life at Harvard, *Lady Baltimore*, a novel about aristocratic Southerners in Charleston, and two collections of stories. His nonfiction work included *How Doth the Simple Spelling Bee*, a criticism of the simple spelling movement, and *Indispensable Information for Infants*, concerned with educational matters. He wrote three books on international affairs—*The Pentecost of Calamity* (about the causes of World War I); *A Straight Deal* (on Anglo-American relations); and *Neighbors Henceforth* (dealing with European reconstruction)—as well as biographies of three presidents: George Washington, Ulyssess Grant, and Theodore Roosevelt, the last drawn from personal reminiscences. He also wrote a farcical play called *Watch Your Thirst* (produced at the Tavern Club during Prohibition) and one book for young readers, *The*

*New Swiss Family Robinson.* His collected works were published in eleven volumes in 1928, a decade before his death. Wister married Mary Channing Wister, a cousin, of Philadelphia in 1898, and the couple had six children.

Owen Wister's papers are in the Library of Congress and the University of Wyoming Library.

PRINCIPAL WORKS: *Novels*—The Dragon of Wantley, 1892; The Virginian, 1902; Philosophy 4, 1903; A Journey in Search of Christmas, 1904; Lady Baltimore, 1906; Mother, 1907; Padre Ignacio, 1911. *Short stories*—Red Men and White, 1958; Lin McLean, 1898; The Jimmyjohn Boss, 1900; Members of the Family, 1911; When West Was West, 1928. *Nonfiction*—Ulysses S. Grant, 1900; The Seven Ages of Washington, 1907; How Doth the Simple Spelling Bee, 1907; The Pentecost of Calamity, 1915; A Straight Deal; or, The Ancient Grudge, 1920; Indispensable Information for Infants, 1921; Neighbors Henceforth, 1922; Roosevelt: The Story of a Friendship, 1930; Owen Wister's West (ed. R. M. Davis) 1987 (articles). *Drama*—Watch Your Thirst, 1923. *Juvenile*—The New Swiss Family Robinson, 1882. *Journals and correspondence*—Owen Wister Out West (ed. F. K. Wister) 1958; My Dear Wister: The Frederic Remington-Owen Wister Letters (ed. B. M. Vorpahl) 1972; That I May Tell You (eds. S. B. Wister and F. K. Wister) 1979. *Collections*—The Writings of Owen Wister, 11 vols., 1928.

ABOUT: Cobbs, J. L. Owen Wister, 1984; Etulain, R. W. Owen Wister, 1973; Payne, D. Owen Wister, 1985; Rush, N. O. The Diversions of a Westerner, 1979; Stokes, F.K.W. My Father Owen Wister, 1952; White, G. E. The Eastern Establishment and the Western Experience, 1968. *Periodicals*—American Heritage February/March 1981; American Literary Realism Winter 1974; American Literature May 1954; American Quarterly Fall 1960; American West September 1965, September 1970, January/February 1984; Atlantic May 1955, June 1955; New Republic September 2, 1972; New York Times July 22, 1938; PMLA January 1987; Saturday Review of Literature August 12, 1944; South Atlantic Quarterly October 1930, Winter 1986; South Dakota Review Spring 1971; Southwest Review Summer 1951; Times (London) July 22, 1938; Western American Literature Summer 1971.

**\*WODEHOUSE, P(ELHAM) G(RENVILLE)** (October 15, 1881–February 14, 1975), English novelist, short story writer, and playwright, was

born in Guildford, Surrey, England to Henry Ernest Wodehouse and Eleanor (Deane) Wodehouse. Henry Wodehouse worked as a British judge in Hong Kong, and, until the age of four, Pelham Grenville (known as "Plum" to friends and family) lived in Hong Kong with his parents and three older brothers. Returning to England, Wodehouse first attended boarding schools, receiving his secondary education at Dulwich College. There he distinguished himself as an outstanding classics scholar and as editor of the school magazine, the *Alleynian*. When he graduated in 1900, his father, who could not afford to send him on to Oxford, found him a position at the Hong Kong & Shanghai Bank in London. Wodehouse was unsuited for the duties of a bank clerk and struggled through the days so that he could get home and write. During his two-year tenure at the bank, he contributed eighty articles of humorous verse and

° WOOD house

fiction to such publications as *School Magazine*, *The Captain*, *Tit-bits*, and *Answers.*

In 1901, Wodehouse learned that one of his old teachers, William Beach-Thomas, was working as an assistant to Harold Begbie, the writer of the London *Globe*'s humorous "By the Way" column. Wodehouse asked Beach-Thomas if he could write for the *Globe* as well. One year later, Wodehouse was asked to fill in for a vacationing Begbie and took a week off from his job at the bank to write the "By the Way" column. He had already received an offer from the publisher A&C Black, which wanted to issue his serial *The Pothunters* as a novel. A career as a professional writer was fast becoming a reality, and, in September of 1902, Wodehouse resigned from the Bank to work as a freelance writer.

Wodehouse succeeded Beach-Thomas in 1903, and one year later he was the sole writer of the "By the Way" column for the *Globe*. Between columns, he wrote a series of juvenile novels about prep school life, including *The Head of Kays* (1905) and *Mike* (1909). In *Mike* the character Psmith was introduced. Arguably, the emergence of this self-important rhetorician marks the real beginning of Wodehouse's distinctive style. As Evelyn Waugh remarked, when "Psmith appears . . . the light was kindled which has burned with glowing brilliance for half a century."

Wodehouse also had profitable career in the theater as a writer of musical scores. In 1904 he was asked by the well-known playwright Owen Hall to write a song for Hall's play *Sergeant Brue*. The song was successful, and by 1906 Wodehouse had written two more songs, this time with Jerome Kern. Nine years later, when Wodehouse was working as a drama critic for *Vanity Fair*, Kern and Wodehouse met Guy Bolton. The three formed what would become a legendary collaboration in musical comedy, beginning by revising a musical entitled *Pom Pom*. Immediately thereafter they were hired to rewrite the operetta *Miss Springtime*, which received highly favorable reviews and became a huge commercial success. Wodehouse, Bolton, and Kern went on to write Broadway hits throughout the teens and twenties, including *Oh Boy* (1916), *Leave it to Jane* (1917), and *Sally* (1920). By the end of what would become a nearly fifty-year involvement with the theater, Wodehouse wrote, both alone and in collaboration with Bolton and Kern, the lyrics for twenty-eight musical plays, working with such figures as Florenz Ziegfeld, George and Ira Gershwin, Oscar Hammerstein, and Cole Porter.

Wodehouse's Broadway fame partly resulted from his long-held belief that America, not England, held the promise of true success. In 1909, Wodehouse moved to Greenwich Village, New York City. He immediately sold two short stories to *Cosmopolitan* and *Collier's* for a sum far more considerable than he had ever been paid in England, but a year later he was forced to go back to England and resume writing the "By the Way" column.

In 1914, Wodehouse returned to the United

States, still confident that he would succeed there as a writer. The *Saturday Evening Post* purchased several of Wodehouse's short stories, as well as the serialization rights for *Something New*, the first of his books to center on the comedic happenings at Blandings Castle. Reviewers immediately praised the book, calling it "the liveliest and most amusing of yarns." He was launched. A long succession followed, all very much alike, which suited Wodehouse's readers, who wanted more of the same.

Wodehouse would revisit the setting and characters of *Something New* many times throughout his prolific writing career. In 1929 he wrote *Fish Preferred*, a novel about two romances that occur in Blandings Castle. Reviews of the novel indicate that by this time Wodehouse was seen as a proven writer who could be depended upon to deliver entertaining fiction. *Fish Preferred* was described as "all in the best Wodehouse manner, and those who know Wodehouse need be told no more." Without resorting to overt satire, Wodehouse was able to mix comedy with a sensitive understanding of human foibles. Some forty years later he was still writing about Blandings Castle with a freshness and ebullience that appealed to a new generation of readers. In 1970 reviewers hailed *No Nudes Is Good Nudes* as "new and delightful" and its stock themes and characters as of a "fresh immediacy."

Wodehouse's most lasting literary creations are probably Bertie Wooster, the accident-prone young man about town, and Jeeves, his inceturbable valet. Jeeves and Bertie are the most famous literary duo since Holmes and Watson and seem likely to be as enduring. Wodehouse invented Wooster and Jeeves in his early short stories, later collected in *My Man Jeeves* (1919), *Jeeves* (1923), and *Carry On, Jeeves* (1927). The first novel centering on Wooster and Jeeves, entitled *Thank You, Jeeves*, was immediately greeted as "one of his very best."

The plots of these novels are usually intricate, Rube Goldberg contraptions (perfectly clear to the reader, however), but the real humor lies in the narrative voice: Wodehouse's comedy, like Damon Runyon's, is largely dependent upon language—in this case the argot of eager, well-bred nitwits who course through the higher reaches of British society, exclaiming, declaiming, always slightly in retard of the facts. Only Jeeves, it appears, can see life steadily and see it whole; only Jeeves, who speaks with a quiet, oily correctness, can arrange Bertie's hairbreadth escapes from irate elders, vicious pets, scheming blackguards, and a never-ending procession of energetic young women determined to make a proper husband of him. The result, in much the same fashion as the Blandings Castle stories, is a series of novels with relatively similar plots but that retain enough freshness and spontaneity to capture one of the most loyal readerships literature has ever known.

By 1934, Wodehouse was living in both England and Le Touquet, France. When France fell to the Nazis in 1940, Wodehouse was taken prisoner and moved from Le Touquet to various prisons and internment camps. Owing to the publicity surrounding Wodehouse's capture, he and his wife were eventually taken to Berlin and kept in a comfortable hotel. As the United States was not yet at war with Germany, Wodehouse was asked by the Americans to tape several broadcasts to the American people. He did so, taping five broadcasts from Berlin. The broadcasts were humorous reflections on his experiences as an internee, and included a word of gratitude to his captors for treating him decently. However, Britain was at war with Germany, and Wodehouse was still a British subject. The mere fact that he had transmitted over German airwaves made him liable to charges of treason. Wodehouse felt the repercussions of his actions in the form of attacks on him in the English newspapers, the expunging of his name from his alma mater's (Dulwich) records and the removal of his books from many libraries. While he had intended no harm, having little interest in political affairs, he was not able to return to England for fear of prosecution and was forced to settle in the United States. As time went on, his books had less and less to do with an actual England; increasingly they were set in a timeless fictional fantasy-world. In 1952, Wodehouse bought a ten-acre estate on Long Island, becoming an American citizen in 1956. English animosity towards him because of his wartime broadcasts had dissipated by this time, and Wodehouse was subsequently awarded a D.Litt from Oxford University.

The world in which Wodehouse's novels are set is strongly tied to the Victorian world in which he grew up; his plots also involve some fairly hoary devices and stock complications. But Wodehouse revised his language incessantly, polishing it and perfecting it so that it remained fresh and new. He was not a satirist, as his humor was often too light and slapstick to support the bite of satire. He published ninety-seven novels under his own name, sixteen plays, and many short stories and musical scores.

PRINCIPAL WORKS: *Fiction*—The Pethunters, 1902; The Gold Bat, 1904; William Tell Told Again, 1904; The Head of Kays, 1905; The White Feather, 1907; Love Among the Chickens, 1909; Mike, A Public School Story, 1909; Mike and Psmith, 1909; The Swoop! Or, How Clarence Saved England: A Tale of the Great Invasion, 1909; The Intrusion of Jimmy, 1910; Prince and Betty, 1912; Little Nugget, 1914; The Golf Omnibus, 1914; The Man Upstairs, and Other Stories, 1914; Something Fresh (in U.S.: Something New), 1915; Psmith, Journalist, 1916; Piccadilly Jim 1917; The Man With Two Left Feet, and Other Stories, 1917; Damsel in Distress, 1919; Their Mutual Child, 1919; The Little Warrior, 1920; Indiscretions of Archie, 1921; The Clicking of Cuthbert, 1922; The Girl on the Boat, 1922; Three Men and a Maid, 1922; Jeeves, 1923; The Adventures of Sally (in U.S.: Mostly Sally), 1923; Tales of St. Austins, 1923; A Prefects Uncle, 1924; Golf Without Tears, 1924; Leave It to Psmith, 1924; Bill the Conqueror, 1925; Sam the Sudden (in U.S.: Sam in the Suburbs), 1925; He Rather Enjoyed It, 1926; The Heart of a Goof, 1926; Carry on, Jeeves (in U.S.: Carry on, Jeeves!), 1927; Divots, 1927; Small Bachelor, 1927; Meet Mr. Mulliner, 1928; Money for Nothing, 1928; Fish Preferred, 1929; Little Warrior, 1929; Mr. Mulliner Speaking, 1930; Very Good, Jeeves, 1930; Big Money, 1931; If I Were You, 1931; Doctor Sally, 1932; Hot Water, 1932; Nothing but Wodehouse, 1932; Heavy Weather, 1933; Mulliner Nights, 1933; Brinkley Manor: A Novel About Jeeves, 1934; Thank You, Jeeves!, 1934; Blandings Castle and Elsewhere (in U.S.: Blandings Castle), 1935; Enter Psmith (in U.S.: Enter Smith), 1935; Trouble Down at Tudsleigh, 1925; Laughing Gas, 1936; The Luck of the Bedkins, 1936; Young Men in Spats, 1936;

Crime Wave at Blandings, 1937; Summer Moonshine, 1937; Lord Emsworth and Others, 1937; The Code of the Woosters, 1938; Uncle Fred in the Springtime, 1939; . . . Dudley is Back to Normal, 1940; Eggs, Beans, and Crumpets, 1940; Quick Service, 1940; Wodehouse on Golf, 1940; Money in the Bank, 1942; Joy in the Morning, 1946; Full Moon, 1947; Spring Fever, 1948; Uncle Dynamite, 1948; Mating Season, 1949; Nothing Serious, 1951; The Old Reliable, 1951; Angel Cake, 1952; Barmie in Wonderland, 1952; Pigs Have Wings, 1952; Mike at Wrykyn, 1953; Bring on the Girls!, 1953; Return to Jeeves, 1954; Jeeves and the Feudal Spirit, 1954; Bertie Wooster Sees It Through, 1955; America, I Like You, 1956; The Butler Did It, 1957; Cocktail Time, 1958; Few Quick Ones, 1959; French Leave, 1960; Jeeves in the Offing, 1960; The Ice in the Bedroom, 1961; The Most of P. G. Wodehouse, 1961; A Gentleman of Leisure, 1962; Author! Author!, 1962; Service With a Smile, 1962; Stiff Upper Lip, 1963; Biffens Millions, 1964; Frozen Assets, 1964; Plum Pie, 1967; The Purloined Paperweight, 1967; Do Butlers Burgle Banks? 1968; No Nudes is Good Nudes, 1970; The Girl in Blue, 1971; Jeeves and the Tie that Binds, 1971; Much Obliged, Jeeves, 1971; A Prefects Uncle, 1972; Pearls, Girls, and Monty Bodkin, 1972; Aunts Arent Gentlemen, 1974; The Plot That Thickened, 1973; The Bachelors Anonymous, 1974; The Cat-Nappers, 1975; Sunset at Blandings, 1978. Correspondence—Performing Flea: A Self-Portrait in Letters (intro. by W. Townend), 1953; Author! Author! (selections from Performing Flea), 1962. As editor—A Century of Humour, 1934; The Best of Modern Humor (general introduction to collection co-edited with S. Meredith), 1952; P. G. Wodehouse Selects the Best of Humor (co-ed., S. Meredith), 1965. Drama—(with J. Stapleton) A Gentleman of Leisure, 1911; (with J. Stapleton) A Thief for the Night, 1913; (with H. Westbrook) Brother Alfred, 1913; (with C. Bovill and F. Tours) Nuts and Wine, 1914; (with G. Bolton and H. Reynolds), Miss Springtime, 1916; (with G. Bolton) Ringtime, 1917; (with G. Bolton) Have a Heart, 1917; (with G. Bolton) Oh, Boy, 1919; (with G. Bolton) The Riviera Girl, 1917; (with G. Bolton) Oh! Lady, Lady!, 1918; (with G. Bolton) TheGirl Behind the Gun, 1918; (with F. Thompson) The Golden Moth, 1921; (with G. Bolton) Sitting Pretty, 1924; (with others) Showboat, 1927; (with I. Gershwin) Rosalie, 1928; The Plays The Thing (adapted from work by F. Molnar), 1927; (with V. Wyngate) Her Cardboard Lover, 1927; Good Morning, Bill (adapted from work by L. Fodor), 1928; (with I. Hay) A Damsel in Distress, 1930; (with I. Hay) Baa, Baa, Black Sheep, 1930; (with I. Hay) Leave it to Psmith, 1932; Candle-light: A Comedy in Three Acts (adapted from work by S. Gayer), 1934; (with G. Bolton) Whos Who, 1934; The Inside Stand, 1935; (with G. Bolton, H. Lindsay, R. Crouse) Anything Goes, 1936; (with G. Grossmith) The Three Musketeers, 1937; (with G. Bolton) Don't Listen, Ladies, 1948; (with G. Bolton) Carry On, Jeeves, 1956. Collections—Jeeves Omnibus, 1931; Louder and Funnier, 1932; Nothing but Wodehouse (ed. O. Nash), 1932; P. G. Wodehouse (ed. E. Knox), 1934; Mulliner Omnibus, 1935; The Week-End Wodehouse, 1939; The Best of Wodehouse (ed. S. Meredith), 1949; The Most of P. G. Wodehouse, 1960; Selected Stories, 1958; A Few Quick Ones, 1959; Plum Pie, 1966; Right Ho, Jeeves [and] Carry On, Jeeves (intro. M. Muggeridge), 1970; The Golf Omnibus, Thirty-one Golfing Short Stories, 1973; The World of Psmith, 1974; The World of Ukridge, 1975; The World of Blandings, 1976; Jeeves, 1976; The Uncollected Wodehouse (ed. D. Jasen, foreword by M. Muggeridge), 1976; Vintage Wodehouse (ed. R. Usborne), 1977; Wodehouse at Work to the End (ed. R. Usborne), 1977; Wodehouse on Crime: A Dozen Tales of Fiendish Cunning (ed. D. Benson), 1981; The World of Uncle Fred, 1983; The World of Wodehouse Clergy, 1984; The Hollywood Omnibus, 1985 Autobiography—Over Seventy: An Autobiography With Digressions, 1957; Wodehouse on Wodehouse, 1980.

ABOUT: Aldridge, J. Time to Murder and Create, 1966; Cazalet-Keir, T. Homage to P. G. Wodehouse, 1973; Current Biography, 1971; Dictionary of Literary Biography, vol. 34, 1985; French, R. B. D., P. G. Wodehouse, 1967; Green, B. P. G. Wodehouse: A Literary Biography, 1981; Heineman, J. and D. Benson (eds.) P. G. Wodehouse: A Centenary Celebration, 1881–1981, 1981; Jasen, D. A Bibliography and a Readers Guide to the First Editions of P. G. Wodehouse, 1970; Jasen,

D. P. G. Wodehouse: A Portrait of a Master, 1974; Sproat, I. Wodehouse at War, 1981; Usborne, R. Wodehouse at Work, 1961. Periodicals—Best Sellers March 15, 1970; Chicago Tribune October 15, 1981; New York Times February 15, 1975; October 18, 1981; November 12, 1984; November 7, 1985; October 20, 1987; March 23, 1989; New Yorker May 15, 1971; Paris Review Winter 1975; Times (London) November 24, 1983; June 21, 1984; June 29, 1985; July 9, 1987.

\*WOESTIJNE, KAREL VAN DE (March 10, 1878–August 24, 1929), Belgian (Flemish) poet, short story writer, and literary and art critic, was born and educated at Ghent. At the University there he studied Germanic philology. Soon after that he became the center of an artistic group; then he was a teacher in schools in the area, then a journalist and government official, until at last his literary fame enabled him in 1921 to acquire the chair of Dutch literature at his old university, a post he held until his premature death of tuberculosis.

In his early twenties Van de Woestijne came under the direct influence of, and associated with, the Van nu en Straaks movement, whose thus entitled magazine (meaning "Today and Tomorrow"), started in the 1890s, aimed to take a more or less moribund Flemish literature into the new century.

But Van de Woestijne had begun, at a very young age, as the center of a group of Flemish artists, which included his brother Gustave, and the sculptor George Minne, that gathered around him at the village of Laethem St. Martin: the group's aim was to combine piety, simplicity, and harmony with nature; later Laethem St. Martin was to become the center of Belgian expressionist painting, and to nurture the genius of Frits van den Berghe and Gustave de Smet. But the simplicity proved too much for Van de Woestijne, for he was a complex "decadent" par excellence, a partaker of some of the many and various fin de siècle manifestations, such as world-weariness (and "the heat-death of the universe"), distrust and/or hatred of convention, a blend of religiosity and atheism (or satanism), tormentedly heavy drinking, venereal disease, anguished self-indulgence, neurasthenia, and general unhappiness. It was a climate of thought influenced by, among others, Nietzsche, Oscar Wilde, Maeterlinck's Serre chaudes (1889), all the various symbolist movements, and even the early Rilke. The vast majority of those called decadents were minor writers—the more of the characteristics of decadence they possessed the more minor, no doubt, they were; however, such as Ernest Dowson and George Bacovia were also among them. And, reinforced by magic, and gnosticism as it was then understood, decadence could accommodate major artists too: the Russian composer Alexander Scriabin was one of these. Van de Woestijne was such another.

Therefore, like others thus characterized, the cosmopolitan Van de Woestijne was a highly original writer who operated self-consciously within a decadent context: Flemish literature has not yet had a poet of such high stature, and in the twentieth century in Dutch or Afrikaans, only Achterberg, and, to a lesser extent, Slauerhoff can rival him. Well known, and translated, in France, the cosmo-
°vuss TINE nuh

politan Van de Woestijne has yet to be fully introduced to an English-language audience. The initial
influences on his work include specific symbolist
recommendations of Baudelaire, the so-called
"sensitivism" of the Dutch *Nieuwe Gids* group,
Maurice Rollinat's *Les Névroses* (1883, The neuras-
thenics), and the poetry of Stefan George and Rilke—but also the neo-classicism of the Greek
Frenchman Jean Moreas.

*Het Vaderhuis* (1903, literally, "the father-
house") is not yet mature, but still highly individual. In a series of languorous poems Van de
Woestijne transmutes his recollections of childhood
into a strictly symbolic record. Two more mature
books are autobiographical in this way: *De Boom-
gaard der Vogelen der Fruchten* (1905, The orchard of birds and fruit), on his love affair and
marriage, and *De Gulden Schaduw* (1910, The
golden shadow), on his family life in Ghent. In
them, Van de Woestijne celebrates, with a deliberately decelerated lyricism, the beauties of nature
and the temptations of the Rubens-like beloved. He
saw himself as lustfully dissolving beauty: as, writes
Martin Seymour-Smith, quoting from one of his poems, "a hazel nut, and, simultaneously, as greedy
worm within it; as it devours his robust center he
becomes 'emptiness that does not speak or heed';
but, touched by a child's hand, he sings." There is,
writes Paul van Aken in the *Columbia Dictionary*
(1980) "no absolute victory of the spiritual over
matter in [his] work."

Van de Woestijne's greatest achievement in poetry is to be found in the latter two books mentioned above, although there are deeply moving
passages in the later poetry, such as, in particular,
the profoundly bitter *De Modderen Man* (1920,The
mud man) which begins a trilogy completed by
*God aan Zee* (1926, God by the sea) and *Het Berg-
meer* (1928, The mountain lake). The epics *Interlu-
dien* (1912–14) and *Zon in den Rug* (1924, Sun on
the back), consciously constructed on classical models in order to illustrate his critical beliefs, in a sort
of synthesis of classicism and symbolism, are impressive but far less good. As a whole the poetry is
sharply metaphysical despite its romantic and decadent trappings. To appreciate it requires hard
work on the part of the reader—thus Van de Woestijne has even been called "a poet's poet." He was
a learned man, and had insight into all his neurasthenic and emotional tendencies. But it repays such
work as it demands, and, in particular, it demands
response to a complex set of symbols through which
the poet refers to sexual matters about which, at
that time, he could not be explicit.

As a prose writer—art critic, story writer and essayist—Van de Woestijne made a leading contribution to Flemish letters. His book on the Laethem St.
Martin experience (1902) is illuminating. He came
under the influence, in both his later poetry and in
his prose, of the ornate style of the Spanish baroque
poet Luis de Gongora (one of the chief inspirations
for Lorca, Cernuda, and others), who resembled
him in a number of ways, especially since the Span-
iard's lush style is intellectually informed and very
consciously attained. In such erudite works as *Janus*

*met het dubbele voorhoofd* (1908, Split-Faced Janus—this was translated into German, *Janus mit
dem Zwiegesicht* in 1948) Van de Woestijne mixed
classical and Flemish folklore with medieval lore—
some of it obscure—in powerful books that were
fascinatingly baroque, and highly attractive in
principle but not so easy to read because of their
density.

A guide to his work may be found in his celebrated brief story, the most affirmative of all his writings, "De Boer de Sterft" (1918, translated and
published in Amsterdam as *The Peasant, Dying* in
1965). In Holland and Belgium this is a much-loved
classic. In this tale, five women, representing the
faculties of touch, taste, smell, hearing, and sight,
persuade a dying peasant that his life has not after
all been in vain.

Van de Woestijne's works have been twice collected, and Flemish and French critics have continued to write about him. A useful selection is one
translated into French by M. Lecomte, *Poèmes
choisis* (1964).

PRINCIPAL WORKS IN ENGLISH TRANSLATION: Twenty-One poems
(translated by C. and F. Stilman) in Jeune Belgique, 1950; The
Peasant, Dying (tr. J. Cantre), 1965.

ABOUT: Columbia Dictionary of Modern European Literature,
1947, 1980; Seymour-Smith, M. Macmillan Guide to Modern
World Literature, 1986.

**WOLFE, HUMBERT** (January 5, 1885–January
5, 1940), British higher civil servant, poet, translator, lampoonist, playwright, and essayist, wrote:
"Born Via Fattebenefratelli, Milan, Italy . . .
Brought to Bradford Grammar School . . . had the
great fortune, in Mr. Battersby and Mr. Barton, of
being under the care of two distinguished men of
letters, both in their own way poets. Left Bradford
for Wadham College, Oxford, and there started
writing verse, but was disturbed by metaphysics . . . entered the Civil Service by examination
in 1908 in the Board of Trade. Married two years
later to Jessie Chalmers Graham of Edinburgh.
Have one daughter. In the years 1910 to 1914 . . .
wrote a certain number of poems never published,
except occasionally . . . and a novel called "The
Count of Saldeyne," consistently refused until 1915
by all publishers, and then put away.

"During the war an ardent disciple of militarism,
and an official of the Ministry of Munitions, suffering violent change of heart when it was fashionable
to do so immediately af-
ter the Armistice. Recov-
ered a part of his
wandered soul . . . pub-
lished his first book, *London Sonnets* . . . A
certain amount of re-
viewing . . . in the *Saturday Review*
encouraged the continu-
ance of literary activities,
not wholly prevented by
writing for the Carnegie Foundation *Labour Supply and Regulation*. In 1921 . . . a second and
equally unsuccessful book of verse, *Shylock Reasons*

*With Mr. Chesterton. . . .* This was followed in 1922 by *Circular Saws*, which cut no wood or ice.

"The Author having now attained a position in which he is violently attacked by some of his brother poets, we may assume that he has reached the point fixed enough to suggest that he should be disestablished. His only merit is that of a hard worker, but the results of his work do not necessarily indicate that this is a merit. He is, of course, of Jewish birth and of no political creed, except that his general view is that money and its possessors should be abolished."

---

As a man of letters Humbert Wolfe was more of a short-lived phenomenon than a memorable poet in his own right. But while he lived he made news.

Wolfe, who changed his name from Umberto Wolff in 1918, was the younger son and third child of Martin Wolff, a German wool-merchant from Mecklenburg-Schwerin, and his Italian wife, the former Consola Terracini, from Genoa. The family came to Bradford to pursue its business. Wolfe was a brilliant scholar, and attained a first-class degree in classics in 1907. He went first to the Board of Trade, where he soon distinguished himself as a progressive civil servant by force of his flamboyant personality and his grasp of detail. With William Beveridge and others he was responsible for the creation of labor exchanges and unemployment insurance schemes. After representing Great Britain at conferences on international labor matters at Geneva, and acting as head of the department of employment and training in Great Britain (1934–1938), he became Deputy Secretary at the Ministry of Labour. His work in raising manpower for defense was notable.

In their time Wolfe's poems were very popular and widely read, but they do not survive now, even in historical anthologies. The *Oxford Companion to Twentieth Century Poetry* has this to say about him: "a quintessentially middle-brow poet, with some small lyric talent ('The dust on Agamemnon's shield' is a typical line), but no genius. His poems are almost always brief and to the point, and in their way well made. His sharpest work is concerned with the prejudice he encountered as a 'clever Jew'; he wrote an effective pamphlet attacking G. K. Chesterton for his anti-Semitism."

Wolfe's *Labour Supply and Regulation* (1923) remains in print, as a document of some importance in the economic history of World War I. The *Spectator* wrote of it that the author had "performed the incredibly difficult feat of presenting an orderly narrative of the confused efforts of various Ministers and various departments to find and retain workers for the munitions industry without depriving the Army of able-bodied men," and the *Times Literary Supplement* pronounced it "essential" to "future historians." It is likely that Wolfe's place in history will be secured by his work for the civil service, for which he deserves to be remembered. His memoirs are lively and interesting documents; but his essays in criticism, although often graceful and appreciative, lack sufficient substance to have survived their immediate occasion.

PRINCIPAL WORKS: *Poetry*—Shylock Reasons with Mr. Chesterton, 1920; London Sonnets, 1920; Journey's End, 1922; Circular Saws, 1923; Kensington Gardens, 1924; Lampoons, 1925; The Unknown Goddess, 1925; Humoresque, 1926; News of the Devil, 1926; The Silver Cat, 1927; Requiem, 1927; Cursory Rhymes, 1927; This Blind Rose, 1928; The Moon and Mrs. Smith, 1928; Dialogues and Monologues, 1928; Troy, 1928; English Verse, 1929; Early Poems, 1930; The Uncelestial City, 1930; Snow, 1931; Truffle Eater, 1933; The Fourth of August, 1935; Stings and Wings, 1935; Out of Great Tribulation, 1939; Kensington Gardens in Wartime, 1940. *Criticism*—The Craft of Verse, 1928; Notes on English Verse Satire, 1929; Tennyson, 1930; George Moore, 1931; Signpost to Poetry, 1931; Romantic and Unromantic Poetry, 1933; Ronsard and French Romantic Poetry, 1935. *Drama*—Reverie of Policemen, 1933; Don J. Ewan, 1937. *As translator*—Others Abide, 1928; Homage to Meleager, 1930; Ronsard's Sonnets pour Hélène, 1934; Heltai's The Silent Knight, 1937; Rostand's Cyrano de Bergerac, 1941. *Memoirs*—Now a Stranger, 1933; Portraits by Inference, 1934; P. L. M.: Peoples, Landfalls, Mountains, 1936; The Upward Anguish, 1939. *Historical*—Labour Supply and Regulation, 1923.

ABOUT: The autobiographical material quoted above was written for Twentieth Century Authors, 1942. Current Biography 1940; Dictionary of National Biography, 1920–1941, 1949; Hamilton, I. (ed.) The Oxford Companion to Twentieth Century Poetry, 1994; Sisson, C. H. Collected Poems, 1984; Wolfe, H. Now a Stranger, 1933; Wolfe, H. P. L. M., 1936; Wolf, H. The Upward Anguish, 1939. *Periodicals*—New York Times January 6, 1940; Poetry March, 1940; Spectator August 23, 1923; Times (London) January 6, 1940; Times Literary Supplement August 9, 1923.

**WOLFE, LINNIE (MARSH)** (1881–September 15, 1945), American biographer, was born in Michigan and educated in Idaho and at Whitman College (Washington) and Radcliffe. She taught in high schools in Washington and worked as a librarian in California. It was as a librarian in Los Angeles that Wolfe first became interested in studying the great naturalist, geologist, and explorer John Muir. Later, after she had gone to live

in Contra Costa Country, she met Muir's eldest daughter, Wanda Muir Hanna, and some of his old friends. Wolfe began to organize pilgrimages of school children to Muir's former home; she also gave a number of radio talks about him. In 1937 she was asked by the Muir heirs to prepare for publication some of his unpublished journals and notes. The work was offered the following year as *John of the Mountains*.

On the invitation of Alfred A. Knopf, Wolfe then undertook the writing of Muir's biography. The research for this work took her across the continent, searching, sifting, and evaluating. The resulting volume, *Son of the Wilderness: The Life of John Muir*, was published in 1945. The portrait of Muir won the 1946 Pulitzer Prize for biography. Not all reviewers accorded it unqualified praise: it was suggested, for example, that her enthusiasm for Muir was uncritical. But the book was both "lovingly researched" and "carefully written," as the cultural historian Richard Hofstadter conceded (*New York Times*). It is still in print.

PRINCIPAL WORKS: *As editor*—Memories of Pioneer Childhood (by E. White) 1936; John of the Mountains: The Unpublished Journals of John Muir, 1938; Son of the Wilderness: The Life of John Muir, 1945.

ABOUT: *Periodicals*—New York Times July 29, 1945; Time July 30, 1945; Weekly Book Review July 15, 1945.

## WOLFE, MARY E. See MADELEVA, SISTER MARY

## WOLFE, MORGAN DE. See WILLIAMSON, THAMES ROSS

**WOLFE, THOMAS** (October 3, 1900–September 15, 1938), American novelist, was born in Asheville, North Carolina, the son of William Oliver Wolfe, a stonecutter, and Julia Elizabeth (Westall) Wolfe, his third wife. Wolfe's parents separated when he was six years old, and he lived with his mother in the boardinghouse she owned and ran. He attended public school in Asheville until he was eleven. Because of his academic progress and potential he was enrolled at the North State Fitting School, a private institution, for the next four years. At fifteen he entered the University of North Carolina, intent on becoming a dramatist. His first play, a melodrama called *The Return of Buck Gavin*, was produced on campus by the Carolina Playmakers in 1919. He also edited the college newspaper and the literary magazine, before graduating with a B.A. degree in 1920. The success of his attempts at playwriting led him to enroll at Harvard University as a graduate student to study with Professor George Pierce Baker in his celebrated 47 Workshop. The group staged two of his plays—*The Mountains* and *Welcome to Our City*—but Wolfe was unable to find a New York producer interested in his work. He headed to the city anyway, and taught English at New York University intermittently from 1924 to 1930.

For several months in 1924–1925 Wolfe traveled in England, France, Italy, and Germany, keeping a detailed record of his impressions and attempting

to write short stories. In Paris he made the acquaintance of the novelists Sinclair Lewis and F. Scott Fitzgerald, and aboard ship returning to New York he met Aline Bernstein, a set designer for the Theatre Guild. Successful, married, and twenty years older, she offered Wolfe encouragement, understanding, and advice and was his lover for the next five years. During the summer of 1926 they traveled together in England. There, advised by her, he set aside his dreams of the theater and began work on a novel. Later in New York City she supported him financially while he struggled to complete it. The massive manuscript was submitted in 1928 to a number of publishers, who were daunted by the book's seemingly unmanageable length. Finally it came to the attention of Scribner's editor, Maxwell Perkins, who recognized its promise. He

cabled Wolfe that Scribner's would publish the book after major cutting, editing, and reshaping of the text. With a dedication to Aline Bernstein, *Look Homeward, Angel* was published to enthusiastic reviews and sold well. Its autobiographical contents, however, outraged residents of Asheville, who detected unflattering portraits of themselves, as well as Southerners who regarded the entire work as an insult to their traditions. The novel depicts the coming of age of Eugene Gant—a representation of the author—focusing on his North Carolina youth. Ultimately he vows to fulfill himself as an artist, and to experience life on his own, free from his roots and family. Reviewing it in the *New York Times* in 1929, Margaret Wallace wrote: "It is a book of great drive and vigor, of profound originality, of rich and variant color. . . . Wolfe has a very great gift—the ability to find in simple events and in humble, unpromising lives the whole meaning and poetry of human existence. . . . His style is sprawling, fecund, subtly rhythmic and amazingly vital."

With the royalties he received from sales of the book and a Guggenheim Fellowship he was given in 1930, Wolfe resigned from his New York University teaching job and sailed for France. He planned a sequel to *Look Homeward, Angel* which would delineate Eugene Gant's drive for fulfillment in Europe and his ultimate return home, his search accomplished. In Paris in 1930 he lived frugally, wrote continuously, and mingled with fellow expatriate writers. Before he started work on the projected sequel he completed a novella entitled *A Portrait of Bascom Hawke*. In 1931 he returned to the United States and rented a cheap apartment in Brooklyn to work on *Of Time and the River*. Living for the most part on coffee, beans, and cigarettes, he wrote steadily for the next few years. By 1934 he and Perkins were editing a manuscript larger and more digressive and episodic than *Look Homeward, Angel* had been. Perkins would cut lengthy sections, and Wolfe would supply new—but longer—passages. Without the author's final approval, Perkins sent the manuscript to the printer. Reviews were mixed: some critics objected to its excessive length and emotion; others saw its earnest lyricism as the appropriate balance to its seeming formlessness. Malcolm Cowley wrote in the *New Republic* in 1935 that the book was "better and worse than I have dared to say—richer, shriller, more exasperating. Cut down by half, it would be twice as good." Bernard De Voto, in a *Saturday Review of Literature* article entitled "Genius Is Not Enough," attacked Wolfe's failure in craftsmanship and judgment, noting that he presented all of the episodes of his thinly concealed autobiography as if they had the same importance. "Works of art cannot be assembled like a carburetor," he added, "they must be grown like a plant." But for all of this criticism, *Of Time and the River* was a best-seller. It was followed that same year with a collection of short stories, *From Death to Morning*, which were actually long sections that Perkins had excised from the manuscripts of Wolfe's two novels.

In July 1935 Wolfe attended a writers' conference in Boulder, Colorado. He gave a lecture (later published as *The Story of a Novel*) which described his writing habits and theories, and acknowledged his debt to his editor. But within a few months he broke with Perkins and left Scribner's, largely because he was upset over comments that Perkins's editorial acumen was the real basis for his commercial success. He spent several months of 1936 in Germany, but he was dismayed by the rise of Nazism. In the summer of 1937 he rented a cottage near Asheville and worked on his next novel, part of another grandiose fiction project whose autobiographical hero was to be called George Webber. During the winter he continued to write in New York. Before he left for a tour of western national parks in the summer, he gave Edward Aswell, his editor at Harper's, his new publisher, a draft of his book as well as a huge crate containing his papers. At Purdue University he gave a speech (later published as *Writing and Living*) in which he admitted that his previous fiction had been too egocentric and promised to focus more on social issues in his new work. He was traveling in the Pacific Northwest in July when he caught pneumonia. After initial treatment in Seattle his condition became complicated by tuberculosis, which he had apparently unknowingly contracted as a child. Despite a series of operations at Johns Hopkins Hospital in Baltimore, he died in September, a couple of weeks before his thirty-eighth birthday. He was buried in Asheville.

From the material that Wolfe had left in Aswell's care, Harper's extracted a pair of novels about George Webber—*The Web and the Rock* and *You Can't Go Home Again*—as well as a volume of short stories (*The Hills Beyond*) which deal with his forebears. Like Perkins before him, Aswell exercised considerable editorial license in molding Wolfe's fiction. These two novels reworked many of the themes and subjects of Wolfe's earlier books.

Wolfe's papers also included thirty-five notebooks and journals, working outlines and summaries for completed and planned novels, plays, and poems. Over the years most of this material has been published, as well as portions of his correspondence. His merit as a novelist has remained an issue of debate. In *You Can't Go Home Again* he wrote that he intended "to use myself to the top of my bent. To use everything. To milk the udder dry, squeeze out the last drop, until there is nothing left." In doing so without real regard for conventional literary technique, form, or style, Wolfe's output and outlook are suggestive of Walt Whitman's. As Alfred Kazin remarked: "Though he used his life and art interchangeably, they were, taken together, a reflection of Wolfe's conviction that he himself was a prime symbol of American experience and of a perpetual American ambition."

Thomas Wolfe's papers are in the Houghton Library at Harvard University, the University of North Carolina Library, and the Pack Memorial Public Library in Asheville, North Carolina.

PRINCIPAL WORKS: *Fiction*—Look Homeward, Angel, 1929; A Portrait of Bascom Hawke, 1932 (novella); Of Time and the River, 1935; From Death Morning, 1935 (stories); The Web and the Rock, 1939; A Note on Experts: Dexter Vespasian Joyner, 1939 (fragment); You Can't Go Home Again, 1940; The Hills Beyond, 1941 (stories); The Good Child's River (ed. S. Stutman) 1991 (fragment); The Lost Boy (ed. J. W. Clark) 1992 (novella). *Drama*—Third Night, 1919; The Mountains; 1921 Welcome to Our City, 1923; The Return of Buck Gavin: The Tragedy of a Mountain Outlaw, 1924; Gentlemen of the Press, 1942; Mannerhouse, 1948; The Streets of Durham, 1982; The Hound of Darkness (ed. J. L. Idol, Jr.) 1986. *Poetry*—A Stone, A Leaf, A Door (ed. J. S. Barnes) 1945. *Nonfiction*—The Crisis in Industry, 1919 (essay). *Memoirs*—The Story of a Novel, 1936; Thomas Wolfe's Purdue Speech: Writing and Living (ed. W. Braswell and L. Field) 1964; The Autobiography of an American Novelist (contains The Story of a Novel and Writing and Living; ed. L. Field) 1983. *Journals and notebooks*—A Western Journal: A Daily Log of the Great Parks Trip [1938] 1951; The Notebooks of Thomas Wolfe (ed. R. S. Kennedy and P. Reeves) 1970; Thomas Wolfe's Composition Books (ed. A. R. Cotten) 1990. *Correspondence*—Thomas Wolfe's Letters to His Mother (ed. J. S. Terry) 1943 (rev. as The Letters of Thomas Wolfe to His Mother; ed. C. H. Holman and S. F. Ross, 1968); The Correspondence of Thomas Wolfe and Homer Andrew Watt (ed. O. Cargill and T. C. Pollock) 1954; Letters of Thomas Wolfe (ed. E. Nowell) 1956; Dear Mabel: Letters of Thomas Wolfe to His Sister, Mabel Wolfe Wheaton (ed. M. L. Thornton) 1961; Beyond Love and Loyalty: The Letters of Thomas Wolfe and Elizabeth Nowell (ed. R. S. Kennedy) 1983; My Other Loneliness: Letters of Thomas Wolfe and Aline Bernstein (ed. S. Stutman) 1983; Holding on for Heaven: The Cables and Postcards of Thomas Wolfe and Aline Bernstein (ed. S. Stutman) 1985. *Collections*—The Face of a Nation (ed. J. H. Wheelock) 1939 (poetical passages); The Portable Thomas Wolfe (ed. M. Geismar) 1946; Short Novels (ed. C. H. Holman) 1961; The Thomas Wolfe Reader (ed. C. H. Holman) 1962; K-19: Salvaged Pieces (ed. J. L. Idol, Jr.) 1983; The Complete Short Novels (ed. F. E. Skipp) 1987.

ABOUT: Austin, N. F. A Biography of Thomas Wolfe, 1968; Berger, B. Thomas Wolfe, 1984; Bloom, H. (ed.) Thomas Wolfe, 1987; Cowley, M. Second Flowering, 1973; Doll, M. A. (ed.) In the Shadow of the Giant, Thomas Wolfe, 1988; Donald, D. H. Look Homeward: A Life of Thomas Wolfe, 1987; Evans, E. Thomas Wolfe, 1984; Field, L. Thomas Wolfe and His Editors, 1987; Field, L. (ed.) Thomas Wolfe: Three Decades of Criticism, 1968; Harper, M. M. The Aristocracy of Art in Joyce and Wolfe, 1990; Holman, C. H. Thomas Wolfe, 1960; Idol, J. L., Jr. A Thomas Wolfe Companion, 1987; Kazin, A. On Native Grounds, 1942; Kennedy, R. S. The Window of Memory: The Literary Career of Thomas Wolfe, 1962; Magi, A. P. and Walser, R. (eds.) Thomas Wolfe Interviewed, 1985; McElderry, B. R. Thomas Wolfe, 1964; Muller, H. Thomas Wolfe, 1947; Nowell, E. Thomas Wolfe, 1960; Phillipson, J. S. (ed.) Critical Essays on Thomas Wolfe, 1985; Pollock, T. C. and Cargill, O. Thomas Wolfe at Washington Square, 1954; Raynolds, R. Thomas Wolfe, 1965; Reeves, P. (ed.) Thomas Wolfe: The Critical Reception, 1974; Reeves, P. (ed.) Thomas Wolfe and the Glass of Time, 1971; Rubin, L. D. Thomas Wolfe, 1955; Rubin, L. D. (ed.) Thomas Wolfe: A Collection of Critical Essays, 1973; Snyder, W. U. Thomas Wolfe, 1971; Teicher, M. I. Looking Homeward: A Thomas Wolfe Photo Album, 1993; Turnbull, A. Thomas Wolfe, 1967; Walser, R. Thomas Wolfe, Undergraduate, 1977; Walser, R. (ed.) The Enigma of Thomas Wolfe, 1953; Wheaton, M. Thomas Wolfe and His Family, 1961. *Bibliography*—Johnston, C. Thomas Wolfe: A Descriptive Bibliography, 1987; Phillipson, J. S. (ed.) Thomas Wolfe: A Reference Guide, 1977. *Periodicals*—American Literature March 1989; Atlantic January 1940, November 1950, November 1957; Commentary January 1952; Harper's May 1958, April 1968; Journal of Modern Literature March 1984, July 1984; Life September 17 and 24, 1956; MELUS Summer 1987; Mississippi Quarterly Winter 1989/1990, Winter 1991/1992; New Republic March 20, 1935; March 23, 1987; New York Review of Books September 24, 1987; New York Times October 27, 1929; September 16, 1938; New York Times Magazine December 15, 1957; New Yorker February 9, 1957; April 12, 1958; Saturday Review of Literature August 17, 1935; Sewanee Review Spring 1989; Southern Review Fall 1982, Spring 1987.

**WOLFERT, IRA** (November 1, 1908– ), American journalist and novelist, was born in New York City, the son of Moses and Sophie (Seidl) Wol-

fert, and was educated in the New York public schools. He began his newspaper career as a copyboy in 1923. Three years later he enrolled in the Columbia University School of Journalism, and paid for this tuition by working as a streetcar motorman and taxi driver. In 1931 he and Helen Herschdorfer, a poet and writer whom he had married in 1928, went to Europe, where he found a position with the Berlin bureau of the *New York Post*. Seeing that the rise of Hitler was inevitable, they returned to New York the following year, and Wolfert became a correspondent for the North American Newspaper Alliance.

In the course of his career as a journalist, Wolfert wrote almost every kind of story—sports, drama criticism, interviews, and feature articles. What brought him fame, however, and established him as an author, was his battlefield reporting. His first book, *Battle for the Solomons*, which won the Pulitzer Prize in 1943, was based on his dispatches from the Solomon Islands during the fighting of October and November of 1942. P. J. Searles, in the *New York Herald Tribune Books*, called it "a keen, intelligent and brave reporter's story of as bitter, bloody fighting as the world has seen." Similar things were said of Wolfert's other accounts of military actions: a *New Yorker* critic wrote of *Torpedo 8*, the story of an American bomber squadron that survived the Battle of Midway, "Wolfert tells the story with a rapid, colorful vitality and an intelligent regard for scene and weather, and for the operation of men's minds in battle."

*American Guerilla in the Philippines*, an account of Navy Lieutenant I. D. Richardson's exploits behind enemy lines on the island of Leyte, was probably the most praised of Wolfert's three books about World War II. "Although successive episodes crowd each other, Wolfert has built up a suspense that will permit the reader only with the greatest reluctance to lay this book aside before reaching the end," wrote Donald Armstrong in the *Saturday Review of Literature* (1945). "The story of [Richardson's] and the guerrillas' activities will fascinate the reader. It is a story of courageous initiative, inventiveness, and cunning."

Wolfert's three novels were more ambitious, and less well achieved, than his nonfiction books. The first, *Tucker's People*, described the workings of the "numbers" racket in New York City during the Depression and its crushing effect on the people who got caught in it. "*Tucker's People* is slow getting under way, needs pruning in general, and there are overripe passages that badly misfire," wrote George Mayberry in the *New Republic*. "But the faults, like the virtues of the book, are the result of generosity and eagerness." *An Act of Love* was

a character study of a Navy pilot recovering from his physical and psychic wounds on a small Pacific island after his ship had sunk. By general consensus, the novel, though excellent in parts, was something of a mess, but the revised version, published six years later, gave Wolfert the chance (according to Norman Cousins in the *Saturday Review of Literature* [1954], "to do what almost every serious novelist who ever lived has dreamed of being able to do: to give added growth and dimension to a book apparently beyond reach."

At over one thousand pages, Wolfert's last novel, *Married Men*, was overwhelmed by its ambitions. Reviewers considered this story of a grasping entrepreneur and his effect on one community over the course of four generations a notable disaster. However, J. W. Aldridge, writing in the *Nation*, disagreed: "*Married Men* may be a crashing bore and a nearly crashing failure," he wrote. "But even at its most boring it is always serious, and even in its failure it testifies in a major way to the high quality of Mr. Wolfert's intent, the continued purity of his aspiration."

Wolfert's last book, *An Epidemic of Genius*, was a paean to advances in modern technology. Although it received favorable reviews, it was criticized for being overoptimistic.

PRINCIPAL WORKS: *Journalism*—Battle for the Solomons, 1943; Torpedo 8: The Story of Swede Larsen's Bomber Squadron, 1943; American Guerrilla in the Philippines, 1945; An Epidemic of Genius, 1960. *As told to*—One-Man Air Force (by D. S. Gentile) 1944. *Novels*—Tucker's People, 1943; An Act of Love, 1948, rev. ed. 1954; Married Men, 1953.

ABOUT: Current Biography 1943; Warfel, H. R. American Novelists of Today, 1951. *Periodicals*—Nation October 17, 1953; New Republic May 3, 1943; New York Herald Tribune Books January 24, 1943; New Yorker July 17, 1943; Saturday Review of Literature April 21, 1945; August 14, 1954.

**WOLFF, MARITTA MARTIN** (December 25, 1918– ), American novelist, was born in Grass Lake, Michigan, the daughter of Joseph and Ivy (Ellis) Wolff. "I was a

very lonely child," she wrote, "and seldom played with other children. I attended a one-room rural school, after the best American tradition, and began to write as soon as I grasped the essentials of penmanship—plays, poems, short stories. My greatest interest as far back as I can remember was in people—anything and everything happening to them." She also added: "I simply wrote down all that I picked up here and there about life and people in various small towns in Michigan."

At the University of Michigan, from which she graduated Phi Beta Kappa in 1940, she switched her major from journalism to English and won two awards for her short stories. Wolff wrote a novel in her senior year that was published by Random House the following season. *Whistle Stop*, the story of a large, impoverished family living on the outskirts of a Michigan town, was a much grittier novel than readers in 1941 might have expected from a twenty-two-year-old woman, and it attracted praise from reviewers. Its technical flaws were obvious, but its powerful realism won over most reviewers. The *New York Times Book Review* wrote: "Though it falters and fumbles very frequently, her book has a rich, raw vitality. . . . *Whistle Stop*, in short, is a most disturbing novel. It is also a very good one. . . . In its force, in its vividness, in its lack of sentimentality, in its refusal to compromise with the reader's natural squeamishness, *Whistle Stop* is brilliantly different from the average."

*Night Shift*, which followed *Whistle Stop* by one year, was a similarly grim chronicle of American family life, this time centering on a Michigan woman who struggles to support her children while her husband is in a mental institution. Despite some disclaimers regarding her lack of psychological penetration, the *Saturday Review of Literature* concluded that Wolff was "vigorous, talented, a brilliant observer, a ruthless realist—naturalist would be the better word—and best of all, master of a wealth of knowledge and material that she has only begun to turn over. In *Night Shift* all of these qualities are displayed with marvelous ease."

Wolff's remaining four novels seldom strayed from the vein of earthy (some would have said sordid) realism that she employed in her first two books, and although it was felt that she never fulfilled the promise of *Whistle Stop*, her later works continued to earn her respectful reviews. For example, a critic in the *New York Herald Tribune Book Review* wrote of *Back of Town*, the story of a man's involvement with three women in a small midwestern town, "If you read *Whistle Stop* and *Night Shift* you have, in a sense, read *Back of Town*. The story and the characters are different, of course, but this is the same murky, bleak, rich, coarse, brilliant, sordid section on the edge of town where life is an unceasing struggle relieved by only occasional flashes of softness."

Wolff's most recent novel, *Buttonwood*, appeared in 1962. Virtually nothing has been written about her since then, and all her books have gone out of print.

PRINCIPAL WORKS: *Novels*—Whistle Stop, 1941; Night Shift, 1942; About Liddy Thomas, 1947; Back of Town, 1952; The Big Nickelodeon, 1956; Buttonwood, 1962.

ABOUT: The autobiographical material quoted above was written for Twentieth Century Authors First Supplement, 1955. Contemporary Authors vols. 17–20, 1976; Current Biography 1941. *Periodicals*—Chicago Sunday Tribune October 28, 1956; New York Herald Tribune Book Review April 6, 1952; New York Times Book Review May 18, 1941; Saturday Review of Literature November 21, 1942.

**WOLFSON, VICTOR** (March 8, 1910–May 23, 1990), American playwright and novelist, was born on New Yorks Lower East Side to Adolph and Rebecca (Hochstein) Wolfson. His father, who was described as "a handsome and eloquent Russian ex-revolutionary," moved the family out of New York City to an upstate farm while Victor was a child. He was educated in New York City, however, at the Ethical Culture School, and helped meet ex-

penses by working backstage at the Neighborhood Playhouse. Determined to make the theater his career, Wolfson enrolled at the University of Wisconsin to study at its experimental theater. He received his B.A. in 1931 and in the following year reached Broadway as assistant stage manager in the highly successful production of Elmer Rice's play *Counsellor-at-Law*. He followed this with other writing, directing, and producing jobs.

From 1933 to 1936 he was on the executive board of the Theatre Union. Later, he was also secretary of the Authors League of America, secretary of the Dramatists Guild, and a lecturer in drama at New York University.

Wolfson's first produced play was his adaptation, with Victor Trivas, of Dostoyevski's *Crime and Punishment*, which opened on Broadway in 1935. He saw his first commercial success a year later with *Bitter Stream*, adaptation fo Silone's *Fontamara*.

His own most successful play, the openly sentimental *Excursion* (1937), takes place on an old Coney Island excursion boat called "Happiness." Its passengers are tempted to evade reality by visiting a magic island. Stark Young, in the *New Republic*, called it "a pretty fable," but said that it "needs . . . a decision in tone." Burns Mantle, however, selected it as one of the ten best plays of the 1937 season.

None of Wolfson's later plays equaled this success. *Pastoral*, a comedy set in the Catskills, saw only a very brief run in 1939; *The Family*, adapted from Nina Fedorovas novel, ran for only seven performances, and *Prides Crossing*, about a vicious servant who seeks to dominate a household, closed after eight performances in 1950. A better reception was accorded *American Gothic*, Wolfsons dramatization of his novel *The Lonely Steeple*. This were produced off-Broadway at the Circle-in-the-Square, under the direction of Jose Quintero in 1953. Two other plays ran outside New York— *Love in the City* in Cleveland (1947) and *A Murder in the Family* at the Berkshire Playhouse (1952)— but more importantly, a number of Wolfsons scripts were aired on radio and television. He contributed regularly to *Alfred Hitchcock Presents*, *Five Star Matinee*, and other programs of the "golden age" of television, and in 1961 won an Emmy Award from the National Academy of Television Arts and Sciences for the episodes he had written for ABC's series *Winston Churchill: The Valiant Years*.

Wolfson also wrote short stories for the *New Yorker*, *Harpers*, and other periodicals. His theatrical experience stood him in good stead in the use of dialogue and the development of suspense. His first novel, *The Lonely Steeple*, published in 1945, was essentially a melodrama about a paranoid New England woman (and became a literal melodrama eight years later, when Wolfson adapted it for the stage). In the Weekly Book Review, Iris Barry called it "more than a tale of poverty and outrage, of incest and murder; it is an intimate analysis of a human being pushed inevitably beyond the borders of sanity." Wolfsons second novel, *Eagle on the Plain*, was a complete change of pace—a "folk story" set in the Appalachian Catskills (where the author had grown up), criticized mainly for being "too consciously mellow." Diana Trilling described it as "a fable of freedom . . . at once truly touching and uncomfortably inflated." Under the pseudonym "Langdon Dodge" he tried his hand at detective fiction in *Midsummer Madness* (1950), without much success. But in 1969 he turned to historical mystery in *The Mayerling Murder* (1969), a reexamination of the famous *liebestod* of Crown Prince Rudolph of Austria-Hungary and his mistress, Marie Vetsera. Wolfson argued that this was not a lovers's suicide at all, but the result of murderous political intrigue. Reviewers found his scenario interesting and even plausible, but not conclusive.

PRINCIPAL WORKS: *Drama*—(with V. Trivas) Crime and Punishment (adaptation of the novel by F. Dostoyevski) 1935; Bitter Stream (adaptation of the novel Fontamara by I. Silone) 1936; Excursion, 1937; Pastoral, 1938; The Family (adaptation of the novel by N. Fedorova) 1943; Love in the City, 1947; Pride's Crossing, 1950; Murder in the Family, 1952; American Gothic (dramatization of his novel The Lonely Steeple) 1953; (with S. Unger) Seventh Heaven, 1955; Boston Love Story, 1958; All in the Family (adapted from the novel by M. Sauvejon) 1959. *Novels*—The Lonely Steeple, 1945; The Eagle on the Plain, 1947; (as "Langdon Dodge") Midsummer Madness, 1950; My Prince! My King!, 1962; The Mayerling Murder, 1969; Cabral, 1972. *Juvenile*—The Man Who Cared: A Life of Harry S. Truman, 1966.

ABOUT: *Periodicals*—Library Journal September 15, 1969; Nation August 23, 1947; New Republic May 26, 1937; New York Herald Tribune April 9, 1950; New York Times September 23, 1945; March 12, 1950; May 8, 1966; May 30, 1990; New Yorker July 26, 1947; Saturday Review of Literature July 26, 1947; Weekly Book Review September 23, 1945.

# WOOD, CHARLES ERSKINE SCOTT (February 20, 1852–January 22, 1944), American poet and essayist, wrote: "I was born in Erie, Pa., the son

of William Maxwell Wood, first Surgeon-General of the United States Navy, and Rose (Carson) Wood. I was appointed to West Point by President Grant in 1870 and graduated in 1874. I was commissioned a second lieutenant and assigned to Company D, 21st Infantry. I served at Fort Bidwell, Calif., and Fort Vancouver, Wash. Late in 1876 I embarked, by Government leave, on an exploration of Alaska, but returned in 1877 to joinmy regiment in the campaign against the Nez Perce Indians under Chief Joseph. I served as Gen. O. O. Howard's aide-de-camp until Joseph's surrender. In 1878 I served through the Bannock and Piute Campaigns and continued with General Howard until he was assigned to West Point. I then served for a time as adjutant of the Military Academy (West Point), but still on Howard's staff; was relieved as adjutant and allowed to enter the School of Law and the School of Political Science of Columbia University. I graduated Ph.B. and LL.B. *cum laude.*

"I had become bitterly opposed to the corruption of the Indian Ring in Washington, which stole the appropriations made for the Indians, and when we ordered out to fight Indians, I felt I was supporting an unworthy cause. I therefore resigned from the army in 1884 [with the rank of colonel] and entered the practice of law at Portland, Ore. I continued until 1918, when I retired from the firm I had established, moving to California to continue the writing I had begun while practicing law.

"My first wife was Nannie Moale Smith, by whom I had six children, four of whom are living. [One daughter, Nan (Wood) Honeycutt, was a Congresswoman from Oregon.] My present wife is Sara Bard Field, the poet, with whom I have lived in our present home, The Cats, Los Gatos, Calif., for many years.

"I have ridden, in the course of my campaigns, over this country from the Rockies to the Pacific, a country which was then scarcely inhabited, and I have seen that vast domain, water, timber, minerals, and arable land, taken by the few with the aid of Congress and secured to their heirs and assigns forever by that relic of the Middle Ages—the fee simple deed. There is not a place for the common man in the covered wagon. The unemployed, the vagrant, and the underfed have increased to an army counted by the million. I am therefore convinced that the politics this country needs is an economic program to return to the people the planetary treasures and monopolies intended for all.

"Now [written in 1940] I am eighty-eight and am spending what time I have in dying and being brought back into this life by modern medical skill- on what I might call sub-lunary mortuary excursions. I am fettered by so many medical injunctions, prohibitions, and commands that I question whether the game is worth the candle.

"I think Poetry the greatest of the Arts-the Immortal Art. I hope you have not scattered your corn before me because of such pleasantries as *Heavenly Discourse* and *Earthly Discourse* rather than *The Poet in the Desert.*"

---

After an active career as an army officer, Indian fighter, and lawyer, Wood began publishing, not tales of bravado, but poems and satires that revealed an idealistic mind searching for truth. A philosophical poet and social satirist, critic of capitalism and crusader for the underclass, he produced his best work during and after World War I, when his natural optimism took on a harder and sometimes bitter edge.

One of his better known works, revised and reprinted in 1918 and in 1929, is *The Poet in the Desert* (1915), a long free-verse poem in which a poet goes deep into the desert for meditation and then holds a dialogue with Truth, who sometimes shares and sometimes disputes his vision of humanity. The influences of Whitman and the Old Testament prophets are evident, as is Wood's deep affection for the desert landscape. "The book cannot be recommended to conventional folk," the *New York Times* observed, "and some of its ideas cannot be commended at all; but it contains both truth and beauty, and its daring will give it zest for the intellectually adventurous."

*Heavenly Discourse* (1927) contains satires on marriage, Prohibition, the church, prayer, censorship, and imperialism, most of which were written for the publication *The Masses. The New York Herald Tribune Books* wrote that the impression made by the book as a whole is that of a sermon delivered by a cultivated, genial, and benign person whose Shavian potentialities are unfortunately at the mercy of his Emersonian limitations.

The economic crisis of the early 1930s prompted Wood to write an anarchistic diatribe, *Too Much Government* (1931), in which he recommended reforming or even completely abolishing many government functions, including the operation and regulation of public utilities, the Mann act, the protective tariff, monopolies, and land tenure. He voiced indignation at Prohibition and war, and he was vehement in his support of absolute freedom of speech.

A prominent fixture in literary San Francisco for many years before his death, Wood died at his estate near Los Gatos, California. Five years later, his wife, the poet Sara Bard Field, with Genevieve Taggard, compiled his *Collected Poems* (1949), which included some previously published and many unpublished poems and a play. Wood was an interesting figure in the history of dissent, but wrote little of enduring literary value. His unfinished autobiography and other papers are housed at the Huntington Library in San Marino, California.

PRINCIPAL WORKS: *Poetry*—A Masque of Love, 1904; The Poet in the Desert, 1915; Maia, 1918; Circe, 1919; Poems from the Ranges, 1929; Sonnets to Sappho, 1940; Collected Poems, 1949. *Prose*—A Book of Tales: Being Myths of the North American Indians, 1901; Heavenly Discourse, 1927; Too Much Government, 1931; Earthly Discourse, 1937.

ABOUT: Bingham, E. R. Charles Erskine Scott Wood, 1990; Dictionary of American Biography 1941–1945; Boston Transcript February 19, 1916; Nation September 18, 1929; May 21, 1949; New York Herald Tribune October 9, 1927; New York Times June 20, 1915; August 18, 1929; March 15, 1931; January 24, 1944; Saturday Review of Literature June 19, 1937; June 4, 1949.

---

## WOOD, CLEMENT (pseudonym "ALAN DU-BOIS") (September 1, 1888–October 26, 1950),

American novelist, critic, historian, and miscellaneous writer, wrote: "Clement Wood was born at Tuscaloosa, Alabama, on both sides of old Southern stock with literary leanings. He was educated at the University of Alabama, A.B. *summa cum laude* (1909) and at Yale University (LL.B. *cum laude* 1911). He practiced law in Birmingham, 1911–1912, with his father, was assistant city attorney in 1912, and chief presiding magistrate of the Central

Recorder's Court (succeeding Justice Hugo Black) in 1913. He was removed for 'lack of the judicial temperament' when he jailed the state's Lieutenant Governor for contempt of court; and ran for president of the City Commission, almost being elected.

"Instead, he bought a one-day ticket to New York, and 'entered literature.' He supported himself by waiting on tables, working for Rockefeller's Vice Commission, and acting as Upton Sinclair's secretary. In 1914 he taught public speaking at Pingry School, Elizabeth, New Jersey; 1915–1920, English and history, Barnard School for Boys, where he became dean; 1920–1922, same subjects, also secretary New York Preparatory Schools and vice-principal Dwight School for Boys. In 1939–1940 he was instructor in versification at New York University, Washington Square Writing Center. Otherwise, he is a free-lance writer, poet, and lecturer.

"In 1914 he married Mildred Mary Cummer, by whom he had a daughter and son. After a divorce, he married Gloria Goddard, poet and novelist, in 1926. They live at Bozenkill in New York State Helderbergs, wintering in New York City or points farther south.

"In 1917 Clement Wood won the Newark 250th Anniversary Prize for his poem, 'The Smithy of God'; in 1920, the Lyric Society's $500 prize for his 'Jehovah.' He has published ten volumes of poetry, eight biographies, six novels, and numerous other works, including *The Complete Rhyming Dictionary* and a *Handbook for Poets* and including also nearly seventy titles on literature and science in the 'Little Blue Book' Series. Among his lyrics set to music by David Guion, Jacques Wolfe, and others, the best known is 'The Glory Road.' He was for two years Mediterranean Cruise Lecturer for the White Star Line. He has hundreds of correspondence course pupils throughout the Americas. He is Assistant Historian General of the Sons of Confederate Veterans and the Order of the Stars and Bars.

"Clement Wood is an enthusiastic devotee of most indoor and outdoor games. He has a powerful baritone, and has given many concerts, especially of Negro spirituals and seculars, as well as being a radio performer in this field. He is a member of the Religious Society of Friends [Quakers], and an independent in politics."

---

In a career notable for its versatility, Clement Wood produced more than fifty books (exclusive of pamphlets) in an extraordinary variety of genres: sonnets, song lyrics, narrative poems, novels, mysteries, biographies, intellectual and political histories, reference works, anthologies, literary criticism, children's stories, dream analyses, and books on games and amusements. As Wood himself admitted, these books varied widely in quality; and only a few earned more than merely respectful reviews.

*Poets of America* is a highly opinionated literary history which includes surveys of Native American and African American poetry years before those subjects were considered worthy of attention. A critic in the *Literary Review of the New York Evening Post* wrote of it, "Full of sound and fury, the pages of *Poets of America* cannot but be impressive. They are written with the earnest conviction of a prophet. . . . He stirs to constant indignation; yet he serves the cause of poetry, for most readers will hurry off to reread the poets, to substantiate and re-establish their opinions after the thundering prejudice of Clement Wood."

Probably Wood's most ambitious work was *The Outline of Man's Knowledge*, a six-hundred-page history that attempted to represent "the thinking achievements of the lifetime of the human race." This undertaking struck some critics as sheer folly, but a hyperbolic *Boston Transcript* reviewer thought Wood showed "imagination, balance and rare power of interpretation. Science is portrayed by him as lucidly as the most prosaic events in history. There is perhaps no more intelligent elucidation of the Einstein theory than that in this volume, and there is the scholarly restraint, in the main, in the presentation of other subjects."

Wood was not always treated so kindly. For example, a reviewer in the *Nation* wrote of *King Henry the Rake*, his biography of Henry VIII, "Writing for an audience whose intellectual capacity is on par with that of school-children, Mr. Wood has merely emphasized what school-children already knew—or guessed. . . . Perhaps his single-mindedness of purpose is commendable; in all other particulars his biography, scholastically speaking, rates from D- to F." Undeterred by such criticism, Wood wrote prolifically until his death.

PRINCIPAL WORKS: *Poetry*—Glad of Earth, 1917; The Earth Turns South, 1919; Jehovah, 1920; The Tide Comes In, 1923; The Eagle Flies: Sonnets, 1925; The Greenwich Village Blues, 1926; The White Peacock, 1928; The Glory Road, 1936; The Eagle Sonnets, 1942; The Eagle Returns, 1947. *Novels*—Mountain, 1920; Nigger, 1922; Folly, 1925; The Shadow from the Bogue, 1928; The Tabloid Murders, 1930; (as "Alan Dubois") Loose Shoulder Straps, 1932; (as Alan Dubois) America's Sweetheart, 1933; (as "Alan Dubois") Other Men's Wives, 1933; (as "Alan Dubois") Artist's Model, 1934; Deep River, 1934; (as "Alan Dubois") Semi-Detached Wife, 1935; The Sensualist: A Novel of the Life and Times of Oscar Wilde, 1942; Death in Ankara, 1944; Death on the Pampas, 1944; The Corpse in the Guest Room, 1945; Double Jeopardy, 1947; Strange Fires, 1951. *Short stories*—Flesh, and Other Stories, 1931; Desire, and Other Stories, 1950. *History, criticism, biography, and other*—Poets of America, 1925; Amy Lowell, 1926; The Outline of Man's Knowledge: The Story of History, Science, Literature, Art, Religion, Philosophy, 1927; (with M. Coleman) Don't Tread on Me: A Study of Aggressive Legal Tactics for Labor, 1928; The Craft of Poetry, 1929; Hunters of Heaven: The American Soul as Revealed by Its Poetry, 1929; King Henry the Rake, 1929; Bernard Macfadden: A Study in Success, 1929; The Woman Who Was Pope: A Biography of Pope Joan, 853–855 A.D., 1931; Dreams: Their Meaning and Practical Application, 1931; Herbert Clark Hoover: An American Tragedy, 1932; The Man Who Killed Kitchener: The Life of Fritz Joubert Duquesne, 1932; Warren Gamaliel Harding: An American Comedy, 1932; The Life of a Man: A Biography of John R. Brinkley, 1934; A Popular History of the World, 1935; The Complete Rhyming Dictionary and Poet's Craft Book, 1936; A Complete History of the United States, 1936; Carelessness: Public Enemy Number One, 1937; (with G. Goddard) Games for Two; or, How to Keep the Reno Wolf away from Your Door, 1937; (with G. Goddard) The Complete Book of Games, 1938; (with G. Goddard) Let's Have a Good

Time Tonight: an Omnibus of Party Games, 1938; Poetry's Handbook, 1940; More Power to Your Words! 1940; (with G. Goddard) The 1941 Quiz Book, 1941; Wood's Unabridged Rhyming Dictionary, 1943; Poet's and Songwriter's Guide: The Complete Book of Scansion for Writers of Poetry, Verse, Song Lyrics and Prose, 1948. *Juvenile*—Tom Sawyer Grows Up, 1939; More Adventures of Huckleberry Fin (Tom Sawyer's Comrade Grows Up) 1940.

ABOUT: The autobiographical material quoted above was written for Twentieth Century Authors, 1942. *Periodicals*—Boston Transcript December 31, 1927; Literary Review of the New York Evening Post May 16, 1925; Nation May 15, 1929; New York Times October 27, 1950.

## WOODBERRY, GEORGE EDWARD (May 12, 1855–January 2, 1930), American critic and poet, was born in Beverly, Massachusetts, the son of Henry Elliott Woodberry and Sarah Dane (Tuck) Woodberry. He was educated at Phillips Exeter Academy and at Harvard University, where he studied under Henry Adams and Charles Eliot Norton and helped edit the *Harvard Advocate*. Before graduating in 1877 he had begun contributing to the *Atlantic Monthly*, and many of his critical essays originally appeared in that magazine and in the *Nation*.

Woodberry's first academic position was as a professor of English at the University of Nebraska (1877–1878 and 1880–1882). The apogee of his academic career was his thirteen years at Columbia University, which began in 1891. He came to Columbia upon the recommendation of Norton and of James Russell Lowell, and a with biography of Edgar Allan Poe to his credit. At Columbia he taught such future scholars as Joel E. Spingarn  and John Erskine; he also produced several of his most substantial works, among them a critical biography of Nathaniel Hawthorne and *The Torch: Eight Lectures on Race Power in Literature*.

The "race" of the title is the human race, which Woodberry imagined as drawn, almost unconsciously, toward ever-greater spiritual development, manifest in literature. Woodberry's critical Platonism—he abjured realism and disparaged such masters of the demotic as Mark Twain, Herman Melville, and Walt Whitman—finds little favor today. When he was writing of Hawthorne, Emerson, Shelley, and other favorites, he was at his best. The *New York Times Book Review* wrote, of *The Torch*, "When Prof. Woodberry leaves the field of theory, or, rather, when he imports into that field specific appreciation and criticism, he is often extremely instructive, and what is more important . . . he is stimulating, satisfying, and quite delightful." But despite the value of his individual appreciations, Woodberry could never make the transition from the nineteenth century to the twentieth. The *Freeman* wrote, as early as 1921, that "Mr. Woodberry is out of date because he did not gear with his own times, but remained aloof and backward-looking and so became the last of the

Lowells instead of the first of the Woodberrys. Mr. Woodberry was old when he was young, and he is an institution before he is dead."

A posthumous edition of Woodberry's letters occasioned several retrospectives on the decline of his influence. Reviewing it in the *New Republic*, Newton Arvin wrote, "His letters express nothing quite so insistently as spiritual fatigue, disenchantment, a sad sense of loneliness and defeat and, finally, the darkest and most sinister views of the world's future. The flame kindled by the elder protestants had flickered feebly, under his ministrations, for many decades; but at last it had sunk down and quite expired. . . . He had inherited the abstract faith of his predecessors, but not their strenuous will."

After being forced to resign from Columbia (1904) when his passion for a student was discovered, Woodberry taught for several years as a visiting professor at Amherst, Cornell, and the Universities of California and Wisconsin. He also traveled extensively in the Mediterranean. Eventually he returned to Beverly. Despite such honors as admission to the American Academy of Arts and Letters and a fellowship in the Royal Society of Literature of England, his last years were unhappy, and he died in the knowledge that a new era had passed him by.

PRINCIPAL WORKS: *Criticism, biography, and other*—A History of Wood-Engraving, 1883; Edgar Allan Poe, 1885; Studies in Letters and Life, 1890; Heart of Man, 1899; Makers of Literature: Being Essays on Shelley, Landor, Browing, Byron, Arnold, Coleridge, Lowell, Whittier, and Others, 1900; Nathaniel Hawthorne, 1902; America in Literature, 1903; The Torch: Eight Lectures on Race Power in Literature, 1905; Swinburne, 1905; Ralph Waldo Emerson, 1907; The Appreciation of Literature, 1907; Great Writers: Cervantes, Scott, Milton, Virgil, Montaigne, Shakespeare, 1907; The Life of Edgar Allan Poe, (2 vols.) 1909; The Inspiration of Poetry, 1910; North Africa and the Desert: Scenes and Moods, 1914; Nathaniel Hawthorne: How to Know Him, 1918; Heart of Man and Other Papers, 1920; The Torch and Other Lectures and Addresses, 1920; Literary Essays, 1920; Studies of a Littérateur, 1921; Literary Memoirs of the Nineteenth Century, 1921; Appreciation of Literature, and America in Literature, 1921. *Poetry*—The North Shore Watch and Other Poems, 1890; The Roamer, 1893; Wild Eden, 1899; Poems: My Country, Wild Eden, The Players' Elegy, The North Shore Watch, Odes and Sonnets, 1903; The Flight and Other Poems, 1914; Ideal Passion: Sonnets, 1903; The Roamer and Other Poems, 1920; Selected Poems of George Edward Woodberry, 1933. *Correspondence*—Selected Letters of George Woodberry, 1933. *As editor*—The Complete Poetical Works of Percy Bysshe Shelley (8 vols.) 1892; (with E. C. Stedman) The Works of Edgar Allan Poe (10 vols.) 1894–1895; Selections from the Poems of Aubrey De Vere, 1894; Tennysons's The Princess, 1896; Poems of the House and Other Poems (by E. M. Olmstead) 1903; The Rime of the Ancient Mariner (by. S. T. Coleridge) 1904; Select Poems of Percy Bysshe Shelley, 1908; The Defence of Poesie; A Letter to Q. Elizabeth; A Defence of Leicester (by P. Sidney) 1908; The Cenci (by P. B. Shelley) 1909; European Years: The Letters of an Idle Man (by H. J. Warner) 1911; New Letters of an Idle Man (by H. J. Warner) 1913.

ABOUT: Dictionary of American Biography, vol. 20 1936; Dictionary of Literary Biography vol. 71 1988; vol. 103 1991; Erskine, J. George Edward Woodberry: An Appreciation, 1930; Pritchard, J. P. Criticism in America: An Account of the Development of Critical Techniques from the Early Period of the Republic to the Middle Years of the Twentieth Century, 1956. *Periodicals*—Dial July 19, 1917; Freeman July 6, 1921; Gay Books Bulletin 7, 1982; Nation July 5, 1933; New Republic July 12, 1933; New York Times January 3, 1930; New York Times Book Review October 28, 1905; Times (London) January 4, 1930.

## WOODHAM-SMITH, CECIL BLANCHE (FITZGERALD)

(April 28, 1896–March 16, 1977), English historian and biographer, was born in Tenby, Wales, the daughter of Colonel James Fitzgerald and Blanche Elizabeth (Philipps) Fitzgerald. On her father's side the family was related to Lord Edward Fitzgerald, the hero of the Irish rising of 1798. Her father had served with his regiment for many years in the In-

dian Army. She was educated at the Royal School for Officers' Daughters in Bath and at a convent in France before she entered St. Hilda's College, Oxford, where she studied English literature, and from which she was briefly suspended for taking part in an Irish demonstration. After her graduation from Oxford in 1917, she went to work for an advertising agency in London until her marriage (1928) to George Iron Woodham-Smith, a solicitor.

While working, and later, while keeping house in London and raising a family, Woodham-Smith turned her hand to writing—mostly articles and short stories published under the name Janet Gordon. Her true interest, however, had always been history, sparked by her father's accounts of military campaigns. She read widely in nineteenth-century English and Irish history and developed a wide and detailed knowledge of the period and its prominent political and military figures.

In 1941, on a suggestion from a British publisher who knew of her historical interests, she embarked on six years of serious research on the life of Florence Nightingale. The challenge was in mastering the formidable collection of materials—letters, documents, state records, family papers. Her job was enormously complicated by the war; papers were scattered all over England, and transportation and normal channels of information were blocked. She did most of her research at the British Museum, sometimes climbing over bomb debris to get there. After more than six years of work, *Florence Nightingale, 1820–1900*, was published. It was awarded the James Tait Black Memorial Prize. Based on contemporary records and family papers never before made public, it was informative, sympathetic yet scrupulously fair, and gracefully written. Its picture of hospital conditions, both in military and civilian life, in mid-nineteenth century England, was greeted with uniform enthusiasm and respect by reviewers on both sides of the Atlantic. Marcia Davenport wrote in the *New York Herald Tribune Book Review* (1951) that Woodham-Smith had produced "a work of glowing vitality and interest, hard to put down, and surely to be cited as one of the important biographies of our time," a view shared by many other reviewers, including Anthony West, Ralph Partridge, Victor Bonham-Carter, and Morton Dauwen Zabel. Writing years later, another British historian, Lady Elizabeth Longford observed that "wit, empathy, and finely sifted information showed what could be done with a Victorian subject conceived on the grand scale. Lytton Strachey had left Florence Nightingale deftly debunked. . . . Cecil Woodham-Smith built her up again into more than a legend; into a living complex woman." However, later readers have found the portrait not all professional historians were impressed.

Her research into the Crimean War for the Nightingale biography led Woodham-Smith to one of the most famous and disastrous episodes of British military history, the charge of the Light Brigade in the Battle of Balaclava of 1854, memorialized in Tennyson's poem. *The Reason Why*, a nonfiction best seller in both England and America, was her examination of the historical events involved in this egregious blunder. More importantly, it was also an absorbing study of the two men most closely involved in the disaster—Lord Raglan, who ordered the charge, and Lord Cardigan, who led it—and of the hopelessly corrupt and decadent military system in which it happened. Describing her thesis, Anthony West wrote in *The New Yorker* that "The cavalry charge in which the Brigade was thrown away was the consequence of a failure of command that Mrs. Woodham-Smith attributed to a clash between the personalities of the officers concerned. Lord Raglan issued an ambiguous order because it was in line with his character; it was garbled in transmission and made into a recipe for disaster because it was passed through a chain of officers who were violently hostile to each other for a variety of reasons." The critical praise for *The Reason Why* equaled, perhaps even surpassed, that accorded to her first book, with qualified military historians such as Michael Howard and Bruce Catton joining in.

In her next work, Woodham-Smith turned to a subject that her *Times* obituary described as "perhaps nearest to her heart, the distress of Ireland." *The Great Hunger* is the story of the Irish potato famine of the 1840s, its causes and its terrible consequences for a nation and its people—over a million Irish died in a five-year period, and hundreds of thousands of others emigrated. Once again Woodham-Smith demonstrated her mastery of source material and her ability to draw from it memorable—and sometimes shocking—scenes. As with her previous efforts, the book was a critical and commercial success, although some historians disputed particular aspects of her account while praising the whole. A. L. Rowse, writing in the *New York Herald Tribune Books* (1963), called *The Great Hunger* "a book of first-rate research and skillfully written" but added that "Cecil Woodham-Smith does not get her subject quite in historical perspective." However, Conor Cruise O'Brien called it "One of the great works not only of Irish nineteenth century history but of nineteenth century history in general."

Cecil Woodham-Smith's final work, a biography of Queen Victoria, is incomplete; she finished the first volume covering the years from the subject's birth until the death of Prince Albert, but died before she could finish the second volume. Elizabeth Longford, the author of an earlier biography of the Queen, wrote, "The death of Woodham-Smith's husband in 1968 took some of the elasticity from her writing and great happiness from her life. Nevertheless, *Queen Victoria: Her Life and Times* . . . showed remarkable feats of research in the Windsor Archives . . . Her account of the Prince's death was the fullest and most moving ever written." *The New Yorker* wrote in 1972 that Woodham-Smith's work "does not replace Lady Longford's one-volume biography, but its minuteness does amplify—and sometimes correct—that more concise and better organized book, and for readers who have the patience, Mrs. Woodham-Smith's Ordinance Survey scale brings us very close to Victoria as a person, and to the persons around her."

In 1960 Cecil Woodham-Smith was made a Commander of the British Empire. She received honorary degrees from the National University of Ireland in 1964 and from St. Andrews University in 1965. She was an honorary fellow of St. Hilda's College Oxford.

PRINCIPAL WORKS: Florence Nightingale, 1820–1900, 1950; Lonely Crusader: The Life of Florence Nightingale, 1951; The Reason Why, 1954; The Great Hunger, 1962; Queen Victoria: Her Life and Times, vol. 1, 1972. As *"Janet Gordon"*—April Sky, 1938; Tennis Star, 1940; Just Off Bond Street, 19.

ABOUT: Longford, E. Dictionary of National Biography 1971–1980. *Periodicals*—New York Herald Tribune Book Review February 25, 1951; May 9, 1954; New York Times March 17, 1977; New Yorker December 9, 1972; Times March 17, 1977.

**WOODWARD, WILLIAM E.** (October 2, 1874–September 27, 1950), American biographer and novelist, wrote: "I was born in Lexington County, South Carolina. My father made his living as a dirt farmer. We were always hard up. When I was six I started my schooling. I was, I suppose, what is known today as a gifted child, though that term was unknown when I went to school. At any rate, I had gone through all the regular classes before I was eleven. At fifteen I entered the South Carolina Military Academy, at Charleston (now known as The Citadel), on a state scholarship. Soon afterwards I lost all desire for learning, and I graduated third from foot of the class. Immediately after my graduation I went into newspaper work. Between 1893 and 1900 I worked on several newspapers—among them the *Atlanta Constitution* and the *New York World*. Around the turn of the century I drifted into the advertising business as a copywriter. For twelve years I was employed by various advertising agencies, and eventually was chief of the copy and planning department of a big agency which I left to become promotion manager

of the Hearst newspapers, until 1916. In 1913 I married Helen Rosen (Helen R. Woodward, a writer).

"In 1916 I went to Wall Street as publicity director of the Industrial Finance corporation. Within two years I had given up the publicity work and had become an executive vice-president and a director of forty-two banks in which the Corporation was interested financially. By 1920 I had grown so bored by banking and finance that I hated the sight of my office, so I quit. I had always wanted to write, and I began almost immediately on a novel. My wife and I went to Paris. In about a year I got tired of Europe—thought I was losing touch with America—and we came back home.

"In 1928 The Citadel awarded me a degree of LL.D. I was not reminded that I had squeezed through third from the foot of my class.

"Though four of my books are novels, my leaning is toward biography and history. I have a consuming curiosity about the doings of people, especially the men and women of the past. I think that most historical writing is dull, insipid, and far too scholarly in style, and my impulse is to present history and biography in such fashion that the subjects are readable and entertaining. I consider *Lottery* my best novel, *Meet General Grant* my best biographical work. In my first book, I invented the word 'debunk,' to my great regret. It has now become thoroughly established in the language, but I do not like the word and have never used it since. My *New American History* has had a phenomenal sale. My purpose in writing it was to clear up some false conceptions concerning American history, and to present the story of the growth of our nation in such form that it would be read by men and women who do not usually read historical works."

---

Although William E. Woodward lamented the fact that he ever invented the word "debunk" it remains the rubric under which his work is best remembered. Only the first of his lively but ephemeral novels is still in print; two of his nonfiction books (on George Washington and on General Grant) are also currently available. The matter is put into its proper context by Samuel Eliot Morison in his *Oxford History of the American People*. Commenting upon the atmosphere of the early 1920's, Morison wrote:

> Widespread distrust of intellectuals is not surprising, for in this era the peculiarly American form of what Julien Benda called *la trahison des clercs*, was to attack American traditions. Charles A. Beard . . . produced his *Rise of American Civilization* to prove that there were no heroes or even leaders in American history, only economic trends. Debunking (the word was coined by William E. Woodward in his novel *Bunk*, 1923) became a literary mode; every American hero from Columbus to Coolidge was successively "debunked"—Woodward himself did it to Washington, Grant, and Lafayette . . . the greatest debunker of all—one who debunked even the debunkers—was H. L. Mencken, "the bad boy of Baltimore."

The ever-generous Carl Van Doren was one of the few reviewers to praise *Bunk* wholeheartedly, describing it (in the *Nation*) as "robust . . . mellow

and learned"; others thought it simply a "trick" which "failed completely." The fact is that everyone was impressed by its mockery of institutions held dear by an unthinking majority. If it has failed to last except as an influential piece of journalism, then this is because it was essentially a topical work, without much literary interest.

Woodward's *Washington: The Image and the Man* was a more seriously intended affair. James Truslow Adams in the *New York Herald Tribune Books* praised it as "genuine effort at interpretation and, in a high degree, a successful one . . . There are a number of minor errors but none of much importance." The *New York Times* (1926) called it "immensely readable," although the reviewer thought that Woodward had "achieved vigor and vividness at the occasional expense of accuracy." Allan Nevins in the *Saturday Review of Literature* (1926) praised it for giving a "vivid and faithful impression" of Washington, but faulted it for being badly proportioned as a biography.

Reviews of the biography of Grant were equally favorable, and, just as in the case of that of Washington, only minor errors were noted. But the *Yale Review*, while calling it "[in] the main perfectly sound," criticized it for its treatment of President Polk and the Mexican War.

Woodward's *New American History* did not fare so well, however: the *Boston Transcript* pronounced that it "could never be used with safety as a textbook"; what praise it did garner was on account of its readability. The "volume as a whole," wrote Arthur M. Schlesinger in the *Saturday Review of Literature* (1936), is "just Woodward." It has not survived.

*New York Herald Tribune Books* commended the Lafayette biography backhandedly, but on the whole in a complimentary manner: "The pageant of impressions, flung together in defiance of sober historical procedure, is often surprisingly authentic." Clifton Fadiman in the *New Yorker* (1938) went further: "at last gives us a picture which makes sense." However, as Crane Brinton made clear in the *Saturday Review of Literature* (1938), it was "certainly not the best life"—not equal to those of Louis Gottschalk or Brand Whitlock. However, Brinton did think that Woodward had given a "realistic view."

That Woodward's books were useful to general readers, if not so much to trained historians, was confirmed by the receipt of *The Way Our People Lived*. The *American Social Review* called it "informal, readable, but not always too accurate." *New England Quarterly* liked it as "engaging" but added that "some of the details which the author paints in with much skill are inaccurate . . . In spite of its defects the book presents social history in a form which is painless to the layman and at the same time inoffensive to the historian."

Woodward's *The Gift of Life: an Autobiography* met with a very mixed reception. *Library Journal* was dismissive and scornful: "Except for scandals included, the present work is conventional and commonplace, a journalistic autobiography of the

old style with no particular insight or penetration."
But the *New Yorker* (1947) found it "very refreshing."

In sum, Woodward must be regarded as a popular historian whose judgments on the whole were sound but never subtle; and, with his biography of Washington, he may be said to have started a necessary period of reappraisal, not by being "right," but by being skeptical. He was in no way as significant as Mencken, but he played his not unimportant part in the "debunking" era.

Woodward's novel *Evelyn Prentice* was made into a successful movie (1934) featuring Myrna Loy and William Powell.

PRINCIPAL WORKS: *Fiction*—Bunk, 1923; Bread and Circuses, 1924; Lottery, 1924; Evelyn Prentice, 1933. *Social history and biography*—George Washington: The Image and the Man, 1926; Meet General Grant, 1928; Money for Tomorrow, 1932; A New American History, 1936; Lafayette, 1938; The Way Our People Lived, 1944; Tom Paine, 1945: Years of Madness, 1951. *Autobiography*—The Gift of Life, 1947.

ABOUT: The autobiographical material quoted above was written for Twentieth Century Authors, 1942. Eliot, S. M. Oxford History of the American People, 1965; Woodward, The Gift of Life, 1947. *Periodicals*—American Social Review December 1944; Boston Transcript December 12, 1936; Library Journal October 15, 1947; Nation October 10, 1923; New England Quarterly December 1944; New York Herald Tribune Books October 10, 1944; November 20, 1938; Newsweek October 9, 1950; New York Times October 24, 1926; September 30, 1950; Newsweek October 9, 1950; Pacific Historical Review November 1983; Saturday Review of Literature December 11, 1926; December 19, 1936; December 3, 1938; Time October 9, 1950; Yale Review Spring 1929.

## WOOLF, LEONARD (SIDNEY) (November 25, 1880–August 14, 1969), English political essayist, editor and publisher, and memoirist, wrote: "I

was born in London. My father [Sidney Woolf] was a barrister, a Queen's Counsel with a family of ten children and a large house in Kensington. When I was twelve my father died suddenly at the height of his powers, leaving my mother to bring up an enormous family on inadequate means. However, I got a scholarship at St. Paul's School and from there a scholarship at Trinity College, Cambridge. I was five years at Cambridge, taking a First Class in the Classical Tripos. In 1904 I went in for the Civil Service Examinations and passed into the Ceylon Civil Service. From 1904 to 1911 I was in Ceylon and for the last two and a half years of that period was in charge of the Hambantota District. . . . Much as I liked Ceylon, I was not prepared to spend my life there, and . . . the position of a semiautocratic ruler was not congenial to me. So when I got my first spell of leave I resigned and stayed in England, hoping to make a living by writing. The first book I wrote was a novel based largely on my experience in Ceylon. But the outbreak of the war led me from fiction into politics and sociology. My views, which had originally been liberal, had become Socialist, and I joined the Fabi-

an Society and the Labour Party. I became convinced of the importance of the Co-operative Movement, made a study of it, and wrote about it. It was through this that I got to know the Webbs and became a regular contributor to the *New Statesman*. The Webbs got me to make a study of international government, and this led me to write a book with that title.

"Towards the end of the [1914–1918] war, H. W. Massingham asked me to become a leader writer on the [London] *Nation*, and when that paper changed hands I became its literary editor for a good many years [1923–1930]. In 1917 my wife, Virginia Woolf, the novelist, and I started as a hobby the Hogarth Press, an amateur publishing business in which we did everything, including the printing. It became so successful that we eventually turned it into a regular publishing business. . . . The management of it, however, always required us to give more time to it than we really wished to give, and [in 1937] my wife retired from it and John Lehmann came in as partner."

---

At Trinity College, Leonard Woolf became a member of the group of Cambridge intellectuals known as the "Apostles"—a group that included Clive Bell, John Maynard Keynes, Lytton Strachey, and Thoby Stephen. In 1904, before going out to Ceylon (equipped with a dog and ninety volumes of Voltaire), he renewed his acquaintance with Stephen's sisters, Vanessa (later Clive Bell's wife) and Virginia; on his return to London in 1911 he became a frequent visitor at their weekly gatherings: the beginning of "Bloomsbury." For some months he lodged on the top floor of the house that Virginia and her younger brother Adrian shared with Keynes and the painter Duncan Grant. By the beginning of the next year Woolf had decided to resign from the Civil Service, and he proposed to Virginia Stephen; in May—after much hesitation, and despite her reservations about marrying "a penniless Jew" (as she described him to a friend), she became Leonard Woolf's wife.

His first book, *The Village in the Jungle*, is a haunting picture of lives lived in great misery and in fear of the dark forces of the jungle. Contemporary reviewers gave it measured praise, but it became a classic in Ceylon, and a later English commentator, Freema Gottlieb, compared it to E. M. Forster's *A Passage to India* in its compassion and breadth of horizon. *Diaries in Ceylon, 1908–1911*, the official record of his administration, was published years later in that country, together with three short stories about Ceylon (retitled *Stories from the East*).

Woolf's second novel, *The Wise Virgins*, is worlds removed. Obviously autobiographical (according to Gottlieb's study of Woolf's attitude toward his Jewish identity), its hero is a young Jew who longs to escape from a stultifying family life in Putney, and to marry a beautiful young woman, a member of the upper classes, who with her father and sister presides over an intellectual salon in Bloomsbury. Life in her set would promise freedom of mind and spirit; he is trapped, however, into marriage within his own philistine milieu. The work has been described by Cynthia Ozick as Leonard Woolf's novel of his life *without* Virginia (*Commentary*). It was not published in America until 1979, at which time Phyllis Grosskurth, writing in the *New York Review of Books*, noted the author's ability to combine satire and sympathy and to convey cultural differences by means of dialogue.

Born into a prosperous Reform Jewish family, Woolf spent his youth—after his father's death—in somewhat reduced circumstances in the Putney of his novel, raised by his mother, Marie (de Jongh) Woolf, the daughter of a Dutch diamond merchant. The anomaly of his position among the elite at Cambridge, in the Civil Service, as part of the Bloomsbury group, and, above all, in his marriage remains a topic of discussion. Although he renounced Judaism at the age of fourteen (and remained opposed to all religions the rest of his life), he was conscious of—and conflicted about—his background. While the mother in *The Wise Virgins* is an unflattering caricature of Woolf's own mother, he drew a sympathetic portrait of Marie Woolf in his autobiography, and described his grandparents with admiration. One of the characters in his early story "The Three Jews," meeting another on a spring day at Kew, comments: "You knew me at once and I knew you. We show up, don't we, under the apple-blossom and this sky. It doesn't belong to us, do you wish it did?" Woolf as an old man, devoted to gardening at his country home, could declare in contrast: "I feel that my roots are here. . . . I have always felt in my bones and brain and heart English" (*Sowing: An Autobiography of the Years 1880–1904*). In the last volume of his autobiography, writing of the time after Virginia Woolf's death, he admits possessing his "full share of the inveterate, the immemorial fatalism of the Jew."

Inevitably, any biography of Leonard Woolf must consider his role in the life of Virginia Woolf: as the critic-adviser to whom she always first submitted her manuscripts, coworker, protector and nurse during her recurrent manic-depressive episodes, and (posthumously) editor of a number of her books. Their relationship is the subject of *A Marriage of True Minds* by George Spater and Ian Parsons; and of Ozick's intriguing and not always well informed speculations in *Commentary* ("Mrs. Virginia Woolf"), in which she questions Leonard Woolf's role, implying that he may have overprotected his wife and that he married her as a way of escape from "Jews in Putney" (Virginia's own disparaging phrase). In any case, his own writing has generally been overshadowed by her achievement.

The concerns addressed in Woolf's political studies are hardly only of historical interest and he continues to be read as a voice of reason, moral commitment, and dedication to humanist ideals. In *International Government* he presents a timely and practical scheme for setting up a world peacekeeping authority. The book served as a blueprint for Britain's proposals for a League of Nations. (He himself had been exempted from service in World War I because of a tremor in one hand, and because

of his wife's illness.) A progressive and optimistic outlook animates *Co-Operation and the Future of Industry*: proposals for the development of a cooperative system that would reconcile the interests of industrialists, workers, and consumers. Two of his other books are indictments of imperialism, on which he could speak with authority. *Empire and Commerce in Africa* documents the "sordid motives and heartless conduct" (*American Economic Review*) of European nations, including his own. W.E.B. Du Bois called it "a book of great value and startling candor [that] will remind some of a Veblen satire but . . . is more concrete and human" (*Survey*). *Imperialism and Civilization* concludes that twentieth-century unrest in Africa and Asia is the legacy of nineteenth-century imperialist control.

Woolf's major political study is perhaps the three-volume *After the Deluge* (a reference to World War I), an examination of the ways people have tried, over the last two centuries, to adjust their political situations to the new society created by the industrial and scientific revolutions. The political scientist Harold Laski praised volume one as a work "of the first importance," written with "a crystal clarity" and evincing wide scholarship (*New Statesman and Nation*). Reviewing the third volume—written after World War II and published under the individual title *Principia Politica*—the *Times Literary Supplement* questioned its relevance to the contemporary world; Leslie Fiedler, too, found "the ideas of this charming book . . . movingly inadequate. . . . [I]ts author still inhabits a blessed world of goodness and rationality which makes him incapable of participating imaginatively in the modern total state" (*New Republic*). In the mid-1930s Woolf did, however, deal with the threat of fascism: *Quack, Quack!*, with mordant Voltairean wit, makes a plea for the restoration of reason in politics. *Barbarians at the Gate* pleads the cause for economic democracy, which, he contends, the Liberals failed to pursue and which can only be attained by socialism.

During the last years of his life Woolf turned to autobiography, giving an account of the ethical and intellectual forces that had shaped him. The first of his five volumes of memoirs, *Sowing*, tells of his youth and education; critics were especially struck with his descriptions of Cambridge life and the nascent Bloomsbury group. *Growing* goes on to describe, often lyrically, his years in Ceylon, drawing not only upon memory but on his diaries and his letters home to Lytton Strachey. (A collection of the letters Woolf wrote throughout his life, including the Strachey correspondence, has been issued with a running biographical commentary by Frederic Spotts.) According to the biographer Leon Edel, *Beginning Again*, winner of the W. H. Smith literary award in 1965, "must have been the most difficult of the [first] three volumes" to write. "Soberly and almost clinically he tells the story of marriage to a woman of genius" who was also profoundly disturbed. (From 1913 on he kept a coded record of the fluctuating states of her health.) The volume is of extraordinary interest, too, in its account of the operation of the Hogarth Press. It was to divert his wife that Woolf bought a small hand printing press and set it up in the dining room of Hogarth House, their home in Richmond. The Woolfs taught themselves how to print, and what started as a hobby became a distinguished and flourishing publishing house. Their first book, in an edition of 150 copies, was *Two Stories*: Virginia Woolf's "Mark on the Wall" and his "Three Jews." Woolf, who proved as able a businessman as he had been a colonial administrator, remained on the board of directors until his death. Among their earlier publications, besides their own writings, were T. S. Eliot's *The Waste Land*; E. M. Forster's *Pharos and Pharillon*; and the first English translation (by James and Alix Strachey) of Sigmund Freud's papers, in the series titled The Psycho-Analytical Library. Offered the manuscript of James Joyce's *Ulysses* in 1918, the Woolfs understandably turned it down as being beyond the technical capacity of the press.

*Downhill All the Way*, volume four of what Edel has characterized as "one of the great intellectual autobiographies of our century" (*Saturday Review*), traces two principal themes: the breakdown of world order, and the disintegration of Virginia Woolf's mind. It serves also as a chronicle of Woolf's years in journalism: literary editor of the *Nation* (a collection of his articles and reviews was published as *Essays on Literature, History, Politics, etc.*); editor of the *International Review* (1919) and the *Contemporary Review* (1920–1921); and, beginning in 1931, joint editor of the *Political Quarterly*. A long-time secretary of the Advisory Committee on Imperial and International Affairs of the Labour party and chairman of the International Section of the Fabian Society Research Bureau, he sought political office only once, in 1920, when he ran unsuccessfully for Parliament as a Labour candidate representing the Combined Universities. *The Journey Not the Arrival Matters* completes the autobiography, and was finished just before his death. Leonard Woolf, who refused a Companion of Honour, held an honorary doctorate from the University of Sussex (1964), where a Woolf archive is maintained. A painting of him by his sister-in-law, Vanessa Bell, hangs in the National Portrait Gallery in London.

PRINCIPAL WORKS: *Fiction*—The Village in the Jungle, 1913; The Wise Virgins: A Story of Words, Opinions, and a Few Emotions, 1914; Three Jews in Two Stories, 1917 (Hogarth Press Publication no. 1); Stories of the East, 1921. *Nonfiction*—International Government: Two Reports . . . for the Fabian Research Department (introd. Bernard Shaw) 1916 (repr. 1971 in The Garland Library of War and Peace, with new introd. by S. J. Stearns); The Future of Constantinople, 1917; Co-Operation and the Future of Industry, 1918; Empire and Commerce in Africa: A Study of Economic Imperialism, 1919 (Labour Research Department report); Economic Imperialism, 1920 (The Swarthmore International Handbooks, 5); Socialism and Co-Operation, 1921 (Social Studies Series, 4); Fear and Politics: A Debate at the Zoo, 1925 (The Hogarth Essays, VII); Essays on Literature, History, Politics, etc., 1927; Hunting the Highbrow, 1927 (The Hogarth Essays, Second Ser., V); Imperialism and Civilization, 1928 (repr. 1972 in The Garland Library of War and Peace, with new introd. by S. Strauss); After the Deluge: A Study of Communal Psychology, 3 vols. [Vol. 3: Principia Politica, 1931–1953; Quack, Quack!, 1935; Barbarians at the Gate, 1939 (in U.S.: Barbarians Within and Without); The War for Peace, 1940 (repr. 1972 in The Garland Library of War and Peace, with new introd. by S. J. Stearns); Sowing: An Autobiography of the Years 1880–1904, 1960; Growing: An Autobiography of the Years 1904–1911, 1961; Diaries in Ceylon, 1908–1911: Records of a Colonial Administrator . . . and Stories from the East: Three Short Stories on Ceylon, 1962 (Ceylon Hist. Journal, vol. 9, July 1959–April 1960, nos. 1–4); Beginning Again: An Autobiography of the Years 1911–1918, 1964; Downhill All the Way: An Autobiography of the years 1919–1939, 1967; The Journey Not the Arrival Matters: An Autobiography of the Years 1939–1969, 1969; In Savage Times: Leonard Woolf on Peace and War, Containing Four Pamphlets, 1973 (The Garland Library of War and Peace with new introd. by S. J. Stearns); Letters of Leonard Woolf (ed. F. Spotts) 1989. *Drama*—The Hotel, 1939. *As editor and compiler*—The Framework of a Lasting Peace, 1917 (repr. 1971 in The Garland Library of War and Peace, with new introd. by S. J. Stearns); Fabian Essays on Co-Operation, 1923; (with others) The Intelligent Man's Way to Prevent War (by Sir N. Angell; introd. by L. Woolf) 1933 (repr. 1973 in The Garland Library of War and Peace, with new introd. by S. J. Stearns); Between the Acts (by V. Woolf) 1941; The Death of the Moth, and Other Essays (by V. Woolf) 1942; A Haunted House, and Other Short Stories (by V. Woolf) 1943; The Moment, and Other Essays (by V. Woolf) 1948; A Writer's Diary; Being Extracts from the Diary of Virginia Woolf, 1953; (with J. Strachey) Letters: Virginia Woolf and Lytton Strachey, 1956; The Hogarth Essays, 1969. *As translator*—(with S. S. Koteliansky) Reminiscences of Leo Nicolayevitch Tolstoi (by M. Gorky) 1920; (with S. S. Koteliansky) Note-Book of Anton Chekhov, 1921; (with S. S. Koteliansky) Reminiscences of Anton Chekhov (by M. Gorky, Alexander Kuprin, and I. A. Bunin) 1921: (with S. S. Koteliansky) The Autobiography of Countess Sophie Tolstoi, 1922; The Gentleman from San Francisco, and Other Stories (by I. A. Bunin) 1923; (with Katherine Mansfield and S. S. Koteliansky) Reminiscences of Tolstoy, Chekhov and Andreev, (by M. Gorky) 1934.

ABOUT: The autobiographical material quoted above was written for Twentieth Century Authors, 1942. Alexander, P. Leonard and Virginia Woolf: A Literary Partnership, 1992; Bell, Q. Virginia Woolf: A Biography, 2 vols., 1972; Contemporary Authors Vols. 25–28, 1977; Current Biography 1965; Dictionary of National Biography, 1961–1970, 1981; Edel, L. Bloomsbury: A House of Lions, 1979; Gottlieb, F. Leonard Woolf's Attitudes to His Jewish Background and to Judaism in Jewish Historical Society of England Transactions, vol. 25 1973–1975, 1977; Kennedy, R. A Boy at the Hogarth Press, 1978; Lehmann, J. In My Own Time: Memoirs of a Literary Life, 1969; Lehmann, J. Thrown to the Woolfs, 1978; Luedeking, L. (with M. Edmonds) Leonard Woolf: A Bibliography 1992; Myerowitz, S. S. Leonard Woolf, 1982; Rhein, D. E. The Handprinted Books of Leonard and Virginia Woolf at the Hogarth Press, 1917–1932, 1985; Spater, G. (with I. M. Parsons) A Marriage of True Minds: An Intimate Portrait of Leonard and Virginia Woolf, 1977; Spotts, F. (ed.) Letters of Leonard Woolf, 1989; Willis, J. H. Leonard and Virginia Woolf as Publishers: The Hogarth Press, 1917–41, 1992; Wilson, Sir D. (with J. Eisenberg) Leonard Woolf: A Political Biography, 1978; Woolf, L. Sowing: An Autobiography of the Years 1880–1904, 1960; Woolf, L. Growing: An Autobiography of the Years 1905–1911, 1961; Woolf, L. Beginning Again: An Autobiography of the Years 1911–1918, 1964; Woolf, L. Downhill All the Way: An Autobiography of the Years 1919–1939, 1967; Woolf, L. The Journey Not the Arrival Matters: An Autobiography of the Years 1939–1969, 1969. *Periodicals*—American Economic Review September 1920; Book Week September 13, 1964; Commentary August 1973; New Republic February 8, 1954; New Statesman and Nation October 17, 1931; New York Review of Books January 24, 1980; New York Times August 15, 1969, February 25, 1979; New Yorker December 23, 1967; Saturday Review November 25, 1967; Survey May 29, 1920; Times (London) August 15, 1969; Times Literary Supplement October 30, 1953, March 2-8, 1990.

**WOOLF, (ADELINE) VIRGINIA (STE-PHEN)** (January 25, 1882–March 28, 1941), English novelist and critic, was born in London.

Virginia Stephen was a member of an upper middle-class family, with interesting antecedents and connections. Her father was Sir Leslie Stephen, critic and first editor of the *Dictionary of National Biography*; her mother, Julia, widow of Herbert Duckworth and niece of the pioneer photographer Julia Margaret Cameron, was his second wife. Virginia, known affectionately to her siblings as "the Goat," was the third of four children, preceded by Vanessa, later a painter and wife of the art critic Clive Bell, and Thoby, who died of typhoid fever in 1906, soon after taking his degree at Cambridge. Thoby's university friends formed the nucleus of the Bloomsbury group, which included the philosopher G. E. Moore, E. M. Forster, and many other notables. The youngest child was Adrian, who eventually became a physician. At one time or another the Stephen household also numbered Sir Leslie's daughter by his first wife, and the three Duckworth children, George, Stella, and Gerald (later the founder of Duckworth and Company Publishers)—who played key roles in Virginia Stephen's early life.

The two Stephen daughters were educated for the most part by their parents, at home, and in her adolescence Virginia was given the run of her father's library. Her hours of reading there were her real education, to some extent a substitute for the university courses she was denied because of her sex. Virginia Stephen's writing career may be said to have begun when she was nine years old and started a weekly paper, *The Hyde Park Gate News*, chronicling family doings in their Kensington home and at Talland House in St. Ives, Cornwall, where they spent their summers from 1882 to 1894. Guests there included, besides family members in great numbers, her father's friends George Meredith, Ralph Waldo Emerson, James Russell Lowell, and Henry James. In one of her news pieces she reports about a trip to the nearby lighthouse, since "there was a prefect tide and wind for going there." As Quentin Bell, in his biography of his aunt, states: "St. Ives provided a treasury of reminiscent gold from which she drew again and again. . . . Cornwall was the Eden of her youth, an unforgettable paradise." It was the setting for *Jacob's Room, The Waves,* and—above all—*To the Lighthouse,* though in the latter the summer home of the Ramsays becomes the Isle of Skye. In Mrs. Ramsay, the woman who holds them all, family and friends, together, the novelist portrayed her mother. In 1895, when Virginia was thirteen, Julia Stephen died. It was at this time that she first suffered symptoms of the recurrent mental illness which was to plague her life.

Woolf suffered from "mixed states " of depres-sion and elation. Sometimes in these troubled years Virginia was disturbed further by the sexual advances of her half-brother George Duckworth. (He remained a tolerated but persistently troublesome presence in her life until she was in her twenties). The extent of his intrusion into her life has, however, been exaggerated by some critics. In the novel *Mrs. Dalloway,* Woolf gives a graphic account of the experience of insanity, through the ramblings of Septimus Warren Smith, whose descent into madness weaves through the events of a summer day in London.

After Stella's death, Virginia was well enough later that year to start the serious study of Greek and Latin, first at King's College, London, and later at home. The death of her father in 1904, however, set off another breakdown and a suicide attempt. "All that summer she was mad," is Quentin Bell's laconic comment.

But that year was, in other respects a watershed one; Vanessa, Virginia, and Adrian Stephen moved into their own home on Gordon Square, in Bloomsbury—the house to which their brother Thoby, in 1905, brought his Cambridge friends to visit. These first "Bloomsbury" gatherings included Clive Bell, Lytton Strachey, and the mysterious "wild man" Leonard Woolf. (The art critic Roger Fry and the novelist E. M. Forster, who became Virginia's particular friends, were drawn into the circle about 1910–11). Also in 1904, thanks to an introduction from her friend Violet Dickinson, Virginia Stephen began to do regular articles and reviews for the *Guardian.* Her first review, of William Dean Howells's *The Son of Royal Langbrigh,* appeared on December 14; an article on the Brontë parsonage appeared the following week. From about the age of fifteen she had been training herself to write professionally, keeping journal notebooks in which she described her round of activities and acquaintances. Seven of these journals (kept up until 1909) have been published under the title *A Passionate Apprentice.* In one of the later entries she declares that she intends in her writing to "achieve a symmetry by means of infinite discords, showing all the traces of the mind's sick passage through the world. . . . " In 1905 she began to write reviews for the *Times Literary Supplement,* and did so for the rest of her life. Toward the end of that year, also, she was invited to teach at Morley College, an institute for working class men and women; until 1907 she lectured informally on English literature and history.

Then once again, in 1906, disaster struck: the death of Thoby (after they had all been on a trip to Greece) and, within days, the announcement of Vanessa's engagement to Clive Bell. Coping successfully with this, she and Adrian took a house on Fitzroy Square.

Leonard Woolf returned from his civil service post in Ceylon, fell deeply in love with Virginia and proposed to her in January 1912; by May—despite doubts about her readiness for marriage, and to "a penniless Jew" (as she described him to Violet Dickinson)—she accepted him. "It was the wisest decision of her life," her nephew concluded.

This was the start of a singular relationship that owed much to Leonard Woolf's understanding and devotion. In the spring of 1913 *The Voyage Out* was finished and accepted by Gerald Duckworth's firm. It is a novel of self-discovery, a voyage *within*. For all its ultimate sadness—sudden death ending Rachell Vinrace's growth of awareness—it has touches of sly humor that became characteristic of Woolf's style—such as a description of Rachel's fellow passengers on the ship bound for South America, as they might look from afar: "lumps on the rigging. Mr. Pepper with all his learning had been mistaken for a cormorant, and then . . . transformed into a cow." Among these passengers is Clarissa Dalloway, the complacent, seemingly assured society wife who becomes the eponymous heroine of one of Woolf's greatest novels. Publication of the book made her excited and ill. After her slow recovery at Asheham, the country home she had bought in Sussex, the Woolfs came back to London and settled at Hogarth House in Richmond (safely distant from "rackety" parties in Bloomsbury), where they lived from 1915 to 1924. Intelligent reviews in the English press (especially by Forster) helped rally her, and by 1918 she was at work on *Night and Day*, and beginning to keep the diary in which she wrote fairly regularly until a few days before her death. These spontaneous jottings, generally penned after teatime, sketch doings and people, and comment on the progress of her writing.

In 1917 Leonard Woolf set up a small hand press at Hogarth House. They both learned how to set type, and in time presided over the growth of a small but distinguished publishing firm, the Hogarth Press, of which Woolf remained a director until his death.

*Night and Day* is dedicated to Vanessa Bell; and the heroine, a young woman born into a family of writers but whose secret passion is mathematics, is in part based on her. It was published about the time the Woolfs took another country home, Monks House, near Rodmell, Sussex—the farmhouse where Vanessa Bell, her children, and her lover the painter Duncan Grant, had been living since 1916. Katherine Mansfield (whose own collection of short stories, *Prelude*, was the second work published by the Hogarth Press) found *Night and Day* "cultivated, distinguished and brilliant" but too deliberate (*Athenaeum*). Forster, whose opinion Woolf always especially valued, was also unsympathetic. With *Jacob's Room*, the first full-length book published by the Hogarth Press, Woolf's later style begins. Plot is nonexistent, metaphor and symbol are substitutes for action, and character is revealed by the flow of interior monologue. Interior reality transcends external events, though Woolf's aim was always to unite them. The impressionistic portrait of Jacob Flanders (a young man with obvious references to Thoby Stephen), from boyhood to death in the war, is built of random reflections: of his room, of character-revealing incidents, of comments by his friends. Many reviewers were left asking what the book was about. John Middleton Murry (Woolf noted in her diary) was sure its writing was a dead end

for her. The book was on the whole a popular success. When Arnold Bennett objected that she could not create living, memorable characters, she replied in a famously angry lecture, "Mr. Bennett and Mrs. Brown," read at Cambridge in 1924 and published in the essay collection *The Captain's Death Bed*. Here she speculates on how the Edwardian writers Bennett, H. G. Wells, and John Galsworthy might describe a hypothetical "Mrs. Brown." None of them, she thought, would get beyond the externals and capture Mrs. Brown's sense of herself. This was to be the mission of Forster, Joyce, D. H. Lawrence, and Woolf herself.

In June 1924 she began *Mrs. Dalloway*; it was finished later that year. A "radial" not "linear" narrative, as the author described it, it spins off in many directions to explore the sources of Clarissa Dalloway's being. The exploration is confined to the events of one day in her life, as she prepares for an evening party, the hours marked by the strokes of Big Ben: the "leaden circles" that "dissolved in the air."

By March 1926 Woolf was at work on *To the Lighthouse*. She found it came more easily than any of her other novels. She told her friend Roger Fry: "I meant *nothing* by it. One has to have a central line drawn down the middle of the book to hold the design together. I saw that all sorts of feelings would accrue to this, but I refused to think them out. . . . I can't manage Symbolism except in this vague, generalised way." The novel, "made from the passions and tragedies of her youth" (Quentin Bell), is a mix of pathos and absurdity, just bordering on satire of some of the Ramsays's famous guests.

Clive Bell gave a dinner party in 1922, at which he introduced Virginia Woolf to Vita Sackville-West. The friendship grew, and somewhere between 1925 and 1929 developed into a love affair. Virginia's letters to Vita are included in volume three of the complete edition of Woolf's letters. Another form of "love letter" (as Nigel Nicolson, Vita's son called it) is *Orlando*, the jeu d'esprit, part masque, part pageant, written for and dedicated to her friend. It is, as Nicolson describes it, an "experimental novel that follows its central character through several centuries and identities"; Vita, as Orlando, plays her part in Sackville family history, an Elizabethan courtier at the start, a modern-day young man at its close. On another level, the book is certainly a spoof of conventional biographies. In any case, it was a commercial success, accepted as a "highbrow" novel that was actually funny and easy to read. The fiction that followed was very different. For some time Woolf struggled with the writing of a book to be called *The Moths*, finally completed as *The Waves*. It is her most difficult book (and in the opinion of Leonard Woolf her greatest), composed of the soliloquies of six friends that reveal their lives over the years. The *Times Literary Supplement* felt it was an admirable technical experiment, but left a sense of void; other critics have been more explicitly negative. Just before this, Woolf had finished the work that is now closely associated with her in the minds of some feminist critics. *A Room of One's Own* began as lectures read at Newnham and Girton colleges, Cambridge, in October 1928. Prefacing it with a story of how, as a woman, she had been turned away from one of the university libraries, she goes on to describe the barriers put in the way of women writers, concluding that to achieve intellectual freedom a woman must have a source of income and a room of her own. *Three Guineas*, published on the eve of World War II, is an outspoken, more general protest on women's place in contemporary English political and social life.

*The Years*, the last novel published during her lifetime, is the story of the Pargiter family, taking them from 1880 to the present. Although plot and character are eschewed (time itself is the chief character), its straightforward narration, mainly in the form of dialogue, appeared to be a regression from the style she had been forging. Her husband, as always her final critic, was disappointed; again, however, it proved popular with readers. As originally drafted, *The Pargiters* alternated narrative with didactic essays on the predicament of women. These are now available in an edition published by the scholar Mitchell A. Leaska, titled *The Pargiters: The Novel-Essay Portion of "The Years"*. Two quite different works followed. *Flush*, a "biography" of Elizabeth Barrett Browning's spaniel, is in fact a description of Wimpole Street and Italy—and of the poet—from a pet's point of view. Flush, according to David Garnett, was "the first animal to become an Eminent Victorian" (*New Statesman and Nation*). *Roger Fry*, a life of the critic who introduced Cézanne and modern art to English viewers, was undertaken at his family's request after his death in 1934. Despite her difficulties with writing about art and about his love affairs, the work turned out to be firm, direct, understanding, and—in view of their long and intimate friendship—surprisingly objective (Herbert Read, *Spectator*). Vanessa Bell is reported to have said of the book: "Now you have given him back to me."

Family and time are again, as always, the center of Virginia Woolf's last novel, *Between the Acts*, completed a month before her death, and to have been titled *Pointz Hall*. Here, in the course of a summer day, an English family and their guests gather at the great house to attend the villagers' historical pageant. Scene and "action" are made manifest by the interior monologues carried on by members of the family.

On March 28, in a fit of depression, Woolf drowned herself in the River Ouse, leaving a note for her husband in which she assured him that "I owe all the happiness of my life to you," and "I don't think two people could have been happier than we have been." Through his devoted efforts, much of her previously unpublished work was issued thereafter, as well as collections of her essays and stories, and her correspondence with Lytton Strachey. Since his death in 1969, an enormous Virginia Woolf bibliography has accumulated; of these at least *A Writer's Diary* and Quentin Bell's detailed biography remain essential. There are now complete editions of her letters and the diaries. The

Bloomsbury group and her relations with it continue to fascinate.

By the 1930s some critics had begun to dismiss Woolf as irrelevant, too distanced from contemporary concerns, overlooking her long commitment to liberal-leftist social causes: women's suffrage, the Women's Co-Operative Guild, pacifism and antifascism. Feminist critics have suggested that anger at male dominance is at the core of her writing. Both she and her husband Leonard refused a Companion of Honor in 1935. She turned down many academic awards, but did accept the Femina-Vie Heureuse Prize in 1938. In his memorial address, given as the Rede Lecture at Cambridge in 1941, E. M. Forster spoke of Woolf's singleness of aesthetic purpose and the joy in her work.

The major collection of Virginia Woolf's manuscripts, drafts, and correspondence is housed in the Berg Collection at the New York Public Library; there are collections of her papers at Monks House and the British Museum.

PRINCIPAL WORKS: *Fiction*—The Voyage Out, 1915, Night and Day, 1919; Monday or Tuesday, 1921. *Short stories*—Jacob's Room, 1922; Mrs. Dalloway; To the Lighthouse, 1927; Orlando, a Biography, 1928; The Waves, 1931; The years, 1937; Between the Acts, 1941; A Haunted House and Other Short stories (Foreword by L. Woolf) 1943; Mrs. Dalloway's Party: A Short Story Sequence (ed. S. McNichol) 1973; The Pargiters: The Novel—Essay Portion of "The Years" (ed. M. A. Leaska) 1977; Pointz Hall: The Earlier and later Transcripts of "Between the Acts" (ed. M. A. Leaska) 1981; Melymbrosia: An Early Version of "The Voyage Out" (ed. L. DeSalvo) 1982; The Complete Shorter Fiction (ed. S. Dick) 1985. *Nonfiction*—The Common Reader, 1925; A Room of One's Own, 1929; The Common Reader: Second Series, 1932 (in U.S.: The Second Common Reader); Flush, a Biography, 1933; Three Guineas, 1938; Roger Fry, a Biography, 1940; The Death of the Moth, and Other Essays (ed. L. Woolf) 1942; The Moment, and Other Essays (ed. L. Woolf) 1947; The Captain's Death Bed, and Other Essays, 1950; A Writer's Diary: Being Extracts from the Diary of Virginia Woolf (ed. L. Woolf) 1953; Letters: Virginia Woolf and Lytton Strachey (ed. L. Woolf and J. Strachey) 1956; Granite and Rainbow: Essays, 1958; Contemporary Writers (pref. by J. Guiguet) 1965; Collected Essys, 4 vols., 1967; The Letters of Virginia Woolf, 6 vols. (ed. N. Nicolson, with J. Trautmann) 1975–80 (vol. 1: 1888–1912, The Flight of the Mind; vol 2: 1912–1922; vol 3: 1923–1928; vol. 4: 1929–1931; vol. 5 1932–1935, The Sickle Side of the Moon; vol. 6: 1936–1941, Leave the Letters Till We're Dead); Moments of Being: Unpublished Autobiographical Writings (ed. J. Schulkind) 1976; The Diary of Virginia Woolf, 4 vols. (ed. O. Bell and A McNellie) 1977–80 (vol. 1; 1915–19, with introd. by Q. Bell; vol. 2: 1920–1924; vol. 3: 1925–1930; vol. 4: 1931–1935); The Essays of Virginia Woolf (ed. A. McNellie) 1986; Congenial Spirits: The Selected Letters of Virginia of Woolf (ed. J. Trautmann Banks) 1990; A Moment's Liberty: The Shorter Diary of Virginia Woolf (ed. A. O. Bell) 1990; A Passionate Apprentice: The Early Journals of Virginia Woolf, 1897–1909 (ed. M. A. Leaska) 1990. *Drama*—Freshwater: A Comedy (ed. L. P. Ruotolo) 1976. *Collection*—The Virginia Woolf Reader: Selections (ed. M. A. Leaska 1984.

ABOUT: Bell, C. Old Friends: Personal Recollections, 1957; Bell, Q. Bloomsbury Recalled, 1996; Bell Q. Virginia Woolf: A Bibliography 2 vols., 1972; Bloom, H. (ed.) Virginia Woolf, 1986; DeSalvo, L. Virginia Woolf's First Voyage: A Novel in the Making, 1980; Dictionary of Literary Biography 36, 1985, 100, 1990, 112, 1991; Dictionary of National Biography 1941–1950, 1959; Dunn, J. A Very Close Conspiracy: Vanessa Bell and Virginia Woolf, 1990; Edel, L. Bloomsbury: A House of Lions, 1979; Encyclopedia of World Literature in the Twentieth Century vol. 4, 1984; Forster, E. M. Virginia Woolf, 1941 (the Rede Lecture . . . Cambridge, May 29, 1941); Haule, J. M. (with P. H. Smith, Jr.) A Concordance to the Novels of Virginia

Woolf, 3 vols., 1991; Homans, M. Virginia Woolf: A Collection of Critical Essays, 1993; Leaska, M. A. The Novels of Virginia Woolf from Beginning to End, 1977; Lee, H. The Novels of Virginia Woolf, 1977; Lehmann, J. Thrown to the Woolfs, 1978; Lehmann, J. Virginia Woolf and Her World, 1976; Lewis, T.S.W. (ed.) Virginia Woolf: A Collection of Criticism, 1975 (Contemporary Studies in Literature); Marcus J. Virginia Woolf: A Feminist Slant, 1983; Marcus, J. Virginia Woolf and Bloomsbury: A Centenary Celebration, 1987; Morris, J. Time and Timelessness in Virginia Woolf, 1977; Nicolson, N. Portrait of a Marriage, 1973; Nobel J. R. (ed.) Recollections of Virginia Woolf by Her Contemporaries (introd. by M. Holroyd) 1975, 1989; O'Brien, Edna. Virginia: A Play. 1981; Pippett, A. The Moth and the Star: A Biography of Virginia Woolf, 1955; Poole, R. The Unknown Virginia Woolf, 4th ed. 1996; Radin, G. Virginia Woolf's "The Years": The Evolution of a Novel, 1981; Raitt, S. Vita and Virginia: The Work and Friendship of V. Sackville-West and Virginia Woolf, 1993; Richter, H. Virginia Woolf: The Inward Voyage, 1970; Rosenman, E. B. The Invisible Presence: Virginia Woolf and the Mother-Daughter Relationship, 1986; Ruddick. L. C. The Seen and the Unseen: Virginia Woolf's To the Lighthouse, 1977; Sackville-West, V. The Letters of Vita Sackville-West to Virginia Woolf (eds. L. A. DeSalvo and M. A. Leaska) 1985; Sharma, V. L. Virginia Woolf as Literary Critic: A Revaluation, 1977; Silver, B. R. Virginia Woolf's Reading Notebooks, 1983; Spater, G. (with I. M. Parsons) A Marriage of True Minds: An Intimate Portrait of Leonard and Virginia Woolf, 1977; Sprague, C. (ed.) Virginia Woolf: A Collection of Critical Essays, 1971; Steele, E. Virginia Woolf's Literary Sources and Allusions: A Guide to the Essays, 1983; Stewart, J. F. Impressionism in the Early Novels of Virginia Woolf in Journal of Modern Literature May 1982; Trautmann, J. The Jessamy Brides: The Friendship of Virginia Woolf and V. Sackville-West, 1973; Woolf, L. Beginning Again: The Autobiography of the Years 1911–1918, 1964. Bibliography—Kirkpatrick, B. J. A. Bibliography of Virginia Woolf, 3d ed. 1980. Periodicals—Athenaeum November 21, 1919; Commentary August 1973; Modern Fiction Studies 18, no. 3, 1972 (Woolf issue); Nation December 16, 1931; New Statesman and Nation October 7, 1933; New York Times April 3, 1941, April 16, 1944, February 21, 1954; New York Tribune July 5, 1925; Spectator November 11, 1922, August 2, 1940; Times (London) April 3, 9. 1941; Times Literary Supplement October 8, 1931.

## WOOLLCOTT, ALEXANDER

(January 19, 1887–January 23, 1943), American drama critic, journalist, essayist, broadcaster and actor, was born

in the former Fourierist socialist commune of Phalanx in Red Bank, New Jersey, the son of Walter Woollcott and Frances Grey (Bucklin) Woollcott. He attended public schools in Kansas City and Philadelphia and won a scholarship to Hamilton College in Clinton, New York, in 1909. At the end of his college years he suffered a severe attack of the mumps, and its complications left him sterile, "in effect a eunuch," according to Edwin P. Hoyt. Hoyt is not the only biographer to have speculated as to the consequences of this for Woollcott's personality. But by 1913 he was well enough to be living in Manhattan and doing postgraduate work at Columbia University, where he remained for a semester.

After a great deal of persuasion, editor Carr Van Anda hired him as a reporter for the New York Times. In 1914 he replaced Adolph Klauber as dra-

ma critic, and a year later he became the center of a controversy with the Shubert brothers, producers who physically barred him from their theaters, claiming he was biased against them. The Times countered by refusing Shubert advertising and filing an injunction allowing Woollcott to review Shubert productions. The courts found in favor of the Shuberts, but they eventually had to readmit Woollcott because they needed to advertise. Woollcott rose to prominence because of this lawsuit. He stayed with the Times until 1922 except for a two-year interruption to serve in World War I as a medical orderly in France, where he was on the staff of Stars and Stripes along with his future New Yorker editor Harold Ross. Before the war, Woollcott's critical writing was saccharine and trite, but by 1919 he realized "the cream-puff reviews he wrote in the past were no longer appropriate drama criticism," wrote Howard Teichmann in Smart Aleck: The Wit, World and Life of Alexander Woollcott (1976). He took a more acidic edge, yet would remain a tireless promoter of those he liked, including Alfred Lunt and Lynne Fontanne, Fred Astaire, Will Rogers, Paul Robeson, Helen Hayes, and Ruth Gordon.

In 1922 he became drama critic of the New York Herald, wrote briefly for the New York Sun, then joined Franklin P. Adams, Heywood Broun and other friends from his Stars and Stripes days at the influential New York World, where he was drama critic until 1928. During those years he eclipsed George Jean Nathan as the most prominent and popular theater critic in America. "Woollcott was immense in his cloak, immaculate in his white tie and tails, and imperious in his hold on the attention of his readers," wrote Teichmann, adding that Woollcott "singly raised the place of the drama critic in America from the role of the harlot to the profession of the journalist." The general belief now, however, is that his critical standards were highly subjective and romantically sentimental, saved only by a command of language and a commendable knowledge of the theater.

A voracious talker, eater, and card player, Woollcott was a well known figure in the New York social scene. He held court as the insulting head of the Algonquin Hotel's infamous Round Table and the poor loser of a companion club, the Thanatopsis Literary and Inside Straight Club, a regular Saturday-night poker game.

When his contract ended at the World, Woollcott turned free-lancer. He started his "Shouts and Murmurs" column for the New Yorker in 1929. It ran for ten years and provided him a forum to discuss his favorite subjects: books and the theater, restaurants and travel, friends and murders. He wrote portraits and gossip articles for Cosmopolitan, Collier's, and other magazines, and a collection of such work became his only bestseller, While Rome Burns (1934), in which he wrote of his conviction "that by faithfully absorbing the imparted wisdom of two Walters (Lippmann and Winchell) I can learn all I really care to know about what is going on in the world."

Radio allowed Woollcott to become the foremost

raconteur and gossip of his day, according to the *New York Times.* "As the town crier of the air, he found a perfect outlet for the enthusiasms and resentment of which his nature was compounded. He could beat the drum with ecstatic glee for the myriad things that pleased him—from anagrams to studies in murder; from Minnie Maddern Fiske to the four Marx brothers. And with a single poisoned phrase, as swift and deadly as a cobra, he could strike down the objects of his scorn."

But perhaps his greatest influence was convincing America's book buyers what was worthy to take home and read. He made bestsellers of books that were otherwise languishing on sellers' shelves, such as James Hilton's *Lost Horizon* and Francis Yeats-Brown's *Lives of a Bengal Lancer.* In the *New York Times,* John Chamberlain called him "an intellectual crooner, bearing about the same relationship to literary criticism that Rudy Vallee or Kate Smith bears to music."

In 1935, he published a collection of his favorite writings, *The Woollcott Reader* (1935), which the *Nation* called "high-grade, streamlined hokum if you will, but hokum. There is not much in *The Woollcott Reader* that any well-known critic of our time except Mr. Woollcott will wish to see preserved. Here is . . . second-rate taste at its most formidable and deceptive, tricked out in its Sunday best, beckoning and easy to take." *Woollcott's Second Reader* (1937) was considered better than the first, and both sold well.

He also took to acting in the 1930s. He played roles that were modeled largely on himself as in S. N. Behrman's *Brief Moment* (1931) and *Wine of Choice* (1938). His most notable performance was as the crotchety, sarcastic critic and "friend of the great," Sheridan Whiteside, in the road company of George S. Kaufman and Moss Hart's *The Man Who Came to Dinner* in 1940 and 1941. Woollcott's acting fared better than his play writing. Two plays written with Kaufman, *The Channel Road* (1929) and *The Dark Tower* (1933) each ran for about four weeks and were blasted by critics.

Woollcott died after suffering a heart attack during a live radio forum on Hitler at CBS studios in New York. A year later, his advisor, manager and close friend, Joseph Hennessey, and another old friend, Beatrice Kaufman, edited and published a selection of his letters arranged chronologically from the age of ten to the end of his life. These were "expertly chosen to paint a delightful portrait of their author and to recreate the building, by slow degrees, of an American legend," according to the *Springfield Republican.* The volume also included reproductions of three of the actual letters, and Russell Maloney wrote in the *New York Times* that he could "imagine Woollcott's plump ghost heaving with laughter at their choice."

*While Rome Burns, Long, Long Ago* and twenty-five other sketches and letters selected by Hennessey were published as *The Portable Woollcott* (1946). Brock Pemberton wrote in the *New York Times* that much of the content is "ephemeral," but "pleasant reading, with here and there a passage still important."

PRINCIPAL WORKS: Mrs. Fiske, 1917; The Command Is Forward, 1919; Mr. Dickens Goes to the Play, 1922; Shouts and Murmurs, 1922; Enchanted Aisles, 1924; The Story of Irving Berlin, 1925; Going to Pieces, 1928; Two Gentlemen and a Lady, 1928; While Rome Burns, 1934; (ed.) The Woollcott Reader, 1935; (ed.) Woollcott's Second Reader, 1937; Long, Long Ago, 1943; (ed.) As You Were (anthology) 1943; Letters (ed. by B. Kaufman & J. Hennessey) 1944; The Portable Woollcott, 1946. *Plays*—The Channel Road (with G. S. Kaufman) 1929; The Dark Tower (with G. S. Kaufman) 1933.

ABOUT: Adams, S. H. Alexander Woollcott, His Life and His World; Burns, M. U. The Dramatic Criticism of Alexander Woollcott; Current Biography 1941; Dictionary of American Biography 1973; Drennan, R. E. (ed.) The Algonquin Wits; Gaines, J. R. Wit's End; Hoyt, E. P. Alexander Woollcott: The Man Who Came to Dinner, 1968; Teichmann, H. Smart Aleck: The Wit, World and Life of Alexander Woollcott; Woollcott, A. While Rome Burns. *Periodicals*—Nation December 18, 1935; New York Times January 24, 1943, July 23, 1944, May 5, 1946; New York Tribune April 5, 1925; New Yorker July 29, 1944; Saturday Review of Literature December 7, 1935; November 20, 1937; Times (London) January 25, 1943.

**WOOLRICH, CORNELL (pseudonym "WILLIAM IRISH")** (December 4, 1906–September 25, 1968), American novelist and short story writer, was born in New York City. His parents' marriage failed and he spent part of his childhood in Mexico, during the revolutions of 1910–1912, with his father, who was a civil engineer. His hobby in those days was collecting used rifle cartridge shells that littered the grounds outside his house. He remembered that "nearly every second night at dinner the lights would fail, which meant either that Villa had captured the town from Carranza or Carranza had captured it from Villa. . . . From my own personal point of view, the revolution was pure velvet, as every time there was a new 'triumphal entry,' the schools would close down for a day or two, until the sporadic shooting had quieted down. I wouldn't have cared if the revolution had never ended."

The revolutions ended for young Woolrich, however, when he was sent back to New York to live with his mother. In 1921 he entered Columbia College and wrote his first novel, *Cover Charge,* in 1925, during an illness that kept him out of school for six months. It was published the following year and tells the story of a young man's rise and fall in the Jazz Age. Woolrich had written it "on one of those stray impulses," and reviews were less than enthusiastic, but he believed he had found his vocation in the written word. His second novel, *Children of the Ritz,* appeared in 1927 and was serialized in *College Humor,* taking a $10,000 prize in a context cosponsored by that magazine. First National Pictures bought the rights and invited Woolrich to Hollywood to work on the script. The film appeared in 1929, but Woolrich continued on as a studio writer.

In his introduction to *The Fantastic Stories of Cornell Woolrich,* Francis M. Nevins, Jr. writes that "by the time of his gritty and cynical third book, *Times Square* (1929), [Woolrich] had begun to develop the headlong story-telling drive and the concern with the torments and the maniacal power of love which were to mark his later suspense fiction." In 1930 Woolrich entered into a marriage, short-lived and never consummated; his diary, later destroyed, indicated that he was homosexual. Nevins states that the "shadow of his desperate need for a relationship with a woman who never was, and never could have been, haunts the pages of his stories like a demon that cannot be exorcised," and goes on to claim that Woolrich's 1932 novel, *Manhattan Love Song*, is "both the best and the most prophetic of his youthful books, anticipating the motifs of his later suspense fiction with its tale of a love-struck young couple cursed by an inexplicable malignant fate which leaves one dead and the other desolate."

After the breakup of his marriage Woolrich returned to his mother in New York, and to an increasingly reclusive life. He continued to write, however. In 1934 he published his first crime story in *Detective Fiction Weekly*. This marked the beginning of a prolific career as a writer of all sorts of crime fiction—ranging from pure detective mysteries to psychological horror stories—published in pulp magazines and as books. The themes of blasted hopes and love gone wrong continue—Woolrich wrote the novel on which *The Bride Wore Black* was based, and Hitchcock's *Rear Window* was derived from one of his stories. He had a gift for the macabre.

PRINCIPAL WORKS: *Novels*—Cover Charge, 1926; Children of the Ritz, 1927; Times Square, 1929; A Young Man's Heart, 1930; The Time of Her Life, 1931; Manhattan Love Song, 1932; The Bride Wore Black, 1940; The Black Curtain, 1941; Black Alibi, 1942; The Black Angel, 1943; (as "George Hopley") Night Has a Thousand Eyes, 1945; (as "George Hopley") Fright, 1950; Savage Bride, 1950; Hotel Room, 1958; Beyond the Night, 1959; Death Is My Dancing Partner: An Original Novel of Terror, 1959; The Doom Stone, 1960. *Short stories*—(as "George Hopely") The Dancing Detective, 1946; Nightmare, 1956; Violence, 1958; The Dark Side of Love: Tales of Love and Death, 1965; The 10 Faces of Cornell Woolrich: An Inner Sanctum Collection of Novelettes and Short Stories, 1965; Nightwebs: A Collection of Stories, 1971; The Fantastic Stories of Cornell Woolrich, 1981; Darkness At Dawn: Early Suspense Classics, 1985. *Memoirs*—Blues of a Lifetime: The Autobiography of Cornell Woolrich, 1991. *As William Irish*—Phantom Lady, 1942; And So To Death, 1943; The Black Path of Fear, 1944; Deadline at Dawn, 1944; Waltz Into Darkness, 1948; I Married a Dead Man, 1948; Rendezvous in Black, 1948; Stranger's Serenade, 1951; I Wouldn't Be In Your Shoes, 1943; After-Dinner Story, 1944; Borrowed Crime, and Other Stories, 1946); Dead Man Blues, 1947; The Blue Ribbon, 1949; Six Nights of Mystery: Tales of Suspense and Intrigue, 1950; Somebody On the Phone, 1950; Eyes That Watch You, 1952.

ABOUT: Nevins, Francis M., Jr. Cornell Woolrich: First You Dream, Then You Die, 1988; Twentieth-Century Crime and Mystery Writers, 1985. *Periodical*—New York Times December 2, 1945.

**\*WOUK, HERMAN** (May 27, 1915– ), American novelist and playwright, wrote: "At thirty-seven I have published three novels and one play. I entered the literary field at thirty. My background was a New York City boyhood, four years at Columbia College, half a dozen years as a radio writer (I wrote mainly for the comedian Fred Allen), and four years as a naval officer of the line in World War II. I briefly served the U.S. government in 1941 as a dollar-a-year man, producing radio broadcasts to sell war bonds. My service in the Navy included three years at sea in the Pacific. The first ship in which I served, the U.S.S. *Zane*, an old de-

°wohk

stroyer-mine-sweeper, received the unit commendation for its service in the Solomons campaign. My last post was second in command (executive officer) of the U.S.S. *Southard*, a ship of the same type.

"*Aurora Dawn*, my first novel, a short satiric extravaganza about big business in New York, was distributed by a popular book club, thereby enabling and encouraging me to continue writing novels. *The City Boy*, a humorous story of boyhood, was made into a movie, and was recently re-issued in an illustrated edition. *The Caine Mutiny*, an account of U.S. Navy life in World War II, was the first of my stories to achieve any general acceptance. It won the Pulitzer prize for fiction, and continues popular in America and abroad. *The Traitor* (1949), a play of atomic spying, drew criticism from some liberals when it first appeared; this was before the convictions of Alger Hiss and Klaus Fuchs, when the idea that Communists are capable of treason was more controversial than it is now. I have also written moving pictures."

"I try for regular work habits, sitting down pen in hand each day to write a few long yellow pages of the story. The first draft, cut down more or less, has been what I have published previously, and I believe this will be true of the next book, which is now (December 1952) partly done. My wife, Betty Sarah, types my manuscripts and is secretary and bookkeeper of the enterprise. I have read to her every word that I have written."

Born into a family of Jewish immigrants from Russia (his parents were Abraham Isaac and Esther [Levine] Wouk), Herman Wouk affectionately evoked his middle-class childhood in the Bronx in his semi-autobiographical novel *The City Boy*. As did his first novel, *Aurora Dawn*, *The City Boy* received some encouraging reviews, but as Wouk remarked, his third book, *The Caine Mutiny*, was the first "to achieve any general acceptance." Indeed, *The Caine Mutiny* and the much later *Winds of War* and *War and Remembrance* constitute an enormous fictional narrative of World War II that stands as his most significant achievement.

*The Caine Mutiny*, which concerns the events leading up to and following from a mutiny onboard a minesweeper captained by an incompetent and cowardly tyrant, was a colossal popular success, and a dramatization of its court martial scenes alone did well on Broadway. To a lesser extent, *The Caine Mutiny* was also a critical success. Edward Weeks wrote of it in the *Atlantic*, "It has the time sense, the enormous boredom, the sense of being hopelessly isolated and cut off from home which every veteran remembers; it has the scope and the skill to reveal how men are tested, exposed, and developed under the long routine of war; finally, it has the slow-fused but inevitably accumulating tension of the mutiny which gives both form and explosive climax to the story." The novel's resolution, in which the deposed Captain Queeg is suddenly seen in a much more favorable light, struck many readers as unconvincing, and revealed problems in Wouk's writing that became increasingly apparent in his later books, such as the immediate successor to *The Caine Mutiny, Marjorie Morningstar*.

This, the story of a beautiful Jewish woman who, after some adolescent confusion and rebellion, finds contentment as a suburban wife and mother, was considered tedious and reactionary by such critics as Edward Weeks and Maxwell Geismar. By then Wouk was dismissed, in most critical quarters, as a hopeless middlebrow, and his next major novel, *Youngblood Hawke*, a sprawling *roman à clef* based on the life of Thomas Wolfe, was heavily criticized for its "toneless prose," "pasteboard characters," and "remorseless prolixity" (*Saturday Review*).

Wouk could not be said to have won over the critics with his return to the subject of World War II in *The Winds of War* and *War and Remembrance*, but his deep engagement with his material impressed even a few skeptics. The two novels encompassed the entirety of the war as witnessed mostly by Captain Victor "Pug" Henry—military man, scholar, translator, and advisor to presidents and statesmen—and various members of his family. The literary deficiencies of the books were not hard to find. Paul Fussell, writing in the *New Republic*, thought the characters and plot of *War and Remembrance* "purely early 1950s Metro-Goldwyn-Mayer. . . . Without typecasting everybody and everything Wouk would be lost in a world more complicated than he and his readers can tolerate. Unable to conceive an original character or to equip anyone with feelings above the commonplace, he must resort wholly to external classifications. His people are devoid of inner life." And yet Fussell, like other critics, expressed some admiration for Wouk's historical and narrative gifts. "As a historian of naval warfare," wrote Fussell, "Wouk is as good as Samuel Eliot Morrison, while as an analytic narrator of land battles . . . he invites comparison with someone like B. H. Liddell Hart. If the idea of 'the novel' had not been his fatal Cleopatra, he could have distinguished himself as a contemporary historian."

As was the case with *The Caine Mutiny* and *Marjorie Morningstar, The Winds of War* and *War and Remembrance* lent themselves readily to cinematic or television adaptation. Wouk himself wrote the screenplays for the ABC television productions of *The Winds of War* in 1983 and *War and Remembrance* in 1988. Whether Wouk's most recent novels, *The Hope* and *The Glory*, will be similarly translated into another medium is not yet known, but these imagined recreations of the founding and development of modern Israel were certainly consistent with Wouk's novelistic practices. The reviews were predictable; Wouk's greatest claim to literary merit clearly was in *The Caine Mutiny*.

Herman Wouk is the recipient of honorary degrees from Yeshiva University in New York, where he was visiting professor of English from 1952 to 1958, and from Clark University in Worcester, Massachusetts. He is the father of three sons and lives in Washington, D.C., with his wife Betty Sarah (Brown) Wouk.

PRINCIPAL WORKS: *Novels*—Aurora Dawn, 1947; The City Boy, 1948; The Caine Mutiny, 1951; Marjorie Morningstar, 1955; Youngblood Hawke, 1962; Don't Stop the Carnival, 1965; The Lomokome Papers, 1968; The Winds of War, 1971; War and Remembrance, 1978; Inside, Outside, 1985; The Hope, 1994; The Glory, 1995. *Drama*—The Traitor: A Play in Two Acts, 1949; The Caine Mutiny Court-Martial, 1954; Nature's Way: A Comedy in Two Acts, 1958. *Other*—This Is My God, 1959.

ABOUT: The autobiographical material quoted above was written for Twentieth Century Authors First Supplement, 1955. Beichman, A. Herman Wouk: The Novelist as Social Historian, 1984; Contemporary Novelists 5th ed., 1991; Current Biography, 1952; Mazzeno, L. W. Herman Wouk, 1994; Twentieth Century Literary Criticism Vol. 7, 1988. *Periodicals*—Atlantic August 1951; New Republic October 14, 1978; New York Times Book Review January 9, 1994; Saturday Review May 19, 1962.

## WREN, PERCIVAL CHRISTOPHER (1885–November 23, 1941), English popular novelist and short story writer, was born in Devonshire, in a house—Burroughs Court—where Charles Kingsley set one of the scenes in *Westward, Ho!* He was a descendant of Matthew Wren, brother of Sir Christopher, the great seventeenth-century architect. P. C. Wren went to Oxford University. He gained his M.A., and was also a heavy-

weight boxer and all-around sportsman, playing cricket, football, and golf.

After his graduation Wren traveled restlessly all over the world, hunting and exploring and working at a great variety of jobs. He was a schoolmaster and a journalist, a navvy and a farm laborer, a tramp and a costermonger in the slums of London. For a time he was a sailor, then a trooper in a British cavalry regiment. Most importantly from the point of view of his literary career, he served in the French Foreign Legion. After five years of adventurous travel, Wren settled down for ten more as assistant director of education and physical training in Bombay. For part of this time he was the fencing champion of western India. His first published works were textbooks for Indian teachers and their pupils. Some of these became standard works—the twenty-third and final edition of his *First Lessons in English Grammar* appeared as recently as 1961. Wren's fiction showed that, like most of his class and education, he accepted absolutely the right of the British Empire to rule much of the world, but also its duty to "civilize" its subjects.

This attitude was evident from the outset. *Dew and Mildew* was a collection of short stories set in India and said to be based on fact. Some of the stories were interrelated. There were several on educational themes, and others concern "William Tom Buggin, Esquire, Member of Parliament for Jews-ditch"—a caricature of the socialist Keir Hardie, who had visited India a few years earlier and spoken out against British rule. The book was praised in the English press for its humor and characterization, and for the accuracy of its portrayal of Indian customs, manners and morals. However, a critic in the *Boston Transcript* was ambivalent: "Few stories dealing with the hybrid Anglo-Indian civilization, as virile, as compelling and as instinct with life have appeared since [Kipling's] *Plain Tales from the Hills.* Their one drawback is the condescension with which the Briton is prone to view all people and all civilizations not his own."

Three novels with Indian settings followed during the war years, when Wren served with the Indian Army in East Africa. He was invalided out with the rank of major in 1917. Married by then, with one son, he became a full-time writer. His books were well enough received—several evoked comparisons with Kipling—but none made much impact until the publication in 1924 of *Beau Geste.* This, his most famous ever, begins with the mysterious disappearance of a precious jewel from an English country house. Suspicion falls on three aristocratic young visitors, the Geste brothers. Quixotically taking the blame upon himself, Beau Geste (French for "noble gesture") runs off and enlists in the French Foreign Legion. He is soon joined by his equally quixotic brothers, and the three earn the grudging respect of the brutal but fearless sergeant. Beau is posted to a desert fortress, Fort Zinderneuf, which is attacked by Arab hordes. The Legionaries fight to the last man (and then fight again, since the dead are propped up in the embrasures as if they were still on duty). Beau's brothers arrive with a relief column to find the fort manned entirely by corpses, Beau's among them. The Gestes set fire to Zinderneuf, giving Beau the "Viking's funeral" they had promised him as children.

The early reviewers of *Beau Geste* were not much impressed, agreeing that the "nobly idiotic" behavior of the brothers was beyond belief. The reading public did not care if it was, and devoured the novel for its mixture of mystery and hair-raising adventure, romantic chivalry and prurient sadism. Its great popularity was increased by the success of a stage adaptation, and much more by Herbert Brenon's silent screen version in 1926, with Ronald Colman as Beau and Noah Beery as the sergeant. William Wellman's 1939 sound version with Gary Cooper became even more successful, thanks to repeated exposure on television. Beau Geste and Fort Zinderneuf have entered popular mythology, receiving the ultimate accolade of endless parodies. The novel itself was much imitated and has never been out of print.

Wren never achieved a comparable triumph, though there were two popular sequels, *Beau Sabreur* and *Beau Ideal,* a collection of stories about the Gestes, and other books with Foreign Legion backgrounds. His later books were extremely uneven in quality. Some were undisguised potboilers, often showing an outrageous reliance on coincidence, and that relish for prolonged scenes of tor-

ture which was a marked feature of English popular fiction in the 1930s. There were also some serious bids for literary respectability, like *Mammon of Righteousness.* A study of sexual enslavement reminiscent of Somerset Maugham's *Of Human Bondage,* it was largely ignored by reviewers expecting quite different things from "Major Wren." *Two Feet from Heaven,* set in the London slums between the wars, and possibly Wren's best novel, is a study of a cowardly and deceitful clergyman.

Affluent enough to live in Albermarle Street, in the most fashionable part of London, Wren was a tall, erect and soldierly figure, complete with monocle and military moustache. Like Sherlock Holmes, he owned a notable collection of pipes. Wren never fully recovered the health he lost during the First World War and was turned down when, visiting Morocco in 1926, he impulsively applied to join the secret service. In 1936 and again in 1938 he was seriously ill with heart disease and muscular rheumatism. He served as a Justice of the Peace in later years.

PRINCIPAL WORKS: *Novels*—Father Gregory, 1913; Smoke and Sword, 1914; Driftwood Spars, 1915; The Wages of Virtue, 1916; Cupid in Africa, 1920; Beau Geste, 1924; Beau Sabreur, 1926; Beau Ideal, 1928; Soldiers of Misfortune, 1929; The Mammon of Righteousness, 1930 (in U.S.: Mammon); Mysterious Waye, 1930; Spring Glory, 1931; Beggars' Horses, 1934 (in U.S.: The Dark Woman); Sinbad the Soldier, 1935; Explosion, 1935; Spanish Maine, 1935 (in U.S.: The Desert Heritage); Bubble Reputation, 1936 (in U.S.: The Cortenay Treasure); The Fort in the Jungle, 1936; The Man of a Ghost, 1937 (in U.S.: The Spur of Pride); Worth Wile, 1937 (in U.S.: To the Hilt); Cardboard Castle, 1938; Paper Prison, 1939 (in U.S.: The Man the Devil Didn't Want); None Are So Blind, 1939; The Disappearance of General Jason, 1940; Two Feet from Heaven, 1940; The Uniform of Glory, 1941. *Short stories*—Dew and Mildew, 1912; The Young Stagers, 1917; Stepsons of France, 1917; The Good Gestes, 1929; Flawed Blades: Tales from the Foreign Legion, 1933; Port o' Missing Men: Strange Tale of the Stranger Regiment, 1934; Rough Shooting: True Tales and Strange Stories, 1938; A Mixed Bag, 1939; The Hunting of Henry, 1944; Stories of the Foreign Legion, 1947; Dead Men's Boots and Other Tales of the Foreign Legion, 1947; Dead Men's Boots and Other Tales of the Foreign Legion, 1949; Odd—But Even So: Stories Stranger than Fiction, 1942. *Nonfiction*—The Indian Teacher's Guide to the Theory and Practice of Mental, Moral and Physical Education, 1910; Indian School Organization . . . Being the Indian Headmaster's Guide, 1911; The "Direct" Teaching of English in Indian Schools, 1911; (with H.E.H. Pratt) Chemistry and First Aid for Standard VII, 1913; (with N. B. Macmillan) Physics and Mechanics, 1914; With the Prince Through Canada, New Zealand and Australia, 1922; First Lesson in English Grammar, 1961. *As editor*—The World and India, 1905; Longman's Science Series for Indian High Schools, 11 vol., 1913–1914; Sowing Glory; The Memoirs of "Mary Ambree," the English Woman Legionary, 1931.

ABOUT: Muldoon, S. J. Psychic Experiences of Famous People, 1947; Vinson, J. (ed.) Twentieth-Century Romance and Gothic Writers, 1982; Who's Who 1941. *Periodicals*—Boston Transcript March 6, 1913; Country Life August 1928; New York Times November 24, 1941; Times (London) November 24, 1941.

**WRIGHT, FRANK LLOYD** (June 8, 1869– April 9, 1959), was born in Richland Center, Wisconsin, the son of William Russell Cary Wright and Anna Lloyd (Jones). His father was a musician and clergyman from New England, his mother a schoolteacher of Welsh descent, with strong roots in the Unitarian faith and community. After a peripatetic childhood, Wright's family settled in Madison, Wisconsin, in 1880. Anna Wright sent Frank to work summers on his uncle's farms in nearby Spring Green. His time spent working in the vast, flat prairie fields of the Middle West shaped his vision of what was to become "organic architecture." In a lecture published in 1935, Wright remarked upon the importance of simplicity and space in forming organic architecture, tracing its origins back to summers on the Lloyd-Jones farmsteads: "You may see in these various feelings all taking the same direction that I was born an American child of the ground and of space, welcoming spaciousness as a modern human need as well as learning to see it as the natural human opportunity."

Wright briefly attended high school in Madison before enrolling at the University of Wisconsin. Since the university offered no degree in architecture, Wright decided to pursue courses in civil engineering, which he did for three largely unfulfilling years. Wright left for Chicago in 1887 and subsequently found work as an $8-a-week draftsman in an architect's office. One year later he secured a position as assistant to the preeminent Chicago architect Louis Sullivan. The Adler-Sullivan firm was the most progressive architectural alliance of its time, and Wright would later acknowledge Sullivan as his "master and inspiration." For the next six years Wright participated in developing works that became landmarks of modern architecture. Sullivan was interested primarily in building skyscrapers, so most commissions for houses received by the firm were given to Wright. Wright married Catherine Tobin in 1889, and as his family began to grow, his debts also accrued, prompting the young architect to undertake domestic projects outside the firm. When Sullivan discovered Wright's private commissions, he dismissed him.

In 1894, when he was just twenty-four, Wright began an independent practice in Chicago. His new innovations and compositions, known as "Prairie" houses, emphasized strong horizontals, a continuous flow of space throughout the interiors, and economical, mass-produced materials. The horizontal line which typified the Prairie School was an attempt to harmonize the buildings with the plains and wide-open vistas originally present on the sites. The spacious, unobstructed interiors and the inexpensive materials were meant to serve the interests of the American family.

After 1900 his work began to be noticed in professional and popular publications—as much in Europe as in America. Over the first decade of the twentieth century, Wright was the chief architect behind such landmark buildings as the Dana House (1902), the Robie House (1906–1910), the Coonley House (1908–1910), the Larkin Building in Buffalo, New York (1902), and the Unity Temple in Oak Park, Illinois (1904).

In 1904 he designed a one-story house in Oak Park, Illinois, for a well-to-do couple and began an affair with the wife, Mamah Borthwick Cheney. It was a serious affair, and by 1908 Wright and Mrs. Cheney had decided to seek divorces from their respective mates so as to marry each other. But although Mr. Cheney was amenable, Mrs. Wright—shocked, hurt, and concerned about the six children—was not. She demanded a year's wait. Wright became increasingly restive and in the fall of 1909 suddenly took off for Europe, where he was soon joined by Mrs. Cheney. Chicago was scandalized. In Europe, however, Wright was well received, and the Wasmuth firm in Berlin agreed to publish his architectural drawings in a seminal monograph informally known as the "Wasmuth Portfolio," issued in 1910 with an introduction by Wright himself. A book of photographs with an essay by a leader of the British Arts and Crafts movement followed (1911). These books, hardly seen in the United States till the 1960s, influenced contemporary European architects and helped create Wright's international reputation. They still constitute a valuable record of his early work and thinking. While preparing the drawings and text, he lived in Fiesole, outside of Florence, in a landscape which seemed to validate his theories: "No really Italian building seems ill at ease in Italy. All are happily content with what ornament and color they carry, as naturally as the rocks and trees and garden slopes which are one with them."

When his work on the books was complete, he moved back to the United States, to a chilly reception and few clients. Mrs. Cheney returned separately. In 1911 Wright undertook the construction of Taliesin, a large farmhouse in Spring Valley, Wisconsin, where they both would live. He wanted a natural house that would not be "on a hill, but rather of the hill." In his autobiography, Wright notes that in his search for the site of Taliesin ("Shining Brow"—the name of a bard in Welsh), he "scanned the hills of the region where the rock came cropping out in strata to suggest buildings." Taliesin became the most personal expression of Wright's theory of domestic architecture. Located on a 600-acre site, the building blended naturally with its wooded hill surroundings, and the buff-colored limestone of its walls was extracted from nearby quarries. In 1913 a crazed servant set fire to the house and murdered Mrs. Cheney, her two children (who were visiting), and four other people. Shattered, Wright began to rebuild the house. His mother came to live with him, and so did a sculptor, Miriam Noel. He and Mrs. Noel then spent five years in Japan, where Wright had been commissioned to build the western-style Imperial Hotel in Tokyo, one of his most famous undertakings. The hotel was constructed between 1915 and 1922 and subsequently withstood the great Tokyo earthquake of 1923, which left much of the city in ruins. Wright's engineering genius and willingness to press on with construction despite the doubts and opposition of Japanese and American colleagues result in a brilliant, beautiful, and structurally innovative building. Its demolition in 1967 was protested in Japan and elsewhere, though its lobby survives, moved brick-by-brick to the Meiji Village architectural preserve.

In 1922 Mrs. Wright agreed to a divorce and Wright married Miriam Noel, but the relationship had already soured and she left him upon their return to America in 1923. Wright spent the ensuing years contesting Noel's claims against him in court and rebuilding Taliesin, which had burned again after a lightning strike. Except for a few commissions in California, where he experimented with concrete, most of his work in this period consisted of plans and drawings for projects that never got built.

By this time, Wright's finances were in terrible shape. He sold a collection of Japanese prints to raise money, but Taliesin was seized by the bank, and his personal and professional affairs became grist for the popular press. He had made a new and happier marriage, to Olgivanna Lazovich, a young Montenegrin, in 1928. In 1929 a group of clients and admirers set up a foundation to protect him from ruin, and in 1932 Wright himself established the Taliesin fellowships, organized as a studioworkshop for apprentices and students who would pay to work and assist in his commissions. The fellowship sustained Wright through the Depression era, allowing him to pursue larger commissions while maintaining a meaningful foundation for his ideas and methods. Much of Wright's time in the 1930s was devoted to writing and lecturing, leading, in time, to the publication of what were to become his most important books. Reviewing his 1931 volume, *Modern Architecture,*a a reviewer for *Books* wrote, "Wright speaks chiefly as a preacher and a poet, in turn brutal and tender, violent and urbane, flippant and intensely serious." Wright spared no invective in his discussions of the "international style" expounded by European Modernists, many of whom, ironically, had cited Wright as a primary influence. "The style internationale," Wright pointed out in *Modern Architecture*, "would soon become a formula any tyro could cliché and it soon became abhorrent to the feelings of the free man everywhere. To eliminate artist individualities inspiring element in favor of the test tube and the mechanical laboratory would be to reduce art to an affair of the brain . . . to leave the human heart and mind, typified by the creative artist, out of its own."

Time and again Wright found himself having to defend organic architecture against currents in modern design and engineering. Architectural tides drastically turned on him as Le Corbusier and the Bauhaus School began to define a new industrial aesthetic congruent with advances in technologies. The machine age marked the ascendancy of function over form, the geometrical over the organic, the rational over the irrational. Wright felt increasingly embattled, the lone exponent of an outmoded aesthetic

His *An Autobiography* was published in 1932 and almost immediately sold out its first printing. It was reprinted in 1938, revised and enlarged in 1943, and eventually published in another revised posthumous edition in 1977. In a review of the 1943 edition, Clifton Fadiman of the *New Yorker* commented, "It is extraordinary that a man whose work is so harmonious, so just, so measured, so serene, and so deeply original should, when he takes up his pen, be so unrestrained, so lopsided, so sentimental, and so ridden with cliches. Yet somehow even his most humorless pomposity can not quite disguise the central magnificence of his professional thought on the subject he knows best." Fadiman's scathing review was not uncommon. Wright's propensity to engage in self-indulgent prose and casually issue pedagogic treatises on American democracy and ethics received less than a gratifying reception. Wright speaks in didactic, often grandiose tones throughout *An Autobiography*, referring to Nature, Truth, Goodness, and Beauty in a turgid, sanctimonious manner. For a time, Wright's self-appointed position as standard-bearer for a uniquely American vision of architecture and design seemed to be obscured.

In 1938, Wright began construction on Taliesin West, a winter retreat in the Arizona desert that featured massive, gently sloping walls built using desert stone masonry. Located on a mesa below the McDowell Mountains, Taliesin West's architecture reflected the environment's, "desert-world examples of hard, savage shapes."

Wright worked and wrote until the time of his death in 1959 at age 89. In 1941 King George of England awarded him the Royal Gold Medal for Architecture. Taliesin West thrived as a workshop for young apprentices, each year attracting a steady flow of brilliant new disciples to study the master's philosophy of organic architecture. Wright was by all accounts invigorated by the fellowships at Taliesin, secure in his abiding faith "man takes positive hand in creation whenever he puts a building upon the earth beneath the sun."

Among the buildings he designed in the final twenty-five years of his life were the S. C. Johnson Administration Building in Racine, Wisconsin (1936–1946), the Kaufmann House (Fallingwater) near Mill Run, Pennsylvania (1936–1939), the Pew House in Shorewood Hills, Wisconsin (1940), the Solomon H. Guggenheim Museum (1945–1959), the Price Tower in Bartlesville, Oklahoma (1956), and the Marin County Civic Center outside San Francisco (1957–1966).

Wright's vision of organic architecture, as articulated in the "Wasmuth Portfolio," has prevailed for the balance of the 20th century. Wright conceived of his work as a search for truth, finding it not in the physical form of a building, but rather in the spaces it contained. In 1994, in the *New York Review of Books*, Martin Filler wrote, "In the 35 years since the death of Frank Lloyd Wright, regard for his immense contribution to architecture has only increased. The present chaotic state of architecture makes Wright seem in hindsight to have been a force for unity."

PRINCIPAL WORKS: Japanese Prints: An Interpretation, 1912 (revised as The Japanese Print, 1967); Modern Architecture, Being the Kahn Lectures . . . , 1931; Two Lectures on Architecture, 1931; An Autobiography, 1932 (revised editions 1943, 1977); The Disappearing City, 1932 (expanded in 1945 as When Democracy Builds, and in 1958 as The Living City); Architecture and Modern Life (with B. Brownell) 1937; An Organic Architecture, the Architecture of Democracy, 1939 (reprinted in The Future of Architecture, 1953); Frank Lloyd Wright on Architecture: Selected Writings 1894–1940 (edited by F. Gutheim) 1941; Genius and the Mobocracy, 1949 (revised edition 1972); The Future of Architecture, 1953; The Natural House, 1954; An American Architecture (edited by E. Kaufmann) 1955; The Story of the Tower, 1956; A Testament, 1957; Writings and Buildings (selected by E. Kaufmann and B. Raeburn) 1960; Plans, Buildings, and Designs, 1963 ("Wasmuth Portfolio" of 1910); Letters to Apprentices (selected by B. B. Pfeiffer) 1982; Collected Writings (edited by B. B. Pfeiffer) 1992– .

ABOUT: Blake, P. The Master Builders, 1960; Brooks, H. A. (ed.) Writings on Wright, 1981; Gill, B. Many Masks: A Life of Frank Lloyd Wright, 1987; Heinz, T. A. Frank Lloyd Wright, 1982; Manson, G. C. Frank Lloyd Wright, vol 1: to 1910, the First Golden Age, 1958; Mumford, L. Roots of Contemporary American Architecture, 1952; Naden, C. J. Frank Lloyd Wright, the Rebel Architect, 1968; Nute, K. Frank Lloyd Wright and Japan, 1994; Pfeiffer, B. B. Frank Lloyd Wright in the Realm of Ideas, 1988; Scully, V. S. Frank Lloyd Wright, 1960; Secrest, M. Frank Lloyd Wright: A Biography, 1992; Smith, N. K. Frank Lloyd Wright: A Study in Architectural Content, 1966; Spencer, B. A. (ed.) The Prairie School Tradition, 1985; Secrest, M. Frank Lloyd Wright: A Biography, 1992; Storrer, W. A. The Frank Lloyd Wright Companion, 1994; Twombley, R. C. Frank Lloyd Wright: His Life and His Architecture, 1979; Willard, C. Frank Lloyd Wright: American Architect, 1972; Wright, J. L. My Father Who Is on Earth, 1946.

**WRIGHT, HAROLD BELL** (May 4, 1872–May 24, 1944), American novelist, wrote: "Harold Bell Wright was born in Rome, N. Y., of an early

American family, in the farmhouse built by his grandfather on the acres cleared by pioneers in the wilderness. His father moved to Whitesboro, N. Y., while the son was still a baby, and later to Sennet, N. Y. His mother died when he was ten, and he was put out to work on a farm. His only schooling was a country school. Before he was twenty-one he learned the trade of house painting and decorating. When he was grown he entered the preparatory department of Hiram College, in Ohio. But after two years a severe attack of pneumonia and serious injury to his eyes from overwork ended his school career.

"When his hopes of gaining a college education ended, he went to Missouri. He became interested in the backwoods people, and to fill a very evident need started preaching in a schoolhouse Sundays and conducted a class in the study of the teachings of Jesus every Friday. Without college or theological seminary training, he spent ten years as pastor of churches in Pierce City, Missouri; Pittsburg, Kansas; Kansas City, Missouri; Lebanon, Missouri; and Redlands, California . . .

"He married Frances E. Long in 1899, and they had three sons (one now deceased). After a divorce, he married Winifred Mary (Potter) Duncan in 1920. . . ."

---

Harold Bell Wright overcame poverty, a lifelong history of bad health, and the universal scorn of critics to write some of America's most popular Western novels of the turn of the century. "I came to my work, not by way of the graded highways of literature but by the rough trails and rutted roads of desperate living," he wrote in To My Sons (1934), an autobiography that covers the first thirty years of his life.

His early years "had been a drama of deprivation, struggle and near oblivion," wrote Lawrence V. Tagg in the 1994 biography Harold Bell Wright. Already ill and impoverished at twenty-two when he set out to convalesce with an uncle in the Ozarks, Wright began a fifty-year ministerial writing journey that brought him fame and fortune through his many scripts for stage plays, numerous magazine articles, and nearly twenty best-selling novels, fifteen of which were made into movies set in the Ozarks, Arizona, and California. His craft was his tonic for coping with his respiratory ailments. "Writing was a form of intoxication, given a pencil and paper I was off on a regular hellbender on words," he wrote in To My Sons.

His name vanished with his death, as his work was too narrowly connected with his era—a time when a significant portion of middle-class Americans bought and relished the sermons and sentiment of his melodramas. These voiced—as John P. Ferre insists in A Gospel for Millions,—a conservative Protestant response to the industrial dislocations and intellectual upheavals of the times. The appeal of Wright's novels rested in their "romanticizing the frontier past by emphasizing morality over belief, and by trusting individuals to solve the problems that they believed were created by social institutions," wrote Ferre, adding that Wright's novels are "a quintessential revealer of pre–World War I American values, particularly religious ones," with an emphasis on "faith in unspoiled nature and a moral code of hard work, clean living and neighborliness."

Originally serialized in the Christian Century, a national religious weekly, Wright's first book, That Printer of Udell's (1903), is a largely autobiographical story of a young itinerant printer that embodies the strong moral-religious theme of all of his fiction—that the church should put aside its piousness to help the least fortunate. Wright usually added a love angle, some masculine conflict, and the flavor of the outdoors to this moral recipe to create the kind of wholesome stories "anybody's sister could read," he told the New York Times.

One of his most popular books was The Shepherd of the Hills (1907), a combination Ozark geography lesson and clean, ends-in-marriage romance, that concentrates on the mental, physical, and spiritual growth of its characters. The start of a trilogy that continued with The Calling of Dan Matthews

(1909) and *God and the Groceryman* (1927), it featured the character Dan Matthews, whose struggle with the ministry paralleled Wright's. John Wayne starred in the 1941 movie adaptation of *The Shepherd of the Hills*.

The substance and purpose of Wright's novels come largely from their settings, as in the once famous but now forgotten *The Winning of Barbara Worth* (1911), a Western-action romance intertwined with the reclamation of the Imperial Valley of California and the struggle with the Colorado River. Also set in California, *The Eyes of the World* (1914) portrays the corruption of Easterners who came West and sold their talents to the highest bidder regardless of moral consequences. It ranked number one on the best-seller list for 1914 despite objections from critics, including H. L. Mencken, who thought Wright was "too sentimental, too romantic, and too unreal in his stories." The *New York Times* called the novel "a yellow-journal sort of sermon"—but it was one that was preached to thirty million readers.

For many years Wright shuttled between Arizona and California. After suffering extensive injuries when he and his horse were struck by a car, settled in Tucson, where he wrote about ranch life and romance in *When a Man's a Man* (1916). But he soon returned to California to write *The Re-creation of Brian Kent* (1919), even while the critics continued their assault on his books. The reading public at the low end of the market were still eagerly buying them. "Fitzgerald's *This Side of Paradise*, brought out within months of Wright's *Brian Kent*, sold fifty-thousand copies while sales of Wright's book neared the million mark," reported Lawrence Tagg. Nonetheless, as the *New York Times* wrote, "It would be difficult to imagine a mushier, more ridiculous mess set forth as a book of fiction." The *Times* was not alone in its indignation. A year later, when Wright's first marriage ended, the *New York Evening Sun* wrote, "Harold Bell Wright, who recently obtained a divorce, complains that his former wife did not appreciate his books. Perhaps she appraised them."

Bothered more by his health than his reviews, an undaunted Wright moved again to Tucson, where he continued to preach to his loyal rural and small-town readers, "anxious not to improve the tone of American letters but the tone of American life," wrote the *New York Times* upon publication of *Helen of the Old House* (1921). Although the Eastern literary establishment viewed him as another Zane Grey low-brow—albeit with fewer guns and less violence in his stories—Hollywood saw his potential at the box office, and in 1922 Paramount Pictures purchased the movie rights to nine of Wright's novels in a deal estimated to involve a million dollars. He continued to churn out best sellers until 1932.

Following an eight-year silence after writing his autobiography, Wright returned to the sub-literary world with *The Man Who Went Away* (1942), the story of a New Yorker who takes refuge in a redwood forest. The underlying theme was that saving a tree saves humanity. It contains the usual city-country dichotomy found in all his work, but "Wright had long ago lost the audience eager for an anti-city social melodrama," Ferre wrote, adding that Wright's moral messages had less impact in a post-war America.

A better preacher than writer, Wright had little ability to bring a vision alive in his books. He "can speak about the past . . . but he has nothing to say for our present," Ferre concluded. Nevertheless, the 1980s and 1990s saw a nostalgic renewal of interest in his work: in 1983, his son, Norman, established the Harold Bell Wright Theater and Museum in Branson, Missouri, and a Harold Bell Wright Society was formed in 1992; many of his books have been reissued in the past twenty years.

PRINCIPAL WORKS: That Printer of Udell's, 1903; The Shepherd of the Hills, 1907; The Calling of Dan Matthews, 1909; The Uncrowned King, 1910; The Winning of Barbara Worth, 1911; Their Yesterdays, 1912; The Eyes of the World, 1914; When a Man's a Man, 1916; The Re-creation of Brian Kent, 1919; Helen of the Old House, 1921; The Mine with the Iron Door, 1923; A Son of His Father, 1925; God and the Groceryman, 1927; Long Ago Told, 1929; Exit, 1930; Ma Cinderella, 1932; The Devil's Highway, 1932; The Man Who Went Away, 1942. Autobiography—To My Sons, 1934.

ABOUT: The autobiographical material quoted above was written for Twentieth Century Authors, 1942. Ferre, J. A Social Gospel for Millions, 1988; Kinkead, J. The Western Sermons of Harold Bell Wright; Tagg, L. Harold Bell Wright: Storyteller to America, 1994. Periodicals—New York Evening Sun August 4, 1920; New York Times August 16, 1914; August 31, 1919; August 28, 1921; May 25, 1944; Times (London) May 26, 1944.

**WRIGHT, RICHARD** (September 4, 1908–November 28, 1960), American novelist, was born on a farm near Roxie, Mississippi, the son of Nathan Wright, a sharecropper and mill worker, and Ella (Wilson) Wright, a schoolteacher. For a couple of years he and his brother lived with their maternal grandparents in Natchez; in 1913 the family moved to Memphis, where his father deserted them and his mother found employ-ment as a cook. Wright attended school for a few months in 1915–1916, but his mother's illness forced him to leave. He and his brother were placed temporarily in an orphanage before joining their grandparents, now living in Jackson, and then for a short time with an aunt in Arkansas. He attended school for several months in 1918–1919, but after his mother's health broke down again he was needed to earn money for the family. In 1919 he went to live with relatives in Greenwood, Mississippi, but by 1920 he was back with his grandparents in Jackson. Although he was a couple of years behind his age group, Wright did well in school. His work as a newspaper delivery boy gave him time to read. During the summer of 1922 he traveled around parts of the rural south as an assistant to an insurance agent. He held a variety of jobs while attending junior high school, yet despite his family's precarious financial situation, he was able to afford decent clothing, school books, and a bicycle. He wrote his first short story, "The Voodoo of Hell's Half-Acre," during the winter of 1923–24; it was published in Jackson's weekly black newspaper, the *Southern Register*. In 1925 Wright graduated junior high school as class valedictorian. He began high school that fall, but quit after a few weeks to seek work. He lived in Memphis from 1925 until 1927, doing menial jobs at an optical company. He read widely, but focused on the writings of H. L. Mencken as well as realist novelists such as Theodore Dreiser, Sherwood Anderson, and Sinclair Lewis. It was at this point in his life that Wright decided to become a writer.

Late in 1927 Wright moved to Chicago and after a while became a post office clerk. The job gave him a steady income, and the opportunity to read and write in his spare time. He joined a local African American literary club but found little to share with its middle-class members. In 1930 he began work on a novel called "Cesspool," later titled *Lawd Today!*, but only published after his death. Naturalistic in outlook, it is the grim story of a Chicago postal worker who brutalizes his wife. The economic depression forced Wright out of his fulltime position, although he worked off and on for the postal service during the early 1930s. In 1931 his story "Superstition" was published in *Abbott's Monthly Magazine*, but he was never paid. Wright held odd jobs during these years: funeral insurance agent, ditch digger, street cleaner. The League of Struggle for Negro Rights attracted his attention in 1931, and in 1933 he joined the Chicago branch of the John Reed Club, a literary organization under Communist party auspices. He joined the party itself the following year. From 1934 to 1937, when he left Chicago, Wright was engaged in a number of literary endeavors directly related to party activities. He wrote leftist poetry for journals such *Left Front*, *Midland Left*, *Anvil*, *International Literature*, *Partisan Review*, and *New Masses*, and contributed articles on avant-garde writing and prizefighting to these magazines. He lectured on black writers and their works, and in so doing attracted the attention of white writers such as James T. Farrell. In 1935 Wright was hired by the Federal Writers' Project (under the Works Progress Administration) to do research on blacks in Chicago for the Illinois volume of the American Guide Series. The following year he became associated with the Negro Federal Theatre (part of the Federal Theater Project) and adapted sections of his unpublished novel for dramatic use. During these years Wright also served on the editorial board of *Left Front*, attended a meeting of the American Writers' Congress in New York City in 1935, was named to the national council of the League of American Writers, and organized a meeting of the National Negro Congress in Chicago in 1936. Despite repeated rejections by publishers of the manuscript of "Cesspool," he continued to write fiction. His story "Big Boy Leaves Home" (later included in *Uncle Tom's Children*) was published in *The New Caravan* and received favorable comments. Over a dispute about the freedom of the writer Wright

stopped participating in party activities in early 1937, and a few months later moved to New York.

Wright settled in Harlem, and was appointed local editor for the *Daily Worker*, a Communist newspaper to which he contributed 200 articles over the next few years. With others he co-founded *New Challenge*, an independent magazine designed to foster in African Americans an awareness of leftist causes and activities. He published "Blueprint for Negro Writing" in the first issue, but the magazine did not survive. His autobiographical sketch "The Ethics of Living Jim Crow" appeared in *American Stuff: WPA Writers' Anthology*; the essay was later added to *Uncle Tom's Children* and reworked into his autobiography. The story "Fire and Cloud," which would also appear in his first collection of short fiction, won first prize in a contest run by *Story Magazine* in 1937 and was given the O. Henry Memorial Award in 1938. Wright rejoined the Federal Writers' Project: he researched the Harlem section of the guide for New York City and wrote parts of *New York Panorama*. The following year Harper and Brothers published four of Wright's stories as *Uncle Tom's Children*. The reviews were generally good. Malcolm Cowley wrote in the *New Republic* in 1938 that he "found these stories both heartening, as evidence of a vigorous new talent, and terrifying as the expression of a racial hatred that has never ceased to grow and gets no chance to die." Some critics, such as Zora Neale Hurston writing in the *Saturday Review of Literature* that year, objected to the book's dominating party line. Hurston added that "Not one act of understanding and sympathy comes to pass in the entire work." Harper reissued the collection two years later in an expanded edition that included six stories and an essay. Wright was also actively engaged in other literary ventures. He was named to the literature editorial board of *New Masses*, won a Guggenheim fellowship, and was denounced by the House Special Committee on Un-American Activities investigating the Federal Writers' Project. He made the acquaintance of many new and established African American writers, notably Langston Hughes, Alain Locke, Arna Bontemps, Countee Cullen, W. E. B. Du Bois, and Ralph Ellison. Also in 1939 Wright married Dhima Rose Meadman, but the relationship lasted less than a year.

Wright wrote the first draft of *Native Son* in 1939 and revised it the following year before it was submitted to Harper. A Book-of-the-Month Club choice, the novel was an explosive best-seller. It is a disturbing case study of a young black murderer. Wright's style is simple and direct, often reaching heights of poetic intensity. The book aroused considerable controversy in that the author placed the blame for the crime mostly on social conditions and environmental factors. Bigger Thomas, with a record of delinquency, gets a job as chauffeur to a rich philanthropist whose daughter, Mary, is a radical. One evening Bigger drives her to a meeting with her Communist friend Jan. The two whites puzzle Bigger by treating him as an equal. In carrying the intoxicated young woman up to her bedroom later than night, Bigger is startled and accidentally smothers her. In panic he burns the body in the furnace and attempts to implicate Jan—but it is not long before he is apprehended for the crime. Bigger's trial becomes an exposition of an individual tragedy that symbolizes the tragedy of a race. His lawyer's defense is that white hatred and suppression led Bigger to commit his actions, and that whites must share Bigger's guilt. But no pleas can save him from execution: "Now I come to think of it, it seems like something that just had to be," Bigger says. "When a man kills, it's for something. . . . I didn't know I was really alive in this world until I felt things hard enough to kill for 'em." For the first time in his life, because he has done things which whites have really noticed, Bigger feels a sense of freedom and power. Yet in prison he eventually comes to terms with the need for a common brotherhood, and before his death this realization redeems him. Wright made a number of deletions and editorial concessions in order to get the book published. It was not until 1991 that the complete text was published, when the Library of America issued its two-volume collection of Wright's most significant writings. Wright was awarded the Spingarn Medal from the National Association for the Advancement of Colored People in 1941 for his "powerful description . . . of the effect of proscription, segregation, and denial of opportunity to the American Negro."

With the money he received from *Native Son* Wright went to Mexico for several months in 1940 to write fiction. During the rest of the year he traveled around the American South and then went to Chicago to work on a nonfictional book, with photographs, about African Americans, later published as *12 Million Black Voices*. He collaborated with Paul Green on a stage adaptation of *Native Son*, sponsored by John Houseman and directed by Orson Welles, which ran successfully on Broadway in 1941–43. He worked on a novel entitled *The Man Who Lived Underground*, which was only published posthumously. With the stature and prominence gained from his successful novel, Wright spoke out against the Roosevelt administration's racial policies. At first Wright was opposed to American involvement in the European conflict, but after United States entry into the war he was supportive. Also in 1941 Wright married Ellen Poplar, a fellow leftist and the daughter of Polish Jewish immigrants, and moved to Brooklyn Heights for a couple of years and then to Greenwich Village. In 1942 he severed ties completely with the Communist party over his continuing claim that it suppressed creative freedom and, additionally, that it did not work hard enough to battle racial discrimination. The following year he began writing his autobiography, to be called *American Hunger*. Harper agreed to publish the first part of the work, telling Wright that the Book-of-the-Month Club would not offer it as a selection if the later parts, about his radical political activities in Chicago, were included. Retitled *Black Boy*, the book was published to highly favorable reviews and sold very well. When later parts of the autobiography appeared in the *Atlantic Monthly* in 1944, Wright was

denounced by the Communist party. The entire second half was published seventeen years after Wright's death, and in 1991 the Library of America issued the correct text of the entire work. In the summer of 1945 Wright was artist-in-residence at the Bread Loaf school for writers in Middlebury, Vermont. In addition, he participated in radio talk programs and toured the country for a couple of months giving lectures.

Wright was in France for several months in 1946. There he met Gertrude Stein, André Gide, Léopold Senghor, Aimé Césaire, and other writers, and helped established the journal *Présence Africaine*. He returned to the United States briefly in 1947 to sell his house and move his family and himself permanently to Europe. He settled in Paris and associated with existentialists such as Jean-Paul Sartre, Simone de Beauvoir, and Albert Camus, and made the acquaintance of fellow black American expatriate writer James Baldwin. The influence of Camus manifested itself in Wright's next literary project, an existential novel of his own called *The Outsider*. He joined associations of writers and intellectuals, attended conferences, and became interested in movements to end European colonialism in Africa and elsewhere in the Third World. In 1949 he joined George Plimpton and others in founding the *Paris Review*, and on his own began working on a screenplay for *Native Son*. He was in the United States briefly that year and the next en route to and from Argentina, where the film was shot, with Wright himself acting the role of Bigger Thomas. Although the film was generally praised overseas, it was substantially cut before its American release in 1951 and received poor reviews. It was also banned in several cities. Wright established the Franco-American Fellowship in 1950 to challenge racial discrimination by American firms and groups operating in France. He continued to work on *The Outsider*, completing the novel in 1952. The book garnered mixed reviews, and sales were modest.

During 1953 Wright traveled extensively in Africa gathering material for a book about the continent entitled *Black Power*. The following year he journeyed around Spain to research another volume of travel impressions, published a couple of years later as *Pagan Spain*. After Harper rejected the manuscript, Avon published a paperback original of his novel *Savage Holiday*. Wright kept quiet about French activities in Algeria, mostly in fear of being deported. But in 1955 he attended the Bandung Conference of nonaligned nations, and recorded his impressions in *The Color Curtain*. In 1956 he adapted Louis Sapin's *Papa Bon Dieu* as *Daddy Goodness*, but it was not until 1959 that the play was produced in Paris. At the inaugural Congress of Negro Artists and Writers, held under the sponsorship of *Présence Africaine*, Wright spoke on "Tradition and Industrialization: The Tragic Plight of the African Elite." He also lectured in Britain, Germany, and Scandinavia on colonial oppression and artistic freedom; these lectures were reworked as essays and collected in *White Man, Listen!*. Later in 1956 he began a novel set in Mississippi, entitled

*The Long Dream.* Although reviews and sales were poor, he immediately started work on a sequel, set in France, called "Island of Hallucinations" (as yet unpublished). In the last years of his life Wright distanced himself from groups he had supported as well as other African Americans living in Paris. He grew more and more suspicious of persecution by the Cental Intelligence Agency. To some extent his feelings were justified: government files released well after his death revealed that his activities were continuously monitored from the 1940s on. Nevertheless he conducted lectures on American literature for the American Cultural Center in Paris and participated in the 1958 meeting of the Congress for Cultural Freedom. He turned down involvement with the next meeting of the organization, however—and it was much later discoverd that the congress had received CIA funding. Wright's poor health (possibly the result of dysentery contracted in Africa), diminishing literary reputation, and financial difficulties led to depression. He made arrangements to move to London, but the British government rejected, without an explanation, his request for a resident visa. He continued to write: his story "Big Black Good Man" was included in *Best American Stories of 1958.* In 1959 he began composing haikus, eventually writing almost four thousand of the short poems. He started a new novel in 1960 but his intestinal problems worsened, despite treatment. He was able to finish work on *Eight Men,* a volume of short stories, before he died of a heart attack at age fifty-two, in November of that year. Mystery about his death remains, with his daughter Julia maintaining that Wright was murdered.

Richard Wright's papers are in the Beinecke Library at Yale University.

PRINCIPAL WORKS: *Fiction*—Lawd Today!, written 1930–37, pub. 1963; Uncle Tom's Children, 1938, expanded ed. 1940 (stories); Native Son, 1940, complete text pub. 1991; The Outsider, 1953; Savage Holiday, 1954; The Long Dream, 1958 (sequel: Island of Hallucinations, written 1958–59, unpub.); Eight Men, 1961 (stories); The Man Who Lived Underground, 1971 (novella). *Drama*—(with P. Green) Native Son, 1941, rev. ed. 1980; Native Son, 1951 (screenplay); Daddy Goodness (adapt. of Papa Bon Dieu by L. Sapin), written 1956, produced 1959. *Nonfiction*—Twelve Million Black Voices: AS Folk History of the Negro in the United States, 1941; Black Power: A Record of Reactions in a Land of Pathos, 1954; The Color Curtain: A Report on the Bandung Conference, 1956; Pagan Spain, 1957; White Man, Listen!, 1957 (essays based on lectures). *Autobiography*—Black Boy: A Record of Childhood and Youth, 1945; American Hunger, 1977; Black Boy (American Hunger), complete text pub. 1991. *As editor*—(and contributor) Quintet, 1961 (stories). *Collections*—A Richard Wright Reader (ed. E. Wright and M. Fabre), 1978; The Life and Work of Richard Wright (ed. D. Ray and R. M. Farnsworth), 1979. The best selection of Wright's writings are available in the Library of America series: Early Works—Lawd Today!, Uncle Tom's Children, Native Son (ed. A. Rampersad), 1991; Later Works—Black Boy (American Hunger), The Outsider (ed. A Rampersad), 1991.

ABOUT: Abcarian, R. (ed.) Richard Wright's Native son: A Critical Handbook, 1970; Baker, H. (ed.) Twentieth Century Interpretations of Native Son, 1972; Bakish, D. Richard Wright, 1973; Baldwin, J. Nobody Knows My Name, 1961; Baldwin, J. Notes of a Native Son, 1955; Bloom, H. (ed.) Bigger Thomas, 1990; Bloom, HJ. (ed.) Richard Wright, 1987; Bloom, H. (ed.) Richard Wright's Black Boy, 1988; Bloom, H. (ed.) Richard Wright;s Native Son, 1988; Bone, R. Richard Wright, 1969; Brignano, R. Richard Wright, 1970; Butler, R. Native Son: The Emergence of a New Black Hero, 1991; Davis, A. P. From the Dark Tower, 1974; Davis, C. T. and Fabre, M. Richard Wright: A Primary Bibliography, 1982; Ellison, R. Shadow and Act, 1964; Fabre, M. From Harlem to Paris: Black American Writers in France, 1991; Fabre, M. Richard Wright: Books and Writers, 1990; Fabre, M. The Unfinished Quest of Richard Wright (tr. I. Barzun), 1973, 2nd ed. 1992; Fabre, M. The World of Richard Wright, 1985; Felgar, R. Richard Wright, 1980; Fishburn, K. Richard Wright's Hero, 1977; Gayle, A. Richard Wright: Ordeal of a Native Son, 1980; Hakutani, Y. (ed.) Critical Essays on Richard Wright, 1982; Joyce, J. A. Richard Wright's Art of Tragedy, 1986; Kinnamon, K. The Emergence of Richard Wright, 1972; Kinnamon, K. (ed.) New Essays on Native Son, 1990; Kinnamon, K. (ed.) A Richard Wright Bibliography, 1988; Macksey, R. and Moorer, F. E. (eds.) Richard Wright: A Collection of Critical Essays, 1984; Margolies, E. The Art of Richard Wright, 1969; McCall, D. The Example of Richard Wright, 1969; Miller, E. E. Voice of a Native Son: The Poetics of Richard Wright, 1990; Ray, D. and Farnsworth, R. M. (eds.) Richard Wright: Impressions and Perspectives, 1973; Reilly, J. M. (ed.) Richard Wright: The Critical Reception, 1978; Urban, J. Richard Wright, 1989; Walker, M. Richard Wright: Daemonic Genius, 1988; Webb, C. Richard Wright, 1968. *Periodicals*—American Literature October 1983; March 1985; May 1985; Antioch Review Summer 1945; Black American Literature Forum Fall 1982; Fall 1984; Winter 1985; Summer 1985; Spring/Summer 1986; Winter 1989; winter 1991; CLA Journal March 1974; September 1977; March 1978; September 1980; December 1983; March 1984; June 1985; June 1986; June 1988; June 1990; September 1990; June 1991; September 1991; Crisis February 1975; Ebony February 1961; February 1989; Essays in Literature Fall 1990; Hudson Review Summer 1992; Journal of American Folklore Summer 1991; Life June 4, 1945; Massachusetts Review Autumn 1977; MELUS Fall 1983; Summer 1985; Mississippi Quarterly Spring 1988; Fall 1989; Modern Fiction Studies Spring 1988; Autumn 1988; Nation January 28, 1961; Negro History Bulletin April 1962; September 1977; New Republic April 6, 1938; April 7, 1941; March 12, 1945; February 13, 1961; March 30, 1992; New York Times November 10, 1960; New York Times Book Review March 3, 1940; March 4, 1945; March 22, 1953; October 7, 1973; December 29, 1991; New York Times Magazine December 7, 1986; Newsweek December 12, 1960; April 1, 1968; Phylon Fall 1960; March 1977; December 1979; June 1986; Reporter March 16, 1961; Saturday Review March 30, 1963; January 21, 1978; Saturday Review of Literature April 2, 1938; March 2, 1940; June 1, 1940; March 3, 1945; March 28, 1953; Sewanee Review Summer 1991; Southern Literary Journal Spring 1984; Southwest Review Winter 1985; Studies in Short Fiction Fall 1986; Texas Studies in Literature and Language Winter 1987; Time March 4, 1940; December 23, 1940; December 12, 1960; March 22, 1968; Time (London) November 30, 1960; Times Literary Supplement November 30, 1990; December 13, 1991.

**WRIGHT, RICHARDSON LITTLE** (June 18, 1886–August 6, 1961), American magazine editor, wrote for more than thirty years on gardening and decorating, as well as on diverse subjects such as Russia, incidental American history, and travel.

Born in Philadelphia, the son of George S. R. Wright and Mary Ann (Wilbraham) Wright, he received his B.A. degree from Trinity College, Hartford, Connecticut, in 1910, returning for his master's in 1924. After graduation, he became Sunday editor of the Knickerbocker Press in Albany, New York, for a year, and then went to Manchuria and Siberia as a special correspondent of the *New York World, Chicago Daily News,* and *London Daily Express.*

After a year in Russia, he returned to the states as literary critic of the *New York Times* and dramatic critic of *Smart Styles*. His first books, written in the nineteen teens, derived from his Russian experiences. *The Russians: An Interpretation* (1917),

was written shortly before the revolution, and was already dated by the time it was published. The following year, with the help of fellow pranksters from the New York Authors Club, Wright contributed to a literary hoax, *Feodor Vladimir Larrovitch: An Appreciation of His Life and Works* (1918) for which Wright served as co-editor and contributed the chapter "The True and False About Larrovitch" in a volume of tributes, critiques, and reminiscences of a fictitious Russian author, complete with a sampling of his works.

In 1914 he was appointed editor of *House and Garden*, a post he held for thirty-five years. Despite his failure to understand why he was chosen for the post, he quickly found his niche as writer and editor of many volumes on gardening and decorating. Besides editing a series of basic working guides, which were updated compilations of the pages of *House and Garden*, Wright went further down the garden path, writing his own more personal accounts that chronicled years of gardening in Connecticut and Cape Cod. Instead of taking a dry textbook approach, his books on gardening, standards in their time, are like having a personal chat with a horticultural expert, sharing practical advice, tips, and trivia in a casual yet absorbing manner, thanks to his evident humor and first-hand experiences with trowel and trellis. "Richardson Wright speaks with authority on any question connected with gardens and flowers," wrote the *New York Times* in reviewing his *Flowers for Cutting and Decoration* (1923).

The wisdom of Wright's experience comes through in *Greedy Gardeners* (1954), a miscellany where humor grows among the lilacs and lilies, with the aim being "to help gardeners avoid horticultural mediocrity," he wrote. Inspired by his "friend and master," Ernest Henry Wilson, and fellow gardening writers Louise Beebe Wilder and Gertrude Jekyll, Wright's humility was obvious when he advised, "Consult all the experts; read as many how-to-garden books as you will: the final knowledge, like all wisdom, comes only from working out your own problems on your own ground."

While Wright was principally concerned with was telling people how to grow their gardens and decorate their homes, away from the wisteria and wallpaper he pursued "the things that crop up when you are searching for something else," as he wrote in *Grandfather Was Queer* (1939). He combined a love of curious and forgotten lore with an easy conversational style to write a serious of bedtime books, little literary midnight snacks.

*Hawkers and Walkers in Early America* (1927), a survey of vagabondage for which Wright dug up tales of strolling peddlers, preachers, players, and others from pre–Civil War days, was the first of

three books he wrote on little-known American history. "No book of recent times . . . has given so much of the flavor and gusto of the early days of America," wrote Morris Markey in *Literary Review*.

He continued indulging his passion for obscure history with *Forgotten Ladies* (1928), a remembrance of such oddball women as Deborah Sampson, who fought in the Revolutionary Army disguised as a man; Belle Boyd, a Virginia Confederate spy who later became an actress; Kate Fox, who at the age of six discovered that she could snap her toe bones and make spiritualistic rappings; and Maria Monk, whose volume of "Awful Disclosures" contributed to the xenophobic and anti-Catholic movement of the 1840s called "Know-Nothingism." His next labor of love, again gleaned from old playbills, newspaper squibs, and forgotten biographies, was *Revels in Jamaica 1682–1838* (1937), an account of the social and artistic life of the island, with emphasis on the theater, the balls and dinners of high society, tumblers and conjurers, cockfights and mummers.

Wright's *Grandfather Was Queer* (1939) was a brief history of eccentricity in America. He wrote in its introduction that he was writing in a time of "flag-pole sitters, champion hog-hollerers, lady vaudeville preachers, candidates who attain gubernatorial office with hill-billy bands, debutantes who pursue sweet charity to get their photographs in newspapers, and yokels who reap national notoriety by spitting tobacco juice the admirable distance of eighteen feet six inches—such an age would seem likely to produce enough queer bits and pieces to make its own crazy quilt without dipping into the scrap-bag of the past."

Wright was in great demand as a lecturer and served for twenty years as chairman of the International Flower Show in New York, where he was also president of the Wine and Food Society and chairman of the board of the Horticultural Society.

Principal Works: Through Siberia: An Empire in the Making (with G. B. Digby) 1913; The Open Door, 1914; (ed.) Inside the Home of Good Taste, 1915; (ed.) Low Cost Suburban Homes, 1916; The Russians: An Interpretation, 1917; Letters to the Mother of a Soldier, 1918; (ed. with W. G. Jordan) Feodor Vladimir Larrovitch, 1918; (ed.) House & Garden's Book of Houses, 1919; (ed.) House & Garden's Book of Interiors, 1920; (ed.) House & Garden's Book of Gardens, 1921; Truly Rural, 1922; Flowers for Cutting and Decoration, 1923; The Practical Book of Outdoor Flowers, 1924; A Small House and Large Garden, 1924; Hawkers & Walkers in Early America, 1927; Forgotten Ladies, 1928; The Gardener's Bed-Book, 1929; (ed.) House & Garden's Book of Color Schemes, 1929; The Bed-Book of Travel, 1931; Another Gardener's Bed-Book, 1933; The Story of Gardening, 1934; The Winter Diversions of a Gardener, 1934; Revels in Jamaica, 1682–1838, 1937; The Gardener's Day-Book, 1938; Grandfather Was Queer, 1939; (ed.) House & Garden's Complete Guide to Interior Decoration, 1941; The Bed-Book of Eating and Drinking, 1943; The Gardener's Tribute, 1949; A Book of Days for Christians, 1951; A Sower Went Forth, 1953; Greedy Gardeners, 1954.

About: Wright, R. L. Grandfather Was Queer, 1939; Wright, R. L. Greedy Gardeners. *Periodicals*—Books May 10, 1931; Literary Review February 26, 1927; New York Herald Tribune December 4, 1949; New York Times June 17, 1923; October 22, 1933; December 24, 1939; August 7, 1961; Publishers Weekly August 28, 1961.

## WRIGHT, WILLARD HUNTINGTON (pseudonym "S. S. VAN DINE") (October 15, 1887–April 11, 1939), American detective fiction

writer, art critic, editor, and journalist, had two distinct literary careers. Willard Huntington Wright was a literary and art critic, a modern art scholar and author of several aesthetic and philological works. S. S. Van Dine, a pseudonym Wright created after suffering a lengthy illness in the mid-1920s, wrote popular detective novels featuring Philo Vance, an erudite sleuth fashioned after his creator. Vance quickly snooped his way through twelve best selling novels that were translated into eleven languages and sold more than a million copies by the end of the 1920s. John Loughery, in his biography *Alias S. S. Van Dine* (1992), wrote that Van Dine—"like a character out of a Fitzgerald short story" with his Van Dyke beard, pearl-handled cane and palatial New York penthouse full of modern paintings and Chinese ceramics—was one of the most interviewed and affluent American authors of the 1920s.

Born in Charlottesville, Virginia, the son of Archibald Davenport Wright and Annie (Van Vranken) Wright, he was educated at St. Vincent and Pomona Colleges in California, and took postgraduate courses at Harvard University under Charles Townsend Copeland. His application to Harvard in 1906 marks the beginning of a pattern of serious public deceptions. Wright listed writer W. C. Morrow as a tutor and reference, though he had never met him. He was nudged out of the university in 1907 and went back to California, where after a brief stint as a ticket-taker, he became literary editor and art critic for the *Los Angeles Times.* The 1910 anarchist bombing of the Times building by the radical McNamara brothers provided Wright with another opportunity to embellish the truth. In interviews for years to come he would tell of his narrow escape from death, claiming that he had fortuitously left the office because of a migraine headache and witnessed the explosion from his cab. He was really at home asleep, and nowhere near the scene.

While still at the *Times,* he concurrently held the same position with *Town Topics* from 1910 to 1914, and at the recommendation of H. L. Mencken, became editor of *Smart Set* from 1912 to 1914, where he was, wrote Loughery, a prolific columnist and critic "loud in his defense of controversial realists like Dreiser and Zola, shameless in his disdain for female novelists and relentlessly cranky about most best sellers." Wright's volume of art criticism, *Modern Painting* (1915), emphasized Cézanne and tried to explain the philosophy behind modernism. Loughery called it "a feisty, impassioned book in a period of impossibly dull criticism . . . a remarkably lopsided treatise with an outlook that was both astute and narrow."

Wright's only attempt at serious fiction was also largely overlooked, despite H. L. Mencken's writing in the *Forum* that *Man of Promise* (1916) is "incomparably above the common run of fiction in English." The book failed to earn Wright his desired reputation as a pre-eminent American realist and did not allow him to leap from art critic to artist. Largely autobiographical, blunt and "profoundly misogynistic," according to Loughery, the novel is "a Nietzschean tract and a fantasy of the way in which the author wanted to perceive his life. It tells the story of a young man with grandiose ambitions . . . confronted by many obstacles to his growth and worldly advancement. And all of the obstacles are female." Reissued in 1930 when S. S. Van Dine was at the height of popularity, the novel again still failed to sell.

Wright suffered a breakdown in 1923 and stayed in bed for two years, where he read more than 2,000 volumes of detective fiction and criminology. He arose from his convalescence as S. S. Van Dine, seeking a cloak of anonymity in his new literary territory. "Van Dine" was not, as he claimed, an old family name on his mothers side, nor is there any particular reason to believe that he derived his "S. S." from "steamship," as he also claimed; some have seen in the initials an allusion to his *Smart Set* days—his happiest period.

The first two Philo Vance novels are based on notorious murders—*The Benson Murder Case* (1926) on the Joseph Bowne Elwell case and *The Canary Murder Case* (1927) on the "Dot" King case—and all twelve contain intricate plots with clues rooted in a range of intellectual arcana—Ibsen plays, chess moves, mathematical theories. The final novel in the series, *The Winter Murder Case* (1939) was written as a plot idea for a Twentieth Century–Fox B movie before it became a novel, and *The Gracie Allen Murder Case* (1938) took the same backwards approach to publication and was considered trash written to order.

The shift toward greater realism in detective fiction had a damaging effect on Wright's sales. No American writer of comparable fame and wealth in his day suffered so abrupt an eclipse in the public mind, Loughery wrote. He was out-of-print in the 1950s and all but forgotten by the 1960s.

PRINCIPAL WORKS: As *"Willard Huntington Wright"*—Songs of Youth, 1913; Europe After 8:15 (with H. L. Mencken and G. J. Nathan) 1914; What Nietzsche Taught, 1915; Modern Painting: Its Tendency and Meaning, 1915; The Creative Will, 1916; The Man of Promise (novel) 1916; Informing a Nation, 1917; Misinforming a Nation, 1917; The Great Modern French Stories (ed.) 1918; The Future of Painting, 1923; The Great Detective Stories (ed.) 1927; As *"S. S. Van Dine"*—The Benson Murder Case, 1926; The Canary Murder Case, 1927; The Greene Murder Case, 1928; The Bishop Murder Case, 1929; The Scarab Murder Case, 1930; The Kennel Murder Case, 1932; The Dragon Murder Case, 1933; The Casino Murder Case, 1934; The Garden Murder Case, 1935; The Kidnap Murder Case, 1936; The Gracie Allen Murder Case, 1938; The Winter Murder Case (posthumous) 1939.

ABOUT: Dictionary of American Biography Vol. 22; Loughery, J. Alias S. S. Van Dine; Reilly, J. (ed.) Twentieth Century Crime and Mystery Writers; Wright, W. H. (ed.) The Great Detective Stories. Periodicals—Forum April 1916; London Times April 13, 1939; New York Times April 13, 1939.

**WURDEMANN, AUDREY** (January 1, 1911–
May 18, 1960), American poet, was the youngest
poet ever to receive the prize. Born in Seattle,
Washington, the daughter of Dr. Harry Wurdemann, an eye surgeon and author of several technical books in his field, and May Audrey (Flynn)
Wurdemann, she was the great-great granddaughter of Percy Bysshe Shelley on her mother's side.

A child prodigy who began writing verse almost
as soon as she could write at all, Wurdemann did
not attend elementary school but was taught at
home by private tutors. When she entered high
school at eleven, she had already sold her first poem
to a local newspaper, and by age fourteen, having
finished high school in three years, she had seen
dozens of poems printed in newspapers and magazines.

Poet George Sterling noticed her work and sponsored her first privately printed book of verse, *The
House of Silk* (1927), when Wurdemann was sixteen. Nelson Antrim Crawford wrote, prophetical-
ly, in *Poetry* that while there was no doubt of
Wurdemann's ability, "the case for genius or even
great poetic talent, such as the author's sponsors intimate, is unproved."

Wurdemann went on to the University of Washington and graduated with honors in three years.
After traveling throughout the United States and
the Far East, she settled
in Seattle and contribut-
ed to *Poetry* and other
magazines. In *Poetry*, she
found and admired the
poems of Joseph Aus-
lander, a professor of
English at Columbia Uni-
versity, and she asked the
editor for an introduction
to the man. He was four-
teen years her senior, but
after a short courtship they were married, in 1933.
They lived in New York City until Auslander became a consultant to the Library of Congress in
1937, when they moved to Washington, D.C.

Her second collection of poems, *Bright Ambush*,
published when she was only twenty-three, won the
Pulitzer Prize for poetry in 1935. Neatly rhymed,
devoid of passion, limited in philosophy, and filled
with praise for nature, her lyrical verse struck most
reviewers as the graceful work of an accomplished
beginner who had yet to develop a strong voice of
her own. The decision to award her the Pulitzer was
controversial. In his book, *The Pulitzer Prizes*, J.
Hohenberg wrote that the judges "had been dis-
posed that year to give the prize to Edwin Arlington Robinson's *Amaranth*, but decided against it
because he had already won three times. The critics
had a field day . . . with Malcom Cowley leading
the pack against Miss Wurdemann." In a review in
the *New Republic*, Cowley wrote, "You would suspect from reading her that she was born somewhere
in a provincial library, that she had moved no farther than from Elizabeth Barrett Browning to A. E.
Housman, and that she sank every night into tender
dreams after wrapping herself in the proofsheets of

Edna St. Vincent Millay. Her book is written on the
margins of others."

Possibly in response to such attacks, Wurdeman-
ns next book focussed on the seven deadly sins, each
personified by one of seven brothers, whose grim
stories are told in dramatic narrative poems. Reviewers were unconvinced, and Wurdemann returned to lyric verse in her next two books. In 1943
she collaborated with her husband on *The Unconquerables* (1943), a book of poems hailing the heroism of the occupied countries during World War II,
and on two nostalgic novels. *My Uncle Jan* (1948)
told of the Americanization of a Czech family in
Wisconsin in the 1890s, including "a little Bohemian madness, much American common sense and
a number of songs, bright and dark," wrote Jessamyn West in the *New York Herald Tribune Weekly Book Review*. *The Islanders* (1951) told in poetic
prose of a Greek family adjusting to life in Florida.

PRINCIPAL WORKS: *Poetry*—House of Silk, 1927; Bright Ambush, 1934; The Seven Sins, 1935; Splendour in the Grass,
1936; Testament of Love: A Sonnet Sequence, 1938; (with J.
Auslander) The Unconquerables, 1943. *Novels*—(with J. Auslander) My Uncle Jan, 1948; (with J. Auslander) The Islanders,
1951.

ABOUT: Hohenberg, J. The Pulitzer Prizes; New Republic May
22, 1935; New York Herald Tribune March 28, 1948; New
York Times December 1, 1935, May 20, 1960; Newsweek May
30, 1960; Poetry January 1928; January 1935; March 1937; Saturday Review of Literature March 10, 1934; May 11, 1935;
January 7, 1939; Time May 30, 1960.

**WYCLIFFE, JOHN.** See **BEDFORD-JONES,
HENRY**

**WYLIE, ELINOR (HOYT)** (September 7, 1885–
December 16, 1928), American novelist and poet,
was born in Somerville, New Jersey, the daughter
of Henry Martyn Hoyt, later a solicitor general of
the United States, and Anne (McMichael) Hoyt. She
attended private schools in Bryn Mawr and Washington, D.C., and studied drawing at the Corcoran
Gallery of Art. Her summers were spent on the
coast of Maine. She traveled to Europe for a season
in Paris and London when she was eighteen and
met a number of the leading social and artistic figures. Two years later she married Philip Hichborn,
a wealthy Washingtonian. They had one son, and
for three years her life was fashionable and without
incident, until she suddenly eloped with Horace
Wylie, fifteen years her senior and also married.
Unlike Hichborn, who was a sportsman, Wylie was
an intellectual—a trait that clearly appealed to Elinor. For the next five years they lived quietly in
England and vacationed in France as "Mr. and Mrs.
Waring." In 1912 Philip Hichborn committed suicide. That same year Elinor's mother financed the
publication of a small volume of her daughter's
verse entitled *Incidental Numbers*. The "Warings"
returned to America in 1915: in 1915: life in England and on the continent had become difficult because of the war; but Wylie's wife finally granted
him a divorce. He and Elinor were married in
1916—only to be divorced in 1923.

Wylie's first substantial book of poems, *Nets to
Catch the Wind*, attracted praise for its technical
skill and its sensitivity. Her next two collections—

*Black Armour* and *Trivial Breath*—maintained these standards but now seem thin and artificial. In her posthumously published works, however, critics saw a greater depth of feeling with no loss of her characteristic control.

In 1923 Wylie married the poet and editor William Rose Benét, a widower. During the mid-1920s she also kept an apartment in Greenwich Village,

spent her summers at the MacDowell Colony in New Hampshire, and made a number of trips to Europe. She also began writing fiction. Her first novel, *Jennifer Lorn*, was an extravagant variation on the eighteenth-century English novel. *The Venetian Glass Nephew* was a fanatastic jeu desprit about artifice itself, brought off, reviewers agreed, by the authors faultless sense of style. In *The Orphan Angel*, a popular book in its day, although it has not lasted, she had a Yankee clipper rescue the poet Shelley from drowning off the Italian coast and described the "continuation" of his life in the United States. Henry Seidel Canby wrote in the *Saturday Review of Literature* in 1926 that "as a novel, it belongs with the not too many which have dealt successfully with realized genius. As a romance, it is a new and piquant rendering of the American theme for sophisticated readers seeking . . . for savour and ideas more than for story or verisimilitude."

Wylie's fourth novel, *Mr. Hodge and Mr. Harzard*, set in the early nineteenth century, portrayed a sensitive, idealistic poet who is destroyed by a blunt vulgarian.

While in England in 1927 Wylie received severe injuries from a fall; shortly afterwards, back in America, she died from a stroke.

Wylie's poems no longer attract the attention of serious critics, although her final sonnet-sequence of love poems, "One Person" (in her posthumous *Angels and Earthly Creatures*) is still read by members of an older generation, and a few of her lyrics are perennial anthology pieces. At its best, her work has a formidable polish and a certain cold fire, but its range is extremely limited. Her papers are in the Berg Collection of the New York Public Library and in the Beinecke Library at Yale University.

PRINCIPAL WORKS: *Poetry*—Incidental Numbers, 1912; Nets to Catch the Wind, 1921; Black Armour, 1923; Trivial Breath, 1928; Angels and Earthly Creatures, 1929; Collected Poems (ed. W. R. Benét) 1932; Last Poems, 1943. *Fiction*—Jennifer Lorn, 1923; The Venetian Glass Nephew, 1925; The Orphan Angel, 1926 (in U.K.: Mortal Image); Mr. Hodge and Mr. Hazard, 1928; Collected Prose, 1933.

ABOUT: Benét, W. R. The Prose and Poetry of Elinor Wylie, 1934; Clark E. Innocence Abroad, 1931; Colum, M. Life and the Dream, 1947; Farr, J. The Life and Art of Elinor Wylie, 1983; Gould, J. American Women Poets, 1980; Gray, T. A. Elinor Wylie, 1969; Hoyt, N. Elinor Wylie: The Portrait of an Unknown Lady, 1935; Monroe, H. Poets and Their Art, 1926, rev. ed. 1932; Olson, S. Elinor Wylie: A Life Apart, 1979; Sergeant, E. Fire under the Andes, 1927; Untermeyer, L. From Another World, 1939; Van Doren, C. Three Worlds, 1936;

Wilson, E. Shores of Light, 1952. *Periodicals*—American Scholar Summer 1969; Explicator Fall 1984, Spring 1986; Harper's Magazine September 1936; New York Times December 17, 1928; Poetry February 1929, August 1932; Saturday Review of Literature November 13, 1926; December 29, 1928; May 21, 1932; December 2, 1933; March 23, 1935; Women's Studies vol. 15, no. 4 1988.

**WYLIE, IDA ALEXA ROSS** (1885–November 5, 1959) British novelist and short story writer, wrote: "I was born in Melbourne, Australia; my father, a barrister-at-law, was a Scotsman. Soon after my birth he went to England, where he proposed resuming his profession. My mother died soon afterwards and from thence onwards I entered on the business of living—almost literally 'on my own.' At the age of ten I was already an ex-

perienced traveler, and, thanks to my father's odd ideas on education, was fully capable of managing myself under most usual and great many unusual circumstances. My father remarried from time to time but I continued to be left to my own devices. Until I was fourteen I received practically no education. But I had read every book in my father's extensive and liberal library, and I had already begun to write and had no other idea but that I should be an author when my time came.

"At fourteen I was shipped, rather ironically, to a finishing school in Brussels, where I lingered three years and acquired great French fluency with a 'marked English accent.' At seventeen I was sent to Cheltenham Ladies College to have my education begun, and after two years there was sent to Karlsruhe, Germany, for a Teutonic finishing. There I wrote my first official stories, which were at once accepted for the incredible price of five pounds apiece by English magazines, and from then on I was self-supporting.

"Since my father and I differed violently on every subject under the sun, I cut myself loose, and having no other home, I stayed on in Germany with a friend for eight years, thereby acquiring perfect German and an insight into the German mentality which made me impervious to surprise at anything the Germans have done since. It also enabled me to write my first successful novel, *Toward Morning*.

"I came home to England in 1911, was violently active in the Suffrage Movement, and lived through the war in London, doing some war work in France. In 1917 I came to America for the first time and stayed for a year. After that I became a transatlantic commuter, and was now what is known as an 'alien resident.'

"I have written over two hundred short stories and some fifteen novels. The only ones which I like at all to remember are *Towards Morning*, *The Silver Virgin*, *To the Vanquished*, *Furious Young Man*, and *A Feather in Her Hat*. I have traveled over a great part of Europe and the United States, mostly by motor car. My favorite recreations are writing, riding, motoring, and dancing. I collect English bull-terriers and have recently [in 1942] purchased a farm in New Jersey and expect to live and die there, but hope, when the present war is over, to resume my yearly visits to my native land."

———

Wylie's father, Alexander Coghill Wylie, really was an eccentric. Although he never had enough money for himself, he supplied his ten-year-old daughter with the funds to travel throughout England and Europe. She drew on her experience to write perceptively of differing cultural attitudes.

Her first book, *The Germans*, was a very lightly fictionalized account of what she saw during her stay in Karlsruhe, when she was nineteen. Not surprisingly, reviewers thought it occasionally naive, but the *Literary Digest* found that "the book reads easily and the subjects chosen for illumination are such as to be universally interesting and instructive."

Wylie then put her experience to work in *Dividing Waters*, which dramatized national divisions through the story of a marriage between a German army officer and an English woman. "[The author's] knowledge of German manners and social usages is considerable," said a reviewer for *Spectator*, "she has a fluent and graceful pen and a sincere desire to render justice to both countries." A string of books followed which used similar situations to examine cultural differences. Thus, *The Daughter of Brahma*, set like several of Wylie's novels in India, tells of a young Englishman who falls in love with a Brahman priestess.

The novel that Wylie cites as her first success, *Towards Morning*, is the story of a painful coming of age for a boy growing up in war-torn Germany. Brutalized by three years in the army, Helmut Felde finally redeems himself when he refuses to do "a foul and evil thing" in the name of the Fatherland, and so loses his life. In the words of the *Nation*, "The story is told with a simplicity, a sureness of touch, a depth of feeling rarely found, hitherto, in novels of the war" (1918).

Among Wylie's more notable novels was *The Silver Virgin*. It centers on Gale and Justin, an English couple who meet at the shrine of the Silver Virgin in Spain, and what happens to their marriage when Justin returns maimed from the war. Reviewers praised the author's ability to move her readers without resorting to sentimentality: "*The Silver Virgin* is a good example of the best type of morbid, realistic school of writing . . . there is beauty in the novel—beauty of reality rather than that of poetry—and an excellent magic plot" (*Outlook*). Indeed, her novels, though now almost forgotten, always received good notices.

Wylie continued to travel, finding settings for her later novels ranging from Central America to Russia, Africa to the United States. She was generally credited with a sympathetic understanding of assorted peoples, and much skill in conveying the look and feel of the places they lived in. Her talent as a storyteller was seldom questioned, although her plots often verged on melodrama.

Wylie's novels remained popular until the end of her life, as did her short stories. In volumes such as *The Mad Busman* she collected expert little tales which demonstrated her "gift for narrative, the faculty of the born story-teller" (*Literary Review*). Most successful was *Some Other Beauty*, a collection of six stories in each of which a protagonist rises above adversarial circumstances. Several of the stories were filmed, and Wylie herself spent a year in Hollywood, working on films, including *Keeper of the Flame* and *Phone Call from a Stranger*.

*Flight to England* was a touching record of the trip Wylie made to England in 1942. She also wrote an account of her eight years in Germany and an autobiography, *My Life With George*. "George" was the name she gave to what she thought was her subconscious mind, and in the book she tells how "he" helped her to convert experiences in every country in which she lived into fiction.

Wylie's books were both better known and better received in the U.S. than in England, and she adopted the American way of life as her own: "I love England as my native land" she once said; "I love Americans as my people."

PRINCIPAL WORKS: Novels—The Germans, 1910 (in U.K.: My German Year); The Native Born, 1910 (in U.K.: The Rajah's People); In Different Keys, 1911; Dividing Waters, 1911; The Daughter of Brahma, 1912; The Red Mirage, 1912; The Paupers of Portman Square, 1913; Five Years to find Out, 1914; The Temple of Dawn, 1915; Hermit Doctor of Gaya, 1915 (in U.K.: Tristram Sahib); The Shining Heights, 1917; The Duchess in Pursuit, 1918; Towards Morning, 1918; Children of Storm, 1920 (in U.K.: Brodie and the Deep Sea); Rogues and Company, 1921; The Dark House, 1922; Ancient Fires, 1924; Black Harvest, 1925; The Silver Virgin, 1929; A Feather in her Hat, 1934; To the Vanquished, 1934; Prelude to Richard, 1935; Furious Young Man, 1936; The Young in Heart, 1938; Strangers are Coming, 1941; Keeper of the Flame, 1942; Ho, the Fair Wind, 1945; Where No Birds Sing, 1947; Candles For Therese, 1951; The Undefeated, 1957; Claire Serrat, 1959 (in U.K.: Home are the Hunted). Short stories—Happy Endings, 1915; Armchair Stories, 1916; All Sorts, 1919; Holy Fire, and Other Stories, 1920; The Mad Busman, and Other Stories, 1926; Some Other Beauty, and Other Stories, 1930; the Thing We Do, and Other Stories, 1932; Storm in April, 1946. Autobiography—My Life With George: An Unconventional Autobiography, 1940. Other—Rambles in the Black Forest, 1911; Eight Years in Germany, 1914; Flight to England, 1943.

ABOUT: The autobiographical material quoted above was written for Twentieth Century Authors, 1942. Blain, V. and others. The Feminist Companion to Literature in English, 1990; Ward, A. C. Longman Companion to Twentieth Century Literature, 3rd ed., 1981; Webster's Biographical Dictionary, 1943; Who's Who 1959; Wylie, I.A.R. Eight Years in Germany, 1914; Wylie, I.A.R. My Life With George, 1940; Wylie, I.A.R. Flight to England, 1943. Periodicals—Catholic World August 1934; Dial July 1, 1913; Literary Digest November 11, 1911; Literary Review August 28, 1926; Nation November 30, 1911; September 7, 1918; New York Herald Tribune Books June 15, 1930; New York Times November 24, 1940; November 5, 1959; Newsweek November 16, 1959; Outlook January 30, 1929; Publishers Weekly November 23, 1959; Spectator April 29, 1911; Time November 16, 1959; Times (London) November 5, 1959; Wilson Library Bulletin 1960.

**WYLIE, PHILIP** (May 12, 1902–October 25, 1971), American novelist, essayist and short story writer, wrote: "My full name is Philip Gordon Wylie. I was born in Beverly, Massachusetts. My father is a Presbyterian minister. My mother, Edna Edwards, was a fiction writer. My brother Max and my late half-brother, Edmund K. Wylie, have both published several books. I was educated at the Montclair, N.J., High School, and I attended Princeton University for three years, leaving at the end of that time because I found no satisfaction in its attitude or its curriculum. Since then I have worked as a press agent, as the advertising manager for a publisher, as one of the editors of the *New Yorker*, and as a studio writer in the movies. Before that time I worked on farms, in Manhattan stores, in factories, on ships, and elsewhere. I sold my first 'piece'—a poem—when I was twelve years old. Since that time I have been selling more pieces—at varying intervals. Inasmuch as I had intended to become a doctor, my education was largely scientific, and I have kept up with science, spending considerable time as a visiting observer in the California Institute of Technology, various commercial and foundation laboratories, the Columbia-Presbyterian Medical Center, and elsewhere. I have traveled in most of Europe and in Russia. I speak French and German and some Russian. I have developed a side interest in psychology and psychiatry and written some technical and some lay papers upon those subjects. My hobbies, indulged in sporadically, are rather varied: playing a piano-accordion, oil-painting, fishing, swimming, diving, canoeing, exploring and making maps, carpentry, gardening, bridge, golf, abstract mathematics. For some time I conducted a newspaper column for a syndicate. Several of my books were written in collaboration with Edwin Balmer, the editor of *Redbook Magazine*, and several were anonymous or written under a pseudonym. . . . I have, as a reviewer once said of me, 'written more pot-boilers than any other two Americans in the same period of time.' I live in Miami Beach, Florida, nine months of the year and wander about in the North in the summer. I have been married twice: in 1928 to Sally Ondeck, one daughter, divorced 1937; in 1938 to Federica Ballard."

---

Philip Wylie was a prolific author who worked quickly. His output included nearly thirty novels and scores of short stories, as well as essays, newspaper columns, scientific papers, advertising copy, screenplays, and radio programs. His reputation, however, as an author of controversial critiques of American values—"full of choler about human stupidity and full, too, of egotism" (*New York Times* 1971)—was based on only a couple of volumes of essays and a relatively few novels.

As a young novelist, Wylie relied upon personal experience as much as the polemicism for which he was to become known. He had rejected the rigid morality of his father's brand of Christianity, and, in his debut, *Heavy Laden*, he explores this generational conflict through the relationship between a puritanical Presbyterian minister and his forward-thinking, hedonistic daughter. Reviewers praised the book's energy and originality: "It is a spectacular first novel. Bursting with vitality it sputters and thunders by turns" (*New York Times Book Review* 1928). It established a pattern, however, and such library contributors as Robert MacDougall were "sure that the novel will be misunderstood. And the fault will be not entirely the reader's, for Mr. Wylie is bitter and he is brutal" (*Saturday Review of Literature* 1928). His second novel, *Babes and Sucklings*, drew on Wylie's troubled relationship with his first wife, and in so doing brought into question the validity of the institution of marriage as a social structure. The *New York Times* (1929) was typical in describing it as smacking "too much of a case history chart to be fully artistic."

More run-of-the-mill novels followed, including *Gladiator*, the story of a superhumanly strong but otherwise ordinary man—claimed, probably erroneously, to have been the model for the character of Superman—and five works of mystery and science fiction written in collaboration with Edwin Balmer.

*Finnley Wren*, the record of the life and loves of a cuckolded young protagonist, experiments with narrative in the discourse between Wren and the author himself. Characteristically, the author uses his hero to rail against the follies inherent in every conceivable aspect of American life. T. F. Keefer, in his *Philip Wylie*, claimed that "*Finnley Wren* lives on, a furious, magnificent act of creation that is . . . not just a clever satire of the absurdities of the day; it is a man's outraged cry against those things that outlast all topicality: man's ineradicable stupidity, cruelty and selfishness." Posterity has failed to agree.

Wylie's best-known, and most sensational book, *A Generation of Vipers*, expresses the same views directly in essay form. This attack on American civilization, derived from Wylie's idiosyncratic reading of Freudian and Jungian theory and depicted a lost nation that was both sex-obsessed and sexually inadequate, and entirely without personal or governmental direction. It demonstrated Wylie's wholesale distrust of prevailing intellectual and religious authority and a fundamental belief in the selfishness and misguidedness of humankind. His intention, as expounded in the introduction, was to "prevent the needless . . . death of a great, free people" and instil the view that "it is time for man to make a new appraisal of himself." The tract was not without a certain short-lived influence. In a chapter entitled "Common Women" Wylie coined the term "Momism" to described the debilitating effects on American society of an unquestioning adoration of the possessive mother figure. This "megaloid momworship" rendered men psychologically impotent, and implemented a model of the feminine as a bitter, helpless form of whoredom. The author longs for a time when someone might exclaim, "Gentlemen, Mom is a jerk." Although this discussion took up only nineteen pages of the volume, and Wylie subsequently insisted such misogynistic posturing had been in jest, the term brought his name into common currency for a decade or so to come. "Although revered by some and reviled by others, few can deny . . . the impact of his style," claimed Clifford Bendau in his study of the author.

In Wylie's second collection, *An Essay on Morals*, he concentrated on dismantling the constructs of organized religion, depicting a world "inhabited by a rabble of two billion God-owned zealots and patriots" and concluding in Jungian terms that man is an animal whom sexual demystification might save. These were concerns he had explored in *Night unto Night*, a philosophical novel cradling a religious drama within the framework of conventional romance fiction. A group of characters come together during a hot Florida summer, and reach various conclusions regarding the nature of their Christianity and their sexuality, of life and death. R. G. Davis found that "along with the slick and fictional goes a real sense of psychic breadth" (*New York Times* 1944), and Thomas Sugrue agreed that "what it says has meaning for everyone who expects to live another day" (*Weekly Book Review*). *Night unto Night* was filmed by Warner Brothers in 1949—one of several Wylie novels adapted for the screen.

Wylie was keenly interested in the environment and concerned about the potential effects on it should an atomic war occur, a not wholly implausible scenario during those Cold War years. This concern was reflected in a series of novels, including *Tomorrow!* and *Triumph*, both of which deal with atomic war. The books were intended to scare, and contained much horrific detail, but were generally considered to be propagandist tracts, managed "at the expense of credibility and readability" (*New York Herald Tribune Books* 1963). Nonetheless, as Wylie's obituarist pointed out in the *New York Times* (1971), if "he was not always taken seriously by critics, it was true that he was very often ahead of his time."

It was quite a different Wylie who produced the gentle tales of Crunch and Des, and their adventures while deep-sea finishing off the coast of southern Florida. Fishing was Wylie's own first love, and his enthusiasm is reflected in his entertaining narratives: "each new chapter is as exhilarating as a fresh cast" said Fred Feldkamp of *Salt Water Daffy* (*Books* 1941). A television series, *Crunch and Des*, was broadcast between 1955 and 1959.

PRINCIPAL WORKS: *Novels*—Heavy Laden, 1928; Babes and Sucklings, 1929; Gladiator, 1930; Footprint of Cinderella, 1931 (published as Nine Rittenhouse Square, 1967); The Murderer Invisible, 1931; The Savage Gentleman, 1932; (with E. Balmer) Five Fatal Words, 1932; (with E, Balmer) When Worlds Collide, 1933; (with E. Balmer) After Worlds Collide, 1934; Finnley Wren, 1934; (with E. Balmer) The Golden Hoard, 1934; (with E. Balmer) The Shield of Silence, 1936; As They Reveled, 1936; Too Much of Everything, 1936; An April Afternoon, 1938; Danger Mansion, 1940; The Other Horseman, 1942; The Corpses at Indian Stones, 1943; Night unto Night, 1944; Opus 21, 1949; The Disappearance, 1951; Tomorrow 1954; The Answer, 1956; Triumph, 1963; They Both Were Naked, 1965; Autumn Romance, 1967; The Spy Who Spoke Porpoise, 1969; The End of a Dream, 1972. *Short stories*—The Big Ones Get Away!, 1940; Salt Water Daffy, 1941; Fish and Tin Fish; Crunch and Des Strike Back, 1944; Crunch and Des; Sto-

ries of Florida Fishing, 1948; Three to be Read, 1952; The Best of Crunch and Des, 1954; Treasure Cruise, and Other Crunch and Des Stories, 1956. *Essays*—A Generation of Vipers, 1942; An Essay on Morals, 1947; Denizens of the Deep: True Tales of the Deep-Sea Fishing, 1953; Innocent Ambassadors, 1957; The Magic Animal: Man Revisited, 1968; Sons and Daughters of Mom, 1970. *Screenplays*—(with W. Young) Island of Lost Souls, 1932; Murders in the Zoo, 1933; (with F. Niblo, Jr) King of the Jungle, 1933. *As contributor*—Fifth Mystery Book, 1944; American Thought, 1947. *Other*—(with W. Muir) The Army Way, 1940.

ABOUT: The autobiographical material quoted above was written for Twentieth Century Authors, 1942. Bendau, C. P. Still Worlds Collide; Philip Wylie and the End of the American Dream, 1980; Burke, W. J. And Howe, W. D. American Authors and Books, 1972; Contemporary Authors vols. 21–22, 1969; vols. 33–36, 1973; Contemporary Literary Criticism vol. 43 1987; Dictionary of Literary Biography vol. 9 1981; Herzberg, M. J. The Reader's Encyclopedia of American Literature, 1962; Keefer, T. F. Philip Wylie, 1977; Moskowitz, S. Explorers of the Infinite, 1963; Warfel, H. R. American Novelists of Today, 1951. *Periodicals*—Detroit Free Press October 26, 1971; Nation June 11, 1949; New York Herald Tribune Book Review January 14, 1951; October 7, 1951; December 13, 1953; January 31, 1954; New York Tribune Books April 21, 1929; January 26, 1941; January 10, 1943; April 21, 1963; New York Times April 14, 1929; September 24, 1944; February 4, 1971; October 25, 1971; New York Times Book Review April 1, 1928; July 3, 1949; February 21, 1954; August 11, 1968; Newsweek November 8, 1971; Publishers Weekly, November 1, 1971; Saturday Review of Literature June 9, 1928; March 8, 1947; May 21, 1949; Science Fiction Studies July 1995; Time January 18, 1943; November 5, 1965; November 8, 1971; Times (London) October 26, 1971; Washington Post October 26, 1971; Weekly Book Review September 24, 1944.

**WYNDHAM, GEORGE** (August 29, 1863–June 8, 1913), English politician and critic, translator, and man of letters, was born in London, the elder son of the Hon. Percy Scawen Wyndham and his wife, Madeleine, a granddaughter of Lord Edward Fitzgerald. Wyndham was educated at Eton, and then the military college at Sandhurst (the English equivalent of West Point), from which he graduated in 1882. He joined the Coldstream Guards and served in Egypt until 1885. In 1887 he married Sibyl Mary, the widow of Earl Grosvenor, with whom he had one son. Later that same year Wyndham became Earl Balfour's private secretary in Ireland. He became conservative MP for Dover (1889) and held minor posts until 1900, when he became Chief Secretary for Ireland, a post which he relinquished five years later.

Wyndham's literary career began in 1892, when he met the poet and editor W. E. Henley. He contributed pieces to Henley's *National Observer*, and introduced North's *Plutarch* in Henley's "Tudor Classics" series.

Wyndham's *Ronsard and La Pléiade* was followed by several selections from Ronsard's work, and graceful translation from the latter and from members of *The Pléiade*. These, his most enduring works, were well received and caused Arthur Symons to praise him (in the *Saturday Review*) for demonstrating "the astonishing fact that it is possible to be a politician and yet to have the instinct of the poet."

PRINCIPAL WORKS: Introduction to North's Plutarch, 1895; Shakespeare's Poems, 1898; Ronsard and La Pléiade, 1906; Essays in Romantic Literature, 1919.

ABOUT: Dictionary of National Biography, 1901–1921, 1927; Who's Who 1912. *Periodicals*—Athenaeum November 24, 1906; Nation November 24, 1907; New York Times June 10, 1913; Saturday Review November 3, 1906; Times (London) June 10, 1913; Times Literary Supplement January 30, 1919.

## YARMOLINSKY, AVRAHM (January 13, 1890–September 28, 1975), American biographer, scholar, librarian, and editor, wrote:

"Avrahm Yarmolinsky was born in the town of Haisin in the Ukraine, Russia, and spent his childhood and youth in Kishinev, Bessarabia. He got his schooling there, and for a while attended the Psychoneurological Institute at St. Peterburg [Leningrad] and the University of Neuchatel, Switzerland. In 1913 he came to the United States, and subsequently became a citizen of this country. In 1916 he graduated from the College of the City of New York, and received his Ph.D. from Columbia University in 1921. He has acted as instructor in Russian at the evening session of the College of the City of New York since 1917, and was instructor in the Russian language and literature in the extension division of Columbia in 1919–20. Since 1918 he has held the post of Chief of the Slavonic Division of the New York Public Library. He was married to Babette Deutsch in 1921, and is the father of two sons.

"In addition to his own books, he has edited Dostoievsky, Pushkin, Gorky, and Count Witte; has edited three anthologies, two of Russian and one of German poetry; and has translated Alexander Blok (in colaboration with Babette Deutsch) and a number of other Russian writers. He has also published several bibliographical monographs, and a number of articles and reviews in literary periodicals.

"In 1939 he received from the Associated Alumni of the College of the City of New York the Townsend Harris Medal for having 'enriched and broadened American culture by his 'contribution to a highly specialized field of knowledge.'

In 1955, Yarmolinsky added: "In 1940 Avrahm Yarmolinsky became an alumnus member of Phi Beta Kappa. He lives in New York with his wife, his sons pursuing their careers elsewhere."

---

Much of Yarmolinsky's literary work was done in collaboration with his wife, the poet and translator Babette Deutsch. In 1922 they jointly produced a useful, if not very inspired anthology of *Modern Russian Poetry*, which included a critical introduction and biographical index. They revised the book periodically, the final edition appearing in 1966,

under the title *Two Centuries of Russian Verse.* Other books resulting from this collaboration included an anthology of *Contemporary German Poetry* and a collection of Russian and Central Asian folk-tales, *Tales of Faraway Folk.*

In addition to editing and writing introductions for numerous editions of Russian literature, including *The Portable Chekhov* and a selection of Chekhov's letters, Yarmolinsky was the author of two biographies. His biography of Turgenev was the first of its subject when it appeared in 1925; when a revised edition was published in 1959 Newton Arvin in the *New York Times Book Review* said, "Mr. Yarmolinsky's book has long been known as a serious, painstaking, and perceptive work; and in its revised form it should still have a long and honorable life before it."

The other biography was *Dostoevsky, a Life*, published in 1934, which, at the time, was the most comprehensive and reliable available. Yarmolinsky's cool, scholarly presentation of the life was admired by reviewers; his analysis of the novels was thought less successful.

Yarmolinsky played an important role in introducing the American reading public to a new range of literature. An edition of his Turgenev biography last appeared in 1977; several of the works which he edited were still in print more recently. He also produced a number of scholarly and specialist bibliographies for the New York Public Library.

PRINCIPAL WORKS: Turgenev, 1926 (2nd ed. 1959); The Jews and Other Minor Nationalities Under the Russians, 1928; Dostoevsky, a Life, 1934 (2nd ed. 1957); Road to Revolution, 1957; Literature Under Communism, 1960; The Russian Literary Imagination, 1969. *As editor*—The Works of Alexander Pushkin, 1936; A Book of Short Stories by Maxim Gorki, 1939; A Treasury of Great Russian Stories, 1944; The Portable Chekhov, 1947; The Unknown Chekhov, 1954; Soviet Short Stories, 1960; A Treasury of Great Russian Stories, 1960; Russians Then and Now, 1963. *With B. Deutsch*—Contemporary German Poetry, 1923; Modern Russian Poetry, 1923, 1927; Eugene Onegin by Alexander Pushkin, 1943; A Treasury of Russian Verse, 1949; Tales of Faraway Folk, 1953; An Anthology of Russian Verse, 1962; More Tales of Faraway Folk, 1963; Two Centuries of Russian Verse, 1966.

ABOUT: Contemporary Author's New Revision Series, 1982; New York Public Library Bulletin March 1955; Yachnin, R. Avrahm Yarmolinsky: A List of His Published Writings 1955–1967, 1968. *Periodicals*—New York Times September 29, 1975; New York Times Book Review May 10, 1959.

## YATES, DORNFORD. See MERCER, CECIL WILLIAM

## YATES, ELIZABETH (December 6, 1905– ), American writer for children and novelist, wrote: "It was in Buffalo, New York, that I was born and there I went to school—the Franklin School from kindergarten through the twelfth grade. The memorable days of my childhood were the long summers spent on my father's farm in the rich rolling country south of Buffalo. Next to the youngest of seven children, there were always playmates for me as well as horses and dogs; and there were always tasks. The house was filled with books, and being alone or being read to by my mother was part of our life. I used to go off on my horse for a day at a time, rambling through the countryside, a sand-

wich in my pocket and the knowledge that any stream would give us both drink; I was never lonely, for there was the horse to talk with and in my head I was writing stories. A year at boarding school followed graduation from the Franklin, a summer abroad, and then three years of work in New York City. During those years I had various jobs, gradually arriving at more and more writing. In the summers I taught riding at girls' camps.

"At twenty-three I married William McGreal, an American whose business was in London. Ten years in England followed with frequent travel in the British Isles and on the Continent. In 1939 we returned to the United States to live in Peterborough, New Hampshire. There we found an old farmhouse which adapted itself happily to our needs, and a farm of fields and woodland which we are endeavoring to bring back to usefulness and production. There are mountains near to climb, forest lakes to swim in, and lovely white villages strong with New England tradition. The garden is my joy; the vegetables, especially, which grow in such abundance that there is always plenty to share with friends, and neighbors. I love good talk, I love the wide warm circle of friends which keeps expanding with the years, but I still love to be alone and it is the hours of working in the garden or the woods that help me to think out stories.

"Morning hours of work are relatively uninterrupted; the rest of the day goes in care of home and family and various oddments of activity. Reading is still my job—books about nature, biography, philosophy; while my mentors of earlier days— Traherne and Blake, Hardy, George Eliot and the Bible—still have much to say to me. There are occasional trips to Boston and New York, to the seashore and the high mountains, to Durham every summer to teach at the Writers' Conference of the University of New Hampshire, or to some city or town to give a talk on books or writing; but it is a quiet life we lead and in it there is time to think— time to enjoy the things that have always meant much: friends, books and the countryside."

---

Elizabeth Yates was the daughter of Harry Yates and the former Mary Duffy. She began her career writing book reviews and articles in New York. While she was in England she did editorial work for the Oxford University Press. Her first book was published in 1938.

In all of her work Elizabeth Yates combines respect and love for the natural world, with belief in the fundamental nobility both of humans and animals. Her moral idealism, her concern for the downtrodden, and a clear, gentle style won her a faithful following, particularly for her children's books.

The stories often focus on the outdoor pursuits of their protagonists. *Haven for the Brave* tells of the adventures—including mountain climbing and a forest fire—of a teenaged brother and sister sent to America during World War I. *Mountain Born* is a gentle pastoral centering on a young shepherd boy. Its sequel, *A Place for Peter*, details the everyday emergencies he faces when left in charge of a farm. A reviewer for *Horn Book* commented: "Miss Yates is at her best when describing life in the country . . . perhaps because she loves it all so much herself" (1952).

A novel for young readers, *Patterns on the Wall*, was inspired by the discovery of some stenciling done by a nineteenth-century journeyman on the walls of her own New Hampshire farmhouse. Her novel depicts a sensitive young man, Jared Austin, who grows up to become a famous artist.

Yates's most significant contribution to literature for children was *Amos Fortune: Free Man*, the true story of an African prince who was brought to America as a slave in 1825 and, at the age of fifty, bought his freedom. He died in 1701, a man of property. Although a reviewer for *Kirkus* found it "an unpleasant, grim story," most felt, like the *New York Times* (1950), that this was "a moving story, underlaid with deep religious feeling, which thoughtful young people will find absorbing and full of meaning today." It won the Newbery Award of the American Library Association, the *New York Herald Tribune* Spring Festival Award, and the William Allen White Children's Book Award. Another biography for young readers centered on Prudence Crandall, a young Quaker who fought for the equal education of black and white girls in the school she established.

Among Yates's books for adults were biographies of the American author Dorothy Canfield Fisher, and of Howard Thurman, who rose from poverty to the post of Dean of the Chapel at Boston University. Her novels include *Wind of Spring*, the story of a Victorian servant's life as it is affected by three wars.

Yates's books have been translated into numerous languages, including Hebrew and Sinhalese. She was awarded seven honorary doctorates between 1965 and 1981. She was a staff member at writer's conferences in three American universities, and an instructor at Christian Writers and Editors conferences in Green Lake, Wisconsin. Her husband once commented that "usefulness seems to be the yardstick of her philosophy."

PRINCIPAL WORKS: *Juvenile*—High Holiday, 1938; Hans and Frieda, 1939; Quest in the North-Land, 1940 (in the U.K.: Climbing Higher); Haven for the Brave, 1941; Around the Year in Iceland, 1942; Under the Little Fir, 1942; Patterns on the Wall, 1943; Mountain Born, 1943; Joseph, 1947; Once in the Year, 1947; The Young Traveler in the USA, 1948; The Christmas Story, 1949; Amos Fortune: Free Man, 1950; Children of the Bible, 1950; David Livingstone, 1952; A Place for Peter 1952; Prudence Crandall, Woman of Courage, 1955; Gifts of True Love, 1958; Someday You'll Write, 1962; Up the Golden Stair, 1966; Sam's Secret Journal, 1964; Carolina's Courage, 1964 (in U.K.: Carolina's and the Indian Doll, 1965;) An Easter Story, 1967; With Pipe, Paddle and Song, 1968; Sara Whitcher's Story, 1971; We, the People 1974; The Seventh One, 1978; (with T. Carroll) The Lost Christmas Star, 1979; Silver Lining, 1981; Sound Friendships. The Story of Willa and

Her Hearing Ear Dog, 1987. *Novels*—Wind of Spring, 1945; Nearby, 1947; Beloved Bondage, 1948; Guardian Heart, 1950; Brave Interval, 1952; Hue and Cry, 1953; The Carey Girl, 1956; The Next Fine Day, 1961; On That Night, 1969. *Biography*—Pebbles in a Pool; The Widening Circle of Dorothy Canfield Fisher's Life, 1958 (also published as The Lady From Vermont; Dorothy Canfield Fisher's Life and World, 1971); Howard Thurman, Portrait of a Practical Dreamer, 1964. *Autobiography*—The Lighted Heart, 1960; My Diary—My World, 1981; My Widening World, 1983; One Writer's Way, 1984. *As editor*—Gathered Grace, 1938; Tregarthen, Enys, Piskey Folk, 1940; Tregarthen, Enys, The Doll Who Came Alive, 1942; Tregarthen, Enys, The White Ring, 1949; Your Prayers, and Mine, 1953; Macdonald, George, Sir Gibbie, 1963; MacDonald, George, The Lost Princess; or, The Wise Woman, 1965. *Other*—Rainbow Round the World: A Story of UNICEF, 1954; Is There a Doctor in the Barn? A Day in the Life of Forrest F. Tenney, DVM, 1966; New Hampshire, 1969; Skeezer, Dog with a Mission, 1972; The Road through Sandwich Notch, 1972; A Book of Hours, 1976.

ABOUT: The autobiographical material quoted above was written for Twentieth Century Authors First Supplement, 1955. Burke, W. J. and others, American Authors and Books, 1972; Commire, A. Something about the Author, 1973; Contemporary Authors vols. 1–4, 1962; Contemporary Authors New Revision Series 6 1982; vol. 21 1987; Current Biography 1948; Herzberg, M. J. The Reader's Encyclopedia of American Literature, 1962; Hopkins, L. B. More Books by More People, 1974; Kunitz, S. J. and Haycraft, H. (eds.) Junior Book of Authors, 2nd rev. ed., 1951; Miller, B. E. and Field E. W. (eds.) Newbery Medal Books 1922–1955, 1955; Oxford Companion to Children Writers 3rd ed., 1989; Ward, M. E. and Marquardt, D. A. Authors of Books for Young People, 1964; Who's Who in America, 1948–1949; Yates, E. The Lighted Heart, 1960; Yates, E. My Diary—My World, 1981; Yates E. One Writer's Way, 1984. *Periodicals*—Chicago Sunday Tribune September 27, 1953; Christian Science Monitor October 28, 1950; November 10, 1955; Horn Book January 1948, July 1951; October 1952; Kirkus July 1, 1946; April 15, 1950; Library Journal April 5, 1951; New York Herald Tribune Book Review October 8, 1950, New York Times June 13, 1953; March 25, 1945; April 16, 1950; Publishers Weekly March 10, 1951; Wilson Library Bulletin February 1948.

**\*YBARRA, THOMAS RUSSELL** (October 8, 1880– ), American journalist and biographer, was born in Boston. His mother, Ellen Taylor Russell,

was the daughter of Judge Thomas Russell; his father, General Alejandro Ybarra, hailed from Caracas, Venezuela, the country which he served, when not in political exile, as Minister of War and Foreign Affairs. During his childhood, Ybarra paid many visits to Venezuela (and the first of his two autobiographical volumes, entitled *Young Man of Caracas*, gives a detailed picture of life there), but he was educated at schools in Boston and at Harvard University. After graduating in 1905 he joined the staff of the *New York Times*.

His first book, *Davy Jones's Yarns and Other Salted Songs*, published in 1908 and containing humorous verses, proved untypical. For the next several years he concentrated on journalism and in the 1920s became, still for the *New York Times*, a European correspondent, first based in Berlin, then in London; ultimately he worked under a traveling brief. He then published three biographies in as

°i BAR rah

many years. They were all romantic, journalistic, and enthusiastic accounts.

In 1931 he began a spell of six years as European editor of *Collier's*, but he worked additionally and busily as a free-lance contributor to other magazines and newspapers. *America Faces South*, a book in which he showed himself both personally and professionally conversant with his subject-matter, proved to be a timely study of his country's Latin-American neighbors. Ybarra himself described it as a "hodgepodge."

*Young Man of Caracas*, a first volume of autobiography, appeared in 1941 and told the story of his life up to the age of twenty. It was entertainingly presented and, at least in America, where Ybarra was well-known for his journalism, was commercially successful. The second volume, *Young Man of the World*, took up the story with his years at Harvard and then became an account of his life as a foreign correspondent. A tourist guide to Peru and Bolivia, titled *Lands of the Andes*, was followed by a return to biography. His last two books had musical subjects. Both were fast-paced, and uncritically partisan. Ernest Newmann, writing in the *New York Times*, remarked of *Verdi, Miracle Man Of Opera*: "In spite . . . of his passion for turning on the full orchestra when the string quartet or even a solo flute would do he has produced a book that will be of the greatest service to the ordinary reader." Ybarra had no pretensions to be writing for any other audience.

He also translated an edition of the memoirs of the German Emperor, Wilhelm II, published as *The Kaiser's Memoirs* (1922).

PRINCIPAL WORKS: Davy Jones's Yarns and Other Salted Songs, 1908; (as translated) The Kaiser's Memoirs, 1922; Bolivar the Passionate Warrior, 1929; Cervantes, 1931; Hindenburg the Man with Three Lives, 1932; America Faces South, 1939; Young Man of Caracas, 1941; Young Man of the World, 1942; Lands of the Andes, 1947; Caruso, 1953; Verdi, Miracle Man of Opera, 1955.

ABOUT: The autobiographical material quoted above was written for Twentieth Century Authors, 1942 and Twentieth Century Authors First Supplement, 1955. Current Biography 1940; Ybarra T. Young Man of Caracas 1941, Young Man of the World 1942. *Periodicals*—New York Times November 5, 1939; November 8, 1953; March 27, 1955.

**YEATS, WILLIAM BUTLER** (June 13, 1865– January 28, 1939), Irish poet, dramatist, and memoirist, was born in Sandymount, Dublin, the son of John Butler Yeats, a

lawyer turned painter who had carved out a considerable reputation for himself. Yeats's mother was the former Susan Pollexfen. Yeats's grandfather, and his father before him, were Anglican clergymen. Most of the people in Yeats's position regarded themselves as

English "born in Ireland" but Yeats thought of himself as an Irishman first and foremost. He also thought of himself from an early age as an artist

(and, in that sense, a member of a special and privileged elite). As a boy he had first (he wrote) been attracted to the Far East; but not long afterwards he became convinced that "I should never go for the scenery of a poem to any country but my own."

Just two years after his birth John Butler Yeats wished to fulfill his potential as an artist, and so moved to Fitzroy Road in Regent's Park, London. Yeats spent his childhood, however, in both County Sligo and London. In 1874 when the family moved to Edith Villas in West Kensington (London), the boy attended the nearby Godolphin School in Hammersmith. After another London move, to Bedford Park, the family returned to Ireland, to Howth in County Dublin; Yeats was fifteen. From 1881 until 1883 he attended the Erasmus High School in Dublin. In the latter year he went to study at the Metropolitan School of Art in Kildare Street, Dublin; his colleagues there included Æ.

It was in March 1885, at twenty, that Yeats published his first poetry, in the *Dublin University Review*. When his family moved back to London (1887) he joined the Theosophical Society there. His own family was religiously skeptical, but he soon became interested in esoteric philosophy, and in 1890 was initiated into the Hermetic Order of the Golden Dawn. Meanwhile he had started an intensive study of the poet William Blake, particularly into the vexed meaning of his Prophetic Books. With his friend Edwin J. Ellis he edited *The Works of William Blake* (1893).

Yeats's creative life can conveniently be divided into three distinct periods. In the first he lived in London and was a member of the group of quite important so-called "decadent" poets, among whom were numbered Ernest Dowson, Lionel Johnson, and Arthur Symons. He founded (with Ernest Rhys) the Rhymers' Club, and had published six volumes by his thirtieth year. He dabbled in every form of the occult, and has thus attracted much criticism. But the right question here, in the case of an indubitably major poet is not "what does it mean" (much of it is low-grade and unscholarly) but, rather, "what did he mean by it?" Rhys described him as he appeared then: "very pale . . . thin, a raven lock over his forehead . . . luminous black eyes."

Yeats then entered into a more mature period. After sharing apartments with Symons in London, and witnessing (in Paris) a performance of Alfred Jarry's *Ubu Roi*, he made a tour of western Ireland with Symons. He returned in 1896 to stay at Coole Park with Lady Gregory, whose studies in Irish folklore made her a prime contributor to the Irish literary renaissance. In 1899, Yeats proposed marriage to Maude Gonne, an occultist and passionate Irish nationalist, but in 1903 she married Major John MacBride. This episode he described as "the troubling of my life"; it inspired his poem "No Second Troy".

Under Lady Gregory's influence he rapidly became more practical, although he continued to pursue his mystical interests. He became established as one of the leaders of the Irish renaissance; he introduced John Millington Synge to Ireland as a playwright, and worked with George Moore and many others. In 1902 with Lady Gregory he founded the Irish National Theater Society, of which he became president. He found that he was an effective poetic playwright, and wrote plays for the Abbey Theater, whose first performance (December 27, 1904) was of his *On Baile's Strand*. In 1907 Synge's *Playboy of the Western World* was produced, creating a scandal that he memorialized in one of his most famous poems. During these years of his "second" period, to 1910, he met Joyce (1902) and Pound (1908).

His poetry began to enter its final phase with *The Green Helmet* in 1910, and then with *Responsibilities* in 1914. He made another failed married proposal, this time to Maud Gonne's daughter Iseult, and in 1917 married George Hyde-Lees, with whom he had a son and a daughter. With her he lived for brief periods in a Norman tower near Coole, at Ballylee. It was never his home, but he started to restore it in 1916. That was the year of the Easter Rising, after which Major MacBride was executed by the British—events that very deeply affected him.

Yeats's wife had the gift of being able to do mediumistic "automatic writing." They did more than four hundred sessions together, and from the raw material Yeats formulated his ideas about life and history. He was influenced by astrology, particularly by the astrology of his friend Cyril Fagan. As a consequence, the mystic in Yeats, always ready to be awakened, especially in view of the tragic events of 1916, did spring to full life again. Yet from 1922 until 1928 he became a "smiling public man," a member (by invitation) of the Senate (defending Protestant interests), and taking a pro-Treaty stance against the Republicans. In 1923 he received the Nobel prize (when first informed of the news, he asked—as any author might—"how much?"); in 1926 he became an advisor to the Minister of Finance on a suitable coinage for the Irish Republic. His health was not generally good, but he tried, apparently unsuccessfully, to rejuvenate at least his sexual powers through surgical means. His 1936 visit in the company of an Indian swami to the Balearic island of Majorca, where Robert Graves refused to meet him, became a famous instance of an old man trying to be young—yet the poetry he wrote on the subject is among the greatest ("An aged man is but a paltry thing / A tattered coat upon a stick, unless / Soul clap its hands and sing, and louder sing / For every tatter in its mortal dress."). He was by now a famous figure, derided for his "occult" beliefs yet also accepted as one of the world's leading living poets. In his final years he worked on the last version of his notorious book *A Vision*, which brought him much derision from many quarters. Yet his remarks on such literary figures as he had known in his distant past in London—on, for example, Lionel Johnson—are often exquisitely informative in their quality. He died in Menton where he had gone for his health but, owing to the outbreak of World War II, could not be buried in Ireland until 1948, when his remains were interred at Drumcliff in Sligo.

In his very early poetry Yeats had power, but, as Denis Donoghue writes in his useful brief study, "he did not know what to do with it." In *A Vision* he wrote of his "instructors," who identified "consciousness with conflict, not with knowledge"—yet Yeats needed it to bring out his full genius. And after all, from the earliest poems onwards. It is also probably true, though, as Conor Cruse O'Brien controversially argued, that Yeats's choices were always governed by his desire to be a "great poet."

Yeats made himself a leader among writers of the general revolt against small-mindedness and narrow-minded nationalism, as he demonstrated in his dignified, telling, and intelligent defense of Synge. Many prefer the clarity of the "middle period" poems to the slight cloudiness of some of the later.

It is unlikely that there will ever be complete agreement about the worth of Yeats in the pantheon of major poets. Yvor Winters thought that his views of the occult made his poetry "nonsense"; but that is the opinion of a sometimes idiosyncratic critic. Yeats's contribution as a verse playwright has probably been underrated on account of its Irish nature. There is much controversy about his texts, and, while Jeffares's editions (*Collected Poems, Yeats's Poems*) come nearest to being definitive, they are by no means universally accepted as such.

PRINCIPAL WORKS: *Collections*—Collected Works in Verse and Prose, 7 vols, 1970; Allt, P. and Alspach, R. (eds.) Variorum Edition of the Poems, 1957, Variorum Edition of the Plays, 1966; Jeffares, A. N. Poems, Prose, Plays and Criticism, 4 vols. 1966, Yeats's Poems, 1990; Allbright, D. (ed.) W. B. Yeats: The Poems, 1990. *Poetry*—Masada, 1886; The Wanderings of Oisin, 1889; Poems, 1895 (rev. 1899, 1901, 1912, 1927); The Wind Among the Reeds, 1899; In The Seven Woods, 1903; Poems 1899-1905, 1906; The Poetical Works 2 vols, 1906 (rev. 1912); Poems: Second Series, 1910; The Green Helmet, 1912; Responsibilities, 1914 (rev. 1916); Michael Robartes and the Dancer, 1921; The Tower, 1928; The Winding Stair, 1929 (rev. 1933); Poems, 1935; A Full Moon In March, 1935; New Poems, 1938. *Drama*—The Land of the Heart's Desire, 1894; The Countess Kathleen, 1912; (with George Moore) Diarmuid and Grania, 1951; Where There Is Nothing, 1987; On Baile's Strand, 1903; The Hour Glass, 1903; The King's Threshold, 1904; Deidre, 1907; The Golden Helmet, 1908; (with Lady Gregory) The Travelling Man, 1910; The Words Upon the Window Pane, 1934; Purgatory, 1985; The Herne's Egg, 1991. *As adapter*—Sophocles's King Oedipus, 1928. *Fiction*—John Sherman, 1990; The Table of the Law, 1904; The Secret Rose, 1897 (ed. Variorum ed. as The Secret Rose: Stories by W. B. Yeats, 1992); Stories of Red Hanrahan, with The Secret Rose and Rosa Alchemica, 1914. *Autobiographies and diaries*—Reveries over Childhood and Youth, 1916; Four Years, 1921; The Trembling of the Veil, 1922; Autobiographies, 1927 (rev. and enlarged 1955); Donaghue, D. (ed.,) Memoirs, 1972. *As editor*—The Oxford Book of Modern verse, 1936. *Letters*—Letters on Poetry from W. B. Yeats to Dorothy Wellesley, 1940; W. B. Yeats and T. Sturge Moore: Their Correspondence, 1953; Some Letters of W. B. Yeats to John O'Leary and His Sister, 1953; Letters of W. B. Yeats to Katharine Tynan, 1953; Wade, A. (ed.) The Letters of W. B. Yeats, 1954 (by no means complete); Ah, Sweet dancer: W. B. Yeats and Margot Ruddock, 1970; The Correspondence of Robert Bridges and W. B. Yeats, 1977; Kelly, J. and Domville, E. (eds.) The Collected Letters of W. B. Yeats, volume I, 1986; The Gonne-Yeats letters, 1992.

ABOUT: O'Connor, U. The Yeats Companion, 1990. Archibald, D. Yeats, 1983; Bloom, H. Yeats, 1970; Bradley, A. William Butler Yeats, 1979; Domville, E. A Concordance to the Plays, 1972; Donoghue, D. Yeats, 1971; Ellmann, R. The Identity of Yeats, 1964, Yeats: The Man and the Masks, 1961; Finneran,

R. J. Editing Yeats's Poems,1990; Hone, J. W. B. Yeats, 1965; Jeffares, A. N. W. B. Yeats: Man and Poet, 1966; Parrish, S. M. A Concordance to the Poems, 1963; Vendler, H. Yeats's "Vision" and the Later Plays, 1963; Warren, A. Rage for Order, 1948. *Bibliography*—Jochum, J. B. S., A Classified Bibliography, 1978.

**\*YEATS-BROWN, FRANCIS CHARLES CLAYPON** (August 15, 1886–December 19, 1944), British travel writer, memoirist, adventurer, editor, journalist, and popular exponent of Indian yoga philosophy, was born in Genoa, Italy, the third son of the British Consul there, Montagu Yeats-Brown and his wife, the former Agnes Matilda Bellingham. He was sent to Harrow School, and went on to the British equivalent of  West Point, the Royal Military College at Sandhurst. At twenty he received a commission as second lieutenant in his brother's regiment, the Royal Rifle Corps, then stationed at Bareilly in India. In the following year, 1907, he was posted to the 17th Cavalry of the Indian Army. In 1913 he became adjutant.

Yeats-Brown was in England on leave when World War I broke out. In this he served with distinction, with the 5th Royal Irish lancers and with the Mesopotamian Flight of the Royal Flying Corps (then a part of the British Army). He won the Distinguished Flying Cross and was twice mentioned in dispatches. His experiences at the hands of the Turks between November 1915 and 1918 provided him with the material for two of his most vivid and successful books, *Caught by the Turks* and the later *Golden Horn*. He made two unsuccessful attempts to escape from the prison camp to which he was confined; on the third, in 1918, he was successful.

On his safe return Yeats-Brown did secret work at Constantinople until the end of the war, and then returned to the Indian Army, until he retired, as a major, on a pension at the end of 1925. He was an assistant editor of the *Spectator* (1926–1928), and later edited, for a short period (September–November 1933), the "corporatist" magazine *Everyman*, which advocated a Great Britain governed by one "strong man," along the lines of, but not identical to, Italian Fascism. He acted as a correspondent in Germany and Italy, and met—and was enthusiastic about—both Mussolini and Hitler.

By far the best known book Yeats-Brown wrote was *Lives of a Bengal Lancer*, published in 1930. The poet Rabindranath Tagore, then the most famous Bengali in the world, himself called it, in the *Chicago Daily Tribune*, one "of the most remarkable books in modern literature. I have known no other instance of a genuine psychological record of any intimate touch of a Western mind with the mind of the East."

This book, although less profound than vivid and sincere, is certainly a classic description of the im-
*YATES-BROWN

pact of India upon a sympathetic if essentially im-
perialistic British mentality. The anti-fascist
Leonard Woolf, who had been a magistrate in India, and was all too well aware of Yeats-Brown's enthusiasm for Mussolini, felt constrained to write, in
the *Nation and Athenaeum*, that Major Yeats-
Brown could "write well" and had "considerable
powers of describing scenes and incidents in his
past with remarkable vividness. . . . His accounts
of a polo match and of pig-sticking are much the
best things in the book, and the whole of the first
part in which he describes life in the Bengal Lancers is admirable. I could have wished that he had
devoted his whole book to that life, for I do not
think he is nearly so successful with his war adventures or his mysticism. But it is only fair to him and
the book to say that many people will not and do
not agree with me."

Yeats-Brown never equalled *Bengal Lancer*—
which was made into a spectacular Hollywood
movie—although he wrote many more books, some
of them including passages as colorful as those that
distinguish most of that one. Perhaps unfortunately, he devoted himself to support for Mussolini and
Hitler, and for a British fascism akin to theirs. As
late as 1942 he wrote to the fascist novelist Henry
Williamson: "Am I an optimist to believe that what
was good in Nazism will survive, and that the Jews
will not rule the world, and that this country will
be regenerated?"

Yeats-Brown was by no means a cruel man or
one with a psychopathic streak, such as were many
(like Oswald Mosley) who were attracted to fascism; but he took a very paternalistic view of the
plight of what were then called the working classes
and he was misguided about what was actually going on in Italy and Germany. He was also a guileless
anti-Semite, who sincerely believed in his own and
others' fantasies of international conspiracies of
grasping communist Jews. Thus the *Boston Transcript* was able truthfully to state, of his *The European Jungle* (1939), that he was "fine material for
the confused emotionalism of Sir Oswald Mosley,
and brilliantly illustrates the truth that a little learning is a dangerous thing." Even the *London Times
Literary Supplement*, then notorious for its policy
of appeasement and of qualified admiration for
Hitler, thought that Yeats-Brown's judgment was
"not always as convincing as his prose."

Yeats-Brown's fundamentally humane attitude
did in fact rescue him from the worst excesses of the
British inter-war fascists. He did not like or trust
Mosley personally, and although he always believed that the Germans had been treated badly at
Versailles, was prepared to go to war with them in
1939. However, he tempered this patriotism by declaring that "we must not be involved in a war to
make the world safe for Stalin" and, he felt impelled to add, "international Jewry." Yet he had
written, not long before, how the Nazis' treatment
of the Jews haunted his conscience: "The way the
Germans have treated their Jews is disgusting."

Yeats-Brown's mystical works have not lasted.
*Yoga Explained* was greeted with respect, but
many, some of these themselves adepts, felt as the

*Saturday Review of Literature* that "parts of his
book, at least to those who have not tried Yoga,
must seem pure wish-fantasy." And the Irish poet
Monk Gibbon, writing in the *Spectator*, thought
that the "popular style" seemed at times "a little in-
congruous." However, Yeats-Brown was impressive
in his many lectures on this subject, which he used
to illustrate by standing on his head for protracted
periods of time.

In 1938 Yeats-Brown married Olga Zoueff Phillips, the widow of a Royal Air Force officer, and in
the following year made a return visit to India.

PRINCIPAL WORKS: Caught by the Turks, 1919; Bengal Lancer,
1930 (in U.S.: Lives of a Bengal Lancer); Bloody Years, 1932;
Golden Horn, 1932; The Eight Steps to Yoga, 1933; Dogs of
War!, 1934; Lancer at Large, 1936; Yoga Explained, 1937; Eu-
ropean Jungle, 1939; The Army from September 1939 to De-
cember 1940: A Complete Record in Text and Pictures, 1941;
Indian Pageant, 1942; Martial India, 1945. *As editor*—Escape:
A Book of Escapes, 1933.

ABOUT: Current Biography 1945; Griffiths, R. Fellow Travellers of the Right: British Enthusiasts for Nazi Germany, 1980;
Wrench, J. E. Francis Yeats-Brown 1886–1944, 1948; Yeats-
Brown, F. Caught by the Turks, 1919; Bengal Lancer, 1930;
Lancer at Large, 1936. *Periodicals*—Boston Transcript January 6, 1940; Chicago Daily Tribune December 13, 1930; Nation and Athenaeum August 2, 1930; New York Times
December 21, 1944; Saturday Review of Literature January
1938; Times Literary Supplement May 20, 1939.

**YERBY, FRANK** (September 5, 1916–November
29, 1991), African-American novelist, wrote: "The
biographical facts are as follows: Born in Augusta
Ga., son of Rufus G. Yer-
by and Wilhelmina Smy-
the Yerby—two brothers,
one sister; education at
Haines Institute, Paine
College, A.B. 1937 (both
Augusta, Ga.); Fisk Uni-
versity, Nashville, Tenn.
M.A. 1938; additional
postgraduate study, Uni-
versity of Chicago. Mar-
ried March 1, 1941 at
New Orleans, La., Flora Helen Claire Williams;
four children—Jacques Loring, Nikki Ethlyn,
Faune Ellena, and Jan Keith. Taught, Florida Agricultural and Mechanical College, Tallahassee, Fla.,
1939–40, Southern University, Baton Rouge, La.,
1940–41. Worked for Ford Motor Company, Detroit, then Fairchild Aircraft, Jamaica, Long Island,
during entire war.

"Writing—won special O. Henry Award for first
published short story, 'Health Card' in 1944. *Foxes
of Harrow* published 1946, has sold to date more
than two million copies in English; translations of
it and my other novels now number more than
twelve languages exclusive of such English editions
as Great Britain, New Zealand, Australia."

Frank Yerby's first published story, "The Health
Card," was a tense account of the mistreatment of
a black soldier and his wife in the South, at the
hands of military police during World War II. Failing to find a publisher for a full-length novel about

racial oppression, Yerby resolved to become a popular writer of romantic costume drama. He set out, unashamedly, to make money, and he did.

*The Foxes of Harrow* established the formula for its successors—dashing young hero and naive heroine in the antebellum South, and a melodramatic storyline involving the protagonist's rise to power and wealth against all adversity. Here a young Irish-American, Stephen Fox, makes his fortune and finds romance as manager of a Louisiana plantation during the late nineteenth century. Like its successors, *The Foxes of Harrow* was marked by colorful language, profuse and often violent action, and a wealth of minor characters. Arna Bontemps was hopeful that Yerby's "touch of very elementary magic" would bring "a flush of new vitality to a slightly worn and inbred form of storytelling" (*Book Week*). The book was certainly a huge popular success, and so was the film starring Rex Harrison and Maureen O'Hara. Yerby hated the film, but his reputation was established.

A string of more Southern romances set during the nineteenth century followed, including a sequel, *The Vixens*. This story of the life and loves of an aristocrat named Laird Fournois was fast-paced and brimming over with the necessary components of "lust and blood and enormous vitality" (*Kirkus*). As a reviewer for *Time* noted, "Vulgarity at the level of *The Vixens* has a polish that almost absolves it; literary standards are irrelevant to its high sheen and jet propulsion" (1947). At the same time, Yerby was producing picaresque adventures such as *The Golden Hawk*, a swashbuckler set in the seventeenth century, and other novels with a European flavor.

Yerby was at the height of his success during the early 1950s. He was publishing a novel every year, each conforming to a tried and tested recipe regardless of its time or geographical location. Discussing his treatment of the French Revolution, one reviewer commented: "*The Devil's Laughter*, like all of Mr. Yerby's books, is full of action. It also contains a little history, a great deal of sex and no conviction" (*New York Herald Tribune Book Review*, 1953). A formulaic family saga, *Benton's Row*, was written with the kind of care that prompted reviewers such as Richard Match to speculate that the author might be "a pretty good novelist if he ever got his mind off the neckline and cash register" (*New York Times*, 1954).

The inevitable attacks upon Yerby's work have been double-edged: he has been criticized both for neglecting the African-American experience and for writing money-motivated narratives unworthy of his skills. Robert A. Bone, writing in *The Negro Novel in America*, dubbed him "the prince of pulpsters," and concluded that "If the Negro novel were really integrated, Frank Yerby would be taken no more seriously than Mickey Spillane." A few responded by claiming that the secondary treatment of racial issues in the novels of the South and the weighty ideas that "writhe behind the soap-opera facade of his fiction" (*The Black Novelist*) had significance. Hugh Gloster asserted that Yerby's chief contribution "has been to shake himself free of the

shackles of race and to use the treasure-trove of American experience rather than restrictively Negro experience as his literary province" (*Crisis*).

Yerby himself defended his approach, stating in a well-known article in *Harper's* that "novels written with the deliberate intention to amuse and entertain have—or should have—a very real place in contemporary literature." As time passed, however, he attempted more authentic portraits, with what he hoped was a more substantial intellectual foundation. A reviewer for the *Times Literary Supplement* commented on the author's "panoramic ambitions" in novels like *An Odor of Sanctity*; Yerby went on to experiment with narratives set much earlier in time and farther afield. *Goat Song* details the trials of Ariston, an illegitimate Spartan-Macedonian living in the fifth century B.C., and *Judas, My Brother* is the story of a fictional thirteenth disciple, Nathan bar Yehudah. Neither was found convincing.

Racial injustice is directly confronted both in *Speak Now*, a study of contemporary interracial relationships, and *The Dahomean*, which chronicles Nyasanu Hwesu's transition from African chief to American slave and deals exclusively with black characters. Yerby's intention, as outlined in a prefatory note, was "to correct, as far as possible, the Anglo-Saxon reader's historical perspective" on black history. The story was moving, and written with care and control—as his *Times* obituarist noted, it was "a thousand miles away from his melodramatic costume pieces." Darwin Turner concluded: "Yerby is at his best when he envelopes his plot with a history he has unearthed painstakingly, and with a serious or satirical but always devastating debunking of historical legends and myths. That achievement is superior in *The Dahomean*." Although Yerby's later work improved and novels such as *The Dahomean* received better notices, he never regained the levels of success he had enjoyed in the forties and fifties, when he was America's most popular black author. His total sales, however, exceeded sixty million dollars, and his books were translated into thirty languages.

During the 1950s, Yerby lived in France while his children were being educated in Switzerland. His first marriage having ended in divorce, he met and married Blanca Calle-Perez during a visit to Madrid, Spain, in 1955, and settled there.

Yerby received honorary doctorates from Fisk University and Paine College.

PRINCIPAL WORKS: *Novels*—The Foxes of Harrow, 1946; The Vixens, 1947; The Golden Hawk, 1948; Pride's Castle, 1949; Floodtide, 1950; A Woman Called Fancy, 1951; The Saracen Blade, 1952; The Devil's Laughter, 1953; Bride of Liberty, 1954; Benton's Row, 1954; The Treasure of Pleasant Valley, 1955; Captain Rebel, 1956; Fairoaks, 1957; The Serpent and the Staff, 1958; Jarrett's Jade, 1959; Gillian, 1960; The Garfield Honor, 1961; Griffins Way, 1962; The Old Gods Laugh; A Modern Romance, 1964; An Odor of Sanctity: A Novel of Medieval Moorish Spain, 1965; Goat Song: A Novel of Ancient Greece, 1967; Judas, My Brother: The Story of the Thirteenth Disciple, 1968; Speak Now: A Modern Novel, 1969; The Dahomean: An Historical Novel, 1971 (in U.K.: The Man from Dahomey); The Girl from Storyville: A Victorian Novel, 1972; The Voyage Unplanned, 1974; Tobias and the Angel, 1975; A Rose for Ana Maria, 1976; Hail the Conquering Hero, 1977;

A Darkness at Ingraham's Crest: A Tale of the Slaveholding South, 1979; Western: A Saga of the Great Plains, 1982; Devilseed, 1984; McKenzies Hundred, 1985. As contributor—Fisher, J. and Silvers, R. B. (ed.) Writing in America, 1960; Hughes, L. (ed.) The Best Short Stories by Negro Writers, 1967; Turner, D. T. (ed.) Black American Literature, 1969; Goff, G. (ed.) Voices of Man/This Is Just to Say, 1969; Benedict, S. H. (ed.) Blacklash, 1970; White, E. and Others (ed.) Understanding Literature, 1970; Singh, R. K. And Fellowes. P. (ed.) Black Literature in America: A Casebook, 1970; McAuliffe, C. (ed.) Re-Action, 1971.

ABOUT: The autobiographical material quoted above was written for Twentieth Century Authors First Supplement, 1955. Bain, R. and others Southern Writers: A Biographical Dictionary, 1979; Black Literature Criticism vol.3, 1992; Bone, R. A. The Negro Novel in American, (rev. ed.) 1965; Breit, H. The Writer Observed, 1956; Burke, W. J. and others American Authors and Books, 1972; Collins, L. M. (ed.) The Annual Obituary 1991, 1993; Contemporary Authors vols. 11–12, 1965; vol. 136 1992; Contemporary Literary Criticism vol. 1 1973; vol. 7 1977; vol. 22 1982; Contemporary Novelists, (3rd ed.) 1982; Current Biography 1949; Hemenway, R. (ed.) The Black Novelist, 1970; Novelists and Prose Writers, 1979; Nye, R. B. The Unembarrassed Muse, 1970; Oxford Companion to American Literature, 1983; Ryan, B. Major 20th Century Writers, 1991; Twentieth Century American Literature 1980; Twentieth Century Fiction, 1983; Vinson, J. (ed.) Twentieth Century Romance and Gothic Writers, 1982; Warfel, H. R. American Novelists of Today, 1951; Who's Who 1992; Who's Who Among Black Americans, 6th ed. 1990. Periodicals—Black World February 1972; Book Week February 10, 1946; Chicago Sunday Tribune April 6, 1952; September 21, 1958; Chicago Tribune January 12, 1992; Crisis January 1948; Harpers October 1959; Kirkus March 1947; Los Angeles Times January 1, 1992; New York Herald Tribune Book Review October 4, 1953; November 28, 1954; New York Times December 5, 1954; January 8, 1992; New York Times Book Review May 13, 1951; June 13, 1982; Time May 5, 1947; November 29, 1954; Times (London) January 11, 1992; Times Literary Supplement July 28, 1966; U.S. News and World Report January 20, 1992; Weekly Book Review February 24, 1946.

**\*YEZIERSKA, ANZIA** (1885–November 21, 1970), American novelist and short story writer, the daughter of Paruch Yezierska, a Talmudic scholar,

was born in a small town in Russian Poland. The family joined other Jewish immigrants and settled in the Lower East Side of New York City some time in the 1890s. (The early years of Yezierska's life are difficult to document. Some sources give her year of birth as 1880, others 1883; 1885 is the most commonly accepted.) Because her father continued to spend his time in study, the burden of supporting the home fell on the females of the household. Anzia spent several years working in sweatshops and as a waitress and laundress. After attending night-school she enrolled, in 1901, at the Teachers College of Columbia University and was awarded a diploma in domestic science in 1904.

Several years of teaching were followed by marriage to Jacob Gordon, an attorney, in 1910. The marriage lasted only months. She remarried the following year, and a daughter, Louise, was born in 1912. But Yezierska felt imprisoned by married

°yeh ZY ER skah

life. She moved to California with her daughter until, in 1916, agreeing to end the marriage formally, she put Louise in the care of her father, Arnold Levitas.

By this time Yezierska was set on pursuing a literary career. Her first story, "Free Vacation House," was published in 1915 in an issue of Forum. Soon afterwards she met the pragmatist and educator John Dewey, and through this connection worked as a translator for a project among Polish-speaking people in Philadelphia. Dewey and Yezierska enjoyed a brief emotional relationship which inspired Dewey to compose, in secret, several romantic poems and Yezierska to continue writing with new purpose. The extent of the relationship has been open to speculation (see Mary V. Dearborn's Love in the Promised Land), but it is generally accepted that it was a true love affair.

One of Yezierska's stories, "The Fat of the Land," was included in Best Short Stories of 1919, edited by Edward O'Brien, and was later selected as winner of the O. Henry Award for best short story of the year. It was included in her first full collection Hungry Hearts, and it descibes a journey which Yezierska was to recount many times—the rise from poverty to affluence, and a corresponding discovery of hollowness at the heart of the American dream. All the narratives in the collection were told with an unrestrained passion and color which too often toppled over into sentiment and vulgarity.

Initially the book sold only moderately, and Yezierska found herself living a desolate life. (Dewey was, by then, away in China.) But a newspaper article brought her to the attention of Sam Goldwyn, and out of the blue she was offered $10,000 for the movie rights. Suddenly she was successful, and dubbed the "sweatshop Cinderella." She went to Hollywood but found the life and atmosphere there distasteful. Returning east she set about writing a novel. Based on the real-life marriage between a millionaire, James Phelps Graham Stokes, and his Jewish immigrant bride, Salome of the Tenements tells the story of a fiery, scheming heroine whose passions prove too much for her paler, more placid husband. However, both the characterization and narrative were judged too hysterical to be convincing; she continued to be read mainly for her vivid reconstructions of immigrant life.

Subsequent books were all attempts to recreate the same world. Breadgivers, her second novel, while pandering a little to her Cinderella reputation (it was publicized as being autobiographical), contained more controlled characterization—the patriarchal Reb Smolinsky is vividly drawn—but Yezierska's attempts to represent Yiddish by broken English rendered much of the dialogue ridiculous, particularly to her Jewish readers, many of whom resented the caricature effect.

After the next two novels, Arrogant Beggar and All I Could Never Be, Yezierska's reputation went into decline, and she lost her savings in the Depression. For nearly twenty years she was unpublished—until 1950, when a volume of autobiography, Red Ribbon on a White Horse ap-

peared, with an introduction by W. H. Auden. Yezierska prided herself on her transparency of style,
some would call it stylelessness, and she somewhat
resented Auden's intellectual interpretation of her
themes. But the introduction was helpful in restor-
ing interest in her work, and during the final two
decades of her life she also benefited from a general
wave of interest in Jewish-American literature. She
wrote regularly on Jewish subjects for the *New
York Times*.

In the 1960s her sight began to fail, and at the
time of her death she was living in a home for the
elderly in California. Her papers, which are held by
the Boston University Library, include work not
published in her lifetime. Some of this appeared in
*The Open Cage* (1979), a volume which included
an afterword by her daughter, Louise Henriksen,
who also published a biography of her mother in
1988. A collected edition of her stories, *How I
Found America*, was published in 1991.

PRINCIPAL WORKS: Hungry Hearts, 1920; Salome of the Tene-
ments, 1923; Children of Loneliness, 1923; Bread Givers, 1925;
Arrogant Beggar, 1927; All I Could Never Be, 1932; Red Ribbon on a White Horse, 1950; The Open Cage, 1979; How I
Found America, 1991.

ABOUT: Dearborn, M. Love in the Promised Land, 1988; Henriksen, L. Anzia Yezierska, a Writer's Life, 1988; Rosen, N.
John and Anzia, an American Romance, 1989; Schoen, C. Anzia Yezierska, 1982. *Periodical*—New York Times November
23, 1970.

**YORKE, HENRY VINCENT.** See **GREEN,
HENRY**

**YOUNG, ELLA** (December 26, 1867–July 24,
1956), Irish mythologist and poet, wrote: "I was
born in the little village of Fenagh, County Antrim,
Ireland. The Youngs have held Antrim land since
early in the seventeenth century when a Young
from Scotland purchased estates there; perhaps it is
for this reason that I feel a close tie with the head-
lands and cliffs of Antrim. I came away as a small
child and lived in Southern Ireland until I left for
America.

"From childhood I heard tales of ghosts, ban-
shees, haunted castles, mischievous and friendly
sprites, snatches of ballads, and political arguments.

As I grew older, there
were tales of national heroes: William Wallace,
William Tell, Hereward
the Wake and others.
'Have we no heroes? I
asked my parents. They
thought not. I made a
mental note that heroes
belonged to foreign coun-
tries and felt cheated. It
was left for a nursemaid
to give me my first glimpse of Irish history: 'Brian
Boru was a great man entirely. He drove the Danes
out of Ireland. The Danes were little black men
with tails. Brian cut off their tails and drove them
out of Ireland for good and all!

"My sisters and I knew Shakespeare, Milton, and
Bunyan at an early age. Later came Plato and the

Norse sagas; also, sandwiched in a few lines of Irish
history, I surprised the name of Cuchulain. I felt
that sagas and poems belonged to this man, but no
one could tell me of them. "It was not until I came
to Dublin and met Standish O'Grady, Æ, and Kuno
Meyer that I realized what a heritage waited for me
in Celtic literature. I read every translation I could
get, learned Irish, and betook myself to Gaelic Ireland where, by turf fires, I could hear poems of the
Fianna recited by people who had not forgotten the
name of Lugh, the sun-god, and who remembered
Aunya, the mother-goddess. These people knew
lakes where the Great Piast still raised a crested
head. They had seen the white Water-Horses that
rear and plunge in dark whirlpools. They had heard
the faery music and had danced in faery circles.
They were folk who maintained a comrade-ship
with mountains and trees, and did not forget to put
out bowls of milk and bowls of ripened grain, on
proper occasions, for Puck, or as he is known in Ireland, the Pooka.

"From such folk I gathered the tales of the Gob-
han Saor which later I put together in *The Wonder-
Smith and His Son*. They were recounted to me, at
times, on mountain-sides; at times, in sailing-boats,
with the ploughed wave sliding greenly under the
keel; always with bright air, sharp scents of bog-
land, sound of sea-strongholds, or the warm aromatic whiff of a peat fire about them, and a sense
of the centuries that went to the making of the
proud and tameless people who had treasured
them.

"A thing that counted greatly in my life was the
Rising in Ireland—this is not the place to write of
it!

"I came to America in 1925, as a lecturer, landing at New York. Later, in California, I held the
Phelan Memorial Lectureship on Celtic Mythology
and Literature in the University of California. I am
living now near the great dunes at Oceano where
I can hear the sound of the sea. I believe that the
two books which I wrote in California, *The Tangle-
Coated Horse* and *The Unicorn with Silver Shoes*,
have gained something from the rhythm of the Pacific and the weird beauty of the Mojave Desert.

"*Celtic Wonder Tales* embodies the Celtic Myth
of Creation, and in it I have used some of the most
splendid material known to the old Saga makers.

"What books I have written, are written for children (and grown-ups) who hunger as I did for a lost
inheritance, who are fain to catch a glimpse of the
Fortunate Islands; to learn that golden apples still
grow in the Garden of the Hesperides; and that Angus moves yet in a cloud of bird-wings, immortally
young, though Tara is ruined."

―――――――

Ella Young went to Dublin to study political
economy, law, and history at the Royal University.
She met George William Russell when she joined
his Hermetical Society—devoted to mysticism and
theology—and was encouraged by him to pursue
her interest in both Irish mythology and politics. A
staunch Republican, Young began writing for Sinn

Féin, and from 1912 was involved in gun-running for the Irish Republican Army from a rented farmhouse in Wicklow. She was blacklisted at the time of the Rising and went for a while to Connemara. There she heard that many of her friends had been executed. She returned to Dublin in 1919, and stayed until her move to America in 1925.

However, political concerns are entirely absent from her poetry and prose. Her work weaves around the Celtic myths and legends for which she had such affection.

*The Tangle-Coated Horse,* a collection of Fenian tales, is marred by an excessive adherence to original sources, in this case the Fenian saga, but was nonetheless well-received.

Young's most popular book for children was *The Unicorn with Silver Shoes.* It tells of the adventures of Ballor's son and his friend Flame of Joy in the Land of the Ever Young.

*Flowering Dusk,* Young's final prose work, constituted random recollections of her life in Ireland and America, and of the people she encountered, including W. B. Yeats, Lady Gregory, Maude Gonne, and Padraic Colum. Although a reviewer for the *New Yorker* warned that some readers "may find the atmosphere of other-worldliness much too rarified at times," others considered *Flowering Dusk* "an enchanting, intimate . . . book by, and about, one of the most sensitive literary artists of our time" (*Book Week*).

PRINCIPAL WORKS: *Juvenile*—The Coming of Lugh, 1909; Celtic Wonder Tales, 1910; The Wonder-Smith and His Son, 1927; The Tangle-Coated Horse, 1929; The Unicorn with Silver Shoe, 1932. *Poetry*—Poems, 1906; The Rose of Heaven, 1918; The Weird of Fionavar, 1922; To the Little Princess, 1930; Marzilian, 1938; Seed of the Pomegranate, 1949; Smoke of Myrrh, 1950. *Autobiography*—Flowering Dusk; Things Remembered Accurately and Inaccurately, 1945.

ABOUT: The autobiographical material quoted above was written for Twentieth Century Authors, 1942. Kunitz, S. J. and Haycraft, H. (eds.) The Junior Book of Authors, 2nd ed., 1951; Macmillan Dictionary of Irish Literature, 1979; Ward, M. E. and Marquardt, D. A. Authors of Books for Young People, 1964; Young E. Flowering Dusk, 1945. *Periodicals*—Atlantic Bookshelf December, 1932; Booklist May 1927; Book Week July 1, 1945; Horn Book May-June 1939; Library Journal April 15, 1945; New Yorker June 30, 1945; New York Herald Tribune Books March 13, 1927; November 17, 1929; New York Times November 13, 1932; July 25, 1956; New York World November 3, 1929; Publisher's Weekly September 3, 1956; Wilson Library Bulletin September, 1956.

# YOUNG, E(MILY) H(ILDA)

(1880–August 8, 1949), English novelist, was born in Northumberland, the third child of William Michael Young, a wealthy shipbroker, and his wife Frances Jane. She received a sound middle-class education, at Gateshead High School and at Penrhos College, a girl's boarding school in Colwyn Bay, North Wales.

In 1902 Young met and married J. A. H. Daniells, a Bristol solicitor, and moved to that city. During the First World War she worked in a munitions factory and as a groom. Her husband died in action at Ypres in 1917, and Young went to live with her lover, and his wife, in London. Although Ralph Henderson had been one of her husband's closest friends and was well-known—as headmaster of Alleyn's School in Dulwich—this *ménage à trois* escaped public attention. Young, who was always addressed as Mrs. Daniells, had her own apartment in the Henderson household, and the relationship was effectively concealed.

Young first achieved notice with *William,* a study of relationships as they are affected by societal codes. *The Vicar's Daughter,* which followed, was a comedy of errors.  L. P. Hartley found this story of the dubious parentage of a servant girl "clever, complicated and, above all, improbable" (*Saturday Review*). *Miss Mole* centers on Hannah Mole, a seemingly colorless, middle-aged housekeeper who has in fact lived a life which is "not hampered by man's conventional morality," When rumors about her begin to escalate, she is saved by one Mr. Blenkinsop, and "an unexpected romance . . . makes a surprisingly moving climax to a beautiful and witty book" (*New Statesman*). Although critics found and continue to find her subject matter "unimportant and unexciting" (*New Republic*), some reviewers liked it. *Miss Mole* was awarded the James Tait Black Memorial Prize in 1930 and remains her best-known novel.

*Jenny Wren,* and its sequel *The Curate's Wife,* deal with two very different daughters of a man who has "married beneath himself" and the marriages they themselves make. Gentle character studies in the Austen vein, they display insight and wit. Dramatic tension, as V. S. Pritchett pointed out, "lies in the skill with which the characters are thoroughly built up and illumined."

Young's final novel *Chatterton Square,* is a study of the contrast between two neighboring families, set like many of her books in Radstowe, her name for Bristol. Centering on a middle-aged woman who is liberated by a reappraisal of her pompous husband, it was commended for its charm, delicacy, and fine characterization.

It was recently claimed that E. H. Young is an undeservedly neglected novelist. She was, as her obituarist in the *Times* said, "a novelist of rare quality, possessed of a singular clarity of imaginative sympathy with the springs of normal character and experience." Although "she stood aside from the tendency of most of her contemporaries . . . she saw life steadily and saw it whole." However, Virago's reprints of some of her novels have sold disappointingly, and no respectable critic has been able to give her more than her due as a worthy writer of her time.

Upon Ralph Henderson's retirement in 1940, he and Young went alone to live in Bradford-on-Avon, Wiltshire. She was active in Civil Defence during World Ward II. An accomplished rock-climber, she spent her summers climbing in Wales, Switzerland, and the Dolomites.

PRINCIPAL WORKS: *Novels*—A Corn of Wheat, 1910; Yonder,

1912; Moor Fires, 1916; The Bridge Dividing (in 1927 as The Misses Mallett, and in U.S.: The Mallets), 1922; William, 1925; The Vicar's Daughter, 1928; Miss Mole, 1930; Jenny Wren, 1932; The Curate's Wife, 1934; Celia, 1937; Chatterton Square, 1947. *Juvenile*—Caravan Island, 1940; River Holiday, 1942.

ABOUT: Blain, V. and Others, The Feminist Companion to Literature in English, 1990; Lawrence, M. We Write as Woman, 1937; Longman Companion to Twentieth Century Literature, 3rd ed., 1981; Oxford Guide to British Women Writers, 1993; Parker, P. (ed.) The Reader's Companion to the Twentieth Century Novel, 1994. Who's Who 1949. *Periodicals*—Bookman October, 1930; Catholic World December, 1947; illustrated London News August 20, 1949; New Republic November 19, 1930; New Statesman July 5, 1930; New Statesman and Nation November 26, 1932; New York Herald Tribune Weekly Book Review September 28, 1947; New York Tribune September 20, 1925; Outlook October 8, 1930; Publisher's Weekly September 17, 1949; Saturday Review September 29, 1928; Saturday Review of Literature January 28, 1950; Spectator May 30, 1925; Times (London) August 10, 1949.

## YOUNG, FRANCIS BRETT (June 29, 1884–

March 28, 1954), English novelist, was born at Halesowen, Worcestershire (the region in which much of his later fiction is set), the eldest son of T. Brett Young, a doctor. After attending school at Epsom College he took a medical degree at the University of Birmingham, where he was a Sands Cox scholar, and then set up in practice in Brixham, Devon.

His publishing career began in 1913 with the appearance of a short critical study of the poetry of Robert Bridges—Young, who was an accomplished

pianist, set several of Bridges's songs to music—and also a novel, *Undergrowth*, which he wrote in collaboration with his younger brother, E. Brett Young. The next novel, *Deep Sea*, which Young wrote on his own, was set in Brixham. It was followed by *The Dark Tower*, considered by Young's obituarist in the London *Times* to exhibit "an almost Jamesian subtlety of narrative method."

During the war he served with the Royal Army Medical Corps in East Africa, with the rank of Major. Afterwards, weakened by malaria, he was unable to return to medical practice and moved to Capri, where he and his wife stayed for the next decade. His experiences in the East African campaign found their way into *Marching on Tanga*, his narrative account of the campaign under General Smuts. After this, despite the fact that he was then living abroad, he began to set his novels in the English West Midlands, otherwise known as the Black Country. "North Bromwich" is his fictional representation of Birmingham. Publishing at the rate of a book a year during the twenties, Young finally began to achieve a higher profile when he was awarded the James Tait Black Memorial Prize for 1927 with *Love Is Enough* (published in England as *Portrait of Claire*). The book's leisurely and enthralling narrative style led people to begin lauding Young as the new Galsworthy. Six years later, in 1933,

Young's name came top in a poll aimed at identifying future literary giants. When citing this fact, John Sutherland, in a 1990 article in the *Times Literary Supplement*, commented: "Young's posthumous fame now seems somewhat less than gigantic." However, his undisputed contemporary popularity was founded in his firm handling of family chronicles and his representation of the Worcestershire landscape as England in microcosm. William Plomer, reviewing Young's 1934 novel *The Little World*, wrote in *The Spectator*: "Everything is worked out most satisfactorily, and it becomes more and more likely that in the long run all is for the best in the best of all possible little worlds—provided they are English, and seen with conventional, middle-class, good-natured, and slightly sentimental eyes. . . . It is not a book for highbrows or proletarians, but it cannot fail to please many people whose conception of the English village and its inhabitants it will do nothing to heighten or disturb."

The Youngs returned from Capri to England in 1932 but later moved to live in South Africa. Several of his later novels have African settings—these include *They Seek a Country* and its sequel, *The City of Gold*, about the founding of Johannesburg. Young's final book, *In South Africa*, was a nonfiction guide for tourists and settlers.

The writing of a verse epic had been a coveted ambition of Young's for most of his life, and he achieved this with publication of *The Island*, a vast panorama of English history, deploying different verse forms for different periods and scenes. But the effort, which went largely unappreciated, exhausted him, and he wrote no more novels. He died in a Cape Town nursing home, aged seventy.

PRINCIPAL WORKS: *Fiction*—(with E. Brett Young) Undergrowth, 1913; Deep Sea, 1914; The Dark Tower, 1915; The Iron Age, 1916; The Crescent Moon, 1918; The Young Physician, 1919; The Tragic Bride, 1920; The Black Diamond, 1921; The Red Knight, 1921; Pilgrim's Rest, 1922; Cold Harbour, 1924; Woodsmoke, 1924; Sea Horses, 1925; Portrait of Clare, 1927 (in U.S.: Love Is Enough); The Key of Life, 1928; My Brother Jonathan, 1928; Black Roses, 1929; Jim Redlake, 1930 (in U.S.: The Redlakes); Mr. and Mrs. Pennington, 1931; Blood Oranges, 1932; The House under the Water, 1932; The Cage Bird and Other Stories, 1933; This Little World, 1934; White Ladies, 1935; Far Forest, 1936; They Seek a Country, 1937; The Christmas Box, 1938; Doctor Bradley Remembers, 1938; The City of Gold, 1939; Cotswolds Honey and Other Stories, 1940 (in U.S.: The Ship's Surgeon's Yarn); The Happy Highway, 1940; Mr. Lucton's Freedom, 1940; A Man about the House, 1942. *Nonfiction*—Robert Bridges, a Critical Study, 1914; Marching on Tanga, 1917; Portrait of a Village, 1937; In South Africa, 1952. *Drama*—Captain Swing, 1919; (with W. Armstrong) The Furnace, 1928. *Poetry*—Five Degrees South, 1917; Poems 1916–1918, 1919; The Island, 1944.

ABOUT: Dictionary of National Biography, 1951–1960; Who's Who 1954; Young J. Brett Francis Brett Young: A Biography, 1962. *Periodicals*—Illustrated London News April 3, 1954; New York Times March 29, 1954; Spectator August 3, 1934; Times (London) March 29, 1954; Times Literary Supplement April 27, 1990.

**YOUNG, STARK** (October 11, 1881–January 6, 1963), American novelist playwright, translator, and dramatic critic, was born in Como, Mississippi, the son of Alfred Alexander Young and Mary (Starks) Young. At the early age of fourteen he entered the University of Mississippi, from which he graduated when he was twenty. After postgraduate study at Columbia University he became (1902) a reporter for the Brooklyn *Standard and Union.* After a year of this he went back to the South. First he taught in a military school, then at the University of Mississippi. Later he held appointment at the University of Texas (where he founded the Curtain Club) and at Amherst College.

In 1921 Young gave up teaching for journalism. He worked for the *New Republic* (1921–1924) and briefly became drama critic for the *New York Times* (1924–1925) before taking the same position with the *New Republic*, for which he wrote until 1947.

Young made his most lasting contributions to American letters in this period. His creative writing was never much more than worthy, but as a keeper of standards, and as a critic of high aesthetic standards, he was invaluable and respected. He wrote in the tradition of the so-called New Criticism, which had sprung up in the 1920s in challenge to poor standards of criticism. Like such critics as John Crowe Ransom and R. P. Blackmur he directed his attention to texts, to structure, and to the way form reinforced content.

As a drama critic he was considered a particularly astute judge of actors' performances, and was, Herbert Gorman said in his *New York Times* review of *Flower In Drama: A Book of Papers on the Theater* (1923), "the sort of critic who manages to get to authentic meat of his subject and is not upset by the excitement of the moment . . . He seizes upon fundamentals, and one reason why he manages to do this is undoubtedly because he possesses well-grounded standards."

Another of his volumes on the art of acting, *Glamour: Essays on the Art of the Theatre* (1925), brought similar praise from the *Theatre Arts Monthly*, which spoke of Young's "uncanny comprehension of the actor's problems and the actor's art, and [he] writes of them in a style at once so glamorous, revealing and precise, that the volume is lifted to that lean shelf reserved for the few permanently contributive books on the theatre."

A judicious selection from Young's many years of theater reviews was compiled in *Immortal Shadows: A Book of Dramatic Criticism* (1948). His general guide, *The Theater* (1927), which discussed plays, actors, setting, directors and audiences, was reissued in 1986. "Few drama critics have had so much practical experience in the theatre as did Young," wrote John Pilkington in the introduction to *Stark Young: A Life in the Arts: Letters 1900–*

*1962* (1973). In the course of his career, he wrote three one-act plays, a collection of plays for children, two full-length plays (produced off-Broadway and in London), a vehicle for his friends Alfred Lunt and Lynne Fontanne, and a play for Maria Ouspenskaya. As director he was in charge of the French playwright Henri René Lenormand's production of *The Failures*, and of Eugene O'Neill's little-known *Welded.* He translated Chekhov's *The Sea Gull* for a Lunt-Fontanne production, as well as *The Three Sisters, The Cherry Orchard* and *Uncle Vanya*—all produced off-Broadway.

As a novelist he is probably best remembered for his epic Civil War tale *So Red the Rose* (1934). Like Margaret Mitchell's *Gone with the Wind* (1936), it painted a romanticized picture of the aristocratic graciousness of the old South. Although eclipsed by *Gone with the Wind*, it managed to sell well for two decades and was made into a motion picture by Paramount in 1935. "The total effect of *So Red the Rose* is that of a dream—long, luscious, and finally cloying," wrote Mary McCarthy in the *Nation.*

As a loosely affiliated member of the Southern Agrarian, or Fugitive, group of writers, which notably included Ransom, Allen Tate, and Robert Penn Warren, Young contributed to *I'll Take My Stand: The South and the Agrarian Tradition; by Twelve Southerners* (1930). He "advocated," wrote Pilkington, "a modern humanism in place of the materialism he deplored as the common denominator of twentieth-century life. . . . Although his stand was often labeled 'Southern,' its fundamental premise was an assertion of the role of culture and tradition in modern life."

Young's attempt to bridge the cultures of the old and new South is clear in his other novels. In *Torches Flare* (1928) a young Southern woman returns to Mississippi from Greenwich Village because of illness in her family. Like his narrator, Hal Boardman, Young "is restrained and wise; alive to shades, nuances, tone and texture; and a trifle academic in the way he stands off from life," wrote the *New York Times* (1928). In *The River House* (1929), Southern newlyweds of a new generation return to the old homestead in a small Mississippi town to find conflict with the family patriarch, Major Dandridge, and spinster aunts. "It is a fascinating picture of Southern life, a novel of first rank, a mature and civilized book," wrote Lyle Saxon in *Saturday Review of Literature.*

Young, who never married, took up painting in 1942 after his retirement. He exhibited in New York, Philadelphia, and Chicago.

In 1951 he published his memoirs, *The Pavilion*, in which he recalled not only his early years in the South but his theater days in New York. It was commended for its modesty, grace, and simple elegance.

PRINCIPAL WORKS: *Criticism*—The Flower in Drama, 1923; Glamour: Essays on the Art of the Theatre, 1925; Theatre Practice, 1926; Encaustics, 1926; The Theatre, 1927; Immortal Shadows, 1948. *Novels*—Heaven Trees, 1926; The Torches Flare, 1928; The River House, 1929; So Red the Rose, 1934. *Drama*—Guenevere, 1906; Addio, Madretta and Other Plays,

1912; The Colonnade, 1924; The Saint, 1925; Sweet Times and The Blue Policeman: A Book of Children's Plays, 1925; Artemise, 1942. *Other*—The Blind Man at the Window and Other Poems, 1906; The Three Fountains, 1924; The Street of the Islands, 1930 (stories); (as contributor) I'll Take My Stand: The South and the Agrarian Tradition; by Twelve Southerners, 1930; Feliciana, 1935 (stories); The Pavilion: Of People and Times Remembered, of Stories and Places, 1951. *As editor*—A Southern Treasury of Art and Literature, 1937; Sidney Lanier, Selected Poems, 1947; The Best Plays of Chekhov, 1956.

ABOUT: Dictionary of American Biography, 1961–1965; Pilkington, J. (ed.) Stark Young: A Life in the Arts: Letters 1900–1962. *Periodicals*—Chicago Daily Tribune August 4, 1934; Nation August 8, 1934; New Republic January 26, 1963; New York Times March 18, 1923; May 11, 1924; May 13, 1928; January 7, 1963; Saturday Review of Literature December 7, 1929; Theatre Arts Monthly June 1925; Times (London) January 9, 1973.

## YU-T'ANG, LIN. See LIN YU-TANG

**ZABEL, MORTON DAUWEN** (August 10, 1901–April 27, 1964), American critic and editor, wrote: "I was born in southern Minnesota (Minnesota Lake), my grandparents and their families having come to that part of America in the early and middle decades of the nineteenth century from Europe, some of them by way of New York and the East, some by way of New Orleans and the Mississippi Valley in the early pioneer years of the Middle West. It was there, a short distance south of Minneapolis, that I spent my childhood, had my early schooling, lost my father when I was thirteen, and prepared for college, first with the intention of going to one of the Eastern universities, but after my father's death with the decision to go to schools nearer home. For three years I attended the Military College of St. Thomas at St. Paul, Minnesota, and then went on to the University of Minnesota, where I took the Master of Arts Degree in 1922. I first planned to study medicine, and in fact completed the work of the pre-medical course for the medical school at the University of Minnesota; but it soon became apparent that my real interests lay not in science but in literary and humanistic studies, so at Minnesota I changed and took the master's degree in English literature, studying there under such men as Cecil A. Moore, Joseph Warren Beach, Frederick Klaeber, Richard Burton, E. E. Stoll, and other professors of literature who formed the distinguished department of English at that time. In 1922 I moved to Chicago, to teach, and to continue doctoral studies at the University of Chicago, where I specialized in nineteenth century literature, English and European. I also spent periods of research at Harvard and Columbia. I took the Ph.D. degree in 1933, at Chicago, with a dissertation on *The Romantic Idealism of Art in England*. . . . Meanwhile I taught for a considerable number of years at Loyola University, Chicago, where in 1928 I became chairman of the department of English; but I also filled visiting professorships at the Universities of Chicago, California, and Northwestern, and lectured at a good many other American universities and colleges.

"My first trip to Europe came in 1922, and others followed in 1924, 1928, 1935, and after the Second World War, in 1951 and 1954. Some of these were long visits, with study and research work in London and Paris, and travels in most of the western and southern Continental countries. My work as a writer began around 1924, and has continued steadily ever since. This work was in poetry and, at one point, in fiction, but chiefly it was in literary and art criticism, and in scholarship. In 1926 I became acquainted with Harriet Monroe, the founder and editor of *Poetry: A Magazine of Verse*.  I began contributing verse and criticism to *Poetry*, and in 1928 Miss Monroe asked me to become her associate editor. This was a fruitful and rewarding association; it brought me the acquaintance of many writers; I contributed, for about twelve years, to every issue of the magazine—editorials, reviews, reports on American and European periodicals, as well as verse. When Miss Monroe died (1926) . . . I took over the editorship of *Poetry* and carried it through a difficult year of problems and adjustments. Then, because writings and teaching had first claims, I decided to withdraw from the editorship and its inevitable insecurity. I continued writing for the journals to which I had been contributing. I also served as visiting professor at Chicago, at Northwestern, and at the University of California in Berkeley. I published *Literary Opinion in America* and other books in the following years. And in 1943 a new chapter opened.

"The Department of State in Washington had negotiated with the government of Brazil for the installation of a Chair of North American Literature at the National University of Brazil in Rio de Janeiro. At the instigation of the Rockefeller Foundation, I was chosen for the post. I had never seriously sent my thoughts in the direction of Latin America, but I decided to undertake the venture. Early in 1944, I went by air—four days of flying in those wartime years—to Rio de Janeiro and saw that fabulous city for the first time. I inaugurated the *cadeira* and began to make the acquaintance of a new world of writers, friends, and scenes. I had gone to Brazil for nine months; I stayed for two years; and besides my work at the university and at the Instituto Brasil-Estados Unidos, I visited and lectured in São Paulo, Belo Horizonte, Ouro Preto, Porto Alegre, Bahia, and other Brazilian cities. When the two memorable Brazilian years and the delightful experience of living in Rio were over, I spent another five months flying to other South American and Central American countries, lecturing in universities and cultural institutes, and making acquaintance with the whole panorama of Latin American life—Uruguay, Argentina, Chile, Peru, Ecuador, Columbia, Venezuela, Panama, Guatemala, and Mexico. I count this as one of the most revealing and impressive experiences of my life. It was renewed in the summer of 1953, when, again on a cultural mission for the State Department, I returned for three months to Brazil (Rio, São Paulo, Bahia, Belo Horizonte, Ouro Preto, Florianopolis, Porto Alegre), as well as to Argentina, Uruguay, and Peru. And in 1954 I was invited by the Brazilian authorities to return to act as United States delegate to the International Congress of Writers in August, held in connection with the Fourth Centenary Exposition of the city of São Paulo. My fellow American delegates were William Faulkner and Robert Frost. This time I flew to Brazil from Europe, where I was spending a year in travel, lecturing, and research, and had three weeks in São Paulo and Rio to renew old friendships, as well as delightful weeks in Portugal and Spain on my return to London. Thus South America, and particularly Brazil, has become a distinct part of my work and experience. I left behind there two books on American literature—*A Literatura dos Estados Unidos*, in Portuguese, published in Rio (1947), and *Historia de la Literatura Norteamericana*, in Spanish, published in Buenos Aires (1951)—as a record of my work and as books now widely used in the schools and universities of the southern hemisphere; as well as many articles in the literary journals and reviews, and two anthologies of American literature.

"In 1944 I was awarded a Guggenheim fellowship to aid my literary studies, and in 1955 a $1000 Award from the National Institute of Arts and Letters. I have tried in my works as a writer to combine the study of literature with social and historical studies, as well as with a lifelong interest in art and music. My particular literary heroes, in the nineteenth and twentieth centuries at least, have been writers like Coleridge, Dickens, Arnold, Flaubert, Conrad, Yeats, and Henry James; the poets have claimed my attention as much as the critics and novelists. I became professor of English Literature at the University of Chicago on my return from South America in 1946. I see the critical spirit, the enquiring intelligence, as central to all great literature, imaginative or otherwise, and have made it my object to trace its workings among the western literatures in whatever form it manifests itself."

---

Morton Dauwen Zabel was a critic and editor whose Viking Portables of Henry James, Joseph Conrad, and the poet Edwin Arlington Robinson brought new audiences to these authors. The verdict of the *New York Herald Tribune Books* on the selection of essays he edited in 1938, *Literary Opinion in America*, perhaps gives a clue as to why his own criticism has failed to last; of these essays selected by Zabel the reviewer had to say: "Gusto yields almost completely to justice." The critic and literary historian Harry Levin, reviewing the same book in the *Nation*, was even more precise in his criticism: "To so uncertain and fitful a subject as contemporary American criticism the mere appearance of a book like this lends a harmony and a dignity that are somewhat specious. Interesting as they are, none of these fifty essays seems an inevitable choice. It would be easy to suggest critics who could have been included: it would be impolite to

point to articles that might have been left out. It might be possible to compile several other volumes of the same size and scope without duplicating material. . . . As a former editor of *Poetry* and a Catholic professor contributing to journals, Morton Dauwen Zabel can be depended on to do a tactful job. But the situation calls for detachment rather than tact."

Zabel revised and expanded this collection in 1951, when Harvey Breit in the *New York Times* (1951) commented that the book, which he called a "colossus of criticism," had been edited with "taste and intelligence." But, he added, "the totality is something else again. It is all too much probing, poking, thinking, analyzing. The mind is enriched, but life is the loser. . . . " G. F. Whicher in the *New York Herald Tribune Book Review* welcomed it as "a masterly survey" and "substantially improved."

Of Zabel's *Craft and Character: Texts, Method and Vocation in Modern Fiction*, the *Manchester Guardian* said that it failed to do its author justice: "too much repetition." But most reviewers, grouping him with the moral rather than with the "new" critics, praised him when he was at his best, and drew attention to the breadth of his knowledge. The *New Yorker* even thought that his prose was "a joy to read."

Zabel's selection from the poems of Robinson (published posthumously, and with an introduction by the poet James Dickey) came at the time when interest in this important poet was beginning to revive. R. D. Spector, in the *Saturday Review*, wrote: " I should like to see greater critical interest in . . . Robinson. Yet I believe neither the late Morton Zabel's judicious selection from Robinson's massive output nor the shrewd comments of James Dickey's introduction can make fashionable a style and manner that in our climate seem like poetry from another planet." *American Literature* came to the real point: a "greatly needed selection . . . well chosen, [but] with an Introduction which should be immediately displaced by an essay from the hand of someone who really knows Robinson's work." However, the selection was reprinted in 1989 and has proved useful in introducing Robinson to new readers.

PRINCIPAL WORKS: The Romantic Idealism of Art 1800–1848: Aspects of English Aesthetics in the Nineteenth Century Before Ruskin and the Pre-Raphaelites, 1933; The Critical Background of Art in England, 1937; Craft and Character: Texts, Methods and Vocation in Modern Fiction, 1957; The Art of Ruth Draper: Her Dramas and Characters, 1960. As editor— (with H. Monroe) A book of Poems for Every Mood, 1933; Literary Opinion in America, 1938, rev. and exp. 1951; The Portable Conrad, 1947 (rev. by F. Karl, 1977); The Portable Henry James, 1951 (rev. by L. H. Powers, 1968); Charles Dickens's Bleak House, 1956; Edwin Arlington Robinson: Selected Poems, 1965.

ABOUT: The autobiographical material quoted above was written for Twentieth Century Authors First Supplement 1955. *Periodicals*—American Literature January 1966; Manchester Guardian November 5, 1957; Nation February 16, 1938; New York Herald Tribune Book Review March 20, 1938; August 5, 1951; New York Times June 3, 1951; April 30, 1964; New Yorker June 29, 1957; Saturday Review February 19, 1966.

## ZAMACOIS, (Y QUINTANA) EDUARDO (DE)

(February 17, 1878–January 9, 1972), Spanish novelist, dramatist, and essayist, was born of a

Cuban mother and a Basque father in Piña del Río in Cuba. He arrived in Madrid at the age of fifteen, having spent much of his time traveling in the wake of his father, a musician, in Seville, Paris, and Cuba. Throughout his life he was as ardent a traveler as he was a philanderer. His final revision of his colorful memoirs, *Un hombre que se va* (A man on the way out, 1964), detail his travels. He spent much time in Latin America, in various European countries (chiefly France), and in the United States.

Zamacois is an example of a somewhat rare breed: the novelist whose work becomes more serious as he gets older. He began as a mischievous, almost journalistic novelist, without literary pretensions. However, after re-reading and studying carefully the French Naturalists, in particular Zola, he became a pioneer of Spanish naturalism. He was nowhere as historically important or as gifted as Benito Peréz Galdós, nor does he rival Emilia Pardo Bazán, but his best fiction has been underrated.

After some struggles in his early career, he founded the Barcelona weekly journal *Vida galante* in order, he wrote, to "capture the bedroom aroma that perfumes French literature of the eighteenth century." *Vida galante* was successful and popular. Nor were Zamacois's own spicy bedroom romances, such as *El seductor* (modeled on Maupassant's *Bel Ami*) and *Incesto* (Incest), badly done, although he makes no effort in them beyond pleasing an easily titillated public.

Not so long before Zamacois began to cover World War I as Western-Front correspondent for *La Tribuna* of Madrid, he became more serious minded. With *El Altro*, 1910, readers saw a different novelist: ironic, sarcastic, and determined to enjoy his task of exposing life as it really was. Much of his later fiction is simply documentary, but in the trilogy *Las raíces*, consisting of *Las raíces* (translated as *Roots*, 1929), *Los vivos muertos* (The living dead), and *El delito de todos* (Everyone's crime), he achieved a certain power. This tragedy of hatred on a Cain Abel theme, set in the plains of Castille, drew praise from Basil Davenport (*Saturday Review of Literature*): "a brutally vivid and absorbing book." Davenport thought that its atmosphere was "strikingly similar" to O'Neill's play *Desire Under the Elms*, but that it was at times "overwritten" and that the Cain figure, Leandro, was "vague" in conception. The *New York Times*, though, found it "one of the most important contributions to belles-lettres we have had from Spain since the war [World War I]," and the reviewer compared it to the work of André Gide.

A few years earlier Zamacois had impressed English language readers with the two novels translated by an enthusiast, George Allen England, who provided an appreciative preface and introduction, in a single volume: *Their Son; The Necklace*. The first, inspired by Zola's famous *La Bête humaine*, is about a locomotive-driver who marries a beautiful young girl; she deceives him with a friend, and he kills the latter in a duel; released from prison after twenty years, he achieves prosperity, but then fate takes a hand in destroying him once again—he is killed by the "son who is not his son." The second tale, "The Necklace," harks back a little to Zamacois's erotic period: a high-class prostitute wields power over a young student. These stories are not much more than exercises in naturalist gloom, but they are well done examples of the genre.

Zamacois's sentimental one-act drama *Los Reyes pasan* (translated as *The Passing of the Magi*, 1912) was written and produced at just the time when he was changing from frivolous eroticist to serious naturalist; however, like his other plays—once taken as important—this play about an unhappy widow who runs away with her lover adds little to his stature.

Zamacois wrote essays, many more novels, books on such subjects as the connections between mysticism and hallucinations, travel and war chronicles, autobiographical works, farces, and dramas; his *Obras Completas* (Complete works), appearing in the early 1920s, took up more than a score of volumes. He was less prolific in the latter half of his long life, but continued to produce novels, stories, and, in particular, autobiographies. An *Obras selectas*, edited by Federico Carlos de Sáinz de Robles, and with a useful introduction, was published in Barcelona in the year before his death—it contained two of the novels from the *Roots* trilogy, and "Their Son." Not on the level of the most famous of his realist-naturalist contemporaries, Vicente Blasco Ibáñez (about whom he wrote a book), Zamacois remains an interesting minor writer whose work improved as he grew older.

PRINCIPAL WORKS IN ENGLISH TRANSLATION: *Fiction*—Their Son; The Necklace (tr. with a preface by G. A. England) 1920; Roots (tr. Eliseo Vivas) 1929. *Drama*—The Passing of the Magi in Turrell, C. A. (ed. and tr.) Contemporary Spanish Dramatists, 1919.

ABOUT: Columbia Dictionary of Modern European Literature, 1980; Seymour-Smith, M. Macmillan Guide to Modern World Literature, 1986. *Periodicals*—Nation April 10, 1920; New York Times December 1, 1929; Saturday Review of Literature December 14, 1929.

## ZAMYATIN, YEVGENY (IVANOVICH)

(February 1, 1884–March 10, 1937), Russian novelist, short story writer, critic, essayist, dramatist, and editor, was born in the provincial town of Lebedyan (in Tambov province), overlooking the River Don, at a distance of about two hundred miles south of Moscow. His birthplace (wrote Alex M. Shane in his introduction to *A Soviet Heretic*) "was known for its swindlers, gypsies, horsefairs and robust Russian speech." He was the son of an Orthodox priest who was also a schoolmaster. His mother, Zamyatin wrote, was a "fine musician." The best account of his childhood and youth is his own (partly translated in *A Soviet Heretic*). After attending the gymnasium at Voronezh he went on to study naval architecture at the Polytechnic Institute in St. Petersburg. This involved the study of advanced mathematics, with which he remained concerned for the whole of his life, and which considerably influenced his literary work.

As a young Bolshevik, he had taken part in the 1905 Revolution and had been briefly imprisoned and exiled. As a promising student, he was permitted to return to his studies, and he graduated in 1908. He went to the Department of Naval Architecture, and taught there until 1911, when he was again imprisoned and exiled for revolutionary activity. In 1913 he published his first book (the official Soviet Communist "critics" were later obliged to pronounce it his "best"), *Uyezdnoye* (*A Provincial Tale*—a *povest*, or "long short story," translated in *The Dragon*). A wholehearted satire on the brutality and primitivism of Russian small-town lower-middle-class life, its publication secured him a reputation among those critical of the regime. His next work, *Na kulichkakh* (At the end of the world, 1914), a scarifying account of the drunken and debauched life of soldiers in a Siberian garrison on the Pacific, was suppressed for "criticism of the Army" (it was reissued in 1922).

Immediately after having taken advantage of the general amnesty that had been offered (1913) by the government, he was a member of the group of writers who contributed to the magazine *Zavety* ("Behests"). This group included the so-called neo-realists, Remizov and Prishvin; and the critic Invanov-Razumnik, a leading sponsor of the so-called "Scythian" movement. This fellow-traveling group, one of the precursors of the Serapion Brotherhood, influentially posited a Russia halfway between the Asiatic and the Western—in essence it was a plea for Russians to affirm their Asiatic mentality. In his half-ironic and subtly written essay "Scythians?" (translated in *A Soviet Heretic*), Zamyatin hails the ideal Scythian as one who "will not bow to anything." Zamyatin wrote: "This is the tragedy and the bitter, racking happiness of the true Scythian: he can never rest on laurels, he will never be with the practical victors, with those who rejoice and sing 'Glory Be.' The lot of the true Scythian is the thorns of the vanquished. His faith is heresy. His destiny is the destiny of Ahasuerus. His work is not for the near but for the distant future. And this work has at all times, under the laws of all monarchies and republics, including the Soviet republics, been rewarded only by a lodging at government expense—prison."

Zamyatin continues to employ this "Scythian" metaphor throughout his writings. This attitude, no doubt seeming to echo Groucho Marx's song "Whatever it is, I'm against it," offers the key to Zamyatin, who has therefore seemed really important only to those few genuine heretics who have followed him. In his most famous critical essay, of 1923, "On Literature, Revolution, Entropy, and Other Matters" (translated in *A Soviet Heretic*), he wrote that artists tended to sink into "satiated slumber in forms once invented and twice perfect-

ed. . . . Of course, to wound oneself is difficult, even dangerous. But for those who are alive, living today as yesterday and yesterday as today is still more difficult." It is easy in the light of this to see why the Revolution failed to satisfy him, and why he commented that it represented no more than a "realignment of elites."

For two years (1916–1918), Zamyatin was in England, at Newcastle-upon-Tyne, supervising the construction of Russian icebreakers. Although in Russia he was known as "the Englishman" because of his reserved manner, English-style moustache, and neat tweed suits, his two books about England are exceedingly caustic (and still very funny): *Ostrovityane* (translated as *The Islanders*) and *Lovets chelovekov* (translated as *A Fisher of Men* in *The Dragon*). The former book he freely dramatized in *Obshchestvo pochotnykhn zvonarei* (The society of honorary bellringers, 1926).

Upon his return to Russia, just before the October Revolution, Zamyatin entered into the literary life. But, since he was an individualist (on the grounds that, as he wrote, "the surest way to destroy is to canonize one given form and one philosophy"), he was not welcome by anyone who possessed political or literary power. His enormous stage success, *Blokha*—a folk play based on Leskov's folk-story "Levsha" ("The Left-Handed Smith")—was quickly taken off the stage by nervous cultural officials. Eventually, in 1929, when the establishment turned against him, all his plays were banned.

Zamyatin was the inspiration behind the Serapion Brotherhood, a group crucially important in the development of that element in the Soviet literature which strove to be imaginatively free rather than to achieve "careers" (Zamyatin was bitingly sarcastic about the careerists, and he paid for it). The group's choice of the name "Serapion"—E. T. A. Hoffmann's hermit—indicated their resolution to be free and humane individuals. They did not aspire to found a school (thus reflecting Zamyatin's insistence that schools destroy themselves), and so dedicated themselves to each other as individual brothers united only in creative freedom. The group of ten men (not including Zamyatin) and four women emerged as an entity on February 1, 1921. The best-known among them were Kaverin, Fedin (the great disappointment, who eventually sold out to the Party), the short-lived Lev Lunts (whose masterpieces were suppressed for more than fifty years by Stalinist "literary" bureaucrats), Slonimsky, Tikhonov, the humorist Zoshchenko, and the poet Elizaveta Poloskaya. The group's meeting place was the St. Petersburg House of Arts—and there they listened to Zamyatin lecture. "I used to come from Karpovka to talk to them about language, plot, rhythm. . . . None of us older writers," wrote Zamyatin in his essay "The Serapion Brethren" (translated in *A Soviet Heretic*), "had gone through such a school. We are all self-taught. And, of course, there is always, in such a school, the danger of goose-stepping, uniformed ranks. But the Serapion Brethren have already, it seems to me, outgrown this danger. Each of them has his own individuality and his own handwriting. The common thing they have derived from the studio is the art of writing with ninety-proof ink, the art of eliminating everything which is superfluous, which is, perhaps, more difficult than writing."

Zamyatin, despite continuing lack of official favor (he was arrested in 1922 and put into the same cell as the Tzarist police had put him in 1905), played a vital part in the Soviet literary activity of the 1920s. He edited many magazines and anthologies, and drew attention to the virtues of many western writers (H. G. Wells, Romain Rolland, O. Henry, Jack London, and Anatole France among them). His chief offense in the eyes of Stalin was his novel *Mi* (translated as *We*). He did not try to publish it, but it was translated into French and then English, and a copy found its way into a Czech emigré magazine in a garbled version in 1927. This led to Zamyatin's exile to Paris (1931), where he would not associate with the other exiles (although it is possible that he met Trotsky). He probably owed his survival and the permission for him and his wife to emigrate to Maxim Gorky. Suffering from poverty, severe angina, and clinical depression, he persevered with a final (unfinished) novel, *Bich Bozhii* (The scourge of god). Ostensibly set in the reign of Attila the Hun, it examines the parallels between the fourth and twentieth centuries. Developed from a play he wrote on the theme of Attila, it might—now that Zamyatin is once again being carefully looked at both in and out of Russia—still prove to be one of the neglected masterpieces of the twentieth century. In Russia itself he remained unknown until the late 1980s—but he was remembered by such writers as Shklovsky, Kaverin, and Leonov.

*We*, written in 1920, is a dystopia. The time is one thousand years hence. The world consists of "One State," which is constructed of glass so that each person may be observed. The ruler is The Benefactor. The plight of the diarist and protagonist, D-503, is pursued in detail until he has "The Operation" (which involves the removal of his imagination), after which he is "normal" and knows that "rationality will conquer."

It was only after the dissolution of the Soviet Union that *We* began to be recognized as one of the greatest dystopias—and as one of the dozen or so indisputable masterpieces of its century. Both Orwell's *1984* and, more particularly, Huxley's *Brave New World*—not to speak of many more inferior works classified as "science fiction"—are very severely diminished in the light of it. George Orwell confessed his debt; Aldous Huxley pretended not to have read it.

*We* is not superior to some of Zamyatin's later stories, but it is the only complete full-length novel he wrote. It is most usefully viewed in the light of his earlier tales. By the time he came to publish in book form in 1913, his style was fairly well established. Shane has written that the early fiction was characterized by an "ornamental prose style [incorporating] grotesque synthesis, impressionistic animal imagery, and *skaz* narration."

*Skaz* is a paradoxical term—from the Russian

*skazat*, to tell, but also from *skazka*, magic, unreal, fantastic. Zamyatin saw *skaz* in the better stories of O. Henry ("his, however, is not that ultimate, complete *skaz* form in which the author is absent, in which the author is but another character"). In its now nascent international sense, there are examples of *skaz* in every language—but Russian is rich in it.

As the critic and novelist Yury Tynyanov controversially claimed, *skaz* in its written form conjures up in the reader his or her own imagined oral performance in uncomfortable circumstances. Zamyatin understood the connection between the *skaz* technique and the profound equality of the relationship between the writer and his "common reader."

In Zamyatin's initial prose this technique was sometimes rather artificial and experimental, and often seemed grotesque. This made him inaccessible to the vexed Soviet officials, and has tended to cut him off from some western critics, who did not understand his complex and teasing prose. Zamyatin had also learned the humorous virtues of Empiricism from the English, whom he appreciated as well as laughed at. In his famous letter to Stalin requesting permission to emigrate he mentioned Joseph Conrad ("perhaps I shall be able, like the Pole Joseph Conrad, to become for a time an English writer"), whose own withering ironies he undoubtedly loved.

*We*, which makes references to the Bible and in particular to the Genesis myth, is a kind of *skaz*, but it is an ironic *skaz* such as what Orwell more famously called *newspeak*. The style continually presses home the message that "the heretic is the only remedy against the entropy of human thought"; victims of entropy "must not be allowed to sleep, or it will be their final sleep, death." The allusion to the teachings of Gurdjieff is obvious—and indeed, one of Zamyatin's acknowledged masters, the novelist Andrei Bely, became a follower of Rudolph Steiner, whose "anthroposophy" has much in common with Gurdjieff's "system." While it is true that *We* owes much to Dostoevsky's "critique of collectivist ideals" considering Russian mysticism and gnosticism of the early 1900s, Zamyatin anatomized the Stalinist state, and he did so by achieving what he called "synthesis, which [includes] simultaneously the microscope of Realism, and the telescopic lenses of Symbolism, leading off into infinities."

*We* is the greatest of the twentieth-century dystopias because it so potently and subtly demonstrates that human sexuality is the main factor that "disrupts" totalitarian regimes. Zamyatin followed Conrad in recognizing the fundamentally oxymoronic nature of "non-official" language when the mechanical is imposed upon the living, when the inert is imposed upon the vital. He justifies the remark of Oscar Wilde, who influenced the Russian writers of Zamyatin's generation: "the way of paradoxes is the way of truth." Zamyatin, too, takes into account the mystico-humorous traditions of the Jews when he alludes to the Abraham-Isaac myth: the knife is poised to strike when God says, "Don't trouble yourself! I was only joking!" The text of *We* is a savage exposure of the Soviet system—from a man who had even welcomed some aspects of the Revolution. It remains one of its century's most disturbing analyses of the age of technology.

In his stories of the late 1920s Zamyatin achieved a "simple" style that further offended the Bolshevik literati, who rightly suspected that he was poking fun at their naive faith (or pretense) that human nature could ever be adapted to the "Soviet system." His fantastic and exasperated "Raskaz o samom glavnom" (1924, translated as "A Story About the Most Important Thing"), one of the great short stories in world literature, rejects the notion that there can be any "rational" solution to human difficulties.

What Zamyatin wrote in 1921 in "I Am Afraid" is still cruelly relevant: "The writer who cannot be nimble must trudge to an office with a briefcase if he wants to stay alive. In our day Gogol would be running with a briefcase to the theater section; Turgenev would undoubtedly be translating Balzac and Flaubert for *World Literature* . . . Chekhov would be working for the Commissariat of Public Health . . . Turgenev would have to turn out three *Father and Sons* every two months. . . . The work of a literary artist who 'embodies his ideas in bronze' with pain and joy, and the work of a prolific windbag . . . are today appraised in the same way: by the yard, by the sheet. . . . To the genuine writer or poet the choice is clear."

PRINCIPAL WORKS IN ENGLISH TRANSLATION: *Fiction*—We (tr. G. Zilboorg) 1924 (tr. B. G. Cuerney, 1970, and, M. Ginsburg, 1972). *Short stories*—"Mamai," 1933; "God," 1953; The Dragon (tr. M. Ginsburg) 1967. *Criticism and reminiscence*—A Soviet Heretic (tr. M. Ginsburg) 1970. *Drama*—The Collected Plays (tr. M. Ginsburg) 1972. *Other*—The Islanders (tr. M. Ginsburg) 1972.

ABOUT: Brown, E. J. Brave New World, 1984, and We: An Essay on Anti-Utopia: Zamyatin and English Literature, 1976; Collins, C. Evgenji Zamyatin: An Interpretative Study, 1973; Columbia Dictionary of Modern Literature, 1947, 1980; Edwards, T. R. N. Three Russian Writers, and the Irrational: Zamyatin, Pilnyak and Bulgakov, 1982; Kern, G. (ed.) Zamyatin's We: A Collection of Critical Essays, 1988; Richards, D. J. Zamyatin, 1962; Seymour-Smith, M. Who's Who in Twentieth Century Literature, 1926; Seymour-Smith, M. An Introduction to 50 European Novels, 1979; Seymour-Smith, M. Macmillan Guide to Modern World Literature, 1986; Shane, A. M. The Life and Works of Evgeny Zamyatin, 1968; Slonim, M. Soviet Russian Literature, 1964; Struve, G. Russian Literature Under Lenin and Stalin 1917–1953, 1971. *Periodicals*—Extrapolation 24 I 1983; Journal of General Education 28, 1986; Papers on Language and Literature 10 1974; Slavonic Review 64 1956.

**ZANGWILL, ISRAEL** (February 14, 1864–August 1, 1926), English novelist, dramatist, and essayist, was born in Whitechapel, London. His father was a Russian exile who had escaped to England from a sentence of death in 1848, and his mother was a refugee from Poland. Israel Zangwill attended a primary school in Bristol (up to the age of nine) and then, after his parents returned to the East End of London, the East London Jews' Free School. To all intents and purposes, however, he was self-educated—well enough to become a teacher in his own right at the age of fourteen. Through independent study, he was able to obtain a degree from London University. He began to write during his late teens and early twenties, starting with short, humorous stories. In 1888 he gave up teaching to write full time, contributing a weekly column to *The Jewish Standard*. In the same year he had his first novel published. *The Premier and the Painter: A Fantastic Romance* was written in collaboration with Louis Cowen and published under a pseudonym (circumstances that Zangwill explained in *The Idler* in a piece entitled "My First Book"), but after that he worked alone.

He quickly established a reputation as a Jewish writer of significance and influence, and among other things as an early adherent of Zionism. His article "English Judaism: A Criticism and Classification," published in the *Jewish Quarterly Review*, led to his being commissioned—by the American jurist Mayer Sulzberger—to write a novel with an explicitly Jewish theme. Up to that time, Zangwill had written fiction in a light-hearted vein. He edited and contributed to the humorous paper *Ariel* and had published two volumes of extravagant tales and character sketches in *The Bachelors' Club* and *The Old Maids' Club*. Sulzberger's commission set the stage for a new departure.

*Children of the Ghetto* was a realistic novel depicting the conditions of London's poorest Jews. Combining pathos, humor, and an indictment of social injustice, it gained Zangwill a reputation as "the Dickens of the ghetto," a reputation cemented by his subsequent "ghetto" titles—*Ghetto Tragedies*, *Ghetto Comedies*, and *Grandchildren of the Ghetto*—as well as *Dreamers of the Ghetto*, a collection of essays about notable Jewish figures from the sixteenth to the nineteenth century. Along with his more serious fiction, he continued to produce works of pure entertainment like *The King of Schnorrers*, set among Sephardic Jews in late eighteenth-century London, and *The Big Bow Mystery*, a very early example of the "locked room" dilemma.

*Children of the Ghetto* was dramatized in 1899 and was especially popular in America, where it was produced in both English and Yiddish. Encouraged by this success, Zangwill wrote a number of plays during the early 1900s, most notably *The Melting Pot* (1908), a drama about immigrants. In America President Theodore Roosevelt attended the opening night, and Zangwill's metaphoric title—the image of a crucible fusing people of different backgrounds into one nation—entered the language permanently. His other plays included *Too Much Money* (1918), *The Cockpit* (1922), and finally *We Moderns* (1924), a rather tired comedy that starred Helen Hayes, then in her prime as an actress.

Zangwill had added his voice to the nascent Zionist movement in the 1890s. He met Theodor Herzl in 1896 and became a devoted follower. After Herzl's death eight years later, Zangwill founded the Jewish Territorial Organisation for the Settlement of Jews Within the British Empire and was for a while the chief advocate of the "Uganda Plan," a proposal to provide the Jews with a homeland in Africa rather than Palestine. Toward the end of his life, however, he became disillusioned with the Zionist movement and increasingly pessimistic about his people's prospects. On a speaking tour of America in 1923, he startled the audience at Carnegie Hall with a controversial lecture entitled "Watchman, What of the Night?" in which he declared the movement dead. He was disillusioned with America too, critical of the lifestyle of its wealthy Jews and convinced that Europe would have been better off had the United States never entered World War I.

Married in 1903, Zangwill had two sons and a daughter and made his home in Sussex. Throughout his career, he was a well-known figure both in Britain and the United States. A painting of him by Sir Bernard Partridge is held by the National Portrait Gallery in London. At one time a fourteen-volume set of his works was in print, and during the 1970s and 1980s, following a period of neglect, several of his titles were reissued. His brother Louis also published novels, some under the pseudonym "Z. Z."

PRINCIPAL WORKS: Fiction—(with L. Cowen, pseud. J. Freeman Bell), The Premier and the Painter 1888; The Bachelors' Club, 1891; The Old Maids' Club, 1892; Children of the Ghetto, 1892; The King of Schnorrers, 1894; The Big Bow Mystery, 1895; Ghetto Tragedies, 1897; The Celibates' Club 1898 (combines The Bachelors' Club and The Old Maids' Club); The Mantle of Elijah, 1900; The Grey Wig, 1903; Ghetto Comedies, 1907; The Grandchildren of the Ghetto, 1917; Jinny the Carrier, 1919. Drama—Merely Mary Ann, 1903; The Man of Iron, 1909; The Melting Pot, 1909; The War God, 1911; The Next Religion, 1912; Plaster Saints, 1914; The Cockpit, 1921; The Forcing-House, 1922; Too Much Money; 1924; We Moderns, 1924. Other—Without Prejudice, 1896; Dreamers of the Ghetto, 1898; Blind Children 1903; (poems), Italian Fantasies, 1910; The War for the World, 1916; Chosen Peoples, 1918; The Voice of Jerusalem, 1920.

ABOUT: Adams, E. B. Israel Zangwill, 1971; Contemporary Authors vol. 109; Dictionary of National Biography 1922–1930, 1937; Sutherland, J. Victorian Fiction, 1988; Udelson, J. H. Dreamer of the Ghetto, 1990; Who's Who 1926. Periodicals—New York Times April 27, 1919; August 2, 1926; Times (London) August 2, 1926; Vanity Fair February 25, 1897.

---

**"ZARA, LOUIS" (pseudonym of LOUIS ROSENFELD)** (August 2, 1910–    ), American novelist, born in New York, grew up and received

his education in Chicago. He wrote: "Born in New York City. Lived in Buffalo 1914–16. Moved to Chicago and was educated there: Crane Technical High School, Crane Junior College, and University of Chicago. Worked in a candy factory, haberdashery, tried to sell magazine subscriptions and failed; studied in a Hebrew theological school and resigned; served an apprenticeship in a print shop and have respected printer's ink ever since. Did not stay for a university degree; the de-

pression and biology caught up with me. [Married Bertha Robbins, 1930; three sons.]

"First short story in print in H. L. Mencken's American Mercury in 1932. Wrote experimental novelette, which unfortunately destroyed. Did not publish for two years, then appeared in Story and Esquire. First novel was picked by the Nation as one of the Fifty Notables of 1935. Summoned to Hollywood in 1936 for a short turn at scenario writing; collaborated with Willis Cooper. Back in Chicago to write political novel, Some for the Glory. Historical novel, This Land Is Ours, published in 1940.

"The Chicago Foundation for Literature presented me with its 1940 Prose Award for 'distinctive' work in the field of the novel. Story in Edward J. O'Brien's Best Short Stories of 1940. In 1940 we lived in the Ozarks thirteen weeks while I was writing a radio network show in collaboration with George Milburn. Finished my first play in the fall of 1940. Have written some fifty short stories and as many articles; many reprinted, as my essay on 'Intelligent Reading' in Freshman Prose Annual. Have also lectured on various topics. Have written a few short poems which I have never shown. My wife is my editorial secretary. "Interests: typography, travel, nature study. Sports: fishing, bowling, baseball." In 1955 Zara added: "Since 1947 I have been associated with the Ziff-Davis Publishing Company, first in Chicago, now in New York City. I started as the executive editor, was promoted to director of the book division, then to a vice-presidency in the firm. I was editor-in-chief of Ziff-Davis' unique experiment in popular art, the publication Masterpieces: The Home Collection of Great Art, now suspended. Since the company no longer publishes books, I am now in charge of various new magazine projects.

"For one year, 1947–47, I was a member of the panel of the 'Stump the Authors' show, which I helped to originate for the American Broadcasting Company network. We did it on radio for twenty-six weeks and also for another twenty-six weeks on television. I was the third member of the storytelling panel.

"At present, in addition to my normal duties, I am planning a new novel, have published a number of new short stories, and have just completed two historical plays: Cleopatra the Queen and Caesar."

---

He attended Crane Technical High School and Crane Junior College. He enrolled at the University of Chicago in 1930 but did not remain long enough to take a degree. Marriage (to Bertha Robbins) and the Depression persuaded him that it was best to seek immediate employment. He took various paid jobs while working at short stories. The first of these appeared in H. L. Mencken's American Mercury in 1932; further success two years later, with stories printed in Story and Esquire, encouraged him to persevere with his first novel, an earlier novelette having been destroyed in a fit of dissatisfaction.

Blessed Is the Man, a rags-to-riches story about

a Jewish immigrant, Jake Krakauer, was enthusiastically received. Mary McCarthy, writing in the *Nation*, thought it "as exciting and as promising a first novel as one will find" and, on the wave of similar expressions of admiration, Zara was listed in the *Nation* as one of the Fifty Notables of 1935. His second novel, *Give Us This Day*, despite exhibiting a propensity for solidity and solemnity, was also greeted in a manner to suggest that a major talent had arrived. Alfred Kazin, in *Books*, thought Zara "a writer who is deeply responsive to the unpleasant facts of life, but who has so sharp an ear and so droll and tender a flavor that his sensibility seems unique." *Some for the Glory*, Zara's third novel, and political in theme, completed a trio of imagined fictions. From this point on Zara's work was based on historical or biographical research.

*This Land Is Ours*, a huge panorama published with end-maps, told the story of westward expansion in eighteenth-century America. His next book, *Against This Rock*, turned to a European theme, a fictionalized biography of emperor Charles V. Other historical subjects used by Zara included an 1862 raid by federal soldiers on the Chatanooga line (*Rebel Run*), the life of Philip II of Spain (*In The House of the King*) and the life of Stephen Crane (*Dark Rider*). An exception was his 1946 novel *Ruth Middleton*, a birth-to-grave story about a midwestern girl. However, Zara chose to tell the story as if Ruth Middleton had actually existed, and his novel was her biography. Several reviewers remarked upon its cold detachment. In the *New York Times*, reference was made to "episodes told in a clinical tone that is chilling."

The nearest Zara came to fulfilling the promise of his early work was in *Blessed Is the Land*, a companion novel to his first book *Blessed Is the Man*. It took the Jewish immigrant theme back to its pioneering beginnings and was told in the form of a diary kept by Ashur Levy, a seventeenth-century arrival.

Zara worked in publishing with the Ziff-Davis company from 1946 to 1953 and with Follet Publishing Company from 1962 to 1965. In the 1940s he appeared on the panel of the radio and television show *Stump the Authors*. After *Dark Rider* his fiction career faded. He concentrated on his hobby, coin collecting (he was a fellow of both the American Numismatic Society and the Royal Numismatic Society), and wrote a number of nonfiction titles.

PRINCIPAL WORKS: Blessed Is the Man, 1935; Give Us This Day, 1935; Some for the Glory, 1937; This Land Is Ours, 1940; Against This Rock, 1943; Ruth Middleton, 1946; Rebel Run, 1951; In the House of the King, 1952; Blessed Is the Land, 1954; Dark Rider, 1961.

ABOUT: *Periodicals*—Books May 17, 1936; Nation June 19, 1935; New York Times June 2, 1946.

**\*ZATURENSKA, MARYA (ALEXANDROVNA)** (September 12, 1902–January 19, 1982), American poet, critic, and biographer, wrote: "I was born in Kiev, Russia, and came to the United States at the age of eight. My mother's family came from Poland, and for generations were in the em-

°zah tur EN ska

ploy of the Radziwill family. My father served in the Russian army during the Russo-Japanese War and was with the Russian army of occupation in China during the Boxer uprising. I was educated in the New York public schools, had to leave at an early age, graduated from night high school, between odd jobs in a factory, then worked in a bookshop and was a feature writer for a New York newspaper for a year, and I received a  scholarship in 1922 to Valparaiso University, studied there for a year, and then in 1923 went to Wisconsin University on a Zona Gale scholarship. Served on the literary magazine at Wisconsin; my previous co-editors had been Horace Gregory, Kenneth Fearing, Marquis W. Childs, Robert S. Allen, and Margery Latimer. I specialized in library school work and graduated from the Wisconsin Library School in 1925. I married Horace Gregory, the poet and critic, in 1925. . . .

"I wrote poetry ever since I can remember, and as a child was always particularly moved by Polish and Russian folk-songs and music. I composed poems to these tunes before I could read or write. My first printed poems appeared when I was in my teens, in *Poetry* and elsewhere. It was not till my first book appeared (1934) that I felt I was beginning to find myself. This book I have always thought of as a series of finger exercises; it was a sort of introduction to my second book, which received the Pulitzer Poetry Award in 1938. . . .

"My husband and I have traveled a number of times in England and Ireland, and I have developed a great admiration, affection, and respect for the English people, whose tradition of justice, tolerance, and fair play still means a great deal to the future of democracy. Last but not least in importance to me are my son and daughter. Aside from poetry my chief interest lies in music."

Marya Zaturenska's tradition-bound lyric poetry varied little from the beginning to the end of her career. The throbbing, somewhat vague musicality of her verse recalled that of the Pre-Raphaelites; and she was herself the author of a once much admired biography of Christina Rossetti. Randall Jarrell, reviewing her third collection, *The Listening Landscape*, contrasted her "curious literalness," her satisfaction "with the stalest romantic diction," with her "obvious virtues: force, emotion, sweep, some amount of form; her poems often have a real subject, are recognizably hers, really get somewhere. . . . Poems like 'The White Dress' or 'Forest of Arden' show her at her rather disquieting best; they are rough and evitable successes—the work of a poet who has a real talent, but not for words."

Although Zaturenska was no mere poetaster, and possessed taste and technique, her faults presented an obstacle to succeeding generations of readers. Although her last collection, *The Hidden Waterfall*, received generally polite reviews, her "poetic language," wrote *Poetry*, was "surely not contemporary." According to Robert Phillips in the *New Criterion*, Zaturenska in her last decades lived in the shadow of her husband the American poet Horace Gregory: "He was a grand old man of letters, she a figure from the past." Furthermore, the highly critical, extremely idiosyncratic *A History of American Poetry, 1900–1946* that she and Gregory published in 1946 alienated many of their colleagues. Delmore Schwartz, one of the many targets of Zaturenska's personal animosity, wrote of that volume in the *Nation*, "The Gregorys indulge in a systematic wrongness of praise and dispraise. Most of the important and famous poets of the period consistently receive the damnation of faint praise; and at the same time minor, mediocre, and bad poets are equally damned by being overpraised. Most difficult to make clear is the margin of inexactness involved in the Gregorys use of comparison."

In the end, wrote Phillips, "Marya simply spent too many hours alone with her thoughts, rehearsing literary grudges and neglect." The Gregorys' home in Palisades, New York, was often visited by such friends as James T. Farrell, Joseph Campbell, and Dudley Fitts, but it was there also that Phillips listened to Zaturenska's repeated denunciations of "Blab-it Deutsch" (Babette Deutsch), "La Bogan" (Louise Bogan), "Robert Pen Wiper" (Robert Penn Warren), and other real or imagined enemies. "Laughter and amusement were rare in her later life," wrote Phillips. The *History*, however—despite the sometimes unfair criticism it attracted by those it did not praise—remains a modestly useful book for students of poetry.

PRINCIPAL WORKS: *Poetry*—Threshold and Hearth, 1934; Cold Morning Sky, 1937; The Listening Landscape, 1941; The Golden Mirror, 1944; Selected Poems, 1954; Terraces of Light, 1960; Collected Poems, 1965; The Hidden Waterfall, 1974. *Criticism and biography*—(with H. Gregory) A History of American Poetry, 1900–1940, 1946; Christina Rossetti: A Portrait with Background, 1949. *As editor*—(with H. Gregory) The Mentor Book of Religious Verse, 1957; (with H. Gregory) The Crystal Cabinet: An Invitation to Poetry, 1962; The Collected Poems of Sara Teasdale, 1966; (with H. Gregory) The Silver Swan: Poems of Romance and Mystery, 1966; (with H. Gregory) Selected Poems of Christina Rossetti, 1970.

ABOUT: The autobiographical material quoted above was written for Twentieth Century Authors, 1942. American Women Writers, vol. 4 1982; Contemporary Literary Criticism vol. 6 1976; vol. 11 1979; Contemporary Poets, 3rd ed., 1980; Jarrell, R. Kipling, Auden and Co.: Essays and Reviews, 1935–1964, 1980; Untermeyer, L. Modern American Poetry, enlarged ed., 1962. *Periodicals*—Nation December 7, 1946; New Criterion September 1900; New York Times January 21, 1982; Poetry May 1975.

**ŻEROMSKI, STEFAN** (November 1, 1864–November 20, 1925), Polish novelist, storywriter, translator, prose-poet, and dramatist—for long regarded as Poland's "national conscience" and "last bard"—was born at Strawczyna, in the Kielce district of Russian Poland, into a noble family in which the tradition of Polish nationalism had long been ingrained. Like Joseph Conrad, who he trans-

lated into Polish, he grew up in the wake of the catastrophic 1863 uprising, which left an indelible mark upon his literary output and led to his family's impoverishment. (His novel *Wierna rzeka*, translated as *The Faithful River*, deals with this event.) Żeromski was the best-known and most representative writer of the romantic Młoda Polska (Young Poland) movement, and his name was put forward for the Nobel Prize. However,

his work is perhaps of too Polish a character to take easily in foreign soil, and to date he has been undertranslated. His circumstances made him into a writer who always had two purposes: one political, the other artistic. That is one of the reasons for which Joseph Conrad left Poland: he wished, as he himself carefully expressed it, to "attend to his business" as a writer without being committed to anything else, especially a political program. Yet, like Żeromski, the program to which Conrad was at least initially attracted was not one of the "left" or of the "right," but simply the necessary matter of getting the Russians out of Poland. Like Conrad, too, Żeromski soon became disenhanted with the violent results of revolution.

Żeromski's rehabilitation in the west—as possessor of an undoubted literary genius which would have expressed itself in the complex mode now usually called "decadent" had it been unimpeded by his desire for Polish freedom—can only be a matter of time, opportunity and the right critic. Like all his contemporaries, he was early prey to three very different movements: romanticism, positivism, and naturalism. His circumstances hardly allowed him to resolve these in his own way; yet a kind of resolution of them is there, for an enterprising critic to trace, in his works as they stand: this is now perhaps the most fruitful way of approaching them. His intimate diaries (*Dziennik podrózy*, 1933; *Dziennik z lat 1882–1890*, 1964), published in Poland in 1933, and then more fully after World War II, have greatly added to his stature as a man agonizedly in quest of full self-awareness.

Both Żeromski's parents died while he was still at school, and he could only pursue his studies sporadically as a result. A brilliant pupil, he nonetheless failed to graduate from the Kielce Gymnasium. He reacted too strongly against the absolute "Russification" policy in force. He had to give lessons to his fellow-pupils and to receive help from relatives, which he found hard to accept. The first of his novels, the semi-autobiographical *Syzyfowe prace* (Sisyphean labors) published in 1898, deals with this period of his life, and in particular with the vain efforts of the craven Polish school authorities to "Russify" their pupils. The novel has been described as a *Nicholas Nickleby* of Polish fiction. It is certainly Żeromski's only book to exhibit much sense of humor. While still at school, Żeromski made and published translations of the Russian poet Lermontov, and published his own youthful stories and poems in various periodicals.

Żeromski studied only briefly at the Warsaw School of Veterinarians (he loved animals and nature, and his books abound in evocative descriptions of these), which he attended briefly in 1886, owing to further financial difficulties and because he found he was suffering from tuberculosis. For some six years he tutored the sons of various landed gentry in his native area of Poland. He had already served time in the Citadel prison in Warsaw for conspiring with Roman Dmowski (later a leader of Polish nationalism) and now had to be careful of what he said and did and whom he met.

The years between 1892 (in which year he married) and 1896 Żeromski spent traveling in Europe, and working as a librarian at the National Museum of Polish immigrants at Rapperschwil, on Lake Zurich in Switzerland. He was also librarian of the Zamosyki Library in Warsaw (1897–1904).

By then he was well known. His reputation began with the publication of two collections of his stories (some of which he had written ten years earlier) in 1895, published in two separate places. In both cases he used the name "Maurycy Zych." The Warsaw collection was called Opowiadania (Tales), the Cracow one Rozdziobiq nas kruki, wrony (Ravens and crows will tear us asunder). The latter was openly critical of the Russians. As Jerzy Peterkiewicz writes in his entry on Żeromski in the Penguin Companion to Literature: "This illustrates the evasive methods of literature under foreign censorship," but, he adds, "in Żeromski's case such a duality of purpose seems to run through his writing."

Peterkiewicz also outlines the contradictions in Żeromski, who was in his lifetime often described as "demonic": "he wrote a pamphlet against snobbery, but had a weakness for aristocratic heroes; he tackled epic themes in a diffuse lyrical language." However, the power which he displayed in his descriptions of the great social ills of his country was entirely genuine, and was confirmed in the novel that made him truly famous: Ludzie bezdomi (The homeless, 1900). Although the appearance of the book quickly became a national as well as a literary event, it has never been translated into English. Quite apart from its literary merits, this tale of the defeat of the idealistic but also "sensual" Doctor Judym is an important historical document, with its vivid portrayal of the various social classes of its time. In it Żermoski dealt with his own problem of politico-social commitment versus personal desire: Judym is seen as destroyed by the conflict, although many of Żeromski's readers outside Poland have missed this point, and have perhaps failed to see the reason why Żeromski's impassioned and lyrical style so often seems to run counter to its polemic subtext.

Żeromski followed The Homeless with his best-known novel, the massive and epic Popioly (1940, translated into English as The Ashes). This is an ostensibly historical treatment of the Polish struggle for independence beginning in the Napoleonic period and ending in 1912. Generations of Poles were brought up on this account of what Żeromski called an area of "heroic conflict"; the "ashes" from which Poland is seen to arise are those of a nation as yet unconscious of its identity. American and British reviewers found the American translation to be "formless" but impressive. The Times Literary Supplement claimed it as "a piece of imaginative literature of a high order" but thought that it might have gained by "being more severely condensed in the translation."

Ashes is an uneven tapestry of public events interspersed with a private love story in which Żeromski explores his more strictly artistic (and erotic) interests. The battle scenes are finely done, but the style is sometimes undistinguished. Later Polish critics have deplored the too-rapid recourse to rhetoric of a writer all too obviously capable of better. M. A. Michael's translation of some of the high points in the book in Introduction to Polish Literature, however, clearly demonstrates it to be a vivid, beautifully observed and unforgettable panorama of period. Nowhere is Żeromski's hatred of war and his generous humanitarianism more eloquently expressed than in this book. The work as a whole is stamped with narrative authority, and is as enthralling to read today as it was to Poles in 1904. The Ashes is also a remarkable anticipation of what would become, under the Nazis and then under the Soviets, a time-honored technique: the presentation of topical issues under a "historical" rubric. Żeromski could never bring himself to become a wholehearted advocate of a military solution, since he did not believe in results achieved by such means; Ashes, therefore, is a genuinely dialectical work, in which views are set against one another.

Dzieje grzechu (History of a sin, 1906), in some ways Żeromski's most personal novel, or at least the one he most enjoyed writing, caused enormous controversy among conservative-minded readers and led to violent attacks on his "morality." Based loosely on incidents in his own life and in that of his sister Olesia, it deals with the disintegration of a woman under the influence of crime, despair, and social hypocrisy. The Faithful River tells two tales in parallel: of a poor young woman of noble stock's doomed love for an aristocrat, against the background of the 1863 uprising and its failure. The massive and ambitious three-volume Walka z Szatanem (Struggles against Satan, 1916–1919) blends the two themes of the lonely Promethean hero and the necessity of social justice. As always in Żeromski, reform is seen as being achievable only at the cost of personal happiness.

After Poland gained its independence in 1919, Żeromski soon became disillusioned. He produced much prose poetry about his native region, such as Puszcza jodlowa (Fir forest), a rhapsodic description of the Holy Cross Mountains, and wrote the best of his plays: Uciela mi przepióeczka (A quail escaped me), whose theme is exactly that of his novel The Homeless. But his chief work in those years, perhaps his greatest, was the complex and scarifying novel Przedwiósnie (Before the spring). This book, often criticized for confusion and false ending, has also been favorably compared with Zamyatin's *We*, Wells's *Mr. Blettsworthy on Rampole Island*, Huxley's *Brave New World*, and Orwell's *1984*. It begins with a powerful but horrific description of the Bolshevik revolution; yet many supporters of Pilsudski, Poland's leader, believed it was pro-communist. Żeromski died, in Warsaw, in the middle of the controversy. The authorities gave him a state funeral, attended by a relieved Pilsudski.

Like Conrad, Żeromski discovered that he could not write major poetry but,' unlike Conrad, he perhaps needed to be able to do so to express his paradoxical genius to the full. The only Polish writer of his generation who was able to do this was Jan Kaprowicz—a greater artist who did not deal with the theme of Polish liberation. Żeromski was the kind of author a country struggling for its identity always needs. Ironically, he may have sacrificed unequivocal greatness as a writer in fulfilling such a role. Some of his novels untranslated into English are available in French, German, and Spanish translations. The notorious *History of a Sin* was made into an Italian silent movie in 1919, and there have been at least four more Polish films based on his work.

PRINCIPAL WORKS IN ENGLISH TRANSLATION: The Ashes (tr. H. S. Zan) 1928; The Faithful River (tr. S. Garry) 1943; Gillon, A. and Krzyzanowski, L. (ed.) Introduction to Polish Literature, 1964.

ABOUT: Kridl, M. A Survey of Polish Literature and Culture, 1956; Krzyzanski, J. A History of Polish Literature, 1978; Milosz, C. The History of Polish Literature, 1969; Penguin Companion to Literature: European, 1969; Seymour-Smith, M. Macmillan Guide to Modern World Literature, 1986. *Periodicals*—Slavonic Review 41 1936; Times Literary Supplement March 28, 1929.

**ZILAHY, LAJOS** (March 27, 1891–December 1, 1974), Hungarian-born American novelist and playwright (writing in his native tongue), was born  at Nagyszalonta, the son of a well-to-do lawyer who worked in a government department, and who was a member of the Austro-Hungarian petty nobility. Zilahy contributed verse to Budapest literary magazines as a boy, studied law—in a desultory way—at Budapest University, and was called up into the Austrian army at the age of twenty-three. He was sent to the Russian front (1915), was wounded and then deserted. His first book, of pacifist and nationalist verse, was published in 1915, just before he left the army.

Although for a short time there was a price on Zilahy's head for his desertion, he was freed from this burden when the Austrian Empire was dissolved and Hungary became independent. His sarcastic and ironic voice soon became well known as he became a prominent journalist, edited a daily newspaper, *Magyarország*, and associated himself with *Híd* (Bridge), a literary periodical devoted to

Hungarian writing. His essays, stories, and verse were published throughout Hungary. The section on Hungarian literature in the revised version of the *Columbia Dictionary of Modern European Literature* states that he first became known as a "conservative raconteur," but thereafter became a "reformist mediator between the government and the young populists." He wrote two novels, both successful in Hungary (the much-discussed first one was *Halálas tavasz*, *Fatal Spring*, made into a Hungarian movie in 1947 by László Komor), and a number of essentially light but skillfully wrought plays. His third novel, *Két fogoly*, translated as *Two Prisoners*, gave him a modest international reputation.

The two prisoners of the title are a bank clerk, Peter Takács, and his wife Miette, who are initially separated by the outbreak of World War I and by the drafting of Peter into the army, and then—even more decisively—by his falling into the hands of the Russians and being sent to a prison camp in Siberia. Each partner finds consolation elsewhere, and ultimately Peter, when given the opportunity, decides not to return to Budapest; he dies in Russia.

This book did not attract much attention from British or American critics; but a few reviewers were enthusiastic. The *New Statesman* believed that Zilahy had "made a long, deeply felt, satisfying novel . . . the inner life of wartime captivities could hardly be more convincingly conjured up than in his pictures of Peter's life . . . the climax has a restrained boldness of irony that rounds off the tragedy in a moving manner." Among the complaints, however, were its excessive length and its "tediousness."

The success of *Two Prisoners* led to the translation of Zilahy's earlier, more autobiographical novel, *A szökevény (The Deserter)*. Zilahy here presented a version of his younger self in the figure of István Komlóssy, son of a provincial minister, who grows up an ardent nationalist, deserts from the Austrian army, becomes a Communist, and dies in a fight. This was not as well received as *Two Prisoners*. Reviewers found it "uneven" and "capable rather than brilliant." The *New York Times* (1932) reviewer wrote: "We are given to understand that this is an important book in Hungary. That may well be, if its importance is political rather than literary. The American reader, unless he is well fortified with an understanding of Hungarian politics, will find difficulty in following the historical action and the motives of the characters." The *Spectator* simply dismissed it on the grounds that the author was unable to create character: "the story abounds in vivid incidents, but they happen to an effigy." Zilahy was never in fact much interested in the psychology of his characters, which may explain in part why his work has failed to last.

Zilahy, not a major novelist compared to Krúdy or Sándor Márai, was a lucid, competent writer whose skillful handling of his plots won him deserved popularity. He was also a generous and courageous man, who in 1942, after his villa in Budapest had been destroyed by Russian bombs, gave away his fortune to the Hungarian nation to found what he called the Zilahy Institute. He then wrote: "Following the example of my forefathers [his mother's ancestors included Protestant ministers], I seek to preach the Gospel, and it is impossible to preach the Gospel while accumulating wealth in the process." The Institute did preach the Gospel, and did not prosper, but it attracted some admiring attention in America, and hostility from the then German-controlled government of Hungary. In 1944 the occupying German forces tried to arrest Zilahy, but he managed to evade them: he and his wife and son hid in a cellar while the battle for Budapest was raging.

Zilahy was quickly labeled a traitor ("a slave to the values of bourgeois liberalism") by the Communists after World War II. He settled with his wife and son in New York in 1947 and became, for a time, one of the best-known Hungarian writers on the international scene. By far the best of his novels, Ararát, written in Hungary, was published in translation in 1949 as The Dukays. The book covered the family history of the Dukay family from 1868 up to the outbreak of World War II, and displayed both the author's intimate knowledge of the fate of the Hungarian aristocracy and his ability to handle the panoramic sweeps of the story. Some American reviewers, misled by Zilahy's picture of the aristocracy as decadent and self-indulgent, seemed to take the book as Communist propaganda, and Catholic World even went so far as to pronounce it as more "dangerous reading" than "the lascivious D. H. Lawrence's Lady Chatterley's Lover." This and other such fulminations greatly increased the book's sales, but it never received truly favorable reviews. It was generally faulted for crude sensationalism, overstatement, and lack of convincing characterization. The sequel The Angry Angel (which did not appear in Hungarian) fared no better with the reviewers, who were irritated by Zilahy's strident sarcasm. The later Century in Scarlet (also dealing with the Dukays, this time after Napoleon's fall) is a markedly inferior, although commercially competent work.

Zilahy's achievement has been viewed (in the Encyclopedia of World Literature in the 20th Century) as that of an "important popular novelist" whose main theme was that of "man's struggle for justice on both the personal and social planes." It also describes Zilahy's fiction as "rich in characters." Many may prefer the judgment implied in the poet and critic Chad Walsh's notice of Century in Scarlet in Book Week: "The book is infused with so passionate a love of freedom that the author seems a contemporary of Garibaldi or Kossuth. Mr. Zilahy is more successful on the large scale than the small. So long as the events he depicts are pageant-like he presents them in all their glittering magnificence. . . . His men and women are created to strike heroic gestures and to triumph or perish with bugle calls and a roll of drums. When he shows them in the dining room or the bed chamber, however, they are less convincing. . . . The characters are two-dimensional and their psychology is only dimly explored."

Zilahy's well-made plays had immediate appeal, but are in no way central to his achievement. Firebird was produced at the Playhouse in London, and at the Empire in New York, in 1932. He died in Yugoslavia while working on a film of one of his stories.

PRINCIPAL WORKS IN ENGLISH TRANSLATION: Two Prisoners (trs. J. Collins and I. Zeitlin) 1931; The Deserter (tr. G. Halasz) 1932; The Guns Look Back (tr. L. Wolfe) 1938; The Dukays (tr. J. Pauker) 1949; The Angry Angel (tr. T. L. Harsner) 1953; Century in Scarlet (tr. J. Pauker) 1965.

ABOUT: Columbia Dictionary of Modern European Literature, 1980; Encyclopedia of World Literature in the 20th Century, 1970; Klaniczay, T. History of Hungarian Literature, 1964; Remenyi, J. Hungarian Writers and Literature, 1964; Seymour-Smith, M. Macmillan Guide to Modern World Literature, 1986. Periodicals—Book Week May 30, 1965; Catholic World April 6, 1949; New Statesman June 20, 1931; New Yorker May 21, 1949; New York Times April 3, 1932; December 1, 1974; Spectator September 17, 1932.

**ZILBOORG, GREGORY** (December 25, 1890–September 17, 1959), American psychiatrist, was born in Kiev, Russia, the son of Moses Zilboorg and Anne (Braun) Zilboorg.  After graduating from the gymnasium in Kiev in 1911, he attended the Psycho-neurological Institute in St. Petersburg, receiving his M.D. degree in 1917. He interrupted his studies to serve as a physician in the Russian Army (1915–1916). He took part in the Russian revolution of March 1917 and became secretary to the Ministry of Labor in the cabinets of Prince Lvov and of Alexander Kerensky. Thrown out of office by the Bolshevik coup that November, he edited a daily newspaper in Kiev until 1918.

When the Bolshevik dictatorship became entrenched, Zilboorg left for the United States in 1919, where he supported himself by lecturing, writing, and translating for the theater while studying for a medical degree at Columbia University, from which he graduated in 1926. In 1931 he began practice of psychoanalysis and psychiatry in New York City.

In 1935 Zilboorg was Noguchi lecturer on the history of medicine at Johns Hopkins University. His lectures were published as The Medical Man and the Witch During the Renaissance (1935). He was among the first writers to show how the medical treatment of the fifteenth and sixteenth centuries mixed with beliefs in witchcraft. Zilboorg also put forward the case for the Dutch physician Johann Weyer as a founder of modern psychiatry.

In 1936 Zilboorg helped to found the Committee for the Study of Suicide, organized to make a world-wide study of self-annihilation as a preventable disease. From thousands of examinations of suicidal patients, the committee issued a four-volume handbook on the subject in 1939.

A confirmed Freudian, and specialist in the history of psychiatry, Zilboorg was considered one of the best known and most versatile practicing psychiatrists in the United States in the 1940s, although he seldom gets mentioned today—there is no place for him, for example, in Sheldon and Alexander's *History of Psychiatry*. However, David Stafford-Clarks, in *Psychiatry Today* (1963), paid tribute to his inspiration in the first chapter of his book. His exhaustive and very popular *A History of Medical Psychology* (1941) was the first to present an introductory historical survey of medical psychology. Zilboorg concluded, "The history of psychiatry is essentially the history of humanism."

*Mind, Medicine and Man* (1943), another of Zilboorg's primers on psychology for laymen, traced the history of mental illness, its treatment and its applications to problems of society, law, and religion. E. R. Groves in *Social Forces* called it an "extraordinary, persuasive, and wideminded exposition of the Freudian contribution through psychoanalysis." Of *Sigmund Freud: His Exploration of the Mind of Man* (1951), a book that describes Freud's discovery of the dynamic power of the unconscious, the role of free associations, and his defense of humanism, Patrick Mullahy wrote in the *Saturday Review of Literature*: "Throughout, Zilboorg attempts to clarify and correct misunderstandings, as well as refute criticisms of Freud. But he never comes to grips with most of the important major criticisms made of Freud's ideas by philosophers, psychoanalytic 'dissidents,' and anthropologists."

Zilboorg, although born of Orthodox Jewish parents, became a Roman Catholic in 1954, and, later, an Episcopalian. He wrote frequently on religious issues and, like other Christian analysts, took Freud to task for his attitude to religion as a neurosis. Zilboorg spent many of his final years trying to reconcile the conflict between psychoanalysis—to whose tenets he remained faithful—and religion. He believed that the discipline could contribute to the understanding of religion.

Zilboorg was a charter member of the New York Psycho-analytic Institute in 1931, and a co-founder of *Psychoanalytic Quarterly* in 1932. As well as serving as chairman of the Consulting Delegation of Criminology to the UN, Zilboorg held many lecturing posts.

PRINCIPAL WORKS: The Medical Man and the Witch During the Renaissance, 1935; (with G. W. Henry) A History of Medical Psychology, 1941; Mind, Medicine, and Man, 1943: Sigmund Freud: His Exploration of the Mind of Man, 1951; The Psychology of the Criminal Act and Punishment, 1954; Psychoanalysis and Religion, 1962.

ABOUT: Current Biography 1941; Dictionary of American Biography, Stafford-Clark, D. Psychiatry Today, 1963. *Periodicals*—American Journal of Psychiatry 1960; New York Herald Tribune Books December 28, 1941; New York Times May 16, 1943; October 14, 1951; May 16, 1954; September 18, 1959; May 2, 1962; Saturday Review of Literature November 10, 1951; Social Forces December 1943.

## ZINSSER, HANS

(November 17, 1878-September 4, 1940), American physician, bacteriologist, and writer, was born in New York City, the youngest of the four sons of August and Marie Theresia (Schmidt) Zinsser. Both parents had come from Germany. His father was a chemist and an ag-

nostic who idolized Goethe and carried a copy of *Faust* in the pocket of each of his suits. His mother had been educated in a convent in the Black Forest and came to the United States to be married. Au-

gust Zinsser's chemical business prospered, and the younger Zinsser was brought up in comfortable circumstances in Westchester, where he enjoyed many of the privileges of suburban life, including learning his favorite sport, horseback riding.

Zinsser was tutored at home before being sent to school in Germany for a year while his parents were traveling. Upon his return to the United States, he enrolled at Julius Sachss school in New York before entering Columbia College in 1895. His education, which had been marked by frequent trips to Europe, had given him an appreciation for fine art and the classical European traditions, and his first aspirations were literary. Inspired by his Columbia literature professor, George Edward Woodberry, Zinsser began to write poetry, and continued to do so throughout his life. But after taking biology courses, his primary interest shifted to science and then to medicine. From Columbia he received his A.B. in 1899, and his A.M. and M.D. in 1903. From 1905 to 1907, as an intern at Roosevelt Hospital, Zinsser often rode an ambulance, witnessing first hand the crime, poverty, and disease of New York City's slums. The experience would stick with him and influence his future writing.

Zinsser was instructor of bacteriology and hygiene at Columbia Medical School from 1907 to 1910, and then, for three years, associate professor of bacteriology at Stanford University, before returning to Columbia in 1913 as full professor—a position he would keep for the next ten years. In the spring of 1915 he went to Serbia with the Red Cross Typhus Commission. While a Colonel in the Medical Corps, he wrote a standard manual for sanitation in the field, and he received the Distinguished Service Medal. In 1923 Zinsser was invited by the League of Nations to go to Russia as Sanitary Commissioner on cholera, and in 1931 he went to Mexico to study a prison epidemic of typhus. From these and other experiences, Zinsser gathered material for his over 160 scientific papers as well as reviews, articles, and books on medical and general education and on public health.

His first books, *Text-Book of Bacteriology* (1911) and *Infection and Resistance* (1913), were both important undergraduate resources, though both are no longer in print. *Rats, Lice and History*, a work based on his time in Russia, was much more accessible to the average reader and was widely reviewed. The *New York Herald Tribune* described it as "a racy book, a witty book, a profound book despite a few professorial witticisms," and the *Saturday Review of Literature* proclaimed that the book was "likely to be quite popular, and deservedly so."

Elements of poetry, romanticism, and imagination pervaded Zinsser's work. His posthumously published *Spring, Summer, and Autumn* collected many poems previously published in *Atlantic*. His well-reviewed autobiography, *As I Remember Him*, appeared the year of his death.

PRINCIPAL WORKS: *Nonfiction*—Text-Book of Bacteriology, 1911; Infection and Resistance, 1914; Rats, Lice and History, 1935. *Autobiography*—As I Remember Him, 1940. Spring, Summer and Autumn, 1942.

ABOUT: Current Biography 1940; Dictionary of American Biography, 1958; Whos Who in America 1938–1939, 1938. *Periodicals*—New York Herald Tribune February 8, 1935; New York Times June 8, 1940; Saturday Review of Literature February 9, 1935.

## ZUCKMAYER, KARL (or CARL) (December 27, 1896–January 18, 1977), German playwright, novelist, and poet, wrote: "Carl Zuckmayer was born in Nackenheim-am-Rhein, where his father was a manufacturer [he owned a bottling factory]. He attended the high school [*Gymnasium*] in Mainz until the outbreak of war in 1914, and soon after took part in the war as a volunteer. He was a soldier in France from 1914 to 1918. His first literary works, mainly lyrical poems, were produced during the last years of the war. Immediately after the war he devoted his time to dramatic art. A course of studies in biology at the University of Heidelberg was interrupted in 1920 by the production of his play, *Kreuzweg* (*The way of the cross*) at the Berlin State Theatre. This play was not a box office success, but opened his literary and theatrical career. After some years of practical work as a play reader [with, among others, Brecht], director, and actor, he produced in 1925 the comedy *Der Froehliche Weinberg* (*The happy vineyard*), which was a very great success. It won the Kleist Prize. From that time onward his works were produced by theatres all over Europe until Adolf Hitler banned them from the German-speaking stage. Apart from *Der Froehliche Weinberg* the best known of his works is *Der Hauptmann von Köpenick* (*The Captain of Köpenick*), which was produced for the first time at the Deutsches Theater in Berlin in 1931. This historical comedy represented an attempt to warn the German nation of the dangers which were threatening by the rise of the National Socialist movement.

"After 1925 Carl Zuckmayer lived in Austria, where he had a small farm near Salzburg. He left Austria in 1938 after the *Anschluss*. After one year's sojourn in Switzerland, he emigrated in 1939 to the United States.

"Occasionally Carl Zuckmayer has worked for the films. Amongst other things he wrote the German manuscript for *The Blue Angel*, as well as the manuscripts for the English films *Rembrandt* and *Escape Me Never*. He also adapted *What Price Glory* to the German stage, and dramatized Ernest Hemingway's *Farewell to Arms*."

---

Karl Zuckmayer, a major German dramatist, novelist, screenwriter, memoirist, and poet, did not mention above that he had been decorated for valor during his war service, and seriously wounded in 1918. He began as a poet—his first poems appeared in *Die Aktion* while he was at the front—and remained notable as such, although his frequently ironic work was always in a modest key. As a young radical Zuckmayer worked at a variety of menial jobs—in a coal mine, as editor of a revolutionary periodical, and even, briefly, as a drug-pusher. His first play, *Kreuzweg*, was in the shrill expressionistic mode popular at that time, but, while Zuckmayer learned a great deal about theater from writing it, this style was not suited to his temperament. An adaptation of the Latin playwright Terence's *Eunuchus* (1923) was closed by the police after just one performance. Zuckmayer subsequently worked at odd jobs in various provincial theaters, as well as in Berlin and Vienna; he learned most from Max Reinhardt, whose Deutsches Theater he joined in 1924.

The Rabelaisian *Der Froehliche Weinberg* (1925), which put him at a stroke in the forefront of young German dramatists, has never been translated, but remains one of the most hilarious German comedies of the twentieth century. It won its author the Kleist Prize—and the hatred of the Nazis, since Zuckmayer (who had some Jewish as well as Italian blood) mocked anti-Semitism in it. In the play, simple, decent and earthy rural values are contrasted with crooked and authoritarian city ones. These latter are personified by pompous proto-Nazi *Corpsstudent* Knuzius, who ends drunk on top of a pile of manure. Meanwhile the pretty village girl, Klächen Gunderloch, whose father won't consent to her marriage until her prospective suitor has got her pregnant, gets the sailor she wants. It is a well-written rural farce that owed much to the playwright Zuckmayer admired most: Gerhart Hauptmann.

With the sudden success of his comedy, the hitherto bohemian Zuckmayer was able to become "respectable": he left Berlin and went to live in Austria, at Henndorf, in the province of Salzburg. In 1926 he met and was much affected by Gerhart Hauptmann. The older man, who had won the Nobel Prize for literature in 1912, came to regard Zuckmayer as his spiritual heir. Zuckmayer later completed Hauptmann's pacifist play *Herbert Engelmann* (1952), which Hauptmann had left unfinished in 1924.

From his retreat, Zuckmayer wrote more successful plays, including the one some believe to be his masterpiece, *Der Hauptmann von Köpenick*, "A German Fairy Tale in Three Acts," which was translated into English in 1932 as *The Captain of Köpenick*. This is perennially revived, and has been made into two German movies (by Richard Oswald in 1931 and by Helmut Käutner in 1957). There is little doubt that, with the exception of the comedies by Hauptmann in his naturalistic period, this is Germany's greatest comedy of the twentieth century. It is firmly in the tradition that Hauptmann invented and perhaps the most good-tempered indictment of Prussian bureaucracy and militarism ever undertaken. It tells of the exploits of a cobbler, Wilhelm Voight, and his outwitting of the authorities. It mocked all that the Nazis held dear, and in 1933, when they took power, they instantly banned all Zuckmayer's works from performance.

In the successful *Schinderhannes*, based on the exploits of Johann Bückler, a Robin Hood-like figure of the time of the Napoleonic Wars, Zuckmayer paid homage to the technique of his fellow-Hessian Georg Büchner. Jealous theatrical columnists tried to undermine his circus comedy, *Katharina Knie* (1928), which was in Rheinish dialect, but the public enjoyed it. In *Bellman* (later revised as *Ulla Winblad*), Zuckmayer treated the life of a Swedish vagabond-poet and songster in a markedly autobiographical manner. In the period of his residence in Austria, Zuckmayer went to London, both to present his adaptation of an Indian play, *The Golden Toy* (at the Coliseum), and to work on the script of the Alexander Korda film of *Rembrandt* (featuring Charles Laughton as the Dutch painter). He also did some work on the script of the famously never-made *I, Claudius*. In 1929 Zuckmayer had written the script for one of the most celebrated films of all time: Josef von Sternberg's *Der blaue Engel* (The Blue Angel), based on Heinrich Mann's novel *Professor Unrat*.

*Bellman* was being rehearsed in Austria when the Nazis entered the country. Some of Zuckmayer's belongings were seized by a Gestapo eager to pay him back for his jokes at their expense, but he himself eluded them by fleeing to Switzerland, and then, via France, to America. In 1939 the Nazis deprived him of his German citizenship. He lived in the States for six years, helping in the Allied war effort, working in Hollywood, teaching theater at the New School for Social Research in New York, and working at his villa in Vermont, where Zuckmayer wrote a vivid account of recent events in the autobiographical *Second Wind* (in English only, and introduced by Dorothy Thompson).

It was in Vermont, too, while cut completely off from events in Germany, that Zuckmayer wrote one of the finest popular plays of the twentieth century: *Des Teufels General* (known worldwide as *The Devil's General*, although there appears to be no published translation of it). For the author himself, who took the play back to Germany with him in 1945, this was a memorial to his friend, the World War I air ace Ernst Udet, who reluctantly served the Nazis and died in 1941 in an unexplained "accident." Zuckmayer's General Harras is loosely modeled on Udet. Harras is first seen mocking the Minister of Culture, who "translates" his sour and dangerous remarks into official clichés; when Harras is asked why he serves the Nazis, whom he hates, he admits that it has come about only through his love of flying. Later, fully convinced that he has been "the Devil's General," he crashes in a plane he knows to be sabotaged.

There was much controversy about *The Devil's General* (premiered in Switzerland, it became a movie, directed again by Helmut Käutner) because in it a man who served the Nazis is portrayed sympathetically. But this was no more than conceding that some of the servants of the Nazis were morally superior to others: that some at least did not believe in their bestial precepts. Zuckmayer portrayed a fundamentally decent man who could purge his guilt only by killing himself; when he takes his final fatal flight it is to protect the chief saboteur, his own chief engineer.

Zuckmayer was awarded the Goethe Prize in 1952, and then the National Prize for Literature in 1955. His postwar plays have worn a little less well than his earlier ones, but all of them were solid and thoughtful. Outstanding among them is *Das kalte Licht* (translated as *The Cold Light* ), about a scientist who betrays the secret of the atom bomb to the Russians.

Zuckmayer was for a time the only really accomplished dramatist in postwar West Germany, and he had a great deal to do with the revival of the theater there, which was weak compared to that of East Germany. He eventually went to live in Switzerland, near Visp, where he died.

All that is available of Zuckmayer's distinguished poetry in English translation seems to be Leonard Forster's literal prose rendering of "An Die Rotweinfelcken auf dem Tischtuch in einem französischen Restaurant" (To the Red Winestains on the Table-Cloth in a French Restaurant, 1936) in his *Penguin Book of German Verse* (1959), but this single poem testifies to his high quality as a poet.

Zuckmayer's fiction, not much translated—there were several novels and short novels, and a few Novellen—was of a similarly high quality. The semi-Gothic romance *Salwàre oder Die Magdalena von Bozen* (translated as *The Moons Ride Over*), an eerie tale of a strangely united brother and sister living in a castle in the Tyrol told by an ancient-mariner sort of narrator, showed a completely unfamiliar side of its author. In the *New York Times* (1937) an uncomprehending Alfred Kazin sneered at it as mystical, but was forced to concede that it was written in "exquisite prose" and to commend its "loving descriptions of nature." The reviewer for *Saturday Review of Literature* praised its psychology, and noted that it avoided the "strained and artificial atmosphere of 'intellectual' fiction."

Zuckmayer had a further success with his autobiography *Als Wär's ein Stück von mir* (1966, abridged in English as *A Part of Myself*). The *New Yorker* found it written with "beguiling freshness" and said that the author had a "talent for happiness." This account of his life warmly and convincingly demonstrates how Zuckmayer returned to religion in his last years; it also shows how nature, and in particular landscape, affected his work.

Zuckmayer was married to Alice von Herden, with whom he had a daughter.

PRINCIPAL WORKS IN ENGLISH TRANSLATION: *Drama*—The Captain of Köpenick (tr. D. Portman) 1932; The Cold Night (tr. E. Montagu) 1958. *Novels*—The Moons Ride Over (tr. M. Firth; in U.K.: Moon in the South), Carnival Confession (tr. J. and N. Mander) 1961. *Memoirs*—Second Wind (tr. E. R. Hapgood) 1940; A Part of Myself (abridged and tr. R. C. Winston) 1970.

ABOUT: The autobiographical material quoted above was written for Twentieth Century Authors, 1942. Balinken, A. The Central Women Figures in Carl Zuckmayer's Dramas, 1978; Bauer, A. Carl Zuckmayer (tr. E. Simmons) 1976; Bromley, G. (ed. and tr.) Karl Barth and Carl Zuckmayer: Late Friendship,

1982; Finke, M. Carl Zuckmayer's Germany, 1990; Garten, H. F. Modern German Drama, 1964; Mews, S. Carl Zuckmayer, 1981; Natan, A. (ed.) German Men of Letters III, 1964; Seymour-Smith, M. Macmillian Guide to Modern World Literature, 1986; Wagener, H. Carl Zuckmayer's Criticism, 1995; Zuckmayer, C. A Part of Myself, 1970. *Periodicals*—Modern Language Review, LXIII, 1968; Newsweek December 28, 1970; New Yorker January 2, 1971; New York Times February 7, 1937; January 19, 1977; Saturday Review of Literature March 20, 1937; Time January 31, 1977; Times (London) January 19, 1977.

**ZUGSMITH, LEANE** (January 18, 1903– October 13, 1969), American novelist, short story writer, and journalist, wrote: "I was born in Louisville, Kentucky, the daughter of Albert Zugsmith and Gertude (Appel) Zugsmith. Most of my early years were spent in Atlantic City, which used to give the world hoofers and swimmers. I don't shine at either trade and can't recommend Atlantic City as an admirable all-year-round residence for young people. I spent one year apiece at Goucher, the University of Pennsylvania, and Columbia, and got my real education afterward, although I wouldn't blame that on any faculty. Since 1924, I've been living in New York—counting out one year spent abroad, chiefly in France and Italy, and a few months recently in Hollywood, where I was supposed to be a screen writer for the Goldwyn studio. For about eight years I wrote at night (not every one) and over week-ends, since I had a job during the day. I have worked as a copy editor for woodpulp magazines, such as *Detective Stories* and *Western Story Magazine*, and later ascended to writing advertising copy and publicity for, first Putnam's, and later—and last—Horace Liveright. Close association with material destined for the pulps fortunately didn't affect me in any way at all beyond getting me an inadequate salary. I don't think my work was affected by Putnam or Liveright authors, either, except that encounters with some of them made me vow never to be a nuisance in any department of my publishers, and I think I've kept the oath.

"My first novel *All Victories Are Alike*, was published in 1929. I don't know who influenced it, but I wish someone had been able to influence me not

to let it be published. Ditto for the next one, *Goodbye and Tomorrow*, 1931—except that this one was shamelessly derivative of Virginia Woolf. It's difficult to trace my development so far as influences were concerned. I know I went through and survived the conventional periods, at the conventional times, of Cabell and D. H. Lawrence and Aldous Huxley and H. L. Mencken and then Joyce and Proust. I am still a staunch admirer of Balzac, Chekhov, Stendhal, Jane Austen, and Dostoievsky; but I am equally interested in contemporary creative writing: Malraux's and Thomas Mann's for example. In America, I think Lillian Hellman ranks about tops as a playwright; Albert

Maltz and Irwin Shaw are two first-class short story writers, in my opinion; and I think Josephine Herbst is a fine novelist. These aren't my only nominations. I think that writing should, first of all, be about human beings, and should illumine them for readers. However, it seems to me to be increasingly difficult to write illuminatingly about human beings without regarding their social circumstances.

"As to my political convictions, I am anti-Fascist and for democracy, not merely a political democracy but also an economic democracy. I try to do what I can to work with others toward such a goal, through organizations like the League of Women Shoppers and the League of American Writers."

———

Leane Zugsmith's social protest novels epitomized the political views of the literary left during the Great Depression and, together with her beauty, spirit, and conversational talents, prompted Matthew Josephson in *Southern Review* to refer to her as "Miss 1930s." After attending high school with Lillian Hellman in Atlantic City and making a pilgrimage to Europe, Zugsmith settled in comfortably to New York bohemia in the mid-1920s "as a liberated young woman writing stories and novels about liberated young women." Many of her stories appeared in the *New Yorker, Harper's, Atlantic*, and other magazines and were often a part of annual short story collections.

Despite her own misgivings, her first two novels, *All Victories Are Alike* (1929) and *Goodbye and Tomorrow* (1931), received some encouraging remarks as many reviewers found promise in the author's clarity, honesty, and intelligence in documenting the mores of the young and the free in the 1920s. After the stock market had crashed and hard times hit home, she veered away from writing about the yearnings of struggling downtown artists into more serious themes. An aspiring sculptor was no longer as relevant as the troubled youngster from the slums in *The Reckoning* (1934), who served as human evidence that legal and social systems did not work for the lower classes of a big city in the down cycle. And instead of speakeasy ladies, she focused on striking store workers in *A Time to Remember* (1936). Zugsmith first unveiled her more socially conscious and sometimes almost preachy tone in *Never Enough* (1932), in which, in the style of Jules Romains, she introduces characters in individual narratives, then meshes them into a kaleidoscope of mainly blue tones that showed the interconnection of eight lives in an urban struggle against economic gloom.

Her strike novel, *A Time to Remember*, romanticized the labor movement and showed great empathy toward the disenfranchised white-collar workers in a major New York department store. Alfred Kazin in the *New York Times* praised its "immediacy" and "insight," and Louis Kronenberger, writing in the *Nation*, considered it not only her best novel, "but one of the best social-minded novels that anybody has written," adding that in terms of a leftist tract, "this is an exemplary novel to set before an open-minded reader because, starting from scratch, he would have no choice but to end up in a partisan mood."

In the meantime, ten short stories from magazines were published in the collection *Home is Where You Hang Your Childhood* (1937), many of which echoed back to Zugsmith's middle-class upbringing, years that were a fight for freedom from the constraints of overprotective parents. In "The New York Visit," a Midwestern girl of fifteen intends to go to the city alone and stay with relatives in order to be with her boyfriend, only to find that her father decides he must chaperone and ruin everything for the now-seething young rebel. Siding with the underdog came easy for Zugsmith. In "Room in the World," she tells with admirable economy of an apartment building janitor fired without cause during the depression and thus forced to cede the cellar that served as a home for his family.

"She excelled in her short stories, which were written by one who was observant and listened closely to the speech of people in the street or in the subway. Rereading them you found the human condition of those crisis years reported by one who sought out the painful truth and yet told it with compassionate humor," wrote Josephson. A short novel, *The Summer Soldier* (1938), showed more structure and irony than previous works; it was the result of her trip to an Alabama mill town in the midst of a labor conflict. "If Leane Zugsmith's novels have not been monuments, they have been milestones along the U.S. road. This novel . . . indicates that she is still headed in the proper direction, up-hill, going places," wrote *Time*. Where she headed was to the Far East with her husband, the journalist Carl Randau, on assignment with the New York newspaper, *PM*, for which she served as a special feature writer. The couple returned home from Japan and Occupied China on the eve of the attack on Pearl Harbor, two of the last American civilians to travel through the Pacific before war was declared, and wrote their impressions of the region in the journalistic work, *The Setting Sun of Japan* (1942), which was considered a colorful and lively account.

While Zugsmith enjoyed a decade of relative success as a novelist, short story writer, consumer boycott organizer, and salon keeper, by the mid-1940s she had begun to eclipse. She and her husband moved to a small beach house in Madison, Connecticut, to economize. They weathered the rising post-war storm of political conservatism and McCarthyism by collaborating on detective fiction that was serialized in popular magazines, and she replaced her political activism with gardening. The Randau's collaborated again on *The Visitor* (1944), a psychological melodrama and surprising mystery in that the authors unobtrusively and cleverly slip in a murder toward the end. Produced as a Broadway play in 1944, it received less than enthusiastic reviews but was purchased by Universal Pictures, with Zugsmith's brother, Albert Zugsmith, Jr., hired to produce the film.

PRINCIPAL WORKS: All Victories Are Alike, 1929; Goodbye and Tomorrow, 1931; Never Enough, 1932; The Reckoning, 1934;

A Time to Remember, 1936; Home Is Where You Hang Your Childhood (short stories) 1937; The Summer Soldier, 1938; The Setting Sun of Japan (with C. Randau) 1942; The Visitor (with C. Randau) 1944.

ABOUT: The autobiographical material quoted above was written for Twentieth Century Authors, 1942. Contemporary Authors vol. 115; Nation August 12, 1936, March 28, 1942; New York Times September 13, 1936; October 14, 1969; Publishers Weekly November 3, 1969; Southern Review July 1975; Time August 29, 1938.

## ZUVIRIA, GUSTAVO MARTÍNEZ. See MARTÍNEZ ZUVIRIA, GUSTAVO

**ZWEIG, ARNOLD** (November 10, 1887–November 26, 1968), German novelist, playwright, and essayist, was born in Grosz-Glogau, Silesia (now Poland), the son of Adolf Zweig, a saddler. After an early education at a school in Kattowitz, Upper Silesia (where the family had been forced to move in 1896 by a decree forbidding Jews from dealing with the Russian forces), Zweig studied at a number of German universities, including Breslau, Munich, Berlin, and Göttingen.

His early work consisted of short stories. 'Vorfrühling' was printed in 1909, in a student magazine of which he was co-editor. The hero, Karl Magnus, is a twenty-two-year-old psychologist marooned in a coldly intellectual mindset. Three years later *Die Novellen um Claudia* appeared. Although purporting to be a novel, the book is really a series of seven linked stories. There are only five characters, the two principal ones being  Claudia Eggeling and Walter Rohme. Their love affair and marriage are depicted with a degree of psychological analysis which was rare in other fiction of the time. A volume of war stories, *Die Bestie*, followed in 1914. The title story in this collection is about a Belgian farmer who, finding himself host to three German soldiers, gets them drunk, then cuts their throats and feeds their insides to his pigs.

Zweig was soon embroiled in the actual agony of war, including being present at the Battle of Verdun. Eventually he was moved to the eastern front, serving in the public information office. Wartime camaraderie influenced him in an increasing shift towards socialism. After demobilization (he had married in 1916), Zweig attempted to build a reputation as freelance essayist and didactic playwright, creating an early version (in 1921) of the character, Sergeant Grischa, upon whom his surviving reputation is deemed to rest.

Zweig's plays and essays—the latter written mainly for the Zionist journal *Jöische Rundschau* and the left-wing *Die Weltböne*—won him only a local reputation. But in 1927 the appearance of *Der Streit um den Sergeanten Grischa* brought him to the attention of an international audience. This book is still considered one of the best anti-war novels of the century. Ironically depicting a bureaucratic connivance in the inevitable descent towards heartlessness, Zweig tells a gripping story which involves the reader in the fate of Grischa, who is eventually put to death despite having his innocence established. It was based on a true story, as told to Zweig in a cafe in Kovno towards the end of the War, about a Russian prisoner who had escaped, was recaptured and shot.

Something important had happened to Zweig during the conversion of the Grischa story from play to novel. He had discovered Freud, and he reworked the earlier material under the influence of the discovery. The novel was first published as 'Alle gegen einen' in serial form in the Frankfurter Zeitung. When it appeared as a book it was an immediate success. The detail with which Zweig portrayed the German army was instantly accepted as authentic and, when the book was translated, reviewers outside Germany responded warmly to the convincing characterization. L. P. Hartley, writing in the *Saturday Review*, echoed others when he said that the book was "extraordinarily impartial and capable, sensitive alike to general tendencies and individual emotions. It is one of the best novels about the war." In the same review he also suggested that the book was "too drawn out," but the *New York Times* reviewer, while agreeing that it was "painfully slow in gathering momentum at the start," decided that this gradual accretion of detail was an essential element in the novel's power. "Some experiences in literature are unforgettable and this is one," he wrote.

Zweig then set out to publish a tetralogy of novels about the war. The second book to appear was *Junge Frau von 1914*, the story of Lenore Wahl and her lover, Werner Bertin. Lionel Trilling, writing in the *Nation*, expressed what has proved to be the longer-term view. "Zweig is a writer considerably but not supremely endowed with novelistic skill; it was his strong intelligence playing over the confused aspects of a great theme, the problem of human justice, that made *The Case of Sergeant Grischa* so fine a book." He did not think the theme of the new book brought Zweig's intelligence adequately into play, and Martin Seymour-Smith, writing in *Guide to Modern World Literature*, found that the book's "criticism of the pre-war society, although justified, is too angry to be altogether good for the fiction."

The other books in the series—*Erziehung vor Ver dun* (in which Werner Bertin is once again a main character) and *Einsetzung eines Königs*—Seymour-Smith describes as "competent but doctrinaire." Zweig had been influenced intellectually by Martin Buber, and emotionally by the East European Jews he had met while on active service. His Zionism was expressed in several plays and essays, including *Das Neue Kanaan* (1925), in which his socialist views were also prominently argued. After the Nazi takeover he was forced to flee Berlin. He left on the morning of March 14, 1933, traveling first to Prague. By the end of the year he was in Palestine, where he remained in exile at Haifa until 1948. He continued to write both fiction and essays. However, his influence on the course of Zionism and the eventual establishment of the state of Israel was limited by his failure to acquire Hebrew, and by the increasing vehemence of his left-wing views. Returning to Germany in 1948, he settled in East Berlin where, for the most part, he showed himself to be at ease with the communist regime, was made president of the East German Academy of Arts (1950–1953), and accepted the Lenin Peace Prize in 1958. At the time of the Six Day War he refused to sign a petition, circulated by communist intellectuals, condemning the Israelis. An eye condition possibly contracted during his miltary service led to loss of sight, and for the last forty years of his life his work was dictated. Much of his later work did not appear in English translation, but a modest edition of his stories appeared in 1959, under the title *A Bit of Blood and Other Stories*.

PRINCIPAL WORKS IN ENGLISH TRANSLATION: (tr. E. Sutton) The Case Of Sergeant Grischa, 1928; Claudia, 1930; Young Woman of 1914, 1932; De Vriendt Goes Home, 1933; Playthings of Time, 1935; Education Before Verdun, 1936; The Crowning of a King, 1938; The Axe of Wandsbek, 1947; A Bit of Blood and Other Stories, 1961; The Time Is Ripe (tr. K. Banerji and M. Wharton); The Letters of Sigmund Freud and Arnold Zweig, 1970.

ABOUT: Columbia Dictionary of Modern European Literature, 1980; Salomon G. Arnold Zweig, 1975; Seymour-Smith, M. Guide to Modern World Literature, 1985; Who's Who 1968. *Periodicals*—Nation January 18, 1933; New York Times December 2, 1928; November 27, 1968; Saturday Review December 1, 1928; Times (London) November 27, 1968.

**ZWEIG, STEFAN** (November 28, 1881–February 23, 1942), Austrian biographer and novelist, wrote: "I was born in Vienna. After leaving school I went to the university, where I studied history, literature, and philosophy, my dissertation dealing with Taine. By that time I had developed an increasing desire to travel and see the world, and undertook several long voyages which took me as far as India, in those times an  adventurous and extremely fascinating journey. During these voyages I continued my literary work, which I had already begun at school. The Great War of 1914 ended the first period of my life and transformed my whole outlook on life. The tragedy, *Jeremiah*, which I wrote in 1917 (it was produced in New York in 1939), expressed my pacifistic ideas on war and its problems. It was produced in Switzerland, a neutral country, being forbidden, naturally, in the belligerent countries. During the last year of the war I had managed to go to Switzerland, where I met a group of writers of all countries who had come there to fight against war and its consequences of exaggerated and one-sided nationalism, the leader of that group being Romain Rolland. I must emphasize, however, that even in the belligerent countries we were then allowed a measure of criticism and of free expression of thought which would have been impossible in most European countries during more recent years.

"After the war I went back to Austria, where I lived in Salzburg for nearly twenty years, although traveling a good deal. I continued my literary work, and gradually my books became known all over the world and were translated into many languages. I left Salzburg and Austria early in 1934 and came to live in London, at first in order to do research work, for the book on Mary, Queen of Scots, which I was then preparing. Then I stayed on because I was pessimistic about the ultimate fate of Austria as an independent state and because I wished to live in a country where individual freedom and liberty of thought were still possible.

"In order to get better acquainted with the United States, I undertook a lecture tour in 1938 which took me right across the country, from New York down to Texas and over to California, and although the time was too short for detailed study and exploration of the country, it gave me a very vivid picture of present-day life in the United States and its growing development in all educational, artistic, and scientific matters.

"My main interest in writing has always been the psychological representation of personalities and their lives and this was also the reason which prompted me to write various essays and biographical studies of well-known personalities. I also take a very great interest in studying the way of working of famous musicians and painters as well as scientists; and that is why my main interest besides my work has always been collecting autograph manuscripts and studying the lives of the great men of all ages. It is a source of personal joy and pride that I have met most of the great artists of our time and that I may count among my personal friends men like Romain Rolland, Toscanini, Bruno Walter, and, until his death, Freud."

———

After becoming a British citizen in 1940, Stefan Zweig left London for New York. Together with his young wife, Charlotte ("Lotte") Elizabeth Altmann, he committed suicide in Persepolis, near Rio de Janeiro in Brazil. Lotte was the secretary whom he had married (in Bath, England, in 1939) after his first wife, Friderike Maria von Winternitz.

Tired and feeling too old to continue a useful life in exile, he left a letter reading: "After I saw the country of my own language fall, and my spiritual land—Europe—destroying itself . . . It would require immense strength to reconstruct my life . . . my energy is exhausted. . . . I believe it is time to end a life which was dedicated only to spiritual work, considering human liberty and my own as the greatest wealth in the world." Like Arthur Koestler and his wife, nearly fifty years afterwards, Zweig and his twenty-eight-year-old wife were found together after having drunk poison in a suicide pact.

In 1930 Zweig was reckoned to be the most widely translated author in the world. He is no longer widely read. However, unlike many such writers whose reputations have faded out with time, or who have become simply cult figures, he stands to receive some measure of rehabilitation. He surely deserves a place in German and, indeed, in European literature. Zweig was a historical figure of great interest. So famous was he at the time of his death that Brazil's populist dictator, Getulio Vargas, the oppressor of his own country's best writers, ordered that his burial expenses should be paid for by the state.

Zweig, whose cry was always "Freiheit!" (Freedom!), decided that he had found it at the university in Berlin. He soon discovered Dostoevsky's quest for redemption through suffering, and so devoted himself to a similar fate. By 1904 he had earned a doctorate from Vienna University and had absorbed Dostoevsky's febrile style as well as he could from German translations.

At this time Zweig was a lyrical symbolist poet first and foremost. In his role, as a highly skilled, speedy, and fluent translator of Verlaile, Baudelaine, and Verhaeren, Zweig was influential on the German-speaking public. But his original verse, seen in retrospect, has little more to offer than the taste of Viennese *Jungwien* impressionism under the sway of French symbolism. He wrote with sensitivity and understanding of himself at this period in his autobiography, *Die Welt von Gestern* (1943; translated as *The World of Yesterday*), which has claims to be his best book. It is still an invaluable source of knowledge about the early world of Freud, Wittgenstein, Otto Weininger, Schnitzler, Musil, Kraus, and many more.

Zweig's first really notable action was to become the ardent disciple of the Belgian poet Émil Verhaeren, then at the height of his fame, and greatly influential all over Europe. He translated him into German, and followed him to most of the many countries which he visited. He mastered five languages, including French and English, at an early age. Thus Zweig met and became intimate with Romain Rolland, Rilke, Freud, and Tagor, whom he visited in India in 1910.

In 1901 Friderike von Winternitz began to send him fan mail; this culminated (1914) in marriage, and Zweig and she lived together, with her two daughters by her first marriage, in a large mansion near Salzburg. Zweig's guests included Ravel, Toscanini, Gorky, and Bartok.

In these years at Salzburg with Friderike, Zweig began to see Hitler's persecution of Jews as directed at him personally. Friderike's introduction of Lotte set off a predictable train of events. Zweig was able to analyze himself (along Freudian lines), and to find refuge in hard work; but he was never to recover from his paranoia. His Austrian friends began to ostracize him, even before the *Anschluss*, and after the invasion his house was searched by police and his books burned.

Zweig himself believed in his poetry and drama, and in particular in the play *Jeremias* (1917), of which a translation was made by Eliot and Cedar Paul in 1922. It was popular in the German-speaking countries, in which its earnest rhetoric was more or less routine, but, despite the respectful reviews, it has been largely forgotten. His best and most widely performed play was an adaptation of Ben Jonson's *Volpone* (he also did the libretto for Strauss's opera *Die Schweigsame Frau*). Aside from his final book, it is for his historical essays and biographies, and for some of his fiction, that Zweig will be remembered.

Outstanding among his fiction are the short novel *Amok* (translated under that title) and his only full-length novel, *Ungeduld des Herzens* (translated as *Beware of Pity*). Both of these tales were filmed, the former memorably in French by Fedor Ozep (1934). *Amok* is the story of a doctor in the Dutch East Indies driven to suicide by his refusal of help to a woman who had sought his aid. *Beware of Pity* deals with a young army officer who, just before the outbreak of World War I, pledges himself to a young crippled girl—only to panic and run away. *Beware of Pity* is memorable enough in its light-hearted way. The critic John Mair, author of *Never Come Back*, wrote the most penetrating of all the contemporary reviews of the English version in the *New Statesman*: "The formula is that of the . . . woman's magazine, and only Herr Zweig's admirable style and polished philosophizings lay claim to anything better. . . . If Herr Zweig was a chronicler one would praise his skill in making the unlikely credible; as he sets out to be a creator one must rather deplore this lack of imagination. Perhaps his historical studies are the real cause of the trouble; the biographer is so dependent on events that he tends to see his characters only in their picturesque superficials."

*Schachnovelle* (Chess story, translated as *The Royal Game*) ingeniously uses two games of chess played aboard an ocean liner on its way from New York to Brazil to illustrate the horrors of Nazism. The unfinished *Clarissa* is an account of a girl who marries an odious Austrian because he can give her and her illegitimate child respectability. The last work might have become Zweig's subtlest and most self-critical novel.

Zweig's many biographies and character studies made use of psychoanalytical concepts. They are probably all useful as general and occasionally insightful introductions to their subjects. The analyses are always along the lines of emotional tension and, even when the subjects were historical, are suspiciously "modern." Those who called them "psychodramas" were not far off the mark. In some ways the earliest were the worst: *Verhaeren* was a useful monograph, but (as all the reviewers of the translation said) marred by high-flown rhetoric. The biography *Romain Rolland* even elicited from the *Boston Transcript* reviewer the remark that it should have been "Rolland's prayer to be saved from his biographer": it contained "extravagant . . . preposterous praise."

But by the time of *Drei Dichter ihres Lebens: Casanova, Stendhal, Tolstoy* (translated as *Adepts in Self-Portraiture*), Zweig was receiving almost universal praise instead of condemnation. The *New York Times* said of *Adepts*: "Not only is Zweig successful in his realization of these great egoists, but

he likewise is able to kindle a desire to reread or read more of the works of these. . . . In Zweig we have a critic extending the function of criticism and revivifying it." The similar studies of Fouché, Balzac, Nietzsche, Verlaine, Mary Queen of Scots, Mesmer, Mary Baker Eddy, Freud, Marie Antoinette, Erasmus, Magellan and many others only served to reinforce such an impression. And in parts they are indeed vivid and memorable (the picture of Nietzsche's struggle with migraine headaches and general ill-health is particularly truthful and moving).

But the vogue for Zweig's biographies has gradually died out. By general consent the best of them are contained in *Baumeister der Welt* (translated as *Master Builders*). Several of them have been reprinted, and some are still in print; they are no longer widely read. Martin Seymour-Smith's ungrammatical verdict on them is that while they are "vulgar" and only "superb journalism" they do "have the marvellous quality of driving the reader to further investigation of their subject, even if they find that Zweig was not strictly accurate. It is a rare virtue, tainted though it may be with sensationalism. . . . the promising *Jungwien* poet and dramatist was destroyed by the disintegration of his world. . . . if he is to be remembered it will be for such examples [of his shorter fiction] as *Amok*."

Also in print is his *Jewish Legends*. Interest in Zweig will continue; he perhaps awaits a truly balanced critic, who will be able to place him convincingly in his historical role. A *Complete Works* in English translation by E. and C. Paul (including all their previous versions) was initiated in 1949, but was never quite completed. Probably the best known of all the nine movies made from his work was Max Ophuls' elegant version of *Letter from an Unknown Woman* (1947), featuring Joan Fontaine and Louis Jourdain.

PRINCIPAL WORKS IN ENGLISH TRANSLATION: *Fiction*—Passion and Pain (tr. E. and C. Paul) 1925; Conflicts (tr. E. and C. Paul) 1927; Amok (tr. E. and C. Paul) 1931; Letter from an Unknown Woman (tr. E. and C. Paul) 1932; Kaleidoscope (tr. E. and C. Paul) 1934; The Buried Candelabrum (tr. E. and C. Paul) 1937; The Royal Game (tr. B. W. Huebsch) 1944. *Novel*—Beware of Pity (tr. P. and T. Blewitt) 1953. *Biography*—Verhaeren (tr. J. Bithell) 1914; Romain Rolland (tr. E. and C. Paul) 1921; Adepts in Self-Portraiture: Casanova, Stendhal, Tolstoy (tr. E. and C. Paul) 1928; Joseph Fouché (tr. E. and C. Paul) 1930; Three Masters (tr. E. and C. Paul) 1930; Mental Healers (tr. E. and C. Paul) 1932; Marie Antoinette (tr. E. and C. Paul) 1933; Erasmus of Rotterdam (tr. E. and C. Paul) 1938; Master Builders: A Typology of the Spirit (tr. E. and C. Paul) 1939; Mary Queen of Scotland (tr. E. and C. Paul) 1935; The Right to Heresy (tr. E. and C. Paul) 1936; The Tide of Fortune: Twelve Historical Miniatures (tr. E. and C. Paul) 1940; Amerigo (tr. A. St. James) 1940. *Autobiography*—Brazil (tr. A. St. James) 1941; The World Of Yesterday (tr. E. and C. Paul) 1943. *Drama*—Jeremiah (tr. E. and C. Paul) 1922; Volpone (tr. R. Langer) 1928. *Other*—Jewish Legends, 1987. *Correspondence*—H. G. Alsberg (ed.) Stefan and Frederike Zweig: Their Correspondence 1912–1942 (tr. E. McArthur) 1954; A Confidential Matter: The Letters of Richard Strauss and Stefan Zweig 1931–1933 (tr. M. Knight) 1977; The Correspondence of Stefan Zweig with Raoul Auernheimer, 1983.

ABOUT: The autobiographical material quoted above was written for Twentieth Century Authors, 1942. Allday, E. Stefan Zweig: A Critical Biography, 1972; Arens, H. (ed.) Stefan Zweig: A Tribute, 1951; Columbia Dictionary of Modern European Literature, 1947, 1980; Prater, D. A European of Yesterday: A Biography of Stefan Zweig, 1972; Seymour-Smith, M. Macmillan Guide to Modern World Literature, 1986; Spitzer L. Lives in Between, 1990; Turner, D. Moral Values and the Human Zoo: The Novellen of Stefan Zweig, F. W. Stefan Zweig (tr. E. McAruthur) 1946; Greatness Revisited (in English) 1971; Zweig, S. The World of Yesterday, 1943. *Bibliography*—Klawiter, R. J. An International Bibliography, 1964, rev. ed. 1991. *Periodicals*—Boston Transcript November 2, 1921; German Quarterly May 1952; Jewish Quarterly 1962; Journal of European Studies June 1976; Literature and Psychology 1/2 1994; Modern Language Notes April 1947; Modern Language Review April 1989; Music and Letters November 1993; New Statesman May 20, 1939; New York Times November 11, 1928; February 24, 1942; Opera News July 1988; Times Literary Supplement May 3, 1991; Unesco Courier July 1992.

# Picture Credits

*Abbott, Eleanor Hallowell*: courtesy of S. W. Woodward
*Abdullah, Achmed*: courtesy of Oggiano
*Adamic, Louis*: courtesy of Oggiano
*Adams, Franklin Pierce*: courtesy of Joseph Cummings Chase
*Adams, James Truslow*: courtesy of P. MacDonald
*Adams, John Cranford*: courtesy of Fabian Bachrach
*Adler, Mortimer Jerome*: courtesy of Halsman
*Agar, Herbert*: courtesy of Pinchot
*Agee, James*: courtesy of Walker Evans
*Aldington, Richard*: courtesy of Blackstone
*Aldrich, Bess*: courtesy of Blackstone
*Aldridge, James*: courtesy of Cosmo-Sileo
*Algren, Nelson*: courtesy of Robert McCullough
*Allen, Hervey*: courtesy of Pinchot
*Amory, Cleveland*: courtesy of Archive
*Anderson, Maxwell*: courtesy of Vandamm
*Andrews, Charles McLean*: courtesy of Bachrach
*Anthony, Katharine Susan*: courtesy of Dexter
*Appel, Benjamin*: courtesy of Pinchot
*Ardrey, Robert*: courtesy of Sam Perkins
*Armstrong, Hamilton Fish*: courtesy of Kazanjian
*Arp, Jean*: courtesy of Archive/Archive France
*Arvin, Newton*: courtesy of Eric Stahlberg
*Asch, Sholem*: courtesy of Pinchot
*Atkinson, Brooks*: courtesy of Oggiano
*Auden, W. H.*: courtesy of Archive
*Auslander, Joseph*: courtesy of Pinchot
*Aymé, Marcel*: courtesy of Studio Lipnitzki

*Bacheller, Irving*: courtesy of Blackstone
*Bacon, Josephine Dodge*: courtesy of George M. Kesslere
*Bacovia, George*: courtesy of Minerva Publishing
*Bailey, Temple*: courtesy of Harris C. Ewing
*Baker, George Pierce*: courtesy of D. Keller
*Baker, Ray Stannard*: courtesy of Blackstone
*Baldwin, Faith*: courtesy of Archive
*Balfour, Arthur James*: courtesy of Underwood
*Banning, Margaret Culkin*: courtesy of Pinchot
*Barker, A. L.*: courtesy of Mary Marney
*Beard, Mary R.*: courtesy of Underwood
*Beauvoir, Simone de*: courtesy of Elliott Erwitt

*Becker, Carl L.*: courtesy of Kaiden-Kazanjian
*Becker, May Lamberton*: courtesy of Oggiano
*Beebe, William*: courtesy of H. Mitchell
*Belasco, David*: courtesy of Abbe
*Bell, Bernard Iddings*: courtesy of Wide World
*Bellah, James Warner*: courtesy of Pinchot
*Bellamann, Henry*: courtesy of M. Horowitz
*Bellow, Saul*: courtesy of Victoria Lidov
*Benefield, Barry*: courtesy of Bachrach
*Benét, William Rose*: courtesy of Delar
*Benson, Sally*: courtesy of John Engstead
*Bercovici, Konrad*: courtesy of Oggiano
*Berto, Giuseppe*: courtesy of Rome Meldolesi
*Beston, Henry*: courtesy of Bachrach
*Betjeman, John*: courtesy of Cecil Beaton
*Binns, Archie*: courtesy of Pinchot
*Bishop, Elizabeth*: courtesy of Joseph Breitenbach
*Blackmur, R. P.*: courtesy of W. Pierce
*Bliven, Bruce*: courtesy of Associated News
*Blum, Léon*: courtesy of Archive
*Bodenheim, Maxwell*: courtesy of Pinchot
*Bodkin, Maud*: courtesy of Lionel Wood
*Bok, Edward William*: courtesy of Chandler
*Bonsal, Stephen*: courtesy of Edward Burks
*Borgese, Giuseppe Antonio*: courtesy of Moffet
*Botkin, Benjamin Albert*: courtesy of Viola Kantrowitz
*Bourne, Randolph*: courtesy of Bloomfield Public Library
*Bowers, Claude Gernade*: courtesy of Harris & Ewing
*Boyd, Ernest Augustus*: courtesy of Pinchot
*Boyd, James*: courtesy of Pinchot
*Boyd, Thomas*: courtesy of Bachrach
*Boynton, Percy Holmes*: courtesy of Underwood
*Bradford, Gamaliel*: courtesy of D. Ullman
*Bradford, Roark*: courtesy of Pinchot
*Brande, Dorothea*: courtesy of Pinchot
*Brecht, Bertolt*: courtesy of Archive
*Breton, André*: courtesy of French Embassy
*Brinig, Myron*: courtesy of Disraeli
*Brinton, Crane*: courtesy of Bachrach
*Brisbane, Arthur*: courtesy of International
*Brogan, Denis W.*: courtesy of British Broadcasting Corp
*Brooke, Jocelyn*: courtesy of W. Fisk-Moore
*Brooks, Cleanth*: courtesy of Fonville Winans
*Brooks, Van Wyck*: courtesy of V. Semler

Brown, Harry: courtesy of G. M. Kesslere
Brown, John Mason: courtesy of Oggiano
Brownell, William Crary: courtesy of P. MacDonald
Bruce, William Cabell: courtesy of Salisbury
Bryson, Lyman: courtesy of Pach
Buck, Paul Herman: courtesy of Bachrach
Bulosan, Carlos: courtesy of F. Belandres
Burke, Kenneth: photo by Nancy Rica Schiff
Burman, Ben Lucien: courtesy of Oggiano
Burnett, Whit: courtesy of Pinchot
Burt, Maxwell Struthers: courtesy of Allied News-Photo

Caldwell, Erskine: courtesy of M. Bourke-White
Calverton, Victor Francis: courtesy of Pach
Canby, Henry Seidel: courtesy of Oggiano
Cantwell, Robert: courtesy of Pinchot
Capote, Truman: courtesy of Cecil Beaton
Carroll, Gladys: courtesy of Pinchot
Carson, Rachel: courtesy of Brooks
Carus, Paul: courtesy of E. W. Reiss
Cather, Willa: courtesy of N. Muray
Céline, Louis-Ferdinand.: courtesy of E. Schaal
Chase, Stuart: courtesy of E. Schaal
Chevigny, Hector: courtesy of Pete Martin
Chidester, Ann: courtesy of Lotte Jacobi
Childs, Marquis William: courtesy of James R. Dunlop
Christie, Agatha: courtesy of Archive
Churchill, Winston: courtesy of Haesler
Chute, Marchette Gaylord: courtesy of Morrice A. Baer
Clapp, Margaret: courtesy of Underwood & Underwood
Clark, Barrett Harper: courtesy of Newspictures
Clark, Eleanor: courtesy of Lotte Jacobi
Clark, Kenneth: courtesy of Fayer
Cleghorn, Sarah N.: courtesy of C. Naar
Clutton-Brock, Arthur: courtesy of W. Rothenstein
Cobb, Humphrey: courtesy of Pinchot
Cocteau, Jean: courtesy of Archive
Coffin, Robert Peter Tristram: courtesy of Pinchot
Collingwood, R. G.: courtesy of Lafayette
Collins, Norman: courtesy of Howard Coster
Collis, Stewart Maurice: courtesy of Baron
Colum, Padraic: courtesy of Pinchot
Commager, Henry Steele: courtesy of Manny Warman
Compton-Burnett, Ivy: courtesy of Walter Bird
Connolly, Cyril: courtesy of Larry Burrows
Corbett, Elizabeth Frances: courtesy of Underwood
Costain, Thomas B.: courtesy of Ottawa Karsh

Cournos, John: courtesy of Oggiano
Cowley, Malcolm: courtesy of Newspictures
Cozzens, James Gould: courtesy of E. Schaal
Crane, Hart: courtesy of W. Evans
Cross, Wilbur Lucius: courtesy of K. Hart
Crouse, Russell: courtesy of Kesslere
Croy, Homer: courtesy of Davart
Cuppy, Will: courtesy of Delar

Dabney, Virginius: courtesy of Foster Studio
Daniels, Jonathan: courtesy of Globe
Davidson, David: courtesy of Vandamm
Davis, Owen: courtesy of White
Davis, Richard Harding: courtesy of P. MacDonald
Dell, Floyd: courtesy of Pinchot
Deutsch, Babette: courtesy of Bachrach
Dimnet, Ernst: courtesy of Pinchot
Dos Passos, John: courtesy of E. Schaal
Douglas, William O.: courtesy of Harris & Ewing
Dupee, F. W.: courtesy of Erich Hartmann
Durrell, Lawrence: courtesy of Archive
Dutourd, Jean: courtesy of British Broadcasting Corp

Eaton, Evelyn Sybil Mary: courtesy of Yolla Niclas
Eberhart, Richard: courtesy of Henri Cartier-Bresson
Edman, Irwin: courtesy of Donaldson
Eliot, George Fielding: courtesy of Louelle
Eliot, T. S.: courtesy of Archive
Eluard, Paul: courtesy of French Embassy
Ervine, St. John Greer: courtesy of Pinchot

Fante, John: courtesy of W. Gail
Farson, Negley: courtesy of Pinchot
Fast, Howard: courtesy of Pinchot
Faure, Elie: courtesy of D. Rivera
Faure, Raoul Cohen: courtesy of Emmett E. Smith
Faÿ, Bernard: courtesy of Bachrach
Fay, Sidney Bradshaw: courtesy of Bachrach
Ferber, Edna: courtesy of N. Muray
Fergusson, Harvey: courtesy of White
Ficke, Arthur Davison: courtesy of Bachrach
Field, Rachel Lyman: courtesy of Pinchot
Field, Sara Bard: courtesy of A. Arkatov
Finney, Charles G.: courtesy of Pereira
Firbank, Ronald: courtesy of A. John
Fisher, Dorothy Canfield: courtesy of E. Schaal
Flavin, Martin: courtesy of Keystone
Fletcher, John Gould: courtesy of Pinchot
Forbes, Esther: courtesy of E. Schaal
Forster, E. M.: courtesy of Archive
Fosdick, Harry Emerson: courtesy of Pach
Franck, Harry A.: courtesy of Pinchot

*Frankenberg, Lloyd*: courtesy of M. Morehouse
*Freeman, Joseph*: courtesy of A. Albee
*Fremantle, Anne*: courtesy of Bertrand de Geofroy
*Frennsen, Gustav*: courtesy of N. Yontoff
*Fry, Christopher*: courtesy of Pix
*Fuess, Claude Moore*: courtesy of Nation-Wide

*Gaither, Frances Ormond*: courtesy of Lotte Jacobi
*Gallico, Paul*: courtesy of Arn Glantz
*Gannett, Lewis*: courtesy of Pinchot
*Gardner, Erle Stanley*: courtesy of Whitesell
*Gaunt, William*: courtesy of London Roye
*Gellhorn, Martha Ellis*: courtesy of Blackstone
*Gill, Brendan*: courtesy of Lotte Jacobi
*Gilman, Lawrence*: courtesy of Pinchot
*Giono, Jean*: courtesy of Schreiber
*Gironella, Jose Maria*: courtesy of Basabe
*Glass, Montague*: courtesy of NBC
*Glenn, Isa*: courtesy of Harris & Ewing
*Godden, Rumer*: courtesy of K. Vaughan
*Gordon, Charles William*: courtesy of P. MacDonald
*Graham, Dorothy*: courtesy of D. Carpenter
*Grant, Robert*: courtesy of E. C. Tarbell
*Graves, Robert*: courtesy of W. Hutchinson
*Greenberg, Clement*: courtesy of Jerry Cooke
*Greene, Graham*: courtesy of Archive
*Greene, Ward*: courtesy of E. Schaal
*Gregory, Horace*: courtesy of L. Jacobi
*Guérard, Albert J.*: courtesy of Walter R. Fleischer
*Gurdjieff, Georges Ivanovitch*: courtesy of Archive
*Gustafson, Ralph Baker*: courtesy of Ottawa Karsh

*Hamilton, Cosmo*: courtesy of J. M. Flagg
*Hamilton, Mary Agnes*: courtesy of C. Harris
*Hammond, Percy*: courtesy of M. Goldberg
*Hapgood, Hutchins*: courtesy of Bouchard
*Hapgood, Norman*: courtesy of Harris & Ewing
*Harris, Seymour Edwin*: courtesy of John Brook
*Hart, Moss*: courtesy of Vandamm
*Hartley, L. P.*: courtesy of Pearl Freeman
*Hartmann, Sadakichi*: courtesy of Rivera Library, University of California/Riverside
*Hauptmann, Gerhart*: courtesy of Times Studios
*Hayakawa, S. I.*: courtesy of Leroy Sylverst
*Haydn, Hiram Collins*: courtesy of Glidden
*Hayes, Alfred*: courtesy of Rose Wolfe
*Hayes, Carlton Joseph Huntley*: courtesy of Blackstone

*Hays, Hoffman Reynolds*: courtesy of Shelburne
*Hecht, Ben*: courtesy of A. Petersen
*Hellman, Lillian*: courtesy of Pinchot
*Hendrick, Burton Jesse*: courtesy of Disraeli
*Herbst, Josephine*: courtesy of C. Fenn
*Herschberger, Ruth*: courtesy of G. Herschberger
*Hersey, John*: courtesy of E. M. M. Warburg
*Highet, Gilbert*: courtesy of Elliott Erwitt
*Hillyer, Robert Silliman*: courtesy of J. Durup
*Hodgson, Ralph*: courtesy of W. Rothenstein
*Hoffenstein, Samuel*: courtesy of Kesslere
*Holliday, Robert Cortes*: courtesy of Pinchot
*Holmes, John Haynes*: courtesy of Editta Sherman
*Hooton, Ernest Albert*: courtesy of Bachrach
*Howe, Helen Huntington*: courtesy of John Erwin
*Hudson, Jay William*: courtesy of Blackstone
*Hudson, Stephen*: courtesy of M. Beerbohm
*Hughes, Rupert*: courtesy of Pach Bros.
*Huie, William Bradford*: courtesy of Fabian Bachrach
*Hummel, George Frederick*: courtesy of Pinchot
*Hurst, Fannie*: courtesy of Oggiano

*Inge, William*: courtesy of Talbot
*Isherwood, Christopher*: courtesy of Disraeli

*Jacks, L. P.*: courtesy of Underwood
*James, Henry*: courtesy of Archive
*James, Will*: courtesy of Apeda
*Janeway, Elizabeth*: courtesy of Leonard
*Jarrell, Randall*: courtesy of R. Thorne McKenna
*Jastrow, Joseph*: courtesy of Keystone
*Jeffers, Robinson*: courtesy of E. Weston
*Johnson, Gerald White*: courtesy of Stanislav Rembski
*Johnson, Pamela Hansford*: courtesy of Elliott Erwitt
*Jonas, Carl*: courtesy of Cosmo-Sileo
*Jones, Rufus Matthew*: courtesy of Hans Roth
*Josephson, Matthew*: courtesy of B. Abbott
*Joyce, James*: courtesy of B. Abbott

*Kang, Younghill*: courtesy of O. Garber
*Katz, H. W.*: courtesy of Wolff
*Kaufman, George S.*: courtesy of White
*Kaye-Smith, Sheila*: courtesy of Pinchot
*Kazin, Alfred*: courtesy of Arni
*Kelly, George*: courtesy of N. Muray
*Kent, Louise*: courtesy of Bradford Bachrach
*Kent, Rockwell*: courtesy of B. Martinson
*Kerr, Sophie*: courtesy of Buschke
*Keyes, Frances Parkinson*: courtesy of

Bachrach
*Kittredge, George Lyman*: courtesy of
Bachrach
*Klein, Abraham Moses*: courtesy of Garcia
Studios
*Koch, Vivienne*: courtesy of Talbot
*Koestler, Arthur Habdank*: courtesy of Erich
Hartmann
*Komroff, Manuel*: courtesy of L. Nelson
*Korzybski, Alfred*: courtesy of Lotte Jacobi
*Kramm, Joseph*: courtesy of Peter Perri
*Krey, Laura Lettie*: courtesy of G. Garrett
*Kreymborg, Alfred*: courtesy of R. L. Jackson

*La Farge, Oliver*: courtesy of D. Ulmann
*Lagerkvist, Pär*: courtesy of Atelje Ugglaaf
*Lancaster, Osbert*: courtesy of Cecil Beaton
*Langner, Lawrence*: courtesy of M. Stein
*Lasswell, Harold Dwight*: courtesy of Yale
News Bureau
*Latourette, Kenneth*: courtesy of Yale News
Bureau
*Lawrence, Josephine*: courtesy of H. Phyfe
*Lawson, John Howard*: courtesy of Harris &
Ewing
*Lea, Tom*: courtesy of McElroy
*Leaf, Munro*: courtesy of Pinchot
*Leighton, Clare*: courtesy of Disraeli
*Lengyel, Emil*: courtesy of Bachrach
*Lerner, Max*: courtesy of Harris & Ewing
*Lewis, Alun*: courtesy of John Petts
*Lewis, Sinclair*: courtesy of H. Stein
*Ley, Willy*: courtesy of Olga Ley
*Liebling, A. J.*: courtesy of Ray Platnik
*Lincoln, Victoria Endicott*: courtesy of
Blackstone
*Lindbergh, Anne Morrow*: courtesy of P.
Cordes
*Lindsay, Vachel*: courtesy of Harris & Ewing
*Linton, Ralph*: courtesy of White Studio
*Lippmann, Walter*: courtesy of R. L. Jackson
*Locke, Alain*: courtesy of J. L. Allen
*Lockridge, Richard* and *Frances Louise*: cour-
tesy of D. Rolph
*Lovejoy, Arthur Oncken*: courtesy of John
Hopkins Magazine
*Lovelace, Maud* and *Delos Wheeler*: courtesy
of Pinchot
*Lovett, Robert Morss*: courtesy of Acme
*Lowell, Robert*: courtesy of Arni
*Lowes, John Livingston*: courtesy of D.
Ulmann
*Luce, Clare Boothe*: courtesy of Archive
*Lustgarten, Edgar Marcus*: courtesy of
Douglas Glass
*Lynd, Robert Staughton*: courtesy of Steiner-
Morris

*MacInnes, Helen*: courtesy of Dorothy Wilding
*MacIver, R. M.*: courtesy of Manny Warman
*Mackintosh, Elizabeth*: courtesy of Angus
McBean
*Maclean, Catherine Macdonald*: courtesy of H.
N. van Wadenoyen
*MacLeish, Archibald*: courtesy of Washington
Press-Photo
*MacLennan, Hugh*: courtesy of Montreal
Nakash
*MacManus, Seumas*: courtesy of Witzel
*Madeleva, Sister Mary*: courtesy of Harris &
Ewing
*Mailer, Norman*: courtesy of Archive
*Malone, Dumas*: courtesy of Blackstone
*Maltz, Albert*: courtesy of Talbot
*Manfred, Frederick Feikema*: courtesy of
Marilyn Bruette
*Mann, Erika*: courtesy of S. Deutch
*Mann, Thomas*: courtesy of F. Warschauer
*Mantle, Burns*: courtesy of Oggiano
*Marquand, John Phillips*: courtesy of Bachrach
*Marshall, Edison*: courtesy of Vernon Gould
*Martin du Gard, Roger*: courtesy of F.
Margaritis
*Martínez Zuviria, Gustavo*: courtesy of Pinchot
*Mason, F. Van Wyck*: courtesy of Globe
*Masters, Edgar Lee*: courtesy of Pinchot
*Masters, John*: courtesy of George Cserna
*Matthiessen, F. O.*: courtesy of Bachrach
*Maugham, Robin*: courtesy of Fayer
*Mayo, Katherine*: courtesy of K. S. Woerner
*McCarthy, Mary*: courtesy of Kevin McCarthy
*McFee, William*: courtesy of Gorska-Hill
*McHugh, Vincent*: courtesy of Pinchot
*McKenney, Ruth*: courtesy of E. Schaal
*McKeon, Richard*: courtesy of Kay Carrington
*McLaverty, Michael*: courtesy of Charles H.
Halliday
*Mead, Margaret*: courtesy of Blackstone
*Mencken, H. L.*: courtesy of Pinchot
*Merz, Charles*: courtesy of N. Y. Times Studio
*Michaux, Henri*: courtesy of Gisèle Freund
*Michener, James Albert*: courtesy of Blackstone
*Miles, Josephine*: courtesy of Estelle Keech
*Millar, George Reid*: courtesy of John Vickers
*Miller, Caroline*: courtesy of Pinchot
*Miller, Henry*: courtesy of C. Van Vechten
*Miller, Mary Britton*: courtesy of Leja Gorska
*Miller, Perry Gilbert Eddy*: courtesy of Havard
Crimson
*Mills, Enos Abijah*: courtesy of Harris &
Ewing
*Mitchell, Margaret*: courtesy of Asasno
*Mitford, Nancy*: courtesy of Dorothy Wilding
*Mizener, Arthur*: courtesy of Fran Hall
*Molloy, Robert*: courtesy of Larry Colwell
*Moore, Marianne*: courtesy of Archive

Moore, Merrill: courtesy of Fabian Bachrach
Morand, Paul: courtesy of A. Abbott
More, Paul Elmer: courtesy of O. J. Turner
Morison, Samuel Eliot: courtesy of U.S. Navy
  Photo
Morley, Christopher: courtesy of Disraeli
Morrison, Theodore: courtesy of John Brook
Morrow, Honore Willsie: courtesy of Pinchot
Motley, Willard: courtesy of Lee
Murray, Gilbert: courtesy of P. Smith
Murray, T. C.: courtesy of Dublin Lafayette
Myers, Gustavus: courtesy of Wide World

Nabokov, Vladimir: courtesy of Clayton Smith
Nathan, George Jean: courtesy of Oggiano
Nevins, Allan: courtesy of Wide World
Newbolt, Henry John: courtesy of W.
  Rothenstein
Newby, P. H.: courtesy of Robin Adler
Nims, John Frederick: courtesy of James Harjie
  Connelly
Nin, Anaïs: courtesy of Soichi Sunami
Nock, Albert Jay: courtesy of E. Stevenson
Norman, Charles: courtesy of M. Morehouse
North, Sterling: courtesy of Pinchot
Northrop, F. S. C.: courtesy of Yale News
  Bureau

O'Casey, Sean: courtesy of Pinchot
O'Connor, Frank: courtesy of Louis Faurer
O'Grady, Standish James: courtesy of J. B.
  Yeats
O'Hara, Mary: courtesy of Marion Stevenson
Oliver, John Rathbone: courtesy of Bachrach
O'Neill, Eugene: courtesy of Pinchot
Oursler, Fulton: courtesy of Oggiano
Overstreet, Harry A.: courtesy of Oggiano
Overton, Grant Martin: courtesy of P.
  MacDonald

Page, Elizabeth: courtesy of L. Costello
Palmer, Frederick: courtesy of Blank & Stoller
Parker, Dorothy: courtesy of M. Goldberg
Parshley, Howard Madison: courtesy of E.
  Stahlberg
Parsons, Geoffrey: courtesy of Pinchot
Patchen, Kenneth: courtesy of R. Carson
Paton, Alan: courtesy of Blackstone
Pearson, Drew: courtesy of Hessler
Pearson, Edmund Lester: courtesy of Bachrach
Pearson, Hesketh: courtesy of Robin Adler
Pearson, Karl: courtesy of F. A. de Biden
  Footner
Peel, Doris: courtesy of D. Ulmann
Pennell, Joseph Stanley: courtesy of John
  Engstead
Percy, William Alexander: courtesy of Wynn
  Richards

Peterkin, Julia: courtesy of D. Ulmann
Peterson, Houston: courtesy of Blackstone
Pinckney, Josephine: courtesy of Arni
Plievier, Theodor: courtesy of Photo Maywald
Plunkett, Joseph Mary: courtesy of G. Plunkett
Pollock, Channing: courtesy of H. Mitchell
Porter, Katherine Anne: courtesy of G. P. Lynes
Potter, Stephen: courtesy of Baron
Pottle, Frederick A.: courtesy of Yale News
  Bureau
Pound, Ezra: courtesy of Archive
Powell, Dawn: courtesy of Pinchot
Powers, J. F.: courtesy of Carl Fritz
Praed, Rose Caroline: courtesy of J. M. Jopling
Pratt, E. J.: courtesy of Ralph MacDonald
Pratt, Fletcher: courtesy of Erich Hartmann
Prescott, Hilda Frances Margaret: courtesy of
  Ramsey & Muspratt
Pringle, Henry Fowles: courtesy of Price
Pritchett, Victor Sawdon: courtesy of Elliott
  Erwitt
Pusey, Merlo J.: courtesy of Harris & Ewing
Putnam, Samuel: courtesy of Joseph Stella

Queen, Ellery: courtesy of Oggiano for both
Quick, Herbert: courtesy of Apeda

Rahv, Philip: courtesy of Sylvia Salmi
Repplier, Agnes: courtesy of Moffett
Reynolds, Quentin: courtesy of R. D. Englund
Rice, Elmer: courtesy of Pinchot
Rich, Louise Dickinson: courtesy of Eric
  Schaal
Richardson, Dorothy M.: courtesy of Beinecke
  Library, Yale Un
Ridge, Lola: courtesy of M. Content
Rilke, Rainer Maria: courtesy of C. J. Naar
Rittenhouse, Jessie B.: courtesy of Underwood
Roberts, Cecil: courtesy of Oggiano
Roberts, Elizabeth Madox: courtesy of W.
  Kelly
Roberts, Kenneth: courtesy of H. Stein
Robinson, Henry Morton: courtesy of Halsman
Rodgers, W. R.: courtesy of Nigel Henderson
Rodman, Selden: courtesy of Maja
  Wojciechowska
Rohmer, Sax: courtesy of White
Ross, Alan: courtesy of Thea Umlauff
Ross, Nancy: courtesy of Marcus Blechman
Rosten, Leo: courtesy of J. Schulman
Rourke, Constance Mayfield: courtesy of H.
  Taylor
Roy, Gabrielle: courtesy of Annette & Basil
  Zarov
Rukeyser, Muriel: courtesy of Chidnoff
Russell, George William: courtesy of E.
  Harrison
Russell, Mary Annette: courtesy of E. Schaal

Salinger, J. D.: courtesy of Lotte Jacobi
Sandburg, Carl: courtesy of E. Schaal
Sarett, Lew R.: courtesy of D. Loving
Saroyan, William: courtesy of E. Schaal
Sarton, George Alfred Léon: courtesy of Fabian Bachrach
Sarton, May: courtesy of Peter Rossiter
Schlesinger, Arthur Meier: courtesy of Bachrach
Schorer, Mark: courtesy of Philip Fein
Schriftgiesser, Karl: courtesy of Cosmo Sileo
Scott, Duncan: courtesy of Karsh
Seabrook, William Buehler: courtesy of E. Schaal
Seaver, Edwin: courtesy of Eliascheff
Seldes, George: courtesy of Pinchot
Sharp, Margery: courtesy of Pinchot
Shaw, George Bernard: courtesy of Fox Movietone
Sherman, Stuart Pratt: courtesy of P. MacDonald
Shuster, George Nauman: courtesy of Kaiden-Keystone
Siegfried, André: courtesy of B. Abbott
Simonds, Frank Herbert: courtesy of Harris & Ewing
Simonov, Konstantin: courtesy of Sovfoto
Simpson, George Gaylord: courtesy of Fabian Bachrach
Skinner, Constance Lindsay: courtesy of Pinchot
Slade, Caroline: courtesy of Gustave Lorey
Slaughter, Frank G.: courtesy of Underwood & Underwood
Slesinger, Tess: courtesy of Pinchot
Slichter, Sumner Huber: courtesy of Michael L. Meier
Smedley, Agnes: courtesy of H. Ansorge
Smith, H. A.: courtesy of Editta Sherman
Smith, Logan Pearsall: courtesy of W. Rothenstein
Snow, Edgar Parks: courtesy of J. A. Piver
Soule, George Henry: courtesy of S. Salmi
Spearman, Frank Hamilton: courtesy of Moffatt
Spencer, Theodor: courtesy of Fabian Bachrach
Speyer, Leonora: courtesy of Phyfe
Stafford, Jean: courtesy of Erich Hartmann
Starrett, Vincent: courtesy of D. Loving
Stauffer, Donald A.: courtesy of Orren Jack Turner
Stearns, Harold E.: courtesy of Bachrach
Stefánsson, Vilhjalmur: courtesy of Times Studio
Stegner, Wallace: courtesy of Bachrach
Sterling, George: courtesy of International Newsreel
Sterne, Emma: courtesy of Bachrach

Stowe, Leland: courtesy of Stephen Fay
Strachey, John: courtesy of Wide World
Street, James: courtesy of Editta Sherman
Stribling, T. S.: courtesy of Pinchot
Suckow, Ruth: courtesy of Bachrach
Sykes, Gerald: courtesy of Buffie Johnson
Sylvester, Harry: courtesy of Stephen Baldanza

Taggard, Genevieve: courtesy of Prix
Tagore, Rabindranath: courtesy of M. Vos
Tallant, Robert: courtesy of Philip Stiegman
Tarbell, Ida Minerva: courtesy of A. C. Johnston
Taylor, Deems: courtesy of Kesslere
Teale, Edwin Way: courtesy of Bachrach
Teasdale, Sara: courtesy of N. Muray
Thomas, Dylan: courtesy of A. John
Thomas, Lowell Jackson: courtesy of Phyfe
Thomson, Virgil Garnett: courtesy of Toppo
Tietjens, Eunice: courtesy of T. Averi
Tinker, Chauncey Brewster: courtesy of Kaiden-Kazanjian
Todd, Ruthven: courtesy of Laura Beaujon
Toller, Ernst: courtesy of L. Jacobs
Trilling, Lionel: courtesy of Robert Christie
Trumbo, Dalton: courtesy of Baskerville
Turnbull, Agnes: courtesy of Bachrach

Underhill, Evelyn: courtesy of H. Smith
Upfield, Arthur William: courtesy of Austin-Murcott

Valle-Inclán, Ramón María Del: courtesy of Eliason
Vallentin, Antonina: courtesy of C. Hess
Van Doren, Mark: courtesy of Fitzsimmons
Van Druten, John William: courtesy of J. Leyda
Van Vechten, Carl: courtesy of N. Muray
Veiller, Bayard: courtesy of C. Van Vechten
Viereck, Peter Robert Edwin: courtesy of Eric Stahlberg
Vizetelly, Frank: courtesy of Apeda
Vollmer, Lula: courtesy of Kesslere
Von Hagen, Victor Wolfgang: courtesy of Charles Daugherty

Waddell, Helen: courtesy of Boals
Walkley, Arthur Bingham: courtesy of K. Shackleton
Warburg, James P.: courtesy of Raymond K. Martin
Ward, Barbara: courtesy of Dorothy Wilding
Warner, Sylvia Townsend: courtesy of Pinchot
Wassermann, Jacob: courtesy of Apeda
Watkins, Vernon Philips: courtesy of Tal Jones
Weaver, John Van Alstyn: courtesy of Kesslere
Weiskopf, Franz Carl: courtesy of Fred Stein
Welles, Sumner: courtesy of Ottawa Karsh

*Welty, Eudora*: courtesy of Kay Bell
*Wendt, Gerald*: courtesy of Oggiano
*Wertham, Frederic*: courtesy of Gordon Parks
*Wescott, Glenway*: courtesy of C. P. Lynes
*West, Anthony*: courtesy of Madame Yevonde
*West, Jessamyn*: courtesy of Kay Bell
*Weygandt, Cornelius*: courtesy of Photo-
  Crafters
*Wharton, Edith*: courtesy of Bonney
*Whibley, Charles*: courtesy of P. Evans
*White, Walter Francis*: courtesy of Irwin &
  Langen
*White, William Lindsay*: courtesy of Arni
*Whitehead, Alfred North*: courtesy of Wide
  World
*Widdemer, Margaret*: courtesy of Underwood
*Wilbur, Richard*: courtesy of Walter R.
  Fleischer
*Wilkins, Vaughan*: courtesy of Howard Coster
*Williams, Ben Ames*: courtesy of Bachrach
*Williams, Emlyn*: courtesy of Acme
*Williams, Michael*: courtesy of Kaiden-
  Keystone
*Williams, William Carlos*: courtesy of C.
  Scheeler
*Willingham, Calder*: courtesy of Hella Heyman
*Wilson, Angus*: courtesy of Paul Moor
*Wilson, Charles Morrow*: courtesy of Affiliated
  Photo
*Winterich, John Tracy*: courtesy of Bachrach
*Winwar, Frances*: courtesy of Blackstone
*Wodehouse, P. G.*: courtesy of Times Wide
  World
*Wolfe, Thomas*: courtesy of Pinchot
*Wolff, Maritta Martin*: courtesy of Ghealey
*Wolfson, Victor*: courtesy of Halsman
*Woollcott, Alexander*: courtesy of R. C. Wood
*Wouk, Herman*: courtesy of Editta Sherman
*Wurdemann, Audrey*: courtesy of Pinchot
*Wylie, Philip*: courtesy of V. Egginton

*Ybarra, Thomas Russell*: courtesy of Arni
*Yeats, William Butler*: courtesy of M. Vos
*Yerby, Frank*: courtesy of Sam Langford
*Yezierska, Anzia*: courtesy of Underwood
*Young, Stark*: courtesy of P. & A.

*Zaturenska, Marya*: courtesy of Oggiano
*Zinsser, Hans*: courtesy of Bachrach